ANNOTATED GUIDE TO THE INSOLVENCY LEGISLATION

Insolvency Acts 1986 and 2000
Insolvency Rules 1986 with 2010 Amendments
Enterprise Act 2002

Thirteenth Edition

Volume 1

Len Sealy MA LLM PhD, Barrister and Solicitor (NZ)

SJ Berwin Professor Emeritus of Corporate Law,
University of Cambridge

David Milman LLB PhD

Professor of Law
Law School
Lancaster University

SWEET & MAXWELL   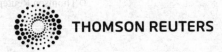 THOMSON REUTERS

Published in 2010 by Thomson Reuters (Legal) Limited
(Registered in England and Wales, Company No. 1679046.
Registered Office and address for service:
100 Avenue Road, London, NW3 3PF)
trading as Sweet and Maxwell

For further information on our products and services, visit
www.sweetandmaxwell.co.uk

Typeset by Interactive Sciences Ltd, Gloucester
Printed and bound in Great Britain by Ashford Colour Press Ltd, Gosport, Hants

No natural forests were destroyed to make this product; only farmed timber was used and replanted.

A CIP catalogue record for this book is available from the British Library

ISBN 978-0-414-04372-5

ANNOTATED
GUIDE TO THE INSOLVENCY LEGISLATION

THIRTEENTH EDITION

VOLUME 1

PREFACE TO THE THIRTEENTH EDITION

On April 6, 2010 the Insolvency Rules 1986 will be extensively altered when the Insolvency (Amendment) Rules 2010 (SI 2010/686) come into force and, on the same day, the Legislative Reform (Insolvency) (Miscellaneous Amendments) Order 2010 (SI 2010/18), which makes some significant changes to the Insolvency Act 1986, will also become operative. These two legislative measures, which run to over 200 pages in total, are a major step in the government's programme for the modernisation of Insolvency Law, following upon the relaxed advertising regime which was introduced in April 2009. The project will reach its culmination in the consolidation of the Insolvency Rules into a single piece of legislation that is planned to become operative on April 6, 2011, together with a consolidation of the rest of insolvency secondary legislation into various instruments to come into force at the same time.

The amending Rules in their final form were only published on March 10, 2010 and it has required a major effort, particularly on the part of our publishers' editorial team, to get the work into print so that it will be available to our readers as soon as possible after the operative date. The task was made all the more challenging because the government on March 12, 2010 announced that the new Rules were to be corrected and in some places clarified by a further statutory instrument which became the Insolvency (Amendment) (No.2) Rules 2010 (SI 2010/734), and that the Insolvency (Scotland) Rules 1986 were also to be amended with effect from April 6, 2010. This was done by the Insolvency (Scotland) Amendment Rules 2010 (SI 2010/688 (S 2)). We have been able to incorporate both of these additional measures into the text of this edition.

The amendments to the Rules will make much of the text and commentary in the current twelfth edition of this work obsolete, and so we have decided to bring forward the publication of this edition of the work to the spring of 2010 rather than delay it until our customary annual date in October. For this purpose the text of the Insolvency Rules 1986 has been fully updated, incorporating all the amendments made by the 2010 legislation and the annotations to the Rules have been revised to explain the reforms that have been made. In other parts of both volumes the commentary has been reviewed to ensure that full account is taken of the effect of the changes made by the new Rules, and cross-references have been altered where necessary to bring them into line with both the substance and the numeration of the rules as amended.

Among the innovations which have been introduced by the amending rules are:

- provisions facilitating the holding of meetings without the physical presence of the participants, e.g. by telephone conference or electronic means;

- elimination in most cases of the use of affidavits and their replacement by witness statements or statements of truth;

- provisions allowing pre-administration and costs as expense of the administration;

- authorisation of the use of electronic means and websites for the communication of information and the sending and service of documents;

- new provisions on block transfer orders;

- further clarification of the linkage with the Civil Procedure Rules; and

- a new Part 12A (dealing with matters of general effect).

Not all of these changes have retrospective effect, so as to apply to insolvencies which are ongoing on April 6, 2010. So practitioners should be aware that they will continue to need to refer to the old rules and that it will be wise to keep their copy of the twelfth edition when they buy the new one!

In addition, the text of the Insolvency Act 1986 has been amended to take account of the changes made by the 2010 Legislative Reform Order, and all of the other legislation reproduced in both volumes of the work has been brought up to date.

The amending Rules are extensive in their range and add considerably to the length and bulk of the Rules as a whole, and this has put such pressure on space in Volume 1 that we have reluctantly had to move the EC Regulation on Insolvency Proceedings into Volume 2, at least for the present edition. We hope that this will not cause too much inconvenience to our readers.

Necessarily, the amount of new case-law to be incorporated into the commentary has been reduced because there has been a shorter period between this edition and the previous one, but even so readers will find a good number of cases of significance, including *Re Bernard L Madoff Investment Securities Ltd* [2009] EWHC 442 (Ch), *Re Lehman Brothers International (Europe)* [2010] EWHC 47 (Ch), *Masri v Consolidated Contractors International (UK) Ltd* [2009] UKHL 43, *Nationwide Building Society v Wright* [2009] EWCA Civ 811 and *Official Receiver v McKay* [2009] EWCA Civ 467.

It is a pleasure once again to express our thanks to our friend and colleague Peter Bailey for his help and support, and to thank our publishers and their staff for their help at all stages of production. We would like also to thank those of our readers who have sent us comments and queries, brought some unreported judgments to our notice and drawn our attention to errors. These contributions are always most welcome. We are grateful also to the officials of the Policy Unit of the Insolvency Service, particularly for having made available early drafts of the amending Rules which enabled us to make a start on revising the work several weeks in advance of the publication of the final text.

Apart from the changes made by the amendments to the Insolvency Rules and the Scottish Insolvency Rules mentioned above, the law is stated as at February 28, 2010, although some later developments have been added at proof stage where space permits.

Len Sealy
David Milman
March 2010

ABOUT THE AUTHORS

Len Sealy MA, LLM, PhD, Barrister and Solicitor (NZ) is SJ Berwin Professor Emeritus of Corporate Law at the University of Cambridge. He is an eminent commentator on company and commercial law, having written and lectured extensively in these areas and is General Editor of British Company Law and Practice.

David Milman LLB, PhD is Professor of Law at Lancaster University. He is also Co-Author of Corporate Insolvency: Law and Practice and Co-General Editor of Insolvency Intelligence.

ABBREVIATIONS

The following abbreviations are used in this work:

BA 1914	Bankruptcy Act 1914
B(A)A 1926	Bankruptcy (Amendment) Act 1926
BR 1952	Bankruptcy Rules 1952
BRO	Bankruptcy restrictions order
BRU	Bankruptcy restrictions undertaking
CA	Companies Act (e.g. CA 2006 = Companies Act 2006)
CBIR	Cross-Border Insolvency Regulations 2006
CDDA 1986	Company Directors Disqualification Act 1986
CFCSA 1972	Companies (Floating Charges and Receivers) (Scotland) Act 1972
CDO	Competition Disqualification Order
CDU	Competition Disqualification Undertaking
CJA	Criminal Justice Act (e.g. CJA 1988 = Criminal Justice Act 1988)
COMI	Centre of main interests
Cork Report	*Report of the Review Committee on Insolvency Law and Practice* (Cmnd.8558, 1982)
CPR	Civil Procedure Rules
CVA	Company voluntary arrangement
DBERR	Department for Business, Enterprise and Regulatory Reform
DBIS	Department for Business, Innovation and Skills
DRO	Debt relief order
DRRO	Debt relief restrictions order
DRRU	Debt relief restrictions undertaking
DTI	Department of Trade and Industry
EA 2002	Enterprise Act 2002
EC Regulation	EC Regulation on Insolvency Proceedings 2000
FA	Finance Act (e.g. FA 1985 = Finance Act 1985)
Finality Regulations	Financial Markets and Insolvency (Settlement Finality) Regulations 1999 (SI 1999/2979)
FSA 1986	Financial Services Act 1986
FSMA 2000	Financial Services and Markets Act 2000
G to E	Model Law on Cross-Border Insolvency Guide to Enactment
IA	Insolvency Act (e.g. IA 1985 = Insolvency Act 1985)
IPA	Income payments agreement
IR 1986	Insolvency Rules 1986
I(A)R	Insolvency (Amendment) Rules (e.g. I(A)R 1993 = Insolvency Amendment Rules 1993)
IVA	Individual voluntary arrangement

Judgments Regulation	Council Regulation (EC) 44/2001 of December 22, 2000 on jurisdiction and the recognition and enforcement of judgments in civil and commercial matters
LLP	Limited liability partnership
LLPA 2000	Limited Liability Partnerships Act 2000
LLPR 2001	Limited Liability Partnerships Regulations 2001 (SI 2001/1090)
LPA 1925	Law of Property Act 1925
LRO 2010	Legislative Reform (Insolvency) (Miscellaneous Amendments) Order 2010
OR	Official receiver
POCA 2002	Proceeds of Crime Act 2002
RSC	Rules of the Supreme Court
TCEA 2007	Tribunals, Courts and Enforcement Act 2007
TUPE Regulations	Transfer of Undertakings (Protection of Employment) Regulations 2006
White Paper	*A Revised Framework for Insolvency Law* (Cmnd.9175, 1984)

Appendix I and Appendix II list the words and phrases which are given a special statutory definition or used in a particular sense in the legislation or the Rules, and give references to the provisions in which they and the accompanying commentary can be found.

CONTENTS

Case Table

References within square brackets are located in Volume 2.

The following abbreviations are used in the tables to denote the location of entries in all tables:

[CBIR]	Cross-Border Insolvency Regulations 2006
[CDDA]	Company Directors Disqualification Act 1986
EA	Enterprise Act 2002
[ER]	EC Regulation on Insolvency Proceedings 2000
IA	Insolvency Act 1986
IA 2000	Insolvency Act 2000
IR	Insolvency Rules 1986
[UML]	UNCITRAL Model Law on Cross-Border Insolvency

Provision

A

4Eng Ltd v Harper [2009] EWHC 2633 (Ch); [2010] B.P.I.R. 1, Ch D ...... IA 423(1)–(3), 425(1)

A Straume (UK) Ltd v Bradlor Developments Ltd [2000] B.C.C. 333, Ch D .... [IA 11(3)]

A&C Group Services Ltd, Re [1993] B.C.L.C. 1297, Ch D .... [CDDA 9(1)]

A&C Supplies Ltd, Re; sub nom. Sutton (Removal of Liquidator), Re [1998] B.C.C. 708, Ch D .... IA 29(2), 45(1), (2), 172(1), (2)

A&J Fabrications (Batley) Ltd v Grant Thornton (A Firm) (No.1) [1999] B.C.C. 807, Ch D .... IA 212(1)

ACLI Metals (London) Ltd, Re (1989) 5 B.C.C. 749, Ch D .... IA 168(5)

AA Mutual International Insurance Co Ltd, Re [2004] EWHC 2430 (Ch), Ch D (Companies Ct) .... IA Pt II, Sch.B1, paras 9, 11

AE Farr Ltd, Re [1992] B.C.C. 150, Ch D (Companies Ct) .... IA 236

AES Barry Ltd v TXU Europe Energy Trading (In admin.) [2004] EWHC 1757 (Ch), Ch D .... [IA 11(3)]

AET v Kermanshahchi. *See* Anglo Eastern Trust Ltd v Kermanshahchi

AG (Manchester) Ltd (formerly The Accident Group Ltd) (In liq.), Re; sub nom. Official Receiver v Langford; Official Receiver v Watson

Provision

[2008] EWHC 64 (Ch); [2008] B.C.C. 497, Ch D (Manchester) .... [CDDA 9(1)]

AE Realisations (1985) Ltd, Re [1988] 1 W.L.R. 200; (1987) 3 B.C.C. 136, Ch D .... IA 179, 181(1)–(3)

AI Levy (Holdings) Ltd, Re [1964] Ch. 19, Ch D .... IA 127

AIB Finance Ltd v Alsop; sub nom. AIB Finance Ltd v Debtors [1998] 2 All E.R. 929; ; [1998] B.C.C. 780, CA (Civ Div) .... IR 6.5

AJ Adams (Builders) Ltd, Re [1991] B.C.C. 62, Ch D (Companies Ct) ... IA 108, 171(4)

AMEC Properties Ltd v Planning Research & Systems Plc [1992] 1 E.G.L.R. 70, CA (Civ Div) .... IA 37(1), (2), 44(1), (2)

AMF International Ltd, Re [1995] B.C.C. 439, Ch D .... IR 4.139– 4.148E

AMF International Ltd (No.2), Re; sub nom. Cohen v Ellis [1996] 1 W.L.R. 77; [1996] B.C.C. 335, Ch D .... IA 212(3)

AMP Enterprises Ltd v Hoffman; sub nom. AMP Music Box Enterprises Ltd v Hoffman [2002] EWHC 1899 (Ch); [2002] B.C.C. 996, Ch D (Companies Ct) .... IA 108

ANC Ltd v Clark Goldring & Page Ltd [2001] B.C.C. 479, CA (Civ Div) ... IA Sch.4 para.6

ARV Aviation Ltd, Re (1988) 4 B.C.C. 708, Ch D .... [IA 15]

Case Table

	Provision		Provision

Provision   **Provision**

EWHC 1410 (Ch); [2005] B.P.I.R.
1472, Ch D (Companies Ct) . . . . IA 245(3)–(5),
Sch.B1 para.74

Unigreg Ltd (In admin.), Re [2005]
B.P.I.R. 220, Ch D . . . . IA 238(4)

Unit 2 Windows Ltd (In liq.), Re [1985]
1 W.L.R. 1383; (1985) 1 B.C.C. 99,
489, Ch D . . . . IA 59(1), (2)

Uno Plc, Re [2004] EWHC 933 (Ch);
[2006] B.C.C. 725, Ch D . . . . [CDDA 9(1)]

Upton v Taylor [1999] B.P.I.R. 168, Ch
D . . . . IR 6.138

V

Valentine v Bangla TV Ltd; sub nom.
Bangla Television Ltd (In liq.), Re
[2006] EWHC 2292 (Ch); [2007] 1
B.C.L.C. 609, Ch D (Companies Ct) . IA 238(4)

Valentine v Bangla TV Ltd; sub nom.
Bangla Television Ltd (In liq.), Re
[2009] EWHC 1632 (Civ); [2010]
B.C.C. 143, Ch D . . . . IA 214

Vedmay Ltd, Re [1994] 1 B.C.L.C. 676;
(1994) 26 H.L.R. 70, Ch D . . . . IA 181(1)–(3),
182(4)

Verby Print for Advertising Ltd, Re; sub
nom. Verby Print for Advertising Ltd
v Secretary of State for Trade and
Industry; Fine v Secretary of State for
Trade and Industry [1998] B.C.C.
652, Ch D (Companies Ct) . . . . [CDDA 1, 1(1),
7(1)]

Victoria Society, Knottingley, Re
[1913] 1 Ch. 167, Ch D . . . . IA Pt IV

Vidyarthi v Clifford [2004] EWHC
2084 (Ch); [2005] B.P.I.R. 233, Ch D IA 238A

Vintage Hallmark Plc, Re; sub nom.
Secretary of State for Trade and
Industry v Grove [2006] EWHC
2761 (Ch); [2008] B.C.C. 150, Ch D
(Companies Ct) . . . . [CDDA 9(1)]

Vlieland-Boddy v Dexter Ltd [2003]
EWHC 2592 (Ch); [2004] B.P.I.R.
235, Ch D . . . . IA 257(1), 262

Vocalion (Foreign) Ltd, Re [1932] 2 Ch.
196, Ch D . . . . IA 183

Vos (Deceased), Re. *See* Dick v Kendall
Freeman

W

W&A Glaser Ltd, Re [1994] B.C.C.
199, Ch D (Companies Ct) . . . . IR 4.152–4.155,
4.156–4.159,
4.172A, 7.47

WBSL Realisations 1992 Ltd, Re; sub
nom. Ward Group Plc, Re [1995]
B.C.C. 1118, Ch D . . . . IA Sch.1,
[IA 11(5)]

WF Fearman Ltd, Re (1988) 4 B.C.C.
139, Ch D (Companies Ct) . . . . [IR 2.1–2.3]

WF Fearman Ltd, Re (No.2) (1988) 4
B.C.C. 141, Ch D (Companies Ct) . . 115, 135, 177,
IR 4.218(1)–(3),
[IA 9(4), (5)]

WGS and MSLS v United Kingdom
(App. No. 38172/97) [2000] B.C.C.
719, ECHR . . . . [CDDA]

WH Smith Ltd v Wyndham Investments
Ltd [1994] B.C.C. 699, Ch D . . . . . . IR 4.187–4.194

Wake-Walker v AKG Group Ltd; sub
nom. Martyn Rose Ltd v AKG Group
Ltd [2003] EWCA Civ 375, CA (Civ
Div) . . . . IA Pt VI

Walker Morris (A Firm) v Khalastchi
[2001] 1 B.C.L.C. 1, Ch D
(Companies Ct) . . . . IA 234(1), (2)

Walker v Secretary of State for Trade
and Industry; sub nom. Secretary of
State for Trade and Industry v Walker
[2003] EWHC 175 (Ch), Ch D
(Companies Ct) . . . . [CDDA 6(1)]

Wallace v Shoa Leasing (Singapore)
PTE Ltd; sub nom. Japan Leasing
(Europe) Plc, Re [1999] B.P.I.R. 911;
[2000] W.T.L.R. 301, Ch D . . . . IA 107

Wallace Smith Trust Co Ltd, Re [1992]
B.C.C. 707, Ch D (Companies Ct) . . IA 131, 235(5)

Walter L Jacob & Co Ltd, Re (1989) 5
B.C.C. 244, CA (Civ Div) . . . . IA 124A,
IR 4.25–4.31

Walter L Jacob & Co Ltd, Re; sub nom.
Official Receiver v Jacob [1993]
B.C.C. 512, Ch D (Companies Ct) . . [CDDA 6(2),
7(2)]

Warley Continental Services Ltd (In
Compulsory Liquidation) v Johal
[2004] B.P.I.R. 353, Ch D . . . . IA 376

Warner v Verfides; sub nom. Rivkin, Re
[2008] EWHC 2609 (Ch) . . . . [CBIR]

Watts v Newham LBC [2009] EWHC
377 (Ch); [2009] B.P.I.R. 718, Ch D . IA 282(1), (3)

Wavern Engineering Co Ltd, Re (1987)
3 B.C.C. 3, Ch D (Companies Ct) . . . IA 124(1)

Webb Distributors (Aust) Pty Ltd v
Victoria (1993) 11 A.C.S.R. 731 . . . . IA 74(2)(f)

Webb Electrical Ltd, Re (1988) 4
B.C.C. 230; [1989] P.C.C. 379; Ch D IA 127

Weddell v JA Pearce & Major (A Firm)
[1988] Ch. 26, Ch D . . . . IA Sch.5

Statutes Table

Statutory Instruments Table

Introduction

The insolvency legislation of 1985 and 1986

The Insolvency Act 1985 was a major piece of new legislation, implementing the most comprehensive review of the subjects of bankruptcy and corporate insolvency for over a century. Its provisions were based largely on the recommendations contained in the Cork Report (see below), after publication of a White Paper entitled *A Revised Framework for Insolvency Law*, Cmnd.9175 (1984). Although it received the Royal Assent and became law on October 30, 1985, the Government decided to delay implementation of all but a few of its provisions and to draw up a new Act, consolidating its provisions with those parts of the Companies Act 1985 dealing with receivership and winding up. This became the Insolvency Act 1986. At the same time a separate Bill was prepared to consolidate the law relating to the disqualification of company directors, which became the Company Directors Disqualification Act 1986. The two consolidating Acts received Royal Assent on July 25, 1986 and were brought into force together on December 29, 1986. On the same date the Insolvency Rules 1986 became operative, replacing the Companies (Winding up) Rules 1949 and the Bankruptcy Rules 1952.

The Cork Report

The main inspiration for the reforms made by the Insolvency Act 1985 was the *Report of the Review Committee on Insolvency Law and Practice*, the chairman of which was the late Sir Kenneth Cork ("the Cork Report", Cmnd.8558 (1982)). This committee was appointed in January 1977 with a wide-ranging brief, and its Report, published in June 1982, made proposals for extensive and radical changes in the law and practice of bankruptcy and corporate insolvency, amounting virtually to the introduction of a completely new code.

Later legislation

There have been a number of changes made to the Act of 1986 since it came into force and, in addition, new legislation in related areas. Among these may be noted the following:

Extension to insolvent partnerships
By the Insolvent Partnerships Order 1994 (SI 1994/2421) the 1986 Act was modified so as to make its provisions applicable to insolvent partnerships as from December 1, 1994. This Order has since been extensively amended. For the full text, as amended, see Vol.2 of this *Guide*.

Extension to building societies
The Building Societies Act 1986 was amended in 1989 so as to provide that where a building society is being wound up, the Insolvency Act 1986 (and the corresponding legislation for Northern Ireland) are to apply: see below, Introductory note to Part IV. Other insolvency procedures were made available to building societies by the Building Societies Act 1997 s.39(1).

Disapplication of insolvency legislation to "market contracts" and "market charges"
The Companies Act 1989 Pt VII modified the application of insolvency law and the enforcement of certain rights and remedies in relation to certain contracts on the financial markets. These are contracts connected with "recognised investment exchanges" and "recognised clearing houses" (CA 1989 s.155), with certain overseas investment exchanges and clearing houses (s.170), with certain money market institutions (s.171) and with settlement arrangements provided by the Bank of England (s.172). Part VII

has effect in three principal ways: (1) it gives effect to contractual settlement procedures in the various financial markets, displacing the normal rules of insolvency law, where one of the contracting parties becomes insolvent (see the notes to ss.107 and 328, below); (2) it preserves (and, in some cases, enhances) the priority of a chargee where a charge has been taken to secure obligations and liabilities arising under a market contract (see the notes to ss.10(1), 11(2), 11(3), 15(1), 15(2), 43, 61, 127 and 284, below); and (3) it safeguards rights and remedies in relation to property provided as cover for margin in relation to market contracts and market charges (see CA 1989 ss.177–181, and note in particular s.180(2), which provides that an investment exchange, clearing house or chargee may authorise the commencement or continuation of enforcement proceedings by an unsecured creditor against property held as margin "notwithstanding any provision of IA 1986"). The order-making powers of Pt VII were brought into force on March 25, 1991 and the remaining provisions (except ss.169(4), 170–172, 176, 178 and 181) became operative on April 25, 1991. The Financial Markets and Insolvency Regulations 1991 (SI 1991/880), which contain important modifications to the provisions of Pt VII, also came into force on the latter date. A number of statutory instruments have since amended or extended this legislation: for details, see the relevant parts of CA 1989 reproduced in Vol.2. Amendments have also been made by EA 2002 Sch.17 paras 43–47 to extend the above disapplication provisions to companies entering into administration under the new administration regime established by IA 1986 Sch.B1.

The insolvency legislation is similarly disapplied in relation to payment and securities settlement systems by the Financial Markets and Insolvency (Settlement Finality) Regulations 1999 (SI 1999/2979), discussed below.

Insolvency Act 1994

The ruling of the Court of Appeal in *Powdrill v Watson, Re Paramount Airways Ltd (No.3)* [1995] 2 A.C. 394 (see below, annotations to ss.19 and 44) caused immediate concern amongst insolvency practitioners because of their possible exposure to personal liability in claims brought by former employees of companies which were, or had been, in administration or administrative receivership. The Insolvency Act 1994 was passed to clarify the question of the liability of office-holders in such circumstances, with effect from March 15, 1994 (but not retrospectively). See the notes to ss.19 and 44, below.

Insolvency (No.2) Act 1994

This short Act amending the Insolvency Act 1986 was also passed in 1994, on the initiative of the Law Society, primarily to remove doubts about the position of a person who purchases unregistered land in a transaction which is challenged as a transaction at an undervalue or a preference under IA 1986 ss.238–241 or 339–342 (or the corresponding provisions in the Northern Ireland insolvency legislation). See the notes to ss.241 and 342, below.

Human Rights Act 1998

The United Kingdom has been a party to the European Convention for the Protection of Human Rights and Fundamental Freedoms since its inception in 1950, but the Convention was only given force in UK domestic law by the Human Rights Act 1998, which became fully operative on October 2, 2000. In consequence, issues of human rights may now be raised before our own courts, rather than having to be litigated before the European Court of Human Rights in Strasbourg.

While the Act does not directly amend the insolvency legislation in any way, it is of significance because (a) the courts are directed to have regard to the established case law of the European Court and opinions and decisions of the European Commission of Human Rights and the Committee of Ministers (s.2); (b) domestic legislation must, so far as possible, be construed in a way which is compatible with Convention rights (s.3); (c) it is unlawful for a public authority (e.g. the Secretary of State or the Insolvency Service) to act in a way which is incompatible with a Convention right (s.6); and (d) in the preparation of new legislation, the draftsman is necessarily concerned to ensure that it is compatible with Convention rights. There will therefore be occasion to refer to the Convention and the Act of 1998 at various times in the discussion which follows.

Civil Procedure Rules 1998

These Rules (commonly known as the CPR) came into force on April 26, 1999. On the same date amendments to the Insolvency Rules 1986 were brought into effect, so as to apply all those provisions of the CPR and such practice of the High Court and County Court as is not inconsistent with IR 1986 to insolvency proceedings, and to bring the terminology used in the Rules into line with the CPR.

Disapplication of insolvency legislation to payment and securities settlement systems

The Financial Markets and Insolvency (Settlement Finality) Regulations 1999 (SI 1999/2979) (the "Finality Regulations"), which became operative on December 11, 1999, were enacted in order to implement Directive 98/26 of the European Community ([1998] O.J. L166/45) into the law of the United Kingdom. The object of the Directive is to reduce the risks associated with participation in payment and securities settlement systems by minimising the disruption caused if insolvency proceedings are brought against a participant in such a system. For this purpose, a settlement system must be specifically designated by the Financial Services Authority or the Bank of England, and "insolvency proceedings" refers to a court order for bankruptcy, sequestration (in Scotland) or winding up, or administration or a creditors' voluntary winding up. These Regulations were extended to Northern Ireland by SI 2006/50.

Regulations 13 to 19 modify the law of insolvency so far as it applies to transfer orders effected through a designated system and to collateral security provided in connection with participation in such a system. But the normal rules of insolvency apply to a transfer order which is entered into a designated system *after* the making of the court order or passing of a winding-up resolution, unless the transfer order is carried out on the same day as the court order or resolution and the relevant person (e.g. the settlement agent or clearing house) does not have notice of the insolvency at the time of settlement (reg.20).

Where a transaction is both a market contract or market charge (as defined for the purposes of Pt VII of the Companies Act 1989 (see above)) and a transfer order or a collateral security charge under the Finality Regulations, certain provisions of the 1989 Act are disapplied, so that the Regulations govern the situation (reg.21). For the text of the Regulations, as amended, see Vol.2.

Insolvency Act 2000

This Act received the Royal Assent on November 30, 2000. The two principal reforms were (a) provision for a moratorium in voluntary arrangements for small companies (s.1 and Sch.1); and (b) the introduction of a formal scheme of disqualification undertakings entered into under an administrative procedure in lieu of disqualification orders made by a court (ss.5–8). Other amendments included: improvements to the procedure for an individual voluntary arrangement (s.3 and Sch.3), new rules relating to the prosecution of delinquent officers and members of a company in a compulsory winding up, designed to bring the law into conformity with the Human Rights Act 1998 (s.11), and a power conferred on the Secretary of State (by s.14) to give effect to the UNCITRAL Model Law on Cross-Border Insolvency (discussed below, in the annotation to s.14 of IA 2000 and, for the text, see Vol.2).

Section 14 (the enabling provision relating to the Model Law) came into operation with the passing of the Act. Other parts of the Act were brought into force in stages, implementation being finally completed on January 1, 2003.

Extension to limited liability partnerships

The Limited Liability Partnerships Act 2000 introduced a new form of incorporated body, the limited liability partnership (LLP), into the law of Great Britain, and provided for the recognition of similar bodies incorporated or established outside the jurisdiction, which are referred to in the Act as "oversea limited liability partnerships". Section 14 of this Act authorised provision to be made by regulation about the insolvency and winding up of LLPs and oversea LLPs by applying or incorporating, with such modifications as might appear appropriate, Pts I to IV, VI and VII of IA 1986. This was done by the Limited Liability Partnership Regulations 2001 (SI 2001/1090), which are reproduced (as amended) in Vol.2. The Act and Regulations came into force on April 6, 2001.

EC Regulation on Insolvency Proceedings 2000

This Regulation (Regulation 1346/2000, [2000] O.J. L160/1) sets out common rules on cross-border insolvency proceedings within the European Union. It came into force on May 31, 2002. As a Regulation, it has direct applicability (i.e. it does not need to be implemented by domestic legislation).

The background to this legislation is set out in Vol.2, where the full text of the Regulation is reproduced with an accompanying commentary.

This Regulation was amended by Regulations 603/2005, 694/2006, 681/2007 and 788/2008 to reflect enlargement of the EU and changes in national insolvency regimes in the intervening period.

Extension of administration procedure to insurance companies

The administration procedure was not available to insurance companies under IA 1986, as originally enacted. However, this has since been made possible by special legislation. See the note to IA 1986 Sch.B1 para.9.

Enterprise Act 2002

This Act followed a number of initiatives and consultations by the DTI and the Treasury between 1999 and 2001 which culminated in the publication of a White Paper published by the Insolvency Service on July 31, 2001, entitled *Productivity and Enterprise: Insolvency—A Second Chance*. Its main proposals concerning corporate insolvency were (a) that the right to appoint an administrative receiver be restricted to holders of floating charges granted in connection with transactions in the capital markets; (b) that the Crown's standing as a preferential creditor be abolished; (c) that the administration procedure be streamlined by reducing its considerable formalities; and (d) to simplify the transition from an administration to a winding up where it was likely that there would be funds available for distribution to unsecured creditors. In regard to bankruptcy law, various reforms which had been outlined in a White Paper of February 13, 2000 would be introduced, together with the abolition of Crown preference in personal insolvencies, and a system of "bankruptcy restriction orders", on analogy with director disqualification orders, would be instituted for the more culpable debtors. It was also proposed to extend the director disqualification regime by adding the disqualification of directors as an additional sanction for breaches of the competition laws.

The ensuing Act, which in a number of respects went further than the White Paper, received Royal Assent as the Enterprise Act 2002 on November 7, 2002. The provisions of this Act relating to corporate insolvency and the abolition of the Crown's preferential status, together with supporting statutory instruments (principally the Insolvency (Amendment) Rules 2003 (SI 2003/1730)), were brought into force on September 15, 2003. The remaining sections dealing with the bankruptcy of individuals became effective from April 1, 2004.

The Enterprise Act 2002 s.255 also gives power to the Treasury, with the concurrence of the Secretary of State, to make orders extending legislative provisions governing CVAs and administrations to bodies such as industrial and provident societies and friendly societies.

Proceeds of Crime Act 2002

This Act provides for the confiscation of assets of persons convicted of criminal offences. Part 9 of the Act, which became operative on March 24, 2003, deals with the potential conflicts which may arise between the criminal law confiscation rules and the insolvency regimes of bankruptcy, sequestration (in Scotland), winding up and receivership. It also applies in the insolvency of limited liability partnerships. The impact of this legislation, relevant parts of which are reproduced in Vol.2, is discussed at appropriate places in the text which follows.

Financial Collateral Arrangements (No.2) Regulations 2003

These Regulations (SI 2003/3226, revoking and replacing SI 2003/3112, which was not brought into force because of a drafting error) became operative on December 26, 2003. They implement the Directive of the EU Parliament and Council 2002/47, and (inter alia) disapply various provisions of domestic insolvency legislation in relation to financial collateral arrangements, giving priority, for instance, to close-out netting provisions in such an arrangement over the rules which would otherwise prevail in a winding up.

Credit Institutions (Reorganisation and Winding Up) Regulations 2004

These Regulations (SI 2004/1945, effective May 5, 2004) implement the Directive of the EU Parliament and Council 2001/24, and provide for the recognition and co-ordination of proceedings for the reorganisation and winding up of banking and other credit institutions throughout the EEA.

Cross-Border Insolvency Regulations 2006

As noted above, the IA 2000 s.14 made provision for the enactment in this country of legislation based on the Model Law on Cross-Border Insolvency, which had been adopted by the United Nations Commission on International Trade Law (UNCITRAL) on May 30, 1997 and later formally agreed by the UN General Assembly on December 15 of the same year. Following the publication by the DTI of a consultation paper and a draft of the proposed legislation in August 2005 the Cross-Border Insolvency Regulations 2006 (SI 2006/1030) were signed into law on April 3, 2006 and came into force on the following day. The Regulations embody (in Sch.1) a modified form of the Model Law, specifically adapted to relate to Great Britain and its existing legislation. The text is reproduced in Vol.2, accompanied by a full annotation. Applied to Northern Ireland by SR 2007/115 as from April 12, 2007.

Companies Act 2006

This Act (the largest ever passed in Parliamentary history) received the Royal Assent on November 8, 2006, and finally came fully into force on October 1, 2009. The legislation both reforms and consolidates much of the existing Companies Act 1985. Note that the law on investigations by the Department of Business remains in the 1985 Act for the moment. For the most part its provisions do not directly impact upon insolvency practice in the sense of making real changes. But note s.193(1)(b) (extending the concession on the need for substantial property transactions approvals to disposals made by administrators) and s.1282 (which reverses *Leyland DAF* [2004] UKHL 9; [2004] 2 A.C. 298). Note also that the Companies Act 2006 applies to Northern Ireland. A number of statutory instruments came into force with the Act on October 1, 2009. In consequence of the Act, extensive amendments were made to the Insolvency Act 1986 and the other legislation which is annotated in this work. All the changes of substance have been noted at the appropriate places, but there are many minor textual changes (e.g. those which simply replace section numbers of CA 1985 with the corresponding numbers of CA 2006, or are purely verbal or cosmetic), and these amendments have been made without annotation.

Fraud Act 2006

This Act came into force on January 15, 2007. Among other reforms, it extends the law relating to fraudulent trading (IA 1986 s.213) to sole traders and other persons participating in fraudulent business, and increases the penalties for persons convicted of fraudulent trading.

Demise of the Department of Trade and Industry

In the course of the Cabinet reshuffle following the resignation of Mr Blair as Prime Minister, the Department of Trade and Industry (formerly the longstanding Board of Trade) was replaced by the Department for Business, Enterprise and Regulatory Reform (BERR). In June 2009 it was replaced by the Department for Business, Innovation and Skills (BIS), commonly abbreviated to the Department for Business. All matters relating to individual bankruptcy and corporate insolvency remain within the brief of the new Department.

Tribunals, Courts and Enforcement Act 2007

This received the Royal Assent on July 19, 2007. A number of elements of this legislation will be relevant to insolvency practitioners, particularly those engaged in personal insolvency work. The most significant development will be the introduction of the "NINA" scheme for debtors with "no income and no assets" (see s.108 and Schs 17 and 18 of the Act). This reform, which necessitates the insertion of Pt 7A and new Schs 4ZA and 4ZB into the Insolvency Act 1986, was brought into force by the Tribunals, Courts and Enforcement Act 2007 (Commencement No.7) Order 2009 (SI 2009/382) with effect from April 6, 2009. It will provide a bureaucratic means of debt relief outside the parameters of bankruptcy or IVA regimes. Linked to this are debt relief restriction orders and undertakings, which are designed to combat abuse by debtors (Sch.19). These reforms produce consequential amendments in the Insolvency Act 1986 (see Sch.20 to the 2007 Act). The 2007 Act also contains many reforms relating to various debt enforcement procedures (Pts 3 and 4); changes are made to the county court administration procedure (s.106); regulations are set in place for debt management schemes (ss.109 et seq.), enforcement restriction orders are introduced (s.107); abolition of the common law right of distress for rent is at last implemented (s.71). In June 2009 the Ministry of Justice announced that Pt 4 of the 2007 Act (relating to attachment of earnings orders, charging orders and information requests and orders) was not to be brought into force. Apart from this, it is understood that the remaining provisions of the Act will not come into force for many months and therefore the affected legislation in this text has not been changed for this edition, though annotations do in some cases anticipate the reforms on the horizon.

Banking Act 2009

New insolvency and administration regimes for banking companies were introduced by the Banking Act 2009, which received the Royal Assent on February 12, 2009 and came into force on February 21. This legislation is intended to strengthen the statutory framework for financial stability and depositor protection when banking companies encounter financial difficulties. Part 1 of the Act introduces the "Special Resolution Regime" (SRR), which provides three stabilisation options: transfer to a purchaser in the private sector, transfer to a bridge bank and transfer to temporary public sector ownership. The SRR may also apply to building societies, and there is power also to apply it to credit unions. Part 2 of the Act establishes a new insolvency procedure called a "bank insolvency order" based on existing liquidation provisions to provide for the orderly winding up, pursuant to a court order, of a failed bank and to facilitate rapid payments under the Financial Services Compensation Scheme to eligible claimants (or to transfer such accounts to another financial institution). Part 3 establishes a new administration procedure (again following the making of a court order) to deal with the remaining assets where there has been a partial transfer of business from a failing bank. The powers conferred by this legislation have already been used to cope with some recent bank failures. The provisions of the Insolvency Act 1986 and the Insolvency Rules 1986 are modified for the purposes of this legislation by the Act itself and by the swathe of secondary legislation which has followed in its wake. Relevant statutory instruments include the Banking Act 2009 (Bank Administration) (Modification for Application to Banks in Temporary Public Ownership) Regulations 2009 (SI 2009/312); the Banking Act 2009 (Bank Administration) (Modification for Application to Multiple Transfers) Regulations 2009 (SI 2009/313); the Banking Act 2009 (Sharing Information) Regulations 2009 (SI 2009/314); the Banking Act 2009 (Parts 2 and 3 Consequential Amendments) Order 2009 (SI 2009/317); the Banking Act 2009 (Third Party Compensation Arrangements for Partial Property Transfers) Regulations 2009 (SI 2009/319); the Banking Act 2009 (Restriction of Partial Property Transfers) Order 2009 (SI 2009/322); the Bank Insolvency (Scotland) Rules 2009 (SI 2009/350); the Bank Administration (Scotland) Rules 2009 (SI 2009/357); the Bank Insolvency (England and Wales) Rules 2009 (SI 2009/356), the Bank Administration (England and Wales) Rules 2009 (SI 2009/357) and the Scottish and Northern Ireland Banknote Regulations 2009 (SI 2009/3056). This legislation generally came into force on February 21, 2009. As regards building societies, see the Building Societies (Insolvency and Special Administration) Order 2009 (SI 2009/805), effective March 29, 2009.

This legislation is too voluminous to be included in the present work and since, in those insolvencies where it is applicable, it specifies variations and modifications for a very large number of provisions of the Act and the Rules, to annotate each provision and rule in detail would take up much space, references to the special case of banking insolvencies and administrations will not normally be given.

For a commentary on this legislation, see R. Tomasic (2009) Insolv. Int. 65, 81.

Introduction

Insolvency Service consultation on company rescue
The Insolvency Service on June 15, 2009 began a consultation exercise on revising the insolvency legislation to encourage corporate rescue. The main proposals are:

- to extend the CVA moratorium, currently available only to a restricted category of small companies, to companies generally;

- to introduce a court-sanctioned moratorium for all companies of up to three months, where the court is satisfied that creditors will be properly safeguarded;

- to improve access by distressed companies to funding by according priority to new money lent to companies subject to a CVA or in administration.

Revision of the Insolvency Rules and consolidation of secondary legislation
In September 2005 the Insolvency Service began a project to review, consolidate and simplify the Insolvency Rules and nine other statutory instruments:

The Insolvent Partnerships Order 1994 (SI 1994/2421)
The Insolvency Regulations 1994 (SI 1994/2507)
The Insolvency Proceedings (Fees) Order 2004 (SI 2004/593)
The Insolvency Proceedings (Monetary Limits) Order 1986 (SI 1986/1996)
The Administration of Insolvent Estates of Deceased Persons Order 1986 (SI 1986/1999)
The Insolvency Practitioners and Insolvency Services Account (Fees) Order 2003 (SI 2003/3363)
The Insolvent Companies (Disqualification of Unfit Directors) Proceedings Rules 1987 (SI 1987/2023)
The Insolvent Companies (Reports on Conduct of Directors) Rules 1996 (SI 1996/1909)
The Companies (Disqualification Orders) Regulations 2001 (SI 2001/967)

The first landmark in this major exercise was reached with the enactment in February 2010 of the Insolvency (Amendment) Rules 2010 (SI 2010/686) and the Insolvency (Amendment) (No.2) Rules 2010 (SI 2010/734), which are to come into force on April 6, 2010. The amending rules (which extend to nearly 200 pages) have among their objects the simplification of procedures (for instance abolishing the use of affidavits and the routine filing of copies of documents with the court) and the use of modern techniques for the communication of information (websites and other electronic means) in place of paper documents and for the holding of meetings without personal attendance. For a more detailed account of these changes, see the Introductory note to the Insolvency Rules 1986 below at p.683. In anticipation of this measure Parliament authorised the making on January 6, 2010 by the Secretary of State for Business, Innovation and Skills of a Legislative Reform Order, the Legislative Reform (Insolvency) (Miscellaneous Provisions) Order 2010 (SI 2010/18, operative from April 6, 2010) ("LRO 2010") which made a number of amendments to the Insolvency Act 1986 to pave the way for the making of the amending Rules. The principal amendments made by this Order are described below at p.9.

This is but the first step in the overall revision programme. In the coming year it is planned to consolidate the original 1986 Rules with these amendments into a single enactment, to come into force on April 6, 2011, and at the same time to make new statutory instruments replacing those listed in the preceding paragraph.

The Insolvency Act 1986

On its enactment, the Insolvency Act 1986 brought into one composite Act the whole of the provisions of the Insolvency Act 1985 (except for ss.12–14, 16, 18 and Sch.2, which were separately consolidated into CDDA 1986) and ss.467–650 and 659–674 of CA 1985, together with certain parts of other ancillary legislation. It deals with both corporate insolvency and the bankruptcy of individuals, but in this context "corporate insolvency" has to be understood in a much wider sense than normal, for the Act is concerned with the winding up and receivership of all companies, whether "solvent" (meaning financially viable) or not, and also with voluntary arrangements, administration and associated matters. Insolvent partnerships are also dealt with by subordinate legislation made under s.420 of the Act, and limited liability partnerships by the Limited Liability Partnerships Regulations 2001 (SI 2001/1090). The Act applies also, with modifications where necessary, in the insolvency of other bodies such as building societies, friendly societies and industrial and provident societies, either by virtue of the particular legislation governing them or because they are treated as "unregistered companies" under IA 1986 Pt V. The Act applies to England and Wales and to Scotland in relation to corporate insolvency, but only to England and Wales in regard to the bankruptcy of individuals. (Responsibility for Scottish liquidations and receiverships has since been devolved to the Scottish Executive, but other procedures (i.e. administrations and CVAs) remain with the Insolvency Service.) The corresponding bankruptcy provisions for Scotland were revised separately by the Bankruptcy (Scotland) Act 1985. Only a few sections of IA 1986 apply to Northern Ireland. (See the note to s.441.) The corresponding law for that jurisdiction is to be found in the separate legislation which is listed in the note to s.441, below. However the law in Northern Ireland so closely mirrors that of Great Britain that this annotation should be of assistance to practitioners in Northern Ireland when grappling with the interpretation and application of their own insolvency legislative system.

Most Acts of Parliament, or at least the larger ones, are divided into Parts, and the Parts subdivided into Chapters, with yet further subdivisions marked by italic subheadings. The present Act has one further tier in this hierarchy: the Parts are collected into three "Groups of Parts". The "First Group of Parts" comprises "Company Insolvency" and "Companies Winding Up"—once again, we notice the ambivalence in the use of the word "insolvency"—and is broken into Pts I–VII; the Group has its own definition sections in Pt VII. The Second Group deals with "Insolvency of Individuals" and "Bankruptcy" and contains four Parts, continuing in numerical sequence from VIII to XI, again with separate interpretation provisions. The Third Group, which comprises Pts XII–XIX, is concerned with the administration of the Act and miscellaneous matters affecting all types of insolvency.

The Act has been amended in minor respects by later legislation, and more substantially by IA 2000, which came into force on various dates between November 30, 2000 and January 1, 2003, and the Enterprise Act 2002, which became operative as regards corporate insolvency and the abolition of Crown preference on September 15, 2003, and in relation to the bankruptcy of individuals on April 1, 2004. In January, 2010 the Secretary of State for Business, Innovation and Skills made a Legislative Reform Order, the Legislative Reform (Insolvency) (Miscellaneous Provisions) Order 2010 (SI 2010/18, operative from April 6, 2010) which amended the Insolvency Act 1986 in a number of respects in order to facilitate the making of the Insolvency (Amendment) Rules 2010 described below.

The principal amendments made to IA 1986 by this Order are as follows:

- authorising the holding of meetings without physical attendance (ss.246A, 379A);

- authorising the use of websites as a means of communication (ss.246B, 379B);

- clarifying reference to things "in writing" and "post" to remove uncertainty about the use of electronic communication, subject to some exceptions where hard copy continues to be required (s.436B);

- removal of the use of affidavits (in England and Wales);

- removal of the requirement for annual meetings in voluntary liquidations, and their replacement by progress reports (in England and Wales) (ss.92A, 104A);

- removal of the requirement for certain documents to be filed in court in IVAs;

- removal of the requirement for sanction for certain compromises in a winding up (in England and Wales) (Sch.4) and bankruptcy (Sch.6).

Some of these reforms apply to existing insolvencies as well as insolvencies commencing after April 6, 2010, while others are subject to transitional provisions contained in LRO art.12. We have endeavoured to draw attention to this aspect of the particular reforms in the commentary.

Of the subordinate legislation promulgated under IA 1986, the Insolvency Rules 1986 (see pp.664 et seq.) are by far the most significant. These Rules replaced the Winding-up Rules and the former Bankruptcy Rules and, like the Acts themselves, became operative on December 29, 1986. Detailed amendments to IR 1986 were made by I(A)R 1987, which came into force on January 11, 1988, and by various other measures since. These amendments have been incorporated into the text of the principal Rules. More recently, the Insolvency Service has conducted a major revision of the Rules, culminating in the enactment of the Insolvency (Amendment) Rules 2010 (SI 2010/686), which are to come into force on April 6, 2010, as a preparatory step towards the consolidation of all the Rules into one measure, planned to be brought into force on April 6, 2011. Note also the Insolvency (Amendment) (No.2) Rules 2010 (SI 2010/734, also effective April 6, 2010), which make a number of corrections to SI 2010/686. All of these amendments have been incorporated into the text of the principal Rules, which is set out later in this volume with full annotation.

The IA 1985, apart from a few sections which had already become operative, was brought into force immediately before the consolidating legislation, and was then at once repealed by the latter Acts (see SI 1986/1924 (C. 71)). This brief moment of existence was sufficient to activate repeals which swept away many special features of insolvency law that had been familiar for over a century: the doctrine of relation back, acts of bankruptcy, winding up subject to the supervision of the court, and many more. Attention has been drawn to these changes at appropriate points in the discussion which follows.

The IA 1985 and the consolidating Acts introduced a good deal of special terminology. It is not practicable to give a repeated explanation of these terms every time that they occur in the text, and so they have been listed in App.I which refers the reader to the appropriate provision of the Act, where the relevant commentary also appears. In App.II there is a similar list for expressions used in the Insolvency Rules.

The Insolvency Act 1986

(1986 Chapter 45)

ARRANGEMENT OF SECTIONS

The Insolvency Act 1986

(1986 Chapter 45)

An Act to consolidate the enactments relating to company insolvency and winding up (including the winding up of companies that are not insolvent, and of unregistered companies); enactments relating to the insolvency and bankruptcy of individuals; and other enactments bearing on those two subject matters, including the functions and qualification of insolvency practitioners, the public administration of insolvency, the penalisation and redress of malpractice and wrongdoing, and the avoidance of certain transactions at an undervalue.

[25th July 1986]

THE FIRST GROUP OF PARTS: COMPANY INSOLVENCY; COMPANIES WINDING UP

Introductory note to the First Group of Parts
The First Group of Parts deals with insolvency procedures in relation to companies (including the winding up of solvent companies), while the Second Group is concerned with the bankruptcy of individuals. "Company" is normally defined for this purpose by CA 2006 ss.1(1), 1171 (see the note to s.73, below.) Some Parts of the Act (and, in particular, Pt IV, dealing with winding up) are extended so as to apply to bodies and associations other than "companies", including partnerships: see the Introductory note to Part IV preceding s.73, below. However, in the absence of any provision to this effect, the First Group of Parts applies only to companies within the statutory definition. Accordingly, where a society incorporated under the Industrial and Provident Societies Act 1965 is in receivership, the creditors who would be entitled to preferential payment in the case of a company have no priority: *Re Devon & Somerset Farmers Ltd* [1994] Ch. 57; [1993] B.C.C. 410. Exceptionally, the European Regulation on Insolvency Proceedings 2000 may confer jurisdiction under IA 1986 where the body concerned has its centre of main interests within the UK, even though it does not fall within the statutory definition: see the note to art.3 of the Regulation. But note the impact of the Insolvency Act 1986 (Amendment) Regulations 2005 (SI 2005/879) on this issue: see s.1(4) below.

PART I

COMPANY VOLUNTARY ARRANGEMENTS

Introductory note to Part I
Part I of IA 1986, which replaces IA 1985 ss.20–26, introduced an entirely new procedure into UK company law, the "Company Voluntary Arrangement"—a term which is commonly abbreviated to "CVA".

The original CVA regime as contained in Pt I of the Insolvency Act 1986 has been the subject of major statutory elaboration through the mechanism of ss.1, 2 of, and Schs 1, 2 to, the Insolvency Act 2000. The effect of these changes has been to introduce a new optional CVA model with moratorium for small eligible companies. (For further guidance on eligibility see the Insolvency Act 1986 (Amendment) (No.3) Regulations 2002 (SI 2002/1990).) There are also amendments to the general CVA model.

The Cork Committee (*Report*, paras 400–403) considered it a weakness of the former company law that a company, unlike an individual, could not enter into a binding arrangement with its creditors for the composition of its indebtedness by some relatively simple procedure. Unless it could obtain the separate consent of every creditor, the only options previously available to a company were the formal statutory procedures of:

(1) a scheme of liquidation and reconstruction under CA 1985 s.582 (formerly CA 1948 s.287);

(2) a scheme of compromise or arrangement under CA 1985 ss.425–427 (CA 1948 ss.206–208); and

(3) the little-used "binding arrangement" under CA 1985 s.601 (CA 1948 s.306).

Each of these methods was too slow, cumbersome and costly to be at all useful in practice.

The present sections introduce a simpler scheme, more or less along the lines recommended by the Cork Committee. The CVA has proved to be of limited utility in practice, however, for two reasons. First, it cannot be made binding upon a secured or preferential creditor without his consent, and secondly, until the enactment of s.1A there was no provision in the Act for obtaining a moratorium while the proposal for an arrangement is being drawn up and considered (contrast the "interim order" available in the case of an insolvent individual: see ss.252–254).

However, a moratorium could be achieved if a proposal for a voluntary arrangement is combined with an application to the court for the appointment of an administrator under Sch.B1: this is, of course, a more elaborate and costly procedure.

In view of these considerations, it is not surprising that the CVA procedure has been relatively little used (especially when compared with the much larger number of individual voluntary arrangements). In the first few years after the 1986 Act, the average number was under 100 per year, and although the figure has now crept up somewhat, the overall picture has been disappointing. In the light of this experience the Government suggested modifications to the CVA procedure in order to improve its effectiveness (and appeal). In particular it favoured the introduction of an optional moratorium facility for CVAs involving small eligible companies. This reform was enacted by the Insolvency Act 2000 s.1 with detailed provision being made in the accompanying Sch.A1. Unfortunately, there was a delay in bringing this reform into effect; this delay was apparently caused by concerns in the City over the impact of the new CVA moratorium on certain specialised corporate financing schemes. The new model came into force only on January 1, 2003—see the Insolvency Act 2000 (Commencement No.3 and Transitional Provisions) Order 2002 (SI 2002/2711 (C. 83)). Since December 1, 1994, a voluntary arrangement procedure modelled upon the CVA has been available for an insolvent partnership: see the Insolvent Partnerships Order 1994 (SI 1994/2421) art.5 and Sch.1. It is a prerequisite that the partnership be unable to pay its debts. As with a CVA, there is no provision for an interim order during which a stay of proceedings operates, although this can be achieved by applying at the same time for an administration order. Alternatively, if the partners are individuals, they may enter into individual voluntary arrangements, which will have much the same effect.

The CVA procedure has been extended to building societies by s.90A of the Building Societies Act 1986 (inserted by the Building Societies Act 1997 s.39, effective December 1, 1997). A foreign company may be permitted to use a CVA by exploiting the facility of s.426, IA 1986—*Re Television Trade Rentals Ltd* [2002] EWHC 211 (Ch); [2002] B.C.C. 807. NHS Foundation Trusts can take advantage of the CVA procedure (with or without moratorium)—the Independent Regulator of NHS Foundation Trusts is given power by s.53 of the National Health Service Act 2006 to direct foundation trustees to exploit this recovery procedure.

The initiative in setting up a CVA is taken by the directors or, if the company is being wound up or is subject to an administration order, by the liquidator or administrator as the case may be. A "proposal" is formulated for consideration by meetings of the company's members and creditors: if the proposal is accepted at the respective meetings, the scheme becomes operative and binding upon the company and all of its creditors—even those who did not support the proposal. Thereafter, it is administered by a "supervisor" who must be qualified to act as an insolvency practitioner in relation to the company. The arrangement is conducted throughout under the aegis of the court, but the court itself is not involved in a judicial capacity unless there is some difficulty or disagreement.

It is not a prerequisite for the application of this Part of the Act that the company should be "insolvent" or "unable to pay its debts" within the statutory definitions of those terms.

A related reform effected by IA 1985 (see Sch.10 Pt II) was the repeal of CA 1985 s.615(2), a provision of ancient origin which stated that any general assignment by a company of its property for the benefit of its creditors was "void to all intents".

The provision which prohibits a company from giving financial assistance in the acquisition of its own shares (CA 1985 s.151 [CA 2006 s.678]) does not apply to anything done under a voluntary arrangement: see CA 1985 s.153(3)(g) (as amended) [CA 2006 s.681(2)(g)]. The abolition of the financial assistance bar for private companies will reduce the significance of this point.

CVAs fall within the ambit of the EC Regulation on Insolvency Proceedings (1346/2000) and the new Cross-Border Insolvency Regulations (SI 2006/1030).

Although the EC Regulation on Insolvency Proceedings (1346/2000) does apply to CVA cases it was held by Lloyd L.J. (sitting as a Judge of the Chancery Division) in *Oakley v Ultra Vehicle Design Ltd* [2005] EWHC 872 (Ch); [2006] B.C.C. 115 that it did not apply if the CVA had been initiated prior to the coming into effect of the EC Regulation.

A CVA is not an "agreement" for the purposes of s.203 of the Employment Rights Act 1996—*Re Britannia Heat Transfer Ltd* [2007] B.P.I.R. 1038. This is because it was a statutory construct established under a specified procedure. This interpretation by H.H.J. Norris Q.C. has served to protect CVAs from being avoided under s.203, thereby protecting their value as a reorganisation tool for distressed businesses.

The fact that the successful party under an arbitration award is undergoing a CVA does not deny that party the possibility of enforcing that award by summary judgment—see *Mead General Building Ltd v Dartmoor Properties Ltd* [2009] B.P.I.R. 516 (Coulson J.).

On the interpretation of CVA terms see *Appleyard Ltd v Ritecrown Ltd* [2009] B.P.I.R. 235 and *Tucker and Spratt v Gold Fields Mining LLC* [2009] EWCA Civ 173; [2009] B.P.I.R. 704. The latter case is an important precedent dealing with the lodging of late claims.

For the corresponding provisions relating to voluntary arrangements for insolvent individuals, see ss.252–263. There is a close parallel between the two sets of provisions, and so cases decided under the individual voluntary arrangement sections may well be relevant in CVA proceedings, and vice versa.

The Act contemplates that a system will be set up by subordinate legislation for the registration of voluntary arrangements in a register open to public inspection: see Sch.8 para.6. The rules make provision for registration with the registrar of companies: IR 1986 rr.1.24(5), 1.29(3).

For the rules relating to CVAs, see IR 1986 Pt 1.

At present there are reform proposals undergoing a public consultation process. This consultation document, a copy of which is available on the Insolvency Service website, was launched by the Insolvency Service in June 2009. Essentially it is opening up for discussion a number ideas designed to reinvigorate corporate rescue. A number of proposals are relevant to the CVA models. These include: extending the Sch.A1 procedure to larger and medium-sized companies; introducing a court-initiated moratorium for CVAs; and improving the position with regard to securing rescue finance. For a summary of these proposals see [2009] 255 Sweet & Maxwell's Company Law Newsletter 1.

The proposal

1 Those who may propose an arrangement

1(1) **[Directors]** The directors of a company (other than one which is in administration or being wound up) may make a proposal under this Part to the company and to its creditors for a composition in satisfaction of its debts or a scheme of arrangement of its affairs (from here on referred to, in either case, as a "voluntary arrangement").

1(2) **[Interpretation]** A proposal under this part is one which provides for some person ("the nominee") to act in relation to the voluntary arrangement either as trustee or otherwise for the purpose of supervising its implementation; and the nominee must be a person who is qualified to act as an insolvency practitioner or authorised to act as nominee, in relation to the voluntary arrangement.

1(3) **[Administrator, liquidator]** Such a proposal may also be made–

(a) where the company is in administration, by the administrator, and

(b) where the company is being wound up, by the liquidator.

1(4) **["Company" in Pt 1]** In this Part "company" means–

(a) a company registered under the Companies Act 2006 in England and Wales or Scotland,

(b) a company incorporated in an EEA State other than the United Kingdom; or

(c) a company not incorporated in an EEA State but having its centre of main interests in a member State other than Denmark.

1(5) **[Presumption of COMI]** In subsection (4), in relation to a company, "centre of main interests" has the same meaning as in the EC Regulation and, in the absence of proof to the contrary, is presumed to be the place of its registered office (within the meaning of that Regulation).

1(6) **[Northern Ireland]** If a company incorporated outside the United Kingdom has a principal place of business in Northern Ireland, no proposal under this Part shall be made in relation to it unless it also has a principal place of business in England and Wales or Scotland (or both in England and Wales or Scotland).

GENERAL NOTE

In any case where the company is not subject to an administration order or being wound up, the initiative in proposing a voluntary arrangement is taken by the directors, and the more elaborate procedure laid down by s.2 applies. An insolvency practitioner who is "qualified" to act in relation to the company must be brought in as "nominee" to report on the directors' proposals and to organise the meetings, etc. by which the scheme is to be implemented. (In practice, the directors will in most cases have consulted the proposed nominee in advance and invoked his help in drawing up the proposal.) Where, however, there is an administrator or liquidator already in office, he will normally himself act as the nominee and may then proceed directly to summon meetings of the company and its creditors under s.3.

Neither creditors nor members of a company have standing to propose a voluntary arrangement. Section 1(2) was modified by s.2 and Sch.2 to IA 2000 to recognise the fact that, under IA 2000, turnaround specialists may act as nominees or supervisors. The language of ss.1(1) and 1(3) was recast by s.248 of and Sch.17 to EA 2002 to reflect the fact that it is no longer strictly accurate to refer to administration *orders*.

S.1(1)

The directors have power to act only when the company is not in liquidation or subject to administration.

There is no statutory definition of "creditor" for the purposes of this Part of the Act. It would be normal to give the word its dictionary meaning, "one to whom a debt is owing"—a phrase which would exclude a prospective or contingent creditor and a person whose claim was for unliquidated damages (see Roy Goode, *Principles of Corporate Insolvency Law*, 3rd edn (2005), at 2.13). This view is reinforced by the fact that the concepts of "debt" and "provable debt" are extended to include these wider categories of claim by IR 1986 rr.13.12, 12.3; but this provision is confined to the winding up of companies. It is also noteworthy that although contingent and prospective creditors are expressly given the same rights as creditors elsewhere in the Act (see, e.g. ss.9, 124 (standing to present petition for administration or winding-up order)), there is no similar provision here in Pt I. It would therefore be reasonable to assume that the term "creditor" does not have the wider meaning in this section. However, r.1.17(3) indicates the contrary by referring (in the context of voluntary arrangements) to "a debt for an unliquidated amount" and a "debt whose value is not ascertained". Fortunately, any doubts that there might have been on this question have now been resolved. In *Doorbar v Alltime Securities Ltd* [1996] 1 W.L.R. 456; [1995] B.C.C. 1,149 the Court of Appeal (affirming Knox J. [1994] B.C.C. 994) held that rent under a lease becoming due in the future was capable of being included in an individual voluntary arrangement under s.258 of the Act, and this ruling has since been applied in the context of a CVA in *Re Cancol Ltd* [1996] 1 All E.R. 37; [1995] B.C.C. 1,133; and *Re Sweatfield Ltd* [1997] B.C.C. 744; and in *Beverley Group plc v McClue* [1995] B.C.C. 751 a person with a claim for an unliquidated amount was held entitled to vote as a creditor. Of course, it is possible that the terms of a scheme of voluntary arrangement should be so drawn up as to exclude future or contingent creditors from its operation. This was the case in *Burford Midland Properties Ltd v Marley Extrusions Ltd* [1994] B.C.C. 604 (a case which contains a useful discussion of the terms "future", "contingent" and "prospective" liabilities).

In *Re FMS Financial Management Services Ltd* (1989) 5 B.C.C. 191, former clients of the company who appeared to have good claims against it for damages for misrepresentation were not treated as creditors for the purposes of a CVA; but an order was made by the court, after the scheme had been approved, directing that they should be admitted to prove on the same terms as the company's creditors.

The terms "composition" and "scheme of arrangement" are not synonymous. The latter involves something less than the release or discharge of a creditor's debts—e.g. a moratorium. Thus, in *IRC v Adam & Partners Ltd* [2000] B.P.I.R. 986 a proposed moratorium which offered nothing to creditors was not sufficient to constitute a "composition" but could amount to a "scheme of arrangement". See also the discussion in *March Estates plc v Gunmark Ltd* [1996] 2 B.C.L.C. 1.

S.1(2)

The Act obviously contemplates that in most cases the "nominee" himself will in due course administer the scheme (e.g. by acting as a trustee for the benefit of the company's creditors), although it is possible in certain circumstances for someone other than the original nominee to be appointed instead (see ss.2(4), 4(2)). When it is finally settled who it is that is to have charge of the scheme, the Act (by s.7(2)) designates him "the supervisor". This tends to obscure the fact that in the great majority of situations "the supervisor" will be the same person as "the nominee" and, where the company is the subject of an administration order or is being wound up, also the same person as the administrator or liquidator. By whatever means he is chosen, however, the "supervisor" must be a person who is qualified to act as an insolvency practitioner in relation to the company; and in this way the legislation ensures that no voluntary scheme can be implemented without independent professional approval and supervision.

The criteria by which a person is deemed to be "qualified" to act as an insolvency practitioner "in relation to" a particular company are laid down in ss.388–398 and 419, below.

The section provides for the nominee or supervisor to act "as trustee or otherwise". In *Re Leisure Study Group Ltd* [1994] 2 B.C.L.C. 65, Harman J. held that funds in the hands of a supervisor were held on trust for the company's unsecured creditors, and had been put out of reach of the security conferred by a floating charge; see the note on s.7(4).

Nothing in this Part of the Act gives the supervisor, as such, power to perform any act in the name of the company or makes him an officer of the company: whatever authority he has must come from the terms of the voluntary arrangement itself, or from the fact that he is also the company's administrator or liquidator. It has been assumed by the draftsman that a decision of the company in general meeting under s.4(1) will be competent, as a matter of company law, to give wide powers of management to a supervisor regardless of the terms of the company's articles. We must probably infer from the general tenor of the Act that the terms of a voluntary arrangement are capable of overriding the articles if necessary. The position would have been less uncertain if the supervisor had been given certain statutory powers and a more clearly defined authority.

The nominee (and, later, the supervisor) is referred to throughout in the singular. There is nothing to prevent the appointment of joint nominees or supervisors, however: see the note to s.7(6) below.

S.1(3)

In the two situations referred to in this subsection, the proposal not only may but (by virtue of the bracketed words in s.1(1)) must be made by the administrator or liquidator. In this case, the administrator or liquidator may appoint himself to be the nominee and proceed immediately to summon meetings under s.3. If for any reason he appoints someone else, the more elaborate procedure under s.2 must be followed. A bank liquidator may propose a CVA—see s.113 of the Banking Act 2009.

For the rules which apply when the application is made under this subsection, see IR 1986 rr.1.10 et seq.

S.1(4)–(6)

Subsection (4) was originally inserted by the Insolvency Act 1986 (Amendment) (No.2) Regulations 2002 (SI 2002/1240) as part of the implementation strategy for the EC Regulation on Insolvency Proceedings (1346/2000). However, because of the way the 2002 Regulations had been drafted an unintentional consequence arose in that in *Re Salvage Association* [2003] EWHC 1028 (Ch); [2003] B.C.C. 504 Blackburne J. held that CVAs were now available for corporate bodies which did not qualify as "companies" within the meaning of the Companies Act 1985. Apparently this caused concerns in the City of London about the potential impact on niche financing transactions— see G. Moss, [2005] 18 Insolv. Int. 92. Accordingly, subs.(4) was replaced and new subs.(5) inserted by the Insolvency Act 1986 (Amendment) Regulations 2005 (SI 2005/879) to neutralise this unintended consequence whilst allowing companies incorporated in EEA states and those having a centre of main interests in Member States (except Denmark) to access the CVA procedure. Subsection (6) deals with non-UK companies having a principal place of business in Northern Ireland. Note the amendment to subs.(4)(a) introduced by the Companies Act 2006 (Consequential Amendments, Transitional Provisions and Savings) Order 2009 (SI 2009/1941) with effect from October 1, 2009. This clarifies the meaning of the word "company" in the light of the Companies Act 2006.

1A Moratorium

1A(1) **[Directors]** Where the directors of an eligible company intend to make a proposal for a voluntary arrangement, they may take steps to obtain a moratorium for the company.

1A(2) **[Applicability of Sch.A1]** The provisions of Schedule A1 to this Act have effect with respect to–

(a) companies eligible for a moratorium under this section,

(b) the procedure for obtaining such a moratorium,

(c) the effects of such a moratorium, and

(d) the procedure applicable (in place of sections 2 to 6 and 7) in relation to the approval and implementation of a voluntary arrangement where such a moratorium is or has been in force.

GENERAL NOTE

This introduces the new Sch.A1 which offers a moratorium facility for the CVA in circumstances where the company is classed as "small" and "eligible". The criteria governing eligibility were added to by Insolvency (Amendment) Regulations 2002 (SI 2002/1990—inserting additional paras 4A–4K into Sch.A1). See further the discussion under Sch.A1. Note in particular that a company cannot be regarded as eligible if it has incurred a liability of £10 million or more under an agreement which is part of a capital market arrangement (Sch.A1 para.4C). The new CVA model came into operation on January 1, 2003—see Insolvency Act 2000 (Commencement No.3) and Transitional Provisions Order 2002 (SI 2002/2711).

Full discussion of this CVA variant is to be found at Sch.A1. Early indications suggest that it is not being used extensively and, with the advent of the out of court administration entry model, that pattern is likely to persist.

2 Procedure where nominee is not the liquidator or administrator

2(1) [Application] This section applies where the nominee under section 1 is not the liquidator or administrator of the company and the directors do not propose to take steps to obtain a moratorium under s.1A for the company.

2(2) [Report to court] The nominee shall, within 28 days (or such longer period as the court may allow) after he is given notice of the proposal for a voluntary arrangement, submit a report to the court stating–

    (a) whether, in his opinion, the proposed voluntary arrangement has a reasonable prospect of being approved and implemented,

    (aa) whether, in his opinion, meetings of the company and of its creditors should be summoned to consider the proposal, and

    (b) if in his opinion such meetings should be summoned, the date on which, and time and place at which, he proposes the meetings should be held.

2(3) [Information to nominee] For the purposes of enabling the nominee to prepare his report, the person intending to make the proposal shall submit to the nominee–

    (a) a document setting out the terms of the proposed voluntary arrangement, and

    (b) a statement of the company's affairs containing–

        (i) such particulars of its creditors and of its debts and other liabilities and of its assets as may be prescribed, and

        (ii) such other information as may be prescribed.

2(4) [Replacement of nominee by court] The court may–

    (a) on an application made by the person intending to make the proposal, in a case where the nominee has failed to submit the report required by this section or has died, or

    (b) on an application made by that person or the nominee, in a case where it is impracticable or inappropriate for the nominee to continue to act as such,

direct that the nominee be replaced as such by another person qualified to act as an insolvency practitioner, or authorised to act as nominee, in relation to the voluntary arrangement.

GENERAL NOTE

The wording of s.2(1) and (2) was modified by IA 2000 s.2 and Sch.2. Section 2(4) was also substituted by those provisions.

S.2(1)

Section 2 will necessarily apply where the proposal is made by the directors under s.1(1); and it will also apply when an administrator or liquidator designates someone other than himself as nominee.

S.2(2)

No step towards implementing the proposal can be taken under this section until a report has first been submitted by the nominee to the court. The court's role is, however, primarily an administrative one, and it will not be involved judicially except when there is some dispute or difficulty. The procedure which the section envisages is as follows:

    (1) The directors decide to propose an arrangement, and themselves find an insolvency practitioner who is qualified to act as nominee and who is willing, at least in principle, to do so (see IR 1986 r.1.3(2)(p)). As has been mentioned above, it is likely in most cases that the directors will seek the intended nominee's professional assistance in preparing the proposal in advance. The routine contemplated by the Act will then be largely a formality.

    (2) The directors give notice of the proposal for a voluntary arrangement to the nominee, and submit to him a document setting out the terms of the proposed arrangement and a statement of the company's affairs

(s.2(3)(a), (b)). (It is not clear from the section itself whether the "notice" referred to in s.2(2) is constituted by the formal submission of the document and statement of affairs specified in s.2(3) or is some separate and earlier notification. The former interpretation is plainly the one intended, since the 28-day period referred to in s.2(2) only starts to run from the receipt of the document: see IR 1986 r.1.4(3).) The court may permit the statement of affairs to be censored—see IR r.1.56.

(3)　The nominee has 28 days (or longer, if the court allows) to prepare and submit a report to the court. This will ensure that a scheme always has the benefit of a preliminary opinion from a professional insolvency practitioner.

(4)　If the nominee forms the view that the proposed scheme should go ahead, he reports to the court his opinion that meetings of the company and its creditors should be summoned, and he must himself fix their date, time and place. (On the formalities for summoning meetings, see the comment to s.3(1) and (2), below.)

(5)　Under s.3(1), it will normally then be the nominee's role to summon the meetings.

(6)　If the nominee considers that the proposed scheme should not be taken further, s.2(2) appears to suggest that he should submit a negative report to the court, and this is confirmed by IR 1986 r.1.7(2). However, nothing is made to depend on the filing of such a report, and the company is not barred from seeking a second opinion from another nominee.

(7)　Where the initiative is not taken by the directors but by an administrator or liquidator who elects not to nominate himself, the responsibility for selecting the intended nominee and preparing the documentation specified in s.2(3) falls upon that person and not on the directors.

Necessarily, the nominee is heavily reliant on the information provided by the debtor company and there is therefore a consequential need for complete candour on the part of the latter. Where the nominee has doubts about the accuracy and reliability of this information, he has a responsibility to satisfy himself, within the resources available to him, by further inquiries. See the position discussed (in the context of an individual voluntary arrangement) in *Re a Debtor (No.140 IO of 1995)* [1996] 2 B.C.L.C. 429.

S.2(3)
This subsection gives details of the two documents on which the nominee is to base his report to the court.

It is made clear by the rules (IR 1986 r.1.4(3)) (as noted above (s.2(2)) that a nominee is not to be considered as having been "given notice" of a proposal until he has received the document referred to in para.(a) of this subsection. The "statement of the company's affairs" must be delivered to him at the same time: IR 1986 r.1.5(1).

The "statement of the company's affairs" referred to is similar to the statement which must be submitted to an administrator (s.22), an administrative receiver (ss.47, 66) and a liquidator (ss.99, 131). On this topic, see the note to s.131.

S.2(4)
If, after the expiration of the 28 days or longer period provided for by s.2(2), the nominee has not submitted a report either in favour of or against proceeding with the proposal, this subsection allows the directors (or the administrator or liquidator, where appropriate) to invoke the court's help and have an alternative nominee appointed. However, there appears to be no reason why an intended proposal should not be aborted without the court's involvement, for at this stage no creditor will have been affected by the scheme or even have been made aware of it, and the court itself will not yet be in the picture. This course should certainly be permissible if the first intended nominee consents; if he does not, however, a professional code of conduct might possibly inhibit a colleague from replacing him against his wishes, and in that case the court's aid would be necessary.

For details of the procedure prescribed for the purpose of this section, see IR 1986 rr.1.3–1.9.

3　Summoning of meetings

3(1)　[Meetings in accordance with report] Where the nominee under section 1 is not the liquidator or administrator, and it has been reported to the court that such meetings as are mentioned in section 2(2) should be summoned, the person making the report shall (unless the court otherwise directs) summon those meetings for the time, date and place proposed in the report.

3(2)　[Where nominee liquidator or administrator] Where the nominee is the liquidator or administrator, he shall summon meetings of the company and of its creditors to consider the proposal for such a time, date and place as he thinks fit.

3(3) **[Persons summoned]** The persons to be summoned to a creditors' meeting under this section are every creditor of the company of whose claim and address the person summoning the meeting is aware.

GENERAL NOTE

A voluntary arrangement comes into effect under s.5 when the proposal has been approved by both a meeting of the company and a meeting of its creditors (unless s.4A(2)(b) applies).

Both s.2(2)(b) and s.3(2) appear to leave it to the nominee's discretion to fix such matters as the time and date of the meetings, the length of notice which is to be given and the order in which the two meetings are to be held. However such discretion as is given to the nominee by ss.2(2)(b) and 3(2) is exercisable only within the constraints imposed by the rules: see IR 1986 rr.1.9, 1.13, 1.21.

S.3(1)

Where the nominee is not the liquidator or administrator, no step can be taken to summon meetings until he has made a favourable report to the court under s.2(2). Once he has done so, it becomes his duty to summon the meetings (without any court order or other formality) in accordance with his own proposals.

No guidance is given by the section as to the basis on which the court might "otherwise direct", or as to who (apart from the nominee himself) might have standing to apply for such a direction.

S.3(2)

Where the nominee is the liquidator or administrator, the procedure outlined in s.2 is bypassed. He himself proceeds straight to the summoning of the meetings, and at this stage nothing is notified or reported to the court. There appears to be no power under this subsection for the court to "direct otherwise".

A nominee who is himself the liquidator or administrator will have received, or be entitled to receive, a "statement of affairs" under ss.22, 99 or 131. This document, or a summary of it, must be sent, with a list of the company's creditors and the amounts of their debts, with the notices summoning the meetings: see IR 1986 r.1.11(2).

For the appropriate rules, see IR 1986 rr.1.10, 1.11.

S.3(3)

A nominee who has prepared a report under s.2(2) will have been given particulars of the company's creditors under s.2(3)(b). A liquidator or administrator who has appointed himself as nominee will receive this information with the "statement of affairs". The question of who might be a "creditor" and hence a party to a CVA was considered by David Richards J. in one instalment of the *Re T & N Ltd* saga (see *Re T & N Ltd* [2005] EWHC 2870 (Ch); [2006] B.P.I.R. 532). The judge held that individuals who may have suffered latent injury through exposure to asbestos could be treated as creditors for CVA purposes. Such future potential tort claimants as the law then stood would not be regarded as creditors enjoying provable debts on liquidation (see IR 1986 rr.12.3 and 13.12). This significant judgment paved the way for a subsequent relaxation of the aforementioned Insolvency Rules (see annotations thereto).

Consideration and implementation of proposal

4 Decisions of meetings

4(1) **[Decision]** The meetings summoned under section 3 shall decide whether to approve the proposed voluntary arrangement (with or without modifications).

4(2) **[Modifications]** The modifications may include one conferring the functions proposed to be conferred on the nominee on another person qualified to act as an insolvency practitioner or authorised to act as nominee, in relation to the voluntary arrangement.

But they shall not include any modification by virtue of which the proposal ceases to be a proposal such as is mentioned in section 1.

4(3) **[Limitation on approval]** A meeting so summoned shall not approve any proposal or modification which affects the right of a secured creditor of the company to enforce his security, except with the concurrence of the creditor concerned.

4(4) **[Further limitation]** Subject as follows, a meeting so summoned shall not approve any proposal or modification under which–

(a) any preferential debt of the company is to be paid otherwise than in priority to such of its debts as are not preferential debts, or

(b) a preferential creditor of the company is to be paid an amount in respect of a preferential debt that bears to that debt a smaller proportion than is borne to another preferential debt by the amount that is to be paid in respect of that other debt.

However, the meeting may approve such a proposal or modification with the concurrence of the preferential creditor concerned.

4(5) **[Meeting in accordance with rules]** Subject as above, each of the meetings shall be conducted in accordance with the rules.

4(6) **[Report to court, notice]** After the conclusion of either meeting in accordance with the rules, the chairman of the meeting shall report the result of the meeting to the court, and, immediately after reporting to the court, shall give notice of the result of the meeting to such persons as may be prescribed.

4(7) **[Interpretation]** References in this section to preferential debts and preferential creditors are to be read in accordance with section 386 in Part XII of this Act.

GENERAL NOTE

The terms of the scheme, when approved by the meetings, bind every member and creditor (see s.5(2)).

No provision appears to be made for any subsequent modification of the scheme unless that modification is put forward by the person who made the original proposal (see s.6(4)). The only opportunity, therefore, for any of the company's members or creditors to seek to have the proposal modified will be at the meetings themselves.

S.4(1)

The scheme can only go ahead in a modified form if both of the meetings approve the same modifications (but see the qualification in s.4A).

S.4(2)

The modifications may include the substitution of a different nominee to administer the scheme; but no modification may take the proceedings outside the scope of s.1 altogether (i.e. amount to a wholly different course of action, such as putting the company into liquidation). Note that s.4(2) was modified by IA 2000 s.2 and Sch.2 to reflect the fact that a wider group of professionals can now act as nominees/supervisors.

S.4(3)

No voluntary arrangement can affect the rights of a secured creditor without his consent. In *March Estates plc v Gunmark Ltd* [1996] 2 B.C.L.C. 1 Lightman J. held that a landlord's right of forfeiture was to be treated as a security for this purpose, but in the latter case of *Razzaq v Pala* [1998] B.C.C. 66 at 71 the same judge said that this ruling had been given without full argument and that, on reconsideration, he should have held otherwise. In *Thomas v Ken Thomas Ltd* [2006] EWCA Civ 1504; [2007] B.P.I.R. 959 the Court of Appeal held that, on the construction of the particular CVA before it, the landlord's right to forfeit had indeed been surrendered in exchange for rights under the CVA. Neuberger L.J., who read the main judgment, disagreed both with Hoffmann J. in *Re Naeem* [1990] 1 W.L.R. 48; and Lightman J. in *March Estates v Gunmark plc* [1996] 2 B.C.L.C. 1 on this particular point. This disagreement was not merely based upon the facts of this particular CVA, but was more general in nature. Reference also was made to the importance of the rescue culture which is prioritised over the rights of individual creditors including landlords. See also *Re The Cotswold Co Ltd* [2009] 2 B.C.L.C. 371.

S.4(4)

The rights of preferential creditors (as defined in s.4(7)) are similarly protected, as regards both their priority vis-à-vis all other debts and their right to rank equally with each other. There is no provision which obliges the preferential creditors to accept a decision made by a majority of them, even if it is passed at a separate class meeting (contrast CA 1985 s.425 [CA 2006 s.895]).

Apart from this and the preceding subsection, there is nothing in the Act which restricts the arrangements which a proposal may make, or requires creditors to be given equal treatment. It is thus permissible, e.g. for small creditors to be given more favourable treatment than larger ones.

The meaning of s.4(4)(a) was considered by the Court of Appeal in *IRC v Wimbledon FC* [2004] EWCA Civ 655; [2004] B.C.C. 638. Here it was held that a restructuring scheme designed to save a football club which involved the introduction of third party funds to repay certain creditors ("the football creditors") in full where other preferential creditors merely received a dividend did not contravene this prohibition in s.4(4)(a) because it only applied to restrict the use of the company's assets for repayment purposes under the proposed arrangement and did not encompass use of third party assets outside the arrangement strictly speaking. Having made that distinction, the Court of Appeal added that had there been a breach of s.4 the court would have had no option but to strike down the arrangement.

S.4(5)

Although this subsection refers in terms only to the conduct of the meetings (and not, e.g. to their summoning) it is plain that the rules apply to all aspects of such meetings: see the note to s.3 above.

For the appropriate rules, see IR 1986 rr.1.13 et seq.

S.4(6)

The chairman of the meetings will be appointed or selected in accordance with the rules (see IR 1986 r.1.14). The rules contemplate that the same person will be chairman of both meetings. It is perhaps odd that it is the chairman, rather than the nominee, who is required to report to the court, but the report must be filed in court very quickly (within four days: see IR 1986 r.124(3)), and difficulties could arise, if, e.g. the nominee was abroad. The subsection implies that separate reports of the result of each meeting are to be prepared, but the rules are less clear: see IR 1986 r.1.24 and Form 1.1. IR 1986 r.1.24(5) provides that if the voluntary arrangement is approved by the meetings, the supervisor must send a copy of the chairman's report to the registrar of companies.

The making of the chairman's report to the court and the giving of the prescribed notices have no direct legal consequences (although time is made to run for various purposes, e.g. the stay of a winding-up order, from the date that the report is made to the court). The voluntary arrangement itself takes effect as a result of the meetings alone, and the court plays no active part in the proceedings at any stage.

S.4(7)

"Preferential debts" and "preferential creditors" are defined for the purpose of this Part of the Act by s.386 and Sch.6, below. The list of preferential creditors is settled by reference to a "relevant date", which determines both the existence and the amount of a preferential debt. To ascertain the "relevant date" for the purpose of the present section, see s.387(3A).

The section makes no reference to the possibility that a voluntary arrangement and a receivership might co-exist. In such a case, there would also be a list of preferential creditors who were entitled to rank in priority to the charge-holder in the receivership. There would then be two lists of preferential debts defined by reference to different "relevant dates"; but those relating to the receivership would have no significance for the purposes of this Part of the Act.

4A   Approval of arrangement

4A(1)   [Application] This section applies to a decision, under section 4, with respect to the approval of a proposed voluntary arrangement.

4A(2)   [Decision to be in accordance with rules] The decision has effect if, in accordance with the rules–

(a)   it has been taken by both meetings summoned under section 3, or

(b)   (subject to any order made under subsection (4)) it has been taken by the creditors' meeting summoned under that section.

4A(3)   [Application to court] If the decision taken by the creditors' meeting differs from that taken by the company meeting, a member of the company may apply to the court.

4A(4)   [Application under s.4A(3)] An application under subsection (3) shall not be made after the end of the period of 28 days beginning with–

(a)   the day on which the decision was taken by the creditors' meeting, or

(b)   where the decision of the company meeting was taken on a later day, that day.

4A(5)   [Regulated companies] Where a member of a regulated company, within the meaning given by paragraph 44 of Schedule A1, applies to the court under subsection (3), the Financial Services Authority is entitled to be heard on the application.

4A(6)   **[Court powers]** On an application under subsection (3), the court may–

    (a)   order the decision of the company meeting to have effect instead of the decision of the creditors' meeting, or

    (b)   make such other order as it thinks fit.

GENERAL NOTE

This new section was introduced by s.2 of, and Sch.2 to, the Insolvency Act 2000 with effect from January 1, 2003. It seeks to provide more detailed guidance on the effect of a CVA being approved.

S.4A(1)
This identifies the applicability of s.4A.

S.4A(2), (3), (4), (6)
The main point to grasp from these subsections is that, if there is a mismatch between the decisions taken at the creditors' and members' meetings, the former decision will prevail. In such circumstances a member can apply to the court within 28 days to challenge this effect. On such an application the court enjoys wide powers under subs.(6).

S.4A(5)
This provision is not of general application.

5   Effect of approval

5(1)   **[Operation]** This section applies where a decision approving a voluntary arrangement has effect under section 4A.

5(2)   **[Effect of composition or scheme]** The voluntary arrangement–

    (a)   takes effect as if made by the company at the creditors' meeting, and

    (b)   binds every person who in accordance with the rules–

        (i)   was entitled to vote at that meeting (whether or not he was present or represented at it), or

        (ii)   would have been so entitled if he had had notice of it,

    as if he were a party to the voluntary arrangement.

5(2A)   **[Amounts payable upon cessation]** If–

    (a)   when the arrangement ceases to have effect any amount payable under the arrangement to a person bound by virtue of subsection (2)(b)(ii) has not been paid, and

    (b)   the arrangement did not come to an end prematurely,

the company shall at that time become liable to pay to that person the amount payable under the arrangement.

5(3)   **[Court powers]** Subject as follows, if the company is being wound up or is in administration, the court may do one or both of the following, namely–

    (a)   by order stay or sist all proceedings in the winding up or provide for the appointment of the administrator to cease to have effect;

    (b)   give such directions with respect to the conduct of the winding up or the administration as it thinks appropriate for facilitating the implementation of the voluntary arrangement.

5(4)   **[Limit on s.5(3)(a)]** The court shall not make an order under subsection (3)(a)–

    (a)   at any time before the end of the period of 28 days beginning with the first day on which each of the reports required by section 4(6) has been made to the court, or

    (b)   at any time when an application under the next section or an appeal in respect of such an application is pending, or at any time in the period within which such an appeal may be brought.

GENERAL NOTE

The former regime under which both meetings had to approve the proposal has been mitigated by s.4A(2). Section 5(2), however, quite clearly makes the time of the creditors' meeting the critical time for the scheme to take effect, and not that of the later of the two meetings. The rules in fact require both meetings to be held on the same day and in the same place, with the creditors' meeting fixed for an earlier time: see IR 1986 r.1.13(3). Alternatively, they may be held together (r.1.21(1)).

It appears that the scheme takes effect at once and continues to be effective even though a challenge is mounted under s.6; but this is subject to any directions which may be given by the court under s.6(6).

Although the effect of a CVA is to establish a statutory "contract" between the company and its creditors it has been held by H.H.J. Norris Q.C. in *Re Britannia Heat Transfer Ltd* [2007] B.C.C. 470 that it does not constitute an "agreement" for the purposes of s.203 of the Employment Rights Act 1996.

On the pragmatic correct approach towards the construction of the terms of a CVA see *Simpson v Bowker* [2007] EWCA Civ 772.

S.5(2)

The word "approved" was deleted by Sch.5 to IA 2000 by authority of s.15(1). For consideration of the former wording of s.5(2) see *Wood v Heart Hospital* [2009] B.P.I.R. 1538.

For the rules relating to the right to vote and the requisite majorities at the meeting of creditors and members, see IR 1986 rr.1.17–1.20.

This subsection makes the scheme binding on all the company's creditors entitled to vote, including absentees and dissentients.

"Notice" in the context of s.5(2)(b) was given a broad interpretation in *Beverley Group plc v McClue* [1995] B.C.C. 751: a formal notice which had been sent had not been received by the creditor, but he had learned of the creditors' meeting indirectly and had also attended the members' meeting.

A voluntary arrangement does not bind a person who was not entitled to vote at the creditors' meeting, and such a person cannot take advantage of the arrangement: *R A Securities Ltd v Mercantile Credit Co Ltd* [1994] B.C.C. 598. However where a creditor who was entitled to vote assigns the benefit of his contract with the company, the assignee takes that benefit as modified by the arrangement; and where land is leased to the debtor company and the reversion is assigned, the assignee is bound by the arrangement as a matter of property law: *Burford Midland Properties Ltd v Marley Extrusions Ltd* [1994] B.C.C. 604. The position of a landlord on a CVA was further considered in *Re The Cotswold Co Ltd* [2009] 2 B.C.L.C. 371. Claims not brought within the arrangement can still be pursued by a participating creditor—*Alman v Approach Housing Ltd* [2001] B.P.I.R. 203.

On the position of creditors whose claims are future or contingent or for an unliquidated amount, see the note to IR 1986 r.1.17(3). See also note to s.3(3) on future tort claimants.

The release of the debtor company from liability under a voluntary arrangement does not also release a solvent co-debtor who is not a party to the arrangement: *March Estates plc v Gunmark Ltd* [1996] 2 B.C.L.C. 1; *Johnson v Davies* [1998] 2 B.C.L.C. 252, although in the latter case the Court of Appeal stated that in principle there is no reason why a term in an agreement could not have the effect of releasing a co-debtor depending on the construction of the agreement, the surrounding circumstances and any terms that could be implied.

Note that the approval of a scheme brings into operation the provisions of s.233, which prevent the suppliers of gas, electricity, etc. from imposing certain terms as to payment as a condition of making a supply available: see s.233(1)(c).

S.5(2)(b)

This was substituted by s.2 of and Sch.2 to IA 2000. It binds in unknown creditors.

S.5(2A)

This was inserted by s.2 of and Sch.2 to IA 2000.

S.5(3), (4)

The word "approved" was removed from s.5(3)(b) by Sch.5 to IA 2000 on the authority of s.15(1). The phraseology used here was modified by s.248 of and Sch.17 to EA 2002 to cater for the change in nature of the administration regime.

If the company is being wound up or is in administration, the court is empowered to stay (or in Scotland, sist) the winding-up order or to terminate the administration, or to give directions short of taking either of these steps which will facilitate the implementation of the scheme; but it may not make an order under s.5(3)(a) until 28 days after the later of the chairman's reports has been made to the court under s.4(6), nor while a hearing or an appeal from a ruling under s.6 is pending. For the interaction of s.5(3) with s.147 see *McGruther v James Scott Ltd* [2004] S.C. 514.

6   Challenge of decisions

6(1)   [Application to court] Subject to this section, an application to the court may be made, by any of the persons specified below, on one or both of the following grounds, namely–

(a)   that a voluntary arrangement which has effect under section 4A unfairly prejudices the interests of a creditor, member or contributory of the company;

(b)   that there has been some material irregularity at or in relation to either of the meetings.

6(2)   [Applicants] The persons who may apply under this section are–

(a)   a person entitled, in accordance with the rules, to vote at either of the meetings;

(aa) a person who would have been entitled, in accordance with the rules, to vote at the creditors' meeting if he had had notice of it;

(b)   the nominee or any person who has replaced him under section 2(4) or 4(2); and

(c)   if the company is being wound up or is in administration, the liquidator or administrator.

6(3)   [Time for application] An application under this section shall not be made–

(a)   after the end of the period of 28 days beginning with the first day on which each of the reports required by section 4(6) has been made to the court; or

(b)   in the case of a person who was not given notice of the creditors' meeting, after the end of the period of 28 days beginning with the day on which he became aware that the meeting had taken place,

but (subject to that) an application made by a person within subsection (2)(aa) on the ground that the voluntary arrangement prejudices his interests may be made after the arrangement has ceased to have effect, unless it came to an end prematurely.

6(4)   [Powers of court] Where on such an application the court is satisfied as to either of the grounds mentioned in subsection (1), it may do one or both of the following, namely–

(a)   revoke or suspend any decision approving the voluntary arrangement which has effect under section 4A or, in a case falling within subsection (1)(b), any decision taken by the meeting in question which has effect under that section;

(b)   give a direction to any person for the summoning of further meetings to consider any revised proposal the person who made the original proposal may make or, in a case falling within subsection (1)(b), a further company or (as the case may be) creditors' meeting to reconsider the original proposal.

6(5)   [Revocation or suspension of approval] Where at any time after giving a direction under subsection (4)(b) for the summoning of meetings to consider a revised proposal the court is satisfied that the person who made the original proposal does not intend to submit a revised proposal, the court shall revoke the direction and revoke or suspend any decision approving the voluntary arrangement which has effect under section 4A.

6(6)   [Supplemental directions] In a case where the court, on an application under this section with respect to any meeting–

(a)   gives a direction under subsection (4)(b), or

(b)   revokes or suspends an approval under subsection (4)(a) or (5),

the court may give such supplemental directions as it thinks fit and, in particular, directions with respect to things done under the voluntary arrangement since it took effect.

6(7)   [Effect of irregularity] Except in pursuance of the preceding provisions of this section, a decision taken at a meeting summoned under section 3 is not invalidated by any irregularity at or in relation to the meeting.

GENERAL NOTE

Section 6 lays down a procedure whereby the various interested persons who are listed in s.6(2) may apply to the court to challenge the fairness or regularity of a voluntary arrangement which has been approved under the preceding sections and also, it would seem (under s.6(1)(b)), the regularity of a creditors' or members' meeting in the case where such approval was not forthcoming. If a person does not come within any of the categories of applicants listed in s.6(2) (e.g. because he or she was not "a person entitled to vote"), there may be available the alternative possibility of an appeal under IR 1986 r.1.17A(3) see *Re Cranley Mansions Ltd, Saigol v Goldstein* [1994] 1 W.L.R. 1610; [1994] B.C.C. 576. By implication, and in part by the express words of s.6(3) and (7), a scheme of voluntary arrangement, once approved, is probably not open to challenge by any other procedure or on any other grounds than are set out here.

The section is obviously modelled on CA 1985 s.459 [CA 2006 s.994], a provision which allows the court to grant a remedy to a member of a company who establishes that the company's affairs are being or have been conducted in a manner which is unfairly prejudicial to the interests of some or all of the members or that some act or omission of the company is or would be so prejudicial. Similar language is used also in IA 1986 s.27; but compare Sch.B1 para.74. Decisions under these related provisions may be helpful in the interpretation of s.6.

Section 6 is concerned only with the events leading up to the implementation of an arrangement and not with complaints about the conduct of the scheme of voluntary arrangement by the supervisor: this is dealt with by a different procedure under s.7(3).

The scope of the power of intervention under s.6 was considered by Warren J. as part of his lengthy judgment in *Sisu Capital Fund Ltd v Tucker* [2005] EWHC 2170 (Ch); [2005] EWHC 2321 (Ch); [2006] B.P.I.R. 154. This was a complex case involving a group of companies with interlocking CVAs and administrations. Here the proposals under attack contained releases for office holders in respect of possible claims that might have been brought against them. In view of the speculative nature of these claims it was held that this was neither unreasonable nor unfairly prejudicial. It was not the role of the court to impose terms which might have been more advantageous to those accepted by creditors. The court could not say that a CVA was unfair simply because the petitioning creditors might have been better protected under a scheme of arrangement constructed under s.425 of the Companies Act 1985. Even if the releases were unfairly prejudicial the court would in any event exercise its discretion under s.6 to refuse to make an order. This conclusion is entirely consistent with judicial thinking in the field.

For the procedure on the making of an order under s.6, see IR 1986 r.1.25.

Note that it is an offence for an officer or former officer of a company to make a false representation or commit any other fraud for the purpose of obtaining the approval of the members or creditors to a proposal: IA 1986 s.6A. An officer would also, in principle, be civilly liable to the company or any other person who could prove damage resulting from such a fraud.

The text of s.6 was substantially amended by s.2 of, and Sch.2 to, IA 2000 to cater for changes brought in by that legislation. Minor linguistic changes were made to s.6(2)(c) by s.248 of, and Sch.17 to, EA 2002 to acknowledge the fact that it is no longer accurate to speak of administration *orders*.

For an unsuccessful attempt to invoke s.6 see *Swindon Town Properties v Swindon Town FC* [2003] B.P.I.R. 253.

S.6(1)

Although the word "may" appears to be permissive, it would probably be construed by a court in the sense "may and may only be" so as to make this the only procedure for challenging a scheme once it has been approved.

It may not be unfairly prejudicial to make a differentiation in the treatment of members of the same class (*Re Cancol Ltd* [1996] 1 All E.R. 37; [1995] B.C.C. 1,133). A rare successful challenge under s.6(1)(a) occurred in *Prudential Assurance Co Ltd v PRG Powerhouse Ltd* [2007] EWHC 1002 (Ch); [2007] B.C.C. 500 which was concerned with the common practice of "guarantee stripping" where a guarantor of a tenant company's rent obligations is relieved of liability via a CVA of the tenant company. Here Etherton J., after full consideration of a large number of authorities, concluded that the CVA did relieve the guarantor of its obligations but in so doing unfairly prejudiced the interests of the landlords. For discussion of this important authority see Chalkiadis, (2007) 219 Sweet & Maxwell's Company Law Newsletter 1; and Swain (2008) 20 Insolv. Int. 123. On the question of "material irregularity" (a phrase which is used also in IR 1986 r.1.17(7)), see the same case and also *Re Cranley Mansions Ltd, Saigol v Goldstein* [1994] 1 W.L.R. 1610; [1994] B.C.C. 576; and *Re Sweatfield Ltd* [1997] B.C.C. 744. In *Re Newlands (Seaford) Educational Trust* [2006] B.C.C. 195 an attempt to challenge under s.6(1)(b) the decision of the chair of the creditors' meeting when valuing a claim was unsuccessful before Sir Andrew Morritt C.

S.6(2)

For the meaning of the phrase "a person entitled, in accordance with the rules, to vote" see the notes to s.5(2) and IR 1986 r.1.17. The FSA can apply or be heard on an application under s.6—Financial Services and Markets Act 2000 s.356 as amended by s.15(2) of the Insolvency Act 2000.

S.6(3)

The time limit here specified is the same as that stipulated in s.5(4). On the calculation of this time, see the note to that subsection and *Re Bournemouth and Boscombe AFC Co Ltd* [1998] B.P.I.R. 183 which confirms that this 28-day limit cannot be extended. The 28-day time limit was reasserted in *Wood v Heart Hospital* [2009] B.P.I.R. 1538. The time limit for making applications under s.6 cannot be waived by invoking CPR r.3.2(a)—on this see *Re Beloit Walmsley Ltd* [2008] B.P.I.R. 1445. For discussion of the powers of the court under s.6 and any discretion given to supervisors to accept late claims see *Tucker and Spratt v Gold Fields Mining LLC* [2009] EWCA Civ 173; [2009] B.P.I.R. 704.

S.6(4)

The court may revoke or suspend the approvals given by the meetings, or one of the meetings, with or without giving directions as to the summoning of further meetings. If it decides to revoke but gives no such directions, it is of course always open to any of the persons mentioned in s.1(1) or (3) to put forward a fresh scheme. However, there is probably no power to reopen the original proposal (with or without modifications) otherwise than by direction of the court under s.6(4)(b).

Under s.6(4)(b), the court may direct "any person" (not necessarily the nominee) to summon the further meetings. However, only the person who made the original proposal may draw up a revised one: this will be the liquidator or administrator of the company if s.1(3) applies, and the directors if it does not. (If this person declines to co-operate, s.6(5) applies and the arrangement falls through.)

The court seems to have no power to make any decision other than those set out in this subsection: it cannot, e.g. approve a proposal subject to modifications of its own devising, or even remit a proposal with such modifications to the meetings for reconsideration. (See, however, the note to s.7(4), below.)

S.6(5)

If it appears that the directors, the liquidator or the administrator, as the case may be (see s.6(4)), do not intend to submit a revised scheme, the matter can proceed no further.

S.6(6)

An arrangement is effective as soon as the two meetings have given their approval (s.5). It is not suspended while an application under s.6 is pending. This subsection empowers the court, in the event of a successful challenge, to give supplemental directions to cover acts done under an arrangement before the court gave its ruling.

S.6(7)

An approval given at a meeting is not open to challenge as irregular otherwise than by proceeding under s.6 itself. Once the 28 days laid down by s.6(3) have elapsed, therefore, the approval is irrebuttably deemed valid for all purposes.

6A   False representations, etc.

6A(1)   [Offence] If, for the purpose of obtaining the approval of the members or creditors of a company to a proposal for a voluntary arrangement, a person who is an officer of the company–

(a)   makes any false representation, or

(b)   fraudulently does, or omits to do, anything,

he commits an offence.

6A(2)   [Application of s.6A(1)] Subsection (1) applies even if the proposal is not approved.

6A(3)   ["Officer"] For purposes of this section "officer" includes a shadow director.

6A(4)   [Penalties] A person guilty of an offence under this section is liable to imprisonment or a fine, or both.

GENERAL NOTE

This addition was introduced via s.2 of, and Sch.2 to, the IA 2000 with effect from January 1, 2003. It seeks to prevent abuse of the CVA mechanism by instilling a degree of integrity reinforced by the criminal law.

S.6A(1)

The bare bones of the offence of seeking to obtain the approval of a CVA by false misrepresentations are outlined.

S.6A(2)

It is no defence that the CVA was voted down by creditors.

S.6A(3)

The offence applies to officers and shadow directors—see the note to s.206(3).

S.6A(4)

This specifies the sanction, though the details are to be found in Sch.10.

7   Implementation of proposal

7(1)   **[Application]** This section applies where a voluntary arrangement has effect under section 4A.

7(2)   **[Supervisor of composition or scheme]** The person who is for the time being carrying out in relation to the voluntary arrangement the functions conferred–

    (a)   on the nominee by virtue of the approval given at one or both of the meetings summoned under section 3,

    (b)   by virtue of section 2(4) or 4(2) on a person other than the nominee,

shall be known as the supervisor of the voluntary arrangement.

7(3)   **[Application to court]** If any of the company's creditors or any other person is dissatisfied by any act, omission or decision of the supervisor, he may apply to the court; and on the application the court may–

    (a)   confirm, reverse or modify any act or decision of the supervisor,

    (b)   give him directions, or

    (c)   make such other order as it thinks fit.

7(4)   **[Application for directions by supervisor]** The supervisor–

    (a)   may apply to the court for directions in relation to any particular matter arising under the voluntary arrangement, and

    (b)   is included among the persons who may apply to the court for the winding up of the company or for an administration order to be made in relation to it.

7(5)   **[Court appointment powers]** The court may, whenever–

    (a)   it is expedient to appoint a person to carry out the functions of the supervisor, and

    (b)   it is inexpedient, difficult or impracticable for an appointment to be made without the assistance of the court,

make an order appointing a person who is qualified to act as an insolvency practitioner or authorised to act as supervisor, in relation to the voluntary arrangement, either in substitution for the existing supervisor or to fill a vacancy.

7(6)   **[Limit on s.7(5) power]** The power conferred by subsection (5) is exercisable so as to increase the number of persons exercising the functions of supervisor or, where there is more than one person exercising those functions, so as to replace one or more of those persons.

S.7(1), (2)

The wording of these subsections was modified by IA 2000 s.2 and Sch.2. As soon as a scheme of voluntary arrangement takes effect, the nominee (or his replacement appointed under ss.2(4) or 4(2)) is redesignated the "supervisor". The supervisor holds funds collected by him on trust for the creditors entitled under the arrangement. These funds cannot be seized by a subsequently appointed receiver: *Re Leisure Study Group Ltd* [1994] 2 B.C.L.C. 65. On s.7(2) for the duties of the supervisor see *Appleyard Ltd v Ritecrown Ltd* [2009] B.P.I.R. 235 (duty of supervisor is to carry out terms of CVA, not to act as champion for unsecured creditors). This case is also significant for making the point that a supervisor of a CVA is an officer of the court and therefore in principle subject to the ethical duties imposed by the rule in *Ex p. James* (1873–74) L.R. 9 Ch. App. 609.

For the rules relating to the implementation of the arrangement and the duties of the supervisor, see IR 1986 rr.1.22–1.23, 1.26A et seq. Note also new IR r.1.55 (time recording).

S.7(3)

The court is given wide—indeed, unlimited—powers to oversee the conduct of the arrangement by the supervisor; and anyone at all (subject, no doubt, to his being able to show that he has some interest in the matter) may invoke the jurisdiction under this section. As to whether a creditor can apply under s.7(3) where the company is also undergoing administration see *Holdenhurst Securities plc v Cohen* [2001] 1 B.C.L.C. 460. The right of application under s.7(3) does not exclude a direct action by a creditor unless the terms of the CVA preclude this—*Alman v Approach Housing Ltd* [2001] 1 B.C.L.C. 530. For an application by the company under s.7(3) see *County Bookshops Ltd v Grove* [2002] EWHC 1160 (Ch); [2002] B.P.I.R. 772. For passing mention of s.7(3) see *Re Hellard and Goldfarb (Joint Supervisors of Pinson Wholesale Ltd)* [2007] B.P.I.R. 1323 (a case concerned with an application for directions with regard to the right of remuneration of CVA supervisors).

S.7(4)

The supervisor (like a liquidator, administrator, trustee, and others discharging comparable functions) may apply to the court for directions. Although the Act nowhere states explicitly that the court may give directions which modify the scheme or extend it to include persons who have not taken part in the meetings, this was in fact done in *Re FMS Financial Management Services Ltd* (1989) 5 B.C.C. 191. Here a voluntary arrangement had been agreed to by both the members and various groups of creditors, but not by another group composed of former clients of the company who appeared to have good claims against the company for damages for misrepresentation. Hoffmann J. directed that they should be treated as creditors and be given the benefit of the scheme, with the consequence that the other creditors received a substantially smaller dividend. The power to seek directions does not enable the court to modify the terms of a CVA—*Re Alpa Lighting Ltd* [1997] B.P.I.R. 341. For an important case involving an application for directions under s.7(4) see *Re Federal-Mogul Aftermarket Ltd* [2008] B.P.I.R. 846.

The supervisor may also apply for an administration order or a winding-up order (para.(b)), but is not listed in either s.9 or s.124 among the categories of persons who are entitled to petition for those orders. This difficulty has to be overcome by having the supervisor petition in the name of the company, on analogy with IR 1986 r.4.7(7)(a). In the case of a petition for an administration order, this would be consistent with r.2.1(4) (which states that the petition is to be treated as if it were the petition of the company); but it is less appropriate in relation to a winding-up petition, for r.4.7(9) declares that this shall be treated as if it were a petition filed by contributories. On winding-up petitions presented by supervisors, see *Re Leisure Study Group Ltd* [1994] 2 B.C.L.C. 65.

A supervisor may apply for a winding-up order under s.7(4)(b) even though he is no longer "carrying out the functions" under the CVA: this wording (in s.7(2)) is descriptive only and not restrictive: *Re Arthur Rathbone Kitchens Ltd* [1998] B.C.C. 450.

Difficult issues arise where a company undergoing the CVA procedure then goes into liquidation. What is the effect of the liquidation on the CVA and what happens to the funds collected by the CVA supervisor? In spite of the relative scarcity of CVAs on the ground we now have a substantial body of case law to grapple with: *Re Halson Packaging Ltd* [1997] B.P.I.R. 194 (H.H.J. Maddocks); *Re Arthur Rathbone Kitchens Ltd* [1997] 2 B.C.L.C. 280 (Roger Kaye Q.C.); *Re Excalibur Airways Ltd* [1998] 1 B.C.L.C. 436 (Jonathan Parker J.); *Re Maple Environmental Services Ltd* [2000] B.C.C. 93 (H.H.J. Boggis); *Welsby v Brelec Installations* [2000] 2 B.C.L.C. 576 (Blackburne J.); and *Re Kudos Glass Ltd* [2000] 1 B.C.L.C. 390 (Richard McCombe Q.C.). This confusing corpus of first-instance case law arguably establishes certain propositions: a CVA can survive subsequent liquidation and the funds collected may be insulated from the residual assets of the company now undergoing the distributional process of winding up. However, whether these twin consequences will apply in an individual case depends to some extent upon the language of the CVA and also upon the circumstances under which the liquidation was commenced. The leading authority now is *Re NT Gallagher & Son Ltd* [2002] EWCA Civ 404; [2002] 1 W.L.R. 2380. Here a civil engineering company had fallen into financial difficulties in 1995 partly because of a substantial contractual dispute which was the subject of litigation initiated by the company ("the Mercury claim"). The CVA was designed to allow the company to continue trading pending the resolution of this substantial claim. Post-CVA creditors were to be paid out of cash flow. Under the CVA monthly payments were to be made by the company to the supervisors for the benefit of participating creditors; the language of "trust" was not used in relation to these payments. As is normal practice the supervisors were *required* to petition for the winding up of the company in the event of failure to comply with the terms of the CVA. By March 1997 the company had failed to keep up with the schedule of payments under the arrangement but the supervisors, after consulting the creditors, decided not to petition for winding up. In so deciding they concluded that they were not subject to an obligation to seek the winding up but were merely vested with a discretionary power; a conclusion, although not contested in the litigation, the correctness of which was viewed as "dubious" by the Court of Appeal (para.20). In any event, the problems of the company grew and in 1997 it was eventually placed into creditors' voluntary winding up with the agreement of the directors and supervisors. The Mercury claim had not been resolved by this date. The mathematics of the insolvency were interesting; the supervisors retained a sum of in excess of £500,000, but the post-CVA liabilities amounted to approximately £2.5 million. Total liabilities exceeded £5 million. The residual assets of the company amounted to £98,000 plus two causes of action (the Mercury claim and one other claim). At first instance (see [2001] B.P.I.R. 1088) H.H.J. Howarth held that both the sums retained by the supervisors and the Mercury claim were held on trust for the CVA creditors and further concluded that those trusts were not terminated by the subsequent liquidation. The CVA creditors could prove in the liquidation of the company provided they surrendered their "security" in respect of the Mercury claim. The liquidators appealed but the Court of Appeal dismissed this appeal, though it varied part of the order of H.H.J. Howarth by allowing the CVA creditors to prove in the liquidation after giving credit for any dividends received from the supervisors. Thus, the analogy used by the trial judge under which the Mercury claim was treated as tantamount to a security (which could be surrendered) did not find favour in the Court of Appeal.

In reaching these conclusions, the Court of Appeal, through Peter Gibson L.J., recognised the unsatisfactory nature of the present law, resting as it does on fine distinctions: "It makes little sense for the form of the liquidation to affect the question of the effect of liquidation on trusts created by a CVA" (para.43). Again, Peter Gibson L.J. stated:

> "We would question whether the mere fact that a supervisor presents a petition entails that the CVA or IVA creditors have elected to terminate the CVA or IVA trust in their favour. Even if there is evidence that all the CVA or IVA creditors supported the presentation of a petition, it does not follow that they were thereby evincing an intention that the trust should come to an end and that the trust assets should revert to the company or debtor" (para.43).

The real significance of this ruling from the Court of Appeal lies in the guidelines for future cases. The following principles have now been established (see para.54). These general rules apply equally to cases of voluntary and compulsory liquidation. Moreover, the question of whether the petitioner is the supervisor or not is immaterial; what mattered is the solution specified in the arrangement.

The governing principles are:

1. Funds collected by the supervisor would, provided the terms of the arrangement made this clear, be held on trust exclusively for the benefit of the CVA participants. The fact that the language of "trust" is not employed in the CVA proposal is immaterial (see para.29).

2. The fate of the CVA trust depends upon the terms under which that arrangement was entered into. On this see the later case of *Re Zebra Industrial Products Ltd* [2004] EWHC 549 (Ch); [2005] B.C.C. 104.

3. The stated effect of liquidation on the CVA should be respected. The contractual foundation of voluntary arrangements is thus reiterated.

4. It is perfectly possible for a CVA to come to an end but for the underlying trust to survive. In this context Peter Gibson L.J. declared: "We do not therefore accept that to treat a trust created by a CVA as continuing notwithstanding the liquidation of the company is productive of such unfairness that the court should conclude that liquidation brings the trust to an end" (para.49). In the absence of express provision the following default rule will, according to Peter Gibson L.J., operate:

> "Further, as a matter of policy, in the absence of any provision in the CVA as to what should happen to trust assets on liquidation of the company, the court should prefer a default rule which furthers rather than hinders what might be taken to be the statutory purpose of Part I of the Act. Parliament plainly intended to encourage companies and creditors to enter into CVAs so as to provide creditors with a means of recovering what they are owed without recourse to the more expensive means provided by winding up or administration, thereby giving many companies the opportunity to continue to trade" (para.50).

5. CVA creditors who have not been fully reimbursed by the trust moneys can prove for the balance in the liquidation.

It is clear from the approach taken by the Court of Appeal in *Gallagher* that the contractual basis of the CVA is now the dominant perspective and thus CVA documentation should be reviewed. This ruling will prove a considerable boost to company voluntary arrangements by offering strong protection (with a commensurate incentive) to those creditors who choose to participate in the CVA as a way of recovering their debts, albeit over a more protracted timeframe than their original contractual rights provided for. The Court of Appeal has confirmed that at heart CVAs are a matter of contract and that this contract can have a negative impact upon the general creditors outside the scheme by establishing a resilient trust of corporate funds. From the perspective of those counterparties who continue to deal with a company undergoing a CVA the dangers of dealing with such a business are exacerbated; not surprisingly, the extension of credit to such a company will be a matter of some considerable risk requiring prudent countermeasures. At the very least some inquiries as to the financial status of the company would be wise (see here para.49). The problem here is that it is quite possible to deal with a company already undergoing the CVA process without realising it (see paras 45 and 49). The end result, therefore, of *Gallagher* is that it may indeed encourage the setting of a CVA, but may have a negative impact upon the day-to-day operation of such arrangements by obstructing the flow of new credit.

S.7(5)

This is a rather puzzling provision, for none of the preceding sections appears to give the meetings of shareholders and creditors, acting either together or independently, a power to fill a vacancy in the office of supervisor or to replace a supervisor once appointed: it seems that once the meetings have approved a proposal under s.4A, they have no further role. So the reference in para.(b) to appointing a substitute supervisor "without the assistance of the court" is strange. Since no power appears to be conferred on the meetings by the rules, it seems that the only way in which a vacancy can be filled or a replacement supervisor appointed is by invoking the jurisdiction of the court under this subsection. See *Clements v Udal* [2001] B.P.I.R. 454. The wording of s.7(5) was modified by IA 2000 s.2 and Sch.2.

S.7(6)

This is the only reference in the Act to the possibility of appointing several persons as joint supervisors (or as joint nominees), although other "office-holders" are specifically covered by s.231. It appears, however, that the general statutory assumption applies, so that words in the singular include the plural (Interpretation Act 1978 s.6); and this construction may be applied throughout this Part of the Act. The rules deal with the appointment of joint supervisors in IR 1986 r.1.22(1).

7A   Prosecution of delinquent officers of company

7A(1)   [Application] This section applies where a moratorium under section 1A has been obtained for a company or the approval of a voluntary arrangement in relation to a company has taken effect under section 4A or paragraph 36 of Schedule A1.

7A(2)   [Procedure for reporting offence to "the appropriate authority"] If it appears to the nominee or supervisor that any past or present officer of the company has been guilty of any offence in connection with the moratorium or, as the case may be, voluntary arrangement for which he is criminally liable, the nominee or supervisor shall forthwith–

(a)   report the matter to the appropriate authority, and

(b)   provide the appropriate authority with such information and give the authority such access to and facilities for inspecting and taking copies of documents (being information or documents in the possession or under the control of the nominee or supervisor and relating to the matter in question) as the authority requires.

In this subsection, "the appropriate authority" means–

(i)   in the case of a company registered in England and Wales, the Secretary of State, and

(ii)   in the case of a company registered in Scotland, the Lord Advocate.

7A(3)   [Powers exercisable by Secretary of State] Where a report is made to the Secretary of State under subsection (2), he may, for the purpose of investigating the matter reported to him and such other matters relating to the affairs of the company as appear to him to require investigation, exercise any of the powers which are exercisable by inspectors appointed under section 431 or 432 of the Companies Act 1985 to investigate a company's affairs.

7A(4)   [Obligations to assist Secretary of State] For the purpose of such an investigation any obligation imposed on a person by any provision of the Companies Acts to produce documents or give information to, or otherwise to assist, inspectors so appointed is to be regarded as an obligation similarly to assist the Secretary of State in his investigation.

7A(5) **[Answers as evidence in investigation]** An answer given by a person to a question put to him in exercise of the powers conferred by subsection (3) may be used in evidence against him.

7A(6) **[Answers as evidence in criminal proceedings]** However, in criminal proceedings in which that person is charged with an offence to which this subsection applies–

(a) no evidence relating to the answer may be adduced, and

(b) no question relating to it may be asked,

by or on behalf of the prosecution, unless evidence relating to it is adduced, or a question relating to it is asked, in the proceedings by or on behalf of that person.

7A(7) **[Offences under s.7A(6)]** Subsection (6) applies to any offence other than–

(a) an offence under section 2 or 5 of the Perjury Act 1911 (false statements made on oath otherwise than in judicial proceedings or made otherwise than on oath), or

(b) an offence under section 44(1) or (2) of the Criminal Law (Consolidation) (Scotland) Act 1995 (false statements made on oath or otherwise than on oath).

7A(8) **[Assistance to be given to prosecuting authority]** Where a prosecuting authority institutes criminal proceedings following any report under subsection (2), the nominee or supervisor, and every officer and agent of the company past and present (other than the defendant or defender), shall give the authority all assistance in connection with the prosecution which he is reasonably able to give.

For this purpose–

"agent" includes any banker or solicitor of the company and any person employed by the company as auditor, whether that person is or is not an officer of the company,

"prosecuting authority" means the Director of Public Prosecutions, the Lord Advocate or the Secretary of State.

7A(9) **[Court directions under s.7A(8)]** The court may, on the application of the prosecuting authority, direct any person referred to in subsection (8) to comply with that subsection if he has failed to do so.

GENERAL NOTE

Introduced by s.2 of, and Sch.2 to, the Insolvency Act 2000 with effect from January 1, 2003.

S.7A(1)
This defines the circumstances under which s.7A applies—i.e. to both types of CVA.

S.7A(2)
Here we have a formal "whistleblowing" obligation imposed on the nominee/supervisor. This is a significant departure from the previous position with regard to CVAs where insolvency practitioners were not expected to discharge such a public service duty. The absence of such a duty may well have been one of the attractions in the CVA model for company directors. On procedures for reporting suspected criminality see *Dear IP*, December 2007.

S.7A(3), (4), (5)
This explains the powers available to the Secretary of State to follow up any report made under subs.(3). The power of investigation is bolstered by the provisions of subss.(4) and (5). Note the amendment to subs.(3) and (4) by the Companies Act 2006 (Consequential Amendments, Transitional Provisions and Savings) Order 2009 (SI 2009/1941) (effective from October 1, 2009). This takes account of the enactment of the Companies Act 2006.

S.7A(6)
This qualifies subs.(5), though in turn this qualification is limited by subs.(7).

S.7A(8), (9)
These deal with follow up matters resulting from a prosecution instituted as a result of a report made under subs.(2).

7B   Arrangements coming to an end prematurely

7B   For the purposes of this Part, a voluntary arrangement the approval of which has taken effect under section 4A or paragraph 36 of Schedule A1 comes to an end prematurely if, when it ceases to have effect, it has not been fully implemented in respect of all persons bound by the arrangement by virtue of section 5(2)(b)(i) or, as the case may be, paragraph 37(2)(b)(i) of Schedule A1.

GENERAL NOTE

This is a curious definitional provision which seeks to identify when a CVA comes to an end prematurely. It needs to be read in the light of ss.5(2A)(a) and 6(3).

PART II

ADMINISTRATION

IMPORTANT

There are now two administration regimes, each governed by what is referred to in the legislation as "Part II" of IA 1986. The "original" Pt II, along with the associated Rules, with annotations, have been transferred to Vol.2 of this edition for reasons of space. The "new" Pt II is to be found in Sch.B1 to the Act, below at pp.520 et seq. The "new" Pt II applies to all administrations commenced after September 15, 2003, except in the relatively few cases to which EA 2002 s.249 (see below, p.650) applies. In order to distinguish between the original and the new Parts, the statutory text of the former has been set in italics, and the same distinction is made in the corresponding Rules.

8   Administration

8   Schedule B1 to this Act (which makes provision about the administration of companies) shall have effect.

Introductory note to the new Part II

Part 10 of the EA 2002, the relevant provisions of which were brought into effect from September 15, 2003 by the Enterprise Act 2002 (Commencement No.4 and Transitional Provisions and Savings) Order 2003 (SI 2003/2093 (C. 85)) art.2(1) and Sch.1, introduced a wholly new administration regime for companies. This was done by declaring (in s.248) that a new Pt II, now to be found set out in Sch.B1 to IA 1986, is to be "substituted" for that contained in IA 1986 as originally drafted and since amended. The side-note to s.248 refers to the "replacement" of Pt II. So the natural inference which the reader might have drawn was that the former Pt II had been consigned to oblivion, subject only to whatever transitional provisions might be needed to deal with companies which were in administration when s.248 was brought into force. But this is not so. In the immediately following section (s.249) it is provided that s.248 "shall have no effect" in relation to a number of categories of public-utility company and to building societies. So, so far as concerns these bodies, the former Pt II survives. It survives also where a petition for an administration order was presented to the court before September 15, 2003 (SI 2003/2093 art.3(2)).

In consequence, we now have two versions of Pt II, one in ss.8–27 and another in Sch.B1; and as if that were not confusing enough, we have two different sections each numbered s.8! Section 8 of the "new" Pt II is set out above.

Because our readers will need to have access to the original ss.8–27 in relation to both companies which were in administration on September 15, 2003 and the other bodies listed above, we continue to include both versions of Pt II in the present edition. We refer to the one as "the original" administration regime, or "Pt II as originally enacted" and the other as "the new" regime and "the new" Pt II. Necessarily, there will be some repetition and much cross-referencing between the two commentaries. However, the cross-references should be read with caution, since the language and some of the statutory definitions in the two Parts are not always the same.

The draftsman has endeavoured to make Sch.B1 largely self-standing, and in doing so has removed references to administration and administrators from many sections in other parts of the Act (e.g. in s.212, the well-known "misfeasance" section). In order to cope with situations involving administrators appointed under the original regime, the former references are reinstated by the Enterprise Act 2002 (Commencement No.4 and Transitional Provisions and Savings) Order 2003 (SI 2003/2093 (C. 85)) arts 3(2), (3). This saving provision applies in cases where a petition for an administration order was presented before September 15, 2003. In the case of building societies and the utility companies mentioned in s.249, the original wording of the Act is preserved because EA 2002 s.249 disapplies Sch.B1 in regard to these bodies.

The administration procedure has been made available to bodies other than companies. Provision was made for building societies by the Building Societies Act 1986 s.90A (inserted by the Building Societies Act 1997 s.39, effective December 1, 1997): as noted above, the original Pt II applies. In the application of Pt II of IA 1986 to Building Societies it is to be read subject to the modifications set out in the Building Societies Act 1986 Sch.15A paras 10 et seq. The original Pt II was also extended to insolvent partnerships by the Insolvent Partnerships Order 1994 (SI 1994/2421) art.6 and Sch.2, which in turn was superseded by the Insolvent Partnerships (Amendment) Order 2005 (SI 2005/1516, effective July 1, 2005), substituting a modified IA 1986 Sch.B1 and so introducing the new Pt II regime. The Limited Liability Partnerships Regulations 2001 (SI 2001/1090) were amended by the Limited Liability Partnerships (Amendment) Regulations 2005 (SI 2005/1989) reg.3 and Sch.3, as from October 1, 2005 so as to make the new Pt II available to LLPs.

The new administration regime has also been applied with special modifications to various types of company governed by separate legislation, e.g. energy companies and railway companies—the main object being to ensure that supplies and services are not interrupted: see, e.g. the Railways Act 1993 ss.59 et seq. and the Energy Administration Rules 2005 (SI 2005/2483). However, in regard to other public-utility companies the original Pt II continues to apply (see above).

The administration procedure was formerly not available to insurance companies. However, by the Financial Services and Markets Act 2000 (Administration Orders Relating to Insurers) Order 2002 (SI 2002/1242), which came into force on May 31, 2002, this became possible for the first time. The Schedule to this statutory instrument listed a series of modifications to IA 1986 Sch.B1 in the application of that regime to insurers. However, much of the 2002 Regulations has since been twice superseded: first, by the Insurers (Reorganisation and Winding Up) Regulations 2003 (SI 2003/1102), which became effective on April 20, 2003, and secondly by the Insurers (Reorganisation and Winding Up) Regulations 2004 (SI 2004/353), effective February 18, 2004 which repealed and replaced the latter. The 2003 Regulations were enacted in order to implement EC Directive 2001/17 and the 2004 Regulations in order to take account of the changes to insolvency law brought about by EA 2002. In addition to making provision for the recognition in this country of insolvency proceedings instituted elsewhere in the EEA, the 2004 Regulations make a number of important changes to the substance of the administration regime so far as it affects UK insurers. In particular, such an undertaking may be put into administration only by court order (even under the new Pt II), and preferential status is accorded to insurance debts ahead of all other debts. The particular Regulations applicable in a particular case will depend on the period within the successive effective dates that the insolvency proceeding falls. The 2000 and 2004 Regulations are reproduced in Vol.2. For a case under the 2004 Regulations, see *Re AA Mutual International Insurance Co Ltd* [2004] EWHC 2430 (Ch); [2005] 2 B.C.L.C. 8. Lloyd's was excluded from the provisions of the above legislation, but comparable provision has now brought it within the net: see the Insurers (Reorganisation and Winding Up) (Lloyd's) Regulations 2005 (SI 2005/1998, effective August 10, 2005).

For the same reason, banks and other "authorised institutions" under the banking legislation were excluded by the Act as originally drafted. However, by the Banks (Administration Proceedings) Order 1989 (SI 1989/1276), effective from August 23, 1989, the original Pt II of the Act was extended so as to apply in relation to banks and the other bodies mentioned in the original s.8(5)(b) which were companies within the meaning of CA 1985 s.735 [CA 2006 ss.1(1), 1171]; but this statutory instrument has since been revoked, subject to transitional arrangements, and the new Pt II now applies to these bodies instead (see the Banks (Former Authorised Institutions) Order 2006 (SI 2006/3107), effective December 15, 2006). The reference to s.8(5)(b) is replaced by a reference to IA 1986 s.422(1). The 2006 Order, art.3 and Sch., provides that certain modifications shall be applied to Pt II in relation to the application of the administration procedure to these institutions. In particular, these modifications confer rights on the Financial Services Authority to participate in the proceedings. In contrast with the legislation governing insurance companies, these bodies may be put into administration without a court order (but the consent of the FSA must be obtained and filed in court (Sch. para.5)). The Credit Institutions (Reorganisation and Winding Up) Regulations 2004 (SI 2004/1045, effective May 5, 2004), which are also reproduced in Vol.2, inter alia prohibit courts in the UK from making an administration order in regard to a credit institution based elsewhere in the EEA and require the notification of UK administration proceedings in other EEA jurisdictions, but do not otherwise affect the 1989 Order. On the special administration regime established by the Banking Act 2009 where there has been government intervention in the affairs of a failing bank, see above, p.6.

The Insolvency (Amendment) Rules 2003 (SI 2003/1730), which also came into force on September 15, 2003, supplement the new legislation by providing a new set of Rules which govern administrations under the new regime. But the rules in force prior to September 15, 2003 continue to apply to administrations under the original Pt II: see

I(A)R 2003 r.5(2)–(4).

Confusingly, both sets of rules are referred to as "Pt 2" of the Rules, and these use similar but not corresponding numbering. Accordingly, it has been necessary to include both versions of Pt 2 in this edition. Part 2 of the new rules is to be found below at p.716, while Pt 2 of the original rules is included in Vol.2 at p.95. References from the annotations to the original Pt II will be to Pt 2 of the original rules, and from the new Pt II to Pt 2 of the new rules (except where there is risk of confusion, when the appropriate label will be added). To aid in distinguishing between the two, the text of the original legislation and rules have been set in italics.

PART III

RECEIVERSHIP

Introductory note to Part III
The Companies Acts have not previously contained many provisions dealing with receivership, at least in relation to England and Wales; matters were left to the general law and the terms of the instrument under or by which the receiver was appointed. The Cork Committee (*Report*, Ch.8) recommended that the law should be amended so that in many respects it was placed on a statutory basis. The recommendations were broadly followed by IA 1985 Ch.IV, which is now consolidated along with a few sections of CA 1985 into the present Act.

Among the principal changes made are the introduction of the new concept of "administrative receiver" (s.29(2)), and the requirement that an administrative receiver be a qualified insolvency practitioner. The date on which a receiver takes office and the extent to which agency rules apply have been clarified, and new provisions ensure that other creditors are kept in the picture regarding the progress of the receivership. The administrative receiver is given the statutory powers set out in Sch.1, and other specific powers including power to dispose of encumbered property (s.43). In many other respects an administrative receivership is placed on a similar footing to a liquidation—e.g. in regard to a statement of affairs, the appointment of a committee of creditors, and the removal of the receiver.

To all intents and purposes these days appointments of receivers to enforce security are effected out of court in pursuance of a contractual power vested in the debenture holder to make such an appointment. The advantage in this course of action is speed and lack of cost. There is, however, always the facility of applying to the court for such an appointment, but this is rare because of the cost and the delay—for an unusual example see *Bank of Credit and Commerce International SA v BRS Kumar Bros Ltd* [1994] B.C.L.C. 211. Cases decided in relation to these other forms of receiver may have a wider value. For an important statement of principle on the right of a receiver to claim remuneration from the receivership assets see *Capewell v HMRC* [2007] UKHL 2; [2007] B.P.I.R. 678.

On the question of the compatibility of a receivership designed to enforce a confiscation order and the requirements of art.1 of the First Protocol ECHR see also *Hansford v Southampton Magistrates Court* [2006] EWHC 67 (Admin); [2008] B.P.I.R. 379.

On the power of the court to appoint a receiver by way of equitable execution over future receipts from a defined foreign asset—see *Masri v Consolidated Contractors International UK Ltd* [2008] EWCA Civ 303; [2008] B.P.I.R. 531.

It must be remembered that a receiver appointed to enforce a fixed charge may be subject to the old established provisions of LPA 1925. For consideration of this statutory code see *Phoenix Properties v Wimpole Street Nominees Ltd* [1992] 1 B.C.L.C. 737; and *Sargent v C & E Commissioners* [1995] 2 B.C.L.C. 34. Specialised statutory regimes also exist for certain types of receivership involving (for example) companies incorporated by statute or as part of statutory insolvency regimes, but these are not our concern in this work.

The institution of receivership was unknown in Scotland until the enactment of CFCSA 1972. In the present Act the provisions of that legislation are consolidated, incorporating certain modifications made by IA 1985. Comparable provisions dealing with receivers and administrative receivers in Northern Ireland are to be found in the Insolvency (Northern Ireland) Order 1989 (SI 1989/2405) (NI 19) arts 40–59 (as amended).

Receivership has enjoyed a renaissance over the past two years in a niche context as a device to deal with distressed hedge funds—see *Re Cheyne Finance plc (No.1)* [2008] 1 B.C.L.C. 732; *Re Cheyne Finance plc (No.2)* [2008] B.C.C. 182 and *Re Whistlejacket Capital Ltd* [2008] 2 B.C.L.C. 683. Note also Milman, [2009] 247 Sweet & Maxwell's Company Law Newsletter 1.

Although the following provisions provide some statutory framework for the mechanism of an administrative receivership there is still a substantial body of rules derived from decisions of the courts. These court-derived principles continue to be important.

Part III applies to limited liability partnerships by virtue of the Limited Liability Partnerships Regulations 2001 (SI 2001/1090) reg.5(1)(a) as from April 6, 2001 subject to reg.5(2) and (3).

Many key issues are not addressed by the legislation. For example, what is the effect of the appointment of a receiver on the power of the directors to litigate on behalf of the company? Compare here *Newhart Developments v Cooperative Commercial Bank* [1978] Q.B. 814 with *Tudor Grange Holdings v Citibank* [1992] Ch. 53; the Irish High Court case of *Lascomme Ltd v United Dominions Trust (Ireland)* [1994] I.L.R.M. 227 and *Independent Pension Trustee v LAW Construction, The Times* Scots Law Report, November 1, 1996. For discussion see Doyle, (1996) 17 Co Law 131. *Newhart* was followed most recently by the Court of Appeal in *Sutton v GE Capital Commercial Finance* [2004] EWCA Civ 315; [2004] 2 B.C.L.C. 662. The Court of Appeal ruled in *Mills v Birchall* [2008] B.P.I.R. 607 that a receiver who conducts litigation on behalf of a company in receivership as part of the security enforcement process does not normally do so at the risk of personal liability for costs under a third party costs order if the litigation is unsuccessful. The defendant in such proceedings is advised to seek an early security for costs order against the claimant company.

The duties of a director to his company may be enforced by an administrative receiver and those duties are not discharged on the company entering administrative receivership—on this see *Simtel Communications Ltd v Rebak* [2006] 2 B.C.L.C. 571.

The question of whether a receiver owes a duty of care to the company (and those claiming through it) when managing and realising the assets has also been left for the courts to grapple with. For a generous treatment of receivers' duties by the Privy Council in this scenario see *Downsview Nominees v First City Corporation Ltd* [1993] A.C. 295; [1993] B.C.C. 46. Here it was held that the responsibilities of receivers are essentially equitable in nature and there was no room for superimposing common law duties of care in negligence. This case is difficult to reconcile with earlier authorities such as *Standard Chartered Bank v Walker* [1982] 1 W.L.R. 1410 and *Knight v Lawrence* [1991] B.C.C. 411 and is best viewed as part of a general retreat on the part of the courts in the areas of economic loss and professional liability. See generally Berg, [1993] J.B.L. 213 and Fealy, [1994] 45 N.I.L.Q. 61. Most commentators have been critical of the approach of the Privy Council but for rare support see Rajak, (1997) 21 Insolv. L. 7. Those commentators who have been critical of the aforementioned Privy Council ruling will have welcomed the subsequent clarification of the law by the Court of Appeal in *Medforth v Blake* [2000] Ch. 86; [1999] B.C.C. 711. In this case it was held that a receiver taking control of a farming business had no obligation to continue to operate the farm, but if that course of action was taken, the receiver should take reasonable steps to ensure that the business was conducted as profitably as possible and, in particular, that the customary discounts on bulk purchase of livestock feed be obtained. The Court of Appeal felt able to reconcile *Downsview* by indicating that this duty to take reasonable care could be seen as part of the obligation to act in good faith. This decision is far more in tune with prevailing professional standards. For comment see Frisby, (2000) 63 M.L.R. 413. The issue of the duties owed by receivers (or mortgagees) when managing, selling or considering the sale of charged property have continued to trouble the courts over the past two years—see for example *Hadjipanayi v Yeldon* [2001] B.P.I.R. 487; *Worwood v Leisure Merchandising* [2002] 1 B.C.L.C. 249; *Cohen v TSB Bank* [2002] 2 B.C.L.C. 32; and *Silven Properties Ltd v Royal Bank of Scotland* [2003] EWCA Civ 764. At the end of the day each case does turn on its own peculiar facts and most claims alleging breach of duty tend to fail. Another vexed issue concerns both the timing of a sale and the selection of a purchaser where the mortgagor wishes to buy the property. In *Lloyds Bank v Cassidy* [2002] EWCA Civ 1427; [2003] B.P.I.R. 425 the Court of Appeal felt that these were issues in need of clarification. In *Bell v Long* [2008] B.P.I.R. 1211 the court ruled that a receiver (or a mortgagee) is entitled to choose the timing of sale even if that works to the disadvantage of the debtor. If a duty of care is owed by selling receivers that duty is owed to any party having an interest in the equity of redemption—*Raja v Austin Gray (a firm)* [2002] EWCA Civ 1965; [2003] B.P.I.R. 725.

Other jurisdictions have had the foresight to address this issue through legislation—see Irish Companies Act 1963 s.311A (introduced in 1990) and the New Zealand Receiverships Act 1993 s.19. In both cases a statutory duty of care when selling company assets has been imposed. In Canada s.247 of the Bankruptcy and Insolvency Act 1992 requires receivers to deal with the security in a commercially reasonable manner.

The rules on set-off on receivership are also within the province of common law: *John Dee Group Ltd v W M H (21) Ltd* [1998] B.C.C. 972.

The effect of the appointment of an administrative receiver was considered by Judge Weeks Q.C. in *Chesterton International Group plc v Deka Immobilien Inv GmbH* [2005] EWHC 656 (Ch); [2005] B.P.I.R. 1103. Here it was held that once an administrative receiver had been validly appointed by a debenture holder it would not then be possible to seek the appointment of an administrator unless that debenture holder consented. This was the position as outlined in para.39(1) of Sch.B1 to the IA 1986.

The relationship between the various corporate insolvency regimes is interesting. It has been clear from the earliest of days that the right of a secured creditor to have a receiver appointed would be protected by the law. Thus, although receivership and liquidation can run concurrently, in practice the liquidator must wait in the wings, at least so far as concerns the property covered by the charge, until the receiver has fulfilled his functions. This is so even though the agency character of the receiver's role changes: *Sowman v David Samuel Trust Ltd* [1978] 1 W.L.R. 22 or even if liquidation precedes receivership: *Re First Express Ltd* [1991] B.C.C. 782. The advent of the administration order regime posed little threat to the rights of the secured creditor in that a right of veto was created by IA 1986 s.9 in favour of a person having the power to appoint an administrative receiver (i.e. a creditor whose security includes a general floating charge) see *Re Croftbell Ltd* [1990] B.C.C. 781. However, if this veto was not exercised, the administrator did enjoy the power to interfere with the rights of the secured creditor (see IA 1986 s.15). The new administration regime under EA 2002 offers good protection to the qualifying floating charge holder. A secured creditor who waits for a CVA to be put in place before appointing a receiver may also be in difficulties: *Re Leisure Study Group Ltd* [1994] 2 B.C.L.C. 65.

Where a receiver pursues litigation on behalf of the company as part of the security realisation process and such litigation is unsuccessful it is unlikely that the receiver will be made subject of a third party costs order pursuant to s.51 of the Supreme Court Act 1981, now rebranded Senior Court Act 1981, according to the Court of Appeal in *Mills v Birchall* [2008] EWCA Civ 385; [2008] B.P.I.R. 607—see annotation to s.37.

Neither receivership nor administrative receivership constitute collective insolvency proceedings for the purposes of either the EC Regulation on Insolvency Proceedings (1346/2000) or the UNCITRAL Cross-Border Insolvency Regulations (SI 2006/1030).

Note the limitations imposed upon a receiver's power of realisation where s.430 of POCA 2002 applies.

As an institution the future of receivership is likely to be a diminished one. This is a result of the changes introduced by EA 2002 limiting the option of administrative receivership to pre-commencement floating charges and to other specialised corporate financing situations—see the note to ss.72A et seq. The relevant provisions barring administrative receivership do not apply to floating charges created before September 15, 2003—see the Enterprise Act 2002 (Commencement No.4 and Transitional Provisions and Savings) Order 2003 (SI 2003/2093 (C. 85)). Having said that, the controversial ruling of the House of Lords in *Re Leyland DAF Ltd* [2004] UKHL 9; [2004] B.C.C. 214 to the effect that liquidation expenses could not be made payable out of assets held by receivers for the floating charge holder should maintain a degree of competitive edge for the institution of receivership, in particular when compared to administration. Note also the Crown Statement of June 2005 on this subject—see R3 Technical Bulletin 71.2 and App.IX in Vol.2. *Leyland DAF* (above) was partially reversed when s.1282 of Companies Act 2006 was brought into force in April 2008. This reversal applies only to English law and Northern Ireland—there are no signs of a reversal of *Leyland DAF* in Scots law.

CHAPTER I

RECEIVERS AND MANAGERS (ENGLAND AND WALES)

Preliminary and general provisions

28 Extent of this Chapter

28(1) ["Company" in Pt 3 Ch.1] In this Chapter **"company"** means a company registered under the Companies Act 2006 in England and Wales or Scotland.

28(2) [Non-application of Pt 3 Ch.2] This Chapter does not apply to receivers appointed under Chapter 2 of this Part (Scotland).

GENERAL NOTE

This emphasises that ss.28–49 only apply to receivers and managers appointed under English law. The Scots have their own rules: see ss.50–71. However, Ch.1 applies to building societies subject to certain modifications: see Sch.15A as inserted by Sch.6 and s.39 of the Building Societies Act 1997.

The changes made to the law relating to receivers and managers by IA 1985 and IA 1986 are not retrospective: see Sch.11 para.2(2).

Note the change made by the Companies Act 2006 (Consequential Amendments, Transitional Provisions and Savings) Order 2009 (SI 2009/1941) with effect from October 1, 2009. This change involves the substitution of a new s.28 in the light of the enactment of the Companies Act 2006.

29 Definitions

29(1) [Interpretation] It is hereby declared that, except where the context otherwise requires–

    (a) any reference in this Act to a receiver or manager of the property of a company, or to a receiver of it, includes a receiver or manager, or (as the case may be) a receiver of part only of that property and a receiver only of the income arising from the property or from part of it; and

(b)   any reference in this Act to the appointment of a receiver or manager under powers contained in an instrument includes an appointment made under powers which, by virtue of any enactment, are implied in and have effect as if contained in an instrument.

29(2)   [**"Administrative receiver"**] In this Chapter **"administrative receiver"** means–

(a)   a receiver or manager of the whole (or substantially the whole) of a company's property appointed by or on behalf of the holders of any debentures of the company secured by a charge which, as created, was a floating charge, or by such a charge and one or more other securities; or

(b)   a person who would be such a receiver or manager but for the appointment of some other person as the receiver of part of the company's property.

S.29(1)

This section defines "receiver and manager" in such a way as to include partial receiverships. Receivers of income appointed under LPA 1925 (see above) are included under the term "receiver".

Note the amendment introduced into subs.(1) via the Companies Act 2006 (Consequential Amendments, Transitional Provisions and Savings) Order 2009 (SI 2009/1941) with effect from October 1, 2009.

S.29(2)

This seeks to cast light upon the unhappy term "administrative receiver", a label first introduced in 1985. It is important to distinguish an administrative receiver from his untitled fellows because, inter alia, ss.42–49, the rules on officeholders and the mitigating provisions in s.2 of IA 1994 only apply to administrative receivers. Moreover, it is only a person having the right to appoint an administrative receiver who can veto the appointment of an administrator (see IA 1986 s.9 and *Re Croftbell Ltd* [1990] B.C.C. 781).

In view of the importance attached to the status of being an administrative receiver it is unfortunate that this provision was not drafted in clearer terms. A number of uncertainties exist:

(1)   Can there be multiple concurrent administrative receivers? The better view here would appear to be "no": see Oditah, [1991] J.B.L. 49.

(2)   Can a court-appointed receiver enjoy this status? The consensus here appears to deny this: see Gordon Stewart, *Administrative Receivers and Administrators* (CCH, 1987), p.13; but compare Schumacher, (1993) 9 I.L. & P. 43 for an interesting counter-argument. In *Re A & C Supplies Ltd* [1998] B.C.C. 708 Blackburne J. indicated that the court did not enjoy the power to appoint an administrative receiver.

(3)   Can an administrative receiver be appointed over the assets of a foreign company? The general rule of interpretation of companies legislation is that the word "company" does not encompass foreign companies; however, this rule can be displaced by the context. Such a displacement was accepted in the context of s.29(2) by Mummery J. in *Re International Bulk Commodities Ltd* [1993] Ch. 77; [1992] B.C.C. 463. This ruling has not escaped criticism and the later judgment in *Re Devon and Somerset Farmers Ltd* [1994] Ch. 57; [1993] B.C.C. 410 to the effect that an industrial and provident society cannot go into administrative receivership (because it is not a "company") sits uneasily alongside it. An equally restrictive view was taken in *Re Dairy Farmers of Britain Ltd* [2009] EWHC 1389 (Ch) where Henderson J. indicated that an industrial and provident society fell outside the administrative receivership regime; indeed such a body did not come within the scope of Pts I–III of the IA 1986. The view that it is now not possible to have an administrative receiver appointed over the assets of a foreign company has been reinforced by consequential amendments introduced in the wake of the introduction of the Companies Act 2006. In particular, the new definition of "company" introduced into s.28 of IA 1986 (see above) would appear to rule out this option. For explanation and critique see Moss, Segal and Fletcher [2010] 23 Insolv. Int. 57.

(4)   Can an administrative receiver be appointed by a fixed chargee? The answer to this is also negative. Moreover, even if the chargee enjoys a hybrid security comprising fixed and floating charges, the appointment must be made under the floating charge element in order for an administrative receivership to result: *Meadrealm Ltd v Transcontinental Golf Construction* (1991) (Vinelott J., unreported) noted by Marks in (1993) 6 Insolv. Int. 41. See also Marks and Emmett, [1994] J.B.L. 1.

30   Disqualification of body corporate from acting as receiver

30   A body corporate is not qualified for appointment as receiver of the property of a company, and any body corporate which acts as such a receiver is liable to a fine.

GENERAL NOTE

This provision continues the rather curious bar on corporate receivers. If a corporate receiver is appointed, a fine will be incurred and the appointment is also invalid. On penalties, see s.430 and Sch.10. Corporations are also barred from being qualified to act as insolvency practitioners: see s.390(1).

31 Disqualification of bankrupt or person in respect of whom a debt relief order is made

31(1) **[Offence]** A person commits an offence if he acts as receiver or manager of the property of a company on behalf of debenture holders while–

(a) he is an undischarged bankrupt,

(aa) a moratorium period under a debt relief order applies in relation to him, or

(b) a bankruptcy restrictions order or a debt relief restrictions order is in force in respect of him.

31(2) **[Sanction]** A person guilty of an offence under subsection (1) shall be liable to imprisonment, a fine or both.

31(3) **[Non-application to court appointee]** This section does not apply to a receiver or manager acting under an appointment made by the court.

GENERAL NOTE

Schedule 21 to EA 2002 substituted a new s.31 into IA 1986 to cater for the advent of bankruptcy restrictions orders in April 2004.

S.31(1), (3)

Undischarged bankrupts or persons subject to a BRO (or BRU) are prohibited from acting as receivers and managers unless the court makes the appointment—hardly likely! Note amendment by Pt 1 para.2 of Sch.20 to the Tribunals, Courts and Enforcement Act 2007 to cater for advent of debt relief orders.

S.31(2)

This indicates the sanction, full details of which are to be found in Sch.10.

32 Power for court to appoint official receiver

32 Where application is made to the court to appoint a receiver on behalf of the debenture holders or other creditors of a company which is being wound up by the court, the official receiver may be appointed.

GENERAL NOTE

If a company is in liquidation, the court, in those rare cases where debenture holders apply to it to have a receiver appointed, may appoint the official receiver. For further details see ss.399–401.

Receivers and managers appointed out of court

33 Time from which appointment is effective

33(1) **[Effect of appointment]** The appointment of a person as a receiver or manager of a company's property under powers contained in an instrument–

(a) is of no effect unless it is accepted by that person before the end of the business day next following that on which the instrument of appointment is received by him or on his behalf, and

(b) subject to this, is deemed to be made at the time at which the instrument of appointment is so received.

33(2) **[Joint receivers or managers]** This section applies to the appointment of two or more persons as joint receivers or managers of a company's property under powers contained in an instrument, subject to such modifications as may be prescribed by the rules.

S.33(1)

The appointment of a receiver and manager out of court takes effect when he receives the letter of appointment, provided that he accepts the office before the end of the next business day. For administrative receivers see also IR 1986 r.3.1.

S.33(2)

The above rule applies to joint receivers, subject to the modifications made by the rules: see also IR 1986 r.3.1.

34   Liability for invalid appointment

34   Where the appointment of a person as the receiver or manager of a company's property under powers contained in an instrument is discovered to be invalid (whether by virtue of the invalidity of the instrument or otherwise), the court may order the person by whom or on whose behalf the appointment was made to indemnify the person appointed against any liability which arises solely by reason of the invalidity of the appointment.

GENERAL NOTE

This permits the court to order that the appointor of a receiver indemnify the latter against liability in trespass, where the appointment turns out to be invalid. Invalidity may be the result of the debenture charge being unregistered or being avoided under IA 1986 s.245. This provision will prove useful because challenges to appointments are becoming more common: see, e.g. *Shamji v Johnson Matthey Bankers Ltd* (1986) 2 B.C.C. 98,910 where the challenge proved unsuccessful. Short notice appointments are permitted under "on demand" debentures: *Sheppard and Cooper Ltd v TSB Bank (No.2)* [1996] B.C.C. 965. The courts will refuse to hear belated complaints about the initiation of the receivership: see *Secretary of State v Jabble* [1998] B.C.C. 39 for an optimistic attempt to challenge the propriety of the receivership in consequential director disqualification proceedings! In *Re Asset Visions Ltd* [2003] B.P.I.R. 305 an attempt to challenge an appointment of a receiver on the grounds that the terms of the debenture governing the appointment were allegedly qualified by a verbal agreement did not appeal to the court. A rare recent authority on the appointment of administrative receivers is *Brampton Manor (Leisure) Ltd v McLean* [2006] EWHC 2983 (Ch) where the point was made by Evans-Lombe J. that provided events had occurred justifying the appointment of an administrative receiver the fact that the debenture had relied on other grounds to support the appointment would not induce the court to conclude that the appointment was invalid. The issue of the legal consequences of an appointment of receivers which was found to be invalid was considered by the Court of Appeal in *OBG Ltd v Allan* [2005] EWCA Civ 106. Here it was held (somewhat surprisingly) that the tort of wrongful interference with contractual relations could not be used to render invalidly appointed receivers liable for their acts in terminating a number of the company's contracts in the wake of their appointment. The Court of Appeal was reluctant to extend the scope of this economic tort in circumstances where the receivers had no wilful intention to procure a breach of contract. On the question whether the invalid appointment of the receivers involved the receivers committing the tort of conversion with regard to the contractual rights of the company placed in receivership, it was held that there was no tort of conversion of a chose in action recognised in English law. Mance L.J. stressed that counsel had agreed that the actions of an improperly appointed receiver remain valid by virtue of s.232 of the IA 1986. This case proceeded to the House of Lords as part of a joined appeal with two other cases, not concerned with the same subject matter. In its judgment *OBG Ltd v Allan* [2007] UKHL 21; [2007] 2 W.L.R. 920 the House of Lords issued some important guidance on the status various economic torts in English law. At the end of the day the claim against the receivers failed and the appeal was dismissed. There was unanimity that the receivers did not intend to induce the company in receivership to breach its contractual obligations and therefore the tort of unlawful interference with contractual relations was not established. The House split on the conversion issue but, bearing in mind the strict liability aspect of this tort, the majority ruled that it could only apply to conversion of chattels and not conversion of choses in action. The courts should not take the initiative in extending the parameters of this tort; such action should be for the prerogative of Parliament. Lord Hoffmann, whose judgment was supported by the majority, reiterated that the receivers had not been negligent and that there was no justification for extending the scope of conversion and thereby holding them responsible on a strict liability basis. These comments will reassure the insolvency practitioner profession.

35   Application to court for directions

35(1)   **[Application]** A receiver or manager of the property of a company appointed under powers contained in an instrument, or the persons by whom or on whose behalf a receiver or manager has been so appointed, may apply to the court for directions in relation to any particular matter arising in connection with the performance of the functions of the receiver or manager.

35(2)   **[Order, directions by court]** On such an application, the court may give such directions, or may make such order declaring the rights of persons before the court or otherwise, as it thinks just.

S.35(1)

This allows a receiver, or his appointor, to apply to the court for directions in the event of legal uncertainty arising. The latter was only given this facility by IA 1985, as a result of the recommendations of the Cork Committee (*Report,* para.828). This provision is to be widely interpreted and enables guidance to be sought on remuneration: *Re Therm-a-Stor Ltd* [1997] B.C.C. 301; and *Munns v Perkins* [2002] B.P.I.R. 120. Such guidance may be welcome in the light of the more stringent regime ushered in by Ferris J. in *Mirror Group Newspapers v Maxwell* [1998] B.C.C. 324. For an important commercial precedent delivered in response to a s.35 application for directions see *Re Cheyne Finance plc* [2007] EWHC 2402 (Ch); [2008] B.C.C. 182.

The FSA may, in an appropriate case, be heard on such an application—FSMA 2000 s.363(2).

S.35(2)
The court enjoys general discretion as to any declaration it may make on such an application.

36   Court's power to fix remuneration

36(1)   [Remuneration] The court may, on an application made by the liquidator of a company, by order fix the amount to be paid by way of remuneration to a person who, under powers contained in an instrument, has been appointed receiver or manager of the company's property.

36(2)   [Extent of court's power] The court's power under subsection (1), where no previous order has been made with respect thereto under the subsection–

(a)   extends to fixing the remuneration for any period before the making of the order or the application for it,

(b)   is exercisable notwithstanding that the receiver or manager has died or ceased to act before the making of the order or the application, and

(c)   where the receiver or manager has been paid or has retained for his remuneration for any period before the making of the order any amount in excess of that so fixed for that period, extends to requiring him or his personal representatives to account for the excess or such part of it as may be specified in the order.

But the power conferred by paragraph (c) shall not be exercised as respects any period before the making of the application for the order under this section, unless in the court's opinion there are special circumstances making it proper for the power to be exercised.

36(3)   [Variation, amendment of order] The court may from time to time on an application made either by the liquidator or by the receiver or manager, vary or amend an order made under subsection (1).

S.36(1)
This allows the court to determine the remuneration of a receiver and manager appointed out of court where the liquidator of the company asks for this to be done. Such applications in the past have been rare, if only because of the courtesy that exists between fellow insolvency practitioners. For a recent but unsuccessful application, see *Re Potters Oils Ltd (No.2)* [1986] 1 W.L.R. 201; (1985) 1 B.C.C. 99,593. With a more questioning era looming with regard to professional remuneration levels applications under this provision may become more commonplace. In *Munns v Perkins* [2002] B.P.I.R. 120 a fee amounting to 4.2 per cent of the value of assets realised was deemed reasonable.

The High Court in *Re Delberry Ltd* [2008] B.P.I.R. 1277 indicated that the investigatory mechanism under s.236 could be used to facilitate a s.36 claim by procuring the delivery up of documents relating to the conduct of the receivership.

S.36(2)
This provides further details of the powers of the court where an application has been made to it under s.36(1).

S.36(3)
The court can vary any order it makes fixing remuneration.

37   Liability for contracts, etc.

37(1)   [Personal liability, indemnity] A receiver or manager appointed under powers contained in an instrument (other than an administrative receiver) is, to the same extent as if he had been appointed by order of the court–

(a) personally liable on any contract entered into by him in the performance of his functions (except in so far as the contract otherwise provides) and on any contract of employment adopted by him in the performance of those functions, and

(b) entitled in respect of that liability to indemnity out of the assets.

37(2) [Interpretation of s.37(1)(a)] For the purposes of subsection (1)(a), the receiver or manager is not to be taken to have adopted a contract of employment by reason of anything done or omitted to be done within 14 days after his appointment.

37(3) [Extent of s.37(1)] Subsection (1) does not limit any right to indemnity which the receiver or manager would have apart from it, nor limit his liability on contracts entered into without authority, nor confer any right to indemnity in respect of that liability.

37(4) [Vacation of office] Where at any time the receiver or manager so appointed vacates office–

(a) his remuneration and any expenses properly incurred by him, and

(b) any indemnity to which he is entitled out of the assets of the company,

shall be charged on and paid out of any property of the company which is in his custody or under his control at that time in priority to any charge or other security held by the person by or on whose behalf he was appointed.

S.37(1), (2)

Receivers appointed out of court are personally liable on contracts entered into by them (unless they have contracted out), and existing contracts of employment adopted by them, although they have 14 days' grace to decide whether to adopt or not. This latter provision is designed to cope with the problems thrown up by *Nicoll v Cutts* (1985) 1 B.C.C. 99,427. Where a receiver adopts a contract of employment under s.37(1)(a) the case will be caught by the rule in *Re Paramount Airways Ltd (No.3)* [1994] B.C.C. 172 (*Powdrill v Watson* [1995] 2 A.C. 394) and this adoption will impose all accrued employment liabilities on the receiver. (See the notes to ss.19 and 44.) The relief extended by s.2 of IA 1994 to mitigate this rule has (for unconvincing reasons) deliberately not been extended to non-administrative receivers, though the Government was supposed to be reconsidering this matter: see DTI Press Notice P/94/319. Such receivers may have to adopt contracts of employment if they are enforcing a fixed charge over, say, a hotel and they wish to retain staff pending a sale of the hotel as a going concern. It is implicit in s.37(1)(a) that a receiver is entitled not to adopt existing contracts of the company. Where he chooses this option as a rule no injunction will lie against him to enforce observance of the contract: see *Airlines Airspares Ltd v Handley Page Ltd* [1970] Ch. 193. However, in some cases the contract may be enforced: see *Freevale Ltd v Metrostore (Holdings) Ltd* [1984] Ch. 199; *Amec Properties v Planning Research and Systems* [1992] 13 E.G. 109; the discussion in *Astor Chemical Ltd v Synthetic Technology Ltd* [1990] B.C.C. 97; and *Ash & Newman v Creative Devices Research Ltd* [1991] B.C.L.C. 403. The uncertainties in this area have continued through cases like *Transtec Automotive (Campsie) Ltd* [2001] B.C.C. 403; and *Land Rover Group v UPF (UK) Ltd* [2002] EWHC 3183 (QB); [2003] 2 B.C.L.C. 222.

For an abortive attempt to make receivers (and their appointing debenture holder) personally liable in costs in the event of unsuccessful litigation brought in the company's name see *Mills v Birchall* [2008] EWCA Civ 385; [2008] B.P.I.R. 607. The action here was merely to enforce a contractual right forming part of the security—it was properly characterised as an action by the company and neither by the receivers nor the debenture holder. The receivers were the agents of the company as both the debenture and s.109(2) of the Law of Property Act 1925 made clear. The debenture holder did not fund the action which had been financed by the receivers out of realisations. In a normal case like this it would be inappropriate to render either the receivers or the debenture holder personally responsible for the costs of the other side even though the litigation had been unsuccessful.

This provision was held not to apply in *Re Dairy Farmers of Britain Ltd* [2009] EWHC 1389 (Ch).

S.37(3)

The receiver's statutory indemnity in respect of contractual liability under s.37(1)(b) is not exhaustive. On the other hand, it does not apply to contracts entered into by him without authority.

S.37(4)

This accords high priority status to the receiver's right to remuneration and indemnity. However it is important to remember that this priority only extends to the proceeds of assets caught by the security. The right to remuneration cannot be charged against assets encompassed by a prior security: *Choudhri v Palta* [1992] B.C.C. 787. Furthermore, in cases where the receiver has realised sufficient funds to repay the debenture holder and also (arguably) to satisfy his own claim to remuneration, etc. the court might intervene and offer interlocutory relief to prevent further sales until the quantum of remuneration has been settled: *Rottenberg v Monjack* [1992] B.C.C. 688.

38 Receivership accounts to be delivered to registrar

38(1) **[Where appointment under powers in instrument]** Except in the case of an administrative receiver, every receiver or manager of a company's property who has been appointed under powers contained in an instrument shall deliver to the registrar of companies for registration the requisite accounts of his receipts and payments.

38(2) **[Time for delivering accounts]** The accounts shall be delivered within one month (or such longer period as the registrar may allow) after the expiration of 12 months from the date of his appointment and of every subsequent period of 6 months, and also within one month after he ceases to act as receiver or manager.

38(3) **[Form of accounts]** The requisite accounts shall be an abstract in the prescribed form showing–

(a) receipts and payments during the relevant period of 12 or 6 months, or

(b) where the receiver or manager ceases to act, receipts and payments during the period from the end of the period of 12 or 6 months to which the last preceding abstract related (or, if no preceding abstract has been delivered under this section, from the date of his appointment) up to the date of his so ceasing, and the aggregate amount of receipts and payments during all preceding periods since his appointment.

38(4) **["Prescribed"]** In this section **"prescribed"** means prescribed by regulations made by statutory instrument by the Secretary of State.

38(5) **[Penalty on default]** A receiver or manager who makes default in complying with this section is liable to a fine and, for continued contravention, to a daily default fine.

S.38(1), (2)
Receivers or managers other than administrative receivers must periodically submit accounts to Cardiff.

S.38(3), (4)
These regulate the form of the accounts. For building societies see para.25 of Sch.15A as inserted by s.39, and Sch.6 to the Building Societies Act 1997.

S.38(5)
Criminal sanctions are imposed on the receiver in the event of default. On penalties, see s.430 and Sch.10. Note also the enforcement procedures laid down in s.41.
    For administrative receivers, see IR 1986 r.3.32.

Provisions applicable to every receivership

39 Notification that receiver or manager appointed

39(1) **[Statement in invoices etc.]** Where a receiver or manager of the property of a company has been appointed–

(a) every invoice, order for goods or services, business letter or order form (whether in hard copy, electronic or any other form) issued by or on behalf of the company or the receiver or manager or the liquidator of the company; and

(b) all the company's websites,

must contain a statement that a receiver or manager has been appointed.

39(2) **[Penalty on default]** If default is made in complying with this section, the company and any of the following persons, who knowingly and wilfully authorises or permits the default, namely, any officer of the company, any liquidator of the company and any receiver or manager, is liable to a fine.

S.39(1)

Invoices, business letters, etc. must disclose the fact that a receiver and manager has been appointed. A new s.39(1) was substituted by the Companies (Trading Disclosures) (Insolvency) Regulations 2008 (SI 2008/1897) (as amended by SI 2009/218) with effect from October 1, 2008. This change was necessary to comply with EC Directive 2003/58 and seeks to promote disclosure where electronic invoices are used and where the company has a website. Note also that under CA 1985 s.405(1) [CA 2006 s.871(1)] the fact of the appointment must be notified to Cardiff, and by virtue of IA 1986 s.46, notice must be given to creditors. Where a secured creditor intends to enforce security in the case of a railway company special advance notification requirements have been imposed by s.62(7) of the Railways Act 1993. For building societies see para.26 of Sch.15A as inserted by s.39 of and Sch.6 to the Building Societies Act 1997.

S.39(2)

Criminal sanctions may be imposed on various named persons in the event of a breach of s.39(1). On penalties, see s.430 and Sch.10.

40 Payment of debts out of assets subject to floating charge

40(1) [Application] The following applies, in the case of a company, where a receiver is appointed on behalf of the holders of any debentures of the company secured by a charge which, as created, was a floating charge.

40(2) [Payment of preferential debts] If the company is not at the time in course of being wound up, its preferential debts (within the meaning given to that expression by section 386 in Part XII) shall be paid out of the assets coming to the hands of the receiver in priority to any claims for principal or interest in respect of the debentures.

40(3) [Recoupment of payments] Payments made under this section shall be recouped, as far as may be, out of the assets of the company available for payment of general creditors.

S.40(1), (2)

These subsections impose an obligation on every receiver appointed to enforce a floating charge to pay preferential claims (see s.386 and Sch.6). However, this obligation does not extend to receivers of industrial and provident societies: *Re Devon and Somerset Farmers Ltd* [1994] Ch. 57; [1993] B.C.C. 410. This is a positive obligation (*IR Commissioners v Goldblatt* [1972] Ch. 498) and a continuing responsibility that is not discharged simply because the debenture holder has been repaid: *Re Pearl Maintenance Services Ltd* [1995] B.C.C. 657. Note that the fact that the charge may have crystallised prior to the appointment of the receiver does not take the case outside the scope of s.40. This follows from the revised definition of "floating charge" which was introduced by IA 1985 (see now IA 1986 s.251), and which is incorporated into the wording of s.40(1). For the significance of this change in the law see *Re Brightlife Ltd* [1987] Ch. 200; (1986) 2 B.C.C. 99,359. The duty imposed by s.40 is limited by s.11(5) but the fact that the company may go into liquidation during the currency of the receivership does not relieve the receiver of his obligation to pay preferential claims: *Re Eisc Teo Ltd* [1991] I.L.R.M. 760. The determination of whether a charge is floating or fixed is clearly of considerable importance for the purposes of s.40—see here *Chalk v Kahn* [2000] 2 B.C.L.C. 361. All authorities on this vexed issue of security characterisation must be read in the light of the advice of the Privy Council in *Agnew v CIR (Re Brumark Investments Ltd)* [2001] UKPC 28; [2001] 2 A.C. 710. For comment see Sealy, [2001] 76 Company Law Newsletter 1. This latter ruling upset established receivership practice and created real worries for practitioners who may have made distributions on the basis of a misinterpretation of the law (relying on the discredited authority of *Re New Bullas Trading Ltd* [1994] 1 B.C.L.C. 485). These concerns were somewhat alleviated by a Crown Departments Statement offering in effect an amnesty for erroneous distributions made prior to June 5, 2001 (i.e. the date when the Privy Council handed down its judgment). For comment see Milman, [2002] Insolv. L. 77. For a further judicial authority in this field see *Re BHT (UK) Ltd* [2004] EWHC 201 (Ch), where an attempt to unwind pre-June 5, 2001 distributions under a now "suspect" fixed charge failed. Further confirmation of the vulnerability of "fixed charges" to judicial recharacterisation is provided by the ruling of Sir Andrew Morritt V.C. in *Re Spectrum Plus Ltd* [2004] EWHC 9 (Ch); [2004] B.C.C. 51 where a standard debenture fixed charge modelled upon that upheld by Slade J. in *Siebe Gorman & Co Ltd v Barclays Bank* [1979] 2 Lloyd's Rep. 142 was in fact held only to create a floating charge. This decision of Morritt V.C. was surprisingly reversed by the Court of Appeal (see [2004] EWCA Civ 670; [2004] B.C.C. 660) which laid great store on the importance of the contractual relationship between the lending bank and the borrower and also on the fact that as *Siebe Gorman* (above) was an established authority that had stood for two decades legitimate expectations in commercial practice required reassurance. These lines of reasoning were greeted with some scepticism in many quarters—see for example

Milman, [2004] 17 Insolv. Int. 116; and Smart, [2004] 17 Insolv. Int. 118. The issue, which it has been estimated is of relevance to some 500 insolvencies worth at least £200 million collectively, was then referred to the House of Lords which sat as a full panel of seven members. That panel unanimously ruled (*National Westminster Bank v Spectrum Plus Ltd* [2005] UKHL 41; [2005] 3 W.L.R. 58; [2005] B.C.C. 694) that *Siebe Gorman* (above) should be overruled and that the standard bank debenture that was the subject of the litigation in fact created only a floating and not a fixed charge. Moreover, the House of Lords refused to mitigate the potentially dire consequences of this ruling for banks by giving it only prospective effect. One might therefore anticipate a number of challenges by those acting on behalf of preferential creditors to require banks to regurgitate funds which were paid to them under mistake as to the status of the *Siebe Gorman*-type debenture. Equally receivers who have made such distributions in error should look to their indemnity arrangements with debenture holders.

For comment see Berg, [2006] J.B.L. 22. Some of the difficulties have been mitigated by the Crown Statement of July 2005, which is reproduced as App.X of Vol.2 of this *Guide*. The Crown Departments are still active in dealing with the consequences of *Brumark* (above) and *Spectrum* (above). This is apparent from *Dear IP*, March 2008. The House of Lords ruling in *Spectrum* (above) was applied by the court in *Re Beam Tube Products Ltd* [2006] B.C.C. 615 to recharacterise a charge described as "fixed" to merely floating status. But compare *Russell Cooke Trust Co Ltd v Elliott* [2007] EWHC 1443 (Ch), where, somewhat bizarrely, the opposite conclusion was arrived at (i.e. a "floating charge" judged to be a fixed charge) when the security documentation was deconstructed. Both cases merely confirm the legal adage that labels are to be treated with caution.

For the difficult questions of interpretation posed by s.40 see *Re H & K Medway Ltd* [1997] 1 W.L.R. 1422; [1997] B.C.C. 853; not following *Griffiths v Yorkshire Bank* [1994] 1 W.L.R. 1427 (discussed by Cooke in (1995) 11 I.L. & P. 163). In the former case Neuberger J. explains the relationship between s.40 and CA 1985 s.196 [CA 2006 s.754]. See also Waller, [1997–98] 3 R.A.L.Q. 131. For a rare discussion of CA 1985 s.196 (now CA 2006 s.754) see *HMRC v Royal Bank of Scotland (Re Oval 1742 Ltd)* [2007] EWCA Civ 1262; [2008] B.C.C. 135, where the relationship with IA 1986 s.175 was also reviewed. Here both the judge at first instance and the Court of Appeal felt justified in adopting a wide view of the concept of "taking possession" and in so doing concentrated upon the substance of the matter under review rather than the form.

The receiver's obligation to cater for preferential claims will be mitigated when the full consequences of the abolition of Crown preferential debt (introduced via EA 2002 s.251) are felt. However, not all preferential debts will disappear. Moreover, receivers will in future have to take account of the special reserve fund for unsecured creditors, which was introduced by EA 2002 s.252 (see IA 1986 s.176A and IR 1986 rr.3.39–3.40). This does not apply to floating charges created before September 15, 2003. Holders of floating charges created before this date thus gain from this package of reforms.

These provisions are inapplicable to building society receiverships as the floating charge is not permitted: see para.27 of Sch.15A as inserted by s.39 and Sch.6 to the Building Societies Act 1997. Note also s.111 of the Building Societies Act 1997.

S.40(3)

This makes it clear that the real burden of meeting the claims of preferential creditors falls on the unsecured creditors.

41   Enforcement of duty to make returns

41(1)   [Court order re defaults] If a receiver or manager of a company's property–

   (a) having made default in filing, delivering or making any return, account or other document, or in giving any notice, which a receiver or manager is by law required to file, deliver, make or give, fails to make good the default within 14 days after the service on him of a notice requiring him to do so, or

   (b) having been appointed under powers contained in an instrument, has, after being required at any time by the liquidator of the company to do so, failed to render proper accounts of his receipts and payments and to vouch them and pay over to the liquidator the amount properly payable to him,

the court may, on an application made for the purpose, make an order directing the receiver or manager (as the case may be) to make good the default within such time as may be specified in the order.

41(2)   [Application for order] In the case of the default mentioned in subsection (1)(a), application to the court may be made by any member or creditor of the company or by the registrar of companies; and in the case of the default mentioned in subsection (1)(b), the application shall be made by the liquidator.

In either case the court's order may provide that all costs of and incidental to the application shall be borne by the receiver or manager, as the case may be.

41(3) [Other enactments] Nothing in this section prejudices the operation of any enactment imposing penalties on receivers in respect of any such default as is mentioned in subsection (1).

S.41(1)
This subsection sets out an enforcement procedure to deal with receivers who fail to submit accounts, returns, etc.

S.41(2)
Applicants to the court for an enforcement order are identified. Applicants may be indemnified against costs thereby arising. The FSA may apply where appropriate—FSMA 2000 s.363(3).

S.41(3)
Sanctions imposed by individual sections creating obligations to file returns, etc. are not prejudiced by s.41.

Administrative receivers: general

42 General powers

42(1) [Powers in Sch.1] The powers conferred on the administrative receiver of a company by the debentures by virtue of which he was appointed are deemed to include (except in so far as they are inconsistent with any of the provisions of those debentures) the powers specified in Schedule 1 to this Act.

42(2) [Interpretation of Sch.1] In the application of Schedule 1 to the administrative receiver of a company–

(a) the words "he" and "him" refer to the administrative receiver, and

(b) references to the property of the company are to the property of which he is or, but for the appointment of some other person as the receiver of part of the company's property, would be the receiver or manager.

42(3) [Deemed capacity] A person dealing with the administrative receiver in good faith and for value is not concerned to inquire whether the receiver is acting within his powers.

S.42(1)
A model list of 23 implied powers for an administrative receiver (for the definition of this term, see s.29(2)) is set out by Sch.1 to this Act. These are commonly found in most standard commercial debentures. These 23 implied powers would appear to cover almost every eventuality, particularly when one bears in mind the general nature of power number 23. The implied powers are the same as those accorded to an administrator. The exercise of these powers may be subject to constraints imposed by companies legislation: see for example *Demite Ltd v Protec Health Ltd* [1998] B.C.C. 638 where the power to sell was subjected to the restrictions imposed by s.320 of CA 1985 [CA 2006 s.190]. The position here will remain unchanged under the Companies Act 2006. It is clear from the extent of these powers that once a company goes into administrative receivership the control of its management passes from the directors to the receiver. For the implications of this see *Re Joshua Shaw & Sons Ltd* (1989) 5 B.C.C. 188. The powers conferred on an administrative receiver (whether conferred by the debenture or by statutory provision) are given to assist in the realisation of assets. Powers should not be used to further the interests of the debenture holder in litigation with third parties—*Sutton v GE Capital Commercial Finance* [2004] EWCA Civ 315; [2004] 2 B.C.L.C. 662.

S.42(2)
This is an interpretation provision designed to smooth out any difficulties in the application of Sch.1.

S.42(3)
This statutory provision is an extension of the basic company law philosophy contained in *Royal British Bank v Turquand* (1856) 6 E. & B. 327; and in CA 1985 ss.35A and 35B [CA 2006 s.40].

43 Power to dispose of charged property, etc.

43(1) [Application to court] Where, on an application by the administrative receiver, the court is satisfied that the disposal (with or without other assets) of any relevant property which is subject to a security would be likely to promote a more advantageous realisation of the company's assets than would otherwise be effected, the court may by order authorise the administrative receiver to dispose of the property as if it were not subject to the security.

43(2)   [Application of s.43(1)] Subsection (1) does not apply in the case of any security held by the person by or on whose behalf the administrative receiver was appointed, or of any security to which a security so held has priority.

43(3)   [Conditions for order] It shall be a condition of an order under this section that–

(a)   the net proceeds of the disposal, and

(b)   where those proceeds are less than such amount as may be determined by the court to be the net amount which would be realised on a sale of the property in the open market by a willing vendor, such sums as may be required to make good the deficiency,

shall be applied towards discharging the sums secured by the security.

43(4)   [Where two or more securities] Where a condition imposed in pursuance of subsection (3) relates to two or more securities, that condition shall require the net proceeds of the disposal and, where paragraph (b) of that subsection applies, the sums mentioned in that paragraph to be applied towards discharging the sums secured by those securities in the order of their priorities.

43(5)   [Copy of order to registrar] A copy of an order under this section shall, within 14 days of the making of the order, be sent by the administrative receiver to the registrar of companies.

43(6)   [Penalty for non-compliance] If the administrative receiver without reasonable excuse fails to comply with subsection (5), he is liable to a fine and, for continued contravention, to a daily default fine.

43(7)   ["Relevant property"] In this section **"relevant property"**, in relation to the administrative receiver, means the property of which he is or, but for the appointment of some other person as the receiver of part of the company's property, would be the receiver or manager.

GENERAL NOTE

This section applies to England and Wales only (see s.440(2)(a)).

Section 43 does not apply in relation to the enforcement of "market charges" (as defined by CA 1989 s.173): see s.175 of that Act (as qualified by the Financial Markets and Insolvency Regulations 1991 (SI 1991/880, amended by SI 1995/586 and SI 1998/27)), and the introductory note at p.3, above.

S.43(1), (2)

These provisions create a novel facility for administrative receivers by allowing them to apply to the court for the disposal of property that is subject to a prior charge (normally a fixed charge). The court must be satisfied that such disposal would promote a more advantageous realisation of the company's assets. The word "likely" in this context would probably be construed by the courts as meaning "a reasonable prospect": see *Re Harris Simons Construction Ltd* [1989] 1 W.L.R. 368; (1989) 5 B.C.C. 11. A similar power is given to an administrator by s.15, but the power under s.15 is wider in that it covers property subject to title retention.

"Relevant property" is defined in s.43(7).

For further details, see IR 1986 r.3.31.

S.43(3), (4)

If the court orders a disposal, the net proceeds are to be paid to discharge the prior security or securities (see s.43(4)). If the court decides that the sale was at an undervalue, the deficiency must be made good.

S.43(5), (6)

A copy of the disposal order must be registered at Cardiff within 14 days or else the administrative receiver may incur criminal sanctions. Note the minor amendment introduced in subs.(5) by the Companies Act 2006 (Consequential Amendments, Transitional Provisions and Savings) Order 2009 (SI 2009/1941) with effect from October 1, 2009.

On penalties, see s.430 and Sch.10.

S.43(7)
This is an interpretation provision and is best understood in relation to s.29(2)(b).

44   Agency and liability for contracts

44(1)   **[Position of administrative receiver]** The administrative receiver of a company–

(a)   is deemed to be the company's agent, unless and until the company goes into liquidation;

(b)   is personally liable on any contract entered into by him in the carrying out of his functions (except in so far as the contract otherwise provides) and, to the extent of any qualifying liability, on any contract of employment adopted by him in the carrying out of those functions; and

(c)   is entitled in respect of that liability to an indemnity out of the assets of the company.

44(2)   **[Interpretation]** For the purposes of subsection (1)(b) the administrative receiver is not to be taken to have adopted a contract of employment by reason of anything done or omitted to be done within 14 days after his appointment.

44(2A)   **[Interpretation of s.44(1)(b)]** For the purposes of subsection (1)(b), a liability under a contract of employment is a qualifying liability if–

(a)   it is a liability to pay a sum by way of wages or salary or contribution to an occupational pension scheme,

(b)   it is incurred while the administrative receiver is in office, and

(c)   it is in respect of services rendered wholly or partly after the adoption of the contract.

44(2B)   **[Further interpretation of s.44(1)(b)]** Where a sum payable in respect of a liability which is a qualifying liability for the purposes of subsection (1)(b) is payable in respect of services rendered partly before and partly after the adoption of the contract, liability under subsection (1)(b) shall only extend to so much of the sum as is payable in respect of services rendered after the adoption of the contract.

44(2C)   **[Interpretation of s.44(2A), (2B)]** For the purposes of subsections (2A) and (2B)–

(a)   wages or salary payable in respect of a period of holiday or absence from work through sickness or other good cause are deemed to be wages or (as the case may be) salary in respect of services rendered in that period, and

(b)   a sum payable in lieu of holiday is deemed to be wages or (as the case may be) salary in respect of services rendered in the period by reference to which the holiday entitlement arose.

44(2D)   **[Interpretation of s.44(2C)(a)]** In subsection (2C)(a), the reference to wages or salary payable in respect of a period of holiday includes any sums which, if they had been paid, would have been treated for the purposes of the enactments relating to social security as earnings in respect of that period.

44(3)   **[Effect on other rights]** This section does not limit any right to indemnity which the administrative receiver would have apart from it, nor limit his liability on contracts entered into or adopted without authority, nor confer any right to indemnity in respect of that liability.

S.44(1), (2)
By virtue of s.44(1)(a), an administrative receiver is deemed to be the company's agent, provided that the company has not gone into liquidation, whereupon the agency relationship terminates. This is merely a statutory declaration of the standard agency provision found in most commercial debentures. For the position on winding up, see *Gosling v Gaskell and Grocott* [1897] A.C. 575; and the article by Turing in (1994) 9 I.L. & P. 163. One implication of the agency relationship was illustrated in *Brown v City of London Corp* [1996] 1 W.L.R. 1070 (also reported as *Re Sobam BV* [1996] B.C.C. 351) where it was held that a receiver was not liable for rates during his period of occupation. The termination of this agency relationship does not result in a change of occupation for rating purposes—*Re Beck Foods Ltd* [2001] EWCA Civ 1934; [2002] B.C.C. 495. These developments represent a further blow for local authorities which no longer enjoy preferential status with respect to unpaid rates and who additionally have difficulty in protecting their interests through distress, as was confirmed by *Re ELS Ltd* [1994] B.C.C. 449.

An agent is not normally liable personally on a contract which he makes for his principal, and in the light of this, para.(b) may seem somewhat surprising—especially when it is contrasted with s.14(5), which deems an administrator to be the company's agent without a similar qualification. The explanation is that a receiver is entitled to stipulate for an indemnity from the charge holder as a term of his accepting office, contracting out of this liability. For a case where such contracting out would have found favour with the courts see *Amec Properties v Planning Research and Systems* [1992] 13 E.G. 109. For the practical significance of this indemnity see *Lipe Ltd v Leyland DAF Ltd* [1993] B.C.C. 385.

Sections 44(1)(a) and 44(2) now need to be read in the light of amendments made by IA 1994. The background to these amendments can be traced back ultimately to the case of *Nicoll v Cutts* (1985) 1 B.C.C. 99,427 where it was held that a receiver who continued to retain the services of company employees during the receivership did not thereby adopt their contracts of employment. This decision was immediately counteracted by an express statutory provision extending the personal contractual liability of administrative receivers to cases of adopted contracts of employment. Insolvency practitioners sought to neutralise this statutory intervention by sending all employees whose services were being retained a letter to the effect that their contracts of employment were not being adopted nor was the administrative receiver undertaking personal liability thereon. This practice drew its support from the unreported ruling of Harman J. in *Re Specialised Mouldings Ltd* (February 13, 1987). The ability of insolvency practitioners to avoid the effect of the statutory rules imposing liability in cases of adoption was reviewed by the Court of Appeal in *Re Paramount Airways Ltd (No.3)* [1994] B.C.C. 172 (see the note to s.19 above). Here the Court of Appeal held (confirming the first instance ruling of Evans-Lombe J.) that adoption could occur simply by retaining staff without changing the terms of their employment. A transparent ploy such as sending a *"Specialised Mouldings"* letter was of no effect. As a result of this pronouncement from the Court of Appeal administrative receivers who retained staff after the initial 14-day period for reflection did so on the basis that they became personally liable for all accrued and current rights arising under the relevant contracts of employment. Not surprisingly, administrative receivers were reluctant to assume such personal risk, even though it would be covered by their indemnity. Debenture holders would be less willing to wait for their money by allowing the receiver to generate it through a corporate rescue but would instead insist on an immediate sale.

The economic and political consequences of abandoning a corporate rescue strategy were so great that the government was persuaded to legislate immediately. This legislation takes the form of IA 1994 which applies to contracts of employment adopted on or after March 15, 1994 (this legislation is to this extent retrospective as Royal Assent was only given on March 24, 1994). Under s.2 of this Act where a contract of employment is adopted by an administrative receiver he will only become personally responsible for "qualifying liabilities". These are defined in the new ss.44(2A)–(2D) (inserted by IA 1994 s.2(1), (3), (4)) as certain liabilities accruing only after the date when the contract was adopted. The government has indicated that it will not be persuaded to extend the retrospective effect of this legislation beyond March 15, 1994: see DTI Press Notice P/95/282.

The issue was revisited when *Paramount* (and the direct appeals in *Re Leyland DAF* and *Re Ferranti International* [1994] B.C.C. 654) reached the House of Lords (reported sub nom. *Powdrill v Watson* [1995] 2 A.C. 394; [1995] B.C.C. 319). Their Lordships were of course concerned to clarify the law pre-March 15, 1994 and in essence they approved of the approach of the Court of Appeal with regard to adoption. However they took a more restrictive view of the extent of liabilities incurred in cases of adoption. For a review of the whole saga see Mudd, (1994) 10 I.L. & P. 38 and (1995) 11 I.L. & P. 78. Pre-1994 claims still continue to trouble receivers, as is clear from the Scottish case of *Jamieson, Petitioners*, 1997 S.C. 195; [1997] B.C.C. 682. On whether adoption can occur by error, see *Re Antal International Ltd* [2003] EWHC 1339 (Ch); [2003] 2 B.C.L.C. 406 a case on administration.

In s.44(1)(b) the words ", to the extent of any qualifying liability," were inserted after "provides) and" by IA 1994 s.2(1), (2), (4).

For discussion of what might be viewed as "wages or salary" in the context of administration see *Re Allders Department Stores Ltd* [2005] EWHC 172 (Ch); [2005] B.C.C. 289. See annotation to Sch.B1 para.99.

For further comment on s.44 and the possibility of personal liability of administrative receivers see *Legends Surf Shops plc v Sun Life Assurance Society plc* [2005] EWHC 1438 (Ch); [2006] B.C.C. 204 (Laddie J.), a case involving an application for relief against forfeiture brought by administrative receivers of the tenant company.

S.44(3)
This, in effect, merely extends s.37(3) to administrative receivers.

45 Vacation of office

45(1) [Removal by court, resignation] An administrative receiver of a company may at any time be removed from office by order of the court (but not otherwise) and may resign his office by giving notice of his resignation in the prescribed manner to such persons as may be prescribed.

45(2) **[Vacation of office]** An administrative receiver shall vacate office if he ceases to be qualified to act as an insolvency practitioner in relation to the company.

45(3) **[Effect of vacation of office]** Where at any time an administrative receiver vacates office–

(a) his remuneration and any expenses properly incurred by him, and

(b) any indemnity to which he is entitled out of the assets of the company,

shall be charged on and paid out of any property of the company which is in his custody or under his control at that time in priority to any security held by the person by or on whose behalf he was appointed.

45(4) **[Notice to registrar]** Where an administrative receiver vacates office otherwise than by death, he shall, within 14 days after his vacation of office, send a notice to that effect to the registrar of companies.

45(5) **[Penalty for non-compliance]** If an administrative receiver without reasonable excuse fails to comply with subsection (4), he is liable to a fine and, for continued contravention, to a daily default fine.

S.45(1), (2)

These subsections outline the situations where the tenure of an administrative receiver comes to an end. Note that (as a result of a change in the law made by IA 1985) he can only be removed by debenture holders if they successfully apply to the court. This will make it clear that he is not entirely the minion of the debenture holders who appointed him. If he loses his qualification as an insolvency practitioner (see Pt XIII) he must also vacate office. Although the court has the power to remove an administrative receiver it does not enjoy the consequential power of appointing a replacement: *Re A & C Supplies Ltd* [1998] B.C.C. 708. Such a replacement can only be effected by a debenture holder enjoying a floating charge.

S.45(3)

This subsection protects the priority status of the administrative receiver's right to remuneration and indemnity.

S.45(4), (5)

On vacating office the administrative receiver must notify Cardiff within 14 days or incur a fine. A similar obligation is imposed by CA 1985 s.405(2). Note prospective amendment in s.45(5): the words "and, for continued contravention, to a daily default fine" are to be repealed by CA 1989 Schs 16 and 24 from a day to be appointed.

On penalties, see s.430 and Sch.10.

On payment of unclaimed dividends by a former administrative receiver of a now dissolved company into the Insolvency Services Account see the Insolvency (Amendment) Regulations 2008 (SI 2008/670), which insert a new reg.3C into the Insolvency Regulations 1994 (SI 1994/2507).

For further information, see IR 1986 rr.3.33–3.35.

Administrative receivers: ascertainment and investigation of company's affairs

46 Information to be given by administrative receiver

46(1) **[Notices]** Where an administrative receiver is appointed, he shall–

(a) forthwith send to the company and publish in the prescribed manner a notice of his appointment, and

(b) within 28 days after his appointment, unless the court otherwise directs, send such a notice to all the creditors of the company (so far as he is aware of their addresses).

46(2) **[Non-application]** This section and the next do not apply in relation to the appointment of an administrative receiver to act–

(a) with an existing administrative receiver, or

(b) in place of an administrative receiver dying or ceasing to act,

except that, where they apply to an administrative receiver who dies or ceases to act before they have been fully complied with, the references in this section and the next to the administrative receiver include (subject to the next subsection) his successor and any continuing administrative receiver.

46(3) **[Where company being wound up]** If the company is being wound up, this section and the next apply notwithstanding that the administrative receiver and the liquidator are the same person, but with any necessary modifications arising from that fact.

46(4) **[Penalty for non-compliance]** If the administrative receiver without reasonable excuse fails to comply with this section, he is liable to a fine and, for continued contravention, to a daily default fine.

S.46(1), (4)
These provisions impose obligations on the administrative receiver to give notice of his appointment to various named parties. Criminal sanctions are imposed in the event of default (on penalties, see s.430 and Sch.10). Note also s.39, and CA 1985 s.405(1) (entry of appointment in register of charges) [CA 2006 s.871(1)].

S.46(2), (3)
Qualifications to the above obligations are imposed. Compliance with s.46(1) is a once and for all requirement. Provision is made for the case where the company is in liquidation and the administrative receiver is also the liquidator.

For further details, see IR 1986 r.3.2.

47   Statement of affairs to be submitted

47(1) **[Duty of administrative receiver]** Where an administrative receiver is appointed, he shall forthwith require some or all of the persons mentioned below to make out and submit to him a statement in the prescribed form as to the affairs of the company.

47(2) **[Contents of statement]** A statement submitted under this section shall be verified by a statement of truth by the persons required to submit it and shall show–

    (a)   particulars of the company's assets, debts and liabilities;

    (b)   the names and addresses of its creditors;

    (c)   the securities held by them respectively;

    (d)   the dates when the securities were respectively given; and

    (e)   such further or other information as may be prescribed.

47(3) **[Persons in s.47(1)]** The persons referred to in subsection (1) are–

    (a)   those who are or have been officers of the company;

    (b)   those who have taken part in the company's formation at any time within one year before the date of the appointment of the administrative receiver;

    (c)   those who are in the company's employment, or have been in its employment within that year, and are in the administrative receiver's opinion capable of giving the information required;

    (d)   those who are or have been within that year officers of or in the employment of a company which is, or within that year was, an officer of the company.

In this subsection **"employment"** includes employment under a contract for services.

47(4) **[Time for statement]** Where any persons are required under this section to submit a statement of affairs to the administrative receiver, they shall do so (subject to the next subsection) before the end of the period of 21 days beginning with the day after that on which the prescribed notice of the requirement is given to them by the administrative receiver.

47(5) **[Release, extension of time]** The administrative receiver, if he thinks fit, may–

    (a)   at any time release a person from an obligation imposed on him under subsection (1) or (2), or

    (b)   either when giving notice under subsection (4) or subsequently, extend the period so mentioned;

and where the administrative receiver has refused to exercise a power conferred by this subsection, the court, if it thinks fit, may exercise it.

47(6) **[Penalty for non-compliance]** If a person without reasonable excuse fails to comply with any obligation imposed under this section, he is liable to a fine and, for continued contravention, to a daily default fine.

S.47(1), (2), (4)

A statement of affairs containing the information outlined in s.47(2) and the rules must be submitted to the administrative receiver within 21 days of his requiring it (or longer, if s.47(5) is activated). Amended by LRO 2010 (SI 2010/18).

S.47(3), (5), (6)

The persons who may be required by the administrative receiver to participate in the submission of the statement of affairs are identified by s.47(3), although they may be excused either by the administrative receiver or the courts. Criminal sanctions are imposed on defaulters. On penalties, see s.430 and Sch.10.

For further information, see IR 1986 rr.3.3–3.7. For enforcement by the administrative receiver, see IR 1986 r.7.20.

48   Report by administrative receiver

48(1) **[Duty of administrative receiver]** Where an administrative receiver is appointed, he shall, within 3 months (or such longer period as the court may allow) after his appointment, send to the registrar of companies, to any trustees for secured creditors of the company and (so far as he is aware of their addresses) to all such creditors a report as to the following matters, namely–

(a)   the events leading up to his appointment, so far as he is aware of them;

(b)   the disposal or proposed disposal by him of any property of the company and the carrying on or proposed carrying on by him of any business of the company;

(c)   the amounts of principal and interest payable to the debenture holders by whom or on whose behalf he was appointed and the amounts payable to preferential creditors; and

(d)   the amount (if any) likely to be available for the payment of other creditors.

48(2) **[Copies of report]** The administrative receiver shall also, within 3 months (or such longer period as the court may allow) after his appointment, either–

(a)   send a copy of the report (so far as he is aware of their addresses) to all unsecured creditors of the company; or

(b)   publish in the prescribed manner a notice stating an address to which unsecured creditors of the company should write for copies of the report to be sent to them free of charge,

and (in either case), unless the court otherwise directs, lay a copy of the report before a meeting of the company's unsecured creditors summoned for the purpose on not less than 14 days' notice.

48(3) **[Conditions for s.48(2) direction]** The court shall not give a direction under subsection (2) unless–

(a)   the report states the intention of the administrative receiver to apply for the direction, and

(b)   a copy of the report is sent to the persons mentioned in paragraph (a) of that subsection, or a notice is published as mentioned in paragraph (b) of that subsection, not less than 14 days before the hearing of the application.

48(4) **[Where company in liquidation]** Where the company has gone or goes into liquidation, the administrative receiver–

(a) shall, within 7 days after his compliance with subsection (1) or, if later, the nomination or appointment of the liquidator, send a copy of the report to the liquidator, and

(b) where he does so within the time limited for compliance with subsection (2), is not required to comply with that subsection.

48(5) **[Report to include summary of statement]** A report under this section shall include a summary of the statement of affairs made out and submitted to the administrative receiver under section 47 and of his comments (if any) upon it.

48(6) **[Limit on report only]** Nothing in this section is to be taken as requiring any such report to include any information the disclosure of which would seriously prejudice the carrying out by the administrative receiver of his functions.

48(7) **[Application of s.46(2)]** Section 46(2) applies for the purposes of this section also.

48(8) **[Penalty for non-compliance]** If the administrative receiver without reasonable excuse fails to comply with this section, he is liable to a fine and, for continued contravention, to a daily default fine.

S.48(1), (4), (7)
These subsections require an administrative receiver to submit a report (normally within three months of his appointment) to various named parties, including the liquidator (see s.48(4)) and the FSA where appropriate—FSMA 2000 s.363(4). The contents of the report are also detailed. It is clear from s.48(7) that this obligation does not apply to an administrative receiver succeeding another or assisting an incumbent administrative receiver.
    Note also the whistleblowing duty imposed by FSMA 2000 s.364.

S.48(2), (3)
More widespread publication of the report is required by s.48(2). Unsecured creditors, in particular, are to be given access to this report. A meeting of unsecured creditors must also be called at which this report is presented. The court can relieve an administrative receiver from this latter obligation, provided that the conditions in s.48(3) are satisfied.

S.48(5), (6)
These provisions go into further detail on the administrative receiver's report. It should contain a summary of the statement of affairs submitted to him, but need not include "any information, the disclosure of which would seriously prejudice the carrying out by the administrative receiver of his functions". It is not clear whether the test to be applied here is subjective or objective. See also *Gomba Holdings UK Ltd v Homan & Bird* [1986] 1 W.L.R. 1301; (1986) 2 B.C.C. 99,102.

S.48(8)
Again, criminal sanctions are imposed on a defaulting administrative receiver. On penalties, see s.430 and Sch.10.
    Section 48 is amplified by IR 1986 rr.3.8–3.15. Note new r.3.11A.

49   Committee of creditors

49(1) **[Meeting may establish committee]** Where a meeting of creditors is summoned under section 48, the meeting may, if it thinks fit, establish a committee (**"the creditors' committee"**) to exercise the functions conferred on it by or under this Act.

49(2) **[Committee may summon administrative receiver]** If such a committee is established, the committee may, on giving not less than 7 days' notice, require the administrative receiver to attend before it at any reasonable time and furnish it with such information relating to the carrying out by him of his functions as it may reasonably require.

S.49(1)
This empowers the unsecured creditors in their meeting called under s.48(2) to set up a committee. An FSA representative may attend where appropriate—FSMA 2000 s.363(5).

S.49(2)
The committee of creditors can request information from the administrative receiver. The test of reasonableness is presumably designed to protect information of the type envisaged by s.48(6).
    Further details on the constitution, role and working of this committee are provided by IR 1986 rr.3.16–3.30A.

CHAPTER II

RECEIVERS (SCOTLAND)

50 Extent of this Chapter

50 This Chapter extends to Scotland only.

GENERAL NOTE

Scottish debenture holders were only given the remedy of receivership in 1972 and, since that date, their law of receivership has developed separately from the English counterpart, although on similar lines. There have been problems in fitting this new remedy into the general system of Scottish corporate insolvency law, and problems of statutory interpretation have troubled the Scottish courts on a number of occasions. For the floating charge in Scotland, see Bankruptcy and Diligence etc. (Scotland) Act 2007 Pt 2 (ss.37–49) which repeals Pt XVIII (which includes ss.462–466) of the CA 1985; and the discussion in the House of Lords in *Sharp v Woolwich Building Society* [1998] B.C.C. 115 (often referred to as *Sharp v Thomson* 1997 S.C. (HL) 66). This particular case has caused real difficulties in practice and, as a result, has attracted the attention of both the Scottish Law Commission (see SLC Report No.208, December 2007) and the Scottish Executive (see Scottish Executive Papers No.242). Reference should also be made to the Receivers (Scotland) Regulations 1986 (SI 1986/1917 (S 141)).

The changes made in this area of the law by IA 1985 and IA 1986 do not operate retrospectively; see Sch.11 para.3(2).

Sections 50–71 apply to LLPs with suitable modifications—see Limited Liability Partnerships (Scotland) Regulations 2001 (SI 2001/128) reg.4, Sch.2.

51 Power to appoint receiver

51(1) **[Floating charge holder may appoint receiver]** It is competent under the law of Scotland for the holder of a floating charge over all or any part of the property (including uncalled capital), which may from time to time be comprised in the property and undertaking of an incorporated company (whether a company registered under the Companies Act 2006 or not) which the Court of Session has jurisdiction to wind up, to appoint a receiver of such part of the property of the company as is subject to the charge.

51(2) **[Appointment by court on application]** It is competent under the law of Scotland for the court, on the application of the holder of such a floating charge, to appoint a receiver of such part of the property of the company as is subject to the charge.

51(2A) **[Application of s.51(1), (2)]** Subsections (1) and (2) are subject to section 72A.

51(3) **[Those disqualified]** The following are disqualified from being appointed as receiver–

   (a)   a body corporate;

   (b)   an undischarged bankrupt; and

   (ba) a person subject to a bankruptcy restrictions order;

   (c)   a firm according to the law of Scotland.

51(4) **[Scottish firm]** A body corporate or a firm according to the law of Scotland which acts as a receiver is liable to a fine.

51(5) **[Undischarged bankrupt]** An undischarged bankrupt or a person subject to a bankruptcy restrictions order who so acts is liable to imprisonment or a fine, or both.

51(6) **["Receiver"]** In this section, **"receiver"** includes joint receivers and

"bankruptcy restrictions order" means–

   (a)   a bankruptcy restrictions order made under section 56A of the Bankruptcy (Scotland) Act 1985 (c. 66);

(b)   a bankruptcy restrictions undertaking entered into under section 56G of that Act;

(c)   a bankruptcy restrictions order made under paragraph 1 of Schedule 4A to this Act; or

(d)   a bankruptcy restrictions undertaking entered into under paragraph 7 of that Schedule.

S.51(1), (2)

These provisions authorise the holder of a floating charge in Scotland (for the meaning of this term, see IA 1986 s.70) to appoint a receiver out of court or to apply to the court for such an appointment. For the meaning of "property" within subs.(1) see *Hawking v Hafton House Ltd*, 1990 S.L.T. 496. A number of technical amendments are made to subsections (3), (5) and (6) of s.51 by the Bankruptcy and Diligence etc. (Scotland) Act 2007. Note the Companies Act 2006 (Consequential Amendments, Transitional Provisions and Savings) Order 2009 (SI 2009/1941) (effective from October 1, 2009) which amends s.51 by introducing a reference to the Companies Act 2006.

S.51(2A)

This was inserted by s.248 of and Sch.17 to EA 2002 to reflect the new restrictive approach towards administrative receivership (or receivership in Scotland). See the commentary on s.72A. See Patrick, [2003] 16 Insolv. Int. 65 for comment.

S.51(3)–(5)

These subsections deal with the question of disqualification and mirror the English provisions to a large extent. However, note that Scottish partnerships, which possess legal personality, are also disqualified. A Scottish receiver will have to be a qualified insolvency practitioner within the meaning of IA 1986 Pt XIII, if he is an administrative receiver, as will commonly be the case (see IA 1986 s.251). On penalties, see s.430 and Sch.10. See note above on amendments.

S.51(6)

Joint receivers are permissible under Scottish law. See note above on amendments.

52   Circumstances justifying appointment

52(1)   [Events for s.51(1) appointment] A receiver may be appointed under section 51(1) by the holder of the floating charge on the occurrence of any event which, by the provisions of the instrument creating the charge, entitles the holder of the charge to make that appointment and, in so far as not otherwise provided for by the instrument, on the occurrence of any of the following events, namely–

(a)   the expiry of a period of 21 days after the making of a demand for payment of the whole or any part of the principal sum secured by the charge, without payment having been made;

(b)   the expiry of a period of 2 months during the whole of which interest due and payable under the charge has been in arrears;

(c)   the making of an order or the passing of a resolution to wind up the company;

(d)   the appointment of a receiver by virtue of any other floating charge created by the company.

52(2)   [Events for s.51(2) appointment] A receiver may be appointed by the court under section 51(2) on the occurrence of any event which, by the provisions of the instrument creating the floating charge, entitles the holder of the charge to make that appointment and, in so far as not otherwise provided for by the instrument, on the occurrence of any of the following events, namely–

(a)   where the court, on the application of the holder of the charge, pronounces itself satisfied that the position of the holder of the charge is likely to be prejudiced if no such appointment is made;

(b)   any of the events referred to in paragraphs (a) to (c) of subsection (1).

S.52(1)

This subsection provides a model list of grounds (which can be varied by the debenture) under which a Scots receiver can be appointed out of court by a holder of a floating charge.

S.52(2)

A receiver can be appointed by the court on the occurrence of any of the events specified in s.52(1) or on grounds of prejudice (a Scottish synonym for "jeopardy").

53 Mode of appointment by holder of charge

53(1) **[Instrument of appointment]** The appointment of a receiver by the holder of the floating charge under section 51(1) shall be by means of an instrument subscribed in accordance with the Requirements of Writing (Scotland) Act 1995 (**"the instrument of appointment"**), a copy (certified in the prescribed manner to be a correct copy) whereof shall be delivered by or on behalf of the person making the appointment to the registrar of companies for registration within 7 days of its execution and shall be accompanied by a notice in the prescribed form.

53(2) **[Penalty on default]** If any person without reasonable excuse makes default in complying with the requirements of subsection (1), he is liable to a fine and, for continued contravention, to a daily default fine.

53(3) (Ceased to have effect and repealed by Law Reform (Miscellaneous Provisions) (Scotland) Act 1990 s.74, Sch.8 para.35 and Sch.9 as from December 1, 1990.)

53(4) **[Execution on behalf of floating charge holders]** If the receiver is to be appointed by the holders of a series of secured debentures, the instrument of appointment may be executed on behalf of the holders of the floating charge by any person authorised by resolution of the debenture-holders to execute the instrument.

53(5) **[Entry on register]** On receipt of the certified copy of the instrument of appointment in accordance with subsection (1), the registrar shall, on payment of the prescribed fee, enter the particulars of the appointment in the register of charges.

53(6) **[Effect of appointment]** The appointment of a person as a receiver by an instrument of appointment in accordance with subsection (1)–

(a) is of no effect unless it is accepted by that person before the end of the business day next following that on which the instrument of appointment is received by him or on his behalf, and

(b) subject to paragraph (a), is deemed to be made on the day on and at the time at which the instrument of appointment is so received, as evidenced by a written docquet by that person or on his behalf;

and this subsection applies to the appointment of joint receivers subject to such modifications as may be prescribed.

53(7) **[Attachment of charge]** On the appointment of a receiver under this section, the floating charge by virtue of which he was appointed attaches to the property then subject to the charge; and such attachment has effect as if the charge was a fixed security over the property to which it has attached.

S.53(1), (2), (5)
Section 53(1) specifies the exclusive method by which a receiver can be appointed out of court. Note that, as in English law (CA 2006 s.871), a notice in proper form of the appointment must be delivered for registration to the Scottish Companies Registry in Edinburgh, whereupon the registrar must register it: see s.53(1). Criminal sanctions are imposed for default. A textual amendment to subs.(1) was made by the Requirements of Writing (Scotland) Act 1995 s.14(1) and Sch.4 para.58(a). Section 53(1) was modified by the Scotland Act 1998 s.125(1) and Sch.8 para.23(1)–(3) so that anything done by the registrar of companies in Scotland or the assistant registrar of friendly societies for Scotland by virtue of s.53(1) as applied in relation to friendly societies, industrial and provident societies or building societies may be done to or by the Accountant in Bankruptcy as from July 1, 1999 (see SI 1998/3178 (C. 79) art.2). Note prospective amendment in s.53(2): the words "and, for continued contravention, to a daily default fine" are to be repealed by CA 1989 Schs 16 and 24 from a day to be appointed. On penalties, see s.430 and Sch.10. For the prescribed form under s.53(1), see the Receivers (Scotland) Regulations 1986 (SI 1986/1917 (S 141)) Form 1 (Scot). Note that s.436B is inapplicable.

S.53(3)
This subsection was repealed by the Law Reform (Miscellaneous Provisions) (Scotland) Act 1990 s.74 and Sch.9: see SI 1990/2328 (C. 60) art.3.
The reference to s.36B was substituted by CA 1989 s.130(7) and Sch.17 para.10.

S.53(4)

This subsection, which was substituted by s.14(1) and Sch.4 para.58(b) to the Requirements of Writing (Scotland) Act 1995, deals with the way in which the instrument of appointment is executed. For the meaning of "holder of the floating charge" and "series of secured debentures" in s.53(4), see s.70.

S.53(6), (7)

The time of the appointment is fixed (for the English position, see IA 1986 s.33(1)). The appointment of the receiver causes crystallisation by converting the charge into a fixed security, but this does not render it immune from attack under IA 1986 s.245, nor from the preferential claims regime. See the Receivers (Scotland) Regulations 1986 (SI 1986/1917 (S 141)). On s.53(7) see *Myles J. Callaghan Ltd (in receivership) v City of Glasgow District Council* (1987) 3 B.C.C. 337; *Scottish and Newcastle plc, Petitioners* [1993] B.C.C. 634; and *Sharp v Woolwich Building Society* [1998] B.C.C. 115.

54 Appointment by court

54(1) **[Petition to court]** Application for the appointment of a receiver by the court under section 51(2) shall be by petition to the court, which shall be served on the company.

54(2) **[Issue of interlocutor]** On such an application, the court shall, if it thinks fit, issue an interlocutor making the appointment of the receiver.

54(3) **[Copy of interlocutor to registrar, penalty on default]** A copy (certified by the clerk of the court to be a correct copy) of the court's interlocutor making the appointment shall be delivered by or on behalf of the petitioner to the registrar of companies for registration, accompanied by a notice in the prescribed form, within 7 days of the date of the interlocutor or such longer period as the court may allow.

If any person without reasonable excuse makes default in complying with the requirements of this subsection, he is liable to a fine and, for continued contravention, to a daily default fine.

54(4) **[Entry on register]** On receipt of the certified copy interlocutor in accordance with subsection (3), the registrar shall, on payment of the prescribed fee, enter the particulars of the appointment in the register of charges.

54(5) **[Date of appointment]** The receiver is to be regarded as having been appointed on the date of his being appointed by the court.

54(6) **[Attachment of charge]** On the appointment of a receiver under this section, the floating charge by virtue of which he was appointed attaches to the property then subject to the charge; and such attachment has effect as if the charge were a fixed security over the property to which it has attached.

54(7) **[Rules of court re urgent cases]** In making rules of court for the purposes of this section, the Court of Session shall have regard to the need for special provision for cases which appear to the court to require to be dealt with as a matter of urgency.

S.54(1), (2)

These provisions outline the procedure by which a receiver can be appointed by the court in Scotland.

S.54(3), (4)

The court's order (interlocutor) is to be registered at Edinburgh, normally within seven days. Criminal sanctions are imposed for failure to submit the order for registration. Section 54(3) modified by Scotland Act 1998 s.125(1) and Sch.8 para.23(1)–(3) so that anything done by the registrar of companies in Scotland or the assistant registrar of friendly societies for Scotland by virtue of s.54(3) as applied in relation to friendly societies, industrial and provident societies or building societies may be done to or by the Accountant in Bankruptcy as from July 1, 1999 (see SI 1998/3178 (C. 79) art.2). Note prospective amendment in s.54(3): the words "and, for continued contravention, to a daily default fine" are to be repealed by CA 1989 Schs 16 and 24 from a day to be appointed. On penalties, see s.430 and Sch.10. For the notice in prescribed form under s.54(3), see Form 2 (Scot) in the Receivers (Scotland) Regulations 1986 (SI 1986/1917 (S 141)).

S.54(5), (6)

These subsections regulate the timing and the effect of the appointment.

S.54(7)
Special rules of court may be devised to expedite urgent cases.

55 Powers of receiver

55(1) [Powers in instrument] Subject to the next subsection, a receiver has in relation to such part of the property of the company as is attached by the floating charge by virtue of which he was appointed, the powers, if any, given to him by the instrument creating that charge.

55(2) [Powers in Sch.2] In addition, the receiver has under this Chapter the powers as respects that property (in so far as these are not inconsistent with any provision contained in that instrument) which are specified in Schedule 2 to this Act.

55(3) [Restriction on powers] Subsections (1) and (2) apply–

(a) subject to the rights of any person who has effectually executed diligence on all or any part of the property of the company prior to the appointment of the receiver, and

(b) subject to the rights of any person who holds over all or any part of the property of the company a fixed security or floating charge having priority over, or ranking pari passu with, the floating charge by virtue of which the receiver was appointed.

55(4) [Enquiry as to authority not necessary] A person dealing with a receiver in good faith and for value is not concerned to enquire whether the receiver is acting within his powers.

S.55(1), (2)
Scottish receivers enjoy the 23 implied powers listed in Sch.2 to the Act. These can be added to by the debenture. For the English position, see s.42 and Sch.1. For a recent authority here, see *Myles J. Callaghan Ltd (in receivership) v City of Glasgow District Council* (1987) 3 B.C.C. 337. The powers of the receiver do not extend to assets which cannot be regarded as the "property" of the company: see *Hawking v Hafton House Ltd*, 1990 S.L.T. 496.

S.55(3), (4)
The rights of third parties, such as holders of a fixed security (for definition, see s.70) and execution creditors, vis-à-vis the receiver in the exercise of his powers are regulated. Third parties need not check to see that the receiver is acting within his powers. See *Iona Hotels Ltd, Petitioners*, 1991 S.L.T. 11.

56 Precedence among receivers

56(1) [Order of precedence] Where there are two or more floating charges subsisting over all or any part of the property of the company, a receiver may be appointed under this Chapter by virtue of each such charge; but a receiver appointed by, or on the application of, the holder of a floating charge having priority of ranking over any other floating charge by virtue of which a receiver has been appointed has the powers given to a receiver by section 55 and Schedule 2 to the exclusion of any other receiver.

56(2) [Where floating charges rank equally] Where two or more floating charges rank with one another equally, and two or more receivers have been appointed by virtue of such charges, the receivers so appointed are deemed to have been appointed as joint receivers.

56(3) [Receivers to act jointly] Receivers appointed, or deemed to have been appointed, as joint receivers shall act jointly unless the instrument of appointment or respective instruments of appointment otherwise provide.

56(4) [Suspension of receiver's powers] Subject to subsection (5) below, the powers of a receiver appointed by, or on the application of, the holder of a floating charge are suspended by, and as from the date of, the appointment of a receiver by, or on the application of, the holder of a floating charge having priority of ranking over that charge to such extent as may be necessary to enable the receiver second mentioned to exercise his powers under section 55 and Schedule 2; and any powers so suspended take effect again when the floating charge having priority of ranking ceases to attach to the property then subject to the charge, whether such cessation is by virtue of section 62(6) or otherwise.

56(5) **[Effect of suspension]** The suspension of the powers of a receiver under subsection (4) does not have the effect of requiring him to release any part of the property (including any letters or documents) of the company from his control until he receives from the receiver superseding him a valid indemnity (subject to the limit of the value of such part of the property of the company as is subject to the charge by virtue of which he was appointed) in respect of any expenses, charges and liabilities he may have incurred in the performance of his functions as receiver.

56(6) **[Floating charge remains attached]** The suspension of the powers of a receiver under subsection (4) does not cause the floating charge by virtue of which he was appointed to cease to attach to the property to which it attached by virtue of section 53(7) or 54(6).

56(7) **[Same receiver by several charges]** Nothing in this section prevents the same receiver being appointed by virtue of two or more floating charges.

S.56(1), (2), (3)
Two competing receivers may be appointed over the same company's assets, but only the one with priority can exercise the statutory powers conferred on receivers. In the event of a "tie" they are deemed to have been appointed as joint receivers, and must act jointly.

S.56(4), (5), (6)
These subsections deal with the situation where the receiver who was appointed first has to give way to a receiver appointed subsequently, but enjoying priority. This is a matter not dealt with by any English statutory provision. The first receiver's powers are suspended until the latter has fulfilled his role. However, he should not hand over property to the latter until he has received an indemnity from him. Furthermore, the mere fact that a receiver's powers have been suspended does not cause the floating charge under which he was appointed to refloat.

S.56(7)
To make matters easier, the same receiver can act for competing chargees, although this may produce conflicts of interest.

57   Agency and liability of receiver for contracts

57(1) **[Receiver deemed agent]** A receiver is deemed to be the agent of the company in relation to such property of the company as is attached by the floating charge by virtue of which he was appointed.

57(1A) **[Further qualification re receiver as agent]** Without prejudice to subsection (1), a receiver is deemed to be the agent of the company in relation to any contract of employment adopted by him in the carrying out of his functions.

57(2) **[Personal liability]** A receiver (including a receiver whose powers are subsequently suspended under section 56) is personally liable on any contract entered into by him in the performance of his functions, except in so far as the contract otherwise provides, and, to the extent of any qualifying liability, on any contract of employment adopted by him in the carrying out of those functions.

57(2A) **[Interpretation of s.57(2)]** For the purposes of subsection (2), a liability under a contract of employment is a qualifying liability if–

(a)   it is a liability to pay a sum by way of wages or salary or contribution to an occupational pension scheme,

(b)   it is incurred while the receiver is in office, and

(c)   it is in respect of services rendered wholly or partly after the adoption of the contract.

57(2B) **[Further interpretation of s.57(2)]** Where a sum payable in respect of a liability which is a qualifying liability for the purposes of subsection (2) is payable in respect of services rendered partly before and partly after the adoption of the contract, liability under that subsection shall only extend to so much of the sum as is payable in respect of services rendered after the adoption of the contract.

57(2C)   **[Interpretation of s.57(2A), (2B)]** For the purposes of subsections (2A) and (2B)–

(a)   wages or salary payable in respect of a period of holiday or absence from work through sickness or other good cause are deemed to be wages or (as the case may be) salary in respect of services rendered in that period, and

(b)   a sum payable in lieu of holiday is deemed to be wages or (as the case may be) salary in respect of services rendered in the period by reference to which the holiday entitlement arose.

57(2D)   **[Interpretation of s.57(2C)(a)]** In subsection (2C)(a), the reference to wages or salary payable in respect of a period of holiday includes any sums which, if they had been paid, would have been treated for the purposes of the enactments relating to social security as earnings in respect of that period.

57(3)   **[Indemnity]** A receiver who is personally liable by virtue of subsection (2) is entitled to be indemnified out of the property in respect of which he was appointed.

57(4)   **[Contracts before appointment]** Any contract entered into by or on behalf of the company prior to the appointment of a receiver continues in force (subject to its terms) notwithstanding that appointment, but the receiver does not by virtue only of his appointment incur any personal liability on any such contract.

57(5)   **[Interpretation of s.57(2)]** For the purposes of subsection (2), a receiver is not to be taken to have adopted a contract of employment by reason of anything done or omitted to be done within 14 days after his appointment.

57(6)   **[Effect]** This section does not limit any right to indemnity which the receiver would have apart from it, nor limit his liability on contracts entered into or adopted without authority, nor confer any right to indemnity in respect of that liability.

57(7)   **[Continuation of contract]** Any contract entered into by a receiver in the performance of his functions continues in force (subject to its terms) although the powers of the receiver are subsequently suspended under section 56.

S.57(1)

As in English law, this subsection makes the receiver the company's agent. Indeed, it goes further, because it would appear to confer such status on court-appointed receivers. In view of this agency relationship there is no change of occupation when a receiver takes possession of the company's premises, and the receiver does not become personally liable for rates accruing on such premises: *McKillop and Watters, Petitioners* [1994] B.C.C. 677. Having said that, it may well be in the case of certain statutory provisions that the court might find a receiver to be in joint occupation. Such a conclusion was arrived at in *Lord Advocate v Aero Technologies Ltd*, 1991 S.L.T. 134 in the context of s.23 of the Explosives Act 1875.

S.57(1A), (2A)–(2D)

These were inserted by IA 1994 (s.3(1), (2), (4), (5)) to counteract the problems posed for Scottish receivers by the ruling of the Court of Appeal in *Re Paramount Airways Ltd (No.3)* [1994] B.C.C. 172; see the discussions on ss.19, 37 and 44 above. A receiver's personal liability under s.57(2) on adoption was distinct from the company's liability under s.60—*Lindop v Stewart Noble & Sons Ltd*, 1999 S.C.L.R. 889 which is discussed by Lewis, [1999] Insolv. L. 303.

S.57(2), (4), (5)

These provisions reproduce the position in English law by making the receiver personally liable on contracts entered into by him and on existing contracts of employment adopted by him, although the circumstances where adoption will occur are limited by s.57(5). Apart from contracts of employment adopted by the receiver, he is not personally liable on the company's existing contracts. For discussion of s.57(2) see *Hill Samuel & Co Ltd v Laing* [1991] B.C.C. 665. In s.57(2) the words, "to the extent of any qualifying liability," inserted after the words "provides, and" by IA 1994 s.3(1), (3), (5) in relation to contracts of employment adopted on or after March 15, 1994. For judicial support for the policy behind IA 1994 reforms in this area see *Lindop v Stuart Noble & Sons Ltd*, 1999 S.C.L.R. 889.

S.57(3), (6)

These subsections deal with the receiver's indemnity against personal liability, and make it clear that it does not extend to unauthorised contracts.

S.57(7)

If a receiver's powers are suspended under s.56, contracts entered into by the receiver will normally remain in force.

58   Remuneration of receiver

58(1)   [Remuneration by agreement] The remuneration to be paid to a receiver is to be determined by agreement between the receiver and the holder of the floating charge by virtue of which he was appointed.

58(2)   [Where remuneration not specified or disputed] Where the remuneration to be paid to the receiver has not been determined under subsection (1), or where it has been so determined but is disputed by any of the persons mentioned in paragraphs (a) to (d) below, it may be fixed instead by the Auditor of the Court of Session on application made to him by–

  (a)   the receiver;

  (b)   the holder of any floating charge or fixed security over all or any part of the property of the company;

  (c)   the company; or

  (d)   the liquidator of the company.

58(3)   [Accounting for excess] Where the receiver has been paid or has retained for his remuneration for any period before the remuneration has been fixed by the Auditor of the Court of Session under subsection (2) any amount in excess of the remuneration so fixed for that period, the receiver or his personal representatives shall account for the excess.

S.58(1)

This subsection states the general rule that the receiver's remuneration is to be fixed by agreement with the debenture holder who appointed him.

S.58(2), (3)

This is a fall-back provision, permitting the Auditor of the Court of Session, on the application of any of various named parties, to fix remuneration in cases where there is no agreement within the meaning of s.58(1), or where there is a dispute as to the level of remuneration. It is interesting to note that CA 1985 s.474 fixed a time-limit for such an application and also specified the correct procedure to be followed—this has been omitted in s.58. Presumably this could be dealt with in the rules: see Sch.8 para.15. Section 58(3) deals with the position when a receiver has received remuneration which turns out to be excessive: surplus amounts have to be repaid.

59   Priority of debts

59(1)   [Certain debts to be paid in priority out of assets] Where a receiver is appointed and the company is not at the time of the appointment in course of being wound up, the debts which fall under subsection (2) of this section shall be paid out of any assets coming to the hands of the receiver in priority to any claim for principal or interest by the holder of the floating charge by virtue of which the receiver was appointed.

59(2)   [Preferential debts] Debts falling under this subsection are preferential debts (within the meaning given by section 386 in Part XII) which, by the end of a period of 6 months after advertisement by the receiver for claims in the *Edinburgh Gazette* and in a newspaper circulating in the district where the company carries on business either–

  (i)   have been intimated to him, or

  (ii)   have become known to him.

59(3)   [Recoupment of payments] Any payments made under this section shall be recouped as far as may be out of the assets of the company available for payment of ordinary creditors.

S.59(1), (2)

These subsections impose a positive obligation on the receiver to meet the preferential claims listed in Sch.6 to the Act. The position in Scottish law differs from its English counterpart in that claims must be submitted to the receiver within six months of an advertisement being placed in the *Gazette*. A further difference exists between English and Scottish law with regard to preferential debts on receivership. Where the Crown wishes to exercise a set-off and has total debts owed to it which have both unsecured and preferential elements, it can exercise the set-off with respect to the unsecured debts without rateably setting off preferential debts. The effect of this is to enhance its overall priority position by preserving its preferential status: see *Turner, Petitioner* [1993] B.C.C. 299. For the approach in English law see *Re Unit 2 Windows Ltd* (1985) 1 B.C.C. 99,489.

For the potential impact of *Re Leyland DAF Ltd* [2004] UKHL 9; [2004] B.C.C. 214 in Scotland see R3 Technical Bulletin 63.6.5 (April 2004). *Leyland DAF* (ibid.) will be reversed by s.1282 in the Companies Act 2006. How that change in the law will be introduced in Scotland is not clear at present.

S.59(3)

As with s.40(3), this makes it clear that the burden of meeting the preferential claims will ultimately fall on the unsecured creditors.

60   Distribution of moneys

60(1)   [Payment of moneys by receiver] Subject to the next section, and to the rights of any of the following categories of persons (which rights shall, except to the extent otherwise provided in any instrument, have the following order of priority), namely–

(a)   the holder of any fixed security which is over property subject to the floating charge and which ranks prior to, or pari passu with, the floating charge;

(b)   all persons who have effectually executed diligence on any part of the property of the company which is subject to the charge by virtue of which the receiver was appointed;

(c)   creditors in respect of all liabilities, charges and expenses incurred by or on behalf of the receiver;

(d)   the receiver in respect of his liabilities, expenses and remuneration, and any indemnity to which he is entitled out of the property of the company; and

(e)   the preferential creditors entitled to payment under section 59,

the receiver shall pay moneys received by him to the holder of the floating charge by virtue of which the receiver was appointed in or towards satisfaction of the debt secured by the floating charge.

60(2)   [Balance of moneys] Any balance of moneys remaining after the provisions of subsection (1) and section 61 below have been satisfied shall be paid in accordance with their respective rights and interests to the following persons, as the case may require–

(a)   any other receiver;

(b)   the holder of a fixed security which is over property subject to the floating charge;

(c)   the company or its liquidator, as the case may be.

60(3)   [Doubt as to person entitled] Where any question arises as to the person entitled to a payment under this section, or where a receipt or a discharge of a security cannot be obtained in respect of any such payment, the receiver shall consign the amount of such payment in any joint stock bank of issue in Scotland in name of the Accountant of Court for behoof of the person or persons entitled thereto.

S.60(1)

This subsection outlines a priority ranking for claims against the assets of a company which is in receivership. There is no parallel provision in English law. When presented in this way it is not surprising that banks have become uneasy about the protection offered by the floating charge. However, EA 2002 does offer them some comfort in that it radically reduces the categories of preferential claim. For the meaning of "fixed security" in subs.(1)(a), see s.70. The position under subs.(1)(c) was considered by the Court of Session (Inner House) in *Lindop v Stuart Noble & Sons Ltd*, 1999 S.C.L.R. 889 in the context of an employee whose contract of employment had initially been adopted by the receiver and then who had subsequently been dismissed. The claim based upon s.60(1)(c) for preferential treatment in respect of salary in lieu of notice was rejected; only new contracts made by receivers were covered by s.60(1)(c). In rejecting this claim the court was mindful not to allow the policy of IA 1994 limiting a receiver's liabilities to "qualifying liabilities" to be circumvented. See also *Scottish and Newcastle plc, Petitioners* [1993] B.C.C. 634 for further guidance on the operation of s.60.

S.60(2)
This provision maps out the fate of any surplus moneys in the hands of the receiver, after the claims listed in s.60(1) have been met.

S.60(3)
In the event of a dispute over whether a claim should be met or not, the receiver should pay an appropriate sum of money into a recognised Scottish bank in the name of the Accountant of Court, pending the resolution of the dispute.

61   Disposal of interest in property

61(1)   [Application to court] Where the receiver sells or disposes, or is desirous of selling or disposing, of any property or interest in property of the company which is subject to the floating charge by virtue of which the receiver was appointed and which is–

(a)   subject to any security or interest of, or burden or encumbrance in favour of, a creditor the ranking of which is prior to, or pari passu with, or postponed to the floating charge, or

(b)   property or an interest in property affected or attached by effectual diligence executed by any person,

and the receiver is unable to obtain the consent of such creditor or, as the case may be, such person to such a sale or disposal, the receiver may apply to the court for authority to sell or dispose of the property or interest in property free of such security, interest, burden, encumbrance or diligence.

61(1A)   [Inhibition after creation of floating charge] For the purposes of subsection (1) above, an inhibition which takes effect after the creation of the floating charge by virtue of which the receiver was appointed is not an effectual diligence.

61(1B)   [When arrestment an effectual diligence] For the purposes of subsection (1) above, an arrestment is an effectual diligence only where it is executed before the floating charge, by virtue of which the receiver was appointed, attaches to the property comprised in the company's property and undertaking.

61(2)   [Authorisation by court] Subject to the next subsection, on such an application the court may, if it thinks fit, authorise the sale or disposal of the property or interest in question free of such security, interest, burden, encumbrance or diligence, and such authorisation may be on such terms or conditions as the court thinks fit.

61(3)   [Condition for authorisation] In the case of an application where a fixed security over the property or interest in question which ranks prior to the floating charge has not been met or provided for in full, the court shall not authorise the sale or disposal of the property or interest in question unless it is satisfied that the sale or disposal would be likely to provide a more advantageous realisation of the company's assets than would otherwise be effected.

61(4)   [Condition for s.61(3)] It shall be a condition of an authorisation to which subsection (3) applies that–

(a)   the net proceeds of the disposal, and

(b)   where those proceeds are less than such amount as may be determined by the court to be the net amount which would be realised on a sale of the property or interest in the open market by a willing seller, such sums as may be required to make good the deficiency, shall be applied towards discharging the sums secured by the fixed security.

61(5)   [Where s.61(4) condition re several securities] Where a condition imposed in pursuance of subsection (4) relates to two or more such fixed securities, that condition shall require the net proceeds of the disposal and, where paragraph (b) of that subsection applies, the sums mentioned in that paragraph to be applied towards discharging the sums secured by those fixed securities in the order of their priorities.

61(6)   [Copy of authorisation to registrar] A copy of an authorisation under subsection (2) shall, within 14 days of the granting of the authorisation, be sent by the receiver to the registrar of companies.

61(7)   [Penalty for non-compliance] If the receiver without reasonable excuse fails to comply with subsection (6), he is liable to a fine and, for continued contravention, to a daily default fine.

61(8)   [Receiver to give document to disponee] Where any sale or disposal is effected in accordance with the authorisation of the court under subsection (2), the receiver shall grant to the purchaser or disponee an appropriate document of transfer or conveyance of the property or interest in question, and that document has the effect, or, where recording, intimation or registration of that document is a legal requirement for completion of title to the property or interest, then that recording, intimation or registration (as the case may be) has the effect, of–

(a)   disencumbering the property or interest of the security, interest, burden or encumbrance affecting it, and

(b)   freeing the property or interest from the diligence executed upon it.

61(9)   [Ranking of creditor in winding up] Nothing in this section prejudices the right of any creditor of the company to rank for his debt in the winding up of the company.

S.61(1), (2)
These subsections allow a receiver to apply to the court for the sale of property subject to a fixed charge, or over which diligence has been effectually executed.
   Editors' note: a subs.(1A) was inserted by s.155(2) of the Bankruptcy and Diligence, etc. (Scotland) Act 2007. A new subs.(1B) was also inserted by Sch.5 para.14(2) of the Bankruptcy and Diligence etc. (Scotland) Act 2007. The purpose of these new subsections is to clarify the meaning of provisions in subs.(1).
   Section 61 does not apply in relation to the enforcement of "market charges" (as defined by CA 1989 s.173): see s.175 of that Act (as qualified by the Financial Markets and Insolvency Regulations 1991 (SI 1991/880)) (as amended by SI 1995/2049 and SI 1998/27), and the introductory note at p.1, above.

S.61(3), (4), (5)
If the receiver has not set aside a sufficient sum to meet the claim of the holder of the "fixed security" (for the meaning of this term, see s.70), the court should only assent to the sale if it would promote a more effective realisation of the company's assets. Even where assent is given, the actual net proceeds (or a reasonable amount, if the sale was at an undervalue) must be set aside for the fixed chargee (or chargees).

S.61(6), (7)
If the court permits the sale to go ahead, the receiver must register the fact at Edinburgh, or incur a default fine. On penalties, see s.430 and Sch.10. Section 61(6) modified by Scotland Act 1998 s.125(1) and Sch.8 para.23(1)–(3) so that anything done by the registrar of companies in Scotland or the assistant registrar of friendly societies for Scotland by virtue of s.61(6) as applied in relation to friendly societies, industrial and provident societies or building societies may be done to or by the Accountant in Bankruptcy as from July 1, 1999 (see SI 1998/3178 (C. 79) art.2). Note the Companies Act 2006 (Consequential Amendments, Transitional Provisions and Savings) Order 2009 (SI 2009/1941) (effective from October 1, 2009) which omits a reference to certification by the clerk of the court.

S.61(8)
This subsection provides a mechanism for assuring the purchaser under the forced sale that he can acquire an effective title from the receiver.

S.61(9)
This is a saving provision allowing a person who has been deprived of his claim against specific property to rank instead as a creditor of the company on winding up.

62 Cessation of appointment of receiver

62(1) [Removal, resignation] A receiver may be removed from office by the court under subsection (3) below and may resign his office by giving notice of his resignation in the prescribed manner to such persons as may be prescribed.

62(2) [Cessation of qualification] A receiver shall vacate office if he ceases to be qualified to act as an insolvency practitioner in relation to the company.

62(3) [Removal on application] Subject to the next subsection, a receiver may, on application to the court by the holder of the floating charge by virtue of which he was appointed, be removed by the court on cause shown.

62(4) [On vacation of office] Where at any time a receiver vacates office–

(a) his remuneration and any expenses properly incurred by him, and

(b) any indemnity to which he is entitled out of the property of the company,

shall be paid out of the property of the company which is subject to the floating charge and shall have priority as provided for in section 60(1).

62(5) [Notice of cessation to registrar, penalty on default] When a receiver ceases to act as such otherwise than by death he shall, and, when a receiver is removed by the court, the holder of the floating charge by virtue of which he was appointed shall, within 14 days of the cessation or removal (as the case may be) give the registrar of companies notice to that effect, and the registrar shall enter the notice in the register of charges.

If the receiver or the holder of the floating charge (as the case may require) makes default in complying with the requirements of this subsection, he is liable to a fine and, for continued contravention, to a daily default fine.

62(6) [Cessation of attachment of charge] If by the expiry of a period of one month following upon the removal of the receiver or his ceasing to act as such no other receiver has been appointed, the floating charge by virtue of which the receiver was appointed–

(a) thereupon ceases to attach to the property then subject to the charge, and

(b) again subsists as a floating charge;

and for the purposes of calculating the period of one month under this subsection no account shall be taken of any period during which the company is in administration under Part II of this Act.

S.62(1)–(3)
These subsections deal with the situations where a receiver will vacate office. Note that he can only be removed by the court on the application of the holder of the floating charge (for the meaning of this term, see s.70), and not out of court by the holder of the floating charge who appointed him. As to the qualification as an insolvency practitioner, see Pt XIII. For the relevant notice of resignation under s.62(1), see the Receivers (Scotland) Regulations 1986 (SI 1986/1917 (S 141)).

S.62(4)
This protects the priority of the receiver's right to indemnity and remuneration.

S.62(5)
Notification must be given to Edinburgh of the receiver leaving office: see Form 3 (Scot) under the Receivers (Scotland) Regulations 1986 (SI 1986/1917 (S 141)). The person responsible for giving notice will incur criminal sanctions in the event of default. On penalties, see s.430 and Sch.10. Section 62(5) was modified by the Scotland Act 1998 s.125(1) and Sch.8 para.23(1)–(3) so that anything done by the registrar of companies in Scotland or the assistant registrar of friendly societies for Scotland by virtue of s.62(5) as applied in relation to friendly societies, industrial and provident societies or building societies may be done to or by the Accountant in Bankruptcy as from July 1, 1999 (see SI 1998/3178 (C. 79) art.2). Note prospective amendment: the words "and, for continued contravention, to a daily default fine" are to be repealed by CA 1989 Schs 16 and 24 from a day to be appointed.

S.62(6)
This provides for the "refloating" of the floating charge on the expiry of one month after the receiver leaves office. Note the semantic change made by the Enterprise Act 2002 (Insolvency) Order 2003 (SI 2003/2096).

63 Powers of court

63(1)   **[Directions, on application]** The court on the application of–

(a)   the holder of a floating charge by virtue of which a receiver was appointed, or

(b)   a receiver appointed under section 51,

may give directions to the receiver in respect of any matter arising in connection with the performance by him of his functions.

63(2)   **[Where receiver's appointment invalid]** Where the appointment of a person as a receiver by the holder of a floating charge is discovered to be invalid (whether by virtue of the invalidity of the instrument or otherwise), the court may order the holder of the floating charge to indemnify the person appointed against any liability which arises solely by reason of the invalidity of the appointment.

S.63(1)
This provision, like its English counterpart (IA 1986 s.35), allows both the receiver or the holder of the floating charge (for definition, see s.70) under which he was appointed to apply to the court for guidance. Such an application was the basis for the litigation in *McKillop and Watters, Petitioners* [1994] B.C.C. 677. Prior to IA 1985, only the appointor (and not the receiver) could make such an application. The power of the Scottish courts to give directions is more limited than the power of their English counterparts under s.35: see here *Jamieson, Petitioners*, 1997 S.C. 195; [1997] B.C.C. 682.
    The FSA may in an appropriate case be heard on a s.63 application—FSMA 2000 s.363(2).

S.63(2)
This allows the court to excuse a receiver from trespass liability arising out of an invalid appointment, and instead to impose that liability on his appointor. For the English counterpart, see s.34.

64 Notification that receiver appointed

64(1)   **[Statement in invoices etc.]** Where a receiver has been appointed–

(a)   every invoice, order for goods or services, business letter or order form (whether in hard copy, electronic or any other form) issued by or on behalf of the company or the receiver or the liquidator of the company; and

(b)   all the company's websites,

must contain a statement that a receiver has been appointed.

64(2)   **[Penalty on default]** If default is made in complying with the requirements of this section, the company and any of the following persons who knowingly and wilfully authorises or permits the default, namely any officer of the company, any liquidator of the company and any receiver, is liable to a fine.

S.64(1)
Invoices, business letters, etc. must disclose the fact that a receiver has been appointed. The English equivalent is to be found in s.39. A new s.64(1) was substituted by the Companies (Trading Disclosures) (Insolvency) Regulations 2008 (SI 2008/1897) with effect from October 1, 2008. This substitution was necessary to comply with EC Directive 2003/58. It extends the disclosure requirement to electronic invoices and company websites.

S.64(2)
Criminal sanctions are imposed on various named parties for breach of s.64(1). On penalties, see s.430 and Sch.10.

65 Information to be given by receiver

65(1)   **[Notification of appointment]** Where a receiver is appointed, he shall–

(a)   forthwith send to the company and publish notice of his appointment, and

(b)   within 28 days after his appointment, unless the court otherwise directs, send such notice to all the creditors of the company (so far as he is aware of their addresses).

65(2)   [Restriction] This section and the next do not apply in relation to the appointment of a receiver to act–

(a)   with an existing receiver, or

(b)   in place of a receiver who has died or ceased to act,

except that, where they apply to a receiver who dies or ceases to act before they have been fully complied with, the references in this section and the next to the receiver include (subject to subsection (3) of this section) his successor and any continuing receiver.

65(3)   [If company being wound up] If the company is being wound up, this section and the next apply notwithstanding that the receiver and the liquidator are the same person, but with any necessary modifications arising from that fact.

65(4)   [Penalty for non-compliance] If a person without reasonable excuse fails to comply with this section, he is liable to a fine and, for continued contravention, to a daily default fine.

S.65(1), (2), (4)
These subsections provide for a receiver on taking up his appointment to give notice to the company and its creditors. See note to s.62(5). This obligation, once complied with, does not have to be fulfilled by successor receivers, or a later appointed joint receiver. Criminal sanctions are imposed in the event of default. On penalties, see s.430 and Sch.10. For the notice under s.65(1)(a) see Form 4 (Scot) in the Receivers (Scotland) Regulations 1986 (SI 1986/1917 (S 141)).

S.65(3)
This caters for the situation where the receiver and liquidator are the same person. It also applies to s.66.

66   Company's statement of affairs

66(1)   [Duty of receiver] Where a receiver of a company is appointed, the receiver shall forthwith require some or all of the persons mentioned in subsection (3) below to make out and submit to him a statement in the prescribed form as to the affairs of the company.

66(2)   [Contents of statement] A statement submitted under this section shall be verified by affidavit by the persons required to submit it and shall show–

(a)   particulars of the company's assets, debts and liabilities;

(b)   the names and addresses of its creditors;

(c)   the securities held by them respectively;

(d)   the dates when the securities were respectively given; and

(e)   such further or other information as may be prescribed.

66(3)   [Persons in s.66(1)] The persons referred to in subsection (1) are–

(a)   those who are or have been officers of the company;

(b)   those who have taken part in the company's formation at any time within one year before the date of the appointment of the receiver;

(c)   those who are in the company's employment or have been in its employment within that year, and are in the receiver's opinion capable of giving the information required;

(d)   those who are or have been within that year officers of or in the employment of a company which is, or within that year was, an officer of the company.

In this subsection **"employment"** includes employment under a contract for services.

66(4)   [Time for statement] Where any persons are required under this section to submit a statement of affairs to the receiver they shall do so (subject to the next subsection) before the end of the period of 21 days beginning with the day after that on which the prescribed notice of the requirement is given to them by the receiver.

66(5)   [Release, extension re statement] The receiver, if he thinks fit, may–

  (a)   at any time release a person from an obligation imposed on him under subsection (1) or (2), or

  (b)   either when giving the notice mentioned in subsection (4) or subsequently extend the period so mentioned,

and where the receiver has refused to exercise a power conferred by this subsection, the court, if it thinks fit, may exercise it.

66(6)   [Penalty for non-compliance] If a person without reasonable excuse fails to comply with any obligation imposed under this section, he is liable to a fine and, for continued contravention, to a daily default fine.

S.66(1), (2)
These provisions require the receiver to ask persons listed in s.66(3) for a statement of the company's affairs in the prescribed form (see s.70), containing details specified in s.66(2). For the relevant form of the statement, see Form 5 (Scot) in the Receivers (Scotland) Regulations 1986 (SI 1986/1917 (S 141)).

S.66(3)–(6)
Section 66(3) identifies the persons who may be required to contribute towards the submission of the statement of affairs, which must normally be submitted within 21 days of a request for it. Criminal sanctions are imposed to deal with defaults. On penalties, see s.430 and Sch.10.

  The receiver enjoys discretion under s.66(5) to release certain persons from their obligations in respect of the statement of affairs or to extend the deadline for submission.

67   Report by receiver

67(1)   [Duty of receiver] Where a receiver is appointed under section 51, he shall within 3 months (or such longer period as the court may allow) after his appointment, send to the registrar of companies, to the holder of the floating charge by virtue of which he was appointed and to any trustees for secured creditors of the company and (so far as he is aware of their addresses) to all such creditors a report as to the following matters, namely–

  (a)   the events leading up to his appointment, so far as he is aware of them;

  (b)   the disposal or proposed disposal by him of any property of the company and the carrying on or proposed carrying on by him of any business of the company;

  (c)   the amounts of principal and interest payable to the holder of the floating charge by virtue of which he was appointed and the amounts payable to preferential creditors; and

  (d)   the amount (if any) likely to be available for the payment of other creditors.

67(2)   [Copies of report] The receiver shall also, within 3 months (or such longer period as the court may allow) after his appointment, either–

  (a)   send a copy of the report (so far as he is aware of their addresses) to all unsecured creditors of the company, or

  (b)   publish in the prescribed manner a notice stating an address to which unsecured creditors of the company should write for copies of the report to be sent to them free of charge, and (in either case), unless the court otherwise directs, lay a copy of the report before a meeting of the company's unsecured creditors summoned for the purpose on not less than 14 days' notice.

67(3) **[Condition for court direction in s.67(2)]** The court shall not give a direction under subsection (2) unless–

(a) the report states the intention of the receiver to apply for the direction, and

(b) a copy of the report is sent to the persons mentioned in paragraph (a) of that subsection, or a notice is published as mentioned in paragraph (b) of that subsection, not less than 14 days before the hearing of the application.

67(4) **[Where company in liquidation]** Where the company has gone or goes into liquidation, the receiver–

(a) shall, within 7 days after his compliance with subsection (1) or, if later, the nomination or appointment of the liquidator, send a copy of the report to the liquidator, and

(b) where he does so within the time limited for compliance with subsection (2), is not required to comply with that subsection.

67(5) **[Report to involve summary of statement of affairs]** A report under this section shall include a summary of the statement of affairs made out and submitted under section 66 and of his comments (if any) on it.

67(6) **[Information not to be disclosed]** Nothing in this section shall be taken as requiring any such report to include any information the disclosure of which would seriously prejudice the carrying out by the receiver of his functions.

67(7) **[Section 65(2)]** Section 65(2) applies for the purposes of this section also.

67(8) **[Penalty for non-compliance]** If a person without reasonable excuse fails to comply with this section, he is liable to a fine and, for continued contravention, to a daily default fine.

67(9) **["Secured creditor"]** In this section **"secured creditor"**, in relation to a company, means a creditor of the company who holds in respect of his debt a security over property of the company, and **"unsecured creditor"** shall be construed accordingly.

S.67(1), (5), (6)
These subsections require the receiver to prepare a report which must be submitted to various named parties (including the FSA in an appropriate case—FSMA 2000 s.363(4)). The report should include certain specified details but need not disclose "prejudicial" information (see s.67(6)). It should also include a summary of the statement of affairs submitted to him under s.66, plus any comments he wishes to make. Section 67(1) was modified by the Scotland Act 1998 s.125(1) and Sch.8 para.23(1)–(3) so that anything done by the registrar of companies in Scotland or the assistant registrar of friendly societies for Scotland by virtue of s.67(1) as applied in relation to friendly societies, industrial and provident societies or building societies may be done to or by the Accountant in Bankruptcy as from July 1, 1999 (see SI 1998/3178 (C. 79) art.2).

S.67(2)–(4)
These provisions relate to the dissemination of the receiver's report to creditors and liquidator (if applicable). The report is to be submitted to a meeting of the company's creditors, unless the court rules to the contrary. With regards to s.67(2) see the Receivers (Scotland) Regulations 1986 (SI 1986/1917 (S 141)). Note that s.436B does not apply.

S.67(7), (9)
These are merely interpretation provisions. Section 65(2) dispenses with the need for a report when an additional receiver is appointed to act with an existing receiver, or a new receiver to replace one who has ceased to act.

S.67(8)
The receiver will incur criminal sanctions for failure to fulfil any of the stated obligations. On penalties, see s.430 and Sch.10.

68   Committee of creditors

68(1)   **[Creditors' meeting may establish committee]** Where a meeting of creditors is summoned under section 67, the meeting may, if it thinks fit, establish a committee (**"the creditors' committee"**) to exercise the functions conferred on it by or under this Act.

68(2)   **[Powers of committee]** If such a committee is established, the committee may on giving not less than 7 days' notice require the receiver to attend before it at any reasonable time and furnish it with such information relating to the carrying out by him of his functions as it may reasonably require.

S.68(1)

A meeting of creditors summoned under s.67(2) may set up a committee of creditors. In an appropriate case an FSA representative can attend—FSMA 2000 s.363(5).

S.68(2)

This committee can make reasonable requests for information from the receiver. It may be unreasonable to request information covered by s.67(6).

69   Enforcement of receiver's duty to make returns, etc.

69(1)   **[Court order re receiver's default]** If any receiver–

(a)   having made default in filing, delivering or making any return, account or other document, or in giving any notice, which a receiver is by law required to file, deliver, make or give, fails to make good the default within 14 days after the service on him of a notice requiring him to do so; or

(b)   has, after being required at any time by the liquidator of the company so to do, failed to render proper accounts of his receipts and payments and to vouch the same and to pay over to the liquidator the amount properly payable to him,

the court may, on an application made for the purpose, make an order directing the receiver to make good the default within such time as may be specified in the order.

69(2)   **[Application to court]** In the case of any such default as is mentioned in subsection (1)(a), an application for the purposes of this section may be made by any member or creditor of the company or by the registrar of companies; and, in the case of any such default as is mentioned in subsection (1)(b), the application shall be made by the liquidator; and, in either case, the order may provide that all expenses of and incidental to the application shall be borne by the receiver.

69(3)   **[Other enactments]** Nothing in this section prejudices the operation of any enactments imposing penalties on receivers in respect of any such default as is mentioned in subsection (1).

S.69(1)

The court can compel a receiver to submit returns, etc. if he fails to comply with a notice to do so. For the English counterpart, see s.41.

S.69(2)

This subsection identifies the applicants for an enforcement order under s.69(1). The FSA may apply in an appropriate case—FSMA 2000 s.363(3).

S.69(3)

This enforcement mechanism is in addition to any criminal sanctions that may be imposed by individual provisions.

70   Interpretation for Chapter II

70(1)   **[Definitions]** In this Chapter, unless the contrary intention appears, the following expressions have the following meanings respectively assigned to them–

     "company" means an incorporated company (whether or not a company registered under the Companies Act 2006) which the Court of Session has jurisdiction to wind up;

"fixed security", in relation to any property of a company, means any security, other than a floating charge or a charge having the nature of a floating charge, which on the winding up of the company in Scotland would be treated as an effective security over that property, and (without prejudice to that generality) includes a security over that property, being a heritable security within the meaning of the Conveyancing and Feudal Reform (Scotland) Act 1970;

"instrument of appointment" has the meaning given by section 53(1);

"prescribed" means prescribed by regulations made under this Chapter by the Secretary of State;

"receiver" means a receiver of such part of the property of the company as is subject to the floating charge by virtue of which he has been appointed under section 51;

"register of charges" means the register kept by the registrar of companies for the purposes of Chapter 2 of Part 25 of the Companies Act 2006;

"secured debenture" means a bond, debenture, debenture stock or other security which, either itself or by reference to any other instrument, creates a floating charge over all or any part of the property of the company, but does not include a security which creates no charge other than a fixed security; and

"series of secured debentures" means two or more secured debentures created as a series by the company in such a manner that the holders thereof are entitled pari passu to the benefit of the floating charge.

70(2) **[Reference to holder of floating charge]** Where a floating charge, secured debenture or series of secured debentures has been created by the company, then, except where the context otherwise requires, any reference in this Chapter to the holder of the floating charge shall–

(a) where the floating charge, secured debenture or series of secured debentures provides for a receiver to be appointed by any person or body, be construed as a reference to that person or body;

(b) where, in the case of a series of secured debentures, no such provision has been made therein but–

    (i) there are trustees acting for the debenture-holders under and in accordance with a trust deed, be construed as a reference to those trustees, and

    (ii) where no such trustees are acting, be construed as a reference to–

        (aa) a majority in nominal value of those present or represented by proxy and voting at a meeting of debenture-holders at which the holders of at least one-third in nominal value of the outstanding debentures of the series are present or so represented, or

        (bb) where no such meeting is held, the holders of at least one-half in nominal value of the outstanding debentures of the series.

70(3) **[Reference to floating charge etc.]** Any reference in this Chapter to a floating charge, secured debenture, series of secured debentures or instrument creating a charge includes, except where the context otherwise requires, a reference to that floating charge, debenture, series of debentures or instrument as varied by any instrument.

70(4) **[Reference to instrument]** References in this Chapter to the instrument by which a floating charge was created are, in the case of a floating charge created by words in a bond or other written acknowledgement, references to the bond or, as the case may be, the other written acknowledgement.

General Note

These are general interpretation provisions for the purposes of ss.50–71 and their main aim is to link these provisions dealing with Scottish receiverships with the sections in CA 1985 regulating the floating charge in Scotland, and also with the general rules of Scots law. Note the Companies Act 2006 (Consequential Amendments, Transitional Provisions and Savings) Order 2009 (SI 2009/1941), which took effect on October 1, 2009. This Order amends s.70 by making reference to the Companies Act 2006. Note that s.436B does not apply.

71 Prescription of forms, etc.; regulations

71(1) **[Prescribed forms]** The notice referred to in section 62(5), and the notice referred to in section 65(1)(a) shall be in such form as may be prescribed.

71(2) **[Regulations]** Any power conferred by this Chapter on the Secretary of State to make regulations is exercisable by statutory instrument; and a statutory instrument made in the exercise of the power so conferred to prescribe a fee is subject to annulment in pursuance of a resolution of either House of Parliament.

S.71(1)

The notice of a receiver taking office or ceasing to act is in a form prescribed by the Receivers (Scotland) Regulations 1986 (SI 1986/1917 (S 141)). See note to ss.62, 65.

S.71(2)

The Secretary of State may make regulations, but where the power involves the prescribing of a fee it is subject to annulment by either the House of Lords or the Commons. See the regulations referred to above.

CHAPTER III

RECEIVERS' POWERS IN GREAT BRITAIN AS A WHOLE

72 Cross-border operation of receivership provisions

72(1) **[Receivers' powers]** A receiver appointed under the law of either part of Great Britain in respect of the whole or any part of any property or undertaking of a company and in consequence of the company having created a charge which, as created, was a floating charge may exercise his powers in the other part of Great Britain so far as their exercise is not inconsistent with the law applicable there.

72(2) **["Receiver"]** In subsection (1) **"receiver"** includes a manager and a person who is appointed both receiver and manager.

GENERAL NOTE

This section allows a receiver appointed in England to act in Scotland, and vice versa, in so far as this is not inconsistent with local law. This provision, which can be traced back to 1970, is less important now that the Scots have a system of receivership running along similar lines to the English regime. For the utility of s.72 see *Norfolk House v Repsol Petroleum*, 1992 S.L.T. 235.

CHAPTER IV

PROHIBITION OF APPOINTMENT OF ADMINISTRATIVE RECEIVER

72A Floating charge holder not to appoint administrative receiver

72A(1) **[Prohibition]** The holder of a qualifying floating charge in respect of a company's property may not appoint an administrative receiver of the company.

72A(2) **[Scotland]** In Scotland, the holder of a qualifying floating charge in respect of a company's property may not appoint or apply to the court for the appointment of a receiver who on appointment would be an administrative receiver of property of the company.

72A(3) **[Meanings in s.72A(1), (2)]** In subsections (1) and (2)–

"holder of a qualifying floating charge in respect of a company's property" has the same meaning as in paragraph 14 of Schedule B1 to this Act, and

"administrative receiver" has the meaning given by section 251.

72A(4) **[Application of section]** This section applies–

(a)   to a floating charge created on or after a date appointed by the Secretary of State by order made by statutory instrument, and

(b)   in spite of any provision of an agreement or instrument which purports to empower a person to appoint an administrative receiver (by whatever name).

72A(5) **[Provision in order]** An order under subsection (4)(a) may–

(a)   make provision which applies generally or only for a specified purpose;

(b)   make different provision for different purposes;

(c)   make transitional provision.

72A(6) **[Exceptions]** This section is subject to the exceptions specified in sections 72B to 72GA.

GENERAL NOTE

This new section, and those following, were added by s.250 of EA 2002. That provision was modified by the Insolvency Act 1986 (Amendment) (Administrative Receivership and Urban Regeneration etc.) Order 2003 (SI 2003/1832) to take effect immediately on the coming into force of s.72A on September 15, 2003. Note also the insertion by s.250(2) and Sch.18 of Sch.2A into the 1986 Act to further bolster these provisions. Schedule 2A was also modified by the Insolvency Act 1986 (Amendment) (Administrative Receivership and Capital Market Arrangements) Order 2003 (SI 2003/1468).

Perhaps the most high profile of all of the changes introduced by EA 2002 was the curtailing of the floating charge holder's entitlement to enforce security through the appointment of an "administrative receiver" (see IA 1986 s.29). After some debate the Government was convinced by the argument that administrative receivership was not a rescue procedure in keeping with the spirit of collectivism but rather a selfish and largely unaccountable recovery mechanism. It therefore decided to curtail its usage, though as a concession to the banking community it offered the option of appointing an administrator out of court.

This change was not retrospective—i.e. it does not deprive this option of installing an administrative receiver from those creditors covered by a floating charge created before the operational date. This point was conceded early on in the gestation of the Enterprise Bill—DTI Press Notice P/2001/629). The Government may have been concerned to head off challenges by banks alleging infringement of their property rights under art.1 of the First Protocol of the ECHR. Moreover, administrative receivership is to survive for certain specialised financing arrangements; these mirror the exceptions to the CVA *cum moratorium* procedure in IA 2000.

S.72A(1), (3)
This outlines the basic prohibition—note again that the wording (albeit obtusely) allows existing floating charges to retain this traditional enforcement mode.

S.72A(2), (3)
Administrative receivership is not a term recognised in Scotland; the institution in that jurisdiction uses the clearer denomination of receivership. Hence the need for separate legislative treatment.

S.72A(4)
This reinforces the prospective-only nature of the reform. However, its restrictive effect cannot be overridden by provision in any debenture. The date appointed under s.72A(4)(a) is September 15, 2003—see the Insolvency Act 1986, Section 72A (Appointed Day) Order 2003 (SI 2003/2095).

S.72A(5), (6)
These rules may be modified by secondary legislation and are qualified by later statutory provisions. Note subs.(6) was modified slightly by the Insolvency Act 1986 (Amendment) (Administrative Receivership and Urban Regeneration etc.) Order 2003 (SI 2003/1832).

72B   First exception: capital market

72B(1) **[Conditions for capital market arrangement]** Section 72A does not prevent the appointment of an administrative receiver in pursuance of an agreement which is or forms part of a capital market arrangement if–

(a)   a party incurs or, when the agreement was entered into was expected to incur, a debt of at least £50 million under the arrangement, and

(b)   the arrangement involves the issue of a capital market investment.

72B(2)   ["Capital market arrangement", "capital market investment"] In subsection (1)–

"capital market arrangement" means an arrangement of a kind described in paragraph 1 of Schedule 2A, and

"capital market investment" means an investment of a kind described in paragraph 2 or 3 of that Schedule.

S.72B(1), (2)

This exception relates to capital market agreements. The exclusion of general insolvency principles from this area of commerce has precedents—witness Companies Act 1989 Pt VII.

72C   Second exception: public-private partnership

72C(1)   [Requirement of step-in rights] Section 72A does not prevent the appointment of an administrative receiver of a project company of a project which–

(a)   is a public-private partnership project, and

(b)   includes step-in rights.

72C(2)   ["Public-private partnership project"] In this section "public-private partnership project" means a project–

(a)   the resources for which are provided partly by one or more public bodies and partly by one or more private persons, or

(b)   which is designed wholly or mainly for the purpose of assisting a public body to discharge a function.

72C(3)   ["Step-in rights", "project company"] In this section–

"step-in rights" has the meaning given by paragraph 6 of Schedule 2A, and

"project company" has the meaning given by paragraph 7 of that Schedule.

S.72C(1), (2), (3)

These provide the continuance of administrative receivership for certain public finance initiative agreements containing "step in" rights as defined by subs.(3).

72D   Third exception: utilities

72D(1)   [Requirement of step-in rights] Section 72A does not prevent the appointment of an administrative receiver of a project company of a project which–

(a)   is a utility project, and

(b)   includes step-in rights.

72D(2)   ["Utility project", "regulated business", "Step-in rights", "project company"] In this section–

(a)   "utility project" means a project designed wholly or mainly for the purpose of a regulated business,

(b)   "regulated business" means a business of a kind listed in paragraph 10 of Schedule 2A,

(c)   "step-in rights" has the meaning given by paragraph 6 of that Schedule, and

(d)   "project company" has the meaning given by paragraph 7 of that Schedule.

S.72D(1), (2)
The creation of discrete insolvency regimes for utilities is now well established—witness the special administration regime under the Railways Act 1993.

72DA Exception in respect of urban regeneration projects

72DA(1) [Administrative receiver of project company] Section 72A does not prevent the appointment of an administrative receiver of a project company of a project which–

(a) is designed wholly or mainly to develop land which at the commencement of the project is wholly or partly in a designated disadvantaged area outside Northern Ireland, and

(b) includes step-in rights.

72DA(2) ["Develop"] In subsection (1) "develop" means to carry out–

(a) building operations,

(b) any operation for the removal of substances or waste from land and the levelling of the surface of the land, or

(c) engineering operations in connection with the activities mentioned in paragraph (a) or (b).

72DA(3) [Meanings] In this section–

"building" includes any structure or erection, and any part of a building as so defined, but does not include plant and machinery comprised in a building,

"building operations" includes–

(a) demolition of buildings,

(b) filling in of trenches,

(c) rebuilding,

(d) structural alterations of, or additions to, buildings and

(e) other operations normally undertaken by a person carrying on business as a builder,

"designated disadvantaged area" means an area designated as a disadvantaged area under section 92 of the Finance Act 2001,

"engineering operations" includes the formation and laying out of means of access to highways,

"project company" has the meaning given by paragraph 7 of Schedule 2A,

"step-in rights" has the meaning given by paragraph 6 of that Schedule,

"substance" means any natural or artificial substance whether in solid or liquid form or in the form of a gas or vapour, and

"waste" includes any waste materials, spoil, refuse or other matter deposited on land.

S.72DA(1)–(3)
This additional exception was created by the Insolvency Act 1986 (Amendment) (Administrative Receivership and Urban Regeneration etc.) Order 2003 (SI 2003/1832) for reasons of social policy.

72E Fourth exception: project finance

72E(1) [Requirement of step-in rights] Section 72A does not prevent the appointment of an administrative receiver of a project company of a project which–

(a) is a financed project, and

(b)   includes step-in rights.

72E(2)   ["Financed", "project company", "step-in rights"] In this section–

(a)   a project is "financed" if under an agreement relating to the project a project company incurs, or when the agreement *is* entered into is expected to incur, a debt of at least £50 million for the purposes of carrying out the project,

(b)   "project company" has the meaning given by paragraph 7 of Schedule 2A, and

(c)   "step-in rights" has the meaning given by paragraph 6 of that Schedule.

S.72E(1), (2)

This fourth exception deals with certain project finance agreements containing "step in" rights. In *Cabvision Ltd v Feetum* [2005] EWCA Civ 1601; [2006] B.C.C. 340 the Court of Appeal (confirming the first instance decision of Lewison J.) rejected a contention that the s.72A bar on the appointment of administrative receivers over the undertaking of an LLP was disapplied by s.72E ("the project finance exception"). On the issue of construction raised in connection with the project finance exception the judge was correct in his interpretation as to whether this was a financed project. The Court of Appeal found that on the facts the critical agreement to consider was the facility agreement and not the earlier software licensing agreement. This project under the terms of the facility agreement did not involve the LLP incurring indebtedness *of at least* £50 million. With regard to the further issue of whether this debenture created step-in rights (within the meaning of Sch.2A para.6) it was inconceivable that Parliament would have intended that the mere right to appoint an administrative receiver under the terms of a debenture constituted step-in rights. Such an interpretation would have the effect of rendering the s.72A bar nugatory. Accordingly, the exception provided for by s.72E did not apply. For comment see Yeowart, [2006] 19 Insolv. Int. 36.

72F   Fifth exception: financial market

72F   Section 72A does not prevent the appointment of an administrative receiver of a company by virtue of–

(a)   a market charge within the meaning of section 173 of the Companies Act 1989 (c. 40),

(b)   a system-charge within the meaning of the Financial Markets and Insolvency Regulations 1996 (S.I. 1996/1469),

(c)   a collateral security charge within the meaning of the Financial Markets and Insolvency (Settlement Finality) Regulations 1999 (S.I. 1999/2979).

GENERAL NOTE

This section deals specifically with the financial markets.

72G   Sixth exception: registered social landlord

72G   Section 72A does not prevent the appointment of an administrative receiver of a company which is registered as a social landlord under Part I of the Housing Act 1996 (c. 52) or under Part 3 of the Housing (Scotland) Act 2001 (asp 10).

GENERAL NOTE

This section deals with the possibility of administrative receivership in the case of a registered social landlord.

72GA   Exception in relation to protected railway companies etc.

72GA   Section 72A does not prevent the appointment of an administrative receiver of–

(a)   a company holding an appointment under Chapter I of Part II of the Water Industry Act 1991,

(b)   a protected railway company within the meaning of section 59 of the Railways Act 1993 (including that section as it has effect by virtue of section 19 of the Channel Tunnel Rail Link Act 1996, or

(c)   a licence company within the meaning of section 26 of the Transport Act 2000.

GENERAL NOTE

This further exception relating to "protected companies" was created by the Insolvency Act 1986 (Amendment) (Administrative Receivership and Urban Regeneration etc.) Order 2003 (SI 2003/1832).

72H   Sections 72A to 72G: supplementary

72H(1)   [Conditions for capital market arrangement] Schedule 2A (which supplements sections 72B to 72G) shall have effect.

72H(2)   [Order-making power] The Secretary of State may by order–

(a)   insert into this Act provision creating an additional exception to section 72A(1) or (2);

(b)   provide for a provision of this Act which creates an exception to section 72A(1) or (2) to cease to have effect;

(c)   amend section 72A in consequence of provision made under paragraph (a) or (b);

(d)   amend any of sections 72B to 72G;

(e)   amend Schedule 2A.

72H(3)   [Statutory instrument] An order under subsection (2) must be made by statutory instrument.

72H(4)   [Provision in order] An order under subsection (2) may make–

(a)   provision which applies generally or only for a specified purpose;

(b)   different provision for different purposes;

(c)   consequential or supplementary provision;

(d)   transitional provision.

72H(5)   [Procedure for order] An order under subsection (2)–

(a)   in the case of an order under subsection (2)(e), shall be subject to annulment in pursuance of a resolution of either House of Parliament,

(b)   in the case of an order under subsection (2)(d) varying the sum specified in section 72B(1)(a) or 72E(2)(a) (whether or not the order also makes consequential or transitional provision), shall be subject to annulment in pursuance of a resolution of either House of Parliament, and

(c)   in the case of any other order under subsection (2)(a) to (d), may not be made unless a draft has been laid before and approved by resolution of each House of Parliament.

S.72H(1)
This directs us to Sch.2A.

S.72H(2)–(5)
Subsection (2) creates a power to make delegated rules. This order making power lead to the Insolvency Act 1986 (Amendment) (Administrative Receivership and Capital Market Arrangements) Order 2003 (SI 2003/1468) and the Insolvency Act 1986 (Amendment) (Administrative Receivership and Urban Regeneration) Order 2003 (SI 2003/1832), both of which modify primary provisions inserted by EA 2002—see Sch.2A. For legal aspects of such delegated rules the position is outlined by subss.(3)–(5).

PART IV

WINDING UP OF COMPANIES REGISTERED UNDER THE COMPANIES ACTS

Introductory note to Part IV
This Part of the Act deals with the winding up of all registered companies, whether solvent or insolvent. For this purpose, the term "company" (or "registered company") is defined by the Companies Acts (see the note to s.73(1)

below). The winding-up provisions are extended to unregistered companies by Pt V of the Act: for the definition of "unregistered company", see s.220. Insolvent partnerships may also be wound up under Pt V of the Act as unregistered companies by virtue of the Insolvent Partnerships Order 1994 (SI 1994/2421): see the note to s.420. But the winding up of limited liability partnerships is governed by IA 1986 Pt IV, by virtue of LLPR 2001 reg.5(1)(a), as modified by reg.5(2) and (3).

Part IV applies generally to Scotland as well as to England and Wales, apart from particular sections which are noted as they occur.

The former Companies (Winding Up) Rules 1949 have been replaced by IR 1986 Pt 4.

The changes made to the law by IA 1985 and IA 1986 do not generally apply retrospectively, so as to affect liquidations which were already in progress when these Acts came into force: Sch.11 para.4. The few exceptions to this (Sch.11 paras 5–9) are noted at the appropriate places in the text which follows.

Where a building society is being wound up under Pt X of the Building Societies Act 1986 Pts IV, VI, VII, XII and XIII of the present Act (and, for Northern Ireland, Pt XX of the Companies (Northern Ireland) Order 1986) apply, subject to the modifications made by Sch.15 to that Act: see Building Societies Act 1986 s.90 and Sch.15, as amended by CA 1989 s.211(1), (2) and Sch.24. Note that the amendments made by CA 1989: (i) require the liquidator of a building society to be a qualified insolvency practitioner under Pt XIII of IA 1986 (s.211(2)(a)); and (ii) extend the concept of "shadow director" to building societies (s.211(2)(b)). Transitional provisions contained in SI 1990/1392 (C. 41) art.7, protect the position of liquidators appointed prior to the commencement of CA 1989 s.211(2)(a), i.e. July 31, 1990.

Special regimes established by the Banking Act 2009 apply where a banking company or building society which is in financial difficulties is the subject of government intervention. See the note on p.6.

The provisions of IA 1986 are made to apply to the winding up of an industrial and provident society (such as a co-operative) by the Industrial and Provident Societies Act 1965 s.55(a) (as amended by IA 1986 s.439(2) and Sch.14), subject to the modifications which are set out in that Act. Other bodies, such as friendly societies, which are not provided for by specific legislation, may be wound up as unregistered companies under Pt V of IA 1986: see *Re Victoria Society, Knottingley* [1913] 1 Ch. 167.

The winding up of insurance undertakings is the subject of a special regime: see the Insurers (Winding Up) Rules 2001 (SI 2001/3635), the Insurers (Reorganisation and Winding up) Regulations 2004 (SI 2004/353) and, as regards Lloyd's, the Insurers (Reorganisation and Winding Up) (Lloyd's) Regulations 2005 (SI 2005/1998).

CHAPTER I

PRELIMINARY

Introductory

73 Scheme of this Part

73(1) [Application of Pt 4] This Part applies to the winding up of a company registered under the Companies Act 2006 in England and Wales or Scotland.

73(2) [Types of winding up] The winding up may be either–

(a) voluntary (see Chapters 2 to 5), or

(b) by the court (see Chapter 6).

73(3) [Application of Chs 1, 7–10] This Chapter and Chapters 7 to 10 relate to winding up generally, except where otherwise stated.

GENERAL NOTE

This section was substituted by the Companies Act 2006 (Consequential Amendments, Transitional Provisions and Savings) Order 2009 (SI 2009/1941) art.2 and Sch.1 para.75(2) as from October 1, 2009. This makes no change of substance.

Prior to the coming into force of IA 1986, there were three modes of winding up: (1) voluntary; (2) by the court; and (3) subject to the supervision of the court. The last of these methods was little used, and was abolished by IA

1985 s.235(3) and Sch.10 Pt II. A voluntary winding up is commenced by the passing of a resolution (usually a special resolution) by the company in general meeting (see s.84): it may be either a "members' voluntary winding up", conducted under the control of the members, if the directors are able to make a declaration of solvency under s.89, or a "creditors' voluntary winding up", if the directors do not make such a declaration, in which case the creditors have control (see ss.89, 90). A winding up by the court (or "compulsory winding up"), as the name suggests, follows from the making of a court order (see ss.122 et seq.).

The Insolvency Act 1986 contains no definition of "company", either generally or for the purposes of this section (although there are some sections which give the term a particular definition for their own specific purpose). Instead, the expression "a company registered under the Companies Act 2006" is used, as in s.73(1), which in effect directs the reader to that Act and, in particular to ss.1(1) and 1171. There we find that the phrase "registered under this Act" is not limited to companies incorporated under CA 2006 but includes also companies formed and registered under earlier Acts and, indeed, companies which "are to be treated" as if formed and registered under the 2006 Act. The relevant sections read as follows:

1   Companies

1(1)   In the Companies Acts, unless the context otherwise requires–

"company" means a company formed and registered under this Act, that is–

(a)   a company so formed and registered after the commencement of this Part, or

(b)   a company that immediately before the commencement of this Part–

(i)   was formed and registered under the Companies Act 1985 (c. 6) or the Companies (Northern Ireland) Order 1986 (S.I. 1986/1032 (N.I. 6)), or

(ii)   was an existing company for the purposes of that Act or that Order,

(which is to be treated on commencement as if formed and registered under this Act).

1171   The former Companies Acts

In the Companies Acts–

"the former Companies Acts" means–

(a)   the Joint Stock Companies Acts, the Companies Act 1862 (c. 89), the Companies (Consolidation) Act 1908 (c. 69), the Companies Act 1929 (c. 23), the Companies Act (Northern Ireland) 1932 (c. 7 (N.I.)), the Companies Acts 1948 to 1983, the Companies Act (Northern Ireland) 1960 (c. 22 (N.I.)), the Companies (Northern Ireland) Order 1986 (S.I. 1986/1032 (N.I. 6)) and the Companies Consolidation (Consequential Provisions) (Northern Ireland) Order 1986 (S.I. 1986/1035 (N.I. 9)), and

(b)   the provisions of the Companies Act 1985 (c. 6) and the Companies Consolidation (Consequential Provisions) Act 1985 (c. 9) that are no longer in force;

"the Joint Stock Companies Acts" means the Joint Stock Companies Act 1856 (c. 47), the Joint Stock Companies Acts 1856, 1857 (20 & 21 Vict. c. 14), the Joint Stock Banking Companies Act 1857 (c. 49), and the Act to enable Joint Stock Banking Companies to be formed on the principle of limited liability (1858 c. 91), but does not include the Joint Stock Companies Act 1844 (c. 110).

The term "existing company", referred to in s.1(1)(b)(ii), was defined by CA 1985 s.735(1)(b), (c) as follows:

(b)   **"existing company"** means a company formed and registered under the former Companies Acts, but does not include a company registered under the Joint Stock Companies Acts, the Companies Act 1862 or the Companies (Consolidation) Act 1908 in what was then Ireland;

(c)   **"the former Companies Acts"** means the Joint Stock Companies Acts, the Companies Act 1862, the Companies (Consolidation) Act 1908, the Companies Act 1929 and the Companies Acts 1948 to 1983.

The definition of "the Joint Stock Companies Acts" (s.735(3)) was identical with that in CA 2006 s.1171.

Contributories

74   Liability as contributories of present and past members

74(1)   [Liability to contribute] When a company is wound up, every present and past member is liable to contribute to its assets to any amount sufficient for payment of its debts and liabilities, and the expenses of the winding up, and for the adjustment of the rights of the contributories among themselves.

74(2)   [Qualifications to liability] This is subject as follows–

(a)   a past member is not liable to contribute if he has ceased to be a member for one year or more before the commencement of the winding up;

(b)   a past member is not liable to contribute in respect of any debt or liability of the company contracted after he ceased to be a member;

(c)   a past member is not liable to contribute, unless it appears to the court that the existing members are unable to satisfy the contributions required to be made by them;

(d)   in the case of a company limited by shares, no contribution is required from any member exceeding the amount (if any) unpaid on the shares in respect of which he is liable as a present or past member;

(e)   nothing in the Companies Acts or this Act invalidates any provision contained in a policy of insurance or other contract whereby the liability of individual members on the policy or contract is restricted, or whereby the funds of the company are alone made liable in respect of the policy or contract;

(f)   a sum due to any member of the company (in his character of a member) by way of dividends, profits or otherwise is not deemed to be a debt of the company, payable to that member in a case of competition between himself and any other creditor not a member of the company, but any such sum may be taken into account for the purpose of the final adjustment of the rights of the contributories among themselves.

74(3)   [Company limited by guarantee] In the case of a company limited by guarantee, no contribution is required from any member exceeding the amount undertaken to be contributed by him to the company's assets in the event of its being wound up; but if it is a company with a share capital, every member of it is liable (in addition to the amount so undertaken to be contributed to the assets), to contribute to the extent of any sums unpaid on shares held by him.

S.74(1)

A "contributory" is a member or past member of the company who is liable to contribute to the assets of the company in a winding up (s.79). This includes a member whose shares are fully paid: *Re Anglesea Colliery Company* (1866) L.R. 1 Ch. 555; and a former member: *Re Consolidated Goldfields of New Zealand Ltd* [1953] Ch. 689. However the court has power to order the rectification of the register of members with retrospective effect, where it is satisfied that a person has never been a member: see *Barbor v Middleton* (1988) 4 B.C.C. 681.

S.74(2)

This provision defines the extent to which both present and past members are liable to contribute to the assets. The principle of limited liability will, where appropriate, apply so as to restrict the amount payable (para.(d)). A past member is liable only in the circumstances listed in paras (a)–(c).

Paragraph (f) subordinates any sums payable by the company to any member qua member (e.g. a dividend declared but not paid) to the company's obligations to its general creditors. The member cannot set off these sums directly against his own contribution.

S.74(2)(f)

In *Soden v British & Commonwealth Holdings plc (in admin.)* [1998] A.C. 298; [1997] B.C.C. 952 the House of Lords held that sums due to a member "in his character of a member" were only those sums the right to which was based on a cause of action on the statutory contract contained in s.14 of CA 1985 [now CA 2006 s.33(1)] and other rights imposed by the Companies Acts. The expression did not include damages awarded to a person who had acquired shares in the company by purchase from an existing member in reliance on a misrepresentation by the company. In contrast, damages for misrepresentation or breach of warranty awarded to a person who had obtained the shares by subscription from the company have been held to be within the section (*Re Addlestone Linoleum Co* (1887) 37 Ch. D. 191; *Webb Distributors (Australia) Pty Ltd v State of Victoria* (1993) 11 A.C.L.C. 1178). The question may, however, be open to reargument in view of CA 2006 s.655, which overrides part of the ratio decidendi of the *Addlestone Linoleum* case.

S.74(3)

This states the limit of the liability of a contributory where a company is limited by guarantee.

75   Directors, etc. with unlimited liability

75 [Omitted by the Companies Act 2006 (Consequential Amendments, Transitional Provisions and Savings) Order 2009 (SI 2009/1941) art.2 and Sch.1 para.75(4) from October 1, 2009, subject to savings in art.9(a).]

GENERAL NOTE

CA 1985 s.306 [now repealed], which was virtually never used in practice, enabled a limited company to provide by its memorandum for its directors and managers to have unlimited liability. This section has now been repealed.

76   Liability of past directors and shareholders

76(1)   **[Application]** This section applies where a company is being wound up and–

(a) it has under Chapter 5 of Part 18 of the Companies Act 2006 (acquisition by limited company of its own shares: redemption or purchase by private company out of capital) made a payment out of capital in respect of the redemption or purchase of any of its own shares (the payment being referred to below as **"the relevant payment"**), and

(b) the aggregate amount of the company's assets and the amounts paid by way of contribution to its assets (apart from this section) is not sufficient for payment of its debts and liabilities, and the expenses of the winding up.

76(2)   **[Contribution of past shareholders, directors]** If the winding up commenced within one year of the date on which the relevant payment was made, then–

(a) the person from whom the shares were redeemed or purchased, and

(b) the directors who signed the statutory declaration made in accordance with section 741(1) to (3) of the Companies Act 2006 for purposes of the redemption or purchase (except a director who shows that he had reasonable grounds for forming the opinion set out in the declaration),

are, so as to enable that insufficiency to be met, liable to contribute to the following extent to the company's assets.

76(3)   **[Amount payable]** A person from whom any of the shares were redeemed or purchased is liable to contribute an amount not exceeding so much of the relevant payment as was made by the company in respect of his shares; and the directors are jointly and severally liable with that person to contribute that amount.

76(4)   **[Application to court]** A person who has contributed any amount to the assets in pursuance of this section may apply to the court for an order directing any other person jointly and severally liable in respect of that amount to pay him such amount as the court thinks just and equitable.

76(5)   **[Non-application of s.74]** Section 74 does not apply in relation to liability accruing by virtue of this section.

76(6)   [Omitted by the Companies Act 2006 (Consequential Amendments, Transitional Provisions and Savings) Order 2009 (SI 2009/1941) art.2 and Sch.1 para.73(5)(d).]

When a payment has been made out of capital by a private company in connection with a redemption or repurchase of shares under CA 2006 s.709, and the company is wound up insolvent within one year of the payment, this section applies so as to make the recipient of the payment liable to refund it in whole or part and, in some circumstances also, the directors jointly and severally liable with him.

Note that although the persons liable under this section fall within the definition of "contributory" for the purposes of this Act, they will not normally be regarded as "contributories" when construing a company's articles (see s.79(3)).

77   Limited company formerly unlimited

77(1)   **[Application]** This section applies in the case of a company being wound up which was at some former time registered as unlimited but has re-registered as a limited company.

77(2)   **[Contribution by past members]** Notwithstanding section 74(2)(a) above, a past member of the company who was a member of it at the time of re-registration, if the winding up commences within the period of 3 years beginning with the day on which the company was re-registered, is liable to contribute to the assets of the company in respect of debts and liabilities contracted before that time.

77(3)   **[If no past members existing members]** If no persons who were members of the company at that time are existing members of it, a person who at that time was a present or past member is liable to contribute as above notwithstanding that the existing members have satisfied the contributions required to be made by them.

This applies subject to section 74(2)(a) above and to subsection (2) of this section, but notwithstanding section 74(2)(c).

77(4)   **[No limitation on contribution]** Notwithstanding section 74(2)(d) and (3), there is no limit on the amount which a person who, at that time, was a past or present member of the company is liable to contribute as above.

The provisions of the Companies Acts mentioned in s.77(1) enable an unlimited company to re-register as limited, but the unlimited liability of both present and past members continues if a winding up ensues within three years of the date of re-registration. The present section deals with the liability of these persons as contributories.

78   Unlimited company formerly limited

78(1)   **[Application]** This section applies in the case of a company being wound up which was at some former time registered as limited but has been re-registered as unlimited.

78(2)   **[Limitation on contribution]** A person who, at the time when the application for the company to be re-registered was lodged, was a past member of the company and did not after that again become a member of it is not liable to contribute to the assets of the company more than he would have been liable to contribute had the company not been re-registered.

When a limited company is converted to an unlimited company under CA 2006 s.102, the limited liability of past members is preserved by this provision.

79   Meaning of "contributory"

79(1)   **["Contributory"]** In this Act the expression **"contributory"** means every person liable to contribute to the assets of a company in the event of its being wound up, and for the purposes of all proceedings for determining, and all proceedings prior to the final determination of, the persons who are to be deemed contributories, includes any person alleged to be a contributory.

79(2) **[Qualification]** The reference in subsection (1) to persons liable to contribute to the assets does not include a person so liable by virtue of a declaration by the court under section 213 (imputed responsibility for company's fraudulent trading) or section 214 (wrongful trading) in Chapter X of this Part.

79(3) **[Reference in articles]** A reference in a company's articles to a contributory does not (unless the context requires) include a person who is a contributory only by virtue of section 76.

GENERAL NOTE

This section defines the term "contributory" for the purposes of both the present Act. It incorporates (by s.79(2)) an amendment made by IA 1985 Sch.6 para.5 which makes it plain that a person is not deemed a contributory merely because he has been ordered by the court to contribute to the company's assets following a finding of fraudulent or wrongful trading under ss.213, 214.

See also the note to s.74(1).

80   Nature of contributory's liability

80   The liability of a contributory creates a debt (in England and Wales in the nature of an ordinary contract debt) accruing due from him at the time when his liability commenced, but payable at the times when calls are made for enforcing the liability.

GENERAL NOTE

"Due" in this section is equivalent to "owing", or "constituting a debt", in contrast with "payable", which is the relevant date for the purposes of the Statutes of Limitation. The words "an ordinary contract debt" were substituted for the former words "a specialty" with effect from October 1, 2009: see the Companies Act 2006 (Consequential Amendments, Transitional Provisions and Savings) Order 2009 art.2 and Sch.1 para.75(9), subject to savings in art.11. In consequence, the period of limitation is now six years.

81   Contributories in case of death of a member

81(1)   **[Personal representative liable]** If a contributory dies either before or after he has been placed on the list of contributories, his personal representatives, and the heirs and legatees of heritage of his heritable estate in Scotland, are liable in a due course of administration to contribute to the assets of the company in discharge of his liability and are contributories accordingly.

81(2)   **[Where personal representatives on list of contributories]** Where the personal representatives are placed on the list of contributories, the heirs or legatees of heritage need not be added, but they may be added as and when the court thinks fit.

81(3)   **[Where default in payment]** If in England and Wales the personal representatives make default in paying any money ordered to be paid by them, proceedings may be taken for administering the estate of the deceased contributory and for compelling payment out of it of the money due.

GENERAL NOTE

This section provides that on the death of a contributory, his personal representatives (or their Scottish counterparts) are substituted for him as contributories.

82   Effect of contributory's bankruptcy

82(1)   **[Application]** The following applies if a contributory becomes bankrupt, either before or after he has been placed on the list of contributories.

82(2)   **[Trustee in bankruptcy a contributory]** His trustee in bankruptcy represents him for all purposes of the winding up, and is a contributory accordingly.

82(3)   [Trustee called on to admit to proof] The trustee may be called on to admit to proof against the bankrupt's estate, or otherwise allow to be paid out of the bankrupt's assets in due course of law, any money due from the bankrupt in respect of his liability to contribute to the company's assets.

82(4)   [Estimated value of liability to future calls] There may be proved against the bankrupt's estate the estimated value of his liability to future calls as well as calls already made.

S.82(1), (2)
The trustee in bankruptcy is deemed a contributory and represents the bankrupt for all purposes of the winding up. It was held under the virtually identical wording of CA 1948 s.216 that this section does not empower a contributory's trustee in bankruptcy to present a winding-up petition (unless the trustee has been registered as a member), since its provisions only become effective once a winding up is in place: *Re H L Bolton (Engineering) Co Ltd* [1956] Ch. 577 at 582–583. In Scotland, however, the wording of the Bankruptcy (Scotland) Act 1985 s.31 is sufficiently wide to empower a trustee to petition: *Taylor, Petitioner; Cumming's Trustee v Glenrinnes Farms Ltd* [1993] B.C.C. 829.

S.82(3), (4)
These subsections deal with the proof against the bankrupt's estate of his liability to the company as a contributory.

83   Companies registered but not formed under the Companies Act 2006

83(1)   [Application] The following applies in the event of a company being wound up which is registered but not formed under the Companies Act 2006.

83(2)   [Contributories re debts and liabilities before registration] Every person is a contributory, in respect of the company's debts and liabilities contracted before registration, who is liable–

(a)   to pay, or contribute to the payment of, any debt or liability so contracted, or

(b)   to pay, or contribute to the payment of, any sum for the adjustment of the rights of the members among themselves in respect of any such debt or liability, or

(c)   to pay, or contribute to the amount of, the expenses of winding up the company, so far as relates to the debts or liabilities above-mentioned.

83(3)   [Amounts liable to be contributed] Every contributory is liable to contribute to the assets of the company, in the course of the winding up, all sums due from him in respect of any such liability.

83(4)   [Death etc. of contributory] In the event of the death, bankruptcy or insolvency of any contributory, provisions of this Act, with respect to the personal representatives, to the heirs and legatees of heritage of the heritable estate in Scotland of deceased contributories and to the trustees of bankrupt or insolvent contributories respectively, apply.

GENERAL NOTE

As explained in the note to s.73, Pt 4 of the Act is expressed to apply to companies "registered under CA 2006", but that phrase includes some companies formed under certain very early Acts which are only "to be treated as if" formed and registered under the 2006 Act (CA 2006 s.1(1)(c)(ii)). This section deals with these rare cases.

CHAPTER II

VOLUNTARY WINDING UP (INTRODUCTORY AND GENERAL)

Resolutions for, and commencement of, voluntary winding up

84   Circumstances in which company may be wound up voluntarily

84(1)   [Circumstances] A company may be wound up voluntarily–

(a)   when the period (if any) fixed for the duration of the company by the articles expires, or the event (if any) occurs, on the occurrence of which the articles provide that the company is to be dissolved, and the company in general meeting has passed a resolution requiring it to be wound up voluntarily;

(b) if the company resolves by special resolution that it be wound up voluntarily;

(c) [Repealed.]

84(2) [Definition] In this Act the expression **"a resolution for voluntary winding up"** means a resolution passed under either of the paragraphs of subsection (1).

84(2A) [Written notice to holder of qualifying floating charge] Before a company passes a resolution for voluntary winding up it must give written notice of the resolution to the holder of any qualifying floating charge to which section 72A applies.

84(2B) [Where written notice given] Where notice is given under subsection (2A) a resolution for voluntary winding up may be passed only–

(a) after the end of the period of five business days beginning with the day on which the notice was given, or

(b) if the person to whom the notice was given has consented in writing to the passing of the resolution.

84(3) [Copy of resolution to registrar] Chapter 3 of Part 3 of the Companies Act 2006 (resolutions affecting a company's constitution) applies to a resolution under paragraph (a) of subsection (1) as well as a special resolution under paragraph (b).

General Note

An insurance company may be wound up voluntarily, either as a members' or creditors' winding up: see the Insurers (Reorganisation and Winding Up) Regulations 2004 (SI 2004/353) regs 7, 9(4).

S.84(1)

Paragraph (a) calls for a "resolution" (i.e. an *ordinary* resolution) and para.(b) for a *special* resolution. The former para.(c) provided for an *extraordinary* resolution where the company was insolvent, but this category of resolution has not survived the enactment of CA 2006 and a special resolution is now required in such a case. The Companies Act 2006 (Commencement No.3, Consequential Amendments, Transitional Provisions and Savings) Order 2007 (SI 2007/2194) art.10(1) and Sch.4 para.39, effective October 1, 2007 accordingly repeals s.84(1)(c) and amends s.84(2) and (3).

S.84(2A), (2B)

These provisions (inserted by SI 2003/2096 from September 15, 2003) give the charge holder a brief opportunity to appoint an administrator, failing which his right to do so will be lost.

A resolution for voluntary winding up cannot be passed conditionally upon the happening of some other event, e.g. the discharge of an administration order: *Re Norditrack (UK) Ltd* [2000] B.C.C. 441.

S.84(3)

Section 29(1)(a) of CA 2006 provides for the registration of all special resolutions, and the requirement to register is extended to resolutions falling within s.84(1)(a) by this provision. The liquidator, for the purposes of these provisions, is deemed to be an officer of the company and liable accordingly to penal sanctions for non-compliance (CA 2006 s.30(4)).

85   Notice of resolution to wind up

85(1) [Notice in Gazette] When a company has passed a resolution for voluntary winding up, it shall, within 14 days after the passing of the resolution, give notice of the resolution by advertisement in the Gazette.

85(2) [Penalty on default] If default is made in complying with this section, the company and every officer of it who is in default is liable to a fine and, for continued contravention, to a daily default fine.

For purposes of this subsection the liquidator is deemed an officer of the company.

GENERAL NOTE

It is the responsibility of the company and its officers (including the liquidator: s.85(2)) to see that notice of the resolution to wind up is gazetted. The liquidator, when appointed, is under a separate obligation to publish notice of his appointment in the *Gazette*: see s.109.

S.85(2)
On penalties, see s.430 and Sch.10.

86 Commencement of winding up

86 A voluntary winding up is deemed to commence at the time of the passing of the resolution for voluntary winding up.

GENERAL NOTE

The "commencement" of a winding up is significant for many purposes under this Act and, previously, the Companies Acts. For the corresponding provision in relation to a winding up by the court, see s.129.

It should be noted that this section refers to the "time" of commencement, as does s.129. In contrast, s.278, the corresponding provision in bankruptcy, states that a bankruptcy "commences *with the day* on which the order is made"—an expression which clearly relates back to the preceding midnight—while other sections of the Act and provisions in the rules refer to the "date" of an event (see, e.g. s.183(2)(a): "date on which he had notice"; "date of commencement of the winding up"; s.240(3): "date of the commencement of the winding up"; and r.4.91(1): "date when the company went into liquidation"). It must be inferred that the draftsmen used these different wordings deliberately, so that where the word "time" is used the normal convention that "the law takes no account of part of a day" (*Trow v Ind Coope (West Midlands) Ltd* [1967] 2 Q.B. 899) is ousted, and an event is to be pinpointed to the precise time of the day when it occurred. This could be an important consideration in some areas of commerce (e.g. financial dealing rooms), where even seconds can count.

The EC Regulation refers to the "time of the opening" of insolvency proceedings. In the case of a creditors' voluntary winding up, this will be the time of the passing of the shareholders' resolution. See the note to the Regulation art.2(f). See also *Secretary of State for Trade and Industry v Slater* [2008] B.C.C. 70 where the court rejected an argument that, for the purposes of the TUPE Regulations 2006, a creditors' voluntary liquidation had commenced at a date earlier than the meetings of the company and creditors.

Consequences of resolution to wind up

87 Effect on business and status of company

87(1) **[Cessation of business]** In case of a voluntary winding up, the company shall from the commencement of the winding up cease to carry on its business, except so far as may be required for its beneficial winding up.

87(2) **[Continuation of corporate state etc.]** However, the corporate state and corporate powers of the company, notwithstanding anything to the contrary in its articles, continue until the company is dissolved.

S.87(1)
In the case of a compulsory winding up, the liquidator may carry on the company's business, "so far as may be necessary for its beneficial winding up" (see s.167(1)(a) and Sch.IV para.5 and, in Scotland, s.169), but normally only with the sanction of the court or the liquidation committee. In a voluntary winding up the question whether it is beneficial to continue the business is a matter for the liquidator's own bona fide judgment.

S.87(2)
The corporate personality of the company in a compulsory winding up also continues until dissolution, although this is not expressly stated in the Act. It follows that acts must be done by the liquidator in the name of the company, and not in his own name. However, where the Act empowers a liquidator (or other office-holder) to institute litigation (e.g. to recover property under s.234 or to have a transaction at an undervalue or a preference set aside under ss.238–239), he should bring the claim in his own name: *Re Cosslett Contractors Ltd (No.2), Smith v Bridgend BC* [2001] UKHL 58; [2002] 1 A.C. 336; [2001] B.C.C. 740 at [32].

88   Avoidance of share transfers, etc. after winding-up resolution

88   Any transfer of shares, not being a transfer made to or with the sanction of the liquidator, and any alteration in the status of the company's members, made after the commencement of a voluntary winding up, is void.

GENERAL NOTE

In a compulsory winding up, a transfer of shares made after the commencement of the winding up is similarly void, but can be validated only by order of the court: see s.127.

Declaration of solvency

89   Statutory declaration of solvency

89(1)   [Declaration by directors] Where it is proposed to wind up a company voluntarily, the directors (or, in the case of a company having more than two directors, the majority of them) may at a directors' meeting make a statutory declaration to the effect that they have made a full inquiry into the company's affairs and that, having done so, they have formed the opinion that the company will be able to pay its debts in full, together with interest at the official rate (as defined in section 251), within such period, not exceeding 12 months from the commencement of the winding up, as may be specified in the declaration.

89(2)   [Requirements for declaration] Such a declaration by the directors has no effect for purposes of this Act unless–

(a)   it is made within the 5 weeks immediately preceding the date of the passing of the resolution for winding up, or on that date but before the passing of the resolution, and

(b)   it embodies a statement of the company's assets and liabilities as at the latest practicable date before the making of the declaration.

89(3)   [Declaration to registrar] The declaration shall be delivered to the registrar of companies before the expiration of 15 days immediately following the date on which the resolution for winding up is passed.

89(4)   [Offence, penalty] A director making a declaration under this section without having reasonable grounds for the opinion that the company will be able to pay its debts in full, together with interest at the official rate, within the period specified is liable to imprisonment or a fine, or both.

89(5)   [Presumption] If the company is wound up in pursuance of a resolution passed within 5 weeks after the making of the declaration, and its debts (together with interest at the official rate) are not paid or provided for in full within the period specified, it is to be presumed (unless the contrary is shown) that the director did not have reasonable grounds for his opinion.

89(6)   [Penalty for non-compliance with s.89(3)] If a declaration required by subsection (3) to be delivered to the registrar is not so delivered within the time prescribed by that subsection, the company and every officer in default is liable to a fine and, for continued contravention, to a daily default fine.

GENERAL NOTE

The category of a voluntary winding up (members' or creditors': see s.90), and the legal rules which apply to it in consequence, depend on whether a statutory declaration of solvency has been made under this section. The responsibility for assessing the likely solvency of the company is placed squarely on the directors (or a majority of them): if they make the declaration, the matter proceeds as a members' voluntary winding up under the control of the members; if they do not, the creditors take over. The severe penalties and reversed onus of proof prescribed by s.89(4) and (5) provide directors with a strong deterrent against making a declaration of solvency irresponsibly.

There is no obligation upon the directors to make a statutory declaration when the company is insolvent or not believed to be solvent: the matter simply proceeds as a creditors' voluntary winding up.

S.89(1)

A statutory declaration is a formal declaration made before a justice of the peace or commissioner for oaths, and is equivalent to an oath for most legal purposes, including the law of perjury. The declaration here required must be made at a directors' meeting, held before the shareholders' meeting at which the resolution for winding up is to be passed, and within the time specified in s.89(2).

The directors must themselves fix the period, not exceeding 12 months from the commencement of the winding up, within which they predict that the company will be able to pay its debts in full. Since the directors' declaration must be made with reference to a future date, they should plainly take into account any prospective and contingent liabilities of which they are aware. On the other hand, it should be noted that they are not required to assert that the company itself is, or will be, "solvent": if the directors have a firm commitment from a third party (such as parent company) that it will meet any liabilities that the company cannot discharge from its own resources, they may well be justified in making a declaration and allowing the liquidation to proceed as a members' voluntary winding up.

Minor inaccuracies in a statement of assets and liabilities on which the directors had relied in making a declaration of solvency were held insufficient to invalidate the declaration in *Re New Millennium Experience Co Ltd* [2003] EWHC 1823 (Ch); [2004] 1 All E.R. 689; [2004] 1 B.C.L.C. 19.

S.89(2)

The five-week period is reckoned back from the date of the winding-up resolution, and the declaration must be based on a financial statement which is as up-to-date as practicable.

S.89(3)

Form 4.70 should be used.

S.89(4)–(6)

The penalties under s.89(4) are stringent—up to two years' imprisonment and an unlimited fine, if the proceedings are on indictment (see Sch.10). If a director's prediction of solvency turns out in the event to be wrong, s.89(5) reverses the normal burden of proof and requires him to show that in fact he had reasonable grounds for making it.

On penalties, see s.430 and Sch.10.

90 Distinction between "members' " and "creditors' " voluntary winding up

90 A winding up in the case of which a directors' statutory declaration under section 89 has been made is a **"members' voluntary winding up"**; and a winding up in the case of which such a declaration has not been made is a **"creditors' voluntary winding up"**.

GENERAL NOTE

In the sections of the Act which follow, Chapter III (ss.91–96) applies only to a members' voluntary winding up and Chapter IV (ss.97–106) only to a creditors' voluntary winding up, while Chapter V (ss.107–116) applies to a voluntary winding up of either kind. This was formerly made clear in the Companies Acts by introductory sections in each case (e.g. CA 1985 ss.579, 587, 596); in the present Act it is left (with the exception of Chapter IV) to be inferred from the title to the chapter in question. (On the relevance of chapter titles in the construction of statutes, see the comment preceding s.230.)

CHAPTER III

MEMBERS' VOLUNTARY WINDING UP

Introductory note to Part IV, Chapter III
Members' voluntary liquidations are discussed in Totty and Moss, *Insolvency*, paras E1–04 et seq.

91 Appointment of liquidator

91(1) [Appointment by general meeting] In a members' voluntary winding up, the company in general meeting shall appoint one or more liquidators for the purpose of winding up the company's affairs and distributing its assets.

91(2) **[Cessation of directors' powers]** On the appointment of a liquidator all the powers of the directors cease, except so far as the company in general meeting or the liquidator sanctions their continuance.

S.91(1)

For the relevant rules, see IR 1986 rr.4.139, 4.141.

S.91(2)

On the making of a winding-up order *by the court* the appointments of all the directors are terminated automatically: *Measures Brothers Ltd v Measures* [1910] 2 Ch. 248. It appears from this subsection that a resolution for voluntary winding up does not of itself operate to remove the directors from office, for if this were the case it would not be possible to sanction the continuance of their powers. This view is, perhaps, confirmed by some reported cases concerning employees, e.g. *Midland Counties District Bank Ltd v Attwood* [1905] 1 Ch. 357, although there are dicta in other cases to the contrary (e.g. *Reigate v Union Manufacturing Co (Ramsbottom) Ltd* [1918] 1 K.B. 592 at 606). It is also endorsed by s.114(2), (3).

92   Power to fill vacancy in office of liquidator

92(1) **[Filling of vacancy]** If a vacancy occurs by death, resignation or otherwise in the office of liquidator appointed by the company, the company in general meeting may, subject to any arrangement with its creditors, fill the vacancy.

92(2) **[Convening of general meeting]** For that purpose a general meeting may be convened by any contributory or, if there were more liquidators than one, by the continuing liquidators.

92(3) **[Manner of holding meeting]** The meeting shall be held in manner provided by this Act or by the articles, or in such manner as may, on application by any contributory or by the continuing liquidators, be determined by the court.

S.92(3)

The reference to "this Act" is probably a slip: fairly obviously, it should have been to CA 1985, as was the case in the pre-consolidation provision (CA 1985 s.581(3)). The present Act contains no provisions regulating the holding of meetings in a members' voluntary winding up (apart from s.194, which deals with resolutions passed at adjourned meetings). The subject is not dealt with in the rules apart from IR 1986 r.4.139, concerning the appointment of the liquidator. In all other respects, the procedure will be the normal one for company meetings laid down by the company's articles and CA 2006 Pt 13.

92A   Progress report to company at year's end (England and Wales)

92A(1) **[Duty of liquidator]** Subject to sections 96 and 102, in the event of the winding up of a company registered in England and Wales continuing for more than one year, the liquidator must–

(a)   for each prescribed period produce a progress report relating to the prescribed matters; and

(b)   within such period commencing with the end of the period referred to in paragraph (a) as may be prescribed send a copy of the progress report to–

(i)   the members of the company; and

(ii)   such other persons as may be prescribed.

92A(2) **[Penalty]** A liquidator who fails to comply with this section is liable to a fine.

GENERAL NOTE

Section 92A was inserted by LRO 2010 (SI 2010/18) art.5(2) from April 6, 2010. The requirement to hold annual meetings has been removed (in England and Wales) by the amendment of s.93. This coincides with the introduction of a provision for the liquidator in that jurisdiction to produce annual progress reports, corresponding to the similar obligation for administrations (where, however, the intervals are six-monthly). For the prescribed matters, see IR 1986 r.4.49C and, for related matters, rr.4.49D–4.49E.

93   General company meeting at each year's end (Scotland)

93(1)   [If winding up for more than one year] Subject to sections 96 and 102, in the event of the winding up of a company registered in Scotland continuing for more than one year, the liquidator shall summon a general meeting of the company at the end of the first year from the commencement of the winding up, and of each succeeding year, or at the first convenient date within 3 months from the end of the year or such longer period as the Secretary of State may allow.

93(2)   [Account by liquidator] The liquidator shall lay before the meeting an account of his acts and dealings, and of the conduct of the winding up, during the preceding year.

93(3)   [Penalty for non-compliance] If the liquidator fails to comply with this section, he is liable to a fine.

GENERAL NOTE

This section now applies in Scotland only, following amendments made by LRO 2010 (SI 2010/18) art.6(2) as from April 6, 2010. There is no longer a requirement to hold AGMs in England and Wales. See the note to s.92A. On the holding of meetings during a winding up, see the note to s.92(3).

S.93(3)
On penalties, see s.430 and Sch.10.

94   Final meeting prior to dissolution

94(1)   [Account of winding up, final meeting] As soon as the company's affairs are fully wound up, the liquidator shall make up an account of the winding up showing how it has been conducted and the company's property has been disposed of, and thereupon shall call a general meeting of the company for the purpose of laying before it the account, and giving an explanation of it.

94(2)   [Advertisement in Gazette] The meeting shall be called by advertisement in the Gazette, specifying its time, place and object and published at least one month before the meeting.

94(3)   [Copy of account etc. to registrar] Within one week after the meeting, the liquidator shall send to the registrar of companies a copy of the account, and shall make a return to him of the holding of the meeting and of its date.

94(4)   [Penalty on default] If the copy is not sent or the return is not made in accordance with subsection (3), the liquidator is liable to a fine and, for continued contravention, to a daily default fine.

94(5)   [If no quorum at meeting] If a quorum is not present at the meeting, the liquidator shall, in lieu of the return mentioned above, make a return that the meeting was duly summoned and that no quorum was present; and upon such a return being made, the provisions of subsection (3) as to the making of the return are deemed complied with.

94(6)   [Penalty if no general meeting called] If the liquidator fails to call a general meeting of the company as required by subsection (1), he is liable to a fine.

GENERAL NOTE

When the liquidator has sent to the registrar his final account and return under this section, dissolution of the company follows automatically three months after the return is registered, unless the court makes an order deferring the date: see s.201(2), (3). For the relevant rule, see r.4.126A.

S.94(4), (6)
On penalties, see s.430 and Sch.10.

S.94(5)
This provision enables the liquidator to cut short the statutory formalities if the meeting, when summoned, is inquorate.

95   Effect of company's insolvency

95(1)   [Application] This section applies where the liquidator is of the opinion that the company will be unable to pay its debts in full (together with interest at the official rate) within the period stated in the directors' declaration under section 89.

95(2)   [Duties of liquidator of Scottish company] In the case of the winding up of a company registered in Scotland, the liquidator shall–

(a)   summon a meeting of creditors for a day not later than the 28th day after the day on which he formed that opinion;

(b)   send notices of the creditors' meeting to the creditors by post not less than 7 days before the day on which that meeting is to be held;

(c)   cause notice of the creditors' meeting to be advertised once in the Gazette and once at least in 2 newspapers circulating in the relevant locality (that is to say the locality in which the company's principal place of business in Great Britain was situated during the relevant period); and

(d)   during the period before the day on which the creditors' meeting is to be held, furnish creditors free of charge with such information concerning the affairs of the company as they may reasonably require;

and the notice of the creditors' meeting shall state the duty imposed by paragraph (d) above.

95(2A)   [Duties of a liquidator of English company] In the case of the winding up of a company registered in England and Wales, the liquidator–

(a)   shall summon a meeting of creditors for a day not later than the 28th day after the day on which he formed that opinion;

(b)   shall send notices of the creditors' meeting to the creditors not less than 7 days before the day on which that meeting is to be held;

(c)   shall cause notice of the creditors' meeting to be advertised once in the Gazette;

(d)   may cause notice of the meeting to be advertised in such other manner as he thinks fit; and

(e)   shall during the period before the day on which the creditors' meeting is to be held, furnish creditors free of charge with such information concerning the affairs of the company as they may reasonably require;

and the notice of the creditors' meeting shall state the duty imposed by paragraph (e) above.

95(3)   [Duties of liquidator re statement of affairs] The liquidator shall also–

(a)   make out a statement in the prescribed form as to the affairs of the company;

(b)   lay that statement before the creditors' meeting; and

(c)   attend and preside at that meeting.

95(4)   [Contents of statement of affairs] The statement as to the affairs of the company shall show–

(a)   particulars of the company's assets, debts and liabilities;

(b)   the names and addresses of the company's creditors;

(c)   the securities held by them respectively;

(d)   the dates when the securities were respectively given; and

(e)   such further or other information as may be prescribed.

95(4A)   [Verification of statement of affairs by liquidator] The statement as to the affairs of the company shall be verified by the liquidator–

(a) in the case of a winding up of a company registered in England and Wales, by a statement of truth; and

(b) in the case of a winding up of a company registered in Scotland, by affidavit.

95(5) [Where principal place of business in different places] Where the company's principal place of business in Great Britain was situated in different localities at different times during the relevant period, the duty imposed by subsection (2)(c) applies separately in relation to each of those localities.

95(6) [Where no place of business in Great Britain] Where the company had no place of business in Great Britain during the relevant period, references in subsections (2)(c) and (5) to the company's principal place of business in Great Britain are replaced by references to its registered office.

95(7) ["The relevant period"] In this section **"the relevant period"** means the period of 6 months immediately preceding the day on which were sent the notices summoning the company meeting at which it was resolved that the company be wound up voluntarily.

95(8) [Penalty for non-compliance] If the liquidator without reasonable excuse fails to comply with this section, he is liable to a fine.

General Note

The earlier law had for a long time been criticised as unsatisfactory (see, e.g. the Cork Committee's *Report*, paras 674–676). The repealed section in the Companies Act required the liquidator in a members' voluntary winding up, if he formed the opinion that the company was insolvent, to summon a meeting of the creditors and inform them of the position. However, the Act made no further provision, and so all that the creditors could then do was petition the court for a compulsory winding-up order to replace the voluntary liquidation. The new section empowers the creditors, without applying to the court, to convert the liquidation into a creditors' voluntary winding up and, if they wish, to substitute a liquidator of their own choice.

Section 95(2A)(b) amended by LRO 2010 (SI 2010/18) art.7 as from April 6, 2010; s.95(4) amended and s.95(4A) inserted by LRO 2010 art.5(2) also from April 6, 2010 (the latter amendments with retrospective effect).

S.95(1)

The reference is to the directors' statutory declaration of solvency by virtue of which the liquidation proceeded initially as a members' voluntary winding up: see s.89(1).

S.95(2), (2A)

Section 95(2) amended, and s.95(2A) inserted, by the Legislative Reform (Insolvency) (Advertising Requirements) Order 2009 art.3(1), as from April 6, 2009. A liquidator in England and Wales is no longer required to advertise notice of the creditors' meeting in a newspaper in addition to publication in the *Gazette*, but instead has a discretion whether or not to undertake additional advertising. The notices no longer need to be sent "by post" (for liquidations commencing after April 6, 2010), following the amendment by LRO 2010 (above). (See further the note to s.98(1).)

S.95(2)(c)

Where the company's principal place of business was situated in different localities at different times within the relevant period, s.95(5) applies; and where the company had no place of business in Great Britain during the relevant period, s.95(6) applies. For the meaning of "the relevant period", see s.95(7).

S.95(3), (4)

The "statement of affairs" provision is parallel to that which applies in a creditors' voluntary winding up (see the comments to s.99 and s.131), except that in the present situation the responsibilities in connection with the statement are imposed on the liquidator and not the directors.

For the rules and forms prescribed for the purposes of this section, see IR 1986 rr.4.34 et seq., 4.49.

S.95(6)

The question whether a company has established a place of business within the jurisdiction had normally arisen in relation to the registration requirements of CA 1985 ss.409 and 691 [CA 2006, no equivalent]. The meaning of the phrase "established a place of business" has been the subject of judicial determination in a number of cases, e.g. *South India Shipping Corporation Ltd v The Export-Import Bank of Korea* [1985] 1 W.L.R. 585; (1985) 1 B.C.C. 99,350; *Re Oriel Ltd* [1986] 1 W.L.R. 180; (1985) 1 B.C.C. 99,444; *Cleveland Museum of Art v Capricorn Art International SA* (1989) 5 B.C.C. 860.

S.95(8)
On penalties, see s.430 and Sch.10.

96 Conversion to creditors' voluntary winding up

96 As from the day on which the creditors' meeting is held under section 95, this Act has effect as if–

(a) the directors' declaration under section 89 had not been made; and

(b) the creditors' meeting and the company meeting at which it was resolved that the company be wound up voluntarily were the meetings mentioned in section 98 in the next Chapter;

and accordingly the winding up becomes a creditors' voluntary winding up.

GENERAL NOTE

It will, of course, be competent for the creditors at their meeting to appoint a liquidator of their own choosing and to establish a liquidation committee under ss.100 and 101, respectively, by virtue of the general provisions of the present section.

Section 97(2) makes it clear that the meeting of creditors held under s.95(2)–(3) and the statement of affairs prepared under s.95(4) are deemed equivalent to the meeting and statement required respectively by ss.98 and 99, so that there is no need to duplicate either of these exercises. This is also confirmed by s.102.

CHAPTER IV

CREDITORS' VOLUNTARY WINDING UP

Introductory note to Part IV, Chapter IV
Creditors' voluntary liquidations are discussed in Totty and Moss, *Insolvency*, paras E1–22 et seq.

97 Application of this Chapter

97(1) [Application] Subject as follows, this Chapter applies in relation to a creditors' voluntary winding up.

97(2) [Non-application of ss.98, 99] Sections 98 and 99 do not apply where, under section 96 in Chapter III, a members' voluntary winding up has become a creditors' voluntary winding up.

S.97(1)
Chapter IV applies in every voluntary winding up where the directors do not make a statutory declaration of solvency under s.89(1).

A creditors' voluntary winding up is a "collective insolvency proceeding" within the scope of the EC Regulation: see the note to the Regulation art.1(1). In order to secure recognition of the winding up in other EU Member States, a certificate of confirmation must be obtained from the court: see Annex A of the Regulation and IR 1986 rr.7.62–7.63.

S.97(2)
See the note to s.96, above.

98 Meeting of creditors

98(1) [Duty of Scottish company] In the case of the winding up of a company registered in Scotland, the company shall–

(a) cause a meeting of its creditors to be summoned for a day not later than the 14th day after the day on which there is to be held the company meeting at which the resolution for voluntary winding up is to be proposed;

(b) cause the notices of the creditors' meeting to be sent by post to the creditors not less than 7 days before the day on which that meeting is to be held; and (c)　cause notice of the creditors' meeting to be advertised once in the Gazette and once at least in two newspapers circulating in the relevant locality (that is to say the locality in which the company's principal place of business in Great Britain was situated during the relevant period).

98(1A)　[Duties of English company] In the case of the winding up of a company registered in England and Wales, the company–

(a)　shall cause a meeting of its creditors to be summoned for a day not later than the 14th day after the day on which there is to be held the company meeting at which the resolution for voluntary winding up is to be proposed;

(b)　shall cause the notices of the creditors' meeting to be sent to the creditors not less than 7 days before the day on which that meeting is to be held;

(c)　shall cause notice of the creditors' meeting to be advertised once in the Gazette; and

(d)　may cause notice of the meeting to be advertised in such other manner as the directors think fit.

98(2)　[Contents of notice of meeting] The notice of the creditors' meeting shall state either–

(a)　the name and address of a person qualified to act as an insolvency practitioner in relation to the company who, during the period before the day on which that meeting is to be held, will furnish creditors free of charge with such information concerning the company's affairs as they may reasonably require; or

(b)　a place in the relevant locality where, on the two business days falling next before the day on which that meeting is to be held, a list of the names and addresses of the company's creditors will be available for inspection free of charge.

98(3)　[Where principal place of business in different places, etc.] Where the company's principal place of business in Great Britain was situated in different localities at different times during the relevant period, the duties imposed by subsections (1)(c) and (2)(b) above apply separately in relation to each of those localities.

98(4)　[Where no place of business in Great Britain] Where the company had no place of business in Great Britain during the relevant period, references in subsections (1)(c) and (3) to the company's principal place of business in Great Britain are replaced by references to its registered office.

98(5)　["The relevant period"] In this section **"the relevant period"** means the period of 6 months immediately preceding the day on which were sent the notices summoning the company meeting at which it was resolved that the company be wound up voluntarily.

98(6)　[Penalty for non-compliance] If the company without reasonable excuse fails to comply with subsection (1), (1A) or (2), it is guilty of an offence and liable to a fine.

GENERAL NOTE

The provisions governing the convening of a creditors' meeting, after the passing by the members of the resolution for voluntary winding up, were extensively redrafted by IA 1985 s.85, which is consolidated in this and the next section. Under the former law, the creditors' meeting was required to be held on the same day as the members' meeting or the day after, and this meant that it had to be summoned before the shareholders' meeting had been held, with little time to prepare information which would put the creditors properly in the picture. Furthermore, by the device known as "centrebinding" (see the note to s.166), the directors were sometimes able to contrive to dispose of the company's assets, or a substantial part of them, before the creditors had a chance to consider their position at all. The present law is designed to ensure that the decisive say in a creditors' voluntary winding up really does lie with the creditors' meeting, that they have proper information on which to base their decisions, and that no action which could be adverse to their interests can be taken before their meeting is held, except to a restricted extent through the agency of a qualified insolvency practitioner (see s.166(3), and also s.114(3)).

　For the rules relating to this section, see IR 1986 rr.4.49, 4.53 et seq., 4.62.

S.98(1), (1A), (6)
Section 98(1) amended, s.98(1A) inserted, and s.98(6) amended, by the Legislative Reform (Insolvency) (Advertising Requirements) Order 2009 art.3(2), as from April 6, 2009. In England and Wales, the company is no longer required to advertise notice of the creditors' meeting in a newspaper in addition to publication in the *Gazette*, but instead the directors have a discretion whether or not to undertake additional advertising. The Insolvency Service has explained (*Dear IP*, March 2009) that the reason for these changes is to achieve better targeted publicity in insolvency proceedings and that if there are resulting savings in the cost of administering insolvencies it is expected that they will be passed on to creditors by way of better returns. The Service does not expect the discretion to be used routinely in run-of-the-mill cases but only where clear benefits or a business need can be identified. Where there is a strong public interest in a particular case, additional publicity may be justified, but in such a situation the expense should be weighed against the likely benefit to be achieved. Advertising in addition to notice in the *Gazette* is no longer restricted to newspaper advertisement but all forms of media advertising may be considered. Section 98(1A)(b) amended by LRO 2010 (SI 2010/18) art.7 as from April 6, 2010. The notices in England and Wales no longer need to be sent "by post" (for liquidations commencing after April 6, 2010).

S.98(1)
The 14-day period replaces the former requirement that the creditors' meeting be held on the same day as the company meeting or the next day. This longer interval enables the directors to prepare properly the information which must be laid before the creditors' meeting under s.99. The directors have very restricted powers to act in relation to the company's property during the period between the two meetings (see s.114) and so it will normally be necessary for the members to appoint an insolvency practitioner to act as liquidator on a provisional basis. He will be empowered to act within the limits prescribed by s.166, and will be able also to make available to creditors the information referred to in s.98(2)(a).

Where the company has had more than one "principal place of business" in Great Britain during the "relevant period", s.98(3) will apply; and if it had no place of business in this country, s.98(4) applies instead. The "relevant period" is defined in s.98(5).

S.98(2)
The directors are, in effect, given a choice. They may either hand over the task of furnishing the creditors with such information as they may require to a person qualified to act as an insolvency practitioner (for the meaning of this expression, see ss.388 et seq.), or they must arrange for a list of all the company's creditors to be kept available for inspection. It is not necessary that this insolvency practitioner should be the liquidator, if a liquidator has been appointed by the members on a provisional basis under s.166; but it will obviously be convenient that he should be, and the requirements of this section will be something of an inducement to appoint a liquidator.

S.98(3)–(5)
See the note to the corresponding s.95(5)–(7).

S.98(6)
On penalties, see s.430 and Sch.10.

99   Directors to lay statement of affairs before creditors

99(1)   [Duty of directors] The directors of the company shall–

(a)   make out a statement in the prescribed form as to the affairs of the company;

(b)   cause that statement to be laid before the creditors' meeting under section 98; and

(c)   appoint one of their number to preside at that meeting;

and it is the duty of the director so appointed to attend the meeting and preside over it.

99(2)   [Contents of statement] The statement as to the affairs of the company shall show–

(a)   particulars of the company's assets, debts and liabilities;

(b)   the names and addresses of the company's creditors;

(c)   the securities held by them respectively;

(d)   the dates when the securities were respectively given; and

(e) such further or other information as may be prescribed.

99(2A) **[Verification of statement of affairs by directors]** The statement as to the affairs of the company shall be verified by some or all of the directors–

(a) in the case of a winding up of a company registered in England and Wales, by a statement of truth; and

(b) in the case of a winding up of a company registered in Scotland, by affidavit.

99(3) **[Penalty for non-compliance]** If–

(a) the directors without reasonable excuse fail to comply with subsection (1), (2) or (2A); or

(b) any director without reasonable excuse fails to comply with subsection (1), so far as requiring him to attend and preside at the creditors' meeting,

the directors are or (as the case may be) the director is guilty of an offence and liable to a fine.

GENERAL NOTE

By this provision the Act imposes an obligation on those who have had control of an insolvent company to make full disclosure of its affairs in a creditors' voluntary winding up. The "statement of affairs" is called for in other situations: for detailed discussion, see the note to s.131.

Section 99(2), (3) was amended and s.99(2A) inserted by LRO 2010 (SI 2010/18) art.5(3) as from April 6, 2010 (with retrospective effect).

For the rules and forms prescribed for the purposes of this section, see IR 1986 rr.4.34 et seq.

If a liquidator has been nominated by the shareholders at their meeting, he is required by s.166(4) to attend the creditors' meeting and report to it on any exercise of his powers during the period between the two meetings.

S.99(1)

If the designated director fails to attend the creditors' meeting, it is open to the creditors to appoint someone else to preside, and a meeting so conducted will be valid: *Re Salcombe Hotel Development Co Ltd* (1989) 5 B.C.C. 807.

S.99(3)

On penalties, see s.430 and Sch.10.

100 Appointment of liquidator

100(1) **[Nomination of liquidator at meetings]** The creditors and the company at their respective meetings mentioned in section 98 may nominate a person to be liquidator for the purpose of winding up the company's affairs and distributing its assets.

100(2) **[Person who is liquidator]** The liquidator shall be the person nominated by the creditors or, where no person has been so nominated, the person (if any) nominated by the company.

100(3) **[Where different persons nominated]** In the case of different persons being nominated, any director, member or creditor of the company may, within 7 days after the date on which the nomination was made by the creditors, apply to the court for an order either–

(a) directing that the person nominated as liquidator by the company shall be liquidator instead of or jointly with the person nominated by the creditors, or

(b) appointing some other person to be liquidator instead of the person nominated by the creditors.

GENERAL NOTE

Although the section uses the word "nominate" rather than "appoint", the nomination is immediately effective in that nothing more is needed to empower the person so chosen to act. This is confirmed by s.166, which deals with the exercise by the members' nominee of his powers as liquidator during the interval between the two meetings.

The person nominated must be qualified to act in relation to the company as an insolvency practitioner: see ss.388, 389. A liquidator appointed under this section is not an officer of the court: *Re T H Knitwear (Wholesale) Ltd* [1988] Ch. 275; (1988) 4 B.C.C. 102.

For the relevant rules, see IR 1986 rr.4.101 et seq.; and in regard to the liquidator's remuneration, rr.4.127 et seq.

Note prospective insertion of new s.100(4) by EA 2002 s.248 and Sch.17 para.14. The holder of a "qualifying" floating charge (for definition, see Sch.B1 para.14(2)–(3)) is to be given the power to select the liquidator unless the court thinks the circumstances exceptional.

101 Appointment of liquidation committee

101(1)   **[Creditors may appoint committee]** The creditors at the meeting to be held under section 98 or at any subsequent meeting may, if they think fit, appoint a committee (**"the liquidation committee"**) of not more than 5 persons to exercise the functions conferred on it by or under this Act.

101(2)   **[Members appointed by company]** If such a committee is appointed, the company may, either at the meeting at which the resolution for voluntary winding up is passed or at any time subsequently in general meeting, appoint such number of persons as they think fit to act as members of the committee, not exceeding 5.

101(3)   **[Creditors may object to members appointed by company]** However, the creditors may, if they think fit, resolve that all or any of the persons so appointed by the company ought not to be members of the liquidation committee; and if the creditors so resolve–

(a)   the persons mentioned in the resolution are not then, unless the court otherwise directs, qualified to act as members of the committee; and

(b)   on any application to the court under this provision the court may, if it thinks fit, appoint other persons to act as such members in place of the persons mentioned in the resolution.

101(4)   **[Scotland]** In Scotland, the liquidation committee has, in addition to the powers and duties conferred and imposed on it by this Act, such of the powers and duties of commissioners on a bankrupt estate as may be conferred and imposed on liquidation committees by the rules.

GENERAL NOTE

The designation of the committee as the "liquidation committee" is a novelty introduced by the draftsman of the consolidating legislation. Under CA 1948, such a committee was given the traditional name, "committee of inspection"; the new name is to reflect the fact that "inspection" of the company's affairs is no longer the primary function of such a committee.

Provision is made for comparable committees by s.26 (administration), ss.49, 68 (administrative receivership) and ss.141, 142 (winding up by the court).

S.101(1)

In addition to the functions conferred on the liquidation committee by the Act itself (see, e.g. s.103), further provisions about its functions, membership and proceedings are contained in the rules: see IR 1986 rr.4.151 et seq.

102 Creditors' meeting where winding up converted under s.96

102   Where, in the case of a winding up which was, under section 96 in Chapter III, converted to a creditors' voluntary winding up, a creditors' meeting is held in accordance with section 95, any appointment made or committee established by that meeting is deemed to have been made or established by a meeting held in accordance with section 98 in this Chapter.

GENERAL NOTE

This section applies when the company in a members' voluntary winding up proves to be insolvent and the liquidation has been converted into a creditors' voluntary winding up under ss.95, 96. Its purpose is to remove any doubts that might otherwise arise about the standing and functions of a liquidator appointed or a liquidation committee established in such a case.

103 Cesser of directors' powers

103 On the appointment of a liquidator, all the powers of the directors cease, except so far as the liquidation committee (or, if there is no such committee, the creditors) sanction their continuance.

GENERAL NOTE

The appointment of a liquidator does not operate of itself to remove the directors from office: see the note to s.91(2).

104 Vacancy in office of liquidator

104 If a vacancy occurs, by death, resignation or otherwise, in the office of a liquidator (other than a liquidator appointed by, or by the direction of, the court), the creditors may fill the vacancy.

GENERAL NOTE

Where the appointment of the previous liquidator was made by or under a court order (see s.100(3)), it appears that a further application to the court is required to fill the vacancy.

104A Progress report to company and creditors at year's end (England and Wales)

104A(1) **[Duty of liquidator]** If the winding up of a company registered in England and Wales continues for more than one year, the liquidator must–

- (a) for each prescribed period produce a progress report relating to the prescribed matters; and
- (b) within such period commencing with the end of the period referred to in paragraph (a) as may be prescribed send a copy of the progress report to–
    - (i) the members and creditors of the company; and
    - (ii) such other persons as may be prescribed.

104A(2) **[Penalty]** A liquidator who fails to comply with this section is liable to a fine.

GENERAL NOTE

Section 104A was inserted by LRO 2010 (SI 2010/18) art.5(3) from April 6, 2010. The requirement to hold annual meetings has been removed (in England and Wales) by the amendment of s.105. This coincides with the introduction of a provision for the liquidator in that jurisdiction to produce annual progress reports, corresponding to the similar obligation for administrations (where, however, the intervals are six-monthly). For the prescribed matters, see IR 1986 r.4.49C and, for related matters, rr.4.49D–4.49E.

105 Meetings of company and creditors at each year's end (Scotland)

105(1) **[Liquidator to summon meetings]** If the winding up of a company registered in Scotland continues for more than one year, the liquidator shall summon a general meeting of the company and a meeting of the creditors at the end of the first year from the commencement of the winding up, and of each succeeding year, or at the first convenient date within 3 months from the end of the year or such longer period as the Secretary of State may allow.

105(2) **[Liquidator to lay account]** The liquidator shall lay before each of the meetings an account of his acts and dealings and of the conduct of the winding up during the preceding year.

105(3) **[Penalty for non-compliance]** If the liquidator fails to comply with this section, he is liable to a fine.

105(4) **[Qualification to requirement]** Where under section 96 a members' voluntary winding up has become a creditors' voluntary winding up, and the creditors' meeting under section 95 is held 3 months or less before the end of the first year from the commencement of the winding up, the liquidator is not required by this section to summon a meeting of creditors at the end of that year.

This section now applies in Scotland only, following amendments made by LRO 2010 (SI 2010/18) art.6(4) as from April 6, 2010. There is no longer a requirement to hold AGMs in England and Wales. See the note to s.104A.

S.105(1)
The corresponding provision in the case of a members' voluntary winding up is s.93; under that section, however, the liquidator is required to report only to the members.

S.105(3)
On penalties, see s.430 and Sch.10.

S.105(4)
This subsection is linked with the procedure prescribed by ss.95, 96 for the situation when a company in a members' voluntary winding up proves to be insolvent. In that case, a creditors' meeting will have been held quite recently, under s.95(2), and there would be little point in summoning a second one so soon afterwards. A general meeting of the company under s.105(1) must, however, still be convened.

106 Final meeting prior to dissolution

106(1) [Account of winding up, meetings] As soon as the company's affairs are fully wound up, the liquidator shall make up an account of the winding up, showing how it has been conducted and the company's property has been disposed of, and thereupon shall call a general meeting of the company and a meeting of the creditors for the purpose of laying the account before the meetings and giving an explanation of it.

106(2) [Advertisement in Gazette] Each such meeting shall be called by advertisement in the Gazette specifying the time, place and object of the meeting, and published at least one month before it.

106(3) [Copy of account, return to registrar] Within one week after the date of the meetings (or, if they are not held on the same date, after the date of the later one) the liquidator shall send to the registrar of companies a copy of the account, and shall make a return to him of the holding of the meetings and of their dates.

106(4) [Penalty on default re s.106(3)] If the copy is not sent or the return is not made in accordance with subsection (3), the liquidator is liable to a fine and, for continued contravention, to a daily default fine.

106(5) [If quorum not present at either meeting] However, if a quorum is not present at either such meeting, the liquidator shall, in lieu of the return required by subsection (3), make a return that the meeting was duly summoned and that no quorum was present; and upon such return being made the provisions of that subsection as to the making of the return are, in respect of that meeting, deemed complied with.

106(6) [Penalty if no meetings called] If the liquidator fails to call a general meeting of the company or a meeting of the creditors as required by this section, he is liable to a fine.

This section corresponds with s.94, which deals with a members' voluntary winding up; but in that case no meeting of the creditors is required.

The affairs of a company may be "fully wound up" even though the company continues to hold property, if the liquidator has done all that he can do to wind up the company: *Re Wilmott Trading Ltd* [2000] B.C.C. 321. The property in that case was a waste management licence. Neuberger J. held that on the subsequent dissolution of the company the licence would cease to exist.

See generally the notes to s.94.

For the relevant rules, see IR 1986 r.4.126.

On penalties, see s.430 and Sch.10.

CHAPTER V

PROVISIONS APPLYING TO BOTH KINDS OF VOLUNTARY WINDING UP

107 Distribution of company's property

107 Subject to the provisions of this Act as to preferential payments, the company's property in a voluntary winding up shall on the winding up be applied in satisfaction of the company's liabilities pari passu and, subject to that application, shall (unless the articles otherwise provide) be distributed among the members according to their rights and interests in the company.

GENERAL NOTE

This section refers to "preferential payments", and not merely to "preferential debts", and thus includes, e.g. the expenses of the winding up (including the liquidator's remuneration) which are given priority by s.115, as well as the preferential debts defined by ss.386, 387.

The company's "property" or "assets" which it is the liquidator's duty to get in and apply under this section is property which is beneficially owned by the company (although where the company holds property on trust, it may also be the duty of the liquidator to see to the due administration of the trust: see the *Berkeley Applegate* cases, discussed in the note to s.115, below). Property which the company does not own beneficially does not form part of the insolvent estate (see, e.g. *Re Global Trader Europe Ltd* [2009] EWHC 602 (Ch); [2009] 2 B.C.L.C. 18). Similarly, it is not caught by a floating charge in a receivership. In a number of cases (of which the best known are perhaps *Barclays Bank Ltd v Quistclose Investments Ltd* [1970] A.C. 567; *Re Kayford Ltd* [1975] 1 W.L.R. 279; *Chase Manhattan Bank NA v Israel–British Bank (London) Ltd* [1979] 3 All E.R. 1025; and *Carreras Rothmans Ltd v Freeman Matthews Treasure Ltd* [1985] 1 All E.R. 155), sums which might have been thought to be recoverable from the company as a debt or in other common-law proceedings have been held to be subject to a trust in the company's hands, with the consequence that the party beneficially entitled could claim the sum in full rather than be obliged to prove as a creditor. Recent cases applying these precedents include *Re Japan Leasing (Europe) plc* [1999] B.P.I.R. 911; *Re Niagara Mechanical Services International Ltd* [2001] B.C.C. 393; *Twinsectra Ltd v Yardley* [2002] UKHL 12; [2002] 2 A.C. 164; and *Re Margaretta Ltd* [2005] EWHC 582 (Ch); [2005] B.C.C. 506. See also *Re Farepak Food and Gifts Ltd* [2006] EWHC 3272 (Ch); [2008] B.C.C. 22; *Cooper v PRG Powerhouse Ltd* [2008] EWHC 498 (Ch); [2008] B.C.C. 588, and contrast *Re BA Peters plc* [2008] EWHC 2205 (Ch); [2008] B.P.I.R. 1180, where the existence of a trust was not established.

The order of application of the assets in the hands of the liquidator will therefore be:

(1)   the expenses of the winding up, including the liquidator's remuneration (s.115);

(2)   the preferential debts, as defined by ss.386, 387 and Sch.6 (s.175);

(3)   any preferential charge on goods distrained that arises under s.176(3);

(4)   the company's general creditors;

(5)   any debts or other sums due from the company to its members qua members (s.74(2)(f));

(6)   the members generally, in accordance with their respective rights and interests (s.107).

Secured creditors will, in principle, be entitled to be paid out of the proceeds of their security (so far as it extends) ahead of all other claims. However, where the security is by way of floating charge, the debts which are preferential debts in the liquidation must be paid first (s.175(2)(b)) and, where s.176A applies, the unsecured creditors will rank ahead of the charge holder in respect of the "prescribed part": see the note to that section. In *Re Leyland DAF Ltd, Buchler v Talbot* [2004] UKHL 9; [2004] 2 A.C. 298; [2004] B.C.C. 214 the House of Lords held that a liquidator was not entitled to claim his expenses in priority to the rights of the holder of a floating charge, and that it was immaterial whether or not the charge had crystallised before the commencement of the liquidation. This overruled the decision in *Re Barleycorn Enterprises Ltd* [1970] Ch. 465, which had been followed in a number of cases including *Re Portbase Clothing Ltd, Mond v Taylor* [1993] Ch. 388; [1993] B.C.C. 96. However, the ruling in *Leyland DAF* has since been reversed by statute: see CA 2006 s.1282, inserting new s.176ZA into IA 1986 with effect from April 6, 2008. See the notes to s.176ZA and rr.4.218A–4.218E.

The statutory order for the application of assets may not be varied by contractual arrangements between the parties concerned, such as a pooling or clearing-house arrangement: *British Eagle International Air Lines Ltd v Cie Nationale Air France* [1975] 1 W.L.R. 758. A pooling arrangement may, however, be structured in a way which does not breach this principle: *North Atlantic Insurance Co Ltd v Nationwide General Insurance Co* [2004] EWCA Civ 423; [2004] 2 All E.R. (Comm) 351. Note that the *British Eagle* case has not been followed, on similar facts, by the High Court of Australia: *International Air Transport Association v Ansett Australia Holdings Ltd* [2008] HCA 3; [2008] B.P.I.R. 57.

The rule in the *British Eagle* case is part of a wider principle, which declares it to be against public policy to displace the insolvency laws by any provision in a contract or other transaction inter partes, e.g. by a term that in the event of one party's bankruptcy a specified asset should become the property of the other (*Ex p. Mackay* (1873) L.R. 8 Ch. App. 643), or by a purported redemption of shares in a company in liquidation by way of a set-off against a judgment debt (*Hague v Nam Tai Electronics Inc* [2006] UKPC 52; [2007] 2 B.C.L.C. 194). But in *Money Markets International Stockbrokers Ltd v London Stock Exchange Ltd* [2001] 2 B.C.L.C. 347 it was held that this principle was not infringed where the rules of a mutual company provided that a member's share should be transferred to a trustee without consideration on his ceasing to be a member, and the member's insolvency was an event leading to the termination of his membership. The share in these circumstances was not a free-standing asset but merely something incidental to his membership rights. The principle in *Ex p. Mackay* was held to apply in *Fraser v Oystertec plc* [2003] EWHC 2787 (Ch); [2004] B.C.C. 233 to an agreement which provided that, in the event of its insolvency, legal ownership of a patent held by a company should pass to a named individual. It was held that such a "divestiture" provision was not merely void as against the company's creditors in any insolvency proceedings which might ensue, but totally void. Contrast *Perpetual Trustee Co Ltd v BNY Corporate Trustee Services Ltd* [2009] EWHC 1912 (Ch); [2009] 2 B.C.L.C. 400, where a security document provided that monies received by the trustee of the collateral in connection its realisation or enforcement of the security should be applied in a specified order of priority unless an event of default (which included the liquidation of the company concerned) should occur, in which case the defaulting party was to lose its priority. This was construed as the grant of a limited and conditional interest in the property which continued only for so long as the latter party was not in default, and not as a divestiture provision prohibited under the *British Eagle* principle.

There are legitimate ways by which creditors of a company may agree that in the event of an insolvency some debts should be subordinated to others, without infringing the principle of the *British Eagle* case, by (for instance) incorporating an undertaking not to prove in respect of the "postponed" debts, and/or a declaration that any moneys received towards payment of such debts should be held on trust for the creditor or creditors having priority, until the latter have been paid in full: *Re SSSL Realisations (2002) Ltd* [2006] EWCA Civ 7; [2006] Ch. 610; [2006] B.C.C. 233.

Moreover, it should be noted that both CA 1989 Pt VII and the Finality Regulations remove various arrangements and transactions altogether from the scope of the insolvency legislation, and specifically disapply particular provisions of the latter legislation in relation to market transactions or payment or settlement systems which come within their ambit. (See also the general reversal of the *British Eagle* principle in the Finality Regulations reg.14.) The impact of these provisions is noted at the relevant places in this *Guide*.

Special regimes are made to apply in particular cases by other legislation, e.g. as regards insurance companies (Insurers (Reorganisation and Winding Up) Regulations 2004 (SI 2004/353)) and the "owner" of regulated covered bonds (Regulated Covered Bonds Regulations 2008 (SI 2008/346)) (both reproduced in Vol.2 of this *Guide*).

Property subject to a restraint order or other order under POCA 2002 is also excluded from the assets available for distribution by the liquidator: see s.426 of that Act. But once the company is in liquidation, the powers under the 2002 Act may not be exercised in relation to property which belonged to the company at the time when it went into liquidation (see s.426(4)–(6), (9)).

A creditor or contributory has no legal or equitable interest in the property of the company held by the liquidator, but only a right to have the assets duly administered by him: *Banque Nationelle de Paris plc v Montman Ltd* [2000] 1 B.C.L.C. 576.

Provision is made for the proof and payment of debts in a members' voluntary winding up by IR 1986 r.4.182A, and in a creditors' voluntary winding up by rr.4.73 et seq., 4.180.

For the application of assets in a winding up by the court, see s.148 and IR 1986 r.4.181.

108 Appointment or removal of liquidator by the court

108(1) [If no liquidator acting] If from any cause whatever there is no liquidator acting, the court may appoint a liquidator.

108(2) [Removal, replacement] The court may, on cause shown, remove a liquidator and appoint another.

GENERAL NOTE

The power of the court supplements the power of the members under s.92 (members' voluntary winding up) and that of the creditors under s.104 (creditors' voluntary winding up) to fill any such vacancy themselves. A liquidator once appointed, however, may be removed only by the court "on cause shown" under s.108(2). The case of *Re Keypak Homecare Ltd* (1987) 3 B.C.C. 558 contains a useful review of the principles upon which the court will act in exercising its power to remove a liquidator under s.108(2). In *Re Bridgend Goldsmiths Ltd* [1995] B.C.C. 226 the court exercised its powers under s.108(1) to appoint a new liquidator when the previous liquidator had ceased to be qualified to act as an insolvency practitioner. An application to remove liquidators was refused in *AMP Music Box Enterprises Ltd v Hoffman* [2002] EWHC 1899 (Ch); [2002] B.C.C. 996, where their conduct had, in the past, been open to the criticism that they had not pursued certain claims very actively but the court considered that they had more recently given the matter more attention. Other cases illustrating the exercise of the court's discretion include *Fielding v Seery* [2004] B.C.C. 315; *Re Buildlead Ltd (No.2)* [2004] EWHC 2443 (Ch); [2005] B.C.C. 138; and *Sisu Capital Fund Ltd v Tucker* [2005] EWHC 2170 and 2321 (Ch); [2006] B.C.C. 463; [2006] B.P.I.R. 154.

In *Re Sankey Furniture Ltd Ex p. Harding* [1995] 2 B.C.L.C. 594 the court declined to use its power under s.108(2) to remove a liquidator (who wished to resign) where this would by-pass the statutory requirement that a meeting of creditors be called to consider whether or not to accept the resignation: the fact that this would save the expense of a meeting was not sufficient to justify the court intervening in a matter which was for the creditors to decide. However, it is now well established that where an insolvency practitioner seeks to resign from multiple offices and be replaced (usually by other members of the same firm), the court is willing to make orders without these statutory formalities: see the note to s.172(1), (2).

An application may be made under s.108 by anyone whom the court considers proper, e.g. a former liquidator who has ceased to be qualified to act in relation to the company (*Re A J Adams (Builders) Ltd* [1991] B.C.C. 62) or the recognised professional body of which such a person was once a member (*Re Stella Metals Ltd (in liq.)* [1997] B.C.C. 626). But the court will not remove the liquidator of an insolvent company on the application of a contributory: *Deloitte & Touche AG v Johnson* [1999] B.C.C. 992.

Save in very exceptional cases, notice of the application should be given to the liquidator whom it is sought to remove, in order to give him an opportunity to be heard: *Clements v Udal* [2001] B.C.C. 658.

For the relevant rules, see IR 1986 rr.4.103, 4.140.

109 Notice by liquidator of his appointment

109(1) [Notice in Gazette and to registrar] The liquidator shall, within 14 days after his appointment, publish in the Gazette and deliver to the registrar of companies for registration a notice of his appointment in the form prescribed by statutory instrument made by the Secretary of State.

109(2) [Penalty on default] If the liquidator fails to comply with this section, he is liable to a fine and, for continued contravention, to a daily default fine.

S.109(1)

The duty of the liquidator to give notice of his appointment under this section is additional to his duty to notify creditors under IR 1986 rr.4.103, 4.139 and 4.140 and also to the obligation imposed by s.85 on the company and its officers (including the liquidator) to notify the passing of the resolution for voluntary winding up by advertisement in the *Gazette*. Further advertising and registration requirements are imposed by r.4.106A.

The gazetting of the liquidator's appointment under this section constitutes an "official notification" of the event for the purposes of CA 2006 ss.1077–1079. If there has not been an official notification, or (in some circumstances) if the official notification is less than 15 days old, s.1079(1) provides that the company "is not entitled to rely against other persons on the happening" of the appointment of the liquidator. This provision has its origin in the EC First Company Law Directive; its meaning and effect (so far as English law is concerned) is obscure. What matters under the Act is the fact that the company has gone into liquidation: nothing turns on the appointment of the liquidator, as such.

The Insolvency Service has confirmed that the requirements of s.109 must be followed where a creditors' voluntary liquidation follows an administration under Sch.B1 para.83: see *Dear IP*, March 2006.

The relevant forms are Forms 600 and 600a set out in Sch.2 Pt II to the Companies (Forms) (Amendment) Regulations 1987 (SI 1987/752).

S.109(2)

On penalties, see s.430 and Sch.10.

110 Acceptance of shares, etc., as consideration for sale of company property

110(1) [Application] This section applies, in the case of a company proposed to be, or being, wound up voluntarily, where the whole or part of the company's business or property is proposed to be transferred or sold–

(a) to another company (**"the transferee company"**), whether or not the latter is a company registered under the Companies Act 2006, or

(b) to a limited liability partnership (the **"transferee limited liability partnership"**).

110(2) [Shares etc. in compensation for transfer] With the requisite sanction, the liquidator of the company being, or proposed to be, wound up (**"the transferor company"**) may receive, in compensation or part compensation for the transfer or sale–

(a) in the case of the transferee company, shares, policies or other like interests in the transferee company for distribution among the members of the transferor company, or

(b) in the case of the transferee limited liability partnership, membership in the transferee limited liability partnership for distribution among the members of the transferor company.

110(3) [Sanction for s.110(2)] The sanction requisite under subsection (2) is–

(a) in the case of a members' voluntary winding up, that of a special resolution of the company, conferring either a general authority on the liquidator or an authority in respect of any particular arrangement, and

(b) in the case of a creditors' voluntary winding up, that of either the court or the liquidation committee.

110(4) [Alternative to s.110(2)] Alternatively to subsection (2), the liquidator may (with that sanction) enter into any other arrangement whereby the members of the transferor company may–

(a) in the case of the transferee company, in lieu of receiving cash, shares, policies or other like interests (or in addition thereto) participate in the profits of, or receive any other benefit from, the transferee company, or

(b) in the case of the transferee limited liability partnership, in lieu of receiving cash or membership (or in addition thereto), participate in some other way in the profits of, or receive any other benefit from, the transferee limited liability partnership.

110(5) [Sale binding on transferors] A sale or arrangement in pursuance of this section is binding on members of the transferor company.

110(6) [Special resolution] A special resolution is not invalid for purposes of this section by reason that it is passed before or concurrently with a resolution for voluntary winding up or for appointing liquidators; but, if an order is made within a year for winding up the company by the court, the special resolution is not valid unless sanctioned by the court.

General Note

This section deals with a corporate "reconstruction", under which the whole or part of the business of a company in liquidation is sold by the liquidator to another company or limited liability partnership and the members of the first company agree to accept shares or other securities in the purchasing company instead of the cash distribution to which they would normally be entitled. Provided that the sanction referred to in s.110(3) is obtained, the scheme is binding on all the members except those who dissent in writing under s.111(1).

Rule 4.49F requires a liquidator who makes a distribution in specie to members in a reconstruction under s.110 to give specified details of the basis of the valuation of the property concerned, in progress reports and in his reports to members and creditors at final meetings and any meeting to receive a liquidator's resignation.

Subsections (1), (2) and (4) were amended by the Limited Liability Partnerships Regulations 2001 (SI 2001/1090, effective April 6, 2001) to make possible the use of a limited liability partnership as the transferee.

S.110(1)

For the definition of "company" referred to, see CA 2006 ss.1(1) and 1171, and the note to s.73 above. The "transferee company" may be a company outside this definition—e.g. a company incorporated overseas.

S.110(2), (4)

The consideration which the members agree to accept normally consists of or includes shares in the transferee company, or corresponding interests in an LLP, but it may take other forms.

S.110(3)

The consolidation has introduced an ambiguity into the section by running together two provisions which were formerly stated separately in CA 1985 s.582(2) and s.593. As it stands, para.(b) of the new subsection appears to read as an *alternative* to para.(a), but it should be an *additional* requirement; i.e. in a members' voluntary winding up, only the sanction in para.(a) is needed, but in a creditors' winding up, *both* para.(a) and para.(b) apply. If this were not so, the members could be obliged to accept shares without their consent, and s.111 would not apply at all!

S.110(5)

This should be read subject to the right of a member to dissent under s.111. In fact, although the arrangement may be "binding" under this provision, in the sense that a dissenting member cannot prevent the deal from going ahead, nothing can oblige him to become a member of the transferee company without his consent. It is necessary in practice therefore for a scheme of reconstruction to make express provision for recalcitrant but inactive shareholders, e.g. by creating a trust to hold the new shares on their behalf.

S.110(6)

The sanction of the court is not required before the liquidator puts a scheme of reconstruction into effect.

111   Dissent from arrangement under s.110

111(1)   [Application] This section applies in the case of a voluntary winding up where, for the purposes of section 110(2) or (4), there has been passed a special resolution of the transferor company providing the sanction requisite for the liquidator under that section.

111(2)   [Objections by members of transferor company] If a member of the transferor company who did not vote in favour of the special resolution expresses his dissent from it in writing, addressed to the liquidator and left at the company's registered office within 7 days after the passing of the resolution, he may require the liquidator either to abstain from carrying the resolution into effect or to purchase his interest at a price to be determined by agreement or by arbitration under this section.

111(3)   [Where liquidator purchases member's interest] If the liquidator elects to purchase the member's interest, the purchase money must be paid before the company is dissolved and be raised by the liquidator in such manner as may be determined by special resolution.

111(4)   [Arbitration] For purposes of an arbitration under this section, the provisions of the Companies Clauses Consolidation Act 1845 or, in the case of a winding up in Scotland, the Companies Clauses Consolidation (Scotland) Act 1845 with respect to the settlement of disputes by arbitration are incorporated with this Act, and–

(a)   in the construction of those provisions this Act is deemed the special Act and **"the company"** means the transferor company, and

(b)   any appointment by the incorporated provisions directed to be made under the hand of the secretary or any two of the directors may be made in writing by the liquidator (or, if there is more than one liquidator, then any two or more of them).

GENERAL NOTE

This section confers on a dissenting member the right to have his shareholding in the company bought out in cash, provided that he takes the prompt action prescribed by s.111(2). The notice of dissent and (in the case of a company registered in Scotland) the appointment under s.111(4)(b) must be in hard copy (s.436B(2)(d), (e)).

112   Reference of questions to court

112(1)   **[Application to court]** The liquidator or any contributory or creditor may apply to the court to determine any question arising in the winding up of a company, or to exercise, as respects the enforcing of calls or any other matter, all or any of the powers which the court might exercise if the company were being wound up by the court.

112(2)   **[Court order]** The court, if satisfied that the determination of the question or the required exercise of power will be just and beneficial, may accede wholly or partially to the application on such terms and conditions as it thinks fit, or may make such other order on the application as it thinks just.

112(3)   **[Copy of order to registrar]** A copy of an order made by virtue of this section staying the proceedings in the winding up shall forthwith be forwarded by the company, or otherwise as may be prescribed, to the registrar of companies, who shall enter it in his records relating to the company.

S.112(1), (2)

The powers of the court in a winding up by the court are contained in Chapter VI of the Act, and more specifically in ss.147 et seq.

    Where a company is an "authorised person" under FSMA 2000, the Financial Services Authority may apply to the court or participate in the proceedings: FSMA 2000 s.365.

S.112(2)

The court's powers are discretionary. It may refuse to permit proceedings under this provision where some other procedure is more appropriate: *Re Stetzel Thomson & Co Ltd* (1988) 4 B.C.C. 74, or when the applicant would not have standing to invoke some other, more appropriate, procedure: *Re James McHale Automobiles Ltd* [1997] B.C.C. 202. It is not a complete bar to the exercise of discretion that the applicant is using the procedure to obtain a collateral advantage: *Re Movitex Ltd* [1992] B.C.C. 101. The court's powers under this section were invoked to make various orders facilitating co-operation under the CBIR between the provisional liquidators in a UK liquidation and the US trustee in bankruptcy of an associated company in *Re Bernard L Madoff Investment Securities LLC* [2009] EWHC 442 (Ch); [2009] 2 B.C.L.C. 78.

S.112(3)

No rules appear to have been prescribed for the purposes of this section.

113   Court's power to control proceedings (Scotland)

113   If the court, on the application of the liquidator in the winding up of a company registered in Scotland, so directs, no action or proceeding shall be proceeded with or commenced against the company except by leave of the court and subject to such terms as the court may impose.

114   No liquidator appointed or nominated by company

114(1)   **[Application]** This section applies where, in the case of a voluntary winding up, no liquidator has been appointed or nominated by the company.

114(2)   **[Limit on exercise of directors' powers]** The powers of the directors shall not be exercised, except with the sanction of the court or (in the case of a creditors' voluntary winding up) so far as may be necessary to secure compliance with sections 98 (creditors' meeting) and 99 (statement of affairs), during the period before the appointment or nomination of a liquidator of the company.

114(3)   **[Non-application of s.114(2)]** Subsection (2) does not apply in relation to the powers of the directors–

(a)   to dispose of perishable goods and other goods the value of which is likely to diminish if they are not immediately disposed of, and

(b)   to do all such other things as may be necessary for the protection of the company's assets.

114(4)   **[Penalty for non-compliance]** If the directors of the company without reasonable excuse fail to comply with this section, they are liable to a fine.

GENERAL NOTE

This section is designed as a counter to the practice of "centrebinding" which was condemned as unsatisfactory by the Cork Committee (*Report*, paras 666 et seq.), and should be read in conjunction with the notes to s.166 below. The Committee drew attention to the fact that there was in every voluntary liquidation a period of time during which the directors remained in control of the company but, until the necessary meetings had been convened and a liquidator appointed, the company's assets and the interests of creditors were most inadequately protected. This period could be extended if the appointment of the liquidator was not made at the same time as the passing of the resolution for winding up but deferred until a later occasion. The Committee's recommendation was that a voluntary liquidation should commence as soon as the *directors* had decided that, because of its liabilities, the company could not carry on business, and that they should be obliged immediately to appoint a provisional liquidator who would assume effective control and safeguard the position until the appropriate meeting had made a permanent appointment.

The legislature did not accept this recommendation of the Committee, and so it remains the law that a voluntary winding up commences when the company's special resolution is passed. This section does, however, in part curb the abuse to which the report drew attention, by providing that the directors should have only very limited powers, restricted to the preservation of the company's assets, until a liquidator has been appointed. The weakness of the section is, however, that it operates only *after* the voluntary winding up has commenced: the directors will still be in full control during the period which must elapse while the meeting of the company is being convened.

S.114(1), (2)

In a members' voluntary winding up, the liquidator is appointed by the company in general meeting under s.91. These provisions should ensure that an appointment is made promptly, whereupon the powers of the directors will normally cease (see s.91(2)). Section 114(2) should also encourage the members to nominate a liquidator promptly in the case of a creditors' voluntary winding up. In this event, it may be inferred from the wording of s.166 that, once the company has nominated a liquidator, he automatically takes office and is vested with the powers and duties set out in that section.

S.114(3)

The very limited powers which the directors retain are confined to the disposal of perishable goods and the protection of assets. They will not extend to continuing to manage the business in any general sense. (Note that para.(a) is confined in its scope to *goods*. Other property which may be likely to diminish in value (e.g. shares in a bear market) is not covered by this paragraph, although some actions of the directors in relation to such property may be justified under para.(b).)

S.114(4)

A contract entered into in breach of s.114 would, at least prima facie, be illegal and void. However it is possible that a third party who has dealt with the directors in good faith and without knowledge of the resolution could enforce the transaction on the basis of the directors' ostensible authority: *Re a Company (No.006341 of 1992) Ex p. B Ltd* [1994] 1 B.C.L.C. 225.

On penalties, see s.430 and Sch.10.

115 Expenses of voluntary winding up

115 All expenses properly incurred in the winding up, including the remuneration of the liquidator, are payable out of the company's assets in priority to all other claims.

GENERAL NOTE

The expenses of the winding up rank ahead of the claims of the preferential creditors who are given priority by ss.175, 176.

In the case of a creditors' voluntary winding up (including one which has commenced as a members' winding up but later proves to be insolvent), the order of priority as between the different categories of expenses is set out in IR 1986 r.4.218, but the court has power to vary these general rules by virtue of ss.112(1) and 156 and r.4.220.

The ruling in *Re Barleycorn Enterprises Ltd* [1970] Ch. 465 (which was followed in a number of cases including *Re Portbase Clothing Ltd, Mond v Taylor* [1993] Ch. 388; [1993] B.C.C. 96) that for the purposes of s.115, the company's "assets" include assets covered by a floating charge, was overruled by the House of Lords in *Re Leyland DAF Ltd, Buchler v Talbot* [2004] UKHL 9; [2004] 2 A.C. 298; [2004] B.C.C. 214, but has since been reinstated by legislation: see s.176ZA, below.

This section does not declare that all expenses properly incurred by a liquidator are payable out of the company's assets, but only that expenses which *are* so payable should have priority to other claims.

In a number of cases, e.g. *Re M C Bacon Ltd (No.2)* [1991] Ch. 127; [1990] B.C.C. 430; *Re RS & M Engineering Co Ltd, Mond v Hammond Suddards (a firm)* [2000] Ch. 40; [2000] B.C.C. 445; and *Re Floor Fourteen Ltd, Lewis v Inland Revenue Commissioner* [2001] 3 All E.R. 449; [2002] B.C.C. 198, it was held that a liquidator's costs in pursuing claims under ss.238 (transaction at an undervalue), 239 (preference), or 214 (wrongful trading), however properly the litigation may have been brought, were not payable out of the company's assets. However, the effect of these rulings has been reversed by an amendment made to IR 1986 r.4.218 by the Insolvency (Amendment) (No.2) Rules 2002 (SI 2002/2712, effective January 1, 2003, subject to transitional provisions contained in r.4(2)). Rule 4.218 now specifies as expenses of the liquidation expenses or costs which are properly chargeable or incurred by the official receiver or liquidator "relating to the conduct of any legal proceedings which he has power to bring or defend whether in his own name or the name of the company". This puts beyond doubt any contention that such expenses do not fall within s.115. However, damages awarded against a liquidator who, in pursuing such a claim, committed a breach of contract were held not to be "costs of the litigation" within r.4.218(1) in *Re SSSL Realisations (2002) Ltd* [2004] EWHC 1760 (Ch); [2005] 1 B.C.L.C. 1. There was no appeal on this point: see [2006] EWCA Civ 7; [2006] Ch. 610; [2006] B.C.C. 233.

Pre-liquidation expenses, other than those specifically incurred for the purpose of enabling the company to pass the winding-up resolution and take other steps required by statute, cannot ordinarily be claimed under this section: *Re A V Sorge & Co Ltd* (1986) 2 B.C.C. 99,306; *Re Sandwell Copiers Ltd* (1988) 4 B.C.C. 227; *Re W F Fearman Ltd (No.2)* (1988) 4 B.C.C. 141.

Corporation tax on post-liquidation profits is payable in priority as a liquidation expense, even if the income in question has not been, and never will be, received: *Kahn v Inland Revenue Commissioners, Re Toshoku Finance (UK) plc* [2002] UKHL 6; [2002] 1 W.L.R. 671; [2002] B.C.C. 110. In the same case it was also held that rates and similar local taxes will also come within the definition of liquidation expenses (at paras 34, 40–41, overruling *Re Kentish Homes Ltd* [1993] B.C.C. 212). Contrast *Re Allders Department Stores Ltd* [2005] EWHC 172 (Ch); [2005] B.C.C. 289 (redundancy payments not "necessary disbursements" in an administration); and see Lyons and Birch, (2005) 18 Insolv. Int. 150.

In *Re Berkeley Applegate (Investment Consultants) Ltd (No.2)* (1988) 4 B.C.C. 279, a liquidator had done substantial work in relation to assets in which, after investigation, the company proved to have no beneficial interest. It was held, in the circumstances, that he was entitled to be paid his proper expenses and remuneration as a charge on those assets, even though they were not "the company's assets" within s.115. (See further *Re Berkeley Applegate (Investment Consultants) Ltd (No.3)* (1989) 5 B.C.C. 803; and compare *Re Eastern Capital Futures Ltd* (1989) 5 B.C.C. 223; *Re Rusjon Ltd* [2007] EWHC 2943 (Ch); [2008] 2 B.C.L.C. 234.)

In relation to the financial markets and securities settlement systems, s.175 has effect subject to the priority accorded to the claim of a participant or central bank to collateral security by the Finality Regulations reg.14(5), (6), unless the terms on which the collateral security was provided expressly state that the expenses, remuneration or preferential debts are to have priority: see the note on p.2.

On the general rules regarding the distribution of assets in a voluntary winding up, see the note to s.107.

116   Saving for certain rights

116   The voluntary winding up of a company does not bar the right of any creditor or contributory to have it wound up by the court; but in the case of an application by a contributory the court must be satisfied that the rights of the contributories will be prejudiced by a voluntary winding up.

GENERAL NOTE

The court has, in any case, a discretion under s.125 to refuse a winding-up order, even where the application is made by a creditor. The wishes of a majority of the company's creditors will be taken into account, but will not be regarded as decisive: see *Re Home Remedies Ltd* [1943] Ch. 1; *Re Southard & Co Ltd* [1979] 1 W.L.R. 1198; *Re Medisco Equipment Ltd* (1983) 1 B.C.C. 98,944.

CHAPTER VI

WINDING UP BY THE COURT

Introductory note to Part IV, Chapter VI
Winding up by the court is discussed in Totty and Moss, *Insolvency*, paras E1–71 et seq.

117 High Court and county court jurisdiction

117(1) **[High Court]** The High Court has jurisdiction to wind up any company registered in England and Wales.

117(2) **[County court]** Where the amount of a company's share capital paid up or credited as paid up does not exceed £120,000, then (subject to this section) the county court of the district in which the company's registered office is situated has concurrent jurisdiction with the High Court to wind up the company.

117(3) **[Increase, reduction of s.117(2) sum]** The money sum for the time being specified in subsection (2) is subject to increase or reduction by order under section 416 in Part XV.

117(4) **[Exclusion of jurisdiction for county court]** The Lord Chancellor may, with the concurrence of the Lord Chief Justice, by order in a statutory instrument exclude a county court from having winding-up jurisdiction, and for the purposes of that jurisdiction may attach its district, or any part thereof, to any other county court, and may by statutory instrument revoke or vary any such order.

In exercising the powers of this section, the Lord Chancellor shall provide that a county court is not to have winding-up jurisdiction unless it has for the time being jurisdiction for the purposes of Parts VIII to XI of this Act (individual insolvency).

117(5) **[Extent of winding-up jurisdiction]** Every court in England and Wales having winding-up jurisdiction has for the purposes of that jurisdiction all the powers of the High Court; and every prescribed officer of the court shall perform any duties which an officer of the High Court may discharge by order of a judge of that court or otherwise in relation to winding up.

117(6) **["Registered office"]** For the purposes of this section, a company's **"registered office"** is the place which has longest been its registered office during the 6 months immediately preceding the presentation of the petition for winding up.

117(7) **[Applicability of EC Regulation]** This section is subject to Article 3 of the EC Regulation (jurisdiction under EC Regulation).

117(8) **[Nomination of judicial office holder]** The Lord Chief Justice may nominate a judicial office holder (as defined in section 109(4) of the Constitutional Reform Act 2005) to exercise his functions under this section.

GENERAL NOTE

For the corresponding provisions relating to Scotland, see ss.120, 121.

In the present Act, the word "court", when used in relation to a company, means the court having jurisdiction to wind up the company: see IA 1986 s.251. [There is a different definition in CA 2006 s.1156(1), but that in IA 1986 is preserved by s.1156(2).] This will be the appropriate court as defined by this section. The relevant date for determining the question of jurisdiction is that when the proceedings in question are commenced (which in some contexts may be a date later than that on which the company in fact went into liquidation): *Re Lichfield Freight Terminal Ltd* [1997] B.C.C. 11.

Where a matter is already the subject of proceedings in a county court, application should be made to that court and not to the High Court. The latter may, however, allow such an application to continue under IR 1986 r.7.12: *Re Sankey Furniture Ltd Ex p. Harding* [1995] 2 B.C.L.C. 594.

Winding-up proceedings are a form of "suit and legal process", but are not a method of "enforcing a judgment or arbitration award": *Re International Tin Council* [1989] Ch. 309; (1988) 4 B.C.C. 653 CA; affirming [1987] Ch. 419; (1987) 3 B.C.C. 103. A creditor who has presented a winding-up petition is "pursuing a course of action" which confers jurisdiction on the court to grant appropriate interim relief (e.g. a freezing order): *Revenue and Customs Commissioners v Egleton* [2006] EWHC 2313 (Ch); [2007] B.C.C. 78. However where, as in the case itself, the freezing order is sought against third parties it is a provisional liquidator and not the petitioning creditor who should pursue this course.

S.117(7)

Article 3 of the EC Regulation, which is supplemented by the Insolvency Act 1986 (Amendment) (No.2) Regulations 2002 (SI 2002/1240, effective May 31, 2002), empowers the courts of a Member State to open insolvency proceedings only if the centre of the debtor's main interests (COMI) is situated within its territory (in the case of "main" proceedings) or—subject to certain limitations—if it possesses an establishment within that territory (in the case of "secondary" or "territorial" proceedings). (See the note to the Regulation art.3.) Although there is a presumption that a company's COMI is the place of its registered office, there will be some exceptional cases where a company incorporated in England and Wales and having its registered office here has its COMI in another Member State. In that event, our courts will have no jurisdiction at all to open main proceedings and will be able to open secondary or territorial proceedings only if the company possesses an establishment here. These questions of jurisdiction are discussed more fully in the note to art.3 referred to above.

118   Proceedings taken in wrong court

118(1)   [Wrong court] Nothing in section 117 invalidates a proceeding by reason of its being taken in the wrong court.

118(2)   [Continuation] The winding up of a company by the court in England and Wales, or any proceedings in the winding up, may be retained in the court in which the proceedings were commenced, although it may not be the court in which they ought to have been commenced.

GENERAL NOTE

It would appear that this provision may be invoked to validate proceedings which have been mistakenly brought in a court which has no insolvency jurisdiction at all: *Re Pleatfine Ltd* (1983) 1 B.C.C. 98,942.

119   Proceedings in county court; case stated for High Court

119(1)   [Special case] If any question arises in any winding-up proceedings in a county court which all the parties to the proceedings, or which one of them and the judge of the court, desire to have determined in the first instance in the High Court, the judge shall state the facts in the form of a special case for the opinion of the High Court.

119(2)   [Transmission] Thereupon the special case and the proceedings (or such of them as may be required) shall be transmitted to the High Court for the purposes of the determination.

Jurisdiction (Scotland)

120   Court of Session and sheriff court jurisdiction

120(1)   [Court of Session] The Court of Session has jurisdiction to wind up any company registered in Scotland.

120(2)   [Vacation judge] When the Court of Session is in vacation, the jurisdiction conferred on that court by this section may (subject to the provisions of this Part) be exercised by the judge acting as vacation judge.

120(3)   [Concurrent jurisdiction of sheriff court] Where the amount of a company's share capital paid up or credited as paid up does not exceed £120,000, the sheriff court of the sheriffdom in which the company's registered office is situated has concurrent jurisdiction with the Court of Session to wind up the company; but–

(a)   the Court of Session may, if it thinks expedient having regard to the amount of the company's assets to do so–

   (i)   remit to a sheriff court any petition presented to the Court of Session for winding up such a company, or

   (ii)   require such a petition presented to a sheriff court to be remitted to the Court of Session; and

(b) the Court of Session may require any such petition as above-mentioned presented to one sheriff court to be remitted to another sheriff court; and

(c) in a winding up in the sheriff court the sheriff may submit a stated case for the opinion of the Court of Session on any question of law arising in that winding up.

120(4) ["Registered office"] For the purposes of this section, the expression **"registered office"** means the place which has longest been the company's registered office during the 6 months immediately preceding the presentation of the petition for winding up.

120(5) [Increase, reduction of s.120(3) sum] The money sum for the time being specified in subsection (3) is subject to increase or reduction by order under section 416 in Part XV.

120(6) [Applicability of EC Regulation] This section is subject to Article 3 of the EC Regulation (jurisdiction under EC Regulation).

General Note

This section lays down provisions for Scotland which correspond generally with those made for England and Wales by s.117. There are, however, no Scottish counterparts to ss.118 and 119.

Section 120(6) is the counterpart for Scotland of s.117(7): see the note to that subsection.

121 Power to remit winding up to Lord Ordinary

121(1) [Remission to Lord Ordinary] The Court of Session may, by Act of Sederunt, make provision for the taking of proceedings in a winding up before one of the Lords Ordinary; and, where provision is so made, the Lord Ordinary has, for the purposes of the winding up, all the powers and jurisdiction of the court.

121(2) [Report by Lord Ordinary] However, the Lord Ordinary may report to the Inner House any matter which may arise in the course of a winding up.

Grounds and effect of winding-up petition

122 Circumstances in which company may be wound up by the court

122(1) [Circumstances] A company may be wound up by the court if–

(a) the company has by special resolution resolved that the company be wound up by the court,

(b) being a public company which was registered as such on its original incorporation, the company has not been issued with a trading certificate under section 761 of the Companies Act 2006 (requirement as to minimum share capital) and more than a year has expired since it was so registered,

(c) it is an old public company, within the meaning of Schedule 3 to the Companies Act 2006 (Consequential Amendments, Transitional Provisions and Savings) Order 2009,

(d) the company does not commence its business within a year from its incorporation or suspends its business for a whole year,

(e) except in the case of a private company limited by shares or by guarantee, the number of members is reduced below 2,

(f) the company is unable to pay its debts,

(fa) at the time at which a moratorium for the company under section 1A comes to an end, no voluntary arrangement approved under Part I has effect in relation to the company,

(g) the court is of the opinion that it is just and equitable that the company should be wound up.

122(2) **[Scotland]** In Scotland, a company which the Court of Session has jurisdiction to wind up may be wound up by the Court if there is subsisting a floating charge over property comprised in the company's property and undertaking, and the court is satisfied that the security of the creditor entitled to the benefit of the floating charge is in jeopardy.

For this purpose a creditor's security is deemed to be in jeopardy if the Court is satisfied that events have occurred or are about to occur which render it unreasonable in the creditor's interests that the company should retain power to dispose of the property which is subject to the floating charge.

S.122(1)

The court has in all cases a discretion whether to make a winding-up order or not. This is implicit in the opening words of the section, and is confirmed by s.125.

Paragraphs (b) and (c) were introduced in conjunction with the redefinition of the public company and the enactment of new statutory rules applicable to such companies by CA 1980. The remaining paragraphs of this subsection are of long standing, except that the minimum number of members for a public company was seven until 1980.

In s.122(1)(e) the words "except in the case of a private company limited by shares or by guarantee" were inserted by the Companies (Single Member Private Limited Companies) Regulations 1992 (SI 1992/1699) reg.1 and Sch. para.8, as from July 15, 1992. These regulations implemented the EC Twelfth Company Law Directive. Section 122(1)(b) was amended by the Companies Act 2006 (Consequential Amendments etc.) Order 2008 (SI 2008/948) arts 2, 3 and Sch.1 para.102, effective April 6, 2008.

Paragraph (f) is elaborated by the presumptions set out in s.123. If a creditor establishes that a company is unable to pay its debts, he is normally entitled to have a winding-up order made as of course, unless the court considers that there is some special reason why it should not do so. One consideration which would incline the court to refuse an order would be that a majority of the company's creditors were opposed to the making of an order; but if the opposing creditors are not independent outsiders but are associated with the directors their views are likely to be discounted: *Re Lummus Agricultural Services Ltd* [1999] B.C.C. 953.

Paragraph (fa) was inserted by the Insolvency Act 2000 s.1, Sch.1 paras 1, 6 with effect from January 1, 2003. The addition of this ground will obviate the need to prove insolvency under s.123. But in most cases the alternative of a creditors' voluntary winding up will be preferred. A petition on this ground may be presented only by one or more creditors: s.124(3A).

Paragraph (g) has been the subject of interpretation in a considerable number of cases, among the best known of which are *Re German Date Coffee Company* (1882) 20 Ch. D. 169 (failure of object); *Re T E Brinsmead & Sons* [1897] 1 Ch. 406 (fraud); *Re Yenidje Tobacco Co Ltd* [1916] 2 Ch. 426 (deadlock); *Loch v John Blackwood Ltd* [1924] A.C. 783 (impropriety); and *Ebrahimi v Westbourne Galleries Ltd* [1973] A.C. 360 (breakdown of confidence). The last-mentioned case established that in the exercise of its jurisdiction on the "just and equitable" ground the court is not restricted by the rights and wrongs of the position as a matter of law but may have regard to wider considerations, such as the expectation of a member of a small "quasi-partnership" company that he will have a say in matters of management. For further illustrations on this point, see *Re Zinotty Properties Ltd* [1984] 1 W.L.R. 1249; (1984) 1 B.C.C. 99,139; *Tay Bok Choon v Tahansan Sdn Bhd* [1987] 1 W.L.R. 413; (1987) 3 B.C.C. 132. Failure on the part of the directors to pay reasonable dividends is in theory capable of supporting a winding-up petition on the "just and equitable" ground, although such a case would be extremely difficult to prove: *Re a Company (No.00370 of 1987)* [1988] 1 W.L.R. 1068; (1988) 4 B.C.C. 506.

The jurisdiction under s.122(1)(g) may not be invoked to protect interests of the petitioner other than his interests as a member: *Re J E Cade & Son Ltd* [1991] B.C.C. 360 (petitioner seeking to assert rights as freeholder of land in occupation of company). Nor is it appropriate to rely on s.122(1)(g) to seek to have a company wound up on public interest grounds (even where the petitioner is a local authority who alleges the dishonest misapplication of public money): the intention of Parliament is that all such cases should be brought by the Secretary of State under s.124A: *Re Millennium Advanced Technology Ltd* [2004] EWHC 711 (Ch); [2004] 4 All E.R. 465; [2004] 2 B.C.L.C. 77.

There is in practice a considerable overlap between the jurisdiction to grant a winding-up order under s.122(1)(g) and that for relief on the ground of unfairly prejudicial conduct under CA 2006 s.994, and it has been common for a petition to seek orders under each of these provisions in the alternative. In *Practice Direction—Order under section 127 Insolvency Act 1986* [2007] B.C.C. 839 (reproduced in App.V to this *Guide*), attention is drawn to the undesirability of asking as a matter of course for a winding-up order unless that is the relief which the petitioner would prefer or may be the only relief to which he may be entitled. The Practice Direction also requires a person presenting a petition under s.122(1)(g) to state whether he consents to an order under IA 1986 s.127: see the note to that section.

Where the dispute in a petition for winding up under s.122(1)(g) is essentially one which involves only rival factions of shareholders, it is a misfeasance for those in control of the company to spend its money in the proceedings, except in relation to matters in which the company, as such, is concerned, e.g. in making disclosure of documents in the possession of the company, or in connection with an application under s.127 (below) to validate a disposition of the company's property or sanction the continuance of its business pending the hearing of the petition: *Re Milgate Developments Ltd* [1991] B.C.C. 24; *Re a Company (No.004502 of 1988) Ex p. Johnson* [1991] B.C.C. 234.

It is an abuse of the process of the court to present a winding-up petition for an improper purpose, e.g. to bring pressure on the directors to register share transfers (*Charles Forte Investments Ltd v Amanda* [1964] Ch. 240), but this will not necessarily be the case where the complainant has no other remedy: *CVC/Opportunity Equity Partners Ltd v Demarco Almeida* [2002] UKPC 16; [2002] B.C.C. 684.

S.122(2)

This provision can be traced back to s.4 of the Companies (Floating Charges) (Scotland) Act 1961, the Act which first introduced the floating charge to Scotland, where it was unknown at common law. At that time, however, it was not possible in Scotland to enforce a floating charge by the appointment of a receiver, and so winding up was the only remedy which the law could provide for in a case when the security was in jeopardy. The present subsection is arguably no longer required, now that receivership is available: see s.52(2) above.

123 Definition of inability to pay debts

123(1) [Inability to pay debts] A company is deemed unable to pay its debts–

(a) if a creditor (by assignment or otherwise) to whom the company is indebted in a sum exceeding £750 then due has served on the company, by leaving it at the company's registered office, a written demand (in the prescribed form) requiring the company to pay the sum so due and the company has for 3 weeks thereafter neglected to pay the sum or to secure or compound for it to the reasonable satisfaction of the creditor, or

(b) if, in England and Wales, execution or other process issued on a judgment, decree or order of any court in favour of a creditor of the company is returned unsatisfied in whole or in part, or

(c) if, in Scotland, the induciae of a charge for payment on an extract decree, or an extract registered bond, or an extract registered protest, have expired without payment being made, or

(d) if, in Northern Ireland, a certificate of unenforceability has been granted in respect of a judgment against the company, or

(e) if it is proved to the satisfaction of the court that the company is unable to pay its debts as they fall due.

123(2) [Proof that assets less than liabilities] A company is also deemed unable to pay its debts if it is proved to the satisfaction of the court that the value of the company's assets is less than the amount of its liabilities, taking into account its contingent and prospective liabilities.

123(3) [Increase, reduction of sum in s.123(1)(a)] The money sum for the time being specified in subsection (1)(a) is subject to increase or reduction by order under section 416 in Part XV.

GENERAL NOTE

The question of a company's inability to pay its debts may be determined by the court as a matter of fact (s.123(1)(e)) or settled by the application of a number of presumptions, four of which (s.123(1)(a)–(d)) turn purely on the evidence, while the fifth (s.123(2)) involves a judicial assessment of the position.

On the meaning of the term "debt" in the present context, see IR 1986 r.13.12. See also the discussion of the related term "creditor" in the note to s.1(1). It is sufficient to give a creditor standing to petition that he should have a legal title to the debt, even though the beneficial interest may be in another person: *Bell Group Finance (Pty) Ltd (in liq.) v Bell Group (UK) Holdings Ltd* [1996] B.C.C. 505.

A winding-up order will not be made on the basis of a debt which is genuinely disputed: *Re LHF Wools Ltd* [1970] Ch. 27; *Re Trinity Insurance Co Ltd* [1990] B.C.C. 235; *Re Janeash Ltd* [1990] B.C.C. 250; *Re a Company (No.0010656 of 1990)* [1991] B.C.L.C. 464; *Re Richbell Strategic Holdings Ltd* [1997] 2 B.C.L.C. 429; *Re a*

Company (No.2634 of 2002) [2002] EWHC 944 (Ch); [2002] 2 B.C.L.C. 591; *Re MCI WorldCom Ltd* [2002] EWHC 2436 (Ch); [2003] 1 B.C.L.C. 330; *Re UK (Aid) Ltd, Glaxosmithkline Export Ltd v UK (Aid) Ltd* [2003] EWHC 1090 (Ch); [2003] 2 B.C.L.C. 351; *Favermead Ltd v FPD Savills Ltd* [2005] EWHC 626 (Ch); [2005] B.P.I.R. 715; *Jubilee International Ltd v Farlin Timbers Pte Ltd* [2005] EWHC 3331 (Ch); [2006] B.P.I.R. 765; contrast *Southern Cross Group plc v Deka Immobilien Investment* [2005] B.P.I.R. 1103 (prior opportunity to litigate not taken). This is also the case where the company has a genuine and serious cross-claim for an amount which exceeds the petition debt (or which, if successful, would reduce the company's net indebtedness below the statutory minimum of £750): *Re Bayoil SA* [1998] B.C.C. 988; *Richbell Information Services Inc v Atlantic General Investments Trust Ltd* [1999] B.C.C. 871; *Re Latreefers Inc* [1999] 1 B.C.L.C. 271; *Greenacre Publishing Group v The Manson Group* [2000] B.C.C. 11; *Orion Media Marketing Ltd v Media Brook Ltd* [2002] 1 B.C.L.C. 184; *Re Ringinfo Ltd* [2002] 1 B.C.L.C. 210; *Montgomery v Wanda Modes Ltd* [2002] 1 B.C.L.C. 289; *Re VP Developments Ltd* [2005] EWHC 259 (Ch); [2005] B.C.C. 393; *Penwith D.C. v VP Developments Ltd* [2005] EWHC 259 (Ch); [2005] B.P.I.R. 1010; *Re a Company (No.2272 of 2004)* [2005] EWHC 422 (Ch); [2005] B.P.I.R. 1251. However a petition will not be struck out or dismissed merely because the company alleges that the debt is disputed; the court must be satisfied that there is a genuine dispute founded on substantial grounds: *Re a Company (No.006685 of 1996)* [1997] B.C.C. 830; compare *Re a Company (No.001946 of 1991) Ex p. Fin Soft Holding SA* [1991] B.C.L.C. 737. If the debt is disputed, the court will normally strike out the petition, leaving the question of its validity to be determined in other proceedings. However this is a rule of practice and not of law, and so may be departed from, in the court's discretion, in an appropriate case—e.g. where, in the case of a foreign company, the petitioner would otherwise be without a remedy; *Re Russian & English Bank* [1932] Ch. 663; *Re Claybridge Shipping Co SA* [1981] Com. L.R. 107n; cf. *Re UOC Corp, Alipour v Ary* [1997] 1 W.L.R. 534; [1997] B.C.C. 377; *Jubilee International Ltd v Farlin Timbers Pte Ltd* (above); *Parmalat Capital Finance Ltd v Food Holdings Ltd* [2008] UKPC 23; [2009] 1 B.C.L.C. 274. Although it would not normally be appropriate to make a winding-up order on the basis of a judgment debt when an appeal against the judgment debt is pending (see, however, *El Ajou v Dollar Land (Manhattan) Ltd* [2005] EWHC 2861 (Ch); [2007] B.C.C. 953), the legislation relating to Value Added Tax, exceptionally, authorises the enforcement of an assessment for VAT by winding-up proceedings even though an appeal against the liability has not been disposed of: *Re D & D Marketing (UK) Ltd* [2002] EWHC 660 (Ch); [2003] B.P.I.R. 539; cf. *Re The Arena Corporation Ltd* [2004] EWCA Civ 371; [2004] B.P.I.R. 415; *Hall v Poolman* [2008] B.P.I.R. 892 (Australia); and contrast *Customs & Excise Commissioners v Anglo Overseas Ltd* [2004] EWHC 2198 (Ch); [2005] B.P.I.R. 137. Where the company is solvent, it is an abuse of the process of the court to present a petition for winding up based on a disputed debt, which the court will restrain by injunction and may penalise in costs, possibly on an indemnity basis: *Re a Company (No.0012209 of 1991)* [1991] 1 W.L.R. 351; *Re a Company (No.2507 of 2003)* [2003] EWHC 1484 (Ch); [2003] 2 B.C.L.C. 346; *Glaxosmithkline v UK (Aid) Ltd* [2003] EWHC 1383 (Ch); [2004] B.P.I.R. 528; *Re Realstar Ltd* [2007] EWHC 2921 (Ch); [2008] B.P.I.R. 1391. A winding-up order made on the basis of a debt which might have been disputed at the time remains in force unless and until it is rescinded by a later order: *Wilson v Specter Partnership* [2007] EWHC 133 (Ch); [2007] B.P.I.R. 649. In the case of a prospective debt which has not yet fallen due, the court may take the view that the matter should be resolved when the petition is heard rather than on an application to strike out: *Securum Finance Ltd v Camswell Ltd* [1994] B.C.C. 434. (On petitions by a prospective or contingent creditor, see further *Re a Company (No.003028 of 1987)* (1987) 3 B.C.C. 575 at 585; and *JSF Finance & Currency Exchange Co Ltd v Akma Solutions Inc* [2001] 2 B.C.L.C. 307.)

Where the company has a cross-claim against the petitioner pending in another court, the court has a discretion whether to make a winding-up order or to dismiss the petition: *Re FSA Business Software Ltd* [1990] B.C.C. 465.

A dispute as to the genuineness of a debt may also be relevant to determine the standing of a person claiming to be a creditor who seeks a winding-up order on grounds other than the company's insolvency. In this case the question is necessarily one for the court to determine: *Morrice (or Rocks) v Brae Hotel (Shetland) Ltd* [1997] B.C.C. 670 (but compare *Baker Hughes Ltd v CCG Contracting International Ltd*, 2005 S.C. 65 (petition dismissed as a serious abuse of process where standing as creditor not shown)).

A petition may not be presented based on a statute-barred debt: *Re Karnos Property Co Ltd* (1989) 5 B.C.C. 14. But a judgment debt is not subject to any statutory limitation: *Ridgeway Motors (Isleworth) Ltd v ALTS Ltd* [2005] EWCA Civ 92; [2005] B.C.C. 496.

Where a company or other body is, or has been, an "authorised person" or "authorised representative" under FSMA 2000, or is or has been carrying on a "regulated activity" in contravention of s.19 of that Act, there is a special provision in s.367(4) of that Act setting out (presumably, additional) circumstances in which such a body is to be deemed unable to pay its debts.

Under the EC Regulation art.27, where "main" insolvency proceedings have been opened in the Member State where the debtor has his centre of main interests, his insolvency is to be taken as conclusively established for the purposes of any secondary proceedings. In such a situation it would not be necessary or, indeed, relevant to invoke the provisions of the present section. In contrast, the CBIR art.31 states that recognition of a foreign main proceeding is, for the purpose of commencing a proceeding under British insolvency law, presumptive (but not conclusive) proof that the debtor is unable to prove his debts (or the Scottish equivalent, "apparently insolvent").

S.123(1)

Paragraphs (a) to (d) correspond with events which would, in the case of an individual, have been acts of bankruptcy prior to the passing of the present Act, and survive as grounds for the making of a bankruptcy order (ss.267, 268). Paragraph (a) was modified by IA 1985 by the addition of the words "in the prescribed form", so that an informal demand will now no longer be sufficient for the purpose of this provision.

In *Re a Debtor (No.544/SD/98)* [2000] 1 B.C.L.C. 103 at 116, Robert Walker L.J. drew attention to a significant difference between the function of the statutory demand in the individual and corporate insolvency regimes respectively. In the former, it merely provides one means of establishing a company's inability to pay its debts, but in bankruptcy it is not the debtor's general inability to pay his debts that is crucial but his apparent inability to pay the debt which is the subject of the statutory demand.

Section 123(1)(a) specifies only one method for the service of a statutory demand, viz. by leaving it at the company's registered office. In *Re a Company* [1985] B.C.L.C. 37 Nourse J. held that a demand sent by telex was not a good statutory demand; but when Morritt J. in *Re a Company (No.008790 of 1990)* [1992] B.C.C. 11 was asked to follow this ruling in relation to a demand which had been sent by registered post, he held that, once it was admitted that the demand had been received at the office (albeit through the post), it had been "left at" the office and therefore properly served. Proof of posting alone, however, would not have been sufficient. It is not clear whether a similar interpretation could be applied to the case of a demand sent by telex, fax or electronic means which had admittedly been received.

Under the previous legislation an inaccuracy in the statutory demand, such as an overstatement of the sum due, was normally regarded as fatal, but there have now been several rulings under s.268 of the present Act which mark a departure from the earlier law, and have not treated a defective statutory demand as invalid: see the notes to that section. It is likely that a similar approach will be taken in regard to a statutory demand under s.123.

For the form and rules relating to the statutory demand, see IR 1986 rr.4.4 et seq. A statutory demand must be in hard copy (s.436B(2)(f)).

Paragraph (e) (as CA 1985 s.518(1)(e)) formerly read: "if it is proved to the satisfaction of the court that the company is unable to pay its debts (and, in determining that question, the court shall take into account the company's contingent and prospective liabilities)". This formula was unhelpful in that it ran together two issues: (1) the question whether current debts could be met as they fell due, i.e. "commercial" solvency; and (2) the question whether the company would ultimately prove solvent if its future as well as its present liabilities were brought into the reckoning. The confusion was resolved by the amendment made by IA 1985: contingent and prospective liabilities are not (at least normally) for the purposes of para.(e), while insolvency calculated on a balance-sheet basis becomes a separate test under s.123(2). However, in Australia (where the statutory definition of insolvency is based on the commercial test), it is well established by the case law that reference may be made to debts which will fall due in the future, and in *Re Cheyne Finance plc* [2007] EWHC 2402 (Ch); [2008] B.C.C. 182, where the term "insolvency event" in a document was defined by reference to the commercial test, this approach was followed.

In *R. v Commissioners of HM Treasury* [2009] EWHC 227 (Admin); [2009] B.C.C. 251 the court discussed the question of insolvency in the special case of a banking company. The view was expressed that insolvency in this context referred primarily to balance-sheet, rather than cash-flow, insolvency but that a lack of liquidity on the part of a (balance-sheet) solvent company, if sufficiently serious, could mean that the company was insolvent for the purposes of IA 1986.

It has been held that failure to pay a debt which is due and not disputed is of itself evidence of insolvency under s.123(1)(e), even though there is other evidence showing a substantial surplus of assets over liabilities (*Cornhill Insurance plc v Improvement Services Ltd* [1986] 1 W.L.R. 114; (1986) 2 B.C.C. 98,942), and even though a statutory demand has not been served under s.123(1)(e) (*Re Taylor's Industrial Flooring Ltd* [1990] B.C.C. 44).

S.123(2)

It is not clear from the language of this provision whether the presumption implied by the word "deemed" may be rebutted by proof that the company is in fact able to meet all its current debts. The issue might in any case be resolved by the court deciding in its discretion (see ss.122, 125) not to make a winding-up order.

124   Application for winding up

124(1)   [Application to court] Subject to the provisions of this section, an application to the court for the winding up of a company shall be by petition presented either by the company, or the directors, or by any creditor or creditors (including any contingent or prospective creditor or creditors), contributory or contributories, or by a liquidator (within the meaning of Article 2(b) of the EC Regulation) appointed in proceedings by virtue of Article 3(1) of the EC Regulation or a temporary administrator (within the meaning of Article 38 of the EC Regulation) or by the designated officer for a magistrates' court in the exercise of the power conferred by section 87A of the Magistrates' Courts Act 1980 (enforcement of fines imposed on companies), or by all or any of those parties, together or separately.

124(2)   **[Conditions for contributory to present winding-up petition]** Except as mentioned below, a contributory is not entitled to present a winding-up petition unless either–

    (a)   the number of members is reduced below 2, or

    (b)   the shares in respect of which he is a contributory, or some of them, either were originally allotted to him, or have been held by him, and registered in his name, for at least 6 months during the 18 months before the commencement of the winding up, or have devolved on him through the death of a former holder.

124(3)   **[Non-application of s.124(2)]** A person who is liable under section 76 to contribute to a company's assets in the event of its being wound up may petition on either of the grounds set out in section 122(1)(f) and (g), and subsection (2) above does not then apply; but unless the person is a contributory otherwise than under section 76, he may not in his character as contributory petition on any other ground.

124(3A)   **[Petition on s.122(1)(fa) ground]** A winding-up petition on the ground set out in section 122(1)(fa) may only be presented by one or more creditors.

124(4)   **[Petition by Secretary of State]** A winding-up petition may be presented by the Secretary of State–

    (a)   if the ground of the petition is that in section 122(1)(b) or (c), or

    (b)   in a case falling within section 124A or 124B below.

124(4AA)   **[Petition by Financial Services Authority]** A winding up petition may be presented by the Financial Services Authority in a case falling within section 124C(1) or (2).

124(4A)   **[Petition by Regulator of Community Interest Companies]** A winding-up petition may be presented by the Regulator of Community Interest Companies in a case falling within section 50 of the Companies (Audit, Investigations and Community Enterprise) Act 2004.

124(5)   **[Petition by official receiver]** Where a company is being wound up voluntarily in England and Wales, a winding-up petition may be presented by the official receiver attached to the court as well as by any other person authorised in that behalf under the other provisions of this section; but the court shall not make a winding-up order on the petition unless it is satisfied that the voluntary winding up cannot be continued with due regard to the interests of the creditors or contributories.

GENERAL NOTE

This section lists the persons who have standing to present a winding-up petition; but it is not exhaustive, for the Attorney-General may petition in the case of a charitable company (Charities Act 1993 s.63), the Financial Services Authority may do so in the case of various bodies carrying on investment business: FSMA 2000 s.367, and the Director of Public Prosecutions and other prosecuting authorities are empowered to petition to have a company wound up on public interest grounds following a conviction for breach of a serious crime prevention order (Serious Crime Act 2007 s.27).

    The Act empowers the supervisor of an IVA (s.7(4)(b)) to apply to the court for a winding-up order and by Sch.1 para.21, states that an administrator and an administrative receiver may present a petition for winding up; but (no doubt as a result of a drafting slip) no mention is made of these office-holders in s.124(1). A partial attempt has been made to overcome this difficulty without amendment of s.124(1) by an alteration made to the rules in 1987: r.4.7(7)(a) declares that an administrator's petition shall be expressed to be "the petition of the company by its administrator". There is no corresponding provision for an administrative receiver, but it appears that the court is prepared to accept a similar practice in this case, i.e. a petition presented by the receiver as the company's agent and in its name: see *Re Television Parlour plc* (1988) 4 B.C.C. 95 at 98; and for a case before the present Act (which could well still govern the situation where the receiver is not an administrative receiver) *Re Emmadart Ltd* [1979] Ch. 540. The supervisor of a voluntary arrangement should probably also petition in the name of the company, although this is nowhere spelt out in the legislation: see the note to s.7(4)(b).

The terms "liquidator" and "temporary administrator" have special meanings for the purposes of the EC Regulation: see the notes to the Regulation arts 2(b) and 38. In particular, "liquidator" extends to the office-holder in most forms of insolvency proceeding (apart from receivership). A "liquidator" appointed under art.3(1) will have been appointed in "main" proceedings in a Member State other than the UK and, as such, is empowered by art.29(a) to request the opening of secondary proceedings (i.e. apply for a winding-up order) in this jurisdiction if the debtor possesses an establishment here. See generally the notes to the articles referred to. Similarly, the CBIR art.9, provides that a "foreign representative" of an insolvency proceeding abroad is entitled to apply directly to a court in Great Britain (for this or any other purpose). A foreign representative (defined in art.2(j)) includes one appointed on an interim basis and is not restricted to a representative in a "main" proceeding. It is not a precondition that the foreign proceeding should have been recognised under art.15. No special formalities apply (other than a translation, where required). Article 13 accords to foreign creditors (including the tax and social security authorities) the same rights regarding the commencement of, and participation in, a British proceeding as creditors in Great Britain.

As a general rule, a winding-up order may only be made on the basis of a petition presented under this section: *Re Brooke Marine Ltd* [1988] B.C.L.C. 546. However, the court may in a proper case make an order of its own motion (*Lancefield v Lancefield* [2002] B.P.I.R. 1108), and an exception has now also been made by Sch.B1 para.13(1)(e): on an application for an administration order made under para.12 of that Schedule, the court may treat the application as a winding-up petition and make any order which the court could make under s.125.

For the procedure on an application for winding up, see IR 1986 rr.4.7 et seq.

Although a winding-up petition is a species of legal proceedings, it is not a "claim or counterclaim" within the Arbitration Act 1996 s.9: *Best Beat Ltd v Rossall* [2006] EWHC 1494 (Comm); [2006] B.P.I.R. 1387.

An application to restrain the presentation or advertisement of a winding-up petition should be made direct to the judge by the issue of an originating application: see the *Practice Direction: Insolvency Proceedings* [2007] B.C.C. 842 (reproduced in App.IV of this *Guide*), paras 5.1(3), 8.1.

S.124(1)

The directors are empowered to present a petition for the winding up of their company, as a result of a change made by IA 1985. This has overcome a difficulty revealed in *Re Emmadart Ltd* [1979] Ch. 540, in which the court ruled that the practice of allowing a company to present a petition on the strength of a resolution of the directors, which had been tolerated for many years, was irregular (at least in the absence of an enabling provision in the company's articles). The amendments make it possible in cases of urgency for a petition to be presented without the delay necessarily involved in summoning a general meeting of the company. Where the petition is presented by the directors, they petition in their own names, rather than that of the company; and—at least in the absence of a formal board resolution—they must act unanimously: *Re Instrumentation Electrical Services Ltd* (1988) 4 B.C.C. 301. However, where a proper resolution has been passed by a majority of the directors at a board meeting, it becomes the duty of all its directors, including those who took no part in the meeting and those who voted against the resolution, to implement it; and thereafter any director has authority to present a petition on behalf of all of them: *Re Equiticorp International plc* [1989] 1 W.L.R. 1010; (1989) 5 B.C.C. 599 (a case decided on the similar wording of IA 1986 s.9(1)).

Under the former law, a contingent or prospective creditor could not be heard on a petition until he had given security for costs and had established that he had a prima facie case. This requirement was repealed by IA 1985 Sch.10 Pt II. On contingent creditors, see *Re T&N Ltd* [2005] EWHC 2870 (Ch); [2005] B.C.C. 982 and the note to r.13.12. A contingent creditor may present a petition on the "just and equitable" ground (s.122(1)(g)): *Re a Company (No.003028 of 1987)* (1987) 3 B.C.C. 575; compare *Re Dollar Land Holdings plc* [1993] B.C.C. 823. Where there has been an equitable assignment of a debt by way of security, the assignor's equity of redemption gives him sufficient interest as a creditor to petition, and the assignee need not be joined as petitioner: *Parmalat Capital Finance Ltd v Food Holdings Ltd* [2008] UKPC 23; [2009] 1 B.C.L.C. 274.

On the standing of a person claiming to be a creditor where his debt is disputed by the company, see the note to s.123. Administrators whose remuneration was yet to be paid were held to be creditors entitled to petition in *Re Lafayette Electronics Europe Ltd* [2006] EWHC 1005, 1006 (Ch); [2007] B.C.C. 890.

Where a person has been compelled to pay a debt owed by a company to a third party, the company is under an obligation at common law to reimburse the person who made the payment, and the latter is a prospective creditor of the company with standing to present a petition for its winding up: *Re Healing Research Trustee Co Ltd* [1991] B.C.L.C. 716.

Where a creditor seeks to withdraw a petition, another creditor may apply to be substituted as petitioner. In *Re Wavern Engineering Co Ltd* (1987) 3 B.C.C. 3 leave was given by the court to a creditor to withdraw a petition in the mistaken belief that no other creditor was willing to support the petition. The court rescinded the leave to withdraw and made an order substituting another creditor as petitioner.

A person who has agreed to take a transfer of shares but whose name has not been entered on the register of members has no standing as a "contributory" to present a winding-up petition: *Re a Company (No.003160 of 1986)* (1986) 2 B.C.C. 99, 276, *Re Quickdome Ltd* (1988) 4 B.C.C. 296. As regards the trustee in bankruptcy of a member, see the note to s.82, above.

Where the petitioner's status as a contributory is in dispute, it was formerly the practice that his standing to petition should be established in separate proceedings: *Re J N 2 Ltd* [1978] 1 W.L.R. 183; but it is now accepted that this is not an inflexible rule and that it may be departed from in the interests of justice: *Re UOC Corp Ltd, Alipour v Ary* [1997] 1 W.L.R. 534; [1997] B.C.C. 377; further proceedings [2002] EWHC 937 (Ch); [2002] 2 B.C.L.C. 770.

S.124(2)–(4A)

These provisions restrict the circumstances in which winding-up proceedings may be instituted by a contributory: generally speaking, he must have been a member of at least six months' standing. Supplementing this statutory rule is the principle, long settled at common law, under which the court will dismiss a petition brought by a contributory unless he shows that he will have a financial interest in the outcome of the liquidation, so that, e.g. the holder of fully paid shares may not seek an order for the winding up of a wholly insolvent company (*Re Rica Gold Washing Company* (1879) 11 Ch. D. 36; *Re Chesterfield Catering Co Ltd* [1977] Ch. 373; *Re Martin-Coulter Enterprises Ltd* (1988) 4 B.C.C. 210). Exceptionally, where the petition (on the "just and equitable" ground) is based on or alleges a failure to supply accounts, and by reason of the company's default insufficient accounts are available to tell whether there will in fact be a surplus for contributories, the petitioner is not required to prove that he has a tangible interest in the outcome: *Re Wessex Computer Stationers Ltd* [1992] B.C.L.C. 366; *Re a Company (No.007936 of 1994)* [1995] B.C.C. 705. The question whether the *Rica Gold* principle applied to LLPs was left open in *Charit-email Technology Partnership LLP v Vermillion International Investments Ltd* [2009] EWHC 388 (Ch); [2009] B.P.I.R. 762. The persons liable under s.76 are (1) former shareholders whose shares have been redeemed or repurchased out of capital by a company which is subsequently wound up insolvent within a year of the transaction; and (2) directors made jointly and severally liable with such former shareholders.

Section 124(2)(a) does not apply where the company has always had only one shareholder (*Re Pimlico Capital Ltd* [2002] EWHC 878 (Ch); [2002] 2 B.C.L.C. 544); indeed, it is arguable that it applies only where the ground on which the petition is based is s.122(1)(e).

Section 124(3A) was inserted by IA 2000 s.1, Sch.1 paras 1, 6 with effect from January 1, 2003, when the ground of winding up under s.122(1)(fa) was also introduced. Section 124(4A) was inserted by the Companies (Audit, Investigations and Community Enterprise) Act 2004 s.50(1), (3) as from July 1, 2005. Section 124(3) was amended by the Companies Act 2006 (Consequential Amendments, Transitional Provisions and Savings) Order 2009 (SI 2009/1941) art.2(1) and Sch.1 para.73(13) as from October 1, 2009.

S.124(5)

An example of this jurisdiction occurred in May 1988 when the official receiver obtained High Court orders appointing him provisional liquidator of some 53 companies in the Manchester area, replacing three named accountants in whose hands the liquidations had been progressing. The official receiver was directed to take possession of papers relating to 200 companies being administered by the accountants, with a view to bringing proceedings on the ground that the voluntary liquidations could not be continued with due regard to the interests of creditors and shareholders as required by s.124(5).

In the exercise of its discretion under this provision the court will normally have regard to the wishes of a majority in value of the company's creditors, where the company is insolvent, but will not necessarily be bound by this: *Re Southard & Co Ltd* [1979] 1 W.L.R. 1198; *Re Medisco Equipment Ltd* (1983) 1 B.C.C. 98,944; *Re Falcon R J Developments Ltd* (1987) 3 B.C.C. 146; *Re M C H Services Ltd* (1987) 3 B.C.C. 179; *Re Hewitt Brannan (Tools) Co Ltd* [1990] B.C.C. 354. The case for a court order will be stronger where there is a suspicion of sharp practice calling for an impartial investigation of the company's affairs: *Re Gordon & Breach Science Publishers Ltd* [1995] B.C.C. 261.

124A   Petition for winding up on grounds of public interest

124A(1)   [Power of Secretary of State] Where it appears to the Secretary of State from–

(a)   any report made or information obtained under Part XIV (except section 448A) of the Companies Act 1985 (company investigations, &c.),

(b) any report made by inspectors under–

    (i) section 167, 168, 169 or 284 of the Financial Services and Markets Act 2000, or

    (ii) where the company is an open-ended investment company (within the meaning of that Act), regulations made as a result of section 262(2)(k) of that Act;

(bb) any information or documents obtained under section 165, 171, 172, 173 or 175 of that Act,

(c) any information obtained under section 2 of the Criminal Justice Act 1987 or section 52 of the Criminal Justice (Scotland) Act 1987 (fraud investigations), or

(d) any information obtained under section 83 of the Companies Act 1989 (powers exercisable for purpose of assisting overseas regulatory authorities),

that it is expedient in the public interest that a company should be wound up, he may present a petition for it to be wound up if the court thinks it just and equitable for it to be so.

124A(2) **[Non-application]** This section does not apply if the company is already being wound up by the court.

GENERAL NOTE

For examples of the exercise of this jurisdiction, see *Re Walter L Jacob & Co Ltd* (1989) 5 B.C.C. 244; *Re Market Wizard Systems (UK) Ltd* [1998] 2 B.C.L.C. 282; *Secretary of State for Trade & Industry v Leyton Housing Trustees Ltd* [2000] 2 B.C.L.C. 808; *Re Equity & Provident Ltd* [2002] EWHC 188 (Ch); [2002] 2 B.C.L.C. 78; *Re Delfin International (SA) Ltd* [2000] 1 B.C.L.C. 71 (where a foreign company was ordered to be wound up under the section); *Re Drivertime Recruitment Ltd* [2004] EWHC 1637 (Ch); [2005] 1 B.C.L.C. 411; *Re UK-Euro Group plc* [2006] EWHC 2102 (Ch); [2007] 1 B.C.L.C. 812; and *Re The Inertia Partnership LLP* [2007] EWHC 539 (Ch); [2007] B.C.C. 656; *Secretary of State for Business, etc. v Art IT plc* [2008] EWHC 258 (Ch); [2009] 1 B.C.L.C. 262 and of a refusal to exercise it; *Re Secure & Provide plc* [1992] B.C.C. 405; *Re Forrester & Lamego Ltd* [1997] 2 B.C.L.C. 155; and *Secretary of State for Trade & Industry v Travel Time (UK) Ltd* [2000] B.C.C. 792. See also *Re ForceSun Ltd* [2002] EWHC 443 (Ch); [2002] 2 B.C.L.C. 302; and *Re Alpha Club (UK) Ltd* [2002] EWHC 884 (Ch); [2004] B.C.C. 754, where the court ruled it appropriate to make a winding-up order under s.124A even though the company was already in voluntary liquidation. In *Re a Company (No.007816 of 1994)* [1997] 2 B.C.L.C. 685 and *Re Titan International Inc* [1998] 1 B.C.L.C. 102 the court declined to order the winding up of foreign companies on public interest grounds for want of evidence of a sufficient connection with the jurisdiction or of prejudice to the public interest in this country.

Note that proceedings under s.124A do not fall within the scope of the EC Regulation, even where the company in question is insolvent: *Re Marann Brooks CSV Ltd* [2003] B.C.C. 239; or the Brussels Convention (now the Judgments Regulation 44/2001): *Re Senator Hanseatische Verwaltungsgesellschaft mbH* [1997] B.C.C. 112.

It may be expedient to order that a company should be wound up in the public interest even though it has not acted unlawfully: *Re S H V Senator Hanseatische Verwaltungs Gesellschaft mbH* [1997] 1 W.L.R. 515; [1997] B.C.C. 112.

In *Re Portfolios of Distinction Ltd* [2006] EWHC 782 (Ch); [2006] 2 B.C.L.C. 261 it was said that while in some cases the public would be seen to be affected where a company was committing offences, in others it would be expedient in the public interest to protect members of the public who had dealt with a company whose business was "inherently objectionable", i.e. that it caused members of the public inevitable loss, whether that derived from illegal activity or not. On the balance of probabilities it was held that the Secretary of State's case had not been made out.

A petition on public interest grounds may only be brought under this section and only by the Secretary of State: *Re Millennium Advanced Technology Ltd* [2004] EWHC 711 (Ch); [2004] 4 All E.R. 465; [2004] 2 B.C.L.C. 77. Where the Secretary of State decided not to pursue a petition on public interest grounds under s.124A, Harman J. declined an application by contributories of the company to be substituted as petitioners: the existing evidence, he said, would not be material to the revised petition, which would be on different grounds (*Re Xyllyx plc (No.1)* [1992] B.C.L.C. 376).

The Financial Services and Markets Act 2000 s.367 authorises the FSA to petition for the winding up of a body specified in that section on the ground (inter alia) that it is just and equitable that it should be wound up. This jurisdiction may be exercised analogously with s.124A: *Re Inertia Partnership LLP* (above).

In *Re Supporting Link Ltd* [2004] EWHC 523 (Ch); [2004] B.C.C. 764 the company had offered undertakings which, it contended, would make it unnecessary for the court to make a winding-up order, but it was held that, unless the Secretary of State was content to accept the undertakings, the court should be very slow indeed to accede to such a request, and a winding-up order was duly made. An offer of undertakings was refused in *Re London Citylink Ltd*

[2005] EWHC 2875 (Ch). In contrast, in *Secretary of State for Business, etc. v Amway (UK) Ltd* [2008] EWHC 1054 (Ch); [2008] B.C.C. 713, where the court held that the company's business was not inherently unlawful or objectionable but its merits had been oversold in its promotional material and it had used improper techniques to recruit customers, a winding-up petition was dismissed on undertakings by the company to adhere to a new business model. This ruling was affirmed on appeal [2009] EWCA Civ 32; [2009] B.C.C. 781.

In *Secretary of State for Trade and Industry v Bell Davies Trading Ltd* [2004] EWCA Civ 1066; [2005] 1 All E.R. 324; [2005] B.C.C. 564 the Court of Appeal (at [110] and [111]) gave the following guidance on the approach to be adopted on this question:

"[110] A valuable review of the authorities on the proper approach of the court to s 124A public interest petitions, in general, and to the practice relating to the acceptance of undertakings, in particular, was carried out by the Vice-Chancellor in his judgment in *Re Supporting Link Ltd* [2004] EWHC 523 (Ch); [2004] B.C.C. 764; [2004] 1 W.L.R. 1549. The judge has a discretion whether or not to make a winding-up order. As for undertakings, the court has a discretion whether or not to accept them if they are proffered and whether or not to make the giving of them a condition of dismissing the petition. In considering the exercise of his discretion the willingness or otherwise of the Secretary of State to accept undertakings, which have to be policed by the Department of Trade and Industry, is an important factor.

[111] Thus, in the exercise of the discretion, the judge is entitled (a) to dismiss the petition on undertakings if, for example, he is satisfied that the offending business has ceased or if the undertakings are acceptable to the Secretary of State; or (b) to dismiss the petition on undertakings, even if that course is opposed by the Secretary of State, although that will be unusual; or (c) to refuse to accept undertakings and to wind the company up, if, for example, he is not satisfied that those giving the undertakings can be trusted."

A petition presented under this section on public interest grounds is required to be advertised in the same way as a creditor's petition, unless the court directs otherwise under IR 1986 r.4.11(1). For a discussion of the considerations affecting the exercise of the court's discretion in this respect, see *Re a Company (No.007923 of 1994), Re a Company (No.007924 of 1994)* [1995] B.C.C. 634 and 641.

In *Secretary of State for Trade and Industry v Aurum Marketing Ltd* [2002] B.C.C. 31, where a company which had operated a swindle was ordered to be wound up on public interest grounds, its sole director was ordered to pay both the applicant's and the company's costs personally. Costs were also awarded against directors personally in *Re North West Holdings plc* [2001] EWCA Civ 67; [2002] B.C.C. 441, where the Court of Appeal held that, although it was the normal rule that directors should not be ordered to pay their company's costs, an exception should be made where the directors had no bona fide belief that the company had an arguable defence and that it was in the interests of the public to advance that defence. A similar order was made against a majority shareholder in *Secretary of State for Trade and Industry v Liquid Acquisitions Ltd* [2002] EWHC 180 (Ch); [2003] 1 B.C.L.C. 375.

Section 124A(1)(b) was substituted and s.124A(1)(bb) inserted by the Financial Services and Markets Act 2000 (Consequential Amendments and Repeals) Order 2001 (SI 2001/3649) as from December 1, 2001.

Generally on s.124A, see Keay, (1999) 20 Co. Law. 296.

124B   Petition for winding up of SE

124B(1)   [Right to present petition] Where–

(a) an SE whose registered office is in Great Britain is not in compliance with Article 7 of Council Regulation (EC) No 2157/2001 on the Statute for a European company (the **"EC Regulation"**) (location of head office and registered office), and

(b) it appears to the Secretary of State that the SE should be wound up, he may present a petition for it to be wound up if the court thinks that it is just and equitable for it to be so.

124B(2)   [Disapplication of s.124B] This section does not apply if the SE is already being wound up by the court.

124B(3)   ["SE"] In this section **"SE"** has the same meaning as in the EC Regulation.

GENERAL NOTE

Section 124B was inserted by the European Public Limited-Liability Company Regulations 2004 (SI 2004/2326) reg.73(3), as from October 8, 2004. The EC Regulation on the *Societas Europaea* requires that an SE should have its head office in the Member State in which its registered office is situated. Where an SE no longer complies with this, the Member State having the registered office is required by art.64 of the Regulation to take appropriate measures to have the SE regularise its position, failing which it must be liquidated.

124C   Petition for winding up of SCE

124C(1)   [Breach of European Cooperative Society Regulation] Where, in the case of an SCE whose registered office is in Great Britain–

    (a)   there has been such a breach as is mentioned in Article 73(1) of Council Regulation (EC) No 1435/2003 on the Statute for a European Cooperative Society (SCE) (the "European Cooperative Society Regulation") (winding up by the court or other competent authority), and

    (b)   it appears to the Financial Services Authority that the SCE should be wound up,

the Authority may present a petition for the SCE to be wound up if the court thinks it is just and equitable for it to be so.

124C(2)   [Non-compliance with European Cooperative Society Regulation art.6] Where, in the case of an SCE whose registered office is in Great Britain–

    (a)   the SCE is not in compliance with Article 6 of the European Cooperative Society Regulation (location of head office and registered office, and

    (b)   it appears to the Financial Service Authority that the SCE should be wound up,

the Authority may present a petition for the SCE to be wound up if the court thinks it is just and equitable for it to be so.

124C(3)   [Non-application of s.124C] This section does not apply if the SCE is already being wound up by the court.

124C(4)   ["SCE"] In this section **"SCE"** has the same meaning as in the European Cooperative Society Regulation.

125   Powers of court on hearing of petition

125(1)   [Extent of powers] On hearing a winding-up petition the court may dismiss it, or adjourn the hearing conditionally or unconditionally, or make an interim order, or any other order that it thinks fit; but the court shall not refuse to make a winding-up order on the ground only that the company's assets have been mortgaged to an amount equal to or in excess of those assets, or that the company has no assets.

125(2)   [Just and equitable winding up] If the petition is presented by members of the company as contributories on the ground that it is just and equitable that the company should be wound up, the court, if it is of opinion–

    (a)   that the petitioners are entitled to relief either by winding up the company or by some other means, and

    (b)   that in the absence of any other remedy it would be just and equitable that the company should be wound up,

shall make a winding-up order; but this does not apply if the court is also of the opinion both that some other remedy is available to the petitioners and that they are acting unreasonably in seeking to have the company wound up instead of pursuing that other remedy.

S.125(1)

This provision gives the court the widest discretion. For instance, in *Re Internet Investment Corp Ltd* [2009] EWHC 2744 a compulsory winding up was preferred to a voluntary liquidation because the director's conduct necessitated a thorough investigation.

There is no established rule, comparable with that applicable in the case of a contributory petitioner (see the note to s.124(2) above), that a creditor's petition will be dismissed unless he can show that he will have a tangible benefit from the liquidation (*Re Crigglestone Coal Co Ltd* [1906] 2 Ch. 327): the court's discretion is unfettered, except by the concluding words of the subsection. For recent cases in which the court reviewed the authorities and discussed the basis on which the discretion will be exercised, where a petition is opposed by some creditors, see *Re Television Parlour plc* (1988) 4 B.C.C. 95; *Re H J Tomkins & Son Ltd* [1990] B.C.L.C. 76; *Re Leigh Estates (UK) Ltd* [1994] B.C.C. 292; *Re Lummus Agricultural Services Ltd* [1999] B.C.C. 953; and *Re Demaglass Holdings Ltd* [2001] 2 B.C.L.C. 633. In *Bell Group Finance (Pty) Ltd v Bell Group (UK) Holdings Ltd* [1996] B.C.C. 505 it was held to be a good reason for the making of a winding-up order that it would allow an investigation to take place into the affairs of a hopelessly insolvent company. An argument that the only proper procedure in such a case was the Secretary of State petitioning on the grounds of public interest, and not a creditor petitioning on the grounds of insolvency, was rejected by the court.

One basis for the exercise of the court's discretion to dismiss a winding-up petition (or to grant a stay of the winding-up proceedings under s.147) has traditionally been that of *forum non conveniens*, i.e. that it is more appropriate that the matter be dealt with by a court in some other jurisdiction. In *Re Harrods (Buenos Aires) Ltd* [1992] Ch. 72; [1991] B.C.C. 249, a petition was presented for the winding up of an English-registered company which carried on business exclusively in Argentina. The Court of Appeal ruled that the courts of Argentina were the appropriate forum, and ordered a stay of the English proceedings. However, the ECJ has ruled that such a decision is inconsistent with art.2 of the Brussels Convention: *Owusu v Jackson* (C-281/02) [2005] Q.B. 801, and so the *Harrods* case must now be treated as overruled.

For the procedure on the making of a winding-up order, see IR 1986 rr.4.20 et seq.

It is the usual practice, where a creditor's petition is dismissed because the debt on which it is based has been paid in full, for the court in its discretion to order the company to pay the petitioner's costs, whether or not the company appears at the hearing. See this matter discussed fully in *Re Nowmost Co Ltd* [1997] B.C.C. 105.

The jurisdiction conferred by s.125 is confined to the disposal of the petition. The section does not confer on the court jurisdiction to deal with other matters, such as a claim for damages in tort for the malicious institution of proceedings: *Partizan Ltd v O J Kilkenny & Co Ltd* [1998] B.C.C. 912.

S.125(2)

It is not sufficient for the purposes of this provision simply to show that the petitioner has alternative remedies open to him; he must also be acting unreasonably in not pursuing them.

In *Re a Company (No.002567 of 1982)* [1983] 1 W.L.R. 927, this subsection was relied on to refuse relief to a petitioner who had agreed to sell his shares to the majority shareholders at an independent valuation and had then reneged on this arrangement. A similar ruling was given in *Fuller v Cyracuse Ltd* [2001] B.C.C. 806, where the petitioner had refused to accept an offer by the company to buy his shares at an independent valuation. In contrast, it was held not unreasonable to refuse a similar offer in *Re Data Online Transactions (UK) Ltd, Apcar v Aftab* [2003] B.C.C. 510.

This was a minority shareholder's petition on the "just and equitable" ground, where it is common to seek in the alternative an order under CA 2006 s.994 [formerly CA 1985 s.459], on the grounds of "unfair prejudice". In this situation the court is frequently asked to exercise its discretion under s.125(2) on the ground that the petitioner is unreasonably refusing to pursue some other form of relief or to accept some other remedy. On the exercise of the court's discretion, see, e.g. *Re a Company (No.003028 of 1987)* (1987) 3 B.C.C. 575; *Re a Company (No.003843 of 1986)* (1987) 3 B.C.C. 624; *Re a Company (No.003096 of 1987)* (1988) 4 B.C.C. 80; *Re a Company (No.001363 of 1988)* (1989) 5 B.C.C. 18; *Vujnovich v Vujnovich* (1989) 5 B.C.C. 740; *Re Abbey Leisure Ltd* [1990] B.C.C. 60; *Re a Company (No.00330 of 1991) Ex p. Holden* [1991] B.C.C. 241; *Re Copeland & Craddock Ltd* [1997] B.C.C. 294; *Re a Company (No.004415 of 1996)* [1997] 1 B.C.L.C. 479; *CVC/Opportunity Equity Partners Ltd v Demarco Almeida* [2002] UKPC 16; [2002] 2 B.C.L.C. 108; *Re Woven Rugs Ltd* [2008] B.C.C. 903.

In a Practice Direction (see *Practice Direction—Order under section 127 Insolvency Act 1986* [2007] B.C.C. 839 (reproduced as App.V to this *Guide*)) the attention of practitioners is drawn to the undesirability of including "as a matter of course" a prayer for winding up as an alternative to an order under CA 2006 s.994. It should be included only if that is the relief which the petitioner prefers or if it is considered that it may be the only relief to which he is entitled. This may be seen as an attempt to discourage the use of an alternative prayer for winding up as a tactical device to put pressure on the company and its controllers. (See further the notes to s.127 below.)

126   Power to stay or restrain proceedings against company

126(1)   **[Exercise of power]** At any time after the presentation of a winding-up petition, and before a winding-up order has been made, the company, or any creditor or contributory, may–

(a)   where any action or proceeding against the company is pending in the High Court or Court of Appeal in England and Wales or Northern Ireland, apply to the court in which the action or proceeding is pending for a stay of proceedings therein, and

(b)   where any other action or proceeding is pending against the company, apply to the court having jurisdiction to wind up the company to restrain further proceedings in the action or proceeding;

and the court to which application is so made may (as the case may be) stay, sist or restrain the proceedings accordingly on such terms as it thinks fit.

126(2)   [Where company registered but not formed under CA 2006] In the case of a company registered but not formed under the Companies Act 2006, where the application to stay, sist or restrain is by a creditor, this section extends to actions and proceedings against any contributory of the company.

<small>GENERAL NOTE</small>

The making of a winding-up order operates automatically to stay all actions and proceedings against the company, as does also the appointment of a provisional liquidator, unless the court directs otherwise (see s.130(2)). This section empowers the court to make interim orders during the period when the hearing of a winding-up application is pending.

S.126(2)
See the notes to ss.73, 83 regarding these companies.

In relation to the financial markets, nothing in s.126 affects any action taken by an exchange or clearing house for the purpose of its default proceedings: CA 1989 s.161(4).

127   Avoidance of property dispositions, etc.

127(1)   [Dispositions etc. void after commencement of winding up] In a winding up by the court, any disposition of the company's property, and any transfer of shares, or alteration in the status of the company's members, made after the commencement of the winding up is, unless the court otherwise orders, void.

127(2)   [No effect on administrator while petition suspended] This section has no effect in respect of anything done by an administrator of a company while a winding-up petition is suspended under paragraph 40 of Schedule B1.

<small>GENERAL NOTE</small>

When an order is made for the winding up of a company by the court, it is deemed for various statutory purposes to have commenced from the time of the presentation of the petition or an even earlier time: see s.129. This section accordingly operates with retrospective effect to avoid the property dispositions and other legal events mentioned, unless the court orders otherwise. It is not necessary that the company should be insolvent. There is a good deal of similarity between s.127 and s.284 (which restricts post-petition dispositions of property made by a person who is adjudged bankrupt). But there are differences between the two regimes, so that decisions given under the one section will not necessarily be binding under the other: *Pettit v Novakovic* [2007] B.C.C. 462.

An application may be made to the court under this section for the prospective validation of a transaction before a winding-up order has been made: see, e.g. *Re A I Levy (Holdings) Ltd* [1964] Ch. 19.

Application may be made to the court by the company itself or by any interested person, such as the disponee of the property: *Re Argentum Reductions (UK) Ltd* [1975] 1 W.L.R. 186. The principles upon which the court will act in exercising its discretion under this section are well settled. The leading case is *Re Gray's Inn Construction Co Ltd* [1980] 1 W.L.R. 711. Where the company is insolvent, the primary purpose of the section is to ensure that all creditors are paid pari passu. A transaction which has, or is likely to have, the effect of reducing the assets available to creditors will not be validated; but if there is no serious risk to creditors or if the company is likely to improve the position of its creditors by trading profitably pending the hearing of the petition, the discretion may be exercised. Payments into or out of the company's bank account were held (or in some respects conceded) to be "dispositions of the company's property" for the purposes of this section, both when the account was in credit and when it was overdrawn, in *Re Gray's Inn Construction Co Ltd* (above); and in *Re McGuinness Bros (UK) Ltd* (1987) 3 B.C.C. 571

at 574; and this view was upheld in the case of an overdrawn account in *Re Tain Construction Ltd, Rose v AIB Group (UK) plc* [2003] EWHC 1737 (Ch); [2003] 1 W.L.R. 2791; [2004] B.C.C. 11. But other cases suggest that this view is too wide. In *Re Barn Crown Ltd* [1994] 1 W.L.R. 147; [1994] B.C.C. 381 payments into an account which was in credit were held not to be within the section—a ruling which has been criticised by Professor Goode, *Principles of Corporate Insolvency Law*, 3rd edn (2005), at 11.128. Professor Goode (ibid., at 11.130) also considers that *Re Gray's Inn Construction Co Ltd* is wrong (save in certain exceptional cases) in so far as it supports the view that payments out of an account which is overdrawn involve a disposition of the company's property. And in *Bank of Ireland v Hollicourt (Contractors) Ltd* [2001] Ch. 555; [2000] B.C.C. 1210 the Court of Appeal, endorsing the ruling of Lightman J. in *Coutts & Co v Stock* [2000] 1 W.L.R. 906; [2000] B.C.C. 247, held that payments made by cheque out of a company's bank account to a third party involve no disposition of the company's property to the bank—which merely acts as the company's agent in making a disposition in favour of the third party—and that this is so whether the account is in credit or overdrawn. [Note that *Hollicourt* was distinguished in *Pettit v Novakovic* (above), a case on s.284 which imposes similar restrictions on post-petition dispositions in bankruptcy.] For other decisions under the section, see *Re a Company (No.007523 of 1986)* (1987) 3 B.C.C. 57 (order refused—company currently trading at a loss); *Re Sugar Properties (Derisley Wood) Ltd* (1987) 3 B.C.C. 88 (order granted authorising sale of shares in racehorses); *Re French's Wine Bar Ltd* (1987) 3 B.C.C. 173 (completion of agreement to sell leasehold property sanctioned); *Re Tramway Building & Construction Co Ltd* [1988] Ch. 293; (1987) 3 B.C.C. 443 (transfer of land validated: no reduction of assets); *Re Webb Electrical Ltd* (1988) 4 B.C.C. 230 (repayment of advance made by director to company not validated: no benefit to company); *Re Fairway Graphics Ltd* [1991] B.C.L.C. 468 (order refused: benefit to creditors not shown); *Re Rafidain Bank* [1992] B.C.C. 376 (order sought for benefit of one creditor only: refused); *Re S A & D Wright Ltd, Denney v John Hudson & Co Ltd* [1992] B.C.C. 503 (fuel oil supplied to company which enabled it to continue its business; seller's requirement in usual course of trading that payment for previous supplies be made as a condition for delivery of new supplies: held not a preference, and order made validating such payments); *Richbell Information Services Inc v Atlantic General Investments Ltd* [1999] B.C.C. 871 (a funding arrangement to enable litigation to be conducted to pursue a claim to recover assets claimed by the company, which would ultimately involve a disposition of proceeds of the litigation: validating order made); *Re Airfreight Express (UK) Ltd* [2005] B.P.I.R. 250; *Re Albany Building Ltd* [2007] B.C.C. 591 (sales of property on advantageous terms). In *Re Tain Construction Ltd, Rose v AIB Group* [2003] EWHC 1737 (Ch); [2003] 1 W.L.R. 2791; [2004] B.C.C. 11 it was held to be material, but not decisive, that (i) the petition had not been advertised and the payee bank was unaware that it had been presented; and (ii) the payments had been made in the ordinary course of business. Even where the parties had acted in good faith a validation order might be refused if there were grounds for thinking that the transaction was an attempt to prefer the disponee or a guarantor of the overdraft. The bank in that case also sought to argue that it had changed its position to its detriment. While not ruling out the possibility that this might be a factor going to the exercise of the court's discretion, the judge regarded it as more relevant to the restitutionary claim which followed from the disponee's failure to obtain a validating order; however, in the case itself the defence of change of position failed on the evidence.

Where the company is solvent, the same considerations do not arise. The court will be concerned to avoid paralysing the company's business, and will normally give leave for it to continue trading, the onus being on the person opposing the grant of leave to justify refusal (*Re Burton & Deakin Ltd* [1977] 1 W.L.R. 390). But the fact that the company is solvent is not determinative: in *Re a Company (No.007130 of 1988)* [2000] 1 B.C.L.C. 582 the court refused to authorise payments out of the bank account of a solvent company which was the subject of a petition to wind it up on public interest grounds, there being evidence of irregularities in the conduct of the company's management.

"The company's property", in s.127, means property beneficially owned by the company: *Re Margart Pty Ltd, Hamilton v Westpac Banking Corp* (1984) 2 A.C.L.C. 709; *Re Branston & Gothard Ltd* [1999] B.P.I.R. 466. Where a company has entered into a binding and unconditional contract for the sale of an interest in land (or, probably, any other specifically enforceable contract to alienate property) before the presentation of a winding-up petition against it, it will in most cases already have disposed of the beneficial interest in the property concerned, and so, strictly speaking, the completion of the transaction by the conveyance of the legal title after the presentation of the petition is not a "disposition" within s.127. However, in practice it may be prudent to seek an order from the court that, in so far as the completion may involve any disposition of the property of the company, it should be treated as valid and effective: *Re French's Wine Bar Ltd* (above).

Where property is recovered by a liquidator under s.127 and the company's assets are subject to a floating charge, the charge attaches to the property, which is deemed to have remained all along the property of the company: *Re R S & M Engineering Co Ltd, Mond v Hammond Suddards* [2000] Ch. 40 at 50; [2000] B.C.C. 445 at 451. However the liquidator cannot assign to a third party the right to bring proceedings to have a disposition declared void under s.127 and to recover the property from the recipient: *Re Ayala Holdings Ltd (No.2)* [1996] 1 B.C.L.C. 467. (This ruling may be open to question (although no doubt correct on the facts of the case itself), for no right to bring proceedings is specifically conferred on the liquidator. It is hard to see why an assignment in favour of a person having a charge over the company's assets should not be effective—or, for that matter, why such a chargee could not institute proceedings in his own right.)

Expenditure of the company's money on litigating the disputes of an individual member will not be condoned by the court: *Re Crossmore Electrical and Civil Engineering Ltd* (1989) 5 B.C.C. 37; *Re a Company (No.005685 of 1988)* (1989) 5 B.C.C. 79.

The section applies in the winding up of a foreign company: *Re Sugar Properties (Derisley Wood) Ltd* (above).

It has been common practice for a shareholder petitioning for relief on the grounds of unfair prejudice (CA 2006 s.994) to add an alternative prayer for the winding up of the company. This automatically brings into operation the provisions of s.127 so that, unless the court gives leave, the company's business will be paralysed, usually to the prejudice of all concerned. Accordingly, in a Practice Direction (*Practice Direction—Order under section 127 of the Insolvency Act 1986* [2007] B.C.C. 839) attention is drawn to the undesirability of asking as a matter of course for a winding-up order as an alternative to relief under that provision; and whenever a winding-up order is asked for in any petition by a contributory the petitioner is required to state in advance whether he consents or objects to a s.127 order in the standard form which is appended to the Practice Direction. If he is prepared to consent, the registrar will normally make an order without further inquiry. The relevant part of the Practice Direction (including the standard form of order) is reproduced at App.V of this *Guide*.

Where a winding-up petition has been presented and the company wishes to apply for a validating order under s.127, a further *Practice Note—Validation Orders* [2007] B.C.C. 91 gives directions as to (i) who may hear the application; (ii) to whom notice of the application should be given; (iii) what evidence is required in support of the application; (iv) urgent cases; and (v) the standard of proof. The *Practice Note* is reproduced as App.XI to this *Guide*.

The court's discretion can extend to validating a transaction to which the company is not a party, but only in special circumstances. In *Re Dewrun Ltd* [2002] B.C.C. 57 the company had transferred freehold property to another company which had given a charge to its bank. An order was made validating the transaction to the limited extent of confirming the bank's charge.

In *Re J Smiths Haulage Ltd* [2007] B.C.C. 135 an administrator was appointed by the holder of a floating charge and immediately disposed of the company's business, unaware that a winding-up petition had been presented some five weeks earlier. It was held that, since the effect of the appointment was to suspend (rather than stay) the winding-up order (IA 1986 Sch.B1 para.40(1)(b)), the petition was without legal effect for the period of the administration and so s.127 did not apply to avoid the disposition.

A provision similar to s.127 is made in relation to a voluntary winding up by s.88, except that it applies only to transfers of shares and alterations in the status of the company's members; and in this case the sanction of the liquidator and not the leave of the court is needed to validate the transaction.

In the context of the financial markets, s.127 does not apply to a market contract or any disposition of property in pursuance of such a contract, the provision of margin in relation to market contracts, a market charge, and certain other transactions: see CA 1989 ss.163(4), 175(3)–(5). A similar dispensation applies in relation to financial and securities settlement systems: s.127 does not apply to a disposition of property as a result of which the property becomes subject to a collateral security charge, or any transactions pursuant to which that transaction is made: Finality Regulations reg.19(3). Section 127 is also disapplied in relation to a transfer order or a contract for the purpose of realising security in such systems: reg.16(1). See the notes on pp.2–3.

Section 127 continues to apply even although the winding-up order is subsequently discharged (e.g. under Sch.B1 para.37(3)(a)): *Re Albany Building Ltd* [2007] B.C.C. 591, and so any post-petition transactions are avoided unless the court orders otherwise.

Note that there is no scope for the application of s.127 in the case where the court exercises the new power (conferred by Sch.B1 para.13(1)(e)) to order a winding up instead of making an administration order, since in that case the winding up is deemed to commence on the making of the order: see s.129(1A).

S.127(2)

This provision was inserted (and the former s.127 renumbered as s.127(1)) by EA 2002 s.248 and Sch.17 para.15, with effect from September 15, 2003. See further the notes to Sch.B1 para.40.

128   Avoidance of attachments, etc.

128(1)   [Attachments etc. void] Where a company registered in England and Wales is being wound up by the court, any attachment, sequestration, distress or execution put in force against the estate or effects of the company after the commencement of the winding up is void.

128(2)   **[Application to Scotland]** This section, so far as relates to any estate or effects of the company situated in England and Wales, applies in the case of a company registered in Scotland as it applies in the case of a company registered in England and Wales.

GENERAL NOTE

In spite of the apparently unqualified wording of s.128, it has been held that the court may override the effect of the section by an order made under s.126(1) or s.130(2): see, e.g. *The Constellation* [1966] 1 W.L.R. 272.

    There is no provision in the Act which avoids attachments, etc. in a similar way in a voluntary winding up; but the liquidator may apply to the court under either s.126(1) or s.130(2) to have such a process stayed or set aside, by virtue of the powers conferred on the court by s.112(1).

    Further sections of the Act deal with the question of executions, etc. which have been begun but not completed at the time when the winding up of the company is deemed to commence: see ss.183, 184.

    Section 176 of the Act is expressed to be without prejudice to this section. Section 176 imposes a charge on goods which have been distrained in the three months before a winding-up order (or their proceeds, if they have been sold) for the benefit of the company's preferential creditors.

    In relation to the financial markets, nothing in s.128 affects any action taken by an exchange or clearing house for the purpose of its default proceedings: CA 1989 s.161(4).

Commencement of winding up

129   Commencement of winding up by the court

129(1)   **[Time of passing of resolution]** If, before the presentation of a petition for the winding up of a company by the court, a resolution has been passed by the company for voluntary winding up, the winding up of the company is deemed to have commenced at the time of the passing of the resolution; and unless the court, on proof of fraud or mistake, directs otherwise, all proceedings taken in the voluntary winding up are deemed to have been validly taken.

129(1A)   **[Winding-up order on administration application]** Where the court makes a winding-up order by virtue of paragraph 13(1)(e) of Schedule B1, the winding up is deemed to commence on the making of the order.

129(2)   **[Time of presentation of petition]** In any other case, the winding up of a company by the court is deemed to commence at the time of the presentation of the petition for winding up.

GENERAL NOTE

The effect of s.192(1), (2) is to backdate the operation of the winding-up order, for the operation of certain statutory provisions, to the time when the petition for winding up was presented (or, if the company was then already in voluntary liquidation, to the time when the resolution for voluntary winding up was passed).

    On the significance of the word "time", see the note to s.86.

    A voluntary liquidation commences at the time of the passing of the resolution for voluntary winding up: see s.86.

    The term "commencement of the winding up" is defined differently for the purposes of s.185 (effect of diligence in Scotland): see s.185(3).

    Subsection (1A) was inserted by EA 2002 s.248 and Sch.17 para.16, with effect from September 15, 2003. Under Sch.B1 para.13(1)(e) the court is empowered, in hearing an application for an administration order, to treat the application as a winding-up petition and order the company to be wound up. In this case, the commencement of the winding up is not back-dated.

    In the application of the EC Regulation, the critical point for many purposes is the "time of the opening of proceedings", which is defined by art.2(f) as "the time at which the judgment opening proceedings becomes effective, whether it is a final judgment or not". This will (at least prima facie) refer to the time when the court pronounces its order, except in the case where the company is already in creditors' voluntary liquidation, when it would be the time of the passing of the shareholders' resolution. However, where the issue for the court is the determination of the debtor's "centre of main interests" (COMI), it may be necessary to examine the position at some earlier time, e.g. on the hearing of an application to serve the proceedings abroad: see the discussion of *Shierson v Vlieland-Boddy* [2005] EWCA Civ 974; [2005] B.C.C. 949 in the note to art.3(1) of the Regulation, below. In *Re Eurofood IFSC Ltd* [2005] B.C.C. 1,021 the Advocate General (at para.93) thought that a statutory provision equivalent to s.129, defining the "commencement of the winding up" was conclusive to fix the "time of the opening of the proceedings". However, this is to give too wide a meaning to the former phrase: in practice, the definition is applied only for the purposes of other sections of the Act which use the same expression (e.g. s.127), and not for other purposes such as the proving of debts. Moreover, the Advocate General's opinion overlooks the fact that s.129(c) has effect only if a winding-up order is eventually made. (The EC Court in its judgment [2006] B.C.C. 397 (at para.59) found it unnecessary to examine this question, in the light of its ruling that the appointment of a provisional liquidator (coincidentally on the same day that the petition was presented) settled the matter. But the Court would surely have considered it critical that s.129 on its own does not have the effect of divesting the company of its assets as from the presentation of the petition.)

It has been held that the periods of limitation prescribed by the Limitation Act 1980 cease to run on the making of a winding-up order, and not (except as against the petitioning creditor) at the time when the winding-up petition is presented: *Re Cases of Taff's Well Ltd* [1992] Ch. 179; [1991] B.C.C. 582; and see *Financial Services Compensation Scheme Ltd v Larnell (Insurances) Ltd* [2005] EWCA Civ 1408; [2006] B.C.C. 690. Accordingly, in the case of a six-year period of limitation, the liquidator in a winding up by the court is at liberty to distribute the assets of the company without regard to the claims of creditors which accrued more than six years before the making of the winding-up order. In the same case the judge expressed the view, obiter, that an administration order would not prevent time running against a creditor of the company.

130 Consequences of winding-up order

130(1) [Copy of order to registrar] On the making of a winding-up order, a copy of the order must forthwith be forwarded by the company (or otherwise as may be prescribed) to the registrar of companies, who shall enter it in his records relating to the company.

130(2) [Actions stayed on winding-up order] When a winding-up order has been made or a provisional liquidator has been appointed, no action or proceeding shall be proceeded with or commenced against the company or its property, except by leave of the court and subject to such terms as the court may impose.

130(3) [Actions stayed re companies registered but not formed under CA 2006] When an order has been made for winding up a company registered but not formed under the Companies Act 2006, no action or proceeding shall be commenced or proceeded with against the company or its property or any contributory of the company, in respect of any debt of the company, except by leave of the court, and subject to such terms as the court may impose.

130(4) [Effect of order] An order for winding up a company operates in favour of all the creditors and of all contributories of the company as if made on the joint petition of a creditor and of a contributory.

GENERAL NOTE

In relation to the financial markets, nothing in s.130 affects any action taken by an exchange or clearing house for the purpose of its default proceedings: CA 1989 s.161(4).

S.130(1)

Under the rules prescribed for the purposes of this provision the court is required to send three copies of the order to the official receiver, who is then charged with the responsibility for serving the company and the registrar and for gazetting and advertising the order: see IR 1986 r.4.21.

Neither the registration of a winding-up order in the Companies Registry nor the gazetting of the fact that a company is in liquidation or of the appointment of a liquidator operates as notice to the world that the company is in liquidation: *Ewart v Fryer* [1901] 1 Ch. 499 (but see more particularly the report in (1900) 82 L.T. 415); affirmed sub nom. *Fryer v Ewart* [1902] A.C. 187; *Official Custodian for Charities v Parway Estates Developments Ltd (in liq.)* [1985] Ch. 151 at 160.

The registrar is required to publish in the *Gazette* notice of the receipt by him of the copy of the winding-up order (CA 2006 s.1078) and this amounts to "official notification" of the making of the winding-up order for the purposes of CA 2006 s.1079. On the effect of "official notification", see the note to s.109, above. It is not easy, however, to reconcile s.1079 with the provisions contained in ss.127–129 above which give a winding-up order retrospective effect: this is a difficult question which awaits judicial determination.

In *Re Calmex Ltd* [1989] 1 All E.R. 485; (1988) 4 B.C.C. 761, a winding-up order had been made against the company in error, and the court exercised its jurisdiction under IR 1986 r.7.47 to rescind it. The registrar of companies took the view that the winding-up order which had been recorded under s.130(1) should remain on his files, but the court ordered it to be removed on the ground that the rescinding order had rendered it a nullity.

S.130(2)

The stay provided for by this subsection is automatic, but only where the order is made by a court in this jurisdiction. Where a foreign court has ordered a winding up (including an order in "main" proceedings under the EC Regulation), the court may order a stay, but this is a matter for its discretion: *Mazur Media Ltd v Mazur Media GmbH* [2004] EWHC 1566 (Ch); [2004] 1 W.L.R. 2966; [2004] B.P.I.R. 1253. The recognition of a foreign proceeding as a "main" proceeding under the CBIR art.17.2(a) also triggers a comparable automatic stay: see the CBIR art.20. There is also a discretionary power conferred on the court to grant a stay or other relief (whether or not the foreign proceeding is recognised as a main proceeding) by art.21.

The power conferred on the court by this subsection complements that provided for in s.126(1), and has been held to qualify the apparently categorical wording of s.128: see the note to that section.

Where the court is asked to give leave to bring an action against a company which is in liquidation, it will seek to do what is right and fair in all the circumstances. In *New Cap Reinsurance Corp Ltd v HIH Casualty & General Insurance Ltd* [2002] EWCA Civ 300; [2002] 2 B.C.L.C. 228 there were issues common to the claim pending against the company and an action between the claimants and third parties, and the hearing of the latter was imminent. The judge's decision to allow the action to proceed was upheld by the Court of Appeal. Leave will be refused if the proposed action raises issues which can with equal convenience and less delay and expense be decided in the liquidation proceedings: *Re Exchange Securities & Commodities Ltd* [1983] B.C.L.C. 186. The court will not undertake any investigation into the merits of the proposed claim or consider the background material to the s.130 application (*Re Bank of Credit and Commerce International SA (No.4)* [1994] 1 B.C.L.C. 419); and accordingly in that case the court declined to make an order for specific discovery of certain documents in favour of the liquidators.

In *Re National Employers' Mutual General Insurance Association* [1995] B.C.C. 774 Rattee J. held that the court could not give leave under this section retrospectively; but in the later case of *Re Saunders (a Bankrupt), Bristol & West Building Society v Saunders* [1997] Ch. 60; [1997] B.C.C. 83 Lindsay J. (after an exhaustive examination of authorities which had not been cited to Rattee J. in the previous case) ruled that this was not so, and that the lack of prior consent was not an absolute bar to the commencement of an action or proceeding. This decision was followed in *Re Linkrealm Ltd* [1998] B.C.C. 478. However, this view may now need reconsideration in the light of the House of Lords' ruling in *Seal v Chief Constable of South Wales Police* [2007] UKHL 31; [2007] 1 W.L.R. 1910: see note to s.285(3), (4).

Leave is not needed where the applicants are not proceeding against either the company or the company's property: *Re Lineas Navieras Bolivianas SAM* [1995] B.C.C. 666 (a case where the Admiralty Court had made an order for the sale of a ship belonging to the company: the effect of this order was to convert the company's interest in the ship into a right on the part of the applicants to have their claims met from the proceeds of sale).

In *Re Swissair Schweizerische Luftverkehr-Aktiengesellschaft, Flightline Ltd v Edwards* [2003] EWCA Civ 63; [2003] 1 W.L.R. 1200; [2003] B.C.C. 361 an action had been begun against the company and the claimant had obtained a freezing order over assets up to the amount being claimed. The freezing order was later discharged when an equivalent sum was paid into an account in the joint names of the parties' solicitors. Neuberger J., at first instance, took the view that the arrangement gave the claimant a security interest in the funds so held, and in the light of that ruling granted leave for the action to continue. The Court of Appeal decided that no security interest had been created and accordingly that leave should be refused.

A criminal prosecution against a company is a "proceeding" within the meaning of this subsection. Accordingly, the leave of the court is required before any prosecution may be brought: *R. v Dickson* [1991] B.C.C. 719.

S.130(3)

See the notes to ss.73, 83 regarding these companies.

Investigation procedures

131   Company's statement of affairs

131(1)   **[Powers of official receiver]** Where the court has made a winding-up order or appointed a provisional liquidator, the official receiver may require some or all of the persons mentioned in subsection (3) below to make out and submit to him a statement in the prescribed form as to the affairs of the company.

131(2) **[Contents of statement]** The statement shall show–

(a) particulars of the company's assets, debts and liabilities;

(b) the names and addresses of the company's creditors;

(c) the securities held by them respectively;

(d) the dates when the securities were respectively given; and

(e) such further or other information as may be prescribed or as the official receiver may require.

131(2A) **[Verification of statement of affairs]** The statement shall be verified by the persons required to submit it–

(a) in the case of an appointment of a provisional liquidator or a winding up by the court in England and Wales, by a statement of truth; and

(b) in the case of an appointment of a provisional liquidator or a winding up by the court in Scotland, by affidavit.

131(3) **[Persons in s.131(1)]** The persons referred to in subsection (1) are–

(a) those who are or have been officers of the company;

(b) those who have taken part in the formation of the company at any time within one year before the relevant date;

(c) those who are in the company's employment, or have been in its employment within that year, and are in the official receiver's opinion capable of giving the information required;

(d) those who are or have been within that year officers of, or in the employment of, a company which is, or within that year was, an officer of the company.

131(4) **[Time for submitting statement]** Where any persons are required under this section to submit a statement of affairs to the official receiver, they shall do so (subject to the next subsection) before the end of the period of 21 days beginning with the day after that on which the prescribed notice of the requirement is given to them by the official receiver.

131(5) **[Release, extension of time]** The official receiver, if he thinks fit, may–

(a) at any time release a person from an obligation imposed on him under subsection (1) or (2) above; or

(b) either when giving the notice mentioned in subsection (4) or subsequently, extend the period so mentioned;

and where the official receiver has refused to exercise a power conferred by this subsection, the court, if it thinks fit, may exercise it.

131(6) **[Definitions]** In this section–

"**employment**" includes employment under a contract for services; and

"**the relevant date**" means–

(a) in a case where a provisional liquidator is appointed, the date of his appointment; and

(b) in a case where no such appointment is made, the date of the winding-up order.

131(7) **[Penalty on default]** If a person without reasonable excuse fails to comply with any obligation imposed under this section, he is liable to a fine and, for continued contravention, to a daily default fine.

131(8) **[Scotland]** In the application of this section to Scotland references to the official receiver are to the liquidator or, in a case where a provisional liquidator is appointed, the provisional liquidator.

GENERAL NOTE

On the making of a winding-up order, the official receiver (in England and Wales) normally becomes liquidator of the company, at least on an interim basis until a liquidator is chosen by the meetings of creditors and contributories under s.139. (The one exception is where the company is already under the control of an administrator or of the supervisor of a voluntary arrangement: see s.140.) In order to put the official receiver in possession of information about the company so that he may make the decisions and discharge the duties which rest upon him under the provisions of the Act which follow, the officers and employees of the company and others specified are required to complete and submit to him a "statement of affairs" under this section. This has long been a feature of a winding up by the court, and it is not simply continued in the present Act but extended to the analogous cases of a CVA (s.2(3)(b)), an administration (s.22 and Sch.B1 para.47), an administrative receivership (ss.47, 66) and a creditors' voluntary winding up, whether originally so constituted (s.99) or converted from a members' voluntary winding up when the company turns out to be insolvent (s.95(3)(a)). Failure by the officers and others concerned to comply with this requirement is sanctioned by criminal penalties (s.131(7)), and untruthfulness in the answers given is punishable as perjury, since s.131(2) stipulates that the statement shall be verified by affidavit.

In *Re Wallace Smith Trust Co Ltd* [1992] B.C.C. 707, the respondent director had failed to submit a statement of affairs after being required by the official receiver to do so; and the official receiver had then sought and obtained an order ex parte for his public examination in order to obtain the information which ought to have been furnished in the statement of affairs. Ferris J. held that, while this course was not an abuse of the process of the court, it would have been more appropriate for a specific order or orders to have been sought under IR 1986 r.7.20 requiring the director to complete and submit the statement of affairs, and possibly also seeking the order for public examination as an alternative in case the court refused to make the specific orders.

The information given by a person in a statement of affairs may (subject to certain safeguards) be used in evidence in subsequent proceedings against him, and also against any other person who concurs in the making of the statement: see s.433.

Where a provisional liquidator has been appointed by the court under s.135 before a winding-up order has been made, the section also comes into operation and the official receiver may proceed to requisition a statement of affairs in anticipation of the making of a winding-up order which may in due course be made.

The provisions of this and the succeeding sections apply whether or not the company is insolvent.

On the office of official receiver, see ss.399 et seq., below.

In Scotland, where there is no official receiver, the functions of the official receiver under this section are conferred by s.131(8) on the liquidator, who is appointed by the court when the winding-up order is made (s.138(1)).

Section 131(2) was amended and s.131(2A) inserted by LRO 2010 (SI 2010/18) art.5(4) as from April 6, 2010 (with retrospective effect).

For the rules and forms prescribed for the purposes of this section, see IR 1986 rr.4.32 et seq. and on enforcement, r.7.20.

S.131(1)

The Act gives the official receiver a discretion, so that he may dispense with the procedure in any case he considers appropriate. One situation where this would be so is where the winding-up order follows the discharge of an administration order (s.140), and the administrator is appointed liquidator by the court. (No similar discretion is given to the supervisor, administrator, etc. in the analogous cases established by ss.2(3)(b), 22, etc. that are referred to in the general note to this section.)

S.131(2)

The information listed here will be required by the official receiver in order that he may make his report to the court under s.132, and may be relevant to the question whether an application to the court under s.133 should be made or granted. Details of the creditors will be needed if a meeting of creditors is to be summoned under s.136(5).

S.131(3)

The terms "employment" and "the relevant date" are defined in s.131(6), below. "Officer" includes a director, manager or secretary: see CA 2006 s.1173(1) and the note to s.206(3).

S.131(5)

The discretion here given to the official receiver supplements the general discretionary terms of s.131(1).

S.131(6)

The inclusion of a person employed under a contract for services gives the section potentially a very wide scope, extending (for example) to an accountant or auditor.

S.131(7)

On penalties, see s.430 and Sch.10.

S.131(8)

As noted above, there is no official receiver in Scotland and so the liquidator or provisional liquidator is empowered to act instead. A liquidator or provisional liquidator will have the full range of discretionary powers conferred by this section on the official receiver.

132 Investigation by official receiver

132(1) **[Duty of official receiver]** Where a winding-up order is made by the court in England and Wales, it is the duty of the official receiver to investigate–

(a) if the company has failed, the causes of the failure; and

(b) generally, the promotion, formation, business, dealings and affairs of the company,

and to make such report (if any) to the court as he thinks fit.

132(2) **[Report prima facie evidence]** The report is, in any proceedings, prima facie evidence of the facts stated in it.

S.132(1)

The official receiver has a discretion to decide whether a report to the court is called for, but has a statutory duty to investigate the matters listed in paras (a) and (b), which applies whether or not he is also the liquidator.

The officers of the company (and its employees and other persons who are specified in s.235(3)) are under a duty to co-operate with the official receiver: see s.235, below.

S.132(2)

The evidentiary presumption applies not only for the purpose of any immediate court hearing, but "in any proceedings".

133 Public examination of officers

133(1) **[Application to court]** Where a company is being wound up by the court, the official receiver or, in Scotland, the liquidator may at any time before the dissolution of the company apply to the court for the public examination of any person who–

(a) is or has been an officer of the company; or

(b) has acted as liquidator or administrator of the company or as receiver or manager or, in Scotland, receiver of its property; or

(c) not being a person falling within paragraph (a) or (b), is or has been concerned, or has taken part, in the promotion, formation or management of the company.

133(2) **[Request to make application]** Unless the court otherwise orders, the official receiver or, in Scotland, the liquidator shall make an application under subsection (1) if he is requested in accordance with the rules to do so by–

(a) one-half, in value, of the company's creditors; or

(b) three-quarters, in value, of the company's contributories.

133(3) **[Court's duties]** On an application under subsection (1), the court shall direct that a public examination of the person to whom the application relates shall be held on a day appointed by the court; and that person shall attend on that day and be publicly examined as to the promotion, formation or management of the company or as to the conduct of its business and affairs, or his conduct or dealings in relation to the company.

133(4) **[Persons taking part]** The following may take part in the public examination of a person under this section and may question that person concerning the matters mentioned in subsection (3), namely–

    (a)   the official receiver;

    (b)   the liquidator of the company;

    (c)   any person who has been appointed as special manager of the company's property or business;

    (d)   any creditor of the company who has tendered a proof or, in Scotland, submitted a claim in the winding up;

    (e)   any contributory of the company.

GENERAL NOTE

The Act makes provision for both a public examination under this section and a private examination under s.236.

Although s.133 is by its terms expressed to apply only in a winding up by the court, s.112 can be invoked to make it apply also in a voluntary liquidation: see *Re Campbell Coverings Ltd (No.2)* [1954] Ch. 225; and *Bishopsgate Investment Management Ltd (in provisional liquidation) v Maxwell, Mirror Group Newspapers plc v Maxwell* [1993] Ch. 1 at 24, 46; [1992] B.C.C. 222 at 232, 249; *Re Pantmaenog Timber Co Ltd, Official Receiver v Wadge, Rapps & Hunt (a firm)* [2003] UKHL 49; [2004] 1 A.C. 158; [2003] B.C.C. 659, at para.56.

Under the present section, the court has power to direct the public examination of an officer of a company in compulsory liquidation who is outside the jurisdiction, and to order service of the order of the court or other relevant document to be effected on him outside the jurisdiction: *Re Seagull Manufacturing Co Ltd (in liq.)* [1993] Ch. 345; [1993] B.C.C. 241; *Re Casterbridge Properties Ltd* [2002] B.C.C. 453; upheld (where this point was not in issue) sub nom. *Jeeves v Official Receiver* (below). See also the discussion of *Seagull Manufacturing* in *Masri v Consolidated Contractors International (UK) Ltd* [2009] UKHL 43 [2009] 2 B.C.L.C. 382, where the House of Lords declined to draw an analogy between s.133 and CPR r.71 in a case where the company concerned was not in liquidation. (For the position in a private examination, see the notes to ss.236, below.)

A person who is subject to examination under s.133 is not entitled to refuse to answer questions on the ground that in doing so he may incriminate himself: this follows by analogy with the cases decided under ss.236, 290 and 366; however, the use that can later be made in criminal proceedings of information obtained under compulsion is now generally prohibited: see *Bishopsgate Investment Management Ltd (in provisional liquidation) v Maxwell* [1993] Ch. 1 at 24, 46, 62; [1992] B.C.C. 222 at 233, 249, 262, and the notes to those sections.

For the rules regarding the procedure for obtaining an order for examination, and the conduct of the examination, see IR 1986 rr.4.211 et seq. The examination is on oath: r.4.215(1). Questions as to the admissibility or otherwise of questions at the examination are a matter for the presiding judge or registrar at the hearing, although the court does have power when ordering the examination to control the form of the examination (as distinct from giving directions as to the conduct of the hearing itself): *Re Richbell Strategic Holdings Ltd* [2001] B.C.C. 409. For the sanctions for nonattendance, see s.134, below.

S.133(1)

The public examination provisions apply also to Scotland (unlike s.132). They may be invoked whether the company is solvent or insolvent.

On the meaning of the term "officer", see the note to s.206(3).

S.133(2), (3)

Section 133(3) appears to give the court no discretion to refuse an order once an application has been made, and this view was upheld, subject to very limited qualification, by the Court of Appeal in *Jeeves v Official Receiver* [2003] EWCA Civ 1246; [2003] B.C.C. 912. Having satisfied itself that the prerequisites of s.133(1) have been met, the court must make an order unless there are no questions which could properly be put to the examinee at the hearing of the examination, or there are no purposes to be served by such an examination. If there are particular questions or areas of inquiry to which objection might be made, this is better raised and debated at the examination itself or, if more convenient, at a preliminary hearing. (The appellant in this case had resisted an order on the ground that if the examination proceeded, he ran the risk of prosecution in another jurisdiction for violation of its confidentiality laws.)

However, under s.133(2) the court is empowered to intervene in order to *prevent* an application from being made to it by the official receiver following a request by the creditors or contributories. The grounds on which the court may make such an order are not stated in the present section, but IR 1986 r.4.213(5) indicates that the official receiver may object that the creditors' request is an unreasonable one. It does, however, appear to be plain from the two subsections, read together, that any other objectors will be out of court if they do not take action before the official receiver does.

In *Jeeves v Official Receiver* it was also noted that, since an application under s.133 would normally be made without notice to the intended examinee, he would have an opportunity to raise matters which he might wish the court to take into account by making an application under r.7.47 to have the order set aside; but this could be done only on one or other of the very limited grounds set out above.

For the procedure, see IR 1986 rr.4.213 et seq.

S.133(4)

It appears that an officer or past officer of the company, though liable himself to be examined under the section, has no right to question those of his colleagues being examined with him unless he falls coincidentally within one of the categories (a)–(e). See further IR 1986 r.4.215.

134   Enforcement of s.133

134(1)   **[Non-attendance]** If a person without reasonable excuse fails at any time to attend his public examination under section 133, he is guilty of a contempt of court and liable to be punished accordingly.

134(2)   **[Warrant etc. re non-attendance]** In a case where a person without reasonable excuse fails at any time to attend his examination under section 133 or there are reasonable grounds for believing that a person has absconded, or is about to abscond, with a view to avoiding or delaying his examination under that section, the court may cause a warrant to be issued to a constable or prescribed officer of the court–

   (a)   for the arrest of that person; and

   (b)   for the seizure of any books, papers, records, money or goods in that person's possession.

134(3)   **[Consequences of warrant]** In such a case the court may authorise the person arrested under the warrant to be kept in custody, and anything seized under such a warrant to be held, in accordance with the rules, until such time as the court may order.

G<small>ENERAL</small> N<small>OTE</small>

This provision deals with the enforcement of s.133. Other details relating to the conduct of the examination and summoning of those required to attend are dealt with in the rules: see IR 1986 rr.4.211 et seq., 7.22.

S.134(2)

A person who appeals unsuccessfully against an order for his arrest under s.134(2)(a) is "singularly close" to being in contempt of court, and may be ordered to pay the official receiver's costs on an indemnity basis: *Re Avatar Communications Ltd* (1988) 4 B.C.C. 473.

Appointment of liquidator

135   Appointment and powers of provisional liquidator

135(1)   **[Time of appointment]** Subject to the provisions of this section, the court may, at any time after the presentation of a winding-up petition, appoint a liquidator provisionally.

135(2)   **[Appointment in England, Wales]** In England and Wales, the appointment of a provisional liquidator may be made at any time before the making of a winding-up order; and either the official receiver or any other fit person may be appointed.

135(3)   **[Appointment in Scotland]** In Scotland, such an appointment may be made at any time before the first appointment of liquidators.

135(4)   **[Provisional liquidator]** The provisional liquidator shall carry out such functions as the court may confer on him.

135(5)   **[Powers of provisional liquidator]** When a liquidator is provisionally appointed by the court, his powers may be limited by the order appointing him.

GENERAL NOTE

The primary reason for appointing a provisional liquidator is normally to ensure the preservation of the company's assets pending the hearing of the winding-up petition. Since an appointment in such circumstances anticipates the eventual making of a winding-up order virtually as a foregone conclusion, it is usually made only with the consent of the company itself or in a clear case of insolvency. But provisional liquidators are also appointed in other situations—as formerly, in the case of an insurance company, when the alternative of administration was not available, as a step towards putting in place a scheme of arrangement under CA 2006 Pt 26 (*Smith v UIC Insurance Co Ltd* [2001] B.C.C. 11 at 20–21); or in order to investigate whether there might be possible claims for fraudulent or wrongful trading under IA 1986, ss.213 or 214 (*Re Latreefers Inc* [2001] B.C.C. 174 at 184–185).

An application for the appointment of a provisional liquidator must be made to a Companies Court judge and, unless otherwise ordered, is held in public. (See *Practice Direction: Insolvency Proceedings* [2007] B.C.C. 842, para.5.1(4) (reproduced as App IV to this *Guide*).) A person applying ex parte for the appointment of a provisional liquidator owes a duty to the court to make full disclosure of all material facts, and any order obtained in breach of this obligation is liable to be set aside: *Re OJSC Ank Yugraneft* [2008] EWHC 2614 (Ch); [2009] 1 B.C.L.C. 298. It is not normally within the duties of a provisional liquidator to realise assets: *Ashborder BV v Green Gas Power Ltd* (January 27, 2005; *British Company Law and Practice New Developments*, para.96-047).

A provisional liquidator must be qualified to act as an insolvency practitioner in relation to the company in question: see s.388(1)(a). In *Re W F Fearman Ltd (No.2)* (1988) 4 B.C.C. 141 it was held to be inappropriate for the court to make an order directly appointing the provisional liquidators, who were already in office, to be the liquidators of the company when the winding-up order was subsequently made, since to do so would deprive the creditors of their say in the selection of a liquidator under s.136. However, a practical solution was found by giving leave to the official receiver to continue to use the services of the former provisional liquidators as special managers.

The appointment of a provisional liquidator automatically revokes the authority of an agent appointed to act on behalf of the company by or on behalf of the directors: *Pacific & General Insurance Ltd (in liq.) v Home & Overseas Insurance Co Ltd* [1997] B.C.C. 400.

For further examples of the exercise of the jurisdiction under this section see *Re Pinstripe Farming Co Ltd* [1996] B.C.C. 913; *Re UOC Corp, Alipour v Ary* [1997] B.C.C. 377; *Re Goodwill Merchant Financial Services Ltd* [2001] 1 B.C.L.C. 259; *Re Namco UK Ltd* [2003] EWHC 989 (Ch); [2003] 2 B.C.L.C. 78; (which also contains a discussion of the powers under s.135(5) which it is appropriate to include in the form of the court's order); and *MHMH Ltd v Carnwood Barker Holdings Ltd* [2004] EWHC 3174 (Ch); [2005] B.C.C. 536. In *Equitas Ltd v Jacob* [2005] EWHC 1440 (Ch); [2005] B.P.I.R. 1312 it was held that s.135(4) empowered the court to circulate certain information about some creditors to other creditors. In *Re Daewoo Motor Co Ltd* [2005] EWHC 2799 (Ch); [2006] B.P.I.R. 415 the court authorised the provisional liquidator of a company to remit the proceeds of realisation of its assets to a receiver overseas, without proceeding to a winding up.

A provisional liquidator is now formally listed in Annex C to the EC Regulation as a "liquidator" for the purposes of art.2(b) of the Regulation. This puts beyond doubt any question whether such an office-holder comes within the statutory definition, even though it does not of itself resolve other difficulties, such as the time when the proceedings in question are opened and whether such proceedings can be "main" proceedings. (See the discussion in the note to art.2(f).) Under the CBIR a provisional liquidator is within the definition of a "British insolvency officeholder" (art.2(b)) and (as "one appointed on an interim basis") also within that of a "foreign representative" (art.2(j)).

On the remuneration and expenses of a provisional liquidator, see the notes to rr.4.30 and 4.218.

For the relevant rules, see IR 1986 rr.4.25 et seq.

136   Functions of official receiver in relation to office of liquidator

136(1) [Application] The following provisions of this section have effect, subject to section 140 below, on a winding-up order being made by the court in England and Wales.

136(2) [Official receiver liquidator] The official receiver, by virtue of his office, becomes the liquidator of the company and continues in office until another person becomes liquidator under the provisions of this Part.

136(3) [Vacancy] The official receiver is, by virtue of his office, the liquidator during any vacancy.

136(4) [Powers of official receiver when liquidator] At any time when he is the liquidator of the company, the official receiver may summon separate meetings of the company's creditors and contributories for the purpose of choosing a person to be liquidator of the company in place of the official receiver.

136(5) **[Duty of official receiver]** It is the duty of the official receiver–

(a) as soon as practicable in the period of 12 weeks beginning with the day on which the winding-up order was made, to decide whether to exercise his power under subsection (4) to summon meetings, and

(b) if in pursuance of paragraph (a) he decides not to exercise that power, to give notice of his decision, before the end of that period, to the court and to the company's creditors and contributories, and

(c) (whether or not he has decided to exercise that power) to exercise his power to summon meetings under subsection (4) if he is at any time requested, in accordance with the rules, to do so by one-quarter, in value, of the company's creditors;

and accordingly, where the duty imposed by paragraph (c) arises before the official receiver has performed a duty imposed by paragraph (a) or (b), he is not required to perform the latter duty.

136(6) **[Contents of s.136(5)(b) notice]** A notice given under subsection (5)(b) to the company's creditors shall contain an explanation of the creditors' power under subsection (5)(c) to require the official receiver to summon meetings of the company's creditors and contributories.

GENERAL NOTE

The official receiver has a discretion to decide whether or not to convene the meetings. He has 12 weeks in which to reach a decision, but the creditors may in any case require him to summon the meetings.

If no meetings are convened, the official receiver continues in office as liquidator. His decision not to convene meetings is therefore, in effect, a decision to keep the liquidation in his own hands.

Section 136 should be read in conjunction with s.137, which alternatively gives the Secretary of State power to appoint a liquidator other than the official receiver.

S.136(1)

Section 140 applies when the company is already subject to administration or a voluntary arrangement. The court is then empowered to make an immediate appointment of the insolvency practitioner who has been the administrator or supervisor to be the liquidator in the winding up.

S.136(2)

If the company is already in voluntary liquidation when a winding-up order is made, the existing liquidator is displaced: see IR 1986 rr.4.136 and 4.147.

S.136(4), (5)

The official receiver must make an initial decision, within the first 12 weeks after the making of the winding-up order, whether to summon meetings or not; and if he decides not to, he must give the notices specified by s.136(5)(b). However, he is free to convene the meetings even after this 12-week period has expired, and the creditors' power to requisition him to call the meetings also continues. This is made clear by the use of the phrase "at any time" in s.136(4) and (5)(c).

For the rules dealing with the summoning of meetings under this section, see IR 1986 rr.4.50 et seq.; and for the official receiver's reporting obligations, see rr.4.43 et seq.: see also r.4.107 (hand-over of assets).

137 Appointment by Secretary of State

137(1) **[Application by official receiver]** In a winding up by the court in England and Wales the official receiver may, at any time when he is the liquidator of the company, apply to the Secretary of State for the appointment of a person as liquidator in his place.

137(2) **[Decision by official receiver]** If meetings are held in pursuance of a decision under section 136(5)(a), but no person is chosen to be liquidator as a result of those meetings, it is the duty of the official receiver to decide whether to refer the need for an appointment to the Secretary of State.

137(3) **[Duty of Secretary of State]** On an application under subsection (1), or a reference made in pursuance of a decision under subsection (2), the Secretary of State shall either make an appointment or decline to make one.

137(4)   **[Notice of appointment by liquidator]** Where a liquidator has been appointed by the Secretary of State under subsection (3), the liquidator shall give notice of his appointment to the company's creditors or, if the court so allows, shall advertise his appointment in accordance with the directions of the court.

137(5)   **[Contents of notice or advertisement]** In that notice or advertisement the liquidator shall–

(a)   state whether he proposes to summon a general meeting of the company's creditors under section 141 below for the purpose of determining (together with any meeting of contributories) whether a liquidation committee should be established under that section, and

(b)   if he does not propose to summon such a meeting, set out the power of the company's creditors under that section to require him to summon one.

GENERAL NOTE

If the official receiver forms the opinion that the conduct of the winding up may be handed over to a private liquidator, he may either invite the creditors and contributories to choose an insolvency practitioner at meetings convened under s.136, or apply under the present section to the Secretary of State to make an appointment. The Secretary of State may decline to do so (s.137(3)), in which case the official receiver is, in effect, directed to continue in office. Since the establishment by the Insolvency Service of the Regional Trustee/Liquidator Units, rather more cases involving a straightforward realisation of assets have been kept within the Service rather than passed over to an insolvency practitioner: see *Dear IP*, June 2007, Ch.3.

There is no provision corresponding to s.136(5)(c) empowering the creditors to require the official receiver to make an application to the Secretary of State under this section, or to apply to him directly themselves.

For the relevant rules, see IR 1986 rr.4.104, 4.107.

S.137(1)

The official receiver may make an application under this section "at any time", and may plainly do so as an alternative to summoning meetings under s.136(4). Once he has called the meetings, however, he is probably bound to go through with that procedure, and could have recourse to his powers under the present section only if the meetings fail to choose a liquidator.

S.137(2)

If the meetings do not choose a liquidator, it is the duty of the official receiver to make a *decision* under this subsection, but he is under no duty to make a *reference*: he may perfectly well decide to stay in office as liquidator himself.

S.137(3)

As has already been observed, a negative decision by the Secretary of State is effectively a direction to the official receiver that he should continue in office himself.

S.137(4), (5)

The court may allow the liquidator to advertise the fact of his appointment rather than notify creditors individually. No guidance is given as to the basis on which the court should exercise this discretion, but fairly obviously it might be used to avoid unjustified expense where there are many creditors, bearing in mind that the only purpose for which the meeting is to be summoned is to decide whether to appoint a liquidation committee.

138   Appointment of liquidator in Scotland

138(1)   **[Appointment]** Where a winding-up order is made by the court in Scotland, a liquidator shall be appointed by the court at the time when the order is made.

138(2)   **[Period of office of interim liquidator]** The liquidator so appointed (here referred to as "the interim liquidator") continues in office until another person becomes liquidator in his place under this section or the next.

138(3)   **[Meetings to be summoned]** The interim liquidator shall (subject to the next subsection) as soon as practicable in the period of 28 days beginning with the day on which the winding-up order was made or such longer period as the court may allow, summon separate meetings of the company's creditors and contributories for the purpose of choosing a person (who may be the person who is the interim liquidator) to be liquidator of the company in place of the interim liquidator.

138(4) **[Qualification to s.138(3)]** If it appears to the interim liquidator, in any case where a company is being wound up on grounds including its inability to pay its debts, that it would be inappropriate to summon under subsection (3) a meeting of the company's contributories, he may summon only a meeting of the company's creditors for the purpose mentioned in that subsection.

138(5) **[If no person appointed at meetings]** If one or more meetings are held in pursuance of this section but no person is appointed or nominated by the meeting or meetings, the interim liquidator shall make a report to the court which shall appoint either the interim liquidator or some other person to be liquidator of the company.

138(6) **[Notification]** A person who becomes liquidator of the company in place of the interim liquidator shall, unless he is appointed by the court, forthwith notify the court of that fact.

GENERAL NOTE

There is no official receiver in Scotland, or any equivalent public officer, and so the liquidator in a Scottish winding up is invariably a private insolvency practitioner. This section provides for the appointment of an "interim liquidator", whose duty it is to take custody of the company's property and to summon meetings, etc. as in a winding up in England or Wales, but he does not enjoy the discretionary powers entrusted to the official receiver under ss.136, 137, and the court is more closely involved throughout the proceedings. The Secretary of State's powers under s.137 do not apply in Scotland.

S.138(5)
In contrast with the position in England and Wales (s.137(2)), the interim liquidator's obligation is mandatory and not discretionary, and the residual power of appointment lies with the court rather than the Secretary of State.

139   Choice of liquidator at meetings of creditors and contributories

139(1) **[Application]** This section applies where a company is being wound up by the court and separate meetings of the company's creditors and contributories are summoned for the purpose of choosing a person to be liquidator of the company.

139(2) **[Nomination of liquidator]** The creditors and the contributories at their respective meetings may nominate a person to be liquidator.

139(3) **[Liquidator]** The liquidator shall be the person nominated by the creditors or, where no person has been so nominated, the person (if any) nominated by the contributories.

139(4) **[Where different persons nominated]** In the case of different persons being nominated, any contributory or creditor may, within 7 days after the date on which the nomination was made by the creditors, apply to the court for an order either–

  (a) appointing the person nominated as liquidator by the contributories to be a liquidator instead of, or jointly with, the person nominated by the creditors; or

  (b) appointing some other person to be liquidator instead of the person nominated by the creditors.

GENERAL NOTE

This section lays down the rules and procedure for the appointment of a liquidator when meetings of the creditors and contributories are convened for the purpose. It is very similar in terms to s.100, which governs a creditors' voluntary winding up. Unlike ss.136, 137, it applies in Scotland as well as England and Wales.

The word "nominate" is used in a sense equivalent to "appoint": see the note to s.100.

In *Re Orient Power Holdings Ltd* [2009] B.C.C. 452 (a decision of the High Court of Hong Kong) companies which had been in receivership were ordered to be wound up. The creditors appointed two independent persons together with one of the receivers (S) as liquidators. The official receiver sought the removal of S on the grounds that there was a risk that he might not be impartial, being the appointee of the secured creditors, but the court confirmed the appointment because the liquidation would benefit from the knowledge of the companies' affairs that S had acquired while receiver, leaving it open to any concerned creditor to have recourse to the court should need arise.

For the relevant rules, see IR 1986 rr.4.100, 4.102.

140   Appointment by the court following administration or voluntary arrangement

140(1)   **[Appointment of administrator]** Where a winding-up order is made immediately upon the appointment of an administrator ceasing to have effect, the court may appoint as liquidator of the company the person whose appointment as administrator has ceased to have effect.

140(2)   **[Appointment of supervisor]** Where a winding-up order is made at a time when there is a supervisor of a voluntary arrangement approved in relation to the company under Part I, the court may appoint as liquidator of the company the person who is the supervisor at the time when the winding-up order is made.

140(3)   **[Position of official receiver]** Where the court makes an appointment under this section, the official receiver does not become the liquidator as otherwise provided by section 136(2), and he has no duty under section 136(5)(a) or (b) in respect of the summoning of creditors' or contributories' meetings.

GENERAL NOTE

This section links in with the procedures for the appointment of an administrator (IA 1986 ss.8 et seq. and Sch.B1) and for instituting a scheme of voluntary arrangement (IA 1986 ss.1 et seq.). If a compulsory winding up follows immediately upon the termination of an administration or a voluntary arrangement, an insolvency practitioner who is fully aware of the company's circumstances will already be in office as the administrator or supervisor of the scheme, and it may make good sense to appoint him to the post of liquidator at the time when the winding-up order is made, so that he can get on with the conduct of the liquidation straightaway. Many of the formalities which are necessary in the case of a normal winding-up order can be bypassed in such a case. In *Re Charnley Davies Business Services Ltd* (1987) 3 B.C.C. 408, the court (with some reluctance) appointed the former administrator as liquidator even though litigation was pending in which his conduct while administrator was to be challenged as irregular.

Subsection (1) was reworded by EA 2002 s.248 and Sch.B1 para.17, to reflect the fact that a company may now be put into administration without a court order. The expression "the appointment of an administrator ceases to have effect" means "the administration is terminated": see Sch.B1 para.1(2)(c), (d).

For the relevant rules, see IR 1986 rr.4.49A, 4.102. Rule 4.49A, inserted by I(A)R 1987, deals with the situation where the existence of further creditors becomes known to the insolvency practitioner who becomes liquidator.

S.140(1), (2)

Section 140 does not empower the court to appoint as liquidator a person who has not previously occupied the position of administrator or supervisor, whether alone or as an additional liquidator (*Re Exchange Travel (Holdings) Ltd* [1992] B.C.C. 954). If an appointment is not made under this section, the normal procedure under ss.136 and 139 must be followed.

Liquidation committees

141   Liquidation committee (England and Wales)

141(1)   **[Meetings may establish committee]** Where a winding-up order has been made by the court in England and Wales and separate meetings of creditors and contributories have been summoned for the purpose of choosing a person to be liquidator, those meetings may establish a committee (**"the liquidation committee"**) to exercise the functions conferred on it by or under this Act.

141(2)   **[Separate meetings may be summoned]** The liquidator (not being the official receiver) may at any time, if he thinks fit, summon separate general meetings of the company's creditors and contributories for the purpose of determining whether such a committee should be established and, if it is so determined, of establishing it.

The liquidator (not being the official receiver) shall summon such a meeting if he is requested, in accordance with the rules, to do so by one-tenth, in value, of the company's creditors.

141(3) **[Where meetings disagree]** Where meetings are summoned under this section, or for the purpose of choosing a person to be liquidator, and either the meeting of creditors or the meeting of contributories decides that a liquidation committee should be established, but the other meeting does not so decide or decides that a committee should not be established, the committee shall be established in accordance with the rules, unless the court otherwise orders.

141(4) **[Committee not to function where official receiver liquidator]** The liquidation committee is not to be able or required to carry out its functions at any time when the official receiver is liquidator; but at any such time its functions are vested in the Secretary of State except to the extent that the rules otherwise provide.

141(5) **[Where no committee etc.]** Where there is for the time being no liquidation committee, and the liquidator is a person other than the official receiver, the functions of such a committee are vested in the Secretary of State except to the extent that the rules otherwise provide.

GENERAL NOTE

Prior to the reforms effected by IA 1985, 1986, the "committee of inspection" had been a feature of the law of bankruptcy and company liquidation for over a century. In the present Act, the title "liquidation committee" has been substituted, both here and in relation to a creditors' voluntary winding up (s.101), while for the purposes of an administration (s.26) and an administrative receivership (ss.49, 68), where it is composed entirely of creditors, it is called the "creditors' committee" or "committee of creditors".

In marked contrast to the detailed provisions of s.101, the present section has nothing to say about the composition of the committee, but this is clarified by the rules. It is stated in IR 1986 r.4.152 that the committee shall consist of between three and five creditors and also (if the company is solvent) up to three contributories. Once the creditors have all been paid in full, the creditor members of the committee cease to be members: r.4.171A.

S.141(1), (2)

The liquidation committee has no role to play while the official receiver is liquidator, as is confirmed by later subsections, and so the machinery for establishing a committee comes into operation only when there is a private liquidator, or when the appointment of a private liquidator is contemplated. The present provisions should be read in conjunction with ss.136(4), 137(5), 139 and 140(3).

Where a liquidator has been appointed by court order under s.140, following upon an administration or voluntary arrangement, s.141(2) will apply, so that he or the creditors may take steps to establish a liquidation committee even though the official receiver is released from his duties in this regard by s.140(3).

S.141(4), (5)

A number of provisions in the Act empower the liquidator to act "with the consent of the liquidation committee" (see, e.g. s.167(1)(a)), while others require him to give notice to the committee of what he has done (see, e.g. s.167(2)). By substituting the Secretary of State for the committee in the circumstances set out, the present subsections enable the liquidator to exercise such powers when there is no committee or none competent to act.

The rules which have been made for the purposes of this section are IR 1986 rr.4.151 et seq. and, for s.141(4), (5) r.4.172. For further guidance, see [2001] Insolv. Int. 61.

142 Liquidation committee (Scotland)

142(1) **[Establishing committees in Scotland]** Where a winding-up order has been made by the court in Scotland and separate meetings of creditors and contributories have been summoned for the purpose of choosing a person to be liquidator or, under section 138(4), only a meeting of creditors has been summoned for that purpose, those meetings or (as the case may be) that meeting may establish a committee ("the liquidation committee") to exercise the functions conferred on it by or under this Act.

142(2) **[Separate meetings may be summoned]** The liquidator may at any time, if he thinks fit, summon separate general meetings of the company's creditors and contributories for the purpose of determining whether such a committee should be established and, if it is so determined, of establishing it.

142(3) **[Meetings to be summoned on request]** The liquidator, if appointed by the court otherwise than under section 139(4)(a), is required to summon meetings under subsection (2) if he is requested, in accordance with the rules, to do so by one-tenth, in value, of the company's creditors.

142(4)   [Where meetings disagree] Where meetings are summoned under this section, or for the purpose of choosing a person to be liquidator, and either the meeting of creditors or the meeting of contributories decides that a liquidation committee should be established, but the other meeting does not so decide or decides that a committee should not be established, the committee shall be established in accordance with the rules, unless the court otherwise orders.

142(5)   [Where no committee etc.] Where in the case of any winding up there is for the time being no liquidation committee, the functions of such a committee are vested in the court except to the extent that the rules otherwise provide.

142(6)   [Powers and duties of committee] In addition to the powers and duties conferred and imposed on it by this Act, a liquidation committee has such of the powers and duties of commissioners in a sequestration as may be conferred and imposed on such committees by the rules.

GENERAL NOTE

This section contains provisions for Scotland similar to those laid down for England and Wales by s.141, and the notes to that section generally apply here also, apart from the references to the official receiver, who of course has no Scottish counterpart.

The liquidator's functions

143   General functions in winding up by the court

143(1)   [Functions] The functions of the liquidator of a company which is being wound up by the court are to secure that the assets of the company are got in, realised and distributed to the company's creditors and, if there is a surplus, to the persons entitled to it.

143(2)   [Duty of liquidator not official receiver] It is the duty of the liquidator of a company which is being wound up by the court in England and Wales, if he is not the official receiver–

(a)   to furnish the official receiver with such information,

(b)   to produce to the official receiver, and permit inspection by the official receiver of, such books, papers and other records, and

(c)   to give the official receiver such other assistance,

as the official receiver may reasonably require for the purposes of carrying out his functions in relation to the winding up.

S.143(1)

The functions of a liquidator in a compulsory winding up are expressed in this subsection rather differently from those of a liquidator in a voluntary liquidation, set out in s.107; but in substance their duties are broadly the same; and similar rules apply regarding the application of assets: see the notes to s.107.

S.143(2)

On the liquidator's duties of care, etc. see the note to s.212; and on enforcement of the liquidator's obligations, see IR 1986 r.7.20.

144   Custody of company's property

144(1)   [Liquidator to take property into custody] When a winding-up order has been made, or where a provisional liquidator has been appointed, the liquidator or the provisional liquidator (as the case may be) shall take into his custody or under his control all the property and things in action to which the company is or appears to be entitled.

144(2)   [In Scotland where no liquidator] In a winding up by the court in Scotland, if and so long as there is no liquidator, all the property of the company is deemed to be in the custody of the court.

S.144(1)

The term "property" has a very comprehensive definition for the purposes of the present Act: see s.436.

It is also the duty of the liquidator to take control of assets held by the company on trust, although such assets are not available for distribution under the winding up. On the question of the liquidator's right to remuneration and his costs and expenses incurred in performing the company's functions as trustee, see the notes to rr.4.127–4.131C.

S.144(2)

There is no equivalent to this provision for England and Wales in view of s.136(2), (3), which ensures that the official receiver holds the office of liquidator if there is any vacancy.

145   Vesting of company property in liquidator

145(1) [Court order] When a company is being wound up by the court, the court may on the application of the liquidator by order direct that all or any part of the property of whatsoever description belonging to the company or held by trustees on its behalf shall vest in the liquidator by his official name; and thereupon the property to which the order relates vests accordingly.

145(2) [Action re property by liquidator] The liquidator may, after giving such indemnity (if any) as the court may direct, bring or defend in his official name any action or other legal proceeding which relates to that property or which it is necessary to bring or defend for the purpose of effectually winding up the company and recovering its property.

GENERAL NOTE

The estate of a bankrupt individual vests automatically in his trustee by operation of law: see s.306. In contrast, the property of a company which is in liquidation remains vested in it unless an order is sought under the present section.

S.145(1)

It is normally unnecessary to have a vesting order made, in view of the wide powers conferred on the liquidator to act in the company's name (see Sch.4). However, an order may be needed in special circumstances: e.g. where the company is a foreign company which has already been wound up or dissolved in its home jurisdiction; or where the body is unincorporated and is being wound up as an "unregistered company" under ss.220 et seq.

When it receives a letter of request from a foreign court, the court has a wide discretionary jurisdiction at common law, including power to make a vesting order in favour of the person or persons nominated in the letter of request: *Cambridge Gas Transport Corp v Official Committee of Unsecured Creditors (of Navigator Holdings plc)* [2006] UKPC 26; [2006] B.C.C. 962.

S.145(2)

The liquidator would normally bring and defend actions in the name of the company: see Sch.4 para.4.

146   Duty to summon final meeting

146(1) [Summoning final meeting] Subject to the next subsection, if it appears to the liquidator of a company which is being wound up by the court that the winding up of the company is for practical purposes complete and the liquidator is not the official receiver, the liquidator shall summon a final general meeting of the company's creditors which–

(a)   shall receive the liquidator's report of the winding up, and

(b)   shall determine whether the liquidator should have his release under section 174 in Chapter VII of this Part.

146(2) [Time for notice] The liquidator may, if he thinks fit, give the notice summoning the final general meeting at the same time as giving notice of any final distribution of the company's property but, if summoned for an earlier date, that meeting shall be adjourned (and, if necessary, further adjourned) until a date on which the liquidator is able to report to the meeting that the winding up of the company is for practical purposes complete.

146(3) **[Retention of sums]** In the carrying out of his functions in the winding up it is the duty of the liquidator to retain sufficient sums from the company's property to cover the expenses of summoning and holding the meeting required by this section.

GENERAL NOTE

This section applies only where a company is being wound up by the court and the liquidator is not the official receiver. It introduces a marked change from the former procedure under CA 1985 s.545, by which the liquidator obtained his release. Previously, the liquidator had to apply for a release to the Secretary of State. He is now required instead to report to the meeting of creditors on the completion of the liquidation and it is left to that meeting to determine whether he should have his release. The creditors are thus kept in the picture throughout the winding up and the liquidator made accountable to them, and at the same time the Secretary of State is relieved from the burden of examining the liquidator's accounts, etc. in order to determine whether he is entitled to his release. The present provision complements, and in part runs parallel to, ss.94 and 106 which apply respectively in a members' and creditors' voluntary winding up. The court may dispense with the obligation to hold a final meeting where it would serve no useful purpose, e.g. where the winding up is ancillary to another liquidation and all known assets have been realised and sent to the liquidator in the primary proceedings: *Morris, Petitioner* [2007] CSOH 165; 2007 S.L.T. 1149; [2009] B.C.C. 307.

S.146(1)

Where the official receiver is the liquidator, the question of his release is for the Secretary of State to determine: see s.174(3). The procedure governing the summoning and conduct of the meeting is in IR 1986 r.4.125.

S.146(2), (3)

It is clear that the winding up must in fact be completed and the company's property finally distributed (apart from what needs to be retained under s.146(3)): the meeting cannot grant the liquidator a prospective or conditional release.

The liquidator must give notice to the court and the registrar of companies that the meeting has been held and report what decisions were made: see s.172(8).

General powers of court

147　Power to stay or sist winding up

147(1) **[Court may order stay on application]** The court may at any time after an order for winding up, on the application either of the liquidator or the official receiver or any creditor or contributory, and on proof to the satisfaction of the court that all proceedings in the winding up ought to be stayed or sisted, make an order staying or sisting the proceedings, either altogether or for a limited time, on such terms and conditions as the court thinks fit.

147(2) **[Report by official receiver]** The court may, before making an order, require the official receiver to furnish to it a report with respect to any facts or matters which are in his opinion relevant to the application.

147(3) **[Copy of order to registrar]** A copy of every order made under this section shall forthwith be forwarded by the company, or otherwise as may be prescribed, to the registrar of companies, who shall enter it in his records relating to the company.

S.147(1)

An order for the stay (or, in Scotland, sist) of the winding-up proceedings may be made either for a limited time, or "altogether". In the latter case, the order for liquidation is, in effect, terminated; the liquidator will then be entitled to a discharge and the directors reinstated in control. For the principles on which the court will grant or refuse a stay, see *Re Lowston Ltd* [1991] B.C.L.C. 570; and *McGruther v James Scott Ltd*, 2004 S.C. 514.

Prior to the 1986 legislation, it was not possible to rescind a winding-up order altogether: the nearest possible thing was the grant of a permanent stay. The consequence was that, technically, the company remained subject to the order, although its operation was suspended. In this situation, a copy of the winding-up order remains on the file at Companies House (see IA 1986 s.130(1)), where it can be the source of misunderstanding (e.g. in relation to credit references). It is now possible, however, for the court to rescind a winding-up order under IR 1986 r.7.47(1) (e.g. on the ground of mistake), and declare it to have been a nullity. The registrar is then bound to remove the order from his files: *Re Calmex Ltd* [1989] 1 All E.R. 485; (1988) 4 B.C.C. 761. However, the jurisdiction to rescind is to be exercised very cautiously, and only to correct an obvious injustice (*Leicester v Stevenson* [2003] 2 B.C.L.C. 97); and see *Re Turnstem Ltd* [2004] EWHC 1765 (Ch); [2005] 1 B.C.L.C. 388. See also the *Practice Direction* [2007] B.C.C. 842 (reproduced as App. IV to this *Guide*), para.7. On the question of standing to apply for the rescission of a winding-up order. see r.7.47 and J. Curl, [2009] Insolv. Int. 145.

A stay may be granted on the ground of *forum non conveniens*, i.e. that the courts of another jurisdiction are more appropriately placed to deal with the proceedings: see the note to s.125(1).

S.147(2)

The officers of the company and its employees and others specified are under a duty to co-operate with the official receiver: see s.235.

S.147(3)

No regulations appear to have been prescribed for the purposes of this section; but IR 1986 r.4.48 empowers the court to impose requirements as to notification.

148 Settlement of list of contributories and application of assets

148(1) [Court's duties] As soon as may be after making a winding-up order, the court shall settle a list of contributories, with power to rectify the register of members in all cases where rectification is required, and shall cause the company's assets to be collected, and applied in discharge of its liabilities.

148(2) [Court may dispense with list] If it appears to the court that it will not be necessary to make calls on or adjust the rights of contributories, the court may dispense with the settlement of a list of contributories.

148(3) [Distinction between types of contributories] In settling the list, the court shall distinguish between persons who are contributories in their own right and persons who are contributories as being representatives of or liable for the debts of others.

S.148(1)

On the meaning of contributories, and their liability, see the note to s.74 above.

The powers conferred by this section have been delegated to the liquidator by rules made under s.160, below; but the power to rectify the register of members may be exercised by the liquidator only with the special leave of the court: s.160(2). For the relevant rules, see IR 1986 rr.4.195 et seq.

The general power of the court to rectify the register of members (e.g. in the case of omission or mistake) is contained in CA 2006 s.125.

The principles governing the application of assets in a voluntary winding up (s.107) and in a winding up by the court under this section are substantially equivalent. See further the note to that section.

On the order of priority of the expenses of a liquidation *inter se*, see IR 1986 rr.4.218–4.220, and the note to s.156.

S.148(2)

This would apply, in particular, where the shares are fully paid.

S.148(3)

The categories of contributories are known as the "A List" and "B List" contributories. The circumstances in which the latter are liable to contribute are set out in s.74(2); see also ss.75, 76.

149 Debts due from contributory to company

149(1) [Court may order payment from contributory] The court may, at any time after making a winding-up order, make an order on any contributory for the time being on the list of contributories to pay, in manner directed by the order, any money due from him (or from the estate of the person who he represents) to the company, exclusive of any money payable by him or the estate by virtue of any call.

149(2) [Allowances and set-offs] The court in making such an order may–

   (a) in the case of an unlimited company, allow to the contributory by way of set-off any money due to him or the estate which he represents from the company on any independent dealing or contract with the company, but not any money due to him as a member of the company in respect of any dividend or profit, and

(b) in the case of a limited company, make to any director or manager whose liability is unlimited or to his estate the like allowance.

149(3) [Money due to contributory may be allowed when creditors paid] In the case of any company, whether limited or unlimited, when all the creditors are paid in full (together with interest at the official rate), any money due on any account whatever to a contributory from the company may be allowed to him by way of set-off against any subsequent call.

S.149(1)
This provision allows the liquidator to recover in a summary way moneys (other than calls, which are dealt with in s.150) due by a member to the company, thus avoiding the formality of a conventional action. However, it is confined to sums owed by the member qua member, e.g. dividends improperly paid to him, and may not be used to claim an ordinary debt: *Re Marlborough Club Co* (1868) L.R. 5 Eq. 365. One consequence of this is that the contributory loses his normal right as a debtor to set off against such a claim any sums due from the company to him (*Re Whitehouse & Co* (1878) 9 Ch. D. 595), apart from the special case where a contributory's liability is unlimited, which is dealt with in s.149(2).

S.149(2)
The right of set-off in the two situations of unlimited liability referred to is not automatic, but rests in the discretion of the court. No set-off lies in any case in regard to dividends or profits payable to the member, in keeping with the principle expressed in s.74(2)(f).

On the question of set-off generally, see the Introductory note to Part IV, Chapter VIII preceding s.175.

S.149(3)
The restrictions as to set-off described in the notes to s.149(1) and (2) no longer apply once the claims of the general creditors have been fully satisfied.

On the entitlement of a creditor to interest, see the note to s.189.

150 Power to make calls

150(1) [Court may make calls to satisfy debts] The court may, at any time after making a winding-up order, and either before or after it has ascertained the sufficiency of the company's assets, make calls on all or any of the contributories for the time being settled on the list of the contributories to the extent of their liability, for payment of any money which the court considers necessary to satisfy the company's debts and liabilities, and the expenses of winding up, and for the adjustment of the rights of the contributories among themselves, and make an order for payment of any calls so made.

150(2) [Matters to be considered] In making a call the court may take into consideration the probability that some of the contributories may partly or wholly fail to pay it.

S.150(1)
This provision authorises the court to settle the liability of contributories to pay calls, and to enforce this liability in a summary way. The powers of the court have been delegated to the liquidator by regulations made under s.160(1): see IR 1986 rr.4.195, 4.202 et seq. In regard to the making of calls, the rules provide for the liquidator to act with the alternative sanction of the liquidation committee: r.4.203. The liquidator may not act without authorisation unless the court gives special leave: s.160(2).

S.150(2)
The court may take into account the likelihood that some contributories may default, so saving the need for a further call on the remainder. If the amount thus raised is surplus to the liquidator's needs, it is of course returnable under s.154.

151 Payment into bank of money due to company

151(1) [Court may order payment into Bank of England] The court may order any contributory, purchaser or other person from whom money is due to the company to pay the amount due into the Bank of England (or any branch of it) to the account of the liquidator instead of to the liquidator, and such an order may be enforced in the same manner as if it had directed payment to the liquidator.

151(2) **[Moneys in Bank subject to court orders]** All money and securities paid or delivered into the Bank of England (or branch) in the event of a winding up by the court are subject in all respects to the orders of the court.

GENERAL NOTE

The power to order payment to be made direct to the Bank of England is not confined to calls and other sums due from contributories, but may be invoked in relation to any debtor. Little or no use has been made of this provision and the Insolvency Service intends to repeal it when there is an appropriate legislative opportunity.

152 Order on contributory to be conclusive evidence

152(1) **[Order evidence that money due]** An order made by the court on a contributory is conclusive evidence that the money (if any) thereby appearing to be due or ordered to be paid is due, but subject to any right of appeal.

152(2) **[Other matters stated in order]** All other pertinent matters stated in the order are to be taken as truly stated as against all persons and in all proceedings except proceedings in Scotland against the heritable estate of a deceased contributory; and in that case the order is only prima facie evidence for the purpose of charging his heritable estate, unless his heirs or legatees of heritage were on the list of contributories at the time of the order being made.

GENERAL NOTE

This section applies only to orders against contributories, but it is not confined to orders for the payment of calls.

153 Power to exclude creditors not proving in time

153 The court may fix a time or times within which creditors are to prove their debts or claims or to be excluded from the benefit of any distribution made before those debts are proved.

GENERAL NOTE

A creditor who does not prove his debt within the time fixed by the court is excluded from participating in any distribution made before he proves, but his right to prove is not itself affected, and he may be paid out of such assets as remain or later become available. See further IR 1986 rr.4.182(2) and 11.2(2).

The power of the court under this section may be delegated by rules to the liquidator: see s.160(1). There does not appear to have been any specific exercise of this power in IR 1986, but the same result is achieved, in effect, by r.11.2.

A creditor may, of course, be barred from claiming by the operation of the statutes of limitation. In *Re Joshua Shaw & Sons Ltd* (1989) 5 B.C.C. 188 the debts of all the company's unsecured creditors, apart from the Crown, became statute-barred during the course of a long-running receivership. The ironic consequence was that the surplus which was found to exist at the conclusion of the receivership went to the company's shareholders.

154 Adjustment of rights of contributories

154 The court shall adjust the rights of the contributories among themselves and distribute any surplus among the persons entitled to it.

GENERAL NOTE

For the corresponding provision in a voluntary winding up, see s.107.

For the relevant rules, see IR 1986 rr.4.221 et seq.

155 Inspection of books by creditors, etc.

155(1) **[Court may make order for inspection]** The court may, at any time after making a winding-up order, make such order for inspection of the company's books and papers by creditors and contributories as the court thinks just; and any books and papers in the company's possession may be inspected by creditors and contributories accordingly, but not further or otherwise.

155(2)   [Statutory rights of government department] Nothing in this section excludes or restricts any statutory rights of a government department or person acting under the authority of a government department.

155(3)   [Government department includes Scottish Administration] For the purposes of subsection (2) above, references to a government department shall be construed as including references to any part of the Scottish Administration.

S.155(1)

The company's books and papers are not ordinarily accessible even to members while the company is a going concern; and although this section does confer such a right on creditors and contributories in a winding up, subject to the leave of the court, there are dicta which state that the court's leave will in practice be granted only for purposes directly connected with the liquidation: *Re North Brazilian Sugar Factories* (1887) 37 Ch. D. 83; *Re D P R Futures Ltd* [1989] 1 W.L.R. 778; (1989) 5 B.C.C. 603. However, it is understood that the court will in fact grant leave in a suitable case, e.g. where a creditor needs to obtain information to defend a claim under a guarantee, or an insurance company to defend a claim made against it, even though the claim in question may not be so connected. The same cases also held that the court's jurisdiction under s.155 extends only to books and papers in the possession of the company: it cannot, for instance, extend to documents formerly in the custody of the company which have been seized by the Serious Fraud Office.

S.155(2)

The statutory rights most obviously referred to here are those of the Secretary of State, and inspectors appointed by him, under CA 1985 ss.431 et seq. [not affected by CA 2006].

S.155(3)

This subsection was inserted by the Scotland Act 1998 (Consequential Modifications) Order 1999 (SI 1999/1820) arts 1(2), 4 and Sch.2 Pt 1 para.85, effective July 1, 1999.

156   Payment of expenses of winding up

156   The court may, in the event of the assets being insufficient to satisfy the liabilities, make an order as to the payment out of the assets of the expenses incurred in the winding up in such order of priority as the court thinks just.

GENERAL NOTE

On the meaning of "assets" in the context of the present section, see the note to s.115.

The rules contain provisions dealing with the payment of expenses of a winding up in the normal case, but subject to any order of the court: IR 1986 rr.4.218, 4.220. The present section gives the court the power to make such an order where it is appropriate, but the power is limited to varying the order of priority and does not extend to making an order giving priority to costs that are not within the list contained in the above rules: *Re R S & M Engineering Co Ltd* [2000] Ch. 40; [2000] B.C.C. 445; *Re MT Realisations Ltd* [2003] EWHC 2895 (Ch); [2004] 1 B.C.L.C. 119. The court will only in exceptional circumstances exercise its jurisdiction under this section to confer on the liquidator's remuneration, or any part of it, priority over liquidation expenses which would normally rank before it: *Re Linda Marie Ltd (in liq.)* (1988) 4 B.C.C. 463.

In relation to the financial markets and securities settlement systems, s.156 has effect subject to the priority accorded to the claim of a participant or central bank to collateral security by the Finality Regulations reg.14(5), (6), unless the terms on which the collateral security was provided expressly state that the expenses, remuneration or preferential debts are to have priority: see the note on p.3.

157   Attendance at company meetings (Scotland)

157   In the winding up by the court of a company registered in Scotland, the court has power to require the attendance of any officer of the company at any meeting of creditors or of contributories, or of a liquidation committee, for the purpose of giving information as to the trade, dealings, affairs or property of the company.

GENERAL NOTE

There is no direct counterpart of this provision for England and Wales.

158   Power to arrest absconding contributory

158   The court, at any time either before or after making a winding-up order, on proof of probable cause for believing that a contributory is about to quit the United Kingdom or otherwise to abscond or to remove or conceal any of his property for the purpose of evading payment of calls, may cause the contributory to be arrested and his books and papers and moveable personal property to be seized and him and them to be kept safely until such time as the court may order.

GENERAL NOTE

The former legislation, after the phrase "for the purpose of evading calls" contained the additional words "or of avoiding examination respecting the company's affairs". These words have been deleted; the point is amply covered elsewhere in the Act: see s.236(5).

159   Powers of court to be cumulative

159   Powers conferred on the court by this Act are in addition to, and not in restriction of, any existing powers of instituting proceedings against a contributory or debtor of the company, or the estate of any contributory or debtor, for the recovery of any call or other sums.

160   Delegation of powers to liquidator (England and Wales)

160(1)   [Delegation by rules] Provision may be made by rules for enabling or requiring all or any of the powers and duties conferred and imposed on the court in England and Wales in respect of the following matters—

     (a)   the holding and conducting of meetings to ascertain the wishes of creditors and contributories,

     (b)   the settling of lists of contributories and the rectifying of the register of members where required, and the collection and application of the assets,

     (c)   the payment, delivery, conveyance, surrender or transfer of money, property, books or papers to the liquidator,

     (d)   the making of calls,

     (e)   the fixing of a time within which debts and claims must be proved,

to be exercised or performed by the liquidator as an officer of the court, and subject to the court's control.

160(2)   [No rectification etc. without special leave] But the liquidator shall not, without the special leave of the court, rectify the register of members, and shall not make any call without either that special leave or the sanction of the liquidation committee.

GENERAL NOTE

For the relevant rules, see IR 1986 rr.4.54 et seq. (meetings); 4.179 et seq. (assets); 4.185 (surrender of books, etc.); 4.195 et seq. (list of contributories); 4.196 (rectifying register); 4.202 et seq. (calls), and see the note to s.153 (time for proving).

Enforcement of, and appeal from, orders

161   Orders for calls on contributories (Scotland)

161(1)   [Court may order calls on contributories on receipt of list] In Scotland, where an order, interlocutor or decree has been made for winding up a company by the court, it is competent to the court, on production by the liquidators of a list certified by them of the names of the contributories liable in payment of any calls, and of the amount due by each contributory, and of the date when that amount became due, to pronounce forthwith a decree against those contributories for payment of the sums so certified to be due, with interest from that date until payment (at 5 per cent per annum) in the same way and to the same effect as if they had severally consented to registration for execution, on a charge of 6 days, of a legal obligation to pay those calls and interest.

161(2)   **[Extraction of decree]** The decree may be extracted immediately, and no suspension of it is competent, except on caution or consignation, unless with special leave of the court.

GENERAL NOTE

The procedure for making calls on contributories in a winding up by the court in England and Wales is prescribed in rather different terms by s.160(1)(d) and the rules made thereunder.

162   Appeals from orders in Scotland

162(1)   **[Appeal from order on winding up]** Subject to the provisions of this section and to rules of court, an appeal from any order or decision made or given in the winding up of a company by the court in Scotland under this Act lies in the same manner and subject to the same conditions as an appeal from an order or decision of the court in cases within its ordinary jurisdiction.

162(2)   **[Orders by judge acting as vacation judge]** In regard to orders or judgments pronounced by the judge acting as vacation judge–

  (a)   none of the orders specified in Part I of Schedule 3 to this Act are subject to review, reduction, suspension or stay of execution, and

  (b)   every other order or judgment (except as mentioned below) may be submitted to review by the Inner House by reclaiming motion enrolled within 14 days from the date of the order or judgment.

162(3)   **[Order in Sch.3 Pt II]** However, an order being one of those specified in Part II of that Schedule shall, from the date of the order and notwithstanding that it has been submitted to review as above, be carried out and receive effect until the Inner House have disposed of the matter.

162(4)   **[Orders by Lord Ordinary]** In regard to orders or judgments pronounced in Scotland by a Lord Ordinary before whom proceedings in a winding up are being taken, any such order or judgment may be submitted to review by the Inner House by reclaiming motion enrolled within 14 days from its date; but should it not be so submitted to review during session, the provisions of this section in regard to orders or judgments pronounced by the judge acting as vacation judge apply.

162(5)   **[Decrees for payment of calls in winding up]** Nothing in this section affects provisions of the Companies Acts or this Act in reference to decrees in Scotland for payment of calls in the winding up of companies, whether voluntary or by the court.

GENERAL NOTE

This section deals with a number of special points of Scottish procedure. It should be read in conjunction with Sch.3, below, which makes more detailed provisions for the purposes of s.162(2) and (3).

CHAPTER VII

LIQUIDATORS

Preliminary

163   Style and title of liquidators

163   The liquidator of a company shall be described–

  (a)   where a person other than the official receiver is liquidator, by the style of "the liquidator" of the particular company, or

(b) where the official receiver is liquidator, by the style of "the official receiver and liquidator" of the particular company;

and in neither case shall he be described by an individual name.

164 Corrupt inducement affecting appointment

164 A person who gives, or agrees or offers to give, to any member or creditor of a company any valuable consideration with a view to securing his own appointment or nomination, or to securing or preventing the appointment or nomination of some person other than himself, as the company's liquidator is liable to a fine.

GENERAL NOTE

It is perhaps surprising that this old provision has survived the reforms made by IA 1985, including the requirement that a liquidator must now be a professional insolvency practitioner.

On penalties, see s.430 and Sch.10.

Liquidator's powers and duties

165 Voluntary winding up

165(1) **[Application]** This section has effect where a company is being wound up voluntarily, but subject to section 166 below in the case of a creditors' voluntary winding up.

165(2) **[Powers in Sch.4 Pt I]** The liquidator may–

(a) in the case of a members' voluntary winding up, with the sanction of a special resolution of the company, and

(b) in the case of a creditors' voluntary winding up, with the sanction of the court or the liquidation committee (or, if there is no such committee, a meeting of the company's creditors),

exercise any of the powers specified in Part I of Schedule 4 to this Act (payment of debts, compromise of claims, etc.).

165(3) **[Powers in Sch.4 Pt II, III]** The liquidator may, without sanction, exercise either of the powers specified in Part II of that Schedule (institution and defence of proceedings; carrying on the business of the company) and any of the general powers specified in Part III of that Schedule.

165(4) **[Other powers]** The liquidator may–

(a) exercise the court's power of settling a list of contributories (which list is prima facie evidence of the liability of the persons named in it to be contributories),

(b) exercise the court's power of making calls,

(c) summon general meetings of the company for the purpose of obtaining its sanction by special resolution or for any other purpose he may think fit.

165(5) **[Duty re payment of debts]** The liquidator shall pay the company's debts and adjust the rights of the contributories among themselves.

165(6) **[Notice to committee re exercise of powers]** Where the liquidator in exercise of the powers conferred on him by this Act disposes of any property of the company to a person who is connected with the company (within the meaning of section 249 in Part VII), he shall, if there is for the time being a liquidation committee, give notice to the committee of that exercise of his powers.

This section deals with the powers and duties of the liquidator in a voluntary winding up. It is to be read in conjunction with Sch.4, in which some powers are set out in detail. Note the limitation on powers of the liquidator to deal with property covered by s.426 of the POCA 2002 (restraint orders, etc.).

Sections 165(2)(a), 165(4)(c) amended by the Companies Act 2006 (Commencement No.3, Consequential Amendments, Transitional Provisions and Savings) Order 2007 (SI 2007/2194 (C. 84)) art.10(1) and Sch.4 para.41(1), as from October 1, 2007.

S.165(1)

The relationship between ss.165 and 166 is a little confusing. Section 165 applies to every voluntary winding up, *including* a creditors' voluntary winding up where the liquidator has been nominated by the company; but s.166 supplements s.165 in the latter case (1) by imposing restrictions on the powers exercisable by the liquidator pending the holding of the creditors' meeting; and (2) by imposing on the liquidator the duty of attending the creditors' meeting (see s.166(4)).

S.165(2)

Schedule 4 is divided into three Parts, listing respectively:

Pt I: powers exercisable with sanction;

Pt II: powers exercisable without sanction in a voluntary winding up, but with sanction in a winding up by the court; and

Pt III: powers exercisable without sanction in any winding up.

The present subsection relates to Pt I of the Schedule and specifies the appropriate sanctioning body in each case.

In *Whitehouse v Wilson* [2005] EWCA Civ 1688; [2007] B.P.I.R. 230 the liquidator sought the court's sanction for the compromise of misfeasance claims against a former director and majority shareholder. Whilst upholding the compromise as being in the best commercial interests of the company, some members of the Court of Appeal expressed the view that the court below ought to have given more consideration to the issue of public interest.

S.165(3)

In the case of a voluntary winding up, no distinction is made between the powers listed in Pt II and those in Pt III of the Schedule. No sanction is required for the exercise of any of these powers.

S.165(4)

These are matters for which, in the case of a winding up by the court, power is in the first instance conferred by the Act upon the court itself, but then normally delegated to the liquidator by rules made under s.160. Note, however, that under the present section the liquidator in a voluntary winding up may make calls without any sanction (para.(b)), in contrast with s.160(2) which stipulates that in a compulsory winding up he may do so only with the special leave of the court.

Reference should be made also to s.112, which empowers the court to determine questions and exercise powers in a voluntary winding up as if the company were being wound up by the court.

S.165(5)

There is some overlap between this provision and s.107. On the application of assets generally, see the note to that section.

S.165(6)

This provision, first introduced by IA 1985, is designed to ensure that, at least in any voluntary winding up where there is a liquidation committee, no property of the company shall be disposed of to someone "connected with" the company unless it is done with the modest amount of disclosure specified. (The legislators have not gone so far as to stipulate for the *sanction* of the committee.) No doubt this requirement is part of the general package of measures aimed at the abuse known as the "phoenix syndrome" (see the note to s.216, below). If there is no liquidation committee, s.141(5) applies, vesting the relevant powers in the Secretary of State.

The category of persons "connected with" a company is very widely defined, and includes a director, employee or controlling shareholder, a close relative of any of these persons, and a company in the same group. See the notes to ss.249 and 435, below.

166 Creditors' voluntary winding up

166(1) [Application] This section applies where, in the case of a creditors' voluntary winding up, a liquidator has been nominated by the company.

166(2) [Non-exercise of s.165 powers] The powers conferred on the liquidator by section 165 shall not be exercised, except with the sanction of the court, during the period before the holding of the creditors' meeting under section 98 in Chapter IV.

166(3) [Non-application of s.166(2)] Subsection (2) does not apply in relation to the power of the liquidator–

(a)   to take into his custody or under his control all the property to which the company is or appears to be entitled;

(b)   to dispose of perishable goods and other goods the value of which is likely to diminish if they are not immediately disposed of; and

(c)   to do all such other things as may be necessary for the protection of the company's assets.

166(4) [Liquidator to attend s.98 meeting] The liquidator shall attend the creditors' meeting held under section 98 and shall report to the meeting on any exercise by him of his powers (whether or not under this section or under section 112 or 165).

166(5) [Where default re ss.98, 99] If default is made–

(a)   by the company in complying with subsection (1), (1A), (2) or (2A) of section 98, or

(b)   by the directors in complying with subsection (1) or (2) of section 99,

the liquidator shall, within 7 days of the relevant day, apply to the court for directions as to the manner in which that default is to be remedied.

166(6) ["The relevant day"] "The relevant day" means the day on which the liquidator was nominated by the company or the day on which he first became aware of the default, whichever is the later.

166(7) [Penalty for non-compliance] If the liquidator without reasonable excuse fails to comply with this section, he is liable to a fine.

GENERAL NOTE

This section should be read in conjunction with ss.98 and 114, above. Taken together, they should ensure (as is undoubtedly intended) that the practice which had become notorious under the name of "centrebinding" is totally stamped out. The abuse takes its name from the case of *Re Centrebind Ltd* [1967] 1 W.L.R. 377, where the members of an insolvent company resolved to go into voluntary liquidation and appointed their own liquidator who, before any creditors' meeting had been held, took immediate steps to restrain the Inland Revenue from proceeding with a distress on the company's assets. Plowman J. held that the liquidator had power to act until the creditors' meeting had been held.

Although the acts of the company and its liquidator in the *Centrebind* case itself were done entirely in good faith, it was not long before the practice developed of calling only a shareholders' meeting in the first instance to pass a winding-up resolution and, although the company was known to be insolvent, deliberately putting off for some time, or perhaps indefinitely, the holding of the creditors' meeting. This, of course, involved a technical breach of the Companies Act (CA 1985 s.588(2)), which required the latter meeting to be held on the same day as the members' meeting or the very next day and, indeed, was a criminal offence. However, it meant that the controllers of a company, with the aid of an unscrupulous liquidator nominated by them, could effectively sell the assets off at a knock-down price to a purchaser closely connected with themselves (e.g. a new company controlled by them), and the creditors were powerless to prevent it.

The introduction by IA 1985 of a mandatory requirement that liquidators shall be of professional standing is probably in itself sufficient to ensure that "centrebinding" will no longer be part of insolvency practice; but the legislature has made doubly sure of this by provisions such as the present.

Note amendment from April 22, 2009 by the introduction of new s.166(1A), removing restrictions on the exercise by a liquidator in Scotland of the power to sell property: Bankruptcy and Diligence etc. (Scotland) Act 2007 s.155(3).

S.166(1)

Where no liquidator has been nominated by the company the directors will remain in control of the company's property, but their powers will be limited to protecting the assets and disposing of perishable goods, unless they obtain the sanction of the court (see s.114).

S.166(2)

The provisions of s.166 operate to qualify s.165 only during the interval between the nomination of a liquidator by the company and the holding of the creditors' meeting—a period which ought not to exceed 14 days (see s.98(1)(a)).

S.166(3)

The restricted powers given to the liquidator (unless he has the sanction of the court under s.166(2)) are, as regards paras (b) and (c), the same as those allowed to directors by s.114(3). In addition he has, by para.(a), the power to take over custody and control of the company's property from the directors. The term "property" is widely defined: see s.436.

S.166(4), (5)

The obligations imposed on the company by s.98 are to convene a creditor's meeting within 14 days of the company's own meeting and to give the appropriate notices; while under s.99 the directors are required to make out a statement of affairs to be laid before the creditors' meeting and to depute one of their number to attend the meeting. The "relevant day" is defined in s.166(6).

The language of s.166(5) is permissive rather than mandatory. There is no obligation on the liquidator to apply for directions where there is no need for them: *Re Salcombe Hotel Development Co Ltd* (1989) 5 B.C.C. 807.

Section 166(5)(a) amended by the Legislative Reform (Insolvency) (Advertising Requirements) Order 2009 art.3(3), as from April 6, 2009, and further amended by LRO 2010 (SI 2010/18) art.5(5) from April 6, 2010 (with retrospective effect).

S.166(7)

On penalties, see s.430 and Sch.10.

167   Winding up by the court

167(1)   [Powers of liquidator] Where a company is being wound up by the court, the liquidator may–

(a)   with the sanction of the court or the liquidation committee, exercise any of the powers specified in Parts I and II of Schedule 4 to this Act (payment of debts; compromise of claims, etc.; institution and defence of proceedings; carrying on of the business of the company), and

(b)   with or without that sanction, exercise any of the general powers specified in Part III of that Schedule.

167(2)   [Duty of liquidator] Where the liquidator (not being the official receiver), in exercise of the powers conferred on him by this Act–

(a)   disposes of any property of the company to a person who is connected with the company (within the meaning of section 249 in Part VII), or

(b)   employs a solicitor to assist him in the carrying out of his functions,

he shall, if there is for the time being a liquidation committee, give notice to the committee of that exercise of his powers.

167(3)   [Control of court] The exercise by the liquidator in a winding up by the court of the powers conferred by this section is subject to the control of the court, and any creditor or contributory may apply to the court with respect to any exercise or proposed exercise of any of those powers.

GENERAL NOTE

The liquidator, in a winding up by the court, is given specific powers and duties by various other sections of the Act. In addition, the present provision confers on him general powers by reference to Sch.4. Note the limitation on the liquidator's powers with regard to property covered by s.426 of POCA 2002 (restraint orders, etc.).

S.167(1)

Although every liquidator has all the powers listed in Sch.4, those of a liquidator in a winding up by the court are more restricted, in that the powers specified in Pt II of the Schedule (instituting and defending proceedings, and carrying on the company's business) are exercisable only with the sanctions specified in para.(a). The rules state that any permission given under this section shall be given in the particular case, and not generally: see IR 1986 r.4.184.

In exercising its powers under s.167(1)(a) the court may have regard to the wishes of creditors and contributories (see s.175), and a creditor or contributory is entitled to be heard on an application by the liquidator: *Re Greenhaven Motors Ltd* [1999] B.C.C. 463. However, the views of those who have no realistic prospect of participating in the ultimate distribution of assets will be disregarded: *Re Barings plc (No.7)* [2002] 1 B.C.L.C. 401. The court will attach considerable weight to the views of the liquidator: *Re Edennote Ltd (No.2)* [1997] 2 B.C.L.C. 89 at 92. But the court is exercising its own discretion and not reviewing a decision of the liquidator (where the basis on which the court will interfere is restricted): see *Re Greenhaven Motors Ltd* (above) and the notes to ss.167(3) and 168(5). Note *Gresham International Ltd v Moonie* [2009] EWHC 1093 (Ch); [2009] 2 B.C.L.C. 256 (failure to obtain sanction did not invalidate liquidator's acts, but liquidator debarred from recovering his costs prior to making application for sanction; court's power to grant retrospective sanction).

S.167(2)

This subsection, apart from para.(b) relating to the employment of a solicitor, is parallel to s.165(6) which applies in a voluntary winding up. (Note that it does not apply where the official receiver is the liquidator.)

A transitional provision extends this power to liquidations existing at the commencement of the Act: see Sch.11 para.6(5).

S.167(3)

There is no provision in the Act directly corresponding to this subsection which applies in a voluntary winding up, but the supervisory powers of the court may be invoked in such a case by an application made under s.112.

The court is traditionally reluctant to interfere in the exercise of discretion by a liquidator, and will not do so where it has been exercised in good faith: see the note to s.168(5), below. This is to be contrasted with the situation where the court is exercising its own discretion, as under s.167(1)(a), above. In *Re Greenhaven Motors Ltd* [1997] B.C.C. 547 at first instance, Harman J. thought that a contributory should not be entitled to make an application under this subsection unless there was a real prospect that there would be assets available to yield him a substantial return, but on appeal ([1999] B.C.C. 463 at 466) this point was left open.

168   Supplementary powers (England and Wales)

168(1)   [Application] This section applies in the case of a company which is being wound up by the court in England and Wales.

168(2)   [Liquidator may summon general meetings] The liquidator may summon general meetings of the creditors or contributories for the purpose of ascertaining their wishes; and it is his duty to summon meetings at such times as the creditors or contributories by resolution (either at the meeting appointing the liquidator or otherwise) may direct, or whenever requested in writing to do so by one-tenth in value of the creditors or contributories (as the case may be).

168(3)   [Liquidator may apply to court for directions] The liquidator may apply to the court (in the prescribed manner) for directions in relation to any particular matter arising in the winding up.

168(4)   [Liquidator to use own discretion] Subject to the provisions of this Act, the liquidator shall use his own discretion in the management of the assets and their distribution among the creditors.

168(5)   [Application to court re acts of liquidator] If any person is aggrieved by an act or decision of the liquidator, that person may apply to the court; and the court may confirm, reverse or modify the act or decision complained of, and make such order in the case as it thinks just.

168(5A)   [Court order re insolvent partnerships] Where at any time after a winding-up petition has been presented to the court against any person (including an insolvent partnership or other body which may be wound up under Part V of the Act as an unregistered company), whether by virtue of the provisions of the Insolvent Partnerships Order 1994 or not, the attention of the court is drawn to the fact that the person in question is a member of an insolvent partnership, the court may make an order as to the future conduct of the insolvency proceedings and any such order may apply any provisions of that Order with any necessary modifications.

168(5B) [Order or directions under s.168(5A)] Any order or directions under subsection (5A) may be made or given on the application of the official receiver, any responsible insolvency practitioner, the trustee of the partnership or any other interested person and may include provisions as to the administration of the joint estate of the partnership, and in particular how it and the separate estate of any member are to be administered.

168(5C) [Sections under which court order made re insolvent partnerships] Where the court makes an order for the winding up of an insolvent partnership under–

(a) section 72(1)(a) of the Financial Services Act 1986;

(b) section 92(1)(a) of the Banking Act 1987; or

(c) section 367(3)(a) of the Financial Services and Markets Act 2000,

the court may make an order as to the future conduct of the winding up proceedings, and any such order may apply any provisions of the Insolvent Partnerships Order 1994 with any necessary modifications.

GENERAL NOTE

This section provides in general terms for consultation between the liquidator and the meetings of creditors and contributories, either on his initiative or on requisition by one-tenth in value of those concerned, and also for the court to give directions and to supervise and control the acts and decisions of the liquidator.

For the rules relating to the summoning of meetings, see IR 1986 rr.4.54 et seq. and as regard applications to the court, rr.7.1 et seq.

S.168(2)

Although this subsection imposes a duty on the liquidator who has received a requisition to summon a meeting, the court has jurisdiction to override that duty by directing him not to comply with it: *Re Barings plc, Hamilton v Law Debenture Trustees Ltd* [2001] 2 B.C.L.C. 159.

S.168(5)

Notwithstanding the width of the words "may … make such order in the case as it thinks just", the court will not normally review the exercise by the liquidator of his powers and discretions in the management and realisation of the corporate property. The court will only interfere with a decision of a liquidator if it was taken in bad faith or if it was so perverse as to demonstrate that no liquidator properly advised could have taken it: *Re a Debtor* [1949] Ch. 236 at 241; *Re Hans Place Ltd* [1992] B.C.C. 737 at 745–746; *Leon v York-o-Matic Ltd* [1966] 1 W.L.R. 1450; *Re Greenhaven Motors Ltd* [1997] B.C.C. 547; *Re Edennote Ltd, Tottenham Hotspur v Ryman* [1996] B.C.C. 718; *Hamilton v Official Receiver* [1998] B.P.I.R. 602.

On the meaning of "person aggrieved", see the remarks of Warner J. (obiter) in *Re ACLI Metals (London) Ltd (AML Holdings Inc v Auger)* (1989) 5 B.C.C. 749 at 754; and *Re Edennote Ltd* (above) at 721–722. Apart from creditors and contributories, those who may apply are not "any outsider" who is dissatisfied with some act or decision of a liquidator, but rather persons directly affected by a power given specifically to a liquidator, such as a landlord following the disclaimer of a lease: *Mahomed v Morris* [2001] B.C.C. 233.

S.168(5A)–(5C)

These subsections were inserted by the Insolvent Partnerships Order 1994 (SI 1994/2421) arts 1, 14(1) with effect from December 1, 1994. Subsection (5C) was briefly repealed by SI 2001/3649 arts 1, 306 as from December 1, 2001 and then reinstated in revised form by SI 2002/1555 arts 1, 15 as from July 3, 2002. They empower the court to make appropriate orders when a winding-up petition has been presented against any person (including a company, partnership or other body) and it appears that that person is a member of an insolvent partnership. Similar provisions apply in regard to bankruptcy petitions: see s.303(2A)–(2C).

169 Supplementary powers (Scotland)

169(1) [Where no liquidation committee] In the case of a winding up in Scotland, the court may provide by order that the liquidator may, where there is no liquidation committee, exercise any of the following powers, namely–

(a)   to bring or defend any action or other legal proceeding in the name and on behalf of the company, or

(b)   to carry on the business of the company so far as may be necessary for its beneficial winding up, without the sanction or intervention of the court.

169(2)   [Liquidator's powers] In a winding up by the court in Scotland, the liquidator has (subject to the rules) the same powers as a trustee on a bankrupt estate.

S.169(1)
This provision allows the court to dispense with the need for its own sanction where there is no liquidation committee. Where there is such a committee, one or other of the sanctions specified in s.167(1)(a) must be obtained.

S.169(2)
For the powers of the trustee on a bankrupt estate in Scotland, see the Bankruptcy (Scotland) Act 1985, especially ss.38 et seq. For the relevant rules see the Insolvency (Scotland) Rules 1986 (SI 1986/1915 (S 139)) r.4.68.

170   Enforcement of liquidator's duty to make returns, etc.

170(1)   [Powers of court if liquidator fails to file returns, etc.] If a liquidator who has made any default–

(a)   in filing, delivering or making any return, account or other document, or

(b)   in giving any notice which he is by law required to file, deliver, make or give,

fails to make good the default within 14 days after the service on him of a notice requiring him to do so, the court has the following powers.

170(2)   [On application court may order to make good default] On an application made by any creditor or contributory of the company, or by the registrar of companies, the court may make an order directing the liquidator to make good the default within such time as may be specified in the order.

170(3)   [Costs] The court's order may provide that all costs of and incidental to the application shall be borne by the liquidator.

170(4)   [Penalties] Nothing in this section prejudices the operation of any enactment imposing penalties on a liquidator in respect of any such default as is mentioned above.

GENERAL NOTE

This section contains provisions parallel to those in CA 2006 s.1113, which deal with the enforcement of such defaults against the company itself and its officers and are, of course, not confined to a winding up. A liquidator is not normally an "officer" for the purposes of the Companies Acts: see the note to s.206(3).

Removal; vacation of office

171   Removal, etc. (voluntary winding up)

171(1)   [Application] This section applies with respect to the removal from office and vacation of office of the liquidator of a company which is being wound up voluntarily.

171(2)   [Removal from office] Subject to the next subsection, the liquidator may be removed from office only by an order of the court or–

(a)   in the case of a members' voluntary winding up, by a general meeting of the company summoned specially for that purpose, or

(b)   in the case of a creditors' voluntary winding up, by a general meeting of the company's creditors summoned specially for that purpose in accordance with the rules.

171(3)   **[Where liquidator appointed by court under s.108]** Where the liquidator was appointed by the court under section 108 in Chapter V, a meeting such as is mentioned in subsection (2) above shall be summoned for the purpose of replacing him only if he thinks fit or the court so directs or the meeting is requested, in accordance with the rules–

    (a)   in the case of a members' voluntary winding up, by members representing not less than one-half of the total voting rights of all the members having at the date of the request a right to vote at the meeting, or

    (b)   in the case of a creditors' voluntary winding up, by not less than one-half, in value, of the company's creditors.

171(4)   **[Vacation of office]** A liquidator shall vacate office if he ceases to be a person who is qualified to act as an insolvency practitioner in relation to the company.

171(5)   **[Resignation]** A liquidator may, in the prescribed circumstances, resign his office by giving notice of his resignation to the registrar of companies.

171(6)   **[Where final meetings held]** Where–

    (a)   in the case of a members' voluntary winding up, a final meeting of the company has been held under section 94 in Chapter III, or

    (b)   in the case of a creditors' voluntary winding up, final meetings of the company and of the creditors have been held under section 106 in Chapter IV,

the liquidator whose report was considered at the meeting or meetings shall vacate office as soon as he has complied with subsection (3) of that section and has given notice to the registrar of companies that the meeting or meetings have been held and of the decisions (if any) of the meeting or meetings.

GENERAL NOTE

This section sets out in detail the manner by which a liquidator in a voluntary winding up may be removed or resign from his office, and the circumstances in which he must vacate it. It complements s.172, which applies in a winding up by the court. Together, the two sections set out the legal position comprehensively and in some detail, in sharp contrast to the situation prior to IA 1985, where the legislation said virtually nothing about the matter (apart from CA 1985 s.599(2), now IA 1986 s.108(2), empowering the court to remove a liquidator "on cause shown"). An important consequence of this change is that the power of the company or of the contributories in general meeting to remove the liquidator in a creditors' voluntary winding up—even a liquidator whom they have themselves appointed—is no longer recognised.

On "block transfers", see the note to s.172.

For the liquidator's duties on vacating office, see IR 1986 rr.4.138, 4.148. A liquidator who ought to have resigned but instead resists an application for his removal may be ordered to pay costs on an indemnity basis: *Shepheard v Lamey* [2001] B.P.I.R. 939.

On a petition for the compulsory winding up of a company which is already in voluntary liquidation, the court may decline to make an order where a more appropriate course would be to allow the voluntary winding up to continue and apply to the court to have the liquidator removed and replaced: see *Re Inside Sports Ltd* [2000] B.C.C. 40 at 43 (where on the special facts of the case a winding-up order was considered more appropriate).

S.171(1), (2)

The members may remove a liquidator only in a members' voluntary winding up. The creditors alone have this power in a creditors' winding up, even where the liquidator was originally appointed by the members under s.100(2).

For the rules prescribed for the purposes of s.171(2)(b), see IR 1986 rr.4.114, 4.120.

S.171(3)

Section 108 empowers the court to appoint a liquidator in a voluntary winding up in the circumstances there set out. A liquidator so appointed may be removed:

    (1)   "on cause shown", by order of the court (s.108(2));

    (2)   by the members or the creditors under s.171(2), if the liquidator himself thinks it "fit" to summon a meeting for the purpose (s.171(3));

(3)   by the members or the creditors under s.171(2) if the court so directs (s.171(3)); or

(4)   by the members or the creditors under s.171(2), if the meeting is requested by members or creditors, as the case may be, having the necessary 50 per cent-plus majority stipulated for by s.171(3)(a) or (b).

An application to have a liquidator removed under this section failed in *SISU Capital Fund Ltd v Tucker* [2005] EWHC 2170 and 2321 (Ch); [2006] B.C.C. 463.

For the relevant rules, see IR 1986 r.4.114.

S.171(4)

The terms "act as an insolvency practitioner in relation to" a particular company, and "qualified to act as an insolvency practitioner" are defined respectively in s.388(1) and s.390.

When a liquidator ceases to be qualified to act as an insolvency practitioner in relation to a company, he vacates office ipso facto and automatically, and does not continue in office until he has complied with his obligations under the rules to notify the registrar, etc. However, the former liquidator in a voluntary liquidation who has vacated office on the ground of disqualification is a proper person to make application to the court under s.108 to have another liquidator appointed in his place (*Re A J Adams (Builders) Ltd* [1991] B.C.C. 62).

For the relevant rules, see IR 1986 rr.4.135, 4.122.

S.171(5)

The circumstances in which a liquidator may resign are defined in IR 1986 rr.4.108(4), 4.142(3). Before resigning his office, the liquidator must summon a meeting of the company or the creditors (depending upon the category of winding up) for the purpose of receiving his resignation (rr.4.108(1), 4.142(1)). (However, the court has an overriding power to make an order dispensing with this requirement: see the note to s.172(1), (2).) The notice to the registrar must be given by the liquidator "as soon as reasonably practicable after the meeting" (r.4.110(2)). The meeting may decline to accept the resignation, in which event the liquidator may apply to the court for leave to resign (r.4.111).

S.171(6)

If the meeting in question was inquorate, so that the liquidator's report could not be considered, s.94(5) and s.106(5) respectively state that the liquidator shall be deemed to have complied with the requirements of the section in question. It would seem therefore that the words "whose report was considered at the meeting" in the present subsection should be taken to include such cases of deemed compliance.

172   Removal, etc. (winding up by the court)

172(1)   [Application] This section applies with respect to the removal from office and vacation of office of the liquidator of a company which is being wound up by the court, or of a provisional liquidator.

172(2)   [Removal from office] Subject as follows, the liquidator may be removed from office only by an order of the court or by a general meeting of the company's creditors summoned specially for that purpose in accordance with the rules; and a provisional liquidator may be removed from office only by an order of the court.

172(3)   [Replacing certain types of liquidator] Where–

(a)   the official receiver is liquidator otherwise than in succession under section 136(3) to a person who held office as a result of a nomination by a meeting of the company's creditors or contributories, or

(b)   the liquidator was appointed by the court otherwise than under section 139(4)(a) or 140(1), or was appointed by the Secretary of State,

a general meeting of the company's creditors shall be summoned for the purpose of replacing him only if he thinks fit, or the court so directs, or the meeting is requested, in accordance with the rules, by not less than one-quarter, in value, of the creditors.

172(4)   [If liquidator appointed by Secretary of State] If appointed by the Secretary of State, the liquidator may be removed from office by a direction of the Secretary of State.

172(5) **[Vacation of office]** A liquidator or provisional liquidator, not being the official receiver, shall vacate office if he ceases to be a person who is qualified to act as an insolvency practitioner in relation to the company.

172(6) **[Resignation]** A liquidator may, in the prescribed circumstances, resign his office by giving notice of his resignation to the court.

172(7) **[Where s.204 order]** Where an order is made under section 204 (early dissolution in Scotland) for the dissolution of the company, the liquidator shall vacate office when the dissolution of the company takes effect in accordance with that section.

172(8) **[Where final meeting under s.146]** Where a final meeting has been held under section 146 (liquidator's report on completion of winding up), the liquidator whose report was considered at the meeting shall vacate office as soon as he has given notice to the court and the registrar of companies that the meeting has been held and of the decisions (if any) of the meeting.

GENERAL NOTE

This section contains provisions, complementary to those in s.171, which apply in a compulsory winding up. The notes to s.171 apply generally to the present section also, subject to the additional points below.

S.172(1), (2)
A provisional liquidator may be removed only by court order.

The exercise by the court of its power to replace the liquidator originally appointed is a matter of discretion for the trial judge, which will not be lightly disturbed on appeal: *Parmalat Capital Finance Ltd v Food Holdings Ltd* [2008] UKPC 23; [2008] B.C.C. 371.

There is nothing in the present section which empowers the shareholders or contributories in general meeting to remove a liquidator, even in cases where the company is demonstrably solvent, and even where the original liquidator was the members' appointee.

Where a liquidator who has been appointed by the creditors wishes to vacate office, the creditors have the right to decide whether to accept his resignation and the court will not exercise its own power to do so without good reason: see *Re Sankey Furniture Ltd Ex p. Harding* [1995] 2 B.C.L.C. 594.

"Block transfer" orders: although r.4.108(1) appears to make it mandatory for the liquidator to call a meeting of creditors before resigning his office, the court has an overriding power to by-pass this procedure and make orders for his removal and replacement without the statutory formalities. This course is particularly appropriate where the insolvency practitioner concerned wishes to be relieved from multiple offices by making a single application. The terms on which such orders have been made in the past were examined by Neuberger J. in *Re Equity Nominees Ltd* [2000] B.C.C. 84 and a new form of order settled, dealing with the information to be given to creditors and the manner in which the outgoing liquidator should deal with the accounts of his administration. The *Practice Direction: Insolvency Proceedings* [2007] B.C.C. 824 (reproduced as App.IV of this *Guide*) para.1.6 was introduced to give practical guidance on the procedure in these cases, and this PD has been augmented (and in some respects varied) by the new Chapter 1A inserted into Pt 7 of the Rules by I(A)R 2010. The changes from the PD are as follows:

- the application may be made to the registrar in the first instance;

- an application may be made to a county court with insolvency jurisdiction where all the cases that are the subject of the application are in the county court; not all of the office-holder's cases need be the subject of the block transfer order;

- the outgoing office-holder's cases may be transferred to more than one replacement office-holder.

See also *Re Alt Landscapes Ltd* [1999] B.P.I.R. 459; *Re A & C Supplies Ltd* [1998] B.C.C. 708; *Clements v Udal* [2002] 2 B.C.L.C. 606; *Customs and Excise Commissioners v Allen* [2003] B.P.I.R. 830; and *Re a Licence Holder, Saville v Gerrard* [2004] EWHC 1363 (Ch); [2005] B.C.C. 433. It appears that such an order cannot be back-dated: *Darrell v Miller* [2003] EWHC 2811 (Ch); [2004] B.P.I.R. 470.

The legal authority for the making of block transfer orders was challenged (in relation to the replacement of a trustee in bankruptcy) in *Donaldson v O'Sullivan* [2008] EWHC 387 (Ch); [2008] B.C.C. 328; on appeal [2008] EWCA Civ 879; [2009] B.C.C. 99. The legitimacy of the procedure was upheld, specifically as regards bankruptcy under s.303(2), and more generally in relation to other insolvencies under the general powers of the court.

A similar procedure for block transfers, by-passing the formalities of the Insolvency (Scotland) Rules 1986 rr.4.28–4.29, has received the blessing of the Scottish courts: *Geddes, Petitioner*, 2006 S.L.T. 664.

A contributory holding fully-paid shares in an insolvent company has no standing to apply to the court for an order removing a liquidator, on the analogy of *Re Rica Gold Washing Co* (1879) 11 Ch. D. 36 (see the note to s.124(2), (3) above): *Re Corbenstoke Ltd (No.2)* (1989) 5 B.C.C. 767.

For the rules prescribed for the purposes of s.172, see IR 1986 rr.4.113 et seq.

S.172(3)
The liquidator may be removed by a general meeting of the creditors without any special formality under s.172(2) above only where:

(1)   he was originally appointed by a meeting of the company's creditors or contributories (s.172(2));

(2)   the official receiver is liquidator in succession to a person who was appointed as in (1) (s.172(3)(a));

(3)   the liquidator was a nominee of the contributories whom the court appointed liquidator either jointly with, or instead of, a nominee of the creditors (ss.139(4)(a), 172(3)(b)); or

(4)   the liquidator was formerly the administrator of the company who was appointed by the court when the winding-up order was made immediately upon the termination of the administration (ss.140(1), 172(3)(b)).

The special preconditions to the summoning of the creditors' general meeting will apply, however, where the official receiver is liquidator otherwise than in (2) above, where the liquidator was appointed by the Secretary of State, or where the liquidator was appointed by the court otherwise than in (3) or (4) above. (Note that this will include, first, a "neutral" liquidator who is appointed on the court's own nomination under s.139(4)(b), following a disagreement between the creditors' and the contributories' meetings, and, secondly, a liquidator appointed by the court under s.140(2), who was formerly the supervisor of a CVA.) In contrast with s.171(3), the percentage of creditors necessary to request a meeting under s.172(2) is one-quarter, rather than "not less than one-half".

The court will not direct a meeting under s.172(3) unless it is satisfied that it is in the best interests of the liquidation to do so: *Managa Properties Ltd v Brittain* [2009] EWHC 157 (Ch); [2009] B.P.I.R. 306.

S.172(4)
This power is additional to that of the court under s.172(2) and that of the creditors under s.172(3)(b). For the relevant rules, see IR 1986 r.4.123.

S.172(5)
For the relevant rules, see IR 1986 rr.4.134, 4.138(1).

S.172(6)
The relevant circumstances are prescribed by IR 1986 r.4.108(4).

S.172(8)
When the liquidator vacates office pursuant to this provision, he must deliver up the company's books and records to the official receiver: see IR 1986 r.4.138(3).

Release of liquidator

173   Release (voluntary winding up)

173(1)   [Application] This section applies with respect to the release of the liquidator of a company which is being wound up voluntarily.

173(2)   [Time of release] A person who has ceased to be a liquidator shall have his release with effect from the following time, that is to say–

(a)   in the case of a person who has been removed from office by a general meeting of the company or by a general meeting of the company's creditors that has not resolved against his release or who has died, the time at which notice is given to the registrar of companies in accordance with the rules that that person has ceased to hold office;

(b)   in the case of a person who has been removed from office by a general meeting of the company's creditors that has resolved against his release, or by the court, or who has vacated office under section 171(4) above, such time as the Secretary of State may, on the application of that person, determine;

   (c)   in the case of a person who has resigned, such time as may be prescribed;

   (d)   in the case of a person who has vacated office under subsection (6)(a) of section 171, the time at which he vacated office;

   (e)   in the case of a person who has vacated office under subsection (6)(b) of that section–

      (i)   if the final meeting of the creditors referred to in that subsection has resolved against that person's release, such time as the Secretary of State may, on an application by that person, determine, and

      (ii)   if that meeting has not resolved against that person's release, the time at which he vacated office.

173(3)   **[Application to Scotland]** In the application of subsection (2) to the winding up of a company registered in Scotland, the references to a determination by the Secretary of State as to the time from which a person who has ceased to be liquidator shall have his release are to be read as references to such a determination by the Accountant of Court.

173(4)   **[Effect of release]** Where a liquidator has his release under subsection (2), he is, with effect from the time specified in that subsection, discharged from all liability both in respect of acts or omissions of his in the winding up and otherwise in relation to his conduct as liquidator.

    But nothing in this section prevents the exercise, in relation to a person who has had his release under subsection (2), of the court's powers under section 212 of this Act (summary remedy against delinquent directors, liquidators, etc.).

S.173(1)

For the corresponding provisions relating to a winding up by the court, see s.174. The effect of a release is stated in s.173(4).

S.173(2), (3)

The times at which the release of a liquidator becomes effective in different circumstances are set out in the various paragraphs of this subsection. For the relevant rules, see IR 1986 rr.4.111(2), 4.114(2), 4.122 and 4.126 (creditors' voluntary winding up) and rr.4.126A, 4.144 and 4.147 (members' voluntary winding up).

    It is open to the members' or creditors' meeting to resolve against the release of a liquidator in the cases mentioned in paras (b) and (e)(i). The question of a release is then a matter for the Secretary of State (or, in Scotland, the Accountant of Court) to determine.

S.173(4)

The terms of this subsection are in all material respects the same as those of s.20(2), (3), relating to the release of an administrator: see, further, the notes to that section.

174   Release (winding up by the court)

174(1)   **[Application]** This section applies with respect to the release of the liquidator of a company which is being wound up by the court, or of a provisional liquidator.

174(2)   **[Where official receiver ceases to be liquidator]** Where the official receiver has ceased to be liquidator and a person becomes liquidator in his stead, the official receiver has his release with effect from the following time, that is to say–

   (a)   in a case where that person was nominated by a general meeting of creditors or contributories, or was appointed by the Secretary of State, the time at which the official receiver gives notice to the court that he has been replaced;

   (b)   in a case where that person is appointed by the court, such time as the court may determine.

174(3)   **[Where official receiver gives notice to Secretary of State]** If the official receiver while he is a liquidator gives notice to the Secretary of State that the winding up is for practical purposes complete, he has his release with effect from such time as the Secretary of State may determine.

174(4) **[Person other than official receiver]** A person other than the official receiver who has ceased to be a liquidator has his release with effect from the following time, that is to say–

    (a) in the case of a person who has been removed from office by a general meeting of creditors that has not resolved against his release or who has died, the time at which notice is given to the court in accordance with the rules that that person has ceased to hold office;

    (b) in the case of a person who has been removed from office by a general meeting of creditors that has resolved against his release, or by the court or the Secretary of State, or who has vacated office under section 172(5) or (7), such time as the Secretary of State may, on an application by that person, determine;

    (c) in the case of a person who has resigned, such time as may be prescribed;

    (d) in the case of a person who has vacated office under section 172(8)–

        (i) if the final meeting referred to in that subsection has resolved against that person's release, such time as the Secretary of State may, on an application by that person, determine, and

        (ii) if that meeting has not so resolved, the time at which that person vacated office.

174(5) **[Provisional liquidator]** A person who has ceased to hold office as a provisional liquidator has his release with effect from such time as the court may, on an application by him, determine.

174(6) **[Effect of release]** Where the official receiver or a liquidator or provisional liquidator has his release under this section, he is, with effect from the time specified in the preceding provisions of this section, discharged from all liability both in respect of acts or omissions of his in the winding up and otherwise in relation to his conduct as liquidator or provisional liquidator.

But nothing in this section prevents the exercise, in relation to a person who has had his release under this section, of the court's powers under section 212 (summary remedy against delinquent directors, liquidators, etc.).

174(7) **[Application to Scotland]** In the application of this section to a case where the order for winding up has been made by the court in Scotland, the references to a determination by the Secretary of State as to the time from which a person who has ceased to be liquidator has his release are to such a determination by the Accountant of Court.

S.174(1)
Section 173 deals with the corresponding questions in a voluntary liquidation.

S.174(2), (3)
These two subsections govern the release of the official receiver as liquidator. Necessarily, of course, they apply only in England and Wales.

    For the relevant rules, see IR 1986 r.4.124.

S.174(4)
The provisions of this subsection are broadly parallel to those of s.173(2). For the rules prescribed for the purposes of s.174, see IR 1986 rr.4.113, 4.121–4.125.

S.174(6)
See the corresponding provisions relating to an administrator (s.20(2), (3)) and a liquidator in a voluntary winding up (s.173(4)).

CHAPTER VIII

PROVISIONS OF GENERAL APPLICATION IN WINDING UP

Introductory note to Part IV, Chapter VIII
Those familiar with the former law relating to company liquidations, as contained in CA 1985 and its predecessors, would naturally expect to find at about this point in the present Act provisions corresponding to CA 1985 ss.611–613.

The first of these sections dealt with the question of debts provable in a liquidation, set-off, and related questions. The debts provable in a liquidation are now dealt with in IR 1986 Chapter 9 (rr.4.73 et seq., and especially r.4.86 et seq.), and rr.12.3 and 13.12, while the questions of mutual credit and set-off are provided for by r.4.90. The corresponding provisions for bankruptcy continue to be set out in primary legislation and are to be found in ss.382 and 323, respectively.

Preferential debts

175   Preferential debts (general provision)

175(1)   **[Payment in priority]** In a winding up the company's preferential debts (within the meaning given by section 386 in Part XII) shall be paid in priority to all other debts.

175(2)   **[Ranking and priority]** Preferential debts–

(a)   rank equally among themselves after the expenses of the winding up and shall be paid in full, unless the assets are insufficient to meet them, in which case they abate in equal proportions; and

(b)   so far as the assets of the company available for payment of general creditors are insufficient to meet them, have priority over the claims of holders of debentures secured by, or holders of, any floating charge created by the company, and shall be paid accordingly out of any property comprised in or subject to that charge.

GENERAL NOTE

Rules giving certain categories of unsecured debt priority in a bankruptcy or winding up have been a feature of the legislation for over a century. However, the impact of this provision (and the corresponding section in bankruptcy, s.328) has been significantly reduced following the abolition of the Crown's priority in regard to PAYE, NIC contributions and VAT, effected by EA 2002 s.251.

Until *Re Leyland DAF Ltd, Buchler v Talbot* [2004] UKHL 9; [2004] 2 A.C. 298; [2004] B.C.C. 214 it was understood that it was not only the preferential debts, but also the expenses of the liquidation, that had to be paid in priority to the holder of a floating charge; but the *Leyland DAF* decision reversed this ruling. The reversal was, however, only temporary, for the Companies Act 2006 s.1282, has reinstated the former interpretation: see s.176ZA, below. In *Re BHT (UK) Ltd* [2004] EWHC 201 (Ch); [2004] B.C.C. 301 the company was in receivership and realisations of the charged property had been paid to the chargee in the belief that the charge was a fixed charge. The question for the court was whether, if the charge was in fact a floating charge, either the company or its liquidator could claim from the chargee the amounts payable to the preferential creditors. The court ruled to the contrary: any claim which the preferential creditors might wish to make could be done by them in their own right.

A further change made by the insolvency legislation of 1985 was to bring into line, not only the law of company insolvency and individual bankruptcy, but also that of CVAs, receiverships and individual voluntary arrangements, so that the same rules set out in Sch.6 apply to them all.

Note that there was no provision for preferential debts in a company administration under the original IA 1986 Pt II, except where the administration was linked with a voluntary arrangement (s.387(2)) or where a winding-up order immediately followed upon the discharge of the administration order (s.387(3)(a)). However, a new subs.(3A) has been added to s.387, which applies to all administrations from September 15, 2003, bringing administrations into line with other insolvency procedures in this respect. See the notes to that provision.

The Companies Act 2006 s.754 makes similar provision for priority to be given to the preferential debts where (if the company is not being wound up) possession is taken by or on behalf of the holder of a floating charge of assets subject to the charge. In *Customs and Excise Commissioners v Royal Bank of Scotland plc, Re Oval 1742 Ltd* [2007] EWCA Civ 1262; [2008] B.C.C. 135 the court adopted a broad approach to the interpretation of this provision, holding that where certain assets were released from the defendant bank's charge and sold by the company, and a substantial part of the proceeds paid to the bank, it had "taken possession" of these proceeds. In substance there had been a realisation of the bank's security. Other proceeds which had been paid to the bank after the company had gone into liquidation were held to rank after the preferential debts in accordance with s.175(2)(b).

In relation to payment and securities settlement systems, where "collateral security" (as defined in the Finality Regulations reg.2(1)) has been provided by a company to which those regulations apply, the claim of a participant or central bank to such security must be paid in priority to the expenses of the winding up, remuneration and preferential debts, unless the terms on which the security was provided expressly state that the expenses, remuneration and preferential debts shall have priority (Finality Regulations reg.14(5), (6)). (See the introductory note at p.3 above.)

S.175(2)(a)
Expenses incurred by a liquidator in pursuing claims under ss.127 (post-petition dispositions), 214 (wrongful trading), 238 (transactions at an undervalue) and 239 (preferences) were held not to be "expenses of the liquidation" in a number of cases, culminating with *Re Floor Fourteen Ltd, Lewis v IRC* [2001] 3 All E.R. 499; [2002] B.C.C. 198. But an amendment to IR 1986 r.4.218 has reversed these rulings: see the note to that rule.

S.175(2)(b)
This important provision continues the rule, laid down in successive Companies Acts, which subordinates the claims of a secured creditor holding a floating charge (but not a fixed charge) to those of the preferential creditors. A similar rule applies in a receivership (ss.40, 59).

However, the application of the rule is now different because the statutory definition of a floating charge has been reworded, so that it includes any charge which, *as created*, was a floating charge (see s.251). In consequence, any charge which was originally a floating charge but has become a fixed charge (e.g. by crystallisation, or by a notice of conversion) before the "relevant date" defined by s.387 will now be subordinated to the preferential debts under the present section. The decisions in *Re Woodroffes (Musical Instruments) Ltd* [1986] Ch. 366; *Re Brightlife Ltd* [1987] Ch. 200; (1986) 2 B.C.C. 99,359; *Stein v Saywell* (1969) 121 C.L.R. 529; and *Re Griffin Hotel Co Ltd* [1941] Ch. 129, which were previously authorities to the contrary, are accordingly no longer good law.

176   Preferential charge on goods distrained

176(1)   [Application] This section applies where a company is being wound up by the court in England and Wales, and is without prejudice to section 128 (avoidance of attachments, etc.).

176(2)   [Where distraining in previous 3 months] Where any person (whether or not a landlord or person entitled to rent) has distrained upon the goods or effects of the company in the period of 3 months ending with the date of the winding-up order, those goods or effects, or the proceeds of their sale, shall be charged for the benefit of the company with the preferential debts of the company to the extent that the company's property is for the time being insufficient for meeting them.

176(3)   [Surrender of goods under s.176(2)] Where by virtue of a charge under subsection (2) any person surrenders any goods or effects to a company or makes a payment to a company, that person ranks, in respect of the amount of the proceeds of sale of those goods or effects by the liquidator or (as the case may be) the amount of the payment, as a preferential creditor of the company, except as against so much of the company's property as is available for the payment of preferential creditors by virtue of the surrender or payment.

S.176(1)
The present section does not apply in the case of a voluntary liquidation; and it will apply only if the distress is not void, under the provisions of s.128, as having been put in force after the commencement of the winding up.

S.176(2)
The effect of the subsection is to make the claims of the preferential creditors a first charge on the goods distrained or their proceeds. Note that the significant date for reckoning the three-month period is that of the winding-up *order*, and not (as in s.128) the date of commencement of the winding up, which will be earlier (see s.129).

S.176(3)
The effect of subss.(2) and (3), taken together, is as follows:

(1)   To the extent that there is property of the company (independently of the proceeds of sale or payment) available for payment of the preferential debts, the preferential creditors participate pari passu.

(2)   In regard to the proceeds of sale or payment, the person who has surrendered the goods or made the payment and the preferential creditors together rank pari passu.

Accordingly, that person is not a "postponed" preferential creditor except as regards the property referred to in para.(1) above: *Re Memco Engineering Ltd* [1986] Ch. 86; (1985) 1 B.C.C. 99,460 (a case on the repealed CA 1985 s.319(7)).

Property subject to floating charge

176ZA   Payment of expenses of winding up (England and Wales)

176ZA(1)   [Priority over floating charge assets] The expenses of winding up in England and Wales, so far as the assets of the company available for payment of general creditors are insufficient to meet them, have priority over any claims to property comprised in or subject to any floating charge created by the company and shall be paid out of any such property accordingly.

176ZA(2)   [Reference in s.176ZA(1) to assets of company, claims to property] In subsection (1)–

    (a)   the reference to assets of the company available for payment of general creditors does not include any amount made available under section 176A(2)(a);

    (b)   the reference to claims to property comprised in or subject to a floating charge is to the claims of–

        (i)   the holders of debentures secured by, or holders of, the floating charge, and

        (ii)   any preferential creditors entitled to be paid out of that property in priority to them.

176ZA(3)   [Rules may restrict s.176ZA(1)] Provision may be made by rules restricting the application of subsection (1), in such circumstances as may be prescribed, to expenses authorised or approved–

    (a)   by the holders of debentures secured by, or holders of, the floating charge and by any preferential creditors entitled to be paid in priority to them, or

    (b)   by the court.

176ZA(4)   [References to the expenses of the winding up] References in this section to the expenses of the winding up are to all expenses properly incurred in the winding up, including the remuneration of the liquidator.

GENERAL NOTE

Section 176ZA was inserted by the Companies Act 2006 s.1282 with effect from April 6, 2008: see the Companies Act 2006 (Commencement No.5, Transitional Provisions and Savings) Order 2007 (SI 2007/3495 (C. 150)) art.3(1)(v) and, for transitional provisions, the Companies Act 2006 (Commencement No.6, Saving and Commencement Nos 3 and 5 (Amendment)) Order 2008 (SI 2008/674 (C. 26)) art.5 and Sch.3 para.6(5).

This section reverses the decision of the House of Lords in *Re Leyland DAF Ltd, Buchler v Talbot* [2004] UKHL 9; [2004] 2 A.C. 298; [2004] B.C.C. 214, in which it was held that a liquidator was not entitled to claim his expenses in priority to the rights of the holder of a floating charge, and that it was immaterial whether or not the charge had crystallised before the commencement of the liquidation. This ruling overruled the decision in *Re Barleycorn Enterprises Ltd* [1970] Ch. 465, which had stood for many years and had been followed in a number of cases including *Re Portbase Clothing Ltd, Mond v Taylor* [1993] Ch. 388; [1993] B.C.C. 96. The priority rule established by *Re Barleycorn* is thus reinstated. Section 1282 was added to the Companies Bill at a late stage and before it was brought into force the Insolvency Service instituted a consultation exercise in August 2007 with a view to introducing rules to restrict the application of s.176ZA in order to provide a better balance between the various stakeholders in a liquidation. The resulting rules are rr.4.218A–4.218E.

S.176ZA(1), (3)

The scope of s.176ZA(1) is limited by the rules referred to above, which require that the liquidator should have obtained authorisation in advance, or subsequent approval, by the floating charge holder and any preferential creditor, for the incurring of expense in certain specified categories of litigation, in order to be entitled to the priority conferred by the section. The court has back-up powers to sanction the incurring of litigation expenses where authorisation or approval has not been given or where the creditor concerned is or is intended to be a defendant in the litigation (r.4.218E). The rules do not apply to litigation expenses which do not exceed £5,000 (r.4.218A(1)(d)(ii)). For further details and the procedure and transitional provisions, see the notes to rr.4.218A–4.218E.

176A   Share of assets for unsecured creditors

176A(1)   [Application of section] This section applies where a floating charge relates to property of a company–

(a) which has gone into liquidation,

(b) which is in administration,

(c) of which there is a provisional liquidator, or

(d) of which there is a receiver.

176A(2) [Prescribed part for unsecured debts] The liquidator, administrator or receiver–

(a) shall make a prescribed part of the company's net property available for the satisfaction of unsecured debts, and

(b) shall not distribute that part to the proprietor of a floating charge except in so far as it exceeds the amount required for the satisfaction of unsecured debts.

176A(3) [Non-application of s.176A(2)] Subsection (2) shall not apply to a company if–

(a) the company's net property is less than the prescribed minimum, and

(b) the liquidator, administrator or receiver thinks that the cost of making a distribution to unsecured creditors would be disproportionate to the benefits.

176A(4) [Disapplication of s.176A(2)] Subsection (2) shall also not apply to a company if or in so far as it is disapplied by–

(a) a voluntary arrangement in respect of the company, or

(b) a compromise or arrangement agreed under Part 26 of the Companies Act 2006 (arrangements and reconstructions).

176A(5) [Non-application by court order] Subsection (2) shall also not apply to a company if–

(a) the liquidator, administrator or receiver applies to the court for an order under this subsection on the ground that the cost of making a distribution to unsecured creditors would be disproportionate to the benefits, and

(b) the court orders that subsection (2) shall not apply.

176A(6) [Net property in s.176A(2), (3)] In subsections (2) and (3) a company's net property is the amount of its property which would, but for this section, be available for satisfaction of claims of holders of debentures secured by, or holders of, any floating charge created by the company.

176A(7) [Provision in order] An order under subsection (2) prescribing part of a company's net property may, in particular, provide for its calculation–

(a) as a percentage of the company's net property, or

(b) as an aggregate of different percentages of different parts of the company's net property.

176A(8) [Procedure for order] An order under this section–

(a) must be made by statutory instrument, and

(b) shall be subject to annulment pursuant to a resolution of either House of Parliament.

176A(9) ["Floating charge", "prescribed"] In this section—**"floating charge"** means a charge which is a floating charge on its creation and which is created after the first order under subsection (2)(a) comes into force, and **"prescribed"** means prescribed by order by the Secretary of State.

176A(10) [Transitional or incidental provision] An order under this section may include transitional or incidental provision.

GENERAL NOTE

This section, introduced by EA 2002 s.252 with effect from September 15, 2003, is one of the major innovations made by the 2002 Act. The measure has some parallel with a recommendation of the Cork Committee (Cmnd.8558 (1982), at para.1538) that a "10 per cent fund" should be set aside out of the net realisations of property subject to a floating charge and that this fund be made available to unsecured creditors upon the insolvency of the company. This is seen by some as a quid pro quo for the abolition of the Crown's preferential status as a creditor: without such a provision, there would simply be a windfall for the charge holder. The "prescribed part" (also referred to as the "special reserved fund" or "ring-fenced sum" for the unsecured creditors) is calculated on the net realisations of property subject to any floating (but not fixed) charge, and will be payable to the charge holder only in so far as anything remains after the unsecured creditors have been paid in full.

The amount of the prescribed part has been fixed as follows:

Where the net property does not exceed £10,000:	50% of that property
Where the net property exceeds £10,000:	50% of the first £10,000, plus 20% of the property which exceeds £10,000, up to a maximum prescribed part of £600,000.

(See the Insolvency Act 1986 (Prescribed Part) Order 2003 (SI 2003/2097), effective September 15, 2003.)

Subsections (3)–(5) set out various situations in which the obligation to set aside a prescribed part does not apply.

Rule 12.2(2) states that the costs associated with the prescribed part shall be paid out of that part. For other relevant rules, see rr.3.39–3.40, 4.43, 4.49, 4.124–4.126A, 7.3A and 7.4A.

On the application of this provision to insolvent partnerships, see the Insolvent Partnerships (Amendment) Order 2006 (SI 2006/622, effective April 6, 2006), which corrects errors contained in earlier legislation.

S.176A(1)

The section only applies where there is a floating charge. Paragraph (d) would therefore not apply to a fixed-charge receivership, but it would apply to any other kind of receivership, including an administrative receivership and a court-appointed receivership (for confirmation, see r.3.39). An administrative receiver is excluded from r.3.39(1)(a) only because he already has reporting obligations under s.48.

There is no obligation to set aside a prescribed part where a charge holder, instead of appointing a receiver, enters into possession (personally or through an agent) under CA 2006 s.754.

S.176A(2), (6)

The office-holder is required by s.176A only to set the prescribed part aside: this section does not authorise him to make a distribution (for which the consent of the court may be required: see, e.g. Sch.B1 para.65(3)). Where there are preferential creditors, the prescribed part is reckoned by reference to net property remaining after their claims have been satisfied, i.e. out of the property which is available to be paid to the floating charge holder.

Section 176A(2)(b) does not make any specific provision for the case where a floating charge secures only part of the debt owed to the charge holder, leaving the remainder of the debt unsecured. Two judicial decisions now make it clear that the charge holder is not entitled to claim any part of the prescribed part in respect of his unsecured surplus: *Re Permacell Finesse Ltd* [2007] EWHC 3233 (Ch); [2008] B.C.C. 208; and *Re Airbase Services (UK) Ltd* [2008] EWHC 124 (Ch); [2008] 1 W.L.R. 1516; [2008] B.C.C. 213. In the latter case Patten J. held that the section applied to all charge holders, whether their charge was floating or fixed, so as to prohibit them from participating in the prescribed part in respect of an unsecured surplus. Both categories of charge holder will, of course, continue to be entitled to prove in the liquidation for the unsecured part of their debt, but this will be of value only in those cases where both the prescribed part and the secured part of the floating charge holder's debt have been fully met and there are still funds available for distribution.

S.176A(3)–(5)

These provisions can be invoked in order to excuse the office-holder from his obligation to set aside the prescribed part in the following situations:

- where the net property is less than the prescribed minimum (fixed by SI 2003/2097 para.2 at £10,000) and he thinks that the cost of making a distribution to the unsecured creditors would be disproportionate to the benefits (for examples of the exercise of this jurisdiction, see *Re Hydroserve Ltd* [2007] EWHC 3026 (Ch); [2008] B.C.C. 175; *Re Courts plc* [2008] EWHC 2339 (Ch); [2008] B.C.C. 917; *Re International Sections Ltd* [2009] EWHC 137 (Ch); [2009] B.C.C. 574);

- where the net property is £10,000 or more and the office-holder applies to the court for an order disapplying subs.(2) on the same ground; or

- where it is disapplied by the terms of a CVA or scheme of compromise or arrangement under CA 2006 Pt 26.

In *Re Courts plc* (above) it was held that there could be no selective disapplication of s.176A(2): the provision must be applied in its entirety to all creditors, or not at all (even if, in the case of smaller creditors, the cost of distribution would exceed what they would receive). In *Re International Sections Ltd* (above), where the distribution would have been under 1.5 pence in the pound, it was said that dispensation under s.176A(5) should be the exception rather than the rule. Permission was refused: it was held that regard should be had to the position of the unsecured creditors as a body and not to the fact that the dividend for each creditor would be small. It was also held that "costs" in IR 1986 r.12.2 included the liquidator's charges for making the distribution.

Rules 7.3A and 7.4A deal with the procedure where application is made to the court under s.176A(5).

S.176A(9)

This section applies only in relation to floating charges that are *created* after the section is brought into force (i.e. on or after September 15, 2003). Where the relevant insolvency proceedings are instituted on or after that date but the charge was created on an earlier date, the charge holder will get the best of both worlds, enjoying the benefit of the abolition of the Crown's preference but not being subject to the deduction of the prescribed part.

Special managers

177   Power to appoint special manager

177(1)   [Power of court] Where a company has gone into liquidation or a provisional liquidator has been appointed, the court may, on an application under this section, appoint any person to be the special manager of the business or property of the company.

177(2)   [Application to court] The application may be made by the liquidator or provisional liquidator in any case where it appears to him that the nature of the business or property of the company, or the interests of the company's creditors or contributories or members generally, require the appointment of another person to manage the company's business or property.

177(3)   [Powers of special manager] The special manager has such powers as may be entrusted to him by the court.

177(4)   [Extent of s.177(3) powers] The court's power to entrust powers to the special manager includes power to direct that any provision of this Act that has effect in relation to the provisional liquidator or liquidator of a company shall have the like effect in relation to the special manager for the purposes of the carrying out by him of any of the functions of the provisional liquidator or liquidator.

177(5)   [Duties of special manager] The special manager shall–

(a)   give such security or, in Scotland, caution as may be prescribed;

(b)   prepare and keep such accounts as may be prescribed; and

(c)   produce those accounts in accordance with the rules to the Secretary of State or to such other persons as may be prescribed.

GENERAL NOTE

The former CA 1985 s.556 provided for the appointment of a special manager when the official receiver became the liquidator or provisional liquidator of a company. The present section extends this facility to all liquidators, and now applies also to Scotland. The appointment of a special manager allows a liquidator to have assistance from someone with particular managerial or commercial expertise that he may not have himself.

A special manager is not required to be qualified to act as an insolvency practitioner: indeed, there may be a particular need to invoke the present section when the skills in question are those which an insolvency practitioner does not normally have. (There is no longer the option of bringing in such an expert in the role of liquidator, or joint liquidator, unless by chance he is also qualified under this Act for appointment.)

In *Re W F Fearman Ltd (No.2)* (1988) 4 B.C.C. 141 the court gave leave to the official receiver to use the services of the outgoing provisional liquidators as special managers, in order to maintain continuity in the administration of the insolvency pending the choice by a creditors' meeting of liquidators on a permanent basis.

S.177(1), (2)
The appointment must in all cases be made by the court, on the application of the liquidator or provisional liquidator himself.

S.177(3), (4)
The powers of a special manager are determined in each case by the court, and they may be made subject to any statutory provision that applies to a liquidator—e.g. an obligation to obtain the consent of the liquidation committee on particular matters.

S.177(5)
The rules prescribed for the purposes of this section are to be found in IR 1986 Ch.18 (rr.4.206 et seq.).

Disclaimer (England and Wales only)

178   Power to disclaim onerous property

178(1)   [Application] This and the next two sections apply to a company that is being wound up in England and Wales.

178(2)   [Disclaimer by liquidator] Subject as follows, the liquidator may, by the giving of the prescribed notice, disclaim any onerous property and may do so notwithstanding that he has taken possession of it, endeavoured to sell it, or otherwise exercised rights of ownership in relation to it.

178(3)   [Onerous property] The following is onerous property for the purposes of this section–

(a)   any unprofitable contract, and

(b)   any other property of the company which is unsaleable or not readily saleable or is such that it may give rise to a liability to pay money or perform any other onerous act.

178(4)   [Effect of disclaimer] A disclaimer under this section–

(a)   operates so as to determine, as from the date of the disclaimer, the rights, interests and liabilities of the company in or in respect of the property disclaimed; but

(b)   does not, except so far as is necessary for the purpose of releasing the company from any liability, affect the rights or liabilities of any other person.

178(5)   [Where notice of disclaimer not to be given] A notice of disclaimer shall not be given under this section in respect of any property if–

(a)   a person interested in the property has applied in writing to the liquidator or one of his predecessors as liquidator requiring the liquidator or that predecessor to decide whether he will disclaim or not, and

(b)   the period of 28 days beginning with the day on which that application was made, or such longer period as the court may allow, has expired without a notice of disclaimer having been given under this section in respect of that property.

178(6)   [Persons sustaining loss etc.] Any person sustaining loss or damage in consequence of the operation of a disclaimer under this section is deemed a creditor of the company to the extent of the loss or damage and accordingly may prove for the loss or damage in the winding up.

GENERAL NOTE

Sections 178–182 enlarge and, in some respects, modify the law regarding disclaimer which was formerly contained in CA 1985 ss.618, 619 and 629. These provisions apply only in England and Wales. They correspond to the bankruptcy rules set out in ss.315 et seq., below.

In the context of the financial markets, s.178 does not apply in relation to a market contract or a contract effected by an exchange or clearing house for the purpose of realising property provided as margin in relation to market contracts: see CA 1989 s.164(1). The section is also disapplied by the Finality Regulations reg.16(1) in relation to a transfer order or a contract for the purpose of realising security in payment and securities settlement systems. (See the notes on pp.2–3 above.)

A waste management licence is "property", or alternatively an interest incidental to property, which may be disclaimed under the section: *Celtic Extraction Ltd & Bluestone Chemicals Ltd v Environment Agency* [2001] Ch. 475; [2000] B.C.C. 487 (overruling *Re Mineral Resources Ltd* [1999] B.C.C. 422, in which Neuberger J. had held that a licence could not be disclaimed because that would be inconsistent with the Environmental Protection Act 1990).

In *Environment Agency v Hillridge Ltd* [2003] EWHC 3023 (Ch); [2004] 2 B.C.L.C. 358 the company had created a trust fund to cover the cost of remedial work at its landfill site after waste tipping ceased. It was held, following the *Celtic Extraction* decision, that the disclaimer of the lease of the site put an end to the company's waste management licence, but that the trusts were not terminated. However, the trust fund did not become repayable to the company or pass to the control of the Environmental Agency: as bona vacantia it reverted to the Crown.

S.178(2)
Under the former law as contained in CA 1985, only the official receiver was empowered to disclaim property on his own authority; any other liquidator was required to obtain the leave of the court. Every liquidator may now exercise the power to disclaim without leave. It is left to the person affected by the proposed disclaimer to take his objection to the court, if he has one. However, the effect of the change in the law removing the requirement of leave is to make the liquidator's decision to disclaim primarily a matter for his discretion, similar to his other powers in the management and realisation of the company's property, which will normally be reviewed by the court only if it has been exercised mala fide or perversely. Cases relating to the granting of leave under the former law are now irrelevant (*Re Hans Place Ltd* [1992] B.C.C. 737).

A notice of disclaimer must now be "in the prescribed form": see IR 1986 r.4.187, and Form 4.53. For the rules regulating the procedure generally, see IR 1986 Ch.15 (rr.4.187 et seq.).

The 12-month time limit which was formerly imposed by CA 1985 s.618(3) has been abolished.

S.178(3)
This is a new and wider definition of "onerous property". The previous specific references in CA 1985 s.618(1) to "land (of any tenure) burdened with onerous covenants" and "shares or stock in companies" have been dropped—though such items are clearly within the wider terms of the new definition—and the former requirement that, to be "onerous", property had to be "unsaleable, or not readily saleable, by reason of its binding its possessor to the performance of any onerous act or to the payment of any sum of money" has now been replaced by s.178(3)(b), in which these attributes are expressed as alternatives.

The term "property" is itself widely defined for the purposes of the present Act by s.436, below. Both this term and the expression "onerous contract" were closely examined by the Court of Appeal in *Re SSSL Realisations (2002) Ltd* [2006] EWCA Civ 7; [2006] Ch. 610; [2006] B.C.C. 233, where the court was concerned with a deed of indemnity which the insolvent company had given as part consideration for a bond provided by the respondents. " 'Property' ", it was said (at [35]), "must involve some element of benefit or entitlement for the person holding it"—a proposition that appears to be confirmed by the descriptive words "unsaleable or not readily saleable". The deed of indemnity did not give rise to a liability to pay money or perform any other onerous act: it simply imposed on the company a disability, preventing it from collecting an asset. This could not be described as "property". On the phrase "onerous contract", Chadwick L.J. adopted five principles derived from a number of Australian authorities and summed up as follows by Chesterman J. in *Transmetro Corporation Ltd v Real Investments Pty Ltd* (1999) 17 A.C.L.C. 1,314 at 1,320:

- A contract is unprofitable … if it imposes on the company continuing financial obligations which may be regarded as detrimental to the creditors, which presumably means that the contract confers no sufficient reciprocal benefit.

- Before a contract may be unprofitable … it must give rise to prospective liabilities.

- Contracts which will delay the winding up of the company's affairs because they are to be performed over a substantial period of time and will involve expenditure that may not be recovered are unprofitable.

- No case has decided that a contract is unprofitable merely because it is financially disadvantageous. The cases focus on the nature and cause of the disadvantage.

- A contract is not unprofitable merely because the company could have made, or could make, a better bargain.

The critical feature, Chadwick L.J. concluded, is that "performance of the future obligations will prejudice the liquidator's obligation to realise the company's property and pay a dividend to creditors within a reasonable time" (at [36]–[54]). Accordingly, the liquidators could not disclaim the deed of indemnity, because it failed to meet these criteria.

S.178(4)

The effect of a disclaimer is, apart from the operation of any vesting order made by the court under the succeeding sections, that the disclaimed property vests in the Crown as bona vacantia (or, in the case of land held in fee simple, by escheat). In *Scmlla Properties Ltd v Gesso Properties (BVI) Ltd* [1995] B.C.C. 793 it was held that a legal charge over a freehold interest in land, and the leases of tenants created out of the freehold, survived a disclaimer of the freehold interest.

A disclaimer should be construed so as to interfere with the rights of third parties as little as possible: thus, although the effect of the disclaimer of a contract is to release the company from its obligations, it does not undo the contract in so far as it has been performed and other parties have acquired rights and interests under it: *Capital Prime Properties plc v Worthgate Ltd* [2000] B.C.C. 525. See also *Groveholt Ltd v Hughes* [2005] EWCA Civ 897; [2005] 2 B.C.L.C. 421.

The disclaimer of a lease does not terminate the liability of a guarantor (including a predecessor who has assigned the lease to the company). See the note to s.181.

S.178(5)

This corresponds with the repealed CA 1985 s.619(2), with the necessary modification that in para.(b) the liquidator must now give an actual notice of disclaimer within the 28-day period, instead of a notice that he intends to apply to the court for leave to disclaim. For the procedure under this subsection, see IR 1986 r.4.191A.

S.178(6)

This is the same as the former CA 1985 s.619(8), with the substitution of the words "sustaining loss or damage" for the less precise term "injured". A sum due to a party under the terms of a contract does not come within this expression: *Groveholt Ltd v Hughes* (above). *Re Park Air Services plc* [2000] 2 A.C. 172; [1999] B.C.C. 135 gives guidance on the method of calculating the loss or damage suffered by a landlord in consequence of the disclaimer of a lease. The company in this case was solvent. The House of Lords held that, following disclaimer, the landlord could not prove in the winding up for future rent but instead had a statutory right to compensation, to be reckoned on the same basis as if he were claiming damages for breach of a contract that had been wrongfully terminated (with an allowance or discount for the accelerated receipt of sums falling due in the future). Interest under s.189 was also allowed.

179 Disclaimer of leaseholds

179(1) [Requirement for disclaimer to take effect] The disclaimer under section 178 of any property of a leasehold nature does not take effect unless a copy of the disclaimer has been served (so far as the liquidator is aware of their addresses) on every person claiming under the company as underlessee or mortgagee and either–

  (a) no application under section 181 below is made with respect to that property before the end of the period of 14 days beginning with the day on which the last notice served under this subsection was served; or

  (b) where such an application has been made, the court directs that the disclaimer shall take effect.

179(2) [Court's directions or orders] Where the court gives a direction under subsection (1)(b) it may also, instead of or in addition to any order it makes under section 181, make such orders with respect to fixtures, tenant's improvements and other matters arising out of the lease as it thinks fit.

GENERAL NOTE

Under the former law, when leave to disclaim had to be sought in every case, the court could require such notices to be given to persons interested as it thought appropriate. The present section, now that the court is no longer involved, makes express provision for notice to be given to underlessees and mortgagees of leasehold property, at least 14 days before the disclaimer can take effect.

The disclaimer of a lease has the effect of destroying any underlease; but the underlessee has the right, if he chooses, to remain in occupation for the term of the underlease, paying the rent reserved by the lease and performing the covenants contained in it: *Re A E Realisations (1985) Ltd* [1988] 1 W.L.R. 200; (1987) 3 B.C.C. 136.

There is no jurisdiction to make a vesting order in favour of a landlord on terms that it shall be subject to and with the benefit of existing subleases: *Re I T M Corp Ltd (in liq.)* [1997] B.C.C. 554.

S.179(1)
An underlessee or mortgagee has 14 days after receiving notice of the proposed disclaimer in which to apply to the court to have a vesting order made in his favour, or such other relief as the court thinks fit.

S.179(2)
This provision confers on the court additional powers to those prescribed by ss.181, 182.

180   Land subject to rentcharge

180(1)   [Application] The following applies where, in consequence of the disclaimer under section 178 of any land subject to a rentcharge, that land vests by operation of law in the Crown or any other person (referred to in the next subsection as **"the proprietor"**).

180(2)   [Liability of proprietor et al.] The proprietor and the successors in title of the proprietor are not subject to any personal liability in respect of any sums becoming due under the rentcharge except sums becoming due after the proprietor, or some person claiming under or through the proprietor, has taken possession or control of the land or has entered into occupation of it.

GENERAL NOTE

The purpose of this section is to ensure that the Crown or any other person in whom land vests as a result of a disclaimer (see the note to s.178(4)) is not made personally liable in respect of the rentcharge unless it (or he) takes possession or control of the land.

181   Powers of court (general)

181(1)   [Application] This section and the next apply where the liquidator has disclaimed property under section 178.

181(2)   [Application to court] An application under this section may be made to the court by–

(a)   any person who claims an interest in the disclaimed property, or

(b)   any person who is under any liability in respect of the disclaimed property, not being a liability discharged by the disclaimer.

181(3)   [Powers of court] Subject as follows, the court may on the application make an order, on such terms as it thinks fit, for the vesting of the disclaimed property in, or for its delivery to–

(a)   a person entitled to it or a trustee for such a person, or

(b)   a person subject to such a liability as is mentioned in subsection (2)(b) or a trustee for such a person.

181(4)   [Limit on court's powers] The court shall not make an order under subsection (3)(b) except where it appears to the court that it would be just to do so for the purpose of compensating the person subject to the liability in respect of the disclaimer.

181(5)   [Relationship with s.178(6)] The effect of any order under this section shall be taken into account in assessing for the purpose of section 178(6) the extent of any loss or damage sustained by any person in consequence of the disclaimer.

181(6)   [Effect of vesting order] An order under this section vesting property in any person need not be completed by conveyance, assignment or transfer.

S.181(1)–(3)

As has been explained above, the liquidator's power to disclaim no longer requires the leave of the court, and so the court becomes involved only if an application is made to it by a person who is interested in the property or otherwise affected by the disclaimer. These subsections deal with the right to make such an application, and set out the general powers of the court in such proceedings. The relevant procedure is laid down by IR 1986 r.4.194. (In regard to vesting orders affecting leasehold property, the provisions of s.182 apply in addition.)

In *Re Vedmay Ltd* [1994] 1 B.C.L.C. 676 it was held that the term "interest" in s.181(2) is not confined to a proprietary interest, and that a subtenant of premises who was in occupation as a statutory tenant had no proprietary interest in the premises, but merely a "status of irremovability"; but even so, since he had a financial interest in the subsistence of the head-lease, he had a sufficient interest for the purpose of s.181. However in *Lloyds Bank SF Nominees v Aladdin Ltd (in liq.)* [1996] 1 B.C.L.C. 720 it was held that a proprietary interest of some kind was essential, so that, if the *Vedmay* decision is to stand, it must be because of the finding that the tenant had a "status of irremovability". The guarantor of a debt secured by a charge over a company's assets similarly has only a financial and not a proprietary interest in those assets: *Re Spirit Motorsport Ltd (in liq.)* [1996] 1 B.C.L.C. 684. See also *Re Ballast plc, St Paul Travelers Insurance Co Ltd v Dargan* [2006] EWHC 3189 (Ch); [2007] B.P.I.R. 117.

In *Stacey v Hill* [1991] 1 K.B. 660 it was held that the disclaimer of a lease brought to an end the obligations of a guarantor or surety in respect of future liabilities under the lease. This ruling was in stark contrast with *Hill v East & West India Dock Co* (1884) 9 App. Cas. 448, in which the House of Lords had held that the disclaimer of a lease which has been assigned does not determine the continuing liability of the original lessee on the covenants in the lease, or the liability of any surety for the original lessee. The anomaly has now been rectified. In *Hindcastle Ltd v Barbara Attenborough Associates Ltd* [1997] A.C. 70; [1996] B.C.C. 636 the House of Lords decided that the two could not stand together and that *Stacey v Hill* should be overruled. It follows that both a guarantor of a lease and an original or former lessee of a lease which has been assigned are "persons under a liability in respect of the disclaimed property, not being a liability discharged by the disclaimer" under s.181(2)(b), and that accordingly they have standing to apply for a vesting order under the present section. See also *Shaw v Doleman* [2009] EWCA Civ 279; [2009] 2 B.C.L.C. 123, where the assignor argued that her liability had been terminated by the disclaimer on the construction of the wording of the assignment, but the *Hindcastle* ruling was followed.

In *Scottish Widows plc v Tripipatkul* [2004] EWHC 1874 (Ch); [2004] B.C.C. 200 the landlord, after the lessee company's liquidator had disclaimed the lease, sold the reversion of the leased property to the claimant. It was held that the benefit of covenants which had been given by the appellant and which survived the disclaimer had been assigned along with the reversion.

The terms of a guarantee sometimes provide that in the event of the lease being disclaimed the guarantor will take a new lease from the landlord for the residue of the term at the same rent. In *Re A E Realisations (1985) Ltd* [1988] 1 W.L.R. 200; (1987) 3 B.C.C. 136, the court declined to make a vesting order in favour of a guarantor because it would have achieved nothing that would not be brought about by the grant of a new lease under the agreement.

Section 1012 of the Companies Act 2006 provides that, when a company is dissolved, all property and rights vested in or held on trust for the company are deemed to be bona vacantia and vest in the Crown (or, where appropriate, the Duchy of Lancaster or the Duke of Cornwall), subject to the possible restoration of the company to the register under ss.1024 et seq. However, the Crown or another appropriate entity may disclaim the property (s.1013). The corresponding sections of the 1985 Act which these provisions replace (CA 1985 ss.656–657) went on to state that ss.178(4) and 179–182 of IA 1986 should apply to such property as if it had been disclaimed by a liquidator; but the 2006 Act makes self-standing provision to essentially the same effect in ss.1015 (for England and Wales and Northern Ireland) and ss.1020–1022 (for Scotland). It is likely that rulings under the insolvency legislation will continue to be of relevance here.

S.181(4)

If a vesting order is made under s.181(3)(b), the beneficiary will not be someone "entitled" to the property in question (compare s.181(3)(a)), but someone who is under a liability in respect of it. A vesting order allows the court to do rough justice by allowing the applicant to take over the property in exchange for the extinction of his liability, provided that the condition in this subsection is met.

S.181(5)

The beneficiary under a vesting order proves in the winding up under s.178(6) for any loss or damage which he may have sustained overall, after bringing into account the effect of the order, which may in itself have left him better or worse off.

S.181(6)

The vesting order operates itself as a conveyance of the property without the need for any other legal act.

182   Powers of court (leaseholds)

182(1)   **[Limit on court's power]** The court shall not make an order under section 181 vesting property of a leasehold nature in any person claiming under the company as underlessee or mortgagee except on terms making that person–

(a)   subject to the same liabilities and obligations as the company was subject to under the lease at the commencement of the winding up, or

(b)   if the court thinks fit, subject to the same liabilities and obligations as that person would be subject to if the lease had been assigned to him at the commencement of the winding up.

182(2)   **[Where order re part of property in lease]** For the purposes of an order under section 181 relating to only part of any property comprised in a lease, the requirements of subsection (1) apply as if the lease comprised only the property to which the order relates.

182(3)   **[Court may vest estate in someone else]** Where subsection (1) applies and no person claiming under the company as underlessee or mortgagee is willing to accept an order under section 181 on the terms required by virtue of that subsection, the court may, by order under that section, vest the company's estate or interest in the property in any person who is liable (whether personally or in a representative capacity, and whether alone or jointly with the company) to perform the lessee's covenants in the lease.

The court may vest that estate and interest in such a person freed and discharged from all estates, incumbrances and interests created by the company.

182(4)   **[Where s.182(1) applies]** Where subsection (1) applies and a person claiming under the company as underlessee or mortgagee declines to accept an order under section 181, that person is excluded from all interest in the property.

GENERAL NOTE

This provision is designed to ensure that persons who have a subordinate interest in leasehold property owned by the company have an opportunity to take over the property itself on the same terms, in effect, as those upon which the company formerly held it.

In *Re I T M Corp Ltd (in liq.)* [1997] B.C.C. 554, a vesting order had been made in favour of a landlord on terms that it should be subject to and with the benefit of existing subleases. On appeal, it was held (1) that the court had no jurisdiction to make an order in favour of a landlord until the interests of all the other relevant parties who could obtain an interest in the property under the statutory mechanism had been cleared away; and (2) that a vesting order in favour of a landlord could only be made freed of the sublessees' interests.

S.182(4)

This provision is limited in its application to persons who have a proprietary interest in the property. It cannot be invoked to determine a statutory tenancy: *Re Vedmay Ltd* [1994] 1 B.C.L.C. 676.

Execution, attachment and the Scottish equivalents

183   Effect of execution or attachment (England and Wales)

183(1)   **[Where creditor seeking benefit of execution or attachment]** Where a creditor has issued execution against the goods or land of a company or has attached any debt due to it, and the company is subsequently wound up, he is not entitled to retain the benefit of the execution or attachment against the liquidator unless he has completed the execution or attachment before the commencement of the winding up.

183(2)   **[Qualifications]** However–

(a)   if a creditor has had notice of a meeting having been called at which a resolution for voluntary winding up is to be proposed, the date on which he had notice is substituted, for the purpose of subsection (1), for the date of commencement of the winding up;

(b) a person who purchases in good faith under a sale by the enforcement officer, or other officer charged with the execution of the writ any goods of a company on which execution has been levied in all cases acquires a good title to them against the liquidator; and

(c) the rights conferred by subsection (1) on the liquidator may be set aside by the court in favour of the creditor to such extent and subject to such terms as the court thinks fit.

183(3)   [Execution, attachment] For purposes of this Act–

(a) an execution against goods is completed by seizure and sale, or by the making of a charging order under section 1 of the Charging Orders Act 1979;

(b) an attachment of a debt is completed by receipt of the debt; and

(c) an execution against land is completed by seizure, by the appointment of a receiver, or by the making of a charging order under section 1 of the Act above mentioned.

183(4)   [Definitions] In this section **"goods"** includes all chattels personal; and **"enforcement officer"** means an individual who is authorised to act as an enforcement officer under the Courts Act 2003.

183(5)   [Scotland] This section does not apply in the case of a winding up in Scotland.

General Note

Section 183 does not have extra-territorial effect, so as to deprive a creditor who has completed an execution process abroad of the assets which he has successfully seized. However the court has a discretion (at least where the creditor in question is amenable to the jurisdiction) to restrain a creditor from bringing or continuing a foreign execution process (*Re Oriental Inland Steam Co Ex p. Scinde Railway Co* (1874) 9 Ch. App. 557; *Re North Carolina Estate Co* (1889) 5 T.L.R. 328; *Re Vocalion (Foreign) Ltd* [1932] 2 Ch. 196); and it also has authority to direct a liquidator to intervene in foreign garnishment proceedings, or to direct him not to do so: *Mitchell v Carter* [1997] B.C.C. 907. Accordingly, it has jurisdiction to decide whether a creditor may retain the fruits of a current or future foreign execution process. (However, in later proceedings (reported as *Re Buckingham International plc (No.2)* [1998] B.C.C. 943) the court declined to make such an order, holding that the circumstances did not justify disturbing the statutory pari passu principle.)

S.183(1)

This section deals with the situation where a creditor has levied execution against the property of a company which then goes into liquidation. Its effect is to deprive him of the benefit of the execution unless it has been "completed" (as that term is defined in s.183(3)) before the commencement of the winding up. Since a winding up may commence at a time earlier than the date of a winding-up order, an execution which has in fact then been completed may be avoided retrospectively.

On the "commencement" of a winding up, see ss.86 and 129. The section may operate even earlier than this time: see s.182(3)(a).

The present provisions are complementary to s.128, which avoids all executions and attachments put in force *after* the commencement of a winding up, but whereas s.128 is restricted to a winding up by the court, s.183 applies to all categories of winding up.

Distress levied against goods by the Revenue for unpaid taxes is not "execution" within s.183: *Re Modern Jet Support Centre Ltd* [2005] EWHC 1611 (Ch); [2005] 1 W.L.R. 3880; [2006] B.C.C. 174.

S.183(2)

Notice of the summoning of a meeting is here, in effect, treated as equivalent to the now discarded "notice of an act of bankruptcy" formerly applicable in the case of an insolvent individual.

The present provision causes the execution creditor to lose the benefit of his execution, but a bona fide purchaser of goods from the enforcement officer is protected by para.(b).

On the significance of the word "date", see the note to s.86.

The court has an overriding jurisdiction: see para.(c).

S.183(3)

These provisions define with precision the point at which an execution or attachment is "completed".

S.183(4)

The definition of "goods" is much wider than, e.g. that in the Sale of Goods Act 1979, and extends to intangible property such as choses in action.

This subsection and parts of s.184 were amended by the Courts Act 2003 s.109(1) and Sch.8 paras 295–296, to reflect the redesignation of the court officers referred to.

S.183(5)

For the position governing the winding up of a company in Scotland, see s.185. Note, however, that where a company registered in England or Wales has assets in Scotland, the provisions of s.185 will apply, presumably to the exclusion of the present section: see s.185(4).

184   Duties of officers charged with execution of writs and other processes (England and Wales)

184(1)   [Application] The following applies where a company's goods are taken in execution and, before their sale or the completion of the execution (by the receipt or recovery of the full amount of the levy), notice is served on the enforcement officer, or other officer, charged with the execution of the writ or process that a provisional liquidator has been appointed or that a winding-up order has been made, or that a resolution for voluntary winding up has been passed.

184(2)   [Enforcement officer to deliver goods and money to liquidator] The enforcement officer or other officer shall, on being so required, deliver the goods and any money seized or received in part satisfaction of the execution to the liquidator; but the costs of execution are a first charge on the goods or money so delivered, and the liquidator may sell the goods, or a sufficient part of them, for the purpose of satisfying the charge.

184(3)   [Costs where goods sold etc.] If under an execution in respect of a judgment for a sum exceeding £500 a company's goods are sold or money is paid in order to avoid sale, the enforcement officer or other officer shall deduct the costs of the execution from the proceeds of sale or the money paid and retain the balance for 14 days.

184(4)   [If within time notice is served] If within that time notice is served on the enforcement officer or other officer of a petition for the winding up of the company having been presented, or of a meeting having been called at which there is to be proposed a resolution for voluntary winding up, and an order is made or a resolution passed (as the case may be), the enforcement officer or other officer shall pay the balance to the liquidator who is entitled to retain it as against the execution creditor.

184(5)   [Liquidator's rights may be set aside by court] The rights conferred by this section on the liquidator may be set aside by the court in favour of the creditor to such extent and subject to such terms as the court thinks fit.

184(6)   [Definitions] In this section, **"goods"** includes all chattels personal; and **"enforcement officer"** means an individual who is authorised to act as an enforcement officer under the Courts Act 2003.

184(7)   [Increase, reduction of s.184(3) sum] The money sum for the time being specified in subsection (3) is subject to increase or reduction by order under section 416 in Part XV.

184(8)   [Scotland] This section does not apply in the case of a winding up in Scotland.

GENERAL NOTE

This section defines the obligations of an enforcement officer where a company's goods are taken in execution, thus facilitating the operation of s.184. For the rules as regards costs, see r.7.36.

S.184(1), (2)

These subsections apply where a notice is served on the officer that the company in question is either actually in liquidation or in the hands of a provisional liquidator. The benefit of the execution must be surrendered to the liquidator, subject to payment of the officer's costs.

S.184(3)–(5)

These provisions deal with the duties of an officer enforcing a judgment debt of over £500. He is required to retain in his hands the net proceeds of the sale, or any money paid to him in order to avoid sale, for 14 days; and if within that time he receives notice that a winding-up petition has been presented or a meeting called to consider a resolution for voluntary winding up, he must continue to hold the money until he learns whether a liquidation has in fact resulted and, if so, hand it to the liquidator (unless the court orders otherwise under s.184(5)).

S.184(6)
The definitions are identical with those in s.183(4).

185   Effect of diligence (Scotland)

185(1)   [Application of Bankruptcy (Scotland) Act] In the winding up of a company registered in Scotland, the following provisions of the Bankruptcy (Scotland) Act 1985–

(a)   subsections (1) to (6) of section 37 (effect of sequestration on diligence); and

(b)   subsections (3), (4), (7) and (8) of section 39 (realisation of estate),

apply, so far as consistent with this Act, in like manner as they apply in the sequestration of a debtor's estate, with the substitutions specified below and with any other necessary modifications.

185(2)   [Substitutions] The substitutions to be made in those sections of the Act of 1985 are as follows–

(a)   for references to the debtor, substitute references to the company;

(b)   for references to the sequestration, substitute references to the winding up;

(c)   for references to the date of sequestration, substitute references to the commencement of the winding up of the company; and

(d)   for references to the trustee, substitute references to the liquidator.

185(3)   [Definition] In this section, **"the commencement of the winding up of the company"** means, where it is being wound up by the court, the day on which the winding-up order is made.

185(4)   [English company with estate in Scotland] This section, so far as relating to any estate or effects of the company situated in Scotland, applies in the case of a company registered in England and Wales as in the case of one registered in Scotland.

GENERAL NOTE

Section 185(2)(d) was amended (by deletion of the word "permanent" before "trustee") by the Bankruptcy and Diligence etc. (Scotland) Act 2007 s.226(2) and Sch.6 as from April 1, 2008. Note prospective amendment of s.185(1)(a) by s.226(1) and Sch.5 para.14 of the same Act.

In relation to the financial markets, nothing in s.185 affects any action taken by an exchange or clearing house for the purpose of its default proceedings: see the note on p.2, and CA 1989 s.161(4).

S.185(1)–(3)
These provisions apply to the winding up of a company in Scotland the rules relating to diligence, etc. (the Scottish equivalent of execution and attachment) in the bankruptcy of an individual. (Note, particularly, the special definition of the term "the commencement of the winding up" for this purpose.)

S.185(4)
It is plain from ss.183(5) and 184(8) that the converse to s.185(4) does not apply: i.e. a company registered in Scotland which has assets in England and Wales will be governed in relation to such property by s.185, and not by those sections.

Miscellaneous matters

186   Rescission of contracts by the court

186(1)   [Power of court] The court may, on the application of a person who is, as against the liquidator, entitled to the benefit or subject to the burden of a contract made with the company, make an order rescinding the contract on such terms as to payment by or to either party of damages for the non-performance of the contract, or otherwise as the court thinks just.

186(2) **[Damages]** Any damages payable under the order to such a person may be proved by him as a debt in the winding up.

GENERAL NOTE

This provision can be traced back to the Bankruptcy Act 1883 and was extended to companies by the Companies Act 1929. It was formerly included as part of the section on disclaimer but is now treated separately. The corresponding provision for bankruptcy is IA 1986 s.345. It is concerned with contracts entered into by the company which are still wholly or partly at an executory stage on the date of liquidation. If the company at that date, or the liquidator subsequently, has committed a repudiatory breach then, on ordinary contractual principles, the other party will be entitled to terminate the contract and claim to the right to damages without recourse to the court. Alternatively, s.186 entitles him to achieve the same result by court order, which will overcome any doubt as to his right to repudiate and quantify the sum for which he can prove in the liquidation.

In the context of the financial markets, s.186 does not apply in relation to a market contract or a contract effected by an exchange or clearing house for the purpose of realising property provided as margin in relation to market contracts: see CA 1989 s.164(1). The section is also disapplied by the Finality Regulations reg.16(1) in relation to a transfer order or a contract for the purpose of realising security in payment and securities settlement systems. (See the notes on pp.2–3 above.)

187   Power to make over assets to employees

187(1) **[CA 2006 s.247 payment on winding up]** On the winding up of a company (whether by the court or voluntarily), the liquidator may, subject to the following provisions of this section, make any payment which the company has, before the commencement of the winding up, decided to make under section 247 of the Companies Act 2006 (power to provide for employees or former employees on cessation or transfer of business).

187(2) **[Power exercisable by liquidator]** The liquidator may, after the winding up has commenced, make any such provision as is mentioned in section 247(1) if–

(a)   the company's liabilities have been fully satisfied and provision has been made for the expenses of the winding up,

(b)   the exercise of the power has been sanctioned by a resolution of the company, and

(c)   any requirements of the company's articles as to the exercise of the power conferred by section 247(1) are complied with.

187(3) **[Source of payment]** Any payment which may be made by a company under this section (that is, a payment after the commencement of its winding up) may be made out of the company's assets which are available to the members on the winding up.

187(4) **[Control by court]** On a winding up by the court, the exercise by the liquidator of his powers under this section is subject to the court's control, and any creditor or contributory may apply to the court with respect to any exercise or proposed exercise of the power.

187(5) **[Effect]** Subsections (1) and (2) above have effect notwithstanding anything in any rule of law or in section 107 of this Act (property of company after satisfaction of liabilities to be distributed among members).

GENERAL NOTE

The provisions of this section and of CA 2006 s.247 were first introduced (as CA 1980 s.74) to negate the common law ruling in *Parke v Daily News Ltd* [1962] Ch. 927. Section 247 applies when the company is a going concern, and the present section when it is being wound up. In *Parke's* case, it was held to be ultra vires for a company which had sold its business to a third party to make substantial ex gratia payments to the employees who were thereby made redundant. Both s.247 and the present section are framed in wide terms, so as not merely to negative any question of ultra vires (abolished by CA 1989 s.108 from February 4, 1991), but to ensure that such payments will not be invalidated on any other grounds.

Section 187(1) amended, and s.187(2) substituted, by the Companies Act 2006 (Commencement No.3, Consequential Amendments, Transitional Provisions and Savings) Order 2007 (SI 2007/2194 (C. 84)) art.10(1) and Sch.4 para.42(2), (3), as from October 1, 2007.

S.187(1)

This subsection applies where the company has already resolved under CA 2006 s.247(4), before the commencement of the winding up, to make a payment to the employees: the liquidator is authorised to implement the resolution and make that payment. This may be made only out of profits of the company which are available for dividend (s.247(7)(b)).

S.187(2)

Once the winding up has commenced, it is still permissible for a company's shareholders to agree to make over assets to the employees, but the restriction to profits available for dividend no longer applies, and instead the payment must be made out of the surplus in the hands of the liquidator after all the company's debts and the costs of the winding up have been met. An ordinary resolution of the shareholders is required or, if the company's memorandum or articles so stipulate, a resolution passed by a larger majority. However, a payment cannot be made on the basis of a decision of the directors alone, even if the memorandum or articles authorise this course, since CA 2006 s.247(4)(b), which permits this prior to the commencement of winding up, is nullified by the present provision.

S.187(3)

This provision is not permissive (as it appears to be), but mandatory: the payment cannot be made out of any assets other than those available to the members.

S.187(4), (5)

The grounds on which the court might interfere to set aside a resolution of the members are not set out. It may be assumed that a plea of ultra vires would not succeed, or an objection that the exercise of power by the majority was not in the best interests of the company (see CA 2006 s.247(2) ("to promote the success of the company")). However, there are clearly circumstances where a minority shareholder might claim that the majority was acting oppressively or mala fide or in a discriminatory way—e.g. perhaps if the majority shareholders were themselves the employees who stood to benefit.

188   Notification that company is in liquidation

188(1)   [Statement in invoices etc.] When a company is being wound up, whether by the court or voluntarily–

(a)   every invoice, order for goods or services, business letter or order form (whether in hard copy, electronic or any other form) issued by or on behalf of the company, or a liquidator of the company or a receiver or manager of the company's property, and

(b)   all the company's websites,

must contain a statement that the company is being wound up.

188(2)   [Penalty on default] If default is made in complying with this section, the company and any of the following persons who knowingly and wilfully authorises or permits the default, namely, any officer of the company, any liquidator of the company and any receiver or manager, is liable to a fine.

GENERAL NOTE

This section has its counterpart in the provisions relating to administration (s.12 and Sch.B1 para.45) and receivership (ss.39, 64). Section 188(1) was substituted by the Companies (Registrar, Languages and Trading Disclosures) Regulations 2006 (SI 2006/3429) reg.7(1), as from January 1, 2007. Section 188(1)(a) was amended by the Companies (Trading Disclosures) (Insolvency) Regulations 2008 (SI 2008/1897) reg.5(1), as from October 1, 2008.

S.188(2)

On penalties, see s.430 and Sch.10.

189   Interest on debts

189(1)   [Payment of interest] In a winding up interest is payable in accordance with this section on any debt proved in the winding up, including so much of any such debt as represents interest on the remainder.

189(2)   [Surplus after payment of debts] Any surplus remaining after the payment of the debts proved in a winding up shall, before being applied for any other purpose, be applied in paying interest on those debts in respect of the periods during which they have been outstanding since the company went into liquidation.

189(3)   [Ranking of interest] All interest under this section ranks equally, whether or not the debts on which it is payable rank equally.

189(4)   [Rate of interest] The rate of interest payable under this section in respect of any debt (**"the official rate"** for the purposes of any provision of this Act in which that expression is used) is whichever is the greater of–

(a)   the rate specified in section 17 of the Judgments Act 1838 on the day on which the company went into liquidation, and

(b)   the rate applicable to that debt apart from the winding up.

189(5)   [Scotland] In the application of this section to Scotland–

(a)   references to a debt proved in a winding up have effect as references to a claim accepted in a winding up, and

(b)   the reference to section 17 of the Judgments Act 1838 has effect as a reference to the rules.

GENERAL NOTE

Before the reform of insolvency legislation in 1985, the legal rules governing the entitlement to interest on debts in a winding up were confused and unsatisfactory (see the Cork Committee's *Report*, Ch.31). On the recommendation of the Committee, all these old rules and the associated anomalies have been done away with and replaced by new provisions. Note that the new law applies in both solvent and insolvent liquidations.

In *Re Empire Paper Ltd* [1999] B.C.C. 406, X Ltd had guaranteed the debt of E Ltd. Both companies were in liquidation. X Ltd had been called upon to pay the debt and, since it was solvent, the debt had been paid with statutory interest under s.189. E Ltd, however, was insolvent, and it was held that this fact prevented X Ltd from proving in the liquidation for the sum which it had paid as interest.

For the relevant rules, see IR 1986 r.4.93.

S.189(1)

Interest at the "official rate" (see s.189(4)) runs on all debts and liabilities proved in the winding up, including any debts representing interest due up to the effective date of proof, and it runs from that date until a final dividend is declared or all the proved debts have been paid in full. The date will be, in a compulsory winding up, that of the winding-up order, and in a voluntary winding up, that of the winding-up resolution: *Re Lines Bros Ltd* [1983] Ch. 1, and compare s.247(2) and IR 1986 r.4.93. Where a creditor proves for loss or damage following a disclaimer by the liquidator, interest runs from the date of the disclaimer: *Re Park Air Services plc* [2000] 2 A.C. 172; [1999] B.C.C. 135.

S.189(2)

Where all the debts have been paid in full, the interest allowed for by this section is payable before any money is returned to shareholders.

In regard to debts payable at a future time, see IR 1986 r.11.13.

S.189(3)

The preferential and non-preferential debts rank equally as regards their right to interest. To give true effect to this provision, it is submitted that no interest should be payable on the preferential debts until the preferential and non-preferential debts have both been paid in full, without interest. Any other construction of the section (e.g. to treat the interest on a preferential debt as being itself simply a non-preferential debt—whether or not the other non-preferential debts are reckoned with interest) would be, in effect, to give the preferential creditors an additional preference in regard to interest.

S.189(4)
The rate of interest payable under the Judgments Act 1838 s.17, is currently 8 per cent (SI 1993/564). If the debt itself carries interest at a higher rate, the latter is payable; but a creditor cannot merely by giving notice impose an obligation to pay interest at a rate higher than that specified in s.189(4)(a): see IR 1986 r.4.93(5), (6) (as amended).

S.189(5)
A rate of 15 per cent is specified in the Insolvency (Scotland) Rules 1986 (SI 1986/1915 (S 139)) r.4.66(2)(b).

190 Documents exempt from stamp duty

190(1) [Application] In the case of a winding up by the court, or of a creditors' voluntary winding up, the following has effect as regards exemption from duties chargeable under the enactments relating to stamp duties.

190(2) [Exempt documents of company registered in England and Wales] If the company is registered in England and Wales, the following documents are exempt from stamp duty–

    (a)   every assurance relating solely to freehold or leasehold property, or to any estate, right or interest in, any real or personal property, which forms part of the company's assets and which, after the execution of the assurance, either at law or in equity, is or remains part of those assets, and

    (b)   every writ, order, certificate, or other instrument or writing relating solely to the property of any company which is being wound up as mentioned in subsection (1), or to any proceeding under such a winding up.

"Assurance" here includes deed, conveyance, assignment and surrender.

190(3) [Exempt document of company registered in Scotland] If the company is registered in Scotland, the following documents are exempt from stamp duty–

    (a)   every conveyance relating solely to property, which forms part of the company's assets and which, after the execution of the conveyance, is or remains the company's property for the benefit of its creditors,

    (b)   any articles of roup or sale, submission and every other instrument and writing whatsoever relating solely to the company's property, and

    (c)   every deed or writing forming part of the proceedings in the winding up.

"Conveyance" here includes assignation, instrument, discharge, writing and deed.

GENERAL NOTE

This section applies only in the case of a winding up by the court or a creditors' voluntary winding up. It exempts from stamp duty all conveyances, etc. which are made to facilitate the winding up and which do not beneficially transfer assets out the hands of the liquidator.

191 Company's books to be evidence

191 Where a company is being wound up, all books and papers of the company and of the liquidators are, as between the contributories of the company, prima facie evidence of the truth of all matters purporting to be recorded in them.

GENERAL NOTE

The presumption which this provision creates applies only "as between the contributories of the company", and is rebuttable.

192   Information as to pending liquidations

192(1)   [Statement to registrar] If the winding up of a company is not concluded within one year after its commencement, the liquidator shall, at such intervals as may be prescribed, until the winding up is concluded, send to the registrar of companies a statement in the prescribed form and containing the prescribed particulars with respect to the proceedings in, and position of, the liquidation.

192(2)   [Penalty on default] If a liquidator fails to comply with this section, he is liable to a fine and, for continued contravention, to a daily default fine.

S.192(1)
The rules prescribed for the purposes of this section were to be found in IR 1986 r.4.223, but this rule has been revoked by I(A)R 2010 (SI 2010/686) as from April 6, 2010 (for liquidations commencing after that date). For existing liquidations (to which the section continues to apply) the "intervals prescribed" by r.4.223 are every six months. It appears that r.4.223 was revoked because of the introduction of the requirement for the liquidator to make annual progress reports (s.92A), a copy of which must be sent to the registrar (rr.4.49B, 4.49C).

S.192(2)
On penalties, see s.430 and Sch.10.
  The liquidator's obligations may also be enforced by seeking an order for compliance under s.170. If a liquidator fails to comply with such an order, he will be in contempt of court and liable to imprisonment: *Re S & A Conversions Ltd* (1988) 4 B.C.C. 384; *Re Allan Ellis (Transport & Packing) Services Ltd* (1989) 5 B.C.C. 835.

193   Unclaimed dividends (Scotland)

193(1)   [Application] The following applies where a company registered in Scotland has been wound up, and is about to be dissolved.

193(2)   [Liquidator to lodge unclaimed money in bank] The liquidator shall lodge in an appropriate bank or institution as defined in section 73(1) of the Bankruptcy (Scotland) Act 1985 (not being a bank or institution in or of which the liquidator is an acting partner, manager, agent or cashier) in the name of the Accountant of Court the whole unclaimed dividends and unapplied or undistributable balances, and the deposit receipts shall be transmitted to the Accountant of Court.

193(3)   [Application of Bankruptcy (Scotland) Act] The provisions of section 58 of the Bankruptcy (Scotland) Act 1985 (so far as consistent with this Act and the Companies Acts) apply with any necessary modifications to sums lodged in a bank or institution under this section as they apply to sums deposited under section 57 of the Act first mentioned.

GENERAL NOTE

Section 58 of the Bankruptcy (Scotland) Act 1985 (as amended) provides that unclaimed dividends in an individual bankruptcy shall be held in a bank in the name of the Accountant in Bankruptcy for a period of seven years, during which they may be claimed by those entitled. After the seven years, the money passes to the Secretary of State who may thereafter pay undisputed claims in his discretion.
  The present section applies the same rules to a company liquidation in Scotland. The Insolvency (Scotland) Rules 1986 r.4.68(1) is to the same effect.

194   Resolutions passed at adjourned meetings

194   Where a resolution is passed at an adjourned meeting of a company's creditors or contributories, the resolution is treated for all purposes as having been passed on the date on which it was in fact passed, and not as having been passed on any earlier date.

GENERAL NOTE

This provision is confirmed in its application to meetings held in connection with a winding up. For other meetings, CA 2006 s.332 lays down a similar rule, reversing the decision at common law in *Neuschild v British Equitorial Oil Co Ltd* [1925] Ch. 346.

195   Meetings to ascertain wishes of creditors or contributories

195(1)   [Power of court] The court may–

   (a)   as to all matters relating to the winding up of a company, have regard to the wishes of the creditors or contributories (as proved to it by any sufficient evidence), and

   (b)   if it thinks fit, for the purpose of ascertaining those wishes, direct meetings of the creditors or contributories to be called, held and conducted in such manner as the court directs, and appoint a person to act as chairman of any such meeting and report the result of it to the court.

195(2)   [Creditors] In the case of creditors, regard shall be had to the value of each creditor's debt.

195(3)   [Contributories] In the case of contributories, regard shall be had to the number of votes conferred on each contributory.

GENERAL NOTE

The use of "may", rather than "shall", in the opening words of the section gives the court a residuary discretion to act without having regard to the wishes of the creditors (or contributories) where there are "special circumstances"—e.g. where it is not practicable to hold meetings because of the complexities of the case and the difficulty of identifying who the creditors are: *Re Bank of Credit & Commerce International SA (No.2)* [1992] B.C.C. 715. However, the court will not lightly disregard or overrule the views of the majority creditors whose interests are at stake: *Re Falcon R J Developments Ltd* (1987) 3 B.C.C. 146: *Re William Thorpe & Son Ltd* (1989) 5 B.C.C. 156. See also the note to s.125(1), above.

The conduct of any meetings directed by the court to be called is dealt with by the rules, as well as being covered in part by the terms of the section itself. For the relevant rules, see IR 1986 rr.4.54 et seq.

196   Judicial notice of court documents

196   In all proceedings under this Part, all courts, judges and persons judicially acting, and all officers, judicial or ministerial, of any court, or employed in enforcing the process of any court shall take judicial notice–

   (a)   of the signature of any officer of the High Court or of a county court in England and Wales, or of the Court of Session or a sheriff court in Scotland, or of the High Court in Northern Ireland, and also

   (b)   of the official seal or stamp of the several offices of the High Court in England and Wales or Northern Ireland, or of the Court of Session, appended to or impressed on any document made, issued or signed under the provisions of this Act or the Companies Acts, or any official copy of such a document.

197   Commission for receiving evidence

197(1)   [Courts for examination of witnesses] When a company is wound up in England and Wales or in Scotland, the court may refer the whole or any part of the examination of witnesses–

   (a)   to a specified county court in England and Wales, or

   (b)   to the sheriff principal for a specified sheriffdom in Scotland, or

   (c)   to the High Court in Northern Ireland or a specified Northern Ireland County Court,

("specified" meaning specified in the order of the winding-up court).

197(2)   [Commissioners for taking evidence] Any person exercising jurisdiction as a judge of the court to which the reference is made (or, in Scotland, the sheriff principal to whom it is made) shall then, by virtue of this section, be a commissioner for the purpose of taking the evidence of those witnesses.

197(3)   [Power of judge or sheriff principal] The judge or sheriff principal has in the matter referred the same power of summoning and examining witnesses, of requiring the production and delivery of documents, of punishing defaults by witnesses, and of allowing costs and expenses to witnesses, as the court which made the winding-up order.

These powers are in addition to any which the judge or sheriff principal might lawfully exercise apart from this section.

197(4)   [Return or report re examination] The examination so taken shall be returned or reported to the court which made the order in such manner as that court requests.

197(5)   [Northern Ireland] This section extends to Northern Ireland.

198   Court order for examination of persons in Scotland

198(1)   [Examination of any person on affairs of company] The court may direct the examination in Scotland of any person for the time being in Scotland (whether a contributory of the company or not), in regard to the trade, dealings, affairs or property of any company in the course of being wound up, or of any person being a contributory of the company, so far as the company may be interested by reason of his being a contributory.

198(2)   [Directions to take examination] The order or commission to take the examination shall be directed to the sheriff principal of the sheriffdom in which the person to be examined is residing or happens to be for the time; and the sheriff principal shall summon the person to appear before him at a time and place to be specified in the summons for examination on oath as a witness or as a haver, and to produce any books or papers called for which are in his possession or power.

198(3)   [Duties of sheriff principal re examination] The sheriff principal may take the examination either orally or on written interrogatories, and shall report the same in writing in the usual form to the court, and shall transmit with the report the books and papers produced, if the originals are required and specified by the order or commission, or otherwise copies or extracts authenticated by the sheriff.

198(4)   [Where person fails to appear for examination] If a person so summoned fails to appear at the time and place specified, or refuses to be examined or to make the production required, the sheriff principal shall proceed against him as a witness or haver duly cited; and failing to appear or refusing to give evidence or make production may be proceeded against by the law of Scotland.

198(5)   [Fees and allowances] The sheriff principal is entitled to such fees, and the witness is entitled to such allowances, as sheriffs principal when acting as commissioners under appointment from the Court of Session and as witnesses and havers are entitled to in the like cases according to the law and practice of Scotland.

198(6)   [Objection by witness] If any objection is stated to the sheriff principal by the witness, either on the ground of his incompetency as a witness, or as to the production required, or on any other ground, the sheriff principal may, if he thinks fit, report the objection to the court, and suspend the examination of the witness until it has been disposed of by the court.

GENERAL NOTE

This section applies in Scotland in addition to ss.133 and 236, which also provide for the judicial examination of persons who have been connected with a company that is in liquidation. There appears to be a considerable degree of overlap. The report to the court under s.198(3) must be in hard copy (LRO 2010 (SI 2010/18) art.4(2)(g)).

199   Costs of application for leave to proceed (Scottish companies)

199   Where a petition or application for leave to proceed with an action or proceeding against a company which is being wound up in Scotland is unopposed and is granted by the court, the costs of the petition or application shall, unless the court otherwise directs, be added to the amount of the petitioner's or applicant's claim against the company.

200   Affidavits etc. in United Kingdom and overseas

200(1)   [Swearing of affidavit] An affidavit required to be sworn under or for the purposes of this Part may be sworn in the United Kingdom, or elsewhere in Her Majesty's dominions, before any court, judge or person lawfully authorised to take and receive affidavits, or before any of Her Majesty's consuls or vice-consuls in any place outside Her dominions.

200(2)   [Judicial notice of signatures etc.] All courts, judges, justices, commissioners and persons acting judicially shall take judicial notice of the seal or stamp or signature (as the case may be) of any such court, judge, person, consul or vice-consul attached, appended or subscribed to any such affidavit, or to any other document to be used for the purposes of this Part.

GENERAL NOTE

This provision is designed to simplify the normal requirements for the taking of evidence abroad, for use in winding-up proceedings.

CHAPTER IX

DISSOLUTION OF COMPANIES AFTER WINDING UP

Introductory note to Part IV, Chapter IX
The dissolution of a company extinguishes its legal personality, so that it goes out of existence for all purposes. Any property and rights formerly vested in it are deemed to belong to the Crown, as bona vacantia (CA 2006 s.1013). (Note, however, that in *Re Wilmott Trading Ltd* [2000] B.C.C. 321 Neuberger J. held that the particular "property" in that case—a waste management licence—did not revert to the Crown on the dissolution of the company, but ceased to exist.)

Under the former provisions of the Companies Acts, different rules regarding dissolution applied in a compulsory winding up and a voluntary winding up, a court order being always required in the former case. The reforms in the law of insolvency which were introduced by IA 1985 dispensed with this need for a court order and so brought the various types of winding up into line. A further innovation was the provision for early dissolution now contained in s.202 below. This enables the official receiver, in a winding up by the court, to apply to the registrar of companies to have the company dissolved at an early stage in the liquidation, when the company is so hopelessly insolvent that it is pointless to proceed further. In Scotland, the liquidator is empowered to make a similar application to the court (s.204). It is possible also for a company which is in administration under IA 1986 Sch.B1 to move directly from administration to dissolution, if the administrator thinks that the company has no property which might permit a distribution to its creditors (Sch.B1 para.84).

In addition to these procedures, a company may be dissolved by having its name struck off the register under CA 2006 s.1000–1011, on the ground that it has ceased to carry on business. The initiative may be taken by the registrar under ss.1000–1002, which provides that after he has made a preliminary inquiry and followed the prescribed procedure (including sending formal notice to the company of his intention to strike off and gazetting the notice) he may strike the company's name off the register after three months. Alternatively, the company itself may apply to have its name struck off (ss.1003–1011). This procedure is now available to all companies (under CA 1985 only private companies could apply). The directors who are making the application must make a declaration that neither s.1004 nor s.1005 prevents the application from being made (see the Registrar of Companies and Applications for Striking Off Regulations 2009 (SI 2009/1803, effective October 1, 2009) reg.2). Section 1004 bans a company from making an application if (inter alia) it has changed its name or carried on business within the previous three months; and s.1005 prevents an application if a scheme of arrangement under CA 2006 Pt 26 or an insolvency proceeding or moratorium is current. The registrar must first publish a notice in the *Gazette* inviting any person to show cause why the name should not be struck off and if there is no response he may then do so after three months. In either case, the company is dissolved by the publication in the *Gazette* of a further notice that the name has been struck off.

A company which has been dissolved may be restored to the register under CA 2006 ss.1024 et seq. Under the former legislation a court order was always needed for this purpose and separate procedures with different time limits applied. The 2006 Act, following a recommendation of the Company Law Review, institutes a simpler mechanism enabling a company which has been struck off (whether or not it has also been dissolved) to be reinstated in many cases by an administrative procedure without the involvement of the court. Application must be made to the registrar by a former member or former director within six years of the dissolution (s.1024). It must be shown that:

- the company was carrying on business at the date when it was struck off,

- if any property or right has vested in the Crown as bona vacantia, the Crown representative has given his written consent to the restoration,

- the applicant has delivered to the registrar such documents as are necessary to bring up to date the records kept by the registrar and paid any outstanding penalties (s.1025).

The general effect of administrative restoration is that the company is deemed to have continued in existence as if it had not been dissolved (s.1028(1)). In other words, reinstatement is retrospective in its effect, so that everything that has been done in the company's name while the company was struck off is automatically validated. This reflects the position under CA 1985 s.653 as decided in *Tyman's Ltd v Craven* [1952] 2 Q.B. 100 (in contrast with the line of cases typified by *Morris v Harris* [1927] A.C. 252, which held that restoration under the now repealed CA 1985 s.652 was not retrospective). The court may give such directions and make such provision (on an application to be made within three years from the date of restoration) as seems just for placing the company and all other persons in the same position (as nearly as may be) as if the company had not been dissolved or struck off (s.1028(3)).

Alternatively, a company that has been struck off (or dissolved or is deemed to have been dissolved) may be restored to the register by court order (s.1029(1)). Section 1029(2) lists the persons who may apply. The six-year time limit also applies here, but there is no limit where the purpose of the application is to bring proceedings against the company for damages for personal injury (s.1030(1)); and if the application is made where the company has been struck off and the registrar has refused reinstatement under s.1024, application may be made within 28 days from the registrar's refusal even if the six-year period has expired (s.1030(5)). The effect and consequences of the restoration are broadly the same as under s.1028 above. Sections 1033 and 1034 contain supplementary provisions dealing with problems which may arise in relation to the company's name (e.g. if another company with the same or a similar name has been registered after it was struck off) or property which was vested in the Crown as bona vacantia has been disposed of.

For cases on the exercise of the jurisdiction under the repealed s.653, see *Shire Court Residents Ltd v Registrar of Companies* [1995] B.C.C. 821; *Re Jayham Ltd* [1996] B.C.C. 224; *Re Priceland Ltd* [1997] B.C.C. 207; *City of Westminster Assurance Co Ltd v Registrar of Companies* [1997] B.C.C. 960; *Re Transocean Equipment Manufacturing & Trading Ltd* [2005] EWHC 2603 (Ch); [2006] B.C.C. 184; *Witherdale Ltd v Registrar of Companies* [2005] EWHC 2964 (Ch); [2008] 1 B.C.L.C. 174.

201 Dissolution (voluntary winding up)

201(1) [Application] This section applies, in the case of a company wound up voluntarily, where the liquidator has sent to the registrar of companies his final account and return under section 94 (members' voluntary) or section 106 (creditors' voluntary).

201(2) [Duty of registrar] The registrar on receiving the account and return shall forthwith register them; and on the expiration of 3 months from the registration of the return the company is deemed to be dissolved.

201(3) [Power of court re deferring date] However, the court may, on the application of the liquidator or any other person who appears to the court to be interested, make an order deferring the date at which the dissolution of the company is to take effect for such time as the court thinks fit.

201(4) [Copy of order to registrar] It is the duty of the person on whose application an order of the court under this section is made within 7 days after the making of the order to deliver to the registrar a copy of the order for registration; and if that person fails to do so he is liable to a fine and, for continued contravention, to a daily default fine.

GENERAL NOTE

The company is automatically dissolved under this section on the expiration of three months from the filing of the liquidator's final return: no further formality is needed.

S.201(3), (4)

The power of the court under subs.(3) is limited to extending the three-month period. "A copy" was substituted for "an office copy" in s.201(4) by the Companies (Registrar, Languages and Trading Disclosures) Regulations 2006 (SI 2006/3429) reg.3(1)(d) as from January 1, 2007.

On penalties, see s.430 and Sch.10.

202   Early dissolution (England and Wales)

202(1)   [Application] This section applies where an order for the winding up of a company has been made by the court in England and Wales.

202(2)   [Official receiver may apply for dissolution] The official receiver, if–

(a)   he is the liquidator of the company, and

(b)   it appears to him–

    (i)   that the realisable assets of the company are insufficient to cover the expenses of the winding up, and

    (ii)   that the affairs of the company do not require any further investigation,

may at any time apply to the registrar of companies for the early dissolution of the company.

202(3)   [Notice by official receiver] Before making that application, the official receiver shall give not less than 28 days' notice of his intention to do so to the company's creditors and contributories and, if there is an administrative receiver of the company, to that receiver.

202(4)   [Effect of notice on official receiver] With the giving of that notice the official receiver ceases (subject to any directions under the next section) to be required to perform any duties imposed on him in relation to the company, its creditors or contributories by virtue of any provision of this Act, apart from a duty to make an application under subsection (2) of this section.

202(5)   [Duty of registrar] On the receipt of the official receiver's application under subsection (2) the registrar shall forthwith register it and, at the end of the period of 3 months beginning with the day of the registration of the application, the company shall be dissolved.

However, the Secretary of State may, on the application of the official receiver or any other person who appears to the Secretary of State to be interested, give directions under section 203 at any time before the end of that period.

GENERAL NOTE

The Cork Committee (*Report*, paras 649–651) recommended that a procedure should be introduced to enable the official receiver to apply to the court for the early dissolution of a company which was in compulsory liquidation and hopelessly insolvent. The legislature has gone one better and dispensed with the need for a court order: the official receiver's application is sent to the registrar of companies and takes effect automatically after three months, unless the Secretary of State intervenes in the meantime. The official receiver (and the taxpayer) is thus spared the pointless expense of completing the winding up. A similar procedure is now available where a company in administration has no property which might permit a distribution to creditors: see Sch.B1 para.84.

S.202(1)

For the corresponding provision for Scotland, see s.204.

S.202(2)

The powers under this section may be exercised only by the official receiver, and only if he is the liquidator.

Paragraph (2)(b)(ii) leaves it to the judgment of the official receiver to decide that the circumstances of the insolvency do not create any suspicion of impropriety, and perhaps even to consider such policy questions as whether the circumstances, though dubious, really justify the expenditure of public money which would be involved in investigating the company's affairs further.

S.202(3), (4)
The official receiver's duties (as liquidator or otherwise) cease as soon as he gives the notice, i.e. even while the 28-day period referred to in s.202(3) and the three-month period in s.202(5) are running, he has no obligation to take further steps in the liquidation.

It seems that the liquidator comes under a *duty* to apply for a dissolution once he has given a notice under s.202(3): if he starts the dissolution process, he must go through with it, and if he has second thoughts he must invoke the powers of the Secretary of State under s.203.

S.202(5)
The dissolution takes effect automatically on the expiry of the three-month period, unless the Secretary of State has directed that a longer period than three months be substituted.

203   Consequence of notice under s.202

203(1)   [Application for directions] Where a notice has been given under section 202(3), the official receiver or any creditor or contributory of the company, or the administrative receiver of the company (if there is one) may apply to the Secretary of State for directions under this section.

203(2)   [Grounds for application] The grounds on which that application may be made are–

(a)   that the realisable assets of the company are sufficient to cover the expenses of the winding up;

(b)   that the affairs of the company do require further investigation; or

(c)   that for any other reason the early dissolution of the company is inappropriate.

203(3)   [Scope of directions] Directions under this section–

(a)   are directions making such provision as the Secretary of State thinks fit for enabling the winding up of the company to proceed as if no notice had been given under section 202(3), and

(b)   may, in the case of an application under section 202(5), include a direction deferring the date at which the dissolution of the company is to take effect for such period as the Secretary of State thinks fit.

203(4)   [Appeal to court] An appeal to the court lies from any decision of the Secretary of State on an application for directions under this section.

203(5)   [Copy of directions etc. to registrar] It is the duty of the person on whose application any directions are given under this section, or in whose favour an appeal with respect to an application for such directions is determined, within 7 days after the giving of the directions or the determination of the appeal, to deliver to the registrar of companies for registration such a copy of the directions or determination as is prescribed.

203(6)   [Penalty on default re s.203(5)] If a person without reasonable excuse fails to deliver a copy as required by subsection (5), he is liable to a fine and, for continued contravention, to a daily default fine.

S.203(1)–(3)
The Secretary of State is empowered by this section to override the official receiver's notice under s.202(3) which initiated the dissolution process, so that the winding up proceeds as before. It also appears from s.203(3)(b) that the Secretary of State may confirm the effect of the notice but delay the dissolution by substituting a longer period than three months for the operation of s.202(5).

S.203(4)
The use of the term "appeal" is significant, since it makes it clear that the court may substitute its own decision on the merits of the case for that of the Secretary of State. For the relevant procedure, see IR 1986 rr.4.224, 4.225.

S.203(5)
The seven-day period is extremely short, especially since it runs from the date of the giving of the directions or determination of the appeal, and not from the day when the applicant is notified of the outcome of his application.

It does not appear that there is any obligation to register a decision on the part of the Secretary of State to give no "directions". (However, there is equally no machinery provided to warn the registrar that an application to the Secretary of State has been made: time will continue to run for the purposes of s.202(5) while such an application is under consideration.)

S.203(6)
On penalties, see s.430 and Sch.10.

204 Early dissolution (Scotland)

204(1) [Application] This section applies where a winding-up order has been made by the court in Scotland.

204(2) [Application by liquidator] If after a meeting or meetings under section 138 (appointment of liquidator in Scotland) it appears to the liquidator that the realisable assets of the company are insufficient to cover the expenses of the winding up, he may apply to the court for an order that the company be dissolved.

204(3) [Court order] Where the liquidator makes that application, if the court is satisfied that the realisable assets of the company are insufficient to cover the expenses of the winding up and it appears to the court appropriate to do so, the court shall make an order that the company be dissolved in accordance with this section.

204(4) [Copy of order to registrar etc.] A copy of the order shall within 14 days from its date be forwarded by the liquidator to the registrar of companies, who shall forthwith register it; and, at the end of the period of 3 months beginning with the day of the registration of the order, the company shall be dissolved.

204(5) [Court may defer dissolution] The court may, on an application by any person who appears to the court to have an interest, order that the date at which the dissolution of the company is to take effect shall be deferred for such period as the court thinks fit.

204(6) [Copy of s.204(5) order to registrar] It is the duty of the person on whose application an order is made under subsection (5), within 7 days after the making of the order, to deliver to the registrar of companies such a copy of the order as is prescribed.

204(7) [Penalty for non-compliance with s.204(4)] If the liquidator without reasonable excuse fails to comply with the requirements of subsection (4), he is liable to a fine and, for continued contravention, to a daily default fine.

204(8) [Penalty for non-compliance with s.204(6)] If a person without reasonable excuse fails to deliver a copy as required by subsection (6), he is liable to a fine and, for continued contravention, to a daily default fine.

GENERAL NOTE

There is no official receiver in Scotland, so that a private liquidator will be in office in every winding up by the court. In the absence of a public officer comparable with the official receiver, it is necessary in Scotland to refer to the court for decision the question whether an early dissolution of the company is justified. This section accordingly modifies the procedure of ss.202, 203 to meet the different circumstances in Scotland.

S.204(2)
There is no obligation in Scotland to give the company's creditors and contributories the 28-day notice required in England and Wales by s.202(3). In Scotland, on the other hand, the liquidator cannot set any steps in motion to bring about an early dissolution until after the meetings of creditors and contributories have been held. It is reasonable to assume that they will have been made aware of the company's hopeless insolvency at the statutory meetings.

S.204(3)–(8)

The whole of the proceedings in an application for early dissolution in Scotland are dealt with by the court. There is no involvement of the Secretary of State at any stage. Apart from this, the comments to ss.202, 203 apply to the present section.

On penalties, see s.430 and Sch.10.

205   Dissolution otherwise than under ss.202–204

205(1)   **[Application]** This section applies where the registrar of companies receives–

    (a)   a notice served for the purposes of section 172(8) (final meeting of creditors and vacation of office by liquidator), or

    (b)   a notice from the official receiver that the winding up of a company by the court is complete.

205(2)   **[Duty of registrar etc.]** The registrar shall, on receipt of the notice, forthwith register it; and, subject as follows, at the end of the period of 3 months beginning with the day of the registration of the notice, the company shall be dissolved.

205(3)   **[Deferral by Secretary of State]** The Secretary of State may, on the application of the official receiver or any other person who appears to the Secretary of State to be interested, give a direction deferring the date at which the dissolution of the company is to take effect for such period as the Secretary of State thinks fit.

205(4)   **[Appeal to court]** An appeal to the court lies from any decision of the Secretary of State on an application for a direction under subsection (3).

205(5)   **[Non-application of s.205(3) in Scotland]** Subsection (3) does not apply in a case where the winding-up order was made by the court in Scotland, but in such a case the court may, on an application by any person appearing to the court to have an interest, order that the date at which the dissolution of the company is to take effect shall be deferred for such period as the court thinks fit.

205(6)   **[Copy of direction etc. to registrar]** It is the duty of the person–

    (a)   on whose application a direction is given under subsection (3);

    (b)   in whose favour an appeal with respect to an application for such a direction is determined; or

    (c)   on whose application an order is made under subsection (5),

within 7 days after the giving of the direction, the determination of the appeal or the making of the order, to deliver to the registrar for registration such a copy of the direction, determination or order as is prescribed.

205(7)   **[Penalty for non-compliance with s.205(6)]** If a person without reasonable excuse fails to deliver a copy as required by subsection (6), he is liable to a fine and, for continued contravention, to a daily default fine.

S.205(1), (2)

Dissolution takes place automatically three months after the registrar has been given the notification by the liquidator or the official receiver required by this section: no court order is required.

S.205(3)–(4)

The Secretary of State, in England and Wales, and the court are given roles under the present section comparable with those which they discharge in relation to the early liquidation procedure under ss.202(5), 203(3)(b) and 203(4): see, further, the notes to those provisions, and for the relevant procedure, see IR 1986 rr.4.224, 4.225.

S.205(5)

Compare s.204(5), and see the notes to that subsection.

S.205(6), (7)

Compare ss.203(5), (6) and 204(6), (8), and for the relevant rule, see IR 1986 r.4.224.

On penalties, see s.430 and Sch.10.

MALPRACTICE BEFORE AND DURING LIQUIDATION; PENALISATION OF COMPANIES AND COMPANY OFFICERS; INVESTIGATIONS AND PROSECUTIONS

Offences of fraud, deception, etc.

206 Fraud, etc. in anticipation of winding up

206(1) **[Offences by officers]** When a company is ordered to be wound up by the court, or passes a resolution for voluntary winding up, any person, being a past or present officer of the company, is deemed to have committed an offence if, within the 12 months immediately preceding the commencement of the winding up, he has–

(a) concealed any part of the company's property to the value of £500 or more, or concealed any debt due to or from the company, or

(b) fraudulently removed any part of the company's property to the value of £500 or more, or

(c) concealed, destroyed, mutilated or falsified any book or paper affecting or relating to the company's property or affairs, or

(d) made any false entry in any book or paper affecting or relating to the company's property or affairs, or

(e) fraudulently parted with, altered or made any omission in any document affecting or relating to the company's property or affairs, or

(f) pawned, pledged or disposed of any property of the company which has been obtained on credit and has not been paid for (unless the pawning, pledging or disposal was in the ordinary way of the company's business).

206(2) **[Further offences]** Such a person is deemed to have committed an offence if within the period above mentioned he has been privy to the doing by others of any of the things mentioned in paragraphs (c), (d) and (e) of subsection (1); and he commits an offence if, at any time after the commencement of the winding up, he does any of the things mentioned in paragraphs (a) to (f) of that subsection, or is privy to the doing by others of any of the things mentioned in paragraphs (c) to (e) of it.

206(3) **["Officer"]** For purposes of this section, **"officer"** includes a shadow director.

206(4) **[Defences]** It is a defence–

(a) for a person charged under paragraph (a) or (f) of subsection (1) (or under subsection (2) in respect of the things mentioned in either of those two paragraphs) to prove that he had no intent to defraud, and

(b) for a person charged under paragraph (c) or (d) of subsection (1) (or under subsection (2) in respect of the things mentioned in either of those two paragraphs) to prove that he had no intent to conceal the state of affairs of the company or to defeat the law.

206(5) **[Offence re person pawning property etc. as in s.206(1)(f)]** Where a person pawns, pledges or disposes of any property in circumstances which amount to an offence under subsection (1)(f), every person who takes in pawn or pledge, or otherwise receives, the property knowing it to be pawned, pledged or disposed of in such circumstances, is guilty of an offence.

206(6) **[Penalty]** A person guilty of an offence under this section is liable to imprisonment or a fine, or both.

206(7) **[Increase, reduction of sums in s.206(1)(a), (b)]** The money sums specified in paragraphs (a) and (b) of subsection (1) are subject to increase or reduction by order under section 416 in Part XV.

S.206(1), (2)

This section makes it an offence for an officer of a company to conceal or remove property, falsify entries in the company's books or perpetrate other similar acts after the commencement of a winding up (s.206(2)), and "deems" an officer or past officer to have committed an offence if he has been guilty of any of these acts and a winding up ensues within the next 12 months (s.206(1)).

The diversion of a debt due to a company into the account of the accused or a third party is equivalent to the "removal" of property for the purposes of s.206(1)(b): *R. v Robinson* [1990] B.C.C. 656.

It may be a defence to a charge under s.206(1) that the liquidator has abandoned the property in question, but this will not be established without proof that the liquidator is aware of its existence—which it will be the duty of the officers of the company (in most cases, the defendants themselves) to declare and deliver up under s.208: *R. v McCredie* [2000] B.C.C. 617.

S.206(3)

The term "officer" is not defined with precision: the definition in CA 2006 s.1173 (which is incorporated into the present Act by the concluding words of s.251) merely states that "officer, in relation to a body corporate, *includes* a director, manager or secretary". A director "includes any person occupying the position of director, by whatever name called" (s.251). A director (in this extended sense) and a secretary plainly will always be "officers". Shadow directors (for definition, see s.251) are frequently declared to be officers for the purposes of a particular provision, as in the present subsection, and so it might be reasonable to infer that where there is no such statement (e.g. as in s.207) the opposite is the case. The same argument would apply in the case of a liquidator: the fact that he is declared to be an officer for the purposes of s.85(2), for example, suggests that he is ordinarily not to be deemed one. This is confirmed by the distinction that appears to be drawn between "officers" on the one hand and liquidators, administrators and receivers on the other (e.g. by ss.133(1) and 212(1), and compare also s.219(3)).

The word "manager", used in CA 2006 s.1173, could well be a source of difficulty. It is not clear whether a person would need to have been appointed to a post carrying managerial responsibilities to come within this concept, or whether it is sufficient that he has taken some part in the management of the company's business, even at a relatively humble level. In *Re a Company (No.00996 of 1979)* [1980] Ch. 138 at 144, Shaw L.J. said:

> "The expression 'manager' should not be too narrowly construed. It is not to be equated with a managing or other director or a general manager … [Any] person who in the affairs of the company exercises a supervisory control which reflects the general policy of the company for the time being or which is related to the general administration of the company is in the sphere of management. He need not be a member of the board of directors. He need not be subject to specific instructions from the board".

A number of provisions in the legislation (e.g. IA 1986 ss.212(1)(c), 216(3), 217(4) and CDDA 1986 ss.1(1)(d), 11, 15(4)) refer to a person "taking part in the management" of a company (and compare "involved in the management": IA 1986 s.217(1), CDDA 1986 ss.2, 15(1)). It would not necessarily follow that a person coming within such a formula was a "manager" for the purposes of the present section, but cases decided under these provisions may be of some relevance: see, e.g. *CCA v Brecht* (1987) 7 A.C.L.C. 40; *Re Clasper Group Services Ltd* (1988) 4 B.C.C. 673; *Drew v Lord Advocate* [1996] S.L.T. 1062; *Re a Company* [1980] Ch. 138; *Re Market Wizard Systems (UK) Ltd* [1998] 2 B.C.L.C. 282; and *R. v Doring* [2002] EWCA Crim 1695; [2002] B.C.C. 838.

Both an administrator and a receiver and manager (including an administrative receiver) discharge functions which can only be described as managerial, but in the leading case of *Re B Johnson & Co (Builders) Ltd* [1955] Ch. 634 a receiver and manager appointed by a debenture-holder was held not to be an "officer" for the purposes of what is now s.212. (The point is now covered by s.212(1)(b).) An administrator has been held to be an "officer" who may be granted relief under the court's discretionary jurisdiction conferred by CA 2006 s.1157: *Re Home Treat Ltd* [1991] B.C.C. 165.

An auditor has been held to be an officer for the purposes of s.212 in a number of cases, e.g. *Re London and General Bank* [1895] 2 Ch. 166; *Re Thomas Gerrard & Son Ltd* [1968] Ch. 455 at 473; and also under other statutory provisions similar to s.206: *R. v Shacter* [1960] 2 Q.B. 252; but the question is not free from doubt: compare CA 2006 s.1157 ("whether or not he is an officer of the company").

Bankers and solicitors and other professional advisers are not, as such, "officers" of the company (*Re Imperial Land Co of Marseilles, Re National Bank* (1870) L.R. 10 Eq. 298), as appears to be confirmed by s.219(3).

S.206(4)

The onus of proof with respect to mens rea is, unusually, put on the defendant. In such a case, the burden of proof on the accused is less than that required at the hands of the prosecution, which must prove the case "beyond reasonable doubt": instead, the burden may be discharged by evidence which satisfies the court on a balance of probabilities: *R. v*

Carr-Briant [1943] K.B. 607; *Morton v Confer* [1963] 1 W.L.R. 763; [1963] 2 All E.R. 765. This, at least, was the view taken before the enactment of the Human Rights Act 1986. In *R. v Carass* [2001] EWCA Crim 2845; [2002] 1 W.L.R. 1714, the Court of Appeal took the view that s.206 imposed only an evidentiary, as opposed to a legal, burden of proof on the defendant and that, on this ground, there was no incompatibility with the Human Rights Act. But in *R. (Griffin) v Richmond Magistrates' Court* [2008] EWHC 84 (Admin); [2008] 1 W.L.R. 1525; [2008] 1 B.C.L.C. 681 (a case on s.208, below) the Divisional Court reviewed the authorities, including the House of Lords' rulings in *Sheldrake v DPP* [2005] 1 All E.R. 237; and *R. v Johnstone* [2003] 3 All E.R. 884, and concluded that *R. v Carass* was wrongly decided: the burden of proof under both ss.206 and 208 is a legal burden and, because of the seriousness of these offences, and this is compatible with the Human Rights Act on the grounds of reasonableness and proportionality. The issue has also been considered by the Court of Appeal in relation to the corresponding bankruptcy offences in *Re Attorney General's Reference (No.1 of 2004)* [2004] EWCA Crim 1025; [2004] B.P.I.R. 1073, discussed in the note to s.352, below.

S.206(5)
In regard to the offence created by this provision, the normal rule as to onus of proof will apply.

S.206(6)
The sanctions fixed by Sch.10 for these offences and the other offences involving dishonesty defined in the following sections are severe: up to seven years' imprisonment; but the maximum has not been increased in line with changes made to other legislation by the Fraud Act 2006.

On penalties, see s.430 and Sch.10.

S.206(7)
See the note to s.206(1), (2) above.

207   Transactions in fraud of creditors

207(1)   **[Offences by officers]** When a company is ordered to be wound up by the court or passes a resolution for voluntary winding up, a person is deemed to have committed an offence if he, being at the time an officer of the company–

   (a)   has made or caused to be made any gift or transfer of, or charge on, or has caused or connived at the levying of any execution against, the company's property, or

   (b)   has concealed or removed any part of the company's property since, or within 2 months before, the date of any unsatisfied judgment or order for the payment of money obtained against the company.

207(2)   **[Exception]** A person is not guilty of an offence under this section–

   (a)   by reason of conduct constituting an offence under subsection (1)(a) which occurred more than 5 years before the commencement of the winding up, or

   (b)   if he proves that, at the time of the conduct constituting the offence, he had no intent to defraud the company's creditors.

207(3)   **[Penalty]** A person guilty of an offence under this section is liable to imprisonment or a fine, or both.

GENERAL NOTE

The offences defined by this section are brought forward from earlier Companies Acts. However, a modification made by IA 1985 has had the effect of reversing the onus of proof of mens rea: the words "with intent to defraud creditors of the company" have been removed from the substantive definition of the crime, and s.207(2)(b) (matching s.206(4) above) has been added.

S.207(1)
There is no definition of "officer", corresponding to ss.206(3) and 208(3), extending the term to include a shadow director for the purposes of this section.

S.207(3)
On penalties, see s.430 and Sch.10.

208   Misconduct in course of winding up

208(1)   [Offences by officers] When a company is being wound up, whether by the court or voluntarily, any person, being a past or present officer of the company, commits an offence if he–

(a)   does not to the best of his knowledge and belief fully and truly discover to the liquidator all the company's property, and how and to whom and for what consideration and when the company disposed of any part of that property (except such part as has been disposed of in the ordinary way of the company's business), or

(b)   does not deliver up to the liquidator (or as he directs) all such part of the company's property as is in his custody or under his control, and which he is required by law to deliver up, or

(c)   does not deliver up to the liquidator (or as he directs) all books and papers in his custody or under his control belonging to the company and which he is required by law to deliver up, or

(d)   knowing or believing that a false debt has been proved by any person in the winding up, fails to inform the liquidator as soon as practicable, or

(e)   after the commencement of the winding up, prevents the production of any book or paper affecting or relating to the company's property or affairs.

208(2)   [Further offences] Such a person commits an offence if after the commencement of the winding up he attempts to account for any part of the company's property by fictitious losses or expenses; and he is deemed to have committed that offence if he has so attempted at any meeting of the company's creditors within the 12 months immediately preceding the commencement of the winding up.

208(3)   ["Officer"] For purposes of this section, **"officer"** includes a shadow director.

208(4)   [Defences] It is a defence–

(a)   for a person charged under paragraph (a), (b) or (c) of subsection (1) to prove that he had no intent to defraud, and

(b)   for a person charged under paragraph (e) of that subsection to prove that he had no intent to conceal the state of affairs of the company or to defeat the law.

208(5)   [Penalty] A person guilty of an offence under this section is liable to imprisonment or a fine, or both.

GENERAL NOTE
The notes to s.206 apply generally to the present section.

S.208(4)
See *R. (Griffin) v Richmond Magistrates' Court* [2008] EWHC 84 (Admin); [2008] 1 W.L.R. 1525; [2008] 1 B.C.L.C. 681, discussed in the note to s.206(4).

209   Falsification of company's books

209(1)   [Offence by officer or contributory] When a company is being wound up, an officer or contributory of the company commits an offence if he destroys, mutilates, alters or falsifies any books, papers or securities, or makes or is privy to the making of any false or fraudulent entry in any register, book of account or document belonging to the company with intent to defraud or deceive any person.

209(2)   [Penalty] A person guilty of an offence under this section is liable to imprisonment or a fine, or both.

The offences which this section defines largely duplicate those specified in s.206(1)(c)–(e), which apply in a winding up by virtue of s.206(2); but those potentially liable include contributories (though not, at least in specific terms, "shadow directors"), and the element of mens rea is expressed differently: compare s.206(4)(b).

210   Material omissions from statement relating to company's affairs

210(1)   [Offence by past or present officer] When a company is being wound up, whether by the court or voluntarily, any person, being a past or present officer of the company, commits an offence if he makes any material omission in any statement relating to the company's affairs.

210(2)   [Offence prior to winding up] When a company has been ordered to be wound up by the court, or has passed a resolution for voluntary winding up, any such person is deemed to have committed that offence if, prior to the winding up, he has made any material omission in any such statement.

210(3)   ["Officer"] For purposes of this section, **"officer"** includes a shadow director.

210(4)   [Defence] It is a defence for a person charged under this section to prove that he had no intent to defraud.

210(5)   [Penalty] A person guilty of an offence under this section is liable to imprisonment or a fine, or both.

The "statement of affairs", which under the Companies Acts was part of the standard procedure in a winding up by the court, has now become a feature of many other forms of insolvency procedure, e.g. administration and receivership (see the note to s.131). The present section is not confined in its scope to the statutory "statement of affairs" so defined, but applies to "any statement in relation to the company's affairs". It is, however, limited to statements made when a company is being wound up, or prior to a winding up; and it is concerned only with omissions. *Positive* misstatements relating to a company's affairs in a winding up will almost certainly amount to one or other of the offences defined in ss.206–209; but similar wrongdoing in other insolvency proceedings may be sanctioned only by the less draconian provisions of s.235, unless of course they are criminal offences apart from the present Act.

Liability under the section is limited to past and present officers of the company (including shadow directors: s.210(3)). On this point and generally, see the notes to s.206.

S.210(4)
See the note to s.206(4).

211   False representations to creditors

211(1)   [Offences by past or present officer] When a company is being wound up, whether by the court or voluntarily, any person, being a past or present officer of the company–

(a)   commits an offence if he makes any false representation or commits any other fraud for the purpose of obtaining the consent of the company's creditors or any of them to an agreement with reference to the company's affairs or to the winding up, and

(b)   is deemed to have committed that offence if, prior to the winding up, he has made any false representation, or committed any other fraud, for that purpose.

211(2)   ["Officer"] For purposes of this section, **"officer"** includes a shadow director.

211(3)   [Penalty] A person guilty of an offence under this section is liable to imprisonment or a fine, or both.

This section applies only to past and present officers (including shadow directors). The notes to s.206 apply generally to s.211; but the onus of establishing fraud is here placed on the prosecution.

Penalisation of directors and officers

212 Summary remedy against delinquent directors, liquidators, etc.

212(1) **[Application]** This section applies if in the course of the winding up of a company it appears that a person who–

(a) is or has been an officer of the company,

(b) has acted as liquidator or administrative receiver of the company, or

(c) not being a person falling within paragraph (a) or (b), is or has been concerned, or has taken part, in the promotion, formation or management of the company,

has misapplied or retained, or become accountable for, any money or other property of the company, or been guilty of any misfeasance or breach of any fiduciary or other duty in relation to the company.

212(2) **[Interpretation]** The reference in subsection (1) to any misfeasance or breach of any fiduciary or other duty in relation to the company includes, in the case of a person who has acted as liquidator of the company, any misfeasance or breach of any fiduciary or other duty in connection with the carrying out of his functions as liquidator of the company.

212(3) **[Examination, orders]** The court may, on the application of the official receiver or the liquidator, or of any creditor or contributory, examine into the conduct of the person falling within subsection (1) and compel him–

(a) to repay, restore or account for the money or property or any part of it, with interest at such rate as the court thinks just, or

(b) to contribute such sum to the company's assets by way of compensation in respect of the misfeasance or breach of fiduciary or other duty as the court thinks just.

212(4) **[Limit on s.212(3) application]** The power to make an application under subsection (3) in relation to a person who has acted as liquidator of the company is not exercisable, except with the leave of the court, after he has had his release.

212(5) **[Exercise of s.212(3) power]** The power of a contributory to make an application under subsection (3) is not exercisable except with the leave of the court, but is exercisable notwithstanding that he will not benefit from any order the court may make on the application.

S.212(1)

This re-enacts, with some amendments introduced by IA 1985, the traditional "misfeasance" section of successive Companies Acts, providing a summary remedy in the liquidation of a company for the restoration of property and the assessment of compensation or damages for breach of duty against its former officers and others. (On the meaning of the term "officer", see the note to s.206(3).) The section applies to shadow directors: *Gemma Ltd v Davies* [2008] EWHC 546 (Ch); [2008] 2 B.C.C. 812, and to de facto directors: *Re Paycheck Services 3 Ltd* [2008] EWHC 2200 (Ch); [2009] B.C.C. 37.

As originally enacted, the section applied to administrators as well as those listed, but all references to administrators were removed by EA 2002 Sch.17 para.18, which came into effect on September 15, 2003. At the same time a separate provision dealing with misfeasance by administrators was enacted in EA 2002 Sch.16, which is now to be found in IA 1986 Sch.B1 para.75, and a saving provision, reinstating s.212 as formerly worded, came into effect under the Enterprise Act 2002 (Commencement No.4 and Transitional Provisions and Savings) Order 2003 (SI 2003/2093 (C. 85)) art.3. This saving provision applies in cases where a petition for an administration order was presented before September 15, 2003, and also in the administration of insolvent partnerships commencing prior to July 1, 2005, limited liability partnerships and bodies which are insurers under FSMA 2002 and SI 2002/1242. There is no mention in the Order of building societies and the public utility companies listed in EA 2002 s.249, but in these cases the original s.212 will continue to apply because s.249 disapplies the new s.8(3) in regard to such bodies. There is also no mention of the supervisor of a CVA, but subs.(2)(c) could no doubt be invoked. The words "breach of trust" in CA 1985 have been replaced by "breach of any fiduciary or other duty", and this also has the effect of extending the coverage of the remedy, for although "breach of trust" and "breach of fiduciary duty" may be regarded as synonymous, it had been held that the former wording did not include claims based on negligence (*Re B Johnson & Co (Builders) Ltd* [1955] Ch. 634). However in *Re D'Jan of London Ltd* [1993] B.C.C. 646 Hoffmann L.J. clearly accepted that the section now covers "breaches of any duty including the duty of care", and applied it in a straightforward case of negligence brought against a director. See also *Re Centralcrest Engineering Ltd* [2000] B.C.C. 727 (where a liquidator was held liable); *Re Westlowe Storage & Distribution Ltd* [2000] B.C.C. 851; *Re Pantone 485 Ltd* (below); *Re Continental Assurance Co of London plc* [2001] B.P.I.R. 733 (a lengthy judgment in which it was held that the case in misfeasance against both the executive and the non-executive directors of the company had not been made out); *Re Transocean Equipment Manufacturing & Trading Ltd* [2005] EWHC 2603 (Ch); [2006] B.C.C. 184 (where the acts of misfeasance took place while the company was dissolved); and *Kinlan v Crimmin* [2006] EWHC 779 (Ch); [2007] B.C.C. 106 (where a repurchase of shares had been carried out under professional advice but without complying with all the statutory formal requirements).

In *Base Metal Trading Ltd v Shamurin* [2004] EWCA Civ 1316; [2005] 1 W.L.R. 1157; [2005] B.C.C. 325, Arden L.J. observed that, in the case of a company incorporated abroad which is being wound up in this country, the content of the duties of directors will be determined by the law of the jurisdiction of incorporation, but s.212 may be invoked to enforce such duties. In *Hague v Nam Tai Electronics Inc* [2008] UKPC 13; [2008] B.C.C. 295 (a misfeasance claim alleging wrongdoing by a liquidator) the Privy Council ruled that, having accepted appointment as liquidator in the jurisdiction of the company's incorporation, it was not open to him to contest the competence of the courts of that jurisdiction to hear the case.

It is well settled that the section creates no new liabilities, but only provides a simpler procedure for the recovery of property or compensation in a winding up. Even here, there are limitations on its use—e.g. it is not available to enforce a contractual debt (*Re Etic Ltd* [1928] Ch. 861), and in *Re Continental Assurance Co of London plc* (above), at 855 it was said to be improper to use it to circumvent the difficulties of establishing a preference claim. Note, however, that the fact that s.212 provides a statutory remedy against a company officer does not in any way exclude the pursuit of common-law remedies in contract and tort against the same person: *A & J Fabrications (Batley) Ltd v Grant Thornton* [1999] B.C.C. 807.

Where a claim is brought under s.212 against directors alleging negligence and/or breach of duty, it is open to them to claim contribution from professional advisers on whose advice they acted, e.g. insolvency practitioners who had advised that they could continue trading before the company went into liquidation: *Re International Championship Management Ltd* [2006] EWHC 768 (Ch); [2007] B.C.C. 95. Contrast the position where the claim is brought under ss.214, 238 or 239, or where the claim is vested by statute in the liquidator (ibid.).

The question whether a claim under s.212 is statute-barred is determined on the same basis as for other claims. So, in *Re Pantone 485 Ltd* [2002] 1 B.C.L.C. 266, where a director used the company's money for his own benefit in a way which rendered him accountable to it as trustee, the claim was held to be within s.21(1)(b) of the Limitation Act 1980 and accordingly not statute-barred. See also *Re Eurocruit Ltd* [2007] EWHC 1433 (Ch); [2007] B.C.C. 916.

Sums or property recovered under this section are the product of a chose in action vested in the company prior to the liquidation and are accordingly "assets of the company" which are capable of being made the subject of a charge (*Re Anglo-Austrian Printing & Publishing Union* [1895] 2 Ch. 891), or of being assigned by it or the liquidator: *Re Oasis Merchandising Services Ltd* [1998] Ch. 170; [1997] B.C.C. 282.

Where directors make payments in breach of duty to one or more of their number, there may be concurrent liability under this section and under such other provisions as s.214 (wrongful trading) and s.239 (preference). In one such case, *Re DKG Contractors Ltd* [1990] B.C.C. 903, it was ordered that liability under the various heads should not be cumulative but that payments made under ss.212 and 239 should go to satisfy the liability under s.214. However, in a later case, *Re Purpoint Ltd* [1991] B.C.C. 121, Vinelott J. made orders against the respondent for the payment of separate sums under ss.212 and 214, being satisfied that there was no injustice in the nature of overlap or "double counting" in making the orders cumulative. See also the calculations in *Re MDA Investment Management Ltd* [2003] EWHC 227 (Ch) and [2004] EWHC 42 (Ch); [2005] B.C.C. 783. For a comprehensive discussion of this and related questions, see Roy Goode, *Principles of Corporate Insolvency Law*, 3rd edn (2005), at 12.41–12.43. See also *Re Krug International (UK) Ltd* [2008] EWHC 2256 (Ch); [2008] B.P.I.R. 1512 (s.423 claim against foreign third party held properly joined with s.212 proceedings against directors).

A sum awarded against a misfeasant officer under s.212 cannot be set off against a debt due to him from the company: *Re Anglo-French Co-operative Society Ex p. Pelly* (1882) 21 Ch. D. 492; *Manson v Smith (liquidator of Thomas Christy Ltd)* [1997] 2 B.C.L.C. 161.

The provisions of s.212 apply to directors (including shadow directors) of building societies: see Building Societies Act 1986 s.90 and Sch.15, as amended by CA 1989 s.211 and Sch.24.

S.212(2)

This provision is probably intended to remove any doubts on the question whether all the duties of a liquidator or administrator are owed to the company. It is curious, but at the same time it may well be significant, that there is no mention of an administrative receiver in this subsection, even though he is mentioned in s.212(1)(b). *Johnson's* case (above) held that a receiver and manager at common law was not concerned to manage the business for the benefit of the company, but only to realise his creditor's security, and that he was under no duty to the company or its contributories to preserve the goodwill and business of the company. This view was confirmed by the Privy Council in *Downsview Nominees Ltd v First City Corporation Ltd* [1993] A.C. 295; [1993] B.C.C. 46, where it was held that a receiver and manager owes no general duty in negligence to, inter alios, the debtor company to use reasonable care in the exercise of his powers. However, it was also stated in the latter case that equity imposes specific duties on such a receiver, including a duty to exercise his powers in good faith; and that, if a receiver decides to sell the charged property, he must take reasonable care to obtain a proper price. (See also *Medforth v Blake* [2000] Ch. 86; [1999] B.C.C. 771, and the Introductory note to Part III.) There is thus potentially scope (albeit of a limited nature) for s.212 to be invoked against an administrative receiver or a receiver and manager.

S.212(3)

Although a creditor has standing to bring proceedings under s.212, the court can only make an order in favour of the company, and not the individual applicant (*Oldham v Kyrris* [2003] EWCA Civ 1506; [2004] B.C.C. 111). This is so even though it may well be arguable, where the defendant is a liquidator, that the duties owed by a liquidator in an insolvent liquidation are owed to the creditors as a class as well as to the company (*Hague v Nam Tai Electronics Inc* (above)). See also *Charalambous v B & C Associates* [2009] EWHC 2601 (Ch) (no duty in tort owed by administrator to unsecured creditor). An assignee of a creditor's claim has standing: *Mullarkey v Broad* [2007] EWHC 3400 (Ch); [2008] 1 B.C.L.C. 638. A contributory's right to make an application is qualified by s.212(5).

The court has a discretion under para.(a) to order the respondent to make restitution in whole or in part, and under para.(b) to order payment of "such sum … as the court thinks just". Clearly, in relation to para.(b), the question of quantum is a matter for the discretion of the court (but even so, it does not extend to enabling the court to disregard the need to establish causation: *Re Simmon Box (Diamonds) Ltd, Cohen v Selby* [2002] B.C.C. 82). In *Re D'Jan of London Ltd* (above) the respondent was ordered to pay a sum which was less than the company's actual loss. However under para.(a) the court (although empowered to order restoration of "all or any part" of the misapplied money or property) does not have a discretion which is similarly unfettered: in particular, it will not reopen a decision as to quantum which has already been settled in the course of the liquidation or in other proceedings: *Re AMF International Ltd* [1996] B.C.C. 335.

Section 1157 of the Companies Act 2006 (formerly CA 1985 s.727) empowers the court, in any proceedings against an officer or auditor of a company for (inter alia) negligence, breach of duty or breach of trust, to relieve the defendant either wholly or partly from liability if he has acted honestly and reasonably and ought, in the circumstances, fairly to be excused. This provision has been invoked in many cases brought under IA 1986 s.212 (and, indeed, it was on this provision that Hoffmann L.J. relied in the *D'Jan* case). Directors who continued trading on professional advice were held not to be liable either for misfeasance under s.212 or wrongful trading under s.214 (*Re Continental Assurance Co of London plc (No.4)* [2007] B.C.L.C. 289); and in *Re Ortega Associates* Ltd [2007] EWHC 2046 (Ch); [2008] B.C.C. 256 a director was held not liable under s.212 for the dishonesty of a fellow director when he had been advised by his solicitor to take no action; the deputy judge went on to hold that even if there had been any breach of duty he should be wholly relieved from liability under s.727. In *Re Marini Ltd* [2003] EWHC 234 (Ch); [2004] B.C.C. 172 it was said that the court would have the greatest difficulty in thinking it ever likely that a defaulting director should be granted relief if the consequence of doing so would be to leave the director enjoying benefits at the expense of creditors which he would never have received but for the default; and in *Re Loquitur Ltd* [2003] EWHC 999 (Ch); [2003] 2 B.C.L.C. 442 Etherton J. said that in view of the terms of CA 1985 s.270 [now CA 2006 s.836] he had no jurisdiction to grant relief under this provision from liability for the wrongful payment of a dividend if the consequence was to leave the company insolvent or potentially so. However, rather paradoxically, his Lordship went on to observe that the court's discretion under s.212 was additional to that under the present section and was not subject to a similar limitation, and in exercise of the former thought it appropriate to limit the amount that the respondents were ordered to pay. See also *Re MDA Investment Management Ltd* [2003] EWHC 227 (Ch) and [2004] EWHC 42 (Ch); [2005] B.C.C. 783, where relief was refused to a director who had acted honestly but not reasonably (reasonableness being an issue to be determined on an objective basis); *PNC Telecom plc v Thomas (No.2)* [2007] EWHC 2157 (Ch); [2008] 2 B.C.L.C. 95. See also *Holland v HM Revenue and Customs* [2009] EWCA Civ 625; [2010] B.C.C. 104, where the Court of Appeal ruled that the discretion conferred by s.212

and CA 1985 s.727 was limited to the relief to be granted and did not extend to create any new defences as to liability.

S.212(4)
For the release of a liquidator, see ss.173, 174, and an administrator, s.20 and Sch.B1 para.98.

S.212(5)
Formerly, a contributory had standing to apply without the leave of the court, but only when he could show that he had an interest in the outcome of the proceedings. The subsection in its present form runs counter to the approach reflected in such decisions as *Re Rica Gold Washing Co* (1879) 11 Ch. D. 36: see the notes to ss.124(2), (3), 172(1), (2) above.

A contributory may not apply for leave unless the company is in liquidation: he must instead use the derivative action procedure: *Wightman v Bennett* [2005] B.P.I.R. 470.

213   Fraudulent trading

213(1)   [Application] If in the course of the winding up of a company it appears that any business of the company has been carried on with intent to defraud creditors of the company or creditors of any other person, or for any fraudulent purpose, the following has effect.

213(2)   [Court may hold persons liable] The court, on the application of the liquidator may declare that any persons who were knowingly parties to the carrying on of the business in the manner above-mentioned are to be liable to make such contributions (if any) to the company's assets as the court thinks proper.

GENERAL NOTE

The Companies Acts have for a long time contained provisions dealing with "fraudulent trading", making it both a criminal offence (CA 2006 s.993) and a ground for imposing personal liability upon those concerned (CA 1985 s.630, now replaced by the present section). Originally, both the criminal and the civil sanctions could be invoked only in a winding up, but the criminal provision has for some years applied without this limitation.

The Cork Committee (*Report*, Ch.44) considered that the previous law in this area was inadequate to deal with irresponsible trading, mainly because the courts have always insisted on the very strict standards of pleading and proof which are invariably applied in cases of fraud. It is not enough, for "fraudulent trading", to show that the company continued to run up debts when the directors knew that it was insolvent; there has to be "actual dishonesty, involving real moral blame" (*Re Patrick and Lyon Ltd* [1933] Ch. 786). (See also *Aktieselskabet Dansk Skibsfinansiering v Brothers* [2001] 2 B.C.L.C. 324; and *Bernasconi v Nicholas Bennett & Co* [2000] B.C.C. 921.)

The Committee recommended that while this should continue to be the approach in criminal proceedings for fraudulent trading, civil liability to pay compensation could arise where loss was suffered as a result of "unreasonable" conduct, which they proposed should be termed "wrongful trading", and that for this purpose the more relaxed standard of proof appropriate to civil proceedings should apply. The former provision creating civil liability for fraudulent trading (CA 1985 s.630) could be subsumed into the new law of wrongful trading.

In the event, the legislators have adopted the Committee's recommendations on wrongful trading in broad terms, but they have done so by creating an *additional* new provision (s.214, below) and left the former law on fraudulent trading intact, with one or two minor amendments (the present section). There will, however, be less reason for liquidators to invoke it, since the concept of wrongful trading, with its less onerous standard of proof, is wide enough to include all cases of fraudulent trading perpetrated by directors, and for all practical purposes the consequences will be the same. However, s.213 will continue to have a role to play where allegations of fraudulent trading are made against other parties, as is dramatically illustrated by the number of cases brought by the liquidators of BCCI: see *Re BCCI, Morris v State Bank of India* [1999] B.C.C. 943; further proceedings [2003] EWHC 1868 (Ch); [2003] B.C.C. 735; and *Morris v Bank of India* [2004] EWHC 528 (Ch); [2004] B.C.C. 404 (and, on appeal, [2005] EWCA Civ 693; [2005] B.C.C. 739); *Morris v Bank of America National Trust* [2000] B.C.C. 1076; *Re BCCI, Banque Arabe Internationale d'Investissement SA v Morris* [2002] B.C.C. 407.

In *Re Overnight Ltd* [2009] EWHC 601 (Ch); [2009] Bus. L.R. 1141 it was ruled that for the purposes of the Statutes of Limitation a cause of action under s.213 arises when the winding-up order is made and not at any earlier date, since the appointment of a liquidator (and not a provisional liquidator) is necessary since only he is authorised to issue proceedings.

The Fraud Act 2006, which came into force on January 15, 2007, increased the maximum penalty for contravention of CA 2006 s.993 from seven to ten years' imprisonment (s.10(1)). It also redefines various offences involving fraud or dishonesty, and in particular extends the scope of the fraudulent trading offence (CA 2006 s.993) so as to include being a party to the fraudulent carrying on of a business by a sole trader or other person who is outside the reach of s.993 (s.9).

S.213(1)

The section, unlike the equivalent criminal provision (see above), applies only in a winding up.

The words "or for any fraudulent purpose" could not be wider, and should not be construed in any limiting way. The wording is certainly wide enough to include frauds committed against potential creditors: see *R. v Kemp* [1988] Q.B. 645; (1988) 4 B.C.C. 203. See also *Re L Todd (Swanscombe) Ltd* [1990] B.C.C. 125 (fraudulent evasion of value added tax). However, in *Morphitis v Bernasconi* [2002] EWCA Civ 289; [2003] Ch. 552; [2003] B.C.C. 540 the Court of Appeal ruled that, although a business may be found to have been carried on with intent to defraud creditors even where only one creditor is shown to have been defrauded, it does not necessarily follow that this is the case whenever a fraud on a creditor has been perpetrated. In such a situation the appropriate remedy may be for the creditor to pursue his own remedy under the general law, and not for the liquidator to seek a contribution to the general assets of the company in the winding up.

In *Bank of India v Morris* [2005] EWCA Civ 693; [2005] B.C.C. 739, the Bank of India was held liable under s.213 on the ground that it had knowingly been a party to frauds committed by officers of BCCI. The Court of Appeal held that it was not necessary to show that any members of the board of the Bank of India had knowledge of the fraud: the appropriate rule of attribution for the purposes of s.213 and its policy was to fix the bank with the knowledge of the employee who had authority to conclude the transactions in question; and it was immaterial that he had acted dishonestly and in breach of his duty to his employer.

A company cannot be treated as "carrying on business" after the date on which a winding-up petition was presented if a winding-up order is subsequently made, and so any transactions made after that date are incapable of constituting fraudulent trading: *Carman v Cronos Group SA* [2005] EWHC 2403 (Ch); [2006] B.C.C. 451. This case is also authority for the following: (a) that the period of fraudulent trading is not interrupted during the time when the company concerned has been struck off but later reinstated, and (b) that where money has been taken from the defendant and wrongfully paid to third parties without resulting in any loss to the company concerned, this does not come within s.213.

S.213(2)

Two changes are made from the former law.

First, it is only the liquidator who has standing to apply for relief under this section. Previously, an individual creditor or contributory could also apply, but this was thought undesirable because it might encourage a creditor to put improper pressure upon directors to settle his claim personally.

Secondly, the order which the court may make declares the wrongdoers "liable to make such contributions (if any) to the company's assets as the court thinks proper". This makes it clear that any sums ordered to be paid must go into the general funds in the hands of the liquidator and be held for the benefit of the whole body of creditors. Under the previous wording, the court had power to order that a defendant should directly reimburse a particular creditor (*Re Cyona Distributors Ltd* [1967] Ch. 889; *Re Gerald Cooper Chemicals Ltd (in liq.)* [1978] Ch. 262). However, a creditor may have a claim for damages directly against a director (e.g. for fraud), independently of s.213: *Contex Drouzhba Ltd v Wiseman* [2007] EWCA Civ 1201; [2008] B.C.C. 301.

In other respects, the law remains the same. Thus, those who may be made liable are "any persons who were knowingly parties" to the fraudulent trading (who need not have any connection with the company itself: *Re BCCI, Banque Arabe Internationale d'Investissement SA v Morris* (above)). This may be contrasted with the wrongful trading provision (s.214) which is limited in its scope to directors and former directors, but pointedly avoids the words "parties to" (and, indeed, "business" or "trading").

In certain cases under the former law it was held appropriate to include a punitive as well as a compensatory element in the court's order, but in *Morphitis v Bernasconi* (above) the Court of Appeal has denied that there is any such power: to make such an award would be foreign to the principle underlying s.213.

Further provisions relating to proceedings for fraudulent trading are contained in s.215, below.

In addition to the civil liability to pay compensation under this section and the criminal sanctions of CA 2006 s.993, a person who is guilty of fraudulent trading may be made the subject of a disqualification order: see CDDA 1986 ss.4, 10.

214 Wrongful trading

214(1) [Declaration by court, on application] Subject to subsection (3) below, if in the course of the winding up of a company it appears that subsection (2) of this section applies in relation to a person who is or has been a director of the company, the court, on the application of the liquidator, may declare that that person is to be liable to make such contribution (if any) to the company's assets as the court thinks proper.

214(2) [Application] This subsection applies in relation to a person if–

(a) the company has gone into insolvent liquidation,

(b) at some time before the commencement of the winding up of the company, that person knew or ought to have concluded that there was no reasonable prospect that the company would avoid going into insolvent liquidation, and

(c) that person was a director of the company at that time;

but the court shall not make a declaration under this section in any case where the time mentioned in paragraph (b) above was before 28th April 1986.

214(3) [Limit on declaration] The court shall not make a declaration under this section with respect to any person if it is satisfied that after the condition specified in subsection (2)(b) was first satisfied in relation to him that person took every step with a view to minimising the potential loss to the company's creditors as (assuming him to have known that there was no reasonable prospect that the company would avoid going into insolvent liquidation) he ought to have taken.

214(4) [Interpretation of s.214(2), (3)] For the purposes of subsections (2) and (3), the facts which a director of a company ought to know or ascertain, the conclusions which he ought to reach and the steps which he ought to take are those which would be known or ascertained, or reached or taken, by a reasonably diligent person having both–

(a) the general knowledge, skill and experience that may reasonably be expected of a person carrying out the same functions as are carried out by that director in relation to the company, and

(b) the general knowledge, skill and experience that that director has.

214(5) [Interpretation of s.214(4)] The reference in subsection (4) to the functions carried out in relation to a company by a director of the company includes any functions which he does not carry out but which have been entrusted to him.

214(6) [Interpretation re insolvent liquidation] For the purposes of this section a company goes into insolvent liquidation if it goes into liquidation at a time when its assets are insufficient for the payment of its debts and other liabilities and the expenses of the winding up.

214(7) ["Director"] In this section **"director"** includes a shadow director.

214(8) [Section 213] This section is without prejudice to section 213.

General Note

For the background to this provision, see the note to s.213 above.

The section, according to the marginal note, is concerned with "wrongful trading"; but it is notable that the word "trading" is not used in the text of the Act. (The marginal note may not be used as an aid for the construction of the text: *Chandler v Director of Public Prosecutions* [1964] A.C. 763.) The section itself is singularly imprecise in defining just what conduct on the part of a director will bring him within its scope.

The Cork Committee (*Report*, para.1806) did put forward its own draft definition of "wrongful trading", the essential part of which read: "… at any time when the company is insolvent or unable to pay its debts as they fall due it incurs further debts or other liabilities to other persons without a reasonable prospect of meeting them in full". However, this definition was explicitly rejected by Parliament when an attempt was made to introduce it as an amendment to the Insolvency Bill 1985, and so it would be wrong to refer to it for guidance on the meaning of the present section. In particular, there may be wrongful trading under s.214 even though the company does not incur further debts: one example mentioned during the parliamentary debate was the case where a company allows its assets to be depleted, e.g. by the payment of excessive directors' fees. It was, presumably, a concern to ensure that this kind of conduct was caught that led the draftsman to omit the word "trading" from his formulation.

The amount of contribution to be ordered is left entirely to the court's discretion, and is not related by the terms of the Act either to any particular period of trading or to the loss suffered by the company or creditors. However, in *Re Produce Marketing Consortium Ltd* (1989) 5 B.C.C. 569 at 597, Knox J. said:

"In my judgment the jurisdiction under sec. 214 is primarily compensatory rather than penal. Prime facie the appropriate amount that a director is declared to be liable to contribute is the amount by which the company's assets can be discerned to have been depleted by the director's conduct which caused the discretion under sec. 214(1) to arise. However Parliament has indeed chosen very wide words of discretion and it would be undesirable to seek to spell out limits on that discretion... The fact that there was no fraudulent intent is not of itself a reason for fixing the amount at a nominal or low figure, for that would amount to frustrating what I discern as Parliament's intention in adding sec. 214 to sec. 213 in the *Insolvency Act* 1986, but I am not persuaded that it is right to ignore that fact totally".

Although the section is silent on the question of causation, it must be shown that if the defendant had complied with his duties to the requisite standard the loss in question would not have resulted (as a matter of probability): *Lexi Holdings plc v Luqman* [2008] EWHC 1639 (Ch); [2008] 2 B.C.L.C. 725 at [40]. In that case the company's managing director, S, had defrauded it of some £60 million. The defendant non-executive directors had remained inactive and (inter alia) had not disclosed to the other directors their knowledge that S had a criminal record. They were held not liable for the loss because the likely result of disclosing this would have been nothing more than the resignation of the other directors.

In *Re Marini Ltd* [2003] EWHC 334 (Ch); [2004] B.C.C. 172, H.H.J. Seymour thought that the powers of the court under s.214 could not arise unless it was demonstrated that the company was, at the date of the actual liquidation, worse off than it would have been if it had ceased trading at the date when the director(s) ought to have realised that insolvent liquidation was inevitable. With respect, this view ignores the relevance of the causation factor. If this can be brought into account in order to reduce the director's liability (see *Re Brian D Pierson (Contractors) Ltd* [1999] B.C.C. 26), it must be just as relevant if the company receives an unexpected windfall which leaves it better off despite the continued wrongful trading.

In the light of the ruling of the Court of Appeal in *Morphitis v Bernasconi* [2002] EWCA Civ 289; [2003] Ch. 552; [2003] B.C.C. 540, it will not be appropriate to include a punitive element in the amount of contribution awarded: see the note to s.213(2), above.

Summary judgment on a s.214 claim was awarded in *Re Bangla Television Ltd* [2009] EWHC 1632 (Ch); [2010] B.C.C. 143.

Where a claim under s.214 is brought against a number of directors, liability is several and not joint and several, that is to say that the position of each individual has to be separately assessed, and payment by one does not discharge the liability of any other: *Re Continental Assurance Co of London plc* [2001] B.P.I.R. 733 at 846–848. However, it was also said in this case that the court may, in its discretion, order that the liability of any two or more directors should be joint and several for the whole or part of the sum which the court has assessed for contribution to the company's assets.

In an appropriate case, an application may be made under s.214 against the foreign directors of a foreign company which is being wound up in this jurisdiction as an unregistered company: *Re Howard Holdings Ltd* [1998] B.C.C. 549.

There will plainly be cases in which claims will be made against the former director of a company both under this section and under some other provisions of the Act, e.g. s.212 (misfeasance) or s.239 (preference). In such a case there may be no injustice in making orders which impose cumulative liability on the defendant: *Re Purpoint Ltd* [1991] B.C.C. 121. However, in *Re DKG Contractors Ltd* [1990] B.C.C. 903 the court ruled that payments made under ss.212 and 239 should go to satisfy the liability under s.214, and that enforcement should be limited to what was necessary to pay the company's creditors and the costs and expenses of the liquidation. On this and related questions, see the note to s.212(1).

It has been ruled that, as a matter of law, CA 2006 s.1157 [formerly CA 1985 s.727] (which empowers the court to relieve a director from liability for breach of duty where he has acted honestly and reasonably and ought fairly to be excused) is not available to a director in s.214 proceedings: *Re Produce Marketing Consortium Ltd (Halls v David)* [1989] 1 W.L.R. 745; (1989) 5 B.C.C. 399.

A claim under s.214 (and, similarly, a claim under s.213) is a "claim for the recovery of a sum recoverable under any enactment" within s.9(1) of the Limitation Act 1980, and the appropriate limitation period is six years, reckoned from the date when the company went into insolvent liquidation: *Re Farmizer (Products) Ltd, Moore v Gadd* [1997] B.C.C. 655. However even if proceedings are commenced within the limitation period, unreasonable delay in prosecuting the claim may justify a striking-out order (ibid.).

The provisions of ss.214–217 apply to the directors of building societies: see the note to CDDA 1986 s.7.

S.214(1)

Four points may be noted:

(1) The section applies only to present and past directors (including shadow directors: s.214(7)). In *Re a Company (No.005009 of 1987)* (1988) 4 B.C.C. 424 (interlocutory proceedings in the saga of *Re M C Bacon Ltd*: see [1990] B.C.C. 78 at 79G) Knox J. ruled that a company's bank which, on becoming apprised of the fact that its client company is in financial difficulties, makes recommendations to its directors as to the future conduct of its business could, in principle, incur liability under the section as a "shadow director"—or, at least, that on the evidence before him the case was not so obviously unsustainable that an allegation to that effect should be struck out without proceeding to trial. A bank would not, however (it is submitted), risk liability as a shadow director if its requirements were expressed as conditions of extending loan facilities to the company rather than as instructions. (Compare the views expressed in *Re PFTZM Ltd (in liq.)* [1995] B.C.C. 280.) In *Re Hydrodan (Corby) Ltd* [1994] B.C.C. 161, Millett J. accepted as correct a concession by counsel that s.214 applies also to de facto directors. (See further on this point the notes to s.251, below.) Proceedings may be brought against the estate of a deceased director: *Re Sherborne Associates Ltd* [1995] B.C.C. 40.

(2) Section 214 applies only in a winding up.

(3) Only the liquidator has standing to bring proceedings.

(4) Any sum paid by a defendant goes into the general assets in the hands of the liquidator. Accordingly, it will not be caught by a charge over the assets of the company (despite the assumption to the contrary made by Knox J. in *Re Produce Marketing Consortium Ltd* (1989) 5 B.C.C. 569 at 598); and it is incapable of assignment (*Re Oasis Merchandising Services Ltd* [1998] Ch. 170; [1997] B.C.C. 282). See the note to Sch.4 paras 6, 13.

The comments to s.213 on these points are also relevant for this subsection.

A person held liable under this section may also have a disqualification order made against him: see CDDA 1986 s.10, although the power appears to be used sparingly (see *Re Brian D Pierson (Contractors) Ltd* [1999] B.C.C. 26). Alternatively, an application under this section may be consolidated with proceedings for a disqualification order, as was done in *Official Receiver v Doshi* [2001] 2 B.C.L.C. 235.

S.214(2)

On the meaning of "has gone into insolvent liquidation" see s.214(6); and for "the commencement of the winding up" see ss.86 and 129.

April 28, 1986 was the date when this provision (as IA 1985 s.15) was first brought into force (SI 1986/463).

The words "knew or ought to have concluded" are to be read in conjunction with s.214(4). See the note to that provision, below.

Note that a director does not contravene the section simply by allowing the company to continue to trade when it is insolvent, or when he knows or ought to know that it is insolvent (on either a balance-sheet or cash-flow test): the question is whether he knows or ought to have concluded that there is no reasonable prospect of avoiding insolvent liquidation: *Re Hawkes Hill Publishing Co Ltd* [2007] B.C.C. 937. Where the liquidator alleges that a respondent knew or ought to have concluded that there was no reasonable prospect of avoiding insolvent liquidation by reference to specific dates, but fails to make out his case as to the dates pleaded, he is not entitled to substitute later dates: *Re Sherborne Associates Ltd* [1995] B.C.C. 40.

S.214(3)

The section, as has been noted, pointedly avoids giving any concrete meaning to the concept of "wrongful trading" or any positive guidance as to the types of conduct which will lead to liability. There is thus a major gap in the law, as framed, which is having to be filled by decisions of the courts in test cases. The only objective facts that need to be established are those relating to the winding up of the company, its insolvency, and that the director held office at the material time (s.214(2)); beyond that, liability turns on his knowledge or imputed knowledge (s.214(2)(b)) and his failure to take "every step with a view to minimising the potential loss to the company's creditors as … he ought to have taken". What a director knows, or must be taken to know, for these purposes is assessed by a mixture of subjective and objective tests (see the note to s.214(4) below).

The phrases "took *every* step" and "*minimising* the potential loss to creditors" seem, at first sight, rather overstated. However, there is no doubt that the use of "every step" was deliberate: a proposed amendment to "every reasonable step" was expressly rejected in Parliament; and on similar reasoning, we must assume that "minimise" was fully intended, rather than, say, "reduce" or "avert".

The bracketed words in the subsection credit a director, for the purpose of determining what he "ought" to have done, with an awareness of the company's financial position and (by virtue of s.214(4)) with a degree of general knowledge, skill and experience which in reality he may not have had. These fictitious assumptions as to the directors' state of mind were invoked against the defendants in *Re Produce Marketing Consortium Ltd* (1989) 5 B.C.C. 569. The company had kept inadequate accounting records, and in consequence the directors were in breach of their statutory duty to prepare accounts for the financial year ending September 30, 1985, which should have been laid before the shareholders and delivered to the registrar of companies by the end of July 1986. Knox J. held that he should assume, for the purposes of s.214, that these financial results were known to the directors at the latter date, at least to the extent of the size of the deficiency of assets over liabilities.

The Act gives no affirmative guidance as to the steps which a director "ought" to take when insolvency is threatening. It was plainly assumed in the Government's White Paper (Cmnd.9175, para.12) that a conscientious director would seek to have the company put into receivership, administration, or voluntary liquidation as soon as possible. There is a clear risk that this may seem the safest course for directors, faced as they are with the threat of personal liability and possible disqualification, even when in their own business judgment there is a good case for carrying on. It is clear that any decision to do so ought to be fully reasoned and documented and, where necessary, made with the benefit of outside professional advice, in order that the requirements of the present subsection can be met if a charge of wrongful trading is brought. It is significant that in *Re Continental Assurance Co of London plc* [2001] B.P.I.R. 733, in which all of the directors concerned were held not to be liable for wrongful trading, management accounts had been prepared (albeit that they may not have been wholly accurate) and two licensed insolvency practitioners were advising the company at the material time. See also *Re Hawkes Hill Publishing Co Ltd* (above).

On principle and, it is submitted, on the language of the section, the onus of proof to show that a director has failed to take every step that he ought to have taken should be on the liquidator. In *Re Sherborne Associates Ltd* (above) it was emphasised that the court should be aware of the danger of making assumptions with the benefit of hindsight, and in the case of a claim against the estate of a deceased director should be particularly astute to recognise the possibility of explanations for his conduct which he might have been able to give had he lived.

S.214(4)

The tests to be applied under this subsection combine both subjective and objective criteria. The director is thus to be judged by the standards of the "reasonable" director, even though he himself is lacking or below average in knowledge, skill or experience, but by his own higher standards if these are above average. In *Re DKG Contractors Ltd* [1990] B.C.C. 903 it was observed: "Patently, [the directors'] own knowledge, skill and experience were hopelessly inadequate for the task they undertook. That is not sufficient to protect them". However, it should be noted that in the *Produce Marketing* case (above), Knox J. accepted a submission that the objective standards fixed by the section do require the court to have regard to the particular company and its business, so that the general knowledge, skill and experience postulated will be much less extensive in a small company in a modest way of business, with simple accounting procedures and equipment, than it will be in a large company with sophisticated procedures. This approach could also give scope for the courts to make some allowances in the case of non-executive and part-time directors. (*Re Continental Assurance Co of London plc* (above) contains an important analysis of the position of non-executive directors in this context.) For a detailed examination of the standards prescribed by s.214(4), see *Rubin v Gunner* [2004] EWHC 316 (Ch); [2004] B.C.C. 684.

In applying objective standards to the conduct of company directors in this way, the Act broke new ground, for the case law had traditionally emphasised the need for honesty and conscientiousness but had not demanded that directors should exercise any particular degree of competence or diligence or skill. However, in *Re D'Jan of London Ltd* [1993] B.C.C. 646, Hoffmann L.J. expressed the view that "the duty of care owed by a director at common law is accurately stated in s.214 of the Insolvency Act 1986", and this view has not only been accepted in later cases but adopted in the statutory statement of directors' duties in the Companies Act 2006.

S.214(5)

The remarks made in the preceding paragraph are underlined by the present subsection, which puts sins of omission into the same category as sins of commission. This, too, is a departure from the common law, which has never had effective sanctions to penalise passive defaults such as non-attendance at board meetings.

S.214(6)

Section 214 applies only in a liquidation; but it is immaterial whether this is a compulsory or voluntary liquidation. The phrase "goes into liquidation" is defined in s.247(2). The test of insolvency applied by s.214(6) is on a "balance sheet" rather than a "liquidity" or "commercial" basis. (The recommendation of the Cork Committee was that *either* should be sufficient.) The definition of "inability to pay debts" in s.123(1)(e) and (2) may be contrasted.

The Act gives no indication whether the company's assets are to be valued for the purpose of s.214 on a "going concern" rather than a "break-up" basis, or whether contingent and future liabilities are to be brought into the reckoning. It is submitted that it would be wrong to judge these matters with the wisdom of hindsight, if it does happen that, e.g. the assets have had to be sold up piecemeal in the winding up which has resulted. The reference to "going into insolvent liquidation" in relation to the making of business judgments in s.214(2)(b) surely indicates that the question of solvency is to be assessed on the basis of going-concern assumptions for all the purposes of the present section.

On the problems of valuation for the purposes of determining "insolvency" under the present section, see the comments of Professor Roy Goode, *Principles of Corporate Insolvency Law*, 3rd edn (2005), at 4.24–4.41.

S.214(7)
For the definition of these terms, see the note to s.206.

S.214(8)
In view of the heavier onus of proof required by s.213, it is unlikely that that section will be invoked in future where a liquidator has a choice of proceeding under either section. The one respect in which the two sections do not overlap, however, is that s.213 applies to persons other than directors and shadow directors, provided that they are knowingly parties to the fraudulent trading.

215   Proceedings under ss.213, 214

215(1)   [Evidence by liquidator] On the hearing of an application under section 213 or 214, the liquidator may himself give evidence or call witnesses.

215(2)   [Further court directions] Where under either section the court makes a declaration, it may give such further directions as it thinks proper for giving effect to the declaration; and in particular, the court may–

(a)   provide for the liability of any person under the declaration to be a charge on any debt or obligation due from the company to him, or on any mortgage or charge or any interest in a mortgage or charge on assets of the company held by or vested in him, or any person on his behalf, or any person claiming as assignee from or through the person liable or any person acting on his behalf, and

(b)   from time to time make such further order as may be necessary for enforcing any charge imposed under this subsection.

215(3)   ["Assignee"] For the purposes of subsection (2), **"assignee"**–

(a)   includes a person to whom or in whose favour, by the directions of the person made liable, the debt, obligation, mortgage or charge was created, issued or transferred or the interest created, but

(b)   does not include an assignee for valuable consideration (not including consideration by way of marriage or the formation of a civil partnership) given in good faith and without notice of any of the matters on the ground of which the declaration is made.

215(4)   [Directions re priority of debts] Where the court makes a declaration under either section in relation to a person who is a creditor of the company, it may direct that the whole or any part of any debt owed by the company to that person and any interest thereon shall rank in priority after all other debts owed by the company and after any interest on those debts.

215(5)   [Sections 213, 214] Sections 213 and 214 have effect notwithstanding that the person concerned may be criminally liable in respect of matters on the ground of which the declaration under the section is to be made.

S.215(4)
The court is empowered to make a declaration, ancillary to an order for contribution, subordinating any debt owed by the company to a respondent so that it ranks after the company's other debts. Such a declaration was made in *Re Purpoint Ltd* [1991] B.C.C. 121.

216　Restriction on re-use of company names

216(1)　[Application] This section applies to a person where a company ("the liquidating company") has gone into insolvent liquidation on or after the appointed day and he was a director or shadow director of the company at any time in the period of 12 months ending with the day before it went into liquidation.

216(2)　[Prohibited name] For the purposes of this section, a name is a prohibited name in relation to such a person if–

(a)　it is a name by which the liquidating company was known at any time in that period of 12 months, or

(b)　it is a name which is so similar to a name falling within paragraph (a) as to suggest an association with that company.

216(3)　[Restriction] Except with leave of the court or in such circumstances as may be prescribed, a person to whom this section applies shall not at any time in the period of 5 years beginning with the day on which the liquidating company went into liquidation–

(a)　be a director of any other company that is known by a prohibited name, or

(b)　in any way, whether directly or indirectly, be concerned or take part in the promotion, formation or management of any such company, or

(c)　in any way, whether directly or indirectly, be concerned or take part in the carrying on of a business carried on (otherwise than by a company) under a prohibited name.

216(4)　[Penalty] If a person acts in contravention of this section, he is liable to imprisonment or a fine, or both.

216(5)　["The court"] In subsection (3) **"the court"** means any court having jurisdiction to wind up companies; and on an application for leave under that subsection, the Secretary of State or the official receiver may appear and call the attention of the court to any matters which seem to him to be relevant.

216(6)　[Interpretation re name] References in this section, in relation to any time, to a name by which a company is known are to the name of the company at that time or to any name under which the company carries on business at that time.

216(7)　[Interpretation re insolvent liquidation] For the purposes of this section a company goes into insolvent liquidation if it goes into liquidation at a time when its assets are insufficient for the payment of its debts and other liabilities and the expenses of the winding up.

216(8)　["Company"] In this section **"company"** includes a company which may be wound up under Part V of this Act.

GENERAL NOTE

This is one of a number of innovations made by IA 1985 which together form a package designed to strike down the "phoenix" phenomenon. This term was used to describe an abuse of the privilege of limited liability which, perhaps more than anything else, showed the inadequacies of the former insolvency law in the corporate sector. A company would be put into receivership (or voluntary liquidation) at a time when it owed large sums to its unsecured creditors. Frequently, the receiver was appointed by a controlling shareholder who had himself taken a floating charge over the whole of the company's undertaking, and there was nothing to stop him from appointing a receiver with whom he could act in collusion. The receiver would sell the entire business as a going concern at a knock-down price to a new company incorporated by the former controllers of the defunct company. As a result, what was essentially the same business would be carried on by the same people in disregard of the claims of the creditors of the first company, who in effect subsidised the launch of the new company debt-free. It was not unknown for the procedure to be repeated several times. The use of nominees or "front men" could add to the confusion and help to deceive future creditors: on the other hand, advantage could sometimes be gained from using a new company name similar to that of the old company, and cashing in on what was left of its goodwill. (On phoenix companies, see the comments of Jacob J. in *Western Intelligence Ltd v KDO Label Printing Machines Ltd* [1998] B.C.C. 472.) The present section is aimed to counter both of these latter aspects of the "phoenix syndrome", but it is so widely drawn that it extends to situations well beyond the phoenix scenario. It is not based on any of the Cork Committee's recommendations, and was introduced at a late stage during the passage of the Insolvency Bill through Parliament in 1985. It simply makes the re-use of the name of a company which has been wound up insolvent a criminal offence in the circumstances defined; but it is not based on any requirement that there should be an attempt to exploit the goodwill of the liquidating company (see the comments of Peter Gibson L.J. in *Thorne v Silverleaf* [1994] B.C.C. 113). It is rather surprisingly confined in its scope to directors and shadow directors of the extinct company, but it is not necessary that the person concerned should hold such a position in the second company (*R. v Doring* [2002] EWCA Crim 1695; [2002] B.C.C. 838). In addition, any such person and any nominee or "front man" through whom he conducts the second business may incur personal liability, without limitation, under s.217. The conditions for liability are stringently drawn, the penalties draconian and both criminal and civil liability are automatic: if they are met, the court has no discretion to absolve the defendant or limit his liability (*Ricketts v Ad Valorem Factors Ltd* [2003] EWCA Civ 1706; [2004] B.C.C. 164).

The civil consequences of a breach of s.216 are spelt out in s.217, and it is usually in proceedings brought under that section by a creditor that such proceedings will be instituted. But a shareholder may plead a breach of s.216 in proceedings under CA 2006 s.994 (unfairly prejudicial conduct): *Re Neath Rugby Club Ltd, Hawkes v Cuddy* [2007] EWHC 1789 (Ch); [2007] B.C.C. 671; on appeal [2007] EWCA Civ 1072; [2008] B.C.C. 125; further proceedings [2008] B.C.C. 390. The subject is discussed by C. Werner, (2009) 22 Insolv. Int. 105.

S.216(1)

Many phrases in this subsection have special meanings. "Company" and "gone into insolvent liquidation" are defined in ss.216(8) and 216(7) respectively; the "appointed day" is the day on which the present Act came into force (December 29, 1986: see ss.436, 443); "director" and "shadow director" have the meanings ascribed to them by s.251.

The prohibition applies to anyone who has been a director or shadow director of the old company within the 12 months prior to its liquidation, and lasts for the period of five years that follows that event (s.216(3)).

S.216(2)

The ban applies to the use of the same name or a similar name: see, further, the note to s.216(6).

It should be emphasised that the present section is not directed against the reuse of an insolvent company's name in itself: there will be no ban on this practice provided that no director of the former company is associated with the second business. It is only directors who can contravene the section, and only directors who are liable to punishment. This explains the phrase "a prohibited name *in relation* to such a person".

S.216(3)

The ban is not restricted to the use of a prohibited name by a newly formed company: an established company (perhaps a member of the same group as the defunct company) may well have a "similar" name already, or may change its name to a "prohibited" name, with the result that its directors may be caught by this section. (Note that IR 1986 r.4.230, may give a director an exemption in the former of these cases.) In *Ricketts v Ad Valorem Factors Ltd* (above), the Court of Appeal drew attention to the hazards which ss.216–217 might pose where one company in a group went into liquidation. (It is understood that in practice Official Receivers allow a three month "period of grace" in order to allow "associated" companies to change their names before taking action for breach of the section.) In *ESS Production Ltd v Sully* [2005] EWCA Civ 554; [2005] B.C.C. 435 the acronym "ESS" had been used informally as a shorthand expression to refer to various companies in which the respondent "S" was a principal shareholder and director. One of these companies had been registered under the name "Electronic Sales Services Ltd" throughout the 12-month qualifying period but had changed its name to "ESS Solutions Ltd" some seven months later. The Court of Appeal held that the informal use of the acronym was sufficient reason to hold that this company had been "known by" a name which linked it to the company that had gone into liquidation, with the result that S was liable for its debts. The test of "similarity" is not to be applied in the abstract, simply by looking at the names in question without regard to the context, but in relation to the circumstances in which they were actually used or likely to be used: *Ricketts v Ad Valorem Factors Ltd* (above); *Revenue and Customs Commissioners v Walsh* [2005] EWHC 1304 (Ch); [2005] EWCA Civ 1291; [2006] B.C.C. 431. The fact that the names of the companies contain a name or surname that is common or well-known (e.g. "Walsh", "William" or "Williams") is irrelevant: *Walsh* (above); *Revenue and Customs Commissioners v Benton-Diggins* [2006] EWHC 793 (Ch); [2006] B.C.C. 769.

Section 216 is infringed where the second company carries on only part of its business under a prohibited name, but in that case civil liability under s.217 is restricted to debts incurred in carrying on that part of the business: *Glasgow City Council v Craig* [2008] CSOH 171; [2009] 1 B.C.L.C. 742.

The court is given power to grant dispensations from the prohibition imposed by this section, which it is likely to do when the insolvency is not linked with any blameworthy conduct on the part of the director concerned. *Re Bonus Breaks Ltd* [1991] B.C.C. 546 is an illustration of such a case. There, the applicant had been a director of a company which had gone into insolvent liquidation, but she had not behaved culpably and had lost substantial sums of her own money. A new company was set up with a capital of £50,000, including £49,000 in redeemable shares. Morritt J. gave leave for her to be a director of the new company against undertakings offered by the applicant that its capital base would be maintained and that it would not redeem any redeemable shares nor purchase its own shares out of distributable profits for a period of two years, unless such action was approved by a director independent of the company's founders. However, in *Penrose v Official Receiver* [1996] 1 W.L.R. 482; [1996] B.C.C. 311, Chadwick J. held that neither the fact that the new company was undercapitalised nor that the applicant was inexperienced and lacked management skills were relevant factors: the object of the section is to prevent abuses of the "phoenix" variety, and therefore the appropriate questions are whether there is any risk to the creditors of the new company beyond that permitted under the law relating to the incorporation of limited liability companies, or any substantial risk that people would be confused by the similarity of names. (See also *Re Lightning Electrical Contractors Ltd* [1996] B.C.C. 950 and *Re Bowman Power Systems Ltd*, October 26, 2004, Sweet & Maxwell's *British Company Law and Practice New Developments*, para.96–031.) In this case it was also held that it is wrong in principle to treat an applicant for leave under s.216 as if he were a person who has been disqualified on the grounds of unfitness from acting as a director under CDDA 1986—at least without evidence of misconduct. (However, a contravention of s.216 may be evidence of "unfitness" justifying disqualification: *Re Migration Services International Ltd* [2000] B.C.C. 1095.) Leave may be granted in respect of "dormant" companies, provided that they are specified; but the court will not give a blanket permission to use the prohibited name in respect of any company to be formed in the future: *Re Lightning Electrical Contractors Ltd* [1996] B.C.C. 950.

The court's leave could not be granted retrospectively, since this would have the effect of decriminalising the director's past conduct: see the notes to CDDA 1986 s.1. But a person who has been acting as a director in breach of s.216 could seek leave for the future, as was accepted by both courts in *Re Neath Rugby Club Ltd* (above).

The rules also specify three sets of circumstances where the section will not apply: see IR 1986 rr.4.228 et seq. These are (1) where the whole, or substantially the whole, of the business of an insolvent company is acquired by a successor company and the liquidator (or equivalent office-holder) of the insolvent company gives notice to its creditors under r.4.228 (as amended); (2) for an interim period, where an application is made to the court within seven days of the liquidation and the court grants leave not later than six weeks from that date (r.4.229); and (3) where the second company has been known by the name in question for at least 12 months prior to the liquidation and has not been a dormant company (r.4.230). All other cases will have to go to the court for authorisation: the relevant rules are rr.4.226, 4.227A. (See the note to r.4.228 for discussion of the recent amendment to this rule.)

Paragraphs (b) and (c), by the use of the term "indirectly", will be effective to stop a person from controlling another company or carrying on a new business through others as "front" men. In addition, para.(c) makes it clear that it will be an offence to use a prohibited name even where no second company is involved, but in this case the civil consequences prescribed by s.217 will not be applicable.

The phrase "be concerned or take part in the management of a company" is not defined, but the note to s.217 is relevant in this context.

S.216(4)

Note that it is only a person who was a director or shadow director of the liquidating company who can be convicted of an offence under this section. In contrast, the civil liability imposed by s.217 extends also to persons who act on the instructions of such ex-directors.

The offence under this section is one of strict liability: mens rea need not be shown; *R. v Cole, Lees & Birch* [1998] B.C.C. 87. In the same case it was held that a sentence of community service is not inappropriate in this context. (See also *R. v McCredie* [2000] B.C.C. 617; and *R. v Doring* (above).)

On penalties, see s.430 and Sch.10.

S.216(5)

For the courts having jurisdiction to wind up companies, see ss.117 and 120. It is clear that "the court" need not be the same court as that which may have been involved in the liquidation of the old company.

S.216(6)

This provision should be read with s.216(2) above. In addition to forbidding the use of an identical name, the section bans a name "so similar as to suggest an association with" the former company. It is likely that this will catch the common and, in many ways, convenient practice of calling a new company by a name such as "John Smith (2002) Ltd", after the original John Smith Ltd has gone out of business. (There will, of course, be no objection to this so long as the first company was wound up solvent.)

The offence is not confined to the use of a prohibited name by a company: an unincorporated business is caught as well (s.216(3)(c)). Further, the prohibition is not confined to a company's registered name. A company may carry on business under another name. Thus, for example, John Smith Ltd, before it went into solvent liquidation, may have used the trade name of "City Autos". It will be an offence for a former director of the company to take part in the management of any business using the name "John Smith", or "City Autos", or any name similar to either. It will also be an offence for him to be a director of any company having the registered name "John Smith Ltd" or "City Autos Ltd" and also of any other company, X Ltd, if it trades under the name "John Smith" or "City Autos"—or a similar name in each case.

It is the last of these possibilities that it is most likely to mislead creditors and members of the public generally, i.e. the use of the same trade name by a succession of limited companies.

S.216(7)

This subsection defines "goes into insolvent liquidation" in terms identical to s.214(6). See the note to that provision and, for the meaning of "goes into liquidation", s.247(2).

S.216(8)

The effect of this provision is to include "unregistered" as well as registered companies within the section. See the note to s.220.

217　Personal liability for debts, following contravention of s.216

217(1)　[Personal liability] A person is personally responsible for all the relevant debts of a company if at any time–

(a)　in a contravention of section 216, he is involved in the management of the company, or

(b)　as a person who is involved in the management of the company, he acts or is willing to act on instructions given (without the leave of the court) by a person whom he knows at that time to be in contravention in relation to the company of section 216.

217(2)　[Joint and several liability] Where a person is personally responsible under this section for the relevant debts of a company, he is jointly and severally liable in respect of those debts with the company and any other person who, whether under this section or otherwise, is so liable.

217(3)　[Relevant debts of company] For the purposes of this section the relevant debts of a company are–

(a)　in relation to a person who is personally responsible under paragraph (a) of subsection (1), such debts and other liabilities of the company as are incurred at a time when that person was involved in the management of the company, and

(b)　in relation to a person who is personally responsible under paragraph (b) of that subsection, such debts and other liabilities of the company as are incurred at a time when that person was acting or was willing to act on instructions given as mentioned in that paragraph.

217(4)　[Person involved in management] For the purposes of this section, a person is involved in the management of a company if he is a director of the company or if he is concerned, whether directly or indirectly, or takes part, in the management of the company.

217(5)　[Interpretation] For the purposes of this section a person who, as a person involved in the management of a company, has at any time acted on instructions given (without the leave of the court) by a person whom he knew at that time to be in contravention in relation to the company of section 216 is presumed, unless the contrary is shown, to have been willing at any time thereafter to act on any instructions given by that person.

217(6)　["Company"] In this section **"company"** includes a company which may be wound up under Part V.

GENERAL NOTE

This section imposes personal liability on a person who contravenes s.216 by reusing a prohibited company name. In addition, it makes similarly liable anyone who allows himself to be used as a "front" man or nominee in breach of that section. Since the criminal liability prescribed by s.216 affects only directors and shadow directors, the category of those who are potentially liable on a civil basis is wider than those who may be convicted of the statutory offence.

In *Thorne v Silverleaf* [1994] B.C.C. 109, summary judgment was given in favour of the plaintiff against a director who had infringed s.216. The Court of Appeal held that it was irrelevant that the plaintiff had allegedly aided and abetted the director in the commission of this offence. It was immaterial that he was aware of the facts, and even that he was aware both of the facts and that they constituted a contravention of s.216. It was also held on the evidence that the plaintiff had not waived his right to seek recovery against the director under s.217.

IRC v Nash [2003] EWHC 686 (Ch); [2004] B.C.C. 150; *Archer Structures Ltd v Griffiths* [2003] EWHC 957 (Ch); [2004] B.C.C. 156; and *Ricketts v Ad Valorem Factors Ltd* [2003] EWCA Civ 1706; [2004] B.C.C. 164 suggest that increasing use is being made of this remedy (not least by the Revenue). See further Milman, [2005] Sweet & Maxwell's Company Law Newsletter 2. There is some parallel with CDDA 1986 ss.11, 15.

S.217(1)

Many of the terms used in this provision are defined or explained in the following subsections, and in particular "relevant debts", "involved in the management of a company", "is willing to act" and "company".

For a person to be made liable under para.(b), it will be necessary to show that he knew all the facts which are relevant to a contravention of s.216.

Liability under the section is automatic, not requiring a special application to the court or court order of any sort and, for a case coming within para.(a), not requiring a prior conviction of the director concerned. The court has no power under CA 2006 s.1157 to relieve a director from liability under s.217: *First Independent Factors & Finance Ltd v Mountford* [2008] EWHC 835 (Ch); [2008] B.C.C. 598.

S.217(2)

A person liable under this section is primarily liable, jointly and severally with the company and others concerned, and not in any secondary way. In *HM Revenue and Customs v Yousef* [2008] EWHC 423 (Ch); [2008] B.C.C. 805 it was held that there was no right of indemnity as between persons liable for the company's debts under s.217, or as between them and the company, either by reason of s.217 itself or under the Civil Liability (Contribution) Act 1978.

S.217(3)

Liability extends not only to debts in the narrow sense but also to all other obligations, such as claims for damages; and it applies to all debts and obligations arising during the relevant time and not merely those incurred *by* the acts of the person in question. The assignee of a debt has standing to sue a director under s.217: *First Independent Factors & Finance Ltd v Mountford* (above).

The phrase "willing to act" is explained in s.217(5).

S.217(4)

A director is irrebuttably presumed to be "involved in the management" of the company.

In regard to other persons, the best guide to the meaning of the phrase may be found in cases where the courts have construed closely similar, but not identical, provisions such as "take part in" or "be concerned in" the management of a company. For a full discussion, see the note to s.206(3).

S.217(5)

This provision creates a presumption against a person who is proved at any one time to have acted on the instructions of another whom he then knew to be contravening s.216. Once this is shown, he is rebuttably presumed to have been "willing to act" on the other's instructions at any time afterwards.

S.217(6)

"Unregistered" companies are included by this formula. See the note to s.220.

Investigation and prosecution of malpractice

218   Prosecution of delinquent officers and members of company

218(1)   [Court may direct matter to be referred for prosecution] If it appears to the court in the course of a winding up by the court that any past or present officer, or any member, of the company has been guilty of any offence in relation to the company for which he is criminally liable, the court may (either on the application of a person interested in the winding up or of its own motion) direct the liquidator to refer the matter–

(a)   in the case of a winding up in England and Wales, to the Secretary of State, and

(b)   in the case of a winding up in Scotland, to the Lord Advocate.

218(2)   [Deleted.]

218(3)   [Report—winding up by court] If in the case of a winding up by the court in England and Wales it appears to the liquidator, not being the official receiver, that any past or present officer of the company, or any member of it, has been guilty of an offence in relation to the company for which he is criminally liable, the liquidator shall report the matter to the official receiver.

218(4)   [Report—voluntary winding up] If it appears to the liquidator in the course of a voluntary winding up that any past or present officer of the company, or any member of it, has been guilty of an offence in relation to the company for which he is criminally liable, he shall forthwith report the matter–

(a)   in the case of a winding up in England and Wales, to the Secretary of State, and

(b)   in the case of a winding up in Scotland, to the Lord Advocate,

and shall furnish to the Secretary of State or (as the case may be) the Lord Advocate, such information and give to him such access to and facilities for inspecting and taking copies of documents (being information or documents in the possession or under the control of the liquidator and relating to the matter in question) as the Secretary of State or (as the case may be) the Lord Advocate requires.

218(5)   [Reference to Secretary of State] Where a report is made to the Secretary of State under subsection (4) he may, for the purpose of investigating the matter reported to him and such other matters relating to the affairs of the company as appear to him to require investigation, exercise any of the powers which are exercisable by inspectors appointed under section 431 or 432 of the Companies Act 1985 to investigate a company's affairs.

218(6)   [Court may direct liquidator to make report] If it appears to the court in the course of a voluntary winding up that–

(a)   any past or present officer of the company, or any member of it, has been guilty as abovementioned, and

(b)   no report with respect to the matter has been made by the liquidator under subsection (4),

the court may (on the application of any person interested in the winding up or of its own motion) direct the liquidator to make such a report.

On a report being made accordingly, this section has effect as though the report had been made in pursuance of subsection (4).

GENERAL NOTE

This provision establishes a reporting chain through which suspected criminal offences uncovered in the course of a winding up may be referred to the appropriate persons for investigation and, where appropriate, prosecution. This section and s.219 were amended by IA 2000 s.10 as from April 2, 2001 as a streamlining measure. Reports in England and Wales now go directly to the Secretary of State and not as previously in the first instance to the Director of Public Prosecutions. (For transitional provisions, see the Insolvency Act 2000 (Commencement No.1 and Transitional Provisions) Order 2001 (SI 2001/766) art.3(4).) The former s.218(2) became redundant and was accordingly repealed.

S.218(1)

In a winding up by the court, the court is empowered to take the initial step when an offence is suspected, by directing the liquidator to refer the matter to the Secretary of State or the Lord Advocate. The court may act of its own motion or on the application of "a person interested in the winding up". In England and Wales, if the liquidator (not being the official receiver) himself suspects wrongdoing, he is obliged to report the matter to the official receiver (s.218(3));

but it is unclear whether that provision by implication debars him from making an application to the court on his own initiative under s.218(1). In Scotland, where s.218(3) does not apply, it would seem to be clear that the liquidator should make application to the court in all cases.

On the meaning of "officer", see the note to s.206(3).

S.218(3)

The section is oddly silent as to what the official receiver should do, both in the case when he is not the liquidator and receives a report of a suspected offence, and in the case where, as liquidator, he suspects an offence himself. It must be intended that he shall (either with or without conducting his own investigation into the matter) refer the case to the prosecuting authority without the need for any intervention by the court. This is confirmed by *R. v Brady* [2004] EWCA Crim 1763; [2005] B.C.C. 357. In this case it was also observed that s.218 is not exhaustive: it says nothing about assisting criminal investigators or prosecutors who might approach the official receiver or liquidator directly, or what he is to do if he becomes aware of apparent criminal behaviour himself; but here, too it would seem that he is entitled to pass on information which he holds to the relevant prosecuting authority.

S.218(4), (6)

In a voluntary winding up, the liquidator's duty is to report the matter himself directly to the Secretary of State or the Lord Advocate, and thereafter to co-operate with the authority as described, and also give the further assistance referred to in s.219(3). The court has, under s.218(6), a further power to give the liquidator directions to this effect.

S.218(5)

The Secretary of State's powers of investigation under CA 1985 ss.431, 432, are far-reaching, and under those sections are not restricted to pursuing inquiries in connection with suspected criminal offences. [These sections are not affected by CA 2006.] Additional provisions governing an investigation by the Secretary of State under the present subsection are laid down by s.219 below.

219   Obligations arising under s.218

219(1)   [Assistance to investigation by Secretary of State] For the purpose of an investigation by the Secretary of State in consequence of a report made to him under section 218(4), any obligation imposed on a person by any provision of the Companies Act 1985 to produce documents or give information to, or otherwise to assist, inspectors appointed as mentioned in section 218(5) is to be regarded as an obligation similarly to assist the Secretary of State in his investigation.

219(2)   [Answer may be used as evidence] An answer given by a person to a question put to him in exercise of the powers conferred by section 218(5) may be used in evidence against him.

219(2A)   [Use of evidence in criminal proceedings] However, in criminal proceedings in which that person is charged with an offence to which this subsection applies–

(a)   no evidence relating to the answer may be adduced, and

(b)   no question relating to it may be asked,

by or on behalf of the prosecution, unless evidence relating to it is adduced, or a question relating to it is asked, in the proceedings by or on behalf of that person.

219(2B)   [Offences to which s.219(2A) not applicable] Subsection (2A) applies to any offence other than–

(a)   an offence under section 2 or 5 of the Perjury Act 1911 (false statements made on oath otherwise than in judicial proceedings or made otherwise than on oath), or

(b)   an offence under section 44(1) or (2) of the Criminal Law (Consolidation) (Scotland) Act 1995 (false statements made on oath or otherwise than on oath).

219(3)   [Liquidator and officer to assist, where criminal proceedings instituted] Where criminal proceedings are instituted by the Director of Public Prosecutions, the Lord Advocate or the Secretary of State following any report or reference under section 218, it is the duty of the liquidator and every officer and agent of the company past and present (other than the defendant or defender) to give to the Director of Public Prosecutions, the Lord Advocate or the Secretary of State (as the case may be) all assistance in connection with the prosecution which he is reasonably able to give.

For this purpose **"agent"** includes any banker or solicitor of the company and any person employed by the company as auditor, whether that person is or is not an officer of the company.

219(4)   [Direction by court re assistance] If a person fails or neglects to give assistance in the manner required by subsection (3), the court may, on the application of the Director of Public Prosecutions, the Lord Advocate or the Secretary of State (as the case may be) direct the person to comply with that subsection; and if the application is made with respect to a liquidator, the court may (unless it appears that the failure or neglect to comply was due to the liquidator not having in his hands sufficient assets of the company to enable him to do so) direct that the costs shall be borne by the liquidator personally.

GENERAL NOTE

The provisions of this section are designed to facilitate the investigations which may be made by the various officials and authorities when a suspected criminal offence is reported to them under the preceding section. The company's bankers, solicitors and auditors are specifically included among those obliged to assist (s.219(3)).

Changes were made to the wording of s.219(1), (3) and (4) by IA 2000 s.10(7) with effect from April 2, 2001 consequentially upon the reform of s.218: see the note to that section.

Section 11 of the same Act inserted the new subss.(2A) and (2B) as from the same date. These provisions limit the use of evidence obtained under compulsion in subsequent criminal prosecutions. A similar reform was made by the Youth Justice and Criminal Evidence Act 1999 s.55 and Sch.3, covering most of the provisions in the companies and insolvency legislation dealing with the use of such evidence, but this provision did not include s.219. See further the notes to ss.236 and 433.

PART V

WINDING UP OF UNREGISTERED COMPANIES

220   Meaning of "unregistered company"

220(1)   ["Unregistered company"] For the purposes of this Part, **"unregistered company"** includes any association and any company, with the exception of a company registered under the Companies Act 2006 in any part of the United Kingdom.

220(2)   [Former references to trustee savings banks, now repealed.]

GENERAL NOTE

This section was replaced as from October 1, 2009, but without any change of substance, by the Companies Act 2006 (Consequential Amendments, Transitional Provisions and Savings) Order 2009 Sch.1 para.76.

The earliest companies legislation that enabled companies to acquire corporate status by registration was accompanied by Winding-up Acts which provided machinery for the winding up of companies which had not registered. Part V of the present Act, which consolidates CA 1985 Pt XXI, is what survives today of that legislation. There are almost certainly, however, no "unregistered companies" in the old sense still around; and for practical purposes it is probably true to say that Pt V will be applied to two or three other types of "unregistered" company—(1) statutory companies incorporated by private Act of Parliament; (2) foreign companies which have been carrying on business in Great Britain or have some other relevant connection with this jurisdiction; and (3) other bodies, such as unregistered friendly societies, for which provision for winding up is not made by specific legislation. Obsolete references to partnerships and limited partnerships contained in CA 1985 s.665, were repealed by IA 1985 Sch.10 Pt II; but paradoxically this Part of the Act is now made to apply to the winding up of insolvent partnerships: see the note to s.420. (Limited liability partnerships, in contrast, are wound up under Pt IV.)

English courts have exercised jurisdiction to wind up foreign companies under the present section or its predecessors for a very long period: s.225, which expressly refers to companies incorporated outside Great Britain but applies in limited circumstances only, is a relative newcomer which has rarely, if ever, been invoked.

Sections 220 and 221 give no guidance as to the criteria which will justify an English court in assuming jurisdiction. The matter has been left to the discretion of the courts. In practice, it is normally considered a sufficient nexus for the company to have, or have had, a place of business or branch office within the jurisdiction, or to have assets here (*Banque des Marchands de Moscou (Koupetschesky) v Kindersley* [1951] Ch. 112; [1950] 2 All E.R. 549), but other factors may also be regarded as relevant, e.g. the fact that a claim may be brought by the company against an insurer in England (*Re Compania Merabello San Nicholas SA* [1973] Ch. 75; [1972] 3 All E.R. 448), that a winding-up order will entitle former employees of the company to claim statutory redundancy payments (*Re Eloc Electro-Optieck and Communicatie BV* [1982] Ch. 43; [1981] 2 All E.R. 1111), or that the debt upon which the petition is founded was incurred here (*Re a Company (No.00359 of 1987)* [1988] Ch. 210; (1987) 3 B.C.C. 160 (also known as *Re Okeanos Maritime Corp*)). It is not necessary that the company should have assets within the jurisdiction: *Re a Company (No.003102 of 1991) Ex p. Nyckeln Finance Co Ltd* [1991] B.C.L.C. 539. However the court must be satisfied that there is a reasonable possibility that the winding-up order will benefit those applying for it, and the court must be able to exercise jurisdiction over one or more persons interested in the distribution of the company's assets: *Re Real Estate Development Co* [1991] B.C.L.C. 210; *Atlantic & General Investment Trust Ltd v Richbell Information Services Inc* [2000] B.C.C. 111; *Re Latreefers Inc* [2001] B.C.C. 174; *Re Westminster Property Management Ltd, Official Receiver v Stern (No.2)* [2001] B.C.C. 305; *Re OJSC Ank Yugraneft* [2008] EWHC 2614 (Ch); [2009] 1 B.C.L.C. 298. These cases may be contrasted with *Banco Nacional de Cuba v Cosmos Trading Corp* [2000] B.C.C. 910, where an order was refused because the connection with the UK was minimal and no benefit to the creditors could realistically be expected.

Everything in the preceding paragraph must now be reconsidered in the light of the EC Regulation, which became effective on May 31, 2002, so far as concerns companies which have their "centre of main interests" (COMI) in another EU Member State. The Regulation confers exclusive jurisdiction to open "main" insolvency proceedings upon the State where the COMI is situated—which is rebuttably presumed to be the place of its registered office (art.3(1)). In regard to "secondary" and "territorial" proceedings—where the COMI is in another Member State—art.3(2) stipulates that the local courts have jurisdiction only if the debtor "possesses an establishment" within the territory of the latter. The effect of secondary or territorial proceedings is restricted to the assets of the debtor situated in that territory. If main proceedings have already been opened, the ancillary proceedings are termed "secondary", and they must be winding-up proceedings. If main proceedings have not yet been opened, the proceedings are "territorial", and another Member State has jurisdiction in only two cases: (a) where main proceedings cannot be opened because of conditions laid down by the law of the "main" State; or (b) where the opening of territorial proceedings is requested by a creditor who has his domicile, habitual residence or registered office within the territory in question, or whose claim arises from the operation of that establishment. These questions of jurisdiction are discussed more fully in the note to the EC Regulation art.3; but it will be apparent that where the Regulation applies, the UK courts' jurisdiction under s.220 is more limited than that described above.

The CBIR does not impose similar jurisdictional limitations where the COMI is in a foreign state. Article 28 does state that, after the formal recognition by a British court of a foreign proceeding as a main proceeding, the *effects* of a proceeding under British insolvency law in relation to the debtor shall, in so far as the assets of that debtor are concerned, be restricted to assets that are located in Great Britain (and to other assets for certain purposes), but this wording does not restrict the jurisdiction of the court as such.

The court, having exercised its discretion to hold that it has jurisdiction in respect of the particular company, has a further discretion whether or not to make an order, and if so upon what terms: see the notes to s.221.

The object of s.220(1)(b) appears fairly plainly to be to ensure that a company registered in one part of the UK may be wound up only in that jurisdiction, e.g. a company registered in England and Wales may only be wound up by the High Court or the county court (s.117), and a company registered in Scotland only by the Court of Session or a sheriff court (s.120). However this is not the case so far as concerns a company registered in Northern Ireland. In *Re Normandy Marketing Ltd* [1993] B.C.C. 879 Morritt J. held that by virtue of s.220 and s.441, read together, the court in England had jurisdiction to wind up a company registered in Northern Ireland, on the petition of the Secretary of State under s.124A, provided that it had a principal place of business in England or Wales. In an appropriate case, s.225 could also be invoked to give a court in Great Britain jurisdiction over a Northern Ireland company. Otherwise, the allocation of jurisdiction over a foreign company as between the different parts of the UK is dealt with by s.221(2), (3).

The Judgments Regulation (Council Regulation (EC) 44/2001 of December 22, 2000 on jurisdiction and the enforcement of judgments in civil and commercial matters), which largely supersedes the Brussels Convention of 1968, does not apply to the winding up of insolvent companies (art.2(b)). In regard to solvent foreign companies, art.22(2) has the effect of denying a British court jurisdiction where the company has its "seat" in a contracting state other than the UK. However, conversely, a solvent company which is incorporated abroad in a contracting state will be subject to jurisdiction here under Pt V of IA 1986 if it has its "seat" in this country.

An unregistered company can be wound up only by order of the court: s.221(4)—except where the European Regulation applies: see the note to s.221(4).

Various other statutory provisions refer to "a company liable to be wound up under the Insolvency Act 1986". For example, CA 2006 s.895 uses this definition in relation to the scope of its provisions relating to reconstructions and arrangements. In such a context it may not always be appropriate to apply the case law which has been established for the purposes of the court's winding-up jurisdiction. In *Re Drax Holdings Ltd* [2003] EWHC 2743 (Ch); [2004] B.C.C. 334, the judgment of Lawrence Collins J. discusses the principles which will guide the court in the exercise of its discretion to assume jurisdiction in such a case. It is necessary that there should be a sufficient connection with the jurisdiction, but other preconditions which would apply in an insolvency (e.g. likelihood of benefit to those applying for a winding-up order) might not be relevant. The *Drax Holdings* judgment was followed in *Re La Mutuelles du Mans Assurances IARD* [2005] EWHC 1599 (Ch); [2006] B.C.C. 11; and in *Re DAP Holding NV* [2005] EWHC 2092 (Ch); [2006] B.C.C. 48 and *Re Sovereign Marine and General Insurance Co Ltd* [2006] EWHC 1335 (Ch); [2006] B.C.C. 774, in which it was held that the UK court had jurisdiction to sanction schemes of arrangement involving insurance companies based elsewhere in the EU, in the light of the construction of the relevant EC legislation.

A European grouping of territorial cooperation ("EGTC") which has its registered office in the United Kingdom is to be wound up as an unregistered company under Pt V of the Act (or the Northern Ireland equivalent): European Grouping of Territorial Cooperation Regulations 2007 (SI 2007/1949, effective August 1, 2007) reg.7; and IR 1986 will apply with the modifications set out in Pts 2 and 3 of the Schedule to those Regulations.

S.220(1)
The term "association" has been held to mean only an association formed for gain or profit: *Re St James's Club* (1852) 2 De G.M. & G. 383; *Re The Bristol Athenaeum* (1889) 43 Ch. D. 236. These decisions may have turned, in part, upon the special wording of the earlier legislation; but the ruling in the former case was given renewed authority when it was endorsed by the Court of Appeal in *Re International Tin Council* [1989] Ch. 309; (1988) 4 B.C.C. 653. The Council was an organisation formed by international treaty with the legal character, status and capacities of a corporate body. In holding that it was not within CA 1985 s.665 (the precursor of the present section), the court adopted the broad test laid down in *Re St James's Club* (above): was the association one which Parliament could reasonably have intended should be subject to the winding-up process? If any state, whether a member of the Council or not, could subject that enterprise to its own domestic law, the independence and international character of the organisation would be fragmented and destroyed. Accordingly, an English court would not assume jurisdiction under s.665. The ruling in *Re St James's Club* was applied to a professional football club in *Re Witney Town Football and Social Club* [1993] B.C.C. 874. For the same reason s.220 does not confer jurisdiction to wind up a trade union: *Re National Union of Flint Glassworkers* [2006] B.C.C. 828.

Note, however, that the court also has power under its general equitable jurisdiction to order the winding up of an unincorporated association, independently of this Part of IA 1986, and to give powers to those administering the winding up similar to those conferred on liquidators by Sch.4: *Butts Park Ventures (Coventry) Ltd v Bryant Homes Central Ltd* [2003] EWHC 2487 (Ch); [2004] B.C.C. 207. In *National Union of Flint Glassworkers* (above) an order was made in the exercise of this jurisdiction for the dissolution of the union concerned.

221 Winding up of unregistered companies

221(1) [Application of winding-up provisions] Subject to the provisions of this Part, any unregistered company may be wound up under this Act; and all the provisions of this Act and about winding up apply to an unregistered company with the exceptions and additions mentioned in the following subsections.

221(2) [Principal place of business in Northern Ireland] If an unregistered company has a principal place of business situated in Northern Ireland, it shall not be wound up under this Part unless it has a principal place of business situated in England and Wales or Scotland, or in both England and Wales and Scotland.

221(3) [Deemed registration, registered office] For the purpose of determining a court's winding-up jurisdiction, an unregistered company is deemed–

(a) to be registered in England and Wales or Scotland, according as its principal place of business is situated in England and Wales or Scotland, or

(b) if it has a principal place of business situated in both countries, to be registered in both countries;

and the principal place of business situated in that part of Great Britain in which proceedings are being instituted is, for all purposes of the winding up, deemed to be the registered office of the company.

221(4)　[No voluntary winding up] No unregistered company shall be wound up under this Act voluntarily, except in accordance with the EC Regulation.

221(5)　[Circumstances for winding up] The circumstances in which an unregistered company may be wound up are as follows–

(a)　if the company is dissolved, or has ceased to carry on business, or is carrying on business only for the purpose of winding up its affairs;

(b)　if the company is unable to pay its debts;

(c)　if the court is of opinion that it is just and equitable that the company should be wound up.

221(6)　(Repealed as from July 21, 1986—Trustee Savings Bank Act 1985 s.4(3) and SI 1986/1223 (C. 36).)

221(7)　[Scotland] In Scotland, an unregistered company which the Court of Session has jurisdiction to wind up may be wound up by the court if there is subsisting a floating charge over property comprised in the company's property and undertaking, and the court is satisfied that the security of the creditor entitled to the benefit of the floating charge is in jeopardy.

For this purpose a creditor's security is deemed to be in jeopardy if the court is satisfied that events have occurred or are about to occur which render it unreasonable in the creditor's interests that the company should retain power to dispose of the property which is subject to the floating charge.

GENERAL NOTE

On the question when the court will exercise jurisdiction to wind up a foreign company, see the note to s.220.

The court has an unrestricted discretion to make or refuse an order, or to make an order subject to conditions. Thus, in the case of an overseas company, it may decline to order a winding up, or grant a stay of proceedings here, on the ground that insolvency proceedings already instituted in another jurisdiction are capable of dealing with the matter (*New Hampshire Insurance Co v Rush & Tompkins Group plc* [1998] 2 B.C.L.C. 417). Alternatively, it may direct that the local winding up be conducted on a basis ancillary to a principal liquidation elsewhere (see *Re Commercial Bank of South Australia* (1886) 33 Ch. D. 174; *Re Hibernian Merchants Ltd* [1958] Ch. 76). (Note also in this connection the CBIR art.28, on the effect of the recognition of a foreign proceeding as a "main" proceeding.) In *Lancefield v Lancefield* [2002] B.P.I.R. 1108 it was held that the court could of its own motion make a winding-up order under s.220 even though no petition had been presented.

S.221(4)

The words "except in accordance with the EC Regulation" were added by the Insolvency Act 1986 (Amendment) (No.2) Regulations 2002 (SI 2002/1240, effective May 31, 2002). It is thus now possible for a company incorporated elsewhere in the EU which has its centre of main interests in England to be wound up in England under a creditors' voluntary winding up: see *Re TXU Europe German Finance BV* [2005] B.C.C. 90. The administration of such a liquidation will be governed by English law.

S.221(5)

The grounds for the winding up of an unregistered company which are set out in this subsection are more restricted than those for registered companies: see s.122.

The court has jurisdiction to wind up a foreign company under this subsection even though it has no assets here, provided that a sufficiently close connection can be shown, e.g. that the debt upon which the petition is founded was incurred here: *Re a Company (No.00359 of 1987)* [1988] Ch. 210; (1987) 3 B.C.C. 160. However, this will not be the case where the EC Regulation applies.

S.221(6)

This was repealed as from July 21, 1986—Trustee Savings Bank Act 1985 s.4(3) and SI 1986/1223 (C. 36).

S.221(7)

See the note to s.122(2).

222   Inability to pay debts: unpaid creditor for £750 or more

222(1)   [Deemed inability to pay debts] An unregistered company is deemed (for the purposes of section 221) unable to pay its debts if there is a creditor, by assignment or otherwise, to whom the company is indebted in a sum exceeding £750 then due and–

(a)   the creditor has served on the company, by leaving at its principal place of business, or by delivering to the secretary or some director, manager or principal officer of the company, or by otherwise serving in such manner as the court may approve or direct, a written demand in the prescribed form requiring the company to pay the sum due, and

(b)   the company has for 3 weeks after the service of the demand neglected to pay the sum or to secure or compound for it to the creditor's satisfaction.

222(2)   [Increase or reduction of s.222(1) sum] The money sum for the time being specified in subsection (1) is subject to increase or reduction by regulations under section 417 in Part XV; but no increase in the sum so specified affects any case in which the winding-up petition was presented before the coming into force of the increase.

GENERAL NOTE

This provision modifies the definition of "inability to pay debts" contained in s.123(1)(a) above to meet the case of an unregistered company. See further the notes to that section.

S.222(1)(a)
The demand must be "in the prescribed form", and also in hard copy (LRO 2010 (SI 2010/18) art.4(2)(h)). For details, see IR 1986 rr.4.5 et seq. and Form 4.1.

223   Inability to pay debts: debt remaining unsatisfied after action brought

223   An unregistered company is deemed (for the purposes of section 221) unable to pay its debts if an action or other proceeding has been instituted against any member for any debt or demand due, or claimed to be due, from the company, or from him in his character of member, and–

(a)   notice in writing of the institution of the action or proceeding has been served on the company by leaving it at the company's principal place of business (or by delivering it to the secretary, or some director, manager or principal officer of the company, or by otherwise serving it in such manner as the court may approve or direct), and

(b)   the company has not within 3 weeks after service of the notice paid, secured or compounded for the debt or demand, or procured the action or proceeding to be stayed or sisted, or indemnified the defendant or defender to his reasonable satisfaction against the action or proceeding, and against all costs, damages and expenses to be incurred by him because of it.

GENERAL NOTE

There is no provision corresponding directly to this section in the case of a registered company. The notice under s.223(a) must be in hard copy (LRO 2010 (SI 2010/18) art.4(2)(i)).

224   Inability to pay debts: other cases

224(1)   [Deemed inability to pay debts] An unregistered company is deemed (for purposes of section 221) unable to pay its debts–

(a)   if in England and Wales execution or other process issued on a judgment, decree or order obtained in any court in favour of a creditor against the company, or any member of it as such, or any person authorised to be sued as nominal defendant on behalf of the company, is returned unsatisfied;

(b)   if in Scotland the induciae of a charge for payment on an extract decree, or an extract registered bond, or an extract registered protest, have expired without payment being made;

(c) if in Northern Ireland a certificate of unenforceability has been granted in respect of any judgment, decree or order obtained as mentioned in paragraph (a);

(d) it is otherwise proved to the satisfaction of the court that the company is unable to pay its debts as they fall due.

224(2) [Deemed inability—another situation] An unregistered company is also deemed unable to pay its debts if it is proved to the satisfaction of the court that the value of the company's assets is less than the amount of its liabilities, taking into account its contingent and prospective liabilities.

GENERAL NOTE

The provisions of this section correspond with those of s.123(1)(b)–(e), (2): see the notes to that section.

225 Company incorporated outside Great Britain may be wound up though dissolved

225(1) [Extent] Where a company incorporated outside Great Britain which has been carrying on business in Great Britain ceases to carry on business in Great Britain, it may be wound up as an unregistered company under this Act, notwithstanding that it has been dissolved or otherwise ceased to exist as a company under or by virtue of the laws of the country under which it was incorporated.

225(2) [Applicability EC Regulation] This section is subject to the EC Regulation.

GENERAL NOTE

The jurisdiction of the court to wind up a foreign company is not, of course, limited to the circumstances set out in this section. In practice, the more widely drawn provisions of s.221 are normally relied on: s.225 derives originally from CA 1928 s.91, which was enacted to remove a doubt as to the court's jurisdiction which arose in connection with the dissolution of Russian banks following the revolution of 1917; it did not confer any new power to wind up companies (per Megarry J. in *Re Compania Merabello San Nicholas SA* [1973] Ch. 75 at 85, 86; and per Morritt J. in *Re Normandy Marketing Ltd* [1993] B.C.C. 879 at 883).

S.225(2)
This subsection was added by the Insolvency Act 1986 (Amendment) (No.2) Regulations 2002 (SI 2002/1240, effective May 31, 2002), in parallel with the amendment to s.221(4). See the note to that section.

226 Contributories in winding up of unregistered company

226(1) [Deemed contributory] In the event of an unregistered company being wound up, every person is deemed a contributory who is liable to pay or contribute to the payment of any debt or liability of the company, or to pay or contribute to the payment of any sum for the adjustment of the rights of members among themselves, or to pay or contribute to the payment of the expenses of winding up the company.

226(2) [Liability for contribution] Every contributory is liable to contribute to the company's assets all sums due from him in respect of any such liability as is mentioned above.

226(3) [Unregistered company re mines in stannaries] In the case of an unregistered company engaged in or formed for working mines within the stannaries, a past member is not liable to contribute to the assets if he has ceased to be a member for 2 years or more either before the mine ceased to be worked or before the date of the winding-up order.

226(4) [Omitted by the Companies Act 2006 (Consequential Amendments, Transitional Provisions and Savings) Order 2009 Sch.1 para.76(5).]

GENERAL NOTE

The reference in s.226(3) to "the stannaries" is to certain Cornish tin-mining companies, which were formerly governed by separate legislation.

227 Power of court to stay, sist or restrain proceedings

227 The provisions of this Part with respect to staying, sisting or restraining actions and proceedings against a company at any time after the presentation of a petition for winding up and before the making of a winding-up order extend, in the case of an unregistered company, where the application to stay, sist or restrain is presented by a creditor, to actions and proceedings against any contributory of the company.

GENERAL NOTE

Compare *Phillips & Harland v Symes* [2006] EWHC 2595 (Ch); [2008] B.P.I.R. 212.

228 Actions stayed on winding-up order

228 Where an order has been made for winding up an unregistered company, no action or proceeding shall be proceeded with or commenced against any contributory of the company in respect of any debt of the company, except by leave of the court, and subject to such terms as the court may impose.

229 Provisions of this Part to be cumulative

229(1) **[Part V in addition to Pt IV]** The provisions of this Part with respect to unregistered companies are in addition to and not in restriction of any provisions in Part IV with respect to winding up companies by the court; and the court or liquidator may exercise any powers or do any act in the case of unregistered companies which might be exercised or done by it or him in winding up companies registered under the Companies Act 2006 in England and Wales or Scotland.

229(2) [Omitted by the Companies Act 2006 (Consequential Amendments, Transitional Provisions and Savings) Order 2009 Sch.1 para.76(6)(b).]

PART VI

MISCELLANEOUS PROVISIONS APPLYING TO COMPANIES WHICH ARE INSOLVENT OR IN LIQUIDATION

Introductory note to Part VI
The heading to this Part is likely to give rise to confusion, because of the phrase "companies which are insolvent". The natural inference to be drawn from this would be that nothing in ss.230–246 applies to a company which is solvent (in a financial sense) so that, for instance, an officer of a company is not under a duty to co-operate with an administrative receiver if the company in question is in fact solvent. The possible confusion is made worse by the absence of any statutory definition of "insolvent" company, though there is a definition of "insolvency" in s.247(1) (and of "onset of insolvency" in ss.240(3) and 245(5), of "goes into insolvent liquidation" in ss.214(6) and 216(7), and of "becomes insolvent" in CDDA 1986 s.6(2)). "Insolvency" in ss.247(1), 240(3) and 245(5) plainly refers to the various types of insolvency *proceedings* (liquidation, administration, administrative receivership, etc.) while "insolvent" in ss.214(6), 214(7) and CDDA 1986 s.6(2) is concerned with the company's financial state. (To add to the confusion, "insolvent" is given yet another special meaning in two chapters of the rules: see IR 1986 rr.4.151, 4.173(2).)

In the heading to this Part, the words "which are insolvent" should probably be taken as meaning "which are the subject of insolvency proceedings"; and "insolvency" could then be construed in accordance with the definition in s.247(1). This may violate to a degree the more natural connotation of the word "insolvent"; but it does mean that the whole of Pt VI can be applied without qualification. The alternative is to take "insolvent" as meaning "not financially viable", which raises serious problems because (1) no definition of "insolvent" is given in the body of this Part, and the word admits of many interpretations (see the note to s.123); and (2) the whole of Pt VI would be subject to limitations which the text of the Act does not specify.

It is generally understood that headings within a statute (in contrast to marginal notes) may be looked at to resolve an ambiguity in the sections that are grouped under them (Halsbury, *Laws of England*, 4th edn, Vol.44, para.818); but it would be unusual to import into the text of an Act qualifications (and ambiguities) which appear only from the words of a heading.

It is therefore submitted that Pt VI applies to *all* companies, whether financially "solvent" or "insolvent", and that "insolvent" must be read analogously with the definition of "insolvency" in s.247(1)—that is, as meaning "which are the subject of insolvency proceedings".

On the scope of the EC Regulation on Insolvency Proceedings 2000, see the Introductory note to the Regulation in Vol.2.

Various definitions of insolvency are found in other legislation: see, e.g. Sale of Goods Act 1979 s.61(4); Employment Rights Act 1996 s.183 (on which, see *Secretary of State for Trade and Industry v Key* [2004] B.P.I.R. 214). The term may also call for construction when used in a document (e.g. "insolvency event"), as in *Martyn Rose Ltd v AKG Group Ltd* [2003] EWCA Civ 375; [2003] 2 B.C.L.C. 102; and *Centre Reinsurance International Co v Curzon Insurance Ltd* [2004] EWHC 200 (Ch); [2006] 1 B.C.L.C. 187. (Note that this case went to appeal, ultimately to the House of Lords ([2006] 1 W.L.R. 2863; [2006] UKHL 45; [2006] B.C.C. 971), but there was no appeal on this point.) See also *Re Cheyne Finance plc* [2007] EWHC 2402 (Ch); [2008] B.C.C. 182; *Merrill Lynch International Bank Ltd v Winterthur Swiss Insurance Co* [2007] EWHC 893 (Comm); [2008] B.P.I.R.129, and the note to s.123.

Office-holders

230   Holders of office to be qualified insolvency practitioners

230(1)   (Section 230(1) ceased to have effect and repealed by the Enterprise Act 2002 s.248(3), Sch.17 para.9, 19 and s.278(2), Sch.26 as from September 15, 2003.)

230(2)   [Administrative receiver] Where an administrative receiver of a company is appointed, he must be a person who is so qualified.

230(3)   [Liquidator] Where a company goes into liquidation, the liquidator must be a person who is so qualified.

230(4)   [Provisional liquidator] Where a provisional liquidator is appointed, he must be a person who is so qualified.

230(5)   [Official receiver] Subsections (3) and (4) are without prejudice to any enactment under which the official receiver is to be, or may be, liquidator or provisional liquidator.

GENERAL NOTE

This section requires that a person appointed to any of the various offices mentioned shall be qualified to act as an insolvency practitioner in relation to the company in question. The term "act as an insolvency practitioner" (in relation to a company) is defined by s.388(1), and "qualified" and "qualified … in relation to" by s.390(2) and s.390(3) respectively. It is an offence under s.389 for a person to act as an insolvency practitioner in relation to a company at a time when he is not qualified to do so.

Section 230(1), which required an administrator to be qualified to act as an insolvency practitioner in relation to the company, was repealed by EA 2002 Sch.17 para.19 with effect from September 15, 2003. The point, so far as concerns administrators appointed under IA 1986 Sch.B1, is now covered by para.6 of the latter Schedule. At the same time a separate provision dealing with this category of administrators was enacted in EA 2002 Sch.16, which is now to be found in IA 1986 Sch.B1 para.75, and a saving provision, reinstating s.230(1), came into effect under the Enterprise Act 2002 (Commencement No.4 and Transitional Provisions and Savings) Order 2003 (SI 2003/2093 (C. 85)) art.3. This saving provision applies in cases where a petition for an administration order was presented before September 15, 2003, and also in the administration of insolvent partnerships commencing prior to July 1, 2005, limited liability partnerships and bodies which are insurers under FSMA 2002 and SI 2002/1242. There is no mention in the Order of building societies and the public utility companies listed in EA 2002 s.249 but in these cases the original s.230 will continue to apply because s.249 disapplies the new s.8(3) in regard to such bodies.

See also the note to s.212(1).

There is no reference in s.230 to the nominee or the supervisor of a voluntary arrangement under Pt I of the Act, which is a little odd since each of these is required also to be a "qualified" insolvency practitioner (see ss.1(2), 2(4), 4(2), 7(5)).

A receiver who is not an administrative receiver is not required to be a qualified insolvency practitioner, but there are specific prohibitions in ss.30, 31, 51(3) on the appointment of corporate bodies and undischarged bankrupts as receivers.

Section 388 defines the expression "acts as an insolvency practitioner", and (in s.388(6)) disapplies that section in relation to insolvency proceedings under the EC Regulation in a Member State other than the UK. The CBIR reg.8 similarly disapplies s.388 as regards anything done by a foreign representative under or by virtue of the CBIR or in relation to relief granted or co-operation or co-ordination provided under those Regulations.

S.230(5)

The official receiver is an officer of the court and is responsible directly to it and to the Secretary of State (see s.400(2)). He is not subject to the regulatory regime introduced by this Act for private insolvency practitioners.

231   Appointment to office of two or more persons

231(1)   [Application] This section applies if an appointment or nomination of any person to the office of administrative receiver, liquidator or provisional liquidator–

(a)   relates to more than one person, or

(b)   has the effect that the office is to be held by more than one person.

231(2)   [Declaration in appointment or nomination] The appointment or nomination shall declare whether any act required or authorised under any enactment to be done by the administrative receiver, liquidator or provisional liquidator is to be done by all or any one or more of the persons for the time being holding the office in question.

GENERAL NOTE

There are very few references in the present Act to joint appointments, but under the normal rules of statutory interpretation words in the singular may be taken to include the plural (Interpretation Act 1978 s.6(c)), and (if it were needed) this section adds further confirmation.

Section 231 makes no reference to the possibility of making a joint appointment to the post of nominee or supervisor of a voluntary arrangement, but it appears from s.7(6) that this, too, is contemplated by the Act: see the note to that provision.

The word "administrator" has been omitted from subss.(1) and (2) by EA 2002 Sch.17 para.20. The point is now covered by IA 1986 Sch.B1 paras 100 et seq. for administrators appointed under that Schedule, and in other cases by s.249 and the Enterprise Act 2002 (Commencement No.4 and Transitional Provisions and Savings) Order 2003 (SI 2003/2093 (C. 85)) art.3. See the notes to ss.212(1) and 230.

232   Validity of office-holder's acts

232   The acts of an individual as administrative receiver, liquidator or provisional liquidator of a company are valid notwithstanding any defect in his appointment, nomination or qualifications.

GENERAL NOTE

This is a standard-form provision, similar to that applicable to directors (CA 2006 s.161). It could not operate, however, to protect acts done where there was no power to appoint at all—e.g. where an administrative receiver is purportedly appointed under an invalid instrument. (See, on this latter point, s.34 above, and on void appointments generally, *Morris v Kanssen* [1946] A.C. 459; *Rolled Steel Products (Holdings) Ltd v British Steel Corporation* [1986] Ch. 246; (1984) 1 B.C.C. 99,158.)

The protection conferred by s.232 is confined to acts done by an *individual*. A body corporate is not qualified to act as an insolvency practitioner (s.390(1)), and it is extremely unlikely that in future there would ever be an attempt to appoint one to hold any of the offices listed in s.232. It is probably correct to infer from the express limitation of s.232 to individuals that any act done by such a corporate appointee would be wholly void. In the case of a receiver (not necessarily an administrative receiver), s.30 adds a further statutory ban on corporate appointments, and it is established that acts done by a receiver appointed in breach of this provision are totally ineffective: see *Portman Building Society v Gallwey* [1955] 1 W.L.R. 96.

The word "administrator" has been omitted from s.232 by EA 2002 Sch.17 para.21. The point is now covered by IA 1986 Sch.B1 para.104 for administrators appointed under that Schedule, and in other cases by EA 2002 s.249 and the Enterprise Act 2002 (Commencement No.4 and Transitional Provisions and Savings) Order 2003 (SI 2003/2093 (C. 85)) art.3. See the notes to ss.212(1) and 230.

There is again no reference in this section to the acts of a person as the nominee or supervisor of a voluntary arrangement. The explanation must be that such a person's role and functions are not statutory, but depend in each case upon the terms of the arrangement.

Management by administrators, liquidators, etc.

233   Supplies of gas, water, electricity, etc.

233(1)   [Application] This section applies in the case of a company where–

(a)   the company enters administration, or

(b)   an administrative receiver is appointed, or

(ba)   a moratorium under section 1A is in force, or

(c)   a voluntary arrangement approved under Part I, has taken effect, or

(d)   the company goes into liquidation, or

(e)   a provisional liquidator is appointed;

and **"the office-holder"** means the administrator, the administrative receiver, the nominee, the supervisor of the voluntary arrangement, the liquidator or the provisional liquidator, as the case may be.

233(2)   [If request by office-holder] If a request is made by or with the concurrence of the office-holder for the giving, after the effective date, of any of the supplies mentioned in the next subsection, the supplier–

(a)   may make it a condition of the giving of the supply that the office-holder personally guarantees the payment of any charges in respect of the supply, but

(b)   shall not make it a condition of the giving of the supply, or do anything which has the effect of making it a condition of the giving of the supply, that any outstanding charges in respect of a supply given to the company before the effective date are paid.

233(3)   [Supplies in s.233(2)] The supplies referred to in subsection (2) are–

(a)   a supply of gas by a gas supplier within the meaning of Part I of the Gas Act 1986,

(b)   a supply of electricity by an electricity supplier within the meaning of Part I of the Electricity Act 1989,

(c)   a supply of water by a water undertaker or, in Scotland, Scottish Water,

(d)   a supply of communications services by a provider of a public electronic communications service.

233(4)   [Effective date] **"The effective date"** for the purposes of this section is whichever is applicable of the following dates–

(a)   the date on which the company entered administration,

(b)   the date on which the administrative receiver was appointed (or, if he was appointed in succession to another administrative receiver, the date on which the first of his predecessors was appointed),

(ba)   the date on which the moratorium came into force,

(c)   the date on which the voluntary arrangement took effect,

(d)   the date on which the company went into liquidation,

(e)   the date on which the provisional liquidator was appointed.

233(5)   [Definitions] The following applies to expressions used in subsection (3)–

(a)   [Repealed.]

(b)   [Repealed.]

(c)   [Repealed.]

(d) **"communications services"** do not include electronic communications services to the extent that they are used to broadcast or otherwise transmit programme services (within the meaning of the Communications Act 2003).

GENERAL NOTE

This section (and its counterpart in bankruptcy, s.372 below) implements a recommendation of the Cork Committee (*Report*, para.1462). Prior to the present Act, a supplier of goods like gas or water or services such as the telephone was able, by virtue of its monopoly position, to compel the payment of an account incurred before the commencement of a liquidation or receivership by threatening to cut off the connection unless the arrears were paid in full or payment was personally guaranteed by the liquidator or receiver. If the supply was essential for the preservation of the company's assets (e.g. livestock or frozen food), there was little choice but to pay, and so the supplier could have its debt paid in priority even to the statutory preferential creditors. The legality of this practice was upheld in *Wellworth Cash & Carry (North Shields) Ltd v North Eastern Electricity Board* (1986) 2 B.C.C. 99,265. This section prohibits further resort to this practice. The supplier may require the "office-holder" to undertake personal responsibility for payment for any new supply, but may not make the provision of a new supply conditional upon receiving payment or security for the old.

S.233(1)

The section extends to a voluntary arrangement under Pt I, provided that it has taken effect, as well as to the other situations listed, and "office-holder" is accordingly defined to include the supervisor of such a scheme. Formerly, there was no equivalent protection during the period prior to the holding of the statutory meetings, but amendments made by IA 2000 s.1 and Sch.1 paras 1, 8(1), (2) as from January 1, 2003 (by the insertion of para.(ba) into subss.(1) and (4)) now meet that need for companies which are eligible for a moratorium. Other companies may be well advised to consider the alternative of administration.

S.233(2)

The "effective date" is defined by s.233(4).

S.233(3)

Some of the terms used in this subsection are explained in s.233(5). The scope of the section is confined to statutory undertakers and similar bodies which are under a legal obligation to provide a service to the public: a private supplier of, e.g. gas or water is not affected.

S.233(4)

The phrase "go into liquidation" is defined in s.247(2): see the note to that subsection.

S.233(5)(a), (b)

The definitions formerly set out here became redundant when s.233(3)(a), (b) was reworded by the Gas Act 1995 s.16(1) and Sch.4 para.14(1), as from March 1, 1996 and the Utilities Act 2000 s.108 and Sch.6 para.47(1), (2)(a) as from October 1, 2001, respectively. The substance of s.233 is unchanged.

234   Getting in the company's property

234(1)   [Application] This section applies in the case of a company where–

(a)   the company enters administration, or

(b)   an administrative receiver is appointed, or

(c)   the company goes into liquidation, or

(d)   a provisional liquidator is appointed;

and **"the office-holder"** means the administrator, the administrative receiver, the liquidator or the provisional liquidator, as the case may be.

234(2)   [Court's powers] Where any person has in his possession or control any property, books, papers or records to which the company appears to be entitled, the court may require that person forthwith (or within such period as the court may direct) to pay, deliver, convey, surrender or transfer the property, books, papers or records to the office-holder.

234(3)   [Application of s.234(4)] Where the office-holder–

(a)   seizes or disposes of any property which is not property of the company, and

(b)   at the time of seizure or disposal believes, and has reasonable grounds for believing, that he is entitled (whether in pursuance of an order of the court or otherwise) to seize or dispose of that property,

the next subsection has effect.

234(4)   [Liability of office-holder] In that case the office-holder–

(a)   is not liable to any person in respect of any loss or damage resulting from the seizure or disposal except in so far as that loss or damage is caused by the office-holder's own negligence, and

(b)   has a lien on the property, or the proceeds of its sale, for such expenses as were incurred in connection with the seizure or disposal.

S.234(1), (2)

The present section replaces CA 1985 s.551, which applied only to a winding up by the court, and extends its provisions to every kind of winding up and to all other "insolvency" procedures except a voluntary arrangement. The office-holder may invoke the assistance of the court to get possession of the company's property and records. However, the powers conferred by ss.234–236 may be used only for the due exercise of the office-holder's statutory functions (and, in the case of an administrative receiver, such additional functions as are given to him by the charge instrument): *Sutton v GE Capital Commercial Finance Ltd* [2004] EWCA Civ 315; [2004] 2 B.C.L.C. 662. In that case an administrative receiver had requested a firm of solicitors to deliver up documents in order to assist the debenture holder in an action against a third party. The Court of Appeal ruled that this was beyond his statutory powers, which were limited to enabling him to get in, protect and realise the mortgaged property for the benefit of the debtor company and its creditors.

An order under s.234 should not be sought ex parte, except perhaps in very exceptional circumstances: *Re First Express Ltd* [1991] B.C.C. 782. The application should be brought in the name of the office-holder, rather than that of the company: *Re Cosslett (Contractors) Ltd (No.2), Smith v Bridgend County Borough Council* [2001] UKHL 58; [2002] 1 A.C. 336; [2001] B.C.C. 740 at [32].

Under earlier provisions corresponding to the present section, the courts had held that its procedure was not appropriate to determine questions of disputed ownership, but in *Re London Iron & Steel Co Ltd* [1990] B.C.C. 159 Warner J. held that the words "to which the company appears to be entitled", coupled with the comprehensive rules laid down in Pt 7 of IR 1986, are of sufficient scope to enable the court to settle such matters; and it now seems that the courts entertain such questions as a matter of course: see *Euro Commercial Leasing Ltd v Cartwright & Lewis* [1995] B.C.C. 830 (solicitor's lien); *Re Cosslett (Contractors) Ltd* [1998] Ch. 495; [1997] B.C.C. 724 (plant on construction site). However the court has no such power where the question of ownership falls to be determined by a foreign court: *Re Leyland DAF Ltd, Talbot v Edcrest Ltd* [1994] B.C.C. 166.

In *Walker Morris v Khalastchi* [2001] 1 B.C.L.C. 1 the applicants, who had been requested by the liquidator to hand over files of documents relating to the company, wished to impose conditions that the liquidator should not release any of the documents or disclose their contents to the Revenue without an order of the court, but it was ruled that, since the files were the property of the company, the liquidator was entitled to possession of them and that it was for the liquidator to decide whether to make voluntary disclosure of the documents.

In a winding up by the court, the powers conferred on the court by this section are exercisable by the liquidator or provisional liquidator: see IR 1986 r.4.185. The liquidator is thus empowered to impose the requirement on his own authority.

No sanction is spelt out either in the Act or in the rules for a failure to comply with a requirement imposed under this subsection. No doubt such a failure could be dealt with under the inherent powers of the court, even in the case where the requirement is imposed by a liquidator.

S.234(3), (4)

These provisions give an immunity to the office-holder (and a lien for his expenses) where he mistakenly but bona fide seizes or disposes of property which does not belong to the company. The protection is given whether or not he has acted in pursuance of a court order granted under s.234(2)—although such an order would go a long way towards establishing his good faith.

The immunity is "in respect of any loss or damage resulting from the seizure or sale" (negligence apart). It does not appear to extend to liability for the wrongful interference per se, and so the owner would not be prevented from suing to establish his right to the return of the property itself or the proceeds of its sale.

It was held in *Welsh Development Agency Ltd v Export Finance Co* [1992] B.C.C. 270 that (notwithstanding the wide definition of "property" in s.436) the protection given to office-holders by these subsections extends only to the seizure and disposal of tangible property, and that they do not apply to wrongful dealings with choses in action.

On the liability of an administrator or other office holder where this statutory defence does not apply, see E. Goodwin, (2009) 22 Insolv. Int. 4.

235 Duty to co-operate with office-holder

235(1) **[Application]** This section applies as does section 234; and it also applies, in the case of a company in respect of which a winding-up order has been made by the court in England and Wales, as if references to the office-holder included the official receiver, whether or not he is the liquidator.

235(2) **[Duty to give information etc.]** Each of the persons mentioned in the next subsection shall–

(a) give to the office-holder such information concerning the company and its promotion, formation, business, dealings, affairs or property as the office-holder may at any time after the effective date reasonably require, and

(b) attend on the office-holder at such times as the latter may reasonably require.

235(3) **[Persons in s.235(2)]** The persons referred to above are–

(a) those who are or have at any time been officers of the company,

(b) those who have taken part in the formation of the company at any time within one year before the effective date,

(c) those who are in the employment of the company, or have been in its employment (including employment under a contract for services) within that year, and are in the office-holder's opinion capable of giving information which he requires,

(d) those who are, or have within that year been, officers of, or in the employment (including employment under a contract for services) of, another company which is, or within that year was, an officer of the company in question, and

(e) in the case of a company being wound up by the court, any person who has acted as administrator, administrative receiver or liquidator of the company.

235(4) **["The effective date"]** For the purposes of subsections (2) and (3), **"the effective date"** is whichever is applicable of the following dates–

(a) the date on which the company entered administration,

(b) the date on which the administrative receiver was appointed or, if he was appointed in succession to another administrative receiver, the date on which the first of his predecessors was appointed,

(c) the date on which the provisional liquidator was appointed, and

(d) the date on which the company went into liquidation.

235(5) **[Penalty for non-compliance]** If a person without reasonable excuse fails to comply with any obligation imposed by this section, he is liable to a fine and, for continued contravention, to a daily default fine.

GENERAL NOTE

In imposing on the former officers and employees of the company, and others, a statutory duty to co-operate with the liquidator or other office-holder by giving him such information as he may reasonably require (and to attend for this purpose on the office-holder), this section supplements the traditional powers to have such persons examined either publicly (s.133) or privately (s.236) before the court. No court order is required under the present provisions.

Information and documents obtained by the office-holder pursuant to this section may properly be disclosed to the Secretary of State so that he may determine whether director disqualification proceedings should be brought. This is so even though the office-holder has given an assurance that the information or documents will be used only for the purposes of the administration, since such disclosure is within "the purposes of the administration" (*Re Polly Peck International plc Ex p. the joint administrators* [1994] B.C.C. 15). The use of statements obtained under s.235 in disqualification proceedings does not in itself involve a breach of the European Convention on Human Rights (or, by inference, of the Human Rights Act 1998): *Re Westminster Property Management Ltd, Official Receiver v Stern* [2000] 1 W.L.R. 2230; [2001] B.C.C. 121. The question whether the use of such statements is unfair is to be determined by the trial judge.

In *Re Bernard L Madoff Investment Securities LLC* [2009] EWHC 442 (Ch); [2009] 2 B.C.L.C. 78 a US company and an associated English company were both in liquidation and the court granted an application for an order under the Data Protection Act 1998 authorising the transfer by the English liquidator to his American counterpart of certain specified information; but it declined to make an order under s.235 authorising the US trustee to ask questions about the American company because the section could not be used as a shortcut to an application by him under art.21 of the CBIR. It also directed that the s.235 interview should be restricted to questions about the English company.

S.235(1)
The situations to which the section applies, and the consequent definition of "office-holder", are the same as are described in s.234(1). A voluntary arrangement is excluded. Where the liquidator in a winding up by the court in England and Wales is not the official receiver, the official receiver as well as the private liquidator has the powers conferred by the section.

S.235(2), (3)
The "effective date" is defined in s.235(4) below.

For the meaning of the term "officer", see the note to s.206(3).

The extension of "employment" to include employment under a contract for services is wide enough to include solicitors, accountants and others who have rendered professional services to the company. A bank or financial institution which provided services to the company (as distinct from being simply a lender) could well fall within the definition.

The phrases "as the office-holder may reasonably require" and "in the office-holder's opinion" are matters left by the statute to the office-holder's discretion, but would no doubt be subject to the general powers of the court to control an office-holder if he were acting unreasonably; and in any event the question of reasonableness could be raised as a defence if a prosecution were brought.

S.235(4)
A company "goes into liquidation" at the times described in s.247(2): see the note to that subsection.

S.235(5)
On penalties, see s.430 and Sch.10.

The duty imposed by this section may also be enforced by court order—e.g. where a director has failed to submit a statement of affairs when required by an office-holder to do so: see IR 1986 r.7.20, and *Re Wallace Smith Trust Co Ltd* [1992] B.C.C. 707. For other relevant rules, see rr.4.39 et seq.

236   Inquiry into company's dealings, etc.

236(1)   [Application] This section applies as does section 234; and it also applies in the case of a company in respect of which a winding-up order has been made by the court in England and Wales as if references to the office-holder included the official receiver, whether or not he is the liquidator.

236(2)   [Court's powers] The court may, on the application of the office-holder, summon to appear before it–

(a)   any officer of the company,

(b)   any person known or suspected to have in his possession any property of the company or supposed to be indebted to the company, or

(c)   any person whom the court thinks capable of giving information concerning the promotion, formation, business, dealings, affairs or property of the company.

236(3) **[Powers re account, production]** The court may require any such person as is mentioned in subsection (2)(a) to (c) to submit to the court an account of his dealings with the company or to produce any books, papers or other records in his possession or under his control relating to the company or the matters mentioned in paragraph (c) of the subsection.

236(3A) **[Where s.236(3) account to be contained]** An account submitted to the court under subsection (3) must be contained in–

(a) a witness statement verified by a statement of truth (in England and Wales), and

(b) an affidavit (in Scotland).

236(4) **[Application of s.236(5)]** The following applies in a case where–

(a) a person without reasonable excuse fails to appear before the court when he is summoned to do so under this section, or

(b) there are reasonable grounds for believing that a person has absconded, or is about to abscond, with a view to avoiding his appearance before the court under this section.

236(5) **[Court's power re warrant]** The court may, for the purpose of bringing that person and anything in his possession before the court, cause a warrant to be issued to a constable or prescribed officer of the court–

(a) for the arrest of that person, and

(b) for the seizure of any books, papers, records, money or goods in that person's possession.

236(6) **[Court authorisation re custody]** The court may authorise a person arrested under such a warrant to be kept in custody, and anything seized under such a warrant to be held, in accordance with the rules, until that person is brought before the court under the warrant or until such other time as the court may order.

GENERAL NOTE

This power of the court to summon persons to appear before it for examination was formerly provided for by CA 1985 s.561, but that section was confined in its scope to a winding up by the court. It is now extended to other forms of corporate "insolvency" proceedings, although not to a voluntary arrangement. An examination conducted under this section is private, in contrast to the public examination of officers and others which may be ordered under s.133.

The court's discretion under this section is unfettered, although it is generally exercised along fairly well-settled lines. There are overriding requirements that the examination should be necessary in the interests of the winding up, and that it should not be oppressive or unfair to the respondent (*Re Embassy Art Products Ltd* (1987) 3 B.C.C. 292; *Re Adlards Motor Group Holding Ltd* [1990] B.C.L.C. 68; and see also *British & Commonwealth Holdings plc (Joint Administrators) v Spicer & Oppenheim, Re British & Commonwealth Holdings plc (No.2)* [1993] A.C. 426; [1992] B.C.C. 977). The onus of establishing a case is on the office-holder, but the views of office-holders that an examination should be ordered "are normally entitled to a good deal of weight" (*Joint Liquidators of Sasea Finance Ltd v KPMG* [1998] B.C.C. 216 at 220; contrast *Re XL Communications Group plc* [2005] EWHC 2413 (Ch)). The section is not to be used just to give the office-holder special advantages in ordinary litigation: *Re Atlantic Computers plc* [1998] B.C.C. 200; *Re Sasea Finance Ltd* [1999] B.C.C. 103. As a general (but not invariable) rule, an office-holder may not apply for examination if he has made a firm decision to commence proceedings against the respondent (*Re Castle New Homes Ltd* [1979] 1 W.L.R. 1075; [1979] 2 All E.R. 775; as explained in *Cloverbay Ltd (Joint Administrators) v Bank of Credit and Commerce International SA (Re Cloverbay Ltd (No.2))* [1991] Ch. 90; [1990] B.C.C. 414); and see *Re RBG Resources plc* [2002] EWCA Civ 1624; [2002] B.C.C. 1005. However even the fact that criminal charges have already been brought against the respondent does not constitute an absolute bar to the making of an order (*Re Arrows Ltd (No.2)* [1992] B.C.C. 446). The court has to balance the importance to the office-holder of obtaining the information against the degree of oppression to the person sought to be examined, bearing in mind that the office-holder's views should be afforded great weight but are not determinative. The fact that proceedings are pending against the respondent including very serious allegations of fraud and dishonesty could make it oppressive to order his examination in advance of the trial, but this consideration may be outweighed by the liquidator's need for information to enable him to get on with his primary function of identifying and getting in the company's assets; and an examination may nevertheless be ordered: *Daltel Europe Ltd v Makki* [2004] EWHC 726 (Ch); [2005] 1 B.C.L.C. 594. The case for making an order against an officer or former officer of the company will usually be stronger than it would be against a third party (see *Re Westmead Consultants Ltd* [2002] 1 B.C.L.C. 384); and an order for oral examination is much more likely to be oppressive than an order for the production of documents (*Cloverbay Ltd*, above). However (even in the case of a third party) an application is not necessarily unreasonable because it is inconvenient for the respondent or may cause him considerable work, or may make him vulnerable to future claims (*British & Commonwealth Holdings*, above). In *Re Trading Partners Ltd* [2002] 1 B.C.L.C. 655 an order was made in favour of liquidators against receivers for the production of material which had been collected by the receivers at their debenture-holders' expense, despite objections based on a possible conflict of interest, the only restriction placed by the court being on documents which might disclose the strategy proposed to be adopted for the receivership. It may be oppressive to seek an order for examination without prior notice to the respondents or without first having asked for the information by letter or some similar means, although such a course of action would be justified in some exceptional cases (*Re Embassy Art Products Ltd*, above). In *Re an Inquiry into Mirror Group Newspapers plc* [2000] B.C.C. 217 inspectors appointed under CA 1985 ss.432 and 442 wished to put extensive questions to the respondent on matters on which he had already been questioned at length under (inter alia) s.236, and had been questioned in cross-examination in a criminal trial: in all, he had undergone interrogations over a total of 61 days. The court directed the inspectors to do their best to avoid questioning him on topics on which he had been questioned before, and so far as possible to rely on the answers which he had already given in the course of the earlier procedures.

In *Re Bank of Credit & Commerce International SA* [1997] B.C.C. 561, where the office-holders in the BCCI liquidation applied to have the production by members of the Bank of America Group of an extensive list of books and documents set out under 12 heads, the court ordered disclosure subject to staging periods spread out between 14 and 84 days, and expressed the tentative view that the costs of compliance with the order (involving, inter alia, air freighting 100 boxes of documents from San Francisco to London) should be costs in the liquidation.

In *Re Delberry Ltd* [2008] EWHC 925 (Ch); [2008] B.C.C. 653 administrative receivers had sold the company's business within a few days of their appointment pursuant to a "pre-pack" agreement. In a subsequent liquidation the liquidator applied to the court to have the receivers produce documents relating to their receivership and their pre-receivership work in order to see whether the remuneration which they had been paid was open to challenge and also whether they might be liable for breach of duty or misfeasance. The court held that these objects were within the scope of s.236.

Any doubts which there might have been on the question whether a respondent could be excused from complying with an order under s.236 on the ground of self-incrimination were set at rest by a series of cases in 1992—at least in the case where he is an officer or former officer of the insolvent company. The relevant cases are: *Re Jeffrey S Levitt Ltd* [1992] Ch. 457; [1992] B.C.C. 137; not following *Re Barlow Clowes (Gilt Managers) Ltd (No.2)* (Ferris J., unreported, July 31, 1990); *Re A E Farr Ltd* [1992] B.C.C. 150 (where Ferris J. decided not to follow his earlier judgment); and *Bishopsgate Investment Management Ltd (in provisional liquidation) v Maxwell (Re Bishopsgate Investment Management Ltd, Mirror Group Newspapers plc v Maxwell)* [1993] Ch. 1; [1992] B.C.C. 222. It has been confirmed that the position is the same in Scotland: *Liquidator of Tay Square Properties Ltd, Noter*, 2005 S.L.T. 469. However, the fact that the privilege against self-incrimination has been impliedly abrogated by statute is a factor which can be taken into account when the court exercises its discretion whether or not to make an order ([1993] Ch. 1 at 63; [1992] B.C.C. 222 at 262). Where the person concerned is not an officer or former officer, the plea of self-incrimination may be available (see the Australian case *O'Toole v Mitcham* (1978) C.L.C. para.40–429). However, it should be noted that these cases were decided before the ruling, discussed below, in *Saunders v United Kingdom* (1997) 23 E.H.R.R. 313; [1997] B.C.C. 872 in which it was held that the *use* in later criminal proceedings of statements obtained under compulsion was contrary to the European Convention on Human Rights, and in practice the use of such statements was discontinued and is now banned by law. This development would suggest that an objection on the ground of self-incrimination is now even less likely to be upheld. For further proceedings, see *R. v Lyons* [2002] UKHL 44; [2003] 1 A.C. 976; [2002] B.C.C. 968.

The ruling in *Saunders v UK* (above) was followed in *Kansal v United Kingdom* [2004] B.P.I.R. 740.

In *Re Pantmaenog Timber Co Ltd, Official Receiver v Wadge Rapps & Hunt (a firm)* [2003] UKHL 49; [2004] 1 A.C. 158; [2003] B.C.C. 659 the House of Lords, reversing the Court of Appeal, ruled that the Official Receiver could make an application under s.236 even when his sole purpose was to obtain information for the purposes of instituting disqualification proceedings against a director on the ground of unfitness under CDDA 1986 s.6. The Court of Appeal had held that the Official Receiver's powers in this regard were limited to those conferred by CDDA 1986 s.7(4), but the House of Lords said that the two provisions should be seen as complementary to each other. It was also open to an office-holder, such as a liquidator, to invoke s.236 for the same purpose—his functions were not confined to the administration of the insolvent company's estate—and the Official Receiver could do so whether or not he was the company's liquidator.

Although information collected under s.236 is confidential (because obtained through a process of compulsion), the confidentiality is not absolute and may be outweighed by considerations of public interest, so that (for instance) if it reveals evidence of tax fraud it may be passed to the Revenue's prosecuting authority: *R. v Brady* [2004] EWCA Crim 1763; [2005] B.C.C. 357. The decision whether or not to disclose is, however, for the official receiver and not for the court. An office-holder should similarly, it appears, take his own advice about the use of information obtained under s.236 rather than ask the court for directions: *Re PNC Telecom plc* [2003] EWHC 2220 (Ch); [2004] B.P.I.R. 314.

In *Bellmex International Ltd v Green* [2001] B.C.C. 253 it was said that the s.236 power should not normally be used to deal with factual issues arising on a proof of debt.

In *Re Brook Martin & Co (Nominees) Ltd* [1993] B.C.L.C. 328, the directors of the company against whom a s.236 order was sought were also the company's solicitors, and they raised a plea of professional privilege. Vinelott J. held that no privilege could be asserted in respect of documents which belonged to the company itself. In regard to documents where the privilege arose through acts done on behalf of other clients, he left open the question whether it could, in exceptional circumstances, be overridden by an order under s.236. In *Re Galileo Group Ltd* [1998] B.C.C. 228 an order was refused where the information which was being sought had been given in confidence.

The transcripts of the examination of a person under this section attract legal professional privilege (*Dubai Bank Ltd v Galadari* (1989) 5 B.C.C. 722), but this is subject to the powers of the court to allow inspection under r.9.5(2).

The object of an order under s.236 was said by Browne-Wilkinson V.C. in the *Cloverbay Ltd* case ([1991] Ch. 90 at 102; [1990] B.C.C. 415 at 419–420) to be limited to enabling the office-holder "to get sufficient information to reconstitute the state of knowledge that the company should possess. In my judgment its purpose is not to put the company in a better position than it would have enjoyed if liquidation or administration had not supervened". However, in *British & Commonwealth Holdings plc (Joint Administrators) v Spicer & Oppenheim (Re British & Commonwealth Holdings plc (No.2))* [1993] A.C. 426; [1992] B.C.C. 977, the House of Lords rejected this narrow approach, holding that an order could properly be made extending to all documents (and, it would appear, all information) which the office-holder reasonably required to have to carry out his functions.

In some early cases decided under the section, an order was made on terms that the record should not be used in subsequent criminal proceedings, or disclosed to the Serious Fraud Office (e.g. *Re Arrows Ltd (No.2)* [1992] B.C.C. 125; and *Re Arrows Ltd (No.4)* (at first instance) [1992] B.C.C. 987). However, in the light of the rulings in *Rank Film Distributors Ltd v Video Information Centre* [1982] A.C. 380; and *AT & T Istel Ltd v Tully* [1992] Q.B. 315 (cases decided on analogous statutory provisions), it was later accepted that the civil courts have no jurisdiction to impose a condition on the use by prosecuting authorities in criminal proceedings of evidence given in the civil proceedings, such as a condition of the kind described: see the *Bishopsgate Investment Management Ltd* case [1992] Ch. 1 at 19; [1992] B.C.C. 222 at 228; and *Re Arrows Ltd (No.4); Hamilton v Naviede* in the House of Lords [1995] 2 A.C. 75; [1994] B.C.C. 641. However, these rulings must now be reconsidered in the light of the decision of the European Court of Human Rights in *Saunders v United Kingdom* (1997) 23 E.H.R.R. 313; [1997] B.C.C. 872, which held that the use of self-incriminating statements obtained under compulsion (in that case, by DTI inspectors acting under CA 1985 s.432) in subsequent criminal proceedings was unfair and a breach of art.6(1) of the European Convention on Human Rights. In the light of this ruling, the practice of using such statements in criminal proceedings was discontinued, and the Youth Justice and Criminal Evidence Act 1999 s.59 and Sch.3 now forbids prosecutors from doing so by statute. (But such statements may be used in disqualification proceedings: *R. v Secretary of State for Trade and Industry Ex p. McCormick* [1998] B.C.C. 379.) Moreover, the Convention has since been incorporated into the domestic law of the United Kingdom by the Human Rights Act 1998.

In *Re Headington Investments Ltd Ex p. Maxwell* [1993] B.C.C. 500, the Court of Appeal held that there was no public interest immunity to prevent the disclosure of s.236 transcripts to the prosecution or regulatory authorities and that, if such disclosure is made, a person facing actual or potential prosecution was not entitled to have simultaneous disclosure made to him: the material would in due course be made available to him in the criminal proceedings, and any question of unfairness or prejudice was a matter for the judge at trial.

For the rules and procedure governing the examinations, see IR 1986 rr.9.1 et seq. Application is made to the court by the office-holder. Although in many, if not most, cases it may be appropriate for the application to be made ex parte, Vinelott J. in *Re Maxwell Communications Corporation plc, Homan v Vogel* [1994] B.C.C. 741 said that some good reason must be shown to justify this course: if the person affected is given notice it may enable the scope of the order to be clarified and in this and in other ways save time and expense. See also on this issue *Re Embassy Art Products Ltd* (1987) 3 B.C.C. 292; and *Re PFTZM Ltd (in liq.)* [1995] B.C.C. 280 (where an order obtained ex parte was set aside on the ground that it was oppressive). In *Miller v Bain* [2002] B.C.C. 899 the respondent director had failed to co-operate with the liquidator by attending for interview and proposed to absent himself for over a year. The liquidator applied ex parte for an order requiring him to attend for a private examination, and was awarded costs of the ex parte application in view of the respondent's recalcitrant attitude. Costs were also awarded in *Hunt v Renzland* [2008] B.P.I.R. 1380.

The application to the court must be in writing, specifying the grounds on which it is being made (r.9.2(1)). This document is confidential, and may not be inspected by anyone, without an order of the court, other than the persons mentioned in r.9.5(2). It had been the invariable practice since *Re Gold Co* (1879) 12 Ch. D. 77 that this document should not be disclosed to the person against whom the order was sought—i.e. that the court would never exercise its discretion to allow inspection by such a person. However, in *Re British & Commonwealth Holdings plc (No.1)* [1992] Ch. 342; [1992] B.C.C. 165, the Court of Appeal decided to depart from this practice, and ruled instead that where an application has been made to have the order set aside, inspection of the document should prima facie be allowed if the court is of the opinion that otherwise it might be unable fairly or properly to dispose of the application. It is for the office-holder to satisfy the court that confidentiality in whole or in part would nevertheless be appropriate. See further on this question *Re Bishopsgate Investment Management Ltd (No.2)* [1994] B.C.C. 732.

In *Re Seagull Manufacturing Co Ltd (in liq.)* [1993] Ch. 345; [1993] B.C.C. 241 the Court of Appeal, affirming Mummery J. [1992] Ch. 128; [1991] B.C.C. 550, held that the public examination provisions of s.133 have extra-territorial effect, and Mummery J. in particular contrasted s.133 with the powers under ss.236, 237 which, he said, did not extend beyond the jurisdiction. However, the Court of Session in *McIsaac, Petitioners; Joint Liquidators of First Tokyo Index Trust Ltd* [1994] B.C.C. 410, rejected a submission that a s.236 order could not be made against a person resident in New York. (See also *Miller v Bain* [2003] B.P.I.R. 959.) The issue is examined in detail by Burton J. in *Re Casterbridge Properties Ltd* [2002] B.C.C. 453 at 475 et seq. Here, it was held that while s.236 undoubtedly has extra-territorial effect to the extent that the court may order the private examination of a person based in a foreign country if the examination is to be held abroad, the question whether an order may be made for such a person to be examined within the UK remains unresolved. In *Re Anglo American Insurance Co Ltd* [2002] B.C.C. 715 the alternative course was adopted of applying for letters of request to courts in Bermuda and the United States, and Neuberger J. held that for this purpose the rules governing the exercise of the s.236 jurisdiction, set out in IR 1986 Pt 9, reflected the way in which the court would exercise its inherent jurisdiction where an application is made for letters of request. In *Re Mid East Trading Ltd, Phillips v Lehman Brothers* [1998] B.C.C. 726, the Court of Appeal held that an order could be made under s.236 in respect of documents situated abroad, where the company in question was being wound up as an unregistered company under IA 1986 Pt V. However, it was emphasised in that case that the court's power extended only to order the production of documents relating to the particular company which was in liquidation. In *Re a Company (No.003318 of 1987) (Oriental Credit Ltd)* [1988] Ch. 204; (1987) 3 B.C.C. 564 it was held that the court has the power to grant an order restraining a person from leaving the jurisdiction pending the holding of an examination under this section.

It has been held that where a foreign court seeks the co-operation of a court in the United Kingdom to have a person who is resident here examined for the purposes of an insolvency proceeding in the foreign jurisdiction, the considerations which might inhibit an English court from making an order under s.236 should not be taken into account: see the notes to s.426, below.

In *Re Barlow Clowes Gilt Managers Ltd* [1992] Ch. 208; [1991] B.C.C. 608, statements had been given voluntarily by various persons to a representative of the liquidators of a company under the threat, express or implicit, that if they did not do so voluntarily the liquidators would have recourse to their powers under ss.236, 237. Other persons, who had been charged with criminal offences in connection with the affairs of the company, sought to have access to the transcripts of these interviews; but Millett J. held that the information contained in the transcripts could be used only for purposes connected with the liquidation. The liquidators had, in this instance, given the interviewees assurances of confidentiality which would not have been needed had the information been obtained under s.236; but even so, information obtained in a private examination under the statute could also have been disclosed only to the extent that it was for the benefit of the liquidation. (On the giving of undertakings by office-holders, see further *McIsaac, Petitioners* [1994] B.C.C. 410.)

Information or documents obtained by an office-holder pursuant to s.236 are subject to an obligation of confidentiality, but this may in an appropriate case be waived by the court: *Re a Company (No.005374 of 1993)* [1993] B.C.C. 734. In that case administrative receivers were allowed to disclose information to the bank which had appointed them. Information may also be disclosed to the Secretary of State for the purpose of considering whether to bring disqualification proceedings: see the notes to s.235, above.

The court has no jurisdiction to authorise anyone other than the applicant (or a solicitor or counsel instructed by him) to examine the witness, except in the rare case where there are two office-holders and IR 1986 r.9.4(2) applies: *Re Maxwell Communications Corporation plc, Homan v Vogel* [1994] B.C.C. 741.

An order under s.236 becomes inoperative if the office-holder in whose favour it has been granted ceases to hold office: *Re Kingscroft Insurance Co Ltd* [1994] B.C.C. 343.

In *Re Galileo Group Ltd* [1998] B.C.C. 228, Lightman J. expressed the view that s.236 was, at least primarily, designed to protect the interests of creditors in an insolvent liquidation: it was not intended to gain a windfall for shareholders in a solvent liquidation. This was a factor that the court might take into account in deciding whether, in its discretion, to grant an order under s.236.

Section 236 binds the Crown, so that it may be ordered to disclose information obtained in the form of transcripts of evidence under the powers of investigation conferred by CA 1985 s.432, subject to prior disclosure to the witnesses whose evidence was covered by the order and subject also to any application by them to have the order set aside: *Soden v Burns* [1996] 1 W.L.R. 1512; [1997] B.C.C. 308.

S.236(1)

This provision is identical with s.235(1): see the note to that subsection.

S.236(2)

Only the office-holder has standing to make application to the court: *Re James McHale Automobiles Ltd* [1997] B.C.C. 202. The former legislation was not so restricted and other persons, such as contributories, were commonly allowed to apply.

The list of persons who may be summoned is shorter than that in s.235(2), but it is potentially of wider scope in view of the discretion given to the court by para.(c). In *Joint Liquidators of Sasea Finance Ltd v KPMG* [1998] B.C.C. 216 at 222 it was said that a company's auditors were "most probably" officers within s.236(2)(a). In *Re Trading Partners Ltd, Akers v Lomas* [2002] 1 B.C.L.C. 655 an order was made for the inspection of working papers and litigation documents held by the administrative receivers of companies related to the company in liquidation.

The question whether costs awarded against an office-holder (e.g. for delay in proceeding with an application) should be on an indemnity basis is discussed in *Re New China Hong Kong Capital Ltd* [2003] EWHC 1573 (Ch); [2003] B.P.I.R. 1176.

S.236(3), (3A)

Section 236(3) was amended and s.236(3A) inserted by LRO 2010 (SI 2010/18) art.5(6) from April 6, 2010 (with retrospective effect).

S.236(4)–(6)

These provisions, especially when read in conjunction with s.237, are more extensive and detailed than the former CA 1985 s.561(4), which was confined to the apprehension of the person summoned, and also stipulated that he had to be tendered a reasonable sum for his expenses. The repealed section also stated (s.561(3)) that if a person (e.g. a solicitor) who was ordered to produce a document relating to the company claimed a lien on it, such production should be without prejudice to the lien. The present section does not reproduce this provision. In many cases the lien will now be unenforceable by virtue of s.246, which will allow the office-holder to demand possession of the document and so make the need for an order for its production superfluous. However even in those cases where s.246 does not apply (e.g. where the office-holder is an administrative receiver, or where the document gives a title to property and is held as such (s.246(3)), an order for production under s.236 will not affect the lien: *Ex p. Bramble* (1880) 13 Ch. D. 885; *Re Aveling Barford Ltd* [1989] 1 W.L.R. 360; (1988) 4 B.C.C. 548).

In *Re Bank of Credit & Commerce International (No.7)* [1994] 1 B.C.L.C. 455 an order made under s.236 against a person domiciled abroad was buttressed by a requirement that he should give security in the sum of £500,000 as a condition of being allowed to leave the country.

For relevant rules, see IR 1986 rr.7.23, 7.24.

237   Court's enforcement powers under s.236

237(1)   [Order to deliver property] If it appears to the court, on consideration of any evidence obtained under section 236 or this section, that any person has in his possession any property of the company, the court may, on the application of the office-holder, order that person to deliver the whole or any part of the property to the office-holder at such time, in such manner and on such terms as the court thinks fit.

237(2)   [Order to pay money due] If it appears to the court, on consideration of any evidence so obtained, that any person is indebted to the company, the court may, on the application of the office-holder, order that person to pay to the office-holder, at such time and in such manner as the court may direct, the whole or any part of the amount due, whether in full discharge of the debt or otherwise, as the court thinks fit.

237(3)   **[Order re examination of persons]** The court may, if it thinks fit, order that any person who if within the jurisdiction of the court would be liable to be summoned to appear before it under section 236 or this section shall be examined in any part of the United Kingdom where he may for the time being be, or in a place outside the United Kingdom.

237(4)   **[Examination on oath etc.]** Any person who appears or is brought before the court under section 236 or this section may be examined on oath, either orally or (except in Scotland) by interrogatories, concerning the company or the matters mentioned in section 236(2)(c).

GENERAL NOTE

Most of these detailed provisions supplementing s.236 had no counterpart in earlier legislation. There is some overlap with s.234.

Adjustment of prior transactions (administration and liquidation)

GENERAL NOTE

The topic of antecedent transactions is discussed in Totty and Moss, *Insolvency*, Ch.H4.

238   Transactions at an undervalue (England and Wales)

238(1)   **[Application]** This section applies in the case of a company where–

  (a)   the company enters administration, or

  (b)   the company goes into liquidation;

and **"the office-holder"** means the administrator or the liquidator, as the case may be.

238(2)   **[Application to court by office-holder]** Where the company has at a relevant time (defined in section 240) entered into a transaction with any person at an undervalue, the office-holder may apply to the court for an order under this section.

238(3)   **[Court order]** Subject as follows, the court shall, on such an application, make such order as it thinks fit for restoring the position to what it would have been if the company had not entered into that transaction.

238(4)   **[Interpretation]** For the purposes of this section and section 241, a company enters into a transaction with a person at an undervalue if–

  (a)   the company makes a gift to that person or otherwise enters into a transaction with that person on terms that provide for the company to receive no consideration, or

  (b)   the company enters into a transaction with that person for a consideration the value of which, in money or money's worth, is significantly less than the value, in money or money's worth, of the consideration provided by the company.

238(5)   **[Restriction on court order]** The court shall not make an order under this section in respect of a transaction at an undervalue if it is satisfied–

  (a)   that the company which entered into the transaction did so in good faith and for the purpose of carrying on its business, and

  (b)   that at the time it did so there were reasonable grounds for believing that the transaction would benefit the company.

GENERAL NOTE

To put the present section into context, it is necessary to discuss briefly the reforms made by IA 1985 in response to the recommendations made in Ch.28 of the Cork Committee's *Report*, which appear in the present Act under the headings "transactions at an undervalue"; "preferences"; and "provisions against debt avoidance" (see respectively ss.238 and 339; ss.239 and 340; and ss.423 et seq.). The concern of the Committee was to state the law more logically and accurately and remove doubts as to its scope, to make the law relating to corporate insolvency and individual bankruptcy broadly the same, and to remove the former emphasis on fraud which was implicit in the traditional terms "fraudulent conveyance" and "fraudulent preference".

The new concept of "transactions at an undervalue" is based on the former BA 1914 s.42, which declared void against the trustee in bankruptcy settlements of property made by a person who became bankrupt within a stated period thereafter. This section has been replaced, in the case of an individual bankrupt, by the broader provisions of IA 1986 s.339, and (in accordance with the recommendations of the Cork Committee (*Report*, para.1237)) applied to corporate insolvency as well as bankruptcy by the present section.

The former rules relating to "fraudulent preferences" (BA 1914 s.44; CA 1985 s.615) are redefined (under the neutral title of "preferences") by IA 1986 s.239 for company insolvencies and s.340 for bankruptcies. As is indicated by the new designation, the law has been changed so that it is no longer necessary to show a dominant and improper intention to give the creditor in question a preference over creditors generally.

Finally, the law governing "fraudulent conveyances", which can be traced back to a statute of Elizabeth I, has been brought up to date and appears in IA 1986 as ss.423 et seq., which apply to both companies and individuals. Once again, the word "fraudulent" has been pointedly dropped from the present statutory provision.

There is a considerable overlap between the three topics here discussed, and particularly, as regards transactions at an undervalue, between ss.238 and 423 et seq. The distinguishing features of the latter sections are: (1) they are not confined to situations where a company is in liquidation or subject to an administration order, or an individual is bankrupt; (2) there is no time limit; and (3) application may be made to the court by any "victim" of the transaction, and not merely the "office-holder" or trustee in bankruptcy; but (4) the requisite intention to put assets out of reach of creditors or prejudice their interests must be shown.

Sections 238–241 deal with transactions at an undervalue and preferences involving companies incorporated in England and Wales: see s.440(2)(a). Equivalent provision is made for Scotland, with the distinctive labels "gratuitous alienations" and "unfair preferences", by ss.242, 243; but these sections follow in detail the rather different bankruptcy law of Scotland.

The provisions of ss.238–243 do not operate retrospectively so as to invalidate a transaction which occurred before the present Act came into force, unless it could have been invalidated under the corresponding provisions of the former law: see Sch.11 para.9.

For the purposes of the Limitation Act 1980, applications to set aside transactions under ss.238–241 are generally actions on a speciality within s.8(1) of that Act, to which a 12-year period of limitation applies, but where the substance of the claim is not to set aside a transaction but to recover a sum by virtue of these sections the period is six years: *Re Priory Garage (Walthamstow) Ltd* [2001] B.P.I.R. 144.

Sections 238 and 239 (and also ss.423 et seq.) are to be construed as having extraterritorial effect, so that an order may be made against a person who is outside the jurisdiction: *Re Paramount Airways Ltd (in admin.)* [1993] Ch. 223; [1992] B.C.C. 416. There are, however, two safeguards: first, the court has a discretion under the sections as to the order which it may make. If a foreign element is involved, it will have to be satisfied that, in respect of the relief sought against him, the respondent is a person sufficiently connected with this jurisdiction for it to be just and proper to make the order. Secondly, a person who wishes to serve the proceedings has to obtain the leave of the court to do so under IR 1986 r.12.20A.

The right of a liquidator to institute proceedings to set aside a transaction at an undervalue or a preference under ss.238 and 239 does not form part of the company's property at the commencement of the liquidation so as to be capable of being charged by the company before the winding up or of being sold by the liquidator afterwards: *Re Yagerphone Ltd* [1935] Ch. 392; *Re Oasis Merchandising Services Ltd* [1998] Ch. 170; [1997] B.C.C. 282: see the note to s.214(1). It had also been held that the liquidator could not recoup the costs of such litigation out of the general assets in the liquidation: *Re Floor Fourteen Ltd, Lewis v IRC* [2001] 3 All E.R. 499; [2002] B.C.C. 198, but this ruling has been nullified as a result of changes made to IR 1986 r.4.218: see the note to s.115.

In the context of the financial markets, no order may be made under s.238 in relation to a market contract to which a recognised investment exchange or clearing house is a party or which is entered into under its default rules, or a disposition of property in pursuance of such a market contract: see CA 1989 s.165. It is also disapplied in relation to payment and securities settlement systems by the Finality Regulations 1999 reg.17. (See the introductory notes at pp.2–3 above.)

A transaction may be the subject of a challenge under ss.238–243 and at the same time open to objection as a "tainted gift" under POCA 2002. In that case, s.427 of the latter Act provides that no order or decree may be made under ss.238, 239, 242, 243 or 423 at a time when the recipient of the tainted gift is the subject of a restraint order or confiscation order under the 2002 Act, and any order or decree made under the above sections after the POCA order is discharged shall take into account any realisation made of property held by the recipient.

S.238(1)
This and the next three sections apply in a narrower range of situations than do earlier sections in this Part, i.e. only to company administrations and liquidations, and "office-holder" means the administrator or liquidator. It does not appear that the official receiver, where he is not the liquidator, is given standing also, as he is by s.235.

For the meaning of "goes into liquidation", see s.247(2).

S.238(2)
Only the office-holder, as defined in s.238(1), may make application. This may be contrasted with the wider category permitted to apply for an order under s.423: see s.424(1).

A "relevant time" for the purposes of this section is defined by reference not only to the calendar but also to the company's solvency: see s.240.

S.238(3)
This subsection (and the corresponding s.239(3) relating to preferences) is curiously worded. On the face of it, the use of the word "shall" and the concluding phrase "for restoring the position to what it would have been if the company had not entered into that transaction" would appear to tie the court's hands, so that (subject only to s.238(5)) it *must* make an order, and then only an order which restores the status quo. However the words "as it thinks fit" and the many and varied examples of possible orders (set out in s.241) which it is open to the court to make clearly indicate that the applicant is not entitled to demand any particular form of order as of right, and this consideration, coupled with the fact that the court's jurisdiction in this sphere is equitable in origin, must lead to the conclusion that the court may in its discretion decline to make any order at all. In *Re Paramount Airways Ltd (in admin.)* [1993] Ch. 223 at 239; [1992] B.C.C. 416 at 425, Nicholls V.C. endorsed this view, and in relation to the corresponding provision in bankruptcy (s.339), the court in *Singla v Brown* [2007] EWHC 405; [2008] Ch. 357 declined to make any order even though the conditions for the application of that section had been satisfied. In the case of *Re MDA Investment Management Ltd* [2003] EWHC 2277 (Ch) and [2004] EWHC 42 (Ch); [2005] B.C.C. 783 the court declined to make an order because the company had been on the verge of collapse at the time that the company entered into the transaction and to restore it to that position would have conferred no benefit on it. See also *Re Parkside International Ltd* [2008] EWHC 3554 (Ch); [2009] B.P.I.R. 549. The exercise of the discretion in regard to third parties may have to be even more flexible. In *Lord v Sinai Securities Ltd* [2004] EWHC 1764 (Ch); [2004] B.C.C. 986 Hart J. said that the primary concern under s.238(3) is with the restoration of the company's position, and indicated that the remedy of any other party would necessarily have to be subordinated to that.

S.238(4)
A "transaction at an undervalue" may include an outright gift (para.(a)), but otherwise must involve some form of dealing between the parties (*Re Taylor Sinclair (Capital) Ltd* [2001] 2 B.C.L.C. 176), and where consideration is given, the discrepancy in value must be "significant" (para.(b)).

In the leading case of *Re M C Bacon Ltd* [1990] B.C.C. 78 Millett J. held that the creation of security over a company's assets was not a transaction at an undervalue. Section 238(4)(b), he said, requires a comparison to be made between the value obtained by the company for the transaction and the value of the consideration provided by the company. Both values have to be measurable in money or money's worth and have to be considered from the company's point of view. The mere creation of security over the company's assets does not deplete them or diminish their value. Loss by the company of the ability to apply the proceeds of the assets otherwise than in satisfaction of the secured debt is not capable of valuation in money terms, nor is the consideration received by the company in return. The ruling in *Re Mistral Finance Ltd* [2001] B.C.C. 27 is to the same effect. But this aspect of the ruling in *Re M C Bacon Ltd* has recently been questioned. In *Hill v Spread Trustee Co Ltd* [2006] EWCA Civ 542; [2006] B.C.C. 646 (a case on s.423) Arden L.J. thought that the value to the creditor of the right to have recourse to his security should not invariably be left out of account when assessing the respective considerations given by the parties.

Similar reasoning would very possibly be applicable to a guarantee given by a company of another's indebtedness. In the Northern Ireland case of *Levy McCallum Ltd v Allen* [2007] N.I. Ch. 3 Treacy J. declined to hold that a guarantee provided by a company to another company in the same group was liable to be set aside as a transaction at an undervalue under the corresponding section in that jurisdiction.

In *Phillips v Brewin Dolphin Bell Lawrie Ltd* [2001] 1 W.L.R. 143; [2001] B.C.C. 864 the House of Lords was concerned with a complex series of linked transactions, in one of which the company had sold its business, worth £1.05 million, to B Ltd for a nominal consideration of £1 and the assumption by B Ltd of redundancy costs of £325,000, and by a contract executed contemporaneously B Ltd's parent company had agreed to lease computers from the company for four quarterly payments of £312,500. The Court of Appeal had considered that the only "transaction" to be considered under s.238 was that for the sale of the business and that no account should be taken of the related contracts; but the House of Lords held that there was no reason why the consideration for a transaction should not be provided by a third party and that, on the facts, the agreement for the sale of the business had been entered into for a consideration which included the benefit of the leasing agreement. The leasing agreement turned out to be worthless but one payment of £312,500 had been made in advance. It followed that credit ought to be given both for this sum and for the £325,000 in determining the amount which the court should order to be repaid to the company's liquidator under s.238.

In *Barber v CI Ltd* [2006] B.C.C. 927 it was held that a payment which is itself open to challenge as a preference cannot constitute valuable consideration so as to take a transaction outside the scope of s.238. The decision was the subject of criticism by Look Chan Ho and Mokal in (2006) 22 I.L. & P. 183. This article was drawn to the attention of the court when the case went to appeal (*Re Sonatacus Ltd* [2007] EWCA Civ 31; [2007] B.C.C. 186) where the point was left open because a decision on the basis of preference (s.239) was sufficient to conclude the case.

In *Re Lewis's of Leicester Ltd* [1995] B.C.C. 514 a company trading as a department store, in anticipation of closing down its operations, had segregated moneys received from several of its concessionaires and placed them in separate bank accounts in circumstances which, the court held, established a trust in their favour. It was further held that the creation of a trust in this way was not a transaction at an undervalue, since the company's assets were not diminished by what was in substance an arrangement for accelerated payment of sums which would in any event become due to the concessionaires in the future.

See also *Re Barton Manufacturing Co Ltd* [1998] B.C.C. 827 (alleged loans to directors held to be gratuitous payments); *Re Shapland Inc* [2000] B.C.C. 106 (retrospective conversion of interest-free loan to interest-bearing loan); and *Re Thoars (decd)* [2002] EWHC 2416 (Ch); [2003] 1 B.C.L.C. 499 (possibility of taking into account events after the transaction in assessing the value of property or consideration). For later proceedings—sub nom. *Ramlort Ltd v Reid* [2004] EWCA Civ 800; [2004] B.P.I.R. 985. See further *Re Bangla Television Ltd* [2006] EWHC 2292 (Ch); [2007] 1 B.C.L.C. 609 (past consideration disregarded); *Re Unigreg Ltd* [2005] B.P.I.R. 220 (summary judgment given against foreign defendants); *Clements v Henry Hadaway Organisation Ltd* [2007] EWHC 2953 (Ch); [2008] 1 B.C.L.C. 223 (excessive management charges).

S.238(5)

These provisions bear a distinct resemblance to the "three-fold test" of Eve J. in *Re Lee, Behrens and Co Ltd* [1932] 2 Ch. 46, which had a chequered history in the context of the doctrine of ultra vires (and, in that context, was later declared to be largely inappropriate: see *Rolled Steel Products (Holdings) Ltd v British Steel Corporation* [1986] Ch. 246; (1984) 1 B.C.C. 99,158). It may well be that s.238(5) will prove most difficult to apply in relation to the very types of transaction illustrated by the facts of the two cases mentioned: the payment of gratuities and pensions to employees and their dependants, and the giving of guarantees (especially within corporate groups). There may be problems, too, with regard to the "genuineness" of directors' remuneration (compare *Re Halt Garage (1964) Ltd* [1982] 3 All E.R. 1016), but it is very likely that the present section will make it easier to impeach such transactions.

239   Preferences (England and Wales)

239(1)   **[Application]** This section applies as does section 238.

239(2)   **[Application to court by office-holder]** Where the company has at a relevant time (defined in the next section) given a preference to any person, the office-holder may apply to the court for an order under this section.

239(3)   **[Court order]** Subject as follows, the court shall, on such an application, make such order as it thinks fit for restoring the position to what it would have been if the company had not given that preference.

239(4)   **[Interpretation]** For the purposes of this section and section 241, a company gives a preference to a person if—

  (a)   that person is one of the company's creditors or a surety or guarantor for any of the company's debts or other liabilities, and

  (b)   the company does anything or suffers anything to be done which (in either case) has the effect of putting that person into a position which, in the event of the company going into insolvent liquidation, will be better than the position he would have been in if that thing had not been done.

239(5)   **[Restriction on court order]** The court shall not make an order under this section in respect of a preference given to any person unless the company which gave the preference was influenced in deciding to give it by a desire to produce in relation to that person the effect mentioned in subsection (4)(b).

239(6) **[Presumption]** A company which has given a preference to a person connected with the company (otherwise than by reason only of being its employee) at the time the preference was given is presumed, unless the contrary is shown, to have been influenced in deciding to give it by such a desire as is mentioned in subsection (5).

239(7) **[Interpretation re preference]** The fact that something has been done in pursuance of the order of a court does not, without more, prevent the doing or suffering of that thing from constituting the giving of a preference.

GENERAL NOTE

The former law relating to "fraudulent preferences", as contained in CA 1985 s.615 and earlier Companies Acts, had long been thought unsatisfactory and, in particular, as the Cork Committee pointed out (*Report*, para.1244), the word "fraudulent" was both inaccurate and misleading. The Committee recommended that the term "fraudulent preference" should be replaced by "voidable preference". The draftsman, however, has rejected this suggestion (and the expression "undue preference", which is common in Australia) in favour of simply "preference", except in Scotland, for which "unfair preference" has been chosen. These differences over terminology are unimportant. The object of the change, at least in regard to England and Wales, is to remove the implication that an improper motive approaching fraud must be shown (and proved to the high standard which that charge requires), and to reflect the fact that under the redefined law it is not necessary for the liquidator even to show that the *dominant* intention of the company was to give the one creditor a preference. It need now only be established that the company was "influenced by a desire" to bring about a preference, and in some cases the burden of proof on this point is reversed (see s.239(5), (6)).

In the first reported case under the new section, *Re M C Bacon Ltd* [1990] B.C.C. 78, Millett J. "emphatically protested" against the citation of cases decided under the old law: these, he said, could not be of any assistance in construing the language of the new statute, which had been so completely and deliberately changed.

On the question whether the right of a liquidator to institute proceedings under s.239 is capable of being charged or assigned, and whether the costs of litigation under the section may be recouped from the general assets in the liquidation, see the general note to s.238.

In the context of the financial markets, no order may be made under s.239 in relation to a market contract to which a recognised investment exchange or clearing house is a party or which is entered into under its default rules, or a disposition of property in pursuance of such a market contract: see CA 1989 s.165. It is also disapplied in relation to payment and securities settlement systems by the Finality Regulations 1999 reg.17. (See the introductory notes at pp.2–3 above.) Note again the potential impact of s.427 of the POCA 2002.

For the corresponding provisions in bankruptcy, see s.340; and for the position in Scotland, see s.243.

In *Re Parkside International Ltd* [2008] EWHC 3554 (Ch); [2009] B.P.I.R. 549 the insolvent company A and two other companies, B and C, were members of the same group. Shortly before A was put into administration B had assigned to C a debt owed to it by A. It was held that this was not a transaction "suffered" by A, being an act over which A had no control, and that this was so even though the three companies had common directors and, further, that although there may have been a desire to improve the position of the group as a whole, this was not the same as a desire to prefer one set of creditors over others.

S.239(1)

Section 238, which is referred to, restricts the jurisdiction to cases where a company is in administration or liquidation, and defines "office-holder" accordingly.

S.239(2)

"Relevant time" refers both to the period within which the preference is given and to the company's solvency: see s.240(2). This is the time when the decision to enter into the transaction is taken, and not the time when the transaction is effected (see *Re M C Bacon Ltd* (above) at 88). The terms "preference" and "any person" are explained in s.239(4).

S.239(3)

The court's powers are similar to those conferred by s.238(3) and include the power to decline to make any order: see the note to that subsection and *Re Parkside International Ltd* [2008] EWHC 3554 (Ch); [2009] B.P.I.R. 549. In *Re Kayford Ltd* [1975] 1 W.L.R. 279 a mail-order company in anticipation of possible insolvency had placed money sent as prepayments by its customers into a special bank account, and it was held that these sums were impressed with a trust which took them out of the insolvent estate when the company was later wound up. Under the law as it then stood, no question of fraudulent preference arose, but such an arrangement could now fall within s.239. If this were so, the circumstances might well justify the court in refusing to make an order. In *Re Lewis's of Leicester Ltd* [1995] B.C.C. 514 a somewhat similar arrangement in favour of certain concessionaires was made by a department store in anticipation of closing down its trading operations; but the court held that the company's desire was not to give the concessionaires a preference but to prevent the store from looking "more like a morgue than a market during its final weeks of trading".

S.239(4)

Examples of a preference given by the Cork Committee in its *Report* (para.1208) were: paying the whole or part of a debt, providing security or further security for an existing debt, and returning goods which have been delivered but not paid for. In *Re Mistral Finance Ltd* [2001] B.C.C. 27 the giving of security to secure an existing debt was struck down as a preference, but a clause which accelerated the obligations of both parties in the event of a liquidation, in consequence of which the creditor acquired a right of set-off, was held not to be open to challenge.

The phrase "going into insolvent liquidation" is not expressly defined for the purposes of the present section as it is for ss.214 and 216. That may, however, be a more helpful definition than anything that can be inferred from ss.240 and 247.

In *Re Thirty-Eight Building Ltd* [1999] B.C.C. 260 the transaction which was challenged was a transfer of the beneficial interest in certain assets to the trustees of a pension fund. It was held that the "creditor" who had to be identified under s.239(4) was the person who was the transferee in law (in this case the trustees and not the beneficiaries under the trust), and it was that person who had to receive a preference. The question was left open whether different considerations would apply where the trustees and the beneficiaries were the same individuals.

A transfer of funds held by the company on trust does not amount to a preference: *Re Branston & Gothard Ltd* [1999] B.P.I.R. 466.

In *Re Shapland Inc* [2000] B.C.C. 106 it was argued that even if the transaction in question was a preference, no order should be made because it would result in advantage to a secured creditor, rather than the company's unsecured creditors whose interests it was understood the legislation was intended to benefit. The court, although holding that the submission was not borne out by the facts of the case, thought it very doubtful that it was correct.

S.239(5)

The phrase "was influenced ... by a desire to produce" replaces language contained in BA 1914 s.44(1) which had been construed as requiring the person who sought to have the payment or other transaction avoided to show that it had been made "with the dominant intention to prefer" the particular creditor. The Cork Committee (*Report*, paras 1248–1258), by a majority, took the view that the requirement of an intention (or dominant intention) to prefer should be retained, and rejected the alternative (established in Australia and the US and adopted in Scotland: see s.243) that it should be sufficient that the conduct in question had the *effect* of giving a preference.

In *Re M C Bacon Ltd* [1990] B.C.C. 78 at 87, Millett J. held that it is no longer necessary to establish a dominant intention to prefer, nor is it sufficient to establish an *intention*: there must be a desire to produce the effect mentioned in the section. "Intention is objective, desire is subjective. A man can choose the lesser of two evils without desiring either ... A man is not to be taken as *desiring* all the necessary consequences of his actions ... It will still be possible to provide assistance to a company in financial difficulties provided that the company is actuated only by proper commercial considerations. Under the new regime a transaction will not be set aside as a voidable preference unless the company positively wished to improve the creditor's position in the event of its own insolvent liquidation." Accordingly, in that case, it was held that a decision by a company to give its bank a charge to secure existing borrowings (when the only alternative, if the bank withdrew its support, was liquidation) was not voidable as a preference under the present section.

The Cork Committee (*Report*, para.1256) took the view that pressure for payment by the creditor should continue, as under the former law, to afford a defence to a claim for the avoidance of a preference. The decision in *Re M C Bacon Ltd* (above) suggests that the new section will be so interpreted "unless the company positively wished to improve the creditor's position in the event of its own insolvency".

S.239(6)

This important change, introduced on the recommendation of the Cork Committee, reverses the burden of proof in regard to intention when the beneficiary of the preference is a person "connected with" the company. This phrase is defined by s.249 and is fully discussed in the note to that section (but the special exception of employees in the present provision should be noted). The effect of s.239(6)—not least when s.240(2) is also taken into account—will make it very difficult for directors and controlling shareholders and their relatives, and other companies in the same group (all of which are "connected persons"), to retain the benefit of a preferential payment under the new legislation. For cases where the statutory presumption against connected persons was held to have been rebutted on the evidence, see *Re Beacon Leisure Ltd* [1991] B.C.C. 213; and *Re Fairway Magazines Ltd* [1992] B.C.C. 924. These may be contrasted with *Re DKG Contractors Ltd* [1990] B.C.C. 903; *Weisgard v Pilkington* [1995] B.C.C. 1,108; *Re Brian D*

Pierson (Contractors) Ltd [1999] B.C.C. 26; *Wills v Corfe Joinery Ltd (in liq.)* [1997] B.C.C. 511; *Re Transworld Trading Ltd* [1999] B.P.I.R. 628; *Katz v McNally* [1999] B.C.C. 291; *Re Shapland Inc* [2000] B.C.C. 106; *Re Conegrade Ltd* [2002] EWHC 2411 (Ch); [2003] B.P.I.R. 358; *Barber v C.I. Ltd* [2006] B.C.C. 927 (affirmed on appeal sub nom. *Re Sonatacus Ltd* [2007] EWCA Civ 31; [2007] B.C.C. 186) and *Re Cityspan Ltd* [2007] EWHC 751 (Ch); [2008] B.C.C. 60, where the presumption was applied. In *Re Oxford Pharmaceuticals Ltd* [2009] EWHC 1753; [2009] 2 B.C.L.C. 485 the respondent succeeded in rebutting the presumption as regards some payments but not others. The judgment also contains a discussion of the overlap between preference and misfeasance proceedings. In *Phillips v McGregort-Paterson* [2009] EWHC 2385 (Ch) it was ruled that it was not appropriate to dispose of a s.239 claim on a summary basis because it was necessary to hear evidence in order to determine issues such as the company's insolvency and a desire to prefer.

240 "Relevant time" under ss.238, 239

240(1) **[Relevant time]** Subject to the next subsection, the time at which a company enters into a transaction at an undervalue or gives a preference is a relevant time if the transaction is entered into, or the preference given–

(a) in the case of a transaction at an undervalue or of a preference which is given to a person who is connected with the company (otherwise than by reason only of being its employee), at a time in the period of 2 years ending with the onset of insolvency (which expression is defined below),

(b) in the case of a preference which is not such a transaction and is not so given, at a time in the period of 6 months ending with the onset of insolvency,

(c) in either case, at a time between the making of an administration application in respect of the company and the making of an administration order on that application, and

(d) in either case, at a time between the filing with the court of a copy of notice of intention to appoint an administrator under paragraph 14 or 22 of Schedule B1 and the making of an appointment under that paragraph.

240(2) **[Where not relevant time]** Where a company enters into a transaction at an undervalue or gives a preference at a time mentioned in subsection (1)(a) or (b), that time is not a relevant time for the purposes of section 238 or 239 unless the company–

(a) is at that time unable to pay its debts within the meaning of section 123 in Chapter VI of Part IV, or

(b) becomes unable to pay its debts within the meaning of that section in consequence of the transaction or preference;

but the requirements of this subsection are presumed to be satisfied, unless the contrary is shown, in relation to any transaction at an undervalue which is entered into by a company with a person who is connected with the company.

240(3) **[Onset of insolvency]** For the purposes of subsection (1), the onset of insolvency is–

(a) in a case where section 238 or 239 applies by reason of an administrator of a company being appointed by administration order, the date on which the administration application is made,

(b) in a case where section 238 or 239 applies by reason of an administrator of a company being appointed under paragraph 14 or 22 of Schedule B1 following filing with the court of a copy of a notice of intention to appoint under that paragraph, the date on which the copy of the notice is filed,

(c) in a case where section 238 or 239 applies by reason of an administrator of a company being appointed otherwise than as mentioned in paragraph (a) or (b), the date on which the appointment takes effect,

(d) in a case where section 238 or 239 applies by reason of a company going into liquidation either following conversion of administration into winding up by virtue of Article 37 of the EC

Regulation or at the time when the appointment of an administrator ceases to have effect, the date on which the company entered administration (or, if relevant, the date on which the application for the administration order was made or a copy of the notice of intention to appoint was filed), and

(e) in a case where section 238 or 239 applies by reason of a company going into liquidation at any other time, the date of the commencement of the winding up.

GENERAL NOTE

Both ss.238 and 239 apply only to a transaction or preference which takes place at a "relevant time". This section explains that term. Two factors may be in issue in determining the question whether a time is a "relevant time": (1) whether the transaction takes place within one of the four periods set out in s.240(1); and (2) whether the company is, at that time, insolvent, or becomes insolvent as a result of the transaction.

Once again, as with s.239(6), the burden of proof (this time, of "insolvency") varies with the position of the other party to the transaction: it is on the liquidator or administrator in the normal case, but on that other party if he is a person "connected with" the company (s.240(2)). Moreover, in the case of a preference, the period by reference to which a "relevant time" is reckoned is increased from six months to two years if the other party is a "connected person" (s.240(1)(a), (b)). In regard to a transaction at an undervalue, the period is two years in all cases (s.240(1)(a)).

On the meaning of "connected person", see the notes to ss.249 and 435. It is, in principle, possible for a company's bank to come within the definition of a "connected person" for the purposes of the present group of sections, if its involvement in the company's affairs is such as to make it a "shadow director": see *Re a Company (No.005009 of 1987)* (1988) 4 B.C.C. 424 and ss.249(a), 251. However where a bank or other creditor of a company simply makes terms for the continuation of credit in the light of threatened default, the court will not infer that its directors are accustomed to act in accordance with its directions so as to make it a shadow director: *Re PFTZM Ltd (in liq.)* [1995] B.C.C. 280.

Section 240 is disapplied in relation to payment and securities settlement systems by the Finality Regulations reg.17. (See the introductory note at p.3 above.)

S.240(1), (3)

The periods for the purposes of ss.238, 239 are determined by reference to a date which is defined by s.240(3) and is very misleadingly called "the onset of insolvency". This has nothing whatever to do with the company's inability to pay its debts (although, to add to the confusion, that issue does matter for the wholly unrelated questions raised by s.240(2)). The "onset of insolvency" is to be determined by reference to the various dates set out in s.240(3).

(On the "commencement" of a winding up, see the notes to ss.86 and 129, where the reference is, more precisely, to the "time" rather than the "date" of commencement. It must be assumed that this variation in language is deliberate: see the note to s.86.)

The requirement that the company should go into liquidation *immediately* upon the discharge of an administration order for s.240(3)(a) to apply calls for a measure of procedural ingenuity if it is proposed that the winding up should be a voluntary winding up, where the order was made under the original Pt II. See *Re Norditrack (UK) Ltd* [2000] 1 W.L.R. 343; [2000] B.C.C. 441, and the notes to s.18.

Subsection (1)(c) was reworded and subs.(1)(d) added, and subs.(3)(a)–(e) substituted for the former sub-s.(3)(a)–(b) by EA 2002 Sch.17 para.26, with effect from September 15, 2003, to take account of the fact that applications for an administration order under IA 1986 Sch.B1 are not made by petition and that appointments may also be made out of court. However, the former wording (which referred to the time or date of the presentation of a petition for an administration order), has been reinstated for cases not coming within Sch.B1 by EA 2002 s.249 and the Enterprise Act 2002 (Commencement No.4 and Transitional Provisions and Savings) Order 2003 (SI 2003/2093 (C. 85)), art.3. See the notes to ss.212 and 230(1).

Section 240(3)(d) (as the former s.240(3)(aa)) was inserted by the Insolvency Act 1986 (Amendment) (No.2) Regulations 2002 (SI 2002/1240, effective May 31, 2002). Article 37 of the EC Regulation empowers the "liquidator" in "main" insolvency proceedings in one Member State to apply to have an administration in another Member State (which will be "secondary" or "territorial" proceedings) converted into a winding up. For the meaning of these technical terms, see the notes to the Regulation arts 2, 3.

The "relevant time" is a time within the six-month or two-year period ending with the "onset of insolvency" as defined in s.240(3). The period will be two years for all undervalue-transactions (s.240(1)(a)); in the case of a preference, it will be two years if the recipient of the preference is a "connected person", and six months if he is not; but employees are again not treated as "connected persons" for this purpose (s.240(1)(a), (b)).

S.240(2)

Section 240(1) and (3) are concerned only with the calculation of time, in the ordinary sense. However, s.240(2) introduces a further factor: a "time" will not be a "relevant" time (and therefore a transaction at an undervalue or a preference will not be liable to be set aside) unless the company is then unable to pay its debts, or becomes unable to pay its debts as a result of the impugned transaction. In other words, a company may enter into any transaction at an undervalue that it chooses or give any creditor a preference without violating ss.238 or 239, so long as it is solvent or so long as the event takes place outside the period leading up to its being put into administration or liquidation that is specified in s.240(1): only if both these conditions are satisfied will the transaction have occurred at a "relevant time" so as to bring those sections into play. (Note, however, that s.423 may be applicable if the necessary intent can be proved.)

The definition of "unable to pay its debts", for the purpose of s.240(2), is the same as in s.123, that is, either (1) deemed unable to pay because of an unpaid statutory demand for over £750 or an unsatisfied execution; or (2) proved unable in either a "commercial" or a "balance-sheet" sense. Inability may also be inferred from the fact that the company has invoices which it has not paid: *Re DKG Contractors Ltd* [1990] B.C.C. 903. For further discussion, see the note to s.123.

Finally, as regards inability to pay debts, there is the question of the burden of proof. This, in relation to a transaction at an undervalue, lies on the liquidator or administrator when the other party is not a "connected person", but on that other party if he is. (There is no similar provision in relation to a preference, but the question of the company's solvency will be relevant, at least indirectly, to the question of intention for which s.239(6) places the burden of proof on the "connected person".) On the meaning of "connected person", see the note to s.249; but note that s.240(2) rather oddly does not repeat the exception for employees which appears in ss.239(6) and 240(1)(a). (This may be a drafting error, in that the former provision corresponding to ss.238–240, IA 1985 s.101, applied the employee exception to all connected persons in the provision: see IA 1985 s.101(11).)

241   Orders under ss.238, 239

241(1)   [Extent of orders] Without prejudice to the generality of sections 238(3) and 239(3), an order under either of those sections with respect to a transaction or preference entered into or given by a company may (subject to the next subsection)–

(a)   require any property transferred as part of the transaction, or in connection with the giving of the preference, to be vested in the company,

(b)   require any property to be so vested if it represents in any person's hands the application either of the proceeds of sale of property so transferred or of money so transferred,

(c)   release or discharge (in whole or in part) any security given by the company,

(d)   require any person to pay, in respect of benefits received by him from the company, such sums to the office-holder as the court may direct,

(e)   provide for any surety or guarantor whose obligations to any person were released or discharged (in whole or in part) under the transaction, or by the giving of the preference, to be under such new or revived obligations to that person as the court thinks appropriate,

(f)   provide for security to be provided for the discharge of any obligation imposed by or arising under the order, for such an obligation to be charged on any property and for the security or charge to have the same priority as a security or charge released or discharged (in whole or in part) under the transaction or by the giving of the preference, and

(g)   provide for the extent to which any person whose property is vested by the order in the company, or on whom obligations are imposed by the order, is to be able to prove in the winding up of the company for debts or other liabilities which arose from, or were released or discharged (in whole or in part) under or by, the transaction or the giving of the preference.

241(2)   [Restriction on orders] An order under section 238 or 239 may affect the property of, or impose any obligation on, any person whether or not he is the person with whom the company in question entered into the transaction or (as the case may be) the person to whom the preference was given; but such an order–

(a) shall not prejudice any interest in property which was acquired from a person other than the company and was acquired in good faith and for value, or prejudice any interest deriving from such an interest, and

(b) shall not require a person who received a benefit from the transaction or preference in good faith and for value to pay a sum to the office-holder, except where that person was a party to the transaction or the payment is to be in respect of a preference given to that person at a time when he was a creditor of the company.

241(2A) [Presumption re good faith in s.241(2)] Where a person has acquired an interest in property from a person other than the company in question, or has received a benefit from the transaction or preference, and at the time of that acquisition or receipt–

(a) he had notice of the relevant surrounding circumstances and of the relevant proceedings, or

(b) he was connected with, or was an associate of, either the company in question or the person with whom that company entered into the transaction or to whom that company gave the preference,

then, unless the contrary is shown, it shall be presumed for the purposes of paragraph (a) or (as the case may be) paragraph (b) of subsection (2) that the interest was acquired or the benefit was received otherwise than in good faith.

241(3) [Relevant surrounding circumstances in s.241(2A)(a)] For the purposes of subsection (2A)(a), the relevant surrounding circumstances are (as the case may require)–

(a) the fact that the company in question entered into the transaction at an undervalue; or

(b) the circumstances which amounted to the giving of the preference by the company in question;

and subsections (3A) to (3C) have effect to determine whether, for those purposes, a person has notice of the relevant proceedings.

241(3A) [Notice of administration proceedings] Where section 238 or 239 applies by reason of a company's entering administration, a person has notice of the relevant proceedings if he has notice that–

(a) an administration application has been made,

(b) an administration order has been made,

(c) a copy of a notice of intention to appoint an administrator under paragraph 14 or 22 of Schedule B1 has been filed, or

(d) notice of the appointment of an administrator has been filed under paragraph 18 or 29 of that Schedule.

241(3B) [Notice of liquidation following administration] Where section 238 or 239 applies by reason of a company's going into liquidation at the time when the appointment of an administrator of the company ceases to have effect, a person has notice of the relevant proceedings if he has notice that–

(a) an administration application has been made,

(b) an administration order has been made,

(c) a copy of a notice of intention to appoint an administrator under paragraph 14 or 22 of Schedule B1 has been filed,

(d) notice of the appointment of an administrator has been filed under paragraph 18 or 29 of that Schedule, or

(e) the company has gone into liquidation.

241(3C) **[Notice where liquidation at other times]** In a case where section 238 or 239 applies by reason of the company in question going into liquidation at any other time, a person has notice of the relevant proceedings if he has notice–

(a) where the company goes into liquidation on the making of a winding-up order, of the fact that the petition on which the winding-up order is made has been presented or of the fact that the company has gone into liquidation;

(b) in any other case, of the fact that the company has gone into liquidation.

241(4) **[Application of ss.238–241]** The provisions of sections 238 to 241 apply without prejudice to the availability of any other remedy, even in relation to a transaction or preference which the company had no power to enter into or give.

GENERAL NOTE

The present section sets out in detail various orders which the court is empowered to make when avoiding a preference or a transaction at an undervalue under ss.238, 239, although it is not intended to limit the general powers of the court. It is designed in part to meet defects in the former law which the Cork Committee (*Report*, paras 1270–1276) identified as likely to arise when a company's obligation is backed by a surety or guarantor. For example, a payment may have been made to a creditor with a view to releasing the surety or guarantor rather than preferring the creditor, and the creditor may have released the guarantee and returned any security given before the payment is struck down as a preference. The creditor would then in all probability have had no remedy against the guarantor.

Section 241 was amended by the Insolvency (No.2) Act 1994 ss.1(1) and 6, with effect from July 26, 1994, as follows:

(1) in s.241(2), in both para.(a) and para.(b), the words "in good faith and for value" were substituted for the former wording, "in good faith, for value and without notice of the relevant circumstances";

(2) new subs.(2A) was inserted; and

(3) new subss.(3), (3A), (3B) and (3C) were substituted for the former subs.(3).

The amendments have effect only in relation to interests acquired and benefits received after the 1994 Act came into force (s.6(3)). For the corresponding provisions in relation to bankruptcy, see s.342 below (as amended).

The amendment, which stems from a recommendation of the Law Society, was designed to get over a perceived difficulty in relation to unregistered land, where a bona fide purchaser might have been taken to have had notice of a transaction that was liable to be set aside under either ss.238 or 239 in the event of a later insolvency. By removing the references to notice from s.241(2), a buyer of unregistered land is put into the same position as a buyer of registered land.

In subss.(3A) and (3B) the reference was formerly to the making of an administration order. The new wording was substituted by EA 2002 Sch.17 para.26, with effect from September 15, 2003, to take account of the fact that applications are no longer made by petition, and that appointments may also be made out of court. However, orders under the original IA 1986 Pt II are made on a petition, and where that regime continues to apply the original wording of the two subsections remains effective.

S.241(1)

Section 241(1) is "subject to the next subsection", which protects bona fide purchasers for value.

The court's discretion extends to refusing to make any order: see the note to s.238(3). In an appropriate case it may appoint a receiver and manager pending trial: *Walker v WA Personnel Ltd* [2002] B.P.I.R. 621. On the question whether the discretion may be exercised so as to benefit the holder of a security, rather than the company's unsecured creditors, see the remarks of Neuberger J., obiter, in *Ciro Citterio Menswear plc v Thakrar* (July 10, 2002, referred to by P. Fleming, in [2003] Insolv. Int. 33 at 34).

Paragraphs (e) and (f) will empower the court to impose revived or new obligations on a guarantor or surety if his former obligations were released or discharged by the transaction which is later impugned, and to reinstate a security with the same priority as a former security or charge.

S.241(2)

This subsection allows third parties to be brought into the proceedings and orders to be made against them or their property instead of, or as well as, against the party with whom the company has dealt in the transaction under challenge. In particular, it will enable an order for repayment to be made directly against a surety or guarantor when the real object of a payment made by the company to a particular creditor was to release the guarantee rather than prefer the creditor. Bona fide third parties acquiring property or benefits for value will, however, be protected. Nevertheless, the concluding words of para.(b) indicate that the person who was the actual counterparty to a transaction at an undervalue or who himself, as a creditor, received the benefit of a preference will not be protected merely because he acted in good faith and for value. (This is in keeping with the traditional view taken in relation to fraudulent preferences, that it is the intention of the company to give an improper preference which is crucial, and that the state of mind of the creditor himself is immaterial.) Although s.241(2) does specifically envisage the making of orders against third parties (i.e. parties who have not in fact been preferred themselves), this is only appropriate if such an order is required as part of the process of restoring the position to what it would otherwise have been: *Re Oxford Pharmaceuticals Ltd* [2009] EWHC 1753; [2009] 2 B.C.L.C. 485.

S.241(2A)–(3C)
These subsections, which were substituted for the former s.241(3) as described above, relate to two categories of person who have acquired an interest in property otherwise than from the company itself: (1) one who had notice of the "relevant surrounding circumstances" *and* of the "relevant proceedings" at the material time; and (2) one who was "connected with" or an "associate" of the company or the counterparty to the transaction. (For the meaning of the terms "connected with" and "associate", see ss.249 and 435, below.) As against such a person, there is a (rebuttable) statutory presumption of a lack of good faith. (In *Re Sonatacus Ltd* [2007] EWCA Civ 31; [2007] B.C.C. 186 the Court of Appeal said that "it was obvious" that the onus of proving good faith lay on the third party in any event.) The requirement in s.241(2A)(a) that the person (if not a "connected person" or "associate") should have notice of the insolvency proceedings as well as of the relevant surrounding circumstances is the major change effected by the 1994 reform.

Sections 241(3)–(3C) clarify the meaning of the terms "the relevant surrounding circumstances" and "notice of the relevant proceedings" used in s.241(2A).

S.241(4)
The phrase "a transaction which the company had no power to enter into or give" is, no doubt, a reference to the common-law doctrine of ultra vires, which was abolished for almost all purposes by CA 1989 s.108 (which inserted a revised s.35(1) into CA 1985 with effect from February 4, 1991 (see SI 1991/2569 (C. 68) art.4(a), 7) [and see now CA 2006 s.39]). However, the question of corporate capacity still has some relevance in relation to charitable companies (see CA 1989 s.111, amending Charities Act 1960 by the insertion of a new s.30B, effective from the same date, now replaced by Charities Act 1993 s.65), and so the doctrine of ultra vires could apply in this restricted area. It is possible also that s.241(1) could be construed as extending to illegal transactions, e.g. those in contravention of the "financial assistance" provisions contained in CA 2006 ss.678 et seq. This subsection will allow the court to override the general law by, e.g. ordering the recipient of an ultra vires loan or gift to give security for its due repayment (s.241(1)(f)).

242 Gratuitous alienations (Scotland)

242(1) [Challenge to alienations] Where this subsection applies and–

(a) the winding up of a company has commenced, an alienation by the company is challengeable by–

(i) any creditor who is a creditor by virtue of a debt incurred on or before the date of such commencement, or

(ii) the liquidator;

(b) a company enters administration, an alienation by the company is challengeable by the administrator.

242(2) [Application of s.242(1)] Subsection (1) applies where–

(a) by the alienation, whether before or after 1st April 1986 (the coming into force of section 75 of the Bankruptcy (Scotland) Act 1985), any part of the company's property is transferred or any claim or right of the company is discharged or renounced, and

(b) the alienation takes place on a relevant day.

242(3) **[Interpretation of s.242(2)(b)]** For the purposes of subsection (2)(b), the day on which an alienation takes place is the day on which it becomes completely effectual; and in that subsection **"relevant day"** means, if the alienation has the effect of favouring–

(a) a person who is an associate (within the meaning of the Bankruptcy (Scotland) Act 1985) of the company, a day not earlier than 5 years before the date on which–

   (i) the winding up of the company commences, or

   (ii) as the case may be, the company enters administration; or

(b) any other person, a day not earlier than 2 years before that date.

242(4) **[Duties of court on challenge under s.242(1)]** On a challenge being brought under subsection (1), the court shall grant decree of reduction or for such restoration of property to the company's assets or other redress as may be appropriate; but the court shall not grant such a decree if the person seeking to uphold the alienation establishes–

(a) that immediately, or at any other time, after the alienation the company's assets were greater than its liabilities, or

(b) that the alienation was made for adequate consideration, or

(c) that the alienation–

   (i) was a birthday, Christmas or other conventional gift, or

   (ii) was a gift made, for a charitable purpose, to a person who is not an associate of the company,

   which, having regard to all the circumstances, it was reasonable for the company to make:

Provided that this subsection is without prejudice to any right or interest acquired in good faith and for value from or through the transferee in the alienation.

242(5) **["Charitable purpose" in s.242(4)]** In subsection (4) above, **"charitable purpose"** means any charitable, benevolent or philanthropic purpose, whether or not it is charitable within the meaning of any rule of law.

242(6) **[Interpretation]** For the purposes of the foregoing provisions of this section, an alienation in implementation of a prior obligation is deemed to be one for which there was no consideration or no adequate consideration to the extent that the prior obligation was undertaken for no consideration or no adequate consideration.

242(7) **[Rights of challenge]** A liquidator and an administrator have the same right as a creditor has under any rule of law to challenge an alienation of a company made for no consideration or no adequate consideration.

242(8) **[Scotland only]** This section applies to Scotland only.

GENERAL NOTE

This section deals with the setting aside of transactions at an undervalue (or the granting of "other redress": s.242(4)) in Scotland. It differs on a number of points of substance from s.238, following in these respects the Bankruptcy (Scotland) Act 1985 s.34.

The rights of creditors under Scots common law, including the right to challenge a debtor's action as a gratuitous alienation, survive the present legislation: see *Bank of Scotland v Pacific Shelf (Sixty Two) Ltd* (1988) 4 B.C.C. 457. On the present section, see *Henderson v 3052775 Nova Scotia Ltd*, 2005 S.C. 325 (whether assumption of debt by company was part of consideration).

In subss.(1)(b) and (3)(a)(ii) the reference was formerly to the making of an administration order. The new wording was substituted by EA 2002 Sch.17 para.28, with effect from September 15, 2003, to take account of the fact that applications are no longer made by petition, and that appointments may also be made out of court. However, orders under the original IA 1986 Pt II are made on a petition, and where that regime continues to apply the original wording of the two subsections remains effective.

In the context of the financial markets, no decree may be granted under s.242 in relation to a market contract to which a recognised investment exchange or clearing house is a party or which is entered into under its default rules, or a disposition of property in pursuance of such a market contract: see CA 1989 s.165. Section 242 is also disapplied in relation to payment and securities settlement systems by the Finality Regulations reg.17. (See the introductory notes at pp.2–3 above.)

An application under s.242 formed the backdrop to the litigation reported as *Henderson v 3052775 Nova Scotia Ltd* [2006] UKHL 21, though the proceedings reported are concerned with procedural aspects of Scottish law rather than substantive consideration of s.242.

S.242(1)

In the case of a liquidation, a creditor is given standing to challenge under para.(a)(i), in contrast with s.238(2), which restricts the right to the "office-holder". A liquidator does not require sanction under s.167 to commence s.242 proceedings—see *Dyer v Hislop* [1994] S.C.L.R. 171. Such proceedings are not taken on behalf of or in the name of the company.

S.242(2), (3)

The periods of five years and two years fixed by s.242(3) are different from those prescribed for England and Wales by s.240(1), but correspond with those that apply in the bankruptcy of an individual in Scotland: see the Bankruptcy (Scotland) Act 1985 s.34. The meaning of "associate" under the Bankruptcy (Scotland) Act 1985 s.74, is similar to, but not co-extensive with, that of "associate" as defined for the purposes of this Act: see s.435 and the note to that section. For England and Wales, the term used by s.240(1) is "connected person", which is slightly wider in scope: see s.249.

S.242(4)

"Gratuitous alienation" includes a transaction for consideration at an undervalue (para.(b)); "reasonable" gifts and charitable donations may be justified (para.(c)). The requirement as to solvency is here more logically placed with the substantive aspects of the statutory provision, rather than linked to the definition of "relevant day": contrast s.240(2). See *McLuckie Bros Ltd v Newhouse Contracts Ltd*, 1993 S.L.T. 641.

243   Unfair preferences (Scotland)

243(1)   [Application of s.243(4)] Subject to subsection (2) below, subsection (4) below applies to a transaction entered into by a company, whether before or after 1st April 1986, which has the effect of creating a preference in favour of a creditor to the prejudice of the general body of creditors, being a preference created not earlier than 6 months before the commencement of the winding up of the company or the company enters administration.

243(2)   [Non-application of s.243(4)] Subsection (4) below does not apply to any of the following transactions–

(a) a transaction in the ordinary course of trade or business;

(b) a payment in cash for a debt which when it was paid had become payable, unless the transaction was collusive with the purpose of prejudicing the general body of creditors;

(c) a transaction whereby the parties to it undertake reciprocal obligations (whether the performance by the parties of their respective obligations occurs at the same time or at different times) unless the transaction was collusive as aforesaid;

(d) the granting of a mandate by a company authorising an arrestee to pay over the arrested funds or part thereof to the arrester where–

   (i)   there has been a decree for payment or a warrant for summary diligence, and

   (ii) the decree or warrant has been preceded by an arrestment on the dependence of the action or followed by an arrestment in execution.

243(3)   [Interpretation of s.243(1)] For the purposes of subsection (1) above, the day on which a preference was created is the day on which the preference became completely effectual.

243(4) **[Persons who may challenge]** A transaction to which this subsection applies is challengeable by–

   (a) in the case of a winding up–

      (i) any creditor who is a creditor by virtue of a debt incurred on or before the date of commencement of the winding up, or

      (ii) the liquidator; and

   (b) where the company has entered administration, the administrator.

243(5) **[Duties of court on s.243(4) challenge]** On a challenge being brought under subsection (4) above, the court, if satisfied that the transaction challenged is a transaction to which this section applies, shall grant decree of reduction or for such restoration of property to the company's assets or other redress as may be appropriate:

Provided that this subsection is without prejudice to any right or interest acquired in good faith and for value from or through the creditor in whose favour the preference was created.

243(6) **[Rights of challenge]** A liquidator and an administrator have the same right as a creditor has under any rule of law to challenge a preference created by a debtor.

243(7) **[Scotland only]** This section applies to Scotland only.

GENERAL NOTE

The law relating to unfair preferences in the bankruptcy of individuals is contained in the Bankruptcy (Scotland) Act 1985 s.36. The present section substantially follows that provision and differs in material respects from s.239—most notably in not requiring any proof of a desire to prefer. For the survival of the common law, see *Bank of Scotland v Pacific Shelf (Sixty Two) Ltd* (1988) 4 B.C.C. 457.

In subss.(1) and (4)(b) the reference was formerly to the making of an administration order. The new wording was substituted by EA 2002 Sch.17 para.29, with effect from September 15, 2003, to take account of the fact that applications are no longer made by petition, and that appointments may also be made out of court. However, the former wording has been reinstated for cases not coming within Sch.B1 by EA 2002 s.249 and by the Enterprise Act 2002 (Commencement No.4 and Transitional Provisions and Savings) Order 2003 (SI 2003/2093 (C. 85)) art.3. See the notes to ss.212 and 230(1).

A payment made by a company is not within the section unless it has completely divested itself of the funds within the relevant period: *Craiglaw Developments Ltd v Wilson* [1998] B.C.C. 530.

In the context of the financial markets, no decree may be granted under s.243 in relation to a market contract to which a recognised investment exchange or clearing house is a party or which is entered into under its default rules, or a disposition of property in pursuance of such a market contract. Section 243 is also disapplied in relation to payment and securities settlement systems by the Finality Regulations reg.17. (See the introductory notes at pp.2–3 above.)

S.243(1), (2)

The vital factor, in contrast with the subjective requirement regarding intent in s.239(1), (5), is whether the transaction has the effect of creating a preference: the intention of the parties is not relevant, unless there is collusion (s.243(2)(b), (c)). For the purposes of s.243(2)(c) there must be a strict equivalence of reciprocal obligations: *Nicoll v Steelpress (Supplies) Ltd*, 1993 S.L.T. 533.

S.243(4)

As with s.242, a creditor has standing to bring proceedings in the case of a winding up.

244 Extortionate credit transactions

244(1) **[Application]** This section applies as does section 238, and where the company is, or has been, a party to a transaction for, or involving, the provision of credit to the company.

244(2) **[Court order re extortionate transaction]** The court may, on the application of the office-holder, make an order with respect to the transaction if the transaction is or was extortionate and was entered into in the period of 3 years ending with the day on which the company entered administration or went into liquidation.

244(3)   **[Extortionate transaction—interpretation]** For the purposes of this section a transaction is extortionate if, having regard to the risk accepted by the person providing the credit–

     (a)   the terms of it are or were such as to require grossly exorbitant payments to be made (whether unconditionally or in certain contingencies) in respect of the provision of the credit, or

     (b)   it otherwise grossly contravened ordinary principles of fair dealing;

and it shall be presumed, unless the contrary is proved, that a transaction with respect to which an application is made under this section is or, as the case may be, was extortionate.

244(4)   **[Extent of court order]** An order under this section with respect to any transaction may contain such one or more of the following as the court thinks fit, that is to say–

     (a)   provision setting aside the whole or part of any obligation created by the transaction,

     (b)   provision otherwise varying the terms of the transaction or varying the terms on which any security for the purposes of the transaction is held,

     (c)   provision requiring any person who is or was a party to the transaction to pay to the office-holder any sums paid to that person, by virtue of the transaction, by the company,

     (d)   provision requiring any person to surrender to the office-holder any property held by him as security for the purposes of the transaction,

     (e)   provision directing accounts to be taken between any persons.

244(5)   **[Exercise of powers]** The powers conferred by this section are exercisable in relation to any transaction concurrently with any powers exercisable in relation to that transaction as a transaction at an undervalue or under section 242 (gratuitous alienations in Scotland).

GENERAL NOTE

Section 66 of BA 1914, which was formerly applied in the winding up of insolvent companies by CA 1985 s.612, restricted the rate of interest that could be proved for in a liquidation, in the case of a debt carrying interest, to five per cent p.a. In keeping with the recommendations of the Cork Committee (*Report*, para.1380), s.66 has now been repealed (see the note to s.189). The removal of s.66, without more, would allow proofs in a winding up to include sums representing exorbitant rates of interest; and accordingly the court is given power by this section to reopen credit agreements on the application of a liquidator or administrator. This is in keeping with a recommendation of the Cork Committee (*Report*, para.1381). The section is modelled on ss.137–140 of the Consumer Credit Act 1974 (now superseded).

     For the corresponding provision in bankruptcy, see s.343.

S.244(1)

Section 238 applies to companies that are in liquidation or administration. Although s.238 is confined to England and Wales, it is submitted that the present section extends also to Scotland, for otherwise the reference to Scotland in s.244(5) would be pointless. This means that the word "applies" in s.244(1) must be construed with reference only to the different forms of insolvency proceedings and not to questions of geography or jurisdiction (even though the wording of s.245(1) would suggest the contrary). This interpretation is supported by s.440(2).

     "Credit" is not defined.

S.244(2)

There is a three-year time limit for the retrospective re-opening of transactions under this section. (Note, however, that the time is reckoned from the date when the company "went into liquidation", in the case of a liquidation, and not from the "commencement of the winding up".)

S.244(3)

The onus of proof that a transaction was not extortionate is put in every case on to the person who gave the credit.

S.244(4)
The orders which the court is empowered to make include orders affecting third parties, e.g. sureties.

S.244(5)
On transactions at an undervalue, see ss.238, 240, 241.

245 Avoidance of certain floating charges

245(1) [Application] This section applies as does section 238, but applies to Scotland as well as to England and Wales.

245(2) [Invalidity of floating charge] Subject as follows, a floating charge on the company's undertaking or property created at a relevant time is invalid except to the extent of the aggregate of–

(a) the value of so much of the consideration for the creation of the charge as consists of money paid, or goods or services supplied, to the company at the same time as, or after, the creation of the charge,

(b) the value of so much of that consideration as consists of the discharge or reduction, at the same time as, or after, the creation of the charge, of any debt of the company, and

(c) the amount of such interest (if any) as is payable on the amount falling within paragraph (a) or (b) in pursuance of any agreement under which the money was so paid, the goods or services were so supplied or the debt was so discharged or reduced.

245(3) [Relevant time] Subject to the next subsection, the time at which a floating charge is created by a company is a relevant time for the purposes of this section if the charge is created–

(a) in the case of a charge which is created in favour of a person who is connected with the company, at a time in the period of 2 years ending with the onset of insolvency,

(b) in the case of a charge which is created in favour of any other person, at a time in the period of 12 months ending with the onset of insolvency,

(c) in either case, at a time between the making of an administration application in respect of the company and the making of an administration order on that application, or

(d) in either case, at a time between the filing with the court of a copy of notice of intention to appoint an administrator under paragraph 14 or 22 of Schedule B1 and the making of an appointment under that paragraph.

245(4) [Qualification to s.245(3)(b)] Where a company creates a floating charge at a time mentioned in subsection (3)(b) and the person in favour of whom the charge is created is not connected with the company, that time is not a relevant time for the purposes of this section unless the company–

(a) is at that time unable to pay its debts within the meaning of section 123 in Chapter VI of Part IV, or

(b) becomes unable to pay its debts within the meaning of that section in consequence of the transaction under which the charge is created.

245(5) [Onset of insolvency in s.245(3)] For the purposes of subsection (3), the onset of insolvency is–

(a) in a case where this section applies by reason of an administrator of a company being appointed by administration order, the date on which the administration application is made,

(b) in a case where this section applies by reason of an administrator of a company being appointed under paragraph 14 or 22 of Schedule B1 following filing with the court of a copy of notice of intention to appoint under that paragraph, the date on which the copy of the notice is filed,

(c)   in a case where this section applies by reason of an administrator of a company being appointed otherwise than as mentioned in paragraph (a) or (b), the date on which the appointment takes effect, and

(d)   in a case where this section applies by reason of a company going into liquidation, the date of the commencement of the winding up.

245(6)   [Value of goods, services etc. in s.245(2)(a)] For the purposes of subsection (2)(a) the value of any goods or services supplied by way of consideration for a floating charge is the amount in money which at the time they were supplied could reasonably have been expected to be obtained for supplying the goods or services in the ordinary course of business and on the same terms (apart from the consideration) as those on which they were supplied to the company.

GENERAL NOTE

Under CA 1985 s.617, which this section replaces, a floating charge was declared invalid if it was created within 12 months of the commencement of a winding up (unless it could be proved that the company, immediately after the creation of the charge, was solvent), except to the amount of any cash paid to the company at the time of, or subsequently to the creation of, and in consideration for, the charge. In other words, a floating charge could not be created within that time to secure past indebtedness, but only an advance of "new money".

The present Act not only formulates more elaborate provisions to apply in such circumstances, but introduces several major changes:

(1)   "floating charge" is redefined so as to include any charge which was originally created as a floating charge but has since become a fixed charge (s.251);

(2)   the provisions apply in an administration as well as a liquidation;

(3)   the section expressly covers some benefits conferred on the company otherwise than by the payment of "cash";

(4)   the 12-month period is extended to two years if the chargee is a person "connected with" the company; and

(5)   the exception where the company is proved at the material time to have been solvent will not be available to a chargee who is a person "connected with" the company.

The provisions of s.245 do not apply to invalidate a charge created before the Act came into force, except to the extent that it could have been invalidated under the previous law: see Sch.11 para.9.

In subss.(3) and (5) the references were formerly to the presentation of a petition for an administration order and the making of such an order. The new wording was substituted by EA 2002 Sch.17 para.31, with effect from September 15, 2003, to take account of the fact that the procedure is now by application and appointments may be made out of court. However, the former wording has been reinstated for cases not coming within Sch.B1 by EA 2002 s.249 and the Enterprise Act 2002 (Commencement No.4 and Transitional Provisions and Savings) Order 2003 (SI 2003/2093 (C. 85)) art.3. See the notes to ss.212 and 230(1).

S.245(1)

The section applies where a company is in liquidation or is in administration.

S.245(2)

A charge will not be invalidated by this section to the extent that the chargee has increased the company's assets in any of the ways described. The extended wording removes doubts about the scope of the former phrase "cash paid to the company" by stipulating that goods or services supplied to the company or the release of a debt in whole or part will be as good as "new money". Whether paras (a) and (b) will themselves be open to a restrictive interpretation is unclear: it is hard to see why other forms of valuable consideration (e.g. the transfer of land or shares) were not included within the reform that was made.

The question whether the payment of money or the supply of goods or services is made "at the same time as" the execution of a charge is one of fact and degree—*Re Shoe Lace Ltd, Power v Sharp Investments Ltd* [1993] B.C.C. 609. In that case, money was advanced in four payments on different dates in April, May, June and on July 16, following a resolution of the company's directors to grant the debenture in March; but the debenture was not executed until July 24. The Court of Appeal, affirming Hoffmann J. [1992] B.C.C. 367, held that the payments could not be said to have been made at the same time as the execution of the debenture. Sir Christopher Slade, giving the leading judgment, said (at 620):

"In a case where no presently existing charge has been created by any agreement or company resolution preceding the execution of the formal debenture, then … no moneys paid before the execution of the debenture will qualify for exemption under the subsection, unless the interval between payment and execution is so short that it can be regarded as minimal and payment and execution can be regarded as contemporaneous".

However, where a promise to execute a debenture creates a present equitable right to a security, and moneys are advanced in reliance on it, any delay between the advances and the execution of the formal instrument of charge is immaterial: the charge has already been "created" and is immediately registrable, so that other creditors of the company will have had the opportunity to learn of its existence (ibid. at 619).

In *Re Fairway Magazines Ltd* [1992] B.C.C. 924 it was held, following *Re Orleans Motor Co Ltd* [1911] 2 Ch. 41, that payments made by the lender directly to the company's bank which reduced its overdraft (and consequently the lender's liability under a personal guarantee) were not payments made "to the company" within the meaning of the section: the money never became available to the company to be used as it liked.

Interest was allowable under the repealed CA 1985 s.617, as it is under para.(c).

S.245(3)–(5)

These provisions are similar to s.240, both in their effect and in the very confusing language which is used. For more detailed comment, see the notes to that section: it is necessary to give the reminder that the phrase "the onset of insolvency" is not used with reference to the company's financial state but only with the question whether an administration or liquidation is deemed to have "commenced"; the issue of its financial well-being (or otherwise) is separately dealt with in s.245(4) in language which avoids the words "solvent" and "insolvent".

To sum up these provisions:

- a floating charge can be retrospectively invalidated within a two-year period for a "connected" chargee, and a 12-month period in other cases; further, if there is, or has been, an administration order in force, the period is extended to include the time between the making of an application for an administration order and the administration order, or the filing of a notice of intention to appoint an administrator and the making of an appointment under Sch.B1 paras 14 or 22;

- the "new consideration" exception applies whether the chargee is a connected person or not; and

- the "solvency" exception will now apply only where the chargee is not a connected person (using the term "solvency" in its everyday sense). The burden of establishing "solvency" under CA 1985 s.617, was put on the person seeking to uphold the charge. This is presumably still the case, although the section does not make the point clear.

The various technical expressions which appear in these provisions are discussed in more detail in the note to s.240.

On the meaning of "connected person", see the notes to ss.249 and 435. It is, in principle, possible for a company's bank to come within the definition of a "connected person" for the purposes of the present section, if its involvement in the company's affairs is such as to make it a "shadow director": see *Re a Company (No.005009 of 1987)* (1988) 4 B.C.C. 424 and ss.249(a), 251. See also *Unidare plc v Cohen* [2005] EWHC 1410 (Ch); [2006] Ch. 489; [2006] 2 B.C.L.C. 140 (discussed in the note to s.435).

All the references to time in s.245(2) are to the time of creation of the charge. So it would seem that a floating charge created in favour of A will attract all the disadvantages associated with "connected" chargees if A was a "connected person" at that time, and it will be immaterial that he has since ceased to be so connected. Conversely, if A was not a connected person at the time of creation, but becomes "connected" within the two-year period, his charge will have the more favourable treatment accorded by s.245(3)(b) and (4). [See *Unidare plc v Cohen* (above).] Again, if a floating charge is created in favour of A and is later assigned to B, the only relevant question will be whether A was, at the time of creation, a "connected person": it will not matter whether B was then, or was at the time of the assignment, or has since become, a "connected person". There are clearly advantages, if one is a "connected person", of taking a charge by assignment rather than directly and, if one is not, of re-financing with a new charge rather than taking an assignment of a charge from a "connected" chargee—unless in either case the whole arrangement could be challenged as evasive.

S.245(6)

This subsection deals with the position where goods or services, rather than "new money", is the consideration provided for a charge. It is made clear that it is the true value of the goods or services that counts, and not the price or valuation that the parties themselves have agreed on as the consideration for the supply. The chargee cannot defeat the object of the Act by having the company credit him with an unrealistic sum.

246   Unenforceability of liens on books, etc.

246(1)   [Application] This section applies in the case of a company where–

(a)   the company enters administration, or

(b)   the company goes into liquidation, or

(c)   a provisional liquidator is appointed;

and **"the office-holder"** means the administrator, the liquidator or the provisional liquidator, as the case may be.

246(2)   [Lien etc. unenforceable] Subject as follows, a lien or other right to retain possession of any of the books, papers or other records of the company is unenforceable to the extent that its enforcement would deny possession of any books, papers or other records to the office-holder.

246(3)   [Non-application] This does not apply to a lien on documents which give a title to property and are held as such.

GENERAL NOTE

This section ensures that a liquidator or administrator is not prevented from taking possession of any of the company's books, etc. because a lien is claimed over them (e.g. by a solicitor or accountant for outstanding fees). It relates only to liens on "books, papers and other records" and not to liens on other categories of goods, and operates to extinguish the lien (or, at the least, to render it unenforceable to the extent specified in s.246(2)). Liens not caught by the section remain valid, but in the case of an administration will not be enforceable without the leave of the court under s.11(3): *Bristol Airport plc v Powdrill* [1990] Ch. 744 at 762 (reported as *Re Paramount Airways Ltd* [1990] B.C.C. 130 at 150).

In subs.(1)(a) the reference was formerly to the making of an administration order. The new wording was substituted by EA 2002 Sch.17 para.32, with effect from September 15, 2003, to take account of appointments made out of court.

Note that s.246 does not apply in favour of an administrative receiver or the supervisor of a voluntary arrangement.

Section 246 does not apply to Scotland (see s.440(2)(a)); but the corresponding provisions of the Bankruptcy (Scotland) Act 1985 s.38(4), which are more limited in scope, have been extended to company liquidations by the rules: see the Insolvency (Scotland) Rules 1986 (SI 1986/1915 (S 139)) r.4.22(1).

S.246(3)

The exception created by s.246(3) is not limited to the case where the person claiming the lien does so by reason of the fact that the documents in question confer "a title to property" upon him. The words "as such" mean "in circumstances which are such as to give rise to a lien". In other words, it is sufficient that the person has a lien over the documents, and the documents are of a kind which give a title to property to somebody: *Re SEIL Trade Finance Ltd* [1992] B.C.C. 538. See also the case of *Re Carter Commercial Developments Ltd* [2002] B.C.C. 803; [2002] B.P.I.R. 1053, noted by S. Unwin in [2003] Insolv. Int. 4.

Remote attendance at meetings

246A   Remote attendance at meetings

246A(1)   [Application of section] Subject to subsection (2), this section applies to–

(a)   any meeting of the creditors of a company summoned under this Act or the rules, or

(b)   any meeting of the members or contributories of a company summoned by the office-holder under this Act or the rules, other than a meeting of the members of a company in a members' voluntary winding up.

246A(2)   [Non-application to appointment of receiver, Scottish winding up] This section does not apply where–

(a)   a company is being wound up in Scotland, or

(b)   a receiver is appointed under section 51 in Chapter 2 of Part 3.

246A(3)   [Attendance at meeting by persons not present together] Where the person summoning a meeting ("the convener") considers it appropriate, the meeting may be conducted and held in such a way that persons who are not present together at the same place may attend it.

246A(4)   [Attendance at meeting by exercise of right to speak and vote] Where a meeting is conducted and held in the manner referred to in subsection (3), a person attends the meeting if that person is able to exercise any rights which that person may have to speak and vote at the meeting.

246A(5)   [When exercising right to speak and vote] For the purposes of this section–

(a)   a person is able to exercise the right to speak at a meeting when that person is in a position to communicate to all those attending the meeting, during the meeting, any information or opinions which that person has on the business of the meeting; and

(b)   a person is able to exercise the right to vote at a meeting when–

(i)   that person is able to vote, during the meeting, on resolutions put to the vote at the meeting, and

(ii)   that person's vote can be taken into account in determining whether or not such resolutions are passed at the same time as the votes of all the other persons attending the meeting.

246A(6)   [Duty of convener to make arrangements] The convener of a meeting which is to be conducted and held in the manner referred to in subsection (3) shall make whatever arrangements the convener considers appropriate to–

(a)   enable those attending the meeting to exercise their rights to speak or vote, and

(b)   ensure the identification of those attending the meeting and the security of any electronic means used to enable attendance.

246A(7)   [Where unnecessary or inexpedient to specify place for meeting] Where in the reasonable opinion of the convener–

(a)   a meeting will be attended by persons who will not be present together at the same place, and

(b)   it is unnecessary or inexpedient to specify a place for the meeting, any requirement under this Act or the rules to specify a place for the meeting may be satisfied by specifying the arrangements the convener proposes to enable persons to exercise their rights to speak or vote.

246A(8)   [Convener to regard legitimate interests of the creditors etc. for s.246A(6), (7)(b)] In making the arrangements referred to in subsection (6) and in forming the opinion referred to in subsection (7)(b), the convener must have regard to the legitimate interests of the creditors, members or contributories and others attending the meeting in the efficient despatch of the business of the meeting.

246A(9)   [Request for convener to specify place for meeting] If–

(a)   the notice of a meeting does not specify a place for the meeting,

(b)   the convener is requested in accordance with the rules to specify a place for the meeting, and

(c)   that request is made–

(i)   in the case of a meeting of creditors or contributories, by not less than ten percent in value of the creditors or contributories, or

   (ii) in the case of a meeting of members, by members representing not less than ten percent of the total voting rights of all the members having at the date of the request a right to vote at the meeting, it shall be the duty of the convener to specify a place for the meeting.

246A(10)   **["The office-holder"]** In this section, "the office-holder", in relation to a company, means–

   (a) its liquidator, provisional liquidator, administrator, or administrative receiver, or

   (b) where a voluntary arrangement in relation to the company is proposed or has taken effect under Part 1, the nominee or the supervisor of the voluntary arrangement.

GENERAL NOTE

Section 246A was inserted by LRO 2010 (SI 2010/18) art.3(1) as from April 6, 2010 (with retrospective effect). It applies with the limitations set out in subsection (2). The section removes any doubt that a "meeting" under the Act or the Rules may be held without the participants being physically present, whether it takes place by video-link, telephone conference or electronic means. It is no longer necessary to specify any place where the meeting is to be held. Other sections of the legislation (e.g. r.2.61) provide for the passing of resolutions without the holding of any meeting—e.g. where assent is recorded by post or email.

Use of websites

246B   **Use of websites**

246B(1)   **[Provision of notice by website]** Subject to subsection (2), where any provision of this Act or the rules requires the office-holder to give, deliver, furnish or send a notice or other document or information to any person, that requirement is satisfied by making the notice, document or information available on a website–

   (a) in accordance with the rules, and

   (b) in such circumstances as may be prescribed.

246B(2)   **[Non-application to appointment of receiver, Scottish winding up]** This section does not apply where–

   (a) a company is being wound up in Scotland, or

   (b) a receiver is appointed under section 51 in Chapter 2 of Part 3.

246B(3)   **["The office-holder"]** In this section, "the office-holder" means–

   (a) the liquidator, provisional liquidator, administrator, or administrative receiver of a company, or

   (b) where a voluntary arrangement in relation to a company is proposed or has taken effect under Part 1, the nominee or the supervisor of the voluntary arrangement.

GENERAL NOTE

Section 246B was inserted by LRO 2010 (SI 2010/18) art.3(1) as from April 6, 2010 (with retrospective effect). It applies with the limitations set out in subsection (2). The section allows an office-holder who is required by the Act to give notice or send any document to any person to do so by means of a website (unless personal service is required). The rules which have been made for the purpose are rr.12A.11–12A.12. The person must be notified that the document is available for viewing and downloading and be given details for accessing the website, and is entitled to request a hard copy. This must be sent within five business days (r.12A.11). Rule 12A.12 provides for the case where a number of notices are to be sent and the cost of complying with r.12A.11 on each occasion would be disproportionate because of the number of persons entitled to receive them: the court may authorise the sending of one notice to cover all the circumstances. The documents must remain available on the website for at least 12 months.

PART VII

INTERPRETATION FOR FIRST GROUP OF PARTS

247 "Insolvency" and "go into liquidation"

247(1) **["Insolvency"]** In this Group of Parts, except in so far as the context otherwise requires, **"insolvency"**, in relation to a company, includes the approval of a voluntary arrangement under Part I, or the appointment of an administrator or administrative receiver.

247(2) **[Company in liquidation]** For the purposes of any provision in this Group of Parts, a company goes into liquidation if it passes a resolution for voluntary winding up or an order for its winding up is made by the court at a time when it has not already gone into liquidation by passing such a resolution.

247(3) **[Resolution following administration or voluntary arrangement]** The reference to a resolution for voluntary winding up in subsection (2) includes a reference to a resolution which is deemed to occur by virtue of–

(a) paragraph 83(6)(b) of Schedule B1, or

(b) an order made following conversion of administration or a voluntary arrangement into winding up by virtue of Article 37 of the EC Regulation.

S.247(1)
This meaning of "insolvency" is discussed in the Introductory note to Part VI, preceding s.230, above, where attention is drawn to the fact that the Act uses the term to describe the various *proceedings*, such as winding up, administration and receivership, which are the subject of the present Act, and not to describe a company's adverse financial situation. The related word "insolvent" is not defined by this section, and at times it appears to be used in the Act in the everyday sense (e.g. "goes into insolvent liquidation": s.214(6)) rather than analogously with the definition of "insolvency" in the present section.

S.247(2)
The time when a company "goes into liquidation" is to be distinguished from the time when its winding up *commences*: see the notes to ss.86 and 129. The phrase was the subject of judicial consideration (in connection with the construction of a trust deed) in *Mettoy Pension Trustees Ltd v Evans* [1991] 2 All E.R. 513, where a meaning in conformity with the definition in the present subsection was approved.

S.247(3)
This subsection was amended by EA 2002 Sch.17 para.33(3), with effect from September 15, 2003, by the insertion of the reference to para.83(6)(b).

Section 247(3), in its original form, was inserted by the Insolvency Act 1986 (Amendment) (No.2) Regulations 2002 (SI 2002/1240, effective May 31, 2002). Where "main" insolvency proceedings have been opened in the Member State where the company in question has its centre of main interests, and the company is already subject to a CVA or administration in "territorial" proceedings in this country, art.37 empowers its "liquidator" to apply to a UK court to have these proceedings converted to a winding up. (For the meaning of these technical terms, see the notes to the EC Regulation arts 2, 3.) The intention behind s.247(3) might have been thought to be to back-date the time of "going into liquidation" to that when the CVA or administration took effect, but even so the reference to a "resolution" which is "deemed to occur" is, at first sight, baffling, particularly as regards a company in administration. For elucidation, we must look to IR 1986 rr.1.31–1.33 and rr.2.59–2.61. This rules out any question of back-dating. The court making an order for conversion under these rules may (inter alia) order that the company be wound up "as if a resolution for a voluntary winding up under s.184 were passed on the day on which the order was made". Unless, therefore, the court were to assume jurisdiction to make an order to the contrary, the time of "going into liquidation" will not be retrospective.

248 "Secured creditor", etc.

248(1) In this Group of Parts, except in so far as the context otherwise requires–

(a) **"secured creditor"**, in relation to a company, means a creditor of the company who holds in respect of his debt a security over property of the company, and **"unsecured creditor"** is to be read accordingly; and

(b) **"security"** means–

(i) in relation to England and Wales, any mortgage, charge, lien or other security, and

(ii) in relation to Scotland, any security (whether heritable or moveable), any floating charge and any right of lien or preference and any right of retention (other than a right of compensation or set off).

GENERAL NOTE

The term "security" as here defined does not include the owner's rights under a hire-purchase, conditional sale, chattel leasing or retention of title agreement, although for some purposes (e.g. s.15(2)) these rights are treated analogously with security interests.

In *Bristol Airport plc v Powdrill* [1990] Ch. 744 (reported as *Re Paramount Airways Ltd* [1990] B.C.C. 130) it was held that the statutory right of an airport under the Civil Aviation Act 1982 s.88, to detain an aircraft for failure to pay outstanding aircraft charges was a "lien or other security" within s.248(b)(i). In *Exchange Travel Agency Ltd v Triton Property Trust plc* [1991] B.C.C. 341 a landlord's right of re-entry on non-payment of rent was held to be a "security", and this ruling was followed by Lightman J. in *March Estates plc v Gunmark Ltd* [1996] 2 B.C.L.C. 1; but in *Razzaq v Pala* [1998] B.C.C. 66 the same judge, after hearing full argument, said that he had been wrong to do so, and this was confirmed by the House of Lords on appeal (sub nom. *Re Park Air Services plc* [2000] 2 A.C. 172 at 186; [1999] B.C.C. 135 at 142). Later cases (notably *Re Lomax Leisure Ltd* [2000] B.C.C. 352) have endorsed the latter ruling. The position thus appears to be settled as a matter of general law, but for practical purposes the agreed view has been reversed as regards IA 1986 ss.10 and 11 by the amendments made to those sections by IA 2000 s.9. See the detailed discussion in the notes to ss.10(1) and 11(3). Corresponding provisions now also apply in CVAs (see Sch.A1 para.12(1)(f)), administrations under the new Pt II (Sch.B1 paras 43(4), 44(5)) and IVAs (s.252(2)(aa)).

249 "Connected" with a company

249 For the purposes of any provision in this Group of Parts, a person is connected with a company if–

(a) he is a director or shadow director of the company or an associate of such a director or shadow director, or

(b) he is an associate of the company;

and **"associate"** has the meaning given by section 435 in Part XVIII of this Act.

GENERAL NOTE

The meaning of "associate" (a term which the Act applies in the bankruptcy of individuals as well as in the winding up, etc. of companies) is defined at length in s.435. The phrase "connected with" a company is used largely to put it beyond doubt that a director or shadow director is always included for the purposes of the statutory provision in question. So, also, will be the "associates" of such a director or shadow director.

It is, in principle, possible for a company's bank to come within the definition of a "connected person", if its involvement in the company's affairs is such as to make it a "shadow director": see *Re a Company (No.005009 of 1987)* (1988) 4 B.C.C. 424.

For the meaning of "associate", see the note to s.435; and for "director" and "shadow director", see s.251. The concepts of "connected person" and "associate" are examined in detail by D. Pollard in (2009) 22 Insolv. Int. 33.

250 "Member" of a company

250 For the purposes of any provision in this Group of Parts, a person who is not a member of a company but to whom shares in the company have been transferred, or transmitted by operation of law, is to be regarded as a member of the company, and references to a member or members are to be read accordingly.

GENERAL NOTE

"Member" is defined for the purposes of the Companies Acts by CA 2006 s.112, and under that definition the term is confined to (1) the subscribers to the memorandum; and (2) those who have agreed to become members and whose names are entered in the register of members. The present provision is designed to include the transferees of shares under unregistered transfers, and the personal representatives of deceased members and others to whom shares have been transmitted by operation of law. It is wide enough, however, to include other categories of person, e.g. holders of share warrants to bearer.

This section was no doubt inserted with the benign intention of ensuring that an unregistered transferee of shares should enjoy the same rights as a member—for instance, to petition for a winding-up order and to vote at meetings of contributories. It appears to be wide enough, however, to impose burdens upon an unregistered transferee as well—for instance, if the shares are not fully paid, to render him directly liable to the company as a contributory for calls on the shares under s.74. Whether the legislators intended to effect such a radical change in the law by a side-wind must be open to question.

251   Expressions used generally

251   In this Group of Parts, except in so far as the context otherwise requires–

"administrative receiver" means–

(a)   an administrative receiver as defined by section 29(2) in Chapter I of Part III, or

(b)   a receiver appointed under section 51 in Chapter II of that Part in a case where the whole (or substantially the whole) of the company's property is attached by the floating charge;

"agent" does not include a person's counsel acting as such;

"books and papers" and **"books or papers"** includes accounts, deeds, writing and documents;

"business day" means any day other than a Saturday, a Sunday, Christmas Day, Good Friday or a day which is a bank holiday in any part of Great Britain;

"chattel leasing agreement" means an agreement for the bailment or, in Scotland, the hiring of goods which is capable of subsisting for more than 3 months;

"contributory" has the meaning given by section 79;

"the court", in relation to a company, means a court having jurisdiction to wind up the company;

"director" includes any person occupying the position of director, by whatever name called;

"document" includes summons, notice, order and other legal process, and registers;

"floating charge" means a charge which, as created, was a floating charge and includes a floating charge within section 462 of the Companies Act (Scottish floating charges);

"the Gazette" means–

(a)   as respects companies registered in England and Wales, the London Gazette;

(b)   as respects companies registered in Scotland, the Edinburgh Gazette;

"officer", in relation to a body corporate, includes a director, manager or secretary;

"the official rate", in relation to interest, means the rate payable under section 189(4);

"prescribed" means prescribed by the rules;

"receiver", in the expression **"receiver or manager"**, does not include a receiver appointed under section 51 in Chapter II of Part III;

"retention of title agreement" means an agreement for the sale of goods to a company, being an agreement–

(a)   which does not constitute a charge on the goods, but

(b) under which, if the seller is not paid and the company is wound up, the seller will have priority over all other creditors of the company as respects the goods or any property representing the goods;

"the rules" means rules under section 411 in Part XV; and

"shadow director", in relation to a company, means a person in accordance with whose directions or instructions the directors of the company are accustomed to act (but so that a person is not deemed a shadow director by reason only that the directors act on advice given by him in a professional capacity).

GENERAL NOTE

Most of the definitions listed here are self-explanatory. For a discussion of terms defined by reference to other sections, see the notes to those sections. The closing words of s.251 were substituted by the Companies Act 2006 (Commencement No.3, Consequential Amendments, Transitional Provisions and Savings) Order 2007 (SI 2007/2194 (C. 84)) art.10 and Sch.4 para.43 as from October 1, 2007.

The term "administrative receiver" may include a receiver of the property of a foreign company: see *Re International Bulk Commodities Ltd* [1993] Ch. 77; [1992] B.C.C. 463 and the notes to s.29(2), above.

The definition of "business day" in the Act differs from that in the rules, at least in some contexts. See the note to IR 1986 r.13.13(1).

The definition of "floating charge" was introduced by the 1986 Act. The change is discussed in the notes to ss.175(2)(b) and 245.

A shadow director is to be distinguished from a de facto director: the terms do not overlap, but are alternatives, and in most if not all cases are mutually exclusive. A de facto director is a person who assumes to act as a director and is held out as such by the company, and who claims and purports to be a director, although never actually or validly appointed as such. A shadow director, in contrast, claims not to be a director but claims that others are the directors to the exclusion of himself. An allegation that a person has acted as a de facto or shadow director, without distinguishing between the two, is embarrassing: *Re Hydrodan (Corby) Ltd* [1994] B.C.C. 161. For a more detailed discussion of the two terms, see the note to CDDA 1986 s.22(5).

If a parent company is a shadow director of its subsidiary, it does not follow that the directors of the parent company are also, without more, its shadow directors. However where the director of a company is a body corporate, there must be an inference that it is accustomed to act on the directions of others, who will be shadow directors (*Re Hydrodan (Corby) Ltd*, above). There is no assumption that a director who is the nominee of a particular shareholder or creditor is the agent of his appointor or acts under his directions or instructions (*Kuwait Asia Bank EC v National Mutual Life Nominees Ltd* [1991] 1 A.C. 187; [1990] B.C.C. 567).

In *Re Tasbian Ltd (No.3)* [1992] B.C.C. 358 there was held to be an arguable case that a person appointed as a consultant to a company by an outside investor was a shadow director. The dividing line between the position of a watchdog or adviser and a shadow director was difficult to draw, but there was a serious question to be tried whether the respondent might have crossed over it.

Note insertion of new definitions of "agent", "books and papers", "court", "document" and "the Gazette" by Companies Act 2006 (Consequential Amendments, Transitional Provisions and Savings) Order 2009 (2009/1941) Sch.1 para.77(1), (2) as from October 1, 2009.

THE SECOND GROUP OF PARTS: INSOLVENCY OF INDIVIDUALS; BANKRUPTCY

Introductory note to the Second Group of Parts
Bankruptcy legislation in England can be traced back to 1542, and the system with which practitioners will be familiar was contained in BA 1914 (as amended in 1926 and 1976). This system was the product of the 1883 reforms pushed through by Gladstone and Joseph Chamberlain. For a superb historical review outlining the violent policy swings in the nineteenth century see Lester, *Victorian Insolvency* (1995). In view of the changed social conditions and altered political economy in the twentieth century it is not surprising that both the Blagden Committee (Cmnd.221) in 1957 and the Cork Committee (Cmnd.8558) in 1982 felt that major revision was long overdue. Part III of IA 1985 did put the law on a modern footing, although its changes were less radical than the Cork Committee had hoped for. IA 1986 ss.252–385 remodel the 1985 legislation mainly by fragmenting its more cumbersome provisions into several sections. Most of the provisions in the 1985 Act relating to bankruptcy never came into force. Cases under the 1914 Act still came before the courts for many years after 1986—see for example *Re Dent* [1994] 1 W.L.R. 956; *Re Dennis* [1996] Ch. 80, discussed by Tee in (1996) 55 C.L.J. 21; *Trustee of F C Jones v Jones* [1996] B.P.I.R. 644; *Re Ross* [1998] B.C.C. 29.

What were the most obvious reforms introduced by the 1985 Act and now found in the 1986 Act? The bankruptcy procedure was greatly simplified, with the abolition of the concept of the act of bankruptcy and the intermediate stage of the receiving order. An attempt was made wherever possible to harmonise bankruptcy procedures with those of company liquidations, although unlike many jurisdictions there is still a distinction between corporate and personal insolvency law. Another reform which is more symbolic than significant in practice was the abolition of the concept of reputed ownership in bankruptcy law (it did not operate on corporate insolvency). Other changes worthy of mention were the rules giving increased protection to the family home (see ss.336–338), the attempt to produce a viable alternative to bankruptcy via voluntary arrangements (ss.252–263), plus a host of minor measures designed to streamline and improve the effectiveness of bankruptcy procedures. The liberalising trend dating back to the Justice Report of 1975 and IA 1976 is again apparent, particularly with the provisions on discharge (ss.279 and 280). This trend has continued with EA 2002.

Criticisms can be made of the 1986 Act. It was heavily dependent on IR 1986. On the other hand it must be conceded that the 1914 Act was considerably supplemented by BR 1952. The drafting of the provisions of Pt III of the 1985 Act left much to be desired, and Muir Hunter Q.C., a leading commentator on bankruptcy law, predicted that this deficiency would lead to an increase in litigation. The drafting of the 1986 Act was much improved. In its 1994 Report entitled *Insolvency Law: An Agenda for Reform* Justice identified a number of weaknesses with the post-1986 bankruptcy regime. Concerns were expressed about the increasing use of bankruptcy to recover small debts and the considerable amount of litigation surrounding the use of statutory demands. Many of these problems could be traced back to the failure of government to implement the changes to the county court administration order procedure which were enacted in 1990.

Finally, it should be noted that ss.252–385 of IA 1986 are not the sole source of law on debt and personal insolvency. Parts XII and XIX of the Act also contain provisions that will be important in practice. Criminal bankruptcy (so far as concerns orders which are still in force: see the notes to ss.264 and 277) is dealt with by the Powers of the Criminal Courts Act 1973. The Deeds of Arrangement Act 1914 survives largely intact, though the number of deeds entered into each year has been miniscule with none recorded in recent years. Accordingly the Deeds of Arrangement Act 1914 has been excised from Vol.2 of this edition. Administration orders against judgment debtors remain governed by the County Courts Act 1984 (as amended). Indeed there are still provisions of the Debtors Act 1869 which may return to haunt debtors—see for example s.13 (offence to make a gift to defeat creditors). Thus in *Woodley v Woodley (No.2)* [1994] 1 W.L.R. 1167 a debtor (who subsequently became bankrupt on his own petition) was threatened with imprisonment by a judge under s.5 of the 1869 Act for wilfully refusing to pay a judgment debt where he had the means to do so prior to his bankruptcy. On appeal, the committal order was quashed by the Court of Appeal because there was a sufficient degree of doubt as to whether he was deliberately defying the law or had been confused as to his obligations. For a more recent case involving s.5 of the Debtors Act 1869 see *L v L* [1997] 2 F.L.R. 252. Note also Insolvent Debtors Relief Act 1729 as discussed in *Aectra Refining v Exmar, The Times*, August 15, 1994.

The personal insolvency provisions in the 1986 legislation have been amended considerably by IA 2000 and EA 2002 (see below). For comment see Frieze, [2005] 18 Insolv. Int. 57.

The law on personal insolvency in Scotland (or sequestration, as it is termed) is to be found in the Bankruptcy (Scotland) Act 1985 (as amended by the Bankruptcy (Scotland) Act 1993) and associated delegated legislation. In 1997 there were 2,502 sequestrations in Scotland. The personal insolvency reforms in EA 2002 were not made applicable to Scotland—for reform prospects in Scotland see McKenzie-Skene, [2004] J.B.L. 171 and our Introduction. Comparable provisions dealing with personal insolvency in Northern Ireland are now contained in the Insolvency (Northern Ireland) Order 1989 (SI 1989/2405) (NI 19), arts 226–345 in particular. The EA 2002 reforms were introduced into the Province by SI 2005/1455 (NI 10). See note to s.441.

For a general review of the subject see Milman, *Personal Insolvency Law, Regulation and Policy* (2005). For a perceptive analysis of the live issues and reform options in consumer bankruptcy law in Britain (covering both English and Scots law) see McKenzie-Skene and Walters (2006) 80 Am. Banky Law Jo. 477.

PART 7A

DEBT RELIEF ORDERS

Introductory note to Part 7A
These new debt relief provisions are introduced by Pt 5 of the Tribunals, Courts and Enforcement Act 2007. Part 7A (ss.251A–251X) inserted by the Tribunals, Courts and Enforcement Act 2007 s.108(1) and Sch.17 as from February 24, 2009, for the purpose of making rules, regulations and orders and from April 6, 2009, for all other purposes (see Tribunals, Courts and Enforcement Act 2007 (Commencement No.7) Order 2009 (SI 2009/382) art.2).

The background to this reform lies in the fact that existing regimes for dealing with personal insolvency are unable to cater efficiently for the small-scale insolvent with debts of less than £15k. The problem has been made worse by the lack of usage of the county court administration order procedure, which itself is remodelled by the 2007 Act (see s.106 and Sch.16). Accordingly, it was felt that there was a need for a new low cost procedure designed to enable small debtors to clear their debts. Proposals to this effect first appeared in 2004. The proposals were labelled "NINA"—"no income, no assets"—and were specifically designed for debtors with few realisable possessions and little in the way of surplus income. Such individuals could not be effectively dealt with either through bankruptcy or an IVA. The proposals were firmed up in 2005/2006 and then included in the Tribunals, Courts and Enforcement Bill. Similar reforms were introduced in New Zealand via the "No Assets Procedure". Debt relief schemes of a similar ilk have been operating in parts of Europe for some time. In *Back v Finland* [2005] B.P.I.R. 1 the European Court of Human Rights upheld a similar debt adjustment scheme, concluding that it did not unfairly diminish the rights of creditors in a manner contrary to art.1 of the First Protocol ECHR.

Section 108(1) of the 2007 Act directs us to Sch.17, which inserts a new Pt 7A into the Insolvency Act 1986. This Part comprises ss.251A–251X, a substantial corpus of law. Part 7A is also be supported by new Schs 4ZA and 4ZB, which are inserted by Schs 18 and 19 of the 2007 Act. These provisions inserted into the 1986 Act are in turn supplemented by new provisions added to the Insolvency Rules 1986 by the Insolvency (Amendment) Rules 2009 (SI 2009/642). Note in particular the new IR rr.5A.1–5A.27. Supplementary provisions on debt relief restriction orders and undertakings are found in IR rr.6.252–6.263.

The instruction of DROs and associated paraphernalia has also required a number of discrete statutory instruments—see the Insolvency Proceedings (Monetary Limits) (Amendment) Order 2009 (SI 2009/465) which provides financial criteria for the purposes of obtaining a DRO.

Preliminary

251A   Debt relief orders

251A(1)   [Application re qualifying debts] An individual who is unable to pay his debts may apply for an order under this Part ("a debt relief order") to be made in respect of his qualifying debts.

251A(2)   ["Qualifying debt" in Pt 7A] In this Part **"qualifying debt"** means (subject to subsection (3)) a debt which–

(a)   is for a liquidated sum payable either immediately or at some certain future time; and

(b)   is not an excluded debt.

251A(3)   [Secured debt not qualifying debt] A debt is not a qualifying debt to the extent that it is secured.

251A(4)   ["Excluded debt" in Pt 7A] In this Part **"excluded debt"** means a debt of any description prescribed for the purposes of this subsection.

General Note

This describes the concept of a debt relief order (DRO). A DRO is potentially available to a debtor with qualifying debts. It cannot be used to wipe the slate clean of secured debt (s.251A(3)) or debts which are viewed as "excluded"—see s.251A(4)) and IR r.5A.2 here. It follows from Sch.4ZA that a debtor cannot take advantage of this procedure if an undischarged bankrupt, or subject to an IVA or if subject to a bankruptcy petition (but see IR r.5A.23 here).

Applications for a debt relief order

251B   Making of application

251B(1)   [Application to official receiver through approved intermediary] An application for a debt relief order must be made to the official receiver through an approved intermediary.

251B(2) **[Contents of application]** The application must include–

(a) a list of the debts to which the debtor is subject at the date of the application, specifying the amount of each debt (including any interest, penalty or other sum that has become payable in relation to that debt on or before that date) and the creditor to whom it is owed;

(b) details of any security held in respect of any of those debts; and

(c) such other information about the debtor's affairs (including his creditors, debts and liabilities and his income and assets) as may be prescribed.

251B(3) [Further provision in rules] The rules may make further provision as to–

(a) the form of an application for a debt relief order;

(b) the manner in which an application is to be made; and

(c) information and documents to be supplied in support of an application.

251B(4) [When application made] For the purposes of this Part an application is not to be regarded as having been made until–

(a) the application has been submitted to the official receiver; and

(b) any fee required in connection with the application by an order under section 415 has been paid to such person as the order may specify.

GENERAL NOTE

The procedure for applying for a DRO is explained. Electronic submission is *required*—IR r.5A. 4. The debtor must apply to the official receiver via an approved intermediary—see s.251U and IR r.5A.5. For further detail on the contents of the application see IR r.5A.3.

251C   Duty of official receiver to consider and determine application

251C(1) [Application of s.251C] This section applies where an application for a debt relief order is made.

251C(2) [Stay of application] The official receiver may stay consideration of the application until he has received answers to any queries raised with the debtor in relation to anything connected with the application.

251C(3) [Determination of application] The official receiver must determine the application by–

(a) deciding whether to refuse the application;

(b) if he does not refuse it, by making a debt relief order in relation to the specified debts he is satisfied were qualifying debts of the debtor at the application date;

but he may only refuse the application if he is authorised or required to do so by any of the following provisions of this section.

251C(4)   [Discretionary refusal] The official receiver may refuse the application if he considers that–

(a) the application does not meet all the requirements imposed by or under section 251B;

(b) any queries raised with the debtor have not been answered to the satisfaction of the official receiver within such time as he may specify when they are raised;

(c) the debtor has made any false representation or omission in making the application or on supplying any information or documents in support of it.

265

251C(5) **[Mandatory refusal]** The official receiver must refuse the application if he is not satisfied that–

(a) the debtor is an individual who is unable to pay his debts;

(b) at least one of the specified debts was a qualifying debt of the debtor at the application date;

(c) each of the conditions set out in Part 1 of Schedule 4ZA is met.

251C(6) **[Requirement for Sch.4ZA Pt 2 conditions]** The official receiver may refuse the application if he is not satisfied that each condition specified in Part 2 of Schedule 4ZA is met.

251C(7) **[Notification of reasons for refusal]** If the official receiver refuses an application he must give reasons for his refusal to the debtor in the prescribed manner.

251C(8) **["Specified debt"]** In this section **"specified debt"** means a debt specified in the application.

GENERAL NOTE

The role of the official receiver on an application for a DRO is outlined. The important point to note is that the official receiver is not to be seen as a rubber stamp. The official receiver should adopt a questioning approach (but see s.251D). The official receiver must be satisfied that the conditions laid down in Sch.4ZA have been met. On verification checks see IR r.5A.7. Note also the financial criteria mapped out in the Insolvency Proceedings (Monetary Limits) (Amendment) Order 2009 (SI 2009/465). See also IR r.5A.6. The geographical link must be established. There must have been no preferences or transactions at an undervalue within the previous two years. The debts must not exceed the prescribed amount (£15k). The debtor's monthly surplus income must not exceed the prescribed amount (£50)—see IR r.5A.8. The debtor must not have property in excess of the prescribed maximum amount (£300)—see IR rr.5A.9 and 5A.10 (which deal with excluded items). Note that vehicles with a realisable value of less than £1000 are excluded—IR r.5A.10(1)(b) and (4).

251D   Presumptions applicable to the determination of an application

251D(1) **[Presumptions]** The following presumptions are to apply to the determination of an application for a debt relief order.

251D(2) **[Debtor an individual unable to pay debts]** The official receiver must presume that the debtor is an individual who is unable to pay his debts at the determination date if–

(a) that appears to the official receiver to be the case at the application date from the information supplied in the application and he has no reason to believe that the information supplied is incomplete or inaccurate; and

(b) he has no reason to believe that, by virtue of a change in the debtor's financial circumstances since the application date, the debtor may be able to pay his debts.

251D(3) **[Specified debt a qualifying debt]** The official receiver must presume that a specified debt (of the amount specified in the application and owed to the creditor so specified) is a qualifying debt at the application date if–

(a) that appears to him to be the case from the information supplied in the application; and

(b) he has no reason to believe that the information supplied is incomplete or inaccurate.

251D(4) **[Schedule 4ZA para.1 condition of domiciled or resident]** The official receiver must presume that the condition specified in paragraph 1 of Schedule 4ZA is met if–

(a) that appears to him to be the case from the information supplied in the application;

(b) any prescribed verification checks relating to the condition have been made; and

(c) he has no reason to believe that the information supplied is incomplete or inaccurate.

251D(5) [Other Sch.4ZA conditions] The official receiver must presume that any other condition specified in Part 1 or 2 of Schedule 4ZA is met if–

(a) that appears to him to have been the case as at the application date from the information supplied in the application and he has no reason to believe that the information supplied is incomplete or inaccurate;

(b) any prescribed verification checks relating to the condition have been made; and

(c) he has no reason to believe that, by virtue of a change in circumstances since the application date, the condition may no longer be met.

251D(6) [References to information supplied] References in this section to information supplied in the application include information supplied to the official receiver in support of the application.

251D(7) ["Specified debt" in s.251D] In this section **"specified debt"** means a debt specified in the application.

GENERAL NOTE

This explains presumptions which the official receiver should make use of when dealing with an application for a DRO. The effect of these presumptions is to water down the questioning approach to be taken by the official receiver when dealing with an application for a DRO. See IR r.5A.7. In effect one might characterise the official receiver as a watchdog and not a bloodhound when performing this role. In view of the potential numbers of applications for DROs, this is inevitable.

Making and effect of debt relief order

251E Making of debt relief orders

251E(1) [Application of s.251C] This section applies where the official receiver makes a debt relief order on determining an application under section 251C.

251E(2) [Order in prescribed form] The order must be made in the prescribed form.

251E(3) [Contents of order] The order must include a list of the debts which the official receiver is satisfied were qualifying debts of the debtor at the application date, specifying the amount of the debt at that time and the creditor to whom it was then owed.

251E(4) [Duty of official receiver re order] The official receiver must–

(a) give a copy of the order to the debtor; and

(b) make an entry for the order in the register containing the prescribed information about the order or the debtor.

251E(5) [Provision in rules] The rules may make provision as to other steps to be taken by the official receiver or the debtor on the making of the order.

251E(6) [Notification to creditors in rules] Those steps may include in particular notifying each creditor to whom a qualifying debt specified in the order is owed of–

(a) the making of the order and its effect,

(b) the grounds on which a creditor may object under section 251K, and

(c) any other prescribed information.

251E(7) ["The effective date"] In this Part the date on which an entry relating to the making of a debt relief order is first made in the register is referred to as "the effective date".

This describes the effect of a DRO made by an official receiver. For form of DRO see IR r.5A.11. On notification see IR rr.5A.12 and 5A.13. For entry on the individual insolvency register see IR r.6A.5A.

251F   Effect of debt relief order on other debt management arrangements

251F(1)   [Application of s.251F] This section applies if–

(a)   a debt relief order is made, and

(b)   immediately before the order is made, other debt management arrangements are in force in respect of the debtor.

251F(2)   [Other debt management arrangements to cease] The other debt management arrangements cease to be in force when the debt relief order is made.

251F(3)   ["Other debt management arrangements"] In this section **"other debt management arrangements"** means–

(a)   an administration order under Part 6 of the County Courts Act 1984;

(b)   an enforcement restriction order under Part 6A of that Act;

(c)   a debt repayment plan arranged in accordance with a debt management scheme that is approved under Chapter 4 of Part 5 of the Tribunals, Courts and Enforcement Act 2007.

This details the effect of a DRO on other debt management arrangements, such as an administration order, an enforcement restrictions order and a debt repayment plan. Basically a DRO will trump these.

251G   Moratorium from qualifying debts

251G(1)   [Moratorium on specified qualifying debts] A moratorium commences on the effective date for a debt relief order in relation to each qualifying debt specified in the order ("a specified qualifying debt").

251G(2)   [Effect of moratorium] During the moratorium, the creditor to whom a specified qualifying debt is owed–

(a)   has no remedy in respect of the debt, and

(b)   may not–

(i)   commence a creditor's petition in respect of the debt, or

(ii)   otherwise commence any action or other legal proceedings against the debtor for the debt,

except with the permission of the court and on such terms as the court may impose.

251G(3)   [Effect on existing petition, action or proceeding] If on the effective date a creditor to whom a specified qualifying debt is owed has any such petition, action or other proceeding as mentioned in subsection (2)(b) pending in any court, the court may–

(a)   stay the proceedings on the petition, action or other proceedings (as the case may be), or

(b)   allow them to continue on such terms as the court thinks fit.

251G(4)   [Debt in s.251G(2)(a), (b) to include] In subsection (2)(a) and (b) references to the debt include a reference to any interest, penalty or other sum that becomes payable in relation to that debt after the application date.

251G(5)   **[Right of secured creditor to enforce]** Nothing in this section affects the right of a secured creditor of the debtor to enforce his security.

GENERAL NOTE

The moratorium associated with the DRO is explained. The moratorium will only have effect as against those creditors owed qualifying debts. Once the DRO is in place leave will be required to enforce a qualifying debt. There is an exception provided for in the case of the moratorium being terminated early by the official receiver under s.251H or by the court under s.251M.

251H   The moratorium period

251H(1)   **[Duration of moratorium]** The moratorium relating to the qualifying debts specified in a debt relief order continues for the period of one year beginning with the effective date for the order, unless–

  (a)   the moratorium terminates early; or

  (b)   the moratorium period is extended by the official receiver under this section or by the court under section 251M.

251H(2)   **[Grounds for extension of moratorium period]** The official receiver may only extend the moratorium period for the purpose of–

  (a)   carrying out or completing an investigation under section 251K;

  (b)   taking any action he considers necessary (whether as a result of an investigation or otherwise) in relation to the order; or

  (c)   in a case where he has decided to revoke the order, providing the debtor with the opportunity to make arrangements for making payments towards his debts.

251H(3)   **[Permission of court for s.251G(2)(a) extension]** The official receiver may not extend the moratorium period for the purpose mentioned in subsection (2)(a) without the permission of the court.

251H(4)   **[Extension no to exceed three months]** The official receiver may not extend the moratorium period beyond the end of the period of three months beginning after the end of the initial period of one year mentioned in subsection (1).

251H(5)   **[Extensions to be made before end of moratorium]** The moratorium period may be extended more than once, but any extension (whether by the official receiver or by the court) must be made before the moratorium would otherwise end.

251H(6)   **[Moratorium terminating early]** References in this Part to a moratorium terminating early are to its terminating before the end of what would otherwise be the moratorium period, whether on the revocation of the order or by virtue of any other enactment.

GENERAL NOTE

This details the duration of the DRO moratorium. The moratorium is to last for one year subject to extension or early termination. On the effect of the death of the debtor during the moratorium period see IR r.5A.27.

251I   Discharge from qualifying debts

251I(1)   **[Discharge at end of moratorium]** Subject as follows, at the end of the moratorium applicable to a debt relief order the debtor is discharged from all the qualifying debts specified in the order (including all interest, penalties and other sums which may have become payable in relation to those debts since the application date).

251I(2)   **[No discharge if early termination]** Subsection (1) does not apply if the moratorium terminates early.

251I(3)   **[No discharge for fraud]** Subsection (1) does not apply in relation to any qualifying debt which the debtor incurred in respect of any fraud or fraudulent breach of trust to which the debtor was a party.

251I(4)   **[Other persons not released]** The discharge of the debtor under subsection (1) does not release any other person from–

(a)   any liability (whether as partner or co-trustee of the debtor or otherwise) from which the debtor is released by the discharge; or

(b)   any liability as surety for the debtor or as a person in the nature of such a surety.

251I(5)   **[No discharge on s.251M revocation of order]** If the order is revoked by the court under section 251M after the end of the moratorium period, the qualifying debts specified in the order shall (so far as practicable) be treated as though subsection (1) had never applied to them.

GENERAL NOTE

At the end of the DRO moratorium period the debtor is relieved from liability to pay for qualifying debts. This discharge effect does not apply in cases of early termination. Sureties of the debtor are not relieved from liability.

Duties of debtor

251J   **Providing assistance to official receiver etc**

251J(1)   **[When s.251J duties apply]** The duties in this section apply to a debtor at any time after the making of an application by him for a debt relief order.

251J(2)   **[Scope of debtor's duty]** The debtor must–

(a)   give to the official receiver such information as to his affairs,

(b)   attend on the official receiver at such times, and

(c)   do all such other things,

as the official receiver may reasonably require for the purpose of carrying out his functions in relation to the application or, as the case may be, the debt relief order made as a result of the application.

251J(3)   **[Debtor's duty to notify official receiver]** The debtor must notify the official receiver as soon as reasonably practicable if he becomes aware of–

(a)   any error in, or omission from, the information supplied to the official receiver in, or in support of, the application;

(b)   any change in his circumstances between the application date and the determination date that would affect (or would have affected) the determination of the application.

251J(4)   **[Duration of s.251J duties]** The duties under subsections (2) and (3) apply after (as well as before) the determination of the application, for as long as the official receiver is able to exercise functions of the kind mentioned in subsection (2).

251J(5)   **[Further duty to notify official receiver]** If a debt relief order is made as a result of the application, the debtor must notify the official receiver as soon as reasonably practicable if–

(a)   there is an increase in his income during the moratorium period applicable to the order;

(b)   he acquires any property or any property is devolved upon him during that period;

(c)   he becomes aware of any error in or omission from any information supplied by him to the official receiver after the determination date.

251J(6) **[Prescribed particulars of s.251J(3), (5) notification]** A notification under subsection (3) or (5) must give the prescribed particulars (if any) of the matter being notified.

GENERAL NOTE

A debtor who obtains a DRO has certain duties to provide assistance to the official receiver. These duties are similar to those owed by a bankrupt to the official receiver/trustee in bankruptcy. Note also IR r.5A.17 and the duty to notify OR of an increase in income or acquisition of property.

Objections, investigations and revocation

251K   Objections and investigations

251K(1) **[Creditors' right to object]** Any person specified in a debt relief order as a creditor to whom a specified qualifying debt is owed may object to–

(a)   the making of the order;

(b)   the inclusion of the debt in the list of the debtor's qualifying debts; or

(c)   the details of the debt specified in the order.

251K(2) **[Conditions for objection]** An objection under subsection (1) must be–

(a)   made during the moratorium period relating to the order and within the prescribed period for objections;

(b)   made to the official receiver in the prescribed manner;

(c)   based on a prescribed ground;

(d)   supported by any information and documents as may be prescribed;

and the prescribed period mentioned in paragraph (a) must not be less than 28 days after the creditor in question has been notified of the making of the order.

251K(3) **[Official receiver to consider objections]** The official receiver must consider every objection made to him under this section.

251K(4) **[Official receiver's power of investigation]** The official receiver may–

(a)   as part of his consideration of an objection, or

(b)   on his own initiative,

carry out an investigation of any matter that appears to the official receiver to be relevant to the making of any decision mentioned in subsection (5) in relation to a debt relief order or the debtor.

251K(5) **[Purpose of investigation]** The decisions to which an investigation may be directed are–

(a)   whether the order should be revoked or amended under section 251L;

(b)   whether an application should be made to the court under section 251M; or

(c)   whether any other steps should be taken in relation to the debtor.

251K(6) **[Duration of investigation power]** The power to carry out an investigation under this section is exercisable after (as well as during) the moratorium relating to the order.

251K(7) **[Official receiver's power to require information]** The official receiver may require any person to give him such information and assistance as he may reasonably require in connection with an investigation under this section.

251K(8)   [Investigation as official receiver thinks fit] Subject to anything prescribed in the rules as to the procedure to be followed in carrying out an investigation under this section, an investigation may be carried out by the official receiver in such manner as he thinks fit.

GENERAL NOTE

This is an important quality control mechanism in that it allows creditors with qualifying debts to object to the DRO, whereupon the official receiver must investigate. In certain circumstances the official receiver may investigate on his own initiative. See IR rr.5A.14 and 5A.15. The right of objection is available during the moratorium period but must be made within 28 days of notification of the DRO—IR r.5A.14(3). On the response options of the OR see IR r.5A.15.

251L   Power of official receiver to revoke or amend a debt relief order

251L(1)   [Power exercisable during moratorium] The official receiver may revoke or amend a debt relief order during the applicable moratorium period in the circumstances provided for by this section.

251L(2)   [Grounds for revocation] The official receiver may revoke the order on the ground that–

    (a)   any information supplied to him by the debtor–

        (i)   in, or in support of, the application, or

        (ii)   after the determination date,

    was incomplete, incorrect or otherwise misleading;

    (b)   the debtor has failed to comply with a duty under section 251J;

    (c)   a bankruptcy order has been made in relation to the debtor; or

    (d)   the debtor has made a proposal under Part 8 (or has notified the official receiver of his intention to do so).

251L(3)   [Revocation where official receiver should not have been satisfied] The official receiver may revoke the order on the ground that he should not have been satisfied–

    (a)   that the debts specified in the order were qualifying debts of the debtor as at the application date;

    (b)   that the conditions specified in Part 1 of Schedule 4ZA were met;

    (c)   that the conditions specified in Part 2 of that Schedule were met or that any failure to meet such a condition did not prevent his making the order.

251L(4)   [Revocation where Sch.4ZA paras 1 and 8 conditions not met] The official receiver may revoke the order on the ground that either or both of the conditions in paragraphs 7 and 8 of Schedule 4ZA (monthly surplus income and property) are not met at any time after the order was made.

For this purpose those paragraphs are to be read as if references to the determination date were references to the time in question.

251L(5)   [Date revocation takes effect] Where the official receiver decides to revoke the order, he may revoke it either–

    (a)   with immediate effect, or

    (b)   with effect from such date (not more than three months after the date of the decision) as he may specify.

251L(6)   [Duty of official receiver to consider] In considering when the revocation should take effect the official receiver must consider (in the light of the grounds on which the decision to revoke was made and all the other circumstances of the case) whether the debtor ought to be given the opportunity to make arrangements for making payments towards his debts.

251L(7)   [Revocation may be changed immediate effect] If the order has been revoked with effect from a specified date the official receiver may, if he thinks it appropriate to do so at any time before that date, revoke the order with immediate effect.

251L(8)   [Power to amend to correct error or omission] The official receiver may amend a debt relief order for the purpose of correcting an error in or omission from anything specified in the order.

251L(9)   [Amending power cannot add to qualifying debts] But subsection (8) does not permit the official receiver to add any debts that were not specified in the application for the debt relief order to the list of qualifying debts.

251L(10)   [Provision in rules] The rules may make further provision as to the procedure to be followed by the official receiver in the exercise of his powers under this section.

General Note

An official may revoke or amend a DRO. See further IR r.5A.16. Various grounds for revocation are identified—these include provision of incomplete/misleading information, failure to cooperate, the making of a bankruptcy order or the making of a proposal for an IVA. On registration see IR r.6A.5B.

Role of the court

251M   Powers of court in relation to debt relief orders

251M(1)   [Application to court by any person] Any person may make an application to the court if he is dissatisfied by any act, omission or decision of the official receiver in connection with a debt relief order or an application for such an order.

251M(2)   [Application for directions, or order re any matter] The official receiver may make an application to the court for directions or an order in relation to any matter arising in connection with a debt relief order or an application for such an order.

251M(3)   [Section 251M(2) matters include compliance with s.251J duty] The matters referred to in subsection (2) include, among other things, matters relating to the debtor's compliance with any duty arising under section 251J.

251M(4)   [Application at any time] An application under this section may, subject to anything in the rules, be made at any time.

251M(5)   [Power of court to extend moratorium period] The court may extend the moratorium period applicable to a debt relief order for the purposes of determining an application under this section.

251M(6)   [Power of court on application] On an application under this section the court may dismiss the application or do one or more of the following–

(a)   quash the whole or part of any act or decision of the official receiver;

(b)   give the official receiver directions (including a direction that he reconsider any matter in relation to which his act or decision has been quashed under paragraph (a));

(c)   make an order for the enforcement of any obligation on the debtor arising by virtue of a duty under section 251J;

(d)   extend the moratorium period applicable to the debt relief order;

(e)   make an order revoking or amending the debt relief order;

(f)   make an order under section 251N; or

(g)   make such other order as the court thinks fit.

251M(7)   [Section 251M(6)(e) revocation order] An order under subsection (6)(e) for the revocation of a debt relief order–

(a)   may be made during the moratorium period applicable to the debt relief order or at any time after that period has ended;

(b)   may be made on the court's own motion if the court has made a bankruptcy order in relation to the debtor during that period;

(c)   may provide for the revocation of the order to take effect on such terms and at such a time as the court may specify.

251M(8)   [Section 251M(6)(e) amendment order] An order under subsection (6)(e) for the amendment of a debt relief order may not add any debts that were not specified in the application for the debt relief order to the list of qualifying debts.

GENERAL NOTE

Another safety mechanism lies in the fact that a dissatisfied person may apply to court for it to overrule the official receiver. See IR r.5A.19. By comparing the counterpart provision in bankruptcy law one would imagine that most challenges will fail. The official receiver can also apply if the debtor fails to cooperate. Under IR r.5A.20 the court can extend the moratorium period whilst considering such an application. For the appropriate court for the application see IR r.5A.21.

251N   Inquiry into debtor's dealings and property

251N(1)   [Application by official receiver] An order under this section may be made by the court on the application of the official receiver.

251N(2)   [Persons who may be summoned to appear] An order under this section is an order summoning any of the following persons to appear before the court–

(a)   the debtor;

(b)   the debtor's spouse or former spouse or the debtor's civil partner or former civil partner;

(c)   any person appearing to the court to be able to give information or assistance concerning the debtor or his dealings, affairs and property.

251N(3)   [Requirement for persons in s.251N(2)(c)] The court may require a person falling within subsection (2)(c)–

(a)   to provide a written account of his dealings with the debtor; or

(b)   to produce any documents in his possession or under his control relating to the debtor or to the debtor's dealings, affairs or property.

251N(4)   [Application of s.251N(5)] Subsection (5) applies where a person fails without reasonable excuse to appear before the court when he is summoned to do so by an order under this section.

251N(5)   [Warrant for arrest or seizure] The court may cause a warrant to be issued to a constable or prescribed officer of the court–

(a)   for the arrest of that person, and

(b)   for the seizure of any records or other documents in that person's possession.

251N(6)   [Custody of person or holding of records etc.] The court may authorise a person arrested under such a warrant to be kept in custody, and anything seized under such a warrant to be held, in

274

accordance with the rules, until that person is brought before the court under the warrant or until such other time as the court may order.

GENERAL NOTE

The court (see IR r.5A.21 here) can order an investigation into the debtor's dealings or property. Third parties can be ordered to provide information. The court enjoys power to order arrest for non co-operation.

Offences

251O   False representations and omissions

251O(1)   [Applicant knowingly or recklessly making representation or omission] A person who makes an application for a debt relief order is guilty of an offence if he knowingly or recklessly makes any false representation or omission in making the application or providing any information or documents to the official receiver in support of the application.

251O(2)   [Applicant intentionally failing to comply with s.251J(3) duty] A person who makes an application for a debt relief order is guilty of an offence if–

(a)   he intentionally fails to comply with a duty under section 251J(3) in connection with the application; or

(b)   he knowingly or recklessly makes any false representation or omission in providing any information to the official receiver in connection with such a duty or otherwise in connection with the application.

251O(3)   [Immaterial for s.251O(3) offence whether order made] It is immaterial for the purposes of an offence under subsection (1) or (2) whether or not a debt relief order is made as a result of the application.

251O(4)   [Intentionally failing to comply with s.251J(5) duty after order] A person in respect of whom a debt relief order is made is guilty of an offence if–

(a)   he intentionally fails to comply with a duty under section 251J(5) in connection with the order; or

(b)   he knowingly or recklessly makes any false representation or omission in providing information to the official receiver in connection with such a duty or otherwise in connection with the performance by the official receiver of functions in relation to the order.

251O(5)   [Immaterial matters for s.251O(4) offence] It is immaterial for the purposes of an offence under subsection (4)–

(a)   whether the offence is committed during or after the moratorium period; and

(b)   whether or not the order is revoked after the conduct constituting the offence takes place.

GENERAL NOTE

This offence is similar to that found with regard to those who falsely procure IVAs (see Insolvency Act 1986 s.262A). The offence may still be committed even if the DRO is never obtained.

251P   Concealment or falsification of documents

251P(1)   [Offence] A person in respect of whom a debt relief order is made is guilty of an offence if, during the moratorium period in relation to that order–

(a)   he does not provide, at the request of the official receiver, all his books, papers and other records of which he has possession or control and which relate to his affairs;

   (b)   he prevents the production to the official receiver of any books, papers or other records relating to his affairs;

   (c)   he conceals, destroys, mutilates or falsifies, or causes or permits the concealment, destruction, mutilation or falsification of, any books, papers or other records relating his affairs;

   (d)   he makes, or causes or permits the making of, any false entries in any book, document or record relating to his affairs; or

   (e)   he disposes of, or alters or makes any omission in, or causes or permits the disposal, altering or making of any omission in, any book, document or record relating to his affairs.

251P(2)   **[Effective dates for s.251P(1)(b)–(e) offences]** A person in respect of whom a debt relief order is made is guilty of an offence if–

   (a)   he did anything falling within paragraphs (c) to (e) of subsection (1) during the period of 12 months ending with the application date; or

   (b)   he did anything falling within paragraphs (b) to (e) of subsection (1) after that date but before the effective date.

251P(3)   **[Defence if no intent to defraud or conceal]** A person is not guilty of an offence under this section if he proves that, in respect of the conduct constituting the offence, he had no intent to defraud or to conceal the state of his affairs.

251P(4)   **[Application of s.251P(2)(a) to trading record]** In its application to a trading record subsection (2)(a) has effect as if the reference to 12 months were a reference to two years.

251P(5)   **["Trading record"]** In subsection (4) **"trading record"** means a book, document or record which shows or explains the transactions or financial position of a person's business, including–

   (a)   a periodic record of cash paid and received,

   (b)   a statement of periodic stock-taking, and

   (c)   except in the case of goods sold by way of retail trade, a record of goods sold and purchased which identifies the buyer and seller or enables them to be identified.

251P(6)   **[Immaterial to offence if order revoked after conduct]** It is immaterial for the purposes of an offence under this section whether or not the debt relief order in question is revoked after the conduct constituting the offence takes place (but no offence is committed under this section by virtue of conduct occurring after the order is revoked).

GENERAL NOTE

There are some parallels here with bankrupts who conceal/falsify information (see Insolvency Act 1986 s.355). The offence applies to activities occurring within the moratorium period.

251Q   Fraudulent disposal of property

251Q(1)   **[Offence]** A person in respect of whom a debt relief order is made is guilty of an offence if he made or caused to be made any gift or transfer of his property during the period between–

   (a)   the start of the period of two years ending with the application date; and

   (b)   the end of the moratorium period.

251Q(2)   **[Transfer of property includes execution against it]** The reference in subsection (1) to making a transfer of any property includes causing or conniving at the levying of any execution against that property.

251Q(3) **[Defence if no intent to defraud or conceal]** A person is not guilty of an offence under this section if he proves that, in respect of the conduct constituting the offence, he had no intent to defraud or to conceal the state of his affairs.

251Q(4) **[Proof of lack of intention]** For the purposes of subsection (3) a person is to be taken to have proved that he had no such intent if–

(a) sufficient evidence is adduced to raise an issue as to whether he had such intent; and

(b) the contrary is not proved beyond reasonable doubt.

251Q(5) **[Immaterial to offence if order revoked after conduct]** It is immaterial for the purposes of this section whether or not the debt relief order in question is revoked after the conduct constituting an offence takes place (but no offence is committed by virtue of conduct occurring after the order is revoked).

GENERAL NOTE

Again the parallel here is to be found in bankruptcy law, notably Insolvency Act 1986 s.357. The court will look at events occurring within the two-year period prior to the making of the application for the DRO. Presumably, the law is seeking here to combat the practice whereby a would-be DRO applicant seeks to reduce assets in order to qualify for a DRO.

251R **Fraudulent dealing with property obtained on credit**

251R(1) **[Offence]** A person in respect of whom a debt relief order is made is guilty of an offence if during the relevant period he disposed of any property which he had obtained on credit and, at the time he disposed of it, had not paid for it.

251R(2) **[Offence by person acquiring or receiving property]** Any other person is guilty of an offence if during the relevant period he acquired or received property from a person in respect of whom a debt relief order was made (the "debtor") knowing or believing–

(a) that the debtor owed money in respect of the property, and

(b) that the debtor did not intend, or was unlikely to be able, to pay the money he so owed.

251R(3) **["Relevant period"]** In subsections (1) and (2) **"relevant period"** means the period between–

(a) the start of the period of two years ending with the application date; and

(b) the determination date.

251R(4) **[Defence of ordinary course of business]** A person is not guilty of an offence under subsection (1) or (2) if the disposal, acquisition or receipt of the property was in the ordinary course of a business carried on by the debtor at the time of the disposal, acquisition or receipt.

251R(5) **[Regard to price in ordinary course of business]** In determining for the purposes of subsection (4) whether any property is disposed of, acquired or received in the ordinary course of a business carried on by the debtor, regard may be had, in particular, to the price paid for the property.

251R(6) **[Defence if no intent to defraud or conceal]** A person is not guilty of an offence under subsection (1) if he proves that, in respect of the conduct constituting the offence, he had no intent to defraud or to conceal the state of his affairs.

251R(7) **[Disposing or acquiring include pawning or pledging]** In this section references to disposing of property include pawning or pledging it; and references to acquiring or receiving property shall be read accordingly.

251R(8) **[Immaterial to offence if order revoked after conduct]** It is immaterial for the purposes of this section whether or not the debt relief order in question is revoked after the conduct constituting an offence takes place (but no offence is committed by virtue of conduct occurring after the order is revoked).

GENERAL NOTE

The disposition of goods acquired on credit where those goods have not be paid for is a practice that should not be facilitated by the obtaining of a DRO. The disposal must have occurred within the two-year period prior to the application for the DRO even if the goods were obtained earlier than that period. Note the disponee might incur criminal liability under subs.(2). Of the defences, note the trading defence where the disposal is in the ordinary course of business.

251S   Obtaining credit or engaging in business

251S(1) [Offence] A person in respect of whom a debt relief order is made is guilty of an offence if, during the relevant period–

(a)   he obtains credit (either alone or jointly with any other person) without giving the person from whom he obtains the credit the relevant information about his status; or

(b)   he engages directly or indirectly in any business under a name other than that in which the order was made without disclosing to all persons with whom he enters into any business transaction the name in which the order was made.

251S(2)   [Relevant information as to status in s.251S(1)(a)] For the purposes of subsection (1)(a) the relevant information about a person's status is the information that–

(a)   a moratorium is in force in relation to the debt relief order,

(b)   a debt relief restrictions order is in force in respect of him, or

(c)   both a moratorium and a debt relief restrictions order is in force,

as the case may be.

251S(3)   ["Relevant period"] In subsection (1) **"relevant period"** means–

(a)   the moratorium period relating to the debt relief order, or

(b)   the period for which a debt relief restrictions order is in force in respect of the person in respect of whom the debt relief order is made,

as the case may be.

251S(4)   [Disapplication of s.251S(1)(a) if credit below prescribed amount] Subsection (1)(a) does not apply if the amount of the credit is less than the prescribed amount (if any).

251S(5)   [Further examples of obtaining credit] The reference in subsection (1)(a) to a person obtaining credit includes the following cases–

(a)   where goods are bailed to him under a hire-purchase agreement, or agreed to be sold to him under a conditional sale agreement;

(b)   where he is paid in advance (in money or otherwise) for the supply of goods or services.

GENERAL NOTE

This duty of disclosure applies to a person who is subject to a DRO or a DRRO. The figure for the purposes of subs.(4) is £500—see the Insolvency Proceedings (Monetary Limits) (Amendment) Order 2009 (SI 2009/465). For a comparable restriction on obtaining credit, see IA 1986 s.360.

251T   Offences: supplementary

251T(1)   [Proceedings instituted by Secretary of State for DPP] Proceedings for an offence under this Part may only be instituted by the Secretary of State or by or with the consent of the Director of Public Prosecutions.

251T(2)   [Conduct outside jurisdiction not a defence] It is not a defence in proceedings for an offence under this Part that anything relied on, in whole or in part, as constituting the offence was done outside England and Wales.

251T(3)   [Penalty] A person guilty of an offence under this Part is liable to imprisonment or a fine, or both (but see section 430).

GENERAL NOTE

This is a supplementary provision. Note the extraterritorial aspect in subs.(2).

Supplementary

251U   Approved intermediaries

251U(1)   ["Approved intermediary"] In this Part **"approved intermediary"** means an individual for the time being approved by a competent authority to act as an intermediary between a person wishing to make an application for a debt relief order and the official receiver.

251U(2)   ["Competent authority"] In this section **"competent authority"** means a person or body for the time being designated by the Secretary of State for the purposes of granting approvals under this section.

251U(3)   [Limitation of competent authority] Designation as a competent authority may be limited so as to permit the authority only to approve persons of a particular description.

251U(4)   [Power to make regulations] The Secretary of State may by regulations make provision as to–

(a)   the procedure for designating persons or bodies as competent authorities;

(b)   descriptions of individuals who are ineligible to be approved under this section;

(c)   the procedure for granting approvals under this section;

(d)   the withdrawal of designations or approvals under this section;

and provision made under paragraph (a) or (c) may include provision requiring the payment of fees.

251U(5)   [Provision in rules] The rules may make provision about the activities to be carried out by an approved intermediary in connection with an application for a debt relief order, which may in particular include–

(a)   assisting the debtor in making the application;

(b)   checking that the application has been properly completed;

(c)   sending the application to the official receiver.

251U(6)   [Provision about other activities in rules] The rules may also make provision about other activities to be carried out by approved intermediaries.

251U(7)   [No fee for approved intermediary] An approved intermediary may not charge a debtor any fee in connection with an application for a debt relief order.

251U(8) **[No liability in damages for approved intermediary]** An approved intermediary is not liable to any person in damages for anything done or omitted to be done when acting (or purporting to act) as an approved intermediary in connection with a particular application by a debtor for a debt relief order.

251U(9) **[Non-application of s.251U(8)]** Subsection (8) does not apply if the act or omission was in bad faith.

251U(10) **[Regulations under s.251U(4)]** Regulations under subsection (4) shall be made by statutory instrument subject to annulment in pursuance of a resolution of either House of Parliament.

GENERAL NOTE

This framework section deals with matters of relevance to the key operational feature of the DRO scheme, namely the channelling of applications though approved intermediaries. There is no direct right of access to a DRO—instead applications will in effect be filtered by professionals including insolvency practitioners.

For the rules relating to the designation of competent authorities see the Debt Relief Orders (Designation of Competent Authorities) Regulations 2009 (SI 2009/457). These regulations (amended by SI 2009/1553) also provide information on how the designated authorities should approve intermediaries.

251V   Debt relief restrictions orders and undertakings

251V Schedule 4ZB (which makes provision about debt relief restrictions orders and debt relief restrictions undertakings) has effect.

GENERAL NOTE

This keys in Sch.4ZB which deals with DRRO and DRRU and interim orders. Further detail is provided by IR rr.6.252–6.263. The grounds on which a DRRO may be obtained are identified in para.2(2) of the Schedule. If a debtor was an undischarged bankrupt within the previous six years he may come in for special attention.

251W   Register of debt relief orders etc

251W The Secretary of State must maintain a register of matters relating to–

(a)   debt relief orders;

(b)   debt relief restrictions orders; and

(c)   debt relief restrictions undertakings.

GENERAL NOTE

DROs, DRROs, and DRRUs, like bankruptcies and IVAs, will be in the public domain. For the public register (entries and deletion of entries) see IR rr.6A.5A, 6A.5B, 6A.7A and 6A.7B. But note the privacy concession in IR r.5A.18.

251X   Interpretation

251X(1) **[Definitions in Pt 7A]** In this Part–

"the application date", in relation to a debt relief order or an application for a debt relief order, means the date on which the application for the order is made to the official receiver;

"approved intermediary" has the meaning given in section 251U(1);

"debt relief order" means an order made by the official receiver under this Part;

"debtor" means–

(a)   in relation to an application for a debt relief order, the applicant; and

(b) in relation to a debt relief order, the person in relation to whom the order is made;

"debt relief restrictions order" and **"debt relief restrictions undertaking"** means an order made, or an undertaking accepted, under Schedule 4ZB;

"the determination date", in relation to a debt relief order or an application for a debt relief order, means the date on which the application for the order is determined by the official receiver;

"the effective date" has the meaning given in section 251E(7);

"excluded debt" is to be construed in accordance with section 251A;

"moratorium" and **"moratorium period"** are to be construed in accordance with sections 251G and 251H;

"qualifying debt", in relation to a debtor, has the meaning given in section 251A(2);

"the register" means the register maintained under section 251W;

"specified qualifying debt" has the meaning given in section 251G(1).

251X(2) **[Creditor in debt relief order]** In this Part references to a creditor specified in a debt relief order as the person to whom a qualifying debt is owed by the debtor include a reference to any person to whom the right to claim the whole or any part of the debt has passed, by assignment or operation of law, after the date of the application for the order.

GENERAL NOTE

This is a general interpretation division.

PART VIII

INDIVIDUAL VOLUNTARY ARRANGEMENTS

Introductory note to Part VIII
The provisions of Pt VIII deal with voluntary arrangements entered into by debtors as an alternative to bankruptcy. A debtor can select a "nominee" to put his proposals into effect. Prior to 1985, a debtor who wished to make an arrangement with his creditors to avoid the consequences of bankruptcy could use the Deeds of Arrangement Act 1914 much of which has survived IA 1986. The problem with a deed of arrangement made under this 1914 legislation was that it could easily be frustrated by a dissenting creditor petitioning for bankruptcy, especially as the mere execution of a deed of arrangement was construed as an act of bankruptcy. Consequently, such deeds of arrangement came to be increasingly under-employed (there were only 51 in 1984). Deeds of arrangement have not been abolished, but rather have been left to wither on the vine. Deeds of arrangement and individual voluntary arrangements are mutually exclusive: see s.260(3) below. There were two deeds of arrangement entered into in 1992, though this figure had leaped to four for 1997. Since then the deed of arrangement has become extinct. The annual report of the Secretary of State made under s.379 must disclose statistics concerning the Deeds of Arrangement Act 1914. Under BA 1914 ss.16, 17, and 21 there was provision for schemes of composition or arrangement once bankruptcy proceedings had started (and even after adjudication). These provisions were little used and have now been supplanted by the more flexible system of voluntary arrangements established by the 1985 Act, and now to be found in the 1986 legislation. The Cork Committee (*Report*, para.399) called for the introduction of a more effective system of voluntary arrangements. Although IA 1986 has not adopted the specific Cork proposal for debts arrangement orders, the general policy of the Cork Committee has been followed.

The original IVA regime as set forth in Pt VIII of the Insolvency Act 1986 has been the subject of significant changes introduced through the medium of s.3 of and Sch.3 to the Insolvency Act 2000. The IVA regime has undergone change as a result of IA 2000. Procedural modifications have been introduced, including the decoupling of the IVA institution from the interim order. An IVA can come into being without the need for an interim order in an appropriate case. These reforms took effect on January 1, 2003.

A number of further changes were also introduced into the IVA mechanism via the provisions of EA 2002. These latter reforms, which include the "fast-track IVA", did not take effect until April 2004.

Individual voluntary arrangements have proved popular with debtors. For background discussion see Williams, (1986) 2 I.L. & P. 11. The impact of the new system of individual voluntary arrangements is covered by Pond in (1988) 4 I.L. & P. 66, 104; (1989) 5 I.L. & P. 73; [1995] J.B.L. 118. There were 44,332 IVAs entered into in 2006 (as compared to 62,956 bankruptcies). This increasing popularity may be attributed to a number of factors. The moratorium initiated by the interim order does allow a period of calm during which a debtor can seek to come to a mutually beneficial arrangement with his creditors without fear of an impatient creditor throwing a spanner in the works by petitioning for bankruptcy. Statistics do show that creditors achieve a higher rate of return under an IVA because the administration costs are so much lower—rates of return double those found in bankruptcy cases are sometimes cited. An increasingly important advantage for the debtor is that in avoiding bankruptcy he also avoids the attendant restrictions and disqualifications—e.g. the bar on becoming a company director. For the impact of an IVA on a debtor's right to litigate see *Envis v Thakkar* [1997] B.P.I.R. 189. For general discussion see Mullarkey, (1993) 137 S.J. 192; Oditah, [1994] L.M.C.L.Q. 210; and Pond, (1993) 9 Insolv. L. 9; (1994) 10 Insolv. L. 2. See Tonge, [2006] 19 Insolv. Int. 53.

Although the IVA has proved a statistical success there are concerns with regard to its operation. It can be relatively expensive to operate (though not so expensive as bankruptcy). Critics have said that it is over-legalistic. R3 has responded by introducing model IVA terms but these are not compulsory. The IVA does also have a high failure rate, which might suggest that it is inefficient or being used in unsuitable cases. For a review of these operational and wider policy issues see the report by Michael Green, *Individual Voluntary Arrangements: Over-indebtedness and the Insolvency Regime* (November 2002) (short report mounted on Insolvency Service website). At the end of the day Green concludes that if the IVA is reformed to neutralise its deficiencies it should become the premier model for dealing with personal insolvency, thereby relegating bankruptcy to a secondary role. As a result of concerns about potential misselling of IVAs the IVA Forum agreed an IVA Protocol in January 2008. This is essentially a guide to best practice. Details of the background to this initiative and associated document can be accessed via *Dear IP*, March 2008. The Insolvency Service produced proposals in 2005 for a deregulated IVA model (or models) denominated SIVA 1 and SIVA 2 (simplified IVAs). The intention behind these is to cut down on bureaucracy and thereby to reduce costs. Essentially SIVAs would not permit modifications of proposals which would be offered to creditors on a "take it, or leave it" basis. The thinking on the SIVA proposals was contained in an Insolvency Service consultative document (posted on its website) which was published in March 2006. See generally Barc, (2005) 21 I.L. & P. 168. The move towards the introduction of simplified IVAs took a step forward with the publication of a consultative document by the Insolvency Service in May 2007 (see Insolvency Service Press Notice May 4, 2007). Under these proposals simplified IVAs would be available to those debtors owing less than £75k. A simplified IVA can be entered into by procuring the support of only a simple majority of creditors. Meetings as such are not to be held; voting will be by post. Creditors claims are to be filed with the IP within 90 days. Many of the more formal procedural/filing/reporting rules relating to IVAs will be waived. Turnaround specialists would be able to supervise IVAs and s.389A will be amended to make this clear. Deeds of arrangement will finally be abolished. There will also be a general restructuring of Pt VIII to make it easier to understand. It was intended to introduce the SIVA and these other reforms via a legislative reform order under the Legislative and Regulatory Reform Act 2006 with the changes to be introduced at some stage in 2008. For discussion of these proposals see Pond [2007] 20 Insolv. Int. 9. In December 2008 the Government suddenly announced that it was abandoning plans to introduce the SIVA model through a legislative reform order. The reason given for this policy change was the success of the IVA Protocol, which had been agreed earlier that year between IPs, major creditors and the Insolvency Service. This Protocol had reduced costs associated with IVAs, one of the main reasons behind the introduction of SIVAs.

The IVA procedure does not apply in Scotland (see s.440(2)). However, a somewhat comparable procedure, known as the debt arrangement scheme, was introduced via the Debt Arrangement and Attachment (Scotland) Act 2002. This Scottish Act has spawned a considerable quantity of secondary legislation including the Debt Arrangement Scheme (Scotland) Regulations 2004 (SSI 2004/468) (as amended by SSI 2004/470); The Debt Arrangement and Attachment (Scotland) Act 2002 (Transfer of Functions to the Accountant in Bankruptcy) Order 2004 (SSI 2004/448); Act of Sederunt (Debt Arrangement and Attachment (Scotland) Act 2002) Amendment (The Debt Arrangement Scheme (Scotland) Regulations 2004) 2004 (SSI 2004/505); and the Act of Sederunt (Sheriff Court Bankruptcy Rules) 1996 Amendment 2004 (SSI 2004/534).

Part VIII of the Act is supplemented by IR 1986 rr.5.1–5.68 and by *Practice Direction (Bankruptcy: Voluntary Arrangements)* [1992] 1 W.L.R. 120. Note in particular that it is a crime fraudulently to procure a voluntary arrangement: IA 1986 s.262A. Although IVAs are provided with a statutory framework, the fact that they are at heart contracts must not be forgotten—*Raja v Rubin* [1999] B.P.I.R. 575. As to who might qualify as a creditor for the purposes of an IVA see *Legal Services Commission v Thipthorpe* [2009] B.P.I.R. 1399.

The Insolvency Service estimates that only 3 per cent of IVAs are post bankruptcy IVAs including fast track IVAs—see Insolvency Service Consultative Document May 2007 para.30.

Moratorium for insolvent debtor

252   Interim order of court

252(1)   [Power of court] In the circumstances specified below, the court may in the case of a debtor (being an individual) make an interim order under this section.

252(2)   [Effect of interim order] An interim order has the effect that, during the period for which it is in force–

(a)   no bankruptcy petition relating to the debtor may be presented or proceeded with,

(aa) no landlord or other person to whom rent is payable may exercise any right of forfeiture by peaceable re-entry in relation to premises let to the debtor in respect of a failure by the debtor to comply with any term or condition of his tenancy of such premises, except with the leave of the court, and

(b)   no other proceedings, and no execution or other legal process, may be commenced or continued and no distress may be levied against the debtor or his property except with the leave of the court.

S.252(1)

In effect, this section allows for an application for an interim order in circumstances described in s.253. On the exercise of discretion see s.255. Prior to the coming into force of the Insolvency Act 2000 the making of an interim order was an essential prerequisite to any valid IVA—*Fletcher v Vooght* [2000] B.P.I.R. 435.

S.252(2)

The effect of an interim order is to impose a moratorium on proceedings *against* an insolvent debtor (see *Frost v Unity Trust Bank* [1998] B.P.I.R. 459). The aim of this provision is to prevent a viable proposal being destroyed by a selfish creditor. For an early illustration of an interim order being used to prevent a sheriff acting on behalf of judgment creditors from completing the execution process, see *Re Peake* [1987] C.L.Y. 215 (Blackburn County Court). An attempt to use an interim order to continually block bankruptcy proceedings proved unsuccessful before Scott J. in *Re a Debtor (No.83 of 1988)* [1990] 1 W.L.R. 708 (this case is reported as *Re Cove (a Debtor)* in [1990] 1 All E.R. 949).

In *Re M (Restraint Order)* [1992] 2 W.L.R. 340 Otton J. held that the making of an interim order under s.252 did not affect the right of the prosecution to make an application for a receiver of realisable property of a person against whom a restraint order had already been made under s.8 of the Drug Trafficking Offences Act 1986. The effect of the interim order was only to protect assets not already covered by the restraint order. Assets covered by the restraint order could no longer be considered as part of the debtor's estate until the defendant was either acquitted, in which case the restraint order would be discharged, or convicted whereupon the restraint order would be converted into a confiscation order. See also *R. v Barnet Justices Ex p. Phillippou* [1997] B.P.I.R. 134, where the court concluded that an interim order did not offer protection against the enforcement of a criminal compensation order which was viewed as being akin to a fine.

The wording of s.252(2) was modified by s.3 of and Sch.3 to IA 2000 to strengthen the moratorium by the amendment of subs.(2)(b). Note the addition of subpara.2(2)(aa) covering forfeiture by a landlord and the inclusion of distress within the moratorium. Thus *Re A Debtor (No.13A IO and 14A IO of 1994)* [1995] 1 W.L.R. 1127; [1996] B.C.C. 57 is no longer representative of the law. The latter amendment of subs.(2)(b) counteracts *McMullen & Sons v Cerrone* [1994] B.C.C. 25.

For the consequences of non-compliance with s.252(2) see *Clarke v Coutts & Co (a firm)* [2002] EWCA Civ 943; [2002] B.P.I.R. 916.

253   Application for interim order

253(1)   [Where application made] Application to the court for an interim order may be made where the debtor intends to make a proposal under this Part, that is, a proposal to his creditors for a composition in satisfaction of his debts or a scheme of arrangement of his affairs (from here on referred to, in either case, as a "voluntary arrangement").

253(2)   **[Nominee]** The proposal must provide for some person ("the nominee") to act in relation to the voluntary arrangement either as trustee or otherwise for the purpose of supervising its implementation and the nominee must be a person who is qualified to act as an insolvency practitioner, or authorised to act as nominee, in relation to the voluntary arrangement.

253(3)   **[Applicants]** Subject as follows, the application may be made–

(a)   if the debtor is an undischarged bankrupt, by the debtor, the trustee of his estate, or the official receiver, and

(b)   in any other case, by the debtor.

253(4)   **[Notice for s.253(3)(a)]** An application shall not be made under subsection (3)(a) unless the debtor has given notice of the proposal to the official receiver and, if there is one, the trustee of his estate.

253(5)   **[When application not to be made]** An application shall not be made while a bankruptcy petition presented by the debtor is pending, if the court has, under section 273 below, appointed an insolvency practitioner to inquire into the debtor's affairs and report.

GENERAL NOTE

A number of relatively minor textual amendments were made to s.253(1), (2) and (4) by s.3 of and Sch.3 to IA 2000. The amendment to subs.(2) reflects the fact that in future a wider category of professionals may be permitted to act as nominees/supervisors of voluntary arrangements.

S.253(1)–(3)

These provisions define the essence of the proposal for a voluntary arrangement, to implement which the interim order is sought, and they identify who may apply for an interim order. In an appropriate case the FSA may be heard on such an application—FSMA 2000 s.357(1). For further details, see IR 1986 rr.5.2–5.6. It seems that an interim order may be sought in respect of partnership debts: *Re Cupit (Note)* [1996] B.P.I.R. 560. A discharged bankrupt cannot access the IVA procedure by seeking an interim order—*Wright v Official Receiver* [2001] B.P.I.R. 196. Compare *Re Ravichandran* [2004] B.P.I.R. 814—same result where discharge came *after* interim order but *before* IVA agreed.

S.253(4)

Where the debtor is an undischarged bankrupt two business days' notice is required: see IR 1986 r.5.7(4).

S.253(5)

This provision restricts an application for an interim order where a bankruptcy petition is pending and the affairs of the debtor are being investigated under s.273. This is because the court can on its own initiative, in such circumstances, grant an interim order.

254   Effect of application

254(1)   **[Stay pending interim order]** At any time when an application under section 253 for an interim order is pending–

(a)   no landlord or other person to whom rent is payable may exercise any right of forfeiture by peaceable re-entry in relation to premises let to the debtor in respect of a failure by the debtor to comply with any term or condition of his tenancy of such premises, except with the leave of the court, and

(b)   the court may forbid the levying of any distress on the debtor's property or its subsequent sale, or both, and stay any action, execution or other legal process against the property or person of the debtor.

254(2)   **[Stay or continuance]** Any court in which proceedings are pending against an individual may, on proof that an application under that section has been made in respect of that individual, either stay the proceedings or allow them to continue on such terms as it thinks fit.

General Note

Where an application for an interim order is pending, the court can take immediate steps to protect the debtor and his assets from legal action. (For the meaning of "the court", see s.385(1).) Indeed, any court in which proceedings are pending can also take such protective steps. The effect of the application has been broadened by s.3 of and Sch.3 to IA 2000 to enable the court to place restrictions on forfeiture and distress.

255 Cases in which interim order can be made

255(1) [Conditions for order] The court shall not make an interim order on an application under section 253 unless it is satisfied–

(a) that the debtor intends to make a proposal under this Part;

(b) that on the day of the making of the application the debtor was an undischarged bankrupt or was able to petition for his own bankruptcy;

(c) that no previous application has been made by the debtor for an interim order in the period of 12 months ending with that day; and

(d) that the nominee under the debtor's proposal is willing to act in relation to the proposal.

255(2) [Order to facilitate consideration and implementation of proposal] The court may make an order if it thinks that it would be appropriate to do so for the purpose of facilitating the consideration and implementation of the debtor's proposal.

255(3) [Where debtor is undischarged bankrupt] Where the debtor is an undischarged bankrupt, the interim order may contain provision as to the conduct of the bankruptcy, and the administration of the bankrupt's estate, during the period for which the order is in force.

255(4) [Extent of s.255(3) provision] Subject as follows, the provision contained in an interim order by virtue of subsection (3) may include provision staying proceedings in the bankruptcy or modifying any provision in this Group of Parts, and any provision of the rules in their application to the debtor's bankruptcy.

255(5) [Limit to interim order] An interim order shall not, in relation to a bankrupt, make provision relaxing or removing any of the requirements of provisions in this Group of Parts, or of the rules, unless the court is satisfied that that provision is unlikely to result in any significant diminution in, or in the value of, the debtor's estate for the purposes of the bankruptcy.

255(6) [When order ceases to have effect] Subject to the following provisions of this Part, an interim order made on an application under section 253 ceases to have effect at the end of the period of 14 days beginning with the day after the making of the order.

S.255(1), (2)

These subsections deal with the circumstances under which the court may make an interim order. Note the minor textual change to subs.(1) by IA 2000 s.3 and Sch.3. Section 255(2) gives general discretion provided the order would facilitate the consideration and implementation of the proposals. Section 255(1) cuts down this discretion by establishing a series of pre-conditions. For the criteria applied by the court when exercising its discretion under s.255(2) of the Insolvency Act 1986 see *Davidson v Stanley* [2004] EWHC 2595 (Ch); [2005] B.P.I.R. 279. Here an interim order was refused as the debtor's proposal was wholly unrealistic. The reference in s.255(1)(d) to the nominee being qualified was removed by Sch.5 to IA 2000 on the authority of s.15(1). The debtor must not have applied for a similar order within the previous 12 months. This restriction cannot be circumvented by an application under s.375—*Hurst v Bennett (No.2)* [2002] B.P.I.R. 102.

The proposal must be viable: *Cooper v Fearnley* [1997] B.P.I.R. 20; *Hook v Jewson Ltd* [1997] B.C.C. 752; *Knowles v Coutts & Co* [1998] B.P.I.R. 96. It appears that this "viability" requirement permits the court to review the proposed fee for the nominee—*Re Julie O'Sullivan* [2001] B.P.I.R. 534.

S.255(3)–(5)

These provisions deal with supplementary matters that may be included in the interim order where the applicant is an undischarged bankrupt—but such a provision in an interim order must not reduce the value of the debtor's estate.

S.255(6)

The interim order will normally expire within 14 days of the order. Unfortunately, the wording of s.255(6) is not reflected in Form 5.2. The Insolvency Service has picked up this error (see *Dear IP*, March 2008) but the Form cannot be changed until the Insolvency Rules are themselves amended.

256   Nominee's report on debtor's proposal

256(1)   **[Report to court]** Where an interim order has been made on an application under section 253, the nominee shall, before the order ceases to have effect, submit a report to the court stating–

     (a)   whether, in his opinion, the voluntary arrangement which the debtor is proposing has a reasonable prospect of being approved and implemented,

     (aa)   whether, in his opinion, a meeting of the debtor's creditors should be summoned to consider the debtor's proposal, and

     (b)   if in his opinion such a meeting should be summoned, the date on which, and time and place at which, he proposes the meeting should be held.

256(2)   **[Information to nominee]** For the purpose of enabling the nominee to prepare his report the debtor shall submit to the nominee–

     (a)   a document setting out the terms of the voluntary arrangement which the debtor is proposing, and

     (b)   a statement of his affairs containing–

         (i)   such particulars of his creditors and of his debts and other liabilities and of his assets as may be prescribed, and

         (ii)   such other information as may be prescribed.

256(3)   **[Directions by court]** The court may–

     (a)   on an application made by the debtor in a case where the nominee has failed to submit the report required by this section or has died, or

     (b)   on an application made by the debtor or the nominee in a case where it is impracticable or inappropriate for the nominee to continue to act as such, direct that the nominee shall be replaced as such by another person qualified to act as an insolvency practitioner, or authorised to act as nominee, in relation to the voluntary arrangement.

256(3A)   **[Further directions]** The court may, on an application made by the debtor in a case where the nominee has failed to submit the report required by this section, direct that the interim order shall continue, or (if it has ceased to have effect) be renewed, for such further period as the court may specify in the direction.

256(4)   **[Extension of period of interim order]** The court may, on the application of the nominee, extend the period for which the interim order has effect so as to enable the nominee to have more time to prepare his report.

256(5)   **[Extension for consideration by creditors]** If the court is satisfied on receiving the nominee's report that a meeting of the debtor's creditors should be summoned to consider the debtor's proposal, the court shall direct that the period for which the interim order has effect shall be extended, for such further period as it may specify in the direction, for the purpose of enabling the debtor's proposal to be considered by his creditors in accordance with the following provisions of this Part.

256(6)   **[Discharge of interim order]** The court may discharge the interim order if it is satisfied, on the application of the nominee–

     (a)   that the debtor has failed to comply with his obligations under subsection (2), or

(b)   that for any other reason it would be inappropriate for a meeting of the debtor's creditors to be summoned to consider the debtor's proposal.

S.256(1)

The nominee of the debtor must, before the interim order has expired (see s.255(6)), report to the court whether in his opinion it is worth calling a creditors' meeting to consider the debtor's proposal. For the nominee's responsibilities when evaluating the proposal see *Greystoke v Hamilton-Smith* [1997] B.P.I.R. 24; and *Shah v Cooper* [2003] B.P.I.R. 1018. The wording of subs.(1) was subsequently amended by IA 2000 s.3 and Sch.3 by the insertion of a new sub-para.(a) requiring the nominee to attest to the viability of the proposal, thus reflecting the standards previously developed at common law. For general discussion of the responsibilities of nominees, see *Prosser v Castle Sanderson (a firm)* [2002] EWCA Civ 1140; [2003] B.C.C. 440. This provision was considered in *Tradition (UK) Ltd v Ahmed* [2009] B.P.I.R. 626. See in general IR 1986 rr.5.2, 5.3, 5.11, 5.12.

S.256(2)

To facilitate the nominee making his report, the debtor must submit to him details of his proposal and statement of affairs. See IR 1986 rr.5.5, 5.6.

S.256(3), (3A)

Subsection (3) has been replaced and subs.(3A) inserted by s.3 of and Sch.3 to IA 2000. If the nominee fails to submit a report the debtor can apply to the court to have him replaced, and the interim order may be extended in such a situation. See IR 1986 r.5.12.

S.256(4)

This also allows for the extension of the order where the nominee requires more time to prepare his report.

S.256(5)

If, after receiving the nominee's report, the court is satisfied that a meeting of creditors should be summoned, the court can again extend the interim order. Note also IR 1986 rr.5.10, 5.12. Several such extensions can be granted but the patience of the court is not limitless: *Re a Debtor (No.83 of 1988)* [1990] 1 W.L.R. 708.

S.256(6)

The interim order can be discharged by the court if the debtor has failed to play his part or if it would be inappropriate to call a creditors' meeting.

Procedure where no interim order made

256A   Debtor's proposal and nominee's report

256A(1)   [Application] This section applies where a debtor (being an individual)–

(a)   intends to make a proposal under this Part (but an interim order has not been made in relation to the proposal and no application for such an order is pending), and

(b)   if he is an undischarged bankrupt, has given notice of the proposal to the official receiver and, if there is one, the trustee of his estate,

unless a bankruptcy petition presented by the debtor is pending and the court has, under section 273, appointed an insolvency practitioner to inquire into the debtor's affairs and report.

256A(2)   [Duty of debtor] For the purpose of enabling the nominee to prepare a report under subsection (3), the debtor shall submit to the nominee–

(a)   a document setting out the terms of the voluntary arrangement which the debtor is proposing, and

(b)   a statement of his affairs containing–

    (i)   such particulars of his creditors and of his debts and other liabilities and of his assets as may be prescribed, and

    (ii)   such other information as may be prescribed.

256A(3)   [Report of nominee] If the nominee is of the opinion that the debtor is an undischarged bankrupt, or is able to petition for his own bankruptcy, the nominee shall, within 14 days (or such longer period as the court may allow) after receiving the document and statement mentioned in subsection (2), submit a report to the debtor's creditors stating–

   (a)   whether, in his opinion, the voluntary arrangement which the debtor is proposing has a reasonable prospect of being approved and implemented,

   (b)   whether, in his opinion, a meeting of the debtor's creditors should be summoned to consider the debtor's proposal, and

   (c)   if in his opinion such a meeting should be summoned, the date on which, and time and place at which, he proposes the meeting should be held.

256A(4)   **[Court response]** The court may–

   (a)   on an application made by the debtor in a case where the nominee has failed to submit the report required by this section or has died, or

   (b)   on an application made by the debtor or the nominee in a case where it is impracticable or inappropriate for the nominee to continue to act as such,

direct that the nominee shall be replaced as such by another person qualified to act as an insolvency practitioner, or authorised to act as nominee, in relation to the voluntary arrangement.

256A(5)   **[Time limit extended]** The court may, on an application made by the nominee, extend the period within which the nominee is to submit his report.

GENERAL NOTE

This new provision was introduced by IA 2000 s.3 and Sch.3 with effect from January 1, 2003. It is designed to decouple the IVA procedure from the need to have an interim order. Under the original model a purported IVA constructed without an interim order was a nullity—*Fletcher v Vooght* [2000] B.P.I.R. 435. See IR rr.5.2, 5.14A, 5.14B.

S.256A(1)
This defines where s.256A applies.

S.256A(2)
This indicates the information required of the debtor.

S.256A(3), (5)
Note that the reporting obligation was amended by LRO 2010 (SI 2010/18). Where the nominee reaches certain conclusions on the documentation furnished to him he makes a report to creditors on whether an IVA is suitable. The 14-day period may be extended—subs.(5).

S.256A(4)
This provides a protective mechanism for the debtor where the nominee has failed to act in accordance with subs.(4).

S.256A(5)
The court can extend the time-limit specified in subs.(3).

Creditors' meeting

257   Summoning of creditors' meeting

257(1)   **[Meeting to be summoned]** Where it has been reported to the court under section 256 or to the debtor's creditors under section 256A that a meeting of debtor's creditors should be summoned, the nominee (or the nominee's replacement under section 256(3) or 256A(4)) shall summon that meeting for the time, date and place proposed in the nominee's report unless, in the case of a report to which section 256 applies, the court otherwise directs.

257(2)   **[Persons summoned to meeting]** The persons to be summoned to the meeting are every creditor of the debtor of whose claim and address the person summoning the meeting is aware.

257(3)   [Creditors of debtor] For this purpose the creditors of a debtor who is an undischarged bankrupt include–

(a)   every person who is a creditor of the bankrupt in respect of a bankruptcy debt, and

(b)   every person who would be such a creditor if the bankruptcy had commenced on the day on which notice of the meeting is given.

S.257(1)

Subsection (1) was substituted by LRO 2010 (SI 2010/18). This deals with reporting obligations. This provision requires the nominee to summon the meeting of creditors in accordance with his report, unless the court has directed otherwise. In *Re a Debtor (No.83 of 1988)* [1990] 1 W.L.R. 708, Scott J. held that this provision (in appropriate circumstances) enables the court to discharge any previous order directing that a creditors' meeting be convened. In order for the approval of the IVA to be binding the meeting must be summoned strictly in accordance with the report to the court—*Re N (a Debtor)* [2002] B.P.I.R. 1024. Minor textual changes were made by IA 2000 s.3 and Sch.3 to cater for the advent of s.256A.

In *Vlieland-Boddy v Dexter Ltd* [2003] EWHC 2592 (Ch); [2004] B.P.I.R. 235 the High Court indicated that if the registrar was not satisfied that a creditors' meeting under s.257 should be called then any such meeting that was held could not be regarded as a valid meeting for the purposes of Pt VIII of the Insolvency Act 1986.

In *Re Plummer* [2004] B.P.I.R. 767 it was held by Registrar Baister that for IVA modifications to become binding it must be proved that the debtor assented to them. Therefore a report by the chairman of the creditors' meeting held under s.257 that an IVA had been proved was inaccurate and the purported IVA was a total nullity.

S.257(2), (3)

These subsections identify which creditors are to be summoned to the meeting—this will depend on whether the debtor is an undischarged bankrupt or not. An FSA representative may attend in an appropriate case—FSMA 2000 s.357(3).

For further information, reference should be made to IR 1986 rr.5.17–5.24.

Consideration and implementation of debtor's proposal

258   Decisions of creditors' meeting

258(1)   [Decision re approval] A creditors' meeting summoned under section 257 shall decide whether to approve the proposed voluntary arrangement.

258(2)   [Approval with modifications] The meeting may approve the proposed voluntary arrangement with modifications, but shall not do so unless the debtor consents to each modification.

258(3)   [Extent of modifications] The modifications subject to which the proposed voluntary arrangement may be approved may include one conferring the functions proposed to be conferred on the nominee on another person qualified to act as an insolvency practitioner or authorised to act as nominee, in relation to the voluntary arrangement.

But they shall not include any modification by virtue of which the proposal ceases to be a proposal under this Part.

258(4)   [Certain modifications not to be approved] The meeting shall not approve any proposal or modification which affects the right of a secured creditor of the debtor to enforce his security, except with the concurrence of the creditor concerned.

258(5)   [Other modifications not to be approved] Subject as follows, the meeting shall not approve any proposal or modification under which–

(a)   any preferential debt of the debtor is to be paid otherwise than in priority to such of his debts as are not preferential debts, or

(b)   a preferential creditor of the debtor is to be paid an amount in respect of a preferential debt that bears to that debt a smaller proportion than is borne to another preferential debt by the amount that is to be paid in respect of that other debt.

However, the meeting may approve such a proposal or modification with the concurrence of the preferential creditor concerned.

258(6) **[Meeting in accordance with rules]** Subject as above, the meeting shall be conducted in accordance with the rules.

258(7) **[Definitions]** In this section **"preferential debt"** has the meaning given by section 386 in Part XII; and **"preferential creditor"** is to be construed accordingly.

S.258(1)

The meeting of creditors can either approve or reject the composition which is being put to them. No mention is made of any required majority—under BA 1914 ss.16(2) and 21(1) it was three-fourths in value of the debtor's creditors: IR 1986 r.5.23 essentially retains the position, although it actually specifies a majority *in excess of* three-quarters. The decision of the meeting is final: *Kent Carpets Ltd v Symes* [1996] B.C.C. 137.

S.258(2)–(5)

These provisions deal with modifications to the proposed scheme. Textual changes were made to subs.(3) by s.3 of, and Sch.3 to, IA 2000. The debtor must assent to any modification and the modification may involve a change of nominee, but the basic proposal must still fall within s.253. A modified IVA that does not have the support of the debtor is void—*Reid v Hamblin* [2001] B.P.I.R. 929. Changes affecting the rights of secured creditors are only permitted in so far as the secured creditors agree, see *Khan v Permayer* [2001] B.P.I.R. 95 where the secured creditor waived his security in favour of a dividend. See also *Rey v FNCB Ltd* [2006] EWHC 1386 (Ch). On who is a secured creditor for these purposes see *Re a Debtor (No.10 of 1992)* [1995] Ch. 525, reported as *Peck v Craighead* [1995] B.C.C. 525. Similar protection is available to consolidate the priority enjoyed by preferential creditors on bankruptcy. This confirms the position under BA 1914 s.16(19).

S.258(6)

The meeting must be conducted according to the rules: see IR 1986 rr.5.17–5.24.

S.258(7)

This defines preferential debts, etc. for the purposes of this provision.

259   Report of decisions to court

259(1) **[Notice of result of meeting; report to court]** After the conclusion in accordance with the rules of the meeting summoned under section 257, the chairman of the meeting shall–

(a)   give notice of the result of the meeting to such persons as may be prescribed, and

(b)   where the meeting was summoned under section 257 pursuant to a report to the court under section 256(1)(aa), report the result of it to the court.

259(2) **[Discharge of interim order]** If the report is that the meeting has declined (with or without modifications) to approve the voluntary arrangement proposed under section 256, the court may discharge any interim order which is in force in relation to the debtor.

GENERAL NOTE

Subsection (1) was substituted and subs.(2) amended by LRO 2010 (SI 2010/18). The change relates to reporting obligations. The chairman of the creditors' meeting must report its decision to the court and give notice to prescribed persons. If the creditors have completely rejected the debtor's proposals, the court may discharge any interim order.
    For further obligations imposed on the chairman, see IR 1986 rr.5.19–5.24.

260   Effect of approval

260(1) **[Effect]** This section has effect where the meeting summoned under section 257 approves the proposed voluntary arrangement (with or without modifications).

260(2) **[Effect of approved composition or scheme]** The approved arrangement–

(a)   takes effect as if made by the debtor at the meeting, and

(b)   binds every person who in accordance with the rules–

     (i)   was entitled to vote at the meeting (whether or not he was present or represented at it), or

     (ii)   would have been so entitled if he had had notice of it,

as if he were a party to the arrangement.

260(2A)   [Amounts payable under s.260(2)(b)(ii)] If–

(a)   when the arrangement ceases to have effect any amount payable under the arrangement to a person bound by virtue of subsection (2)(b)(ii) has not been paid, and

(b)   the arrangement did not come to an end prematurely, the debtor shall at that time become liable to pay to that person the amount payable under the arrangement.

260(3)   [Deeds of Arrangement Act] The Deeds of Arrangement Act 1914 does not apply to the approved voluntary arrangement.

260(4)   [Certain interim orders to cease] Any interim order in force in relation to the debtor immediately before the end of the period of 28 days beginning with the day on which the report with respect to the creditors' meeting was made to the court under section 259 ceases to have effect at the end of that period.

This subsection applies except to such extent as the court may direct for the purposes of any application under section 262 below.

260(5)   [Bankruptcy petition stayed by s.260(4) interim order] Where proceedings on a bankruptcy petition have been stayed by an interim order which ceases to have effect under subsection (4), that petition is deemed, unless the court otherwise orders, to have been dismissed.

S.260(1), (2), (2A)

Subsection 2(b) was replaced and subs.(2A) was inserted by IA 2000 s.3 and Sch.3. These modifications deal with the position of unknown creditors and their rights in cesser of the arrangement in circumstances where they have still not been paid. Where the creditors' meeting approves the debtor's proposal (whether modified or not), this will bind every person falling within s.260(2)(b). A creditor can split a debt and be bound by the IVA only in respect of part of the sums owing: *Re Hoare* [1997] B.P.I.R. 683. The legislation does not fully bring out the contractual foundation of a voluntary arrangement. That has been illustrated by court decisions. For example, in *Welburn v Dibb Lupton Broomhead* [2002] EWCA Civ 1601; [2003] B.P.I.R. 768, the court indicated that whether a cause of action had become one of the "trust assets" was essentially a matter of contractual construction.

A secured creditor who accepts a dividend on a voluntary arrangement does not necessarily waive rights of security—*Whitehead v Household Mortgage Corp* [2002] EWCA Civ 1657.

Note that court approval is not required to make the scheme binding, unlike under s.16 of the 1914 Act. Notwithstanding approval of a scheme by creditors under s.260, an aggrieved creditor may apply to the court under s.262 if the scheme unfairly prejudices him in his capacity as a creditor: see here *Re Naeem (a Bankrupt) (No.18 of 1988)* [1990] 1 W.L.R. 48.

For the effect of s.260 in releasing old debts and creating new obligations see *Re Wisepark Ltd* [1994] B.C.C. 221 at 223. On the effect of an IVA on sureties see *Johnson v Davies* [1998] 1 B.C.L.C. 580; *Greene King plc v Stanley* [2001] EWCA Civ 1966; [2002] B.P.I.R. 491; *Lombard Natwest Factors Ltd v Koutrouzas* [2002] EWHC 1084 (QB); [2003] B.P.I.R. 444; and *Lloyds Bank v Ellicott* [2002] EWCA Civ 1333; [2003] B.P.I.R. 632. A creditor with a non-provable matrimonial debt can be bound by an IVA—*JP v A Debtor* [1999] B.P.I.R. 206. On future tort claims see annotation to s.3 above.

On whether a post-IVA creditor can become bound see *Re Goldspan Ltd* [2003] B.P.I.R. 93.

On what debts are covered by an IVA see *Cornelius v Casson* [2008] B.P.I.R. 504, which confirms that each case turns upon the individual terms of the particular IVA.

A minor case management point arose in *Grimme Landmaschinenfabrik GmbH v Scott* [2009] B.P.I.R. 506 where the fact that the defendant was undergoing an IVA was deemed by Kitchin J. to be a relevant consideration in determining the time required to prepare a defence in patent proceedings.

S.260(3)

The Deeds of Arrangement Act 1914 does not apply to the approved scheme. There have been no deeds of arrangement recorded in recent years. Registration of voluntary arrangements is provided for by IR 1986 r.6A.2A.

S.260(4), (5)

Interim orders automatically lapse within 28 days of the chairman's report to the court. One effect of this is that if the interim order has "blocked" a bankruptcy petition, the petition is now to be treated as having been dismissed.

261   Additional effect on undischarged bankrupt

261(1)   [Application of section] This section applies where–

(a)   the creditors' meeting summoned under section 257 approves the proposed voluntary arrangement (with or without modifications), and

(b)   the debtor is an undischarged bankrupt.

261(2)   [Annulment of bankruptcy order] Where this section applies the court shall annul the bankruptcy order on an application made–

(a)   by the bankrupt, or

(b)   where the bankrupt has not made an application within the prescribed period, by the official receiver.

261(3)   [When application for annulment not to be made] An application under subsection (2) may not be made–

(a)   during the period specified in section 262(3)(a) during which the decision of the creditors' meeting can be challenged by application under section 262,

(b)   while an application under that section is pending, or

(c)   while an appeal in respect of an application under that section is pending or may be brought.

261(4)   [Court to give directions] Where this section applies the court may give such directions about the conduct of the bankruptcy and the administration of the bankrupt's estate as it thinks appropriate for facilitating the implementation of the approved voluntary arrangement.

GENERAL NOTE

This was replaced and reconstituted by EA 2002 s.264 and Sch.22.

S.261(1)

This explains the ambit of this section. The Court of Appeal considered the issue of an IVA post bankruptcy in *Demarco v Perkins and Bulley Davey* [2006] EWCA Civ 188; [2006] B.P.I.R. 645. This case involved allegations of professional negligence in that insolvency advisers had failed to get a bankruptcy annulled pursuant to s.261(1)(a) before the debtor was automatically discharged from bankruptcy with the result that a valid IVA could not then be embarked upon. The Court of Appeal gave guidance on the quantum of liability in such cases.

S.261(2)

If an IVA is made under this provision the court should annul the extant bankruptcy order. See IR 1986 rr.5.51 and 5.54. In *Re Johnson* [2006] B.P.I.R. 987 (H.H.J. Roger Kaye Q.C. sitting in the Leeds County Court) a question arose as to whether a discharged bankrupt who previously had had an IVA approved could seek an annulment under s.261 of the IA 1986. It was held that a person whose bankruptcy had been automatically discharged could still be regarded as a "bankrupt" for the purposes of seeking an annulment under this provision. The term "bankrupt" when used in s.261 could include a former bankrupt. This conclusion is plausible because it is clear from s.282(3) that a discharged bankrupt could seek an annulment under s.282 but it is difficult to square with the heading of s.261 which is "Additional Effect on Undischarged Bankrupt". Having raised that doubt, it is possible to square this conclusion with the assumptions made in *Demarco v Perkins and Bulley Davey* [2006] EWCA Civ 188 (IVA not possible because bankruptcy had already been discharged), because in *Re Johnson* (above) the IVA was agreed *before* the discharge occurred.

S.261(3)

This explains when an application can be made under this provision.

S.261(4)

This outlines the wide consequential powers of the court.

262   Challenge of meeting's decision

262(1)   [Application to court] Subject to this section, an application to the court may be made, by any of the persons specified below, on one or both of the following grounds, namely–

(a)   that a voluntary arrangement approved by a creditors' meeting summoned under section 257 unfairly prejudices the interests of a creditor of the debtor;

(b)   that there has been some material irregularity at or in relation to such a meeting.

262(2)   [Applicants] The persons who may apply under this section are–

(a)   the debtor;

(b)   a person who–

   (i)   was entitled, in accordance with the rules, to vote at the creditors' meeting, or

   (ii)   would have been so entitled if he had had notice of it;

(c)   the nominee (or his replacement under section 256(3), 256A(4) or 258(3)); and

(d)   if the debtor is an undischarged bankrupt, the trustee of his estate or the official receiver.

262(3)   [Time for application] An application under this section shall not be made

(a)   after the end of the period of 28 days beginning with the day on which the report of the creditors' meeting was made to the court under section 259; or

(b)   in the case of a person who was not given notice of the creditors' meeting, after the end of the period of 28 days beginning with the day on which he became aware that the meeting had taken place, but (subject to that) an application made by a person within subsection (2)(b)(ii) on the ground that the arrangement prejudices his interests may be made after the arrangement has ceased to have effect, unless it has come to an end prematurely.

262(4)   [Court's powers] Where on an application under this section the court is satisfied as to either of the grounds mentioned in subsection (1), it may do one or both of the following, namely–

(a)   revoke or suspend any approval given by the meeting;

(b)   give a direction to any person for the summoning of a further meeting of the debtor's creditors to consider any revised proposal he may make or, in a case falling within subsection (1)(b), to reconsider his original proposal.

262(5)   [Revocation of direction, approval] Where at any time after giving a direction under subsection (4)(b) for the summoning of a meeting to consider a revised proposal the court is satisfied that the debtor does not intend to submit such a proposal, the court shall revoke the direction and revoke or suspend any approval given at the previous meeting.

262(6)   [Further direction] Where the court gives a direction under subsection (4)(b), it may also give a direction continuing or, as the case may require, renewing, for such period as may be specified in the direction, the effect in relation to the debtor of any interim order.

262(7)   [Supplemental directions] In any case where the court, on an application made under this section with respect to a creditors' meeting, gives a direction under subsection (4)(b) or revokes or suspends an approval under subsection (4)(a) or (5), the court may give such supplemental directions as it thinks fit, and, in particular, directions with respect to–

(a) things done since the meeting under any voluntary arrangement approved by the meeting, and

(b) such things done since the meeting as could not have been done if an interim order had been in force in relation to the debtor when they were done.

262(8) **[Effects of irregularity at meeting]** Except in pursuance of the preceding provisions of this section, an approval given at a creditors' meeting summoned under section 257 is not invalidated by any irregularity at or in relation to the meeting.

GENERAL NOTE

Modifications to s.262 were made by IA 2000 s.3 and Sch.3. Of these modifications the provisions dealing with unidentified (and therefore unnotified) creditors are the most significant. Under s.16 of BA 1914, it was the task of the court to approve the scheme, and it had to consider whether it was reasonable and for the benefit of the general creditors. Under the 1986 Act, the court's role is reduced and it will assume such a paternal posture only if the decision of the majority of creditors is challenged under s.262. The court will consider whether the interests of some creditors have been unfairly prejudiced and will be less concerned with an overview of the scheme—it will assume that it is beneficial to the creditors if the majority support it. It is important to grasp that the remedy is only available to protect the complainant's interests as a creditor and not ulterior interests, a point confirmed in *Doorbar v Alltime Securities Ltd (No.2)* [1995] B.C.C. 1,149. Furthermore, the court has more discretion under s.262 to secure the revision of the scheme to meet any objections. In *Re Naeem (a Bankrupt) (No.18 of 1988)* [1990] 1 W.L.R. 48 a landlord successfully exploited s.262 before a registrar to block a scheme on the ground that it unfairly prejudiced his interests, but on appeal to Hoffmann J. the scheme was reinstated as no unfair prejudice to his interests as a creditor could be established. This case is also instructive on the question of who pays the costs of a s.262 application. See also *March Estates v Gunmark* [1996] B.P.I.R. 439.

Challenges under the s.262 procedure are only required where an IVA has come into existence (albeit with some irregularity). Where the flaw (whether it be procedural or substantive) is so serious as to render the purported IVA a nullity the time limits specified in s.262(3) become irrelevant—*IRC v Bland and Sargent* [2003] EWHC 1068 (Ch); [2003] B.P.I.R. 1274; *Vlieland-Boddy v Dexter Ltd* [2003] EWHC 2592 (Ch); [2004] B.P.I.R. 235; *Re Plummer* [2004] B.P.I.R. 767.

A success for s.262 was notched up in *Re a Debtor (No.222 of 1990) Ex p. Bank of Ireland (No.2)* [1993] B.C.L.C. 233 where Harman J. found that as the nominee/chairman had conducted the IVA meeting in a materially irregular way by denying certain creditors a vote (see the earlier proceedings reported in [1992] B.C.L.C. 137) he should be personally liable for the costs of the IVA which had to be set aside. It is difficult not to feel some sympathy for the unfortunate insolvency practitioner here as the right to vote on an IVA in certain contentious cases is less than clear. See also *Fender v IRC* [2003] B.P.I.R. 1304. For another s.262 application that resulted in difficulties for the insolvency practitioner concerned, see *Re N (a Debtor)* [2002] B.P.I.R. 1024. A s.262 application on the grounds of unfair prejudice also succeeded in *Re A Debtor (No.1 of 1999)* [2000] B.P.I.R. 998.

By way of comparison a s.262 application failed in *Re a Debtor (No.259 of 1990)* [1992] 1 W.L.R. 226 where the court made the point that the alleged unfairness must emanate from the scheme itself. For another unsuccessful petition alleging unfair prejudice see *National Westminster Bank v Scher* [1998] B.P.I.R. 224.

For consequential procedural aspects of an application under s.262, see IR 1986 r.5.30. Note also *Re a Debtor (No.87 of 1993) (No.1)* [1996] B.C.C. 74 (hearsay evidence not admissible).

A challenge by a creditor under s.262 provided the basis for the complex litigation reported as *Smurthwaite v Simpson-Smith* [2006] EWCA Civ 1183. The report in question throws little light on the substantive aspects of the provision in that it deals with preliminary issues linked to disclosure of documents and costs incurred in respect of applications to seek disclosure, though once again it does show the difficulties faced by the chairman of the creditors meeting in dealing with disputed debts.

In *Coutts & Co v Passey* [2007] B.P.I.R. 323 the issue was whether a material irregularity had occurred in that the applicant creditor had not been allowed to vote for the full amount which it claimed was due. The disputed element in the debt related to legal costs incurred by the applicant bank in seeking to recover its lending to a client. Under the terms of the lending agreement there was an express provision that the client would be liable for recovery costs. The court felt that this fact provided sufficient grounds to distinguish *Glenister v Rowe* [2000] Ch. 76.

For further consideration of s.262 and its relationship with IR r.5.22 see *Monecor (London) Ltd v Ahmed* [2008] B.P.I.R. 458. This case provides an up to date interpretation of the concept of material irregularity and considers the options open to the court under s.262(4). A number of aspects of IVA procedure were reviewed by the court in *Tradition (UK) Ltd v Ahmed* [2009] B.P.I.R. 626.

S.262(1)–(3), (8)

Within 28 days of the chairman's report to the court a dissenter may apply to the court to challenge the scheme. Section 262(2) allows the debtor, creditors, nominee, trustee or official receiver to make such an application. As to who is a creditor, see *Sea Voyager Maritime Inc v Bielecki* [1999] 1 All E.R. 628. The FSA may apply (and be heard on the application of another) in an appropriate case—FSMA 2000 s.357(5) and (6). The grounds for the challenge are that the scheme unfairly prejudices the interests of a creditor, or that there has been some *material* irregularity in relation to the meeting. The test for material irregularity is the same under the Act and the Rules: *Re Sweatfield Ltd* [1997] B.C.C. 744. Irregularity will not be regarded as material unless it would be likely to affect the outcome of the vote: *Doorbar v Alltime Securities* [1995] B.C.C. 1,149. The irregularity need not be at the meeting as such but may occur in the preparatory documentation: *Re a Debtor (No.87 of 1993) (No.2)* [1996] B.C.C. 80. In *Fender v IRC* [2003] B.P.I.R. 1304 the court indicated that a material irregularity might occur in the proposal, the statement of affairs the nominee's report or in the nominee's chairmanship of the creditors' meeting. See also *IRC v Duce* [1999] B.P.I.R. 189. In *Roberts v Pinnacle Entertainment Ltd* [2003] EWHC 2394 (Ch); [2004] B.P.I.R. 208 a misguided refusal by the chair of the creditors' meeting to admit a major creditor to voting was held to be a material irregularity within s.262(1)(b). Material irregularity can arise even though no party can be said to be at blame: *Great Yarmouth BC v Alterman* (unreported county court ruling noted in *Current Law Week* April 17, 1998).

Unless there has been a successful challenge under this section, irregularities will not invalidate the scheme—see s.262(8).

The 28-day period for challenge can be extended: *Tager v Westpac Banking Corp* [1998] B.C.C. 73. In *Tanner v Everitt* [2004] EWHC 1130 (Ch); [2004] B.P.I.R. 1026 the court indicated that there might be some flexibility with regard to challenges outside the 28 day limit but that did not extend to an attempt to use s.262 some 13 years after the event!

Warren J. considered various aspects of the s.262 jurisdiction in *Re Timothy* [2005] EWHC (Ch); [2005] B.P.I.R. 329. An application made under s.376 of the IA 1986 to extend time for a s.262 application was rejected because of an unjustifiable 9 month delay after the IVA was agreed. It was important that parties to an IVA feel reassured that it not be set aside out of time. Moreover, the underlying complaint of unfair prejudice, although arguable, was not bound to succeed.

S.262(4)–(7)

These provisions outline what the court may do where a scheme is challenged. It may revoke or suspend the approval or call for further meetings to be held—i.e. to reconsider the proposals or to consider revised proposals. If the debtor does not intend to put revised proposals the court can simply revoke or suspend its support for the scheme, although it can direct the interim relief to continue and also make supplementary directions. The court refused to give a direction under s.262(4)(b) for a further meeting in *Re A Debtor (No.101 of 1999) (No.2)* [2001] B.P.I.R. 996. See also *Monecor (London) Ltd v Ahmed* [2008] B.P.I.R. 458. On directions under s.262(7) see *IRC v Duce* [1999] B.P.I.R. 189. For the scope of the jurisdiction under s.262(7) see *Re a Debtor (No.83 of 1988)* [1990] 1 W.L.R. 708. On revoking see *Re Cardona* [1997] B.C.C. 697.

262A False representations etc.

262A(1) [Offence] If for the purpose of obtaining the approval of his creditors to a proposal for a voluntary arrangement, the debtor–

(a) makes any false representation, or

(b) fraudulently does, or omits to do, anything,

he commits an offence.

262A(2) [Unapproved proposal] Subsection (1) applies even if the proposal is not approved.

262A(3) [Penalty] A person guilty of an offence under this section is liable to imprisonment or a fine, or both.

GENERAL NOTE

Introduced by IA 2000 s.3 and Sch.3 with effect from January 1, 2003, this new provision seeks to introduce a new sanction for those debtors who make false representations to seek creditor approval for a voluntary arrangement.

S.262A(1), (2)

These define the extent of the offence—the fact that the IVA is voted down by creditors is immaterial. See the note to s.6A.

S.262A(3)

The sanction is hereby specified, though details of this can only be discovered by reference to Sch.10.

262B   Prosecution of delinquent debtors

262B(1)   [Application] This section applies where a voluntary arrangement approved by a creditors' meeting summoned under section 257 has taken effect.

262B(2)   [Whistleblowing obligation] If it appears to the nominee or supervisor that the debtor has been guilty of any offence in connection with the arrangement for which he is criminally liable, he shall forthwith–

(a)   report the matter to the Secretary of State, and

(b)   provide the Secretary of State with such information and give the Secretary of State such access to and facilities for inspecting and taking copies of documents (being information or documents in his possession or under his control and relating to the matter in question) as the Secretary of State requires.

262B(3)   [Consequences] Where a prosecuting authority institutes criminal proceedings following any report under subsection (2), the nominee or, as the case may be, supervisor shall give the authority all assistance in connection with the prosecution which he is reasonably able to give.

For this purpose, "prosecuting authority" means the Director of Public Prosecutions or the Secretary of State.

262B(4)   [Power of court] The court may, on the application of the prosecuting authority, direct a nominee or supervisor to comply with subsection (3) if he has failed to do so.

GENERAL NOTE

This again reflects a desire to combat IVA abuse by imposing a "whistleblowing" obligation on the nominee/supervisor.

S.262B(1)

This indicates the applicability of this section.

S.262B(2)

The details of the whistleblowing obligation are specified. For procedures on reporting suspected criminality see *Dear IP*, December 2007.

S.262B(3), (4)

These deal with consequential matters where a prosecution of a debtor is instituted in the wake of a report made under subs.(2).

262C   Arrangements coming to an end prematurely

262C For the purposes of this Part, a voluntary arrangement approved by a creditors' meeting summoned under section 257 comes to an end prematurely if, when it ceases to have effect, it has not been fully implemented in respect of all persons bound by the arrangement by virtue of section 260(2)(b)(i).

GENERAL NOTE

This explains when an IVA can be said to come to an end prematurely. This new provision was inserted by IA 2000 s.3 and Sch.3 with effect from January 1, 2003. Its importance can be gleaned by reference to s.260(2A).

263   Implementation and supervision of approved voluntary arrangement

263(1)   [Application] This section applies where a voluntary arrangement approved by a creditors' meeting summoned under section 257 has taken effect.

263(2)   [Supervisor of voluntary arrangement] The person who is for the time being carrying out, in relation to the voluntary arrangement, the functions conferred by virtue of the approval on the nominee (or his replacement under section 256(3), 256A(4) or 258(3)) shall be known as the supervisor of the voluntary arrangement.

263(3)   [Application to court re actions of supervisor] If the debtor, any of his creditors or any other person is dissatisfied by any act, omission or decision of the supervisor, he may apply to the court; and on such an application the court may–

(a)   confirm, reverse or modify any act or decision of the supervisor,

(b)   give him directions, or

(c)   make such other order as it thinks fit.

263(4)   [Application for directions] The supervisor may apply to the court for directions in relation to any particular matter arising under the voluntary arrangement.

263(5)   [Court may fill supervisor vacancy etc.] The court may, whenever–

(a)   it is expedient to appoint a person to carry out the functions of the supervisor, and

(b)   it is inexpedient, difficult or impracticable for an appointment to be made without the assistance of the court,

make an order appointing a person who is qualified to act as an insolvency practitioner or authorised to act as supervisor in relation to the voluntary arrangement, either in substitution for the existing supervisor or to fill a vacancy.

This is without prejudice to section 41(2) of the Trustee Act 1925 (power of court to appoint trustees of deeds of arrangement).

263(6)   [Exercise of s.263(5) power] The power conferred by subsection (5) is exercisable so as to increase the number of persons exercising the functions of the supervisor or, where there is more than one person exercising those functions, so as to replace one or more of those persons.

GENERAL NOTE

Minor textual amendments were made to s.263(3) and (5) by IA 2000 s.3 and Sch.3. In s.263(5) the amendment reflects the possibility of non-IPs in future acting as nominees/supervisors.

S.263(1), (2)
Once the scheme has taken effect the "nominee" will be transformed into the "supervisor" of the composition or scheme. On the standards of competence expected of the nominee/supervisor see *Heritage Joinery v Krasner* [1999] B.P.I.R. 683; and *Pitt v Mond* [2001] B.P.I.R. 624. Compare *Harmony Carpets v Chaffin-Laird* [2000] B.P.I.R. 61. On the need for the insolvency practitioner to maintain independence see the comments of Jacob L.J. in *Smurthwaite v Simpson-Smith* [2006] B.P.I.R. 1504 at 1524 (para.[33]).

S.263(3)
This allows for the court to interfere with decisions of the supervisor which have been objected to. Compare IA 1986 s.303(1). For an application that failed largely on procedural grounds see *Timmins v Conn* [2004] EWCA Civ 1761; [2005] B.P.I.R. 647. For a direction under para.(b) see *Ing Lease (UK) Ltd v Griswold* [1998] B.C.C. 905. Creditors have no private rights of action outside s.263 to enforce a supervisor's duties—*King v Anthony* [1999] B.P.I.R. 73. In *Timmins v Conn* [2004] EWCA Civ 1761; [2005] B.P.I.R. 647 the Court of Appeal on an application by a creditor under s.263(3) had to grapple with the difficulties in interpreting IVA terms, and in particular with whether certain assets (the debtor's interest in the family home) had been excluded from the IVA. The Court of Appeal concluded that the debtor's share in the family home had formed part of the IVA assets from the outset. The suggestion that it had been formally excluded by the supervisor did not stand up. As this share in the family home had not been realised it

could not be said that the IVA had been successfully completed. However, the court could not grant the applicant a declaration to the above effect as it would impact upon the debtor who was not a party to the proceedings. The case is therefore of some procedural significance. The court felt unable to make a compensation order against the supervisor partly because it would be impossible to quantify damage as the unrealised asset in question might still be traceable.

S.263(4)

The supervisor may apply to the court for directions, as can a trustee in bankruptcy under IA 1986 s.303(2). For an example see *Re a Debtor (No.638 IO of 1994), The Times*, December 3, 1998; and *Horrocks v Broome* [1999] B.P.I.R. 66. This power to seek directions does not authorise the court to vary the IVA—*Re Alpa Lighting Ltd* [1997] B.P.I.R. 341; *Raja v Rubin* [1999] B.P.I.R. 575.

S.263(5), (6)

The court can fill vacancies, appoint substitutes or increase the number of supervisors. On this jurisdiction see *Re Bridgend Goldsmiths* [1995] B.C.C. 226 (a questionable authority); *Re Bullard & Taplin* [1996] B.C.C. 973; *Re Stella Metals Ltd* [1997] B.C.C. 626 (professional body can apply for replacement where original appointee ceases to be qualified); *Re Abbott* [1997] B.C.C. 666 (original appointment made by county court therefore case had to be transferred High Court to enable it to replace); and *Clements v Udal* [2001] B.P.I.R. 454.

For further provisions on the implementation of the voluntary arrangement and the role of the supervisor, see IR 1986 rr.5.26, 5.31A, 5.32 and 5.34. Note that an IVA may expire automatically by effluxion of time—*Strongmaster Ltd v Kaye* [2002] EWHC 444 (Ch); [2002] B.P.I.R. 1259.

It is disappointing that the IVA legislation does not address the scenario where an IVA established under Pt VIII of IA 1986 fails and the debtor is declared bankrupt. We are told by s.264(1)(c) that a supervisor may present a bankruptcy petition but bankruptcy may occur in other circumstances—e.g. by default towards post-IVA creditors. What is the impact of bankruptcy upon the earlier IVA? More importantly, what happens to the funds collected by the IVA supervisor—are they reserved exclusively for the IVA participants or can they be claimed by the trustee in bankruptcy for the benefit of the creditors at large? The case law here is voluminous: *Re McKeen* [1995] B.C.C. 412 (Morritt J.); *Re Bradley-Hole* [1995] 1 W.L.R. 1097 (Rimer J.); *Davis v Martin-Sklan* [1995] 2 B.C.L.C. 483 (Blackburne J.); *Kings v Cleghorn* [1998] B.P.I.R. 463 (H.H.J. Behrens); and *Re Coath* [2000] B.P.I.R. 981 (DJ Field). A useful analysis of some of the earlier of these authorities is provided by Bailey in [1995–96] 2 R.A.L.Q. 87 and Walton, [1997–98] 3 R.A.L.Q. 277. Some clarity in the law has now been introduced by the Court of Appeal ruling in *Re N.T. Gallagher & Son Ltd* [2002] EWCA Civ 404. Although this case is concerned with CVAs the principles developed in that case were expressly intended to apply mutatis mutandis to IVAs. In short it is clear that an IVA may survive subsequent bankruptcy and that funds collected by the supervisor may be retained and kept out of the hands of the trustee in bankruptcy. The IVA documentation will be important here. For a full discussion of these principles see note to s.7 above.

Fast-track voluntary arrangement

263A   Availability

263A   Section 263B applies where an individual debtor intends to make a proposal to his creditors for a voluntary arrangement and–

(a)   the debtor is an undischarged bankrupt,

(b)   the official receiver is specified in the proposal as the nominee in relation to the voluntary arrangement, and

(c)   no interim order is applied for under section 253.

GENERAL NOTE

This group of provisions was added by EA 2002 s.264 and Sch.22 with effect from April 1, 2004. It establishes yet another IVA variant—namely the "fast-track IVA" which can be used by undischarged bankrupts and managed by the official receiver. The criteria for application are mapped out in s.263A. One concern about this new procedure is whether it will appeal to undischarged bankrupts, who in future are going to be discharged after one year in any case. Other debtors in a position to avoid bankruptcy by proposing an IVA to creditors are clearly not going to be caught by the net because they will not enter bankruptcy in the first place.

263B Decision

263B(1) [Documents to official receiver] The debtor may submit to the official receiver–

(a) a document setting out the terms of the voluntary arrangement which the debtor is proposing, and

(b) a statement of his affairs containing such particulars as may be prescribed of his creditors, debts, other liabilities and assets and such other information as may be prescribed.

263B(2) [Invitation to creditors to approve] If the official receiver thinks that the voluntary arrangement proposed has a reasonable prospect of being approved and implemented, he may make arrangements for inviting creditors to decide whether to approve it.

263B(3) ["Creditor"] For the purposes of subsection (2) a person is a "creditor" only if–

(a) he is a creditor of the debtor in respect of a bankruptcy debt, and

(b) the official receiver is aware of his claim and his address.

263B(4) [Arrangements under s.236B] Arrangements made under subsection (2)–

(a) must include the provision to each creditor of a copy of the proposed voluntary arrangement,

(b) must include the provision to each creditor of information about the criteria by reference to which the official receiver will determine whether the creditors approve or reject the proposed voluntary arrangement, and

(c) may not include an opportunity for modifications to the proposed voluntary arrangement to be suggested or made.

263B(5) [When no interim order to be made] Where a debtor submits documents to the official receiver under subsection (1) no application under section 253 for an interim order may be made in respect of the debtor until the official receiver has–

(a) made arrangements as described in subsection (2), or

(b) informed the debtor that he does not intend to make arrangements (whether because he does not think the voluntary arrangement has a reasonable prospect of being approved and implemented or because he declines to act).

S.263B(1)
The onus is on the undischarged bankrupt to initiate this procedure. On notification a deposit of £335 is payable (Insolvency Proceedings (Fees) Order 2004 (SI 2004/593)).

S.263B(2), (3)
The official receiver acts as facilitator. For bankruptcy debt see s.382.

S.263B(4), (5)
These deal with various operational issues.

263C Result

263C As soon as is reasonably practicable after the implementation of arrangements under section 263B(2) the official receiver shall notify the Secretary of State whether the proposed voluntary arrangement has been approved or rejected.

GENERAL NOTE

The only role of the court up to this stage is to be notified of the creditors' decision. A minor amendment made by LRO 2010 (SI 2010/18) with regard to reporting obligations.

263D   Approval of voluntary arrangement

263D(1)   [Application of section] This section applies where the official receiver notifies the Secretary of State under section 263C that a proposed voluntary arrangement has been approved.

263D(2)   [Binding effect of arrangement] The voluntary arrangement–

(a)   takes effect,

(b)   binds the debtor, and

(c)   binds every person who was entitled to participate in the arrangements made under section 263B(2).

263D(3)   [Bankruptcy order to be annulled] The court shall annul the bankruptcy order in respect of the debtor on an application made by the official receiver.

263D(4)   [When no application to annul to be made] An application under subsection (3) may not be made–

(a)   during the period specified in section 263F(3) during which the voluntary arrangement can be challenged by application under section 263F(2),

(b)   while an application under that section is pending, or

(c)   while an appeal in respect of an application under that section is pending or may be brought.

263D(5)   [Directions] The court may give such directions about the conduct of the bankruptcy and the administration of the bankrupt's estate as it thinks appropriate for facilitating the implementation of the approved voluntary arrangement.

263D(6)   [Non-application of Deeds of Arrangement Act 1914] The Deeds of Arrangement Act 1914 (c. 47) does not apply to the voluntary arrangement.

263D(7)   [Reference to voluntary arrangement] A reference in this Act or another enactment to a voluntary arrangement approved under this Part includes a reference to a voluntary arrangement which has effect by virtue of this section.

S.263D(1), (2)
These are the usual consequences attendant upon VA approval. A minor amendment is made by LRO 2010 (SI 2010/18) with regard to reporting obligations.

S.263D(3)
This is more specific and requires the court to annul the bankruptcy order.

S.263D(4)
This qualifies subs.(3).

S.263D(5)
In spite of what was said above, the court may have a continuing role to deal with transition from bankruptcy to IVA.

S.263D(6)
This is true of all IVAs, not that it matters with the dearth of deeds of arrangement these days.

S.263D(7)
This is purely explanatory.

263E   Implementation

263E   Section 263 shall apply to a voluntary arrangement which has effect by virtue of section 263D(2) as it applies to a voluntary arrangement approved by a creditors' meeting.

GENERAL NOTE
This applies s.263 to fast-track IVAs.

263F   Revocation

263F(1)   [Grounds for revocation] The court may make an order revoking a voluntary arrangement which has effect by virtue of section 263D(2) on the ground–

(a)   that it unfairly prejudices the interests of a creditor of the debtor, or

(b)   that a material irregularity occurred in relation to the arrangements made under section 263B(2).

263F(2)   [Applicant for revocation order] An order under subsection (1) may be made only on the application of–

(a)   the debtor,

(b)   a person who was entitled to participate in the arrangements made under section 263B(2),

(c)   the trustee of the bankrupt's estate, or

(d)   the official receiver.

263F(3)   [Period when application may not be made] An application under subsection (2) may not be made after the end of the period of 28 days beginning with the date on which the official receiver notifies the Secretary of State his report to the court under section 263C.

263F(4)   [Where creditor not aware of arrangement] But a creditor who was not made aware of the arrangements under section 263B(2) at the time when they were made may make an application under subsection (2) during the period of 28 days beginning with the date on which he becomes aware of the voluntary arrangement.

S.263F(1), (2)
This confers wide intervention powers on the court provided the applicant qualifies under subs.(2).

S.263F(3), (4)
This is the standard 28-day time-limit subject to extension if the conditions in subs.(4) are met. A minor amendment is made by LRO 2010 (SI 2010/18) with regard to reporting obligations.

263G   Offences

263G(1)   [False representations etc.] Section 262A shall have effect in relation to obtaining approval to a proposal for a voluntary arrangement under section 263D.

263G(2)   [Prosecution of delinquent debtors] Section 262B shall have effect in relation to a voluntary arrangement which has effect by virtue of section 263D(2) (for which purposes the words "by a creditors' meeting summoned under section 257" shall be disregarded).

S.263G(1)
This extends the offence in s.262A to fast-track IVAs.

S.263G(2)
This makes provision for s.262B to apply to fast-track IVAs.

PART IX

BANKRUPTCY

Introductory note to Part IX
Before embarking upon the analysis of the provisions of IA 1986 with regard to bankruptcy a caveat ought to be issued with regard to usage of statutory predecessors. Where this is appropriate the legislative origins of particular provisions are identified in the following text. However, care must be taken in handling these former provisions (which are largely from BA 1914) for it is now clear that the courts are minded to interpret the bankruptcy sections of IA 1986 in their own light and are not necessarily going to take advantage of earlier interpretations of similar

provisions in the 1914 Act. Thus in *Re a Debtor (No.1 of 1987)* [1989] 1 W.L.R. 271, a leading case on statutory demands, Nicholls L.J. declared:

> "I do not think that on this the new bankruptcy code simply incorporates and adopts the same approach as the old code. The new code has made many changes in the law of bankruptcy, and the court's task, with regard to the new code, must be to construe the new statutory provisions in accordance with the ordinary canons of construction, unfettered by previous authorities." (ibid., at 276.)

More recently in the House of Lords' ruling in *Smith v Braintree District Council* [1990] 2 A.C. 215, which was concerned with the interpretation of IA 1986 s.285, Lord Jauncey (at 237–238) reinforced this view on the modus operandi of interpretation:

> "... the Act of 1986, although re-enacting many provisions from earlier statutes, contains a good deal of fresh material derived from the Insolvency Act 1985. In particular, the legislation now emphasises the importance of the rehabilitation of the individual insolvent, it provides for automatic discharge from bankruptcy in many cases, and it abolishes mandatory public examinations as well as enabling a bankrupt to be discharged without public examination. Thus not only has the legislative approach to individual bankruptcy altered since the mid-19th century, but social views as to what conduct involves delinquency, as to punishment and as to the desirability of imprisonment have drastically changed ... In these circumstances, I feel justified in construing section 285 of the Act of 1986 as a piece of new legislation without regard to 19th century authorities or similar provisions of repealed Bankruptcy Acts ...".

See also *Official Receiver v McKay* [2009] B.P.I.R. 1061 where the Court of Appeal discarded an old precedent on annulment.

These are important statements of principle that should be borne in mind when trying to attach meaning to the new statutory provisions in bankruptcy law. Having said that, there are instances where pre-1985 law has been important and therefore generalisations must be treated with caution.

It should also be borne in mind that there are significant principles of common law in bankruptcy which have never been embodied in legislation. For example the rule against double proof and the curious duty imposed on trustees to act honourably as devised in *Ex p. James* (1874) L.R. 9 Ch. App. 609, which for once was applied in *Patel v Jones* [2001] B.P.I.R. 919. However, increasingly courts permit trustees to act so as to maximise returns to creditors even where they may be viewed as taking advantage—see the comparable Scottish authority of *Burnett's Trustee v Grainger* [2004] UKHL 8; [2004] S.L.T. 513. For recent discussion of the rule in *Ex p. James* (1873–74) L.R. 9 Ch. App. 609 and its application to trustees in bankruptcy see *Bank of Baroda v Patel* [2009] B.P.I.R. 255.

The similarities/differences between governing principles of personal and corporate insolvency law are well illuminated by the judgment of David Richards J. in *Re T & N Ltd* [2005] EWHC 2870 (Ch); [2006] B.P.I.R. 532. In discussing the different rules relating to proof of debt by future tort claimants (for bankrupts s.382 of the Act and for companies IR 1986 r.13.12) the judge concluded that the principle of disallowing proof was the same for both cases, but for companies the social consequences of applying the principle were more serious by virtue of the fact that for an insolvent company liquidation was the end of the matter, whereas for an individual the possibility of pursuing the claim after discharge of the bankrupt was real. At the end of the day IR 1986 r.13.12 was amended by SI 2006/1272 to allow future tort claims to be proved on corporate insolvency whereas s.382 has remained unamended for the present. A substantive difference has thus emerged, though in view of the point made by David Richards J. that difference may in this instance be justified. There are still significant differences between the bankruptcy and winding up procedures; for instance, bankruptcy petitions are not advertised as such.

It should be remembered that in addition to the Act and the Rules and the underlying common law, there are a number of relevant practice directions governing bankruptcy cases. Some of these are referred to in connection with the relevant legislative provisions. Most, however, have now been overtaken by the *Practice Direction: Insolvency Proceedings* [2000] B.C.C. 927 (reproduced as App.IV to this *Guide* in Vol.2) which can also be found reported in [1999] B.P.I.R. 441 (as revised in [2000] B.P.I.R. 647). A case of general significance in bankruptcy litigation is *Hocking v Walker* [1997] B.P.I.R. 93, where the Court of Appeal held that a bankrupt may be required to give security for costs when appealing against a bankruptcy order.

The provisions in Pt IX of IA 1986 have been substantially amended by Pt 10 of EA 2002. Most of these changes took effect in April 2004. Transitional provisions are contained in s.256 of and Sch.19 to EA 2002. The purpose of these amending provisions was to liberalise bankruptcy law in this country. The thinking behind this reform was that by removing some of the unpleasantness associated with business failure individuals would be more inclined to undertake entrepreneurial risk. The problem with this reasoning is that the majority of bankrupts these days are consumer debtors taking no part whatsoever in the risks associated with trade. Having said that, consumer credit is now a key feature of our economy and any government is naturally concerned with the downside of such an economic facility deemed so vital to the health of the national economy. The 2002 Act changes bankruptcy topography in a number of ways. First, automatic discharge will now be available after a maximum of one year (EA 2002 s.256). Official receivers will no longer be subject to a statutory obligation to investigate the causes of every bankruptcy (EA 2002 s.258). Disqualifications of bankrupts will be relaxed in a variety of ways (see EA 2002 ss.265–268). Certain bankruptcy offences will be decriminalised (EA 2002 s.263). The rights of bankrupts and their families over the home will be further strengthened by requiring a trustee to take firm action within three years or lose entitlement to this major asset (s.261). To compensate for these changes the concept of a bankruptcy restriction order (or undertaking) is introduced to deal with those bankrupts whose conduct is not beyond reproach (s.257 and Schs 20, 21). Other changes introduced by the 2002 Act include reforms to the income payments regime (ss.259, 260). Each of these reforms will be considered below at the appropriate statutory point in the amended 1986 Act.

Illuminating details of the profile of the modern bankrupt are contained in an Insolvency Service report, *The Characteristics of a Bankrupt* (March 2006—see IS Press Notice March 27, 2006 for a summary). From this we learn that the average age of a bankrupt is falling (to age 41 at present). Male bankrupts still predominate, but the female population of bankrupts is growing. The proportion of bankrupts aged under 30 is nearly 19 per cent and rising. Another recommended source of data and insights is the *Bankruptcy Courts Survey*, a pilot study carried out in 2005 for the Insolvency Service by John Tribe of the Centre for Insolvency Law and Policy at Kingston University, details of which are available on the Insolvency Service website under "Insolvency Research" (personal research resources) section—for comment see editorial, (2006) 22 I.L. & P. 1.

The long term future of bankruptcy as the premier legal institution for dealing with personal insolvency is in question. Apart from the increasing significance of IVAs (which now comprise nearly 50 per cent of all personal insolvencies) the advent of debt relief orders and other debt-related procedures under the Tribunals, Courts and Enforcement Act 2007 is likely to have a significant impact on bankruptcy usage, though the precise timescale for the introduction of these new procedures is still unpredictable.

The huge increase in self generated bankruptcies by means of debtor petitions has lead to a rethink on whether such largely uncontested cases should be taken out of the court system—see Insolvency Service Consultative Document (October 2007) entitled *"Bankruptcy: Proposals for Reform of the Debtor Petition Process"*. At the time of submission of manuscript there was no further news on whether this reform would indeed proceed.

For a general overview of modern developments in bankruptcy and personal insolvency law in the context of an enterprise-driven economy see Milman, (2008) 20 Singapore Academy of Law Journal 438.

The English courts have said that art.6 ECHR has no relevance to delay in the completion of the bankruptcy process by the trustee as that administrative process does not itself determine the civil rights of the bankrupt—*Holtham v Kelmanson* [2006] EWHC 2588 (Ch); [2006] B.P.I.R. 1422, *Foyle v Turner* [2007] B.P.I.R. 43. But one interpretation of *Skurcak v Slovakia* [2007] B.P.I.R. 440 might be to suggest that the matter is not entirely free of doubt. Much may depend upon the operation of the particular bankruptcy regime operating in each adhering State.

CHAPTER I

BANKRUPTCY PETITIONS; BANKRUPTCY ORDERS

Introductory note to Part IX, Chapter I

The 1985 Act implemented the recommendation of Cork (*Report*, para.529), that acts of bankruptcy should be abolished. The presentation of a bankruptcy petition is not "an action on a judgment" for the purposes of s.24 of the Limitation Act 1980—*Ridgeway Motors (Isleworth) Ltd v ALTS Ltd* [2005] EWCA Civ 92; [2005] 2 All E.R. 304. But see also *HMRC v Morris* [2007] EWHC 3345 (Ch); [2008] B.P.I.R. 391 where the court held that a bankruptcy petition is an available method of enforcement of obligations arising under EC Council Directive 76/308 (which deals with European agricultural levies and customs).

HMRC can use bankruptcy petitions to recover tax arrears, even though it has no explicit statutory authorisation to do so—see the comments of Lord Walker in *Total Network SL v HMRC* [2008] B.P.I.R. 699.

Bankruptcy proceedings cannot be used to unpick tax assessments as there are dedicated procedures to achieve that goal—*Lam v IRC* [2009] B.P.I.R. 301.

In a growing number of cases local government ombudsmen have ruled that the mechanistic use of bankruptcy proceedings to collect council tax arrears without regard to the personal circumstances of the debtor or the possibility of using alternative recovery methods could constitute maladministration—see *Ford v Wolverhampton CC* [2008] B.P.I.R. 1304; *Re An Investigation into Complaint 07/A/12661 Against Camden LBC* [2008] B.P.I.R. 1572 and *Report of an Investigation into Complaint 08 002 300 v Exeter CC* [2009] B.P.I.R. 598. These rulings are beginning to have an impact on bankruptcy litigation—see *Hunt v Fylde BC* [2008] B.P.I.R. 1368.

The courts are becoming increasingly irritated by parties to a divorce seeking to use the bankruptcy procedure as a tactical tool—see the comments of the court in *Ella v Ella* [2009] B.P.I.R. 441.

Preliminary

264 Who may present a bankruptcy petition

264(1) **[Presentation of petition]** A petition for a bankruptcy order to be made against an individual may be presented to the court in accordance with the following provisions of this Part–

(a) by one of the individual's creditors or jointly by more than one of them,

(b) by the individual himself,

(ba) by a temporary administrator (within the meaning of Article 38 of the EC Regulation),

(bb) by a liquidator (within the meaning of Article 2(b) of the EC Regulation) appointed in proceedings by virtue of Article 3(1) of the EC Regulation,

(c) by the supervisor of, or any person (other than the individual) who is for the time being bound by, a voluntary arrangement proposed by the individual and approved under Part VIII, or

(d) where a criminal bankruptcy order has been made against the individual, by the Official Petitioner or by any person specified in the order in pursuance of section 39(3)(b) of the Powers of Criminal Courts Act 1973.

264(2) **[Power of court to make order]** Subject to those provisions, the court may make a bankruptcy order on any such petition.

GENERAL NOTE

This section describes the persons who may present a bankruptcy petition and authorises the court to make an order on such a petition. In *Mahmood v Penrose* [2005] B.P.I.R. 170 a petitioner in whose favour a costs award had been made jointly was held to have locus standi for the purposes of s.264(1)(a). Sub-subsections (1)(ba) and (bb) were introduced to cater for the advent of EC Council Regulation 1346/2000 with effect from May 31, 2002. See also Insolvency Proceedings (Fees) Amendment Order 2005 (SI 2005/544). For the "Official Petitioner" in s.264(1)(d) see s.402. The FSA may petition in an appropriate case—for the position here see s.372 of FSMA 2000. See Peat, (2006) 22 I.L. & P. 7. It may also be heard on a s.264 petition presented by any other party—see FSMA 2000 s.374(2). Creditors with separate debts can join together and present a single bankruptcy petition: *Re Allen (Re a Debtor 367 of 1992)* [1998] B.P.I.R. 319. A creditor with a non-provable bankruptcy debt is entitled to present a petition, though the court is unlikely to accede to it unless there are exceptional circumstances—*Russell v Russell* [1998] B.P.I.R. 259. Such exceptional circumstances were present in *Wheatley v Wheatley* [1999] B.P.I.R. 431. On the general issue of petitions and non-provable debts see *Levy v Legal Services Commission* [2000] B.P.I.R. 1065.

A default petition can be presented under s.264(1)(c) even though the specified duration for the IVA has expired—*Harris v Gross* [2001] B.P.I.R. 586. In *Clarke v Birkin* [2006] EWHC 340 (Ch); [2006] B.P.I.R. 632 Evans-Lombe J. upheld a bankruptcy ruling made by a Registrar on a petition by IVA-participating creditors for the bankruptcy of the applicant pursuant to s.264(1)(c) of the IA 1986 on the grounds that the debtor had failed to comply with his obligations under the arrangement. The debtor did not deny that he had been in default in making payments, but he argued that it was not a material default. Evans-Lombe J. held that as the Registrar had properly considered all relevant factors in this case when making the bankruptcy order there were no grounds for interfering with that order which was a proper exercise of his discretion. Indeed there was a term in the IVA making it clear that failure to pay instalments on time could not be remedied by subsequent payment. As to who should be appointed trustee on such a petition see *Landsman v de Concilio* [2005] EWHC 267 (Ch); [2005] B.P.I.R. 829.

Note prospective amendment: s.264(1)(d) and the word "or" immediately preceding it are to be repealed by CJA 1988 s.170(2) and Sch.16 as from a day to be appointed. (The power to make criminal bankruptcy orders has been abolished by s.101 of this Act, with effect from April 3, 1989 (see SI 1989/264 (C. 8)), but this and other provisions of IA 1986 and IR 1986 remain in force for the time being to govern orders already existing: see further the note to s.277.)

In the future, once s.115 of the Tribunals, Courts and Enforcement Act 2007 is commenced, the right of an unsecured creditor with a qualifying debt to petition will be restricted if the debtor has entered a debt repayment scheme under the 2007 Act. In such circumstances the creditor cannot petition for bankruptcy during the currency of such a scheme.

The fee for a creditor's petition is now £190, with a debtor's petition costing £150: see the Civil Proceedings Fees Order 2008 (SI 2008/1053 (L. 5)). The relevant deposits for petitions presented under s.264(1) are £600 for petitions presented under para.(a), (c) and (d) and £450 for petitions presented by debtors under para.(b) (from April 6, 2010—see the Insolvency Proceedings (Fees) (Amendment) Order 2010 (SI 2010/732).

265 Conditions to be satisfied in respect of debtor

265(1) [Conditions for presentation of petition] A bankruptcy petition shall not be presented to the court under section 264(1)(a) or (b) unless the debtor–

(a) is domiciled in England and Wales,

(b) is personally present in England and Wales on the day on which the petition is presented, or

(c) at any time in the period of 3 years ending with that day–

   (i) has been ordinarily resident, or has had a place of residence, in England and Wales, or

   (ii) has carried on business in England and Wales.

265(2) [Interpretation] The reference in subsection (1)(c) to an individual carrying on business includes–

(a) the carrying on of business by a firm or partnership of which the individual is a member, and

(b) the carrying on of business by an agent or manager for the individual or for such a firm or partnership.

265(3) [EC Regulation] This section is subject to Article 3 of the EC Regulation.

GENERAL NOTE

This section largely repeats provisions to the same effect in BA 1914 s.1(2). The purpose of these provisions is to establish a geographic connection between the debtor and the English bankruptcy system. For an instructive authority here, see *Re Brauch* [1978] Ch. 316. In *Re Thulin* [1995] 1 W.L.R. 165 a non-resident Swede was bankrupted by the English courts to facilitate the international collection of his assets. For the purposes of s.265(1)(c)(ii) a person does not cease to carry on business until arrangements have been made to settle business debts: see *Re a Debtor (No.784 of 1991)* [1992] Ch. 554 where Hoffmann J. followed *Theophile v Solicitor General* [1950] A.C. 186. Note also *Wilkinson v IRC* [1998] B.P.I.R. 418. The issue of the jurisdiction of the English courts under s.265 was considered in *Barlow Clowes International Ltd v Henwood* [2008] EWCA Civ 577. At first instance it was held that there was a lack of jurisdiction because the domicile of origin had been replaced first by a domicile of choice in the Isle of Man and then by a domicile of choice in Mauritius. This latter conclusion was disputed on the facts. On appeal, the Court of Appeal ruled that where the debtor had abandoned his domicile of choice in the Isle of Man without acquiring a new domicile of choice in Mauritius then the original domicile of origin was revived. This judgment contains an excellent review of the rules on domicile insofar as they may be relevant for the purposes of s.265.

Subsection (3) was inserted by Insolvency Act 1986 (Amendment) (No.2) Regulations 2002 (SI 2002/1240) reg.14 with effect from May 31, 2002. Article 3 of the EC Regulation overrides s.265(1) where the debtor has his centre of main interests in another EU Member State—our local courts enjoy only limited jurisdiction to open a local bankruptcy—see Vol 2, pp.125 et seq. On when COMI is to be determined—*Shierson v Vlieland-Boddy* [2005] EWCA Civ 974. Where there is no COMI within an EU Member State, s.265 retains its importance to found jurisdiction—*Geveran Trading Co v Skjevesland* [2003] B.C.C. 209 (confirmed on appeal [2002] EWHC 2898 (Ch); [2003] B.C.C. 391). See also the approach taken by Lewison J. in *Cross Construction (Sussex) Ltd v Tseliki* [2006] EWHC 1056 (Ch).

266 Other preliminary conditions

266(1) [Treatment of petition] Where a bankruptcy petition relating to an individual is presented by a person who is entitled to present a petition under two or more paragraphs of section 264(1), the petition is to be treated for the purposes of this Part as a petition under such one of those paragraphs as may be specified in the petition.

266(2)   [Limit on withdrawal of petition] A bankruptcy petition shall not be withdrawn without the leave of the court.

266(3)   [Power of dismissal or stay] The court has a general power, if it appears to it appropriate to do so on the grounds that there has been a contravention of the rules or for any other reason, to dismiss a bankruptcy petition or to stay proceedings on such a petition; and, where it stays proceedings on a petition, it may do so on such terms and conditions as it thinks fit.

266(4)   [Where criminal bankruptcy order] Without prejudice to subsection (3), where a petition under section 264(1)(a), (b) or (c) in respect of an individual is pending at a time when a criminal bankruptcy order is made against him, or is presented after such an order has been so made, the court may on the application of the Official Petitioner dismiss the petition if it appears to it appropriate to do so.

S.266(1)
A person may be entitled to present a petition under two or more paragraphs of s.264(1), but he must specify which paragraph he is relying on.

S.266(2)
The leave of the court is required before a petition can be withdrawn. This repeats BA 1914 ss.5(7) and 6(2).

S.266(3), (4)
The court has general discretion to stay or dismiss petitions, as was the case under BA 1914 s.113. This discretion is to be kept flexible: *TSB Bank v Platts* [1997] B.P.I.R. 151. See also *Oxted Financial Services v Gordon* [1998] B.P.I.R. 231; and *Re Micklethwait* [2002] EWHC 1123 (Ch); [2003] B.P.I.R. 101 where the court refused to invoke s.266(3). Compare *Re Ross (No.2)* [2000] B.P.I.R. 636. See also *Westminster CC v Parkin* [2001] B.P.I.R. 1156, where the court refused to intervene even where the petition debt was subject to appeal because it did not believe that the appeal had a reasonable prospect of success. Note *Shepherd v LSC* [2003] B.P.I.R. 140 where a bankruptcy order was made notwithstanding the fact that it was conceded by all sides that there were no assets to realise. In *John Lewis v Pearson Burton* [2004] B.P.I.R. 70 Pumfrey J. held that it had been incorrect for a district judge to have dismissed a bankruptcy petition by using discretion vested by s.266(3) because the creditor had been entitled to refuse an offer from the debtor to repay the debt over a seven year period. Furthermore, the fact that the creditor had not exhausted all other remedies instead of bankruptcy was immaterial. The case was remitted for reconsideration. Section 266(3) was considered by Rimer J. in *HMRC v Crossman* [2007] EWHC 1585 (Ch); [2007] B.P.I.R. 1068. Here the court refused to exercise its discretion to dismiss the petition. Section 266(4) ensures that if there is a possibility of a petition based on a criminal bankruptcy order, that should receive priority treatment. For the role of the official petitioner, see s.402.

Note prospective amendment: s.266(4) is to be repealed by CJA 1988 s.170(2) and Sch.16 as from a day to be appointed: see the note to s.264.

Creditor's petition

267   Grounds of creditor's petition

267(1)   [Requirements] A creditor's petition must be in respect of one or more debts owed by the debtor, and the petitioning creditor or each of the petitioning creditors must be a person to whom the debt or (as the case may be) at least one of the debts is owed.

267(2)   [Conditions for presentation of petition] Subject to the next three sections, a creditor's petition may be presented to the court in respect of a debt or debts only if, at the time the petition is presented–

(a)   the amount of the debt, or the aggregate amount of the debts, is equal to or exceeds the bankruptcy level,

(b)   the debt, or each of the debts, is for a liquidated sum payable to the petitioning creditor, or one or more of the petitioning creditors, either immediately or at some certain, future time, and is unsecured,

(c) the debt, or each of the debts, is a debt which the debtor appears either to be unable to pay or to have no reasonable prospect of being able to pay, and

(d) there is no outstanding application to set aside a statutory demand served (under section 268 below) in respect of the debt or any of the debts.

267(3) [Interpretation] A debt is not to be regarded for the purposes of subsection (2) as a debt for a liquidated sum by reason only that the amount of the debt is specified in a criminal bankruptcy order.

267(4) ["The bankruptcy level"] "The bankruptcy level" is £750; but the Secretary of State may by order in a statutory instrument substitute any amount specified in the order for that amount or (as the case may be) for the amount which by virtue of such an order is for the time being the amount of the bankruptcy level.

267(5) [Approval of order by Parliament] An order shall not be made under subsection (4) unless a draft of it has been laid before, and approved by a resolution of, each House of Parliament.

S.267(1), (2)

These provisions explain what debts can be used as the basis of a creditor's petition. Basically, the debt must be undisputed and for a liquidated sum in excess of the bankruptcy level (see s.267(4)). In *Coulter v Chief of Dorset Police* [2004] EWCA Civ 1259; [2005] B.P.I.R. 62 the Court of Appeal reiterated that for the purposes of s.267 a petitioner must be a creditor who must have a debt which is payable immediately or at some future time. An unliquidated claim cannot provide the basis for a petition—*Hope v Premierpace (Europe) Ltd* [1999] B.P.I.R. 695. On whether a debt is unliquidated or disputed see *TSB v Platts (No.2)* [1998] B.P.I.R. 284. In *Dubai Aluminium Co Ltd v Salaam* [2007] B.P.I.R. 690 Registrar Simmonds held that the reference to "debt" in s.267 must be taken to mean unsecured debt. Here it was held that where the debtor had paid the debt cited in the petition it would be wrong to allow that petition to be amended to include some other debt. The proper approach in such cases was to present a new statutory demand. The debtor must appear to be unable to pay or have no reasonable prospect of paying this debt. If an application is pending to set aside the statutory demand for payment of this debt, it falls outside the category of qualifying debts. For what constitutes an outstanding set-aside application see *Ariyo v Sovereign Leasing* [1998] B.P.I.R. 177. A statute-barred debt cannot form the basis for a statutory demand: *Jelly v All Type Roofing* [1997] B.C.C. 465; *Bruton v IRC* [2000] B.P.I.R. 946. Compare *Times Newspapers Ltd v Chohan* [2001] B.P.I.R. 943; *Global Finance Recoveries Ltd v Jones* [2000] B.P.I.R. 1029; and *West Bromwich Building Society v Crammer* [2002] EWHC 2618 (Ch); [2003] B.P.I.R. 783.

For full consideration of the requirements that must be established for the tort of malicious presentation of a bankruptcy petition see *Jacob v Vockrodt* [2007] EWHC 2403 (QB); [2007] B.P.I.R. 1568.

See also *Rio Properties Inc v Al-Midani* [2003] B.P.I.R. 128 where the court held that a foreign gaming debt which had apparently been settled via an English law compromise could form the basis of a bankruptcy petition.

In *Klamer v Kyriakides and Braier (a firm)* [2005] B.P.I.R. 1115 Mr Registrar Simmonds held that a solicitor's bill that had not been assessed was not a liquidated debt capable of forming the basis of a statutory demand/bankruptcy petition for the purposes of s.267(2)(b) of the IA 1986. In *Truex v Toll* [2009] EWHC 396 (Ch); [2009] B.P.I.R. 692 Proudman J. ruled that an untaxed solicitor's bill was not a liquidated debt for the purposes of s.267. Here it could not be said that the client had admitted liability to pay the invoice because the alleged admission was not unequivocal and was not supported by consideration.

A sum due under an interim payments order made under CPR r.25.6 is a "debt" for these purposes: *Maxwell v Bishopsgate Investment Management Ltd* [1993] T.L.R. 67. In so deciding Chadwick J. noted that the abolition of acts of bankruptcy had produced this change in the law—a final judgment was not necessary under the new bankruptcy code to justify a statutory demand. A taxed costs order can found a statutory demand—*Galloppa v Galloppa* [1999] B.P.I.R. 352. A debt arising under a regulated hire purchase agreement can found the basis for a statutory demand: *Mills v Grove Securities Ltd* [1997] B.P.I.R. 243. A joint debt owed by a partner also falls within s.267(1) according to *Schooler v Customs and Excise Commissioners* [1996] B.P.I.R. 207. Non-provable bankruptcy debts can provide the basis for a petition—*Levy v Legal Services Commission* [2000] B.P.I.R. 1065. On the status of unpaid community charge see *Re Wood* [1994] 1 C.L. 257 (1993, Tamworth County Court). The debt can be a sum due in a foreign currency according to Morritt J. in *Re a Debtor (51/SD/1991)* [1992] 1 W.L.R. 1294.

Presumably the rule in *Re McGreavy* [1950] Ch. 269, that an unpaid rates demand is a "debt" for the purposes of a bankruptcy petition, is preserved by s.267. For discussion of the position with regard to unpaid community charges see *Preston BC v Riley* [1999] B.P.I.R. 284 (an authority on county court administration orders).

A council tax liability order is a "debt" for the purposes of s.267—see Peter Smith J. in *Smolen v Tower Hamlets LBC* [2007] B.P.I.R. 448. A reduction in the amount of liability (provided the reduction does not take the liability to a sum under £750) does not affect that position.

A statutory demand can be issued in respect of a consumer credit debt notwithstanding the provisions of s.141 of the Consumer Credit Act 1974—*Omokwe v HFC Bank Ltd* [2007] B.P.I.R. 1157.

For guidance on preparing the petition see *Practice Direction: Insolvency Proceedings* [2000] B.C.C. 927 (reproduced in [2007] B.C.C. 842—see App.IV in Vol.2).

The criteria in s.267(2)(a) and (b) were *not* satisfied in *Dean & Dean v Angel Airlines SA* [2009] EWHC 447 (Ch) [2009] B.P.I.R. 409.

For the scope of s.267(2)(d) see *Ahmad v Commissioners of Inland Revenue* [2004] EWHC 2292 (Ch); [2005] B.P.I.R. 541. Section 267(2)(d) must, in the opinion of Mummery J., be read as being subject to s.270: see *Re a Debtor (No.22 of 1993)* [1994] 1 W.L.R. 46 (sometimes cited as *Focus Insurance v A Debtor*).

S.267(3)

This narrows the definition of a liquidated sum to exclude amounts of debts specified in criminal bankruptcy orders.

Note prospective amendment: s.267(3) is to be repealed by CJA 1988 s.170(2) and Sch.16 as from a day to be appointed: see the note to s.264.

S.267(4), (5)

The current bankruptcy level is £750, although the Secretary of State can increase it. On whether this amount must still be outstanding at the date of the hearing: *Re Patel* [1986] 1 W.L.R. 221 (a case decided under the 1914 Act). Whether this case would be followed under the new regime is questionable—*Lilley v American Express (Europe) Ltd* [2000] B.P.I.R. 70. The courts are not favourably disposed to bankruptcy proceedings brought to recover debts slightly in excess of £750: *City Electrical Factors Ltd v Hardingham* [1996] B.P.I.R. 541. Where there is an undisputed debt clearly in excess of the statutory minimum but a balance that is disputed the petition can proceed: *TSB Bank v Platts (No.2)* [1998] B.P.I.R. 284.

268 Definition of "inability to pay", etc.; the statutory demand

268(1) **[Interpretation of s.267(2)(c)]** For the purposes of section 267(2)(c), the debtor appears to be unable to pay a debt if, but only if, the debt is payable immediately and either–

(a) the petitioning creditor to whom the debt is owed has served on the debtor a demand (known as "the statutory demand") in the prescribed form requiring him to pay the debt or to secure or compound for it to the satisfaction of the creditor, at least 3 weeks have elapsed since the demand was served and the demand has been neither complied with nor set aside in accordance with the rules, or

(b) execution or other process issued in respect of the debt on a judgment or order of any court in favour of the petitioning creditor, or one or more of the petitioning creditors to whom the debt is owed, has been returned unsatisfied in whole or in part.

268(2) **[Further interpretation]** For the purposes of section 267(2)(c) the debtor appears to have no reasonable prospect of being able to pay a debt if, but only if, the debt is not immediately payable and–

(a) the petitioning creditor to whom it is owed has served on the debtor a demand (also known as "the statutory demand") in the prescribed form requiring him to establish to the satisfaction of the creditor that there is a reasonable prospect that the debtor will be able to pay the debt when it falls due,

(b) at least 3 weeks have elapsed since the demand was served, and

(c) the demand has been neither complied with nor set aside in accordance with the rules.

GENERAL NOTE

This section defines "inability to pay" and "statutory demand", terms featuring in s.267. A debtor will be deemed unable to pay a debt if he fails to meet a demand in the prescribed form served on him within three weeks—under the previous law the debtor was given only 10 days' grace—or an execution for a judgment debt has been returned unsatisfied. In *Re a Debtor (No.1 of 1987)* [1989] 1 W.L.R. 271 the Court of Appeal, confirming a ruling of Warner J., took a relaxed view of a statutory demand that contained errors as to the amount owed. The Court of Appeal refused to set aside this demand as no injustice had been done to the debtor. In so deciding the Court of Appeal departed from the position under the pre-1985 bankruptcy law and indicated that the new provisions had to be interpreted in their own context. This case is a watershed authority marking a fundamental change in attitude on the part of the courts to procedural errors in the bankruptcy process. Formerly, in the case of a defect in a bankruptcy notice the whole proceedings would be invalidated. Now that bankruptcy is viewed as a more user-friendly regime for the debtor the courts feel justified in adopting a more pragmatic stance. For a full discussion of this relaxation of judicial attitudes see Milman, [1994] Conv. 289–298. Thus if the debt mentioned in the demand is overstated this will not invalidate the demand (provided the undisputed element exceeds the minimum bankruptcy level): see here *Re a Debtor (490/SD/1991)* [1992] 1 W.L.R. 507 where Hoffmann J. disclaimed his earlier contrary view in *Re a Debtor (No.10 of 1988)* [1989] 1 W.L.R. 405. Similar principles would appear to apply if part of the debt is disputed but there is an undisputed balance—failure to highlight the dispute may not be critical (*Re a Debtor (657/SD/1991)* [1993] B.C.L.C. 1280, per Ferris J.). Equally errors as to the degree of security enjoyed by the creditor might be overlooked: see *Re a Debtor (No.106 of 1992)*, *The Independent*, April 20, 1992.

Bankruptcy proceedings cannot be used to go behind a determination of the Revenue General Commissioners— *Cullinane v IRC* [2000] B.P.I.R. 996.

An important point to note is that a statutory demand is a document issued by a creditor. Unlike the old bankruptcy notice it is not issued by the court and does not form part of court proceedings. This can have implications. Thus in *Re a Debtor (No.190 of 1987)*, *The Times*, May 21, 1988 Vinelott J. held that the relieving jurisdiction in r.7.55 was inapplicable—but in view of the more liberal attitude of the courts to procedural irregularities this hardly matters. Equally it was held in *Re a Debtor (No.88 of 1991)* [1993] Ch. 286 that the presentation of a statutory demand is not an "action" within the meaning of s.69 of the Solicitors Act 1974 and so the one month moratorium imposed on solicitors seeking to recover fees from debtor clients does not apply (though the moratorium would extend to the presentation of the petition). For discussion see Start, (1992) 142 N.L.J. 1121 and Simmonds, (1992) 26 Law. Soc. Gaz. 18. See also *Shalson v DF Keane Ltd* [2003] EWHC 599 (Ch); [2003] B.P.I.R. 1045 where it was held that the mere service of a statutory demand did not constitute the commencement of legal proceedings so as to trigger the stay on such proceedings under the terms of s.9 of the Arbitration Act 1996.

On issue estoppel and failed set-aside applications note *Eberhardt & Co v Mair* [1995] B.C.C. 845.

On what constitutes an unsatisfied execution within s.268(1)(b) see *Re a Debtor (No.340 of 1992)* [1996] 2 All E.R. 211; and *Skarzynski v Chalford Property Co Ltd* [2001] B.P.I.R. 673.

In *Dubai Aluminium v Salaam* [2007] B.P.I.R. 690 Registrar Simmonds ruled that where a bankruptcy petition referred to unsecured and secured debts and the unsecured debts had been paid off the creditor could not then amend its petition and revalue its security to create a new unsecured debt. In such a case the requirements of s.268 were not satisfied and a new statutory demand would have to be served.

Where council tax arrears liability orders are relied upon by local authorities to form the basis of a statutory demand the amounts in question should be precise and itemised—the courts have expressed their irritation at being asked to accede to a bankruptcy petition on the basis of imprecise information about the debtor's status with regard to council tax arrears—*London Borough of Lambeth v Simon* [2007] B.P.I.R. 1629. Indeed on March 31, 2008 a local government ombudsman has gone so far as to suggest that for a local authority (in this case Wolverhampton City Council) to present a bankruptcy petition for council tax arrears of £1,105 without fully considering other options (such as a charging order) could amount to maladministration. Other local authorities have been criticised for similar practices—see p.303 above.

If the requirements of s.268 are satisfied it is no defence for the debtor to establish that he was solvent at the time. A solvent debtor can be made subject to a bankruptcy order—*Johnson v Tandrige DC* [2008] B.P.I.R. 405. See also the discussion in *Evans v Clarke Willmott & Clarke* [2007] EWHC 852 (Ch); [2008] B.P.I.R. 37.

A statutory demand does not constitute a formal demand under a guarantee—rather it is a prescribed form solely designed for the purposes of bankruptcy law—*TS & S Global Ltd v Fithian-Franks* [2007] EWHC 1401 (Ch); [2007] B.P.I.R. 424.

For further details on the statutory demand, see IR 1986 rr.6.1–6.5 and *Practice Direction: Insolvency Proceedings* [2000] B.C.C. 927, which is reproduced in [2007] B.C.C. 842 and included in App.IV.

For security as to costs where s.268(2) is relied upon see IR 1986 r.6.17.

269   Creditor with security

269(1)   [Where debt not unsecured] A debt which is the debt, or one of the debts, in respect of which a creditor's petition is presented need not be unsecured if either–

(a) the petition contains a statement by the person having the right to enforce the security that he is willing, in the event of a bankruptcy order being made, to give up his security for the benefit of all the bankrupt's creditors, or

(b) the petition is expressed not to be made in respect of the secured part of the debt and contains a statement by that person of the estimated value at the date of the petition of the security for the secured part of the debt.

269(2)   **[Debt in s.269(1)(b)]** In a case falling within subsection (1)(b) the secured and unsecured parts of the debt are to be treated for the purposes of sections 267 to 270 as separate debts.

GENERAL NOTE

Secured debts can form the basis of a creditor's petition, provided the creditor is willing to give up his security or if the petition is in respect of an unsecured part of the same debt. See *Zandfarid v BCCI* [1996] B.P.I.R. 501. In *Barclays Bank v Mogg* [2003] EWHC 2645 (Ch); [2004] B.P.I.R. 259 David Richards J. held that a failure to comply with the requirements of s.269, although a serious procedural flaw, might not be fatal to the success of the petition where the debtor was not misled and had suffered no prejudice. Drawing on authorities dealing with the 1914 Act it was held that the court retained discretion to permit the petition to be amended. Note also s.383 here (definition of "secured debt", etc.). For the linkage between s.269 and ss.267 and 268 see *Dubai Aluminium v Salaam* [2007] B.P.I.R. 690.

See also IR 1986 rr.6.115–6.119.

270   Expedited petition

270   In the case of a creditor's petition presented wholly or partly in respect of a debt which is the subject of a statutory demand under section 268, the petition may be presented before the end of the 3-week period there mentioned if there is a serious possibility that the debtor's property or the value of any of his property will be significantly diminished during that period and the petition contains a statement to that effect.

GENERAL NOTE

The three weeks' grace given to the debtor by s.268 can be cut short and the petition presented prematurely if the petition alleges that there is a serious possibility of a significant fall in value of the debtor's assets. The power to expedite the petition under s.270 can only be invoked if the statutory demand has been served—*Wehmeyer v Wehmeyer* [2001] B.P.I.R. 548. This procedure can still be invoked even though there is an extant set-aside application with respect to the statutory demand: see the ruling of Mummery J. in *Re a Debtor (No.22 of 1993)* [1994] 1 W.L.R. 46 (sometimes cited as *Focus Insurance v A Debtor*). However, should the set-aside application succeed at the end of the day the creditor might be exposed to some sort of personal claim by the debtor, a point considered by Mummery J.

271   Proceedings on creditor's petition

271(1)   **[Conditions for bankruptcy order]** The court shall not make a bankruptcy order on a creditor's petition unless it is satisfied that the debt, or one of the debts, in respect of which the petition was presented is either–

(a) a debt which, having been payable at the date of the petition or having since become payable, has been neither paid nor secured or compounded for, or

(b) a debt which the debtor has no reasonable prospect of being able to pay when it falls due.

271(2)   **[Where petition contains s.270 statement]** In a case in which the petition contains such a statement as is required by section 270, the court shall not make a bankruptcy order until at least 3 weeks have elapsed since the service of any statutory demand under section 268.

271(3)   **[Dismissal of petition]** The court may dismiss the petition if it is satisfied that the debtor is able to pay all his debts or is satisfied–

(a)   that the debtor has made an offer to secure or compound for a debt in respect of which the petition is presented,

(b)   that the acceptance of that offer would have required the dismissal of the petition, and

(c)   that the offer has been unreasonably refused;

and, in determining for the purposes of this subsection whether the debtor is able to pay all his debts, the court shall take into account his contingent and prospective liabilities.

271(4)   **[Interpretation]** In determining for the purposes of this section what constitutes a reasonable prospect that a debtor will be able to pay a debt when it falls due, it is to be assumed that the prospect given by the facts and other matters known to the creditor at the time he entered into the transaction resulting in the debt was a reasonable prospect.

271(5)   **[Powers of court to amend etc.]** Nothing in sections 267 to 271 prejudices the power of the court, in accordance with the rules, to authorise a creditor's petition to be amended by the omission of any creditor or debt and to be proceeded with as if things done for the purposes of those sections had been done only by or in relation to the remaining creditors or debts.

GENERAL NOTE

If a petition is granted under IA 1986 it is followed by a bankruptcy order. The previous intermediate stage of a receiving order (BA 1914 s.3) has been abolished. Note also IR 1986 rr.6.18, 6.22 and 6.25 and 6.33. Note that bankruptcy petitions, unlike winding up petitions, are not advertised.

S.271(1), (2), (4)

The power of the court to make a bankruptcy order is qualified by these provisions. For an explicit assertion of the jurisdiction of the court under s.271 see *Potter v HMRC* (unreported 2008). Where the bankruptcy petition is contested the court should consider whether the defence raises a genuinely triable issue (even if it is improbable)— *Markham v Karsten* [2007] EWHC 1509 (Ch); [2007] B.P.I.R. 1109. See *Lambeth LBC v Simon* [2007] B.P.I.R. 1629 for a strong assertion by the bankruptcy court of its right (and in some cases its duty) to go behind judgments triggering bankruptcy proceedings. In *Smolen v Tower Hamlets LBC* [2007] B.P.I.R. 448 Peter Smith J. confirmed that ss.271(1)(a) and 271(1)(b) are alternatives and not cumulative. Note that in the event of a petition presented prematurely the court must wait until the three weeks have elapsed before making the order. Unsuccessful arguments which have been run on a failed set aside application with regard to the statutory demand should not generally be revisited when the petition is being heard—on this see *Adams v Mason Bullock (a firm)* [2005] B.P.I.R. 241. However, if the argument was not considered on its merits at that earlier stage it can be raised when the petition is being heard—see *IRC v Lee-Phipps* [2003] B.P.I.R. 803. Moreover in *Barnes v Whitehead* [2004] B.P.I.R. 693 the court ruled that an earlier failure by the debtor to raise a dispute as to the existence of the debt by seeking to have the statutory demand set aside did not preclude the debtor from raising this very issue at a later date when the petition was being heard. The court had to be satisfied under s.271 that an undisputed debt existed. See also further discussion of these issues in *Adams v Mason Bullock (a firm)* (above). The definition of when a debtor has a "reasonable prospect" of paying a debt certainly leaves a lot to be desired. On s.271(1)(a) see the *Practice Direction* in [1986] 3 All E.R. 864; and *Artman v Artman* [1996] B.P.I.R. 511. On whether joint debts have been compounded see *Re a Bankrupt (No.622 of 1995), The Times*, June 27, 1996.

     The existence of discretion under s.271 was emphasised in *HMRC v Potter* [2008] B.P.I.R. 1033, where the court was not satisfied that the petition debt was owed by the defendant—the debt may have been owed by a company which she controlled. The petition was therefore dismissed.

     Again in *Dean & Dean v Angel Airlines SA* [2009] EWHC 447 (Ch); [2009] B.P.I.R. 409 Patten J. refused to make a bankruptcy order against a party because he was not satisfied that a debt was owing within the terms of s.267(2)(a) and (b).

S.271(3)

This provision states that the court may dismiss the petition if the debtor is able to meet his debts, or has made a proposal to the creditor to secure or compound the debt and it has been unreasonably refused. For discussion of the operation of this provision see *Re Gilmartin (a Bankrupt)* [1989] 1 W.L.R. 513 where Harman J. concluded that the registrar had been correct in deciding that an offer had not been unreasonably refused by the petitioner and the supporting creditors. In *Re a Debtor (No.32 of 1993)* [1994] 1 W.L.R. 899; [1994] B.C.C. 438 it was held by Timothy Lloyd Q.C. (sitting as a deputy High Court judge) that a debtor can offer to secure or compound within the meaning of s.271(3) where there is just a single creditor involved. However, in determining whether the creditor's refusal of the offer was unreasonable it must be established to the satisfaction of the court that no reasonable hypothetical creditor would have rejected the debtor's offer; the fact that some creditors might have accepted it is not conclusive. In *Inland Revenue Commissioners v A Debtor* [1995] B.C.C. 971 the court could not be persuaded that the refusal of tax officers to accept security for a debt was unreasonable. In *Evans v Clarke, Willmott & Clarke* [2007] EWHC 852 (Ch); [2008] B.P.I.R. 37 the creditor was held not to have behaved unreasonably in rejecting the debtor's offer as no clear and satisfactory offer had in fact been made. On s.271(3) generally see *Re a Debtor (No.415/SD/1993)* [1994] 1 W.L.R. 917; and *King v IRC* [1996] B.P.I.R. 414. In *Re a Debtor (No.2389 of 1989)* [1991] Ch. 326 Vinelott J. held that the proposal of a voluntary arrangement by the debtor under Pt VIII of the Act cannot be regarded as an "offer" for the purposes of s.271(3) in that the decision on acceptance is not solely a matter for the petitioning creditor. The consequences of acceptance or refusal of such a proposal are dealt with exclusively by Pt VIII. For discussion, see Griffiths (1991) 135 S.J. 598.

The court also has discretion to adjourn the petition but this discretion must be carefully watched—*Harrison v Seggar* [2005] EWHC 411 (Ch); [2005] B.P.I.R. 583. Having made a bankruptcy order under s.271 the court has jurisdiction to stay the order if appropriate—*Emap Active Ltd v Hill* [2007] EWHC 1592 (Ch); [2007] B.P.I.R. 1228. Putative bankrupts frequently fail to turn up for the hearing of the petition against them. Provided they have been served with the petition and given appropriate notice the mere fact that the judge decides to hear the petition in their absence does not necessarily involve a contravention of art.6 ECHR—*Manyan v Dewar Hogan* [2004] EWHC 3107 (Ch); [2006] B.P.I.R. 71.

Note also IR 1986 r.5A.23—possibility of a debt relief order.

S.271(5)

This protects the discretion of the court to amend petitions, etc. Presumably this would permit consolidation of petitions or changes in the carriage of proceedings (compare the repealed BA 1914 ss.110 and 111). See *Re Purvis* [1998] B.P.I.R. 153.

Debtor's petition

272   Grounds of debtor's petition

272(1)   [Presentation to court] A debtor's petition may be presented to the court only on the grounds that the debtor is unable to pay his debts.

272(2)   [Statement of debtor's affairs] The petition shall be accompanied by a statement of the debtor's affairs containing–

(a)   such particulars of the debtor's creditors and of his debts and other liabilities and of his assets as may be prescribed, and

(b)   such other information as may be prescribed.

GENERAL NOTE

This again is, in many senses, a new provision, though the break with the past is not as radical as it might appear at first sight. A debtor could file for his own bankruptcy under the old law—indeed, this was an act of bankruptcy. For further guidance on a debtor's petition see IR 1986 rr.6.37–6.50. The fee for such a petition is £150—see Civil Proceedings Fees Order 2004 (SI 2004/3121 (L. 23)). A deposit of £450 is also payable to cover the costs of the official receiver—see SI 2010/732. This deposit requirement does not deprive the debtor of a fundamental right of access to the court—*R. v Lord Chancellor Ex p. Lightfoot* [2000] B.P.I.R. 120. A debtor who petitions for his own bankruptcy does not thereby make a disposition of his property contrary to s.37 of the Matrimonial Causes Act 1973: *Woodley v Woodley (No.2)* [1994] 1 W.L.R. 1167.

At the moment it is taking up to three months to process some debtor petitions—this has lead the Insolvency Service to consider handing over the processing of debtor petitions to the Official Receiver, thus taking them out of the court system entirely—see Insolvency Service Consultative Document, "Bankruptcy: Proposals for Reform of the Debtor Petition Procedure" (October 2007). Further developments in this area are awaited.

S.272(1)

This provision preserves a debtor's right to petition for his own bankruptcy. Note that no minimum debt is required here. The test for inability to pay debts here appears to be based upon current liquidity: *Re Coney* [1998] B.P.I.R. 333.

The scenario of a husband/debtor presenting a bankruptcy petition allegedly in order to frustrate his wife's claim to matrimonial relief surfaced in *Paulin v Paulin* [2009] EWCA Civ 221; [2009] B.P.I.R. 572. Here the Court of Appeal followed *Re Coney* (above) and confirmed that for the purposes of s.272 a commercial solvency criterion, rather than a balance sheet test, was to be applied.

S.272(2)

This provision details the content of the petition. The rules are important for clarification purposes here: see IR 1986 rr.6.38, 6.39.

273 Appointment of insolvency practitioner by the court

273(1) **[Where court not to make bankruptcy order]** Subject to the next section, on the hearing of a debtor's petition the court shall not make a bankruptcy order if it appears to the court–

(a) that if a bankruptcy order were made the aggregate amount of the bankruptcy debts, so far as unsecured, would be less than the small bankruptcies level,

(b) that if a bankruptcy order were made, the value of the bankrupt's estate would be equal to or more than the minimum amount,

(c) that within the period of 5 years ending with the presentation of the petition the debtor has neither been adjudged bankrupt nor made a composition with his creditors in satisfaction of his debts or a scheme of arrangement of his affairs, and

(d) that it would be appropriate to appoint a person to prepare a report under section 274.

"The minimum amount" and **"the small bankruptcies level"** mean such amounts as may for the time being be prescribed for the purposes of this section.

273(2) **[Appointment of person to prepare report]** Where on the hearing of the petition, it appears to the court as mentioned in subsection (1), the court shall appoint a person who is qualified to act as an insolvency practitioner in relation to the debtor–

(a) to prepare a report under the next section, and

(b) subject to section 258(3) in Part VIII, to act in relation to any voluntary arrangement to which the report relates either as trustee or otherwise for the purpose of supervising its implementation.

GENERAL NOTE

This provision reflects the strategy of the Cork Committee, which was to use bankruptcy only as a last resort, especially where the amounts involved were small.

S.273(1)

The power of the court to make a bankruptcy order on a debtor's petition is restricted. Where the court is satisfied that the debts do not exceed the "small bankruptcies level" (£40,000), the estate's value exceeds the "minimum amount" £4,000 (see the Insolvency Proceedings (Monetary Limits) (Amendment) Order 2004 (SI 2004/547)), and the debtor has not been in serious financial difficulties within the previous five years, it may feel it more appropriate to ask for a report as described below.

S.273(2)

If the conditions in s.273(1) are satisfied, the court can appoint a qualified insolvency practitioner to prepare a s.274 report, and to act as supervisor of a voluntary arrangement. The fee here was increased to £450 by the Insolvency Proceedings (Fees) (Amendment) Order 2010 (SI 2010/732) with effect from April 6, 2010.

See also IR 1986 r.6.44.

274 Action on report of insolvency practitioner

274(1) **[Report to court]** A person appointed under section 273 shall inquire into the debtor's affairs and, within such period as the court may direct, shall submit a report to the court stating whether the debtor is willing, for the purposes of Part VIII, to make a proposal for a voluntary arrangement.

274(2)   [Contents of report] A report which states that the debtor is willing as above mentioned shall also state–

(a)   whether, in the opinion of the person making the report, a meeting of the debtor's creditors should be summoned to consider the proposal, and

(b)   if in that person's opinion such a meeting should be summoned, the date on which, and time and place at which, he proposes the meeting should be held.

274(3)   [Powers of court] On considering a report under this section the court may–

(a)   without any application, make an interim order under section 252, if it thinks that it is appropriate to do so for the purpose of facilitating the consideration and implementation of the debtor's proposal, or

(b)   if it thinks it would be inappropriate to make such an order, make a bankruptcy order.

274(4)   [Cessation of interim order] An interim order made by virtue of this section ceases to have effect at the end of such period as the court may specify for the purpose of enabling the debtor's proposal to be considered by his creditors in accordance with the applicable provisions of Part VIII.

274(5)   [Summoning of meeting] Where it has been reported to the court under this section that a meeting of the debtor's creditors should be summoned, the person making the report shall, unless the court otherwise directs, summon that meeting for the time, date and place proposed in his report.

The meeting is then deemed to have been summoned under section 257 in Part VIII, and subsections (2) and (3) of that section, and sections 258 to 263 apply accordingly.

S.274(1), (2)
If the court makes a s.273 appointment, the appointee must investigate the debtor's affairs to see whether a viable proposal for a voluntary arrangement (see ss.252–263, above) can be constructed and, if so, whether a creditors' meeting should be held. Where the court appoints an insolvency practitioner under s.273(2) to prepare and submit a report under s.274 the court must, on submission of that report, pay to the practitioner a fee of £360 (which is inclusive of VAT): see the Insolvency Proceedings (Fees) (Amendment) Order 2009 (SI 2009/645).

A copy of an s.274 must be sent to the FSA where appropriate—FSMA 2000 s.374(3).

S.274(3)
This maps out the court's options on receiving the above report—these are to make either an interim order with a view to facilitating a voluntary arrangement or a bankruptcy order.

S.274(4)
This provision describes the duration of an interim order made under s.274(3).

S.274(5)
This makes provision for any meeting of creditors which has to be held to consider the voluntary arrangement.

274A   Debtor who meets conditions for a debt relief order

274A(1)   [Application of s.274A] This section applies where, on the hearing of a debtor's petition–

(a)   it appears to the court that a debt relief order would be made in relation to the debtor if, instead of presenting the petition, he had made an application under Part 7A; and

(b)   the court does not appoint an insolvency practitioner under section 273.

274A(2)   [Referral to approved intermediary for debt relief order] If the court thinks it would be in the debtor's interests to apply for a debt relief order instead of proceeding on the petition, the court may refer the debtor to an approved intermediary (within the meaning of Part 7A) for the purposes of making an application for a debt relief order.

274A(3)   [Stay of bankruptcy petition] Where a reference is made under subsection (2) the court shall stay proceedings on the petition on such terms and conditions as it thinks fit; but if following the reference a debt relief order is made in relation to the debtor the court shall dismiss the petition.

Note insertion of s.274A by para.3 of Pt 1 of Sch.20 to the Tribunals, Courts and Enforcement Act 2007. This new section will enable the court to direct debtors who present their own bankruptcy petitions to the new debt relief order procedure introduced by the 2007 Act. The current mechanism of appointing an insolvency practitioner under s.273 to look at an IVA possibility has not been widely used, and one wonders whether this well-intentioned measure will have any greater utility.

See IR r.5A.22.

275　Summary administration [Repealed.]

GENERAL NOTE

Editors' note—summary administration was repealed from April 1, 2004—see s.269 of and Sch.23 to EA 2002.

Other cases for special consideration

276　Default in connection with voluntary arrangement

276(1)　[Conditions for s.264(1)(c) bankruptcy order] The court shall not make a bankruptcy order on a petition under section 264(1)(c) (supervisor of, or person bound by, voluntary arrangement proposed and approved) unless it is satisfied–

(a)　that the debtor has failed to comply with his obligations under the voluntary arrangement, or

(b)　that information which was false or misleading in any material particular or which contained material omissions–

　(i)　was contained in any statement of affairs or other document supplied by the debtor under Part VIII to any person, or

　(ii)　was otherwise made available by the debtor to his creditors at or in connection with a meeting summoned under that Part, or

(c)　that the debtor has failed to do all such things as may for the purposes of the voluntary arrangement have been reasonably required of him by the supervisor of the arrangement.

276(2)　[Expenses] Where a bankruptcy order is made on a petition under section 264(1)(c), any expenses properly incurred as expenses of the administration of the voluntary arrangement in question shall be a first charge on the bankrupt's estate.

S.276(1)

This allows the court to make a bankruptcy order where a debtor has failed to fulfil his obligations under a voluntary arrangement set up by virtue of ss.252–263. The jurisdiction here is discretionary and if appropriate the court may permit the IVA to continue—*Kaye v Bourne* [2004] EWHC 3236 (Ch); [2005] B.P.I.R. 590. Material omissions in the proposal, etc. may also justify this course of action—*Re Tack* [2000] B.P.I.R. 164. On s.276(1)(b) and the continuing duty of disclosure see *Somji v Cadbury Schweppes plc* [2001] B.P.I.R. 172. The fact that the debtor is not to blame for the failure of the IVA is irrelevant: *Re Keenan* [1998] B.P.I.R. 205. Nor indeed is it a bar to a s.276 petition that the debtor has remedied the default by the time the petition is heard—*Carter-Knight v Peat* [2000] B.P.I.R. 268. A default petition can be presented by the supervisor even though the time period specified in the IVA has expired—*Harris v Gross* [2001] B.P.I.R. 586. In *Bradburn v Kaye* [2006] B.P.I.R. 605 Mr Recorder Hodge Q.C. (sitting as a Deputy Judge of the High Court) held that an IVA could be set aside under s.276(1)(b) of the IA 1986 and a bankruptcy order substituted on the grounds of non disclosure of the full extent of potential liabilities to the Revenue. It was material non disclosure because had the Revenue been treated as a creditor for the full amount it would have been in a position to block the IVA. There was no need to show that the non disclosure was culpable. Moreover, the existence of a waiver provision in the IVA terms excusing default or non disclosure could not override the statutory jurisdiction under s.276. On the other hand, the alternative grounds put forward by the supervisor (i.e. failure to obtain consent before incurring further credit contrary to the IVA terms) for setting aside were rejected. Although in engaging the services of accountants the debtor technically had incurred further credit in breach of the IVA that alone would not have persuaded this court to exercise its jurisdiction under s.276(1)(a) to set aside the IVA because this was a technical breach and the IVA was delivering the promised payments on time to creditors. Where an IVA is set aside under s.276 it is not a nullity ab initio—see *Cooper v Official Receiver* [2002] EWHC 1970 (Ch); [2003] B.P.I.R. 55.

S.276(2)
Where the court takes this drastic step, the expenses already incurred in connection with the scheme become a first charge on the bankrupt's estate.

277   Petition based on criminal bankruptcy order

277(1)   [Duty of court] Subject to section 266(3), the court shall make a bankruptcy order on a petition under section 264(1)(d) on production of a copy of the criminal bankruptcy order on which the petition is based.

This does not apply if it appears to the court that the criminal bankruptcy order has been rescinded on appeal.

277(2)   [Effect of appeal pending] Subject to the provisions of this Part, the fact that an appeal is pending against any conviction by virtue of which a criminal bankruptcy order was made does not affect any proceedings on a petition under section 264(1)(d) based on that order.

277(3)   [When appeal is pending] For the purposes of this section, an appeal against a conviction is pending–

(a)   in any case, until the expiration of the period of 28 days beginning with the date of conviction;

(b)   if notice of appeal to the Court of Appeal is given during that period and during that period the appellant notifies the official receiver of it, until the determination of the appeal and thereafter for so long as an appeal to the Supreme Court is pending within the meaning of subsection (4).

277(4)   [When appeal to Supreme Court pending] For the purposes of subsection (3)(b) an appeal to the Supreme Court shall be treated as pending until any application for leave to appeal is disposed of and, if leave to appeal is granted, until the appeal is disposed of; and for the purposes of this subsection an application for leave to appeal shall be treated as disposed of at the expiration of the time within which it may be made, if it is not made within that time.

GENERAL NOTE

This section deals with petitions arising out of criminal bankruptcy orders. Criminal bankruptcy orders were first introduced in 1972, and the legislation currently in force is the Powers of the Criminal Courts Act 1973 ss.39, 40. However, the power to make such orders was abolished by CJA 1988 s.101, with effect from April 3, 1989 (see SI 1989/264 (C. 8)), and so it is most unlikely that there will be any occasion to invoke the provisions of s.264(1)(d) or s.277 in the future.

Commencement and duration of bankruptcy; discharge

278   Commencement and continuance

278   The bankruptcy of an individual against whom a bankruptcy order has been made–

(a)   commences with the day on which the order is made, and

(b)   continues until the individual is discharged under the following provisions of this Chapter.

GENERAL NOTE

Bankruptcy commences at the date of the order (and not when the petition was presented), and lasts until discharge. See IR 1986 rr.6.34 and 6.46.

279   Duration

279(1)   [Discharge from bankruptcy in one year] A bankrupt is discharged from bankruptcy at the end of the period of one year beginning with the date on which the bankruptcy commences.

279(2)   [Earlier discharge on official receiver's notice] If before the end of that period the official receiver files with the court a notice stating that investigation of the conduct and affairs of the bankrupt under section 289 is unnecessary or concluded, the bankrupt is discharged when the notice is filed.

279(3)   [Order that discharge period ceases to run] On the application of the official receiver or the trustee of a bankrupt's estate, the court may order that the period specified in subsection (1) shall cease to run until–

(a)   the end of a specified period, or

(b)   the fulfilment of a specified condition.

279(4)   [When order may be made] The court may make an order under subsection (3) only if satisfied that the bankrupt has failed or is failing to comply with an obligation under this Part.

279(5)   ["Condition" in s.279(3)(b)] In subsection (3)(b) "condition" includes a condition requiring that the court be satisfied of something.

279(6)   [Non-application of s.279(1)–(5)] In the case of an individual who is adjudged bankrupt on a petition under section 264(1)(d)–

(a)   subsections (1) to (5) shall not apply, and

(b)   the bankrupt is discharged from bankruptcy by an order of the court under section 280.

279(7)   [Power of court to annul bankruptcy order] This section is without prejudice to any power of the court to annul a bankruptcy order.

GENERAL NOTE

These new provisions on discharge, which were introduced by s.256 of EA 2002, came into effect in April 2004. These provisions must be read in the light of Sch.19 to EA 2002 which makes transitional provisions.

Automatic discharge, which was pioneered in 1976 is now widely accepted as a feature of bankruptcy regulation, in spite of concerns raised by the Cork Committee (Cmnd.8558, para.607).

For further provisions on discharge see IR 1986 rr.6.215–6.222.

S.279(1)

This introduces the new one-year maximum period before discharge takes effect. It is a significant reduction on the existing three-year period, though not as great as the government intended when it initially proposed six months! When assessing this discharge period it must be borne in mind that discharge does not for the most part mean that the powers of the trustee vis-à-vis the estate have come to an end. Realisation powers and income payments matters can continue for some time thereafter.

S.279(2)

Discharge can take place before the one year is up if the official receiver gives the green light. On early discharge procedures see *Dear IP* Issue 25 (December 2005).

S.279(3)–(5)

These deal with the converse situation where the trustee or official receiver wish to extend the one-year period for a specified period or until a condition is satisfied. This will only happen if the bankrupt has failed to fulfil his obligations. Cases decided under the former s.279(3) will continue to be instructive—see here *Hardy v Focus Insurance Co Ltd* [1997] B.P.I.R. 77; *Holmes v Official Receiver* [1996] B.C.C. 246; *Jacobs v Official Receiver* [1999] 1 W.L.R. 619; and *Bagnall v Official Receiver* [2004] EWCA Civ 1925; [2004] B.P.I.R. 445 where the Court of Appeal adopted a purposive view on whether interim orders could in principle be made suspending discharge pending a full hearing. Late applications for such an order were not to be encouraged and the lateness of any application might persuade the court not to grant the order sought. On circumstances where suspension of automatic discharge might be appropriate see *Shierson v Rastogi* [2007] EWHC 1266 (Ch); [2007] B.P.I.R. 864.

S.279(6)

This deals with a special (and extremely rare) case involving criminal bankruptcy.

S.279(7)

This provision governing discharge does not affect the power of the court to annul a bankruptcy order—see s.282.

280 Discharge by order of the court

280(1)   [Application to court] An application for an order of the court discharging an individual from bankruptcy in a case falling within section 279(6) may be made by the bankrupt at any time after the end of the period of 5 years beginning with the date on which the bankruptcy commences.

280(2)   [Powers of court] On an application under this section the court may–

(a)   refuse to discharge the bankrupt from bankruptcy,

(b)   make an order discharging him absolutely, or

(c)   make an order discharging him subject to such conditions with respect to any income which may subsequently become due to him, or with respect to property devolving upon him, or acquired by him, after his discharge, as may be specified in the order.

280(3)   [Commencement of effect of order] The court may provide for an order falling within subsection (2)(b) or (c) to have immediate effect or to have its effect suspended for such period, or until the fulfilment of such conditions (including a condition requiring the court to be satisfied as to any matter), as may be specified in the order.

General Note

Tracking back through s.279(6) and 264(1)(d) it becomes apparent on closer examination that s.280 only applies to cases of criminal bankruptcy. The headnote could be more explicit here. Minor textual changes were made by s.269 of and Sch.23 to EA 2002.

S.280(1)

This provision deals with the situation where an undischarged bankrupt applies to the court for his discharge. Automatic discharge is not available where a person was made bankrupt as a result of a criminal bankruptcy order or where he had experienced an earlier bankruptcy within the 15 years prior to the commencement of the present bankruptcy. In these cases he must wait for five years after the commencement of the bankruptcy to elapse before applying to the court for his discharge. See also IR 1986 rr.6.215–6.223.

There is no provision in the present Act for the automatic review of cases every five years by the official receiver, as was required by IA 1976 s.8. However, this is immaterial, as automatic discharge under s.279 is now the general rule.

S.280(2), (3)

On such an application the court has a variety of options open to it, including the grant of conditional or suspended discharges. The Secretary of State can appeal against a discharge order, see IR 1986 r.7.48.

281   Effect of discharge

281(1)   [Discharge qualified release] Subject as follows, where a bankrupt is discharged, the discharge releases him from all the bankruptcy debts, but has no effect–

(a)   on the functions (so far as they remain to be carried out) of the trustee of his estate, or

(b)   on the operation, for the purposes of the carrying out of those functions, of the provisions of this Part;

and, in particular, discharge does not affect the right of any creditor of the bankrupt to prove in the bankruptcy for any debt from which the bankrupt is released.

281(2)   [Enforcement of security] Discharge does not affect the right of any secured creditor of the bankrupt to enforce his security for the payment of a debt from which the bankrupt is released.

281(3)   [Fraud etc.] Discharge does not release the bankrupt from any bankruptcy debt which he incurred in respect of, or forbearance in respect of which was secured by means of, any fraud or fraudulent breach of trust to which he was a party.

281(4)   [Fines, other penalties] Discharge does not release the bankrupt from any liability in respect of a fine imposed for an offence or from any liability under a recognisance except, in the case of a penalty imposed for an offence under an enactment relating to the public revenue or of a recognisance, with the consent of the Treasury.

281(4A)   [Confiscation order] In subsection (4) the reference to a fine includes a reference to a confiscation order under Part 2, 3 or 4 of the Proceeds of Crime Act 2002.

281(5)   [Debts re damages etc.] Discharge does not, except to such extent and on such conditions as the court may direct, release the bankrupt from any bankruptcy debt which–

(a)   consists in a liability to pay damages for negligence, nuisance or breach of a statutory, contractual or other duty, or to pay damages by virtue of Part I of the Consumer Protection Act 1987, being in either case damages in respect of personal injuries to any person, or

(b)   arises under any order made in family proceedings or under a maintenance calculation made under the Child Support Act 1991.

281(6)   [Other bankruptcy debts] Discharge does not release the bankrupt from such other bankruptcy debts, not being debts provable in his bankruptcy, as are prescribed.

281(7)   [Liability as surety] Discharge does not release any person other than the bankrupt from any liability (whether as partner or co-trustee of the bankrupt or otherwise) from which the bankrupt is released by the discharge, or from any liability as surety for the bankrupt or as a person in the nature of such a surety.

281(8)   [Definitions] In this section–

"family proceedings" means–

(a)   family proceedings within the meaning of the Magistrates' Courts Act 1980 and any proceedings which would be such proceedings but for section 65(1)(ii) of that Act (proceedings for variation of order for periodical payments); and

(b)   family proceedings within the meaning of Part V of the Matrimonial and Family Proceedings Act 1984.

"fine" means the same as in the Magistrates' Courts Act 1980; and

"personal injuries" includes death and any disease or other impairment of a person's physical or mental condition.

S.281(1)

As a general rule, discharge releases the bankrupt from liability in respect of "bankruptcy debts" (see s.382). However, any residual functions of the trustee are not to be affected, and creditors in respect of whose debts the bankrupt has been released by the discharge may still prove in the bankruptcy. See further IR 1986 r.6.223. A discharged bankrupt cannot escape the attentions of a trustee by seeking an IVA as at this stage he is no longer a "debtor" for the purposes of s.253—see *Wright v Official Receiver* [2001] B.P.I.R. 196.

Note also the effect of discharge on disqualifications, see for example s.427(2)(a).

As to what constitutes a bankruptcy debt for the purposes of a s.281 discharge see *Secretary of State for Work and Pensions v Balding* [2007] EWCA Civ 1327; [2007] B.P.I.R. 1669. See also *Casson and Wales v Law Society* [2009] EWHC 1943 (Admin)—liability not discharged by bankruptcy because it did not qualify as a contingent liability at time of bankruptcy order and so was not a bankruptcy debt. See also s.382.

Discharge prevents a creditor from pursuing a debtor who is now a discharged bankrupt, but it does not destroy any underlying cause of action—see *Law Society v OR and Shah* [2007] EWHC 2841 (Ch); [2007] B.P.I.R. 1595. This can have consequences in relation to the Third Parties (Rights Against Insurers) Act 1930.

Note also *Arnold v Williams* [2008] EWHC 218 (Ch); [2008] B.P.I.R. 247.

S.281(2)–(6), (8)

In s.281(5)(a) the words "or to pay damages by virtue of Part I of the Consumer Protection Act 1987, being in either case" have been substituted by the Consumer Protection Act 1987. Subsection (5) has been amended by the Children Act 1989 which removed the words "or in domestic proceedings" from the original text. Subsection (8) now has a new definition of "family proceedings" provided by the Children Act 1989.

These provisions deal with the exceptions to the general release in s.281(1). Note especially IR 1986 r.6.223 to explain the word "prescribed" in s.281(6). Security enforcement rights are preserved notwithstanding the release of the debt. Debts connected with fraud or breach of trust survive, as does liability in respect of a fine (see s.281(8)) or similar penalty (note the exception for fines, etc. in respect of public revenue offences). On the meaning of "fraud" for the purposes of s.281(3) see *Masters v Leaver* [2000] B.P.I.R. 284; *Mander v Evans* [2001] B.P.I.R. 902; and *Woodland Ferrari v UCL Group Retirement Benefits Scheme* [2002] B.P.I.R. 1270. Note here *Anglo Manx Group Ltd v Aitken* [2002] B.P.I.R. 215 where the significance of limitation periods continuing to run throughout the period of bankruptcy was emphasised. Liability to pay damages in respect of personal injuries (see s.281(8)), or liability arising from family or domestic proceedings (see s.281(8)) is not released unless the court so directs. There is also no release in respect of debts not provable in bankruptcy. Note that the list of exceptions in BA 1914 s.28 has been widened. The Cork Committee recommended that there should be no release of fines on discharge, but by a majority voted against allowing claims for personal injury to survive—see the *Report*, paras 1330 and 1333 respectively. Both items, however, have been added to the list of exceptions. Liability in respect of student loans is not discharged—Higher Education Act 2004 s.42 and reg.5 of the Education (Student Support) (No.2) Regulations 2002 (Amendment) (No.3) Regulations 2004 (SI 2004/2041).

Section 281(4) has effect as if the reference to a fine included a reference to a confiscation order (an extended meaning introduced by CJA 1988). Section 281(4A) was inserted by POCA 2002 Sch.11 para.16(2).

S.281(7)

Although the bankrupt may be released from liability for a debt, any co-obligor (e.g. a partner of the bankrupt, or co-trustee, etc.) and any person liable as surety for him is not so released.

281A   Post-discharge restrictions

281A   Schedule 4A to this Act (bankruptcy restrictions order and bankruptcy restrictions undertaking) shall have effect.

GENERAL NOTE

This new provision is introduced via s.257 of EA 2002 with effect from April 2004. It directs our attention to the new Sch.4A. In order to reassure the public concerned about the risks posed by early discharge the Government introduced a degree of balance in the form of a bankruptcy restriction order which will be applied to those bankrupts deemed not to be "honest" or, more accurately, those whose conduct falls within subparas (a)–(m) of para.2(2) in Sch.4A. We thus have a return to a former manifestation in bankruptcy law under which legal distinctions were drawn between types of bankrupt. Looking at (a)–(m) there are some predictable *indiciae* of misbehaviour—note the reappearance of now decriminalised conduct in (a) and (j). Of the other *indiciae* one can envisage a flood of litigation clarifying the ambit of these provisions—para.(k) looks a prime candidate. Subparagraph (e) will raise many concerns and guidance may have to be drawn from any jurisprudence under s.342A. Serial bankrupts will fall foul of para.2(3).

Applications for a BRO must normally be made within one year of the bankruptcy, though the court can grant an extension. The possibility of an interim order is provided for by para.5 for extreme cases.

Where the court grants a BRO against a bankrupt a series of restrictions will be applied for a period of not less than 2 years and up to 15 years after the grant of the order (see Sch.21 to the 2002 Act). In anticipation of a flood of cases disabling the courts the possibility of securing restrictions via an undertakings procedure is provided for by para.7. Actually very few BROs (or BRUs for that matter) were made in the first year of operation of the new scheme but the numbers are steadily increasing.

All BROs and BRUs should be listed in a public register—Sch.4A para.12.

282   Court's power to annul bankruptcy order

282(1)   **[Power of annulment]** The court may annul a bankruptcy order if it at any time appears to the court–

(a) that, on any grounds existing at the time the order was made, the order ought not to have been made, or

(b) that, to the extent required by the rules, the bankruptcy debts and the expenses of the bankruptcy have all, since the making of the order, been either paid or secured for to the satisfaction of the court.

282(2)   [Where petition under s.264(1)(a), (b), (c)] The court may annul a bankruptcy order made against an individual on a petition under paragraph (a), (b) or (c) of section 264(1) if it at any time appears to the court, on an application by the Official Petitioner–

(a) that the petition was pending at a time when a criminal bankruptcy order was made against the individual or was presented after such an order was so made, and

(b) no appeal is pending (within the meaning of section 277) against the individual's conviction of any offence by virtue of which the criminal bankruptcy order was made;

and the court shall annul a bankruptcy order made on a petition under section 264(1)(d) if it at any time appears to the court that the criminal bankruptcy order on which the petition was based has been rescinded in consequence of an appeal.

282(3)   [Annulment whether or not discharged] The court may annul a bankruptcy order whether or not the bankrupt has been discharged from the bankruptcy.

282(4)   [Effect of annulment] Where the court annuls a bankruptcy order (whether under this section or under section 261 or 263D in Part VIII)–

(a) any sale or other disposition of property, payment made or other thing duly done, under any provision in this Group of Parts, by or under the authority of the official receiver or a trustee of the bankrupt's estate or by the court is valid, but

(b) if any of the bankrupt's estate is then vested, under any such provision, in such a trustee, it shall vest in such person as the court may appoint or, in default of any such appointment, revert to the bankrupt on such terms (if any) as the court may direct;

and the court may include in its order such supplemental provisions as may be authorised by the rules.

282(5)   [Repealed from April 1, 2004.]

S.282(1), (3)
The court can annul a bankruptcy order if it should never have been made (compare here *Re a Bankrupt (No.622 of 1995), The Times,* June 27, 1996; *Henwood v Customs and Excise Commissioners* [1998] B.P.I.R. 339; and *Hope v Premierpace (Europe) Ltd* [1999] B.P.I.R. 695) and also if the bankrupt has paid all his debts and bankruptcy expenses to the extent required by the rules: see IR 1986 r.6.211. In *Paulin v Paulin* [2009] B.P.I.R. 572 the Court of Appeal stressed that, where a wife applies for the annulment of her husband's bankruptcy and alleges that he procured his own bankruptcy as a tactic in a divorce dispute, the onus is on her to show that he was not insolvent at the time the bankruptcy order was made. The burden of proof is the ordinary burden expected in civil cases but, if she can establish he was not insolvent in terms of his balance sheet, then he falls under an evidential burden to show that he was insolvent on a commercial basis. This case is also significant with regard to the question as to whether the court can revisit its own judgment on the question of annulment. The question of annulment rests upon the discretion of the court: *Askew v Peter Dominic Ltd* [1997] B.P.I.R. 163; *Re Coney* [1998] B.P.I.R. 333; *Skarzynski v Chalford Property Co Ltd* [2001] B.P.I.R. 673. Annulment is discretionary and therefore establishing grounds for annulment is no guarantee that the court will annul—*Omokwe v HFC Bank* [2007] B.P.I.R. 1157 (per Chief Registrar Baister). But the court stressed in *Royal Bank of Scotland v The Debtor* [1996] B.P.I.R. 478 that there is no inherent power of annulment beyond the statutory power. Moreover the s.375 review jurisdiction cannot be used to circumvent the stringent conditions of s.282—*IRC v Robinson* [1999] B.P.I.R. 329. For the distinction between rescission and annulment see *Hoare v IRC* [2002] EWHC 755 (Ch); [2002] B.P.I.R. 986. For discussion of the role of the court under these distinct jurisdictions see *Hunt v Peasegood* [2001] B.P.I.R. 76. The relationship between ss.282 and 375 was further reviewed in *Ahmed v Mogul Eastern Foods* [2005] EWHC 3532 (Ch) by Patten J. Points of similarity and areas of difference in these two jurisdictions were highlighted. In particular Patten J. was disinclined to allow the

rule in *Ladd v Marshall* [1954] 1 W.L.R. 1489 to intrude into the s.282 jurisdiction. For the wide power of the court under s.282(1) and its relationship with the s.375 review jurisdiction see *Snopek v Urang Ltd* [2008] B.P.I.R. 1416. On s.282 and its relationship with the s.375 review jurisdiction see also *HMRC v Cassells* [2009] B.P.I.R. 284. On the facts here an annulment was not a realistic possibility. Annulment can be granted even though discharge has occurred—though it may not be in the interests of the former bankrupt in such a case to seek annulment—*Owo-Samson v Barclays Bank (No.1)* [2003] EWCA Civ 714; [2003] B.P.I.R. 1373. The Secretary of State can appeal against an annulment order, see IR 1986 r.7.48. An annulment of a bankruptcy order was refused by Warner J. in *Re Robertson (a Bankrupt)* [1989] 1 W.L.R. 1139 where there had been failure to prove all debts. See also *Artman v Artman* [1996] B.P.I.R. 511 (annulment refused). The court can annul conditionally—*Engel v Peri* [2002] EWHC 799 (Ch); [2002] B.P.I.R. 961; *Hirani v Rendle* [2004] B.P.I.R. 274; *Thornhill v Atherton* [2004] EWCA Civ 1858; [2005] B.P.I.R. 437. For general analysis of annulment see Brockman and French, [2006] 19 Insolv. Int. 62 and 93.

Harman J. considered the nature of the jurisdiction to annul in *Re a Debtor (No.68 of 1992)* [1993] T.L.R. 69. Here the point was made that on an annulment hearing under s.282 it was not possible for the court to consider evidence which had been unavailable to the court which had made the bankruptcy in the first place. Relevant considerations on an annulment application were discussed in *Lloyds v Waters* [2001] B.P.I.R. 698. For an unsuccessful s.282 application see *Shamash v IRC* [2002] B.P.I.R. 189. In dealing with an annulment application the court should take into account material events occurring after the date of the bankruptcy order—see *Watts v Newham LBC* [2009] B.P.I.R. 718.

Bankruptcy is a class remedy and the court should not annul without a proper investigation of the facts—*Housiaux v Customs and Excise Commissioners* [2003] EWCA Civ 257; [2003] B.P.I.R. 858; *Leicester v Plumtree Farms* [2004] B.P.I.R. 296.

On going behind a default judgment for the purposes of s.282(1)(a) see *Royal Bank of Scotland v Farley* [1996] B.P.I.R. 638; and *Hunter v Lex Vehicle Finance* [2005] EWHC 223 (Ch); [2005] B.P.I.R. 586. In *Re a Debtor (No.169 of 1997)* (unreported but noted in *Current Law Week*, August 14, 1998) a county court judge annulled a bankruptcy order under s.282(1)(a) because the consent order upon which the petition has been based should never have been made.

In *Whig v Whig* [2007] EWHC 1856 (Fam); [2007] B.P.I.R. 1418 Munby J. on the application of a wife refused to annul a bankruptcy order made against her insolvent husband on his own petition. The effect of that bankruptcy order had been to frustrate the wife's claims to ancillary relief, but the court held that, as the husband was insolvent and bad faith on his part could not be established, annulment under s.282(1)(a) was not justified. In the light of *Paulin v Paulin* [2009] EWCA Civ 221 this authority must be treated with some caution.

On liability for the trustee's costs of the bankruptcy on an annulment application see *Tetteh v Lambeth LBC* [2008] B.P.I.R. 241. Where the annulment is made pursuant to s.282(1)(a) the starting point is that the petitioning creditor is liable for the bankruptcy costs but that presumption may be rebutted on the facts of each case.

In *Hunt v Fylde BC* [2008] B.P.I.R. 1368 the court ordered annulment under s.282(1)(a) because it uncovered circumstances not apparent at the time when the bankruptcy order was made. The bankruptcy was annulled under s.282(1)(a) in *Official Receiver v Mitterfellner* [2009] B.P.I.R. 1075 because the debtor did not have a genuine COMI in the jurisdiction so as to justify the making of the bankruptcy order by the English court.

Although there is no fixed limitation period in which annulment must be sought the longer the bankrupt waits the more difficult it may be to ensure that the creditors can be contacted to enable them to be repaid in full for the purposes of s.282(1)(b)—*Gill v Quinn* [2004] EWHC 883 (Ch); [2005] B.P.I.R. 129. For the general principles relevant when considering whether to annul see *Harper v Buchler* [2004] B.P.I.R. 724. For later proceedings in this case see *Harper v Buchler (No.2)* [2005] B.P.I.R. 577 where the court indicated that it would be unlikely to exercise its discretion to annul a bankruptcy order made a decade ago unless statutory interest was paid. For further consideration of whether (and to what extent) statutory interest should be paid see *Wilcock v Duckworth* [2005] B.P.I.R. 682. For an instructive review of these questions see Pomeroy, [2005] 18 Insolv. Int. 90. On the question of solicitors' undertakings and s.282(1)(b) annulments see *Halabi v Camden LBC* [2008] EWHC 322 (Ch); [2008] B.P.I.R. 370. Here the county court practice of granting an annulment by reference to a solicitors' undertaking was ruled to be undesirable and should in future by replaced by a practice involving annulment orders conditional upon certain events occurring to the satisfaction of the official receiver. There was no prospect of an annulment under s.282(1)(b) in *Dadourian Group v Simms* [2008] B.P.I.R. 508.

In *OR v McKay* [2009] B.P.I.R. 1061 the Court of Appeal departed from an old precedent when seeking to give a modern meaning to s.282(1)(b).

An annulment application cannot be used to relitigate issues determined in the bankruptcy proceedings—*Balendran v Law Society* [2004] EWHC 495 (Ch); [2004] B.P.I.R. 859.

On annulment and disputed debts see *Guinan III v Caldwell Associates Ltd* [2004] EWHC 3348 (Ch); [2004] B.P.I.R. 531.

An annulment application alleging procedural unfairness was rejected in *Simmons v Mole Valley* [2004] EWHC 475 (Ch); [2004] B.P.I.R. 1022 because the bankrupt had not bothered to attend the hearing of the bankruptcy petition.

There is no provision in s.282 requiring the annulment order to be gazetted and published in a local paper, as was necessary under BA 1914 s.29(3): now see IR 1986 r.6.212. Formerly an application for annulment had to be supplemented with a request for rescission of the receiving order under what is now s.375(1). With the abolition of receiving orders this is no longer necessary. For a Court of Appeal authority on rescission of receiving orders, which might have some impact on judicial practice in cases of annulment of bankruptcy orders, see *Re a Debtor (No.707 of 1985), The Times*, January 21, 1988.

Under BA 1914 s.29, the application for annulment had to be made by "any person interested". This requirement, which caused problems in *Re Beesley Ex p. Beesley v The Official Receiver* [1975] 1 All E.R. 385, has been dropped. See here *F v F* [1994] 1 F.L.R. 359 (application by wife of debtor). For discussion, see Miller, (1994) 10 I.L. & P. 66. A similar change has been made with regard to s.375.

For further provisions on annulment, see IR 1986 rr.6.206–6.214. In *Howard v Savage* [2006] EWHC 3693 (Ch); [2007] B.P.I.R. 1097 Lewison J. stressed the link between the requirements of s.282(1)(b) and IR 6.206 et seq. For an illuminating review of this jurisdiction see Briggs and Sims, [2002] Insolv. L. 2.

Local authorities which through maladministration have improperly sought the bankruptcy of a council tax defaulter are increasingly being called upon to seek a remedial annulment in the wake of an adverse ruling from local government ombudsmen.

S.282(2)
This provision confirms the supremacy of the system of criminal bankruptcy over ordinary bankruptcy cases. The subsection also allows the court to annul a bankruptcy order which was granted on a petition based on a criminal bankruptcy order if that latter order has been rescinded on appeal.

Note prospective amendment: s.282(2) is to be repealed by CJA 1988 s.170(2) and Sch.16 as from a day to be appointed; see the note to s.264.

S.282(4)
This deals with the practical effects of annulment—dispositions of property, etc. carried out by a trustee are valid. On annulment, the court can order the revesting of the property in the former bankrupt or some other person. For the rules on liability for costs of the trustee where the bankruptcy is annulled see *Butterworth v Soutter* [2000] B.P.I.R. 582. Where a bankruptcy is annulled under s.282(1)(a) the trustee is entitled to claim payment of costs and expenses where the annulment is postponed pending payment of such items—*Thornhill v Atherton (No.2)* [2008] B.P.I.R. 691. In such a case the trustee can realise estate assets to recover payment. For the effect of annulment on prosecutions for bankruptcy offices, see s.350(2). However, in the case of offences not covered by s.350(2) annulment of a bankruptcy order does not "whitewash" any crimes that may have been committed whilst the individual was bankrupt, for example, the offence of acting as a director whilst being an undischarged bankrupt contrary to s.11 of the CDDA 1986—for discussion see *Inland Revenue Commissioners v McEntaggart* [2004] EWHC 3431 (Ch); [2006] B.P.I.R. 750. On annulment a bankruptcy petition does not necessarily lapse—*Choudhury v IRC* [2000] B.P.I.R. 246. This conclusion was reached notwithstanding the terms of r.6.213.

For the effect of annulment upon unknown debts see *London Borough of Lambeth v Simon* [2007] B.P.I.R. 1629. On the interpretation of agreements between bankrupts and third parties designed to facilitate the obtaining of an annulment see *Schweppe v Harper* [2008] B.P.I.R. 1090.

On the consequences of annulment for any claim by trustees for remuneration and costs see *Ella v Ella* [2009] B.P.I.R. 441.

S.282(5)
This provision (which dealt with the implications of annulment) was repealed by EA 2002 s.269 and Sch.23 with effect from April 1, 2004.

CHAPTER II

PROTECTION OF BANKRUPT'S ESTATE AND INVESTIGATION OF HIS AFFAIRS

283   Definition of bankrupt's estate

283(1)   [Bankrupt's estate] Subject as follows, a bankrupt's estate for the purposes of any of this Group of Parts comprises–

    (a)   all property belonging to or vested in the bankrupt at the commencement of the bankruptcy, and

    (b)   any property which by virtue of any of the following provisions of this Part is comprised in that estate or is treated as falling within the preceding paragraph.

283(2) **[Non-application of s.283(1)]** Subsection (1) does not apply to–

    (a)   such tools, books, vehicles and other items of equipment as are necessary to the bankrupt for use personally by him in his employment, business or vocation;

    (b)   such clothing, bedding, furniture, household equipment and provisions as are necessary for satisfying the basic domestic needs of the bankrupt and his family.

This subsection is subject to section 308 in Chapter IV (certain excluded property reclaimable by trustee).

283(3) **[Further non-application of s.283(1)]** Subsection (1) does not apply to–

    (a)   property held by the bankrupt on trust for any other person, or

    (b)   the right of nomination to a vacant ecclesiastical benefice.

283(3A) **[Further non-application of s.283(1)]** Subject to section 308A in Chapter IV, subsection (1) does not apply to–

    (a)   a tenancy which is an assured tenancy or an assured agricultural occupancy, within the meaning of Part I of the Housing Act 1988, and the terms of which inhibit an assignment as mentioned in section 127(5) of the Rent Act 1977, or

    (b)   a protected tenancy, within the meaning of the Rent Act 1977, in respect of which, by virtue of any provision of Part IX of that Act, no premium can lawfully be required as a condition of assignment, or

    (c)   a tenancy of a dwelling-house by virtue of which the bankrupt is, within the meaning of the Rent (Agriculture) Act 1976, a protected occupier of the dwelling-house, and the terms of which inhibit an assignment as mentioned in section 127(5) of the Rent Act 1977, or

    (d)   a secure tenancy, within the meaning of Part IV of the Housing Act 1985, which is not capable of being assigned, except in the cases mentioned in section 91(3) of that Act.

283(4) **[References to property]** References in any of this Group of Parts to property, in relation to a bankrupt, include references to any power exercisable by him over or in respect of property except in so far as the power is exercisable over or in respect of property not for the time being comprised in the bankrupt's estate and–

    (a)   is so exercisable at a time after either the official receiver has had his release in respect of that estate under section 299(2) in Chapter III or a meeting summoned by the trustee of that estate under section 331 in Chapter IV has been held, or

    (b)   cannot be so exercised for the benefit of the bankrupt;

and a power exercisable over or in respect of property is deemed for the purposes of any of this Group of Parts to vest in the person entitled to exercise it at the time of the transaction or event by virtue of which it is exercisable by that person (whether or not it becomes so exercisable at that time).

283(5) **[Property in bankrupt's estate]** For the purposes of any such provision in this Group of Parts, property comprised in a bankrupt's estate is so comprised subject to the rights of any person other than the bankrupt (whether as a secured creditor of the bankrupt or otherwise) in relation thereto, but disregarding–

(a)   any rights in relation to which a statement such as is required by section 269(1)(a) was made in the petition on which the bankrupt was adjudged bankrupt, and

(b)   any rights which have been otherwise given up in accordance with the rules.

283(6)   [Other enactments] This section has effect subject to the provisions of any enactment not contained in this Act under which any property is to be excluded from a bankrupt's estate.

GENERAL NOTE

The major change effected by this provision is the abolition of the doctrine of reputed ownership. This doctrine, which could trace its origins back to 1623, stated that if the debtor appeared to be in possession of property which secretly belonged to another, that would boost his creditworthiness, and therefore his creditors should be entitled to treat that property as part of the bankrupt's estate. The rationale of this doctrine, which applied only to traders who became bankrupt, was criticised by Parke B. long ago in *Belcher v Bellamy* (1848) 2 Exch. 303. It did not reflect commercial practices and it appeared particularly inappropriate with the growth of hire-purchase and consumer credit in the twentieth century. Both the courts and Parliament began to curtail the scope of the doctrine: see, e.g. Consumer Credit Act 1974 s.192(3) and Sch.4 para.6. The doctrine did not apply in Ireland and many Commonwealth jurisdictions. Accordingly, calls for abolition were made by the Cork Committee (*Report*, 1093) and the White Paper, para.116. Incidentally, the abolition of the doctrine may throw up difficulties—the problem of title retention clauses which has troubled corporate insolvency law over the past decade might now raise its ugly head. The doctrine of reputed ownership which applied only to personal and not corporate insolvency law at least served to keep that problem at bay in the law of bankruptcy. The doctrine of "relation back" of the trustee's title to the date of the act of bankruptcy has also been abandoned in the wake of the new procedures for bankruptcy. See *Re Dennis* [1996] B.P.I.R. 106 for the significance of this change. For general discussion of the new rules on the bankrupt's estate see Milman, (1988) 4 I.L. & P. 71. For a general analysis of the bankruptcy estate see Brown, (2007) 11 Jo of S. Pacific Law 89. On the entitlement of the estate to claim windfalls see *Trustee of F C Jones v Jones* [1996] B.P.I.R. 644. Note that property subject to a restraint, etc. order under the Proceeds of Crime Act 2002 is also excluded from the estate—POCA 2002 s.417.

S.283(1)

This section identifies the bankrupt's estate. Note the possible impact of ss.307–309 here and the general definition of "property" in s.436. Notwithstanding the wide terms of s.283(1)(a) personal correspondence of the debtor does not vest in the trustee—*Haig v Aitken* [2000] B.P.I.R. 462. In *Malcolm v Benedict Mackenzie* [2004] EWCA Civ 1748; [2005] B.P.I.R. 176 the Court of Appeal reaffirmed that the rules relating to the vesting of personal pension rights in the estate did not infringe the European Convention on Human Rights. In particular in this case the bankrupt fell under the old rules applying to bankruptcies commenced pre-May 29, 2000 and the fact that his position was materially worse than a later bankrupt did not constitute an infringement of art.14 of the Convention. The possibility of foreign property vesting in the estate was also considered in *Thornhill v Atherton (No.2)* [2008] B.P.I.R. 691.

For the commencement of the bankruptcy, see s.278(a).

S.283(2), (3)

These provisions list those items that are excluded from the estate. Section 283(2) again reflects a change in the law. See *Hill v Secretary of State* [2005] EWHC 696 (Ch); [2006] 1 B.C.L.C. 601. It was felt that a bankrupt ought to be allowed to keep a greater range of personal possessions than BA 1914 permitted—see the Cork *Report*, para.1113. Thus, the £250 limit has been dropped. It had been overtaken by inflation and discriminated against debtors with capital-intensive businesses. Vehicles are now included among the exceptions, as are general items of business equipment. Thus the old restrictive authorities on "tools" such as *Re Sherman* [1916] W.N. 26 have lost much of their importance. On the other hand, such property may now be "replaced" by the trustee under s.308. Trust property is not included in the estate: see *Re Tout & Finch Ltd* [1954] 1 W.L.R. 178; and *Re McKeown* [1974] N.I. 226. Funds held on trust for IVA creditors all come within this exception—*Re Coath* [2000] B.P.I.R. 981. See also *Abrahams v Trustee of Property of Abrahams* [1999] B.P.I.R. 637 (bankrupt holds lottery win on resulting trust for ticket purchaser). For a more complex question relating to a possible trust see *Rooney v Cardona* [1999] B.P.I.R. 291. Where the trustee in bankruptcy realises trust property with the consent of the beneficiary he may be entitled to realisation costs out of the trust fund—*Re Sobey* [1999] B.P.I.R. 1009. Section 283(3) repeats BA 1914 s.38(b).

Certain "personal" claims may also be excluded from the estate—for discussion see *Collins v Official Receiver* [1996] B.P.I.R. 552; *Lang v McKenna* [1997] B.P.I.R. 340; *Re Bell* [1998] B.P.I.R. 26. Compare *Cork v Rawlins* [2001] B.P.I.R. 222.

Note that pensions benefits can be excluded from the estate if they have been lawfully forfeited. For the position at common law see *Aitchison and Tuivaiti v NZI Life Superannuation Nominees* [1996] B.P.I.R. 215; and *Re The Trusts of the Scientific Investment Pension Plan* [1998] B.P.I.R. 410. The position here is now governed by the Pensions Act 1995 and the Pensions and Welfare Reform Act 1999.

S.283(3A)

Subsection (3A) was introduced into s.283 by s.117(1) of the Housing Act 1988. Its effect is to add assured tenancies, protected tenancies, protected occupancies of dwelling houses and secure tenancies to the list of exclusions from the bankrupt's estate. Continuation tenancies are outside this exclusion—*Rothschild v Bell* [1999] B.P.I.R. 300. This provision has to be read however in the light of the newly introduced s.308A which enables the trustee to claim such tenancies by giving notice to the bankrupt.

S.283(4)

This deals with rights to exercise powers over the property of others. Note *Clarkson v Clarkson* [1994] B.C.C. 921.

S.283(5)

Third-party rights over the bankrupt's property are preserved, unless those rights have been surrendered. Rights in this context means property rights (including equitable interests)—*Mountney v Treharne* [2002] EWCA Civ 1174. On the potential impact of the s.283(5) exclusion see *Roberts v Nunn and Tiffany* [2004] EWHC 114 (Ch); [2004] B.P.I.R. 623 (consent order had it been made with jurisdiction would have excluded pension rights from estate). For an abortive attempt to rely on s.283(5) see *Avis v Turner* [2007] EWCA Civ 748; [2007] B.P.I.R. 663. On s.283(5) see also *Burke v Chapman and Chubb* [2008] B.P.I.R. 266.

S.283(6)

Property may be excluded from the estate by other statutes. For example statute now provides that student loans are specifically excluded from the estate—Higher Education Act 2004, s.42 and reg.5 of the Education (Student Support) (No.2) Regulations 2002 (Amendment No.3) Regulations 2004 (SI 2004/2041)—these provisions amend s.22 of the Teaching and Higher Education Act 1998 and reg.39 of the Education (Student Support) (No.2) Regulations 2002 (SI 2002/3200) with September 1, 2004 being specified as the cut off date for the new regime. For student loans made under earlier regimes, e.g. the Education (Student Loans) Act 1990 Sch.2 para.5(1) transitional provision apply.

283A   Bankrupt's home ceasing to form part of estate

283A(1)   **[Application of section]** This section applies where property comprised in the bankrupt's estate consists of an interest in a dwelling-house which at the date of the bankruptcy was the sole or principal residence of–

(a) the bankrupt,

(b) the bankrupt's spouse or civil partner, or

(c) a former spouse or former civil partner of the bankrupt.

283A(2)   **[Interest to vest in bankrupt]** At the end of the period of three years beginning with the date of the bankruptcy the interest mentioned in subsection (1) shall–

(a) cease to be comprised in the bankrupt's estate, and

(b) vest in the bankrupt (without conveyance, assignment or transfer).

283A(3)   **[Non-application of s.283A(2)]** Subsection (2) shall not apply if during the period mentioned in that subsection–

(a) the trustee realises the interest mentioned in subsection (1),

(b) the trustee applies for an order for sale in respect of the dwelling-house,

(c) the trustee applies for an order for possession of the dwelling-house,

(d) the trustee applies for an order under section 313 in Chapter IV in respect of that interest, or

(e) the trustee and the bankrupt agree that the bankrupt shall incur a specified liability to his estate (with or without the addition of interest from the date of the agreement) in consideration of which the interest mentioned in subsection (1) shall cease to form part of the estate.

283A(4) [Where application for order dismissed] Where an application of a kind described in subsection (3)(b) to (d) is made during the period mentioned in subsection (2) and is dismissed, unless the court orders otherwise the interest to which the application relates shall on the dismissal of the application–

(a) cease to be comprised in the bankrupt's estate, and

(b) vest in the bankrupt (without conveyance, assignment or transfer).

283A(5) [Effect of late notification of interest] If the bankrupt does not inform the trustee or the official receiver of his interest in a property before the end of the period of three months beginning with the date of the bankruptcy, the period of three years mentioned in subsection (2)–

(a) shall not begin with the date of the bankruptcy, but

(b) shall begin with the date on which the trustee or official receiver becomes aware of the bankrupt's interest.

283A(6) [Power of court to substitute longer period] The court may substitute for the period of three years mentioned in subsection (2) a longer period–

(a) in prescribed circumstances, and

(b) in such other circumstances as the court thinks appropriate.

283A(7) [Provision in rules for shorter period] The rules may make provision for this section to have effect with the substitution of a shorter period for the period of three years mentioned in subsection (2) in specified circumstances (which may be described by reference to action to be taken by a trustee in bankruptcy).

283A(8) [Other provision in rules] The rules may also, in particular, make provision–

(a) requiring or enabling the trustee of a bankrupt's estate to give notice that this section applies or does not apply;

(b) about the effect of a notice under paragraph (a);

(c) requiring the trustee of a bankrupt's estate to make an application to the Chief Land Registrar.

283A(9) [Rules concerning notice of disapplication of section] Rules under subsection (8)(b) may, in particular–

(a) disapply this section;

(b) enable a court to disapply this section;

(c) make provision in consequence of a disapplication of this section;

(d) enable a court to make provision in consequence of a disapplication of this section;

(e) make provision (which may include provision conferring jurisdiction on a court or tribunal) about compensation.

GENERAL NOTE

This important reform is introduced by s.261 of EA 2002. In the debate on the powers of a trustee in bankruptcy concerns were expressed about the practice adopted by certain trustees of not realising family homes immediately but allowing the matter to lie dormant, only acting many years after discharge where the value of the property had increased due to inflation. This was seen as unjust, a criticism accepted by the Government, which permitted a late amendment of the Bill. For judicial comment on the thinking behind the new policy here see Lawrence Collins J. in *Re Byford (decd)* [2003] EWHC 1267 (Ch); [2003] B.P.I.R. 1089. We thus move over to a regime under which the trustee in dealing with the bankrupt's home must "use it or lose it".

The three year time limit imposed on trustees wishing to realise the family home did not apply retrospectively to bankruptcies commencing before s.283A took effect—*Vidyarthi v Clifford* [2005] B.P.I.R. 233. For other transitional matters see EA 2002 s.261 and *Dear IP* Issue 25 (December 2005).

In *Lewis v Metropolitan Property Realizations Ltd* [2009] B.P.I.R. 79 Proudman J. took a flexible view on the word "realisation" by holding that a property was realised where the trustee took a deferred consideration. On appeal ([2009] EWCA Civ 448), however, the Court of Appeal preferred a more traditional construction of the word and ruled that the taking of deferred consideration did not constitute "realisation". Although this interpretation may accord with a literal approach, it will do nothing to aid the position of a trustee in bankruptcy when considering the best options to convert the estate interest in the debtor's property.

In *Pannell v Official Receiver* [2008] B.P.I.R. 629 the court concluded that the three year "use it or lose it" rule only applied to bankruptcies occurring after December 29, 1986 based upon petitions presented on or after that date. That said one would imagine difficulties with ECHR in the case of realisations of property of individuals declared bankrupt prior to that date.

In *Re Byford* [2003] EWHC 1267 (Ch); [2003] B.P.I.R. 1089 Lawrence Collins J. made the point that s.283A does not oblige the trustee to go for an immediate sale of the family home; rather he has a three year window of opportunity in which to act.

The Insolvency Service has offered guidance on the interaction between s.283A, IR 6.237 and Form 6.83—see *Dear IP*, September 2007.

S.283A(1)

This defines the type of property covered by this new restrictive provision. The interest must be in a dwelling house that is the sole or principal residence of the bankrupt, the bankrupt's spouse or former spouse. Note the additional reference to civil partners by Sch.27 to the Civil Partnership Act 2004. Thus the provision does not protect interests in second homes purchased for investment or recreation purposes. However, one could envisage a situation where two or even three properties were caught by this provision if for example the bankrupt was divorced and was also living apart from a second spouse. Thus, low value dwelling 1 was occupied by the bankrupt, low value dwelling 2 was occupied by current (but separated) spouse, and low value property 3 was occupied by former spouse.

S.283A(2), (3), (4)

If the trustee fails to take the specified action within three years the property will revest in the bankrupt. The specified courses of action which the trustee must take are identified in subs.(3). Note the qualification dealt with by subs.(4)—early unsuccessful action by the trustee might result in the *immediate* revesting of the dwelling in the bankrupt.

S.283A(5), (6)

The three-year period does not begin to run until the trustee has been informed of the bankrupt's interest where notification has not occurred within the initial three months. This provision suggests that if a bankrupt waits until the three months are nearly expired before notifying the interest then the trustee in effect has only two years and nine months to take action. Generally, the three-year period may be extended according to subs.(6) and one would imagine that this power might be used in cases where the bankrupt is seen as trying to exploit this potential loophole.

S.283A(7)–(9)

These deal with the potential content of secondary rules.

284 Restrictions on dispositions of property

284(1) [Where person adjudged bankrupt] Where a person is adjudged bankrupt, any disposition of property made by that person in the period to which this section applies is void except to the extent that it is or was made with the consent of the court, or is or was subsequently ratified by the court.

284(2) [Application of s.284(1) to payment] Subsection (1) applies to a payment (whether in cash or otherwise) as it applies to a disposition of property and, accordingly, where any payment is void by virtue of that subsection, the person paid shall hold the sum paid for the bankrupt as part of his estate.

284(3) [Relevant period] This section applies to the period beginning with the day of the presentation of the petition for the bankruptcy order and ending with the vesting, under Chapter IV of this Part, of the bankrupt's estate in a trustee.

284(4) [Limit to effect of s.284(1)–(3)] The preceding provisions of this section do not give a remedy against any person–

(a) in respect of any property or payment which he received before the commencement of the bankruptcy in good faith, for value and without notice that the petition had been presented, or

(b) in respect of any interest in property which derives from an interest in respect of which there is, by virtue of this subsection, no remedy.

284(5) [Debt after commencement of bankruptcy] Where after the commencement of his bankruptcy the bankrupt has incurred a debt to a banker or other person by reason of the making of a payment which is void under this section, that debt is deemed for the purposes of any of this Group of Parts to have been incurred before the commencement of the bankruptcy unless–

(a) that banker or person had notice of the bankruptcy before the debt was incurred, or

(b) it is not reasonably practicable for the amount of the payment to be recovered from the person to whom it was made.

284(6) [Property not in bankrupt's estate] A disposition of property is void under this section notwithstanding that the property is not or, as the case may be, would not be comprised in the bankrupt's estate; but nothing in this section affects any disposition made by a person of property held by him on trust for any other person.

GENERAL NOTE

In the context of the financial markets, s.284 does not apply to a market contract or any disposition of property in pursuance of such a contract, the provision of margin in relation to market contracts, a market charge, and certain other transactions: see CA 1989 ss.163(4), 175(3)–(5), and the note on p.3.

A new set of guidelines contained in *Practice Note: Validation Orders (Sections 127 and 284 of the Insolvency Act 1986)* has been issued by Sir Andrew Morritt C.—see [2007] B.P.I.R. 94. The effect of this new judicial guidance is to clarify procedures where leave is sought.

Although authorities decided under s.127 may be of assistance in interpreting s.284 the point has been made by H.H.J. Norris Q.C. in *Pettit v Novakovic* [2007] B.C.C. 462 that authorities cannot automatically be transposed as the statutory language may differ and the purposes of the two provisions had subtle differences.

Some consideration was given to this provision by the court in *OR v Bathurst* [2008] B.P.I.R. 1548.

S.284(1)–(3), (6)

Any disposition of property or payment of money by the debtor after the date of the petition will be void unless approved by the court, either at the time or subsequently. This is so even if the property would not have formed part of the bankrupt's estate under s.283. Moreover, it would appear that a transfer of an interest in the matrimonial home pursuant to a consent order made under s.24 of the Matrimonial Causes Act 1973 constitutes a "disposition" for these purposes and is therefore void. This startling conclusion was arrived at by Nicholas Stewart Q.C. (sitting as a deputy judge of the High Court) in *Re Flint* [1993] Ch. 319. This case once again illustrates that where a conflict occurs between rules of family law and principles of bankruptcy law the latter are often victorious. This critical view of the law is reinforced by *Woodley v Woodley (No.2)* [1994] 1 W.L.R. 1167 where the Court of Appeal held that the presentation of a bankruptcy petition by a debtor husband is not a disposition for the purposes of s.37 of the Matrimonial Causes Act 1973 and cannot be challenged as an attempt to avoid an order for matrimonial relief. *Re Flint* (above) is inconsistent with *Burton v Burton* [1986] 2 F.L.R. 419 and was not followed by Jonathan Parker J. in *Beer v Higham* [1997] B.P.I.R. 349. However, see *Harper v O'Reilly* [1997] B.P.I.R. 656; and *Mountney v Treharne* [2002] EWCA Civ 1174; [2002] B.P.I.R. 1126 for continuing problems of uncertainty on the interface between matrimonial law and insolvency law. *Beer v Higham* (above) is no longer good law. For comment on the unpredictability of *Mountney v Treharne* (above) see *Burke v Chapman & Chubb* [2008] EWHC 341 (QB); [2008] B.P.I.R. 266 at [57]. In spite of the criticism levelled at *Re Flint* (above) it was followed by Lindsay J. in *Treharne and Sand v Forrester* [2004] EWHC 2784 (Ch); [2004] B.P.I.R. 338. Thus a matrimonial property transfer order made after the presentation of the bankruptcy petition could be viewed as a void disposition by the debtor for the purposes of s.284. The argument that the court might be viewed as the disponor was specifically rejected.

This provision compensates for the abolition of the doctrine of "relation back" of title and the end of the protection offered by receiving orders.

Note that s.284 allows the court some discretion with regard to avoidance—the provision in BA 1914 allowed no such flexibility. Leave was granted in *Rio Properties Inc v Al-Midani* [2003] B.P.I.R. 128 to enable funds to be used as payment for legal advice. On s.284(6) and sums akin to trust moneys see *Re Mordant* [1996] B.P.I.R. 302.

As to what constitutes a "payment" for the purposes of s.284(2) see *Pettit v Novakovic* [2007] B.C.C. 462.

On s.284(6) see *Power v Brown* [2009] B.P.I.R. 340, where the court ruled that the provision did not apply on the facts of the case.

A transaction in breach of s.284 is void and not merely voidable—see *Bateman v Hyde* [2009] B.P.I.R. 737. In this case the court found that s.284(6) was not applicable.

S.284(4)

This offers protection to third parties, especially bona fide purchasers for value without notice of the petition.

S.284(5)

This provision deals with payments by the bankrupt avoided under this section, thus leaving the bankrupt indebted to the payee. If the sum of money can be recovered from the payee he will be treated as a pre-bankruptcy creditor unless he had notice of the petition at the time the debt was incurred.

285 Restriction on proceedings and remedies

285(1) [Court's power to stay] At any time when proceedings on a bankruptcy petition are pending or an individual has been adjudged bankrupt the court may stay any action, execution or other legal process against the property or person of the debtor or, as the case may be, of the bankrupt.

285(2) [Where proceedings pending against individual] Any court in which proceedings are pending against any individual may, on proof that a bankruptcy petition has been presented in respect of that individual or that he is an undischarged bankrupt, either stay the proceedings or allow them to continue on such terms as it thinks fit.

285(3) [Limit on creditors' actions] After the making of a bankruptcy order no person who is a creditor of the bankrupt in respect of a debt provable in the bankruptcy shall–

(a) have any remedy against the property or person of the bankrupt in respect of that debt, or

(b) before the discharge of the bankrupt, commence any action or other legal proceedings against the bankrupt except with the leave of the court and on such terms as the court may impose.

This is subject to sections 346 (enforcement procedures) and 347 (limited right to distress).

285(4) [Right of secured creditor] Subject as follows, subsection (3) does not affect the right of a secured creditor of the bankrupt to enforce his security.

285(5) [Where goods of undischarged bankrupt held by pledge etc.] Where any goods of an undischarged bankrupt are held by any person by way of pledge, pawn or other security, the official receiver may, after giving notice in writing of his intention to do so, inspect the goods.

Where such a notice has been given to any person, that person is not entitled, without leave of the court, to realise his security unless he has given the trustee of the bankrupt's estate a reasonable opportunity of inspecting the goods and of exercising the bankrupt's right of redemption.

285(6) [Interpretation] References in this section to the property or goods of the bankrupt are to any of his property or goods, whether or not comprised in his estate.

GENERAL NOTE

In relation to the financial markets, nothing in s.285 affects any action taken by an exchange or clearing house for the purpose of its default proceedings: CA 1989 s.161(4).

S.285(1)

This provision authorises the court (for definition, see s.385) to stay actions, executions, etc. where a bankruptcy petition is pending or, indeed, after the grant of the order. The Blagden Committee (Cmnd.221 (1957)), paras 19–20, called for the insertion of a provision *ex abundanti cautela* to the effect that High Court proceedings could be stayed under this provision. This has not been done, presumably because the existing language was deemed sufficiently wide. In *Re Smith (a Bankrupt) Ex p. Braintree District Council* [1990] 2 A.C. 215, the House of Lords held that this provision did enable it to stay proceedings for committal for non-payment of rates. There was no justification for excluding such proceedings from the scope of s.285. See also *Lewis v Ogwr BC* [1996] Rating Appeals 124. Compare *R. v Secretary of State for Social Security Ex p. Taylor* [1997] B.P.I.R. 505 (authorities' right to deduct benefits at source not prejudiced by s.285(3)). In *Harlow District Council v Hall* [2006] EWCA Civ 156; [2006] B.P.I.R. 712 the Court of Appeal (Civil Division) held that there was no breach of s.285 of the IA 1986 where the court had ordered the surrender of a secure tenancy pursuant to s.79 of the Housing Act 1985, such surrender of possession to be completed the day before the bankruptcy petition was presented by the debtor. At the commencement of the bankruptcy the local authority were not seeking to enforce a remedy against the property of the bankrupt under the terms of s.285. The remedy had already been granted. The court also expressed the view that the same result would probably have been arrived at had the bankruptcy order predated the ending of possession. This view seems to have been taken because it was common ground between the parties that the secure tenancy would not have vested in the trustee on bankruptcy and so there was no estate to be protected within the spirit of s.285.

On various aspects of s.285 see also *Arnold v Williams* [2008] EWHC 218 (Ch); [2008] B.P.I.R. 247.

S.285(2)
Any court may exercise such staying powers on proof that a bankruptcy petition is pending. On this see *Re Eileen Davies* [1997] B.P.I.R. 619 and *Godfrey v Torpy, The Times* May 16, 2007.

S.285(3), (4)
This compels unsecured creditors of the bankrupt to look solely to bankruptcy procedures as a remedy to secure payment of their debts once the bankruptcy order has been made. This general rule is qualified by ss.346, 347. Secured creditors do not suffer such a disability, unless s.285(5) below applies. Subsection (3) only protects against the enforcement of provable debts—*Re X* [1996] B.P.I.R. 494. As to which debts are provable see IR 1986 r.12.3. Landlords exercising powers of re-entry are also not hindered by this provision: *Razzaq v Pala* [1998] B.C.C. 66.

One view is that s.285(3) is to be interpreted in a purposive manner: *Bristol and West Building Society v Saunders* [1997] Ch. 60; [1997] B.C.C. 83 and leave can therefore be granted retrospectively. For factors relevant to the grant of leave *nunc pro tunc* see *Bristol and West Building Society v Back and Melinek* [1997] B.P.I.R. 358. However this liberal approach is now questionable. *Saunders* (above) was not followed by H.H.J. Kershaw in *Re Taylor* [2007] B.P.I.R. 175; [2007] 1 Ch. 150 and the court therefore refused to grant a retrospective validation under s.285(3)(c). Proceedings instituted without leave were *void* and could not retrospectively be validated. This latter, more draconian, interpretation is in line with the approach of the majority of the House of Lords in *Seal v Chief Constable of South Wales Police* [2007] UKHL 31; [2007] 1 W.L.R. 1910 to this issue in general in civil procedure.

On the operation of s.285(3) see *Dadourian Group International v Simms* [2008] EWHC 723 (Ch); [2008] B.P.I.R. 508. The court here stressed that creditors with provable debts cannot lay claim to particular assets—they merely have a right of proof in the bankruptcy and must look to the general pool of realised assets to satisfy that right.

A council tax liability order was quashed in *R. (Mohammed) v Southwark LBC* [2009] B.P.I.R. 882 in view of the failure of the local authority to obtain permission under s.285.

S.285(5)
This allows the official receiver to inspect any of the bankrupt's goods which have been used as security and to redeem them if necessary. The person holding the goods cannot enforce his security without the leave of the court.

S.285(6)
This gives the words "property" and "goods" a meaning that is not restricted by s.283.

286   Power to appoint interim receiver

286(1)   **[Court's power]** The court may, if it is shown to be necessary for the protection of the debtor's property, at any time after the presentation of a bankruptcy petition and before making a bankruptcy order, appoint the official receiver to be interim receiver of the debtor's property.

286(2)   **[Appointment of person instead of official receiver]** Where the court has, on a debtor's petition, appointed an insolvency practitioner under section 273 and it is shown to the court as mentioned in subsection (1) of this section, the court may, without making a bankruptcy order, appoint that practitioner, instead of the official receiver, to be interim receiver of the debtor's property.

286(3)   [Rights, powers etc. of interim receiver] The court may by an order appointing any person to be an interim receiver direct that his powers shall be limited or restricted in any respect; but, save as so directed, an interim receiver has, in relation to the debtor's property, all the rights, powers, duties and immunities of a receiver and manager under the next section.

286(4)   [Contents of court order] An order of the court appointing any person to be an interim receiver shall require that person to take immediate possession of the debtor's property or, as the case may be, the part of it to which his powers as interim receiver are limited.

286(5)   [Duties of debtor] Where an interim receiver has been appointed, the debtor shall give him such inventory of his property and such other information, and shall attend on the interim receiver at such times, as the latter may for the purpose of carrying out his functions under this section reasonably require.

286(6)   [Application of s.285(3)] Where an interim receiver is appointed, section 285(3) applies for the period between the appointment and the making of a bankruptcy order on the petition, or the dismissal of the petition, as if the appointment were the making of such an order.

286(7)   [Ceasing to be interim receiver] A person ceases to be interim receiver of a debtor's property if the bankruptcy petition relating to the debtor is dismissed, if a bankruptcy order is made on the petition or if the court by order otherwise terminates the appointment.

286(8)   [Interpretation] References in this section to the debtor's property are to all his property, whether or not it would be comprised in his estate if he were adjudged bankrupt.

S.286(1), (2)
The court may appoint the official receiver as an interim receiver after the presentation of the bankruptcy petition if such an appointment is necessary to protect the debtor's property. In *Gibson Dunn & Crutcher v Rio Properties Inc* [2004] EWCA Civ 1043; [2004] B.P.I.R. 1203 the Court of Appeal indicated that it was possible to appoint some other suitably qualified person apart from the official receiver to act as an interim receiver pursuant to s.286. The interim receiver has a company law counterpart in the provisional liquidator (IA 1986 s.135). As an alternative to the official receiver, the person appointed on a debtor's petition under s.273(2) to make a report on the possibility of a rescue plan can be given the role of interim receiver. For the powers and role of an interim receiver vis-à-vis the debtor see *Re Baars* [2002] EWHC 2159 (Ch); [2003] B.P.I.R. 523.
    The law on interim receivers can be expanded by the rules—see Sch.9 paras 9, 30. The key provisions are IR 1986 rr.6.51–6.57.

S.286(3)
This describes the role of such an interim receiver—note the degree of control over him exercised by the court.

S.286(4), (8)
The interim receiver should normally take immediate possession of the debtor's assets—even those assets which would not subsequently form part of the bankrupt's estate.

S.286(5)
This requires the debtor to accede to the interim receiver's demands for assistance.

S.286(6)
During this interim receivership the debtor's assets enjoy the same protection as if a bankruptcy order had been made.

S.286(7)
This deals with termination of the interim receivership.

287   Receivership pending appointment of trustee

287(1)   [Official receiver, receiver and manager] Between the making of a bankruptcy order and the time at which the bankrupt's estate vests in a trustee under Chapter IV of this Part, the official receiver is the receiver and (subject to section 370 (special manager)) the manager of the bankrupt's estate and is under a duty to act as such.

287(2)   [Function and powers of official receiver] The function of the official receiver while acting as receiver or manager of the bankrupt's estate under this section is to protect the estate; and for this purpose–

(a) he has the same powers as if he were a receiver or manager appointed by the High Court, and

(b) he is entitled to sell or otherwise dispose of any perishable goods comprised in the estate and any other goods so comprised the value of which is likely to diminish if they are not disposed of.

287(3)   [Steps re protecting property] The official receiver while acting as receiver or manager of the estate under this section–

(a) shall take all such steps as he thinks fit for protecting any property which may be claimed for the estate by the trustee of that estate,

(b) is not, except in pursuance of directions given by the Secretary of State, required to do anything that involves his incurring expenditure,

(c) may, if he thinks fit (and shall, if so directed by the court) at any time summon a general meeting of the bankrupt's creditors.

287(4)   [Liability of official receiver] Where–

(a) the official receiver acting as receiver or manager of the estate under this section seizes or disposes of any property which is not comprised in the estate, and

(b) at the time of the seizure or disposal the official receiver believes, and has reasonable grounds for believing, that he is entitled (whether in pursuance of an order of the court or otherwise) to seize or dispose of that property,

the official receiver is not liable to any person in respect of any loss or damage resulting from the seizure or disposal except in so far as that loss or damage is caused by his negligence; and he has a lien on the property, or the proceeds of its sale, for such of the expenses of the bankruptcy as were incurred in connection with the seizure or disposal.

287(5)   [Non-application] This section does not apply where by virtue of section 297 (appointment of trustee; special cases) the bankrupt's estate vests in a trustee immediately on the making of the bankruptcy order.

S.287(1), (2), (5)
The official receiver is to act as receiver and manager of the bankrupt's estate between the date of the bankruptcy order and when the trustee takes control. If the estate has vested immediately in the trustee by virtue of s.297, then s.287 does not apply. His role is of a caretaker nature (like a court-appointed receiver and manager), although he may sell perishables, etc. For the nature of the receivership in the hands of the official receiver operating under s.287(1) see *Dadourian Group International v Simms* [2008] EWHC 723 (Ch); [2008] B.P.I.R. 508.

Under BA 1914 s.10, the official receiver could, in the period before the receiving order and the trustee taking over, appoint a manager—under s.287 it seems that the official receiver must fulfil this role himself. The court can, however, appoint a special manager under s.370 instead of the official receiver.

Further details on the role of the official receiver as receiver and manager may be provided by regulations which may be made by the Secretary of State under the rules: see Sch.9 paras 10, 30 and IR 1986 r.12.1(1), (2).

S.287(3)
These paragraphs detail further the obligations of the official receiver while acting as receiver and manager. His duty to protect the assets is stressed, although he cannot incur expenditure unless directed to do so by the Secretary of State. He may, and, if directed by the court, must, call meetings of creditors.

S.287(4)
This offers protection from liability for wrongful seizure of assets where the official receiver has acted reasonably and without negligence. Moreover, he has a lien over any proceeds of the wrongful sale to cover his expenses.

288   Statement of affairs

288(1)   [Submission of statement to official receiver] Where a bankruptcy order has been made otherwise than on a debtor's petition, the bankrupt shall submit a statement of his affairs to the official receiver before the end of the period of 21 days beginning with the commencement of the bankruptcy.

288(2)   [Contents of statement] The statement of affairs shall contain–

(a)   such particulars of the bankrupt's creditors and of his debts and other liabilities and of his assets as may be prescribed, and

(b)   such other information as may be prescribed.

288(3)   [Powers of official receiver] The official receiver may, if he thinks fit–

(a)   release the bankrupt from his duty under subsection (1), or

(b)   extend the period specified in that subsection;

and where the official receiver has refused to exercise a power conferred by this section, the court, if it thinks fit, may exercise it.

288(4)   [Penalty for non-compliance] A bankrupt who–

(a)   without reasonable excuse fails to comply with the obligation imposed by this section, or

(b)   without reasonable excuse submits a statement of affairs that does not comply with the prescribed requirements,

is guilty of a contempt of court and liable to be punished accordingly (in addition to any other punishment to which he may be subject).

S.288(1), (3)

Where a bankruptcy order has been made on the initiative of a creditor, the bankrupt normally has 21 days to submit a statement of affairs to the official receiver. A bankrupt may be released from this obligation by the official receiver (see IR 1986 r.6.62 and r.6.76), who may also extend the 21-day period. If the official receiver refuses to exercise his discretion the court may intervene. This provision differs from its predecessor in a number of respects. The time period mentioned in BA 1914 s.14 was seven days. Furthermore, under the 1914 Act a statement of affairs was required within three days where the debtor had petitioned for his own bankruptcy: the position now is governed by s.272(2).

S.288(2)

This specifies the contents of the statement of affairs. The rules amplify these requirements: see IR 1986 rr.6.58–6.66.

For the evidential status of such a statement, see s.433.

S.288(4)

Non-compliance can result in liability for contempt of court.

289   Investigatory duties of official receiver

289(1)   [Investigation and report] The official receiver shall–

(a)   investigate the conduct and affairs of each bankrupt (including his conduct and affairs before the making of the bankruptcy order), and

(b)   make such report (if any) to the court as the official receiver thinks fit.

289(2)   [Non-application of s.289(1)] Subsection (1) shall not apply to a case in which the official receiver thinks an investigation under that subsection unnecessary.

289(3)   [Where application for discharge] Where a bankrupt makes an application for discharge under section 280–

(a)   the official receiver shall make a report to the court about such matters as may be prescribed, and

(b)   the court shall consider the report before determining the application.

289(4)   [Report prima facie evidence of facts] A report by the official receiver under this section shall in any proceedings be prima facie evidence of the facts stated in it.

GENERAL NOTE

This substituted provision was introduced by s.258 of EA 2002 with effect from April 2004.

S.289(1)
This in effect repeats the current position suggesting that all bankrupts should be investigated by the OR.

S.289(2)
This is the key change, removing the mandatory obligation to investigate in circumstances where the OR deems this "unnecessary". No criteria are given for the making of this judgment, but reference to the grounds for the making of a BRO in Sch.4A might provide a useful pointer. One would imagine that the Insolvency Service would produce its own internal guidelines for official receivers. One effect of not having an investigation would be the reduction in bankruptcy administration costs.

S.289(3)
This deals with reports to the court where the bankrupt makes a discharge application under s.280.

S.289(4)
This outlines the evidential status of any report made by the OR.

290   Public examination of bankrupt

290(1)   [Application to court] Where a bankruptcy order has been made, the official receiver may at any time before the discharge of the bankrupt apply to the court for the public examination of the bankrupt.

290(2)   [Duty of official receiver to make application] Unless the court otherwise orders, the official receiver shall make an application under subsection (1) if notice requiring him to do so is given to him, in accordance with the rules, by one of the bankrupt's creditors with the concurrence of not less than one-half, in value, of those creditors (including the creditor giving notice).

290(3)   [Direction re public examination] On an application under subsection (1), the court shall direct that a public examination of the bankrupt shall be held on a day appointed by the court; and the bankrupt shall attend on that day and be publicly examined as to his affairs, dealings and property.

290(4)   [Persons taking part in examination] The following may take part in the public examination of the bankrupt and may question him concerning his affairs, dealings and property and the causes of his failure, namely–

(a)   the official receiver and, in the case of an individual adjudged bankrupt on a petition under section 264(1)(d), the Official Petitioner,

(b)   the trustee of the bankrupt's estate, if his appointment has taken effect,

(c)   any person who has been appointed as special manager of the bankrupt's estate or business,

(d)   any creditor of the bankrupt who has tendered a proof in the bankruptcy.

290(5)   [Penalty re non-attendance] If a bankrupt without reasonable excuse fails at any time to attend his public examination under this section he is guilty of a contempt of court and liable to be punished accordingly (in addition to any other punishment to which he may be subject).

Under BA 1914 s.15, a public examination was required in every case of bankruptcy. This was unfortunate because it seemed unnecessary to ask every bankrupt to undergo such an ordeal and, in some cases, public examinations caused embarrassment to third parties not directly concerned with the bankruptcy. The most notorious example of this was provided by the public examination of John Poulson in 1972. Accordingly, IA 1976 s.6 permitted the official receiver to ask the court to relieve certain bankrupts of this onerous procedure.

The Bankruptcy Rules 1952 rr.188–196 contained additional material on public examinations and the relevant provisions are now IR 1986 rr.6.172–6.177.

S.290(1), (2)

The position now is that a public examination will only be held where the official receiver asks for one. However, his hand can be forced by a majority of the bankrupt's creditors. It was held by the Court of Appeal in *Re Seagull Manufacturing Co Ltd* [1993] Ch. 345; [1993] B.C.C. 241 that the court has jurisdiction in the case of a public examination under s.133 to order a person resident outside the jurisdiction to attend for examination. (For the position in a private examination, see the notes to s.236, above.)

S.290(3), (5)

The court fixes the date of the public examination and the bankrupt must attend or face liability for contempt. Self-incrimination is no excuse for refusal to answer questions (*Re Paget* [1927] 2 Ch. 85). That said, the use of information gleaned from a public examination in criminal proceedings in English law is tightly controlled as a result of the requirements of the ECHR. Indeed, the court can adjourn a public examination and direct that further proceedings be conducted in private where there are real concerns that the transcript of a public examination might jeopardise the position of the bankrupt with regard to foreign criminal proceedings—for discussion on this point see *Rottmann v Official Receiver* [2009] B.P.I.R. 617—confirmed in [2009] EWCA Civ 473.

S.290(4)

This determines who may attend and participate in the public examination. This means that the authority of *Re Stern (a Bankrupt)* [1982] 1 W.L.R. 860 has been superseded.

291 Duties of bankrupt in relation to official receiver

291(1) [Duties where bankruptcy order made] Where a bankruptcy order has been made, the bankrupt is under a duty–

(a) to deliver possession of his estate to the official receiver, and

(b) to deliver up to the official receiver all books, papers and other records of which he has possession or control and which relate to his estate and affairs (including any which would be privileged from disclosure in any proceedings).

291(2) [Property not capable of delivery to official receiver] In the case of any part of the bankrupt's estate which consists of things possession of which cannot be delivered to the official receiver, and in the case of any property that may be claimed for the bankrupt's estate by the trustee, it is the bankrupt's duty to do all such things as may reasonably be required by the official receiver for the protection of those things or that property.

291(3) [Non-application of s.291(1), (2)] Subsections (1) and (2) do not apply where by virtue of section 297 below the bankrupt's estate vests in a trustee immediately on the making of the bankruptcy order.

291(4) [Bankrupt to give information] The bankrupt shall give the official receiver such inventory of his estate and such other information, and shall attend on the official receiver at such times, as the official receiver may reasonably require–

(a) for a purpose of this Chapter, or

(b) in connection with the making of a bankruptcy restrictions order.

291(5) [Application of s.291(4)] Subsection (4) applies to a bankrupt after his discharge.

291(6)   [Penalty for non-compliance] If the bankrupt without reasonable excuse fails to comply with any obligation imposed by this section, he is guilty of a contempt of court and liable to be punished accordingly (in addition to any other punishment to which he may be subject).

S.291(1)–(3)
This lists some of the obligations of the bankrupt towards the official receiver—this includes handing over property in his possession, assisting the recovery of other items and delivering up all relevant books and records. These obligations do not apply to the special cases covered by s.297.

S.291(4), (5)
Subsection (4) was reconstituted by EA 2002 s.269 and Sch.23 with effect from April 1, 2004. This imposes an additional obligation on the bankrupt to provide information and be prepared to assist the official receiver where this is reasonably requested. The obligation continues to apply after discharge.

S.291(6)
Failure to comply with the above obligations results in liability for contempt of court.

CHAPTER III

TRUSTEES IN BANKRUPTCY

Tenure of office as trustee

292   Power to make appointments

292(1)   [Exercise of power] The power to appoint a person as trustee of a bankrupt's estate (whether the first such trustee or a trustee appointed to fill any vacancy) is exercisable–

(a)   by a general meeting of the bankrupt's creditors;

(b)   under section 295(2), 296(2) or 300(6) below in this Chapter, by the Secretary of State; or

(c)   under section 297, by the court.

292(2)   [Qualification for trustee] No person may be appointed as trustee of a bankrupt's estate unless he is, at the time of the appointment, qualified to act as an insolvency practitioner in relation to the bankrupt.

292(3)   [Joint trustees] Any power to appoint a person as trustee of a bankrupt's estate includes power to appoint two or more persons as joint trustees; but such an appointment must make provision as to the circumstances in which the trustees must act together and the circumstances in which one or more of them may act for the others.

292(4)   [Requirement of acceptance of appointment] The appointment of any person as trustee takes effect only if that person accepts the appointment in accordance with the rules. Subject to this, the appointment of any person as trustee takes effect at the time specified in his certificate of appointment.

292(5)   [Effect] This section is without prejudice to the provisions of this Chapter under which the official receiver is, in certain circumstances, to be trustee of the estate.

S.292(1)
This determines who may appoint a trustee in bankruptcy. Normally it will be a decision for the creditors, although there are situations whether the Secretary of State, or the court, may assume responsibility for the appointment. Section 292 is not exhaustive of the circumstances in which a trustee in bankruptcy may be appointed—*Donaldson v O'Sullivan* [2008] EWHC 387 (Ch); [2008] B.P.I.R. 288 which was confirmed in [2008] EWCA Civ 879. A reference to summary administration was deleted by EA 2002 s.269 and Sch.23 with effect from April 1, 2004. See generally IR 1986 rr.6.120–6.125.

S.292(2)
Under BA 1914 s.19 the trustee had to be a "fit person"—now he must be properly qualified under Pt XIII.

S.292(3)
This restates BA 1914 s.77 which permitted the appointment of joint trustees.

S.292(4)
For the appointment to take effect the trustee must accept the post in accordance with the rules (see IR 1986 r.6.124).
The date of the appointment is specified in the certificate of appointment.

S.292(5)
The aforementioned provisions do not apply where the official receiver acts as trustee: see ss.293(3), 295(4), 297 and 300(2).

293   Summoning of meeting to appoint first trustee

293(1)   [Duty of official receiver] Where a bankruptcy order has been made, it is the duty of the official receiver, as soon as practicable in the period of 12 weeks beginning with the day on which the order was made, to decide whether to summon a general meeting of the bankrupt's creditors for the purpose of appointing a trustee of the bankrupt's estate.

This section does not apply where the bankruptcy order was made on a petition under section 264(1)(d) (criminal bankruptcy); and it is subject to the provision made in sections 294(3) and 297(6) below.

293(2)   [Duty if no meeting summoned] Subject to the next section, if the official receiver decides not to summon such a meeting, he shall, before the end of the period of 12 weeks above mentioned, give notice of his decision to the court and to every creditor of the bankrupt who is known to the official receiver or is identified in the bankrupt's statement of affairs.

293(3)   [Official receiver trustee from s.293(2) notice] As from the giving to the court of a notice under subsection (2), the official receiver is the trustee of the bankrupt's estate.

S.293(1)
The official receiver must within 12 weeks of the bankruptcy order decide whether to call a general meeting of the bankrupt's creditors in order to appoint a trustee. The reference to summary administration in subs.(1) was deleted with effect from April 1, 2004 by EA 2002 s.269 and Sch.23.

Note prospective amendment: in s.293(1) the words "does not apply where the bankruptcy order was made on a petition under section 264(1)(d) (criminal bankruptcy) and it" are to be repealed by CJA 1988 s.170(2) and Sch.16 as from a day to be appointed. See the note to s.264.

S.293(2), (3)
If he decides not to summon such a meeting he must inform the court and every known creditor of his decision. He thereupon becomes a trustee of the estate.

The BA 1914 Sch.1 contained details of creditors' meetings; such matters are now dealt with by the rules (Sch.9 para.12): see IR 1986 rr.6.79–6.95.

294   Power of creditors to requisition meeting

294(1)   [Request to official receiver] Where in the case of any bankruptcy the official receiver has not yet summoned, or has decided not to summon, a general meeting of the bankrupt's creditors for the purpose of appointing the trustee any creditor of the bankrupt may request the official receiver to summon such a meeting for that purpose.

294(2)   [Duty to summon meeting on request] If such a request appears to the official receiver to be made with the concurrence of not less than one-quarter, in value, of the bankrupt's creditors (including the creditor making the request), it is the duty of the official receiver to summon the requested meeting.

294(3)   [Where s.294(2) duty has arisen] Accordingly, where the duty imposed by subsection (2) has arisen, the official receiver is required neither to reach a decision for the purposes of section 293(1) nor (if he has reached one) to serve any notice under section 293(2).

S.294(1), (2)
In a normal bankruptcy case a creditor can ask the official receiver to call a creditors' meeting, with a view to appointing a trustee. Indeed, he *must* summon such a meeting if the request is backed by creditors owed 25 per cent

of the bankrupt's debts. (This percentage was reduced from the original figure of 50 per cent at the Report Stage of the 1985 Bill.) The reference to summary administration in subs.(1)(b) was deleted with effect from April 1, 2004 by s.269 of and Sch.23 to EA 2002.

S.294(3)
Where the creditors have forced the official receiver's hand in this way, he is excused his obligations under s.293.
  See also IR 1986 r.6.83.

295   Failure of meeting to appoint trustee

295(1)   [Duty of official receiver] If a meeting summoned under section 293 or 294 is held but no appointment of a person as trustee is made, it is the duty of the official receiver to decide whether to refer the need for an appointment to the Secretary of State.

295(2)   [Duty of Secretary of State] On a reference made in pursuance of that decision, the Secretary of State shall either make an appointment or decline to make one.

295(3)   [Notice to court] If–

  (a)   the official receiver decides not to refer the need for an appointment to the Secretary of State, or

  (b)   on such a reference the Secretary of State declines to make an appointment,

the official receiver shall give notice of his decision or, as the case may be, of the Secretary of State's decision to the court.

295(4)   [As from notice official receiver trustee] As from the giving of notice under subsection (3) in a case in which no notice has been given under section 293(2), the official receiver shall be trustee of the bankrupt's estate.

S.295(1), (2)
Where the creditors in meeting fail to appoint a trustee, the official receiver must decide whether to refer the matter to the Secretary of State, who has discretion whether to appoint a trustee or not. The value of the bankrupt's estate will clearly be relevant in such cases even if the small bankruptcies level (see s.273) has been exceeded.

S.295(3)
If the official receiver has decided not to refer the matter to the Secretary of State, or the Secretary of State has decided not to make an appointment, the official receiver must notify the court.

S.295(4)
Where the official receiver has decided not to call on the assistance of the Secretary of State or the latter has failed to make an appointment, the official receiver will become the trustee.
  See also IR 1986 r.6.122.

296   Appointment of trustee by Secretary of State

296(1)   [Application for appointment instead of official receiver] At any time when the official receiver is the trustee of a bankrupt's estate by virtue of any provision of this Chapter (other than section 297(1) below) he may apply to the Secretary of State for the appointment of a person as trustee instead of the official receiver.

296(2)   [Duty of Secretary of State] On an application under subsection (1) the Secretary of State shall either make an appointment or decline to make one.

296(3)   [Making of application] Such an application may be made notwithstanding that the Secretary of State has declined to make an appointment either on a previous application under subsection (1) or on a reference under section 295 or under section 300(4) below.

296(4)   [Notice etc., re appointment] Where the trustee of a bankrupt's estate has been appointed by the Secretary of State (whether under this section or otherwise), the trustee shall give notice to the bankrupt's creditors of his appointment or, if the court so allows, shall advertise his appointment in accordance with the court's directions.

296(5)   [Contents of notice] In that notice or advertisement the trustee shall–

(a)   state whether he proposes to summon a general meeting of the bankrupt's creditors for the purpose of establishing a creditors' committee under section 301, and

(b)   if he does not propose to summon such a meeting, set out the power of the creditors under this Part to require him to summon one.

S.296(1)–(3)

This permits the official receiver when acting as a trustee to seek another appointment in his stead. He cannot do this where he is acting as a trustee in case of summary administration or a bankruptcy initiated as the result of a criminal bankruptcy order. On the other hand, he is not precluded from making such an application by the fact that he has previously made unsuccessful applications under ss.295, 296(1) or 300(4). On an application by the official receiver the Secretary of State has discretion whether to appoint a trustee or not. See also IR 1986 r.6.122.

S.296(4), (5)

Any appointment of a trustee by the Secretary of State must be notified to the creditors by the trustee or, if the court permits, be advertised with a view to informing the creditors whether a committee should be set up under s.301. See also IR 1986 r.6.124 for the advertisement of the appointment.

297   Special cases

297(1)   [Where s.264(1)(d) bankruptcy order] Where a bankruptcy order is made on a petition under section 264(1)(d) (criminal bankruptcy), the official receiver shall be trustee of the bankrupt's estate.

297(2)   [Repealed.]

297(3)   [Repealed.]

297(4)   [Person who made s.274 report may be appointed trustee] Where a bankruptcy order is made in a case in which an insolvency practitioner's report has been submitted to the court under section 274, the court, if it thinks fit, may on making the order appoint the person who made the report as trustee.

297(5)   [Where there is supervisor] Where a bankruptcy order is made (whether or not on a petition under section 264(1)(c)) at a time when there is a supervisor of a voluntary arrangement approved in relation to the bankrupt under Part VIII, the court, if it thinks fit, may on making the order appoint the supervisor of the arrangement as trustee.

297(6)   [Exception re s.293(1) duty] Where an appointment is made under subsection (4) or (5) of this section, the official receiver is not under the duty imposed by section 293(1) (to decide whether or not to summon a meeting of creditors).

297(7)   [Notice where trustee appointed by court] Where the trustee of a bankrupt's estate has been appointed by the court, the trustee shall give notice to the bankrupt's creditors of his appointment or, if the court so allows, shall advertise his appointment in accordance with the directions of the court.

297(8)   [Contents of notice] In that notice or advertisement he shall–

(a)   state whether he proposes to summon a general meeting of the bankrupt's creditors for the purpose of establishing a creditors' committee under section 301 below, and

(b)   if he does not propose to summon such a meeting, set out the power of the creditors under this Part to require him to summon one.

S.297(1)

These provisions deal with cases where the official receiver is to act as trustee: e.g. on bankruptcy initiated as the result of a criminal bankruptcy order. These are not the only instances where the official receiver acts as trustee: see ss.293(3) and 295(4).

   Note prospective amendment: s.297(1) is to be repealed by CJA 1988 s.170(2) and Sch.16 as from a day to be appointed; see the note to s.264.

S.297(2), (3)

These subsections were deleted by s.269 of and Sch.23 to EA 2002 with effect from April 1, 2004. They dealt with summary administration.

S.297(4)

This deals with another special case. Where in a small bankruptcy case the court can select the person who made the crucial report to it under s.274(1) as trustee. See also IR 1986 r.6.121.

S.297(5)

If bankruptcy has been initiated notwithstanding the existence of a composition or scheme (see ss.252–263) the court may appoint the supervisor as trustee. See also IR 1986 r.6.121.

S.297(6)

In cases covered by s.297(4) and (5) the official receiver is not under a duty to decide whether to call a general meeting of creditors for the purpose of appointing a trustee.

S.297(7), (8)

This mirrors s.296(4) and (5), although the appointor here is the court and not the Secretary of State.

298   Removal of trustee; vacation of office

298(1)   [Removal by court order or creditors' meeting] Subject as follows, the trustee of a bankrupt's estate may be removed from office only by an order of the court or by a general meeting of the bankrupt's creditors summoned specially for that purpose in accordance with the rules.

298(2)   [Where official receiver trustee under s.297(1)] Where the official receiver is trustee by virtue of section 297(1), he shall not be removed from office under this section.

298(3)   [Deleted.]

298(4)   [Where official receiver trustee under s.293(3), 295(4)] Where the official receiver is trustee by virtue of section 293(3) or 295(4) or a trustee is appointed by the Secretary of State or (otherwise than under section 297(5)) by the court, a general meeting of the bankrupt's creditors shall be summoned for the purpose of replacing the trustee only if–

   (a)   the trustee thinks fit, or

   (b)   the court so directs, or

   (c)   the meeting is requested by one of the bankrupt's creditors with the concurrence of not less than one-quarter, in value, of the creditors (including the creditor making the request).

298(5)   [Where trustee appointed by Secretary of State] If the trustee was appointed by the Secretary of State, he may be removed by a direction of the Secretary of State.

298(6)   [Vacation of office] The trustee (not being the official receiver) shall vacate office if he ceases to be a person who is for the time being qualified to act as an insolvency practitioner in relation to the bankrupt.

298(7)   [Resignation] The trustee may, in the prescribed circumstances, resign his office by giving notice of his resignation to the court.

298(8)   [Vacation on s.331 notice] The trustee shall vacate office on giving notice to the court that a final meeting has been held under section 331 in Chapter IV and of the decision (if any) of that meeting.

298(9)   [When bankruptcy order annulled] The trustee shall vacate office if the bankruptcy order is annulled.

S.298(1), (2)

Trustees may as a general rule only be removed by the court or the general meeting of creditors. However, this does not apply where the official receiver is trustee. See also IR r.6.129. There has been a lack of guidance on the principles to be applied in the context of this provision—see *Smedley v Brittain* [2008] B.P.I.R. 219.

S.298(3)
This was deleted by s.269 of and Sch.23 to EA 2002 as from April 1, 2004. It covered summary administration.

S.298(4)
The drafting of this provision is complex. It covers the official receiver acting as trustee by virtue of ss.293(3) or 295(4), and trustees appointed by the Secretary of State, or by the court (but not under s.297(5)). This allows a meeting to be called to dismiss the trustee—either the trustee himself, the court or creditors owed 25 per cent of the bankrupt's debts can call for this. This was reduced from 50 per cent in the original 1985 Bill.

S.298(5)
The Secretary of State can remove his own appointees.

S.298(6)
A trustee must vacate office if he ceases to be qualified to act: see Pt XIII and r.6.144(1).

S.298(7)
Resignation in the circumstances prescribed is permitted. See IR 1986 r.6.126.

S.298(8)
The trustee shall vacate office after giving notice to the court of the outcome of the final meeting of creditors (see s.331).

S.298(9)
Annulment of the bankruptcy order will cause the trustee to vacate office.
    For further details on removal and vacation of office, see IR 1986 rr.6.126–6.135.

299   Release of trustee

299(1)   **[Time of release for official receiver]** Where the official receiver has ceased to be the trustee of a bankrupt's estate and a person is appointed in his stead, the official receiver shall have his release with effect from the following time, that is to say–

    (a)   where that person is appointed by a general meeting of the bankrupt's creditors or by the Secretary of State, the time at which the official receiver gives notice to the court that he has been replaced, and

    (b)   where that person is appointed by the court, such time as the court may determine.

299(2)   **[Time of release if notice given by official receiver]** If the official receiver while he is the trustee gives notice to the Secretary of State that the administration of the bankrupt's estate in accordance with Chapter IV of this Part is for practical purposes complete, he shall have his release with effect from such time as the Secretary of State may determine.

299(3)   **[Time of release for person not official receiver]** A person other than the official receiver who has ceased to be the trustee shall have his release with effect from the following time, that is to say–

    (a)   in the case of a person who has been removed from office by a general meeting of the bankrupt's creditors that has not resolved against his release or who has died, the time at which notice is given to the court in accordance with the rules that that person has ceased to hold office;

    (b)   in the case of a person who has been removed from office by a general meeting of the bankrupt's creditors that has resolved against his release, or by the court, or by the Secretary of State, or who has vacated office under section 298(6), such time as the Secretary of State may, on an application by that person, determine;

    (c)   in the case of a person who has resigned, such time as may be prescribed;

    (d)   in the case of a person who has vacated office under section 298(8)–

       (i)   if the final meeting referred to in that subsection has resolved against that person's release, such time as the Secretary of State may, on an application by that person, determine; and

       (ii)   if that meeting has not so resolved, the time at which the person vacated office.

299(4)   [Time of release where bankruptcy order annulled] Where a bankruptcy order is annulled, the trustee at the time of the annulment has his release with effect from such time as the court may determine.

299(5)   [Effect of release] Where the official receiver or the trustee has his release under this section, he shall, with effect from the time specified in the preceding provisions of this section, be discharged from all liability both in respect of acts or omissions of his in the administration of the estate and otherwise in relation to his conduct as trustee.

But nothing in this section prevents the exercise, in relation to a person who has had his release under this section, of the court's powers under section 304.

S.299(1), (2)
These provisions deal with the release of an official receiver who has been acting as trustee. The procedure to be followed depends on whether he is being replaced or whether he has simply completed the administration of the estate.

For the equivalent provision for the release of liquidators, see s.174. As to the possibility of a release being set aside, see *Re Munro Ex p. Singer v Trustee in Bankruptcy* [1981] 1 W.L.R. 1358. Release is also dealt with by IR 1986 rr.6.136, 6.137.

S.299(3)
This fixes the date of release for trustees other than the official receiver. Again, the date will vary according to the circumstances of the case—a comprehensive list of possibilities is provided for.

S.299(4)
Where release is the result of the annulment of the bankruptcy order the court will fix the date of release. See *Dear IP* Issue 26 (March 2006).

S.299(5)
This is a general provision dealing with the *effect* of a release: it serves as a discharge of liabilities, unless an action is subsequently brought under s.304.

300   Vacancy in office of trustee

300(1)   [Application] This section applies where the appointment of any person as trustee of a bankrupt's estate fails to take effect or, such an appointment having taken effect, there is otherwise a vacancy in the office of trustee.

300(2)   [Official receiver trustee] The official receiver shall be trustee until the vacancy is filled.

300(3)   [Summoning creditors' meeting] The official receiver may summon a general meeting of the bankrupt's creditors for the purpose of filling the vacancy and shall summon such a meeting if required to do so in pursuance of section 314(7) (creditors' requisition).

300(4)   [If no meeting summoned within 28 days] If at the end of the period of 28 days beginning with the day on which the vacancy first came to the official receiver's attention he has not summoned, and is not proposing to summon, a general meeting of creditors for the purpose of filling the vacancy, he shall refer the need for an appointment to the Secretary of State.

300(5)   [Deleted.]

300(6)   [Duty of Secretary of State re s.300(4), (5)] On a reference to the Secretary of State under subsection (4) the Secretary of State shall either make an appointment or decline to make one.

300(7)   [If no appointment on s.300(4), (5) reference] If on a reference under subsection (4) no appointment is made, the official receiver shall continue to be trustee of the bankrupt's estate, but without prejudice to his power to make a further reference.

300(8)   [Interpretation] References in this section to a vacancy include a case where it is necessary, in relation to any property which is or may be comprised in a bankrupt's estate, to revive the trusteeship of that estate after the holding of a final meeting summoned under section 331 or the giving by the official receiver of notice under section 299(2).

S.300(1), (2)

Where the appointment of a trustee fails to take effect (e.g. because he refuses the appointment) or a casual vacancy occurs, the official receiver must act as trustee during the interregnum.

S.300(3), (4)

The official receiver may (and, in cases under s.314(7), must) call a general meeting to fill this vacancy. If he fails to act within 28 days he must refer the matter to the Secretary of State. See IR 1986 r.6.122.

S.300(5)

This was deleted by s.269 of and Sch.23 to EA 2002 with effect from April 1, 2004. It dealt with summary administration.

S.300(6), (7)

Where a casual vacancy has been referred to the Secretary of State he has discretion whether to fill it or not. If the vacancy is not filled the official receiver must act as trustee pending the resolution of the matter.

S.300(8)

This defines what is meant by a "vacancy" for the purposes of the present section.

Control of trustee

301   Creditors' committee

301(1)   **[Meeting may establish committee]** Subject as follows, a general meeting of a bankrupt's creditors (whether summoned under the preceding provisions of this Chapter or otherwise) may, in accordance with the rules, establish a committee (known as "the creditors' committee") to exercise the functions conferred on it by or under this Act.

301(2)   **[Exception]** A general meeting of the bankrupt's creditors shall not establish such a committee, or confer any functions on such a committee, at any time when the official receiver is the trustee of the bankrupt's estate, except in connection with an appointment made by that meeting of a person to be trustee instead of the official receiver.

S.301(1)

This enables the general meeting of creditors to establish a committee to supervise the trustee. Under the 1914 Act this committee was known as a "committee of inspection" but this title has now been dropped on the recommendation of the Cork Committee (*Report*, para.932). The role and general position of the committee is now governed by the Rules—see now IR 1986 rr.6.150–6.166. Under BA 1914 many of these details were spelled out in the provisions of the Act itself. Under BA 1914 s.79(1) the committee had general power to give directions to the trustee. This power was not re-enacted in the 1986 Act and therefore the role of the committee is more limited. Members of this committee occupy a fiduciary position vis-à-vis the bankrupt's estate: *Re Bulmer Ex p. Greaves* [1937] Ch. 499.

An FSA representative can attend where appropriate—FSMA 2000 s.374(4).

S.301(2)

The committee has no role where the official receiver is trustee—he is supervised by the Secretary of State under s.302.

This could apply to cases of criminal bankruptcy.

302   Exercise by Secretary of State of functions of creditors' committee

302(1)   **[Where official receiver trustee]** The creditors' committee is not to be able or required to carry out its functions at any time when the official receiver is trustee of the bankrupt's estate; but at any such time the functions of the committee under this Act shall be vested in the Secretary of State, except to the extent that the rules otherwise provide.

302(2)   **[Where no committee]** Where in the case of any bankruptcy there is for the time being no creditors' committee and the trustee of the bankrupt's estate is a person other than the official receiver, the functions of such a committee shall be vested in the Secretary of State, except to the extent that the rules otherwise provide.

S.302(1)

This reiterates that the committee established under s.301 cannot exercise any control functions when the official receiver is acting as trustee. Instead, control in such cases must be exercised by the Secretary of State. See IR 1986 r.6.166.

S.302(2)

For the relevant rules, see IR 1986 r.6.166.

303 General control of trustee by the court

303(1)   [Application to court] If a bankrupt or any of his creditors or any other person is dissatisfied by any act, omission or decision of a trustee of the bankrupt's estate, he may apply to the court; and on such an application the court may confirm, reverse or modify any act or decision of the trustee, may give him directions or may make such other order as it thinks fit.

303(2)   [Application by trustee for directions] The trustee of a bankrupt's estate may apply to the court for directions in relation to any particular matter arising under the bankruptcy.

303(2A)   [Insolvent partnerships] Where at any time after a bankruptcy petition has been presented to the court against any person, whether under the provisions of the Insolvent Partnerships Order 1994 or not, the attention of the court is drawn to the fact that the person in question is a member of an insolvent partnership, the court may make an order as to the future conduct of the insolvency proceedings and any such order may apply any provisions of that Order with any necessary modifications.

303(2B)   [Court power to consolidate s.303(2A) proceedings] Where a bankruptcy petition has been presented against more than one individual in the circumstances mentioned in subsection (2A) above, the court may give such directions for consolidating the proceedings, or any of them, as it thinks just.

303(2C)   [Order or directions under s.303(2A), (2B)] Any order or directions under subsection (2A) or (2B) may be made or given on the application of the official receiver, any responsible insolvency practitioner, the trustee of the partnership or any other interested person and may include provisions as to the administration of the joint estate of the partnership, and in particular how it and the separate estate of any member are to be administered.

S.303(1)

This permits any person (including a discharged bankrupt—*Osborn v Cole* [1999] B.P.I.R. 251 or a person whose bankruptcy has been annulled—*Engel v Peri* [2002] EWHC 799 (Ch); [2002] B.P.I.R. 961) who is dissatisfied with a decision of a trustee in bankruptcy to apply to the court for relief. On such an application the court enjoys general discretion to deal with the matter. This is a useful reserve control power, but in practice, as the Cork Committee observed (*Report*, para.779), such applications rarely succeed: see, for an example of an unsuccessful application, *Re a Debtor Ex p. The Debtor v Dodwell (The Trustee)* [1949] Ch. 236. See also *Canty v Boyden* [2006] EWCA Civ 194; [2006] B.P.I.R. 624. In *Osborn v Cole* (above) this difficulty was exemplified by requiring proof that the trustee was acting in a manner in which no reasonable trustee would act. On the appropriate test to be applied by the court under s.303 see *Bank of Baroda v Patel* [2009] B.P.I.R. 255, a case where *Osborne v Cole* (above) was followed. In *Supperstone v Hurst (No.3)* [2006] EWHC 2147 (Ch); [2006] B.P.I.R. 1263 the strict test for interference with the actions of the trustee was applied by Warren J. In effect we are looking at *Wednesbury* unreasonableness. It was not surprising therefore that the application under s.303 was dismissed. *Miller v Bayliss* [2009] B.P.I.R. 1438 provides yet another example of the reluctance of the court to intervene in respect of the actions of the trustee. This case is also significant for casting light upon the issue of locus standi under s.303. Certainly this provision cannot be used to challenge the exercise of public law functions by an official receiver: *Hardy v Focus Insurance Co Ltd* [1997] B.P.I.R. 77. The fact that the courts are reluctant to direct a trustee to engage in speculative litigation is apparent from the comments of the Court of Appeal in *James v Rutherford-Hodge* [2005] EWCA Civ 1580; [2006] B.P.I.R. 973. In *Shepherd v Official Receiver* [2007] B.P.I.R. 101 Gabriel Moss Q.C. refused to exercise the s.303 jurisdiction to order an official receiver to investigate further the possibility of a claim being brought against the Legal Services Commission. See *Law Society v OR and Shah* [2007] EWHC 2841 (Ch); [2007] B.P.I.R. 1595 for an example of a case where usage of s.303 was deemed not to be appropriate because the conduct of the trustees did not amount to *Wednesbury* unreasonableness. Interestingly, the jurisdiction of the court under s.363 was held not to be so limited.

It is uncertain whether the change from "aggrieved" in BA 1914 to "dissatisfied" will produce any practical differences. In *Osborn v Cole* (above) the old law was found to be of some value. Note also IR 1986 Pt 7. Section 303 is not an appropriate tool to use to fix the trustee's remuneration—*Engel v Peri* [2002] EWHC 799 (Ch); [2002] B.P.I.R. 961. In *Woodbridge v Smith* [2004] B.P.I.R. 247 Registrar Baister held that the wife of a bankrupt had standing s.303 to apply to the court to extract information from the trustee giving a breakdown on his claim for fees and expenses. Although s.303 could not be used to fix the remuneration and charges of the trustee it could be used in this indirect fashion to facilitate that goal. There is still dispute as to whether the court can utilise s.303 to determine the remuneration and expenses of the trustee—*Re Cooper* [2005] N.I. Ch. 1; [2007] B.P.I.R. 219 (a case involving the equivalent statutory provision in Northern Ireland). On the use of s.303 as a means of challenging the remuneration of a trustee see *Barker v Bajjon* [2008] B.P.I.R. 771. The potential usage of s.303 by a bankrupt disgruntled at the composition of a creditors' committee was noted by Nicholas Strauss Q.C. in *Foenander v Allan* [2006] B.P.I.R. 1392.

Those lawyers looking for a more liberal use of this control facility will have been disappointed by the comments of Harman J. in *Port v Auger* [1994] 1 W.L.R. 862 at 873–874. Although Harman J. appeared to accept that the change in terminology from "aggrieved" to "dissatisfied" may have indicated an intention on the part of the legislature to widen access to the court he expressed the view that the applicant must have some substantial interest that has been adversely affected and then went on to suggest that the s.303 jurisdiction should not be invoked lightly by the court for fear of inflicting unnecessary expense on the insolvent estate. For a case which pushed the s.303 jurisdiction to the limit see *Re Cook* [1999] B.P.I.R. 881. In *Re Shettar* [2003] B.P.I.R. 1055 Park J. on an application under s.303 refused to direct the trustee to assign a statute-barred cause of action back to the bankrupt because in so doing the trustee might expose himself to potential liability for costs if the bankrupt unsuccessfully pursued that claim.

In *Heath v Tang* [1993] 1 W.L.R. 1421 it was suggested by the court that this provision might prove useful if the trustee refuses to pursue a claim of action belonging to the debtor but now vested in the estate. On this see also the notes on ss.285(3) and 306.

In *Skeete v Pick* [2007] EWHC 2211 (Ch) the court indicated that in principle s.303 might be engaged where a trustee acknowledged a third party interest in the bankrupt's property which the bankrupt disputed.

There is a good account of the case law governing the s.303 jurisdiction in *Smedley v Brittain* [2008] B.P.I.R. 219.

On the interface between s.303 and s.304 see *Brown v Beat* [2002] B.P.I.R. 421.

S.303(2)

This is a useful facility in that it allows a trustee in bankruptcy to apply to the court for guidance on a difficult matter. For an illustration of the court giving such directions see *Re a Debtor (No.26A of 1975)* [1985] 1 W.L.R. 6. Other interested parties may also apply—*Supperstone v Auger* [1999] B.P.I.R. 152. Subsection (2) of this provision may provide the jurisdiction to appoint a trustee in bankruptcy under a block transfer order—*Donaldson v O'Sullivan* [2008] EWCA Civ 879.

S.303(2A)–(2C)

For insolvent partners there are modifications in the form of subss.(2A)–(2C) inserted by the Insolvent Partnerships Order 1994 (SI 1994/2421) art.14. These are reproduced in Vol.2. On the usage of s.303(2A)–(2C) in the context of an insolvent partnership see *Official Receiver v Hollens* [2007] EWHC 754 (Ch); [2007] B.P.I.R. 830 where the court gave directions to facilitate the appropriate handling of the partnership assets.

304   Liability of trustee

304(1)   [Powers of court on application] Where on an application under this section the court is satisfied–

(a)   that the trustee of a bankrupt's estate has misapplied or retained, or become accountable for, any money or other property comprised in the bankrupt's estate, or

(b)   that a bankrupt's estate has suffered any loss in consequence of any misfeasance or breach of fiduciary or other duty by a trustee of the estate in the carrying out of his functions,

the court may order the trustee, for the benefit of the estate, to repay, restore or account for money or other property (together with interest at such rate as the court thinks just) or, as the case may require, to pay such sum by way of compensation in respect of the misfeasance or breach of fiduciary or other duty as the court thinks just.

This is without prejudice to any liability arising apart from this section.

304(2)   **[Applicants]** An application under this section may be made by the official receiver, the Secretary of State, a creditor of the bankrupt or (whether or not there is, or is likely to be, a surplus for the purposes of section 330(5) (final distribution)) the bankrupt himself.

But the leave of the court is required for the making of an application if it is to be made by the bankrupt or if it is to be made after the trustee has had his release under section 299.

304(3)   **[Limit on liability]** Where–

(a)   the trustee seizes or disposes of any property which is not comprised in the bankrupt's estate, and

(b)   at the time of the seizure or disposal the trustee believes, and has reasonable grounds for believing, that he is entitled (whether in pursuance of an order of the court or otherwise) to seize or dispose of that property,

the trustee is not liable to any person (whether under this section or otherwise) in respect of any loss or damage resulting from the seizure or disposal except in so far as that loss or damage is caused by the negligence of the trustee; and he has a lien on the property, or the proceeds of its sale, for such of the expenses of the bankruptcy as were incurred in connection with the seizure or disposal.

GENERAL NOTE

The Cork Committee (*Report*, paras 777–788) called for the introduction of a statutory duty of care imposed on trustees. This section goes some way towards this, and towards rationalising the law on the liability of trustees.

S.304(1)
This allows the court to impose liability on the trustee for misfeasance or misapplication of money belonging to the estate, etc. The remedy is at the discretion of the court, and it is worth noting that interest can be awarded against the trustee. The comparable provision in company law is to be found in s.212. See *Green v Satsangi* [1998] B.P.I.R. 55 where an order made against a trustee under s.304 was quashed on appeal.

S.304(2)
This determines who can apply for relief under s.304(1). Note that if the bankrupt applies, or the application is made after the date of the trustee's release, the leave of the court must first be obtained. See here *Brown v Beat* [2002] B.P.I.R. 421.

S.304(3)
This is not a new provision, but rather a reformulation of BA 1914 s.61. It is designed to protect a trustee who innocently seizes or disposes of property belonging to a third party. Note that this protection is lost if he acts negligently. The problem of a trustee seizing property which does not belong to the bankrupt may arise more frequently in the future with the abolition of the concept of reputed ownership.

CHAPTER IV

ADMINISTRATION BY TRUSTEE

Preliminary

305   **General functions of trustee**

305(1)   **[Application of Ch.IV]** This Chapter applies in relation to any bankruptcy where either–

(a)   the appointment of a person as trustee of a bankrupt's estate takes effect, or

(b)   the official receiver becomes trustee of a bankrupt's estate.

305(2)   **[Function of trustee]** The function of the trustee is to get in, realise and distribute the bankrupt's estate in accordance with the following provisions of this Chapter; and in the carrying out of that function and in the management of the bankrupt's estate the trustee is entitled, subject to those provisions, to use his own discretion.

305(3) **[Duties of trustee]** It is the duty of the trustee, if he is not the official receiver–

(a) to furnish the official receiver with such information,

(b) to produce to the official receiver, and permit inspection by the official receiver of, such books, papers and other records, and

(c) to give the official receiver such other assistance,

as the official receiver may reasonably require for the purpose of enabling him to carry out his functions in relation to the bankruptcy.

305(4) **[Official name of trustee]** The official name of the trustee shall be "the trustee of the estate of…, a bankrupt" (inserting the name of the bankrupt); but he may be referred to as "the trustee in bankruptcy" of the particular bankrupt.

S.305(1)

Sections 305–335 apply to cases where the trustee's appointment is effective or where the official receiver is acting as trustee.

S.305(2)

This describes the general role of the trustee and confers considerable residual discretion upon him. On the implications of s.305(2) see *Foyle v Turner* [2007] B.P.I.R. 43. The courts are minded to maximise his room for manoeuvre: *Judd v Brown* [1997] B.P.I.R. 470 at 476–477. It is important that the trustee retains professional independence and is not seen to be acting as a hired gun for a major creditor—*Re Ng* [1997] B.C.C. 507, per Lightman J., a comment which was approved by the Court of Appeal in *Trustee in Bankruptcy of Bukhari v Bukhari* [1999] B.P.I.R. 157. With regard to s.305(2) note the comments of the court in *Thornhill v Atherton (No.2)* [2008] B.P.I.R. 691 to the effect that it was not a misuse of the power of realisation for a trustee to carry out that role simply to generate funds to repay his claim for remuneration and costs.

Note the new whistleblowing duty imposed in appropriate cases by s.373 of FSMA 2000.

S.305(3)

This provision makes the trustee subordinate to the official receiver. Further details of the relationship can be seen in IR 1986 r.6.149.

S.305(4)

This describes the official name of the trustee and repeats BA 1914 s.76, although his powers are not mentioned in the new provision.

Acquisition, control and realisation of bankrupt's estate

306 Vesting of bankrupt's estate in trustee

306(1) **[Time of vesting]** The bankrupt's estate shall vest in the trustee immediately on his appointment taking effect or, in the case of the official receiver, on his becoming trustee.

306(2) **[Mode of vesting]** Where any property which is, or is to be, comprised in the bankrupt's estate vests in the trustee (whether under this section or under any other provision of this Part), it shall so vest without any conveyance, assignment or transfer.

GENERAL NOTE

This section provides that the bankrupt's property shall vest in the trustee, on his appointment taking effect, or in the official receiver where he becomes trustee. No conveyance, etc. is required. A trustee takes assets subject to equities—*Avis v Turner* [2007] B.P.I.R. 663.

In *Dadourian Group International v Simms* [2008] EWHC 723 (Ch); [2008] B.P.I.R. 508 Warren J. made the point that automatic vesting under s.306 only applied on the appointment of a trustee in bankruptcy, whether it be a private trustee or the official receiver—until that happened the estate remained vested in the bankrupt.

This automatic vesting is to be compared with the position under s.145 where the court may direct that some or all of the company's property shall vest in the liquidator in a compulsory liquidation. The bankrupt retains no immediate beneficial interest in this property until a surplus has been determined—*Ram v Ram (No.2)* [2004] EWCA Civ 1684;

[2005] B.P.I.R. 628. Once the estate has vested in the trustee the bankrupt merely has a contingent right to participate in any eventual surplus that might materialise; that did not confer an immediate beneficial right—on this see *James v Rutherford-Hodge* [2005] EWCA Civ 1580; [2006] B.P.I.R. 973. The earlier decision of Peter Smith J. in *Phillips v Symes* [2005] EWHC 2867 (Ch); [2006] B.P.I.R. 1430 (on the meaning of s.330(5)) is difficult to reconcile with this view.

The property does not have to be located within the jurisdiction to vest: *Singh v Official Receiver* [1997] B.P.I.R. 530; *Pollard v Ashurst* [2001] B.P.I.R. 131. It follows from *Thornhill v Atherton (No.2)* [2008] B.P.I.R. 691 that foreign assets form part of the estate.

For the meaning of "property" within s.306(2) see *London City Corp v Bown, The Times*, October 11, 1989, where it was held by the Court of Appeal that a non-assignable secure periodic tenancy within the meaning of the Housing Act 1985 confers only personal rights and therefore could not be regarded as "property" for these purposes. Similarly in *Re Rae* [1995] B.C.C. 102; and *Griffiths v Civil Aviation Authority* [1997] B.P.I.R. 50 personal and non-transferable rights to hold a licence did not vest in the trustee. Compare *Cork v Rawlins* [2001] B.P.I.R. 222 (insurance policies). See *Re Pritchard* [2007] B.P.I.R. 1385 (automatic vesting of interests under a life policy). Transferable licences of value may on the other hand be regarded as property: *Environment Agency v Stout* [1998] B.P.I.R. 576. Personal injury compensation also cannot be claimed by the trustee for the estate: *Lang v McKenna* [1996] B.P.I.R. 419; and [1997] B.P.I.R. 340; and *Rahall v McLennan* [2000] B.P.I.R. 140. The generality of this latter statement was questioned in *Re Bell* [1998] B.P.I.R. 26 where it was held that compensation for personal injury leading to damage to assets of economic value might form part of the estate; see also *Davis v Trustee in Bankruptcy of Davis* [1998] B.P.I.R. 572. If the claim is hybrid (i.e. contains an element relating to an allegation of damage to assets of the bankrupt coupled with a personal claim) the claim vests in the trustee, but any proceeds of action relating to the personal element are held on trust for the bankrupt—see here *Ord v Upton* [2000] 2 W.L.R. 755. The difficulty in distinguishing these issues was reflected by *Mulkerrins v PricewaterhouseCoopers* [2003] UKHL 41; [2003] 1 W.L.R. 1937. In *Grady v Prison Service* [2003] EWCA Civ 527 a claim for unfair dismissal was held to be "personal" and therefore did not vest within the estate. For further consideration of the difficulties posed by the issue of hybrid claims see *Kaberry v Freethcartwright* [2003] EWCA Civ 1077; [2003] B.P.I.R. 1144. In the curious decision in *Khan v Trident Safeguards Ltd* [2004] EWCA Civ 624; [2004] B.P.I.R. 881 the Court of Appeal held that a bankrupt could recharacterise claims alleging racial discrimination by restricting the remedy sought to a declaration and compensation for injured feelings, thereby removing such claims from the category of "hybrid" claims to be pursued by the trustee in bankruptcy. This decision will cause many practical difficulties and is undoubtedly influenced by the laudable desire to see that claims of discrimination are not stifled by the technicalities of bankruptcy law. Ironically, the court indicated that the proceeds of such a claim might be treated as being encompassed within that estate. By way of contrast in *Saini v Petroform Ltd* [1997] B.P.I.R. 515 the right to seek a new business tenancy under the Landlord and Tenant Act 1954 was held to be property. Again in *Performing Rights Society v Rowland* [1998] B.P.I.R. 128 the personal right to receive royalties from the PRS vested in the trustee as property as did the right of a lawyer to receive professional fees under a contingency fee agreement in *Royal Bank of Canada and Burlingham Associates v Chetty* [1997] B.P.I.R. 137. One can only conclude that the dividing line between personal rights which are outside the estate and property rights which the trustee can lay claim to is unclear. On current trends the courts are inclined to treat assets of value as being proprietorial and therefore caught by s.306.

The rights of action possessed by the debtor at the time of his bankruptcy form part of the estate under the control of the trustee: see *Heath v Tang* [1993] 1 W.L.R. 1421; *Nelson v Nelson* [1997] B.P.I.R. 702. *Heath v Tang* (above) was applied in *Dadourian Group International Inc v Simms* [2008] EWHC 723 (Ch); [2008] B.P.I.R. 508. The issue of whether rights of appeal pass to the trustee or are retained by the bankrupt has generated much controversy but again the courts are inclined to treat these as forming part of the estate: *Wordsworth v Dixon* [1997] B.P.I.R. 337; *Church of Scientology v Scott* [1997] B.P.I.R. 418; *Cummings and Fuller v Claremont Petroleum* [1998] B.P.I.R. 187; and see *Boyd and Hutchinson v Foenander* [2003] EWCA Civ 1516; [2004] B.P.I.R. 20. See also *Seven Eight Six Properties Ltd v Ghafoor* B.P.I.R. 519 (right to resist possession proceedings forms part of estate); *Hunt v Peasegood* [2001] B.P.I.R. 76.

The position with regard to pension benefits has undergone considerable change in recent years. For bankruptcies commencing prior to May 29, 2000 personal and occupational pension benefits automatically vest in the estate—*Re Landau* [1998] Ch. 223; *Krasner v Dennison* [2001] Ch. 76; *Patel v Jones* [2001] B.P.I.R. 919; and *Rowe v Sanders* [2002] EWCA Civ 242; [2002] B.P.I.R. 847. In the latter case the Court of Appeal has confirmed that there is no infringement of fundamental rights expectations as a result of this automatic vesting. Moreover, in view of this vesting there is no need to seek an income payments order in respect of pension benefits. For bankruptcies commencing after May 29, 2000 the position is governed by ss.11 and 12 of the Welfare Reform and Pensions Act 1999 which seeks to exclude certain specified pensions from the estate, subject to the clawback provisions in ss.342A–342C of the 1986 Act. More detailed legislative provision on the new scheme is found in the Occupational and Personal Pension Schemes (Bankruptcy) Regulations 2002 (SI 2002/427). This establishes machinery to enable a bankrupt to seek a court order to exclude pension benefits from his estate or to facilitate agreements between the trustee and the bankrupt as to pension rights. In *Malcolm v Benedict Mackenzie* [2004] EWCA Civ 1748; [2005] B.P.I.R. 176 the Court of Appeal held that the differential treatment for vesting purposes of personal pensions of pre- and post-May 29, 2000 bankrupts did not infringe art.14 ECHR.

Provisions seeking to forfeit personal pension rights on bankruptcy (and thereby to circumvent bankruptcy law) are ineffective—Welfare Reform and Pensions Act 1999 s.14 (which inserts a new s.159A into the Pension Schemes Act 1993).

Income-related social security benefits do not form part of the estate: *Mulvey v Secretary of State for Social Security* [1997] B.P.I.R. 696.

306A   Property subject to restraint order

306A(1)   [Application] This section applies where–

- (a)   property is excluded from the bankrupt's estate by virtue of section 417(2)(a) of the Proceeds of Crime Act 2002 (property subject to a restraint order),

- (b)   an order under section 50, 128 or 198 of that Act has not been made in respect of the property, and

- (c)   the restraint order is discharged.

306A(2)   [Vesting] On the discharge of the restraint order the property vests in the trustee as part of the bankrupt's estate.

306A(3)   [Non-application of s.306A(2)] But subsection (2) does not apply to the proceeds of property realised by a management receiver under section 49(2)(d) or 197(2)(d) of that Act (realisation of property to meet receiver's remuneration and expenses).

306B   Property in respect of which receivership or administration order made

306B(1)   [Application] This section applies where–

- (a)   property is excluded from the bankrupt's estate by virtue of section 417(2)(b), (c) or (d) of the Proceeds of Crime Act 2002 (property in respect of which an order for the appointment of a receiver or administrator under certain provisions of that Act is in force),

- (b)   a confiscation order is made under section 6, 92 or 156 of that Act,

- (c)   the amount payable under the confiscation order is fully paid, and

- (d)   any of the property remains in the hands of the receiver or administrator (as the case may be).

306B(2)   [Vesting] The property vests in the trustee as part of the bankrupt's estate.

306C   Property subject to certain orders where confiscation order discharged or quashed

306C(1)   [Application] This section applies where–

- (a)   property is excluded from the bankrupt's estate by virtue of section 417(2)(a), (b), (c) or (d) of the Proceeds of Crime Act 2002 (property in respect of which a restraint order or an order for the appointment of a receiver or administrator under that Act is in force),

- (b)   a confiscation order is made under section 6, 92 or 156 of that Act, and

- (c)   the confiscation order is discharged under section 30, 114 or 180 of that Act (as the case may be) or quashed under that Act or in pursuance of any enactment relating to appeals against conviction or sentence.

306C(2)   [Vesting] Any such property in the hands of a receiver appointed under Part 2 or 4 of that Act or an administrator appointed under Part 3 of that Act vests in the trustee as part of the bankrupt's estate.

306C(3)   **[Non-application of s.306C]** But subsection (2) does not apply to the proceeds of property realised by a management receiver under section 49(2)(d) or 197(2)(d) of that Act (realisation of property to meet receiver's remuneration and expenses).

GENERAL NOTE

S.306A–C

Note insertion of ss.306A, 306B and 306C by Sch.11 to the Proceeds of Crime Act 2002. The 2002 Act deals with the interface between insolvency law and criminal proceeds recovery proceedings. Generally speaking, a bankrupt's estate will not include assets which are the subject of a criminal recovery action (s.417 of the 2002 Act) but the three new prospective sections deal with the return to the estate of such assets if the relevant criminal proceedings order is discharged, or liability extinguished through the confiscation process or the order quashed. In such circumstances the excluded assets are returned to the estate.

307   After-acquired property

307(1)   **[Power of trustee]** Subject to this section and section 309, the trustee may by notice in writing claim for the bankrupt's estate any property which has been acquired by, or has devolved upon, the bankrupt since the commencement of the bankruptcy.

307(2)   **[Limit on s.307(1) notice]** A notice under this section shall not be served in respect of–

    (a)   any property falling within subsection (2) or (3) of section 283 in Chapter II,

    (aa)   any property vesting in the bankrupt by virtue of section 283A in Chapter II,

    (b)   any property which by virtue of any other enactment is excluded from the bankrupt's estate, or

    (c)   without prejudice to section 280(2)(c) (order of court on application for discharge), any property which is acquired by, or devolves upon, the bankrupt after his discharge.

307(3)   **[Vesting on service of notice]** Subject to the next subsection, upon the service on the bankrupt of a notice under this section the property to which the notice relates shall vest in the trustee as part of the bankrupt's estate; and the trustee's title to that property has relation back to the time at which the property was acquired by, or devolved upon, the bankrupt.

307(4)   **[Outsiders]** Where, whether before or after service of a notice under this section–

    (a)   a person acquires property in good faith, for value and without notice of the bankruptcy, or

    (b)   a banker enters into a transaction in good faith and without such notice,

the trustee is not in respect of that property or transaction entitled by virtue of this section to any remedy against that person or banker, or any person whose title to any property derives from that person or banker.

307(5)   **[Interpretation]** References in this section to property do not include any property which, as part of the bankrupt's income, may be the subject of an income payments order under section 310.

S.307(1)

This enables the trustee to take the initiative and claim property vesting in the bankrupt after the commencement of the bankruptcy (as defined in s.278(a)). Under BA 1914 s.28(a) such property *automatically* vested in the trustee: see *Re Pascoe* [1944] Ch. 219. Prior to 1944 it was generally believed that positive intervention by the trustee was required. The Cork Committee (*Report*, para.1152) felt that it would be more flexible if the trustee could be allowed to choose whether the estate wanted such property. The advantage in such a change is highlighted by the White Paper, para.112—it saves the trustee from wasting his time in having to disclaim onerous after-acquired property. See also IR 1986 rr.6.200–6.202. The operation of this provision does depend on the bankrupt being honest with his trustee, as he is required to be by ss.333(2) and 353. The bankrupt must tell the trustee within 21 days of the acquisition of the property: see IR 1986 r.6.200(1).

For s.307 at work see *Pike v Cork Gully* [1997] B.P.I.R. 723; and *Re Mathew* (unreported, but noted in *Current Law Week*, September 20, 1996). This latter case involved a trustee laying claim to a legacy where the bankrupt had not kept the trustee fully informed. See also *Hill v Secretary of State* [2005] EWHC 696 (Ch); [2006] 1 B.C.L.C. 601.

S.307(2), (5)

Certain after-acquired property cannot be claimed by the trustee: property which would not be included in the estate in any case, and property acquired after the date of discharge. Section 307(2)(aa) was inserted by s.261 of EA 2002 with effect from April 1, 2004. Note also that income which may be caught by s.310 cannot fall under s.307. See *Supperstone v Lloyds Names Working Party* [1999] B.P.I.R. 832. In *Arnold v Williams and HMRC* [2008] EWHC 218 (Ch); [2008] B.P.I.R. 247 it was confirmed that s.307(2)(c) does not apply after discharge. This case provides an interesting discussion as to whether a trustee can use s.307 to compel a bankrupt to appeal post-bankruptcy tax assessments made in the period before discharge.

S.307(3)

On service of the trustee's notice the property vests in the trustee. The trustee has 42 days to claim the property after receiving notice of it from the bankrupt, see IA 1986 s.309(1)(a), or else it can be disposed of by the bankrupt.

S.307(4)

This protects bona fide purchasers (for value, without notice...) of after-acquired property from the bankrupt. It is based on BA 1914 s.47 which, in turn, confirmed the rule in *Cohen v Mitchell* (1890) 25 Q.B.D. 262. For a comparable Australian authority see *Rimar Pty Ltd v Pappas* (1986) 60 A.L.J.R. 309. However, the third party loses his protection if he has notice of the bankruptcy order: thus, *Hunt v Fripp* [1898] 1 Ch. 675 is reversed. If the disponee is not protected the trustee can recover the property under IR 1986 r.6.201.

308 Vesting in trustee of certain items of excess value

308(1) **[Claim by trustee in writing]** Subject to section 309, where–

(a) property is excluded by virtue of section 283(2) (tools of trade, household effects, etc.) from the bankrupt's estate, and

(b) it appears to the trustee that the realisable value of the whole or any part of that property exceeds the cost of a reasonable replacement for that property or that part of it,

the trustee may by notice in writing claim that property or, as the case may be, that part of it for the bankrupt's estate.

308(2) **[Vesting on service of s.308(1) notice]** Upon the service on the bankrupt of a notice under this section, the property to which the notice relates vests in the trustee as part of the bankrupt's estate; and, except against a purchaser in good faith, for value and without notice of the bankruptcy, the trustee's title to that property has relation back to the commencement of the bankruptcy.

308(3) **[Application of funds by trustee]** The trustee shall apply funds comprised in the estate to the purchase by or on behalf of the bankrupt of a reasonable replacement for any property vested in the trustee under this section; and the duty imposed by this subsection has priority over the obligation of the trustee to distribute the estate.

308(4) **[Reasonable replacement]** For the purposes of this section property is a reasonable replacement for other property if it is reasonably adequate for meeting the needs met by the other property.

GENERAL NOTE

This is a new provision which implements the recommendations of the Cork Committee (*Report*, para.1101). This section is supplemented by IR 1986 rr.6.187, 6.188.

S.308(1), (4)

The trustee is allowed to claim certain property, which would normally not be included in the bankrupt's estate by virtue of s.283(2), if that property can be reasonably replaced (as defined in s.308(4), producing a surplus for the estate. See *Pike v Cork Gully* [1997] B.P.I.R. 723. Note the 42-day limit in s.309. The provision is designed to prevent bankrupts with large debts from continuing to live a life of luxury surrounded by expensive cars and consumer durables. A bankrupt who objects to replacement can complain to the court under s.303. A third party can pay off the trustee to avert replacement: IR 1986 r.6.188. A minor change has been made to subs.(1) to accommodate the insertion of s.308A: see Housing Act 1988 Sch.17 para.73.

S.308(2)
Once the trustee has given notice, the property in question will vest in the trustee, subject to the rights of any bona fide purchaser.

S.308(3)
The cost of the replacement is to be met out of the estate funds and the defrayment of this cost takes priority over the trustee's obligation to distribute. The replacement may occur before or after the sale of the original item, see IR 1986 r.6.187.

S.308(4)
It would appear from the link with subs.(1) that the test as to what is "reasonable" is likely to be applied subjectively, i.e. does the trustee believe it is reasonable? Provided his decision is not totally erratic, the court would not intervene.

308A Vesting in trustee of certain tenancies

308A Upon the service on the bankrupt by the trustee of a notice in writing under this section, any tenancy–

(a) which is excluded by virtue of section 283(3A) from the bankrupt's estate, and

(b) to which the notice relates,

vests in the trustee as part of the bankrupt's estate; and, except against a purchaser in good faith, for value and without notice of the bankruptcy, the trustee's title to that tenancy has relation back to the commencement of the bankruptcy.

309 Time-limit for notice under s.307 or 308

309(1) **[Timing of notice]** Except with the leave of the court, a notice shall not be served–

(a) under section 307, after the end of the period of 42 days beginning with the day on which it first came to the knowledge of the trustee that the property in question had been acquired by, or had devolved upon, the bankrupt;

(b) under section 308 or section 308A, after the end of the period of 42 days beginning with the day on which the property or tenancy in question first came to the knowledge of the trustee.

309(2) **[Deemed knowledge]** For the purposes of this section–

(a) anything which comes to the knowledge of the trustee is deemed in relation to any successor of his as trustee to have come to the knowledge of the successor at the same time; and

(b) anything which comes (otherwise than under paragraph (a)) to the knowledge of a person before he is the trustee is deemed to come to his knowledge on his appointment taking effect or, in the case of the official receiver, on his becoming trustee.

GENERAL NOTE

The trustee must claim the property or seek replacement (under ss.307, 308 or 308A) within 42 days after it has come to his notice, as defined by s.309(2). The court refused to permit a s.307 notice to be served out of time in *Solomons v Williams* [2001] B.P.I.R. 112. In *Franses v Oomerjee* [2005] B.P.I.R. 1320 the court refused to accept a notice given under s.307 in view of the delays involved. The notice was given by a trustee in bankruptcy some 15 weeks after his appointment, that appointment having been made in November 2004 with respect to a bankruptcy commencing as long ago as 1991. The bankrupt had notified the official receiver in 1997 of the after acquired-property but no action was taken. No explanation could be given for the delays in serving the s.307 notice in this case and in view of the prejudice to the bankrupt permission to claim the after-acquired property was refused. Note the minor changes made to subs.1(b) by s.117(3) of the Housing Act 1988.

310   Income payments orders

310(1)   [Order by court] The court may, make an order ("an income payments order") claiming for the bankrupt's estate so much of the income of the bankrupt during the period for which the order is in force as may be specified in the order.

310(1A)   [Applicant for order] An income payments order may be made only on an application instituted–

   (a)   by the trustee, and

   (b)   before the discharge of the bankrupt.

310(2)   [Limit on order] The court shall not make an income payments order the effect of which would be to reduce the income of the bankrupt when taken together with any payments to which subsection (8) applies below what appears to the court to be necessary for meeting the reasonable domestic needs of the bankrupt and his family.

310(3)   [Extent of order] An income payments order shall, in respect of any payment of income to which it is to apply, either–

   (a)   require the bankrupt to pay the trustee an amount equal to so much of that payment as is claimed by the order, or

   (b)   require the person making the payment to pay so much of it as is so claimed to the trustee, instead of to the bankrupt.

310(4)   [Power to discharge or vary attachment of earnings] Where the court makes an income payments order it may, if it thinks fit, discharge or vary any attachment of earnings order that is for the time being in force to secure payments by the bankrupt.

310(5)   [Sums part of estate] Sums received by the trustee under an income payments order form part of the bankrupt's estate.

310(6)   [Period of order] An income payments order must specify the period during which it is to have effect; and that period–

   (a)   may end after the discharge of the bankrupt, but

   (b)   may not end after the period of three years beginning with the date on which the order is made.

310(6A)   [Variation of order] An income payments order may (subject to subsection (6)(b)) be varied on the application of the trustee or the bankrupt (whether before or after discharge).

310(7)   [Income of the bankrupt] For the purposes of this section the income of the bankrupt comprises every payment in the nature of income which is from time to time made to him or to which he from time to time becomes entitled, including any payment in respect of the carrying on of any business or in respect of any office or employment and (despite anything in section 11 or 12 of the Welfare Reform and Pensions Act 1999) any payment under a pension scheme but excluding any payment to which subsection (8) applies.

310(8)   [Application] This subsection applies to–

   (a)   payments by way of guaranteed minimum pension; and

   (b)   payments giving effect to the bankrupt's protected rights as a member of a pension scheme.

310(9) **[Definitions]** In this section, **"guaranteed minimum pension"** and **"protected rights"** have the same meaning as in the Pension Schemes Act 1993.

GENERAL NOTE

One of the defects in BA 1914 was that it did not have an effective mechanism to enable the trustee to appropriate the income of the bankrupt for the benefit of the estate. BA 1914 s.51 was largely ineffective, especially where the bankrupt was self-employed. The Cork Committee (*Report*, paras 591–598) recommended a change in the law which would enable creditors to be paid off out of future income rather than the proceeds of a forced sale. Although s.310 introduces such a mechanism the evidence is that income payment orders have not been widely used: see Justice, *Insolvency Law: An Agenda for Reform* (1994) at para.4.30.

For the relationship with s.306 see *Re Landau* [1998] Ch. 223, a case of major significance on pension rights and the unreported 1994 county court case of *Carman v Baron*, which is noted by Greenstreet in (1996) 12 I.L. & P. 60. Section 310 does not apply to a pension which has automatically vested in the trustee—*Lesser v Lawrence* [2000] B.P.I.R. 410; and *Rowe v Sanders* [2002] EWCA Civ 242; [2002] B.P.I.R. 847. In the context of income payments orders and pensions note also s.91 of the Pensions Act 1995 and the amendments effected by Sch.3 para.15. On the role of s.310 in matrimonial proceedings note *Albert v Albert* [1996] B.P.I.R. 232; and *Re X* [1996] B.P.I.R. 494.

For an application for an income payments order in a cross border insolvency see *C Brooks Thurmond III v Rajapakse* [2008] B.P.I.R. 283. This case is interesting in that it confirms that lump sums may be made subject to an income payments order and considers the susceptibility of pensions to the income payments regime.

S.310(1), (1A), (2)

In subs.(1) the phrase "on the application of the trustee" was deleted by EA 2002 s.259 with effect from April 2004. Subsection (1A) was added by that same provision. Section 310 permits an application to court for an income payments order, but the court cannot appropriate so great a proportion of the bankrupt's income as to reduce him and his family to penury. This restriction existed at common law: *Re Roberts* [1900] 1 Q.B. 122. Note the amendment introduced into subs.(2) by Sch.3 para.15 to the Pensions Act 1995. The bankrupt must be given 28 days' notice of the application, see IR 1986 r.6.189. Reasonable domestic need is to be determined by reference to the circumstances of each case and may include private school fees where removal from a school might be detrimental to the children: *Re Rayatt* [1998] B.P.I.R. 495. In *Scott v Davis* [2003] B.P.I.R. 1009 the issue of private school fees was revisited and the court stressed the importance of there being evidence that on the facts of the particular case that they were a reasonable domestic need. For further discussion of this subsection see *Kilvert v Flackett* [1998] B.P.I.R. 721; and *Malcolm v Official Receiver* [1999] B.P.I.R. 97. In *Boyden v Watson* [2004] B.P.I.R. 1131 the court rejected an application for an income payments in the most scathing of terms. The bankrupt had insufficient funds once his reasonable domestic needs had been met.

S.310(3)–(5)

These provisions deal with the effect of an income payments order. Either the bankrupt or some third party can be directed to make payments to the trustee, the sums thereby received forming part of the estate. On making such an order the court can modify any attachment of earnings order relating to the bankrupt's income. Note that s.310(3) is amplified by the rules: see Sch.9 para.15 and IR 1986 rr.6.189–6.193. The order may be reviewed on the application of either party or varied on the application of the trustee. The latter might occur where the bankrupt's income increases. Note here the obligation to notify the trustee within 21 days (s.332(2) and r.6.200(1)).

S.310(6), (6A)

Subsection (6) was reconstituted by s.259 of EA 2002 with effect from April 2004.

Subsection (6A), which deals with variation of IPOs, was inserted by s.259 of EA 2002 with effect from April 2004.

S.310(7)

This defines "income" in wide terms and emphasises that it covers the income of a self-employed person. Presumably payments in the nature of capital are not covered by s.310 unless such payments could be treated as a single surge of income, as was the subject of discussion in the case of *Kilvert v Flackett* (above). See also *Supperstone v Lloyds Names Working Party* [1999] B.P.I.R. 832. Again the text of this subsection has been supplemented by Sch.3 para.15 to the Pensions Act 1995 and s.18 coupled with Sch.2 to the Welfare Reform and Pensions Act 1999 with effect from May 29, 2000 (see Welfare Reform and Pensions Act 1999 (Commencement No.7) Order 2000 (SI 2000/1382 (C. 41))). Note the limitation on income identified in *Dear IP* Issue 24 (September 2005).

S.310(8), (9)

These completely new subsections were introduced by the Pensions Act 1995 (Sch.3 para.15).

310A Income payments agreement

310A(1) ["Income payments agreement"] In this section "income payments agreement" means a written agreement between a bankrupt and his trustee or between a bankrupt and the official receiver which provides–

(a) that the bankrupt is to pay to the trustee or the official receiver an amount equal to a specified part or proportion of the bankrupt's income for a specified period, or

(b) that a third person is to pay to the trustee or the official receiver a specified proportion of money due to the bankrupt by way of income for a specified period.

310A(2) [Enforceability of agreement] A provision of an income payments agreement of a kind specified in subsection (1)(a) or (b) may be enforced as if it were a provision of an income payments order.

310A(3) [Discharge or variation of attachment of earnings order] While an income payments agreement is in force the court may, on the application of the bankrupt, his trustee or the official receiver, discharge or vary an attachment of earnings order that is for the time being in force to secure payments by the bankrupt.

310A(4) [Application of s.310(5), (7)–(9)] The following provisions of section 310 shall apply to an income payments agreement as they apply to an income payments order–

(a) subsection (5) (receipts to form part of estate), and

(b) subsections (7) to (9) (meaning of income).

310A(5) [Period of agreement] An income payments agreement must specify the period during which it is to have effect; and that period–

(a) may end after the discharge of the bankrupt, but

(b) may not end after the period of three years beginning with the date on which the agreement is made.

310A(6) [Variation of agreement] An income payments agreement may (subject to subsection (5)(b)) be varied–

(a) by written agreement between the parties, or

(b) by the court on an application made by the bankrupt, the trustee or the official receiver.

310A(7) [Power to vary] The court–

(a) may not vary an income payments agreement so as to include provision of a kind which could not be included in an income payments order, and

(b) shall grant an application to vary an income payments agreement if and to the extent that the court thinks variation necessary to avoid the effect mentioned in section 310(2).

GENERAL NOTE

This innovation (which took effect in April 2004) came about as a result of the enactment of s.260 of EA 2002. The aim is to put in place a legally binding income payments scheme without the need for a formal court order. Once again the underlying policy goal is to reduce administration costs, a particularly important consideration bearing in mind the inefficiencies involved in the IPO procedure. Further provision for IPAs is to be found in IR 1986 rr.6.193A–C.

S.310A(1)
This defines what is meant by an income payments agreement (IPA). The agreement must be in writing. IPAs can be used to divert sums due to the bankrupt from a third party.

S.310A(2), (4)
The effect of an IPA is equivalent to that of an IPO. This is reinforced by subs.(4).

S.310A(3), (6), (7)
Variation and discharge of IPAs is hereby provided for. Note also the variation possibilities covered by subs.(6), including variation by agreement in writing and the limitations on the court imposed by subs.(7).

S.310A(5)
This regulates the duration of an IPA. It can last beyond the date of discharge but cannot persist for more than three years after the agreement date.

311 Acquisition by trustee of control

311(1) **[Trustee to take possession]** The trustee shall take possession of all books, papers and other records which relate to the bankrupt's estate or affairs and which belong to him or are in his possession or under his control (including any which would be privileged from disclosure in any proceedings).

311(2) **[Trustee like receiver]** In relation to, and for the purpose of acquiring or retaining possession of, the bankrupt's estate, the trustee is in the same position as if he were a receiver of property appointed by the High Court; and the court may, on his application, enforce such acquisition or retention accordingly.

311(3) **[Where estate includes transferable property]** Where any part of the bankrupt's estate consists of stock or shares in a company, shares in a ship or any other property transferable in the books of a company, office or person, the trustee may exercise the right to transfer the property to the same extent as the bankrupt might have exercised it if he had not become bankrupt.

311(4) **[Where estate includes things in action]** Where any part of the estate consists of things in action, they are deemed to have been assigned to the trustee; but notice of the deemed assignment need not be given except in so far as it is necessary, in a case where the deemed assignment is from the bankrupt himself, for protecting the priority of the trustee.

311(5) **[Where goods held by pledge]** Where any goods comprised in the estate are held by any person by way of pledge, pawn or other security and no notice has been served in respect of those goods by the official receiver under subsection (5) of section 285 (restriction on realising security), the trustee may serve such a notice in respect of the goods; and whether or not a notice has been served under this subsection or that subsection, the trustee may, if he thinks fit, exercise the bankrupt's right of redemption in respect of any such goods.

311(6) **[Effect of s.311(5) notice]** A notice served by the trustee under subsection (5) has the same effect as a notice served by the official receiver under section 285(5).

S.311(1)
This describes the most basic duty of a trustee, which is to collect the bankrupt's property together. For the impact of this provision on privileged documents see *Re Konigsberg (a Bankrupt)* [1989] 1 W.L.R. 1257. The right to take papers is limited to business or financial records and does not include personal correspondence even if it has an economic value—see *Haig v Aitken* [2000] B.P.I.R. 462 where the possibility that seizure of such documents might infringe art.8 ECHR (right of privacy) was also considered by the court. In *Boyden v Canty (No.2)* [2007] EWCA Civ 241; [2007] B.P.I.R. 299 the court indicated that failure to comply with obligations under s.311 could be regarded as contempt justifying committal.

S.311(2)
While carrying out the above function the trustee will be treated as if he were a court-appointed receiver and will, for example, enjoy the protection of the law of contempt.

S.311(3), (4)
These provisions deal with the trustee's rights in respect of certain intangible forms of property, such as shares or choses in action.

S.311(5), (6)

These provisions, based on BA 1914 s.59 deal with the situation where the bankrupt's goods have been given as security to some other person. The trustee may (if the official receiver has not already done so) serve a notice on the third party in order to redeem the goods. Such a notice has the same effect as a notice served by the official receiver under s.285(5).

312 Obligation to surrender control to trustee

312(1) [Bankrupt to surrender property] The bankrupt shall deliver up to the trustee possession of any property, books, papers or other records of which he has possession or control and of which the trustee is required to take possession.

This is without prejudice to the general duties of the bankrupt under section 333 in this Chapter.

312(2) [Other persons in possession] If any of the following is in possession of any property, books, papers or other records of which the trustee is required to take possession, namely–

(a) the official receiver,

(b) a person who has ceased to be trustee of the bankrupt's estate, or

(c) a person who has been the supervisor of a voluntary arrangement approved in relation to the bankrupt under Part VIII,

the official receiver or, as the case may be, that person shall deliver up possession of the property, books, papers or records to the trustee.

312(3) [Bankers, agents et al. of bankrupt] Any banker or agent of the bankrupt or any other person who holds any property to the account of, or for, the bankrupt shall pay or deliver to the trustee all property in his possession or under his control which forms part of the bankrupt's estate and which he is not by law entitled to retain as against the bankrupt or trustee.

312(4) [Penalty for non-compliance] If any person without reasonable excuse fails to comply with any obligation imposed by this section, he is guilty of a contempt of court and liable to be punished accordingly (in addition to any other punishment to which he may be subject).

S.312(1)

This provision obliges the bankrupt, in addition to his general duty to assist the trustee, to hand over possession of his property, books, etc. to the trustee.

S.312(2), (3)

This obligation extends to official receivers, former trustees, supervisors of a voluntary arrangement, bankers and agents of the bankrupt, although the latter two groups may have certain rights of retention as against the trustee.

S.312(4)

The above obligations are reinforced by the law of contempt.

313 Charge on bankrupt's home

313(1) [Application to court by trustee] Where any property consisting of an interest in a dwelling house which is occupied by the bankrupt or by his spouse or former spouse or by his civil partner or former civil partner is comprised in the bankrupt's estate and the trustee is, for any reason, unable for the time being to realise that property, the trustee may apply to the court for an order imposing a charge on the property for the benefit of the bankrupt's estate.

313(2) [Benefit of charge] If on an application under this section the court imposes a charge on any property, the benefit of that charge shall be comprised in the bankrupt's estate and is enforceable, up to the charged value from time to time, for the payment of any amount which is payable otherwise than to the bankrupt out of the estate and of interest on that amount at the prescribed rate.

313(2A)   [Meaning of charged value in s.313(2)] In subsection (2) the charged value means–

(a)   the amount specified in the charging order as the value of the bankrupt's interest in the property at the date of the order, plus

(b)   interest on that amount from the date of the charging order at the prescribed rate.

313(2B)   [Court's duty in valuing interest] In determining the value of an interest for the purposes of this section the court shall disregard any matter which it is required to disregard by the rules.

313(3)   [Provision in order] An order under this section made in respect of property vested in the trustee shall provide, in accordance with the rules, for the property to cease to be comprised in the bankrupt's estate and, subject to the charge (and any prior charge), to vest in the bankrupt.

313(4)   [Effect of Charging Orders Act] Subsections (1) and (2) and (4) to (6) of section 3 of the Charging Orders Act 1979 (supplemental provisions with respect to charging orders) have effect in relation to orders under this section as in relation to charging orders under that Act.

313(5)   [No power to vary a charged value] But an order under section 3(5) of that Act may not vary a charged value.

GENERAL NOTE

This is a new provision which would probably be better located next to ss.336–338, which also deal with the matrimonial home. This new package of provisions, which was recommended by the Cork Committee (*Report*, paras 1114–1131), is designed to tilt the balance more in favour of the bankrupt and his family when it comes to selling the family home. This provision, unlike the others dealing with the matrimonial home, was included in the original Insolvency Bill of 1895. For a general view of the operation of s.313 in practice see Hill, (1990) 6 I.L. & P. 12. Section 313 is amended with effect from April 1, 2004 by s.260 of EA 2002. The effect is to improve the rights of bankrupts where orders under s.313 are utilised. An important issue of principle was determined in *Gotham v Doodes* [2006] EWCA Civ 1080. Here it had been held by Lindsay J. (reluctantly overturning a ruling of Chief Registrar Baister) that a trustee was prevented from enforcing a charging order through sale because of the expiry of a limitation period of 12 years running from the date when the charging order had been granted. In so deciding the judge had felt compelled to follow an obscure Court of Appeal precedent dealing, arguably, with an analogous situation. However, in this case the Court of Appeal held that the limitation period under s.20 of the Limitation Act 1980 only began to run from the order permitting sale and not from when the charging order originally had been granted. Only when sale was permitted did the right to receive the income from the charged property arise. This ruling will reassure trustees who use charging orders as a mode of protecting the interest of the estate in the family home.

S.313(1)
If the trustee cannot sell the bankrupt's interest in the "dwelling house" (for the definition, see s.385) occupied by him or his family he may apply to a court for a charging order on that interest. Note the insertion of the reference to civil partners by the Civil Partnership Act 2004 Sch.27.

S.313(2)–(4)
These provisions deal with the effect of the court granting such a charging order. It attaches to the property in question until enforced, although the property ceases to vest in the trustee and will revert to the bankrupt (subject to the charge). Certain parts of s.3 of the Charging Orders Act 1979 will apply to such an order made by the court under s.313(1).

Amendments to ss.313(2), 313(2A) and 313(2B) here are designed to ensure that where the value of the charged property increases over time the benefit accrues to the bankrupt and not to the estate. This in effect is achieved by providing for the value of the bankrupt's interest in the charged property to be identified on application; that charged value then gets the benefit of any inflationary uplift.

Editors' note: the wording of s.313(4) will be amended by s.93(5) of the Tribunals, Courts and Enforcement Act 2007 from a date yet to be determined.

The rules provide more details of the conditions which may be attached to such a charge: see IR 1986 r.6.237.

S.313(5)
Inserted by s.260 of EA 2002 with effect from April 1, 2004 this prevents a charging order from undermining the protective effect of s.313(2A).

313A   Low value home: application for sale, possession or charge

313A(1)   [Application of section] This section applies where–

(a) property comprised in the bankrupt's estate consists of an interest in a dwelling-house which at the date of the bankruptcy was the sole or principal residence of–

    (i)   the bankrupt,

    (ii)   the bankrupt's spouse or civil partner, or

    (iii)   a former spouse or former civil partner of the bankrupt, and

(b) the trustee applies for an order for the sale of the property, for an order for possession of the property or for an order under section 313 in respect of the property.

313A(2)   [Court's duty to dismiss application] The court shall dismiss the application if the value of the interest is below the amount prescribed for the purposes of this subsection.

313A(3)   [Court's duty to disregard matters prescribed by order] In determining the value of an interest for the purposes of this section the court shall disregard any matter which it is required to disregard by the order which prescribes the amount for the purposes of subsection (2).

General Note

Again introduced by s.261(3) of EA 2002 this deals with the realisation of low value properties. The feeling is that the marginal benefit to creditors from realising such an asset is outweighed by the disproportionate suffering imposed upon the bankrupt by the loss of his home. This provision came into effect on April 1, 2004.

S.313A(1)
This seeks to identify what is meant by an interest in a low value home for the purposes of this section. The problem of multiple low value homes might have to be addressed—see the comments on s.283A. Note the insertion of the reference to civil partners by the Civil Partnership Act 2004 Sch.27.

S.313A(2)
The trustee is hereby in effect debarred from taking specified realisation action in respect of an interest in a dwelling covered by subs.(1). The minimum amount prescribed is £1,000 (Insolvency Proceedings (Monetary Limits) (Amendment) Order 2004 (SI 2004/547)), though that valuation figure is then qualified by art.3 of that Order.

S.313(A)(3)
This deals further with the question of valuation and inclusion within this restrictive mechanism.

314   Powers of trustee

314(1)   [Powers in Sch.5 Pt I and II] The trustee may–

(a) with the permission of the creditors' committee or the court, exercise any of the powers specified in Part I of Schedule 5 to this Act, and

(b) without that permission, exercise any of the general powers specified in Part II of that Schedule.

314(2)   [Powers of appointment re bankrupt] With the permission of the creditors' committee or the court, the trustee may appoint the bankrupt–

(a) to superintend the management of his estate or any part of it,

(b) to carry on his business (if any) for the benefit of his creditors, or

(c) in any other respect to assist in administering the estate in such manner and on such terms as the trustee may direct.

314(3)   [Permission in s.314(1)(a), (2)] A permission given for the purposes of subsection (1)(a) or (2) shall not be a general permission but shall relate to a particular proposed exercise of the power in question; and a person dealing with the trustee in good faith and for value is not to be concerned to enquire whether any permission required in either case has been given.

314(4)   [Where no permission under s.314(1)(a), (2)] Where the trustee has done anything without the permission required by subsection (1)(a) or (2), the court or the creditors' committee may, for the purpose of enabling him to meet his expenses out of the bankrupt's estate, ratify what the trustee has done.

But the committee shall not do so unless it is satisfied that the trustee has acted in a case of urgency and has sought its ratification without undue delay.

314(5)   [Powers in Sch.5 Pt III] Part III of Schedule 5 to this Act has effect with respect to the things which the trustee is able to do for the purposes of, or in connection with, the exercise of any of his powers under any of this Group of Parts.

314(6)   [Notice to committee] Where the trustee (not being the official receiver) in exercise of the powers conferred on him by any provision in this Group of Parts–

(a)   disposes of any property comprised in the bankrupt's estate to an associate of the bankrupt, or

(b)   employs a solicitor,

he shall, if there is for the time being a creditors' committee, give notice to the committee of that exercise of his powers.

314(7)   [Power to summon general meeting of creditors] Without prejudice to the generality of subsection (5) and Part III of Schedule 5, the trustee may, if he thinks fit, at any time summon a general meeting of the bankrupt's creditors.

Subject to the preceding provisions in this Group of Parts, he shall summon such a meeting if he is requested to do so by a creditor of the bankrupt and the request is made with the concurrence of not less than one-tenth, in value, of the bankrupt's creditors (including the creditor making the request).

314(8)   [Capacity of trustee] Nothing in this Act is to be construed as restricting the capacity of the trustee to exercise any of his powers outside England and Wales.

S.314(1), (2), (6)
A trustee may exercise the powers listed in Pt II of Sch.5 without obtaining permission of the committee of creditors (see s.301). This list of powers is derived from BA 1914 s.55. No major changes have been made to these basic powers. Note, however, that if property is disposed of to an "associate" of the bankrupt (for the meaning of this term see s.435), the committee of creditors must be told. Section 314(2) refers to Pt I of Sch.5, which describes powers which the trustee may exercise only with the consent of the committee of creditors. These powers are based on BA 1914 ss.56, 57. The sanction requirement is to protect the bankrupt's estate, see *Re a Debtor (No.26A of 1975)* [1985] 1 W.L.R. 6. See *Re Don Basil Williams* [2002] EWHC 1393 (Ch); [2003] B.P.I.R. 545 where the court sanctioned a compromise favoured by the trustee. The requirement that the trustee should obtain permission before employing a solicitor or agent, contained formerly in s.56(3), has been dropped—but if he does this he must now give notice to the committee according to s.314(6)(b). The meaning of "compromise" and "sale" within the meaning of paras 7 and 9 of Sch.5 was considered in by the court in *Power v Brown* [2009] B.P.I.R. 340.

S.314(3), (4)
These provisions deal with the question of permission as required by s.314(2) and (7) above. It must be specific. Bona fide purchasers for value dealing with the trustee need not investigate to see that it has been given: this is in line with the general policy of s.377 validating the acts of the trustee.

S.314(5)
This provision refers to Pt III of Sch.5, which gives a general account of the trustee's powers (e.g. to hold property and make contracts) that may be exercised in his "official name" (see s.305(4)).

S.314(7)
This deals with the calling of a general meeting of creditors by the trustee. Note that he must call such a meeting if asked to do so by creditors owed one-tenth of the bankrupt's total debts. The figure fixed by BA 1914 s.79(2) was one-sixth in value of the total debts.

S.314(8)

The trustee may exercise his powers outside England and Wales. This is increasingly important as the problems of cross-border insolvency increase. See here *Re Hayward* [1997] Ch. 45 where the trustee was required by virtue of the European Convention on Jurisdiction and Enforcement of Judgments in Civil Matters to pursue a claim to Spanish real estate in Spain and not in England. Rattee J. concluded that the claim was not primarily concerned with insolvency, but with title to immoveable property, and therefore the Spanish courts enjoyed exclusive jurisdiction under the Convention. See also *Pollard v Ashurst* [2001] B.P.I.R. 131. The entry into effect of the EC Regulation on Insolvency Proceedings will improve matters considerably.

Disclaimer of onerous property

315 Disclaimer (general power)

315(1) **[Power of trustee to disclaim]** Subject as follows, the trustee may, by the giving of the prescribed notice, disclaim any onerous property and may do so notwithstanding that he has taken possession of it, endeavoured to sell it or otherwise exercised rights of ownership in relation to it.

315(2) **[Onerous property]** The following is onerous property for the purposes of this section, that is to say–

(a) any unprofitable contract, and

(b) any other property comprised in the bankrupt's estate which is unsaleable or not readily saleable, or is such that it may give rise to a liability to pay money or perform any other onerous act.

315(3) **[Effect of disclaimer]** A disclaimer under this section–

(a) operates so as to determine, as from the date of the disclaimer, the rights, interests and liabilities of the bankrupt and his estate in or in respect of the property disclaimed, and

(b) discharges the trustee from all personal liability in respect of that property as from the commencement of his trusteeship,

but does not, except so far as is necessary for the purpose of releasing the bankrupt, the bankrupt's estate and the trustee from any liability, affect the rights or liabilities of any other person.

315(4) **[Where notice of disclaimer not to be given]** A notice of disclaimer shall not be given under this section in respect of any property that has been claimed for the estate under section 307 (after-acquired property) or 308 (personal property of bankrupt exceeding reasonable replacement value) or 308A, except with the leave of the court.

315(5) **[Persons sustaining loss or damage]** Any person sustaining loss or damage in consequence of the operation of a disclaimer under this section is deemed to be a creditor of the bankrupt to the extent of the loss or damage and accordingly may prove for the loss or damage as a bankruptcy debt.

GENERAL NOTE

This section, and the ones immediately following it, deal with the power of the trustee to disclaim onerous property, and the role of the court in the event of disclaimer. The Cork Committee (*Report*, paras 1182–1199) felt that this power, which has existed since 1869, should be modified to enable the trustee to utilise it more effectively. The comparable provisions relating to disclaimers by liquidators are to be found in ss.178–182. A disclaimer is deemed to have been validly exercised unless the contrary is established: see IR 1986 r.6.185. For historical background see *Hindcastle v Barbara Attenborough Associates* [1997] A.C. 70; [1996] B.C.C. 636.

In the context of the financial markets, s.315 does not apply in relation to a market contract or a contract effected by an exchange or clearing house for the purpose of realising property provided as margin in relation to market contracts: see CA 1989 s.164(1), and the note on p.2.

S.315(1), (2)

This authorises disclaimer of onerous property even though the trustee may have already tried to sell it. As to what is an unprofitable contract see *Re SSSL Realisations (2002) Ltd*, sub nom. *Squires v AIG Europe (UK) Ltd* [2006]

EWCA Civ 7; [2006] B.C.C. 233. For the form of the notice see IR 1986 r.6.178 and Form 6.61. Communication of this notice is covered by rr.6.179–6.181A. Property which may be so disclaimed is defined in s.315(2). For the meaning of "property" here see *London City Corporation v Bown, The Times*, October 11, 1989 where a secure periodic tenancy was not so regarded. A cause of action may be disclaimed—*Khan-Ghauri v Dunbar Bank plc* [2001] B.P.I.R. 618. Note that the 12-month cut-off period for disclaimer in BA 1914 s.54(1) has been dropped, against the wishes of the Cork Committee (*Report*, para.1195).

S.315(3), (5)

The effect of disclaimer is explained here. Note that third-party rights are only to be prejudiced in so far as that is absolutely necessary, and anyone suffering losses as a result of a disclaimer can prove in the bankruptcy in respect of it (but see s.320(5) here). On the effect of disclaimer see *MEPC plc v Scottish Amicable Life Assurance Society* [1996] B.P.I.R. 447; and *Hindcastle v Barbara Attenborough Associates* [1997] A.C. 70; [1996] B.C.C. 636.

S.315(4)

Notices of disclaimer are restricted by this provision. Leave of the court is required before the trustee may disclaim after-acquired property which has already been claimed for the estate (s.307), or property claimed under ss.308 or 308A (added by the Housing Act 1988 s.117(3)) with a view to replacement. For the leave procedure, see IR 1986 r.6.182.

These rules on disclaimer are supplemented by IR 1986 rr.6.178–6.186.

316 Notice requiring trustee's decision

316(1) [Where notice not to be given] Notice of disclaimer shall not be given under section 315 in respect of any property if–

(a) a person interested in the property has applied in writing to the trustee or one of his predecessors as trustee requiring the trustee or that predecessor to decide whether he will disclaim or not, and

(b) the period of 28 days beginning with the day on which that application was made has expired without a notice of disclaimer having been given under section 315 in respect of that property.

316(2) [Deemed adoption] The trustee is deemed to have adopted any contract which by virtue of this section he is not entitled to disclaim.

GENERAL NOTE

If the trustee, having been required to make a choice, decides not to disclaim, he cannot later change his mind. Failure to disclaim constitutes adoption. The 28-day period during which the trustee must make his decision has been retained from BA 1914 s.54(4). For the form of a s.316 application see IR 1986 r.6.183. The trustee can force a person to declare his interest in disclaimable property by using IR 1986 r.6.184 and Form 6.63.

Note also IR 1986 rr.6.178–6.186.

317 Disclaimer of leaseholds

317(1) [Disclaimer of leasehold property] The disclaimer of any property of a leasehold nature does not take effect unless a copy of the disclaimer has been served (so far as the trustee is aware of their addresses) on every person claiming under the bankrupt as underlessee or mortgagee and either–

(a) no application under section 320 below is made with respect to the property before the end of the period of 14 days beginning with the day on which the last notice served under this subsection was served, or

(b) where such an application has been made, the court directs that the disclaimer is to take effect.

317(2) [Where court gives s.317(1)(b) direction] Where the court gives a direction under subsection (1)(b) it may also, instead of or in addition to any order it makes under section 320, make such orders with respect to fixtures, tenant's improvements and other matters arising out of the lease as it thinks fit.

GENERAL NOTE

These provisions deal with disclaimers in respect of onerous land. In the case of leasehold property, both underlessees and mortgagees must be served with notices of disclaimer. Note here IR 1986 rr.6.178–6.186.

Formerly, disclaimers of leases required the consent of the court: BA 1914 s.54(3). Now the court will only be involved if an application is made to it within 14 days under s.320. The trustee, after serving notice, must wait for the 14 days to elapse before the disclaimer can take effect. If application to the court has been made, obviously the trustee must wait for the outcome of the application.

The court, if it permits disclaimer, can make special provision for fixtures, etc.

318 Disclaimer of dwelling house

318 Without prejudice to section 317, the disclaimer of any property in a dwelling house does not take effect unless a copy of the disclaimer has been served (so far as the trustee is aware of their addresses) on every person in occupation of or claiming a right to occupy the dwelling house and either–

(a) no application under section 320 is made with respect to the property before the end of the period of 14 days beginning with the day on which the last notice served under this section was served, or

(b) where such an application has been made, the court directs that the disclaimer is to take effect.

GENERAL NOTE

In the case of dwelling houses (for definition, see s.385), all occupiers must be notified. This is a new provision, which substantially mirrors s.317 in many procedural respects.

319 Disclaimer of land subject to rentcharge

319(1) **[Application]** The following applies where, in consequence of the disclaimer under section 315 of any land subject to a rentcharge, that land vests by operation of law in the Crown or any other person (referred to in the next subsection as "the proprietor").

319(2) **[Limit on liability]** The proprietor, and the successors in title of the proprietor, are not subject to any personal liability in respect of any sums becoming due under the rentcharge, except sums becoming due after the proprietor, or some person claiming under or through the proprietor, has taken possession or control of the land or has entered into occupation of it.

GENERAL NOTE

These are highly specialised provisions relating to disclaimers of land subject to a rentcharge. The person in whom the land vests subsequently is not subject to the normal rentcharge obligations.

320 Court order vesting disclaimed property

320(1) **[Application]** This section and the next apply where the trustee has disclaimed property under section 315.

320(2) **[Application to court]** An application may be made to the court under this section by–

(a) any person who claims an interest in the disclaimed property,

(b) any person who is under any liability in respect of the disclaimed property, not being a liability discharged by the disclaimer, or

(c) where the disclaimed property is property in a dwelling house, any person who at the time when the bankruptcy petition was presented was in occupation of or entitled to occupy the dwelling house.

320(3) **[Order by court]** Subject as follows in this section and the next, the court may, on an application under this section, make an order on such terms as it thinks fit for the vesting of the disclaimed property in, or for its delivery to–

(a) a person entitled to it or a trustee for such a person,

  (b)   a person subject to such a liability as is mentioned in subsection (2)(b) or a trustee for such a person, or

  (c)   where the disclaimed property is property in a dwelling house, any person who at the time when the bankruptcy petition was presented was in occupation of or entitled to occupy the dwelling house.

320(4)   [Limit to s.320(3)(b)] The court shall not make an order by virtue of subsection (3)(b) except where it appears to the court that it would be just to do so for the purpose of compensating the person subject to the liability in respect of the disclaimer.

320(5)   [Effect of order in s.315(5) assessment] The effect of any order under this section shall be taken into account in assessing for the purposes of section 315(5) the extent of any loss or damage sustained by any person in consequence of the disclaimer.

320(6)   [Mode of vesting re order] An order under this section vesting property in any person need not be completed by any conveyance, assignment or transfer.

S.320(1)–(4)

Where a trustee has disclaimed onerous property, certain persons have the right to apply to the court for relief. Note the three-month time limit for applications, see IR 1986 r.6.186. Note that occupiers of dwelling houses have now been given this right. The type of relief which the court may grant is described by these provisions. Vesting and delivery orders may be made according to the general discretion of the court. See *Lee v Lee* [1999] B.P.I.R. 926 for an unusual case. On s.320(2)(a) see *Hackney LBC v Crown Estates Commissioners* [1996] B.P.I.R. 428.

S.320(5), (6)

Where a vesting order is made, no conveyance, etc. is required to effect it. If disclaimed property is vested in a person who has suffered loss as a result of the disclaimer, that vesting is to be taken into account when assessing compensation.

    Note here IR 1986 r.6.186.

321   Order under s.320 in respect of leaseholds

321(1)   [Terms of order re leasehold property] The court shall not make an order under section 320 vesting property of a leasehold nature in any person, except on terms making that person–

  (a)   subject to the same liabilities and obligations as the bankrupt was subject to under the lease on the day the bankruptcy petition was presented, or

  (b)   if the court thinks fit, subject to the same liabilities and obligations as that person would be subject to if the lease had been assigned to him on that day.

321(2)   [Where order re part of property in lease] For the purposes of an order under section 320 relating to only part of any property comprised in a lease, the requirements of subsection (1) apply as if the lease comprised only the property to which the order relates.

321(3)   [Where no person accepts order in s.320 case] Where subsection (1) applies and no person is willing to accept an order under section 320 on the terms required by that subsection, the court may (by order under section 320) vest the estate or interest of the bankrupt in the property in any person who is liable (whether personally or in a representative capacity and whether alone or jointly with the bankrupt) to perform the lessee's covenants in the lease.

    The court may by virtue of this subsection vest that estate and interest in such a person freed and discharged from all estates, incumbrances and interests created by the bankrupt.

321(4)   [Exclusion from interest in property] Where subsection (1) applies and a person declines to accept any order under section 320, that person shall be excluded from all interest in the property.

GENERAL NOTE

Section 321(1) deals with applications in respect of leasehold property—the person in whom the leasehold property is vested must assume the same obligations as the lessee was subject to prior to his bankruptcy. If only part of the leasehold property is so vested, the order must take this into account when determining the obligations to impose. Section 321(2) and (3) deal with cases where persons decline to accept orders made under s.320—the court may make adjustments to interests in the property concerned. This includes exclusion from all interest in the property in question (s.321(4)).

Distribution of bankrupt's estate

322   Proof of debts

322(1)   **[Proof in accordance with rules]** Subject to this section and the next, the proof of any bankruptcy debt by a secured or unsecured creditor of the bankrupt and the admission or rejection of any proof shall take place in accordance with the rules.

322(2)   **[Where bankruptcy debt bears interest]** Where a bankruptcy debt bears interest, that interest is provable as part of the debt except in so far as it is payable in respect of any period after the commencement of the bankruptcy.

322(3)   **[Estimation of debt]** The trustee shall estimate the value of any bankruptcy debt which, by reason of its being subject to any contingency or contingencies or for any other reason, does not bear a certain value.

322(4)   **[Where estimate under s.303, 322(3)]** Where the value of a bankruptcy debt is estimated by the trustee under subsection (3) or, by virtue of section 303 in Chapter III, by the court, the amount provable in the bankruptcy in respect of the debt is the amount of the estimate.

S.322(1)

The procedure governing proof of "bankruptcy debts" (see s.382) is governed by the rules: see in particular IR 1986 rr.6.96–6.114. For further discussion see *Arnold v Williams* [2008] EWHC 218 (Ch); [2008] B.P.I.R. 247.

    For the question of proof by secured creditors see s.383. For a case where contingent tax penalties were held provable, see *Re Hurren (a Bankrupt)* [1983] 1 W.L.R. 183. Fines were provable debts under the old law: *Re Pascoe Ex p. Trustee of the Bankrupt v Lords Commissioners of His Majesty's Treasury* [1944] Ch. 310. It is not clear from the Act itself whether the recommendation of the Cork Committee (*Report*, para.1330), that this rule should be reversed, has been implemented. However, the fact that fines are not provable is apparent from IR 1986 r.12.3.

S.322(2)

Under BA 1914 s.66 there were severe restrictions on proving in respect of interest. These restrictions, which were heavily criticised by the Cork Committee (*Report*, para.1381), have been largely removed except with regard to interest accruing after the commencement of the bankruptcy. It should also be remembered that s.343 may be relevant here.

S.322(3), (4)

This allows the trustee to estimate the value of contingent or uncertain debts. For the costs of the trustee see IR 1986 r.6.100(2). Under BA 1914 s.30 there was a facility allowing a creditor to appeal against any estimate made by a trustee. This is not specifically recreated by s.322 but possibly a disappointed creditor could make use of s.303. This provision for estimates will be doubly useful now that the old restriction, formerly contained in BA 1914 s.30(1), banning proof in respect of unliquidated claims, has been abolished: see s.382(3). The Cork Committee (*Report*, para.1318) favoured this change partly because the restriction did not apply to a corporate insolvency: *Re Berkeley Securities (Property) Ltd* [1980] 1 W.L.R. 1589—but this had been the subject of some uncertainty. The change in bankruptcy law will be welcomed if it avoids such confusion.

323   Mutual credit and set-off

323(1)   **[Application]** This section applies where before the commencement of the bankruptcy there have been mutual credits, mutual debts or other mutual dealings between the bankrupt and any creditor of the bankrupt proving or claiming to prove for a bankruptcy debt.

323(2)   **[Account to be taken]** An account shall be taken of what is due from each party to the other in respect of the mutual dealings and the sums due from one party shall be set off against the sums due from the other.

323(3) **[Qualification to s.323(2)]** Sums due from the bankrupt to another party shall not be included in the account taken under subsection (2) if that other party had notice at the time they became due that a bankruptcy petition relating to the bankrupt was pending.

323(4) **[Balance to trustee]** Only the balance (if any) of the account taken under subsection (2) is provable as a bankruptcy debt or, as the case may be, to be paid to the trustee as part of the bankrupt's estate.

GENERAL NOTE

There is little change here. The rules are those in BA 1914 s.31, which in turn reflected common-law authorities such as *Foster v Wilson* (1843) 12 M. & W. 191. The only changes in s.323 are of a terminological or consequential nature reflecting the demise of concepts such as acts of bankruptcy and receiving orders. Notwithstanding the apparent desire of the legislature to reaffirm the old rules on set-off, in *Stein v Blake* [1996] A.C. 243; [1995] B.C.C. 543 the House of Lords concluded that it was possible for a trustee in bankruptcy to assign the net balance of a claim vested in the estate once a self-executing right of set off has been accounted for. This decision of the House of Lords can be seen as one of a number of recent authorities favouring an "estate maximisation" policy on the part of the judiciary. *Stein v Blake* (above) was followed in Australia in *Re Bankrupt Estate of Cirillo* [1997] B.P.I.R. 574. For a review of insolvency set off which involved the House of Lords taking a wide view of its availability see *Secretary of State for Trade and Industry v Frid* [2004] UKHL 24; [2004] B.P.I.R. 841.

It is worth noting that s.323 does not implement the recommendation of the Cork Committee (*Report*, para.1342) that the decision in *National Westminster Bank Ltd v Halesowen Presswork & Assemblies Ltd* [1972] A.C. 785, banning contracting out of the statutory rules, be reversed. However, there is a special exception allowing contracting out on the financial markets: see CA 1989 ss.159, 163, and the note on p.2, above.

For interpretation of the statutory set off provision see the comments of H.H.J. Kershaw in *Re Taylor (a Bankrupt)* [2007] B.P.I.R. 175 at [67]–[68].

For an instance where s.323 was held to be inapplicable see *Bateman v Williams* [2009] B.P.I.R. 973.

For the exclusion of set-off in respect of post-insolvency VAT credits, see FA 1988 s.21 (as amended by FA 1994 s.47).

On s.323(3) see *Coe v Ashurst* [1999] B.P.I.R. 662.

324   Distribution by means of dividend

324(1) **[Duty to declare and distribute]** Whenever the trustee has sufficient funds in hand for the purpose he shall, subject to the retention of such sums as may be necessary for the expenses of the bankruptcy, declare and distribute dividends among the creditors in respect of the bankruptcy debts which they have respectively proved.

324(2) **[Notice of intention to declare and distribute]** The trustee shall give notice of his intention to declare and distribute a dividend.

324(3) **[Notice of dividend etc.]** Where the trustee has declared a dividend, he shall give notice of the dividend and of how it is proposed to distribute it; and a notice given under this subsection shall contain the prescribed particulars of the bankrupt's estate.

324(4) **[Calculation and distribution of dividend]** In the calculation and distribution of a dividend the trustee shall make provision–

(a) for any bankruptcy debts which appear to him to be due to persons who, by reason of the distance of their place of residence, may not have had sufficient time to tender and establish their proofs,

(b) for any bankruptcy debts which are the subject of claims which have not yet been determined, and

(c) for disputed proofs and claims.

S.324(1)–(3)

These provide for the declaration of dividends to creditors when the trustee has sufficient funds at his disposal for that purpose, once expenses have been taken into account. Notice of the dividend must be given to creditors. Under BA 1914 s.62(2) the trustee had, as a general rule, to declare the first dividend within four months of the first meeting of creditors; this specific deadline has been dropped.

For further details on declaration of dividends, see IR 1986 Pt 11. For the mechanics of payment, see the Insolvency Regulations 1994 (SI 1994/2507) reg.23.

S.324(4)

This is a good housekeeping provision. The trustee should set aside funds to cover disputed claims or claims by persons who have not yet lodged proofs.

If the trustee proposes to pay an interim dividend at a time when an application to the court to challenge the admission or rejection of a proof is outstanding, the leave of the court is required under IR 1986 r.11.5(2).

325 Claims by unsatisfied creditors

325(1) **[Entitlements of creditors]** A creditor who has not proved his debt before the declaration of any dividend is not entitled to disturb, by reason that he has not participated in it, the distribution of that dividend or any other dividend declared before his debt was proved, but–

   (a)   when he has proved that debt he is entitled to be paid, out of any money for the time being available for the payment of any further dividend, any dividend or dividends which he has failed to receive; and

   (b)   any dividend or dividends payable under paragraph (a) shall be paid before that money is applied to the payment of any such further dividend.

325(2) **[Order re payment of dividend]** No action lies against the trustee for a dividend, but if the trustee refuses to pay a dividend the court may, if it thinks fit, order him to pay it and also to pay, out of his own money–

   (a)   interest on the dividend, at the rate for the time being specified in section 17 of the Judgments Act 1838, from the time it was withheld, and

   (b)   the costs of the proceedings in which the order to pay is made.

S.325(1)

Late claimants cannot upset properly declared dividends, but they may make a claim on any surplus available.

S.325(2)

This curiously worded provision is derived from BA 1914 s.68. On the one hand, it states that no action shall lie against a trustee for a dividend, but then it permits the court to order the trustee to pay one, and, indeed, to pay interest and costs out of his own pocket.

Compare IR 1986 r.11.8.

326 Distribution of property in specie

326(1) **[Division of unsaleable property]** Without prejudice to sections 315 to 319 (disclaimer), the trustee may, with the permission of the creditors' committee, divide in its existing form amongst the bankrupt's creditors, according to its estimated value, any property which from its peculiar nature or other special circumstances cannot be readily or advantageously sold.

326(2) **[Permission under s.326(1)]** A permission given for the purposes of subsection (1) shall not be a general permission but shall relate to a particular proposed exercise of the power in question; and a person dealing with the trustee in good faith and for value is not to be concerned to enquire whether any permission required by subsection (1) has been given.

326(3) **[Where no permission under s.326(1)]** Where the trustee has done anything without the permission required by subsection (1), the court or the creditors' committee may, for the purpose of enabling him to meet his expenses out of the bankrupt's estate, ratify what the trustee has done.

But the committee shall not do so unless it is satisfied that the trustee acted in a case of urgency and has sought its ratification without undue delay.

S.326(1)

This authorises the trustee to make distributions in specie of the property which is difficult to realise. This is a new facility without precedent in the 1914 Act.

S.326(2), (3)

The trustee must obtain specific permission to exercise his power to make an in specie distribution under s.326(1) above. Unauthorised distributions may, in certain circumstances, be ratified by the creditors' committee.

327   Distribution in criminal bankruptcy

327   Where the bankruptcy order was made on a petition under section 264(1)(d) (criminal bankruptcy), no distribution shall be made under sections 324 to 326 so long as an appeal is pending (within the meaning of section 277) against the bankrupt's conviction of any offence by virtue of which the criminal bankruptcy order on which the petition was based was made.

GENERAL NOTE

In cases of criminal bankruptcy no distribution is to be made until the final appeal in the criminal case is heard.

Note prospective amendment: s.327 is to be repealed by CJA 1988 s.170(2) and Sch.16 as from a day to be appointed; see the note to s.264.

328   Priority of debts

328(1)   **[Preferential debts to be paid first]** In the distribution of the bankrupt's estate, his preferential debts (within the meaning given by section 386 in Part XII) shall be paid in priority to other debts.

328(2)   **[Ranking of preferential debts]** Preferential debts rank equally between themselves after the expenses of the bankruptcy and shall be paid in full unless the bankrupt's estate is insufficient for meeting them, in which case they abate in equal proportions between themselves.

328(3)   **[Debts neither preferential nor under s.329]** Debts which are neither preferential debts nor debts to which the next section applies also rank equally between themselves and, after the preferential debts, shall be paid in full unless the bankrupt's estate is insufficient for meeting them, in which case they abate in equal proportions between themselves.

328(4)   **[Surplus after payment]** Any surplus remaining after the payment of the debts that are preferential or rank equally under subsection (3) shall be applied in paying interest on those debts in respect of the periods during which they have been outstanding since the commencement of the bankruptcy; and interest on preferential debts ranks equally with interest on debts other than preferential debts.

328(5)   **[Rate of interest under s.328(4)]** The rate of interest payable under subsection (4) in respect of any debt is whichever is the greater of the following–

(a)   the rate specified in section 17 of the Judgments Act 1838 at the commencement of the bankruptcy, and

(b)   the rate applicable to that debt apart from the bankruptcy.

328(6)   **[Other enactments]** This section and the next are without prejudice to any provision of this Act or any other Act under which the payment of any debt or the making of any other payment is, in the event of bankruptcy, to have a particular priority or to be postponed.

GENERAL NOTE

This section has dropped what was formerly BA 1914 s.33(6), dealing with payment of debts in the case of partnership insolvency: see s.420 now. The provision relating to insolvent estates of deceased persons has also not been retained—see s.421. The text of BA 1914 s.33(4) is now included in s.347. See also IR 1986 rr.6.224 and 11.2 in this context.

S.328(1), (2)

These provisions deal with preferential debts. Those debts described as preferential by ss.386, 387 and by Sch.6 to this Act are to be paid in priority to other debts (but not the expenses of the bankruptcy: see Sch.9 para.22). In the event of a shortfall they are to abate in equal proportions. Note that the list of preferential debts has been pruned radically by Sch.6 after considerable pressure had been exerted on the government. This issue is considered fully in the note to s.386 below.

S.328(3)

Ordinary debts—i.e. those which are neither preferential nor deferred—rank equally between themselves and abate rateably in the event of a shortfall.

S.328(4), (5)

These provisions deal with the payment of interest on debts which has accrued since the commencement of the bankruptcy (for the meaning of this phrase, see s.278). It is to be paid only after both the preferential and ordinary creditors have been satisfied in full. Interest on preferential debts receives no special treatment. Section 328(5) specifies the maximum rate of interest allowed (currently 8 per cent (see SI 1993/564)). Note the use of the contract interest rate alternative in subs.(5)—this does not appear to have featured in the statutory predecessor (BA 1914 s.33(8))—for discussion see Cork Committee (Cmnd.8558 paras 1383 et seq.).

S.328(6)

The general law on deferred creditors is preserved—for example, a creditor whose case falls within s.3 of the Partnership Act 1890.

329   Debts to spouse

329(1)   [Application] This section applies to bankruptcy debts owed in respect of credit provided by a person who (whether or not the bankrupt's spouse or civil partner at the time the credit was provided) was the bankrupt's spouse or civil partner at the commencement of the bankruptcy.

329(2)   [Ranking, payment] Such debts–

   (a)   rank in priority after the debts and interest required to be paid in pursuance of section 328(3) and (4), and

   (b)   are payable with interest at the rate specified in section 328(5) in respect of the period during which they have been outstanding since the commencement of the bankruptcy;

and the interest payable under paragraph (b) has the same priority as the debts on which it is payable.

GENERAL NOTE

This section differs from its predecessor in the 1914 Act in a number of respects. For example, BA 1914 s.36 related only to a loan in connection with a business or trade carried on by the bankrupt (where the lender was a husband), but not if it was lent by a wife. Note the insertion of the reference to civil partners by the Civil Partnership Act 2004 Sch.27.

330   Final distribution

330(1)   [Notice re dividend, etc.] When the trustee has realised all the bankrupt's estate or so much of it as can, in the trustee's opinion, be realised without needlessly protracting the trusteeship, he shall give notice in the prescribed manner either–

   (a)   of his intention to declare a final dividend, or

   (b)   that no dividend, or further dividend, will be declared.

330(2)   [Contents of notice] The notice under subsection (1) shall contain the prescribed particulars and shall require claims against the bankrupt's estate to be established by a date ("the final date") specified in the notice.

330(3)   [Postponement of final date] The court may, on the application of any person, postpone the final date.

330(4)   [Trustee's duties after final date] After the final date, the trustee shall–

   (a)   defray any outstanding expenses of the bankruptcy out of the bankrupt's estate, and

(b) if he intends to declare a final dividend, declare and distribute that dividend without regard to the claim of any person in respect of a debt not already proved in the bankruptcy.

330(5) [Where surplus] If a surplus remains after payment in full and with interest of all the bankrupt's creditors and the payment of the expenses of the bankruptcy, the bankrupt is entitled to the surplus.

330(6) [Applicability of EC Regulation] Subsection (5) is subject to Article 35 of the EC Regulation (surplus in secondary proceedings to be transferred to main proceedings).

S.330(1)–(3)
Where the trustee has realised all that can be converted into money he should notify the creditors whether he is in a position to declare a final dividend. This notice must indicate a final date for claims. This final date can be extended by the court.

S.330(4)
Once the final date is passed the trustee should pay his final dividend, but not before the costs of the bankruptcy (which often represent a considerable figure) have been defrayed out of the proceeds of realisation.

There appears to be no provision dealing with unclaimed dividends to replace BA 1914 s.153. Generally see IR 1986 Pt 11.

S.330(5)
Any surplus goes to the bankrupt. Subsection (5) was considered in *Phillips v Symes* [2005] EWHC 2867 (Ch); [2006] B.P.I.R. 1430. Here Peter Smith J. made the point that the trustee holds the estate on trust for the bankrupt against the possibility of a surplus arising at the end of the day. That being so, an immediate charging order could be granted against the bankrupt's interest in the potential surplus even before such surplus was ascertained. This case may need to be viewed in the light of the later Court of Appeal ruling in *James v Rutherford-Hodge* [2005] EWCA Civ 1580; [2006] B.P.I.R. 973 (mentioned in the annotation to s.306 above).

S.330(6)
This was inserted by Insolvency Act 1986 (Amendment) (No.2) Regulations 2002 (SI 2002/1240) reg.15 with effect from May 31, 2002.

331 Final meeting

331(1) [Application] Subject as follows in this section and the next, this section applies where–

(a) it appears to the trustee that the administration of the bankrupt's estate in accordance with this Chapter is for practical purposes complete, and

(b) the trustee is not the official receiver.

331(2) [Duty of trustee] The trustee shall summon a final general meeting of the bankrupt's creditors which–

(a) shall receive the trustee's report of his administration of the bankrupt's estate, and

(b) shall determine whether the trustee should have his release under section 299 in Chapter III.

331(3) [Time for notice] The trustee may, if he thinks fit, give the notice summoning the final general meeting at the same time as giving notice under section 330(1); but, if summoned for an earlier date, that meeting shall be adjourned (and, if necessary, further adjourned) until a date on which the trustee is able to report to the meeting that the administration of the bankrupt's estate is for practical purposes complete.

331(4) [Expenses] In the administration of the estate it is the trustee's duty to retain sufficient sums from the estate to cover the expenses of summoning and holding the meeting required by this section.

S.331(1), (2)
These provisions require a trustee (but not an official receiver) to call a final meeting of creditors to report on how things went. This appears to be an innovation.

S.331(3)

To save money, notice of the final meeting can be sent out along with notice of the final dividend, but the meeting cannot be held until the final dividend has been paid.

S.331(4)

This is a reminder to the trustees to set aside sufficient funds to cover the cost of this final meeting.

332   Saving for bankrupt's home

332(1)   **[Application]** This section applies where–

    (a)   there is comprised in the bankrupt's estate property consisting of an interest in a dwelling house which is occupied by the bankrupt or by his spouse or former spouse or by his civil partner or former civil partner, and

    (b)   the trustee has been unable for any reason to realise that property.

332(2)   **[Conditions for s.331 meeting]** The trustee shall not summon a meeting under section 331 unless either–

    (a)   the court has made an order under section 313 imposing a charge on that property for the benefit of the bankrupt's estate, or

    (b)   the court has declined, on an application under that section, to make such an order, or

    (c)   the Secretary of State has issued a certificate to the trustee stating that it would be inappropriate or inexpedient for such an application to be made in the case in question.

GENERAL NOTE

This again is a new provision. It states that as a general rule there should be no summoning of a final meeting where the bankrupt's interest in a "dwelling house" (for definition, see s.385) has not been realised. Exceptions to this general rule are: (1) where a s.313 charge has been imposed on the property; (2) where the court has refused to grant a s.313 charge; or (3) where the Secretary of State has certified that it would be inappropriate for the trustee to apply for a s.313 charge. Note the insertion of the reference to civil partners by Sch.27 to the Civil Partnership Act 2004. On s.332(2)(c) see *Dear IP* Issue 26 (March 2006).

Supplemental

333   Duties of bankrupt in relation to trustee

333(1)   **[Duties]** The bankrupt shall–

    (a)   give to the trustee such information as to his affairs,

    (b)   attend on the trustee at such times, and

    (c)   do all such other things,

as the trustee may for the purposes of carrying out his functions under any of this Group of Parts reasonably require.

333(2)   **[Notice re after-acquired property]** Where at any time after the commencement of the bankruptcy any property is acquired by, or devolves upon, the bankrupt or there is an increase of the bankrupt's income, the bankrupt shall, within the prescribed period, give the trustee notice of the property or, as the case may be, of the increase.

333(3)   **[Application of s.333(1)]** Subsection (1) applies to a bankrupt after his discharge.

333(4)   **[Penalty for non-compliance]** If the bankrupt without reasonable excuse fails to comply with any obligation imposed by this section, he is guilty of a contempt of court and liable to be punished accordingly (in addition to any other punishment to which he may be subject).

S.333(1), (3)

These provisions impose duties on a bankrupt, up to and after the date of his discharge, to provide information and assistance to enable the *trustee* to carry out his duties. The comparable provision describing the bankrupt's duties towards the *official receiver* is to be found in s.291. On the nature of the respective duties of bankrupt and trustee see *Morris v Murjani* [1996] B.P.I.R. 458. A bankrupt who fails to comply with his obligations under s.333 runs the risk of having his automatic discharge suspended—*Shierson v Rastogi* [2007] EWHC 1266 (Ch); [2007] B.P.I.R. 891. In *Re Caldwell* (unreported decision of registrar, 1998) the court felt able to bolster this duty to co-operate by exercising its powers under s.39(1) of the Supreme Court Act 1981 and authorising the trustee to execute a power of attorney on behalf of the bankrupt in order to gain access to financial information from foreign authorities: see Archer, (1998) 142 S.J. 596. For passing comment on s.333 see *Arnold v Williams* [2008] EWHC 218 (Ch); [2008] B.P.I.R. 247.

Note also the bankrupt's more specific duties in regard to property, records, etc. under s.312.

S.333(2)

The obligation to provide information about the property and income is a continuing one. Such an obligation is essential for the operation of ss.307 and 310. The prescribed period is 21 days: see IR 1986 r.6.200(1). For the unintended consequences that might flow from a bankrupt failing to comply with the obligation of disclosure under s.333(2) see *Barrett v Barrett* [2008] EWHC 1061 (Ch).

S.333(4)

A bankrupt may be held liable for contempt if he breaches any of the above obligations.

334 Stay of distribution in case of second bankruptcy

334(1) **[Application, definitions]** This section and the next apply where a bankruptcy order is made against an undischarged bankrupt; and in both sections–

(a) **"the later bankruptcy"** means the bankruptcy arising from that order,

(b) **"the earlier bankruptcy"** means the bankruptcy (or, as the case may be, most recent bankruptcy) from which the bankrupt has not been discharged at the commencement of the later bankruptcy, and

(c) **"the existing trustee"** means the trustee (if any) of the bankrupt's estate for the purposes of the earlier bankruptcy.

334(2) **[Certain distributions void]** Where the existing trustee has been given the prescribed notice of the presentation of the petition for the later bankruptcy, any distribution or other disposition by him of anything to which the next subsection applies, if made after the giving of the notice, is void except to the extent that it was made with the consent of the court or is or was subsequently ratified by the court.

This is without prejudice to section 284 (restrictions on dispositions of property following bankruptcy order).

334(3) **[Application of s.334(2)]** This subsection applies to–

(a) any property which is vested in the existing trustee under section 307(3) (after-acquired property);

(b) any money paid to the existing trustee in pursuance of an income payments order under section 310; and

(c) any property or money which is, or in the hands of the existing trustee represents, the proceeds of sale or application of property or money falling within paragraph (a) or (b) of this subsection.

GENERAL NOTE

This provision is, of necessity, more sophisticated than its predecessor as a result of the advent of the new rules on after-acquired property and income payments orders.

S.334(1)

Where a petition for bankruptcy is issued against an undischarged bankrupt who is already undergoing the bankruptcy process, his existing trustee, on receiving notice of the petition, must not make any further distributions or dispositions without the consent of the court. However, this only applies to property covered by s.334(3).

S.334(3)

Section 334(3) applies to after-acquired property or money from any income payments order, or the proceeds thereof. Note also IR 1986 rr.6.225–6.228.

335   Adjustment between earlier and later bankruptcy estates

335(1)   **[Matters in bankrupt's estate]** With effect from the commencement of the later bankruptcy anything to which section 334(3) applies which, immediately before the commencement of that bankruptcy, is comprised in the bankrupt's estate for the purposes of the earlier bankruptcy is to be treated as comprised in the bankrupt's estate for the purposes of the later bankruptcy and, until there is a trustee of that estate, is to be dealt with by the existing trustee in accordance with the rules.

335(2)   **[Sums paid under s.310]** Any sums which in pursuance of an income payments order under section 310 are payable after the commencement of the later bankruptcy to the existing trustee shall form part of the bankrupt's estate for the purposes of the later bankruptcy; and the court may give such consequential directions for the modification of the order as it thinks fit.

335(3)   **[Charge re bankruptcy expenses]** Anything comprised in a bankrupt's estate by virtue of subsection (1) or (2) is so comprised subject to a first charge in favour of the existing trustee for any bankruptcy expenses incurred by him in relation thereto.

335(4)   **[Property not in estate]** Except as provided above and in section 334, property which is, or by virtue of section 308 (personal property of bankrupt exceeding reasonable replacement value) or section 308A (vesting in trustee of certain tenancies) is capable of being, comprised in the bankrupt's estate for the purposes of the earlier bankruptcy, or of any bankruptcy prior to it, shall not be comprised in his estate for the purposes of the later bankruptcy.

335(5)   **[Creditors of earlier bankruptcies]** The creditors of the bankrupt in the earlier bankruptcy and the creditors of the bankrupt in any bankruptcy prior to the earlier one, are not to be creditors of his in the later bankruptcy in respect of the same debts; but the existing trustee may prove in the later bankruptcy for–

(a) the unsatisfied balance of the debts (including any debt under this subsection) provable against the bankrupt's estate in the earlier bankruptcy;

(b) any interest payable on that balance; and

(c) any unpaid expenses of the earlier bankruptcy.

335(6)   **[Priority of amounts in s.335(5)]** Any amount provable under subsection (5) ranks in priority after all the other debts provable in the later bankruptcy and after interest on those debts and, accordingly, shall not be paid unless those debts and that interest have first been paid in full.

S.335(1)–(3)

Such items, on the commencement of the second bankruptcy, must be treated as part of the estate for the purpose of that second bankruptcy. The same is true of any money paid to the first trustee under an income payments order after the date of the commencement of the second bankruptcy. Indeed, the income payments order can be modified. However, the first trustee may be entitled to a charge over such property to cover any expenses incurred in relation to it.

S.335(4)

Other property comprised in the bankrupt's estate in the first bankruptcy does not pass to the estate on the second bankruptcy. A minor insertion has been made by the Housing Act 1988 Sch.17 para.74.

S.335(5), (6)

These provisions deal with the status of creditors in the first bankruptcy vis-à-vis the second bankruptcy: any residual claims they may have can be proved for in the second bankruptcy, but they only enjoy deferred status in this respect. This implements the recommendation of the Blagden Committee (Cmnd.221, para.114). Note also IR 1986 rr.6.225–6.228. Note also r.6.96.

CHAPTER V

EFFECT OF BANKRUPTCY ON CERTAIN RIGHTS, TRANSACTIONS, ETC.

Rights under trusts of land

335A   Rights under trusts of land

335A(1)   [Application for order for sale of land] Any application by a trustee of a bankrupt's estate under section 14 of the Trusts of Land and Appointment of Trustees Act 1996 (powers of court in relation to trusts of land) for an order under that section for the sale of land shall be made to the court having jurisdiction in relation to the bankruptcy.

335A(2)   [Interests considered before order] On such an application the court shall make such order as it thinks just and reasonable having regard to–

   (a) the interests of the bankrupt's creditors;

   (b) where the application is made in respect of land which includes a dwelling house which is or has been the home of the bankrupt or the bankrupt's spouse or civil partner or former spouse or former civil partner–

      (i) the conduct of the spouse, civil partner, former spouse or former civil partner, so far as contributing to the bankruptcy,

      (ii) the needs and financial resources of the spouse, civil partner, former spouse or former civil partner, and

      (iii) the needs of any children; and

   (c) all the circumstances of the case other than the needs of the bankrupt.

335A(3)   [Assumption by court re interests of creditors] Where such an application is made after the end of the period of one year beginning with the first vesting under Chapter IV of this Part of the bankrupt's estate in a trustee, the court shall assume, unless the circumstances of the case are exceptional, that the interests of the bankrupt's creditors outweigh all other considerations.

335A(4)   [Exercise of powers conferred on court] The powers conferred on the court by this section are exercisable on an application whether it is made before or after the commencement of this section.

GENERAL NOTE

This and the following three sections are part of a package to redress the balance of rights between the trustee, on the one hand, and the bankrupt and his family on the other hand, over what will probably represent the bankrupt's most valuable asset, his family home. This is a problem that has troubled the law for many years—witness the decision in *Bendall v McWhirter* [1952] 2 Q.B. 466, which created a "deserted wife's equity" capable of prevailing over the trustee's rights, and its rejection by the House of Lords in *National Provincial Bank Ltd v Ainsworth* [1965] A.C. 1175. This decision, in turn, was reversed by the Matrimonial Homes Act 1967, a piece of legislation consolidated by the Matrimonial Homes Act 1983 which in turn was replaced by the Family Law Act 1996. Notwithstanding this, it was felt that the family's right to a roof over its head required greater protection in the event of the breadwinner becoming bankrupt: see the Cork *Report*, paras 1114–1131. These provisions on the family home were a late insertion in the Insolvency Bill 1985. For the background to this legislation, see Miller, (1986) 50 Conv. 393; and Cretney, (1991) 107 L.Q.R. 177. For further discussion of this area see Creasey and Doyle, (1992) 136 S.J. 920. For a summary of the Joint Insolvency Committee Insolvency Guidance Paper on the family home (2005) see [2006] 19 Insolv. Int. 42.

Where a trustee in bankruptcy makes an application for sale under these provisions an issue will frequently arise as to the allocation of proceeds between the estate and the non-bankrupt party. In such a scenario general equitable principles governing the determination of beneficial interests will be applied, as explained by the House of Lords in *Stack v Dowden* [2007] UKHL 17; [2007] 2 W.L.R. 831. In addition, questions may arise as to whether the trustee can invoke equitable accounting principles and charge an "occupation rent" to be paid by the non-bankrupt party.

There is a body of precedent governing this scenario—see *Re Gorman* [1990] 1 W.L.R. 616; *Re Pavlou* [1993] 1 W.L.R. 1046; *Re Byford* [2003] B.P.I.R. 1089; and *French v Barcham* [2008] EWHC 1505 (Ch). Uncertainty has crept in as a result of *Murphy v Gooch* [2007] EWCA Civ 603; [2007] B.P.I.R. 1123 where the view was taken that the common law principles of equitable accounting have been replaced by the statutory criteria listed in ss.12–15 of the TLATA 1996, but this view was questioned by Blackburne J. in *French v Barcham* (above), where the residual discretion enjoyed by the court was championed. Blackburne J. ruled that the principles of equitable accounting were not displaced by the House of Lords precedent of *Stack v Dowden* [2007] UKHL 17. This question is likely to be revisited in the years to come.

Section 335A was inserted by s.25(1) of and Sch.3 para.23 to the Trusts of Land and Appointment of Trustees Act 1996 with effect from January 1, 1997. For its significance see the note to s.336 below. Early interpretation on the meaning of s.335A is provided by the Court of Appeal in *Judd v Brown* [1999] B.P.I.R. 517 where the point was made that it may be proper to order a sale even if the prime beneficiary would be a secured creditor. In *Re Raval* [1998] B.P.I.R. 389 Blackburne J. was faced with the question of whether exceptional circumstances existed for the purposes of s.335A(3). Again the issue centred upon the ill-health of the wife. The registrar had decided that this did constitute an exceptional circumstance but was only prepared to delay the sale of the family home for six months to enable arrangements to be made in the light of the wife's condition. Although Blackburne J. agreed with the interpretation of the registrar on whether this was an exceptional circumstance he did not feel that appropriate weight had been given to it when making the order and therefore postponed the sale for just over one year. General principles governing the s.335A jurisdiction were laid down by the High Court in *Harrington v Bennett* [2000] B.P.I.R. 630. Exceptional circumstances within s.335A(3) were present in *Claughton v Charalamabous* [1998] B.P.I.R. 558. In *Barca v Mears* [2005] B.P.I.R. 15 the High Court reluctantly followed *Re Citro* [1991] Ch. 142 but questioned whether the narrow approach used for determining "exceptional circumstances" for the purposes of s.335A(3) was consistent with the requirements of the European Convention on Human Rights and, in particular, with art.8 (right to family life).

A lucid exposition of the principles to be applied under s.335A(ii) and (iii) was provided by Lawrence Collins J. in *Dean v Stout* [2005] EWHC 3315 (Ch); [2005] B.P.I.R. 1113. In particular the flexible and open-ended nature of the concept of exceptional circumstances was stressed. The fact that a wife and children will lose the family home is a normal incidence of many bankruptcies and therefore not exceptional. Simply because the proceeds of sale will be swallowed up by bankruptcy expenses does not make the circumstances exceptional. This judgment very much reflects traditional judicial attitudes.

In *Awoyemi v Bowell* [2005] EWHC 2138 (Ch); [2006] B.P.I.R. 1, yet another case on s.335A, Evans-Lombe J. stressed that it was very much a matter of discretion as to whether the trustee decided to enforce a possession order granted under s.335A and the court would be reluctant to interfere with that discretion.

In *Donohoe v Ingram* [2006] B.P.I.R. 417 Stuart Isaacs Q.C. (sitting as a Deputy Judge in the High Court) supported a ruling from the District Judge that a sale should be ordered under s.335A notwithstanding the fact that there were still children in the house. A suggestion that sale should be delayed until the youngest child reached 16 was rejected. As more than a year had elapsed since the commencement of the bankruptcy the presumption favoured sale and the mere presence of children in the family home did not constitute exceptional circumstances. Once again the issue whether a narrow construction of "exceptional circumstances" does involve an infringement of the right to family life as conferred by art.8 ECHR was left open. As a small crumb of comfort in the interests of common humanity sale was deferred for three months.

This continues to be the most litigated aspect of bankruptcy.

The case of *Re Karia* [2006] B.P.I.R. 1226 (which was decided in 2001) shows that the courts will not infer exceptional circumstances exist simply because the proceeds of sale will be swallowed up in meeting the expenses of the bankruptcy. Rights conferred by art.8 had to be balanced against the rights of creditors; that balance here favoured sale.

Again in *Nicholls v Lan* [2006] B.P.I.R. 1243 the High Court held that s.335A was consistent with art.8 ECHR because it sought to balance family interests against those of creditors. The order of the district judge in this case clearly did that to the extent of deferring a sale for 18 months and therefore on appeal the High Court would not interfere. For discussion see Pawlowski, [2007] Conv. 78.

In *Foenander v Allan* [2006] B.P.I.R. 1392 the court took the view that even if art.8 had shifted the goalposts for the purposes of s.335A the registrar had been correct in finding no exceptional circumstances on the facts of the case. Ill-health on the part of the brother of the bankrupt who had an interest in and lived in the property did not justify a delay in the realisation of what was the estate's only real asset.

The court in *Foyle v Turner* [2007] B.P.I.R. 43 felt that there was no inconsistency between art.8 and s.335A. According to Judge Norris exceptional circumstances might arise out of prolonged and inordinate delay between initial vesting and application for sale; but in this case a delay of some 13 years was not inordinate. The point was made that the application was made within the new three year period introduced by s.283A which came into effect on April 1, 2004.

The court in *Turner v Avis* [2008] B.P.I.R. 1143 undertook a significant review of the authorities in order to explain what was meant by "exceptional circumstances". In *Everitt v Budhram, The Times,* July 14, 2009 Mr Justice Henderson indicated that the word "needs" in s.335A(2) was to be widely interpreted and could encompass financial, medical, emotional and mental needs.

Avis v Turner [2007] EWCA Civ 748 confirms the point that s.335A applies where s.14 of Trusts of Land and Appointment of Trustees Act 1996 would operate. Whereas in *Holtham v Kelmanson* [2006] B.P.I.R. 1422 it was held that s.335A did not apply if the applicant trustee was solely interested in the property.

The presumption in s.335A(3) was applied in *Avis v Turner* [2007] EWCA Civ 748; [2007] B.P.I.R. 663.

For discussion of this area see Davey, [2001] Insolv. L. 2 at 12.

These provisions must be read in the light of s.283A (inserted by EA 2002 from April 1, 2004).

S.335A(2)
Note the amendments introduced by the Civil Partnership Act 2004 Sch.27. On "needs" see *Everitt v Budhram, The Times,* July 14, 2009.

Rights of occupation

336   Rights of occupation etc. of bankrupt's spouse or civil partner

336(1)   [Family Law Act 1996] Nothing occurring in the initial period of the bankruptcy (that is to say, the period beginning with the day of the presentation of the petition for the bankruptcy order and ending with the vesting of the bankrupt's estate in a trustee) is to be taken as having given rise to any home rights under Part IV of the Family Law Act 1996 in relation to a dwelling house comprised in the bankrupt's estate.

336(2)   [Where spouse or civil partner's home rights charge on estate] Where a spouse's or civil partner's home rights under the Act of 1996 are a charge on the estate or interest of the other spouse or civil partner, or of trustees for the other spouse or civil partner, and the other spouse is adjudged bankrupt–

(a)   the charge continues to subsist notwithstanding the bankruptcy and, subject to the provisions of that Act, binds the trustee of the bankrupt's estate and persons deriving title under that trustee, and

(b)   any application for an order under section 33 of that Act shall be made to the court having jurisdiction in relation to the bankruptcy.

336(3)   (Repealed by Trusts of Land and Appointment of Trustees Act 1996 Pt III s.25(2), 27 and Sch. 4 as from January 1, 1997.)

336(4)   [Court orders] On such an application as is mentioned in subsection (2) the court shall make such order under section 33 of the Act of 1996 as it thinks just and reasonable having regard to–

(a)   the interests of the bankrupt's creditors,

(b)   the conduct of the spouse or former spouse or civil partner or former civil partner, so far as contributing to the bankruptcy,

(c)   the needs and financial resources of the spouse or former spouse, or civil partner or former civil partner,

(d)   the needs of any children, and

(e)   all the circumstances of the case other than the needs of the bankrupt.

336(5)   [Assumption by court re interests of creditors] Where such an application is made after the end of the period of one year beginning with the first vesting under Chapter IV of this Part of the bankrupt's estate in a trustee, the court shall assume, unless the circumstances of the case are exceptional, that the interests of the bankrupt's creditors outweigh all other considerations.

GENERAL NOTE

For the definitions of "family" and "dwelling house", see s.385.

S.336(1)
This prevents a spouse's matrimonial home rights under the Family Law Act 1996 arising during the period after the date of the petition and up to the time when the property vests in the trustee.

S.336(2)
Where the spouse of a bankrupt has acquired statutory rights of occupation representing a charge on the house owned by the bankrupt, that charge is effective as against the trustee. Any applications made under s.33 of the Family Law Act 1996 (i.e. to have the spouse evicted or to enable him or her to regain possession), however, must be made to the appropriate bankruptcy court. Note that s.336(4), commented on below, applies to such an application.

S.336(3)–(5)
These provisions cover the situation where the spouses or former spouses are joint owners of the property, and a trust for sale has arisen. Any application under s.30 of LPA 1925 or s.14 of the Trusts of Land and Appointment of Trustees Act 1996 (which substantially remodelled the provision in the 1925 Act) to the court by the trustee in bankruptcy of one of the spouses or ex-spouses for an enforced sale is to be made to the relevant bankruptcy court. In the past in cases under s.30 of the 1925 Act, the courts have normally acceded to the trustee's request for sale, although the family interests have been considered: see *Re Solomon* [1967] Ch. 573; *Re Turner* [1974] 1 W.L.R. 1556; *Re Densham* [1975] 1 W.L.R. 1519; *Re Bailey* [1977] 1 W.L.R. 278; *Re Lowrie* [1981] 3 All E.R. 353; *Re Citro (a Bankrupt)* [1991] Ch. 142; *Zandfarid v BCCI* [1996] 1 W.L.R. 1420; and *Re Ng* [1997] B.C.C. 507. A decision which went against the grain and resulted in the sale of the matrimonial home being postponed for several years until the children had finished their education was *Re Holliday* [1981] Ch. 405. A similar more "caring" approach was taken by Hoffmann J. in the poorly reported *Re Mott* [1987] C.L.Y. 212 where the sick mother of the bankrupt was allowed to postpone the sale of the house until after her death. In *Re Bremner* [1999] B.P.I.R. 185 a sale was postponed for a short period to allow a terminally ill bankrupt the dignity of dying in his own home. For a comparable problem posed by novel facts see *Re Gorman (a Bankrupt)* [1990] 1 All E.R. 717. In *Re Haghighat* [2009] B.P.I.R. 268 the court found the presence of exceptional circumstances because the property was occupied by a disabled child.

The extent to which the case law under LPA 1925 s.30 retains value is unclear because in future cases where an application is made under s.14 of the Trusts of Land and Appointment of Trustees Act 1996 the factors which the court shall have regard to in non-bankruptcy cases include the intentions of the settlor, the purposes of the trust, the welfare of minors in occupation and the interests of secured creditors of the beneficiary (s.15 of the Trusts of Land and Appointment of Trustees Act 1996). Where the application for sale is by the trustee in bankruptcy the matter is governed by IA 1986 s.335A, which identifies relevant considerations. In spite of this statutory intrusion one suspects that the courts will be reluctant to cast aside all previous jurisprudence on this difficult subject.

Now, if such an application is made, the court has general discretion and can consider all the circumstances (including the interests of the family and creditors and the contribution of either party towards the bankruptcy); but if it is made more than one year after the vesting of the property in the trustee in bankruptcy, it will be the interests of the creditors which will prevail unless there are exceptional counterbalancing factors: see s.335A(3). There is a question as to when the one period presumption in favour of the spouse begins to run. Does it run from the date of the bankruptcy order or from when the estate vests in the trustee? This issue may require clarification through litigation.

There is some discussion of s.336(5) in *Re Citro (a Bankrupt)* (above) where the point is made that many of the old bankruptcy cases (which are discussed above) will be relevant to its interpretation. It is also stressed that this provision will only operate within the context of a marriage (and not to cohabitees). Exceptional circumstances were found to be present in *Judd v Brown* [1997] B.P.I.R. 470 where the illness of the wife was sufficient to persuade the court to refuse an application for sale. Further discussion of s.336(5) is to be found in *Trustee of the Estate of Bowe v Bowe* [1997] B.P.I.R. 747 where Jonathan Parker J. found that there was an absence of exceptional circumstances. The fact that the sale of the property might produce no immediate benefit for creditors because the proceeds were to be used to defray the costs of the bankruptcy was not in itself a reason to block the sale. See also *Barca v Mears* [2005] B.P.I.R. 15 and the discussion on s.335A above. The "exceptional circumstances" test used in s.336 has been held not to be inconsistent with the protection offered by art.8 ECHR—*Hosking v Michaelides* [2006] B.P.I.R. 1192. The court in this case ruled that under s.336(4) the voice of creditors should now prevail and the exceptional circumstances as such only justified a postponement of six months in the sale. Section 336(5) does not apply where the spouse has a proprietary interest in the property—*Avis v Turner* [2007] B.P.I.R. 6.

In *Official Receiver for Northern Ireland v Rooney and Paulson* [2009] B.P.I.R. 536 the importance of the ECHR requirements was stressed by Weir J. in a case of protracted realisation. Here there had been a 12-year hiatus between the start of the bankruptcy and the request of the official receiver to sell the family home. The court cited both arts 6 and 8 ECHR to deny this application as there was evidence that the wives of the bankrupts had been lulled into a false sense of security by the inactivity of the authorities.

For similar problems of social priority encountered under s.40 of the Bankruptcy (Scotland) Act 1985 see *Gourlay's Trustee v Gourlay*, 1995 S.L.T. (Sh Ct) 7; *Hunt's Trustee v Hunt*, 1995 S.C.L.R. 969; *McMahon's Trustee, The Times*, March 26, 1997, and *Ritchie v Burns* [2001] B.P.I.R. 666.

Note the textual amendments made to s.336 by s.66(1) of and Sch.8 para.57 to the Family Law Act 1996 and the repeal in its entirety of subs.(3) and minor repeal in subs.(4) effected by Sch.4 to the Trusts of Land and Appointment of Trustees Act 1996.

337   Rights of occupation of bankrupt

337(1)   [Application] This section applies where–

   (a)   a person who is entitled to occupy a dwelling house by virtue of a beneficial estate or interest is adjudged bankrupt, and

   (b)   any persons under the age of 18 with whom that person had at some time occupied that dwelling house had their home with that person at the time when the bankruptcy petition was presented and at the commencement of the bankruptcy.

337(2)   [Rights of occupation, etc.] Whether or not the bankrupt's spouse or civil partner (if any) has home rights under Part IV of the Family Law Act 1996–

   (a)   the bankrupt has the following rights as against the trustee of his estate–

      (i)   if in occupation, a right not to be evicted or excluded from the dwelling house or any part of it, except with the leave of the court,

      (ii)   if not in occupation, a right with the leave of the court to enter into and occupy the dwelling house, and

   (b)   the bankrupt's rights are a charge, having the like priority as an equitable interest created immediately before the commencement of the bankruptcy, on so much of his estate or interest in the dwelling house as vests in the trustee.

337(3)   [Application of Family Law Act] The Act of 1996 has effect, with the necessary modifications, as if–

   (a)   the rights conferred by paragraph (a) of subsection (2) were home rights under that Act,

   (b)   any application for such leave as is mentioned in that paragraph were an application for an order under section 33 of that Act, and

   (c)   any charge under paragraph (b) of that subsection on the estate or interest of the trustee were a charge under that Act on the estate or interest of a spouse or civil partner.

337(4)   [Application to court] Any application for leave such as is mentioned in subsection (2)(a) or otherwise by virtue of this section for an order under section 33 of the Act of 1996 shall be made to the court having jurisdiction in relation to the bankruptcy.

337(5)   [Court order under s.337(4)] On such an application the court shall make such order under section 33 of the Act of 1996 as it thinks just and reasonable having regard to the interests of the creditors, to the bankrupt's financial resources, to the needs of the children and to all the circumstances of the case other than the needs of the bankrupt.

337(6)   [Assumption re interests of creditors] Where such an application is made after the end of the period of one year beginning with the first vesting (under Chapter IV of this Part) of the bankrupt's estate in a trustee, the court shall assume, unless the circumstances of the case are exceptional, that the interests of the bankrupt's creditors outweigh all other considerations.

S.337(1), (2)

These provisions protect the rights of occupation of the bankrupt who has dependent children living with him: he cannot be evicted from the family home without a court order and can apply to the court to regain entry if out of possession. His rights under these provisions are in the nature of an equitable interest binding on the trustee. A number of textual changes have been introduced by the Family Law Act 1996 (see Sch.8 para.58).

S.337(3)

This extends certain provisions in the Family Law Act 1996 relating to matrimonial home rights to bankruptcy situations. The substitution of the original subs.(3) was effected by Sch.8 para.58 to the 1996 Act with effect from October 1, 1997.

S.337(4)–(6)

Applications for leave under s.337(2)(a) must be made to the relevant bankruptcy court. On such an application the court should adopt a similar approach to that specified in s.336(4) and (5) above (although the criteria are different), with the creditors' interests having priority where the application is made more than a year after the property has vested in the trustee. On "exceptional circumstances" in s.337(6) see *Barca v Mears* [2005] B.P.I.R. 15 and the discussion on s.335A above. Subsection (6) was the focus of consideration in *Martin-Sklan v White* [2007] B.P.I.R. 76. Exceptional circumstances were found to exist in this case—those circumstances consisted of the fact that there were children of the bankrupt in the house who needed the support network of neighbours, family and local schools because of the ill health/frequent absence of their mother. A postponement of the sale until a date when the youngest child reached 16 was decreed. In this case the application was made five days short of the 12 month deadline specified by s.337(6) and so the case should have been covered by s.337(5) but it was held that this made no real difference to the ultimate disposition of the case by the court. Further discussion of this provision was undertaken in *Re Haghighat* [2009] B.P.I.R. 268 where the court found that exceptional circumstances did exist because the family home was occupied by a disabled child. Minor textual changes were made to subs.(4) by Sch.8 para.50 to the Family Law Act 1996.

338   Payments in respect of premises occupied by bankrupt

338   Where any premises comprised in a bankrupt's estate are occupied by him (whether by virtue of the preceding section or otherwise) on condition that he makes payments towards satisfying any liability arising under a mortgage of the premises or otherwise towards the outgoings of the premises, the bankrupt does not, by virtue of those payments, acquire any interest in the premises.

GENERAL NOTE

This provision clarifies the position where a bankrupt is allowed to remain in occupation of premises provided that he pays the mortgage, etc. Any such payment will not result in his acquiring an interest in the property.

Compare this provision with s.1(7) of the Matrimonial Homes Act 1983.

Adjustment of prior transactions, etc.

339   Transactions at an undervalue

339(1)   [Application to court] Subject as follows in this section and sections 341 and 342, where an individual is adjudged bankrupt and he has at a relevant time (defined in section 341) entered into a transaction with any person at an undervalue, the trustee of the bankrupt's estate may apply to the court for an order under this section.

339(2)   [Order by court] The court shall, on such an application, make such order as it thinks fit for restoring the position to what it would have been if that individual had not entered into that transaction.

339(3)   [Where transaction is at undervalue] For the purposes of this section and sections 341 and 342, an individual enters into a transaction with a person at an undervalue if–

(a)   he makes a gift to that person or he otherwise enters into a transaction with that person on terms that provide for him to receive no consideration,

(b)   he enters into a transaction with that person in consideration of marriage or the formation of a civil partnership, or

(c) he enters into a transaction with that person for a consideration the value of which, in money or money's worth, is significantly less than the value, in money or money's worth, of the consideration provided by the individual.

GENERAL NOTE

Sections 339–341 are new provisions designed to rationalise and update their outmoded predecessors in BA 1914. They were substantially amended at the Report Stage of the 1985 Bill. For the views of the Cork Committee on the former law, see its *Report*, paras 1226, 1285 and 1287. Unfortunately, ss.339–341 are of Byzantine complexity. Corresponding provisions for corporate insolvency are to be found in ss.238 et seq. Note also that these sections are supplemented by the more general avoidance provision in s.423.
    See further the notes to ss.238–243.
    In the context of the financial markets, no order may be made under s.339 in relation to a market contract to which a recognised investment exchange or clearing house is a party or which is entered into under its default rules, or a disposition of property in pursuance of such a market contract: see CA 1989 s.165, and the note on p.2.

S.339(1)–(3)

These provisions allow the trustee to apply to the court for relief where a person who is subsequently made bankrupt has entered into a transaction at an undervalue, at the "relevant time". The transaction must have been carried out by the debtor—*Re Brabon* [2000] B.P.I.R. 537. Section 339(3) defines what is meant by a transaction at an undervalue, e.g. gifts, marriage settlements, etc. The meaning of the key phrase "relevant time" is supplied by s.341 and was considered in *Clarkson v Clarkson* [1994] B.C.C. 921. This avoidance facility was successfully invoked by the trustee in *Re Kumar* [1993] 1 W.L.R. 224 where a transfer of an interest in a matrimonial home from debtor husband to wife was set aside by Ferris J. The interest in the equity that was given to the wife far exceeded in value the size of the mortgage commitments that she had taken over from the husband. Notwithstanding this ruling Ferris J. refused to make an immediate sale order under s.30 of LPA 1925—separate issues had to be tried here. See also *Simms v Oakes* [2002] B.P.I.R. 1244. Section 339 was successfully engaged in *Ramlort Ltd v Reid* [2004] EWCA Civ 800; [2004] B.P.I.R. 985. Here the courts were creative in determining differentials in value and were also quite flexible in terms of the final order granted to restore the position. For another successful application of s.339 see *Hocking v Canyon Holdings Ltd* [2005] B.P.I.R. 160.
    For unsuccessful s.339 claims see *Doyle v Saville and Hardwick* [2002] B.P.I.R. 947; and *Mears v Latif* [2005] EWHC 1146 (Ch); [2006] B.P.I.R. 80. For another failed application under s.339 see *Papanicola v Fagan* [2009] B.P.I.R. 320 (debtor was solvent at time of disputed transaction and wife/transferee gave consideration by promising not to pursue a divorce). In *Re Marsh* [2009] B.P.I.R. 834 the application by the trustee under s.339 failed because it could not be established that the sale of an asset was at a significant undervalue, nor was there evidence that the debtor was insolvent at the relevant time.
    The Court of Appeal is to review the question of whether a transaction carried out pursuant to an order from the Family Division could be challenged under s.339—*Jackson v Bell* [2001] EWCA Civ 387; [2001] B.P.I.R. 612. In the high profile case of *Hill v Haines* [2007] EWHC 1012 (Ch) the High Court held that a matrimonial property order made after contested proceedings, but prior to the commencement of the bankruptcy, could be characterised as a transaction at an undervalue if no consideration was given to the husband who later became bankrupt. See S. Frieze, [2007] Insol. Int. 109 for discussion. This case, which was apparently followed by Robin Knowles Q.C. in the unreported case of *Segal v Pasram* (2007), was subject to an appeal. On appeal the Court of Appeal took a different view—see *Haines v Hill* [2007] EWCA Civ 1284; [2007] B.P.I.R. 1280. Although the Court of Appeal was undoubtedly correct in concluding that the wife gave some consideration in giving up claims to ancillary relief, it is unfortunate that there was no full analysis of whether this consideration was significantly less than the consideration received from the husband. Leave to appeal to the House of Lords was refused apparently because no issue of general public importance was raised and the issues had been well tested in the courts below. One cannot help suspecting that the final outcome in *Haines v Hill* (above) owes more to public policy considerations relating to the need to promote finality of divorce settlements than to pure legal logic. As a result of this controversial Court of Appeal ruling first instance authorities such as *Shah v Baverstock* [2007] B.P.I.R. 1191; *Segal v Pasram* [2007] B.P.I.R. 881; and *Re Rich* [2008] B.P.I.R. 485 must now be viewed with doubt. That said, the issues raised in *Haines v Hill* (above) will not go away. In particular, the Court of Appeal left open the possibility of a challenge where the matrimonial property order was "collusive" or where the court had been misled. However, in *Re Jones* [2008] B.P.I.R. 1051 Chief Registrar Baister refused to set aside a matrimonial property consent order on the grounds of collusion. This concept it seems is to be narrowly interpreted and does not cover a scenario where the collateral effect of a matrimonial property settlement is to prejudice creditors.

In *Re Peppard* [2009] B.P.I.R. 331 a s.339 application succeeded—the argument that the transferee gave good consideration by waiving repayment of a debt was rejected by the court because repayment could have been challenged as a preference.

For discussion of the recent judicial pronouncements in this field and critique of *Haines v Hill* (above) see Briggs, [2008] 21 Insolv. Int. 90; Daniels, [2008] 1 Corp. Res. and Insolv. 82.

For general discussion of s.339 see *Re Share* [2002] B.P.I.R. 194. See also *Stow v Stow* [2008] EWHC 495 (Ch); [2008] B.P.I.R. 673—possibility of a trustee challenging a family trust settlement by using s.339 considered in passing.

On the difficult issue of valuation of consideration where the transferee has benefited from a statutory discount made only available to the bankrupt see *Pozzuto v Iacovides* [2003] EWHC 431 (Ch); [2003] B.P.I.R. 999.

A s.339 claim must be brought within the appropriate limitation period (see *Re Priory Garage (Walthamstow) Ltd* [2001] B.P.I.R. 144) and even then can be struck out for want of prosecution—*Hamblin v Field* [2000] B.P.I.R. 621. Further consideration of the limitation issue is to be found in *Re Yates* [2005] B.P.I.R. 476. A 12-year limitation period applies to claims under s.339—*Segal v Pasram* (above).

The ruling of Thomas Ivory Q.C. in *Singla v Brown* [2007] B.P.I.R. 424 confirms the view taken in *Re Paramount Airways Ltd (No.2)* [1993] Ch. 223 that the court has discretion in exceptional cases to make "no order", even though it has found that a breach of s.339 has occurred.

In s.339(3)(b) note the insertion of the reference to civil partners by the Civil Partnership Act 2004 Sch.27.

340   Preferences

340(1)   **[Application to court]** Subject as follows in this and the next two sections, where an individual is adjudged bankrupt and he has at a relevant time (defined in section 341) given a preference to any person, the trustee of the bankrupt's estate may apply to the court for an order under this section.

340(2)   **[Order by court]** The court shall, on such an application, make such order as it thinks fit for restoring the position to what it would have been if that individual had not given that preference.

340(3)   **[Where preference given]** For the purposes of this and the next two sections, an individual gives a preference to a person if–

  (a)   that person is one of the individual's creditors or a surety or guarantor for any of his debts or other liabilities, and

  (b)   the individual does anything or suffers anything to be done which (in either case) has the effect of putting that person into a position which, in the event of the individual's bankruptcy, will be better than the position he would have been in if that thing had not been done.

340(4)   **[Where court not to make order]** The court shall not make an order under this section in respect of a preference given to any person unless the individual who gave the preference was influenced in deciding to give it by a desire to produce in relation to that person the effect mentioned in subsection (3)(b) above.

340(5)   **[Preference to associate]** An individual who has given a preference to a person who, at the time the preference was given, was an associate of his (otherwise than by reason only of being his employee) is presumed, unless the contrary is shown, to have been influenced in deciding to give it by such a desire as is mentioned in subsection (4).

340(6)   **[Things done under court order]** The fact that something has been done in pursuance of the order of a court does not, without more, prevent the doing or suffering of that thing from constituting the giving of a preference.

GENERAL NOTE

In the context of the financial markets, no order may be made under s.340 in relation to a market contract to which a recognised investment exchange or clearing house is a party or which is entered into under its default rules, or a disposition of property in pursuance of such a market contract: see CA 1989 s.165, and the note on p.2.

S.340(1), (2)

These provisions mirror s.339(1) and (2), although of course they relate to preferences.

S.340(3)

This defines what is meant by the term "preference". See *Re Ledingham-Smith* [1993] B.C.L.C. 635. An actual preference must be established in order for the avoidance provision to operate: see here *Lewis v Hyde* [1997] B.C.C. 976. A preference can arise where an unsecured creditor is discharged out of a fund belonging exclusively to a secured creditor—*G & M Aldridge Pty Ltd v Walsh* [2002] B.P.I.R. 482.

S.340(4), (5)

Preferences can only be challenged if the bankrupt was influenced by a desire to achieve the effect stated in s.340(3)(b). This would appear to be a looser test than that required under the old law, which stated that the act in question must have been done "with a view" to effecting the preference. Thus under the new law an incidental or subsidiary motive to prefer could lead to the transaction being avoided. This will be presumed where the beneficiary is an "associate" (for the meaning of this term, see s.435, as qualified here by s.340(5)), although it is open for this presumption to be rebutted. The Cork Committee *Report*, paras 1256–1258) favoured this overall solution. In *Pick v Goel* [2006] EWHC 833 (Ch); [2006] B.P.I.R. 827 the court (confirming a ruling from Deputy Registrar Schaffer) indicated that an agreement for the transfer of a vehicle registration mark was potentially a preference contrary to s.340 of the IA 1986. As the purported transfer had occurred outside the specified six month period in order for the claimant to succeed in the claim it had to be shown that the respondent was an associate of the bankrupt. This was established on the facts. As it happened the preference issue became irrelevant because the registration mark was found to be an asset of the bankrupt at the date of his bankruptcy. The agreement to transfer the mark to the respondent had not been executed at that date and the court would not grant specific performance after the bankruptcy had commenced. Section 340 will be interpreted in the same light as s.239 and therefore the comments of Millett J. in *Re M C Bacon Ltd* [1990] B.C.C. 78 must be taken cognisance of. This fact is apparent from the case of *Re Ledingham-Smith* [1993] B.C.L.C. 635. Here a payment by a debtor of arrears of fees due to a firm of accountants within the susceptible period was held not to be avoidable under s.340. In following *Re M C Bacon Ltd* (above) Morritt J. held that the debtor was not influenced by a desire to prefer but rather by a desire to retain the services of the said firm of accountants so that they would continue to advise him during his period of financial difficulties. See also *Rooney v Das* [1999] B.P.I.R. 404 where the trustee again failed at this hurdle. The Court of Appeal is to review the question of whether a transaction carried out pursuant to an order of the Family Division can be challenged under s.340—*Jackson v Bell* [2001] EWCA Civ 387; [2001] B.P.I.R. 612. The possibility of challenging a matrimonial property consent order as a preference is diminished by virtue of the fact that a spouse, having some expectation of ancillary relief on divorce, a possibility which is given up in return for the matrimonial property order, is not a "creditor" for the purposes of s.340—see *Re Jones* [2008] B.P.I.R. 1051 where Chief Registrar Baister refused to follow *Re Rich* [2008] B.P.I.R. 485 on this point. The decision in *Re Rich* [2008] B.P.I.R. 485 must, in any case, now be treated with caution generally as it predates the Court of Appeal ruling in *Haines v Hill* [2007] EWCA Civ 1284 on the effectiveness of property arrangements between spouses where assets are exchanged for the surrender of rights to ancillary relief and where one spouse then is adjudicated bankrupt. See the discussion in the annotation to s.339 above. The court made a finding of a preference in *Cork v Gill* [2004] EWHC 2536 (Ch); [2005] B.P.I.R. 272. Having concluded in favour of the trustee's application the court should normally require the respondent to the application to pay the trustee's costs.

S.340(6)

A preference can arise out of a court order.

341   "Relevant time" under ss.339, 340

341(1)   **[Where relevant time]** Subject as follows, the time at which an individual enters into a transaction at an undervalue or gives a preference is a relevant time if the transaction is entered into or the preference given–

  (a)   in the case of a transaction at an undervalue, at a time in the period of 5 years ending with the day of the presentation of the bankruptcy petition on which the individual is adjudged bankrupt,

  (b)   in the case of a preference which is not a transaction at an undervalue and is given to a person who is an associate of the individual (otherwise than by reason only of being his employee), at a time in the period of 2 years ending with that day, and

  (c)   in any other case of a preference which is not a transaction at an undervalue, at a time in the period of 6 months ending with that day.

341(2) **[Conditions for relevant time]** Where an individual enters into a transaction at an undervalue or gives a preference at a time mentioned in paragraph (a), (b) or (c) of subsection (1) (not being, in the case of a transaction at an undervalue, a time less than 2 years before the end of the period mentioned in paragraph (a)), that time is not a relevant time for the purposes of sections 339 and 340 unless the individual–

(a)   is insolvent at that time, or

(b)   becomes insolvent in consequence of the transaction or preference;

but the requirements of this subsection are presumed to be satisfied, unless the contrary is shown, in relation to any transaction at an undervalue which is entered into by an individual with a person who is an associate of his (otherwise than by reason only of being his employee).

341(3) **[Insolvent individual under s.341(2)]** For the purposes of subsection (2), an individual is insolvent if–

(a)   he is unable to pay his debts as they fall due, or

(b)   the value of his assets is less than the amount of his liabilities, taking into account his contingent and prospective liabilities.

341(4) **[Where person later bankrupt under s.264(1)(d)]** A transaction entered into or preference given by a person who is subsequently adjudged bankrupt on a petition under section 264(1)(d) (criminal bankruptcy) is to be treated as having been entered into or given at a relevant time for the purposes of sections 339 and 340 if it was entered into or given at any time on or after the date specified for the purposes of this subsection in the criminal bankruptcy order on which the petition was based.

341(5) **[Where appeal pending]** No order shall be made under section 339 or 340 by virtue of subsection (4) of this section where an appeal is pending (within the meaning of section 277) against the individual's conviction of any offence by virtue of which the criminal bankruptcy order was made.

S.341(1)

This provides a general definition of "relevant time", for the purposes of ss.339, 340 above. In the case of transactions at an undervalue, it covers a five-year period prior to the presentation of the petition. Formerly, a ten-year period was prescribed. For preferences, it is six months (this was favoured by the Cork Committee: *Report*, para.1260), but this period is extended to two years prior to the petition where the beneficiary is an "associate" of the bankrupt (as defined by s.435, although note the qualification in s.340(5)). See *Re Marsh* [2009] B.P.I.R. 834 (discussed in annotation to s.339).

S.341(2), (3)

The time periods given in s.341(1) are qualified by the fact that in most cases (but not a transaction at an undervalue within two years of the petition), it is necessary that the person entering the transaction should either have been insolvent at the time or reduced to insolvency by the transaction. Normally the onus of proving insolvency is on the trustee, but this is not so where the beneficiary of the transaction is an "associate" (see s.435 as qualified by s.340(5)). Note the special definition of insolvency in s.341(3) which now also covers balance-sheet insolvency—this was a late amendment at the Report Stage of the 1985 Bill.

S.341(4), (5)

These provisions modify the above rules where a person was made bankrupt as a result of a petition based on a criminal bankruptcy order. Special provision is made where an appeal is pending against the criminal conviction.

   Note prospective amendment: s.341(4) and (5) are to be repealed by CJA 1988 s.170(2) and Sch.16 as from a day to be appointed; see the note to s.264.

342   Orders under ss.339, 340

342(1) **[Extent of order]** Without prejudice to the generality of section 339(2) or 340(2), an order under either of those sections with respect to a transaction or preference entered into or given by an individual who is subsequently adjudged bankrupt may (subject as follows)–

(a) require any property transferred as part of the transaction, or in connection with the giving of the preference, to be vested in the trustee of the bankrupt's estate as part of that estate;

(b) require any property to be so vested if it represents in any person's hands the application either of the proceeds of sale of property so transferred or of money so transferred;

(c) release or discharge (in whole or in part) any security given by the individual;

(d) require any person to pay, in respect of benefits received by him from the individual, such sums to the trustee of his estate as the court may direct;

(e) provide for any surety or guarantor whose obligations to any person were released or discharged (in whole or in part) under the transaction or by the giving of the preference to be under such new or revived obligations to that person as the court thinks appropriate;

(f) provide for security to be provided for the discharge of any obligation imposed by or arising under the order, for such an obligation to be charged on any property and for the security or charge to have the same priority as a security or charge released or discharged (in whole or in part) under the transaction or by the giving of the preference; and

(g) provide for the extent to which any person whose property is vested by the order in the trustee of the bankrupt's estate, or on whom obligations are imposed by the order, is to be able to prove in the bankruptcy for debts or other liabilities which arose from, or were released or discharged (in whole or in part) under or by, the transaction or the giving of the preference.

342(2)   [Effect of order] An order under section 339 or 340 may affect the property of, or impose any obligation on, any person whether or not he is the person with whom the individual in question entered into the transaction or, as the case may be, the person to whom the preference was given; but such an order–

(a) shall not prejudice any interest in property which was acquired from a person other than that individual and was acquired in good faith and for value, or prejudice any interest deriving from such an interest, and

(b) shall not require a person who received a benefit from the transaction or preference in good faith and for value to pay a sum to the trustee of the bankrupt's estate, except where he was a party to the transaction or the payment is to be in respect of a preference given to that person at a time when he was a creditor of that individual.

342(2A)   [Presumption re good faith in s.342(2)] Where a person has acquired an interest in property from a person other than the individual in question, or has received a benefit from the transaction or preference, and at the time of that acquisition or receipt–

(a) he had notice of the relevant surrounding circumstances and of the relevant proceedings, or

(b) he was an associate of, or was connected with, either the individual in question or the person with whom that individual entered into the transaction or to whom that individual gave the preference,

then, unless the contrary is shown, it shall be presumed for the purposes of paragraph (a) or (as the case may be) paragraph (b) of subsection (2) that the interest was acquired or the benefit was received otherwise than in good faith.

342(3)   [Sums to be paid to trustee] Any sums required to be paid to the trustee in accordance with an order under section 339 or 340 shall be comprised in the bankrupt's estate.

342(4)   [Relevant surrounding circumstances in s.342(2A)(a)] For the purposes of subsection (2A)(a), the relevant surrounding circumstances are (as the case may require)–

(a) the fact that the individual in question entered into the transaction at an undervalue; or

(b) the circumstances which amounted to the giving of the preference by the individual in question.

342(5)   [Notice of relevant proceedings in s.342(2A)(a)] For the purposes of subsection (2A)(a), a person has notice of the relevant proceedings if he has notice–

(a)   of the fact that the petition on which the individual in question is adjudged bankrupt has been presented; or

(b)   of the fact that the individual in question has been adjudged bankrupt.

342(6)   [Application of s.249] Section 249 in Part VII of this Act shall apply for the purposes of subsection (2A)(b) as it applies for the purposes of the first Group of Parts.

S.342(1)

Sections 339(2) and 340(2) confer general discretion on the court where the trustee applies for relief. However, we are here given a non-exhaustive list of the possible forms of relief which the court may grant. On how the claim for relief can affect limitation periods see *Re Priory Garage (Walthamstow) Ltd* [2001] B.P.I.R. 144; and *Re Yates* [2005] B.P.I.R. 476. Note the limitations imposed by s.419 of POCA 2002.

S.342(2)

This subsection was amended by s.2(1) of the Insolvency (No.2) Act 1994 to clarify the degree of protection offered to third parties. Comparable changes have been made in the corporate context: see the annotations to s.241. The Bill leading to this Act was sponsored by the Law Society which was concerned by the uncertainty created by the original version of s.342 in the context of property purchases of unregistered land. Later purchasers in a chain started off by an undervalue transfer might theoretically be prejudiced and therefore be reluctant to transact with that risk in mind until the five-year limitation period had expired. This was creating further problems in the already depressed domestic property market by generating delays or additional cost caused by the necessity of taking out title insurance. For general discussion see Potterton and Cullen, (1994) 138 S.J. 710.

Thus the words "in good faith, for value and without notice of the relevant circumstances" have been replaced by "in good faith and for value" with the question of notice now being dealt with by a new subs.(2A). Note that these changes only apply to interests acquired and benefits received after the coming into force of the 1994 Act—i.e. July 26, 1994 (see s.6 (ibid.)). Transactions occurring before that date will be governed by the original wording of s.342.

S.342(2A)

This subsection was introduced by s.2(2) of the Insolvency (No.2) Act 1994 and seeks to provide guidance on what is "good faith" for the purposes of the amended subs.(2) above. The burden of proving good faith switches to the person acquiring an interest in the property if he knows of the relevant surrounding circumstances *and* of the relevant proceedings. A similar reversal of the onus of proof occurs where the acquirer is an associate or connected person (see subs.(6) below). Further guidance on the relevant surrounding circumstances and notice of the relevant proceedings is provided by new subss.(4) and (5), also introduced by the 1994 Act.

S.342(3)

This is unaffected by the 1994 changes.

S.342(4), (5)

See the note to subs.(2A) above.

S.342(6)

This was inserted by s.2(3) of the Insolvency (No.2) Act 1994 and merely renders applicable the standard definitions of associates and connected persons as found in IA 1986.

342A   Recovery of excessive pension contributions

342A(1)   [Trustee to apply for order] Where an individual who is adjudged bankrupt–

(a)   has rights under an approved pension arrangement, or

(b)   has excluded rights under an unapproved pension arrangement,

the trustee of the bankrupt's estate may apply to the court for an order under this section.

342A(2)   [Court Order] If the court is satisfied–

(a)   that the rights under the arrangement are to any extent, and whether directly or indirectly, the fruits of relevant contributions, and

(b)   that the making of any of the relevant contributions ("the excessive contributions") has unfairly prejudiced the individual's creditors,

the court may make such order as it thinks fit for restoring the position to what it would have been had the excessive contributions not been made.

342A(3)   [Application of s.342A(4)] Subsection (4) applies where the court is satisfied that the value of the rights under the arrangement is, as a result of rights of the individual under the arrangement or any other pension arrangement having at any time become subject to a debit under section 29(1)(a) of the Welfare Reform and Pensions Act 1999 (debits giving effect to pension-sharing), less than it would otherwise have been.

342A(4)   [Extent of contributions] Where this subsection applies–

(a)   any relevant contributions which were represented by the rights which became subject to the debit shall, for the purposes of subsection (2), be taken to be contributions of which the rights under the arrangement are the fruits, and

(b)   where the relevant contributions represented by the rights under the arrangement (including those so represented by virtue of paragraph (a)) are not all excessive contributions, relevant contributions which are represented by the rights under the arrangement otherwise than by virtue of paragraph (a) shall be treated as excessive contributions before any which are so represented by virtue of that paragraph.

342A(5)   ["Relevant contributions"] In subsections (2) to (4) "relevant contributions" means contributions to the arrangement or any other pension arrangement–

(a)   which the individual has at any time made on his own behalf, or

(b)   which have at any time been made on his behalf.

342A(6)   [Court considerations in determination] The court shall, in determining whether it is satisfied under subsection (2)(b), consider in particular–

(a)   whether any of the contributions were made for the purpose of putting assets beyond the reach of the individual's creditors or any of them, and

(b)   whether the total amount of any contributions–

(i)   made by or on behalf of the individual to pension arrangements, and

(ii)   represented (whether directly or indirectly) by rights under approved pension arrangements or excluded rights under unapproved pension arrangements,

is an amount which is excessive in view of the individual's circumstances when those contributions were made.

342A(7)   [Excluded rights] For the purposes of this section and sections 342B and 342C ("the recovery provisions"), rights of an individual under an unapproved pension arrangement are excluded rights if they are rights which are excluded from his estate by virtue of regulations under section 12 of the Welfare Reform and Pensions Act 1999.

342A(8)   ["Approved pension arrangement", "unapproved pension arrangement"] In the recovery provisions—**"approved pension arrangement"** has the same meaning as in section 11 of the Welfare Reform and Pensions Act 1999; **"unapproved pension arrangement"** has the same meaning as in section 12 of that Act.

General Note

These clawback provisions originated in s.95 of the Pensions Act 1995, which in turn sought to implement the recommendations of the Goode Committee on Pension Law Review. The 1995 Act provisions were never brought into force. In view of the criticisms generated by cases like *Re Landau* [1998] Ch. 223 and with the advent of the policy in favour of pensions sharing between spouses, Parliament took the opportunity to revisit the area of interface between pensions law and bankruptcy law (see ss.324D–F below for the new provisions on pensions sharing). As part of an overall package ss.342A–342C were reformulated by s.15 of the Welfare Reform and Pensions Act 1999. These provisions were brought into force with effect from May 29, 2000—Welfare Reform and Pensions Act 1999 (Commencement No.7) Order 2000 (SI 2000/1382). Comparable provisions have been made for Scotland by ss.13 and 16 of the 1999 Act.

Sections 342A–342C must be read in the light of other changes made by the 1999 Act, namely the reversal of *Re Landau* (above) by ss.11 and 12 of that Act (which enables the Secretary of State to make regulations to exclude pension rights from the bankrupt's estate) and s.14 which prevents personal pension rights being forfeited in the event of the pensioner becoming bankrupt.

S.342A(1), (2), (5)
This enables the trustee to apply to the court to claw back for the benefit of the estate excessive contributions to pension schemes which unfairly prejudice creditors. Subsection (5) is a definition provision.

S.342A(3), (4)
These deal with the interface between the clawback and pension-sharing arrangements introduced also by the 1999 Act.

S.342A(6)
This is an important provision which seeks to assist the court in exercising its discretion under subs.2 in determining whether contributions were excessive in the circumstances.

S.342A(7), (8)
These are further definition provisions linked to ss.342B and 342C.

342B   Orders under section 342A

342B(1)   [Contents of order] Without prejudice to the generality of section 342A(2), an order under section 342A may include provision–

(a) requiring the person responsible for the arrangement to pay an amount to the individual's trustee in bankruptcy,

(b) adjusting the liabilities of the arrangement in respect of the individual,

(c) adjusting any liabilities of the arrangement in respect of any other person that derive, directly or indirectly, from rights of the individual under the arrangement,

(d) for the recovery by the person responsible for the arrangement (whether by deduction from any amount which that person is ordered to pay or otherwise) of costs incurred by that person in complying in the bankrupt's case with any requirement under section 342C(1) or in giving effect to the order.

342B(2)   [Adjusting liabilities in s.342B(1)] In subsection (1), references to adjusting the liabilities of the arrangement in respect of a person include (in particular) reducing the amount of any benefit or future benefit to which that person is entitled under the arrangement.

342B(3)   [Liabilities in s.342B(1)(c)] In subsection (1)(c), the reference to liabilities of the arrangement does not include liabilities in respect of a person which result from giving effect to an order or provision falling within section 28(1) of the Welfare Reform and Pensions Act 1999 (pension sharing orders and agreements).

342B(4)   [Maximum amount payable] The maximum amount which the person responsible for an arrangement may be required to pay by an order under section 342A is the lesser of–

(a) the amount of the excessive contributions, and

(b) the value of the individual's rights under the arrangement (if the arrangement is an approved pension arrangement) or of his excluded rights under the arrangement (if the arrangement is an unapproved pension arrangement).

342B(5)   [Provisions in "restoration amount"] An order under section 342A which requires the person responsible for an arrangement to pay an amount ("the restoration amount") to the individual's trustee in bankruptcy must provide for the liabilities of the arrangement to be correspondingly reduced.

342B(6)   [Liabilities in s.342B(5)] For the purposes of subsection (5), liabilities are correspondingly reduced if the difference between–

(a)   the amount of the liabilities immediately before the reduction, and

(b)   the amount of the liabilities immediately after the reduction,

is equal to the restoration amount.

342B(7)   [Effect of s.342A order] An order under section 342A in respect of an arrangement–

(a)   shall be binding on the person responsible for the arrangement, and

(b)   overrides provisions of the arrangement to the extent that they conflict with the provisions of the order.

GENERAL NOTE

This was introduced by s.15 of the Welfare Reform and Pensions Act 1999 with effect from May 29, 2000.

S.342B(1)
This identifies examples of the type of order the court may make under s.342A.

S.342B(2), (3)
These provide further clarification on the precise effect of certain s.342A orders.

S.342B(4)
This caps the maximum amount of an order.

S.342B(5)–(7)
These deal with pension-sharing arrangements.

342C   Orders under section 342A: supplementary

342C(1)   [Provision of information under s.342A] The person responsible for–

(a)   an approved pension arrangement under which a bankrupt has rights,

(b)   an unapproved pension arrangement under which a bankrupt has excluded rights, or

(c)   a pension arrangement under which a bankrupt has at any time had rights,

shall, on the bankrupt's trustee in bankruptcy making a written request, provide the trustee with such information about the arrangement and rights as the trustee may reasonably require for, or in connection with, the making of applications under section 342A.

342C(2)   [Non-applicable provisions] Nothing in–

(a)   any provision of section 159 of the Pension Schemes Act 1993 or section 91 of the Pensions Act 1995 (which prevent assignment and the making of orders that restrain a person from receiving anything which he is prevented from assigning),

(b)   any provision of any enactment (whether passed or made before or after the passing of the Welfare Reform and Pensions Act 1999) corresponding to any of the provisions mentioned in paragraph (a), or

(c)   any provision of the arrangement in question corresponding to any of those provisions,

applies to a court exercising its powers under section 342A.

342C(3)   [Bankrupt's estate] Where any sum is required by an order under section 342A to be paid to the trustee in bankruptcy, that sum shall be comprised in the bankrupt's estate.

342C(4) **[Provisions re calculation and verification etc.]** Regulations may, for the purposes of the recovery provisions, make provision about the calculation and verification of–

(a)   any such value as is mentioned in section 342B(4)(b);

(b)   any such amounts as are mentioned in section 342B(6)(a) and (b).

342C(5) **[Powers conferred by s.342A]** The power conferred by subsection (4) includes power to provide for calculation or verification–

(a)   in such manner as may, in the particular case, be approved by a prescribed person; or

(b)   in accordance with guidance from time to time prepared by a prescribed person.

342C(6) **[Persons responsible for pension arrangements]** References in the recovery provisions to the person responsible for a pension arrangement are to–

(a)   the trustees, managers or provider of the arrangement, or

(b)   the person having functions in relation to the arrangement corresponding to those of a trustee, manager or provider.

342C(7) **[Meaning in ss.342A, 342B and 342C]** In this section and sections 342A and 342B–

    "prescribed" means prescribed by regulations;

    "the recovery provisions" means this section and sections 342A and 342B;

    "regulations" means regulations made by the Secretary of State.

342C(8) **[Scope of regulations]** Regulations under the recovery provisions may–

(a)   make different provision for different cases;

(b)   contain such incidental, supplemental and transitional provisions as appear to the Secretary of State necessary or expedient.

342C(9) **[Making of regulations]** Regulations under the recovery provisions shall be made by statutory instrument subject to annulment in pursuance of a resolution of either House of Parliament.

General Note

This was introduced by s.15 of the Welfare Reform and Pensions Act 1999 with effect from May 29, 2000.

S.342C(1), (6)
This is an important provision enabling the trustee in bankruptcy to gain access to the full details of the bankrupt's pension arrangement. Subsection (6) clarifies who is responsible for the provision of such information.

S.342C(2)
This is a saving provision.

S.342C(3)
Any sums clawed back under s.342A form part of the estate.

S.342C(4), (5), (8), (9)
These deal with the power of the Secretary of State to make delegated legislation. See now the Occupational and Personal Pension Schemes (Bankruptcy) (No.2) Regulations 2002 (SI 2002/836) which repealed the similarly-named SI 2002/427 and came into force on April 6, 2002.

342D **Recovery of excessive contributions in pension-sharing cases**

342D(1) **[Meaning of pension-sharing transaction]** For the purposes of sections 339, 341 and 342, a pension-sharing transaction shall be taken–

(a)   to be a transaction, entered into by the transferor with the transferee, by which the appropriate amount is transferred by the transferor to the transferee; and

(b)   to be capable of being a transaction entered into at an undervalue only so far as it is a transfer of so much of the appropriate amount as is recoverable.

342D(2)   [Further meaning] For the purposes of sections 340 to 342, a pension-sharing transaction shall be taken–

(a)   to be something (namely a transfer of the appropriate amount to the transferee) done by the transferor; and

(b)   to be capable of being a preference given to the transferee only so far as it is a transfer of so much of the appropriate amount as is recoverable.

342D(3)   [Determination of recoverability] If on an application under section 339 or 340 any question arises as to whether, or the extent to which, the appropriate amount in the case of a pension-sharing transaction is recoverable, the question shall be determined in accordance with subsections (4) to (8).

342D(4)   ["Personal contributions"] The court shall first determine the extent (if any) to which the transferor's rights under the shared arrangement at the time of the transaction appear to have been (whether directly or indirectly) the fruits of contributions ("personal contributions")–

(a)   which the transferor has at any time made on his own behalf, or

(b)   which have at any time been made on the transferor's behalf,

to the shared arrangement or any other pension arrangement.

342D(5)   ["The unfair contributions"] Where it appears that those rights were to any extent the fruits of personal contributions, the court shall then determine the extent (if any) to which those rights appear to have been the fruits of personal contributions whose making has unfairly prejudiced the transferor's creditors ("the unfair contributions").

342D(6)   [Circumstances where not recoverable] If it appears to the court that the extent to which those rights were the fruits of the unfair contributions is such that the transfer of the appropriate amount could have been made out of rights under the shared arrangement which were not the fruits of the unfair contributions, then the appropriate amount is not recoverable.

342D(7)   [Circumstances where recoverable] If it appears to the court that the transfer could not have been wholly so made, then the appropriate amount is recoverable to the extent to which it appears to the court that the transfer could not have been so made.

342D(8)   [Court considerations in determination] In making the determination mentioned in subsection (5) the court shall consider in particular–

(a)   whether any of the personal contributions were made for the purpose of putting assets beyond the reach of the transferor's creditors or any of them, and

(b)   whether the total amount of any personal contributions represented, at the time the pension-sharing transaction was made, by rights under pension arrangements is an amount which is excessive in view of the transferor's circumstances when those contributions were made.

342D(9)   [Definitions] In this section and sections 342E and 342F–

"**appropriate amount**", in relation to a pension-sharing transaction, means the appropriate amount in relation to that transaction for the purposes of section 29(1) of the Welfare Reform and Pensions Act 1999 (creation of pension credits and debits);

"**pension-sharing transaction**" means an order or provision falling within section 28(1) of the Welfare Reform and Pensions Act 1999 (orders and agreements which activate pension-sharing);

"**shared arrangement**", in relation to a pension-sharing transaction, means the pension arrangement to which the transaction relates;

"transferee", in relation to a pension-sharing transaction, means the person for whose benefit the transaction is made;

"transferor", in relation to a pension-sharing transaction, means the person to whose rights the transaction relates.

GENERAL NOTE

This was inserted by para.71 of Sch.12 to the Welfare Reform and Pensions Act 1999.
S.342D(1) and (2)
These define a pension-sharing transaction for the purposes of ss.339–342.

S.342D(3)–(8)
These provisions explain what is the appropriate amount recoverable on applications under ss.339 or 340 of the 1986 Act. Essentially the law is seeking to create some sort of balance between the rights of the parties to the pension-sharing arrangement but not at the expense of unfairness to the bankrupt transferor's creditors. The critical issue is the quantum of personal contributions by the transferor and whether the making of those contributions unfairly prejudiced his creditors.

S.342D(9)
This is a definition provision.

342E   Orders under section 339 or 340 in respect of pension-sharing transactions

342E(1)   **[Application]** This section and section 342F apply if the court is making an order under section 339 or 340 in a case where–

(a) the transaction or preference is, or is any part of, a pension-sharing transaction, and

(b) the transferee has rights under a pension arrangement ("the destination arrangement", which may be the shared arrangement or any other pension arrangement) that are derived, directly or indirectly, from the pension-sharing transaction.

342E(2)   **[Contents of order]** Without prejudice to the generality of section 339(2) or 340(2), or of section 342, the order may include provision–

(a) requiring the person responsible for the destination arrangement to pay an amount to the transferor's trustee in bankruptcy,

(b) adjusting the liabilities of the destination arrangement in respect of the transferee,

(c) adjusting any liabilities of the destination arrangement in respect of any other person that derive, directly or indirectly, from rights of the transferee under the destination arrangement,

(d) for the recovery by the person responsible for the destination arrangement (whether by deduction from any amount which that person is ordered to pay or otherwise) of costs incurred by that person in complying in the transferor's case with any requirement under section 342F(1) or in giving effect to the order,

(e) for the recovery, from the transferor's trustee in bankruptcy, by the person responsible for a pension arrangement, of costs incurred by that person in complying in the transferor's case with any requirement under section 342F(2) or (3).

342E(3)   **[Adjusting liabilities in s.342E(2)]** In subsection (2), references to adjusting the liabilities of the destination arrangement in respect of a person include (in particular) reducing the amount of any benefit or future benefit to which that person is entitled under the arrangement.

342E(4)   **[Maximum amount payable]** The maximum amount which the person responsible for the destination arrangement may be required to pay by the order is the smallest of–

(a) so much of the appropriate amount as, in accordance with section 342D, is recoverable,

(b) so much (if any) of the amount of the unfair contributions (within the meaning given by section 342D(5)) as is not recoverable by way of an order under section 342A containing provision such as is mentioned in section 342B(1)(a), and

(c) the value of the transferee's rights under the destination arrangement so far as they are derived, directly or indirectly, from the pension-sharing transaction.

342E(5) **[Provision on "restoration amount"]** If the order requires the person responsible for the destination arrangement to pay an amount ("the restoration amount") to the transferor's trustee in bankruptcy it must provide for the liabilities of the arrangement to be correspondingly reduced.

342E(6) **[Liabilities in s.342E(5)]** For the purposes of subsection (5), liabilities are correspondingly reduced if the difference between–

(a) the amount of the liabilities immediately before the reduction, and

(b) the amount of the liabilities immediately after the reduction,

is equal to the restoration amount.

342E(7) **[Effect of order]** The order–

(a) shall be binding on the person responsible for the destination arrangement, and

(b) overrides provisions of the destination arrangement to the extent that they conflict with the provisions of the order.

GENERAL NOTE

This was inserted by para.71 of Sch.12 to the Welfare Reform and Pensions Act 1999.

S.342E(1) and (2)

These explain the remedial powers of the court in pension-sharing cases where ss.339 or 340 have been successfully invoked. Subsection (1) defines the parameters of the provision. The provisions in subs.(2) are not intended to prejudice the flexibility enjoyed by the court.

S.342E(3)–(6)

These are technical provisions explaining various mechanics involving in a remedial order where there is a pension-sharing scenario.

S.342E(7)

This makes is clear that the provisions of any remedial court order prevail over the terms of a pension-sharing agreement.

342F   Orders under section 339 or 340 in pension-sharing cases: supplementary

342F(1) **[Provision of information: destination arrangement]** On the transferor's trustee in bankruptcy making a written request to the person responsible for the destination arrangement, that person shall provide the trustee with such information about–

(a) the arrangement,

(b) the transferee's rights under it, and

(c) where the destination arrangement is the shared arrangement, the transferor's rights under it, as the trustee may reasonably require for, or in connection with, the making of applications under sections 339 and 340.

342F(2) **[Provision of information: no destination arrangement]** Where the shared arrangement is not the destination arrangement, the person responsible for the shared arrangement shall, on the transferor's trustee in bankruptcy making a written request to that person, provide the trustee with such information about–

(a)   the arrangement, and

(b)   the transferor's rights under it,

as the trustee may reasonably require for, or in connection with, the making of applications under sections 339 and 340.

342F(3)   [Provision of information: no immediate arrangement] On the transferor's trustee in bankruptcy making a written request to the person responsible for any intermediate arrangement, that person shall provide the trustee with such information about–

(a)   the arrangement, and

(b)   the transferee's rights under it,

as the trustee may reasonably require for, or in connection with, the making of applications under sections 339 and 340.

342F(4)   ["Intermediate arrangement"] In subsection (3) "intermediate arrangement" means a pension arrangement, other than the shared arrangement or the destination arrangement, in relation to which the following conditions are fulfilled–

(a)   there was a time when the transferee had rights under the arrangement that were derived (directly or indirectly) from the pension-sharing transaction, and

(b)   the transferee's rights under the destination arrangement (so far as derived from the pension-sharing transaction) are to any extent derived (directly or indirectly) from the rights mentioned in paragraph (a).

342F(5)   [Non-applicable provisions] Nothing in–

(a)   any provision of section 159 of the Pension Schemes Act 1993 or section 91 of the Pensions Act 1995 (which prevent assignment and the making of orders which restrain a person from receiving anything which he is prevented from assigning),

(b)   any provision of any enactment (whether passed or made before or after the passing of the Welfare Reform and Pensions Act 1999) corresponding to any of the provisions mentioned in paragraph (a), or

(c)   any provision of the destination arrangement corresponding to any of those provisions,

applies to a court exercising its powers under section 339 or 340.

342F(6)   [Provisions for calculation and verification etc.] Regulations may, for the purposes of sections 339 to 342, sections 342D and 342E and this section, make provision about the calculation and verification of–

(a)   any such value as is mentioned in section 342E(4)(c);

(b)   any such amounts as are mentioned in section 342E(6)(a) and (b).

342F(7)   [Powers conferred by s.342F(6)] The power conferred by subsection (6) includes power to provide for calculation or verification–

(a)   in such manner as may, in the particular case, be approved by a prescribed person; or

(b)   in accordance with guidance from time to time prepared by a prescribed person.

342F(8)   [Persons responsible for pension arrangements] In section 342E and this section, references to the person responsible for a pension arrangement are to–

(a)   the trustees, managers or provider of the arrangement, or

(b)   the person having functions in relation to the arrangement corresponding to those of a trustee, manager or provider.

342F(9) **[Meanings in s.342F]** In this section–

"**prescribed**" means prescribed by regulations;

"**regulations**" means regulations made by the Secretary of State.

342F(10) **[Scope of regulations]** Regulations under this section may–

(a) make different provision for different cases;

(b) contain such incidental, supplemental and transitional provisions as appear to the Secretary of State necessary or expedient.

342F(11) **[Making of regulations]** Regulations under this section shall be made by statutory instrument subject to annulment in pursuance of a resolution of either House of Parliament.

GENERAL NOTE

This was inserted by para.71 of Sch.12 to the Welfare Reform and Pensions Act 1999.

S.342F(1)–(3)
These provisions enable a trustee in bankruptcy to secure information about pensions where there is a pensions-sharing arrangement. This is a prelude to the exercise of avoidance powers.

S.342F(4)
This is a technical definition provision explaining a concept central to subs.(3).

S.342F(5)
This is a saving provision preserving the powers of the court notwithstanding an apparent conflict with other legislative provisions under pensions law.

S.342F(6), (7), (10) and (11)
These deal with the making of secondary rules.

S.342F(8) and (9)
These again are interpretation provisions.

343 Extortionate credit transactions

343(1) **[Application]** This section applies where a person is adjudged bankrupt who is or has been a party to a transaction for, or involving, the provision to him of credit.

343(2) **[Order by court]** The court may, on the application of the trustee of the bankrupt's estate, make an order with respect to the transaction if the transaction is or was extortionate and was not entered into more than 3 years before the commencement of the bankruptcy.

343(3) **[Extortionate transaction]** For the purposes of this section a transaction is extortionate if, having regard to the risk accepted by the person providing the credit–

(a) the terms of it are or were such as to require grossly exorbitant payments to be made (whether unconditionally or in certain contingencies) in respect of the provision of the credit, or

(b) it otherwise grossly contravened ordinary principles of fair dealing;

and it shall be presumed, unless the contrary is proved, that a transaction with respect to which an application is made under this section is or, as the case may be, was extortionate.

343(4) **[Extent of order]** An order under this section with respect to any transaction may contain such one or more of the following as the court thinks fit, that is to say–

(a) provision setting aside the whole or part of any obligation created by the transaction;

(b) provision otherwise varying the terms of the transaction or varying the terms on which any security for the purposes of the transaction is held;

(c) provision requiring any person who is or was party to the transaction to pay to the trustee any sums paid to that person, by virtue of the transaction, by the bankrupt;

(d) provision requiring any person to surrender to the trustee any property held by him as security for the purposes of the transaction;

(e) provision directing accounts to be taken between any persons.

343(5)   **[Sums to trustee]** Any sums or property required to be paid or surrendered to the trustee in accordance with an order under this section shall be comprised in the bankrupt's estate.

343(6)   **[Application under Consumer Credit Act]** But the powers conferred by this section are exercisable in relation to any transaction concurrently with any powers exercisable under this Act in relation to that transaction as a transaction at an undervalue.

GENERAL NOTE

This is a new provision enabling the trustee in bankruptcy to reopen a credit bargain made by a bankrupt, on the grounds that it was extortionate vis-à-vis the bankrupt. The Cork Committee (*Report*, para.1381) called for such a provision, and its introduction in some senses can be viewed as a quid pro quo for the repeal of BA 1914 s.66, which placed restrictions on a lender proving for interest: see the White Paper, para.87.

A corresponding provision has been introduced for corporate insolvency: see s.244.

S.343(1), (2)

These permit the trustee to reopen extortionate credit bargains entered into by the bankrupt for the provision of credit to him within three years of the commencement of his bankruptcy (see s.278).

S.343(3)

The onus is on the other party to show that the bargain was not "extortionate" within the meaning of this subsection.

S.343(4)

This explains what the court may do if the bargain is extortionate—again this provision has been borrowed from the Consumer Credit Act 1974.

S.343(5)

Any "proceeds" of such an action become part of the bankrupt's estate.

S.343(6)

Formerly this subsection contained in its first paragraph reference to s.139(1)(a) of the Consumer Credit Act 1974 in that it denied a trustee in bankruptcy/undischarged bankrupt access to that particular transactional avoidance mechanism. That particular section in the 1974 Act was repealed and replaced by a new regime governing unfair consumer credit relationships which is contained in the Consumer Credit Act 2006 ss.19–22. Hence the repeal of the first paragraph of s.343(6) by Sch.4 to the 2006 Act. Subsection 6 still reminds us, however, that the transaction may also be challenged under s.339.

344   Avoidance of general assignment of book debts

344(1)   **[Application]** The following applies where a person engaged in any business makes a general assignment to another person of his existing or future book debts, or any class of them, and is subsequently adjudged bankrupt.

344(2)   **[Certain assignments void against trustee]** The assignment is void against the trustee of the bankrupt's estate as regards book debts which were not paid before the presentation of the bankruptcy petition, unless the assignment has been registered under the Bills of Sale Act 1878.

344(3)   **[Definitions]** For the purposes of subsections (1) and (2)–

(a) **"assignment"** includes an assignment by way of security or charge on book debts, and

(b) **"general assignment"** does not include–

    (i) an assignment of book debts due at the date of the assignment from specified debtors or of debts becoming due under specified contracts, or

(ii) an assignment of book debts included either in a transfer of a business made in good faith and for value or in an assignment of assets for the benefit of creditors generally.

344(4) **[Registration under Bills of Sales Act]** For the purposes of registration under the Act of 1878 an assignment of book debts is to be treated as if it were a bill of sale given otherwise than by way of security for the payment of a sum of money; and the provisions of that Act with respect to the registration of bills of sale apply accordingly with such necessary modifications as may be made by rules under that Act.

S.344(1), (2)
This provides that a general assignment of book debts by a trader shall be void on bankruptcy unless registered under the Bills of Sale Act 1878. Note the word "general" is now used in the text of subs.(1)—in s.43 of the 1914 Act this word merely appeared in the marginal note. For a rare authority on the effect of s.344(2) see *Hills v Alex Lawrie Factors* [2001] B.P.I.R. 1038.

S.344(3)
This provision clarifies s.344(1) by stressing that assignments by way of security are covered but not specific assignments of specific book debts, nor assignments connected with a bona fide transfer of a business for value, nor a general assignment of assets for the benefit of creditors generally.

S.344(4)
This provision describes the mechanics of registration under the 1878 Act.

345 Contracts to which bankrupt is a party

345(1) **[Application]** The following applies where a contract has been made with a person who is subsequently adjudged bankrupt.

345(2) **[Court order on application]** The court may, on the application of any other party to the contract, make an order discharging obligations under the contract on such terms as to payment by the applicant or the bankrupt of damages for non-performance or otherwise as appear to the court to be equitable.

345(3) **[Damages as bankruptcy debt]** Any damages payable by the bankrupt by virtue of an order of the court under this section are provable as a bankruptcy debt.

345(4) **[Where joint contract]** Where an undischarged bankrupt is a contractor in respect of any contract jointly with any person, that person may sue or be sued in respect of the contract without the joinder of the bankrupt.

GENERAL NOTE

In the context of the financial markets, s.345 does not apply in relation to a market contract or a contract effected by an exchange or clearing house for the purpose of realising property provided as margin in relation to market contracts: see CA 1989 s.164(1), and the note on p.2.

S.345(1)–(3)
At common law the general rule, as laid down in *Brooke v Hewitt* (1796) 3 Ves. 253, was that the bankruptcy of a party to a contract did not terminate that contract. Hence the need to confer on trustees a power to disclaim onerous contracts. There is no need to have recourse to s.345 if the contract provides that bankruptcy is a terminating event—on this common provision and the consequences of bankruptcy in general see *Cadogan Estates v McMahon* [2001] B.P.I.R. 17. Section 345(2) in effect redresses the balance as far as the other contracting party is concerned. He can now apply to the court to have contractual obligations discharged. The court enjoys general discretion and can order compensation payments to be paid by either party. If the bankrupt is ordered to pay compensation, that sum constitutes a provable debt.

S.345(4)
This repeats BA 1914 s.118 and allows a person who has entered into a contract jointly with a bankrupt to sue the other party to the contract without the joinder of the bankrupt to the proceedings.

346   Enforcement procedures

346(1)   [Creditor's execution against bankrupt] Subject to section 285 in Chapter II (restrictions on proceedings and remedies) and to the following provisions of this section, where the creditor of any person who is adjudged bankrupt has, before the commencement of the bankruptcy–

(a)   issued execution against the goods or land of that person, or

(b)   attached a debt due to that person from another person,

that creditor is not entitled, as against the official receiver or trustee of the bankrupt's estate, to retain the benefit of the execution or attachment, or any sums paid to avoid it, unless the execution or attachment was completed, or the sums were paid, before the commencement of the bankruptcy.

346(2)   [Where goods taken in execution] Subject as follows, where any goods of a person have been taken in execution, then, if before the completion of the execution notice is given to the enforcement officer or other officer charged with the execution that that person has been adjudged bankrupt–

(a)   the enforcement officer or other officer shall on request deliver to the official receiver or trustee of the bankrupt's estate the goods and any money seized or recovered in part satisfaction of the execution, but

(b)   the costs of the execution are a first charge on the goods or money so delivered and the official receiver or trustee may sell the goods or a sufficient part of them for the purpose of satisfying the charge.

346(3)   [Balance of sale proceeds] Subject to subsection (6) below, where–

(a)   under an execution in respect of a judgment for a sum exceeding such sum as may be prescribed for the purposes of this subsection, the goods of any person are sold or money is paid in order to avoid a sale, and

(b)   before the end of the period of 14 days beginning with the day of the sale or payment the enforcement officer or other officer charged with the execution is given notice that a bankruptcy petition has been presented in relation to that person, and

(c)   a bankruptcy order is or has been made on that petition,

the balance of the proceeds of sale or money paid, after deducting the costs of execution, shall (in priority to the claim of the execution creditor) be comprised in the bankrupt's estate.

346(4)   [Duty of enforcement officer re sum in s.346(3)] Accordingly, in the case of an execution in respect of a judgment for a sum exceeding the sum prescribed for the purposes of subsection (3), the enforcement officer or other officer charged with the execution–

(a)   shall not dispose of the balance mentioned in subsection (3) at any time within the period of 14 days so mentioned or while there is pending a bankruptcy petition of which he has been given notice under that subsection, and

(b)   shall pay that balance, where by virtue of that subsection it is comprised in the bankrupt's estate, to the official receiver or (if there is one) to the trustee of that estate.

346(5)   [Completion of execution or attachment] For the purposes of this section–

(a)   an execution against goods is completed by seizure and sale or by the making of a charging order under section 1 of the Charging Orders Act 1979;

(b)   an execution against land is completed by seizure, by the appointment of a receiver or by the making of a charging order under that section;

(c)   an attachment of a debt is completed by the receipt of the debt.

346(6)   **[Setting aside of s.346(1)–(3) rights by court]** The rights conferred by subsections (1) to (3) on the official receiver or the trustee may, to such extent and on such terms as it thinks fit, be set aside by the court in favour of the creditor who has issued the execution or attached the debt.

346(7)   **[Acquisition in good faith]** Nothing in this section entitles the trustee of a bankrupt's estate to claim goods from a person who has acquired them in good faith under a sale by an enforcement officer or other officer charged with an execution.

346(8)   **[Non-application of s.346(2), (3)]** Neither subsection (2) nor subsection (3) applies in relation to any execution against property which has been acquired by or has devolved upon the bankrupt since the commencement of the bankruptcy, unless, at the time the execution is issued or before it is completed–

(a)   the property has been or is claimed for the bankrupt's estate under section 307 (after-acquired property), and

(b)   a copy of the notice given under that section has been or is served on the enforcement officer or other officer charged with the execution.

346(9)   **["Enforcement officer"]** In this section **"enforcement officer"** means an individual who is authorised to act as an enforcement officer under the Courts Act 2003.

GENERAL NOTE

The former references to the "sheriff" were replaced by "enforcement officer" by Sch.8 to the Courts Act 2003.

S.346(1), (5)

Where a creditor has begun an execution process before the commencement of the bankruptcy (see s.278(a)), but has failed to complete before that date, he will not be allowed to proceed further and any proceeds received after the commencement of the bankruptcy must be handed over to the estate. The stages at which the various execution processes are deemed to be completed are described by s.346(5). In *Nationwide Building Society v Wright* [2009] B.P.I.R. 1047 the Court of Appeal held that it was not the intention of s.346 to defeat a creditor who had obtained a final charging order prior to the making of the bankruptcy order.

     Executions may also be restrained under s.285. The court retains the power to set aside a garnishee order notwithstanding the provisions of s.346—*Industrial Diseases Compensation Ltd v Marrons* [2001] B.P.I.R. 600.

S.346(2)

This deals with the position of an enforcement officer who has seized goods in execution. The goods must be handed over to the estate, although the enforcement officer's costs are a first charge on such goods. Note also IR 1986 r.12A.28. For the enforcement officer's costs see r.7.36.

S.346(3), (4)

These provisions deal with the situation where the enforcement officer has received the proceeds of sale of goods seized in execution of a judgment for a "prescribed amount" (see s.418), or has been paid not to sell them. The amount is £1,000 under the Insolvency Proceedings (Monetary Limits) (Amendment) Order 2004 (SI 2004/547) operating from April 1, 2004. If, within 14 days thereafter, the sheriff is given notice of the bankruptcy petition, the balance of the proceeds after deducting costs must be paid to the estate if the petition succeeds. The enforcement officer therefore under a duty to retain proceeds for the required period, just in case this obligation is activated.

     On s.346(3)(b) see IR 1986 r.12A.28.

S.346(6)

The court has discretion to set aside the rights of the estate in favour of the execution creditor. On the exercise of discretion under s.346(6) see *Tagore Investments v Official Receiver* [2009] B.P.I.R. 392. In this case the unusual circumstances justified the court departing from the pari passu rule and allowing the execution to proceed.

S.346(7)

Bona fide purchasers from the enforcement officer are protected.

S.346(8)

This provision lays down special rules for execution against property acquired by the bankrupt after the commencement of the bankruptcy.

347 Distress, etc.

347(1) [Limit on distraining goods] The right of any landlord or other person to whom rent is payable to distrain upon the goods and effects of an undischarged bankrupt for rent due to him from the bankrupt is available (subject to sections 252(2)(b) and 254(1) above and subsection (5) below) against goods and effects comprised in the bankrupt's estate, but only for 6 months' rent accrued due before the commencement of the bankruptcy.

347(2) [Distraining where order later made] Where a landlord or other person to whom rent is payable has distrained for rent upon the goods and effects of an individual to whom a bankruptcy petition relates and a bankruptcy order is subsequently made on that petition, any amount recovered by way of that distress which–

(a)   is in excess of the amount which by virtue of subsection (1) would have been recoverable after the commencement of the bankruptcy, or

(b)   is in respect of rent for a period or part of a period after the distress was levied,

shall be held for the bankrupt as part of his estate.

347(3) [Proceeds of sale re goods not held under s.347(2)] Where any person (whether or not a landlord or person entitled to rent) has distrained upon the goods or effects of an individual who is adjudged bankrupt before the end of the period of 3 months beginning with the distraint, so much of those goods or effects, or of the proceeds of their sale, as is not held for the bankrupt under subsection (2) shall be charged for the benefit of the bankrupt's estate with the preferential debts of the bankrupt to the extent that the bankrupt's estate is for the time being insufficient for meeting those debts.

347(4) [Where surrender under s.347(3)] Where by virtue of any charge under subsection (3) any person surrenders any goods or effects to the trustee of a bankrupt's estate or makes a payment to such a trustee, that person ranks, in respect of the amount of the proceeds of the sale of those goods or effects by the trustee or, as the case may be, the amount of the payment, as a preferential creditor of the bankrupt, except as against so much of the bankrupt's estate as is available for the payment of preferential creditors by virtue of the surrender or payment.

347(5) [Rights of landlord after discharge] A landlord or other person to whom rent is payable is not at any time after the discharge of a bankrupt entitled to distrain upon any goods or effects comprised in the bankrupt's estate.

347(6) [Restriction of landlord's rights] Where in the case of any execution–

(a)   a landlord is (apart from this section) entitled under section 1 of the Landlord and Tenant Act 1709 or section 102 of the County Courts Act 1984 (claims for rent where goods seized in execution) to claim for an amount not exceeding one year's rent, and

(b)   the person against whom the execution is levied is adjudged bankrupt before the notice of claim is served on the enforcement officer or other officer charged with the execution,

the right of the landlord to claim under that section is restricted to a right to claim for an amount not exceeding 6 months' rent and does not extend to any rent payable in respect of a period after the notice of claim is so served.

347(7) [Limit to s.347(6)] Nothing in subsection (6) imposes any liability on an enforcement officer or other officer charged with an execution to account to the official receiver or the trustee of a bankrupt's estate for any sums paid by him to a landlord at any time before the enforcement officer or other officer was served with notice of the bankruptcy order in question.

But this subsection is without prejudice to the liability of the landlord.

347(8) [Rights to distrain other than for rent] Subject to sections 252(2)(b) and 254(1) above, nothing in this Group of Parts affects any right to distrain otherwise than for rent; and any such right is at any time exercisable without restriction against property comprised in a bankrupt's estate, even if that right is expressed by any enactment to be exercisable in like manner as a right to distrain for rent.

347(9)   **[Exercise of right]** Any right to distrain against property comprised in a bankrupt's estate is exercisable notwithstanding that the property has vested in the trustee.

347(10)   **[Landlord's right to prove]** The provisions of this section are without prejudice to a landlord's right in a bankruptcy to prove for any bankruptcy debt in respect of rent.

347(11)   **[Enforcement officer]** In this section "enforcement officer" means an individual who is authorised to act as an enforcement officer under the Courts Act 2003.

S.347(1), (2), (5), (9)
This continues the favoured treatment of landlords. A landlord may still distrain on the goods of an undischarged bankrupt (even if they have vested in the trustee—s.347(9)), but only for a maximum of six months' rent accruing before the commencement of the bankruptcy. There is a similar rule where an administration order is in force: see County Courts Act 1984 s.116. Where distress is levied after the petition but before the order, the landlord must hand over any proceeds in excess of the amount of rent referred to in s.347(1). Distress cannot be levied after the discharge of the bankrupt. Subsection (1) was subject to minor amendment by IA 2000 Sch.3.
Editors' note: amendments are to be made to s.347(1),(2) and (5) by Sch.14 to the Tribunals, Courts and Enforcement Act 2007 from a date yet to be determined. These changes relate to the new commercial rent arrears recovery procedures.

S.347(3), (4)
These make special provision out of the proceeds of a distress for the preferential creditors (see s.328) in so far as the estate is insufficient to meet their claims. However, the landlord who loses out as a result of this provision is then subrogated to the claims of the preferential creditors against the general estate of the bankrupt.

S.347(6), (7)
These provisions deal with special forms of distress. Although normally 12 months' rent can be claimed, this is reduced to six months' rent in the event of bankruptcy. Special protection is offered to enforcement officers who inadvertently breach this provision, but the landlord himself may still incur liability. The ancient title of sheriff was replaced by enforcement officer by Sch.8 to the Courts Act 2003 with effect from September 1, 2004.

S.347(8)
Distress otherwise than for rent is not hampered by bankruptcy. Again, note amendment by IA 2000 Sch.3.

S.347(10)
As an alternative to levying distress for rent, a landlord can of course prove for the unpaid amount in the bankruptcy.

S.347(11)
Inserted by Sch.8 to the Courts Act 2003.
Editors' note: see prospective repeal of subss.(6), (7) and (11) by Sch.23 to the Tribunals, Courts and Enforcement Act 2007. No commencement for this repeal has been set.

348   Apprenticeships, etc.

348(1)   **[Application]** This section applies where–

(a) a bankruptcy order is made in respect of an individual to whom another individual was an apprentice or articled clerk at the time when the petition on which the order was made was presented, and

(b) the bankrupt or the apprentice or clerk gives notice to the trustee terminating the apprenticeship or articles.

348(2)   **[Discharge etc.]** Subject to subsection (6) below, the indenture of apprenticeship or, as the case may be, the articles of agreement shall be discharged with effect from the commencement of the bankruptcy.

348(3) **[If money paid]** If any money has been paid by or on behalf of the apprentice or clerk to the bankrupt as a fee, the trustee may, on an application made by or on behalf of the apprentice or clerk, pay such sum to the apprentice or clerk as the trustee thinks reasonable, having regard to–

    (a) the amount of the fee,

    (b) the proportion of the period in respect of which the fee was paid that has been served by the apprentice or clerk before the commencement of the bankruptcy, and

    (c) the other circumstances of the case.

348(4) **[Priority of s.348(3) power]** The power of the trustee to make a payment under subsection (3) has priority over his obligation to distribute the bankrupt's estate.

348(5) **[Instead of s.348(3) payment]** Instead of making a payment under subsection (3), the trustee may, if it appears to him expedient to do so on an application made by or on behalf of the apprentice or clerk, transfer the indenture or articles to a person other than the bankrupt.

348(6) **[Where s.348(5) transfer]** Where a transfer is made under subsection (5), subsection (2) has effect only as between the apprentice or clerk and the bankrupt.

S.348(1)
This section applies where a principal is declared bankrupt and notice is given to terminate a contract of apprenticeship or articled clerkship. Either party can give notice to terminate.

S.348(2)
The effect of such notice is to discharge the contract from the date of the commencement of the bankruptcy (for the meaning of this term, see s.278(a)).

S.348(3), (4)
The trustee can repay any fee paid by the apprentice or articled clerk in whole or in part. Factors such as the duration of the apprenticeship which is unexpired and the general circumstances of the case are relevant here. The approach will be similar to that taken with regard to premiums under s.40 of the Partnership Act 1890. The sum of money repaid under s.348(3) ranks as a pre-preferential debt.

S.348(5), (6)
As an alternative, the trustee can transfer the apprenticeship, etc. to another principal if the apprentice, etc. so wishes. The continuity of the apprenticeship in such a case will not be disrupted by s.348(2). This latter provision clarifies the former law under BA 1914 s.34.

349 Unenforceability of liens on books, etc.

349(1) **[Unenforceability]** Subject as follows, a lien or other right to retain possession of any of the books, papers or other records of a bankrupt is unenforceable to the extent that its enforcement would deny possession of any books, papers or other records to the official receiver or the trustee of the bankrupt's estate.

349(2) **[Non-application of s.349(1)]** Subsection (1) does not apply to a lien on documents which give a title to property and are held as such.

GENERAL NOTE

This section renders ineffective liens, etc. on the books and records of a bankrupt in so far as they would deny possession of them to the official receiver or trustee. Liens on documents of title are not affected. Here the public interest is accorded priority over private security rights.

    See also s.333(4) for another indication of how liens on books require special treatment from the law. Regulations made by the Secretary of State pursuant to the rules may allow the trustee wide powers to deal with, and dispose of, the bankrupt's books: see IR 1986 r.12.1(1)(c). Note also the Insolvency Regulations 1994 (SI 1994/2507) reg.30.

S.349(2)
On the interpretation of this provision, see the note to s.246(3).

349A   Arbitration agreements to which bankrupt is party

349A(1)   [Application of section] This section applies where a bankrupt had become party to a contract containing an arbitration agreement before the commencement of his bankruptcy.

349A(2)   [If contract adopted by trustee] If the trustee in bankruptcy adopts the contract, the arbitration agreement is enforceable by or against the trustee in relation to matters arising from or connected with the contract.

349A(3)   [If contract not adopted by trustee] If the trustee in bankruptcy does not adopt the contract and a matter to which the arbitration agreement applies requires to be determined in connection with or for the purposes of the bankruptcy proceedings–

(a)   the trustee with the consent of the creditors' committee, or

(b)   any other party to the agreement,

may apply to the court which may, if it thinks fit in all the circumstances of the case, order that the matter be referred to arbitration in accordance with the arbitration agreement.

349A(4)   ["Arbitration agreement", "the court"] In this section–

"arbitration agreement" has the same meaning as in Part I of the Arbitration Act 1996; and

"the court" means the court which has jurisdiction in the bankruptcy proceedings.

CHAPTER VI

BANKRUPTCY OFFENCES

Preliminary

350   Scheme of this Chapter

350(1)   [Application] Subject to section 360(3) below, this Chapter applies where the court has made a bankruptcy order on a bankruptcy petition.

350(2)   [Effect of annulment of bankruptcy] This Chapter applies whether or not the bankruptcy order is annulled, but proceedings for an offence under this Chapter shall not be instituted after the annulment.

350(3)   [Liability of bankrupt after discharge] Without prejudice to his liability in respect of a subsequent bankruptcy, the bankrupt is not guilty of an offence under this Chapter in respect of anything done after his discharge; but nothing in this Group of Parts prevents the institution of proceedings against a discharged bankrupt for an offence committed before his discharge.

350(3A)   [Effect of bankruptcy restrictions order] Subsection (3) is without prejudice to any provision of this Chapter which applies to a person in respect of whom a bankruptcy restrictions order is in force.

350(4)   [Where not defence] It is not a defence in proceedings for an offence under this Chapter that anything relied on, in whole or in part, as constituting that offence was done outside England and Wales.

350(5)   [Institution of proceedings for offence] Proceedings for an offence under this Chapter or under the rules shall not be instituted except by the Secretary of State or by or with the consent of the Director of Public Prosecutions.

350(6)   [Penalty] A person guilty of any offence under this Chapter is liable to imprisonment or a fine, or both.

GENERAL NOTE

The Cork Committee (*Report*, para.1900) called for greater use to be made of the criminal law in controlling fraud in bankruptcy. In addition, it recommended a cautious tidying up of the offences (para.1883), and this has been to some extent implemented by the following provisions in the Act. Incidentally, the Blagden Committee (Cmnd.221 (1957) paras 206–213) also suggested that the criminal law should be applied more strictly to control fraudulent bankrupts. Note that the rules themselves create several offences, the punishments for which are prescribed by Sch.5 to the rules. For an analysis of the new regime of bankruptcy offences see Griffiths, (1986) 2 I.L. & P. 73.

S.350(1), (2)

These are new provisions dealing with bankruptcy offences in general. In particular, s.350(2) makes it clear that the subsequent annulment of the bankruptcy is relevant only in so far as a prosecution cannot be instituted after this date. But see *Inland Revenue Commissioners v McEntaggart* [2004] EWHC 341 (Ch); [2006] B.P.I.R. 750.

S.350(3)

This repeats the provision under the 1914 Act—the bankrupt cannot be guilty for acts done after his discharge, but he can be prosecuted after his discharge for earlier misconduct.

S.350(3A)

This was inserted by EA 2002 s.257 and Sch.21 with effect from April 1, 2004 to deal with the effect of BROs.

S.350(4)

By way of contrast, it is not a defence to show that the conduct complained of was done outside England and Wales.

S.350(5)

This is a new general provision replacing the fragmentary approach of the 1914 Act. Prosecutions now require the consent of the Director of Public Prosecutions or the Secretary of State. Formerly, the court's consent was needed for certain prosecutions.

S.350(6)

For details of penalties, see s.430 and Sch.10.

351   Definitions

351   In the following provisions of this Chapter–

(a)   references to property comprised in the bankrupt's estate or to property possession of which is required to be delivered up to the official receiver or the trustee of the bankrupt's estate include any property which would be such property if a notice in respect of it were given under section 307 (after-acquired property), section 308 (personal property and effects of bankrupt having more than replacement value) or section 308A (vesting in trustee of certain tenancies);

(b)   **"the initial period"** means the period between the presentation of the bankruptcy petition and the commencement of the bankruptcy; and

(c)   a reference to a number of months or years before petition is to that period ending with the presentation of the bankruptcy petition.

GENERAL NOTE

This section contains definitions of three concepts and phrases which recur throughout ss.352–362:

(a)   "property": see ss.353, 354, 356, 357, 358, 359, 362;

(b)   "initial period": see ss.354, 355, 356, 358, 359, 362 (for further explanation, see s.278(a));

(c)   "before petition": see ss.354, 355, 356, 358, 359, 361, 362.

In s.351(a) the words relating to s.308A inserted and consequential amendment made by the Housing Act 1988 Sch.17 para.75.

352 Defence of innocent intention

352 Where in the case of an offence under any provision of this Chapter it is stated that this section applies, a person is not guilty of the offence if he proves that, at the time of the conduct constituting the offence, he had no intent to defraud or to conceal the state of his affairs.

GENERAL NOTE

This is an important new general defence. If the bankrupt is charged with certain offences in ss.353–362, he has a defence if he can prove that he had not intended to defraud or conceal his affairs. The provisions creating the offences state whether s.352 applies. On the burden of proof see *R. v Daniel* [2002] EWCA Crim 959; [2002] B.P.I.R. 1193.

In *Attorney General's Reference (No.1 of 2004)* [2004] EWCA Crim 1025; [2004] B.P.I.R. 1074 the Court of Appeal sought to explain the relationship between ss.352, 353 and 357 in the context of the requirements of art.6 of the European Convention on Human Rights. According to the court only an evidential burden of proof (as opposed to a legal burden) is generated by the interaction of the statutory provisions in ss.352 and 357 and accordingly there is no breach of art.6. When s.352 is read with s.353 even if a legal burden is created there is no breach of art.6. See also *R. (Griffin) v Richmond Magistrates Court* [2008] B.P.I.R. 468 (a case on s.208).

Wrongdoing by the bankrupt before and after bankruptcy

353 Non-disclosure

353(1) **[Offence]** The bankrupt is guilty of an offence if–

(a) he does not to the best of his knowledge and belief disclose all the property comprised in his estate to the official receiver or the trustee, or

(b) he does not inform the official receiver or the trustee of any disposal of any property which but for the disposal would be so comprised, stating how, when, to whom and for what consideration the property was disposed of.

353(2) **[Exception to s.353(1)(b)]** Subsection (1)(b) does not apply to any disposal in the ordinary course of a business carried on by the bankrupt or to any payment of the ordinary expenses of the bankrupt or his family.

353(3) **[Application of s.352]** Section 352 applies to this offence.

S.353(1), (2)
This makes it an offence for the bankrupt to fail to disclose items of "property" (for definition, see s.351(a)) to his trustee or official receiver. Moreover, certain disposals of property which have resulted in a diminution of the estate must also be revealed. Note the positive nature of the obligations imposed here. There is a defence for bona fide business and domestic transactions.

For the appropriate penalty, see ss.350, 430 and Sch.10.

S.353(3)
The general defence in s.352 applies here. See the note to s.352.

354 Concealment of property

354(1) **[Offence of concealment etc.]** The bankrupt is guilty of an offence if–

(a) he does not deliver up possession to the official receiver or trustee, or as the official receiver or trustee may direct, of such part of the property comprised in his estate as is in his possession or under his control and possession of which he is required by law so to deliver up,

(b)   he conceals any debt due to or from him or conceals any property the value of which is not less than the prescribed amount and possession of which he is required to deliver up to the official receiver or trustee, or

(c)   in the 12 months before petition, or in the initial period, he did anything which would have been an offence under paragraph (b) above if the bankruptcy order had been made immediately before he did it.

Section 352 applies to this offence.

354(2)   [Offence re removal of property] The bankrupt is guilty of an offence if he removes, or in the initial period removed, any property the value of which was not less than the prescribed amount and possession of which he has or would have been required to deliver up to the official receiver or the trustee.
Section 352 applies to this offence.

354(3)   [Offence re failure to account for loss] The bankrupt is guilty of an offence if he without reasonable excuse fails, on being required to do so by the official receiver, the trustee or the court–

(a)   to account for the loss of any substantial part of his property incurred in the 12 months before petition or in the initial period, or

(b)   to give a satisfactory explanation of the manner in which such a loss was incurred.

S.354(1)
This is a related offence of failing to hand over "property" (for definition, see s.351(a)), or concealing debts or property which is not less than the "prescribed amount" (see s.418). The amount is £1,000 under the Insolvency Proceedings (Monetary Limits) (Amendment) Order 2004 (SI 2004/547) (which operates from April 1, 2004). Note that, in the case of concealment, conduct in the "initial period" (i.e. between the petition and order: see s.351(b)) and, indeed, in the 12 months "before petition" (see s.351(c)), is covered.
   The general defence in s.352 applies. See *R. v Daniel* [2002] EWCA Crim 959; [2002] B.P.I.R. 1193.
   For penalties, see ss.350, 430 and Sch.10.

S.354(2)
Removal of "property" from the estate after the order or in the "initial period" is unlawful where the property exceeds the "prescribed amount" (£1,000—see the note to s.354(1)). The general defence in s.352 applies. Settling a nonprovable debt during the period in question is an offence under s.354: *Woodley v Woodley (No.2)* [1994] 1 W.L.R. 1167.

S.354(3)
Failure to provide explanations for substantial losses of "property" dating back to 12 months "before petition", or in the "initial period", is unlawful, unless there is a reasonable excuse for this. The words ", the trustee" were inserted by s.269 of and Sch.23 to EA 2002 with effect from April 1, 2004. The existence of the offence under s.354(3)(a) does not infringe fundamental human rights expectations—*R. v Kearns (Nicholas Gary)* [2002] EWCA Crim 748; [2002] B.P.I.R. 1213. The time limit referred to in s.354(3) is the same as that in BA 1914, in spite of recommendations from the Cork Committee (*Report*, para.1888) that it should be extended to two years.

355   Concealment of books and papers; falsification

355(1)   [Offence re non-delivery of books etc.] The bankrupt is guilty of an offence if he does not deliver up possession to the official receiver or the trustee, or as the official receiver or trustee may direct, of all books, papers and other records of which he has possession or control and which relate to his estate or his affairs.
Section 352 applies to this offence.

355(2)   [Offence re destruction, concealment etc.] The bankrupt is guilty of an offence if–

(a)   he prevents, or in the initial period prevented, the production of any books, papers or records relating to his estate or affairs;

(b) he conceals, destroys, mutilates or falsifies, or causes or permits the concealment, destruction, mutilation or falsification of, any books, papers or other records relating to his estate or affairs;

(c) he makes, or causes or permits the making of, any false entries in any book, document or record relating to his estate or affairs; or

(d) in the 12 months before petition, or in the initial period, he did anything which would have been an offence under paragraph (b) or (c) above if the bankruptcy order had been made before he did it.

Section 352 applies to this offence.

355(3)   **[Offence re disposal, alteration etc.]** The bankrupt is guilty of an offence if–

(a) he disposes of, or alters or makes any omission in, or causes or permits the disposal, altering or making of any omission in, any book, document or record relating to his estate or affairs, or

(b) in the 12 months before petition, or in the initial period, he did anything which would have been an offence under paragraph (a) if the bankruptcy order had been made before he did it.

Section 352 applies to this offence.

355(4)   **[Application of s.355(2)(d), (3)(b)]** In their application to a trading record subsections (2)(d) and (3)(b) shall have effect as if the reference to 12 months were a reference to two years.

355(5)   **["Trading record"]** In subsection (4) **"trading record"** means a book, document or record which shows or explains the transactions or financial position of a person's business, including–

(a) a periodic record of cash paid and received,

(b) a statement of periodic stock-taking, and

(c) except in the case of goods sold by way of retail trade, a record of goods sold and purchased which identifies the buyer and seller or enables them to be identified.

GENERAL NOTE

This involved provision is somewhat tautological.

For penalties, see ss.350, 430 and Sch.10, and for defences, see s.352. Note that, in the case of those basic records described by s.361(3), the 12-month periods referred to in s.355 are extended to two years: see s.361(4).

S.355(1), (2)

Failure to deliver up books and records is an offence. Moreover, if one prevents such books and records being produced, or conceals, destroys or falsifies them, this will also be unlawful. Note that for concealment and falsification, the relevant period is extended to 12 months "before petition" (see s.351(c)), plus the "initial period" (see s.351(b)).

S.355(3)

It is unlawful for a bankrupt to dispose of or alter books or records—this again extends to the 12 months "before petition" and the "initial period".

S.355(4), (5)

These were added by EA 2002 s.269 and Sch.23 with effect from April 1, 2004. They clarify the position.

356   False statements

356(1)   **[Offence re material omission]** The bankrupt is guilty of an offence if he makes or has made any material omission in any statement made under any provision in this Group of Parts and relating to his affairs.

Section 352 applies to this offence.

356(2)   [Offence re failing to inform etc.] The bankrupt is guilty of an offence if–

(a) knowing or believing that a false debt has been proved by any person under the bankruptcy, he fails to inform the trustee as soon as practicable; or

(b) he attempts to account for any part of his property by fictitious losses or expenses; or

(c) at any meeting of his creditors in the 12 months before petition or (whether or not at such a meeting) at any time in the initial period, he did anything which would have been an offence under paragraph (b) if the bankruptcy order had been made before he did it; or

(d) he is, or at any time has been, guilty of any false representation or other fraud for the purpose of obtaining the consent of his creditors, or any of them, to an agreement with reference to his affairs or to his bankruptcy.

S.356(1)
This is a general offence derived from BA 1914 s.154(6), prohibiting the bankrupt from making false statements by omission. The statement must relate to his "affairs" (for definition, see s.385(2)).

Section 356(1) (unlike s.356(2)) does not, on its face, require any intent to cheat or defraud, but of course the general defence under s.352 can be utilised to offer a defence to the innocent bankrupt.

S.356(2)
This provision specifies certain prohibited forms of conduct involving falsehoods. Such behaviour was an offence under BA 1914 s.154(1), (7), (12), and (16). For definitions of "property", "before petition" and "initial period", see the note to s.351.

The penalties for the above offences are dealt with by ss.350, 430 and Sch.10.

357   Fraudulent disposal of property

357(1)   [Offence re transfer] The bankrupt is guilty of an offence if he makes or causes to be made, or has in the period of 5 years ending with the commencement of the bankruptcy made or caused to be made, any gift or transfer of, or any charge on, his property.

Section 352 applies to this offence.

357(2)   [Interpretation] The reference to making a transfer of or charge on any property includes causing or conniving at the levying of any execution against that property.

357(3)   [Offence re concealment or removal of property] The bankrupt is guilty of an offence if he conceals or removes, or has at any time before the commencement of the bankruptcy concealed or removed, any part of his property after, or within 2 months before, the date on which a judgment or order for the payment of money has been obtained against him, being a judgment or order which was not satisfied before the commencement of the bankruptcy.

Section 352 applies to this offence.

S.357(1), (3)
Based partly on BA 1914 s.156 and partly on s.6 of the 1926 Act, this provision prohibits fraudulent disposal by the bankrupt of any "property" (see s.351(a)) within five years of his bankruptcy commencing (for the definition of "commencement", see s.278(a)). It also covers attempts to defeat judgments by concealment of property. For sanctions see *R. v Mungroo* [1998] B.P.I.R. 784.

S.357(2)
This is a supplementary provision, based partly on s.6 of the 1926 Act. It indicates that the bankrupt commits an offence under s.357(1) if he causes or connives at the levying of execution on his "property".

A bankrupt charged with offences under this section can rely on the general defence in s.352. For the issue of reverse burdens of proof and compliance with ECHR see *Attorney General's Reference (No.1 of 2004)* [2004] EWCA Crim 1025; [2004] B.P.I.R. 1074 and the annotation to s.352 above. The relevant penalties are specified by ss.350, 430 and Sch.10.

358 Absconding

358 The bankrupt is guilty of an offence if–

(a) he leaves, or attempts or makes preparations to leave, England and Wales with any property the value of which is not less than the prescribed amount and possession of which he is required to deliver up to the official receiver or the trustee, or

(b) in the 6 months before petition, or in the initial period, he did anything which would have been an offence under paragraph (a) if the bankruptcy order had been made immediately before he did it.

Section 352 applies to this offence.

GENERAL NOTE

This largely repeats BA 1914 s.159, although the previous arbitrary figure of £250 has been dropped—unfortunately, in favour of another arbitrary figure to be fixed under s.418. The figure from April 1, 2004 is £1,000: see the Insolvency Proceedings (Monetary Limits) (Amendment) Order 2004 (SI 2004/547). For a critique of this, see the Cork *Report*, para.1889. Note that the offence covers absconding, etc. within the six months prior to the petition.

The s.352 defence applies here. For penalties, see ss.350, 430 and Sch.10. The terms "property", "before petition" and "initial period" are all defined in s.351.

359 Fraudulent dealing with property obtained on credit

359(1) [Offence re disposal of property obtained on credit] The bankrupt is guilty of an offence if, in the 12 months before petition, or in the initial period, he disposed of any property which he had obtained on credit and, at the time he disposed of it, had not paid for.

Section 352 applies to this offence.

359(2) [Offence re knowingly dealing with bankrupt] A person is guilty of an offence if, in the 12 months before petition or in the initial period, he acquired or received property from the bankrupt knowing or believing–

(a) that the bankrupt owed money in respect of the property, and

(b) that the bankrupt did not intend, or was unlikely to be able, to pay the money he so owed.

359(3) [Disposals etc. in ordinary course of business] A person is not guilty of an offence under subsection (1) or (2) if the disposal, acquisition or receipt of the property was in the ordinary course of a business carried on by the bankrupt at the time of the disposal, acquisition or receipt.

359(4) [Ordinary course of business] In determining for the purposes of this section whether any property is disposed of, acquired or received in the ordinary course of a business carried on by the bankrupt, regard may be had, in particular, to the price paid for the property.

359(5) [Interpretation] In this section references to disposing of property include pawning or pledging it; and references to acquiring or receiving property shall be read accordingly.

S.359(1)

Based on BA 1914 s.154(1), (15), this provision prohibits a bankrupt from disposing of "property" (for definition, see s.351(a)) obtained on credit, where the disposal occurs within 12 months "before petition" (see s.351(c)), or in the "initial period" (see s.351(b)).

The s.352 defence applies here.

On penalties for the offences in this and the following subsections, see ss.350, 430 and Sch.10.

S.359(2)

Derived from s.154(3), this penalises the knowing recipient of property obtained on credit and unlawfully disposed of under s.359(1). Note again the definitions in s.351.

A defence for the innocent recipient is built into this subsection.

S.359(3), (4)

These are saving provisions for disposals and receipts of "property" in the ordinary course of business. In determining whether this saving facility can operate, the price paid for the property is clearly relevant.

S.359(5)

This provision defines disposal of "property" so as to include pawns and pledges.

360   Obtaining credit; engaging in business

360(1)   [Offence re credit, non-disclosure of bankruptcy] The bankrupt is guilty of an offence if–

(a) either alone or jointly with any other person, he obtains credit to the extent of the prescribed amount or more without giving the person from whom he obtains it the relevant information about his status; or

(b) he engages (whether directly or indirectly) in any business under a name other than that in which he was adjudged bankrupt without disclosing to all persons with whom he enters into any business transaction the name in which he was so adjudged.

360(2)   [Cases of bankrupt obtaining credit] The reference to the bankrupt obtaining credit includes the following cases–

(a) where goods are bailed to him under a hire-purchase agreement, or agreed to be sold to him under a conditional sale agreement, and

(b) where he is paid in advance (whether in money or otherwise) for the supply of goods or services.

360(3)   [Scotland or Northern Ireland] A person whose estate has been sequestrated in Scotland, or who has been adjudged bankrupt in Northern Ireland, is guilty of an offence if, before his discharge, he does anything in England and Wales which would be an offence under subsection (1) if he were an undischarged bankrupt and the sequestration of his estate or the adjudication in Northern Ireland were an adjudication under this Part.

360(4)   [Information for s.360(1)(a)] For the purposes of subsection (1)(a), the relevant information about the status of the person in question is the information that he is an undischarged bankrupt or, as the case may be, that his estate has been sequestrated in Scotland and that he has not been discharged.

360(5)   [Application of section] This section applies to the bankrupt after discharge while a bankruptcy restrictions order is in force in respect of him.

360(6)   [Relevant information] For the purposes of subsection (1)(a) as it applies by virtue of subsection (5), the relevant information about the status of the person in question is the information that a bankruptcy restrictions order is in force in respect of him.

S.360(1)

This prevents an undischarged bankrupt from obtaining credit to the extent of the prescribed amount, either solely or jointly, without disclosing the relevant information about his status. It also prohibits him from carrying on a business under a name which was not the name by which he was declared bankrupt. Note that a person who enters into an individual voluntary arrangement is not subject to these disabilities. The figure from April 1, 2004 is £500 under the Insolvency Proceedings (Monetary Limits) (Amendment) Order 2004 (SI 2004/547) made under s.418. The offence under s.360(1) is one of strict liability (see *R. v Scott* [1998] B.P.I.R. 471) and the general defence under s.352 does not apply, although the offence would not operate where credit is obtained for an independent third person: *R. v Godwin* (1980) 71 Cr. App. Rep. 97.

The sanction for breach of s.360 is specified by ss.350, 430 and Sch.10.

S.360(2)

This represents a change in the law by extending the meaning of "obtaining credit" to cover receipt of goods under a hire-purchase agreement and receiving payment in advance for goods or services. Thus, authorities such as *R. v Miller* [1977] 3 All E.R. 986; and *Fisher v Raven* [1964] A.C. 210 are no longer good law on this point.

S.360(3)
This applies the above offence to a person whose estate is sequestrated in Scotland or who is declared bankrupt in Northern Ireland and who obtains credit in England and Wales.

S.360(4)
This provision defines the "relevant information" for the purposes of s.360(1).

S.360(5), (6)
This was inserted by s.257 of and Sch.21 to EA 2002 with effect from April 1, 2004 to deal with the effect of BROs.

361   Failure to keep proper accounts of business [Repealed.]

GENERAL NOTE

This offence of failing to keep accounts was repealed by EA 2002 s.263 with effect from April 1, 2004. However such conduct might justify a BRO.

362   Gambling [Repealed.]

GENERAL NOTE

This offence of gambling, etc., was repealed by s.263 of EA 2002 with effect from April 2004. Such behaviour is, however, still frowned upon and may form the basis for a bankruptcy restrictions order.

CHAPTER VII

POWERS OF COURT IN BANKRUPTCY

363   General control of court

363(1)   [Power of court] Every bankruptcy is under the general control of the court and, subject to the provisions in this Group of Parts, the court has full power to decide all questions of priorities and all other questions, whether of law or fact, arising in any bankruptcy.

363(2)   [Bankrupt to do as directed] Without prejudice to any other provision in this Group of Parts, an undischarged bankrupt or a discharged bankrupt whose estate is still being administered under Chapter IV of this Part shall do all such things as he may be directed to do by the court for the purposes of his bankruptcy or, as the case may be, the administration of that estate.

363(3)   [Application for directions] The official receiver or the trustee of a bankrupt's estate may at any time apply to the court for a direction under subsection (2).

363(4)   [Contempt of court] If any person without reasonable excuse fails to comply with any obligation imposed on him by subsection (2), he is guilty of a contempt of court and liable to be punished accordingly (in addition to any other punishment to which he may be subject).

S.363(1)
This confers on "the court" (see ss.373 and 385) the power to resolve all disputes in bankruptcy matters. The breadth of the jurisdiction of the court under s.363 was underlined in *Law Society v Shah* [2007] EWHC 2841 (Ch); [2007] B.P.I.R. 1595. See also *Engel v Peri* [2002] EWHC 799 (Ch); [2002] B.P.I.R. 961 where the point was made that the s.363 jurisdiction is still available notwithstanding the fact that the bankruptcy may already have been annulled. For the use of s.363(1) in the context of an annulment see *Howard v Savage* [2006] EWHC 3693 (Ch); [2007] B.P.I.R. 1097. In *Re Colgate* [1986] Ch. 439, the court used the predecessor of this provision to fix the remuneration of a trustee where this was in dispute. Section 363 may also be of use in fixing the remuneration of the trustee—*Re Cooper* [2005] N.I. Ch. 1; [2007] B.P.I.R. 1206 (Weatherup J. in High Court of Northern Ireland dealing with the equivalent statutory provision in that jurisdiction). Note also *Woodbridge v Smith* [2004] B.P.I.R. 247. Appointment of an additional trustee might also be a suitable use of this power—*Clements v Udal* [2001] B.P.I.R. 454. This provision may be utilised to appoint a trustee in bankruptcy pursuant to a block transfer order—*Donaldson v*

411

O'Sullivan [2008] EWCA Civ 879. See also *Barker v Bajjon* [2008] B.P.I.R. 771. The rules are also relevant here: see IR 1986 r.6.141 and Pt 7.

S.363(2), (4)

This places an undischarged bankrupt squarely under the thumb of the court: see *Hardy v Buchler* [1997] B.P.I.R. 643. If he unreasonably fails to obey its instructions he could be liable for contempt; see *Official Receiver v Cummings-John* [2000] B.P.I.R. 320. In *Boyden v Canty (No.2)* [2007] EWCA Civ 241; [2007] B.P.I.R. 299 failure to comply with s.363 (and other obligations) justified the bankrupt being committed to prison for six months.

An order was made under s.363(2) in *Buchler v Al Midani (No.3)* [2006] EWHC 170 (Ch); [2006] B.P.I.R. 881 to prevent a bankrupt from frustrating the realisation of assets located in Spain by interfering in legal proceedings taking place in that jurisdiction.

Subsection (2) was at issue in *Holtham v Kelmanson* [2006] B.P.I.R. 1422. Here Evans-Lombe J. indicated that a former bankrupt who was the absolute owner of land could be ordered under this provision to deliver up property to a trustee and that it was not necessary to consider an application under s.335A or s.14 of the Trusts of Land and Appointment of Trustees Act 1996.

Form 7.16 is no longer to be used for contempt proceedings, but see now Form 7.15. This change was effected by I(A)R 1987 (SI 1987/1919) r.3(1), Sch. Pt 2 para.159.

S.363(3)

The trustee or official receiver may apply to the court for a direction that the undischarged bankrupt behave in a certain way. This must not be confused with the power to apply for directions under s.303(2).

364   Power of arrest

364(1)   [Court's power re warrant] In the cases specified in the next subsection the court may cause a warrant to be issued to a constable or prescribed officer of the court–

  (a)   for the arrest of a debtor to whom a bankruptcy petition relates or of an undischarged bankrupt, or of a discharged bankrupt whose estate is still being administered under Chapter IV of this Part, and

  (b)   for the seizure of any books, papers, records, money or goods in the possession of a person arrested under the warrant,

and may authorise a person arrested under such a warrant to be kept in custody, and anything seized under such a warrant to be held, in accordance with the rules, until such time as the court may order.

364(2)   [Where s.364(1) powers exercisable] The powers conferred by subsection (1) are exercisable in relation to a debtor or undischarged or discharged bankrupt if, at any time after the presentation of the bankruptcy petition relating to him or the making of the bankruptcy order against him, it appears to the court–

  (a)   that there are reasonable grounds for believing that he has absconded, or is about to abscond, with a view to avoiding or delaying the payment of any of his debts or his appearance to a bankruptcy petition or to avoiding, delaying or disrupting any proceedings in bankruptcy against him or any examination of his affairs, or

  (b)   that he is about to remove his goods with a view to preventing or delaying possession being taken of them by the official receiver or the trustee of his estate, or

  (c)   that there are reasonable grounds for believing that he has concealed or destroyed, or is about to conceal or destroy, any of his goods or any books, papers or records which might be of use to his creditors in the course of his bankruptcy or in connection with the administration of his estate, or

  (d)   that he has, without the leave of the official receiver or the trustee of his estate, removed any goods in his possession which exceed in value such sum as may be prescribed for the purposes of this paragraph, or

(e)   that he has failed, without reasonable excuse, to attend any examination ordered by the court.

S.364(1)
This provides for the issue of warrants for the arrest of debtors or undischarged bankrupts and for seizure of their books. In *Hickling v Baker* [2007] EWCA Civ 287; [2007] B.P.I.R. 346, the Court of Appeal stressed that in exercising jurisdiction to commit under s.364 the court should seek to conform with the protections guaranteed by art.5 ECHR. The purpose of s.364 was not to punish as such, but to compel a bankrupt to comply with his legal obligations. Although notice of the application was not essential under s.364 it would be normal to expect notice of the application to be given to the bankrupt. Where an application is made without notice the application should explain why that is so. Where a person is arrested under s.364 he should be brought before the court as soon as possible. This case is highly significant in outlining good practice with regard to s.364 committals so as to ensure that there is no breach of art.5 ECHR.

S.364(2)
The court can issue such a warrant if any of the five facts listed in (a)–(e) appear to it to be present. Under BA 1914 s.23 there were only four paras ((a)–(d)), but in substance the grounds have not been added to. The grounds are aimed at debtors who are likely to abscond, avoid public examination or hide assets. What is now para.(d) used to include an arbitrary minimum amount of £60 but this has been scrapped, as the Blagden Committee recommended; but alas in favour of another random figure fixed under s.418. From April 1, 2004 under the Insolvency Proceedings (Monetary Limits) (Amendment) Order 2004 (SI 2004/547) the figure is £1,000.

Note also IR 1986 rr.7.21, 7.22.

365   Seizure of bankrupt's property

365(1)   [Court's power re warrant] At any time after a bankruptcy order has been made, the court may, on the application of the official receiver or the trustee of the bankrupt's estate, issue a warrant authorising the person to whom it is directed to seize any property comprised in the bankrupt's estate which is, or any books, papers or records relating to the bankrupt's estate or affairs which are, in the possession or under the control of the bankrupt or any other person who is required to deliver the property, books, papers or records to the official receiver or trustee.

365(2)   [Power to break open premises etc.] Any person executing a warrant under this section may, for the purpose of seizing any property comprised in the bankrupt's estate or any books, papers or records relating to the bankrupt's estate or affairs, break open any premises where the bankrupt or anything that may be seized under the warrant is or is believed to be and any receptacle of the bankrupt which contains or is believed to contain anything that may be so seized.

365(3)   [Power of court re search] If, after a bankruptcy order has been made, the court is satisfied that any property comprised in the bankrupt's estate is, or any books, papers or records relating to the bankrupt's estate or affairs are, concealed in any premises not belonging to him, it may issue a warrant authorising any constable or prescribed officer of the court to search those premises for the property, books, papers or records.

365(4)   [Execution of s.365(3) warrant] A warrant under subsection (3) shall not be executed except in the prescribed manner and in accordance with its terms.

S.365(1), (2)
These provisions allow the court to issue a warrant for the seizure of the bankrupt's property even though it may be in the possession of a third party. Forcing entry into premises or breaking open "receptacles" is permitted when executing such a warrant.

S.365(3), (4)
A search warrant (in the prescribed form) for a third party's premises may also be obtained under this section, although the court must be satisfied that the bankrupt's property, etc. is concealed there. Fishing expeditions will not be permitted.

Note also IR 1986 rr.7.21, 7.25.

366 Inquiry into bankrupt's dealings and property

366(1) [Power of court to summon bankrupt to appear] At any time after a bankruptcy order has been made the court may, on the application of the official receiver or the trustee of the bankrupt's estate, summon to appear before it–

(a) the bankrupt or the bankrupt's spouse or former spouse or civil partner or former civil partner,

(b) any person known or believed to have any property comprised in the bankrupt's estate in his possession or to be indebted to the bankrupt,

(c) any person appearing to the court to be able to give information concerning the bankrupt or the bankrupt's dealings, affairs or property.

The court may require any such person as is mentioned in paragraph (b) or (c) to submit a witness statement verified by a statement of truth to the court containing an account of his dealings with the bankrupt or to produce any documents in his possession or under his control relating to the bankrupt or the bankrupt's dealings, affairs or property.

366(2) [Application of s.366(3)] Without prejudice to section 364, the following applies in a case where–

(a) a person without reasonable excuse fails to appear before the court when he is summoned to do so under this section, or

(b) there are reasonable grounds for believing that a person has absconded, or is about to abscond, with a view to avoiding his appearance before the court under this section.

366(3) [Issue of warrant re non-appearance] The court may, for the purpose of bringing that person and anything in his possession before the court, cause a warrant to be issued to a constable or prescribed officer of the court–

(a) for the arrest of that person, and

(b) for the seizure of any books, papers, records, money or goods in that person's possession.

366(4) [Power re custody etc.] The court may authorise a person arrested under such a warrant to be kept in custody, and anything seized under such a warrant to be held, in accordance with the rules, until that person is brought before the court under the warrant or until such other time as the court may order.

S.366(1)

Amended by LRO 2010 (SI 2010/18). This permits the trustee or official receiver to ask the court to examine the bankrupt privately (or his spouse, or former spouse, or third parties believed to be in possession of the bankrupt's property or of information about his affairs). Civil partners and former civil partners fall within this section by virtue of Sch.27 to the Civil Partnership Act 2004. On the meaning of "affairs", see s.385(2). The power to direct the bankrupt to attend for examination survives discharge: *Oakes v Simms* [1997] B.P.I.R. 499. On the linkage between ss.366 and 364 see *Hickling v Baker* [2007] EWCA Civ 287; [2007] B.P.I.R. 346.

This changes the previous law in a number of respects. The BA 1914 provision referred to the bankrupt's "wife", which made an assumption which can no longer be justified in an age of sexual equality. The new provision also allows the court to require affidavits from the persons mentioned in para.(a) and (b). This reform, which was recommended by the Cork *Report*, para.903, reverses the rule in *Ex p. Reynolds* (1882) 21 Ch. D. 601.

On the relationship between s.366 and professional privilege see *Re Murjani* [1996] 1 W.L.R. 1498; [1996] B.C.C. 278; and *Re Ouvaroff* [1997] B.P.I.R. 712. Where inquiries are made of a bank concerning a client's affairs, major issues of confidentiality can arise—*Christofi v Barclays Bank plc* [1999] B.P.I.R. 855.

It was held in *Re Tucker (a Bankrupt) Ex p. Tucker* [1990] Ch. 148 that the court had no jurisdiction under s.25(6) of BA 1914 (the precursor of the present section) over British subjects resident abroad. In *Re Seagull Manufacturing Co Ltd* [1992] Ch. 128 at 137; [1991] B.C.C. 550 at 555 Mummery J. expressed the view that there was little doubt that, on the authority of *Re Tucker*, the court would construe ss.366 and 367 as subject to the same territorial limitation. In the Court of Appeal in the same case, [1993] Ch. 345; [1993] B.C.C. 241, no opinion was expressed on this point. The potential extraterritorial effect of s.366 was considered by Patten J. in *Buchler v Al Midani (No.2)* [2005] EWHC 3183 (Ch); [2006] B.P.I.R. 867. The English courts would take note of the attitude of foreign courts before exercising discretion under s.366 to make a disclosure order against a party based abroad. Contrast the position in regard to a public examination under s.133: see the notes to that section and to s.236. The position may be different where s.426 can be called into aid: *McIsaac, Petitioners* [1994] B.C.C. 410.

For the principles governing the exercise of discretion under s.366 see the comments of Rimer J. in *Long v Farrer & Co* [2004] EWHC 1774 (Ch); [2004] B.P.I.R. 1218.

On s.366 generally see *Albert v Albert* [1996] B.P.I.R. 232; and *Bird v Hadkinson* [1999] B.P.I.R. 653. Further provisions on s.366 examinations are contained in the rules: see IR 1986 rr.9.1–9.6. For an illuminating review see Frith, (2005) 21 I.L. & P. 141.

S.366(2)–(4)
The court can order the arrest of absconders, plus the seizure of property. Note also IR 1986 rr.7.21, 7.23.

367   Court's enforcement powers under s.366

367(1) [Power to order delivery] If it appears to the court, on consideration of any evidence obtained under section 366 or this section, that any person has in his possession any property comprised in the bankrupt's estate, the court may, on the application of the official receiver or the trustee of the bankrupt's estate, order that person to deliver the whole or any part of the property to the official receiver or the trustee at such time, in such manner and on such terms as the court thinks fit.

367(2) [Power to order payment from bankrupt debtor] If it appears to the court, on consideration of any evidence obtained under section 366 or this section, that any person is indebted to the bankrupt, the court may, on the application of the official receiver or the trustee of the bankrupt's estate, order that person to pay to the official receiver or trustee, at such time and in such manner as the court may direct, the whole or part of the amount due, whether in full discharge of the debt or otherwise as the court thinks fit.

367(3) [Place of examination] The court may, if it thinks fit, order that any person who if within the jurisdiction of the court would be liable to be summoned to appear before it under section 366 shall be examined in any part of the United Kingdom where he may be for the time being, or in any place outside the United Kingdom.

367(4) [Examination on oath] Any person who appears or is brought before the court under section 366 or this section may be examined on oath, either orally or by interrogatories, concerning the bankrupt or the bankrupt's dealings, affairs and property.

S.367(1), (2)
If, as a result of information gleaned from the examination, it appears that the bankrupt's property is in the possession of a third party, the court can order it to be handed over. Debts owing to the bankrupt can also be ordered to be paid.

S.367(3)
Examinations under s.366 do not have to be held in the UK. In *Re Tucker (a Bankrupt) Ex p. Tucker* [1990] Ch. 148 (decided under BA 1914 s.25(6)), the Court of Appeal refused to exercise its discretion to allow examination of a witness in Belgium, since it was not possible to compel him to attend such examination. On the question whether ss.366–367 extend to the examinations of witnesses abroad, see the notes to s.366.

S.367(4)
This deals with the form of the examination under s.366. Note also IR 1986 rr.9.1–9.6.

368   Provision corresponding to s.366, where interim receiver appointed

368 Sections 366 and 367 apply where an interim receiver has been appointed under section 286 as they apply where a bankruptcy order has been made, as if–

   (a) references to the official receiver or the trustee were to the interim receiver, and

   (b) references to the bankrupt and to his estate were (respectively) to the debtor and his property.

GENERAL NOTE

This extends ss.366 and 367 to situations where the debtor has not yet been declared bankrupt, but an interim receiver has been appointed after presentation of the petition under s.286.

369 Order for production of documents by inland revenue

369(1) **[Power of court]** For the purposes of an examination under section 290 (public examination of bankrupt) or proceedings under sections 366 to 368, the court may, on the application of the official receiver or the trustee of the bankrupt's estate, order an inland revenue official to produce to the court–

(a) any return, account or accounts submitted (whether before or after the commencement of the bankruptcy) by the bankrupt to any inland revenue official,

(b) any assessment or determination made (whether before or after the commencement of the bankruptcy) in relation to the bankrupt by any inland revenue official, or

(c) any correspondence (whether before or after the commencement of the bankruptcy) between the bankrupt and any inland revenue official.

369(2) **[Order re disclosure of document]** Where the court has made an order under subsection (1) for the purposes of any examination or proceedings, the court may, at any time after the document to which the order relates is produced to it, by order authorise the disclosure of the document, or of any part of its contents, to the official receiver, the trustee of the bankrupt's estate or the bankrupt's creditors.

369(3) **[Condition for s.369(1) order]** The court shall not address an order under subsection (1) to an inland revenue official unless it is satisfied that that official is dealing, or has dealt, with the affairs of the bankrupt.

369(4) **[Where s.369(1) document not in official's possession]** Where any document to which an order under subsection (1) relates is not in the possession of the official to whom the order is addressed, it is the duty of that official to take all reasonable steps to secure possession of it and, if he fails to do so, to report the reasons for his failure to the court.

369(5) **[Where document held by another official]** Where any document to which an order under subsection (1) relates is in the possession of an inland revenue official other than the one to whom the order is addressed, it is the duty of the official in possession of the document, at the request of the official to whom the order is addressed, to deliver it to the official making the request.

369(6) **["Inland revenue official"]** In this section **"inland revenue official"** means any inspector or collector of taxes appointed by the Commissioners of Inland Revenue or any person appointed by the Commissioners to serve in any other capacity.

369(7) **[Non-application]** This section does not apply for the purposes of an examination under sections 366 and 367 which takes place by virtue of section 368 (interim receiver).

S.369(1), (3), (6)
The court can order Inland Revenue officials (as defined by s.369(6)) to hand over tax documents relating to the bankrupt's financial affairs to assist examinations under ss.290 or 366. Only officials dealing with the bankrupt can be so directed.

S.369(2)
The court can order the disclosure of any document ordered to be produced under s.369(1) to the official receiver or the trustee.

S.369(4), (5)
Where the court makes an order under s.369(1), an Inland Revenue official must use his best efforts to obtain the documents in question, and this may involve securing possession of them from another Inland Revenue official.

S.369(7)

This states that s.369 does not apply where the debtor has not been declared bankrupt and where there is merely an examination under ss.366, 367 at the request of his interim receiver under s.368.

For further information, see IR 1986 rr.6.194–6.196.

370   Power to appoint special manager

370(1)   [Power of court] The court may, on an application under this section, appoint any person to be the special manager–

   (a)   of a bankrupt's estate, or

   (b)   of the business of an undischarged bankrupt, or

   (c)   of the property or business of a debtor in whose case the official receiver has been appointed interim receiver under section 286.

370(2)   [Application to court] An application under this section may be made by the official receiver or the trustee of the bankrupt's estate in any case where it appears to the official receiver or trustee that the nature of the estate, property or business, or the interests of the creditors generally, require the appointment of another person to manage the estate, property or business.

370(3)   [Powers of special manager] A special manager appointed under this section has such powers as may be entrusted to him by the court.

370(4)   [Powers included in s.370(3)] The power of the court under subsection (3) to entrust powers to a special manager includes power to direct that any provision in this Group of Parts that has effect in relation to the official receiver, interim receiver or trustee shall have the like effect in relation to the special manager for the purposes of the carrying out by the special manager of any of the functions of the official receiver, interim receiver or trustee.

370(5)   [Duties of special manager] A special manager appointed under this section shall–

   (a)   give such security as may be prescribed,

   (b)   prepare and keep such accounts as may be prescribed, and

   (c)   produce those accounts in accordance with the rules to the Secretary of State or to such other persons as may be prescribed.

S.370(1), (2)

The court can appoint a special manager of the bankrupt's estate or business, or indeed of a debtor's estate or business where an interim receiver has been installed. The application may be made by the official receiver or trustee where it appears that it is in the interests of the creditors that such an appointment be made. Under s.10 of the 1914 Act the official receiver made the appointment.

For the question of remuneration see Sch.9 para.20.

This section should be read in conjunction with s.287 and IR 1986 rr.6.167–6.171.

371   Re-direction of bankrupt's letters, etc.

371(1)   [Power of court] Where a bankruptcy order has been made, the court may from time to time, on the application of the official receiver or the trustee of the bankrupt's estate, order a postal operator (within the meaning of the Postal Services Act 2000) to re-direct and send or deliver to the official receiver or trustee or otherwise any postal packet (within the meaning of that Act) which would otherwise be sent or delivered by the operator concerned to the bankrupt at such place or places as may be specified in the order.

371(2)   [Duration of court order] An order under this section has effect for such period, not exceeding 3 months, as may be specified in the order.

S.371(1)

This provision allows the court on an application from the official receiver or trustee to order a postal operator to redirect the bankrupt's mail after a bankruptcy order has been made. The mail can then be opened by the official receiver or trustee (see s.365). This provision dates back to s.85 of the Debtors Act 1869. Unfortunately there are questions as to its legality in the light of art.8 ECHR and its relationship with the Interception of Communications Act 1985: see Jaconelli, [1994] Conv. 370 on these intriguing issues. In *Foxley v UK* [2000] B.P.I.R. 1009 the European Court of Human Rights held that a s.371 order does not per se breach art.8 ECHR provided its terms are strictly observed and it is not used in a disproportionate manner. Interception of communications between a bankrupt and his lawyers is not acceptable. Further consideration to the issue of redirection of post was given by the European Court of Human Rights in *Narinen v Finland* [2004] B.P.I.R. 914. Here it was stressed that any interference with a debtor's correspondence would only be permitted under a precise legal authority. For authoritative advice on the correct procedure to be adopted see *Singh v Official Receiver* [1997] B.P.I.R. 530. Note also the newly introduced IR r.6.235A. For the most recent analysis of this provision see *Smedley v Brittain* [2008] B.P.I.R. 219, where the question of compliance with art.8 of the ECHR was fully considered.

Note that the power to open the bankrupt's mail does not extend to outgoing mail. Moreover, a debtor who enters into an individual voluntary arrangement to settle his debts cannot have his mail opened under this provision.

In s.371(1) the words "a postal operator (within the meaning of the Postal Services Act 2000)" substituted for the words "the Post Office", the words "that Act" substituted for the words "the Post Office Act 1953" and the words "the operator concerned" substituted for the word "them" by the Postal Services Act 2000 s.127(4), Sch.8 para.20 as from March 26, 2001 (see the Postal Service Act 2000 (Commencement No.4 and Transitional and Savings Provisions) Order 2001 (SI 2001/1148 (C. 37)) art.2(2), Sch. Note that the commencement date of March 26, 2001 had previously been set by the Postal Services Act 2000 (Commencement No.1 and Transitional Provisions) Order 2000 (SI 2000/2957 (C. 88)) art.2(3), Sch.3, but that implementation was revoked by art.43 of SI 2001/1148 (C. 37).

S.371(2)

The maximum period of interference permitted by the order is three months, as was the case previously.

PART X

INDIVIDUAL INSOLVENCY: GENERAL PROVISIONS

372   Supplies of gas, water, electricity, etc.

372(1)   [Application] This section applies where on any day (**"the relevant day"**)–

(a)   a bankruptcy order is made against an individual or an interim receiver of an individual's property is appointed, or

(b)   a voluntary arrangement proposed by an individual is approved under Part VIII, or

(c)   a deed of arrangement is made for the benefit of an individual's creditors;

and in this section **"the office-holder"** means the official receiver, the trustee in bankruptcy, the interim receiver, the supervisor of the voluntary arrangement or the trustee under the deed of arrangement, as the case may be.

372(2)   [Where s.372(3) request] If a request falling within the next subsection is made for the giving after the relevant day of any of the supplies mentioned in subsection (4), the supplier–

(a)   may make it a condition of the giving of the supply that the office-holder personally guarantees the payment of any charges in respect of the supply, but

(b)   shall not make it a condition of the giving of the supply, or do anything which has the effect of making it a condition of the giving of the supply, that any outstanding charges in respect of a supply given to the individual before the relevant day are paid.

372(3)   [Type of request] A request falls within this subsection if it is made–

(a)   by or with the concurrence of the office-holder, and

(b) for the purposes of any business which is or has been carried on by the individual, by a firm or partnership of which the individual is or was a member, or by an agent or manager for the individual or for such a firm or partnership.

372(4)   **[Supplies in s.372(2)]** The supplies referred to in subsection (2) are–

(a) a supply of gas by a gas supplier within the meaning of Part I of the Gas Act 1986,

(b) a supply of electricity by an electricity supplier within the meaning of Part I of the Electricity Act 1989,

(c) a supply of water by a water undertaker,

(d) a supply of communications services by a provider of a public electronic communications service.

372(5)   **[Definitions]** The following applies to expressions used in subsection (4)–

(a) [Repealed.]

(b) [Repealed.]

(c) **"communications services"** do not include electronic communications services to the extent that they are used to broadcast or otherwise transmit programme services (within the meaning of the Communications Act 2003).

GENERAL NOTE

This section represents a late change of mind by the government in that it did not appear in the early forms of the 1985 Bill. It is designed to stop public utilities "blackmailing" the trustee in bankruptcy, etc. of an insolvent individual into paying arrears in respect of public utility supplies as a precondition to receiving supplies in the future. It was not clear at common law whether a public utility could behave in such a way: see *Re Flack* [1900] 2 Q.B. 32—but the Cork Committee (*Report*, para.1466) favoured legislation to outlaw expressly such "priority gaining".

For the corresponding provisions in corporate insolvencies, see s.233.

S.372(1)–(3)

These provisions enable an office-holder (as defined by s.372(1)) to request a supply from a public utility. The supplier, although he may require the office-holder to guarantee future payments personally, cannot require arrears to be paid as a precondition to the making of the supply.

S.372(4), (5)

These provisions list the public utilities that are covered by this section—gas, electricity, water and tele-communications (but not cable services). Subsections (4) and (5) have been amended to cope with utility privatisation legislation. Section 372(4)(d) substituted by the Communications Act 2003 Sch.17 para.82(3)(a) as from July 25, 2003 (see Communications Act 2003 (Commencement No.1) Order 2003 (SI 2003/1900 (C. 77)) art.2(1) and Sch.1).

Previously in s.372(4) para.(a) substituted by the Gas Act 1995 s.16(1), Sch.4 para.14(3) as from March 1, 1996 (see Gas Act 1995 (Appointed Day and Commencement) Order 1996 (SI 1996/218 (C. 4)) art.2).

Paragraph (b) substituted by the Utilities Act 2000 s.108 Sch.6 Pt III para.47(3)(b) as from October 1, 2001 (see Utilities Act 2000 (Commencement No.6 and Transitional Provisions) Order 2001 (SI 2001/3266 (C. 106)) arts 1 and 2 and Sch.), subject to transitional provisions.

Previously para.(b) substituted by the Electricity Act 1989 s.112(1) and Sch.16 para.35(1), (3)(a) as from March 31, 1990 (see Electricity Act 1989 s.113(2) and SI 1990/117 (C. 4)).

373   Jurisdiction in relation to insolvent individuals

373(1)   **[High Court and county courts]** The High Court and the county courts have jurisdiction throughout England and Wales for the purposes of the Parts in this Group.

373(2)   **[Powers of county court]** For the purposes of those Parts, a county court has, in addition to its ordinary jurisdiction, all the powers and jurisdiction of the High Court; and the orders of the court may be enforced accordingly in the prescribed manner.

373(3) **[Exercise of jurisdiction]** Jurisdiction for the purposes of those Parts is exercised–

(a) by the High Court in relation to the proceedings which, in accordance with the rules, are allocated to the London insolvency district, and

(b) by each county court in relation to the proceedings which are so allocated to the insolvency district of that court.

373(4) **[Operation of s.373(3)]** Subsection (3) is without prejudice to the transfer of proceedings from one court to another in the manner prescribed by the rules; and nothing in that subsection invalidates any proceedings on the grounds that they were initiated or continued in the wrong court.

S.373(1)

This vests bankruptcy jurisdiction in the High Court and the county courts in the case of England and Wales. See also Pt 7 of the rules here. For the fees in county court proceedings see the County Court Fees (Amendment No.2) Order 1986 (SI 1986/2143).

S.373(2)

In bankruptcy matters county courts are to have all the powers of the High Court. This was the case under BA 1914 s.103. See here *Re a Debtor (No.2A of 1980)* [1981] Ch. 148.

S.373(3)

This provision allocates cases between the High Court and county courts—much will depend upon the "insolvency districts" which are described in s.374.

S.373(4)

The transfer of proceedings from one court to another is permitted. Note IR 1986 rr.7.11–7.15. See also IR 1986 Sch.2, for insolvency courts.

374 Insolvency districts

374(1) **[Order by Lord Chancellor]** The Lord Chancellor may with the concurrence of the Lord Chief Justice by order designate the areas which are for the time being to be comprised, for the purposes of the Parts in this Group, in the London insolvency district and the insolvency district of each county court; and an order under this section may–

(a) exclude any county court from having jurisdiction for the purposes of those Parts, or

(b) confer jurisdiction for those purposes on any county court which has not previously had that jurisdiction.

374(2) **[Incidental provisions etc.]** An order under this section may contain such incidental, supplemental and transitional provisions as may appear to the Lord Chancellor and the Lord Chief Justice necessary or expedient.

374(3) **[Order by statutory instrument]** An order under this section shall be made by statutory instrument and, after being made, shall be laid before each House of Parliament.

374(4) **[Relevant districts]** Subject to any order under this section–

(a) the district which, immediately before the appointed day, is the London bankruptcy district becomes, on that day, the London insolvency district;

(b) any district which immediately before that day is the bankruptcy district of a county court becomes, on that day, the insolvency district of that court, and

(c) any county court which immediately before that day is excluded from having jurisdiction in bankruptcy is excluded, on and after that day, from having jurisdiction for the purposes of the Parts in this Group.

374(5) **[LCJ nominee]** The Lord Chief Justice may nominate a judicial office holder (as defined in section 109(4) of the Constitutional Reform Act 2005) to exercise his functions under this section.

S.374(1), (4), (5)

The Lord Chancellor may by order designate the insolvency districts—certain county courts can be prevented from handling bankruptcy matters, whereas others may be given this jurisdiction for the first time. See for example the Civil Courts (Amendment No.3) Order 1992 (SI 1992/1810), the Civil Courts (Amendment) Order 1998 (SI 1998/1880), the Civil Courts (Amendment) (No.2) Order 1998 (SI 1998/2910) and the Civil Courts (Amendment) Order 2006 (SI 2006/1542). Subject to this power, existing jurisdictional patterns are to be retained. For alternative county courts see Sch.2 to IR 1986 (as amended).

Subsections (1) and (2) were amended and a new subs.(5) inserted by the Constitutional Reform Act 2005 s.15 and Sch.4 Pt I para.187.

S.374(2), (3)

These provisions permit any order by the Lord Chancellor to deal with ancillary matters and regulate the mode by which such orders are to be made.

See IR 1986 r.6.40A(5) and Sch.2.

375 Appeals etc. from courts exercising insolvency jurisdiction

375(1)   [Review, rescission etc.] Every court having jurisdiction for the purposes of the Parts in this Group may review, rescind or vary any order made by it in the exercise of that jurisdiction.

375(2)   [Appeals] An appeal from a decision made in the exercise of jurisdiction for the purposes of those Parts by a county court or by a registrar in bankruptcy of the High Court lies to a single judge of the High Court; and an appeal from a decision of that judge on such an appeal lies to the Court of Appeal.

375(3)   [No other appeals] A county court is not, in the exercise of its jurisdiction for the purposes of those Parts, to be subject to be restrained by the order of any other court, and no appeal lies from its decision in the exercise of that jurisdiction except as provided by this section.

S.375(1)

This confers a general "safety valve" power on the courts to review, rescind or vary orders on bankruptcy matters. The equivalent in corporate insolvency law is r.7.47 and broadly speaking similar principles should be applied: *Midrome Ltd v Shaw* [1993] B.C.C. 659. This review jurisdiction must be kept flexible but must not be allowed to become a gateway for late appeals or to undermine the principle of *res judicata: Re Debtors (No.VA7 and VA8) Ex p. Stevens* [1996] B.P.I.R. 101; and *Brillouet v Hachette Magazines* [1996] B.P.I.R. 518 or to avoid other restrictions on applications to the court—*Hurst v Bennett (No.2)* [2002] B.P.I.R. 102. It is not appropriate to allow s.375 to be used as a further appeal mechanism where the bankrupt has exhausted his appeal rights—*Egleton v IRC* [2003] EWHC 3226 (Ch); [2004] B.P.I.R. 476. If a bankrupt persists in making applications under s.375 to reopen issues finally determined the court might be prepared to grant a civil restraint order—*Hurst v Bennett* [2004] EWCA Civ 230; [2004] B.P.I.R. 732. For a successful attempt to invoke the jurisdiction see *Fitch v Official Receiver* [1996] 1 W.L.R. 242, CA; [1996] B.C.C. 328. For a very unusual case where the s.375 jurisdiction was used to procure an annulment see *Amihyia v Official Receiver* [2005] B.P.I.R. 264.

A comprehensive review of the s.375 review mechanism was conducted by Laddie J. in *Papanicola (as trustee in bankruptcy for Mak) v Humphreys* [2005] EWHC 335 (Ch); [2005] 2 All E.R. 418. Key points to emerge from the judgment include:

–   discretionary nature of the jurisdiction;

–   onus on applicant to persuade court to exercise this exceptional discretion;

–   ability of court to weigh up wide range of circumstances including events occurring after original court order and facts not brought to the attention of the court (subject to satisfactory explanation);

–   a better presentation of matters put before the original hearing was not something that the review jurisdiction was intended to encourage;

–   CPR 39.3(3)–(5), although not formally engaged by s.375, was relevant when exercising the review jurisdiction.

In *Skeete v Pick* [2007] EWHC 2211 (Ch) the court identified circumstances in which the bankrupt might consider invoking the s.375 jurisdiction (though it was careful to stress that it was not indicating whether such an application would succeed).

In *Hurst v Supperstone (No.2)* [2007] EWHC 865 (Ch), [2007] B.P.I.R. 1104 the court refused to permit the s.375 jurisdiction to be used to review a costs order. This refusal was based on the facts but it was accepted in principle that costs orders fell within the s.375 purview if a cogent case could established for a costs order review.

In *Snopek v Urang* [2008] B.P.I.R. 1416 the court indicated that on a s.375 review it could consider evidence that had materialised after the date of the making of the bankruptcy order which was under review.

On the exercise of discretion under s.375 see *HMRC v Cassells* [2009] B.P.I.R. 284.

An application under s.375 also failed in *Re Haghighat (No.2)* [2009] B.P.I.R. 785 where the difficulty of the burden of proof facing the applicant was emphasised.

S.375(2)

In s.375(2) the words, "with the leave of the judge or of the Court of Appeal," formerly appearing after the words "on such an appeal lies" repealed by Access to Justice Act 1999 ss.106, 108(3)(f), Sch.15 Pt III as from September 27, 1999.

This provision deals with the question of appeals, whether against a decision of the county court or High Court. Under s.55 of the Access to Justice Act 1999 a "second appeal" to the Court of Appeal is only permitted with the leave of the Court of Appeal and on restricted grounds.

In *Re a Debtor (No.32/SD/1991)* [1993] 1 W.L.R. 314 Millett J. indicated that in a s.375(1) review the court can hear fresh evidence not available at the original hearing. Such a review therefore differs fundamentally from a simple appeal where this would not be permitted. By way of contrast a case brought under s.375(2) is a true appeal: *Vadher v Weisgard* [1997] B.C.C. 219. For the inconsistencies on the admission of fresh evidence see *Purvis v Customs and Excise Commissioners* [1999] B.P.I.R. 396 at 398, per Hazel Williamson Q.C. Vinelott J. further considered the nature of the court's jurisdiction under s.375 in later proceedings in *Re a Debtor (No.32/SD/1991) (No.2)* [1994] B.C.C. 524. According to his Lordship (at 528G) it was an exceptional reserve jurisdiction only to be resorted to in the most extreme of cases. It existed to prevent "miscarriages of justice" in the field of bankruptcy law where a person's reputation and freedom of action was at stake.

Section 375(2) and its relationship with insolvency appeals procedures was reviewed in *Bailey v Dargue* [2009] B.P.I.R. 1.

Note also *Practice Direction (Insolvency Proceedings)* [2007] B.C.C. 842.

S.375(3)

This complements s.373(2) by conferring jurisdictional integrity on the county courts.

See further IR 1986 r.7.48.

376 Time-limits

376 Where by any provision in this Group of Parts or by the rules the time for doing anything is limited, the court may extend the time, either before or after it has expired, on such terms, if any, as it thinks fit.

GENERAL NOTE

This provision once again emphasises the general control of the court over bankruptcy proceedings by allowing it to extend time-limits. For the primacy of s.376 see *Tager v Westpac Banking Corporation* [1998] B.C.C. 73. For guidance on how the discretion under s.376 should be exercised see *Warley Continental Services v Johal* [2004] B.P.I.R. 353 (extension of time refused where time limit under s.262 IA 1986 had expired).

377 Formal defects

377 The acts of a person as the trustee of a bankrupt's estate or as a special manager, and the acts of the creditors' committee established for any bankruptcy, are valid notwithstanding any defect in the appointment, election or qualifications of the trustee or manager or, as the case may be, of any member of the committee.

GENERAL NOTE

This provision displays a liberal attitude towards procedural defects in the appointment or qualifications of the trustee, etc. Corresponding sections in the case of company officers and office-holders are s.232 above and CA 1985 s.285 [CA 2006 s.161]. It is necessary to instil confidence in third parties and to preclude the need to investigate that correct procedures have been followed. Note that the predecessor of s.377 only covered situations where the trustee, etc. acted in good faith, but this is not mentioned in s.377. Under BA 1914 s.147(1), which is not specifically repeated in IA 1986, other defects in bankruptcy proceedings could be excused by the court unless substantial and irreparable injustice has been caused by the irregularity. Presumably such cases could now be dealt with under ss.363(1) and 375(1). Finally it should be remembered that the question of a trustee's qualifications must be viewed in the light of the requirements of Pt XIII. This section was considered in *Foenander v Allan* [2006] B.P.I.R. 1392, where it was held that alleged defects in the membership of the creditors' committee which had appointed a trustee could not invalidate the actions of said trustee.

Schedule 9 para.32 states that non-compliance with the rules may be made a criminal offence.

Compare also IR 1986 r.7.55.

378   Exemption from stamp duty

378   Stamp duty shall not be charged on–

  (a)   any document, being a deed, conveyance, assignment, surrender, admission or other assurance relating solely to property which is comprised in a bankrupt's estate and which, after the execution of that document, is or remains at law or in equity the property of the bankrupt or of the trustee of that estate,

  (b)   any writ, order, certificate or other instrument relating solely to the property of a bankrupt or to any bankruptcy proceedings.

GENERAL NOTE

This section offers welcome relief from the operation of stamp duty on documents connected with bankruptcy matters.

379   Annual report

379   As soon as practicable after the end of 1986 and each subsequent calendar year, the Secretary of State shall prepare and lay before each House of Parliament a report about the operation during that year of so much of this Act as is comprised in this Group of Parts, and about proceedings in the course of that year under the Deeds of Arrangement Act 1914.

GENERAL NOTE

This section requires the Secretary of State to lay before Parliament an annual report on the working of IA 1986 and the Deeds of Arrangement Act 1914. This is not a new obligation. The 1984 annual report (published in November 1985) is a mine of statistical information on the working of the old bankruptcy legislation.

This provision, unlike its predecessor, makes no mention of the obligation imposed on bankruptcy officers to provide the raw statistics to the Department of Trade and Industry to facilitate the preparation of this report.

Remote attendance at meetings

379A   Remote attendance at meetings

379A(1)   **[Application of section]** Where–

  (a)   a bankruptcy order is made against an individual or an interim receiver of an individual's property is appointed, or

  (b)   a voluntary arrangement in relation to an individual is proposed or is approved under Part 8, this section applies to any meeting of the individual's creditors summoned under this Act or the rules.

379A(2)   **[Attendance at meeting by persons not present together]** Where the person summoning a meeting ("the convener") considers it appropriate, the meeting may be conducted and held in such a way that persons who are not present together at the same place may attend it.

379A(3)   **[Attendance at meeting by exercise of right to speak and vote]** Where a meeting is conducted and held in the manner referred to in subsection (2), a person attends the meeting if that person is able to exercise any rights which that person may have to speak and vote at the meeting.

379A(4)   **[When exercising right to speak and vote]** For the purposes of this section–

(a)   a person exercises the right to speak at a meeting when that person is in a position to communicate to all those attending the meeting, during the meeting, any information or opinions which that person has on the business of the meeting; and

(b)   a person exercises the right to vote at a meeting when–

     (i)   that person is able to vote, during the meeting, on resolutions put to the vote at the meeting, and

     (ii)   that person's vote can be taken into account in determining whether or not such resolutions are passed at the same time as the votes of all the other persons attending the meeting.

379A(5)   **[Duty of convener to make arrangements]** The convener of a meeting which is to be conducted and held in the manner referred to in subsection (2) may make whatever arrangements the convener considers appropriate to–

(a)   enable those attending the meeting to exercise their rights to speak or vote, and

(b)   ensure the identification of those attending the meeting and the security of any electronic means used to enable attendance.

379A(6)   **[Where unnecessary or inexpedient to specify place for meeting]** Where in the reasonable opinion of the convener–

(a)   a meeting will be attended by persons who will not be present together at the same place, and

(b)   it is unnecessary or inexpedient to specify a place for the meeting, any requirement under this Act or the rules to specify a place for the meeting may be satisfied by specifying the arrangements the convener proposes to enable persons to exercise their rights to speak or vote.

379A(7)   **[Convener to regard legitimate interests of the creditors etc. for s.379A(5), (6)(b)]** In making the arrangements referred to in subsection (5) and in forming the opinion referred to in subsection (6)(b), the convener must have regard to the legitimate interests of the creditors and others attending the meeting in the efficient despatch of the business of the meeting.

379A(8)   **[Request for convener to specify place for meeting]** If–

(a)   the notice of a meeting does not specify a place for the meeting,

(b)   the convener is requested in accordance with the rules to specify a place for the meeting, and

(c)   that request is made by not less than ten percent in value of the creditors, it shall be the duty of the convener to specify a place for the meeting.

GENERAL NOTE

Introduced by LRO 2010 (SI 2010/18). This provision is designed to give the convener of a creditors' meeting (whether in bankruptcy or an IVA) discretion as to whether it should be held remotely using advances in communications technology. It mirrors s.246A. See IR 1986 rr.12A.22 and 12A.23.

Use of websites

379B   Use of websites

379B(1)   [Application of section; meaning of "the office-holder"] This section applies where–

(a)   a bankruptcy order is made against an individual or an interim receiver of an individual's property is appointed, or

(b)   a voluntary arrangement in relation to an individual is proposed or is approved under Part 8, and "the office-holder" means the official receiver, the trustee in bankruptcy, the interim receiver, the nominee or the supervisor of the voluntary arrangement, as the case may be.

379B(2)   [Provision of notice by website] Where any provision of this Act or the rules requires the office-holder to give, deliver, furnish or send a notice or other document or information to any person, that requirement is satisfied by making the notice, document or information available on a website–

(a)   in accordance with the rules, and

(b)   in such circumstances as may be prescribed.

GENERAL NOTE

Introduced by LRO 2010 (SI 2010/18) this allows the office-holder to make use of a website in communications with stakeholders. It mirrors s.246B. See IR 1986 r.12A.12.

PART XI

INTERPRETATION FOR SECOND GROUP OF PARTS

380   Introductory

380   The next five sections have effect for the interpretation of the provisions of this Act which are comprised in this Group of Parts; and where a definition is provided for a particular expression, it applies except so far as the context otherwise requires.

GENERAL NOTE

This introduces the bankruptcy interpretation sections. Meanings attributed in ss.381–385 can be excluded by the context. Note also Pt XVIII of the Act and IR 1986 Pt 13.

381   "Bankrupt" and associated terminology

381(1)   ["Bankrupt"] "Bankrupt" means an individual who has been adjudged bankrupt and, in relation to a bankruptcy order, it means the individual adjudged bankrupt by that order.

381(2)   ["Bankruptcy order"] "Bankruptcy order" means an order adjudging an individual bankrupt.

381(3)   ["Bankruptcy petition"] "Bankruptcy petition" means a petition to the court for a bankruptcy order.

GENERAL NOTE

These common phrases are hereby defined.

382   "Bankruptcy debt", etc.

382(1)   ["Bankruptcy debt"] "Bankruptcy debt", in relation to a bankrupt, means (subject to the next subsection) any of the following–

(a)   any debt or liability to which he is subject at the commencement of the bankruptcy,

(b) any debt or liability to which he may become subject after the commencement of the bankruptcy (including after his discharge from bankruptcy) by reason of any obligation incurred before the commencement of the bankruptcy,

(c) any amount specified in pursuance of section 39(3)(c) of the Powers of Criminal Courts Act 1973 in any criminal bankruptcy order made against him before the commencement of the bankruptcy, and

(d) any interest provable as mentioned in section 322(2) in Chapter IV of Part IX.

382(2) [Liability in tort] In determining for the purposes of any provision in this Group of Parts whether any liability in tort is a bankruptcy debt, the bankrupt is deemed to become subject to that liability by reason of an obligation incurred at the time when the cause of action accrued.

382(3) [References to debtor liability] For the purposes of references in this Group of Parts to a debt or liability, it is immaterial whether the debt or liability is present or future, whether it is certain or contingent or whether its amount is fixed or liquidated, or is capable of being ascertained by fixed rules or as a matter of opinion; and references in this Group of Parts to owing a debt are to be read accordingly.

382(4) ["Liability"] In this Group of Parts, except in so far as the context otherwise requires, **"liability"** means (subject to subsection (3) above) a liability to pay money or money's worth, including any liability under an enactment, any liability for breach of trust, any liability in contract, tort or bailment and any liability arising out of an obligation to make restitution.

S.382(1), (2)

These provisions define a bankruptcy debt. It would appear from the comments of David Richards J. in *Re T & N Ltd* [2005] EWHC 2870 (Ch); [2006] B.P.I.R. 532 that future tort claims would not rank as bankruptcy debts under s.382 of the IA 1986. Having said that, the judge made the point that after discharge such claimants could still pursue the erstwhile bankrupt.

Note prospective amendment: s.382(1)(c) is to be repealed by CJA 1988 s.170(2) and Sch.16 as from a day to be appointed; see the note to s.264.

S.382(3), (4)

These provisions make liability in tort a bankruptcy debt and make it clear that both contingent and unliquidated liabilities are capable of forming the basis of a bankruptcy debt. On the latter point, this is a change in the law, which the Cork Committee (*Report*, para.1318) called for. In *Re Wisepark Ltd* [1994] B.C.C. 221 it was held that a claim for costs was not a contingent liability within s.382 because it did not exist until the court made an order for costs. This was confirmed by the Court of Appeal in *Glenister v Rowe* [1999] B.P.I.R. 674. Therefore a person having such a claim could not vote on a voluntary arrangement but conversely was not bound by its terms and could pursue the debtor if the costs order was eventually made in his favour. *Glenister v Rowe* [2000] Ch. 76 was followed by the High Court of Australia in *Foots v Southern Cross Mine Management Pty Ltd* [2007] HCA 56; [2007] B.P.I.R. 1498. In *R. (on the application of Steele) v Birmingham City Council and Secretary of State for Work and Pensions* [2005] EWCA Civ 1824; [2006] B.P.I.R. 856, the Court of Appeal was concerned with clawback of overpaid social security benefits from a former bankrupt "S" and in particular whether the possibility of clawback of the overpayment pursuant to s.71 of the Social Security Administration Act 1992 constituted a contingent liability so as render it a bankruptcy debt for the purposes of discharge. The precise question to be determined was whether the potential liability to repay the overpaid job-seekers allowance was a "contingent liability" and therefore a "bankruptcy debt" within the meaning of s.382 of the IA 1986 at the commencement of the bankruptcy. If so, that liability to repay would be discharged with other bankruptcy debts at the conclusion of the bankruptcy. The Court of Appeal held that the liability to repay was *not* a contingent liability and therefore survived bankruptcy discharge. At the commencement of the bankruptcy there was merely a *possibility* that the Secretary of State would make a repayment determination against S under the statutory procedure laid down in the Act. The Secretary of State was entitled to, but not obliged to, recover overpayments. That possibility, which was not a formality, did not constitute a contingent liability on the part of S and therefore there was no bankruptcy debt to be discharged. *Glenister v Rowe* [1999] B.P.I.R. 674 was accordingly followed. Moreover, there was no scope for S (in order to circumvent the above conclusion) introducing the notion of a common law restitutionary liability to repay, as this had been superseded by the statutory repayment mechanism once the claim for benefit had been made. This ruling is consistent with current authority. This issue was revisited in *Casson and Wales v Law Society* [2009] EWHC 1943 (Admin) where the view was taken that a liability which may or may not be imposed upon a solicitor by the regulatory authorities could not be regarded as a contingent liability giving rise to a bankruptcy debt because of the uncertainty that existed at the time of the making of the bankruptcy order. Subsection (4) was mentioned in *R. (Balding) v Secretary of State for Work and Pensions* [2007] EWHC 759 (Admin). Here the Divisional Court ruled that the liability to repay overpaid social security benefit where that liability had been determined prior to bankruptcy was to be regarded as a bankruptcy debt. As such, on discharge from bankruptcy of the recipient that liability was extinguished and deductions could not be made in respect of it from future benefit payments. On appeal the Court of Appeal upheld this ruling and confirmed that the liability to repay the overpayment (which had been adjudicated prior to bankruptcy) was a bankruptcy debt which was released on discharge from bankruptcy—see *Secretary of State for Work and Pensions v Balding* [2007] EWCA Civ 1327; [2007] B.P.I.R. 1669. Mummery L.J. sympathised with the difficulties that this conclusion would cause for the public exchequer, but the solution lay in the hands of Parliament by introducing amending legislation. A debt arising in respect of a lump sum payable under matrimonial proceedings is a bankruptcy debt (*Russell v Russell* [1998] B.P.I.R. 259) but until recently was not a provable debt. On the significance of this see *Woodley v Woodley (No.2)* [1994] 1 W.L.R. 1167; and *Levy v LSC* [2000] B.P.I.R. 1065. The court will only grant a bankruptcy order on the basis of a non-provable debt if the circumstances are exceptional—*Wehmeyer v Weymeyer* [2001] B.P.I.R. 548. Lump sums in matrimonial proceedings were made provable debts by the Insolvency (Amendment) Rules 2005 (SI 2005/527). As to whether a wife's putative claims to ancillary relief on divorce are contingent debts compare *Re Rich* [2008] B.P.I.R. 485 with *Re Jones* [2008] B.P.I.R. 1051. It is submitted that the latter decision is more likely to be representative of the law in the wake of *Haines v Hill* [2007] EWCA Civ 1284; [2007] B.P.I.R. 1280.

In *Smurthwaite v Simpson-Smith and Mond (No.2)* [2006] B.P.I.R. 1483 the court considered the application of s.382—but comments here need to be viewed in the context of the appeal in this complex litigation see *Smurthwaite v Simpson-Smith and Mond (No.2)* [2006] B.P.I.R. 1504. In *El Ajou v Stern* [2006] EWHC 3067 (Ch); [2007] B.P.I.R. 693 (an IVA case) there was further consideration of what constitutes a bankruptcy debt for the purposes of s.382.

For the corresponding definitions in corporate insolvency, see the note to Sch.8 paras 12, 14.

Note that bankruptcy debts are not always provable: see the note to IR 1986 r.12.3.

383   "Creditor", "security", etc.

383(1)   ["Creditor"] "Creditor"–

(a)   in relation to a bankrupt, means a person to whom any of the bankruptcy debts is owed (being, in the case of an amount falling within paragraph (c) of the definition in section 382(1) of **"bankruptcy debt"**, the person in respect of whom that amount is specified in the criminal bankruptcy order in question), and

(b)   in relation to an individual to whom a bankruptcy petition relates, means a person who would be a creditor in the bankruptcy if a bankruptcy order were made on that petition.

383(2)   [Securing of debt] Subject to the next two subsections and any provision of the rules requiring a creditor to give up his security for the purposes of proving a debt, a debt is secured for the purposes of this Group of Parts to the extent that the person to whom the debt is owed holds any security for the debt (whether a mortgage, charge, lien or other security) over any property of the person by whom the debt is owed.

383(3)   [Where s.269(1)(a) statement made] Where a statement such as is mentioned in section 269(1)(a) in Chapter I of Part IX has been made by a secured creditor for the purposes of any bankruptcy petition and a bankruptcy order is subsequently made on that petition, the creditor is deemed for the purposes of the Parts in this Group to have given up the security specified in the statement.

383(4)   [Qualification to s.383(2)] In subsection (2) the reference to a security does not include a lien on books, papers or other records, except to the extent that they consist of documents which give a title to property and are held as such.

S.383(1)

This defines "creditor".

Note prospective amendment: in s.383(1)(a) the words from "(being," to "question)" are to be repealed by CJA 1988 s.170(2) and Sch.16 as from a day to be appointed; see the note to s.264.

S.383(2)–(4)

These provisions deal with the security and secured creditors. Section 383(2) defines "security", but this must be read in the light of s.383(4), excluding liens over books, etc. As to what constitutes "security" for the purposes of s.383(2) see *Fagg v Rushton* [2007] EWHC 657 (Ch); [2007] B.P.I.R. 1059. A landlord's right of re-entry is not regarded as security for these purposes: *Razzaq v Pala* [1998] B.C.C. 66. See also *Re a Debtor (No.310 of 1988)* [1989] 1 W.L.R. 452. Section 383(3) would be better located in s.269, to which it relates.

Section 383 was also considered in *Re Jones* [2008] B.P.I.R. 1051.

384   "Prescribed" and "the rules"

384(1)   **[Definitions]** Subject to the next subsection and sections 342C(7) and 342F(9) in Chapter V of Part IX, **"prescribed"** means prescribed by the rules; and **"the rules"** means rules made under section 412 in Part XV.

384(2)   **[Interpretation]** References in this Group of Parts to the amount prescribed for the purposes of any of the following provisions–

section 251S(4);

section 273;

section 313A;

section 346(3);

section 354(1) and (2);

section 358;

section 360(1);

section 361(2);

section 364(2)(d),

paragraphs 6 to 8 of Schedule 4ZA,

and references in those provisions to the prescribed amount are to be read in accordance with section 418 in Part XV and orders made under that section.

GENERAL NOTE

This section defines "prescribed" and "the rules" and must be read in the light of ss.418 and 412 respectively. A textual modification to s.384(1) was made by para.71 of Sch.12 to the Welfare Reform and Pensions Act 1999. The reference to s.313A was introduced by EA 2002 s.261(4).

Note amendment by Pt 1 para.4 of Sch.20 to the Tribunals, Courts and Enforcement Act 2007.

385   Miscellaneous definitions

385(1)   **[Definitions]** The following definitions have effect–

"the court", in relation to any matter, means the court to which, in accordance with section 373 in Part X and the rules, proceedings with respect to that matter are allocated or transferred;

"creditor's petition" means a bankruptcy petition under section 264(1)(a);

"criminal bankruptcy order" means an order under section 39(1) of the Powers of Criminal Courts Act 1973;

"debt" is to be construed in accordance with section 382(3);

"the debtor"–

    (za) in relation to a debt relief order or an application for such an order, has the same meaning as in Part 7A,

(a) in relation to a proposal for the purposes of Part VIII, means the individual making or intending to make that proposal, and

(b) in relation to a bankruptcy petition, means the individual to whom the petition relates;

"debtor's petition" means a bankruptcy petition presented by the debtor himself under section 264(1)(b);

"debt relief order" means an order made by the official receiver under Part 7A;

"dwelling house" includes any building or part of a building which is occupied as a dwelling and any yard, garden, garage or outhouse belonging to the dwelling house and occupied with it;

"estate", in relation to a bankrupt is to be construed in accordance with section 283 in Chapter II of Part IX;

"family", in relation to a bankrupt, means the persons (if any) who are living with him and are dependent on him;

"insolvency administration order" means an order for the administration in bankruptcy of the insolvent estate of a deceased debtor (being an individual at the date of his death);

"insolvency administration petition" means a petition for an insolvency administration order;

"secured" and related expressions are to be construed in accordance with section 383;

"the Rules" means the Insolvency Rules 1986; and

"the trustee", in relation to a bankruptcy and the bankrupt, means the trustee of the bankrupt's estate.

385(2) **[Interpretation]** References in this Group of Parts to a person's affairs include his business, if any.

S.385(1)

This provides general definitions of words commonly appearing in the Second Group of Parts. There are differences from its statutory predecessor. Thus, for example, references to resolutions passed at creditors' meetings have been omitted, as have other terms which have become obsolete. On the other hand, new terms have been included, such as "dwelling house" and "family" (note its extended meaning). Note also ss.382 and 383, and ss.435, 436.

Note prospective amendment: in s.385(1) the definition of "criminal bankruptcy order" is to be repealed by CJA 1988 s.170(2) and Sch.16 as from a day to be appointed; see the note to s.264.

S.385(2)

This is inserted *ex abundanti cautela*—a person's "affairs" would cover his business.

Note amendment by Pt 1 para.5 of Sch.20 to the Tribunals, Courts and Enforcement Act 2007.

THE THIRD GROUP OF PARTS: MISCELLANEOUS MATTERS BEARING ON BOTH COMPANY AND INDIVIDUAL INSOLVENCY; GENERAL INTERPRETATION; FINAL PROVISIONS

Introductory note to the Third Group of Parts

Parts XII–XIX of IA 1986 consist of a great variety of matters. Apart from the usual "mechanical" provisions (interpretation, short title, commencement, etc.), there is a group of sections, namely ss.386–387, which substantially reduce the significance of preferential claims in insolvency law. EA 2002 s.251 further reduces these by removing preferential status from Crown debts. The provisions on the qualification of insolvency practitioners are to be found in Pt XIII. There is also reference to official receivers (happily retained for corporate and personal insolvencies), the official petitioner, the Insolvency Rules Committee, insolvency service finance, insolvent estates of deceased persons and insolvent partnerships. The connection of other sections within Pt XVII with insolvency law is more indirect—thus there are provisions dealing with Parliamentary disqualification and restrictive trade practices.

Scholars of legislative history should note ss.423–425, which revamp s.172 of LPA 1925, a provision which can trace its own ancestry back to 1571!

PART XII

PREFERENTIAL DEBTS IN COMPANY AND INDIVIDUAL INSOLVENCY

Introductory note to Part XII

Preferential claims have been a part of insolvency law for nearly a hundred years. A preferential claim is essentially an unsecured one that is given especially favourable treatment by the legislature. Although the legislature is at liberty to create new preferential claims it seems clear that the courts will not do so on their own initiative: see here *Re Rafidain Bank* [1992] B.C.C. 376. It is not surprising, therefore, that the state has been the main preferential claimant. In the context of corporate insolvency law, this means that preferential claims are to be satisfied out of a company's assets subject to a floating charge in priority to the debenture holder enjoying that charge. They do not rank ahead of the claims of a debenture holder secured by a fixed charge: *Re Lewis Merthyr Consolidated Collieries Ltd* [1929] 1 Ch. 498; *Re G L Saunders Ltd* [1986] 1 W.L.R. 215. Although preferential claims enjoy no inherent priority over a fixed charge, such a priority can arise if the fixed chargee surrenders priority in respect of the charged asset to a floating chargee and fails to do so via a subrogation mechanism. A simple postponement agreement can lead to the fixed chargee inadvertently also surrendering priority to preferential claims: see *Re Portbase (Clothing) Ltd* [1993] Ch. 388; [1993] B.C.C. 96.

The proliferation of preferential claims since 1945 has worried banks enjoying the security of a floating charge and has led them to seek increased security in the form of the highly artificial fixed charge over future assets. The end result of these trends has been to make the position of unsecured creditors even more unhappy.

After reviewing the evidence, the Cork Committee (*Report*, para.1450) called for a radical reduction in the number of preferential claims:

"We unhesitatingly reject the argument that debts owed to the community ought to be paid in priority to debts owed to private creditors. A bad debt owed to the State is likely to be insignificant, in terms of total Government receipts; the loss of a similar sum by a private creditor may cause substantial hardship, and bring further insolvencies in its train" (para.1410).

In the early drafts of the Insolvency Bill 1985, the Government refused to act on this proposal because of the implications for the public exchequer. Reluctantly, however, it included provisions in IA 1985 (s.89 and Sch.4) which did reduce its own preferential position, and it is these provisions which have found their way into IA 1986.

The continued survival of preferential claims under English law was the subject of constant debate. It is interesting to note that the Crown's preferential rights have been entirely swept away in Australia by the 1992 amendments to the Corporations Law and in Canada have been significantly reduced by the Bankruptcy and Insolvency Act 1992. In view of these developments in other jurisdictions it came as no surprise when the Government indicated that it was intending to abolish Crown preferential debt. That process of abolition was completed by s.251 of EA 2002 with effect from September 15, 2003. Thus a number of preferential items are removed from the list in Sch.6. The underlying intention was that this sacrifice on the part of the state would compensate floating charge holders for the new burden created by the reserved fund for unsecured creditors (see s.176A). Although this is a significant change its impact must not be overestimated; other preferential claims will continue to survive for the foreseeable future.

Part XII applies to limited liability partnerships by virtue of the Limited Liability Partnerships Regulations 2001 (SI 2001/1090) reg.5(1)(b) as from April 6, 2001 subject to reg.5(2) and (3). For transitional provision see SI 2003/2093 (C. 85) art.4 and SI 2003/2332. Note also *Jackson and Long, Noters* [2004] S.C. 474.

Re application of Pt XII to insolvent partnerships, see the Insolvent Partnerships Order 1994 (SI 1994/2421), especially arts 10, 11, Sch.7.

386   Categories of preferential debts

386(1)   [Debts listed in Sch.6] A reference in this Act to the preferential debts of a company or an individual is to the debts listed in Schedule 6 to this Act (contributions to occupational pension schemes; remuneration, &c. of employees; levies on coal and steel production); and references to preferential creditors are to be read accordingly.

386(2)   ["The debtor"] In that Schedule **"the debtor"** means the company or the individual concerned.

386(3)   [Interpretation of Sch.6] Schedule 6 is to be read with Schedule 4 to the Pension Schemes Act 1993 (occupational pension scheme contributions).

GENERAL NOTE

These provisions, allied to Sch.6, reduce the number of preferential claims to a bare minimum. Note Banking Act 2009 ss.103 and 145.

S.386(3)

The reference to Sch.4 to the Pension Schemes Act 1993 was substituted for the former reference to Sch.3 to the Social Security Pensions Act 1975 by s.190 of and Sch.8 para.18 to the 1993 Act.

387 "The relevant date"

387(1) **[Explanation of Sch.6]** This section explains references in Schedule 6 to the relevant date (being the date which determines the existence and amount of a preferential debt).

387(2) **[Part I s.4]** For the purposes of section 4 in Part I (meetings to consider company voluntary arrangement), the relevant date in relation to a company which is not being wound up is–

(a) if the company is in administration, the date on which it entered administration, and

(b) if the company is not in administration, the date on which the voluntary arrangement takes effect.

387(2A) **[Schedule A1 para.31]** For the purposes of paragraph 31 of Schedule A1 (meetings to consider company voluntary arrangement where a moratorium under section 1A is in force), the relevant date in relation to a company is the date of filing.

387(3) **[Company being wound up]** In relation to a company which is being wound up, the following applies–

(a) if the winding up is by the court, and the winding-up order was made immediately upon the discharge of an administration order, the relevant date is the date on which the company entered administration;

(aa) if the winding up is by the court and the winding-up order was made following conversion of administration into winding up by virtue of Article 37 of the EC Regulation, the relevant date is the date on which the company entered administration;

(ab) if the company is deemed to have passed a resolution for voluntary winding up by virtue of an order following conversion of administration into winding up under Article 37 of the EC Regulation, the relevant date is the date on which the company entered administration;

(b) if the case does not fall within paragraph (a), (aa) or (ab) and the company–

(i) is being wound up by the court, and

(ii) had not commenced to be wound up voluntarily before the date of the making of the winding-up order,

the relevant date is the date of the appointment (or first appointment) of a provisional liquidator or, if no such appointment has been made, the date of the winding-up order;

(ba) if the case does not fall within paragraph (a), (aa), (ab) or (b) and the company is being wound up following administration pursuant to paragraph 83 of Schedule B1, the relevant date is the date on which the company entered administration;

(c) if the case does not fall within paragraph (a), (aa), (ab), (b) or (ba), the relevant date is the date of the passing of the resolution for the winding up of the company.

387(3A) **[Company in administration]** In relation to a company which is in administration (and to which no other provision of this section applies) the relevant date is the date on which the company enters administration.

387(4) **[Company in receivership]** In relation to a company in receivership (where section 40 or, as the case may be, section 59 applies), the relevant date is–

(a)   in England and Wales, the date of the appointment of the receiver by debenture-holders, and

(b)   in Scotland, the date of the appointment of the receiver under section 53(6) or (as the case may be) 54(5).

387(5)   [Part VIII s.258] For the purposes of section 258 in Part VIII (individual voluntary arrangements), the relevant date is, in relation to a debtor who is not an undischarged bankrupt–

(a)   where an interim order has been made under section 252 with respect to his proposal, the date of that order, and

(b)   in any other case, the date on which the voluntary arrangement takes effect.

387(6)   [Bankrupt] In relation to a bankrupt, the following applies–

(a)   where at the time the bankruptcy order was made there was an interim receiver appointed under section 286, the relevant date is the date on which the interim receiver was first appointed after the presentation of the bankruptcy petition;

(b)   otherwise, the relevant date is the date of the making of the bankruptcy order.

GENERAL NOTE

The purpose of these provisions is to explain the meaning of the phrase "the relevant date", used extensively in Sch.6. The timing for assessment of preferential claims depends on the particular insolvency regime involved, and whether corporate or individual.

Paragraphs (aa) and (ab) were inserted into subs.(3) by the Insolvency Act 1986 (Amendment) (No.2) Regulations 2002 (SI 2002/1240) reg.16 with effect from May 31, 2002. This insertion made necessary consequential amendments in the remainder of this subsection.

Subsection (2) was replaced, subs.(3) amended and subs.(3A) inserted by Sch.17 to EA 2002. Subsection (2A) was inserted by IA 2000 Sch.1.

Note Banking Act 2009 ss.103 and 145.

PART XIII

INSOLVENCY PRACTITIONERS AND THEIR QUALIFICATION

Introductory note to Part XIII

A major recommendation of the Cork Committee (*Report*, Chs 15–17) was that every insolvency practitioner should be a member of a recognised professional body, or at least have some minimum professional qualification, and that all practitioners should be subject to compulsory bonding to secure the due performance of their obligations. This, it was hoped, would curb the abuses associated in the past with "cowboy" liquidators, often people with no practical experience or relevant qualifications, who engaged in dubious practices to the detriment of creditors, sometimes in league with the controllers of the defunct company whose irresponsibility (and perhaps fraud) had brought about its collapse.

These proposals were accepted by the government in its White Paper (paras 8–11), and the framework for the new professional regime was set up by IA 1985 ss.1–11, now Pt XIII of the present Act. Much of its detail, however, has been left to be prescribed in the form of rules: see the Insolvency Practitioners Regulations 2005 (SI 2005/524). The 2005 Regulations repeal the 1990 Regulations (SI 1990/439) of the same name. The law now requires every insolvency practitioner either to be a member of a recognised professional body, or to be personally authorised to act by the Secretary of State (s.390(2)).

The Committee accepted that some concessionary arrangements would need to be made for established practitioners with substantial experience and a good record who lacked a professional qualification. However, since April 1, 1990, (the date when the now repealed 1990 Regulations referred to above came into effect), it has been necessary for persons applying to the Secretary of State for authorisation to have passed the examination set by the Joint Insolvency Examination Board or to have a similar overseas qualification, unless they already hold a current authorisation.

The introduction of professional standards for all insolvency practitioners has allowed some relaxation of the law, e.g. in such matters as the need to obtain the consent of the court before action is taken; and many of the functions which were formerly entrusted only to the official receiver have now been devolved upon private insolvency practitioners.

The policy towards insisting on a compulsory professional qualification limited to insolvency practitioners took a strange turn with the enactment and implementation of s.4 of IA 2000, which permitted other authorised persons to act as nominees or supervisors of voluntary arrangement. For background comment, see the note to s.389A below.

When the winding-up provisions of IA 1986 were extended to apply to building societies by the Building Societies Act 1986 Pt XIII was not specifically included. This oversight has since been corrected by CA 1989 s.211(2)(a). See the general note to Pt IV, preceding s.73, above. Part XIII applies to limited liability partnerships by virtue of the Limited Liability Partnerships Regulations 2001 (SI 2001/1090) reg.5(1)(b) as from April 6, 2001 subject to reg.5(2) and (3).

On the application of Pt XIII to insolvent partnerships, see the Insolvent Partnerships Order 1994 (SI 1994/2421), especially arts 10, 11, Sch.7.

In November 1996, the DTI Insolvency Service and the recognised professional bodies established a Working Party with terms of reference to review the state of regulation of the insolvency profession and to consider whether the regulation could be made more efficient and effective. The Working Party in December 1997 issued a consultation document inviting comments on such matters as the qualifications for entry into the profession, the scope and effectiveness of the regulatory regime, and its complaints procedures, and published its report on February 24, 1999. The report recommended the establishment of a new Insolvency Practices Council, to consist of a majority of lay members together with representatives from the professions to provide expertise and informed comment. The Council's remit includes to set professional and ethical standards and to promote efficiency, transparency and independence while at the same time assisting insolvency practice to respond to changing demands. The first chairman of the Council was appointed on December 21, 1999. The IPC funds strategic research. For example, it funded an empirical study produced by Adrian Walters and Mary Seneviratne of Nottingham Trent University in 2008 into Complaints Handling Procedures—see IPC *2007 Annual Report* at p.9 for full details.

In October 2001 the Insolvency Service issued a publication giving guidance on the making of complaints about insolvency practitioners.

Major changes to the rules governing the authorisation of and responsibilities owed by insolvency practitioners were made by the Insolvency Practitioners Regulations 2005 (SI 2005/524). These regulations, which took effect on April 1, 2005, repeal and replace the existing regulatory matrix founded upon the 1990 Regulations. In particular SI 1990/439, SI 1993/221, SI 2002/2710, SI 2002/2748 and SI 2004/473 are all repealed. Under the 2005 Regulations, broadly speaking, an insolvency practitioner must be an authorised person within the meaning of Pt 2 of the 2005 Regulations. Regulation 6 deals with the criteria for determining whether a candidate for authorisation is a fit and proper person. Apart from issues of personal integrity, there are detailed requirements mapped out in reg.7 as to requisite experience and training. Continuing professional development is compulsory (reg.9). Details on annual returns by authorised persons to the Secretary of State are outlined in reg.11.

Insolvency practitioners must lodge a bond in the form of a security or caution to cover potential liabilities to the insolvent estate in cases where duties are not properly performed (see Pt 3 of the 2005 Regulations which refers to Sch.2). The terms of the bond, amount of cover and penalties thereunder are dealt with by Sch.2.

Responsibilities with regard to maintaining records are dealt with by Pt 4 of the 2005 Regulations with the details of the minimum information required being specified in Sch.3 to those Regulations. Provision is made for identifying the location of such records (reg.14) and inspection procedures (regs 15–17). These records should contain information on the insolvency practitioner, the insolvent, details of bonding, information on meetings of creditors, the basis upon which remuneration is to be calculated and details on distributions.

Restrictions on unqualified persons acting as liquidator, trustee in bankruptcy, etc.

388 Meaning of "act as insolvency practitioner"

388(1) **[Acting as insolvency practitioner re company]** A person acts as an insolvency practitioner in relation to a company by acting–

(a) as its liquidator, provisional liquidator, administrator or administrative receiver, or

(b) where a voluntary arrangement in relation to the company is proposed or approved under Part I, as nominee or supervisor.

388(2) **[Acting as insolvency practitioner re individual]** A person acts as an insolvency practitioner in relation to an individual by acting–

(a) as his trustee in bankruptcy or interim receiver of his property or as permanent or interim trustee in the sequestration of his estate; or

(b) as trustee under a deed which is a deed of arrangement made for the benefit of his creditors or, in Scotland, a trust deed for his creditors; or

(c) where a voluntary arrangement in relation to the individual is proposed or approved under Part VIII, as nominee or supervisor;

(d) in the case of a deceased individual to the administration of whose estate this section applies by virtue of an order under section 421 (application of provisions of this Act to insolvent estates of deceased persons), as administrator of that estate.

388(2A) **[Acting as insolvency practitioner re insolvent partnership]** A person acts as an insolvency practitioner in relation to an insolvent partnership by acting–

(a) as its liquidator, provisional liquidator or administrator, or

(b) as trustee of the partnership under article 11 of the Insolvent Partnerships Order 1994, or

(c) as supervisor of a voluntary arrangement approved in relation to it under Part I of this Act.

388(2B) **[Acting as nominee re voluntary arrangement]** In relation to a voluntary arrangement proposed under Part I or VIII, a person acts as nominee if he performs any of the functions conferred on nominees under the Part in question.

388(3) **[Interpretation]** References in this section to an individual include, except in so far as the context otherwise requires, references to a partnership and to any debtor within the meaning of the Bankruptcy (Scotland) Act 1985.

388(4) **[Definitions]** In this section–

"administrative receiver" has the meaning given by section 251 in Part VII;

"company" means–

(a) a company registered under the Companies Act 2006 in England and Wales or Scotland, or

(b) a company that may be wound up under Part 5 of this Act (unregistered companies);

"interim trustee" and **"permanent trustee"** mean the same as in the Bankruptcy (Scotland) Act 1985.

388(5) **[Application]** Nothing in this section applies to anything done by–

(a) the official receiver; or

(b) the Accountant in Bankruptcy (within the meaning of the Bankruptcy (Scotland) Act 1985).

388(6) **[Applicability of EC Regulation]** Nothing in this section applies to anything done (whether in the United Kingdom or elsewhere) in relation to insolvency proceedings under the EC Regulation in a member State other than the United Kingdom.

GENERAL NOTE

The first step in establishing the statutory requirement that every insolvency practitioner should be professionally qualified is taken in this section, which defines the phrase "acts as an insolvency practitioner". This is not a *general* definition describing the work or activities of such a practitioner in the abstract, but a *specific* definition of what amounts to acting as an insolvency practitioner *in relation to* a particular company or individual. The Act does not make it an offence to carry on an insolvency practitioner's business without the requisite qualification, but rather to act "in relation to" a company or individual when the statutory requirements are not met (s.389).

An important point to bear in mind is that it is possible to "act as an insolvency practitioner" in relation to a person who is not insolvent—and to do so in breach of the Act will be just as much an offence as in a case of actual insolvency. Thus, the liquidator appointed by a company in a members' voluntary winding up "acts as an insolvency practitioner" even where the company has a large cash surplus and has never been in trading difficulties.

Most of the expressions used in this section are defined or explained either in the section itself or elsewhere in the Act: for reference, see App.I.

Section 388 is disapplied to a limited extent by the Cross-Border Insolvency Regulations 2006 (SI 2006/1030).

S.388(1), (2)
Note the amendments by IA 2000 s.4.

S.388(2A)
Section 388(2A) was inserted and the words "to a partnership and" in s.388(3) were omitted for the purposes of the Insolvent Partnerships Order 1994 (SI 1994/2421) art.15 as from December 1, 1994.

S.388(2B)
This was inserted by IA 2000 s.4.

S.388(4)
A receiver who is not an administrative receiver (i.e. a receiver of less than a "substantial" part of the company's property (ss.29(2), 251)) is not required to be qualified to act, but certain categories of person are disqualified from acting by ss.30, 31, 51(3).

Note the amendment made to subs.(4) by the Companies Act 2006 (Consequential Amendments, Transitional Provisions and Savings) Order 2009 (SI 2009/1941), which took effect on October 1, 2009. This amendment provides a new definition of "company". For the meaning of "company", see further the note to s.73(1). On "unregistered companies", see s.220. An insolvent partnership is treated as an unregistered company for the purposes of Pt V: see subs.(2A) above and the note to s.420.

Part XIII of IA 1986 was extended to apply to the winding up of building societies by CA 1989 s.211(2)(a) with effect from July 31, 1990, thus remedying an omission made when building societies were first made subject to the winding-up provisions by the Building Societies Act 1986.

S.388(5)
The official receiver, as the holder of a public office, is not required to be qualified to act as an insolvency practitioner. This will include a deputy official receiver (see s.401).

S.388(6)
This was added by Insolvency Act 1986 (Amendment) (No.2) Regulations 2002 (SI 2002/1240) reg.17 with effect from May 31, 2002.

389   Acting without qualification an offence

389(1)   **[Penalty]** A person who acts as an insolvency practitioner in relation to a company or an individual at a time when he is not qualified to do so is liable to imprisonment or a fine, or to both.

389(1A)   **[Limitation]** This section is subject to section 389A.

389(2)   **[Non-application to official receiver]** This section does not apply to the official receiver or the Accountant in Bankruptcy (within the meaning of the Bankruptcy (Scotland) Act 1985).

S.389(1)
The word "qualified" refers not simply to a professional qualification (which may or may not be required: see s.390(2)(b)), but to a complex set of requirements, some of them specifically related to the company or individual concerned.

On penalties, see s.430 and Sch.10. Note Banking Act 2009 ss.103 and 145.

S.389(1A)
Inserted by IA 2000 s.4.

389A   Authorisation of nominees and supervisors

389A(1)   **[Non-application of s.389]** Section 389 does not apply to a person acting, in relation to a voluntary arrangement proposed or approved under Part I or Part VIII, as nominee or supervisor if he is authorised so to act.

389A(2) [Requirements for authorisation] For the purposes of subsection (1) and those Parts, an individual to whom subsection (3) does not apply is authorised to act as nominee or supervisor in relation to such an arrangement if–

(a) he is a member of a body recognised for the purpose by the Secretary of State or of a body recognised for the purpose of Article 348A(2)(a) of the Insolvency (Northern Ireland) Order 1989 by the Department of Enterprise, Trade and Investment for Northern Ireland, and

(b) there is in force security (in Scotland, caution) for the proper performance of his functions and that security or caution meets the prescribed requirements with respect to his so acting in relation to the arrangement.

389A(3) [Bars to authorisation] This subsection applies to a person if–

(a) he has been adjudged bankrupt or sequestration of his estate has been awarded and (in either case) he has not been discharged,

(b) he is subject to a disqualification order made or a disqualification undertaking accepted under the Company Directors Disqualification Act 1986 or the Company Directors Disqualification (Northern Ireland) Order 2002,

(c) he is a patient within the meaning of section 329(1) of the Mental Health (Care and Treatment) (Scotland) Act 2003, or

(d) he lacks capacity (within the meaning of the Mental Capacity Act 2005) to act as nominee or supervisor.

389A(4) [Order by Secretary of State] The Secretary of State may by order declare a body which appears to him to fall within subsection (5) to be a recognised body for the purposes of subsection (2)(a).

389A(5) [Bodies recognised] A body may be recognised if it maintains and enforces rules for securing that its members–

(a) are fit and proper persons to act as nominees or supervisors, and

(b) meet acceptable requirements as to education and practical training and experience.

389A(6) [Members of a body] For the purposes of this section, a person is a member of a body only if he is subject to its rules when acting as nominee or supervisor (whether or not he is in fact a member of the body).

389A(7) [Revocation of s.389A(4) order] An order made under subsection (4) in relation to a body may be revoked by a further order if it appears to the Secretary of State that the body no longer falls within subsection (5).

389A(8) [Effect of order] An order of the Secretary of State under this section has effect from such date as is specified in the order; and any such order revoking a previous order may make provision for members of the body in question to continue to be treated as members of a recognised body for a specified period after the revocation takes effect.

GENERAL NOTE

This new section was added by s.4 of IA 2000. It allows a wider range of practitioners to service voluntary arrangements, and in particular those turnaround specialists who may be authorised by the Secretary of State. For discussion of the role of turnaround practitioners see Finch, [2005] J.B.L. 690. According to an Insolvency Service Consultative Document on Proposed Changes to the IVA Regime (issued in May 2007) this provision is likely to be modified by legislative reform order to make it absolutely clear that non-IPs can apply to operate IVAs, CVAs or both. This is a recognition that the current wording of s.389A is unclear. The timescale for such a reform is unclear.

S.389A(1)
This disapplies s.389 in the case of voluntary arrangements.

S.389A(2), (3)
These need to be read together. Note the amendment made to subs.(3)(b) by the Companies Act 2006 (Consequential Amendments, Transitional Provisions and Savings) Order 2009 (SI 2009/1941) (operational from October 1, 2009).

S.389A(4)
This authorises the Secretary of State to recognise bodies of practitioners who are not licensed insolvency practitioners—e.g. turnaround specialists.

S.389A(5)
This maps out the criteria for recognition under subs.(4).

S.389A(6)
This defines member in a regulatory fashion requiring compliance with rules of the recognised body when acting as nominee/supervisor.

S.389A(7), (8)
These deal with the status and effect of orders made under subs.(4).

389B   Official receiver as nominee or supervisor

389B(1)   [Voluntary arrangement where debtor undischarged bankrupt] The official receiver is authorised to act as nominee or supervisor in relation to a voluntary arrangement approved under Part VIII provided that the debtor is an undischarged bankrupt when the arrangement is proposed.

389B(2)   [Power of Secretary of State] The Secretary of State may by order repeal the proviso in subsection (1).

389B(3)   [Procedure for s.389B(2) order] An order under subsection (2)–

(a)   must be made by statutory instrument, and

(b)   shall be subject to annulment in pursuance of a resolution of either House of Parliament.

S.389B(1)
Introduced by EA 2002 s.264 and Sch.22, this enables the official receiver to acts as nominee/supervisor of a "fast track IVA" agreed under s.263A. This is an innovation—previously the role of servicing IVAs was restricted to private insolvency practitioners.

S.389B(2), (3)
These provide future flexibility for the Secretary of State.

The requisite qualification, and the means of obtaining it

390   Persons not qualified to act as insolvency practitioners

390(1)   [Must be individual] A person who is not an individual is not qualified to act as an insolvency practitioner.

390(2)   [Authorisation necessary] A person is not qualified to act as an insolvency practitioner at any time unless at that time–

(a)   he is authorised so to act by virtue of membership of a professional body recognised under section 391 below, being permitted so to act by or under the rules of that body, or

(b)   he holds an authorisation granted by a competent authority under section 393; or

(c)   he holds an authorisation granted by the Department of Enterprise, Trade and Investment for Northern Ireland under Article 352 of the Insolvency (Northern Ireland) Order 1989.

390(3)   [Security as condition required] A person is not qualified to act as an insolvency practitioner in relation to another person at any time unless–

(a)   there is in force at that time security or, in Scotland, caution for the proper performance of his functions, and

(b) that security or caution meets the prescribed requirements with respect to his so acting in relation to that other person.

390(4)   [Disqualification] A person is not qualified to act as an insolvency practitioner at any time if at that time–

(a) he has been adjudged bankrupt or sequestration of his estate has been awarded and (in either case) he has not been discharged,

(aa) a moratorium period under a debt relief order applies in relation of him,

(b) he is subject to a disqualification order made or a disqualification undertaking accepted under the Company Directors Disqualification Act 1986 or the Company Directors Disqualification (Northern Ireland) Order 2002,

(c) he is a patient within the meaning of section 125(1) of the Mental Health (Scotland) Act 1984 or has had a guardian appointed to him under the Adults with Incapacity (Scotland) Act 2000 (asp 4), or

(d) he lacks capacity (within the meaning of the Mental Capacity Act 2005) to act as an insolvency practitioner.

390(5)   [Disqualification where bankruptcy restrictions order] A person is not qualified to act as an insolvency practitioner while a bankruptcy restrictions order or a debt relief restrictions order is in force in respect of him.

GENERAL NOTE

As explained above, the Act uses the one term "qualified" with reference both to the general eligibility of the person to act as a practitioner and also to his specific eligibility to act vis-à-vis a particular company or individual. This section deals mainly with the general requirement, except for the statement in s.390(3)(b) that the practitioner's bonding obligation must relate to the person or company whose affairs he is administering. However, the subject of "qualification" is further dealt with in subordinate legislation made under s.419(2)(b). Reference should be made to the Insolvency Practitioners Regulations 2005 (SI 2005/524), which consolidate and replace earlier regulations dating from 1990.

Each of the regulatory bodies (see the note to s.391(1)), and also the Insolvency Practitioners' Association and the Association of Business Recovery Professionals publishes a guide to professional conduct and ethics, which sets out guiding principles relating to the conduct of insolvency practitioners in regard to accepting appointment as a trustee or office-holder, etc.

For the potential effect of EU Directive 2005/36 on the recognition of professional qualifications of insolvency practitioners who had qualified outside the UK see *Dear IP*, September 2007. This Directive is implemented in the UK by the EC (Recognition of Professional Qualifications) Regulations 2007 (SI 2007/2781).

Note Banking Act 2009 ss.103 and 145.

S.390(1)

The disqualification of corporate bodies is an extension of the prohibition that formerly applied in the case of a liquidator (CA 1985 s.634) and still applies to a receiver (not necessarily an administrative receiver): see ss.30 and 51(3)(a), (c). An act purportedly done by a corporate receiver has been held to be a nullity: see the note to s.232.

On the question of joint appointments, see s.231.

S.390(2)

The Cork Committee recommended (*Report*, para.758) that an insolvency practitioner should be required in all cases to be a member of an "approved" professional body and to have been in general practice for five years before being eligible to act. (Transitional arrangements would have allowed experienced individuals who were not professionally qualified to obtain direct authorisation to act from the Secretary of State.) The Government in its White Paper (para.43) broadly endorsed this view, but in the Insolvency Bill as originally published in 1984 went further, and provided that every insolvency practitioner, whether a member of a profession or not, should be required to hold a certificate issued to him personally by the Secretary of State before he was eligible to act. The legislation in its final form, however, returns to a compromise position: those who are under the supervision of a recognised professional body are to be permitted or authorised to act by that body, and will not be directly licensed or controlled by the

Secretary of State, while others may be authorised as individuals to act, either by the Secretary of State or by a "competent authority" to which this function may be delegated (s.392). The "direct licensing" provisions of the Act do not appear, however, to have been purely a transitional arrangement as the Cork Committee envisaged.

Schedule 11 para.21 provides that a person who was already in office (e.g. as a liquidator) when the Act came into force could continue to discharge the functions of that particular office, and so complete the liquidation, etc. without the need for acquiring a qualification under s.390(2) or (3).

S.390(3)

This subsection provides for the bonding of insolvency practitioners, which is a mandatory requirement for all officeholders. The security may be provided either generally or specially for a particular insolvency, and provides a safeguard for creditors and other interested persons who may suffer loss as a result of breach by the insolvency practitioner of the duties and obligations imposed on him by the legislation. The surety's liability is limited to a sum equivalent to the losses caused by the fraud or dishonesty of the practitioner, whether acting alone or in collusion with others; for the maximum amount for which any bond must be given see the Insolvency Practitioners Regulations 2005 (SI 2005/524).

On the question of transitional provisions for persons holding office when the Act came into force, see the note to s.390(2) above.

S.390(4)

In s.390(4)(c) the words "or has had a guardian appointed to him under the Adults with Incapacity (Scotland) Act 2000 (asp 4)" inserted at the end by the Adults with Incapacity (Scotland) Act 2000 s.88(2), Sch.5 para.18 as from April 1, 2002 (Adults with Incapacity (Scotland) Act 2000 (Commencement No.1) Order 2001 (SI 2000/81 (C. 2)) art.3, Sch.2). Subsection (4) was amended by Sch.6 to the Mental Capacity Act 2005 and by the Tribunals, Courts and Enforcement Act 2007.

Note the amendment made to subs.(4)(b) by the Companies Act 2006 (Consequential Amendments, Transitional Provisions and Savings) Order 2009 (SI 2009/1941), which came into effect on October 1, 2009.

If a person comes under any of the disabilities mentioned, his disqualification is automatic, and does not depend upon the withdrawal of his authorisation under s.393. Acts done by a disqualified person may, however, be valid by virtue of s.232: see the note to that section.

S.390(5)

This was inserted by EA 2002 Sch.21 to respond to the advent of BROs from April 2004.

Note prospective amendment by para.6 of Pt 1 of Sch.20 to the Tribunals, Courts and Enforcement Act 2007. The amendment is not included in the statutory text above as it is not yet in force.

391 Recognised professional bodies

391(1) **[Order by Secretary of State]** The Secretary of State may by order declare a body which appears to him to fall within subsection (2) below to be a recognised professional body for the purposes of this section.

391(2) **[Bodies recognised]** A body may be recognised if it regulates the practice of a profession and maintains and enforces rules for securing that such of its members as are permitted by or under the rules to act as insolvency practitioners–

(a)   are fit and proper persons so to act, and

(b)   meet acceptable requirements as to education and practical training and experience.

391(3) **[Interpretation]** References to members of a recognised professional body are to persons who, whether members of that body or not, are subject to its rules in the practice of the profession in question.

The reference in section 390(2) above to membership of a professional body recognised under this section is to be read accordingly.

391(4) **[Revocation of order]** An order made under subsection (1) in relation to a professional body may be revoked by a further order if it appears to the Secretary of State that the body no longer falls within subsection (2).

391(5) **[Effect of order]** An order of the Secretary of State under this section has effect from such date as is specified in the order; and any such order revoking a previous order may make provision whereby members of the body in question continue to be treated as authorised to act as insolvency practitioners for a specified period after the revocation takes effect.

GENERAL NOTE

This section provides the machinery for "recognising" professional bodies whose members will be authorised to act as insolvency practitioners under s.390(2)(a), and also for the withdrawal of such recognition. For application and ongoing fees see the Insolvency Practitioners and Insolvency Services Account (Fees) Order 2003 (SI 2003/3363) as amended by SI 2004/476, SI 2005/523, SI 2005/3524 and SI 2007/133. Note Banking Act 2009 ss.103 and 145.

S.391(1)

The relevant order is the Insolvency Practitioners (Recognised Professional Bodies) Order 1986 (SI 1986/1764) under which the following bodies are recognised:

- The Chartered Association of Certified Accountants,
- The Institute of Chartered Accountants in England and Wales,
- The Institute of Chartered Accountants of Scotland,
- The Institute of Chartered Accountants in Ireland,
- The Insolvency Practitioners Association,
- The Law Society of Scotland,
- The Law Society.

S.391(2)

Membership of the professional body is not in itself sufficient (nor, in some cases, even necessary: see s.391(3)): the person must be specifically permitted by the rules of the body to act as an insolvency practitioner. This enables the professional body to restrict eligibility to those of its members who are able to satisfy prescribed requirements as to examinations and practical experience. If the professional body withdraws a member's licence to act as an insolvency practitioner he ceases, of course, to be qualified to act. This the body may do without prior notice to the member if this is thought necessary in order to protect the public: *R. v Institute of Chartered Accountants, ex rel Eliades* [2001] B.P.I.R. 363. The importance of the professional regulatory body following correct procedures in exercising its regulatory powers was stressed by Collins J. in *Mond v ACCA* [2005] EWHC 1414 (Admin); [2006] B.P.I.R. 94. Although disciplinary regulations should not be interpreted in an over-technical manner the law did require them and any charges made under them to be properly drawn up. The criterion of fairness had to be observed.

S.391(3)

Persons who are subject to the rules of a professional body without having the full status and privileges of "membership" may be authorised under this section.

S.391(4)

The only power specifically conferred on the Secretary of State is to withdraw recognition from the body concerned. He is not given power to exercise detailed control over the activities of the professional body or to give it directions about the way it conducts its affairs. Nevertheless, the fact that the ultimate sanction of revocation is in his hands enables him to ensure that a body is kept up to the mark in such matters as, e.g. the enforcement of its disciplinary rules. This is important, because neither the Secretary of State nor the tribunal established under s.396 has direct jurisdiction over an individual member of a recognised professional body, or power to revoke his authorisation.

S.391(5)

The period of grace which the Secretary of State may allow has enabled some liquidations, etc. to be completed by the existing office-holder. It also gave the individual insolvency practitioners affected by the order time to apply for direct authorisation under s.392, or seek to become a member of another professional body.

392   Authorisation by competent authority

392(1)   [Application] Application may be made to a competent authority for authorisation to act as an insolvency practitioner.

392(2)　[Competent authorities] The competent authorities for this purpose are–

(a)　in relation to a case of any description specified in directions given by the Secretary of State, the body or person so specified in relation to cases of that description, and

(b)　in relation to a case not falling within paragraph (a), the Secretary of State.

392(3)　[Application] The application–

(a)　shall be made in such manner as the competent authority may direct,

(b)　shall contain or be accompanied by such information as that authority may reasonably require for the purpose of determining the application, and

(c)　shall be accompanied by the prescribed fee; and the authority may direct that notice of the making of the application shall be published in such manner as may be specified in the direction.

392(4)　[Additional information] At any time after receiving the application and before determining it the authority may require the applicant to furnish additional information.

392(5)　[Requirements may differ] Directions and requirements given or imposed under subsection (3) or (4) may differ as between different applications.

392(6)　[Forms] Any information to be furnished to the competent authority under this section shall, if it so requires, be in such form or verified in such manner as it may specify.

392(7)　[Withdrawal of application] An application may be withdrawn before it is granted or refused.

392(8)　[Sums received] Any sums received under this section by a competent authority other than the Secretary of State may be retained by the authority; and any sums so received by the Secretary of State shall be paid into the Consolidated Fund.

392(9)　[No fee under s.392(3)(c) in applications to Secretary of State] Subsection (3)(c) shall not have effect in respect of an application made to the Secretary of State (but this subsection is without prejudice to section 415A).

S.392(1)
Most insolvency practitioners become qualified to act by being members of a recognised professional body under s.391. However, these professions do not have a monopoly over insolvency work. The present section allows any individual to obtain authorisation personally, either from the Secretary of State or from a "competent authority" which may be designated to discharge this function. A person who is a member of a recognised professional body is not excluded from seeking direct authorisation under this section rather than authorisation from that body.

For the regulations relating to applications for authorisation under these provisions: see the Insolvency Practitioners Regulations 2005 (SI 2005/524). On fees see SI 2003/3363 as amended by SI 2004/476, SI 2005/523 and SI 2007/133.

S.392(2)
The Secretary of State is himself a "competent authority" and will always have a residuary power to deal with cases not specified under para.(a), and also during times when no alternative competent authority exists.

No competent authority has been specified in directions given under this section, and so for the time being the only competent authority is the Secretary of State.

S.392(3)–(7)
"Directions" relating to applications do not take the form of legislation but are made by the competent authority itself, i.e. at present, the Secretary of State.

S.392(8)
This provision enables an authority other than the Secretary of State to be wholly or partly self-funded.

S.392(9)
This was added by EA 2002 s.270(3) with effect from September 15, 2003.

393   Grant, refusal and withdrawal of authorisation

393(1)   [Power to grant, refuse application] The competent authority may, on an application duly made in accordance with section 392 and after being furnished with all such information as it may require under that section, grant or refuse the application.

393(2)   [Granting application] The authority shall grant the application if it appears to it from the information furnished by the applicant and having regard to such other information, if any, as it may have–

(a)   that the applicant is a fit and proper person to act as an insolvency practitioner, and

(b)   that the applicant meets the prescribed requirements with respect to education and practical training and experience.

393(3)   [Duration of authorisation] An authorisation granted under this section, if not previously withdrawn, continues in force for one year.

393(3A)   [Duty to grant further authorisation] But where an authorisation is granted under this section the competent authority must, before its expiry (and without a further application made in accordance with section 392) grant a further authorisation under this section taking effect immediately after the expiry of the previous authorisation, unless it appears to the authority that the subject of the authorisation no longer complies with subsection (2)(a) and (b).

393(4)   [Withdrawal of authorisation] An authorisation granted under this section may be withdrawn by the competent authority if it appears to it–

(a)   that the holder of the authorisation is no longer a fit and proper person to act as an insolvency practitioner, or

(b)   without prejudice to paragraph (a), that the holder–

(i)   has failed to comply with any provision of this Part or of any regulations made under this Part or Part XV, or

(ii)   in purported compliance with any such provision, has furnished the competent authority with false, inaccurate or misleading information.

393(5)   [Withdrawal on request] An authorisation granted under this section may be withdrawn by the competent authority at the request or with the consent of the holder of the authorisation.

393(6)   [Effect of withdrawal of authorisation] Where an authorisation granted under this section is withdrawn–

(a)   subsection (3A) does not require a further authorisation to be granted, or

(b)   if a further authorisation has already been granted at the time of the withdrawal, the further authorisation is also withdrawn.

GENERAL NOTE

The regulations relating to the grant and refusal of authorisation in force from April 1, 2005 are the Insolvency Practitioners Regulations 2005 (SI 2005/524, as amended) which replace the 1990 Regulations. On fees see the Insolvency Practitioners and Insolvency Services Account (Fees) Order 2003 (SI 2003/3363) as amended by SI 2004/476 and SI 2005/523.

S.393(1)
The Secretary of State is the only competent authority for the time being: see the note to s.392(2).

S.393(2)
The regulations referred to above set out in some detail the matters which are to be taken into account in determining whether an applicant is a fit and proper person, ranging from his personal integrity and history as a law-abiding

citizen to the adequacy of the systems of control and record-keeping in his business practice: see SI 2005/524. Practical training and experience is demanded of all applicants: see regs 7 and 8.

S.393(3), (3A)
See Provision of Services (Insolvency Practitioners) Regulations 2009 (SI 2009/3081).

S.393(4)
The procedure for appeal from the withdrawal, or the refusal, of an authorisation is set out in ss.394–398.

394 Notices

394(1) [Notice to applicant re grant] Where a competent authority grants an authorisation under section 393, it shall give written notice of that fact to the applicant, specifying the date on which the authorisation takes effect.

394(2) [Notice re proposed refusal, withdrawal] Where the authority proposes to refuse an application, or to withdraw an authorisation under section 393(4), it shall give the applicant or holder of the authorisation written notice of its intention to do so, setting out particulars of the grounds on which it proposes to act.

394(3) [Date to be stated re withdrawal] In the case of a proposed withdrawal the notice shall state the date on which it is proposed that the withdrawal should take effect.

394(4) [Notice to give details re rights] A notice under subsection (2) shall give particulars of the rights exercisable under the next two sections by a person on whom the notice is served.

S.394(1)
Without authorisation, the person will not be "qualified" under s.390(2)(a), and will be automatically liable to criminal prosecution under s.389 if he acts as an insolvency practitioner; but this does not affect any appointment which he already held when the Act came into force: see Sch.11 para.21.

S.394(2)–(4)
It would appear from the repeated use of the word "propose" that a decision to refuse or withdraw an authorisation does not take effect until the applicant or holder is informed of his rights to make representations under s.395(1) and to refer the matter for consideration to the Insolvency Practitioners Tribunal under s.396, and given an opportunity to do so. It is submitted that the word "decision" in s.396(2)(b) must mean "provisional decision", to be consistent with this view. There is no indication in s.394(3) whether the authority is free to specify any date it chooses as the effective date, but it would seem that, to make sense of the scheme of the Act as a whole, the date should be fixed at least 28 days ahead, and the notice should probably state in addition "or such later date as the authority may subsequently fix, if steps are taken by the holder to have the case reconsidered or reviewed under s.395 or s.396".

395 Right to make representations

395(1) [Right exercisable within 14 days] A person on whom a notice is served under section 394(2) may within 14 days after the date of service make written representations to the competent authority.

395(2) [Representations to be considered] The competent authority shall have regard to any representations so made in determining whether to refuse the application or withdraw the authorisation, as the case may be.

GENERAL NOTE

In addition to his right to have the case referred directly to the tribunal under s.396, the person affected by a proposed refusal or withdrawal may ask the authority itself to reconsider its decision. This will not prevent him from seeking a review by the tribunal if he is notified that the authority's earlier decision stands; and indeed he may apparently ask for a reconsideration under the present section and then change his mind and have the matter taken to the tribunal without waiting for the authority to complete its reconsideration.

396 Reference to Tribunal

396(1) [Application of Sch.7] The Insolvency Practitioners Tribunal (**"the Tribunal"**) continues in being; and the provisions of Schedule 7 apply to it.

396(2) [Person served with notice] Where a person is served with a notice under section 394(2), he may–

(a) at any time within 28 days after the date of service of the notice, or

(b) at any time after the making by him of representations under section 395 and before the end of the period of 28 days after the date of the service on him of a notice by the competent authority that the authority does not propose to alter its decision in consequence of the representations,

give written notice to the authority requiring the case to be referred to the Tribunal.

396(3) [Reference] Where a requirement is made under subsection (2), then, unless the competent authority–

(a) has decided or decides to grant the application or, as the case may be, not to withdraw the authorisation, and

(b) within 7 days after the date of the making of the requirement, gives written notice of that decision to the person by whom the requirement was made,

it shall refer the case to the Tribunal.

S.396(1)

The Insolvency Practitioners Tribunal was established by IA 1985 s.8(6) to discharge the functions set out in ss.396, 397 of the present Act. For further discussion, see the note to Sch.7 and the Insolvency Practitioners Tribunal (Conduct of Investigations) Rules 1986 (SI 1986/952) which continue in force. The Insolvency Practitioners Tribunal is a "tribunal" for the purposes of s.30 of the Tribunals, Courts and Enforcement Act 2007 (see Sch.6 Pt 4 to the 2007 Act).

S.396(2)

The present section provides a procedure which is in part alternative to s.395 and in part supplementary to it. A person who has been notified by an authority that it proposes to refuse his application or withdraw his authorisation may invoke the jurisdiction of the tribunal *either* (1) immediately and directly, *or* (2) after the authority's own procedure for reconsideration has run its course and the decision adverse to him is confirmed; and it appears that he may also interrupt the latter procedure and have the matter referred to the tribunal without waiting for a second decision. He must act within 28 days of being notified of the authority's provisional decision (in case (1)) or of its confirmed decision (in case (2)). The case is then referred by the authority itself to the tribunal for review.

S.396(3)

On receipt of a notice, the authority has seven days in which to change its mind and notify the person of its revised decision; failing this, it must refer the matter to the tribunal (though not necessarily within that seven-day period).

397 Action of Tribunal on reference

397(1) [Duties of Tribunal] On a reference under section 396 the Tribunal shall–

(a) investigate the case, and

(b) make a report to the competent authority stating what would in their opinion be the appropriate decision in the matter and the reasons for that opinion,

and it is the duty of the competent authority to decide the matter accordingly.

397(2) [Copy of report to applicant] The Tribunal shall send a copy of the report to the applicant or, as the case may be, the holder of the authorisation; and the competent authority shall serve him with a written notice of the decision made by it in accordance with the report.

397(3) [Publication of report] The competent authority may, if he thinks fit, publish the report of the Tribunal.

The tribunal makes its own investigation of the case but does not itself make a decision: instead, it gives directions to the authority (which are binding), supported by its reasons. The requirement that the tribunal should give a reasoned ruling plainly contemplates that it is open to a dissatisfied applicant to seek judicial review of a decision.

398 Refusal or withdrawal without reference to Tribunal

398 Where in the case of any proposed refusal or withdrawal of an authorisation either–

(a) the period mentioned in section 396(2)(a) has expired without the making of any requirement under that subsection or of any representations under section 395, or

(b) the competent authority has given a notice such as is mentioned in section 396(2)(b) and the period so mentioned has expired without the making of any such requirement,

the competent authority may give written notice of the refusal or withdrawal to the person concerned in accordance with the proposal in the notice given under section 394(2).

GENERAL NOTE

If a person who has been notified under s.394(2) of a proposal to refuse his application or withdraw his authorisation does not take the appropriate action within 28 days, he cannot prevent the refusal or withdrawal from taking effect. Whether this happens automatically, or whether a written notice must be given, depends upon whether the word "may" is to be read in a permissive or a mandatory sense. The stipulation that the notice shall be written probably indicates the latter: the point will be important only in regard to a withdrawal.

PART XIV

PUBLIC ADMINISTRATION (ENGLAND AND WALES)

Official Receivers

399 Appointment, etc. of official receivers

399(1) **[Official receiver]** For the purposes of this Act the official receiver, in relation to any bankruptcy, winding up, individual voluntary arrangement, debt relief order or application for such an order, is any person who by virtue of the following provisions of this section or section 401 below is authorised to act as the official receiver in relation to that bankruptcy, winding up, individual voluntary arrangement, debt relief order or application for such an order.

399(2) **[Power of appointment by Secretary of State]** The Secretary of State may (subject to the approval of the Treasury as to numbers) appoint persons to the office of official receiver, and a person appointed to that office (whether under this section or section 70 of the Bankruptcy Act 1914)–

(a) shall be paid out of money provided by Parliament such salary as the Secretary of State may with the concurrence of the Treasury direct,

(b) shall hold office on such other terms and conditions as the Secretary of State may with the concurrence of the Treasury direct, and

(c) may be removed from office by a direction of the Secretary of State.

399(3) **[Attachment to particular court]** Where a person holds the office of official receiver, the Secretary of State shall from time to time attach him either to the High Court or to a county court having jurisdiction for the purposes of the second Group of Parts of this Act.

399(4) **[Person authorised to act as official receiver]** Subject to any directions under subsection (6) below, an official receiver attached to a particular court is the person authorised to act as the official receiver in relation to every bankruptcy, winding up, individual voluntary arrangement, debt relief order or application for such an order falling within the jurisdiction of that court.

399(5) [Each court to have official receiver] The Secretary of State shall ensure that there is, at all times, at least one official receiver attached to the High Court and at least one attached to each county court having jurisdiction for the purposes of the second Group of Parts; but he may attach the same official receiver to two or more different courts.

399(6) [Directions by Secretary of State] The Secretary of State may give directions with respect to the disposal of the business of official receivers, and such directions may, in particular–

(a) authorise an official receiver attached to one court to act as the official receiver in relation to any case or description of cases falling within the jurisdiction of another court;

(b) provide, where there is more than one official receiver authorised to act as the official receiver in relation to cases falling within the jurisdiction of any court, for the distribution of their business between or among themselves.

399(7) [Continuation of official receiver] A person who at the coming into force of section 222 of the Insolvency Act 1985 (replaced by this section) is an official receiver attached to a court shall continue in office after the coming into force of that section as an official receiver attached to that court under this section.

GENERAL NOTE

The government in its zeal for public expenditure economies originally wanted to remove official receivers from personal insolvency law and to hive off their functions to the private sector—see its Green Paper on Bankruptcy (Cmnd.7967 (July 1980)), para.8. The outcry that this proposal attracted, not least from the Cork Committee (*Report*, para.723), was sufficient to force a rethink. The IA 1986 retains the role of the official receivers in bankruptcy law, although their involvement is now restricted to the more serious cases. For further guidance on official receivers, see IR 1986 Pt 10 and r.7.52 (rights of audience). Note amendment to subss.(1) and (4) by para.7 of Pt 1 to Sch.20 of the Tribunals, Courts and Enforcement Act 2007.

S.399(1)

This confirms that official receivers will continue to act both in individual and corporate insolvency cases. Reference to IVAs was inserted by EA 2002 Sch.23. A similar change was also made in subs.(4).

S.399(2)

The question of appointment, remuneration and tenure is to be determined by the Secretary of State. For the remuneration of the official receiver, see the Insolvency Regulations 1994 (SI 1994/2507) reg.35 as inserted by the Insolvency (Amendment) Regulations 2005 (SI 2005/512). The present position is reviewed by Ferris J. in *Mirror Group Newspapers v Maxwell* [1998] B.C.C. 324 at 337 and in the Working Party chaired by Ferris J. which reported in 1998—see Ferris, [1999] Ins. Law. 48.

S.399(3)–(5)

It is the responsibility of the Secretary of State to attach official receivers to the various courts having insolvency jurisdiction. Every court must have at least one official receiver attached to it, although that court may not be his sole responsibility.

S.399(6)

This provision authorises the Secretary of State to give directions to facilitate the disposal of business by official receivers.

S.399(7)

This is a transitional provision designed to ensure continuity.

400   Functions and status of official receivers

400(1) [Functions] In addition to any functions conferred on him by this Act, a person holding the office of official receiver shall carry out such other functions as may from time to time be conferred on him by the Secretary of State.

400(2)   [Status] In the exercise of the functions of his office a person holding the office of official receiver shall act under the general directions of the Secretary of State and shall also be an officer of the court in relation to which he exercises those functions.

400(3)   [Death or ceasing to hold office] Any property vested in his official capacity in a person holding the office of official receiver shall, on his dying, ceasing to hold office or being otherwise succeeded in relation to the bankruptcy or winding up in question by another official receiver, vest in his successor without any conveyance, assignment or transfer.

S.400(1)
The persons holding office as official receivers will have their functions governed either by the 1986 Act or by directions from the Secretary of State.

S.400(2)
This provision confirms that the Secretary of State has general control over official receivers although, as was the case under BA 1914 s.70(1), it is emphasised that they are also officers of the court. The effect of this is that any wrongful interference with them will constitute contempt of court. For the legal position relating to immunity for actions see *Mond v Hyde* [1999] Q.B. 1097. The immunity from suit of the official receiver was upheld by the European Court of Human Rights in *Mond v UK* [2003] B.P.I.R. 1347 where it was held that by maintaining this immunity English law did not breach the rights of the injured party under art.6 ECHR.

An official receiver can be a litigant in person—*Official Receiver v Brunt* [1999] B.P.I.R. 560 where the Court of Appeal gives detailed consideration to the nature of the office.

S.400(3)
The aim of this provision is to secure continuity of property ownership if an official receiver leaves office prematurely.

401   Deputy official receivers and staff

401(1)   [Deputy official receiver] The Secretary of State may, if he thinks it expedient to do so in order to facilitate the disposal of the business of the official receiver attached to any court, appoint an officer of his department to act as deputy to that official receiver.

401(2)   [Same status and functions] Subject to any directions given by the Secretary of State under section 399 or 400, a person appointed to act as deputy to an official receiver has, on such conditions and for such period as may be specified in the terms of his appointment, the same status and functions as the official receiver to whom he is appointed deputy.

Accordingly, references in this Act (except section 399(1) to (5)) to an official receiver include a person appointed to act as his deputy.

401(3)   [Termination of appointment] An appointment made under subsection (1) may be terminated at any time by the Secretary of State.

401(4)   [Staff] The Secretary of State may, subject to the approval of the Treasury as to numbers and remuneration and as to the other terms and conditions of the appointments, appoint officers of his department to assist official receivers in the carrying out of their functions.

S.401(1)
To facilitate the despatch of business by official receivers, the Secretary of State may appoint deputy official receivers.

Under BA 1914 s.71, the deputy could be appointed on application from an official receiver but only for a two-month period at most. The present Act appears to be more flexible on this matter.

S.401(2), (3)
A deputy enjoys the same status as an official receiver, fulfils the same functions and can be dismissed in the same way by the Secretary of State. References in IA 1986 to official receivers include references to deputies.

S.401(4)
The Secretary of State may also appoint civil servants from his department to assist official receivers, although the consent of the Treasury must first be obtained.

402　Official Petitioner

402(1)　[Continuation of officer] There continues to be an officer known as the Official Petitioner for the purpose of discharging, in relation to cases in which a criminal bankruptcy order is made, the functions assigned to him by or under this Act; and the Director of Public Prosecutions continues, by virtue of his office, to be the Official Petitioner.

402(2)　[Functions] The functions of the Official Petitioner include the following–

(a)　to consider whether, in a case in which a criminal bankruptcy order is made, it is in the public interest that he should himself present a petition under section 264(1)(d) of this Act;

(b)　to present such a petition in any case where he determines that it is in the public interest for him to do so;

(c)　to make payments, in such cases as he may determine, towards expenses incurred by other persons in connection with proceedings in pursuance of such a petition; and

(d)　to exercise, so far as he considers it in the public interest to do so, any of the powers conferred on him by or under this Act.

402(3)　[Discharge of functions on authority] Any functions of the Official Petitioner may be discharged on his behalf by any person acting with his authority.

402(4)　[Inability] Neither the Official Petitioner nor any person acting with his authority is liable to any action or proceeding in respect of anything done or omitted to be done in the discharge, or purported discharge, of the functions of the Official Petitioner.

402(5)　["Criminal bankruptcy order"] In this section **"criminal bankruptcy order"** means an order under section 39(1) of the Powers of Criminal Courts Act 1973.

S.402(1), (3)

This section preserves the post of official petitioner which will continue to be held by the Director of Public Prosecutions. The DPP can authorise junior officials to act in his stead.

S.402(2), (5)

These provisions describe his functions, the most obvious of which is to present a petition under s.264(1)(d) where a criminal bankruptcy order (as defined by s.402(5)) has been made, although he does have discretion to present petitions in the public interest in other cases.

S.402(4)

This confers immunity on the official petitioner for acts done in the discharge of his duties.

　　See also IR 1986 r.6.230.

　　Note prospective amendment: s.402 is to be repealed by CJA 1988 s.170(2) and Sch.16 as from a day to be appointed; see the note to s.264.

Insolvency Service finance, accounting and investment

403　Insolvency Services Account

403(1)　[Payment into Account] All money received by the Secretary of State in respect of proceedings under this Act as it applies to England and Wales shall be paid into the Insolvency Services Account kept by the Secretary of State with the Bank of England; and all payments out of money standing to the credit of the Secretary of State in that account shall be made by the Bank of England in such manner as he may direct.

403(2)　[Where excess amount] Whenever the cash balance standing to the credit of the Insolvency Services Account is in excess of the amount which in the opinion of the Secretary of State is required for the time being to answer demands in respect of bankrupts' estates or companies' estates, the Secretary of State shall–

(a) notify the excess to the National Debt Commissioners, and

(b) pay into the Insolvency Services Investment Account (**"the Investment Account"**) kept by the Commissioners with the Bank of England the whole or any part of the excess as the Commissioners may require for investment in accordance with the following provisions of this Part.

403(3) **[Where invested money required]** Whenever any part of the money so invested is, in the opinion of the Secretary of State, required to answer any demand in respect of bankrupts' estates or companies' estates, he shall notify to the National Debt Commissioners the amount so required and the Commissioners–

(a) shall thereupon repay to the Secretary of State such sum as may be required to the credit of the Insolvency Services Account, and

(b) for that purpose may direct the sale of such part of the securities in which the money has been invested as may be necessary.

S.403(1)
Fees, etc. collected in England and Wales by the Secretary of State in respect of proceedings under this Act (see ss.414, 415) are to be paid into the Insolvency Services Account at the Bank of England.

S.403(2), (3)
These subsections regulate investment of surplus moneys from the above Account in the Investment Account at the Bank of England. See also the Insolvency Regulations 1994 (SI 1994/2507), as amended by SI 2004/472 and SI 2005/512.

404   Investment Account

404   Any money standing to the credit of the Investment Account (including any money received by the National Debt Commissioners by way of interest on or proceeds of any investment under this section) may be invested by the Commissioners, in accordance with such directions as may be given by the Treasury, in any manner for the time being specified in Part II of Schedule 1 to the Trustee Investments Act 1961.

GENERAL NOTE

This section restricts investment of money placed in the Investment Account under s.403(2).

405   [Repealed.]

GENERAL NOTE

These provisions provided for the transfer of sums to the Consolidated Fund from the Investment Account and vice versa, where it is appropriate to adjust balances. They were repealed by EA 2002 s.272 with effect from April 1, 2004.

406   Interest on money received by liquidators or trustees in bankruptcy and invested

406   Where under rules made by virtue of paragraph 16 of Schedule 8 to this Act (investment of money received by company liquidators) or paragraph 21 of Schedule 9 to this Act (investment of money received by trustee in bankruptcy) a company or a bankrupt's estate has become entitled to any sum by way of interest, the Secretary of State shall certify that sum and the amount of tax payable on it to the National Debt Commissioners; and the Commissioners shall pay, out of the Investment Account–

(a) into the Insolvency Services Account, the sum so certified less the amount of tax so certified, and

(b) to the Commissioners of Inland Revenue, the amount of tax so certified.

GENERAL NOTE

Where a liquidator or trustee has paid sums into the Insolvency Services Account which have been invested, and these sums have earned interest, s.406 provides a mechanism for allocating these sums between those entitled, including the Revenue in respect of tax payable on the interest. In s.406 the words "or paragraph 21 of Schedule 9 to this Act (investment of money received by trustee in bankruptcy) a company or a bankrupt's estate" substituted for the words "a company" and the sidenote substituted for the former sidenote "Interest on money received by liquidators and invested" by IA 2000 s.13(2) as from April 2, 2001 (see SI 2001/766 (C. 27) arts 1, 2(1)(b)). This change was part of a package to benefit estates of bankrupts, which were otherwise providing an unjustified source of income for the State—a fact deplored by the Cork Committee (Cmnd.8558, para.857).

407 Unclaimed dividends and undistributed balances

407(1) **[Duty of Secretary of State]** The Secretary of State shall from time to time pay into the Consolidated Fund out of the Insolvency Services Account so much of the sums standing to the credit of that Account as represents–

(a) dividends which were declared before such date as the Treasury may from time to time determine and have not been claimed, and

(b) balances ascertained before that date which are too small to be divided among the persons entitled to them.

407(2) **[Sums to credit of Insolvency Services Account]** For the purposes of this section the sums standing to the credit of the Insolvency Services Account are deemed to include any sums paid out of that Account and represented by any sums or securities standing to the credit of the Investment Account.

407(3) **[Power of Secretary of State]** The Secretary of State may require the National Debt Commissioners to pay out of the Investment Account into the Insolvency Services Account the whole or part of any sum which he is required to pay out of that account under subsection (1); and the Commissioners may direct the sale of such securities standing to the credit of the Investment Account as may be necessary for that purpose.

GENERAL NOTE

This section states that unclaimed dividends, etc. are to be moved periodically by the Secretary of State from the Insolvency Services Account (or the Investment Account, where appropriate) to the Consolidated Fund. Investments in securities may need to be realised to achieve this end.

408 Adjustment of balances

408(1) **[Payments by Treasury out of Consolidated Fund]** The Treasury may direct the payment out of the Consolidated Fund of sums into–

(a) the Insolvency Services Account;

(b) the Investment Account.

408(2) **[Certification of reason for payment]** The Treasury shall certify to the House of Commons the reason for any payment under subsection (1).

408(3) **[Payments by Secretary of State into consolidated fund]** The Secretary of State may pay sums out of the Insolvency Services Account into the Consolidated Fund.

408(4) **[Payments by National Debt Commissioners into consolidated fund]** The National Debt Commissioners may pay sums out of the Investment Account into the Consolidated Fund.

GENERAL NOTE

This provision was introduced by s.272(2) of the Enterprise Act 2002 in substitution for the original s.408, which dealt with recourse to the Consolidated Fund. This substitution took place on April 1, 2004.

S.408(1)

This permits the Treasury to direct an adjustment of balances from the Consolidated Fund into the Insolvency Services Account and Investment Account. With regard to the Investment Account note the repeal of s.405 by s.272(1) of EA 2002.

S.408(2)

Directions given under subs.(1) must be reasoned.

S.408(3)

This permits payments out of the Insolvency Services Account into the Consolidated Fund.

S.408(4)

Payments from the Investment Fund into the Consolidated Account are hereby authorised.

409   Annual financial statement and audit

409(1)   **[Preparation of statement]** The National Debt Commissioners shall for each year ending on 31st March prepare a statement of the sums credited and debited to the Investment Account in such form and manner as the Treasury may direct and shall transmit it to the Comptroller and Auditor General before the end of November next following the year.

409(2)   **[Duty of Secretary of State]** The Secretary of State shall for each year ending 31st March prepare a statement of the sums received or paid by him under section 403 above in such form and manner as the Treasury may direct and shall transmit each statement to the Comptroller and Auditor General before the end of November next following the year.

409(3)   **[Additional information]** Every such statement shall include such additional information as the Treasury may direct.

409(4)   **[Examination etc. of statement]** The Comptroller and Auditor General shall examine, certify and report on every such statement and shall lay copies of it, and of his report, before Parliament.

GENERAL NOTE

This section lays down a framework for annual financial statements in respect of the Investment Account and the Insolvency Services Account, and the auditing thereof.

Supplementary

410   Extent of this Part

410   This Part of this Act extends to England and Wales only.

GENERAL NOTE

Sections 399–409 do not apply in Scotland, nor in Northern Ireland. This is confirmed by ss.440 and 441.

PART XV

SUBORDINATE LEGISLATION

General insolvency rules

411   Company insolvency rules

411(1)   **[Rules re Pts 1–7 or EC Regulation]** Rules may be made–

(a)   in relation to England and Wales, by the Lord Chancellor with the concurrence of the Secretary of State and, in the case of rules that affect court procedure, with the concurrence of the Lord Chief Justice, or

(b)   in relation to Scotland, by the Secretary of State,

for the purpose of giving effect to Parts I to VII of this Act or the EC Regulation.

411(1A)   **[Rules re Banking Act 2009 Pt 2]** Rules may also be made for the purpose of giving effect to Part 2 of the Banking Act 2009 (bank insolvency orders); and rules for that purpose shall be made–

(a)   in relation to England and Wales, by the Lord Chancellor with the concurrence of–

(i)   the Treasury, and

(ii)   in the case of rules that affect court procedure, the Lord Chief Justice, or

(b)   in relation to Scotland, by the Treasury.

411(1B)   **[Rules re Banking Act 2009 Pt 3]** Rules may also be made for the purpose of giving effect to Part 3 of the Banking Act 2009 (bank administration); and rules for that purpose shall be made–

(a)   in relation to England and Wales, by the Lord Chancellor with the concurrence of–

(i)   the Treasury, and

(ii)   in the case of rules that affect court procedure, the Lord Chief Justice, or

(b)   in relation to Scotland, by the Treasury.

411(2)   **[Contents of rules]** Without prejudice to the generality of subsection (1), (1A) or (1B) or to any provision of those Parts by virtue of which rules under this section may be made with respect to any matter, rules under this section may contain–

(a)   any such provision as is specified in Schedule 8 to this Act or corresponds to provision contained immediately before the coming into force of section 106 of the Insolvency Act 1985 in rules made, or having effect as if made, under section 663(1) or (2) of the Companies Act (old winding-up rules), and

(b)   such incidental, supplemental and transitional provisions as may appear to the Lord Chancellor or, as the case may be, the Secretary of State or the Treasury necessary or expedient.

411(2A)   **[Applicability of EC Regulation]** For the purposes of subsection (2), a reference in Schedule 8 to this Act to doing anything under or for the purposes of a provision of this Act includes a reference to doing anything under or for the purposes of the EC Regulation (in so far as the provision of this Act relates to a matter to which the EC Regulation applies).

411(2B)   **[Rules not to create an offence]** Rules under this section for the purpose of giving effect to the EC Regulation may not create an offence of a kind referred to in paragraph 1(1)(d) of Schedule 2 to the European Communities Act 1972.

411(2C)   **[Section 411(2) purposes: Sch.8 reference includes Banking Act 2009 Pt 2]** For the purposes of subsection (2), a reference in Schedule 8 to this Act to doing anything under or for the purposes of a provision of this Act includes a reference to doing anything under or for the purposes of Part 2 of the Banking Act 2009.

411(2D)   **[Section 411(2) purposes: Sch.8 reference includes Banking Act 2009 Pt 3]** For the purposes of subsection (2), a reference in Schedule 8 to this Act to doing anything under or for the purposes of a provision of this Act includes a reference to doing anything under or for the purposes of Part 3 of the Banking Act 2009.

411(3)   **[Interpretation of Sch.8]** In Schedule 8 to this Act "liquidator" includes a provisional liquidator or bank liquidator or administrator; and references above in this section to Parts I to VII of this Act or Part 2 or 3 of the Banking Act 2009 are to be read as including the Companies Acts so far as relating to, and to matters connected with or arising out of, the insolvency or winding up of companies.

411(3A)   **[References in s.411 to Banking Act 2009]** In this section references to Part 2 or 3 of the Banking Act 2009 include references to those Parts as applied to building societies (see section 90C of the Building Societies Act 1986).

411(4)   **[Rules by statutory instrument etc.]** Rules under this section shall be made by statutory instrument subject to annulment in pursuance of a resolution of either House of Parliament.

411(5)   **[Regulations]** Regulations made by the Secretary of State or the Treasury under a power conferred by rules under this section shall be made by statutory instrument and, after being made, shall be laid before each House of Parliament.

411(6)   **[Rules of court]** Nothing in this section prejudices any power to make rules of court.

411(7)   **[LCJ nominee]** The Lord Chief Justice may nominate a judicial office holder (as defined in section 109(4) of the Constitutional Reform Act 2005) to exercise his functions under this section.

S.411(1), (1A), (1B), (2), (2A), (2B), (2C), (2D), (7)
These subsections provide for the making of company insolvency rules which may include, for example, the matters specified in Sch.8 to this Act, or former corresponding matters. Note Banking Act 2009 s.100(7). Subsection (1) was amended and subss.(2A) and (2B) added by the Insolvency Act 1986 (Amendment) Regulations 2002 (SI 2002/1037) reg.3 with effect from May 3, 2002. See the Insolvency (Amendment) Regulations 2008 (SI 2008/670). The Insolvency Rules 1986 (IR 1986) (SI 1986/1925), as amended, are to be found below, commencing at p.664. Subsection (1)(a) was amended and subs.(7) inserted by the Constitutional Reform Act 2005 s.15 and Sch.4 Pt I para.188. The Banking Act 2009 ss.125 and 160 makes a number of amendments including the insertion of subss.(1A), (1B), (2C) and (2D).

Note the change to subs.(2)(a) by the Companies Act 2006 (Consequential Amendments, Transitional Provisions and Savings) Order 2009 (SI 2009/1941) (effective from October 1, 2009). This is in consequence of the enactment of the Companies Act 2006.

For recent secondary rules made under s.411 see for example the Energy Administration Rules 2005 (SI 2005/2483), the Energy Administration (Scotland) Rules 2006 (SI 2006/772 (S 8)), the Insolvency (Scotland) Amendment Rules 2006 (SI 2006/734 (S 6)), the Insolvency (Scotland) Amendment Rules 2007 (SI 2007/2537 (S 5)), the PPI Administration Order Rules 2007 (SI 2007/3141) and the Insolvency (Scotland) Amendment Rules 2009 (SI 2009/662 (S 1)).

S.411(3)
This is an interpretation provision, amplifying terms used in Sch.8 and s.411(1) and (2). Amendment by the Companies Act 2006 (Commencement No.3, Consequential Amendments, Transitional Provisions and Savings) Order 2007 (SI 2007/2194 (C. 84)) art.10 and Sch.4 para.44 as from October 1, 2007, recognises the Companies Act 2006. Note amendments by ss.125 and 160 of the Banking Act 2009.

S.411(4), (5)
These provisions explain how company insolvency rules and regulations may be made. The regulations are the Insolvency Regulations 1994 (SI 1994/2507) as amended, most recently by SI 2004/472. Note amendments by ss.125 and 160 of the Banking Act 2009.

S.411(6)
This is a saving provision mirrored by s.412(5).

412   **Individual insolvency rules (England and Wales)**

412(1)   **[Rules by Lord Chancellor]** The Lord Chancellor may, with the concurrence of the Secretary of State and, in the case of rules that affect court procedure, with the concurrence of the Lord Chief Justice, make rules for the purpose of giving effect to Parts 7A to 11 of this Act or the EC Regulation.

412(2)   **[Contents of rules]** Without prejudice to the generality of subsection (1), or to any provision of those Parts by virtue of which rules under this section may be made with respect to any matter, rules under this section may contain–

   (a)   any such provision as is specified in Schedule 9 to this Act or corresponds to provision contained immediately before the appointed day in rules made under section 132 of the Bankruptcy Act 1914; and

(b) such incidental, supplemental and transitional provisions as may appear to the Lord Chancellor necessary or expedient.

412(2A) **[Applicability of EC Regulation]** For the purposes of subsection (2), a reference in Schedule 9 to this Act to doing anything under or for the purposes of a provision of this Act includes a reference to doing anything under or for the purposes of the EC Regulation (in so far as the provision of this Act relates to a matter to which the EC Regulation applies).

412(2B) **[Rules not to create an offence]** Rules under this section for the purpose of giving effect to the EC Regulation may not create an offence of a kind referred to in paragraph 1(1)(d) of Schedule 2 to the European Communities Act 1972.

412(3) **[Rules to be made by statutory instrument]** Rules under this section shall be made by statutory instrument subject to annulment in pursuance of a resolution of either House of Parliament.

412(4) **[Regulations]** Regulations made by the Secretary of State under a power conferred by rules under this section shall be made by statutory instrument and, after being made, shall be laid before each House of Parliament.

412(5) **[Rules of court]** Nothing in this section prejudices any power to make rules of court.

412(6) **[LCJ nominee]** The Lord Chief Justice may nominate a judicial office holder (as defined in section 109(4) of the Constitutional Reform Act 2005) to exercise his functions under this section.

S.412(1), (2), (2A), (2B), (6)
These subsections give authority to the Lord Chancellor, with the agreement of the Secretary of State, to make new rules which replace the 1952 rules. These are the Insolvency Rules 1986 (SI 1986/1925) (see below, p.664). Schedule 9 to the Act provides guidelines on the matters which may be dealt with by the rules—e.g. role of the insolvency courts; notices; registration of voluntary arrangements; role of interim receivers and receivers and managers; meetings of creditors; other matters concerned with the administration of the bankrupt's estate; financial provisions; information and records; powers of the court; and miscellaneous and supplementary matters. Subsection (1) was amended and subss.(2A) and (2B) were added by the Insolvency Act 1986 (Amendment) Regulations 2002 (SI 2002/1037) reg.3 with effect from May 3, 2002. Subsection (1) was amended and subs.(6) inserted by the Constitutional Reform Act 2005 s.15 and Sch.4 Pt I para.189.
   Note amendment to subs.(1) by para.8 of Pt 1 of Sch.20 to the Tribunals, Courts and Enforcement Act 2007.
   The scope of the Lord Chancellor's rule making power under this provision was considered in *Trustee in Bankruptcy of St John Poulton v Ministry of Justice* [2009] B.P.I.R. 1512—but see now [2010] EWCA Civ 392.

S.412(3), (4)
These provisions govern how the Lord Chancellor may make rules under s.412 and how the Secretary of State may exercise powers by regulations under the said rules (see the Insolvency Regulations 1994 (SI 1994/2507). See also the Insolvency (Amendment) Regulations 2004 (SI 2004/472), Insolvency (Amendment) Regulations 2005 (SI 2005/512) and the Insolvency (Amendment) Regulations 2009 (SI 2009/482).

S.412(5)
The power of the court to make its own rules is not to be prejudiced by this provision.

413 Insolvency Rules Committee

413(1) **[Continuation of committee]** The committee established under section 10 of the Insolvency Act 1976 (advisory committee on bankruptcy and winding-up rules) continues to exist for the purpose of being consulted under this section.

413(2) **[Consultation by Lord Chancellor]** The Lord Chancellor shall consult the committee before making any rules under section 411 or 412 other than rules which contain a statement that the only provision made by the rules is provision applying rules made under section 411, with or without modifications, for the purposes of provision made by any of sections 23 to 26 of the Water Industry Act 1991 or Schedule 3 to that Act or by any of sections 59 to 65 of, or Schedule 6 or 7 to, the Railways Act 1993.

413(3) **[Members of committee]** Subject to the next subsection, the committee shall consist of–

(a) a judge of the High Court attached to the Chancery Division;

(b) a circuit judge;

(c) a registrar in bankruptcy of the High Court;

(d) the registrar of a county court;

(e) a practising barrister;

(f) a practising solicitor; and

(g) a practising accountant;

and the appointment of any person as a member of the committee shall be made in accordance with subsection (3A) or (3B).

413(3A) **[LCJ consults]** The Lord Chief Justice must appoint the persons referred to in paragraphs (a) to (d) of subsection (3), after consulting the Lord Chancellor.

413(3B) **[LC consults]** The Lord Chancellor must appoint the persons referred to in paragraphs (e) to (g) of subsection (3), after consulting the Lord Chief Justice.

413(4) **[Additional members]** The Lord Chancellor may appoint as additional members of the committee any persons appearing to him to have qualifications or experience that would be of value to the committee in considering any matter with which it is concerned.

413(5) **[LCJ nominee]** The Lord Chief Justice may nominate a judicial office holder (as defined in section 109(4) of the Constitutional Reform Act 2005) to exercise his functions under this section.

S.413(1)
This provides for the continuance of the Insolvency Rules Committee established under IA 1976 s.10. This is not to be confused with the Insolvency Court Users' Committee set up by the Vice Chancellor, Sir Nicolas Browne-Wilkinson, in April 1987 to advise on improvements to court practices: see *The Times*, April 8, 1987. In *Woodley v Woodley (No.2)* [1994] 1 W.L.R. 1167 Balcombe L.J. (at 1179D) formally invited the Insolvency Rules Committee to consider whether lump sum payments arising out of matrimonial proceedings should be made provable debts under r.12.3 of the Insolvency Rules and so restore the pre-1986 position. A similar, more successful, request was made in *Ram v Ram* [2004] EWCA Civ 1452; [2005] B.P.I.R. 396. See note to IR 1986 r.12.3. See also *Re Austintel Ltd* [1997] B.C.C. 362.
   For an excellent review of the role and constitution of the Insolvency Rules Committee see Davis, [2007] 20 Insolv. Int. 65.

S.413(2)
This Committee must normally be consulted before the Lord Chancellor makes any insolvency rules under s.411 or under s.412. Note the provisions in Banking Act 2009 ss.125(8) and 160(6).

S.413(3), (3A), (3B), (4) and (5)
These provisions regulate the composition of the Committee. Like s.413(1) and (2) they represent no real change in the law. Note the amendment to subs.(3) and the insertion of subss.(3A), (3B) and (5) by the Constitutional Reform Act 2005 s.15 and Sch.4 Pt I para.190.

Fees orders

414 Fees orders (company insolvency proceedings)

414(1) **[Fees]** There shall be paid in respect of–

(a) proceedings under any of Parts I to VII of this Act, and

(b) the performance by the official receiver or the Secretary of State of functions under those Parts,

such fees as the competent authority may with the sanction of the Treasury by order direct.

414(2)   **[Security for fees]** That authority is–

(a)   in relation to England and Wales, the Lord Chancellor, and

(b)   in relation to Scotland, the Secretary of State.

414(3)   **[Order by Treasury]** The Treasury may by order direct by whom and in what manner the fees are to be collected and accounted for.

414(4)   **[Security for fees]** The Lord Chancellor may, with the sanction of the Treasury, by order provide for sums to be deposited, by such persons, in such manner and in such circumstances as may be specified in the order, by way of security for fees payable by virtue of this section.

414(5)   **[Incidental matter under order]** An order under this section may contain such incidental, supplemental and transitional provisions as may appear to the Lord Chancellor, the Secretary of State or (as the case may be) the Treasury necessary or expedient.

414(6)   **[Order by statutory instrument etc.]** An order under this section shall be made by statutory instrument and, after being made, shall be laid before each House of Parliament.

414(7)   **[Payment into Consolidated Fund]** Fees payable by virtue of this section shall be paid into the Consolidated Fund.

414(8)   **[Interpretation]** References in subsection (1) to Parts I to VII of this Act are to be read as including the Companies Acts so far as relating to, and to matters connected with or arising out of, the insolvency or winding up of companies.

414(8A)   **[Application to Banking Act 2009 Pt 2]** This section applies in relation to Part 2 of the Banking Act 2009 (bank insolvency) as in relation to Parts I to VII of this Act.

414(8B)   **[Application to Banking Act 2009 Pt 3]** This section applies in relation to Part 3 of the Banking Act 2009 (bank administration) as in relation to Parts I to VII of this Act.

414(8C)   **[References in s.414(8A), (8B) to Banking Act 2009]** In subsections (8A) and (8B) the reference to Parts 2 and 3 of the Banking Act 2009 include references to those Parts as applied to building societies (see section 90C of the Building Societies Act 1986).

414(9)   **[Rules of court, Scotland]** Nothing in this section prejudices any power to make rules of court; and the application of this section to Scotland is without prejudice to section 2 of the Courts of Law Fees (Scotland) Act 1895.

S.414(1), (2)

These subsections govern the fixing of company insolvency fees in England and Wales, and in Scotland. Note the role of the Treasury in such matters. See the Insolvency Fees Order 2004 (SI 2004/593) as amended by SI 2005/544. A general updating of these fees was carried out by the Insolvency Fees (Amendment) Order 2007 (SI 2007/521). See also the Civil Proceedings Fees Order 2008 (SI 2008/1053 (L. 5)).

S.414(3), (7)

These provisions deal with the manner of collection and payment into the Consolidated Fund.

S.414(4)

Deposits by way of security may also be provided for.

S.414(5)

This is a safety valve mechanism designed to build flexibility into the system.

S.414(6)

This describes the parliamentary procedure to be used for orders fixing company insolvency fees.

S.414(8), (8A), (8B), (9)

These subsections provide an interpretation facility and a saving mechanism. Amendment of subs.(8) by the Companies Act 2006 (Commencement No.3, Consequential Amendments, Transitional Provisions and Savings)

Order 2007 (SI 2007/2194 (C. 84)) art.10 and Sch.4 para.44 as from October 1, 2007, recognises the Companies Act 2006. Subsection (8A) was inserted by ss.126 of the Banking Act 2009. Subsection (8B) was inserted by s.161 of the Banking Act 2009.

415   Fees orders (individual insolvency proceedings in England and Wales)

415(1)   [Payment of fees] There shall be paid in respect of–

(za) the costs of persons acting as approved intermediaries under Part 7A,

(a)   proceedings under Parts 7A to 11 of this Act, and

(b)   the performance by the official receiver or the Secretary of State of functions under those Parts,

such fees as the Lord Chancellor may with the sanction of the Treasury by order direct.

415(2)   [Order by Treasury] The Treasury may by order direct by whom and in what manner the fees are to be collected and accounted for.

415(3)   [Security for fees] The Lord Chancellor may, with the sanction of the Treasury, by order provide for sums to be deposited, by such persons, in such manner and in such circumstances as may be specified in the order, by way of security for–

(a)   fees payable by virtue of this section, and

(b)   fees payable to any person who has prepared an insolvency practitioner's report under section 274 in Chapter I of Part IX.

415(4)   [Incidental provisions etc. of order] An order under this section may contain such incidental, supplemental and transitional provisions as may appear to the Lord Chancellor or, as the case may be, the Treasury, necessary or expedient.

415(5)   [Order by statutory instrument etc.] An order under this section shall be made by statutory instrument and, after being made, shall be laid before each House of Parliament.

415(6)   [Payment into Consolidated Fund] Fees payable by virtue of this section shall be paid into the Consolidated Fund.

415(7)   [Rules of court] Nothing in this section prejudices any power to make rules of court.

S.415(1)–(3)
These subsections permit the Lord Chancellor, with the assent of the Treasury, to fix fees for bankruptcy proceedings and for tasks carried out by the official receiver or Secretary of State. Deposits which, e.g. represent advance payment of fees may also be similarly prescribed. See also the Civil Proceedings Fees Order 2008 (SI 2008/1053 (L. 5)). See the Insolvency Proceedings (Fees) (Amendment) Order 2008 (SI 2008/714) which came into effect on April 6, 2008. This amends SI 2004/593, SI 2006/561 and SI 2007/521 and revokes SIs 1984/880, 1985/1784, whilst partially revoking SI 1986/2030. Note Insolvency Proceedings (Fees) (Amendment) Order 2009 (SI 2009/645) which introduced new fees with regard to debt relief orders and increased other fees with effect from April 6, 2009.
  For the company law counterpart, see s.414. For further details, see Sch.9.
  Note amendment by Sch.20 to the Tribunals, Courts and Enforcement Act 2007 Pt 1 para.9.

S.415(4), (5)
These provisions deal with the procedural prerequisites of such an order from the Lord Chancellor and with supplementary matters which may be included therein.

S.415(6)
Fees collected under this provision are paid into the Consolidated Fund.

S.415(7)
This preserves the inherent power of the court to make rules of court.

415A   Fees orders (general)

415A(A1) [Fee by competent authority under s.251U re debt relief orders] The Secretary of State–

(a)   may by order require a person or body to pay a fee in connection with the grant or maintenance of a designation of that person or body as a competent authority under section 251U, and

(b)   may refuse to grant, or may withdraw, any such designation where a fee is not paid.

415A(1)   [Fee by recognised professional bodies] The Secretary of State–

(a)   may by order require a body to pay a fee in connection with the grant or maintenance of recognition of the body under section 391, and

(b)   may refuse recognition, or revoke an order of recognition under section 391(1) by a further order, where a fee is not paid.

415A(2)   [Fee by applicant as insolvency practitioner] The Secretary of State–

(a)   may by order require a person to pay a fee in connection with the grant or maintenance of authorisation of the person under section 393, and

(b)   may disregard an application or withdraw an authorisation where a fee is not paid.

415A(3)   [Insolvency Services Account] The Secretary of State may by order require the payment of fees in respect of–

(a)   the operation of the Insolvency Services Account;

(b)   payments into and out of that Account.

415A(4)   [Application of s.414(3), (5)–(7), (9)] The following provisions of section 414 apply to fees under this section as they apply to fees under that section–

(a)   subsection (3) (manner of payment),

(b)   subsection (5) (additional provision),

(c)   subsection (6) (statutory instrument),

(d)   subsection (7) (payment into Consolidated Fund), and

(e)   subsection (9) (saving for rules of court).

GENERAL NOTE

This additional provision was introduced by s.270 of EA 2002. The Secretary of State has made the following order under s.415A—the Insolvency Practitioners and Insolvency Services Account (Fees) Order 2003 (SI 2003/3363) as amended by SI 2004/476, SI 2005/523, SI 2005/3524, SI 2007/133 and SI 2009/487. This Order provides for payment of fees in connection with the authorisation of insolvency practitioners and the recognition of bodies under ss.391, 392, 393. Payment of fees in connection with transactions with the ISA is also prescribed.

The Insolvency Practitioners and Insolvency Services Account (Fees) (Amendment) Order 2007 (SI 2007/133) which amends SI 2003/3363 came into effect on April 1, 2007. See also the Insolvency Practitioners and Insolvency Services Account (Fees) (Amendment) Order 2008 (SI 2008/3) and the Insolvency Practitioners and Insolvency Services Account (Fees) (Amendment) (No.2) Order 2008 (SI 2008/672).

Note amendment by Sch.20 to the Tribunals, Courts and Enforcement Act 2007 Pt 1 para.10.

S.415A(1), (2)
The Secretary of State may charge a fee for recognising certain bodies under s.391 or persons under s.393 and may remove recognition if the appropriate fee is not paid.

S.415A(3)
Fees may be charged in respect of the operation of the Insolvency Services Account.

S.415A(4)

This extends various provisions in s.414 to s.415A.

Specification, increase and reduction of money sums relevant in the operation of this Act

416   Monetary limits (companies winding up)

416(1)   [Increase or reduction of certain provisions] The Secretary of State may by order in a statutory instrument increase or reduce any of the money sums for the time being specified in the following provisions in the first Group of Parts–

section 117(2) (amount of company's share capital determining whether county court has jurisdiction to wind it up);

section 120(3) (the equivalent as respects sheriff court jurisdiction in Scotland);

section 123(1)(a) (minimum debt for service of demand on company by unpaid creditor);

section 184(3) (minimum value of judgment, affecting sheriff's duties on levying execution);

section 206(1)(a) and (b) (minimum value of company property concealed or fraudulently removed, affecting criminal liability of company's officer).

416(2)   [Transitional provisions] An order under this section may contain such transitional provisions as may appear to the Secretary of State necessary or expedient.

416(3)   [Approval by Parliament] No order under this section increasing or reducing any of the money sums for the time being specified in section 117(2), 120(3) or 123(1)(a) shall be made unless a draft of the order has been laid before and approved by a resolution of each House of Parliament.

416(4)   [Annulment of statutory instrument] A statutory instrument containing an order under this section, other than an order to which subsection (3) applies, is subject to annulment in pursuance of a resolution of either House of Parliament.

S.416(1)

This provision allows the Secretary of State to use statutory instruments to increase or reduce various figures specified in the First Group of Parts without recourse to primary legislation.

In relation to Scotland, s.416(1) applies (with modifications) to limited liability partnerships by virtue of the Limited Liability Partnerships (Scotland) Regulations 2001 (SI 2001/128) reg.4(1), (2) and Sch.2 as from April 6, 2001.

S.416(2)

The statutory instrument may provide for transitional matters.

S.416(3), (4)

The basic parliamentary procedure to be used is mapped out by s.416(4), although this is qualified by s.416(3) in respect of the variation of certain figures. In relation to Scotland, s.416(4) applies (with modifications) to limited liability partnerships by virtue of the Limited Liability Partnerships (Scotland) Regulations 2001 (SI 2001/128) reg.4(1), (2) and Sch.2 as from April 6, 2001.

417   Money sum in s.222

417 The Secretary of State may by regulations in a statutory instrument increase or reduce the money sum for the time being specified in section 222(1) (minimum debt for service of demand on unregistered company by unpaid creditor); but such regulations shall not be made unless a draft of the statutory instrument containing them has been approved by resolution of each House of Parliament.

GENERAL NOTE

This section provides a procedure for modifying the minimum debt for a statutory demand (currently £750).

417A Money sums (company moratorium)

417A(1) [Change of sums] The Secretary of State may by order increase or reduce any of the money sums for the time being specified in the following provisions of Schedule A1 to this Act–

paragraph 17(1) (maximum amount of credit which company may obtain without disclosure of moratorium);

paragraph 41(4) (minimum value of company property concealed or fraudulently removed, affecting criminal liability of company's officer).

417A(2) [Transitional matters] An order under this section may contain such transitional provisions as may appear to the Secretary of State necessary or expedient.

417A(3) [Procedure] An order under this section shall be made by statutory instrument subject to annulment in pursuance of a resolution of either House of Parliament.

GENERAL NOTE

This was introduced by Sch.1 to IA 2000 with effect from January 1, 2003. It enables monetary figures mentioned in connection with the new CVA moratorium procedure to be modified by the Secretary of State.

418 Monetary limits (bankruptcy)

418(1) [Powers of Secretary of State] The Secretary of State may by order prescribe amounts for the purposes of the following provisions in the second Group of Parts–

section 251S(4) (maximum amount of credit which a person in respect of whom a debt relief order is made may obtain without disclosure of his status);

section 273 (minimum value of debtor's estate determining whether immediate bankruptcy order should be made; small bankruptcies level);

section 313A (value of property below which application for sale, possession or charge to be dismissed);

section 346(3) (minimum amount of judgment, determining whether amount recovered on sale of debtor's goods is to be treated as part of his estate in bankruptcy);

section 354(1) and (2) (minimum amount of concealed debt, or value of property concealed or removed, determining criminal liability under the section);

section 358 (minimum value of property taken by a bankrupt out of England and Wales, determining his criminal liability);

section 360(1) (maximum amount of credit which bankrupt may obtain without disclosure of his status);

section 361(2) (exemption of bankrupt from criminal liability for failure to keep proper accounts, if unsecured debts not more than the prescribed minimum);

section 364(2)(d) (minimum value of goods removed by the bankrupt, determining his liability to arrest);

paragraphs 6 to 8 of Schedule 4ZA (maximum amount of a person's debts, monthly surplus income and property for purposes of obtaining a debt relief order);

and references in the second Group of Parts to the amount prescribed for the purposes of any of those provisions, and references in those provisions to the prescribed amount, are to be construed accordingly.

418(2) [Transitional provisions] An order under this section may contain such transitional provisions as may appear to the Secretary of State necessary or expedient.

418(3) [Order by statutory instrument etc.] An order under this section shall be made by statutory instrument subject to annulment in pursuance of a resolution of either House of Parliament.

S.418(1)

This provision authorises the Secretary of State to fix monetary amounts for a number of provisions in the Second Group of Parts. For example, he can determine the "minimum amount" and the "small bankruptcies level" for the purposes of s.273, the minimum judgment for s.364(3), property values for the purposes of s.354, and so on. This represents a trend away from mentioning specific figures in the statutory provision itself to a more flexible regime suited to coping with inflation. The reference to s.313A was made by EA 2002 s.261(6). See Insolvency Proceedings (Monetary Limits) (Amendment) Order 2004 (SI 2004/547). See also the Insolvency Proceedings (Monetary Limits) (Amendment) Order 2009 (SI 2009/465).

Note amendment of subs.(1) by para.11 of Pt 1 of Sch.20 to the Tribunals, Courts and Enforcement Act 2007.

S.418(2), (3)

These deal with ancillary matters and the form of any order made by the Secretary of State under s.418(1).

Insolvency practice

419   Regulations for purposes of Part XIII

419(1)   [Power to make regulations] The Secretary of State may make regulations for the purpose of giving effect to Part XIII of this Act; and **"prescribed"** in that Part means prescribed by regulations made by the Secretary of State.

419(2)   [Extent of regulations] Without prejudice to the generality of subsection (1) or to any provision of that Part by virtue of which regulations may be made with respect to any matter, regulations under this section may contain–

(a)   provision as to the matters to be taken into account in determining whether a person is a fit and proper person to act as an insolvency practitioner;

(b)   provision prohibiting a person from so acting in prescribed cases, being cases in which a conflict of interest will or may arise;

(c)   provision imposing requirements with respect to–

(i)   the preparation and keeping by a person who acts as an insolvency practitioner of prescribed books, accounts and other records, and

(ii)   the production of those books, accounts and records to prescribed persons;

(d)   provision conferring power on prescribed persons–

(i)   to require any person who acts or has acted as an insolvency practitioner to answer any inquiry in relation to a case in which he is so acting or has so acted, and

(ii)   to apply to a court to examine such a person or any other person on oath concerning such a case;

(e)   provision making non-compliance with any of the regulations a criminal offence; and

(f)   such incidental, supplemental and transitional provisions as may appear to the Secretary of State necessary or expedient.

419(3)   [Power exercisable by statutory instrument etc.] Any power conferred by Part XIII or this Part to make regulations, rules or orders is exercisable by statutory instrument subject to annulment by resolution of either House of Parliament.

419(4)   [Different provisions for different cases] Any rule or regulation under Part XIII or this Part may make different provision with respect to different cases or descriptions of cases, including different provision for different areas.

S.419(1), (2)

This section provides for regulations to be made by the Secretary of State in order to achieve the aims of Pt XIII (qualification of insolvency practitioners). Examples of the matters which may be provided for are listed. It would perhaps have been more appropriate to include these provisions within Pt XIII itself. For the relevant regulations see the Insolvency Practitioners Regulations 2005 (SI 2005/524) which replace the 1990 Regulations as amended.

S.419(3)
This lays down the parliamentary procedure to be used for creating such regulations.

S.419(4)
This subsection, coupled with the generality of s.419(1), gives the Secretary of State considerable freedom for manoeuvre.

Other order-making powers

420   Insolvent partnerships

420(1)   [Application to insolvent partnerships] The Lord Chancellor may, by order made with the concurrence of the Secretary of State and the Lord Chief Justice provide that such provisions of this Act as may be specified in the order shall apply in relation to insolvent partnerships with such modifications as may be so specified.

420(1A)   [Provision re EC Regulation] An order under this section may make provision in relation to the EC Regulation.

420(1B)   [Provision must not create an offence] But provision made by virtue of this section in relation to the EC Regulation may not create an offence of a kind referred to in paragraph 1(1)(d) of Schedule 2 to the European Communities Act 1972.

420(2)   [Incidental provisions etc.] An order under this section may make different provision for different cases and may contain such incidental, supplemental and transitional provisions as may appear to the Lord Chancellor and the Lord Chief Justice necessary or expedient.

420(3)   [Order by statutory instrument etc.] An order under this section shall be made by statutory instrument subject to annulment in pursuance of a resolution of either House of Parliament.

420(4)   [LCJ nominee] The Lord Chief Justice may nominate a judicial office holder (as defined in section 109(4) of the Constitutional Reform Act 2005) to exercise his functions under this section.

S.420(1)
This allows the provisions of the Act to be extended (with suitable modifications) to deal with situations where insolvent partnerships are being wound up or are subject to various other insolvency regimes. Note the insertion of subss.(1A) and (1B) by the Insolvency Act 1986 (Amendment) Regulations 2002 (SI 2002/1037) reg.3 with effect from May 3, 2002. Note amendment of subs.(1) by the addition of the reference to the Lord Chief Justice by the Constitutional Reform Act 2005 s.15 and Sch.4 Pt I para.191. The Lord Chancellor originally exercised his power under subs.(1) to make the Insolvent Partnerships Order 1986 (SI 1986/2142), which has been replaced by the Insolvent Partnerships Order 1994 (SI 1994/2421). The 1994 Order provides the details of the necessary procedures with the modified primary legislation being reproduced *in extenso* in the Schedules to the Order. Appropriate forms are also appended. In the case of insolvency orders made before the coming into force of the 1994 Order (December 1, 1994) the provisions of the 1986 Order will continue to apply. Transitional matters are dealt with by art.19 of the 1994 Order. For discussion of the 1994 Order see Frith and Jones, (1995) 11 I.L. & P. 14.

The 1986 Order replaced the provisions in BA 1914 which dealt with insolvent partnerships: e.g. ss.114, 116, 119 and 127, plus rr.279–297 of BR 1952. For analysis of art.15(3) of the original 1986 Order see *Schooler v Customs and Excise Commissioners* [1996] B.P.I.R. 207. The 1986 Order in turn has been completely replaced by the 1994 Order. There were a number of factors which led to the introduction of the new Order. Amongst these were:

(1)   a desire to promote rescue procedures for insolvent partnerships;

(2)   the need to enhance the presentation of the relevant provisions to enable practitioners to interpret them more easily;

(3)   the necessity of dealing with the problems of conflict between the Act and the 1986 Order as revealed by the case of *Re Marr* [1990] Ch. 773;

(4)   the desirability of implementing the recommendations of the Cork Committee on distribution of assets of joint and several estates (see *Report*, paras 1685–1690);

(5)   the attractions of streamlining unnecessary procedures in order to reduce running costs.

For a fuller insight into the motivation leading to the introduction of the 1994 Order, see the Insolvency Service's Consultation Document of November 1992.

Under the 1994 Order a partnership continues to be treated as an unregistered company and therefore the provisions of Pt V of IA 1986 are made applicable (with necessary modifications). The purpose of the new rules is to facilitate combined insolvency proceedings against both the firm and its members, where the business is insolvent. If the business is solvent, but an individual partner is in financial difficulties, then the general procedures relating to personal or corporate insolvency, as contained in the 1986 Act, must be used instead.

The 1994 Order (in force from December 1, 1994) deals with a number of distinct insolvency situations:

A voluntary arrangement in respect of the firm (a partnership voluntary arrangement or PVA) (art.4). Full details of how Pt I of the Act is to be modified to deal with such a case are provided by Sch.1 to the Order. For analysis of a PVA see Bacon, (1994) 10 I.L. & P. 166.

A voluntary arrangement in respect of the members of an insolvent partnership (art.5). This was already a possibility before 1994, but art.5 clarifies the position (especially where both the firm and the partners are participating in voluntary arrangements).

An administration order in respect of the firm (art.6). Details of the modus operandi here are found in Sch.2 to the Order. See *Re Kyrris (No.1)* [1998] B.P.I.R. 103 and *Re Kyrris (No.2)* [1998] B.P.I.R. 111.

The winding up of the partnership firm (arts 7 and 9). Here, the partnership is treated as an unregistered company with the effect that the procedures contained in Pt V of the Act relating to the winding up of such companies are made applicable. The main ground for a winding-up petition is that the firm is unable to pay its debts. Such a petition may be presented by a creditor, or, where the firm consists of not less than eight partners by any member of the partnership. Separate provision is made for petitions presented by creditors (art.7 and Sch.3) and by members (art.9 and Sch.5).

The 1994 Order extends the availability of this winding-up procedure to the case of the winding up by creditor's petition of insolvent partnerships where the partnership has a place of business in England or Wales—it is not necessary that the principal place of business be so located. Thus certain overseas partnerships can now be brought within this regime.

Concurrent insolvency proceedings against the firm and individual partners (arts 8 and 10). Here, it is possible to present consolidated petitions against both the partnership firm and one or more partners in that firm (whether they be individuals or companies). The petitions will be presented to and heard by the same court. The petition against the firm is treated as the principal petition. A creditor can present a petition in such a case on the ground that the partnership is unable to pay its debts. The aim of this procedure is to facilitate the concurrent insolvency regimes—thus normally a single insolvency practitioner will handle the winding up of the firm and the insolvency proceedings against the individual members. A single public examination may be used to kill two birds with one stone. The partnership assets are to be used primarily to settle partnership liabilities; the old bankruptcy rule that the separate estates of the individual partners must first be utilised towards satisfying the claims of their own individual creditors has given way to a system under which creditors of the firm who have not been able to obtain satisfaction out of the firm's assets are entitled to equal treatment in any distribution of the separate estates. Thus the rule in s.33(6) of BA 1914 is abolished and English law is brought into line with Scottish law.

The other main changes introduced by the 1994 Order in this hybrid scenario are as follows:

- this procedure can be used where only one of the members (as opposed to the previous requirement of two) is facing insolvency proceedings concurrently with the partnership;

- special amendments are made to s.271 of the Act to reduce the difficulties encountered in *Re Marr* (above);

- procedural changes are made to cut costs (e.g. by removing the requirement for meetings that may be deemed to be unnecessary).

A joint bankruptcy petition covering all of the partners (art.11). It is possible for all of the partners to petition jointly for their own bankruptcy, or alternatively for some of the partners with the concurrence of the others to do this. In such a case, the trustee acting for the insolvent partners has authority to wind up the partnership firm even though no petition has been presented against it. This form of proceedings can only be initiated by the partners themselves, on the ground that the firm is unable to meet its debts, and it cannot be used if there are corporate partners or partners who dissent from this course of action.

Winding up an unregistered company where an insolvent partnership is a member (art.12). Here the insolvent partnership is treated as if it were a corporate member of the unregistered company.

In addition to the above procedural changes the 1994 Order also makes changes, for the purposes of the Order, to ss.168 and 303 of the Act (supplemental powers of court) and to s.388 (meaning of "act as insolvency practitioner"): see the notes to those sections.

A further amendment to the discrete insolvency regime for partnerships was introduced by the Insolvent Partnerships (Amendment) Order 1996 (SI 1996/1308). The main effect of this amendment was to allow the Bank of England and the Securities and Investments Board (now the FSA) to present winding up petitions in certain circumstances.

The Insolvent Partnerships (Amendment) Order 2001 (SI 2001/767) applies additional provisions inserted into CDDA 1986 to insolvent partnerships where appropriate.

The Insolvent Partnerships (Amendment) Order 2002 (SI 2002/1308) makes further changes into the legal regime governing insolvent partnerships. Essentially this Order caters for the introduction of the EC Regulation (1346/2000) by amending various procedural requirements relating to petitions and providing new forms which must be used for petitions presented after May 31, 2002. Note also SI 2002/2708.

The Insolvent Partnerships (Amendment) Order 2005 (SI 2005/1516) makes a number of significant changes to the regime for insolvent partnerships as based in the 1994 Order. These changes are introduced to cater for general reforms both to personal and corporate insolvency law made by the Enterprise Act 2002. Amongst the more significant reforms introduced by the 1995 Order are the application of the new administration procedure laid down in Sch.B1 to the 1986 Act to insolvent partnerships (see art.3). The new financial criteria governing Sch.A1 CVAs are now applied to insolvent partnerships (art.6(4)). The abolition of summary administration in bankruptcy law is also carried over to insolvent partnerships (art.5). However the rules on the prescribed part (see s.176A) are explicitly *not* extended to insolvent partnerships (art.4).

Note further changes have been made by the Insolvent Partnerships (Amendment) Order 2006 (SI 2006/622). Minor amendments to the 1994 Order were also made by the Lord Chancellor (Transfer of Functions and Supplementary Provisions) Order 2006 (SI 2006/680).

For technical provisions in the area of pensions see the Pension Protection Fund (Insolvent Partnerships) (Amendment of Insolvency Events) Order 2005 (SI 2005/2893).

S.420(2), (3), (4)

These subsections provide for flexibility of application, transitional matters and the procedure by which delegated legislation is to be made under this section. Subsection (2) was amended and subs.(4) inserted by the Constitutional Reform Act 2005 s.15 and Sch.4 Pt I para.191.

421   Insolvent estates of deceased persons

421(1)   **[Order by Lord Chancellor]** The Lord Chancellor may, by order made with the concurrence of the Secretary of State and the Lord Chief Justice, provide that such provisions of this Act as may be specified in the order shall apply in relation to the administration of the insolvent estates of deceased persons with such modifications as may be so specified.

421(1A)   **[Provision re EC Regulation]** An order under this section may make provision in relation to the EC Regulation.

421(1B)   **[Provision must not create an offence]** But provision made by virtue of this section in relation to the EC Regulation may not create an offence of a kind referred to in paragraph 1(1)(d) of Schedule 2 to the European Communities Act 1972.

421(2)   **[Incidental provisions etc.]** An order under this section may make different provision for different cases and may contain such incidental, supplemental and transitional provisions as may appear to the Lord Chancellor and the Lord Chief Justice necessary or expedient.

421(3)   **[Order by statutory instrument]** An order under this section shall be made by statutory instrument subject to annulment in pursuance of a resolution of either House of Parliament.

421(4)   **[Interpretation]** For the purposes of this section the estate of a deceased person is insolvent if, when realised, it will be insufficient to meet in full all the debts and other liabilities to which it is subject.

421(5) **[LCJ nominee]** The Lord Chief Justice may nominate a judicial office holder (as defined in section 109(4) of the Constitutional Reform Act 2005) to exercise his functions under this section.

S.421(1), (1A), (1B), (2)

This authorises the Lord Chancellor, with the agreement of the Secretary of State and Lord Chief Justice—see Constitutional Reform Act 2005 s.15 and Sch.4 Pt I para.192—to extend the provisions of IA 1986 to the insolvent estates of deceased persons, subject to any modifications deemed necessary. A minor textual change was made by s.12(2) IA 2000 with effect from April 2, 2001. See SI 2001/766 (C. 27). Subsections (1A) and (1B) were inserted by the Insolvency Act 1986 (Amendment) Regulations 2002 (SI 2002/1037) with effect from May 3, 2002.

The BA 1914 laid down considerable detail on the administration of estates of deceased insolvents, whereas the present Act clearly leaves much to the rules in delegated legislation: see Sch.9 para.19 and the Administration of Insolvent Estates of Deceased Persons Order 1986 (SI 1986/1999).

Orders granted under s.421 and the 1986 Order are extremely rare. The relationship between the Act, the Order and certain common law presumptions was the subject of judicial comment in *Re Palmer* [1994] Ch. 316. Here it was held by the Court of Appeal that the general legal presumption that a judicial act is deemed to have occurred at the earliest moment from the day on which it was done cannot be used to provide an interpretation of the Order that would make it inconsistent with the Act or make the Order ultra vires s.421. Thus an administration order made by the court in respect of the estate of a deceased insolvent could not by using judicial fictions be deemed to have been made during the lifetime of that person. In so deciding the Court of Appeal rejected the approach adopted by Vinelott J. at first instance: see [1994] Ch. 316.

Another case where this regime was considered, albeit in a Northern Irish context, was *McAteer v Lismore (No.1)* [2002] B.P.I.R. 804. Here Girvan J. held that the modus operandi of various transactional avoidance provisions which sought to avoid transactions from the date of the death rather than from the actual date of the commencement of the insolvency administration would have to be reviewed by the court in the light of the right to peaceable enjoyment of one's property as conferred by art.1 of the First Protocol of the European Convention on Human Rights.

In *Re Vos (decd)* [2006] B.P.I.R. 348 Registrar Baister was confronted with another case involving the administration of the estate of deceased insolvent. The issue at stake here was whether payment for professional services rendered to the estate of the deceased insolvent before insolvency was declared could be treated as automatically void by virtue of the operation of s.284 of the IA 1986 (as modified by the Administration of Estates of Deceased Insolvents Order 1986 so as to apply to dispositions on behalf of deceased insolvents with effect from the date of the death). The professional firm involved contended that this provision did not apply and that, even if it did, such payments should be ratified by the court as they were made bona fide in return for beneficial services rendered to the estate. Registrar Baister held that by adopting a purposive approach to interpretation the modified s.284 applied so as to render automatically void any payments made out of the estate of the deceased from the date of the death up to the date of the insolvency order, notwithstanding the fact that the insolvency order was not made until many years after the death. The protective provisions of the Human Rights Act 1998 relating to expropriation of property were not engaged so as to protect the position of the payee. However, the court enjoyed the power to ratify certain payments made prior to any realisation that the estate might be insolvent and would do so here to mitigate to a limited extent the liability to reimburse the estate. This is a cautionary tale.

The regime governing the administration of estates of deceased insolvents was modified with effect from May 31, 2002 by the Administration of Insolvent Estates of Deceased Persons (Amendment) Order 2002 (SI 2002/1309). This piece of delegated legislation owes its existence to EC Council Regulation 1346/2000 on Insolvency Proceedings. The effect of these changes is to facilitate cross-border insolvency administration by providing new forms (instead of those found in the 1986 Order) which are to be used where the EC Regulation applies.

S.421(3)

This describes the modus operandi of such extension.

S.421(4)

This determines when the estate of a deceased person is insolvent.

S.421(5)

This was inserted by para.192 of Sch.4 Pt I of the Constitutional Reform Act 2005.

421A Insolvent estates: joint tenancies

421A(1) **[Application]** This section applies where–

(a) an insolvency administration order has been made in respect of the insolvent estate of a deceased person,

(b) the petition for the order was presented after the commencement of this section and within the period of five years beginning with the day on which he died, and

(c) immediately before his death he was beneficially entitled to an interest in any property as joint tenant.

421A(2) [Power of court] For the purpose of securing that debts and other liabilities to which the estate is subject are met, the court may, on an application by the trustee appointed pursuant to the insolvency administration order, make an order under this section requiring the survivor to pay to the trustee an amount not exceeding the value lost to the estate.

421A(3) [Duty of court] In determining whether to make an order under this section, and the terms of such an order, the court must have regard to all the circumstances of the case, including the interests of the deceased's creditors and of the survivor; but, unless the circumstances are exceptional, the court must assume that the interests of the deceased's creditors outweigh all other considerations.

421A(4) [Terms, etc. of order] The order may be made on such terms and conditions as the court thinks fit.

421A(5) [Sums to be comprised in the estate] Any sums required to be paid to the trustee in accordance with an order under this section shall be comprised in the estate.

421A(6) [Section 421 modifications] The modifications of this Act which may be made by an order under section 421 include any modifications which are necessary or expedient in consequence of this section.

421A(7) ["Survivor"] In this section, "survivor" means the person who, immediately before the death, was beneficially entitled as joint tenant with the deceased or, if the person who was so entitled dies after the making of the insolvency administration order, his personal representatives.

421A(8) [Multiple survivors] If there is more than one survivor–

(a) an order under this section may be made against all or any of them, but

(b) no survivor shall be required to pay more than so much of the value lost to the estate as is properly attributable to him.

421A(9) [Definitions] In this section–

"insolvency administration order" has the same meaning as in any order under section 421 having effect for the time being,

"value lost to the estate" means the amount which, if paid to the trustee, would in the court's opinion restore the position to what it would have been if the deceased had been adjudged bankrupt immediately before his death.

GENERAL NOTE

Introduced by s.12 of IA 2000 with effect from April 2, 2001, this introduces a new s.421A whose effect is to reverse the inconvenient decision of the Court of Appeal in *Re Palmer (decd)* [1994] Ch. 316 which cast doubt upon the effectiveness of secondary legislation made under s.421. Here the Court of Appeal ruled that the Administration of Insolvent Estates of Deceased Persons Order 1986 (SI 1986/1999) did not have the effect that it was apparently intended to have and in particular where a joint tenant of property died insolvent his or her interest in the property passed automatically to the other joint tenant and did not form part of the insolvent estate for distribution amongst creditors. This ruling was seen to favour spouses in particular at the expense of creditors. There are admittedly very few cases where an administration of an estate of a deceased insolvent is required, but the problem was deemed sufficiently serious to require legislative correction. The original clause in the Bill had to be rewritten to counteract unintended consequences with regard to the marketability of property and the final provision arose out of the work of HC Standing Committee B (for explanation see *Hansard*, HL Vol.619, cols 1345–1350).

Under s.421A the survivor can be ordered to pay value to the estate; there is no transfer of property rights as such. The court enjoys discretion to deal with the matter, but as in insolvency generally the interests of creditors prevail unless the case is exceptional. The jurisprudence under s.336 of IA 1986 is likely to be influential here. Subsections (7) and (9) of the new s.421A are definitional.

Concerns were raised as to whether this provision would have retrospective effect. This was eventually conceded by the government, who argued that the limited degree of retroactivity struck the right balance—see *Hansard*, HL Vol.619, cols 1348–9. On closer examination of s.421A(1) the position is that this new provision can only operate if the petition for the administration order was brought within five years of the death and after the coming into force of the section. Therefore there may be some retrospectivity at work depending on commencement dates though the danger here looks to be more theoretical than real.

A recent authority dealing with s.421A is *Wicks v Russell and Parkes* [2009] B.P.I.R. 194, which looks at the interaction between the regime set up by s.421A and the meaning of ss.267(2) and 382.

422 Formerly authorised banks

422(1) [Order by Secretary of State] The Secretary of State may by order made with the concurrence of the Treasury and after consultation with the Financial Services Authority provide that specified provisions in the first Group of Parts shall apply with specified modifications in relation to any person who–

(a) has a liability in respect of a deposit which he accepted in accordance with the Banking Act 1979 (c. 37) or 1987 (c. 22), but

(b) does not have permission under Part IV of the Financial Services and Markets Act 2000 (c. 8) (regulated activities) to accept deposits.

422(1A) [Where no permission under Financial Services and Markets Act 2000] Subsection (1)(b) shall be construed in accordance with–

(a) section 22 of the Financial Services and Markets Act 2000 (classes of regulated activity and categories of investment),

(b) any relevant order under that section, and

(c) Schedule 2 to that Act (regulated activities).

422(2) [Incidental provisions etc.] An order under this section may make different provision for different cases and may contain such incidental, supplemental and transitional provisions as may appear to the Secretary of State necessary or expedient.

422(3) [Order by statutory instrument etc.] An order under this section shall be made by statutory instrument subject to annulment in pursuance of a resolution of either House of Parliament.

S.422(1), (1A)
Subsection (1) was replaced by EA 2002 s.248 and Sch.17. Subsection (1A) was also inserted in this manner. It replaces an earlier version of subs.(1A) inserted by SI 2002/1555 which was then omitted by the Enterprise Act 2002 (Insolvency) Order 2003 (SI 2003/2096).

S.422(2), (3)
These provisions regulate procedural and transitional matters.

Part XVI

Provisions Against Debt Avoidance (England and Wales Only)

423 Transactions defrauding creditors

423(1) [Transaction at undervalue] This section relates to transactions entered into at an undervalue; and a person enters into such a transaction with another person if–

(a) he makes a gift to the other person or he otherwise enters into a transaction with the other on terms that provide for him to receive no consideration;

(b) he enters into a transaction with the other in consideration of marriage or the formation of a civil partnership; or

(c) he enters into a transaction with the other for a consideration the value of which, in money or money's worth, is significantly less than the value, in money or money's worth, of the consideration provided by himself.

423(2) [Order by court] Where a person has entered into such a transaction, the court may, if satisfied under the next subsection, make such order as it thinks fit for–

(a) restoring the position to what it would have been if the transaction had not been entered into, and

(b) protecting the interests of persons who are victims of the transaction.

423(3) [Conditions for court order] In the case of a person entering into such a transaction, an order shall only be made if the court is satisfied that it was entered into by him for the purpose–

(a) of putting assets beyond the reach of a person who is making, or may at some time make, a claim against him, or

(b) of otherwise prejudicing the interests of such a person in relation to the claim which he is making or may make.

423(4) ["The court"] In this section **"the court"** means the High Court or–

(a) if the person entering into the transaction is an individual, any other court which would have jurisdiction in relation to a bankruptcy petition relating to him;

(b) if that person is a body capable of being wound up under Part IV or V of this Act, any other court having jurisdiction to wind it up.

423(5) [Interpretation] In relation to a transaction at an undervalue, references here and below to a victim of the transaction are to a person who is, or is capable of being, prejudiced by it; and in the following two sections the person entering into the transaction is referred to as **"the debtor"**.

GENERAL NOTE

The purpose of this section and those immediately following it is to revamp s.172 of LPA 1925, which was used to avoid fraudulent conveyances. The Cork Committee wanted this provision widened, and, in particular, to cover payments of money: see the *Report*, para.1238. This has been done. There has been a provision along these lines in English law since 1571, and ultimately it can trace its ancestry back to the Paulian action of Roman law. This provision applies to both individuals and companies alike: *Re Shilena Hosiery Co Ltd* [1980] Ch. 219. The great utility of this provision lies in the fact that no time-limit for avoidance is fixed, in contrast with the case of ss.238, 239 and 339, 340. However, this advantage may be more illusory than real in that the courts are reluctant to reopen transactions going back many years—*The Law Society v Southall* [2001] EWCA Civ 2001; [2002] B.P.I.R. 336. There may also be limitation considerations—see *Re Yates* [2005] B.P.I.R. 476 and now *Re Nurkowski* [2006] EWCA Civ 542; [2006] B.P.I.R. 789 (which is discussed below). (For further points of comparison, see the note to s.238.) See generally Milman and Parry, (1997) 48 N.I.L.Q. 24; and Keay, [1998] J.B.L. 515.

For guidance on various procedural aspects of a s.423 application see *Godfrey v Torpy*, *The Times* May 16, 2007. Note Banking Act 2009 ss.103 and 145.

S.423(1)–(3)

These provisions allow the court to set aside transactions at an undervalue designed to put assets out of reach of creditors. They explain what a transaction at an undervalue is. The definition is similar to that in ss.238(4) and 339(3). Section 423(1)(b) was amended by the Civil Partnership Act 2004 Sch.27. On identification of the relevant "transaction" see *National Westminster Bank v Jones* [2001] EWCA Civ 1541; [2002] B.P.I.R. 361. The broad remedy which the court should have in mind is stated in s.423(2), although the specifics are detailed in s.425. Section 423(3) makes it clear that the transaction must have been intended to have a prejudicial effect.

Section 423 was the basis of a successful application by a creditor in *Arbuthnot Leasing International Ltd v Havelet Leasing Ltd (No.2)* [1990] B.C.C. 636. In acceding to the application Scott J. held that the fact that the debtor had acted on legal advice did not exclude the debtor having the purpose specified in s.423(3)(a). Where there is a prima facie breach of s.423 the court may lift the veil of professional privilege to ascertain motives: *Barclays Bank v Eustice* [1995] 1 W.L.R. 1238; [1995] B.C.C. 978. See also *Re Schuppan* [1997] B.P.I.R. 271.

In *Chohan v Saggar* [1992] B.C.C. 306 (on appeal, [1994] B.C.C. 134) it was held that the requirements of subs.(3) are satisfied provided the dominant purpose of the debtor was to achieve one of the prohibited aims. This analysis sits uneasily alongside the approach the courts have taken to s.238 (see above). Indeed, in *Royscot Spa Leasing Ltd v Lovett* [1995] B.C.C. 502 the Court of Appeal was prepared to accept a test based upon substantial (rather than dominant) purpose, though it did stress that it was important to distinguish between the purpose behind a transaction and the result of it. The dominant purpose test was favoured by Lightman J. in *Banca Carige v Banco Nacional de Cuba* [2001] B.P.I.R. 407. The opposite view was taken by the Court of Appeal in *Hashmi v IRC* [2002] EWCA Civ 981 and that now represents the accepted view—*Kubiangha v Ekpenyong* [2002] EWHC 1567 (Ch); [2002] 2 B.C.L.C. 597. The mental state of the recipient is not relevant when trying to determine the purpose of the debtor when entering into the transaction: *Moon v Franklin* [1996] B.P.I.R. 196. The court stressed the importance of *purpose* in *Papanicola v Fagan* [2009] B.P.I.R. 320. Here it was clear that the *result* of the transaction would be to defeat creditors but the *purpose* of the transaction was to help to preserve the debtor's marriage. A detailed consideration of this provision is found in the judgment of Sales J. in *4Eng Ltd v Harper* [2009] EWHC 2633 (Ch). Amongst the various points made was the support for the substantial purpose test. Some consideration was also given to the relevance of the state of mind of the transferee.

In *Agricultural Mortgage Corp plc v Woodward* [1994] B.C.C. 688 a transaction falling within s.423(1)(c) was encountered. Here the Court of Appeal found that a grant of an agricultural tenancy by a farmer to his wife just before the mortgagee of the farm was intending to enforce the security was a transaction at an undervalue and should be set aside. Although a fair market rent had been charged by the husband, that rent did not take into account the fact that the wife as tenant could effectively hold the mortgagee to ransom by denying it vacant possession and thus preventing it enforcing its security. Looking at the transaction as a whole the arrangement was designed to defeat the interests of the mortgagee and the wife received real benefits outside the formal tenancy agreement that had not been paid for. In *Midland Bank v Wyatt* [1996] B.P.I.R. 288 a sham family trust established to protect assets in the event of business failure was avoided under s.423. Note also *Re Schuppan* [1997] B.P.I.R. 271 where an attempt by a wife to argue that nothing of value had been transferred was unsuccessful. A successful s.423 case was found in *Trowbridge v Trowbridge* [2003] B.P.I.R. 258. A s.423 application succeeded in *Beckenham MC Ltd v Centralex Ltd* [2004] EWHC 1287 (Ch); [2004] B.P.I.R. 1112 where a property transfer had been carried out in order to defeat the possible grant of a charging order against that property. Another successful s.423 application was exemplified by *Gil v Baygreen Properties Ltd* [2004] EWHC 1732 (Ch); [2005] B.P.I.R. 95. See also *AET v Kermanshahchi* [2003] EWHC 1939 (Ch); [2003] B.P.I.R. 1229; and *Pena v Coyne* [2004] B.P.I.R. 1286. For cases falling on the other side of the line see *Menzies v National Bank of Kuwait SAK* [1994] B.C.C. 119; *Pinewood Joinery v Starelm Properties Ltd* [1994] B.C.C. 569; *Re Brabon* [2000] B.P.I.R. 537; *Re Taylor Sinclair (Capital) Ltd* [2002] B.P.I.R. 203. On s.423 note also *Ashe v Mumford* [2001] B.P.I.R. 1.

In *Feakins v DEFRA* [2005] EWCA Civ 1513; [2006] B.P.I.R. 895 the jurisdiction under s.423 came under the judicial microscope in the Court of Appeal. As is now consistent with modern authority a wide view of these provisions was adopted. In particular the concept of a "transaction" was applied flexibly to include any arrangement whether it be a formal agreement or informal understanding. The court also adopted a "commercial" view when determining any differential in consideration exchanged between the parties as part of the transaction.

Furthermore, the Court of Appeal in *Re Nurkowski (Hill v Spread Trustee Co Ltd)* [2006] EWCA Civ 542; [2006] B.P.I.R. 789 made a number of important observations on ss.423–425. First, the Inland Revenue could be a "victim" for the purposes of these provisions where property transactions had occurred with the substantial purpose of misleading the tax authorities as to potential capital gains tax liability. The concept should be interpreted flexibly; a party could be a potential victim at one date, cease to be a victim at another and then revert to victim status at some later time. A claim under s.423 that involved a settlement of property being set aside was subject to a 12-year limitation period with time running from the date of the bankruptcy order. The Court of Appeal also took the opportunity to express the view (without finally determining the matter) that the grant of security might constitute a transaction at an undervalue, thereby doubting *Re M C Bacon Ltd* [1991] Ch. 127 on this point. This is interesting as a somewhat differently constituted Court of Appeal in *Feakins v DEFRA* (above) did not express such doubts. This issue is likely to be revisited in future litigation.

In *Sands v Clitheroe* [2006] B.P.I.R. 1000 further consideration was given to the question of who might invoke s.423. Here Registrar Jaques held that a party could in principle invoke s.423 to challenge a transaction entered into many years previously if the substantive requirements of the section were met. The fact that the particular claimant was not in the contemplation of the transferor at the time of the transaction was immaterial. All that was required was that the claimant was prejudiced by the transaction albeit at some later date. This, along with other rulings noted above, will expand the potential of transaction avoidance under s.423.

When assessing differences in the value of consideration the court is concerned with real economic benefits and not artificial book values—*Pena v Coyne (No.1)* [2004] EWHC 2684 (Ch); [2004] 2 B.C.L.C. 703.

Further consideration of s.423 is to be found in *Kali Ltd v Chawla* [2007] EWHC 1989 (Ch); [2007] EWHC 2357 (Ch); [2008] B.P.I.R. 415. Section 423 was invoked successfully in *Griffin v Awoderu* [2008] B.P.I.R. 877, where the court (D. Phillips Q.C.) reviewed its options in redressing the position. A s.423 claim brought on behalf of the Crown succeeded in *HM Treasury Solicitor v Doveton* [2009] B.P.I.R. 352. Here a will was found to be forged and as a result dispositions made under it were avoided and property became bona vacantia. *Barnett v Semenyuk* [2008] B.P.I.R. 1427 provides another illustration of a successful s.423 claim.

For further consideration of the interface between s.423 and the Limitation Act 1980 see *Giles v Rhind* [2008] EWCA Civ 118; [2008] B.P.I.R. 342 where the Court of Appeal indicated that a s.423 claim involved an allegation of "breach of duty" for the purposes of s.32(2) of the Limitation Act 1980.

Note also *Stow v Stow* [2008] EWHC 495 (Ch); [2008] B.P.I.R. 673 where the potential utility of s.423 to the HMRC was commented upon. On the potential for a s.423 claim see *Brittain v Courtway Estates* [2008] B.P.I.R. 1229.

S.423(4), (5)

These provisions define "court" and "victim" (see ss.423(2)(b), 424(1)(a)–(c), 424(2)). The latter term was not used in IA 1985. In *Moon v Franklin* (above) the victims were persons who were suing the debtor for professional negligence. See also *Pinewood Joinery v Starelm Properties* (above); and *Jyske Bank (Gibraltar) v Spjeldnaes (No.2)* [1999] B.P.I.R. 525.

Section 423 can be invoked by a plaintiff in any part of the High Court provided the claim does not form part of proceedings being conducted in the Bankruptcy Court or the Companies Court: *TSB Bank plc v Katz* [1997] B.P.I.R. 147. On extraterritoriality see *Jyske Bank (Gibraltar) Ltd v Spjeldnaes (No.2),* (above). In *Banca Carige v Banco Nacional de Cuba* [2001] B.P.I.R. 407 Lightman J. stressed that leave is required in order to serve a s.423 claim abroad.

424   Those who may apply for an order under s.423

424(1)   [Conditions for s.423 application] An application for an order under section 423 shall not be made in relation to a transaction except–

(a)   in a case where the debtor has been adjudged bankrupt or is a body corporate which is being wound up or is in administration, by the official receiver, by the trustee of the bankrupt's estate or the liquidator or administrator of the body corporate or (with the leave of the court) by a victim of the transaction;

(b)   in a case where a victim of the transaction is bound by a voluntary arrangement approved under Part I or Part VIII of this Act, by the supervisor of the voluntary arrangement or by any person who (whether or not so bound) is such a victim; or

(c)   in any other case, by a victim of the transaction.

424(2)   [Treatment of application] An application made under any of the paragraphs of subsection (1) is to be treated as made on behalf of every victim of the transaction.

GENERAL NOTE

These provisions explain who may make a s.423 application (see the annotation to s.423 above for further analysis). A minor textual change to subs.(1)(a) was made by Sch.17 to EA 2002. Note the leave requirement is s.424(1)(a). As to whether leave can be granted retrospectively see the discussion in *Dora v Simper* [2000] 2 B.C.L.C. 561. In *Godfrey v Torpey (No.2)* [2007] EWHC 919 (Ch); [2007] B.P.I.R. 1538 the court held that retrospective leave could be granted where a victim commences a s.423 action without leave. But this appears to be inconsistent with the general approach adopted by the House of Lords in *Seal v Chief Constable of South Wales* [2007] UKHL 31. If the person entering into the transaction was a company, then it may be challenged under this provision by the liquidator or administrator. If it was an individual, then the official receiver or trustee may bring the proceedings. Supervisors of voluntary arrangements may also apply in certain cases (most avoidance provisions are not available in the cases of a company or individual voluntary arrangement), as may "victims" (for definition see s.423(5)), who may bring an action either individually or in a representative capacity. See *Moon v Franklin* [1996] B.P.I.R. 196 for an example of a victim making the application. A creditor of an insolvent company can be a victim: *Re Ayala Holdings Ltd* [1993] B.C.L.C. 256. See also *Pinewood Joinery v Starelm Properties Ltd* [1994] B.C.C. 569.

Note that the FSA may apply in an appropriate case—FSMA 2000 s.375. The Pensions Regulator may also invoke s.423—see Pensions Act 2004 s.58.

425 Provision which may be made by order under s.423

425(1) [Scope of order] Without prejudice to the generality of section 423, an order made under that section with respect to a transaction may (subject as follows)–

(a) require any property transferred as part of the transaction to be vested in any person, either absolutely or for the benefit of all the persons on whose behalf the application for the order is treated as made;

(b) require any property to be so vested if it represents, in any person's hands, the application either of the proceeds of sale of property so transferred or of money so transferred;

(c) release or discharge (in whole or in part) any security given by the debtor;

(d) require any person to pay to any other person in respect of benefits received from the debtor such sums as the court may direct;

(e) provide for any surety or guarantor whose obligations to any person were released or discharged (in whole or in part) under the transaction to be under such new or revived obligations as the court thinks appropriate;

(f) provide for security to be provided for the discharge of any obligation imposed by or arising under the order, for such an obligation to be charged on any property and for such security or charge to have the same priority as a security or charge released or discharged (in whole or in part) under the transaction.

425(2) [Limit to order] An order under section 423 may affect the property of, or impose any obligation on, any person whether or not he is the person with whom the debtor entered into the transaction; but such an order–

(a) shall not prejudice any interest in property which was acquired from a person other than the debtor and was acquired in good faith, for value and without notice of the relevant circumstances, or prejudice any interest deriving from such an interest, and

(b) shall not require a person who received a benefit from the transaction in good faith, for value and without notice of the relevant circumstances to pay any sum unless he was a party to the transaction.

425(3) [Relevant circumstances] For the purposes of this section the relevant circumstances in relation to a transaction are the circumstances by virtue of which an order under section 423 may be made in respect of the transaction.

425(4) ["Security"] In this section **"security"** means any mortgage, charge, lien or other security.

S.425(1)

This gives illustrations of the types of order the court may make under s.423. This is similar to ss.241(1) and 342(1), but with the omission of para.(g). A declaration was the basis of the relief granted in *Moon v Franklin* [1996] B.P.I.R. 196. Interim relief may be available: *Aiglon Ltd v Gau Shan Co Ltd* [1993] 1 Lloyd's Rep. 164. In *Re Krug International (UK) Ltd* [2008] B.P.I.R. 1512 H.H.J. Purle Q.C. indicated the scope of potential remedies under s.423 were the avoidance claim to prove successful. For an example of monetary compensation being the preferred remedy under s.425 on the particular facts of the case see *Pena v Coyne (No.2)* [2004] EWHC 2685 (Ch); [2004] 2 B.C.L.C. 730. The remedial jurisdiction of the court when acceding to a s.423 application was considered by Sales J. in *4Eng Ltd v Harper* [2009] EWHC 2633 (Ch). Here the judge made the point that the court was under no obligation to seek to maintain the standard of living of the transferee where a breach of s.423 had been established. For an order given extraterritorial effect see *Jyske Bank (Gibraltar) Ltd v Spjeldnaes (No.2)* [1999] B.P.I.R. 525. Note the limitation imposed on any relief by POCA 2002 s.419.

S.425(2), (3)

Although third-party rights may be affected, there is protection for bona fide purchasers, for value and without notice, who have taken without notice of the relevant circumstances, as defined by s.425(3). The relief granted in *Arbuthnot Leasing International Ltd v Havelet Leasing Ltd (No.2)* [1990] B.C.C. 636 (see the note to s.423, above) took the form of an order that the assets improperly transferred should be held on trust for the transferor, but without prejudice to the claims of those who had become creditors of the transferee since the date of the transfer. In *Chohan v Saggar* [1994] B.C.C. 134 the Court of Appeal considered the aim of an order under s.425. Although the order should seek to restore the original pre-transaction position, sometimes the need to protect third parties may prevent a complete restoration. Partial invalidation of transactions may therefore be the best answer to the problem of balancing the competing interests of creditors and bona fide third parties.

For the difficult balancing exercise that often arises when determining the precise scope of an order under s.425 see *Griffin v Awoderu* [2008] EWHC 349 (Ch).

S.425(4)

This is an interpretation provision relevant to s.425(1)(c) and (f).

PART XVII

MISCELLANEOUS AND GENERAL

426   Co-operation between courts exercising jurisdiction in relation to insolvency

426(1)   [Enforcement in other parts of UK] An order made by a court in any part of the United Kingdom in the exercise of jurisdiction in relation to insolvency law shall be enforced in any other part of the United Kingdom as if it were made by a court exercising the corresponding jurisdiction in that other part.

426(2)   [Limit to s.426(1)] However, without prejudice to the following provisions of this section, nothing in subsection (1) requires a court in any part of the United Kingdom to enforce, in relation to property situated in that part, any order made by a court in any other part of the United Kingdom.

426(3)   [Order by Secretary of State] The Secretary of State, with the concurrence in relation to property situated in England and Wales of the Lord Chancellor, may by order make provision for securing that a trustee or assignee under the insolvency law of any part of the United Kingdom has, with such modifications as may be specified in the order, the same rights in relation to any property situated in another part of the United Kingdom as he would have in the corresponding circumstances if he were a trustee or assignee under the insolvency law of that other part.

426(4)   [Assistance between courts] The courts having jurisdiction in relation to insolvency law in any part of the United Kingdom shall assist the courts having the corresponding jurisdiction in any other part of the United Kingdom or any relevant country or territory.

426(5)   [Request under s.426(4)] For the purposes of subsection (4) a request made to a court in any part of the United Kingdom by a court in any other part of the United Kingdom or in a relevant country or territory is authority for the court to which the request is made to apply, in relation to any matters specified in the request, the insolvency law which is applicable by either court in relation to comparable matters falling within its jurisdiction.

In exercising its discretion under this subsection, a court shall have regard in particular to the rules of private international law.

426(6)   [Claim by trustee or assignee] Where a person who is a trustee or assignee under the insolvency law of any part of the United Kingdom claims property situated in any other part of the United Kingdom (whether by virtue of an order under subsection (3) or otherwise), the submission of that claim to the court exercising jurisdiction in relation to insolvency law in that other part shall be treated in the same manner as a request made by a court for the purpose of subsection (4).

426(7)   [Application of Criminal Law Act] Section 38 of the Criminal Law Act 1977 (execution of warrant of arrest throughout the United Kingdom) applies to a warrant which, in exercise of any jurisdiction in relation to insolvency law, is issued in any part of the United Kingdom for the arrest of a person as it applies to a warrant issued in that part of the United Kingdom for the arrest of a person charged with an offence.

426(8)   [Powers in subordinate legislation] Without prejudice to any power to make rules of court, any power to make provision by subordinate legislation for the purpose of giving effect in relation to companies or individuals to the insolvency law of any part of the United Kingdom includes power to make provision for the purpose of giving effect in that part to any provision made by or under the preceding provisions of this section.

426(9)   [Section 426(3) order by statutory instrument etc.] An order under subsection (3) shall be made by statutory instrument subject to annulment in pursuance of a resolution of either House of Parliament.

426(10)   ["Insolvency law"] In this section **"insolvency law"** means–

(a)   in relation to England and Wales, provision extending to England and Wales and made by or under this Act or sections 1A, 6 to 10, 12 to 15, 19(c) and 20 (with Schedule 1) of the Company Directors Disqualification Act 1986 and sections 1 to 17 of that Act as they apply for the purposes of those provisions of that Act;

(b)   in relation to Scotland, provision extending to Scotland and made by or under this Act, sections 1A, 6 to 10, 12 to 15, 19(c) and 20 (with Schedule 1) of the Company Directors Disqualification Act 1986 and sections 1 to 17 of that Act as they apply for the purposes of those provisions of that Act, Part XVIII of the Companies Act or the Bankruptcy (Scotland) Act 1985;

(c)   in relation to Northern Ireland, provision made by or under the Insolvency (Northern Ireland) Order 1989 or the Company Directors Disqualification (Northern Ireland) Order 2002;

(d)   in relation to any relevant country or territory, so much of the law of that country or territory as corresponds to provisions falling within any of the foregoing paragraphs;

and references in this subsection to any enactment include, in relation to any time before the coming into force of that enactment the corresponding enactment in force at that time.

426(11)   ["Relevant country or territory"] In this section **"relevant country or territory"** means–

(a)   any of the Channel Islands or the Isle of Man, or

(b)   any country or territory designated for the purposes of this section by the Secretary of State by order made by statutory instrument.

426(12)   [Application to Northern Ireland] In the application of this section to Northern Ireland–

(a)   for any reference to the Secretary of State there is substituted a reference to the Department of Economic Development in Northern Ireland;

(b)   in subsection (3) for the words "another part of the United Kingdom" and the words "that other part" there is substituted the words "Northern Ireland";

(c)   for subsection (9) there is substituted the following subsection–

"(9) An order made under subsection (3) by the Department of Economic Development in Northern Ireland shall be a statutory rule for the purposes of the Statutory Rules (Northern Ireland) Order 1979 and shall be subject to negative resolution within the meaning of section 41(6) of the Interpretation Act (Northern Ireland) 1954."

426(13)   [Bank insolvency in Banking Act 2009 s.129 as "insolvency law"] Section 129 of the Banking Act 2009 provides for provisions of that Act about bank insolvency to be "insolvency law" for the purposes of this section.

426(14)   [Banking administration in Banking Act 2009 s.165 as "insolvency law"] Section 165 of the Banking Act 2009 provides for provisions of that Act about bank administration to be "insolvency law" for the purposes of this section.

GENERAL NOTE

Section 426 bears some resemblance to s.122 of the Bankruptcy Act 1914, which dealt with co-operation in bankruptcy matters between the courts of the UK and colonial territories. This former provision in English law has been held by the Privy Council in *Al Sabah v Grupo Torras SA* [2005] UKPC 1; [2005] 2 W.L.R. 904 to have continuing effect vis-á-vis the Cayman Islands as it had never been repealed with respect to that jurisdiction. The advice of the Privy Council contains a useful historical perspective on s.426. The Cork *Report*, Ch.49, called for the rationalisation and improvement of co-operation between the insolvency courts in the UK. This section represents a step in that direction. However there are problems of interpretation particularly concerned with the freedom of action enjoyed by the English courts and these have troubled the judiciary in a number of recent cases discussed below.

Various aspects of the s.426 jurisdiction were considered by the courts in the *Fourie v Le Roux* sequence of cases. Blackburn J. held in *Fourie v Le Roux* [2004] EWHC 2557 (Ch); [2005] B.P.I.R. 723 that under s.426(5) of the IA 1986 the co-operative jurisdiction under s.426 could only be engaged if the foreign requesting court (here a South African court) specified what assistance it was seeking from the English court. In *Fourie v Le Roux* [2005] EWCA Civ 204; [2005] B.P.I.R. 756 the Court of Appeal had nothing to add on the narrow s.426 point and an appeal from this ruling was dismissed by the House of Lords in *Fourie v Le Roux* [2007] UKHL 1. But when the case came back before Blackburne J. in *Fourie v Le Roux* [2004] EWHC 2557 (Ch); [2005] B.P.I.R. 779 a new letter of request from the South African courts fell to be considered. In this latest instalment Blackburne J. held that jurisdiction to assist the foreign court existed under s.426 to assist the foreign court even if the assistance would impact upon a party outside the jurisdiction of the requesting court. However this fact was relevant to the question as to whether the English court should exercise its discretion to assist. Moreover, the procedure for serving claims outside the jurisdiction as specified in IR 1986 r.12.12 did not apply to requests for assistance made under s.426. Service in such cases was governed by CPR Pt 6.20.

A number of countries and territories were designated for the purposes of s.426 by the Co-operation of Insolvency Courts (Designation of Relevant Countries and Territories) Order 1986 (SI 1986/2123), effective December 29, 1986. These were: Anguilla, Australia, the Bahamas, Bermuda, Botswana, Canada, Cayman Islands, Falkland Islands, Gibraltar, Hong Kong, the Republic of Ireland, Montserrat, New Zealand, St Helena, Turks and Caicos Islands, Tuvalu and the Virgin Islands. Malaysia and South Africa were added by SI 1996/253. Brunei was included by SI 1998/2766. In consequence, the courts of these countries and territories have the right to request assistance in matters of insolvency from courts having jurisdiction in insolvency in any part of the UK.

Subsections (4), (5), (10) and (11) of s.426 were extended to the Bailiwick of Guernsey by the Insolvency Act 1986 (Guernsey) Order 1989 (SI 1989/2409), with the modifications specified in the Schedule to that Order, as from February 1, 1990. Accordingly, a co-operative insolvency regime is now established between Guernsey (including Alderney and Sark) and the UK. Note the modifications to s.426(10) by para.16(3) of Sch.4 to the IA 2000.

In relation to the financial markets (see the note on p.2), the provisions of s.426 are subject to the limitations set out in CA 1989 s.183. Part XVII applies to limited liability partnerships by virtue of the Limited Liability Partnerships Regulations 2001 (SI 2001/1090) reg.5(1)(b) as from April 6, 2001 subject to reg.5(2) and (3).

In future s.426 will have to be read alongside s.14 of IA 2000 and regulations made thereunder. Section 14 permits the Secretary of State to adopt the UNICITRAL Model Law on Cross-Border Insolvency Proceedings and to modify existing rules (including s.426) and this was achieved by SI 2006/1060—see Vol.2. On an EU level judicial comity in insolvency matters is to be promoted by EC Council Regulation 1346/2000 on insolvency proceedings. See the discussion in Vol 2, p.125.

Readers should note that there is always the possibility of judicial comity operating via the common law—on this see *Cambridge Gas Transport Corp v The Official Committee of Unsecured Creditors of Navigator Holdings* [2006] UKPC 26; [2006] B.C.C. 962. *Cambridge Gas* (above) was followed by Registrar Jaques in *Re Phoenix Kapitaldienst GmbH* [2008] B.P.I.R. 1082.

S.426(1), (2)

This allows for general enforcement of court orders throughout the UK, although there are limitations expressed with regard to enforcement of court orders against property in different parts of the UK.

S.426(3), (9)

Assimilation of the powers of a trustee, etc. in the different UK jurisdictions is provided for here. The Secretary of State may use statutory instruments to do this.

S.426(4), (5), (11)

The UK courts must on a matter of insolvency law co-operate with each other, and indeed with courts from the Isle of Man, Channel Isles or from any jurisdiction specified by the Secretary of State. These provisions permit the court to offer assistance to courts in other parts of the UK or in other "relevant" countries, as defined in s.426(11). With the increased incidence of cross-border insolvency in recent years the UK courts have increasingly been faced with requests for assistance. For a review of this jurisdiction see Smart, (1996) 112 L.Q.R. 397; (1998) 114 L.Q.R. 46; and Fletcher, [1997] J.B.L. 470.

In *Re Gerrard (Trustee in the Bankruptcy of Hynd)* [2009] B.P.I.R. 1374 the Scottish courts offered assistance to an English trustee by invoking its jurisdiction under s.426(4). Lord Glennie noted that the Cross-Border Insolvency Regulations 2006 (SI 2006/1030) were not applicable to this scenario.

In spite of the apparent statutory obligation to lend assistance the Court of Appeal confirmed in *Hughes v Hannover-Rucksversicherungs AG* [1997] B.C.C. 921 that the court continues to enjoy discretion in such applications and may think it appropriate to reject the request for assistance. Indeed it chose this course of action in that particular case because the circumstances had changed materially since the date of the request. In *Re Focus Insurance Co Ltd* [1996] B.C.C. 659 Scott V.C. refused assistance to foreign liquidators who had successfully petitioned for the respondent to be bankrupted in England. To offer the assistance sought would involve complicating and possibly undermining the English bankruptcy which the applicants themselves had initiated. Again in *Re J N Taylor Pty Ltd* [1998] B.P.I.R. 347 the primary request for assistance was also rejected because to have acceded to it would result in company officers being subjected to examination by an Australian liquidator in circumstances where no such examination would have been permitted under English law. This decision must be of questionable authority in view of the later Court of Appeal ruling in *England v Smith (Re Southern Equities Corp)* [2001] Ch. 419; [2000] B.P.I.R. 28. Here it was held that the policy of judicial comity was the starting point on any s.426 request. Thus it was possible for the English courts to accede to a request to interview a party under the machinery of Australian insolvency law even though such an interview would not have been allowed had this been an entirely domestic case. Differences in the substantive law between nations on individual statutory provisions did not necessarily mean that one system was fairer than another. The whole picture required consideration. Subsequently, a similar approach was taken by Jonathan Parker J. in *Duke Group Ltd v Carver* [2001] B.P.I.R. 459 where an Australian judge was permitted to examine a witness in England pursuant to Australian law. The point was made that it would require something extraordinary to refuse a request for assistance and it was not for the English courts to water down the assistance requested. In *Re Trading Partners Ltd* [2002] B.P.I.R. 606 Patten J. acceded to a request from the courts of the British Virgin Islands to allow liquidators of a company to take advantage of s.236 of IA 1986 in order to gain access to documents in the possession of administrative receivers of a related company. In *Re Television Trade Rentals Ltd* [2002] EWHC 211 (Ch); [2002] B.C.C. 807 s.426 was used to apply the CVA procedure to companies incorporated in the Isle of Man. A request to do this retrospectively was refused.

When considering whether to offer assistance the court has a range of options available. According to the Court of Appeal in *Hughes v Hannover-Rucksversicherungs AG* (above) the courts can apply their own inherent general jurisdiction, substantive English insolvency law or the substantive insolvency law of the foreign jurisdiction. Flexibility is the order of the day.

An order was made under s.426(4) in the case of *Re Dallhold Estates (UK) Pty Ltd* [1992] B.C.C. 394. Here the courts of Western Australia sought help from the English courts to protect the assets of an Australian company having property in this jurisdiction. Although it seems that it is not possible for the English courts to grant an administration order in respect of a foreign company on their own initiative they can in effect do this if they receive a request under s.426. Accordingly the administration order was granted. In *Re Bank of Credit and Commerce International SA* [1993] B.C.C. 787 Rattee J. held that when faced with a request for assistance (in this case from the Grand Court of the Cayman Islands) the English courts were not restricted to rendering applicable procedural facilities of English law but could also declare principles of substantive English insolvency law applicable in the particular case. In *Re Business City Express Ltd* [1997] B.C.C. 826 relief was offered by Rattee J. to facilitate a rescue plan mounted by the examiner of an Irish company. Although the request involved some departure from normal distribution rules on insolvency the circumstances were such as to justify this on utilitarian grounds.

In the major case of *McGrath v Riddell* [2008] UKHL 21; [2008] B.C.C. 349 the House of Lords on an application under s.426 authorised English provisional liquidators to hand over assets collected in an ancillary winding up in this country to Australian liquidators. This was in spite of the fact that there existed a difference between Australian and English law on pari passu distribution. Although all of their Lordships agreed with this outcome there was an unresolved disagreement between Lord Hoffmann, who argued that there was inherent jurisdiction to do this, and

Lord Scott, who maintained that this could only be done within the terms of s.426. This disagreement might have implications in the case of liquidations conducted in jurisdictions not recognised under s.426. What is apparent from this case is that there is an emerging common law principle of international comity in cross border insolvency developing outside the confines of s.426.

S.426(6)

This subsection allows trustees, etc. to claim property situated in other parts of the UK by calling on the assistance of the courts where the property is situated.

S.426(7)

This applies s.38 of the Criminal Law Act 1977 to warrants for arrest in connection with insolvency law matters.

S.426(8)

Delegated legislation can be used to achieve the aim of co-operation as contained in s.426: see the Co-operation of Insolvency Courts (Designation of Relevant Countries and Territories) Order 1986 (SI 1986/2123).

S.426(10), (11), (12)

These provisions define "insolvency law" and "relevant country or territory" for the purposes of this section and these definitions are exhaustive: see *Hughes v Hannover-Rucksversicherungs AG* [1997] B.C.C. 921 here. Provision is also made for Northern Ireland. Subsection (10) was amended and subs.(12) added by Sch.9 to the Insolvency (Northern Ireland) Order 1989 (SI 1989/2045 (NI 19)).

S.426(13), (14)

Inserted by the Banking Act 2009.

426A Disqualification from Parliament (England and Wales)

426A(1) **[Bankruptcy restrictions or debt relief restrictions orders]** A person in respect of whom a bankruptcy restrictions order or a debt relief restrictions order has effect shall be disqualified–

(a) from membership of the House of Commons,

(b) from sitting or voting in the House of Lords, and

(c) from sitting or voting in a committee of the House of Lords or a joint committee of both Houses.

426A(2) **[MP to vacate seat]** If a member of the House of Commons becomes disqualified under this section, his seat shall be vacated.

426A(3) **[Election return void]** If a person who is disqualified under this section is returned as a member of the House of Commons, his return shall be void.

426A(4) **[No writ to member of House of Lords]** No writ of summons shall be issued to a member of the House of Lords who is disqualified under this section.

426A(5) **[Notification of Speaker of various orders]** If a court makes a bankruptcy restrictions order or interim order, or a debt relief restrictions order or an interim debt relief restrictions order, in respect of a member of the House of Commons or the House of Lords the court shall notify the Speaker of that House.

426A(6) **[Notification of Speaker of various undertakings]** If the Secretary of State accepts a bankruptcy restrictions undertaking or a debt relief restrictions undertaking made by a member of the House of Commons or the House of Lords, the Secretary of State shall notify the Speaker of that House.

GENERAL NOTE

Sections 426A–C were introduced by s.266 of EA 2002 as part of a policy of removing automatic restrictions from the shoulders of bankrupts. This policy has lead to the removal of the automatic bar on being a JP (see EA 2002 s.265), a local government member (EA 2002 s.267) and to the introduction of a general power to relax such disqualifications (EA 2002 s.268). Section 426A addresses specifically the position of MPs and members of the House of Lords. These sections took effect in April 2004.

Note amendment to subss.(1), (5) and (6) by para.12 of Pt 1 of Sch.20 to the Tribunals, Courts and Enforcement Act 2007.

S.426A(1)

Those individuals who are the subject of a BRO or BRU are disqualified from Parliament.

S.426A(2)–(4)

These provisions amplify the consequences of disqualification.

S.426A(5), (6)

This imposes an additional obligation on a court making a BRO or interim order or on the Secretary of State accepting a BRU. It is unlikely to be onerous in view of the rarity of the situation.

426B Devolution

426B(1) [Various orders in Scotland, Northern Ireland, Wales] If a court makes a bankruptcy restrictions order or interim order in respect of a member of the Scottish Parliament, the Northern Ireland Assembly or the National Assembly for Wales, or makes a debt relief restrictions order or interim debt relief order in respect of such a member, the court shall notify the presiding officer of that body.

426B(2) [Various undertakings in Scotland, Northern Ireland, Wales] If the Secretary of State accepts a bankruptcy restrictions undertaking or a debt relief restrictions undertaking made by a member of the Scottish Parliament, the Northern Ireland Assembly or the National Assembly for Wales, the Secretary of State shall notify the presiding officer of that body.

S.426B(1), (2)

These make special provision for disqualification attendant upon a BRO or BRU or interim order granted in respect of a member of a dissolved assembly.

Note amendment to subss.(1) and (2) by para.13 of Pt 1 of Sch.20 to the Tribunals, Courts and Enforcement Act 2007.

426C Irrelevance of privilege

426C(1) [No effect of Parliamentary privilege on insolvency enactment] An enactment about insolvency applies in relation to a member of the House of Commons or the House of Lords irrespective of any Parliamentary privilege.

426C(2) ["Enactment"] In this section "enactment" includes a provision made by or under–

(a) an Act of the Scottish Parliament, or

(b) Northern Ireland legislation.

S.426C(1), (2)

Parliamentary privilege does not protect Members of Parliament, etc. from the consequences of insolvency prescribed by legislation.

427 Parliamentary disqualification

427(1) [Disqualification of bankrupt] Where a court in Northern Ireland adjudges an individual bankrupt or a court in Scotland awards sequestration of an individual's estate, the individual is disqualified–

(a) for sitting or voting in the House of Lords,

(b) for being elected to, or sitting or voting in, the House of Commons, and

(c) for sitting or voting in a committee of either House.

427(2) [When disqualification ceases] Where an individual is disqualified under this section, the disqualification ceases–

(a) except where the adjudication is annulled or the award recalled or reduced without the individual having been first discharged, on the discharge of the individual, and

(b)   in the excepted case, on the annulment, recall or reduction, as the case may be.

427(3)   [Disqualified peer] No writ of summons shall be issued to any lord of Parliament who is for the time being disqualified under this section for sitting and voting in the House of Lords.

427(4)   [Disqualified MP] Where a member of the House of Commons who is disqualified under this section continues to be so disqualified until the end of the period of 6 months beginning with the day of the adjudication or award, his seat shall be vacated at the end of that period.

427(5)   [Certification of s.427(1) award etc.] A court which makes an adjudication or award such as is mentioned in subsection (1) in relation to any lord of Parliament or member of the House of Commons shall forthwith certify the adjudication or award to the Speaker of the House of Lords or, as the case may be, to the Speaker of the House of Commons.

427(6)   [Further certification after s.427(5)] Where a court has certified an adjudication or award to the Speaker of the House of Commons under subsection (5), then immediately after it becomes apparent which of the following certificates is applicable, the court shall certify to the Speaker of the House of Commons–

(a)   that the period of 6 months beginning with the day of the adjudication or award has expired without the adjudication or award having been annulled, recalled or reduced, or

(b)   that the adjudication or award has been annulled, recalled or reduced before the end of that period.

427(6A)   [Members of the Scottish Parliament] Subsections (4) to (6) have effect in relation to a member of the Scottish Parliament but as if–

(a)   references to the House of Commons were to the Parliament and references to the Speaker were to the Presiding Officer, and

(b)   in subsection (4), for "under this section" there were substituted "under section 15(1)(b) of the Scotland Act 1998 by virtue of this section".

427(6B)   [Members of the National Assembly for Wales] Subsections (4) to (6) have effect in relation to a member of the National Assembly for Wales but as if–

(a)   references to the House of Commons were to the Assembly and references to the Speaker were to the presiding officer, and

(b)   in subsection (4), for "under this section" there were substituted "under section 16(2) of the Government of Wales Act 2006 by virtue of this section".

427(6C)   [Members of the Northern Ireland Assembly] Subsection (1), as applied to a member of the Northern Ireland Assembly by virtue of section 36(4) of the Northern Ireland Act 1998, has effect as if "or Northern Ireland" were omitted; and subsections (4) to (6) have effect in relation to such a member as if–

(a)   references to the House of Commons were to the Assembly and references to the Speaker were to the Presiding Officer; and

(b)   in subsection (4), for "under this section" there were substituted "under section 36(4) of the Northern Ireland Act 1998 by virtue of this section".

**427(7)   ** [Repealed by EA 2002 s.266(2) with effect from April 1, 2004.]

S.427(1), (2)
Where a person has been adjudged bankrupt in Scotland or Northern Ireland he is disqualified from both Houses of Parliament until he is discharged or the order is annulled. Similar provision is made for Scotland and Northern Ireland. Local government councillors face a similar bar: Local Government Act 1972 s.80. The former reference to England and Wales was dropped by EA 2002 s.266(2).

S.427(3)

A writ of summons must not be issued in respect of any person so disqualified who is a member of the House of Lords.

S.427(4)

A Member of Parliament who is so disqualified has six months to vacate his seat.

S.427(5), (6)

Where a court makes a bankruptcy order, etc. the Speaker of the appropriate House of Parliament must be notified. Further, the court must notify the Speaker of the Commons of the elapse of the six-month period mentioned in s.427(4) or of any annulment in the meantime.

S.427(6A), (6B), (6C)

These subsections were inserted respectively by the Scotland Act 1998 s.125(1) and Sch.8 para.23 as from November 19, 1998, the Government of Wales Act 2006 s.160 as of May 3, 2007 and the Northern Ireland Act, in order to take account of the devolution of legislative powers to the regional assemblies.

S.427(7)

Repealed by EA 2002 s.266(2).

428   Exemptions from Restrictive Trade Practices Act

428(1, 2)   [Repealed.]

428(3)   [**"Insolvency services"**] In this section **"insolvency services"** means the services of persons acting as insolvency practitioners or carrying out under the law of Northern Ireland functions corresponding to those mentioned in section 388(1) or (2) in Part XIII, in their capacity as such.

GENERAL NOTE

Formerly s.428 sought to exclude agreements relating to fees charged for insolvency services, etc. being made subject to the Restrictive Trade Practices Act 1976, especially Pt III of that Act. Schedule 14 also adds insolvency services to the list of exempt services described in Sch.1 to the Restrictive Trade Practices Act 1976, such as legal services, medical services, accountancy services and many other professional services. This is in accord with the general policy of the Act, and in particular Pt XIII, which requires insolvency practitioners to be professionals. The Restrictive Trade Practices Act was repealed by the Competition Act 1998 which introduced a new competition regime on the intended date of March 1, 2000.

429   Disabilities on revocation of administration order against an individual

429(1)   [**Application**] The following applies where a person fails to make any payment which he is required to make by virtue of an administration order under Part VI of the County Courts Act 1984.

429(2)   [**Power of court**] The court which is administering that person's estate under the order may, if it thinks fit–

(a)   revoke the administration order, and

(b)   make an order directing that this section and section 12 of the Company Directors Disqualification Act 1986 shall apply to the person for such period, not exceeding 1 year, as may be specified in the order.

429(3)   [**Restrictions**] A person to whom this section so applies shall not–

(a)   either alone or jointly with another person, obtain credit to the extent of the amount prescribed for the purposes of section 360(1)(a) or more, or

(b)   enter into any transaction in the course of or for the purposes of any business in which he is directly or indirectly engaged,

without disclosing to the person from whom he obtains the credit, or (as the case may be) with whom the transaction is entered into, the fact that this section applies to him.

429(4)   [Person obtaining credit] The reference in subsection (3) to a person obtaining credit includes–

(a)   a case where goods are bailed or hired to him under a hire-purchase agreement or agreed to be sold to him under a conditional sale agreement, and

(b)   a case where he is paid in advance (whether in money or otherwise) for the supply of goods or services.

429(5)   [Penalty] A person who contravenes this section is guilty of an offence and liable to imprisonment or a fine, or both.

S.429(1)

This section applies where a debtor has failed to comply with his obligations under an administration order granted under Pt VI of the County Courts Act 1984 (as amended by s.13 of the Courts and Legal Services Act 1990).

S.429(2)–(4)

The court has discretion to revoke the administration order and instead apply the following restrictions for a maximum period of one year—subs.(2)(b) was changed by Sch.23 to EA 2002 by the substitution of one year for two years. Prior to IA 1985 there was a similar provision in IA 1976 s.11, allowing for the revocation of administration orders and substitution of receiving orders. The new restrictions are more flexible.

The restrictions that may be imposed by the court where an administration order is revoked are then outlined. Thus, the debtor can be banned from acting as company director, liquidator or promoter, etc. (see CDDA 1986 s.12(2)). Furthermore, he can be made subject to restrictions which are similar to the s.360 curbs—e.g. restrictions on obtaining credit (widely defined by s.429(4)), or, indeed, entering into business transactions without disclosing his true status. The Cork Committee (*Report*, para.317) was in favour of such restrictions.

S.429(5)

The sanctions for the breach of this provision are the same as for contravening s.360: see s.430 and Sch.10.

Editors' note: amendments are to be made to s.429 by Sch.16 para.3 to the Tribunals, Courts and Enforcement Act 2007 from a date yet to be determined.

430   Provision introducing Schedule of punishments

430(1)   [Schedule 10] Schedule 10 to this Act has effect with respect to the way in which offences under this Act are punishable on conviction.

430(2)   [First, second and third columns of Schedule] In relation to an offence under a provision of this Act specified in the first column of the Schedule (the general nature of the offence being described in the second column), the third column shows whether the offence is punishable on conviction on indictment, or on summary conviction, or either in the one way or the other.

430(3)   [Fourth column] The fourth column of the Schedule shows, in relation to an offence, the maximum punishment by way of fine or imprisonment under this Act which may be imposed on a person convicted of the offence in the way specified in relation to it in the third column (that is to say, on indictment or summarily), a reference to a period of years or months being to a term of imprisonment of that duration.

430(4)   [Fifth column] The fifth column shows (in relation to an offence for which there is an entry in that column) that a person convicted of the offence after continued contravention is liable to a daily default fine; that is to say, he is liable on a second or subsequent conviction of the offence to the fine specified in that column for each day on which the contravention is continued (instead of the penalty specified for the offence in the fourth column of the Schedule).

430(5)   ["Officer who is in default"] For the purpose of any enactment in this Act whereby an officer of a company who is in default is liable to a fine or penalty, the expression **"officer who is in default"** means any officer of the company who knowingly and wilfully authorises or permits the default, refusal or contravention mentioned in the enactment.

S.430(1)
This directs the reader to Sch.10 for a comprehensive list of punishments for offences created by the Act. For offences under the rules and their punishment see IR 1986 r.12.21 and Sch.5.

Note Banking Act 2009 ss.103 and 145.

S.430(2)–(4)
These subsections provide a guide to the use of Sch.10. This schedule is similar in form to CA 1985 Sch.24.

S.430(5)
This defines the common phrase "officer who is in default" in the same terms as CA 1985 s.730(5).

431 Summary proceedings

431(1)   [Taking of summary proceedings] Summary proceedings for any offence under any of Parts I to VII of this Act may (without prejudice to any jurisdiction exercisable apart from this subsection) be taken against a body corporate at any place at which the body has a place of business, and against any other person at any place at which he is for the time being.

431(2)   [Time for laying information] Notwithstanding anything in section 127(1) of the Magistrates' Courts Act 1980, an information relating to such an offence which is triable by a magistrates' court in England and Wales may be so tried if it is laid at any time within 3 years after the commission of the offence and within 12 months after the date on which evidence sufficient in the opinion of the Director of Public Prosecutions or the Secretary of State (as the case may be) to justify the proceedings comes to his knowledge.

431(3)   [Time for commencement of summary proceedings in Scotland] Summary proceedings in Scotland for such an offence shall not be commenced after the expiration of 3 years from the commission of the offence. Subject to this (and notwithstanding anything in section 136 of the Criminal Procedure (Scotland) Act 1995), such proceedings may (in Scotland) be commenced at any time within 12 months after the date on which evidence sufficient in the Lord Advocate's opinion to justify the proceedings came to his knowledge or, where such evidence was reported to him by the Secretary of State, within 12 months after the date on which it came to the knowledge of the latter; and subsection (3) of that section applies for the purpose of this subsection as it applies for the purpose of that section.

431(4)   [Certificate by DPP et al. conclusive evidence] For purposes of this section, a certificate of the Director of Public Prosecutions, the Lord Advocate or the Secretary of State (as the case may be) as to the date on which such evidence as is referred to above came to his knowledge is conclusive evidence.

S.431(1), (2), (4)
These subsections regulate summary proceedings under this Act in England and Wales. The phrase "a place of business" is much wider than "an established place of business", which is the formula used in CA 1985 s.409, for example.

Note Banking Act 2009 ss.103 and 145.

S.431(3), (4)
Summary proceedings in Scotland are provided for.

432 Offences by bodies corporate

432(1)   [Application] This section applies to offences under this Act other than those excepted by subsection (4).

432(2)   [Consent or connivance of various persons] Where a body corporate is guilty of an offence to which this section applies and the offence is proved to have been committed with the consent or connivance of, or to be attributable to any neglect on the part of, any director, manager, secretary or other similar officer of the body corporate or any person who was purporting to act in any such capacity he, as well as the body corporate, is guilty of the offence and liable to be proceeded against and punished accordingly.

432(3) **[Where affairs managed by members]** Where the affairs of a body corporate are managed by its members, subsection (2) applies in relation to the acts and defaults of a member in connection with his functions of management as if he were a director of the body corporate.

432(4) **[Offences excepted]** The offences excepted from this section are those under sections 30, 39, 51, 53, 54, 62, 64, 66, 85, 89, 164, 188, 201, 206, 207, 208, 209, 210 and 211 and those under paragraphs 16(2), 17(3)(a), 18(3)(a), 19(3)(a), 22(1) and 23(1)(a) of Schedule A1.

S.432(1)–(3)

Here there is a repetition of CA 1985 s.733. Where an offence under this Act has been committed by a body corporate, any officer who was a party to or responsible for the offence is subject to criminal liability, as well as the body corporate. De facto officers are similarly liable. "Body corporate" is not defined for the purposes of this Part of IA 1986; the definition contained in CA 1985 s.740 applies only to Pts I–VII (see s.251). It is therefore likely that a Scottish firm and a foreign corporation would be within the scope of this provision, even though they are not within s.740.

Note Banking Act 2009 ss.103 and 145.

S.432(3)

Some corporations, and in particular some incorporated by Royal Charter, have no body equivalent to a board of directors and are managed by their members. This is also true of a Scottish firm, if it is within the present provision. In such cases the members may incur personal liability under this section.

S.432(4)

Offences under certain named sections of the Act are excluded from the operation of s.432. Note the addition made by IA 2000 Sch.1.

433 Admissibility in evidence of statements of affairs, etc.

433(1) **[General rule on admissibility of statements]** In any proceedings (whether or not under this Act)–

(a) a statement of affairs prepared for the purposes of any provision of this Act which is derived from the Insolvency Act 1985,

(aa) a statement made in pursuance of a requirement imposed by or under Part 2 of the Banking Act 2009 (bank insolvency),

(ab) a statement made in pursuance of a requirement imposed by or under Part 3 of that Act (bank administration), and

(b) any other statement made in pursuance of a requirement imposed by or under any such provision or by or under rules made under this Act,

may be used in evidence against any person making or concurring in making the statement.

433(2) **[Limits on use of statement in criminal proceedings]** However, in criminal proceedings in which any such person is charged with an offence to which this subsection applies–

(a) no evidence relating to the statement may be adduced, and

(b) no question relating to it may be asked,

by or on behalf of the prosecution, unless evidence relating to it is adduced, or a question relating to it is asked, in the proceedings by or on behalf of that person.

433(3) **[Offences to which s.433(2) applies]** Subsection (2) applies to any offence other than–

(a) an offence under section 22(6), 47(6), 48(8), 66(6), 67(8), 95(8), 98(6), 99(3)(a), 131(7), 192(2), 208(1)(a) or (d) or (2), 210, 235(5), 353(1), 354(1)(b) or (3) or 356(1) or (2)(a) or (b) or paragraph 4(3)(a) of Schedule 7;

(b) an offence which is–

(i) created by rules made under this Act, and

(ii) designated for the purposes of this subsection by such rules or by regulations made by the Secretary of State;

(c) an offence which is–

(i) created by regulations made under any such rules, and

(ii) designated for the purposes of this subsection by such regulations;

(d) an offence under section 1, 2 or 5 of the Perjury Act 1911 (false statements made on oath or made otherwise than on oath); or

(e) an offence under section 44(1) or (2) of the Criminal Law (Consolidation) (Scotland) Act 1995 (false statements made on oath or otherwise than on oath).

433(4) [Procedure for making regulations] Regulations under subsection (3)(b)(ii) shall be made by statutory instrument and, after being made, shall be laid before each House of Parliament.

GENERAL NOTE

Section 433 was expanded considerably by the addition of three new subss.(2)–(4) via the Youth Justice and Criminal Evidence Act 1999 (ss.59, 68(3) and Sch.3 para.7(2) and (3)) with effect from April 14, 2000. Note Banking Act 2009 ss.103 and 145.

S.433(1)

Amended by ss.128 and 162 of the Banking Act 2009. It declares that any statement of affairs or other statement made in pursuance of a requirement under the insolvency legislation may be used in evidence against the person making it. See *R. v Kansal* [1993] Q.B. 244; [1992] B.C.C. 615; and *Hamilton v Naviede (Re Arrows Ltd (No.4))* [1995] 2 A.C. 75; [1994] B.C.C. 641. On the meaning of what is now s.433(1)(b) see *R. v Sawtell* [2001] B.P.I.R. 381. This wide evidential provision became suspect in view of the ruling of the European Court of Human Rights in *Saunders v UK* (1997) 23 E.H.R.R. 313 on the oppressive usage of compelled evidence in criminal prosecutions. Hence the need for modification by the introduction of subss.(2)–(4) in the Youth Justice and Criminal Evidence Act 1999. Note also *R. v Faryab* [1999] B.P.I.R. 569. On reopening "safe" convictions see *R. v Kansal* [2001] UKHL 62; [2002] B.P.I.R. 370—eventually this particular case proceeded to the European Court of Human Rights where it was held in *Kansal v UK* [2004] B.P.I.R. 740 that the use in a prosecution of transcripts obtained from an interrogation where the suspect was denied the right of silence did infringe the right to a fair trial under art.6 ECHR.

In *Rottmann v Official Receiver* [2009] B.P.I.R. 617 the bankrupt applied under IR r.6.175(6) for the public examination to be suspended lest it prejudice his position with respect to criminal proceedings against him in Germany. The court noted that s.433 only protected the bankrupt's right to silence with respect to proceedings under English law. However, it was observed that the guarantees under ECHR might operate in a protective fashion in the German proceedings. In the circumstances, the court felt that justice would be best served by suspending the public examination and substituting a private examination.

S.433(2)–(4)

Significant limitations are placed by the new provisions introduced via the 1999 Act upon the use by the prosecution of evidence made available pursuant to subs.(1) in a whole range of prosecutions unless the offence falls within the list prescribed by subs.(3). This list may, according to subs.(4), be modified by delegated legislation. See *Attorney General's Reference (No.7 of 2000)* [2001] EWCA Civ 888; [2001] 1 W.L.R. 1879.

434 Crown application

434 For the avoidance of doubt it is hereby declared that provisions of this Act which derive from the Insolvency Act 1985 bind the Crown so far as affecting or relating to the following matters, namely–

(a) remedies against, or against the property of, companies or individuals;

(b) priorities of debts;

(c) transactions at an undervalue or preferences;

(d) voluntary arrangements approved under Part I or Part VIII, and

(e)   discharge from bankruptcy.

GENERAL NOTE

This section makes it clear that specified provisions of the Act, whether they relate to companies or individuals, bind the Crown. Indeed, certain sections are specifically designed to take away Crown privileges—e.g. s.386 and Sch.6.

PART 17A

SUPPLEMENTARY PROVISIONS

434A   Introductory

434A   The provisions of this Part have effect for the purposes of–

(a)   the First Group of Parts, and

(b)   sections 411, 413, 414, 416 and 417 in Part 15.

434B   Representation of corporations at meetings

434B(1)   [Authorisation of representative] If a corporation is a creditor or debenture-holder, it may by resolution of its directors or other governing body authorise a person or persons to act as its representative or representatives–

(a)   at any meeting of the creditors of a company held in pursuance of this Act or of rules made under it, or

(b)   at any meeting of a company held in pursuance of the provisions contained in a debenture or trust deed.

434B(2)   [Power exercised by one person] Where the corporation authorises only one person, that person is entitled to exercise the same powers on behalf of the corporation as the corporation could exercise if it were an individual creditor or debenture-holder.

434B(3)   [Power exercised by more than one person] Where the corporation authorises more than one person, any one of them is entitled to exercise the same powers on behalf of the corporation as the corporation could exercise if it were an individual creditor or debenture-holder.

434B(4)   [Section 434B(3) power exercised differently] Where the corporation authorises more than one person and more than one of them purport to exercise a power under subsection (3)–

(a)   if they purport to exercise the power in the same way, the power is treated as exercised in that way;

(b)   if they do not purport to exercise the power in the same way, the power is treated as not exercised.

434C   Legal professional privilege

434C   In proceedings against a person for an offence under this Act nothing in this Act is to be taken to require any person to disclose any information that he is entitled to refuse to disclose on grounds of legal professional privilege (in Scotland, confidentiality of communications).

434D   Enforcement of company's filing obligations

434D(1)   [Application of s.434D] This section applies where a company has made default in complying with any obligation under this Act–

(a)   to deliver a document to the registrar, or

(b)   to give notice to the registrar of any matter.

434D(2) **[Power to notify company to comply with requirement]** The registrar, or any member or creditor of the company, may give notice to the company requiring it to comply with the obligation.

434D(3) **[Power to apply to court for failure to comply]** If the company fails to make good the default within 14 days after service of the notice, the registrar, or any member or creditor of the company, may apply to the court for an order directing the company, and any specified officer of it, to make good the default within a specified time.

434D(4) **[Court order re costs (Scotland: expenses)]** The court's order may provide that all costs (in Scotland, expenses) of or incidental to the application are to be borne by the company or by any officers of it responsible for the default.

434D(5) **[Section not to affect statutory penalties]** This section does not affect the operation of any enactment imposing penalties on a company or its officers in respect of any such default.

434E Application of filing obligations to overseas companies

434E The provisions of this Act requiring documents to be forwarded or delivered to, or filed with, the registrar of companies apply in relation to an overseas company that is required to register particulars under section 1046 of the Companies Act 2006 as they apply in relation to a company registered under that Act in England and Wales or Scotland.

GENERAL NOTE

This additional Part was inserted by the Companies Act (Consequential Amendments etc.) Order 2008 (SI 2008/948). Section 434B deals with the representation of companies and other corporations at meetings of creditors, etc. This provision reflects general provisions operating in corporate law. Section 434C protects legal professional privilege in proceedings for an alleged offence under this Act.

S.434D
This new transparency enforcement provision was inserted by the Companies Act 2006 (Consequential Amendments, Transitional Provisions and Savings) Order 2009 (SI 2009/1941) (operational from October 1, 2009). Its intention is to enable creditors, etc. to gain access to information, which should have been filed. Note that directors may be required personally to meet the costs of an application to secure such information.

S.434E
This new provision, which is specifically applicable to overseas companies, was inserted by the Companies Act 2006 (Consequential Amendments, Transitional Provisions and Savings) Order 2009 (SI 2009/1941) with effect from October 1, 2009.

PART XVIII

INTERPRETATION

435 Meaning of "associate"

435(1) **[Determination of whether associate]** For the purposes of this Act any question whether a person is an associate of another person is to be determined in accordance with the following provisions of this section (any provision that a person is an associate of another person being taken to mean that they are associates of each other).

435(2) **[Associate of individual]** A person is an associate of an individual if that person is–

(a) the individual's husband or wife or civil partner,

(b) a relative, of–

   (i) the individual, or

   (ii) the individual's husband or wife or civil partner, or

   (c)   the husband or wife or civil partner of a relative of–

      (i)   the individual, or

      (ii)   the individual's husband or wife or civil partner.

435(3)   **[Associate of partner]** A person is an associate of any person with whom he is in partnership, and of the husband or wife or civil partner or a relative of any individual with whom he is in partnership; and a Scottish firm is an associate of any person who is a member of the firm.

435(4)   **[Associate of employee, employer]** A person is an associate of any person whom he employs or by whom he is employed.

435(5)   **[Associate of trustee]** A person in his capacity as trustee of a trust other than–

   (a)   a trust arising under any of the second Group of Parts or the Bankruptcy (Scotland) Act 1985, or

   (b)   a pension scheme or an employees' share scheme,

is an associate of another person if the beneficiaries of the trust include, or the terms of the trust confer a power that may be exercised for the benefit of, that other person or an associate of that other person.

435(6)   **[Company associate of another company]** A company is an associate of another company–

   (a)   if the same person has control of both, or a person has control of one and persons who are his associates, or he and persons who are his associates, have control of the other, or

   (b)   if a group of two or more persons has control of each company, and the groups either consist of the same persons or could be regarded as consisting of the same persons by treating (in one or more cases) a member of either group as replaced by a person of whom he is an associate.

435(7)   **[Company associate of another person]** A company is an associate of another person if that person has control of it or if that person and persons who are his associates together have control of it.

435(8)   **[Person relative of individual]** For the purposes of this section a person is a relative of an individual if he is that individual's brother, sister, uncle, aunt, nephew, niece, lineal ancestor or lineal descendant, treating–

   (a)   any relationship of the half blood as a relationship of the whole blood and the stepchild or adopted child of any person as his child, and

   (b)   an illegitimate child as the legitimate child of his mother and reputed father;

and references in this section to a husband or wife include a former husband or wife and a reputed husband or wife and references to a civil partner include a former civil partner and a reputed civil partner.

435(9)   **[Director employee]** For the purposes of this section any director or other officer of a company is to be treated as employed by that company.

435(10)   **[Person with control]** For the purposes of this section a person is to be taken as having control of a company if–

   (a)   the directors of the company or of another company which has control of it (or any of them) are accustomed to act in accordance with his directions or instructions, or

   (b)   he is entitled to exercise, or control the exercise of, one third or more of the voting power at any general meeting of the company or of another company which has control of it;

and where two or more persons together satisfy either of the above conditions, they are to be taken as having control of the company.

435(11)   **["Company"]** In this section **"company"** includes any body corporate (whether incorporated in Great Britain or elsewhere); and references to directors and other officers of a company and to voting power at any general meeting of a company have effect with any necessary modifications.

GENERAL NOTE

Part XVIII applies to limited liability partnerships by virtue of the Limited Liability Partnerships Regulations 2001 (SI 2001/1090) reg.5(1)(b) as from April 6, 2001 subject to reg.5(2) and (3).

Re application of Pt XVIII to insolvent partnerships, see the Insolvent Partnerships Order 1994 (SI 1994/2121), especially arts 10, 11, Sch.7.

S.435(1)

This is a new and complex provision defining the word "associate" for the purposes of the Act. It will be particularly relevant to ss.314(6) and 340(5), and to the definition of "connected person" (s.249), a term extensively used in Pts I–VII.

S.435(2), (8)

Close family connections are sufficient to make one person an associate of another.

S.435(3)

Partnership links with an individual, or his close family, are sufficient to give rise to an "associate" relationship.

S.435(4)

Employers and employees are associates. However, see ss.239(6), 240(1)(a), 340(5).

S.435(5)

Certain trust relationships are caught by the net, where the insolvent or his or its associates could benefit from the trust. Note the change to subs.(5)(b) by the Companies Act 2006 (Consequential Amendments, Transitional Provisions and Savings) Order 2009 (SI 2009/1941) (with effect from October 1, 2009). This reflects the coming into force of the Companies Act 2006.

S.435(6), (7), (9)–(11)

These deal with the concept of "associate" in relation to companies (including companies incorporated outside Great Britain: see s.435(11)). A company can become an associate if it is controlled by the person in question or by his associate. Control can be determined by reference to a third of voting power at shareholders' meetings or by whether the directors normally act in accordance with his instructions. In *Unidare plc v Cohen* [2005] EWHC 1410 (Ch); [2005] 3 All E.R. 730, it was held that where shares are held on a bare trust it is the beneficiary and not the registered shareholder who has voting "power" for the purposes of s.435(10). Directors and officers are to be treated as being employed by their companies—this will be relevant in connection with s.435(4). In *Smurthwaite v Simpson-Smith and Mond (No.2)* [2006] B.P.I.R. 1483 there was consideration at first instance of what was meant by the term "reputed wife" for the purposes of s.435(8). But these comments need to be viewed in the light of the appeal in this case reported sub nom. *Smurthwaite v Simpson-Smith and Mond (No.2)* [2006] B.P.I.R. 1504 (where s.435(8) does not appear to have been at issue).

436   Expressions used generally

436(1)   [Definitions] In this Act, except in so far as the context otherwise requires (and subject to Parts VII and XI)–

"the appointed day" means the day on which this Act comes into force under section 443;

"associate" has the meaning given by section 435;

"body corporate" includes a body incorporated outside Great Britain, but does not include–

(a)   a corporation sole, or

(b)   a partnership that, whether or not a legal person, is not regarded as a body corporate under the law by which it is governed;

"business" includes a trade or profession;

"the Companies Acts" means the Companies Acts (as defined in section 2 of the Companies Act 2006) as they have effect in Great Britain;

"conditional sale agreement" and **"hire-purchase agreement"** have the same meanings as in the Consumer Credit Act 1974;

"the EC Regulation" means Council Regulation (EC) No. 1346/2000;

"EEA State" means a state that is a Contracting Party to the Agreement on the European Economic Area signed at Oporto on 2nd May 1992 as adjusted by the Protocol signed at Brussels on 17th March 1993;

"employees' share scheme" means a scheme for encouraging or facilitating the holding of shares in or debentures of a company by or for the benefit of–

 (a) the bona fide employees or former employees of–

   (i) the company,

   (ii) any subsidiary of the company, or

   (iii) the company's holding company or any subsidiary of the company's holding company, or

 (b) the spouses, civil partners, surviving spouses, surviving civil partners, or minor children or step-children of such employees or former employees.

"modifications" includes additions, alterations and omissions and cognate expressions shall be construed accordingly;

"property" includes money, goods, things in action, land and every description of property wherever situated and also obligations and every description of interest, whether present or future or vested or contingent, arising out of, or incidental to, property;

"records" includes computer records and other non-documentary records;

"subordinate legislation" has the same meaning as in the Interpretation Act 1978; and

"transaction" includes a gift, agreement or arrangement, and references to entering into a transaction shall be construed accordingly.

436(2) **[Definitions in Companies Acts]** The following expressions have the same meaning in this Act as in the Companies Acts–

"articles", in relation to a company (see section 18 of the Companies Act 2006);

"debenture" (see section 738 of that Act);

"holding company" (see sections 1159 and 1160 of, and Schedule 6 to, that Act);

"the Joint Stock Companies Acts" (see section 1171 of that Act);

"overseas company"(see section 1044 of that Act);

"paid up" (see section 583 of that Act);

"private company" and **"public company"** (see section 4 of that Act);

"registrar of companies" (see section 1060 of that Act);

"share" (see section 540 of that Act);

"subsidiary" (see sections 1159 and 1160 of, and Schedule 6 to, that Act).

GENERAL NOTE

This is general interpretation provision for the Act. It should be read in the light of Pts VII, XI and s.435. Note that the general meaning given to words by s.436 can be excluded where the context demands this.

 The "appointed day" was December 29, 1986: see the note to s.443.

 The reference to the EC Regulation was inserted by the Insolvency Act 1986 (Amendment) Regulations 2002 (SI 2002/1037) reg.4 with effect from May 3, 2002. The EEA State definition was inserted by the Insolvency Act 1986 (Amendment) Regulations 2005 (SI 2005/879). Note amendment by the Companies Act 2006 (Consequential Amendments, Transitional Provisions and Savings) Order 2009 (SI 2009/1941) (effective from October 1, 2009). This makes a number of changes, some of which result from the enactment of the Companies Act 2006.

Revised definition of "the Companies Acts" by the Companies Act 2006 (Commencement No.3, Consequential Amendments, Transitional Provisions and Savings) Order 2007 (SI 2007/2194 (C. 84)) art.10 and Sch.4 para.45 as from October 1, 2007, recognises the Companies Act 2006.

A company's interest as lessee under a lease of a chattel (an aircraft) was held to be "property" within the statutory definition contained in this section in *Bristol Airport plc v Powdrill; Re Paramount Airways Ltd* [1990] Ch. 744; [1990] B.C.C. 130. An expectation to receive a payment from the Criminal Injuries Compensation Board is not property: *Re a Bankrupt (No.145 of 1995)* [1996] B.P.I.R. 238. Compare *Re Rae* [1995] B.C.C. 102; and *Performing Rights Society v Rowland* [1998] B.P.I.R. 128. In *Official Receiver v Environment Agency* [1999] B.P.I.R. 986 the Court of Appeal held that a waste management licence was property for the purposes of s.436. In *Dear v Reeves* [2001] EWCA Civ 277; [2001] B.P.I.R. 577 a right of pre-emption was held to constitute "property" as were occupational benefits in *Patel v Jones* [2001] B.P.I.R. 919. In *Re Hemming (decd)* [2009] B.P.I.R. 50 the court (Richard Snowden Q.C.) held that the right of a residuary legatee (who had become bankrupt) to have the estate of the deceased properly administered was "property" for the purposes of s.436. This again is consistent with a broad interpretation of this pivotal concept in bankruptcy law.

See *Thornhill v Atherton (No.2)* [2008] B.P.I.R. 691 (foreign property).

A definition of "distress" is to be introduced by Sch.13 para.85 to the Tribunals, Courts and Enforcement Act 2007.

436A Proceedings under EC Regulation: modified definition of property

436A In the application of this Act to proceedings by virtue of Article 3 of the EC Regulation, a reference to property is a reference to property which may be dealt with in the proceedings.

GENERAL NOTE

Section 436A was inserted by Insolvency Act 1986 (Amendment) (No.2) Regulations 2002 (SI 2002/1240) reg.18 with effect from May 31, 2002. This limitation is needed to comply with the EC Regulation on Insolvency Proceedings, where the jurisdiction is sometimes restricted to local assets.

436B References to things in writing

436B(1) **[References include things in electronic form]** A reference in this Act to a thing in writing includes that thing in electronic form.

436B(2) **[Non-application of s.436B(1)]** Subsection (1) does not apply to the following provisions–

(a) section 53 (mode of appointment by holder of charge),

(b) section 67(2) (report by receiver),

(c) section 70(4) (reference to instrument creating a charge),

(d) section 111(2) (dissent from arrangement under s. 110),

(e) in the case of a winding up of a company registered in Scotland, section 111(4),

(f) section 123(1) (definition of inability to pay debts),

(g) section 198(3) (duties of sheriff principal as regards examination),

(h) section 222(1) (inability to pay debts: unpaid creditor for £750 or more), and

(i) section 223 (inability to pay debts: debt remaining unsatisfied after action brought).

GENERAL NOTE

Introduced by LRO 2010 (SI 2010/18). This provides (subject to exceptions specified in subs.(2)), that, where the Act requires something to be done in writing, it can now be done via electronic communication.

PART XIX

FINAL PROVISIONS

437 Transitional provisions, and savings

437 The transitional provisions and savings set out in Schedule 11 to this Act shall have effect, the Schedule comprising the following Parts–

Part I: company insolvency and winding up (matters arising before appointed day, and continuance of proceedings in certain cases as before that day);

Part II: individual insolvency (matters so arising, and continuance of bankruptcy proceedings in certain cases as before that day);

Part III: transactions entered into before the appointed day and capable of being affected by orders of the court under Part XVI of this Act;

Part IV: insolvency practitioners acting as such before the appointed day; and

Part V: general transitional provisions and savings required consequentially on, and in connection with, the repeal and replacement by this Act and the Company Directors Disqualification Act 1986 of provisions of the Companies Act 1985, the greater part of the Insolvency Act 1985 and other enactments.

GENERAL NOTE

This, coupled with Sch.11, makes transitional provisions and savings.

The significant transitional provisions have been noted at the relevant places in the text. Note the amendment by the Companies Act 2006 (Consequential Amendments, Transitional Provisions and Savings) Order 2009 (SI 2009/1941) with effect from October 1, 2009). This merely recognises the fact that there are now multiple Companies Acts.

438 Repeals

438 The enactments specified in the second column of Schedule 12 to this Act are repealed to the extent specified in the third column of that Schedule.

GENERAL NOTE

This section refers the reader to Sch.12, which lists the provisions repealed by IA 1986. Included amongst the repeals are a large number of provisions in CA 1985, plus virtually the entirety of IA 1985. See also Sch.4 to CDDA 1986.

439 Amendment of enactments

439(1) **[Amendment of Companies Act]** The Companies Act is amended as shown in Parts I and II of Schedule 13 to this Act, being amendments consequential on this Act and the Company Directors Disqualification Act 1986.

439(2) **[Enactments in Sch.14]** The enactments specified in the first column of Schedule 14 to this Act (being enactments which refer, or otherwise relate, to those which are repealed and replaced by this Act or the Company Directors Disqualification Act 1986) are amended as shown in the second column of that Schedule.

439(3) **[Consequential modifications of subordinate legislation]** The Lord Chancellor may by order make such consequential modifications of any provision contained in any subordinate legislation made before the appointed day and such transitional provisions in connection with those modifications as appear to him necessary or expedient in respect of–

(a)   any reference in that subordinate legislation to the Bankruptcy Act 1914;

(b) any reference in that subordinate legislation to any enactment repealed by Part III or IV of Schedule 10 to the Insolvency Act 1985; or

(c) any reference in that subordinate legislation to any matter provided for under the Act of 1914 or under any enactment so repealed.

439(4) **[Order by statutory instrument etc.]** An order under this section shall be made by statutory instrument subject to annulment in pursuance of a resolution of either House of Parliament.

S.439(1), (2)

These subsections refer to Schs 13 and 14 which respectively make consequential amendments to CA 1985 and other legislation. Most of the consequential amendments of CA 1985 are purely minor textual changes. A new s.196 of CA 1985 is enacted to apply the new preferential claims regime to the situation where the holder of a floating charge, instead of putting in a receiver, takes possession of the charged property. The consequential amendments effected by Sch.14 are also of a minor nature.

440　Extent (Scotland)

440(1) **[Extension to Scotland except where stated]** Subject to the next subsection, provisions of this Act contained in the first Group of Parts extend to Scotland except where otherwise stated.

440(2) **[Provisions not extending to Scotland]** The following provisions of this Act do not extend to Scotland–

(a) in the first Group of Parts–

section 43;

sections 238 to 241; and

section 246;

(b) the second Group of Parts;

(c) in the third Group of Parts–

sections 399 to 402,

sections 412, 413, 415, 415A(3), 418, 420 and 421,

sections 423 to 425, and

section 429(1) and (2); and

(d) in the Schedules–

Parts II and III of Schedule 11; and

Schedules 12 and 14 so far as they repeal or amend enactments which extend to England and Wales only.

GENERAL NOTE

This section identifies those provisions in IA 1986 which apply to Scotland. Most of the provisions on corporate insolvency apply equally to Scotland, except for certain receivership provisions (Scotland has its own receivership system in ss.50–71), the rules on preferences and transactions at an undervalue (again the Scots have their own rules in ss.242, 243 and also s.246). The rules on personal insolvency do not apply to Scotland, which has its own system contained in the Bankruptcy (Scotland) Act 1985. Note also the Debt Arrangement and Attachment (Scotland) Act 2002. Bearing in mind this point, it is not surprising that certain named miscellaneous provisions in the Third Group of Parts and the Schedules do not operate north of the border. The reference to s.415A(3) in subs.(2)(c) was added by EA 2002 s.270(4).

441   Extent (Northern Ireland)

441(1)   [Provisions extending to Northern Ireland] The following provisions of this Act extend to Northern Ireland–

(a)   sections 197, 426, 427 and 428; and

(b)   so much of section 439 and Schedule 14 as relates to enactments which extend to Northern Ireland.

441(2)   [Most of provisions not extending to Northern Ireland] Subject as above, and to any provision expressly relating to companies incorporated elsewhere than in Great Britain, nothing in this Act extends to Northern Ireland or applies to or in relation to companies registered or incorporated in Northern Ireland.

GENERAL NOTE

The Act, generally speaking, does not apply to Northern Ireland, which has its own distinct systems of corporate and personal insolvency law. Certain exceptional provisions do apply in Northern Ireland, however—e.g. s.426, which provides for co-operation between the various UK insolvency courts and s.427, which deals with parliamentary disqualification.

However, legislation has since been enacted which has made the insolvency law of Northern Ireland broadly similar to that of England and Wales. New rules relating to the disqualification of company directors were introduced with effect from September 24, 1986 by the Companies (Northern Ireland) Order 1986 (SI 1986/1032 (NI 6)); and these have since been re-enacted and extended by Pt II of the Companies (Northern Ireland) Order 1989 (SI 1989/2404 (NI 18)). In consequence, legislation equivalent to CDDA 1986 is now in place in Northern Ireland. The 1989 Order was brought into force with effect from October 1, 1991 by the Companies Act (1989 Order) (Commencement No.2) Order (Northern Ireland) 1991 (SR 1991/410 (C. 19)). The Insolvency (Northern Ireland) Order 1989 (SI 1989/2405 (NI 19)) is the counterpart for Northern Ireland of IA 1986. The object of the order is to bring the insolvency legislation, both personal and corporate, of that jurisdiction into line with that of England and Wales. This order was made on December 19, 1989, and was brought into operation in full on October 1, 1991 by the Insolvency (1989 Order) (Commencement No.4) Order (Northern Ireland) 1991 (SR 1991/411 (C. 20)). Previous Commencement Orders were of minimal impact. Note also SI 2002/3152 (NI 6) (SR 2003/545 and SR 2003/546). Other provisions which have been put into force as part of the new insolvency regime in Northern Ireland include the Insolvency Practitioners (Recognised Practitioners Regulations (Northern Ireland) 1991 (SR 1991/302 as amended by SR 2003/547); the Insolvency Rules (Northern Ireland) 1991 (SR 1991/364 as amended by SR 2000/247, SR 2003/549 and SR 2008/118); the Insolvency (Deposits) Order (Northern Ireland) 1991 (SR 1991/384); the Insolvency (Monetary Limits) Order (Northern Ireland) 1991 (SR 1991/386); the Insolvency (Fees) Order (Northern Ireland) 1991 (SR 1991/385); the Insolvency Regulations (Northern Ireland) 1991 (SR 1991/388); the Financial Markets and Insolvency Regulations (Northern Ireland) 1991 (SR 1991/443); and the Insolvency Practitioners Order (Northern Ireland) 1995 (SR 1995/225, (as amended by SR 1996/472)). Note also Occupational and Personal Pension Schemes (Bankruptcy) Regulations (Northern Ireland) 2002 (SR 2002/127); the Insolvency Regulations (Northern Ireland) 1996 (Electronic. Communications) Order (Northern Ireland) 2006 (SR 2006/461) which amends SR 1996/574.

The IA 1994, which amended the law relating to the "adoption" of contracts of employment by administrators and administrative receivers, also amends the law applicable in Northern Ireland: see s.4 of and Sch.1 to that Act. There is also an Insolvent Partnerships (Northern Ireland) Order 1991 (SR 1991/366 most recently amended by SI 2003/144 and SR 2003/550) and specific regulations dealing with proceedings and reports arising out of the disqualification of directors (see SR 1991/367, 1991/368, 1991/413 and SR 2003/345–347). Administration of estates of deceased insolvents in Northern Ireland is covered by SR 1991/365 as amended by SR 2003/103. Many of these provisions have since been the subject of amending legislation: see, e.g. SR 1992/398, 1993/302, 1993/454, 1994/26, 1995/291, 1996/471, 1996/574–577, 1997/1072, SR 2002/334.

The reforms introduced in English law by the EA 2002 were incorporated into Northern Ireland by the Insolvency (Northern Ireland) Order 2005 (SI 2005/1455 (NI 10)). For commencement see the Insolvency (2005 Order) (Commencement No.1) Order (Northern Ireland) 2006 (SI 2006/21 (C. 1)). Associated measures linked to the advent of the 2005 Order are contained in the Insolvency (2005 Order) (Transitional Provision and Savings) Order (Northern Ireland) 2006 (SR 2006/22); the Insolvency (Amendment) Regulations (Northern Ireland) 2005 (SR 2006/23); the Insolvency (Northern Ireland) Order 1989 Article 59A (Appointed Date) Order (Northern Ireland) 2006 (SR 2006/24); the Insolvency (Northern Ireland) Order 1989 (Prescribed Part) Order (Northern Ireland) 2006 (SR

2006/25); the Insolvency (Monetary Limits) (Amendment) Order (Northern Ireland) 2006 (SR 2006/26); the Insolvency Practitioners Regulations (Northern Ireland) 2006 (SR 2006/33); the Insolvency (Northern Ireland) Order 2005 (Minor and Consequential Amendments) Order (Northern Ireland) 2006 (SR 2006/61). The advent of the 2005 Order has made it necessary to amend the Credit Institutions (Reorganisation and Winding Up) Regulations 2004 (SI 2004/1045) to cater for the new administration procedure now operating in Northern Ireland—see SI 2007/830; the Insolvent Partnerships (Amendment) Order (Northern Ireland) 2006 (SR 2006/515). For further instances of recent secondary legislation see the Insolvency Practitioners and Insolvency Account (Fees) Order (Northern Ireland) 2006 (SR 2006/53); the Insolvency (Fees) Order (Northern Ireland) 2006 (SR 2006/54). On director disqualification note the Insolvent Companies (Disqualification of Unfit Directors) Proceedings (Amendment) Rules (Northern Ireland) 2005 (SI 2005/517); the Company Directors Disqualification (Amendment) 2005 Order (SI 2005/1454 (NI 9)). See also the Insolvency (Disqualification from Office: General) Order (Northern Ireland) 2008 (SR 2008/94). Note also the Financial Markets and Insolvency (Settlement Finality) (Amendment) Regulations 2006 (SI 2006/50) which extend SI 1999/2979 to Northern Ireland. These regulations were amended by SI 2007/832.

Changes to Northern Irish insolvency laws can be made via UK statutory instruments—see for example the Companies (Trading Disclosures) (Insolvency) Regulations 2008 (SI 2008/1897) which were introduced to ensure compliance with EC Directive 2003/58. These regulations amend art.49, art.159, Sch.A1 para.27 and Sch.B1 para.46 to the 1989 Order with effect from October 1, 2008. Note the Companies Act 2006 (Consequential Amendments, Transitional Provisions and Savings) Order 2009 (SI 2009/1941) (effective from October 1, 2009), which made a number of amendments to Northern Irish insolvency law.

Note the statement in para.84 of the Companies Act 2006 (Consequential Amendments, Transitional Provisions and Savings) Order 2009 (SI 2009/1941) which is reproduced below. This is effective from October 1, 2009.

"Nothing in the amendments of the Insolvency Act 1986 made by this Schedule is to be read as qualifying the generality of section 441(2) of that Act (which provides that, with certain exceptions, nothing in the Act extends to Northern Ireland or applies to or in relation to companies registered or incorporated in Northern Ireland)."

Section 441(2) was considered by the court in *Re Normandy Marketing Ltd* [1993] B.C.C. 879. Here it was held that s.221 was wide enough to cover Northern Ireland companies and therefore such a company could be wound up under English law under s.124A of IA 1986 on the grounds that it was in the public interest to do so.

For a review of insolvency litigation in the Province see Capper, [2001] Ins. Law 119; [2003] Ins. Law 132; [2005] 18 Insolv. Int. 81; and [2008] 21 Insolv. Int. 59.

442   Extent (other territories)

442   Her Majesty may, by Order in Council, direct that such of the provisions of this Act as are specified in the Order, being provisions formerly contained in the Insolvency Act 1985, shall extend to any of the Channel Islands or any colony with such modifications as may be so specified.

GENERAL NOTE

This provides for the extension of the Act by Order in Council to any of the Channel Islands or any colony. The Isle of Man is not included. Note *Re Television Trade Rentals Ltd* [2002] EWHC 211 (Ch); [2002] B.C.C. 807 where s.426 of IA 1986 was used to extend the CVA provisions in Pt I of the Act to companies incorporated in the Isle of Man.

The Insolvency Act 1986 (Guernsey) Order 1989 (SI 1989/2409) makes provision for co-operation between the courts of the Bailiwick of Guernsey (including Alderney and Sark) and the courts of the UK: see the note to s.426.

443   Commencement

443   This Act comes into force on the day appointed under section 236(2) of the Insolvency Act 1985 for the coming into force of Part III of that Act (individual insolvency and bankruptcy), immediately after that part of that Act comes into force for England and Wales.

GENERAL NOTE

This odd formula ties the commencement date of IA 1986 to the commencement date of Pt III of IA 1985: see SI 1986/1924 (C. 71) and the general note to s.439 above. The date was December 29, 1986. Certain other provisions in the 1985 Act, relating to corporate insolvency and the licensing of insolvency practitioners, had already been put into force (and now form part of the 1986 consolidation).

444 Citation

444 This Act may be cited as the Insolvency Act 1986.

SCHEDULE A1

MORATORIUM WHERE DIRECTORS PROPOSE VOLUNTARY ARRANGEMENT

PART I

INTRODUCTORY

Interpretation

1 In this Schedule–

"the beginning of the moratorium" has the meaning given by paragraph 8(1),

"the date of filing" means the date on which the documents for the time being referred to in paragraph 7(1) are filed or lodged with the court,

"hire-purchase agreement" includes a conditional sale agreement, a chattel leasing agreement and a retention of title agreement,

"market contract" and **"market charge"** have the meanings given by Part VII of the Companies Act 1989,

"moratorium" means a moratorium under section 1A,

"the nominee" includes any person for the time being carrying out the functions of a nominee under this Schedule,

"the settlement finality regulations" means the Financial Markets and Insolvency (Settlement Finality) Regulations 1999,

"system-charge" has the meaning given by the Financial Markets and Insolvency Regulations 1996.

Eligible companies

2(1) A company is eligible for a moratorium if it meets the requirements of paragraph 3, unless–

    (a)   it is excluded from being eligible by virtue of paragraph 4, or

    (b)   it falls within sub-paragraph (2).

2(2) A company falls within this sub-paragraph if–

    (a)   it effects or carries out contracts of insurance, but is not exempt from the general prohibition, within the meaning of section 19 of the Financial Services and Markets Act 2000, in relation to that activity,

    (b)   it has permission under Part IV of that Act to accept deposits,

    (bb) it has a liability in respect of a deposit which it accepted in accordance with the Banking Act 1979 (c. 37) or 1987 (c. 22),

    (c)   it is a party to a market contract or any of its property is subject to a market charge or a system-charge, or

    (d)   it is a participant (within the meaning of the settlement finality regulations) or any of its property is subject to a collateral security charge (within the meaning of those regulations).

494

2(3) Paragraphs (a), (b) and (bb) of sub-paragraph (2) must be read with–

(a) section 22 of the Financial Services and Markets Act 2000;

(b) any relevant order under that section; and

(c) Schedule 2 to that Act.

3(1) A company meets the requirements of this paragraph if the qualifying conditions are met–

(a) in the year ending with the date of filing, or

(b) in the financial year of the company which ended last before that date.

3(2) For the purposes of sub-paragraph (1)–

(a) the qualifying conditions are met by a company in a period if, in that period, it satisfies two or more of the requirements for being a small company specified for the time being in section 382(3) of the Companies Act 2006, and

(b) a company's financial year is to be determined in accordance with that Act.

3(3) Section 382(4), (5) and (6) of that Act apply for the purposes of this paragraph as they apply for the purposes of that section.

3(4) A company does not meet the requirements of this paragraph if it is a parent company of a group of companies which does not qualify as a small group or a medium-sized group in relation to the financial year of the company which ended last before the date of filing.

3(5) For the purposes of sub-paragraph (4)–

(a) "group" has the same meaning as in Part 15 of the Companies Act 2006 (see section 474(1) of that Act); and

(b) a group qualifies as small in relation to a financial year if it so qualifies under section 383(2) to (7) of that Act, and qualifies as medium-sized in relation to a financial year if it so qualifies under section 466(2) to (7) of that Act.

3(6) Expressions used in this paragraph that are defined expressions in Part 15 of the Companies Act 2006 (accounts and reports) have the same meaning in this paragraph as in that Part.

4(1) A company is excluded from being eligible for a moratorium if, on the date of filing–

(a) the company is in administration,

(b) the company is being wound up,

(c) there is an administrative receiver of the company,

(d) a voluntary arrangement has effect in relation to the company,

(e) there is a provisional liquidator of the company,

(f) a moratorium has been in force for the company at any time during the period of 12 months ending with the date of filing and–

(i) no voluntary arrangement had effect at the time at which the moratorium came to an end, or

(ii) a voluntary arrangement which had effect at any time in that period has come to an end prematurely, or

(fa) an administrator appointed under paragraph 22 of Schedule B1 has held office in the period of 12 months ending with the date of filing,

(g) a voluntary arrangement in relation to the company which had effect in pursuance of a proposal under section 1(3) has come to an end prematurely and, during the period of 12 months ending with the date of filing, an order under section 5(3)(a) has been made.

4(2) Sub-paragraph (1)(b) does not apply to a company which, by reason of a winding-up order made after the date of filing, is treated as being wound up on that date.

Capital market arrangement

4A A company is also excluded from being eligible for a moratorium if, on the date of filing, it is a party to an agreement which is or forms part of a capital market arrangement under which–

(i) a party has incurred, or when the agreement was entered into was expected to incur, a debt of at least £10 million under the arrangement, and

(ii) the arrangement involves the issue of a capital market investment.

Public private partnership

4B A company is also excluded from being eligible for a moratorium if, on the date of filing, it is a project company of a project which–

(i) is a public-private partnership project, and

(ii) includes step-in rights.

Liability under an arrangement

4C(1) A company is also excluded from being eligible for a moratorium if, on the date of filing, it has incurred a liability under an agreement of £10 million or more.

4C(2) Where the liability in sub-paragraph (1) is a contingent liability under or by virtue of a guarantee or an indemnity or security provided on behalf of another person, the amount of that liability is the full amount of the liability in relation to which the guarantee, indemnity or security is provided.

4C(3) In this paragraph–

(a) the reference to "liability" includes a present or future liability whether, in either case, it is certain or contingent,

(b) the reference to "liability" includes a reference to a liability to be paid wholly or partly in foreign currency (in which case the sterling equivalent shall be calculated as at the time when the liability is incurred).

Interpretation of capital market arrangement

4D(1) For the purposes of paragraph 4A an arrangement is a capital market arrangement if–

(a) it involves a grant of security to a person holding it as trustee for a person who holds a capital market investment issued by a party to the arrangement, or

(b) at least one party guarantees the performance of obligations of another party, or

(c) at least one party provides security in respect of the performance of obligations of another party, or

(d) the arrangement involves an investment of a kind described in articles 83 to 85 of the Financial Services and Markets Act 2000 (Regulated Activities) Order 2001 (S.I. 2001/544) (options, futures and contracts for differences).

4D(2) For the purposes of sub-paragraph (1)–

  (a)   a reference to holding as trustee includes a reference to holding as nominee or agent,

  (b)   a reference to holding for a person who holds a capital market investment includes a reference to holding for a number of persons at least one of whom holds a capital market investment, and

  (c)   a person holds a capital market investment if he has a legal or beneficial interest in it.

4D(3) In paragraph 4A, 4C, 4J and this paragraph–

"agreement" includes an agreement or undertaking effected by–

  (a)   contract,

  (b)   deed, or

  (c)   any other instrument intended to have effect in accordance with the law of England and Wales, Scotland or another jurisdiction, and

"party" to an arrangement includes a party to an agreement which–

  (a)   forms part of the arrangement,

  (b)   provides for the raising of finance as part of the arrangement, or

  (c)   is necessary for the purposes of implementing the arrangement.

Capital market investment

4E(1) For the purposes of paragraphs 4A and 4D, an investment is a capital market investment if–

  (a)   it is within article 77 of the Financial Services and Markets Act 2000 (Regulated Activities) Order 2001 (S.I. 2001/544) (debt instruments) and

  (b)   it is rated, listed or traded or designed to be rated, listed or traded.

4E(2) In sub-paragraph (1)–

"listed" means admitted to the official list within the meaning given by section 103(1) of the Financial Services and Markets Act 2000 (c. 8) (interpretation),

"rated" means rated for the purposes of investment by an internationally recognised rating agency,

"traded" means admitted to trading on a market established under the rules of a recognised investment exchange or on a foreign market.

4E(3) In sub-paragraph (2)–

"foreign market" has the same meaning as "relevant market" in article 67(2) of the Financial Services and Markets Act 2000 (Financial Promotion) Order 2001 (S.I. 2001/1335) (foreign markets),

"recognised investment exchange" has the meaning given by section 285 of the Financial Services and Markets Act 2000 (recognised investment exchange).

4F(1) For the purposes of paragraphs 4A and 4D an investment is also a capital market investment if it consists of a bond or commercial paper issued to one or more of the following–

  (a)   an investment professional within the meaning of article 19(5) of the Financial Services and Markets Act 2000 (Financial Promotion) Order 2001,

  (b)   a person who is, when the agreement mentioned in paragraph 4A is entered into, a certified high net worth individual in relation to a communication within the meaning of article 48(2) of that order,

   (c)   a person to whom article 49(2) of that order applies (high net worth company, &c),

   (d)   a person who is, when the agreement mentioned in paragraph 4A is entered into, a certified sophisticated investor in relation to a communication within the meaning of article 50(1) of that order, and

   (e)   a person in a State other than the United Kingdom who under the law of that State is not prohibited from investing in bonds or commercial paper.

4F(2)   For the purposes of sub-paragraph (1)–

   (a)   in applying article 19(5) of the Financial Services and Markets Act 2000 (Financial Promotion) Order 2001 for the purposes of sub-paragraph (1)(a)–

      (i)   in article 19(5)(b), ignore the words after "exempt person",

      (ii)   in article 19(5)(c)(i), for the words from "the controlled activity" to the end substitute "a controlled activity", and

      (iii)   in article 19(5)(e) ignore the words from "where the communication" to the end, and

   (b)   in applying article 49(2) of that order for the purposes of sub-paragraph (1)(c), ignore article 49(2)(e).

4F(3)   In sub-paragraph (1)–

"bond" shall be construed in accordance with article 77 of the Financial Services and Markets Act 2000 (Regulated Activities) Order 2001 (S.I. 2001/544), and

"commercial paper" has the meaning given by article 9(3) of that order.

Debt

4G   The debt of at least £10 million referred to in paragraph 4A–

   (a)   may be incurred at any time during the life of the capital market arrangement, and

   (b)   may be expressed wholly or partly in a foreign currency (in which case the sterling equivalent shall be calculated as at the time when the arrangement is entered into).

Interpretation of project company

4H(1)   For the purposes of paragraph 4B a company is a "project company" of a project if–

   (a)   it holds property for the purpose of the project,

   (b)   it has sole or principal responsibility under an agreement for carrying out all or part of the project,

   (c)   it is one of a number of companies which together carry out the project,

   (d)   it has the purpose of supplying finance to enable the project to be carried out, or

   (e)   it is the holding company of a company within any of paragraphs (a) to (d).

4H(2)   But a company is not a "project company" of a project if–

   (a)   it performs a function within sub-paragraph (1)(a) to (d) or is within sub-paragraph (1)(e), but

   (b)   it also performs a function which is not–

      (i)   within sub-paragraph (1)(a) to (d),

      (ii)   related to a function within sub-paragraph (1)(a) to (d), or

      (iii)   related to the project.

4H(3) For the purposes of this paragraph a company carries out all or part of a project whether or not it acts wholly or partly through agents.

Public-private partnership project

4I(1) In paragraph 4B "public-private partnership project" means a project–

    (a) the resources for which are provided partly by one or more public bodies and partly by one or more private persons, or

    (b) which is designed wholly or mainly for the purpose of assisting a public body to discharge a function.

4I(2) In sub-paragraph (1) "resources" includes–

    (a) funds (including payment for the provision of services or facilities),

    (b) assets,

    (c) professional skill,

    (d) the grant of a concession or franchise, and

    (e) any other commercial resource.

4I(3) In sub-paragraph (1) "public body" means–

    (a) a body which exercises public functions,

    (b) a body specified for the purposes of this paragraph by the Secretary of State, and

    (c) a body within a class specified for the purposes of this paragraph by the Secretary of State.

4I(4) A specification under sub-paragraph (3) may be–

    (a) general, or

    (b) for the purpose of the application of paragraph 4B to a specified case.

Step-in rights

4J(1) For the purposes of paragraph 4B a project has "step-in rights" if a person who provides finance in connection with the project has a conditional entitlement under an agreement to–

    (i) assume sole or principal responsibility under an agreement for carrying out all or part of the project, or

    (ii) make arrangements for carrying out all or part of the project.

4J(2) In sub-paragraph (1) a reference to the provision of finance includes a reference to the provision of an indemnity.

Person

4K For the purposes of paragraphs 4A to 4J, a reference to a person includes a reference to a partnership or another unincorporated group of persons.

5 The Secretary of State may by regulations modify the qualifications for eligibility of a company for a moratorium.

PART II

OBTAINING A MORATORIUM

Nominee's statement

6(1)   Where the directors of a company wish to obtain a moratorium, they shall submit to the nominee–

   (a)   a document setting out the terms of the proposed voluntary arrangement,

   (b)   a statement of the company's affairs containing–

      (i)   such particulars of its creditors and of its debts and other liabilities and of its assets as may be prescribed, and

      (ii)   such other information as may be prescribed, and

   (c)   any other information necessary to enable the nominee to comply with sub-paragraph (2) which he requests from them.

6(2)   The nominee shall submit to the directors a statement in the prescribed form indicating whether or not, in his opinion–

   (a)   the proposed voluntary arrangement has a reasonable prospect of being approved and implemented,

   (b)   the company is likely to have sufficient funds available to it during the proposed moratorium to enable it to carry on its business, and

   (c)   meetings of the company and its creditors should be summoned to consider the proposed voluntary arrangement.

6(3)   In forming his opinion on the matters mentioned in sub-paragraph (2), the nominee is entitled to rely on the information submitted to him under sub-paragraph (1) unless he has reason to doubt its accuracy.

6(4)   The reference in sub-paragraph (2)(b) to the company's business is to that business as the company proposes to carry it on during the moratorium.

Documents to be submitted to court

7(1)   To obtain a moratorium the directors of a company must file (in Scotland, lodge) with the court–

   (a)   a document setting out the terms of the proposed voluntary arrangement,

   (b)   a statement of the company's affairs containing–

      (i)   such particulars of its creditors and of its debts and other liabilities and of its assets as may be prescribed, and

      (ii)   such other information as may be prescribed,

   (c)   a statement that the company is eligible for a moratorium,

   (d)   a statement from the nominee that he has given his consent to act, and

   (e)   a statement from the nominee that, in his opinion–

      (i)   the proposed voluntary arrangement has a reasonable prospect of being approved and implemented,

      (ii)   the company is likely to have sufficient funds available to it during the proposed moratorium to enable it to carry on its business, and

500

(iii) meetings of the company and its creditors should be summoned to consider the proposed voluntary arrangement.

7(2) Each of the statements mentioned in sub-paragraph (1)(b) to (e), except so far as it contains the particulars referred to in paragraph (b)(i), must be in the prescribed form.

7(3) The reference in sub-paragraph (1)(e)(ii) to the company's business is to that business as the company proposes to carry it on during the moratorium.

7(4) The Secretary of State may by regulations modify the requirements of this paragraph as to the documents required to be filed (in Scotland, lodged) with the court in order to obtain a moratorium.

Duration of moratorium

8(1) A moratorium comes into force when the documents for the time being referred to in paragraph 7(1) are filed or lodged with the court and references in this Schedule to "the beginning of the moratorium" shall be construed accordingly.

8(2) A moratorium ends at the end of the day on which the meetings summoned under paragraph 29(1) are first held (or, if the meetings are held on different days, the later of those days), unless it is extended under paragraph 32.

8(3) If either of those meetings has not first met before the end of the period of 28 days beginning with the day on which the moratorium comes into force, the moratorium ends at the end of the day on which those meetings were to be held (or, if those meetings were summoned to be held on different days, the later of those days), unless it is extended under paragraph 32.

8(4) If the nominee fails to summon either meeting within the period required by paragraph 29(1), the moratorium ends at the end of the last day of that period.

8(5) If the moratorium is extended (or further extended) under paragraph 32, it ends at the end of the day to which it is extended (or further extended).

8(6) Sub-paragraphs (2) to (5) do not apply if the moratorium comes to an end before the time concerned by virtue of–

(a) paragraph 25(4) (effect of withdrawal by nominee of consent to act),

(b) an order under paragraph 26(3), 27(3) or 40 (challenge of actions of nominee or directors), or

(c) a decision of one or both of the meetings summoned under paragraph 29.

8(7) If the moratorium has not previously come to an end in accordance with sub-paragraphs (2) to (6), it ends at the end of the day on which a decision under paragraph 31 to approve a voluntary arrangement takes effect under paragraph 36.

8(8) The Secretary of State may by order increase or reduce the period for the time being specified in sub-paragraph (3).

Notification of beginning of moratorium

9(1) When a moratorium comes into force, the directors shall notify the nominee of that fact forthwith.

9(2) If the directors without reasonable excuse fail to comply with sub-paragraph (1), each of them is liable to imprisonment or a fine, or both.

10(1) When a moratorium comes into force, the nominee shall, in accordance with the rules–

(a) advertise that fact forthwith, and

    (b)   notify the registrar of companies, the company and any petitioning creditor of the company of whose claim he is aware of that fact.

10(2)   In sub-paragraph (1)(b), "petitioning creditor" means a creditor by whom a winding-up petition has been presented before the beginning of the moratorium, as long as the petition has not been dismissed or withdrawn.

10(3)   If the nominee without reasonable excuse fails to comply with sub-paragraph (1)(a) or (b), he is liable to a fine.

Notification of end of moratorium

11(1)   When a moratorium comes to an end, the nominee shall, in accordance with the rules–

    (a)   advertise that fact forthwith, and

    (b)   notify the court, the registrar of companies, the company and any creditor of the company of whose claim he is aware of that fact.

11(2)   If the nominee without reasonable excuse fails to comply with sub-paragraph (1)(a) or (b), he is liable to a fine.

PART III

EFFECTS OF MORATORIUM

Effect on creditors, etc.

12(1)   During the period for which a moratorium is in force for a company–

    (a)   no petition may be presented for the winding up of the company,

    (b)   no meeting of the company may be called or requisitioned except with the consent of the nominee or the leave of the court and subject (where the court gives leave) to such terms as the court may impose,

    (c)   no resolution may be passed or order made for the winding up of the company,

    (d)   no administration application may be made in respect of the company,

  (da) no administrator of the company may be appointed under paragraph 14 or 22 of Schedule B1,

    (e)   no administrative receiver of the company may be appointed,

    (f)   no landlord or other person to whom rent is payable may exercise any right of forfeiture by peaceable re-entry in relation to premises let to the company in respect of a failure by the company to comply with any term or condition of its tenancy of such premises, except with the leave of the court and subject to such terms as the court may impose,

    (g)   no other steps may be taken to enforce any security over the company's property, or to repossess goods in the company's possession under any hire-purchase agreement, except with the leave of the court and subject to such terms as the court may impose, and

    (h)   no other proceedings and no execution or other legal process may be commenced or continued, and no distress may be levied, against the company or its property except with the leave of the court and subject to such terms as the court may impose.

12(2)   Where a petition, other than an excepted petition, for the winding up of the company has been presented before the beginning of the moratorium, section 127 shall not apply in relation to any disposition of property, transfer of shares or alteration in status made during the moratorium or at a time mentioned in paragraph 37(5)(a).

12(3) In the application of sub-paragraph (1)(h) to Scotland, the reference to execution being commenced or continued includes a reference to diligence being carried out or continued, and the reference to distress being levied is omitted.

12(4) Paragraph (a) of sub-paragraph (1) does not apply to an excepted petition and, where such a petition has been presented before the beginning of the moratorium or is presented during the moratorium, paragraphs (b) and (c) of that sub-paragraph do not apply in relation to proceedings on the petition.

12(5) For the purposes of this paragraph, "excepted petition" means a petition under–

(a) section 124A or 124B of this Act,

(b) section 72 of the Financial Services Act 1986 on the ground mentioned in subsection (1)(b) of that section, or

(c) section 92 of the Banking Act 1987 on the ground mentioned in subsection (1)(b) of that section.

(d) section 367 of the Financial Services and Markets Act 2000 on the ground mentioned in subsection 3(b) of that section.

13(1) This paragraph applies where there is an uncrystallised floating charge on the property of a company for which a moratorium is in force.

13(2) If the conditions for the holder of the charge to give a notice having the effect mentioned in sub-paragraph (4) are met at any time, the notice may not be given at that time but may instead be given as soon as practicable after the moratorium has come to an end.

13(3) If any other event occurs at any time which (apart from this sub-paragraph) would have the effect mentioned in sub-paragraph (4), then–

(a) the event shall not have the effect in question at that time, but

(b) if notice of the event is given to the company by the holder of the charge as soon as is practicable after the moratorium has come to an end, the event is to be treated as if it had occurred when the notice was given.

13(4) The effect referred to in sub-paragraphs (2) and (3) is–

(a) causing the crystallisation of the floating charge, or

(b) causing the imposition, by virtue of provision in the instrument creating the charge, of any restriction on the disposal of any property of the company.

13(5) Application may not be made for leave under paragraph 12(1)(g) or (h) with a view to obtaining–

(a) the crystallisation of the floating charge, or

(b) the imposition, by virtue of provision in the instrument creating the charge, of any restriction on the disposal of any property of the company.

14 Security granted by a company at a time when a moratorium is in force in relation to the company may only be enforced if, at that time, there were reasonable grounds for believing that it would benefit the company.

Effect on company

15(1) Paragraphs 16 to 23 apply in relation to a company for which a moratorium is in force.

15(2) The fact that a company enters into a transaction in contravention of any of paragraphs 16 to 22 does not–

(a)   make the transaction void, or

(b)   make it to any extent unenforceable against the company.

Company invoices, etc.

16(1)   Every invoice, order for goods or services, business letter or order form (whether in hard copy, electronic or any other form) issued by or on behalf of the company, and all the company's websites, must also contain the nominee's name and a statement that the moratorium is in force for the company.

16(2)   If default is made in complying with sub-paragraph (1), the company and (subject to sub-paragraph (3)) any officer of the company is liable to a fine.

16(3)   An officer of the company is only liable under sub-paragraph (2) if, without reasonable excuse, he authorises or permits the default.

Obtaining credit during moratorium

17(1)   The company may not obtain credit to the extent of £250 or more from a person who has not been informed that a moratorium is in force in relation to the company.

17(2)   The reference to the company obtaining credit includes the following cases–

(a)   where goods are bailed (in Scotland, hired) to the company under a hire-purchase agreement, or agreed to be sold to the company under a conditional sale agreement, and

(b)   where the company is paid in advance (whether in money or otherwise) for the supply of goods or services.

17(3)   Where the company obtains credit in contravention of sub-paragraph (1)–

(a)   the company is liable to a fine, and

(b)   if any officer of the company knowingly and wilfully authorised or permitted the contravention, he is liable to imprisonment or a fine, or both.

17(4)   The money sum specified in sub-paragraph (1) is subject to increase or reduction by order under section 417A in Part XV.

Disposals and payments

18(1)   Subject to sub-paragraph (2), the company may only dispose of any of its property if–

(a)   there are reasonable grounds for believing that the disposal will benefit the company, and

(b)   the disposal is approved by the committee established under paragraph 35(1) or, where there is no such committee, by the nominee.

18(2)   Sub-paragraph (1) does not apply to a disposal made in the ordinary way of the company's business.

18(3)   If the company makes a disposal in contravention of sub-paragraph (1) otherwise than in pursuance of an order of the court–

(a)   the company is liable to a fine, and

(b)   if any officer of the company authorised or permitted the contravention, without reasonable excuse, he is liable to imprisonment or a fine, or both.

19(1)   Subject to sub-paragraph (2), the company may only make any payment in respect of any debt or other liability of the company in existence before the beginning of the moratorium if–

(a) there are reasonable grounds for believing that the payment will benefit the company, and

(b) the payment is approved by the committee established under paragraph 35(1) or, where there is no such committee, by the nominee.

19(2) Sub-paragraph (1) does not apply to a payment required by paragraph 20(6).

19(3) If the company makes a payment in contravention of sub-paragraph (1) otherwise than in pursuance of an order of the court–

(a) the company is liable to a fine, and

(b) if any officer of the company authorised or permitted the contravention, without reasonable excuse, he is liable to imprisonment or a fine, or both.

Disposal of charged property, etc.

20(1) This paragraph applies where–

(a) any property of the company is subject to a security, or

(b) any goods are in the possession of the company under a hire-purchase agreement.

20(2) If the holder of the security consents, or the court gives leave, the company may dispose of the property as if it were not subject to the security.

20(3) If the owner of the goods consents, or the court gives leave, the company may dispose of the goods as if all rights of the owner under the hire-purchase agreement were vested in the company.

20(4) Where property subject to a security which, as created, was a floating charge is disposed of under sub-paragraph (2), the holder of the security has the same priority in respect of any property of the company directly or indirectly representing the property disposed of as he would have had in respect of the property subject to the security.

20(5) Sub-paragraph (6) applies to the disposal under sub-paragraph (2) or (as the case may be) sub-paragraph (3) of–

(a) any property subject to a security other than a security which, as created, was a floating charge, or

(b) any goods in the possession of the company under a hire-purchase agreement.

20(6) It shall be a condition of any consent or leave under sub-paragraph (2) or (as the case may be) sub-paragraph (3) that–

(a) the net proceeds of the disposal, and

(b) where those proceeds are less than such amount as may be agreed, or determined by the court, to be the net amount which would be realised on a sale of the property or goods in the open market by a willing vendor, such sums as may be required to make good the deficiency,

shall be applied towards discharging the sums secured by the security or payable under the hire-purchase agreement.

20(7) Where a condition imposed in pursuance of sub-paragraph (6) relates to two or more securities, that condition requires–

(a) the net proceeds of the disposal, and

(b) where paragraph (b) of sub-paragraph (6) applies, the sums mentioned in that paragraph,

to be applied towards discharging the sums secured by those securities in the order of their priorities.

20(8) Where the court gives leave for a disposal under sub-paragraph (2) or (3), the directors shall, within 14 days after leave is given, send a copy of the order giving leave to the registrar of companies.

20(9)   If the directors without reasonable excuse fail to comply with sub-paragraph (8), they are liable to a fine.

21(1)   Where property is disposed of under paragraph 20 in its application to Scotland, the company shall grant to the disponee an appropriate document of transfer or conveyance of the property, and

(a)   that document, or

(b)   where any recording, intimation or registration of the document is a legal requirement for completion of title to the property, that recording, intimation or registration,

has the effect of disencumbering the property of, or (as the case may be) freeing the property from, the security.

21(2)   Where goods in the possession of the company under a hire-purchase agreement are disposed of under paragraph 20 in its application to Scotland, the disposal has the effect of extinguishing, as against the disponee, all rights of the owner of the goods under the agreement.

22(1)   If the company–

(a)   without any consent or leave under paragraph 20, disposes of any of its property which is subject to a security otherwise than in accordance with the terms of the security,

(b)   without any consent or leave under paragraph 20, disposes of any goods in the possession of the company under a hire-purchase agreement otherwise than in accordance with the terms of the agreement, or

(c)   fails to comply with any requirement imposed by paragraph 20 or 21,

it is liable to a fine.

22(2)   If any officer of the company, without reasonable excuse, authorises or permits any such disposal or failure to comply, he is liable to imprisonment or a fine, or both.

Market contracts, etc.

23(1)   If the company enters into any transaction to which this paragraph applies–

(a)   the company is liable to a fine, and

(b)   if any officer of the company, without reasonable excuse, authorised or permitted the company to enter into the transaction, he is liable to imprisonment or a fine, or both.

23(2)   A company enters into a transaction to which this paragraph applies if it–

(a)   enters into a market contract,

(b)   gives a transfer order,

(c)   grants a market charge or a system-charge, or

(d)   provides any collateral security.

23(3)   The fact that a company enters into a transaction in contravention of this paragraph does not–

(a)   make the transaction void, or

(b)   make it to any extent unenforceable by or against the company.

23(4)   Where during the moratorium a company enters into a transaction to which this paragraph applies, nothing done by or in pursuance of the transaction is to be treated as done in contravention of paragraphs 12(1)(g), 14 or 16 to 22.

23(5) Paragraph 20 does not apply in relation to any property which is subject to a market charge, a system-charge or a collateral security charge.

23(6) In this paragraph, "transfer order", "collateral security" and "collateral security charge" have the same meanings as in the settlement finality regulations.

PART IV

NOMINEES

Monitoring of company's activities

24(1) During a moratorium, the nominee shall monitor the company's affairs for the purpose of forming an opinion as to whether–

(a) the proposed voluntary arrangement or, if he has received notice of proposed modifications under paragraph 31(7), the proposed arrangement with those modifications has a reasonable prospect of being approved and implemented, and

(b) the company is likely to have sufficient funds available to it during the remainder of the moratorium to enable it to continue to carry on its business.

24(2) The directors shall submit to the nominee any information necessary to enable him to comply with sub-paragraph (1) which he requests from them.

24(3) In forming his opinion on the matters mentioned in sub-paragraph (1), the nominee is entitled to rely on the information submitted to him under sub-paragraph (2) unless he has reason to doubt its accuracy.

24(4) The reference in sub-paragraph (1)(b) to the company's business is to that business as the company proposes to carry it on during the remainder of the moratorium.

Withdrawal of consent to act

25(1) The nominee may only withdraw his consent to act in the circumstances mentioned in this paragraph.

25(2) The nominee must withdraw his consent to act if, at any time during a moratorium–

(a) he forms the opinion that–

(i) the proposed voluntary arrangement or, if he has received notice of proposed modifications under paragraph 31(7), the proposed arrangement with those modifications no longer has a reasonable prospect of being approved or implemented, or

(ii) the company will not have sufficient funds available to it during the remainder of the moratorium to enable it to continue to carry on its business,

(b) he becomes aware that, on the date of filing, the company was not eligible for a moratorium, or

(c) the directors fail to comply with their duty under paragraph 24(2).

25(3) The reference in sub-paragraph (2)(a)(ii) to the company's business is to that business as the company proposes to carry it on during the remainder of the moratorium.

25(4) If the nominee withdraws his consent to act, the moratorium comes to an end.

25(5) If the nominee withdraws his consent to act he must, in accordance with the rules, notify the court, the registrar of companies, the company and any creditor of the company of whose claim he is aware of his withdrawal and the reason for it.

25(6)   If the nominee without reasonable excuse fails to comply with sub-paragraph (5), he is liable to a fine.

Challenge of nominee's actions, etc.

26(1)   If any creditor, director or member of the company, or any other person affected by a moratorium, is dissatisfied by any act, omission or decision of the nominee during the moratorium, he may apply to the court.

26(2)   An application under sub-paragraph (1) may be made during the moratorium or after it has ended.

26(3)   On an application under sub-paragraph (1) the court may–

   (a)   confirm, reverse or modify any act or decision of the nominee,

   (b)   give him directions, or

   (c)   make such other order as it thinks fit.

26(4)   An order under sub-paragraph (3) may (among other things) bring the moratorium to an end and make such consequential provision as the court thinks fit.

27(1)   Where there are reasonable grounds for believing that–

   (a)   as a result of any act, omission or decision of the nominee during the moratorium, the company has suffered loss, but

   (b)   the company does not intend to pursue any claim it may have against the nominee,

any creditor of the company may apply to the court.

27(2)   An application under sub-paragraph (1) may be made during the moratorium or after it has ended.

27(3)   On an application under sub-paragraph (1) the court may–

   (a)   order the company to pursue any claim against the nominee,

   (b)   authorise any creditor to pursue such a claim in the name of the company, or

   (c)   make such other order with respect to such a claim as it thinks fit,

unless the court is satisfied that the act, omission or decision of the nominee was in all the circumstances reasonable.

27(4)   An order under sub-paragraph (3) may (among other things)–

   (a)   impose conditions on any authority given to pursue a claim,

   (b)   direct the company to assist in the pursuit of a claim,

   (c)   make directions with respect to the distribution of anything received as a result of the pursuit of a claim,

   (d)   bring the moratorium to an end and make such consequential provision as the court thinks fit.

27(5)   On an application under sub-paragraph (1) the court shall have regard to the interests of the members and creditors of the company generally.

Replacement of nominee by court

28(1)   The court may–

   (a)   on an application made by the directors in a case where the nominee has failed to comply with any duty imposed on him under this Schedule or has died, or

(b) on an application made by the directors or the nominee in a case where it is impracticable or inappropriate for the nominee to continue to act as such,

direct that the nominee be replaced as such by another person qualified to act as an insolvency practitioner, or authorised to act as nominee, in relation to the voluntary arrangement.

28(2) A person may only be appointed as a replacement nominee under this paragraph if he submits to the court a statement indicating his consent to act.

PART V

CONSIDERATION AND IMPLEMENTATION OF VOLUNTARY ARRANGEMENT

Summoning of meetings

29(1) Where a moratorium is in force, the nominee shall summon meetings of the company and its creditors for such a time, date (within the period for the time being specified in paragraph 8(3)) and place as he thinks fit.

29(2) The persons to be summoned to a creditors' meeting under this paragraph are every creditor of the company of whose claim the nominee is aware.

Conduct of meetings

30(1) Subject to the provisions of paragraphs 31 to 35, the meetings summoned under paragraph 29 shall be conducted in accordance with the rules.

30(2) A meeting so summoned may resolve that it be adjourned (or further adjourned).

30(3) After the conclusion of either meeting in accordance with the rules, the chairman of the meeting shall report the result of the meeting to the court, and, immediately after reporting to the court, shall give notice of the result of the meeting to such persons as may be prescribed.

Approval of voluntary arrangement

31(1) The meetings summoned under paragraph 29 shall decide whether to approve the proposed voluntary arrangement (with or without modifications).

31(2) The modifications may include one conferring the functions proposed to be conferred on the nominee on another person qualified to act as an insolvency practitioner, or authorised to act as nominee, in relation to the voluntary arrangement.

31(3) The modifications shall not include one by virtue of which the proposal ceases to be a proposal such as is mentioned in section 1.

31(4) A meeting summoned under paragraph 29 shall not approve any proposal or modification which affects the right of a secured creditor of the company to enforce his security, except with the concurrence of the creditor concerned.

31(5) Subject to sub-paragraph (6), a meeting so summoned shall not approve any proposal or modification under which–

(a) any preferential debt of the company is to be paid otherwise than in priority to such of its debts as are not preferential debts, or

(b) a preferential creditor of the company is to be paid an amount in respect of a preferential debt that bears to that debt a smaller proportion than is borne to another preferential debt by the amount that is to be paid in respect of that other debt.

509

31(6)   The meeting may approve such a proposal or modification with the concurrence of the preferential creditor concerned.

31(7)   The directors of the company may, before the beginning of the period of seven days which ends with the meetings (or either of them) summoned under paragraph 29 being held, give notice to the nominee of any modifications of the proposal for which the directors intend to seek the approval of those meetings.

31(8)   References in this paragraph to preferential debts and preferential creditors are to be read in accordance with section 386 in Part XII of this Act.

Extension of moratorium

32(1)   Subject to sub-paragraph (2), a meeting summoned under paragraph 29 which resolves that it be adjourned (or further adjourned) may resolve that the moratorium be extended (or further extended), with or without conditions.

32(2)   The moratorium may not be extended (or further extended) to a day later than the end of the period of two months which begins–

  (a)   where both meetings summoned under paragraph 29 are first held on the same day, with that day,

  (b)   in any other case, with the day on which the later of those meetings is first held.

32(3)   At any meeting where it is proposed to extend (or further extend) the moratorium, before a decision is taken with respect to that proposal, the nominee shall inform the meeting–

  (a)   of what he has done in order to comply with his duty under paragraph 24 and the cost of his actions for the company, and

  (b)   of what he intends to do to continue to comply with that duty if the moratorium is extended (or further extended) and the expected cost of his actions for the company.

32(4)   Where, in accordance with sub-paragraph (3)(b), the nominee informs a meeting of the expected cost of his intended actions, the meeting shall resolve whether or not to approve that expected cost.

32(5)   If a decision not to approve the expected cost of the nominee's intended actions has effect under paragraph 36, the moratorium comes to an end.

32(6)   A meeting may resolve that a moratorium which has been extended (or further extended) be brought to an end before the end of the period of the extension (or further extension).

32(7)   The Secretary of State may by order increase or reduce the period for the time being specified in sub-paragraph (2).

33(1)   The conditions which may be imposed when a moratorium is extended (or further extended) include a requirement that the nominee be replaced as such by another person qualified to act as an insolvency practitioner, or authorised to act as nominee, in relation to the voluntary arrangement.

33(2)   A person may only be appointed as a replacement nominee by virtue of sub-paragraph (1) if he submits to the court a statement indicating his consent to act.

33(3)   At any meeting where it is proposed to appoint a replacement nominee as a condition of extending (or further extending) the moratorium–

  (a)   the duty imposed by paragraph 32(3)(b) on the nominee shall instead be imposed on the person proposed as the replacement nominee, and

  (b)   paragraphs 32(4) and (5) and 36(1)(e) apply as if the references to the nominee were to that person.

34(1)   If a decision to extend, or further extend, the moratorium takes effect under paragraph 36, the nominee shall, in accordance with the rules, notify the registrar of companies and the court.

34(2)   If the moratorium is extended, or further extended, by virtue of an order under paragraph 36(5), the nominee shall, in accordance with the rules, send a copy of the order to the registrar of companies.

34(3)   If the nominee without reasonable excuse fails to comply with this paragraph, he is liable to a fine.

Moratorium committee

35(1)   A meeting summoned under paragraph 29 which resolves that the moratorium be extended (or further extended) may, with the consent of the nominee, resolve that a committee be established to exercise the functions conferred on it by the meeting.

35(2)   The meeting may not so resolve unless it has approved an estimate of the expenses to be incurred by the committee in the exercise of the proposed functions.

35(3)   Any expenses, not exceeding the amount of the estimate, incurred by the committee in the exercise of its functions shall be reimbursed by the nominee.

35(4)   The committee shall cease to exist when the moratorium comes to an end.

Effectiveness of decisions

36(1)   Sub-paragraph (2) applies to references to one of the following decisions having effect, that is, a decision, under paragraph 31, 32 or 35, with respect to–

   (a)   the approval of a proposed voluntary arrangement,

   (b)   the extension (or further extension) of a moratorium,

   (c)   the bringing of a moratorium to an end,

   (d)   the establishment of a committee, or

   (e)   the approval of the expected cost of a nominee's intended actions.

36(2)   The decision has effect if, in accordance with the rules–

   (a)   it has been taken by both meetings summoned under paragraph 29, or

   (b)   (subject to any order made under sub-paragraph (5)) it has been taken by the creditors' meeting summoned under that paragraph.

36(3)   If a decision taken by the creditors' meeting under any of paragraphs 31, 32 or 35 with respect to any of the matters mentioned in sub-paragraph (1) differs from one so taken by the company meeting with respect to that matter, a member of the company may apply to the court.

36(4)   An application under sub-paragraph (3) shall not be made after the end of the period of 28 days beginning with–

   (a)   the day on which the decision was taken by the creditors' meeting, or

   (b)   where the decision of the company meeting was taken on a later day, that day.

36(5)   On an application under sub-paragraph (3), the court may–

   (a)   order the decision of the company meeting to have effect instead of the decision of the creditors' meeting, or

   (b)   make such other order as it thinks fit.

Effect of approval of voluntary arrangement

37(1)   This paragraph applies where a decision approving a voluntary arrangement has effect under paragraph 36.

37(2)   The approved voluntary arrangement–

(a)   takes effect as if made by the company at the creditors' meeting, and

(b)   binds every person who in accordance with the rules–

   (i)   was entitled to vote at that meeting (whether or not he was present or represented at it), or

   (ii)   would have been so entitled if he had had notice of it,

as if he were a party to the voluntary arrangement.

37(3)   If–

(a)   when the arrangement ceases to have effect any amount payable under the arrangement to a person bound by virtue of sub-paragraph (2)(b)(ii) has not been paid, and

(b)   the arrangement did not come to an end prematurely,

the company shall at that time become liable to pay to that person the amount payable under the arrangement.

37(4)   Where a petition for the winding up of the company, other than an excepted petition within the meaning of paragraph 12, was presented before the beginning of the moratorium, the court shall dismiss the petition.

37(5)   The court shall not dismiss a petition under sub-paragraph (4)–

(a)   at any time before the end of the period of 28 days beginning with the first day on which each of the reports of the meetings required by paragraph 30(3) has been made to the court, or

(b)   at any time when an application under paragraph 38 or an appeal in respect of such an application is pending, or at any time in the period within which such an appeal may be brought.

Challenge of decisions

38(1)   Subject to the following provisions of this paragraph, any of the persons mentioned in sub-paragraph (2) may apply to the court on one or both of the following grounds–

(a)   that a voluntary arrangement approved at one or both of the meetings summoned under paragraph 29 and which has taken effect unfairly prejudices the interests of a creditor, member or contributory of the company,

(b)   that there has been some material irregularity at or in relation to either of those meetings.

38(2)   The persons who may apply under this paragraph are–

(a)   a person entitled, in accordance with the rules, to vote at either of the meetings,

(b)   a person who would have been entitled, in accordance with the rules, to vote at the creditors' meeting if he had had notice of it, and

(c)   the nominee.

38(3)   An application under this paragraph shall not be made–

(a)   after the end of the period of 28 days beginning with the first day on which each of the reports required by paragraph 30(3) has been made to the court, or

(b) in the case of a person who was not given notice of the creditors' meeting, after the end of the period of 28 days beginning with the day on which he became aware that the meeting had taken place,

but (subject to that) an application made by a person within sub-paragraph (2)(b) on the ground that the arrangement prejudices his interests may be made after the arrangement has ceased to have effect, unless it came to an end prematurely.

38(4) Where on an application under this paragraph the court is satisfied as to either of the grounds mentioned in sub-paragraph (1), it may do any of the following–

(a) revoke or suspend–

    (i) any decision approving the voluntary arrangement which has effect under paragraph 36, or

    (ii) in a case falling within sub-paragraph (1)(b), any decision taken by the meeting in question which has effect under that paragraph,

(b) give a direction to any person–

    (i) for the summoning of further meetings to consider any revised proposal for a voluntary arrangement which the directors may make, or

    (ii) in a case falling within sub-paragraph (1)(b), for the summoning of a further company or (as the case may be) creditors' meeting to reconsider the original proposal.

38(5) Where at any time after giving a direction under sub-paragraph (4)(b)(i) the court is satisfied that the directors do not intend to submit a revised proposal, the court shall revoke the direction and revoke or suspend any decision approving the voluntary arrangement which has effect under paragraph 36.

38(6) Where the court gives a direction under sub-paragraph (4)(b), it may also give a direction continuing or, as the case may require, renewing, for such period as may be specified in the direction, the effect of the moratorium.

38(7) Sub-paragraph (8) applies in a case where the court, on an application under this paragraph–

(a) gives a direction under sub-paragraph (4)(b), or

(b) revokes or suspends a decision under sub-paragraph (4)(a) or (5).

38(8) In such a case, the court may give such supplemental directions as it thinks fit and, in particular, directions with respect to–

(a) things done under the voluntary arrangement since it took effect, and

(b) such things done since that time as could not have been done if a moratorium had been in force in relation to the company when they were done.

38(9) Except in pursuance of the preceding provisions of this paragraph, a decision taken at a meeting summoned under paragraph 29 is not invalidated by any irregularity at or in relation to the meeting.

Implementation of voluntary arrangement

39(1) This paragraph applies where a voluntary arrangement approved by one or both of the meetings summoned under paragraph 29 has taken effect.

39(2) The person who is for the time being carrying out in relation to the voluntary arrangement the functions conferred–

(a) by virtue of the approval of the arrangement, on the nominee, or

(b) by virtue of paragraph 31(2), on a person other than the nominee,

shall be known as the supervisor of the voluntary arrangement.

39(3)   If any of the company's creditors or any other person is dissatisfied by any act, omission or decision of the supervisor, he may apply to the court.

39(4)   On an application under sub-paragraph (3) the court may–

(a)   confirm, reverse or modify any act or decision of the supervisor,

(b)   give him directions, or

(c)   make such other order as it thinks fit.

39(5)   The supervisor–

(a)   may apply to the court for directions in relation to any particular matter arising under the voluntary arrangement, and

(b)   is included among the persons who may apply to the court for the winding up of the company or for an administration order to be made in relation to it.

39(6)   The court may, whenever–

(a)   it is expedient to appoint a person to carry out the functions of the supervisor, and

(b)   it is inexpedient, difficult or impracticable for an appointment to be made without the assistance of the court,

make an order appointing a person who is qualified to act as an insolvency practitioner, or authorised to act as supervisor, in relation to the voluntary arrangement, either in substitution for the existing supervisor or to fill a vacancy.

39(7)   The power conferred by sub-paragraph (6) is exercisable so as to increase the number of persons exercising the functions of supervisor or, where there is more than one person exercising those functions, so as to replace one or more of those persons.

PART VI

MISCELLANEOUS

Challenge of directors' actions

40(1)   This paragraph applies in relation to acts or omissions of the directors of a company during a moratorium.

40(2)   A creditor or member of the company may apply to the court for an order under this paragraph on the ground–

(a)   that the company's affairs, business and property are being or have been managed by the directors in a manner which is unfairly prejudicial to the interests of its creditors or members generally, or of some part of its creditors or members (including at least the petitioner), or

(b)   that any actual or proposed act or omission of the directors is or would be so prejudicial.

40(3)   An application for an order under this paragraph may be made during or after the moratorium.

40(4)   On an application for an order under this paragraph the court may–

(a)   make such order as it thinks fit for giving relief in respect of the matters complained of,

(b)   adjourn the hearing conditionally or unconditionally, or

(c)   make an interim order or any other order that it thinks fit.

40(5) An order under this paragraph may in particular–

(a) regulate the management by the directors of the company's affairs, business and property during the remainder of the moratorium,

(b) require the directors to refrain from doing or continuing an act complained of by the petitioner, or to do an act which the petitioner has complained they have omitted to do,

(c) require the summoning of a meeting of creditors or members for the purpose of considering such matters as the court may direct,

(d) bring the moratorium to an end and make such consequential provision as the court thinks fit.

40(6) In making an order under this paragraph the court shall have regard to the need to safeguard the interests of persons who have dealt with the company in good faith and for value.

40(7) Sub-paragraph (8) applies where–

(a) the appointment of an administrator has effect in relation to the company and that appointment was in pursuance of–

    (i) an administration application made, or

    (ii) a notice of intention to appoint filed,

before the moratorium came into force, or

(b) the company is being wound up in pursuance of a petition presented before the moratorium came into force.

40(8) No application for an order under this paragraph may be made by a creditor or member of the company; but such an application may be made instead by the administrator or (as the case may be) the liquidator.

Offences

41(1) This paragraph applies where a moratorium has been obtained for a company.

41(2) If, within the period of 12 months ending with the day on which the moratorium came into force, a person who was at the time an officer of the company–

(a) did any of the things mentioned in paragraphs (a) to (f) of sub-paragraph (4), or

(b) was privy to the doing by others of any of the things mentioned in paragraphs (c), (d) and (e) of that sub-paragraph,

he is to be treated as having committed an offence at that time.

41(3) If, at any time during the moratorium, a person who is an officer of the company–

(a) does any of the things mentioned in paragraphs (a) to (f) of sub-paragraph (4), or

(b) is privy to the doing by others of any of the things mentioned in paragraphs (c), (d) and (e) of that sub-paragraph,

he commits an offence.

41(4) Those things are–

(a) concealing any part of the company's property to the value of £500 or more, or concealing any debt due to or from the company, or

(b) fraudulently removing any part of the company's property to the value of £500 or more, or

(c)   concealing, destroying, mutilating or falsifying any book or paper affecting or relating to the company's property or affairs, or

(d)   making any false entry in any book or paper affecting or relating to the company's property or affairs, or

(e)   fraudulently parting with, altering or making any omission in any document affecting or relating to the company's property or affairs, or

(f)   pawning, pledging or disposing of any property of the company which has been obtained on credit and has not been paid for (unless the pawning, pledging or disposal was in the ordinary way of the company's business).

41(5)   For the purposes of this paragraph, "officer" includes a shadow director.

41(6)   It is a defence–

(a)   for a person charged under sub-paragraph (2) or (3) in respect of the things mentioned in paragraph (a) or (f) of sub-paragraph (4) to prove that he had no intent to defraud, and

(b)   for a person charged under sub-paragraph (2) or (3) in respect of the things mentioned in paragraph (c) or (d) of sub-paragraph (4) to prove that he had no intent to conceal the state of affairs of the company or to defeat the law.

41(7)   Where a person pawns, pledges or disposes of any property of a company in circumstances which amount to an offence under sub-paragraph (2) or (3), every person who takes in pawn or pledge, or otherwise receives, the property knowing it to be pawned, pledged or disposed of in circumstances which–

(a)   would, if a moratorium were obtained for the company within the period of 12 months beginning with the day on which the pawning, pledging or disposal took place, amount to an offence under sub-paragraph (2), or

(b)   amount to an offence under sub-paragraph (3), commits an offence.

41(8)   A person guilty of an offence under this paragraph is liable to imprisonment or a fine, or both.

41(9)   The money sums specified in paragraphs (a) and (b) of sub-paragraph (4) are subject to increase or reduction by order under section 417A in Part XV.

42(1)   If, for the purpose of obtaining a moratorium, or an extension of a moratorium, for a company, a person who is an officer of the company–

(a)   makes any false representation, or

(b)   fraudulently does, or omits to do, anything, he commits an offence.

42(2)   Sub-paragraph (1) applies even if no moratorium or extension is obtained.

42(3)   For the purposes of this paragraph, "officer" includes a shadow director.

42(4)   A person guilty of an offence under this paragraph is liable to imprisonment or a fine, or both.

Void provisions in floating charge documents

43(1)   A provision in an instrument creating a floating charge is void if it provides for–

(a)   obtaining a moratorium, or

(b)   anything done with a view to obtaining a moratorium (including any preliminary decision or investigation), to be an event causing the floating charge to crystallise or causing restrictions which would not otherwise apply to be imposed on the disposal of property by the company or a ground for the appointment of a receiver.

43(2) In sub-paragraph (1), "receiver" includes a manager and a person who is appointed both receiver and manager.

Functions of the Financial Services Authority

44(1) This Schedule has effect in relation to a moratorium for a regulated company with the modifications in sub-paragraphs (2) to (16) below.

44(2) Any notice or other document required by virtue of this Schedule to be sent to a creditor of a regulated company must also be sent to the Authority.

44(3) The Authority is entitled to be heard on any application to the court for leave under paragraph 20(2) or 20(3) (disposal of charged property, etc.).

44(4) Where paragraph 26(1) (challenge of nominee's actions, etc.) applies, the persons who may apply to the court include the Authority.

44(5) If a person other than the Authority applies to the court under that paragraph, the Authority is entitled to be heard on the application.

44(6) Where paragraph 27(1) (challenge of nominee's actions, etc.) applies, the persons who may apply to the court include the Authority.

44(7) If a person other than the Authority applies to the court under that paragraph, the Authority is entitled to be heard on the application.

44(8) The persons to be summoned to a creditors' meeting under paragraph 29 include the Authority.

44(9) A person appointed for the purpose by the Authority is entitled to attend and participate in (but not to vote at)–

(a) any creditors' meeting summoned under that paragraph,

(b) any meeting of a committee established under paragraph 35 (moratorium committee).

44(10) The Authority is entitled to be heard on any application under paragraph 36(3) (effectiveness of decisions).

44(11) Where paragraph 38(1) (challenge of decisions) applies, the persons who may apply to the court include the Authority.

44(12) If a person other than the Authority applies to the court under that paragraph, the Authority is entitled to be heard on the application.

44(13) Where paragraph 39(3) (implementation of voluntary arrangement) applies, the persons who may apply to the court include the Authority.

44(14) If a person other than the Authority applies to the court under that paragraph, the Authority is entitled to be heard on the application.

44(15) Where paragraph 40(2) (challenge of directors' actions) applies, the persons who may apply to the court include the Authority.

44(16) If a person other than the Authority applies to the court under that paragraph, the Authority is entitled to be heard on the application.

44(17) This paragraph does not prejudice any right the Authority has (apart from this paragraph) as a creditor of a regulated company.

44(18)   In this paragraph–

"the Authority" means the Financial Services Authority, and

"regulated company" means a company which–

(a)   is, or has been, an authorised person within the meaning given by section 31 of the Financial Services and Markets Act 2000,

(b)   is, or has been, an appointed representative within the meaning given by section 39 of that Act, or

(c)   is carrying on, or has carried on, a regulated activity, within the meaning given by section 22 of that Act, in contravention of the general prohibition within the meaning given by section 19 of that Act.

Subordinate legislation

45(1)   Regulations or an order made by the Secretary of State under this Schedule may make different provision for different cases.

45(2)   Regulations so made may make such consequential, incidental, supplemental and transitional provision as may appear to the Secretary of State necessary or expedient.

45(3)   Any power of the Secretary of State to make regulations under this Schedule may be exercised by amending or repealing any enactment contained in this Act (including one contained in this Schedule) or contained in the Company Directors Disqualification Act 1986.

45(4)   Regulations (except regulations under paragraph 5) or an order made by the Secretary of State under this Schedule shall be made by statutory instrument subject to annulment in pursuance of a resolution of either House of Parliament.

45(5)   Regulations under paragraph 5 of this Schedule are to be made by statutory instrument and shall only be made if a draft containing the regulations has been laid before and approved by resolution of each House of Parliament.

GENERAL NOTE

On close examination of Sch.A1, we find that this moratorium facility is restricted to "eligible" companies, i.e. small companies, excluding companies such as banks, insurance companies, companies involved with the performance of market contracts. A small company is defined by s.247(3) of CA 1985 as one which fulfils two of the following three conditions:

(a)   turnover less than £6.5 million;

(b)   balance sheet total less than £3.26 million; and

(c)   having fewer than 50 employees.

These criteria (which apply to any filing after April 6, 2008) may be changed in the future through delegated legislation. The new criteria are specified in the Companies Act 2006 (Amendment) (Account and Reports) Regulations 2008 (SI 2008/393). Possible changes in eligibility might bring larger companies within the catchment and deal with the technical issue of "special purpose vehicle companies" for whom this reform has posed difficulties (see Livingston, (2000) 16 I.L. & P. 189). This latter problem has been recognised by the Government (see *Hansard*, HC Vol.355, cols 163–4)—note the further exceptions introduced via paras 4A–4K (see note to s.1A). For consideration of step in rights (para.4K) see *Cabvision Ltd v Feetum* [2005] EWCA Civ 1601; [2006] B.C.C. 340 (a ruling on s.72E).

The new CVA with moratorium also cannot operate where the company is already undergoing administration, administrative receivership or liquidation (including provisional liquidation). The moratorium is also denied to a company currently undergoing a CVA and also to one which has already had recourse to such protection in the previous 12 months. It is estimated that some 38 per cent of all companies may access this new CVA moratorium model. Notwithstanding this potential constituency the procedure has hardly been used.

In order to obtain the CVA moratorium the directors must prepare documents and submit these to the nominee. Subsequently, these documents, accompanied by the nominee's statement, must be submitted by the directors to the court. The nominee must state whether there is a reasonable prospect of the purpose being approved and implemented. The test of "reasonable prospect" for these purposes will presumably be the same as that laid down in administration order cases in *Re Harris Simons Construction Ltd* [1989] 1 W.L.R. 368. The nominee in promoting the proposal is entitled to rely on information provided by the directors and it is an offence for company officers to seek to obtain a moratorium by false representations (para.42). The filing of these documents triggers an initial moratorium (para.8) that will last 28 days or until the creditors' meeting is held. Extensions for a further two months are possible under para.32. No court order as such is required to initiate the moratorium. The moratorium is to be advertised and any creditor who has petitioned for winding up must be personally notified.

The moratorium has the standard incidents found in corporate insolvency law of excluding most hostile actions against the company (see para.12). Proceedings on extant winding-up petitions are stayed and the disabling effect of s.127 of IA 1986 does not operate, though certain restrictions are imposed on the directors' freedom of action during the currency of the moratorium. However, petitions presented to wind up a company in the public interest are not to be obstructed. The effect of the moratorium upon the rights of the floating-charge holder is dealt with in some detail by para.13. Debenture provisions allowing a floating charge to crystallise on the taking of preparatory steps to obtain a moratorium are void (para.43). In this sense this legislation is to have retrospective effect. There is an interesting contrast with administration where the floating charge holder has a right of veto—see *Re Croftbell Ltd* [1990] B.C.C. 781. The exclusion of traditional remedies exercised by secured creditors in the new CVA moratorium has aroused concern, but in practice banks often choose not to exercise such remedies. See Milman and Chittenden, *Corporate Rescue—CVAs and the Challenge of Small Companies*, ACCA Research Report No.44 (1995). This abstinence has become even more noticeable since the advent of the Bankers' Code of Practice in July 1997 under which banks undertake to support business rescues. In any case, banks may still exert considerable influence because they are not obliged to offer continued funding; if the funding for the rescue is not available the nominee must terminate the moratorium (see *Hansard*, HL Vol.613, CWH 13). In addition to the curbs on security enforcement, one effect of the moratorium is that security rights may be overridden with the leave of the court (see para.20). Section 233 of IA 1986 is extended forward to prevent "blackmail" by utility suppliers during the preliminary moratorium period (this prohibition already operates once the CVA has been agreed).

The directors may provide additional security during the moratorium but this will only be enforceable if it is for the benefit of the company (e.g. it has produced rescue funding).

An interesting feature of the moratorium is that it constrains managerial actions on obtaining credit of more than £250 (unless the credit provider has been informed of the moratorium) and also when disposing of property. With regard to the obtaining of credit the case law under IA 1986 s.360 may be relevant. There must be reasonable grounds for believing that the disposal will benefit the company and the nominee (or creditors' committee appointed under para.35) must give approval. Where the directors exceed their limited powers during this period the transaction is not rendered unenforceable (see para.15), though the directors may incur penalties (para.18(3)). Certain other prejudicial conduct by directors in the 12 months prior to the moratorium may be subject to criminal sanction (para.41). The figure of £500 in para.41(4) has been the subject of much parliamentary debate and has been criticised for being arbitrary. Although the Government has stoutly defended its usage, it has nevertheless indicated that the figure could be revised if a problem arose (*Hansard*, HC Standing Committee B, November 2, 2000, col.75). The actions of directors may be challenged by creditors on the grounds of unfair prejudice (para.40). These provisions are clearly designed to prevent abuse of the moratorium facility. Moreover, the nominee is expected to assume a monitoring role during this critical period (para.24).

The actions of the nominee during the moratorium are open to challenge (paras 26 and 27). Nominees must withdraw their consent to act under certain conditions set out in para.25. The court can also replace the nominee.

Part V deals with the consideration and implementation of the proposed CVA. These provisions mirror those found in Pt I of IA 1986.

Paragraph 3(2) was amended in 2008 to drop the reference to s.247 of the Companies Act 1985 and instead to substitute a reference to s.382 of the Companies Act 2006—see the Companies Act 2006 (Consequential Amendments, etc.) Order 2008 (SI 2008/948).

Note the Companies Act 2006 (Consequential Amendments, Transitional Provisions and Savings) Order 2009 (SI 2009/1941) amended para.3(6) to cater for the enactment of the Companies Act 2006. Effective from October 1, 2009.

Paragraph 12(1)(d), (da) substituted for the former para.12(1)(d) by the Enterprise Act 2002 s.248(3) Sch.17 paras 9, 37(1), (3) as from September 15, 2003 (see the Enterprise Act 2003 (Commencement No.4 and Transitional

Provisions and Savings) Order 2003 (SI 2003/2093 (C. 85)) art.2(1), Sch.1), subject to transitional provisions in SI 2003/2093 (C. 85), art.3. The amendment has no effect in relation to certain companies by virtue of the Enterprise Act 2002 s.249(1).

Paragraph 12(1)(b) modified as from December 26, 2003 by the Financial Collateral Arrangements (No.2) Regulations 2003 (SI 2003/3226) reg.8(5).

In para.12(5)(a) the words "or 124B" inserted by the European Public Limited-Liability Company Regulations (SI 2004/2326) reg.73(4)(b) as from October 8, 2004.

Paragraph 12(5)(d) inserted by the Financial Services and Markets Act 2000 (Consequential Amendments) Order 2002 (SI 2002/1555) arts 1, 30 as from July 3, 2002.

Paragraph 16(1) was replaced by the Companies (Trading Disclosures) (Insolvency) Regulations 2008 with effect from October 1, 2008. This substitution was necessary to ensure compliance with EC Directive 2003/58 and is intended to promote disclosure where invoices are in electronic form and where the company has a website.

Paragraphs 20(8) and 34(2) were subject to a minor amendment by the Companies Act 2006 (Consequential Amendments, Transitional Provisions and Savings) Order 2009 (SI 2009/1941). Effective from October 1, 2009.

Paragraph 40(7)(a) was amended by the Enterprise Act 2002 (Insolvency) Order 2004 (SI 2004/2312) from October 15, 2004 to reflect the new administration procedure.

SCHEDULE B1

ADMINISTRATION

Introductory note to Schedule B1

Schedule B1 was inserted into IA 1986 by EA 2002 s.248, (1), (2), with effect from September 15, 2003 (see the Enterprise Act 2002 (Commencement No.4 and Transitional Provisions and Savings) Order 2003 (SI 2003/2093 (C. 85)) art.2(1) and Sch.(1), introducing a new Pt II and inaugurating a wholly new corporate administration regime—or range of regimes. Section 248 states that the new Pt II shall "be substituted" for the original Pt II, but this does not mean that the original Pt II is repealed, for s.249, immediately following, reinstates the latter for many purposes. (See the Introductory note to the new Part II on pp.40–42.) The original Pt II and the accompanying rules, with annotations, are now to be found in Vol.2.

The Insolvency (Amendment) Rules 2003 (SI 2003/1730, also effective September 15, 2003) r.5 complements Sch.B1 by substituting a new Pt 2 of the Rules for the original Pt 2 of IR 1986. However, as with Pt II of the Act, the original Pt 2 of the Rules is preserved for those cases where a company or other body is put into administration under the original Pt II. (For a list of the bodies concerned, see I(A)R 2003 para.5(2)–(4)). There are thus two sets of rules governing corporate administrations; and, confusingly, the rules of each Pt 2 are similarly (but not correspondingly) numbered. All references to the rules in this annotation to Sch.B1 are to the substituted rules, unless otherwise stated.

In *William Hare Ltd v Shepherd Construction Ltd* [2009] EWHC 1603 (TCC); [2009] Bus.L.R. 447 an administration under Sch.B1 was held to fall within the phrase "the making of an administration order by the court under the Insolvency Act 1986 Part II" in a construction contract, even though the administration had been initiated out of court.

Although Sch.B1 applies both in England and Wales and in Scotland, a company can only enter administration, by any of the statutory procedures, in the jurisdiction of its incorporation (i.e. a Scottish company must do so in Scotland): *Re Brownridge Plastics Ltd* (unreported), referred to in *Dear IP*, December 2005.

Schedule B1 applies (with modifications) to insurance companies, except that the appointment of an administrator can only be made by court order: see the Insurers (Reorganisation and Winding Up) Regulations Order 2004 (SI 2004/353) reg.52 and the note to para.9 and, as an example, *Re AA Mutual International Insurance Co Ltd* [2004] EWHC 2430 (Ch); [2005] 2 B.C.L.C. 8.

The Insolvency Service early in 2003 issued a consultation paper proposing that the new Pt II regime should be extended to insolvent partnerships, and this was done by the Insolvent Partnerships (Amendment) Order 2005 (SI 2005/1516), operative from July 1, 2005. Administrations of insolvent partnerships which took effect before that date will continue to be governed by the original Pt II. Similar amendments to the Limited Liability Partnerships Regulations 2001 were made by SI 2005/1989 with effect from October 1, 2005.

Banks and the other bodies mentioned in IA 1986 s.422(1) which are companies within the meaning of CA 2006 ss.1(1), 1171 have also now been brought within the new Pt II (see the Banks (Former Authorised Institutions) (Insolvency) Order 2006 (SI 2006/3107), effective December 15, 2006). Previously the original Pt II had governed administrations relating to these bodies by virtue of the Banks (Administration Proceedings) Order 1989 (SI 1989/1276, as amended). The 2006 Order art.3 and Sch., provides that certain modifications shall be applied to Pt II in relation to the application of the administration procedure to these institutions. In particular, these modifications confer rights on the Financial Services Authority to participate in the proceedings. In contrast with the legislation governing insurance companies, these bodies may be put into administration without a court order (but the consent of the FSA must be obtained and filed in court (Sch. para.5)). The Banking Act 2009 introduces a special form of administration where a bank or building society encounters financial difficulties leading to government intervention. This new procedure may be put in place by court order to deal with the remaining assets where there has been a partial transfer of business from a failing bank. The Act and the Rules are extensively modified for the purposes of this legislation. See further pp.6–7 above.

The Energy Act 2004 s.159 and Schs 20, 21 establishes a special administration regime for bodies licensed to supply energy under that Act, and extends the provisions of Sch.B1 (with modifications) to such bodies. This regime is designed to ensure that energy supplies are maintained where a licensee becomes insolvent. A modified administration regime has also been introduced to cater for public–private partnerships: see the PPP Administration Order Rules 2007 (SI 2007/3141), effective November 30, 2007 and, for a case not brought under these rules but under the Greater London Authority Act 1999 Sch.15, *Re Metronet Rail BCV Ltd* [2008] 1 B.C.L.C. 760.

The administration regime does not apply to Industrial and Provident Societies: *Re Dairy Farmers of Great Britain Ltd* [2009] EWHC 1389 (Ch); [2009] Bus.L.R. 1627.

The new administration regime has not only succeeded in displacing administrative receivership as the primary method available to a floating charge holder to enforce his security, but is also proving to be a popular alternative to a creditors' voluntary winding up in the insolvency of smaller companies, because of its flexibility and informality.

As was to be expected when a new and complex regime was introduced, Sch.B1 has encountered a number of teething problems. These have been met, and generally resolved, by judges adopting a bold and purposive approach, as (for instance) by Blackburne J. in *Re Ballast plc* [2004] EWHC 2356 (Ch); [2005] B.C.C. 96; by Lawrence Collins J. in *Re Transbus International Ltd* [2004] EWHC 932 (Ch); [2004] B.C.C. 401; and by rulings on paras 83–84.

NATURE OF ADMINISTRATION

Administration

1(1) For the purposes of this Act **"administrator"** of a company means a person appointed under this Schedule to manage the company's affairs, business and property.

1(2) For the purposes of this Act–

(a) a company is **"in administration"** while the appointment of an administrator of the company has effect,

(b) a company **"enters administration"** when the appointment of an administrator takes effect,

(c) a company ceases to be in administration when the appointment of an administrator of the company ceases to have effect in accordance with this Schedule, and

(d) a company does not cease to be in administration merely because an administrator vacates office (by reason of resignation, death or otherwise) or is removed from office.

GENERAL NOTE

The original legislation, s.8(2) contains definitions of "administration order" and "administrator" ("an administration order is an order directing that … the affairs, business and property of the company shall be managed by a person ('the administrator') appointed for the purpose by the court"). While the definition of "administrator" remains essentially the same, the new definitions introduced by subpara.(2) are necessary because an administrator can in many cases be appointed under the present Schedule without a court order.

These definitions are confined to administrators "appointed under this Schedule". In other cases, the original definitions of "administration order" and "administrator" will continue to apply, by virtue of EA 2002 s.249 and the saving provisions of the Enterprise Act 2002 (Commencement No.4 and Transitional Provisions and Savings) Order 2003 (SI 2003/2093 (C. 85)). See the Introductory note to the new Part II, on pp.40–42.

Para.1(2)(c), (d)

It is particularly important to note the use of this wording in later provisions of the Schedule, since it is likely to be the source of confusion. The draftsman has throughout chosen to avoid terms such as the "termination" of an administration, or an administration "coming to an end", or a company "ceasing to be in administration" (except in the marginal notes). Instead, in subpara.(2)(c), the circumlocution "the appointment of an administrator ceases to have effect" has been preferred. As is explained in subpara.(2)(d), this does not refer to the ending of the appointment of the particular individual as administrator, but to the ending of the administration itself: in contrast, in the former case, the *office* of administrator continues in being, even though it may for the time being be unoccupied.

2   A person may be appointed as administrator of a company–

(a)   by administration order of the court under paragraph 10,

(b)   by the holder of a floating charge under paragraph 14, or

(c)   by the company or its directors under paragraph 22.

GENERAL NOTE

Under the original legislation, an administrator could only be appointed by court order. The alternative of a direct appointment without application to the court under paras 14 and 22 clearly saves time and expense and has become the norm in the great majority of cases. However, where the administration has a cross-border element there may be uncertainty whether an administrator appointed out of court will be recognised in a foreign jurisdiction, and if there is doubt in this respect it may be thought prudent to obtain a court appointment. But there should no longer be any such doubts in regard to jurisdictions governed by the EC Regulation, since Annexes A and B have been amended to make it clear that out-of-court appointments are included. The same is true of out-of-court appointments under the CBIR, with this difference: whereas other EU Member States are bound under the EC Regulation to accord recognition to such appointments, nothing in the CBIR imposes any equivalent obligation on a foreign court (unless the country concerned has also enacted the Model Law). It may be helpful in these circumstances to take a course similar to that followed in *Re MG Rover España SA* [2005] B.P.I.R. 1192, and have the court make a supplemental order summarising the effect of an administration order and the administrator's responsibilities and powers.

A practice has developed which is not expressly sanctioned by the legislation and, indeed, might have been regarded as of doubtful legitimacy—the "pre-pack" administration. The pre-pack is not altogether a new concept, since it has regularly been used in receiverships for some time. In a pre-pack, the insolvency practitioner who, it is intended, is to become the administrator is involved in planning in advance an arrangement under which the business of the company is to be sold immediately after his appointment, bypassing the statutory procedure of a creditors' meeting, and without any direction from the court. The pre-pack is most appropriate where the insolvency is such that there will be no surplus available for distribution to the company's unsecured creditors and the proposed sale is likely to be advantageous by comparison with what might be yielded if all the statutory formalities were followed.

The main advantage of the procedure is the saving of time and expense and the avoidance of possibly adverse publicity which the statutory formalities would involve. The continuity of the business may preserve goodwill and save jobs, and for this reason may enable the business to be sold for a better price. However, two aspects of the pre-pack have given rise to a degree of concern: in most cases, the company's unsecured creditors are likely to receive no dividend and, secondly, they will usually have had no advance notice of the pre-arranged sale and no opportunity to have a say in the decision-making process. These circumstances are all the more likely to arouse suspicion where, as in many cases, the sale is to the existing management or other "connected" persons. Despite these objections, the pre-pack is now regarded as firmly established. Its legitimacy has been upheld in *DKLL Solicitors v HM Revenue and Customs* [2007] EWHC 2067 (Ch); [2007] B.C.C. 908, *Innovate Logistics Ltd v Sunberry Properties Ltd* [2008] EWCA Civ 1321; [2009] B.C.C. 164, *Re Kayley Vending Ltd* [2009] B.C.C. 578 and *Re Hellas Telecommunications (Luxembourg) II SCA* [2009] EWHC 3199 (Ch).

In January 2009 the Insolvency Service sought to address these concerns, which had begun to attract adverse public comment, by issuing a Statement of Insolvency Practice (SIP 16) which requires insolvency practitioners to adhere to an extra-statutory scheme for the regulation of pre-packs. (The SIP applies only to administration pre-packs.) The principal criticisms were that the process did not allow for the business to be fully marketed, that the directors of a failing company might be influenced to put the company into administration by a desire to purchase the business themselves, free of existing debts, and that there was a lack of transparency, especially so far as creditors were concerned. The SIP obliges the company's administrator to send detailed information to creditors at the earliest opportunity (normally when notifying them of the administration) and to forward a copy to the Insolvency Service. Disclosure is required of information set out in the SIP under 17 bullet points. The document also gives directions to practitioners as to the manner in which the work preparatory to their appointment should be conducted (and if the directors are to acquire an interest under the pre-pack sale, requires the directors to be encouraged to take independent advice); and it reminds them of their statutory duties and general legal liabilities. In *Re Hellas Telecommunications (Luxembourg) II SCA* (above) Lewison J. required, as a matter of good practice, that the court should be given the same information (or as much of it as possible) when it was considering an application for the making of an administration order in the context of a pre-pack sale. The Insolvency Service monitors the operation of SIP 16 and has published two Reports.

The Rules now make provision for the remuneration and expenses incurred by an insolvency practitioner prior to the appointment of an administrator to be paid as an expense of the administration which follows, if approved by the creditors or creditors' committee (r.2.67A). In *Re Kayley Vending Ltd* (above) such a payment was authorised by the court under Sch.B1 para.13; but in *Re Johnson Machine and Tool Co Ltd* [2010] EWHC 582 (Ch) H.H.J. Purle Q.C. disallowed similar claims and ruled that the court should authorise payment only if the balance of advantage in putting the company into administration as in the creditors' favour.

In the *DKLL Solicitors* case (above) an insolvent firm of solicitors was faced with a winding-up petition issued by the Revenue, its largest creditor. Two partners in the firm applied to the court for an administration order under para.11 of Sch.B1 which, if made by the court, would involve the dismissal of the Revenue's petition. It had been arranged in advance that, immediately on their appointment, the business of the firm would be sold by the administrators to a newly incorporated limited liability partnership for a consideration which would enable the business to be continued without further funding (which would otherwise not be available). The court approved the proposal and made an administration order.

On pre-pack administrations, see further S. Frisby, (2007) 23 I.L. & P. 152 and 227 Sweet & Maxwell's Company Law Newsletter 1; 246 ibid. 1, (2008) 21 Insolv. Int. 154 and 259 Sweet & Maxwell's Company Law Newsletter 1.

Para.2(b)
The power of the holder of a floating charge to appoint an administrative receiver has generally been abrogated by IA 1986 s.72A as from September 15, 2003 (but not with retrospective effect): see the note to that section. Charges created after that date will normally be enforced by the appointment of an administrator under para.14.

Purpose of administration

3(1)   The administrator of a company must perform his functions with the objective of–

    (a)   rescuing the company as a going concern, or

    (b)   achieving a better result for the company's creditors as a whole than would be likely if the company were wound up (without first being in administration), or

    (c)   realising property in order to make a distribution to one or more secured or preferential creditors.

3(2)   Subject to sub-paragraph (4), the administrator of a company must perform his functions in the interests of the company's creditors as a whole.

3(3)   The administrator must perform his functions with the objective specified in sub-paragraph (1)(a) unless he thinks either–

    (a)   that it is not reasonably practicable to achieve that objective, or

    (b)   that the objective specified in sub-paragraph (1)(b) would achieve a better result for the company's creditors as a whole.

3(4)   The administrator may perform his functions with the objective specified in sub-paragraph (1)(c) only if–

    (a)   he thinks that it is not reasonably practicable to achieve either of the objectives specified in sub-paragraph (1)(a) and (b), and

    (b)   he does not unnecessarily harm the interests of the creditors of the company as a whole.

GENERAL NOTE

This paragraph contains one of the major changes introduced by the new administration regime. Under the original regime an order may specify one or more of four alternatives: (a) the survival of the company, and the whole or any part of its undertaking, as a going concern; (b) the approval of a voluntary arrangement under IA 1986 Pt I; (c) the sanctioning of a scheme of arrangement or compromise under CA 1985 s.425 [now CA 2006 Pt 26]; and (d) a more advantageous realisation of the company's assets than would be effected on a winding up. For the new regime this formulation has been entirely replaced, and the new wording is significant in a number of respects. First, and most importantly, there is no longer a choice of alternative purposes but a single hierarchy of objects. All administrations, whether instituted by court order or out of court, and regardless of the purpose of the person seeking or making the appointment of the administrator, are to have the same statutory objectives. The rescue of the company is made a matter of priority, and it is only if the administrator is of the opinion that this is not reasonably practicable or that a better result can be achieved for the company's creditors by pursuing some other course that he is permitted to disregard that primary objective.

Next, there is a repeated emphasis in all four subparagraphs on the interests of "the company's creditors as a whole". The purpose of this is not so much to make any change in the law governing administrations as to underline the contrast between administration and receivership, and particularly administrative receivership. It is well established that a receiver's duties are owed primarily to the secured creditor who has appointed him, and that all other interests are subordinated to the obligation to safeguard and enforce that security. Subject only to the statutory rights of the company's preferential creditors, his obligations in respect of the "prescribed part" under s.176A and a duty to act in good faith, a receiver is generally free to realise sufficient assets to pay off the secured debt without any concern for the interests of the company itself or its other creditors. Moreover, the holder of a floating charge over all, or substantially all, of the company's assets has the power under the original law to veto the appointment of an administrator and appoint an administrative receiver instead. EA 2002 no longer gives these secured creditors the whip hand: not only does it remove this power of veto (subject to certain specific exceptions and some transitional provisions: see the note to IA 1986 s.72A), so obliging the holder of a floating charge to appoint an administrator rather than a receiver if he wishes to enforce his security, but it lumps the company's secured and preferential creditors together with all the other creditors and requires the administrator to act in the interests of them all. It is only if the requirements of subpara.(4)(a) can be met that the administrator is permitted to realise assets in order to pay off the preferential and secured creditors (para.(1)(c)), and even then only on condition that he does not unnecessarily harm the interests of the creditors as a whole. The priority traditionally attaching to receivership is thus virtually stood on its head.

Para.3(1), (3)
The formula "rescuing the company as a going concern" may be contrasted with the wording under the original legislation, "the survival of *the company, and* the whole or any part of its undertaking, as a going concern". The emphasis placed on the rescue or survival of the company (as distinct from its business or undertaking) is rather curious, for the Cork Committee was firmly of the view that it was only the latter that really mattered. In *Re Rowbotham Baxter Ltd* [1990] B.C.C. 113 at 115, Harman J. stated that a proposal involving the sale of a "hived down" company formed to take over part of a company's business could not be brought within the original wording, in view of the words which have been italicised above; and even more plainly it could not come within the new formulation. However, this may in fact make it easier for an administrator to conclude that it is not reasonably practicable to achieve a rescue of the company and so move on to the second statutory objective (achieving a better result for the company's creditors as a whole than would be likely under an immediate winding up).

Paragraph 3(1)(b) was relied on in *Re Logitext UK Ltd* [2004] EWHC 2899 (Ch); [2005] 1 B.C.L.C. 326, where the company had no tangible assets but stood a chance of recovering funds by pursuing claims against alleged wrongdoers. The applicant was an unsecured creditor who was prepared to put up funding to enable the administrator to investigate the case and undertake the litigation, but no similar source of funding was likely if the company were put into liquidation. In *Doltable Ltd v Lexi Holdings plc* [2005] EWHC 1804 (Ch); [2006] B.C.C. 918 the company sought an administration order with a view to preventing a secured creditor from selling the secured property (allegedly) at an undervalue. Any surplus would benefit the members. It was held that this was outside the statutory purposes and an order was refused. In *Re British American Racing (Holdings) Ltd* [2004] EWHC 2947 (Ch); [2005] B.C.C. 110 it was argued that a petition presented by a creditor which also held 89 per cent of the company's issued share capital was an abuse of the process of the court because administration would lead to the exclusion of the minority shareholders. This contention was rejected: the applicant, as a creditor, was entitled to proceed on the basis that the company's shares were valueless and a sale of its assets by administrators was likely to achieve a better result for the company's creditors as a whole (in which the applicant would participate in the same way as any other creditor).

Para.3(2), (4)
As noted above, the administrator, unlike a receiver, is not subject to an overriding obligation to have regard to the interests of the company's secured and preferential creditors: he must have regard to the interests of the company's creditors as a whole. Once a receiver has paid off the secured charge, his functions are completed: he must hand over control of the company's property to its directors or liquidator. Apart from the statutory obligations to pay the preferential creditors and set aside the prescribed part under s.176A, it is not his concern to see that any of the other creditors' debts are paid, and he owes them no duties either at law or in equity. An administrator, in contrast, is now by these subparagraphs bound to perform his functions in the interests of the company's creditors as a whole: paying

off the secured creditors ranks last in the statutory objectives, and in doing so he is under a positive duty not to harm the company's other creditors. A creditor has standing to complain of a breach of this duty under para.74.

4   The administrator of a company must perform his functions as quickly and efficiently as is reasonably practicable.

GENERAL NOTE

This provision may have been inserted to meet criticisms that, in contrast with receivership, the administration procedure (involving meetings of creditors, etc.) is relatively more slow, formal and expensive. It may be thought rather too vague to establish a positive legal duty remediable in damages: the most obvious sanction would be an application to the court to have the defaulting administrator removed and replaced, and for this purpose para.74(2) may help to smooth the path.

Status of administrator

5   An administrator is an officer of the court (whether or not he is appointed by the court).

GENERAL NOTE

As an officer of the court (like the liquidator in a compulsory liquidation), an administrator is bound by the rule in *Ex p. James* (1874) L.R. 9 Ch. App. 609, which imposes a rather ill-defined obligation to act honourably and fairly. He also enjoys the protection of the law of contempt of court if there is any interference with the performance of his duties.

General restrictions

6   A person may be appointed as administrator of a company only if he is qualified to act as an insolvency practitioner in relation to the company.

GENERAL NOTE

The expression "qualified to act as an insolvency practitioner in relation to the company" refers not only to the requirement that the individual concerned should have the appropriate professional qualification but also to his specific eligibility to act vis-à-vis the particular company. See the note to s.390.

7   A person may not be appointed as administrator of a company which is in administration (subject to the provisions of paragraphs 90 to 97 and 100 to 103 about replacement and additional administrators).

GENERAL NOTE

There cannot be two administrations simultaneously in existence, e.g. one appointed on the initiative of the directors and another by the holder of a floating charge. But it is possible to have administrators representing such different interests appointed to act jointly or concurrently in the same administration: see the notes to paras 90–97 and 100–103.

8(1)   A person may not be appointed as administrator of a company which is in liquidation by virtue of–

(a)   a resolution for voluntary winding up, or

(b)   a winding-up order.

8(2)   Sub-paragraph (1)(a) is subject to paragraph 38.

8(3)   Sub-paragraph (1)(b) is subject to paragraphs 37 and 38.

GENERAL NOTE

A company which is in liquidation cannot at the same time be put into administration. But paras 37 and 38 empower the court, on the application respectively of a floating charge holder or the liquidator, to order that administration be substituted for a winding up. And in the special case where a winding-up order is made on public interest grounds in relation to a company which is already in administration, the court may order the administration to continue under para.82. See further the notes to those paragraphs.

9(1)   A person may not be appointed as administrator of a company which–

(a)   has a liability in respect of a deposit which it accepted in accordance with the Banking Act 1979 (c. 37) or 1987 (c. 22), but

(b)   is not an authorised deposit taker.

9(2)   A person may not be appointed as administrator of a company which effects or carries out contracts of insurance.

9(3)   But sub-paragraph (2) does not apply to a company which–

(a)   is exempt from the general prohibition in relation to effecting or carrying out contracts of insurance, or

(b)   is an authorised deposit taker effecting or carrying out contracts of insurance in the course of a banking business.

9(4)   In this paragraph–

"authorised deposit taker" means a person with permission under Part IV of the Financial Services and Markets Act 2000 (c. 8) to accept deposits, and

"the general prohibition" has the meaning given by section 19 of that Act.

9(5)   This paragraph shall be construed in accordance with–

(a)   section 22 of the Financial Services and Markets Act 2000 (classes of regulated activity and categories of investment),

(b)   any relevant order under that section, and

(c)   Schedule 2 to that Act (regulated activities).

GENERAL NOTE

Under IA 1986 as originally enacted, banking and insurance companies were excluded from the administration regime. But Pt II of the Act was extended to apply (with certain modifications) to banks and the other bodies mentioned in para.9(1)(a), if they were companies within the meaning of CA 1985 s.735, by the Banks (Administration Proceedings) Order 1989 (SI 1989/1276) with effect from August 23, 1989; and similarly the administration procedure was made available to insurance companies by the Financial Services and Markets Act 2000 (Administration Orders Relating to Insurers) Order 2002 (SI 2002/1242) from May 31, 2002. This paragraph brings forward those provisions so that the categories of banking and insurance companies identified may be made subject to the new administration regime, (but, in regard to insurance companies, a company can only be put into administration by court order: see the Financial Services and Markets Act 2000 (Administration Orders Relating to Insurers) Order 2002 (SI 2002/1242, as amended by SI 2003/2134 and SI 2004/353 reg.52, as from February 18, 2004)). However, the Enterprise Act 2002 (Commencement No.4 and Transitional Provisions and Savings) Order 2003 (SI 2003/2093, effective September 15, 2003) art.3(3) provides that the original IA 1986 Pt II will continue to apply insofar as is necessary to give effect to the above order of 2002, so that, for administrations already current on that date, it is the provisions of the original Pt II and not the present Schedule that govern the position. In regard to Northern Ireland, see the Financial Services and Markets Act 2000 (Administration Orders Relating to Insurers) (Northern Ireland) Order 2007 (SI 2007/846), effective April 6, 2007.

The Banks (Administration Proceedings) Order 1989, referred to above, has been revoked and replaced by the Banks (Former Authorised Institutions) (Insolvency) Order 2006 (SI 2006/3107, effective December 15, 2006): see the note preceding para.1. This Order makes the administration regime under Sch.B1 available to banks and analogous institutions. These orders are supplemented by the Credit Institutions (Reorganisation and Winding Up) Regulations 2004 (SI 2004/1045, effective May 5, 2004), which deny our courts jurisdiction in respect of credit institutions based elsewhere in the EEA and impose certain requirements where the administration involves creditors in other EEA States. On the special administration regime established by the Banking Act 2009 where there has been government intervention in the affairs of a failing bank, see above, p.6.

In regard to insurers, SI 2002/1242 is supplemented by the Insurers (Reorganisation and Winding Up) Regulations 2004 (SI 2004/353, effective February 18, 2004). These latter Regulations apply to all UK insurers except Lloyd's and, as regards Lloyd's, the Insurers (Reorganisation and Winding Up) (Lloyd's) Regulations 2005 (SI 2005/1998), effective August 10, 2005, equivalent provision has since been made. An administration order was made against an insurer in *Re AA Mutual International Insurance Co Ltd* [2004] EWHC 2430 (Ch); [2005] 2 B.C.L.C. 8.

APPOINTMENT OF ADMINISTRATOR BY COURT

Administration order

10 An administration order is an order appointing a person as the administrator of a company.

GENERAL NOTE

Under the original Pt II regime, a company can be put into administration only by court order. Paragraphs 14–34 now authorise the alternative of making an appointment extra-judicially, which will be the procedure used in the great majority of cases because of the saving in time, formality and expense. It is only in cases where the initiative is taken by a person other than the company or its directors or the holder of a "qualifying" floating charge (see the note to para.14(2)) that it will be obligatory to use the court procedure. (Note also that for building societies and the categories of company mentioned in EA 2002 s.249 and the bodies mentioned in the next paragraph, the only way to have the company put into administration is by court order, but in this case it is the regime under the unamended IA 1986 Pt II which will apply.)

For court appointments under the new regime (i.e. where the application for an order is presented to the court on or after September 15, 2003), the relevant rules are to be found in the new Pt 2 of Sch.1 to the Rules: see I(A)R 2003 para.5(1) and below, pp.716 et seq. For appointments under the original regime (including appointments made on petitions presented before that date, and all applications under EA 2002 s.249(2), the Insolvent Partnerships Order 1994 made prior to July 1, 2005, the Limited Liability Partnerships Regulations 2001 and the Financial Services and Markets Act 2000 (Administration Orders relating to Insurers) Order 2002 (as amended)), the original Pt 2 of the rules applies: see I(A)R 2003 para.5(2)–(4) and Vol.2, pp.95 et seq. The Insolvent Partnerships (Amendment) Order 2005 (SI 2005/1516) introduced a modified regime based on Sch.B1 for administrations of insolvent partnerships as from July 1, 2005.

Conditions for making order

11 The court may make an administration order in relation to a company only if satisfied–

 (a) that the company is or is likely to become unable to pay its debts, and

 (b) that the administration order is reasonably likely to achieve the purpose of administration.

GENERAL NOTE

As under the original IA 1986 s.*8(1)*, there are here two preconditions for the making of an administration order: (a) actual or likely insolvency; and (b) the likely achievement of the purpose of the administration. But under that section there was for a time considerable judicial disagreement as to the degree of probability and the appropriate standard of proof to be applied in construing such expressions as "satisfied" and "likely". The decisions under that provision are no doubt apt to give guidance in the construction of the present paragraph, but a note of caution must be expressed because the wording of the two statutory provisions is not identical.

So far as concerns the phrase "satisfied ... that the company is or is likely to become unable to pay its debts", however, the language is the same. In *Re COLT Telecom Group plc* [2002] EWHC 2815 (Ch); [2003] B.P.I.R. 324 Jacob J. ruled that "likely" in this context meant "more probable than not". It was not enough for the petitioner to give evidence sufficient to satisfy some lesser test, e.g. that there was a "real prospect" of insolvency (as had been held to be the case in regard to the same word, "likely" where it appeared later in the original subsection: see below). "Satisfied" thus means "satisfied on a balance of probabilities". The term "unable to pay its debts" has the meaning given by IA 1986 s.123, i.e. insolvent on either a "cash-flow" or a "balance-sheet" basis: see para.111(1) and the notes to s.123.

There is a slight change in the wording used in para.11(b): the court must now be "satisfied" that "the administration order is reasonably likely to achieve the purpose of the administration", whereas the original s.*8(1)(b)* reads "considers that the making of an order under this section would be likely to achieve one or more of the purposes mentioned below". Thus "is satisfied" replaces "considers" and "likely" becomes "reasonably likely". In *Re Harris Simons Construction Ltd* [1989] 1 W.L.R. 368; (1989) 5 B.C.C. 11, Hoffmann J. held that it was sufficient that the court should consider that there was "a real prospect" that one or more of the statutory purposes might be achieved, and later cases (e.g. *Re Lomax Leisure Ltd* [2000] B.C.C. 352 at 363) have consistently applied the "real prospect" test: see the note to the original IA 1986 s.*8(1), (2)*. In construing the new provision, the phrase "is satisfied" may be thought to impose a more stringent standard than "considers", but this appears to be balanced by the insertion of the word "reasonably" before "likely". In *Re AA Mutual International Insurance Co Ltd* [2004] EWHC 2430 (Ch); [2005] 2 B.C.L.C. 8 Lewison J. confirmed that the new wording replicates the distinction made under the original Pt II: that under para.11(a) the test is "more probable than not", while for para.11(b) it is "a real prospect". In *Auto Management Services Ltd v Oracle Fleet UK Ltd* [2007] EWHC 392 (Ch); [2008] B.C.C. 761 Warren J. said that if an administration could be shown in all but the most unlikely circumstances to produce a result no worse than a liquidation and there were reasonably likely circumstances where the result would be better, that would be significant in influencing the court towards making an order and, in the light of an impression that an administration would be more cost-effective than a liquidation, decided in favour of an administration.

An order will be refused if the application is not made for a proper purpose (i.e. not within the statutory definition): see the note to para.3(1), (3). However, it is not necessary for the applicant to identify which of the statutory purposes it is intended should be attained: *Hammonds v Pro-Fit USA Ltd* [2007] EWHC 1998 (Ch); [2008] 2 B.C.L.C. 159.

On the meaning of "debts", see IR 1986 r.13.12(5).

It should be noted that para.11(a) does not apply—i.e. insolvency or near-insolvency is not a prerequisite—where the applicant is the holder of a "qualifying" floating charge and satisfies the court that it is in a position to appoint an administrator under para.14 (see para.35). This reflects the fact that there is no similar prerequisite where the charge holder makes an out-of-court appointment.

Administration application

12(1) An application to the court for an administration order in respect of a company (an **"administration application"**) may be made only by–

(a)   the company,

(b)   the directors of the company,

(c)   one or more creditors of the company,

(d)   the designated officer for a magistrates' court in the exercise of the power conferred by section 87A of the Magistrates' Courts Act 1980 (c. 43) (fine imposed on company), or

(e)   a combination of persons listed in paragraphs (a) to (d).

12(2) As soon as is reasonably practicable after the making of an administration application the applicant shall notify–

(a)   any person who has appointed an administrative receiver of the company,

(b)   any person who is or may be entitled to appoint an administrative receiver of the company,

(c)   any person who is or may be entitled to appoint an administrator of the company under paragraph 14, and

(d)   such other persons as may be prescribed.

12(3) An administration application may not be withdrawn without the permission of the court.

12(4) In sub-paragraph (1) **"creditor"** includes a contingent creditor and a prospective creditor.

12(5) Sub-paragraph (1) is without prejudice to section 7(4)(b).

GENERAL NOTE

The former procedure, involving a petition to the court, has been replaced by an "administration application" in Form 2.1B. For the relevant rules, see IR 1986 rr.2.2 et seq.

The court can only make an administration order on an application made under this provision.

Para.12(1), (4)

These subparagraphs cover essentially the same ground as the original *s.9(1)*. The notes to that section may be relevant here. It should be noted that the following, in addition to those listed in this subparagraph, the following (inter alios) also have standing to apply:

- the liquidator of the company (see para.38);

- the supervisor of a CVA (see para.12(5) and s.7(4)(b));

- the Financial Services Authority, under FSMA 2000 s.359 (as amended by EA 2002 Sch.17 para.55).

An application by the supervisor of a CVA is treated as if it were an application by the company: see r.2.2(4). The holder of a "qualifying" floating charge is also singled out for special mention in Form 2.1B as a separate category of applicant. This is no doubt a matter of administrative convenience: of course, the holder of any charge will in any case have standing as a creditor under para.12(1)(c).

Under the original *s.9(1)*, there was uncertainty for a time regarding an application made by "the directors": could they act informally, and must they be unanimous? Happily, for the purposes of the present Schedule para.105 states that they may act by a majority and imposes no formal requirement.

In the case of a petition for a winding-up order, the court will not entertain an application by a creditor whose debt is the subject of a genuine dispute or cross-claim. The validity of the debt must first be established in separate proceedings. In *Re Simoco Digital UK Ltd* [2004] EWHC 209 (Ch); [2004] 1 B.C.L.C. 541 it was accepted by counsel and the court that this rule would apply also to applications for an administration order. However, in *Hammonds v Pro-Fit USA Ltd* [2007] EWHC 1998; [2008] 2 B.C.L.C. 159 Warren J took a different view: in an administration application the court could make an order if it was "likely" that the company would become insolvent in the future even if it was not shown to be currently insolvent, and in this situation the court could in its discretion make an order on the basis of a disputed debt. But para.12(1)(c) does not extend to contingent or prospective creditors. In *Re British American Racing (Holdings) Ltd* [2004] EWHC 2947 (Ch); [2005] B.C.C. 110 objection was taken that the debt was not presently payable, but this argument failed on the facts. See also *El Ajou v Dollar Land (Manhattan) Ltd* [2005] EWHC 2861 (Ch); [2007] B.C.C. 953 (judgment debt not a disputed debt even though appeal pending).

Para.12(2)

The list of persons who must be given notice has been extended by the inclusion of subpara.(2)(c): this is now necessary because EA 2002 s.250, inserting new s.72A into IA 1986, means that the holder of a floating charge can no longer prevent the appointment of an administrator by putting the company into administrative receivership. But, even so, the holder of such a charge may wish to take action under para.14 or para.36 in order to ensure that, if the company is to be put into administration, the administrator will be a person of whom he approves. However, since s.250 is not retrospective, and is also subject to the exceptions set out in ss.72B–72H, it has been necessary to continue to include subparas.(a) and (b).

For the persons prescribed for the purposes of subpara.(2)(d), see rr.2.6(3), 2.7.

In cases brought under the original Pt II the court has been prepared in a situation of urgency to hear an application without observing the formalities as to notice, etc. required by the Act: see the note to *s.9(1)*.

Para.12(5)

This subparagraph was inserted by the Enterprise Act 2002 (Insolvency) Order 2003 (SI 2003/2096) arts 1, 2(1), (2), effective September 15, 2003.

Powers of court

13(1) On hearing an administration application the court may–

    (a) make the administration order sought;

    (b) dismiss the application;

    (c) adjourn the hearing conditionally or unconditionally;

    (d) make an interim order;

    (e) treat the application as a winding-up petition and make any order which the court could make under section 125;

    (f) make any other order which the court thinks appropriate.

13(2)   An appointment of an administrator by administration order takes effect–

(a)   at a time appointed by the order, or

(b)   where no time is appointed by the order, when the order is made.

13(3)   An interim order under sub-paragraph (1)(d) may, in particular–

(a)   restrict the exercise of a power of the directors or the company;

(b)   make provision conferring a discretion on the court or on a person qualified to act as an insolvency practitioner in relation to the company.

13(4)   This paragraph is subject to paragraph 39.

GENERAL NOTE

This paragraph corresponds broadly to the original s.*9(4)–(5)*, with certain additions and modifications, and the notes to those provisions may be relevant here. However, the power conferred by subpara.(1)(e) to make a winding-up order in lieu of an administration order is new: previously, in *Re Brooke Marine Ltd* [1988] B.C.L.C. 546 it was ruled that a winding-up order could only be made on a petition presented under s.124.

For the rules and prescribed forms governing an application for an administration order and the supporting documents which must be filed with the application, see rr.2.2 et seq. Among these documents is a statement by the proposed administrator (in Form 2.2B) that he consents to act, and that in his opinion the purpose of the administration is reasonably likely to be achieved.

Para.13(1), (3)
As noted above, the power conferred on the court by subpara.(1)(e) to make a winding-up order in lieu of an administration order had no counterpart in the former legislation. A winding-up order was made under this provision against a Delaware corporation in *Re Ci4net.com Inc* [2004] EWHC 1941 (Ch); [2005] B.C.C. 277.

In *GP Noble Trustees Ltd v Directors of Berkeley Berry Birch plc* [2006] EWHC 982 (Ch); [2007] B.P.I.R. 1271, the applicant's choice of administrators was disputed by the company's directors but was upheld by the court. In *Oracle (North West) Ltd v Pinnacle Services (UK) Ltd* [2008] EWHC 1920 (Ch); [2009] B.C.C. 159, where there is a dispute as to the choice of an administrator, the creditors' nominee was preferred by the court.

Where the court makes an order under para.13(1)(d) or (f), it must give directions regarding the giving of notice of the order under r.2.14(3).

On the "commencement" of a winding up under para.13(1)(e), see IA 1986 s.129(1A).

Para.13(2)
There was no counterpart to this provision in the former legislation: it makes clear that the court has power to fix a time other than that of the order for it to take effect.

Where the court fixes a time later than that of its order, the interim moratorium which will have been in place under para.44(1)(a) is continued under para.44(1)(b).

Para.13(4)
Paragraph 39 preserves the position under the former law, viz. that an administration cannot co-exist with an administrative receivership. It follows that where the holder of a floating charge continues to have the power to appoint an administrative receiver (see the note to IA 1986 s.72A), he can effectively veto the appointment of an administrator. See further the note to para.39.

APPOINTMENT OF ADMINISTRATOR BY HOLDER OF FLOATING CHARGE

Power to appoint

14(1)   The holder of a qualifying floating charge in respect of a company's property may appoint an administrator of the company.

14(2)   For the purposes of sub-paragraph (1) a floating charge qualifies if created by an instrument which–

(a)   states that this paragraph applies to the floating charge,

(b)   purports to empower the holder of the floating charge to appoint an administrator of the company,

(c)   purports to empower the holder of the floating charge to make an appointment which would be the appointment of an administrative receiver within the meaning given by section 29(2), or

(d)   purports to empower the holder of a floating charge in Scotland to appoint a receiver who on appointment would be an administrative receiver.

14(3)   For the purposes of sub-paragraph (1) a person is the holder of a qualifying floating charge in respect of a company's property if he holds one or more debentures of the company secured–

(a)   by a qualifying floating charge which relates to the whole or substantially the whole of the company's property,

(b)   by a number of qualifying floating charges which together relate to the whole or substantially the whole of the company's property, or

(c)   by charges and other forms of security which together relate to the whole or substantially the whole of the company's property and at least one of which is a qualifying floating charge.

GENERAL NOTE

The power which the holder of a floating charge has enjoyed in the past to appoint an administrative receiver has been abrogated by EA 2002 s.250 (although not with retrospective effect, and subject to the exceptions set out in IA 1986 ss.72B–72H: see the notes to ss.72A–72H, EA 2002 s.250 and para.39, below). The legislature now contemplates that a charge holder will normally enforce his security by putting the company into administration, and in consequence (a) the objective of an administration now expressly includes "realising property in order to make a distribution to one or more secured or preferential creditors" (para.3(1)(c) above); and (b) the holder of a "qualifying" floating charge, as defined in para.14(2), is now given the power to appoint an administrator directly, without the need to apply to the court for an order. However, from the charge holder's point of view, his position is considerably less advantageous than would be the case in a receivership: first, because the administrator not only has to act in the interests of the company's creditors as a whole (para.3(2)), rather than primarily in the interests of the charge holder; secondly, because satisfying the charge holder's security ranks last in the hierarchy of objectives of an administration—even when the charge holder has appointed the administrator under this paragraph; and thirdly because, even under the new administration regime, the procedure is more formal and elaborate than a receivership, and consequently slower and more expensive. In an appropriate case, however, it may be possible to use a "pre-pack" arrangement (see the note to para.2) to streamline the procedure.

The holder of a floating charge may still enforce his security by appointing a non-administrative receiver (i.e. a receiver of less than a substantial part of the company's assets), but if the company is then put into administration on the initiative of some other party the receiver may be required to vacate office under para.41(2).

For a charge holder to be able to make an appointment under para.14, it is necessary that a default or other event should have occurred which entitles him to enforce the charge (para.16); but it is not a prerequisite that the company should be, or be likely to become, insolvent.

Where the appointment of an administrator is to be made under para.14, there will be an interim moratorium only if the charge holder files a notice of intention to appoint an administrator under para.44(2), (3): see the note to those provisions.

For the relevant rules and prescribed forms, see rr.2.15 et seq.

Para.14(2), (3)

It is only if the charge is a "qualifying" floating charge that the holder has the power to appoint an administrator under this paragraph: the holder of any other charge (e.g. a floating charge over part only of the company's assets) will have to apply for a court order. The essential characteristics of a qualifying floating charge, elaborated in more detail in these subparagraphs, are: (a) that the charge must by its terms give the holder power to appoint an administrator (or an administrative receiver); and (b) the charge (or that and other charges taken together) must relate to the whole or substantially the whole of the company's property. So far as concerns characteristic (a), there is a variety of terminology which may be used in the charge instrument: subparas (2)(a)–(d) are alternatives. In the first place, the draftsman may simply refer to para.14 or he may expressly give the charge holder power to appoint an administrator. Alternatively, if he has not brought his precedents up to date to take account of EA 2002 s.250 or (more realistically) if the document was executed before that Act came into force, and the powers conferred on the charge holder include a power to appoint a receiver who would be an administrative receiver as defined by IA 1986 s.29(2), this also will enable the chargee to appoint an administrator directly under this provision.

Paragraph 14(3)(c) will cover the common case where a chargee takes security by way of a fixed charge over parts of a company's property and a floating charge over all or substantially all of the remainder, and this will be so whether there is one charge instrument or several. It would also seem, at least tacitly, to affirm the effectiveness of what is commonly referred to as a "lightweight" floating charge, which was upheld in *Re Croftbell Ltd* [1990] B.C.C. 781 (see the note to IA 1986 s.9(3)): the holder of such a charge will be able to appoint an administrator directly if it is in his interests to do so. However, it may well make more sense to enforce the fixed-charge elements of the security by other means.

The position where there is more than one floating charge over a company's property is dealt with in para.15.

In *Lovett v Carson Country Homes Ltd* [2009] EWHC 1143 (Ch) the appointment of administrators was upheld even though the signature of one of the company's directors to the charge instrument was a forgery. The document had been held out to the charge bank as genuine by the company secretary, and this was sufficient to estop the company from disowning responsibility.

Restrictions on power to appoint

15(1) A person may not appoint an administrator under paragraph 14 unless–

(a) he has given at least two business days' written notice to the holder of any prior floating charge which satisfies paragraph 14(2), or

(b) the holder of any prior floating charge which satisfies paragraph 14(2) has consented in writing to the making of the appointment.

15(2) One floating charge is prior to another for the purposes of this paragraph if–

(a) it was created first, or

(b) it is to be treated as having priority in accordance with an agreement to which the holder of each floating charge was party.

15(3) Sub-paragraph (2) shall have effect in relation to Scotland as if the following were substituted for paragraph (a)–

> "(a) it has priority of ranking in accordance with section 464(4)(b) of the Companies Act 1985 (c. 6) [CA 2006, no equivalent],".

General Note

This paragraph deals with the position where there are two or more charges, each being or including a floating charge, over the company's property: a junior-ranking chargee who wishes to appoint an administrator must give at least two days' notice to those having priority, or alternatively secure their written consent. Priority is determined by reference to the time of creation, or any agreement between the charge holders (para.15(2)). Curiously, the obligation to give notice is imposed only by reference to the criteria set out in para.14(2), and not also to those in para.14(3): what matters is whether there is a power to appoint an administrator directly conferred on the senior chargee by his charge instrument rather than whether his charge is over the whole or substantially the whole of the company's property. From one point of view, this is unimportant, for there will effectively be no power to make an appointment unless the charge is "substantial". But from another viewpoint para.15((1) poses a problem for a junior chargee, since it may be difficult for him to find out whether the instrument creating the senior-ranking charge contains any of the clauses referred to in para.14(2). The particulars registered in Companies House will not include them unless the company has gratuitously volunteered to file the information, and while in theory he has a right under CA 2006 s.877 to inspect the charge instrument itself at the company's registered office, it is a notorious fact that few companies bother to comply with these particular statutory obligations. The best advice for the holder of a junior-ranking charge is that he should give notice to his superior counterparts in any case, without concerning himself whether or not para.14(2) applies.

Note that notice must be given to a senior chargee even if his charge is not currently enforceable. This view has been confirmed in *Re OMP Leisure Ltd* [2008] B.C.C. 67, where notice had not been given to a senior charge holder but it was probable that that charge had been discharged—in which case it would never be enforceable. Because there was doubt on this point the appointment of the administrators was made subject to the condition that notice should be given to the senior chargee, but H.H.J. Hodge Q.C. expressed the view that there was no obligation to notify a senior chargee whose charge would never become enforceable. On the "giving" of notice, see the note to para.26.

The options available to a senior chargee who receives such a notice are limited. He would have no right to prevent the holder of the later charge from enforcing his security unless he could persuade the court to intervene on the ground that the appointment was being sought mala fide or for an improper purpose. Most obviously, he could take steps (either by negotiation or by making an appointment himself) to ensure that the proposed administrator was a practitioner of his own choosing, or that such a person should be appointed an additional administrator to act jointly or concurrently with the junior chargee's nominee.

Para.15(1)

Although it is not necessary that the notice to the charge holder should be in a prescribed form, Form 2.5B must be used for filing in court in order to obtain a moratorium. This embodies a form of consent which the recipient has the option of using. In contrast with the position under paras 26–27, there is no obligation to file a copy of the notice with the court, although if this is done the charge holder will enjoy the benefit of a five-day moratorium under para.44(2).

Para.15(2)

Oddly, there is no mention of the case where a number of charges rank pari passu. Prudence would dictate that notice should be given anyway, and also to the trustee of any trust deed.

16 An administrator may not be appointed under paragraph 14 while a floating charge on which the appointment relies is not enforceable.

GENERAL NOTE

The power of a floating charge holder to appoint an administrator out of court arises only if a default or other event has occurred which entitles him to enforce the charge. If this is not so, he would still have standing, as a creditor, to apply or to join with other creditors in applying to the court for an order under para.12.

This paragraph can also be read as confirming the obvious point that if the charge is invalid or void (e.g. because the charge instrument was not properly executed or particulars of the charge have not been duly registered) it cannot confer any powers on the holder. If the holder purports to appoint an administrator without the power to do so, the administrator will be liable to the company as a trespasser but will be entitled to an indemnity under para.21.

17 An administrator of a company may not be appointed under paragraph 14 if–

(a)   a provisional liquidator of the company has been appointed under section 135, or

(b)   an administrative receiver of the company is in office.

GENERAL NOTE

It would obviously create difficulties to have two office-holders in post at the same time administering the company's affairs with conflicting objectives. It would, of course, be open to the charge holder to apply to the court under r.4.31 to have the appointment of a provisional liquidator terminated and the company put into administration instead, e.g. with a view to rescuing the company as a going concern.

This paragraph may be contrasted with para.25, which bars a company or its directors from appointing an administrator out of court while a petition for a winding-up order or an application to the court for the appointment of an administrator is pending. Neither of these limitations applies to an appointment by the holder of a floating charge under para.14. If an appointment is made under para.14, any petition for winding up is suspended while the company is in administration, unless it is a petition based on public interest grounds (para.40(1)(b), (2)).

Although IA 1986 s.72A now generally prevents a charge holder from appointing an administrative receiver, this provision is not retrospective so as to apply to charges already created before September 15, 2003, and so there will continue to be cases where para.17(b) will apply.

Notice of appointment

18(1)   A person who appoints an administrator of a company under paragraph 14 shall file with the court–

(a)   a notice of appointment, and

(b)   such other documents as may be prescribed.

18(2)   The notice of appointment must include a statutory declaration by or on behalf of the person who makes the appointment–

(a)   that the person is the holder of a qualifying floating charge in respect of the company's property,

(b)   that each floating charge relied on in making the appointment is (or was) enforceable on the date of the appointment, and

(c)   that the appointment is in accordance with this Schedule.

18(3)   The notice of appointment must identify the administrator and must be accompanied by a statement by the administrator–

(a)   that he consents to the appointment,

(b)   that in his opinion the purpose of administration is reasonably likely to be achieved, and

(c)   giving such other information and opinions as may be prescribed.

18(4)   For the purpose of a statement under sub-paragraph (3) an administrator may rely on information supplied by directors of the company (unless he has reason to doubt its accuracy).

18(5)   The notice of appointment and any document accompanying it must be in the prescribed form.

18(6)   A statutory declaration under sub-paragraph (2) must be made during the prescribed period.

18(7)   A person commits an offence if in a statutory declaration under sub-paragraph (2) he makes a statement–

(a)   which is false, and

(b)   which he does not reasonably believe to be true.

GENERAL NOTE

The appointment of the administrator under para.14 takes effect only when the requirements of this paragraph have been satisfied (para.19). The completion of all the necessary formalities, even with the co-operation of everyone concerned, is bound to take some time—a situation which may be thought disadvantageous from the viewpoint of the floating charge holder in comparison with the speed and simplicity of appointing a receiver. The legislators have taken some steps to meet concerns on this score: first, it is possible at least in some circumstances for the charge holder to secure an interim moratorium for up to five business days by filing a notice of intention to appoint with the court under para.44(2), using Form 2.5B and, secondly, provision has been made by r.2.19 for the appointment of an administrator under para.14 to take effect even when the court is closed, by allowing notice of the appointment to be sent by fax or email: see the note to that rule.

In an appropriate case, however, it may be possible to use a "pre-pack" arrangement (see the note to para.2) to streamline the procedure.

For the relevant rules and prescribed forms, see rr.2.15 et seq.

Para.18(2), (6)
Form 2.6B is prescribed for the statutory declaration: it must be made not more than five business days before it is filed with the court (r.2.16(3)).

Para.18(3)
The same form (Form 2.2B) is used for the administrator's written statement in all proceedings under Sch.B1. It also requires the proposed administrator to certify that he is authorised to act, and to give details of any prior professional relationship with the company.

Para.18(5)
Form 2.6B has been prescribed for the notice of appointment, Form 2.2B for the administrator's written statement and Form 2.6B for the statutory declaration. If notice of intention to appoint is to be given to the court under para.44(2), the form that may be used is Form 2.5B. Further requirements are set out in rr.2.15–2.17. Note that where a notice of appointment is to be sent by fax, Form 2.7B and not Form 2.6B is to be used.

Para.18(7)

On penalties, see s.430 and Sch.10. The same penalties are prescribed by the Perjury Act 1911 s.5.

Commencement of appointment

19   The appointment of an administrator under paragraph 14 takes effect when the requirements of paragraph 18 are satisfied.

GENERAL NOTE

This provision may be contrasted with the appointment of an administrator by the court, which takes effect from or under the court's order (para.13(2)), and with the appointment of a receiver, where the court is not involved in any way and s.33 applies.

The requirements of para.18 are not satisfied until the relevant documents are filed with the court. The fact that the statutory declaration was made on an earlier date is irrelevant: *Fliptex Ltd v Hogg* [2004] EWHC 1280 (Ch); [2004] B.C.C. 870.

At any time when the court is closed (but not otherwise), r.2.19 allows a notice of appointment to be filed by fax or email, using Form 2.7B. The notice must be either faxed to a designated telephone number or sent as an attachment to a designated email address, provided by the Court Service for that purpose. This number and address are published on the Insolvency Service's website and may also be obtained from it on request. The telephone number currently published is 020 7947 6607, and the email address is rcjcompanies.orders@hmcourts-service-gsi.gov.uk. For Scottish administrations, reference should be made to the website *http://www.scotcourts.gov.uk*. If sent by email, a hard copy of the email must be created detailing its time and date and the address to which it was sent, and containing a copy of the document sent as an attachment. The appointor must retain the report or hard copy. The copy of the faxed notice of appointment, or the email (or a hard copy of the email) containing the notice of appointment, as (in either case) received by the Court Service must be forwarded as soon as reasonably practicable to the court specified in the notice as the court having jurisdiction in the case, to be placed on the relevant court file. The appointment takes effect from the date and time of sending the fax or email, and this is rebuttably presumed to be the date and time shown on the transmission report or hard copy. The appointor must notify the administrator, as soon as reasonably practicable, that the notice has been filed. He must also take three copies of the notice, together with the transmission report or hard copy of the email, and all the necessary supporting documents listed on Form 2.7B, to the court on the next day that it is open for business. (If he fails to so within that time, the administrator's appointment ceases to have effect.) There must be attached to these documents a statement providing, inter alia, "full reasons for the out of hours filing of the notice of appointment, including why it would have been damaging to the company and/or its creditors not to have so acted" (r.2.19(8)). While the point, and indeed the legitimacy, of this last requirement may be questioned, it should not be too difficult to find a suitable form of words to meet the case. The court seals the copy notices, endorsed with the date and time when the notice was faxed or sent (according to the report or hard copy) and also with the date when the notice and accompanying documents were delivered to the court. It then issues two of the sealed copies of the notice to the person making the appointment, who must as soon as reasonably practicable send one sealed copy to the administrator.

On the possibility of putting an interim moratorium in place pending compliance with para.19, see the note to para.44(2).

20   A person who appoints an administrator under paragraph 14–

  (a) shall notify the administrator and such other persons as may be prescribed as soon as is reasonably practicable after the requirements of paragraph 18 are satisfied, and

  (b) commits an offence if he fails without reasonable excuse to comply with paragraph (a).

GENERAL NOTE

It will be in the interests of all concerned (and not least the administrator himself) for para.18 to be complied with expeditiously, since until this is done he will have no power or authority to act. However, it is immaterial for this purpose whether he has been given the notice required by para.20(a).

Rule 2.17(2) requires that the administrator should be sent a copy of the notice of appointment bearing the seal of the court and endorsed with the date and time of filing. It is no doubt intended that this should be the way in which the administrator should be "notified" under para.20(a), although this is not stated in specific terms.

For the "other persons" prescribed by para.20(a), see r.2.18: if the charge holder appoints an administrator in reliance on para.14 after he has received notice that an application has been made to the court for the appointment of an administrator, he must send a copy of the notice of appointment to the applicant and to the court in which the application has been made.

The administrator himself has obligations to give various notices under para.46(2).

On penalties, see s.430, Sch.10 and para.106(2).

Invalid appointment: indemnity

21(1)   This paragraph applies where–

(a)   a person purports to appoint an administrator under paragraph 14, and

(b)   the appointment is discovered to be invalid.

21(2)   The court may order the person who purported to make the appointment to indemnify the person appointed against liability which arises solely by reason of the appointment's invalidity.

GENERAL NOTE

The purported appointment of an administrator may be invalid for any number of reasons: for instance, the charge instrument may be void, e.g. for want of due execution or registration under CA 2006 Pt 25 the charge may not come within the definition of a "qualifying" floating charge under para.14 above; or the conditions rendering the charge enforceable may not have been met. The court has a discretionary power under this provision to order the charge holder (or, indeed, any person) who made the purported appointment to indemnify the appointee against any liability in trespass, etc. that he may have incurred. But there is no power conferred on the court to validate the appointment. There is a parallel with s.34, which deals with the invalid appointment of a receiver. Of course, the parties may in any case have entered into a contract of indemnity, in which case no question of the court's discretion will arise.

In *Hans Brochier Holdings Ltd v Exner* [2006] EWHC 2594 (Ch); [2007] B.C.C. 127 the directors had appointed administrators in England in the belief, reasonably held, that the company's COMI was in England. Shortly afterwards insolvency proceedings were commenced in Germany and on further inquiry it was accepted that the COMI was in Germany. This meant that no main proceedings could be instituted in England and the administrators' appointment (at least as it stood) was invalid. However, it was arguable that the English administration might be continued as territorial proceedings. In that event para.21(2) would not be applicable.

APPOINTMENT OF ADMINISTRATOR BY COMPANY OR DIRECTORS

Power to appoint

22(1)   A company may appoint an administrator.

22(2)   The directors of a company may appoint an administrator.

GENERAL NOTE

As has been noted, under IA 1986 Pt II as originally enacted, a company could be put into administration only by order of the court. The reforms made by EA 2002 not only empower the holder of a floating charge to appoint an administrator without the involvement of the court, but confer a similar power on the company itself or its directors. These innovations will obviate the need for the involvement of the court (except as a repository of documents) in the great majority of cases.

For the relevant rules, see rr.2.20 et seq.

Para.22(1)

The company may take this step by resolution of the shareholders passed at a general meeting (or a unanimous informal agreement which is equivalent to such a resolution either at common law or under CA 2006 ss.288–289). An ordinary resolution appears to be sufficient.

Para.22(2)

The directors for this purpose may act by a majority, and it does not appear to be necessary that they should do so at a formal meeting: see para.105. This is confirmed by r.2.22, which refers to "a copy of the *resolution* of the company", but "a record of the *decision* of the directors".

Restrictions on power to appoint

23(1)   This paragraph applies where an administrator of a company is appointed–

(a)   under paragraph 22, or

(b)   on an administration application made by the company or its directors.

23(2)   An administrator of the company may not be appointed under paragraph 22 during the period of 12 months beginning with the date on which the appointment referred to in sub-paragraph (1) ceases to have effect.

GENERAL NOTE

If a company has already been put into administration on the initiative of the company itself or its directors (either out of court under para.22 or by a court order made on its or their application), this provision places a ban on the company being put into administration for a second time under para.22 unless a 12-month period has elapsed since the first appointment "ceased to have effect" (i.e. the administration terminated: see para.1(2)(c)). We may see a parallel here with the similar ban imposed upon a company from entering into a second CVA less than 12 months after it has had the benefit of a moratorium following a proposal for an earlier CVA: see Sch.A1 para.4(1)(f), (g). Note, however, that this restriction only applies to a second appointment made under para.22, i.e. out of court: there is no prohibition on the company or its directors making an application to the court for the appointment of a second administrator within the 12-month period.

24(1)   If a moratorium for a company under Schedule A1 ends on a date when no voluntary arrangement is in force in respect of the company, this paragraph applies for the period of 12 months beginning with that date.

24(2)   This paragraph also applies for the period of 12 months beginning with the date on which a voluntary arrangement in respect of a company ends if–

(a)   the arrangement was made during a moratorium for the company under Schedule A1, and

(b)   the arrangement ends prematurely (within the meaning of section 7B).

24(3)   While this paragraph applies, an administrator of the company may not be appointed under paragraph 22.

GENERAL NOTE

As noted above, the legislation imposes a ban upon a company from entering into a second CVA less than 12 months after it has had the benefit of a moratorium following a proposal for an earlier CVA (Sch.A1 para.4(1)(f), (g)). This paragraph similarly prohibits the company or its directors from appointing an administrator out of court within that period—although they are not prevented from making an application to the court for an administration order.

See further the note to Sch.A1 para.4(1).

25   An administrator of a company may not be appointed under paragraph 22 if–

(a)   a petition for the winding up of the company has been presented and is not yet disposed of,

(b)   an administration application has been made and is not yet disposed of, or

(c)   an administrative receiver of the company is in office.

GENERAL NOTE

These limitations are more extensive than those which apply where an out-of-court appointment is made by the holder of a floating charge under para.14: see para.17. Once again, the restrictions imposed by this paragraph apply only to the appointment of an administrator by a company or its directors out of court: there is nothing to prevent them from making an application to the court for an appointment, although if there is an administrative receiver in office, para.39 will apply.

A petition is "presented" when it is delivered to the court, and not when it is later sealed and issued: *Re Blights Builders Ltd* [2006] EWHC 3549 (Ch); [2007] B.C.C. 712. A purported appointment of an administrator made after that time is a nullity and cannot be rectified under IR 1986 r.7.55. On the difficulties which may arise where a winding-up petition has been presented to the court but not yet served on the company, see (2009) 22 Insolv. Int. 31.

The reference in subpara.(b) to the making of an application, taken literally, would arguably not cover proceedings instituted by petition under the original Pt II—e.g. a petition presented but not disposed of on September 15, 2003. But it would be within the court's powers to restrain the making of an appointment under para.22.

Notice of intention to appoint

26(1)   A person who proposes to make an appointment under paragraph 22 shall give at least five business days' written notice to–

(a)   any person who is or may be entitled to appoint an administrative receiver of the company, and

(b)   any person who is or may be entitled to appoint an administrator of the company under paragraph 14.

26(2)   A person who proposes to make an appointment under paragraph 22 shall also give such notice as may be prescribed to such other persons as may be prescribed.

26(3)   A notice under this paragraph must–

(a)   identify the proposed administrator, and

(b)   be in the prescribed form.

GENERAL NOTE

Regrettably, this section of the Schedule makes baffling reading because it does not draw attention to what is omitted. It does not mention all the possible situations. The logical approach is as follows. (1) If there is no secured creditor who has, or might have, the right to appoint an administrator under para.14 or an administrative receiver, and there is also no person to whom notice of intention to appoint is required to be given under para.26(2), the company or directors may proceed to make an appointment out of court without giving notice of intention to appoint to anyone, or being required to file such a notice with the court. Form 2.10B confirms this. In this situation there is no interim moratorium. It would be reasonable to suppose that a moratorium could be secured for a few days by filing with the court a notice of intention to appoint even though it there is no person to whom it is obligatory to give notice: see the note to para.44(2); but para.27(1) seems to apply only if a notice of intention has been given under para.26, i.e. only if there are persons entitled to be given such notice. (2) If there is a secured creditor with a "qualifying" floating charge (whether or not it is currently enforceable), five business days' notice under para.26(1) must be given before an appointment can be made, and a moratorium comes into force under para.44(4) from the time when a copy of the notice is filed with the court. Any appointment must be made within ten business days after the specified documents have been filed. (3) If there is no such charge holder but some other person is entitled to notice under para.26(2), notice of intention must be given but the five-day period of notice does not apply; a copy of the notice must be filed, but there appears to be nothing to stop the company or directors proceeding to an immediate appointment, in which case no moratorium would be needed. (Form 2.9B would need minor modification.) Once again, any appointment must be made within ten days of the filing (para.28(2)).

If there is no floating charge holder with the power to appoint an administrative receiver or administrator, para.28 does not apply and paras 27 and 29 are modified: see para.30. And notice must still be given to any person entitled to receive it under para.26(2) in such a case.

The giving of notice is now dealt with by Pt 12A of the Rules. Personal delivery of a document is always permissible (r.12A.2), and unless the Act provides otherwise, the use of the post in accordance with CPR Pt 6 is authorised as an alternative and has effect as specified in those Rules (r.12A.3)). Under the CPR, a document sent by first class post is deemed to have been served no later than the second day after posting (or the first day after that if it is not a business day). However, the requirement in para.26(1) that the recipient should be given "at least five business days' written notice" may be intended to mean that the notice should be actual notice, without regard to any presumption if the post is used. The decision in *Re Sporting Options plc* [2004] EWHC 3128 (Ch); [2005] B.C.C. 88 clearly rules out the use of email.

Para.26(1)

This provision enables the charge holder, if he is not content for the administration to proceed under the control of the person proposed by the company or the directors, to appoint an insolvency practitioner of his own choice as administrative receiver or administrator, or negotiate to have such a person appointed instead of or in addition to the company's or directors' nominee. The charge holder would have time, also, to apply to the court to have the latter restrained from proceeding with their application, if he could show that this was inappropriate or for an improper purpose.

The use of the phrase "is or may be" makes it plain that notice must be given even though the charge is not currently enforceable.

Para.26(2), (3)

Form 2.8B is to be used. Unhappily, this form has been drafted in order to serve a multiplicity of purposes, and this could be a source of confusion. Most persons reading the form will assume that all of its requirements must be completed, including the statutory declaration and attachments, in order to give the statutory notice to those entitled under para.26(1) and (2), and yet it appears from para.27(2) that it is only the copy filed in court that must be accompanied by the statutory declaration. Arguably, therefore, notice could be validly given to the persons entitled under para.26 without any accompanying documents. However, since para.26(3) requires that the notice should be "in the prescribed form", it is recommended that all the paragraphs on this form should be completed, so far as they are applicable, in order to avoid the risk that the effectiveness of the notice might be subsequently challenged.

For the relevant rules, see rr.2.20 et seq. and rr.2.2–2.8(6). A copy of the notice of intention to appoint must be filed with the court (para.27), and written notice must be given also to the following persons as well as those mentioned in para.26(1):

- any sheriff who is known to be charged with execution or other legal process against the company;

- any person who is known to have distrained against the company or its property;

- any supervisor of a CVA;

- the company, if it is not the company that is intending to make the appointment (r.2.20(2)).

27(1) A person who gives notice of intention to appoint under paragraph 26 shall file with the court as soon as is reasonably practicable a copy of–

    (a) the notice, and

    (b) any document accompanying it.

27(2) The copy filed under sub-paragraph (1) must be accompanied by a statutory declaration made by or on behalf of the person who proposes to make the appointment–

    (a) that the company is or is likely to become unable to pay its debts,

    (b) that the company is not in liquidation, and

    (c) that, so far as the person making the statement is able to ascertain, the appointment is not prevented by paragraphs 23 to 25, and

    (d) to such additional effect, and giving such information, as may be prescribed.

27(3) A statutory declaration under sub-paragraph (2) must–

    (a) be in the prescribed form, and

    (b) be made during the prescribed period.

27(4) A person commits an offence if in a statutory declaration under sub-paragraph (2) he makes a statement–

    (a) which is false, and

    (b) which he does not reasonably believe to be true.

Where there is a "qualifying" floating charge holder, compliance with this paragraph is a prerequisite to the making of an effective appointment, and the appointment must be made within the following ten business days: see para.28. Filing the notice triggers an interim moratorium: see para.44(4). Where there is no such charge holder, whether or not there is any person entitled to notice under para.26(2), the company or directors may proceed to an immediate appointment: see the note to para.26.

Para.27(1)
As well as the statutory declaration referred to in para.27(2), the notice must be accompanied by one or other of the documents referred to in r.2.22.

Para.27(2), (3)
An appointment by the company or its directors may only be made if the company is insolvent, or nearly so. For the definition of "unable to pay its debts", see the notes to paras 11, 111(1) and s.123.

As noted above, Form 2.8B is prescribed both for the purpose of giving notice to the floating charge holder(s) (if any) and other persons under para.26(1) and (2) and for the purpose of filing with the court under para.27, and it incorporates the statutory declaration required by para.27(2). The prescribed period is five business days (r.2.21).

Para.27(4)
See the note to para.18(7).

28(1)　An appointment may not be made under paragraph 22 unless the person who makes the appointment has complied with any requirement of paragraphs 26 and 27 and–

(a)　the period of notice specified in paragraph 26(1) has expired, or

(b)　each person to whom notice has been given under paragraph 26(1) has consented in writing to the making of the appointment.

28(2)　An appointment may not be made under paragraph 22 after the period of ten business days beginning with the date on which the notice of intention to appoint is filed under paragraph 27(1).

The time limits imposed by this provision impose a tight framework within which the necessary action must be taken. But para.28(1) only applies where there are persons who must be given notice under para.26(1): if not, an immediate appointment may be made.

Notice of appointment

29(1)　A person who appoints an administrator of a company under paragraph 22 shall file with the court–

(a)　a notice of appointment, and

(b)　such other documents as may be prescribed.

29(2)　The notice of appointment must include a statutory declaration by or on behalf of the person who makes the appointment–

(a)　that the person is entitled to make an appointment under paragraph 22,

(b)　that the appointment is in accordance with this Schedule, and

(c)　that, so far as the person making the statement is able to ascertain, the statements made and information given in the statutory declaration filed with the notice of intention to appoint remain accurate.

29(3)　The notice of appointment must identify the administrator and must be accompanied by a statement by the administrator–

(a)　that he consents to the appointment,

(b)   that in his opinion the purpose of administration is reasonably likely to be achieved, and

(c)   giving such other information and opinions as may be prescribed.

29(4)   For the purpose of a statement under sub-paragraph (3) an administrator may rely on information supplied by directors of the company (unless he has reason to doubt its accuracy).

29(5)   The notice of appointment and any document accompanying it must be in the prescribed form.

29(6)   A statutory declaration under sub-paragraph (2) must be made during the prescribed period.

29(7)   A person commits an offence if in a statutory declaration under sub-paragraph (2) he makes a statement–

(a)   which is false, and

(b)   which he does not reasonably believe to be true.

GENERAL NOTE

The requirements of this paragraph closely parallel those of para.18: see the note to that provision. The appointment of the administrator takes effect from the time of the filing of the notice of appointment under this provision (para.31).
    For the prescribed forms and other prescribed matter, see rr.2.23 et seq.
    Where notice of intention to appoint under para.26 has been given, Form 2.9B is to be used. Where there is no charge holder entitled to notice under para.26(1), an immediate appointment may be made, using Form 2.10B. In that event, para.30, which disapplies para.29(2)(c), should be noted, and the notice must be accompanied by one or other of the documents specified in r.2.22 (r.2.25).

Para.29(2), (6)
Note that this statutory declaration is additional to that required by para.27(2) to accompany a notice of intention to appoint. The prescribed period is not more than five business days before the notice is filed with the court (r.2.24).

Para.29(7)
See the note to para.18(7).

30   In a case in which no person is entitled to notice of intention to appoint under paragraph 26(1) (and paragraph 28 therefore does not apply)–

(a)   the statutory declaration accompanying the notice of appointment must include the statements and information required under paragraph 27(2), and

(b)   paragraph 29(2)(c) shall not apply.

GENERAL NOTE

Where there is no floating charge holder entitled to notice of intention to appoint under para.26(1), the various time limits set out in paras 26–28(1) do not apply; but the statements and information which would otherwise have accompanied the notice of intention must be given with the notice of appointment, and the filing and notification obligations imposed by para.29 (except for para.29(2)(c)) must still be complied with. Although the words in brackets indicate that para.28 does not apply where the only persons entitled to notice of intention to appoint fall within para.26(2), this is contradicted by paras 27(1) and 28(2), read together, from which it would follow that the ten-day time limit imposed by para.28(2) applies in such a case.

Commencement of appointment

31   The appointment of an administrator under paragraph 22 takes effect when the requirements of paragraph 29 are satisfied.

GENERAL NOTE

As is the case with an out-of-court appointment by a floating charge holder (see para.19), the administrator cannot exercise any powers until the statutory filing and notification requirements have been complied with.

32 A person who appoints an administrator under paragraph 22–

(a) shall notify the administrator and such other persons as may be prescribed as soon as is reasonably practicable after the requirements of paragraph 29 are satisfied, and

(b) commits an offence if he fails without reasonable excuse to comply with paragraph (a).

GENERAL NOTE

A copy of the notice of appointment sealed by the court must be sent to the administrator as soon as reasonably practicable (r.2.26(2)). No other persons appear to have been prescribed under para.32(a).

On penalties, see s.430, para.106 and Sch.10.

33 If before the requirements of paragraph 29 are satisfied the company enters administration by virtue of an administration order or an appointment under paragraph 14–

(a) the appointment under paragraph 22 shall not take effect, and

(b) paragraph 32 shall not apply.

GENERAL NOTE

An appointment by the court or an out-of-court appointment made by a floating charge holder has preference over one made by the company or its directors, but only if the charge in either of the former categories "takes effect" first: see the definition of "enters administration" in para.1(2). In any event, the company or directors will not have been free to proceed to an appointment if an application is before the court and has not yet been disposed of (para.25(b)).

Invalid appointment: indemnity

34(1) This paragraph applies where–

(a) a person purports to appoint an administrator under paragraph 22, and

(b) the appointment is discovered to be invalid.

34(2) The court may order the person who purported to make the appointment to indemnify the person appointed against liability which arises solely by reason of the appointment's invalidity.

GENERAL NOTE

This paragraph is in identical terms to para.20. See the note to that paragraph.

ADMINISTRATION APPLICATION—SPECIAL CASES

Application by holder of floating charge

35(1) This paragraph applies where an administration application in respect of a company–

(a) is made by the holder of a qualifying floating charge in respect of the company's property, and

(b) includes a statement that the application is made in reliance on this paragraph.

35(2) The court may make an administration order–

(a) whether or not satisfied that the company is or is likely to become unable to pay its debts, but

(b) only if satisfied that the applicant could appoint an administrator under paragraph 14.

GENERAL NOTE

It is generally a prerequisite for the making of an administration order that the company should be, or be likely to become, insolvent (para.11); but an appointment may be made out of court by the holder of a qualifying floating charge even in the case of a solvent company: see the note to para.14. The present provision makes an exception to para.11 if the following conditions are satisfied:

- the applicant for the order must be the holder of a qualifying floating charge, as defined in para.14(2);
- the application must expressly state that it is made in reliance on para.35; and
- an event must have occurred or a condition been met which would entitle the charge holder to make an out-of-court appointment under para.14.

If these conditions cannot all be met, the holder of a floating charge (whether or not a qualifying charge) may still apply to the court for an administration order, but the company must be shown to be insolvent or nearly so.

Intervention by holder of floating charge

36(1)   This paragraph applies where–

(a)   an administration application in respect of a company is made by a person who is not the holder of a qualifying floating charge in respect of the company's property, and

(b)   the holder of a qualifying floating charge in respect of the company's property applies to the court to have a specified person appointed as administrator (and not the person specified by the administration applicant).

36(2)   The court shall grant an application under sub-paragraph (1)(b) unless the court thinks it right to refuse the application because of the particular circumstances of the case.

GENERAL NOTE

This provision enables the holder of a qualifying floating charge to intervene, where an application to the court for an administration order has been made by someone else and he would prefer a different person to be appointed as administrator from the one who has been nominated. The charge holder must produce to the court:

- the written consent of all holders of any prior qualifying floating charge;
- a statement in Form 2.2B by the proposed administrator; and
- sufficient evidence to satisfy the court that he is entitled to appoint an administrator under para.14 (r.2.10(1)).

This last requirement no doubt requires proof that the charge is immediately enforceable (para.16).

    The court is required to accede to the charge holder's request unless the particular circumstances of the case dictate otherwise. Costs will normally be an expense of the administration (r.2.10(2)).

    Where it is proposed to make an out-of-court appointment of an administrator who does not have the approval of the charge holder, he may take his own steps under para.14: see the note to para.26.

Application where company in liquidation

37(1)   This paragraph applies where the holder of a qualifying floating charge in respect of a company's property could appoint an administrator under paragraph 14 but for paragraph 8(1)(b).

37(2)   The holder of the qualifying floating charge may make an administration application.

37(3)   If the court makes an administration order on hearing an application made by virtue of sub-paragraph (2)–

(a)   the court shall discharge the winding-up order,

(b)   the court shall make provision for such matters as may be prescribed,

(c)   the court may make other consequential provision,

(d)   the court shall specify which of the powers under this Schedule are to be exercisable by the administrator, and

(e)   this Schedule shall have effect with such modifications as the court may specify.

Paragraph 8(1) imposes a general ban on the appointment of an administrator while a company is being wound up. However, the present provision empowers the court to substitute an administration for the liquidation where (a) the winding up is by court order; and (b) application is made by the holder of a "qualifying" floating charge who would, but for the winding up, be in a position to appoint an administrator out of court under para.14. Paragraph 37(3) ("If the court makes an administration order…") makes it plain that the court is not bound to accede to the application.

Rule 2.11 applies, specifying the matters which must be contained in the affidavit in support of the application.

Note the court's discretionary powers under para.37(3)(c)–(e). The matters prescribed for the purposes of para.37(3)(b) appear in r.2.13.

For the effects on employees of a winding-up order under this provision, see *Dear IP*, December 15, 2003, p.11.4.

Para.37(3)(a)–(c)

An order for the discharge of a winding-up order is not the same as a rescission of the order and does not operate retrospectively, and so a disposition of the company's property after the winding-up petition was presented comes within s.127 and is void unless the court orders otherwise. An administrator has standing to apply under s.127 for the validation of the disposition. (*Re Albany Building Ltd* [2007] B.C.C. 591.) Alternatively, this may be done in exercise of the discretion under para.37(3)(b), (c).

38(1)   The liquidator of a company may make an administration application.

38(2)   If the court makes an administration order on hearing an application made by virtue of sub-paragraph (1)–

(a)   the court shall discharge any winding-up order in respect of the company,

(b)   the court shall make provision for such matters as may be prescribed,

(c)   the court may make other consequential provision,

(d)   the court shall specify which of the powers under this Schedule are to be exercisable by the administrator, and

(e)   this Schedule shall have effect with such modifications as the court may specify.

Paragraph 8, which bans the appointment of the administrator of a company which is in liquidation, is made subject to this paragraph when the company is in voluntary or compulsory liquidation (para.8(2), (3)). The administration can only be instituted by court order, and only the liquidator may make the application.

For the effects on employees of a winding-up order under this provision, see *Dear IP*, December 15, 2003, p.11.4.

Para.38(2)

This subparagraph is in similar terms to para.37(3): the court has a discretion whether to make an order or not. But if it does decide to make an order, it must discharge any winding-up order. If the company is in voluntary liquidation, it would be open to the court to grant a stay of the proceedings under s.147.

Rule 2.11 applies, specifying the matters which must be contained in the affidavit in support of the application. The matters prescribed for the purposes of para.38(2)(b) appear in r.2.13.

Effect of administrative receivership

39(1)   Where there is an administrative receiver of a company the court must dismiss an administration application in respect of the company unless–

(a)   the person by or on behalf of whom the receiver was appointed consents to the making of the administration order,

(b)   the court thinks that the security by virtue of which the receiver was appointed would be liable to be released or discharged under sections 238 to 240 (transaction at undervalue and preference) if an administration order were made,

(c) the court thinks that the security by virtue of which the receiver was appointed would be avoided under section 245 (avoidance of floating charge) if an administration order were made, or

(d) the court thinks that the security by virtue of which the receiver was appointed would be challengeable under section 242 (gratuitous alienations) or 243 (unfair preferences) or under any rule of law in Scotland.

39(2) Sub-paragraph (1) applies whether the administrative receiver is appointed before or after the making of the administration application.

GENERAL NOTE

This provision is in similar terms to s.*9(3)*, which applies in the original administration regime. But in some respects the drafting is different: under that section the court was not to dismiss the petition unless it was "*satisfied* … that, if an administration order were made, any security by virtue of which the receiver was appointed would be liable to be released or discharged" under IA 1986 ss.238–240 (or be avoided under s.245 or be challengeable under s.242). It is open to debate whether the phrase "the court thinks" is intended to set a lower standard of proof than "satisfied". (Compare the construction put on the words "if the court … *considers* that the making of an order under this section would be likely…" in the original s.*8(1)(b)* in *Re Harris Simons Construction Ltd* [1989] 1 W.L.R. 368; (1989) 5 B.C.C. 11: see the note to s.*8(1), (2)*.) In *Chesterton International Group plc v Deka Immobilien Inv GmbH* [2005] EWHC 656 (Ch); [2005] B.P.I.R. 1103 administrative receivers were already in post when an application was made to the court for an order. The judge held that, without the consent of the receivers and in the absence of circumstances rendering the security suspect, the court lacked jurisdiction.

EFFECT OF ADMINISTRATION

Dismissal of pending winding-up petition

40(1) A petition for the winding up of a company–

(a) shall be dismissed on the making of an administration order in respect of the company, and

(b) shall be suspended while the company is in administration following an appointment under paragraph 14.

40(2) Sub-paragraph (1)(b) does not apply to a petition presented under–

(a) section 124A (public interest), or

(aa) section 124B (SEs),

(b) section 367 of the Financial Services and Markets Act 2000 (c. 8) (petition by Financial Services Authority).

40(3) Where an administrator becomes aware that a petition was presented under a provision referred to in sub-paragraph (2) before his appointment, he shall apply to the court for directions under paragraph 63.

Para.40(1)

Where a petition for winding up has been made to the court but not yet heard or disposed of, it is to be dismissed if the company is put into administration by order of the court, and suspended if an administrator is appointed out of court by a floating charge holder. (An out-of-court appointment cannot be made by the company or its directors at such a time: see para.25(a).) When a winding-up petition is "suspended", it is without legal effect for the period of the administration, and so provisions such as s.127 do not apply: *Re J Smiths Haulage Ltd* [2007] B.C.C. 135.

Para.40(2)

Although the Act does not generally allow a company to be in administration and in liquidation at the same time (see paras 8, 37, 38 and 42(4)), the possibility is recognised in the case of a winding up on public-interest grounds. If a winding-up order is made in respect of a company which is already in administration, para.82(3)(b) empowers the court to direct that the administration shall continue to have effect, and to give consequential directions.

    Paragraph 40(2)(aa) was inserted by the European Public Limited-Liability Company Regulations 2004 (SI 2004/2326) reg.73(4)(c), as from October 8, 2004.

Dismissal of administrative or other receiver

41(1)   When an administration order takes effect in respect of a company any administrative receiver of the company shall vacate office.

41(2)   Where a company is in administration, any receiver of part of the company's property shall vacate office if the administrator requires him to.

41(3)   Where an administrative receiver or receiver vacates office under sub-paragraph (1) or (2)–

(a)   his remuneration shall be charged on and paid out of any property of the company which was in his custody or under his control immediately before he vacated office, and

(b)   he need not take any further steps under section 40 or 59.

41(4)   In the application of sub-paragraph (3)(a)–

(a)   **"remuneration"** includes expenses properly incurred and any indemnity to which the administrative receiver or receiver is entitled out of the assets of the company,

(b)   the charge imposed takes priority over security held by the person by whom or on whose behalf the administrative receiver or receiver was appointed, and

(c)   the provision for payment is subject to paragraph 43.

General Note

This provision covers the same ground as s.*11(1), (2), (4), (5)* which applies under the original administration regime and, although the drafting is in many respects different, there appears to be no change of substance. Paragraph 41(1) necessarily applies only where the company is put into administration by court order, but para.41(2) applies in all administrations. (An out-of-court appointment cannot be made if an administrative receiver is already in office: see paras 17(b) and 25(c).)

Para.41(4)(c)

This is the counterpart of s.*11(4)* of the original legislation, which is expressly made subject to s.*11(3)*. Although the legislation makes special provision to secure payment of the outgoing receiver's remuneration and expenses, the moratorium imposed by para.43 will prevent him from enforcing payment during the currency of the administration except with the consent of the administrator or the court.

Moratorium on insolvency proceedings

42(1)   This paragraph applies to a company in administration.

42(2)   No resolution may be passed for the winding up of the company.

42(3)   No order may be made for the winding up of the company.

42(4)   Sub-paragraph (3) does not apply to an order made on a petition presented under–

(a)   section 124A (public interest), or

(aa)   section 124B (SEs),

(b)   section 367 of the Financial Services and Markets Act 2000 (c. 8) (petition by Financial Services Authority).

42(5)   If a petition presented under a provision referred to in sub-paragraph (4) comes to the attention of the administrator, he shall apply to the court for directions under paragraph 63.

Para.42(1)–(3)

Unless para.42(4) applies, a company cannot be put into liquidation either voluntarily or compulsorily while it is in administration. If winding up is to supersede an administration, it is necessary for the administration to be terminated either before or simultaneously with the transition. Voluntary liquidation is likely to be preferred in most cases because it can be carried out more cheaply and quickly and with less formality. The new legislation makes express provision for this in para.83 below, so avoiding many of the difficulties experienced under the original regime. Alternatively, the court may make an order under para.79, bringing the administration to an end.

Paragraph 42(4)(aa) was inserted by the European Public Limited-Liability Company Regulations 2004 (SI 2004/2326) reg.73(4)(c), as from October 8, 2004.

Para.42(4), (5)

Once again, winding up on public interest grounds is made an exception, mirroring para.40(2), (3). If the court is satisfied that a winding-up order should be made, it is not required that the administration should be immediately terminated. There might be a case for leaving the administrator in post for a brief period, for instance, if he was in the process of realising security for the benefit of a charge holder. Paragraph 82(3)(b) makes provision for this to be done.

Moratorium on other legal process

43(1)   This paragraph applies to a company in administration.

43(2)   No step may be taken to enforce security over the company's property except–

(a)   with the consent of the administrator, or

(b)   with the permission of the court.

43(3)   No step may be taken to repossess goods in the company's possession under a hire-purchase agreement except–

(a)   with the consent of the administrator, or

(b)   with the permission of the court.

43(4)   A landlord may not exercise a right of forfeiture by peaceable re-entry in relation to premises let to the company except–

(a)   with the consent of the administrator, or

(b)   with the permission of the court.

43(5)   In Scotland, a landlord may not exercise a right of irritancy in relation to premises let to the company except–

(a)   with the consent of the administrator, or

(b)   with the permission of the court.

43(6)   No legal process (including legal proceedings, execution, distress and diligence) may be instituted or continued against the company or property of the company except–

(a)   with the consent of the administrator, or

(b)   with the permission of the court.

43(6A)   An administrative receiver of the company may not be appointed.

43(7)   Where the court gives permission for a transaction under this paragraph it may impose a condition on or a requirement in connection with the transaction.

43(8)   In this paragraph **"landlord"** includes a person to whom rent is payable.

GENERAL NOTE

The provisions of the present paragraph correspond to parts of s.*11(3)* of the original administration regime. They apply once the appointment of an administrator has taken effect: see para.1(2)(a). An interim moratorium may already be in place under para.44 below. For a detailed commentary, see the note to s.*11(3)*.

Paragraph 43(6A) was inserted by the Enterprise Act 2002 (Insolvency) Order 2003 (SI 2003/2096 arts 1, 2(1), (3)) as from September 15, 2003.

The statutory prohibition on the institution of proceedings contained in para.43(6) does not have extra-territorial effect. However, the jurisdiction of the court is not restricted by the territoriality of this provision, because an administration, like a liquidation, imposes a trust of the assets for the benefit of creditors, and this results effectively in an extra-territorial jurisdiction, which may be exercised (in the discretion of the court) to prevent a creditor taking the benefit of a foreign attachment: *Harms Offshore AHT "Taurus" GmbH & Co KG v Bloom* [2009] EWCA Civ 632; [2010] 2 W.L.R. 349.

Para.43(6)

Leave to commence proceedings under this provision was granted in *Hammonds v Thomas Muckle & Sons Ltd* [2006] B.P.I.R. 704 and in *Funding Corp Block Discounting Ltd v Lexi Holdings plc* [2008] EWHC 985 (Ch); [2008] 2 B.C.L.C. 596. In *Metro Nominees (Wandsworth) (No.1) Ltd v Rayment* [2008] B.C.C. 40, where a landlord sought leave to exercise a right of re-entry against a company in administration, it was held that where the exercise of the right would not impede the purpose of the administration leave should normally be given: the court in deciding whether to grant leave should conduct a balancing exercise on principles similar to those set out by the Court of Appeal in *Re Atlantic Computer Systems plc* [1992] Ch. 505; [1990] B.C.C. 859, weighing the proprietary interests of the landlord against those of the company's unsecured creditors. See also *Fashoff (UK) Ltd v Linton* [2008] EWHC 537 (Ch); [2008] B.C.C. 542, where leave to repossess goods was refused because of the delay in bringing the application; it was also held that the goods had not been shown to be in either the actual or constructive possession of the administrator at the relevant time; and *Innovate Logistics Ltd v Sunberry Properties Ltd* [2008] EWCA Civ 1321; [2009] B.C.C. 164, where the Court of Appeal held that a landlord should be refused permission to seek repossession of premises which were necessary for the continuation of the company's business during the administration.

Interim moratorium

44(1) This paragraph applies where an administration application in respect of a company has been made and–

  (a) the application has not yet been granted or dismissed, or

  (b) the application has been granted but the administration order has not yet taken effect.

44(2) This paragraph also applies from the time when a copy of notice of intention to appoint an administrator under paragraph 14 is filed with the court until–

  (a) the appointment of the administrator takes effect, or

  (b) the period of five business days beginning with the date of filing expires without an administrator having been appointed.

44(3) Sub-paragraph (2) has effect in relation to a notice of intention to appoint only if it is in the prescribed form.

44(4) This paragraph also applies from the time when a copy of notice of intention to appoint an administrator is filed with the court under paragraph 27(1) until–

  (a) the appointment of the administrator takes effect, or

  (b) the period specified in paragraph 28(2) expires without an administrator having been appointed.

44(5) The provisions of paragraphs 42 and 43 shall apply (ignoring any reference to the consent of the administrator).

44(6) If there is an administrative receiver of the company when the administration application is made, the provisions of paragraphs 42 and 43 shall not begin to apply by virtue of this paragraph until the person by or on behalf of whom the receiver was appointed consents to the making of the administration order.

44(7) This paragraph does not prevent or require the permission of the court for–

  (a) the presentation of a petition for the winding up of the company under a provision mentioned in paragraph 42(4),

  (b) the appointment of an administrator under paragraph 14,

    (c)   the appointment of an administrative receiver of the company, or

    (d)   the carrying out by an administrative receiver (whenever appointed) of his functions.

GENERAL NOTE

Under the original administration regime, a company can be put into administration only by order of the court—a process which necessarily takes some time. In order to protect the company's assets during this period, provision is made by s.*10* for an automatic moratorium to operate from the time of the presentation of a petition to the court. The present provision gives corresponding protection in the case where the appointment of an administrator is sought by court order under para.10, and also establishes a brief moratorium pending the taking effect of an out-of-court appointment.

Para.44(1)

Under the original regime there is no provision corresponding to that in para.13(2)(a) which expressly empowers the court to specify a time other than that of the order from which the appointment of an administrator is to take effect. Paragraph 44(1)(b) ensures that the interim moratorium continues where a time later that that of the order is fixed by the court. In an appropriate case the court has power under paras 13(1)(f) or 43(7) to modify the terms of the moratorium.

Paras 44(2)–(4)

Where the appointment of an administrator is being made out of court, it does not take effect until the filing and notice requirements of paras 18 or 26 have been complied with (see paras 19, 31). Paragraph 44(2) applies where a floating charge holder intending to appoint an administrator files a notice of intention to appoint with the court. (The prescribed form is Form 2.5B: r.2.15.) Paragraph 44(4) establishes a moratorium where it is the company or its directors who make an out-of-court appointment, for a period which at a maximum cannot exceed ten days (see r.2.20 and Form 2.8B). The main difference between paras 44(2) and 44(4) is that the filing of a notice of intention to appoint is optional in the former case but obligatory in the latter—at least where there is a holder of a qualifying floating charge or other person to whom notice must be given under para.26(1). It does not appear that a moratorium could be obtained in either case simply by filing a notice of intention to appoint with the court when there is nobody who is required by the Act to be given notice: the general tenor of the Act, rules and prescribed forms (and especially the requirement that it is in every case a *copy* of the notice that is to be filed) suggests otherwise. In some circumstances the charge holder or the company or its directors may proceed to make an immediate appointment, in which case there will be no interim moratorium: see the note to paras 14 and 26. The position where an appointment is made by the company or its directors and the only persons entitled to notice of intention to appoint are those specified under para.26(2) is unclear. If the appointment takes effect immediately upon the filing of the copy notice, there will be no need for a moratorium, but if there is any intervening period of delay para.44(4) would appear to indicate that a moratorium comes into operation.

Para.44(5)

Under paras 42 and 43 a dispensation from a restriction imposed by the (permanent) statutory moratorium may be granted by either the administrator or the court. Since the appointment of the administrator will not have taken effect when para.44 applies, it is only the court which will have power to grant the necessary leave.

Para.44(6)

This subparagraph refers to an "administration application", and so applies only where an appointment is sought by court order. Paragraph 39 gives the person who has appointed an administrative receiver a veto over a court appointment unless he is willing to consent to an order under para.39(1(a). If an administrative receiver is in office when an application for an administration order is made to the court, the interim moratorium will not take effect unless and until the charge holder decides to give his consent.

Para.44(7)

This subparagraph applies only during an interim moratorium. Paragraph 43 will normally prevent similar action being taken against a company once a permanent moratorium has come into effect. Paragraph 44(7)(d) would allow the administrative receiver to continue to act until the court order is made, even where the charge-holder has signified his intention to consent to the order.

Publicity

45(1)   While a company is in administration, every business document issued by or on behalf of the company or the administrator, and all the company's websites, must state–

(a) the name of the administrator, and

(b) that the affairs, business and property of the company are being managed by the administrator.

45(2) Any of the following persons commits an offence if without reasonable excuse the person authorises or permits a contravention of sub-paragraph (1)–

(a) the administrator,

(b) an officer of the company, and

(c) the company.

45(3) In sub-paragraph (1) **"business document"** means–

(a) an invoice,

(b) an order for goods or services,

(c) a business letter, and

(d) an order form,

whether in hard copy, electronic or any other form.

GENERAL NOTE

This is a parallel provision to those requiring notification of the appointment of a receiver (ss.39, 64) and notification that the company is in liquidation (s.188). It restates in different wording the original s.12. Paragraph 45 was amended by the Companies (Trading Disclosures) (Insolvency) Regulations 2008 (SI 2008/1897) reg.4(1), as from October 1, 2008. The policy reasons for making the company itself liable for this offence are not obvious.

On penalties, see s.430 and Sch.10.

PROCESS OF ADMINISTRATION

Announcement of administrator's appointment

46(1) This paragraph applies where a person becomes the administrator of a company.

46(2) As soon as is reasonably practicable the administrator shall–

(a) send a notice of his appointment to the company, and

(b) publish a notice of his appointment in the prescribed manner.

46(3) As soon as is reasonably practicable the administrator shall–

(a) obtain a list of the company's creditors, and

(b) send a notice of his appointment to each creditor of whose claim and address he is aware.

46(4) The administrator shall send a notice of his appointment to the registrar of companies before the end of the period of 7 days beginning with the date specified in sub-paragraph (6).

46(5) The administrator shall send a notice of his appointment to such persons as may be prescribed before the end of the prescribed period beginning with the date specified in sub-paragraph (6).

46(6) The date for the purpose of sub-paragraphs (4) and (5) is–

(a) in the case of an administrator appointed by administration order, the date of the order,

(b) in the case of an administrator appointed under paragraph 14, the date on which he receives notice under paragraph 20, and

(c)   in the case of an administrator appointed under paragraph 22, the date on which he receives notice under paragraph 32.

46(7)   The court may direct that sub-paragraph (3)(b) or (5)–

(a)   shall not apply, or

(b)   shall apply with the substitution of a different period.

46(8)   A notice under this paragraph must–

(a)   contain the prescribed information, and

(b)   be in the prescribed form.

46(9)   An administrator commits an offence if he fails without reasonable excuse to comply with a requirement of this paragraph.

GENERAL NOTE

This is an extended version of the original s.21, adjusted to take account of cases where the administrator is appointed out of court. However, the time limits have been altered as noted below. For the relevant rules and forms prescribed for the purposes of this paragraph, see r.2.27. On the giving of notice, see IR 1986 Pt 12A. The notice of appointment may not be sent by email (*Re Sporting Options plc* [2004] EWHC 3128 (Ch); [2005] B.C.C. 88), but in the same case the court, in order to save expense, allowed the administrator to send by post a short indication of the website at which his proposals could be found and indicated that this would be regarded as sufficient service of the proposals.

Para.46(2)
Form 2.12B is to be used where the notice of appointment is to be sent to any person, and Form 2.11B for the published notices. The latter must be published once in the *Gazette* and once in an appropriate newspaper (r.2.27(1)). Where the appointment has been made by the company under para.22, para.46(2)(a) would seem superfluous, since the company will already have sent a notice to him under para.32(a)!

Para.46(3)
"As soon as reasonably practicable" has been substituted for "within 28 days after the making of the order" under the original regime.

Para.46(4), (6)
The period under the original Pt II is 14 days from the making of the order. Note that subpara.(a) refers to the date of the order, not the date when the order takes effect (so placing a duty on the administrator before his appointment is effective).

Para.46(5)
The prescribed persons are:

- any receiver or administrative receiver;
- the petitioner under any pending winding-up petition, and any provisional liquidator;
- any sheriff charged with execution or other legal process against the company;
- any person who has distrained against the company or its property;
- the supervisor of any CVA (r.2.27(2)).

No specific period is prescribed: r.2.27(2) simply states that notice shall be given "as soon as reasonably practicable".

Para.46(9)
On penalties, see s.430, Sch.B1 para.106(2) and Sch.10.

Statement of company's affairs

47(1)   As soon as is reasonably practicable after appointment the administrator of a company shall by notice in the prescribed form require one or more relevant persons to provide the administrator with a statement of the affairs of the company.

47(2) The statement must–

(a) be verified by a statement of truth in accordance with Civil Procedure Rules,

(b) be in the prescribed form,

(c) give particulars of the company's property, debts and liabilities,

(d) give the names and addresses of the company's creditors,

(e) specify the security held by each creditor,

(f) give the date on which each security was granted, and

(g) contain such other information as may be prescribed.

47(3) In sub-paragraph (1) **"relevant person"** means–

(a) a person who is or has been an officer of the company,

(b) a person who took part in the formation of the company during the period of one year ending with the date on which the company enters administration,

(c) a person employed by the company during that period, and

(d) a person who is or has been during that period an officer or employee of a company which is or has been during that year an officer of the company.

47(4) For the purpose of sub-paragraph (3) a reference to employment is a reference to employment through a contract of employment or a contract for services.

47(5) In Scotland, a statement of affairs under sub-paragraph (1) must be a statutory declaration made in accordance with the Statutory Declarations Act 1835 (c. 62) (and sub-paragraph (2)(a) shall not apply).

GENERAL NOTE

This paragraph corresponds to s.22 in the original Pt II. The "statement of affairs", which had long been a feature of the liquidation procedure in a compulsory winding up (see s.131), was made a requirement by IA 1986 in administration and a number of other insolvency proceedings. For further comment, see the notes to s.131.

For the relevant rules, forms and other matters prescribed for the purposes of this paragraph, see rr.2.28 et seq.

Para.47(1)

"As soon as reasonably practicable" has been substituted for "forthwith" in the original Pt II. The notice is to be in Form 2.13B, and must contain the information specified in r.2.28(3). In addition, the administrator must furnish each recipient with the forms required for the preparation of the statement of affairs (r.2.28(4)).

Para.47(2), (5)

The statement must be in Form 2.14B. A "statement of truth" has been substituted for the affidavit which is required by the original Pt II. The administrator may require any "relevant person" to submit a statement of concurrence (in Form 2.15B) stating that he concurs in the statement of affairs (r.2.29(1), (2)). In this event:

- the person making the statement of affairs must be informed;
- that person must deliver a copy of the statement of affairs to the other "relevant person (or persons)";
- the latter then has five business days to submit the statement of concurrence to the administrator;
- a statement of concurrence may be qualified in certain events;
- every statement of concurrence is to be verified by a statement of truth;
- every statement of concurrence is to be filed together with the statement of affairs with the court and sent to the registrar of companies (r.2.29).

Form 2.16B is to be used for the purposes of filing and registration. There is provision in r.2.30 for the court to order that limited disclosure only should be made, or no disclosure at all, where the administrator thinks that disclosure would prejudice the conduct of the administration, and a right given to a creditor by r.2.30(4) to apply for an order that the administrator should disclose the statement or part of it notwithstanding such an order.

A person making a statement of affairs may be reimbursed expenses which he has incurred (r.2.32).

Para.47(3), (4)
The expression "officer", in relation to a company, includes a director, manager or secretary (CA 2006 s.1121), and at least in some contexts may extend to the holders of other offices: see the note to s.206(3). The wide definition of "employment" used here could include professionals such as the company's auditors and bankers.

48(1)   A person required to submit a statement of affairs must do so before the end of the period of 11 days beginning with the day on which he receives notice of the requirement.

48(2)   The administrator may–

(a)   revoke a requirement under paragraph 47(1), or

(b)   extend the period specified in sub-paragraph (1) (whether before or after expiry).

48(3)   If the administrator refuses a request to act under sub-paragraph (2)–

(a)   the person whose request is refused may apply to the court, and

(b)   the court may take action of a kind specified in sub-paragraph (2).

48(4)   A person commits an offence if he fails without reasonable excuse to comply with a requirement under paragraph 47(1).

GENERAL NOTE

This paragraph corresponds to s.22(4)–(6) of the original regime. For the relevant rules, see rr.2.29 et seq.

Para.48(1)
The period was formerly 21 days. Note that the period is 11 days, not 11 business days. Form 2.14B is to be used for the statement of affairs.

Para.48(2), (3)
The language used in para.48(2)(a) is rather less clear than that in s.22(5), although the meaning is no doubt meant to be the same. Section 22(5) empowers the administrator to "release a person from an obligation imposed on him" to submit a statement of affairs, and also to extend the period, and continues: "where the administrator has refused to exercise a power conferred by this subsection, the court, if it thinks fit, may exercise it". Rule 2.31 (which uses similar language) sets out the procedure as regards both the grant of a release and an extension of time.

Para.48(4)
On penalties, see s.430, para.106(2) and Sch.10.

Administrator's proposals

49(1)   The administrator of a company shall make a statement setting out proposals for achieving the purpose of administration.

49(2)   A statement under sub-paragraph (1) must, in particular–

(a)   deal with such matters as may be prescribed, and

(b)   where applicable, explain why the administrator thinks that the objective mentioned in paragraph 3(1)(a) or (b) cannot be achieved.

49(3)   Proposals under this paragraph may include–

(a)   a proposal for a voluntary arrangement under Part I of this Act (although this paragraph is without prejudice to section 4(3));

(b)   a proposal for a compromise or arrangement to be sanctioned under Part 26 of the Companies Act 2006 (arrangements and reconstructions).

49(4) The administrator shall send a copy of the statement of his proposals–

(a) to the registrar of companies,

(b) to every creditor of the company of whose claim and address he is aware, and

(c) to every member of the company of whose address he is aware.

49(5) The administrator shall comply with sub-paragraph (4)–

(a) as soon as is reasonably practicable after the company enters administration, and

(b) in any event, before the end of the period of eight weeks beginning with the day on which the company enters administration.

49(6) The administrator shall be taken to comply with sub-paragraph (4)(c) if he publishes in the prescribed manner a notice undertaking to provide a copy of the statement of proposals free of charge to any member of the company who applies in writing to a specified address.

49(7) An administrator commits an offence if he fails without reasonable excuse to comply with sub-paragraph (5).

49(8) A period specified in this paragraph may be varied in accordance with paragraph 107.

GENERAL NOTE

The equivalent provision under the original regime is s.*23*. The most notable change is that the period allowed for the administrator to formulate his proposals has been shortened from three months to eight weeks. Rule 2.33 sets out in considerable detail the matters required to be dealt with (in addition to those prescribed by para.49) in the statement of proposals, which must be sent as directed by para.49(4).

A new r.2.33A introduced by I(A)R 2010 empowers the administrator to apply to the court for an order authorising him to make limited disclosure of any specified part of the para.49 statement where he thinks that it would prejudice the conduct of the administration or be prejudicial to the interests of a creditor to disclose all the matters specified in r.2.33(2)(h) and (j). Such an order directs that some or all of the specified part must not be sent to the registrar of companies and the members and creditors. The persons listed in para.49(4) must then be sent the para.49 statement to the extent provided by the order and an indication of the nature of the matter in relation to which the order was made. A creditor may apply to the court for an order requiring disclosure of a part of the statement covered by the order and the court on such an application may make the order subject to conditions as to confidentiality, etc. as it sees fit. If there is a material change of circumstances after an order for limited disclosure has been made which renders the limit unnecessary the administrator must apply to the court for the order to be rescinded in whole or in part.

Para.49(2)

Paragraph 3 of Sch.B1 ranks the statutory objectives of an administration in a definite sequence: (1) corporate rescue; (2) a better result for the creditors as a whole than would be likely in a winding up without prior administration; and (3) satisfying the claims of preferential and secured creditors. Subparagraph (2)(b) is a reminder that the administrator cannot lightly disregard this hierarchy, e.g. by treating the administration as in effect a receivership and proceeding immediately to discharge the claims in category (3).

Para.49(3)

These are two of the statutory purposes for which an administration order can be sought under the original regime. Although they have been given no place in the structured "objectives" of the new regime (see above), this is an indication that they have not been wholly forgotten. There will now be less occasion to have recourse to the former practice of combining an administration with a CVA in order to obtain a moratorium, in view of the enactment of Sch.A1, but of course a moratorium is available only for "eligible" companies; and in any case there may sometimes be advantages in a CVA which administration alone could not secure—e.g. if it is desired to involve the members as well as the creditors in the proposals.

Section 4(3) preserves the rights of secured creditors to enforce their security, unless they agree otherwise. (Note also the protection given to secured and preferential creditors by para.73.)

There is at present no statutory provision for a moratorium for the period in which a scheme of arrangement under CA 2006 Pt 26 is formulated and sanctioned, but this can be achieved by putting a scheme together under the protective umbrella of an administration. Again, this may make it possible to achieve rather more than under administration alone, e.g. a restructuring involving more than one company of which some are not insolvent.

Para.49(4)–(8)

As noted, the former period of three months has been shortened to eight weeks. Under para.107, the court (or the administrator with the "consent" of the creditors, as there defined) may vary this period: see the note to that paragraph. If the court grants an extension of time, the persons referred to in para.49(4) must be notified, using Form 2.18B (r.2.33(4)).

Rule 2.33(5)–(8) deals with the situations where the administrator thinks that no meeting of creditors need be called (para.52), where he thinks that the purpose of the administration has been sufficiently achieved before he has sent a statement of his proposals to creditors (para.80) and where he chooses the alternative course of publishing a notice relating to the proposals under para.49(6) rather than sending a statement to every member.

On penalties, see s.430, para.106(2) and Sch.10.

Creditors' meeting

50(1)   In this Schedule **"creditors' meeting"** means a meeting of creditors of a company summoned by the administrator–

(a)   in the prescribed manner, and

(b)   giving the prescribed period of notice to every creditor of the company of whose claim and address he is aware.

50(2)   A period prescribed under sub-paragraph (1)(b) may be varied in accordance with paragraph 107.

50(3)   A creditors' meeting shall be conducted in accordance with the rules.

GENERAL NOTE

This paragraph refers to all creditors' meetings. For the matters prescribed and the relevant rules, see rr.2.34 et seq. The prescribed period of notice is 14 days (r.2.35(4)), but this may be varied by the court in accordance with para.107, or by the administrator with the consent of the creditors under para.108: see the notes to those provisions. Notice of certain meetings (i.e. those summoned under paras 51, 52(2), 54(2), 56(1) and 62) must be in Form 2.20B (r.2.35(1), (2)) and must be gazetted (r.2.35(4A)).

Proxy forms (in Form 8.2) must also be sent (r.2.35(4)(c)).

An administrator may also call a meeting of the company's members, although there is no statutory requirement that the members should be involved in an administration. Rule 2.49 applies to such meetings.

The court may order that notice of any meeting be given by public advertisement rather than by individual notice to the persons concerned, e.g. on the grounds of cost (r.2.37A).

Requirement for initial creditors' meeting

51(1)   Each copy of an administrator's statement of proposals sent to a creditor under paragraph 49(4)(b) must be accompanied by an invitation to a creditors' meeting (an **"initial creditors' meeting"**).

51(2)   The date set for an initial creditors' meeting must be–

(a)   as soon as is reasonably practicable after the company enters administration, and

(b)   in any event, within the period of ten weeks beginning with the date on which the company enters administration.

51(3)   An administrator shall present a copy of his statement of proposals to an initial creditors' meeting.

51(4)   A period specified in this paragraph may be varied in accordance with paragraph 107.

51(5)   An administrator commits an offence if he fails without reasonable excuse to comply with a requirement of this paragraph.

GENERAL NOTE

Under the original regime, the administrator is required to summon a creditors' meeting on not less than 14 days' notice sent within the period of three months from the date of the administration order (IA 1986 s.*13(1)(b)*). The ten-week limit here specified reflects the shortening of the three-month period to eight weeks (see the note to para.49(4)–(8) above). This may be varied by the court under para.107 or the administrator with the consent of the creditors under para.108: see the notes to those provisions. Where the court orders an extension under para.107, notice in Form 2.18B must be sent to all the persons listed in para.49(4): see r.2.34(3).

Notice of the initial creditors' meeting must normally be advertised in accordance with r.2.34(1), gazetted and sent (in Form 2.19B) to those present and past directors and officers of the company whose presence the administrator thinks is required (r.2.34(2)). One or more adjournments for not more than 14 days in total is possible, subject to any direction by the court (r.2.34(4), (5)). For the circumstances in which a meeting need not be called, see para.52(1).

Note also that the administrator may dispense with the need to call a meeting of creditors where he thinks that the purpose of the administration has already been sufficiently achieved (see para.80 and r.2.33(5)) or if he decides that the company should move from administration to dissolution under para.84.

Para.51(5)
On penalties, see s.430, para.106(2) and Sch.10.

52(1) Paragraph 51(1) shall not apply where the statement of proposals states that the administrator thinks–

   (a) that the company has sufficient property to enable each creditor of the company to be paid in full,

   (b) that the company has insufficient property to enable a distribution to be made to unsecured creditors other than by virtue of section 176A(2)(a), or

   (c) that neither of the objectives specified in paragraph 3(1)(a) and (b) can be achieved.

52(2) But the administrator shall summon an initial creditors' meeting if it is requested–

   (a) by creditors of the company whose debts amount to at least 10% of the total debts of the company,

   (b) in the prescribed manner, and

   (c) in the prescribed period.

52(3) A meeting requested under sub-paragraph (2) must be summoned for a date in the prescribed period.

52(4) The period prescribed under sub-paragraph (3) may be varied in accordance with paragraph 107.

GENERAL NOTE

Paragraph 52(1) authorises the administrator to dispense with the need to summon an initial creditors' meeting. In essence, it applies in circumstances where there is likely to be nothing of substance that a creditors' meeting could decide. These circumstances are:

- that there are sufficient assets to enable all the company's creditors to be paid in full;

- that there will be insufficient assets to enable anything to be paid to the unsecured creditors (apart from anything that may come to them from the "prescribed part", set aside following the realisation of assets subject to a floating charge: see the notes to s.176A); or

- that the only objective of the administration which the administrator thinks is capable of achievement is "realising property in order to make a distribution to one or more secured or preferential creditors" (para.3(1)(c)).

There is obviously an overlap between the latter two situations, but the third would apply and not the second where there was no floating charge or where there are only sufficient assets to make a part payment to the unsecured creditors.

Para.52(2)–(4)
Rule 2.37 applies. The request must be in Form 2.21B. The period prescribed is 12 days from the date on which the administrator's proposals are sent out, and the meeting must be held within 28 days of the request being received by the administrator. Security must be given for the expenses of summoning and holding the meeting. Notice of the meeting must be in Form 2.20B (r.2.35(2)). The 12-day period may be varied by the court under para.107.

Business and result of initial creditors' meeting

53(1)   An initial creditors' meeting to which an administrator's proposals are presented shall consider them and may–

(a)   approve them without modification, or

(b)   approve them with modification to which the administrator consents.

53(2)   After the conclusion of an initial creditors' meeting the administrator shall as soon as is reasonably practicable report any decision taken to–

(a)   the court,

(b)   the registrar of companies, and

(c)   such other persons as may be prescribed.

53(3)   An administrator commits an offence if he fails without reasonable excuse to comply with sub-paragraph (2).

GENERAL NOTE

This provision has its counterpart in s.*24(2), (4)* of the original regime.

The administrator's freedom to act in the exercise of his functions is limited by the scope of the proposals, once approved (see para.68(1))—apart from "insubstantial" deviations (para.54(1)(c)); and so it is important, from his point of view, that they should not be too restrictively drawn. Indeed, in *Re Dana (UK) Ltd* [1999] 2 B.C.L.C. 239 Neuberger J. thought that it would make good sense for the proposals put before an initial meeting to include a mechanism empowering the largest and/or representative creditors to approve future decisions or variations of decisions of the administrator. In any event the court may, in exceptional circumstances, authorise the administrator to depart from the approved scheme: see the note to para.54, below.

For the rules governing the conduct of the meeting, see rr.2.36, 2.38 et seq. Note that the rules invalidate any resolution of the creditors which is opposed by a majority of the creditors who are not "connected with" the company: see r.2.43(2) and, on the meaning of "connected with", s.249.

On the persons prescribed for the purposes of para.53(2)(c), see r.2.46. Form 2.23B is to be used.

On penalties, see s.430, para.106(2) and Sch.10.

Revision of administrator's proposals

54(1)   This paragraph applies where–

(a)   an administrator's proposals have been approved (with or without modification) at an initial creditors' meeting,

(b)   the administrator proposes a revision to the proposals, and

(c)   the administrator thinks that the proposed revision is substantial.

54(2)   The administrator shall–

(a)   summon a creditors' meeting,

(b)   send a statement in the prescribed form of the proposed revision with the notice of the meeting sent to each creditor,

(c)   send a copy of the statement, within the prescribed period, to each member of the company of whose address he is aware, and

(d)   present a copy of the statement to the meeting.

54(3)   The administrator shall be taken to have complied with sub-paragraph (2)(c) if he publishes a notice undertaking to provide a copy of the statement free of charge to any member of the company who applies in writing to a specified address.

54(4)   A notice under sub-paragraph (3) must be published–

   (a)   in the prescribed manner, and

   (b)   within the prescribed period.

54(5)   A creditors' meeting to which a proposed revision is presented shall consider it and may–

   (a)   approve it without modification, or

   (b)   approve it with modification to which the administrator consents.

54(6)   After the conclusion of a creditors' meeting the administrator shall as soon as is reasonably practicable report any decision taken to–

   (a)   the court,

   (b)   the registrar of companies, and

   (c)   such other persons as may be prescribed.

54(7)   An administrator commits an offence if he fails without reasonable excuse to comply with sub-paragraph (6).

GENERAL NOTE

This paragraph corresponds to IA 1986 s.25, which applies under the original regime. Its wording often repeats provisions to be found elsewhere, e.g. in paras 49, 51 and 53, and it may be helpful to refer to the notes to those provisions.

The administrator is bound to adhere to the course of action agreed to by the creditors at their initial meeting (except that he may, apparently, make "insubstantial" deviations: see para.54(1)(c)). If he wishes to work to a different strategy, he must go back to the creditors for approval of revised proposals. However, in exceptional circumstances (e.g. where the delay involved in summoning a creditors' meeting to consider a revised scheme could cause substantial loss) the court has power under para.68(3)(c)) to authorise an administrator to depart from an approved scheme: cf. *Re Smallman Construction Ltd* (1988) 4 B.C.C. 784; and *Re Dana (UK) Ltd* [1999] 2 B.C.L.C. 239.

Para.54(2)–(4)
Rules 2.35 et seq. and more particularly r.2.45 apply. Form 2.22B is to be used, with a statement attached setting out the proposed revisions. Members must be sent copies of the statement within five days of sending the statement to creditors, unless s.54(3) applies, when the administrator must publish a notice in accordance with r.2.45(4).

Para.54(6)
Rule 2.45 applies, and Form 2.23B is to be used.

Para.54(7)
On penalties, see s.430, para.106(2) and Sch.10.

Failure to obtain approval of administrator's proposals

55(1)   This paragraph applies where an administrator reports to the court that–

   (a)   an initial creditors' meeting has failed to approve the administrator's proposals presented to it, or

   (b)   a creditors' meeting has failed to approve a revision of the administrator's proposals presented to it.

55(2)   The court may–

   (a)   provide that the appointment of an administrator shall cease to have effect from a specified time;

   (b)   adjourn the hearing conditionally or unconditionally;

   (c)   make an interim order;

(d) make an order on a petition for winding up suspended by virtue of paragraph 40(1)(b);

(e) make any other order (including an order making consequential provision) that the court thinks appropriate.

GENERAL NOTE

This provision gives discretionary powers to the court in the event that proposals or revised proposals are not approved at the creditors' meeting. Although the administrator is required to report the failure to gain approval to the court, it does not appear to be essential that he should seek any ruling from the court: in particular, if revised proposals are not approved, he is surely free to continue to act under the original proposals or to draw up a new set of revised proposals and summon a further creditors' meeting. But despite the wide wording of para.(2)(e), the court's powers must be of a limited nature: it could not, for example, impose on the creditors a set of proposals to which they have not agreed.

Further creditors' meetings

56(1) The administrator of a company shall summon a creditors' meeting if–

(a) it is requested in the prescribed manner by creditors of the company whose debts amount to at least 10% of the total debts of the company, or

(b) he is directed by the court to summon a creditors' meeting.

56(2) An administrator commits an offence if he fails without reasonable excuse to summon a creditors' meeting as required by this paragraph.

GENERAL NOTE

There appears to be no restriction on the circumstances in which the creditors may exercise this power to have a meeting summoned, or on their reasons or motivation, except that such a meeting probably could not be called before the initial creditors' meeting.

Para.56(2)
On penalties, see s.430, para.106(2) and Sch.10.

Creditors' committee

57(1) A creditors' meeting may establish a creditors' committee.

57(2) A creditors' committee shall carry out functions conferred on it by or under this Act.

57(3) A creditors' committee may require the administrator–

(a) to attend on the committee at any reasonable time of which he is given at least seven days' notice, and

(b) to provide the committee with information about the exercise of his functions.

GENERAL NOTE

The appointment of a creditors' or liquidation committee is a feature of most insolvency proceedings: see, e.g. ss.49, 68, 101 and 141–142. For the rules relating to the creditors' committee, see rr.2.50 et seq. The business of the committee may be conducted otherwise than at a meeting (r.2.61): see the note to the next paragraph.

Correspondence instead of creditors' meeting

58(1) Anything which is required or permitted by or under this Schedule to be done at a creditors' meeting may be done by correspondence between the administrator and creditors–

(a)   in accordance with the rules, and

(b)   subject to any prescribed condition.

58(2)   A reference in this Schedule to anything done at a creditors' meeting includes a reference to anything done in the course of correspondence in reliance on sub-paragraph (1).

58(3)   A requirement to hold a creditors' meeting is satisfied by conducting correspondence in accordance with this paragraph.

GENERAL NOTE

This provision is new. Plainly, it can operate only where the number of creditors is small. For the relevant rule, see r.2.48. "Correspondence" includes correspondence by telephonic or other electronic means (para.111(1)). A notice in Form 2.25B must be sent to every creditor entitled to notice of a creditors' meeting. If no valid Forms 2.25B are received by the administrator by the specified time he must call a creditors' meeting (r.2.48(6)). A creditor or creditors whose debt(s) amount to at least 10 per cent of the total debts of the company may require a meeting to be summoned in the normal way (r.2.48(7)). For guidance on the use of correspondence, see *Dear IP,* October 2004.

Section 246A, introduced by LRO 2010 (SI 2010/18), now provides more generally for the holding of meetings without the participants being physically present together. See the note to that section.

FUNCTIONS OF ADMINISTRATOR

General powers

59(1)   The administrator of a company may do anything necessary or expedient for the management of the affairs, business and property of the company.

59(2)   A provision of this Schedule which expressly permits the administrator to do a specified thing is without prejudice to the generality of sub-paragraph (1).

59(3)   A person who deals with the administrator of a company in good faith and for value need not inquire whether the administrator is acting within his powers.

GENERAL NOTE

The powers of an administrator under the original regime are set out in IA 1986 ss.14–16, which correspond broadly to paras 59–72 of this Schedule. The court will not readily give directions to the administrator in regard to matters which it is his responsibility to deal with: *RAB Capital plc v Lehman Brothers (International) Europe* [2008] EWHC 2335 (Ch); [2008] B.C.C. 915. The court will not order the removal of an administrator who has made a commercial judgment that a creditor considers to be unfair to him: *Re Zegna III Holdings Inc* [2009] EWHC 2994 (Ch).

Para.59(1), (2)
The powers are here conferred in the widest terms. These powers are not, however, restricted to the management of the company's business (as is normally the case with the board of directors). This is indicated by the use of the word "affairs", and appears also from some of the particular matters mentioned in this Schedule and in Sch.1, e.g. the power to remove a director (para.61). The administrator may summon a meeting of shareholders: see r.2.49.

The notes to s.14(1) will be generally applicable, since the wording is very similar.

Para.59(3)
This provision is probably only inserted out of caution, since a third party would almost certainly be protected by the ordinary rules of agency.

60   The administrator of a company has the powers specified in Schedule 1 to this Act.

GENERAL NOTE

The powers conferred by Sch.1, which are common to both administrators and administrative receivers, also apply under the original regime. See the notes to s.*14* and Sch.1.

61   The administrator of a company–

(a)   may remove a director of the company, and

(b)   may appoint a director of the company (whether or not to fill a vacancy).

GENERAL NOTE

This provision has its counterpart in s.*14(2)(a)*. See the note to s.*14(2)*.

62   The administrator of a company may call a meeting of members or creditors of the company.

63   The administrator of a company may apply to the court for directions in connection with his functions.

GENERAL NOTE

This provision corresponds to s.*14(3)* of the original regime. See the note to that provision.

64(1)   A company in administration or an officer of a company in administration may not exercise a management power without the consent of the administrator.

64(2)   For the purpose of sub-paragraph (1)–

(a)   **"management power"** means a power which could be exercised so as to interfere with the exercise of the administrator's powers,

(b)   it is immaterial whether the power is conferred by an enactment or an instrument, and

(c)   consent may be general or specific.

GENERAL NOTE

This paragraph corresponds to IA 1986 s.*14(4)*, which applies under the original regime. See the note to that provision.

The definition of "management power" extends to functions which are wider than those usually associated with management—e.g. the appointment of directors by the company in general meeting.

It is clear that the proposals, or the administrator himself, may leave some functions in the hands of the company's directors or other officers, but not of course so as to absolve the administrator from his own responsibilities.

Distribution

65(1)   The administrator of a company may make a distribution to a creditor of the company.

65(2)   Section 175 shall apply in relation to a distribution under this paragraph as it applies in relation to a winding up.

65(3)   A payment may not be made by way of distribution under this paragraph to a creditor of the company who is neither secured nor preferential unless the court gives permission.

GENERAL NOTE

There is no counterpart to this provision under the original regime.

It is left to the proposals as approved by the creditors to determine when and how payments are to be made to those entitled. Chapter 10 of the Rules (rr.2.68–2.105) deals in detail with the making of distributions to creditors: with the proving of debts, quantification of claims, mutual credit and set-off, interest, proof by secured creditors, etc. These largely mirror the provisions which apply in a winding up (rr.4.73–4.99).

Para.65(1)

The term "distribution" is not defined for the purposes of this Schedule or for the Act as a whole, although it is used also in the context of liquidations (ss.107, 143, 146, etc.) and personal bankruptcy (ss.324, 330, etc.). The term necessarily relates only to pre-administration creditors. Unsecured creditors rank *inter se* on a pari passu basis (r.2.69). The rules regarding the declaration and payment of a dividend are rr.2.97 et seq.

However, the term "distribution" is capable of a wider construction, and is not applicable only to payments to be made on a rateable basis to the unsecured creditors as a whole. In *Re HPJ UK Ltd* [2007] B.C.C. 284 the company's administrators were authorised under para.65 to make a single payment to the Revenue, reached as a compromise in settlement of a disputed claim. This cleared the way for the administrators to attend to the interests of the remaining creditors (who had approved the settlement).

Para.65(2)

Section 175 gives priority the company's preferential creditors ahead of the claims of any floating charge holder (but not the holder of a fixed charge). Note also that s.176A directs that a "prescribed part" of the company's net property shall be made available for the satisfaction of its unsecured debts and paid in priority to the holder of a floating charge. Under IA 1986 Pt II, as originally drafted, there was no statutory category of preferential debts in an administration, unless the administration was followed immediately by a winding up. The new regime introduced by Sch.B1, and in particular this subparagraph, now makes provision for preferential debts to have priority, and s.387 has been amended so as to make the date on which the company enters into administration the relevant date to determine the existence and amount of such debts. The categories of preferential debts are the same as those in other insolvency proceedings, as defined in Sch.6.

Section 175(2)(a) also states that the preferential debts shall rank after the expenses of the winding up. By analogy, the same priority is accorded to the expenses of the administration (including the administrator's remuneration), and those expenses (amplified by the debts referred to in para.99(4) and (5)) will be given priority over the claim of any floating charge holder—or at least those to which para.70 applies (see para.99(3)(b)).

Paragraph 65(2) has not been amended to include a reference to the new s.176ZA, which (reversing the decision of the House of Lords in *Re Leyland DAF Ltd, Buchler v Talbot* [2004] UKHL 9; [2004] 2 A.C. 298; [2004] B.C.C. 214) directs that the expenses of a winding up shall have priority over claims to property comprised in or subject to a floating charge. The corresponding position in an administration under Sch.B1 was not referred to in the judgments in *Leyland DAF* (although paras 69 and 95 were mentioned in argument), and it is probable that the draftsman of s.176ZA took the view that these two paragraphs already gave the expenses of an administration the same priority as s.176ZA now does. Although an argument might still be advanced that in some circumstances the *Leyland DAF* reasoning survives despite paras 69 and 95, it is unlikely to find favour at a time when the "rescue culture" holds sway.

Para.65(3)

This provision applies even though the claims of the secured and preferential creditors have been fully met, and (it would seem) even in relation to the "prescribed part" to which unsecured creditors are entitled under s.176A. Note, however, the special power given to the administrator by para.66. The section gives no guidance as to the criteria that the court should apply in considering whether or not to grant permission. In *Re GHE Realisations Ltd* [2005] EWHC 2400 (Ch); [2006] 1 W.L.R. 287; [2006] B.C.C. 139 Rimer J. said that the principal consideration which should ultimately govern the matter was "the interests of the company's creditors as a whole". In *Re MG Rover Belux SA/NV* [2007] B.C.C. 446 H.H.J. Norris, Q.C. listed a number of further factors which he considered material, including (i) that the proposed distribution should be conducive to the achievement of the then current objectives of the administration; (ii) that proper provision has been made for secured and preferential creditors; (iii) what realistic alternatives there might be; (iv) the basis on which the administration has been conducted so far as the creditors were concerned, and whether they had approved (or not objected to) any proposal concerning the relevant distribution; and (v) the impact of the distribution on any proposed exit route from the distribution.

66 The administrator of a company may make a payment otherwise than in accordance with paragraph 65 or paragraph 13 of Schedule 1 if he thinks it likely to assist achievement of the purpose of administration.

GENERAL NOTE

This provision would, for example, allow the administrator, without reference to the court, to pay off arrears owed to a creditor who made such a payment a condition of making further essential supplies, e.g. of fuel or raw materials. So far as concerns para.13 of Sch.1, it is not easy to think of a payment "likely to assist achievement of the purpose of administration" which is not also "necessary or incidental to the performance of his functions".

In *Re MG Rover España SA* [2006] B.C.C. 599 the view was expressed that para.66 could be invoked to empower administrators to make payments to employees under the national laws of EU Member States over and above their entitlement under English law, so avoiding the need to open secondary proceedings (which would necessarily be winding-up proceedings) in each national territory where employee rights were greater than under English law. A similar point was made by Lindsay J. in *Re Collins & Aikman Europe SA* [2006] EWHC 1343 (Ch); [2006] B.C.C.

861, where the relationship between paras 65 and 66, IA 1986 Sch.1 para.13 and the court's inherent jurisdiction to authorise payments by an administrator (as an officer of the court) is examined in some detail. See also *Re MG Rover Belux SA/NV* [2007] B.C.C. 446, where the court approved payments to Belgian creditors of a Belgian-registered company which was in administration in England, so indirectly applying rules of Belgian insolvency law.

General duties

67   The administrator of a company shall on his appointment take custody or control of all the property to which he thinks the company is entitled.

GENERAL NOTE

This provision corresponds to IA 1986 s.*17(1)*, which applies under the original regime, but the phrase "to which he thinks the company is entitled" has been substituted for "to which the company is or appears to be entitled", so making the administrator's subjective belief the critical factor.

68(1)   Subject to sub-paragraph (2), the administrator of a company shall manage its affairs, business and property in accordance with–

   (a)   any proposals approved under paragraph 53,

   (b)   any revision of those proposals which is made by him and which he does not consider substantial, and

   (c)   any revision of those proposals approved under paragraph 54.

68(2)   If the court gives directions to the administrator of a company in connection with any aspect of his management of the company's affairs, business or property, the administrator shall comply with the directions.

68(3)   The court may give directions under sub-paragraph (2) only if–

   (a)   no proposals have been approved under paragraph 53,

   (b)   the directions are consistent with any proposals or revision approved under paragraph 53 or 54,

   (c)   the court thinks the directions are required in order to reflect a change in circumstances since the approval of proposals or a revision under paragraph 53 or 54, or

   (d)   the court thinks the directions are desirable because of a misunderstanding about proposals or a revision approved under paragraph 53 or 54.

GENERAL NOTE

This provision is comparable with IA 1986 s.*17(2)*, but is more elaborately expressed. See the note to that subsection.

Para.68(1)
The Act gives few directions as to the functions of an administrator: it is the proposals approved by the creditors which instruct him what he is to do. He may depart from these proposals only in a respect which he does not consider substantial (subpara.(1)(b)), and even the court's power to depart from the approved proposals appears to be strictly limited by para.68(3).

Para.68(2), (3)
The apparent breadth of para.68(2) is misleading: it is severely cut down by para.68(3).
   The Act sets out an elaborate procedure which an administrator must follow before his terms of reference are eventually settled by the creditors' approval of the proposals which he has drawn up on the basis of the statement of affairs which he has obtained from the company's officers. This process will necessarily take the best part of two or three months—hence the need to give him interim powers to act under subpara.(3)(a), under the direction of the court. But the Act does not expressly authorise him to set about his task of seeking the rehabilitation of the company at once, on his own initiative.
   However the legislation, as worded for the original regime (IA 1986 s.*17(2)(a)*), which has a slightly different emphasis, has been interpreted by the courts as empowering an administrator to take immediate steps, in advance of

the creditors' meeting and without reference to the court, if he considers that to do so is in the best interests of the company and its creditors. (See the note to that provision.) Although the language of para.68(2)–(3) is not the same as that of s.*17(2)(a)*, and arguably leaves less scope for an interpretation similar to that of Vinelott J. (discussed in the note to s.*17(2)(a)*), it was held by Lawrence Collins J. in *Re Transbus International Ltd* [2004] EWHC 932 (Ch); [2004] 1 W.L.R. 2654; [2004] B.C.C. 401 that a similar meaning is to be given to the new wording: there are many cases in which an administrator will be justified in by-passing the statutory procedure and proceeding to an immediate sale, without the direction of the court—e.g. where the unsecured creditors are likely to be paid in full, or to receive no payment, or where neither of the first two objectives set out in para.3(1) can be achieved.

It may be relevant to note that r.2.33(6) contemplates that the purposes of an administration may be achieved before a statement of proposals has been sent to creditors.

These factors have led to the development of the practice known as "pre-pack" administrations where, prior to the company or its directors taking steps to make an out-of-court appointment of an administrator, detailed plans are worked out on the advice and with the co-operation of the insolvency practitioner concerned for the prompt sale of the business soon after he takes office, without the formalities of meetings, etc. contemplated by the Act. This is likely to be practicable only when the assets will not permit any distribution to unsecured creditors. See further on this topic the general note to para.2.

Paragraph 68(3)(c) and (d) expressly give the court power to act in circumstances which might have given rise to doubts under the former legislation, although in *Re Smallman Construction Ltd* (1988) 4 B.C.C. 784; and *Re Dana (UK) Ltd* [1999] 2 B.C.L.C. 239 the court considered that the general power conferred by s.14(3) (now para.63) was sufficiently wide to enable it to authorise the departure from an approved scheme. In view of the new statutory language, it is uncertain whether the court could still act in this way, relying on the residual jurisdiction conferred by para.63.

Administrator as agent of company

69   In exercising his functions under this Schedule the administrator of a company acts as its agent.

GENERAL NOTE

This provision corresponds with s.*14(5)*, which applies under the original regime. See the note to that subsection.

Charged property: floating charge

70(1)   The administrator of a company may dispose of or take action relating to property which is subject to a floating charge as if it were not subject to the charge.

70(2)   Where property is disposed of in reliance on sub-paragraph (1) the holder of the floating charge shall have the same priority in respect of acquired property as he had in respect of the property disposed of.

70(3)   In sub-paragraph (2) **"acquired property"** means property of the company which directly or indirectly represents the property disposed of.

GENERAL NOTE

This provision is similar to s.*15(1), (3), (4)*, which applies under the original regime. See the note to that section. The disapplication provisions in relation to market charges, etc. there referred to also apply to administrations under Sch.B1: see EA 2002 Sch.17 para.47.

Charged property: non-floating charge

71(1)   The court may by order enable the administrator of a company to dispose of property which is subject to a security (other than a floating charge) as if it were not subject to the security.

71(2)   An order under sub-paragraph (1) may be made only–

(a)   on the application of the administrator, and

(b)   where the court thinks that disposal of the property would be likely to promote the purpose of administration in respect of the company.

71(3)   An order under this paragraph is subject to the condition that there be applied towards discharging the sums secured by the security–

(a)   the net proceeds of disposal of the property, and

(b)   any additional money required to be added to the net proceeds so as to produce the amount determined by the court as the net amount which would be realised on a sale of the property at market value.

71(4)   If an order under this paragraph relates to more than one security, application of money under sub-paragraph (3) shall be in the order of the priorities of the securities.

71(5)   An administrator who makes a successful application for an order under this paragraph shall send a copy of the order to the registrar of companies before the end of the period of 14 days starting with the date of the order.

71(6)   An administrator commits an offence if he fails to comply with sub-paragraph (5) without reasonable excuse.

GENERAL NOTE

This provision is similar to s.*15(2),(3),(5)–(8)* which applies under the original regime. See the note to that section. The disapplication provisions in relation to market charges, etc. there referred to also apply to administrations under Sch.B1: see EA 2002 Sch.17 para.47.

Rule 2.66 governs the application to the court. "Market value" is defined in para.111(1).

Para.71(6)
On penalties, see s.430, para.106(2) and Sch.10.

Hire-purchase property

72(1)   The court may by order enable the administrator of a company to dispose of goods which are in the possession of the company under a hire-purchase agreement as if all the rights of the owner under the agreement were vested in the company.

72(2)   An order under sub-paragraph (1) may be made only–

(a)   on the application of the administrator, and

(b)   where the court thinks that disposal of the goods would be likely to promote the purpose of administration in respect of the company.

72(3)   An order under this paragraph is subject to the condition that there be applied towards discharging the sums payable under the hire-purchase agreement–

(a)   the net proceeds of disposal of the goods, and

(b)   any additional money required to be added to the net proceeds so as to produce the amount determined by the court as the net amount which would be realised on a sale of the goods at market value.

72(4)   An administrator who makes a successful application for an order under this paragraph shall send a copy of the order to the registrar of companies before the end of the period of 14 days starting with the date of the order.

72(5)   An administrator commits an offence if he fails without reasonable excuse to comply with sub-paragraph (4).

In s.*15*, which applies under the original regime, the power conferred upon an administrator, with the leave of the court, to dispose of (a) property subject to a security and (b) property in the possession of the company under a hire-purchase or similar agreement is dealt with in the same section. The two are now treated separately in paras 71 and 72. The notes to paras 70 and 71 are therefore relevant here. See also the note to s.*15*. The disapplication provisions in relation to market charges, etc. there referred to also apply to administrations under Sch.B1: see EA 2002 Sch.17 para.47.

Rule 2.66 governs the application to the court. "Hire-purchase agreement" extends to retention of title, etc. transactions by virtue of the definition in para.111(1), where "market value" is also defined.

On the role of the judge in assessing the market value, see *Stanley J Holmes & Sons Ltd v Davenham Trust plc* [2006] EWCA Civ 1568.

Para.72(5)
On penalties, see s.430, para.106(2) and Sch.10.

Protection for secured or preferential creditor

73(1)   An administrator's statement of proposals under paragraph 49 may not include any action which–

(a)   affects the right of a secured creditor of the company to enforce his security,

(b)   would result in a preferential debt of the company being paid otherwise than in priority to its non-preferential debts, or

(c)   would result in one preferential creditor of the company being paid a smaller proportion of his debt than another.

73(2)   Sub-paragraph (1) does not apply to–

(a)   action to which the relevant creditor consents,

(b)   a proposal for a voluntary arrangement under Part I of this Act (although this sub-paragraph is without prejudice to section 4(3)),

(c)   a proposal for a compromise or arrangement to be sanctioned under Part 26 of the Companies Act 2006 (arrangements and reconstructions), or

(d)   a proposal for a cross-border merger within the meaning of regulation 2 of the Companies (Cross-Border Mergers) Regulations 2007.

73(3)   The reference to a statement of proposals in sub-paragraph (1) includes a reference to a statement as revised or modified.

There was no provision corresponding to this paragraph in the Pt II regime, as originally drafted. There were no preferential creditors; and any secured creditor who felt himself disadvantaged by the proposals could take his complaint to the court under s.27. This paragraph is modelled on s.4(3), (4) and Sch.A1 para.31(4), (5), which apply in a CVA, and the notes to those provisions may be relevant here.

Paragraph 73(2)(b) and (c) amended and para.73(2)(d) inserted by the Companies (Cross-Border Mergers) Regulations 2007 (SI 2007/2974) reg.65, as from December 15, 2007.

Para.73(1)(a)
The question whether a landlord seeking to exercise rights of forfeiture, etc. for non-payment of rent is a secured creditor has been the subject of much debate: see the note to s.*11(3)*. Although the issue has been resolved for the purposes of that section by legislation, the cases referred to in that note remain relevant generally.

Para.73(2)(b)
A secured creditor will in any case have similar protection under s.*4(3)*. It is surprising that there is no reference to the corresponding provisions in Sch.A1 para.31(4)–(6). The intention may be to pass the consideration of all the issues that may arise to the CVA meetings.

Para.73(2)(c)

A scheme under CA 2006 Pt 26 may involve the variation or abrogation of the rights of secured and preferential creditors, and will be effective (and binding on minorities) if carried at the relevant class meetings and confirmed by the court. Paragraph 73(1) is not to affect this well-sanctioned procedure.

Challenge to administrator's conduct of company

74(1)   A creditor or member of a company in administration may apply to the court claiming that–

(a)   the administrator is acting or has acted so as unfairly to harm the interests of the applicant (whether alone or in common with some or all other members or creditors), or

(b)   the administrator proposes to act in a way which would unfairly harm the interests of the applicant (whether alone or in common with some or all other members or creditors).

74(2)   A creditor or member of a company in administration may apply to the court claiming that the administrator is not performing his functions as quickly or as efficiently as is reasonably practicable.

74(3)   The court may–

(a)   grant relief;

(b)   dismiss the application;

(c)   adjourn the hearing conditionally or unconditionally;

(d)   make an interim order;

(e)   make any other order it thinks appropriate.

74(4)   In particular, an order under this paragraph may–

(a)   regulate the administrator's exercise of his functions;

(b)   require the administrator to do or not do a specified thing;

(c)   require a creditors' meeting to be held for a specified purpose;

(d)   provide for the appointment of an administrator to cease to have effect;

(e)   make consequential provision.

74(5)   An order may be made on a claim under sub-paragraph (1) whether or not the action complained of–

(a)   is within the administrator's powers under this Schedule;

(b)   was taken in reliance on an order under paragraph 71 or 72.

74(6)   An order may not be made under this paragraph if it would impede or prevent the implementation of–

(a)   a voluntary arrangement approved under Part I,

(b)   a compromise or arrangement sanctioned under Part 26 of the Companies Act 2006 (arrangements and reconstructions),

(ba)   a cross-border merger within the meaning of regulation 2 of the Companies (Cross-Border Mergers) Regulations 2007, or

(c)   proposals or a revision approved under paragraph 53 or 54 more than 28 days before the day on which the application for the order under this paragraph is made.

GENERAL NOTE

This provision corresponds to s.27, which applies under the original regime. The notes to that provision may be relevant. An application under this provision to have the administrators replaced was unsuccessful in *SISU Capital Fund Ltd v Tucker* [2005] EWHC 2170 and 2371 (Ch); [2006] B.C.C. 463.

The procedure under para.74 is not appropriate to review a reasonable decision of administrators, even if influenced by a mistake (to convert the administration into a creditors' voluntary liquidation), or a decision to reject a proof: *Unidare plc v Cohen* [2005] EWHC 1410 (Ch); [2006] Ch. 489; [2006] 2 B.C.L.C. 140. Nor will the court use its powers, either under this section or more generally, to give directions to an administrator in the day-to-day management of the administration, e.g. to require him to direct resources to provide information sought by one particular group of creditors: *Four Private Investment Funds v Lomas* [2008] EWHC 2869 (Ch); [2009] 1 B.C.L.C. 161. In *Re Lehman Brothers International (Europe)* [2009] EWHC 2869 (Ch); [2009] B.C.C. 632 a group of creditors applied under para.74 for an order requiring the administrators to disclose more information than had already been given to them in respect of securities held by them. The administrators were carrying out their functions in accordance with the Act and with proposals which had been approved by a meeting of creditors. The court refused relief, holding that the administrators should not be required to devote more time and resources in order to answer the applicants' questions than they had already done, and that any harm alleged by the applicants could not be said to be "unfair".

Paragraph 74(6)(b) amended and para.74(6)(ba) inserted by the Companies (Cross-Border Mergers) Regulations 2007 (SI 2007/2974) reg.65, as from December 15, 2007.

Para.74(1)
Surprisingly, the draftsman has chosen to abandon the time-honoured expression "unfairly prejudicial to the interests" (familiar to company lawyers from its use in CA 2006 s.994) in favour of "unfairly to harm the interests". It will be a matter for judicial interpretation whether any different meaning is intended.

Para.74(2)
This provision is new, and reflects the duty to act expeditiously specifically imposed on an administrator by para.4.

Para.74(5)(a)
This provision has no counterpart in the original s.27. As with s.994, the fact that an act is lawful and within the actor's powers does not prevent the court from having regard to wider considerations of an equitable nature in determining whether it is unfairly harmful.

Para.74(5)(b), (6)
The comments made (respectively) in the notes to ss.27(5), 27(3) apply here.

Misfeasance

75(1)   The court may examine the conduct of a person who–

(a)   is or purports to be the administrator of a company, or

(b)   has been or has purported to be the administrator of a company.

75(2)   An examination under this paragraph may be held only on the application of–

(a)   the official receiver,

(b)   the administrator of the company,

(c)   the liquidator of the company,

(d)   a creditor of the company, or

(e)   a contributory of the company.

75(3)   An application under sub-paragraph (2) must allege that the administrator–

(a)   has misapplied or retained money or other property of the company,

(b)   has become accountable for money or other property of the company,

(c)   has breached a fiduciary or other duty in relation to the company, or

    (d)   has been guilty of misfeasance.

75(4)   On an examination under this paragraph into a person's conduct the court may order him–

    (a)   to repay, restore or account for money or property;

    (b)   to pay interest;

    (c)   to contribute a sum to the company's property by way of compensation for breach of duty or misfeasance.

75(5)   In sub-paragraph (3) **"administrator"** includes a person who purports or has purported to be a company's administrator.

75(6)   An application under sub-paragraph (2) may be made in respect of an administrator who has been discharged under paragraph 98 only with the permission of the court.

GENERAL NOTE

The "misfeasance" section applicable generally in corporate insolvency proceedings is s.212. In the Act as originally drafted, an administrator was listed in s.212(1)(b) as an office-holder who could be made accountable under the section. All references to an administrator have been removed from s.212 by EA 2002 s.278 and Sch.26, and the present paragraph will now apply instead to an administrator appointed under the new regime. The main difference from s.212 is that it is not necessary that the company should be in liquidation. The only other change of significance appears to be the inclusion of a person who has purported to be an administrator. In other respects, the notes to s.212 may be treated as applicable.

ENDING ADMINISTRATION

Automatic end of administration

76(1)   The appointment of an administrator shall cease to have effect at the end of the period of one year beginning with the date on which it takes effect.

76(2)   But–

    (a)   on the application of an administrator the court may by order extend his term of office for a specified period, and

    (b)   an administrator's term of office may be extended for a specified period not exceeding six months by consent.

GENERAL NOTE

Paragraphs 76–86 deal with the ending, or termination, of an administration. However, in these provisions the draftsman prefers to refer to "the appointment of an administrator ceasing to have effect", in keeping with the definition in para.1(2).

    The automatic termination of an administration after one year is a novel feature introduced by the 2002 reforms, emphasising the legislature's concern that matters should be dealt with expeditiously that is also reflected in para.4. The administration may, however, be extended by court order or (subject to a limit of six months) by consent of the creditors in accordance with para.78. The factors relied on by the court in granting an extension of the administration are discussed by Ridgway, (2005) Insolv. Int. 25 at 28. An extension was granted in *Re Top Marques Car Rental* [2006] EWHC 746 (Ch); [2006] B.P.I.R. 1328. In *Re Taylor Made Foods plc* (unreported, February 28, 2010) the term of office of the administrators had terminated at a weekend. Henderson J. allowed an application for an extension under paras 76 and 77(1)(b) to be made on the Monday, the next day that the Court Office was open.

    In *Dear IP* (October 2008, p.1.28) attention is drawn to the practice of including among the administrator's proposals a "blanket resolution" authorising the administrator to extend the period of the administration without calling a further meeting. The Insolvency Service expresses the view that this practice is questionable and that such a provision should only be included in cases where it is "necessary" (within r.2.33(2)(q)). This could be so where it is reasonably foreseeable that the administration may need to run for more than 12 months, e.g. where there are large book debt collections which cannot realistically be completed within a year.

Rules 2.110–2.112 apply in regard to paras 76–78.

77(1)   An order of the court under paragraph 76–

(a)   may be made in respect of an administrator whose term of office has already been extended by order or by consent, but

(b)   may not be made after the expiry of the administrator's term of office.

77(2)   Where an order is made under paragraph 76 the administrator shall as soon as is reasonably practicable notify the registrar of companies.

77(3)   An administrator who fails without reasonable excuse to comply with sub-paragraph (2) commits an offence.

Para.77(1)

The maximum period for which an administration may be extended out of court is six months (para.76(2)(b)), and there can be only one such an extension (para.78(4)). However, the court may grant a further extension without regard to these restrictions. Even so, there can be no retrospective extension once an administrator's term of office has expired. Exceptionally, in *Re TT Industries Ltd* [2006] B.C.C. 372, H.H.J. Norris, Q.C., sitting as a deputy judge of the High Court at Birmingham, held that an extension of the administration could be ordered, notwithstanding the lapse of the administrator's appointment, where an application for extension had been made before the administration expired and there were grounds to indicate that the delay was at least in part due to the way the application had been handled by the court staff. See also *Re E-Squared Ltd* [2006] EWHC 532 (Ch); [2006] B.C.C. 379, noted below, para.83.

Para.77(2), (3)

On penalties, see s.430, para.106(2) and Sch.10.

78(1)   In paragraph 76(2)(b) **"consent"** means consent of–

(a)   each secured creditor of the company, and

(b)   if the company has unsecured debts, creditors whose debts amount to more than 50% of the company's unsecured debts, disregarding debts of any creditor who does not respond to an invitation to give or withhold consent.

78(2)   But where the administrator has made a statement under paragraph 52(1)(b) "consent" means–

(a)   consent of each secured creditor of the company, or

(b)   if the administrator thinks that a distribution may be made to preferential creditors, consent of–

     (i)   each secured creditor of the company, and

     (ii)   preferential creditors whose debts amount to more than 50% of the preferential debts of the company, disregarding debts of any creditor who does not respond to an invitation to give or withhold consent.

78(3)   Consent for the purposes of paragraph 76(2)(b) may be–

(a)   written, or

(b)   signified at a creditors' meeting.

78(4)   An administrator's term of office–

(a)   may be extended by consent only once,

(b)   may not be extended by consent after extension by order of the court, and

(c)   may not be extended by consent after expiry.

78(5)   Where an administrator's term of office is extended by consent he shall as soon as is reasonably practicable–

    (a)   file notice of the extension with the court, and

    (b)   notify the registrar of companies.

78(6)   An administrator who fails without reasonable excuse to comply with sub-paragraph (5) commits an offence.

Para.78(1)–(3)

Paragraph 78 defines "consent" in various ways for the purposes of the one-off extension of an administration which can be made out of court under para.76(2)(b). The alternatives depend on whether the administrator has included in his proposals a statement under para.52(1)(b) that he thinks that the company has insufficient property to enable a distribution to be made to unsecured creditors (other than what they might be entitled to under the "prescribed part" provisions of s.176A). If he has not, and the company has unsecured creditors, the consent must be that of each secured creditor of the company and over 50 per cent in value of the company's unsecured creditors. If he has made such a statement, the consent must be *either* that of each secured creditor of the company *or*, if the administrator thinks that a distribution may be made to the company's preferential creditors, the consent of each secured creditor and over 50 per cent in value of the preferential creditors. There are thus three possible scenarios. The debts of creditors who abstain or choose not to respond are ignored. Consent may be obtained either at a creditors' meeting or in writing (which may be in electronic form: s.436B) from each individual creditor.

Para.78(4)

Note these further limitations on the power to extend an administration by consent.

Para.78(5), (6)

On penalties, see s.430, para.106(2) and Sch.10.

Court ending administration on application of administrator

79(1)   On the application of the administrator of a company the court may provide for the appointment of an administrator of the company to cease to have effect from a specified time.

79(2)   The administrator of a company shall make an application under this paragraph if–

    (a)   he thinks the purpose of administration cannot be achieved in relation to the company,

    (b)   he thinks the company should not have entered administration, or

    (c)   a creditors' meeting requires him to make an application under this paragraph.

79(3)   The administrator of a company shall make an application under this paragraph if–

    (a)   the administration is pursuant to an administration order, and

    (b)   the administrator thinks that the purpose of administration has been sufficiently achieved in relation to the company.

79(4)   On an application under this paragraph the court may–

    (a)   adjourn the hearing conditionally or unconditionally;

    (b)   dismiss the application;

    (c)   make an interim order;

    (d)   make any order it thinks appropriate (whether in addition to, in consequence of or instead of the order applied for).

GENERAL NOTE

This paragraph deals with the ending of the administration by order of the court. Paragraph 79(2) applies in all administrations, while para.79(3) is applicable only where the administrator was appointed by the court.
   Rules 2.114 and 2.116 apply in this case.

Para.79(2)
It appears that in these three situations the administrator *must* make an application. But he may also do so in other circumstances, e.g. where the administration is to be replaced by a compulsory liquidation, as in *Re J Smiths Haulage Ltd* [2007] B.C.C. 135. *Re TM Kingdom Ltd* [2007] B.C.C. 480 confirms that the jurisdiction under para.79(1) is not confined to the situations listed in para.79(2), (3). One reason why a company might fall within para.79(2)(b) would be if it is proved to have been solvent all along.

Para.79(3)
If the administrator was appointed by the court, the administration can only be terminated under this paragraph. If he was appointed out of court and he thinks that the purpose of the administration has been sufficiently achieved, he may follow the alternative procedure under para.80.

Termination of administration where objective achieved

80(1) This paragraph applies where an administrator of a company is appointed under paragraph 14 or 22.

80(2) If the administrator thinks that the purpose of administration has been sufficiently achieved in relation to the company he may file a notice in the prescribed form–

    (a) with the court, and

    (b) with the registrar of companies.

80(3) The administrator's appointment shall cease to have effect when the requirements of sub-paragraph (2) are satisfied.

80(4) Where the administrator files a notice he shall within the prescribed period send a copy to every creditor of the company of whose claim and address he is aware.

80(5) The rules may provide that the administrator is taken to have complied with sub-paragraph (4) if before the end of the prescribed period he publishes in the prescribed manner a notice undertaking to provide a copy of the notice under sub-paragraph (2) to any creditor of the company who applies in writing to a specified address.

80(6) An administrator who fails without reasonable excuse to comply with sub-paragraph (4) commits an offence.

GENERAL NOTE

Where the administrator has been appointed out of court and he thinks that he has sufficiently achieved the objective of the administration, this paragraph provides a simple and informal way for him to sign off and bring the administration to an end.
    Rules 2.110 and 2.113 apply, and Form 2.32B is prescribed.

Para.80(1)–(5)
The notice must be sent to creditors (or published under para.80(5)) within five business days (r.2.113(5)). The obligation to notify creditors ensures that any of them who disagree with the administrator's decision may take appropriate action, but this will necessarily only happen after the administration has been terminated pursuant to para.80(3) and it would appear that the court has no power to reinstate the administration.

Para.80(6)
On penalties, see s.430, para.106(2) and Sch.10.

Court ending administration on application of creditor

81(1) On the application of a creditor of a company the court may provide for the appointment of an administrator of the company to cease to have effect at a specified time.

81(2)   An application under this paragraph must allege an improper motive–

(a)   in the case of an administrator appointed by administration order, on the part of the applicant for the order, or

(b)   in any other case, on the part of the person who appointed the administrator.

81(3)   On an application under this paragraph the court may–

(a)   adjourn the hearing conditionally or unconditionally;

(b)   dismiss the application;

(c)   make an interim order;

(d)   make any order it thinks appropriate (whether in addition to, in consequence of or instead of the order applied for).

GENERAL NOTE

A creditor may apply to the court to have the administration terminated, but only on the limited grounds set out in para.81(2). Rule 2.115 applies.

Public interest winding-up

82(1)   This paragraph applies where a winding-up order is made for the winding up of a company in administration on a petition presented under–

(a)   section 124A (public interest), or

(aa) section 124B (SEs),

(b)   section 367 of the Financial Services and Markets Act 2000 (c. 8) (petition by Financial Services Authority).

82(2)   This paragraph also applies where a provisional liquidator of a company in administration is appointed following the presentation of a petition under any of the provisions listed in sub-paragraph (1).

82(3)   The court shall order–

(a)   that the appointment of the administrator shall cease to have effect, or

(b)   that the appointment of the administrator shall continue to have effect.

82(4)   If the court makes an order under sub-paragraph (3)(b) it may also–

(a)   specify which of the powers under this Schedule are to be exercisable by the administrator, and

(b)   order that this Schedule shall have effect in relation to the administrator with specified modifications.

GENERAL NOTE

It is only where a winding-up order is made, or a provisional liquidator appointed, on public interest grounds under one of the provisions mentioned in para.82(1) that an administrator can hold office concurrently with a liquidator or provisional liquidator: see para.40(2). The court is here given power either to terminate the administration or to allow it to continue and allocate responsibilities between the two office-holders.

Paragraph 82(1)(aa) was inserted by the European Public Limited-Liability Company Regulations 2004 (SI 2004/2326) reg.73(4)(c), as from October 8, 2004.

Moving from administration to creditors' voluntary liquidation

83(1)   This paragraph applies in England and Wales where the administrator of a company thinks–

(a)   that the total amount which each secured creditor of the company is likely to receive has been paid to him or set aside for him, and

(b)   that a distribution will be made to unsecured creditors of the company (if there are any).

83(2)   This paragraph applies in Scotland where the administrator of a company thinks–

(a)   that each secured creditor of the company will receive payment in respect of his debt, and

(b)   that a distribution will be made to unsecured creditors (if there are any).

83(3)   The administrator may send to the registrar of companies a notice that this paragraph applies.

83(4)   On receipt of a notice under sub-paragraph (3) the registrar shall register it.

83(5)   If an administrator sends a notice under sub-paragraph (3) he shall as soon as is reasonably practicable–

(a)   file a copy of the notice with the court, and

(b)   send a copy of the notice to each creditor of whose claim and address he is aware.

83(6)   On the registration of a notice under sub-paragraph (3)–

(a)   the appointment of an administrator in respect of the company shall cease to have effect, and

(b)   the company shall be wound up as if a resolution for voluntary winding up under section 84 were passed on the day on which the notice is registered.

83(7)   The liquidator for the purposes of the winding up shall be–

(a)   a person nominated by the creditors of the company in the prescribed manner and within the prescribed period, or

(b)   if no person is nominated under paragraph (a), the administrator.

83(8)   In the application of Part IV to a winding up by virtue of this paragraph–

(a)   section 85 shall not apply,

(b)   section 86 shall apply as if the reference to the time of the passing of the resolution for voluntary winding up were a reference to the beginning of the date of registration of the notice under sub-paragraph (3),

(c)   section 89 does not apply,

(d)   sections 98, 99 and 100 shall not apply,

(e)   section 129 shall apply as if the reference to the time of the passing of the resolution for voluntary winding up were a reference to the beginning of the date of registration of the notice under sub-paragraph (3), and

(f)   any creditors' committee which is in existence immediately before the company ceases to be in administration shall continue in existence after that time as if appointed as a liquidation committee under section 101.

GENERAL NOTE

Under the original Pt II of IA 1986 it is possible for a company to move more or less seamlessly from administration to compulsory winding up, but various obstacles stand in the way of a move to voluntary liquidation, which have only been overcome with some difficulty: see the note to s.*18(1),(2)*. In the new regime these obstacles are eliminated, and a straightforward procedure is laid down by the present provision to facilitate such a move. Paragraph 83(1), (2) lays down preconditions: first, provision must have been made to ensure that all secured creditors will be paid off and secondly, after that, there must be something remaining available for the unsecured creditors. The simple act of filing a notice with the registrar of companies is then all that is needed to transform the administration into a creditors' voluntary winding up, with an insolvency practitioner chosen by the creditors or the former administrator as liquidator (para.83 (6)(a), (7)). Necessarily, a certain amount of "deeming" is required to take account of the fact that this creditors' voluntary liquidation has not come into being by the usual procedure.

In *Re E-Squared Ltd* [2006] EWHC 532 (Ch); [2006] 1 W.L.R. 3414; [2006] B.C.C. 379 the administrators had sent the notices under para.83 to the registrar while they were still in office but the notices were not registered until after a date when their appointments had ceased to have effect. It was held that the companies had been wound up on the date of registration and that the (by then) former administrators were its liquidators.

This procedure is available whether the administrator has been appointed by the court or out of court. It is not necessary for a court-appointed administrator to seek any order of the court (e.g. under para.79) beforehand: the decision to send a notice under para.83(3) rests entirely at his discretion (*Re Ballast plc* [2004] EWHC 2356 (Ch); [2005] B.C.C. 96). Where the administrator was appointed by court order, he must, however, seek an order if he wishes to obtain his discharge.

Where a company enters administration before April 6, 2010 and is converted into a creditors' involuntary liquidation on or after that date the amendments to IR 1986 made by I(A)R 2010 will apply, providing for progress reports and removing the requirements to hold annual meetings: see I(A)R (No.2) 2010 r.13. Rule 2.117A applies.

Para.83(6)(b)
The draftsman has used the phrase "on the day" rather than "at the time" (as in s.86). The winding up will therefore be deemed to have commenced as from the preceding midnight: see the note to s.86.

Para.83(7)
The appointment, if made by the creditors, follows the procedure in r.2.33(2)(m) or r.2.45(2)(g), and takes effect by the creditors approving the administrator's proposals or revised proposals (r.2.117A(4)).

Moving from administration to dissolution

84(1)   If the administrator of a company thinks that the company has no property which might permit a distribution to its creditors, he shall send a notice to that effect to the registrar of companies.

84(2)   The court may on the application of the administrator of a company disapply sub-paragraph (1) in respect of the company.

84(3)   On receipt of a notice under sub-paragraph (1) the registrar shall register it.

84(4)   On the registration of a notice in respect of a company under sub-paragraph (1) the appointment of an administrator of the company shall cease to have effect.

84(5)   If an administrator sends a notice under sub-paragraph (1) he shall as soon as is reasonably practicable–

(a)   file a copy of the notice with the court, and

(b)   send a copy of the notice to each creditor of whose claim and address he is aware.

84(6)   At the end of the period of three months beginning with the date of registration of a notice in respect of a company under sub-paragraph (1) the company is deemed to be dissolved.

84(7)   On an application in respect of a company by the administrator or another interested person the court may–

(a)   extend the period specified in sub-paragraph (6),

(b)   suspend that period, or

(c)   disapply sub-paragraph (6).

84(8)   Where an order is made under sub-paragraph (7) in respect of a company the administrator shall as soon as is reasonably practicable notify the registrar of companies.

84(9) An administrator commits an offence if he fails without reasonable excuse to comply with sub-paragraph (5).

GENERAL NOTE

This is a new provision which has no counterpart in the original IA 1986 Pt II. It is modelled on the "early dissolution" procedure (ss.202–204) that enables a company in compulsory liquidation to move to dissolution without further formality if it has no assets worth realising. All that is required is for the administrator to send the requisite notice to the registrar of companies and notify the court and the creditors. Unless the court orders otherwise under para.84(7), dissolution follows automatically three months later.

Para.84(1), (2)
It would appear from the wording of these subparagraphs, taken together, that once the administrator has reached a conclusion that the property is insufficient he has no discretion to do otherwise than proceed to a dissolution: only the court can determine that the administration should continue. One situation where this might be appropriate would be where there are circumstances suggesting misconduct which require investigation.

Although on a first reading this paragraph would appear to apply only in the case where there never has been property of the company in the hands of the administrator which would permit a distribution to its creditors, it has come to be used in practice as a convenient exit route from administration after the administrator has distributed such assets as he has been able to and there is nothing more in his hands—in other words, para.84(1) is read as if it included the words "or no remaining property which might permit a further distribution to its creditors". This practice has received the blessing of the Insolvency Service: see *Dear IP*, March 2005, para.6 and endorsement by the courts: *Re Preston & Duckworth Ltd* [2006] B.C.C. 133; *Re GHE Realisations Ltd* [2005] EWHC 2400 (Ch); [2006] 1 W.L.R. 287; [2006] B.C.C. 139.

Paragraph 84 applies to both court-appointed and out-of-court administrations, and no court order is necessary at any stage (*Re Ballast plc* [2004] EWHC 2356 (Ch); [2005] B.C.C. 96).

Rule 2.117A applies, and Form 2.34B is prescribed for the notice.

Para.84(4)
The administration comes to an end on registration. There would appear to be no power to reinstate the administration once this has been done.

Para.84(6)
Should it be necessary to revive the company (e.g. if unknown assets belonging to the company come to light), CA 2006 ss.1029 et seq. empowers the court to declare the dissolution void and restore the company to the register if application is made within the ensuing six years.

Para.84(7)
The powers of the court under this subparagraph apply only to para.84(6), i.e. to the anticipated dissolution of the company, and not to the ending of the administration under para.84(4).

Para.84(8), (9)
Form 2.36B should be used. On penalties, see s.430, para.106(2) and Sch.10.

Discharge of administration order where administration ends

85(1) This paragraph applies where–

(a) the court makes an order under this Schedule providing for the appointment of an administrator of a company to cease to have effect, and

(b) the administrator was appointed by administration order.

85(2) The court shall discharge the administration order.

GENERAL NOTE

This paragraph applies only where the administrator was appointed by court order. Under the original Pt II, it is the discharge of the order which brings the administration to an end. Under Sch.B1, the sequence is reversed.

Notice to Companies Registrar where administration ends

86(1) This paragraph applies where the court makes an order under this Schedule providing for the appointment of an administrator to cease to have effect.

86(2) The administrator shall send a copy of the order to the registrar of companies within the period of 14 days beginning with the date of the order.

86(3) An administrator who fails without reasonable excuse to comply with sub-paragraph (2) commits an offence.

GENERAL NOTE

This provision, again, is not concerned with the situation where an individual administrator ceases to hold office, but with the termination of the administration itself. In contrast with para.85, it is not confined to the case of an administrator appointed by the court: there are other provisions (e.g. para.81) empowering the court to order that an administration should come to an end.

Rule 2.116 applies, and Form 2.33B is prescribed.

Para.86(3)
On penalties, see s.430, para.106(2) and Sch.10.

REPLACING ADMINISTRATOR

Resignation of administrator

87(1) An administrator may resign only in prescribed circumstances.

87(2) Where an administrator may resign he may do so only–

(a) in the case of an administrator appointed by administration order, by notice in writing to the court,

(b) in the case of an administrator appointed under paragraph 14, by notice in writing to the holder of the floating charge by virtue of which the appointment was made,

(c) in the case of an administrator appointed under paragraph 22(1), by notice in writing to the company, or

(d) in the case of an administrator appointed under paragraph 22(2), by notice in writing to the directors of the company.

GENERAL NOTE

The circumstances in which an administrator may resign his office are prescribed by r.2.119. Forms 2.37B and 2.38B (respectively) are to be used for the notice of intention to resign and the notice of resignation: see rr.2.120–121, which give further details regarding the giving of notice and its filing with the court and the registrar of companies.

On the question when a notice of resignation takes effect, see the note to s.19(1).

Removal of administrator from office

88 The court may by order remove an administrator from office.

GENERAL NOTE

This provision applies to any administrator under the new regime, however appointed. Both the administration itself, and the office of administrator, continue in being: see para.1(2)(d). An application under this provision and para.74 succeeded in *Clydesdale Financial Services Ltd v Smailes* [2009] EWHC 1745 (Ch); [2009] B.C.C. 810 but failed in *SISU Capital Fund Ltd v Tucker* [2005] EWHC 2170 and 2321 (Ch); [2006] B.C.C. 463. For a subsequent application, see *Clydesdale Financial Services v Smailes* [2009] EWHC 1745 (Ch). Costs may be awarded against the administrator: *Coyne v DRC Distribution Ltd* [2008] EWCA Civ 488; [2008] B.C.C. 612. Rule 2.122 applies.

Administrator ceasing to be qualified

89(1)   The administrator of a company shall vacate office if he ceases to be qualified to act as an insolvency practitioner in relation to the company.

89(2)   Where an administrator vacates office by virtue of sub-paragraph (1) he shall give notice in writing–

(a)   in the case of an administrator appointed by administration order, to the court,

(b)   in the case of an administrator appointed under paragraph 14, to the holder of the floating charge by virtue of which the appointment was made,

(c)   in the case of an administrator appointed under paragraph 22(1), to the company, or

(d)   in the case of an administrator appointed under paragraph 22(2), to the directors of the company.

89(3)   An administrator who fails without reasonable excuse to comply with sub-paragraph (2) commits an offence.

GENERAL NOTE

An administrator will "cease to be qualified to act" in relation to the company if at any time he fails to meet the criteria set out in s.390. "Shall vacate office" may be read as meaning either something that happens automatically or something which depends on the administrator taking action to step aside. It is probably the former that is intended, the giving of notice under para.89(2) being merely consequential.

Notice must also be given to the registrar of companies, using Form 2.39B (r.2.123).

Para.89(3)
On penalties, see s.390, para.106(2) and Sch.10.

Supplying vacancy in office of administrator

90   Paragraphs 91 to 95 apply where an administrator–

(a)   dies,

(b)   resigns,

(c)   is removed from office under paragraph 88, or

(d)   vacates office under paragraph 89.

GENERAL NOTE

Paragraphs 91–95 apply only if the office of administrator has become vacant. The substitution of one administrator by another is dealt with in paras 96–97, and the appointment of one or more additional administrators in paras 100–103.

Rules 2.12 et seq. apply in these cases.

91(1)   Where the administrator was appointed by administration order, the court may replace the administrator on an application under this sub-paragraph made by–

(a)   a creditors' committee of the company,

(b)   the company,

(c)   the directors of the company,

(d)   one or more creditors of the company, or

(e)   where more than one person was appointed to act jointly or concurrently as the administrator, any of those persons who remains in office.

91(2)   But an application may be made in reliance on sub-paragraph (1)(b) to (d) only where–

(a)   there is no creditors' committee of the company,

(b)   the court is satisfied that the creditors' committee or a remaining administrator is not taking reasonable steps to make a replacement, or

(c)   the court is satisfied that for another reason it is right for the application to be made.

GENERAL NOTE

This paragraph applies only where the administrator who has vacated office was appointed by the court. Where the administrator was appointed out of court, a replacement will normally be appointed out of court under paras 92–94, but the court has back-up and, where appropriate, overriding powers in the circumstances set out in para.95.

Rules 2.125 et seq. give details of the procedure and notification requirements.

Para.91(1)

It does not appear that the outgoing administrator may make an application under this provision. But there are situations where this would be appropriate, perhaps particularly where it is sought to replace an insolvency practitioner who holds multiple offices in a single application and appoint replacements, e.g. one or more members of the same firm, as in *Re Equity Nominees Ltd* [2000] B.C.C. 84. (On "block" transfer orders, see the note to s.171(1), (2).) The court would no doubt allow the application to be made under some other provision, e.g. para.63.

Para.91(2)

The persons listed in subparas (1)(b)–(d) must stand aside and allow the creditors' committee, if there is one, or a remaining administrator where there were joint or concurrent appointments, to have first bite at the cherry (not necessarily by applying to the court), subject to the court's discretion under para.91(2)(c).

92   Where the administrator was appointed under paragraph 14 the holder of the floating charge by virtue of which the appointment was made may replace the administrator.

GENERAL NOTE

This provision applies only where the office of administrator has become vacant: for the replacement of an administrator currently in office, see paras 87–97. The right of the holder of the floating charge to replace his own appointee is unqualified, although no doubt this could be challenged under para.95(b) if good reason could be shown.

Rules 2.126, 2.129 apply.

93(1)   Where the administrator was appointed under paragraph 22(1) by the company it may replace the administrator.

93(2)   A replacement under this paragraph may be made only–

(a)   with the consent of each person who is the holder of a qualifying floating charge in respect of the company's property, or

(b)   where consent is withheld, with the permission of the court.

GENERAL NOTE

The initial appointment of an administrator by the company under para.22(1) may be made only after giving five days' notice to the holder of a qualifying floating charge under para.26, so enabling the latter to make his own appointment instead. The present paragraph to some extent echoes para.26, giving the charge holder an opportunity to have some say in the choice of a replacement, but stops short of giving him an outright veto.

Rules 2.126, 2.129 apply.

94(1)   Where the administrator was appointed under paragraph 22(2) the directors of the company may replace the administrator.

94(2)   A replacement under this paragraph may be made only–

(a)   with the consent of each person who is the holder of a qualifying floating charge in respect of the company's property, or

(b)   where consent is withheld, with the permission of the court.

GENERAL NOTE

This provision is in similar terms to para.93. See the comment to that paragraph.

95   The court may replace an administrator on the application of a person listed in paragraph 91(1) if the court–

(a)   is satisfied that a person who is entitled to replace the administrator under any of paragraphs 92 to 94 is not taking reasonable steps to make a replacement, or

(b)   that for another reason it is right for the court to make the replacement.

GENERAL NOTE

This provision gives the court back-up powers to deal with situations of inertia or dispute. Only those persons listed in para.91(1) have standing to apply. If anyone else (e.g. an outgoing administrator) wishes to have the court make a replacement, application would have to be made under some other provision, such as para.63. Rule 2.125 applies to the application. See the note to para.91(1).
    Rules 2.126, 2.129 apply.

Substitution of administrator: competing floating charge-holder

96(1)   This paragraph applies where an administrator of a company is appointed under paragraph 14 by the holder of a qualifying floating charge in respect of the company's property.

96(2)   The holder of a prior qualifying floating charge in respect of the company's property may apply to the court for the administrator to be replaced by an administrator nominated by the holder of the prior floating charge.

96(3)   One floating charge is prior to another for the purposes of this paragraph if–

(a)   it was created first, or

(b)   it is to be treated as having priority in accordance with an agreement to which the holder of each floating charge was party.

96(4)   Sub-paragraph (3) shall have effect in relation to Scotland as if the following were substituted for paragraph (a)–

"(a) it has priority of ranking in accordance with section 464(4)(b) of the Companies Act 1985 (c. 6) [CA 2006, no equivalent],".

GENERAL NOTE

In contrast with paras 87–95, this provision appears to apply whether or not there is a vacancy in the office of administrator. It deals with the situation where an administrator is or has been in office who has been appointed by the holder of a junior-ranking floating charge. When the initial appointment was made, the charge holder making the appointment would have been required to notify or secure the consent of any senior-ranking charge holder(s) under para.15(1), and it is assumed that the latter took no steps at that time to block the appointment. The present provision allows the holder of a senior-ranking charge to apply to the court subsequently to request that a different person be appointed administrator in place of the junior charge-holder's appointee. No guidance is given to the court as to the basis on which it should exercise its discretion to accede to such a request, although prima facie the holder of a senior-ranking charge would expect the court to support his choice of nominee.
    On the meaning of "qualifying" floating charge, see para.14(2). The court would surely also require the senior-ranking charge to be enforceable at the time the application is made, in keeping with para.16, although this is not stated in para.96.
    Rules 2.126, 2.129 apply.

Substitution of administrator appointed by company or directors: creditors' meeting

97(1) This paragraph applies where–

(a) an administrator of a company is appointed by a company or directors under paragraph 22, and

(b) there is no holder of a qualifying floating charge in respect of the company's property.

97(2) A creditors' meeting may replace the administrator.

97(3) A creditors' meeting may act under sub-paragraph (2) only if the new administrator's written consent to act is presented to the meeting before the replacement is made.

GENERAL NOTE

As with para.96, this provision appears to apply whether or not there is a vacancy in the office of administrator but, in contrast with that paragraph, no application to the court is needed. If there is a vacancy, the company or the directors (as the case may be) will also have the power to appoint a replacement under paras 93 or 94, but it would make no sense for either of them to do so if there is opposition from the creditors' committee, since it could use its power under the present paragraph to override their appointment.

Rules 2.126, 2.129 apply.

Vacation of office: discharge from liability

98(1) Where a person ceases to be the administrator of a company (whether because he vacates office by reason of resignation, death or otherwise, because he is removed from office or because his appointment ceases to have effect) he is discharged from liability in respect of any action of his as administrator.

98(2) The discharge provided by sub-paragraph (1) takes effect–

(a) in the case of an administrator who dies, on the filing with the court of notice of his death,

(b) in the case of an administrator appointed under paragraph 14 or 22, at a time appointed by resolution of the creditors' committee or, if there is no committee, by resolution of the creditors, or

(c) in any case, at a time specified by the court.

98(3) For the purpose of the application of sub-paragraph (2)(b) in a case where the administrator has made a statement under paragraph 52(1)(b), a resolution shall be taken as passed if (and only if) passed with the approval of–

(a) each secured creditor of the company, or

(b) if the administrator has made a distribution to preferential creditors or thinks that a distribution may be made to preferential creditors–

(i) each secured creditor of the company, and

(ii) preferential creditors whose debts amount to more than 50% of the preferential debts of the company, disregarding debts of any creditor who does not respond to an invitation to give or withhold approval.

98(4) Discharge–

(a) applies to liability accrued before the discharge takes effect, and

(b) does not prevent the exercise of the court's powers under paragraph 75.

This provision corresponds to IA 1986 s.*20*, which applies in the original regime. It uses the expression "he is discharged from liability" instead of "he has his release", but once s.*20(2)* is taken into account, the net result appears to be the same. The comment to s.*20* may be helpful.

The phrase "the appointment of an administrator ceases to have effect" is used by the draftsman as equivalent to "the administration comes to an end" or "is terminated": see, e.g. paras 76, 80, 81. The present provision thus applies both in the case where an administrator is replaced and also where the administration has come to an end.

Para.98(1)

The discharge is not automatic, but takes effect only from the time specified in subpara.(2).

Para.98(2)

Paragraph 98(2)(c) corresponds to s.*20(1)(b)*, except that the latter states "in any *other* case". It is thus conceivable that the court could fix a time other than those mentioned in subpara.(2)(a) and (b), although the court would not normally be involved in either of these cases.

Where the administrator in question was appointed out of court under paras 14 or 22, it is left to the creditors' committee or creditors to decide when the discharge should take effect. There is some parallel with s.173, which deals with the release of a liquidator in a voluntary winding up, but there is no provision in the present paragraph for the relevant meeting to resolve against a discharge. If the meeting is unwilling to set a date from which the discharge is to take effect, and the contention above is correct, recourse could be had to the court to resolve the matter.

Para.98(3)

Paragraph 52(1)(b) applies where the administrator thinks that the company has insufficient property to enable a distribution to be made to the company's unsecured creditors (apart from anything they may get through the "prescribed part" provisions of s.176A). In such circumstances it is inappropriate that the decision on the administrator's discharge should be in the hands of the creditors' committee or the creditors at large, most of whom will have no interest in the outcome of the administration: hence the need for the consents required by this sub-paragraph.

Para.98(4)

See the note to s.*20(2), (3)*.

Vacation of office: charges and liabilities

99(1) This paragraph applies where a person ceases to be the administrator of a company (whether because he vacates office by reason of resignation, death or otherwise, because he is removed from office or because his appointment ceases to have effect).

99(2) In this paragraph–

> **"the former administrator"** means the person referred to in sub-paragraph (1), and

> **"cessation"** means the time when he ceases to be the company's administrator.

99(3) The former administrator's remuneration and expenses shall be–

    (a) charged on and payable out of property of which he had custody or control immediately before cessation, and

    (b) payable in priority to any security to which paragraph 70 applies.

99(4) A sum payable in respect of a debt or liability arising out of a contract entered into by the former administrator or a predecessor before cessation shall be–

    (a) charged on and payable out of property of which the former administrator had custody or control immediately before cessation, and

    (b) payable in priority to any charge arising under sub-paragraph (3).

99(5) Sub-paragraph (4) shall apply to a liability arising under a contract of employment which was adopted by the former administrator or a predecessor before cessation; and for that purpose–

(a) action taken within the period of 14 days after an administrator's appointment shall not be taken to amount or contribute to the adoption of a contract,

(b) no account shall be taken of a liability which arises, or in so far as it arises, by reference to anything which is done or which occurs before the adoption of the contract of employment, and

(c) no account shall be taken of a liability to make a payment other than wages or salary.

99(6) In sub-paragraph (5)(c) **"wages or salary"** includes–

(a) a sum payable in respect of a period of holiday (for which purpose the sum shall be treated as relating to the period by reference to which the entitlement to holiday accrued),

(b) a sum payable in respect of a period of absence through illness or other good cause,

(c) a sum payable in lieu of holiday,

(d) in respect of a period, a sum which would be treated as earnings for that period for the purposes of an enactment about social security, and

(e) a contribution to an occupational pension scheme.

GENERAL NOTE

This provision broadly corresponds to s.*19(4)–(10)*, including the reforms made by IA 1994 in consequence of the ruling of the Court of Appeal in *Powdrill v Watson; Re Paramount Airways Ltd (No.3)* [1994] 2 All E.R. 513; [1994] B.C.C. 172. Note that although the paragraph is expressed to apply only where a person ceases to be the administrator, it is well recognised that many of the payments referred to will, in the ordinary case, be paid in the course of the administration: see the note to s.*19(3)–(6)*. Note, however, that under the original administration regime there was no provision in the rules corresponding to r.2.67, and certain decisions under the former law have not been followed in cases under the new Sch.B1 regime: see the notes to para.99(3)–(4) below and r.2.67.

In *Re Lafayette Electronics Europe Ltd* [2006] EWHC 1005, 1006 (Ch); [2007] B.C.C. 890 the administration had, by an oversight, been allowed to expire at a time when the administrators' fees were outstanding. H.H.J. Norris Q.C. approved an application by the administrators for them to be appointed provisional liquidators pending the hearing of a winding-up petition which they had presented as creditors in respect of the petition. The only qualification made was that they should have no power to sanction their own fees and to decide upon their own release.

On the effect in this context of the ruling of the House of Lords in *Re Leyland DAF Ltd, Buchler v Talbot* [2004] UKHL 9; [2004] 2 A.C. 298; [2004] B.C.C. 214 and its reversal by statute, see the note to para.65.

Para.99(3)–(4)
In *Exeter City Council v Bairstow* [2007] EWHC 400 (Ch); [2007] B.C.C. 236 (the *"Trident Fashions"* case) David Richards J. drew attention to the differences between the provisions governing an administrator's expenses and disbursements under s.*19* and those in the new regime, to which the present paragraph and r.2.67 apply. (There is no corresponding rule where s.*19* applies.) In particular, an administrator's liability to defray non-domestic rates levied against the company were held to be necessary disbursements (and thus entitled to priority), in contrast with the position under s.*19*. The rates with which that case was concerned had been levied in respect of premises occupied by the company while in administration. The decision has left the question regarding the priority accorded to such rates in a somewhat paradoxical situation. Rates accruing on premises occupied by a company while in liquidation are payable as an expense of the liquidation: *Re Toshoku Finance (UK) plc* [2002] UKHL 6; [2002] 1 W.L.R. 671; [2002] B.C.C. 110. If the company is in administration under the original Pt II, the rates were not payable as an expense of the administration: *Freakley v Centre Reinsurance International Co* [2006] UKHL 45; [2006] 1 W.L.R. 2863; [2006] B.C.C. 971. If, however, the company is in administration under Sch.B1, the position is the same as in a liquidation and the rates rank as an expense of the administration by virtue of r.2.67. But, following the decision, the position was less clear in relation to rates payable on unoccupied property. These were not payable in a liquidation by virtue of the special exemption conferred by the Non-Domestic Rating (Unoccupied Property) Regulations 1989 (SI 1989/2261). In the absence of any comparable legislative exemption, David Richards J. in *Exeter City Council v Bairstow* expressed the view that these also had priority as an expense of a Sch.B1 administration under r.2.67. This observation gave rise to considerable concern and has led to a change in the law, bringing administration into line with liquidation. By the Non-Domestic Rating (Unoccupied Property) (England) Regulations 2008 (SI 2008/386, effective April 1, 2008) the 1989 Regulations are revoked (in their application to England) and a new exemption regime has been introduced which applies both in a liquidation (reg.4(k)) and an administration (whether under the

Thank you for purchasing the 13th edition of **Sealy & Milman Annotated Guide to the Insolvency Legislation**

ADD SEALY & MILMAN TO YOUR WESTLAW UK SUBSCRIPTION
Sealy & Milman Annotated Guide to the Insolvency Legislation is now available as an add-on to a Westlaw UK subscription.

QUICKER ACCESS TO MORE UP-TO-DATE INFORMATION
This gives you weekly online updates to search using Westlaw UK's easy to use website. Much more than just a copy of the book online, Westlaw UK helps you join-up your research with direct links to primary law and all related materials.

START YOUR FREE TRIAL TODAY
Sign-up for a Free Trial today and see the way that having the most current information can help you make a difference.

Complete your details below and a member of our Customer Support Team will be in touch to discuss your requirements.

Please note we are unable to offer free trials to students. If you would like to access Westlaw UK, please contact your Law Librarian.

WESTLAW UK FREE TRIAL
I would like a free trial of:

☐ **Westlaw UK and Sealy & Milman Annotated Guide to the Insolvency Legislation**

☐ **Sealy & Milman Annotated Guide to the Insolvency Legislation added to my Westlaw UK subscription**

OTHER SWEET & MAXWELL SERVICES
I am also interested in the following Sweet & Maxwell online services:

☐ **Lawtel**

☐ **Lawtel Precedents**

☐ **Localaw UK**

☐ **I do not wish to receive any information about other relevant Sweet & Maxwell products and services.**

☐ **Please use my email for relevant marketing and informational material**

Title	**Name**
Organisation	
Job title	
Address	
Postcode	
Telephone	
Email	
S&M account number (if known)	
PO number	

All orders are accepted subject to the terms of this order form and our Terms of Trading (see www.sweetandmaxwell.co.uk). By submitting this order form I confirm that I accept these terms and I am authorised to sign on behalf of the customer.

Signed	**Job Title**
Print Name	**Date**

(LBU004) V7EX (04.2010) SC / LV

SWEET & MAXWELL

 THOMSON REUTERS

SWEET & MAXWELL

FREEPOST

PO BOX 2000

ANDOVER

SP10 9AH

UNITED KINGDOM

original Pt II or Sch.B1) (reg.4(l)). (There is also a curious reference to IA 1986 ss.112 and 146 in reg.4(m).) For Scotland, the exemption has been extended to both administration regimes by the Non-Domestic Rating (Unoccupied Property) (Scotland) Amendment Regulations 2008 (SSI 2008/83) as from April 1, 2008 and, for Wales, by the Non-Domestic Rating (Unoccupied Property) (Wales) Regulations 2008 (SI 2008/2499 (W 217) as from November 1, 2008. See further the note to r.2.67.

Pre-administration costs approved under r.2.67A now rank along with the administrator's remuneration (r.2.67(1)(h)).

Para.99(4)

The estate for the purpose of ascertaining the respective entitlements of the creditors under the statutory charge created by this provision consists only of the property of which the former administrator had control on the date of his cessation of office. Payments already made to creditors coming within the para.99(4) description prior to that date remain undisturbed and should not be brought into account. (*Re Sports Betting Media Ltd* [2007] EWHC 2085 (Ch); [2008] B.C.C. 177.) In the case where there has been a change of administrator, the creditors entitled to the benefit of the charge under the prior administrator's term of office must pay the new administrator the reasonable cost of realising the assets constituting the fund.

Para.99(5)–(6)

The liabilities which are payable by virtue of para.99 in priority to the administrator's expenses are those liabilities which have been adopted after 14 days of appointment and which are "wages or salary". These do not include redundancy payments or unfair dismissal payments of employees who have not been kept on: *Re Allders Department Stores Ltd* [2005] EWHC 172 (Ch); [2005] B.C.C. 289 (discussed by Lyons and Birch, (2005) 18 Insolv. Int. 150); *Re Leeds United Association Football Club Ltd* [2007] EWHC 1761 (Ch); [2008] B.C.C. 11. Nor are such payments entitled to priority under r.2.67(1)(f)–(g): see the note to r.2.67.

Although the drafting of para.99 follows a different style from that of s.*19(6)–(10)*, it might have been assumed that no change of substance was intended to be made in the law, and indeed that view was confirmed by statements made in Parliament. However, in *Krasner v McMath* [2005] EWHC 1682 (Ch); [2005] B.C.C. 896, Peter Smith J. held that payments in lieu of notice and protective awards made in a redundancy situation under the Trade Union and Labour Relations Act 1992 s.188 were entitled to priority over the administrator's remuneration and expenses, in effect reversing the amendments made to s.*19* in 1994. This view was based in part on the fact that para.99(6)(d) omits the words "payable in respect of a period of holiday" which are to be found in s.*19(10)*. Happily, when the case was taken to appeal (in a joined appeal with another from the decision in *Re Ferrotech Ltd and Re Granville Technology Group Ltd* [2005] EWHC 1848 (Ch); [2005] B.C.C. 905, in which Etherton J. had declined to follow this ruling), the Court of Appeal held that (subject to a minor exception where the employee is required to take "garden leave") neither payments in lieu of notice nor protective awards have such priority: see *Re Huddersfield Fine Worsteds Ltd, Re Ferrotech Ltd and Re Granville Technology Group Ltd* [2005] EWCA Civ 1072; [2005] B.C.C. 915. In particular, protective awards are excluded because they arise under statute and not under the contract of employment. (On protective awards, see also *Haine v Day* [2008] EWCA Civ 626; [2008] 2 B.C.L.C. 517 and the note to r.13.12.)

GENERAL

Joint and concurrent administrators

100(1)   In this Schedule–

(a)   a reference to the appointment of an administrator of a company includes a reference to the appointment of a number of persons to act jointly or concurrently as the administrator of a company, and

(b)   a reference to the appointment of a person as administrator of a company includes a reference to the appointment of a person as one of a number of persons to act jointly or concurrently as the administrator of a company.

100(2)   The appointment of a number of persons to act as administrator of a company must specify–

(a)   which functions (if any) are to be exercised by the persons appointed acting jointly, and

(b)   which functions (if any) are to be exercised by any or all of the persons appointed.

GENERAL NOTE

It is well established that expressions in the singular in legislation are to be read as including the plural (Interpretation Act 1978 s.6), but this and the ensuing paragraphs go further, providing that where an appointment is made of more than one person as administrators, they may empowered to act either jointly or concurrently, identifying the functions which each may exercise. Note that the Act does not require the appointment, as such, to be of administrators empowered to act either jointly or concurrently in everything that they do—although these options are permitted. Rather, the appointment must name the persons as administrators and then specify which functions are to be exercised jointly and which may be exercised by any or all (or fewer than all, e.g. authorising cheques to be signed by any two): para.100(2).

Rule 2.127 applies where a joint administrator is appointed.

101(1)   This paragraph applies where two or more persons are appointed to act jointly as the administrator of a company.

101(2)   A reference to the administrator of the company is a reference to those persons acting jointly.

101(3)   But a reference to the administrator of a company in paragraphs 87 to 99 of this Schedule is a reference to any or all of the persons appointed to act jointly.

101(4)   Where an offence of omission is committed by the administrator, each of the persons appointed to act jointly–

(a)   commits the offence, and

(b)   may be proceeded against and punished individually.

101(5)   The reference in paragraph 45(1)(a) to the name of the administrator is a reference to the name of each of the persons appointed to act jointly.

101(6)   Where persons are appointed to act jointly in respect of only some of the functions of the administrator of a company, this paragraph applies only in relation to those functions.

GENERAL NOTE

It would be an affront to the intelligence of the reader to add any comment to the astonishing verbosity of this paragraph.

102(1)   This paragraph applies where two or more persons are appointed to act concurrently as the administrator of a company.

102(2)   A reference to the administrator of a company in this Schedule is a reference to any of the persons appointed (or any combination of them).

GENERAL NOTE

For the position where administrators are appointed to act jointly, see para.101.

103(1)   Where a company is in administration, a person may be appointed to act as administrator jointly or concurrently with the person or persons acting as the administrator of the company.

103(2)   Where a company entered administration by administration order, an appointment under sub-paragraph (1) must be made by the court on the application of–

(a)   a person or group listed in paragraph 12(1)(a) to (e), or

(b)   the person or persons acting as the administrator of the company.

103(3)   Where a company entered administration by virtue of an appointment under paragraph 14, an appointment under sub-paragraph (1) must be made by–

(a)   the holder of the floating charge by virtue of which the appointment was made, or

(b)   the court on the application of the person or persons acting as the administrator of the company.

103(4) Where a company entered administration by virtue of an appointment under paragraph 22(1), an appointment under sub-paragraph (1) above must be made either by the court on the application of the person or persons acting as the administrator of the company or–

(a) by the company, and

(b) with the consent of each person who is the holder of a qualifying floating charge in respect of the company's property or, where consent is withheld, with the permission of the court.

103(5) Where a company entered administration by virtue of an appointment under paragraph 22(2), an appointment under sub-paragraph (1) must be made either by the court on the application of the person or persons acting as the administrator of the company or–

(a) by the directors of the company, and

(b) with the consent of each person who is the holder of a qualifying floating charge in respect of the company's property or, where consent is withheld, with the permission of the court.

103(6) An appointment under sub-paragraph (1) may be made only with the consent of the person or persons acting as the administrator of the company.

GENERAL NOTE

There may be situations in which it is thought advisable or necessary to appoint one or more additional administrators to act jointly or concurrently with the administrator(s) already in office: the task may call for more manpower than was originally envisaged, or a creditor who holds a "qualifying" floating charge may feel happier if his own appointee joins the person or persons already in office who have been appointed by somebody else. This paragraph spells out the procedure to be followed. The court has overall control but, subject to that, deference must be shown to floating charge holders. Since the administrator currently in office may have an interest in what is proposed, he is given standing to apply to the court and also a veto on the proposed appointment.

Para.103(6)
This provision applies in each of the cases covered by para.103(2)–(5). It ensures that anyone already in office is not to have wished on to him a newcomer that he does not feel happy to work with—even where the new appointment is made by the court.

Presumption of validity

104 An act of the administrator of a company is valid in spite of a defect in his appointment or qualification.

GENERAL NOTE

This is a standard provision, which under the original Pt II is catered for by s.232: see the note to that section. However, it may not be relied on where the appointment was a nullity (e.g. because the correct procedure had not been followed); but the difficulty may be overcome if the court makes an order for the administrator to be appointed with retrospective effect: *Re G-Tech Construction Ltd* [2007] B.P.I.R. 1275.

Majority decision of directors

105 A reference in this Schedule to something done by the directors of a company includes a reference to the same thing done by a majority of the directors of a company.

GENERAL NOTE

This is a novel and welcome provision: references in earlier legislation to an act done by the directors have been construed as requiring either that the directors should act unanimously or that a meeting be duly convened at which a decision is reached by the requisite majority: see the notes to ss.9(1) and 124(1). Under the present provision a meeting is not required.

Penalties

106(1)   A person who is guilty of an offence under this Schedule is liable to a fine (in accordance with section 430 and Schedule 10).

106(2)   A person who is guilty of an offence under any of the following paragraphs of this Schedule is liable to a daily default fine (in accordance with section 430 and Schedule 10)–

(a)   paragraph 20,

(b)   paragraph 32,

(c)   paragraph 46,

(d)   paragraph 48,

(e)   paragraph 49,

(f)   paragraph 51,

(g)   paragraph 53,

(h)   paragraph 54,

(i)   paragraph 56,

(j)   paragraph 71,

(k)   paragraph 72,

(l)   paragraph 77,

(m)   paragraph 78,

(n)   paragraph 80,

(o)   paragraph 84,

(p)   paragraph 86, and

(q)   paragraph 89.

GENERAL NOTE

For the amounts payable as fines for each of these offences, see Sch.10 and comments.

Extension of time limit

107(1)   Where a provision of this Schedule provides that a period may be varied in accordance with this paragraph, the period may be varied in respect of a company–

(a)   by the court, and

(b)   on the application of the administrator.

107(2)   A time period may be extended in respect of a company under this paragraph–

(a)   more than once, and

(b)   after expiry.

GENERAL NOTE

The scope of this paragraph is limited by the words "varied in accordance with this paragraph". Those paragraphs which refer to para.107 are paras 49, 50, 51, However, it is unlikely that this limitation would override the court's powers under more general provisions such as para.55(2)(e).

Some of the statutory time periods may also be varied by the administrator with the creditors' consent under para.108.

108(1) A period specified in paragraph 49(5), 50(1)(b) or 51(2) may be varied in respect of a company by the administrator with consent.

108(2) In sub-paragraph (1) **"consent"** means consent of–

(a) each secured creditor of the company, and

(b) if the company has unsecured debts, creditors whose debts amount to more than 50% of the company's unsecured debts, disregarding debts of any creditor who does not respond to an invitation to give or withhold consent.

108(3) But where the administrator has made a statement under paragraph 52(1)(b) "consent" means–

(a) consent of each secured creditor of the company, or

(b) if the administrator thinks that a distribution may be made to preferential creditors, consent of–

    (i) each secured creditor of the company, and

    (ii) preferential creditors whose debts amount to more than 50% of the total preferential debts of the company, disregarding debts of any creditor who does not respond to an invitation to give or withhold consent.

108(4) Consent for the purposes of sub-paragraph (1) may be–

(a) written, or

(b) signified at a creditors' meeting.

108(5) The power to extend under sub-paragraph (1)–

(a) may be exercised in respect of a period only once,

(b) may not be used to extend a period by more than 28 days,

(c) may not be used to extend a period which has been extended by the court, and

(d) may not be used to extend a period after expiry.

GENERAL NOTE

The time limits prescribed by the three paragraphs referred to may be varied by the administrator without a court order if the consent of the secured and unsecured creditors is obtained in accordance with this provision. Note the limitations imposed by para.108(5): in these cases there is no alternative but to apply to the court under para.107. Reference may be made also to the notes to paras 76–78, which are drafted in similar language.

Para.108(4)
"Written" includes the use of electronic means: s.436B.

109 Where a period is extended under paragraph 107 or 108, a reference to the period shall be taken as a reference to the period as extended.

Amendment of provision about time

110(1) The Secretary of State may by order amend a provision of this Schedule which–

(a) requires anything to be done within a specified period of time,

(b) prevents anything from being done after a specified time, or

(c) requires a specified minimum period of notice to be given.

110(2)   An order under this paragraph–

(a)   must be made by statutory instrument, and

(b)   shall be subject to annulment in pursuance of a resolution of either House of Parliament.

GENERAL NOTE

The power conferred by this paragraph will allow for adjustments to be made to time provisions specified for the new regime if they prove to be inconvenient in practice, or if it is decided as a matter of policy to set shorter time-limits in order to speed up the rescue process.

Interpretation

111(1)   In this Schedule–

"administrative receiver" has the meaning given by section 251,

"administrator" has the meaning given by paragraph 1 and, where the context requires, includes a reference to a former administrator,

"correspondence" includes correspondence by telephonic or other electronic means,

"creditors' meeting" has the meaning given by paragraph 50,

"enters administration" has the meaning given by paragraph 1,

"floating charge" means a charge which is a floating charge on its creation,

"in administration" has the meaning given by paragraph 1,

"hire-purchase agreement" includes a conditional sale agreement, a chattel leasing agreement and a retention of title agreement,

"holder of a qualifying floating charge" in respect of a company's property has the meaning given by paragraph 14,

"market value" means the amount which would be realised on a sale of property in the open market by a willing vendor,

"the purpose of administration" means an objective specified in paragraph 3, and

"unable to pay its debts" has the meaning given by section 123.

111(1A) In this Schedule, **"company"** means–

(a)   a company registered under the Companies Act 2006 in England and Wales or in Scotland,

(b)   a company incorporated in an EEA State other than the United Kingdom, or

(c)   a company not incorporated in an EEA State but having its centre of main interests in a member State other than Denmark.

111(1B) In sub-paragraph (1A), in relation to a company, **"centre of main interests"** has the same meaning as in the EC Regulation and, in the absence of proof to the contrary, is presumed to be the place of its registered office (within the meaning of that Regulation).

111(2)   [Repealed by LRO 2010 (SI 2010/18) art.4(2) (with retrospective effect).]

111(3)   In this Schedule a reference to action includes a reference to inaction.

GENERAL NOTE

The definitions here set out apply only for the purposes of the present Schedule. This limitation may create some difficulties—for instance, the word "administrator" will have one meaning for the purposes of the Schedule and another where the original s.8 applies. By way of example, does the term "a former administrator" in the definition in para.111(1) include an administrator who was appointed under s.8?

Other definitions may be found in ss.247 et seq. and 435 et seq.

Para.111(1), 111(1A), 111(1B)

Note the rather surprising extension of the scope of para.111(1A)(b) to the whole of the EEA rather than those EU Member States that are within the EC Regulation. The "additional" countries (including Denmark) are thus brought within the jurisdiction of Sch.B1, but without any need to have regard to the provisions of the EC Regulation: questions as to the COMI, whether proceedings are "main", "secondary" or "territorial", etc. do not arise. In sub-para.(c), in contrast, "member State" must refer to countries within the EU.

Paragraph 111(1) formerly contained a definition of "company" which read: " 'Company' includes a company which may enter administration by virtue of Article 3 of the EC Regulation". This definition was revoked, and paras 111(1A) and 111(1B) inserted, by the Insolvency Act 1986 (Amendment) Regulations 2005 (SI 2005/879) regs 2(1), 4(a), as from April 13, 2005, in order to reverse the effect of the ruling in *Re The Salvage Association* [2003] EWHC 1028 (Ch); [2004] 1 W.L.R. 174; [2003] B.C.C. 504 (see the note to s.8(1), (2).) It follows that a company incorporated in this jurisdiction by Royal Charter may not be put into administration under Sch.B1. In *Re Dairy Farmers of Great Britain Ltd* [2009] EWHC 1389 (Ch); [2009] Bus.L.R. 1627 it was held that Industrial and Provident Societies were not "companies" within this definition. On Northern Ireland, see Moss, (2005) 18 Insolv. Int. 107; but quaere whether this view is consistent with *Re Brownridge Plastics Ltd*, referred to in the Introductory note to Schedule B1?

For a case on the repealed para.111(1) (but which would now come within s.111(1A)), see *Re Sendo Ltd* [2005] EWHC 1604 (Ch); [2006] 1 B.C.L.C. 395.

"Correspondence": this definition is clearly intended to include communications by email, etc. in written form, but clearer language would surely be needed if it were meant to extend to oral conversations by telephone.

"Floating charge": compare the definition in IA 1986 s.251. It is not obvious why different wording has been used.

Paragraph 111(2), which provided that "a reference to a thing in writing includes a reference to a thing in electronic form" is now superseded by the more general provisions of s.436B.

Non-UK companies

111A A company incorporated outside the United Kingdom that has a principal place of business in Northern Ireland may not enter administration under this Schedule unless it also has a principal place of business in England and Wales or Scotland (or both in England and Wales and in Scotland).

GENERAL NOTE

Section 111A was inserted, by the Insolvency Act 1986 (Amendment) Regulations 2005 (SI 2005/879) regs 2(1), 4(c), as from April 13, 2005.

Scotland

112 In the application of this Schedule to Scotland–

    (a)   a reference to filing with the court is a reference to lodging in court, and

    (b)   a reference to a charge is a reference to a right in security.

(See General Note after para.116.)

113 Where property in Scotland is disposed of under paragraph 70 or 71, the administrator shall grant to the disponee an appropriate document of transfer or conveyance of the property, and–

    (a)   that document, or

    (b)   recording, intimation or registration of that document (where recording, intimation or registration of the document is a legal requirement for completion of title to the property),

has the effect of disencumbering the property of or, as the case may be, freeing the property from, the security.

(See General Note after para.116.)

114   In Scotland, where goods in the possession of a company under a hire-purchase agreement are disposed of under paragraph 72, the disposal has the effect of extinguishing as against the disponee all rights of the owner of the goods under the agreement.

(See General Note after para.116.)

115(1)   In Scotland, the administrator of a company may make, in or towards the satisfaction of the debt secured by the floating charge, a payment to the holder of a floating charge which has attached to the property subject to the charge.

115(2)   In Scotland, where the administrator thinks that the company has insufficient property to enable a distribution to be made to unsecured creditors other than by virtue of section 176A(2)(a), he may file a notice to that effect with the registrar of companies.

115(3)   On delivery of the notice to the registrar of companies, any floating charge granted by the company shall, unless it has already so attached, attach to the property which is subject to the charge and that attachment shall have effect as if each floating charge is a fixed security over the property to which it has attached.

(See General Note after para.116.)

116   In Scotland, the administrator in making any payment in accordance with paragraph 115 shall make such payment subject to the rights of any of the following categories of persons (which rights shall, except to the extent provided in any instrument, have the following order of priority)–

   (a)   the holder of any fixed security which is over property subject to the floating charge and which ranks prior to, or pari passu with, the floating charge,

   (b)   creditors in respect of all liabilities and expenses incurred by or on behalf of the administrator,

   (c)   the administrator in respect of his liabilities, expenses and remuneration and any indemnity to which he is entitled out of the property of the company,

   (d)   the preferential creditors entitled to payment in accordance with paragraph 65,

   (e)   the holder of the floating charge in accordance with the priority of that charge in relation to any other floating charge which has attached, and

   (f)   the holder of a fixed security, other than one referred to in paragraph (a), which is over property subject to the floating charge.

GENERAL NOTE TO PARAS 112–116

These paragraphs make minor modifications to the provisions of Sch.B1 in its application to Scotland. Some of these are purely terminological. Others reflect differences in conveyancing practice and property law, and the fact that the floating charge is based on statute rather than common law in Scots law.
   Paragraphs 115–116 supplement para.99.

SCHEDULE 1

POWERS OF ADMINISTRATOR OR ADMINISTRATIVE RECEIVER

Sections 14, 42

1   Power to take possession of, collect and get in the property of the company and, for that purpose, to take such proceedings as may seem to him expedient.

2   Power to sell or otherwise dispose of the property of the company by public auction or private contract or, in Scotland, to sell, hire out or otherwise dispose of the property of the company by public roup or private bargain.

3   Power to raise or borrow money and grant security therefor over the property of the company.

4   Power to appoint a solicitor or accountant or other professionally qualified person to assist him in the performance of his functions.

5   Power to bring or defend any action or other legal proceedings in the name and on behalf of the company.

6   Power to refer to arbitration any question affecting the company.

7   Power to effect and maintain insurances in respect of the business and property of the company.

8   Power to use the company's seal.

9   Power to do all acts and to execute in the name and on behalf of the company any deed, receipt or other document.

10   Power to draw, accept, make and endorse any bill of exchange or promissory note in the name and on behalf of the company.

11   Power to appoint any agent to do any business which he is unable to do himself or which can more conveniently be done by an agent and power to employ and dismiss employees.

12   Power to do all such things (including the carrying out of works) as may be necessary for the realisation of the property of the company.

13   Power to make any payment which is necessary or incidental to the performance of his functions.

14   Power to carry on the business of the company.

15   Power to establish subsidiaries of the company.

16   Power to transfer to subsidiaries of the company the whole or any part of the business and property of the company.

17   Power to grant or accept a surrender of a lease or tenancy of any of the property of the company, and to take a lease or tenancy of any property required or convenient for the business of the company.

18   Power to make any arrangement or compromise on behalf of the company.

19   Power to call up any uncalled capital of the company.

20   Power to rank and claim in the bankruptcy, insolvency, sequestration or liquidation of any person indebted to the company and to receive dividends, and to accede to trust deeds for the creditors of any such person.

21   Power to present or defend a petition for the winding up of the company.

22   Power to change the situation of the company's registered office.

23   Power to do all other things incidental to the exercise of the foregoing powers.

GENERAL NOTE

This Schedule applies to all administrators, whether appointed under the original Pt II or under Sch.B1, and to administrative receivers.

Under CA 1985, the powers of a receiver (or receiver and manager) appointed out of court were left to be settled almost entirely by the provisions of the instrument under which he was appointed and the terms of the appointment itself. The Cork Committee (*Report*, para.494) recommended that the general powers of a receiver should be set out in a statute, so that it would not be necessary for a person dealing with him to refer to the particular debenture to find out what powers he could exercise in the circumstances. (This was, in fact, already the case in Scotland under

Companies (Floating Charges and Receivers) (Scotland) Act 1972 s.15.) The present Schedule and IA 1986 s.42 implement those recommendations, which apply in every *administrative* receivership, and—no doubt reflecting the fact that the administration order regime set up by ss.8 et seq. was modelled on the institution of receivership—the Schedule is made by s.14 and Sch.B1 para.60 to apply to an administrator as well. An administrator has, in addition, the general statutory powers set out in s.14(1)(a) and para.59, and the specific powers given by ss.14(2) and 15 and paras 70–72.

The disposal of a "substantial property" by an administrator does not require approval by the company's members under CA 2006 s.190: see s.193(1)(b) of that Act. On the power of an administrator to sell the business or its property prior to the holding of a creditors' meeting, see the notes to s.17(2) and Sch.B1 para.68.

The powers of an administrative receiver listed in this Schedule may be overridden by the terms of the debenture under which he is appointed, but a person dealing with him in good faith and for value is not concerned to inquire whether he is acting within his powers (s.42(3)). The Act, by s.43, also confers special powers on an administrative receiver to dispose of charged property, etc.

A receiver who is not an administrative receiver is not affected by the provisions described above, and Sch.1 does not apply in such a case.

The Schedule applies in Scotland in the case of an administrator, but not an administrative receiver; all Scottish receivers, however, have the powers set out in s.55 and Sch.2.

The specific powers listed in Sch.1 do not, on the whole, call for detailed comment, apart from para.21 (power to present or defend a winding-up petition), which has clarified doubts regarding a receiver's ability to present such a petition at common law, and removes the limitations upon such powers as he may have had: compare *Re Emmadart Ltd* [1979] Ch. 540. A petition by an administrator or administrative receiver is presented in the name of the company: see the note to s.124. The power of a receiver to present a winding-up petition was also the subject of comment in *Re Anvil Estates Ltd* (unreported, 1993)—discussed by Pugh and Ede in (1994) 10 I.L. & P. 48. The case was actually decided on the basis of the right of the secured creditor (as opposed to the receiver) to petition but there is some useful general discussion in the judgment. The power of an administrative receiver to oppose a winding-up petition presented by another creditor was considered in *Re Leigh Estates (UK) Ltd* [1994] B.C.C. 292.

In some earlier cases, it was held that para.13 is expressed in sufficiently wide terms as to permit a distribution of assets to be made on the same basis as would have applied if the company had been put into liquidation on the date of the administration order, so giving priority to those creditors whose debts would have been preferential on a winding up: *Re WBSL Realisations 1992 Ltd* [1995] B.C.L.C. 576, and also to authorise an administrator to pay all the company's pre-administration creditors in full: *Re John Slack Ltd* [1995] B.C.C. 1,116. However, in *Re The Designer Room Ltd* [2004] B.C.C. 904 Rimer J. held that para.13 could only be construed as giving such powers if, on the particular facts, the making of such payments was necessary or incidental to the performance by the administrators of their functions as such. The mere fact that to do so would achieve the distribution of the assets in question more cheaply did not satisfy this test. Nor could the court authorise the administrators to make such payments in exercise of its inherent jurisdiction. These decisions must now be reconsidered in the light of the ruling of the Court of Appeal in *Re Lune Metal Products Ltd* [2006] EWCA Civ 1720; [2007] B.C.C. 217, where Neuberger L.J. drew attention to the differences between Sch.1 and Sch.4 (powers of liquidators), and in particular to the absence in Sch.1 of any power for an administrator to make distributions. Such payments can now only be made where a discharge of the administration is to be followed by a striking off of the companies concerned. See the discussion in the note to s.*18(1), (2)*. For distributions and other payments by administrators under Sch.B1 see paras 65 and 66.

In *Re TXU UK Ltd* [2002] EWHC 2784 (Ch); [2003] 2 B.C.L.C. 341 para.13 was relied on to authorise administrators to compromise certain future claims (so giving them a priority which they would not receive if the company later went into liquidation), on the ground that this course would achieve a benefit to the administration as a whole.

As noted below (see the note to Sch.4 para.6) the statutory authority given to a liquidator to sell any of the company's property enables him to assign a cause of action vested in the company without infringing the common-law rule which declares transactions involving maintenance or champerty to be illegal. A similar protection is given to a trustee in bankruptcy by Sch.6 para.9, and to an administrator by s.14 and para.1 of this Schedule. However, the position as regards an administrative receiver may be different, for the power is derived from s.42, which does not confer the power by virtue of the statute itself but instead by deeming it to have been included in the charge instrument under which the receiver has been appointed. As a mere term in a contract it would not be sufficient to displace the common-law rule.

Where an administration order is in force in relation to an insurance company, the powers of the administrator include the power to make certain payments to a creditor in advance of the holding of a meeting under IA 1986 s.23: see the Financial Services and Markets Act 2000 (Administration Orders Relating to Insurers) Order 2002 (SI 2002/1242) Sch. para.8.

SCHEDULE 2

POWERS OF A SCOTTISH RECEIVER (ADDITIONAL TO THOSE CONFERRED ON HIM BY THE INSTRUMENT OF CHARGE)

Section 55

1 Power to take possession of, collect and get in the property from the company or a liquidator thereof or any other person, and for that purpose, to take such proceedings as may seem to him expedient.

2 Power to sell, hire out or otherwise dispose of the property by public roup or private bargain and with or without advertisement.

3 Power to raise or borrow money and grant security therefor over the property.

4 Power to appoint a solicitor or accountant or other professionally qualified person to assist him in the performance of his functions.

5 Power to bring or defend any action or other legal proceedings in the name and on behalf of the company.

6 Power to refer to arbitration all questions affecting the company.

7 Power to effect and maintain insurances in respect of the business and property of the company.

8 Power to use the company's seal.

9 Power to do all acts and to execute in the name and on behalf of the company any deed, receipt or other document.

10 Power to draw, accept, make and endorse any bill of exchange or promissory note in the name and on behalf of the company.

11 Power to appoint any agent to do any business which he is unable to do himself or which can more conveniently be done by an agent, and power to employ and dismiss employees.

12 Power to do all such things (including the carrying out of works), as may be necessary for the realisation of the property.

13 Power to make any payment which is necessary or incidental to the performance of his functions.

14 Power to carry on the business of the company or any part of it.

15 Power to grant or accept a surrender of a lease or tenancy of any of the property, and to take a lease or tenancy of any property required or convenient for the business of the company.

16 Power to make any arrangement or compromise on behalf of the company.

17 Power to call up any uncalled capital of the company.

18 Power to establish subsidiaries of the company.

19 Power to transfer to subsidiaries of the company the business of the company or any part of it and any of the property.

20 Power to rank and claim in the bankruptcy, insolvency, sequestration or liquidation of any person or company indebted to the company and to receive dividends, and to accede to trust deeds for creditors of any such person.

21 Power to present or defend a petition for the winding up of the company.

22 Power to change the situation of the company's registered office.

23 Power to do all other things incidental to the exercise of the powers mentioned in section 55(1) of this Act or above in this Schedule.

GENERAL NOTE

This Schedule provides a model list of powers for a Scottish receiver appointed by a holder of a floating charge. The list, although modified, dates back to the introduction of receivership in Scotland in 1972. The 23 implied powers mirror those of an English administrative receiver set out in Sch.1, with only slight changes in the order. For further comment, see s.55.

SCHEDULE 2A

EXCEPTIONS TO PROHIBITION ON APPOINTMENT OF ADMINISTRATIVE RECEIVER: SUPPLEMENTARY PROVISIONS

1 Capital market arrangement

1(1) For the purposes of section 72B an arrangement is a capital market arrangement if—

(a) it involves a grant of security to a person holding it as trustee for a person who holds a capital market investment issued by a party to the arrangement, or

(aa) it involves a grant of security to—

    (i) a party to the arrangement who issues a capital market investment, or

    (ii) a person who holds the security as trustee for a party to the arrangement in connection with the issue of a capital market investment, or

(ab) it involves a grant of security to a person who holds the security as trustee for a party to the arrangement who agrees to provide finance to another party, or

(b) at least one party guarantees the performance of obligations of another party, or

(c) at least one party provides security in respect of the performance of obligations of another party, or

(d) the arrangement involves an investment of a kind described in articles 83 to 85 of the Financial Services and Markets Act 2000 (Regulated Activities) Order 2001 (SI 2001/544) (options, futures and contracts for differences).

1(2) For the purposes of sub-paragraph (1)—

(a) a reference to holding as trustee includes a reference to holding as nominee or agent,

(b) a reference to holding for a person who holds a capital market investment includes a reference to holding for a number of persons at least one of whom holds a capital market investment, and

(c) a person holds a capital market investment if he has a legal or beneficial interest in it, and

(d) the reference to the provision of finance includes the provision of an indemnity.

1(3) In section 72B(1) and this paragraph "party" to an arrangement includes a party to an agreement which—

(a) forms part of the arrangement,

(b) provides for the raising of finance as part of the arrangement, or

(c) is necessary for the purposes of implementing the arrangement.

2 Capital market investment

2(1) For the purposes of section 72B an investment is a capital market investment if it—

(a) is within article 77 of the Financial Services and Markets Act 2000 (Regulated Activities) Order 2001 (SI 2001/544) (debt instruments), and

(b)   is rated, listed or traded or designed to be rated, listed or traded.

2(2)   In sub-paragraph (1)–

"rated" means rated for the purposes of investment by an internationally recognised rating agency,

"listed" means admitted to the official list within the meaning given by section 103(1) of the Financial Services and Markets Act 2000 (c. 8) (interpretation), and

"traded" means admitted to trading on a market established under the rules of a recognised investment exchange or on a foreign market.

2(3)   In sub-paragraph (2)–

"recognised investment exchange" has the meaning given by section 285 of the Financial Services and Markets Act 2000 (recognised investment exchange), and

"foreign market" has the same meaning as "relevant market" in article 67(2) of the Financial Services and Markets Act 2000 (Financial Promotion) Order 2001 (SI 2001/1335) (foreign markets).

3(1)   An investment is also a capital market investment for the purposes of section 72B if it consists of a bond or commercial paper issued to one or more of the following–

(a)   an investment professional within the meaning of article 19(5) of the Financial Services and Markets Act 2000 (Financial Promotion) Order 2001,

(b)   a person who is, when the agreement mentioned in section 72B(1) is entered into, a certified high net worth individual in relation to a communication within the meaning of article 48(2) of that order,

(c)   a person to whom article 49(2) of that order applies (high net worth company, &c.),

(d)   a person who is, when the agreement mentioned in section 72B(1) is entered into, a certified sophisticated investor in relation to a communication within the meaning of article 50(1) of that order, and

(e)   a person in a State other than the United Kingdom who under the law of that State is not prohibited from investing in bonds or commercial paper.

3(2)   In sub-paragraph (1)–

"bond" shall be construed in accordance with article 77 of the Financial Services and Markets Act 2000 (Regulated Activities) Order 2001 (SI 2001/544), and

"commercial paper" has the meaning given by article 9(3) of that order.

3(3)   For the purposes of sub-paragraph (1)–

(a)   in applying article 19(5) of the Financial Promotion Order for the purposes of sub-paragraph (1)(a)–

(i)   in article 19(5)(b), ignore the words after "exempt person",

(ii)   in article 19(5)(c)(i), for the words from "the controlled activity" to the end substitute "a controlled activity", and

(iii)   in article 19(5)(e) ignore the words from "where the communication" to the end, and

(b)   in applying article 49(2) of that order for the purposes of sub-paragraph (1)(c), ignore article 49(2)(e).

4 "Agreement"

4 For the purposes of sections 72B and 72E and this Schedule **"agreement"** includes an agreement or undertaking effected by–

(a) contract,

(b) deed, or

(c) any other instrument intended to have effect in accordance with the law of England and Wales, Scotland or another jurisdiction.

5 Debt

5 The debt of at least £50 million referred to in section 72B(1)(a) or 72E(2)(a)–

(a) may be incurred at any time during the life of the capital market arrangement or financed project, and

(b) may be expressed wholly or partly in foreign currency (in which case the sterling equivalent shall be calculated as at the time when the arrangement is entered into or the project begins).

6 Step-in rights

6(1) For the purposes of sections 72C to 72E a project has "step-in rights" if a person who provides finance in connection with the project has a conditional entitlement under an agreement to–

(a) assume sole or principal responsibility under an agreement for carrying out all or part of the project, or

(b) make arrangements for carrying out all or part of the project.

6(2) In sub-paragraph (1) a reference to the provision of finance includes a reference to the provision of an indemnity.

7 Project company

7(1) For the purposes of sections 72C to 72E a company is a "project company" of a project if–

(a) it holds property for the purpose of the project,

(b) it has sole or principal responsibility under an agreement for carrying out all or part of the project,

(c) it is one of a number of companies which together carry out the project,

(d) it has the purpose of supplying finance to enable the project to be carried out, or

(e) it is the holding company of a company within any of paragraphs (a) to (d).

7(2) But a company is not a "project company" of a project if–

(a) it performs a function within sub-paragraph (1)(a) to (d) or is within sub-paragraph (1)(e), but

(b) it also performs a function which is not–

(i) within sub-paragraph (1)(a) to (d),

(ii) related to a function within sub-paragraph (1)(a) to (d), or

(iii) related to the project.

7(3) For the purposes of this paragraph a company carries out all or part of a project whether or not it acts wholly or partly through agents.

8   "Resources"

8   In section 72C **"resources"** includes–

(a)   funds (including payment for the provision of services or facilities),

(b)   assets,

(c)   professional skill,

(d)   the grant of a concession or franchise, and

(e)   any other commercial resource.

9   "Public body"

9(1)   In section 72C **"public body"** means–

(a)   a body which exercises public functions,

(b)   a body specified for the purposes of this paragraph by the Secretary of State, and

(c)   a body within a class specified for the purposes of this paragraph by the Secretary of State.

9(2)   A specification under sub-paragraph (1) may be–

(a)   general, or

(b)   for the purpose of the application of section 72C to a specified case.

10   Regulated business

10(1)   For the purposes of section 72D a business is regulated if it is carried on–

(a)   [Repealed.]

(b)   in reliance on a licence under section 7 or 7A of the Gas Act 1986 (c. 44) (transport and supply of gas),

(c)   in reliance on a licence granted by virtue of section 41C of that Act (power to prescribe additional licensable activity),

(d)   in reliance on a licence under section 6 of the Electricity Act 1989 (c. 29) (supply of electricity),

(e)   by a water undertaker,

(f)   by a sewerage undertaker,

(g)   by a universal service provider within the meaning given by section 4(3) and (4) of the Postal Services Act 2000 (c. 26),

(h)   by the Post Office company within the meaning given by section 62 of that Act (transfer of property),

(i)   by a relevant subsidiary of the Post Office Company within the meaning given by section 63 of that Act (government holding),

(j)   in reliance on a licence under section 8 of the Railways Act 1993 (c. 43) (railway services),

(k)   in reliance on a licence exemption under section 7 of that Act (subject to sub-paragraph (2) below),

(l)   by the operator of a system of transport which is deemed to be a railway for a purpose of Part I of that Act by virtue of section 81(2) of that Act (tramways, &c.),

(m)   by the operator of a vehicle carried on flanged wheels along a system within paragraph (l), or

    (n)   in reliance on a European licence granted pursuant to a provision contained in any instrument made for the purpose of implementing Council Directive 1995/18/EC dated 19th June 1995 on the licensing of railway undertakings, as amended by Directive 2001/13/EC dated 26th February 2001 and Directive 2004/49/EC dated 29th April 2004, both of the European Parliament and of the Council, or pursuant to any action taken by an EEA State for that purpose.

10(2)   Sub-paragraph (1)(k) does not apply to the operator of a railway asset on a railway unless on some part of the railway there is a permitted line speed exceeding 40 kilometres per hour.

10(2A)   For the purposes of section 72D a business is also regulated to the extent that it consists in the provision of a public electronic communications network or a public electronic communications service.

10(2B)   In sub-paragraph (1)(n), an "EEA State" means a member State, Norway, Iceland or Liechtenstein.

11   "Person"

11   A reference to a person in this Schedule includes a reference to a partnership or another unincorporated group of persons.

General Note

This was inserted by EA 2002 s.250(2) and Sch.8 to further supplement the provisions in ss.72A–H with particular reference to those exceptional situations where the appointment of an administrative receiver is still possible notwithstanding the general bar on that remedy. Before the provisions of Sch.2A came into force they were then modified by the Insolvency Act 1986 (Amendment) (Administrative Receivership and Capital Market Arrangements) Order 2003 (SI 2003/1468) by the addition of paras 1(1)(aa), 1(1)(ab) and 1(2)(d). Essentially, Sch.2A serves as a complex interpretation provision. These provisions took effect on September 15, 2003. Curiously para.10(1)(a) was omitted and 10(2A) inserted by the Communications Act 2003 with effect from July 25, 2003. On "step in" rights under para.6 see *Cabvision Ltd v Feetum* [2005] EWCA Civ 1601; [2006] B.C.C. 340.

SCHEDULE 3

ORDERS IN COURSE OF WINDING UP PRONOUNCED IN VACATION (SCOTLAND)

Section 162

PART I

ORDERS WHICH ARE TO BE FINAL

Orders under section 153, as to the time for proving debts and claims.

Orders under section 195 as to meetings for ascertaining wishes of creditors or contributories.

Orders under section 198, as to the examination of witnesses in regard to the property or affairs of a company.

PART II

ORDERS WHICH ARE TO TAKE EFFECT UNTIL MATTER DISPOSED OF BY INNER HOUSE

Orders under section 126(1), 130(2) or (3), 147, 227 or 228, restraining or permitting the commencement or the continuance of legal proceedings.

Orders under section 135(5), limiting the powers of provisional liquidators.

Orders under section 108, appointing a liquidator to fill a vacancy.

Orders under section 167 or 169, sanctioning the exercise of any powers by a liquidator, other than the powers specified in paragraphs 1, 2 and 3 of Schedule 4 to this Act.

Orders under section 158, as to the arrest and detention of an absconding contributory and his property.

Schedule 4

Powers of Liquidator in a Winding Up

Sections 165, 167

Part I

Powers Exercisable with Sanction

1   Power to pay any class of creditors in full.

2   Power to make any compromise or arrangement with creditors or persons claiming to be creditors, or having or alleging themselves to have any claim (present or future, certain or contingent, ascertained or sounding only in damages) against the company, or whereby the company may be rendered liable.

3   In the case of a winding up in Scotland, power to compromise, on such terms as may be agreed–

(a)   all calls and liabilities to calls, all debts and liabilities capable of resulting in debts, and all claims (present or future, certain or contingent, ascertained or sounding only in damages) subsisting or supposed to subsist between the company and a contributory or alleged contributory or other debtor or person apprehending liability to the company, and

(b)   all questions in any way relating to or affecting the assets or the winding up of the company,

and take any security for the discharge of any such call, debt, liability or claim and give a complete discharge in respect of it.

3A   Power to bring legal proceedings under section 213, 214, 238, 239, 242, 243 or 423.

Part II

Powers Exercisable without Sanction in Voluntary Winding Up, with Sanction in Winding Up by the Court

4   Power to bring or defend any action or other legal proceeding in the name and on behalf of the company.

5   Power to carry on the business of the company so far as may be necessary for its beneficial winding up.

Part III

Powers Exercisable Without Sanction in any Winding Up

6   Power to sell any of the company's property by public auction or private contract, with power to transfer the whole of it to any person or to sell the same in parcels.

6A   In the case of a winding up in England and Wales, power to compromise, on such terms as may be agreed–

(a) all calls and liabilities to calls, all debts and liabilities capable of resulting in debts, and all claims (present or future, certain or contingent, ascertained or sounding only in damages) subsisting or supposed to subsist between the company and a contributory or alleged contributory or other debtor or person apprehending liability to the company, and

(b) subject to paragraph 2 in Part 1 of this Schedule, all questions in any way relating to or affecting the assets or the winding up of the company, and take any security for the discharge of any such call, debt, liability or claim and give a complete discharge in respect of it.

7 Power to do all acts and execute, in the name and on behalf of the company, all deeds, receipts and other documents and for that purpose to use, when necessary, the company's seal.

8 Power to prove, rank and claim in the bankruptcy, insolvency or sequestration of any contributory for any balance against his estate, and to receive dividends in the bankruptcy, insolvency or sequestration in respect of that balance, as a separate debt due from the bankrupt or insolvent, and rateably with the other separate creditors.

9 Power to draw, accept, make and indorse any bill of exchange or promissory note in the name and on behalf of the company, with the same effect with respect to the company's liability as if the bill or note had been drawn, accepted, made or indorsed by or on behalf of the company in the course of its business.

10 Power to raise on the security of the assets of the company any money requisite.

11 Power to take out in his official name letters of administration to any deceased contributory, and to do in his official name any other act necessary for obtaining payment of any money due from a contributory or his estate which cannot conveniently be done in the name of the company.

In all such cases the money due is deemed, for the purpose of enabling the liquidator to take out the letters of administration or recover the money, to be due to the liquidator himself.

12 Power to appoint an agent to do any business which the liquidator is unable to do himself.

13 Power to do all such other things as may be necessary for winding up the company's affairs and distributing its assets.

GENERAL NOTE

The powers of a liquidator in a winding up by the court were formerly set out in CA 1985 s.539(1), (2), and those in a voluntary winding up in CA 1985 s.598(1), (2). Many of these powers are now conveniently collected together and arranged in tabulated form in this Schedule, which (unless otherwise stated) applies both in England and Wales and in Scotland. Paragraph 3 was amended and para.6A inserted by LRO 2010 (SI 2010/18) art.10 as from April 6, 2010.

A liquidator in a winding up by the court has also the supplementary powers listed in s.168 (England and Wales) and s.169 (Scotland); and further powers are given to a voluntary liquidator by ss.165, 166.

Schedule 4 does not apply in the case of a provisional liquidator. However, the court has jurisdiction under s.135(4) to confer powers on a provisional liquidator which may include powers corresponding to those set out in Sch.4: *Re Hawk Insurance Co Ltd* [2001] B.C.C. 57.

Forms of application for the court's sanction are available on the Insolvency Service's website.

Para.1

The Insolvency Service takes the view that the court's sanction is not required before paying the preferential creditors in full, since the liquidator has a *duty* to do so under IA 1986 s.175: see *Dear IP*, Ch.17(2).

Para.2, 3

By virtue of the LRO 2010 amendments (above), para.3 now applies only in Scotland. For England and Wales, para.6A now applies, so that the power to compromise calls and other liabilities to the company no longer requires sanction.

It was held in *Taylor, Noter* [1992] B.C.C. 440 that the corresponding provisions of CA 1948 empowered the liquidator of a company, with the necessary sanction, to enter into any compromise or arrangement that might have been entered into by the company itself. In that case the affairs of a number of companies controlled by the same person had been treated as one, and the liquidator had found it impossible to determine which creditors had claims against the particular companies and which had claims against the individual controller, who was now bankrupt. A scheme was agreed for a single scheme of ranking and division of all the assets and creditors. This case was followed by the Court of Appeal in England in somewhat similar circumstances in *Re Bank of Credit & Commerce International SA (No.2)* [1992] B.C.C. 715. The compromise powers include power to depart from the general rule that creditors are entitled to participate in the estate on a pari passu basis (above). If the creditors' committee refuses its sanction, the court may override the refusal: *Re Andrew Rhodes Ltd* (March 15, 2005, noted (2005) 21 I.L. & P. 63).

Para.3A

This paragraph was inserted by EA 2002 s.253, with effect from September 15, 2003. It is part of the package of reforms designed to reverse the effect of decisions such as *Re Floor Fourteen Ltd, Lewis v IRC* [2001] 3 All E.R. 499; [2002] B.C.C. 198, which held that a liquidator pursuing claims under the sections referred to could not claim his costs as expenses of the liquidation. This has now been rectified by an amendment to IR 1986 r.4.218 but, in order to ensure that liquidators do not make such claims at the expense of the creditors, they may not do so without their approval (or, alternatively, the leave of the court). See further the notes to s.115 and r.4.218.

Para.6

The liquidator's power to sell "any of the company's property" enables him to assign any causes of action which were vested in the company at the time of the winding up, including the right to bring misfeasance proceedings under IA 1986 s.212. The rule of law which would normally prohibit such an assignment—at least an assignment to a third party who had no interest otherwise in the litigation—on the ground that it would be champertous and illegal is displaced by this statutory authority: *Re Park Gate Waggon Works Co* (1881) 17 Ch. D. 234. Such a sale may be made for any consideration, including a share of any proceeds of the action if it is successful. The fact that the company (or the liquidator) is not eligible for legal aid but the assignee may be entitled to it is not a ground for the court to declare the assignment unlawful, but a matter for consideration by the Legal Aid Board (*Norglen Ltd (in liq.) v Reeds Rains Prudential Ltd* [1999] 2 A.C. 1; [1998] B.C.C. 44). This provision does not, however, empower the liquidator to assign a right of action which arises only in the event of a liquidation and is vested in him by statute, e.g. the right to bring proceedings to recover a preference (IA 1986 s.239) or compensation for fraudulent or wrongful trading (ss.213, 214) or to set aside a transaction at an undervalue (s.238) or have a disposition of the company's property after the commencement of the winding up declared void under s.127, or a floating charge declared void under s.245. (See *Re Oasis Merchandising Services Ltd* [1998] Ch. 170; [1997] B.C.C. 282; *Re Ayala Holdings Ltd (No.2)* [1996] 1 B.C.L.C. 467). However, if the assignee has a genuine interest in the outcome of the litigation (e.g. as a creditor of the company), an assignment of the "fruits" of such litigation may not be unlawful at common law, at least if the liquidator is left free to conduct the litigation without interference by the assignee; and there is certainly no objection to such a creditor simply putting the liquidator in funds to conduct the litigation on terms that any proceeds shall go in the first instance towards reimbursing him (*Katz v McNally* [1997] B.C.C. 784). See also *Empire Resolution Ltd v MPW Insurance Brokers Ltd* [1999] B.P.I.R. 486; *Farmer v Moseley (Holdings) Ltd* [2001] 2 B.C.L.C. 572 and the analysis of the present state of the law put forward by counsel and approved by the Court of Appeal (as "a valuable aid to clarification of the position") in *ANC Ltd v Clark Goldring & Page Ltd* [2001] B.C.C. 479. The ruling of Lightman J. in *Grovewood Holdings plc v James Capel & Co Ltd* [1995] Ch. 80; [1995] B.C.C. 760, that a sale for a consideration which included a provision for the purchaser to finance the litigation was champertous has been much criticised and is probably open to reconsideration: see the *Oasis* judgment [1998] Ch. 170 at 179; [1997] B.C.C. 282 at 288; and *Farmer v Moseley (Holdings) Ltd* [2002] B.P.I.R. 473.

The disposal of a "substantial property" by a liquidator does not require approval by the company's members under CA 2006 s.190 (except in a members' voluntary liquidation): see s.193(1)(a) of that Act.

On the liquidator's power to assign where contractual restrictions have been imposed see *Ruttle Plant Ltd v DEFRA* [2007] EWHC 2870 (TCC); [2007] B.P.I.R. 1652. In later proceedings sub nom. *Ruttle Plant Ltd v DEFRA (No.2)* [2008] EWHC 238 (TCC); [2009] 1 All E.R. 448; [2008] B.C.C. 790 there is to be found an excellent review of the power of the liquidator to assign fruits of legal claims and restrictions upon such power.

A prohibition on assignment by a company of a claim arising out of a contract is binding on its liquidator: *Quadmost Ltd v Reprotech (Pebsham) Ltd* [2001] B.P.I.R. 349. The fact that the intended defendant has a cross-claim for a larger amount, which can be set off in the liquidation under IR 1986 r.4.90, is also effectively a bar to the assignment of a cause of action by a liquidator: *Craig v Humberclyde Industrial Finance Group Ltd* [1999] B.C.C. 378.

In an article in Sweet & Maxwell's Company Law Newsletter (October 31, 2005), Sir Gavin Lightman draws attention to the risks inherent in the giving or taking of an assignment of a cause of action by an insolvency office-holder. See also *Hopkins v TL Dallas Group Ltd* [2005] 1 B.C.L.C. 543 at [105].

SCHEDULE 4ZA

CONDITIONS FOR MAKING A DEBT RELIEF ORDER

PART 1

CONDITIONS WHICH MUST BE MET

Connection with England and Wales

1(1) The debtor–

(a) is domiciled in England and Wales on the application date; or

(b) at any time during the period of three years ending with that date–

    (i) was ordinarily resident, or had a place of residence, in England and Wales; or

    (ii) carried on business in England and Wales.

1(2) The reference in sub-paragraph (1)(b)(ii) to the debtor carrying on business includes–

(a) the carrying on of business by a firm or partnership of which he is a member;

(b) the carrying on of business by an agent or manager for him or for such a firm or partnership.

Debtor's previous insolvency history

2 The debtor is not, on the determination date–

(a) an undischarged bankrupt;

(b) subject to an interim order or voluntary arrangement under Part 8; or

(c) subject to a bankruptcy restrictions order or a debt relief restrictions order.

3 A debtor's petition for the debtor's bankruptcy under Part 9–

(a) has not been presented by the debtor before the determination date;

(b) has been so presented, but proceedings on the petition have been finally disposed of before that date; or

(c) has been so presented and proceedings in relation to the petition remain before the court at that date, but the court has referred the debtor under section 274A(2) for the purposes of making an application for a debt relief order.

4 A creditor's petition for the debtor's bankruptcy under Part 9–

(a) has not been presented against the debtor at any time before the determination date;

(b) has been so presented, but proceedings on the petition have been finally disposed of before that date; or

(c) has been so presented and proceedings in relation to the petition remain before the court at that date, but the person who presented the petition has consented to the making of an application for a debt relief order.

5 A debt relief order has not been made in relation to the debtor in the period of six years ending with the determination date.

Limit on debtor's overall indebtedness

6(1) The total amount of the debtor's debts on the determination date, other than unliquidated debts and excluded debts, does not exceed the prescribed amount.

6(2) For this purpose an unliquidated debt is a debt that is not for a liquidated sum payable to a creditor either immediately or at some future certain time.

Limit on debtor's monthly surplus income

7(1) The debtor's monthly surplus income (if any) on the determination date does not exceed the prescribed amount.

7(2) For this purpose "monthly surplus income" is the amount by which a person's monthly income exceeds the amount necessary for the reasonable domestic needs of himself and his family.

7(3) The rules may–

   (a)   make provision as to how the debtor's monthly surplus income is to be determined;

   (b)   provide that particular descriptions of income are to be excluded for the purposes of this paragraph.

Limit on value of debtor's property

8(1) The total value of the debtor's property on the determination date does not exceed the prescribed amount.

8(2) The rules may–

   (a)   make provision as to how the value of a person's property is to be determined;

   (b)   provide that particular descriptions of property are to be excluded for the purposes of this paragraph.

PART 2

OTHER CONDITIONS

9(1) The debtor has not entered into a transaction with any person at an undervalue during the period between–

   (a)   the start of the period of two years ending with the application date; and

   (b)   the determination date.

9(2) For this purpose a debtor enters into a transaction with a person at an undervalue if–

   (a)   he makes a gift to that person or he otherwise enters into a transaction with that person on terms that provide for him to receive no consideration;

   (b)   he enters into a transaction with that person in consideration of marriage or the formation of a civil partnership; or

   (c)   he enters into a transaction with that person for a consideration the value of which, in money or money's worth, is significantly less than the value, in money or money's worth, of the consideration provided by the individual.

10(1) The debtor has not given a preference to any person during the period between–

  (a) the start of the period of two years ending with the application date; and

  (b) the determination date.

10(2) For this purpose a debtor gives a preference to a person if–

  (a) that person is one of the debtor's creditors to whom a qualifying debt is owed or is a surety or guarantor for any such debt, and

  (b) the debtor does anything or suffers anything to be done which (in either case) has the effect of putting that person into a position which, in the event that a debt relief order is made in relation to the debtor, will be better than the position he would have been in if that thing had not been done.

GENERAL NOTE

Introduced by s.108(2) of, and Sch.18 to, the Tribunals, Courts and Enforcement Act 2007 with effect from April 6, 2009, this is an important set of preconditions that must be met before a debtor can qualify for a DRO. These criteria are supplemented by the Insolvency Proceedings (Monetary Limits) (Amendment) Order 2009 (SI 2009/465) which specifies maximum indebtedness of 15k, maximum monthly surplus income of £50 and maximum property value of £300. The jurisdiction boxes that must be ticked are the same as those traditionally applied to would be bankrupts under IA 1986 s.265. A DRO is not available to a debtor already undergoing a personal insolvency procedure. Financial criteria are mapped out by paras 6, 7 and 8 subject to clarification by secondary legislation. A DRO is not available to a person who has undertaken a transaction at an undervalue or a preference within the past two years. See IA 1986 Pt 7A and IR 1986 rr.5A.1–5A.27.

SCHEDULE 4ZB

DEBT RELIEF RESTRICTIONS ORDERS AND UNDERTAKINGS

Debt relief restrictions order

1(1) A debt relief restrictions order may be made by the court in relation to a person in respect of whom a debt relief order has been made.

1(2) An order may be made only on the application of–

  (a) the Secretary of State, or

  (b) the official receiver acting on a direction of the Secretary of State.

Grounds for making order

2(1) The court shall grant an application for a debt relief restrictions order if it thinks it appropriate to do so having regard to the conduct of the debtor (whether before or after the making of the debt relief order).

2(2) The court shall, in particular, take into account any of the following kinds of behaviour on the part of the debtor–

  (a) failing to keep records which account for a loss of property by the debtor, or by a business carried on by him, where the loss occurred in the period beginning two years before the application date for the debt relief order and ending with the date of the application for the debt relief restrictions order;

  (b) failing to produce records of that kind on demand by the official receiver;

(c) entering into a transaction at an undervalue in the period beginning two years before the application date for the debt relief order and ending with the date of the determination of that application;

(d) giving a preference in the period beginning two years before the application date for the debt relief order and ending with the date of the determination of that application;

(e) making an excessive pension contribution;

(f) a failure to supply goods or services that were wholly or partly paid for;

(g) trading at a time, before the date of the determination of the application for the debt relief order, when the debtor knew or ought to have known that he was himself to be unable to pay his debts;

(h) incurring, before the date of the determination of the application for the debt relief order, a debt which the debtor had no reasonable expectation of being able to pay;

(i) failing to account satisfactorily to the court or the official receiver for a loss of property or for an insufficiency of property to meet his debts;

(j) carrying on any gambling, rash and hazardous speculation or unreasonable extravagance which may have materially contributed to or increased the extent of his inability to pay his debts before the application date for the debt relief order or which took place between that date and the date of the determination of the application for the debt relief order;

(k) neglect of business affairs of a kind which may have materially contributed to or increased the extent of his inability to pay his debts;

(l) fraud or fraudulent breach of trust;

(m) failing to cooperate with the official receiver.

2(3) The court shall also, in particular, consider whether the debtor was an undischarged bankrupt at some time during the period of six years ending with the date of the application for the debt relief order.

2(4) For the purposes of sub-paragraph (2)–

"excessive pension contribution" shall be construed in accordance with section 342A;

"preference" shall be construed in accordance with paragraph 10(2) of Schedule 4ZA;

"undervalue" shall be construed in accordance with paragraph 9(2) of that Schedule.

Timing of application for order

3 An application for a debt relief restrictions order in respect of a debtor may be made–

(a) at any time during the moratorium period relating to the debt relief order in question, or

(b) after the end of that period, but only with the permission of the court.

Duration of order

4(1) A debt relief restrictions order–

(a) comes into force when it is made, and

(b) ceases to have effect at the end of a date specified in the order.

4(2) The date specified in a debt relief restrictions order under sub-paragraph (1)(b) must not be–

(a) before the end of the period of two years beginning with the date on which the order is made, or

(b)   after the end of the period of 15 years beginning with that date.

Interim debt relief restrictions order

5(1)   This paragraph applies at any time between–

(a)   the institution of an application for a debt relief restrictions order, and

(b)   the determination of the application.

5(2)   The court may make an interim debt relief restrictions order if the court thinks that–

(a)   there are prima facie grounds to suggest that the application for the debt relief restrictions order will be successful, and

(b)   it is in the public interest to make an interim debt relief restrictions order.

5(3)   An interim debt relief restrictions order may only be made on the application of–

(a)   the Secretary of State, or

(b)   the official receiver acting on a direction of the Secretary of State.

5(4)   An interim debt relief restrictions order–

(a)   has the same effect as a debt relief restrictions order, and

(b)   comes into force when it is made.

5(5)   An interim debt relief restrictions order ceases to have effect–

(a)   on the determination of the application for the debt relief restrictions order,

(b)   on the acceptance of a debt relief restrictions undertaking made by the debtor, or

(c)   if the court discharges the interim debt relief restrictions order on the application of the person who applied for it or of the debtor.

6(1)   This paragraph applies to a case in which both an interim debt relief restrictions order and a debt relief restrictions order are made.

6(2)   Paragraph 4(2) has effect in relation to the debt relief restrictions order as if a reference to the date of that order were a reference to the date of the interim debt relief restrictions order.

Debt relief restrictions undertaking

7(1)   A debtor may offer a debt relief restrictions undertaking to the Secretary of State.

7(2)   In determining whether to accept a debt relief restrictions undertaking the Secretary of State shall have regard to the matters specified in paragraph 2(2) and (3).

8   A reference in an enactment to a person in respect of whom a debt relief restrictions order has effect (or who is "the subject of" a debt relief restrictions order) includes a reference to a person in respect of whom a debt relief restrictions undertaking has effect.

9(1)   A debt relief restrictions undertaking–

(a)   comes into force on being accepted by the Secretary of State, and

(b)   ceases to have effect at the end of a date specified in the undertaking.

9(2)   The date specified under sub-paragraph (1)(b) must not be–

(a)   before the end of the period of two years beginning with the date on which the undertaking is accepted, or

(b)   after the end of the period of 15 years beginning with that date.

9(3)   On an application by the debtor the court may–

(a)   annul a debt relief restrictions undertaking;

(b)   provide for a debt relief restrictions undertaking to cease to have effect before the date specified under sub-paragraph (1)(b).

Effect of revocation of debt relief order

10   Unless the court directs otherwise, the revocation at any time of a debt relief order does not–

(a)   affect the validity of any debt relief restrictions order, interim debt relief restrictions order or debt relief restrictions undertaking which is in force in respect of the debtor;

(b)   prevent the determination of any application for a debt relief restrictions order, or an interim debt relief restrictions order, in relation to the debtor that was instituted before that time;

(c)   prevent the acceptance of a debt relief restrictions undertaking that was offered before that time; or

(d)   prevent the institution of an application for a debt relief restrictions order or interim debt relief restrictions order in respect of the debtor, or the offer or acceptance of a debt relief restrictions undertaking by the debtor, after that time.

GENERAL NOTE

Introduced by s.108(2) to, and Sch.19 of, the Tribunals, Courts and Enforcement Act 2007 with effect from April 6, 2009, these provisions, which are anticipated by s.251V, clarify what is a debt relief restrictions order (DRRO) and the grounds for the making of such an order. The criteria that the court should have regard to mirror those relevant for a bankruptcy restrictions order. DRROs can run for a maximum of 15 years. Interim DRROs are a possibility and there is the predictable alternative of a debt relief restrictions undertaking (DRRU). Note that both DRROs and DRRUs should appear on a public register (s.251W). Further relevant provisions are to be found in IR 1986 rr.6.252–6.263.

SCHEDULE 4A

BANKRUPTCY RESTRICTIONS ORDER AND UNDERTAKING

1   Bankruptcy restrictions order

1(1)   A bankruptcy restrictions order may be made by the court.

1(2)   An order may be made only on the application of–

(a)   the Secretary of State, or

(b)   the official receiver acting on a direction of the Secretary of State.

2   Grounds for making order

2(1)   The court shall grant an application for a bankruptcy restrictions order if it thinks it appropriate having regard to the conduct of the bankrupt (whether before or after the making of the bankruptcy order).

2(2)   The court shall, in particular, take into account any of the following kinds of behaviour on the part of the bankrupt–

   (a)   failing to keep records which account for a loss of property by the bankrupt, or by a business carried on by him, where the loss occurred in the period beginning 2 years before petition and ending with the date of the application;

   (b)   failing to produce records of that kind on demand by the official receiver or the trustee;

   (c)   entering into a transaction at an undervalue;

   (d)   giving a preference;

   (e)   making an excessive pension contribution;

   (f)   a failure to supply goods or services which were wholly or partly paid for which gave rise to a claim provable in the bankruptcy;

   (g)   trading at a time before commencement of the bankruptcy when the bankrupt knew or ought to have known that he was himself to be unable to pay his debts;

   (h)   incurring, before commencement of the bankruptcy, a debt which the bankrupt had no reasonable expectation of being able to pay;

   (i)   failing to account satisfactorily to the court, the official receiver or the trustee for a loss of property or for an insufficiency of property to meet bankruptcy debts;

   (j)   carrying on any gambling, rash and hazardous speculation or unreasonable extravagance which may have materially contributed to or increased the extent of the bankruptcy or which took place between presentation of the petition and commencement of the bankruptcy;

   (k)   neglect of business affairs of a kind which may have materially contributed to or increased the extent of the bankruptcy;

   (l)   fraud or fraudulent breach of trust;

   (m) failing to cooperate with the official receiver or the trustee.

2(3)   The court shall also, in particular, consider whether the bankrupt was an undischarged bankrupt at some time during the period of six years ending with the date of the bankruptcy to which the application relates.

2(4)   For the purpose of sub-paragraph (2)–

   "before petition" shall be construed in accordance with section 351(c),

   "excessive pension contribution" shall be construed in accordance with section 342A,

   "preference" shall be construed in accordance with section 340, and

   "undervalue" shall be construed in accordance with section 339.

3   Timing of application for order

3(1)   An application for a bankruptcy restrictions order in respect of a bankrupt must be made–

   (a)   before the end of the period of one year beginning with the date on which the bankruptcy commences, or

   (b)   with the permission of the court.

3(2)   The period specified in sub-paragraph (1)(a) shall cease to run in respect of a bankrupt while the period set for his discharge is suspended under section 279(3).

4 Duration of order

4(1) A bankruptcy restrictions order–

  (a) shall come into force when it is made, and

  (b) shall cease to have effect at the end of a date specified in the order.

4(2) The date specified in a bankruptcy restrictions order under sub-paragraph (1)(b) must not be–

  (a) before the end of the period of two years beginning with the date on which the order is made, or

  (b) after the end of the period of 15 years beginning with that date.

5 Interim bankruptcy restrictions order

5(1) This paragraph applies at any time between–

  (a) the institution of an application for a bankruptcy restrictions order, and

  (b) the determination of the application.

5(2) The court may make an interim bankruptcy restrictions order if the court thinks that–

  (a) there are prima facie grounds to suggest that the application for the bankruptcy restrictions order will be successful, and

  (b) it is in the public interest to make an interim order.

5(3) An interim order may be made only on the application of–

  (a) the Secretary of State, or

  (b) the official receiver acting on a direction of the Secretary of State.

5(4) An interim order–

  (a) shall have the same effect as a bankruptcy restrictions order, and

  (b) shall come into force when it is made.

5(5) An interim order shall cease to have effect–

  (a) on the determination of the application for the bankruptcy restrictions order,

  (b) on the acceptance of a bankruptcy restrictions undertaking made by the bankrupt, or

  (c) if the court discharges the interim order on the application of the person who applied for it or of the bankrupt.

6(1) This paragraph applies to a case in which both an interim bankruptcy restrictions order and a bankruptcy restrictions order are made.

6(2) Paragraph 4(2) shall have effect in relation to the bankruptcy restrictions order as if a reference to the date of that order were a reference to the date of the interim order.

7 Bankruptcy restrictions undertaking

7(1) A bankrupt may offer a bankruptcy restrictions undertaking to the Secretary of State.

7(2) In determining whether to accept a bankruptcy restrictions undertaking the Secretary of State shall have regard to the matters specified in paragraph 2(2) and (3).

8 A reference in an enactment to a person in respect of whom a bankruptcy restrictions order has effect (or who is "the subject of" a bankruptcy restrictions order) includes a reference to a person in respect of whom a bankruptcy restrictions undertaking has effect.

9(1)   A bankruptcy restrictions undertaking–

    (a)   shall come into force on being accepted by the Secretary of State, and

    (b)   shall cease to have effect at the end of a date specified in the undertaking.

9(2)   The date specified under sub-paragraph (1)(b) must not be–

    (a)   before the end of the period of two years beginning with the date on which the undertaking is accepted, or

    (b)   after the end of the period of 15 years beginning with that date.

9(3)   On an application by the bankrupt the court may–

    (a)   annul a bankruptcy restrictions undertaking;

    (b)   provide for a bankruptcy restrictions undertaking to cease to have effect before the date specified under sub-paragraph (1)(b).

10   Effect of annulment of bankruptcy order

10   Where a bankruptcy order is annulled under section 282(1)(a) or (2)–

    (a)   any bankruptcy restrictions order, interim order or undertaking which is in force in respect of the bankrupt shall be annulled,

    (b)   no new bankruptcy restrictions order or interim order may be made in respect of the bankrupt, and

    (c)   no new bankruptcy restrictions undertaking by the bankrupt may be accepted.

11   Where a bankruptcy order is annulled under section 261, 263D or 282(1)(b)–

    (a)   the annulment shall not affect any bankruptcy restrictions order, interim order or undertaking in respect of the bankrupt,

    (b)   the court may make a bankruptcy restrictions order in relation to the bankrupt on an application instituted before the annulment,

    (c)   the Secretary of State may accept a bankruptcy restrictions undertaking offered before the annulment, and

    (d)   an application for a bankruptcy restrictions order or interim order in respect of the bankrupt may not be instituted after the annulment.

12   Registration

12   The Secretary of State shall maintain a register of–

    (a)   bankruptcy restrictions orders,

    (b)   interim bankruptcy restrictions orders, and

    (c)   bankruptcy restrictions undertakings.

GENERAL NOTE

This was inserted by EA 2002 s.257 and Sch.20 to further supplement the rules on BROs and BRUs. See the notes to s.281A above. Details of the use of BROs and BRUs in practice are mounted on the Insolvency Service website under Press Notices.

Cases involving bankruptcy restrictions orders are beginning to be reported. In *Randhawa v Official Receiver* [2006] B.P.I.R. 1435 the court was at pains to stress the common heritage of the BRO regime with the director disqualification procedure. Once the court had concluded that the conduct in question merited a BRO it was obliged to make such an order; this was consistent with the approach taken by the court in the director disqualification case of *Re Grayan Building Services Ltd* [1995] Ch. 241. BROs were intended both to protect the public and also to have a deterrent effect. The three-tier classification in *Re Sevenoaks Stationers Ltd* [1991] Ch. 164 governing the duration of a director disqualification could be adopted for determining the length of the BRO. The three year BRO was upheld. In concluding his judgment Launcelot Henderson Q.C. expressed disquiet that nowhere in Sch.4A was there any indication of the consequences that would ensue if a BRO were breached. If the conduct of the bankrupt is found to fall below the required standard the court *must* impose a BRO at least for the minimum two-year period—*Official Receiver v May* [2008] B.P.I.R. 1562.

Another reported case is *Official Receiver v Merchant* [2006] B.P.I.R. 1525 where Chief Registrar Baister dismissed an application for an interim BRO. The point was made that different considerations applied to the making of an interim order. General guidance was given on procedural aspects where an application for an interim BRO was sought.

In *Official Receiver v Doganci* [2007] B.P.I.R. 87 Chief Registrar Baister refused to grant a BRO because it could not be said that the bankrupt's explanation for the loss of property, although implausible, was untruthful. The bankrupt deserved the benefit of the doubt.

In *OR v Pyman* [2007] EWHC 1150; [2007] B.P.I.R. 1150 on appeal a bankruptcy restrictions order was doubled to seven years because the trial judge had underestimated the degree of culpability of the individual concerned (who had been bankrupted previously). The fact of a previous bankruptcy experience should have alerted the defendant to his responsibilities under bankruptcy law. The advanced age of the defendant was not relevant, unless there was evidence of infirmity.

Where a bankruptcy has been annulled under s.282(1)(b) on the ground that all debts have been paid the court can still grant a BRO provided the application was made before the annulment and within a year of the commencement of the bankruptcy—*Jenkins v OR* [2007] EWHC 1402 (Ch); [2007] B.P.I.R. 740. In this case it was held that in considering whether to make a BRO the court could take into account the fact that the individual whilst an undischarged bankrupt was continuing to act as a company director without leave.

A BRO was refused in *Official Receiver v Southey* [2009] B.P.I.R. 89 because the court was not satisfied that the bankrupt when incurring the debt in question had no reasonable prospect of repaying it. It took this generous view because the bankrupt had lived a precarious financial existence in the past and had always managed to repay his credit.

The issue of the cut off period for applications for a BRO was examined in *Official Receiver v Baars* [2009] B.P.I.R. 524. Here the bankruptcy had been discharged in late 2005 but the application for the BRO was not made to the court for more than two years after that date. The justification for the late application was the allegation that the former bankrupt had not disclosed his assets and this non-disclosure had not come to light until seven months before the application. In the light of these circumstances the court allowed the application to proceed.

A nine-year BRO was imposed by the court in *Official Receiver v Bathurst* [2008] B.P.I.R. 1548. Here the court at first instance had imposed a three-year restriction, but this was substantially increased by Sir Andrew Morritt CVO on appeal.

Most cases involving bankruptcy restrictions will be dealt with through the undertakings procedure.

For comment see Taylor, [2007] 20 Insolv. Int. 90.

SCHEDULE 5

POWERS OF TRUSTEE IN BANKRUPTCY

Section 314

PART I

POWERS EXERCISABLE WITH SANCTION

1 Power to carry on any business of the bankrupt so far as may be necessary for winding it up beneficially and so far as the trustee is able to do so without contravening any requirement imposed by or under any enactment.

2 Power to bring, institute or defend any action or legal proceedings relating to the property comprised in the bankrupt's estate.

2A Power to bring legal proceedings under section 339, 340 or 423.

3   Power to accept as the consideration for the sale of any property comprised in the bankrupt's estate a sum of money payable at a future time subject to such stipulations as to security or otherwise as the creditors' committee or the court thinks fit.

4   Power to mortgage or pledge any part of the property comprised in the bankrupt's estate for the purpose of raising money for the payment of his debts.

5   Power, where any right, option or other power forms part of the bankrupt's estate, to make payments or incur liabilities with a view to obtaining, for the benefit of the creditors, any property which is the subject of the right, option or power.

6   [Deleted.]

7   Power to make such compromise or other arrangement as may be thought expedient with creditors, or persons claiming to be creditors, in respect of bankruptcy debts.

8   Power to make such compromise or other arrangement as may be thought expedient with respect to any claim arising out of or incidental to the bankrupt's estate made or capable of being made on the trustee by any person.

PART II
GENERAL POWERS

9   Power to sell any part of the property for the time being comprised in the bankrupt's estate, including the goodwill and book debts of any business.

9A   Power to refer to arbitration, or compromise on such terms as may be agreed, any debts, claims or liabilities subsisting or supposed to subsist between the bankrupt and any person who may have incurred any liability to the bankrupt.

9B   Power to make such compromise or other arrangement as may be thought expedient with respect to any claim arising out of or incidental to the bankrupt's estate made or capable of being made by the trustee on any person.

10   Power to give receipts for any money received by him, being receipts which effectually discharge the person paying the money from all responsibility in respect of its application.

11   Power to prove, rank, claim and draw a dividend in respect of such debts due to the bankrupt as are comprised in his estate.

12   Power to exercise in relation to any property comprised in the bankrupt's estate any powers the capacity to exercise which is vested in him under Parts VIII to XI of this Act.

13   Power to deal with any property comprised in the estate to which the bankrupt is beneficially entitled as tenant in tail in the same manner as the bankrupt might have dealt with it.

PART III
ANCILLARY POWERS

14   For the purposes of, or in connection with, the exercise of any of his powers under Parts VIII to XI of this Act, the trustee may, by his official name–

(a)   hold property of every description,

(b)   make contracts,

(c)   sue and be sued,

(d)   enter into engagements binding on himself and, in respect of the bankrupt's estate, on his successors in office,

   (e)   employ an agent,

   (f)   execute any power of attorney, deed or other instrument;

and he may do any other act which is necessary or expedient for the purposes of or in connection with the exercise of those powers.

GENERAL NOTE

This schedule, allied to s.314, lists the powers of a trustee in bankruptcy. Like Sch.2, it has been hived off from the mainstream of the legislation. The crucial distinguishing factor is the need to obtain the sanction of the committee of creditors (see s.301) before the powers listed in Pt I can be exercised. Paragraph 2A was inserted by s.262 of EA 2002 to ensure that recovery actions were properly sanctioned as the costs of such actions can now be treated as a winding-up expense, see IR 1986 r.6.224.

   For a recent decision on the effect of the power now contained in Sch.5 para.3, see *Weddell v Pearce (JA) & Major* [1988] Ch. 26. This case involved the assignment of a cause of action by the trustee for future consideration without obtaining the requisite sanction. It was held by Scott J. that notwithstanding this failure to obtain sanction, the assignment took effect in equity. This ruling is in line with the philosophy now expressed in ss.314(3) and 377 of IA 1986. The power to assign was also reviewed by the Australian courts in *Re Cirillo* [1997] B.P.I.R. 166. On the power to employ a solicitor see *Re Schuppan* [1996] B.P.I.R. 486. On the meaning of "compromise" and "sale" within paras 7 and 9 respectively see the judgment of Gabriel Moss Q.C. in *Power v Brown* [2009] B.P.I.R. 340.

   Note the deletion of para.6, amendment of para.8 and the insertion of paras 9A and 9B by LRO 2010 (SI 2010/18). The net effect of this is to extend the powers of the trustee by removing the need to obtain sanction before exercising the specified powers.

   For further guidance on this Schedule see the note to s.314.

SCHEDULE 6

THE CATEGORIES OF PREFERENTIAL DEBTS

Section 386

Category 1: Debts due to Inland Revenue

[Deleted.]

Category 2: Debts due to Customs and Excise

[Deleted.]

Category 3: Social Security Contributions

[Deleted.]

Category 4: Contributions to Occupational Pension Schemes, etc.

8   Any sum which is owed by the debtor and is a sum to which Schedule 4 to the Pension Schemes Act 1993 applies (contributions to occupational pension schemes and state scheme premiums).

Category 5: Remuneration, etc., of Employees

9   So much of any amount which–

   (a)   is owed by the debtor to a person who is or has been an employee of the debtor, and

(b)   is payable by way of remuneration in respect of the whole or any part of the period of 4 months next before the relevant date,

as does not exceed so much as may be prescribed by order made by the Secretary of State.

10   An amount owed by way of accrued holiday remuneration, in respect of any period of employment before the relevant date, to a person whose employment by the debtor has been terminated, whether before, on or after that date.

11   So much of any sum owed in respect of money advanced for the purpose as has been applied for the payment of a debt which, if it had not been paid, would have been a debt falling within paragraph 9 or 10.

12   So much of any amount which–

(a)   is ordered (whether before or after the relevant date) to be paid by the debtor under the Reserve Forces (Safeguard of Employment) Act 1985, and

(b)   is so ordered in respect of a default made by the debtor before that date in the discharge of his obligations under that Act,

as does not exceed such amount as may be prescribed by order made by the Secretary of State.

Interpretation for Category 5

13(1)   For the purposes of paragraphs 9 to 12, a sum is payable by the debtor to a person by way of remuneration in respect of any period if–

(a)   it is paid as wages or salary (whether payable for time or for piece work or earned wholly or partly by way of commission) in respect of services rendered to the debtor in that period, or

(b)   it is an amount falling within the following sub-paragraph and is payable by the debtor in respect of that period.

13(2)   An amount falls within this sub-paragraph if it is–

(a)   a guarantee payment under Part III of the Employment Rights Act 1996 (employee without work to do);

(b)   any payment for time off under section 53 (time off to look for work to arrange training) or section 56 (time off for ante-natal care) of that Act or under section 169 of the Trade Union and Labour Relations (Consolidation) Act 1992 (time off for carrying out trade union duties etc.);

(c)   remuneration on suspension on medical grounds, or on maternity grounds, under Part VII of the Employment Rights Act 1996; or

(d)   remuneration under a protective award under section 189 of the Trade Union and Labour Relations (Consolidation) Act 1992 (redundancy dismissal with compensation).

14(1)   This paragraph relates to a case in which a person's employment has been terminated by or in consequence of his employer going into liquidation or being adjudged bankrupt or (his employer being a company not in liquidation) by or in consequence of–

(a)   a receiver being appointed as mentioned in section 40 of this Act (debenture-holders secured by floating charge), or

(b)   the appointment of a receiver under section 53(6) or 54(5) of this Act (Scottish company with property subject to floating charge), or

(c)   the taking of possession by debenture-holders (so secured), as mentioned in section 754 of the Companies Act 2006.

14(2)   For the purposes of paragraphs 9 to 12, holiday remuneration is deemed to have accrued to that person in respect of any period of employment if, by virtue of his contract of employment or of any enactment, that remuneration would have accrued in respect of that period if his employment had continued until he became entitled to be allowed the holiday.

14(3)   The reference in sub-paragraph (2) to any enactment includes an order or direction made under an enactment.

15   Without prejudice to paragraphs 13 and 14–

(a)   any remuneration payable by the debtor to a person in respect of a period of holiday or of absence from work through sickness or other good cause is deemed to be wages or (as the case may be) salary in respect of services rendered to the debtor in that period, and

(b)   references here and in those paragraphs to remuneration in respect of a period of holiday include any sums which, if they had been paid, would have been treated for the purposes of the enactments relating to social security as earnings in respect of that period.

Category 6: Levies on Coal and Steel Production

15A   Any sums due at the relevant date from the debtor in respect of–

(a)   the levies on the production of coal and steel referred to in Articles 49 and 50 of the E.C.S.C. Treaty, or

(b)   any surcharge for delay provided for in Article 50(3) of that Treaty and Article 6 of Decision 3/52 of the High Authority of the Coal and Steel Community.

Orders

16   An order under paragraph 9 or 12–

(a)   may contain such transitional provisions as may appear to the Secretary of State necessary or expedient;

(b)   shall be made by statutory instrument subject to annulment in pursuance of a resolution of either House of Parliament.

GENERAL NOTE

This Schedule, which is brought into play by s.386, largely reflects the preferential claims regime as suggested by the Cork Committee (Cmnd.8558, para.1450) and further pruned by EA 2002. Categories 1, 2 and 3 (Crown debts) were abolished by s.251 of EA 2002 effective September 15, 2003. (For transitional provisions, see SI 2003/2093 art.4.)

For the meaning of the phrase "the relevant date", see s.387. For further comment, see the general note to Pt XII. The amount for paras 9 and 12 is fixed at £800: see the Insolvency Proceedings (Monetary Limits) Order 1986 (SI 1986/1996) art.4.

Para.8
A minor textual amendment was made here by the Pension Schemes Act 1993 Sch.8 para.18.

Para.13
A new subpara.(2) was added by para.29 of Sch.1 to the Employment Rights Act 1996 to facilitate the recent changes in employment legislation.

Para.14
A minor change was made to para.14(1) by the Companies Act 2006 (Consequential Amendments) Order 2008 (SI 2008/948) to convert references in the Companies Act 1985 into their counterparts in the Companies Act 2006.

SCHEDULE 7

INSOLVENCY PRACTITIONERS TRIBUNAL

Section 396

Panels of Members

1(1) The Secretary of State shall draw up and from time to time revise–

(a) a panel of persons who

    (i) satisfy the judicial-appointment eligibility condition on a 5-year basis;

    (ii) are advocates or solicitors in Scotland of at least 5 years' standing, and are nominated for the purpose by the Lord Chancellor or the Lord President of the Court of Session, and

(b) a panel of persons who are experienced in insolvency matters;

and the members of the Tribunal shall be selected from those panels in accordance with this Schedule.

1(2) The power to revise the panels includes power to terminate a person's membership of either of them, and is accordingly to that extent subject to section 7 of the Tribunals and Inquiries Act 1992 (which makes it necessary to obtain the concurrence of the Lord Chancellor and the Lord President of the Court of Session to dismissals in certain cases).

Remuneration of Members

2 The Secretary of State may out of money provided by Parliament pay to members of the Tribunal such remuneration as he may with the approval of the Treasury determine; and such expenses of the Tribunal as the Secretary of State and the Treasury may approve shall be defrayed by the Secretary of State out of money so provided.

Sittings of Tribunal

3(1) For the purposes of carrying out their functions in relation to any cases referred to them, the Tribunal may sit either as a single tribunal or in two or more divisions.

3(2) The functions of the Tribunal in relation to any case referred to them shall be exercised by three members consisting of–

(a) a chairman selected by the Secretary of State from the panel drawn up under paragraph 1(1)(a) above, and

(b) two other members selected by the Secretary of State from the panel drawn up under paragraph 1(1)(b).

Procedure of Tribunal

4(1) Any investigation by the Tribunal shall be so conducted as to afford a reasonable opportunity for representations to be made to the Tribunal by or on behalf of the person whose case is the subject of the investigation.

4(2) For the purposes of any such investigation, the Tribunal–

(a) may by summons require any person to attend, at such time and place as is specified in the summons, to give evidence or to produce any books, papers and other records in his possession or under his control which the Tribunal consider it necessary for the purposes of the investigation to examine, and

(b)   may take evidence on oath, and for the purpose administer oaths, or may, instead of administering an oath, require the person examined to make and subscribe a declaration of the truth of the matter respecting which he is examined;

but no person shall be required, in obedience to such a summons, to go more than ten miles from his place of residence, unless the necessary expenses of his attendance are paid or tendered to him.

4(3)   Every person who–

(a)   without reasonable excuse fails to attend in obedience to a summons issued under this paragraph, or refuses to give evidence, or

(b)   intentionally alters, suppresses, conceals or destroys or refuses to produce any document which he may be required to produce for the purpose of an investigation by the Tribunal,

is liable to a fine.

4(4)   Subject to the provisions of this paragraph, the Secretary of State may make rules for regulating the procedure on any investigation by the Tribunal.

4(5)   In their application to Scotland, sub-paragraphs (2) and (3) above have effect as if for any reference to a summons there were substituted a reference to a notice in writing.

General Note

The Insolvency Practitioners Tribunal, which was established under IA 1985 s.8(6) and is confirmed by s.396(1) of the present Act, is empowered to review the decisions of the Secretary of State (or other "competent authority") to refuse an application for authorisation or withdraw an authorisation to act as an insolvency practitioner: see the note to s.396 and the Insolvency Practitioners Tribunal (Conduct of Investigations) Rules 1986 (SI 1986/952). It is not concerned with decisions about authorisation made by professional bodies under ss.390(2)(a) and 391, since those bodies have their own reviewing procedures.

This Schedule contains details about the membership and procedure of the tribunal, which consists, for the hearing of any case, of two insolvency experts and a legally qualified chairman. Although the power of selection, and also largely that of nomination, of members rests with the Secretary of State, the tribunal is intended to function as an independent body.

SCHEDULE 8

PROVISIONS CAPABLE OF INCLUSION IN COMPANY INSOLVENCY RULES

Section 411

Courts

1   Provision for supplementing, in relation to the insolvency or winding up of companies, any provision made by or under section 117 of this Act (jurisdiction in relation to winding up).

2(1)   Provision for regulating the practice and procedure of any court exercising jurisdiction for the purposes of Parts I to VII of this Act or the Companies Acts so far as relating to, and to matters connected with or arising out of, the insolvency or winding up of companies, being any provision that could be made by rules of court.

2(2)   Rules made by virtue of this paragraph about the consequence of failure to comply with practice or procedure may, in particular, include provision about the termination of administration.

Notices, etc.

3   Provision requiring notice of any proceedings in connection with or arising out of the insolvency or winding up of a company to be given or published in the manner prescribed by the rules.

4   Provision with respect to the form, manner of serving, contents and proof of any petition, application, order, notice, statement or other document required to be presented, made, given, published or prepared under any enactment or subordinate legislation relating to, or to matters connected with or arising out of, the insolvency or winding up of companies.

5   Provision specifying the persons to whom any notice is to be given.

Registration of Voluntary Arrangements

6   Provision for the registration of voluntary arrangements approved under Part I of this Act, including provision for the keeping and inspection of a register.

7   Provision as to the manner in which a provisional liquidator appointed under section 135 is to carry out his functions.

Conduct of Insolvency

8   Provision with respect to the certification of any person as, and as to the proof that a person is, the liquidator, administrator or administrative receiver of a company.

9   The following provision with respect to meetings of a company's creditors, contributories or members–

  (a)   provision as to the manner of summoning a meeting (including provision as to how any power to require a meeting is to be exercised, provision as to the manner of determining the value of any debt or contribution for the purposes of any such power and provision making the exercise of any such power subject to the deposit of a sum sufficient to cover the expenses likely to be incurred in summoning and holding a meeting);

  (b)   provision specifying the time and place at which a meeting may be held and the period of notice required for a meeting;

  (c)   provision as to the procedure to be followed at a meeting (including the manner in which decisions may be reached by a meeting and the manner in which the value of any vote at a meeting is to be determined);

  (d)   provision for requiring a person who is or has been an officer of the company to attend a meeting;

  (e)   provision creating, in the prescribed circumstances, a presumption that a meeting has been duly summoned and held;

  (f)   provision as to the manner of proving the decisions of a meeting.

10(1)   Provision as to the functions, membership and proceedings of a committee established under section 49, 68, 101, 141 or 142 of, or paragraph 57 of Schedule B1 to, this Act.

10(2)   The following provision with respect to the establishment of a committee under section 101, 141 or 142 of this Act, that is to say–

  (a)   provision for resolving differences between a meeting of the company's creditors and a meeting of its contributories or members;

  (b)   provision authorising the establishment of the committee without a meeting of contributories in a case where a company is being wound up on grounds including its inability to pay its debts; and

(c)   provision modifying the requirements of this Act with respect to the establishment of the committee in a case where a winding-up order has been made immediately upon the discharge of an administration order.

11   Provision as to the manner in which any requirement that may be imposed on a person under any of Parts I to VII of this Act by the official receiver, the liquidator, administrator or administrative receiver of a company or a special manager appointed under section 177 is to be so imposed.

12   Provision as to the debts that may be proved in a winding up, as to the manner and conditions of proving a debt and as to the manner and expenses of establishing the value of any debt or security.

13   Provision with respect to the manner of the distribution of the property of a company that is being wound up, including provision with respect to unclaimed funds and dividends.

14   Provision which, with or without modifications, applies in relation to the winding up of companies any enactment contained in Parts VIII to XI of this Act or in the Bankruptcy (Scotland) Act 1985.

14A   Provision about the application of section 176A of this Act which may include, in particular–

(a)   provision enabling a receiver to institute winding-up proceedings;

(b)   provision requiring a receiver to institute winding-up proceedings.

Administration

14B   Provision which–

(a)   applies in relation to administration, with or without modifications, a provision of Parts IV to VII of this Act, or

(b)   serves a purpose in relation to administration similar to a purpose that may be served by the rules in relation to winding up by virtue of a provision of this Schedule.

Financial Provisions

15   Provision as to the amount, or manner of determining the amount, payable to the liquidator, administrator or administrative receiver of a company or a special manager appointed under section 177, by way of remuneration for the carrying out of functions in connection with or arising out of the insolvency or winding up of a company.

16   Provision with respect to the manner in which moneys received by the liquidator of a company in the course of carrying out his functions as such are to be invested or otherwise handled and with respect to the payment of interest on sums which, in pursuance of rules made by virtue of this paragraph, have been paid into the Insolvency Services Account.

16A   Provision enabling the Secretary of State to set the rate of interest paid on sums which have been paid into the Insolvency Services Account.

17   Provision as to the fees, costs, charges and other expenses that may be treated as the expenses of a winding up.

18   Provision as to the fees, costs, charges and other expenses that may be treated as properly incurred by the administrator or administrative receiver of a company.

19   Provision as to the fees, costs, charges and other expenses that may be incurred for any of the purposes of Part I of this Act or in the administration of any voluntary arrangement approved under that Part.

20   Provision requiring registrars and other officers of courts having jurisdiction in England and Wales in relation to, or to matters connected with or arising out of, the insolvency or winding up of companies–

(a)   to keep books and other records with respect to the exercise of that jurisdiction, and

(b)   to make returns to the Secretary of State of the business of those courts.

21   Provision requiring a creditor, member or contributory, or such a committee as is mentioned in paragraph 10 above, to be supplied (on payment in prescribed cases of the prescribed fee) with such information and with copies of such documents as may be prescribed.

22   Provision as to the manner in which public examinations under sections 133 and 134 of this Act and proceedings under sections 236 and 237 are to be conducted, as to the circumstances in which records of such examinations or proceedings are to be made available to prescribed persons and as to the costs of such examinations and proceedings.

23   Provision imposing requirements with respect to–

(a)   the preparation and keeping by the liquidator, administrator or administrative receiver of a company, or by the supervisor of a voluntary arrangement approved under Part I of this Act, of prescribed books, accounts and other records;

(b)   the production of those books, accounts and records for inspection by prescribed persons;

(c)   the auditing of accounts kept by the liquidator, administrator or administrative receiver of a company, or the supervisor of such a voluntary arrangement; and

(d)   the issue by the administrator or administrative receiver of a company of such a certificate as is mentioned in section 22(3)(b) of the Value Added Tax Act 1983 (refund of tax in cases of bad debts) and the supply of copies of the certificate to creditors of the company.

24   Provision requiring the person who is the supervisor of a voluntary arrangement approved under Part I, when it appears to him that the voluntary arrangement has been fully implemented and that nothing remains to be done by him under the arrangement–

(a)   to give notice of that fact to persons bound by the voluntary arrangement, and

(b)   to report to those persons on the carrying out of the functions conferred on the supervisor of the arrangement.

25   Provision as to the manner in which the liquidator of a company is to act in relation to the books, papers and other records of the company, including provision authorising their disposal.

26   Provision imposing requirements in connection with the carrying out of functions under section 7(3) of the Company Directors Disqualification Act 1986 (including, in particular, requirements with respect to the making of periodic returns).

General

27   Provision conferring power on the Secretary of State or the Treasury to make regulations with respect to so much of any matter that may be provided for in the rules as relates to the carrying out of the functions of the liquidator, administrator or administrative receiver of a company.

28   Provision conferring a discretion on the court.

29   Provision conferring power on the court to make orders for the purpose of securing compliance with obligations imposed by or under section 47, 66, 131, 143(2) or 235 of, or paragraph 47 of Schedule B1 to, this Act or section 7(4) of the Company Directors Disqualification Act 1986.

30 Provision making non-compliance with any of the rules a criminal offence.

31 Provision making different provision for different cases or descriptions of cases, including different provisions for different areas.

GENERAL NOTE

Much of the detail of the insolvency regime which IA 1985 introduced and IA 1986 consolidated was left to be spelt out in subordinate legislation by regulations made under ss.411 et seq. This Schedule outlines some of the matters which may be the subject of rules relating to company insolvency. The Companies (Winding-Up) Rules 1949 were superseded by IR 1986, which were brought into force contemporaneously with the commencement of the Act itself; but the Schedule is by no means confined in scope to matters which have traditionally been part of winding-up rules.

Numerous amendments to this Schedule were made by EA 2002. Note that in this Schedule, "liquidator" includes a provisional liquidator (s.411(3)). Attention should also be drawn to IR 1986 r.12.1, which authorises the Secretary of State (pursuant to Sch.8 para.27 and Sch.9 para.30) to make regulations in regard to various matters, supplementary to the Insolvency Rules made under s.411.

Among the items listed which cannot be regarded as purely procedural or are not self-explanatory the following may be noted.

Para.2

Amendment by the Companies Act 2006 (Commencement No.3, Consequential Amendments, Transitional Provisions and Savings) Order 2007 (SI 2007/2194 (C. 84)) art.10(1) and Sch.4 para.44, as from October 1, 2007, recognises the Companies Act 2006.

Para.6

There is no mention in the body of the Act of any registration procedure for a CVA, although certain matters must be reported to the court (see, e.g. ss.2(2), 4(6)). The present paragraph has been implemented by IR 1986 r.1.24(5), which provides for registration with the registrar of companies.

Paras 12, 14

The Parts of the Act dealing with company insolvency contain no definition of "debts" and no provisions relating to proofs of debts, in marked contrast to those relating to the bankruptcy of individuals (see ss.322, 382), and, indeed, to the repealed CA 1985 s.611. It is only by subordinate legislation made under these paragraphs of the present Schedule that such important matters as the nature of provable debts, the quantification of such debts, allowances for mutual credit and set-off, etc. are established for company liquidations and some (but not all) analogous proceedings. This has been done by IR 1986 rr.4.73 et seq., 4.86 et seq. and 12.3.

For further discussion of the term "debts", see the notes to s.1(1) and IR 1986 r.13.12.

The Companies Acts prior to the present legislation always included a substantive provision (e.g. CA 1985 s.612) which incorporated specified aspects of bankruptcy law into the law governing the winding up of *insolvent* companies. Paragraph 14 of this Schedule is potentially of wider scope, since it applies to solvent liquidations as well.

See further the introductory note to Pt IV, Ch.VIII, following s.174.

Para.27

For the relevant regulations see the Insolvency Regulations 1994 (SI 1994/2507, operative October 24, 1994, as amended by SI 2000/485, effective March 31, 2000 and SI 2001/762, effective April 2, 2001); SI 2004/472 (effective April 1, 2004); SI 2005/512 (effective April 1, 2005); and SI 2008/670 (effective April 6, 2008). Paragraph 27 was amended by the Banking Act 2009 s.125(7) as from February 21, 2009.

SCHEDULE 9

PROVISIONS CAPABLE OF INCLUSION IN INDIVIDUAL INSOLVENCY RULES

Section 412

Courts

1 Provision with respect to the arrangement and disposition of the business under Parts 7A to 11 of this Act of courts having jurisdiction for the purpose of those Parts, including provision for the allocation of proceedings under those Parts to particular courts and for the transfer of such proceedings from one court to another.

2 Provision for enabling a registrar in bankruptcy of the High Court or a registrar of a county court having jurisdiction for the purposes of those Parts to exercise such of the jurisdiction conferred for those purposes on the High Court or, as the case may be, that county court as may be prescribed.

3 Provision for regulating the practice and procedure of any court exercising jurisdiction for the purposes of those Parts, being any provision that could be made by rules of court.

4 Provision conferring rights of audience, in courts exercising jurisdiction for the purposes of those Parts, on the official receiver and on solicitors.

Notices etc.

5 Provision requiring notice of any proceedings under Parts 7A to 11 of this Act or of any matter relating to or arising out of a proposal under Part VIII or a bankruptcy to be given or published in the prescribed manner.

6 Provision with respect to the form, manner of serving, contents and proof of any petition, application, order, notice, statement or other document required to be presented, made, given, published or prepared under any enactment contained in Parts 7A to 11 or subordinate legislation under those Parts or Part XV (including provision requiring prescribed matters to be verified by affidavit).

7 Provision specifying the persons to whom any notice under Parts 7A to 11 is to be given.

Debt relief orders

7A Provision as to the manner in which the official receiver is to carry out his functions under Part 7A.

7B Provision as to the manner in which any requirement that may be imposed by the official receiver on a person under Part 7A is to take effect.

7C Provision modifying the application of Part 7A in relation to an individual who has died at a time when a moratorium period under a debt relief order applies in relation to him.

Debt relief restrictions orders and undertakings

7D Provision about debt relief restrictions orders, interim orders and undertakings, including provision about evidence.

Register of debt relief orders and debt relief restrictions orders etc

7E Provision about the register required to be maintained by section 251W and the information to be contained in it, including provision–

(a) enabling the amalgamation of the register with another register;

(b) enabling inspection of the register by the public.

Registration of Voluntary Arrangements

8 Provision for the registration of voluntary arrangements approved under Part VIII of this Act, including provision for the keeping and inspection of a register.

Official Receiver Acting on Voluntary Arrangement

8A Provision about the official receiver acting as nominee or supervisor in relation to a voluntary arrangement under Part VIII of this Act, including–

(a) provision requiring the official receiver to act in specified circumstances;

(b) provision about remuneration;

(c) provision prescribing terms or conditions to be treated as forming part of a voluntary arrangement in relation to which the official receiver acts as nominee or supervisor;

(d) provision enabling those terms or conditions to be varied or excluded, in specified circumstances or subject to specified conditions, by express provision in an arrangement.

Interim Receiver

9 Provision as to the manner in which an interim receiver appointed under section 286 is to carry out his functions, including any such provision as is specified in relation to the trustee of a bankrupt's estate in paragraph 21 or 27 below.

Receiver or Manager

10 Provision as to the manner in which the official receiver is to carry out his functions as receiver or manager of a bankrupt's estate under section 287, including any such provision as is specified in relation to the trustee of a bankrupt's estate in paragraph 21 or 27 below.

Administration of Individual Insolvency

11 Provision with respect to the certification of the appointment of any person as trustee of a bankrupt's estate and as to the proof of that appointment.

12 The following provision with respect to meetings of creditors–

(a) provision as to the manner of summoning a meeting (including provision as to how any power to require a meeting is to be exercised, provision as to the manner of determining the value of any debt for the purposes of any such power and provision making the exercise of any such power subject to the deposit of a sum sufficient to cover the expenses likely to be incurred in summoning and holding a meeting);

(b) provision specifying the time and place at which a meeting may be held and the period of notice required for a meeting;

(c) provision as to the procedure to be followed at such a meeting (including the manner in which decisions may be reached by a meeting and the manner in which the value of any vote at a meeting is to be determined);

(d) provision for requiring a bankrupt or debtor to attend a meeting;

(e) provision creating, in the prescribed circumstances, a presumption that a meeting has been duly summoned and held; and

(f) provision as to the manner of proving the decisions of a meeting.

13 Provision as to the functions, membership and proceedings of a creditors' committee established under section 301.

14 Provision as to the manner in which any requirement that may be imposed on a person under Parts VIII to XI of this Act by the official receiver, the trustee of a bankrupt's estate or a special manager appointed under section 370 is to be so imposed and, in the case of any requirement imposed under section 305(3) (information etc. to be given by the trustee to the official receiver), provision conferring power on the court to make orders for the purpose of securing compliance with that requirement.

15 Provision as to the manner in which any requirement imposed by virtue of section 310(3) (compliance with income payments order) is to take effect.

16 Provision as to the terms and conditions that may be included in a charge under section 313 (dwelling house forming part of bankrupt's estate).

17 Provision as to the debts that may be proved in any bankruptcy, as to the manner and conditions of proving a debt and as to the manner and expenses of establishing the value of any debt or security.

18 Provision with respect to the manner of the distribution of a bankrupt's estate, including provision with respect to unclaimed funds and dividends.

19 Provision modifying the application of Parts VIII to XI of this Act in relation to a debtor or bankrupt who has died.

Financial Provisions

20 Provision as to the amount, or manner of determining the amount, payable to an interim receiver, the trustee of a bankrupt's estate or a special manager appointed under section 370 by way of remuneration for the performance of functions in connection with or arising out of the bankruptcy of any person.

21 Provision with respect to the manner in which moneys received by the trustee of a bankrupt's estate in the course of carrying out his functions as such are to be invested or otherwise handled and with respect to the payment of interest on sums which, in pursuance of rules made by virtue of this paragraph, have been paid into the Insolvency Services Account.

21A Provision enabling the Secretary of State to set the rate of interest paid on sums which have been paid into the Insolvency Services Account.

22 Provision as to the fees, costs, charges and other expenses that may be treated as the expenses of a bankruptcy.

23 Provision as to the fees, costs, charges and other expenses that may be incurred for any of the purposes of Part VIII of this Act or in the administration of any voluntary arrangement approved under that Part.

Information and Records

24 Provision requiring registrars and other officers of courts having jurisdiction for the purposes of Parts VIII to XI–

    (a) to keep books and other records with respect to the exercise of that jurisdiction and of jurisdiction under the Deeds of Arrangement Act 1914, and

    (b) to make returns to the Secretary of State of the business of those courts.

25 Provision requiring a creditor or a committee established under section 301 to be supplied (on payment in prescribed cases of the prescribed fee) with such information and with copies of such documents as may be prescribed.

26 Provision as to the manner in which public examinations under section 290 and proceedings under sections 366 to 368 are to be conducted, as to the circumstances in which records of such examinations and proceedings are to be made available to prescribed persons and as to the costs of such examinations and proceedings.

27 Provision imposing requirements with respect to–

(a) the preparation and keeping by the trustee of a bankrupt's estate, or the supervisor of a voluntary arrangement approved under Part VIII, of prescribed books, accounts and other records;

(b) the production of those books, accounts and records for inspection by prescribed persons; and

(c) the auditing of accounts kept by the trustee of a bankrupt's estate or the supervisor of such a voluntary arrangement.

28 Provision requiring the person who is the supervisor of a voluntary arrangement approved under Part VIII, when it appears to him that the voluntary arrangement has been fully implemented and that nothing remains to be done by him under it–

(a) to give notice of that fact to persons bound by the voluntary arrangement, and

(b) to report to those persons on the carrying out of the functions conferred on the supervisor of it.

29 Provision as to the manner in which the trustee of a bankrupt's estate is to act in relation to the books, papers and other records of the bankrupt, including provision authorising their disposal.

Bankruptcy Restrictions Orders and Undertakings

29A Provision about bankruptcy restrictions orders, interim orders and undertakings, including–

(a) provision about evidence;

(b) provision enabling the amalgamation of the register mentioned in paragraph 12 of Schedule 4A with another register;

(c) provision enabling inspection of that register by the public.

General

30 Provision conferring power on the Secretary of State to make regulations with respect to so much of any matter that may be provided for in the rules as relates to the carrying out of the functions of an interim receiver appointed under section 286, of the official receiver while acting as a receiver or manager under section 287 or of a trustee of a bankrupt's estate.

31 Provision conferring a discretion on the court.

32 Provision making non-compliance with any of the rules a criminal offence.

33 Provision making different provision for different cases, including different provision for different areas.

GENERAL NOTE

This provides a useful guide to the matters which may be provided for by the rules. Authority to make these rules is given by s.412, and the note on that section should be referred to. Paragraphs 8A and 29A were inserted by EA 2002 s.269 and Sch.23 to deal with the advent of fast-track IVAs and BROs. The utility of para.17 was illustrated in *Woodley v Woodley (No.2)* [1994] 1 W.L.R. 1167. For the text of the Insolvency Rules (1986/1925) as amended see below, at pp.664 et seq. For the regulations referred to in para.30 see the Insolvency Regulations 1994 (SI 1994/2507), operative October 24, 1994, replacing the original Insolvency Regulations 1986 (SI 1986/1994), as amended.

In para.21 the words "invested or otherwise handled and with respect to the payment of interest on sums which, in pursuance of rules made by virtue of this paragraph, have been paid into the Insolvency Services Account" substituted for the word "handled" by the Insolvency Act 2000 (s.13(1) as from April 2, 2001 (see SI 2001/766 (C. 27) arts 1, 2(1)(b)). See note to s.406.

Note amendment of various paras in Sch.9 by para.14 of Pt 1 of Sch.20 to the Tribunals, Courts and Enforcement Act 2007. Paragraphs 7A to 7E have been inserted.

SCHEDULE 10

PUNISHMENT OF OFFENCES UNDER THIS ACT

Section 430

Note: In the fourth and fifth columns of this Schedule, **"the statutory maximum"** means–

- (a) in England and Wales, the prescribed sum under section 32 of the Magistrates' Courts Act 1980 (c. 43), and

- (b) in Scotland, the prescribed sum under section 289B of the Criminal Procedure (Scotland) Act 1975 (c. 21).

Section of Act creating offence	General nature of offence	Mode of prosecution	Punishment	Daily default fine (where applicable)
6A(1)	False representation or fraud for purpose of obtaining members' or creditors' approval of proposed voluntary arrangement.	1. On indictment. 2. Summary.	7 years or a fine, or both. 6 months or the statutory maximum, or both.	
12(2)	Company and others failing to state in correspondence etc. that administrator appointed.	Summary.	One-fifth of the statutory maximum.	
15(8)	Failure of administrator to register office copy of court order permitting disposal of charged property.	Summary.	One-fifth of the statutory maximum.	One-fiftieth of the statutory maximum.
18(5)	Failure of administrator to register office copy of court order varying or discharging administration order.	Summary.	One-fifth of the statutory maximum.	One-fiftieth of the statutory maximum.
21(3)	Administrator failing to register administration order and give notice of appointment.	Summary.	One-fifth of the statutory maximum.	One-fiftieth of the statutory maximum.
22(6)	Failure to comply with provisions relating to statement of affairs, where administrator appointed.	1. On indictment. 2. Summary.	A fine. The statutory maximum.	One-tenth of the statutory maximum.
23(3)	Administrator failing to send out, register and lay before creditors statement of his proposals.	Summary.	One-fifth of the statutory maximum.	One-fiftieth of the statutory maximum.
24(7)	Administrator failing to file court order discharging administration order under s.24.	Summary.	One-fifth of the statutory maximum.	One-fiftieth of the statutory maximum.
27(6)	Administrator failing to file court order discharging administration order under s.27.	Summary.	One-fifth of the statutory maximum.	One-fiftieth of the statutory maximum.
30	Body corporate acting as receiver.	1. On indictment. 2. Summary.	A fine. The statutory maximum.	
31	Bankrupt or a person in respect of whom a debt relief order is made acting as receiver or manager.	1. On indictment. 2. Summary.	2 years or a fine, or both. 6 months or the statutory maximum, or both.	
38(5)	Receiver failing to deliver accounts to registrar.	Summary.	One-fifth of the statutory maximum.	One-fiftieth of the statutory maximum.
39(2)	Company and others failing to state in correspondence that receiver appointed.	Summary.	One-fifth of the statutory maximum.	One-fiftieth of the statutory maximum.
43(6)	Administrative receiver failing to file copy of order permitting disposal of charged property.	Summary.	One-fifth of the statutory maximum.	One-fiftieth of the statutory maximum.
45(5)	Administrative receiver failing to file notice of vacation of office.	Summary.	One-fifth of the statutory maximum.	One-fiftieth of the statutory maximum.

Section of Act creating offence	General nature of offence	Mode of prosecution	Punishment	Daily default fine (where applicable)
46(4)	Administrative receiver failing to give notice of his appointment.	Summary.	One-fifth of the statutory maximum.	One-fiftieth of the statutory maximum.
47(6)	Failure to comply with provisions relating to statement of affairs where administrative receiver appointed.	1. On indictment. 2. Summary.	A fine. The statutory maximum.	One-tenth of the statutory maximum.
48(8)	Administrative receiver failing to comply with requirements as to his report.	Summary.	One-fifth of the statutory maximum.	One-fiftieth of the statutory maximum.
51(4)	Body corporate or Scottish firm acting as receiver.	1. On indictment. 2. Summary.	A fine. The statutory maximum.	
51(5)	Undischarged bankrupt acting as receiver (Scotland).	1. On indictment. 2. Summary.	2 years or a fine, or both. 6 months or the statutory maximum, or both.	
53(2)	Failing to deliver to registrar copy of instrument of appointing of receiver	Summary.	One-fifth of the statutory maximum.	One-fiftieth of the statutory maximum.
54(3)	Failing to deliver to registrar the court's interlocutor appointing receiver.	Summary.	One-fifth of the statutory maximum.	One-fiftieth of the statutory maximum.
61(7)	Receiver failing to send registrar certified copy of court order authorising disposal of charged property.	Summary.	One-fifth of the statutory maximum.	One-fiftieth of the statutory maximum.
62(5)	Failing to give notice to registrar of cessation or removal of receiver.	Summary.	One-fifth of the statutory maximum.	One-fiftieth of the statutory maximum.
64(2)	Company and others failing to state on correspondence etc. that receiver appointed.	Summary.	One-fifth of the statutory maximum.	One-fiftieth of the statutory maximum.
65(4)	Receiver failing to send or publish notice of his appointment.	Summary.	One-fifth of the statutory maximum.	One-fiftieth of the statutory maximum.
66(6)	Failing to comply with provisions concerning statement of affairs where receiver appointed.	1. On indictment. 2. Summary.	A fine. The statutory maximum.	One-tenth of the statutory maximum.
67(8)	Receiver failing to comply with requirements as to his report.	Summary.	One-fifth of the statutory maximum.	One-fiftieth of the statutory maximum.
85(2)	Company failing to give notice in Gazette of resolution for voluntary winding up.	Summary.	One-fifth of the statutory maximum.	One-fiftieth of the statutory maximum.
89(4)	Director making statutory declaration of company's solvency without reasonable grounds for his opinion.	1. On indictment. 2. Summary.	2 years or a fine, or both. 6 months or the statutory maximum, or both	

Section of Act creating offence	General nature of offence	Mode of prosecution	Punishment	Daily default fine (where applicable)
89(6).........	Declaration under s.89 not delivered to registrar within prescribed time.	Summary.	One-fifth of the statutory maximum.	One-fiftieth of the statutory maximum.
92A(2).........	Liquidator failing to send progress report to members at year's end.	Summary.	Level 3 on the standard scale.	
93(3).........	Liquidator failing to summon general meeting of company at each year's end.	Summary.	One-fifth of the statutory maximum.	One-fiftieth of the statutory maximum.
94(4).........	Liquidator failing to send to registrar a copy of account of winding up and return of final meeting.	Summary.	One-fifth of the statutory maximum.	
94(6).........	Liquidator failing to call final meeting.	Summary.	One-fifth of the statutory maximum.	
95(8).........	Liquidator failing to comply with s.95, where company insolvent.	Summary.	The statutory maximum.	
98(6).........	Company failing to comply with s.98 in respect of summoning and giving notice of creditors' meeting.	1. On indictment. 2. Summary.	A fine. The statutory maximum.	
99(3).........	Directors failing to attend and lay statement in prescribed form before creditors' meeting.	1. On indictment. 2. Summary.	A fine. The statutory maximum.	
104A(2).........	Liquidator failing to send progress report to members and creditors at year's end.	Summary.	Level 3 on the standard scale.	
105(3).........	Liquidator failing to summon company general meeting and creditors' meeting at each year's end.	Summary.	One-fifth of the statutory maximum.	
106(4).........	Liquidator failing to send to registrar account of winding up and return of final meetings.	Summary.	One-fifth of the statutory maximum.	One-fiftieth of the statutory maximum.
106(6).........	Liquidator failing to call final meeting of company or creditors.	Summary.	One-fifth of the statutory maximum.	One-fiftieth of the statutory maximum.
109(2).........	Liquidator failing to publish notice of his appointment.	Summary.	The statutory maximum.	One-fifth of the statutory maximum.
114(4).........	Directors exercising powers in breach of s.114, where no liquidator.	Summary.	The statutory maximum.	One-tenth of the statutory maximum.
131(7).........	Failing to comply with requirements as to statement of affairs, where liquidator appointed.	1. On indictment. 2. Summary.	A fine. The statutory maximum.	
164.........	Giving, offering etc. corrupt inducement affecting appointment of liquidator.	1. On indictment. 2. Summary.	A fine. The statutory maximum.	
166(7).........	Liquidator failing to comply with requirements of s.166 in creditors' voluntary winding up.	Summary.	The statutory maximum.	
188(2).........	Default in compliance with s.188 as to notification that company being wound up.	Summary.	One-fifth of the statutory maximum.	

Section of Act creating offence	General nature of offence	Mode of prosecution	Punishment	Daily default fine (where applicable)
192(2)	Liquidator failing to notify registrar as to progress of winding up.	Summary.	One-fifth of the statutory maximum.	One-fiftieth of the statutory maximum.
201(4)	Failing to deliver to registrar copy of court order deferring dissolution.	Summary.	One-fifth of the statutory maximum.	One-fiftieth of the statutory maximum.
203(6)	Failing to deliver to registrar copy of directions or result of appeal under s.203.	Summary.	One-fifth of the statutory maximum.	One-fiftieth of the statutory maximum.
204(7)	Liquidator failing to deliver to registrar copy of court order for early dissolution.	Summary.	One-fifth of the statutory maximum.	One-fiftieth of the statutory maximum.
204(8)	Failing to deliver to registrar copy of court order deferring early dissolution.	Summary.	One-fifth of the statutory maximum.	One-fiftieth of the statutory maximum.
205(7)	Failing to deliver to registrar copy of Secretary of State's directions or court order deferring dissolution.	Summary.	One-fifth of the statutory maximum.	One-fiftieth of the statutory maximum.
206(1)	Fraud etc. in anticipation of winding up.	1. On indictment. 2. Summary.	7 years or a fine, or both. 6 months or the statutory maximum, or both	
206(2)	Privity to fraud in anticipation of winding up; fraud or privity to fraud, after commencement of winding up.	1. On indictment. 2. Summary.	7 years or a fine, or both. 6 months or the statutory maximum, or both.	
206(5)	Knowingly taking in pawn or pledge, or otherwise receiving, company property.	1. On indictment. 2. Summary.	7 years or a fine, or both. 6 months or the statutory maximum, or both.	
207	Officer of company entering into transaction in fraud of company's creditors.	1. On indictment. 2. Summary.	2 years or a fine, or both. 6 months or the statutory maximum, or both.	
208	Officer of company misconducting himself in course of winding up.	1. On indictment. 2. Summary.	7 years or a fine, or both. 6 months or the statutory maximum, or both.	
209	Officer or contributory destroying, falsifying, etc. company's books.	1. On indictment. 2. Summary.	7 years or a fine, or both. 6 months or the statutory maximum, or both.	
210	Officer of company making material omission from statement relating to company's affairs.	1. On indictment. 2. Summary.	7 years or a fine, or both. 6 months or the statutory maximum, or both.	

Section of Act creating offence	General nature of offence	Mode of prosecution	Punishment	Daily default fine (where applicable)
211............	False representation or fraud for purpose of obtaining creditors' consent to an agreement in connection with winding up.	1. On indictment. 2. Summary.	7 years or a fine, or both. 6 months or the statutory maximum, or both.	
216(4)............	Contravening restrictions on re-use of name of company in insolvent liquidation.	1. On indictment. 2. Summary.	2 years or a fine, or both. 6 months or the statutory maximum, or both.	
235(5)............	Failing to co-operate with office-holder.	1. On indictment. 2. Summary.	A fine. The statutory maximum.	One-tenth of the statutory maximum.
251O(1)............	False representations or omissions in making an application for a debt relief order.	1. On indictment 2. Summary	7 years or a fine, or both. 12 months or the statutory maximum, or both.	
251O(2)(a)............	Failing to comply with duty in connection with an application for a debt relief order.	1. On indictment 2. Summary	2 years or a fine, or both. 12 months or the statutory maximum, or both.	
251O(2)(b)............	False representations or omissions in connection with duty in relation to an application for a debt relief order.	1. On indictment 2. Summary	7 years or a fine, or both. 12 months or the statutory maximum, or both.	
251O(4)(a)............	Failing to comply with duty in connection with a debt relief order.	1. On indictment 2. Summary	2 years or a fine, or both. 12 months or the statutory maximum, or both.	
251O(4)(b)............	False representations or omissions in connection with a duty in relation to a debt relief order.	1. On indictment 2. Summary	7 years or a fine, or both. 12 months or the statutory maximum, or both.	
251P(1)............	Failing to deliver books, records and papers to official receiver, concealing or destroying them or making false entries in them by person in respect of whom a debt relief order is made.	1. On indictment 2. Summary	7 years or a fine, or both. 12 months or the statutory maximum, or both.	
251P(2)............	Person in respect of whom debt relief order is made doing anything falling within paragraphs (c) to (e) of section 251P(1) during the period of 12 months ending with the application date or doing anything falling within paragraphs (b) to (e) of section 251P(1) after that date but before the effective date.	1. On indictment 2. Summary	7 years or a fine, or both. 12 months or the statutory maximum, or both.	
251Q(1)............	Fraudulent disposal of property by person in respect of whom a debt relief order is made.	1. On indictment 2. Summary	2 years or a fine, or both. 12 months or the statutory maximum, or both.	

Section of Act creating offence	General nature of offence	Mode of prosecution	Punishment	Daily default fine (where applicable)
251R(1)	Disposal of property that is not paid for by person in respect of whom a debt relief order is made.	1. On indictment 2. Summary	7 years or a fine, or both. 12 months or the statutory maximum, or both.	
251R(2)	Obtaining property in respect of which money is owed by a person in respect of whom a debt relief order is made.	1. On indictment 2. Summary	7 years or a fine, or both. 12 months or the statutory maximum, or both.	
251S(1)	Person in respect of whom a debt relief order is made obtaining credit or engaging in business without disclosing his status or name.	1. On indictment 2. Summary	2 years or a fine, or both. 12 months or the statutory maximum, or both.	
262A(1)	False representation or fraud for purpose of obtaining creditors' approval of proposed voluntary arrangement.	1. On indictment. 2. Summary.	7 years or a fine, or both. 6 months or the statutory maximum, or both.	
353(1)	Bankrupt failing to disclose property or disposals to official receiver or trustee.	1. On indictment. 2. Summary.	7 years or a fine, or both. 6 months or the statutory maximum, or both.	
354(1)	Bankrupt failing to deliver property to, or concealing property from, official receiver or trustee.	1. On indictment. 2. Summary.	7 years or a fine, or both. 6 months or the statutory maximum, or both.	
354(2)	Bankrupt removing property which he is required to deliver to official receiver or trustee.	1. On indictment. 2. Summary.	7 years or a fine, or both. 6 months or the statutory maximum, or both.	
354(3)	Bankrupt failing to account for loss of substantial part of property.	1. On indictment. 2. Summary.	2 years or a fine, or both. 6 months or the statutory maximum, or both	
355(1)	Bankrupt failing to deliver books, papers and records to official receiver or trustee.	1. On indictment. 2. Summary.	7 years or a fine, or both. 6 months or the statutory maximum, or both.	
355(2)	Bankrupt concealing, destroying etc. books, papers or records, or making false entries in them.	1. On indictment. 2. Summary.	7 years or a fine, or both. 6 months or the statutory maximum, or both.	
355(3)	Bankrupt disposing of, or altering, books, papers or records relating to his estate or affairs.	1. On indictment. 2. Summary.	7 years or a fine, or both. 6 months or the statutory maximum, or both.	
356(1)	Bankrupt making material omission in statement relating to his affairs.	1. On indictment. 2. Summary.	7 years or a fine, or both. 6 months or the statutory maximum, or both.	

Section of Act creating offence	General nature of offence	Mode of prosecution	Punishment	Daily default fine (where applicable)
356(2)	Bankrupt making false statement, or failing to inform trustee, where false debt proved.	1. On indictment. 2. Summary.	7 years or a fine, or both. 6 months or the statutory maximum, or both.	
357	Bankrupt fraudulently disposing of property.	1. On indictment. 2. Summary.	2 years or a fine, or both. 6 months or the statutory maximum, or both	
358	Bankrupt absconding with property he is required to deliver to official receiver or trustee.	1. On indictment. 2. Summary.	2 years or a fine, or both. 6 months or the statutory maximum, or both.	
359(1)	Bankrupt disposing of property obtained on credit and not paid for.	1. On indictment. 2. Summary.	7 years or a fine, or both. 6 months or the statutory maximum, or both.	
359(2)	Obtaining property in respect of which money is owed by a bankrupt.	1. On indictment. 2. Summary.	7 years or a fine, or both. 6 months or the statutory maximum, or both.	
360(1)	Bankrupt obtaining credit or engaging in business without disclosing his status or name in which he was made bankrupt.	1. On indictment. 2. Summary.	2 years or a fine, or both. 6 months or the statutory maximum, or both.	
360(3)	Person made bankrupt in Scotland or Northern Ireland obtaining credit, etc. in England and Wales.	1. On indictment. 2. Summary.	2 years or a fine, or both. 6 months or the statutory maximum, or both.	
389	Acting as insolvency practitioner when not qualified.	1. On indictment. 2. Summary.	2 years or a fine, or both. 6 months or the statutory maximum, or both.	
429(5)	Contravening s.429 in respect of disabilities imposed by county court on revocation of administration order.	1. On indictment. 2. Summary.	2 years or a fine, or both. 6 months or the statutory maximum, or both.	
Sch.A1, para.9(2)	Directors failing to notify nominee of beginning of moratorium.	1. On indictment. 2. Summary.	2 years or a fine, or both. 6 months or the statutory maximum, or both.	
Sch.A1, para.10(3)	Nominee failing to advertise or notify beginning of moratorium.	Summary.	One-fifth of the statutory maximum.	
Sch.A1, para.11(2)	Nominee failing to advertise or notify end of moratorium.	Summary.	One-fifth of the statutory maximum.	
Sch.A1, para.16(2)	Company and officers failing to state in correspondence etc. that moratorium in force.	Summary.	One-fifth of the statutory maximum.	

Section of Act creating offence	General nature of offence	Mode of prosecution	Punishment	Daily default fine (where applicable)
Sch.A1, para.17(3)(a)............	Company obtaining credit without disclosing existence of moratorium.	1. On indictment. 2. Summary.	A fine. The statutory maximum.	
Sch.A1, para.17(3)(b)	Obtaining credit for company without disclosing existence of moratorium.	1. On indictment. 2. Summary.	2 years or a fine, or both. 6 months or the statutory maximum, or both.	
Sch.A1, para.18(3)(a)............	Company disposing of property otherwise than in ordinary way of business.	1. On indictment. 2. Summary.	A fine. The statutory maximum.	
Sch.A1, para.18(3)(b)	Authorising or permitting disposal of company property.	1. On indictment. 2. Summary.	2 years or a fine, or both. 6 months or the statutory maximum, or both.	
Sch.A1, para.19(3)(a)............	Company making payments in respect of liabilities existing before beginning of moratorium.	1. On indictment. 2. Summary.	A fine. The statutory maximum.	
Sch.A1, para.19(3)(b)	Authorising or permitting such a payment.	1. On indictment. 2. Summary.	2 years or a fine, or both. 6 months or the statutory maximum, or both.	
Sch.A1, para.20(9)	Directors failing to send to registrar copy of court order permitting disposal of charged property.	Summary.	One-fifth of the statutory maximum.	
Sch.A1, para.22(1)	Company disposing of charged property.	1. On indictment. 2. Summary.	A fine. The statutory maximum.	
Sch.A1, para.22(2)	Authorising or permitting such a disposal.	1. On indictment. 2. Summary.	2 years or a fine, or both. 6 months or the statutory maximum, or both.	
Sch.A1, para.23(1)(a)............	Company entering into market contract, etc.	1. On indictment. 2. Summary.	A fine. The statutory maximum	
Sch.A1, para.17(3)(a)............	Company obtaining credit without disclosing existence of moratorium.	1. On indictment. 2. Summary.	A fine. The statutory maximum.	
Sch.A1, para.23(1)(b)	Authorising or permitting company to do so.	1. On indictment. 2. Summary.	2 years or a fine, or both. 6 months or the statutory maximum, or both.	
Sch.A1, para.25(6)............	Nominee failing to give notice of withdrawal of consent to act.	Summary.	One-fifth of the statutory maximum.	
Sch.A1, para.34(3)............	Nominee failing to give notice of extension of moratorium.	Summary.	One-fifth of the statutory maximum.	

Section of Act creating offence	General nature of offence	Mode of prosecution	Punishment	Daily default fine (where applicable)
Sch.A1, para.41(2)	Fraud or privity to fraud in anticipation of moratorium.	1. On indictment. 2. Summary.	7 years or a fine, or both. 6 months or the statutory maximum, or both.	
Sch.A1, para.41(3)	Fraud or privity to fraud during moratorium.	1. On indictment. 2. Summary.	7 years or a fine, or both. 6 months or the statutory maximum, or both.	
Sch.A1, para.41(7)	Knowingly taking in pawn or pledge, or otherwise receiving, company property.	1. On indictment. 2. Summary.	7 years or a fine, or both. 6 months or the statutory maximum, or both.	
Sch.A1, para.42(1)	False representation or fraud for purpose of obtaining or extending moratorium.	1. On indictment. 2. Summary.	7 years or a fine, or both. 6 months or the statutory maximum, or both.	
Sch.B1, para.18(7)	Making false statement in statutory declaration where administrator appointed by holder of floating charge.	1. On indictment. 2. Summary.	2 years, or a fine or both. 6 months, or the statutory maximum or both.	One-tenth of the statutory maximum.
Sch.B1, para.20	Holder of floating charge failing to notify administrator or others of commencement of appointment.	1. On indictment. 2. Summary.	2 years, or a fine or both. 6 months, or the statutory maximum or both.	
Sch.B1, para.27(4)	Making false statement in statutory declaration where appointment of administrator proposed by company or directors.	1. On indictment. 2. Summary.	2 years, or a fine or both. 6 months, or the statutory maximum or both.	
Sch.B1, para.29(7)	Making false statement in statutory declaration where administrator appointed by company or directors.	1. On indictment. 2. Summary.	2 years, or a fine or both. 6 months, or the statutory maximum or both.	
Sch.B1, para.32	Company or directors failing to notify administrator or others of commencement of appointment.	1. On indictment. 2. Summary.	2 years, or a fine or both. 6 months, or the statutory maximum or both.	One-tenth of the statutory maximum.
Sch.B1, para.45(2)	Administrator, company or officer failing to state in business document that administrator appointed.	Summary.	One-fifth of the statutory maximum.	
Sch.B1, para.46(9)	Administrator failing to give notice of his appointment.	Summary.	One-fifth of the statutory maximum. A fine.	One-fiftieth of the statutory maximum.
Sch.B1, para.48(4)	Failing to comply with provisions about statement of affairs where administrator appointed.	1. On indictment. 2. Summary.	The statutory maximum.	One-tenth of the statutory maximum.

Section of Act creating offence	General nature of offence	Mode of prosecution	Punishment	Daily default fine (where applicable)
Sch.B1, para.49(7)	Administrator failing to send out statement of his proposals.	Summary.	One-fifth of the statutory maximum.	One-fiftieth of the statutory maximum.
Sch.B1, para.51(5)	Administrator failing to arrange initial creditors' meeting.	Summary.	One-fifth of the statutory maximum.	One-fiftieth of the statutory maximum.
Sch.B1, para.53(3)	Administrator failing to report decision taken at initial creditors' meeting.	Summary.	One-fifth of the statutory maximum.	One-fiftieth of the statutory maximum.
Sch.B1, para.54(7)	Administrator failing to report decision taken at creditors' meeting summoned to consider revised proposal.	Summary.	One-fifth of the statutory maximum.	One-fiftieth of the statutory maximum.
Sch.B1, para.56(2)	Administrator failing to summon creditors' meeting.	Summary.	One-fifth of the statutory maximum.	One-fiftieth of the statutory maximum.
Sch.B1, para.71(6)	Administrator failing to file court order enabling disposal of charged property.	Summary.	One-fifth of the statutory maximum.	One-fiftieth of the statutory maximum.
Sch.B1, para.72(5)	Administrator failing to file court order enabling disposal of hire-purchase property.	Summary.	One-fifth of the statutory maximum.	One-fiftieth of the statutory maximum.
Sch.B1, para.77(3)	Administrator failing to notify Registrar of Companies of automatic end of administration.	Summary.	One-fifth of the statutory maximum.	One-fiftieth of the statutory maximum.
Sch.B1, para.78(6)	Administrator failing to give notice of extension by consent of term of office.	Summary.	One-fifth of the statutory maximum.	One-fiftieth of the statutory maximum.
Sch.B1, para.45(2)	Administrator, company or officer failing to state in business document that administrator appointed.	Summary.	One-fifth of the statutory maximum.	
Sch.B1, para.46(9)	Administrator failing to give notice of his appointment.	Summary.	One-fifth of the statutory maximum.	One-fiftieth of the statutory maximum.
Sch.B1, para.48(4)	Failing to comply with provisions about statement of affairs where administrator appointed.	1. On indictment. 2. Summary.	A fine. The statutory maximum.	One-tenth of the statutory maximum.
Sch.B1, para.49(7)	Administrator failing to send out statement of his proposals.	Summary.	One-fifth of the statutory maximum.	One-fiftieth of the statutory maximum.
Sch.B1, para.51(5)	Administrator failing to arrange initial creditors' meeting.	Summary.	One-fifth of the statutory maximum.	One-fiftieth of the statutory maximum.
Sch.B1, para.53(3)	Administrator failing to report decision taken at initial creditors' meeting.	Summary.	One-fifth of the statutory maximum.	One-fiftieth of the statutory maximum.

Section of Act creating offence	General nature of offence	Mode of prosecution	Punishment	Daily default fine (where applicable)
Sch.B1, para.54(7)	Administrator failing to report decision taken at creditors' meeting summoned to consider revised proposal.	Summary.	One-fifth of the statutory maximum.	One-fiftieth of the statutory maximum.
Sch.B1, para.56(2)	Administrator failing to summon creditors' meeting.	Summary.	One-fifth of the statutory maximum.	One-fiftieth of the statutory maximum.
Sch.B1, para.71(6)	Administrator failing to file court order enabling disposal of charged property.	Summary.	One-fifth of the statutory maximum.	One-fiftieth of the statutory maximum.
Sch.B1, para.72(5)	Administrator failing to file court order enabling disposal of hire-purchase property.	Summary.	One-fifth of the statutory maximum.	One-fiftieth of the statutory maximum.
Sch.B1, para.77(3)	Administrator failing to notify Registrar of Companies of automatic end of administration.	Summary.	One-fifth of the statutory maximum.	One-fiftieth of the statutory maximum.
Sch.B1, para.78(6)	Administrator failing to give notice of extension by consent of term of office.	Summary.	One-fifth of the statutory maximum.	One-fiftieth of the statutory maximum.
Sch.B1, para.80(6)	Administrator failing to give notice of termination of administration where objective achieved.	Summary.	One-fifth of the statutory maximum.	One-fiftieth of the statutory maximum.
Sch.B1, para.84(9)	Administrator failing to comply with provisions where company moves to dissolution.	Summary.	One-fifth of the statutory maximum.	One-fiftieth of the statutory maximum.
Sch.B1, para.86(3)	Administrator failing to notify Registrar of Companies where court terminates administration.	Summary.	One-fifth of the statutory maximum.	One-fiftieth of the statutory maximum.
Sch.B1, para.89(3)	Administrator failing to give notice on ceasing to be qualified.	Summary.	One-fifth of the statutory maximum.	One-fiftieth of the statutory maximum.
Sch.7, para.4(3)	Failure to attend and give evidence to Insolvency Practitioners Tribunal; suppressing, concealing, etc. relevant documents.	Summary.	Level 3 on the standard scale within the meaning given by section 75 of the Criminal Justice Act 1982.	

GENERAL NOTE

This technique of using a Schedule of punishments is used by CA 1985 and CA 2006, but not by IA 1985. Guidance on the use of Sch.10 is provided by s.430. Sections 431 and 432 are also of assistance when applying Sch.10.

The "statutory maximum" referred to in the introductory note to the Schedule and in cols 4 and 5 is at present £5,000 (but £2,000 in respect of offences committed before October 1, 1992): see CJA 1991 s.17 and SI 1992/333, SI 1993/2118. In the application of those entries in relation to offences committed before the commencement of s.154(1) of the CJA 2003 (C. 44) (limit on magistrates' court powers to impose imprisonment), the references in the fourth column to "12 months" are to be read as references to "6 months".

Schedule 10 was substantially modified by IA 2000 and EA 2002 Sch.17.

Note amendments by para.15 of Pt 1 of Sch.20 to the Tribunals, Courts and Enforcement Act 2007. Note amendments made by LRO 2010 (SI 2010/18).

SCHEDULE 11

TRANSITIONAL PROVISIONS AND SAVINGS

SCHEDULE 12

ENACTMENTS REPEALED

SCHEDULE 13

CONSEQUENTIAL AMENDMENTS OF COMPANIES ACT 1985

SCHEDULE 14

CONSEQUENTIAL AMENDMENTS OF OTHER ENACTMENTS

[Schedules 11–14 have not been reproduced in the present edition of the *Guide*. The full text may be found in *British Companies Legislation*, pp.56,604 et seq., or in the official version of IA 1986 published by The Stationery Office.]

The Insolvency Act 2000

This Act is now fully in force. In particular, those parts dealing with director disqualification (ss.5–13 and Sch.4) became effective on April 2, 2001, and those dealing with voluntary arrangements on January 1, 2003. In so far as the Act amends IA 1986 and CDDA 1986, the amendments have been taken into account in the text to those Acts. The remaining, "free-standing" provisions (e.g. s.14) are annotated in this section of the *Guide*.

The Insolvency Act 2000

(2000 Chapter 39)

An Act to amend the law about insolvency; to amend the Company Directors Disqualification Act 1986; and for connected purposes.

[30th November 2000]

Introductory note to the Act

This legislation was finally brought fully into force on January 1, 2003. As many of the provisions operate as amendments to the 1986 Act and CDDA 1986 they are not reproduced below but rather at the appropriate location within those Acts. However, a number of the provisions could be regarded as "free-standing" and are included below with comment where appropriate.

This chapter in the reform of insolvency law has modest aims as was immediately conceded by the Government spokesman when the Bill was given its Second Reading in the House of Lords. The Bill was famously put down by Rt Hon. Tony Benn, MP on October 23, 2000, the day before the Bill had its Second Reading in the Commons (see *Hansard*, HC Vol.355, col.12 and the retort from Kim Howells MP *Hansard*, HC Vol.355, col.160). While recognising that it may not have major constitutional implications, it does deal with significant matters in the regulation of commerce. Essentially it is intended to improve debtor rehabilitation procedures, both in personal and corporate insolvency law. Thus, there are reforms to the company voluntary arrangement procedure (CVA), (contained in Pt I of IA 1986) to permit the proposal for an arrangement to enjoy the benefit of a moratorium whilst the CVA is being constructed and approved (s.1 and Sch.1). Conversely, the IVA procedure (Pt VIII of IA 1986) is modified to introduce a variant which can operate without the protection of an interim order (s.3 and Sch.3). There are general changes to both the CVA and IVA procedures (see ss.2 and 3) and the moratorium applying in case of company administration is extended by s.9 to encompass a landlord's right of re-entry.

Another aim of the Act (see s.6), is to formalise a system whereby the authorities can accept a legally binding undertaking from a director facing disqualification proceedings, rather than pursuing him (or her) at great cost through the courts under the provisions of CDDA 1986. This reform is to some extent designed to save public expenditure, but it is also intended to speed up the process of disqualification, which can take as much as three years to complete. As a result, this might have been contrary to the right of a speedy trial enshrined by art.6 of the European Convention on Human Rights (now incorporated by the Human Rights Act 1998 (C. 42)).

The Insolvency Act 2000 addresses other areas of concern. The prosecution and investigation of those suspected of committing offences under insolvency law is the subject of attention in ss.10 and 11. A technical difficulty in the law relating to the administration of estates of deceased insolvents is resolved by s.12. The legislation permits (in s.13) trustees in bankruptcy greater flexibility in exploiting funds paid into the Insolvency Services Account. Section 14 enables the authorities to implement the United Nations Commission on International Trade Law (UNCITRAL) Convention on Cross Border Insolvency Proceedings and to amend domestic law to promote the aim of judicial co-operation in cross-border insolvency matters. The powers conferred by this provision were exercised in the Cross-Border Insolvency Regulations 2006 (SI 2006/1030). A curious reform is the introduction by s.4 of the possibility of nonqualified insolvency practitioners acting as nominees and supervisors for voluntary arrangements. This mirrors the growth of the "turnaround specialist" but it does represent a reversal of the policy enshrined in the IA 1986 of compulsory qualification as the norm for all insolvency practitioners. This is a development that will have to be watched carefully lest it provides a Trojan horse for cowboy operators in insolvency practice.

The matters dealt with in this Act have undergone considerable discussion. The issue of improving the CVA procedure via the introduction of a moratorium was the subject of a number of Insolvency Service consultation exercises in the 1990s (see *Company Voluntary Arrangements and Administration Orders* (October 1993); *Revised Proposals for a New Company Voluntary Arrangement Procedure* (April 1995); *Review of Company Rescue and Business Reconstruction Mechanisms* (September 1999)).

Voluntary arrangements

1 Moratorium where directors propose voluntary arrangement

1 Schedule 1 (which–

(a) enables the directors of a company to obtain an initial moratorium for the company where they propose a voluntary arrangement under Part I of the Insolvency Act 1986,

(b) makes provision about the approval and implementation of such a voluntary arrangement where a moratorium is obtained, and

(c) makes consequential amendments),

is to have effect.

[Amends IA 1986 by inserting s.1A and Sch.A1: see the notes to those provisions. Minor consequential amendments are made to other parts of the Act.]

2 Company voluntary arrangements

2 Schedule 2 (which–

(a) amends the provisions about company voluntary arrangements under Part I of the Insolvency Act 1986, and

(b) in consequence of Schedule 1 and those amendments, makes amendments of the Building Societies Act 1986),

is to have effect.

GENERAL NOTE

This makes applicable the general CVA reform provisions in Sch.2. For example, the nominee is now required to state in the report to the court whether the proposal has a reasonable prospect of being approved and implemented. This addresses issues raised in cases such as *Greystoke v Hamilton-Smith* [1997] B.P.I.R. 24 where the court made it clear that the nominee should reassure himself about the viability of the proposal before promoting it. There are also technical changes in the provisions relating to the approval of CVAs. Members lose their automatic veto over an arrangement that meets with the approval of creditors, though a member may have recourse to the courts (new s.4A). A facility under which the CVA will bind unknown creditors is introduced (new s.5(2)(b)). Nominees are also now required to "blow the whistle" on directors suspected of committing offences during the moratorium period. This change (contained in s.7A) will reassure those commentators who suspect that voluntary arrangements are simply being used by unscrupulous directors to buy time for a failing business. A new s.6A also creates an offence of seeking to obtain a CVA by false representations.

Schedule 2 Pt II, makes a number of changes in the context of building societies, which can exploit the CVA option but are prevented from benefiting from the moratorium. This is consistent with the treatment of banks with regard to the moratorium variation. Some of the provisions that deal with investigations carried out by inspectors appointed by the Building Societies Commission would appear to have more in common with the reforms introduced under ss.10 and 11.

3 Individual voluntary arrangements

3 Schedule 3 (which enables the procedure for the approval of individual voluntary arrangements under Part VIII of the Insolvency Act 1986 to be started without an initial moratorium for the insolvent debtor and makes other amendments of the provisions about individual voluntary arrangements) is to have effect.

4 Qualification or authorisation of nominees and supervisors

[Amends IA 1986 ss.388–389 in various respects and inserts s.389A. See the notes to those sections.]

Disqualification of company directors etc.

[Sections 5–8 make amendments to CDDA 1986, and are dealt with in that appropriate location.]

5 Disqualification orders

6 Disqualification undertakings

7 Effect of Northern Irish disqualifications

8 Amendments

Miscellaneous

9 Administration orders

[Inserts new ss.10(1)(aa) and 11(3)(ba) into CDDA 1986 repealed by Sch.26 to EA 2002.]

10 Investigation and prosecution of malpractice

[Amends ss.218, 219 of IA 1986: see the notes to those sections.]

11 Restriction on use of answers obtained under compulsion

[Inserts s.219(2A) into IA 1986: see the note to that subsection.]

12 Insolvent estates of deceased persons

[Amends s.421(1) and inserts new s.421A into IA 1986: see the note to those sections.]

13 Bankruptcy: interest on sums held in Insolvency Services Account

[Amends s.406 of and Sch.9 para.21 to IA 1986: see the note to s.406.]

14 Model law on cross-border insolvency

14(1) **[Adoption of model law]** The Secretary of State may by regulations make any provision which he considers necessary or expedient for the purpose of giving effect, with or without modifications, to the model law on cross-border insolvency.

14(2) **[Scope of regulations]** In particular, the regulations may–

(a) apply any provision of insolvency law in relation to foreign proceedings (whether begun before or after the regulations come into force),

(b) modify the application of insolvency law (whether in relation to foreign proceedings or otherwise),

(c) amend any provision of section 426 of the Insolvency Act 1986 (co-operation between courts),

and may apply or, as the case may be, modify the application of insolvency law in relation to the Crown.

14(3) **[Special cases]** The regulations may make different provision for different purposes and may make–

(a) any supplementary, incidental or consequential provision, or

(b) any transitory, transitional or saving provision,

which the Secretary of State considers necessary or expedient.

14(4) **[Definitions]** In this section–

"foreign proceedings" has the same meaning as in the model law on cross-border insolvency,

"insolvency law" has the same meaning as in section 426(10)(a) and (b) of the Insolvency Act 1986,

"the model law on cross-border insolvency" means the model law contained in Annex I of the report of the 30th session of UNCITRAL.

14(5) **[Procedure]** Regulations under this section are to be made by statutory instrument and may only be made if a draft has been laid before and approved by resolution of each House of Parliament.

14(6) **[Approval]** Making regulations under this section requires the agreement–

(a) if they extend to England and Wales, of the Lord Chancellor,

(b) if they extend to Scotland, of the Scottish Ministers.

GENERAL NOTE

The problem of cross-border insolvency has become more vexed with globalised trading, ease of foreign travel and advances in communications technology. These developments have compelled national authorities to introduce tailored judicial comity mechanisms (see for example, s.426 of IA 1986). They have also led to changes at EU level (see the EC Regulation 2000/1346 (Vol 2, pp.125 et seq.), which superseded the abortive Bankruptcy Convention and came into effect in May 2002). At a truly international level, UNCITRAL in 1997 sponsored a Model Law on Cross Border Insolvency and a number of leading economies have already adopted this (USA, Japan, South Africa, Australia). Other participants include Eritrea, Poland, Romania, BVI, Mexico and Montenegro. The Model Law is set out in Vol.2 of this *Guide*.

For a background discussion see Fletcher, [2000] 13 Insolv. Int. 57 and 68; Dawson, [2000] 4 R.A.L.Q. 147; and Omar, [2000] Insolv. L. 211.

Section 14 came into force on November 30, 2000, the date of Royal Assent: see s.16(2).

S.14(1)

This permits the Secretary of State to implement the UNCITRAL Model Law on Cross Border Insolvency by Regulation. There need not be exact replication: the Secretary of State is given discretion to modify incorporation. The UNCITRAL convention was implemented in English law by the Cross-Border Insolvency Regulations 2006 (SI 2006/1030) as amended by the Companies Act 2006 (Consequential Amendments, Transitional Provisions and Savings) Order 2009 (SI 2009/1941). These Regulations are reproduced in Vol.2. For discussion see Sealy, [2006] (7) Sweet and Maxwell's Company Law Newsletter 1; Fletcher, (2006) 19 Insolv. Int. 86.

Comparable provision for Scotland with suitable modifications was made by the Act of Sederunt (Sheriff Court Bankruptcy Rules 1996) Amendment (UNCITRAL Model Law on Cross-Border Insolvency) 2006 (SSI 2006/197);

Act of Sederunt (Sheriff Court Caveat Rules) 2006 (SSI 2006/198); Act of Sederunt (Rules of the Court of Session Amendment No.2) (UNCITRAL Model Law on Cross-Border Insolvency) 2006 (SSI 2006/1999); and the Act of Sederunt (Sheriff Court Company Insolvency Rules 1986) Amendment (UNCITRAL Model Law on Cross-Border Insolvency) 2006 (SSI 2006/2000).

The Model Law was extended to Northern Ireland by the Cross-Border Insolvency Regulations (Northern Ireland) 2007 (SR 2007/115) with effect from April 12, 2007.

An early example of the Cross Border Insolvency Regulations coming into play is afforded by *Re Rajapakse (Note)* [2007] B.P.I.R. 99 where Registrar Nicholls offered some valuable procedural guidance on recognition applications. In later proceedings (sub nom. *C Brooks Thurmond III v Rajapakse* [2008] B.P.I.R. 283) Registrar Nicholls granted an income payments order as art.21 relief on the application of the foreign trustee.

S.14(2) and (3)
The Secretary of State enjoys considerable flexibility in so doing and may amend the terms of s.426 (e.g. by extending the number of friendly jurisdictions covered beyond the current list of mainly Commonwealth countries).

S.14(4)
This is a dedicated definition facility, a rarity in what is an amendment Act.

S.14(5) and (6)
These deal with operational matters.

General

15 Amendments of Financial Services and Markets Act 2000 and repeals

[Not reproduced.]

16 Commencement

16(1) [Commencement orders] The preceding provisions of this Act (including the Schedules) are to come into force on such day as the Secretary of State may by order made by statutory instrument appoint.

16(2) [Section 14] Subsection (1) does not apply to section 14 (which accordingly comes into force on the day on which this Act is passed).

16(3) [Special cases] An order under this section may make different provision for different purposes and may make–

    (a)   any supplementary, incidental or consequential provision, and

    (b)   any transitory, transitional or saving provision,

which the Secretary of State considers necessary or expedient.

S.16(1) and (2)
This clarifies commencement dates with the enabling s.14 coming immediately into effect on Royal Assent.

S.16(3)
Technical aspects of commencement orders are explained.

17 Extent

17 This Act, except section 15(3), Part II of Schedule 2 and paragraphs 16(3) and 22 of Schedule 4, does not extend to Northern Ireland.

GENERAL NOTE

The Act generally does not apply to Northern Ireland, which has its own distinctive system of insolvency law.

18 Short title

18 This Act may be cited as the Insolvency Act 2000.

SCHEDULES

[Schedules 1–5 are not reproduced. The amendments made to IA 1986 and CDDA 1986 by these Schedules, which are all in force, have been noted at appropriate places in the text.]

SCHEDULE 1

MORATORIUM WHERE DIRECTORS PROPOSE VOLUNTARY ARRANGEMENT

SCHEDULE 2

COMPANY VOLUNTARY ARRANGEMENTS

SCHEDULE 3

INDIVIDUAL VOLUNTARY ARRANGEMENTS

SCHEDULE 4

MINOR AND CONSEQUENTIAL AMENDMENTS ABOUT DISQUALIFICATION OF COMPANY DIRECTORS ETC.

[Note repeals made by the Companies Act 2006 (Consequential Amendments, Transitional Provisions and Savings) Order 2009 (SI 2009/1941). In operation from October 1, 2009.]

SCHEDULE 5

REPEALS

The Enterprise Act 2002

(2002 Chapter 40)

ARRANGEMENT OF SECTIONS

Introductory note to the Enterprise Act 2002

The Enterprise Act 2002 received the Royal Assent on November 7, 2002. Part 10 of that Act clearly will have a major impact upon the operation of insolvency practice in the years to come. It could also have a significant influence on social attitudes to debt and on the appropriate legislative response to that condition.

Casual observers might find the inclusion of insolvency law under the banner of an Enterprise Act curious. It may be that the opportunity was taken to "thumb a lift" on a passing statute but a more serious study would reveal potential points of interface between "enterprise" and "insolvency". The history of this legislative change can be traced via a number of documents emanating from the Insolvency Service and the DTI. Reform of corporate rescue has been on the cards since the DTI/Treasury Review Group document *A Review of Company Rescue and Business Reconstruction Mechanisms* was published in the summer of 2000. These proposals were also heralded by the 2001 White Paper, *Productivity and Enterprise: Insolvency—A Second Chance* (Cm. 5234). Equally, it has been clear beyond doubt since the White Paper, *Opportunity for All in a World of Change* (2001) (Cm. 5052) that the Government intended to liberalise the law on bankruptcy. This change in the approach towards bankruptcy was also apparent in *A Second Chance* (above), which gave more detail on possible reforms. The thinking was that a more liberal law of bankruptcy would encourage risk taking and hence stimulate a sense of enterprise. A more probable connection between bankruptcy reform and enterprise lies in the fact that UK commercial life is now founded upon consumer spending derived from consumer credit. An earlier indication of the shape of things to come can be found in the *Bankruptcy—A Fresh Start* Consultative Document of April 2000—see editorial in [2000] Ins. L. 147 for a full account.

The Enterprise Bill was published in March 2002 with full Explanatory Notes. It was introduced into the House of Commons on March 26, 2002. For comment on the Bill see editorial in [2002] Ins. L. 119.

For corporate recovery practitioners the most important feature of the Act will be the scaling back of administrative receivership (see s.250 inserting new ss.72A–H into the 1986 Act) and introduction of the new style administration regime. This new insolvency model is introduced by s.248 and then described in detail by Sch.16 (which becomes Sch.B1 to the 1986 Act). Part II of the Insolvency Act 1986 is thus of reduced significance. This new regime marks a serious departure from the former administration mechanism both in terms of availability and operation. The advent of a dedicated fund for unsecured creditors by s.252 (inserting s.176A into the 1986 Act) is an enlightened move. More certainty is provided by s.251 which abolishes Crown preferential debts; no quibbles about this long overdue change in the law. The curious provision in s.253 on the need for a liquidator to obtain sanction before the commencement of certain recovery actions only makes sense in the light of the reform of IR 1986 r.4.218 and IR r.6.224 by treating costs incurred in such actions as liquidation expenses—on this see SI 2002/2712. These changes to corporate insolvency law took effect on September 15, 2003.

The reforms to personal insolvency law are in many senses more radical. Thus, we see significant modifications to the IVA scheme with the introduction of post bankruptcy IVA operated by the official receiver (s.264 and Sch.22), the relaxation of bankruptcy discharge procedures to permit discharge after one year (s.256) unless the bankrupt is unfortunate enough to fall within the bankruptcy restrictions regime detailed in Schs 20–21 to the Act and introduced by s.257. The official receiver will now have a *discretion* (rather than an obligation) to investigate bankrupts (s.258). The procedures for the use of income to settle a bankrupt's debts have been made more flexible (ss.259–260). Powers of trustees over the bankrupt's home are circumscribed via a late amendment of the Bill (supported by the Government from June 2002) and as a result this asset will automatically cease to form part of the estate after three years unless the trustee takes action in regard to it (s.261). Certain outmoded bankruptcy offences (such as gambling) are abolished by s.263, though such behaviour may continue to be relevant for the purposes of a bankruptcy restriction order. Such reforms will certainly liberalise the bankruptcy laws in this country, though the consequences of such a change are less predictable. Will there be a future for the IVA mechanism if bankruptcy becomes too gentle? What impact will these changes have on the growing social problem of consumer debt? These are important issues that will only be capable of being assessed objectively in several years time as the bankruptcy reforms were only implemented in April 1, 2004.

The Enterprise Act, like all modern legislation depends upon secondary legislation to supplement it. The major statutory instrument in English law was the Insolvency (Amendment) Rules 2003 (SI 2003/1730) but more focused delegated legislation was required to deal with the future of administrative receivership and the reserve fund for unsecured creditors. Scots lawyers have had to navigate equivalent masses of secondary legislation in order to make sense of the Enterprise Act—note in particular the Insolvency (Scotland) Amendment Rules 2003 (SI 2003/2111 (s.9)). EA 2002 s.277 confers power to make consequential amendments. For delegated legislation made pursuant to s.277(1) see the Insolvency (Scotland) Amendment Order 2006 (SI 2006/735) (S 7). This came into force on April 6, 2006 and amended SI 1986/1915. The Insolvency Service website has been an invaluable source of information on the evolution of this secondary legislation.

Part 10 of this legislation introduces major reform into the areas of corporate and personal insolvency law. For the most part these reforming provisions are cast as amendments to provisions in the IA 1986 and accordingly our commentary is located at the point of amendment in the primary legislation. However, there are a number of sections (or mere subsections) that do not take this form, but rather are viewed as free standing. These are reproduced below with appropriate annotations. For commencement of this legislation see the Enterprise Act 2002 (Commencement No.4 and Transitional Provisions and Savings) Order 2003 (SI 2003/2093 (C. 85)). Generally speaking, the corporate insolvency reforms took effect on September 15, 2003, with the personal insolvency law changes being deferred to April 1, 2004.

Equivalent provisions to EA 2002 were introduced into Northern Ireland by the Insolvency (Northern Ireland) Order 2005 (SI 2005/1455 (NI 10)).

PART 10

INSOLVENCY ACT

248 Replacement of Part II of Insolvency Act 1986

[Not reproduced—see discussion under Sch.B1 to IA 1986.]

249 Special administration regimes

249(1) **[Where s.248 not to have effect]** Section 248 shall have no effect in relation to–

(a) a company holding an appointment under Chapter I of Part II of the Water Industry Act 1991 (c. 56) (water and sewerage undertakers), (aa) a qualifying licensed water supplier within the meaning of subsection (6) of section 23 of the Water Industry Act 1991 (meaning and effect of special administration order),

(b) a protected railway company within the meaning of section 59 of the Railways Act 1993 (c. 43) (railway administration order) (including that section as it has effect by virtue of section 19 of the Channel Tunnel Rail Link Act 1996 (c. 61) (administration)),

(c) a licence company within the meaning of section 26 of the Transport Act 2000 (c. 38) (air traffic services),

(d) a public-private partnership company within the meaning of section 210 of the Greater London Authority Act 1999 (c. 29) (public-private partnership agreement), or

(e) a building society within the meaning of section 119 of the Building Societies Act 1986 (c. 53) (interpretation).

249(2) [Reference in Acts in s.249(1) to Pt II of 1986 Act] A reference in an Act listed in subsection (1) to a provision of Part II of the Insolvency Act 1986 (or to a provision which has effect in relation to a provision of that Part of that Act) shall, in so far as it relates to a company or society listed in subsection (1), continue to have effect as if it referred to Part II as it had effect immediately before the coming into force of section 248.

249(3) [Effect of s.249(2) modified] But the effect of subsection (2) in respect of a particular class of company or society may be modified by order of–

(a) the Treasury, in the case of building societies, or

(b) the Secretary of State, in any other case.

249(4) [Order under s.249(3)] An order under subsection (3) may make consequential amendment of an enactment.

249(5) [Procedure for order] An order under subsection (3)–

(a) must be made by statutory instrument, and

(b) may not be made unless a draft has been laid before and approved by resolution of each House of Parliament.

249(6) [Financial markets] An amendment of the Insolvency Act 1986 (c. 45) made by this Act is without prejudice to any power conferred by Part VII of the Companies Act 1989 (c. 40) (financial markets) to modify the law of insolvency.

S.249(1)
This preserves special administration regimes for various utility companies, etc.

S.249(2), (3)
These deal with modifications and transitional matters.

S.249(4), (5)
These are standard operational provisions.

S.249(6)
This is a special saving provision.

250 Prohibition of appointment of administrative receiver

[Not reproduced—see discussion under Chapter IV of Pt III of IA 1986.]

251 Abolition of Crown preference

[Not reproduced—see discussion under Sch.6 to IA 1986.]

252 Unsecured creditors

[Not reproduced—see discussion under IA 1986 s.176A.]

253 Liquidator's powers

[Not reproduced—see discussion under Sch.4 to IA 1986.]

254 Application of insolvency law to foreign company

254(1) [Power to make order] The Secretary of State may by order provide for a provision of the Insolvency Act 1986 to apply (with or without modification) in relation to a company incorporated outside Great Britain.

254(2) [Effect of order] An order under this section–

(a) may make provision generally or for a specified purpose only,

(b) may make different provision for different purposes, and

(c) may make transitional, consequential or incidental provision.

254(3) [Procedure for order] An order under this section–

(a) must be made by statutory instrument, and

(b) shall be subject to annulment in pursuance of a resolution of either House of Parliament.

S.254(1)
This enables the Secretary of State to make orders extending provisions in the Insolvency Act 1986 to apply to foreign companies. At present such application is not possible (see *Felixstowe Dock and Rwy Co v United States Lines Inc* [1989] Q.B. 360) and as a result in individual cases requests to make English law provisions apply have to be channelled through the cumbersome judicial comity procedure laid down in IA 1986 s.426 (see, e.g. *Re Dallhold Estates (UK) Pty Ltd* [1992] B.C.C. 394).

S.254(2), (3)
These are standard operational provisions.

255 Application of law about company arrangement or administration to non-company

255(1) [Power to make order] The Treasury may with the concurrence of the Secretary of State by order provide for a company arrangement or administration provision to apply (with or without modification) in relation to–

(a) a society registered under the Industrial and Provident Societies Act 1965 (c. 12),

(b) a society registered under section 7(1)(b), (c), (d), (e) or (f) of the Friendly Societies Act 1974 (c. 46),

(c) a friendly society within the meaning of the Friendly Societies Act 1992 (c. 40), or

(d) an unregistered friendly society.

255(2) ["Company arrangement or administration provision"] In subsection (1) "company arrangement or administration provision" means–

(a) a provision of Part I of the Insolvency Act 1986 (company voluntary arrangements),

(b) a provision of Part II of that Act (administration), and

(c) Part 26 of the Companies Act 2006 (compromise or arrangement with creditors).

255(3) [Order not to apply to social landlord] An order under this section may not provide for a company arrangement or administration provision to apply in relation to a society which is registered as a social landlord under Part I of the Housing Act 1996 (c. 52) or under Part 3 of the Housing (Scotland) Act 2001 (asp 10).

255(4) **[Scope of order]** An order under this section–

(a) may make provision generally or for a specified purpose only,

(b) may make different provision for different purposes, and

(c) may make transitional, consequential or incidental provision.

255(5) **[Transitional, consequential or incidental provision in order]** Provision by virtue of subsection (4)(c) may, in particular–

(a) apply an enactment (with or without modification);

(b) amend an enactment.

255(6) **[Procedure for order]** An order under this section–

(a) must be made by statutory instrument, and

(b) shall be subject to annulment in pursuance of a resolution of either House of Parliament.

S.255(1), (2)

These enable the Treasury, with the approval of the Secretary of State, to extend provisions relating to CVAs, schemes of arrangement and administration to incorporated bodies such as industrial and provident societies and friendly societies.

A minor change was made to s.255(2)(c) by the Companies Act 2006 (Consequential Amendments) Order 2008 (SI 2008/948) to convert references in the Companies Act 1985 into their counterparts in the Companies Act 2006.

S.255(3)

Societies acting as social landlords are excluded from being subject to the aforementioned legislative power. Such activities are frequently subject to discrete insolvency regulation in view of the public interest element involved.

S.255(4)–(6)

These are standard operational provisions governing the exercise of this power to make secondary legislation.

256 Duration of bankruptcy

[Subsection (1) is not reproduced—see IA 1986 s.279.]

256(2) **[Transitional provision]** Schedule 19 (which makes transitional provision in relation to this section)–

(a) shall have effect, and

(b) is without prejudice to the generality of section 276.

S.256(2)

This refers us to Sch.19 (see pp.661–662, below).

257 Post-discharge restrictions

[Subsection (1) is not reproduced—see IA 1986 s.281A.]

257(2) **[Insertion of Sch.4A into 1986 Act]** The Schedule 4A set out in Schedule 20 to this Act shall be inserted after Schedule 4 to the Insolvency Act 1986.

257(3) **[Amendments]** The amendments set out in Schedule 21 (which specify the effect of a bankruptcy restrictions order or undertaking) shall have effect.

S.257(2), (3)

These refer us to Sch.20 (Sch.4A to IA 1986) and Sch.21, which supplement the law on BROs.

258 Investigation by official receiver

[Not reproduced—see IA 1986 s.289.]

259 Income payments order

[Not reproduced—see IA 1986 s.310.]

260 Income payments agreement

[Not reproduced—see IA 1986 s.310A.]

261 Bankrupt's home

[Subsections (1)–(6) not reproduced—see IA 1986 ss.283A, 313 and 313A.]

261(7) [Definitions in s.261(8)] In subsection (8)–

(a) "pre-commencement bankrupt" means an individual who is adjudged bankrupt on a petition presented before subsection (1) above comes into force, and

(b) "the transitional period" is the period of three years beginning with the date on which subsection (1) above comes into force.

261(8) [Interest in dwelling-house] If a pre-commencement bankrupt's estate includes an interest in a dwelling-house which at the date of the bankruptcy was the sole or principal residence of him, his spouse or a former spouse of his, at the end of the transitional period that interest shall–

(a) cease to be comprised in the estate, and

(b) vest in the bankrupt (without conveyance, assignment or transfer).

261(9) [Application of s.261(8)] But subsection (8) shall not apply if before or during the transitional period–

(a) any of the events mentioned in section 283A(3) of the Insolvency Act 1986 (c. 45) (inserted by subsection (1) above) occurs in relation to the interest or the dwelling-house, or

(b) the trustee obtains any order of a court, or makes any agreement with the bankrupt, in respect of the interest or the dwelling-house.

261(10) [Effect of s.283A(4)–(9) of 1986 Act] Subsections 283A(4) to (9) of that Act shall have effect, with any necessary modifications, in relation to the provision made by subsections (7) to (9) above; in particular–

(a) a reference to the period mentioned in section 283A(2) shall be construed as a reference to the transitional period,

(b) in the application of section 283A(5) a reference to the date of the bankruptcy shall be construed as a reference to the date on which subsection (1) above comes into force, and

(c) a reference to the rules is a reference to rules made under section 412 of the Insolvency Act 1986 (for which purpose this section shall be treated as forming part of Parts VIII to XI of that Act).

GENERAL NOTE

This is a curious statutory provision. The bulk of it consists of transplants into IA 1986, and in particular the new ss.283A and 313A dealing with the realisation of the family home. These provisions are dealt with at the appropriate destination. Subsections (7)–(10) however are free-standing and require comment here, though sense can only be made of these provisions by referring to s.283A.

S.261(7)

This is an interpretation provision.

S.261(8)–(10)

These deal with transitional matters flowing from the significant changes in the law on the bankrupt's family home introduced by s.261 of EA 2002.

262   Powers of trustee in bankruptcy

[Not reproduced—see Sch.5 to IA 1986.]

263   Repeal of certain bankruptcy offences

[Not reproduced—see IA 1986 ss.361 and 362.]

264   Individual voluntary arrangement

264(1)   [Schedule 22 to have effect] Schedule 22 (which makes provision about individual voluntary arrangements) shall have effect.

264(2)   [Power to make order] The Secretary of State may by order amend the Insolvency Act 1986 so as to extend the provisions of sections 263B to 263G (which are inserted by Schedule 22 and provide a fasttrack procedure for making an individual voluntary arrangement) to some or all cases other than those specified in section 263A as inserted by Schedule 22.

264(3)   [Procedure for order] An order under subsection (2)–

(a)   must be made by statutory instrument, and

(b)   may not be made unless a draft has been laid before and approved by each House of Parliament.

264(4)   [Effect of order] An order under subsection (2) may make–

(a)   consequential provision (which may include provision amending the Insolvency Act 1986 or another enactment);

(b)   transitional provision.

S.264

This introduces Sch.22, which makes amendments to IVA law and in particular introduces the fast track IVA for undischarged bankrupts. The Secretary of State is given power by subs.(2) to extend this fast track procedure to a wider range of applications by using secondary rules.

265   Disqualification from office: justice of the peace [Repealed.]

S.265

This provision, which repealed s.65 of the Justices of the Peace Act 1997 furthered the new policy of removing automatic restrictions from bankrupts holding certain public offices. Bankrupts will no longer automatically be disqualified from holding this minor judicial office. Section 265 was itself repealed by the Courts Act 2003.

266   Disqualification from office: Parliament

[Subsections (1)–(2) not reproduced—see IA 1986 ss.426A–C and 427.]

266(3)   [Power to make order] The Secretary of State may by order–

(a)   provide for section 426A or 426B of that Act (as inserted by subsection (1) above) to have effect in relation to orders made or undertakings accepted in Scotland or Northern Ireland under a system which appears to the Secretary of State to be equivalent to the system operating under Schedule 4A to that Act (as inserted by section 257 of this Act);

(b)   make consequential amendment of section 426A or 426B of that Act (as inserted by subsection (1) above);

(c) make other consequential amendment of an enactment.

266(4) **[Effect of order]** An order under this section may make transitional, consequential or incidental provision.

266(5) **[Procedure for order]** An order under this section–

(a) must be made by statutory instrument, and

(b) may not be made unless a draft has been laid before and approved by resolution of each House of Parliament.

S.266

Subsections (1) and (2) insert new provisions into IA 1986 and are dealt with in the commentary to ss.426A, 426B and 427. Subsections (3)–(6) are however "free-standing" and permit the creation of secondary rules to extend ss.426A and 426B of IA 1986 to Scotland or Northern Ireland.

267 Disqualification from office: local government

267(1) **[Substitution of Local Government Act 1972 s.80(1)(b)]** The following shall be substituted for section 80(1)(b) of the Local Government Act 1972 (c. 70) (disqualification for membership of local authority: bankrupt)–

"(b) is the subject of a bankruptcy restrictions order or interim order;".

267(2) **[Cessation of Local Government Act 1972 s.81(1), (2)]** Section 81(1) and (2) of that Act (which amplify the provision substituted by subsection (1) above) shall cease to have effect.

GENERAL NOTE

This again reflects the new "softer" approach towards bankrupts by removing another automatic disqualification from their shoulders.

S.267(1), (2)

The disqualification from holding local government office will now only apply if a bankruptcy restrictions order or interim order has been made against the individual. Presumably the same would apply in the case of a BRU—see Sch.4A para.8.

268 Disqualification from office: general

268(1) **[Power to make order]** The Secretary of State may make an order under this section in relation to a disqualification provision.

268(2) **["Disqualification provision"]** A "disqualification provision" is a provision which disqualifies (whether permanently or temporarily and whether absolutely or conditionally) a bankrupt or a class of bankrupts from–

(a) being elected or appointed to an office or position,

(b) holding an office or position, or

(c) becoming or remaining a member of a body or group.

268(3) **[Reference in s.267(2)]** In subsection (2) the reference to a provision which disqualifies a person conditionally includes a reference to a provision which enables him to be dismissed.

268(4) **[Scope of order under s.267(1)]** An order under subsection (1) may repeal or revoke the disqualification provision.

268(5) **[Effect of order]** An order under subsection (1) may amend, or modify the effect of, the disqualification provision–

(a) so as to reduce the class of bankrupts to whom the disqualification provision applies;

(b) so as to extend the disqualification provision to some or all individuals who are subject to a bankruptcy restrictions regime;

(c) so that the disqualification provision applies only to some or all individuals who are subject to a bankruptcy restrictions regime;

(d) so as to make the application of the disqualification provision wholly or partly subject to the discretion of a specified person, body or group.

268(6)   [Discretionary provision in order] An order by virtue of subsection (5)(d) may provide for a discretion to be subject to–

(a) the approval of a specified person or body;

(b) appeal to a specified person or body.

268(7)   [Discretion subject to appeal] An order by virtue of subsection (5)(d) may provide for a discretion to be subject to appeal to a specified court or tribunal; but any such order must–

(a) if it relates to England and Wales, be made with the concurrence of the Lord Chief Justice of England and Wales;

(b) if it relates to Northern Ireland, be made with the concurrence of the Lord Chief Justice of Northern Ireland.

268(8)   [Secretary of State specified] The Secretary of State may specify himself for the purposes of subsection (5)(d) or (6)(a) or (b).

268(9)   ["Bankrupt"] In this section "bankrupt" means an individual–

(a) who has been adjudged bankrupt by a court in England and Wales or in Northern Ireland,

(b) whose estate has been sequestrated by a court in Scotland, or

(c) who has made an agreement with creditors of his for a composition of debts, for a scheme of arrangement of affairs, for the grant of a trust deed or for some other kind of settlement or arrangement.

268(10)   ["Bankruptcy restrictions regime"] In this section "bankruptcy restrictions regime" means an order or undertaking–

(a) under Schedule 4A to the Insolvency Act 1986 (c. 45) (bankruptcy restrictions orders), or

(b) under any system operating in Scotland or Northern Ireland which appears to the Secretary of State to be equivalent to the system operating under that Schedule.

268(11)   ["Body", "provision"] In this section–

"body" includes Parliament and any other legislative body, and

"provision" means–

(a) a provision made by an Act of Parliament passed before or in the same Session as this Act, and

(b) a provision made, before or in the same Session as this Act, under an Act of Parliament.

268(12)   [Scope of order] An order under this section–

(a) may make provision generally or for a specified purpose only,

(b) may make different provision for different purposes, and

(c) may make transitional, consequential or incidental provision.

268(13) **[Procedure for order]** An order under this section–

(a) must be made by statutory instrument, and

(b) may not be made unless a draft has been laid before and approved by resolution of each House of Parliament.

268(14) **[National Assembly of Wales]** A reference in this section to the Secretary of State shall be treated as a reference to the National Assembly for Wales in so far as it relates to a disqualification provision which–

(a) is made by the National Assembly for Wales, or

(b) relates to a function of the National Assembly.

268(15) **[Appeals]** Provision made by virtue of subsection (7) is subject to any order of the Lord Chancellor under section 56(1) of the Access to Justice Act 1999 (c. 22) (appeals: jurisdiction).

268(16) **[LCJ nominee]** The Lord Chief Justice may nominate a judicial office holder (as defined in section 109(4) of the Constitutional Reform Act 2005) to exercise his functions under subsection (7).

268(17) **[LCJ nominee]** The Lord Chief Justice of Northern Ireland may nominate any of the following to exercise his functions under subsection (7)–

(a) the holder of one of the offices listed in Schedule 1 to the Justice (Northern Ireland) Act 2002;

(b) a Lord Justice of Appeal (as defined in section 88 of that Act).

GENERAL NOTE

This introduces the possibility of future flexibility into the area of bankruptcy disqualification. There are at present many numerous disqualifications applied to bankrupts which are not dealt with specifically by EA 2002 and thus s.268 provides an instrument for future reform. The power to make delegated legislation under s.268 was exercised with the making of the Enterprise Act (Disqualification from Office: General) Order 2006 (SI 2006/1722) which removes bankruptcy disqualification in some instances and reinforces it in other cases to cover individuals covered by BROs or BRUs. Note also in this context the Education (Disqualification Provisions: Bankruptcy and Mental Health) (England) Regulations 2006 (SI 2006/2198) which, although not made under s.268, are relevant.

S.268(1), (2), (3), (9), (10)
These define the extent of the power of the Secretary of State to make delegated provision.

S.268(4)–(8), (16) and (17)
These deal with the effect of the exercise of this rule-making power. Subsection (7) was amended and subss.(16) and (17) inserted by the Constitutional Reform Act 2005 s.15 and Sch.4 Pt 1 para.304.

S.268(10), (11)
These are definitional provisions.

S.268(12), (13)
These deal with formal legislative matters.

S.268(14)
This deals with the legislative position in Wales.

S.268(15)
This qualifies subs.(7).

269 Minor and consequential amendments

269 Schedule 23 (minor and consequential amendments relating to individual insolvency) shall have effect.

GENERAL NOTE

This refers us to Sch.23 which makes a number of minor and consequential changes to personal insolvency law.

270 Fees

[Subsection (1) not reproduced—see IA 1986 s.415A.]

270(2) [Order made before s.270 in force] An order made by virtue of subsection (1) may relate to the maintenance of recognition or authorisation granted before this section comes into force.

[Subsections (3) and (4) amend IA 1986 ss.392 and 440 and are not reproduced here.]

GENERAL NOTE

On commencement see Enterprise Act 2002 (Commencement No.5 and Amendment) Order 2003 (SI 2003/3340 (C. 132)).

271 Insolvency Services Account: interest

[Not reproduced—see IA 1986 Schs 8 and 9.]

GENERAL NOTE

On commencement see Enterprise Act 2002 (Commencement No.5 and Amendment) Order 2003 (SI 2003/3340 (C. 132)).

272 Insolvency Services Accounts

[Not reproduced—see IA 1986 ss.405 and 408.]

SCHEDULE 16

SCHEDULE B1 TO INSOLVENCY ACT 1986

[Not reproduced—see Sch.B1 to IA 1986.]

SCHEDULE 17

ADMINISTRATION: MINOR AND CONSEQUENTIAL AMENDMENTS

General

1 In any instrument made before section 248(1) to (3) of this Act comes into force–

(a) a reference to the making of an administration order shall be treated as including a reference to the appointment of an administrator under paragraph 14 or 22 of Schedule B1 to the Insolvency Act 1986 (c. 45) (inserted by section 248(2) of this Act), and

(b) a reference to making an application for an administration order by petition shall be treated as including a reference to making an administration application under that Schedule, appointing an administrator under paragraph 14 or 22 of that Schedule or giving notice under paragraph 15 or 26 of that Schedule.

[Paras 2–59 not reproduced.]

SCHEDULE 18

SCHEDULE 2A TO INSOLVENCY ACT 1986

[Not reproduced—see Sch.2A to IA 1986.]

Schedule 19

Duration of Bankruptcy: Transitional Provisions

Introduction

1 This Schedule applies to an individual who immediately before commencement–

(a) has been adjudged bankrupt, and

(b) has not been discharged from the bankruptcy.

2 In this Schedule–

"commencement" means the date appointed under section 279 for the commencement of section 256, and

"pre-commencement bankrupt" means an individual to whom this Schedule applies.

Neither old law nor new law to apply

3 Section 279 of the Insolvency Act 1986 (c. 45) (bankruptcy: discharge) shall not apply to a pre-commencement bankrupt (whether in its pre-commencement or its post-commencement form).

General rule for discharge from pre-commencement bankruptcy

4(1) A pre-commencement bankrupt is, subject to sub-paragraphs (2) and (3), discharged from bankruptcy at whichever is the earlier of–

(a) the end of the period of one year beginning with commencement, and

(b) the end of the relevant period applicable to the bankrupt under section 279(1)(b) of the Insolvency Act 1986 (duration of bankruptcy) as it had effect immediately before commencement.

4(2) An order made under section 279(3) of that Act before commencement–

(a) shall continue to have effect in respect of the pre-commencement bankrupt after commencement, and

(b) may be varied or revoked after commencement by an order under section 279(3) as substituted by section 256 of this Act.

4(3) Section 279(3) to (5) of that Act as substituted by section 256 of this Act shall have effect after commencement in relation to the period mentioned in sub-paragraph (1)(a) or (b) above.

Second-time bankruptcy

5(1) This paragraph applies to a pre-commencement bankrupt who was an undischarged bankrupt at some time during the period of 15 years ending with the day before the date on which the pre-commencement bankruptcy commenced.

5(2) The pre-commencement bankrupt shall not be discharged from bankruptcy in accordance with paragraph 4 above.

5(3) An order made before commencement under section 280(2)(b) or (c) of the Insolvency Act 1986 (c. 45) (discharge by order of the court) shall continue to have effect after commencement (including any provision made by the court by virtue of section 280(3)).

5(4) A pre-commencement bankrupt to whom this paragraph applies (and in respect of whom no order is in force under section 280(2)(b) or (c) on commencement) is discharged–

661

(a)   at the end of the period of five years beginning with commencement, or

(b)   at such earlier time as the court may order on an application under section 280 of the Insolvency Act 1986 (discharge by order) heard after commencement.

5(5)   Section 279(3) to (5) of the Insolvency Act 1986 as substituted by section 256 of this Act shall have effect after commencement in relation to the period mentioned in sub-paragraph (4)(a) above.

5(6)   A bankruptcy annulled under section 282 shall be ignored for the purpose of sub-paragraph (1).

Criminal bankruptcy

6   A pre-commencement bankrupt who was adjudged bankrupt on a petition under section 264(1)(d) of the Insolvency Act 1986 (criminal bankruptcy)–

(a)   shall not be discharged from bankruptcy in accordance with paragraph 4 above, but

(b)   may be discharged from bankruptcy by an order of the court under section 280 of that Act.

Income payments order

7(1)   This paragraph applies where–

(a)   a pre-commencement bankrupt is discharged by virtue of paragraph 4(1)(a), and

(b)   an income payments order is in force in respect of him immediately before his discharge.

7(2)   If the income payments order specifies a date after which it is not to have effect, it shall continue in force until that date (and then lapse).

7(3)   But the court may on the application of the pre-commencement bankrupt–

(a)   vary the income payments order;

(b)   provide for the income payments order to cease to have effect before the date referred to in sub-paragraph (2).

Bankruptcy restrictions order or undertaking

8   A provision of this Schedule which provides for an individual to be discharged from bankruptcy is subject to–

(a)   any bankruptcy restrictions order (or interim order) which may be made in relation to that individual, and

(b)   any bankruptcy restrictions undertaking entered into by that individual.

GENERAL NOTE

This deals with important transitional matters in bankruptcy law. The reforms in EA 2002 generally speaking will not affect existing bankruptcies commenced prior to April 1, 2004, though a pre-commencement bankrupt may benefit from an earlier discharge—see *Re Johnson* [2006] B.P.I.R. 987. The major exception relates to the powers of the trustee with regard to the recovery actions (see EA 2002 s.262)—the reforms here take effect on September 15, 2003 provided the action was commenced before that date. This point is reinforced by the Enterprise Act 2002 (Commencement No.4 and Transitional Provisions and Savings) Order 2003 (SI 2003/2093 (C. 85)). It is clear from this latter SI that conduct on the part of a person who becomes bankrupt and which occurs prior to April 1, 2004 is not relevant for the purposes of a BRO or BRU. Note the minor amendment to para.4(1) by the Enterprise Act 2002 (Insolvency) Order 2003 (SI 2003/2096).

SCHEDULE 20

SCHEDULE 4A TO INSOLVENCY ACT 1986

[Not reproduced—see above.]

SCHEDULE 21

EFFECT OF BANKRUPTCY RESTRICTIONS ORDER AND UNDERTAKING

[Not reproduced—see amendments to IA 1986.]

SCHEDULE 22

INDIVIDUAL VOLUNTARY ARRANGEMENT

[Not reproduced—see IA 1986 ss.261, 263A–G and 389B.]

SCHEDULE 23

INDIVIDUAL INSOLVENCY: MINOR AND CONSEQUENTIAL AMENDMENTS

[Not reproduced—see amendments to IA 1986.]

SCHEDULE 26

REPEALS AND REVOCATIONS

[Not reproduced.]

The Insolvency Rules 1986

(SI 1986/1925)

Made on 10 November 1986 by the Lord Chancellor under s.411 and 412 of the Insolvency Act 1986. Operative from 29 December 1986.

[**Note**: These Rules are amended by the Insolvency (Amendment) Rules 1987 (SI 1987/1919) as from January 11, 1988; by the Insolvency (Amendment) Rules 1989 (SI 1989/397) as from April 3, 1989; by the Insolvency (Amendment) Rules 1991 (SI 1991/495) as from April 2, 1991; by the Insolvency (Amendment) Rules 1993 (SI 1993/602) as from April 5, 1993; by the Insolvency (Amendment) Rules 1995 (SI 1995/586) as from April 1, 1995; by the Insolvency (Amendment) Rules 1999 (SI 1999/359) as from March 22, 1999; by the Insolvency (Amendment) (No.2) Rules 1999 (SI 1999/1022) as from March 22, 1999; by the Insolvency (Amendment) Rules 2001 (SI 2001/763) as from April 2, 2001; by the Insolvency (Amendment) Rules 2002 (SI 2002/1307) as from May 31, 2002; by the Insolvency (Amendment) (No.2) Rules 2002 (SI 2002/2712) as from January 15 2003; by the Insolvency (Amendment) Rules 2003 (SI 2003/1730), as from September 15, 2003 and April 1, 2004; by the Insolvency (Amendment) Rules 2004 (SI 2004/584) as from April 1, 2004; by the Insolvency (Amendment) (No.2) Rules 2004 (SI 2004/1070) as from May 3, 2004; by the Insolvency (Amendment) Rules 2005 (SI 2005/527), as from April 1, 2005 (for transitional provisions, see SI 2005/527, reproduced in Vol.2 of this *Guide*, Rule 3); by the Insolvency (Amendment) Rules 2006 (SI 2006/1272), as from June 1, 2006; by the Insolvency (Amendment) Rules 2007 (SI 2007/1974), as from August 6, 2007; by the Insolvency (Amendment) Rules 2008 (SI 2008/737), as from April 6, 2008; by the Insolvency (Amendment) Rules 2009 (SI 2009/642), as from April 6, 2009, by the Insolvency (Amendment) (No.2) Rules 2009 (SI 2009/2472), as from October 1, 2009, by the Insolvency (Amendment) Rules 2010 (SI 2010/686) and the Insolvency (Amendment) (No.2) Rules 2010 (SI 2010/734) as from April 6, 2010.

These rules apply in England and Wales only.]

ARRANGEMENT OF RULES

The Insolvency Rules 1986

(SI 1986/1925)

Introductory note to the Insolvency Rules 1986

The rules in this section are prefixed with the figure 0. The remainder of the rules are grouped into Parts, numbered 1, 2, etc. and the rules in each part begin with the same figure, e.g. r.1.1, 1.2, etc. The sequence of Parts broadly follows the scheme of IA 1986.

Where a rule calls for the use of a prescribed form, the reference number of the appropriate form is shown adjacent to the rule in question.

The text incorporates all amendments made to the rules which are currently in force. (See the list of amending statutory instruments on p.664.)

The Rules were drawn up at a time when procedure in the civil courts was regulated by the Rules of the Supreme Court 1986 and the County Court Rules 1981. These two sets of Rules were replaced by the Civil Procedure Rules 1998 (commonly known as the CPR) which came into force on April 26, 1999. Under r.2.1 of the CPR, the new civil procedure does not apply to insolvency proceedings, but by the Insolvency (Amendment) (No.2) Rules 1999 (SI 1999/1022) the Insolvency Rules 1986 are amended, with effect from April 26, 1999, so as to apply all those provisions of the CPR and such practice of the High Court and County Court as is not inconsistent with provisions made by IR 1986 to insolvency proceedings. In addition, detailed amendment is made of such of the latter Rules as use language which has been discarded by the CPR, such as "*ex parte* hearings" and the "taxation" of costs. Again, in order to achieve consistency with the CPR, the amendments bring practice in insolvency proceedings into line with the new civil procedure, for example by providing for the use of witness statements verified by statements of truth in a number of situations where affidavit evidence was formerly obligatory.

The phrase "as soon as reasonably practicable" has been substituted for the word "forthwith" wherever it occurs in the Rules, as from April 6, 2009: see I(A)R 2009 (SI 2009/642) r.5. This has been done in the text which follows (in most instances without annotation).

The Insolvency Rules 1986 have been extensively amended by the Insolvency (Amendment) Rules 2010 (SI 2010/686) (as amended by SI 2010/734) with effect from April 6, 2010. The main changes of substance include:

- changes relating to advertising;
- the introduction of "standard contents" for notices in the Gazette and other notices;
- provisions facilitating the holding of meetings without the physical presence of the participants, e.g. by electronic means;
- changes to the rules regarding eligibility to serve on creditors' and liquidation committees;
- amendments to the disclaimer procedure;
- changes to court procedure and practice;
- changes to the rules on public and private examinations;
- in CVAs and IVAs, removal of the requirement to file copies of documents in court;
- elimination in most cases of the use of affidavits and their replacement by witness statements or statements of truth;
- revision of the rules governing office-holders' remuneration and expenses;
- provisions allowing pre-administration remuneration and costs as expenses of the administration;
- supplementary rules relating to block transfer orders;
- standardised rules limiting the public disclosure of information about creditors;
- authorisation of the communication of information and sending or service of documents by electronic means and the use of websites, including authentication of documents without signatures;
- confidentiality of personal information for persons at risk of physical violence.

These amendments are fully annotated at the appropriate places.

Among other changes which will be important in practice may be mentioned:

- "deponent", "sworn" and other terms associated with "affidavit" replaced by equivalent expressions;

- abolition of the requirement to use prescribed forms in notifications to the registrar of companies;

- generally specifying periods of time for seven days or fewer in "business days" rather than "days";

- hearings by "the registrar in chambers" replaced by "the registrar or district judge".

Some particular points are worthy of special mention.

Scope

The 1986 Rules do not apply in Scotland (*Secretary of State for Trade and Industry v Frid* [2004] UKHL 24; [2004] 2 A.C. 506; [2004] B.C.C. 525 at [31]) or in Northern Ireland. The 2010 amendments are similarly confined in their application to England and Wales.

Retrospectivity

As is normal in the case of amending legislation, many of the above changes will not affect insolvencies that commenced before April 6, 2010. Exceptionally, however, a number of them do affect insolvencies which are in process on that date. The new rules which are to apply "in all cases" are identified in Sch.4, and especially para.2 of that Schedule. Among these are (broadly speaking) the new rules authorising the use of electronic means of communication and websites, the relaxation of the requirement for physical attendance at meetings and abolition of the use of affidavits. Where the distinction may be important we have endeavoured to include a reminder that the former law will continue to apply to existing insolvencies (which will mean that the unamended Rules must be consulted, as found in the 12th edition of this *Guide*). If there is room for doubt, Sch.4 should be referred to.

New Part 12A

A new Pt 12A brings together the rules on (a) the giving of notice and the supply of documents by or to office-holders and the service of court documents, (b) meetings, (c) the giving of notice to enforcement officers, (d) forms and the electronic submission of information in lieu of forms, (e) the contents of notices to be gazetted, (f) the contents of notices advertised otherwise than in the *Gazette*, (g) notifications to the registrar of companies, (h) inspection of documents and the provision of information, (i) computation of time and time limits, (j) insolvency practitioners' security and (k) notice of an order under IA 1986 s.176A.

Business days

Most periods of time are now specified in "business days" rather than "days", at least where the resulting number is below 7: thus 10 days has become 7 business days, and 7 days has become 5 business days. These changes are not retrospective, which may mean that a longer period of time will continue to apply in an existing insolvency. Note also that the definition of "business day" has been altered (and that it is not the same as that in the Act), so that no account is now to be taken of a date that is a bank holiday in Scotland but not in England.

Affidavits

Affidavits are no longer to be used in all proceedings under the Act: instead we have witness statements, statements of truth and certificates of service. But note that this does not apply to proceedings under CDDA 1986 (unless brought under a rule, such as an application under r.7.47), and that affidavits continue to be necessary in Scotland and Northern Ireland.

Old Part II administrations

Special provision as regards retrospectivity is made in Sch.5 for administrations under the original IA 1986 Pt II, i.e. those involving various types of utility company and building societies and pre-Enterprise Act administrations.

Substituted rules and sub-rules

A word of warning here. In many (but not all) cases where a new rule or paragraph of a rule is substituted by a new one, the new rule has not been given the same number as its predecessor, but the same number with the letter A added. Thus r.2.44 is replaced by r.2.44A, and the former is effectively deleted.

Various other changes may be regarded as essentially verbal or cosmetic, or as merely consequential upon some of the amendments listed above, and so involving no change of substance; e.g. (see I(A)R 2010 Sch. para.1):

- "as the court thinks fit" replaced by "as the court thinks just";

- "leave of the court" replaced by "permission of the court";

- "sign" (and associated terms) replaced by "authenticate";

- use of gender-neutral language;

- "*ex parte*" replaced by equivalent English terms;

In these and similar cases the changes have been made in the text of the rules without annotation.

Contemporaneously with the 2010 Rules, the Legislative Reform (Insolvency) (Miscellaneous Provisions) Order 2010 (SI 2010/18) came into force on April 6, 2010, making some changes to the 1986 Act. See the note above, p.7.

INTRODUCTORY PROVISIONS

0.1 Citation and commencement

0.1 These Rules may be cited as the Insolvency Rules 1986 and shall come into force on 29th December 1986.

0.2 Construction and interpretation

0.2(1) [Definitions] In these Rules–

"the Act" means the Insolvency Act 1986 (any reference to a numbered section being to a section of that Act);

"the Companies Act" means the Companies Act 2006;

"CPR" means the Civil Procedure Rules 1998 and **"CPR"** followed by a Part or rule by number means the Part or rule with that number in those Rules;

"RSC" followed by an Order by number means the Order with that number set out in Schedule 1 to the CPR; and

"the Rules" means the Insolvency Rules 1986.

0.2(2) [Omitted by I(A)R 2010 (SI 2010/686) r.2 and Sch. para.2(2) as from April 6, 2010.]

0.2(3) [Part 13] Subject to paragraph (1), Part 13 of the Rules has effect for their interpretation and application.

GENERAL NOTE

Rule 0.2(2) omitted and r.0.2(3) amended by I(A)R 2010 (SI 2010/686) r.2 and Sch. para.2(2), (3) as from April 6, 2010.

0.3 Extent

0.3(1) [Parts 1, 2 and 4] Parts 1, 2, and 4 of the Rules, and Parts 7 to 13 as they relate to company insolvency, apply in relation to companies which the courts in England and Wales have jurisdiction to wind up.

0.3(2) [Application of rr.3.1, 3.39, 3.40, remainder of Pt 3] Rule 3.1 applies to all receivers to whom Part III of the Act applies, Rule 3.39 and 3.40 apply to all receivers who are not administrative receivers, and the remainder of Part 3 of the Rules applies to administrative receivers appointed otherwise than under section 51 (Scottish Receivership).

0.3(3) [Parts 5 and 6] Parts 5 and 6 of the Rules, and Parts 7 to 13 as they relate to individual insolvency, extend to England and Wales only.

GENERAL NOTE

Rule 0.3(2) was replaced by the Insolvency (Amendment) Rules 2003 (SI 2003/1730).

Corresponding subordinate legislation has been enacted for Scotland, principally by the Insolvency (Scotland) Rules 1986 (SI 1986/1915 (S 139)) (as amended).

For the position in Northern Ireland see the Insolvency Rules (Northern Ireland) 1991 (SR 1991/364), (as amended) and the note to IA 1986 s.441.

685

THE FIRST GROUP OF PARTS

COMPANY INSOLVENCY; COMPANIES WINDING UP

Introductory note to the First Group of Parts
Note that, in the absence of special statutory provision, the rules in this Group of Parts do not apply to bodies other than companies (e.g. the rules as to set-off do not apply to building societies).

PART 1

COMPANY VOLUNTARY ARRANGEMENTS

Introductory note to Part 1
The topic of CVAs to which these rules relate is dealt with in IA 1986 ss.1–7. On voluntary arrangements for individual debtors, see IA 1986 ss.252 et seq., and IR 1986 Pt 5.

CHAPTER 1

PRELIMINARY

1.1   Scope of this Part; interpretation

1.1(1)   **[Application of Pt 1 Rules]** The Rules in this Part apply where, pursuant to Part I of the Act, it is intended to make, and there is made, a proposal to a company and its creditors for a voluntary arrangement, that is to say, a composition in satisfaction of its debts or a scheme of arrangement of its affairs.

1.1(2)   **[Application of Chs 2–8]** In this Part–

(a)   Chapter 2 applies where the proposal for the voluntary arrangement is made by the directors of the company and

     (i)   the company is neither in liquidation nor is the company in administration; and

     (ii)   no steps have been taken to obtain a moratorium under Schedule A1 to the Act in connection with the proposal;

(b)   Chapter 3 applies where the company is in liquidation or the company is in administration, and the proposal is made by the liquidator or (as the case may be) the administrator, he in either case being the nominee for the purposes of the proposal;

(c)   Chapter 4 applies in the same case as Chapter 3, but where the nominee is not the liquidator or administrator;

(d)   Chapter 5 applies in all the three cases mentioned in sub-paragraphs (a) to (c) above;

(e)   Chapters 7 and 8 apply to all voluntary arrangements with or without a moratorium; and

(f)   Chapter 9 applies where the proposal is made by the directors of an eligible company with a view to obtaining a moratorium.

1.1(3)   **["The responsible insolvency practitioner" in Chs 3–5]** In Chapters 3, 4 and 5, the liquidator or the administrator is referred to as "the responsible insolvency practitioner".

1.1(4)   **["Eligible company"]** In this Part, a reference to an eligible company is to a company that is eligible for a moratorium in accordance with paragraph 2 of Schedule A1 to the Act.

GENERAL NOTE

This was amended in paras (1) and (2) by the Insolvency (Amendment) (No.2) Rules 2002 (SI 2002/2712) with effect from January 1, 2003 to cater for the coming into operation of the new optional CVA cum moratorium model. It fully reflects the increased complexity of CVA law in the wake of the full range of changes effected by IA 2000. A new para.(4) was added as part of this overhaul.

A further textual amendment came via the Insolvency (Amendment) Rules 2003 (SI 2003/1730) in recognition of the fact that it is not always appropriate to use the phrase "administration order".

GENERAL NOTE

Different procedures must be followed in the three cases listed in r.1.1(2)(a–c): see IA 1986 ss.1, 2. The relevant rules are set out in Chs 2, 3 and 4 respectively. Rule 1.1(2)(d) was amended by the Insolvency (Amendment) Rules 2002 (SI 2002/1307) para.4(1).

CHAPTER 2

PROPOSAL BY DIRECTORS

1.2 Preparation of proposal [Revoked by I(A)R 2010 (SI 2010/686).]

1.3 Contents of proposal

1.3(1) [Explanation why voluntary arrangement desirable] The directors' proposal shall provide a short explanation why, in their opinion, a voluntary arrangement under Part I of the Act is desirable, and give reasons why the company's creditors may be expected to concur with such an arrangement.

1.3(2) [Other matters] The following matters shall be stated, or otherwise dealt with, in the directors' proposal–

(a) the following matters, so far as within the directors' immediate knowledge–

   (i) the company's assets, with an estimate of their respective values,

   (ii) the extent (if any) to which the assets are charged in favour of creditors,

   (iii) the extent (if any) to which particular assets are to be excluded from the voluntary arrangement;

(b) particulars of any property, other than assets of the company itself, which is proposed to be included in the arrangement, the source of such property and the terms on which it is to be made available for inclusion;

(c) the nature and amount of the company's liabilities (so far as within the directors' immediate knowledge), the manner in which they are proposed to be met, modified, postponed or otherwise dealt with by means of the arrangement, and (in particular)–

   (i) how it is proposed to deal with preferential creditors (defined in section 4(7)) and creditors who are, or claim to be, secured,

   (ii) how persons connected with the company (being creditors) are proposed to be treated under the arrangement, and

   (iii) whether there are, to the directors' knowledge, any circumstances giving rise to the possibility, in the event that the company should go into liquidation, of claims under–

section 238 (transactions at an undervalue),

section 239 (preferences),

section 244 (extortionate credit transactions), or

section 245 (floating charges invalid);

and, where any such circumstances are present, whether, and if so how, it is proposed under the voluntary arrangement to make provision for wholly or partly indemnifying the company in respect of such claims;

(ca) an estimate (to the best of the directors' knowledge and belief and subject to paragraph (4)) of–

    (i) the value of the prescribed part, should the company go into liquidation if the proposal for the voluntary arrangement is not accepted, whether or not section 176A is to be disapplied; and

    (ii) the value of the company's net property on the date that the estimate is made.

(d) whether any, and if so what, guarantees have been given of the company's debts by other persons, specifying which (if any) of the guarantors are persons connected with the company;

(e) the proposed duration of the voluntary arrangement;

(f) the proposed dates of distributions to creditors, with estimates of their amounts;

(fa) how it is proposed to deal with the claim of any person who is bound by the arrangement by virtue of section 5(2)(b)(ii);

(g) the amount proposed to be paid to the nominee (as such) by way of remuneration and expenses;

(h) the manner in which it is proposed that the supervisor of the arrangement should be remunerated, and his expenses defrayed;

(j) whether, for the purposes of the arrangement, any guarantees are to be offered by directors, or other persons, and whether (if so) any security is to be given or sought;

(k) the manner in which funds held for the purposes of the arrangement are to be banked, invested or otherwise dealt with pending distribution to creditors;

(l) the manner in which funds held for the purpose of payment to creditors, and not so paid on the termination of the arrangement, are to be dealt with;

(m) the manner in which the business of the company is proposed to be conducted during the course of the arrangement;

(n) details of any further credit facilities which it is intended to arrange for the company, and how the debts so arising are to be paid;

(o) the functions which are to be undertaken by the supervisor of the arrangement;

(p) the name, address and qualification of the person proposed as supervisor of the voluntary arrangement, and confirmation that he is either qualified to act as an insolvency practitioner in relation to the company or is an authorised person in relation to the company;

(q) whether the EC Regulation will apply and, if so, whether the proceedings will be main proceedings, secondary proceedings or territorial proceedings; and

(r) such other matters (if any) as the directors consider appropriate for ensuring that members and creditors are enabled to reach an informed decision on the proposal.

1.3(3) [Amendment of proposal] With the agreement in writing of the nominee, the directors' proposal may be amended at any time up to delivery of the nominee's report to the court under section 2(2).

1.3(4) [Disclosure of information prejudicial] Nothing in paragraph (2)(ca) is to be taken as requiring the estimate referred to in that paragraph to include any information, the disclosure of which could seriously prejudice the commercial interests of the company. If such information is excluded from the calculation the estimate shall be accompanied by a statement to that effect.

(See General Note after r.1.6.) Paragraph 1.3(2)(q) was inserted by the Insolvency (Amendment) Rules 2002 (SI 2002/1307) para.4(2).

GENERAL NOTE

New subpara.(2)(fa) and a revised (2)(p) were added by the Insolvency (Amendment) (No.2) Rules 2002 (SI 2002/2712) with effect from January 1, 2003 to cater for reforms introduced by IA 2000 particularly with regard to unknown creditors and non-IPs acting as supervisors.

This rule was then also further amended by the Insolvency (Amendment) Rules 2003 (SI 2003/1730) to address the implications of the reserved fund for unsecured creditors, though subject to the need to protect commercial confidences.

New para.(2)(r) added by I(A)R 2010 (SI 2010/686).

1.4 Notice to intended nominee

1.4(1) [Written notice] The directors shall give to the intended nominee written notice of their proposal.

1.4(2) [Delivery of notice] The notice, accompanied by a copy of the proposal, shall be delivered either to the nominee himself, or to a person authorised to take delivery of documents on his behalf.

1.4(3) [Endorsement of receipt] If the intended nominee agrees to act, he shall cause a copy of the notice to be endorsed to the effect that it has been received by him on a specified date; and the period of 28 days referred to in section 2(2) then runs from that date.

1.4(4) [Return of endorsed notice] The copy of the notice so endorsed shall be returned by the nominee as soon as reasonably practicable to the directors at an address specified by them in the notice for that purpose.

(See General Note after r.1.6.)

1.5 Statement of affairs

1.5(1) [Delivery of statement] The directors shall, at the same time as the proposal is delivered to the nominee, deliver to him a statement of the company's affairs.

1.5(2) [Particulars in statement] The statement shall comprise the following particulars (supplementing or amplifying, so far as is necessary for clarifying the state of the company's affairs, those already given in the directors' proposal)–

(a) a list of the company's assets, divided into such categories as are appropriate for easy identification, with estimated values assigned to each category;

(b) in the case of any property on which a claim against the company is wholly or partly secured, particulars of the claim and its amount, and of how and when the security was created;

(c) the names and addresses of the company's preferential creditors (defined in section 4(7)), with the amounts of their respective claims;

(d) the names and addresses of the company's unsecured creditors, with the amounts of their respective claims;

(e) particulars of any debts owed by or to the company to or by persons connected with it;

(f) the names and addresses of the company's members, with details of their respective shareholdings;

(g) such other particulars (if any) as the nominee may in writing require to be furnished for the purposes of making his report to the court on the directors' proposal.

1.5(3)   [Relevant date] The statement of affairs shall be made up to a date not earlier than 2 weeks before the date of the notice to the nominee under Rule 1.4.

However, the nominee may allow an extension of that period to the nearest practicable date (not earlier than 2 months before the date of the notice under Rule 1.4); and if he does so, he shall give his reasons in his report to the court on the directors' proposal.

1.5(4)   [Verification of statement] The statement must be verified by a statement of truth made by at least one director.

(See General Note after r.1.6.) See I(A)R 2010 (SI 2010/686)—this tightens up timescales and deregulates matters concerned with statement of truth.

1.6   Additional disclosure for assistance of nominee

1.6(1)   [Nominee may request further information] If it appears to the nominee that he cannot properly prepare his report on the basis of information in the directors' proposal and statement of affairs, he may call on the directors to provide him with–

(a)   further and better particulars as to the circumstances in which, and the reasons why, the company is insolvent or (as the case may be) threatened with insolvency;

(b)   particulars of any previous proposals which have been made in respect of the company under Part I of the Act;

(c)   any further information with respect to the company's affairs which the nominee thinks necessary for the purposes of his report.

1.6(2)   [Information about directors etc.] The nominee may call on the directors to inform him, with respect to any person who is, or at any time in the 2 years preceding the notice under Rule 1.4 has been, a director or officer of the company, whether and in what circumstances (in those 2 years or previously) that person–

(a)   has been concerned in the affairs of any other company (whether or not incorporated in England and Wales) which has become insolvent, or

(b)   has himself been adjudged bankrupt or entered into an arrangement with his creditors.

1.6(3)   [Access to accounts and records] For the purpose of enabling the nominee to consider their proposal and prepare his report on it, the directors must give the nominee such access to the company's accounts and records as the nominee may require.

GENERAL NOTE TO RR.1.2–1.6

The proposal and the statement of affairs will be relied on both by the nominee in the preparation of his report to the court under IA 1986 s.2 and by the meetings of the company and its creditors which are summoned in due course if the proposal goes ahead. These rules seek to ensure that the decisions will be made on a basis of adequate evidence.

There is no prescribed form for the statement of affairs which is required in a voluntary arrangement, in contrast with the position in a liquidation: see rr.4.33, 4.34.

See I(A)R 2010 (SI 2010/686).

1.7   Nominee's report on the proposal

1.7(1)   [Accompanying documents] With his report to the court under section 2 the nominee shall deliver–

(a)   a copy of the directors' proposal (with amendments, if any, authorised under Rule 1.3(3)); and

(b)   a copy or summary of the company's statement of affairs.

1.7(2)   [Nominee's opinion re meetings] If the nominee makes known his opinion that the directors proposal has a reasonable prospect of being approved and implemented and that meetings of the company and its creditors should be summoned under section 3, his report shall have annexed to it his comments on the proposal.

If his opinion is otherwise, he shall give his reasons for that opinion.

1.7(3)   **[Endorsement of date of filing, and right to inspect]** The court shall cause the nominee's report to be endorsed with the date on which it is filed in court. Any director, member or creditor of the company is entitled, at all reasonable times on any business day, to inspect the file.

1.7(4)   **[Copy to company]** The nominee shall send a copy of his report, and of his comments (if any), to the company.

GENERAL NOTE

The court's role is purely an administrative one, unless a challenge is mounted under IA 1986 s.6. Note the amendment of para.(2) by the insertion of the words "that the directors' proposal has a reasonable prospect of being approved and implemented and" via the Insolvency (Amendment) (No.2) Rules 2002 (SI 2002/2712). This reflects the policy for promoting greater quality controls on CVAs as pursued by IA 2000.

1.8   Replacement of nominee

1.8(1)   **[Application by person other than nominee]** Where a person other than the nominee intends to apply to the court under section 2(4) for the nominee to be replaced, (except in any case where the nominee has died) he shall give to the nominee at least 5 business days' notice of his application.

1.8(2)   **[Application by nominee]** Where the nominee intends to apply to the court under section 2(4) of the Act to be replaced, he shall give at least 5 business days' notice of his application to the person intending to make the proposal.

1.8(3)   **[Statement of replacement nominee]** No appointment of a replacement nominee shall be made by the court unless there is filed in court a statement by the replacement nominee–

    (a)   indicating his consent to act, and

        [FORM 1.8]

    (b)   that he is qualified to act as an insolvency practitioner in relation to the company or is an authorised person in relation to the company.

GENERAL NOTE

The provision on replacing nominees was reconstituted in the above version by the Insolvency (Amendment) (No.2) Rules 2002 (SI 2002/2712) with effect from January 1, 2003. It recognises the fact that, in future, nominees may be authorised persons, such as "turnaround specialists", rather than restricted to insolvency practitioners. It also requires the suggested appointee to record his or her assent. See I(A)R 2010 (SI 2010/686), which replaces the seven-day time limit with five business days.

1.9   Summoning of meetings under s.3

1.9(1)   **[Date for meetings]** If in his report the nominee states that in his opinion meetings of the company and its creditors should be summoned to consider the directors' proposal, the date on which the meetings are to be held shall be not more than 28, days from that on which the nominee's report is filed in court under Rule 1.7.

1.9(2)   **[Notices of meetings]** Notices calling the meetings shall be sent by the nominee, at least 14 days before the day fixed for them to be held–

    (a)   in the case of the creditors' meeting, to all the creditors specified in the statement of affairs, and any other creditors of the company of whose address the nominee is otherwise aware; and

    (b)   in the case of the meeting of members of the company, to all persons who are, to the best of the nominee's belief, members of it.

1.9(3) **[Contents etc. of notice]** Each notice sent under this Rule shall specify the court to which the nominee's report under section 2 has been delivered and shall state the effect of Rule 1.19(2), (3) and (4) (requisite majorities (creditors)); and with each notice there shall be sent–

(a) a copy of the directors' proposal;

(b) a copy of the statement of affairs or, if the nominee thinks fit, a summary of it (the summary to include a list of creditors and the amount of their debts); and

(c) the nominee's comments on the proposal.

GENERAL NOTE

The Act is largely silent about the manner of summoning meetings, but it is here made plain that a fairly strict procedure must be followed. See in addition rr.1.13 et seq. See I(A)R 2010 (SI 2010/686).

CHAPTER 3

PROPOSAL BY ADMINISTRATOR OR LIQUIDATOR (HIMSELF THE NOMINEE)

1.10   Preparation of proposal

1.10(1)   [Matters to be specified in proposal] The responsible insolvency practitioner's proposal must specify all such matters as under Rule 1.3 (subject to paragraph (3) below) in Chapter 2 the directors of the company would be required to include in a proposal by them, with the addition, where the company is in administration or liquidation, of the nature and amount of its preferential creditors.

1.10(2)   [Notice to official receiver] Where the company is being wound up by the court, the insolvency practitioner shall give notice of the proposal to the official receiver.

1.10(3)   [Statement of administrator or liquidator in place of estimate] The administrator or liquidator shall include, in place of the estimate required by Rule 1.3(2)(ca), a statement which contains–

(a) to the best of the administrator or liquidator's knowledge and belief–

   (i) an estimate of the value of the prescribed part (whether or not he proposes to make an application to court under section 176A(5) or section 176A(3) applies), and

   (ii) an estimate of the value of the company's net property, and

(b) whether, and, if so, why, the administrator or liquidator proposes to make an application to court under section 176A(5).

1.10(4)   [Disclosure of information prejudicial] Nothing in this Rule is to be taken as requiring any such estimate to include any information, the disclosure of which could seriously prejudice the commercial interests of the company. If such information is excluded from the calculation the estimate shall be accompanied by a statement to that effect.

GENERAL NOTE

This was amended by Insolvency (Amendment) Rules 2003 (SI 2003/1730) to deal both with the advent of new style administration and the implications flowing from the introduction of the special reserve fund for unsecured creditors (see comments on IA 1986 s.176A). Paragraph (1) reworked by I(A)R 2010 (SI 2010/686).

1.11   Summoning of meetings under s.3

1.11(1)   [Venues and notice of meetings] The responsible insolvency practitioner shall fix a venue for the creditors' meeting and the company meeting, and give at least 14 days' notice of the meetings–

(a)   in the case of the creditors' meeting, to all the creditors specified in the company's statement of affairs, and to any other creditors of whose address the insolvency practitioner is otherwise aware; and

(b)   in the case of the company meeting, to all persons who are, to the best of his belief, members of the company.

1.11(2)   [Contents etc. of notice] Each notice sent out under this Rule shall state the effect of Rule 1.19 (1), (3) and (4) (requisite majorities (creditors)); and with it there shall be sent–

(a)   a copy of the responsible insolvency practitioner's proposal, and

(b)   a copy of the statement of affairs or, if he thinks fit, a summary of it (the summary to include a list of creditors and the amounts of their debts).

GENERAL NOTE TO RR.1.10, 1.11

Where the administrator or liquidator is himself to be the nominee, he may proceed directly to summon meetings in accordance with this chapter. On r.11.1(1)(a) see *Re T & N Ltd* [2006] EWHC 842 (Ch); [2006] B.P.I.R. 1268.
   See I(A)R 2010 (SI 2010/686).

CHAPTER 4

PROPOSAL BY ADMINISTRATOR OR LIQUIDATOR (ANOTHER INSOLVENCY PRACTITIONER THE NOMINEE)

1.12   Preparation of proposal and notice to nominee

1.12(1)   [Manner of giving notice etc.] The responsible insolvency practitioner shall give notice to the intended nominee, and prepare his proposal for a voluntary arrangement, in the same manner as is required of the directors, in the case of a proposal by them, under Chapter 2.

1.12(2)   [Application of r.1.2 and 1.4] Rule 1.2 applies to the responsible insolvency practitioner as it applies to the directors; and Rule 1.4 applies as regards the action to be taken by the nominee.

1.12(3)   [Content of proposal] The content of the proposal shall be as required by Rule 1.3 (and, where relevant, Rule 1.10), reading references to the directors as referring to the responsible insolvency practitioner.

1.12(4)   [Application of r.1.6] Rule 1.6 applies in respect of the information to be furnished to the nominee, reading references to the directors as referring to the responsible insolvency practitioner.

1.12(5)   [Copy statement of affairs] With the proposal the responsible insolvency practitioner shall provide a copy of the company's statement of affairs.

1.12(6)   [Copy proposal to official receiver] Where the company is being wound up by the court, the responsible insolvency practitioner shall send a copy of the proposal to the official receiver, accompanied by the name and address of the insolvency practitioner or authorised person who has agreed to act as nominee.

1.12(7)   [Application of rr.1.7–1.9] Rules 1.7 to 1.9 apply as regards a proposal under this Chapter as they apply to a proposal under Chapter 2.

GENERAL NOTE

Where the administrator or liquidator does not propose himself as nominee, the procedure is very similar to that for a directors' proposal.

CHAPTER 5

PROCEEDINGS ON A PROPOSAL MADE BY THE DIRECTORS, OR BY THE ADMINISTRATOR, OR BY THE LIQUIDATOR

Section A: Meetings of company's creditors and members

1.13   Summoning of meetings

1.13(1)   [Nominee to regard convenience of creditors for venue] Subject as follows, in fixing the venue for the creditors' meeting and the company meeting, the nominee must have regard primarily to the convenience of the creditors.

1.13(2)   [Time of meetings] Meetings shall in each case be summoned for commencement between 10.00 and 16.00 hours on a business day.

1.13(3)   [Creditors' meeting in advance of company meeting] The meetings may be held on the same day or on different days. If held on the same day, the meetings shall be held in the same place, but in either case the creditors' meeting shall be fixed for a time in advance of the company meeting.

1.13(4)   [Maximum five business days between meetings] Where the meetings are not held on the same day, they shall be held within 5 business days of each other.

1.13(5)   [Forms of proxy with notice] With every notice summoning either meeting there shall be sent out forms of proxy.

GENERAL NOTE

Paragraph (3) was replaced and para.(4) added by the Insolvency (Amendment) (No.2) Rules 2002 (SI 2002/2712). These changes reflect a need for greater clarity with regard to meetings' procedures and, while introducing some flexibility (subject to a maximum hiatus of five business days between meetings), also recognise the fact that there is no point of having a meeting of members if the creditors have voted down the proposal.

This rule was then further amended in the form of a complete reconstitution by Insolvency (Amendment) Rules 2003 (SI 2003/1730).

See I(A)R 2010 (SI 2010/686) which substitutes five business days for seven days in para.(4).

1.14   The chairman at meetings

1.14(1)   [Nominee must be chairman] Subject as follows, at both the creditors' meeting and the company meeting, and at any combined meeting, the nominee must be chairman.

1.14(2)   [Other nominated chairman] If for any reason he is unable to attend, he may nominate another person to act as chairman in his place; but a person so nominated must be–

    (a)   a person qualified to act as an insolvency practitioner in relation to the company;

    (b)   an authorised person in relation to the company; or

    (c)   an employee of the nominee or his firm who is experienced in insolvency matters.

GENERAL NOTE

A number of amendments were made by Insolvency (Amendment) (No.2) Rules 2002 (SI 2002/2712) with effect from January 1, 2003 to allow greater flexibility as to who should chair the meeting of creditors. See I(A)R 2010 (SI 2010/686).

1.15   The chairman as proxy-holder

1.15   The chairman shall not by virtue of any proxy held by him vote to increase or reduce the amount of the remuneration or expenses of the nominee or the supervisor of the proposed arrangement, unless the proxy specifically directs him to vote in that way.

(See General Note after r.1.21.)

1.16   Attendance by company officers

1.16(1)   [Notice to directors and officers] At least 14 days' notice to attend the meetings shall be given by the nominee–

(a)   to all directors of the company, and

(b)   to any persons in whose case the nominee thinks that their presence is required as being officers of the company, or as having been directors or officers of it at any time in the 2 years immediately preceding the date of the notice.

1.16(2)   [Exclusion of director etc.] The chairman may, if he thinks fit, exclude any present or former director or officer from attendance at a meeting, either completely or for any part of it; and this applies whether or not a notice under this Rule has been sent to the person excluded.

(See General Note after r.1.21.) See I(A)R 2010 (SI 2010/686).

Section B: Voting rights and majorities

1.17   Entitlement to vote (creditors)

1.17(1)   [Entitlement to vote] Subject as follows, every creditor who has notice of the creditors' meeting is entitled to vote at the meeting or any adjournment of it.

1.17(2)   [Calculation of votes] Votes are calculated according to the amount of the creditor's debt as at the date of the meeting or, where the company is being wound up or is in administration, the date of its going into liquidation or (as the case may be) when the company entered administration.

1.17(3)   [Limitation on voting] A creditor may vote in respect of a debt for an unliquidated amount or any debt whose value is not ascertained and for the purposes of voting (but not otherwise) his debt shall be valued at £1 unless the chairman agrees to put a higher value on it.

1.17A   Procedure for admission of creditors' claims for voting purposes

1.17A(1)   [Procedure at creditors' meeting] Subject as follows, at any creditors' meeting the chairman shall ascertain the entitlement of persons wishing to vote and shall admit or reject their claims accordingly.

1.17A(2)   [Chairman's discretion] The chairman may admit or reject a claim in whole or in part.

1.17A(3)   [Appeal from chairman's decision] The chairman's decision on any matter under this Rule or under paragraph (3) of Rule 1.17 is subject to appeal to the court by any creditor or member of the company.

1.17A(4)   [Voting subject to objection] If the chairman is in doubt whether a claim should be admitted or rejected, he shall mark it as objected to and allow votes to be cast in respect of it, subject to such votes being subsequently declared invalid if the objection to the claim is sustained.

1.17A(5)   [Where chairman's decision reversed etc.] If on an appeal the chairman's decision is reversed or varied, or votes are declared invalid, the court may order another meeting to be summoned, or make such order as it thinks just.

  The court's power to make an order under this paragraph is exercisable only if it considers that the circumstances giving rise to the appeal give rise to unfair prejudice or material irregularity.

1.17A(6)   [Time for appeal] An application to the court by way of appeal against the chairman's decision shall not be made after the end of the period of 28 days beginning with the first day on which the report required by section 4(6) has been made to the court.

1.17A(7)   [Costs of appeal] The chairman is not personally liable for any costs incurred by any person in respect of an appeal under this Rule.

Rule 1.17 was replaced by Insolvency (Amendment) (No.2) Rules 2002 (SI 2002/2712) with effect from January 1, 2003. Note the use of the £1 nominal value presumption for unliquidated/unascertained debts—this reflects practice used by insolvency practitioners. In *Re Newlands (Seaford) Educational Trust* [2007] B.C.C. 195 Sir Andrew Morritt C upheld the valuation adopted by the chairman under IR r.1.17(3).

Note the change in terminology with regard to administration introduced by Insolvency (Amendment) Rules 2003 (SI 2003/1730).

R.1.17A

This new addition was made by Insolvency (Amendment) (No.2) Rules 2002 (SI 2002/2712) with effect from January 1, 2003. In effect it contains a number of amended provisions which were formerly contained in the original and cumbersome r.1.17. A challenge under IR r.1.17A(3) failed before Sir Andrew Morritt C. in *Re Newlands (Seaford) Educational Trust* [2007] B.C.C. 195.

1.18 Voting rights (members)

1.18(1) **[Voting rights in accordance with articles]** Subject as follows, members of the company at their meeting vote according to the rights attaching to their shares respectively in accordance with the articles.

1.18(2) [Omitted.]

1.18(3) **[Interpretation]** References in this Rule to a person's shares include any other interest which he may have as a member of the company.

(See General Note after r.1.21.) Rule 1.18(2) was omitted by Insolvency (Amendment) (No.2) Rules 2002 (SI 2002/2712).

1.19 Requisite majorities (creditors)

1.19(1) **[Resolution by majority in value]** Subject to paragraph (2), at the creditors' meeting, a resolution is passed when a majority (in value) of those present and voting in person or by proxy have voted in favour of it.

1.19(2) **[Resolution to approve/modify proposal by three-quarters majority]** A resolution to approve the proposal or a modification is passed when a majority of three quarters or more (in value) of those present and voting in person or by proxy have voted in favour of it.

1.19(3) **[Votes to be left out of account]** In the following cases there is to be left out of account a creditor's vote in respect of any claim or part of a claim–

    (a)   where written notice of the claim was not given, either at the meeting or before it, to the chairman or nominee;

    (b)   where the claim or part is secured;

    (c)   where the claim is in respect of a debt wholly or partly on, or secured by, a current bill of exchange or promissory note, unless the creditor is willing–

        (i)   to treat the liability to him on the bill or note of every person who is liable on it antecedently to the company, and against whom a bankruptcy order has not been made (or in the case of a company, which has not gone into liquidation), as a security in his hands, and

        (ii)   to estimate the value of the security and (for the purpose of entitlement to vote, but not of any distribution under the arrangement) to deduct it from his claim.

1.19(4) **[Voting rendering resolution invalid]** Any resolution is invalid if those voting against it include more than half in value of the creditors, counting in these latter only those–

    (a)   to whom notice of the meeting was sent;

(b)   whose votes are not to be left out of account under paragraph (3); and

(c)   who are not, to the best of the chairman's belief, persons connected with the company.

1.19(5)   [Chairman's powers] It is for the chairman of the meeting to decide whether under this Rule–

(a)   a vote is to be left out of account in accordance with paragraph (3), or

(b)   a person is a connected person for the purposes of paragraph (4)(c);

and in relation to the second of these two cases the chairman is entitled to rely on the information provided by the company's statement of affairs or otherwise in accordance with this Part of the Rules.

1.19(6)   [Use of proxy contrary to r.1.15] If the chairman uses a proxy contrary to Rule 1.15, his vote with that proxy does not count towards any majority under this Rule.

1.19(7)   [Appeal from chairman's decision] The chairman's decision on any matter under this Rule is subject to appeal to the court by any creditor or member and paragraphs (5) to (7) of Rule 1.17A apply as regards such an appeal.

GENERAL NOTE

A replacement for para.(7) was made by the Insolvency (Amendment) (No.2) Rules 2002 (SI 2002/2712)—this was necessitated by the insertion of r.1.17A. See I(A)R 2010 (SI 2010/686) which reformulates the statement of required majority in paras (1) and (2).

1.20   Requisite majorities (members)

1.20(1)   [One-half majority] Subject as follows, and to any express provision made in the articles, at a company meeting any resolution is to be regarded as passed if voted for by more than one-half in value of the members present in person or by proxy and voting on the resolution.

The value of members is determined by reference to the number of votes conferred on each member by the company's articles.

1.20(2)   [Omitted.]

1.20(3)   [Use of proxy contrary to r.1.15] If the chairman uses a proxy contrary to Rule 1.15, his vote with that proxy does not count towards any majority under this Rule.

(See General Note after r.1.21.)

1.21   Proceedings to obtain agreement on the proposal

1.21(1)   [Meetings may be held together] If the chairman thinks fit, the creditors' meeting and the company meeting may be held together.

1.21(2)   [Chairman may adjourn meeting] The chairman may, and shall if it is so resolved at the meeting in question, adjourn that meeting for not more than 14 days.

1.21(3)   [Final adjournment] If there are subsequently further adjournments, the final adjournment shall not be to a day later than 14 days after the date on which the meeting in question was originally held.

1.21(4)   [Notice of adjournment] In the case of a proposal by the directors, if the meetings are adjourned under paragraph (2), notice of the fact shall be given by the nominee as soon as reasonably practicable to the court.

1.21(4A)   [Single suspension without adjournment] Once only in the course of a meeting the chairman may, without an adjournment, declare it suspended for any period up to 1 hour.

1.21(5)   [Deemed rejection of proposal] If following the final adjournment of the creditors' meeting the proposal (with or without modifications) has not been approved by the creditors, it is deemed rejected.

GENERAL NOTE

A new version of r.1.21 was substituted by Insolvency (Amendment) (No.2) Rules 2002 (SI 2002/2712) with effect from January 1, 2003 to reflect the increased flexibility introduced by permitting meetings of creditors and members to be held on different days. See I(A)R 2010 (SI 2010/686)—new para.(4A) inserted.

GENERAL NOTE TO RR.1.13–1.21

The detailed procedure for the summoning and conduct of meetings is here set out, and a number of points which the Insolvency Act appears to leave in doubt are settled.

Although the creditors' meeting must be *fixed* for a time in advance of the company meeting (r.1.13(3)), it need not conclude its business before the company meeting begins (r.1.22(2)); and the meetings may be held together (r.1.21 (1)).

Rules 1.16(1)(b) and 1.16(2) allow the chairman a wide discretion, on the one hand to insist on the attendance of a director whose presence he may consider helpful and, on the other, to exclude any director who may be thought to hinder the proceedings.

Although a contingent or prospective creditor, or a person who has a claim for an unliquidated amount is not, on a strict view, a "creditor", the cases now make it reasonably clear that they should be treated as creditors for the purposes of Pt I of the Act and the Rules (see the note to s.1(1) and the cases there cited). Any such person is therefore entitled to receive notice of the creditors' meeting under r.1.9(2) and (subject to r.1.17(3)) to attend and vote at it. If he has had notice of the meeting and was entitled to vote at it, he is bound by the voluntary arrangement which was approved at the meetings, whether or not he attended the creditors' meeting or voted at it.

In *Beverley Group plc v McClue* [1995] B.C.C. 751 a person who had a claim for an unliquidated amount (and was accordingly held to have been entitled to vote) had been sent formal notice of the meeting by post but this had never reached him. He had, however, learned of the meeting from another source but chose not to attend it. The court ruled that he had had notice of the meeting and was bound by the arrangement.

Rule 1.17(3) allows a creditor whose debt is for an unliquidated amount or whose value is not ascertained to vote at the meeting only if the chairman agrees to put upon the debt an estimated minimum value for the purpose of entitlement to vote. It is now settled that "agrees" does not mean "agrees with the creditor" in the sense that there must be a bilateral consent to the estimated value, but rather "expresses a willingness" to put a value: *Re Cancol Ltd* [1995] B.C.C. 1,133; *Doorbar v Alltime Securities Ltd* [1995] B.C.C. 1,149. The earlier case of *Re Cranley Mansions Ltd* [1994] B.C.C. 576, in which the applicant had refused to accept the chairman's estimate of £1 on a claim for £900,000, would not now be followed on this point (note the use of the £1 valuation prescription). If a person declines to attend the creditors' meeting it is not open to him to object that the chairman has not put an estimated valuation on his debt: see *Beverley Group plc v McClue* (above). On voting entitlement see also *Lombard North Central plc v Brook* [1999] B.P.I.R. 701.

Rule 1.17(A(6)) states categorically that there is a 28-day time-limit for appeals against the chairman's decision, and this limitation was emphasised in *Re Bournemouth & Boscombe AFC Co Ltd* [1998] B.P.I.R. 183 (a case decided under s.6).

The majority required by r.1.19 is reformulated by I(A)R 2010 (SI 2010/686). Note in addition, however, that both this majority and the ordinary majority required by r.1.19(1) are qualified by r.1.19(4), which in effect nullifies the votes of any creditors "connected with" the company (and certain others) who support the proposal. (For the meaning of a "connected" person, see IA 1986 s.249).

The rules assume that the same person will be chairman of both meetings: see r.1.24(1).

Section C: Implementation of the arrangement

1.22   Resolutions to follow approval

1.22(1)   **[Resolution re supervisory acts]** If the voluntary arrangement is approved (with or without modifications) by the creditors' meeting, a resolution must be taken by the creditors, where two or more supervisors are appointed, on the question whether acts to be done in connection with the arrangement may be done by any one or more of them, or must be done by all of them.

1.22(2)   [Deleted.]

1.22(3)   **[Other than nominee to be supervisor]** If at either meeting a resolution is moved for the appointment of some person other than the nominee to be supervisor of the arrangement, there must be produced to the chairman, at or before the meeting–

(a) that person's written consent to act (unless he is present and then and there signifies his consent), and

(b) his written confirmation that he is qualified to act as an insolvency practitioner in relation to the company or is an authorised person in relation to the company.

R.1.22
A significant amendment was made by Insolvency (Amendment) (No.2) Rules 2002 (SI 2002/2712) with effect from January 1, 2003 to address specifically operational issues which may arise where joint supervisors are appointed. See I(A)R 2010 (SI 2010/686).

1.22A　Notice of order made under section 4A(6)

1.22A(1)　[Application] This Rule applies where the court makes an order under section 4A(6).

1.22A(2)　[Service of order] The member of the company who applied for the order shall serve sealed copies of it on–

(a) the supervisor of the voluntary arrangement; and

(b) the directors of the company.

1.22A(3)　[Service on directors] Service on the directors may be effected by service of a single copy on the company at its registered office.

1.22A(4)　[Notice of order] The directors or (as the case may be) the supervisor shall as soon as reasonably practicable after receiving a copy of the court's order, give notice of it to all persons who were sent notice of the creditors' or company meetings or who, not having been sent such notice, are affected by the order.

1.22A(5)　[Office copy to registrar of companies] The person on whose application the order of the court was made shall, within 5 business days of the order, deliver a copy to the registrar of companies.

R.1.22A
This was added by Insolvency (Amendment) (No.2) Rules 2002 (SI 2002/2712) with effect from January 1, 2003. It deals with orders made under s.4A(6)—i.e. orders made by the court directing that the views of members shall prevail over creditors. These are expected to be rare birds. See I(A)R 2010 (SI 2010/686) which substitutes five business days for seven days in para.(5).

1.23　Hand-over of property etc. to supervisor

1.23(1)　[Putting supervisor into possession of assets] Where the decision approving the voluntary arrangement has effect under section 4A–

(a) the directors, or

(b) where the company is in liquidation or is in administration, and a person other than the responsible insolvency practitioner is appointed as supervisor of the voluntary arrangement, the insolvency practitioner,

shall as soon as reasonably practicable do all that is required for putting the supervisor into possession of the assets included in the arrangement.

1.23(2)　[Discharge of insolvency practitioner's remuneration etc.] Where the company is in liquidation or is in administration, the supervisor shall on taking possession of the assets discharge any balance due to the insolvency practitioner by way of remuneration or on account of–

(a) fees, costs, charges and expenses properly incurred and payable under the Act or the Rules, and

(b) any advances made in respect of the company, together with interest on such advances at the rate specified in section 17 of the Judgments Act 1838 at the date on which the company went into liquidation or (as the case may be) entered administration.

1.23(3) **[Undertaking to discharge]** Alternatively, the supervisor must, before taking possession, give the responsible insolvency practitioner a written undertaking to discharge any such balance out of the first realisation of assets.

1.23(4) **[Charge on assets]** The insolvency practitioner has a charge on the assets included in the voluntary arrangement in respect of any sums due as above until they have been discharged, subject only to the deduction from realisations by the supervisor of the proper costs and expenses of such realisations.

1.23(5) **[Discharge of guarantees etc.]** The supervisor shall from time to time out of the realisation of assets discharge all guarantees properly given by the responsible insolvency practitioner for the benefit of the company, and shall pay all the insolvency practitioner's expenses.

1.23(6) **[Interpretation]** References in this Rule to the responsible insolvency practitioner include, where a company is being wound up by the court, the official receiver, whether or not in his capacity as liquidator; and any sums due to the official receiver take priority over those due to a liquidator.

GENERAL NOTE

A minor amendment occurred via Insolvency (Amendment) (No.2) Rules 2002 (SI 2002/2712) to cater for the coming into effect of the Insolvency Act 2000. A further linguistic change was necessitated by the introduction of new style administration—see Insolvency (Amendment) Rules 2003 (SI 2003/1730).

1.24   Report of meetings

1.24(1) **[Chairman to prepare report]** A report of the meetings shall be prepared by the person who was chairman of them.

1.24(2) **[Contents of report]** The report shall–

(a)   state whether the proposal for a voluntary arrangement was approved by the creditors of the company alone or by both the creditors and members of the company and in either case whether such approval was with any modifications;

(b)   set out the resolutions which were taken at each meeting, and the decision on each one;

(c)   list the creditors and members of the company (with their respective values) who were present or represented at the meetings, and how they voted on each resolution;

(ca) state whether, in the opinion of the supervisor, (i) the EC Regulation applies to the voluntary arrangement and (ii) if so, whether the proceedings are main proceedings, secondary proceedings or territorial proceedings; and

(d)   include such further information (if any) as the chairman thinks it appropriate to make known to the court.

1.24(3) **[Copy report to be filed in court]** A copy of the chairman's report shall, within 4 business days of the meetings being held, be filed in court; and the court shall cause that copy to be endorsed with the date of filing.

1.24(4) **[Notice of result]** In respect of each of the meetings, the persons to whom notice of its result is to be sent by the chairman under section 4(6) are all those who were sent notice of the meeting under this Part of the Rules.

The notice shall be sent as soon as reasonably practicable after a copy of the chairman's report is filed in court under paragraph (3).

1.24(5) **[Copy report to registrar of companies]** If the decision approving the voluntary arrangement has effect under section 4A (whether or not in the form proposed), the supervisor shall as soon as reasonably practicable send a copy of the chairman's report to the registrar of companies.

Note the amendments to paras (2) and (5) by Insolvency (Amendment) (No.2) Rules 2002 (SI 2002/2712) with effect from January 1, 2003. These relate to the report to be submitted by the chair to the court and reflect the fact that there is now greater information that has to be reported. *(See General Note after r.1.29.)* Paragraph (ca) was inserted by the Insolvency (Amendment) Rules 2002 (SI 2002/1307) para.4(3)(b). See I(A)R 2010 (SI 2010/686) which amends para.(3) to specify four business days. Note also the reference to "immediately" in para.(4) is watered down to "as soon as reasonably practicable".

1.25 Revocation or suspension of the arrangement

1.25(1) [Application of Rule] This Rule applies where the court makes an order of revocation or suspension under section 6.

1.25(2) [Service of copy orders] The person who applied for the order shall serve sealed copies of it–

(a) on the supervisor of the voluntary arrangement, and

(b) on the directors of the company or the administrator or liquidator (according to who made the proposal for the arrangement).

Service on the directors may be effected by service of a single copy of the order on the company at its registered office.

1.25(3) [Notice re further meetings] If the order includes a direction by the court under section 6(4)(b) for any further meetings to be summoned, notice shall also be given (by the person who applied for the order) to whoever is, in accordance with the direction, required to summon the meetings.

1.25(4) [Notice of order, and of intention re proposal] The directors or (as the case may be) the administrator or liquidator shall–

(a) as soon as reasonably practicable after receiving a copy of the court's order, give notice of it to all persons who were sent notice of the creditors' and company meetings or who, not having been sent that notice, appear to be affected by the order;

(b) within 5 business days of their receiving a copy of the order (or within such longer period as the court may allow), give notice to the court whether it is intended to make a revised proposal to the company and its creditors, or to invite re-consideration of the original proposal.

1.25(5) [Copy order to registrar of companies] The person on whose application the order of revocation or suspension was made shall, within 5 business days after the making of the order, deliver a copy of the order to the registrar of companies.

See I(A)R 2010 (SI 2010/686) which converts the seven-day period specified in paras (4) and (5) to five business days.

1.26 Supervisor's accounts and reports [Deleted by I(A)R 2010 (SI 2010/686) and replaced by IR r.1.26A.]

1.26A Supervisor's accounts and reports

1.26A(1) [Application of r.1.26A(2)] Paragraph (2) applies where the voluntary arrangement authorises or requires the supervisor–

(a) to carry on the business of the company or trade on its behalf or in its name; or

(b) to realise assets of the company; or

(c) otherwise to administer or dispose of any of its funds.

1.26A(2)   **[Obligation to keep accounts etc. including receipts and payments]** The supervisor must keep accounts and records of the supervisor's acts and dealings in, and in connection with, the arrangement, including in particular records of all receipts and payments of money.

1.26A(3)   **[Preservation of other supervisor's accounts etc.]** The supervisor must preserve any accounts and records in paragraph (2) which–

    (a)   were kept by any other person who has acted as supervisor of the arrangement; and

    (b)   are in the supervisor's possession.

1.26A(4)   **[Annual progress report of CVA]** Subject to paragraph (5), the supervisor must in respect of each period of 12 months ending with the anniversary of the commencement of the arrangement send within 2 months of the end of that period a report on the progress and prospects for the full implementation of the voluntary arrangement to–

    (a)   the registrar of companies;

    (b)   the company;

    (c)   all those of the company's creditors who are bound by the voluntary arrangement of whose address the supervisor is aware;

    (d)   subject to paragraph (7) below, the members of the company; and

    (e)   if the company is not in liquidation, the company's auditors (if any) for the time being.

1.26A(5)   **[Release from annual report obligation]** The supervisor is released from an obligation to send a report under paragraph (4), if an obligation to send a final report under Rule 1.29 arises in the period of 2 months mentioned in paragraph (4).

1.26A(6)   **[Report to include abstract of receipts and payments]** Where the supervisor is authorised or required to do any of the things mentioned in paragraph (1)(a) to (c), the report required to be sent pursuant to paragraph (4) must include or be accompanied by–

    (a)   an abstract of receipts and payments required to be recorded by virtue of paragraph (2); or

    (b)   where there have been no such receipts and payments, a statement to that effect.

1.26A(7)   **[Dispensing power of court]** The court may, on application by the supervisor dispense with the sending under this Rule of abstracts or reports to members of the company, either altogether or on the basis that the availability of the abstract or report to members is to be advertised by the supervisor in a specified manner.

GENERAL NOTE

Substituted by I(A)R 2010 (SI 2010/686) for IR r.1.26.

1.27   Production of accounts and records to Secretary of State

1.27(1)   **[Powers of Secretary of State]** The Secretary of State may at any time during the course of the voluntary arrangement or after its completion or termination require the supervisor to produce for inspection–

    (a)   his records and accounts in respect of the arrangement, and

    (b)   copies of abstracts and reports prepared in compliance with Rule 1.26A.

1.27(2)   **[Production and duty to comply]** The Secretary of State may require production either at the premises of the supervisor or elsewhere; and it is the duty of the supervisor to comply with any requirement imposed on him under this Rule.

1.27(3)   [Audit of accounts and records] The Secretary of State may cause any accounts and records produced to him under this Rule to be audited; and the supervisor shall give to the Secretary of State such further information and assistance as he needs for the purposes of his audit.

(See General Note after r.1.29.)

GENERAL NOTE

Note the addition of the words "or termination" in para.(1) by Insolvency (Amendment) (No.2) Rules 2002 (SI 2002/2712) with effect from January 1, 2003. This reflects the fact that CVAs may be brought to an end in a variety of ways post-IA 2000. See I(A)R 2010 (SI 2010/686).

1.28   Fees, costs, charges and expenses

1.28   The fees, costs, charges and expenses that may be incurred for any of the purposes of the voluntary arrangement are–

   (a)   any disbursements made by the nominee prior to the decision approving the arrangement taking effect under section 4A and any remuneration for his services as such agreed between himself and the company (or, as the case may be, the administrator or liquidator);

   (b)   any fees, costs, charges or expenses which–

      (i)   are sanctioned by the terms of the arrangement, or

      (ii)   would be payable, or correspond to those which would be payable, in an administration or winding up.

(See General Note after r.1.29.)

GENERAL NOTE

An amendment to para.(1a) was made by Insolvency (Amendment) (No.2) Rules 2002 (SI 2002/2712) with effect from January 1, 2003 to reflect the consequences of s.4A (which had been introduced by IA 2000) coming into effect.

1.29   Completion or termination of the arrangement

1.29(1)   [Supervisor to send notice] Not more than 28 days after the final completion or termination of the voluntary arrangement, the supervisor shall send to creditors and members of the company who are bound by it a notice that the voluntary arrangement has been fully implemented or (as the case may be) has terminated.

1.29(2)   [Supervisor's report] With the notice there shall be sent to each creditor and member a copy of a report by the supervisor summarising all receipts and payments made by him in pursuance of the arrangement, and explaining in relation to implementation of the arrangement any departure from the proposals as they originally took effect, or (in the case of termination of the arrangement) explaining the reasons why the arrangement has terminated.

1.29(3)   [Copy notice and report to registrar and court] The supervisor shall, within the 28 days mentioned above, send to the registrar of companies and to the court a copy of the notice to creditors and members under paragraph (1), together with a copy of the report under paragraph (2), and the supervisor shall not vacate office until after such copies have been sent.

1.29(4)   [Report to include statement as to prescribed part] In the report under paragraph (2), the supervisor shall include a statement as to the amount paid, if any, to unsecured creditors by virtue of the application of section 176A (prescribed part).

GENERAL NOTE TO RR.1.22–129

The detailed procedure for the implementation of the proposals, if approved, is set out here. The scheme takes effect without further formality from the time of the creditors' meeting, even though under the rules the members' meeting must be fixed for a later time on the same day: see IA 1986 s.5(2)(a).

A new r.1.29 was inserted by Insolvency (Amendment) (No.2) Rules 2002 (SI 2002/2712) with effect from January 1, 2003 to cater for the coming into force of the Insolvency Act 2000 with particular reference to the possibility of termination. This newly substituted rule was then further amended by Insolvency (Amendment) Rules 2003 (SI 2003/1730) to provide information on any distributions made in connection with the s.176A reserve fund.

CHAPTER 6

GENERAL

1.30 False representations, etc. [Repealed.]

GENERAL NOTE

This r.1.30 was repealed by Insolvency (Amendment) (No.2) Rules 2002 (SI 2002/2712). These offences are now more properly dealt with by the primary legislation (i.e. s.6A).

CHAPTER 7

EC REGULATION—CONVERSION OF VOLUNTARY ARRANGEMENT INTO WINDING UP

1.31 Application for conversion into winding up

1.31(1) [Witness statement in support] Where a member State liquidator proposes to apply to the court for conversion of a voluntary arrangement into winding-up proceedings, a witness statement complying with Rule 1.32 must be prepared and filed in court in support of the application.

1.31(1A) ["Conversion into winding-up proceedings" in rr.1.31–1.33] In this Rule, and in Rules 1.32 and 1.33, **"conversion into winding-up proceedings"** means an order under Article 37 of the EC Regulation (conversion of earlier proceedings) that the voluntary arrangement is converted into–

(a) administration proceedings whose purposes are limited to the winding up of the company through administration and are to exclude the purpose contained in paragraph 3(1)(a) of Schedule B1 to the Act;

(b) a creditors' voluntary winding up; or

(c) a winding up by the court.

1.31(2) [Originating application] An application under this Rule shall be by originating application.

1.31(3) [Service of application and witness statement] The application and the witness statement required under this Rule shall be served upon–

(a) the company; and

(b) the supervisor.

GENERAL NOTE

See I(A)R 2010 (SI 2010/686) which substitutes witness statements for affidavits. Note also new para.(1A) inserted.

1.32 Contents of witness statement

1.32(1) [Contents] The witness statement shall state–

(a) that main proceedings have been opened in relation to the company in a member State other than the United Kingdom;

(b) the belief of the person making the statement that the conversion of the voluntary arrangement into winding-up proceedings would prove to be in the interests of the creditors in the main proceedings;

(c)   the opinion of the person making the statement as to whether the company ought to go into voluntary liquidation or be wound up by the court; and

(d)   all other matters that, in the opinion of the member State liquidator, would assist the court–

   (i)   in deciding whether to make such an order, and

   (ii)   if the court were to do so, in considering the need for any consequential provision that would be necessary or desirable.

1.32(2)   [Procedure] A witness statement under this Rule shall be made by, or on behalf of, the member State liquidator.

1.33   Power of court

1.33(1)   [Powers of court] On hearing the application for conversion into winding-up proceedings the court may make such order as it thinks fit.

1.33(2)   [Consequential provisions] If the court makes an order for conversion into winding-up proceedings the order may contain all such consequential provisions as the court deems necessary or desirable.

1.33(3)   [Effect of order made under r.1.33(1)] Without prejudice to the generality of paragraph (1), an order under that paragraph may provide that the company be wound up as if a resolution for voluntary winding up under section 84 were passed on the day on which the order is made.

1.33(4)   [Expenses incurred] Where the court makes an order for conversion into winding-up proceedings under paragraph (1), any expenses properly incurred as expenses of the administration of the voluntary arrangement in question shall be a first charge on the company's assets.

GENERAL NOTE

Chapter 7 (comprising new rr.1.31–1.33) was introduced by the Insolvency (Amendment) Rules 2002 (SI 2002/1307) para.4(4) to cater for the advent of EC Council Regulation on Insolvency Proceedings (1346/2000) with effect from May 31, 2002. See I(A)R 2010 (SI 2010/686) which substitutes witness statements for affidavits and generally tidies up IR rr.1.32 and 1.33.

CHAPTER 8

EC REGULATION—MEMBER STATE LIQUIDATOR

1.34   Interpretation of creditor and notice to member State liquidator

1.34(1)   [Application] This Rule applies where a member State liquidator has been appointed in relation to the company.

1.34(2)   [Notice, copies] Where the supervisor is obliged to give notice to, or provide a copy of a document (including an order of court) to, the court, the registrar of companies or the official receiver, the supervisor shall give notice or provide copies, as appropriate, to the member State liquidator.

1.34(3)   [Duty to cooperate and communicate information] Paragraph (2) is without prejudice to the generality of the obligations imposed by Article 31 of the EC Regulation (duty to cooperate and communicate information).

GENERAL NOTE

Chapter 8 (consisting of r.1.34) was introduced in similar circumstances to Chapter 7.

CHAPTER 9

OBTAINING A MORATORIUM

PROCEEDINGS DURING A MORATORIUM

NOMINEES

CONSIDERATION OF PROPOSALS WHERE MORATORIUM OBTAINED

Section A: Obtaining a moratorium

1.35   Preparation of proposal by directors and submission to nominee

1.35(1)   [Requirements for proposal document] The document containing the proposal referred to in paragraph 6(1)(a) of Schedule A1 to the Act shall–

(a)   be prepared by the directors;

(b)   comply with the requirements of paragraphs (1) and (2) of Rule 1.3 (save that the reference to preferential creditors shall be to preferential creditors within the meaning of paragraph 31(8) of Schedule A1 to the Act); and

(c)   state the address to which notice of the consent of the nominee to act and the documents referred to in Rule 1.38 shall be sent.

1.35(2)   [Amendment of proposal] With the agreement in writing of the nominee, the directors may amend the proposal at any time before submission to them by the nominee of the statement required by paragraph 6(2) of Schedule A1 to the Act.

R.1.35
This explains how directors are to submit their draft proposals to the nominee by itemising the contents of the documentation.

1.36   Delivery of documents to the intended nominee etc.

1.36(1)   [Delivery to nominee or authorised person] The documents required to be delivered to the nominee pursuant to paragraph 6(1) of Schedule A1 to the Act shall be delivered to the nominee himself or to a person authorised to take delivery of documents on his behalf.

1.36(2)   [Acknowledgement of receipt] On receipt of the documents, the nominee shall as soon as reasonably practicable issue an acknowledgement of receipt of the documents to the directors which shall indicate the date on which the documents were received.

R.1.36
This proceeds to describe how the proposed documents are to be delivered.

1.37   Statement of affairs

1.37(1)   [Time for delivery] The statement of the company's affairs required to be delivered to the nominee pursuant to paragraph 6(1)(b) of Schedule A1 to the Act shall be delivered to the nominee at the same time as the delivery to him of the document setting out the terms of the proposed voluntary arrangement.

[FORM 1.6]

1.37(2)   [Particulars in statement] The statement of affairs shall comprise the same particulars as required by Rule 1.5(2) (supplementing or amplifying, so far as is necessary for clarifying the state of the company's affairs, those already given in the directors' proposal).

1.37(3)   [Relevant date] The statement of affairs shall be made up to a date not earlier than 2 weeks before the date of the delivery of the document containing the proposal for the voluntary arrangement to the nominee under Rule 1.36(1).

However, the nominee may allow an extension of that period to the nearest practicable date (not earlier than 2 months before the date of delivery of the documents referred to in Rule 1.36(1)) and if he does so, he shall give a statement of his reasons in writing to the directors.

1.37(4)   [Verification of statement of affairs] The statement of affairs must be verified by a statement of truth made by at least one director.

R.1.37
The directors must, within seven days of delivering the proposals, produce a formal statement of affairs for the nominee. See I(A)R 2010 (SI 2010/686) which tightens up timescales in para.(1) and reformulates the statement of affairs in para.(4).

1.38   The nominee's statement

1.38(1)   [Time for submission of statement] The nominee shall submit to the directors the statement required by paragraph 6(2) of Schedule A1 to the Act within 28 days of the submission to him of the document setting out the terms of the proposed voluntary arrangement.

[FORM 1.5]

1.38(2)   [Nominee's comments, statement of consent] The statement shall have annexed to it–

[FORM 1.8]

(a)   the nominee's comments on the proposal, unless the statement contains an opinion in the negative on any of the matters referred to in paragraph 6(2)(a) and (b) of Schedule A1 to the Act, in which case he shall instead give his reasons for that opinion, and

(b)   where he is willing to act in relation to the proposed arrangement, a statement of his consent to act.

R.1.38
This deals with the nominee's response to the directors.

1.39   Documents submitted to the court to obtain moratorium

1.39(1)   [Required documents, time for delivery] Where pursuant to paragraph 7 of Schedule A1 to the Act the directors file the document and statements referred to in that paragraph in court, those documents shall be delivered together with 4 copies of a schedule listing them within 3 business days of the date of the submission to them of the nominee's statement under paragraph 6(2) of Schedule A1 to the Act.

[FORMS 1.5, 1.7, 1.8 AND 1.9]

1.39(2)   [Additional documents to file] When the directors file the document and statements referred to in paragraph (1), they shall also file–

(a)   a copy of any statement of reasons made by the nominee pursuant to Rule 1.37(3); and

(b)   a copy of the nominee's comments on the proposal submitted to them pursuant to Rule 1.38(2).

1.39(3)   [Endorsement of schedule copies] The copies of the schedule shall be endorsed by the court with the date on which the documents were filed in court and 3 copies of the schedule sealed by the court shall be returned by the court to the person who filed the documents in court.

1.39(4)   [Particulars in statement] The statement of affairs required to be filed under paragraph 7(1)(b) of Schedule A1 to the Act shall comprise the same particulars as required by Rule 1.5(2).

[FORM 1.6]

R.1.39
The documents that need to be filed in court to obtain the moratorium are explained along with the filing procedure. See I(A)R 2010 (SI 2010/686) which replaces the reference to working days in para.(1) with business days.

1.40   Notice and advertisement of beginning of a moratorium

1.40(1)   [Service on nominee and company] After receiving the copies of the schedule endorsed by the court under Rule 1.39(3), the directors shall as soon as reasonably practicable serve 2 of them on the nominee and one on the company.

1.40(2)   [Advertisement by nominee] On receipt of the copies of the schedule pursuant to paragraph (1), the nominee—

(a)   as soon as reasonably practicable shall cause a notice of the coming into force of the moratorium to be gazetted; and

(b)   may advertise the notice in such other manner as the nominee thinks fit.

[FORM 1.10]

1.40(2A)   [Additional contents of r.1.40(2) notice] In addition to the standard contents, the notice under paragraph (2) must state–

(a)   the nature of the business of the company;

(b)   that a moratorium under section 1A has come into force; and

(c)   the date upon which the moratorium came into force.

1.40(3)   [Notice of moratorium commencement date] The nominee shall as soon as reasonably practicable notify the registrar of companies, the company and any petitioning creditor of the company of whose address the nominee is aware of the coming into force of the moratorium and such notification shall specify the date on which the moratorium came into force and the court at which the documents to obtain the moratorium were filed.

1.40(4)   [Further notice requirements] The nominee shall give notice of the coming into force of the moratorium specifying the date on which it came into force to–

(a)   any enforcement officer or other officer who, to his knowledge, is charged with an execution or other legal process against the company or its property; and

(b)   any person who, to his knowledge, has distrained against the company or its property.

R.1.40
The fact that the moratorium has started needs to be advertised. This CVA model is not as discreet as the original CVA alternative. The term "enforcement officer" was substituted for "sheriff" by the Insolvency (Amendment) Rules 2005 (SI 2005/527) and reflects reforms made by the Courts Act 2003. Note the Insolvency (Amendment) Rules 2009 (SI 2009/642) (effective April 6, 2009) which modified the wording of this provision by substituting a new para.(2). See I(A)R 2010 (SI 2010/686) which provides amplification via para.(2A).

1.41   Notice of extension of moratorium

1.41(1)   [Notice of extension etc.] The nominee shall as soon as reasonably practicable notify the registrar of companies and the court of a decision taking effect pursuant to paragraph 36 of Schedule A1 to the Act to extend or further extend the moratorium and such notice shall specify the new expiry date of the moratorium.

[FORM 1.13]

1.41(2)   [Further notice following court order] Where an order is made by the court extending or further extending or renewing or continuing a moratorium, the nominee shall as soon as reasonably practicable after receiving a copy of the same give notice to the registrar of companies and with the notice shall send a copy of the order.

R.1.41
The registrar and court need to be informed if the moratorium has been extended.

1.42 Notice and advertisement of end of moratorium

1.42(1) [Advertisement, notice] After the moratorium comes to an end, the nominee—

(a) as soon as reasonably practicable shall cause a notice of its coming to an end and the date on which it came to an end to be gazetted; and

(b) may advertise the notice in such other manner as the nominee thinks fit.

[FORM 1.10]

1.42(1A) [Additional contents of r.1.42(1) notice] In addition to the standard contents, the notice under paragraph (1) must state–

(a) the nature of the business of the company;

(b) that a moratorium under section 1A has come to an end; and

(c) the date upon which the moratorium came to an end.

1.42(2) [Notice to registrar etc.] The nominee shall as soon as reasonably practicable give notice of the ending of the moratorium to the registrar of companies, the court, the company and any creditor of the company of whose address the nominee is aware and such notice shall specify the date on which the moratorium came to an end.

[FORM 1.15]

R.1.42
Where the moratorium has come to an end that fact must be advertised. Note the change made by the Insolvency (Amendment) Rules 2009 (SI 2009/642) (effective April 6, 2009). This amendment involved substituting a new para.(1). See the clarification introduced via para.(1A) inserted by I(A)R 2010 (SI 2010/686).

Section B: Proceedings during a moratorium

1.43 Disposal of charged property etc. during a moratorium

1.43(1) [Application] This Rule applies in any case where the company makes an application to the court under paragraph 20 of Schedule A1 to the Act for permission to dispose of property of the company which is subject to a security, or goods in possession of the company under an agreement to which that paragraph relates.

1.43(2) [Venue, notice to security holder etc.] The court shall fix a venue for the hearing of the application and the company shall as soon as reasonably practicable give notice of the venue to the person who is the holder of the security or, as the case may be, the owner under the agreement.

1.43(3) [Notice of order] If an order is made, the company shall as soon as reasonably practicable give notice of it to that person or owner.

1.43(4) [Sealed copies of order] The court shall send 2 sealed copies of the order to the company, who shall send one of them to that person or owner.

R.1.43
If directors wish to obtain permission to dispose of company property during the course of the moratorium the requirements of this rule must be met.

1.44   Withdrawal of nominee's consent to act

1.44   Where the nominee withdraws his consent to act he shall, pursuant to paragraph 25(5) of Schedule A1 to the Act, as soon as reasonably practicable give notice of his withdrawal and the reason for withdrawing his consent to act to–

    (a)   the registrar of companies;

    (b)   the court;

[FORM 1.17]

    (c)   the company; and

    (d)   any creditor of the company of whose claim and address the nominee is aware.

R.1.44
This outlines formal requirements where a nominee withdraws consent to act. See I(A)R 2010 (SI 2010/686).

1.45   Replacement of nominee by the court

1.45(1)   [Notice of directors' application] Where the directors intend to make an application to the court under paragraph 28 of Schedule A1 to the Act for the nominee to be replaced, they shall give to the nominee at least 5 business days' notice of their application.

1.45(2)   [Notice of nominee's application] Where the nominee intends to make an application to the court under that paragraph to be replaced, he shall give to the directors at least 5 business days' notice of his application.

1.45(3)   [Replacement nominee's consent and qualification to act] No appointment of a replacement nominee shall be made by the court unless there is filed in court a statement by the replacement nominee indicating that the replacement nominee–

    (a)   consents to act; and

    (b)   is qualified to act as an insolvency practitioner in relation to the company or is an authorised person in relation to the company.

[FORM 1.8]

R.1.45
Procedures governing the replacement of the nominee by the court are explained. See I(A)R 2010 (SI 2010/686) which converts the specified timescale in paras (1) and (2) to five business days.

1.46   Notification of appointment of a replacement nominee

1.46   Where a person is appointed as a replacement nominee, he shall as soon as reasonably practicable give notice of his appointment to–

    (a)   the registrar of companies;

[FORM 1.19]

    (b)   the court (in any case where he was not appointed by the court); and

    (c)   the person whom he has replaced as nominee.

R.1.46
Where a replacement nominee is installed that fact needs to be advertised.

1.47   Applications to court under paragraphs 26 or 27 of Schedule A1 to the Act

1.47   Where any person intends to make an application to the court pursuant to paragraph 26 or 27 of Schedule A1 to the Act, he shall give to the nominee at least 5 business days' notice of his application.

R.1.47

This explains procedures on applications pursuant to paras 26 and 27 of Sch.A1 (i.e. applications to challenge the acts and omissions of the nominee). See I(A)R 2010 (SI 2010/686) which changes the seven-day timescale to five business days.

Section D: Consideration of proposals where moratorium obtained

1.48   Summoning of meetings; procedure at meetings etc.

1.48(1)   [Date for meetings] Where the nominee summons meetings of creditors and the company pursuant to paragraph 29(1) of Schedule A1 to the Act, each of those meetings shall be summoned for a date that is not more than 28 days from the date on which the moratorium came into force.

1.48(2)   [Notices of creditors' meetings] Notices calling the creditors' meetings shall be sent by the nominee to all creditors specified in the statement of affairs and any other creditors of the company of whose address he is aware at least 14 days before the day fixed for the meeting.

1.48(3)   [Notices of company meeting] Notices calling the company meeting shall be sent by the nominee to all persons who are, to the best of the nominee's belief, members of the company at least 14 days before the day fixed for the meeting.

1.48(4)   [What notice to specify and state] Each notice sent under this Rule must–

(a)   specify–

   (i)   the court in which the documents relating to the obtaining of the moratorium were filed and

   (ii)   the court reference; and

(b)   state the effect of paragraphs (2) to (4) of Rule 1.52 (requisite majorities (creditors)).

1.48(4A)   [Additional contents of notice] With each notice there must be sent–

(a)   a copy of the directors' proposal;

(b)   a copy of the statement of affairs or, if the nominee thinks fit, a summary of it (the summary to include a list of creditors and the amount of their debts); and

(c)   the nominee's comments on the proposal.

1.48(5)   [Application of rr.1.13–1.16] The provisions of Rules 1.13 to 1.16 shall apply.

R.1.48

This explains the rules governing the summoning of meetings where the moratorium is in place and the creditors need to vote on the proposal. For amplification of the procedural requirements see I(A)R 2010 (SI 2010/686) which makes changes via new paras (4) and (4A).

1.49   Entitlement to vote (creditors)

1.49(1)   [Entitlement] Subject as follows, every creditor who has notice of the creditors' meeting is entitled to vote at the meeting or any adjournment of it.

1.49(2)   [Calculation of votes] Votes are calculated according to the amount of the creditor's debt as at the beginning of the moratorium, after deducting any amounts paid in respect of that debt after that date.

1.49(3)   [Limitation on voting] A creditor may vote in respect of a debt for an unliquidated amount or any debt whose value is not ascertained and for the purposes of voting (but not otherwise) his debt shall be valued at £1 unless the chairman agrees to put a higher value on it.

R.1.49

This explains creditors' entitlement to vote. The rules here are standard.

1.50   Procedure for admission of creditors' claims for voting purposes

1.50(1)   [Chairman's duty] Subject as follows, at any creditors' meeting the chairman shall ascertain the entitlement of persons wishing to vote and shall admit or reject their claims accordingly.

1.50(2)   [Chairman's discretion] The chairman may admit or reject a claim in whole or in part.

1.50(3)   [Appeal from chairman's decision] The chairman's decision on any matter under this Rule or under paragraph (3) of Rule 1.49 is subject to appeal to the court by any creditor or member of the company.

1.50(4)   [Voting subject to objection] If the chairman is in doubt whether a claim should be admitted or rejected, he shall mark it as objected to and allow votes to be cast in respect of it, subject to such votes being subsequently declared invalid if the objection to the claim is sustained.

1.50(5)   [Where chairman's decision reversed etc.] If on an appeal the chairman's decision is reversed or varied, or votes are declared invalid, the court may order another meeting to be summoned, or make such order as it thinks just.

The court's power to make an order under this paragraph is exercisable only if it considers that the circumstances giving rise to the appeal are such as give rise to unfair prejudice or material irregularity.

1.50(6)   [Time for appeal] An application to the court by way of appeal against the chairman's decision shall not be made after the end of the period of 28 days beginning with the first day on which the report required by paragraph 30(3) of Schedule A1 to the Act has been made to the court.

1.50(7)   [Costs of appeal] The chairman is not personally liable for any costs incurred by any person in respect of an appeal under this Rule.

R.1.50
Admission to voting in this CVA model is governed by r.1.50.

1.51   Voting rights (members)

1.51   Rule 1.18 shall apply.

R.1.51
This sensibly adopts r.1.18.

1.52   Requisite majorities (creditors)

1.52(1)   [Resolution by majority in value] Subject to paragraph (2), at the creditors' meeting, a resolution is passed when a majority (in value) of those present and voting in person or by proxy have voted in favour of it.

1.52(2)   [Resolution to approve/modify proposal by three-quarters majority] A resolution to approve the proposal or a modification is passed when a majority of three quarters or more (in value) of those present and voting in person or by proxy have voted in favour of it.

1.52(3)   [Extension of moratorium, non-application of r.1.52(4)] At a meeting of the creditors for any resolution to pass extending (or further extending) a moratorium, or to bring a moratorium to an end before the end of the period of any extension, there must be a majority in excess of three quarters in value of the creditors present in person or by proxy and voting on the resolution. For this purpose paragraph (4)(b) below shall not apply and a secured creditor is entitled to vote in respect of the amount of his claim without deducting the value of his security.

1.52(4)   [Votes to be left out of account] In the following cases there is to be left out of account a creditor's vote in respect of any claim or part of a claim—

(a)   where written notice of the claim was not given, either at the meeting or before it, to the chairman or nominee;

(b)   where the claim or part is secured;

(c)   where the claim is in respect of a debt wholly or partly on, or secured by, a current bill of exchange or promissory note, unless the creditor is willing–

> (i)   to treat the liability to him on the bill or note of every person who is liable on it antecedently to the company, and against whom a bankruptcy order has not been made (or, in the case of a company, which has not gone into liquidation), as a security in his hands, and

> (ii)   to estimate the value of the security and (for the purpose of entitlement to vote, but not of any distribution under the arrangement) to deduct it from his claim.

1.52(5)   [Voting rendering resolution invalid] Any resolution is invalid if those voting against it include more than half in value of the creditors, counting in these latter only those–

(a)   who have notice of the meeting;

(b)   whose votes are not to be left out of account under paragraph (4); and

(c)   who are not, to the best of the chairman's belief, persons connected with the company.

1.52(6)   [Chairman's powers] It is for the chairman of the meeting to decide whether under this Rule–

(a)   a vote is to be left out of account in accordance with paragraph (4), or

(b)   a person is a connected person for the purposes of paragraph (5)(c);

and in relation to the second of these two cases the chairman is entitled to rely on the information provided by the statement of the company's affairs or otherwise in accordance with this Part of the Rules.

1.52(7)   [Use of proxy contrary to r.1.15] If the chairman uses a proxy contrary to Rule 1.15 as it applies by virtue of Rule 1.48(5), his vote with that proxy does not count towards any majority under this Rule.

1.52(8)   [Chairman's decision subject to appeal] The chairman's decision on any matter under this Rule is subject to appeal to the court by any creditor or member and paragraphs (5) to (7) of Rule 1.50 apply as regards such an appeal.

R.1.52
Voting majorities for creditors are laid down. See I(A)R 2010 (SI 2010/686) which reformulates the statement of required majority. A simple majority is the norm but a three-quarters majority must be obtained for modifications.

1.53   Requisite majorities (members) and proceedings to obtain agreement on the proposal

1.53(1)   [Application of r.1.20] Rule 1.20 shall apply.

1.53(2)   [Chairman's discretion to hold meetings together] If the chairman thinks fit, the creditors' meeting and the company meeting may be held together.

1.53(3)   [Adjournment of meeting] The chairman may, and shall if it is so resolved at the meeting in question, adjourn that meeting, but any adjournment shall not be to a day which is more than 14 days after the date on which the moratorium (including any extension) ends.

1.53(4)   [Notice of adjournment] If the meetings are adjourned under paragraph (3), notice of the fact shall be given by the nominee as soon as reasonably practicable to the court.

1.53(4A)   [Single suspension without adjournment] Once only in the course of a meeting the chairman may, without an adjournment, declare it suspended for any period up to 1 hour.

1.53(5)   [Deemed rejection of proposal] If following the final adjournment of the creditors' meeting the proposal (with or without modifications) has not been approved by the creditors, it is deemed rejected.

R.1.53

This incorporates r.1.20 with some modification. Note the new power of suspension in para.(4A) introduced by I(A)R 2010 (SI 2010/686).

1.54 Implementation of the arrangement

1.54(1) [Putting supervisor in possession of assets] Where a decision approving the arrangement has effect under paragraph 36 of Schedule A1 to the Act, the directors shall as soon as reasonably practicable do all that is required for putting the supervisor into possession of the assets included in the arrangement.

1.54(2) [Application of rr.1.22, 1.22A, 1.24 and 1.29] Subject to paragraph (3), Rules 1.22, 1.22A and 1.24 to 1.29 apply.

1.54(3) [Modified provisions] The provisions referred to in paragraph (2) are modified as follows–

(a) in paragraph (1) of Rule 1.22A the reference to section 4A(6) is to be read as a reference to paragraph 36(5) of Schedule A1 to the Act;

(b) in paragraph (4) of Rule 1.24 the reference to section 4(6) is to be read as a reference to paragraph 30(3) of Schedule A1 to the Act;

(c) in paragraph (5) of Rule 1.24 the reference to section 4A is to be read as a reference to paragraph 36 of Schedule A1 to the Act;

(d) in paragraph (1) of Rule 1.25 the reference to section 6 is to be read as a reference to paragraph 38 of Schedule A1 to the Act and the references in paragraphs (2) and (4) to the administrator or liquidator shall be ignored;

(e) in paragraph (3) of Rule 1.25 the reference to section 6(4)(b) is to be read as a reference to paragraph 38 (4)(b) of Schedule A1 to the Act; and

(f) in sub-paragraph (a) of paragraph (1) of Rule 1.28 the reference to section 4A is to be read as a reference to paragraph 36 of Schedule A1 to the Act.

R.1.54

This explains the responsibilities of the directors vis-à-vis the supervisor to facilitate implementation of the CVA.

GENERAL NOTE TO CHAPTER 9

This major insertion of rr.1.35–1.54 was made by the Insolvency (Amendment) (No.2) Rules 2002 (SI 2002/2712) to cater for the coming into effect of the Insolvency Act 2000. Chapter 9 deals with the new CVA moratorium which is already heavily regulated by Sch.A1.

CHAPTER 10

TIME RECORDING INFORMATION

1.55 Provision by nominee or supervisor of information about time spent on a proposal or voluntary arrangement

1.55(1) [Duty of nominee or supervisor to provide statement] Subject as set out in this Rule, a person ("the relevant person") who has acted or is acting as–

(a) a nominee in respect of a proposed voluntary arrangement; or

(b) a supervisor in respect of a voluntary arrangement

must, on request in writing by any person mentioned in paragraph (2), supply free of charge to that person a statement of the kind described in paragraph (3).

1.55(2)   [Who may request statement] The persons referred to in paragraph (1) are–

(a) any director of the company;

(b) where the proposal has been approved, any creditor or member of the company in respect of the arrangement.

1.55(3)   [Period and content of statement] The statement referred to in paragraph (1)–

(a) must cover the period beginning with the date of the appointment of the relevant person as nominee or supervisor, as the case may be, and ending–

   (i) with the date next before the date of making the request on which the relevant person has completed any period as nominee or supervisor, or both, which is a multiple of 6 months or,

   (ii) where the relevant person has ceased to act as nominee or supervisor, the date upon which the person so cease; and

(b) must comprise the following details–

   (i) the total number of hours spent on the voluntary arrangement by the relevant person whether as nominee or supervisor, or both, and any staff assigned to the voluntary arrangement during that period;

   (ii) for each grade of individual so engaged, the average hourly rate at which any work carried out by individuals in that grade is charged; and

   (iii) the number of hours spent by each grade of staff during that period.

1.55(4)   [Time limit to request statement] No request pursuant to this Rule may be made where more than 2 years has elapsed since the relevant person ceased to act in any capacity in relation to the proposal or any voluntary arrangement arising out of the approval of the proposal.

1.55(5)   [Time limit to supply statement] Any statement required to be provided to any person under this Rule must be supplied within 28 days of the date of the receipt of the request by the person required to supply it.

GENERAL NOTE

Introduced by I(A)R 2010 (SI 2010/686) to provide greater transparency.

CHAPTER 11

OMISSION OF INFORMATION FROM STATEMENT OF AFFAIRS

1.56   Omission of information from Statement of Affairs

1.56   The court, on the application of the nominee, the directors or any person appearing to it to have an interest, may direct that specified information may be omitted from any statement of affairs required to be sent to the creditors where the disclosure of such information would be likely to prejudice the conduct of the voluntary arrangement or might reasonably be expected to lead to violence against any person.

GENERAL NOTE

Introduced by I(A)R 2010 (SI 2010/686) to protect commercially sensitive information and to protect personal safety.

PART 2

Introductory note to Part 2

The rules which follow apply in the new administration regime (Sch.B1, introduced by EA 2002 with effect from September 15, 2003). In those cases where the original regime continues to apply, reference should be made to the original Pt 2 (see Vol. 2).

CHAPTER 1

PRELIMINARY

2.1   Introductory and interpretation

2.1(1)   [Application of Pt 2] In this Part–

(a)   Chapter 2 applies in relation to the appointment of an administrator by the court;

(b)   Chapter 3 applies in relation to the appointment of an administrator by the holder of a qualifying floating charge under paragraph 14;

(c)   Chapter 4 applies in relation to the appointment of an administrator by the company or the directors under paragraph 22;

(d)   The following Chapters apply in all the cases mentioned in sub-paragraphs (a)–(c) above:

— Chapter 5: Process of administration;

— Chapter 6: Meetings and reports;

— Chapter 7: The creditors' committee;

— Chapter 8: Disposal of charged property;

— Chapter 9: Expenses of the administration;

— Chapter 10: Distributions to creditors;

— Chapter 11: The administrator;

— Chapter 12: Ending administration;

— Chapter 13: Replacing administrator;

— Chapter 14: EC Regulation—conversion of administration into winding up;

— Chapter 15: EC Regulation—member State liquidator.

2.1(2)   [Reference to numbered paragraphs] In this Part of these Rules a reference to a numbered paragraph shall, unless otherwise stated, be to the paragraph so numbered in Schedule B1 to the Act.

GENERAL NOTE

The rules in this Part govern administrations where the administrator is appointed under the new IA 1986 Pt II, which is to be found in Sch.B1 to the Act. The appointment may be made by the court under para.11 of Sch.B1, by the holder of a "qualifying" floating charge under para.14, or by the company itself or its directors under para.22. This rule indicates the Chapters of the rules which are to apply in each of these cases.

References to paragraph numbers in the notes which follow are to paragraphs of Sch.B1, and those to section numbers are to sections of IA 1986. Cross-references to other rules, if in italics, are to the original Pt 2 of IR 1986; if in roman type, to the new Pt 2. For definitions of special terms, reference should be made to Apps I and II.

2.2 Witness statement in support of administration application

2.2(1) **[Witness statement required]** Where it is proposed to apply to the court for an administration order to be made in relation to a company, the administration application shall be in Form 2.1B and a witness statement complying with Rule 2.4 must be prepared, with a view to its being filed with the court in support of the application.

[FORM 2.1B]

2.2(2) **[Application by company or directors]** If the administration application is to be made by the company or by the directors, the witness statement shall be made by one of the directors, or the secretary of the company, stating himself to make it on behalf of the company or, as the case may be, on behalf of the directors.

2.2(3) **[Application by creditors]** If the application is to be made by creditors, the witness statement shall be made by a person acting under the authority of them all, whether or not himself one of their number. In any case there must be stated in the witness statement the nature of his authority and the means of his knowledge of the matters to which the witness statement relates.

2.2(4) **[Application by CVA supervisor]** If the application is to be made by the supervisor of a voluntary arrangement under Part I of the Act, it is to be treated as if it were an application by the company.

(See General Note after r.2.9.)

2.3 Form of application

2.3(1) **[Application by company or directors]** If made by the company or by the directors, the application shall state the name of the company and its address for service, which (in the absence of special reasons to the contrary) is that of the company's registered office.

2.3(2) **[Application by directors]** If the application is made by the directors, it shall state that it is so made under paragraph 12(1)(b); but from and after making it is to be treated for all purposes as the application of the company.

2.3(3) **[Application by single creditor]** If made by a single creditor, the application shall state his name and address for service.

2.3(4) **[Application by two or more creditors]** If the application is made by two or more creditors, it shall state that it is so made (naming them); but from and after making it is to be treated for all purposes as the application of only one of them, named in the application as applying on behalf of himself and other creditors. An address for service for that one shall be specified.

2.3(5) **[Statement by proposed administrator]** There shall be attached to the application a written statement which shall be in Form 2.2B by each of the persons proposed to be administrator stating–

[FORM 2.2B]

   (a) that he consents to accept appointment;

   (b) details of any prior professional relationship(s) that he has had with the company to which he is to be appointed as administrator; and

   (c) his opinion that it is reasonably likely that the purpose of administration will be achieved.

(See General Note after r.2.9.)

2.4   Contents of application and witness statement in support

2.4(1)   [Inability to pay debts] The administration application shall contain a statement of the applicant's belief that the company is, or is likely to become, unable to pay its debts, except where the applicant is the holder of a qualifying floating charge and is making the application in reliance on paragraph 35.

2.4(2)   [Company's financial position etc.] There shall be attached to the application a witness statement in support which shall contain–

  (a)   a statement of the company's financial position, specifying (to the best of the applicant's knowledge and belief) the company's assets and liabilities, including contingent and prospective liabilities;

  (b)   details of any security known or believed to be held by creditors of the company, and whether in any case the security is such as to confer power on the holder to appoint an administrative receiver or to appoint an administrator under paragraph 14. If an administrative receiver has been appointed, that fact shall be stated;

  (c)   details of any insolvency proceedings in relation to the company including any petition that has been presented for the winding up of the company so far as within the immediate knowledge of the applicant;

  (d)   where it is intended to appoint a number of persons as administrators, details of the matters set out in paragraph 100(2) regarding the exercise of the function of the administrators; and

  (e)   any other matters which, in the opinion of those intending to make the application for an administration order, will assist the court in deciding whether to make such an order, so far as lying within the knowledge or belief of the applicant.

2.4(3)   [Application by qualifying floating charge-holder] Where the application is made by the holder of a qualifying floating charge in reliance on paragraph 35, he shall give sufficient details in the witness statement in support to satisfy the court that he is entitled to appoint an administrator under paragraph 14.

2.4(4)   [Whether EC Insolvency Proceedings Regulation applies] The witness statement shall state whether, in the opinion of the person making the application, (i) the EC Regulation will apply and (ii) if so, whether the proceedings will be main proceedings, secondary proceedings or territorial proceedings.

(See General Note after r.2.9.)

2.5   Filing of application

2.5(1)   [Filing in court] The application (and all supporting documents) shall be filed with the court, with a sufficient number of copies for service and use as provided by Rule 2.6.

2.5(2)   [Sealed copies] Each of the copies filed shall have applied to it the seal of the court and be issued to the applicant; and on each copy there shall be endorsed the date and time of filing.

2.5(3)   [Venue for hearing endorsed on copies] The court shall fix a venue for the hearing of the application and this also shall be endorsed on each copy of the application issued under paragraph (2).

2.5(4)   [Existence of insolvency proceedings] After the application is filed, it is the duty of the applicant to notify the court in writing of the existence of any insolvency proceedings, and any insolvency proceedings under the EC Regulation, in relation to the company, as soon as he becomes aware of them.

(See General Note after r.2.9.)

2.6   Service of application

2.6(1)   [References to the application] In the following paragraphs of this Rule, references to the application are to a copy of the application issued by the court under Rule 2.5(2) together with the witness statement required by Rule 2.4 and the documents attached to the application.

2.6(2)   [Notification by service] Notification for the purposes of paragraph 12(2) shall be by way of service in accordance with Rule 2.8, verified in accordance with Rule 2.9.

2.6(3)   [Persons to be served] The application shall be served in addition to those persons referred to in paragraph 12(2)–

  (a)   if an administrative receiver has been appointed, on him;

  (b)   if there is pending a petition for the winding-up of the company, on the petitioner (and also on the provisional liquidator, if any);

  (c)   if a member State liquidator has been appointed in main proceedings in relation to the company, on him;

  (d)   on the person proposed as administrator;

  (e)   on the company, if the application is made by anyone other than the company;

  (f)   if a supervisor of a voluntary arrangement under Part I of the Act has been appointed, on him.

(See General Note after r.2.9.)

2.7   Notice to officers charged with execution of writs or other process, etc.

2.7 The applicant shall as soon as reasonably practicable after filing the application give notice of its being made to–

  (a)   any enforcement officer or other officer who to his knowledge is charged with an execution or other legal process against the company or its property; and

  (b)   any person who to his knowledge has distrained against the company or its property.

(See General Note after r.2.9.)

2.8   Manner in which service to be effected

2.8(1)   [Service not less than five days before hearing] Service of the application in accordance with Rule 2.6 shall be effected by the applicant, or his solicitor, or by a person instructed by him or his solicitor, not less than 5 business days before the date fixed for the hearing.

2.8(2)   [How service effected] Service shall be effected as follows–

  (a)   on the company (subject to paragraph (3) below), by delivering the documents to its registered office;

  (b)   on any other person (subject to paragraph (4) below), by delivering the documents to his proper address;

  (c)   in either case, in such other manner as the court may direct.

2.8(3)   [Service to registered office not practicable] If delivery to a company's registered office is not practicable, service may be effected by delivery to its last known principal place of business in England and Wales.

2.8(4)   [Proper address under r.2.8(2)(b)] Subject to paragraph (5), for the purposes of paragraph (2)(b) above, a person's proper address is any which he has previously notified as his address for service;

but if he has not notified any such address, service may be effected by delivery to his usual or last known address.

2.8(5)   [Authorised deposit-taker] In the case of a person who–

(a)   is an authorised deposit-taker or former authorised deposit-taker;

(b)   (i)   has appointed, or is or may be entitled to appoint, an administrative receiver of the company, or

(ii)   is, or may be, entitled to appoint an administrator of the company under paragraph 14; and

(c)   has not notified an address for service,

the proper address is the address of an office of that person where, to the knowledge of the applicant, the company maintains a bank account or, where no such office is known to the applicant, the registered office of that person, or, if there is no such office, his usual or last known address.

2.8(6)   [Omitted by I(A)R 2010 r.2 and Sch. para.38(3) as from April 6, 2010.]

(See General Note after r.2.9.)

2.9   Proof of service

2.9(1)   [Verification by certificate of service] Service of the application must be verified by a certificate of service.

2.9(1A)   [Content of certificate of service] The certificate of service must be sufficient to identify the application served and must specify–

(a)   the name and registered number of the company,

(b)   the address of the registered office of the company,

(c)   the name of the applicant,

(d)   the court to which the application was made and the court reference number,

(e)   the date of the application,

(f)   whether the copy served was a sealed copy,

(g)   the date on which service was effected, and

(h)   the manner in which service was effected.

2.9(2)   [Certificate of service to be filed in court] The certificate of service shall be filed with the court as soon as reasonably practicable after service, and in any event not less than 1 business day before the hearing of the application.

GENERAL NOTE TO RR.2.2–2.9

These rules correspond to rr.*2.1–2.8* which apply in the original regime, but there are many points of difference. The procedure is by way of application rather than by petition.

R.2.3
An application by the directors may be made by a majority, not necessarily at a formal meeting (para.105).
    The "Rule 2.2 report" required to be made under the original regime has been replaced by the simple statement described in r.2.3(5). No witness statement or statement of truth is required.

R.2.4(4)
On the question whether the EC Regulation applies and the different types of proceedings, see the note to art.3 of the Regulation.

R.2.9(1A)
Rule 2.9(1A) inserted by I(A)R 2010 r.2 and Sch. para.39(2) as from April 6, 2010.

2.10 Application to appoint specified person as administrator by holder of qualifying floating charge

2.10(1) [Production to court] Where the holder of a qualifying floating charge applies to the court under paragraph 36(1)(b), he shall produce to the court–

(a) the written consent of all holders of any prior qualifying floating charge;

(b) a written statement in the Form 2.2B made by the specified person proposed by him as administrator; and

(c) sufficient evidence to satisfy the court that he is entitled to appoint an administrator under paragraph 14.

2.10(2) [Costs to be expense of administration] If an administration order is made appointing the specified person, the costs of the person who made the administration application and the applicant under paragraph 36(1)(b) shall, unless the court otherwise orders, be paid as an expense of the administration.

GENERAL NOTE

Where another person has made an application to the court for the appointment of an administrator, para.36 allows the holder of a qualifying floating charge to intervene and request the court to appoint a specified insolvency practitioner as administrator instead of the person nominated in the application. This rule sets out the procedural requirements for such an application.

2.11 Application where company in liquidation

2.11(1) [Content of witness statement in support] Where an administration application is made under paragraph 37 or paragraph 38, the witness statement required by Rule 2.4 shall contain–

(a) full details of the existing insolvency proceedings, the name and address of the liquidator, the date he was appointed and by whom;

(b) the reasons why it has subsequently been considered appropriate that an administration application should be made;

(c) all other matters that would, in the opinion of the applicant, assist the court in considering the need to make provisions in respect of matters arising in connection with the liquidation; and

(d) the details required in Rules 2.4(2) and (4).

2.11(2) [Application by qualifying floating charge-holder] Where the application is made by the holder of a qualifying floating charge he shall set out sufficient evidence in the witness statement required by Rule 2.4 to satisfy the court that he is entitled to appoint an administrator under paragraph 14.

GENERAL NOTE

A company which is in liquidation cannot normally be put into administration (para.8(1)), but exceptions are made by paras 37 and 38. If an order is made, the administration supersedes the liquidation. This rule spells out some procedural requirements.

2.12 The hearing

2.12(1) [Appearances] At the hearing of the administration application, any of the following may appear or be represented–

(a) the applicant;

(b) the company;

(c) one or more of the directors;

(d) if an administrative receiver has been appointed, that person;

(e) any person who has presented a petition for the winding-up of the company;

(f) the person proposed for appointment as administrator;

(g) if a member State liquidator has been appointed in main proceedings in relation to the company, that person;

(h) any person that is the holder of a qualifying floating charge;

(j) any supervisor of a voluntary arrangement under Part I of the Act;

(k) with the permission of the court, any other person who appears to have an interest justifying his appearance.

2.12(2)   [Form of order] If the court makes an administration order, it shall be in Form 2.4B.

[FORM 2.4B]

2.12(3)   [Costs] If the court makes an administration order, the costs of the applicant, and of any person whose costs are allowed by the court, are payable as an expense of the administration.

(See General Note after r.2.14.)

2.13   Where the court makes an administration order in relation to a company upon an application under paragraph 37 or 38, the court shall include in the order–

(a) in the case of a liquidator appointed in a voluntary winding-up, his removal from office;

(b) details concerning the release of the liquidator;

(c) provision for payment of the expenses of the liquidation;

(d) provisions regarding any indemnity given to the liquidator;

(e) provisions regarding the handling or realisation of any of the company's assets in the hands of or under the control of the liquidator;

(f) such provision as the court thinks fit with respect to matters arising in connection with the liquidation; and

(g) such other provisions as the court shall think fit.

(See General Note after r.2.14.)

2.14   Notice of administration order

2.14(1)   [Court to send two sealed copies to applicant] If the court makes an administration order, it shall as soon as reasonably practicable send two sealed copies of the order to the person who made the application.

2.14(2)   [Applicant to send copy to administrator] The applicant shall send a sealed copy of the order as soon as reasonably practicable to the person appointed as administrator.

2.14(3)   [Directions as notice of interim or other order] If the court makes an order under paragraph 13(1)(d) or any other order under paragraph 13(1)(f), it shall give directions as to the persons to whom, and how, notice of that order is to be given.

GENERAL NOTE TO RR.2.12–2.14

For corresponding provisions under the original regime, see rr.*2.9–2.10*. There is, however, no counterpart to r.2.13.

R.2.12(3)

A creditor who unsuccessfully opposes an application may be allowed his costs, but only (and exceptionally) if the court considers it just in all the circumstances: *Re Professional Computer Group Ltd* [2008] EWHC 1541 (Ch);

[2009] B.C.C. 323. In this case it was held that, since the creditor's unsuccessful opposition to the application had significantly increased the company's own costs, he should be ordered under CPR r.48.2 to pay its costs to that extent.

CHAPTER 3

APPOINTMENT OF ADMINISTRATOR BY HOLDER OF FLOATING CHARGE

2.15   Notice of intention to appoint

2.15(1)   [Prescribed form] The prescribed form for the notice of intention to appoint for the purposes of paragraph 44(2) is Form 2.5B.

[FORM 2.5B]

2.15(2)   [Interim moratorium] For the purposes of paragraph 44(2), a copy of Form 2.5B shall be filed with the court at the same time as it is sent in accordance with paragraph 15(1) to the holder of any prior qualifying floating charge.

2.15(3)   [Service] The provisions of Rule 2.8(2) to 2.8(6) shall apply to the sending of a notice under this Rule as they apply to the manner in which service of an administration application is effected under that Rule.

(See General Note after r.2.18.)

2.16   Notice of appointment

2.16(1)   [Form] The notice of appointment for the purposes of an appointment under paragraph 14 shall be in Form 2.6B.

[FORM 2.6B]

2.16(2)   [Copies to be accompanied by] The copies of the notice filed with the court, shall be accompanied by–

  (a)   the administrator's written statement in Form 2.2B; and

  (b)   either–

    (i)   evidence that the person making the appointment has given such notice as may be required by paragraph 15(1)(a); or

    (ii)   copies of the written consent of all those required to give consent in accordance with paragraph 15(1)(b); and

  (c)   a statement of those matters provided for in paragraph 100(2), if applicable.

2.16(3)   [Statutory declaration] The statutory declaration on Form 2.6B shall be made not more than 5 business days before the form is filed with the court.

2.16(4)   [Form of consent by prior qualifying floating charge holder] Written consent may be given by the holder of a prior qualifying floating charge where a notice of intention to appoint an administrator has been given and filed with the court in accordance with Rule 2.15 above, by completing the section provided on Form 2.5B and returning to the appointor a copy of the form.

2.16(5)   [Written consent by prior qualifying floating charge holder] Where the holder of a prior qualifying floating charge does not choose to complete the section provided on Form 2.5B to indicate his consent, or no such form has been sent to him, his written consent shall include–

723

(a) details of the name, address of registered office and registered number of the company in respect of which the appointment is proposed to be made;

(b) details of the charge held by him including the date it was registered and, where applicable, any financial limit and any deeds of priority;

(c) his name and address;

(d) the name and address of the holder of the qualifying floating charge who is proposing to make the appointment;

(e) the date that notice of intention to appoint was given;

(f) the name of the proposed administrator;

(g) statement of consent to the proposed appointment,

and it shall be authenticated and dated.

2.16(6) **[Appointment out of court business hours]** This Rule and the following Rule are subject to Rule 2.19, the provisions of which apply when an appointment is to be made out of court business hours.

(See General Note after r.2.18.)

2.17(1) **[Three copies filed in court]** Three copies of the notice of appointment shall be filed with the court and shall have applied to them the seal of the court and be endorsed with the date and time of filing.

2.17(2) **[Court to issue two sealed copies]** The court shall issue two of the sealed copies of the notice of appointment to the person making the appointment, who shall as soon as reasonably practicable send one of the sealed copies to the administrator.

2.18 Where, after receiving notice that an administration application has been made, the holder of a qualifying floating charge appoints an administrator in reliance on paragraph 14, he shall as soon as reasonably practicable send a copy of the notice of appointment to the person making the administration application and to the court in which the application has been made.

General Note to rr.2.15–2.18

The holder of a "qualifying" floating charge (as defined in para.14(2), (3)) may appoint an administrator out of court under para.14. These rules set out the procedural requirements.

Where there is a prior-ranking qualifying floating charge, para.15 will apply, and either two business days' written notice must be given to the holder or his written consent must be obtained. Paragraph 15 does not specify that the notice to the creditor should be in a prescribed form, but Form 2.5B must be used to file a copy with the court under para.44(2) if it is desired to obtain a moratorium. (Note that filing with the court is not obligatory. On the question whether a notice of intention to appoint can be filed in other circumstances, see the notes to paras 15 and 44.) Where there is no prior-ranking floating charge, the charge holder may proceed to make an appointment immediately, without the need to give or file any notice.

R.2.16(5)
The detailed requirements of this provision make the use of Form 2.5B considerably more attractive.

2.19 Appointment taking place out of court business hours

2.19(1) **[Form when court closed]** The holder of a qualifying floating charge may file a notice of appointment with the court, notwithstanding that the court is not open for public business. When the court is closed (and only when it is closed) a notice of appointment may be filed with the court by faxing that form or sending it as an attachment to an e-mail in accordance with paragraphs (3) and (3A). The notice of appointment shall be in Form 2.7B.

[FORM 2.7B]

2.19(2)   **[Notice of appointment]** The filing of a notice in accordance with this Rule shall have the same effect for all purposes as a notice of appointment filed in accordance with Rule 2.16 with the court specified in the notice as having jurisdiction in the case.

2.19(3)   **[Notice by fax, email]** The notice must be–

(a)   faxed to a designated telephone number, or

(b)   sent as an attachment by e-mail to a designated e-mail address,

which must be provided by the Court Service for that purpose.

2.19(3A)   **[Fax number, email address]** The Secretary of State must publish the designated telephone number and e-mail address on The Insolvency Service website and, on request to The Insolvency Service, make them available in writing.

2.19(4)   **[Fax transmission report, email hard copy]** The appointor shall ensure that–

(a)   a fax transmission report detailing the time and date of the fax transmission and the telephone number to which the notice was faxed and containing a copy of the first page (in part or in full) of the document faxed is created by the fax machine that is used to fax the form, or

(b)   a hard copy of the e-mail is created detailing the time and date of the e-mail and the address to which it was sent and containing a copy of the document sent as an attachment,

as the case may be; and the appointor must retain the report or hard copy.

2.19(5)   **[When appointment effective]** The appointment shall take effect from the date and time of the fax transmission or sending of the e-mail. The appointor shall notify the administrator, as soon as reasonably practicable, that the notice has been filed.

2.19(6)   **[Copy of faxed notice of email to court]** The copy of the faxed notice of appointment, or the e-mail (or a hard copy of the e-mail) containing the notice of appointment, as (in either case) received by the Court Service, shall be forwarded as soon as reasonably practicable to the court specified in the notice as the court having jurisdiction in the case, to be placed on the relevant court file.

2.19(7)   **[Appointor to take copies to court]** The appointor shall take three copies of the notice of appointment that was faxed to the designated telephone number, together with the transmission report or hard copy required by paragraph (4) and all the necessary supporting documents listed on Form 2.7B, to the court on the next day that the court is open for business.

2.19(8)   **[Reasons for out of hours filing]** The appointor shall attach to the notice a statement providing full reasons for the out of hours filing of the notice of appointment, including why it would have been damaging to the company and its creditors not to have so acted.

2.19(9)   **[Copies sealed by court]** The copies of the notice shall be sealed by the court and shall be endorsed with the date and time when, according to the appointor's fax transmission report or hard copy of the e-mail, the notice was faxed or sent and the date when the notice and accompanying documents were delivered to the court.

2.19(10)   **[Cessation of appointment]** The administrator's appointment shall cease to have effect if the requirements of paragraph (7) are not completed within the time period indicated in that paragraph.

2.19(11)   **[Presumption as to date and time of appointment]** Where any question arises in respect of the date and time that the notice of appointment was filed with the court it shall be a presumption capable of rebuttal that the date and time shown on the appointor's fax transmission report or hard copy of the e-mail is the date and time at which the notice was so filed.

2.19(12)   **[Court to issue two sealed copies]** The court shall issue two of the sealed copies of the notice of appointment to the person making the appointment, who shall, as soon as reasonably practicable, send one of the copies to the administrator.

Rule 2.19 amended by I(A)R 2010 r.2 and Sch. para.41 as from April 6, 2010. This amendment allows the use of email as an alternative to fax where an administrator is appointed out of office hours.

There may be occasions when the holder of a floating charge will wish to appoint an administrator at a time when the court office is closed. Since the appointment only takes effect on the filing of a notice of appointment with the court (para.19), it has been necessary to make special provision in this rule, providing for the filing of a notice of appointment by fax or email, with confirmation by the lodgement of physical documents on the next day that the court is open for business. The requirements, spelt out in this rule, are quite strict; and it should be noted that the option of filing by fax or email is available only when the court office is closed.

The fax number is published on the Insolvency Service's website (*http://www.insolvency.gov.uk*) and is currently 020 7947 6607. The email address is rcjcompanies.orders@hmcourts-service-gsi.gov.uk. In Scotland, refer to the Courts website *http://www.scotcourts.gov.uk*. Note the requirement in r.2.19(4) that evidence be preserved in hard copy (in some detail) for filing in court on the first available day.

Rule 2.19(8) carries the implication that a floating charge holder should not use a notice by fax or email, rather than wait for the court office to open on a later date, without good reason. Absurdly, it is suggested that the good reason should relate to the interests of the company and/or its creditors, rather than that of the charge holder himself. However, it should not be beyond the wit of man to devise a formula sufficient to deter anyone minded to challenge the appointment.

CHAPTER 4

APPOINTMENT OF ADMINISTRATOR BY COMPANY OR DIRECTORS

2.20   Notice of intention to appoint

2.20(1)   **[Form of notice]** The notice of intention to appoint an administrator for the purposes of paragraph 26 shall be in Form 2.8B.

[FORM 2.8B]

2.20(2)   **[Copy of notice to be sent to]** A copy of the notice of intention to appoint must, in addition to the persons specified in paragraph 26, be given to–

    (a)   any enforcement officer who, to the knowledge of the person giving the notice, is charged with execution or other legal process against the company;

    (b)   any person who, to the knowledge of the person giving the notice, has distrained against the company or its property;

    (c)   any supervisor of a voluntary arrangement under Part I of the Act; and

    (d)   the company, if the company is not intending to make the appointment.

2.20(3)   **[Application of r.2.8(2)–(5) to notice]** The provisions of Rule 2.8(2) to 2.8(5) shall apply to the sending or giving of a notice under this Rule as they apply to the manner in which service of an administration application is effected under that Rule.

(See General Note after r.2.26.)

2.21   The statutory declaration on Form 2.8B shall be made not more than 5 business days before the notice is filed with the court.

(See General Note after r.2.26.)

2.22   The notice of intention to appoint shall be accompanied by either a copy of the resolution of the company to appoint an administrator (where the company intends to make the appointment) or a record of the decision of the directors (where the directors intend to make the appointment).

(See General Note after r.2.26.)

2.23 Notice of appointment

2.23(1) **[Form of notice]** The notice of appointment for the purposes of an appointment under paragraph 22 shall be in Form 2.9B or Form 2.10B, as appropriate.

[FORM 2.9B, FORM 2.10B]

2.23(2) **[Copy of notice to be filed and accompanied by]** The copies of the notice filed with the court shall be accompanied by–

(a) the administrator's written statement in Form 2.2B;

(b) the written consent of all those persons to whom notice was given in accordance with paragraph 26(1) unless the period of notice set out in paragraph 26(1) has expired; and

(c) a statement of the matters provided for in paragraph 100(2), where applicable.

(See General Note after r.2.26.)

2.24 The statutory declaration on Form 2.9B or Form 2.10B shall be made not more than 5 business days before the notice is filed with the court.

(See General Note after r.2.26.)

2.25 Where a notice of intention to appoint an administrator has not been given, the notice of appointment shall be accompanied by the documents specified in Rule 2.22 above.

(See General Note after r.2.26.)

2.26(1) **[Court to seal and endorse copies]** Three copies of the notice of appointment shall be filed with the court and shall have applied to them the seal of the court and be endorsed with the date and time of filing.

2.26(2) **[Court to issue copies to appointor]** The court shall issue two of the sealed copies of the notice of appointment to the person making the appointment who shall as soon as reasonably practicable send one of the sealed copies to the administrator.

GENERAL NOTE

These rules apply in the appointment of an administrator by a company or its directors out of court under paras 22 et seq.

It is not necessary that the company or directors should give notice of intention to appoint under para.26. If there is no person to whom such a notice needs to be sent, the appointment can be made directly (in which case there will be no moratorium), and the relevant form is Form 2.10B. Whether a notice of intention to appoint can be filed (so securing a brief moratorium) when there is no person entitled to the statutory notice is open to debate: see the note to para.26.

Form 2.8B contains material which is not relevant for the purposes of para.26, but only for para.27 and rr.2.21–2.22 when the copy notice is later filed in court. It is probably not necessary to complete anything other than paras 1 and 2 of the form in order to comply with para.26, but the whole form should no doubt be filled in where possible to avoid any dispute.

A second statutory declaration on Form 2.9B, in addition to that on Form 2.8B, is required, and it too must not be more than five business days old.

CHAPTER 5

PROCESS OF ADMINISTRATION

2.27 Notification and advertisement of administrator's appointment

2.27(1) **[Form of advertisement]** The notice of appointment to be given by the administrator as soon as reasonably practicable after appointment under paragraph 46(2)(b) shall be gazetted and may be advertised in such other manner as the administrator thinks fit.

2.27(1A)   **[Additional contents to r.2.27(1) notice]** In addition to the standard contents, the notice under paragraph (1) must state–

    (a)   that an administrator has been appointed,

    (b)   the date of the appointment, and

    (c)   the nature of the business of the company.

2.27(2)   **[To whom administrator to notify appointment]** The administrator shall, as soon as reasonably practicable after the date specified in paragraph 46(6), give notice of his appointment–

    (a)   if a receiver or an administrative receiver has been appointed, to him;

    (b)   if there is pending a petition for the winding up of the company, to the petitioner (and also to the provisional liquidator, if any);

    (c)   to any enforcement officer who, to the administrator's knowledge, is charged with execution or other legal process against the company;

    (d)   to any person who, to the administrator's knowledge, has distrained against the company or its property; and

    (e)   any supervisor of a voluntary arrangement under Part I of the Act.

2.27(3)   **[Form of notice]** Where, under a provision of Schedule B1 to the Act or these Rules, the administrator is required to send a notice of his appointment to any person other than the registrar of companies he shall do so in Form 2.12B.

[FORM 2.12B]

(See General Note after r.2.32.)

2.28   Notice requiring statement of affairs

2.28(1)   **["Relevant person"]** In this Chapter **"relevant person"** shall have the meaning given to it in paragraph 47(3).

2.28(2)   **[Form of notice]** The administrator shall send notice in Form 2.13B to each relevant person whom he determines appropriate requiring him to prepare and submit a statement of the company's affairs.

[FORM 2.13B]

2.28(3)   **[Content of notice]** The notice shall inform each of the relevant persons–

    (a)   of the names and addresses of all others (if any) to whom the same notice has been sent;

    (b)   of the time within which the statement must be delivered;

    (c)   of the effect of paragraph 48(4) (penalty for non-compliance); and

    (d)   of the application to him, and to each other relevant person, of section 235 (duty to provide information, and to attend on the administrator, if required).

2.28(4)   **[Forms for preparation of statement of affairs]** The administrator shall furnish each relevant person to whom he has sent notice in Form 2.13B with the forms required for the preparation of the statement of affairs.

(See General Note after r.2.32.)

2.29   Verification and filing

2.29(1)   [Form and verification] The statement of the company's affairs shall be in Form 2.14B, contain all the particulars required by that form and be verified by a statement of truth by the relevant person.

[FORM 2.14B]

2.29(2)   [Statement of concurrence] The administrator may require any relevant person to submit a statement of concurrence in Form 2.15B stating that he concurs in the statement of affairs. Where the administrator does so, he shall inform the person making the statement of affairs of that fact.

[FORM 2.15B]

2.29(3)   [Statement of affairs to administrator] The statement of affairs shall be delivered by the relevant person making the statement of truth, together with a copy, to the administrator. The relevant person shall also deliver a copy of the statement of affairs to all those persons whom the administrator has required to make a statement of concurrence.

2.29(4)   [Period for delivery of statement of concurrence] A person required to submit a statement of concurrence shall do so before the end of the period of 5 business days (or such other period as the administrator may agree) beginning with the day on which the statement of affairs being concurred with is received by him.

2.29(5)   [Qualification of statement of concurrence] A statement of concurrence may be qualified in respect of matters dealt with in the statement of affairs, where the maker of the statement of concurrence is not in agreement with the relevant person, or he considers the statement of affairs to be erroneous or misleading, or he is without the direct knowledge necessary for concurring with it.

2.29(6)   [Verification and delivery of statement of concurrence] Every statement of concurrence shall be verified by a statement of truth and be delivered to the administrator by the person who makes it, together with a copy of it.

2.29(7)   [Form of notice of statement of affairs] Subject to Rule 2.30 below, the administrator shall as soon as reasonably practicable send to the registrar of companies a copy of the statement of affairs and any statement of concurrence.

(See General Note after r.2.32.)

2.30   Limited disclosure

2.30(1)   [Administrator may apply to court] Where the administrator thinks that it would prejudice the conduct of the administration or might reasonably be expected to lead to violence against any person for the whole or part of the statement of the company's affairs to be disclosed, he may apply to the court for an order of limited disclosure in respect of the statement, or any specified part of it.

2.30(2)   [Powers of court] The court may, on such application, order that the statement or, as the case may be, the specified part of it, shall not be filed with the registrar of companies.

2.30(3)   [Delivery to registrar of companies] The administrator shall as soon as reasonably practicable send to the registrar of companies a copy of the order and the statement of affairs (to the extent provided by the order) and any statement of concurrence.

2.30(4)   [Application to court by creditor for disclosure] If a creditor seeks disclosure of a statement of affairs or a specified part of it in relation to which an order has been made under this Rule, he may apply to the court for an order that the administrator disclose it or a specified part of it. The application shall be supported by written evidence in the form of a witness statement.

2.30(5)   [Notice of application to administrator] The applicant shall give the administrator notice of his application at least 3 business days before the hearing.

2.30(6) **[Power of court to order disclosure]** The court may make any order for disclosure subject to any conditions as to confidentiality, duration, the scope of the order in the event of any change of circumstances, or other matters as it sees fit.

2.30(7) **[Material change in circumstances]** If there is a material change in circumstances rendering the limit on disclosure or any part of it unnecessary, the administrator shall, as soon as reasonably practicable after the change, apply to the court for the order or any part of it to be rescinded.

2.30(8) **[Filing notice of and statement of affairs]** The administrator shall, as soon as reasonably practicable after the making of an order under paragraph (7) above, file with the registrar of companies a copy of the statement of affairs to the extent provided by the order.

2.30(9) **[Copies of statement of affairs]** When the statement of affairs is filed in accordance with paragraph (8), the administrator shall, where he has sent a statement of proposals under paragraph 49, provide the creditors with a copy of the statement of affairs as filed, or a summary thereof.

2.30(10) **[CPR Pt 31 not to apply]** The provisions of Part 31 of the CPR shall not apply to an application under this Rule.

(See General Note after r.2.32.)

2.31   Release from duty to submit statement of affairs; extension of time

2.31(1) **[Exercise of powers]** The power of the administrator under paragraph 48(2) to give a release from the obligation imposed by paragraph 47(1), or to grant an extension of time, may be exercised at the administrator's own discretion, or at the request of any relevant person.

2.31(2) **[Application to court]** A relevant person may, if he requests a release or extension of time and it is refused by the administrator, apply to the court for it.

2.31(3) **[Powers of court]** The court may, if it thinks that no sufficient cause is shown for the application, dismiss it without a hearing but it shall not do so without giving the relevant person at least 5 business days' notice, upon receipt of which the relevant person may request the court to list the application for a without notice hearing. If the application is not dismissed the court shall fix a venue for it to be heard, and give notice to the relevant person accordingly.

2.31(4) **[Notice of hearing to administrator]** The relevant person shall, at least 14 days before the hearing, send to the administrator a notice stating the venue and accompanied by a copy of the application and of any evidence which he (the relevant person) intends to adduce in support of it.

2.31(5) **[Appearance etc. by liquidator]** The administrator may appear and be heard on the application and, whether or not he appears, he may file a written report of any matters which he considers ought to be drawn to the court's attention.

If such a report is filed, a copy of it shall be sent by the administrator to the relevant person, not later than 5 business days before the hearing.

2.31(6) **[Sealed copies of order]** Sealed copies of any order made on the application shall be sent by the court to the relevant person and the administrator.

2.31(7) **[Applicant's costs]** On any application under this Rule the relevant person's costs shall be paid in any event by him and, unless the court otherwise orders, no allowance towards them shall be made as an expense of the administration.

(See General Note after r.2.32.)

2.32   Expenses of statement of affairs

2.32(1) **[Payment of expenses]** A relevant person making the statement of the affairs of the company or statement of concurrence shall be allowed, and paid by the administrator as an expense of the administration, any expenses incurred by the relevant person in so doing which the administrator considers reasonable.

2.32(2) **[Appeal to court]** Any decision by the administrator under this Rule is subject to appeal to the court.

2.32(3) **[Effect of Rule]** Nothing in this Rule relieves a relevant person from any obligation with respect to the preparation, verification and submission of the statement of affairs, or to the provision of information to the administrator.

GENERAL NOTE TO RR.2.27–2.32

These and the succeeding rules in Pt 2 apply whether the administrator is appointed by the court or out of court. For the corresponding rules under the original regime, see rr.*2.11* et seq. Rule 2.27(1) substituted by I(A)R 2009 (SI 2009/642) r.8 as from April 6, 2009. Rules 2.27(1), (3), 2.29–2.32 amended and r.2.27(1A) inserted by I(A)R 2010 r.2 and Sch. paras 43–47 as from April 6, 2010.

On the standard contents for gazetted notices, see rr.12A.31–12A.33.

On the statement of affairs generally, see the note to para.47.

2.33 Administrator's proposals

2.33(1) **[Statement of administrator's proposals]** The administrator shall, under paragraph 49, make a statement which he shall send to the registrar of companies.

2.33(2) **[Contents of statement]** The statement shall include, in addition to those matters set out in paragraph 49–

  (a) details of the court where the proceedings are and the relevant court reference number;

  (b) the full name, registered address, registered number and any other trading names of the company;

  (c) details relating to his appointment as administrator, including the date of appointment and the person making the application or appointment and, where there are joint administrators, details of the matters set out in paragraph 100(2);

  (d) the names of the directors and secretary of the company and details of any shareholdings in the company they may have;

  (e) an account of the circumstances giving rise to the appointment of the administrator;

  (f) if a statement of the company's affairs has been submitted, a copy or summary of it, with the administrator's comments, if any;

  (g) if an order limiting the disclosure of the statement of affairs (under Rule 2.30) has been made, a statement of that fact, as well as–

    (i) details of who provided the statement of affairs;

    (ii) the date of the order of limited disclosure; and

    (iii) the details or a summary of the details that are not subject to that order;

  (h) if a full statement of affairs is not provided, the names, addresses and debts of the creditors including details of any security held;

  (j) if no statement of affairs has been submitted, details of the financial position of the company at the latest practicable date (which must, unless the court otherwise orders, be a date not earlier than that on which the company entered administration), a list of the company's creditors including their names, addresses and details of their debts, including any security held, and an explanation as to why there is no statement of affairs;

  (k) the basis upon which it is proposed that the administrator's remuneration should be fixed under Rule 2.106;

(ka) a statement complying with paragraph (2B) of any pre-administration costs charged or incurred by the administrator or, to the administrator's knowledge, by any other person qualified to act as an insolvency practitioner;

(l) (except where the administrator proposes a voluntary arrangement in relation to the company and subject to paragraph (3))–

    (i) to the best of the administrator's knowledge and belief–

        (aa) an estimate of the value of the prescribed part (whether or not he proposes to make an application to court under section 176A(5) or section 176A(3) applies); and

        (bb) an estimate of the value of the company's net property; and

    (ii) whether, and, if so, why, the administrator proposes to make an application to court under section 176A(5);

(m) a statement (which must comply with paragraph (2C) where that paragraph applies) of how it is envisaged the purpose of the administration will be achieved and how it is proposed that the administration shall end;

(n) where the administrator has decided not to call a meeting of creditors, his reasons;

(o) the manner in which the affairs and business of the company–

    (i) have, since the date of the administrator's appointment, been managed and financed, including, where any assets have been disposed of, the reasons for such disposals and the terms upon which such disposals were made; and

    (ii) will, if the administrator's proposals are approved, continue to be managed and financed;

(p) whether–

    (i) the EC Regulation applies; and

    (ii) if so, whether the proceedings are main proceedings, secondary proceedings or territorial proceedings; and

(q) such other information (if any) as the administrator thinks necessary to enable creditors to decide whether or not to vote for the adoption of the proposals.

2.33(2A)   **["Pre-administration costs", "unpaid pre-administration costs"]** In this Part–

(a) **"pre-administration costs"** are–

    (i) fees charged, and

    (ii) expenses incurred,

by the administrator, or another person qualified to act as an insolvency practitioner, before the company entered administration but with a view to its doing so; and

(b) **"unpaid pre-administration costs"** are pre-administration costs which had not been paid when the company entered administration.

2.33(2B)   **[Statement of pre-administration costs]** A statement of pre-administration costs complies with this paragraph if it includes–

(a) details of any agreement under which the fees were charged and expenses incurred, including the parties to the agreement and the date on which the agreement was made,

(b) details of the work done for which the fees were charged and expenses incurred,

(c)   an explanation of why the work was done before the company entered administration and how it would further the achievement of an objective in sub-paragraph (1) of paragraph (3) in accordance with sub-paragraphs (2) to (4) of that paragraph,

(d)   a statement of the amount of the pre-administration costs, setting out separately–

   (i)   the fees charged by the administrator,

   (ii)   the expenses incurred by the administrator,

   (iii) the fees charged (to the administrator's knowledge) by any other person qualified to act as an insolvency practitioner (and, if more than one, by each separately), and

   (iv) the expenses incurred (to the administrator's knowledge) by any other person qualified to act as an insolvency practitioner (and, if more than one, by each separately),

(e)   a statement of the amounts of pre-administration costs which have already been paid (set out separately as under sub-paragraph (d),

(f)   the identity of the person who made the payment or, if more than one person made the payment, the identity of each such person and of the amounts paid by each such person set out separately as under sub-paragraph (d),

(g)   a statement of the amounts of unpaid pre-administration costs (set out separately as under sub-paragraph (d)), and

(h)   a statement that the payment of unpaid pre-administration costs as an expense of the administration is–

   (i)   subject to approval under Rule 2.67A, and

   (ii)   not part of the proposals subject to approval under paragraph 53.

2.33(2C)   [Rule 2.33(2)(m) statement where administration to move to CVL] This paragraph applies where it is proposed that the administration will end by the company moving to a creditors' voluntary liquidation; and in that case, the statement required by paragraph (2)(m) must include–

(a)   details of the proposed liquidator;

(b)   where applicable, the declaration required by section 231; and

(c)   a statement that the creditors may, before the proposals are approved, nominate a different person as liquidator in accordance with paragraph 83(7)(a) and Rule 2.117A(2)(b).

2.33(3)   [Non-disclosure of information prejudicial to company's interests] Nothing in paragraph (2) (l) is to be taken as requiring any such estimate to include any information, the disclosure of which could seriously prejudice the commercial interests of the company. If such information is excluded from the calculation the estimate shall be accompanied by a statement to that effect.

2.33(4)   [Notification of extension of time for proposals] Where the court orders, upon an application by the administrator under paragraph 107, an extension of the period of time in paragraph 49(5), the administrator must as soon as reasonably practicable after the making of the order–

(a)   notify in Form 2.18B every creditor of the company and every member of the company of whose address (in either case) the administrator is aware, and

(b)   send a copy of the notification to the registrar of companies.

[FORM 2.18B]

2.33(5)   [Proposals deemed approved] Where the administrator has made a statement under paragraph 52(1) and has not called an initial meeting of creditors, the proposals sent out under this Rule and paragraph 49 will (if no meeting has been requisitioned under paragraph 52(2) within the period set out in Rule 2.37 (1)) be deemed to have been approved by the creditors.

2.33(5A)   **[Notice of deemed approval of proposals]** Where proposals are deemed under paragraph (5) to have been approved, the administrator. must, as soon as reasonably practicable after expiry of the period set out in Rule 2.37(1), give notice of the date on which they were deemed to have been approved to the registrar of companies, the court and the creditors; and a copy of the proposals must be attached to the notice given to the court and to creditors who have not previously received them.

2.33(6)   **[Notice where application for administration to cease]** Where the administrator intends to apply to the court (or file a notice under paragraph 80(2)) for the administration to cease at a time before he has sent a statement of his proposals to creditors in accordance with paragraph 49, he shall, at least 7 business days before he makes such an application (or files such a notice), send to all creditors of the company (so far as he is aware of their addresses) a report containing the information required by paragraphs (2)(a)–(p) of this Rule.

2.33(7)   **[Advertisement of notice for copy of statement of proposals]** Where the administrator wishes to publish a notice under paragraph 49(6), the notice shall be advertised in such manner as the administrator thinks fit.

2.33(7A)   **[Additional contents in r.2.33(7) notice]** In addition to the standard contents, the notice under paragraph (7) must state–

(a)   that members can write for a copy of the statement of proposals for achieving the purpose of administration; and

(b)   the address to which to write.

2.33(8)   **[Time limit for publication of notice]** This notice must be published as soon as reasonably practicable after the administrator sends his statement of proposals to the company's creditors but no later than 8 weeks (or such other period as may be agreed by the creditors or as the court may order) from the date that the company entered administration.

GENERAL NOTE

This rule applies to all administrations under Sch.B1, however initiated. The legislators have embraced the philosophy of disclosure with both hands! At least they have provided administrators with a comprehensive check-list.

R.2.33(2)(j)
It does not appear that the administrator has any discretion not to require a statement of affairs to be submitted (see para.47(1)), but this paragraph could apply if no statement of affairs has been submitted at the time when the proposals are sent out, and conceivably also where nobody formerly connected with the company can be traced.

R.2.33(2)(ka)
Rule 2.33(2)(ka) inserted by I(A)R 2010 r.2 and Sch. para.48(3)(a) as from April 6, 2010.

R.2.33(2)(m)
Rule 2.33(2)(m) amended by I(A)R 2010 r.2 and Sch. para.48(3)(b) as from April 6, 2010.

R.2.33(2)(p)
Rule 2.33(2)(p) amended by I(A)R 2010 r.2 and Sch. para.48(3)(c) as from April 6, 2010.
    On this issue, see the note to art.3 of the Regulation.

R.2.33(2A)–(2C)
Rule 2.33(2A)–(2C) inserted by I(A)R 2010 r.2 and Sch. para.48(4) as from April 6, 2010. These amendments make provision for an administrator (or another qualified insolvency practitioner) to be able to recover remuneration charged and expenses incurred before the formal start of the administration—an innovation which will be of particular importance and value in pre-pack administrations.

R.2.33(4)
Rule 2.33(4) amended by I(A)R 2010 r.2 and Sch. para.48(5) as from April 6, 2010.

R.2.33(5A)
Rule 2.33(5A) inserted by I(A)R 2010 r.2 and Sch. para.48(6) as from April 6, 2010.

R.2.33(6)

Where the company is hopelessly insolvent or has assets which will all go to paying off its secured creditors—or, on the other hand, where it is clear that there are sufficient assets for all the creditors to be paid in full—there is little point in going through with the full statutory routine. In these circumstances, the administrator may be able to sign off at an early stage.

R.2.33(7), (7A)

Rule 2.33(7A) substituted by I(A)R 2010 r.2 and Sch. para.48(6) as from April 6, 2010. Previously r.2.33(7) substituted, and r.2.33(7A) inserted, by I(A)R 2009 (SI 2009/642) r.9 as from April 6, 2009. On the standard contents (for notices other than gazetted notices), see rr.12A.36–12A.39.

2.33A   Limited disclosure of para 49 statement

2.33A(1)   [Application by administrator re creditors] Where the administrator thinks that it would prejudice the conduct of the administration or might reasonably be expected to lead to violence against any person for any of the matters specified in Rule 2.33(2)(h) and (j) to be disclosed, the administrator may apply to the court for an order of limited disclosure in respect of any specified part of the statement under paragraph 49.

2.33A(2)   [Power of court] The court may, on such application, order that some or all of the specified part of the statement must not be sent to the registrar of companies or to creditors or members of the company as otherwise required by paragraph 49(4).

2.33A(3)   [Administrator's duty to send statement] The administrator must as soon as reasonably practicable send to the persons specified in paragraph 49(4) the statement under paragraph 49 (to the extent provided by the order) and an indication of the nature of the matter in relation to which the order was made.

2.33A(4)   [Copy to registrar] The administrator must also send a copy of the order to the registrar of companies.

2.33A(5)   [Application for disclosure by creditor] A creditor who seeks disclosure of a part of a statement under paragraph 49 in relation to which an order has been made under this Rule may apply to the court for an order that the administrator disclose it. The application must be supported by written evidence in the form of a witness statement.

2.33A(6)   [Notice to administrator by applicant] The applicant must give the administrator notice of the application at least 3 business days before the hearing.

2.33A(7)   [Court order] The court may make any order for disclosure subject to any conditions as to confidentiality, duration, the scope of the order in the event of any change of circumstances, or other matters as it sees just.

2.33A(8)   [Change in circumstances: rescission of limitation order] If there is a material change in circumstances rendering the limit on disclosure or any part of it unnecessary, the administrator must, as soon as reasonably practicable after the change, apply to the court for the order or any part of it to be rescinded.

2.33A(9)   [Copy of amended statement] The administrator must, as soon as reasonably practicable after the making of an order under paragraph (8), send to the persons specified in paragraph 49(4) a copy of the statement under paragraph 49 to the extent provided by the order.

2.33A(10)   [Non-application of CPR Pt 31] The provisions of CPR Part 31 do not apply to an application under this Rule.

GENERAL NOTE

Rule 2.33A inserted by I(A)R 2010 r.2 and Sch. para.49 as from April 6, 2010. The 2010 amendments have removed discrepancies in the former rules between the various provisions on limiting the public disclosure of information, so that the same principles are now applied uniformly to all types of insolvency proceedings. On an application by the administrator on the grounds stated in r.2.33A(1), the court may order that information about creditors and the financial position of the company may be omitted from what is filed at Companies House, sent to creditors generally or otherwise given publicity; and a creditor who objects to an order under this rule may apply to the court for an order directing that the information should be disclosed.

CHAPTER 6

MEETINGS AND REPORTS

Section A: Creditors' meetings

2.34 Meetings to consider administrator's proposals

2.34(1)   [Gazetting after notice of initial creditor' meeting] As soon as reasonably practicable after an invitation to the initial creditors' meeting has been sent to the creditors in compliance with the requirements of paragraph 51(1), the administrator must have gazetted a notice which, in addition to the standard contents, must state–

(a)   that an initial creditors' meeting is to take place; and

(b)   the venue fixed for the meeting.

2.34(1A)   [Advertisement of r.2.34(1) information] The information required to be gazetted under paragraph (1) may also be advertised in such other manner as the administrator thinks fit.

2.34(2)   [Notice to directors etc.] Notice in Form 2.19B to attend the meeting shall be sent out at the same time to any directors or officers of the company (including persons who have been directors or officers in the past) whose presence at the meeting is, in the administrator's opinion, required.

[FORM 2.19B]

2.34(3)   [Notice where period for initial meeting extended] Where the court orders an extension to the period set out in paragraph 51(2)(b) the administrator shall send a notice in Form 2.18B to each person to whom he is required to send notice by paragraph 49(4).

2.34(4)   [Adjournment of meeting] If at the meeting there is not the requisite majority for approval of the administrator's proposals (with modifications, if any), the chairman may, and shall if a resolution is passed to that effect, adjourn the meeting for not more than 14 days (subject to any direction by the court).

2.34(5)   [Final adjournment] If there are subsequently further adjournments, the final adjournment must not be to a day later than 14 days after the date on which the meeting was originally held, subject to any direction of the court.

2.34(6)   [Lodging proofs and proxies for adjourned meeting] Where a meeting is adjourned under this Rule, proofs and proxies may be used if lodged at any time up to 12.00 hours on the business day immediately before the adjourned meeting.

(See General Note after r.2.44A.)

2.35 Creditors' meetings generally

2.35(1)   [Application of r.2.35] This Rule applies to creditors' meetings summoned by the administrator under–

(a)   paragraph 51 (initial creditors' meeting);

(b)   paragraph 52(2) (at the request of the creditors);

(c)   paragraph 54(2) (to consider revision to the administrator's proposals);

(d)   paragraph 56(1) (further creditors' meetings); and

(e)   paragraph 62 (general power to summon meetings of creditors).

2.35(2)   [Form of notice] Notice of any of the meetings set out in paragraph (1) above shall be in Form 2.20B.

[FORM 2.20B]

2.35(3)   [Convenience of venue] In fixing the venue for the meeting, the administrator shall have regard to the convenience of creditors and the meeting shall be summoned for commencement between 10.00 and 16.00 hours on a business day, unless the court otherwise directs.

2.35(4)   [Period of notice] Subject to paragraphs (6) and (7) below, at least 14 days' notice of the meeting shall be given to all creditors who are known to the administrator and had claims against the company at the date when the company entered administration unless that creditor has subsequently been paid in full; and the notice shall–

(a)   specify the purpose of the meeting;

(b)   contain a statement of the effect of Rule 2.38 (entitlement to vote); and

(c)   contain the forms of proxy.

[FORM 8.2]

2.35(4A)   [Gazetting of notice with additional contents] As soon as reasonably practicable after notice of the meeting has been given, the administrator must have gazetted a notice which, in addition to the standard contents, must state–

(a)   that a creditors' meeting is to take place;

(b)   the venue fixed for the meeting;

(c)   the purpose of the meeting; and

(d)   a statement of the effect of Rule 2.38 (entitlement to vote).

2.35(5)   [Adjournment where no chairman] If within 30 minutes from the time fixed for commencement of the meeting there is no person present to act as chairman, the meeting stands adjourned to the same time and place in the following week or, if that is not a business day, to the business day immediately following.

2.35(6)   [Omitted.]

2.35(6A)   [Adjournment where no quorum] If within 30 minutes from the time fixed for the commencement of the meeting those persons attending the meeting do not constitute a quorum, the chairman may adjourn the meeting to such time and place as the chairman may appoint.

2.35(6B)   [Single suspension without adjournment] Once only in the course of the meeting the chairman may, without an adjournment, declare the meeting suspended for any period up to 1 hour.

2.35(6C)   [Power to adjourn] The chairman may, and must if the meeting so resolves, adjourn the meeting to such time and place as seems to the chairman to be appropriate in the circumstances.

An adjournment under this paragraph must not be for a period of more than 14 days, subject to the direction of the court.

2.35(6D)   [Final adjournment] If there are subsequently further adjournments, the final adjournment must not be to a day later than 14 days after the date on which the meeting was originally held.

2.35(6E)   [Lodging proofs and proxies for adjourned meeting] Where a meeting is adjourned under this Rule, proofs and proxies may be used if lodged at any time up to 12.00 hours on the business day immediately before the adjourned meeting.

2.35(6F)   **[Application of r.2.35(3) to adjourned meeting]** Paragraph (3) applies with regard to the venue fixed for a meeting adjourned under this Rule.

2.35(7)   [Omitted.]

(See General Note after r.2.44A.)

2.36   The chairman at meetings

2.36(1)   **[Administrator or his nominee to be chairman]** At any meeting of creditors summoned by the administrator, either he shall be chairman, or a person nominated by him in writing to act in his place.

2.36(2)   **[Nominee chairman]** A person so nominated must be either–

     (a)   one who is qualified to act as an insolvency practitioner in relation to the company; or

     (b)   an employee of the administrator or his firm who is experienced in insolvency matters.

2.36(3)   **[Special proxy for resolution not proposed]** Where the chairman holds a proxy which includes a requirement to vote for a particular resolution and no other person proposes that resolution–

     (a)   the chairman must propose it unless the chairman considers that there is good reason for not doing so, and

     (b)   if the chairman does not propose it, the chairman must as soon as reasonably practicable after the meeting notify the principal of the reason why not.

(See General Note after r.2.44A.)

2.37   Meeting requisitioned by creditors

2.37(1)   **[Form of request]** The request for a creditors' meeting under paragraph 52(2) or 56(1) shall be in Form 2.21B. A request for an initial creditors' meeting shall be made within 8 business days of the date on which the administrator's statement of proposals is sent out. A request under paragraph 52(2) or 56(1) shall include–

                                                           [FORM 2.21B]

     (a)   a list of the creditors concurring with the request, showing the amounts of their respective debts in the administration;

     (b)   from each creditor concurring, written confirmation of his concurrence; and

     (c)   a statement of the purpose of the proposed meeting,

but sub-paragraphs (a) and (b) do not apply if the requisitioning creditor's debt is alone sufficient without the concurrence of other creditors.

2.37(2)   **[Period for meeting to be held]** A meeting requested under paragraph 52(2) or 56(1) shall be held within 28 days of the administrator's receipt of the notice requesting the meeting.

2.37(3)   **[Expenses]** The expenses of summoning and holding a meeting at the request of a creditor shall be paid by that person, who shall deposit with the administrator security for their payment.

2.37(4)   **[Deposit as security for expenses]** The sum to be deposited shall be such as the administrator may determine, and he shall not act without the deposit having been made.

2.37(5)   **[Resolution of meeting re expenses]** The meeting may resolve that the expenses of summoning and holding it are to be payable out of the assets of the company as an expense of the administration.

2.37(6) **[Repayment of deposit]** To the extent that any deposit made under this Rule is not required for the payment of expenses of summoning and holding the meeting, it shall be repaid to the person who made it.

(See General Note after r.2.44A.)

2.37A   Notice of meetings by advertisement only

2.37A(1) **[Power of court to order]** The court may order that notice of any meeting be given by advertisement and not by individual notice to the persons concerned.

2.37A(2) **[Matters court to consider]** In considering whether to act under this Rule, the court must have regard to the cost of advertisement, the amount of assets available and the extent of the interest of creditors, members or any particular class of either.

(See General Note after r.2.44A.)

2.38   Entitlement to vote

2.38(1) **[Conditions for voting]** Subject as follows, at a meeting of creditors in administration proceedings a person is entitled to vote only if–

  (a) he has given to the administrator, not later than 12.00 hours on the business day before the day fixed for the meeting, details in writing of the debt which–

      (i) he claims to be due to him from the company; or

      (ii) in relation to a member State liquidator, is claimed to be due to creditors in proceedings in relation to which he holds office;

  (b) the claim has been duly admitted under Rule 2.39 or this Rule; and

  (c) there has been lodged with the administrator any proxy which he intends to be used on his behalf,

and details of the debt must include any calculation for the purposes of Rules 2.40 to 2.42.

2.38(2) **[Voting despite failure to comply with r.2.38(1)(a)]** The chairman of the meeting may allow a creditor to vote, notwithstanding that he has failed to comply with paragraph (1)(a), if satisfied that the failure was due to circumstances beyond the creditor's control.

2.38(3) **[Call for documents to substantiate claim]** The chairman of the meeting may call for any document or other evidence to be produced to him, where he thinks it necessary for the purpose of substantiating the whole or any part of the claim.

2.38(4) **[Calculation of votes]** Votes are calculated according to the amount of a creditor's claim as at the date on which the company entered administration, less any payments that have been made to him after that date in respect of his claim and any adjustment by way of set-off in accordance with Rule 2.85 as if that Rule were applied on the date that the votes are counted.

2.38(5) **[Unliquidated debts]** A creditor shall not vote in respect of a debt for an unliquidated amount, or any debt whose value is not ascertained, except where the chairman agrees to put upon the debt an estimated minimum value for the purpose of entitlement to vote and admits the claim for that purpose.

2.38(6) **[Votes cast only once]** No vote shall be cast by virtue of a claim more than once on any resolution put to the meeting.

2.38(7) **[Creditor's vote priority over member State liquidator]** Where–

  (a) a creditor is entitled to vote under this Rule and Rule 2.39;

  (b) has lodged his claim in one or more sets of other proceedings; and

  (c) votes (either in person or by proxy) on a resolution put to the meeting; and

(d)   the member State liquidator casts a vote in respect of the same claim,

only the creditor's vote shall be counted.

2.38(8)   [Voting in more than one set of proceedings] Where–

(a)   a creditor has lodged his claim in more than one set of other proceedings; and

(b)   more than one member State liquidator seeks to vote by virtue of that claim,

the entitlement to vote by virtue of that claim is exercisable by the member State liquidator in main proceedings, whether or not the creditor has lodged his claim in the main proceedings.

2.38(9)   [Creditor and member State liquidator single claim] For the purposes of paragraph (6), the claim of a creditor and of any member State liquidator in relation to the same debt are a single claim.

2.38(10)   ["Other proceedings"] For the purposes of paragraphs (7) and (8), **"other proceedings"** means main proceedings, secondary proceedings or territorial proceedings in another member State.

(See General Note after r.2.44A.)

2.39   Admission and rejection of claims

2.39(1)   [Power of chairman] At any creditors' meeting the chairman has power to admit or reject a creditor's claim for the purpose of his entitlement to vote; and the power is exercisable with respect to the whole or any part of the claim.

2.39(2)   [Appeal from chairman's decision] The chairman's decision under this Rule, or in respect of any matter arising under Rule 2.38, is subject to appeal to the court by any creditor.

2.39(3)   [Doubtful claim vote admitted marked objected to] If the chairman is in doubt whether a claim should be admitted or rejected, he shall mark it as objected to and allow the creditor to vote, subject to his vote being subsequently declared invalid if the objection to the claim is sustained.

2.39(4)   [If chairman's decision reversed etc.] If on an appeal the chairman's decision is reversed or varied, or a creditor's vote is declared invalid, the court may order that another meeting be summoned, or make such other order as it thinks just.

2.39(5)   [Time limit for appeal] An application to the court by way of appeal under this Rule against a decision of the chairman must be made not later than 21 days after the date of the meeting.

2.39(6)   [Costs of appeal] Neither the administrator nor any person nominated by him to be chairman is personally liable for costs incurred by any person in respect of an appeal to the court under this Rule, unless the court makes an order to that effect.

(See General Note after r.2.44A.)

2.40   Secured creditors

2.40(1)   [Voting entitlement on balance of debt] At a meeting of creditors a secured creditor is entitled to vote only in respect of the balance (if any) of his debt after deducting the value of his security as estimated by him.

2.40(2)   [Voting entitlement for full value of debt] However, in a case where the administrator has made a statement under paragraph 52(1)(b) and an initial creditors' meeting has been requisitioned under paragraph 52(2) then a secured creditor is entitled to vote in respect of the full value of his debt without any deduction of the value of his security.

(See General Note after r.2.44A.)

2.41   Holders of negotiable instruments

2.41   A creditor shall not vote in respect of a debt on, or secured by, a current bill of exchange or promissory note, unless he is willing–

(a)   to treat the liability to him on the bill or note of every person who is liable on it antecedently to the company, and against whom a bankruptcy order has not been made (or, in the case of a company, which has not gone into liquidation), as a security in his hands; and

(b)   to estimate the value of the security and, for the purpose of his entitlement to vote (but not for dividend), to deduct it from his claim.

(See General Note after r.2.44A.)

2.42   Hire-purchase, conditional sale and chattel leasing agreements

2.42(1)   [Entitlement to vote] Subject as follows, an owner of goods under a hire-purchase or chattel leasing agreement, or a seller of goods under a conditional sale agreement, is entitled to vote in respect of the amount of the debt due and payable to him by the company on the date that the company entered administration.

2.42(2)   [Calculating amount of debt] In calculating the amount of any debt for this purpose, no account shall be taken of any amount attributable to the exercise of any right under the relevant agreement, so far as the right has become exercisable solely by virtue of the making of an administration application, a notice of intention to appoint an administrator or any matter arising as a consequence, or of the company entering administration.

(See General Note after r.2.44A.)

2.43   Resolutions

2.43(1)   [Resolution passed by majority in value] Subject to paragraph (2), at a creditors' meeting in administration proceedings, a resolution is passed when a majority (in value) of those present and voting, in person or by proxy, have voted in favour of it.

2.43(2)   [Resolution invalid] Any resolution is invalid if those voting against it include more than half in value of the creditors to whom notice of the meeting was sent and who are not, to the best of the chairman's belief, persons connected with the company.

(See General Note after r.2.44A.)

2.44   Minutes [Deleted by I(A)R 2010 r.2 and Sch. para.58 as from April 6, 2010.]

2.44A   Minutes

2.44A(1)   [Duty of chairman] The chairman of the meeting must cause minutes of its proceedings to be kept.

2.44A(2)   [Authentication and retention by chairman] The minutes must be authenticated by the chairman, and be retained by the chairman as part of the records of the administration.

2.44A(3)   [List of attendees] The chairman must also cause to be made up and kept a list of all the creditors who attended the meeting.

2.44A(4)   [Contents] The minutes must include–

(a)   a list of the names of creditors who attended (personally or by proxy) and their claims,

(b)   if a creditors' committee has been established, the names and addresses of those elected to be members of the committee, and

(c)   a record of every resolution passed.

The corresponding rules which apply in the original regime are rr.*2.18* et seq.

On the meaning of "debt", see r.13.12(5).

Rules 2.34–2.41 amended, rr.2.34(5), (6), 2.35(4A), (6A)–(6F), 2.36(3), 2.37A inserted, r.2.39(5) substituted and r.2.35(6), (7) omitted by I(A)R 2010 r.2 and Sch. paras 50–57; r.2.44A substituted for r.2.44 by r.2 and Sch. para.58 as from April 6, 2010. Previously r.2.34(1) substituted, and r.2.34(1A) inserted, by I(A)R 2009 (SI 2009/642) r.10 as from April 6, 2009.

R.2.34
On the standard contents for gazetted notices, see rr.12A.31–12A.33.

R.2.35
Although this rule refers only to meetings summoned under the five provisions referred to, para.50 defines "creditors' meeting" for the all the purposes of Sch.B1 as a meeting of creditors summoned "in the prescribed manner" and giving "the prescribed period of notice". It would therefore be prudent to follow the procedure set out in this paragraph for any other creditors' meeting. The requirement for gazetting (para.(4A)) and the more detailed provisions governing adjournments (paras (6A)–(6F)) were introduced by the 2010 amendments. On the standard contents for gazetted notices, see rr.12A.31–12A.33.

R.2.37
The requisitioning creditor or creditors must have debts amounting to at least 10 per cent of the total debts of the company (para.52(2)).

R.2.38(5)
On the meaning of "agrees", see the note to r.1.17(3), but note that there is here no equivalent to r.1.17(3) fixing a sum of £1 in the absence of an agreement by the chairman to fix a higher value. Cf. *Re Newlands (Seaford) Educational Trust* [2006] EWHC 1511 (Ch); [2006] B.P.I.R. 1231.

R.2.38(7)–(10)
On voting by a Member State liquidator, see the note to r.*2.29*.

R.2.40(2)
A secured creditor may vote for the amount of his secured debt only where there is insufficient property to enable a distribution to be made to unsecured creditors (apart from the "prescribed part"): see para.52(1)(b).

2.45   Revision of the administrator's proposals

2.45(1)   [Statement of proposed revised proposals] The administrator shall, under paragraph 54, make a statement setting out the proposed revisions to his proposals which he shall attach to Form 2.22B and send to all those to whom he is required to send a copy of his revised proposals.

[FORM 2.22B]

2.45(2)   [Contents of statement] The statement of revised proposals shall include–

(a)   details of the court where the proceedings are and the relevant court reference number;

(b)   the full name, registered address, registered number and any other trading names of the company;

(c)   details relating to his appointment as administrator, including the date of appointment and the person making the administration application or appointment;

(d)   the names of the directors and secretary of the company and details of any shareholdings in the company they may have;

(e)   a summary of the initial proposals and the reason(s) for proposing a revision;

(f)   details of the proposed revision including details of the administrator's assessment of the likely impact of the proposed revision upon creditors generally or upon each class of creditors (as the case may be);

(g)   where a proposed revision relates to the ending of the administration by a creditors' voluntary liquidation and the nomination of a person to be the proposed liquidator of the company,

(i)   details of the proposed liquidator,

(ii)   where applicable, the declaration required by section 231, and

(iii)   a statement that the creditors may, before the proposals are approved,

nominate a different person as liquidator in accordance with paragraph 83(7)(a) and Rule 2.117A(2)(b); and

(h)   any other information that the administrator thinks necessary to enable creditors to decide whether or not to vote for the proposed revisions.

2.45(3)   [Copy of statement to members] Subject to paragraph 54(3), within 5 business days of sending out the statement in paragraph (1) above, the administrator shall send a copy of the statement to every member of the company.

2.45(4)   [Advertisement of notice of revised proposals] Any notice to be published by the administrator acting under paragraph 54(3) shall be advertised in such manner as the administrator thinks fit.

2.45(5)   [Publication and additional contents of notice] The notice must be published as soon as reasonably practicable after the administrator sends the statement to the creditors and in addition to the standard contents must state–

(a)   that members can write for a copy of the statement of revised proposals for the administration; and

(b)   the address to which to write.

GENERAL NOTE

See para.54. There is no equivalent provision in the rules governing the original regime; but the notes to s.25 may be relevant. Rule 2.45(2)(g) and 2.45(4) amended and r.2.45(5) inserted by I(A)R 2010 r.2 and Sch. para.59 as from April 6, 2010. Previously r.2.45(4) amended by I(A)R 2009 (SI 2009/642) r.11 as from April 6, 2009.

On the standard contents (for notices other than gazetted notices), see rr.12A.36–12A.39.

2.46   Notice to creditors

2.46   As soon as reasonably practicable after the conclusion of a meeting of creditors to consider the administrator's proposals or revised proposals, the administrator shall–

(a)   send notice in Form 2.23B of the result of the meeting to every creditor and to every other person who received a copy of the original proposals,

(b)   attach a copy of the proposals considered at the meeting to the notice sent to each creditor who did not receive notice of the meeting but of whose claim the administrator has subsequently become aware, and

(c)   file with the court a copy of the proposals considered at the meeting and notice of the result of the meeting.

(See General Note after r.2.47.)

2.47   Reports to creditors

2.47(1)   ["Progress report"] "Progress report" means a report which includes–

(a)   details of the court where the proceedings are and the relevant court reference number;

(b)   full details of the company's name, address of registered office and registered number;

(c) full details of the administrator's name and address, date of appointment and name and address of appointor, including any changes in office-holder, and, in the case of joint administrators, their functions as set out in the statement made for the purposes of paragraph 100(2);

(d) details of any extensions to the initial period of appointment;

(da) details of the basis fixed for the remuneration of the administrator under Rule 2.106 (or if not fixed at the date of the report, the steps taken during the period of the report to fix it);

(db) if the basis of remuneration has been fixed, a statement of–

    (i) the remuneration charged by the administrator during the period of the report (subject to paragraph (2A)), and

    (ii) where the report is the first to be made after the basis has been fixed, the remuneration charged by the administrator during the periods covered by the previous reports (subject to paragraph (2A)), together with a description of the things done by the administrator during those periods in respect of which the remuneration was charged,

irrespective in either case of whether payment was made in respect of that remuneration during the period of the report;

(dc) a statement of the expenses incurred by the administrator during the period of the report, irrespective of whether payment was made in respect of them during that period;

(e) details of progress during the period of the report, including a receipts and payments account (as detailed in paragraph (2) below);

(f) details of any assets that remain to be realised;

(fa) a statement of the creditors' right to request information under Rule 2.48A and their right to challenge the administrator's remuneration and expenses under Rule 2.109; and

(g) any other relevant information for the creditors.

2.47(2) **[Receipts and payments account]** A receipts and payments account must be in the form of an abstract showing receipts and payments during the period of the report and, where the administrator has ceased to act, must also include a statement as to the amount paid to unsecured creditors by virtue of the application of section 176A.

2.47(2A) **[Basis of remuneration a set amount under r.2.106(2)(c)]** Where the basis for the remuneration is a set amount under Rule 2.106(2)(c), it may be shown as that amount without any apportionment to the period of the report.

2.47(2B) **[Where statement of pre-administration costs under r.2.33(2)(ka)]** Where the administrator has made a statement of pre-administration costs under Rule 2.33(2)(ka)–

(a) if they are approved under Rule 2.67A, the first progress report after the approval must include a statement setting out the date of the approval and the amounts approved;

(b) each successive report, so long as any of the costs remain unapproved, must include a statement either–

    (i) of any steps taken to get approval, or

    (ii) that the administrator has decided, or (as the case may be) another insolvency practitioner entitled to seek approval has told the administrator of that practitioner's decision, not to seek approval.

2.47(3) **[Period of progress report]** The progress report must, except where paragraph (3A) or (3B) applies, cover the period of 6 months commencing on the date on which the company entered administration and every subsequent period of 6 months.

2.47(3A) **[Period to end when administrator ceases to act]** The period to be covered by a progress report ends on the date when an administrator ceases to act, and the period to be covered by each subsequent progress report is each successive period of 6 months beginning immediately after that date (subject to the further application of this paragraph when another administrator ceases to act).

2.47(3B) **[Progress report where extension of administration]** The sending of a progress report to creditors under Rule 2.112 (application for extension of administration) also satisfies paragraph (3) or (3A) of this Rule in respect of the period covered by that report; and the period to be covered by each subsequent progress report under this Rule is each successive period of 6 months beginning with the end of the period covered by the report under Rule 2.112.

2.47(4) **[Copy of progress report to creditors and registrar; not final report]** The administrator must, within 1 month of the end of the period covered by the report, send–

(a) a copy to the creditors attached to Form 2.24B, and

(b) a copy to the registrar of companies;

but this paragraph does not apply when the period covered by the report is that of a final progress report under Rule 2.110.

2.47(5) **[Extension of period to send copies]** The court may, on the administrator's application, extend the period of 1 month mentioned in paragraph (4) above, or make such other order in respect of the content of the report as it thinks fit.

2.47(6) **[Criminal liability of administrator in default of r.2.47]** If the administrator makes default in complying with this Rule, he is liable to a fine and, for continued contravention, to a daily default fine.

GENERAL NOTE TO RR.2.46–2.47

The corresponding rules under the original regime are rr.*2.29–2.30.*

Rule 2.46 amended by I(A)R 2010 r.2 and Sch. para.60 as from April 6, 2010. Rule 2.47(2), (3), (4) amended and r.2.47(1)(da), (2A)–(2C), (3A), (3B), (4) inserted by I(A)R 2010 r.2 and Sch. para.61 as from April 6, 2010. The new paras 2.47(2A)–(2C) require more detailed disclosure relating to the administrator's remuneration and any pre-administration costs, and paras 2.47(3A), (3B) spell out more specifically the required timing of the administrator's progress reports.

2.48 Correspondence instead of creditors' meetings

2.48(1) **[Form of notice for correspondence]** The administrator may seek to obtain the passing of a resolution by the creditors by sending a notice in Form 2.25B to every creditor who is entitled to be notified of a creditors' meeting under Rule 2.35(4).

[FORM 2.25B]

2.48(2) **[Conditions for voting entitlement]** In order to be counted, votes must be received by the administrator by 12.00 hours on the closing date specified on Form 2.25B and must be accompanied by the statement in writing on entitlement to vote required by Rule 2.38 unless it has already been given to the administrator under that Rule.

2.48(3) **[When votes to be disregarded]** If any votes are received without the statement as to entitlement, or the administrator decides that the creditor is not entitled to vote according to Rules 2.38 and 2.39, then that creditor's votes shall be disregarded.

2.48(4) **[Closing date for votes]** The closing date shall be set at the discretion of the administrator. In any event it must not be set less than 14 days from the date of issue of the Form 2.25B.

2.48(5) **[Condition for business to be transacted]** For any business to be transacted the administrator must receive at least 1 valid Form 2.25B by the closing date specified by him.

2.48(6) **[Administrator to call creditors' meeting if condition unsatisfied]** If no valid Form 2.25B is received by the closing date specified then the administrator shall call a meeting of the creditors in accordance with Rule 2.35.

2.48(7) **[Requisition of creditors' meeting]** Any single creditor, or a group of creditors, of the company whose debt(s) amount to at least 10% of the total debts of the company may, within 5 business days from the date of the administrator sending out a resolution or proposals, require him to summon a meeting of creditors to consider the matters raised therein in accordance with Rule 2.37. Any meeting called under this Rule shall be conducted in accordance with Rule 2.35.

2.48(8) [Omitted.]

2.48(9) **[Requirement for creditors' meeting to include course of correspondence]** A reference in these Rules to anything done, or required to be done, at, or in connection with, or in consequence of, a creditors' meeting includes a reference to anything done in the course of correspondence in accordance with this Rule.

2.48A   Creditors' request for further information

2.48A(1) **[Duty of administrator]** If–

   (a)   within 21 days of receipt of a progress report under Rule 2.47–

      (i)   a secured creditor, or

      (ii)   an unsecured creditor with the concurrence of at least 5% in value of the unsecured creditors (including the creditor in question), or

   (b)   with the permission of the court upon an application made within that period of 21 days, any unsecured creditor,

makes a request in writing to the administrator for further information about remuneration or expenses (other than pre-administration costs) set out in a statement required by Rule 2.47(1)(db) or (dc), the administrator must, within 14 days of receipt of the request, comply with paragraph (2).

2.48A(2) **[Compliance by administrator]** The administrator complies with this paragraph by either–

   (a)   providing all of the information asked for, or

   (b)   so far as the administrator considers that–

      (i)   the time or cost of preparation of the information would be excessive, or

      (ii)   disclosure of the information would be prejudicial to the conduct of the administration or might reasonably be expected to lead to violence against any person, or

      (iii)   the administrator is subject to an obligation of confidentiality in respect of the information,

       giving reasons for not providing all of the information.

2.48A(3) **[Application to court by creditor]** Any creditor, who need not be the same as the creditor who requested further information under paragraph (1), may apply to the court within 21 days of–

   (a)   the giving by the administrator of reasons for not providing all of the information asked for, or

   (b)   the expiry of the 14 days provided for in paragraph (1),

and the court may make such order as it thinks just.

2.48A(4) **[Power of court to extend period]** Without prejudice to the generality of paragraph (3), the order of the court under that paragraph may extend the period of 8 weeks provided for in Rule 2.109(1B) by such further period as the court thinks just.

<small>GENERAL NOTE TO RR.2.48–2.48A</small>

"Correspondence" includes correspondence by telephonic or other electronic means (para.111(1)).

   Rule 2.48(2) amended and r.2.48(8) omitted by I(A)R 2010 r.2 and Sch. para.62 as from April 6, 2010. Rule 2.48A inserted by I(A)R 2010 r.2 and Sch. para.63 as from April 6, 2010. This new rule allows a creditor with 10 per cent support of his fellow-creditors to provide further information about his remuneration or expenses, backed if necessary by court order.

Section B: Company meetings

2.49 Venue and conduct of company meeting

2.49(1) [Convenience of venue] Where the administrator summons a meeting of members of the company, he shall fix a venue for it having regard to their convenience.

2.49(2) [Chairman] The chairman of the meeting shall be the administrator or a person nominated by him in writing to act in his place.

2.49(3) [Nominee chairman] A person so nominated must be either–

(a) one who is qualified to act as an insolvency practitioner in relation to the company; or

(b) an employee of the administrator or his firm who is experienced in insolvency matters.

2.49(4) [Adjournment if no chairman] If within 30 minutes from the time fixed for commencement of the meeting there is no person present to act as chairman, the meeting stands adjourned to the same time and place in the following week or, if that is not a business day, to the business day immediately following.

2.49(5) [Omitted.]

2.49(5A) [Law of summoning and conduct of meeting] Subject to anything to the contrary in the Act and these Rules, the meeting must be summoned and conducted–

(a) in the case of a company incorporated–

   (i) in England and Wales, or in Wales, or

   (ii) outside the United Kingdom other than in an EEA state,

   in accordance with the law of England and Wales, including any applicable provision in or made under the Companies Act;

(b) in the case of a company incorporated in an EEA state other than the United Kingdom, in accordance with the law of that state applicable to meetings of the company.

2.49(6) [Omitted.]

2.49(7) [Minutes] The chairman of the meeting shall cause minutes of its proceedings to be entered in the company's minute book.

GENERAL NOTE

There is no obligation placed on an administrator under Sch.B1 to call a shareholders' meeting for any purpose, but he may choose to do so (e.g. if it is proposed to institute a CVA), in which event this rule will apply.

Rule 2.49(5), (6) omitted and r.2.49(5A) inserted by I(A)R 2010 r.2 and Sch. para.64 as from April 6, 2010.

CHAPTER 7

THE CREDITORS' COMMITTEE

2.50 Constitution of committee

2.50(1) [Three to five creditors] Where it is resolved by a creditors' meeting to establish a creditors' committee for the purposes of the administration, the committee shall consist of at least 3 and not more than 5 creditors of the company elected at the meeting.

2.50(2)   [Eligibility of creditors] A person claiming to be a creditor is entitled to be a member of the committee provided that–

(a)   that person's claim has neither been wholly disallowed for voting purposes, nor wholly rejected for the purpose of distribution or dividend; and

(b)   the claim mentioned in sub-paragraph (a) is not fully secured.

2.50(3)   [Body corporate as member] A body corporate may be a member of the committee, but it cannot act as such otherwise than by a representative appointed under Rule 2.55 below.

(See General Note after r.2.65.)

2.51   Formalities of establishment

2.51(1)   [Certificate of due constitution] The creditors' committee does not come into being, and accordingly cannot act, until the administrator has issued a certificate in Form 2.26B of its due constitution.

[FORM 2.26B]

2.51(1A)   [Where chairman at creditors' meeting not the administrator] If the chairman of the creditors' meeting which resolves to establish the committee is not the administrator, the chairman must as soon as reasonably practicable give notice of the resolution to the administrator and inform the administrator of the names and addresses of the persons elected to be members of the committee.

2.51(2)   [Agreement to act] No person may act as a member of the committee unless and until he has agreed to do so and, unless the relevant proxy or authorisation contains a statement to the contrary, such agreement may be given by his proxy-holder present at the meeting establishing the committee or, in the case of a corporation, by its duly appointed representative.

2.51(3)   [Issue of administrator's certificate] The administrator's certificate of the committee's due constitution shall not be issued before the minimum number of members set out in Rule 2.50 elected to be members of the committee have agreed to act and shall be issued as soon as reasonably practicable thereafter.

2.51(4)   [Amended certificate] As and when the others (if any) agree to act, the administrator shall issue an amended certificate in Form 2.26B.

2.51(5)   [Copy of certificate to registrar] The certificate, and any amended certificate, shall be sent to the registrar of companies by the administrator, as soon as reasonably practicable.

2.51(6)   [Change in membership] If after the first establishment of the committee there is any change in its membership, the administrator shall as soon as reasonably practicable report the change to the registrar of companies by filing an amended certificate.

(See General Note after r.2.65.)

2.52   Functions and meetings of the committee

2.52(1)   [Functions] In addition to any functions conferred on the creditors' committee by any provision of the Act, the creditors' committee shall assist the administrator in discharging his functions, and act in relation to him in such manner as may be agreed from time to time.

2.52(2)   [Holding of meetings] Subject as follows, meetings of the committee shall be held when and where determined by the administrator.

2.52(3)   [Calling of first meeting] The administrator must call a first meeting of the committee to take place within 6 weeks of the committee's establishment.

2.52(3A)   [Calling of subsequent meetings] After the calling of the first meeting, the administrator must call a meeting–

(a) if so requested by a member of the committee or the member's representative (the meeting then to be held within 21 days of the request being received by the administrator); and

(b) for a specified date, if the committee has previously resolved that a meeting be held on that date.

2.52(4) **[Notice of venue]** Subject to paragraph (5), the administrator shall give 5 business days' written notice of the venue of any meeting to every member of the committee (or his representative designated for that purpose), unless in any case the requirement of notice has been waived by or on behalf of any member. Waiver may be signified either at or before the meeting.

2.52(5) **[Notice period for remote meeting]** Where the administrator has determined that a meeting should be conducted and held in the manner referred to in Rule 12A.26(2), the notice period mentioned in paragraph (4) is 7 business days.

(See General Note after r.2.65.)

2.53 The chairman at meetings

2.53(1) **[Chairman: administrator or person appointed thereby]** The chairman at any meeting of the creditors' committee must be the administrator, or a person appointed by the administrator in writing to act.

2.53(2) **[Qualification etc. of person appointed]** A person so appointed must be either–

(a) one who is qualified to act as an insolvency practitioner in relation to the company; or

(b) an employee of the administrator or his firm who is experienced in insolvency matters.

(See General Note after r.2.65.)

2.54 Quorum

2.54 A meeting of the committee is duly constituted if due notice of it has been given to all the members, and at least 2 members are present or represented.

(See General Note after r.2.65.)

2.55 Committee-members' representatives

2.55(1) **[Representation]** A member of the committee may, in relation to the business of the committee, be represented by another person duly authorised by him for that purpose.

2.55(2) **[Letter of authority or proxy]** A person acting as a committee-member's representative must hold a letter of authority entitling him so to act (either generally or specially) and authenticated by or on behalf of the committee-member, and for this purpose any proxy in relation to any meeting of creditors of the company shall, unless it contains a statement to the contrary, be treated as a letter of authority to act generally authenticated by or on behalf of the committee-member.

2.55(3) **[Production of letter of authority]** The chairman at any meeting of the committee may call on a person claiming to act as a committee-member's representative to produce his letter of authority, and may exclude him if it appears that his authority is deficient.

2.55(4) **[Who may not represent a member]** No member may be represented by–

(a) another member of the committee;

(b) a person who is at the same time representing another committee member;

(c) a body corporate;

(d) an undischarged bankrupt;

(e) a disqualified director; or

(f)   a person who is subject to a bankruptcy restrictions order (including an interim order), a bankruptcy restrictions undertaking, a debt relief restrictions order (including an interim order) or a debt relief restrictions undertaking.

2.55(5)   [Omitted by I(A)R 2010 r.2 and Sch. para.69(4) as from April 6, 2010.]

2.55(6)   [Authenticating as representative] Where a member's representative authenticates any document on the member's behalf, the fact that he so authenticates must be stated below his authentication.

(See General Note after r. 2.65.)

2.56   Resignation

2.56   A member of the committee may resign by notice in writing delivered to the administrator.

(See General Note after r.2.65.)

2.57   Termination of membership

2.57(1)   [Automatic termination] Membership of the creditors' committee is automatically terminated if the member–

(a)   becomes bankrupt; or

(b)   at 3 consecutive meetings of the committee is neither present nor represented (unless at the third of those meetings it is resolved that this Rule is not to apply in his case); or

(c)   ceases to be a creditor and a period of 3 months has elapsed from the date that that member ceased to be a creditor or is found never to have been a creditor.

2.57(2)   [Trustee in bankruptcy as member] However, if the cause of termination is the member's bankruptcy, his trustee in bankruptcy replaces him as a member of the committee.

(See General Note after r.2.65.)

2.58   Removal

2.58   A member of the committee may be removed by resolution at a meeting of creditors' at least 14 days' notice having been given of the intention to move that resolution.

(See General Note after r.2.65.)

2.59   Vacancies

2.59(1)   [Application of r.2.59] The following applies if there is a vacancy in the membership of the creditors' committee.

2.59(2)   [Agreement not to fill vacancy] The vacancy need not be filled if the administrator and a majority of the remaining members of the committee so agree, provided that the total number of members does not fall below 3.

2.59(3)   [Filling vacancy] The administrator may appoint any creditor (being qualified under the Rules to be a member of the committee) to fill the vacancy, if a majority of the other members of the committee agree to the appointment, and the creditor concerned consents to act.

2.59(4)   [Resolution by creditors] Alternatively, a meeting of creditors may resolve that a creditor be appointed (with that creditor's consent) to fill the vacancy.

2.59(5) **[Report of appointment to administrator if not present]** Where the vacancy is filled by an appointment made by a creditors' meeting at which the administrator is not present, the chairman of the meeting must report to the administrator the appointment which has been made.

(See General Note after r.2.65.)

2.60 Procedure at meetings

2.60(1) **[Voting and resolutions]** At any meeting of the creditors' committee, each member of it (whether present himself, or by his representative) has one vote; and a resolution is passed when a majority of the members present or represented have voted in favour of it.

2.60(2) **[Resolutions recorded, authenticated and kept]** Every resolution passed must be recorded in writing and authenticated by the chairman, either separately or as part of the minutes of the meeting, and the record must be kept with the records of the proceedings.

2.60(3) [Omitted.]

(See General Note after r.2.65.)

2.61 Resolutions of creditors' committee otherwise than at a meeting

2.61(1) **[Proposed resolution sent to committee members]** In accordance with this Rule, the administrator may seek to obtain the agreement of members of the creditors' committee to a resolution by sending to every member (or his representative designated for the purpose) a copy of the proposed resolution.

2.61(2) **[Voting indicated on copy]** Where the administrator makes use of the procedure allowed by this Rule, he shall send out to members of the committee or their representatives (as the case may be) a copy of any proposed resolution on which a decision is sought, which shall be set out in such a way that agreement with or dissent from each separate resolution may be indicated by the recipient on the copy so sent.

2.61(3) **[Member may require meeting]** Any member of the committee may, within 7 business days from the date of the administrator sending out a resolution, require him to summon a meeting of the committee to consider matters raised by the resolution.

2.61(4) **[Deemed passing of resolution]** In the absence of such a request, the resolution is deemed to have been passed by the committee if and when the administrator is notified in writing by a majority of the members that they concur with it.

2.61(5) **[Copy resolution to be kept]** A copy of every resolution passed under this Rule, and a note that the committee's concurrence was obtained, shall be kept with the records of the proceedings.

(See General Note after r.2.65.)

2.62 Information from administrator

2.62(1) **[Notice to administrator]** Where the committee resolves to require the attendance of the administrator under paragraph 57(3)(a), the notice to him shall be in writing authenticated by the majority of the members of the committee for the time being. A member's representative may authenticate for him.

2.62(2) **[Time and place of meeting]** The meeting at which the administrator's attendance is required shall be fixed by the committee for a business day, and shall be held at such time and place as he determines.

2.62(3) **[Chairman not administrator]** Where the administrator so attends, the members of the committee may elect any one of their number to be chairman of the meeting, in place of the administrator or a nominee of his.

(See General Note after r.2.65.)

2.63   Expenses of members

2.63(1)   [Expenses defrayed out of assets] Subject as follows, the administrator shall, out of the assets of the company, defray in the prescribed order of priority any reasonable travelling expenses directly incurred by members of the creditors' committee or their representatives in relation to their attendance at the committee's meetings, or otherwise on the committee's business, as an expense of the administration.

2.63(2)   [Non-application of r.2.63(1)] Paragraph (1) does not apply to any meeting of the committee held within 6 weeks of a previous meeting, unless the meeting in question is summoned at the instance of the administrator.

(See General Note after r.2.65.)

2.64   Members' dealing with the company

2.64(1)   [Dealings to be in good faith] Membership of the committee does not prevent a person from dealing with the company while the company is in administration, provided that any transactions in the course of such dealings are in good faith and for value.

2.64(2)   [Court may set aside transaction] The court may, on the application of any person interested, set aside any transaction which appears to it to be contrary to the requirements of this Rule, and may give such consequential directions as it thinks fit for compensating the company for any loss which it may have incurred in consequence of the transaction.

(See General Note after r.2.65.)

2.65   Formal defects

2.65 The acts of the creditors' committee established for any administration are valid notwithstanding any defect in the appointment, election or qualifications of any member of the committee or any committee-member's representative or in the formalities of its establishment.

General Note to rr.2.50–2.65

Rules 2.51(2)–(6), 2.52(1), (4), 2.53(2), 2.55(2), 2.59(2), 2.61(5), 2.63(1) amended, rr.2.51(1A), 2.52(3A), 2.59(4), (5) inserted, rr.2.50(2), 2.52(3), 2.53(1), 2.55(4), 2.57(1)(c), 2.60(2) substituted, and rr.2.55(5), 2.60(3) omitted, by I(A)R 2010 r.2 and Sch. paras 66–75 as from April 6, 2010.
    The corresponding rules under the original regime are rr.*2.32* et seq. See the note following r.*2.46A*.

CHAPTER 8

DISPOSAL OF CHARGED PROPERTY

2.66(1)   [Application of r.2.66] The following applies where the administrator applies to the court under paragraphs 71 or 72 for authority to dispose of property of the company which is subject to a security (other than a floating charge), or goods in the possession of the company under a hire purchase agreement.

2.66(2)   [Venue and notice] The court shall fix a venue for the hearing of the application, and the administrator shall as soon as reasonably practicable give notice of the venue to the person who is the holder of the security or, as the case may be, the owner under the agreement.

2.66(3)   [Sealed copies of order re non-floating charge or hire-purchase property] If an order is made under paragraphs 71 or 72 the court shall send two sealed copies to the administrator.

2.66(4)   [Copy to holder of security or owner of property] The administrator shall send one of them to that person who is the holder of the security or owner under the agreement.

2.66(5)   **[Copy of sealed order to registrar]** The administrator must send a copy of the sealed order to the registrar of companies.

GENERAL NOTE

Rule 2.66(5) substituted by I(A)R 2010 r.2 and Sch. para.75 as from April 6, 2010.

The leave of the court is not required where the administrator wishes to deal with property that is subject to a floating charge.

"Hire purchase agreement" includes a conditional sale agreement, a chattel leasing agreement and a retention of title agreement (para.111(1)).

CHAPTER 9

EXPENSES OF THE ADMINISTRATION

2.67(1)   **[Priority of expenses]** The expenses of the administration are payable in the following order of priority–

- (a) expenses properly incurred by the administrator in performing his functions in the administration of the company;

- (b) the cost of any security provided by the administrator in accordance with the Act or the Rules;

- (c) where an administration order was made, the costs of the applicant and any person appearing on the hearing of the application and where the administrator was appointed otherwise than by order of the court, any costs and expenses of the appointor in connection with the making of the appointment and the costs and expenses incurred by any other person in giving notice of intention to appoint an administrator;

- (d) any amount payable to a person employed or authorised, under Chapter 5 of this Part of the Rules, to assist in the preparation of a statement of affairs or statement of concurrence;

- (e) any allowance made, by order of the court, towards costs on an application for release from the obligation to submit a statement of affairs or statement of concurrence;

- (f) any necessary disbursements by the administrator in the course of the administration (including any expenses incurred by members of the creditors' committee or their representatives and allowed for by the administrator under Rule 2.63, but not including any payment of corporation tax in circumstances referred to in sub-paragraph (j) below);

- (g) the remuneration or emoluments of any person who has been employed by the administrator to perform any services for the company, as required or authorised under the Act or the Rules;

- (h) the administrator's remuneration the basis of which has been fixed under Chapter 11 of this Part of the Rules and unpaid pre-administration costs approved under Rule 2.67A;

- (j) the amount of any corporation tax on chargeable gains accruing on the realisation of any asset of the company (without regard to whether the realisation is effected by the administrator, a secured creditor, or a receiver or manager appointed to deal with a security).

2.67(2)   **[Priorities where assets insufficient to satisfy liabilities]** The priorities laid down by paragraph (1) of this Rule are subject to the power of the court to make orders under paragraph (3) of this Rule where the assets are insufficient to satisfy the liabilities.

2.67(3)   **[Court's power to alter order of priority]** The court may, in the event of the assets being insufficient to satisfy the liabilities, make an order as to the payment out of the assets of the expenses incurred in the administration in such order of priority as the court thinks just.

2.67(4) [Former administrator's remuneration and expenses] For the purposes of paragraph 99(3), the former administrator's remuneration and expenses shall comprise all those items set out in paragraph (1) of this Rule.

GENERAL NOTE

There is no equivalent to this rule under the original regime. The notes to s.156 and r.4.218 (dealing with the expenses of a liquidation) may be helpful. However, the drafting of this rule is not as detailed as r.4.218 and it may be open to a different construction, e.g. in regard to litigation costs: see Lyons and Roberts, Sweet & Maxwell's Company Law Newsletter 16 (2005, p.1); and Lyons and Birch, (2005) 18 Insolv. Int. 150. In *Re Allders Department Stores Ltd* [2005] EWHC 172 (Ch); [2005] 2 All E.R. 122; [2005] B.C.C. 289 statutory liabilities to make redundancy and unfair dismissal payments were held not to have priority as "expenses properly incurred" by the administrator under r.2.67(1)(a) or "necessary disbursements" under r.2.67(1)(f). In contrast, non-domestic rates payable in respect of rates occupied by a company in administration were held to be "necessary disbursements" and accordingly entitled to priority under Sch.B1 para.99 in *Exeter City Council v Bairstow* [2007] EWHC 400 (Ch); [2007] B.C.C. 236. The court expressed the view that unoccupied property rates would rank similarly, but the law has since been amended so that such rates are no longer payable where the owner of the relevant property is a company in administration, under either the original or the Sch.B1 regime: see the Non-Domestic Rating (Unoccupied Property) (England) Regulations 2008 (SI 2008/386) regs 3, 4(l); and the Non-Domestic Rating (Unoccupied Property) (Scotland) Regulations 2008 (SSI 2008/83) reg.2, both effective April 1, 2008. In regard to Wales, see the Non-Domestic Rating (Unoccupied Property) (Wales) Regulations 2008 (SI 2008/2499 (W 217)).

Rule 2.67(4) was inserted by the Insolvency (Amendment) Rules 2005 (SI 2005/527) r.8, as from April 1, 2005.
Rule 2.67(2) substituted by I(A)R 2010 r.2 and Sch. para.76 as from April 6, 2010.

2.67A Pre-administration costs

2.67A(1) [Creditors' committee may approve for payment] Where the administrator has made a statement of pre-administration costs under Rule 2.33(2)(ka), the creditors' committee may determine whether and to what extent the unpaid pre-administration costs set out in the statement are approved for payment.

2.67A(2) [Application of r.2.67A(3)] But if–

(a)   there is no creditors' committee, or

(b)   there is but it does not make the necessary determination, or

(c)   it does do so but the administrator or other insolvency practitioner who has charged fees or incurred expenses as pre-administration costs considers the amount determined to be insufficient,

paragraph (3) applies.

2.67A(3) [Approval by creditors, secured or preferential creditors] When this paragraph applies, determination of whether and to what extent the unpaid pre-administration costs are approved for payment shall be–

(a)   by resolution of a meeting of creditors other than in a case falling in sub-paragraph (b), or

(b)   in a case where the administrator has made a statement under paragraph 52(1)(b)–

    (i)   by the approval of each secured creditor of the company, or

    (ii) if the administrator has made, or intends to make, a distribution to preferential creditors, by the approval of–

        (aa) each secured creditor of the company, and

        (bb) preferential creditors whose debts amount to more than 50% of the preferential debts of the company, disregarding debts of any creditor who does not respond to an invitation to give or withhold approval.

2.67A(4) **[Creditors' meeting for approval of expenses of other IP]** The administrator must call a meeting of the creditors' committee or of creditors if so requested for the purposes of paragraphs (1) to (3) by another insolvency practitioner who has charged fees or incurred expenses as pre-administration costs; and the administrator must give notice of the meeting within 28 days of receipt of the request.

2.67A(5) **[Application to court by administrator or other IP]** If–

(a) there is no determination under paragraph (1) or (3), or

(b) there is such a determination but the administrator or other insolvency practitioner who has charged fees or incurred expenses as pre-administration costs considers the amount determined to be insufficient,

the administrator (where the fees were charged or expenses incurred by the administrator) or other insolvency practitioner (where the fees were charged or expenses incurred by that practitioner) may apply to the court for a determination of whether and to what extent the unpaid pre-administration costs are approved for payment.

2.67A(6) **[Application of r.2.108 to r.2.67A(5) application]** Paragraphs (2) to (4) of Rule 2.108 apply to an application under paragraph (5) of this Rule as they do to an application under paragraph (1) of that Rule (references to the administrator being read as references to the insolvency practitioner who has charged fees or incurred expenses as pre-administration costs).

2.67A(7) **[Where administrator fails to call meeting under r.2.67A(4)]** Where the administrator fails to call a meeting of the creditors' committee or of creditors in accordance with paragraph (4), the other insolvency practitioner may apply to the court for an order requiring the administrator to do so.

GENERAL NOTE

Rule 2.67A inserted by I(A)R 2010 r.2 and Sch. para.77 as from April 6, 2010. On pre-administration costs, see r.2.33.

CHAPTER 10

DISTRIBUTIONS TO CREDITORS

Section A: Application of Chapter and general

2.68(1) **[Application of Ch.10]** This Chapter applies where the administrator makes, or proposes to make, a distribution to any class of creditors other than secured creditors. Where the distribution is to a particular class of creditors, references in this Chapter to creditors shall, in so far as the context requires, be a reference to that class of creditors only.

2.68(2) **[Notice of intention to declare and distribute dividend]** The administrator shall give notice to the creditors of his intention to declare and distribute a dividend in accordance with Rule 2.95.

2.68(3) **[Where sole or final dividend]** Where it is intended that the distribution is to be a sole or final dividend, the administrator shall, after the date specified in the notice referred to in paragraph (2)–

(a) defray any outstanding expenses of a liquidation (including any of the items mentioned in Rule 4.218) or provisional liquidation that immediately preceded the administration;

(b) defray any items payable in accordance with the provisions of paragraph 99;

(c) defray any amounts (including any debts or liabilities and his own remuneration and expenses) which would, if the administrator were to cease to be the administrator of the company, be payable out of the property of which he had custody or control in accordance with the provisions of paragraph 99; and

    (d)   declare and distribute that dividend without regard to the claim of any person in respect of a debt not already proved.

2.68(4) [Power of court to postpone date] The court may, on the application of any person, postpone the date specified in the notice.

(See General Note after r.2.71.)

2.69 Debts of insolvent company to rank equally

2.69 Debts other than preferential debts rank equally between themselves in the administration and, after the preferential debts, shall be paid in full unless the assets are insufficient for meeting them, in which case they abate in equal proportions between themselves.

(See General Note after r.2.71.)

2.70 Supplementary provisions as to dividend

2.70(1) [What administrator to make provision for] In the calculation and distribution of a dividend the administrator shall make provision for–

    (a)   any debts which appear to him to be due to persons who, by reason of the distance of their place of residence, may not have had sufficient time to tender and establish their proofs;

    (b)   any debts which are the subject of claims which have not yet been determined; and

    (c)   disputed proofs and claims.

2.70(2) [Where creditor has not proved debt] A creditor who has not proved his debt before the declaration of any dividend is not entitled to disturb, by reason that he has not participated in it, the distribution of that dividend or any other dividend declared before his debt was proved, but–

    (a)   when he has proved that debt he is entitled to be paid, out of any money for the time being available for the payment of any further dividend, any dividend or dividends which he has failed to receive; and

    (b)   any dividends payable under sub-paragraph (a) shall be paid before the money is applied to the payment of any such further dividend.

2.70(3) [No action against administrator for dividend] No action lies against the administrator for a dividend; but if he refuses to pay a dividend the court may, if it thinks fit, order him to pay it and also to pay, out of his own money–

    (a)   interest on the dividend, at the rate for the time being specified in section 17 of the Judgments Act 1838, from the time when it was withheld; and

    (b)   the costs of the proceedings in which the order to pay is made.

(See General Note after r.2.71.)

2.71 Division of unsold assets

2.71(1) [Assets not readily or advantageously saleable] The administrator may, with the permission of the creditors' committee, or if there is no creditors' committee, the creditors, divide in its existing form amongst the company's creditors, according to its estimated value, any property which from its peculiar nature or other special circumstances cannot be readily or advantageously sold.

2.71(2) [Value of assets in receipts and payments account] The administrator must–

    (a)   in the receipts and payments account included in the final progress report under Chapter 12 of this Part, state the estimated value of the property divided amongst the creditors of the company during the period to which the report relates, and

(b)   as a note to the account, provide details of the basis of the valuation.

GENERAL NOTE TO RR.2.68–2.71

Rule 2.71(2) inserted by I(A)R 2010 r.2 and Sch. para.79 as from April 6, 2010. Details of the valuation must be provided.

A distribution to creditors is not among the purposes for which an administration order can be made under the original administration regime, and where it is sought to make a distribution the most convenient course is to specify the approval of a CVA among the purposes of the order. The statutory objectives under the new regime do include the making of a distribution (although it is still contemplated that this may be done via a CVA). Where a distribution is to be made under the administration, these rules will apply.

The notes to rr.4.179 et seq. (which apply in a liquidation) may be helpful.

Section B: Machinery of proving a debt

2.72   Proving a debt

2.72(1)   [Claim in writing] A person claiming to be a creditor of the company and wishing to recover his debt in whole or in part must (subject to any order of the court to the contrary) submit his claim in writing to the administrator.

2.72(2)   ["Proving" and "proof"] A creditor who claims is referred to as **"proving"** for his debt and a document by which he seeks to establish his claim is his **"proof"**.

2.72(3)   [Making of proof] Subject to the next paragraph, a proof must–

(a)   be made out by, or under the direction of, the creditor and authenticated by him or a person authorised in that behalf; and

(b)   state the following matters–

    (i)   the creditor's name and address;

    (ia)   if the creditor is a company, its registered number;

    (ii)   the total amount of the creditor's claim (including value added tax) as at the date on which the company entered administration (or, if the company was in liquidation when it entered administration, the date on which it went into liquidation), less any payments made after that date in respect of the claim, any deduction under Rule 2.84 and any adjustment by way of set-off in accordance with Rule 2.85;

    (iii)   whether or not the claim includes outstanding uncapitalised interest;

    (iv), (v)   [Omitted.]

    (vi)   particulars of how and when the debt was incurred by the company;

    (vii)   particulars of any security held, the date on which it was given and the value which the creditor puts on it;

    (viii)   details of any reservation of title in respect of goods to which the debt refers; and

    (ix)   the name, address and authority of the person authenticating the proof (if other than the creditor himself).

2.72(4)   [Substantiating documents] There shall be specified in the proof details of any documents by reference to which the debt can be substantiated; but (subject as follows) it is not essential that such document be attached to the proof or submitted with it.

2.72(5)   [Power of administrator to call for other document] The administrator may call for any document or other evidence to be produced to him, where he thinks it necessary for the purpose of substantiating the whole or any part of the claim made in the proof.

2.72(6) [Where administration preceded by winding up] Where an administration is immediately preceded by a winding up, a creditor proving in the winding up is deemed to have proved in the administration.

(See General Note after r.2.80.)

2.73 Claim established by affidavit [Revoked by I(A)R 2010 r.5 (with retrospective effect).]

2.74 Costs of proving

2.74 Unless the court otherwise orders–

    (a) every creditor bears the cost of proving his own debt, including costs incurred in providing documents or evidence under Rule 2.72(5); and

    (b) costs incurred by the administrator in estimating the quantum of a debt under Rule 2.81 are payable out of the assets as an expense of the administration.

(See General Note after r.2.80.)

2.75 Administrator to allow inspection of proofs

2.75 The administrator shall, so long as proofs lodged with him are in his hands, allow them to be inspected, at all reasonable times on any business day, by any of the following persons–

    (a) any creditor who has submitted a proof of debt (unless his proof has been wholly rejected for purposes of dividend or otherwise);

    (b) any contributory of the company; and

    (c) any person acting on behalf of either of the above.

(See General Note after r.2.80.)

2.76 New administrator appointed

2.76(1) [Proofs and itemised list to new administrator] If a new administrator is appointed in place of another, the former administrator must as soon as reasonably practicable transmit to him all proofs which he has received, together with an itemised list of them.

2.76(2) [Authenticated list returned to former administrator] The new administrator shall authenticate the list by way of receipt for the proofs, and return it to his predecessor.

2.76(3) [Proofs to and retained by new administrator] From then on, all proofs of debt must be sent to and retained by the new administrator.

(See General Note after r.2.80.)

2.77 Admission and rejection of proofs for dividend

2.77(1) [Admission for whole or part] A proof may be admitted for dividend either for the whole amount claimed by the creditor, or for part of that amount.

2.77(2) [Written statement of reasons for rejection] If the administrator rejects a proof in whole or in part, he shall prepare a written statement of his reasons for doing so, and send it as soon as reasonably practicable to the creditor.

(See General Note after r.2.80.)

2.78 Appeal against decision on proof

2.78(1) [Application to court by creditor] If a creditor is dissatisfied with the administrator's decision with respect to his proof (including any decision on the question of preference), he may apply to the court for the decision to be reversed or varied. The application must be made within 21 days of his receiving the statement sent under Rule 2.77(2).

2.78(2)   [Application by member or other creditor] A member or any other creditor may, if dissatisfied with the administrator's decision admitting or rejecting the whole or any part of a proof, make such an application within 21 days of becoming aware of the administrator's decision.

2.78(3)   [Court to fix venue for hearing] Where application is made to the court under this Rule, the court shall fix a venue for the application to be heard, notice of which shall be sent by the applicant to the creditor who lodged the proof in question (if it is not himself) and the administrator.

2.78(4)   [Administrator to file proof and rejection in court] The administrator shall, on receipt of the notice, file with the court the relevant proof, together (if appropriate) with a copy of the statement sent under Rule 2.77(2).

2.78(4A)   [Application by member, surplus assets required] Where the application is made by a member, the court must not disallow the proof (in whole or in part) unless the member shows that there is (or would be but for the amount claimed in the proof), or that it is likely that there will be (or would be but for the amount claimed in the proof), a surplus of assets to which the company would be entitled.

2.78(5)   [Court to return proof to administrator] After the application has been heard and determined, the proof shall, unless it has been wholly disallowed, be returned by the court to the administrator.

2.78(6)   [Costs of application] The administrator is not personally liable for costs incurred by any person in respect of an application under this Rule unless the court otherwise orders.

(See General Note after r.2.80.)

2.79   Withdrawal or variation of proof

2.79   A creditor's proof may at any time, by agreement between himself and the administrator, be withdrawn or varied as to the amount claimed.

(See General Note after r.2.80.)

2.80   Expunging of proof by the court

2.80(1)   [Power of court] The court may expunge a proof or reduce the amount claimed–

(a)   on the administrator's application, where he thinks that the proof has been improperly admitted, or ought to be reduced; or

(b)   on the application of a creditor, if the administrator declines to interfere in the matter.

2.80(2)   [Court to fix venue for hearing] Where application is made to the court under this Rule, the court shall fix a venue for the application to be heard, notice of which shall be sent by the applicant–

(a)   in the case of an application by the administrator, to the creditor who made the proof; and

(b)   in the case of an application by a creditor, to the administrator and to the creditor who made the proof (if not himself).

GENERAL NOTE TO RR.2.72–2.80

References to "lodging a claim" under the original regime (rr.2.22 et seq.) have been changed to "proving a debt" in the present section. On the meaning of "debt", see r.13.12, and especially r.13.12(5). The corresponding rules which apply in a liquidation (rr.4.67 et seq., 4.73 et seq.) may be relevant.

    Rules 2.72(3), 2.78(2) amended and rr.2.72(6), 2.76(3), 2.78(4A) inserted by I(A)R 2010 r.2 and Sch. paras 80–82 as from April 6, 2010.

Section C: Quantification of claims

2.81   Estimate of quantum

2.81(1)   [Administrator to estimate where value uncertain] The administrator shall estimate the value of any debt which, by reason of its being subject to any contingency or for any other reason, does not bear a certain value; and he may revise any estimate previously made, if he thinks fit by reference to any change of circumstances or to information becoming available to him. He shall inform the creditor as to his estimate and any revision of it.

2.81(2)   [Estimate provable] Where the value of a debt is estimated under this Rule, the amount provable in the administration in the case of that debt is that of the estimate for the time being.

(See General Note after r.2.94.)

2.82   Negotiable instruments, etc

2.82   Unless the administrator allows, a proof in respect of money owed on a bill of exchange, promissory note, cheque or other negotiable instrument or security cannot be admitted unless there is produced the instrument or security itself or a copy of it, certified by the creditor or his authorised representative to be a true copy.

(See General Note after r.2.94.)

2.83   Secured creditors

2.83(1)   [Proof for balance of debt if security realised] If a secured creditor realises his security, he may prove for the balance of his debt, after deducting the amount realised.

2.83(2)   [Proof for whole of debt if security surrendered] If a secured creditor voluntarily surrenders his security for the general benefit of creditors, he may prove for his whole debt, as if it were unsecured.

(See General Note after r.2.94.)

2.84   Discounts

2.84   There shall in every case be deducted from the claim all trade and other discounts which would have been available to the company but for its administration except any discount for immediate, early or cash settlement.

(See General Note after r.2.94.)

2.85   Mutual credits and set-off

2.85(1)   [Application of r.2.85] This Rule applies where the administrator, being authorised to make the distribution in question, has, pursuant to Rule 2.95 given notice that he proposes to make it.

2.85(2)   ["Mutual dealings"] In this Rule **"mutual dealings"** means mutual credits, mutual debts or other mutual dealings between the company and any creditor of the company proving or claiming to prove for a debt in the administration but does not include any of the following–

(a)   any debt arising out of an obligation incurred after the company entered administration;

(b)   any debt arising out of an obligation incurred at a time when the creditor had notice that–

    (i)   an application for an administration order was pending; or

    (ii)   any person had given notice of intention to appoint an administrator;

(c)   any debt arising out of an obligation where–

    (i)   the administration was immediately preceded by a winding up; and

(ii) at the time the obligation was incurred the creditor had notice that a meeting of creditors had been summoned under section 98 or a petition for the winding up of the company was pending;

(d) any debt arising out of an obligation incurred during a winding up which immediately preceded the administration; or

(e) any debt which has been acquired by a creditor by assignment or otherwise, pursuant to an agreement between the creditor and any other party where that agreement was entered into–

(i) after the company entered administration;

(ii) at a time when the creditor had notice that an application for an administration order was pending;

(iii) at a time when the creditor had notice that any person had given notice of intention to appoint an administrator;

(iv) where the administration was immediately preceded by a winding up, at a time when the creditor had notice that a meeting of creditors had been summoned under section 98 or that a winding up petition was pending; or

(v) during a winding up which immediately preceded the administration.

2.85(3) [Account of mutual dealings and set-off] An account shall be taken as at the date of the notice referred to in paragraph (1) of what is due from each party to the other in respect of the mutual dealings and the sums due from one party shall be set off against the sums due from the other.

2.85(4) [Sums regarded as due] A sum shall be regarded as being due to or from the company for the purposes of paragraph (3) whether–

(a) it is payable at present or in the future;

(b) the obligation by virtue of which it is payable is certain or contingent; or

(c) its amount is fixed or liquidated, or is capable of being ascertained by fixed rules or as a matter of opinion.

2.85(5) [Application of r.2.81] Rule 2.81 shall apply for the purposes of this Rule to any obligation to or from the company which, by reason of its being subject to any contingency or for any other reason, does not bear a certain value;

2.85(6) [Application of rr.2.86–2.88] Rules 2.86 to 2.88 shall apply for the purposes of this Rule in relation to any sums due to the company which–

(a) are payable in a currency other than sterling;

(b) are of a periodical nature; or

(c) bear interest.

2.85(7) [Application of r.2.105] Rule 2.105 shall apply for the purposes of this Rule to any sum due to or from the company which is payable in the future.

2.85(8) [Only balance provable] Only the balance (if any) of the account owed to the creditor is provable in the administration. Alternatively the balance (if any) owed to the company shall be paid to the administrator as part of the assets except where all or part of the balance results from a contingent or prospective debt owed by the creditor and in such a case the balance (or that part of it which results from the contingent or prospective debt) shall be paid if and when that debt becomes due and payable.

2.85(9) ["Obligation"] In this Rule **"obligation"** means an obligation however arising, whether by virtue of an agreement, rule of law or otherwise.

(See General Note after r.2.94.)

2.86   Debt in foreign currency

2.86(1)   [Conversion into sterling] For the purpose of proving a debt incurred or payable in a currency other than sterling, the amount of the debt shall be converted into sterling at the official exchange rate prevailing on the date when the company entered administration or, if the administration was immediately preceded by a winding up, on the date that the company went into liquidation.

2.86(2)   ["The official exchange rate"] "The official exchange rate" is the middle exchange rate on the London Foreign Exchange Market at the close of business, as published for the date in question. In the absence of any such published rate, it is such rate as the court determines.

(See General Note after r.2.94.)

2.87   Payments of a periodical nature

2.87(1)   [Rent etc.] In the case of rent and other payments of a periodical nature, the creditor may prove for any amounts due and unpaid up to the date when the company entered administration or, if the administration was immediately preceded by a winding up, up to the date that the company went into liquidation.

2.87(2)   [If accruing from day to day] Where at that date any payment was accruing due, the creditor may prove for so much as would have fallen due at that date, if accruing from day to day.

(See General Note after r.2.94.)

2.88   Interest

2.88(A1)   ["The relevant date"] In this Rule, **"the relevant date"** means the date on which the company entered administration or, if the administration was immediately preceded by a winding up, the date on which the company went into liquidation.

2.88(1)   [Where debt bears interest] Where a debt proved in the administration bears interest, that interest is provable as part of the debt except in so far as it is payable in respect of any period after the company entered administration or, if the administration was immediately preceded by a winding up, any period after the relevant date.

2.88(2)   [Where claim may include interest] In the following circumstances the creditor's claim may include interest on the debt for periods before the relevant date, although not previously reserved or agreed.

2.88(3)   [Debt due by written instrument] If the debt is due by virtue of a written instrument, and payable at a certain time, interest may be claimed for the period from that time to the relevant date.

2.88(4)   [Debt due otherwise] If the debt is due otherwise, interest may only be claimed if, before the relevant date, a demand for payment of the debt was made in writing by or on behalf of the creditor, and notice given that interest would be payable from the date of the demand to the date of payment.

2.88(5)   [Claiming interest under r.2.88(4)] Interest under paragraph (4) may only be claimed for the period from the date of the demand to the relevant date and for all the purposes of the Act and the Rules shall be chargeable at a rate not exceeding that mentioned in paragraph (6).

2.88(6)   [Rate of interest under r.2.88(3), (4)] The rate of interest to be claimed under paragraphs (3) and (4) is the rate specified in section 17 of the Judgments Act 1838 on the relevant date.

2.88(7)   [Surplus applied for payment of interest] Any surplus remaining after payment of the debts proved shall, before being applied for any purpose, be applied in paying interest on those debts in respect of the periods during which they have been outstanding since the relevant date.

2.88(8)   [Interest payable under r.2.88(7)] All interest payable under paragraph (7) ranks equally whether or not the debts on which it is payable rank equally.

2.88(9) **[Rate of interest under r.2.88(7)]** The rate of interest payable under paragraph (7) is whichever is the greater of the rate specified under paragraph (6) and the rate applicable to the debt apart from the administration.

(See General Note after r.2.94.)

2.89 Debt payable at future time

2.89 A creditor may prove for a debt of which payment was not yet due on the date when the company entered administration or, if the administration was immediately preceded by a winding up, up to the date that the company went into liquidation, subject to Rule 2.105 (adjustment of dividend where payment made before time).

(See General Note after r.2.94.)

2.90 Value of security

2.90(1) **[Altering value]** A secured creditor may, with the agreement of the administrator or the permission of the court, at any time alter the value which he has, in his proof of debt, put upon his security.

2.90(2) **[Limitation on re-valuation]** However, if a secured creditor–

(a) being the applicant for an administration order or the appointor of the administrator, has in the application or the notice of appointment put a value on his security; or

(b) has voted in respect of the unsecured balance of his debt,

he may re-value his security only with permission of the court.

(See General Note after r.2.94.)

2.91 Surrender for non-disclosure

2.91(1) **[Omission to disclose security]** If a secured creditor omits to disclose his security in his proof of debt, he shall surrender his security for the general benefit of creditors, unless the court, on application by him, relieves him from the effect of this Rule on the ground that the omission was inadvertent or the result of honest mistake.

2.91(2) **[Relief from effect of r.2.91(1)]** If the court grants that relief, it may require or allow the creditor's proof of debt to be amended, on such terms as may be just.

2.91(3) **[Rights protected by art.5 of EC Regulation]** Nothing in this Rule or the following two Rules may affect the rights in rem of creditors or third parties protected under Article 5 of the EC Regulation (third parties' rights in rem).

(See General Note after r.2.94.)

2.92 Redemption by administrator

2.92(1) **[Notice of proposed redemption]** The administrator may at any time give notice to a creditor whose debt is secured that he proposes, at the expiration of 28 days from the date of the notice, to redeem the security at the value put upon it in the creditor's proof.

2.92(2) **[Time for revaluation etc.]** The creditor then has 21 days (or such longer period as the administrator may allow) in which, if he so wishes, to exercise his right to revalue his security (with the permission of the court, where Rule 2.90(2) applies).

If the creditor re-values his security, the administrator may only redeem at the new value.

2.92(3) **[If administrator redeems]** If the administrator redeems the security, the cost of transferring it is payable out of the assets.

2.92(4)   **[Notice to administrator to elect etc.]** A secured creditor may at any time, by a notice in writing, call on the administrator to elect whether he will or will not exercise his power to redeem the security at the value then placed on it; and the administrator then has 3 months in which to exercise the power or determine not to exercise it.

(See General Note after r.2.94.)

2.93   Test of security's value

2.93(1)   **[Offer for sale]** Subject as follows, the administrator, if he is dissatisfied with the value which a secured creditor puts on his security (whether in his proof or by way of re-valuation under Rule 2.92), may require any property comprised in the security to be offered for sale.

2.93(2)   **[Terms of sale]** The terms of sale shall be such as may be agreed, or as the court may direct; and if the sale is by auction, the administrator on behalf of the company, and the creditor on his own behalf, may appear and bid.

2.93(3)   **[Revaluation]** This Rule does not apply if the security has been revalued and the revaluation has been approved by the court.

(See General Note after r.2.94.)

2.94   Realisation of security by creditor

2.94   If a creditor who has valued his security subsequently realises it (whether or not at the instance of the administrator)–

    (a)   the net amount realised shall be substituted for the value previously put by the creditor on the security; and

    (b)   that amount shall be treated in all respects as an amended valuation made by him.

GENERAL NOTE TO RR.2.81–2.94

Rule 2.85 was substituted by the Insolvency (Amendment) Rules 2005 (SI 2005/527) r.9, as from April 1, 2005. The new rule closely follows the equivalent provision in r.4.90, which applies in a winding up. See the note to that rule.
     Rules 2.86(1), 2.87(1), 2.88(1) and 2.89 were amended by the same SI, rr.10–13, also as from April 1, 2005, to deal with the situation where the administration immediately follows a winding up. Rule 2.88(7) was also modified by the omission of the opening words "Subject to r.2.105(3)".
     Rules 2.88 and 2.93(1) amended and rr.2.88(A1), 2.93(3) inserted by I(A)R 2010 r.2 and Sch. paras 83, 84 as from April 6, 2010.
     There are parallels here in the rules governing claims under the original regime (rr.2.24 et seq.) and in a liquidation (rr.4.86 et seq.). The construction of an industry netting agreement was the subject of debate in *Revenue and Customs Commissioners v Enron Europe Ltd* [2006] EWHC 824 (Ch); [2006] B.C.C. 953.

R.2.83

The secured creditor may also prove for the balance of his debt after placing an estimate on the value of his security under rr.2.90 et seq.

R.2.85

The corresponding provision in a liquidation is r.4.90. See the note to that rule.

R.2.88

See the note to s.189.

2.95   Notice of proposed distribution

2.95(1)   **[Period of notice]** Where an administrator is proposing to make a distribution to creditors he shall give notice of that fact.

2.95(2)   **[Contents of notice and to whom sent]** The notice given pursuant to paragraph (1) shall–

    (a)   be sent to–

(i) all creditors whose addresses are known to the administrator; and

(ii) where a member State liquidator has been appointed in relation to the company, to the member State liquidator;

(b) state whether the distribution is to preferential creditors or preferential creditors and unsecured creditors; and

(c) where the administrator proposes to make a distribution to unsecured creditors, state the value of the prescribed part, except where the court has made an order under section 176A(5).

2.95(3) **[Gazetting and advertisement of notice]** Subject to paragraph (5)(b), before declaring a dividend the administrator shall by notice invite the creditors to prove their debts. Such notice–

(a) shall be gazetted; and

(b) may be advertised in such other manner as the administrator thinks fit.

2.95(4) **[Statement etc. in notice]** A notice pursuant to paragraphs (1) or (3) must, in addition to the standard contents–

(a) state that it is the intention of the administrator to make a distribution to creditors within the period of 2 months from the last date for proving;

(b) specify whether the proposed dividend is interim or final;

(c) specify a date up to which proofs may be lodged being a date which–

(i) is the same date for all creditors; and

(ii) is not less than 21 days from that of the notice.

2.95(5) **[To whom r.2.95(1), (3) notices should be sent]** Where a dividend is to be declared for preferential creditors–

(a) the notice pursuant to paragraph (1) need only to be given to those creditors in whose case the administrator has reason to believe that their debts are preferential; and

(b) the notice pursuant to paragraph (3) need only be given if the administrator thinks fit.

(See General Note after r.2.105.)

2.96 Admission or rejection of proofs

2.96(1) **[Duty of administrator]** Unless he has already dealt with them, within 5 business days of the last date for proving, the administrator shall–

(a) admit or reject (whole or in part) proofs submitted to him; or

(b) make such provision in respect of them as he thinks fit.

2.96(2) **[Late proofs]** The administrator is not obliged to deal with proofs lodged after the last date for proving, but he may do so, if he thinks fit.

2.96(3) **[Single payment only in respect of debt]** In the declaration of a dividend no payment shall be made more than once by virtue of the same debt.

2.96(4) **[Creditor and member State liquidator]** Subject to Rule 2.104, where–

(a) a creditor has proved; and

(b) a member State liquidator has proved in relation to the same debt,

payment shall only be made to the creditor.

(See General Note after r.2.105.)

2.96A   Postponement or cancellation of dividend

2.96A   If in the period of 2 months referred to in Rule 2.95(4)(a)–

(a)   the administrator has rejected a proof in whole or in part and application is made to the court for that decision to be reversed or varied, or

(b)   application is made to the court for the administrator's decision on a proof to be reversed or varied, or for a proof to be expunged, or for a reduction of the amount claimed,

the administrator may postpone or cancel the dividend.

(See General Note after r.2.105.)

2.97   Declaration of dividend

2.97(1)   [Duty of administrator] Subject to paragraph (2), within the 2 month period referred to in Rule 2.95(4)(a) the administrator shall proceed to declare the dividend to one or more classes of creditor of which he gave notice.

2.97(2)   [Pending applications] Except with the permission of the court, the administrator shall not declare a dividend so long as there is pending any application to the court to reverse or vary a decision of his on a proof, or to expunge a proof or to reduce the amount claimed.

2.97(3)   [Administrator to make provision] If the court gives permission under paragraph (2), the administrator must make such provision in respect of the proof in question as the court directs.

(See General Note after r.2.105.)

2.98   Notice of declaration of a dividend

2.98(1)   [Notice to all creditors who have proved] Where the administrator declares a dividend he shall give notice of that fact to all creditors who have proved their debts and, where a member State liquidator has been appointed in relation to the company, to the member State liquidator.

2.98(2)   [Particulars in notice] The notice shall include the following particulars relating to the administration–

(a)   amounts raised from the sale of assets, indicating (so far as practicable) amounts raised by the sale of particular assets;

(b)   payments made by the administrator when acting as such;

(c)   where the administrator proposed to make a distribution to unsecured creditors, the value of the prescribed part, except where the court has made an order under section 176A(5);

(d)   provision (if any) made for unsettled claims, and funds (if any) retained for particular purposes;

(e)   the total amount of dividend and the rate of dividend; and

(f)   [Omitted.]

(g)   whether, and if so when, any further dividend is expected to be declared.

(See General Note after r.2.105.)

2.99   Payments of dividends and related matters

2.99(1)   [Simultaneous distribution] The dividend may be distributed simultaneously with the notice declaring it.

2.99(2)   [Method of payment] Payment of dividend may be made by post, or arrangements may be made with any creditor for it to be paid to him in another way, or held for his collection.

2.99(3) **[Endorsement on negotiable instrument]** Where a dividend is paid on a bill of exchange or other negotiable instrument, the amount of the dividend shall be endorsed on the instrument, or on a certified copy of it, if required to be produced by the holder for that purpose.

(See General Note after r.2.105.)

2.100 Notice of no dividend, or no further dividend

2.100 If the administrator gives notice to creditors that he is unable to declare any dividend or (as the case may be) any further dividend, the notice shall contain a statement to the effect either–

(a) that no funds have been realised; or

(b) that the funds realised have already been distributed or used or allocated for defraying the expenses of administration.

(See General Note after r.2.105.)

2.101 Proof altered after payment of dividend

2.101(1) **[If amount claimed in proof increased]** If after payment of dividend the amount claimed by a creditor in his proof is increased, the creditor is not entitled to disturb the distribution of the dividend; but he is entitled to be paid, out of any money for the time being available for the payment of any further dividend, any dividend or dividends which he has failed to receive.

2.101(2) **[Payment under r.2.101(1)]** Any dividend or dividends payable under paragraph (1) shall be paid before the money there referred to is applied to the payment of any such further dividend.

2.101(3) **[Proof withdrawn etc.]** If, after a creditor's proof has been admitted, the proof is withdrawn or expunged, or the amount is reduced, the creditor is liable to repay to the administrator any amount overpaid by way of dividend.

(See General Note after r.2.105.)

2.102 Secured creditors

2.102(1) **[Application of r.2.102]** The following applies where a creditor re-values his security at a time when a dividend has been declared.

2.102(2) **[Reduction of unsecured claim]** If the revaluation results in a reduction of his unsecured claim ranking for dividend, the creditor shall as soon as reasonably practicable repay to the administrator, for the credit of the administration, any amount received by him as dividend in excess of that to which he would be entitled having regard to the revaluation of the security.

2.102(3) **[Reduction of unsecured claim]** If the revaluation results in an increase of his unsecured claim, the creditor is entitled to receive from the administrator, out of any money for the time being available for the payment of a further dividend, before any such further dividend is paid, any dividend or dividends which he has failed to receive, having regard to the revaluation of the security.

However, the creditor is not entitled to disturb any dividend declared (whether or not distributed) before the date of the revaluation.

(See General Note after r.2.105.)

2.103 Disqualification from dividend

2.103 If a creditor contravenes any provision of the Act or the Rules relating to the valuation of securities, the court may, on the application of the administrator, order that the creditor be wholly or partly disqualified from participation in any dividend.

(See General Note after r.2.105.)

2.104 Assignment of right to dividend

2.104(1) [Notice of assignment etc.] If a person entitled to a dividend gives notice to the administrator that he wishes the dividend to be paid to another person, or that he has assigned his entitlement to another person, the administrator shall pay the dividend to that other accordingly.

2.104(2) [Contents of notice] A notice given under this Rule must specify the name and address of the person to whom payment is to be made.

(See General Note after r.2.105.)

2.105 Debt payable at future time

2.105(1) [Entitlement to dividend] Where a creditor has proved for a debt of which payment is not due at the date of the declaration of dividend, he is entitled to dividend equally with other creditors, but subject as follows.

2.105(2) [Calculation of amount of reduction] For the purpose of dividend (and no other purpose) the amount of the creditor's admitted proof (or, if a distribution has previously been made to him, the amount remaining outstanding in respect of his admitted proof) shall be reduced by applying the following formula–

$$\frac{X}{1.05^n}$$

where–

(a) "X" is the value of the admitted proof; and

(b) "n" is the period beginning with the relevant date and ending with the date on which the payment of the creditor's debt would otherwise be due expressed in years and months in a decimalised form.

2.105(3) ["Relevant date"] In paragraph (2) **"relevant date"** means–

(a) in the case of an administration which was not immediately preceded by a winding up, the date that the company entered administration;

(b) in the case of an administration which was immediately preceded by a winding up, the date that the company went into liquidation.

GENERAL NOTE TO RR.2.95–2.105

As noted above, the making of a distribution is not among the purposes which may be specified under the original administration regime. These rules therefore have no counterpart in Pt 2 of the original rules, but they are largely modelled on rr.11.1 et seq.

The deletion of r.2.95(1), (2), (5A) means that (for other than existing insolvencies) it is no longer necessary to give notice individually to creditors entitled to participate in the distribution.

An administrator may not make a distribution to unsecured, non-preferential creditors without the permission of the court (para.65(3)).

Rule 2.105(2) was substituted and the former r.2.105(3) omitted, by the Insolvency (Amendment) Rules 2005 (SI 2005/527) r.14, as from April 1, 2005. The change was designed to meet the criticisms made of the former wording by Lord Millett in *Re Park Air Services plc* [2000] 2 A.C. 172 at 188. The discount is now to be applied to the reducing amount of the debt rather than to the full amount of the admitted proof. A similar change has been made to r.11.13(2). Rules 2.95(3), 2.96 amended, rr.2.95(1), (2), (5)(a), 2.98(2)(f) omitted and rr.2.96A, 2.97(3) inserted by I(A)R 2010 r.2 and Sch. paras 85–89 as from April 6, 2010. Previously r.2.95(3), (5) substituted by I(A)R 2009 (SI 2009/642) r.12 as from April 6, 2009.

CHAPTER 11

THE ADMINISTRATOR

2.106   Fixing of remuneration

2.106(1)   [Entitlement to remuneration] The administrator is entitled to receive remuneration for his services as such.

2.106(2)   [How basis of remuneration fixed] The basis of remuneration shall be fixed–

(a)   as a percentage of the value of the property with which he has to deal; or

(b)   by reference to the time properly given by the insolvency practitioner (as administrator) and his staff in attending to matters arising in the administration; or

(c)   as a set amount.

2.106(3)   [Omitted.]

2.106(3A)   [Different bases for different things done] The basis of remuneration may be fixed as any one or more of the bases set out in paragraph (2), and different bases may be fixed in respect of different things done by the administrator.

2.106(3B)   [Different percentages] Where the basis of remuneration is fixed as set out in paragraph (2)(a), different percentages may be fixed in respect of different things done by the administrator.

2.106(3C)   [Creditors' committee to determine base(s)/percentage(s)] It is for the creditors' committee (if there is one) to determine–

(a)   which of the bases set out in paragraph (2) are to be fixed and (where appropriate) in what combination under paragraph (3A), and

(b)   the percentage or percentages (if any) to be fixed under paragraphs (2)(a) and (3B) and the amount (if any) to be set under paragraph (2)(c).

2.106(4)   [Matters relevant to r.2.106(2) determination] In arriving at that determination, the committee shall have regard to the following matters–

(a)   the complexity (or otherwise) of the case;

(b)   any respects in which, in connection with the company's affairs, there falls on the administrator any responsibility of an exceptional kind or degree;

(c)   the effectiveness with which the administrator appears to be carrying out, or to have carried out, his duties as such; and

(d)   the value and nature of the property with which he has to deal.

2.106(5)   [If no committee or determination and not within r.2.106(5A)] If there is no creditors' committee, or the committee does not make the requisite determination, and the case does not fall within paragraph (5A), the basis of the administrator's remuneration may be fixed (in accordance with paragraphs (2), (3A) and (3B)) by a resolution of a meeting of creditors; and paragraph (4) applies to them as it does to the creditors' committee.

2.106(5A)   [Where no creditors' committee or no determination] In a case where the administrator has made a statement under paragraph 52(1)(b), if there is no creditors' committee, or the committee does not make the requisite determination, the basis of the administrator's remuneration may be fixed (in accordance with paragraphs (2), (3A) and (3B)) by the approval of–

(a)   each secured creditor of the company: or

(b) if the administrator has made or intends to make a distribution to preferential creditors-

    (i) each secured creditor of the company; and

    (ii) preferential creditors whose debts amount to more than 50% of the preferential debts of the company, disregarding debts of any creditor who does not respond to an invitation to give or withhold approval;

and paragraph (4) applies to them as it does to the creditors' committee.

2.106(6) [Application to court] If not fixed as above, the basis of the administrator's remuneration shall, on his application, be fixed by the court and the provisions of paragraphs (2) to (4) apply as they do to the fixing of the basis of remuneration by the creditors' committee; but such an application may not be made by the administrator unless the administrator has first sought fixing of the basis in accordance with paragraph (3), (5) or (5A), and in any event may not be made more than 18 months after the date of the administrator's appointment.

2.106(7) [Where joint administrators] Where there are joint administrators, it is for them to agree between themselves as to how the remuneration payable should be apportioned. Any dispute arising between them may be referred–

(a) to the court, for settlement by order; or

(b) to the creditors' committee or a meeting of creditors, for settlement by resolution.

2.106(8) [Where administrator a solicitor] If the administrator is a solicitor and employs his own firm, or any partner in it, to act on behalf of the company, profit costs shall not be paid unless this is authorised by the creditors' committee, the creditors or the court.

(See General Note after r.2.109C.)

2.107 Recourse to meeting of creditors

2.107(1) [Request for increase by resolution of creditors] If the basis of the administrator's remuneration has been fixed by the creditors' committee, and he considers the rate or amount to be insufficient, or the basis to be inappropriate, the administrator may request that the rate or amount be increased or the basis changed by resolution of the creditors.

2.107(2) [Statement under para.52(1)(b)] In a case where the administrator has made a statement under paragraph 52(1)(b), if the basis of the administrator's remuneration has been fixed by the creditors' committee, and he considers the rate or amount to be insufficient, or the basis to be inappropriate, the administrator may request that the rate or amount be increased or the basis changed by the approval of–

(a) each secured creditor of the company: or

(b) if the administrator has made or intends to make a distribution to preferential creditors-

    (i) each secured creditor of the company; and

    (ii) preferential creditors whose debts amount to more than 50% of the preferential debts of the company, disregarding debts of any creditor who does not respond to an invitation to give or withhold approval.

(See General Note after r.2.109C.)

2.108 Recourse to the court

2.108(1) [Administrator's power to apply to court] If the administrator considers that the basis of remuneration fixed for him by the creditors' committee, or by resolution of the creditors, is insufficient or inappropriate, he may apply to the court for an order changing it or increasing its amount or rate.

2.108(1A) [Statement under para.52(1)(b)] In a case where the administrator has made a statement under paragraph 52(1)(b), if the administrator considers that the basis of remuneration fixed by the approval of the creditors in accordance with Rule 2.107(2) is insufficient or inappropriate, he may apply to the court for an order changing it or increasing its amount or rate.

2.108(1B) [Notice where application under r.2.108A] Where an application is made under paragraph (1A), the administrator must give notice to each of the creditors whose approval was sought under Rule 2.106(5A).

2.108(2) [Notice to creditors' committee] The administrator shall give at least 14 days' notice of his application to the members of the creditors' committee; and the committee may nominate one or more members to appear, or be represented, and to be heard on the application.

2.108(3) [Where no creditors' committee] If there is no creditors' committee, the administrator's notice of his application shall be sent to such one or more of the company's creditors as the court may direct, which creditors may nominate one or more of their number to appear or be represented.

2.108(4) [Costs of application] The court may, if it appears to be a proper case, order the costs of the administrator's application, including the costs of any member of the creditors' committee appearing or being represented on it, or any creditor so appearing or being represented, to be paid as an expense of the administration.

(See General Note after r.2.109C.)

2.109   Creditors' claim that remuneration is or other expenses are excessive

2.109(1) [Which creditors may apply to court] Any secured creditor, or any unsecured creditor with either the concurrence of at least 10% in value of the unsecured creditors (including that creditor) or the permission of the court, may apply to the court for one or more of the orders in paragraph (4).

2.109(1A) [Grounds for application] Application may be made on the grounds that–

(a)   the remuneration charged by the administrator,

(b)   the basis fixed for the administrator's remuneration under Rule 2.106, or

(c)   expenses incurred by the administrator,

is or are, in all the circumstances, excessive or, in the case of an application under sub-paragraph (b), inappropriate.

2.109(1B) [Time limit for application] The application must, subject to any order of the court under Rule 2.48A(4), be made no later than 8 weeks after receipt by the applicant of the progress report which first reports the charging of the remuneration or the incurring of the expenses in question (**"the relevant report"**).

2.109(2) [Power of court to dismiss etc.] The court may, if it thinks that no sufficient cause is shown for a reduction, dismiss it without a hearing but it shall not do so without giving the applicant at least 5 business days' notice, upon receipt of which the applicant may require the court to list the application for a without notice hearing. If the application is not dismissed, the court shall fix a venue for it to be heard, and give notice to the applicant accordingly.

2.109(3) [Notice to administrator] The applicant shall, at least 14 days before the hearing, send to the administrator a notice stating the venue and accompanied by a copy of the application, and of any evidence which the applicant intends to adduce in support of it.

2.109(4) [Court order if application well-founded] If the court considers the application to be well-founded, it must make one or more of the following orders–

(a)   an order reducing the amount of remuneration which the administrator was entitled to charge;

   (b)   an order fixing the basis of remuneration at a reduced rate or amount;

   (c)   an order changing the basis of remuneration;

   (d)   an order that some or all of the remuneration or expenses in question be treated as not being expenses of the administration;

   (e)   an order that the administrator or the administrator's personal representative pay to the company the amount of the excess of remuneration or expenses or such part of the excess as the court may specify;

and may make any other order that it thinks just; but an order under sub-paragraph (b) or (c) may be made only in respect of periods after the period covered by the relevant report.

2.109(5)   **[Costs of application]** Unless the court orders otherwise, the costs of the application shall be paid by the applicant, and are not payable as an expense of the administration.

2.109A   Review of remuneration

2.109A(1)   **[Request by administrator]** Where, after the basis of the administrator's remuneration has been fixed, there is a material and substantial change in the circumstances which were taken into account in fixing it, the administrator may request that it be changed.

2.109A(2)   **[To whom request to be made]** The request must be made–

   (a)   where the creditors' committee fixed the basis, to the committee;

   (b)   where the creditors fixed the basis, to the creditors;

   (c)   where the court fixed the basis, by application to the court;

and Rules 2.106 to 2.109 apply as appropriate.

2.109A(3)   **[Date from when change applies]** Any change in the basis for remuneration applies from the date of the request under paragraph (2) and not for any earlier period.

2.109B   Remuneration of new administrator

2.109B   If a new administrator is appointed in place of another, any determination, resolution or court order in effect under the preceding provisions of this Chapter immediately before the former administrator ceased to hold office continues to apply in respect of the remuneration of the new administrator until a further determination, resolution or court order is made in accordance with those provisions.

2.109C   Apportionment of set fee remuneration

2.109C(1)   **[Former administrator or personal representative]** In a case in which the basis of the administrator's remuneration is a set amount under Rule 2.106(2)(c) and the administrator ("the former administrator") ceases (for whatever reason) to hold office before the time has elapsed or the work has been completed in respect of which the amount was set, application may be made for determination of what portion of the amount should be paid to the former administrator or the former administrator's personal representative in respect of the time which has actually elapsed or the work which has actually been done.

2.109C(2)   **[Who may make application]** Application may be made–

   (a)   by the former administrator or the former administrator's personal representative within the period of 28 days beginning with the date upon which the former administrator ceased to hold office, or

(b) by the administrator for the time being in office if the former administrator or the former administrator's personal representative has not applied by the end of that period.

2.109C(3)   **[To whom application to be made]** Application must be made–

(a) where the creditors' committee fixed the basis, to the committee;

(b) where the creditors fixed the basis, to the creditors for a resolution determining the portion;

(c) where the court fixed the basis, to the court for an order determining the portion.

2.109C(4)   **[Copy of application]** The applicant must give a copy of the application to the administrator for the time being in office or to the former administrator or the former administrator's personal representative, as the case may be ("the recipient").

2.109C(5)   **[Notice to make representations etc.]** The recipient may within 21 days of receipt of the copy of the application give notice of intent to make representations to the creditors' committee or the creditors or to appear or be represented before the court, as the case may be.

2.109C(6)   **[Minimum period for determination]** No determination may be made upon the application until expiry of the 21 days referred to in paragraph (5) or, if the recipient does give notice of intent in accordance with that paragraph, until the recipient has been afforded the opportunity to make representations or to appear or be represented, as the case may be.

2.109C(7)   **[Application to increase portion]** If the former administrator or the former administrator's personal representative (whether or not the original applicant) considers that the portion determined upon application to the creditors' committee or the creditors is insufficient, that person may apply–

(a) in the case of a determination by the creditors' committee, to the creditors for a resolution increasing the portion;

(b) in the case of a resolution of the creditors (whether under paragraph (1) or under sub-paragraph (a)), to the court for an order increasing the portion;

and paragraphs (4) to (6) apply as appropriate.

GENERAL NOTE TO RR.2.106–2.109C

On the remuneration of office-holders generally, see the *Practice Statement: The Fixing and Approval of the Remuneration of Appointees (2004)* [2004] B.C.C. 912 (reproduced as App. VII to this *Guide*) and, for an account of a disputed case (*Re Cabletel Installations Ltd* (April 20, 2004)), see Moss, (2005) 18 Insolv. Int. 61.

Rules 2.106–2.108 were modified by the Insolvency (Amendment) Rules 2005 (SI 2005/527) rr.15–17, as from April 1, 2005. This change was intended to clarify which of the creditors have the responsibility for fixing or increasing the administrator's remuneration in the circumstances described in r.106(5A). Rules 2.106(2),(5)–(6), 2.107(1), (2) amended, r.2.106(3) omitted, r.2.109(1), (4) substituted and rr.2.106(3A)–(3C), 2.108(1A), 2.109(1A), 2.109A–2.109C inserted by I(A)R 2010 r.2 and Sch. paras 90–93 as from April 6, 2010.

New rr.2.109A–2.109C make provision allowing an administrator to seek a review of his remuneration if there has been a change of circumstances.

For the corresponding rules which apply under the original regime, see the original rr.2.47 et seq.

CHAPTER 12

ENDING ADMINISTRATION

2.110   **Final progress reports**

2.110(1)   **[References to progress report]** In this Chapter reference to a progress report is to a report in the form specified in Rule 2.47.

2.110(2)   [Meaning of final progress report] The final progress report means a progress report which includes a summary of–

(a)   the administrator's proposals;

(b)   any major amendments to, or deviations from, those proposals;

(c)   the steps taken during the administration; and

(d)   the outcome.

(See General Note after r.2.118.)

2.111   Notice of automatic end of administration

2.111(1)   [Notice where appointment ceased to have effect] Where the appointment of an administrator has ceased to have effect, and the administrator is not required by any other Rule to give notice of that fact, he shall, as soon as reasonably practicable, and in any event within 5 business days of the date when the appointment has ceased, file a notice of automatic end of administration in Form 2.30B with the court. The notice shall be accompanied by a final progress report.

[FORM 2.30B]

2.111(2)   [Copy to registrar of companies] A copy of the notice and accompanying document shall be sent as soon as reasonably practicable to the registrar of companies, and to all other persons who received a copy of the administrator's proposals.

2.111(3)   [Default fine] If the administrator makes default in complying with this Rule, he is liable to a fine and, for continued contravention, to a daily default fine.

(See General Note after r.2.118.)

2.112   Applications for extension of administration

2.112(1)   [Application accompanied by further progress report] An application to court for an extension of administration shall be accompanied by a progress report for the period since the last progress report (if any) or the date the company entered administration.

2.112(2)   [Extension request by consent of creditors] When the administrator requests an extension of the period of the administration by consent of creditors, his request shall be accompanied by a progress report for the period since the last progress report (if any) or the date the company entered administration.

2.112(3)   [Omitted.]

2.112(4)   [Notice where extension order by court] Where the court makes an order extending the administration, the administrator must give notice of the order to the creditors as soon as reasonably practicable, together with a copy of the progress report which accompanied the application to the court.

2.112(5)   [Notice where extension by consent of creditors] Where the period of the administration has been extended by consent of creditors, the administrator must give notice to the creditors as soon as reasonably practicable.

(See General Note after r.2.118.)

2.113   Notice of end of administration

2.113(1)   [Form of notice etc.] Where an administrator who was appointed under paragraph 14 or 22 gives notice that the purpose of administration has been sufficiently achieved he shall use Form 2.32B. The notice shall be accompanied by a final progress report.

[FORM 2.32B]

2.113(2)   [Copy to registrar of companies] The administrator shall send a copy of the notice to the registrar of companies.

2.113(3) **[Endorsement by court]** Two copies of the notice shall be filed with the court and shall contain a statement that a copy of the notice has been sent to the registrar of companies. The court shall endorse each copy with the date and time of filing. The appointment shall cease to have effect from that date and time.

2.113(4) **[Sealed copy to administrator]** The court shall give a sealed copy of the notice to the administrator.

2.113(5) **[Duty of administrator to notify]** The administrator shall, as soon as reasonably practicable, and within 5 business days, send a copy of the notice of end of administration (and the accompanying report) to every creditor of the company of whose claim and address he is aware, to all those persons (except the registrar of companies – see paragraph (2)) who were notified of his appointment and to the company.

2.113(6) **[Gazetting of notice]** The requirements of paragraph 80(4) shall be taken to be complied with if, within 5 business days of filing the notice of end of administration with the court, the administrator has gazetted a notice undertaking to provide a copy of the notice of the end of administration to any creditor of the company.

2.113(6A) **[Advertisement of r.2.113(6) notice]** The notice under Rule 2.113(6) may be advertised in such other manner as the administrator thinks fit.

2.113(7) **[Additional contents of notice]** In addition to the standard contents, the notice under paragraph (6) must state–

    (a)   the date that the administration ended; and

    (b)   that creditors can write for a copy of the notice of end of administration and the address to which to write.

(See General Note after r.2.118.)

2.114   Application to court by administrator

2.114(1) **[Further progress report etc.]** An application to court under paragraph 79 for an order ending an administration shall have attached to it a progress report for the period since the last progress report (if any) or the date the company entered administration and a statement indicating what the administrator thinks should be the next steps for the company (if applicable).

2.114(2) **[Application at creditors' request]** Where the administrator applies to the court because the creditors' meeting has required him to, he shall also attach a statement to the application in which he shall indicate (giving reasons) whether or not he agrees with the creditors' requirement to him to make the application.

2.114(3) **[Application other than at creditors' request]** When the administrator applies other than at the request of a creditors' meeting, he shall–

    (a)   give notice in writing to the applicant for the administration order under which he was appointed, or the person by whom he was appointed and the creditors of his intention to apply to court at least 5 business days before the date that he intends to makes his application; and

    (b)   attach to his application to court a statement that he has notified the creditors, and copies of any response from creditors to that notification.

2.114(4) **[Application in conjunction with winding-up petition]** Where the administrator applies to court under paragraph 79 in conjunction with a petition under section 124 for an order to wind up the company, he shall, in addition to the requirements of paragraph (3), notify the creditors whether he intends to seek appointment as liquidator.

(See General Note after r.2.118.)

2.115 Application to court by creditor

2.115(1) [Service of application] Where a creditor applies to the court to end the administration a copy of the application shall be served on the administrator and the person who either made the application for the administration order or made the appointment. Where the appointment was made under paragraph 14, a copy of the application shall be served on the holder of the floating charge by virtue of which the appointment was made.

2.115(2) [Period for service; appearance at hearing] Service shall be effected not less than 5 business days before the date fixed for the hearing. The administrator, applicant or appointor, or holder of the floating charge by virtue of which the appointment was made may appear at the hearing of the application.

2.115(3) [Copy of order to amend administration] Where the court makes an order to end the administration, the court shall send a copy of the order to the administrator.

(See General Note after r.2.118.)

2.116 Notification by administrator of court order

2.116(1) [Administrator to notify registrar of companies] Where the court makes an order to end the administration, the administrator must send to the registrar of companies a copy of the court order and a copy of his final progress report.

2.116(2) [Copy of notice and final progress report] As soon as reasonably practicable, the administrator must send a copy of the notice and the final progress report to all other persons who received notice of the administrator's appointment.

(See General Note after r.2.118.)

2.117 Moving from administration to creditors' voluntary liquidation [Deleted.]

2.117A Moving from administration to creditors' voluntary liquidation

2.117A(1) [Former administrator to send final progress report to registrar etc.] As soon as reasonably practicable after the day on which the registrar of companies registers the notice of moving from administration to creditors' voluntary liquidation sent by the administrator for the purposes of paragraph 83(3), the person who at that point ceases to be the administrator must (whether the administrator becomes the liquidator or not) send a final progress report (which must include details of the assets to be dealt with in the liquidation) to the registrar of companies and to all those who received notice of the administrator's appointment.

2.117A(2) [Person nominated by creditors as liquidator for Sch.B1 para.83(7)(a)] For the purposes of paragraph 83(7)(a), a person is nominated by the creditors as liquidator by–

(a) their approval of the statement of the proposed liquidator in the administrator's proposals or revised proposals, or

(b) their nomination of a different person before their approval of the proposals or revised proposals.

2.117A(3) [Different person nominated] Where the creditors nominate a different person, the nomination must, where applicable, include the declaration required by section 231.

(See General Note after r.2.118.)

2.118 Moving from administration to dissolution

2.118(1) [Form of notice with final progress report] Where, for the purposes of paragraph 84(1), the administrator sends a notice of moving from administration to dissolution to the registrar of companies, the administrator must attach to that notice a final progress report.

2.118(2)   **[Copies]** As soon as reasonably practicable a copy of the notice and the attached document shall be sent to all other persons who received notice of the administrator's appointment.

2.118(3)   **[Copy of order for extension, suspension or disapplication of dissolution]** Where a court makes an order under paragraph 84(7) it shall, where the applicant is not the administrator, give a copy of the order to the administrator.

2.118(4)   [Omitted.]

GENERAL NOTE TO RR.2.110–2.118

Paragraphs 76 et seq. of Sch.B1 deal with the various ways in which an administration can come to an end (in the words of the draftsman, "the appointment of an administrator shall cease to have effect"). These rules supplement those provisions by spelling out the procedure to be followed and the forms to be used in each case. Rules 2.111, 2.113, 2.116, 2.118 amended, rr.2.112(3), 2.117, 2.118(4) omitted, rr.2.112(4), (5), 2.116(2), 2.117A inserted and r.2.113(7) substituted by I(A)R 2010 r.2 and Sch. paras 95–100 as from April 6, 2010. Previously r.2.113(6) amended, and r.2.113(6A) inserted, by I(A)R 2009 (SI 2009/642) r.13 as from April 6, 2009.

R.2.111(3)
On penalties, see s.430 and Sch.10.

R.2.112
An application for extension must be made well ahead of time so that it can be heard by the registrar. On October 15, 2008 Mann J. issued a warning that administrators who leave applying until a late date will have their costs disallowed by the applications judge. See also the unreported case *Re Taylor Made Foods plc*, discussed in the note to Sch.B1 paras 76–77.

R.2.113(7)
On the standard contents (for notices other than gazetted notices), see rr.12A.36–12A.39.

CHAPTER 13

REPLACING THE ADMINISTRATOR

2.119   **Grounds for resignation**

2.119(1)   **[Notice of grounds]** The administrator may give notice of his resignation on grounds of ill health or because–

  (a)   he intends ceasing to be in practice as an insolvency practitioner; or

  (b)   there is some conflict of interest, or change of personal circumstances, which precludes or makes impracticable the further discharge by him of the duties of administrator.

2.119(2)   **[Other grounds]** The administrator may, with the permission of the court, give notice of his resignation on grounds other than those specified in paragraph (1).

(See General Note after r.2.129.)

2.120   **Notice of intention to resign**

2.120(1)   **[Form of notice of intention to resign]** The administrator shall in all cases give at least 5 business days' notice in Form 2.37B of his intention to resign, or to apply for the court's permission to do so, to the following persons–

                                                                     [FORM 2.37B]

  (a)   if there is a continuing administrator of the company, to him; and

  (b)   if there is a creditors' committee to it; but

  (c)   if there is no such administrator and no creditors' committee, to the company and its creditors.

2.120(2) **[Notice to member State liquidator]** Where the administrator gives notice under paragraph (1), he shall also give notice to a member State liquidator, if such a person has been appointed in relation to the company.

2.120(3) **[Notice to holders of prior qualifying floating charges etc.]** Where the administrator was appointed by the holder of a qualifying floating charge under paragraph 14, the notice of intention to resign shall also be sent to all holders of prior qualifying floating charges, and to the person who appointed the administrator. A copy of the notice shall also be sent to the holder of the floating charge by virtue of which the appointment was made.

2.120(4) **[Where appointed by company or directors]** Where the administrator was appointed by the company or the directors of the company under paragraph 22, a copy of the notice of intention to resign shall also be sent to the appointor and all holders of a qualifying floating charge.

(See General Note after r.2.129.)

2.121 Notice of resignation

2.121(1) **[Form of notice]** The notice of resignation shall be in Form 2.38B.

[FORM 2.38B]

2.121(2) **[Notice filed; copies]** Where the administrator was appointed under an administration order, the notice shall be filed with the court, and a copy sent to the registrar of companies. A copy of the notice of resignation shall be sent not more than 5 business days after it has been filed with the court to all those to whom notice of intention to resign was sent.

2.121(3) **[Copies where administrator appointed by holder of qualifying floating charge]** Where the administrator was appointed by the holder of a qualifying floating charge under paragraph 14, a copy of the notice of resignation shall be filed with the court and sent to the registrar of companies, and anyone else who received a copy of the notice of intention to resign, within 5 business days of the notice of resignation being sent to the holder of the floating charge by virtue of which the appointment was made.

2.121(4) **[Copies where administrator appointed by company or directors]** Where the administrator was appointed by the company or the directors under paragraph 22, a copy of the notice of resignation shall be filed with the court and sent to the registrar of companies and to anyone else who received notice of intention to resign within 5 business days of the notice of resignation being sent to either the company or the directors that made the appointment.

(See General Note after r.2.129.)

2.122 Application to court to remove administrator from office

2.122(1) **[Grounds]** Any application under paragraph 88 shall state the grounds on which it is requested that the administrator should be removed from office.

2.122(2) **[Service of notice]** Service of the notice of the application shall be effected on the administrator, the person who made the application for the administration order or the person who appointed the administrator, the creditors' committee (if any), the joint administrator (if any), and where there is neither a creditors' committee or joint administrator, to the company and all the creditors, including any floating charge holders not less than 5 business days before the date fixed for the application to be heard. Where the appointment was made under paragraph 14, the notice shall be served on the holder of the floating charge by virtue of which the appointment was made.

2.122(3) **[Order]** Where a court makes an order removing the administrator it shall give a copy of the order to the applicant who as soon as reasonably practicable shall send a copy to the administrator.

2.122(4) **[Copies]** The applicant shall also within 5 business days of the order being made send a copy of the order to all those to whom notice of the application was sent.

2.122(5)   [Copy to registrar of companies] A copy of the order shall also be sent to the registrar of companies within the same time period.

(See General Note after r.2.129.)

2.123   Notice of vacation of office when administrator ceases to be qualified to act

2.123   Where the administrator who has ceased to be qualified to act as an insolvency practitioner in relation to the company gives notice in accordance with paragraph 89, he shall also give notice to the registrar of companies.

(See General Note after r.2.129.)

2.124   Administrator deceased

2.124(1)   [Notice to court] Subject as follows, where the administrator has died, it is the duty of his personal representatives to give notice of the fact to the court, specifying the date of the death. This does not apply if notice has been given under either paragraph (2) or (3) of this Rule.

2.124(2)   [Notice by partner, employee etc.] If the deceased administrator was a partner in or an employee of a firm, notice may be given by a partner in the firm who is qualified to act as an insolvency practitioner, or is a member of any body recognised by the Secretary of State for the authorisation of insolvency practitioners.

2.124(3)   [Notice by others] Notice of the death may be given by any person producing to the court the relevant death certificate or a copy of it.

2.124(4)   [Notice to registrar of companies] Where a person gives notice to the court under this Rule, he shall also give notice to the registrar of companies.

(See General Note after r.2.129.)

2.125   Application to replace

2.125(1)   [Written statement by proposed replacement] Where an application is made to court under paragraphs 91(1) or 95 to appoint a replacement administrator, the application shall be accompanied by a written statement in Form 2.2B by the person proposed to be the replacement administrator.

2.125(2)   [Where administrator appointed under administration order] Where the original administrator was appointed under an administration order, a copy of the application shall be served, in addition to those persons listed in paragraph 12(2) and Rule 2.6(3), on the person who made the application for the administration order.

2.125(3)   [Witness statement of applicant's belief] Where the application to court is made under paragraph 95, the application shall be accompanied by a witness statement setting out the applicant's belief as to the matters set out in that paragraph.

2.125(4)   [Application of r.2.8 to service] Rule 2.8 shall apply to the service of an application under paragraphs 91(1) and 95 as it applies to service in accordance with Rule 2.6.

2.125(5)   [Application of rr.2.9, 2.10, 2.12, 2.14(1), (2)] Rules 2.9, 2.10, 2.12 and 2.14(1) and (2) apply to an application under paragraphs 91(1) and 95.]

(See General Note after r.2.129.)

2.126   Notification and advertisement of appointment of replacement administrator

2.126   Where a replacement administrator is appointed, the same provisions apply in respect of giving notice of, and advertising, the replacement appointment as in the case of the appointment (subject to Rule 2.128), and all statements, consents etc as are required shall also be required in the case of the appointment of a replacement. All forms and notices shall clearly identify that the appointment is of a replacement administrator.

(See General Note after r.2.129.)

2.127 Notification and advertisement of appointment of joint administrator

2.127 Where, after an initial appointment has been made, an additional person or persons are to be appointed as joint administrator the same Rules shall apply in respect of giving notice of and advertising the appointment as in the case of the initial appointment, subject to Rule 2.128.

(See General Note after r.2.129.)

2.128 The replacement or additional administrator shall send notice of the appointment to the registrar of companies.

(See General Note after r.2.129.)

2.129 Administrator's duties on vacating office

2.129(1) **[Delivery of assets, records, books etc.]** Where the administrator ceases to be in office as such, in consequence of removal, resignation or cesser of qualification as an insolvency practitioner, he is under obligation as soon as reasonably practicable to deliver up to the person succeeding him as administrator the assets (after deduction of any expenses properly incurred and distributions made by him) and further to deliver up to that person–

(a) the records of the administration, including correspondence, proofs and other related papers appertaining to the administration while it was within his responsibility; and

(b) the company's books, papers and other records.

2.129(2) **[Default fine]** If the administrator makes default in complying with this Rule, he is liable to a fine and, for continued contravention, to a daily default fine.

GENERAL NOTE TO RR.2.119–2.129

Rules 2.122–2.125, 2.128 amended by I(A)R 2010 r.2 and Sch. paras 103–107 as from April 6, 2010.

Paragraphs 87 et seq. of Sch.B1 deal with the various circumstances in which an administrator can leave office and be replaced by another, with the appointment of one or more additional administrators and with matters consequential upon an administrator leaving office. These rules supplement those provisions by spelling out the procedure to be followed and the forms to be used in each case. On "block transfers" (where it is proposed that an insolvency practitioner who holds multiple offices is to vacate them simultaneously and be replaced by another), see the note to IA 1986 s.172(1), (2); and the *Practice Direction: Insolvency Proceedings* [2007] B.C.C. 842 (reproduced as App.IV of this *Guide*). See also IR rr.7.10A et seq.

CHAPTER 14

EC REGULATION: CONVERSION OF ADMINISTRATION INTO WINDING UP

2.130 Application for conversion into winding up

2.130(1) **[Witness statement in support of application]** Where a member State liquidator proposes to apply to the court for the conversion into winding-up proceedings of an administration, a witness statement complying with Rule 2.131 must be prepared and filed with the court in support of the application.

2.130(1A) **["Conversion into winding-up proceedings" in rr.2.130–2.132]** In this Rule, and in Rules 2.131 and 2.132, **"conversion into winding-up proceedings"** means an order under Article 37 of the EC Regulation (conversion of earlier proceedings) that–

(a) the purposes of the administration are to be limited to the winding up of the company through administration and are to exclude the purpose contained in sub-paragraph (a) of paragraph 3(1);

(b) the administration is converted into a creditors' voluntary winding up; or

(c) the administration is converted into a winding up by the court.

2.130(2) **[Originating application]** An application under this Rule shall be by originating application.

2.130(3) **[On whom application to be served]** The application and the witness statement required under this Rule shall be served upon–

(a) the company; and

(b) the administrator.

(See General Note after r.2.133.)

2.131 Contents of witness statement

2.131(1) **[Contents]** The witness statement shall state–

(a) that main proceedings have been opened in relation to the company in a member State other than the United Kingdom;

(b) the belief of the person making the statement that the conversion of the administration into winding-up proceedings would prove to be in the interests of the creditors in the main proceedings;

(c) the opinion of the person making the statement as to whether the company ought to go into voluntary liquidation or be wound up by the court; and

(d) all other matters that, in the opinion of the member State liquidator, would assist the court–

    (i) in deciding whether to make such an order; and

    (ii) if the court were to do so, in considering the need for any consequential provision that would be necessary or desirable.

2.131(2) **[Member State liquidator to make witness statement]** A witness statement under this rule shall be made by, or on behalf of, the member State liquidator.

(See General Note after r.2.133.)

2.132 Power of court

2.132(1) **[Order]** On hearing the application for conversion into winding-up proceedings the court may make such order as it thinks fit.

2.132(2) **[Consequential provisions]** If the court makes an order for conversion into winding-up proceedings the order may contain all such consequential provisions as the court deems necessary or desirable.

2.132(3) **[Power to make order as if for voluntary winding up]** Without prejudice to the generality of paragraph (1), an order under that paragraph may provide that the company be wound up as if a resolution for voluntary winding up under section 84 were passed on the day on which the order is made.

(See General Note after r.2.133.)

CHAPTER 15

EC REGULATION: MEMBER STATE LIQUIDATOR

2.133 Interpretation of creditor and notice to member State liquidator

2.133(1) **[Application of r.2.133]** This Rule applies where a member State liquidator has been appointed in relation to the company.

2.133(2) **[Member State liquidator deemed creditor for certain Rules]** For the purposes of the Rules referred to in paragraph (3) the member State liquidator is deemed to be a creditor.

2.133(3) **[Rules for purpose of r.2.133(2)]** The Rules referred to in paragraph (2) are Rules 2.34 (notice of creditors' meeting), 2.35(4) (creditors' meeting), 2.37 (requisitioning of creditors' meeting), 2.38 (entitlement to vote), 2.39 (admission and rejection of claims), 2.40 (secured creditors), 2.41 (holders of negotiable instruments), 2.42 (hire-purchase, conditional sale and chattel leasing agreements), 2.46 (notice to creditors), 2.47 (reports to creditors), 2.48 (correspondence instead of creditors' meeting), 2.50(2) (creditors' committee), 2.57(1)(b) and (c) (termination of membership of creditors' committee), 2.59(3) (vacancies in creditors' committee), 2.108(3) (administrator's remuneration—recourse to court) and 2.109 (challenge to administrator's remuneration).

2.133(4) **[Rule 2.133(2), (3) subject to exercise of creditors' rights]** Paragraphs (2) and (3) are without prejudice to the generality of the right to participate referred to in paragraph 3 of Article 32 of the EC Regulation (exercise of creditors' rights).

2.133(5) **[Notice or copies to the member State liquidator]** Where the administrator is obliged to give notice to, or provide a copy of a document (including an order of court) to, the court, the registrar of companies or the official receiver, the administrator shall give notice or provide copies, as the case may be, to the member State liquidator.

2.133(6) **[Rule 2.133(5) subject to co-operate and communicate]** Paragraph (5) is without prejudice to the generality of the obligations imposed by Article 31 of the EC Regulation (duty to co-operate and communicate information).

GENERAL NOTE TO RR.2.130–2.133

These rules follow closely rr.*2.59–2.62* which apply under the original regime. See the notes to those provisions.
  Rules 2.130–2.132 amended by I(A)R 2010 r.2 and Sch. paras 108–110 as from April 6, 2010.

PART 3

ADMINISTRATIVE RECEIVERSHIP

Introductory note to Part 3
These rules are new and they have no counterpart in the previous legislation. The bulk of the rules deal with the creditors' committee which was an innovation introduced by IA 1986. It should be noted that the following rules do not apply to Scottish receiverships or receivers in Northern Ireland.

CHAPTER 1

APPOINTMENT OF ADMINISTRATIVE RECEIVER

3.1 Acceptance and confirmation of acceptance of appointment

3.1(1) **[Two or more persons appointed jointly]** Where two or more persons are appointed as joint receivers or managers of a company's property under powers contained in an instrument, the acceptance of such an appointment shall be made by each of them in accordance with section 33 as if that person were a sole appointee, but the joint appointment takes effect only when all such persons have so accepted and is then deemed to have been made at the time at which the instrument of appointment was received by or on behalf of all such persons.

3.1(2) **[Sole or joint receiver]** Subject to the next paragraph, where a person is appointed as the sole or joint receiver of a company's property under powers contained in an instrument, the appointee shall, if he accepts the appointment, within 5 business days confirm his acceptance in writing to the person appointing him.

3.1(3) **[Non-application of r.3.1(2)]** Paragraph (2) does not apply where an appointment is accepted in writing.

[FORM 3.1]

3.1(4) **[Who may accept or confirm]** Any acceptance or confirmation of acceptance of appointment as a receiver or manager of a company's property, whether under the Act or the Rules, may be given by any person (including, in the case of a joint appointment, any joint appointee) duly authorised for that purpose on behalf of the receiver or manager.

3.1(5) **[Statements in confirmation]** In confirming acceptance the appointee or person authorised for that purpose shall state–

(a)   the time and date of receipt of the instrument of appointment, and

(b)   the time and date of acceptance.

GENERAL NOTE

This rule should be viewed in the light of s.33. It deals with acceptance and confirmation of appointment as receiver or manager (not just an administrative receiver) despite the title of this Part and Chapter of the rules: see r.0.3(2) as amended. See I(A)R 2010 (SI 2010/686) which converts the seven-day period in para.(2) to five business days.

3.2   Notice and advertisement of appointment

3.2(1) **[Notice required by s.46(1)]** This Rule relates to the notice which a person is required by section 46(1) to send and publish, when appointed as administrative receiver.

3.2(2) **[Matters to be stated in notice]** The following matters shall be stated in the notices sent to the company and the creditors–

(a)   the registered name of the company, as at the date of the appointment, and its registered number;

(b)   any other name with which the company has been registered in the 12 months preceding that date;

(c)   any name under which the company has traded at any time in those 12 months, if substantially different from its then registered name;

(d)   the name and address of the administrative receiver, and the date of his appointment;

(e)   the name of the person by whom the appointment was made;

(f)   the date of the instrument conferring the power under which the appointment was made, and a brief description of the instrument;

(g)   a brief description of the assets of the company (if any) in respect of which the person appointed is not made the receiver.

3.2(3) **[Gazetting and advertisement of notice of appointment]** Subject to paragraph (4), the notice of appointment to be given by the administrative receiver under section 46(1)(a) shall be gazetted and may be advertised in such other manner as the administrative receiver thinks fit.

[FORM 3.1A]

3.2(4) **[Additional contents of r.3.2(3) notice]** In addition to the standard contents, the notice under paragraph (3) must state–

(a)   that an administrative receiver has been appointed;

(b)   the date of the appointment;

(c)   the name of the person who made the appointment, and that the appointment was made by that person; and

(d)   the nature of the business of the company.

GENERAL NOTE

Details of the notices required to be given by an administrative receiver under IA 1986 s.46 to the company and the public at large are here provided. Note the change of wording introduced by the Insolvency (Amendment) Rules 2009 (SI 2009/642) with effect from April 6, 2009. This change involved substituting new paras (3) and (4). See I(A)R 2010 (SI 2010/686) which replaces para.(4).

CHAPTER 2

STATEMENT OF AFFAIRS AND REPORT TO CREDITORS

3.3   Notice requiring statement of affairs

3.3(1)   [Notice re s.47 statement] Where the administrative receiver determines to require a statement of the company's affairs to be made out and submitted to him in accordance with section 47, he shall send notice to each of the persons whom he considers should be made responsible under that section, requiring them to prepare and submit the statement.

[FORM 3.1B]

3.3(2)   ["The nominated persons"] The persons to whom the notice is sent are referred to in this Chapter as "the nominated persons".

3.3(3)   [Contents of notice] The notice shall inform each of the nominated persons–

(a)   of the names and addresses of all others (if any) to whom the same notice has been sent;

(b)   of the time within which the statement must be delivered;

(c)   of the effect of section 47(6) (penalty for non-compliance); and

(d)   of the application to him, and to each of the other nominated persons, of section 235 (duty to provide information, and to attend on the administrative receiver if required).

3.3(4)   [Instructions for preparation of statement] The administrative receiver shall, on request, furnish each nominated person with the forms required for the preparation of the statement of affairs.

GENERAL NOTE

This rule fills out the contents of any notice given by an administrative receiver under IA 1986 s.47 to "nominated persons" who must submit a statement of the company's affairs to him.

The receiver *must* demand a statement from someone: his only discretion is in determining who to "require" it from (see s.47 itself). See I(A)R 2010 (SI 2010/686) which replaces deponent with nominated person.

3.4   Verification and filing

3.4(1)   [Form of statement and verification] The statement of affairs shall be in Form 3.2, shall contain all the particulars required by that form and shall be verified by statement of truth by the nominated persons (using the same form).

[FORM 3.2]

3.4(2) **[Statement of concurrence]** The administrative receiver may require any of the persons mentioned in section 47(3) to submit a statement of concurrence, stating that he concurs with the statement of affairs.

3.4(3) **[Statement of concurrence may be qualified]** A statement of concurrence may be qualified in respect of matters dealt with in the statement of affairs, where the maker of the statement of concurrence is not in agreement with the nominated persons, or he considers the statement to be erroneous or misleading, or he is without the direct knowledge necessary for concurring with it.

3.4(4) **[Statement of affairs to receiver]** The statement of affairs shall be delivered to the receiver by the nominated persons making the statement of truth (or by one of them, if more than one), together with a copy of the verified statement.

3.4(5) **[Delivery of statement of concurrence]** Every statement of concurrence shall be delivered by the person who makes it, together with a copy.

3.4(6) **[Retention of copy statement of affairs, etc.]** The administrative receiver shall retain the verified copy of the statement of affairs and the statements of concurrence (if any) as part of the records of the receivership.

GENERAL NOTE

This relates to the form of the statement of affairs submitted under IA 1986 s.47. See I(A)R 2010 (SI 2010/686) which replaces "affidavit" with "statement of truth".

3.5 Limited disclosure

3.5(1) **[Application to court]** Where the administrative receiver thinks that it would prejudice the conduct of the receivership or might reasonably be expected to lead to violence against any person for the whole or part of the statement of affairs to be disclosed, he may apply to the court for an order of limited disclosure in respect of the statement or a specified part of it.

3.5(2) **[Powers of court]** The court may on the application order that the statement, or, as the case may be, the specified part of it, be not open to inspection otherwise than with permission of the court.

3.5(3) **[Directions]** The court's order may include directions as to the delivery of documents to the registrar of companies and the disclosure of relevant information to other persons.

GENERAL NOTE

This allows the administrative receiver to apply to the court to censor the statement of affairs if publication would prejudice his task or endanger persons. Compare IA 1986 s.48(6). See I(A)R 2010 (SI 2010/686) which amends para.(1) to limit disclosure in order to protect personal safety.

3.6 Release from duty to submit statement of affairs; extension of time

3.6(1) **[Exercise of s.47(5) power]** The power of the administrative receiver under section 47(5) to give a release from the obligation imposed by that section, or to grant an extension of time, may be exercised at the receiver's own discretion, or at the request of any nominated person.

3.6(2) **[Application to court]** A nominated person may, if he requests a release or extension of time and it is refused by the receiver, apply to the court for it.

3.6(3) **[Court may dismiss application etc.]** The court may, if it thinks that no sufficient cause is shown for the application, dismiss it; but it shall not do so unless the applicant has had an opportunity to attend the court for a hearing without notice to any other party, of which he has been given at least 5 business days' notice.

If the application is not dismissed under this paragraph, the court shall fix a venue for it to be heard, and give notice to the deponent accordingly.

3.6(4)   [Nominated person to send notice to receiver] The deponent shall, at least 14 days before the hearing, send to the receiver a notice stating the venue and accompanied by a copy of the application, and of any evidence which he (the deponent) intends to adduce in support of it.

3.6(5)   [Appearance etc. by receiver] The receiver may appear and be heard on the application; and, whether or not he appears he may file a written report of any matters which he considers ought to be drawn to the court's attention.

  If such a report is filed, a copy of it shall be sent by the receiver to the deponent, not later than 5 business days before the hearing.

3.6(6)   [Sealed copies of order] Sealed copies of any order made on the application shall be sent by the court to the deponent and the receiver.

3.6(7)   [Costs] On any application under this Rule the applicant's costs shall be paid in any event by him and, unless the court otherwise orders, no allowance towards them shall be made out of the assets under the administrative receiver's control.

GENERAL NOTE

See I(A)R 2010 (SI 2010/686)—"deponent" replaced by "nominated person". Note also the temporal changes made to paras (3) and (5). Further details of any release given by an administrative receiver under IA 1986 s.47(5) are provided by this rule.

3.7   Expenses of statement of affairs

3.7(1)   [Payment of expenses] A nominated person making the statement of affairs and statement of truth shall be allowed, and paid by the administrative receiver out of his receipts, any expenses incurred by the nominated person in so doing which the receiver thinks reasonable.

3.7(2)   [Appeal to court] Any decision by the receiver under this Rule is subject to appeal to the court.

3.7(3)   [Effect of Rule] Nothing in this Rule relieves a nominated person from any obligation with respect to the preparation, verification and submission of the statement of affairs, or to the provision of information to the receiver.

GENERAL NOTE

This allows a "nominated person" (see r.3.3(2)) to recover from the company's assets his expenses incurred in producing the statement of affairs. See I(A)R 2010 (SI 2010/686) which discards terms such as deponent and affidavit in favour of modern terminology.

3.8   Report to creditors

3.8(1)   [Gazetting and advertisement of s.48(2)(b) notice] If an administrative receiver gives notice under section 48(2)(b), the notice–

  (a)   shall be gazetted; and

  (b)   may be advertised in such other manner as the administrative receiver thinks fit.

3.8(1A)   [Additional contents of r.3.8(1) notice] In addition to the standard contents, the notice under paragraph (1) must state that creditors can write for a copy of the report and the address to which to write.

3.8(2)   [No s.48(2) meeting proposed] If he proposes to apply to the court to dispense with the holding of the meeting of unsecured creditors (otherwise required by section 48(2)), he shall in his report to creditors or (as the case may be) in the notice published as above, state the venue fixed by the court for the hearing of the application.

3.8(3)   [Documents to be attached to report] Subject to any order of the court under Rule 3.5, the copy of the receiver's report which under section 48(1) is to be sent to the registrar of companies shall have attached to it a copy of any statement of affairs under section 47, and copies of any statements of concurrence.

3.8(4)   **[Late submission of documents]** If the statement of affairs or statements of concurrence, if any, have not been submitted to the receiver by the time he sends a copy of his report to the registrar of companies, he shall send a copy of the statement of affairs and any statements of concurrence as soon thereafter as he receives them.

3.8(5)   **[Statement in report]** The receiver's report under section 48(1) shall state, to the best of his knowledge and belief–

    (a)   an estimate of the value of the prescribed part (whether or not he proposes to make an application under section 176A(5) or whether section 176A(3) applies); and

    (b)   an estimate of the value of the company's net property.

3.8(6)   **[Non-disclosure of seriously prejudicial information]** Nothing in this Rule is to be taken as requiring any such estimate to include any information, the disclosure of which could seriously prejudice the commercial interests of the company.

If such information is excluded from the calculation the estimate shall be accompanied by a statement to that effect.

3.8(7)   **[Report to state whether application to court under s.176A(5)]** The report shall also state whether, and if so why, the receiver proposes to make an application to court under section 176A(5).

Gᴇɴᴇʀᴀʟ Nᴏᴛᴇ

If the administrative receiver opts to inform creditors under IA 1986 s.48(2) by a notice, then this rule will apply. This rule also deals with other actions of the administrative receiver under IA 1986 s.48.

    This reporting obligation was extended by Insolvency (Amendment) Rules 2003 (SI 2003/1730) by the addition of paras (5)–(7) which deal with the special reserve fund for unsecured creditors set up by s.176A.

    Note the amendment made by the Insolvency (Amendment) Rules 2009 (SI 2009/642) (from April 6, 2009). This amendment substituted a new para.(1).

    See I(A)R 2010 (SI 2010/686)—new para.(1A) inserted.

Cʜᴀᴘᴛᴇʀ 3

Cʀᴇᴅɪᴛᴏʀs' Mᴇᴇᴛɪɴɢ

3.9   Procedure for summoning meeting under s.48(2)

3.9(1)   **[Convenience of venue]** In fixing the venue for a meeting of creditors summoned under section 48(2), the administrative receiver shall have regard to the convenience of the persons who are invited to attend.

3.9(2)   **[Time of meeting]** The meeting shall be summoned for commencement between 10.00 and 16.00 hours on a business day, unless the court otherwise directs.

3.9(3)   **[Notice of venue]** At least 14 days' notice of the venue shall be given to all creditors of the company who are known to the receiver and had claims against the company at the date of his appointment.

3.9(4)   **[Forms of proxy]** With the notice summoning the meeting there shall be sent out forms of proxy.
                        [FORM 8.3]

3.9(5)   **[Statement in notice]** The notice shall include a statement to the effect that creditors whose claims are wholly secured are not entitled to attend or be represented at the meeting.

3.9(6)   [Administrative receiver to gazette and advertise notice of meeting] The administrative receiver–

(a)   as soon as reasonably practicable must also have gazetted a notice of the meeting; and

(b)   may advertise the notice of the meeting in such other manner as the administrative receiver thinks fit.

3.9(6A)   [Additional contents of notice] In addition to the standard contents, the notice under paragraph (6) must–

(a)   state that a meeting under section 48(2) is to take place;

(b)   include the statement required by paragraph (5); and

(c)   state the venue for the meeting.

3.9(7)   [Rule 3.11(1) statement] The notice to creditors and the notice given under paragraph (6) shall contain a statement of the effect of Rule 3.11(1) below (voting rights).

General Note

This outlines the procedure to be followed if the administrative receiver calls a meeting of creditors under IA 1986 s.48(2). For the definition of "venue" and "business day" see rr.13.6 and 13.3(1). Note the change introduced by the Insolvency (Amendment) Rules 2009 (SI 2009/642) (effective from April 6, 2009). This amendment involved substituting a new para.(6) and making a minor consequential change to para.(7). See I(A)R 2010 (SI 2010/686) which reformulates para.(6) and adds para.(6A).

3.10   The chairman at the meeting

3.10(1)   [Receiver or his nominee to be chairman] The chairman at the creditors' meeting shall be the receiver, or a person nominated by him in writing to act in his place.

3.10(2)   [Nominee chairman] A person so nominated must be either–

(a)   one who is qualified to act as an insolvency practitioner in relation to the company, or

(b)   an employee of the receiver or his firm who is experienced in insolvency matters.

General Note

Where the chairman of the meeting is not the administrative receiver, then he must also be qualified as an insolvency practitioner or have experience to satisfy r.3.10(2)(b): see Pt XIII of the Act.

3.11   Voting rights

3.11(1)   [Entitlement to vote] Subject as follows, at the creditors' meeting a person is entitled to vote only if–

(a)   he has given to the receiver, not later than 12.00 hours on the business day before the day fixed for the meeting, details in writing of the debt that he claims to be due to him from the company, and the claim has been duly admitted under Rule 3.12 or this Rule, and

(b)   there has been lodged with the administrative receiver any proxy which the creditor intends to be used on his behalf

and details of the debt must include any calculation for the purposes of paragraphs (6) and (7).

3.11(2)   [Failure to comply with r.3.11(1)(a)] The chairman of the meeting may allow a creditor to vote, notwithstanding that he has failed to comply with paragraph (1)(a), if satisfied that the failure was due to circumstances beyond the creditor's control.

3.11(3) **[Production of documents]** The receiver or (if other) the chairman of the meeting may call for any document or other evidence to be produced to him where he thinks it necessary for the purpose of substantiating the whole or any part of the claim.

3.11(4) **[Calculation of votes]** Votes are calculated according to the amount of a creditor's debt as at the date of the appointment of the receiver, after deducting any amounts paid in respect of that debt after that date.

3.11(5) **[Limitation on voting]** A creditor shall not vote in respect of a debt for an unliquidated amount, or any debt whose value is not ascertained, except where the chairman agrees to put upon the debt an estimated minimum value for the purpose of entitlement to vote and admits the claim for that purpose.

3.11(5A) **[Vote cast only once per resolution]** No vote may be cast by virtue of a claim more than once on any resolution put to the meeting.

3.11(6) **[Secured creditors]** A secured creditor is entitled to vote only in respect of the balance (if any) of his debt after deducting the value of his security as estimated by him.

3.11(7) **[Further limitation on voting]** A creditor shall not vote in respect of a debt on, or secured by, a current bill of exchange or promissory note, unless he is willing–

(a) to treat the liability to him on the bill or note of every person who is liable on it antecedently to the company, and against whom a bankruptcy order has not been made (or, in the case of a company, which has not gone into liquidation), as a security in his hands, and

(b) to estimate the value of the security and, for the purpose of his entitlement to vote (but not for dividend), to deduct it from his claim.

GENERAL NOTE

This regulates the exercise of voting rights at the creditors' meeting. The voting is likely to favour larger creditors. Note the special rules for persons having unliquidated claims in damages, etc. against the company. See I(A)R 2010 (SI 2010/686) which inserts a new restriction via para.(5A).

3.11A Contents of claim

3.11A(1) **[Matters to be stated]** The following matters must be stated in a creditor's claim under Rule 3.11–

(a) the creditor's name and address, and, if a company, its company registration number;

(b) the total amount of the claim (including any Value Added Tax) as at the date of the appointment of the receiver, less all trade and other discounts available to the company, or which would have been available to the company but for the appointment, except for any discount for immediate, early or cash settlement;

(c) whether or not that amount includes outstanding uncapitalised interest;

(d) particulars of how and when the debt was incurred by the company;

(e) particulars of any security held, the date when it was given and the value which the creditor puts upon it;

(f) details of any reservation of title in respect of goods to which the debt refers; and

(g) the name, and address and authority of the person making out the claim (if other than the creditor himself).

3.11A(2) **[Claim to specify substantiating documents]** The claim must specify any documents by reference to which the debt can be substantiated; but it is not essential that such documents be attached to the claim or submitted with it.

GENERAL NOTE

This is a new provision introduced by I(A)R 2010 (SI 2010/686).

3.12   Admission and rejection of claim

3.12(1)   [Power of chairman] At the creditors' meeting the chairman has power to admit or reject a creditor's claim for the purpose of his entitlement to vote; and the power is exercisable with respect to the whole or any part of the claim.

3.12(2)   [Appeal from chairman's decision] The chairman's decision under this Rule, or in respect of any matter arising under Rule 3.11, is subject to appeal to the court by any creditor.

3.12(3)   [Voting subject to objection] If the chairman is in doubt whether a claim should be admitted or rejected, he shall mark it as objected to and allow the creditor to vote, subject to his vote being subsequently declared invalid if the objection to the claim is sustained.

3.12(4)   [If chairman's decision reversed etc.] If on an appeal the chairman's decision is reversed or varied, or a creditor's vote is declared invalid, the court may order that another meeting be summoned, or make such other order as it thinks just.

3.12(4A)   [Time limit for application to appeal] An application to the court by way of appeal under this Rule against a decision of the chairman must be made not later than 21 days after the date of the meeting.

3.12(5)   [Costs of appeal] Neither the receiver nor any person nominated by him to be chairman is personally liable for costs incurred by any person in respect of an appeal to the court under this Rule, unless the court makes an order to that effect.

GENERAL NOTE

The chairman can regulate the acceptance of claims and therefore voting rights. Appeal to the court is possible. See I(A)R 2010 (SI 2010/686) which inserts a new para.(4A).

3.13   Quorum

3.13   [Omitted by the Insolvency (Amendment) Rules 1987 (SI 1987/1919) r.3(1), Sch. Pt 1 para.26 as from January 11, 1988.]

GENERAL NOTE

See now the general provision in r.12A.21.

3.14   Adjournment

3.14(1)   [Chairman's decision] The creditors' meeting shall not be adjourned, even if no quorum is present, unless the chairman decides that it is desirable; and in that case he shall adjourn it to such date, time and place as he thinks fit.

3.14(2)   [Application of r.3.9] Rule 3.9(1) and (2) applies, with necessary modifications, to any adjourned meeting.

3.14(2A)   [Single suspension without adjournment] Once only in the course of a meeting the chairman may, without an adjournment, declare it suspended for any period up to 1 hour.

3.14(3)   [If no quorum or adjournment] If there is no quorum, and the meeting is not adjourned, it is deemed to have been duly summoned and held.

GENERAL NOTE

See I(A)R 2010 (SI 2010/686) which introduces via para.(2A) a new power of suspension.

3.15 Resolutions and minutes

3.15(1) **[Resolution passed by majority in value]** At the creditors' meeting, a resolution is passed when a majority (in value) of those present and voting in person or by proxy have voted in favour of it.

3.15(2) **[Record of proceedings]** The chairman of the meeting shall cause a record to be made of the proceedings (including of every resolution passed) and kept as part of the records of the receivership.

3.15(3) **[Contents of record]** The record shall include a list of the creditors who attended (personally or by proxy) and, if a creditors' committee has been established, the names and addresses of those elected to be members of the committee.

GENERAL NOTE

Resolutions are to be passed by simple majority. See I(A)R 2010 (SI 2010/686).

CHAPTER 4

THE CREDITORS' COMMITTEE

3.16 Constitution of committee

3.16(1) **[Three–five creditors]** Where it is resolved by the creditors' meeting to establish a creditors' committee, the committee shall consist of at least 3 and not more than 5 creditors of the company elected at the meeting.

3.16(2) **[Entitlement to membership of committee]** A person claiming to be a creditor is entitled to be a member of the committee provided that–

(a) that person's claim has not been wholly disallowed for voting purposes; and

(b) the claim mentioned in sub-paragraph (a) is not fully secured.

3.16(3) **[Body corporate as member]** A body corporate may be a member of the committee, but it cannot act as such otherwise than by a representative appointed under Rule 3.21 below.

GENERAL NOTE

This details the constitution and size of any committee set up under IA 1986 s.49. See I(A)R 2010 (SI 2010/686).

3.17 Formalities of establishment

3.17(1) **[Certificate of due constitution]** The creditors' committee does not come into being, and accordingly cannot act, until the administrative receiver has issued a certificate of its due constitution.

3.17(1A) **[Notice of resolution where chairman not administrative receiver]** If the chairman of the creditors' meeting which resolves to establish the committee is not the administrative receiver, the chairman must as soon as reasonably practicable give notice of the resolution to the receiver and inform the receiver of the names and addresses of the persons elected to be members of the committee.

3.17(2) **[Agreement to act]** No person may act as a member of the committee unless and until he has agreed to do so and, unless the relevant proxy or authorisation contains a statement to the contrary, such agreement may be given by his proxy-holder present at the meeting establishing the committee or, in the case of a corporation, by its duly appointed representative.

3.17(2A) **[Issue of certificate]** The receiver's certificate of the committee's due constitution shall not be issued before the minimum number of members set out in Rule 3.16 elected to be members of the committee have agreed to act and must be issued as soon as reasonably practicable thereafter.

3.17(3)   **[Amended certificate]** As and when the others (if any) agree to act, the receiver shall issue an amended certificate.

3.17(4)   **[Certificates to be sent to registrar]** The certificate, and any amended certificate, shall be sent by the receiver to the registrar of companies as soon as reasonably practicable.

3.17(5)   **[Change in membership]** If, after the first establishment of the committee, there is any change in its membership, as soon as reasonably practicable the receiver shall report the change to the registrar of companies.

GENERAL NOTE

It is for the administrative receiver to certify this committee.

Rules 3.17(2) and 3.17(2A) aim to facilitate the establishment of a committee after the creditors' meeting. See I(A)R 2010 (SI 2010/686)—new para.(1A).

3.18   Functions and meetings of the committee

3.18(1)   **[Functions]** In addition to any functions conferred on the creditors' committee by any provision of the Act, the creditors' committee shall assist the administrative receiver in discharging his functions, and act in relation to him in such manner as may be agreed from time to time.

3.18(2)   **[Holding of meetings]** Subject as follows, meetings of the committee shall be held when and where determined by the receiver.

3.18(3)   **[Time limit for first meeting]** The receiver must call a first meeting of the committee to take place within 6 weeks of the committee's establishment.

3.18(3A)   **[Calling of subsequent of meetings]** After the calling of the first meeting, the receiver must call a meeting–

    (a)   if so requested by a member of the committee or the member's representative (the meeting then to be held within 21 days of the request being received by the receiver); and

    (b)   for a specified date, if the committee has previously resolved that a meeting be held on that date.

3.18(4)   **[Notice of venue]** Subject to paragraph (5), the receiver shall give 5 business days' written notice of the venue of any meeting to every member (or his representative designated for that purpose), unless in any case the requirement of notice has been waived by or on behalf of any member.

Waiver may be signified either at or before the meeting.

3.18(5)   **[Notice period for remote meeting]** Where the receiver has determined that a meeting should be conducted and held in the manner referred to in Rule 12A.26(2), the notice period mentioned in paragraph (4) is 7 business days.

GENERAL NOTE

This outlines the role of the committee. The committee's functions are left vague by IA 1986 s.49. For "venue" in r.3.18(4) see r.13.6. There is some reworking carried out by I(A)R 2010 (SI 2010/686), including the commonplace change from seven to five business days in para.(4). Note new paras (3), (3A) and (5).

3.19   The chairman at meetings

3.19(1)   **[Administrative receiver or nominee to be chairman]** The chairman at any meeting of the creditors' committee must be the administrative receiver, or a person appointed by the receiver in writing to act.

3.19(2)   **[Qualification etc. of person appointed]** A person so appointed must be either–

    (a)   one who is qualified to act as an insolvency practitioner in relation to the company, or

    (b)   an employee of the receiver or his firm who is experienced in insolvency matters.

GENERAL NOTE

This is similar to r.3.10. See I(A)R 2010 (SI 2010/686).

3.20 Quorum

3.20 A meeting of the committee is duly constituted if due notice has been given to all the members, and at least 2 members are present or represented.

GENERAL NOTE

The committee's quorum is two.

3.21 Committee-members' representatives

3.21(1) [Representation] A member of the committee may, in relation to the business of the committee, be represented by another person duly authorised by him for that purpose.

3.21(2) [Letter of authority] A person acting as a committee-member's representative must hold a letter of authority entitling him so to act (either generally or specially) and authenticated by or on behalf of the committee-member, and for this purpose any proxy in relation to any meeting of creditors of the company shall, unless it contains a statement to the contrary, be treated as a letter of authority to act generally authenticated by or on behalf of the committee-member.

3.21(3) [Production of letter of authority] The chairman at any meeting of the committee may call on a person claiming to act as a committee-member's representative to produce his letter of authority, and may exclude him if it appears that his authority is deficient.

3.21(4) [Who may not be a representative] No member may be represented by–

(a)   another member of the committee;

(b)   a person who is at the same time representing another committee member;

(c)   a body corporate;

(d)   an undischarged bankrupt;

(e)   a disqualified director; or

(f)   a person who is subject to a bankruptcy restrictions order (including an interim order), a bankruptcy restrictions undertaking, a debt relief restrictions order (including an interim order) or a debt relief restrictions undertaking.

3.21(5) [Omitted.]

3.21(6) [Authenticating as representative] Where a member's representative authenticates any document on the member's behalf, the fact that he so authenticates must be stated below his authentication.

GENERAL NOTE

Committee members may appoint representatives to act for them. Amendments were made to para.(4) by I(A)R 2004 (SI 2004/584) with effect from April 1, 2004 in order inter alia to cater for the exclusion from committee membership of persons subject to BROs, BRUs, etc. and to remove the obsolete reference to persons entering compositions with creditors. See I(A)R 2010 (SI 2010/686) which substitutes a new para.(4) and deletes para.(5).

3.22 Resignation

3.22 A member of the committee may resign by notice in writing delivered to the administrative receiver.

3.23   Termination of membership

3.23(1)   [Automatic termination] Membership of the creditors' committee is automatically terminated if the member–

(a)   becomes bankrupt, or

(b)   at 3 consecutive meetings of the committee is neither present nor represented (unless at the third of those meetings it is resolved that this Rule is not to apply in his case), or

(c)   ceases to be a creditor and a period of 3 months has elapsed from the date that that member ceased to be a creditor or is found never to have been a creditor.

3.23(2)   [Termination on bankruptcy] However, if the cause of termination is the member's bankruptcy, his trustee in bankruptcy replaces him as a member of the committee.

GENERAL NOTE

Note the sanction against absentees. The former reference in para.(1)(a) to compositions and arrangements with creditors was removed by I(A)R 2004 (SI 2004/584) with effect from April 1, 2004. See I(A)R 2010 (SI 2010/686) which clarifies para.(1)(c).

3.24   Removal

3.24   A member of the committee may be removed by resolution at a meeting of creditors, at least 14 days' notice having been given of the intention to move that resolution.

GENERAL NOTE

The committee is thus controlled by the creditors' meeting.

3.25   Vacancies

3.25(1)   [Application of Rule] The following applies if there is a vacancy in the membership of the creditors' committee.

3.25(2)   [Agreement not to fill vacancy] The vacancy need not be filled if the administrative receiver and a majority of the remaining members of the committee so agree, provided that the total number of members does not fall below 3.

3.25(3)   [Filling vacancy] The receiver may appoint any creditor (being qualified under the Rules to be a member of the committee) to fill the vacancy, if a majority of the other members of the committee agree to the appointment and the creditor concerned consents to act.

3.25(4)   [Appointment by creditors' meeting] Alternatively, a meeting of creditors may resolve that a creditor be appointed (with that creditor's consent) to fill the vacancy. In this case at least 14 days' notice must have been given of a resolution to make such an appointment (whether or not of a person named in the notice).

3.25(5)   [Report where appointment by creditors' meeting without receiver] Where the vacancy is filled by an appointment made by a creditors' meeting at which the receiver is not present, the chairman of the meeting must report to the receiver the appointment which has been made.

GENERAL NOTE

Paragraphs (4) and (5) are new, having been introduced by I(A)R 2010 (SI 2010/686).

3.26   Procedure at meetings

3.26(1)   [Votes and passing of resolutions] At any meeting of the committee, each member of it (whether present himself or by his representative) has one vote; and a resolution is passed when a majority of the members present or represented have voted in favour of it.

3.26(2) **[Resolutions to be recorded, authenticated and kept]** Every resolution passed must be recorded in writing and authenticated by the chairman, either separately or as part of the minutes of the meeting and the record must be kept with the records of the proceedings.

GENERAL NOTE

Votes at the committee are passed by a simple majority. There is no weighting of votes here. See I(A)R 2010 (SI 2010/686) which replaces paras (2) and (3) with a new para.(2).

3.27 Resolutions otherwise than at a meeting

3.27(1) **[Proposed resolution sent to members]** In accordance with this Rule, the administrative receiver may seek to obtain the agreement of members of the creditors' committee to a resolution by sending to every member (or his representative designated for the purpose) a copy of the proposed resolution.

3.27(2) **[Copies of proposed resolution]** Where the receiver makes use of the procedure allowed by this Rule, he shall send out to members of the committee or their representatives (as the case may be) a copy of any proposed resolution on which a decision is sought, which shall be set out in such a way that agreement with or dissent from each separate resolution may be indicated by the recipient on the copy so sent.

3.27(3) **[Member may require meeting]** Any member of the committee may, within 7 business days from the date of the receiver sending out a resolution, require him to summon a meeting of the committee to consider the matters raised by the resolution.

3.27(4) **[Deemed passing of resolution]** In the absence of such a request, the resolution is deemed to have been passed by the committee if and when the receiver is notified in writing by a majority of the members that they concur with it.

3.27(5) **[Copy resolution etc. with records]** A copy of every resolution passed under this Rule, and a note that the committee's concurrence was obtained, shall be kept with the records of the receivership.

GENERAL NOTE

Postal voting is acceptable if no member objects.

Rule 3.27(2) was amended in 1988 to prevent duplication of papers and so to save money. See I(A)R 2010 (SI 2010/686).

3.28 Information from receiver

3.28(1) **[Notice to administrative receiver]** Where the committee resolves to require the attendance of the administrative receiver under section 49(2), the notice to him shall be in writing authenticated by the majority of the members of the committee for the time being. A member's representative may authenticate for him.

3.28(2) **[Time and place of meeting]** The meeting at which the receiver's attendance is required shall be fixed by the committee for a business day, and shall be held at such time and place as he determines.

3.28(3) **[Chairman]** Where the receiver so attends, the members of the committee may elect any one of their number to be chairman of the meeting, in place of the receiver or any nominee of his.

GENERAL NOTE

This provides essential procedural guidance on the operation of IA 1986 s.49(2). "Business day" (r.3.28(2)) is defined in r.13.13(1).

3.29   Expenses of members

3.29(1)   [Expenses defrayed out of assets] Subject as follows, the administrative receiver shall out of the assets of the company defray, in the prescribed order of priority, any reasonable travelling expenses directly incurred by members of the creditors' committee or their representatives in relation to their attendance at the committee's meetings, or otherwise on the committee's business, as an expense of the receivership.

3.29(2)   [Non-application of r.3.29(1)] Paragraph (1) does not apply to any meeting of the committee held within 3 months of a previous meeting, unless the meeting in question is summoned at the instance of the administrative receiver.

GENERAL NOTE

See I(A)R 2010 (SI 2010/686).

3.30   Members' dealings with the company [Omitted by I(A)R 2010 (SI 2010/686).]

GENERAL NOTE

This allows committee members to deal with the company in good faith and for value. The court can invalidate transactions entered into in breach of this provision. Surely this power of invalidation would have been better located within the Insolvency Act itself.

3.30A   Formal defects

3.30A   The acts of the creditors' committee established for any administrative receivership are valid notwithstanding any defect in the appointment, election or qualifications of any member of the committee or any committee-member's representative or in the formalities of its establishment.

GENERAL NOTE

Rule 3.30A (which was inserted in 1988) reflects a common philosophy in the new insolvency legislation: see, for example, s.377 of the Act and rr.6.156(7) and 7.55. The insertion of rr.2.46A and 4.172A has a similar rationale.

CHAPTER 5

THE ADMINISTRATIVE RECEIVER (MISCELLANEOUS)

3.31   Disposal of charged property

3.31(1)   [Application of Rule] The following applies where the administrative receiver applies to the court under section 43(1) for authority to dispose of property of the company which is subject to a security.

3.31(2)   [Venue for hearing] The court shall fix a venue for the hearing of the application, and the receiver shall as soon as reasonably practicable give notice of the venue to the person who is the holder of the security.

3.31(3)   [Copies of s.43(1) order to administrative receiver] If an order is made under section 43(1), the court must send two sealed copies to the administrative receiver.

3.31(4)   [Copy of order to security holder] The administrative receiver must send one of them to that person who is the holder of the security.

GENERAL NOTE

This clarifies the position where applications are made by the administrative receiver to the court under IA 1986 s.43(1). For "venue" in r.3.31(2) see r.13.6. Paragraphs (3) and (4) have been reworked by I(A)R 2010 (SI 2010/686).

3.32 Abstract of receipts and payments

3.32(1) [Administrative receiver to send accounts etc.] The administrative receiver shall–

(a) within 2 months after the end of 12 months from the date of his appointment, and of every subsequent period of 12 months, and

(b) within 2 months after he ceases to act as administrative receiver,

send to the registrar of companies, to the company and to the person by whom he was appointed, and to each member of the creditors' committee (if there is one), the requisite accounts of his receipts and payments as receiver.

[FORM 3.6]

3.32(2) [Extension of time] The court may, on the receiver's application, extend the period of 2 months referred to in paragraph (1).

3.32(3) [Form of abstract] The accounts are to be in the form of an abstract showing–

(a) receipts and payments during the relevant period of 12 months, or

(b) where the receiver has ceased to act, receipts and payments during the period from the end of the last 12-month period to the time when he so ceased (alternatively, if there has been no previous abstract, receipts and payments in the period since his appointment as administrative receiver).

3.32(4) [Effect of Rule] This Rule is without prejudice to the receiver's duty to render proper accounts required otherwise than as above.

3.32(5) [Penalty on default] If the administrative receiver makes default in complying with this Rule, he is liable to a fine and, for continued contravention, to a daily default fine.

GENERAL NOTE

This imposes accounting requirements on the administrative receiver. Compare these with the requirements of IA 1986 s.38. Rule 3.32(4) preserves the common-law duty to account: see *Smiths Ltd v Middleton* [1979] 3 All E.R. 842. For the sanction in r.3.32(5), see IR 1986 Sch.5.

3.33 Resignation

3.33(1) [Notice of intention] Subject as follows, before resigning his office the administrative receiver shall give at least 5 business days' notice of his intention to do so to–

(a) the person by whom he was appointed,

(b) the company or, if it is then in liquidation, its liquidator, and

(c) in any case, to the members of the creditors' committee (if any).

3.33(2) [Contents of notice] A notice given under this Rule shall specify the date on which the receiver intends his resignation to take effect.

3.33(3) [Omitted.]

GENERAL NOTE

This expands upon the provisions of IA 1986 s.45. See I(A)R 2010 (SI 2010/686) which changed the period in para.(1) from seven days to five business days. Paragraph (3) is also omitted.

3.34 Receiver deceased

3.34 If the administrative receiver dies, the person by whom he was appointed shall, as soon as reasonably practicable on his becoming aware of the death, give notice of it to–

(a) the registrar of companies,

  (b)   the company or, if it is in liquidation, the liquidator, and

  (c)   in any case, to the members of the creditors' committee (if any).

3.35   Vacation of office

3.35(1)   **[Notice]** The administrative receiver, on vacating office on completion of the receivership, or in consequence of his ceasing to be qualified as an insolvency practitioner, shall as soon as reasonably practicable give notice of his doing so–

  (a)   to the company or, if it is in liquidation, the liquidator, and

  (b)   to the members of the creditors' committee (if any).

3.35(2)   **[Indorsement on notice]** Where the receiver's office is vacated, the notice to the registrar of companies which is required by section 45(4) may be given by means of an indorsement on the notice required by section 871(2) of the Companies Act (notice for the purposes of the register of charges).

GENERAL NOTE

This rule should be viewed in the light of IA 1986 s.45.

CHAPTER 6

VAT BAD DEBT RELIEF

3.36   Issue of certificate of insolvency [Revoked.]

3.37   Notice to creditors [Revoked.]

3.38   Preservation of certificate with company's records [Revoked.]

GENERAL NOTE TO RR.3.36–3.38

Revoked by I(A)R 2010 (SI 2010/686).

CHAPTER 7

SECTION 176A: THE PRESCRIBED PART

3.39   Report to creditors

3.39(1)   **[Application of r.3.39]** This Rule applies where–

  (a)   a receiver (other than an administrative receiver) is appointed by the court or otherwise under a charge which as created was a floating charge; and

  (b)   section 176A applies.

3.39(2)   **[Notice of appointment and report]** Within 3 months (or such longer period as the court may allow) of the date of his appointment the receiver shall send to creditors, details of whose names and addresses are available to him, notice of his appointment and a report which will include the following matters–

  (a)   to the best of the receiver's knowledge and belief–

(i)   an estimate of the value of the prescribed part (whether or not he proposes to make an application to the court under section 176A(5) or section 176A(3) applies); and

(ii)   an estimate of the value of company's net property;

(b)   whether, and if so, why, he proposes to make an application to court under section 176A(5); and

(c)   whether he proposes to present a petition for the winding up of the company.

3.39(3)   [Non-disclosure of seriously prejudicial information] Nothing in this Rule is to be taken as requiring any such estimate to include any information, the disclosure of which could seriously prejudice the commercial interests of the company. If such information is excluded from the calculation the estimate shall be accompanied by a statement to that effect.

3.39(4)   [Gazetting and advertisement of report instead of sending] Where the requirements of paragraph (5) are satisfied, the receiver may, instead of sending the report required under paragraph (2)–

(a)   cause a notice to be gazetted; and

(b)   may advertise the notice in such other manner as the receiver thinks fit.

3.39(4A)   [Additional contents of r.3.39(4) notice] In addition to the standard contents, the notice under paragraph (4) must include a statement of the matters required to be included in the receiver's report under paragraph (2).

3.39(5)   [Requirements for r.3.39(5)] The requirements of this paragraph are that–

(a)   full details of the unsecured creditors of the company are not available to the receiver; or

(b)   the receiver thinks it is otherwise impracticable to send the report.

GENERAL NOTE

See I(A)R 2010 (SI 2010/686) for the insertion of a new para.(4A).

3.40   Receiver to deal with prescribed part

3.40   Where Rule 3.39 applies–

(a)   the receiver may present a petition for the winding up of the company if the ground of the petition is that in section 122(1)(f);

(b)   where a liquidator or administrator has been appointed to the company, the receiver shall deliver up the sums representing the prescribed part to him;

(c)   in any other case, the receiver shall apply to the court for directions as to the manner in which he is to discharge his duty under section 176A(2)(a) and shall act in accordance with such directions as are given by the court.

GENERAL NOTE TO RR.3.39, 3.40

The Insolvency (Amendment) Rules 2003 (SI 2003/1730) inserted a new Chapter 7 to deal with the provision of the prescribed part of the fund for unsecured creditors in cases of receivership. The application of Chapter 7 is defined by r.3.39(1). With the striking down of "fixed charges" using the *Siebe Gorman* precedent by the House of Lords in *National Westminster Bank v Spectrum Plus Ltd* [2005] UKHL 41; [2005] 3 W.L.R. 58; [2005] B.C.C. 694, the significance of this reserved fund will grow.

R.3.39

This rule requires the receiver to keep unsecured creditors informed of the prospects for them of the reserved fund being operated. Note the options where individual notification is not feasible. Note the modification made by the Insolvency (Amendment) Rules 2009 (SI 2009/642) with effect from April 6, 2009. Under this amendment a new para.(4) is substituted and a new para.(5) introduced.

R.3.40

This allows a receiver to present a winding-up petition or take other specified action in order to facilitate the operation of the reserved fund mechanism.

PART 4

COMPANIES WINDING UP

CHAPTER 1

THE SCHEME OF THIS PART OF THE RULES

4.1 Voluntary winding up; winding up by the court

4.1(1) **[Members' voluntary winding up]** In a members' voluntary winding up, the Rules in this Part do not apply, except as follows–

    (a) Rules 4.3 and 4.5 apply in the same way as they apply in a creditors' voluntary winding up;

    (aa) Rules 4.49C, 4.49E and 4.49F apply except so far as it is provided (expressly or by necessary implication) that they do not apply;

    (ab) Rule 4.49G applies only in a members' voluntary winding up, and not otherwise;

    (b) Rule 4.72 (additional provisions concerning meetings in relation to the Financial Services Authority and the scheme manager) applies in the winding up of authorised deposit-takers or former authorised deposit-takers, whether members' or creditors' voluntary or by the court;

    (c) Chapters 9 (proof of debts in a liquidation), 10 (secured creditors), 15 (disclaimer) and 18 (special manager) apply wherever, and in the same way as, they apply in a creditors' voluntary winding up;

    (d) Section F of Chapter 11 (the liquidator) applies only in a members' voluntary winding up, and not otherwise;

    (e) Section G of that Chapter (court's power to set aside certain transactions; rule against solicitation) applies in any winding up, whether members' or creditors' voluntary or by the court;

    (f) Rules 4.126A and 4.182A apply only in a members' voluntary winding up, and not otherwise; and

    (g) Rule 4.223-CVL (liquidator's statements) applies in the same way as it applies in a creditors' voluntary winding up.

4.1(2) **[Creditors' voluntary winding up and winding up by court]** Subject as follows, the Rules in this Part apply both in a creditors' voluntary winding up and in a winding up by the court; and for this purpose a winding up is treated as a creditors' voluntary winding up if, and from the time when, the liquidator forms the opinion that the company will be unable to pay its debts in full, and determines accordingly to summon a creditors' meeting under section 95.

4.1(3) **[Creditors' voluntary winding up]** The following Chapters, or Sections of Chapters, of this Part do not apply in a creditors' voluntary winding up–

    Chapter 2—The statutory demand;

    Chapter 3—Petition to winding-up order;

    Chapter 4—Petition by contributories;

    Chapter 5—Provisional liquidator;

    Chapter 11 (Section F)—The liquidator in a members' voluntary winding up;

800

Chapter 13—The liquidation committee where winding up follows immediately on administration;

Chapter 16—Settlement of list of contributories;

Chapter 17—Calls;

Chapter 19—Public examination of company officers and others; and

Chapter 21 (Section A)—Return of capital;

Chapter 21 (Section C)—Dissolution after winding up.

4.1(4)   ["(NO CVL APPLICATION)"] Where at the head of any Rule, or at the end of any paragraph of a Rule, there appear the words "(NO CVL APPLICATION)", this signifies that the Rule or, as the case may be, the paragraph does not apply in a creditors' voluntary winding up.

However, this does not affect the court's power to make orders under section 112 (exercise in relation to voluntary winding up of powers available in winding up by the court).

4.1(5)   ["CVL"] Where to any Rule or paragraph there is given a number incorporating the letters "CVL", that signifies that the Rule or (as the case may be) the paragraph applies in a creditors' voluntary winding up, and not in a winding up by the court.

4.1(6)   [Provisions of Pt 4 not applicable in CVL following administration] In a voluntary winding-up which is commenced by the registration of a notice under paragraph 83(3) of Schedule B1 to the Act, the following provisions of this Part shall not apply–

Rules 4.34, 4.38, 4.49, 4.51, 4.53, 4.62, 4.101, 4.103, 4.106, 4.152, 4.153, 4.206–4.210.

GENERAL NOTE

The rules in this Part do not apply to a members' voluntary winding up, except as stated in r.4.1(1).

Section F of Chapter 11 (rr.4.139–4.148F) applies only in a members' voluntary winding up.

The remaining rules apply generally to both a winding up by the court *and* a creditors' voluntary winding up (including a creditors' voluntary winding up that begins as a members' winding up but later proves insolvent); but some rules or parts of rules apply only in a winding up by the court, and these are marked NO CVL APPLICATION; while others apply only in a creditors' voluntary winding up, and are marked CVL.

Rule 4.1(1)(b) was substituted by the Financial Services and Markets Act 2000 (Consequential Amendments and Repeals) Order 2001 (SI 2001/3649) as from December 1, 2001.

Paragraph (6) was inserted by the Insolvency (Amendment) Rules 2003 (SI 2003/1730, effective September 15, 2003) Sch.1 para.12. The disapplication of the rules listed is designed as a short cut to the procedure where a creditors' voluntary winding up follows directly upon an administration.

Rule 4.1(1)(a), (f) amended and r.4.1(1)(aa), (ab) inserted by I(A)R 2010 r.2 and Sch. para.138 as from April 6, 2010.

Rule 4.223, referred to in r.4.1(1)(g), was revoked by I(A)R 2010 r.5.

Following the amendments made to the Rules by the Insolvency (Amendment) Rules 2008 (SI 2008/737, effective April 6, 2008), inserting new rr.4.218A–4.218E (which reversed the House of Lords' ruling in *Re Leyland DAF Ltd, Buchler v Talbot* [2004] UKHL 9; [2004] A.C. 298; [2004] B.C.C. 214), changes of a purely verbal nature were made to a considerable number of rules in this Part, e.g. by substituting "as an expense of the liquidation" for "out of the assets": see SI 2008/737 r.7. The wording of these rules has been amended accordingly in the pages which follow, without annotation.

4.2   Winding up by the court: the various forms of petition

(NO CVL APPLICATION)

4.2(1)   [Section 122(1)] Insofar as the Rules in this Part apply to winding up by the court, they apply (subject as follows) whether the petition for winding up is presented under any of the several paragraphs of section 122(1), namely–

paragraph (a)—company special resolution for winding up by the court;

paragraph (b)—public company without certificate under section 761 of the Companies Act;

paragraph (c)—old public company;

paragraph (d)—company not commencing business after formation, or suspending business;

paragraph (e)—number of company's members reduced below 2;

paragraph (f)—company unable to pay its debts;

paragraph (fa)—end of moratorium without approval of voluntary arrangement;

paragraph (g)—court's power under the "just and equitable" rule,

or under any enactment enabling the presentation of a winding-up petition.

4.2(2) [Petitioners] Except as provided by the following two paragraphs or by any particular Rule, the Rules apply whether the petition for winding up is presented by the company, the directors, one or more creditors, one or more contributories, the Secretary of State, the official receiver, or any person entitled under any enactment to present such a petition.

4.2(3) [Application of Ch.2] Chapter 2 (statutory demand) has no application except in relation to an unpaid creditor of the company satisfying section 123(1)(a) (the first of the two cases specified, in relation to England and Wales, of the company being deemed unable to pay its debts within section 122(1)(f)) or section 222(1) (the equivalent provision in relation to unregistered companies).

4.2(4) [Application of Ch.3 and 4] Chapter 3 (petition to winding-up order) has no application to a petition for winding up presented by one or more contributories; and in relation to a petition so presented Chapter 4 has effect.

GENERAL NOTE

Rule 4.2(1) lists all the circumstances in which a company may be wound up by the court, and r.4.2(2) all the possible petitioners: see IA 1986 ss.122, 124. Where a receiver or administrator or the supervisor of a voluntary arrangement petitions, he does so in the name of the company: see the note to s.124.

The reference to para.(fa) of s.122(1) was inserted by the Insolvency (Amendment) (No.2) Rules 2002 (SI 2002/2712, effective January 1, 2003) r.1.4(1) and Sch. Pt 2 para.22.

4.3 Time-limits

4.3 Where by any provision of the Act or the Rules about winding up, the time for doing anything is limited, the court may extend the time, either before or after it has expired, on such terms, if any, as it thinks fit.

GENERAL NOTE

See *Practice Direction: Insolvency Proceedings* [2007] B.C.C. 842 (reproduced in App.IV of this *Guide*).

CHAPTER 2

THE STATUTORY DEMAND (NO CVL APPLICATION)

4.4 Preliminary

4.4(1) [Non-application of Ch.2] This Chapter does not apply where a petition for the winding up of a company is presented under section 124 on or after the date on which the Rules come into force and the petition is based on failure to comply with a written demand served on the company before that date.

4.4(2)   ["The statutory demand"] A written demand served by a creditor on a company under section 123(1)(a) (registered companies) or 222(1)(a) (unregistered companies) is known as **"the statutory demand"**.

4.4(3)   [Must be dated and authenticated] The statutory demand must be dated, and be authenticated either by the creditor himself or by a person stating himself to be authorised to make the demand on the creditor's behalf.

(See General Note after r.4.6.)

4.5   Form and content of statutory demand

4.5(1)   [Form of demand] The statutory demand must state the amount of the debt and the consideration for it (or, if there is no consideration, the way in which it arises).

[FORM 4.1]

4.5(2)   [Interest and accruing charges] If the amount claimed in the demand includes–

(a)   any charge by way of interest not previously notified to the company as included in its liability, or

(b)   any other charge accruing from time to time,

the amount or rate of the charge must be separately identified, and the grounds on which payment of it is claimed must be stated.

In either case the amount claimed must be limited to that which has accrued due at the date of the demand.

(See General Note after r.4.6.)

4.6   Information to be given in statutory demand

4.6(1)   [Explanation of demand generally] The statutory demand must include an explanation to the company of the following matters–

(a)   the purpose of the demand, and the fact that, if the demand is not complied with, proceedings may be instituted for the winding up of the company;

(b)   the time within which it must be complied with, if that consequence is to be avoided;

(c)   the methods of compliance which are open to the company; and

(d)   that the company has the right to make an application to the court for an injunction restraining the creditor from presenting or advertising a petition for the winding up of the company.

4.6(2)   [Information re named individuals] Information must be provided for the company as to how an officer or representative of it may enter into communication with one or more named individuals, with a view to securing or compounding for the debt to the creditor's satisfaction.

In the case of any individual so named in the demand, his address and telephone number (if any) must be given.

GENERAL NOTE TO RR.4.4–4.6

Rules 4.4, 4.6(1) amended by I(A)R 2010 r.2 and Sch. paras 139–140 as from April 6, 2010.

This chapter has no application except in relation to an unpaid creditor of the company satisfying IA 1986 s.123(1)(a) or s.222(1): see r.4.2(3).

Under IA 1986 s.123, a written demand for the payment of a debt must be "in the prescribed form". These rules deal with the form and content of the statutory demand.

A statutory demand may be effective despite some inaccuracy, e.g. in relation to the sum stated to be due: see the note to s.123.

4.6A   Injunction to restrain presentation or advertisement of petition

4.6A   An application by a company for an injunction restraining a creditor from–

(a)   presenting a petition for the winding up of the company must be made to a court having jurisdiction to wind up the company;

(b)   advertising a petition for the winding up of a company must be made to the court in which the petition is pending.

4.7   Presentation and filing of petition

4.7(1)   [Filing with verifying statement of truth] The petition, verified by a statement of truth in accordance with Rule 4.12 below, shall be filed in court.

[FORM 4.2]
[FORM 4.3]

4.7(2)   [When petition not filed] No petition shall be filed unless there is produced on presentation of the petition a receipt for the deposit payable or paragraph (2A) applies.

4.7(2A)   [Notice of alternative arrangements for payment of deposit] This paragraph applies in any case where the Secretary of State has given written notice to the court that the petitioner has made suitable alternative arrangements for the payment of the deposit to the official receiver and such notice has not been revoked in relation to the petitioner in accordance with paragraph (2B).

4.7(2B)   [Revocation of r.4.7(2A) notice] A notice of the kind referred to in paragraph (2A) may be revoked in relation to the petitioner in whose favour it is given by a further notice in writing to the court stating that the earlier notice is revoked in relation to the petitioner.

4.7(3)   [Petitioner other than company] A petitioner who is a person other than the company must also deliver to the court one copy for service on the company.

4.7(4)   [Accompanying documents] There shall in any case be delivered with the petition–

(a)   if the company is in course of being wound up voluntarily, and a liquidator has been appointed, one copy of the petition to be sent to him;

(b)   if the company is in administration, one copy to be sent to the administrator;

(c)   if an administrative receiver has been appointed in relation to the company, one copy to be sent to him;

(d)   if there is in force for the company a voluntary arrangement under Part I of the Act, one copy for the supervisor of the arrangement;

(da) if a member State liquidator has been appointed in main proceedings in relation to the company, one copy to be sent to him; and

(e)   if the company is an authorised deposit-taker or a former authorised deposit-taker and the petitioner is not the Financial Services Authority, one copy to be sent to the Authority.

4.7(5)   [Sealed copies issued to petitioner] Each of the copies delivered shall have applied to it the seal of the court, and shall be issued to the petitioner.

4.7(6)   [Venue for hearing] The court shall fix a venue for the hearing of the petition; and this shall be endorsed on any copy issued to the petitioner under paragraph (5).

4.7(7) [Petition by administrator] Where a petition is filed at the instance of a company's administrator the petition shall–

(a) be expressed to be the petition of the company by its administrator,

(b) state the name of the administrator, the court case number and the date that the company entered administration, and

(c) where applicable, contain an application under paragraph 79 of Schedule B1, requesting that the appointment of the administrator shall cease to have effect.

4.7(8) [Filing if in administration or voluntary arrangement] Any petition filed in relation to a company in respect of which there is in force a voluntary arrangement under Part I of the Act or which is in administration shall be presented to the court to which the nominee's report under section 2 was submitted or the court having jurisdiction for the administration.

4.7(9) [Treatment of petition of administrator or supervisor] Any petition such as is mentioned in paragraph (7) above or presented by the supervisor of a voluntary arrangement under Part I of the Act in force for the company shall be treated as if it were a petition filed by contributories, and Chapter 4 in this Part of the Rules shall apply accordingly.

4.7(10) [Request for appointment under s.140] Where a petition contains a request for the appointment of a person as liquidator in accordance with section 140 (appointment of former administrator or supervisor as liquidator) the person whose appointment is sought shall, not less than 2 business days before the return day for the petition, file in court a report including particulars of–

(a) a date on which he notified creditors of the company, either in writing or at a meeting of creditors, of the intention to seek his appointment as liquidator, such date to be at least 7 business days before the day on which the report under this paragraph is filed, and

(b) details of any response from creditors to that notification, including any objections to his appointment.

(See General Note after r.4.14.)

4.8 Service of petition

4.8(1) [Application of Rule] The following paragraphs apply as regards service of the petition on the company (where the petitioner is other than the company itself); and references to the petition are to a copy of the petition bearing the seal of the court in which it is presented.

4.8(2) [Service] Subject as follows, the petition shall be served at the company's registered office, that is to say–

(a) the place which is specified, in the company's statement delivered under section 9 of the Companies Act as the intended situation of its registered office on incorporation, or

(b) if notice has been given by the company to the registrar of companies under section 87 of that Act (change of registered office), the place specified in that notice or, as the case may be, in the last such notice.

4.8(3) [Means of service] Service of the petition at the registered office may be effected in any of the following ways–

(a) it may be handed to a person who there and then acknowledges himself to be, or to the best of the server's knowledge, information and belief is, a director or other officer, or employee, of the company; or

(b) it may be handed to a person who there and then acknowledges himself to be authorised to accept service of documents on the company's behalf; or

(c)   in the absence of any such person as is mentioned in sub-paragraph (a) or (b), it may be deposited at or about the registered office in such a way that it is likely to come to the notice of a person attending at the office.

4.8(4)   **[Service at registered office not practicable etc.]** If for any reason service at the registered office is not practicable, or the company has no registered office or is an unregistered company, the petition may be served on the company by leaving it at the company's last known principal place of business in such a way that it is likely to come to the attention of a person attending there, or by delivering it to the secretary or some director, manager or principal officer of the company, wherever that person may be found.

4.8(5)   **[Overseas company]** In the case of an overseas company, service may be effected in any manner provided for by section 1139(2) of the Companies Act.

4.8(6)   **[Service in another manner]** If for any reason it is impracticable to effect service as provided by paragraphs (2) to (5), the petition may be served in such other manner as the court may approve or direct.

4.8(7)   **[Application under r.4.8(6)]** Application for permission of the court under paragraph (6) may be made by an application without notice to any other party, supported by a witness statement stating what steps have been taken to comply with paragraphs (2) to (5), and the reasons why it is impracticable to effect service as there provided.

R.4.8(6)
See *Practice Direction: Insolvency Proceedings* [2007] B.C.C. 842 (reproduced in App.IV of this *Guide*).

(See General Note after r.4.14.)

4.9   Proof of service [Deleted.]

4.9A   Proof of service

4.9A(1)   **[Certificate of service]** Service of the petition must be proved by a certificate of service.

4.9A(2)   **[Contents of certificate of service]** The certificate of service must be sufficient to identify the petition served and must specify–

(a)   the name and registered number of the company,

(b)   the address of the registered office of the company,

(c)   the name of the petitioner,

(d)   the court in which the petition was filed and the court reference number,

(e)   the date of the petition,

(f)   whether the copy served was a sealed copy,

(g)   the date on which service was effected, and

(h)   the manner in which service was effected.

4.9A(3)   **[Where substituted service ordered]** Where substituted service has been ordered, the certificate of service must have attached to it a sealed copy of the order.

4.9A(4)   **[Time limit for filing certificate of service in court]** The certificate of service must be filed in court as soon as reasonably practicable after service, and in any event not less than 5 business days before the hearing of the petition.

(See General Note after r.4.14.)

4.10   Other persons to receive copies of petition

4.10(1)   [Company being wound up voluntarily] If to the petitioner's knowledge the company is in course of being wound up voluntarily, a copy of the petition shall be sent by him to the liquidator.

4.10(2)   [Administrative receiver appointed etc.] If to the petitioner's knowledge an administrative receiver has been appointed in relation to the company, or the company is in administration, a copy of the petition shall be sent by him to the receiver or, as the case may be, the administrator.

4.10(3)   [Voluntary arrangement in force] If to the petitioner's knowledge there is in force for the company a voluntary arrangement under Part I of the Act, a copy of the petition shall be sent by him to the supervisor of the voluntary arrangement.

4.10(3A)   [Member State liquidator] If to the petitioner's knowledge, there is a member State liquidator appointed in main proceedings in relation to the company, a copy of the petition shall be sent by him to that person.

This does not apply if the petitioner referred to in this paragraph is a member State liquidator.

4.10(4)   [If company is authorised institution under Banking Act] If the company is an authorised institution or former authorised institution within the meaning of the Banking Act 1987, a copy of the petition shall be sent by the petitioner to the Financial Services Authority.

This does not apply if the petitioner is the Financial Services Authority itself.

4.10(5)   [Time for sending copy of petition] A copy of the petition which is required by this Rule to be sent shall be despatched on the next business day after the day on which the petition is served on the company.

(See General Note after r.4.14.)

4.11   Advertisement of petition

4.11(1)   [Duty of petitioner to give notice] Unless the court otherwise directs, the petitioner shall give notice of the petition.

4.11(2)   [Notice in Gazette] The notice shall be gazetted.

4.11(3)   [Where gazetting not reasonably practical] Where compliance with paragraph (2) is not reasonably practicable, the court may direct that instead of the notice being gazetted, it shall be given in such other manner as the court thinks fit.

4.11(4)   [Time limit for notice] The notice must be made to appear–

(a)   if the petitioner is the company itself, not less than 7 business days before the day appointed for the hearing; and

(b)   otherwise, not less than 7 business days after service of the petition on the company, nor less than 7 business days before the day so appointed.

4.11(5)   [Additional contents of r.4.11(4) notice] In addition to the standard contents, the notice under paragraph (4) must state–

(a)   that a petition has been presented for the winding up of the company;

(b)   in the case of an overseas company, the address at which service of the petition was effected;

(c)   the name and address of the petitioner;

(d)   the date on which the petition was presented;

(e)   the venue fixed for the hearing of the petition;

(f)   the name and address of the petitioner's solicitor (if any); and

(g)   that any person intending to appear at the hearing (whether to support or oppose the petition) must give notice of that intention in accordance with Rule 4.16.

4.11(6)   [Court may dismiss petition] If notice of the petition is not given in accordance with this Rule, the court may dismiss it.

(See General Note after r.4.14.)

4.12   Verification of petition

4.12(1)   [Petition verified by statement of truth] The petition shall be verified by a statement of truth.
[FORM 4.2]

4.12(2)   [Debts due to different creditors] If the petition is in respect of debts due to different creditors, the debts to each creditor must be separately verified.

4.12(3)   [Omitted.]

4.12(3A)   [Statement of truth not contained in petition etc. to specify] A statement of truth which is not contained in or endorsed upon the petition which it verifies must be sufficient to identify the petition and must specify–

(a)   the name and registered number of the company,

(b)   the name of the petitioner, and

(c)   the court in which the petition is to be presented.

4.12(4)   [Who must authenticate statement of truth] The statement of truth must be authenticated–

(a)   by the petitioner (or if there are two or more petitioners, any one of them), or

(b)   by some person such as a director, company secretary or similar company officer, or a solicitor, who has been concerned in the matters giving rise to the presentation of the petition, or

(c)   by some responsible person who is duly authorised to authenticate the statement of truth and has the requisite knowledge of those matters.

4.12(5)   [Where person authenticating statement of truth not petitioner] Where the person authenticating the statement of truth is not the petitioner himself, or one of the petitioners, he must in the statement of truth identify himself and state–

(a)   the capacity in which, and the authority by which, he authenticates it, and

(b)   the means of his knowledge of the matters verified in the statement of truth.

4.12(6)   [Omitted.]

4.12(7)   [Statement of truth verifying more than one petition] A statement of truth verifying more than one petition shall include in its title the names of the companies to which it relates and shall set out, in respect of each company, the statements relied on by the petitioner; and a clear and legible photocopy of the statement of truth must be filed with each petition which it verifies.

4.12(8)   [EC Regulation] The statement of truth shall state whether, in the opinion of the person making the application, (i) the EC Regulation will apply and (ii) if so, whether the proceedings will be main proceedings, secondary proceedings or territorial proceedings.

(See General Note after r.4.14.)

4.13 Persons entitled to copy of petition

4.13 Every director, contributory or creditor of the company is entitled to be furnished by the solicitor for the petitioner (or by the petitioner himself, if acting in person) with a copy of the petition within 2 business days after requiring it, on payment of the appropriate fee.

(See General Note after r.4.14.)

4.14 Certificate of compliance

4.14(1) **[Filing in court]** The petitioner or his solicitor shall, at least 5 business days before the hearing of the petition, file in court a certificate of compliance with the Rules relating to service and advertisement.

[FORM 4.7]

4.14(2) **[Contents of certificate]** The certificate shall show–

(a) the date of presentation of the petition,

(b) the date fixed for the hearing, and

(c) the date or dates on which the petition was served and notice of it was given in compliance with the Rules.

A copy or, where this is not reasonably practicable, a description of the form and content of any notice given shall be filed in court with the certificate.

4.14(3) **[Effect of non-compliance]** Non-compliance with this Rule is a ground on which the court may, if it thinks fit, dismiss the petition.

GENERAL NOTE TO RR.4.7–4.14

These rules deal with the filing, service, advertisement and verification of the petition.

The deposit referred to in r.4.7(2) is fixed at £690 from April 1, 2008. See the Insolvency Proceedings (Fees) Order 2004 (SI 2004/593) art.6(1)(a), as amended.

Any director, contributory or creditor of the company is entitled to a copy of the petition on payment of the appropriate fee (r.4.13).

Rule 4.7(4)(e) was substituted by the Financial Services and Markets Act 2000 (Consequential Amendments and Repeals) Order 2001 (SI 2001/3649) as from December 1, 2001. The draftsman seems to have overlooked the need for similar amendments to r.4.10(4).

Paragraph (da) was inserted into r.4.7 and para.(3A) into r.4.10(3) by the Insolvency (Amendment) Rules 2002 (SI 2002/1307, effective May 31, 2002). Note that the exception to r.4.10(3A) is not confined to the case where the petitioner is a liquidator appointed in "main" proceedings.

Changes were made to r.4.7 paras (4)(b), (7)(b), (7)(c) and 8 and to r.4.10(2) by the Insolvency (Amendment) Rules 2003 (SI 2003/1730, effective September 15, 2003) Sch.1 paras 13, 14 to reflect the fact that administrators may now also be appointed out of court. Further changes to para.(4)(b) were made, and paras (2A), (2B) added, by the Insolvency (Amendment) Rules 2004 (SI 2004/584), effective April 1, 2004. The latter allows alternative arrangements to be made for the payment of the deposit.

Minor changes were made to rr.4.7(7)(c) and 4.11(4)(a) and r.4.12(8) inserted, by the Insolvency (Amendment) Rules 2005 (SI 2005/527) rr.18–20, as from April 1, 2005.

Rule 4.11 and r.4.14(2)(c) substituted by I(A)R 2009 (SI 2009/642) rr.18, 19 as from April 6, 2009.

Rules 4.7–4.8, 4.12 amended, r.4.7(3) substituted, rr.4.9, 4.12(3), (6) omitted and rr.4.9A, 4.12(3A) inserted by I(A)R 2010 r.2 and Sch. paras 142–148 as from April 6, 2010.

Service of the petition is now proved by a certificate rather than an affidavit in all cases. The gazetting of the notice of petition (r.4.11(5)) must now include the standard contents (see rr.12A.31–12A.33) with the further details set out in that paragraph.

In *Re Oakwood Storage Services Ltd* [2003] EWHC 2807 (Ch); [2004] 2 B.C.L.C. 404 service of a winding-up petition was effected at the company's registered office at a time when its directors were barred from attending the premises as a result of action taken by the Customs and Excise. The court held that the directors could not complain that the service was ineffective since it was up to them to have made suitable arrangements to ensure that such documents came to their notice while the ban continued.

The reference in r.4.10(4) to the Banking Act 1987 is obsolete: this Act was repealed by FSMA 2000 and SI 2001/3649, art.3(1)(d) as from December 1, 2001. Banking is now regulated under the FSMA itself.

The court is given a discretion by r.4.11(5) to dismiss the petition if it has not been duly advertised. It has been the practice of the court since the ruling in *Re Signland Ltd* [1982] 2 All E.R. 609 to strike out any petition where the petitioning creditor has not observed the provisions as to time set out in r.4.11(2)(b), and in particular where the petition has been advertised without giving the company the prescribed seven days' notice. This is confirmed by para.2.1 of the *Practice Direction: Insolvency Proceedings* [2007] B.C.C. 842 (reproduced as App.IV to this *Guide*). If the court, in its discretion, grants an adjournment instead of dismissing the petition, this will be on the condition that the petition is advertised in due time for the adjourned hearing, and no further adjournment for the purpose of advertisement will be granted.

Rule 4.14 must be complied with even if the advertisement is defective in any way or if the petitioner decides not to pursue the petition (e.g. on receiving payment) (ibid., para.2(2)). Paragraph 3(1) of the same practice direction extends the time laid down by r.4.14 for filing a certificate of compliance to not later than 4.30pm on the Friday preceding the day on which the petition is to be heard. Applications to file later will only be allowed if good reason is shown for the delay.

The word "advertised" has two meanings: (1) a paid announcement in a general publication; and (2) notifying the existence of the matter in question. Where the court has made an order restraining the advertisement of a winding-up petition, the word is to be construed in a wide sense, and any communication to an unauthorised party (e.g. informing the company's bank) of the fact that the petition has been presented will be a breach of the order: see the note to r.4.23(1)(c). However in rr.4.11 and 4.14 the word refers to publication in the *Gazette*—i.e. is used in the former sense (*S N Group plc v Barclays Bank plc* [1993] B.C.C. 506), and a notification to a third party of the existence of the petition will not in itself be a breach of rr.4.11 or 4.14. The Court of Appeal in *Secretary of State for Trade and Industry v North West Holdings plc* [1998] B.C.C. 997 approved *S N Group v Barclays Bank* and held that press notices by the Department of Trade and Industry stating that a winding-up petition had been presented and provisional liquidator appointed to a company were not in breach of r.4.11, although Chadwick L.J. warned the DTI that if it were in any doubt whether it was appropriate to issue a press notice then directions from the court should be sought. A communication to a third party, may, however be open to condemnation as an abuse of the process of the court, if made for an improper purpose such as putting pressure on the company: if so, the petition may be struck out for this reason (*Re Bill Hennessey Associates Ltd* [1992] B.C.C. 386).

The court has a discretion under r.4.11(1) to restrain or dispense altogether with advertising, which it may do (e.g.) in order to enable presentation of a petition for an administration order (*Re a Company (No.001448 of 1989)* [1989] B.C.L.C. 715) but otherwise, unless the petition is held to constitute an abuse of the process of the court, this discretion will be exercised only in exceptional circumstances: *Applied Data Base Ltd v Secretary of State for Trade & Industry* [1995] 1 B.C.L.C. 272.

The factors which the court will take into account in considering whether to order a restraint on advertisement were examined in *Re a Company (No.007923 of 1994)* [1995] 1 W.L.R. 953; [1995] B.C.C. 634. In addition to satisfying the court that there was not likely to be any significant damage to the company's creditors, contributories and current trading partners, it was held that company needed to show that advertisement might cause serious damage to its reputation and financial stability. See also *James Dolman & Co Ltd v Pedley* [2003] EWCA Civ 1686; [2004] B.P.I.R. 290.

Rule 4.7(7) goes some way to meet drafting deficiencies in the Act, but it does not deal with the case of a petition instituted by an administrative receiver (as might have been expected) or meet all the problems that may arise with a supervisor's petition under IA 1986 s.7(4)(b). See the note to s.124(1).

The procedure on a petition presented by contributories is set out in Ch.4 (rr.4.22 et seq.).

Rule 4.8(4) enables service to be effected more easily on a company which has ceased trading.

An application to restrain the presentation of a winding-up petition should be by originating application made to the judge: see the *Practice Direction* (above) at para.8(1).

4.15   Permission for petitioner to withdraw

4.15   If at least 5 business days before the hearing the petitioner, on an application without notice to any other party, satisfies the court that–

(a)   the petition has not been advertised, and

(b)   no notices (whether in support or in opposition) have been received by him with reference to the petition, and (c)　the company consents to an order being made under this Rule,

the court may order that the petitioner has permission to withdraw the petition on such terms as to costs as the parties may agree.

[FORM 4.8]

GENERAL NOTE

Rule 4.15 amended by I(A)R 2010 r.2 and Sch. para.149 as from April 6, 2010.

The circumstances in which a petition may be withdrawn are limited to those prescribed. See *Practice Direction: Insolvency Proceedings* [2007] B.C.C. 842 (reproduced in App.IV to this *Guide*).

4.16　Notice of appearance

4.16(1)　[Notice of intention] Every person who intends to appear on the hearing of the petition shall give to the petitioner notice of his intention in accordance with this Rule.

[FORM 4.9]

4.16(2)　[Contents of notice] The notice shall specify–

(a)　the name and address of the person giving it, and any telephone number and reference which may be required for communication with him or with any other person (to be also specified in the notice) authorised to speak or act on his behalf;

(b)　whether his intention is to support or oppose the petition; and

(c)　the amount and nature of his debt.

4.16(3)　[Address for sending notice] The notice shall be sent to the petitioner at the address shown for him in the court records, or in the advertisement of the petition required by Rule 4.11; or it may be sent to his solicitor.

4.16(4)　[Time for sending notice] The notice shall be sent so as to reach the addressee not later than 16.00 hours on the business day before that which is appointed for the hearing (or, where the hearing has been adjourned, for the adjourned hearing).

4.16(5)　[Effect of non-compliance] A person failing to comply with this Rule may appear on the hearing of the petition only with the permission of the court.

(See General Note after r.4.21B.)

4.17　List of appearances

4.17(1)　[Petitioner to prepare list] The petitioner shall prepare for the court a list of the persons (if any) who have given notice under Rule 4.16, specifying their names and addresses and (if known to him) their respective solicitors.

[FORM 4.10]

4.17(2)　[Whether creditors support or oppose] Against the name of each creditor in the list it shall be stated whether his intention is to support the petition, or to oppose it.

4.17(3)　[Copy of list handed to court] On the day appointed for the hearing of the petition, a copy of the list shall be handed to the court before the commencement of the hearing.

4.17(4)　[Permission under r.4.16(5)] If any permission is given under Rule 4.16(5), the petitioner shall add to the list the same particulars in respect of the person to whom permission has been given.

(See General Note after r.4.21B.)

4.18 Witness statement in opposition

4.18(1) [Filing in court] If the company intends to oppose the petition, its witness statement in opposition shall be filed in court not less than 5 business days before the date fixed for the hearing.

4.18(2) [Copy to petitioner] A copy of the witness statement shall be sent by the company to the petitioner, as soon as reasonably practicable after filing.

(See General Note after r.4.21B.)

4.18A Adjournment

4.18A(1) [Where adjournment] If the court adjourns the hearing of the petition, the following applies.

4.18A(2) [Notice of order] Unless the court otherwise directs, the petitioning creditor must forthwith send–

(a) to the company, and

(b) where any creditor has given notice under Rule 4.16 but was not present at the hearing, to that creditor,

notice of the making of the order of adjournment. The notice must state the venue for the adjourned hearing.

(See General Note after r.4.21B.)

4.19 Substitution of creditor or contributory for petitioner

4.19(1) [Application of Rule] This Rule applies where a person petitions and is subsequently found not entitled to do so, or where the petitioner–

(a) fails to advertise his petition within the time prescribed by the Rules or such extended time as the court may allow, or

(b) consents to withdraw his petition, or to allow it to be dismissed, consents to an adjournment, or fails to appear in support of his petition when it is called on in court on the day originally fixed for the hearing, or on a day to which it is adjourned, or

(c) appears, but does not apply for an order in the terms of the prayer of his petition.

4.19(2) [Power of court] The court may, on such terms as it thinks just, substitute as petitioner any creditor or contributory who in its opinion would have a right to present a petition, and who is desirous of prosecuting it.

4.19(2A) [Appointment of member State liquidator] Where a member State liquidator has been appointed in main proceedings in relation to the company, without prejudice to paragraph (2), the court may, on such terms as it thinks just, substitute the member State liquidator as petitioner, where he is desirous of prosecuting the petition.

4.19(3) [Making of order] An order of the court under this Rule may, where a petitioner fails to advertise his petition within the time prescribed by these Rules, or consents to withdraw his petition, be made at any time.

GENERAL NOTE

See *Practice Direction: Insolvency Proceedings* [2007] B.C.C. 842 (reproduced in App.IV to this *Guide*). See also General Note after r.4.21B.

Paragraph (2A) was inserted into r.4.19 by the Insolvency (Amendment) Rules 2002 (SI 2002/1307, effective May 31, 2002). It will apply only where the debtor company's centre of main interests is situated in another EU Member State.

4.20 Notice and settling of winding-up order

4.20(1) [Notice to official receiver] When a winding-up order has been made, the court shall as soon as reasonably practicable give notice of the fact to the official receiver.

[FORM 4.11]
[FORM 4.12]
[FORM 4.13]

4.20(2) [Documents to be left at court] The petitioner and every other person who has appeared on the hearing of the petition shall, not later than the business day following that on which the order is made, leave at the court all the documents required for enabling the order to be completed as soon as reasonably practicable.

4.20(3) [Appointment of venue] It is not necessary for the court to appoint a venue for any person to attend to settle the order, unless in any particular case the special circumstances make an appointment necessary.

(See General Note after r.4.21B.)

4.21 Transmission and advertisement of order

4.21(1) [Copy of orders to official receiver] When the winding-up order has been made, 3 copies of it, sealed with the seal of the court, shall be sent as soon as reasonably practicable by the court to the official receiver.

4.21(2) [Service on company etc.] The official receiver shall cause a sealed copy of the order to be served on the company by prepaid letter addressed to it at its registered office (if any) or, if there is no registered office, at its principal or last known principal place of business.

Alternatively, the order may be served on such other person or persons, or in such other manner, as the court directs.

4.21(3) [Copy of order to registrar] The official receiver shall forward to the registrar of companies the copy of the order which by section 130(1) is directed to be so forwarded by the company.

4.21(4) [Gazetting/advertisement of notice of order] The official receiver–

(a) as soon as reasonably practicable shall cause notice of the order to be gazetted; and

(b) may advertise notice of the order in such other manner as the official receiver thinks fit.

4.21(5) [Additional contents of r.4.21(4) notice] In addition to the standard contents a notice under paragraph (4) must state–

(a) that a winding up order has been made in respect of the company; and

(b) the date of the order.

(See General Note after r.4.21B.)

4.21A Expenses of voluntary arrangement

4.21A Where a winding-up order is made and there is at the time of the presentation of the petition in force for the company a voluntary arrangement under Part I of the Act, any expenses properly incurred as expenses of the administration of the arrangement in question shall be payable in priority to any expenses of the liquidation.

4.21B   Petition dismissed

4.21B(1)   [Duty of petitioner to give notice of dismissal] Unless the court otherwise directs, when a petition is dismissed, as soon as reasonably practicable the petitioner shall give notice of the dismissal. Such notice shall be–

(a)   gazetted; or

(b)   advertised in accordance with any directions of the court.

4.21B(2)   [Additional contents of r.4.21B(1) notice] In addition to the standard contents, the notice published under paragraph (1) must state—

(a)   that a petition for the winding up of the company has been dismissed;

(b)   in the case of an overseas company, the address at which service of the petition was effected;

(c)   the name and address of the petitioner;

(d)   the date on which the petition was presented;

(e)   the date on which the petition was gazetted or otherwise advertised; and

(f)   the date of the hearing at which the petition was dismissed.

4.21B(3)   [Notice by company where non-compliance with r.4.21B(1), (2)] Where–

(a)   the petitioner is not the company itself; and

(b)   the petitioner has not complied with paragraphs (1) and (2) within 21 days of the date of the hearing at which the petition was dismissed,

the company may give notice of the dismissal itself. Such notice shall be gazetted.

GENERAL NOTE TO RR.4.16–4.21B

These rules deal with the conduct of the hearing, and the steps which are to be taken once a winding-up order has been made. This includes the registration of a copy of the winding-up order in the Companies Registry.

Where the court orders the rescission of a winding-up order under r.7.47, the registrar of companies may be directed to remove the order from his files; but he may, if he thinks it desirable, record the fact that it has been removed in a note: *Re Calmex Ltd* (1988) 4 B.C.C. 761.

For an example of the exercise of the court's discretion under r.4.16(5), see *Re Dollar Land (Feltham) Ltd* [1995] B.C.C. 740. (Note that "appear" in this paragraph and elsewhere in r.4.16 means "have a right of audience": *Re Piccadilly Property Management Ltd* [2000] B.C.C. 44 at 50.)

A petition presented in the name of a non-existent person is a nullity, but this is to be distinguished from the case where the petitioner exists but is merely misnamed, which can be dealt with by an application to amend: *Re Goldthorpe & Lacey Ltd* (1987) 3 B.C.C. 595—a case which also illustrates the exercise of the court's discretion to substitute a petitioner under r.4.19(2).

Where a winding-up order is made against a company which is subject to a CVA, the funds in the hands of the supervisor will in many cases be subject to a trust in favour of the CVA creditors: see the note to IA 1986 s.7(4). Rule 4.21A does not carry the implication that in all cases the funds in a CVA should pass to the liquidator: the rule is only designed to ensure that the supervisor will obtain his expenses if the effect of a particular winding up is to discharge the CVA and any trust thereunder (see *Re NT Gallagher & Sons Ltd* [2002] EWCA Civ 404; [2002] 1 W.L.R. 2380; [2002] B.C.C. 867).

Rules 4.18A, 4.21(5) inserted and r.4.21B(2) substituted by I(A)R 2010 r.2 and Sch. paras 151–153 as from April 6, 2010. Previously r.1.33(4) (introduced by the Insolvency (Amendment) Rules 2002 (SI 2002/1307, effective May 31, 2002)) makes provision similar to r.4.21A for the case where the court makes an order converting a CVA into a winding up in accordance with the EC Regulation art.37. Rule 4.21(4) substituted, and r.4.21B inserted, by I(A)R 2009 (SI 2009/642) rr.20, 21 as from April 6, 2009.

Both the making of the winding-up order and the dismissal of the petition must be gazetted, incorporating the standard contents (see rr.12A.31–12A.33) and the further information set out in para.4.21(5) or 4.21B(2).

CHAPTER 4

PETITION BY CONTRIBUTORIES (NO CVL APPLICATION)

4.22   Presentation and service of petition

4.22(1)   [Form of petition and filing in court] The petition must or, where the petition is presented under Rule 4.7(9), may specify the grounds on which it is presented and shall be filed in court with one copy for service under this Rule.

[FORM 4.14]

4.22(1A)   [Deposit receipt to be produced] No petition shall be filed unless there is produced with it the receipt for the deposit payable on presentation.

4.22(2)   [Fixing return day] The court shall fix a hearing for a day (**"the return day"**) on which, unless the court otherwise directs, the petitioner and the company shall attend before the registrar or district judge for–

  (a)   directions to be given in relation to the procedure on the petition; or

  (b)   where–

     (i)   the petition is presented under Rule 4.7(9), and

     (ii)   the court considers it just in all the circumstances,

the hearing of the petition.

4.22(3)   [Copy of petition for service] On fixing the return day, the court shall return to the petitioner a sealed copy of the petition for service, endorsed with the return day and time of hearing.

4.22(4)   [Service on company] The petitioner shall, at least 14 days before the return day, serve a sealed copy of the petition on the company.

4.22(5)   [Appointment of member State liquidator] Where a member State liquidator has been appointed in main proceedings in relation to the company, the petitioner shall send a copy of the petition to him.

(See General Note after r.4.24.)

4.23   Return of petition

4.23(1)   [Directions] On the return day, or at any time after it, the court must or, where the petition is presented under Rule 4.7(9), may give such directions as it thinks appropriate with respect to the following matters–

  (a)   service of the petition, whether in connection with the venue for a further hearing, or for any other purpose;

  (b)   whether particulars of claim and defence are to be delivered, and generally as to the procedure on the petition;

  (c)   whether, and if so by what means, the petition is to be advertised;

  (d)   the manner in which any evidence is to be adduced at any hearing before the judge and in particular (but without prejudice to the generality of the above) as to–

     (i)   the taking of evidence wholly or in part by witness statement or orally;

     (ii)   the cross-examination of any persons authenticating witness statements;

     (iii)   the matters to be dealt with in evidence;

(e) any other matter affecting the procedure on the petition or in connection with the hearing and disposal of the petition.

4.23(2) **[Directions under r.4.23(1)(a)]** In giving directions under paragraph (1)(a), the court shall have regard to whether any of the persons specified in Rule 4.10 should be served with a copy of the petition.

(See General Note after r.4.24.)

4.24 Application of Rules in Chapter 3

4.24 The following Rules in Chapter 3 apply, with the necessary modifications–

    Rule 4.16 (notice of appearance);

    Rule 4.17 (list of appearances);

    Rule 4.20 (notice and settling of winding-up order);

    Rule 4.21 (transmission and advertisement of order); and

    Rule 4.21A (expenses of voluntary arrangement)

GENERAL NOTE TO RR.4.22–4.24

The procedure to be followed on a contributory's petition is generally the same as that for other petitions, with the modifications set out here. Directions from the court regarding the service, advertisement and hearing of the petition must be sought in every case. If the petition is advertised prematurely the court may order that the petition be struck out and removed from the court file: *Re a Company (No.007020 of 1996)* [1998] 2 B.C.L.C. 54.

The word "advertised" has two meanings: primarily, a paid announcement in a general publication, but also notifying the existence of the matter in question in any way. Where the court has made an order restraining the advertisement of a winding-up petition under r.4.23(1)(c), the word may be construed in the latter sense, and any communication to an unauthorised party (e.g. informing the company's bank) of the fact that the petition has been presented will be a breach of the order (*Re a Company (No.00687 of 1991)* [1991] B.C.C. 210). It may also be an abuse of the process of the court to engage in premature advertisement of a contributories' petition, e.g. by telling the company's bank and trading partners that a petition has been or will be presented: *Re Doreen Boards Ltd* [1996] 1 B.C.L.C. 501. (See also the note to r.4.11, above.)

Paragraph (5) was inserted into r.4.22 by the Insolvency (Amendment) Rules 2002 (SI 2002/1307, effective May 31, 2002). It will apply only where the debtor company's centre of main interests is situated in another EU Member State. Rules 4.22, 4.23 amended by I(A)R 2010 r.2 and Sch. paras 154, 155 as from April 6, 2010.

CHAPTER 5

PROVISIONAL LIQUIDATOR (NO CVL APPLICATION)

4.25 Appointment of provisional liquidator

4.25(1) **[Who may apply to court]** An application to the court for the appointment of a provisional liquidator under section 135 may be made by–

(a) the petitioner;

(b) a creditor of the company;

(c) a contributory;

(d) the company;

(e) the Secretary of State;

(f) a temporary administrator;

(g) a member State liquidator appointed in main proceedings; or

(h) any person who under any enactment would be entitled to present a petition for the winding up of the company.

4.25(2) **[Supporting witness statement]** The application must be supported by a witness statement stating–

(a) the grounds on which it is proposed that a provisional liquidator should be appointed;

(b) if some person other than the official receiver is proposed to be appointed, that the person has consented to act and, to the best of the applicant's belief, is qualified to act as an insolvency practitioner in relation to the company;

(c) whether or not the official receiver has been informed of the application and, if so, has been furnished with a copy of it;

(d) whether to the applicant's knowledge–

   (i) there has been proposed or is in force for the company a voluntary arrangement under Part I of the Act, or

   (ii) an administrator or administrative receiver is acting in relation to the company, or

   (iii) a liquidator has been appointed for its voluntary winding up; and

(e) the applicant's estimate of the value of the assets in respect of which the provisional liquidator is to be appointed.

4.25(3) **[Copies to official receiver etc.]** The applicant shall send copies of the application and of the witness statement in support to the official receiver, who may attend the hearing and make any representations which he thinks appropriate.

If for any reason it is not practicable to comply with this paragraph, the official receiver must be informed of the application in sufficient time for him to be able to attend.

4.25(4) **[Powers of court]** The court may on the application, if satisfied that sufficient grounds are shown for the appointment, make it on such terms as it thinks fit.

(See General Note after r.4.31.)

4.25A Notice of appointment

4.25A(1) **[Notice to official receiver]** Where a provisional liquidator has been appointed the court shall as soon as reasonably practicable give notice of the fact to the official receiver.

4.25A(2) **[Copy to provisional liquidator]** A copy of that notice shall at the same time be sent by the court to the provisional liquidator where he is not the official receiver.

4.25A(3) **[Gazetting/advertisement of appointment by provisional liquidator]** Unless the court otherwise directs, on receipt of the notice of appointment, as soon as reasonably practicable the provisional liquidator shall give notice of that appointment. Such notice–

(a) shall be gazetted; and

(b) may be advertised in such other manner as the provisional liquidator thinks fit.

[FORM 4.14A]

4.25A(4) **[Additional contents in r.4.25A(3) notice]** In addition to the standard contents, the notice under paragraph (3) must state–

(a) that a provisional liquidator has been appointed; and

(b)   the date of the appointment.

(See General Note after r.4.31.)

4.26   Order of appointment

4.26(1)   [Form of order] The order appointing the provisional liquidator shall specify the functions to be carried out by him in relation to the company's affairs.

[FORM 4.15]

4.26(2)   [Sealed copies] The court shall, as soon as reasonably practicable after the order is made, send sealed copies of the order as follows–

(a)   if the official receiver is appointed, three copies to him;

(b)   if a person other than the official receiver is appointed–

(i)   three copies to that person, and

(ii)   one copy to the official receiver;

(c)   if there is an administrative receiver acting in relation to the company, one copy to him.

4.26(3)   [Distribution of r.4.26(2) copies] Of the three copies of the order sent to the official receiver under paragraph (2)(a), or to another person under paragraph (2)(b)(i)-

(i)   one shall in each case be sent by the recipient to the company, or if a liquidator has been appointed for the company's voluntary winding-up, to him; and

(ii)   one shall be sent to the registrar of companies.

(See General Note after r.4.31.)

4.27   Deposit

4.27(1)   [Security for official receiver's remuneration etc.] Before an order appointing the official receiver as provisional liquidator is issued, the applicant for it shall deposit with him, or otherwise secure to his satisfaction, such sum as the court directs to cover the official receiver's remuneration and expenses.

4.27(2)   [Insufficiency of deposit etc.] If the sum deposited or secured subsequently proves to be insufficient, the court may, on application by the official receiver, order that an additional sum be deposited or secured. If the order is not complied with within 2 business days after service of it on the person to whom it is directed, the court may discharge the order appointing the provisional liquidator.

4.27(3)   [Repayment of deposit etc.] If a winding-up order is made after a provisional liquidator has been appointed, any money deposited under this Rule shall (unless it is required by reason of insufficiency of assets for payment of remuneration and expenses of the provisional liquidator) be repaid to the person depositing it (or as that person may direct) as an expense of the liquidation, in the prescribed order of priority.

(See General Note after r.4.31.)

4.28   Security

4.28(1)   [Application of Rule] The following applies where an insolvency practitioner is appointed to be provisional liquidator under section 135.

4.28(2)   [Cost of providing security] The cost of providing the security required under the Act shall be paid in the first instance by the provisional liquidator; but–

(a) if a winding-up order is not made, the person so appointed is entitled to be reimbursed out of the property of the company, and the court may make an order on the company accordingly, and

(b) if a winding-up order is made, he is entitled to be reimbursed as an expense of the liquidation in the prescribed order of priority.

(See General Note after r.4.31.)

4.29 Failure to give or keep up security

4.29(1) [Powers of court] If the provisional liquidator fails to give or keep up his security, the court may remove him, and make such order as it thinks fit as to costs.

4.29(2) [Directions for replacement] If an order is made under this Rule removing the provisional liquidator, or discharging the order appointing him, the court shall give directions as to whether any, and if so what, steps should be taken for the appointment of another person in his place.

(See General Note after r.4.31.)

4.30 Remuneration

4.30(1) [To be fixed by court] The remuneration of the provisional liquidator (other than the official receiver) shall be fixed by the court from time to time on his application.

4.30(2) [Matters to be taken into account] In fixing his remuneration, the court shall take into account–

(a) the time properly given by him (as provisional liquidator) and his staff in attending to the company's affairs;

(b) the complexity (or otherwise) of the case;

(c) any respects in which, in connection with the company's affairs, there falls on the provisional liquidator any responsibility of an exceptional kind or degree;

(d) the effectiveness with which the provisional liquidator appears to be carrying out, or to have carried out, his duties; and

(e) the value and nature of the property with which he has to deal.

4.30(3) [Source of payment of remuneration etc.] Without prejudice to any order the court may make as to costs, the provisional liquidator's remuneration (whether the official receiver or another) shall be paid to him, and the amount of any expenses incurred by him (including the remuneration and expenses of any special manager appointed under section 177) reimbursed–

(a) if a winding-up order is not made, out of the property of the company; and

(b) if a winding-up order is made, as an expense of the liquidation, in the prescribed order of priority, or, in either case (the relevant funds being insufficient), out of the deposit under Rule 4.27.

4.30(3A) [Power of retention] Unless the court otherwise directs, in a case falling within paragraph (3)(a) above the provisional liquidator may retain out of the company's property such sums or property as are or may be required for meeting his remuneration and expenses.

4.30(4) [Provisional liquidator other than official receiver] Where a person other than the official receiver has been appointed provisional liquidator, and the official receiver has taken any steps for the purpose of obtaining a statement of affairs or has performed any other duty under the Rules, he shall pay the official receiver such sum (if any) as the court may direct.

(See General Note after r.4.31.)

4.31 Termination of appointment

4.31(1) [Termination by court] The appointment of the provisional liquidator may be terminated by the court on his application, or on that of any of the persons specified in Rule 4.25(1).

4.31(2) [Directions on termination] If the provisional liquidator's appointment terminates, in consequence of the dismissal of the winding-up petition or otherwise, the court may give such directions as it thinks fit with respect to the accounts of his administration or any other matters which it thinks appropriate.

4.31(3) [Omitted.]

4.31(4) [Notice: registrar/gazette/advertisement] Notice of termination of the appointment of a provisional liquidator must be given by the provisional liquidator, unless the termination is on the making of a winding-up order or the court otherwise directs. Such notice–

(a)   as soon as reasonably practicable must be sent to the registrar of companies;

(b)   as soon as reasonably practicable must be gazetted; and

(c)   may be advertised in such other manner as the provisional liquidator thinks fit.

4.31(5) [Additional contents in r.4.31(4)(b) or (c) notice] In addition to the standard contents, a notice under paragraph (4)(b) or (c) must state–

(a)   that the appointment as provisional liquidator has been terminated;

(b)   the date of that termination; and

(c)   that the appointment terminated otherwise than on the making of a winding-up order.

GENERAL NOTE TO RR.4.25–4.31

These rules set out the procedure governing an application to the court for the appointment of a provisional liquidator under IA 1986 s.135, and the associated questions of furnishing a deposit (where the official receiver is appointed) or security (where the provisional liquidator is an insolvency practitioner), and the liquidator's remuneration.

Rule 4.25(1) was substituted by the Insolvency (Amendment) Rules 2002 (SI 2002/1307, effective May 31, 2002), so as to include the persons mentioned in subparas (f) and (g).

Rule 4.25A(3) inserted) by I(A)R 2009 (SI 2009/642) r.22 as from April 6, 2009. Former r.4.31(3) omitted by I(A)R 1987 (SI 1987/1919) r.3(1) and Sch. Pt 1 para.44 as from January 11, 1988, and new r.4.31(3) inserted by I(A)R 2009 (SI 2009/642) r.23 as from April 6, 2009.

Rule 4.26 was amended by the Insolvency (Amendment) Rules 2005 (SI 2005/527) r.21, as from April 1, 2005, to provide for the issue of a third copy of the order.

Rule 4.31(3) omitted and rr.4.25A(4), 4.31(4), (5) inserted by I(A)R 2010 r.2 and Sch. paras 157, 160 as from April 6, 2010.

The court may in an appropriate case refer the fixing of remuneration under r.4.30 to one or more assessors: *Re Independent Insurance Co Ltd* [2002] EWHC 1577 (Ch); [2003] EWHC 51 (Ch); [2004] B.C.C. 919. In the latter judgment the principles for the fixing of remuneration and making of interim payments are discussed in detail. The judgment of Peter Smith J. in *Jacob v UIC Insurance Co Ltd* [2006] EWHC 2717 (Ch); [2007] B.C.C.167 discusses many issues relating to the review of the remuneration of provisional liquidators, including (i) the procedure for an appeal under r.7.47 of an assessment made by a registrar; (ii) the reasons for disallowing claims for remuneration on the basis of over-management, the use of staff of too high a grade and of consultants; (iii) the justice of re-opening claims settled or agreed in the past; and (iv) the irrelevance of the fact that the provisional liquidation was successful. (For further proceedings, see *Re UIC Insurance Co Ltd (No.2)* [2007] B.P.I.R. 589.) See also the *Practice Statement* [2004] B.C.C. 912 (reproduced as App.VII to this *Guide*).

There is no provision in the rules governing the priority in which the remuneration and expenses of a provisional liquidator should be paid, either vis-à-vis the company's debts or in relation to each other; but in *Re Grey Marlin Ltd* [2000] B.C.C. 410; and in *Smith v UIC Insurance Co Ltd* [2001] B.C.C. 11 the rules governing a liquidator's remuneration and expenses were applied by analogy.

The provisions in rr.4.28 and 4.30 are directory, although subject to the overall discretion conferred by r.4.31(2); and so a court will not normally make an order that an unsuccessful petitioner should pay the remuneration of a provisional liquidator: *Re Walter L Jacob & Co Ltd* (1987) 3 B.C.C. 532. (See, however, *Re Secure & Provide plc* [1992] B.C.C. 405, where such an order was made against the Secretary of State following the failure of a petition under s.124A; and compare *Re Xyllyx plc (No.2)* [1992] B.C.L.C. 378.)

The court has power under r.4.31(2) to direct that a provisional liquidator who has been discharged before the hearing of the petition shall be paid remuneration out of the company's assets: see *Re U O C Corporation, Alipour v U O C Corporation* [1998] B.C.C. 191.

Rules 4.25A(4) and 4.31(4)–(7) prescribe in detail the required contents of the notice of the provisional liquidator's appointment and its termination. On the standard contents for gazetted notices, see rr.12A.31–12A.33.

A provisional liquidator is now listed in Annex C to the EC Regulation as a "liquidator" referred to in art.2(b) of the Regulation.

CHAPTER 6

STATEMENT OF AFFAIRS AND OTHER INFORMATION

4.32   Notice requiring statement of affairs

(NO CVL APPLICATION)

4.32(1)   **[Application of Rule]** The following applies where the official receiver determines to require a statement of the company's affairs to be made out and submitted to him in accordance with section 131.

[FORM 4.16]

4.32(2)   **[Notice]** He shall send notice to each of the persons whom he considers should be made responsible under that section, requiring them to prepare and submit the statement.

4.32(3)   **["Nominated persons"]** The persons to whom that notice is sent are referred to in this Chapter as **"the nominated persons"**.

4.32(4)   **[Contents of notice]** The notice shall inform each of the nominated persons–

(a)   of the names and addresses of all others (if any) to whom the same notice has been sent;

(b)   of the time within which the statement must be delivered;

(c)   of the effect of section 131(7) (penalty for non-compliance); and

(d)   of the application to him, and to each of the other nominated persons, of section 235 (duty to provide information, and to attend on the official receiver if required).

4.32(5)   **[Instructions for preparation of statement]** The official receiver shall, on request, furnish a nominated person with instructions for the preparation of the statement and with the forms required for that purpose.

(See General Note after r.4.33.)

4.33   Verification and filing

(NO CVL APPLICATION)

4.33(1)   **[Form and verification]** The statement of affairs shall be in Form 4.17, shall contain all the particulars required by that form and shall be verified by a statement of truth by the persons making the statement of affairs (using the same form).

[FORM 4.17]

4.33(2)   **[Statement of concurrence verified by statement of truth]** The official receiver may require any of the persons mentioned in section 131(3) to submit a statement of concurrence verified by a statement of truth, stating that he concurs in the statement of affairs.

4.33(3) **[Statement of concurrence may be qualified]** A statement of concurrence made under paragraph (2) may be qualified in respect of matters dealt with in the statement of affairs, where the maker of the statement of concurrence is not in agreement with the persons making the statement of affairs, or he considers the statement to be erroneous or misleading, or he is without the direct knowledge necessary for concurring in the statement.

4.33(4) **[Delivery of statement of affairs to official receiver]** The statement of affairs shall be delivered to the official receiver by the nominated person (or by one of them, if more than one), together with a copy of the verified statement.

4.33(5) **[Delivery of statement of concurrence]** Every statement of concurrence shall be delivered to the official receiver by the person who makes it, together with a copy.

4.33(6) **[Official receiver to send copies to registrar]** The official receiver must send the verified copy of the statement of affairs and any statements of concurrence to the registrar of companies.

4.33(7) [Omitted.]

GENERAL NOTE TO RR.4.32, 4.33

The statement of affairs referred to in these rules is that which the official receiver may require when an order for winding up or for the appointment of a provisional liquidator has been made.

Rule 4.33(6) substituted and r.4.33(7) omitted by I(A)R 2010 r.2 and Sch. para.162 as from April 6, 2010.

4.34-CVL   Statement of affairs

4.34-CVL(1) **[Application of Rule]** This Rule applies with respect to the statement of affairs made out by the liquidator under section 95(3) or (as the case may be) by the directors under section 99(1).

[FORM 4.18]

[FORM 4.19]

4.34-CVL(2) **[Made out by liquidator]** Where it is made out by the liquidator, the statement of affairs shall be delivered by him to the registrar of companies within 5 business days after the creditors' meeting summoned under section 95(2).

4.34-CVL(3) **[Made out by directors]** Where it is made out by the directors under section 99(1) the statement of affairs shall be delivered by them to the liquidator in office following the creditors' meeting summoned under section 98 as soon as reasonably practicable after that meeting has been held; and he shall, within 5 business days, deliver it to the registrar of companies.

4.34-CVL(4) **[Date where made out by directors]** A statement of affairs under section 99(1) may be made up to a date not more than 14 days before that on which the resolution for voluntary winding up is passed by the company.

4.34-CVL(5) **[Liquidator may require statement of concurrence]** The liquidator may require any of the directors who has not submitted the statement of affairs to submit a statement of concurrence verified by a statement of truth, stating that that director concurs in the statement of affairs.

4.34-CVL(6) **[Qualification of statement of concurrence in r.4.34-CVL(5)]** A statement of concurrence made under paragraph (5) may be qualified in respect of matters dealt with in the statement of affairs, where the maker of the statement of concurrence—

(a) is not in agreement with the persons making the statement of affairs, or

(b) considers the statement to be erroneous or misleading, or

(c) is without the direct knowledge necessary for concurring in the statement.

4.34-CVL(7) **[Delivery of statements of concurrence and copy to liquidator]** Every statement of concurrence must be delivered to the liquidator by the person who makes it, together with a copy.

(See General Note after r.4.34A-CVL.)

4.34A-CVL Copy statement of affairs

4.34A-CVL   Where a liquidator is nominated by the company at a general meeting held on a day prior to that on which the creditors' meeting summoned under section 98 is held, the directors shall as soon as reasonably practicable after his nomination or the making of the statement of affairs, whichever is the later, deliver to him a copy of the statement of affairs.

GENERAL NOTE TO RR.4.34-CVL, 4.34A-CVL

These rules deal with the registration of the statement of affairs made out in a creditors' voluntary winding up.
  Rule 4.34(5)–(7) inserted by I(A)R 2010 r.2 and Sch. para.163 as from April 6, 2010.

4.35   Limited disclosure

4.35(1) **[Official receiver or liquidator may apply to court]** Where the official receiver or liquidator thinks that it would prejudice the conduct of the liquidation or might reasonably be expected to lead to violence against any person for the whole or part of the statement of affairs to be disclosed, he may apply to the court for an order of limited disclosure in respect of the statement, or any specified part of it.

4.35(2) **[Powers of court]** The court may on the application order that the statement or, as the case may be, the specified part of it be not filed with the registrar of companies otherwise than with permission of the court.

4.35(3) **[Copy of order, statement of affairs/concurrence to registrar]** The official receiver or liquidator must as soon as reasonably practicable send to the registrar of companies a copy of the order and the statement of affairs (to the extent provided by the order) and any statement of concurrence.

4.35(4) **[Application of r.4.35 in voluntary winding up]** In a voluntary winding up, this Rule does not apply so far as section 95, 98 or 99 does not permit limited disclosure.

GENERAL NOTE

See *Practice Direction: Insolvency Proceedings* [2007] B.C.C. 842 (reproduced in App.IV to this *Guide*). See also General Note after r.4.37.

4.36   Release from duty to submit statement of affairs; extension of time

(NO CVL APPLICATION)

4.36(1) **[Exercise of s.131(5) power]** The power of the official receiver under section 131(5) to give a release from the obligation imposed by that section, or to grant an extension of time, may be exercised at the official receiver's own discretion, or at the request of any nominated person.

4.36(2) **[Nominated person may apply to court]** A nominated person may, if he requests a release or extension of time and it is refused by the official receiver, apply to the court for it.

4.36(3) **[Court may dismiss application etc.]** The court may, if it thinks that no sufficient cause is shown for the application, dismiss it; but it shall not do so unless the applicant has had an opportunity to attend the court for a hearing, of which he has been given at least 5 business days' notice but which is without notice to any other party.
  If the application is not dismissed under this paragraph, the court shall fix a venue for it to be heard, and give notice to the nominated person accordingly.

4.36(4)   **[Nominated person to send notice to official receiver]** The nominated person shall, at least 14 days before the hearing, send to the official receiver a notice stating the venue and accompanied by a copy of the application, and of any evidence which he (the nominated person) intends to adduce in support of it.

4.36(5)   **[Appearance etc. by official receiver]** The official receiver may appear and be heard on the application; and, whether or not he appears, he may file a written report of any matters which he considers ought to be drawn to the court's attention.

    If such a report is filed, a copy of it shall be sent by the official receiver to the nominated person, not later than 5 business days before the hearing.

4.36(6)   **[Sealed copies of order]** Sealed copies of any order made on the application shall be sent by the court to the nominated person and the official receiver.

4.36(7)   **[Applicant's costs]** On any application under this Rule the applicant's costs shall be paid in any event by him and, unless and to the extent that the court otherwise orders, shall not be an expense of the liquidation.

(See General Note after r.4.37.)

4.37   Expenses of statement of affairs

(NO CVL APPLICATION)

4.37(1)   **[Persons assisting in preparation of statement]** If any nominated person cannot himself prepare a proper statement of affairs, the official receiver may, as an expense of the liquidation, employ some person or persons to assist in the preparation of the statement.

4.37(2)   **[Allowance towards expenses]** At the request of any nominated person, made on the grounds that he cannot himself prepare a proper statement, the official receiver may authorise an allowance, payable as an expense of the liquidation, towards expenses to be incurred by the nominated person in employing some person or persons to assist him in preparing it.

4.37(3)   **[Estimate of expenses]** Any such request by the nominated person shall be accompanied by an estimate of the expenses involved; and the official receiver shall only authorise the employment of a named person or a named firm, being in either case approved by him.

4.37(4)   **[Authorisation subject to conditions]** An authorisation given by the official receiver under this Rule shall be subject to such conditions (if any) as he thinks fit to impose with respect to the manner in which any person may obtain access to relevant books and papers.

4.37(5)   **[Effect of Rule]** Nothing in this Rule relieves a nominated person from any obligation with respect to the preparation, verification and submission of the statement of affairs, or to the provision of information to the official receiver or the liquidator.

4.37(6)   **[Priority of payment out of assets]** Any payment made as an expense of the liquidation under this Rule shall be made in the prescribed order of priority.

4.37(7)   **[Application of r.4.37(2)–(6)]** Paragraphs (2) to (6) of this Rule may be applied, on application to the official receiver by any nominated person, in relation to the making of a statement of concurrence verified by a statement of truth.

GENERAL NOTE TO RR.4.35–4.37

These rules are concerned with various discretionary powers conferred on the official receiver in regard to the statement of affairs: to apply to the court for an order authorising limited disclosure in the statement of affairs, to grant a release or an extension of time, and to provide a deponent with professional help.

4.38-CVL   Expenses of statement of affairs

4.38-CVL(1)   [Payment out of assets] Payment may be made out of the company's assets, either before or after the commencement of the winding up, of any reasonable and necessary expenses of preparing the statement of affairs under section 99.

Any such payment is an expense of the liquidation.

4.38-CVL(2)   [Payment before commencement of winding up] Where such a payment is made before the commencement of the winding up, the director presiding at the creditors' meeting held under section 98 shall inform the meeting of the amount of the payment and the identity of the person to whom it was made.

4.38-CVL(3)   [Payment by liquidator] The liquidator appointed under section 100 may make such a payment (subject to the next paragraph); but if there is a liquidation committee, he must give the committee at least 5 business days' notice of his intention to make it.

4.38-CVL(4)   [No payment by liquidator to himself] Such a payment shall not be made by the liquidator to himself, or to any associate of his, otherwise than with the approval of the liquidation committee, the creditors, or the court.

4.38-CVL(5)   [Powers of court under r.4.219] This Rule is without prejudice to the powers of the court under Rule 4.219 (voluntary winding up superseded by winding up by the court).

GENERAL NOTE

In a creditors' voluntary liquidation, the expenses of preparing the statement may be met from the assets, on the authority of the various persons or bodies mentioned.

4.39   Submission of accounts

(NO CVL APPLICATION)

4.39(1)   [Request to persons specified in s.235(3)] Any of the persons specified in section 235(3) shall, at the request of the official receiver, furnish him with accounts of the company of such nature, as at such date, and for such period, as he may specify.

4.39(2)   [Beginning of specified period] The period specified may begin from a date up to 3 years preceding the date of the presentation of the winding-up petition, or from an earlier date to which audited accounts of the company were last prepared.

4.39(3)   [Accounts for earlier period] The court may, on the official receiver's application, require accounts for any earlier period.

4.39(4)   [Application of r.4.37] Rule 4.37 applies (with the necessary modifications) in relation to accounts to be furnished under this Rule as it applies in relation to the statement of affairs.

4.39(5)   [Verification and delivery] The accounts shall, if the official receiver so requires, be verified by a statement of truth and (whether or not so verified) delivered to him within 21 days of the request under paragraph (1), or such longer period as he may allow.

4.39(6)   [Omitted.]

GENERAL NOTE

The official receiver may call for accounts for up to three years past or up to the date of the last audited accounts, or for a longer period on an order of the court.

Professional assistance may be authorised under r.4.37. The official receiver may call for further disclosure under r.4.42.

Rule 4.39(6) omitted by I(A)R 2010 r.2 and Sch. para.168(3) as from April 6, 2010.

4.40-CVL   Submission of accounts

4.40-CVL(1)   [Request to persons specified in s.235(3)] Any of the persons specified in section 235(3) shall, at the request of the liquidator, furnish him with accounts of the company of such nature, as at such date, and for such period, as he may specify.

4.40-CVL(2)   [Beginning of specified period] The specified period for the accounts may begin from a date up to 3 years preceding the date of the resolution for winding up, or from an earlier date to which audited accounts of the company were last prepared.

4.40-CVL(3)   [Verification and delivery] The accounts shall, if the liquidator so requires, be verified by a statement of truth and (whether or not so verified) delivered to him, with the statement of truth if required, within 21 days from the request under paragraph (1), or such longer period as he may allow.

(See General Note after r.4.41-CVL.)

4.41-CVL   Expenses of preparing accounts

4.41-CVL(1)   [Persons assisting in preparation of accounts] Where a person is required under Rule 4.40-CVL to furnish accounts, the liquidator may, with the sanction of the liquidation committee (if there is one) and as an expense of the liquidation, employ some person or persons to assist in the preparation of the accounts.

4.41-CVL(2)   [Allowance towards expenses] At the request of the person subject to the requirement, the liquidator may, with that sanction, authorise an allowance, payable as an expense of the liquidation, towards expenses to be incurred by that person in employing others to assist him in preparing the accounts.

4.41-CVL(3)   [Estimate of expenses] Any such request shall be accompanied by an estimate of the expenses involved; and the liquidator shall only authorise the employment of a named person or a named firm, being in either case approved by him.

GENERAL NOTE TO RR.4.40-CVL, 4.41-CVL

These rules make provision corresponding to r.4.39, to apply in a creditors' voluntary liquidation. If accounts are required for a period more than three years back, the court's jurisdiction under IA 1986 s.112 may be invoked.

4.42   Further disclosure

(NO CVL APPLICATION)

4.42(1)   [Official receiver may require further information] The official receiver may at any time require the nominated persons, or any one or more of them, to submit (in writing) further information amplifying, modifying or explaining any matter contained in the statement of affairs, or in accounts submitted in pursuance of the Act or the Rules.

4.42(2)   [Verification and delivery] The information shall, if the official receiver so directs, be verified by a statement of truth, and (whether or not so verified) delivered to him within 21 days of the requirement under paragraph (1), or such longer period as he may allow.

4.42(3)   [Omitted.]

GENERAL NOTE

This rule should be read in conjunction with rr.4.32 et seq. (statement of affairs) and r.4.39 (submission of accounts).
    Rule 4.42(3) omitted by I(A)R 2010 r.2 and Sch. para.170(4) as from April 6, 2010.

4.43 Reports by official receiver

(NO CVL APPLICATION)

4.43(1) **[Report on winding-up proceedings and state of affairs]** The official receiver shall, at least once after the making of the winding-up order, send a report to creditors and contributories with respect to the proceedings in the winding up, and the state of the company's affairs.

4.43(1A) **[Contents of report]** The official receiver shall also include in the report under paragraph (1)–

(a) to the best of his knowledge and belief–

    (i) an estimate of the value of the prescribed part (whether or not he proposes to make an application to the court under section 176A(5) or section 176A(3) applies);

    (ii) an estimate of the value of the company's net property; and

(b) whether, and if so, why, he proposes to make an application to court under section 176A(5).

4.43(1B) **[Non-disclosure of seriously prejudicial information]** Nothing in this Rule is to be taken as requiring any such estimate to include any information, the disclosure of which could seriously prejudice the commercial interests of the company. If such information is excluded from the calculation the estimate shall be accompanied by a statement to that effect.

4.43(2) [Omitted.]

(See General Note after r.4.49G.)

4.44 Meaning of "creditors"

4.44 Any reference in this Chapter to creditors is to creditors of the company who are known to the official receiver or (as the case may be) the liquidator.

(See General Note after r.4.49G.)

4.45 Report where statement of affairs lodged

(NO CVL APPLICATION)

4.45(1) **[Report to creditors and contributories]** Where a statement of affairs has been submitted, the official receiver shall send out to creditors and contributories a report containing a summary of the statement (if he thinks fit, as amplified, modified or explained by virtue of Rule 4.42) and such observations (if any) as he thinks fit to make with respect to it, or to the affairs of the company in general.

4.45(2) **[Where no need to comply with r.4.45(1)]** The official receiver need not comply with paragraph (1) if he has previously reported to creditors and contributories with respect to the company's affairs (so far as known to him) and he is of opinion that there are no additional matters which ought to be brought to their attention.

(See General Note after r.4.49G.)

4.46 Statement of affairs dispensed with

(NO CVL APPLICATION)

4.46(1) **[Application of Rule]** This Rule applies where, in the company's case, release from the obligation to submit a statement of affairs has been granted by the official receiver or the court.

4.46(2) **[Report to creditors and contributories]** As soon as may be after the release has been granted, the official receiver shall send to creditors and contributories a report containing a summary of the company's affairs (so far as within his knowledge), and his observations (if any) with respect to it, or to the affairs of the company in general.

4.46(3) **[Where no need to comply with r.4.46(2)]** The official receiver need not comply with paragraph (2) if he has previously reported to creditors and contributories with respect to the company's affairs (so far as known to him) and he is of opinion that there are no additional matters which ought to be brought to their attention.

(See General Note after r.4.49G.)

4.47 General rule as to reporting

(NO CVL APPLICATION)

4.47(1) **[Powers of court]** The court may, on the official receiver's application, relieve him of any duty imposed on him by this Chapter, or authorise him to carry out the duty in a way other than there required.

4.47(2) **[Matters for court to consider]** In considering whether to act under this Rule, the court shall have regard to the cost of carrying out the duty, to the amount of the assets available, and to the extent of the interest of creditors or contributories, or any particular class of them.

GENERAL NOTE

See *Practice Direction: Insolvency Proceedings* [2000] B.C.C. 927 (reproduced in App.IV to this *Guide*). See also General Note after r.4.49G.

4.48 Winding up stayed

(NO CVL APPLICATION)

4.48(1) **[Cessation of official receiver's duty]** If proceedings in the winding up are stayed by order of the court, any duty of the official receiver to send reports under the preceding Rules in this Chapter ceases.

4.48(2) **[Notice of stay]** Where the court grants a stay, it may include in its order such requirements on the company as it thinks fit with a view to bringing the stay to the notice of creditors and contributories.

(See General Note after r.4.49G.)

4.49-CVL Information to creditors and contributories

4.49-CVL(1) **[Report on meeting]** The liquidator shall, within 28 days of a meeting held under section 95 or 98, send to creditors and contributories of the company–

(a) a copy or summary of the statement of affairs, and

(b) a report of the proceedings at the meeting.

4.49-CVL(2) **[Contents of report]** The report under paragraph (1) shall also include–

(a) to the best of the liquidator's knowledge and belief–

(i) an estimate of the value of the prescribed part (whether or not he proposes to make an application to court under section 176A(5) or section 176A(3) applies); and

(ii) an estimate of the value of the company's net property; and

(b) whether, and if so, why, the liquidator proposes to make an application to court under section 176A(5).

4.49-CVL(3) **[Non-disclosure of seriously prejudicial information]** Nothing in this Rule is to be taken as requiring any such estimate to include any information, the disclosure of which could seriously prejudice the commercial interests of the company. If such information is excluded from the calculation the estimate shall be accompanied by a statement to that effect.

(See General Note after r.4.49G.)

4.49A Further information where liquidation follows administration

4.49A Where under section 140 the court appoints as the company's liquidator a person who was formerly its administrator or a person is appointed as liquidator upon the registration of a notice under paragraph 83(3) of Schedule B1 to the Act and that person becomes aware of creditors not formerly known to him in his capacity as administrator, he shall send to those creditors a copy of any statement or report sent by him to creditors under Rule 2.33, so noted as to indicate that it is being sent under this Rule.

4.49B Reports to creditors and members—winding up by the court

(NO CVL APPLICATION)

4.49B(1) **["Progress report"]** "Progress report" means a report which includes–

(a) details of the court where the proceedings are and the relevant court reference number;

(b) full details of the company's name, address of registered office and registered number;

(c) full details of the liquidator's name and address and date of appointment, including any changes in office-holder;

(d) details of the basis fixed for the remuneration of the liquidator under Rule 4.127 (or if not fixed at the date of the report, the steps taken during the period of the report to fix it);

(e) if the basis of remuneration has been fixed, a statement of–

(i) the remuneration charged by the liquidator during the period of the report (subject to paragraph (3)), and

(ii) where the report is the first to be made after the basis has been fixed, the remuneration charged by the liquidator during the periods covered by the previous reports (subject to paragraph (3)), together with a description of the things done by the liquidator during those periods in respect of which the remuneration was charged,

irrespective in either case of whether payment was made in respect of that remuneration during that period;

(f) a statement of the expenses incurred by the liquidator during the period of the report, irrespective of whether payment was made in respect of them during that period;

(g) details of progress during the period of the report, including a receipts and payments account (as detailed in paragraph (2));

(h) details of any assets that remain to be realised;

(j) a statement of the creditors' right to request information under Rule 4.49E and their right to challenge the liquidator's remuneration and expenses under Rule 4.131; and

(k) any other relevant information for the creditors.

4.49B(2) **[Form of receipts and payments account]** A receipts and payments account must be in the form of an abstract showing receipts and payments during the period of the report and, where the liquidator has ceased to act, must also include a statement as to the amount paid to unsecured creditors by virtue of the application of section 176A.

4.49B(3)   [Basis of remuneration] Where the basis for the remuneration is a set amount under Rule 4.127(2)(c), it may be shown as that amount without any apportionment to the period of the report.

4.49B(4)   [Period of progress report] The progress report must, except where paragraph (5) or (6) applies, cover the period of 1 year commencing on the date on which the liquidator is appointed and every subsequent period of 1 year.

4.49B(5)   [End of period of progress report] The period to be covered by a progress report ends on the date when a liquidator ceases to act, and the period to be covered by each subsequent progress report is each successive period of 1 year beginning immediately after that date (subject to the further application of this paragraph when another liquidator ceases to act).

4.49B(6)   [When progress report not required] A progress report is not required for any period which ends after the liquidator has sent a draft report to creditors under Rule 4.49D.

4.49B(7)   [By when and to whom copies of progress report to be sent] The liquidator must send a copy of the progress report within 2 months of the end of the period covered by the report, to the registrar of companies, to the members of the company and to the creditors.

4.49B(8)   [Extension of r.4.49B(7) period] The court may, on the liquidator's application, extend the period of 2 months mentioned in paragraph (7), or make such other order in respect of the content of the report as it thinks just.

4.49B(9)   [Non-application of r.4.49B] This Rule does not apply where the liquidator is the official receiver.

4.49C CVL   Progress reports—voluntary winding up

4.49C-CVL(1)   [Application of r.4.49C] This Rule applies for the purposes of sections 92A and 104A.

4.49C-CVL(2)   [Prescribed period for report] The prescribed period for which the liquidator must produce a progress report, except when the liquidator ceases to act (in which case paragraph (3) applies) and subject to paragraph (4), is the period of 1 year commencing on the date on which the liquidator is appointed and every subsequent period of 1 year.

4.49C-CVL(3)   [Prescribed period when liquidator ceases to act] When a liquidator ceases to act, and subject to paragraph (4)–

(a)   the prescribed period for which the liquidator must produce a progress report ends on the date of that liquidator's ceasing to act, and

(b)   the prescribed period for which the new liquidator (if any) must produce a progress report is the period of 1 year commencing immediately after that date and every subsequent period of 1 year (subject to the further application of this paragraph when that new liquidator ceases to act).

4.49C-CVL(4)   [When report not required] A progress report is not required for any period which ends after the liquidator has sent a draft report to creditors under Rule 4.49D (final report to creditors).

4.49C-CVL(5)   [Prescribed matters for report] The prescribed matters to which a progress report must relate are those set out in Rule 4.49B(1)(b) to (j), (2) and (3); and for that purpose in a members' voluntary winding up–

(a)   the reference in Rule 4.49B(1)(d) to Rule 4.127 is to be read as a reference to Rule 4.148A,

(b)   the reference in Rule 4.49B(1)(j) to–

   (i)   the creditors' right to request information is to be read as a reference to the members' right to request information,

   (ii)   Rule 4.131 is to be read as a reference to Rule 4.148C, and

(c) the reference in Rule 4.49B(3) to Rule 4.127(2)(c) is to be read as a reference to Rule 4.148A(2)(c).

4.49C-CVL(6)   **[Copy to registrar]** The prescribed person (in addition to members and creditors) to whom the liquidator must send a copy of a progress report is the registrar of companies.

4.49C-CVL(7)   **[Time limit for sending copies of report]** The prescribed period commencing with the end of the period prescribed in sub-paragraph (a) or (b) of paragraph (3) within which the liquidator must send a copy of a progress report to members, creditors and the registrar of companies is 2 months.

4.49D   **Final report to creditors**

4.49D(1)   **[Draft report]** The liquidator must, at least 8 weeks before holding a final meeting in accordance with section 106 or 146, send to each creditor known to the liquidator a draft of the report which the liquidator intends to lay before the meeting under Rule 4.125 or 4.126.

4.49D(2)   **[Contents of draft report]** The draft report must–

(a) contain such matters and be in such terms as would comply with Rule 4.125 or 4.126, as the case may be, if the report were to be laid before a meeting as soon as reasonably practicable after the draft had been sent to creditors, and

(b) be accompanied by a statement of the creditors' right to request information under Rule 4.49E and their right to challenge the liquidator's remuneration and expenses under Rule 4.131.

4.49D(3)   **[Notice re dividend to precede draft report]** The liquidator may not send a draft report to creditors under this Rule before giving notice under Rule 4.186 of intention to declare a final dividend or that no dividend or further dividend will be declared.

4.49D(4)   **[Where application under r.4.131 that liquidator's remuneration excessive]** If any creditor has applied to the court under Rule 4.131 and given a copy of the application to the liquidator, the final meeting may not be held until the application (including any appeal) has been disposed of and the liquidator has complied with any order of the court.

4.49D(5)   **[Non-application to official receiver]** This Rule does not apply where the liquidator is the official receiver.

4.49E   **Creditors' and members' request for further information**

4.49E(1)   **[Duty of liquidator re remuneration or expenses]** If–

(a) within the period mentioned in paragraph (2)–

     (i) a secured creditor, or

     (ii) an unsecured creditor with the concurrence of at least 5% in value of the unsecured creditors (including the creditor in question), or

     (iii) members of the company in a members' voluntary winding up with at least 5% of the total voting rights of all the members having the right to vote at general meetings of the company, or

(b) with the permission of the court upon an application made within the period mentioned in paragraph (2)–

     (i) any unsecured creditor, or

     (ii) any member of the company in a members' voluntary winding up,

makes a request in writing to the liquidator for further information about remuneration or expenses set out in a progress report in accordance with Rule 4.49B(1)(e) or (f) (including by virtue of Rule 4.49C(5)) or in a draft report under Rule 4.49D, the liquidator must, within 14 days of receipt of the request, comply with paragraph (3) except to the extent that the request is in respect of matter in a draft report under Rule 4.49D or a progress report required by Rule 4.108 which (in either case) was previously included in a progress report not required by Rule 4.108.

4.49E(2)   [Period for compliance with r.4.49E(1)] The period referred to in paragraph (1)(a) and (b) is–

(a)   7 business days of receipt (by the last of them in the case of an application by more than one member) of the progress report where it is required by Rule 4.108, and

(b)   21 days of receipt (by the last of them in the case of an application by more than one member) of the report or draft report in any other case.

4.49E(3)   [How liquidator to comply] The liquidator complies with this paragraph by either–

(a)   providing all of the information asked for, or

(b)   so far as the liquidator considers that–

　　　(i)   the time or cost of preparation of the information would be excessive, or

　　　(ii)   disclosure of the information would be prejudicial to the conduct of the liquidation or might reasonably be expected to lead to violence against any person, or

　　　(iii)   the liquidator is subject to an obligation of confidentiality in respect of the information,

giving reasons for not providing all of the information.

4.49E(4)   [Application to court by creditors and members] Any creditor, and any member of the company in a members' voluntary winding up, who need not be the same as the creditors or members who asked for the information, may apply to the court within 21 days of–

(a)   the giving by the liquidator of reasons for not providing all of the information asked for, or

(b)   the expiry of the 14 days provided for in paragraph (1),

and the court may make such order as it thinks just.

4.49E(5)   [Court may extend period in rr.4.131(1B), 4.148C(2)] Without prejudice to the generality of paragraph (4), the order of the court under that paragraph may extend the period of 8 weeks or, as the case may be, 4 weeks provided for in Rule 4.131(1B) or 4.148C(2) by such further period as the court thinks just.

4.49E(6)   [Non-application to official receiver] This Rule does not apply where the liquidator is the official receiver.

4.49F   Arrangements under s 110 (acceptance of shares, etc., as consideration for sale of company property)

4.49F(1)   [Duty of liquidator] Where there has been an arrangement under section 110 and a distribution to members has taken place pursuant to subsection (2) or (4) of that section, the liquidator must comply with paragraph (2) in respect of any account or report which the liquidator is required to prepare pursuant to any of the following–

(a)   section 92A (progress report to company at year's end);

(b)   section 94 (final meeting prior to dissolution – members' voluntary winding up);

(c)   section 104A (progress report to company and creditors at year's end);

(d)   section 106 (final meeting prior to dissolution – creditors' voluntary winding up);

(e)   Rule 4.49B (reports to creditors and members – winding up by the court);

(f)   Rule 4.49D (final report to creditors);

(g)   Rule 4.108 (creditors' meeting to receive liquidator's resignation);

(h)   Rule 4.126 (final meeting – creditors' voluntary liquidation);

(j)   Rule 4.142 (company meeting to receive liquidator's resignation).

4.49F(2)   [How liquidator to comply] The liquidator must–

(a)   in any account or summary of receipts and payments which is required to be included in the account or report, state the estimated value of–

    (i)   the property transferred to the transferee;

    (ii)   the property received from the transferee; and

    (iii) the property distributed to members pursuant to section 110(2) or (4),

    during the period to which the account or report relates, and

(b)   as a note to the account or summary of receipts and payments, provide details of the basis of the valuation.

4.49G   Other distributions to members in specie

4.49G(1)   [Duty of liquidator] In a members' voluntary winding up, where there has been a distribution of property to members in its existing form other than pursuant to an arrangement under section 110, the liquidator must comply with paragraph (2) in respect of any account or report which the liquidator is required to prepare pursuant to any of the following–

(a)   section 92A (progress report to company at year's end);

(b)   section 94 (final meeting prior to dissolution);

(c)   Rule 4.142 (company meeting to receive liquidator's resignation).

4.49G(2)   [How liquidator to comply] The liquidator must–

(a)   in any account or summary of receipts and payments which is required to be included in the account or report, state the estimated value of the property distributed amongst the members of the company during the period to which the account or report relates, and

(b)   as a note to the account or summary of receipts and payments, provide details of the basis of the valuation.

GENERAL NOTE TO RR.4.43–4.49G

These rules are designed to ensure that creditors and contributories are kept informed of the state of the company's affairs in the various situations referred to.

Paragraphs (1A) and (1B) of r.4.43 and paras (2) and (3) of r.4.49 were inserted by the Insolvency (Amendment) Rules 2003 (SI 2003/1730, effective September 15, 2003) Sch.1 paras 15, 16. By para.16 of that Schedule r.4.49A was amended, inter alia, by replacing the former reference to r.2.16 to r.2.33. Here, "r.2.16" refers to the original administration regime (which still applies in some administrations) and "r.2.33" to the new regime.

Rule 4.43(2) omitted, r.4.44 amended and rr.4.49B–4.49G inserted by I(A)R 2010 r.2 and Sch. paras 171–174 as from April 6, 2010.

Rules 4.49B–4.49D, introduced by the 2010 amendments, provide for regular progress reports (already a feature of administrations) to be made in a liquidation, but at annual intervals rather than every six months as in administration. The report to be laid before the final meeting of creditors (rr.4.125, 4.126) is brought into line with progress reports, and a draft of the final report must be sent to creditors eight weeks beforehand.

Rule 4.49E empowers one or more creditors with the backing of 10 per cent of their fellow creditors to seek further information relating to the liquidator's remuneration and expenses. If he is unwilling to do so on any of the grounds listed in para.(2)(b) the matter may be resolved by the court.

Rule 4.49F requires a liquidator who makes a distribution in specie to members in a reconstruction under s.110 to give details of the basis of the valuation of the property concerned, and this is also a requirement when the liquidator in a voluntary winding up makes a distribution in specie otherwise than under s.110 (r.4.49G).

Chapter 8

Meetings of Creditors and Contributories

Section A: Rules of general application

4.50 First meetings

(NO CVL APPLICATION)

4.50(1) **[Venue for meetings etc.]** If under section 136(5) the official receiver decides to summon meetings of the company's creditors and contributories for the purpose of nominating a person to be liquidator in place of himself, he shall fix a venue for each meeting, in neither case more than 4 months from the date of the winding-up order.

4.50(2) **[Notice of meetings]** When for each meeting a venue has been fixed, notice of the meetings shall be given–

  (a)   in the case of the creditors' meeting, to every creditor who is known to the official receiver; and

  (b)   in the case of the contributories' meeting, to every person appearing (by the company's books or otherwise) to be a contributory of the company.

4.50(3) **[Time limit for notice]** Notice for each meeting must be given at least 14 days before the date fixed for it.

4.50(4) **[Contents of notice re lodging proofs and proxies]** The notice to creditors must state that proofs and (if applicable) proxies must be lodged at a specified place not later than 12.00 hours on the business day before the date fixed for the meeting in order for creditors to be entitled to vote at the meeting; and the same applies in respect of contributories and their proxies.

4.50(5) **[Notice of meetings]** Notice of the meetings shall be gazetted and may be advertised in such other manner as the official receiver thinks fit.

4.50(5A) **[Additional contents of notice under r.4.50(5)]** In addition to the standard contents, a notice under paragraph (5) must state–

  (a)   that a meeting of the creditors or contributories is to take place;

  (b)   the venue fixed for the meeting; and

  (c)   the time and date by which, and place at which, creditors must lodge proxies and hitherto unlodged proofs in order to be entitled to vote at the meeting.

4.50(6) **[Request by creditors under s.136(5)(c)]** Where the official receiver receives a request by creditors under section 136(5)(c) for meetings of creditors and contributories to be summoned, and it appears to him that the request is properly made in accordance with the Act, he shall–

  (a)   withdraw any notices previously given by him under section 136(5)(b) (that he has decided not to summon such meetings),

  (b)   fix the venue of each meeting for not more than 3 months from his receipt of the creditors' request, and

834

(c) act in accordance with paragraphs (2) to (5) above, as if he had decided under section 136 to summon the meetings.

[FORM 4.21]

4.50(7) **[Names of meetings]** Meetings summoned by the official receiver under this Rule are known respectively as **"the first meeting of creditors"** and **"the first meeting of contributories",** and jointly as **"the first meetings in the liquidation".**

4.50(8) **[Where company is authorised deposit-taker]** Where the company is an authorised deposit-taker or a former authorised deposit-taker, additional notices are required by Rule 4.72.

(See General Note after r.4.71.)

4.51-CVL   First meeting of creditors

4.51-CVL(1) **[Application of Rule]** This Rule applies in the case of a meeting of creditors summoned by the liquidator under section 95 (where, in what starts as a members' voluntary winding up, he forms the opinion that the company will be unable to pay its debts) or a meeting under section 98 (first meeting of creditors in a creditors' voluntary winding up).

4.51-CVL(2) **[Contents of notice]** The notice summoning the meeting shall state the name of the company and the registered number of the company, and specify a venue for the meeting and the time (not earlier than 12.00 hours on the business day before the day fixed for the meeting) by which, and the place at which, creditors must lodge any proofs and proxies necessary to entitle them to vote at the meeting.

4.51-CVL(3) **[Where company is authorised deposit-taker]** Where the company is an authorised deposit-taker or a former authorised deposit-taker, additional notices are required by Rule 4.72.

(See General Note after r.4.71.)

4.52   Business at first meetings in the liquidation

(NO CVL APPLICATION)

4.52(1) **[Limitation on resolutions at first meeting of creditors]** At the first meeting of creditors, no resolutions shall be taken other than the following–

(a) a resolution to appoint a named insolvency practitioner to be liquidator, or two or more insolvency practitioners as joint liquidators;

(b) a resolution to establish a liquidation committee;

(c) (unless it has been resolved to establish a liquidation committee) a resolution specifying the terms on which the liquidator is to be remunerated, or to defer consideration of that matter;

(d) (if, and only if, two or more persons are appointed to act jointly as liquidator) a resolution specifying whether acts are to be done by both or all of them, or by only one;

(e) (where the meeting has been requisitioned under section 136), a resolution authorising payment as an expense of the liquidation, of the cost of summoning and holding the meeting and any meeting of contributories so requisitioned and held;

(f) a resolution to adjourn the meeting;

(g) any other resolution which the chairman thinks it right to allow for special reasons.

4.52(2) **[At first meeting of contributories]** The same applies as regards the first meeting of contributories, but that meeting shall not pass any resolution to the effect of paragraph (1)(c) or (e).

4.52(3) [Omitted.]

4.52(3A) **[Power to adjourn meeting]** The meeting may be adjourned, either in accordance with a resolution under paragraph (1)(f) or if the chairman thinks fit, but for not more than 14 days from the date on which it was fixed to commence, subject to any direction of the court.

4.52(3B) **[Time limit for final adjournment]** If there are subsequently further adjournments, the final adjournment must not be to a day later than 14 days after the date on which the meeting was originally held, subject to any direction of the court.

4.52(3C) **[Proofs and proxies at adjourned meetings]** Where a meeting is adjourned under this Rule, proofs and proxies may be used if lodged at any time up to 12.00 hours on the business day immediately before the adjourned meeting.

(See General Note after r.4.71.)

4.53-CVL   Business at meeting under s.95 or 98

4.53-CVL Rule 4.52(1), except sub-paragraph (e), applies to a creditors' meeting under section 95 or 98.

(See General Note after r.4.71.)

4.53A-CVL   Effect of adjournment of company meeting

4.53A-CVL Where a company meeting at which a resolution for voluntary winding up is to be proposed is adjourned, any resolution passed at a meeting under section 98 held before the holding of the adjourned company meeting only has effect on and from the passing by the company of a resolution for winding up.

(See General Note after r.4.71.)

4.53B-CVL   Report by director, etc.

4.53B-CVL(1) **[State of company's affairs]** At any meeting held under section 98 where the statement of affairs laid before the meeting does not state the company's affairs as at the date of the meeting, the directors of the company shall cause to be made to the meeting, either by the director presiding at the meeting or by another person with knowledge of the relevant matters, a report (written or oral) on any material transactions relating to the company occurring between the date of the making of the statement of affairs and that of the meeting.

4.53B-CVL(2) **[Recorded in minutes]** Any such report shall be recorded in the minutes of the meeting kept under Rule 4.71.

(See General Note after r.4.71.)

4.53C CVL   Additional contents of notices gazetted or advertised under s.95

4.53C CVL In addition to the statement of duty required under subsection (2A) of section 95, and to the standard contents, notices under paragraphs (c) and (d) of that subsection must state–

(a) the purpose of the meeting; and

(b) the venue fixed for the meeting.

4.53D CVL   Additional contents of notices gazetted or advertised under s.98

4.53D CVL In addition to the content required by section 98(2), and the standard contents, notices under section 98(1A) (c) or (d) must state–

(a) the purpose of the meeting; and

(b) the venue fixed for the meeting.

4.54   General power to call meetings

4.54(1) [General power, "the convener"] The official receiver or the liquidator may at any time summon and conduct meetings of creditors or of contributories for the purpose of ascertaining their wishes in all matters relating to the liquidation; and in relation to any meeting summoned under the Act or the Rules, the person summoning it is referred to as "the convener".

4.54(2) [Notice of venue] When (in either case) a venue for the meeting has been fixed, notice of it shall be given by the convener–

  (a) in the case of a creditors' meeting, to every creditor who is known to him; and

                                                              [FORM 4.22]

  (b) in the case of a meeting of contributories, to every person appearing (by the company's books or otherwise) to be a contributory of the company.

                                                              [FORM 4.23]

4.54(3) [Time for giving notice etc.] Notice of the meeting shall be given at least 14 days before the date fixed for it, and shall specify the purpose of the meeting.

4.54(4) [Content of notice re lodging proofs and proxies] The notice must state that proofs and (if applicable) proxies must be lodged at a specified place not later than 12.00 hours on the business day before the date fixed for the meeting in order for creditors to be entitled to vote at the meeting; and the same applies in respect of contributories and their proxies.

(NO CVL APPLICATION)

4.54-CVL(5) [Content of notice re lodging proofs and proxies] The notice must state that proofs and (if applicable) proxies must be lodged at a specified place not later than 12.00 hours on the business day before the date fixed for the meeting in order for creditors to be entitled to vote at the meeting.

4.54(6) [Gazetting/advertisement of meeting] Notice of the meeting–

  (a) shall be gazetted; and

  (b) may be advertised in such other manner as the convenor thinks fit.

4.54(7) [Additional content of notice under r.4.54(6)] In addition to the standard contents, the notice under paragraph (6) must state–

  (a) who summoned the meeting;

  (b) if the meeting was summoned by a creditor, the fact that it was so summoned and the section of the Act under which it was summoned;

  (c) the purpose for which the meeting was summoned;

  (d) the venue fixed for the meeting; and

  (e) the time and date by which, and place at which, creditors must lodge proxies and hitherto unlodged proofs in order to be entitled to vote at the meeting.

(See General Note after r.4.71.)

4.55   The chairman at meetings

(NO CVL APPLICATION)

4.55(1) [Application of Rule] This Rule applies both to a meeting of creditors and to a meeting of contributories.

4.55(2) [Where convener official receiver] Where the convener of the meeting is the official receiver, he, or a person nominated by him, shall be chairman.

A nomination under this paragraph shall be in writing, unless the nominee is another official receiver or a deputy official receiver.

4.55(3)   **[Where convener not official receiver]** Where the convener is other than the official receiver, the chairman shall be he, or a person nominated in writing by him.

A person nominated under this paragraph must be either–

(a) one who is qualified to act as an insolvency practitioner in relation to the company, or

(b) an employee of the liquidator or his firm who is experienced in insolvency matters.

(See General Note after r.4.71.)

4.56-CVL   The chairman at meetings

4.56-CVL(1)   **[Application of Rule]** This Rule applies both to a meeting of creditors (except a meeting under section 95 or 98) and to a meeting of contributories.

4.56-CVL(2)   **[Liquidator or his nominee to be chairman]** The liquidator, or a person nominated by him in writing to act, shall be chairman of the meeting.

A person nominated under this paragraph must be either–

(a) one who is qualified to act as an insolvency practitioner in relation to the company, or

(b) an employee of the liquidator or his firm who is experienced in insolvency matters.

(See General Note after r.4.71.)

4.57   Requisitioned meetings

4.57(1)   **[Documents to accompany creditors' request]** Any request by creditors to the liquidator (whether or not the official receiver) for a meeting of creditors or contributories, or meetings of both, to be summoned shall be accompanied by–

(a) a list of the creditors concurring with the request and the amount of their respective claims in the winding up;

(b) from each creditor concurring, written confirmation of his concurrence; and

(c) a statement of the purpose of the proposed meeting.

Sub-paragraphs (a) and (b) do not apply if the requisitioning creditor's debt is alone sufficient, without the concurrence of other creditors.

                                                        [FORM 4.21]

4.57(2)   **[Liquidator to fix venue]** The liquidator shall, if he considers the request to be properly made in accordance with the Act, fix a venue for the meeting, not more than 28 days from his receipt of the request.

4.57(3)   **[Notice of meeting]** The liquidator shall give 14 days' notice of the meeting, and the venue for it, to creditors.

4.57(4)   **[Application of r.4.57(1)–(3) to contributories' meetings]** Paragraphs (1) to (3) above apply to the requisitioning by contributories of contributories' meetings, with the following modifications–

(a) for the reference in paragraph (1)(a) to the creditors' respective claims substitute the contributories' respective values (being the amounts for which they may vote at any meeting); and

(b) the persons to be given notice under paragraph (3) are those appearing (by the company's books or otherwise) to be contributories of the company.

                                                         [FORM 4.24]

(NO CVL APPLICATION)

(See General Note after r.4.71.)

4.58   Attendance at meetings of company's personnel

4.58(1)   [Application of Rule] This Rule applies to meetings of creditors and to meetings of contributories.

4.58(2)   [Notice to company's personnel] Whenever a meeting is summoned, the convener shall give at least 14 days' notice to such of the company's personnel as he thinks should be told of, or be present at, the meeting.

"**The company's personnel**" means the persons referred to in paragraphs (a) to (d) of section 235(3) (present and past officers, employees, etc.).

4.58(3)   [Notice of adjournment] If the meeting is adjourned, the chairman of the meeting shall, unless for any reason he thinks it unnecessary or impracticable, give notice of the adjournment to such (if any) of the company's personnel as he considers appropriate, being persons who were not themselves present at the meeting.

4.58(4)   [Notice that presence required] The convener may, if he thinks fit, give notice to any one or more of the company's personnel that he is, or they are, required to be present at the meeting, or to be in attendance.

4.58(5)   [Admission to meetings] In the case of any meeting, any one or more of the company's personnel, and any other persons, may be admitted, but–

   (a)   they must have given reasonable notice of their wish to be present, and

   (b)   it is a matter for the chairman's discretion whether they are to be admitted or not, and his decision is final as to what (if any) intervention may be made by any of them.

4.58(6)   [Adjournment for obtaining attendance] If it is desired to put questions to any one of the company's personnel who is not present, the chairman may adjourn the meeting with a view to obtaining his attendance.

4.58(7)   [Chairman's discretion re questions] Where one of the company's personnel is present at a meeting, only such questions may be put to him as the chairman may in his discretion allow.

(See General Note after r.4.71.)

4.59   Notice of meetings by advertisement only

4.59(1)   [Power of court] In the case of any meeting of creditors or contributories to be held under the Act or the Rules, the court may order that notice of the meeting be given by advertisement, and not by individual notice to the persons concerned.

4.59(2)   [Matters for court to consider] In considering whether to act under this Rule, the court shall have regard to the cost of advertisement, to the amount of the assets available, and to the extent of the interest of creditors or of contributories, or any particular class of either of them.

4.59(3)   [Additional content of advertisement] In addition to the standard contents, the advertisement must state–

   (a)   the venue fixed for the meeting;

   (b)   that proofs and (if applicable) proxies must be lodged at a specified place not later than 12.00 hours on the business day before the date fixed for the meeting;

   (c)   the date of the court order or the date of the resolution to wind up.

GENERAL NOTE

See *Practice Direction: Insolvency Proceedings* [2007] B.C.C. 842 (reproduced in App.IV to this *Guide*). See also General Note after r.4.71.

4.60 Venue

4.60(1) [Convenience of venue] In fixing the venue for a meeting of creditors or contributories, the convener shall have regard to the convenience of the persons (other than whoever is to be chairman) who are invited to attend.

4.60(2) [Time of meetings] Meetings shall in all cases be summoned for commencement between the hours of 10.00 and 16.00 hours on a business day, unless the court otherwise directs.

4.60(3) [Forms of proxy] With every notice summoning a meeting of creditors or contributories there shall be sent out forms of proxy.

[FORM 8.4]
or [FORM 8.5]

(See General Note after r.4.71.)

4.61 Expenses of summoning meetings

4.61(1) [Deposit for payment of expenses] Subject as follows, the expenses of summoning and holding a meeting of creditors or contributories at the instance of any person other than the official receiver or the liquidator shall be paid by that person, who shall deposit with the liquidator security for their payment.

4.61(2) [Appropriate security] The sum to be deposited shall be such as the official receiver or liquidator (as the case may be) determines to be appropriate; and neither shall act without the deposit having been made.

4.61(3) [Vote for expenses to be paid out of assets] Where a meeting of creditors is so summoned, it may vote that the expenses of summoning and holding it, and of summoning and holding any meeting of contributories requisitioned at the same time, shall be payable as an expense of the liquidation.

4.61(4) [Contributories' meeting] Where a meeting of contributories is summoned on the requisition of contributories, it may vote that the expenses of summoning and holding it shall be payable as an expense of the liquidation, but subject to the right of creditors to be paid in full, with interest.

4.61(5) [Repayment of deposit] To the extent that any deposit made under this Rule is not required for the payment of expenses of summoning and holding a meeting, it shall be repaid to the person who made it.

(See General Note after r.4.71.)

4.62-CVL Expenses of meeting under s.98

4.62-CVL(1) [Payment out of assets] Payment may be made either before or after the commencement of the winding up, of any reasonable and necessary expenses incurred in connection with the summoning, advertisement and holding of a creditors' meeting under section 98.

Any such payment is an expense of the liquidation.

4.62-CVL(2) [Payment before commencement of winding up] Where such payments are made before the commencement of the winding up, the director presiding at the creditors' meeting shall inform the meeting of their amount and the identity of the persons to whom they were made.

4.62-CVL(3) [Payment by s.100 liquidator] The liquidator appointed under section 100 may make such a payment (subject to the next paragraph); but if there is a liquidation committee, he must give the committee at least 5 business days' notice of his intention to make the payment.

4.62-CVL(4)   [No payment by liquidator to himself] Such a payment shall not be made by the liquidator to himself, or to any associate of his, otherwise than with the approval of the liquidation committee, the creditors, or the court.

4.62-CVL(5)   [Powers of court under r.4.219] This Rule is without prejudice to the powers of the court under Rule 4.219 (voluntary winding up superseded by winding up by the court).

(See General Note after r.4.71.)

4.63   Resolutions

4.63(1)   [Resolution passed by majority in value] Subject as follows, at a meeting of creditors or contributories, a resolution is passed when a majority (in value) of those present and voting, in person or by proxy, have voted in favour of the resolution.

The value of contributories is determined by reference to the number of votes conferred on each contributory by the company's articles.

4.63(2)   [Resolution for appointment of liquidator] In the case of a resolution for the appointment of a liquidator–

  (a)   if on any vote there are two nominees for appointment, the person who obtains the most support is appointed;

  (b)   if there are three or more nominees, and one of them has a clear majority over both or all the others together, that one is appointed; and

  (c)   in any other case, the chairman of the meeting shall continue to take votes (disregarding at each vote any nominee who has withdrawn and, if no nominee has withdrawn, the nominee who obtained the least support last time), until a clear majority is obtained for any one nominee.

4.63(2A)   [Omitted.]

4.63(3)   [Resolution for joint appointment] The chairman may at any time put to the meeting a resolution for the joint appointment of any two or more nominees.

4.63(4)   [Resolution affecting liquidator etc.] Where a resolution is proposed which affects a person in respect of his remuneration or conduct as liquidator, or as proposed or former liquidator, the vote of that person, and of any partner or employee of his, shall not be reckoned in the majority required for passing the resolution.

This paragraph applies with respect to a vote given by a person (whether personally or on his behalf by a proxy-holder) either as creditor or contributory or as proxy-holder for a creditor or a contributory (but subject to Rule 8.6 in Part 8 of the Rules).

(See General Note after r.4.71.)

4.63A   Resolutions by correspondence

4.63A(1)   [Power of liquidator to seek] The liquidator may seek to obtain the passing of a resolution by creditors or contributories without holding a meeting by giving notice of the resolution to every creditor or contributory who is entitled to be notified of a meeting at which the resolution could be passed.

4.63A(2)   [Time limit on closing date for votes] In order to be counted, votes must be received by the liquidator in writing by 12.00 hours on the closing date specified in the notice, and in the case of votes cast by creditors must be accompanied by a proof of debt as required by Rule 4.67(1)(a) unless it has already been lodged under that Rule.

4.63A(3)   [Vote disregarded without proof or entitlement] If any vote cast by a creditor is received without a proof of debt, or the liquidator decides that the creditor or contributory is not entitled to vote according to Rules 4.67 to 4.70, then that creditor's or contributory's vote must be disregarded.

4.63A(4)   **[Time limit for voting closing date]** The closing date shall be set at the discretion of the liquidator; but in any event it must not be set less than 14 days from the giving of notice provided for in paragraph (1).

4.63A(5)   **[Minimum of one valid vote needed]** For the resolution to be passed, the liquidator must receive at least one valid vote by the closing date specified in the notice.

4.63A(6)   **[Where no valid vote received]** If no valid vote is received by the closing date specified, the liquidator must call a meeting of creditors or contributories at which the resolution could be passed.

4.63A(7)   **[Requisition of creditors' meeting]** Creditors whose debts amount to at least 10% of the total debts of the company may, within 5 business days from the giving of notice provided for in paragraph (1), require the liquidator to summon a meeting of creditors to consider the resolution.

4.63A(8)   **[Requisition of contributories' meeting]** Contributories representing at least 10% of the total voting rights of all contributories having the right to vote at a meeting of contributories may, within 5 business days from the giving of notice provided for in paragraph (1), require the liquidator to summon a meeting of contributories to consider the resolution.

4.63A(9)   **[Reference to resolution in Rules]** A reference in these Rules to a resolution passed at a creditors' or contributories' meeting includes a reference to a resolution passed under this Rule.

4.63A(10)   **[Non-application of r.4.63A]** This Rule does not apply in respect of any resolution which the Act requires to be passed at a meeting.

(See General Note after r.4.71.)

4.64   Chairman of meeting as proxy-holder

4.64   Where the chairman at a meeting of creditors or contributories holds a proxy which requires him to vote for a particular resolution, and no other person proposes that resolution–

    (a)   he shall himself propose it, unless he considers that there is good reason for not doing so, and

    (b)   if he does not propose it, he shall as soon as reasonably practicable after the meeting notify his principal of the reason why not.

(See General Note after r.4.71.)

4.65   Suspension and adjournment

4.65(1)   **[Application of Rule]** This Rule applies to meetings of creditors and to meetings of contributories.

4.65(2)   **[Suspension at chairman's discretion]** Once only in the course of any meeting, the chairman may, in his discretion and without an adjournment, declare the meeting suspended for any period up to one hour.

4.65(3)   **[Adjournment]** The chairman at any meeting may in his discretion, and shall if the meeting so resolves, adjourn it to such time and place as seems to him to be appropriate in the circumstances.

    This is subject to Rule 4.113(3) or, as the case may be, 4.114–CVL(3), in a case where the liquidator or his nominee is chairman, and a resolution has been proposed for the liquidator's removal.

4.65(4)   **[Adjourned if inquorate]** If within a period of 30 minutes from the time appointed for the commencement of a meeting a quorum is not present, then the chairman may, at his discretion, adjourn the meeting to such time and place as he may appoint.

4.65(5)   **[Period of adjournment]** An adjournment under this Rule shall not be for a period of more than 14 days; and Rule 4.60(1) and (2) applies.

4.65(6)   **[Omitted.]**

4.65(6A)   [If no chairman] If within 30 minutes from the time appointed for commencement of a meeting there is no person present to act as chairman, the meeting stands adjourned to the same time and place in the following week or, if that is not a business day, to the business day immediately following.

4.65(6B)   [Application of r.4.65(6A) to further adjournment of final meeting] Paragraph (6A) applies to further adjournments of a final meeting.

4.65(6C)   [Further adjournment of any other meeting] In the case of any other meeting, further adjournment must be to the same time and place in the following week or, if either–

(a)   that is not a business day, or

(b)   whether or not it is a business day, it is later than 14 days after the date on which the meeting in question was originally held,

to the same time and place on the business day immediately preceding which is not later than 14 days after the date on which the meeting in question was originally held.

4.65(7)   [Use of proofs and proxies at adjourned meeting] Where a meeting is adjourned under this Rule, proofs and proxies may be used if lodged at any time up to midday on the business day immediately before the adjourned meeting.

(See General Note after r.4.71.)

4.66   Quorum

4.66   [Omitted by the Insolvency (Amendment) Rules 1987 (SI 1987/1919) r.3(1), Sch. Pt 1 para.56 as from January 11, 1988.]

4.67   Entitlement to vote (creditors)

4.67(1)   [Conditions for voting] Subject as follows in this Rule and the next, at a meeting of creditors a person is entitled to vote as a creditor only if–

(a)   there has been duly lodged (by the time and date stated in the notice of the meeting) a proof of the debt

    (i)   claimed to be due to him from the company, or

    (ii)   in relation to a member State liquidator, is claimed to be due to creditors in proceedings in relation to which he holds office,

    and the claim has been admitted under Rule 4.70 for the purpose of entitlement to vote, and

(b)   there has been lodged, by the time and date stated in the notice of the meeting, any proxy requisite for that entitlement.

4.67(2)   [Powers of court] The court may, in exceptional circumstances, by order declare the creditors, or any class of them, entitled to vote at creditors' meetings, without being required to prove their debts.

Where a creditor is so entitled, the court may, on the application of the liquidator, make such consequential orders as it thinks fit (as for example an order treating a creditor as having proved his debt for the purpose of permitting payment of dividend).

4.67(3)   [Limitation on voting] A creditor shall not vote in respect of a debt for an unliquidated amount, or any debt whose value is not ascertained, except where the chairman agrees to put upon the debt an estimated minimum value for the purpose of entitlement to vote and admits his proof for that purpose.

4.67(4)   [Secured creditor] A secured creditor is entitled to vote only in respect of the balance (if any) of his debt after deducting the value of his security as estimated by him.

4.67(5)   [Further limitation on voting] A creditor shall not vote in respect of a debt on, or secured by, a current bill of exchange or promissory note, unless he is willing–

(a)   to treat the liability to him on the bill or note of every person who is liable on it antecedently to the company, and against whom a bankruptcy order has not been made (or, in the case of a company, which has not gone into liquidation), as a security in his hands, and

(b)   to estimate the value of the security and (for the purpose of entitlement to vote, but not for dividend) to deduct it from his proof.

4.67(6)   [Still further limitation on voting] No vote shall be cast by virtue of a debt more than once on any resolution put to the meeting.

4.67(7)   [Creditor's vote] Where–

(a)   a creditor is entitled to vote under this Rule and Rule 4.70 (admission of proof),

(b)   has lodged his claim in one or more sets of other proceedings, and

(c)   votes (either in person or by proxy) on a resolution put to the meeting,

only the creditor's vote shall be counted.

4.67(8)   [Member State liquidator] Where–

(a)   a creditor has lodged his claim in more than one set of other proceedings, and

(b)   more than one member State liquidator seeks to vote by virtue of that claim,

the entitlement to vote by virtue of that claim is exercisable by the member State liquidator in main proceedings, whether or not the creditor has lodged his claim in the main proceedings.

4.67(9)   ["Other proceedings"] For the purposes of paragraphs (7) and (8), **"other proceedings"** means main proceedings, secondary proceedings or territorial proceedings in another member State.

(See General Note after r.4.71.)

4.68   Chairman's discretion to allow vote

4.68   At a creditors' meeting in a creditors' voluntary winding up or a winding up by the court, the chairman may allow a creditor to vote, notwithstanding that he has failed to comply with Rule 4.67(1)(a), if satisfied that the failure was due to circumstances beyond the creditor's control.

(See General Note after r.4.71.)

4.69   Entitlement to vote (contributories)

4.69   At a meeting of contributories, voting rights are as at a general meeting of the company, subject to any provision in the articles affecting entitlement to vote, either generally or at a time when the company is in liquidation.

(See General Note after r.4.71.)

4.70   Admission and rejection of proof (creditors' meeting)

4.70(1)   [Power of chairman] At any creditors' meeting the chairman has power to admit or reject a creditor's proof for the purpose of his entitlement to vote; and the power is exercisable with respect to the whole or any part of the proof.

4.70(2)   [Appeal from chairman's decision] The chairman's decision under this Rule, or in respect of any matter arising under Rule 4.67, is subject to appeal to the court by any creditor or contributory.

4.70(3)   [Voting subject to objection] If the chairman is in doubt whether a proof should be admitted or rejected, he shall mark it as objected to and allow the creditor to vote, subject to his vote being subsequently declared invalid if the objection to the proof is sustained.

4.70(4) [If chairman's decision reversed etc.] If on an appeal the chairman's decision is reversed or varied, or a creditor's vote is declared invalid, the court may order that another meeting be summoned, or make such other order as it thinks just.

4.70(4A)   [Time limit for appeal] An application to the court by way of appeal under this Rule against a decision of the chairman must be made not later than 21 days after the date of the meeting.

4.70(5)   [Costs re application] Neither the official receiver, nor any person nominated by him to be chairman, is personally liable for costs incurred by any person in respect of an application under this Rule; and the chairman (if other than the official receiver or a person so nominated) is not so liable unless the court makes an order to that effect.

(NO CVL APPLICATION)

4.70(6)   [Costs re application] The liquidator or his nominee as chairman is not personally liable for costs incurred by any person in respect of an application under this Rule, unless the court makes an order to that effect.

(See General Note after r.4.71.)

4.71   Record of proceedings

4.71(1)   [Minutes of proceedings] At any meeting, the chairman shall cause minutes of the proceedings to be kept. The minutes shall be authenticated by him, and retained as part of the records of the liquidation.

4.71(2)   [List of creditors or contributories attending] The chairman shall also cause to be made up and kept a list of all the creditors or, as the case may be, contributories who attended the meeting.

4.71(3)   [Record of resolutions, members elected to creditors committee] The minutes of the meeting shall include a record of every resolution passed and if a liquidation committee has been established, the names and addresses of those elected to be members of the committee.

4.71(4)   [Omitted.]

GENERAL NOTE TO RR.4.50–4.71

Rules 4.50(8) and 4.51(3) were substituted by the Financial Services and Markets Act 2000 (Consequential Amendments and Repeals) Order 2001 (SI 2001/3649) as from December 1, 2001. Rules 4.50(5) and 4.54(6) substituted by I(A)R 2009 (SI 2009/642) rr.24, 25 as from April 6, 2009.

Subparagraph (ii) was inserted into r.4.67(1)(a) and paras (6)–(9) added by the Insolvency (Amendment) Rules 2002 (SI 2002/1307, effective May 31, 2002). A "liquidator" in insolvency proceedings which have been opened in any Member State is empowered by the EC Regulation art.32(2), (3) to prove in proceedings in another Member State in respect of claims which have been lodged with him, and to attend meetings, etc. as a creditor. This rule, as amended, confirms his right to vote but includes provisions to ensure that a vote in respect of any particular debt is cast only once. (Note that under the CBIR a foreign representative is not similarly empowered to prove as a creditor in a British insolvency proceeding, although foreign creditors may, of course, prove in their own right.)

Rules 4.50–4.54, 4.57–4.59, 4.62–4.63, 4.65, 4.67–4.68, 4.70–4.71 amended, rr.4.50(3), (4), 4.54(4), (5), 4.65(6) substituted, rr.4.52(3), 4.63(2A), 4.65(6), 4.71(4) omitted, and rr.4.50(5A), 4.52(3A)–(3C), 4.53C, 4.53D, 4.54(7), 4.59(3), 4.63A, 4.65(6A)–(6C), 4.70(4A) inserted by I(A)R 2010 r.2 and Sch. paras 175–190 as from April 6, 2010.

The 2010 reforms have shortened the timetable by seven days in certain respects: the liquidator has 28 rather than 35 days to fix a venue for the meeting (r.4.57(2)), and the periods of notice under rr.4.50(3), 4.57(3), 4.58(2) and 4.65(5) have been reduced from 21 to 14 days. Any adjournment or adjournments of the first meeting of creditors may not extend in all beyond 14 days under the amended rules (unless the court orders otherwise) (r.4.52(3A)–(3C)): the period was formerly three weeks. The previous time-limits will of course continue to apply in existing liquidations.

The notices required under rr.4.50, 4.53C, 4,53D and 4.54 must include the detailed information referred to in the relevant section in addition to the standard contents. On the standard contents for gazetted notices, see rr.12A.31–12A.33. On the standard contents for notices other than gazetted notices, see rr.12A.36–12A.39. Gazetting is not required where the notice is of an annual meeting in a voluntary liquidation: I(A)R 2010 r.6.

Provision is now also made for the liquidator to seek the passing of creditors' and contributories' resolutions by correspondence (s.4.63A).

The official receiver has a discretion under IA 1986 whether to summon first meetings. If he decides to do so, the procedure to be followed in a winding up by the court is set out in rr.4.50 and 4.52; rr.4.51-CVL and 4.53-CVL deal with the first meeting of creditors in a creditors' voluntary winding up.

Voting at creditors' meetings is by a majority in *value* only, instead of the majority in *number* and *value* required under r.134 of the former winding-up rules.

It is well established in company law that one person may constitute a "meeting" when in the class (of shareholders, creditors or directors) that person is the only member, and also that the consent of such a person may be given informally. But the rule does not apply where there is no evidence that the person is the only member of the class. In *Re Altitude Scaffolding Ltd* [2006] EWHC 1401 (Ch); [2006] B.C.C. 904 only one creditor attended a meeting, but his consent was held to be insufficient for this reason.

Note in regard to r.4.57(1), (2) that the statutory power of the creditors and contributories to requisition meetings is contained in IA 1986 s.168(2), which requires the support of at least one-tenth in value of the creditors or contributories, as the case may be.

Before a creditor may vote, a proof of his debt must have been lodged and admitted under r.4.70 (subject to the court's powers under r.4.67(1)); and, if he wishes to vote by proxy, his proxy must also have been duly lodged. The deadline for lodging a proof is fixed, in the case of a winding up by the court, by the notice convening the meeting (r.4.67(1)), but there is no corresponding provision for the case of a creditors' voluntary winding up. It would appear that this may be done at any time up to the taking of the vote, or even (if the chairman exercises his discretion under r.4.68) without lodging a proof at all. The chairman has no similar discretion in a compulsory winding up; but the court has power to grant a dispensation in either kind of winding up under r.4.67(2). Rules 4.50(4), 4.51(2) and 4.54(4) specify varying times by which proxies must be lodged by creditors (and, where appropriate, contributories) for the different meetings.

The identity of a person named as proxy is a procedural matter "of absolutely no significance" and if another person attends the meeting in his place and no objection is taken the requirement may be treated as waived, or the company and the liquidator may be estopped from relying on the point: *Re Shruth Ltd* [2005] EWHC 1293 (Ch); [2007] B.C.C. 960. In the same case it was held that a chairman may reject a proof where the claim is for an unliquidated amount (in the absence of agreement), and is not obliged to allow the creditor to vote subject to objection under r.4.70(3).

Rule 4.53A-CVL brings back into operation a provision equivalent to the repealed CA 1985 s.588(4), and allows the creditors to pass a resolution in anticipation of and conditionally upon the passing in due course of a resolution for winding up at an adjourned shareholders' meeting.

Rule 4.53B-CVL reflects a change in the form relating to the statement of affairs (Form 4.19). Previously, this had to be made up to the date of the creditors' meeting—a requirement which could not be met in practice. The date may now be anything up to 14 days before the meeting; and r.4.53B-CVL imposes an obligation to make a report (which may be oral) to the meeting, bringing the statement up to date.

Rule 4.63(2A) prevents the election of a liquidator on a minority vote in the case where there are several nominees. The exclusion of its application to a creditors' voluntary winding up ensures that a liquidator who has the greatest support among the creditors (even if only a minority of them overall) is preferred to the company's nominee.

The repealed r.4.66 has been replaced by the new r.12.4A.

The language of r.4.67(3) is similar to that formerly used in other rules, e.g. r.1.17(3) and r.5.17(3), and accordingly decisions on those provisions (such as *Re a Debtor (No.222 of 1990) Ex p. Bank of Ireland* [1992] B.C.L.C. 137) are relevant to its interpretation. In *Re Bank of Credit & Commerce International SA (No.5), Sheik Khalid v Bank of Credit & Commerce International SA* [1994] 1 B.C.L.C. 429 the court considered an application by a person claiming to be a creditor before any ruling had been given by the chairman (who had not yet been appointed).

Note that a secured creditor who proves for his debt without mentioning his security is required to surrender his security unless the court otherwise orders: see r.4.96.

A decision to accept a creditor's proof for voting purposes is not binding or conclusive for other purposes: *Re Assico Engineering Ltd* [2002] B.C.C. 481.

In considering an appeal from the decision of the chairman to allow or reject a creditor's proof for voting purposes, the evidence which the court may consider is not confined to that which was available to the chairman at the meeting: *Re a Company (No.004539 of 1993)* [1995] B.C.C. 116. A similar approach was adopted by the court in reviewing the validity of proxies in *Re Philip Alexander Securities & Futures Ltd* [1998] B.C.C. 819. See also *Re Power Builders (Surrey) Ltd* [2008] EWHC 2607 (Ch); [2009] 1 B.C.L.C. 250; and see further the note to rr.4.73–4.85.

Section B: Winding up of recognised banks, etc.

4.72   Additional provisions as regards certain meetings

4.72(1)   [Application of Rule] This Rule applies where a company goes, or proposes to go, into liquidation and it is an authorised deposit-taker or former authorised deposit-taker.

4.72(2)   [Notice re proposed winding up] Notice of any meeting of the company at which it is intended to propose a resolution for its winding up shall be given by the directors to the Financial Services Authority and to the scheme manager established under section 212(1) of the Financial Services and Markets Act 2000.

4.72(3)   [Form of notice] Notice to the Authority and the scheme manager shall be the same as given to members of the company.

4.72(4)   [Where creditors' meeting summoned under s.95 or 98] Where a creditors' meeting is summoned by the liquidator under section 95 or, in a creditors' voluntary winding up, is summoned under section 98, the same notice of the meeting must be given to the Authority and the scheme manager as is given to creditors under Rule 4.51–CVL.

4.72(5)   [Where company being wound up by court] Where the company is being wound up by the court, notice of the first meetings of creditors and contributories shall be given to the Authority and the scheme manager by the official receiver.

4.72(6)   [Where meeting to receive liquidator's resignation etc.] Where in the winding up (whether voluntary or by the court) a meeting of creditors or contributories or of the company is summoned for the purpose of–

(a)   receiving the liquidator's resignation, or

(b)   removing the liquidator, or

(c)   appointing a new liquidator,

the person summoning the meeting and giving notice of it shall also give notice to the Authority and the scheme manager.

4.72(7)   [Representation of scheme manager] The scheme manager is entitled to be represented at any meeting of which it is required by this Rule to be given notice; and Schedule 1 to the Rules has effect with respect to the voting rights of the scheme manager at such a meeting.

GENERAL NOTE

Rules 4.72(1)–(7) were substituted by the Financial Services and Markets Act 2000 (Consequential Amendments and Repeals) Order 2001 (SI 2001/3649) as from December 1, 2001. This rule ensures that the Financial Services Authority and the scheme manager are notified of meetings summoned in connection with the winding-up of an authorised deposit-taker under the Banking Act 1987.

Section A: Procedure for proving

4.73   Meaning of "prove"

4.73(1)   [Winding up by court] Where a company is being wound up by the court, a person claiming to be a creditor of the company and wishing to recover his debt in whole or in part must (subject to any order of the court under Rule 4.67(2)) submit his claim in writing to the liquidator.

(NO CVL APPLICATION)

4.73(2)   [Voluntary winding up] In a voluntary winding up (whether members' or creditors') the liquidator may require a person claiming to be a creditor of the company and wishing to recover his debt in whole or in part, to submit the claim in writing to him.

4.73(3)   ["Proving" and "proof"] A creditor who claims (whether or not in writing) is referred to as **"proving"** for his debt; and a document by which he seeks to establish his claim is his **"proof"**.

4.73(4)   ["Proof of debt"] Subject to the next paragraph, a proof must be in the form known as **"proof of debt"** (whether the form prescribed by the Rules, or a substantially similar form), which shall be made out by or under the directions of the creditor, and authenticated by him or a person authorised in that behalf.

(NO CVL APPLICATION)

[FORM 4.25]

4.73(5)   [Debt due to Crown etc.] Where a debt is due to a Minister of the Crown or a Government Department, the proof need not be in that form, provided that there are shown all such particulars of the debt as are required in the form used by other creditors, and as are relevant in the circumstances.

(NO CVL APPLICATION)

4.73(6)   [Creditor's proof] The creditor's proof may be in any form.

4.73(7)   [Omitted.]

4.73(8)   [Deemed proof in winding up] Where a winding up is immediately preceded by an administration, a creditor proving in the administration shall be deemed to have proved in the winding up.

(See General Note after r.4.85.)

4.74   Supply of forms

(NO CVL APPLICATION)

4.74   A form of proof shall be sent to any creditor of the company by the liquidator where the creditor so requests.

(See General Note after r.4.85.)

4.75   Contents of proof

(NO CVL APPLICATION)

4.75(1)   [Matters to be stated in creditor's proof] Subject to Rule 4.73(5), the following matters shall be stated in a creditor's proof of debt–

   (a)   the creditor's name and address, and, if a company, its company registration number;

(b) the total amount of his claim (including any Value Added Tax) as at the date on which the company went into liquidation (or, if the liquidation was immediately preceded by an administration, the date on which the company entered administration), less any payments made after that date in respect of the claim and any deduction under Rule 4.89;

(c) whether or not that amount includes outstanding uncapitalised interest;

(d) particulars of how and when the debt was incurred by the company;

(e) particulars of any security held, the date when it was given and the value which the creditor puts upon it;

(f) details of any reservation of title in respect of goods to which the debt refers; and

(g) the name, and address and authority of the person authenticating the proof (if other than the creditor himself).

4.75(2) [Specified documents] There shall be specified in the proof any documents by reference to which the debt can be substantiated; but (subject as follows) it is not essential that such documents be attached to the proof or submitted with it.

4.75(3) [Production of documents etc.] The liquidator, or the chairman or convener of any meeting, may call for any document or other evidence to be produced to him, where he thinks it necessary for the purpose of substantiating the whole or any part of the claim made in the proof.

(See General Note after r.4.85.)

4.76-CVL   Particulars of creditor's claim

4.76-CVL   The liquidator, or the convener or chairman of any meeting, may, if he thinks it necessary for the purpose of clarifying or substantiating the whole or any part of a creditor's claim made in his proof, call for details of any matter specified in paragraphs (a) to (h) of Rule 4.75(1), or for the production to him of such documentary or other evidence as he may require.

(See General Note after r.4.85.)

4.77   Claim established by affidavit [Revoked by (I(A)R 2010 r.5 (with retrospective effect).]

(See General Note after r.4.85.)

4.78   Cost of proving

4.78(1) [Creditor bears cost of proving own debt] Subject as follows, every creditor bears the cost of proving his own debt, including such as may be incurred in providing documents or evidence under Rule 4.75(3) or 4.76–CVL.

4.78(2) [Liquidator's costs] Costs incurred by the liquidator in estimating the quantum of a debt under Rule 4.86 (debts not bearing a certain value) are payable as an expense of the liquidation.

4.78(3) [Application of r.4.78(1), (2)] Paragraphs (1) and (2) apply unless the court otherwise orders.

(See General Note after r.4.85.)

4.79   Liquidator to allow inspection of proofs

4.79   The liquidator shall, so long as proofs lodged with him are in his hands, allow them to be inspected, at all reasonable times on any business day, by any of the following persons–

(a) any creditor who has submitted his proof of debt (unless his proof has been wholly rejected for purposes of dividend or otherwise);

(b) any contributory of the company;

(c)   any person acting on behalf of either of the above.

(See General Note after r.4.85.)

4.80   Transmission of proofs to liquidator

(NO CVL APPLICATION)

4.80(1)   [On liquidator's appointment] Where a liquidator is appointed, the official receiver shall as soon as reasonably practicable transmit to him all the proofs which he has so far received, together with an itemised list of them.

4.80(2)   [Receipt for proofs] The liquidator shall authenticate the list by way of receipt for the proofs, and return it to the official receiver.

4.80(3)   [All later proofs to liquidator] From then on, all proofs of debt shall be sent to the liquidator, and retained by him.

(See General Note after r.4.85.)

4.81   New liquidator appointed

4.81(1)   [On appointment] If a new liquidator is appointed in place of another, the former liquidator must as soon as reasonably practicable transmit to him all proofs which he has received, together with an itemised list of them.

4.81(2)   [Receipt for proofs] The new liquidator shall authenticate the list by way of receipt for the proofs, and return it to his predecessor.

4.81(3)   [Proofs to and retained by new liquidator] From then on, all proofs of debt must be sent to and retained by the new liquidator.

(See General Note after r.4.85.)

4.82   Admission and rejection of proofs for dividend

4.82(1)   [Admission] A proof may be admitted for dividend either for the whole amount claimed by the creditor, or for part of that amount.

4.82(2)   [Rejection] If the liquidator rejects a proof in whole or in part, he shall prepare a written statement of his reasons for doing so, and send it as soon as reasonably practicable to the creditor.

(See General Note after r.4.85.)

4.83   Appeal against decision on proof

4.83(1)   [Application by creditor] If a creditor is dissatisfied with the liquidator's decision with respect to his proof (including any decision on the question of preference), he may apply to the court for the decision to be reversed or varied.

The application must be made within 21 days of his receiving the statement sent under Rule 4.82(2).

4.83(2)   [Application by contributory etc.] A contributory or any other creditor may, if dissatisfied with the liquidator's decision admitting or rejecting the whole or any part of a proof, make such an application within 21 days of becoming aware of the liquidator's decision.

4.83(3)   [Venue and notice] Where application is made to the court under this Rule, the court shall fix a venue for the application to be heard, notice of which shall be sent by the applicant to the creditor who lodged the proof in question (if it is not himself) and to the liquidator.

4.83(4)   [Relevant proof etc. to be filed in court] The liquidator shall, on receipt of the notice, file in court the relevant proof, together (if appropriate) with a copy of the statement sent under Rule 4.82(2).

4.83(4A) **[Contributory to show surplus of assets]** Where the application is made by a contributory, the court must not disallow the proof (in whole or in part) unless the contributory shows that there is (or would be but for the amount claimed in the proof), or that it is likely that there will be (or would be but for the amount claimed in the proof), a surplus of assets to which the company would be entitled.

4.83(5) **[Return of proof]** After the application has been heard and determined, the proof shall, unless it has been wholly disallowed, be returned by the court to the liquidator.

4.83(6) **[Costs re application]** The official receiver is not personally liable for costs incurred by any person in respect of an application under this Rule; and the liquidator (if other than the official receiver) is not so liable unless the court makes an order to that effect.

(See General Note after r.4.85.)

4.84 Withdrawal or variation of proof

4.84 A creditor's proof may at any time, by agreement between himself and the liquidator, be withdrawn or varied as to the amount claimed.

(See General Note after r.4.85.)

4.85 Expunging of proof by the court

4.85(1) **[Expunging or reduction of amount]** The court may expunge a proof or reduce the amount claimed–

(a) on the liquidator's application, where he thinks that the proof has been improperly admitted, or ought to be reduced; or

(b) on the application of a creditor, if the liquidator declines to interfere in the matter.

4.85(2) **[Venue and notice]** Where application is made to the court under this Rule, the court shall fix a venue for the application to be heard, notice of which shall be sent by the applicant–

(a) in the case of an application by the liquidator, to the creditor who made the proof, and

(b) in the case of an application by a creditor, to the liquidator and to the creditor who made the proof (if not himself).

GENERAL NOTE TO RR.4.73–4.85

Here are set out the rules governing the proof of debts, the rights of inspection of proofs, appeals against a liquidator's decision with respect to a proof, etc. See generally the comment preceding s.175.

Paragraph (8) was inserted into r.4.73 by the Insolvency (Amendment) Rules 2003 (SI 2003/1730, effective September 15, 2003) Sch.1 para.18. Rules 4.74 and 4.75(1) were substituted by the Insolvency (Amendment) Rules 2004 (SI 2004/584), effective April 1, 2004. The liquidator is no longer obliged to send a form of proof to every creditor, but only to do so if a particular creditor requests. The details to be stated in a creditor's proof of debt have been revised. Where an insolvency practitioner holds a blanket authority from a creditor to act under r.4.75(1)(g), an approved form of authority acceptable to official receivers is to be found in *Dear IP*, October 2008.

Rules 4.75, 4.81(1) amended, r.4.73(7) omitted and rr.4.81(3), 4.83(4A) inserted by I(A)R 2010 r.2 and Sch. paras 192–194 as from April 6, 2010.

The "rule against double proof" forbids more than one proof to be admitted in respect of the same debt (e.g. by a guarantor as well as a principal creditor). See *Re Oriental Commercial Bank* (1871) 7 Ch. App. 99; and the discussion in *Re Polly Peck International plc* [1996] B.C.C. 486; and contrast *Re Parkfield Group plc* [1997] B.C.C. 778.

In a proper case, a liquidator or the court may disallow a proof notwithstanding the fact that a judgment has been obtained in respect of the debt in question; but the court will do so only if it appears that there was some fraud, collusion or miscarriage of justice: *Re Menastar Finance Ltd* [2002] EWHC 2610 (Ch); [2003] B.C.C. 404; *Re Shruth Ltd* [2005] EWHC 1293 (Ch); [2007] B.C.C. 960.

The words "improperly admitted" in r.4.85(1)(a) carry no connotation of impropriety. It is sufficient that the proof was admitted in error, and the burden of proof in establishing this is the balance of probabilities: see *Re Globe Legal Services Ltd* [2002] B.C.C. 858; *Re Allard Holdings Ltd* [2001] 1 B.C.L.C. 404 (in which the relevance of delay is also discussed). If a proof has been improperly rejected, the court may, of course, direct the liquidator to accept it under r.4.83. For an example, see *Re Shruth Ltd* (above).

Where a single claim has been submitted, it is probably correct that that claim can only be increased by variation of the original proof and not by submission of a new proof: *Meisels v Martin* [2005] EWHC 845 (Ch); [2005] B.P.I.R. 1151.

On the application of the Limitation Act 1980 to claims, see the note to s.129.

The proper law of a debt is determined by its *lex situs*, and is not affected by the fact that the debtor is subsequently wound up in another jurisdiction. But if the debt has been discharged under its proper law, it may not be proved in the liquidation: *Wight v Eckhardt Marine GmbH* [2003] UKPC 37; [2004] 1 A.C. 147; [2003] B.C.C. 702.

On the meaning of "went into liquidation", in r.4.75, see IA 1986 s.247.

Section B: Quantification of claim

4.86 Estimate of quantum

4.86(1) [Estimating value of debts etc.] The liquidator shall estimate the value of any debt which, by reason of its being subject to any contingency or for any other reason, does not bear a certain value; and he may revise any estimate previously made, if he thinks fit by reference to any change of circumstances or to information becoming available to him.

He shall inform the creditor as to his estimate and any revision of it.

4.86(2) [Amount provable in winding up] Where the value of a debt is estimated under this Rule, or by the court under section 168(3) or (5), the amount provable in the winding up in the case of that debt is that of the estimate for the time being.

(See General Note after r.4.89.)

4.87 Negotiable instruments, etc.

4.87 Unless the liquidator allows, a proof in respect of money owed on a bill of exchange, promissory note, cheque or other negotiable instrument or security cannot be admitted unless there is produced the instrument or security itself or a copy of it, certified by the creditor or his authorised representative to be a true copy.

(See General Note after r.4.89.)

4.88 Secured creditors

4.88(1) [Proving for balance of debt] If a secured creditor realises his security, he may prove for the balance of his debt, after deducting the amount realised.

4.88(2) [Proving for whole debt] If a secured creditor voluntarily surrenders his security for the general benefit of creditors, he may prove for his whole debt, as if it were unsecured.

(See General Note after r.4.89.)

4.89 Discounts

4.89 There shall in every case be deducted from the claim all trade and other discounts which would have been available to the company but for its liquidation, except any discount for immediate, early or cash settlement.

GENERAL NOTE TO RR.4.86–4.89

These are the rules for assessing a debt for the purposes of proof in the special cases of contingent and secured debts, etc.

R.4.88

A secured creditor who has been paid part of his debt as a result of realising his security may prove for the balance without bringing what he has received into hotchpot: *Cleaver v Delta American Reinsurance Co* [2001] UKPC 6; [2001] 1 B.C.L.C. 482.

4.90 Mutual credits and set-off

4.90(1) [Application of Rule] This Rule applies where, before the company goes into liquidation there have been mutual credits, mutual debts or other mutual dealings between the company and any creditor of the company proving or claiming to prove for a debt in the liquidation.

4.90(2) [Excluded debts] The reference in paragraph (1) to mutual credits, mutual debts or other mutual dealings does not include-

(a) any debt arising out of an obligation incurred at a time when the creditor had notice that-

    (i) a meeting of creditors had been summoned under section 98; or

    (ii) a petition for the winding up of the company was pending;

(b) any debt arising out of an obligation where–

    (i) the liquidation was immediately preceded by an administration; and

    (ii) at the time the obligation was incurred the creditor had notice that an application for an administration order was pending or a person had given notice of intention to appoint an administrator;

(c) any debt arising out of an obligation incurred during an administration which immediately preceded the liquidation; or

(d) any debt which has been acquired by a creditor by assignment or otherwise, pursuant to an agreement between the creditor and any other party where that agreement was entered into-

    (i) after the company went into liquidation;

    (ii) at a time when the creditor had notice that a meeting of creditors had been summoned under section 98;

    (iii) at a time when the creditor had notice that a winding up petition was pending;

    (iv) where the liquidation was immediately preceded by an administration, at a time when the creditor had notice that an application for an administration order was pending or a person had given notice of intention to appoint an administrator; or

    (v) during an administration which immediately preceded the liquidation.

4.90(3) [Account of mutual dealings and set-off] An account shall be taken of what is due from each party to the other in respect of the mutual dealings, and the sums due from one party shall be set off against the sums due from the other.

4.90(4) [Sums regarded as being due] A sum shall be regarded as being due to or from the company for the purposes of paragraph (3) whether–

(a) it is payable at present or in the future;

(b) the obligation by virtue of which it is payable is certain or contingent; or

(c) its amount is fixed or liquidated, or is capable of being ascertained by fixed rules or as a matter of opinion.

4.90(5) [Application of r.4.86] Rule 4.86 shall also apply for the purposes of this Rule to any obligation to or from the company which, by reason of its being subject to any contingency or for any other reason, does not bear a certain value.

4.90(6) [Application of rr.4.91–4.93] Rules 4.91 to 4.93 shall apply for the purposes of this Rule in relation to any sums due to the company which-

(a) are payable in a currency other than sterling;

(b)　are of a periodical nature; or

(c)　bear interest.

4.90(7)　[Application of r.11.13] Rule 11.13 shall apply for the purposes of this Rule to any sum due to or from the company which is payable in the future.

4.90(8)　[Only balance provable] Only the balance (if any) of the account owed to the creditor is provable in the liquidation. Alternatively the balance (if any) owed to the company shall be paid to the liquidator as part of the assets except where all or part of the balance results from a contingent or prospective debt owed by the creditor and in such a case the balance (or that part of it which results from the contingent or prospective debt) shall be paid if and when that debt becomes due and payable.

4.90(9)　["Obligation"] In this Rule **"obligation"** means an obligation however arising, whether by virtue of an agreement, rule of law or otherwise.

GENERAL NOTE

There is no provision in the Insolvency Act itself for the case of mutual credits and set-off in company insolvency corresponding to IA 1986 s.323, which deals with individual bankruptcy. The present rule makes good this shortcoming. See the Introductory note to Part IV, Chapter VIII preceding IA 1986 s.175.

Rule 4.90 (and with it r.2.85) were totally recast by the Insolvency (Amendment) Rules 2005 (SI 2005/527) r.23 (and r.9), as from April 1, 2005. These amendments are designed to provide greater detail and clarity of meaning, to reflect the applicable case law, to remove certain anomalies and to bring the set-off rules for liquidation and administration into line.

Rule 4.90, as originally drafted, removed some uncertainties that were not fully resolved previously. First, it was made clear that the rules as to mutual credits and set-off applied to all liquidations, irrespective of the solvency or otherwise of the company and whether the liquidation was voluntary or compulsory. Secondly, it was also made clear that the relevant date (or time: see the note to s.86) for all purposes of proof and set-off is that when the company went into liquidation. (For the meaning of this expression, see s.247(2).) On the other hand, some difficult questions remained to be resolved. The reforms introduced by the 2005 Rules are intended to deal with the most important of these.

First, the former rule gave inadequate guidance as to the set-off of contingent liabilities, and in particular how such liabilities when owed *to* the company should be quantified. (On this point see Wood, (1987) 8 Co. Law. 262; Roy Goode, *Principles of Corporate Insolvency Law* 3rd edn (2005), Ch.8; *M S Fashions Ltd v Bank of Credit & Commerce International SA (No.2)* [1993] Ch. 425 at 435; [1993] B.C.C. 70 at 75; and, especially, *Stein v Blake* [1996] A.C. 243 at 251 et seq., per Lord Hoffmann. In contrast, the rules did contain provisions dealing with contingent liabilities owed *by* the company.

The revised r.4.90 now puts all contingent liabilities on the same footing, and the new rules assimilate the position for both liquidations and administrations (or, at least, those established under Sch.B1). Those rules which relate to the quantification of debts (i.e. rr.2.81, 2.86–2.88, 2.105, 4.86, 4.91–4.93 and 11.13) are extended to cover debts owed *to* a company, as well as those owed *by* a company. Accordingly, debts owed to the company that are contingent or payable at a future time are to be included in the set-off account, and liquidators and administrators will be able to put a value on such debts.

Other innovations introduced by the new r.4.90 are:

- "Mutual debts" that are not to be included in the set-off account are defined. These include any debt acquired by a creditor by assignment or otherwise, pursuant to an agreement entered into after one of the dates set out in rr.2.85(2)(e) and 4.90(2)(d). But if a creditor acquires or re-acquires a debt after one of those dates as a result of an agreement entered into at an earlier date, it is to be considered a "mutual dealing" for the purposes of the set-off account.

- Rule 4.90(4) now clarifies the question when a sum becomes "due" for set-off purposes, drawing on the definition of "debt or liability" in r.13.12(3). (Note also r.4.90(7).)

- Where, after the calculation of the set-off account, an amount is owed to the company arising from a contingent debt or a sum payable at a future time, that amount only has to be paid to the liquidator if and when it becomes due and payable.

A creditor whose proof has been rejected cannot reassert the debt by claiming to rely on it as a set-off: *Bank of Credit & Commerce International (Overseas) Ltd v Habib Bank Ltd* [1998] 2 B.C.L.C. 459. On similar reasoning, a claim that would be open to objection on the grounds of double proof cannot be set off: *Re Glen Express Ltd* [2000] B.P.I.R. 456. In the *Habib Bank* case it was also held that under r.4.90 the court had to take account of the fact that debts owed to the creditor at the date of the liquidation had subsequently been paid by third parties.

The rules as to set-off in insolvency proceedings apply in both solvent and insolvent liquidations (*Rayden v Edwardo Ltd* [2008] EWHC 2689 (Comm); [2009] B.P.I.R. 892, but are different from those which apply in other contexts (or before such proceedings take effect): see the subject discussed by Lord Hoffmann in *Stein v Blake* (above). The object of the latter is to avoid cross-actions, and their scope is restricted. The former, in contrast, are intended to do substantial justice between the parties, and their application is not limited to particular categories of claim, but apply to all cross-claims provided that they are mutual and measurable in money terms (*Stein v Blake* [1993] B.C.C. 587 at 590, per Balcombe L.J.). Claims are only "mutual" if they are due between the same parties and in the same right—e.g. a debt owed by A to B as trustee for C and a debt owed to A by B personally cannot be set off: *Re ILG Travel Ltd* [1996] B.C.C. 21; *Re Griffin Trading Co* [1999] B.P.I.R. 256. In the converse case, where B alleges that a debt owed by A to C is in fact held by C as trustee for B, the court will allow set-off only where it is satisfied that the debt is clear and ascertained and that B is the sole beneficiary and entitled without further inquiry to demand that the debt be transferred to him: *Ex p. Morier* (1879) 12 Ch. D. 491; *Bank of Credit and Commercial International SA (in liq.) v Prince Fahd Bin Salman Abdul Aziz Al-Saud* [1997] B.C.C. 63. The fact that one debt is secured and the other unsecured is not inconsistent with mutuality: *Re ILG Travel Ltd* (above). But there must have been "dealing" between the parties; and so (for instance) a debt cannot be set off against the creditor's liability to the company in damages for conversion: *Re Cosslett (Contractors) Ltd (No.2), Smith v Bridgend County Borough Council* [2001] UKHL 58; [2002] 1 A.C. 336; [2001] B.C.C. 740. (Contrast *Myles J. Callaghan Ltd (in receivership) v City of Glasgow District Council* (1987) 3 B.C.C. 337, where it was held competent in Scots law for a creditor in a liquidation to set off a claim for damages for breach of a building contract against a claim by the company for the return of its plant and equipment or payment of its value, and to do so notwithstanding the appointment of a receiver.) The rules as to set-off are mandatory and cannot be excluded by agreement between the parties (*National Westminster Bank Ltd v Halesowen Presswork & Assemblies Ltd* [1972] A.C. 785); nor can they be disapplied by the court in the exercise of its discretion: *Re Bank of Credit & Commerce International SA (No.10)* [1997] Ch. 213; [1996] B.C.C. 980. In the *M S Fashions* case (above, affirmed [1993] Ch. 425 at 439, sub nom. *High Street Services Ltd v Bank of Credit & Commerce International SA* [1993] B.C.C. 360), it was held that where several persons were each liable to the company as principal debtors in respect of the same debt, a set-off available against one of them operated automatically to reduce the debt for the benefit of them all. It was not open to a liquidator to seek to avoid this consequence by electing to claim the full amount in the first instance from the other debtors. (For earlier proceedings in the same case, see *M S Fashions Ltd v Bank of Credit & Commerce International SA* [1992] B.C.C. 571.) In contrast, in *Re Bank of Credit & Commerce International SA (No.8), Morris v Rayners Enterprises Inc* [1988] A.C. 214; [1997] B.C.C. 965, the House of Lords held that the bank's liquidators could proceed first against the principal debtors concerned, without bringing into account the amounts of certain deposits made with the bank by other persons and allegedly charged to secure the debts. In this case the depositors had no personal liability for the principal debts, and accordingly there was no sum "due" from them on which a set-off could operate. It was observed that to permit the set-off of claims by third parties, even with their consent, would be to allow the parties by agreement to subvert the fundamental principle of pari passu distribution of assets in an insolvency. Other cases on r.4.90 include *Re a Company (No.1641 of 2003)* [2003] EWHC 2652 (Ch); [2004] 1 B.C.L.C. 211 (debt arising out of unlawful transaction cannot be set off); and *Re Greenport Ltd* [2004] 1 B.C.L.C. 555 (no question of set-off under r.4.90 arises where creditor has a contractual right to make deductions from a deposit and that suffices to determine the rights of the parties).

A debt owed to a company by the Crown for overpaid VAT and a sum which became payable by the company in its liquidation to the Crown for redundancy payments made after the commencement of the liquidation were held to arise out of "mutual dealings" in *Secretary of State for Trade and Industry v Frid, Re West End Networks Ltd* [2004] UKHL 24; [2004] 2 A.C. 506; [2004] B.C.C. 525. It was not necessary that the latter sums should have become due and payable at the date of the liquidation, so long as there was an obligation arising out of a contract, or the commission of a tort, or (as in this case) a statutory provision, by which a debt sounding in money would become payable on the occurrence of some future event. The Crown for this purpose was to be regarded as indivisible.

Rule 4.83 (or, in an administration, r.2.78) provides the means of appeal if a third party disagrees with the valuation that has been placed on a debt that he owes to the company.

A contributory's liability for calls cannot be set off in a liquidation against any liability of the company to him: *Re Overend Gurney, Grissell's case* (1864) 1 Ch. App. 528; *Re Pinecord Ltd* [1995] B.C.C. 483.

The holder of a secured debt is not required by r.4.90 to set off money owed by the company to him against that debt, unless he elects to give up his security and prove his debt in the liquidation: *Re Norman Holding Co Ltd (in liq.)* [1991] 1 W.L.R. 10; [1991] B.C.C. 11.

For a case where a creditor acquired a debt by assignment shortly before the debtor company entered administration and successfully avoided the statutory exclusion corresponding to r.4.90(2)(b)(ii), see *Re Parkside International Ltd* [2008] EWHC 3554 (Ch); [2009] B.P.I.R. 549.

In *Swissport (UK) Ltd v Aer Lingus Ltd* [2007] EWHC 1089 (Ch); [2009] B.C.C. 113 an insolvent company applied for summary judgment in respect of charges for services performed for the defendant, but the latter contended that it had a possible cross-claim which might be set off against that debt under r.4.90 and that in such circumstances summary judgment was inappropriate and leave to defend should always be given, even where the debt was undisputed. The court held that this was not the case and gave summary judgment.

For the exclusion of set-off in respect of post-insolvency VAT credits, see Value Added Tax Act 1994 s.81(4)–(5).

On the application of r.4.90 in the context of payment and securities settlement systems, see the Finality Regulations reg.15.

Under the original administration regime, there is no provision corresponding to r.4.90, and the principle of insolvency set-off is not applicable: *Isovel Contracts Ltd v ABB Building Technologies Ltd* [2002] 1 B.C.L.C. 390.

Note that r.4.90 (like IR 1986 generally) does not apply to bodies other than companies (e.g. building societies), and it applies only in England and Wales. In Scotland set-off is determined by the rules of the common law. (See Lord Hope in *Secretary of State for Trade and Industry v Frid* (above), at [31]).

4.91   Debt in foreign currency

4.91(1)   [Conversion into sterling] For the purpose of proving a debt incurred or payable in a currency other than sterling, the amount of the debt shall be converted into sterling at the official exchange rate prevailing on the date when the company went into liquidation or, if the liquidation was immediately preceded by an administration, on the date that the company entered administration.

4.91(2)   ["The official exchange rate"] "The official exchange rate" is the middle exchange rate on the London Foreign Exchange Market at the close of business, as published for the date in question. In the absence of any such published rate, it is such rate as the court determines.

GENERAL NOTE

This confirms the ruling in *Re Lines Bros Ltd* [1983] Ch. 1 in which comments made (obiter) in the earlier decision of the House of Lords in *Miliangos v George Frank (Textiles) Ltd* [1976] A.C. 443 were not followed. For the meaning of "went into liquidation", see s.247(2). Note that the rule refers to the *date*, rather than the *time*. (On this point, see the note to s.86.)

Rule 4.91(1) was amended by the Insolvency (Amendment) Rules 2005 (SI 2005/527) r.24, as from April 1, 2005, to deal with the case where a liquidation is immediately preceded by an administration. Similar modifications were made to rr.4.92(1), 4.93(1) and 4.94 by rr.25–27 of the 2005 Rules.

4.92   Payments of a periodical nature

4.92(1)   [Rent etc.] In the case of rent and other payments of a periodical nature, the creditor may prove for any amounts due and unpaid up to the date when the company went into liquidation or, if the liquidation was immediately preceded by an administration, up to the date that the company entered administration.

4.92(2)   [If accruing from day to day] Where at that date any payment was accruing due, the creditor may prove for so much as would have fallen due at that date, if accruing from day to day.

4.93   Interest

4.93(A1)   ["The relevant date"] In this Rule, **"the relevant date"** means the date on which the company went into liquidation or, if the liquidation was immediately preceded by an administration, the date on which the company entered administration.

4.93(1)   [Where debt bears interest] Where a debt proved in the liquidation bears interest, that interest is provable as part of the debt except in so far as it is payable in respect of any period after the company went into liquidation or, if the liquidation was immediately preceded by an administration, any period after the relevant date.

4.93(2)   [Where claim may include interest] In the following circumstances the creditor's claim may include interest on the debt for periods before the relevant date, although not previously reserved or agreed.

4.93(3)   [Debt due by written instrument] If the debt is due by virtue of a written instrument, and payable at a certain time, interest may be claimed for the period from that time to the relevant date.

4.93(4)   [Debt due otherwise] If the debt is due otherwise, interest may only be claimed if, before the relevant date, a demand for payment of the debt was made in writing by or on behalf of the creditor, and notice given that interest would be payable from the date of the demand to the date of payment.

4.93(5)   [Claiming r.4.93(4) interest] Interest under paragraph (4) may only be claimed for the period from the date of the demand to the relevant date and for all the purposes of the Act and the Rules shall be chargeable at a rate not exceeding that mentioned in paragraph (6).

4.93(6)   [Rate of interest under r.4.93(3) and (4)] The rate of interest to be claimed under paragraphs (3) and (4) is the rate specified in section 17 of the Judgments Act 1838 on the relevant date.

GENERAL NOTE

Rule 4.93(A1) inserted and r.4.93(1)–(6) amended by I(A)R 2010 r.2 and Sch. para.195 as from April 6, 2010.
   See the notes to IA 1986 s.189.

4.94   Debt payable at future time

4.94   A creditor may prove for a debt of which payment was not yet due on the date when the company went into liquidation or, if the liquidation was immediately preceded by an administration, on the date that the company entered administration, but subject to Rule 11.13 in Part 11 of the Rules (adjustment of dividend where payment made before time).

CHAPTER 10

SECURED CREDITORS

4.95   Value of security

4.95(1)   [Altering value] A secured creditor may, with the agreement of the liquidator or the permission of the court, at any time alter the value which he has, in his proof of debt, put upon his security.

4.95(2)   [Limitation on re-valuation] However, if a secured creditor–

   (a)   being the petitioner, has in the petition put a value on his security, or

   (b)   has voted in respect of the unsecured balance of his debt,

he may re-value his security only with permission of the court. (NO CVL APPLICATION)

(See General Note after r.4.99.)

4.96   Surrender for non-disclosure

4.96(1)   [Omission to disclose security] If a secured creditor omits to disclose his security in his proof of debt, he shall surrender his security for the general benefit of creditors, unless the court, on application by him, relieves him from the effect of this Rule on the ground that the omission was inadvertent or the result of honest mistake.

4.96(2)   [Relief from effect of r.4.96(1)] If the court grants that relief, it may require or allow the creditor's proof of debt to be amended, on such terms as may be just.

4.96(3)   [Rights protected under art.5] Nothing in this Rule or the following two Rules may affect the rights in rem of creditors or third parties protected under Article 5 of the EC Regulation (third parties' rights in rem).

(See General Note after r.4.99.)

4.97   Redemption by liquidator

4.97(1)   [Notice of proposed redemption] The liquidator may at any time give notice to a creditor whose debt is secured that he proposes, at the expiration of 28 days from the date of the notice, to redeem the security at the value put upon it in the creditor's proof.

4.97(2)   [Time for revaluation etc.] The creditor then has 21 days (or such longer period as the liquidator may allow) in which, if he so wishes, to exercise his right to revalue his security (with the permission of the court, where Rule 4.95(2) applies).

   If the creditor re-values his security, the liquidator may only redeem at the new value.

4.97(3)   [If liquidator redeems] If the liquidator redeems the security, the cost of transferring it is payable as an expense of the liquidation.

4.97(4)   [Notice to liquidator to elect etc.] A secured creditor may at any time, by a notice in writing, call on the liquidator to elect whether he will or will not exercise his power to redeem the security at the value then placed on it; and the liquidator then has 3 months in which to exercise the power or determine not to exercise it.

(See General Note after r.4.99.)

4.98   Test of security's value

4.98(1)   [Offer for sale] Subject as follows, the liquidator, if he is dissatisfied with the value which a secured creditor puts on his security (whether in his proof or by way of re-valuation under Rule 4.97), may require any property comprised in the security to be offered for sale.

4.98(2)   [Terms of sale] The terms of sale shall be such as may be agreed, or as the court may direct; and if the sale is by auction, the liquidator on behalf of the company, and the creditor on his own behalf, may appear and bid.

4.98(3)   [Non-application of r.4.98] This Rule does not apply if the security has been revalued and the revaluation has been approved by the court.

(See General Note after r.4.99.)

4.99   Realisation of security by creditor

4.99   If a creditor who has valued his security subsequently realises it (whether or not at the instance of the liquidator)–

   (a)   the net amount realised shall be substituted for the value previously put by the creditor on the security, and

   (b)   that amount shall be treated in all respects as an amended valuation made by him.

GENERAL NOTE TO RR.4.95–4.99

These rules deal with the valuation of his security by a secured creditor, the liquidator's right to redeem the security, the consequences of the realisation of a security, and various related matters. A landlord who had submitted a proof without mentioning his right of distress was ruled to be a secured creditor who had abandoned his security under r.4.96(1) in *LCP Retail Ltd v Segal* [2006] EWHC 2087 (Ch); [2007] B.C.C. 584.

   Rule 4.96(3) was added by the Insolvency (Amendment) Rules 2002 (SI 2002/1307, effective May 31, 2002). The rights in rem referred to are those in respect of assets belonging to the debtor company which are situated within the territory of another Member State at the time of the opening of proceedings. See further the note to the EC Regulation art.5.

Rule 4.97 amended and r.4.98(3) inserted by I(A)R 2010 r.2 and Sch. paras 197, 198 as from April 6, 2010. The period of time within which the liquidator must make his election under r.4.97(4) has been reduced (for liquidations commencing after that date) from six months to three.

CHAPTER 11

THE LIQUIDATOR

Section A: Appointment and associated formalities

4.100   Appointment by creditors or contributories

(NO CVL APPLICATION)

4.100(1)   [Application of Rule] This Rule applies where a person is appointed as liquidator either by a meeting of creditors or by a meeting of contributories.

4.100(2)   [Certification of appointment] The chairman of the meeting shall certify the appointment, but not unless and until the person appointed has provided him with a written statement to the effect that he is an insolvency practitioner, duly qualified under the Act to be the liquidator, and that he consents so to act.

[FORM 4.27]
[FORM 4.28]

4.100(3)   [Date when appointment effective] The liquidator's appointment is effective from the date on which the appointment is certified, that date to be endorsed on the certificate.

4.100(4)   [Certificate to official receiver] The chairman of the meeting (if not himself the official receiver) shall send the certificate to the official receiver.

4.100(5)   [Official receiver to send certificate to liquidator] The official receiver shall in any case send the certificate to the liquidator.

(See General Note after r.4.106A.)

4.101-CVL   Appointment by creditors or by the company

4.101-CVL(1)   [Application of Rule] This Rule applies where a person is appointed as liquidator either by a meeting of creditors or by a meeting of the company.

4.101-CVL(2)   [Certification and effective date of appointment] Subject as follows, the chairman of the meeting shall certify the appointment, but not unless and until the person appointed has provided him with a written statement to the effect that he is an insolvency practitioner, duly qualified under the Act to be the liquidator, and that he consents so to act; the liquidator's appointment takes effect upon the passing of the resolution for that appointment.

[FORM 4.27]
[FORM 4.28]

4.101-CVL(3)   [Certificate to liquidator] The chairman shall send the certificate as soon as reasonably practicable to the liquidator, who shall keep it as part of the records of the liquidation.

4.101-CVL(4)   [Where no need to comply with r.4.101(2), (3)] Paragraphs (2) and (3) need not be complied with in the case of a liquidator appointed by a company meeting and replaced by another liquidator appointed on the same day by a creditors' meeting.

(See General Note after r.4.106A.)

4.101A-CVL   Power to fill vacancy in office of liquidator

4.101A-CVL   Where a vacancy in the office of liquidator occurs in the manner mentioned in section 104 a meeting of creditors to fill the vacancy may be convened by any creditor or, if there were more liquidators than one, by the continuing liquidators.

(See General Note after r.4.106A.)

4.101B   Official receiver not to be appointed liquidator

4.101B   The official receiver may not be appointed as liquidator by any meeting of creditors, contributories or the company.

(See General Note after r.4.106A.)

4.102   Appointment by the court

(NO CVL APPLICATION)

4.102(1)   [Application of Rule] This Rule applies where the liquidator is appointed by the court under section 139(4) (different persons nominated by creditors and contributories) or section 140 (liquidation following administration or voluntary arrangement).

[FORM 4.29]
[FORM 4.30]

4.102(2)   [Issue of court order] The court's order shall not issue unless and until the person appointed has filed in court a statement to the effect that he is an insolvency practitioner, duly qualified under the Act to be the liquidator, and that he consents so to act.

4.102(3)   [Copy of orders to official receiver etc.] Thereafter, the court shall send 2 copies of the order to the official receiver. One of the copies shall be sealed, and this shall be sent to the person appointed as liquidator.

4.102(4)   [Commencement of appointment] The liquidator's appointment takes effect from the date of the order.

4.102(4A)   [Omitted.]

4.102(5)   [Notice to creditors etc.] Within 28 days from appointment, the liquidator shall–

- (a)   give notice of it to all creditors and contributories of the company of whom the liquidator is aware; or
- (b)   advertise it in accordance with any directions given by the court.

4.102(6)   [Contents of notice] In his notice under this Rule the liquidator shall–

- (a)   state whether he proposes to summon meetings of creditors and contributories for the purpose of establishing a liquidation committee, or proposes to summon only a meeting of creditors for that purpose, and
- (b)   if he does not propose to summon any such meeting, set out the powers of the creditors under the Act to require him to summon one.

(See General Note after r.4.106A.)

4.103-CVL   Appointment by the court

4.103-CVL(1)   [Application of Rule] This Rule applies where the liquidator is appointed by the court under section 100(3) or 108.

[FORM 4.29]
[FORM 4.30]

4.103-CVL(2)   [Issue of court order] The court's order shall not issue unless and until the person appointed has filed in court a statement to the effect that he is an insolvency practitioner, duly qualified under the Act to be the liquidator, and that he consents so to act.

4.103-CVL(3)   [Sealed copy to liquidator] Thereafter, the court shall send a sealed copy of the order to the liquidator, whose appointment takes effect from the date of the order.

4.103-CVL(4)   [Notice or advertisement of appointment] Within 28 days from appointment, the liquidator shall–

(a)   give notice of it to all creditors of the company of whom the liquidator is aware; or

(b)   advertise it in accordance with any directions given by the court.

(See General Note after r.4.106A.)

4.104   Appointment by Secretary of State

(NO CVL APPLICATION)

4.104(1)   [Application of Rule] This Rule applies where the official receiver applies to the Secretary of State to appoint a liquidator in place of himself, or refers to the Secretary of State the need for an appointment.

4.104(2)   [Copy of certificates to official receiver etc.] If the Secretary of State makes an appointment, he shall send a copy of the certificate of appointment to the official receiver, who shall transmit it to the person appointed.

4.104(3)   [Content of certificate] The certificate shall specify the date from which the liquidator's appointment is to be effective.

(See General Note after r.4.106A.)

4.105   Authentication of liquidator's appointment

4.105   A copy of the certificate of the liquidator's appointment or (as the case may be) a sealed copy of the court's order or a copy of the notice registered in accordance with paragraph 83(3) of Schedule B1 to the Act, may in any proceedings be adduced as proof that the person appointed is duly authorised to exercise the powers and perform the duties of liquidator in the company's winding up.

(See General Note after r.4.106A.)

4.106   Appointment to be advertised and registered [Deleted.]

4.106A   Appointment to be gazetted and registered

4.106A(1)   [Notice in voluntary winding up] A liquidator appointed in a voluntary winding up in addition to giving notice of the appointment in accordance with section 109(1) may advertise the notice in such other manner as the liquidator thinks fit.

4.106A(2)   [Notice on compulsory winding up] A liquidator appointed in a winding up by the court–

(a)   as soon as reasonably practicable must have gazetted a notice of the appointment; and

(b)   may advertise the notice in such other manner as the liquidator thinks fit.

4.106A(3)   [Additional contents of notice] In addition to the standard contents, the notice must state–

(a)   that a liquidator has been appointed; and

(b)   the date of the appointment.

4.106A(4)   **[Notification to registrar in compulsory winding up]** As soon as reasonably practicable a liquidator appointed in a winding up by the court must notify the appointment to the registrar of companies.

4.106A(5)   **[First instance expense of notice]** At first instance the liquidator must bear the expense of giving notice under this Rule.

4.106A(6)   **[Reimbursement as liquidation expense]** The liquidator is entitled to be reimbursed for such expenditure as an expense of the liquidation.

GENERAL NOTE TO RR.4.100–4.106A

These rules are concerned with the formalities relating to the appointment of a liquidator by the creditors or contributories (rr.4.100, 4.101-CVL), by the court (rr.4.102, 4.103-CVL), and by the Secretary of State (r.4.104), and the certification, registration and notification of the appointment.

Rule 4.105 was amended by the insertion of the reference to the para.83(3) notice by the Insolvency (Amendment) Rules 2003 (SI 2003/1730, effective September 15, 2003) Sch.1 para.20. Rule 4.102(4A) inserted, r.4.102(5) substituted and r.4.102(6) amended by I(A)R 2009 (SI 2009/642) r.26; r.4.103(4) and former r.4.106(1) substituted respectively by rr.27, 28 ibid., all as from April 6, 2009. The liquidator was formerly required to give notice of his appointment in an appropriate newspaper as well as in the *Gazette*. It is now for him to decide in his discretion whether additional advertisement is needed.

Rules 4.100, 4.102, 4.104 amended, r.4.106 deleted and rr.4.101B, 106A inserted by I(A)R 2010 r.2 and Sch. paras 199–203 as from April 6, 2010.

The notice of the liquidator's appointment must include the standard contents and also the details set out in r.4.106A(3). On the standard contents for gazetted notices, see rr.12A.31–12A.33. On the standard contents for notices other than gazetted notices, see rr.12A.36–12A.39.

4.107   Hand-over of assets to liquidator

(NO CVL APPLICATION)

4.107(1)   **[Application of Rule]** This Rule applies only where the liquidator is appointed in succession to the official receiver acting as liquidator.

4.107(2)   **[On liquidator's appointment]** When the liquidator's appointment takes effect, the official receiver shall as soon as reasonably practicable do all that is required for putting him into possession of the assets.

4.107(3)   **[Discharge of balance due to official receiver]** On taking possession of the assets, the liquidator shall discharge any balance due to the official receiver on account of–

(a)   expenses properly incurred by him and payable under the Act or the Rules, and

(b)   any advances made by him in respect of the assets, together with interest on such advances at the rate specified in section 17 of the Judgments Act 1838 at the date of the winding-up order.

4.107(4)   **[Undertaking to discharge]** Alternatively, the liquidator may (before taking office) give to the official receiver a written undertaking to discharge any such balance out of the first realisation of assets.

4.107(5)   **[Official receiver's charge]** The official receiver has a charge on the assets in respect of any sums due to him under paragraph (3). But, where the liquidator has realised assets with a view to making those payments, the official receiver's charge does not extend in respect of sums deductible by the liquidator from the proceeds of realisation, as being expenses properly incurred therein.

4.107(6)   **[Discharge of guarantees etc.]** The liquidator shall from time to time out of the realisation of assets discharge all guarantees properly given by the official receiver for the benefit of the estate, and shall pay all the official receiver's expenses.

4.107(7)   **[Official receiver to give liquidator information]** The official receiver shall give to the liquidator all such information relating to the affairs of the company and the course of the winding up as he (the official receiver) considers to be reasonably required for the effective discharge by the liquidator of his duties as such.

4.107(8) [Copy of Ch.7 report] The liquidator shall also be furnished with a copy of any report made by the official receiver under Chapter 7 of this Part of the Rules.

<small>GENERAL NOTE</small>

This rule applies following the appointment of a private liquidator under IA 1986 ss.136 and 139, or s.137.

Section B: Resignation and removal; vacation of office

4.108   Creditors' meeting to receive liquidator's resignation

4.108(1) [Liquidator must call meeting etc.] Before resigning his office, the liquidator must call a meeting of creditors for the purpose of receiving his resignation.

[FORM 4.22]

4.108(1A) [Notice of meeting] The liquidator must give at least 28 days' notice of the meeting.

4.108(1B) [Content of notice] The notice summoning the meeting must—

(a) indicate that the purpose or one of the purposes of the meeting is to receive the liquidator's resignation; and

(b) draw the attention of the creditors with respect to the liquidator's release to Rule 4.121 or, as the case may be, Rule 4.122.

4.108(2) [Copy of notice to official receiver] A copy of the notice shall at the same time also be sent to the official receiver. (NO CVL APPLICATION)

4.108(3) [Notice accompanied by account] The notice to creditors under paragraph (1A) must be accompanied by an account of the liquidator's administration of the winding up including–

(a) where appropriate, a statement that the liquidator has reconciled the account with that held by the Secretary of State in respect of the winding up; and

(b) a progress report for the period–

    (i) commencing with the later of the date of–

        (aa) the appointment of the liquidator; and

        (bb) the day immediately following the end of the period of the last progress report; and

    (ii) ending with the date of the meeting.

4.108(4) [Grounds for proceeding under Rule] Subject as follows, the liquidator may only proceed under this Rule on grounds of ill health or because–

(a) he intends ceasing to be in practice as an insolvency practitioner, or

(b) there is some conflict of interest or change of personal circumstances which precludes or makes impracticable the further discharge by him of the duties of liquidator.

4.108(5) [Where joint liquidators] Where two or more persons are acting as liquidator jointly, any one of them may proceed under this Rule (without prejudice to the continuation in office of the other or others) on the ground that, in his opinion and that of the other or others, it is no longer expedient that there should continue to be the present number of joint liquidators.

4.108(6) [If no quorum] Except where Rule 4.108A applies, if there is no quorum present at the meeting summoned to receive the liquidator's resignation, the meeting is deemed to have been held, a resolution is deemed to have been passed that the liquidator's resignation be accepted and the creditors are deemed not to have resolved against the liquidator having his release.

4.108(7)   [Application of r.4.108(6)] Where paragraph (6) applies any reference in the Rules to a resolution that the liquidator's resignation be accepted is replaced by a reference to the making of a written statement, authenticated by the person who, had there been a quorum present, would have been chairman of the meeting, that no quorum was present and that the liquidator may resign.

(See General Note after r.4.112.)

4.108A   Resignation (application under Rule 4.131)

4.108A(1)   [Application of Rule] This Rule applies where at the date of a meeting summoned for the purpose of receiving the liquidator's resignation, an application made to the court under Rule 4.131 (including any appeal) has not been disposed of.

4.108A(2)   [No release at meeting] At the meeting no resolution may be put regarding the liquidator's release.

4.108A(3)   [Meeting adjourned if resignation accepted] If at the meeting the liquidator's resignation is accepted, the meeting must be adjourned (notwithstanding anything in Rule 4.65 (suspension and adjournment)) to a day not less than 14 days after the day on which the application under Rule 4.131 (including any appeal) has been disposed of.

4.108A(4)   [Notice of adjourned meeting] The liquidator must give at least 14 days' notice of the meeting adjourned in accordance with paragraph (3) to the creditors.

4.108A(5)   [At adjourned meeting] At the meeting adjourned in accordance with paragraph (3)–

(a)   a revised version of the account which accompanied the notice of the meeting must be laid showing any changes required as a result, or arising out of the application under Rule 4.131; and

(b)   a resolution must be put for the release of the liquidator whose resignation has been accepted.

4.108A(6)   [Where no quorum at adjourned meeting] If there is no quorum present at the adjourned meeting, the meeting is deemed to have been held and the creditors are deemed to have resolved that the liquidator be released.

4.108A(7)   [Certificate and revised account where liquidator released] Where the creditors have resolved at the adjourned meeting that the liquidator be released (or are deemed to have so resolved by virtue of paragraph (5)), the chairman of the meeting (or the person who, had there been a quorum present would have been chairman of the meeting) must send as soon as reasonably practicable a certificate to that effect with a copy of the revised account to–

(a)   the official receiver; and (NO CVL APPLICATION)

(b)   the registrar of companies.

4.108A(8)   [Copy of certificate filed in court] The official receiver must file a copy of the certificate in court.

4.108A(9)   [Where resignation not accepted] If at the meeting the liquidator's resignation is not accepted, the liquidator must not summon any further meeting under Rule 4.108 until the application under Rule 4.131 (including any appeal) has been disposed of.

4.108A(10)   [Where permission to resign granted by court under r.4.111] Paragraph (7) is subject to the powers of the court on an application being made to it by the liquidator under Rule 4.111 (permission to resign granted by the court).

4.108A(11)   [Application of r.4.108 to further meeting] Rule 4.108 applies to any such further meeting with the modification that the progress report required to accompany the notice of the meeting must show any changes from the report which accompanied the notice of the earlier meeting called to receive the liquidator's resignation, and in particular any changes required as a result of the application under Rule 4.131 and any further remuneration charged or expenses incurred.

4.108A(12) [Creditors' rights under rr.4.49E, 4.131] The creditors' rights under Rules 4.49E and 4.131 do not apply in respect of any matter included in that report which—

(a) was included in the report which accompanied the notice of the earlier meeting called to receive the liquidator's resignation; or

(b) was the subject of the order of the court on the application made to it by the liquidator under Rule 4.131.

(See General Note after r.4.112.)

4.109   Action following acceptance of resignation

(NO CVL APPLICATION)

4.109(1) [Application of Rule] This Rule applies where a meeting is summoned to receive the liquidator's resignation.

4.109(2) [Copy of resolutions to official receiver etc.] If the chairman of the meeting is other than the official receiver, and there is passed at the meeting any of the following resolutions–

(a) that the liquidator's resignation be accepted,

(b) that a new liquidator be appointed,

(c) that the resigning liquidator be not given his release,

the chairman shall, within 3 business days of the date of the resolution, send to the official receiver a copy of the resolution.

If it has been resolved to accept the liquidator's resignation, the chairman shall send to the official receiver a certificate to that effect.

4.109(3) [If creditors resolve to appoint new liquidator] If the creditors have resolved to appoint a new liquidator, the certificate of his appointment shall also be sent to the official receiver within that time; and Rule 4.100 shall be complied with in respect of it.

4.109(4) [If liquidator's resignation accepted] If the liquidator's resignation is accepted, the notice of it required by section 172(6) shall be given by him as soon as reasonably practicable after the resolution has been passed; and he shall send a copy of the notice to the official receiver.

The notice shall be accompanied by a copy of the account sent to creditors under Rule 4.108(3).

[FORM 4.32]

4.109(5) [Copy notice] The official receiver shall file a copy of the notice in court.

4.109(6) [Effective date of resignation] The liquidator's resignation is effective as from the date on which the official receiver files the copy notice in court, that date to be endorsed on the copy notice.

(See General Note after r.4.112.)

4.110-CVL   Action following acceptance of resignation

4.110-CVL(1) [Application of Rule] This Rule applies where a meeting is summoned to receive the liquidator's resignation.

4.110-CVL(2) [Section 171(5) notice] If his resignation is accepted, the notice of it required by section 171(5) shall be given by him as soon as reasonably practicable after the resolution has been passed.

4.110-CVL(3)   [Certificate of new liquidator's appointment] Where a new liquidator is appointed in place of the one who has resigned, the certificate of his appointment shall be delivered as soon as reasonably practicable by the chairman of the meeting to the new liquidator.

(See General Note after r.4.112.)

4.111   Permission to resign granted by the court

4.111(1)   [If liquidator's resignation not accepted] If at a creditors' meeting summoned to accept the liquidator's resignation it is resolved that it be not accepted, the court may, on the liquidator's application, make an order giving him permission to resign.

[FORM 4.34]

4.111(2)   [Extent of order under r.4.111(1)] The court's order may include such provision as it thinks fit with respect to matters arising in connection with the resignation, and shall determine the date from which the liquidator's release is effective.

4.111(3)   [Sealed copies of order] The court shall send two sealed copies of the order to the liquidator, who shall send one of the copies as soon as reasonably practicable to the official receiver. (NO CVL APPLICATION)

4.111(4)   [Sealed copies] The court shall send two sealed copies of the order to the liquidator, who shall as soon as reasonably practicable send one of them to the registrar of companies.

4.111(5)   [Copy notice to court and official receiver] On sending notice of his resignation to the court, the liquidator shall send a copy of it to the official receiver.

(NO CVL APPLICATION)

[FORM 4.36]

4.112   Advertisement of resignation

4.112   Where a new liquidator is appointed in place of one who has resigned, the former shall, in giving notice of his appointment, state that his predecessor has resigned and (if it be the case) that he has been given his release.

GENERAL NOTE TO RR.4.108–4.112

Rules 4.108–4.112 amended and rr.4.108(1A), (1B), 4.108A inserted by I(A)R 2010 r.2 and Sch. paras 204–207 as from April 6, 2010.

The circumstances in which a liquidator may resign are set out in r.108(4), (5). These rules detail the procedure to be followed, and the date when the resignation takes effect. However, where an insolvency practitioner holds multiple offices and application is made to the court for a "block transfer" order, to remove him from all the offices and appoint a suitable replacement, the court has jurisdiction to bypass the procedures laid down in these rules (and the corresponding rules for the removal of other office-holders) where it is satisfied that no useful purpose will be served by holding the meetings: see *Re Alt Landscapes Ltd* [1999] B.P.I.R. 459; *Re Equity Nominees Ltd* [2000] B.C.C. 84, and the note to s.172(2). See also the discussion at IR 1986 r.6.126, and, on procedure, App.IV to this *Guide*, para.1.1(6).

The question of the release of the liquidator is covered by rr.4.121, 4.122-CVL.

New r.4.108A deals with the position where a meeting has been summoned to receive the liquidator's resignation for a date when an application under r.131 to review the liquidator's remuneration has not been heard by the court and disposed of. The meeting must be adjourned until this has been completed and the amended procedure set out in r.4.108A(5) followed.

4.113   Meeting of creditors to remove liquidator

(NO CVL APPLICATION)

4.113(1)   [Notice] Where a meeting of creditors is summoned for the purpose of removing the liquidator, the notice summoning it shall indicate that this is the purpose, or one of the purposes, of the meeting; and the notice shall draw the attention of creditors to section 174(4) with respect to the liquidator's release.

[FORM 4.22]

4.113(2)   **[Copy notice to official receiver]** A copy of the notice shall at the same time also be sent to the official receiver.

4.113(3)   **[Chairman; if liquidator chairman etc.]** At the meeting, a person other than the liquidator or his nominee may be elected to act as chairman; but if the liquidator or his nominee is chairman and a resolution has been proposed for the liquidator's removal, the chairman shall not adjourn the meeting without the consent of at least one-half (in value) of the creditors present (in person or by proxy) and entitled to vote.

4.113(4)   **[Copy resolutions to official receiver]** Where the chairman of the meeting is other than the official receiver, and there is passed at the meeting any of the following resolutions–

  (a)   that the liquidator be removed,

  (b)   that a new liquidator be appointed,

  (c)   that the removed liquidator be not given his release,

the chairman shall, within 3 business days, send to the official receiver a copy of the resolution.

    If it has been resolved to remove the liquidator, the chairman shall send to the official receiver a certificate to that effect.

[FORM 4.37]

4.113(5)   **[If creditors resolve to appoint new liquidator]** If the creditors have resolved to appoint a new liquidator, the certificate of his appointment shall also be sent to the official receiver within that time; and Rule 4.100 above shall be complied with in respect of it.

(See General Note after r.4.120-CVL.)

4.114-CVL   Meeting of creditors to remove liquidator

4.114-CVL(1)   **[Section 171(2)(b) meeting requested]** A meeting held under section 171(2)(b) for the removal of the liquidator shall be summoned by him if requested by 25 per cent in value of the company's creditors, excluding those who are connected with it.

4.114-CVL(2)   **[Notice]** The notice summoning the meeting shall indicate that the removal of the liquidator is the purpose, or one of the purposes, of the meeting; and the notice shall draw the attention of creditors to section 173(2) with respect to the liquidator's release.

[FORM 4.22]

4.114-CVL(3)   **[Chairman; if liquidator chairman etc.]** At the meeting, a person other than the liquidator or his nominee may be elected to act as chairman, but if the liquidator or his nominee is chairman and a resolution has been proposed for the liquidator's removal, the chairman shall not adjourn the meeting without the consent of at least one-half (in value) of the creditors present (in person or by proxy) and entitled to vote.

(See General Note after r.4.120-CVL.)

4.115   Court's power to regulate meetings under Rules 4.113, 4.114–CVL

4.115   Where a meeting under Rule 4.113 or 4.114–CVL is to be held, or is proposed to be summoned, the court may, on the application of any creditor, give directions as to the mode of summoning it, the sending out and return of forms of proxy, the conduct of the meeting, and any other matter which appears to the court to require regulation or control under this Rule.

(See General Note after r.4.120-CVL.)

4.116   Procedure on removal

(NO CVL APPLICATION)

4.116(1)   [Certificate of removal to be filed] Where the creditors have resolved that the liquidator be removed, the official receiver shall file in court the certificate of removal.

4.116(2)   [Effective date of removal resolution] The resolution is effective as from the date on which the official receiver files the certificate of removal in court, and that date shall be endorsed on the certificate.

4.116(3)   [Official receiver to send endorsed copy certificate] The official receiver must send a copy of the certificate, so endorsed, as soon as reasonably practicable to–

    (a)   the removed liquidator;

    (b)   the new liquidator (if appointed); and

    (c)   the registrar of companies.

4.116(4)   [Reconciliation of accounts] The official receiver shall not file the certificate in court unless and until the Secretary of State has certified to him that the removed liquidator has reconciled his account with that held by the Secretary of State in respect of the winding up.

(See General Note after r.4.120-CVL.)

4.117-CVL   Procedure on removal

4.117-CVL   Where the creditors have resolved that the liquidator be removed, the chairman of the creditors' meeting shall as soon as reasonably practicable–

    (a)   if at the meeting another liquidator was not appointed, send the certificate of the liquidator's removal to the registrar of companies, and

    (b)   otherwise, deliver the certificate to the new liquidator, who shall send it to the registrar.

(See General Note after r.4.120-CVL.)

4.118   Advertisement of removal

4.118   Where a new liquidator is appointed in place of one removed, the former shall, in giving notice of his appointment, state that his predecessor has been removed and (if it be the case) that he has been given his release.

(See General Note after r.4.120-CVL.)

4.119   Removal of liquidator by the court

(NO CVL APPLICATION)

4.119(1)   [Application of Rule] This Rule applies where application is made to the court for the removal of the liquidator, or for an order directing the liquidator to summon a meeting of creditors for the purpose of removing him.

[FORM 4.39]

4.119(2)   [Court may dismiss application etc.] The court may, if it thinks that no sufficient cause is shown for the application, dismiss it; but it shall not do so unless the applicant has had an opportunity to attend the court for a hearing, of which he has been given at least 5 business days' notice but which is without notice to any other party.

    If the application is not dismissed under this paragraph, the court shall fix a venue for it to be heard.

4.119(3)   **[Deposit or security for costs]** The court may require the applicant to make a deposit or give security for the costs to be incurred by the liquidator on the application.

4.119(4)   **[Notice etc.]** The applicant shall, at least 14 days before the hearing, send to the liquidator and the official receiver a notice stating the venue and accompanied by a copy of the application, and of any evidence which he intends to adduce in support of it.

4.119(5)   **[Costs]** Subject to any contrary order of the court, the costs of the application are not payable as an expense of the liquidation.

4.119(6)   **[Where court removes liquidator]** Where the court removes the liquidator–

   (a)   it shall send copies of the order of removal to him and to the official receiver;

   (b)   the order may include such provision as the court thinks fit with respect to matters arising in connection with the removal; and

   (c)   if the court appoints a new liquidator, Rule 4.102 applies.

(See General Note after r.4.120-CVL.)

4.120-CVL   Removal of liquidator by the court

4.120-CVL(1)   **[Application of Rule]** This Rule applies where application is made to the court for the removal of the liquidator, or for an order directing the liquidator to summon a creditors' meeting for the purpose of removing him.

[FORM 4.39]

4.120-CVL(2)   **[Court may dismiss application etc.]** The court may, if it thinks that no sufficient cause is shown for the application, dismiss it; but it shall not do so unless the applicant has had an opportunity to attend the court for a hearing, of which he has been given at least 5 business days' notice but which is without notice to any other party.

    If the application is not dismissed under this paragraph, the court shall fix a venue for it to be heard.

4.120-CVL(3)   **[Deposit or security for costs]** The court may require the applicant to make a deposit or give security for the costs to be incurred by the liquidator on the application.

4.120-CVL(4)   **[Notice etc.]** The applicant shall, at least 14 days before the hearing, send to the liquidator a notice stating the venue and accompanied by a copy of the application, and of any evidence which he intends to adduce in support of it.

4.120-CVL(5)   **[Costs]** Subject to any contrary order of the court, the costs of the application are not payable as an expense of the liquidation.

4.120-CVL(6)   **[Where court removes liquidator]** Where the court removes the liquidator–

   (a)   it shall send 2 copies of the order of removal to him, one to be sent by him as soon as reasonably practicable to the registrar of companies, with notice of his ceasing to act;

   (b)   the order may include such provision as the court thinks fit with respect to matters arising in connection with the removal; and

   (c)   if the court appoints a new liquidator, Rule 4.103–CVL applies.

GENERAL NOTE TO RR.4.113–4.120-CVL

Rules 4.119, 4.120 amended and r.4.116(3) substituted by I(A)R 2010 r.2 and Sch. paras 209–211 as from April 6, 2010.

    The removal of a liquidator is dealt with in IA 1986 ss.171, 172, which these rules supplement. The exercise of discretion under r.4.120(3) was discussed in *Re Buildlead Ltd* [2003] EWHC 1981 (Ch); [2003] 4 All E.R. 864; [2005] B.C.C. 133; and *Re Buildlead Ltd (No.2)* [2004] EWHC 2443 (Ch); [2005] B.C.C. 138. On the liquidator's release, see rr.4.121, 4.122-CVL. Costs on an indemnity basis may be awarded against a liquidator who unreasonably resists an application for his removal: *Shepheard v Lamey* [2001] B.P.I.R. 939.

On the "block" replacement of office-holders, see the note to s.172(1),(2). See also the note to r.4.112.

4.121   Release of resigning or removed liquidator

(NO CVL APPLICATION)

4.121(1)   [Where liquidator's resignation accepted] Subject to paragraph (1A), where the liquidator's resignation is accepted by a meeting of creditors which has not resolved against his release, he has his release from when his resignation is effective under Rule 4.109.

4.121(1A)   [Where resignation accepted under r.4.108A] Where the liquidator's resignation is accepted under Rule 4.108A, the liquidator's release is effective as from the date on which the official receiver files the copy of the certificate under paragraph (8) of that Rule in court, that date to be endorsed on the copy certificate.

4.121(2)   [Where liquidator removed by meeting] Where the liquidator is removed by a meeting of creditors which has not resolved against his release, the fact of his release shall be stated in the certificate of removal.

4.121(3)   [Application to Secretary of State] Where–

   (a)   the liquidator resigns, and the creditors' meeting called to receive his resignation has resolved against his release, or

   (b)   he is removed by a creditors' meeting which has so resolved, or is removed by the court,

he must apply to the Secretary of State for his release.

[FORM 4.41]

4.121(4)   [Certificate of release] When the Secretary of State gives the release, he shall certify it accordingly, and send the certificate to the official receiver, to be filed in court.

4.121(5)   [Copy of certificate] A copy of the certificate shall be sent by the Secretary of State to the former liquidator, whose release is effective from the date of the certificate.

(See General Note after r.4.122-CVL.)

4.122-CVL   Release of resigning or removed liquidator

4.122-CVL(1)   [Where liquidator's resignation accepted] Subject to paragraph (1A), where the liquidator's resignation is accepted by a meeting of creditors which has not resolved against his release, he has his release from when he gives notice of his resignation to the registrar of companies.

4.122-CVL(1A)   [Where resignation accepted under r.4.108A] Where the liquidator's resignation is accepted under Rule 4.108A, the liquidator's release is effective as from the date of the certificate.

4.122-CVL(2)   [Where liquidator removed by meeting] Where the liquidator is removed by a creditors' meeting which has not resolved against his release, the fact of his release shall be stated in the certificate of removal.

4.122-CVL(3)   [Application to Secretary of State] Where–

   (a)   the liquidator resigns, and the creditors' meeting called to receive his resignation has resolved against his release, or

   (b)   he is removed by a creditors' meeting which has so resolved, or is removed by the court,

he must apply to the Secretary of State for his release.

[FORM 4.41]

4.122-CVL(4) [Certificate of release] When the Secretary of State gives the release, he shall certify it accordingly, and send the certificate to the registrar of companies.

4.122-CVL(5) [Copy of certificate] A copy of the certificate shall be sent by the Secretary of State to the former liquidator, whose release is effective from the date of the certificate.

General Note to rr.4.121, 4.122-CVL

Rules 4.121, 4.122 amended and rr.4.121(1A), 4.122(1A) inserted by I(A)R 2010 r.2 and Sch. paras 212–213 as from April 6, 2010.

These rules deal with the liquidator's release following his resignation or removal. On the question of release following completion of the administration of the winding up, see rr.4.124 et seq.

4.123 Removal of liquidator by Secretary of State

(NO CVL APPLICATION)

4.123(1) [Notice to liquidator etc.] If the Secretary of State decides to remove the liquidator, he shall before doing so notify the liquidator and the official receiver of his decision and the grounds of it, and specify a period within which the liquidator may make representations against implementation of the decision.

4.123(2) [On removal] If the Secretary of State directs the removal of the liquidator, he shall as soon as reasonably practicable–

(a) file notice of his decision in court, and

(b) send notice to the liquidator and the official receiver.

4.123(3) [If liquidator removed] If the liquidator is removed by direction of the Secretary of State–

(a) Rule 4.121 applies as regards the liquidator obtaining his release, as if he had been removed by the court, and

(b) the court may make any such order in his case as it would have power to make if he had been so removed.

General Note

The removal of a liquidator by the Secretary of State is provided for by IA 1986 s.172(4).

Section C: Release on completion of administration

4.124 Release of official receiver

(NO CVL APPLICATION)

4.124(1) [Notice of intention] The official receiver shall, before giving notice to the Secretary of State under section 174(3) (that the winding up is for practical purposes complete), send out notice of his intention to do so to all creditors of which he is aware.

4.124(2) [Accompanying summary of receipts and payments] The notice shall in each case be accompanied by a summary of the official receiver's receipts and payments as liquidator.

4.124(2A) [Summary to include amount paid under prescribed part] The summary of receipts and payments referred to in paragraph (2) shall also include a statement as to the amount paid to unsecured creditors by virtue of the application of section 176A (prescribed part).

4.124(3) [Notice to court of date of release] The Secretary of State, when he has determined the date from which the official receiver is to have his release, shall give notice to the court that he has done so. The notice shall be accompanied by the summary referred to in paragraph (2).

(See General Note after r.4.126-CVL.)

4.125   Final meeting

(NO CVL APPLICATION)

4.125(1)   [Notice to creditors etc.] Where the liquidator is other than the official receiver, he shall give at least 28 days' notice of the final meeting of creditors to be held under section 146. The notice shall be sent to all creditors of which he is aware.

[FORM 4.22]

4.125(1A)   [No final meeting without compliance with r.4.49D] The final meeting must not be held unless Rule 4.49D has been complied with; and if for that reason the meeting is not held–

- (a)   the liquidator must give notice of that fact as soon as reasonably practicable to all to whom notice of the meeting was given, and

- (b)   fresh notice of the meeting complying with this Rule must be given when Rule 4.49D has been complied with.

4.125(1B)   [Liquidator to gazette and advertise notice of meeting] The liquidator–

- (a)   at least 1 month before the meeting is held must have gazetted a notice of the meeting; and

- (b)   may advertise the notice in such other manner as the liquidator thinks fit.

4.125(1C)   [Additional contents of notice under r.4.125(1B)] In addition to the standard contents, the notice under paragraph (1B) must state–

- (a)   who summoned the meeting;

- (b)   if the meeting was summoned at the request of a creditor, the fact that it was so summoned and the section of the Act under which it was requested;

- (c)   the purpose for which the meeting is summoned;

- (d)   the venue fixed for the meeting; and

- (e)   the time and date by which, and place at which, creditors must lodge proxies and hitherto unlodged proofs in order to be entitled to vote at the meeting.

4.125(2)   [Liquidator's report] The liquidator's report laid before the meeting under that section shall contain an account of the liquidator's administration of the winding up, including–

- (a)   a summary of his receipts and payments, including details of remuneration charged and expenses incurred by the liquidator,

- (ab)   details of the basis fixed for the liquidator's remuneration, and

- (b)   a statement by him that he has reconciled his account with that which is held by the Secretary of State in respect of the winding up.

4.125(2A)   [Report to contain amount paid under prescribed part] The liquidator's report shall also contain a statement as to the amount paid to unsecured creditors by virtue of the application of section 176A (prescribed part).

4.125(2B)   [Report where progress report] Where the liquidator has sent a progress report to creditors in accordance with Rule 4.49B, the report to be laid at the final meeting of creditors must also–

- (a)   contain a receipts and payments account in the form of an abstract showing the receipts and payments during the period since the last progress report, and

- (b)   include–

    - (i)   details of the remuneration charged and expenses incurred by the liquidator during that period, and

(ii) a description of the things done by the liquidator during that period in respect of which that remuneration was charged and those expenses incurred.

4.125(2C) [Where basis of liquidator's remuneration not fixed] In any case where the basis of the liquidator's remuneration had not been fixed by the date to which the last progress report was made up, the receipts and payments account required by paragraph (2B)(a) must also include details of the remuneration charged in the period of any preceding progress report in which details of remuneration were not included.

4.125(2D) [Where basis of remuneration a set amount only] Where the basis of remuneration has been fixed as a set amount only, it is sufficient compliance with paragraph (2B)(b) for the liquidator to state the amount which has been set and to supply details of the expenses charged within the period in question.

4.125(3) [Questioning of liquidator] At the final meeting, the creditors may question the liquidator with respect to any matter contained in his report, and may resolve against him having his release.

4.125(4) [Notice to court] The liquidator shall give notice to the court that the final meeting has been held; and the notice shall state whether or not he has been given his release, and be accompanied by a copy of the report laid before the final meeting. A copy of the notice shall be sent by the liquidator to the Secretary of State.

[FORM 4.42]

4.125(5) [No quorum at final meeting] If there is no quorum present at the final meeting, the liquidator shall report to the court that a final meeting was summoned in accordance with the Rules, but there was no quorum present; and the final meeting is then deemed to have been held, and the creditors not to have resolved against the liquidator having his release.

4.125(6) [Release of liquidator] If the creditors at the final meeting have not so resolved, the liquidator is released when the notice under paragraph (4) is filed in court. If they have so resolved, the liquidator must obtain his release from the Secretary of State and Rule 4.121 applies accordingly.

(See General Note after r.4.126-CVL.)

4.125A Rule as to reporting

4.125A(1) [Power of court] The court may, on the liquidator or official receiver's application, relieve him of any duty imposed on him by Rule 4.124 or 4.125, or authorise him to carry out the duty in a way other than there required.

4.125A(2) [Consideration in exercising power] In considering whether to act under this Rule, the court shall have regard to the cost of carrying out the duty, to the amount of the assets available, and to the extent of the interest of creditors or contributories, or any particular class of them.

(See General Note after r.4.126-CVL.)

4.126-CVL Final meeting

4.126-CVL(1) [Notice to creditors] The liquidator shall give at least 28 days' notice of the final meeting of creditors to be held under section 106. The notice shall be sent to all creditors who are known to the liquidators.

[FORM 4.22]

4.126-CVL(1A) [Additional contents of s.106(2) advertisement] In addition to information required by subsection (2) of section 106 and the standard contents, the advertisement required by that subsection must state the time and date by which, and place at which, creditors must lodge proxies and hitherto unlodged proofs in order to be entitled to vote at the meeting.

4.126-CVL(1B)   [Liquidator to advertise notice of meeting] In addition to the notice required by paragraph (1) and the advertisement required by section 106(2), the liquidator may advertise notice of the meeting in such other manner as the liquidator thinks fit.

4.126-CVL(1C)   [Additional contents of r.4.126(1B) notice] In addition to the standard contents, notice under paragraph (1B) must state–

(a)   the purpose of the meeting;

(b)   the venue fixed for the meeting; and

(c)   the time and date by which, and place at which, creditors must lodge proxies and hitherto unlodged proofs in order to be entitled to vote at the meeting.

4.126-CVL(1D)   [No final meeting without compliance with r.4.49D] The final meeting must not be held unless Rule 4.49D has been complied with; and if for that reason the meeting is not held–

(a)   the liquidator must give notice of that fact as soon as reasonably practicable to all to whom notice of the meeting was given, and

(b)   fresh notice of the meeting complying with this Rule must be given when Rule 4.49D has been complied with.

4.126-CVL(1E)   [Liquidator's report at meeting] The liquidator's report laid before the meeting of creditors under section 106 must contain an account of the liquidator's administration of the winding up, including–

(a)   a summary of the liquidator's receipts and payments, including at least the following items separately specified (except where the amount for an item is zero)–

    (i)   the total of all receipts, with separate specification thereunder of–

        (aa) receipts from trading carried on by the liquidator;

        (bb) payments made in the course of trading carried on by the liquidator;

        (cc) the source of all other receipts;

        (dd) payments to redeem securities;

        (ee) costs of execution; and

        (ff) net realisations;

    (ii)   the cost of employing a solicitor;

    (iii) other legal costs;

    (iv)   the liquidator's remuneration;

    (v)   the cost of employing an auctioneer;

    (vi)   the cost of employing a valuer;

    (vii) the costs of taking possession of and maintaining the company's property;

    (viii) the cost of advertising in the Gazette and other newspapers;

    (ix)   incidental outlays;

    (x)   a statement of the total of costs and charges incurred;

    (xi)   the amount paid to holders of debentures of each class of debenture, setting out the amount paid per debenture, the nominal value of each debenture in each class and the total amount paid in respect of each class;

(xii) the aggregate numbers of preferential and unsecured creditors and the aggregate amounts paid out to them, the aggregates for preferential and unsecured creditors set out separately unless all creditors have been paid in full;

(xiii) statements of the aggregate dividend paid on each pound of preferential and of unsecured debt and of the estimate of the value of the company's net property which had been made under Rule 4.49(2)(a)(ii);

(xiv) the amount of interest paid under section 189;

(xv) the amount paid to contributories in respect of each class of share, setting out the amount per share and the nominal value of each share in each class;

(xvi) a statement of the total amount paid to holders of debentures, preferential and unsecured creditors and contributories;

(xvii) a statement of assets which have proved to be unrealisable, including the value of those assets which had been made for the purpose of Rule 4.49(2)(a)(ii);

(xviii) the amounts paid into the Insolvency Services Account, set out separately, in respect of–

(aa) unclaimed dividends payable to creditors in the winding up;

(bb) other unclaimed dividends in the winding up;

(cc) moneys held by the company in trust in respect of dividends or other sums due before the commencement of the winding up to any person as a member of the company;

(b) details of the basis fixed for the liquidator's remuneration and by whom it was fixed;

(c) a statement by the liquidator that the account included in the report has been reconciled with that which is held by the Secretary of State in respect of the winding up;

(d) any other statement which the liquidator thinks it desirable to make.

4.126-CVL(2)   [Questioning of liquidator] At the final meeting, the creditors may question the liquidator with respect to any matter contained in the account required under section 106 or paragraph (4) of this Rule, and may resolve against the liquidator having his release.

4.126-CVL(3)   [Release of liquidator] Where the creditors have so resolved, he must obtain his release from the Secretary of State; and Rule 4.122–CVL applies accordingly.

4.126-CVL(4)   [Account to include amount paid under prescribed part] The account of the winding up required under section 106 shall also include a statement as to the amount paid to unsecured creditors by virtue of the application of section 176A (prescribed part).

4.126-CVL(5)   [Report where progress report] Where the liquidator has sent a progress report to creditors in accordance with section 104A, the report to be laid at the final meeting of creditors must also–

(a) contain a receipts and payments account in the form of an abstract showing the receipts and payments during the period since the last progress report, and

(b) include–

(i) details of the remuneration charged and expenses incurred by the liquidator during that period, and

(ii) a description of the things done by the liquidator during that period in respect of which that remuneration was charged and those expenses incurred.

4.126-CVL(6)   [Where basis of liquidator's remuneration not fixed] In any case where the basis of the liquidator's remuneration had not been fixed by the date to which the last progress report was made up, the receipts and payments account required by paragraph (5)(a) must also include details of the remuneration charged in the period of any preceding progress report in which details of remuneration were not included.

4.126-CVL(7) [Where basis of remuneration a set amount only] Where the basis of remuneration has been fixed as a set amount only, it is sufficient compliance with paragraph (5)(b) for the liquidator to state the amount which has been set and to supply details of the expenses charged within the period in question.

GENERAL NOTE TO RR.4.124–4.126-CVL

These rules deal with the liquidator's release following the completion of his administration of the estate. On the question of his release upon his resignation or removal, see rr.4.121, 4.122-CVL.

New paras (2A) were inserted into rr.4.124 and 4.125, and para.4.126(4) added, by the Insolvency (Amendment) Rules 2003 (SI 2003/1730, effective September 15, 2003) Sch.1 paras 21–23. Rule 4.125A was inserted by the Insolvency (Amendment) Rules 2004 (SI 2004/584) effective April 1, 2004. The Secretary of State was substituted for the official receiver in r.4.125(4) by the Insolvency (Amendment) Rules 2005 (SI 2005/527) r.28, as from April 1, 2005.

Rules 4.125(1), (2), 4.126(1), (2) amended and rr.4.125(1A)–(1C), (2B)–(2D), 4.126(1A)–(1E), (5)–(7) inserted by I(A)R 2010 r.2 and Sch. paras 214, 215 as from April 6, 2010.

The amendments to r.4.125 prohibit the holding of a final meeting unless a draft final report has been sent to creditors in compliance with r.4.49D, and r.4.126(1A)–(1D), (5)–(7) sets out in detail the information which must be provided to creditors for the purposes of the meeting.

Rules 4.125 and 4.126 require the notice of the final meeting to include the information specified in the relevant rule in addition to the standard contents. On the standard contents (for notices other than gazetted notices), see rr.12A.36–12A.39.

4.126A Final meeting in members' voluntary liquidation

(NO CVL APPLICATION)

4.126A(1) [Additional contents of s.94(2) advertisement] In addition to the information required by section 94(2) and the standard contents, the advertisement required by that subsection must state the time and date by which, and place at which, members must lodge proxies in order to be entitled to vote.

4.126A(2) [Liquidator may advertise notice of meeting] In addition to the advertisement required by section 94(2), the liquidator may advertise notice of the meeting in such other manner as the liquidator thinks fit.

4.126A(3) [Additional contents of r.4.126A(2) advertisement] In addition to the standard contents, notice given under paragraph (2) must state–

(a) the purpose of the meeting,

(b) the venue fixed for the meeting, and

(c) the time and date by which, and place at which, members must lodge proxies in order to be entitled to vote at the meeting.

4.126A(4) [Contents of liquidator's report at company meeting] The liquidator's report laid before the meeting of the company under section 94 must contain an account of the liquidator's administration of the winding up, including (except where the amount for an item is zero)–

(a) a summary of the liquidator's receipts and payments, including at least the following items separately specified–

(i) the total of all receipts, with separate specification thereunder of–

(aa) receipts from trading carried on by the liquidator;

(bb) payments made in the course of trading carried on by the liquidator;

(cc) the source of all other receipts;

(dd) payments to redeem securities;

(ee) costs of execution; and

(ff) net realisations;

(ii) the cost of employing a solicitor;

(iii) other legal costs;

(iv) the liquidator's remuneration;

(v) the cost of employing an auctioneer;

(vi) the cost of employing a valuer;

(vii) the costs of taking possession of and maintaining the company's property;

(viii) the cost of advertising in the Gazette and other newspapers;

(ix) incidental outlays;

(x) a statement of the total of costs and charges incurred;

(xi) the amount paid to holders of debentures of each class of debenture, setting out the amount paid per debenture, the nominal value of each debenture in each class and the total amount paid in respect of each class;

(xii) the aggregate amount paid out to creditors;

(xiii) the amount of interest paid under section 189;

(xiv) the amount paid to contributories in respect of each class of share, setting out the amount per share and the nominal value of each share in each class;

(xv) a statement of the total amount paid to holders of debentures, preferential and unsecured creditors and contributories;

(xvi) a statement of assets which have proved to be unrealisable, including the value of those assets which had been made for the purpose of Rule 4.49(2)(a)(ii);

(xvii) the amounts paid into the Insolvency Services Account, set out separately, in respect of–

(aa) unclaimed dividends payable to creditors in the winding up;

(bb) other unclaimed dividends in the winding up;

(cc) moneys held by the company in trust in respect of dividends or other sums due before the commencement of the winding up to any person as a member of the company;

(b) details of the basis fixed for the liquidator's remuneration and by whom it was fixed;

(c) any other statement which the liquidator thinks it desirable to make.

GENERAL NOTE

Rule 4.126A inserted by I(A)R 2010 r.2 and Sch. para.216 as from April 6, 2010. This new rule 4.126A deals with the provision of information to members for the final meeting in a members' voluntary liquidation. On the standard contents (for notices other than gazetted notices), see rr.12A.36–12A.39.

Section D: Remuneration

4.127 Fixing of remuneration

4.127(1) [Entitlement to remuneration] The liquidator is entitled to receive remuneration for his services as such.

4.127(2)   [How fixed] The basis of remuneration shall be fixed–

(a)   as a percentage of the value of the assets which are realised or distributed, or of the one value and the other in combination, or

(b)   by reference to the time properly given by the insolvency practitioner (as liquidator) and his staff in attending to matters arising in the winding up, or

(c)   as a set amount.

4.127(3)   [Deleted.]

4.127(3A)   [Different bases of remuneration] The basis of remuneration may be fixed as any one or more of the bases set out in paragraph (2), and different bases may be fixed in respect of different things done by the liquidator.

4.127(3B)   [Different percentages where different things done] Where the basis of remuneration is fixed as set out in paragraph (2)(a), different percentages may be fixed in respect of different things done by the liquidator.

4.127(3C)   [Determination of basis by liquidation committee] Where the liquidator is other than the official receiver, and subject to paragraph (5A), it is for the liquidation committee (if there is one) to determine–

(a)   which of the bases set out in paragraph (2) are to be fixed and (where appropriate) in what combination under paragraph (3A), and

(b)   the percentage or percentages (if any) to be fixed under paragraphs (2)(a) and (3B) and the amount (if any) to be set under paragraph (2)(c).

4.127(4)   [Matters relevant r.4.127(3) determination] In arriving at that determination, the committee shall have regard to the following matters–

(a)   the complexity (or otherwise) of the case,

(b)   any respects in which, in connection with the winding up, there falls on the insolvency practitioner (as liquidator) any responsibility of an exceptional kind or degree,

(c)   the effectiveness with which the insolvency practitioner appears to be carrying out, or to have carried out, his duties as liquidator, and

(d)   the value and nature of the assets with which the liquidator has to deal.

4.127(5)   [If no committee or no determination] If there is no liquidation committee, or the committee does not make the requisite determination, and subject to paragraph (5A), the liquidator's remuneration may be fixed (in accordance with paragraphs (2), (3A) and (3B)) by a resolution of a meeting of creditors; and paragraph (4) applies to them as it does to the liquidation committee.

4.127(5A)   [Where administrator becomes liquidator] Where–

(a)   a company which is in administration moves into winding up under paragraph 83 of Schedule B1 to the Act and the administrator becomes the liquidator, or

(b)   a winding-up order is made immediately upon the appointment of an administrator ceasing to have effect and the court under section 140(1) appoints as liquidator the person whose appointment as administrator has ceased to have effect,

the basis of remuneration fixed under Rule 2.106 is treated as having been fixed under this Rule and paragraphs (4) and (5) do not apply.

4.127(6)   [Basis of remuneration not otherwise fixed] Where the liquidator is not the official receiver the basis of and his remuneration is not fixed as above within 18 months after the date of the liquidator's appointment, the liquidator shall be entitled to remuneration fixed in accordance with the provisions of Rule 4.127A.

(NO CVL APPLICATION)

4.127-CVL(7) **[Basis of remuneration fixed by court]** If not fixed as above, the basis of the liquidator's remuneration shall, on application by the liquidator, be fixed by the court, and the provisions of paragraphs (2) to (4) apply as they do to the fixing of the basis of remuneration by the liquidation committee; but such an application may not be made by the liquidator unless the liquidator has first sought fixing of the basis in accordance with paragraph (3C) or (5), and in any event may not be made more than 18 months after the date of the liquidator's appointment.

(See General Note after r.4.131C.)

4.127A   Liquidator's entitlement to remuneration where it is not fixed under Rule 4.127

(NO CVL APPLICATION)

4.127A(1) **[Application of r.4.127A]** This Rule applies where the liquidator is not the official receiver and the basis of his remuneration is not fixed or treated as fixed in accordance with Rule 4.127.

4.127A(2) **[Realisation scale in Sch.6]** The liquidator shall be entitled by way of remuneration for his services as such, to such sum as is arrived at by–

(a)   first applying the realisation scale set out in Schedule 6 to the monies received by him from the realisation of the assets of the company (including any Value Added Tax thereon but after deducting any sums paid to secured creditors in respect of their securities and any sums spent out of money received in carrying on the business of the company); and

(b)   then by adding to the sum arrived at under sub-paragraph (a) such sum as is arrived at by applying the distribution scale set out in Schedule 6 to the value of assets distributed to creditors of the company (including payments made in respect of preferential debts) and to contributories.

(See General Note after r.4.131C.)

4.127B   Liquidator's remuneration where the liquidator realises assets on behalf of chargeholder

4.127B(1) **[Application of r.4.127B]** This Rule applies where the liquidator is not the official receiver and realises assets on behalf of a secured creditor.

4.127B(2) **[Mortgage or fixed charge]** Where the assets realised for a secured creditor are subject to a charge which when created was a mortgage or a fixed charge, the liquidator shall be entitled to such sum by way of remuneration as is arrived at by applying the realisation scale set out in Schedule 6 to the monies received by him in respect of the assets realised (including any sums received in respect of Value Added Tax thereon but after deducting any sums spent out of money received in carrying on the business of the company).

4.127B(3) **[Floating charge]** Where the assets realised for a secured creditor are subject to a charge which when created was a floating charge, the liquidator shall be entitled to such sum by way of remuneration as is arrived at by–

(a)   first applying the realisation scale set out in Schedule 6 to monies received by him from the realisation of those assets (including any Value Added Tax thereon but ignoring any sums received which are spent in carrying on the business of the company); and

(b)   then by adding to the sum arrived at under sub-paragraph (a) such sum as is arrived at by applying the distribution scale set out in Schedule 6 to the value of the assets distributed to the holder of the charge and payments made in respect of preferential debts.

4.127B(4) **[Remuneration from proceeds realised]** The sum to which the liquidator is entitled under paragraph (2) or (3) shall be taken out of the proceeds of the realisation effected under that paragraph.

(See General Note after r.4.131C.)

4.128 Other matters affecting remuneration

4.128(1) [Omitted.]

4.128(2) **[Where joint liquidators]** Where there are joint liquidators, it is for them to agree between themselves as to how the remuneration payable should be apportioned. Any dispute arising between them may be referred–

(a) to the court, for settlement by order, or

(b) to the liquidation committee or a meeting of creditors, for settlement by resolution.

4.128(3) **[If liquidator is a solicitor]** If the liquidator is a solicitor and employs his own firm, or any partner in it, to act on behalf of the company, profit costs shall not be paid unless this is authorised by the liquidation committee, the creditors or the court.

(See General Note after r.4.131C.)

4.129 Recourse of liquidator to meeting of creditors [Deleted.]

4.129A Recourse of liquidator to meeting of creditors

4.129A If the basis of the liquidator's remuneration has been fixed by the liquidation committee, or by the creditors' committee under Rule 2.106(3C) in a case falling within Rule 4.127(5A) in which the administrator had not requested an increase under Rule 2.107, and the liquidator considers the rate or amount to be insufficient or the basis to be inappropriate, the liquidator may request that the rate or amount be increased or the basis changed by resolution of the creditors.

(See General Note after r.4.131C.)

4.130 Recourse to the court

4.130(1) **[Liquidator may apply to court]** If the liquidator considers that the basis of remuneration fixed by the liquidation committee, or by resolution of the creditors, or as under Rule 4.127(5A) or (6), is insufficient or inappropriate, the liquidator may apply to the court for an order changing it or increasing its amount or rate.

4.130(2) **[Notice to committee etc.]** The liquidator shall give at least 14 days' notice of his application to the members of the liquidation committee; and the committee may nominate one or more members to appear or be represented, and to be heard, on the application.

4.130(3) **[Where no committee]** If there is no liquidation committee, the liquidator's notice of his application shall be sent to such one or more of the company's creditors as the court may direct, which creditors may nominate one or more of their number to appear or be represented.

4.130(4) **[Costs of application]** The court may, if it appears to be a proper case, order the costs of the liquidator's application, including the costs of any member of the liquidation committee appearing or being represented on it, or any creditor so appearing or being represented, to be paid as an expense of the liquidation.

(See General Note after r.4.131C.)

4.131 Creditors' claim that remuneration is or other expenses are excessive

4.131(1) **[Secured or certain unsecured creditors may apply to court]** Any secured creditor, or any unsecured creditor with either the concurrence of at least 10% in value of the creditors (including that creditor) or the permission of the court, may apply to the court for one or more of the orders in paragraph (4).

4.131(1A) **[Grounds for application]** Application may be made on the grounds that–

(a) the remuneration charged by the liquidator,

(b) the basis fixed for the liquidator's remuneration under Rule 4.127, or

(c) expenses incurred by the liquidator,

is or are, in all the circumstances, excessive or, in the case of an application under sub-paragraph (b), inappropriate.

4.131(1B) **[Time limit for application]** The application must, subject to any order of the court under Rule 4.49E(5), be made no later than 8 weeks (or, in a case falling within Rule 4.108, 4 weeks) after receipt by the applicant of the progress report, or the draft report under Rule 4.49D, which first reports the charging of the remuneration or the incurring of the expenses in question ("the relevant report").

4.131(2) **[Power of court to dismiss etc.]** The court may, if it thinks that no sufficient cause is shown for a reduction, dismiss the application; but it shall not do so unless the applicant has had an opportunity to attend the court for a hearing, of which he has been given at least 5 business days' notice but which is without notice to any other party.

If the application is not dismissed under this paragraph, the court shall fix a venue for it to be heard, and give notice to the applicant accordingly.

4.131(3) **[Notice to liquidator]** The applicant shall, at least 14 days before the hearing, send to the liquidator a notice stating the venue and accompanied by a copy of the application, and of any evidence which the applicant intends to adduce in support of it.

4.131(4) **[Court order]** If the court considers the application to be well-founded, it must make one or more of the following orders–

(a) an order reducing the amount of remuneration which the liquidator was entitled to charge;

(b) an order fixing the basis of remuneration at a reduced rate or amount;

(c) an order changing the basis of remuneration;

(d) an order that some or all of the remuneration or expenses in question be treated as not being expenses of the liquidation;

(e) an order that the liquidator or the liquidator's personal representative pay to the company the amount of the excess of remuneration or expenses or such part of the excess as the court may specify;

and may make any other order that it thinks just; but an order under sub-paragraph (b) or (c) may be made only in respect of periods after the period covered by the relevant report.

4.131(5) **[Costs of application]** Unless the court orders otherwise, the costs of the application shall be paid by the applicant, and are not payable as an expense of the liquidation.

(See General Note after r.4.131C.)

4.131A   Review of remuneration

4.131A(1) **[Power of liquidator to request change]** Where, after the basis of the liquidator's remuneration has been fixed, there is a material and substantial change in the circumstances which were taken into account in fixing it, the liquidator may request that it be changed.

4.131A(2) **[To whom request must be made]** The request must be made–

(a) where the liquidation committee fixed the basis, to the committee;

   (b)   where the creditors fixed the basis, to the creditors;

   (c)   where the court fixed the basis, by application to the court;

   (d)   where the remuneration was determined by application of the realisation scale under Rule 4.127A, to the liquidation committee if there is one or otherwise to the creditors;

and subject to paragraph (3), Rules 4.127 to 4.131 apply as appropriate.

4.131A(3)   **[Where r.4.129A applied with r.4.131A(2)]** Where Rule 4.129A is applied in accordance with paragraph (2) of this Rule, ignore the words "in which the administrator had not requested an increase under Rule 2.107".

4.131A(4)   **[Date when change in basis applies from]** Any change in the basis for remuneration applies from the date of the request under paragraph (2) and not for any earlier period.

4.131A(5)   **[Non-application where liquidator official receiver]** This Rule does not apply where the liquidator is the official receiver.

(See General Note after r.4.131C.)

4.131B   Remuneration of new liquidator

4.131B(1)   **[Basis of remuneration if former liquidator continues]** If a new liquidator is appointed in place of another, any determination, resolution or court order in effect under the preceding provisions of this Section of this Chapter immediately before the former liquidator ceased to hold office continues to apply in respect of the remuneration of the new liquidator until a further determination, resolution or court order is made in accordance with those provisions.

4.131B(2)   **[Non-application where liquidator official receiver]** This Rule does not apply where the new liquidator is the official receiver.

(See General Note after r.4.131C.)

4.131C   Apportionment of set fee remuneration

4.131C(1)   **[Where liquidator ceases to hold office]** In a case in which the basis of the liquidator's remuneration is a set amount under Rule 4.127(2)(c) and the liquidator ("the former liquidator") ceases (for whatever reason) to hold office before the time has elapsed or the work has been completed in respect of which the amount was set, application may be made for determination of what portion of the amount should be paid to the former liquidator or the former liquidator's personal representative in respect of the time which has actually elapsed or the work which has actually been done.

4.131C(2)   **[By who and by when application may be made]** Application may be made–

   (a)   by the former liquidator or the former liquidator's personal representative within the period of 28 days beginning with the date upon which the former liquidator ceased to hold office, or

   (b)   by the liquidator for the time being in office if the former liquidator or the former liquidator's personal representative has not applied by the end of that period.

4.131C(3)   **[To whom application must be made]** Application must be made–

   (a)   where the liquidation committee fixed the basis, to the committee;

   (b)   where the creditors fixed the basis, to the creditors for a resolution determining the portion;

   (c)   where the court fixed the basis, to the court for an order determining the portion.

4.131C(4)   **[Copy of application to recipient]** The applicant must give a copy of the application to the liquidator for the time being in office or to the former liquidator or the former liquidator's personal representative, as the case may be ("the recipient").

4.131C(5)   [Notice of recipient's intention to make representations etc.] The recipient may within 21 days of receipt of the copy of the application give notice of intent to make representations to the liquidation committee or the creditors or to appear or be represented before the court, as the case may be.

4.131C(6)   [Period for determination] No determination may be made upon the application until expiry of the 21 days referred to in paragraph (5) or, if the recipient does give notice of intent in accordance with that paragraph, until the recipient has been afforded the opportunity to make representations or to appear or be represented, as the case may be.

4.131C(7)   [Application to increase portion] If the former liquidator or the former liquidator's personal representative (whether or not the original applicant) considers that the portion determined upon application to the liquidation committee or the creditors is insufficient, that person may apply–

(a)   in the case of a determination by the liquidation committee, to the creditors for a resolution increasing the portion;

(b)   in the case of a resolution of the creditors (whether under paragraph (1) or under sub-paragraph (a)), to the court for an order increasing the portion;

and paragraphs (4) to (6) apply as appropriate.

GENERAL NOTE TO RR.4.127–4.131C

Rules 4.127–4.127B, 4.129–4.131 amended, rr.4.127(3A)–(3C), (5A), (7), 4.131A–4.131C inserted and rr.4.131(4) substituted by I(A)R 2010 r.2 and Sch. paras 217–233 as from April 6, 2010.

Here are set out the provisions relating to fixing the liquidator's remuneration and the various ways in which a decision on this question may be reviewed or challenged. Rule 4.127(6) was amended, new rr.4.127A, 4.127B inserted, and r.4.128(1) omitted by the Insolvency (Amendment) Rules 2004 (SI 2004/584), effective April 1, 2004. The latter rules repeat in substance the provisions formerly set out in relation to the remuneration of official receivers by the Insolvency Regulations 1994 (SI 1994/2507), which have been repealed. Transitional provisions in reg.3 of SI 2004/584 ensure that the former provisions continue to apply to cases which were already on foot on April 1, 2004. The reference to payments made in respect of preferential debts was added to r.4.127B(3)(b) by the Insolvency (Amendment) Rules 2005 (SI 2005/527) r.29, as from April 1, 2005.

Following the 2010 amendments, the liquidator's remuneration may now also be determined as a set amount (r.4.127(2)(c)). Where an administration is converted into a winding up the remuneration fixed under r.2.106 is treated as having been fixed also for the purposes of the liquidation (r.4.127(5A)). Rule 4.131 has been elaborated to deal in more detail with the review of the liquidator's remuneration, and r.4.131A inserted to provide for a review where there has been a material change of circumstances. New rules 4.131B–4.131C have been inserted to cover the case where there has been a change of liquidator.

On the fixing and approval of the liquidator's remuneration, see the *Practice Statement* [2004] B.C.C. 912 (reproduced as App.VII to this *Guide*). See also *Hyndman v Readman*, 2004 S.L.T. 959 and, for an account of a disputed case (*Re Cabletel Installations Ltd* (April 20, 2004)), see Moss, (2005) 18 Insolv. Int. 61. *Jacob v UIC Insurance Co Ltd* [2006] EWHC 2717 (Ch); [2007] B.C.C.167, discussed in the note to r.4.30, is also relevant.

A liquidator may not fix his own remuneration, and has no right to retain remuneration out of the assets if they are insufficient to pay other expenses of the liquidation ranking no lower than the remuneration in question: *Re Salters Hall School Ltd (in liq.)* [1998] B.C.C. 503. For an example of the exercise by the court of its jurisdiction under r.4.130, see *Re Tony Rowse NMC Ltd* [1996] B.C.C. 196. On the remuneration of a liquidator in a members' voluntary winding up, see r.4.148A and, where a compulsory winding up follows a voluntary winding up, r.4.219.

A liquidator may, in an appropriate case, also be paid remuneration and allowed expenses for work done in relation to property which does not form part of the assets in the liquidation, for instance property held by the company on trust, or property subject to a fixed or floating charge where the chargee has not appointed a receiver (see *Re Leyland DAF Ltd, Buchler v Talbot* [2004] UKHL 9; [2004] 2 A.C. 298; [2004] B.C.C. 214 at [63]). In *Re Berkeley Applegate (Investment Consultants) Ltd (No.2)* (1988) 4 B.C.C. 279 the liquidator in a creditors' voluntary winding up discovered, after extensive investigations, that certain assets standing in the name of the company were held by it on trust for people who had paid money to the company for investment. Although there was no statutory authority for payment, the court held that fair compensation could be awarded to the liquidator on general equitable principles. In later proceedings (*Re Berkeley Applegate (Investment Consultants) Ltd (No.3)* (1989) 5 B.C.C. 803), it was held that this remuneration could not properly be charged on the company's assets in the liquidation but only on the trust funds themselves. See also *Rye v Ashfield Nominees Ltd* (August 2, 2001, *British Company Law and Practice New Developments*, para.96–471.

Section E: Supplementary provisions

4.132 Liquidator deceased

(NO CVL APPLICATION)

4.132(1) **[Notice to official receiver]** Subject as follows, where the liquidator (other than the official receiver) has died, it is the duty of his personal representatives to give notice of the fact to the official receiver, specifying the date of the death.

This does not apply if notice has been given under any of the following paragraphs of this Rule.

4.132(2) **[Notice by partner etc.]** If the deceased liquidator was a partner in or an employee of a firm, notice may be given to the official receiver by a partner in the firm who is qualified to act as an insolvency practitioner, or is a member of any body recognised by the Secretary of State for the authorisation of insolvency practitioners.

4.132(3) **[Notice by others]** Notice of the death may be given by any person producing to the official receiver the relevant death certificate or a copy of it.

4.132(4) **[Notice by official receiver]** The official receiver shall give notice to the court, for the purpose of fixing the date of the deceased liquidator's release.

(See General Note after r.4.138.)

4.133-CVL Liquidator deceased

4.133-CVL(1) **[Notice to registrar and committee]** Subject as follows, where the liquidator has died, it is the duty of his personal representatives to give notice of the fact, and of the date of death, to the registrar of companies and to the liquidation committee (if any) or a member of that committee.

4.133-CVL(2) **[Notice by others]** In the alternative, notice of the death may be given–

(a) if the deceased liquidator was a partner in or an employee of a firm, by a partner in the firm qualified to act as an insolvency practitioner or who is a member of any body approved by the Secretary of State for the authorisation of insolvency practitioners, or

(b) by any person, if he delivers with the notice a copy of the relevant death certificate.

(See General Note after r.4.138.)

4.134 Loss of qualification as insolvency practitioner

(NO CVL APPLICATION)

4.134(1) **[Application of Rule]** This Rule applies where the liquidator vacates office on ceasing to be qualified to act as an insolvency practitioner in relation to the company.

4.134(2) **[Notice to official receiver etc.]** He shall as soon as reasonably practicable give notice of his doing so to the official receiver, who shall give notice to the Secretary of State.

The official receiver shall file in court a copy of his notice under this paragraph.

[FORM 4.45]

4.134(3) **[Application of r.4.121]** Rule 4.121 applies as regards the liquidator obtaining his release, as if he had been removed by the court.

(See General Note after r.4.138.)

4.135-CVL Loss of qualification as insolvency practitioner

4.135-CVL(1) **[Application of Rule]** This Rule applies where the liquidator vacates office on ceasing to be qualified to act as an insolvency practitioner in relation to the company.

4.135-CVL(2)   [Notice] He shall as soon as reasonably practicable give notice of his doing so to the registrar of companies and the Secretary of State.

[FORM 4.45]

4.135-CVL(3)   [Application of r.4.122–CVL] Rule 4.122–CVL applies as regards the liquidator obtaining his release, as if he had been removed by the court.

(See General Note after r.4.138.)

4.136-CVL   Vacation of office on making of winding-up order

4.136-CVL   Where the liquidator vacates office in consequence of the court making a winding-up order against the company, Rule 4.122-CVL applies as regards his obtaining his release, as if he had been removed by the court.

(See General Note after r.4.138.)

4.137   Notice to official receiver of intention to vacate office

(NO CVL APPLICATION)

4.137(1)   [Notice to official receiver] Where the liquidator intends to vacate office, whether by resignation or otherwise, he shall give notice of his intention to the official receiver together with notice of any creditors' meeting to be held in respect of his vacation of office, including any meeting to receive his resignation.

4.137(2)   [Time limit for notice] The notice to the official receiver must be given at least 21 days before any such creditors' meeting.

4.137(3)   [Details of property] Where there remains any property of the company which has not been realised, applied, distributed or otherwise fully dealt with in the winding up, the liquidator shall include in his notice to the official receiver details of the nature of that property, its value (or the fact that it has no value), its location, any action taken by the liquidator to deal with that property or any reason for his not dealing with it, and the current position in relation to it.

(See General Note after r.4.138.)

4.138   Liquidator's duties on vacating office

4.138(1)   [Obligation to deliver up assets etc.] Where the liquidator ceases to be in office as such, in consequence of removal, resignation or cesser of qualification as an insolvency practitioner, he is under obligation as soon as reasonably practicable to deliver up to the person succeeding him as liquidator the assets (after deduction of any expenses properly incurred, and distributions made, by him) and further to deliver up to that person–

(a)   the records of the liquidation, including correspondence, proofs and other related papers appertaining to the administration while it was within his responsibility, and

(b)   the company's books, papers and other records.

4.138(2)   [Omitted.]

4.138(3)   [Vacation following creditors' final meeting] Where the liquidator vacates office under section 172(8) (final meeting of creditors), he shall deliver up to the official receiver the company's books, papers and other records which have not already been disposed of in accordance with general regulations in the course of the liquidation. (NO CVL APPLICATION).

GENERAL NOTE TO RR.4.132–4.138

Apart from resignation and removal, which are dealt with in rr.4.108 et seq., the office of liquidator may be vacated by death or disqualification or in consequence of a court order. The present rules are concerned with these situations and with various other matters incidental to vacating office.

Rule 4.138(2) was omitted by the Insolvency (Amendment) Rules 2004 (SI 2004/584), effective April 1, 2004. This amendment relieved the liquidator from the obligation to file proofs of debt in court at the conclusion of his administration, which left official receivers having to deal with assets without access to these proofs. In view of this, practitioners vacating office who notify the official receiver of property which has not been realised, distributed or otherwise dealt with have been requested to forward proofs of debt to him (*Dear IP*, December 2005).

Section F: The liquidator in a members' voluntary winding up

4.139   Appointment by the company

4.139(1)   [Application of Rule] This Rule applies where the liquidator is appointed by a meeting of the company.

4.139(2)   [Certifying appointment etc.] Subject as follows, the chairman of the meeting shall certify the appointment, but not unless and until the person appointed has provided him with a written statement to the effect that he is an insolvency practitioner, duly qualified under the Act to be the liquidator, and that he consents so to act.

[FORM 4.27]
[FORM 4.28]

4.139(3)   [Certificate to liquidator] The chairman shall send the certificate as soon as reasonably practicable to the liquidator, who shall keep it as part of the records of the liquidation.

4.139(4)   [Notice to creditors] Not later than 28 days from his appointment, the liquidator shall give notice of it to all creditors of the company of whom he is aware in that period.

(See General Note after r.4.148E.)

4.140   Appointment by the court

4.140(1)   [Application of Rule] This Rule applies where the liquidator is appointed by the court under section 108.

4.140(2)   [Issue of court order] The court's order shall not issue unless and until the person appointed has filed in court a statement to the effect that he is an insolvency practitioner, duly qualified under the Act to be the liquidator, and that he consents so to act.

[FORM 4.29]
[FORM 4.30]

4.140(3)   [Copy of order to liquidator] Thereafter, the court shall send a sealed copy of the order to the liquidator, whose appointment takes effect from the date of the order.

4.140(4)   [Notice to creditors] Not later than 28 days from his appointment, the liquidator shall give notice of it all creditors of the company of whom he is aware in that period.

(See General Note after r.4.148E.)

4.141   Authentication of liquidator's appointment

4.141 A copy of the certificate of the liquidator's appointment or (as the case may be) a sealed copy of the court's order appointing him may in any proceedings be adduced as proof that the person appointed is duly authorised to exercise the powers and perform the duties of liquidator in the company's winding up.

(See General Note after r.4.148E.)

4.142   Company meeting to receive liquidator's resignation

4.142(1)   **[Liquidator must call meeting etc.]** Before resigning his office, the liquidator must call a meeting of the company for the purpose of receiving his resignation. The notice summoning the meeting shall indicate that this is the purpose, or one of the purposes, of it.

4.142(2)   **[Account of liquidator's administration]** The notice under paragraph (1) must be accompanied by an account of the liquidator's administration of the winding up, including–

   (a)   a summary of his receipts and payments, and

   (b)   a statement by him that he has reconciled his account with that which is held by the Secretary of State in respect of the winding up.

4.142(3)   **[Grounds for proceeding under Rule]** Subject as follows, the liquidator may only proceed under this Rule on grounds of ill health or because–

   (a)   he intends ceasing to be in practice as an insolvency practitioner, or

   (b)   there is some conflict of interest or change of personal circumstances which precludes or makes impracticable the further discharge by him of the duties of liquidator.

4.142(4)   **[Where joint liquidators]** Where two or more persons are acting as liquidator jointly, any one of them may proceed under this Rule (without prejudice to the continuation in office of the other or others) on the ground that, in his opinion or that of the other or others, it is no longer expedient that there should continue to be the present number of joint liquidators.

4.142(4A)   **[If no quorum]** If there is no quorum present at the meeting summoned to receive the liquidator's resignation, the meeting is deemed to have been held.

4.142(5)   **[Section 171(5) notice]** The notice of the liquidator's resignation required by section 171(5) shall be given by him as soon as reasonably practicable after the meeting.

4.142(6)   **[Where new liquidator appointed]** Where a new liquidator is appointed in place of one who has resigned, the former shall, in giving notice of his appointment, state that his predecessor has resigned.

(See General Note after r.4.148E.)

4.143   Removal of liquidator by the court

4.143(1)   **[Application of Rule]** This Rule applies where application is made to the court for the removal of the liquidator, or for an order directing the liquidator to summon a company meeting for the purpose of removing him.

4.143(2)   **[Court may dismiss application etc.]** The court may, if it thinks that no sufficient cause is shown for the application, dismiss it; but it shall not do so unless the applicant has had an opportunity to attend the court for a hearing, of which he has been given at least 5 business days' notice but which is without notice to any other party.

   If the application is not dismissed under this paragraph, the court shall fix a venue for it to be heard.

4.143(3)   **[Deposit or security for costs]** The court may require the applicant to make a deposit or give security for the costs to be incurred by the liquidator on the application.

4.143(4)   **[Notice etc.]** The applicant shall, at least 14 days before the hearing, send to the liquidator a notice stating the venue and accompanied by a copy of the application, and of any evidence which he intends to adduce in support of it.

   Subject to any contrary order of the court, the costs of the application are not payable as an expense of the liquidation.

4.143(5) **[Where court removes liquidator]** Where the court removes the liquidator–

(a) it shall send 2 copies of the order of removal to him, one to be sent by him as soon as reasonably practicable to the registrar of companies, with notice of his ceasing to act;

(b) the order may include such provision as the court thinks fit with respect to matters arising in connection with the removal; and

(c) if the court appoints a new liquidator, Rule 4.140 applies.

[FORM 4.39]

(See General Note after r.4.148E.)

4.144   Release of resigning or removed liquidator

4.144(1) **[Where liquidator resigns]** Where the liquidator resigns, he has his release from the date on which he gives notice of his resignation to the registrar of companies.

4.144(2) **[Where removed by meeting]** Where the liquidator is removed by a meeting of the company, he shall as soon as reasonably practicable give notice to the registrar of companies of his ceasing to act.

4.144(3) **[Where removed by court]** Where the liquidator is removed by the court, he must apply to the Secretary of State for his release.

4.144(4) **[Certifying release etc.]** When the Secretary of State gives the release, he shall certify it accordingly, and send the certificate to the registrar of companies.

4.144(5) **[Copy of certificate]** A copy of the certificate shall be sent by the Secretary of State to the former liquidator, whose release is effective from the date of the certificate.

(See General Note after r.4.148E.)

4.145   Liquidator deceased

4.145(1) **[Duty to give notice]** Subject as follows, where the liquidator has died, it is the duty of his personal representatives to give notice of the fact, and of the date of death, to the company's directors, or any one of them, and to the registrar of companies.

4.145(2) **[Notice by partner or others]** In the alternative, notice of the death may be given–

(a) if the deceased liquidator was a partner in or an employee of a firm, by a partner in the firm qualified to act as an insolvency practitioner or who is a member of any body approved by the Secretary of State for the authorisation of insolvency practitioners, or

(b) by any person, if he delivers with the notice a copy of the relevant death certificate.

(See General Note after r.4.148E.)

4.146   Loss of qualification as insolvency practitioner

4.146(1) **[Application of Rule]** This Rule applies where the liquidator vacates office on ceasing to be qualified to act as an insolvency practitioner in relation to the company.

4.146(2) **[Notice]** He shall as soon as reasonably practicable give notice of his doing so to the registrar of companies and the Secretary of State.

[FORM 4.45]

4.146(3) **[Application of r.4.144]** Rule 4.144 applies as regards the liquidator obtaining his release, as if he had been removed by the court.

(See General Note after r.4.148E.)

4.147   Vacation of office on making of winding-up order

4.147   Where the liquidator vacates office in consequence of the court making a winding-up order against the company. Rule 4.144 applies as regards his obtaining his release, as if he had been removed by the court.

(See General Note after r.4.148E.)

4.148   Liquidator's duties on vacating office

4.148   Where the liquidator ceases to be in office as such, in consequence of removal, resignation or cesser of qualification as an insolvency practitioner, he is under obligation as soon as reasonably practicable to deliver up to the person succeeding him as liquidator the assets (after deduction of any expenses properly incurred, and distributions made, by him) and further to deliver up to that person–

   (a) the records of the liquidation, including correspondence, proofs and other related papers appertaining to the administration while it was within his responsibility, and

   (b) the company's books, papers and other records.

(See General Note after r.4.148E.)

4.148A   Remuneration of liquidator in members' voluntary winding up

4.148A(1)   **[Entitlement]** The liquidator is entitled to receive remuneration for his services as such.

4.148A(2)   **[How fixed]** The basis of remuneration shall be fixed–

   (a) as a percentage of the value of the assets which are realised or distributed, or of the one value and the other in combination, or

   (b) by reference to the time properly given by the insolvency practitioner (as liquidator) and his staff in attending to matters arising in the winding up, or

   (c) as a set amount.

4.148A(2A)   **[Different bases of remuneration]** The basis of remuneration may be fixed as any one or more of the bases set out in paragraph (2), and different bases may be fixed in respect of different things done by the liquidator.

4.148A(2B)   **[Different percentages where different things done]** Where the basis of remuneration is fixed as set out in paragraph (2)(a), different percentages may be fixed in respect of different things done by the liquidator.

4.148A(2C)   **[Company to determine bases, percentages]** It is for the company in general meeting to determine–

   (a) which of the bases set out in paragraph (2) are to be fixed and (where appropriate) in what combination under paragraph (2A), and

   (b) the percentage or percentages (if any) to be fixed under paragraphs (2)(a) and (2B) and the amount (if any) to be set under paragraph (2)(c).

4.148A(3)   **[Matters in determination]** In arriving at that determination the company in general meeting shall have regard to the matters set out in paragraph (4) of Rule 4.127.

4.148A(4)   **[Where remuneration not otherwise fixed]** If not fixed as above, the basis of the liquidator's remuneration shall, on application by the liquidator, be fixed by the court, and the provisions of paragraphs (2) to (3) apply as they do to the fixing of the basis of remuneration by the company in general meeting; but such an application may not be made by the liquidator unless the liquidator has first sought fixing of the basis in accordance with paragraph (2C), and in any event may not be made more than 18 months after the date of the liquidator's appointment.

4.148A(5) **[Application of r.4.128]** Rule 4.128 and Rule 4.127B shall apply in relation to the remuneration of the liquidator in respect of the matters there mentioned and for this purpose references in that Rule to "the liquidation committee" and "a meeting of creditors" shall be read as references to the company in general meeting.

4.148A(6) **[Application to court]** If the liquidator considers that the basis of the remuneration fixed by the company in general meeting is insufficient or inappropriate, the liquidator may apply to the court for an order changing it or increasing its amount or rate.

4.148A(7) **[Notice to contributories]** The liquidator shall give at least 14 days' notice of an application under paragraph (4) or (6) to the company's contributories, or such one or more of them as the court may direct, and the contributories may nominate any one or more of their number to appear or be represented.

4.148A(8) **[Costs of application]** The court may, if it appears to be a proper case, order the costs of the liquidator's application, including the costs of any contributory appearing or being represented on it, to be paid as an expense of the liquidation.

(See General Note after r.4.148E.)

4.148B **Liquidator's remuneration in members' voluntary liquidation where it is not fixed under Rule 4.148A [Revoked by I(A)R 2010 r.5 as from April 6, 2010.]**

4.148C **Members' claim that remuneration is excessive**

4.148C(1) **[Who may apply to the court]** Members of the company with at least 10% of the total voting rights of all the members having the right to vote at general meetings of the company, or any member with the permission of the court, may apply to the court for one or more of the orders in paragraph (6) on the grounds that–

    (a)   the remuneration charged by the liquidator,

    (b)   the basis fixed for the liquidator's remuneration under Rule 4.148A, or

    (c)   expenses incurred by the liquidator,

is or are, in all the circumstances, excessive or, in the case of an application under sub-paragraph (b), inappropriate.

4.148C(2) **[Time limit for application]** Application must, subject to any order of the court under Rule 4.49E(5), be made no later than 8 weeks (or 4 weeks when the liquidator has resigned in accordance with Rule 4.142) after receipt by the applicant of the report or account which first reports the charging of the remuneration or the incurring of the expenses in question **("the relevant report")**.

4.148C(3) **[Power of court to dismiss application]** The court may, if it thinks that no sufficient cause is shown for a reduction, dismiss the application; but it must not do so unless the applicant has had the opportunity to attend the court for a hearing of which the applicant has been given at least 5 business days' notice but which is without notice to any other party.

4.148C(4) **[Court to fix venue for hearing]** If the application is not dismissed under paragraph (3), the court must fix a venue for it to be heard and give notice to the applicant accordingly.

4.148C(5) **[Applicant to notify liquidator of venue etc.]** The applicant must at least 14 days before the hearing send to the liquidator a notice stating the venue and accompanied by a copy of the application and of any evidence which the applicant intends to adduce in support of it.

4.148C(6) **[Court order if application well-founded]** If the court considers the application to be well-founded, it must make one or more of the following orders–

    (a)   an order reducing the amount of remuneration which the liquidator was entitled to charge;

(b) an order fixing the basis of remuneration at a reduced rate or amount;

(c) an order changing the basis of remuneration;

(d) an order that some or all of the remuneration or expenses in question be treated as not being expenses of the liquidation;

(e) an order that the liquidator or the liquidator's personal representative pay to the company the amount of the excess of remuneration or expenses or such part of the excess as the court may specify;

and may make any other order that it thinks just; but an order under sub-paragraph (b) or (c) may be made only in respect of periods after the period covered by the relevant report.

4.148C(7)   [Costs of application] Unless the court orders otherwise, the costs of the application must be paid by the applicant and are not payable as an expense of the liquidation.

(See General Note after r.4.148E.)

4.148D   Remuneration of new liquidator

4.148D   If a new liquidator is appointed in place of another, any determination or court order in effect under Rule 4.148A immediately before the former liquidator ceased to hold office continues to apply in respect of the remuneration of the new liquidator until a further determination or court order is made in accordance with that Rule.

(See General Note after r.4.148E.)

4.148E   Apportionment of fixed fee remuneration

4.148E(1)   [Where liquidator ceases to hold office] In a case in which the basis of the liquidator's remuneration is a set amount under Rule 4.148A(2)(c) and the liquidator ("the former liquidator") ceases (for whatever reason) to hold office before the time has elapsed or the work has been completed in respect of which the amount was set, application may be made for determination of what portion of the amount should be paid to the former liquidator or the former liquidator's personal representative in respect of the time which has actually elapsed or the work which has actually been done.

4.148E(2)   [By whom and by when application may be made] Application may be made–

(a) by the former liquidator or the former liquidator's personal representative within the period of 28 days beginning with the date upon which the former liquidator ceased to hold office, or

(b) by the liquidator for the time being in office if the former liquidator or the former liquidator's personal representative has not applied by the end of that period.

4.148E(3)   [To whom application must be made] Application must be made–

(a) where the company in general meeting fixed the basis, to the company for a resolution determining the portion;

(b) where the court fixed the basis, to the court for an order determining the portion.

4.148E(4)   [Copy of application to the recipient] The applicant must give a copy of the application to the liquidator for the time being in office or to the former liquidator or the former liquidator's personal representative, as the case may be (**"the recipient"**).

4.148E(5)   [Notice of recipient's intention to make representations etc.] The recipient may within 21 days of receipt of the copy of the application give notice of intent to make representations to the company in general meeting or to appear or be represented before the court, as the case may be.

4.148E(6)   [Time for determination] No determination may be made upon the application until expiry of the 21 days referred to in paragraph (5) or, if the recipient does give notice of intent in accordance with that paragraph, until the recipient has been afforded the opportunity to make representations or to appear or be represented, as the case may be.

4.148E(7)   **[Application to court]** If the former liquidator or the former liquidator's personal representative (whether or not the original applicant) considers that the portion determined upon application to the company in general meeting is insufficient, that person may apply to the court for an order increasing the portion; and paragraphs (4) to (6) apply as appropriate.

GENERAL NOTE TO RR.4.139–4.148E

Rules 4.143, 4.145, 4.148A amended, r.4.148(4) substituted and rr.4.148A(2A)–(2C), 4.148C–4.148E inserted by I(A)R 2010 r.2 and Sch. paras 226–229 as from April 6, 2010. There is now the alternative of determining the liquidator's remuneration as a fixed amount, as in other forms of liquidation (r.148A(2)(c)), and the remainder of these amendments parallel the changes made under rr.4.127–4.131C above.

This is the only part of the rules which deals exclusively with a members' voluntary winding up. The rules set out here relate to the questions of the appointment of the liquidator and the vacation of his office, corresponding to earlier sections of this chapter which govern compulsory and insolvent liquidations. Rule 4.148A(4) was amended, and the former r.4.148B inserted, by the Insolvency (Amendment) Rules 2004 (SI 2004/584), effective April 1, 2004. This follows amendments made to the Insolvency Regulations 1994 (SI 1994/2507): see the note to rr.4.127–4.131.

In *Re AMF International Ltd* [1995] B.C.C. 439 a members' voluntary winding up was commenced but proved to be insolvent. A creditor applied to have the liquidator removed by the court, but before the application was heard he was replaced by a meeting of the creditors summoned under s.95 of the Act. The court took the view that the liquidator had acted improperly in paying a contributory before all the creditors' claims had been satisfied and, acting under r.4.143(4), ordered him to bear the costs of all parties personally.

Section G: Rules applying in every winding up, whether voluntary or by the court

4.149   Power of court to set aside certain transactions

4.149(1)   **[Liquidator's transaction with associate]** If in the administration of the estate the liquidator enters into any transaction with a person who is an associate of his, the court may, on the application of any person interested, set the transaction aside and order the liquidator to compensate the company for any loss suffered in consequence of it.

4.149(2)   **[Where r.4.149(1) does not apply]** This does not apply if either–

(a) the transaction was entered into with the prior consent of the court, or

(b) it is shown to the court's satisfaction that the transaction was for value, and that it was entered into by the liquidator without knowing, or having any reason to suppose, that the person concerned was an associate.

4.149(3)   **[Effect of Rule]** Nothing in this Rule is to be taken as prejudicing the operation of any rule of law or equity with respect to a liquidator's dealings with trust property, or the fiduciary obligations of any person.

GENERAL NOTE

This rule imposes statutory duties of a quasi-fiduciary character on a liquidator, supplementing the rules of equity and the common law. For the meaning of "associate", see IA 1986 s.435.

4.150   Rule against solicitation

4.150(1)   **[Power of court]** Where the court is satisfied that any improper solicitation has been used by or on behalf of the liquidator in obtaining proxies or procuring his appointment, it may order that no remuneration be allowed as an expense of the liquidation to any person by whom, or on whose behalf, the solicitation was exercised.

4.150(2)   [Effect of court order] An order of the court under this Rule overrides any resolution of the liquidation committee or the creditors, or any other provision of the Rules relating to the liquidator's remuneration.

GENERAL NOTE

This rule similarly supplements principles of equity and the common law; and see also IA 1986 s.164 (corrupt inducement affecting liquidator's appointment).

CHAPTER 12

THE LIQUIDATION COMMITTEE

4.151   Preliminary

(NO CVL APPLICATION)

4.151   For the purposes of this Chapter–

(a)   an **"insolvent winding up"** is where the company is being wound up on grounds which include inability to pay its debts, and

(b)   a **"solvent winding up"** is where the company is being wound up on grounds which do not include that one.

GENERAL NOTE

Note that this is a special use of the word "solvent": a company which is ordered to be wound up on grounds other than inability to pay debts may well be "insolvent" in any of the normal senses of that word, but the liquidation will be "solvent" within this definition, and conversely. See the general comment to IA 1986 Pt VI, preceding s.230, and the note to IA 1986 s.247.

For the meaning of "inability to pay its debts", see IA 1986 s.123.

For the rules which apply where a winding up follows immediately upon an administration, see rr.4.173 et seq.

4.152   Membership of committee

4.152(1)   [Numbers to be elected] Subject to Rule 4.154 below, the liquidation committee shall consist as follows–

(a)   in any case of at least 3, and not more than 5, creditors of the company, elected by the meeting of creditors held under section 141 of the Act, and

(b)   also, in the case of a solvent winding up, where the contributories' meeting held under that section so decides, of up to 3 contributories, elected by that meeting.

(NO CVL APPLICATION)

4.152(2)   [At least three members] The committee must have at least 3 members before it can be established.

4.152(3)   [Eligibility] Any creditor of the company (other than one whose debt is fully secured) is eligible to be a member of the committee, so long as–

(a)   he has lodged a proof of his debt, and

(b)   his proof has neither been wholly disallowed for voting purposes, nor wholly rejected for purposes of distribution or dividend.

4.152(4)   [No dual membership] No person can be a member as both a creditor and a contributory.

4.152(5)   [Representation of body corporate] A body corporate may be a member of the committee, but it cannot act as such otherwise than by a representative appointed under Rule 4.159.

4.152(6) **["Creditor members", "contributory members"]** Members of the committee elected or appointed to represent the creditors are called **"creditor members"**; and those elected or appointed to represent the contributories are called **"contributory members"**.

4.152(7) **[Additional creditor members]** The following categories of person are to be regarded as additional creditor members–

(a) a representative of the Financial Services Authority who exercises the right under section 371(4)(b) of the Financial Services and Markets Act 2000 to be a member of the committee;

(b) a representative of the scheme manager who exercises the right under section 215(4) of that Act to be a member of the committee.

(See General Note after r.4.155.)

4.153 Formalities of establishment

4.153(1) **[Liquidator's certificate]** The liquidation committee does not come into being, and accordingly cannot act, until the liquidator has issued a certificate of its due constitution.

[FORM 4.47]

4.153(2) **[If chairman of meeting not liquidator]** If the chairman of the meeting which resolves to establish the committee is not the liquidator, he shall as soon as reasonably practicable give notice of the resolution to the liquidator (or, as the case may be, the person appointed as liquidator by that same meeting), and inform him of the names and addresses of the persons elected to be members of the committee.

4.153(3) **[Agreement to act]** No person may act as a member of the committee unless and until he has agreed to do so and, unless the relevant proxy or authorisation contains a statement to the contrary, such agreement may be given by his proxy-holder present at the meeting establishing the committee or, in the case of a corporation, by its duly appointed representative.

4.153(3A) **[No certificate without agreement]** The liquidator's certificate of the committee's due constitution shall not be issued before the minimum number of persons (in accordance with Rule 4.152) who are to be members of the committee have agreed to act and must be issued as soon as reasonably practicable thereafter.

4.153(4) **[Amended certificate]** As and when the others (if any) agree to act, the liquidator shall issue an amended certificate.

4.153(5) [Omitted.]

4.153(6) **[Certificate to registrar]** The certificate, and any amended certificate, shall be sent by the liquidator to the registrar of companies as soon as reasonably practicable.

[FORM 4.47]

4.153(7) [Omitted.]

4.153(8) **[Change in membership]** If after the first establishment of the committee there is any change in its membership, as soon as reasonably practicable the liquidator shall report the change to the registrar of companies.

(See General Note after r.4.155.)

4.154 Committee established by contributories

(NO CVL APPLICATION)

4.154(1) **[Application of Rule]** The following applies where the creditors' meeting under section 141 does not decide that a liquidation committee should be established, or decides that a committee should not be established.

4.154(2)　[Further creditors' meeting] The meeting of contributories under that section may appoint one of their number to make application to the court for an order to the liquidator that a further creditors' meeting be summoned for the purpose of establishing a liquidation committee; and–

(a)　the court may, if it thinks that there are special circumstances to justify it, make that order, and

(b)　the creditors' meeting summoned by the liquidator in compliance with the order is deemed to have been summoned under section 141.

4.154(3)　[Meeting of contributories] If the creditors' meeting so summoned does not establish a liquidation committee, a meeting of contributories may do so.

4.154(4)　[Constitution of committee] The committee shall then consist of at least 3, and not more than 5, contributories elected by that meeting; and Rule 4.153 applies, substituting for the reference in paragraph (3A) of that Rule to Rule 4.152 a reference to this paragraph.

(See General Note after r.4.155.)

4.155　Obligations of liquidator to committee

4.155(1)　[Liquidator's duty to report] Subject as follows, it is the duty of the liquidator to report to the members of the liquidation committee all such matters as appear to him to be, or as they have indicated to him as being, of concern to them with respect to the winding up.

4.155(2)　[Non-compliance with request for information] In the case of matters so indicated to him by the committee, the liquidator need not comply with any request for information where it appears to him that–

(a)　the request is frivolous or unreasonable, or

(b)　the cost of complying would be excessive, having regard to the relative importance of the information, or

(c)　there are not sufficient assets to enable him to comply.

4.155(3)　[Report in summary form] Where the committee has come into being more than 28 days after the appointment of the liquidator, he shall report to them, in summary form, what actions he has taken since his appointment, and shall answer all such questions as they may put to him regarding his conduct of the winding up hitherto.

4.155(4)　[Summary report for subsequent member] A person who becomes a member of the committee at any time after its first establishment is not entitled to require a report to him by the liquidator, otherwise than in summary form, of any matters previously arising.

4.155(5)　[Access to liquidator's records] Nothing in this Rule disentitles the committee, or any member of it from having access to the liquidator's records of the liquidation, or from seeking an explanation of any matter within the committee's responsibility.

GENERAL NOTE TO RR.4.152–4.155

These rules deal with the membership of the liquidation committee in different circumstances (rr.4.152, 4.154), and with the liquidator's reporting obligations (r.4.155). Note that the contributories may be represented on the committee only in the case of a "solvent" winding up (as that term is defined by r.4.151(b)). On the termination of membership, see rr.4.160–4.164 and 4.171A; and for further reporting obligations, see r.4.168.

The amendment to r.153(3) is intended to enable a meeting of the liquidation committee to be held immediately after the meeting at which the liquidator is appointed.

Rule 4.152(7) was substituted by the Financial Services and Markets Act 2000 (Consequential Provisions and Repeals) Order 2001 (SI 2001/3649) as from December 1, 2001. Rule 4.153 amended and r.153(5), (7) omitted by I(A)R 2010 r.2 and Sch. para.230 as from April 6, 2010.

Documents passing between the liquidator and the Department of Trade and Industry concerning possible disqualification of directors are not documents which are within any of the statutory rights of the liquidation committee to inspect, or in respect of which the committee can properly put questions to the liquidator and ask him to report to them: *Re W & A Glaser Ltd* [1994] B.C.C. 199.

4.156 Meetings of the committee

4.156(1) **[Holding of meetings]** Subject as follows, meetings of the liquidation committee shall be held when and where determined by the liquidator.

4.156(2) **[First and subsequent meetings]** The liquidator shall call a first meeting of the committee to take place within 6 weeks of his appointment or of the committee's establishment (whichever is the later); and thereafter he shall call a meeting–

(a)   if so requested by a creditor member of the committee or his representative (the meeting then to be held within 21 days of the request being received by the liquidator), and

(b)   for a specified date, if the committee has previously resolved that a meeting be held on that date.

4.156(3) **[Notice of venue]** Subject to paragraph (4), the liquidator shall give 5 business days' written notice of the venue of a meeting to every member of the committee (or his representative, if designated for that purpose), unless in any case the requirement of the notice has been waived by or on behalf of any member.

Waiver may be signified either at or before the meeting.

4.156(4) **[Notice period for remote meeting]** Where the liquidator has determined that a meeting should be conducted and held in the manner referred to in Rule 12A.26(2), the notice period mentioned in paragraph (3) is 7 business days.

4.156(5) **[Additional functions of committee]** In addition to any functions conferred on a committee by any provision of the Act, a committee must assist the liquidator in discharging the liquidator's functions and act in relation to that liquidator in such manner as may from time to time be agreed.

(See General Note after r.4.159.)

4.157 The chairman at meetings

4.157(1) **[Liquidator or his appointee]** The chairman at any meeting of the liquidation committee shall be the liquidator, or a person appointed by the liquidator in writing to act.

4.157(2) **[Appointed chairman]** A person so appointed must be either–

(a)   one who is qualified to act as an insolvency practitioner in relation to the company, or

(b)   an employee of the liquidator or his firm who is experienced in insolvency matters.

(See General Note after r.4.159.)

4.158 Quorum

4.158(1) **[Two creditor members]** A meeting of the committee is duly constituted if due notice of it has been given to all the members, and at least 2 creditor members are present or represented.

(NO CVL APPLICATION)

4.158(2) **[Two members]** A meeting of the committee is duly constituted if due notice of it has been given to all the members, and at least 2 members are present or represented.

(See General Note after r.4.159.)

4.159 Committee-members' representatives

4.159(1) **[Representation]** A member of the liquidation committee may, in relation to the business of the committee, be represented by another person duly authorised by him for that purpose.

4.159(2) **[Letter of authority]** A person acting as a committee-member's representative must hold a letter of authority entitling him so to act (either generally or specially) and authenticated by or on behalf of the committee-member, and for this purpose any proxy in relation to any meeting of creditors (or, as the case may be, members or contributories) of the company shall, unless it contains a statement to the contrary, be treated as such a letter of authority to act generally authenticated by or on behalf of the committee-member.

4.159(3) **[Production of letter of authority]** The chairman at any meeting of the committee may call on a person claiming to act as a committee-member's representative to produce his letter of authority, and may exclude him if it appears that his authority is deficient.

4.159(4) **[Who may not be a representative]** No member may be represented by–

   (a)   another member of the committee;

   (b)   a person who is at the same time representing another committee member;

   (c)   a body corporate;

   (d)   an undischarged bankrupt;

   (e)   a disqualified director; or

   (f)   a person who is subject to a bankruptcy restrictions order (including an interim order), a bankruptcy restrictions undertaking, a debt relief restrictions order (including an interim order) or a debt relief restrictions undertaking.

4.159(5) [Omitted.]

4.159(6) **[Authenticating as representative]** Where a member's representative authenticates any document on the member's behalf, the fact that he so authenticates must be stated below his authentication.

GENERAL NOTE TO RR.4.156–4.159

Some of the rules regarding the holding and conduct of meetings of the liquidation committee are set out here. The remainder are at rr.4.165–4.168. On the members' expenses, see r.4.169, and on the role of representatives, see *Re W & A Glaser Ltd* [1994] B.C.C. 199 at 208. Rule 4.159(4) was amended by the Insolvency (Amendment) Rules 2004 (SI 2004/584), effective April 1, 2004, by the insertion of the reference to "a disqualified director", and also to take account of the changes made by the new bankruptcy regime.

    Rules 4.156, 4.157, 4.159 amended, r.4.159(4) substituted and r.4.159(5) omitted by I(A)R 2010 r.2 and Sch. paras 231–233 as from April 6, 2010. The liquidator must now call the first meeting of the creditors' committee within six weeks of his appointment (or the establishment of the committee, if later), rather than three months as previously.

4.160   Resignation

4.160 A member of the liquidation committee may resign by notice in writing delivered to the liquidator.

(See General Note after r.4.164.)

4.161   Termination of membership

4.161(1) **[Automatic termination]** A person's membership of the liquidation committee is automatically terminated if–

   (a)   he becomes bankrupt, or

   (b)   at 3 consecutive meetings of the committee he is neither present nor represented (unless at the third of those meetings it is resolved that this Rule is not to apply in his case).

4.161(2)   [Termination on bankruptcy] However, if the cause of termination is the member's bankruptcy, his trustee in bankruptcy replaces him as a member of the committee.

4.161(3)   [Not a creditor] The membership of a creditor member is also automatically terminated if he ceases to be, or is found never to have been, a creditor.

(See General Note after r.4.164.)

4.162   Removal

4.162(1)   [Removal by resolution] A creditor member of the committee may be removed by resolution at a meeting of creditors; and a contributory member may be removed by a resolution of a meeting of contributories.

4.162(2)   [Notice of intention] In either case, 14 days' notice must be given of the intention to move the resolution.

(See General Note after r.4.164.)

4.163   Vacancy (creditor members)

4.163(1)   [Application of Rule] The following applies if there is a vacancy among the creditor members of the committee.

4.163(2)   [Agreement not to fill vacancy] The vacancy need not be filled if the liquidator and a majority of the remaining creditor members so agree, provided that the total number of members does not fall below 3.

4.163(3)   [Appointment by liquidator] The liquidator may appoint any creditor (being qualified under the Rules to be a member of the committee) to fill the vacancy, if a majority of the other creditor members agree to the appointment, and the creditor concerned consents to act.

4.163(4)   [Appointment by resolution] Alternatively, a meeting of creditors may resolve that a creditor be appointed (with his consent) to fill the vacancy. In this case, at least 14 days' notice must have been given of the resolution to make such an appointment (whether or not of a person named in the notice).

4.163(5)   [Report to liquidator] Where the vacancy is filled by an appointment made by a creditors' meeting at which the liquidator is not present, the chairman of the meeting shall report to the liquidator the appointment which has been made.

(See General Note after r.4.164.)

4.164   Vacancy (contributory members)

4.164(1)   [Application of Rule] The following applies if there is a vacancy among the contributory members of the committee.

4.164(2)   [Agreement not to fill vacancy] The vacancy need not be filled if the liquidator and a majority of the remaining contributory members so agree, provided that, in the case of a committee of contributory members only, the total number of members does not fall below 3.

4.164(3)   [Appointment by liquidator] The liquidator may appoint any contributory member (being qualified under the Rules to be a member of the committee) to fill the vacancy, if a majority of the other contributory members agree to the appointment, and the contributory concerned consents to act.

4.164(4)   [Appointment by resolution] Alternatively, a meeting of contributories may resolve that a contributory be appointed (with his consent) to fill the vacancy. In this case, at least 14 days' notice must have been given of the resolution to make such an appointment (whether or not of a person named in the notice).

4.164(5)   [Where contributories make r.4.164(4) appointment] Where the contributories make an appointment under paragraph (4), the creditor members of the committee may, if they think fit, resolve that the person appointed ought not to be a member of the committee; and–

(a)   that person is not then, unless the court otherwise directs, qualified to act as a member of the committee, and

(b)   on any application to the court for a direction under this paragraph the court may, if it thinks fit, appoint another person (being a contributory) to fill the vacancy on the committee.

4.164(6)   [Report to liquidator] Where the vacancy is filled by an appointment made by a contributories' meeting at which the liquidator is not present, the chairman of the meeting shall report to the liquidator the appointment which has been made.

GENERAL NOTE TO RR.4.160–4.164

Note also that the membership of the creditor members of the committee automatically ceases when it is certified that the creditors have been paid in full (r.4.171A).
   Rules 4.163, 4.164 amended by I(A)R 2010 r.2 and Sch. paras 234, 235 as from April 6, 2010.

4.165   Voting rights and resolutions

(NO CVL APPLICATION)

4.165(1)   [Creditor members' votes] At any meeting of the committee, each member of it (whether present himself, or by his representative) has one vote; and a resolution is passed when a majority of the creditor members present or represented have voted in favour of it.

4.165(2)   [Contributory members' votes] Subject to the next paragraph, the votes of contributory members do not count towards the number required for passing a resolution, but the way in which they vote on any resolution shall be recorded.

4.165(3)   [Only contributory members] Paragraph (2) does not apply where, by virtue of Rule 4.154 or 4.171, the only members of the committee are contributories. In that case the committee is to be treated for voting purposes as if all its members were creditors.

4.165(4)   [Record of resolutions] Every resolution passed shall be recorded in writing, either separately or as part of the minutes of the meeting. The record shall be authenticated by the chairman and kept with the records of the liquidation.

(See General Note after r.4.169.)

4.166-CVL   Voting rights and resolutions

4.166-CVL(1)   [Votes etc.] At any meeting of the committee, each member of it (whether present himself, or by his representative) has one vote; and a resolution is passed when a majority of the members present or represented have voted in favour of it.

4.166-CVL(2)   [Record of resolutions] Every resolution passed shall be recorded in writing, either separately or as part of the minutes of the meeting. The record shall be authenticated by the chairman and kept with the records of the liquidation.

(See General Note after r.4.169.)

4.167   Resolutions otherwise than at a meeting

4.167(1)   [Sending proposed resolution] In accordance with this Rule, the liquidator may seek to obtain the agreement of members of the liquidation committee to a resolution by sending to every member (or his representative designated for the purpose) a copy of the proposed resolution.

4.167(2) **[Copy of proposed resolution]** Where the liquidator makes use of the procedure allowed by this Rule, he shall send out to members of the committee or their representatives (as the case may be) a copy of any proposed resolution on which a decision is sought, which shall be set out in such a way that agreement with or dissent from each separate resolution may be indicated by the recipient on the copy so sent.

4.167(3) **[Creditor requiring meeting]** Any creditor member of the committee may, within 7 business days from the date of the liquidator sending out a resolution, require him to summon a meeting of the committee to consider the matters raised by the resolution. (NO CVL APPLICATION)

4.167(4) **[Member requiring meeting]** Any member of the committee may, within 7 business days from the date of the liquidator sending out a resolution, require him to summon a meeting of the committee to consider the matters raised by the resolution.

4.167(5) **[Deemed passing of resolution]** In the absence of such a request, the resolution is deemed to have been passed by the committee if and when the liquidator is notified in writing by a majority of the creditor members that they concur with it. (NO CVL APPLICATION)

4.167(6) **[Deemed passing of resolution where no request]** In the absence of such a request, the resolution is deemed to have been passed by the committee if and when the liquidator is notified in writing by a majority of the members that they concur with it.

4.167(7) **[Copy of resolutions]** A copy of every resolution passed under this Rule, and a note that the committee's concurrence was obtained, shall be kept with the records of the liquidation.

(See General Note after r.4.169.)

4.168   Liquidator's reports

4.168(1) **[Liquidator directed to report]** The liquidator shall, as and when directed by the liquidation committee (but not more often than once in any period of 2 months), send a written report to every member of the committee setting out the position generally as regards the progress of the winding up and matters arising in connection with it, to which he (the liquidator) considers the committee's attention should be drawn.

4.168(2) **[If no directions to report]** In the absence of such directions by the committee, the liquidator shall send such a report not less often than once in every period of 6 months.

4.168(3) **[Effect of Rule]** The obligations of the liquidator under this Rule are without prejudice to those imposed by Rule 4.155.

(See General Note after r.4.169.)

4.169   Expenses of members, etc.

4.169 The liquidator shall defray as an expense of the liquidation, in the prescribed order of priority, any reasonable travelling expenses directly incurred by members of the liquidation committee or their representatives in respect of their attendance at the committee's meetings, or otherwise on the committee's business.

GENERAL NOTE TO RR.4.165–4.169

See also rr.4.155–4.159 and, on the question of priority, r.4.218(1)(m).

Rule 4.167(2), as now worded, removes the former requirement that each resolution be set out on a separate piece of paper. Rule 4.167 amended by I(A)R 2010 r.2 and Sch. para.236 as from April 6, 2010.

In *Re Buildlead Ltd (No.2)* [2004] EWHC 2443 (Ch); [2005] B.C.C. 138 the liquidators had not made the reports required by r.4.168(2) for several years and had used the method of postal ballots permitted by r.4.167 to sanction payment of their fees when, in the view of the court, it would have been more in keeping with the spirit of professional guidance to have held a meeting of the committee and held a full and frank discussion about the level of their fees. This was a material factor influencing the court in its decision to order that the liquidators be removed.

4.170   Dealings by committee-members and others

4.170(1)   [Application of Rule] This Rule applies to–

(a) any member of the liquidation committee,

(b) any committee-member's representative,

(c) any person who is an associate of a member of the committee or a committee-member's representative, and

(d) any person who has been a member of the committee at any time in the last 12 months.

4.170(2)   [Prohibited transactions] Subject as follows, a person to whom this Rule applies shall not enter into any transaction whereby he–

(a) receives as an expense of the liquidation any payment for services given or goods supplied in connection with the administration, or

(b) obtains any profit from the administration, or

(c) acquires any asset forming part of the estate.

4.170(3)   [Permission or sanction for r.4.170(2) transaction] Such a transaction may be entered into by a person to whom this Rule applies–

(a) with the prior permission of the court, or

(b) if he does so as a matter of urgency, or by way of performance of a contract in force before the date on which the company went into liquidation, and obtains the court's permission for the transaction, having applied for it without undue delay, or

(c) with the prior sanction of the liquidation committee, where it is satisfied (after full disclosure of the circumstances) that the person will be giving full value in the transaction.

4.170(4)   [Resolution to sanction transaction] Where in the committee a resolution is proposed that sanction be accorded for a transaction to be entered into which, without that sanction or the permission of the court, would be in contravention of this Rule, no member of the committee, and no representative of a member, shall vote if he is to participate directly or indirectly in the transaction.

4.170(5)   [Powers of court] The court may, on the application of any person interested–

(a) set aside a transaction on the ground that it has been entered into in contravention of this Rule, and

(b) make with respect to it such other order as it thinks fit, including (subject to the following paragraph) an order requiring a person to whom this Rule applies to account for any profit obtained from the transaction and compensate the estate for any resultant loss.

4.170(6)   [Member's or representative's associate] In the case of a person to whom this Rule applies as an associate of a member of the committee or of a committee-member's representative, the court shall not make any order under paragraph (5), if satisfied that he entered into the relevant transaction without having any reason to suppose that in doing so he would contravene this Rule.

4.170(7)   [Costs of application] The costs of an application to the court for permission under this Rule are not payable as an expense of the liquidation, unless the court so orders.

GENERAL NOTE

This rule makes provision to guard against the risks of conflicts of interest on the part of committee members and their associates. (For the meaning of "associate", see IA 1986 s.435.)

4.171   Composition of committee when creditors paid in full [Deleted.]

4.171A   Composition of committee when creditors paid in full

4.171A(1)   [Certificate that creditors paid in full] Where the creditors have been paid in full together with interest in accordance with section 189, the liquidator must–

(a)   issue a certificate to that effect; and

(b)   send to the registrar of companies a notification to that effect together with a copy of the certificate referred to in sub-paragraph (a).

4.171A(2)   [Committee membership ceases on issue of certificate] On the issue of a certificate pursuant to paragraph (1), the creditor members of the liquidation committee cease to be members of the committee.

4.171A(3)   [Status of committee] The committee continues in existence unless–

(a)   it is abolished by a decision of a meeting of contributories; or

(b)   the number of members is less than 3 and 28 days have elapsed since the issue of the liquidator's certificate.

4.171A(4)   [Suspension of committee] At any time in the period referred to in paragraph (3)(b) where the committee consists of less than 3 contributory members it is suspended and cannot act.

4.171A(5)   [Contents of r.4.121A(1)(a) certificate] The certificate referred to in paragraph (1)(a) must include the following information–

(a)   the name of the liquidator; and

(b)   a statement by the liquidator certifying that the creditors of the company have been paid in full together with interest in accordance with section 189;

and must be authenticated and dated by the liquidator.

GENERAL NOTE

The liquidation committee continues in being without creditor members after the creditors have been paid in full, subject to r.4.171A(3).

Rule 4.171 deleted and r.4.171A inserted by I(A)R 2010 r.2 and Sch. para.237 as from April 6, 2010.

4.172   Committee's functions vested in Secretary of State

(NO CVL APPLICATION)

4.172(1)   [Liquidator's notices and reports] At any time when the functions of the liquidation committee are vested in the Secretary of State under section 141(4) or (5), requirements of the Act or the Rules about notices to be given, or reports to be made, to the committee by the liquidator do not apply, otherwise than as enabling the committee to require a report as to any matter.

4.172(2)   [Exercise by official receiver] Where the committee's functions are so vested under section 141(5), they may be exercised by the official receiver.

GENERAL NOTE

IA 1986 s.141(4) applies when the official receiver is liquidator, and s.141(5) where there is for the time being no liquidation committee.

4.172A   Formal defects

4.172A   The acts of the liquidation committee established for any winding up are valid notwithstanding any defect in the appointment, election or qualifications of any member of the committee or any committee-member's representative or in the formalities of its establishment.

This is a standard-form provision designed to prevent technical objections to the constitution of the committee. (See, however, *Re W & A Glaser Ltd* [1994] B.C.C. 199, which makes it clear that the court itself is free to go into this question.)

CHAPTER 13

THE LIQUIDATION COMMITTEE WHERE WINDING UP FOLLOWS IMMEDIATELY ON ADMINISTRATION (NO CVL APPLICATION)

4.173   Preliminary

4.173(1)   [Application of Rules] The Rules in this Chapter apply where–

(a)   the winding-up order has been made by the court upon an application under paragraph 79 of Schedule B1 to the Act,

(b)   the court makes an order under section 140(1) of the Act appointing as liquidator the person who was previously the administrator,

(c)   a creditors' committee was established under paragraph 57 of Schedule B1 to the Act, and

(d)   as at the date of the making of the order under section 140(1) the committee has at least three, but not more than five, members (leaving out of account any member whose debt is fully secured).

4.173(2)   [Definitions] In this Chapter, **"insolvent winding up"**, **"solvent winding up"**, **"creditor member"** and **"contributory member"** mean the same as in Chapter 12.

(See General Note after r.4.178.)

4.174   Continuation of creditors' committee [Deleted.]

4.174A   Continuation of creditors' committee

4.174A   Where a committee of the kind mentioned in Rule 4.173 is in existence in the circumstances mentioned in that Rule–

(a)   that committee is deemed to have been established under section 141;

(b)   no action may be taken under section 141(1) to (3) to establish any other committee;

(c)   in the case of a solvent winding up, the liquidator must, on not less than 14 days' notice summon a meeting of contributories, in order to elect (if it so wishes) contributory members of the liquidation committee, up to 3 in number; and

(d)   pending the issue of the liquidator's certificate referred to in Rule 4.176 the committee is suspended and cannot act.

(See General Note after r.4.178.)

4.175   Membership of committee [Revoked by I(A)R 2010 r.5 as from April 6, 2010.]

4.176   Liquidator's certificate

4.176(1)   [Certificate of continuance] The liquidator must ascertain whether the members of the committee agree to continue to act as members of the committee; and if the minimum number of 3 members required by Rule 4.152 to form a committee have signified their agreement so to act, the

The Insolvency Rules 1986

liquidator must issue a certificate of the liquidation committee's continuance, specifying the person who are, or are to be, members of it.

[FORM 4.52]

4.176(2) **[Contents of certificate]** It shall be stated in the certificate whether or not the liquidator has summoned a meeting of contributories under Rule 4.174A(c), and whether (if so) the meeting has elected contributories to be members of the committee.

4.176(3) [Omitted.]

4.176(4) **[Agreement to act]** No person may act, or continue to act, as a member of the committee unless and until he has agreed to do so.

4.176(5) **[Amended certificate]** As and when the others signify their agreement, the liquidator shall issue an amended certificate.

[FORM 4.52]

4.176(6) **[Liquidator to send certificate to registrar]** The liquidator must send the certificate in paragraph (1) or as the case may be the amended certificate in paragraph (5) to the registrar of companies.

4.176(7) **[Change in membership]** If subsequently there is any change in the committee's membership, the liquidator must send an amended certificate to the registrar of companies.

(See General Note after r.4.178.)

4.177 Obligations of liquidator to committee

4.177(1) **[Liquidator's report]** As soon as reasonably practicable after the issue of the liquidator's certificate under Rule 4.176, the liquidator shall report to the liquidation committee what actions he has taken since the date on which the company went into liquidation.

4.177(2) **[Summary report]** A person who becomes a member of the committee after the date of issue of the liquidator's certificate is not entitled to require a report to him by the liquidator, otherwise than in a summary form, of any matters previously arising.

4.177(3) **[Access to records etc.]** Nothing in this Rule disentitles the committee, or any member of it, from having access to the records of the liquidation (whether relating to the period when he was administrator, or to any subsequent period), or from seeking an explanation of any matter within the committee's responsibility.

(See General Note after r.4.178.)

4.178 Application of Chapter 12

4.178 Except as provided above in this Chapter, Rules 4.155 to 4.172A in Chapter 12 apply to the liquidation committee following the issue of the liquidator's certificate under Rule 4.176, as if it had been established under section 141.

GENERAL NOTE TO RR.4.173–4.178

These rules adapt those generally applicable to the liquidation committee (rr.4.151–4.172A) for the special case where a winding up follows immediately on an administration. The creditors' committee appointed for the purpose of the administration continues in being as the liquidation committee, subject to the right of the contributories (where it is a "solvent" liquidation—see r.4.151) to appoint their own members.

In rr.4.173(1)(a), 4.174A and 4.175(1) references to the original Pt II have been replaced by references to Sch.B1, which will of course apply only in the new administration regime: see the Insolvency (Amendment) Rules 2003 (SI 2003/1730, effective September 15, 2003) Sch.1 paras 24–26. Rules 4.173, 4.176, 4.177 amended, r.4.174 deleted and r.4.174A inserted by I(A)R 2010 r.2 and Sch. paras 238–241 as from April 6, 2010.

CHAPTER 14

COLLECTION AND DISTRIBUTION OF COMPANY'S ASSETS BY LIQUIDATOR

4.179 General duties of liquidator

(NO CVL APPLICATION)

4.179(1) [Officer of the court] The duties imposed on the court by the Act with regard to the collection of the company's assets and their application in discharge of its liabilities are discharged by the liquidator as an officer of the court subject to its control.

4.179(2) [Same powers as a receiver] In the discharge of his duties the liquidator, for the purposes of acquiring and retaining possession of the company's property, has the same powers as a receiver appointed by the High Court, and the court may on his application enforce such acquisition or retention accordingly.

GENERAL NOTE

For the statutory source of this rule, see IA 1986, ss.148(1), 160(1)(b).

4.180 Manner of distributing assets

4.180(1) [Dividends] Whenever the liquidator has sufficient funds in hand for the purpose he shall, subject to the retention of such sums as may be necessary for the expenses of the winding up, declare and distribute dividends among the creditors in respect of the debts which they have respectively proved.

4.180(2) [Notice of intention] The liquidator shall give notice of his intention to declare and distribute a dividend.

4.180(3) [Notice of dividend] Where the liquidator has declared a dividend, he shall give notice of it to the creditors, stating how the dividend is proposed to be distributed. The notice shall contain such particulars with respect to the company, and to its assets and affairs, as will enable the creditors to comprehend the calculation of the amount of the dividend and the manner of its distribution.

(See General Note after r.4.183.)

4.181 Debts of insolvent company to rank equally

(NO CVL APPLICATION)

4.181(1) [Ranking and priority] Debts other than preferential debts rank equally between themselves in the winding up and, after the preferential debts, shall be paid in full unless the assets are insufficient for meeting them, in which case they abate in equal proportions between themselves.

4.181(2) [Application of r.4.181(1)] Paragraph (1) applies whether or not the company is unable to pay its debts.

(See General Note after r.4.183.)

4.182 Supplementary provisions as to dividend

4.182(1) [Calculation and distribution] In the calculation and distribution of a dividend the liquidator shall make provision–

(a) for any debts which appear to him to be due to persons who, by reason of the distance of their place of residence, may not have had sufficient time to tender and establish their proofs,

(b) for any debts which are the subject of claims which have not yet been determined, and

(c) for disputed proofs and claims.

4.182(2) **[Proof after dividend declared]** A creditor who has not proved his debt before the declaration of any dividend is not entitled to disturb, by reason that he has not participated in it, the distribution of that dividend or any other dividend declared before his debt was proved, but–

(a) when he has proved that debt he is entitled to be paid, out of any money for the time being available for the payment of any further dividend, any dividend or dividends which he has failed to receive, and

(b) any dividend or dividends payable under sub-paragraph (a) shall be paid before that money is applied to the payment of any such further dividend.

4.182(3) **[Order for payment etc.]** No action lies against the liquidator for a dividend; but if he refuses to pay a dividend the court may, if it thinks fit, order him to pay it and also to pay, out of his own money–

(a) interest on the dividend, at the rate for the time being specified in section 17 of the Judgments Act 1838, from the time when it was withheld, and

(b) the costs of the proceedings in which the order to pay is made.

(See General Note after r.4.183.)

4.182A   Distribution in members' voluntary winding up

(NO CVL APPLICATION)

4.182A(1) **[Gazetting/advertisement of intention to distribute]** In a members' voluntary winding up the liquidator may give notice of the intention to make a distribution to creditors. Such notice–

(a) shall be gazetted; and

(b) may be advertised in such other manner as the liquidator thinks fit.

4.182A(2) **["The last date for proving"]** In addition to the standard contents, the notice under paragraph (1) must–

(a) state that the liquidator intends to make a distribution to creditors; and

(b) specify a date (**"the last date for proving"**) up to which proofs may be lodged at a specified place, which must be the same date for all creditors and not less than 21 days from that of the notice.

4.182A(3) **[Proofs lodged out of time]** The liquidator is not obliged to deal with proofs lodged after the last date for proving; but he may do so, if he thinks fit.

4.182A(4) **[Distribution not to be disturbed]** A creditor who has not proved his debt before the last date for proving or after that date increases the claim in his proof is not entitled to disturb, by reason that he has not participated in it, either at all or, as the case may be, to the extent that his increased claim would allow, that distribution or any other distribution made before his debt was proved or his claim increased; but when he has proved his debt or, as the case may be, increased his claim, he is entitled to be paid, out of any money for the time being available for the payment of any further distribution, any distribution or distributions which he has failed to receive.

4.182A(5) **[Only or final distribution]** Where the distribution proposed to be made is to be the only or the final distribution in that winding up, the liquidator may, subject to paragraph (6), make that distribution without regard to the claim of any person in respect of a debt not already proved.

4.182A(6) **[Notice in r.4.182A(5)]** Where the distribution proposed to be made is one specified in paragraph (5), the notice given under paragraph (1) shall state the effect of paragraph (5).

(See General Note after r.4.183.)

4.183   Division of unsold assets

4.183(1)   [Power of liquidator to divide assets] Without prejudice to provisions of the Act about disclaimer, the liquidator may, with the permission of the liquidation committee (or if there is no such committee, a meeting of the company's creditors), divide in its existing form amongst the company's creditors, according to its estimated value, any property which from its peculiar nature or other special circumstances cannot be readily or advantageously sold.

4.183(2)   [Duty of liquidator] The liquidator must comply with paragraph (3) in respect of any account or report which the liquidator is required to prepare pursuant to any of the following–

(a)   section 104A (progress report to company and creditors at year's end);

(b)   section 106 (final meeting prior to dissolution – creditors' voluntary winding up);

(c)   section 146 (duty to summon final meeting – winding up by the court);

(d)   Rule 4.49B (reports to creditors and members – winding up by the court);

(e)   Rule 4.49D (final report to creditors);

(f)   Rule 4.108 (creditors' meeting to receive liquidator's resignation);

(g)   Rule 4.125 (final meeting – winding up by the court);

(h)   Rule 4.126 (final meeting – creditors' voluntary liquidation).

4.183(3)   [Value of distributed assets to be stated] The liquidator must–

(a)   in any account or summary of receipts and payments which is required to be included in the account or report, state the estimated value of the property distributed amongst the creditors of the company during the period to which the account or report relates, and

(b)   as a note to the account or summary of receipts and payments, provide details of the basis of the valuation.

GENERAL NOTE TO RR.4.180–4.183

These rules deal with the distribution of dividends and the ranking of debts *inter se*. For further provisions regarding dividends, see rr.4.186 and 11.1 et seq.; and on preferential debts see IA 1986 s.386 and Sch.6.

If the liquidator proposes to pay an interim dividend at a time when an application to the court to challenge the admission or rejection of a proof is outstanding, the leave of the court is required under IR 1986 r.11.5(2).

Rule 4.181 was amended by the addition of para.(2) in 1987, but this amendment seems to have added more confusion that it has dispelled. If the new para.(2) was necessary at all, it ought to have been accompanied by the removal of the reference to insolvency in the heading to the rule. It appears that para.(2) was introduced to refer to the words "shall be paid in full" in para.(1); but there can hardly be any question of the "ranking" of debts that are all to be paid in full.

Rule 4.182A(1) substituted by I(A)R 2009 (SI 2009/642) r.29 as from April 6, 2009. Rules 4.182A, 4.183(1) amended and r.4.183(2), (3) inserted by I(A)R 2010 r.2 and Sch. paras 242, 243 as from April 6, 2010.

The notice required by r.4.182A must contain the information mentioned in r.4128A(2) in addition to the standard contents. On the standard contents for gazetted notices, see rr.12A.31–12A.33. On the standard contents for notices other than gazetted notices, see rr.12A.36–12A.39.

If any assets have been distributed in specie, the liquidator's report must include details of the valuation of the property concerned (r.4.183(3)).

Note that a sum due to a member qua member is not deemed to be a debt, and ranks after the claims of the company's creditors: s.74(2)(f).

Provision equivalent to r.4.181 is made for a voluntary winding up by s.107.

In *Lomax Leisure Ltd* [2007] EWHC 2508 (Ch); [2008] B.C.C. 686 a final dividend had been declared and cheques had been posted to all the creditors who had been admitted to proof. Meantime, a creditor whose proof had been rejected had applied to the court appealing against the rejection of his proof, but notice of his application was not served on the liquidators until after the cheques had been sent out. The liquidators immediately stopped payment on the cheques. It was held that the creditors had no right to enforce payment of the cheques under the Bills of Exchange

Act 1882 s.27, since they had given no consideration sufficient to support the cheques. The court also confirmed that the only remedy of a creditor who wished to enforce payment of a dividend was to apply under r.4.182(3): he could not sue the liquidator directly.

4.184   General powers of liquidator

4.184(1)   **[Particular permission]** Any permission given by the liquidation committee (or if there is no such committee, a meeting of the company's creditors) or the court under section 165(2) or section 167(1)(a), or under the Rules, shall not be a general permission but shall relate to a particular proposed exercise of the liquidator's power in question; and a person dealing with the liquidator in good faith and for value is not concerned to enquire whether any such permission has been given.

4.184(2)   **[Ratification]** Where the liquidator has done anything without that permission, the court or the liquidation committee may, for the purpose of enabling him to meet his expenses out of the assets, ratify what he has done; but neither shall do so unless it is satisfied that the liquidator has acted in a case of urgency and has sought ratification without undue delay.

GENERAL NOTE

The powers referred to in IA 1986 s.167(1)(a) are the payment of debts, the compromise of claims, the institution and defence of proceedings, and the carrying on of the business of the company.

     Minor modifications were made to this rule by the Insolvency (Amendment) Rules 2005 (SI, 2005/527) r.31, as from April 1, 2005.

4.185   Enforced delivery up of company's property

(NO CVL APPLICATION)

4.185(1)   **[Powers under s.234]** The powers conferred on the court by section 234 (enforced delivery of company property) are exercisable by the liquidator or, where a provisional liquidator has been appointed, by him.

4.185(2)   **[Duty to comply]** Any person on whom a requirement under section 234(2) is imposed by the liquidator or provisional liquidator shall, without avoidable delay, comply with it.

GENERAL NOTE

For the statutory source of this rule, see IA 1986 ss.160(1)(c), 234.

4.186   Final distribution

4.186(1)   **[Notice under Pt 11]** When the liquidator has realised all the company's assets or so much of them as can, in his opinion, be realised without needlessly protracting the liquidation, he shall give notice, under Part 11 of the Rules, either–

     (a)   of his intention to declare a final dividend, or

     (b)   that no dividend, or further dividend, will be declared.

4.186(2)   **[Contents of notice]** The notice shall contain all such particulars as are required by Part 11 of the Rules and shall require claims against the assets to be established by a date specified in the notice.

4.186(3)   **[Final dividend]** After that date, the liquidator shall–

     (a)   defray any outstanding expenses of the winding up as an expense of the liquidation, and

     (b)   if he intends to declare a final dividend, declare and distribute that dividend without regard to the claim of any person in respect of a debt not already proved.

4.186(4)   **[Postponement]** The court may, on the application of any person, postpone the date specified in the notice.

GENERAL NOTE
On dividends generally, see rr.4.180–4.183 and 11.1 et seq.

CHAPTER 15

DISCLAIMER

4.187   Liquidator's notice of disclaimer

4.187(1)   [Contents of notice] Where the liquidator disclaims property under section 178, the notice of disclaimer shall contain such particulars of the property disclaimed as enable it to be easily identified.

[FORM 4.53A]

4.187(2)   [Notice to be authenticated and dated] The notice of disclaimer must be authenticated and dated by the liquidator.

4.187(3)   [Omitted.]

4.187(3A)   [Copy of notice to registrar etc.] As soon as reasonably practicable after authenticating the notice of disclaimer, the liquidator must–

(a)   send a copy of the notice to the registrar of companies; and

(b)   in any case where the disclaimer is of registered land as defined in section 132(1) of the Land Registration Act 2002, send a copy of the notice to the Chief Land Registrar.

4.187(4)   [Date of notice] For the purposes of section 178, the date of the prescribed notice is that on which the liquidator authenticated it.

(See General Note after r.4.194.)

4.188   Communication of disclaimer to persons interested

4.188(1)   [Copies of notices] Within 7 business days after the date of the notice of disclaimer, the liquidator shall send or give copies of the notice to the persons mentioned in paragraphs (2) to (4).

[FORM 4.53A]

4.188(2)   [Leasehold property] Where the property disclaimed is of a leasehold nature, he shall send or give a copy to every person who (to his knowledge) claims under the company as underlessee or mortgagee.

4.188(3)   [Giving notice] He shall in any case send or give a copy of the notice to every person who (to his knowledge)–

(a)   claims an interest in the disclaimed property, or

(b)   is under any liability in respect of the property, not being a liability discharged by the disclaimer.

4.188(4)   [Unprofitable contract] If the disclaimer is of an unprofitable contract, he shall send or give copies of the notice to all such persons as, to his knowledge, are parties to the contract or have interests under it.

4.188(5)   [Late communication] If subsequently it comes to the liquidator's knowledge, in the case of any person, that he has such an interest in the disclaimed property as would have entitled him to receive a copy of the notice of disclaimer in pursuance of paragraphs (2) to (4), the liquidator shall then as soon as reasonably practicable send or give to that person a copy of the notice.

But compliance with this paragraph is not required if–

(a)   the liquidator is satisfied that the person has already been made aware of the disclaimer and its date, or

(b) the court, on the liquidator's application, orders that compliance is not required in that particular case.

(See General Note after r.4.194.)

4.189   Additional notices

4.189   The liquidator disclaiming property may, without prejudice to his obligations under sections 178 to 180 and Rules 4.187 and 4.188, at any time send or give copies of the notice of the disclaimer to any persons who in his opinion ought, in the public interest or otherwise, to be informed of the disclaimer.

[FORM 4.53A]

(See General Note after r.4.194.)

4.190   Duty to keep court informed [Revoked by I(A)R 2010 r.5 (with retrospective effect).]

4.190A   Records

4.190A   The liquidator must include in the liquidator's records of the insolvency a record of–

(a) the persons to whom that liquidator has sent or given copies of the notice of disclaimer under the two preceding Rules, showing their names and addresses, and the nature of their respective interests;

(b) the dates on which the copies of the notice of disclaimer were sent or given to those persons;

(c) the date on which, as required by Rule 4.187(3)(a), a copy of the notice of disclaimer was sent to the registrar of companies; and

(d) (where applicable) the date on which, as required by Rule 4.187(3)(b), a copy of the notice was sent to the Chief Land Registrar.

(See General Note after r.4.194.)

4.191   Application by interested party under s.178(5) [Deleted.]

4.191A   Application to interested party under s 178(5)

4.191A(1)   [Where application to liquidator] The following applies where, in the case of any property, application is made to the liquidator by an interested party under section 178(5).

4.191A(2)   [How application to be delivered] The application must be delivered to the liquidator–

(a) personally;

(b) by electronic means in accordance with Part 12A; or

(c) by any other means of delivery which enables proof of receipt of the application by the liquidator to be provided, if requested.

(See General Note after r.4.194.)

4.192   Interest in property to be declared on request

4.192(1)   [Notice to declare interest] If, in the case of property which the liquidator has the right to disclaim, it appears to him that there is some person who claims, or may claim, to have an interest in the property, he may give notice to that person calling on him to declare within 14 days whether he claims any such interest and, if so, the nature and extent of it.

[FORM 4.55]

4.192(2) **[Failing compliance with notice]** Failing compliance with the notice, the liquidator is entitled to assume that the person concerned has no such interest in the property as will prevent or impede its disclaimer.

(See General Note after r.4.194.)

4.193 Disclaimer presumed valid and effective

4.193 Any disclaimer of property by the liquidator is presumed valid and effective, unless it is proved that he has been in breach of his duty with respect to the giving of notice of disclaimer, or otherwise under sections 178 to 180, or under this Chapter of the Rules.

(See General Note after r.4.194.)

4.194 Application for exercise of court's powers under s.181

4.194(1) **[Application of Rule]** This Rule applies with respect to an application by any person under section 181 for an order of the court to vest or deliver disclaimed property.

4.194(2) **[Time for application]** The application must be made within 3 months of the applicant becoming aware of the disclaimer, or of his receiving a copy of the liquidator's notice of disclaimer sent under Rule 4.188, whichever is the earlier.

4.194(3) **[Contents of witness statement]** The applicant shall with his application file a witness statement–

(a) stating whether he applies under paragraph (a) of section 181(2) (claim of interest in the property) or under paragraph (b) (liability not discharged);

(b) specifying the date on which he received a copy of the liquidator's notice of disclaimer, or otherwise became aware of the disclaimer; and

(c) specifying the grounds of his application and the order which he desires the court to make under section 181.

4.194(4) **[Venue for hearing]** The court shall fix a venue for the hearing of the application; and the applicant shall, not later than 5 business days before the date fixed, give to the liquidator notice of the venue, accompanied by copies of the application and the witness statement required by paragraph (3).

4.194(5) **[Directions for notice etc.]** On the hearing of the application, the court may give directions as to other persons (if any) who should be sent or given notice of the application and the grounds on which it is made.

4.194(6) **[Sealed copies of order]** Sealed copies of any order made on the application shall be sent by the court to the applicant and the liquidator.

4.194(7) **[Leasehold property]** In a case where the property disclaimed is of a leasehold nature, and section 179 applies to suspend the effect of the disclaimer, there shall be included in the court's order a direction giving effect to the disclaimer.

This paragraph does not apply if, at the time when the order is issued, other applications under section 181 are pending in respect of the same property.

GENERAL NOTE TO RR.4.187–4.194

The statutory powers of disclaimer are contained in IA 1986 ss.178–182. These rules supplement those provisions. On property "of a leasehold nature", see IA 1986 ss.179, 182.

The period of three months specified in r.4.194(2) may be extended at the discretion of the court: *W H Smith Ltd v Wyndham Investments Ltd* [1994] B.C.C. 699. In the same case it was held that, although a lease becomes ownerless following a disclaimer, it does not disappear, but ceases to exist only on the occurrence of one of the normal means of termination—effluxion of time, surrender or retaking of possession by the landlord.

Rule 4.191 deleted, rr.4.187, 4.189, 4.194 amended, r.4.188(7) substituted and rr.4.190A, 4.191A inserted by I(A)R 2010 r.2 and Sch. paras 244–248 as from April 6, 2010. In consequence of these amendments, it is no longer a requirement that a copy of the liquidator's disclaimer should be filed in court and in due course returned to him endorsed by the court. Instead, a copy must be sent to the registrar of companies and also in an appropriate case to the Chief Land Registrar. The former r.4.190 required the liquidator to keep the court informed regarding the disclaimer. This has been replaced by an obligation to keep certain records (r.4.190A).

CHAPTER 16

SETTLEMENT OF LIST OF CONTRIBUTORIES (NO CVL APPLICATION)

4.195 Preliminary

4.195 The duties of the court with regard to the settling of the list of contributories are, by virtue of the Rules, delegated to the liquidator.

(See General Note after r.4.196.)

4.196 Duty of liquidator to settle list

4.196(1) **[Settling list of contributories]** Subject as follows, the liquidator shall, as soon as may be after his appointment, exercise the court's power to settle a list of the company's contributories for the purposes of section 148 and, with the court's approval, rectify the register of members.

4.196(2) **[Officer of the court]** The liquidator's duties under this Rule are performed by him as an officer of the court subject to the court's control.

GENERAL NOTE TO RR.4.195–4.196

For the statutory source of these rules, see IA 1986 ss.148, 160(1)(b).

4.197 Form of list

4.197(1) **[Contents of list]** The list shall identify–

   (a)   the several classes of the company's shares (if more than one), and

   (b)   the several classes of contributories, distinguishing between those who are contributories in their own right and those who are so as representatives of, or liable for the debts of, others.

4.197(2) **[Further contents]** In the case of each contributory there shall in the list be stated–

   (a)   his address,

   (b)   the number and class of shares, or the extent of any other interest to be attributed to him, and

   (c)   if the shares are not fully paid up, the amounts which have been called up and paid in respect of them (and the equivalent, if any, where his interest is other than shares).

(See General Note after r.4.201.)

4.198 Procedure for settling list

4.198(1) **[Notice]** Having settled the list, the liquidator shall as soon as reasonably practicable give notice, to every person included in the list, that he has done so.

4.198(2) **[Contents of notice]** The notice given to each person shall state–

   (a)   in what character, and for what number of shares or what interest, he is included in the list,

   (b)   what amounts have been called up and paid up in respect of the shares or interest, and

(c) that in relation to any shares or interest not fully paid up, his inclusion in the list may result in the unpaid capital being called.

4.198(3) [Objection to list] The notice shall inform any person to whom it is given that, if he objects to any entry in, or omission from, the list, he should so inform the liquidator in writing within 21 days from the date of the notice.

4.198(4) [Amendment of list] On receipt of any such objection, the liquidator shall within 14 days give notice to the objector either–

(a) that he has amended the list (specifying the amendment), or

(b) that he considers the objection to be not well-founded and declines to amend the list.

The notice shall in either case inform the objector of the effect of Rule 4.199.

(See General Note after r.4.201.)

4.199 Application to court for variation of the list

4.199(1) [Application to court] If a person objects to any entry in, or exclusion from, the list of contributories as settled by the liquidator and, notwithstanding notice by the liquidator declining to amend the list, maintains his objection, he may apply to the court for an order removing the entry to which he objects or (as the case may be) otherwise amending the list.

4.199(2) [Time for application] The application must be made within 21 days of the service on the applicant of the liquidator's notice under Rule 4.198(4).

(See General Note after r.4.201.)

4.200 Variation of, or addition to, the list

4.200 The liquidator may from time to time vary or add to the list of contributories as previously settled by him, but subject in all respects to the preceding Rules in this Chapter.

(See General Note after r.4.201.)

4.201 Costs not to fall on official receiver

4.201 The official receiver is not personally liable for any costs incurred by a person in respect of an application to set aside or vary his act or decision in settling the list of contributories, or varying or adding to the list; and the liquidator (if other than the official receiver) is not so liable unless the court makes an order to that effect.

GENERAL NOTE TO RR.4.197–4.201

Here are set out the rules prescribing the form of the list of contributories and the procedure for settling it. Note that the power to rectify the register of members may be exercised only with the special leave of the court: IA 1986 s.160(2), r.4.196(1).

CHAPTER 17

CALLS (NO CVL APPLICATION)

4.202 Calls by liquidator

4.202 Subject as follows, the powers conferred by the Act with respect to the making of calls on contributories are exercisable by the liquidator as an officer of the court subject to the court's control.

(See General Note after r.4.205.)

4.203   Control by liquidation committee

4.203(1)   **[Meeting to sanction call]** Where the liquidator proposes to make a call, and there is a liquidation committee, he may summon a meeting of the committee for the purpose of obtaining its sanction.

4.203(2)   **[Notice]** At least 5 business days' notice of the meeting shall be given by the liquidator to each member of the committee.

4.203(3)   **[Contents of notice]** The notice shall contain a statement of the proposed amount of the call, and the purpose for which it is intended to be made.

(See General Note after r.4.205.)

4.204   Application to court for permission to make a call

4.204(1)   **[Form of application]** For the purpose of obtaining the permission of the court for the making of a call on any contributories of the company, the liquidator shall apply without notice to any other party, supporting his application by witness statement.

[FORM 4.56]

4.204(2)   **[Contents of application]** There shall in the application be stated the amount of the proposed call, and the contributories on whom it is to be made.

4.204(3)   **[Powers of court]** The court may direct that notice of the order be given to the contributories concerned, or to other contributories, or may direct that the notice be publicly advertised.

[FORM 4.57]

(See General Note after r.4.205.)

4.205   Making and enforcement of the call

4.205(1)   **[Notice of call]** Notice of the call shall be given to each of the contributories concerned, and shall specify–

  (a)   the amount or balance due from him in respect of it, and

  (b)   whether the call is made with the sanction of the court or the liquidation committee.

[FORM 4.58]

4.205(2)   **[Enforcement by order]** Payment of the amount due from any contributory may be enforced by order of the court.

[FORM 4.59]

GENERAL NOTE TO RR.4.202–4.205

For the statutory source of these rules, see IA 1986 ss.150, 160(1)(d). The exercise of the power of the liquidator to make a call requires the special leave of the court or the sanction of the liquidation committee (s.160(2), rr.4.203, 4.204).

CHAPTER 18

SPECIAL MANAGER

4.206   Appointment and remuneration

4.206(1)   **[Liquidator's report]** An application made by the liquidator under section 177 for the appointment of a person to be special manager shall be supported by a report setting out the reasons for the application.

The report shall include the applicant's estimate of the value of the business or property in respect of which the special manager is to be appointed.

4.206(2) [Application of Chapter] This Chapter applies also with respect to an application by the provisional liquidator, where one has been appointed, and references to the liquidator are to be read accordingly as including the provisional liquidator. (NO CVL APPLICATION).

4.206(3) [Duration of appointment] The court's order appointing the special manager shall specify the duration of his appointment, which may be for a period of time, or until the occurrence of a specified event. Alternatively, the order may specify that the duration of the appointment is to be subject to a further order of the court.

[FORM 4.60]

4.206(4) [Renewal] The appointment of a special manager may be renewed by order of the court.

4.206(5) [Remuneration] The special manager's remuneration shall be fixed from time to time by the court.

4.206(6) [Validation of acts] The acts of the special manager are valid notwithstanding any defect in his appointment or qualifications.

(See General Note after r.4.210.)

4.207 Security

4.207(1) [Effect of giving security] The appointment of the special manager does not take effect until the person appointed has given (or, being allowed by the court to do so, undertaken to give) security to the person who applies for him to be appointed.

4.207(2) [Special or general security] It is not necessary that security shall be given for each separate company liquidation; but it may be given either specially for a particular liquidation, or generally for any liquidation in relation to which the special manager may be employed as such.

4.207(3) [Amount of security] The amount of the security shall be not less than the value of the business or property in respect of which he is appointed, as estimated by the applicant in his report under Rule 4.206.

4.207(4) [Certificate of adequacy] When the special manager has given security to the person applying for his appointment, that person shall file in court a certificate as to the adequacy of the security.

4.207(5) [Cost of security] The cost of providing the security shall be paid in the first instance by the special manager; but–

(a) where a winding-up order is not made, he is entitled to be reimbursed out of the property of the company, and the court may make an order on the company accordingly, and

(b) where a winding-up order is made, he is entitled to be reimbursed as an expense of the liquidation in the prescribed order of priority.

(NO CVL APPLICATION)

4.207(6) [Cost of providing security] The cost of providing the security shall be paid in the first instance by the special manager; but he is entitled to be reimbursed as an expense of the liquidation, in the prescribed order of priority.

(See General Note after r.4.210.)

4.208 Failure to give or keep up security

4.208(1) [Failure to give security] If the special manager fails to give the required security within the time stated for that purpose by the order appointing him, or any extension of that time that may be allowed, the liquidator shall report the failure to the court, which may thereupon discharge the order appointing the special manager.

4.208(2)   [Failure to keep up security] If the special manager fails to keep up his security, the liquidator shall report his failure to the court, which may thereupon remove the special manager, and make such order as it thinks fit as to costs.

4.208(3)   [Directions on removal] If an order is made under this Rule removing the special manager, or discharging the order appointing him, the court shall give directions as to whether any, and if so what, steps should be taken for the appointment of another special manager in his place.

(See General Note after r.4.210.)

4.209   Accounting

4.209(1)   [Contents of accounts] The special manager shall produce accounts, containing details of his receipts and payments, for the approval of the liquidator.

4.209(2)   [Period of accounts] The accounts shall be in respect of 3-month periods for the duration of the special manager's appointment (or for a lesser period, if his appointment terminates less than 3 months from its date, or from the date to which the last accounts were made up).

4.209(3)   [When accounts approved] When the accounts have been approved, the special manager's receipts and payments shall be added to those of the liquidator.

(See General Note after r.4.210.)

4.210   Termination of appointment

4.210(1)   [Automatic termination] The special manager's appointment terminates if the winding-up petition is dismissed or if, a provisional liquidator having been appointed, the latter is discharged without a winding-up order having been made. (NO CVL APPLICATION).

4.210(2)   [Application to court] If the liquidator is of opinion that the employment of the special manager is no longer necessary or profitable for the company, he shall apply to the court for directions, and the court may order the special manager's appointment to be terminated.

4.210(3)   [Resolution of creditors] The liquidator shall make the same application if a resolution of the creditors is passed, requesting that the appointment be terminated.

GENERAL NOTE TO RR.4.206–4.210

On the appointment of a special manager, see IA 1986 s.177 and the notes thereto. A special manager need not be qualified to act as an insolvency practitioner. These rules deal with his appointment and remuneration, the furnishing of security, his obligation to keep accounts and the termination of his appointment.

CHAPTER 19

PUBLIC EXAMINATION OF COMPANY OFFICERS AND OTHERS

4.211   Order for public examination

4.211(1)   [Service of copy order] If the official receiver applies to the court under section 133 for the public examination of any person, a copy of the court's order shall, as soon as reasonably practicable after its making, be served on that person.

[FORM 4.61]

4.211(2) **[Official receiver's report]** Where the application relates to a person falling within section 133(1)(c) (promoters, past managers, etc.), it shall be accompanied by a report by the official receiver indicating–

(a) the grounds on which the person is supposed to fall within that paragraph, and

(b) whether, in the official receiver's opinion, it is likely that service of the order on the person can be effected at a known address in accordance with Chapter 3 of Part 12A, (service of court documents), and, if so, by what means.

4.211(3) **[Means of service]** If in his report the official receiver gives it as his opinion that, in a case to which paragraph (2) applies, there is no reasonable certainty that service at a known address in accordance with Chapter 3 of Part 12A will be effective, the court may direct that the order be served by some means other than, or in addition to, service in such manner.

4.211(4) **[Rescission of order]** In a case to which paragraphs (2) and (3) apply, the court shall rescind the order if satisfied by the person to whom it is directed that he does not fall within section 133(1)(c).

(See General Note after r.4.217.)

4.212 Notice of hearing

4.212(1) **[Venue and direction to attend]** The court's order shall appoint a venue for the examination of the person to whom it is directed (**"the examinee"**), and direct his attendance thereat.

4.212(2) **[Notice of hearing]** The official receiver shall give at least 14 days' notice of the hearing–

(a) if a liquidator has been nominated or appointed, to him;

(b) if a special manager has been appointed, to him; and

(c) subject to any contrary direction of the court, to every creditor and contributory of the company who is known to the official receiver.

4.212(3) **[Gazetting/advertisement of notice]** Subject to paragraph (4), where the official receiver thinks fit, notice of the order–

(a) shall be gazetted; and

(b) may be advertised in such other manner as the official receiver thinks fit,

not less than 14 days before the date fixed for the hearing.

4.212(3A) **[Additional contents of notice under r.4.212(3)]** In addition to the standard contents, the notice under paragraph (3) must state–

(a) the purpose of the hearing; and

(b) the venue for the hearing.

4.212(4) **[Publication after notice to examinee]** Where the court's order relates to a person falling within section 133(1)(c), unless the court otherwise directs, there shall be no publication under paragraph (3) before at least 5 business days have elapsed since the examinee was served with the order.

(See General Note after r.4.217.)

4.213 Order on request by creditors or contributories

4.213(1) **[Form of request etc.]** A request to the official receiver by creditors or contributories under section 133(2) shall be made in writing and be accompanied by–

(a) a list of the creditors concurring with the request and the amounts of their respective claims in the liquidation or (as the case may be) of the contributories so concurring, with their respective values, and

(b)   from each creditor or contributory concurring, written confirmation of his concurrence.

This paragraph does not apply if the requisitioning creditor's debt or, as the case may be, requisitioning contributory's shareholding is alone sufficient, without the concurrence of others.

[FORM 4.62]

[FORM 4.63]

4.213(2)   [Further contents] The request must specify the name of the proposed examinee, the relationship which he has, or has had, to the company and a statement of the reasons why his examination is requested.

4.213(3)   [Security for expenses of hearing] Before an application to the court is made on the request, the requisitionists shall deposit with the official receiver such sum as the latter may determine to be appropriate by way of security for the expenses of the hearing of a public examination, if ordered.

4.213(4)   [Time for application] Subject as follows, the official receiver shall, within 28 days of receiving the request, make the application to the court required by section 133(2).

4.213(5)   [Relief from unreasonable request] If the official receiver is of opinion that the request is an unreasonable one in the circumstances, he may apply to the court for an order relieving him from the obligation to make the application otherwise required by that subsection.

4.213(6)   [Notice of relief order etc.] If the court so orders, and the application for the order was made without notice to any other party, notice of the order shall be given as soon as reasonably practicable by the official receiver to the requisitionists. If the application for an order is dismissed, the official receiver's application under section 133(2) shall be made as soon as reasonably practicable on conclusion of the hearing of the application first mentioned.

(See General Note after r.4.217.)

4.214   Examinee unfit for examination

4.214(1)   [Application for stay etc.] Where the examinee is a person who lacks capacity within the meaning of the Mental Capacity Act 2005 (c. 9) or is suffering from any physical affliction or disability rendering him unfit to undergo or attend for public examination, the court may, on an application being made to it under this Rule, either stay the order for his public examination or direct that it shall be conducted in such manner and at such place as it thinks fit.

[FORM 4.64]

4.214(2)   [Who may apply] Application under this Rule shall be made–

(a)   by a person who has been appointed by a court in the United Kingdom or elsewhere to manage the affairs of, or to represent, the examinee, or

(b)   by a relative or friend of the examinee whom the court considers to be a proper person to make the application, or

(c)   by the official receiver.

4.214(3)   [Application not by official receiver] Where the application is made by a person other than the official receiver, then–

(a)   it shall, unless the examinee is a person who lacks capacity within the meaning of the Mental Capacity Act 2005, be supported by the witness statement of a registered medical practitioner as to the examinee's mental and physical condition;

(b)   at least 7 days' notice of the application shall be given to the official receiver and the liquidator (if other than the official receiver); and

(c)   before any order is made on the application, the applicant shall deposit with the official receiver such sum as the latter certifies to be necessary for the additional expenses of any examination that may be ordered on the application.

An order made on the application may provide that the expenses of the examination are to be payable, as to a specified proportion, out of the deposit under sub-paragraph (c), instead of as an expense of the liquidation.

4.214(4)   [Application by official receiver] Where the application is made by the official receiver it may be made without notice to any other party, and may be supported by evidence in the form of a report by the official receiver to the court.

(See General Note after r.4.217.)

4.215   Procedure at hearing

4.215(1)   [Examination on oath] The examinee shall at the hearing be examined on oath; and he shall answer all such questions as the court may put, or allow to be put, to him.

4.215(2)   [Appearances etc.] Any of the persons allowed by section 133(4) to question the examinee may, with the approval of the court (made known either at the hearing or in advance of it), appear by solicitor or counsel; or he may in writing authorise another person to question the examinee on his behalf.

4.215(3)   [Representation of examinee] The examinee may at his own expense employ a solicitor with or without counsel, who may put to him such questions as the court may allow for the purpose of enabling him to explain or qualify any answers given by him, and may make representations on his behalf.

4.215(4)   [Record of examination] There shall be made in writing such record of the examination as the court thinks proper. The record shall be read over either to or by the examinee, authenticated by him, and verified by a statement of truth at a venue fixed by the court.

[FORM 4.65]

4.215(5)   [Record as evidence] The written record may, in any proceedings (whether under the Act or otherwise) be used as evidence against the examinee of any statement made by him in the course of his public examination.

4.215(6)   [Criminal proceedings etc.] If criminal proceedings have been instituted against the examinee, and the court is of opinion that the continuance of the hearing would be calculated to prejudice a fair trial of those proceedings, the hearing may be adjourned.

(See General Note after r.4.217.)

4.216   Adjournment

4.216(1)   [Adjourned by court] The public examination may be adjourned by the court from time to time, either to a fixed date or generally.

[FORM 4.66]

4.216(2)   [Resumption] Where the examination has been adjourned generally, the court may at any time on the application of the official receiver or of the examinee–

(a)   fix a venue for the resumption of the examination, and

(b)   give directions as to the manner in which, and the time within which, notice of the resumed public examination is to be given to persons entitled to take part in it.

[FORM 4.67]

4.216(3)   [Deposit for expenses re application] Where application under paragraph (2) is made by the examinee, the court may grant it on terms that the expenses of giving the notices required by that paragraph shall be paid by him and that, before a venue for the resumed public examination is fixed, he shall deposit with the official receiver such sum as the latter considers necessary to cover those expenses.

(See General Note after r.4.217.)

4.217   Expenses of examination

4.217(1)   [Expenses paid out of r.4.213 deposit] Where a public examination of the examinee has been ordered by the court on a creditors' or contributories' requisition under Rule 4.213, the court may order that the expenses of the examination are to be paid, as to a specified proportion, out of the deposit under Rule 4.213(3), instead of as an expense of the liquidation.

4.217(2)   [Official receiver not liable for costs] In no case do the costs and expenses of a public examination fall on the official receiver personally.

General Note to rr.4.211–4.217

Rule 4.214(1), (3a) amended by the Mental Capacity Act 2005 (Transitional and Consequential Revisions) Order 2007 (SI 2007/1898) art.6 and Sch.1 para.12, as from October 1, 2007. Rule 4.212(3) substituted, and r.4.212(3) added, by I(A)R 2009 (SI 2009/642) r.30 as from April 6, 2009. Rules 4.212, 4.214 amended and r.4.212(3A) inserted by I(A)R 2010 r.2 and Sch. paras 253–255 as from April 6, 2010.

On the standard contents for gazetted notices (r.4.212(3A)), see rr.12A.31–12A.33. On the standard contents for notices other than gazetted notices, see rr.12A.36–12A.39.

The power conferred on the official receiver to have company officers and others attend for public examination is conferred by the 1986 Act in more broadly drawn terms than under the former law: see the note to IA 1986 s.133. If the preconditions of s.133 are satisfied, the court should make an order for the examination except where no useful purpose would be served by it: *Jeeves v Official Receiver* [2003] EWCA Civ 1246; [2004] B.P.I.R. 46. The court has power under r.4.215 to control the form of the examination and to give directions, or at least guidance, as to the hearing, but will not pre-empt questions which are a matter for the judge presiding at the hearing, e.g. as to the admissibility of questions and whether a particular question would be oppressive: *Re Richbell Strategic Holdings Ltd* [2001] B.C.C. 409. However, it was said in *Jeeves v Official Receiver* (above) that if the court was hearing an application under r.7.47 to rescind an order for examination, it was appropriate for that court to consider whether a foreign jurisdiction might make it difficult or oppressive to require the proposed examinee to answer questions.

On the *private* examination of persons connected with an insolvent company, see IA 1986 s.236, and rr.9.1 et seq., and the notes thereto.

Subject to r.4.211(2)(a) and (4), the official receiver is entitled to an order ipso facto, i.e. he need not make out any case to the court.

Chapter 20

Order of Payment of Costs, etc., out of Assets

4.218   General rule as to priority

4.218(1)   [Expenses of the liquidation] All fees, costs, charges and other expenses incurred in the course of the liquidation are to be regarded as expenses of the liquidation.

4.218(2)   [Assets from which expenses payable] The expenses of the liquidation are payable out of–

(a)   assets of the company available for the payment of general creditors, which shall be taken to include proceeds–

(i)   of any legal action which the liquidator has power to bring in his own name or in the name of the company, or

(ii)   arising from any award made under any arbitration or other dispute resolution procedure which the liquidator has power to bring in his own name or in the name of the company,

which shall, for the purposes of this subparagraph, also include–

(iii) any payments made under any compromise or other agreement intended to avoid legal action or recourse to arbitration or to any other dispute resolution procedure, and

(iv) payments made as a result of a settlement of any such action, arrangement or procedure in lieu of or prior to any judgment being given or award being made;

(b) subject as provided in Rules 4.218A to 4.218E, property comprised in or subject to a floating charge created by the company.

4.218(3) [Order of priority] Subject as provided in Rules 4.218A to 4.218E, the expenses are payable in the following order of priority–

(a) expenses which–

    (i) are properly chargeable or incurred by the provisional liquidator in carrying out the functions conferred on him by the court;

    (ii) are properly chargeable or incurred by the official receiver or the liquidator in preserving, realising or getting in any of the assets of the company or otherwise in the preparation or conduct of any legal proceedings, arbitration or other dispute resolution procedures, which he has power to bring in his own name or bring or defend in the name of the company or in the preparation or conduct of any negotiations intended to lead or leading to a settlement or compromise of any legal action or dispute to which the proceedings or procedures relate;

    (iii) relate to the employment of a shorthand writer, if appointed by an order of the court made at the instance of the official receiver in connection with an examination; or

    (iv) are incurred in holding an examination under Rule 4.214 (examinee unfit) where the application for it was made by the official receiver;

(b) any other expenses incurred or disbursements made by the official receiver or under his authority, including those incurred or made in carrying on the business of the company;

(c) the fees payable under any order made under section 414 or section 415A, including those payable to the official receiver (other than the fee referred to in sub-paragraph (d)(i) below), and any remuneration payable to him under general regulations;

(d) (i) the fee payable under any order made under section 414 for the performance by the official receiver of his general duties as official receiver;

    (ii) any repayable deposit lodged under any such order as security for the fee mentioned in sub-paragraph (i);

(e) the cost of any security provided by a provisional liquidator, liquidator or special manager in accordance with the Act or the Rules;

(f) the remuneration of the provisional liquidator (if any);

(g) any deposit lodged on an application for the appointment of a provisional liquidator;

(h) the costs of the petitioner, and of any person appearing on the petition whose costs are allowed by the court;

(j) the remuneration of the special manager (if any);

(k) any amount payable to a person employed or authorised, under Chapter 6 of this Part of the Rules, to assist in the preparation of a statement of affairs or of accounts;

(l) any allowance made, by order of the court, towards costs on an application for release from the obligation to submit a statement of affairs, or for an extension of time for submitting such a statement;

(la)   the costs of employing a shorthand writer in any case other than one appointed by an order of the court at the instance of the official receiver in connection with an examination;

(m)   any necessary disbursements by the liquidator in the course of his administration (including any expenses incurred by members of the liquidation committee or their representatives and allowed by the liquidator under Rule 4.169, but not including any payment of corporation tax in circumstances referred to in sub-paragraph (p) below);

(n)   the remuneration or emoluments of any person who has been employed by the liquidator to perform any services for the company, as required or authorised by or under the Act or the Rules;

(o)   the remuneration of the liquidator, up to any amount not exceeding that which is payable under Schedule 6;

(p)   the amount of any corporation tax on chargeable gains accruing on the realisation of any asset of the company (without regard to whether the realisation is effected by the liquidator, a secured creditor, or a receiver or manager appointed to deal with a security);

(q)   the balance, after payment of any sums due under sub-paragraph (o) above, of any remuneration due to the liquidator;

(r)   any other expenses properly chargeable by the liquidator in carrying out his functions in the liquidation.

(See General Note after r.4.220.)

4.218A   Litigation expenses and property subject to a floating charge—general provisions

4.218A(1)   **[Definitions]** In this Rule and Rules 4.218B to 4.218E–

(a)   "**approval**" and "**authorisation**" respectively mean:

    (i)   where yet to be incurred, the approval, and

    (ii)   where already incurred, the authorisation,

    of expenses specified in section 176ZA(3);

(b)   "**the creditor**" means–

    (i)   a preferential creditor of the company, or

    (ii)   a holder of a debenture secured by, or a holder of, a floating charge created by the company;

(c)   "**legal proceedings**" means–

    (i)   proceedings under sections 212, 213, 214, 238, 239, 244 and 423 and any arbitration or other dispute resolution proceedings invoked for purposes corresponding to those to which the sections relate and any other proceedings, including arbitration or other dispute resolution procedures, which a liquidator has power to bring in his own name for the purpose of preserving, realising, or getting in any of the assets of the company;

    (ii)   legal actions and proceedings, arbitration or any other dispute resolution procedures which a liquidator has power to bring or defend in the name of the company, and

    (iii)   negotiations intended to lead or leading to a settlement or compromise of any action, proceeding or procedure to which subparagraphs (i) or (ii) relate;

(d)   "**litigation expenses**" means expenses of a liquidation which–

    (i)   are properly chargeable or incurred in the preparation or conduct of any legal proceedings, and

(ii)   as expenses in the liquidation, exceed, or in the opinion of the liquidator are likely to exceed (and only in so far as they exceed or are likely to exceed), in the aggregate £5000.

4.218A(2)   [No priority for litigation expenses] Litigation expenses shall not have the priority provided by section 176ZA over any claims to property comprised in or subject to a floating charge created by the company and shall not be paid out of any such property unless and until approved or authorised in accordance with Rules 4.218B to 4.218E.

(See General Note after r.4.220.)

4.218B   Litigation expenses and property subject to a floating charge—requirement for approval or authorisation

4.218B(1)   [Liquidator's opinion] Subject to Rules 4.218C to 4.218E, paragraphs (2) and (3) or (4) apply where, in the course of winding up a company, the liquidator–

(a)   ascertains that property is comprised in or subject to a floating charge;

(b)   has himself instituted or proposes to institute or continue legal proceedings or is in the process of defending or proposes to defend any legal proceeding brought or likely to be brought against the company; and

(c)   prior to or at any stage in those proceedings, is of the opinion that–

(i)   the assets of the company available for payment of general creditors are or will be insufficient to pay litigation expenses; and

(ii)   in order to pay litigation expenses he will have to have recourse to property comprised in or subject to a floating charge created by the company.

4.218B(2)   [Identification of creditors with claim to property] As soon as reasonably practicable after the date on which he forms the opinion referred to in paragraph (1), the liquidator shall identify the creditor who, in his opinion at that time–

(a)   has a claim to property comprised in or subject to a floating charge created by the company, and,

(b)   taking into account the value of that claim and any subsisting property then comprised in or secured by such a charge, appears to the liquidator to be the creditor most immediately likely of any persons having such claims to receive some payment in respect of his claim but whose claim would not be paid in full ("the specified creditor").

4.218B(3)   [Request for approval of litigation expenses: specified creditors] The liquidator shall request from the specified creditor the approval or authorisation of such amount for litigation expenses as the liquidator thinks fit.

4.218B(4)   [Request for approval of litigation expenses: multiple creditors] Where, in the liquidator's opinion, two or more creditors who are holders of debentures secured by, or holders of, floating charges created by the company, meet the condition in paragraph (2), the liquidator is to seek from each of them (**"the specified creditors"**) approval or authorisation of such amount of litigation expenses as the liquidator thinks fit, apportioned between them (**"the apportioned amount"**) according to the value of the property to the extent covered by their charges.

4.218B(5)   [Further requests for litigation expenses] For so long as the conditions specified in paragraph (1) subsist, the liquidator may, in the course of a winding up, make such further requests to the specified creditor or creditors for approval or authorisation of such further amount for litigation expenses as he thinks fit to be paid out of property comprised in or subject to a floating charge created by the company, taking into account any amount for litigation expenses previously approved or authorised and the value of the property comprised in or subject to the floating charge.

(See General Note after r.4.220.)

4.218C   Litigation expenses and property subject to a floating charge—request for approval or authorisation

4.218C(1)   [Details of written requests] All requests made by the liquidator for approval or authorisation shall be in writing whether in Form 4.74 or otherwise, and shall include the following–

    (a)   a statement describing the nature of the legal proceedings, including, where relevant, the statutory provision under which proceedings are or are to be brought and the grounds upon which the liquidator relies;

    (b)   where the power to bring those proceedings is subject to sanction, a statement that the liquidator has sought and been given the relevant permissions or an undertaking that the liquidator will seek the relevant permissions upon authorisation or approval being granted;

    (c)   a statement specifying the amount or apportioned amount of litigation expenses for which approval or authorisation is sought ("the specified amount");

    (d)   notice that approval or authorisation or other reply to the request must be made in writing (whether by way of Form 4.74 or otherwise) within 28 days from the date of its being received ("the specified time limit"); and

    (e)   a statement explaining the consequences of a failure to reply within the specified time limit.

4.218C(2)   [Inclusion of prejudicial information] Where anything in paragraph (1) requires the inclusion of any information, the disclosure of which could be seriously prejudicial to the winding up of the company, the liquidator may–

    (a)   exclude such information from any of the above, provided that it is accompanied by a statement to that effect; or

    (b)   include it on terms–

        (i)   that bind the creditor to keep the information confidential, and

        (ii)   that include an undertaking on the part of the liquidator to apply to the court for an order that so much of the information as may be kept in the files of the court, not be open to public inspection.

4.218C(3)   [Creditor's application for further particulars] The creditor may within the specified time limit apply to the liquidator in writing for such further particulars as is reasonable and in such a case, the time limit specified in paragraph (1)(d) shall apply from the date of the creditor's receipt of the liquidator's response to any such request.

4.218C(4)   [Supplemental details to para.(1) requests] Where the liquidator requires the approval or authorisation of two or more creditors, he shall send a request to each creditor in writing (whether by way of Form 4.74 or otherwise), containing the matters listed in paragraph (1) and also giving–

    (a)   the number of creditors concerned,

    (b)   the total value of their claims, or if not known, as it is estimated to be by the liquidator immediately prior to sending any such request, and

    (c)   to each preferential creditor, notice that approval or authorisation of the specified amount shall be taken to be given where a majority in value of those preferential creditors who respond within the specified time limit are in favour of it, or

(d)   where Rule 4.218B(4) applies, notice to the specified creditors that the amount of litigation expenses will be apportioned between them in accordance with that rule and notice of the value of the portion allocated to, and the identity of, the specified creditors affected by that apportionment.

(See General Note after r.4.220.)

4.218D   Litigation expenses and property subject to a floating charge—grant of approval or authorisation

4.218D(1)   **[Failure to include matters in liquidators request]** Where the liquidator fails to include in his request any one of the matters, statements or notices required to be specified by paragraph (1) or paragraphs (1) and (4), of Rule 4.218C, as the case may be, the request for approval or authorisation shall be treated as not having been made.

4.218D(2)   **[Where approval or authorisation taken to have been given]** Subject to paragraphs (3), (4) and (5), approval or authorisation shall be taken to have been given where the specified amount has been requested by the liquidator, and–

(a)   that amount is approved or authorised within the specified time limit; or

(b)   a different amount is approved or authorised within the specified time limit and the liquidator considers it sufficient.

4.218D(3)   **[Approval or authorisation by creditors]** Where the liquidator requires the approval or authorisation of two or more preferential creditors, approval or authorisation shall be taken to be given where a majority in value of those who respond within the specified time limit approve or authorise–

(a)   the specified amount, or

(b)   a different amount which the liquidator considers sufficient.

4.218D(4)   **[Proposal of different amount]** Where a majority in value of two or more preferential creditors propose an amount other than that specified by the liquidator, they shall be taken to have approved or authorised an amount equal to the lowest of the amounts so proposed.

4.218D(5)   **[Where no written response within time limits]** In any case in which there is no response in writing within the specified time limit to the liquidator's request–

(a)   at all, or

(b)   at any time following the liquidator's provision of further particulars under Rule 4.218C(3),

the liquidator's request shall be taken to have been approved or authorised from the date of the expiry of that time limit.

(See General Note after r.4.220.)

4.218E   Litigation expenses and property subject to a floating charge—application to court by the liquidator

4.218E(1)   **[Court approval or authorisation]** In the circumstances specified below the court may, upon the application of the liquidator, approve or authorise such amount of litigation expenses as it thinks fit.

4.218E(2)   **[Circumstances where application to court can be made]** Save as provided by paragraph (3), application to the court by a liquidator for an order approving or authorising an amount for litigation expenses may only be made where–

(a)   the specified creditor (or, if more than one, any one of them) is or is intended to be a defendant in the legal proceedings in respect of which the litigation expenses have been or are to be incurred; or

(b)   the specified creditor has been requested to approve or authorise the amount specified under Rule 4.218C(1)(c) and has, in any case—

   (i)   declined to approve or authorise, as the case may be, the specified amount; or

   (ii)   has approved or authorised an amount which is less than the specified amount and which lesser amount the liquidator considers insufficient, or

   (iii)   made such application for further particulars or other response to the liquidator's request as is, in the liquidator's opinion, unreasonable.

4.218E(3)   [Application for urgent approval or authorisation] Where the liquidator is of the view that circumstances are such that he requires urgent approval or authorisation of litigation expenses, he may apply to the court for approval or authorisation either–

(a)   without seeking approval or authorisation from the specified creditor; or

(b)   if sought, prior to the expiry of the specified time limit.

4.218E(4)   [Conditions for granting an urgent application] The court may grant such application for approval or authorisation–

(a)   provided that the liquidator satisfies it of the urgency of the case, and

(b)   subject to such terms and conditions as it thinks fit.

4.218E(5)   [Copies of the urgent application] The liquidator shall, at the same time as making any application to the court under this rule, send copies of it to the specified creditor or creditors, unless the court orders otherwise.

4.218E(6)   [Creditor's entitlement to be heard] The specified creditor (including any one or all of them where there are two or more such creditors) is entitled to be heard on any such application unless the court orders otherwise.

4.218E(7)   [Terms and conditions of grant] The court may grant approval or authorisation subject to such terms and conditions as it may think fit, including terms and conditions relating to the amount or nature of the litigation expenses and as to any obligation to make further applications to the court under this Rule.

4.218E(8)   [Cost of liquidator's application] The costs of the liquidator's application under this Rule, including the costs of any specified creditor appearing or represented on it, shall be an expense of the liquidation unless the court orders otherwise.

(See General Note after r.4.220.)

4.219   Winding up commencing as voluntary

4.219   In a winding up by the court which follows immediately on a voluntary winding up (whether members' voluntary or creditors' voluntary), such remuneration of the voluntary liquidator and costs and expenses of the voluntary liquidation as the court may allow are to rank in priority with the expenses specified in Rule 4.218(3)(a).

(See General Note after r.4.220.)

4.220   Saving for powers of the court

4.220(1)   [Powers of court under s.156] In a winding up by the court, the priorities laid down by Rules 4.218 and 4.219 are subject to the power of the court to make orders under section 156, where the assets are insufficient to satisfy the liabilities.

4.220(2)   [Powers of court re costs etc.] Nothing in those Rules applies to or affects the power of any court, in proceedings by or against the company, to order costs to be paid by the company, or the liquidator; nor do they affect the rights of any person to whom such costs are ordered to be paid.

GENERAL NOTE TO RR.4.218–4.220

These rules deal with the expenses of the liquidation, including the liquidator's remuneration, and define the order of priority not only as between the various heads of expenditure incurred by the liquidator but also as between the funds in the liquidator's hands and claims to assets covered by a floating charge.

R.4.218
The present list giving the order of priority for payment of the expenses of the liquidation is longer and more detailed than under the old winding-up rules. The text as shown incorporates changes which have been made by later statutory instruments (most recently by I(A)R 2008 (SI 2008/737) rr.4, 5 as from April 6 2008, amending r.4.218(1) and inserting new rr.4.218A–4.218E).

The rule as now worded makes it plain that the line of cases, from *Re M C Bacon Ltd (No.2)* [1991] Ch. 127; [1990] B.C.C. 430 to *Re Floor Fourteen Ltd, Lewis v IRC* [2001] 3 All E.R. 499; [2002] B.C.C. 198 (in which it was held that the expenses incurred by a liquidator in pursuing claims for wrongful trading and to recover preferences, etc. were not "expenses of the liquidation"), are no longer good law.

An application for the interim reimbursement of costs in proceedings brought by the liquidator against the company's former directors was held to be premature in *Re Romar Engineering Co Ltd* [2003] B.C.C. 535.

Rule 4.218 applies to a creditors' voluntary winding up (including one that was originally a members' winding up): see r.4.1(2).

R.4.218(1)–(3)
The former para.(1)(a) has now been substantially re-enacted as para.(3)(a). The new paras (1) and (2) elaborate the terms "expenses of the liquidation" and the "assets" out of which the expenses are to be paid. In particular, it is expressly provided that the expenses of the liquidation may be paid out of the fruits of any litigation which the liquidator has power to bring or defend in his own name or of any corresponding arbitration or dispute resolution procedures, and any settlement or compromise of a claim or dispute.

The ruling in *Re Barleycorn Enterprises Ltd* [1970] Ch. 465 (which was followed in a number of cases including *Re Portbase Clothing Ltd, Mond v Taylor* [1993] Ch. 388; [1993] B.C.C. 96), that for the purposes of the former r.4.218(1) the company's "assets" include assets covered by a floating charge, was overruled by the House of Lords in *Re Leyland DAF Ltd, Buchler v Talbot* [2004] UKHL 9; [2004] 2 A.C. 298; [2004] B.C.C. 214: see the note to s.107. It followed that the liquidator's claims for expenses ranked behind those of the holder of a floating charge and the preferential creditors.

However, this ruling was considered by government to run contrary to the current philosophy and objectives of insolvency law and a clause was inserted into the Companies Bill to reverse the decision, which in due course became CA 2006 s.1282. This provision has inserted new s.176ZA into IA 1986, which provides that the expenses of a winding up should, so far as necessary, have priority over any claims to property comprised in or subject to a floating charge. There is power in s.176ZA(3) to make rules restricting the application of this rule and new rr.4.218A–4.218E, above, were inserted by the Insolvency (Amendment) Rules 2008 (SI 2008/737, effective April 6, 2008) for this purpose. See further the notes to s.176ZA and rr.4.218A–4.218E.

In *Kahn v Inland Revenue Commissioners, Re Toshoku Finance (UK) plc* [2002] UKHL 6; [2002] 1 W.L.R. 671; [2002] B.C.C. 110 the House of Lords held that corporation tax was payable out of the assets in priority to other claims as an expense of the liquidation even though the "income" in respect of which the tax was assessed had not been (and never would be) received by the company, and the tax debt had not arisen as a result of something done for the purposes of or with a view to obtaining a benefit for the estate. On this case, see Lyons and Birch, (2005) 18 Insolv. Int. 150.

In *Re W F Fearman Ltd (No.2)* (1988) 4 B.C.C. 141 it was held that the costs of an administration petition (although bona fide presented and proving in the event to have been in the interests of the creditors) could not be allowed as a liquidation expense when the administration proceedings were terminated and a winding-up order was made. However, in the later case of *Re Gosscott (Groundworks) Ltd* (1988) 4 B.C.C. 372, an order was made in such circumstances.

In *Re Movitex Ltd* [1990] B.C.C. 491 the liquidators had continued an action, which had been commenced by the company before the winding up, to have certain property transactions set aside on the ground that they had been entered into without authority or in breach of directors' duty. Judgment had been given for the defendants with costs against the company, but the company's assets were insufficient to pay the costs order. It was held that the litigation costs were payable in full to the extent of the company's assets, but only after allowing the liquidators a deduction in respect of their costs in realising those assets. See also *Re MT Realisations Ltd* [2003] EWHC 2895 (Ch); [2004] 1 W.L.R. 678, where the court not only confirmed that costs which had been awarded against the liquidator in litigation were payable in priority to the general expenses of the liquidation but also held that they were not "expenses of the liquidation" within r.4.218 at all, so that the court had no power under IA 1986 s.156 to accord them a lower priority. In *RBG Resources plc v Rastogi* [2005] EWHC 994 (Ch); [2005] 2 B.C.L.C. 592 Lightman J. warned that liquidators should think very carefully before making decisions to bring or continue expensive proceedings against impecunious defendants. The liquidator in that case had been obliged to discontinue an action for want of funds; the normal rule was applied that the claimant should be liable for the defendant's costs on the standard basis, which in the circumstances had to be funded at the expense of the liquidator's remuneration. In *Unadkat & Co (Accountants) Ltd v Bhardwaj* [2006] EWHC 2785 (Ch); [2007] B.C.C. 452 the company had been dissolved, but a creditor had put up funds to have it restored to the register and a new liquidator appointed, so that misfeasance proceedings (which were successfully settled) could be brought against a former director. The judgment contains an interesting discussion of the court's discretionary power to award costs in the restoration proceedings and the status of those costs (as liquidation expenses) under r.4.218.

Where rent is paid by a liquidator who has retained a lease in the hope of realising the company's assets to better advantage (as distinct from preserving the lease as an asset of the company) the rent does not rank as an expense of the liquidation under para.(a) of r.4.218(3) but as a necessary disbursement under para.(m): *Re Linda Marie Ltd (in liq.)* (1988) 4 B.C.C. 463. In the same case, the court declined to exercise its discretion to confer priority on the liquidator's remuneration over the landlord's claim for rent.

A company's liability under a protective award made after the commencement of liquidation was considered not to be a necessary disbursement under the former r.4.218(1)(m) [now r.4.218(3)(m)] in *Day v Haine* [2007] EWHC 2691 (Ch); [2008] B.C.C. 199, on the basis that there was no certainty that the employees would ever have an enforceable claim against the company; but this decision was reversed by the Court of Appeal: *Haine v Day* [2008] EWCA Civ 626. See the note to r.13.12.

A liquidator may seek guidance from the court in anticipation of making any particular expenditure in order to determine whether it will be treated as an expense of the liquidation: *Re Demaglass Ltd* (above).

The court has power under r.4.219 to allow, review or disallow in whole or in part the liquidator's remuneration, costs and expenses. However, if the liquidator seeks an increase of remuneration it is more appropriate to proceed under r.4.130 than r.4.219: *Re Tony Rowse NMC Ltd* [1996] B.C.C. 196.

Where the liquidator administers assets which are outside the scope of the liquidation (e.g. assets held by the company on trust), the court has jurisdiction to allow him access to those funds to recoup his remuneration and expenses: *Re Berkeley Applegate (Investment Consultants) Ltd (No.2)* [1989] Ch. 32; (1988) B.C.C. 279. But it will not do so in relation to assets which are in dispute: *Re London Local Residential Ltd* [2004] EWHC 114 (Ch); [2004] 2 B.C.L.C. 72.

Rr.4.218A–4.218E

The new s.176ZA, inserted by CA 2006 s.1282 with effect from April 6, 2008 (reversing the effect of *Re Leyland DAF Ltd, Buchler v Talbot* [2004] UKHL 9; [2004] 2 A.C. 298; [2004] B.C.C. 214), is expressly made subject to any rules restricting its application in certain circumstances to expenses authorised or approved by (a) floating charge holders; (b) preferential creditors; or (c) the court. These are the relevant rules (inserted by I(A)R 2008 (SI 2008/737) r.5 as from April 6, 2008).

They provide that the litigation expenses incurred in any of the proceedings described in r.4.218A(1)(c) (or corresponding arbitration or dispute resolution proceedings) may not be paid out of property subject to a floating charge without the approval or authorisation of the preferential creditors and charge holders who have claims on it (or, failing such approval or authorisation, of the court). The rules set out the conditions with which the liquidator and the creditors and charge holders must comply. The rules recognise the interest that these parties have in the asset realisations because they are effectively funding the liquidator's litigation. In all other types of litigation the liquidator is free to make his own decisions.

In an explanatory memorandum issued by the Insolvency Service it is acknowledged that insolvency practitioners may be inclined to favour administration (where there are no provisions corresponding to these rules) rather than liquidation because of the relative certainty of recovering their expenses. The rules also impact upon the returns floating charge holders may receive, depending on which insolvency procedure is employed.

Note that authorisation or approval is not required where the litigation expenses do not exceed (or in the liquidator's opinion are not likely to exceed) £5,000 (r.4.218A(1)(d)(ii)).

R.4.218B(2)

The "specified creditor" may be a preferential creditor or a floating charge holder but must be one whose claim will not be paid in full. If all preferential creditors' claims will be paid in full, the next in line will be the floating charge holder or holders. This rule deals expressly with the case where there are two or more floating charge holders, but not with a plurality of preferential creditors. However, it is to be assumed that, following the usual rules of statutory interpretation, it is intended that the singular includes the plural and that where there are several preferential creditors the authorisation of all must be sought. (This is confirmed by rr.4.218C(4)(c) and 4.218D.)

There must needs be a further assumption, namely that the actual or anticipated expenses are to be brought into account by the liquidator in determining whether a creditor's debt is likely to be paid in full. The scenario could be more complex if, having initially secured the necessary authorisation for a specified amount under r.4.218B(3), the liquidator seeks approval for an additional sum under r.4.218B(5). If the new sum is expected to eat into the assets to an extent that a prior-ranking creditor will no longer be paid less than his full claim, he will become the specified creditor under r.4.218B(2)(b) and a new round of authorisation will be necessary, superseding and supplementing the existing one.

If the specified creditor is, or is intended to be, a defendant in the proceedings, application may be made to the court for approval under r.4.218E.

R.4.218B(4)

The assumption is that any preferential creditors will be paid in full. If the floating charges relate to the same property, it must be assumed that the charge holders rank equally: if not, the "specified creditor" will be the first in the priority ranking whose debt will not be fully paid. If, on the other hand, one has a charge over (for instance) the company's book debts and another over other assets, it appears that the apportioned amount will depend on either or both of the value of the respective properties and the amount covered by each charge. The former would be more appropriate where the charge is insufficient to cover all the secured debt; the latter if the debt is fully secured.

R.4.218C

Note the provision in para.(2) for information thought by the liquidator to be confidential.

R.4.218D

This rule contains various default provisions on the basis of which approval will be deemed either to have been made or refused.

R.4.218E

Standing is given to the liquidator by this rule to seek authorisation or approval from the court in the circumstances specified, which include, in effect, an appeal to the court where the specified creditor has declined to approve the requested amount. There is no corresponding right expressly given to a creditor—say a minority creditor who wishes to challenge a decision of the majority—but this would not rule out the court having jurisdiction in an appropriate case.

CHAPTER 21

MISCELLANEOUS RULES

Section A: Return of capital (No CVL Application)

4.221   Application to court for order authorising return

4.221(1)   **[Application of Rule]** This Rule applies where the liquidator intends to apply to the court for an order authorising a return of capital.

4.221(2)   **[Accompanying list]** The application shall be accompanied by a list of the persons to whom the return is to be made.

4.221(3) **[Contents of list]** The list shall include the same details of those persons as appears in the settled list of contributories, with any necessary alterations to take account of matters after settlement of the list, and the amount to be paid to each person.

4.221(4) **[Copy order]** Where the court makes an order authorising the return, it shall send a sealed copy of the order to the liquidator.

(See General Note after r.4.222.)

4.222   Procedure for return

4.222(1) **[Rate of return etc.]** The liquidator shall inform each person to whom a return is made of the rate of return per share, and whether it is expected that any further return will be made.

4.222(2) **[Method of payment]** Any payments made by the liquidator by way of the return may be sent by post, unless for any reason another method of making the payment has been agreed with the payee.

GENERAL NOTE TO RR.4.221–4.222

In a winding up by the court, the court must "adjust the rights of the contributories among themselves and distribute any surplus among the persons entitled to it" (IA 1986 s.154). Although it might have been thought from the language of IA 1986 ss.143(1) and 160(1)(b), (2) that capital could be returned to contributories on the liquidator's own authority, these rules confirm that he must have the sanction of the court.

Section B: Conclusion of winding up

4.223-CVL   Statements to registrar of companies under s.192 [Revoked by I(A)R 2010 r.5 as from April 6, 2010.]

NOTE

This rule formerly elaborated the detailed reporting requirements at the conclusion of a winding up imposed on a liquidator by s.192. The rule has been replaced (for insolvencies commencing after that date) by amendments made elsewhere.

Section C: Dissolution after winding up

4.224   Secretary of State's directions under ss.203, 205

4.224(1) **[Copy of directions]** Where the Secretary of State gives a direction under–

(a) section 203 (where official receiver applies to registrar of companies for a company's early dissolution), or

(b) section 205 (application by interested person for postponement of dissolution),

he shall send two copies of the direction to the applicant for it.

4.224(2) **[Copy to registrar]** Of those copies one shall be sent by the applicant to the registrar of companies, to comply with section 203(5) or, as the case may be, 205(6).

(See General Note after r.4.225.)

4.225   Procedure following appeal under s.203(4) or 205(4)

4.225   Following an appeal under section 203(4) or 205(4) (against a decision of the Secretary of State under the applicable section) the court shall send two sealed copies of its order to the person in whose favour the appeal was determined; and that party shall send one of the copies to the registrar of companies to comply with section 203(5) or, as the case may be, 205(6).

GENERAL NOTE TO RR.4.224–4.225

These rules provide machinery for the exercise of the official receiver's power under IA 1986 ss.202 et seq., to apply to the registrar of companies for the early dissolution of the company where the assets are not worth the expense of administration.

CHAPTER 22

PERMISSION TO ACT AS DIRECTOR, ETC., OF COMPANY WITH PROHIBITED NAME (SECTION 216 OF THE ACT)

4.226   Preliminary

4.226   The Rules in this Chapter–

(a)   relate to the permission required under section 216 (restriction on reuse of name of company in insolvent liquidation) for a person to act as mentioned in section 216(3) in relation to a company with a prohibited name,

(b)   prescribe the cases excepted from that provision, that is to say, those in which a person to whom the section applies may so act without that permission, and

(c)   apply to all windings up to which section 216 applies, whether or not the winding up commenced before the coming into force of the Rules.

(See General Note after r.4.227A.)

4.227   Application for leave under s.216(3) [Deleted.]

4.227A   Application for permission under s 216(3)

4.227A(1)   [Notice to Secretary of State] At least 14 days notice of any application for permission to act in any of the circumstances which would otherwise be prohibited by section 216(3) must be given by the applicant to the Secretary of State, who may–

(a)   appear at the hearing of the application; and

(b)   whether or not appearing at the hearing, make representations.

4.227A(2)   [Power of court to call for liquidator's report] When considering an application for permission under section 216, the court may call on the liquidator, or any former liquidator, of the liquidating company for a report of the circumstances in which that company became insolvent and the extent (if any) of the applicant's apparent responsibility for its doing so.

GENERAL NOTE TO RR.4.226, 4.227A

A former director or shadow director may not reuse a prohibited company name "except with the leave of the court or in such circumstances as may be prescribed" (IA 1986 s.216(3)). Rule 4.227A deals with an application for such leave, while rr.4.228–4.230 specify three sets of circumstances which are to be treated as excepted cases. Rule 4.226(c) makes this chapter co-extensive with s.216, so that the rules apply (for example) to a winding up where the petition was presented before December 29, 1986 (the commencement date for IR 1986) but the winding-up order was not made until after that date.

Rule 4.227 deleted and r.4.227A inserted by I(A)R 2010 r.2 and Sch. para.257 as from April 6, 2010. Notice of an application for leave to act must now be given to the Secretary of State, who may then appear at the hearing or make representations to the court.

4.228 First excepted case

4.228(1) [Application of r.4.228] This Rule applies where–

(a) a person (**"the person"**) was within the period mentioned in section 216(1) a director, or shadow director, of an insolvent company that has gone into insolvent liquidation

(b) the person acts in all or any of the ways specified in section 216(3) in connection with, or for the purposes of, the carrying on (or proposed carrying on) of the whole or substantially the whole of the business of the insolvent company where that business (or substantially the whole of it) is (or is to be) acquired from the insolvent company under arrangements—

    (i) made by its liquidator; or

    (ii) made before the insolvent company entered into insolvent liquidation by an office-holder acting in relation to it as administrator, administrative receiver or supervisor of a voluntary arrangement under Part 1 of the Act.

4.228(2) [Circumstances not contravening s.216] The person, will not be taken to have contravened section 216 if prior to his acting in the circumstances set out in paragraph (1) a notice is, in accordance with the requirements of paragraph (3),–

(a) given by the person, to every creditor of the insolvent company whose name and address—

    (i) is known by him; or

    (ii) is ascertainable by him on the making of such enquiries as are reasonable in the circumstances; and

(b) published in the Gazette.

4.228(3) [Rule 4.228(2) notice] The notice referred to in paragraph (2)–

(a) may be given and published before the completion of the arrangements referred to in paragraph (1)(b) but must be given and published no later than 28 days after that completion;

(b) must state–

    (i) the name and registered number of the insolvent company;

    (ii) the name of the person;

    (iii) that it is his intention to act (or, where the insolvent company has not entered insolvent liquidation, to act or continue to act) in all or any of the ways specified in section 216(3) in connection with, or for the purposes of, the carrying on of the whole or substantially the whole of the business of the insolvent company; and

    (iv) the prohibited name or, where the company has not entered insolvent liquidation, the name under which the business is being, or is to be, carried on which would be a prohibited name in respect of the person in the event of the insolvent company entering insolvent liquidation; and

(c) must in the case of notice given to each creditor of the company be given using Form 4.73.

4.228(4) [Timing of r.4.228(2) notice] Notice may in particular be given under this Rule–

(a) prior to the insolvent company entering insolvent liquidation where the business (or substantially the whole of the business) is, or is to be, acquired by another company under arrangements made by an office-holder acting in relation to the insolvent company as administrator, administrative receiver or supervisor of a voluntary arrangement (whether or not at the time of the giving of the notice the director is a director of that other company); or

(b)   at a time where the person is a director of another company where–

  (i)   the other company has acquired, or is to acquire, the whole, or substantially the whole, of the business of the insolvent company under arrangements made by its liquidator; and

  (ii)   it is proposed that after the giving of the notice a prohibited name should be adopted by the other company.

GENERAL NOTE

This rule in its former wording proved unsatisfactory. It was interpreted in some county court judgments in a way which made it virtually impossible to apply in any case where the director was already working in the management of the successor company (e.g. in a management buy-out situation); and this construction was upheld by the Court of Appeal in *Churchill v First Independent Factors and Finance Ltd* [2006] EWCA Civ 1623; [2007] B.C.C. 45.

  The government responded swiftly to rectify this position. The Insolvency (Amendment) Rules 2007 (SI 2007/1974, effective August 6, 2007) amended r.4.228 (but not with retrospective effect) so as to substitute the above wording. A director will now bring himself within the first excepted case (and so will not require the leave of the court) if the prescribed notice is given in accordance with r.4.228(2)–(4), using Form 4.73. Such a notice may be given before the company enters into insolvent liquidation (e.g. where the company is in administration and it is likely or possible that it will subsequently go into liquidation), or in cases where the successor company has not yet adopted a prohibited name.

4.229   Second excepted case

4.229(1)   [Where director applies for permission] Where a person to whom section 216 applies as having been a director or shadow director of the liquidating company applies for permission of the court under that section not later than 7 business days from the date on which the company went into liquidation, he may, during the period specified in paragraph (2) below, act in any of the ways mentioned in section 216(3), notwithstanding that he has not the permission of the court under that section.

4.229(2)   [Period in r.4.229(1)] The period referred to in paragraph (1) begins with the day on which the company goes into liquidation and ends either on the day falling six weeks after that date or on the day on which the court disposes of the application for permission under section 216, whichever of those days occurs first.

GENERAL NOTE

This exception enables a person who is seeking the leave of the court to act as a director, etc. of a company with a prohibited name for a brief period while his application is awaiting a hearing. Note the strict time limits. The six-week period in r.4.229(2) is intended to avoid the risk that an applicant who is unsuccessful would have unwittingly committed an offence while the hearing of his case was pending.

4.230   Third excepted case

4.230 The court's permission under section 216(3) is not required where the company there referred to, though known by a prohibited name within the meaning of the section–

(a)   has been known by that name for the whole of the period of 12 months ending with the day before the liquidating company went into liquidation, and

(b)   has not at any time in those 12 months been dormant within the meaning of section 1169(1), (2) and (3)(a) of the Companies Act.

GENERAL NOTE

This exception allows a former director to continue to act in the affairs of an established company even though it is known by a prohibited name, provided that it has been using that name for at least a year before his other company went into liquidation. See *ESS Production Ltd v Sully* [2005] EWCA Civ 554; [2005] B.C.C. 435. But the exception applies only where there was a previously established and active business trading with limited liability. It was held not to apply in *First Independent Factors & Finance Ltd v Mountford* [2008] EWHC 835 (Ch); [2008] B.C.C. 598, where the business in question had been carried on by the defendant personally and was then transferred to a dormant company controlled by him.

R.4.230(b)

Section 1169(1), (2) defines a company as dormant during any period in which it has no significant accounting transaction (i.e. a transaction that is required by CA 2006 s.386 to be entered in its accounting records).

CHAPTER 23

EC REGULATION—MEMBER STATE LIQUIDATOR

4.231 Interpretation of creditor and notice to member State liquidator

4.231(1) **[Application]** This Rule applies where a member State liquidator has been appointed in relation to the company.

4.231(2) **[Interpretation]** For the purposes of the Rules referred to in paragraph (3) the member State liquidator is deemed to be a creditor.

4.231(3) **[Rules referred to in r.4.231(2)]** The Rules referred to in paragraph (2) are Rules 4.43(1) (official receiver's report), 4.45(1) (report on statement of affairs), 4.46(2) (report where no statement of affairs), 4.47(2) (general rule on reporting), 4.48(2) (winding up stayed), 4.49 (information to creditors), 4.50(2) (notice of meetings), 4.51(2) (notice of creditors' meeting—CVL), 4.54 (power to call meetings), 4.57(1) (requisitioned meetings), 4.57(3), 4.67 (entitlement to vote (creditors)), 4.68 (chairman's discretion to allow vote—CVL), 4.70 (admission and rejection of proof (creditors' meeting)), 4.73 (meaning of "prove"), 4.74 (supply of forms), 4.75 (contents of proof), 4.76 (particulars of creditor's claim), 4.78 (cost of proving), 4.79 (inspection of proofs), 4.82 (admission and rejection of proofs for dividend), 4.83(1) (appeal against decision in relation to proof), 4.83(2), 4.84 (withdrawal or variation of proof), 4.85(1) (expunging of proof), 4.86 (estimate of quantum), 4.87 (negotiable instruments, etc.), 4.88 (secured creditors), 4.89 (discounts), 4.90 (mutual credit and set-off), 4.91 (debt in foreign currency), 4.92 (payment of a periodical nature), 4.93 (interest), 4.94 (debt payable at future time), 4.101A (power to fill vacancy in office of liquidator), 4.102(5) (appointment by court), 4.103(4) (appointment by court), 4.113(1) (meeting of creditors to remove liquidator), 4.114(1) (meeting of creditors to remove liquidator), 4.115 (regulation of meetings), 4.124(1) (release of official receiver), 4.125(1) (final meeting), 4.125A(2) (rule on reporting), 4.126(1) (final meeting), 4.131(1) (challenge to liquidator's remuneration), 4.152(1) (liquidation committee), 4.152(3) (eligibility for liquidation committee), 4.163(3) (vacancy on liquidation committee), 4.175(1) (liquidation committee), 4.180 (notice of dividend) and 4.212(2) (notice of public examination hearing).

4.231(4) **[Exercise of creditor's rights]** Paragraphs (2) and (3) are without prejudice to the generality of the right to participate referred to in paragraph 3 of Article 32 of the EC Regulation (exercise of creditor's rights).

4.231(5) **[Notice, copies]** Where the liquidator is obliged to give notice to, or provide a copy of a document (including an order of court) to, the court, the registrar of companies or the official receiver, the liquidator shall give notice or provide copies, as the case may be, to the member State liquidator.

4.231(6) **[Duty to cooperate and communicate information]** Paragraph (5) is without prejudice to the generality of the obligations imposed by Article 31 of the EC Regulation (duty to cooperate and communicate information).

Chapter 23 was added by the Insolvency (Amendment) Rules 2002 (SI 2002/1307, effective May 31, 2002). It corresponds in a liquidation to Chapter 8, which makes similar provision for the rights of a Member State "liquidator" in an administration. See the note to r.2.62.

THE SECOND GROUP OF PARTS

INDIVIDUAL INSOLVENCY; BANKRUPTCY

PART 5

INDIVIDUAL VOLUNTARY ARRANGEMENTS

Introductory note to Part 5
A replacement Pt 5 was inserted by the Insolvency (Amendment) (No.2) Rules 2002 (SI 2002/2712) with effect from January 1, 2003 to cater for the significant changes in the IVA regime brought about by IA 2000. This new Pt 5 only applies to IVAs agreed after January 1, 2003—for existing IVAs the old Pt 5 which is covered by the 6th edition of this work applies. Further major changes/additions to Pt 5 were effected by the Insolvency (Amendment) Rules 2003 (SI 2003/1730) in response to the new requirements of EA 2002. Many changes were made by I(A)R 2010 (SI 2010/686).

CHAPTER 1

PRELIMINARY

5.1 Introductory

5.1(1) **[Application of Pt 5 Rules]** The Rules in this Part apply in relation to a voluntary arrangement under Part VIII of the Act, except in relation to voluntary arrangements under section 263A, in relation to which only Chapters 7 and 10 to 14 of this Part shall apply.

5.1(2) **[Application re voluntary arrangements other than under IA 1986 s.263A]** In this Part, in respect of voluntary arrangements other than voluntary arrangements under section 263A–

(a) Chapter 2 applies in all cases;

(b) Chapter 3 applies in cases where an application for an interim order is made;

(c) Chapter 4 applies in cases where no application for an interim order is or is to be made;

(d) except where otherwise stated, Chapters 5 and 6 apply in all cases;

(e) Chapter 8 applies where a bankrupt makes an application under section 261(2)(a); and

(f) Chapter 9 applies where the official receiver makes an application under section 261(2)(b).

5.1(3) **[Application re voluntary arrangements under IA 1986 s.263A]** In this Part, in respect of voluntary arrangements under section 263A–

(a) Chapter 7 applies in all cases; and

(b) Chapter 10 applies where the official receiver makes an application under section 263D(3).

5.1(4) **[Application in all cases]** In this Part, Chapters 11 to 14 apply in all cases.

R.5.1
See general note to Pt 5. Rule 5.1 explains the structure of Pt 5 and reflects the growing complexity of IVA law.
This was further amended by Insolvency (Amendment) Rules 2003 (SI 2003/1730) in order to cater for the additional complications attendant upon reforms to IVA law made by EA 2002.

CHAPTER 2

PREPARATION OF THE DEBTOR'S PROPOSAL

5.2 Preparation of proposal

5.2 The debtor shall prepare for the intended nominee a proposal on which (with or without amendments to be made under Rule 5.3(3) below) to make his report to the court under section 256 or the debtor's creditors under section 256A.

R.5.2
See general note on Pt 5. This rule explains the debtor's responsibilities with regard to the preparation of the IVA proposal. See the clarification in I(A)R 2010 (SI 2010/686).

5.3 Contents of proposal

5.3(1) [Explanation why voluntary arrangement desirable] The debtor's proposal shall provide a short explanation why, in his opinion, a voluntary arrangement under Part VIII is desirable, and give reasons why his creditors may be expected to concur with such an arrangement.

5.3(2) [Other matters] The following matters shall be stated, or otherwise dealt with, in the proposal–

  (a) the following matters, so far as within the debtor's immediate knowledge–

   (i) his assets, with an estimate of their respective values,

   (ii) the extent (if any) to which the assets are charged in favour of creditors,

   (iii) the extent (if any) to which particular assets are to be excluded from the voluntary arrangement;

  (b) particulars of any property, other than assets of the debtor himself, which is proposed to be included in the arrangement, the source of such property and the terms on which it is to be made available for inclusion;

  (c) the nature and amount of the debtor's liabilities (so far as within his immediate knowledge), the manner in which they are proposed to be met, modified, postponed or otherwise dealt with by means of the arrangement and (in particular)–

   (i) how it is proposed to deal with preferential creditors (defined in section 258(7)) and creditors who are, or claim to be, secured,

   (ii) how associates of the debtor (being creditors of his) are proposed to be treated under the arrangement, and

   (iii) in any case where the debtor is an undischarged bankrupt, whether, to the debtor's knowledge, claims have been made under section 339 (transactions at an undervalue), section 340 (preferences) or section 343 (extortionate credit transactions), or where the debtor is not an undischarged bankrupt, whether there are circumstances which would give rise to the possibility of such claims in the event that he should be adjudged bankrupt,

and, where any such circumstances are present, whether, and if so how, it is proposed under the voluntary arrangement to make provision for wholly or partly indemnifying the insolvent estate in respect of such claims;

  (d) whether any, and if so what, guarantees have been given of the debtor's debts by other persons, specifying which (if any) of the guarantors are associates of his;

  (e) the proposed duration of the voluntary arrangement;

  (f) the proposed dates of distributions to creditors, with estimates of their amounts;

(g) how it is proposed to deal with the claims of any person who is bound by the arrangement by virtue of section 260(2)(b)(ii);

(h) the amount proposed to be paid to the nominee (as such) by way of remuneration and expenses;

(j) the manner in which it is proposed that the supervisor of the arrangement should be remunerated, and his expenses defrayed;

(k) whether, for the purposes of the arrangement, any guarantees are to be offered by any persons other than the debtor, and whether (if so) any security is to be given or sought;

(l) the manner in which funds held for the purposes of the arrangement are to be banked, invested or otherwise dealt with pending distribution to creditors;

(m) the manner in which funds held for the purpose of payment to creditors, and not so paid on the termination of the arrangement, are to be dealt with;

(n) if the debtor has any business, the manner in which it is proposed to be conducted during the course of the arrangement;

(o) details of any further credit facilities which it is intended to arrange for the debtor, and how the debts so arising are to be paid;

(p) the functions which are to be undertaken by the supervisor of the arrangement;

(q) the name, address and qualification of the person proposed as supervisor of the voluntary arrangement, and confirmation that he is, so far as the debtor is aware, qualified to act as an insolvency practitioner in relation to him or is an authorised person in relation to him;

(r) whether the EC Regulation will apply and, if so, whether the proceedings will be main proceedings or territorial proceedings.

(s) within the 24 months preceding the date on which the proposal is delivered to the nominee, whether a proposal for an individual voluntary arrangement in respect of the debtor was submitted–

   (i) to a meeting of the debtor's creditors for approval and if so,

      (aa) whether the proposal was approved and the arrangement completed, or

      (bb) whether the proposal was rejected or the arrangement was terminated and if so, in what respects it differs from the proposal in this Rule;

   (ii) to the court in connection with an application for an interim order under section 253 and if so, whether the interim order was made.

5.3(3)   **[Amendment of proposal]** With the agreement in writing of the nominee, the debtor's proposal may be amended at any time up to the delivery of the nominee's report to the court under section 256 or to the debtor's creditors under section 256A.

R.5.3

See general note to Pt 5. Rule 5.3 details the required contents of the proposal—e.g. information on assets, liabilities, duration of IVA, proposed dividends, supervisor's remuneration, etc. See I(A)R 2010 (SI 2010/686) which modifies para.(3).

5.4   Notice to the intended nominee

5.4(1)   **[Written notice]** The debtor shall give to the intended nominee written notice of his proposal.

5.4(2)   **[Delivery of notice]** The notice, accompanied by a copy of the proposal, shall be delivered either to the nominee himself, or to a person authorised to take delivery of documents on his behalf.

5.4(3) **[Endorsement of receipt]** If the intended nominee agrees to act, he shall cause a copy of the notice to be endorsed to the effect that it has been received by him on a specified date.

5.4(4) **[Return of endorsed notice]** The copy of the notice so endorsed shall be returned by the nominee as soon as reasonably practicable to the debtor at an address specified by him in the notice for that purpose.

5.4(5) **[Where debtor undischarged bankrupt]** Where the debtor is an undischarged bankrupt and he gives notice of his proposal to the official receiver and (if any) the trustee, the notice must contain the name and address of the insolvency practitioner or (as the case may be) authorised person who has agreed to act as nominee.

R.5.4
See general note to Pt 5. This deals with the formal communication of the proposal by the debtor to his nominee.

5.5   Statement of Affairs

5.5(1) **[Delivery of statement]** Subject to paragraph (2), the debtor shall, at the same time as the proposal is delivered to the nominee, deliver to the nominee a statement of the debtor's affairs.

5.5(2) **[Non-application of r.5.5(1)]** Paragraph (1) shall not apply where the debtor is an undischarged bankrupt and he has already delivered a statement of affairs under section 272 (debtor's petition) or 288 (creditor's petition) but the nominee may require the debtor to submit a further statement supplementing or amplifying the statement of affairs already submitted.

5.5(3) **[Particulars in statement]** The statement of affairs shall comprise the following particulars (supplementing or amplifying, so far as is necessary for clarifying the state of the debtor's affairs, those already given in his proposal)–

   (a) a list of his assets, divided into such categories as are appropriate for easy identification, with estimated values assigned to each category;

   (b) in the case of any property on which a claim against the debtor is wholly or partly secured, particulars of the claim and its amount, and of how and when the security was created;

   (c) the names and addresses of the debtor's preferential creditors (defined in section 258(7)), with the amounts of their respective claims;

   (d) the names and addresses of the debtor's unsecured creditors, with the amounts of their respective claims;

   (e) particulars of any debts owed by or to the debtor to or by persons who are associates of his;

   (f) such other particulars (if any) as the nominee may in writing require to be furnished for the purposes of making his report on the debtor's proposal to the court or to the debtor's creditors as the case may be.

5.5(4) **[Relevant date]** The statement of affairs shall be made up to a date not earlier than 2 weeks before the date of the notice to the nominee under Rule 5.4.

However, the nominee may allow an extension of that period to the nearest practicable date (not earlier than 2 months before the date of the notice under Rule 5.4); and if he does so, he shall give his reasons in his report on the debtor's proposal.

5.5(5) **[Statement verified by statement of truth]** The statement must be verified by a statement of truth made by the debtor.

R.5.5
See general note to Pt 5. After the proposal has been communicated the debtor has seven days to furnish the nominee with a formal statement of affairs. Rule 5.5 details the contents of this statement. See the modernisation effected by I(A)R 2010 (SI 2010/686). The seven-day period in para.(1) has been cut to delivery at the same time as proposal is delivered to the nominee.

5.6 Additional disclosure for assistance of nominee

5.6(1) [Nominee may request further information] If it appears to the nominee that he cannot properly prepare his report on the basis of information in the debtor's proposal and statement of affairs, he may call on the debtor to provide him with–

(a) further and better particulars as to the circumstances in which, and the reasons why, he is insolvent or (as the case may be) threatened with insolvency;

(aa) further and better particulars of any proposals of the kind, and within the period, referred to in Rule 5.3(2)(s) which have been submitted by the debtor;

(b) particulars of any previous proposals other than those referred to in Rule 5.3(2)(s) which have been made by the debtor at any time under Part VIII of the Act; and

(c) any further information with respect to his affairs which the nominee thinks necessary for the purposes of his report.

5.6(2) [Whether debtor concerned with insolvent company, bankrupt etc.] The nominee may call on the debtor to inform him whether and in what circumstances he has at any time–

(a) been concerned in the affairs of any company (whether or not incorporated in England and Wales) which has become insolvent, or

(b) been adjudged bankrupt, or entered into an arrangement with his creditors.

5.6(3) [Access to accounts and records] For the purpose of enabling the nominee to consider the debtor's proposal and prepare his report on it, the latter must give the nominee such access to the debtor's accounts and records as the nominee may require.

R.5.6
See general note to Pt 5. This allows the nominee to call for further information from the debtor.
See the modernisation by I(A)R 2010 (SI 2010/686).

CHAPTER 3

CASES IN WHICH AN APPLICATION FOR AN INTERIM ORDER IS MADE

5.7 Application for interim order

5.7(1) [Accompanying witness statement] An application to the court for an interim order under Part VIII of the Act shall be accompanied by a witness statement of the following matters–

(a) the reasons for making the application;

(b) particulars of any execution or other legal process or levying of any distress which, to the debtor's knowledge, has been commenced against him;

(c) that he is an undischarged bankrupt or (as the case may be) that he is able to petition for his own bankruptcy;

(d) that no previous application for an interim order has been made by or in respect of the debtor in the period of 12 months ending with the date of the witness statement;

(e) that the nominee under the proposal (naming him) is willing to act in relation to the proposal and is a person who is either qualified to act as an insolvency practitioner in relation to the debtor or is authorised to act as nominee in relation to him; and

(f) whether the debtor has submitted to the official receiver either the document referred to at section 263B(1)(a) or the statement referred to at section 263B(1)(b) and, if so, when and with what result.

5.7(2) **[Rule 5.4 notice and copy proposal to be attached to witness statement]** A copy of the notice to the intended nominee under Rule 5.4, endorsed to the effect that he agrees so to act, and a copy of the debtor's proposal given to the nominee under that Rule, shall be attached to the witness statement.

5.7(3) **[Court to fix venue]** On receiving the application and the witness statement, the court shall fix a venue for the hearing of the application.

5.7(4) **[Notice of hearing]** The applicant shall give at least 2 business days' notice of the hearing–

(a) where the debtor is an undischarged bankrupt, to the bankrupt, the official receiver and the trustee (whichever of those three is not himself the applicant),

(b) where the debtor is not an undischarged bankrupt, to any creditor who (to the debtor's knowledge) has presented a bankruptcy petition against him, and

(c) in either case, to the nominee who has agreed to act in relation to the debtor's proposal.

R.5.7
See general note to Pt 5. This explains the procedure to be followed on an application for an interim order.

This was then further amended in minor respects by Insolvency (Amendment) Rules 2003 (SI 2003/1730) to cater for modifications in the IVA regime made by EA 2002. See I(A)R 2010 (SI 2010/686)—the modernisations here include the removal of references to affidavits. In para.(4) we now to refer to 2 *business* days.

5.8   Court in which application to be made

5.8(1) **[Debtor not undischarged bankrupt]** Except in the case of an undischarged bankrupt, an application to the court under Part VIII of the Act shall be made to a court in which the debtor would be entitled to present his own petition in bankruptcy under Rule 6.40A.

5.8(2) **[Information in application]** The application shall contain sufficient information to establish that it is brought in the appropriate court.

5.8(3) **[Debtor undischarged bankrupt]** In the case of an undischarged bankrupt, such an application shall be made to the court having the conduct of his bankruptcy and shall be filed with the bankruptcy proceedings.

R.5.8
See the general note to Pt 5. This identifies the appropriate court where an application for an interim order is made. See I(A)R 2010 (SI 2010/686).

5.9   Hearing of the application

5.9(1) **[Appearances etc.]** Any of the persons who have been given notice under Rule 5.7(4) may appear or be represented at the hearing of the application.

5.9(2) **[Representations re order]** The court, in deciding whether to make an interim order on the application, shall take into account any representations made by or on behalf of any of those persons (in particular, whether an order should be made containing such provision as is referred to in section 255(3) and (4)).

5.9(3) **[Consideration of nominee's report]** If the court makes an interim order, it shall fix a venue for consideration of the nominee's report. Subject to the following paragraph, the date for that consideration shall be not later than that on which the interim order ceases to have effect under section 255(6).

5.9(4) **[Extension of time under s.256(4)]** If under section 256(4) an extension of time is granted for filing the nominee's report, the court shall, unless there appear to be good reasons against it, correspondingly extend the period for which the interim order has effect.

R.5.9
See the general note to Pt 5. This explains the procedure to be followed on hearing an application for an interim order.

5.10   Action to follow making of order

5.10(1)   [Sealed copies] Where an interim order is made, at least 2 sealed copies of the order shall be sent by the court to the person who applied for it; and that person shall serve one of the copies on the nominee under the debtor's proposal.

[FORM 5.2]

5.10(2)   [Notice of order] The applicant shall also as soon as reasonably practicable give notice of the making of the order to any person who was given notice of the hearing pursuant to Rule 5.7(4) and was not present or represented at it.

R.5.10
See the general note to Pt 5. This rule deals with the dissemination of the fact that an interim order has been made.

5.11   Nominee's report on the proposal

5.11(1)   [Time for delivery] Where the nominee makes his report to the court under section 256, he shall deliver 2 copies of it to the court not less than 2 business days before the interim order ceases to have effect.

5.11(2)   [Accompanying documents] With his report the nominee shall deliver–

(a)   a copy of the debtor's proposal (with amendments, if any, authorised under Rule 5.3(3)); and

(b)   a copy or summary of any statement of affairs provided by the debtor.

5.11(3)   [Nominee's opinion] If the nominee makes known his opinion that the debtor's proposal has a reasonable prospect of being approved and implemented, and that a meeting of the debtor's creditors should be summoned under section 257, his report shall have annexed to it his comments on the debtor's proposal.
If his opinion is otherwise, he shall give his reasons for that opinion.

5.11(4)   [Endorsement of date of filing] The court shall upon receipt of the report cause one copy of the report to be endorsed with the date of its filing in court and returned to the nominee.

5.11(5)   [Omitted.]

5.11(6)   [Where debtor undischarged bankrupt] Where the debtor is an undischarged bankrupt, the nominee shall send to the official receiver and (if any) the trustee–

(a)   a copy of the debtor's proposal,

(b)   a copy of his (the nominee's) report and his comments accompanying it (if any), and

(c)   a copy or summary of the debtor's statement of affairs.

5.11(7)   [Where debtor not undischarged bankrupt] Where the debtor is not an undischarged bankrupt, the nominee shall send a copy of each of the documents referred to in paragraph (6) to any person who has presented a bankruptcy petition against the debtor.

R.5.11
See the general note to Pt 5. This regulates the nominee's report on the debtor's proposal and the communication of his views to the court. Note the right of creditors to inspect the court file. See I(A)R 2010 (SI 2010/686)—para.(5) deleted.

5.12   Replacement of nominee

5.12(1)   [Notice of application] Where the debtor intends to apply to the court under section 256(3) for the nominee to be replaced, he shall give to the nominee at least 5 business days' notice of his application.

5.12(2)   [Replacement nominee to file consent and qualification to act] No appointment of a replacement nominee shall be made by the court unless there is filed in court a statement by the replacement nominee indicating that the replacement nominee–

(a)   consents to act; and

(b)   is qualified to act as an insolvency practitioner in relation to the debtor or is an authorised person in relation to the debtor.

R.5.12
See the general note to Pt 5. This provision supplements s.256(3) on replacement of nominees. See I(A)R 2010 (SI 2010/686) which makes the standard change from seven days to five business days.

5.13   Consideration of nominee's report

5.13(1)   [Appearances etc.] At the hearing by the court to consider the nominee's report, any of the persons who have been given notice under Rule 5.7(4) may appear or be represented.

5.13(2)   [Application of r.5.10] Rule 5.10 applies to any order made by the court at the hearing.

R.5.13
See the general note to Pt 5. This deals with procedural matters where the nominee's report is being considered.

CHAPTER 4

CASES WHERE NO INTERIM ORDER IS TO BE OBTAINED

5.14   Nominee's report to the court [Deleted.]

5.14A   Nominee's report

5.14A(1)   [Application of r.5.14A] This rule applies where the nominee has received the document and statement mentioned in section 256A(2).

5.14A(2)   [Time limit to attach nominee's opinions on proposal] The nominee must within 14 days (or such longer period as the court may allow)–

(a)   if the nominee has the opinions in section 256A(3)(a) and (b), attach to the report the nominee's comments on the debtor's proposal and comply with paragraph (3); or

(b)   if the nominee does not have the opinions in section 256A(3)(a) and (b), comply with paragraph (5).

5.14A(3)   [To whom documents to be delivered] Where paragraph (2)(a) applies, the nominee must deliver the documents in paragraph (4) to–

(a)   each of the debtor's creditors of whose address the nominee is aware;

(b)   where the debtor is an undischarged bankrupt, the official receiver and (if any) the trustee; and

(c)   any person who has presented a bankruptcy petition against the debtor.

5.14A(4)   [Documents to be delivered] The documents are–

(a)   a copy of the report;

(b)   a copy of the nominee's comments attached to the report;

(c)   a copy of the debtor's proposal (with amendments, if any, authorised under Rule 5.3(3));

(d)   a copy or summary of any statement of affairs provided by the debtor; and

(e)   a copy of the notice referred to in Rule 5.4(3), and

(f)   a statement that no application for an interim order under section 253 is to be made.

5.14A(5)   [Documents to be delivered if no opinion] Where paragraph (2)(b) applies the nominee must–

(a)   deliver a copy of the report to each of the debtor's creditors of whose address the nominee is aware; and

(b)   give the reasons for that opinion to the debtor.

GENERAL NOTE

Substituted by I(A)R 2010 (SI 2010/686) to replace IR r.5.14.

5.14B   Applications to the court

5.14B(1)   [Duty to file; appropriate court] Subject to paragraph (2), where a report has been made under section 256A any application relating to a voluntary arrangement or a proposal for a voluntary arrangement must be filed in the court in which the debtor would be entitled to present the debtor's petition in bankruptcy under Rule 6.40A.

5.14B(2)   [Court where debtor undischarged bankrupt] Where the debtor is an undischarged bankrupt, the appropriate court is the court having the conduct of the debtor's bankruptcy and any application must be filed with the bankruptcy proceedings.

5.14B(3)   [Report to identify appropriate court] The report must contain sufficient information to identify the appropriate court in which to file an application relating to a voluntary arrangement or to a proposal for a voluntary arrangement.

5.14B(4)   [Filing other documentation to assist court] Where an application is made to the court in relation to any matter relating to a voluntary arrangement or a proposal for a voluntary arrangement, in addition to the documents in support of the application, the applicant must file in court such other documents required by this Part as the applicant considers may assist the court in determining the application.

5.14B(5)   [Notice of debtor's application to replace nominee] Where the debtor intends to apply to the court under section 256A(4)(a) or (b) for the nominee to be replaced, the debtor must give to the nominee at least 5 business days' notice of the application.

5.14B(6)   [Notice of nominee's application to be replaced to debtor] Where the nominee intends to apply to the court under section 256A(4)(b) to be replaced as nominee, the nominee must give to the debtor at least 5 business days' notice of the application.

5.14B(7)   [Consent of replacement nominee to be filed] The court must not appoint a replacement nominee unless a statement by the replacement nominee indicating consent to act is filed in court.

GENERAL NOTE

Substituted by I(A)R 2010 (SI 2010/686) to replace IR r.5.14.

5.15   Filing of reports made under section 256A—appropriate court [Revoked by I(A)R 2010 (SI 2010/686).]

5.16   Applications to the court [Revoked by I(A)R 2010 (SI 2010/686).]

CHAPTER 5

CREDITORS' MEETINGS

5.17   Summoning of creditors' meeting

5.17(1)   [Date of meeting] If in his report the nominee states that in his opinion a meeting of creditors should be summoned to consider the debtor's proposal, the date on which the meeting is to be held shall be–

(a)   in a case where an interim order has not been obtained, not more than 28 days from that on which the nominee received the document and statement in section 256A(2); and

(b)   in a case where an interim order is in force, not less than 14 days from the date on which the nominee's report is filed in court nor more than 28 days from that on which the report is considered by the court.

5.17(2)   [Notice of meeting] Notices calling the meeting shall be sent by the nominee, at least 14 days before the day fixed for it to be held, to all the creditors of the debtor of whose address the nominee is aware.

5.17(3)   [Contents of notice] Each notice sent under this rule must specify–

(a)   in a case where an interim order has not been obtained, the court to which application must be made under Rule 5.14B(1) or (2) as the case may be; or

(b)   in a case where an interim order is in force, the court in which the nominee's report on the debtor's proposal has been filed under Rule 5.8;

and must state the effect of Rule 5.23(2) to (4) (requisite majorities).

5.17(3A)   [Documents with notice] Unless they have been sent under Rule 5.14A, the following documents must be sent with every notice under paragraph (3)–

(a)   a copy of the proposal;

(b)   a copy of the statement of affairs or, if the nominee thinks fit, a summary of it (the summary to include a list of the creditors and the amounts of their debts); and

(c)   the nominee's report with the comments on the proposal annexed to it.

R.5.17
See the general note to Pt 5. Chapter 5 is devoted to creditor meetings and r.5.17 outlines procedures for summoning such meetings. See the modernisations made by I(A)R 2010 (SI 2010/686). These include the replacement of the original para.(3) with new paras (3) and (3A).

5.18   Creditors' meeting: supplementary

5.18(1)   [Convenience of venue] Subject as follows, in fixing the venue for the creditors' meeting, the nominee shall have regard to the convenience of creditors.

944

5.18(2)　**[Time of meeting]** The meeting shall be summoned for commencement between 10.00 and 16.00 hours on a business day.

5.18(3)　**[Forms of proxy]** With every notice summoning the meeting there shall be sent out forms of proxy.

[FORM 8.1]

R.5.18
See the general note to Pt 5. This rules deals with mundane matters such as venue.

5.19　The chairman at the meeting

5.19(1)　**[Nominee to be chairman]** Subject as follows, the nominee shall be chairman of the creditors' meeting.

5.19(2)　**[Other nominated chairman]** If for any reason the nominee is unable to attend, he may nominate another person to act as chairman in his place; but a person so nominated must be–

(a)　a person qualified to act as an insolvency practitioner in relation to the debtor;

(b)　an authorised person in relation to the debtor; or

(c)　an employee of the nominee or his firm who is experienced in insolvency matters.

R.5.19
See the general note to Pt 5. This particular rule regulates choice of chairman.

5.20　The chairman as proxy-holder

5.20　The chairman shall not by virtue of any proxy held by him vote to increase or reduce the amount of the remuneration or expenses of the nominee or the supervisor of the proposed arrangement, unless the proxy specifically directs him to vote in that way.

R.5.20
See the general note to Pt 5. This is a sensible provision designed to curb any potential for abuse by a chair of a creditors' meeting.

5.21　Entitlement to vote

5.21(1)　**[Entitlement]** Subject as follows, every creditor who has notice of the creditors' meeting is entitled to vote at the meeting or any adjournment of it.

5.21(2)　**[Calculation of votes]** A creditor's entitlement to vote is calculated as follows–

(a)　where the debtor is not an undischarged bankrupt and an interim order is in force, by reference to the amount of the debt owed to him as at the date of the interim order;

(b)　where the debtor is not an undischarged bankrupt and an interim order is not in force, by reference to the amount of the debt owed to him at the date of the meeting; and

(c)　where the debtor is an undischarged bankrupt, by reference to the amount of the debt owed to him as at the date of the bankruptcy order.

5.21(3)　**[Limitation on voting]** A creditor may vote in respect of a debt for an unliquidated amount or any debt whose value is not ascertained, and for the purposes of voting (but not otherwise) his debt shall be valued at £1 unless the chairman agrees to put a higher value on it.

R.5.21
See the general note to Pt 5. This important provision explains the calculation of voting entitlements. Note the nominal £1 valuation for unliquidated/unascertained debts.

5.22   Procedure for admission of creditors' claims for voting purposes

5.22(1)   [Procedure at creditors' meeting] Subject as follows, at the creditors' meeting the chairman shall ascertain the entitlement of persons wishing to vote and shall admit or reject their claims accordingly.

5.22(2)   [Chairman's discretion] The chairman may admit or reject a claim in whole or in part.

5.22(3)   [Appeal from chairman's decision] The chairman's decision on any matter under this Rule or under paragraph (3) of Rule 5.21 is subject to appeal to the court by any creditor or by the debtor.

5.22(4)   [Voting subject to objection] If the chairman is in doubt whether a claim should be admitted or rejected, he shall mark it as objected to and allow votes to be cast in respect of it, subject to such votes being subsequently declared invalid if the objection to the claim is sustained.

5.22(5)   [When chairman's decision reversed etc.] If on an appeal the chairman's decision is reversed or varied, or votes are declared invalid, the court may order another meeting to be summoned, or make such order as it thinks just.

The court's power to make an order under this paragraph is exercisable only if it considers that the circumstances giving rise to the appeal are such as give rise to unfair prejudice or material irregularity.

5.22(6)   [Time for appeal] An application to the court by way of appeal against the chairman's decision shall not be made after the end of the period of 28 days beginning with the first day on which–

(a)   where the creditors' meeting was summoned under section 257 pursuant to a report to the debtor's creditors under section 256A(3), the notice of the result of the meeting required by section 259(1)(a) has been given; or

(b)   where the creditors' meeting was summoned under section 257 pursuant to a report to a court under section 256(1)(aa), the report required by section 259(1)(b) is made to the court.

5.22(7)   [Costs of appeal] The chairman is not personally liable for any costs incurred by any person in respect of an appeal under this Rule.

R.5.22

See the general note to Pt 5. This deals with the sensitive matter of managing entitlement to vote. This has triggered much litigation in the past. IR 1986 rr.5.21 and 5.22, and the duties/powers of the chairman under these rules, were considered in *Smurthwaite v Simpson-Smith and Mond (No.2)* [2006] B.P.I.R. 1483—but any such consideration must be viewed in the light of the appeal proceedings reported in [2006] B.P.I.R. 1504. See *Monecor (London) Ltd v Ahmed* [2008] B.P.I.R. 458. Rule 5.22 was reviewed by the court in *Tradition (UK) Ltd v Ahmed* [2009] B.P.I.R. 626.

There is some discussion of r.5.22 and analogous insolvency rules by Lewison J. in *Power v Petrus Estates Ltd* [2009] B.P.I.R. 141.

See the clarification made by I(A)R 2010 (SI 2010/686) to para.(6).

5.23   Requisite majorities

5.23(1)   [Resolution by majority in value] Subject to paragraph (2), at the creditors' meeting, a resolution is passed when a majority (in value) of those present and voting in person or by proxy have voted in favour of it.

5.23(2)   [Resolution to approve proposal/modification by three-quarters in value] A resolution to approve the proposal or a modification is passed when a majority of three-quarters or more (in value) of those present and voting in person or by proxy have voted in favour of it.

5.23(3)   [Votes to be left out of account] In the following cases there is to be left out of account a creditor's vote in respect of any claim or part of a claim–

(a)   where written notice of the claim was not given, either at the meeting or before it, to the chairman or the nominee;

(b)   where the claim or part is secured;

(c) where the claim is in respect of a debt wholly or partly on, or secured by, a current bill of exchange or promissory note, unless the creditor is willing–

(i) to treat the liability to him on the bill or note of every person who is liable on it antecedently to the debtor, and against whom a bankruptcy order has not been made (or, in the case of a company, which has not gone into liquidation), as a security in his hands, and

(ii) to estimate the value of the security and (for the purpose of entitlement to vote, but not of any distribution under the arrangement) to deduct it from his claim.

5.23(4) [Votes rendering resolution invalid] Any resolution is invalid if those voting against it include more than half in value of the creditors, counting in these latter only those–

(a) who have notice of the meeting;

(b) whose votes are not to be left out of account under paragraph (3); and

(c) who are not, to the best of the chairman's belief, associates of the debtor.

5.23(5) [Chairman's powers] It is for the chairman of the meeting to decide whether under this Rule–

(a) a vote is to be left out of account in accordance with the paragraph (3), or

(b) a person is an associate of the debtor for the purposes of paragraph (4)(c);

and in relation to the second of these cases the chairman is entitled to rely on the information provided by the debtor's statement of affairs or otherwise in accordance with this Part of the Rules.

5.23(6) [Chairman's use of proxy] If the chairman uses a proxy contrary to Rule 5.20, his vote with that proxy does not count towards any majority under this Rule.

5.23(7) [Chairman's decision subject to appeal] The chairman's decision on any matter under this Rule is subject to appeal to the court by any creditor or by the debtor and paragraphs (5) to (7) of Rule 5.22 apply as regards such an appeal.

R.5.23
See the general note to Pt 5. The proposal must attract the support of the holders of 75 per cent of the debt and of more than 50 per cent of the independent debt. The voting position where debts are secured is also explained. Creditors who have not notified their claim before the meeting cannot vote. See I(A)R 2010 (SI 2010/686) which reworks the statement of the required majority.

5.24 Proceedings to obtain agreement on the proposal

5.24(1) [Adjournments] On the day on which the creditors' meeting is held, it may from time to time be adjourned.

5.24(2) [Failure to obtain requisite majority] If on that day the requisite majority for the approval of the voluntary arrangement (with or without modifications) has not been obtained, the chairman may, and shall if it is so resolved, adjourn the meeting for not more than 14 days.

5.24(3) [Final adjournment] If there are subsequently further adjournments, the final adjournment shall not be to a day later than 14 days after that on which the meeting was originally held.

5.24(4) [Notice of adjournment] If the meeting is adjourned under paragraph (2), notice of the fact shall be given by the chairman as soon as reasonably practicable to the court.

5.24(4A) [Single suspension of meeting without adjournment] Once only in the course of a meeting the chairman may, without an adjournment, declare it suspended for any period up to 1 hour.

5.24(5) [Deemed rejection of proposal] If following any final adjournment of the meeting the proposal (with or without modifications) is not agreed to, it is deemed rejected.

R.5.24
See the general note to Pt 5. This deals with the possibility of adjournment, which is a common happening, in order to amend the proposal and win over doubters. Any adjournment(s) can only last for a maximum of 14 days after the initial meeting. This rule was considered in *Tradition (UK) Ltd v Ahmed* [2009] B.P.I.R. 626.

See the new para.(4A) introduced by I(A)R 2010 (SI 2010/686) which confers a power of suspension.

CHAPTER 6

IMPLEMENTATION OF THE ARRANGEMENT

5.25   Resolutions to follow approval

5.25(1)   [Resolution re supervisory acts] If the voluntary arrangement is approved (with or without modifications), a resolution must be taken by the creditors, where two or more individuals are appointed to act as supervisor, on the question whether acts to be done in connection with the arrangement may be done by any one of them, or must be done by both or all.

5.25(2)   [Where supervisor to be other than nominee] If at the creditors' meeting a resolution is moved for the appointment of some person other than the nominee to be supervisor of the arrangement, there must be produced to the chairman, at or before the meeting–

(a)   that person's written consent to act (unless he is present and then and there signifies his consent), and

(b)   his written confirmation that he is qualified to act as an insolvency practitioner in relation to the debtor or is an authorised person in relation to the debtor.

R.5.25
See the general note to Pt 5. Chapter 6 deals with matters consequent upon approval of an IVA, including the powers of joint supervisors. See I(A)R 2010 (SI 2010/686) which makes para.(1) more restrictive than its previous formulation.

5.26   Hand-over of property, etc to supervisor

5.26(1)   [Putting supervisor into possession of assets] As soon as reasonably practicable after the approval of the voluntary arrangement, the debtor or, where the debtor is an undischarged bankrupt, the official receiver or the debtor's trustee, shall do all that is required for putting the supervisor into possession of the assets included in the arrangement.

5.26(2)   [Discharge of official receiver's remuneration etc.] On taking possession of the assets in any case where the debtor is an undischarged bankrupt, the supervisor shall discharge any balance due to the official receiver and (if other) the trustee by way of remuneration or on account of–

(a)   fees, costs, charges and expenses properly incurred and payable under the Act or the Rules, and

(b)   any advances made in respect of the insolvent estate, together with interest on such advances at the rate specified in section 17 of the Judgments Act 1838 at the date of the bankruptcy order.

5.26(3)   [Undertaking to discharge etc.] Alternatively where the debtor is an undischarged bankrupt, the supervisor must, before taking possession, give the official receiver or the trustee a written undertaking to discharge any such balance out of the first realisation of assets.

5.26(4)   [Charge on assets] Where the debtor is an undischarged bankrupt, the official receiver and (if other) the trustee has a charge on the assets included in the voluntary arrangement in respect of any sums due as above until they have been discharged, subject only to the deduction from realisations by the supervisor of the proper costs and expenses of realisation.

Any sums due to the official receiver take priority over those due to a trustee.

948

5.26(5)   [Discharge of guarantees etc.] The supervisor shall from time to time out of the realisation of assets discharge all guarantees properly given by the official receiver or the trustee for the benefit of the estate, and shall pay all their expenses.

R.5.26

See the general note to Pt 5. Chapter 6 deals with the implementation of the approved arrangement. Rule 5.26 addresses various matters consequential to approval, including the handing over of property to the supervisor. A properly drafted arrangement should carefully identify such property in order for it to become a trust asset protected from the claims of creditors outside the IVA.

5.27   Report of creditors' meeting

5.27(1)   [Chairman to prepare report] A report of the creditors' meeting shall be prepared by the chairman of the meeting.

5.27(2)   [Contents of report] The report shall–

(a)   state whether the proposal for a voluntary arrangement was approved or rejected and, if approved, with what (if any) modifications;

(b)   set out the resolutions which were taken at the meeting, and the decision on each one;

(c)   list the creditors (with their respective values) who were present or represented at the meeting, and how they voted on each resolution;

(d)   whether in the opinion of the supervisor,

(i)   the EC Regulation applies to the voluntary arrangement, and

(ii)   if so, whether the proceedings are main proceedings or territorial proceedings; and

(e)   include such further information (if any) as the chairman thinks it appropriate to make known to the court or the debtor's creditors as the case may be.

5.27(3)   [Copy of report to be filed in court] Where the creditors' meeting was summoned under section 257 pursuant to a report to a court under section 256(1)(aa), a copy of the chairman's report shall, within 4 business days of the meeting being held, be filed in court; and the court shall cause that copy to be endorsed with the date of filing.

5.27(4)   [To whom notice of result to be sent] The persons to whom notice of the result is to be given, under section 259(1), are all those who were sent notice of the meeting under this Part of the Rules and any other creditor of whose address the chairman is aware, and where the debtor is an undischarged bankrupt, the official receiver and (if any) the trustee.

5.27(4A)   [Time limit for notice to be sent] The notice must be sent–

(a)   where the creditors' meeting was summoned under section 257 pursuant to a report to a court under section 256(1)(aa), as soon as reasonably practicable after a copy of the chairman's report is filed in court;

(b)   where the creditors' meeting was summoned under section 257 pursuant to a report to creditors under section 256A(3), within 4 business days of the meeting being held.

5.27(5)   [Where no interim order obtained] In a case where no interim order has been obtained the court shall not consider the chairman's report unless an application is made to the court under the Act or the Rules in relation to it.

R.5.27

See the general note to Pt 5. This rules explains the contents of the chairman's report on the creditors' meeting—this report, which has become more fulsome with successive reforms, must be filed in court within four days. See the modernisations effected by I(A)R 2010 (SI 2010/686)—new para.(4A) introduced.

5.28   Register of voluntary arrangements [Omitted.]

R.5.28

See the general note to Pt 5. A register of IVAs was to be maintained by the Secretary of State and be open for public inspection.

[This rule was then omitted by the Insolvency (Amendment) Rules 2003 (SI 2003/1730)—this register is now provided for by Pt 6A.]

5.29   Reports to Secretary of State

5.29(1)   [Chairman to send information] As soon as reasonably practicable, and in any event, within the period of 14 days after a report that the creditors' meeting has approved the voluntary arrangement has been filed in court or sent to the creditors as the case may be, the chairman of the creditors' meeting must send to the Secretary of State the following information–

    (a)   the name and address of the debtor;

    (b)   the date on which the arrangement was approved by the creditors;

    (c)   the name and address of the supervisor;

    (d)   the debtor's gender;

    (e)   the debtor's date of birth; and

    (f)   any name by which the debtor was or is known, not being the name in which the debtor has entered into the voluntary arrangement.

5.29(2)   [Notice of appointment as supervisor etc.] A person who is appointed to act as supervisor of an individual voluntary arrangement (whether in the first instance or by way of replacement of another person previously appointed) shall as soon as reasonably practicable give written notice to the Secretary of State of his appointment.

If he vacates office as supervisor, he shall as soon as reasonably practicable give written notice of that fact also to the Secretary of State.

R.5.29

See the general note to Pt 5. In addition to notifying the court the chairman of the creditors' meeting must notify approved voluntary arrangements to the Secretary of State. This is necessary to enable the latter to maintain the public register (see Pt 6A). The supervisor must also notify his appointment to the Secretary of State. Modernised by I(A)R 2010 (SI 2010/686).

5.30   Revocation or suspension of the arrangement

5.30(1)   [Application] This Rule applies where the court makes an order of revocation or suspension under section 262.

5.30(2)   [Service of sealed copies] The person who applied for the order shall serve sealed copies of it–

    (a)   in a case where the debtor is an undischarged bankrupt, on the debtor, the official receiver and the trustee;

    (b)   in any other case, on the debtor; and

    (c)   in either case, on the supervisor of the voluntary arrangement.

5.30(3)   [Notice re further creditors' meeting] If the order includes a direction by the court under section 262(4)(b) for any further creditors' meeting to be summoned, notice shall also be given (by the person who applied for the order) to whoever is, in accordance with the direction, required to summon the meeting.

5.30(4)   [Notice of order and of intention re proposal] The debtor or (where the debtor is an undischarged bankrupt) the trustee or (if there is no trustee) the official receiver shall–

(a) as soon as reasonably practicable after receiving a copy of the court's order, give notice of it to all persons who were sent notice of the creditors' meeting which approved the voluntary arrangement or who, not having been sent that notice, are affected by the order;

(b) within 5 business days of their receiving a copy of the order (or within such longer period as the court may allow), give notice to the court whether it is intended to make a revised proposal to creditors, or to invite reconsideration of the original proposal.

5.30(5) [Notice to Secretary of State] The person on whose application the order of revocation or suspension was made shall, within 5 business days after the making of the order, give written notice of it to the Secretary of State and shall, in the case of an order of suspension, within 5 business days of the expiry of any suspension order, given written notice of such expiry to the Secretary of State.

R.5.30
See the general note to Pt 5. This particular rule deals with revocation or suspension of the IVA under the terms of s.262. Various consequential matters are addressed including the requirement imposed on the successful applicant to notify the Secretary of State. See I(A)R 2010 (SI 2010/686)—note the change in paras (4)(b) and (5) from seven days to five business days.

5.31 Supervisor's accounts and reports [Deleted.]

5.31A Supervisor's accounts and reports

5.31A(1) [Application of r.5.31A(2)] Paragraph (2) applies where the voluntary arrangement authorises or requires the supervisor–

(a) to carry on the business of the debtor or trade on behalf of or in the name of the debtor; or

(b) to realise assets of the debtor or (in a case where the debtor is an undischarged bankrupt) belonging to the estate; or

(c) otherwise to administer or dispose of any funds of the debtor or the estate.

5.31A(2) [Duty to keep accounts and records including receipts and payments] The supervisor must keep accounts and records of the supervisor's acts and dealings in, and in connection with, the arrangement, including in particular records of all receipts and payments of money.

5.31A(3) [Duty to preserve predecessor accounts and records] The supervisor must preserve any accounts and records in paragraph (2) which–

(a) were kept by any other person who has acted as supervisor of the arrangement; and

(b) are in the supervisor's possession.

5.31A(4) [Progress report] Subject to paragraph (5), the supervisor must in respect of each period of 12 months ending with the anniversary of the commencement of the arrangement send within 2 months of the end of that period a report on the progress and prospects for the full implementation of the voluntary arrangement to–

(a) the debtor, and

(b) all those of the debtor's creditors who are bound by the voluntary arrangement and of whose address the supervisor is aware.

5.31A(5) [No progress report where final report] The supervisor is released from an obligation to send a report under paragraph (4), if an obligation to send a final report under Rule 5.34 arises in the period of 2 months mentioned in paragraph (4).

5.31A(6) [Abstract of receipts and payments] Where the supervisor is authorised or required to do any of the things mentioned in paragraph (1)(a) to (c) the report required to be sent pursuant to paragraph (2) must include or be accompanied by–

(a) an abstract of receipts and payments required to be recorded by virtue of paragraph (2); or

(b) where there have been no such receipts and payments, a statement to that effect.

GENERAL NOTE

Substituted by I(A)R 2010 (SI 2010/686) for the former IR r.5.31.

5.32 Production of accounts and records to Secretary of State

5.32(1) [Powers of Secretary of State] The Secretary of State may at any time during the course of the voluntary arrangement or after its completion require the supervisor to produce for inspection–

(a) his records and accounts in respect of the arrangement, and

(b) copies of abstracts and reports prepared in compliance with Rule 5.31A.

5.32(2) [Production and duty to comply] The Secretary of State may require production either at the premises of the supervisor or elsewhere; and it is the duty of the supervisor to comply with any requirement imposed on him under this Rule.

5.32(3) [Audit of accounts and records] The Secretary of State may cause any accounts and records produced to him under this Rule to be audited; and the supervisor shall give to the Secretary of State such further information and assistance as he needs for the purposes of his audit.

R.5.32
See the general note to Pt 5. In addition to the general accounting requirements imposed by r.5.31A, the Secretary of State can at any time require further accounts and reports from the supervisor. See I(A)R 2010 (SI 2010/686).

5.33 Fees, costs, charges and expenses

5.33 The fees, costs, charges and expenses that may be incurred for any purposes of the voluntary arrangement are–

(a) any disbursements made by the nominee prior to the approval of the arrangement, and any remuneration for his services as such agreed between himself and the debtor, the official receiver or the trustee;

(b) any fees, costs, charges or expenses which–

(i) are sanctioned by the terms of the arrangement, or

(ii) would be payable, or correspond to those which would be payable, in the debtor's bankruptcy.

R.5.33
See the general note to Pt 5. This identifies the fees and expenses, etc. of an IVA.

5.34 Completion or termination of the arrangement

5.34(1) [Supervisor to send notice] Not more than 28 days after the final completion or termination of the voluntary arrangement, the supervisor shall send to all creditors of the debtor who are bound by the arrangement, and to the debtor, a notice that the arrangement has been fully implemented or (as the case may be) terminated.

5.34(2) [Supervisor's report] With the notice there shall be sent to each of those persons a copy of a report by the supervisor summarising all receipts and payments made by him in pursuance of the arrangement, and explaining any difference in the actual implementation of it as compared with the proposal as approved by the creditors' meeting or (in the case of termination of the arrangement) explaining the reasons why the arrangement has not been implemented in accordance with the proposal as approved by the creditors' meeting.

5.34(3) **[Vacation of office]** The Supervisor must not vacate office until paragraph (3A) has been complied with.

5.34(3A) **[Copy of notice and report]** Within the period in paragraph (1), a copy of the notice under paragraph (1), together with a copy of the report under paragraph (2) must be–

(a)   sent by the supervisor to the Secretary of State; and

(b)   where the creditors' meeting was summoned under section 257 pursuant to a report to a court under section 256(1)(aa), filed with the court by the supervisor.

5.34(4) **[Extension of time]** The court may, on application by the supervisor, extend the period of 28 days under paragraph (1).

R.5.34
See the general note to Pt 5. The supervisor must notify all creditors of completion or termination and also must furnish them with a summary of receipts and payments. The Secretary of State must in addition be notified. The time limit for such notifications is fixed at 28 days. See I(A)R 2010 (SI 2010/686) which replaces para.(3) and inserts new para.(3A).

CHAPTER 7

FAST-TRACK VOLUNTARY ARRANGEMENT

5.35   Application of Chapter

5.35   The Rules in this Chapter apply in relation to an individual debtor who intends to submit a proposal for a voluntary arrangement with his creditors to the official receiver in accordance with the provisions of section 263B.

GENERAL NOTE

This new Chapter 7 dealing with fast-track IVAs was inserted by the Insolvency (Amendment) Rules 2003 (SI 2003/1730) in the wake of the Enterprise Act 2002, which introduced this new IVA variant via s.263B.
   Under this model the official receiver is permitted to act as nominee/supervisor of an IVA proposed by an undischarged bankrupt. This is an exceptional scenario which has raised some concern in the minds of private practitioners but quite frankly its potential usage is likely to be limited particularly with bankruptcy discharge available after only one year. Indeed it appears that this procedure was rarely used in its first year of operation.
   The required contents of the undischarged bankrupt's proposal are mapped out by r.5.37. The official receiver has 28 days to respond (r.5.38). If his response is favourable he must as soon as practicable notify the creditors and the trustee in bankruptcy (r.5.39). Voting is by post (r.5.40) rather than through the medium of a meeting; this will save on costs. Rules on voting entitlements and majorities are detailed in rr.5.41–5.43. There is an opportunity to challenge any approval given to such an IVA proposal (s.263F and r.5.46). Duties of the supervisor (who may be the official receiver) are explained in rr.5.47A–5.50. Paragraphs (3) and (4) of r.5.43 were inserted by I(A)R 2004 (SI 2004/584) with effect from April 1, 2004 to clarify the position on calculating votes for the purposes of requisite majorities. Note the introduction of the standard IVA requirement that the support of the holders of 50 per cent of the independent debt must be obtained. Again note the many changes made by I(A)R 2010 (SI 2010/686).

5.36   Interpretation

5.36   In this Chapter–

   "voluntary arrangement" means an individual voluntary arrangement under section 263A;

   "proposal" means the document setting out the terms of the voluntary arrangement which the debtor is proposing.

(See General Note after r.5.35.)

5.37   Contents of proposal

5.37(1)   [Fees and contents] The debtor's proposal submitted under section 263B(1) shall–

(a)   be accompanied by any fee payable to the official receiver for acting as nominee; and

(b)   contain–

   (i)   a statement that the debtor is eligible to propose a voluntary arrangement;

   (ii)   a short explanation why, in his opinion, a voluntary arrangement is desirable, and give reasons why his creditors may be expected to concur with such an arrangement; and

   (iii)   a statement that the debtor is aware that he commits an offence under section 262A if, for the purpose of obtaining the approval of his creditors to his proposal, he makes any false representation, or fraudulently does, or omits to do, anything.

5.37(2)   [Matters to be stated] The following matters shall be stated, or otherwise dealt with, in the proposal–

(a)   the following matters, so far as within the debtor's immediate knowledge

   (i)   his assets, with an estimate of their respective values;

   (ii)   the extent (if any) to which the assets are charged in favour of creditors; and

   (iii)   the extent (if any) to which particular assets are to be excluded from the voluntary arrangement;

(b)   particulars of any property, other than assets of the debtor himself, which is proposed to be included in the voluntary arrangement, the source of such property and the terms on which it is to be made available for inclusion;

(c)   the nature and amount of the debtor's liabilities (so far as within his immediate knowledge), the manner in which they are proposed to be met, modified, postponed or otherwise dealt with by means of the voluntary arrangement and (in particular)–

   (i)   how it is proposed to deal with preferential creditors (defined in section 258(7)) and creditors who are, or claim to be, secured;

   (ii)   how associates of the debtor (being creditors of his) are proposed to be treated under the voluntary arrangement; and

   (iii)   whether, to the debtor's knowledge, claims have been made under section 339 (transactions at an undervalue), section 340 (preferences), section 343 (extortionate credit transactions), or whether there are circumstances giving rise to the possibility of such claims

   and, where any such circumstances are present, whether, and if so how, it is proposed under the voluntary arrangement to make provision for wholly or partly indemnifying the insolvent estate in respect of such claims;

(d)   whether any, and if so what, guarantees have been given of the debtor's debts by other persons, specifying which (if any) of the guarantors are associates of his;

(e)   the proposed duration of the voluntary arrangement;

(f)   the proposed dates of distributions to creditors, with estimates of their amounts;

(g)   how it is proposed to deal with the claims of any person who is bound by the arrangement by virtue of section 263D(2)(c);

(h)   an estimate of the fees and expenses that will be incurred in connection with the approval and implementation of the voluntary agreement;

(j) whether, for the purposes of the voluntary arrangement, any guarantees are to be offered by any persons other than the debtor and whether (if so) any security is to be given or sought;

(k) the manner in which funds held for the purpose of payment to creditors, and not so paid on the termination of the voluntary arrangement, are to be dealt with;

(l) the functions which are to be undertaken by the supervisor of the voluntary arrangement;

(m) an address of the official receiver to which correspondence with the official receiver is to be sent;

(n) the names and addresses of all the debtor's creditors so far as within his immediate knowledge; and

(o) whether the EC Regulation will apply and, if so, whether the proceedings will be main proceedings or territorial proceedings

and the proposal shall be authenticated by the debtor.

5.37(3)   [Address of official receiver] The official receiver shall on request supply to the debtor the address referred to in paragraph 2(m).

(See General Note after r.5.35.) See I(A)R 2010 (SI 2010/686).

5.38   Requirement for the official receiver's decision

5.38(1)   [Duty of official receiver to notify debtor] Where the official receiver receives a proposal for a voluntary arrangement in accordance with Rule 5.37 he shall, within 28 days of its receipt, serve a notice on the debtor stating that–

(a) he agrees to act as nominee in relation to the proposal;

(b) he declines to act as nominee in relation to the proposal and specifying reasons for his decision; or

(c) on the basis of the information supplied to him he is unable to reach a decision as to whether to act and specifying what further information he requires.

5.38(2)   [Where a decision after further information] Where the debtor, pursuant to a request under paragraph (1)(c), supplies the information requested, the official receiver shall, within 28 days of the receipt of the information, serve a notice on the debtor in accordance with paragraph (1).

(See General Note after r.5.35.)

5.39   Arrangements for approval of fast-track voluntary arrangement

5.39(1)   [Duty of official receiver to creditors and trustee] As soon as reasonably practicable after the official receiver agrees to act as nominee, he shall send to the creditors and any trustee who is not the official receiver–

(a) a copy of the proposal; and

(b) a notice inviting creditors to vote to approve or reject the debtor's proposal and stating that–

    (i) if a majority of three-quarters or more in value of creditors who vote approve the proposal, the official receiver will, as soon as reasonably practicable, notify the Secretary of State that the proposal has been approved;

    (ii) under section 263F–

        (aa) the debtor, a person who was entitled to participate in the arrangements made under section 263B(2), any trustee who is not the official receiver, or the official receiver, has 28 days from the date the official receiver notifies the Secretary of State under section 263C that the proposal has been approved to apply to the court to have the proposal set aside on the grounds set out in section 263F(1);

> (bb) a creditor, who was not made aware of the arrangements under section 263B(2) at the time when they were made, has 28 days from the date on which he becomes aware of the voluntary arrangement, to apply to have the proposal set aside on the grounds set out in section 263F(1); and

> (iii) creditors cannot propose modifications to the debtor's proposal; and

(c) for the creditors, a copy of Form 5.6 for their use.

5.39(2) **[Final date for voting]** The notice shall include a date specified by the official receiver as the final date on which he will accept votes from creditors, being a date not less than 14 days and not more than 28 days from the date of the notice.

(See General Note after r.5.35.) Modernised by I(A)R 2010 (SI 2010/686) which removes the requirement of a report to the court.

5.40   Approval by creditors

5.40(1) **[Forms of notice re proposal]** All creditors who wish to vote shall give notice in Form 5.6 to the official receiver of their decision whether to accept or reject the debtor's proposal. Such notification shall be sent to the official receiver at the address specified in the notice.

[FORM 5.6]

5.40(2) **[Notice by representative of creditor]** That notice may be sent by a representative of a creditor if it is accompanied by a written authority for that representation authenticated by the creditor.

5.40(3) [Omitted.]

(See General Note after r.5.35.) See the modernisations effected by I(A)R 2010 (SI 2010/686).

5.41   Entitlement to vote

5.41(1) **[Entitlement to vote]** Subject as follows, any creditor who is sent a notice by the official receiver is entitled to vote for the approval or rejection of the proposal.

5.41(2) **[Calculation of voting entitlement]** A creditor's entitlement to vote is calculated by reference to the amount of the creditor's debt at the date of the bankruptcy order.

5.41(3) **[Valuation of unliquidated amounts]** A creditor may vote in respect of a debt for an unliquidated amount or any debt whose value is not ascertained, and for the purposes of voting (but not otherwise) his debt shall be valued at £1 unless the official receiver agrees to put a higher value on it.

(See General Note after r.5.35.)

5.42   Procedure for admission of creditors' claims for voting purposes

5.42(1) **[Power of official receiver]** The official receiver has the power to admit or reject a creditor's claim for the purpose of his entitlement to vote, and the power is exercisable with respect to the whole or part of the claim.

5.42(2) **[Appeal]** The official receiver's decision on entitlement to vote is subject to appeal to the court by any creditor or the debtor.

5.42(3) **[Power of court]** If on appeal the official receiver's decision is reversed or varied, or votes are declared invalid, the court may order another vote to be held, or make such order as it thinks just. The court's power to make an order under this paragraph is exercisable only if it considers that the circumstances giving rise to the appeal are such as give rise to unfair prejudice or material irregularity.

5.42(4) **[Time-limit for appeal]** An application to the court by way of appeal against the official receiver's decision shall not be made after the end of the period of 28 days beginning with the day on which the official receiver is required by section 263C to notify the Secretary of State.

5.42(5)   [Liability for costs of appeal] The official receiver is not personally liable for any costs incurred by any person in respect of an appeal under this Rule.

(See General Note after r.5.35.) Reworded by I(A)R 2010 (SI 2010/686).

5.43   Requisite majorities

5.43(1)   [Proposal approved by three-quarters or more of creditors] A proposal is approved by the creditors if three-quarters or more in value of the creditors who vote approve the proposal.

5.43(2)   [Votes to be left out of account] In the following cases there is to be left out of account a creditor's vote in respect of any claim or part of a claim–

(a)   where the claim or part is secured;

(b)   where the claim is in respect of a debt wholly or partly on, or secured by, a current bill of exchange or promissory note, unless the creditor is willing–

    (i)   to treat the liability to him on the bill or note of every person who is liable on it antecedently to the debtor, and against whom a bankruptcy order has not been made (or in the case of a company, which has not gone into liquidation), as a security in his hands and

    (ii)   to estimate the value of the security and (for the purpose of entitlement to vote, but not of any distribution under the arrangement) to deduct it from his claim.

5.43(3)   [Proposal not approved] A proposal is not approved if those voting against it include more than half in value of the creditors, counting in the latter only those–

(a)   who gave notice to the official receiver in accordance with Rule 5.40;

(b)   whose votes are not to be left out of account under paragraph (2); and

(c)   who are not, to the best of the official receiver's belief, associates of the debtor.

5.43(4)   [Whether person associate of debtor] It is for the official receiver to decide whether, under this Rule a person is an associate of the debtor for the purposes of paragraph (3)(c) and in relation to this he is entitled to rely on the information provided by the debtor's statement of affairs or otherwise in accordance with this Part of the Rules.

(See General Note after r.5.35.) The statement of required majority has been reworded by I(A)R 2010 (SI 2010/686).

5.44   Notification to the court [Revoked by I(A)R 2010 (SI 2010/686).]

5.45   Notice of appointment as supervisor etc

5.45(1)   [Duty of official receiver] Where the official receiver is appointed to act as supervisor of a voluntary arrangement, he shall, as soon as reasonably practicable, give written notice of his appointment to the Secretary of State, and all creditors of whose address the official receiver is aware, and the trustee (if any) who is not the official receiver.

5.45(2)   [Duty on vacation of office] If the official receiver vacates office as supervisor he must, as soon as reasonably practicable after doing so, give written notice of that fact to the Secretary of State.

(See General Note after r.5.35.) See I(A)R 2010 (SI 2010/686) for rewording.

5.46   Revocation of the fast-track voluntary arrangement

5.46(1)   [Application of r.5.46] This Rule applies where the court makes an order of revocation under section 263F.

5.46(2)   [Who to serve sealed copy of order] Where the person who applied for the order is–

(a)   the debtor, he shall serve a sealed copy of the order on the supervisor and any trustee of his estate who is not the official receiver;

(b)   the supervisor, he shall serve a sealed copy of the order on the debtor, and any trustee who is not the official receiver;

(c)   a trustee who is not the official receiver, he shall serve a sealed copy of the order on the debtor and the supervisor; and

(d)   a creditor, he shall serve a sealed copy of the order on the debtor, the supervisor and any trustee who is not the official receiver.

5.46(3)   [Duty of supervisor to notify re order] The supervisor shall, as soon as reasonably practicable after receiving a copy of the order, give notice of it, to all persons who were sent a copy of the debtor's proposal under Rule 5.39 and all other persons who are affected by the order.

5.46(4)   [Notice of order to Secretary of State] The person on whose application the order was made shall, within 5 business days after the making of the order, give written notice of it to the Secretary of State.

(See General Note after r.5.35.) See I(A)R 2010 (SI 2010/686).

5.47   Supervisor's accounts and reports [Deleted.]

5.47A   Supervisor's accounts and reports

5.47A(1)   [Duty to keep accounts and records including receipts and payments] The supervisor must keep accounts and records of the supervisor's acts and dealings in, and in connection with, the arrangement including in particular records of all receipts and payments of money.

5.47A(2)   [Progress report] Subject to paragraph (3), the supervisor must in respect of each period of 12 months ending with the anniversary of the commencement of the arrangement send within 2 months of the end of that period a report on the progress and prospects for the full implementation of the voluntary arrangement to–

(a)   the debtor;

(b)   all those of the debtor's creditors who are bound by the voluntary arrangement of whose address the supervisor is aware;

5.47A(3)   [No progress report where final report] The supervisor is released from an obligation to send a report under paragraph (2), if an obligation to send a final report under Rule 5.50 arises in the period of 2 months mentioned in paragraph (2).

GENERAL NOTE

Substituted by I(A)R 2010 (SI 2010/686) for IR r.5.47.

5.48   Fees, costs and expenses in respect of the performance of the functions of the official receiver

5.48   The fees, costs and expenses in respect of the performance by the official receiver of his functions in relation to the bankruptcy and those of the trustee who is not the official receiver (including those in connection with the employment of agents) shall be a first charge on any sums realised under the terms of the voluntary arrangement, and those of the official receiver in relation to the voluntary arrangement, shall be a second charge.

(See General Note after r.5.35.)

5.49 Employment of agents by the supervisor

5.49 The supervisor may employ agents in connection with the realisation of any assets subject to the terms of the voluntary arrangement.

(See General Note after r.5.35.)

5.50 Completion or termination of the fast-track voluntary arrangement

5.50(1) [Duty of supervisor] Not more than 28 days after the final completion or termination of the voluntary arrangement, the supervisor shall send to all creditors of the debtor who are bound by the arrangement, and to the debtor, a notice that the voluntary arrangement has been fully implemented, or (as the case may be) terminated.

5.50(2) [Copy of supervisor's report] With the notice there shall be sent to each of those persons a copy of a report by the supervisor summarising all receipts and payments made by him in pursuance of the voluntary arrangement, and explaining any difference in the actual implementation of it compared with the proposal as approved by the creditors.

5.50(3) [Copies to Secretary of State] The supervisor shall, within the 28 days mentioned above, send to the Secretary of State a copy of the notice under paragraph (1), together with a copy of the report under paragraph (2), and he shall not vacate office until after such copies have been sent.

5.50(4) [Extension of time limits] The court may, on application by the supervisor, extend the period of 28 days under paragraphs (1) and (3).

(See General Note after r.5.35.)

CHAPTER 8

APPLICATION BY A BANKRUPT TO ANNUL A BANKRUPTCY ORDER UNDER SECTION 261(2)(A)

5.51 Application of this Chapter

5.51 The following Rules apply where a bankrupt applies for an annulment of a bankruptcy order under section 261(2)(a).

R.5.51
This new Chapter 8 was inserted by the Insolvency (Amendment) Rules 2003 (SI 2003/1730). It deals with applications to annul a bankruptcy order pursuant to s.261(2)(a) in order to allow an IVA to be promoted. This was modernised by I(A)R 2010 (SI 2010/686).

5.52 Application to court

5.52(1) [Application to specify section made under] An application to the court to annul a bankruptcy order under section 261(2)(a) shall specify the section under which it is made.

5.52(2) [Witness statement in support] The application shall be supported by a witness statement stating–

(a) that the voluntary arrangement has been approved at a meeting of creditors;

(b) the date of the approval by the creditors; and

(c) that the 28 day period in section 262(3)(a) for applications to be made under section 262(1) has expired and no applications or appeal remain to be disposed of.

5.52(3) [Duty of court to fix venue] The application and supporting witness statement shall be filed in court; and the court shall give to the bankrupt notice of the venue fixed for the hearing.

5.52(4) **[Duty of bankrupt to notify official receiver etc.]** The bankrupt shall give notice of the venue, accompanied by copies of the application and witness statement to the official receiver, any trustee who is not the official receiver, and the supervisor of the voluntary arrangement not less than 5 business days before the date of the hearing.

5.52(5) **[Power of official receiver etc. to attend hearing]** The official receiver, the supervisor of the voluntary arrangement and any trustee who is not the official receiver may attend the hearing or be represented and call to the attention of the court any matters which seem to him to be relevant.

5.52(6) **[Court to send copies of annulment order]** Where the court annuls a bankruptcy order, it shall send sealed copies of the order of annulment in Form 5.7 to the bankrupt, the official receiver, the supervisor of the voluntary arrangement and any trustee who is not the official receiver.

[FORM 5.7]

R.5.52

This describes the manner of application and the procedure relating to the hearing of such application. See I(A)R 2010 (SI 2010/686) which replaces "affidavit" with "witness statement".

5.53   Notice to creditors

5.53(1) **[Duty of official receiver]** Where the official receiver has notified creditors of the debtor's bankruptcy, and the bankruptcy order is annulled, he shall, as soon as reasonably practicable, notify them of the annulment.

5.53(2) **[Notification expenses charge on former bankrupt's property]** Expenses incurred by the official receiver in giving notice under this Rule are a charge in his favour on the property of the former bankrupt, whether or not actually in his hands.

5.53(3) **[Where property not in former bankrupt's hands]** Where any property is in the hands of a trustee or any person other than the former bankrupt himself, the official receiver's charge is valid subject only to any costs that may be incurred by the trustee or that other person in effecting realisation of the property for the purpose of satisfying the charge.

R.5.53

This deals with various consequential matters, including notification of the change of situation and expenses thereby incurred.

CHAPTER 9

APPLICATION BY OFFICIAL RECEIVER TO ANNUL A BANKRUPTCY ORDER UNDER SECTION 261(2)(B)

5.54   Application of this Chapter

5.54 The following Rules apply where the official receiver applies for an annulment of a bankruptcy order under section 261(2)(b).

R.5.54

Chapter 9 was inserted by the Insolvency (Amendment) Rules 2003 (SI 2003/1730). It deals with applications to annul bankruptcy orders in cases covered by s.261(2)(b).

5.55   Application to court

5.55(1) **[Application to specify section made under]** An application to the court to annul a bankruptcy order under section 261(2)(b) shall specify the section under which it is made.

5.55(2) **[Time limit]** The official receiver may not make an application under section 261(2)(b) before the expiry of the period of 42 days beginning with the day on which–

(a) where the creditors' meeting was summoned under section 257 pursuant to a report to a court under section 256(1)(aa), the nominee filed the report of the creditors' meeting with the court; or

(b) where the creditors' meeting was summoned under section 257 pursuant to a report to the debtor's creditors under section 256A(3), the result of the creditors' meeting was notified to the creditors.

5.55(3) [Affidavit in support] The application shall be supported by a report stating the grounds on which it is made. It shall also state that–

(a) the time period for application in paragraph (2) above has expired; and

(b) the official receiver is not aware that any application or appeal remains to be disposed of.

5.55(4) [Duty of court to fix venue] The application and the report shall be filed in court and the court shall give to the official receiver notice of the venue fixed for the hearing.

5.55(5) [Duty of official receiver to notify bankrupt] The official receiver shall give notice of the venue, accompanied by copies of the application and the report to the bankrupt not less than 5 business days before the date of the hearing.

5.55(6) [Court to send copies of annulment order] Where the court annuls a bankruptcy order, it shall send sealed copies of the order of annulment in Form 5.7 to the official receiver, any trustee who is not the official receiver, the supervisor of the voluntary arrangement and the bankrupt.

[FORM 5.7]

R.5.55
This details the application procedure. See I(A)R 2010 (SI 2010/686) which changes the time limits. So for instance seven days in para.(5) becomes five business days. Paragraph (2) is also reworked.

5.56 Notice to creditors

5.56(1) [Duty of official receiver] Where the bankruptcy order is annulled, the official receiver shall notify all creditors of whose address the official receiver is aware of the annulment.

5.56(2) [Notification expenses charge on former bankrupt's property] Expenses incurred by the official receiver in giving notice under this Rule are a charge in his favour on the property of the former bankrupt, whether or not actually in his hands.

5.56(3) [Where property not in former bankrupt's hands] Where any property is in the hands of a trustee or any person other than the former bankrupt himself, the official receiver's charge is valid only to any costs that may be incurred by the trustee or that other person in effecting realisation of the property for the purpose of satisfying the charge.

R.5.56
This rule explains the consequences of an annulment order made pursuant to the aforementioned procedure.

CHAPTER 10

APPLICATION BY OFFICIAL RECEIVER TO ANNUL A BANKRUPTCY ORDER UNDER SECTION 263D(3)

5.57 Application of this Chapter

5.57 The following Rules apply where the official receiver applies for an annulment of a bankruptcy order under section 263D(3).

R.5.57
Chapter 10 was inserted by Insolvency (Amendment) Rules 2003 (SI 2003/1730). It deals with applications by the OR to annul bankruptcy orders under s.263D(3) of the Act.

5.58   Application to court

5.58(1)   [Application to specify section made under] An application to the court to annul a bankruptcy order under section 263D(3) shall specify the section under which it is made.

5.58(2)   [Time limit] An application under section 263D(3) shall be made within 21 days of the expiry of the relevant period set out in section 263D(4).

5.58(3)   [Report in support] The application shall be supported by a report stating the grounds on which it is made and a statement by the official receiver that he is not aware that any application or appeal under section 263F remains to be disposed of.

5.58(4)   [To accompany report] The report shall be accompanied by a copy of the proposal for the voluntary arrangement and a copy of the report under section 263C.

5.58(5)   [Duty of court to fix venue] The application, together with the report and the documents in support, shall be filed in court and the court shall give to the official receiver notice of the venue fixed for the hearing.

5.58(6)   [Duty of official receiver to notify bankrupt] The official receiver shall give notice of the venue, accompanied by copies of the application and the report, to the bankrupt not less than 5 business days before the date of the hearing.

5.58(7)   [Court to send copies of annulment order] Where the court annuls a bankruptcy order, it shall send sealed copies of the order of annulment in Form 5.8 to the official receiver and the bankrupt.

[FORM 5.8]

R.5.58
This details the application procedure. Note the 21-day deadline. See I(A)R 2010 (SI 2010/686) which converts the seven-day period in para.(6) to five business days.

5.59   Notice to creditors

5.59(1)   [Duty of official receiver] Where the official receiver has notified creditors of the debtor's bankruptcy, and the bankruptcy order is annulled, he shall, as soon as reasonably practicable, notify them of the annulment.

5.59(2)   [Notification expenses charge on former bankrupt's property] Expenses incurred by the official receiver in giving notice under this Rule are a charge in his favour on the property of the former bankrupt, whether or not actually in his hands.

5.59(3)   [Where property not in former bankrupt's hands] Where any property is in the hands of a trustee or any person other than the former bankrupt himself, the official receiver's charge is valid subject only to any costs that may be incurred by the trustee or that other person in effecting realisation of the property for the purpose of satisfying the charge.

R.5.59
The consequences of a successful application are explained.

CHAPTER 11

OTHER MATTERS ARISING ON ANNULMENTS UNDER SECTIONS 261(2)(A), 261(2)(B) OR 263D(3)

5.60(1)   [Provision in order] In an order under section 261(2)(a), 261(2)(b) or 263D(3) the court shall include provision permitting vacation of the registration of the bankruptcy petition as a pending action, and of the bankruptcy order, in the register of writs and orders affecting land.

5.60(2) **[Notice of order to Secretary of State]** The court shall as soon as reasonably practicable give notice of the making of the order to the Secretary of State.

5.60(3) **[Power of bankrupt require gazetting/advertisement of order]** The former bankrupt may in writing within 28 days of the date of the order require the Secretary of State to give notice of the making of the order. As soon as reasonably practicable the notice shall be–

(a) gazetted; and

(b) advertised in the same manner as the bankruptcy order to which it relates was advertised.

5.60(3A) **[Additional contents of notice under r.5.60(3)]** In addition to the standard contents, the notice under paragraph (3) must state–

(a) the name of the former bankrupt;

(b) the date on which the bankruptcy order was made;

(c) that the bankruptcy order has been annulled;

(d) the date of the annulling order; and

(e) the grounds of the annulment.

5.60(4) [Omitted.]

5.60(5) **[Former bankrupt deceased or unable to manage affairs]** Where the former bankrupt has died, or is a person incapable of managing his affairs (within the meaning of Chapter 7 in Part 7 of the Rules), the references to him in paragraph (3) is to be read as referring to his personal representative or, as the case may be, a person appointed by the court to represent or act for him.

R.5.60

This new Chapter 11 was inserted by the Insolvency (Amendment) Rules 2003 (SI 2003/1730). It deals with general matters relevant to applications made under Chapters 8–10. Rule 5.60 tidies up various loose ends attendant upon a successful application, including the clearing of registered entries and wide dissemination of the annulment. A 28-day time limit was inserted into para.(3) by I(A)R 2004 (SI 2004/584), which also deleted para.4 on the cost of advertisement. Paragraph (5) was amended by the Insolvency (Amendment) Rules 2005 (SI 2005/527) to cater for the earlier omission of para.(4). Note the Insolvency (Amendment) Rules 2009 (SI 2009/642), which has substituted a new para.(3) from April 6, 2009. See I(A)R 2010 (SI 2010/686)—new para.(3A) added.

5.61 Trustee's final account

5.61(1) **[Trustee liable to account]** Where a bankruptcy order is annulled under section 261(2)(a), 261 (2)(b) or 263D(3), this does not of itself release the trustee from any duty or obligation, imposed on him by or under the Act or the Rules, to account for all his transactions in connection with the former bankrupt's estate.

5.61(2) **[Duty of trustee to submit final account]** The trustee shall submit a copy of his final account to the Secretary of State as soon as reasonably practicable after the court's order annulling the bankruptcy order; and he shall file a copy of the final account in court.

5.61(3) **[Contents of final account]** The final account must include a summary of the trustee's receipts and payments in the administration, and contain a statement to the effect that he has reconciled his account with that held by the Secretary of State in respect of the bankruptcy.

5.61(4) **[Release of trustee]** The trustee is released from such time as the court may determine, having regard to whether paragraph (2) of this Rule has been complied with.

R.5.61

The obligation of the trustee to produce a final account is not removed by the fact of annulment.

CHAPTER 12

EC REGULATION: CONVERSION OF VOLUNTARY ARRANGEMENT INTO BANKRUPTCY

5.62 Application for conversion of voluntary arrangement into bankruptcy

5.62(1) **[Application to be supported by witness statement]** Where a member State liquidator proposes to apply to the court for conversion under Article 37 of the EC Regulation (conversion of earlier proceedings) of a voluntary arrangement into a bankruptcy, a witness statement complying with Rule 5.63 must be prepared and sworn, and filed in court in support of the application.

5.62(2) **[Service]** The application and the witness statement required under this Rule shall be served upon–

(a) the debtor; and

(b) the supervisor.

R.5.62
Chapter 12 was inserted by Insolvency (Amendment) Rules 2003 (SI 2003/1730). It deals with the impact of the EC Regulation on Insolvency Proceedings (1346/2000) and covers ground previously dealt with by IR 1986 rr.5.35–5.38 in the former regime. Rule 5.62 deals with conversion of an IVA into a bankruptcy for the purposes of that Regulation. I(A)R 2010 (SI 2010/686) converts references to affidavits to witness statements.

5.63 Contents of witness statement

5.63(1) **[Contents]** The witness statement shall state–

(a) that the main proceedings have been opened in relation to the debtor in a member State other than the United Kingdom;

(b) the belief of the person making the witness statement that the conversion of the voluntary arrangement into a bankruptcy would prove to be in the interests of the creditors in the main proceedings; and

(c) all other matters that, in the opinion of the member State liquidator, would assist the court–

(i) in deciding whether to make an order under Rule 5.64; and

(ii) if the court were to do so, in considering the need for any consequential provision that would be necessary or desirable.

5.63(2) **[Witness statement by member State liquidator]** A witness statement under this Rule shall be made by, or on behalf of, the member State liquidator.

R.5.63
This explains the contents of the witness statement which the member state liquidator must file. See I(A)R 2010 (SI 2010/686) which substitutes references to witness statements for affidavits.

5.64 Power of court

5.64(1) **[Order as thinks fit]** On hearing an application for conversion of a voluntary arrangement into a bankruptcy, the court may make such order as it thinks fit.

5.64(2) **[Consequential provisions]** If the court makes an order for conversion of a voluntary arrangement into a bankruptcy under paragraph (1), the order may contain all such consequential provisions as the court deems necessary or desirable.

5.64(3) **[Expenses incurred]** Where the court makes an order for conversion of a voluntary arrangement into a bankruptcy under paragraph (1), any expenses properly incurred as expenses of the administration of the voluntary arrangement in question shall be a first charge on the bankrupt's estate.

R.5.64

The options open to the court are thus outlined.

5.65 Notices to be given to member State liquidator

5.65(1) [Application of r.5.65] This Rule applies where a member State liquidator has been appointed in relation to the debtor.

5.65(2) [Notice, copies] Where the supervisor is obliged to give notice to, or provide a copy of a document (including an order of the court) to, the court or the official receiver, the supervisor shall give notice or provide copies, as appropriate, to the member State liquidator.

R.5.65

This explains consequential matters resulting from a conversion.

CHAPTER 13

INFORMATION ABOUT TIME SPENT ON A CASE TO BE PROVIDED BY PERSON ACTING AS NOMINEE OR SUPERVISOR

5.66 Provision of information

5.66(1) [Relevant person to supply statement] A person ("the relevant person") who has acted or is acting as–

(a) a nominee in respect of a proposed voluntary arrangement, or

(b) a supervisor in respect of a voluntary arrangement

must, on request in writing by any person mentioned in paragraph (2), supply free of charge to that person a statement complying with paragraph (3).

5.66(2) [Relevant person in r.5.66(1)] The persons mentioned in this paragraph are–

(a) the debtor; and

(b) where the proposal has been approved, any creditor of the debtor in respect of the arrangement.

5.66(3) [Statement in r.5.66(1)] The statement referred to in paragraph (1)–

(a) must cover the period beginning with the date of the appointment of the relevant person as nominee or supervisor, as the case may be, and ending–

    (i) with the date next before the date of making the request on which the relevant person has completed any period as nominee or supervisor, or both, which is a multiple of 6 months, or

    (ii) where the relevant person has ceased to act as nominee or supervisor, the date upon which the person so ceased; and

(b) must comprise the following details–

    (i) the total number of hours spent on the voluntary arrangement by the relevant person whether as nominee or supervisor, or both, and any staff assigned to the voluntary arrangement during that period;

    (ii) for each grade of individual so engaged, the average hourly rate at which any work carried out by individuals in that grade is charged; and

    (iii) the number of hours spent by each grade of staff during that period.

5.66(4) **[Time limit for request]** No request pursuant to this Rule may be made where more than 2 years has elapsed since the relevant person ceased to act in any capacity in relation to the proposal or any voluntary arrangement arising out of the approval of the proposal.

5.66(5) **[Time limit for supply of statement]** Any statement required to be provided to any person under this Rule must be supplied within 28 days of the date of the receipt of the request by the person required to supply it.

GENERAL NOTE

See I(A)R 2010 (SI 2010/686) which introduces this new provision in order to promote transparency. Note the time limit for requests imposed by para.(4).

CHAPTER 14

PERSONS AT RISK OF VIOLENCE

5.67 Persons at risk of violence

5.67(1) **[Application of r.5.67]** The provisions of this Rule apply in any case where disclosure or continuing disclosure to other persons (whether to the public generally or to specific persons) of the current address or whereabouts of a debtor might reasonably be expected to lead to violence against the debtor or against a person who normally resides with the debtor as a member of the debtor's family.

5.67(2) **["Current address", "debtor"]** For the purposes of this Rule–

"current address" means, in relation to any debtor, the address of the debtor's current place of residence and any address at which the debtor currently carries on business;

"debtor" means a debtor who has entered into an individual voluntary arrangement.

5.67(3) **[Power of court]** The court may, on the application of the debtor, the supervisor, the official receiver (whether acting as a supervisor or otherwise) or the Secretary of State, order that–

(a) details of the debtor's current address be removed from any part of the court file of the proceedings in relation to the debtor which is open to inspection and be kept on a separate file not open to inspection;

(b) the details in respect of the debtor to be entered onto the individual insolvency register under Rule 6A.2A in respect of an individual voluntary arrangement must not include details of the debtor's current address; and

(c) that any notice published by the Secretary of State of the making of any order permitting vacation of the registration of a bankruptcy petition referred to in Rule 5.60, must not include details of the bankrupt's address.

5.67(4) **[Further order of court]** Where the court makes an order under paragraph (3), it may further order that the details in respect of the debtor to be entered onto the register referred to in paragraph (3) must instead include such other details of the debtor's addresses or whereabouts as the court thinks just, including details of any address at which the debtor has previously resided or carried on business.

5.67(5) **[Application to be supported by witness statement]** In any case where an application is made in respect of a debtor under or by virtue of this Rule, the application must be accompanied by a witness statement referring to this Rule and containing sufficient evidence to satisfy the court that paragraph (1) of this Rule applies to or in respect of that debtor.

GENERAL NOTE

See I(A)R 2010 (SI 2010/686) which introduces this new provision to promote personal safety.

CHAPTER 15

OMISSION OF INFORMATION FROM STATEMENT OF AFFAIRS

5.68 Omission of information from statement of affairs

5.68 The court, on the application of the nominee, the debtor or any person appearing to it to have an interest, may direct that specified information may be omitted from any statement of affairs required to be sent to the creditors where the disclosure of such information would be likely to prejudice the conduct of the voluntary arrangement or might reasonably be expected to lead to violence against any person.

GENERAL NOTE

Again a new safety-conscious provision inserted by I(A)R 2010 (SI 2010/686).

PART 5A

DEBT RELIEF ORDERS

CHAPTER 1

PRELIMINARY

5A.1 Scope of this part: introductory and interpretation

5A.1 The Rules in this Part apply in relation to debt relief orders and applications for debt relief orders under Part 7A of the Act.

5A.2 Excluded debts

5A.2 For the purposes of that Part of the Act and this Part of the Rules–

"excluded debt" means–

   (a) any fine imposed for an offence and any obligation (including an obligation to pay a lump sum or to pay costs) arising under an order made in family proceedings or any obligation arising under a maintenance assessment made under the Child Support Act 1991

   (b) any obligation arising under a confiscation order made under section 1 of the Drug Trafficking Offences Act 1986 or section 1 of the Criminal Justice (Scotland) Act 1987 or section 71 of the Criminal Justice Act 1988 or under Parts 2, 3 or 4 of the Proceeds of Crime Act 2002;

   (c) any debt or liability to which a debtor is or may become subject in respect of any sum paid or payable to the debtor as a student by way of a loan and which he receives before or after a debt relief order is made in respect of him; and

   (d) any debt which consists in a liability to pay damages for negligence, nuisance or breach of a statutory, contractual or other duty, or to pay damages by virtue of Part 1 of the Consumer Protection Act 1987, being in either case damages in respect of the death of or personal injury (including any disease or other impairment of physical or mental condition) to any person.

"Fine" and **"family proceedings"** have the meanings given by section 281(8) of the Act (which applies the Magistrates' Courts Act 1980 and the Matrimonial and Family Proceedings Act 1984).

"Loan" means a loan made pursuant to–

   (a) regulations made under section 22(1) of the Teaching and Higher Education Act 1998, or

(b) the Education (Student Loans) Act 1990, or that Act as it continues in force by virtue of any savings made, in connection with its repeal by the Teaching and Higher Education Act 1998, by an order made under section 46(4) of that Act,

including any interest on the loan and any penalties or charges incurred in connection with it

GENERAL NOTE

See I(A)R 2010 (SI 2010/686) which inserts a new subpara.(d).

5A.3   Application for a debt relief order—information to be in the application

5A.3(1)   [Matters in r.5A.3(2)–(4)] In addition to the matters referred to in section 251B(2)(a) and (b) of the Act and subject to paragraphs (5) to (11), an application for a debt relief order under section 251A must also state the matters set out in paragraphs (2) to (4) as they subsist at the date of the application.

5A.3(2)   [Contents of application] The application must state–

(a) the debtor's surname, forenames and occupation (if any);

(b) the debtor's gender and date of birth;

(c) the debtor's places of residence during the three years preceding the date of the application;

(d) any name or names used by the debtor for any purpose, if different from the above;

(e) the name, address and nature of any business carried on by the debtor, including any business carried on by–

    (i) a firm or partnership of which the debtor is a member;

    (ii) an agent or manager for the debtor or for such firm or partnership;

(f) any other liabilities (including those imposed by an order of the court) to which the debtor is subject;

(g) the address of the creditor to whom each debt is owed;

(h) the total amount of the debtor's monthly income from any source (see Rule 5A.8(1));

(i) the sources of that income and the amount from each source;

(j) particulars of the expenditure which the debtor claims is necessary to meet the monthly reasonable domestic needs of the debtor and the debtor's family, including the object and the amount of that expenditure (see Rule 5A.8(2));

(k) the total amount available from any source to meet the claimed monthly reasonable domestic needs of the debtor and his or her family (see Rule 5A.8(2)); and

(l) particulars of the debtor's property and its total estimated value (see Rule 5A.9 and 5A.10).

5A.3(3)   [Debtor to state in application] The debtor shall also state in the application–

(a) whether or not the debtor at the date of the application–

    (i) has given a preference to any person during the period of two years prior to and ending with the application date;

    (ii) has entered into a transaction with any person at an undervalue during the period of two years prior to and ending with the application date;

    (iii) is domiciled in England and Wales;

    (iv) at any time during the period of three years ending with the application date, (aa) was ordinarily resident,

(bb) had a place of residence, or

(cc) carried on business, in England and Wales;

(v) is an undischarged bankrupt;

(vi) is subject to a debt relief order;

(vii) has been subject to a debt relief order in the six years preceding the date of the application;

(viii) is subject to an interim order or a voluntary arrangement under Part 8 of the Act; or

(ix) is subject to a bankruptcy restrictions order or undertaking or debt relief restrictions order or undertaking; and

(b) whether at the date of the application–

(i) a bankruptcy petition has been presented by the debtor or by a creditor against the debtor;

(ii) a bankruptcy petition has been presented by the debtor, but the court has referred the debtor for the purpose of making an application for a debt relief order;

(iii) any debt management arrangements (see section 251F) are in force in respect of the debtor; and

(iv) any other legal action has been taken against the debtor in respect of any of the debtor's existing debts.

5A.3(4)   [Further matters debtor to consent, state, request, indicate] In the application, the debtor must also–

(a) consent to checks being made by the official receiver for the purpose of verifying that the debtor complies with the conditions to which the making of a debt relief order is subject;

(b) state that the debtor is unable to pay his or her debts;

(c) request a debt relief order, and

(d) indicate the date on which the application is completed.

5A.3(5)   [Information and documents to approved intermediary] The debtor shall submit to the approved intermediary such information and such documents by reference to which the information in the application, including information about each debt, the amount of the debt and the name and address of the creditor, may be substantiated.

5A.3(6)   [Deduction of trade etc. discounts from debt] In making the application, the debtor must in every case deduct from the amount of the debt all trade and other discounts which are available to the debtor, except any discount for immediate, early or cash settlement.

5A.3(7)   [Debts in foreign currency] Subject to paragraph (8), where a debt was incurred or is payable in a currency other than sterling, the amount of the debt shall be converted into sterling at the official exchange rate prevailing on the application date.

5A.3(8)   [Official exchange rate] The official exchange rate is the middle exchange rate on the London foreign exchange market at the close of business, as published for the date in question or, in the absence of any such published rate for the date in question such rate as the official receiver determines.

5A.3(9)   [Unpaid debts of periodical nature] Where a debt consists of unpaid payments of a periodical nature, the amount of the debt shall consist of any amounts due and unpaid up to the date of the application.

5A.3(10)   [Accrued debts] Where at the application date any payment was accruing due, the debt shall consist of so much as would have fallen due at that date, if accruing from day to day.

5A.3(11) **[Accrued debts not due at application]** A debtor may include a debt of which payment is not yet due at the date of the application, provided that it is for a liquidated sum payable at some certain future time.

5A.4 Application for a debt relief order

5A.4(1) **[Application in electronic form]** Subject to paragraphs (2) and (3), an application for a debt relief order must be completed and sent to the official receiver in electronic form and by electronic means.

5A.4(2) **[Electronic means, electronic form, hard copy form]** In this Rule, an application–

(a) is sent by electronic means, if it is sent initially and received at its destination by means of electronic equipment for the processing (which expression includes digital compression) or storage of data and entirely created, transmitted, conveyed and received by wire, by radio, by optical means or by other electromagnetic means but does not include electronic facsimile transmission or mobile telephonic text messaging;

(b) is completed in electronic form, if it is an application which is created, and sent, by electronic means;

(c) in hard copy form, means an application completed and sent on paper and capable of being read (but is not the product of an electronic facsimile transmission).

5A.4(3) **[Official receiver to acknowledge receipt]** An application in electronic form sent by electronic means shall be treated as not having been submitted unless and until its receipt has been acknowledged by the official receiver in the same form and by the same means.

5A.4(4) **[When hard copy form may be used]** In the event of any malfunction or error in the operation of the electronic form or means referred to, the official receiver shall notify the competent authorities and approved intermediaries–

(a) that approved intermediaries may, for a specified period, complete and send applications in hard copy form; and

(b) of the postal address to which such applications are to be sent and any terms or conditions to which their use is subject.

5A.5 Approved intermediary

5A.5(1) **[Duty to apply for debt relief order]** The approved intermediary, as and when requested by a debtor who proposes to make an application for a debt relief order through him or her, shall create an application for a debt relief order in the name of the debtor.

5A.5(2) **[Power to assist debtor]** The approved intermediary through whom the application for a debt relief order is to be made may assist the debtor–

(a) to identify what information is required to complete the application;

(b) based upon the documentation and information supplied by the debtor, to ascertain whether–

(i) the debtor appears to have debts not exceeding the prescribed amount;

(ii) the debtor's surplus income does not exceed the prescribed amount; and

(iii) the value of the debtor's property does not exceed the prescribed amount; and

(c) to ensure that the application (if any) is completed in full.

5A.5(3) **[What to draw debtor's attention to]** The approved intermediary must draw the debtor's attention to–

(a) all the conditions to which an application for, and the making of, a debt relief order is subject;

(b) the possible consequences of the making by the debtor of any false representation or omission in the debtor's application; and

(c) the fact that verification checks will be made for the purpose of verifying that the debtor complies with the conditions to which the making of a debt relief order is subject and the requirement for the debtor to consent to such checks being made.

5A.5(4)   **[Application to official receiver on debtor's request]** If and when instructed to do so by the debtor, the approved intermediary must send the application to the official receiver on behalf of the debtor.

5A.6   Form, manner and reasons for refusal of application for debt relief order

5A.6(1)   **[Duty of official receiver to notify debtor]** The official receiver must notify the debtor of his or her decision to refuse an application for a debt relief order in accordance with this Rule.

5A.6(2)   **[Notice to debtor]** The official receiver must send a notice in writing to the debtor stating–

(a) that the official receiver has decided to refuse the debtor's application, and

(b) the reason for which it has been refused.

5A.7   Prescribed verification checks—conditions in paragraphs 1 to 8 of Schedule 4ZA

5A.7(1)   **["Credit reference agency"]** In this Rule, "**credit reference agency**" means a person licensed to carry on a business comprising the furnishing of information relevant to the financial standing of individuals.

5A.7(2)   **[Searches or enquiries in r.5A.7(3)–(8) for s.251D(4), (5)]** For the purposes of subsections (4) and (5) of section 251D and the conditions specified in paragraphs 1 to 8 of Schedule 4ZA, the prescribed verification checks are those searches or enquiries specified in relation to the condition in paragraphs (3) to (8) below.

5A.7(3)   **[Debtor's connection with England and Wales]** For the purpose of verifying a debtor's connection with England and Wales on the application date, verification checks made in, or with, one or more of the following–

(a) the electoral registers for the areas in England and Wales in which the debtor in, and at the date of, the debtor's application, claims to reside or to carry on business or to have resided or carried on business;

(b) the individual insolvency register;

(c) the bankruptcy restrictions register;

(d) the debt relief restrictions register;

(e) a credit reference agency.

5A.7(4)   **[Checks in registers for personal insolvency]** For the purpose of verifying that a debtor–

(a) is not, on the determination date–

    (i) an undischarged bankrupt;

    (ii) subject to a bankruptcy restrictions order or undertaking;

    (iii) subject to a debt relief restrictions order or undertaking;

    (iv) subject to an individual voluntary arrangement; or

(b)   has not been the subject of a debt relief order in the period of 6 years ending with the determination date,

verification checks made in one or more of the registers specified in paragraph (5).

5A.7(5)   **[Registers for r.5A.7(4)]** The registers referred to in paragraph (4) are–

(a)   the individual insolvency register;

(b)   the bankruptcy restrictions register;

(c)   the debt relief restrictions register.

5A.7(6)   **[Verification of bankruptcy]** For the purpose of verifying–

(a)   that the debtor is not, on the determination date, subject to an interim order;

(b)   whether a debtor's or creditor's bankruptcy petition has been presented against the debtor prior to the determination date;

(c)   where a bankruptcy petition has been presented against the debtor prior to the determination date, whether proceedings in relation to the petition have finally been disposed of before the determination date;

(d)   where a bankruptcy petition has been presented against the debtor prior to the determination date, the status of the proceedings in relation to the petition and whether the court has referred the debtor under section 274A(2) for the purpose of making an application for a debt relief order;

(e)   where a creditor's bankruptcy petition has been presented against the debtor prior to the determination date, the status of the proceedings in relation to the petition and whether the person who presented the petition has consented to the making of the application for a debt relief order,

verification checks made in, or with one or more of the sources specified in paragraph (7).

5A.7(7)   **[Sources for r.5A.7(6) checks]** The sources are–

(a)   the individual insolvency register;

(b)   county or other court records;

(c)   a credit reference agency.

5A.7(8)   **[Checks with credit reference agency]** For the purpose of verifying that–

(a)   the amount of the debtor's overall indebtedness;

(b)   the amount of the debtor's monthly surplus income; or

(c)   the total value of the debtor's property,

does not exceed the prescribed amount, verification checks made with a credit reference agency.

5A.8   Determination of debtor's monthly surplus income

5A.8(1)   **[Income from business, office, employment or pension]** For the purposes of this Part, the income of a debtor comprises every payment in the nature of income which is from time to time made to him or to which he from time to time becomes entitled, including any payment in respect of the carrying on of any business or in respect of any office or employment and (despite anything in section 11 or 12 of the Welfare Reform and Pensions Act 1999) any payment under a pension scheme.

5A.8(2)   **[Contributions from debtor's family]** In determining the monthly surplus income of a debtor, the official receiver shall take into account any contribution made by any member of the debtor's family to the amount necessary for the reasonable domestic needs of the debtor and his or her family.

5A.9 Determination of value of a debtor's property

5A.9(1) **[Property relevant]** Subject to Rule 5A.10, the official receiver in determining whether the condition in paragraph 8 of Schedule 4ZA to the Act is met shall regard as a debtor's property for the purposes of this Part–

(a) all property belonging to or vested in the debtor on the determination date, and

(b) any property which by virtue of any of the following provisions of this Part is comprised in or is treated as falling within the preceding sub-paragraph.

5A.9(2) **[Property includes power over property]** References in this Part to property, in relation to a debtor, include references to any power exercisable by him or her over or in respect of property except in so far as the power is exercisable over or in respect of property which is not or is deemed not for the time being to be the property of the debtor and cannot be exercised for the benefit of the debtor;

and a power exercisable over or in respect of property is deemed for the purposes of this Part to vest in the person entitled to exercise it at the time of the transaction or event by virtue of which it is exercisable by that person (whether or not it becomes so exercisable at that time).

5A.9(3) **[Rights of secured creditors etc.]** For the purposes of any such provision in this Part, property belonging to or vested in the debtor so belongs or vests in him or her subject to the rights of any person other than the debtor (whether as a secured creditor of the debtor or otherwise) in relation thereto.

5A.10 Particular descriptions of property to be excluded for the purpose of determining the value of a person's property

5A.10(1) **[Property to be disregarded from r.5A.9]** For the purposes of Rule 5A.9, the official receiver shall disregard–

(a) subject to paragraph (2), a single domestic motor vehicle belonging to or vested in the debtor provided that–

    (i) it has been especially adapted for use by him or her because he or she has a physical impairment that has a substantial and long-term adverse effect on his or her ability to carry out normal day-to-day activities; or

    (ii) the maximum potential realisable value of the vehicle is less than the prescribed amount;

(b) subject to paragraph (3), such tools, books and other items of equipment as are necessary to the debtor for use personally by him in his employment, business or vocation;

(c) such clothing, bedding, furniture, household equipment and provisions as are necessary for satisfying the basic domestic needs of the debtor and his or her family;

(d) property held by the debtor on trust for any other person;

(e) the right of nomination to a vacant ecclesiastical benefice;

(f) a tenancy which is an assured tenancy or an assured agricultural occupancy, within the meaning of Part I of the Housing Act 1988, and the terms of which inhibit an assignment as mentioned in section 127(5) of the Rent Act 1977;

(g) a protected tenancy, within the meaning of the Rent Act 1977, in respect of which, by virtue of any provision of Part IX of that Act, no premium can lawfully be required as a condition of assignment;

(h) a tenancy of a dwelling-house by virtue of which the debtor is, within the meaning of the Rent (Agriculture) Act 1976, a protected occupier of the dwelling-house, and the terms of which inhibit an assignment as mentioned in section 127(5) of the Rent Act 1977, or

   (i)   a secure tenancy, within the meaning of Part IV of the Housing Act 1985, which is not capable of being assigned, except in the cases mentioned in section 91(3) of that Act.

5A.10(2)   **[Vehicle where realisable value exceeds replacement cost]** Where–

  (a)   a vehicle is to be disregarded by the official receiver by virtue of paragraph (1)(a)(i) of this Rule (adapted vehicle), and

  (b)   it appears to the official receiver that the realisable value of the vehicle exceeds the cost of a reasonable replacement for it,

the official receiver shall disregard only the value of a reasonable replacement.

5A.10(3)   **[Tools, household effects where realisable value exceeds replacement cost]** Where–

  (a)   property is to be disregarded by the official receiver by virtue of paragraph (1)(b) or (c) of this Rule (tools of trade, household effects, etc), and

  (b)   it appears to the official receiver that the realisable value of the whole or any part of that property exceeds the cost of a reasonable replacement for that property or that part of it,

the official receiver shall disregard only the value of a reasonable replacement.

5A.10(4)   **[Prescribed amount; reasonable replacement in r.5A.10]** For the purposes of this Rule,

  (a)   the prescribed amount is £1000

  (b)   property is a reasonable replacement for other property if it is reasonably adequate for meeting the needs met by the other property.

5A.10(5)   **[Rule 5A.10 subject to exclusion of property by other enactment]** This Rule has effect subject to the provisions of any enactment not contained in these Rules or in the Act under which any property is to be excluded from belonging to or being vested in the debtor for the purposes of the determination of a debt relief order.

5A.11   Making of debt relief order—form of debt relief order

5A.11   A debt relief order must be in writing and include the following particulars–

  (a)   the name and address of the debtor;

  (b)   the date of, and the reference number allocated to, the debtor's application;

  (c)   a list of the debtor's qualifying debts as at the application date, specifying the amount owed and the creditor's name, address and reference (if any); and

  (d)   the date on which the order was made.

5A.12   Other steps to be taken by official receiver or debtor upon making of the order

5A.12(1)   **[Notification to approved intermediary; entry in register]** In addition to giving a copy of the order to the debtor, the official receiver must–

  (a)   notify the approved intermediary through whom the debtor's application was made, of the making and date of the order; and

  (b)   cause an entry to be made in the individual insolvency register in accordance with Rule 6A.5A.

5A.12(2)   **[Notification of other debt management arrangements]** In any case in which there are other debt management arrangements or attachment of earnings orders in force in respect of the debtor, the official receiver must notify the court, or the body, as the case may be, responsible for making the debt management arrangements or orders, of the making of the debt relief order.

5A.13   Prescribed information to be notified to creditor on making of debt relief order

5A.13   The official receiver must notify each creditor to whom a qualifying debt specified in the order is owed, of–

(a)   the making, the date and the reference number of the order and its effect;

(b)   the matters to which a creditor may object under section 251K; and

(c)   the name, address and telephone number of the official receiver sending the notice and the address to which any objection under that section may or must be sent.

5A.14   Creditor's objection

5A.14(1)   ["Creditor"] In this Rule, **"creditor"** means a person specified in a debt relief order as a creditor to whom a specified qualifying debt is owed.

5A.14(2)   [Objection in writing to official receiver] A creditor who wishes to object to–

(a)   the making of an order;

(b)   the inclusion of the debt in the list of the debtor's qualifying debts; or

(c)   the details of the debt specified in the order,

must object in writing to the official receiver in accordance with this Rule.

5A.14(3)   [Period for and contents of objection] For an objection to be considered by the official receiver, it must be made during the moratorium period relating to the order and within 28 days of the date on which the creditor was notified of the making of the order and must include–

(a)   the name and address of the creditor;

(b)   the name of the debtor and the reference number of the order;

(c)   which of the matters under section 251K the creditor objects to;

(d)   a statement indicating at least one or more of the grounds listed in paragraph (4), upon which the creditor relies;

(e)   a statement indicating the facts upon which the creditor relies, and

(f)   information and documents in support of the grounds and the facts upon which the creditor relies.

5A.14(4)   [Grounds for objection] The grounds are that–

(a)   there is an error in, or an omission from, something specified in the debt relief order;

(b)   a bankruptcy order has been made in respect of the debtor;

(c)   the debtor has made a proposal under Part 8 of the Act;

(d)   the official receiver should not have been satisfied that–

   (i)   the debts specified in the order were qualifying debts of the debtor as at the application date;

   (ii)   the conditions specified in Part 1 of Schedule 4ZA to the Act were met;

   (iii) the conditions specified in Part 2 of that Schedule were met or that any failure to meet such condition did not prevent him or her from making the order;

   (iv) the condition in paragraph 7 of that Schedule was not met at any time after the order was made;

   (v)   the condition in paragraph 8 of that Schedule was not met at any time after the order was made.

5A.14(5)   **[References to time in r.5A.14(4)(iv), (v)]** For the purposes of paragraph (4)(d)(iv) and (v) above, paragraph 7 and 8 of Schedule 4ZA to the Act are to be read as if references to the determination date were references to the time in question.

5A.15   Official receiver's response to objection

5A.15(1)   **["The creditor", "the debt relief order", "the debtor"]** For the purposes of this Rule–

"the creditor" means the creditor specified in a debt relief order as a creditor to whom a qualifying debt is owed and who has made an objection in relation to that order under the Act and the Rules;

"the debt relief order" means the debt relief order in which the creditor is specified;

"the debtor" means the person subject to the debt relief order.

5A.15(2)   **[Particulars to debtor]** If, after considering an objection in accordance with section 251K, the official receiver is minded to revoke or amend the debt relief order, he or she shall send to the debtor particulars of–

    (a)   the objection;

    (b)   the grounds and facts upon which the creditor relies; and

    (c)   the address to which the debtor's comments must be sent,

and invite the debtor to comment on them.

5A.15(3)   **[Official receiver to consider comments of debtor]** Before deciding whether to revoke or amend the debt relief order, the official receiver shall consider any comments made by the debtor, provided they are made within 21 days after the particulars were sent to the debtor.

5A.15(4)   **[Official receiver to notify decision to creditor]** The official receiver must–

    (a)   within 14 days of coming to a decision specified in section 251K(5)–

        (i)   send notice to the creditor under and in accordance with Rule 5A.16 of either the revocation or amendment of the debt relief order under section 251L; or

        (ii)   under Rule 5A.19(b), if he or she would not otherwise be treated as such, treat the creditor as a person interested in any application made under section 251M by the official receiver to the court for directions or an order in relation to any matter arising in connection with the debt relief order, to whom notice of the official receiver's application must be sent; or

        (iii)   send notice to the creditor of the official receiver's decision to take other steps in relation to the debtor and of the steps he or she proposes to take; or

    (b)   notify the creditor of the official receiver's decision to do none of the above.

5A.16   Procedure to be followed when revoking or amending a debt relief order

5A.16(1)   **[Notice of decision to revoke]** Subject to Rule 5A.27, the official receiver must as soon as reasonably practicable after deciding to revoke a debt relief order–

    (a)   send notice of the decision to revoke to–

        (i)   the debtor; and

        (ii)   any creditor specified in the debt relief order as a creditor to whom a qualifying debt is owed; and

    (b)   upon the revocation taking effect, provided that information concerning a debt relief order has not been deleted under Rule 6A.5B, cause the entry in the individual insolvency register relating to the debt relief order to be amended accordingly.

5A.16(2)   **[Contents of notice]** The notice of the decision to revoke must–

(a)   identify the debtor and the date and reference number of the debt relief order;

(b)   state the reasons for revocation; and

(c)   specify the date (whether under subsection (5) or (7) of section 251L) on or from which the revocation has effect.

5A.16(3)   **[Notice of early revocation]** Where–

(a)   a revocation is to take effect from a specified date, and

(b)   the official receiver thinks it appropriate to revoke the order under subsection (7) of section 251L with immediate effect at any time before that date,

any debtor or creditor to whom notice of the specified date has already been sent pursuant to paragraph (1), must be notified by the official receiver of the earlier date on which the revocation has effect.

5A.16(4)   **[Notice of amendment]** Upon amendment of a debt relief order, the official receiver shall as soon as reasonably practicable after the amendment–

(a)   send notice of the amendment to–

    (i)   the debtor; and

    (ii)   any creditor specified in the debt relief order as a creditor to whom a qualifying debt is owed;

(b)   in the notice of amendment–

    (i)   identify the debtor and the date and reference number of the debt relief order;

    (ii)   specify the amendment;

    (iii)   specify the date on which the amendment was made; and

    (iv)   state the reasons for it; and

(c)   cause the entry in the individual insolvency register relating to the amended debt relief order to be amended accordingly.

5A.17   Notification of official receiver by debtor of matters in section 251J(3) or (5)

5A.17(1)   **[Duty of debtor to notify error, omission etc. in information]** As soon as reasonably practicable after the debtor becomes aware of–

(a)   an error in, or omission from, the information supplied to the official receiver in, or in support of, the application, he or she must notify the official receiver of–

    (i)   the nature of the error or omission; and

    (ii)   the reason for it;

(b)   a change in his or her circumstances between the application date and the determination date that would affect (or would have affected) the determination of the application, he or she must notify the official receiver of–

    (i)   the nature of the change; and

    (ii)   the date of the change.

5A.17(2)   [Duty where debt relief order made] Where a debt relief order is made and–

(a)   there is an increase in the debtor's income during the moratorium period applicable to the order, the debtor shall notify the official receiver, as soon as reasonably practicable after the date of the increase, of–

    (i)   the amount of the increase;

    (ii)   the reason for it;

    (iii)   the date of the increase; and

    (iv)   its expected duration;

(b)   the debtor acquires any property or any property is devolved upon him during that period, the debtor shall notify the official receiver, as soon as reasonably practicable after the date of the acquisition or the devolution, of–

    (i)   the nature of the acquisition or devolution;

    (ii)   the date of the acquisition or devolution;

    (iii)   the reason for it; and

    (iv)   its value;

(c)   the debtor becomes aware of any error in or omission from any information supplied by him or her to the official receiver after the determination date, the debtor shall notify the official receiver, as soon as reasonably practicable after the date on which the debtor becomes aware of it, of–

    (i)   the nature of the error or omission;

    (ii)   the reason for it; and

    (iii)   the date on which the debtor becomes aware of it.

5A.18   Persons at risk of violence—debt relief orders, debt relief restrictions orders and debt relief restrictions undertakings

5A.18(1)   ["Debtor", "current address"] For the purposes of this Rule–

"debtor" means a person subject to a debt relief order, or a debt relief restrictions order or a debt relief restrictions undertaking; and

"current address" means in relation to any debtor the address of his or her current place of residence and any address at which he or she currently carries on business.

5A.18(2)   [Threat of violence] This Rule applies in any case where disclosure or continuing disclosure to other persons (whether to the public generally or to specific persons) of the current address or whereabouts of a debtor might reasonably be expected to lead to violence against him or her or against a person who normally resides with him or her as a member of his or her family.

5A.18(3)   [Power of court to remove debtor's current address from register, etc.] The court may, subject to paragraph (6)–

(a)   on the application of a debtor subject to a debt relief order or the official receiver in respect of such a debtor, order that–

    (i)   the details in respect of the debtor to be entered onto the individual insolvency register under Rule 6A.5A shall not include details of the debtor's current address; or

    (ii)   the details of the debtor's current address kept on the individual insolvency register under Part 6A shall be removed from such register;

(b)   on the application of a debtor subject to a debt relief restrictions order or the official receiver in respect of such a debtor, order that–

  (i)   details of the debtor's current address shall be removed from any part of the court file of the proceedings in relation to the debtor which is open to inspection and be kept on a separate file not open to inspection;

  (ii)   the full of title of the proceedings shall be amended by the removal of the details of the debtor's current address from the description of the debtor;

  (iii)   the details in respect of the debtor to be entered onto the debt relief restrictions register under Rule 6A.7A shall not include details of the debtor's current address; or

  (iv)   the details of the debtor's current address kept on the debt relief restrictions register under Rule 6A shall be removed from such register;

(c)   on the application of a debtor subject to a debt relief restrictions undertaking or the official receiver in respect of such a debtor, order that–

  (i)   the details of the debtor's current address shall be excluded from the details in respect of the debtor to be entered onto the debt relief restrictions register under Rule 6A.7A; or

  (ii)   the details of the debtor's current address kept on the debt relief restrictions register under Rule 6A shall be removed from such register.

5A.18(4)   [Further order re addresses] Where the court makes an order under paragraph (3), it may further order that–

(a)   the full title of any proceedings; or

(b)   the details in respect of the debtor kept on or to be entered onto the registers referred to in that paragraph,

as the case may be, shall instead include such other details of the debtor's addresses or whereabouts as the court thinks fit, including details of any address at which the debtor has previously resided or carried on business.

5A.18(5)   [Transfer of proceedings under r.7.11] Proceedings under this Rule may be ordered by the court to be transferred under Rule 7.11 on the application of the person in respect of whom the application is being made.

5A.18(6)   [Witness statement in support to refer to r.5A.18] In any case where an application is made by a debtor under or by virtue of this Rule, the application shall be accompanied by a witness statement referring to this Rule and containing sufficient evidence to satisfy the court to which the application was made, that this Rule applies to or in respect of that debtor.

GENERAL NOTE

See I(A)R 2010 (SI 2010/686) which makes the usual change from affidavit to witness statement in para.(6).

5A.19   Application to court under section 251M

5A.19   Where an application is made to the court under section 251M–

(a)   by a person who is dissatisfied by any act, omission or decision of the official receiver in connection with a debt relief order or an application for a debt relief order, if the person making the application–

  (i)   is the debtor, notice of the application to the court must be sent to the official receiver and to any creditor specified in the debt relief order or in the application for a debt relief order; or

(ii) is a person other than the debtor, notice of the application to the court must be sent to the official receiver and to the debtor;

(b) by the official receiver for directions or an order in relation to any matter arising in connection with a debt relief order or an application for such an order, notice of the application must be sent by the official receiver to the debtor and to any person appearing to the official receiver to have an interest in the application.

5A.20   Extension of moratorium period

5A.20   Where the moratorium period applicable to a debt relief order is extended–

(a) notice of the extension, and the period for which it is extended must be sent,

   (i) where extended by the court, to the official receiver, who shall send a copy to the debtor subject to the debt relief order and to the creditors specified in it;

   (ii) where extended by the official receiver, to the debtor subject to the debt relief order and to the creditors specified in it; and

(b) the official receiver shall cause to be entered in the individual insolvency register that–

   (i) such an extension has been made in relation to the debtor;

   (ii) the date on which the extension was made;

   (iii) its duration; and

   (iv) the date of the anticipated end of the moratorium period.

5A.21   Court in which applications under sections 251M (powers of court in relation to debt relief orders) or 251N (inquiry into debtor's dealings and property) to be made

5A.21(1)   **[High Court, county court]** An application to the court by a debtor under section 251M(1) or by the official receiver under section 251M(2) or 251N shall, if the debtor is resident in England and Wales–

(a) be made to the High Court if the debtor has resided or carried on business in the London insolvency district for the greater part of the 6 months immediately preceding the making of the application, or for a longer period in those 6 months than in any other insolvency district, and

(b) in any other case, (subject to paragraph (2)) be made to the debtor's own county court, which is–

   (i) the county court for the insolvency district in which he or she has resided or carried on business for the longest period during those 6 months, or

   (ii) if he or she has for the greater part of those 6 months carried on business in one insolvency district and resided in another, the county court for that in which he or she has carried on business, or

   (iii) if he or she has during those 6 months carried on business in more than one insolvency district, the county court for that in which is, or has been for the longest period in those 6 months, his or her principal place of business.

5A.21(2)   **[Expediting application]** If, in a case not falling within paragraph (1)(a), it is more expedient for the debtor with a view to expediting the application–

(a) it may in any case be made to whichever court is specified by Schedule 2 to the Rules as being, in relation to the debtor's own county court, the nearest full-time court, and

(b) it may alternatively, in a case falling within paragraph (1)(b)(ii), be made to the court for the insolvency district in which he or she has resided for the greater part of the 6 months there referred to.

5A.21(3)   [Debtor no longer resident in England or Wales] If the debtor is not resident in England and Wales but has resided or carried on business in England and Wales within the 6 months immediately preceding the making of the application, the application–

(a) shall be made to the High Court if the debtor has resided or carried on business in the London insolvency district for the greater part of those 6 months, or for a longer period in those 6 months than in any other insolvency district, and

(b) in any other case, may (subject to paragraph (4)) be made either to the debtor's own county court or to the High Court.

5A.21(4)   [Application of r.5A.21(2)] The provisions of paragraph (2) shall apply with any appropriate modifications in any case where in accordance with paragraph (3)(b) the application may be made to the debtor's own county court.

5A.21(5)   [Debtor not resident in England or Wales for six months] If the debtor is not resident in England and Wales and has not resided or carried on business in England and Wales within the 6 months immediately preceding the making of the application, the application shall be made to the High Court.

5A.21(6)   [Application to contain sufficient information to determine court] The application shall contain sufficient information to establish that it is brought in the appropriate court.

5A.22   Referral of debtor, by court, to intermediary under section 274A

5A.22   If, on the hearing of a debtor's bankruptcy petition, the court refers the debtor to an approved intermediary under section 274A for the purposes of making an application for a debt relief order, as soon as reasonably practicable after the making of the order of referral–

(a) the court shall send to the debtor a sealed copy of the order of referral, and

(b) the debtor shall send to the approved intermediary a copy of the order and copies of the debtor's petition and statement of affairs.

5A.23   Creditor's bankruptcy petition—where creditor consents to making of application for a debt relief order

5A.23(1)   [Application of r.5A.23] This Rule applies where prior to the determination of an application, a creditor's petition for bankruptcy has been presented against a debtor and the proceedings in relation to that petition remain before the court.

5A.23(2)   ["The petition", "the debt"] In this Rule,

"the petition" means the creditor's bankruptcy petition; and

"the debt" means the debt to which the creditor's bankruptcy petition relates.

5A.23(3)   [Duty of court and debtor] If, on the hearing of the petition, the petitioner consents to the making by the debtor of an application for a debt relief order in respect of the debt–

(a) the court shall–

(i)   refer the debtor to an approved intermediary (within the meaning of Part 7A) for the purpose of making an application for a debt relief order in relation to the debtor and the debt noting the consent of the creditor on the order for referral;

(ii) stay the proceedings on the petition in relation to the debt on such terms and conditions as it thinks fit; and

(b)   the debtor shall send to the approved intermediary as soon as reasonably practicable after the making of the order of referral,

      (i)   a sealed copy of the order, and

      (ii)   copies of the petition and (if any), of the creditor's statutory demand.

5A.23(4)   **[Duty of approved intermediary]** The approved intermediary shall, on receipt of the order and the copies, as soon as reasonably practicable after the application for a debt relief order has been made, send them to the official receiver endorsed with the name of the debtor and the number of the application to which they relate.

5A.23(5)   **[Petition dismissed if debt relief order made]** If, following the reference by the court, a debt relief order is made in relation to the debt, the petition shall be dismissed in relation to it unless the court otherwise directs.

5A.24   Application for permission under Company Directors Disqualification Act 1986

5A.24(1)   **[Application for permission to be supported by witness statement]** An application by a person–

(a)   in relation to whom a moratorium period under a debt relief order applies, or

(b)   in respect of whom a debt relief restrictions order or undertaking is in force,

for permission (**"the applicant for permission"**), under section 11 of the Company Directors Disqualification Act 1986), to act as director of, or to take part or be concerned in the promotion, formation or management of a company, shall be supported by a witness statement complying with this Rule.

5A.24(2)   **[Contents of witness statement re company concerned]** The witness statement must identify the company and specify–

(a)   the nature of its business or intended business, and the place or places where that business is, or is to be, carried on;

(b)   whether it is, or is to be, a private or a public company;

(c)   the persons who are, or are to be, principally responsible for the conduct of its affairs (whether as directors, shadow directors, managers or otherwise);

(d)   the manner and capacity in which the applicant for permission proposes to take part or be concerned in the promotion or formation of the company or, as the case may be, its management; and

(e)   the emoluments and other benefits to be obtained from the directorship.

5A.24(3)   **[Date of incorporation and capital of company]** If the company is already in existence, the witness statement must specify the date of its incorporation and the amount of its nominal and issued share capital; and if not, it must specify the amount, or approximate amount, of its proposed commencing share capital, and the sources from which that capital is to be obtained.

5A.24(4)   **[Permission for promotion or formation of company]** Where the applicant for permission intends to take part or be concerned in the promotion or formation of a company, the witness statement must contain an undertaking by the applicant for permission that he or she will, within not less than 5 business days of the company being incorporated, file in court a copy of its memorandum of association and certificate of incorporation under section 15 of the Companies Act.

5A.24(5)   **[Court to fix venue for hearing; notice]** The court shall fix a venue for the hearing of the application, and shall give notice to the applicant for permission accordingly.

GENERAL NOTE

References to affidavits have been replaced by references to witness statements as a result of I(A)R 2010 (SI 2010/686). The seven-day period in para.(4) now becomes five business days.

5A.25 Application for permission under Company Directors Disqualification Act 1986—report of official receiver

5A.25(1)   [Applicant to notify official receiver] The applicant for permission shall, not less than 28 days before the date fixed for the hearing, give to the official receiver, notice of the venue, accompanied by copies of the application and the witness statement under Rule 5A.24.

5A.25(2)   [Power of official receiver to draw matters to court's attention] The official receiver may, not less than 14 days before the date fixed for the hearing, file in court a report of any matters which he considers ought to be drawn to the court's attention. A copy of the report shall be sent by him, as soon as reasonably practicable after it is filed, to the applicant for permission.

5A.25(3)   [Power of applicant to deny/dispute official receiver's statements] The applicant for permission may, not later than 5 business days before the date of the hearing, file in court a notice specifying any statements in the official receiver's report which he or she intends to deny or dispute.

5A.25(4)   [Applicant to send copy of notice to official receiver] If he or she gives notice under this paragraph, he or she shall send copies of it, not less than 4 business days before the date of the hearing, to the official receiver.

5A.25(5)   [Power of official receiver to appear at hearing] The official receiver may appear on the hearing of the application, and may make representations and put to the applicant for permission such questions as the court may allow.

GENERAL NOTE

See I(A)R 2010 (SI 2010/686) which makes the usual changes by replacing references in para.(1) to affidavits and converting seven-day period to five business days in para.(3).

5A.26 Application for permission under Company Directors Disqualification Act 1986—court's order on application

5A.26(1)   [Order to specify permission if granted] If the court grants the application for permission under section 11 of the Company Directors Disqualification Act 1986, its order shall specify that which by virtue of the order the applicant has permission to do.

5A.26(2)   [Effect on moratorium or debt relief order] The court may at the same time, having regard to any representations made by the official receiver on the hearing of the application, exercise in relation to the moratorium period or the debt relief order to which the applicant for permission is subject, any power which it has under section 251M.

5A.26(3)   [Copy of order to applicant and official receiver] Whether or not the application is granted, copies of the order shall be sent by the court to the applicant and the official receiver.

5A.27 Death of debtor at a time when a moratorium period under a debt relief order applies in relation to him or her

5A.27(1)   [Application of r.5A.27] This Rule applies where a debtor dies at a time when a moratorium period under a debt relief order applies in relation to him or her.

5A.27(2)   [Official receiver to revoke debt relief order and give notice] The official receiver shall, as soon as reasonably practicable after receiving notice of the death of the debtor–

(a)   revoke the debt relief order;

(b) cause a note of the fact and the date of the death to be entered on the individual insolvency register under Rule 6A.8; and

(c) send notice of the revocation–

   (i) to any creditor specified in the debt relief order as a creditor to whom a qualifying debt is owed, and

   (ii) to the personal representatives of the deceased debtor.

5A.27(3)   [Contents of revocation notice] In the notice of revocation, the official receiver shall–

(a) identify the debtor;

(b) state the reason for the revocation, and

(c) specify the date on which the revocation took effect.

General Note

The Insolvency (Amendment) Rules 2009 (SI 2009/642), introduced via Sch.1 a new Pt 5A (IR rr.5A.1–5A.27) with effect from April 6, 2009. These new rules deal with the process by which a debtor may seek a debt relief order, the consequences of such an order, the rights of creditors and the responsibilities of the debtor and official receiver. In order to obtain a debt relief order a debtor must apply via an approved intermediary to the official receiver. Full discussion of this new aspect of personal insolvency law is to be found in the General Note to Part 7A of the Insolvency Act 1986, which was introduced under the auspices of the Tribunals, Courts and Enforcement Act 2007. On debt relief orders note also Sch.4ZA of the Act. Schedule 4ZB deals with debt relief restriction orders, etc.

PART 6

BANKRUPTCY

CHAPTER 1

THE STATUTORY DEMAND

6.1   Form and content of statutory demand

6.1(1)   [Must be dated and authenticated] A statutory demand under section 268 must be dated, and be authenticated either by the creditor himself or by a person stating himself to be authorised to make the demand on the creditor's behalf.

[FORM 6.1]
or [FORM 6.2]
or [FORM 6.3]

6.1(2)   [Whether s.268(1) or (2)] The statutory demand must specify whether it is made under section 268(1) (debt payable immediately) or section 268(2) (debt not so payable).

6.1(3)   [Further contents] The demand must state the amount of the debt, and the consideration for it (or, if there is no consideration, the way in which it arises) and–

(a) if made under section 268(1) and founded on a judgment or order of a court, it must give details of the judgment or order, and

(b) if made under section 268(2), it must state the grounds on which it is alleged that the debtor appears to have no reasonable prospect of paying the debt.

6.1(4)   [Interest and accruing charges] If the amount claimed in the demand includes–

(a) any charge by way of interest not previously notified to the debtor as a liability of his, or

(b) any other charge accruing from time to time,

the amount or rate of the charge must be separately identified, and the grounds on which payment of it is claimed must be stated.

In either case the amount claimed must be limited to that which has accrued due at the date of the demand.

6.1(5) [If creditor holds security] If the creditor holds any security in respect of the debt, the full amount of the debt shall be specified, but–

(a) there shall in the demand be specified the nature of the security, and the value which the creditor puts upon it as at the date of the demand, and

(b) the amount of which payment is claimed by the demand shall be the full amount of the debt, less the amount specified as the value of the security.

GENERAL NOTE

For practical guidance see Baister, (2006) 22 I.L. & P. 55. On who is an authorised signatory for the purposes of r.6.1(1) see *Horne v Dacorum BC* [2000] B.P.I.R. 1047.

For judicial consideration of this provision see *Re a Debtor (No.310 of 1988)* [1989] 1 W.L.R. 452. Here Knox J. held that the phrase "any security in respect of the debt" when used in r.6.1(5) must have the same meaning as when used in IA 1986 ss.383 and 385(1). Therefore the security that had to be referred to in the statutory demand was security over any property of the alleged debtor and not security provided by a third party. Failure to specify the security held as required under r.6.1(5) may not always be fatal for the creditor, as the court now tends to consider whether the debtor has suffered any real injustice: see *Re a Debtor (No.106 of 1992), The Independent*, April 20, 1992 and the comments on s.268. For the position where the incorrect form is used see *Cartwright v Staffordshire and Moorlands DC* [1998] B.P.I.R. 328.

(See General Note after r.6.2.)

6.2 Information to be given in statutory demand

6.2(1) [Explanation of demand generally] The statutory demand must include an explanation to the debtor of the following matters–

(a) the purpose of the demand, and the fact that, if the debtor does not comply with the demand, bankruptcy proceedings may be commenced against him;

(b) the time within which the demand must be complied with, if that consequence is to be avoided;

(c) the methods of compliance which are open to the debtor; and

(d) his right to apply to the court for the statutory demand to be set aside.

6.2(2) [Information re named individuals] The demand must specify one or more named individuals with whom the debtor may, if he wishes, enter into communication with a view to securing or compounding for the debt to the satisfaction of the creditor or (as the case may be) establishing to the creditor's satisfaction that there is a reasonable prospect that the debt will be paid when it falls due.

In the case of any individual so named in the demand, his address and telephone number (if any) must be given.

GENERAL NOTE TO RR.6.1, 6.2

These rules describe the statutory demand mentioned in IA 1986 s.268(1)(a), (2)(a). The form and contents are detailed. Where the demand is made under s.372(4)(a) of the FSMA 2000 r.6.2 is disapplied (and substitute rules provided) by the Bankruptcy (Financial Services and Markets Act 2000) Rules 2001 (SI 2001/3634) rr.1, 3 and 5 as from December 1, 2001.

6.3   Requirements as to service

6.3(1)   [Effect of r.6.11] Rule 6.11 in Chapter 2 below has effect as regards service of the statutory demand, and proof of that service by a certificate of service to be filed with a bankruptcy petition.

6.3(2)   [Creditor's obligation to effect personal service etc.] The creditor is, by virtue of the Rules, under an obligation to do all that is reasonable for the purpose of bringing the statutory demand to the debtor's attention and, if practicable in the particular circumstances, to cause personal service of the demand to be effected.

6.3(3)   [Advertisement of demand for sum due under judgment etc.] Where the statutory demand is for payment of a sum due under a judgment or order of any court and the creditor knows, or believes with reasonable cause–

(a)   that the debtor has absconded or is keeping out of the way with a view to avoiding service, and

(b)   there is no real prospect of the sum due being recovered by execution or other process,

the creditor may advertise the demand in such manner as the creditor thinks fit; and the time limited for compliance with the demand runs from the date of the advertisement's appearance or (as the case may be) its first appearance.

GENERAL NOTE

The rules as to service of the statutory demand are hereby prescribed. Personal service is normally required, subject to r.6.3(3). See also *Practice Direction: Insolvency Proceedings* [2000] B.C.C. 927 (reproduced in [2007] B.C.C. 842 and included in App.IV of this *Guide*).

In *Re a Debtor (No.234 and 236 of 1991), The Independent*, June 29, 1992 it was confirmed by Blackett-Ord Q.C. (sitting as a judge of the High Court) that in some cases it may be appropriate to serve the statutory demand upon the solicitors of the debtor. In *Regional Collection Services Ltd v Heald* [2000] B.P.I.R. 641 it was held that a creditor had failed to take all reasonable steps to bring the demand to the debtor's attention because it had failed to visit the debtor's business premises. For a case where substituted service was found to be sufficient compliance with IR r.6.3 see *Takavarasha v Newham Borough Council* [2004] EWHC 3232 (Ch); [2006] B.P.I.R. 311 (statutory demand pushed through letter box where debtor had refused to meet process server).

For the obligations of the creditor under IR r.6.3(2) see *Omokwe v HFC Bank Ltd* [2007] B.P.I.R. 1157.

Rule 6.3 is modified so as to apply in relation to a demand made under s.372(4)(a) of FSMA 2000 as if (a) references to the debtors were references to an individual; (b) references (other than in r.6.5(2) and (4)(c) to the creditor were references to the Authority; and (c) references to the creditor in r.6.5(2) and (4)(c) were references to the person to whom the debt is owed by virtue of the Bankruptcy (Financial Services and Markets Act 2000) Rules 2001 (SI 2001/3634) rr.1, 3 and 6(1) as from December 1, 2001.

Note the Insolvency (Amendment) Rules 2009 (SI 2009/642) which has amended IR r.6.3(3) with effect from April 6, 2009. This amendment involved a change of wording in para.(3) to permit more discretion in terms of advertising mode.

Note references to affidavit were replaced with references to certificates of service by I(A)R 2010 (SI 2010/686).

6.4   Application to set aside statutory demand

6.4(1)   [Time for application] The debtor may, within the period allowed by this Rule, apply to the appropriate court for an order setting the statutory demand aside.

[FORM 6.4]

That period is 18 days from the date of the service on him of the statutory demand or, where the demand is advertised pursuant to Rule 6.3, from the date of the advertisement's appearance or (as the case may be) its first appearance.

6.4(2)   [Appropriate court for application] Subject to paragraph (2A), an application to the court under this Rule must be made to the court to which the debtor would in accordance with Rule 6.40A present the petition for the debtor's bankruptcy.

6.4(2A) **[Appropriate court where creditor is Minister]** A debtor may make an application to the High Court where the High Court is not the court to which the debtor would in accordance with Rule 6.40A present the petition for the debtor's bankruptcy if–

(a) the creditor issuing the statutory demand is a Minister of the Crown or a Government Department;

(b) the debt in respect of which the statutory demand is made, or a part of it equal to or exceeding the bankruptcy level (within the meaning of section 267), is the subject of a judgment or order of any court; and

(c) the statutory demand–

   (i) specifies the date of the judgment or order and the court in which it was obtained; and

   (ii) indicates the creditor's intention to present a bankruptcy petition against the debtor in the High Court.

6.4(3) **[Effect of filing application in court]** As from (inclusive) the date on which the application is filed in court, the time limited for compliance with the statutory demand ceases to run, subject to any order of the court under Rule 6.5(6).

6.4(4) **[Witness statement in support]** The debtor's application shall be supported by a witness statement–

(a) specifying the date on which the statutory demand came into his hands, and

(b) stating the grounds on which he claims that it should be set aside.

6.4(5) **[Statutory demand copy to be attached to witness statement]** The witness statement must have attached to it a copy of the statutory demand.

[FORM 6.5]

GENERAL NOTE

The debtor can, by using Forms 6.4 and 6.5, apply to the court to have the statutory demand set aside. He has 18 days after service to make such an application. If an application is made, the three weeks' deadline for compliance with the demand ceases to run. In *HM Revenue and Customs v Soor* [2005] EWHC 3080 (Ch); [2006] B.P.I.R. 429 Warren J. rejected a later application to set aside a statutory demand. There were no grounds for allowing an application for the late setting aside of the statutory demand. The liability, established by court judgment, could not be disputed.

See also *Practice Direction: Insolvency Proceedings* [2000] B.C.C. 927 (the *Practice Direction* was republished in a more up-to-date form in 2007—see *Practice Direction: Insolvency Proceedings* [2007] B.C.C. 842 reproduced in App.IV of this *Guide*); and *Morley IRC* [1996] B.P.I.R. 452. On the need for proper formal requirements to be satisfied see *Ariyo v Sovereign Leasing* [1998] B.P.I.R. 177.

Rule 6.4 is modified so as to apply in relation to a demand made under s.372(4)(a) of FSMA 2000 as if (a) references to the debtor were references to an individual; (b) the words in para.(2), "the creditor issuing the statutory demand is a Minister of the Crown or a Government Department, and" were omitted; and (c) the reference to the creditor in para.(2)(b) was a reference to the Authority, by virtue of the Bankruptcy (Financial Services and Markets Act 2000) Rules 2001 (SI 2001/3634) rr.1, 3 and 7 as from December 1, 2001.

Note the Insolvency (Amendment) Rules 2009 (SI 2009/642) which have removed "in a newspaper" from the original version of IR r.6.4(1).

The changes made by I(A)R 2010 (SI 2010/686) include the substitution of new paras (2) and (2A) to replace former para.(2) and the insertion of new para.(5). The term affidavit has been changed to witness statement.

6.5 Hearing of application to set aside

6.5(1) **[Court may dismiss application etc.]** On receipt of an application under Rule 6.4, the court may, if satisfied that no sufficient cause is shown for it, dismiss it without giving notice to the creditor. As from (inclusive) the date on which the application is dismissed, the time limited for compliance with the statutory demand runs again.

6.5(2) **[Application not dismissed under r.6.5(1)]** If the application is not dismissed under paragraph (1), the court shall fix a venue for it to be heard, and shall give at least 5 business days' notice of it to–

(a) the debtor or, if the debtor's application was made by a solicitor acting for him, to the solicitor,

(b) the creditor, and

(c) whoever is named in the statutory demand as the person with whom the debtor may enter into communication with reference to the demand (or, if more than one person is so named, the first of them).

6.5(3) **[Summary determination or adjournment]** On the hearing of the application, the court shall consider the evidence then available to it, and may either summarily determine the application or adjourn it, giving such directions as it thinks appropriate.

6.5(4) **[Setting aside demand]** The court may grant the application if–

(a) the debtor appears to have a counterclaim, set-off or cross demand which equals or exceeds the amount of the debt or debts specified in the statutory demand; or

(b) the debt is disputed on grounds which appear to the court to be substantial; or

(c) it appears that the creditor holds some security in respect of the debt claimed by the demand, and either Rule 6.1(5) is not complied with in respect of it, or the court is satisfied that the value of the security equals or exceeds the full amount of the debt; or

(d) the court is satisfied, on other grounds, that the demand ought to be set aside.

[FORM 6.6]

6.5(5) **[Under-valued security]** Where the creditor holds some security in respect of his debt, and Rule 6.1(5) is complied with in respect of it but the court is satisfied that the security is under-valued in the statutory demand, the creditor may be required to amend the demand accordingly (but without prejudice to his right to present a bankruptcy petition by reference to the original demand).

6.5(6) **[On dismissal of application]** If the court dismisses the application, it shall make an order authorising the creditor to present a bankruptcy petition either as soon as reasonably practicable, or on or after a date specified in the order.

A copy of the order shall be sent by the court as soon as reasonably practicable to the creditor.

GENERAL NOTE

This rule outlines the hearing procedure for an application made under r.6.4. Note that the seven-day period in para.(2) has been changed to five business days by I(A)R 2010 (SI 2010/686). If the application succeeds, the court's order should be in the style of Form 6.6. If the application fails the court can permit the immediate presentation of the bankruptcy petition. The leading case on r.6.5(4) is *Re a Debtor (No.1 of 1987)* [1989] 1 W.L.R. 271 where the Court of Appeal held that a document purporting to be a statutory demand was to be treated as such until set aside. In cases of setting aside under r.6.5(4)(d) the debtor must not merely convince the court that the demand was perplexing but also prove what the true position was between himself and the creditor. See the general note after s.268. For a useful comparison between the rules relating to set aside of statutory demands in corporate and personal insolvency law see *Re A Debtor (544/SD/98)* [2001] 1 B.C.L.C. 103 (also reported as *Garrow v The Society of Lloyds* [1999] B.P.I.R. 885).

A set-aside application is not a trial on the merits and fresh evidence can be adduced: *Royal Bank of Scotland v Binnell* [1996] B.P.I.R. 352; *Norman Laurier v United Overseas Bank* [1996] B.P.I.R. 635; *Salvidge v Hussein* [1999] B.P.I.R. 410. These cases confirm that the rule in *Ladd v Marshall* [1954] 1 W.L.R. 1489 does not apply. For further discussion in the context of appeals from decisions on set-aside applications see *AIB Finance Ltd v Alsop* [1998] B.C.C. 780. Such appeals are true appeals and subsequent events should not be taken into account—*Cozens v Customs and Excise Commissioners* [2000] B.P.I.R. 252.

The jurisdiction to set aside statutory demands is permissive; the court is under no obligation to act, as was stressed in *Re a Debtor (No.106 of 1992), The Independent*, April 20, 1992. See also *Khan v Breezevale SARL* [1996] B.P.I.R. 190 (failure to refer to security). The fact that a statutory demand may be defective does not guarantee that it will be set aside under r.6.5(4)—*Coulter v Chief of Dorset Police* [2004] EWCA Civ 1259; [2005] B.P.I.R. 62. For a continuation of this saga see *Coulter v Dorset Police (No.2)* [2005] EWCA Civ 1113; [2006] B.P.I.R. 10.

The court cannot make a conditional order on a set-aside application. Either the demand must be set aside or the application rejected: *Re a Debtor (No.90 of 1992)* [1993] T.L.R. 387; and *Re Debtor (No.32 of 1991) (No.2)* [1994] B.C.C. 524. Equally the courts will not allow a petition to be presented and then adjourned simply in order to trigger time periods for transactional avoidance. Thus if the debtor has an arguable cross claim the proper course of action is to set aside the demand and not to allow this issue to be reserved for trial of the petition—*Garrow v The Society of Lloyds* [1999] B.P.I.R. 885. If a set-aside application fails the same issues cannot normally be relitigated on the hearing of the petition—*Turner v Royal Bank of Scotland* [2000] B.P.I.R. 683; *Atherton v Ogunlende* [2003] B.P.I.R. 21. See also *Coulter v Dorset Police (No.2)* [2005] EWCA Civ 1113; [2006] B.P.I.R. 10.

On r.6.5(4)(a) see *Hofer v Strawson* [1999] B.P.I.R. 501; and *Re A Debtor (No.87 of 1999)* [2000] B.P.I.R. 589, which offer guidance on cross claims. The requirements of IR 6.5(4)(a) were found to be satisfied in *Stone v Vallance* [2008] B.P.I.R. 236. For the meaning of a cross demand within r.6.5(4)(a) see *Popely v Popely* [2004] EWCA Civ 463; [2004] B.P.I.R. 778. In determining whether to set aside a statutory demand because of the existence of a potential cross claim the court should ask itself whether there was a "genuinely triable issue" as to the existence of the cross claim. That test was, in effect, the same as that used in the Civil Procedure Rules, where the requirement was for a "real prospect of success"—*Ashworth v Newnote Ltd* [2007] EWCA Civ 793; [2007] B.P.I.R. 1012. An attempt to seek a set aside on the basis of a dubious cross claim failed in *Gustavi v Moore* [2004] B.P.I.R. 268. Any counterclaim must be legally enforceable—*Re A Debtor (No.35 of 2000)* [2002] B.P.I.R. 75. Where there is a counterclaim within r.6.5(4)(a) there appears to be a mutuality requirement—*Hurst v Bennett* [2001] EWCA Civ 182; [2001] B.P.I.R. 287; *Southward v Banham* [2002] B.P.I.R. 1253. In *Chan Sui v Appasamy* [2005] EWHC 3519 (Ch); [2008] B.P.I.R. 18 the court set aside a statutory demand under IR 6.5(4)(a) where there were a series of interlocking cross claims producing a situation that could not be resolved by the court on a summary set aside application. H.H.J. Weeks Q.C. in this case explains the residual role played by IR 6.5(4)(d). In *Ahmed v Landstone Leisure Ltd* [2009] B.P.I.R. 227 the statutory demand was set aside under IR r.6.5(4)(a) by H.H.J. Purle Q.C. because the debtor may have had a counterclaim. For comment see V. Cocks, (2009) 22 Insolv. Int. 108.

In *Re a Debtor (No.960/SD/1992)* [1993] S.T.C. 218 Mummery J. refused to set aside a statutory demand under r.6.5(4)(c) in a case where a tax assessment was being challenged by the taxpayer; the case did not appear to be covered by this provision. See *Fagg v Rushton* [2007] EWHC 657 (Ch); [2007] B.P.I.R. 1059 for the meaning of "security" in IR r.6.5(4)(c).

A set-aside application also proved unsuccessful in *Re a Debtor (No.415/SD/1993)* [1994] 1 W.L.R. 917. Here the debtor was seeking to set aside the demand by arguing that he had made a reasonable offer of security to the creditor. In discussing the meaning of "other grounds" in r.6.5(4)(d) Jacob J. made it clear that set-aside applications were designed to deal with procedural flaws in the demand and were not meant to raise substantive issues of reasonableness—these issues could be considered when the petition was heard. Equally in *Platts v Western Trust and Savings Ltd* [1996] B.P.I.R. 339 the court indicated that it would not investigate such questions as whether the creditor was secured or not as these were issues best dealt with when the petition was heard. However see the comments of the Court of Appeal on r.6.5(4)(d) in *Budge v Budge (Contractors) Ltd* [1997] B.P.I.R. 366. In *Re a Debtor (No.90 of 1997), The Times*, July 1, 1998, the High Court considered the position with regard to setting aside under r.6.5(4)(d) when there were parallel bankruptcy and civil proceedings afoot. The importance of the general discretion vested in the court by r.6.5(4)(d) was clearly illustrated in *City Electrical Factors v Hardingham* [1996] B.P.I.R. 541 where a statutory demand based upon a debt slightly in excess of £750 was set aside. In *Turner v Turner* [2006] EWHC 2023 (Ch); [2006] B.P.I.R. 1531 the court dealt with the factors relevant to the exercise of discretion under r.6.5(4)(d). The factors taken into account should have some relevance/ proximity to the statutory demand.

Some further consideration was given to the criteria governing the exercise of discretion under IR 1986 r.6.5(4)(d) in *TS & S Global Ltd v Fithian-Franks* [2007] EWHC 1401 (Ch). For an interesting discussion on whether it was appropriate to set aside a statutory demand served on a guarantor of a tenant see *Octagon Assets Ltd v Remblance* [2009] B.P.I.R. 1129.

If the creditor bases his petition upon a judgment debt the court will not on a set-aside application look behind the earlier judgment: see Ferris J. in *Re a Debtor (657/SD/1991)* [1993] B.C.L.C. 1280 applying *Practice Direction* [1987] 1 W.L.R. 119. Note also *Neely v IRC* [1996] B.P.I.R. 473; and *Practice Direction: Insolvency Proceedings* [2000] B.C.C. 927, para.12.3 in App.IV of this *Guide* (Vol.2). The *Practice Direction* was republished in a more up-to-date form in 2007—see *Practice Direction: Insolvency Proceedings* [2007] B.C.C. 842.

For the position where the debt is disputed within the context of r.6.5(4)(b), see *Re a Debtor (No.11 of 1987), The Independent*, March 28, 1988; *Re a Debtor (No.10 of 1988)* [1989] 1 W.L.R. 405; and *Cale v Assiudoman KPS (Harrow) Ltd* [1996] B.P.I.R. 245. On the standard of proof see *Kellar v BBR Graphic Engineers Ltd* [2002] B.P.I.R. 544. Another interesting case involving a disputed debt was *Re a Debtor (No.49 and 50 of 1992)* [1995] Ch. 66. Here part of the debt upon which the statutory demand was based was disputed by the debtor. The undisputed element was for an amount less than the statutory minimum upon which a creditor could petition for bankruptcy. In those circumstances the Court of Appeal held that although the demand could not be set aside in its entirety under r.6.5(4)(b) the court could set aside the whole demand using its residual discretion under r.6.5(4)(d). In *Interframe Ltd v Brown* [2005] EWHC 3527 (Ch); [2008] B.P.I.R. 49 Lawrence Collins J. indicated that an overstated debt will not normally justify the setting aside of a statutory demand. For the dangers as to costs of a creditor using a statutory demand in cases where a trial of the action is pending see *Re a Debtor (No. 620 of 1997), The Times*, June 18, 1998.

On the exercise of discretion under r.6.5(6) see *Everard v Lloyds* [2003] B.P.I.R. 1286.

There is authority that the remedial r.7.55 cannot apply in the context of defects in the statutory demand: *Re a Debtor (No.190 of 1987), The Times*, May 21, 1988.

Rule 6.5 is modified so as to apply in relation to a demand made under s.372(4)(a) of FSMA 2000 as if (a) references to the debtor were references to an individual; (b) references (other than in r.6.5(2) and (4)(c)) to the creditor were references to the Authority; and (c) references to the creditor in r.6.5(2) and (4)(c) were references to the person to whom the debt is owed by virtue of the Bankruptcy (Financial Services and Markets Act 2000) Rules 2001 (SI 2001/3634) rr.1, 3 and 6(1) as from December 1, 2001.

CHAPTER 2

BANKRUPTCY PETITION (CREDITOR'S)

6.6 Preliminary

6.6 The Rules in this Chapter relate to a creditor's petition, and the making of a bankruptcy order thereon; and in those Rules **"the debt"** means, except where the context otherwise requires, the debt (or debts) in respect of which the petition is presented.

Those Rules also apply to a petition under section 264(1)(c) (supervisor of, or person bound by, voluntary arrangement), with any necessary modifications.

[FORM 6.7]
or [FORM 6.8]
or [FORM 6.9]
or [FORM 6.10]

GENERAL NOTE

See the guidance in *Practice Note (Bankruptcy: Petition)* [1987] 1 W.L.R. 81; and the *Practice Direction 3/86* noted in (1987) 3 I.L. & P. 101.

6.7 Identification of debtor

6.7(1) **[Contents of petition]** The petition shall state the following matters with respect to the debtor, so far as they are within the petitioner's knowledge–

(a) his name, place of residence and occupation (if any);

(b) the name or names in which he carries on business, if other than his true name, and whether, in the case of any business of a specified nature, he carries it on alone or with others;

(c) the nature of his business, and the address or addresses at which he carries it on;

(d) any name or names, other than his true name, in which he has carried on business at or after the time when the debt was incurred, and whether he has done so alone or with others;

(e) any address or addresses at which he has resided or carried on business at or after that time, and the nature of that business;

(f) whether the debtor has his centre of main interests or an establishment in another member State.

6.7(2) **[Title of proceedings]** The particulars of the debtor given under this Rule determine the full title of the proceedings.

6.7(3) **[Debtor's other names]** If to the petitioner's personal knowledge the debtor has used any name other than the one specified under paragraph (1)(a), that fact shall be stated in the petition.

(See General Note after r.6.8.)

6.8   Identification of debt

6.8(1) **[Contents of petition]** There shall be stated in the petition, with reference to every debt in respect of which it is presented–

  (a)   the amount of the debt, the consideration for it (or, if there is no consideration, the way in which it arises) and the fact that it is owed to the petitioner;

  (b)   when the debt was incurred or became due;

  (c)   if the amount of the debt includes–

    (i)   any charge by way of interest not previously notified to the debtor as a liability of his, or

    (ii)   any other charge accruing from time to time,

    the amount or rate of the charge (separately identified) and the grounds on which it is claimed to form part of the debt, provided that such amount or rate must, in the case of a petition based on a statutory demand, be limited to that claimed in that demand;

  (d)   either–

    (i)   that the debt is for a liquidated sum payable immediately, and the debtor appears to be unable to pay it, or

    (ii)   that the debt is for a liquidated sum payable at some certain, future time (that time to be specified), and the debtor appears to have no reasonable prospect of being able to pay it,

and, in either case (subject to section 269) that the debt is unsecured.

6.8(2) **[Where statutory demand served]** Where the debt is one for which, under section 268, a statutory demand must have been served on the debtor–

  (a)   there shall be specified the date and manner of service of the statutory demand, and

  (b)   it shall be stated that, to the best of the creditor's knowledge and belief–

    (i)   the demand has been neither complied with nor set aside in accordance with the Rules, and

    (ii)   no application to set it aside is outstanding.

6.8(3) **[If case within s.268(1)(b)]** If the case is within section 268(1)(b) (debt arising under judgment or order of court; execution returned unsatisfied), the court from which the execution or other process issued shall be specified, and particulars shall be given relating to the return.

GENERAL NOTE TO RR.6.7, 6.8

These rules outline the contents of a creditor's petition. IR r.6.7(1)(f) was inserted by the Insolvency (Amendment) Rules 2002 (SI 2002/1307) para.8(1) with effect from May 31, 2002. This was required by the advent of EC Council Regulation (1346/2000) on Insolvency Proceedings.

   See *Practice Direction: Insolvency Proceedings* [2000] B.C.C. 927 (reproduced in App.IV of this *Guide*). The *Practice Direction* was republished in a more up-to-date form in 2007—see *Practice Direction: Insolvency Proceedings* [2007] B.C.C. 842. See *Lambeth LBC v Simon* [2007] B.P.I.R. 1629 for a stern reminder of the need to comply with the requirements of this rule. For the remedial effect of r.7.55 in cases where the requirements of r.6.8 have not been met see *Re a Debtor (No.510 of 1997), The Times*, June 18, 1998.

6.9   Court in which petition to be presented [Deleted.]

6.9A   Court in which petition to be presented

6.9A(1)   [Presentation to High Court] If the debtor is resident in England and Wales, the petition must, in the following cases, be presented to the High Court–

   (a)   if the petition is presented by a Minister of the Crown or a Government Department, and either–

       (i)   in any statutory demand on which the petition is based the creditor has indicated the intention to present a bankruptcy petition to that Court, or

       (ii)   the petition is presented under section 268(1)(b);

   (b)   if, for the greater part of the 6 months immediately preceding the presentation of the petition, the debtor–

       (i)   has carried on a business in the London insolvency district; or

       (ii)   has not carried on a business in England and Wales but has resided in the London insolvency district; or

   (c)   if the petitioner is unable to ascertain the debtor's residence or place of business within England and Wales.

6.9A(2)   [County court] Where the debtor is resident in England and Wales and paragraph (1) does not apply, the petition must be presented to the debtor's own county court if the debtor–

   (a)   has carried on a business in England and Wales other than in the London insolvency district, or

   (b)   has not carried on a business in England and Wales and has resided outside the London insolvency district.

6.9A(3)   [Debtor's own county court] In this Rule the debtor's own county court is–

   (a)   where the debtor has carried on a business within the 6 months immediately preceding the presentation of the petition, the county court for the insolvency district where for the greater part of that period of 6 months–

       (i)   the debtor carried on the business, or

       (ii)   the principal place of business was located, if the business was carried on in more than one insolvency district; or

   (b)   where the debtor has not carried on a business in the 6 months immediately preceding the presentation of the petition, the county court for the insolvency district where the debtor resided for the greater part of that 6 month period.

6.9A(4)   [Debtor no longer resident in England and Wales] If the debtor is not resident in England and Wales but was resident or carried on business in England and Wales within the 6 months immediately preceding the presentation of the petition, the petition–

   (a)   must be presented to the High Court if the debtor–

       (i)   carried on a business in the London insolvency district for a longer period in those 6 months than in any other insolvency district, or

       (ii)   did not carry on a business in England and Wales but resided in the London insolvency district for a longer period in those 6 months than in any other insolvency district; and

   (b)   in any other case, may be presented either to the debtor's own county court or to the High Court.

6.9A(5)   [Debtor not resident in England and Wales] The petition must be presented to the High Court if the debtor is not resident in England and Wales and–

(a) has not resided or carried on business in England and Wales within the 6 months immediately preceding the presentation of the petition, or

(b) the petitioner is unable to ascertain the debtor's residence or place of business.

6.9A(6)   [Where IVA in force for debtor] Notwithstanding any other provision of this Rule, where there is in force for the debtor a voluntary arrangement under Part 8 of the Act, the petition must be presented to the court to which the nominee's report under section 256 was submitted.

6.9A(7)   [Petition to establish appropriate court] The petition must contain sufficient information to establish that it is presented in the appropriate court.

General Note

Substituted by I(A)R 2010 (SI 2010/686) for the previous IR r.6.9.

6.10   Procedure for presentation and filing

6.10(1)   [Petition filing and statement of truth] The petition, verified by a statement of truth in accordance with Rule 6.12(1) below, shall be filed in court.

6.10(2)   [When petition not to be filed] No petition shall be filed unless there is produced on presentation of the petition a receipt for the deposit payable or paragraph (2A) applies.

6.10(2A)   [Written notice of alternative arrangements] This paragraph applies in any case where the Secretary of State has given written notice to the court that the petitioner has made suitable alternative arrangements for the payment of the deposit to the official receiver and such notice has not been revoked in relation to the petitioner in accordance with paragraph (2B).

6.10(2B)   [Revocation of r.6.10(2A) notice] A notice of the kind referred to in paragraph (2A) may be revoked in relation to the petitioner in whose favour it is given by a further notice in writing to the court stating that the earlier notice is revoked in relation to the petitioner.

6.10(3)   [Copies of petition] The following copies of the petition shall also be delivered to the court with the petition–

(a) one for service on the debtor, and

(b) [Omitted.]

(c) if there is in force for the debtor a voluntary arrangement under Part VIII of the Act, and the petitioner is not the supervisor of the arrangement, one copy for him.

Each of these copies shall have applied to it the seal of the court, and shall be issued to the petitioner.

6.10(4)   [Endorsing of r.6.10(3) copies] The date and time of filing the petition shall be endorsed on the petition and on any copy issued under paragraph (3).

6.10(5)   [Venue for hearing] The court shall fix a venue for hearing the petition, and this also shall be endorsed on the petition and on any copy so issued.

6.10(6)   [Former supervisor requested as trustee] Where a petition contains a request for the appointment of a person as trustee in accordance with section 297(5) (appointment of former supervisor as trustee) the person whose appointment is sought shall, not less than 2 business days before the day appointed for hearing the petition, file in court a report including particulars of–

(a)   a date on which he gave written notification to creditors bound by the arrangement of the intention to seek his appointment as trustee, such date to be at least 7 business days before the day on which the report under this paragraph is filed, and

(b)   details of any response from creditors to that notice, including any objections to his appointment.

(See General Note after r.6.12.) See I(A)R 2010 (SI 2010/686). The reference to affidavit has been dropped in favour of statement of truth. Paragraph (3)(b) has been omitted.

6.11   Proof of service of statutory demand

6.11(1)   **[Certificate of service]** Where under section 268 the petition must have been preceded by a statutory demand, there must be filed in court, with the petition, a certificate or certificates proving service of the demand.

6.11(2)   **[Certificate to be verified and attached to demand]** Every certificate must be verified by a statement of truth and have attached to it a copy of the demand as served.

6.11(3)   **[Where personal service of demand]** Subject to the next paragraph, if the demand has been served personally on the debtor, the certificate must be authenticated by the person who effected that service.

[FORM 6.11]

6.11(4)   **[If service of demand acknowledged]** If service of the demand (however effected) has been acknowledged in writing either by the debtor himself, or by some person stating himself in the acknowledgement to be authorised to accept service on the debtor's behalf, the certificate must be authenticated either by the creditor or by a person acting on his behalf, and the acknowledgement of service must be exhibited to the certificate.

6.11(5)   **[If neither r.6.11(3) or (4) applies]** If neither paragraph (3) nor paragraph (4) applies, the certificate or certificates must be authenticated by a person or persons having direct personal knowledge of the means adopted for serving the statutory demand, and must–

(a)   give particulars of the steps which have been taken with a view to serving the demand personally, and

(b)   state the means whereby (those steps having been ineffective) it was sought to bring the demand to the debtor's attention, and

(c)   specify a date by which, to the best of the knowledge, information and belief of the person authenticating the certificate, the demand will have come to the debtor's attention.

[FORM 6.12]

6.11(6)   **[Sufficiency of r.6.11(5)(a) particulars]** The steps of which particulars are given for the purposes of paragraph (5)(a) must be such as would have sufficed to justify an order for substituted service of a petition.

6.11(7)   **[Deemed date of service]** If the certificate specifies a date for the purposes of compliance with paragraph (5)(c), then unless the court otherwise orders, that date is deemed for the purposes of the Rules to have been the date on which the statutory demand was served on the debtor.

6.11(8)   **[Certificate following advertisement]** Where the creditor has taken advantage of Rule 6.3(3) (advertisement), the certificate must be authenticated either by the creditor himself or by a person having direct personal knowledge of the circumstances; and there must be specified in the certificate–

(a)   the means of the creditor's knowledge or (as the case may be) belief required for the purposes of that Rule, and

(b) the method by which, and the date or dates on which the statutory demand was advertised under that rule;

and there shall be exhibited to the certificate either a copy of any advertisement of the statutory demand or, where this is not reasonably practicable, the certificate must contain or attach a description of the contents of any such advertisement of the statutory demand.

6.11(9)   [Discharge of r.6.3(2) obligation] The court may decline to file the petition if not satisfied that the creditor has discharged the obligation imposed on him by Rule 6.3(2).

GENERAL NOTE

See *Practice Direction: Insolvency Proceedings* [2000] B.C.C. 927 (reproduced in App.IV of this *Guide*). The *Practice Direction* was republished in a more up-to-date form in 2007—see *Practice Direction: Insolvency Proceedings* [2007] B.C.C. 842. IR 6.11 was noted in passing in *HMRC v Soor* [2005] EWHC 3080 (Ch); [2006] B.P.I.R. 429. See also general note after r.6.12. Rule 6.11 is modified so as to apply in relation to a demand made under s.372(4)(a) of FSMA 2000 as if (a) references to the debtor were references to an individual; (b) references (other than in r.6.5(2) and (4)(c)) to the creditor were references to the Authority; and (c) references to the creditor in r.6.5(2) and (4)(c) were references to the person to whom the debt is owed by virtue of the Bankruptcy (Financial Services and Markets Act 2000) Rules 2001 (SI 2001/3634) rr.1, 3 and 6(1) as from December 1, 2001. Note the changes introduced into para.(8) by Insolvency (Amendment) Rules 2009 (SI 2009/642) with effect from April 6, 2009. The effect of this modification is to amend para.(8) to permit discretionary advertising. Modernised by I(A)R 2010 (SI 2010/686).

6.12   Verification of petition

6.12(1)   [Statement of truth] The petition shall be verified by a statement of truth.

[FORM 6.13A]

6.12(2)   [Debts due to different creditors] If the petition is in respect of debts to different creditors, the debts to each creditor must be separately verified.

6.12(3)   [Omitted.]

6.12(3A)   [Where statement of truth not in petition] A statement of truth which is not contained in or endorsed upon the petition which it verifies must be sufficient to identify the petition and must specify–

(a) the name of the debtor,

(b) the name of the petitioner, and

(c) the court in which the petition is to be presented.

6.12(4)   [Who must authenticate statement of truth] The statement of truth must be authenticated–

(a) by the petitioner (or if there are two or more petitioners, any one of them), or

(b) by some person such as a director, company secretary or similar company officer, or a solicitor, who has been concerned in the matters giving rise to the presentation of the petition, or

(c) by some responsible person who is duly authorised to authenticate the statement of truth and has the requisite knowledge of those matters.

6.12(5)   [Where person authenticating not petitioner] Where the person authenticating the statement of truth is not the petitioner himself, or one of the petitioners, he must in the statement of truth identify himself and state–

(a) the capacity in which, and the authority by which, he authenticates it, and

(b) the means of his knowledge of the matters verified in the statement of truth.

6.12(6)   [Omitted.]

6.12(7)   **[Delay between demand and petition]** If the petition is based upon a statutory demand, and more than 4 months have elapsed between the service of the demand and the presentation of the petition, the petition must include a statement explaining the reasons for the delay.

GENERAL NOTE TO RR.6.10–6.12

The procedure for filing a creditor's petition is described in these rules. The petition should be accompanied by proof of service of the statutory demand, and by a statement of truth. Paragraph (2) of r.6.10 was substituted by paras (2)–(2B) by I(A)R 2004 (SI 2004/584) with effect from April 1, 2004. It introduces additional machinery for dealing with payment of the deposit. The reference to affidavit has been replaced and a new para.(3A) inserted by I(A)R 2010 (SI 2010/686). Paragraph (6) has been omitted.

6.13   Notice to Chief Land Registrar

6.13   When the petition is filed, the court shall as soon as reasonably practicable send to the Chief Land Registrar notice of the petition together with a request that it may be registered in the register of pending actions.

[FORM 6.14]

GENERAL NOTE

Form 6.14 is now contained in modified form in I(A)R 1987 (SI 1987/1919) r.3(1), Sch. Pt 5 s.1. In *Trustee in Bankruptcy of St John Poulton v Ministry of Justice* [2010] EWCA Civ 392 the court held that a failure by the responsible authorities to comply with this rule could not lead to an action for breach of statutory duty.

6.14   Service of petition

6.14(1)   **[Personal service]** Subject as follows, the petition shall be served personally on the debtor by an officer of the court, or by the petitioning creditor or his solicitor, or by a person instructed by the creditor or his solicitor for that purpose; and service shall be effected by delivering to him a sealed copy of the petition.

6.14(2)   **[Substituted service]** If the court is satisfied by a witness statement or other evidence on oath that prompt personal service cannot be effected because the debtor is keeping out of the way to avoid service of the petition or other legal process, or for any other cause, it may order substituted service to be effected in such manner as it thinks fit.

6.14(3)   **[Deemed service]** Where an order for substituted service has been carried out, the petition is deemed duly served on the debtor.

[FORM 6.15A]
[FORM 6.16]

6.14(4)   **[If voluntary arrangement in force]** If to the petitioner's knowledge there is in force for the debtor a voluntary arrangement under Part VIII of the Act, and the petitioner is not himself the supervisor of the arrangement, a copy of the petition shall be sent by him to the supervisor.

6.14(5)   **[Member State liquidator]** If, to the petitioner's knowledge, there is a member State liquidator appointed in main proceedings in relation to the bankrupt, a copy of the petition shall be sent by him to the member State liquidator.

6.14(6)   **[Service outside England and Wales]** A bankruptcy petition may, with the permission of the court, be served outside England and Wales in such manner as the court may direct.

GENERAL NOTE

Personal service of a creditor's petition is required unless it is a case where substituted service may be appropriate: see *Re a Debtor (No.234 and 236 of 1991), The Independent*, June 29, 1992 (Blackett-Ord Q.C. sitting as a judge of the High Court).

See *Practice Direction: Insolvency Proceedings* [2000] B.C.C. 927 (see App.IV of this *Guide*). The *Practice Direction* was republished in a more up-to-date form in 2007—see *Practice Direction: Insolvency Proceedings* [2007] B.C.C. 842. For service outside the jurisdiction see r.12A.20.

IR 1986 6.14(5) was added by the Insolvency (Amendment) Rules 2002 (SI 2002/1307) para.8(2) in consequence of the advent of EC Council Regulation on Insolvency Proceedings (1346/2000) on May 31, 2002.

See I(A)R 2010 (SI 2010/686)—introducing a new para.(6).

6.15 Proof of service [Deleted.]

6.15A Proof of service

6.15A(1)   **[Certificate of service]** Service of the petition must be proved by a certificate of service.

6.15A(2)   **[Content of certificate of service]** The certificate of service must be sufficient to identify the petition served and must specify–

(a) the name of the debtor,

(b) the name of the petitioner,

(c) the court in which the petition was filed and the court reference number,

(d) the date of the petition,

(e) whether the copy served was a sealed copy,

(f) the date on which service was effected, and

(g) the manner in which service was effected.

6.15A(3)   **[Where substituted service]** Where substituted service has been ordered, the certificate of service must have attached to it a sealed copy of the order.

6.15A(4)   **[Time limit for filing certificate of service]** The certificate of service must be filed in court as soon as reasonably practicable after service, and in any event not less than 5 business days before the hearing of the petition.

GENERAL NOTE

Substituted by I(A)R 2010 (SI 2010/686) for the former IR r.6.15.

6.16 Death of debtor before service

6.16   If the debtor dies before service of the petition, the court may order service to be effected on his personal representatives or on such other persons as it thinks fit.

6.17 Security for costs (s. 268(2) only)

6.17(1)   **[Application of Rule]** This Rule applies where the debt in respect of which the petition is presented is for a liquidated sum payable at some future time, it being claimed in the petition that the debtor appears to have no reasonable prospect of being able to pay it.

6.17(2)   **[Debtor's application for security]** The petitioning creditor may, on the debtor's application, be ordered to give security for the debtor's costs.

6.17(3)   **[Court's discretion]** The nature and amount of the security to be ordered is in the court's discretion.

6.17(4)   **[If order made]** If an order is made under this Rule, there shall be no hearing of the petition until the whole amount of the security has been given.

GENERAL NOTE

This imposes additional financial requirements for petitions based on IA 1986 s.268(2).

6.18 Hearing of petition

6.18(1) [Time for hearing] Subject as follows, the petition shall not be heard until at least 14 days have elapsed since it was served on the debtor.

6.18(2) [Expedited hearing] The court may, on such terms as it thinks fit, hear the petition at an earlier date, if it appears that the debtor has absconded, or the court is satisfied that it is a proper case for an expedited hearing, or the debtor consents to a hearing within the 14 days.

6.18(3) [Appearances] Any of the following may appear and be heard, that is to say, the petitioning creditor, the debtor, the supervisor of any voluntary arrangement under Part VIII of the Act in force for the debtor and any creditor who has given notice under Rule 6.23 below.

GENERAL NOTE

Normally, 14 days must elapse between the petition being served and the hearing.

6.19 Petition against two or more debtors

6.19 [Omitted by the Insolvency (Amendment) Rules 1987 (SI 1987/1919) r.3(1), Sch. Pt 1 para.97 as from January 11, 1988.]

GENERAL NOTE

This rule was omitted because it was felt that a joint petition against multiple debtors would create problems. The general rule of one petition for each debtor should prevail.

6.20 Petition by moneylender [Revoked.]

6.21 Petition opposed by debtor

6.21 Where the debtor intends to oppose the petition, he shall not later than 5 business days before the day fixed for the hearing–

  (a) file in court a notice specifying the grounds on which he will object to the making of a bankruptcy order, and

  (b) send a copy of the notice to the petitioning creditor or his solicitor.

[FORM 6.19]

GENERAL NOTE

The reference to seven days has been changed to five business days by I(A)R 2010 (SI 2010/686).

6.22 Amendment of petition

6.22 With the permission of the court (given on such terms, if any, as the court thinks fit to impose), the petition may be amended at any time after presentation.

GENERAL NOTE

For rationale see s.271(5). On the general rules on amendments to petitions laid down by RSC O. 20 r.8: see *Aspinalls Club Ltd v Simone Halabi* [1998] B.P.I.R. 322. See CPR r.17.1. See I(A)R 2010 (SI 2010/686).

6.23 Notice by persons intending to appear

6.23(1) [Notice of intention] Every creditor who intends to appear on the hearing of the petition shall give to the petitioning creditor notice of his intention in accordance with this Rule.

[FORM 6.20]

6.23(2) **[Contents of notice]** The notice shall specify–

  (a) the name and address of the person giving it, and any telephone number and reference which may be required for communication with him or with any other person (to be also specified in the notice) authorised to speak or act on his behalf;

  (b) whether his intention is to support or oppose the petition; and

  (c) the amount and nature of his debt.

6.23(3) **[Time for sending notice]** The notice shall be sent so as to reach the addressee not later than 16.00 hours on the business day before that which is appointed for the hearing (or, where the hearing has been adjourned, for the adjourned hearing).

6.23(4) **[Effect of non-compliance]** A person failing to comply with this Rule may appear on the hearing of the petition only with the permission of the court.

(See General Note after r.6.24.)

6.24 List of appearances

6.24(1) **[Petitioning creditor to prepare list]** The petitioning creditor shall prepare for the court a list of the creditors (if any) who have given notice under Rule 6.23, specifying their names and addresses and (if known to him) their respective solicitors.

[FORM 6.21]

6.24(2) **[Whether creditors support or oppose]** Against the name of each creditor in the list it shall be stated whether his intention is to support the petition, or to oppose it.

6.24(3) **[Copy list handed to court]** On the day appointed for the hearing of the petition, a copy of the list shall be handed to the court before the commencement of the hearing.

6.24(4) **[Permission under r.6.23(4)]** If any permission is given under Rule 6.23(4), the petitioner shall add to the list the same particulars in respect of the person to whom permission has been given.

GENERAL NOTE TO RR.6.23, 6.24

Creditors who wish to attend the hearing must notify the petitioning creditor, informing him of their attitude to the petition. The petitioning creditor must draw up a list of such persons (Form 6.21), and hand it to the court before the start of the hearing.

6.25 Decision on the hearing

6.25(1) **[Bankruptcy order]** On the hearing of the petition, the court may make a bankruptcy order if satisfied that the statements in the petition are true, and that the debt on which it is founded has not been paid, or secured or compounded for.

6.25(2) **[Stay or dismissal]** If the petition is brought in respect of a judgment debt, or a sum ordered by any court to be paid, the court may stay or dismiss the petition on the ground that an appeal is pending from the judgment or order, or that execution of the judgment has been stayed.

[FORM 6.22]

6.25(3) **[Debt over-stated in demand]** A petition preceded by a statutory demand shall not be dismissed on the ground only that the amount of the debt was over-stated in the demand, unless the debtor, within the time allowed for complying with the demand, gave notice to the creditor disputing the validity of the demand on that ground; but, in the absence of such notice, the debtor is deemed to have complied with the demand if he has, within the time allowed, paid the correct amount.

GENERAL NOTE

See *Practice Note (Bankruptcy: Certificate of Debt)* [1987] 1 W.L.R. 120; and *Eberhardt v Mair* [1995] B.C.C. 845. For a review of r.6.25 see *Legal Services Commission v Leonard* [2002] EWCA Civ 744; [2002] B.P.I.R. 994. See also general note after r.6.26. On the power of the court to go behind a judgment debt see *Dawodu v American Express Bank* [2001] B.P.I.R. 983. For the role of the court under r.6.25(1) in satisfying itself that the statements in the petition are true see *Barnes v Whitehead* [2004] B.P.I.R. 693. See *Lambeth LBC v Simon* [2007] B.P.I.R. 1629 for the latitude given to the court by this particular rule when considering whether to accede to a bankruptcy petition. For a review of IR r.6.25(2) see *Rehman v Boardman* [2004] EWHC 505 (Ch); [2004] B.P.I.R. 820. On overstated demands and IR r.6.25(3) see *Mohammed v London Borough of Southwark* [2006] EWHC 305 (Ch); [2006] B.P.I.R. 782.

Rule 6.25 is modified so as to apply in relation to a demand made under s.372(4)(a) of FSMA 2000 as if (a) references to the debtor were references to an individual; (b) references (other than in r.6.5(2) and (4)(c)) to the creditor were references to the Authority; and (c) references to the creditor in r.6.5(2) and (4)(c) were references to the person to whom the debt is owed by virtue of the Bankruptcy (Financial Services and Markets Act 2000) Rules 2001 (SI 2001/3634) rr.1, 3 and 6(1) as from December 1, 2001.

6.26   Non-appearance of creditor

6.26   If the petitioning creditor fails to appear on the hearing of the petition, no subsequent petition against the same debtor, either alone or jointly with any other person, shall be presented by the same creditor in respect of the same debt, without the permission of the court to which the previous petition was presented.

GENERAL NOTE TO RR.6.25, 6.26

These supplement IA 1986 s.271. Note the sanction against non-appearance by a petitioning creditor. For guidance on the exercise of discretion under IR 1986 r.6.26 see *Omgate Ltd v Gordon* [2001] B.P.I.R. 909.

6.27   Vacating registration on dismissal of petition

6.27   If the petition is dismissed or withdrawn by permission of the court, an order shall be made at the same time permitting vacation of the registration of the petition as a pending action; and the court shall send to the debtor two sealed copies of the order.

[FORM 6.22]

GENERAL NOTE

This should be viewed in the light of r.6.13.

6.28   Extension of time for hearing

6.28(1)   **[If petition not served]** The petitioning creditor may, if the petition has not been served, apply to the court to appoint another venue for the hearing.

6.28(2)   **[Why petition not served]** The application shall state the reasons why the petition has not been served.

6.28(3)   **[Costs]** No costs occasioned by the application shall be allowed in the proceedings except by order of the court.

6.28(4)   **[Notification of creditors]** If the court appoints another day for the hearing, the petitioning creditor shall as soon as reasonably practicable notify any creditor who has given notice under Rule 6.23.

GENERAL NOTE

"Venue" in r.6.28(1) is defined in r.13.6. See *Practice Direction (Bankruptcy 1/92)* [1992] 1 All E.R. 704.

6.29 Adjournment

6.29(1) **[Application of Rule]** If the court adjourns the hearing of the petition, the following applies.

[FORM 6.23]

6.29(2) **[Notice of adjournment]** Unless the court otherwise directs, the petitioning creditor shall as soon as reasonably practicable send–

(a) to the debtor, and

(b) where any creditor has given notice under Rule 6.23 but was not present at the hearing, to him, notice of the making of the order of adjournment. The notice shall state the venue for the adjourned hearing.

[FORM 6.24]

GENERAL NOTE

The order for adjournment is to take the style of Form 6.23, whereas Form 6.24 is to be used when giving notice of the adjournment to the debtor. On this rule see *Johnson v Tandrige DC* [2008] B.P.I.R. 405.

6.30 Substitution of petitioner

6.30(1) **[Application of Rule]** This Rule applies where a creditor petitions and is subsequently found not entitled to do so, or where the petitioner–

(a) consents to withdraw his petition or to allow it to be dismissed, or consents to an adjournment, or fails to appear in support of his petition when it is called on in court on the day originally fixed for the hearing, or on a day to which it is adjourned, or

(b) appears, but does not apply for an order in the terms of the prayer of his petition.

6.30(2) **[Substitution]** The court may, on such terms as it thinks just, order that there be substituted as petitioner any creditor who–

(a) has under Rule 6.23 given notice of his intention to appear at the hearing,

(b) is desirous of prosecuting the petition, and

(c) was, at the date on which the petition was presented, in such a position in relation to the debtor as would have enabled him (the creditor) on that date to present a bankruptcy petition in respect of a debt or debts owed to him by the debtor (or in the case of the member State liquidator, owed to creditors in proceedings in relation to which he holds office), paragraphs (a) to (d) of section 267(2) being satisfied in respect of that debt or those debts.

[FORM 6.24A]

GENERAL NOTE

This allows the court to substitute petitioners in appropriate circumstances. The words in brackets in IR 1986 r.6.30(2)(c) were added by Insolvency (Amendment) Rules 2002 (SI 2002/1307) para.8(3) with effect from May 31, 2002 to cater for the advent of EC Council Regulation 1346/2000 on Insolvency Proceedings.

6.31 Change of carriage of petition

6.31(1) **[Application by creditor]** On the hearing of the petition, any person who claims to be a creditor of the debtor, and who has given notice under Rule 6.23 of his intention to appear at the hearing, may apply to the court for an order giving him carriage of the petition in place of the petitioning creditor, but without requiring any amendment of the petition.

6.31(2)   **[Powers of court]** The court may, on such terms as it thinks just, make a change of carriage order if satisfied that–

(a)   the applicant is an unpaid and unsecured creditor of the debtor, and

(b)   the petitioning creditor either–

     (i)   intends by any means to secure the postponement, adjournment or withdrawal of the petition, or

     (ii)   does not intend to prosecute the petition, either diligently or at all.

                                                   [FORM 6.24B]

6.31(3)   **[Where court not to make order]** The court shall not make the order if satisfied that the petitioning creditor's debt has been paid, secured or compounded for by means of–

(a)   a disposition of property made by some person other than the debtor, or

(b)   a disposition of the debtor's own property made with the approval of, or ratified by, the court.

6.31(4)   **[Appearance by petitioning creditor]** A change of carriage order may be made whether or not the petitioning creditor appears at the hearing.

6.31(5)   **[If order made]** If the order is made, the person given the carriage of the petition is entitled to rely on all evidence previously adduced in the proceedings.

GENERAL NOTE

Other creditors can apply to the court for carriage of the petition. A formal amendment of the petition is not required. See *Re Purvis* [1998] B.P.I.R. 153. See I(A)R 2010 (SI 2010/686).

6.32   Petitioner seeking dismissal or permission to withdraw

6.32(1)   **[Witness statement specifying grounds of application]** Where the petitioner applies to the court for the petition to be dismissed, or for permission to withdraw it, the petitioner must, in any case where–

(a)   a creditor of the debtor has given notice under Rule 6.23 of intention to appear at the hearing of the petition, or

(b)   the court so orders,

file with the court a witness statement specifying the grounds of the application and the circumstances in which it is made.

6.32(2)   **[If payment made since petition filed]** If, since the petition was filed, any payment has been made to the petitioner by way of settlement (in whole or in part) of the debt or debts in respect of which the petition was brought, or any arrangement has been entered into for securing or compounding it or them, the witness statement must also state–

(a)   what dispositions of property have been made for the purposes of the settlement or arrangement, and

(b)   whether, in the case of any disposition, it was property of the debtor himself, or of some other person, and

(c)   whether, if it was property of the debtor, the disposition was made with the approval of, or has been ratified by, the court (if so, specifying the relevant court order).

6.32(3)   [No order before hearing] No order giving permission to withdraw a petition shall be given before the petition is heard.

[FORM 6.22]

GENERAL NOTE

This restricts the right of a petitioner to change his mind, so to speak. Bankruptcy proceedings are essentially a class remedy for the benefit of all creditors. There is a new para.(1) substituted by I(A)R 2010 (SI 2010/686).

6.33   Settlement and content of bankruptcy order

6.33(1)   [Order to be settled by court] The bankruptcy order shall be settled by the court.

[FORM 6.25]

6.33(2)   [Contents of order] The order shall–

(a)   state the date of the presentation of the petition on which the order is made, and the date and time of the making of the order, and

(b)   contain a notice referring to the bankrupt's duties in relation to the official receiver under section 291, and in particular to the bankrupt's duty to give the official receiver such inventory of the bankrupt's estate and such other information, and to attend on the official receiver at such times, as the official receiver may reasonably require.

6.33(3)   [Order staying proceedings] Subject to section 346 (effect of bankruptcy on enforcement procedures), the order may include provision staying any action or proceeding against the bankrupt.

6.33(4)   [Where petitioning creditor represented by solicitor] Where the petitioning creditor is represented by a solicitor, the order shall be endorsed with the latter's name, address, telephone number and reference (if any).

GENERAL NOTE

This regulates the form of any bankruptcy order made under IA 1986 s.271. Paragraph (2)(b) has been replaced by I(A)R 2010 (SI 2010/686).

6.34   Action to follow making of order

6.34(1)   [Copies of order to official receiver etc.] At least two sealed copies of the bankruptcy order shall be sent as soon as reasonably practicable by the court to the official receiver, who shall as soon as reasonably practicable send one of them to the bankrupt.

6.34(2)   [Notice of order to Chief Bankruptcy Registrar, etc.] Subject to the next paragraph, on receipt of the sealed copies of the bankruptcy order, the official receiver–

(a)   as soon as reasonably practicable shall–

(i)   send notice of the making of the order to the Chief Land Registrar, for registration in the register of writs and orders affecting land;

(ii)   cause notice of the order to be gazetted; and

(b)   may cause notice of the order to be advertised in such other manner as the official receiver thinks fit.

[FORM 6.26]

6.34(2A)   [Additional contents of notice under r.6.34(2)] In addition to the standard contents, the notice to be gazetted and any notice to be advertised under paragraph (2) must state–

(a)   that a bankruptcy order has been made against the bankrupt;

(b)   the date and time of making of the bankruptcy order;

(c)   the name and address of the petitioning creditor; and

(d)   the date of presentation of the petition.

6.34(3)   [Suspension of action under r.6.34(2)] The court may, on the application of the bankrupt or a creditor, order the official receiver to suspend action under paragraph (2) and Rule 6A.4(2), pending a further order of the court.

An application under this paragraph shall be supported by a witness statement stating the grounds on which it is made.

6.34(4)   [Where order made under r.6.34(3)] Where an order is made under paragraph (3), the applicant for the order shall as soon as reasonably practicable deliver a copy of it to the official receiver.

GENERAL NOTE

This provides for the dissemination, advertisement and gazetting of the bankruptcy order.

R.6.34(2), (2A)
The Insolvency (Amendment) Rules 2009 (SI 2009/642) amended this rule from April 6, 2009 by substituting a new para.(2). Note new para.(2A) here inserted by I(A)R 2010 (SI 2010/686).

R.6.34(3)
Note the addition of the reference to r.6.223(B)(i) by the Insolvency (Amendment) Rules 1999 (SI 1999/359) with effect from March 22, 1999. This reference was then modified to refer to r.6A.4(2) by the Insolvency (Amendment) Rules 2005 (SI 2005/527).

6.35   Amendment of title of proceedings

6.35(1)   [Application for amendment] At any time after the making of a bankruptcy order, the official receiver or the trustee may apply to the court for an order amending the full title of the proceedings.

6.35(2)   [Notice of order to Chief Land Registrar] Where such an order is made, as soon as reasonably practicable the official receiver shall send notice of it to the Chief Land Registrar for corresponding amendment of the register.

6.35(3)   [Gazetting and advertisement of order] If the official receiver thinks fit, notice of the order–

(a)   as soon as reasonably practicable, shall be gazetted; and

(b)   may be advertised in such other manner as the official receiver thinks fit.

6.35(4)   [Additional contents of notice under r.6.35(3)] In addition to the standard contents, the notice under paragraph (3) must–

(a)   state that an amendment to the full title of the proceedings has been made; and

(b)   specify the amendment.

GENERAL NOTE

For comment on IR 1986 r.6.35(1) in an unusual case see *Michael Yee Fun Chu v Price* [2003] EWCA Civ 1744; [2004] B.P.I.R. 603.

The Insolvency (Amendment) Rules 2009 (SI 2009/642), which took effect on April 6, 2009, made a change in this rule by substituting a new para.(2) and adding a new para.(3). Note new para.(4) here inserted by I(A)R 2010 (SI 2010/686).

6.36   Old bankruptcy notices [Revoked by I(A)R 2010 (SI 2010/686).]

CHAPTER 3

BANKRUPTCY PETITION (DEBTOR'S)

6.37   Preliminary

6.37   The Rules in this Chapter relate to a debtor's petition, and the making of a bankruptcy order thereon.

[FORM 6.27]

(See General Note after r.6.39.)

6.38   Identification of debtor

6.38(1)   [Contents of petition] The petition shall state the following matters with respect to the debtor–

(a)   his name, place of residence and occupation (if any);

(b)   the name or names in which he carries on business, if other than his true name, and whether, in the case of any business of a specified nature, he carries it on alone or with others;

(c)   the nature of his business, and the address or addresses at which he carries it on;

(d)   any name or names, other than his true name, in which he has carried on business in the period in which any of his bankruptcy debts were incurred and, in the case of any such business, whether he has carried it on alone or with others; and

(e)   any address or addresses at which he has resided or carried on business during that period, and the nature of that business.

6.38(2)   [Title of proceedings] The particulars of the debtor given under this Rule determine the full title of the proceedings.

6.38(3)   [Debtor's other names] If the debtor has at any time used a name other than the one given under paragraph (1)(a), that fact shall be stated in the petition.

(See General Note after r.6.39.)

6.39   Admission of insolvency

6.39(1)   [Contents of petition] The petition shall contain the statement that the petitioner is unable to pay his debts, and a request that a bankruptcy order be made against him.

6.39(2)   [Particulars in preceding five-year period] If within the period of 5 years ending with the date of the petition the petitioner has been adjudged bankrupt, or has made a composition with his creditors in satisfaction of his debts or a scheme of arrangement of his affairs, or he has entered into any voluntary arrangement or been subject to an administration order under Part VI of the County Courts Act 1984, particulars of these matters shall be given in the petition.

6.39(3)   [If voluntary arrangement in force] If there is at the date of the petition in force for the debtor a voluntary arrangement under Part VIII of the Act, the particulars required by paragraph (2) above shall contain a statement to that effect and the name and address of the supervisor of the arrangement.

GENERAL NOTE TO RR.6.37–6.39

These rules map out the form and the contents of a debtor's petition (see IA 1986 s.272). Form 6.27 should be employed for such a bankruptcy petition.

6.40   Court in which petition to be filed [Deleted.]

6.40A   Court in which petition to be presented

6.40A(1)   [Debtor resident in England and Wales] If the debtor is resident in England and Wales, the petition–

(a)   must be presented to the High Court if, for the greater part of the 6 months immediately preceding the presentation of the petition, the debtor–

    (i)   has carried on a business in the London insolvency district; or

    (ii)   has not carried on a business in England and Wales but has resided in the London insolvency district; or

(b)   must be presented to the debtor's own county court (unless paragraph (5) applies) if the debtor–

    (i)   has carried on a business in England and Wales other than in the London insolvency district, or

    (ii)   has not carried on a business in England and Wales and has resided outside the London insolvency district.

6.40A(2)   [Debtor no longer resident in England and Wales] If the debtor is not resident in England and Wales but was resident or carried on business in England and Wales within the 6 months immediately preceding the presentation of the petition, the petition–

(a)   must be presented to the High Court if the debtor–

    (i)   carried on a business in the London insolvency district for a longer period in those 6 months than in any other insolvency district, or

    (ii)   did not carry on a business in England and Wales but resided in the London insolvency district for a longer period in those 6 months than in any other insolvency district; and

(b)   in any other case, may be presented either to the debtor's own county court or to the High Court.

6.40A(3)   [High Court] In a case not falling within either paragraph (1) or (2), the petition must be presented to the High Court.

6.40A(4)   [Debtor's own county court] For the purposes of this Rule, what constitutes the debtor's own county court is to be determined in accordance with Rule 6.9A(3).

6.40A(5)   [Where not possible to present petition to debtor's own county court] Where, for whatever reason, it is not possible for the petition to be presented to the debtor's own county court, the debtor may, with a view to expediting the presentation of the petition, present the petition–

(a)   where Rule 6.9A(3)(a) applies, to–

    (i)   the court for the insolvency district in which the debtor resides, or

    (ii)   whichever court is specified by Schedule 2 to these Rules as being the nearest full time court in relation to–

        (aa)   the court in Rule 6.9A(3)(a), or

        (bb)   where the court in paragraph (i) is a county court, that court; or

(b)   where Rule 6.9A(3)(b) applies, whichever court is specified by Schedule 2 to these Rules as being the nearest full time court in relation to the court in that paragraph.

6.40A(6)   [Where IVA in force for debtor] Notwithstanding any other provision of this Rule, where there is in force for the debtor a voluntary arrangement under Part 8 of the Act, the petition must be presented to the court to which the nominee's report under section 256 was submitted.

6.40A(7) **[Petition to establish appropriate court]** The petition must contain sufficient information to establish that it is presented to the appropriate court.

GENERAL NOTE

Substituted by I(A)R 2010 (SI 2010/686) for former IR r.6.40.

6.41 Statement of affairs

6.41(1) **[Accompanying statement etc.]** The petition shall be accompanied by a statement of the debtor's affairs, verified by a statement of truth.

[FORM 6.28]

6.41(2) **[Application of Section B of Ch.5]** Section B of Chapter 5 below applies with respect to the statement of affairs.

GENERAL NOTE

This supplements IA 1986 s.272(2). Note also rr.6.67, 6.68. See I(A)R 2010 (SI 2010/686).

6.42 Procedure for presentation and filing

6.42(1) **[Filing in court]** The petition and the statement of affairs shall be filed in court, together with three copies of the petition, and one copy of the statement. No petition shall be filed unless there is produced with it the receipt for the deposit payable on presentation.

6.42(2) **[Powers of court]** Subject to paragraph (2A), the court may hear the petition as soon as reasonably practicable. If it does not do so, it shall fix a venue for the hearing.

6.42(2A) **[If petition refers to voluntary arrangement]** If the petition contains particulars of a voluntary arrangement under Part VIII of the Act in force for the debtor, the court shall fix a venue for the hearing and give at least 14 days' notice of it to the supervisor of the arrangement; the supervisor may appear and be heard on the petition.

6.42(3) **[Copies of petition]** Of the three copies of the petition delivered–

(a) one shall be returned to the petitioner, endorsed with any venue fixed;

(b) another, so endorsed, shall be sent by the court to the official receiver; and

(c) the remaining copy shall be retained by the court, to be sent to an insolvency practitioner (if appointed under section 273(2)).

6.42(4) **[Copy of statement of affairs]** The copy of the statement of affairs shall be sent by the court to the official receiver.

6.42(5) [Omitted.]

6.42(6) **[Documents to official receiver]** Where the court hears a petition as soon as reasonably practicable, or it will in the opinion of the court otherwise expedite the delivery of any document to the official receiver, the court may, instead of sending that document to the official receiver, direct the bankrupt as soon as reasonably practicable to deliver it to him.

6.42(7) **[Former supervisor requested as trustee]** Where a petition contains a request for the appointment of a person as trustee in accordance with section 297(5) (appointment of former supervisor as trustee) the person whose appointment is sought shall, not less than 2 business days before the day appointed for hearing the petition, file in court a report including particulars of–

(a) a date on which he gave written notification to creditors bound by the arrangement of the intention to seek his appointment as trustee, such date to be at least 7 business days before the day on which the report under this paragraph is filed, and

(b) details of any response from creditors to that notice, including any objections to his appointment.

GENERAL NOTE

Rule 6.42 was substantially modified by I(A)R 1987. Paragraph (1) was modified by the Insolvency (Amendment) Rules 2005 (SI 2005/527) to reduce the required copies of the statement of affairs to a single copy. This change in turn meant that para.(4) had to be reconstituted. Note the addition of rr.6.42(2A), 6.42(6) and 6.42(7). Changes made by I(A)R 2010 (SI 2010/686) include the change from 10 to 7 days in para.(7) and the omission of para.(5).

6.43 Notice to Chief Land Registrar

6.43 When the petition is filed, the court shall as soon as reasonably practicable send to the Chief Land Registrar notice of the petition, for registration in the register of pending actions.

[FORM 6.14]

6.44 Report of insolvency practitioner

6.44(1) [If court appoints insolvency practitioner] If the court under section 273(2) appoints an insolvency practitioner to act in the debtor's case, it shall as soon as reasonably practicable–

(a) send to the person appointed–

    (i) a sealed copy of the order of appointment, and

    (ii) copies of the petition and statement of affairs,

(b) fix a venue for the insolvency practitioner's report to be considered, and

(c) send notice of the venue to the insolvency practitioner and the debtor.

[FORM 6.29]

6.44(2) [Insolvency practitioner's report] The insolvency practitioner shall file his report in court and send one copy of it to the debtor, so as to be in his hands not less than 3 business days before the date fixed for consideration of the report, and a further copy to the official receiver.

6.44(3) [Debtor's attendance etc.] The debtor is entitled to attend when the report is considered, and shall attend if so directed by the court. If he attends, the court shall hear any representations which he makes with respect to any of the matters dealt with in the report.

6.44(4) [Omitted by the Insolvency (Amendment) Rules 1987 (SI 1987/1919), r.3(1), Sch., Pt 1, para.101(2) as from January 11, 1988.]

GENERAL NOTE

This adds to IA 1986 s.273(2) (appointment of insolvency practitioner in small bankruptcies). It deals with the form of the court's order (see Form 6.29), and the production of the report under IA 1986 s.274.

    Rule 6.44(2) was amended to give the official receiver early access to the report. See also I(A)R 2010 (SI 2010/686).

6.45 Settlement and content of bankruptcy order

6.45(1) [Order to be settled by court] The bankruptcy order shall be settled by the court.

[FORM 6.30]

6.45(2) [Contents of order] The order shall–

(a) state the date of the presentation of the petition on which the order is made, and the date and time of the making of the order, and

(b) contain a notice referring to the bankrupt's duties in relation to the official receiver under section 291, and in particular to the bankrupt's duty to give the official receiver such inventory of the bankrupt's estate and such other information, and attend on the official receiver at such times, as the official receiver may reasonably require.

6.45(3) **[Order staying proceedings]** Subject to section 346 (effect of bankruptcy on enforcement procedures), the order may include provision staying any action or proceeding against the bankrupt.

6.45(4) **[Where bankrupt represented by solicitor]** Where the bankrupt is represented by a solicitor, the order shall be endorsed with the latter's name, address, telephone number and reference.

GENERAL NOTE

Here the main change made by I(A)R 2010 (SI 2010/686) is the replacing of para.(2)(b).

6.46 Action to follow making of order

6.46(1) **[Copy orders to official receiver etc.]** At least two sealed copies of the bankruptcy order shall be sent as soon as reasonably practicable by the court to the official receiver, who must (unless the official receiver is satisfied that the bankrupt has already received a copy of the order) as soon as reasonably practicable send one of them to the bankrupt.

6.46(2) **[Official receiver to send notice etc.]** Subject to the next paragraph, on receipt of the sealed copies of the bankruptcy order, the official receiver–

(a) as soon as reasonably practicable shall–

   (i) send notice of the making of the order to the Chief Land Registrar, for registration in the register of writs and orders affecting land; and

   (ii) cause notice of the order to be gazetted; and

(b) may cause notice of the order to be advertised in such other manner as the official receiver thinks fit.

[FORM 6.26]

6.46(2A) **[Additional contents of notice under r.6.46(2)(b), (c)]** In addition to the standard contents, the notice to be gazetted under paragraph (2)(b) and any notice to be advertised under paragraph (2)(c) must state–

(a) that a bankruptcy order has been made against the bankrupt;

(b) the date and time of making of the bankruptcy order;

(c) that the bankruptcy order was made on the debtor's own petition; and

(d) the date of presentation of the petition.

6.46(3) **[Suspension of action under r.6.46(2)]** The court may, on the application of the bankrupt or a creditor, order the official receiver to suspend action under paragraph (2) and Rule 6A.4(2), pending a further order of the court.

6.46(3A) **[Application supported by witness statement]** An application under this paragraph must be supported by a witness statement stating the grounds on which it is made.

6.46(4) **[Where order made under r.6.46(3)]** Where an order is made under paragraph (3), the applicant shall as soon as reasonably practicable deliver a copy of it to the official receiver.

GENERAL NOTE

This regulates the dissemination, advertisement and gazetting of the order. Note the use of Form 6.26 and the connection with r.6.43.

The Insolvency (Amendment) Rules 2009 (SI 2009/642) modified this rule with effect from April 6, 2009 by substituting a new para.(2).

The reference in r.6.46(3) to r.6A.4(2) was introduced by the Insolvency (Amendment) Rules 2005 (SI 2005/527) in substitution for the redundant reference to r.6.223(B).

Note insertion of paras (2A) and (3A) by I(A)R 2010 (SI 2010/686).

6.46A   Expenses of voluntary arrangement

6.46A   Where a bankruptcy order is made on a debtor's petition and there is at the time of the petition in force for the debtor a voluntary arrangement under Part VIII of the Act, any expenses properly incurred as expenses of the administration of the arrangement in question shall be a first charge on the bankrupt's estate.

6.47   Amendment of title of proceedings

6.47(1)   [Application for amendment] At any time after the making of the bankruptcy order, the official receiver or the trustee may apply to the court for an order amending the full title of the proceedings.

6.47(2)   [Notice to Chief Land Registrar] Where such an order is made, as soon as reasonably practicable the official receiver shall send notice of it to the Chief Land Registrar for corresponding amendment of the register.

6.47(3)   [Gazetting and advertisement of order] Where the official receiver thinks fit, notice of the order–

   (a)   as soon as reasonably practicable shall be gazetted; and

   (b)   may be advertised in such other manner as the official receiver thinks fit.

6.47(4)   [Additional contents of notice under r.6.47(3)] In addition to the standard contents, the notice under paragraph (3) must–

   (a)   state that an amendment to the full title of the proceedings has been made; and

   (b)   specify the amendment.

GENERAL NOTE

The category of newspapers that can be used for placing notices has been extended by I(A)R 1991 (SI 1991/495). See the comment on r.6.46(2)(b) above. Note the change made by the Insolvency (Amendment) Rules 2009 (SI 2009/642) with effect from April 6, 2009. This change involved substituting a new para.(2) and adding a new para.(3). I(A)R 2010 (SI 2010/686) introduces a new para.(4).

6.48   Certificate of summary administration [Revoked.]

6.49   Duty of official receiver in summary administration [Revoked.]

6.50   Revocation of certificate of summary administration [Revoked.]

GENERAL NOTE TO RR.6.48–6.50

These rules provided guidance on the operation of summary administrations (see IA 1986 s.275). Rule 6.50 was to be viewed in the light of s.275(3). They were revoked by I(A)R 2003 (SI 2003/1730) with effect from April 1, 2004.

CHAPTER 4

THE INTERIM RECEIVER

6.51   Application for appointment of interim receiver

6.51(1)   An application to the court for the appointment of an interim receiver under section 286 may be made by–

(a) a creditor;

(b) the debtor;

(c) an insolvency practitioner appointed under section 273(2);

(d) a temporary administrator, or

(e) a member State liquidator appointed in main proceedings.

6.51(2) [Witness statement in support] The application must be supported by a witness statement stating–

(a) the grounds on which it is proposed that the interim receiver should be appointed,

(b) whether or not the official receiver has been informed of the application and, if so, has been furnished with a copy of it,

(c) whether to the applicant's knowledge there has been proposed or is in force a voluntary arrangement under Part VIII of the Act, and

(d) the applicant's estimate of the value of the property or business in respect of which the interim receiver is to be appointed.

6.51(3) [If insolvency practitioner to be interim receiver] If an insolvency practitioner has been appointed under section 273, and it is proposed that he (and not the official receiver) should be appointed interim receiver, and it is not the insolvency practitioner himself who is the applicant under this Rule, the witness statement under paragraph (2) must state that he has consented to act.

6.51(4) [Copies of application and witness statement] The applicant shall send copies of the application and the witness statement to the person proposed to be appointed interim receiver. If that person is the official receiver and an insolvency practitioner has been appointed under section 273 (and he is not himself the applicant), copies of the application and affidavit shall be sent by the applicant to the insolvency practitioner.

If, in any case where a copy of the application is to be sent to a person under this paragraph, it is for any reason not practicable to send a copy, that person must be informed of the application in sufficient time to enable him to be present at the hearing.

6.51(5) [Appearances] The official receiver and (if appointed) the insolvency practitioner may attend the hearing of the application and make representations.

6.51(6) [Powers of court] The court may on the application, if satisfied that sufficient grounds are shown for the appointment, make it on such terms as it thinks fit.

(See General Note after r.6.57.) IR 6.51(1) was reconstituted by Insolvency (Amendment) Rules 2002 (SI 2002/1307) with effect from May 31, 2002 to cater for the advent of EC Council Regulation 1346/2000 on Insolvency Proceedings. The previous references to affidavits have been replaced by I(A)R 2010 (SI 2010/686).

6.52 Order of appointment

6.52(1) [Contents of order] The order appointing the interim receiver shall state the nature and a short description of the property of which the person appointed is to take possession, and the duties to be performed by him in relation to the debtor's affairs.

[FORM 6.32]

6.52(2) [Sealed copies] The court shall, as soon as reasonably practicable after the order is made, send 2 sealed copies of it to the person appointed interim receiver (one of which shall be sent by him as soon as reasonably practicable to the debtor).

(See General Note after r.6.57.)

6.53 Deposit

6.53(1) **[Security for official receiver's remuneration etc.]** Before an order appointing the official receiver as interim receiver is issued, the applicant for it shall deposit with him, or otherwise secure to his satisfaction, such sum as the court directs to cover his remuneration and expenses.

6.53(2) **[Sufficiency of deposit etc.]** If the sum deposited or secured subsequently proves to be insufficient, the court may, on application by the official receiver, order that an additional sum be deposited or secured. If the order is not complied with within 2 business days after service on the person to whom the order is directed, the court may discharge the order appointing the interim receiver.

6.53(3) **[Repayment etc. of deposit]** If a bankruptcy order is made after an interim receiver has been appointed, any money deposited under this Rule shall (unless it is required by reason of insufficiency of assets for payment of remuneration and expenses of the interim receiver, or the deposit was made by the debtor out of his own property) be repaid to the person depositing it (or as that person may direct) out of the bankrupt's estate, in the prescribed order of priority.

(See General Note after r.6.57.) See I(A)R 2010 (SI 2010/686).

6.54 Security

6.54(1) **[Application of Rule]** The following applies where an insolvency practitioner is appointed to be interim receiver under section 286(2).

6.54(2) **[Cost of providing security]** The cost of providing the security required under the Act shall be paid in the first instance by the interim receiver; but–

(a) if a bankruptcy order is not made, the person so appointed is entitled to be reimbursed out of the property of the debtor, and the court may make an order on the debtor accordingly, and

(b) if a bankruptcy order is made, he is entitled to be reimbursed out of the estate in the prescribed order of priority.

(See General Note after r.6.57.)

6.55 Failure to give or keep up security

6.55(1) **[Powers of court]** If the interim receiver fails to give or keep up his security, the court may remove him, and make such order as it thinks fit as to costs.

6.55(2) **[Directions on removal etc.]** If an order is made under this Rule removing the interim receiver, or discharging the order appointing him, the court shall give directions as to whether any, and if so what, steps should be taken for the appointment of another person in his place.

(See General Note after r.6.57.)

6.56 Remuneration

6.56(1) **[To be fixed by court]** The remuneration of the interim receiver (other than the official receiver) shall be fixed by the court from time to time on his application.

6.56(2) **[Matters to be taken into account]** In fixing the interim receiver's remuneration, the court shall take into account–

(a) the time properly given by him (as interim receiver) and his staff in attending to the debtor's affairs,

(b) the complexity (or otherwise) of the case,

(c) any respects in which, in connection with the debtor's affairs, there falls on the interim receiver any responsibility of an exceptional kind or degree,

(d)   the effectiveness with which the interim receiver appears to be carrying out, or to have carried out, his duties as such, and

(e)   the value and nature of the property with which he has to deal.

6.56(3)   [Source of payment of remuneration etc.] Without prejudice to any order the court may make as to costs, the interim receiver's remuneration (whether the official receiver or another) shall be paid to him, and the amount of any expenses incurred by him (including the remuneration and expenses of any special manager appointed under section 370) reimbursed–

(a)   if a bankruptcy order is not made, out of the property of the debtor, and

(b)   if a bankruptcy order is made, out of the estate in the prescribed order of priority,

or, in either case (the relevant funds being insufficient), out of the deposit under Rule 6.53.

6.56(4)   [Power of retention] Unless the court otherwise directs, in a case falling within paragraph (3)(a) above the interim receiver may retain out of the debtor's property such sums or property as are or may be required for meeting his remuneration and expenses.

(See General Note after r.6.57.)

6.57   Termination of appointment

6.57(1)   [Termination by court] The appointment of the interim receiver may be terminated by the court on his application, or on that of the official receiver, the debtor or any creditor.

6.57(2)   [Directions on termination] If the interim receiver's appointment terminates, in consequence of the dismissal of the bankruptcy petition or otherwise, the court may give such directions as it thinks fit with respect to the accounts of his administration and any other matters which it thinks appropriate.

6.57(3)   [Omitted by the Insolvency (Amendment) Rules 1987 (SI 1987/1919) r.3(1), Sch. Pt 1 para.104 as from January 11, 1988.]

GENERAL NOTE TO RR.6.51–6.57

These rules all deal with the appointment of an interim receiver to protect the debtor's assets under IA 1986 s.286. The application procedure is detailed. The order of appointment takes the style of Form 6.32. A deposit may be required from the applicant. The interim receiver may be required to give security; failure to do so could result in his removal by the court. The court is to determine the remuneration of an interim receiver. The question of the termination of his appointment is governed by r.6.57, which should be cross-referenced to IA 1986 s.286(7).

CHAPTER 5

DISCLOSURE BY BANKRUPT WITH RESPECT TO THE STATE OF HIS AFFAIRS

Section A: Creditor's petition

6.58   Preliminary

6.58   The Rules in this Section apply with respect to the statement of affairs required by section 288(1) to be submitted by the bankrupt, following a bankruptcy order made on a creditor's petition, and the further and other disclosure which is required of him in that case.

(See General Note after r.6.59.)

6.59   The statement of affairs

6.59   The bankrupt's statement of affairs shall be in Form 6.33, and contain all the particulars required by that form.

[FORM 6.33A]

These rules expand upon the provisions of IA 1986 s.288.

6.60   Verification and filing

6.60(1)   [Instructions for preparation of statement] The bankrupt shall be furnished by the official receiver with instructions for the preparation of his statement of affairs, and the forms required for that purpose.

6.60(2)   [Verification and delivery] The statement of affairs shall be verified by a statement of truth and delivered to the official receiver, together with one copy.

6.60(3)   [Filing in court] The official receiver shall file the verified statement in court.

6.60(4)   [Omitted.]

GENERAL NOTE

Paragraph (4) is omitted by I(A)R 2010 (SI 2010/686).

6.61   Limited disclosure

6.61(1)   [Official receiver may apply to court] Where the official receiver thinks that it would prejudice the conduct of the bankruptcy or might reasonably be expected to lead to violence against any person for the whole or part of the statement of affairs to be disclosed, he may apply to the court for an order of limited disclosure in respect of the statement, or any specified part of it.

6.61(2)   [Powers of court] The court may on the application order that the statement or, as the case may be, the specified part of it be not filed in court, or that it is to be filed separately and not be open to inspection otherwise than with permission of the court.

GENERAL NOTE

This is the standard provision in the rules enabling the court to censor sensitive information. Paragraph (1) is extended by I(A)R 2010 (SI 2010/686) to protect personal safety.

6.62   Release from duty to submit statement of affairs; extension of time

6.62(1)   [Exercise of s.288(3) power] The power of the official receiver under section 288(3) to release the bankrupt from his duty to submit a statement of affairs, or to grant an extension of time, may be exercised at the official receiver's own discretion, or at the bankrupt's request.

6.62(2)   [Bankrupt may apply to court] The bankrupt may, if he requests a release or extension of time and it is refused by the official receiver, apply to the court for it.

6.62(3)   [Court may dismiss application etc.] The court may, if it thinks that no sufficient cause is shown for the application, dismiss it; but it shall not do so unless the bankrupt has had an opportunity to attend the court for a hearing, of which he has been given at least 5 business days' notice.

If the application is not dismissed under this paragraph, the court shall fix a venue for it to be heard, and give notice but which is without notice to any other party to the bankrupt accordingly.

6.62(4)   [Bankrupt to send notice to official receiver] The bankrupt shall, at least 14 days before the hearing, send to the official receiver a notice stating the venue and accompanied by a copy of the application, and of any evidence which he (the bankrupt) intends to adduce in support of it.

6.62(5) **[Appearance etc. by official receiver]** The official receiver may appear and be heard on the application; and, whether or not he appears, he may file a written report of any matters which he considers ought to be drawn to the court's attention.

If such a report is filed, a copy of it shall be sent by the official receiver to the bankrupt, not later than 5 business days before the hearing.

6.62(6) **[Sealed copies of order]** Sealed copies of any order made on the application shall be sent by the court to the bankrupt and the official receiver.

6.62(7) **[Bankrupt's costs]** On any application under this Rule the bankrupt's costs shall be paid in any event by him and, unless the court otherwise orders, no allowance towards them shall be made out of the estate.

General Note

This builds upon IA 1986 s.288(3). The references to ex parte hearings have been removed by I(A)R 2010 (SI 2010/686) and the seven-day period has been changed to five business days.

6.63   Expenses of statement of affairs

6.63(1) **[Persons assisting in preparation of statement]** If the bankrupt cannot himself prepare a proper statement of affairs, the official receiver may, at the expense of the estate, employ some person or persons to assist in the preparation of the statement.

6.63(2) **[Allowance towards expenses]** At the request of the bankrupt, made on the grounds that he cannot himself prepare a proper statement, the official receiver may authorise an allowance payable out of the estate (in accordance with the prescribed order of priority) towards expenses to be incurred by the bankrupt in employing some person or persons to assist him in preparing it.

6.63(3) **[Estimate of expenses]** Any such request by the bankrupt shall be accompanied by an estimate of the expenses involved; and the official receiver shall only authorise the employment of a named person or a named firm, being in either case approved by him.

6.63(4) **[Authorisation subject to conditions]** An authorisation given by the official receiver under this Rule shall be subject to such conditions (if any) as he thinks fit to impose with respect to the manner in which any person may obtain access to relevant books and papers.

6.63(5) **[Effect of Rule]** Nothing in this Rule relieves the bankrupt from any obligation with respect to the preparation, verification and submission of his statement of affairs, or to the provision of information to the official receiver or the trustee.

General Note

This deals with the funding of the statement of affairs where the bankrupt is unable to prepare it himself.

6.64   Requirement to submit accounts

6.64(1) **[At request of official receiver]** The bankrupt shall, at the request of the official receiver, furnish him with accounts relating to his affairs of such nature, as at such date and for such period as he may specify.

6.64(2) **[Beginning of specified period]** The period specified may begin from a date up to 3 years preceding the date of the presentation of the bankruptcy petition.

6.64(3) **[Accounts for earlier period]** The court may, on the official receiver's application, require accounts in respect of any earlier period.

6.64(4) **[Application of r.6.63]** Rule 6.63 applies (with the necessary modifications) in relation to accounts to be furnished under this Rule as it applies in relation to the statement of affairs.

(See General Note after r.6.66.)

6.65   Submission and filing of accounts

6.65(1)   [Verification and delivery] The accounts to be furnished under Rule 6.64 shall, if the official receiver so requires, be verified by a statement of truth, and (whether or not so verified) delivered to him within 21 days of the request under Rule 6.64(1), or such longer period as he may allow.

6.65(2) [Omitted.]

(See General Note after r.6.66.) I(A)R 2010 (SI 2010/686) removes para.(2) to ease the regulatory burden.

6.66   Further disclosure

6.66(1)   [Official receiver may require further information] The official receiver may at any time require the bankrupt to submit (in writing) further information amplifying, modifying or explaining any matter contained in his statement of affairs, or in accounts submitted in pursuance of the Act or the Rules.

6.66(2)   [Verification and delivery] The information shall, if the official receiver so directs, be verified by a statement of truth, and (whether or not so verified) delivered to him within 21 days of the requirement under this Rule, or such longer period as he may allow.

6.66(3) [Omitted.]

GENERAL NOTE TO RR.6.64–6.66

These provisions clarify IA 1986 s.288(2)(b). Note how far back the official receiver can request accounts for under r.6.64(2). Rule 6.66(3) was removed by I(A)R 2010 (SI 2010/686) to lighten the regulatory burden.

Section B: Debtor's petition

6.67   Preliminary

6.67   The Rules in this Section apply with respect to the statement of affairs required in the case of a person petitioning for a bankruptcy order to be made against him, and the further disclosure which is required of him in that case.

GENERAL NOTE

This provision and r.6.68 are to be linked with r.6.41.

6.68   Contents of statement

6.68   The statement of affairs required by Rule 6.41 to accompany the debtor's petition shall be in Form 6.28, and contain all the particulars required by that form.

[FORM 6.28]

6.69   Requirement to submit accounts

6.69(1)   [At request of official receiver] The bankrupt shall, at the request of the official receiver, furnish him with accounts relating to his affairs of such nature, as at such date and for such period as he may specify.

6.69(2)   [Beginning of specified period] The period specified may begin from a date up to 3 years preceding the date of the presentation of the bankruptcy petition.

6.69(3)   [Accounts for earlier period] The court may, on the official receiver's application, require accounts in respect of any earlier period.

(See General Note after r.6.72.)

6.70 Submission and filing of accounts

6.70(1) [Verification and delivery] The accounts to be furnished under Rule 6.69 shall, if the official receiver so requires, be verified by a statement of truth, and (whether or not so verified) delivered to him within 21 days of the request under Rule 6.69, or such longer period as he may allow.

6.70(2) [Omitted.]

(See General Note after r.6.72.) Paragraph (2) was removed by I(A)R 2010 (SI 2010/686) as a deregulation measure.

6.71 Expenses of preparing accounts

6.71(1) [Persons assisting in preparation of accounts] If the bankrupt cannot himself prepare proper accounts under Rule 6.69, the official receiver may, at the expense of the estate, employ some person or persons to assist in their preparation.

6.71(2) [Allowance towards expenses] At the request of the bankrupt, made on the grounds that he cannot himself prepare the accounts, the official receiver may authorise an allowance payable out of the estate (in accordance with the prescribed order of priority) towards expenses to be incurred by the bankrupt in employing some person or persons to assist him in their preparation.

6.71(3) [Estimate of expenses] Any such request by the bankrupt shall be accompanied by an estimate of the expenses involved; and the official receiver shall only authorise the employment of a named person or a named firm, being in either case approved by him.

6.71(4) [Authorisation subject to conditions] An authorisation given by the official receiver under this Rule shall be subject to such conditions (if any) as he thinks fit to impose with respect to the manner in which any person may obtain access to relevant books and papers.

6.71(5) [Effect of Rule] Nothing in this Rule relieves the bankrupt from any obligation with respect to the preparation and submission of accounts, or to the provision of information to the official receiver or the trustee.

(See General Note after r.6.72.)

6.72 Further disclosure

6.72(1) [Official receiver may require further information] The official receiver may at any time require the bankrupt to submit (in writing) further information amplifying, modifying or explaining any matter contained in his statement of affairs, or in accounts submitted in pursuance of the Act or the Rules.

6.72(2) [Verification and delivery] The information shall, if the official receiver so directs, be verified by a statement of truth, and (whether or not so verified) delivered to him within 21 days from the date of the requirement under paragraph (1), or such longer period as he may allow.

6.72(3) [Omitted.]

GENERAL NOTE TO RR.6.69–6.72

These provisions largely mirror rr.6.63–6.66. I(A)R 2010 (SI 2010/686) removes r.6.72(3) to ease burdens.

CHAPTER 6

INFORMATION TO CREDITORS

6.73 General duty of official receiver

6.73(1) [Report to creditors] In accordance with this Chapter, the official receiver shall, at least once after the making of the bankruptcy order, send a report to creditors with respect to the bankruptcy proceedings, and the state of the bankrupt's affairs.

6.73(2)   [Omitted.]

GENERAL NOTE

The rules in Chapter 6 impose additional duties upon the official receiver to keep creditors informed. I(A)R 2010 (SI 2010/686) deletes para.(2).

6.74   Those entitled to be informed

6.74   Any reference in this Chapter to creditors is to creditors of the bankrupt who are known to the official receiver.

GENERAL NOTE

This narrows the definition of "creditors". See I(A)R 2010 (SI 2010/686).

6.75   Report where statement of affairs lodged

6.75(1)   **[Report to creditors]** Where the bankrupt has submitted a statement of affairs, the official receiver shall send out to creditors a report containing a summary of the statement (if he thinks fit, as amplified, modified or explained by virtue of Rule 6.66 or 6.72) and such observations (if any) as he thinks fit to make with respect to it or to the bankrupt's affairs generally.

6.75(2)   **[Where no need to comply with r.6.75(1)]** The official receiver need not comply with paragraph (1) if he has previously reported to creditors with respect to the bankrupt's affairs (so far as known to him) and he is of opinion that there are no additional matters which ought to be brought to their attention.

GENERAL NOTE

This develops IA 1986 s.288 and relates to the dissemination of the statement of affairs. See I(A)R 2010 (SI 2010/686).

6.76   Statement of affairs dispensed with

6.76(1)   **[Application of Rule]** This Rule applies where the bankrupt has been released from the obligation to submit a statement of affairs.

6.76(2)   **[Report to creditors]** As soon as may be after the release has been granted, the official receiver shall send to creditors a report containing a summary of the bankrupt's affairs (so far as within his knowledge), and his observations (if any) with respect to it or the bankrupt's affairs generally.

6.76(3)   **[Where no need to comply with r.6.76(2)]** The official receiver need not comply with paragraph (2) if he has previously reported to creditors with respect to the bankrupt's affairs (so far as known to him) and he is of opinion that there are no additional matters which ought to be brought to their attention.

GENERAL NOTE

If IA 1986 s.288(3)(a) has been activated, the official receiver must supply a report to the creditors dealing with the financial position of the bankrupt.

6.77   General rule as to reporting

6.77(1)   **[Powers of court]** The court may, on the official receiver's application, relieve him of any duty imposed on him by this Chapter of the Rules, or authorise him to carry out the duty in a way other than there required.

6.77(2) **[Matters for court to consider]** In considering whether to act as above, the court shall have regard to the cost of carrying out the duty, to the amount of the funds available in the estate, and to the extent of the interest of creditors or any particular class of them.

(See General Note after r.6.78.)

6.78   Bankruptcy order annulled

6.78 If the bankruptcy order is annulled, the duty of the official receiver to send reports under the preceding Rules in this Chapter ceases.

GENERAL NOTE TO RR.6.77, 6.78

These rules modify the above obligations which have been imposed on the official receiver. Note the court's power of waiver under r.6.77.

6.78A   Reports to creditors

6.78A(1) **["Progress report"]** "Progress report" means a report which includes–

(a)   details of the court where the proceedings are and the relevant court reference number;

(b)   the bankrupt's name;

(c)   the title of the proceedings;

(d)   full details of the trustee's name and address and date of appointment, including any changes in office-holder;

(e)   details of the basis fixed for the remuneration of the trustee under Rule 6.138 (or if not fixed at the date of the report, the steps taken during the period of the report to fix it);

(f)   if the basis of remuneration has been fixed, a statement of–

   (i)   the remuneration charged by the trustee during the period of the report (subject to paragraph (2)), and

   (ii)   where the report is the first to be made after the basis has been fixed, the remuneration charged by the trustee during the periods covered by the previous reports (subject to paragraph (2)), together with a description of the things done by the trustee during those periods in respect of which the remuneration was charged,

irrespective in either case of whether payment was made in respect of that remuneration during that period;

(g)   a statement of the expenses incurred by the trustee during the period of the report, irrespective of whether payment was made in respect of them during that period;

(h)   details of progress during the period of the report, including a receipts and payments account in the form of an abstract showing receipts and payments during the period of the report;

(j)   details of any assets that remain to be realised;

(k)   a statement of the creditors' right to request information under Rule 6.78C and their right to challenge the trustee's remuneration and expenses under Rule 6.142; and

(l)   any other relevant information for the creditors.

6.78A(2) **[Where basis of remuneration a set amount]** Where the basis for the remuneration is a set amount under Rule 6.138(2)(c), it may be shown as that amount without any apportionment to the period of the report.

6.78A(3) **[Period of progress report]** The progress report must, except where paragraph (4) or (5) applies, cover the period of 1 year commencing on the date on which the trustee is appointed and every subsequent period of 1 year.

6.78A(4)   [End of period] The period to be covered by a progress report ends on the date when a trustee ceases to act, and the period to be covered by each subsequent progress report is each successive period of 1 year beginning immediately after that date (subject to the further application of this paragraph when another trustee ceases to act).

6.78A(5)   [No progress report after draft final report to creditors] A progress report is not required for any period which ends after the trustee has sent a draft report to creditors under Rule 6.78B (final report to creditors).

6.78A(6)   [Time limit for sending progress reports] The trustee must send a copy of the progress report to the creditors within 2 months of the end of the period covered by the report.

6.78A(7)   [Power of court re time limit and contents] The court may, on the trustee's application, extend the period of 2 months mentioned in paragraph (6), or make such other order in respect of the content of the report as it thinks just.

6.78A(8)   [Non-application to official receiver] This Rule does not apply where the trustee is the official receiver.

GENERAL NOTE

Inserted by I(A)R 2010 (SI 2010/686).

6.78B   Final report to creditors and bankrupt

6.78B(1)   [Time limit for draft final report] The trustee must, at least 8 weeks before holding a final meeting in accordance with section 331, send to each creditor known to the trustee and to the bankrupt a draft of the report which the trustee intends to lay before the meeting under Rule 6.137.

6.78B(2)   [Contents of draft report] The draft report must–

(a)   contain such matters and be in such terms as would comply with Rule 6.137 if the report were to be laid before a meeting as soon as reasonably practicable after the draft had been sent to creditors, and

(b)   be accompanied by a statement of the creditors' right to request information under Rule 6.78C and their right to challenge the trustee's remuneration and expenses under Rule 6.142.

6.78B(3)   [No draft report to be sent before intention to declare dividend] The trustee may not send a draft report to creditors under this Rule before giving notice–

(a)   under Rule 11.2 of intention to declare a final dividend, or

(b)   under Rule 11.7 that no dividend or further dividend will be declared.

6.78B(4)   [No final meeting if application re excessive remuneration outstanding] If any creditor has applied to the court under Rule 6.142 and given a copy of the application to the trustee, the final meeting may not be held until the application (including any appeal) has been disposed of and the trustee has complied with any order of the court.

6.78B(5)   [Non-application to official receiver] This Rule does not apply where the trustee is the official receiver.

GENERAL NOTE

Introduced via I(A)R 2010 (SI 2010/686).

6.78C   Creditors' request for further information

6.78C(1)   [Duty of trustee where request re remuneration/expenses in progress report] If–

(a)   within the period mentioned in paragraph (2)–

(i)   a secured creditor, or

(ii) an unsecured creditor with the concurrence of at least 5% in value of the unsecured creditors (including the creditor in question), or

(b) with the permission of the court upon an application made within the period mentioned in paragraph (2), any unsecured creditor,

makes a request in writing to the trustee for further information about remuneration or expenses set out in a progress report under Rule 6.78A(1)(f) or (g) or in a draft report under Rule 6.78B, the trustee must, within 14 days of receipt of the request, comply with paragraph (3) except to the extent that the request is in respect of matter in a draft report under Rule 6.78B or a progress report required by Rule 6.126 which (in either case) was previously included in a progress report not required by Rule 6.126.

6.78C(2)   [Time limit for request under r.6.78C(1)(a)] The period referred to in paragraph (1)(a) is–

(a) 7 business days of receipt of the progress report where it is required by Rule 6.126, and

(b) 21 days of receipt of the report or draft report in any other case.

6.78C(3)   [Compliance by trustee] The trustee complies with this paragraph by either–

(a) providing all of the information asked for,

(b) so far as the trustee considers that–

(i)   the time or cost of preparation of the information would be excessive, or

(ii) disclosure of the information would be prejudicial to the conduct of the bankruptcy or might reasonably be expected to lead to violence against any person, or

(iii) the trustee is subject to an obligation of confidentiality in respect of the information,

giving reasons for not providing all of the information.

6.78C(4)   [Application by creditor] Any creditor, who need not be the same as the creditor who asked for the information, may apply to the court within 21 days of–

(a) the giving by the trustee of reasons for not providing all of the information asked for, or

(b) the expiry of the 14 days provided for in paragraph (1),

and the court may make such order as it thinks just.

6.78C(5)   [Court order may extend period] Without prejudice to the generality of paragraph (4), the order of the court under that paragraph may extend the period of 8 weeks or, as the case may be, 4 weeks provided for in Rule 6.142(1B) by such further period as the court thinks just.

6.78C(6)   [Non-application to official receiver] This Rule does not apply where the trustee is the official receiver.

GENERAL NOTE

Introduced via I(A)R 2010 (SI 2010/686).

6.78D   Distribution of property in specie

6.78D(1)   [Account or report] Where there has been a distribution of property to creditors under section 326, the trustee must comply with paragraph (2) in respect of any account or report which the trustee is required to prepare pursuant to any of the following–

(a) section 331 (final meeting);

(b) Rule 6.78A (reports to creditors);

(c)   Rule 6.78B (final report to creditors);

(d)   Rule 6.126 (creditors' meeting to receive trustee's resignation);

(e)   Rule 6.137 (final meeting of creditors).

6.78D(2)   [Duty of trustee to state value of property distributed] The trustee must–

(a)   in any account or summary of receipts and payments which is required to be included in the account or report, state the estimated value of the property distributed amongst the creditors during the period to which the account or report relates, and

(b)   as a note to the account or summary of receipts and payments, provide details of the basis of the valuation.

GENERAL NOTE

Inserted by I(A)R 2010 (SI 2010/686).

CHAPTER 7

CREDITORS' MEETINGS

6.79   First meeting of creditors

6.79(1)   [Venue for meeting etc.] If under section 293(1) the official receiver decides to summon a meeting of creditors, he shall fix a venue for the meeting, not more than 4 months from the date of the bankruptcy order.

6.79(2)   [Notice of meeting] When a venue has been fixed, notice of the meeting shall be given to every creditor of the bankrupt who is known to the official receiver.

6.79(3)   [Time limit for notice] Notice must be given at least 14 days before the date fixed for the meeting.

6.79(4)   [Contents of notice] The notice to creditors must state that proofs and (if applicable) proxies must be lodged at a specified place not later than 12.00 hours on the business day before the date fixed for the meeting in order for creditors to be entitled to vote at the meeting.

6.79(5)   [Gazetting/advertisement of notice] As soon as reasonably practicable, notice of the meeting shall also be gazetted and may be advertised in such other manner as the official receiver thinks fit.

6.79(5A)   [Additional contents of r.6.79(5) notice] In addition to the standard contents, the notice under paragraph (5) must state–

(a)   the purpose for which the meeting is summoned;

(b)   the venue fixed for the meeting; and

(c)   the time and date by which, and place at which, creditors must lodge proxies and hitherto unlodged proofs in order to be entitled to vote at the meeting.

6.79(6)   [Request by creditor under s.294] Where the official receiver receives a request by a creditor under section 294 for a meeting of creditors to be summoned, and it appears to him that the request is properly made in accordance with the Act, he shall–

(a)   withdraw any notice already given by him under section 293(2) (that he has decided not to summon such a meeting), and

(b) fix the venue of the meeting for not more than 3 months from his receipt of the creditor's request, and

(c) act in accordance with paragraphs (2) to (5) above, as if he had decided under section 293(1) to summon the meeting.

[FORM 6.34]

6.79(7) **[Name of meeting]** A meeting summoned by the official receiver under section 293 or 294 is known as "the first meeting of creditors".

GENERAL NOTE

If the official receiver decides to call a first meeting of creditors under IA 1986 s.293, it must take place within four months of the date of the bankruptcy order. The meeting must be properly notified to the court (immediately), and to creditors (who should have 21 days' notice). It should also be advertised. The Insolvency (Amendment) Rules 2009 (SI 2009/642) modified this rule with effect from April 6, 2009 by substituting a new para.(5). Creditors should be given an opportunity to lodge proofs. Rule 6.79(6) develops the provisions of IA 1986 s.294. Note the use of Form 6.34 for the purposes of s.294. For the meaning of "venue" see r.13.6. Substantially amended by I(A)R 2010 (SI 2010/686) including the addition of a new para.(5A).

6.80 Business at first meeting

6.80(1) **[Limitation on resolutions]** At the first meeting of creditors, no resolutions shall be taken other than the following–

(a) a resolution to appoint a named insolvency practitioner to be trustee in bankruptcy or two or more named insolvency practitioners as joint trustees;

(b) a resolution to establish a creditors' committee;

(c) (unless it has been resolved to establish a creditors' committee) a resolution specifying the terms on which the trustee is to be remunerated, or to defer consideration of that matter;

(d) (if, and only if, two or more persons are appointed to act jointly as trustee) a resolution specifying whether acts are to be done by both or all of them, or by only one;

(e) (where the meeting has been requisitioned under section 294) a resolution authorising payment out of the estate, as an expense of the bankruptcy, of the cost of summoning and holding the meeting;

(f) a resolution to adjourn the meeting;

(g) any other resolution which the chairman thinks it right to allow for special reasons.

6.80(2) [Omitted.]

6.80(2A) **[Adjournment]** The meeting may be adjourned, either in accordance with a resolution under paragraph (1)(f) or if the chairman thinks fit, but for not more than 14 days from the date on which it was fixed to commence, subject to any direction of the court.

6.80(2B) **[Time limit for subject adjournment]** If there are subsequently further adjournments, the final adjournment must not be to a day later than 14 days after the date on which the meeting was originally held, subject to any direction of the court.

6.80(2C) **[Lodging proofs and proxies before adjourned meeting]** Where a meeting is adjourned under this Rule, proofs and proxies may be used if lodged at any time up to 12.00 hours on the business day immediately before the adjourned meeting.

GENERAL NOTE

This restricts the agenda of the first meeting of creditors. Note the importance of securing the appointment of a trustee. I(A)R 2010 (SI 2010/686) replaces para.(2) with paras (2A) to (2C).

6.81   General power to call meetings

6.81(1)   **[General power, "the convener"]** The official receiver or the trustee may at any time summon and conduct meetings of creditors for the purpose of ascertaining their wishes in all matters relating to the bankruptcy.

In relation to any meeting of creditors, the person summoning it is referred to as "the convener".

6.81(2)   **[Notice of meeting]** When a venue for the meeting has been fixed, notice of the meeting shall be given by the convener to every creditor who is known to him.

The notice shall be given at least 14 days before the date fixed for the meeting.

[FORM 6.35]

6.81(3)   **[Contents of notice]** The notice must specify the purpose for which the meeting is summoned and state that proofs and (if applicable) proxies must be lodged at a specified place not later than 12.00 hours on the business day before the date fixed for the meeting in order for creditors to be entitled to vote at the meeting.

6.81(4)   **[Gazetting/advertisement of notice]** As soon as reasonably practicable after sending notice of the meeting to the creditors under paragraph (2), the convener must give additional notice of the meeting. Such notice–

   (a)   shall be gazetted; and

   (b)   may be advertised in such other manner as the convenor thinks fit.

6.81(5)   **[Additional contents of notice under r.6.81(4)]** In addition to the standard contents, the notice under paragraph (4) must specify–

   (a)   who summoned the meeting;

   (b)   if the meeting was summoned at the request of a creditor, the fact that it was so summoned and the section of the Act under which it was requested;

   (c)   the purpose for which the meeting is summoned;

   (d)   the venue fixed for the meeting; and

   (e)   the time and date by which, and place at which, creditors must lodge proxies and hitherto unlodged proofs in order to be entitled to vote at the meeting.

GENERAL NOTE

Subsequent meetings of creditors are held normally at the discretion of the official receiver, or trustee (subject to requisitions under r.6.83). Note the Insolvency (Amendment) Rules 2009 (SI 2009/642) (operational from April 6, 2009). The amendment made by these rules involves substituting a new para.(4).

Substantially amended by I(A)R 2010 (SI 2010/686)—this includes a new para.(5).

6.82   The chairman at a meeting

6.82(1)   **[Where convener official receiver]** Where the convener of a meeting is the official receiver, he, or a person nominated by him, shall be chairman.

A nomination under this paragraph shall be in writing, unless the nominee is another official receiver or a deputy official receiver.

6.82(2)   **[Where convener other than official receiver]** Where the convener is other than the official receiver, the chairman shall be he, or a person nominated by him in writing to act.

A person nominated under this paragraph must be either–

   (a)   one who is qualified to act as an insolvency practitioner in relation to the bankrupt, or

   (b)   an employee of the trustee or his firm who is experienced in insolvency matters.

GENERAL NOTE

For the qualification of insolvency practitioners, see IA 1986 Pt XIII.

6.83 Requisitioned meetings

6.83(1) **[Documents to accompany creditors' request]** A request by creditors to the official receiver for a meeting of creditors to be summoned shall be accompanied by–

   (a)   a list of the creditors concurring with the request and the amount of their respective claims in the bankruptcy,

   (b)   from each creditor concurring, written confirmation of his concurrence, and

   (c)   a statement of the purpose of the proposed meeting.

Sub-paragraphs (a) and (b) do not apply if the requisitioning creditor's debt is alone sufficient, without the concurrence of other creditors.

[FORM 6.34]

6.83(2) **[Official receiver to fix venue etc.]** The official receiver, if he considers the request to be properly made in accordance with the Act, shall–

   (a)   fix a venue for the meeting, to take place not more than 28 days from the receipt of the request, and

   (b)   give 14 days' notice of the meeting, and of the venue for it, to creditors.

6.83(3) **[Application of Rule]** Where a request for a creditors' meeting is made to the trustee, this Rule applies to him as it does to the official receiver.

6.83(4) This Rule shall not apply to voluntary arrangements under section 263A.

GENERAL NOTE

This qualifies r.6.81. No minimum level of support is specified here: but see IA 1986 s.294. For the meaning of "venue" see r.13.6. A new para.(4) was introduced by the Insolvency (Amendment) Rules 2003 (SI 2003/1730) to exclude voluntary arrangements covered by s.263A. Note that the timescales here have been conflated by I(A)R 2010 (SI 2010/686).

6.84 Attendance at meetings of bankrupt, etc.

6.84(1) **[Notice to bankrupt]** Whenever a meeting of creditors is summoned, the convener shall give at least 14 days' notice of the meeting to the bankrupt.

[FORM 6.36]

6.84(2) **[Notice of adjournment]** If the meeting is adjourned, the chairman of the meeting shall (unless for any reason it appears to him to be unnecessary or impracticable) give notice of the fact to the bankrupt, if the latter was not himself present at the meeting.

6.84(3) **[Notice that presence required]** The convener may, if he thinks fit, give notice to the bankrupt that he is required to be present, or in attendance.

6.84(4) **[Admission to meetings]** In the case of any meeting, the bankrupt or any other person may, if he has given reasonable notice of his wish to be present, be admitted; but this is at the discretion of the chairman.

The chairman's decision is final as to what (if any) intervention may be made by the bankrupt, or by any other person admitted to the meeting under this paragraph.

6.84(5) **[Adjournment for obtaining attendance]** If the bankrupt is not present, and it is desired to put questions to him, the chairman may adjourn the meeting with a view to obtaining his attendance.

6.84(6) **[Chairman's discretion re questions]** Where the bankrupt is present at a creditors' meeting, only such questions may be put to him as the chairman may in his discretion allow.

GENERAL NOTE

This is largely self-explanatory. Form 6.36 is used to notify the bankrupt. Bankrupts may be forced to attend. Note the wide powers of the chairman of the meeting. Note here the shortening of timescale from 21 to 14 days by I(A)R 2010 (SI 2010/686).

6.85   Notice of meetings by advertisement only

6.85(1) **[Power of court]** In the case of any meeting to be held under the Act or the Rules, the court may order that notice of it be given by advertisement, and not by individual notice to the persons concerned.

6.85(2) **[Matters for court to consider]** In considering whether to act under this Rule, the court shall have regard to the cost of advertisement, to the amount of the funds available in the estate, and to the extent of the interest of creditors or any particular class of them.

6.85(3) **[Additional contents of advertisement]** In addition to the standard contents, the advertisement must state–

(a)   the venue fixed for the meeting;

(b)   that proofs and (if applicable) proxies must be lodged at a specified place not later than 12.00 hours on the business day before the date fixed for the meeting; and

(c)   the date of the court order.

GENERAL NOTE

This is an economy measure that the court may adopt in appropriate circumstances. Note here the removal of public advertisement requirement by I(A)R 2010 (SI 2010/686). A new para.(3) has been substituted and there is clarification on contents of notice.

6.86   Venue of meetings

6.86(1) **[Convenience of venue]** In fixing the venue for a meeting of creditors, the person summoning the meeting shall have regard to the convenience of the creditors.

6.86(2) **[Time of meetings]** Meetings shall in all cases be summoned for commencement between the hours of 10.00 and 16.00 hours on a business day, unless the court otherwise directs.

6.86(3) **[Forms of proxy]** With every notice summoning a creditors' meeting there shall be sent out forms of proxy.

[FORM 8.5]

GENERAL NOTE

For the meaning of "venue" and "business day" see rr.13.6 and 13.13(1).

6.87   Expenses of summoning meetings

6.87(1) **[Security for payment of expenses]** Subject to paragraph (3) below, the expenses of summoning and holding a meeting of creditors at the instance of any person other, than the official receiver or the trustee shall be paid by that person, who shall deposit security for their payment with the trustee or, if no trustee has been appointed, with the official receiver.

6.87(2) **[Appropriate security]** The sum to be deposited shall be such as the trustee or (as the case may be) the official receiver determines to be appropriate; and neither shall act without the deposit having been made.

6.87(3) **[Vote for expenses to be paid out of estate]** Where a meeting is so summoned, it may vote that the expenses of summoning and holding it shall be payable out of the estate, as an expense of the bankruptcy.

6.87(4) **[Repayment of deposit]** To the extent that any deposit made under this Rule is not required for the payment of expenses of summoning and holding the meeting, it shall be repaid to the person who made it.

GENERAL NOTE

This serves as a deterrent to persons wishing to requisition meetings under r.6.83. See IR r.12A.22(7).

6.88 Resolutions

6.88(1) **[Resolution passed by majority in value]** Subject as follows, at a meeting of creditors, a resolution is passed when a majority (in value) of those present and voting, in person or by proxy, have voted in favour of the resolution.

6.88(2) **[Resolution for appointment of trustee]** In the case of a resolution for the appointment of a trustee–

(a) if on any vote there are two nominees for appointment, the person who obtains the most support is appointed;

(b) if there are three or more nominees, and one of them has a clear majority over both or all the others together, that one is appointed; and

(c) in any other case the chairman shall continue to take votes (disregarding at each vote any nominee who has withdrawn and, if no nominee has withdrawn, the nominee who obtained the least support last time), until a clear majority is obtained for any one nominee.

6.88(3) **[Resolution for joint appointment]** The chairman may at any time put to the meeting a resolution for the joint appointment of any two or more nominees.

6.88(4) **[Resolution affecting trustee etc.]** Where a resolution is proposed which affects a person in respect of his remuneration or conduct as trustee, or as proposed or former trustee, the vote of that person, and of any partner or employee of his, shall not be reckoned in the majority required for passing the resolution.

This paragraph applies with respect to a vote given by a person (whether personally or on his behalf by a proxy-holder) either as creditor or as proxy-holder for a creditor (but subject to Rule 8.6 in Part 8 of the Rules).

GENERAL NOTE

Simple majorities are required to pass resolutions. I(A)R 2010 (SI 2010/686) changes the calculation by removing the former proviso in para.(2)(a).

6.88A Resolutions by correspondence

6.88A(1) **[Trustee to give notice of resolution without meeting]** The trustee may seek to obtain the passing of a resolution by creditors without holding a meeting by giving notice of the resolution to every creditor who is entitled to be notified of a meeting at which the resolution could be passed.

6.88A(2) **[Time for receipt of votes and proof]** In order to be counted, votes must be received by the trustee in writing by 12.00 hours on the closing date specified in the notice, and must be accompanied by a proof of debt as required by Rule 6.93(1)(a) unless it has already been lodged under that Rule.

6.88A(3) **[Votes to be disregarding]** If any vote cast by a creditor is received without a proof of debt, or the trustee decides that the creditor is not entitled to vote according to Rules 6.93 to 6.94, then that creditor's vote must be disregarded.

6.88A(4) **[Time limit for closing date]** The closing date shall be set at the discretion of the trustee, but in any event it must not be set less than 14 days from the giving of notice provided for in paragraph (1).

6.88A(5) **[Minimum of one vote required for resolution]** For the resolution to be passed, the trustee must receive at least one valid vote by the closing date specified in the notice.

6.88A(6) **[If no valid vote received]** If no valid vote is received by the closing date specified, the trustee must call a meeting of creditors at which the resolution could be passed.

6.88A(7) **[Requisition for meeting]** Creditors whose debts amount to at least 10% of the bankrupt's total debts may, within 5 business days from the giving of notice provided for in paragraph (1), require the trustee to summon a meeting of creditors to consider the resolution.

6.88A(8) **[Reference to resolution passed at a creditors' meeting]** A reference in these Rules to a resolution passed at a creditors' meeting includes a reference to a resolution passed under this Rule.

6.88A(9) **[Non-application of r.6.88A]** This Rule does not apply in respect of any resolution which the Act requires to be passed at a meeting.

GENERAL NOTE

This is a new provision introduced by I(A)R 2010 (SI 2010/686) enabling use of resolutions by post.

6.89   Chairman of meeting as proxy-holder

6.89   Where the chairman at a meeting holds a proxy for a creditor, which requires him to vote for a particular resolution, and no other person proposes that resolution–

   (a)   he shall himself propose it, unless he considers that there is good reason for not doing so, and

   (b)   if he does not propose it, he shall as soon as reasonably practicable after the meeting notify his principal of the reason why not.

6.90   Suspension of meeting

6.90   Once only in the course of any meeting, the chairman may, in his discretion and without an adjournment, declare the meeting suspended for any period up to one hour.

6.91   Adjournment

6.91(1) **[At chairman's discretion]** The chairman at any meeting may, in his discretion, and shall if the meeting so resolves, adjourn it to such time and place as seems to him to be appropriate in the circumstances.

   This is subject to Rule 6.129(3) in a case where the trustee or his nominee is chairman and a resolution has been proposed for the trustee's removal.

6.91(2) **[Adjournment if inquorate]** If within a period of 30 minutes from the time appointed for the commencement of a meeting a quorum is not present, then the chairman may, at his discretion, adjourn the meeting to such time and place as he may appoint.

6.91(3) **[Period of adjournment]** An adjournment under this Rule shall not be for a period of more than 14 days; and Rule 6.86(1) and (2) applies with regard to the venue of the adjourned meeting.

6.91(4)   [Omitted.]

6.91(4A) **[If no chairman]** If within 30 minutes from the time appointed for commencement of a meeting there is no person present to act as chairman, the meeting stands adjourned to the same time and place in the following week or, if that is not a business day, to the business day immediately following.

6.91(4B) **[Application of r.6.91(4A)]** Paragraph (4A) applies to further adjournments of a final meeting.

6.91(4C) **[Time and place of further adjourned meeting]** In the case of any other meeting, further adjournment must be to the same time and place in the following week or, if either–

(a) that is not a business day, or

(b) whether or not it is a business day, it is later than 14 days after the date on which the meeting in question was originally held,

to the same time and place on the business day immediately preceding which is not later than 14 days after the date on which the meeting in question was originally held.

6.91(5) **[Use of proof and proxies at adjourned meeting]** Where a meeting is adjourned under this Rule, proofs and proxies may be used if lodged at any time up to midday on the business day immediately before the adjourned meeting.

GENERAL NOTE

For the meaning of "venue" and "business day" see rr.13.6 and 13.13(1).
   Rule 6.91(2) was amended to allow the chairman discretion to adjourn.
   Substantially amended by I(A)R 2010 (SI 2010/686) with new paras (4A) to (4C) introduced in lieu of para.(4). The period specified in para.(3) has been reduced to 14 days.

6.92 Quorum

6.92 [Omitted by the Insolvency (Amendment) Rules 1987 (SI 1987/1919) r.3(1), Sch. Pt 1 para.109 as from January 11, 1988.]

GENERAL NOTE

See now r.12A.21.

6.93 Entitlement to vote

6.93(1) **[Conditions for voting]** Subject as follows in this Rule and the next, at a meeting of creditors a person is entitled to vote as a creditor only if–

(a) there has been duly lodged, by the time and date stated in the notice of the meeting, a proof of the debt

  (i) claimed to be due to him from the bankrupt, or

  (ii) in relation to a member State liquidator, is claimed to be due to creditors in proceedings in relation to which he holds office, and

  the claim has been admitted under Rule 6.94 for the purpose of entitlement to vote, and

(b) there has been lodged, by that time and date, any proxy requisite for that entitlement.

6.93(2) **[Powers of court]** The court may, in exceptional circumstances, by order declare the creditors, or any class of them, entitled to vote at creditors' meetings, without being required to prove their debts.
   Where a creditor is so entitled, the court may, on the application of the trustee, make such consequential orders as it thinks fit (as for example an order treating a creditor as having proved his debt for the purpose of permitting payment of dividend).

6.93(3) **[Limitation on voting]** A creditor shall not vote in respect of a debt for an unliquidated amount, or any debt whose value is not ascertained, except where the chairman agrees to put upon the debt an estimated minimum value for the purpose of entitlement to vote and admits his proof for that purpose.

6.93(4) **[Secured creditor]** A secured creditor is entitled to vote only in respect of the balance (if any) of his debt after deducting the value of his security as estimated by him.

6.93(5) **[Further limitation on voting]** A creditor shall not vote in respect of a debt on, or secured by, a current bill of exchange or promissory note, unless he is willing–

(a) to treat the liability to him on the bill or note of every person who is liable on it antecedently to the bankrupt, and against whom a bankruptcy order has not been made (or, in the case of a company, which has not gone into liquidation), as a security in his hands, and

(b) to estimate the value of the security and (for the purpose of entitlement to vote, but not for dividend) to deduct it from his proof.

6.93(6) **[Still further limitation on voting]** No vote shall be cast by virtue of a debt more than once on any resolution put to the meeting.

6.93(7) **[Creditor's vote]** Where–

(a) a creditor is entitled to vote under this Rule and Rule 6.94 (admission of proof),

(b) has lodged his claim in one or more sets of other proceedings, and

(c) votes (either in person or by proxy) on a resolution put to the meeting, only the creditor's vote shall be counted.

6.93(8) **[Member State liquidator]** Where–

(a) a creditor has lodged his claim in more than one set of other proceedings, and

(b) more than one member State liquidator seeks to vote by virtue of that claim,

the entitlement to vote by virtue of that claim is exercisable by the member State liquidator in main proceedings, whether or not the creditor has lodged his claim in the main proceedings.

6.93(9) **["Other proceedings"]** For the purposes of paragraphs (7) and (8), "other proceedings" means main proceedings, secondary proceedings or territorial proceedings in another member State.

General Note

As a general rule, only creditors who have lodged proofs which have been admitted can vote. Note the special rules for persons claiming unliquidated amounts, etc. Note the amendment of r.6.93(1)(a) and the insertion of r.6.93(6)–(9) by the Insolvency (Amendment) Rules 2002 (SI 2002/1307) with effect from May 31, 2002 to cater for the advent of EC Council Regulation 1346/2000 on Insolvency Proceedings. See I(A)R 2010 (SI 2010/686).

6.93A **Chairman's discretion to allow vote**

6.93A At a creditors' meeting, the chairman may allow a creditor to vote, notwithstanding that the creditor has failed to comply with Rule 6.93(1)(a), if satisfied that the failure was due to circumstances beyond the creditor's control.

General Note

This is a new provision introduced by I(A)R 2010 (SI 2010/686) to expand the discretion of the chairman.

6.94 **Admission and rejection of proof**

6.94(1) **[Power of chairman]** At any creditors' meeting the chairman has power to admit or reject a creditor's proof for the purpose of his entitlement to vote; and the power is exercisable with respect to the whole or any part of the proof.

6.94(2) **[Appeal from chairman's decision]** The chairman's decision under this Rule, or in respect of any matter arising under Rule 6.93, is subject to appeal to the court by any creditor, or by the bankrupt.

6.94(3) **[Voting subject to objection]** If the chairman is in doubt whether a proof should be admitted or rejected, he shall mark it as objected to and allow the creditor to vote, subject to his vote being subsequently declared invalid if the objection to the proof is sustained.

6.94(4) **[If chairman's decision reversed etc.]** If on an appeal the chairman's decision is reversed or varied, or a creditor's vote is declared invalid, the court may order that another meeting be summoned, or make such other order as it thinks just.

6.94(4A) **[Time limit for appeal application]** An application to the court by way of appeal under this Rule against a decision of the chairman must be made not later than 21 days after the date of the meeting.

6.94(5) **[Costs re application]** Neither the official receiver nor any person nominated by him to be chairman is personally liable for costs incurred by any person in respect of an application to the court under this Rule; and the chairman (if other than the official receiver or a person so nominated) is not so liable unless the court makes an order to that effect.

GENERAL NOTE

Admission of proofs is a matter for the chairman (subject to an appeal to the court). On r.6.94(2) see *Re Gunningham* [2002] B.P.I.R. 302. A new para.(4A) has been inserted here by I(A)R 2010 (SI 2010/686).

6.95 Record of proceedings

6.95(1) **[Minutes of proceedings]** The chairman at any creditors' meeting shall cause minutes of the proceedings at the meeting, authenticated by him, to be retained by him as part of the records of the bankruptcy.

6.95(2) **[List of creditors attending]** He shall also cause to be made up and kept a list of all the creditors who attended the meeting.

6.95(3) **[Record of resolutions, etc.]** The minutes of the meeting shall include a record of every resolution passed; and if a creditors' committee has been established, the names and addresses of those elected to be members of the committee.

GENERAL NOTE

Paragraph (3) here has been amended by I(A)R 2010 (SI 2010/686).

CHAPTER 8

PROOF OF BANKRUPTCY DEBTS

Section A: Procedure for proving

6.96 Meaning of "prove"

6.96(1) **[Claim to be submitted in writing etc.]** A person claiming to be a creditor of the bankrupt and wishing to recover his debt in whole or in part must (subject to any order of the court under Rule 6.93(2)) submit his claim in writing to the official receiver, where acting as receiver and manager, or to the trustee.

6.96(2) **["Proving" and "proof"]** The creditor is referred to as **"proving"** for his debt; and the document by which he seeks to establish his claim is his **"proof"**.

6.96(3) **["Proof of debt"]** Subject to the next two paragraphs, the proof must be in the form known as **"proof of debt"** (whether the form prescribed by the Rules, or a substantially similar form), which shall be made out by or under the directions of the creditor, and authenticated by him or a person authorised in that behalf.

[FORM 6.37]

6.96(4) **[Debt due to Crown etc.]** Where a debt is due to a Minister of the Crown or a Government Department, the proof need not be in that form, provided that there are shown all such particulars of the debt as are required in the form used by other creditors, and as are relevant in the circumstances.

6.96(5) **[Proof under s.335(5)]** Where an existing trustee proves in a later bankruptcy under section 335(5), the proof must be in Form 6.38.

[FORM 6.38]

6.96(6) [Omitted.]

GENERAL NOTE

This supplements IA 1986 s.322. Paragraph (6) here has been omitted by I(A)R 2010 (SI 2010/686).

6.97   Supply of forms

6.97 A form of proof shall be sent to any creditor of the bankrupt by the official receiver or trustee where the creditor so requests.

GENERAL NOTE

This rule, which deals with the supply of debt proof forms, was substituted by I(A)R 2004 (SI 2004/584) with effect from April 1, 2004 with a less complex version.

6.98   Contents of proof

6.98(1) **[Matters to be stated]** Subject to Rule 6.96(4), the following matters shall be stated in a creditor's proof of debt–

(a)   the creditor's name and address, and, if a company, its company registration number;

(b)   the total amount of his claim (including any Value Added Tax) as at the date of the bankruptcy order, less any deduction under Rule 6.110;

(c)   whether or not that amount includes outstanding uncapitalised interest;

(d)   particulars of how and when the debt was incurred by the debtor;

(e)   particulars of any security held, the date when it was given and the value which the creditor puts upon it

(f)   details of any reservation of title in respect of goods to which the debt refers; and

(g)   the name, and address and authority of the person authenticating the proof (if other than the creditor himself).

6.98(2) **[Specified documents]** There shall be specified in the proof any documents by reference to which the debt can be substantiated; but (subject as follows) it is not essential that such documents be attached to the proof or submitted with it.

6.98(3) **[Production of documents etc.]** The trustee, the official receiver, acting as receiver and manager or the convener or chairman of any meeting, may call for any document or other evidence to be produced to him, where he thinks it necessary for the purpose of substantiating the whole or any part of the claim made in the proof.

GENERAL NOTE

A new r.6.98(1) was substituted by the Insolvency (Amendment No.2) Rules 2004 (SI 2004/1070) r.2 with effect from May 3, 2004 in substitution for r.6.98(1) previously substituted by the Insolvency (Amendment) Rules 2004 (SI 2004/584) r.28 as from April 1, 2004. The later substitution was to correct a drafting error which referred to companies rather than bankrupts. I(A)R 2010 (SI 2010/686) qualifies para.(1)(b).

6.99   Claim established by affidavit [Revoked by I(A)R 2010 (SI 2010/686).]

6.100   Cost of proving

6.100(1)   [Creditor bears cost of proving own debt] Subject as follows, every creditor bears the cost of proving his own debt, including such as may be incurred in providing documents or evidence under Rule 6.98(3).

6.100(2)   [Trustee's costs] Costs incurred by the trustee in estimating the value of a bankruptcy debt under section 322(3) (debts not bearing a certain value) fall on the estate, as an expense of the bankruptcy.

6.100(3)   [Application of r.6.100(1), (2)] Paragraphs (1) and (2) apply unless the court otherwise orders.

6.101   Trustee to allow inspection of proofs

6.101   The trustee shall, so long as proofs lodged with him are in his hands, allow them to be inspected, at all reasonable times on any business day, by any of the following persons–

(a)   any creditor who has submitted his proof of debt (unless his proof has been wholly rejected for purposes of dividend or otherwise),

(b)   the bankrupt, and

(c)   any person acting on behalf of either of the above.

GENERAL NOTE

Proofs are available for inspection by the creditors and the bankrupt and their representatives.

6.102   Proof of licensed moneylender [Revoked by I(A)R 2010 (SI 2010/686).]

6.103   Transmissions of proofs to trustee

6.103(1)   [On trustee's appointment] Where a trustee is appointed, the official receiver shall as soon as reasonably practicable transmit to him all the proofs which he has so far received, together with an itemised list of them.

6.103(2)   [Receipt for proofs] The trustee shall authenticate the list by way of receipt for the proofs, and return it to the official receiver.

6.103(3)   [All later proofs to trustee] From then on, all proofs of debt shall be sent to the trustee and retained by him.

GENERAL NOTE

This deals with the transfer of responsibilities from the official receiver to the trustee.

6.103A   New trustee appointed

6.103A(1)   [Former trustee to transmit proofs and itemised list] If a new trustee is appointed in place of another, the former trustee must as soon as reasonably practicable transmit to the new one all proofs which the former trustee has received, together with an itemised list of them.

6.103A(2)   [New trustee to authenticate and return list] The new trustee must authenticate the list by way of receipt for the proofs, and return it to the former trustee.

6.103A(3)   [All further proofs to new trustee] From then on, all proofs of debt must be sent to and retained by the new trustee.

GENERAL NOTE

This is a new provision inserted by I(A)R 2010 (SI 2010/686).

6.104   Admission and rejection of proofs for dividend

6.104(1)   [Admission] A proof may be admitted for dividend either for the whole amount claimed by the creditor, or for part of that amount.

6.104(2)   [Rejection] If the trustee rejects a proof in whole or in part, he shall prepare a written statement of his reasons for doing so, and send it as soon as reasonably practicable to the creditor.

GENERAL NOTE

For dividend distributions see IA 1986 s.324. Note also Pt 11 of the rules.

6.105   Appeal against decision on proof

6.105(1)   [Application by creditor] If a creditor is dissatisfied with the trustee's decision with respect to his proof (including any decision on the question of preference), he may apply to the court for the decision to be reversed or varied.

     The application must be made within 21 days of his receiving the statement sent under Rule 6.104(2).

6.105(2)   [Application by bankrupt etc.] The bankrupt or any other creditor may, if dissatisfied with the trustee's decision admitting or rejecting the whole or any part of a proof, make such an application within 21 days of becoming aware of the trustee's decision.

6.105(3)   [Venue and notice] Where application is made to the court under this Rule, the court shall fix a venue for the application to be heard, notice of which shall be sent by the applicant to the creditor who lodged the proof in question (if it is not himself) and to the trustee.

6.105(4)   [Relevant proof etc. to be filed in court] The trustee shall, on receipt of the notice, file in court the relevant proof, together (if appropriate) with a copy of the statement sent under Rule 6.104(2).

6.105(5)   [Return of proof] After the application has been heard and determined, the proof shall, unless it has been wholly disallowed, be returned by the court to the trustee.

6.105(6)   [Costs re application] The official receiver is not personally liable for costs incurred by any person in respect of an application under this Rule; and the trustee (if other than the official receiver) is not so liable unless the court makes an order to that effect.

GENERAL NOTE

Rejection of proof under r.6.104 may be appealed against to the court. This is not a true appeal—*Cadwell v Jackson* [2001] B.P.I.R. 966. For the meaning of "venue" in r.6.105(3) see r.13.6. For the potential utility of r.6.105 see *Barclays Bank v Henson* [2000] B.P.I.R. 941.

6.106   Withdrawal or variation of proof

6.106   A creditor's proof may at any time, by agreement between himself and the trustee, be withdrawn or varied as to the amount claimed.

GENERAL NOTE

See *Official Receiver v McKay* [2009] B.P.I.R. 1061.

6.107   Expunging of proof by the court

6.107(1)   [Expunging or reduction of amount] The court may expunge a proof or reduce the amount claimed–

     (a)   on the trustee's application, where he thinks that the proof has been improperly admitted, or ought to be reduced; or

     (b)   on the application of a creditor, if the trustee declines to interfere in the matter.

6.107(2)   **[Venue and notice]** Where application is made to the court under this Rule, the court shall fix a venue for the application to be heard, notice of which shall be sent by the applicant–

(a)   in the case of an application by the trustee, to the creditor who made the proof, and

(b)   in the case of an application by a creditor, to the trustee and to the creditor who made the proof (if not himself).

GENERAL NOTE

For the meaning of "venue" in r.6.107(2) see r.13.6. See *Official Receiver v McKay* [2009] B.P.I.R. 1061.

Section B: Quantification of claim

6.108   Negotiable instruments, etc.

6.108   Unless the trustee allows, a proof in respect of money owed on a bill of exchange, promissory note, cheque or other negotiable instrument or security cannot be admitted unless there is produced the instrument or security itself or a copy of it, certified by the creditor or his authorised representative to be a true copy.

6.109   Secured creditors

6.109(1)   **[Proving for balance of debt]** If a secured creditor realises his security, he may prove for the balance of his debt, after deducting the amount realised.

6.109(2)   **[Proving for whole debt]** If a secured creditor voluntarily surrenders his security for the general benefit of creditors, he may prove for his whole debt, as if it were unsecured.

GENERAL NOTE

This should be viewed in the light of IA 1986 ss.269 and 383(2), and also rr.6.15–6.19. For a useful discussion of the operation of this rule see Anderson, (1989) 5 I.L. & P. 180.

6.110   Discounts

6.110   There shall in every case be deducted from the claim all trade and other discounts which would have been available to the bankrupt but for his bankruptcy, except any discount for immediate, early or cash settlement.

6.111   Debt in foreign currency

6.111(1)   **[Conversion into sterling]** For the purpose of proving a debt incurred or payable in a currency other than sterling, the amount of the debt shall be converted into sterling at the official exchange rate prevailing on the date of the bankruptcy order.

6.111(2)   **["The official exchange rate"]** "The official exchange rate" is the middle exchange rate on the London Foreign Exchange Market at the close of business, as published for the date in question. In the absence of any such published rate, it is such rate as the court determines.

GENERAL NOTE

A similar rule applies in company law: *Re Dynamics Corporation of America (No.2)* [1976] 1 W.L.R. 757. Note that conversion into sterling under r.6.111(1) is not required at the stage when a statutory demand is presented: see the ruling of Morritt J. in *Re a Debtor (51/SD/1991)* [1992] 1 W.L.R. 1294. Rule 6.111(2) was modified by I(A)R 2003 (SI 2003/1730) with effect from April 1, 2004.

6.112   Payments of a periodical nature

6.112(1)   **[Rent etc.]** In the case of rent and other payments of a periodical nature, the creditor may prove for any amounts due and unpaid up to the date of the bankruptcy order.

6.112(2)   **[If accruing from day to day]** Where at that date any payment was accruing due, the creditor may prove for so much as would have fallen due at that date, if accruing from day to day.

6.113   Interest

6.113(1)   **[Where claim may include interest]** In the following circumstances the creditor's claim may include interest on the debt for periods before the bankruptcy order, although not previously reserved or agreed.

6.113(2)   **[Debt due by written instrument]** If the debt is due by virtue of a written instrument and payable at a certain time, interest may be claimed for the period from that time to the date of the bankruptcy order.

6.113(3)   **[Debt due otherwise]** If the debt is due otherwise, interest may only be claimed if, before the presentation of the bankruptcy petition, a demand for payment was made in writing by or on behalf of the creditor, and notice given that interest would be payable from the date of the demand to the date of payment and for all the purposes of the Act and the Rules shall be chargeable at a rate not exceeding that mentioned in paragraph (5).

6.113(4)   **[Period of claim]** Interest under paragraph (3) may only be claimed for the period from the date of the demand to that of the bankruptcy order.

6.113(5)   **[Rate of interest]** The rate of interest to be claimed under paragraphs (2) and (3) is the rate specified in section 17 of the Judgments Act 1838 on the date of the bankruptcy order.

GENERAL NOTE

There is a good discussion of this rule and its legislative antecedents in *El Ajou v Stern* [2006] EWHC 3067 (Ch); [2007] B.P.I.R. 693 (which ironically is an IVA case). For further guidance on claims in respect of interest, see IA 1986 s.328(4), (5). Rule 6.113(4) and (5) substituted for the former second paragraph of r.6.113(3) and the former r.6.113(4) by the Insolvency (Amendment) Rules 1987 (SI 1987/1919) r.3(1), Sch. Pt 1 para.112(2) as from January 11, 1988. See also r.4.93.

6.114   Debt payable at future time

6.114   A creditor may prove for a debt of which payment was not yet due at the date of the bankruptcy order, but subject to Rule 11.13 in Part 11 of the Rules (adjustment of dividend where payment made before time).

CHAPTER 9

SECURED CREDITORS

6.115   Value of security

6.115(1)   **[Altering value]** A secured creditor may, with the agreement of the trustee or the permission of the court, at any time alter the value which he has, in his proof of debt, put upon his security.

6.115(2)   **[Limitation on re-valuation]** However, if a secured creditor–

(a)   being the petitioner, has in the petition put a value on his security, or

(b)   has voted in respect of the unsecured balance of his debt,

he may re-value his security only with permission of the court.

(See General Note after r.6.119.) This particular rule was considered by Lightman J. in *Rey v FNCB* [2006] B.P.I.R. 1260 where it was held that the fact that a secured creditor was party to an IVA which made reference to r.6.115 did

not prevent it from relying on its enforcement rights as secured creditor because there was no explicit prohibitory provision to that effect in the IVA.

6.116   Surrender for non-disclosure

6.116(1)   [Omission to disclose security] If a secured creditor omits to disclose his security in his proof of debt, he shall surrender his security for the general benefit of creditors, unless the court, on application by him, relieves him from the effect of this Rule on the ground that the omission was inadvertent or the result of honest mistake.

6.116(2)   [Relief from effect of r.6.116(1)] If the court grants that relief, it may require or allow the creditor's proof of debt to be amended, on such terms as may be just.

6.116(3)   [Third parties' rights in rem] Nothing in this Rule or the following two Rules may affect the rights in rem of creditors or third parties protected under Article 5 of the EC Regulation (third parties' rights in rem).

(See General Note after r.6.119.)
     IR r.6.116(3) was inserted by the Insolvency (Amendment) Rules 2002 (SI 2002/1307) with effect from May 31, 2002 to cater for the advent of the EC Regulation 1346/2000 on Insolvency Proceedings.

6.117   Redemption by trustee

6.117(1)   [Notice of proposed redemption] The trustee may at any time give notice to a creditor whose debt is secured that he proposes, at the expiration of 28 days from the date of the notice, to redeem the security at the value put upon it in the creditor's proof.

6.117(2)   [Time for re-valuation] The creditor then has 21 days (or such longer period as the trustee may allow) in which, if he so wishes, to exercise his right to re-value his security (with the permission of the court, where Rule 6.115(2) applies).
     If the creditor re-values his security, the trustee may only redeem at the new value.

6.117(3)   [If trustee redeems] If the trustee redeems the security, the cost of transferring it is borne by the estate.

6.117(4)   [Notice to trustee to elect etc.] A secured creditor may at any time, by a notice in writing, call on the trustee to elect whether he will or will not exercise his power to redeem the security at the value then placed on it; and the trustee then has 3 months in which to exercise the power or determine not to exercise it.

(See General Note after r.6.119.) The period in para.(4) has been reduced from six to three months by I(A)R 2010 (SI 2010/686).

6.118   Test of security's value

6.118(1)   [Offer for sale] Subject as follows, the trustee, if he is dissatisfied with the value which a secured creditor puts on his security (whether in his proof or by way of re-valuation under Rule 6.117), may require any property comprised in the security to be offered for sale.

6.118(2)   [Terms of sale] The terms of sale shall be such as may be agreed, or as the court may direct; and if the sale is by auction, the trustee on behalf of the estate, and the creditor on his own behalf, may appear and bid.

6.118(3)   [Non-application of Rule] This Rule does not apply if the security has been re-valued and the re-valuation has been approved by the court.

(See General Note after r.6.119.)

6.119   Realisation of security by creditor

6.119   If a creditor who has valued his security subsequently realises it (whether or not at the instance of the trustee)–

(a)   the net amount realised shall be substituted for the value previously put by the creditor on the security, and

(b)   that amount shall be treated in all respects as an amended valuation made by him.

GENERAL NOTE TO RR.6.115–6.119

These rules relate to secured creditors. Revaluation of security is permitted, subject to certain restrictions. Nondisclosure of security can lead to it being forfeited. Security may be redeemed by the trustee. If the secured creditor realises his security, the original valuation is replaced by the amount of the net proceeds of realisation.

CHAPTER 10

THE TRUSTEE IN BANKRUPTCY

Section A: Appointment and associated formalities

6.120   Appointment by creditors' meeting

6.120(1)   [Application of Rule] This Rule applies where a person has been appointed trustee by resolution of a creditors' meeting.

6.120(2)   [Certification of appointment] The chairman of the meeting shall certify the appointment, but not unless and until the person to be appointed has provided him with a written statement to the effect that he is an insolvency practitioner, duly qualified under the Act to act as trustee in relation to the bankrupt, and that he consents so to act.

[FORM 6.40]
or [FORM 6.41]

6.120(3)   [Date when appointment effective] The trustee's appointment is effective from the date on which the appointment is certified, that date to be endorsed on the certificate.

6.120(4)   [Certificate to official receiver] The chairman of the meeting (if not himself the official receiver) shall send the certificate to the official receiver.

6.120(5)   [Certificate to trustee] The official receiver shall in any case send the certificate to the trustee.

GENERAL NOTE

This supplements IA 1986 s.293. Rules 6.120(3)–(5) were substituted to facilitate handovers to insolvency practitioners. See I(A)R 2010 (SI 2010/686)—filing in court is no longer required.

6.120A   Official receiver not to be appointed trustee

6.120A   The official receiver may not be appointed as trustee by resolution of a creditors' meeting.

GENERAL NOTE

This is a new provision inserted by I(A)R 2010 (SI 2010/686).

6.121   Appointment by the court

6.121(1)   [Application of Rule] This Rule applies where the court under section 297 (4) or (5) appoints the trustee.

[FORM 6.42]
or [FORM 6.43]

6.121(2)   [Issue of court order] The court's order shall not issue unless and until the person appointed has filed in court a statement to the effect that he is an insolvency practitioner, duly qualified under the Act to be the trustee, and that he consents so to act.

6.121(3)   [Copies of orders to official receiver etc.] Thereafter, the court shall send 2 copies of the order to the official receiver. One of the copies shall be sealed, and this shall be sent by him to the person appointed as trustee.

6.121(4)   [Commencement of appointment] The trustee's appointment takes effect from the date of the order.

GENERAL NOTE

This rule should be viewed in the light of IA 1986 s.297(3), (4), (5). If the court appoints a trustee under these provisions, Forms 6.42 and 6.43 are to be adopted. Rule 6.121(1) was amended by I(A)R 2003 (SI 2003/1730) with effect from April 1, 2004.

6.122   Appointment by Secretary of State

6.122(1)   [Application of Rule] This Rule applies where the official receiver–

(a)   under section 295 or 300, refers to the Secretary of State the need for an appointment of a trustee, or

(b)   under section 296, applies to the Secretary of State to make the appointment.

6.122(2)   [Copies of certificate to official receiver, etc.] If the Secretary of State makes an appointment he shall send a copy of the certificate of appointment to the official receiver, who shall transmit it to the person appointed.
    The certificate shall specify the date from which the trustee's appointment is to be effective.

GENERAL NOTE

This rule clarifies the provisions of IA 1986 ss.295, 296 and 300. The regulatory burden in para.(2) has been relaxed by I(A)R 2010 (SI 2010/686).

6.123   Authentication of trustee's appointment

6.123   Where a trustee is appointed under any of Rules 6.120, 6.121 and 6.122, a sealed copy of the order of appointment or (as the case may be) a copy of the certificate of his appointment may in any proceedings be adduced as proof that he is duly authorised to exercise the powers and perform the duties of trustee of the bankrupt's estate.

GENERAL NOTE

This relates to rr.6.120–6.122 by providing for the authentication of the trustee's appointment.

6.124   Advertisement of appointment

6.124(1)   [Gazetting/advertisement of notice of appointment] A trustee who is appointed by a creditors' meeting, as soon as reasonably practicable after receiving the certificate of appointment, shall give notice of that appointment. Such notice–

(a)   shall be gazetted; and

(b)   may be advertised in other such manner as the trustee thinks fit.

6.124(1A)   [Additional contents of notice under r.6.124(1)] In addition to the standard contents, the notice under paragraph (1) must state–

(a)   that a trustee has been appointed by a creditors' meeting; and

(b)   the date of the appointment.

6.124(2)   [Expense of giving notice] The expense of giving the notice shall be borne in the first instance by the trustee; but he is entitled to be reimbursed by the estate, as an expense of the bankruptcy.

The same applies also in the case of the notice or advertisement under section 296(4) (appointment of trustee by Secretary of State), and of the notice or advertisement under section 297(7) (appointment by the court).

GENERAL NOTE

The onus is on the trustee to ensure that his appointment is advertised as appropriate and gazetted. Note the change made by the Insolvency (Amendment) Rules 2009 (SI 2009/642) (which took effect on April 6, 2009). This change involved substituting a new para.(1). I(A)R 2010 (SI 2010/686) inserts a new para.(1A).

6.125   Hand-over of estate to trustee

6.125(1)   [Application of Rule] This Rule applies only where–

(a)   the bankrupt's estate vests in the trustee under Chapter IV of Part IX of the Act, following a period in which the official receiver is the receiver and manager of the estate according to section 287, or

(b)   the trustee is appointed in succession to the official receiver acting as trustee.

6.125(2)   [On trustee's appointment] When the trustee's appointment takes effect, the official receiver shall as soon as reasonably practicable do all that is required for putting him into possession of the estate.

6.125(3)   [Discharge of balance due to official receiver] On taking possession of the estate, the trustee shall discharge any balance due to the official receiver on account of–

(a)   expenses properly incurred by him and payable under the Act or the Rules, and

(b)   any advances made by him in respect of the estate, together with interest on such advances at the rate specified in section 17 of the Judgments Act 1838 on the date of the bankruptcy order.

6.125(4)   [Undertaking to discharge] Alternatively, the trustee may (before taking office) give to the official receiver a written undertaking to discharge any such balance out of the first realisation of assets.

6.125(5)   [Official receiver's charge] The official receiver has a charge on the estate in respect of any sums due to him under paragraph (3). But, where the trustee has realised assets with a view to making those payments, the official receiver's charge does not extend in respect of sums deductible by the trustee from the proceeds of realisation, as being expenses properly incurred therein.

6.125(6)   [Discharge of guarantees etc.] The trustee shall from time to time out of the realisation of assets discharge all guarantees properly given by the official receiver for the benefit of the estate, and shall pay all the official receiver's expenses.

6.125(7)   [Official receiver to give trustee information] The official receiver shall give to the trustee all such information, relating to the affairs of the bankrupt and the course of the bankruptcy, as he (the official receiver) considers to be reasonably required for the effective discharge by the trustee of his duties in relation to the estate.

6.125(8)   [Ch.6 report] The trustee shall also be furnished with any report of the official receiver under Chapter 6 of this Part of the Rules.

See IA 1986 ss.287 and 306 for the relevant statutory provisions here.

Section B: Resignation and removal; vacation of office

6.126   Creditors' meeting to receive trustee's resignation

6.126(1)   [Trustee must call meeting etc.] Before resigning his office, the trustee must call a meeting of creditors for the purpose of receiving his resignation.

6.126(1A)   [Minimum notice for meeting] The trustee must give at least 28 days' notice of the meeting.

6.126(1B)   [Contents of notice] The notice summoning the meeting must–

(a)   indicate that the purpose or one of the purposes of the meeting is to receive the trustee's resignation; and

(b)   draw the attention of the creditors to Rule 6.142.

6.126(1C)   [Notice to official receiver and bankrupt at same time] Notice of the meeting must be sent to the official receiver and to the bankrupt at the same time as it is sent to creditors.

6.126(2)   [Notice accompanied by account of trustee's administration] The notice to creditors and the bankrupt must be accompanied by an account of the trustee's administration of the bankrupt's estate, including–

(a)   a statement that the trustee has reconciled the account with that held by the Secretary of State in respect of the bankruptcy; and

(b)   a progress report for the period–

    (i)   commencing with the later of the date of–

        (aa)   the appointment of the trustee; and

        (bb)   the day immediately following the end of the period of the last progress report; and

    (ii)   ending with the date of the meeting.

6.126(3)   [Grounds for proceedings under Rule] Subject as follows, the trustee may only proceed under this Rule on grounds of ill health or because–

(a)   he intends ceasing to be in practice as an insolvency practitioner, or

(b)   there is some conflict of interest or change of personal circumstances which precludes or makes impracticable the further discharge by him of the duties of trustee.

6.126(4)   [Where joint trustees] Where two or more persons are acting as trustee jointly, any one of them may proceed under this Rule (without prejudice to the continuation in office of the other or others) on the ground that, in his opinion and that of the other or others, it is no longer expedient that there should continue to be the present number of joint trustees.

6.126(5)   [If no quorum] Except where Rule 6.126A applies if there is no quorum present at the meeting summoned to receive the trustee's resignation, the meeting is deemed to have been held, a resolution is deemed to have been passed that the trustee's resignation be accepted and the creditors are deemed not to have resolved against the trustee having his release.

6.126(6)   [Application of r.6.126(5)] Where paragraph (5) applies any reference in the Rules to a resolution that the trustee's resignation be accepted is replaced by a reference to the making of a written statement, authenticated by the person who, had there been a quorum present, would have been chairman of the meeting, that no quorum was present and that the trustee may resign.

GENERAL NOTE

The relevant statutory provision here is IA 1986 s.298(7). Note the restriction in r.6.126(3) on the grounds for resignation. The concept of impracticability in r.6.126(3) is to be construed narrowly—*Re Alt Landscapes Ltd* [1999] B.P.I.R. 459 where the court rejected *Re Sankey Furniture Ltd Ex p. Harding* [1995] 2 B.C.L.C. 594. For the facilitation of multiple resignations see *Re Equity Nominees Ltd* [2000] B.C.C. 84. Further explanation is provided by *Customs and Excise Commissioners v Allen* [2003] B.P.I.R. 830. For procedure, see Practice Direction [2007] B.C.C. 842 found in App.IV, para.1.6. I(A)R 2010 (SI 2010/686) inserts new paras (1A) to (1C) and replaces para.(2).

6.126A   Resignation (application under Rule 6.142)

6.126A(1)   **[Application of r.6.126A]** This Rule applies where at the date of a meeting summoned for the purpose of receiving the trustee's resignation, an application made to the court under Rule 6.142 (including any appeal) has not been disposed of.

6.126A(2)   **[No resolution on release of trustee]** At the meeting no resolution may be put regarding the trustee's release.

6.126A(3)   **[Meeting adjourned if resignation accepted]** If at the meeting the trustee's resignation is accepted the meeting must be adjourned (notwithstanding anything in Rule 6.90 (suspension of meeting)) to a day not less than 14 days after the day on which the application under Rule 6.142 (including any appeal) has been disposed of.

6.126A(4)   **[Notice to trustee of adjourned meeting]** The trustee must give at least 14 days' notice of the meeting adjourned in accordance with paragraph (3) to the creditors.

6.126A(5)   **[Proceedings at adjourned meeting]** At the meeting adjourned in accordance with paragraph (3)–

(a) a revised version of the account which accompanied the notice of the meeting must be laid showing any changes required as a result, or arising out of the application under Rule 6.142; and

(b) a resolution for the release of the trustee whose resignation has been accepted must be put.

6.126A(6)   **[If no quorum at adjourned meeting]** If there is no quorum present at the adjourned meeting, the meeting is deemed to have been held and the creditors are deemed to have resolved that the trustee be released.

6.126A(7)   **[Where trustee released]** Where the creditors have resolved at the adjourned meeting that the trustee be released (or are deemed to have so resolved by virtue of paragraph (5))–

(a) the chairman of the meeting (or the person who, had there been a quorum present would have been chairman of the meeting) must send as soon as reasonably practicable a certificate to that effect to the official receiver with a copy of the revised account; and

(b) the official receiver must file a copy of the certificate in court.

6.126A(8)   **[If resignation not accepted]** If at the meeting the trustee's resignation is not accepted, the trustee must not summon any further meeting under Rule 6.126 until the application under Rule 6.142 (including any appeal) has been disposed of.

6.126A(9)   **[Powers of court on trustee being released]** Paragraph (7) is subject to the powers of the court on an application being made to it by the trustee under Rule 6.128 (permission to resign granted by the court).

6.126A(10)   **[Application of r.6.126 to further meeting]** Rule 6.126 applies to any such further meeting with the modification that the account required to accompany the notice of the meeting must show any changes from the account which accompanied the notice of the earlier meeting called to receive the trustee's resignation, and in particular any changes required as a result of the application under Rule 6.142 and any further remuneration charged or expenses incurred.

6.126A(11)   [Non-application of rr.6.78C and 6.142 creditors' rights] The creditors' rights under Rules 6.78C and 6.142 do not apply in respect of any matter included in that account which–

(a)   was included in the account which accompanied the notice of the earlier meeting called to receive the trustee's resignation; or

(b)   was the subject of the order of the court on the application made to it by the trustee under Rule 6.142.

GENERAL NOTE

This is newly inserted by I(A)R 2010 (SI 2010/686).

6.127   Action following acceptance of resignation

6.127(1)   [Omitted.]

6.127(2)   [Omitted.]

6.127(3)   [Where chairman at creditors' meeting other than official receiver] Where the chairman of the creditors' meeting summoned for the purpose of receiving the trustee's resignation is other than the official receiver, and there is passed at the meeting any of the following resolutions–

(a)   that the trustee's resignation be accepted,

(b)   that a new trustee be appointed,

(c)   that the resigning trustee be not given his release,

the chairman shall, within 3 business days of the date of the resolution, send to the official receiver a copy of the resolution.

If it has been resolved to accept the trustee's resignation, the chairman shall send to the official receiver a certificate to that effect.

[FORM 6.44]

6.127(4)   [If creditors resolve to appoint new trustee] If the creditors have resolved to appoint a new trustee, the certificate of his appointment shall also be sent to the official receiver within that time; and Rule 6.120 above shall be complied with in respect of it.

6.127(5)   [If trustee's resignation accepted] If the trustee's resignation is accepted, the notice of it required by section 298(7) shall be given by him as soon as reasonably practicable after the resolution has been passed; and he shall send a copy of the notice to the official receiver.

The notice shall be accompanied by a copy of the account sent to creditors under Rule 6.126(2).

6.127(6)   [Copy of notice] The official receiver shall file a copy of the notice in court.

6.127(7)   [Effective date of resignation] The trustee's resignation is effective as from the date on which the official receiver files the copy notice in court, that date to be endorsed on the copy notice.

GENERAL NOTE

Form 6.44 is to be used by the chairman of the creditors' committee to notify the official receiver of the resignation. The trustee must also notify the court. Paragraphs (1) and (2) are omitted and paras (3), (5) and (7) amended by I(A)R 2010 (SI 2010/686).

6.128   Permission to resign granted by the court

6.128(1)   [If creditors resolve not to accept resignation] If at a creditors' meeting summoned to accept the trustee's resignation it is resolved that it be not accepted, the court may, on the trustee's application, make an order giving him permission to resign.

[FORM 6.45]

6.128(2)   [Extent of order under r.6.128(1)] The court's order under this Rule may include such provision as it thinks fit with respect to matters arising in connection with the resignation, and shall determine the date from which the trustee's release is effective.

6.128(3)   [Sealed copies of order] The court shall send two sealed copies of the order to the trustee, who shall send one of the copies as soon as reasonably practicable to the official receiver.

6.128(4)   [Copy notice to court and official receiver] On sending notice of his resignation to the court, as required by section 298(7), the trustee shall send a copy of it to the official receiver.

[FORM 6.46]

<small>GENERAL NOTE</small>

This allows the court to accept a trustee's resignation notwithstanding opposition from the creditors.

6.129   Meeting of creditors to remove trustee

6.129(1)   [Notice] Where a meeting of creditors is summoned for the purpose of removing the trustee, the notice summoning it shall indicate that this is the purpose, or one of the purposes, of the meeting; and the notice shall draw the attention of creditors to section 299(3) with respect to the trustee's release.

[FORM 6.35]

6.129(2)   [Copy of notice to official receiver] A copy of the notice shall at the same time also be sent to the official receiver.

6.129(3)   [Chairman, if trustee chairman etc.] At the meeting, a person other than the trustee or his nominee may be elected to act as chairman; but if the trustee or his nominee is chairman and a resolution has been proposed for the trustee's removal, the chairman shall not adjourn the meeting without the consent of at least one-half (in value) of the creditors present (in person or by proxy) and entitled to vote.

6.129(4)   [Where chairman other than official receiver] Where the chairman of the meeting is other than the official receiver, and there is passed at the meeting any of the following resolutions–

(a)   that the trustee be removed,

(b)   that a new trustee be appointed,

(c)   that the removed trustee be not given his release,

the chairman shall, within 3 business days, send to the official receiver a copy of the resolution.

If it has been resolved to remove the trustee, the chairman shall send to the official receiver a certificate to that effect.

[FORM 6.47]

6.129(5)   [If creditors resolve to appoint new trustee] If the creditors have resolved to appoint a new trustee, the certificate of his appointment shall also be sent to the official receiver within that time; and Rule 6.120 shall be complied with in respect of it.

<small>GENERAL NOTE</small>

This develops IA 1986 s.298(1). See I(A)R 2010 (SI 2010/686).

6.130   Court's power to regulate meeting under Rule 6.129

6.130   Where a meeting under Rule 6.129 is to be held, or is proposed to be summoned, the court may on the application of any creditor give directions as to the mode of summoning it, the sending out and return of forms of proxy, the conduct of the meeting, and any other matter which appears to the court to require regulation or control.

6.131   Procedure on removal

6.131(1)   **[Certificate of removal to be filed]** Where the creditors have resolved that the trustee be removed, the official receiver shall file the certificate of removal in court.

6.131(2)   **[Effective date]** The resolution is effective as from the date on which the official receiver files the certificate of removal in court, and that date shall be endorsed on the certificate.

6.131(3)   **[Copy of certificate]** A copy of the certificate, so endorsed, shall be sent by the official receiver to the trustee who has been removed and, if a new trustee has been appointed, to him.

6.131(4)   **[Reconciliation of accounts]** The official receiver shall not file the certificate in court until the Secretary of State has certified to him that the removed trustee has reconciled his account with that held by the Secretary of State in respect of the bankruptcy.

6.132   Removal of trustee by the court

6.132(1)   **[Application of Rule]** This Rule applies where application is made to the court for the removal of the trustee, or for an order directing the trustee to summon a meeting of creditors for the purpose of removing him.

[FORM 6.48]

6.132(2)   **[Court may dismiss application etc.]** The court may, if it thinks that no sufficient cause is shown for the application, dismiss it; but it shall not do so unless the applicant has had an opportunity to attend the court for a hearing, of which he has been given at least 5 business days' notice but which is without notice to any other party.

If the application is not dismissed under this paragraph, the court shall fix a venue for it to be heard.

6.132(3)   **[Notice etc.]** The applicant shall, at least 14 days before the hearing, send to the trustee and the official receiver notice stating the venue so fixed; and the notice shall be accompanied by a copy of the application, and of any evidence which the applicant intends to adduce in support of it.

6.132(4)   **[Costs]** Subject to any contrary order of the court, the costs of the application do not fall on the estate.

6.132(5)   **[Where court removes trustee]** Where the court removes the trustee–

(a)   it shall send copies of the order of removal to him and to the official receiver;

(b)   the order may include such provision as the court thinks fit with respect to matters arising in connection with the removal; and

(c)   if the court appoints a new trustee, Rule 6.121 applies.

GENERAL NOTE

The court enjoys power to remove trustees under IA 1986 s.298(1). For the meaning of "venue" in r.6.132(2) and (3), see r.13.6. IR 6.132(5) does not confer jurisdiction to appoint a trustee in bankruptcy—*Donaldson v O'Sullivan* [2008] EWHC 387 (Ch); [2008] B.P.I.R. 288—confirmed in [2008] EWCA Civ 879. Modernised by I(A)R 2010 (SI 2010/686). The period specified in para.(2) is changed from seven to five business days and the references to ex parte hearings have been dropped.

6.133   Removal of trustee by Secretary of State

6.133(1)   **[Notice to trustee etc.]** If the Secretary of State decides to remove the trustee, he shall before doing so notify the trustee and the official receiver of his decision and the grounds of it, and specify a period within which the trustee may make representations against implementation of the decision.

6.133(2)   **[On removal]** If the Secretary of State directs the removal of the trustee, he shall as soon as reasonably practicable–

(a)   file notice of his decision in court, and

(b)   send notice to the trustee and the official receiver.

6.133(3)   [If trustee removed] If the trustee is removed by direction of the Secretary of State, the court may make any such order in his case as it would have power to make if he had been removed by itself.

GENERAL NOTE

See IA 1986 s.298(5).

6.134   Notice of resignation or removal

6.134   Where a new trustee is appointed in place of one who has resigned or been removed, the new trustee shall, in the notice of his appointment, state that his predecessor has resigned or, as the case may be, been removed and (if it be the case) that he has been given his release.

GENERAL NOTE

Note the Insolvency (Amendment) Rules 2009 (SI 2009/642) (effective from April 6, 2009). Under these amendment rules the word "advertisement" is removed from the heading and the rule itself to be replaced by "notice".

6.135   Release of resigning or removed trustee

6.135(1)   [Where trustee's resignation accepted] Subject to paragraph (1A), where the trustee's resignation is accepted by a meeting of creditors which has not resolved against his release, he has his release from when his resignation is effective under Rule 6.127.

6.135(1A)   [Where trustee's resignation accepted under r.6.126A] Where the trustee's resignation is accepted under Rule 6.126A, the trustee's release is effective as from the date on which the official receiver files the copy of the certificate under paragraph (7) of that Rule in court, that date to be endorsed on the copy certificate.

6.135(2)   [Where trustee removed by meeting] Where the trustee is removed by a meeting of creditors which has not resolved against his release, the fact of his release shall be stated in the certificate of removal.

6.135(3)   [Application to Secretary of State] Where–

(a)   the trustee resigns, and the creditor's meeting called to receive his resignation has resolved against his release, or

(b)   he is removed by a creditors' meeting which has so resolved, or is removed by the court, he must apply to the Secretary of State for his release.

[FORM 6.49]

6.135(4)   [Certificate of release] When the Secretary of State gives the release, he shall certify it accordingly, and send the certificate to the official receiver, to be filed in court.

6.135(5)   [Copy of certificate] A copy of the certificate shall be sent by the Secretary of State to the former trustee, whose release is effective from the date of the certificate.

(See General Note after r.6.136.) I(A)R 2010 (SI 2010/686) inserts a new para.(1A).

Section C: Release on completion of administration

6.136   Release of official receiver

6.136(1)   [Notice of intention] The official receiver shall, before giving notice to the Secretary of State under section 299(2) (that the administration of the estate is for practical purposes complete), send out notice of his intention to do so to all creditors of which he is aware, and to the bankrupt.

6.136(2)   [Accompanying summary] The notice shall in each case be accompanied by a summary of the official receiver's receipts and payments as trustee.

6.136(3)   [Notice to court of date of release] The Secretary of State, when he has under section 299(2) determined the date from which the official receiver is to have his release, shall give notice to the court that he has done so. The notice shall be accompanied by the summary referred to in paragraph (2).

GENERAL NOTE

These supplement IA 1986 s.299 (release of trustees). The former reference to creditors proving for their debts has been dropped in favour of a modern terminology. See I(A)R 2004 (SI 2004/584) with effect from April 1, 2004.

6.137   Final meeting of creditors

6.137(1)   [Notice to creditors etc.] Where the trustee is other than the official receiver, he shall give at least 28 days' notice of the final meeting of creditors to be held under section 331. The notice shall be sent to all creditors of which he is aware, and to the bankrupt.

[FORM 6.35]

6.137(1A)   [Gazetting and advertising of notice] The trustee–

(a)   as soon as reasonably practicable after giving notice under paragraph (1) must have gazetted a notice of the final meeting; and

(b)   may advertise notice of the meeting in such other manner as the trustee thinks fit.

6.137(1B)   [Additional contents of notice under r.6.137(1A)] In addition to the standard contents, the notice under paragraph (1A) must state–

(a)   that the trustee has summoned the meeting;

(b)   if the meeting was summoned at the request of a creditor, the fact that it was so summoned and the section of the Act under which it was summoned;

(c)   the purpose for which the meeting was summoned;

(d)   the venue fixed for the meeting; and

(e)   the time and date by which, and place at which, creditors must lodge proxies and hitherto unlodged proofs in order to be entitled to vote at the meeting.

6.137(1C)   [Final meeting not held] The final meeting must not be held unless Rule 6.78B has been complied with; and if for that reason the meeting is not held–

(a)   the trustee must give notice of that fact as soon as reasonably practicable to all to whom notice of the meeting was given, and

(b)   fresh notice of the meeting complying with this Rule must be given when Rule 6.78B has been complied with.

6.137(2)   [Trustee's report] The trustee's report laid before the meeting under that section shall include–

(a)   a summary of his receipts and payments, including details of remuneration charged and expenses incurred by the trustee,

(ab)   details of the basis fixed for the trustee's remuneration, and

(b)   a statement by him that he has reconciled his account with that which is held by the Secretary of State in respect of the bankruptcy.

6.137(2A)   [Where progress report sent] Where the trustee has sent a progress report to creditors in accordance with Rule 6.78A, the report to be laid at the final meeting of creditors must also–

(a)   contain a receipts and payments account in the form of an abstract showing the receipts and payments during the period since the last progress report, and

(b)   include–

   (i)   details of the remuneration charged and expenses incurred by the trustee during that period, and

   (ii)   a description of the things done by the trustee during that period in respect of which that remuneration was charged and those expenses incurred.

6.137(2B)   [Where trustee's remuneration not fixed by last progress report] In any case where the basis of the trustee's remuneration had not been fixed by the date to which the last progress report was made up, the receipts and payments account required by paragraph (2A)(a) must also include details of the remuneration charged in the period of any preceding progress report in which details of remuneration were not included.

6.137(2C)   [Where trustee's remuneration fixed as set amount] Where the basis of remuneration has been fixed as a set amount only, it is sufficient compliance with paragraph (2A)(b) for the trustee to state the amount which has been set and to supply details of the expenses charged within the period in question.

6.137(3)   [Questioning of trustee] At the final meeting, the creditors may question the trustee with respect to any matter contained in his report, and may resolve against him having his release.

6.137(4)   [Notice to court] The trustee shall give notice to the court that the final meeting has been held; and the notice shall state whether or not he has been given his release, and be accompanied by a copy of the report laid before the final meeting. A copy of the notice shall be sent by the trustee to the Secretary of State.

[FORM 6.50]

6.137(5)   [No quorum at final meeting] If there is no quorum present at the final meeting, the trustee shall report to the court that a final meeting was summoned in accordance with the Rules, but there was no quorum present; and the final meeting is then deemed to have been held, and the creditors not to have resolved against the trustee having his release.

6.137(6)   [Release of trustee] If the creditors at the final meeting have not so resolved, the trustee is released when the notice under paragraph (4) is filed in court. If they have so resolved, the trustee must obtain his release from the Secretary of State, as provided by Rule 6.135.

GENERAL NOTE

See IA 1986 s.331. 28 days' notice of the final meeting must be given. The change made by I(A)R 2004 (SI 2004/584) (effective from April 1, 2004) is along the same lines as that made for IR 1986 r.6.136. Substantially amended by I(A)R 2010 (SI 2010/686) with the insertion of new paras (1A) to (1C) and (2A) to (2C).

6.137A   Rule as to reporting

6.137A(1)   [Power of court] The court may, on the trustee or official receiver's application, relieve him of any duty imposed on him by Rules 6.136 or 6.137, or authorise him to carry out the duty in a way other than there required.

6.137A(2)   [Considerations in exercising power] In considering whether to act as above, the court shall have regard to the cost of carrying out the duty, to the amount of the funds available in the estate, and to the extent of the interest of creditors or any particular class of them.

GENERAL NOTE

This new rule was added by I(A)R 2004 (SI 2004/584) with effect from April 1, 2004. It shows an awareness of the need for cost efficiencies by removing the automatic requirement to send out certain notices. The reference to the Secretary of State in para.(4) was made by the Insolvency (Amendment) Rules 2005 (SI 2005/527) to replace a prior reference to the official receiver.

Section D: Remuneration

6.138   Fixing of remuneration

6.138(1)   [Entitlement to remuneration] The trustee is entitled to receive remuneration for his services as such.

6.138(2)   [How fixed] The basis of remuneration shall be fixed–

  (a)   as a percentage of the value of the assets in the bankrupt's estate which are realised or distributed, or of the one value and the other in combination, or

  (b)   by reference to the time properly given by the insolvency practitioner (as trustee) and his staff in attending to matters arising in the bankruptcy, or

  (c)   as a set amount.

6.138(3)   [Omitted.]

6.138(3A)   [Different bases of remuneration] The basis of remuneration may be fixed as any one or more of the bases set out in paragraph (2), and different bases may be fixed in respect of different things done by the trustee.

6.138(3B)   [Different percentages] Where remuneration is fixed as set out in paragraph (2)(a), different percentages may be fixed in respect of different things done by the trustee.

6.138(3C)   [Creditors' committee to determine bases/percentages] Where the trustee is other than the official receiver, it is for the creditors' committee (if there is one) to determine–

  (a)   which of the bases set out in paragraph (2) are to be fixed and (where appropriate) in what combination under paragraph (3A), and

  (b)   the percentage or percentages (if any) to be fixed under paragraphs (2)(a) and (3B) and the amount (if any) to be set under paragraph (2)(c).

6.138(4)   [Matters relevant to r.6.138(3) determination] In arriving at that determination, the committee shall have regard to the following matters–

  (a)   the complexity (or otherwise) of the case,

  (b)   any respects in which, in connection with the administration of the estate, there falls on the insolvency practitioner (as trustee) any responsibility of an exceptional kind or degree,

    (c)   the effectiveness with which the insolvency practitioner appears to be carrying out, or to have carried out, his duties as trustee, and

    (d)   the value and nature of the assets in the estate with which the trustee has to deal.

6.138(5)   **[If no committee or no determination]** If there is no creditors' committee, or the committee does not make the requisite determination, the basis of the trustee's remuneration may be fixed (in accordance with paragraphs (2), (3A) and (3B)) by a resolution of a meeting of creditors; and paragraph (4) applies to them as it does to the creditors' committee.

6.138(6)   **[Otherwise fixed where not the official receiver]** Where the trustee is not the official receiver and the basis of his remuneration is not fixed as above within 18 months after the date of the trustee's appointment, the trustee shall be entitled to remuneration calculated in accordance with Rule 6.138A.

GENERAL NOTE

The IA 1986 is silent on the question of the trustee's remuneration. This provision lays down the general rules for determining the rate of remuneration by the creditors' committee. For the meaning of "general regulations" in r.6.138(6), see r.13.13(5). In a case decided under the 1914 Act the court decided that the use of the official receiver's scale was not suitable to be applied to value the work of a private practitioner—*Upton v Taylor and Colley* [1999] B.P.I.R. 168. For comment on assessment of a trustee's remuneration see *Mirror Group Newspapers v Maxwell* [1998] B.C.C. 324 at 336, per Ferris J. On taxation the claim for fees and disbursements was largely upheld—see the note in [1999] B.C.C. 684 (a rare instance of a determination on a matter of taxation of costs being reported). Matters in this area were reviewed by the Ferris Working Party in 1998 and a revised SIP 9 was published in December 2002. See *Freeburn v Hunt* [2010] B.P.I.R. 325. Paragraph (6) was remodelled by I(A)R 2004 (SI 2004/584) with effect from April 1, 2004. It anticipates the introduction of IR r.6.138A. The move towards greater transparency with regard to remuneration is reflected by the insertion of reg.36A into the Insolvency Regulations 1994 (SI 1994/2507) by the Insolvency (Amendment) Regulations 2005 (SI 2005/512). This new regulation requires trustees (and other insolvency practitioners) to give a breakdown on how fees are calculated by reference to time spent on the case by different categories of staff in the firm if so requested by either the bankrupt or creditors. Substantially amended by I(A)R 2010 (SI 2010/686)—new paras (3A) to (3C) inserted to replace former para.(3). Note in para.(6) that an 18-month limitation period has been introduced.

6.138A   Trustee's remuneration where it is not fixed in accordance with Rule 6.138

6.138A(1)   **[Application of rule]** This Rule applies where the trustee is not the official receiver and his remuneration is not fixed in accordance with Rule 6.138.

6.138A(2)   **[How fixed]** Subject to paragraph (3), the trustee shall be entitled by way of remuneration for his services as such, to such sum as is arrived at by–

    (a)   first applying the realisation scale set out in Schedule 6 to the monies received by him from the realisation of the assets of the bankrupt (including any Value Added Tax thereon but after deducting any sums paid to secured creditors in respect of their securities and any sums spent out of money received in carrying on the business of the bankrupt); and

    (b)   then by adding to the sum arrived at under sub-paragraph (a) such sum as is arrived at by applying the distribution scale set out in Schedule 6 to the value of assets distributed to creditors of the bankrupt (including sums paid in respect of preferential debts).

6.138A(3)   **[Not to exceed bankruptcy debts and expenses]** That part of the trustee's remuneration calculated by reference to the realisation scale shall not exceed such sum as is arrived at by applying the realisation scale to such part of the bankrupt's assets as are required to pay the items referred to in paragraph (4).

6.138A(4)   **[Bankruptcy debts and expenses]** The items referred to in paragraph (3) are–

    (a)   the bankruptcy debts (including any interest payable by virtue of section 328(4)) to the extent required to be paid by these Rules (ignoring those debts paid otherwise than out of the proceeds of the realisation of the bankrupt's assets or which have been secured to the satisfaction of the court);

(b)   the expenses of the bankruptcy other than–

    (i)   fees or the remuneration of the official receiver; and

    (ii)   any sums spent out of money received in carrying on the business of the bankrupt;

(c)   fees payable by virtue of any order made under section 415; and

(d)   the remuneration of the official receiver.

GENERAL NOTE

This new rule was added by I(A)R 2004 (SI 2004/584) with effect from April 1, 2004. It deals with the fixing of remuneration in circumstances not covered by IR 1986 r.6.138. Note the use of the realisation scale mapped out in the new Sch.6.

6.139   Other matters affecting remuneration

6.139(1)   [Where trustee sells for secured creditor] Where the trustee (not being the official receiver) realises assets on behalf of a secured creditor, the trustee is entitled to such sum by way of remuneration as is arrived at by applying the realisation scale set out in Schedule 6 to the monies received by him in respect of the assets realised (including any Value Added Tax thereon).

6.139(2)   [Where joint trustees] Where there are joint trustees, it is for them to agree between themselves as to how the remuneration payable should be apportioned. Any dispute arising between them may be referred–

(a)   to the court, for settlement by order, or

(b)   to the creditors' committee or a meeting of creditors, for settlement by resolution.

6.139(3)   [If trustee is a solicitor] If the trustee is a solicitor and employs his own firm, or any partner in it, to act on behalf of the estate, profit costs shall not be paid unless this is authorised by the creditors' committee, the creditors or the court.

R.6.139(1)
This relates to remuneration where the trustee is really acting for the benefit of a secured creditor. A new para.(1) was substituted by I(A)R 2004 (SI 2004/584) with effect from April 1, 2004. This extends the use of the new Sch.6 realisation scale to circumstances where the realisation is carried out on behalf of a secured creditor.

6.140   Recourse of trustee to meeting of creditors [Deleted.]

6.140A   Recourse of trustee to meeting of creditors

6.140A   If the basis of the trustee's remuneration has been fixed by the creditors' committee and the trustee considers the rate or amount to be insufficient or the basis to be inappropriate, the trustee may request that the rate or amount be increased or the basis changed by resolution of the creditors.

GENERAL NOTE

I(A)R 2010 (SI 2010/686) introduces this to replace former IR r.6.140.

6.141   Recourse to the court

6.141(1)   [Power of trustee to apply for increase] If the trustee considers that the basis of remuneration fixed by the creditors' committee, or by resolution of the creditors, or as under Rule 6.138(6), is insufficient or inappropriate, the trustee may apply to the court for an order changing it or increasing its amount or rate.

6.141(2)   **[Notice to committee etc.]** The trustee shall give at least 14 days' notice of his application to the members of the creditors' committee; and the committee may nominate one or more members to appear or be represented, and to be heard, on the application.

6.141(3)   **[If no committee]** If there is no creditors' committee, the trustee's notice of his application shall be sent to such one or more of the bankrupt's creditors as the court may direct, which creditors may nominate one or more of their number to appear or be represented.

6.141(4)   **[Costs of application]** The court may, if it appears to be a proper case, order the costs of the trustee's application, including the costs of any member of the creditors' committee appearing or being represented on it, or any creditor so appearing or being represented, to be paid out of the estate.

(See General Note after r.6.142.) A new para.(1) is substituted by I(A)R 2010 (SI 2010/686).

6.142   Creditor's claim that remuneration is or other expenses are excessive

6.142(1)   **[Application to court]** Any secured creditor, or any unsecured creditor with either the concurrence of at least 10% in value of the creditors (including that creditor) or the permission of the court, or the bankrupt may apply to the court for one or more of the orders in paragraph (4).

6.142(1A)   **[Grounds of application]** Application by a creditor may be made on the grounds that–

    (a)   the remuneration charged by the trustee,

    (b)   the basis fixed for the trustee's remuneration under Rule 6.138, or

    (c)   expenses incurred by the trustee,

is or are, in all the circumstances, excessive or, in the case of an application under sub-paragraph (b), inappropriate.

6.142(1B)   **[Time limit for application]** Application by a creditor must, subject to any order of the court under Rule 6.78C(5), be made no later than 8 weeks (or in a case falling within Rule 6.126, 4 weeks) after receipt by the applicant of the progress report, or the draft report under Rule 6.78B, which first reports the charging of the remuneration or the incurring of the expenses in question ("the relevant report").

6.142(1C)   **[Application by bankrupt]** Application by the bankrupt may be made only on one or both of the grounds in paragraph (1A)(a) and (c) and no later than–

    (a)   8 weeks after receipt by the bankrupt of the draft report under Rule 6.78B, or

    (b)   in a case falling within Rule 6.126, 4 weeks after receipt by the bankrupt of notice under Rule 6.126(1C).

6.142(2)   **[Power of court on application by creditor]** When the application is made by a creditor, the court may dismiss it if it thinks that no sufficient cause is shown; but it must not do so unless the applicant has had an opportunity to attend the court for a hearing of which the applicant has been given at least 5 business days' notice but which is without notice to any other party.

6.142(2A)   **[Permission of court for application by bankrupt]** Application may be made by the bankrupt only with the permission of the court; and without prejudice to the generality of the matters which the court may take into account, permission must not be given unless the bankrupt shows that there is (or would be but for the remuneration or expenses in question), or that it is likely that there will be (or would be but for the remuneration or expenses in question), a surplus of assets to which the bankrupt would be entitled.

6.142(2B)   **[Court to fix venue for application]** If, as the case may be, the application is not dismissed under paragraph (2) or the bankrupt is given permission under paragraph (2A), the court must fix a venue for the application to be heard.

6.142(3)   [Notice to trustee] The applicant shall, at least 14 days before the hearing, send to the trustee a notice stating the venue so fixed; and the notice shall be accompanied by a copy of the application, and of any evidence which the applicant intends to adduce in support of it.

6.142(4)   [Court order if application well-founded] If the court considers the application to be well-founded, it must make one or more of the following orders–

(a)   an order reducing the amount of remuneration which the trustee was entitled to charge;

(b)   an order fixing the basis of remuneration at a reduced rate or amount;

(c)   an order changing the basis of remuneration;

(d)   an order that some or all of the remuneration or expenses in question be treated as not being bankruptcy expenses;

(e)   an order that the trustee or the trustee's personal representative pay to such person as the court may specify as property comprised in the bankrupt's estate the amount of the excess of remuneration or expenses or such part of the excess as the court may specify;

and may make any other order that it thinks just; but an order under sub-paragraph (b) or (c) may be made only in respect of periods after the period covered by the relevant report.

6.142(5)   [Costs of application] Unless the court orders otherwise, the costs of the application shall be paid by the applicant, and do not fall on the estate.

GENERAL NOTE TO RR.6.141, 6.142

For an example of an application by a trustee under this provision see *Barker v Bajjon* [2008] B.P.I.R. 771. The court will always have the final say on issues of remuneration. If a creditor wishes to challenge the trustee's remuneration he must have the support of 25 per cent in value of the creditors. For governing principles see *Practice Statement: The Fixing and Approval of Remuneration of Appointees* [2004] B.C.C. 912, reproduced as App.VII in Vol.2. The *Practice Statement* was considered by David Richards J. in *Simion v Brown* [2007] B.P.I.R. 412 where a creditor challenged the remuneration claimed by the trustee. The judge made a number of important points. In small bankruptcies the amount of remuneration/expenses will be inevitably appear disproportionately large. A trustee has to carry out certain statutory functions and this has cost implications. The guiding principle under the *Practice Statement* was whether the work undertaken provided value for money. Itemisation of all expenses was to be recommended rather than a general claim for overheads. The court considered the *Practice Statement on the Remuneration of Appointees* [2004] B.C.C. 912 in *Hunt v Yearwood-Grazette* [2009] B.P.I.R. 810 on an application by the trustee under IR r.6.142. See generally *Freeburn v Hunt* [2010] B.P.I.R. 325. Rule 6.142 was virtually rewritten by I(A)R 2010 (SI 2010/686).

6.142A   Review of remuneration

6.142A(1)   [Request by trustee] Where, after the basis of the trustee's remuneration has been fixed, there is a material and substantial change in the circumstances which were taken into account in fixing it, the trustee may request that it be changed.

6.142A(2)   [To whom request made] The request must be made–

(a)   where the creditors' committee fixed the basis, to the committee;

(b)   where the creditors fixed the basis, to the creditors;

(c)   where the court fixed the basis, by application to the court;

(d)   where the remuneration was fixed by application of the realisation scale under Rule 6.138A, to the creditors' committee if there is one or otherwise to the creditors;

and Rules 6.138 to 6.142 apply as appropriate.

6.142A(3)   [Change in basis of remuneration] Any change in the basis for remuneration applies from the date of the request under paragraph (2) and not for any earlier period.

6.142A(4)   [Non-application to official receiver] This Rule does not apply where the trustee is the official receiver.

GENERAL NOTE

Inserted by I(A)R 2010 (SI 2010/686).

6.142B   Remuneration of new trustee

6.142B(1)   [Continuation of remuneration provisions of former trustee] If a new trustee is appointed in place of another, any determination, resolution or court order in effect under the preceding provisions of this Section of this Chapter immediately before the former trustee ceased to hold office continues to apply in respect of the remuneration of the new trustee until a further determination, resolution or court order is made in accordance with those provisions.

6.142B(2)   [Non-application to official receiver] This Rule does not apply where the new trustee is the official receiver.

GENERAL NOTE

Inserted by I(A)R 2010 (SI 2010/686).

6.142C   Apportionment of set fee remuneration

6.142C(1)   [Apportionment of set amount of remuneration of former trustee] In a case in which the basis of the trustee's remuneration is a set amount under Rule 6.138(2)(c) and the trustee ("the former trustee") ceases (for whatever reason) to hold office before the time has elapsed or the work has been completed in respect of which the amount was set, application may be made for determination of what portion of the amount should be paid to the former trustee or the former trustee's personal representative in respect of the time which has actually elapsed or the work which has actually been done.

6.142C(2)   [Application by former trustee or new trustee] Application may be made–

(a)   by the former trustee or the former trustee's personal representative within the period of 28 days beginning with the date upon which the former trustee ceased to hold office, or

(b)   by the trustee for the time being in office if the former trustee or the former trustee's personal representative has not applied by the end of that period.

6.142C(3)   [To whom application made] Application must be made–

(a)   where the creditors' committee fixed the basis, to the committee;

(b)   where the creditors fixed the basis, to the creditors for a resolution determining the portion;

(c)   where the court fixed the basis, to the court for an order determining the portion.

6.142C(4)   [Copy of application to the recipient] The applicant must give a copy of the application to the trustee for the time being in office or to the former trustee or the former trustee's personal representative, as the case may be ("the recipient").

6.142C(5)   [Notice of intent by recipient to make representations] The recipient may within 21 days of receipt of the copy of the application give notice of intent to make representations to the creditors' committee or the creditors or to appear or be represented before the court, as the case may be.

6.142C(6)   [Minimum period for determination] No determination may be made upon the application until expiry of the 21 days referred to in paragraph (5) or, if the recipient does give notice of intent in accordance with that paragraph, until the recipient has been afforded the opportunity to make representations or to appear or be represented, as the case may be.

6.142C(7) **[Application to increase portion]** If the former trustee or the former trustee's personal representative (whether or not the original applicant) considers that the portion determined upon application to the creditors' committee or the creditors is insufficient, that person may apply–

(a) in the case of a determination by the creditors' committee, to the creditors for a resolution increasing the portion;

(b) in the case of a resolution of the creditors (whether under paragraph (1) or under sub-paragraph (a)), to the court for an order increasing the portion,

and paragraphs (4) to (6) apply as appropriate.

GENERAL NOTE

Inserted by I(A)R 2010 (SI 2010/686).

Section E: Supplementary provisions

6.143 Trustee deceased

6.143(1) **[Notice to official receiver]** Subject as follows, where the trustee (other than the official receiver) has died, it is the duty of his personal representatives to give notice of the fact to the official receiver, specifying the date of the death.

This does not apply if notice has been given under any of the following paragraphs of this Rule.

6.143(2) **[Notice by partner etc.]** If the deceased trustee was a partner in or an employee of a firm, notice may be given to the official receiver by a partner in the firm who is qualified to act as an insolvency practitioner, or is a member of any body recognised by the Secretary of State for the authorisation of insolvency practitioners.

6.143(3) **[Notice by others]** Notice of the death may be given by any person producing to the official receiver the relevant death certificate or a copy of it.

6.143(4) **[Notice to court by official receiver]** The official receiver shall give notice to the court, for the purpose of fixing the date of the deceased trustee's release in accordance with section 299(3)(a).

GENERAL NOTE

Note minor modifications are made to para.(2) by I(A)R 2010 (SI 2010/686).

6.144 Loss of qualification as insolvency practitioner

6.144(1) **[Application of Rule]** This Rule applies where the trustee vacates office, under section 298(6), on his ceasing to be qualified to act as an insolvency practitioner in relation to the bankrupt.

6.144(2) **[Notice to official receiver etc.]** The trustee vacating office shall as soon as reasonably practicable give notice of his doing so to the official receiver, who shall give notice to the Secretary of State.

The official receiver shall file in court a copy of his notice under this paragraph.

[FORM 6.51]

6.144(3) **[Application of r.6.135]** Rule 6.135 applies as regards the trustee obtaining his release, as if he had been removed by the court.

GENERAL NOTE

This expands IA 1986 s.298(6). On qualification, see IA 1986 Pt XIII.

6.145 Notice to official receiver of intention to vacate office

6.145(1) **[Notice of official receiver]** Where the trustee intends to vacate office, whether by resignation or otherwise, he shall give notice of his intention to the official receiver together with notice of any creditors' meeting to be held in respect of his vacation of office, including any meeting to receive his resignation.

6.145(2) **[Time limit for notice]** The notice to the official receiver must be given at least 21 days before any such creditors' meeting.

6.145(3) **[Details of property]** Where there remains in the bankrupt's estate any property which has not been realised, applied, distributed or otherwise fully dealt with in the bankruptcy, the trustee shall include in his notice to the official receiver details of the nature of that property, its value (or the fact that it has no value), its location, any action taken by the trustee to deal with that property or any reason for his not dealing with it, and the current position in relation to it.

GENERAL NOTE

Rule 6.145(3) makes it clear that valueless property must now be detailed in the report to the official receiver. The word "assets" used in the previous version of r.6.145 has now been dropped to clarify matters. See also *Dear IP* Issue 25 (December 2005).

6.146 Trustee's duties on vacating office

6.146(1) **[Obligation to deliver any assets etc.]** Where the trustee ceases to be in office as such, in consequence of removal, resignation or cesser of qualification as an insolvency practitioner, he is under obligation as soon as reasonably practicable to deliver up to the person succeeding him as trustee the assets of the estate (after deduction of any expenses properly incurred, and distributions made, by him) and further to deliver up to that person–

(a)   the records of the bankruptcy, including correspondence, proofs and other related papers appertaining to the bankruptcy while it was within his responsibility, and

(b)   the bankrupt's books, papers and other records.

6.146(2) [Omitted.]

GENERAL NOTE

This ties up matters left unresolved by IA 1986 s.298. Paragraph (2) was omitted by I(A)R 2004 (SI 2004/584) with effect from April 1, 2004. Again this appears to be a new cost cutting device.

6.147 Power of court to set aside certain transactions

6.147(1) **[Trustee's transaction with associate]** If in the administration of the estate the trustee enters into any transaction with a person who is an associate of his, the court may, on the application of any person interested, set the transaction aside and order the trustee to compensate the estate for any loss suffered in consequence of it.

6.147(2) **[Where r.6.147(1) does not apply]** This does not apply if either–

(a)   the transaction was entered into with the prior consent of the court, or

(b)   it is shown to the court's satisfaction that the transaction was for value, and that it was entered into by the trustee without knowing, or having any reason to suppose, that the person concerned was an associate.

6.147(3) **[Effect of Rule]** Nothing in this Rule is to be taken as prejudicing the operation of any rule of law or equity with respect to a trustee's dealings with trust property, or the fiduciary obligations of any person.

This power is sufficiently important to have been located within the text of IA 1986. For "associate" see IA 1986 s.435.

6.148   Rule against solicitation

6.148(1)   **[Power of court]** Where the court is satisfied that any improper solicitation has been used by or on behalf of the trustee in obtaining proxies or procuring his appointment, it may order that no remuneration out of the estate be allowed to any person by whom, or on whose behalf, the solicitation was exercised.

6.148(2)   **[Effect of court order]** An order of the court under this Rule overrides any resolution of the creditors' committee or the creditors, or any other provision of the Rules relating to the trustee's remuneration.

6.149   Enforcement of trustee's obligations to official receiver

6.149(1)   **[Powers of court]** The court may, on the application of the official receiver, make such orders as it thinks necessary for enforcement of the duties of the trustee under section 305(3) (information and assistance to be given; production and inspection of books and records relating to the bankruptcy).

6.149(2)   **[Extent of order]** An order of the court under this Rule may provide that all costs of and incidental to the official receiver's application shall be borne by the trustee.

GENERAL NOTE

See IA 1986 s.305(3).

CHAPTER 11

THE CREDITORS' COMMITTEE

6.150   Membership of creditors' committee

6.150(1)   **[Three-five members]** The creditors' committee shall consist of at least 3, and not more than 5, members.

6.150(2)   **[Eligibility]** A person claiming to be a creditor is entitled to be a member of the committee provided that–

  (a)   that person has lodged a proof of debt;

  (b)   the proof mentioned in sub-paragraph (a) has neither been wholly disallowed for voting purposes, nor wholly rejected for the purpose of distribution or dividend; and

  (c)   the debt mentioned in sub-paragraph (a) is not fully secured.

6.150(3)   **[Representation of body corporate]** A body corporate may be a member of the committee, but it cannot act as such otherwise than by a representative appointed under Rule 6.156.

GENERAL NOTE

This develops IA 1986 s.301. *Foenander v Allan* [2006] B.P.I.R. 1392 indicates that for the purposes of IR 1986 r.6.150(2) eligibility is to be determined by proof of debt and not by other unproved claims. Paragraph (2) has been replaced by I(A)R 2010 (SI 2010/686).

6.151   Formalities of establishment

6.151(1)   [Trustee's certificate of due constitution] The creditors' committee does not come into being, and accordingly cannot act, until the trustee has issued a certificate of its due constitution.

[FORM 6.52]

6.151(2)   [If chairman of meeting not trustee] If the chairman of the creditors' meeting which resolves to establish the committee is not the trustee, he shall as soon as reasonably practicable give notice of the resolution to the trustee (or, as the case may be, the person appointed as trustee by that same meeting), and inform him of the names and addresses of the persons elected to be members of the committee.

6.151(3)   [Agreement to act] No person may act as a member of the committee unless and until he has agreed to do so and, unless the relevant proxy or authorisation contains a statement to the contrary, such agreement may be given by his proxy-holder present at the meeting establishing the committee.

6.151(3A)   [No certificate without agreement] The trustee's certificate of the committee's due constitution shall not be issued before the minimum number of members set out in Rule 6.150 elected to be members of the committee have agreed to act and must be issued as soon as reasonably practicable thereafter.

6.151(4)   [Amended certificate] As and when the others (if any) agree to act, the trustee shall issue an amended certificate.

[FORM 6.52]

6.151(5)   [Certificate to be filed] The certificate, and any amended certificate, shall be filed in court by the trustee as soon as reasonably practicable.

6.151(6)   [Change in membership of committee] If after the first establishment of the committee there is any change in its membership, as soon as reasonably practicable the trustee must file with the court notice of the change.

G<small>ENERAL</small> N<small>OTE</small>

This rule was amended to facilitate immediate committee meetings after the creditors' meeting. The original r.6.151(3) has been broken down into (3) and (3A). Modernised by I(A)R 2010 (SI 2010/686).

6.152   Obligations of trustee to committee

6.152(1)   [Trustee's duty to report] Subject as follows, it is the duty of the trustee to report to the members of the creditors' committee all such matters as appear to him to be, or as they have indicated to him as being, of concern to them with respect to the bankruptcy.

6.152(2)   [Non-compliance with request for information] In the case of matters so indicated to him by the committee, the trustee need not comply with any request for information where it appears to him that–

(a)   the request is frivolous or unreasonable, or

(b)   the cost of complying would be excessive, having regard to the relative importance of the information, or

(c)   the estate is without funds sufficient for enabling him to comply.

6.152(3)   [Report in summary form] Where the committee has come into being more than 28 days after the appointment of the trustee, the latter shall report to them, in summary form, what actions he has taken since his appointment, and shall answer such questions as they may put to him regarding his conduct of the bankruptcy hitherto.

6.152(4) **[Summary report for subsequent member]** A person who becomes a member of the committee at any time after its first establishment is not entitled to require a report to him by the trustee, otherwise than in summary form, of any matters previously arising.

6.152(5) **[Access to trustee's records]** Nothing in this Rule disentitles the committee, or any member of it, from having access to the trustee's records of the bankruptcy, or from seeking an explanation of any matter within the committee's responsibility.

GENERAL NOTE

This imposes a duty on the trustee to keep the committee informed (subject to r.6.152(2)). Note also r.6.163.

6.153 Meetings of the committee

6.153(1) **[Holding of meetings]** Subject as follows, meetings of the creditors' committee shall be held when and where determined by the trustee.

6.153(2) **[First and subsequent meetings]** The trustee shall call a first meeting of the committee to take place within 6 weeks of the committee's establishment; and thereafter he shall call a meeting–

(a) if so requested by a member of the committee or his representative (the meeting then to be held within 21 days of the request being received by the trustee), and

(b) for a specified date, if the committee has previously resolved that a meeting be held on that date.

6.153(3) **[Notice of venue]** Subject to paragraph (4), the trustee shall give 5 business days' notice in writing of the venue of any meeting to every member of the committee (or his representative, if designated for that purpose), unless in any case the requirement of the notice has been waived by or on behalf of any member.

Waiver may be signified either at or before the meeting.

6.153(4) **[Notice for remote meeting]** Where the trustee has determined that a meeting should be conducted and held in the manner referred to in Rule 12A.26(2), the notice period mentioned in paragraph (3) is 7 business days.

6.153(5) **[Committee to assist trustee]** In addition to any functions conferred on a committee by any provision of the Act, a committee must assist the trustee in discharging the trustee's functions and act in relation to that trustee in such manner as may from time to time be agreed.

(See General Note after r.6.156.) Modernised by I(A)R 2010 (SI 2010/686). There is the usual change from seven days to five business days. The period in para.(2) is cut from three months to six weeks. New paras (4) and (5) have been added.

6.154 The chairman at meetings

6.154(1) **[Trustee or his nominee]** The chairman at any meeting of the creditors committee shall be the trustee, or a person appointed by him in writing to act.

6.154(2) **[Appointed chairman]** A person so appointed must be either–

(a) one who is qualified to act as an insolvency practitioner in relation to the bankrupt, or

(b) an employee of the trustee or his firm who is experienced in insolvency matters.

(See General Note after r.6.156.)

6.155 Quorum

6.155 A meeting of the committee is duly constituted if due notice of it has been given to all the members and at least 2 of the members are present or represented.

(See General Note after r.6.156.)

6.156   Committee-members' representatives

6.156(1)   **[Representation]** A member of the creditors' committee may, in relation to the business of the committee, be represented by another person duly authorised by him for that purpose.

6.156(2)   **[Letter of authority]** A person acting as a committee-member's representative must hold a letter of authority entitling him so to act (either generally or specially) and authenticated by or on behalf of the committee-member, and for this purpose any proxy in relation to any meeting of creditors of the bankrupt shall, unless it contains a statement to the contrary, be treated as such a letter of authority to act generally authenticated by or on behalf of the committee-member.

6.156(3)   **[Production of letter of authority]** The chairman at any meeting of the committee may call on a person claiming to act as a committee-member's representative to produce his letter of authority, and may exclude him if it appears that his authority is deficient.

6.156(4)   **[Who may not be a representative]** No member may be represented by–

(a)   another member of the committee;

(b)   a person who is at the same time representing another committee member;

(c)   a body corporate;

(d)   an undischarged bankrupt;

(e)   a disqualified director; or

(f)   a person who is subject to a bankruptcy restrictions order (including an interim order), a bankruptcy restrictions undertaking, a debt relief restrictions order (including an interim order) or a debt relief restrictions undertaking.

6.156(5)   [Omitted.]

6.156(6)   **[Authenticating as representative]** Where the representative of a committee-member authenticates any document on the latter's behalf, the fact that he so authenticates must be stated below his authentication.

6.156(7)   **[Validity of acts]** The acts of the committee are valid notwithstanding any defect in the appointment or qualifications of any committee-member's representative.

GENERAL NOTE TO RR.6.153–6.156

These rules regulate meetings of the committee. Note that the quorum is fixed at two members. Committee members may appoint representatives to act on their behalf. The wording of para.(4) was modified by I(A)R 2004 (SI 2004/584) with effect from April 1, 2004 to include reference to disqualified directors and those subject to BROs, etc. The former reference to the exclusion of persons who had entered compositions with creditors was removed. Paragraph (4) has been replaced and para.(5) deleted by I(A)R 2010 (SI 2010/686).

6.157   Resignation

6.157   A member of the creditors' committee may resign by notice in writing delivered to the trustee.

6.158   Termination of membership

6.158(1)   **[Automatic termination]** A person's membership of the creditors committee is automatically terminated if–

(a)   he becomes bankrupt, or

(b)   at 3 consecutive meetings of the committee he is neither present nor represented (unless at the third of those meetings it is resolved that this Rule is not to apply in his case), or

(c)   ceases to be a creditor and a period of 3 months has elapsed from the date that that member ceased to be a creditor or is found never to have been a creditor.

6.158(2)   [Termination on bankruptcy] However, if the cause of termination is the member's bankruptcy, his trustee in bankruptcy replaces him as a member of the committee.

GENERAL NOTE

Note the sanction against absenteeism. The former reference in para.(1)(a) to compositions or arrangements with creditors was removed by I(A)R 2004 (SI 2004/584) with effect from April 1, 2004. Paragraph (1)(c) has been modified by I(A)R 2010 (SI 2010/686).

6.159   Removal

6.159   A member of the creditors' committee may be removed by resolution at a meeting of creditors, at least 14 days' notice having been given of the intention to move that resolution.

6.160   Vacancies

6.160(1)   [Application of Rule] The following applies if there is a vacancy in the membership of the creditors' committee.

6.160(2)   [Agreement not to fill vacancy] The vacancy need not be filled if the trustee and a majority of the remaining committee-members so agree, provided that the number of members does not fall below 3.

6.160(3)   [Appointment by trustee] The trustee may appoint any creditor (being qualified under the Rules to be a member of the committee) to fill the vacancy, if a majority of the other members of the committee agree to the appointment and the creditor concerned consents to act.

6.160(4)   [Appointment by resolution] Alternatively, a meeting of creditors may resolve that a creditor be appointed (with his consent) to fill the vacancy. In this case at least 14 days' notice must have been given of a resolution to make such an appointment (whether or not of a person named in the notice).

6.160(5)   [Report to trustee] Where the vacancy is filled by an appointment made by a creditors' meeting at which the trustee is not present, the chairman of the meeting shall report to the trustee the appointment which has been made.

6.161   Voting rights and resolutions

6.161(1)   [Votes etc.] At any meeting of the committee, each member (whether present himself, or by his representative) has one vote; and a resolution is passed when a majority of the members present or represented have voted in favour of it.

6.161(2)   [Record of resolutions] Every resolution passed shall be recorded in writing, either separately or as part of the minutes of the meeting. The record shall be authenticated by the chairman and kept with the records of the bankruptcy.

GENERAL NOTE

Committee resolutions are to be passed by simple majority and there is to be no weighting of votes.

6.162   Resolutions otherwise than at a meeting

6.162(1)   [Sending proposed resolution] In accordance with this Rule, the trustee may seek to obtain the agreement of members of the creditors' committee to a resolution by sending to every member (or his representative designated for the purpose) a copy of the proposed resolution.

6.162(2)   [Copy of proposed resolution] Where the trustee makes use of the procedure allowed by this Rule, he shall send out to members of the committee or their representatives (as the case may be) a copy of any proposed resolution on which a decision is sought, which shall be set out in such a way that agreement with or dissent from each separate resolution may be indicated by the recipient on the copy so sent.

6.162(3) **[Member requiring meeting]** Any member of the committee may, within 7 business days from the date of the trustee sending out a resolution, require the trustee to summon a meeting of the committee to consider the matters raised by the resolution.

6.162(4) **[Deemed passing of resolution]** In the absence of such a request, the resolution is deemed to have been carried in the committee if and when the trustee is notified in writing by a majority of the members that they concur with it.

6.162(5) **[Copy resolutions]** A copy of every resolution passed under this Rule, and a note that the concurrence of the committee was obtained, shall be kept with the records of the bankruptcy.

GENERAL NOTE

I(A)R 2010 (SI 2010/686) amends heading. This is to make life easy for committee members (and for the trustee). The change to r.6.162(2) is intended to prevent proliferation of documents. Rule 6.162(3) now refers to "business days" (for definition, see r.13.13(1)).

6.163 Trustee's reports

6.163(1) **[Trustee directed to report]** The trustee shall, as and when directed by the creditors' committee (but not more often than once in any period of 2 months), send a written report to every member of the committee setting out the position generally as regards the progress of the bankruptcy and matters arising in connection with it, to which he (the trustee) considers the committee's attention should be drawn.

6.163(2) **[If no directions to report]** In the absence of any such directions by the committee, the trustee shall send such a report not less often than once in every period of 6 months.

6.163(3) **[Effect of Rule]** The obligations of the trustee under this Rule are without prejudice to those imposed by Rule 6.152.

GENERAL NOTE

The trustee can be required to submit two-monthly reports to the committee.

6.164 Expenses of members etc.

6.164 The trustee shall defray out of the estate, in the prescribed order of priority, any reasonable travelling expenses directly incurred by members of the creditors' committee or their representatives in respect of their attendance at the committee's meetings, or otherwise on the committee's business.

6.165 Dealings by committee-members and others

6.165(1) **[Application of Rule]** This Rule applies to–

(a) any member of the creditors' committee,

(b) any committee-member's representative,

(c) any person who is an associate of a member of the committee or a committee-member's representative, and

(d) any person who has been a member of the committee at any time in the last 12 months.

6.165(2) **[Prohibited transactions]** Subject as follows, a person to whom this Rule applies shall not enter into any transaction whereby he–

(a)   receives out of the estate any payment for services given or goods supplied in connection with the estate's administration, or

(b)   obtains any profit from the administration, or

(c)   acquires any asset forming part of the estate.

6.165(3)   [Permission or sanction for r.6.165(2) transaction] Such a transaction may be entered into by a person to whom this Rule applies–

(a)   with the prior permission of the court, or

(b)   if he does so as a matter of urgency, or by way of performance of a contract in force before the commencement of the bankruptcy, and obtains the court's permission for the transaction, having applied for it without undue delay, or

(c)   with the prior sanction of the creditors' committee, where it is satisfied (after full disclosure of the circumstances) that the person will be giving full value in the transaction.

6.165(4)   [Resolution to sanction transaction] Where in the committee a resolution is proposed that sanction be accorded for a transaction to be entered into which, without that sanction or the permission of the court, would be in contravention of this Rule, no member of the committee, and no representative of a member, shall vote if he is to participate directly or indirectly in the transaction.

6.165(5)   [Powers of court] The court may, on the application of any person interested–

(a)   set aside a transaction on the ground that it has been entered into in contravention of this Rule, and

(b)   make with respect to it such other order as it thinks fit, including (subject to the following paragraph) an order requiring a person to whom this Rule applies to account for any profit obtained from the transaction and compensate the estate for any resultant loss.

6.165(6)   [Member's or representative's associate] In the case of a person to whom this Rule applies as an associate of a member of the committee or of a committee-member's representative the court shall not make any order under paragraph (5), if satisfied that he entered into the relevant transaction without having any reason to suppose that in doing so he would contravene this Rule.

6.165(7)   [Costs of application] The costs of an application to the court for permission under this Rule do not fall on the estate, unless the court so orders.

GENERAL NOTE

This imposes strict controls on dealings between committee members, *et al.* and the estate. Full disclosure is required and the permission of the court or of the creditors must first be obtained. The court can set aside transactions contravening these rules. Once again, an important substantive provision like this would have been more appropriately placed in IA 1986 itself. See also *Re Gallard* [1896] 1 Q.B. 68; and *Re Bulmer Ex p. Greaves* [1937] Ch. 499.

6.166   Committee's functions vested in Secretary of State

6.166(1)   [Trustee's notices and reports] At any time when the functions of the creditors' committee are vested in the Secretary of State under section 302(1) or (2), requirements of the Act or the Rules about notices to be given, or reports to be made, to the committee by the trustee do not apply, otherwise than as enabling the committee to require a report as to any matter.

6.166(2)   [Exercise by official receiver] Where the committee's functions are so vested under section 302(2), they may be exercised by the official receiver.

GENERAL NOTE

See IA 1986 s.302.

6.167   Appointment and remuneration

6.167(1)   [Application under s.370 to be supported by report] An application made by the official receiver or trustee under section 370 for the appointment of a person to be special manager shall be supported by a report setting out the reasons for the application.

The report shall include the applicant's estimate of the value of the estate, property or business in respect of which the special manager is to be appointed.

6.167(2)   [Duration of appointment] The court's order appointing the special manager shall specify the duration of his appointment, which may be for a period of time, or until the occurrence of a specified event. Alternatively, the order may specify that the duration of the appointment is to be subject to a further order of the court.

[FORM 6.54]

6.167(3)   [Renewal] The appointment of a special manager may be renewed by order of the court.

6.167(4)   [Remuneration] The special manager's remuneration shall be fixed from time to time by the court.

(See General Note after r.6.171.)

6.168   Security

6.168(1)   [Effect of giving security] The appointment of the special manager does not take effect until the person appointed has given (or, being allowed by the court to do so, undertaken to give) security to the person who applies for him to be appointed.

6.168(2)   [Special or general security] It is not necessary that security shall be given for each separate bankruptcy; but it may be given either specially for a particular bankruptcy, or generally for any bankruptcy in relation to which the special manager may be employed as such.

6.168(3)   [Amount of security] The amount of the security shall be not less than the value of the estate, property or business in respect of which he is appointed, as estimated by the applicant in his report under Rule 6.167(1).

6.168(4)   [Certificate of adequacy] When the special manager has given security to the person applying for his appointment, that person's certificate as to the adequacy of the security shall be filed in court.

6.168(5)   [Cost of providing security] The cost of providing the security shall be paid in the first instance by the special manager; but–

(a)   where a bankruptcy order is not made, he is entitled to be reimbursed out of the property of the debtor, and the court may make an order on the debtor accordingly, and

(b)   where a bankruptcy order is made, he is entitled to be reimbursed out of the estate in the prescribed order of priority.

(See General Note after r.6.171.)

6.169   Failure to give or keep up security

6.169(1)   [Failure to give security] If the special manager fails to give the required security within the time stated for that purpose by the order appointing him, or any extension of that time that may be allowed, the official receiver or trustee (as the case may be) shall report the failure to the court, which may thereupon discharge the order appointing the special manager.

6.169(2) **[Failure to keep up security]** If the special manager fails to keep up his security, the official receiver or trustee shall report his failure to the court, which may thereupon remove the special manager, and make such order as it thinks fit as to costs.

6.169(3) **[Directions on removal]** If an order is made under this Rule removing the special manager, or discharging the order appointing him, the court shall give directions as to whether any, and if so what, steps should be taken for the appointment of another special manager in his place.

(See General Note after r.6.171.)

6.170 Accounting

6.170(1) **[Contents of accounts]** The special manager shall produce accounts, containing details of his receipts and payments, for the approval of the trustee.

6.170(2) **[Period of accounts]** The accounts shall be in respect of 3-month periods for the duration of the special manager's appointment (or for a lesser period, if his appointment terminates less than 3 months from its date, or from the date to which the last accounts were made up).

6.170(3) **[When accounts approved]** When the accounts have been approved, the special manager's receipts and payments shall be added to those of the trustee.

(See General Note after r.6.171.)

6.171 Termination of appointment

6.171(1) **[Automatic termination]** The special manager's appointment terminates if the bankruptcy petition is dismissed or if, an interim receiver having been appointed, the latter is discharged without a bankruptcy order having been made.

6.171(2) **[Application to court]** If the official receiver or the trustee is of opinion that the employment of the special manager is no longer necessary or profitable for the estate, he shall apply to the court for directions, and the court may order the special manager's appointment to be terminated.

6.171(3) **[Resolution of creditors]** The official receiver or the trustee shall make the same application if a resolution of the creditors is passed, requesting that the appointment be terminated.

GENERAL NOTE TO RR.6.167–6.171

These rules develop the provisions of IA 1986 s.370. If the court appoints a special manager, Form 6.54 is to be used. The court fixes his remuneration. Security is required. The special manager must provide three-monthly accounts for the trustee. The circumstances leading to the termination of the appointment of the special manager are mapped out.

CHAPTER 13

PUBLIC EXAMINATION OF BANKRUPT

6.172 Order for public examination

6.172(1) **[Copy of order to bankrupt]** If the official receiver applies to the court, under section 290, for the public examination of the bankrupt, a copy of the court's order shall, as soon as reasonably practicable after its making, be sent by the official receiver to the bankrupt.

[FORM 6.55]

6.172(2) **[Venue and bankrupt's attendance]** The order shall appoint a venue for the hearing, and direct the bankrupt's attendance thereat.

6.172(3) **[Notice of hearing]** The official receiver shall give at least 14 days' notice of the hearing–

(a) if a trustee has been nominated or appointed, to him;

(b) if a special manager has been appointed, to him; and

(c) subject to any contrary direction of the court, to every creditor of the bankrupt who is known to the official receiver.

6.172(4) [Notice of order to be gazetted] Where the official receiver thinks fit, a notice of the order shall be gazetted not less than 14 days before the day fixed for the hearing.

6.172(5) [Advertisement of notice of order] The official receiver may advertise the notice under paragraph (4) of this Rule in such other manner as the official receiver thinks fit.

6.172(5A) [Additional contents of notices under r.6.172(4), (5)] In addition to the standard contents, notices under paragraphs (4) and (5) must state–

(a) the purpose of the hearing; and

(b) the venue fixed for the hearing.

(See General Note after r.6.177.) Note the change made by the Insolvency (Amendment) Rules 2009 (SI 2009/642) with effect from April 6, 2009. This change involved substituting a new para.(4) and adding a new para.(5). Modernised by I(A)R 2010 (SI 2010/686) with the addition of a new para.(5A).

6.173 Order on request by creditors

6.173(1) [Form of request etc.] A request by a creditor to the official receiver, under section 290(2), for the bankrupt to be publicly examined shall be made in writing and be accompanied by–

(a) a list of the creditors concurring with the request and the amount of their respective claims in the bankruptcy,

(b) from each creditor concurring, written confirmation of his concurrence, and

(c) a statement of the reasons why the examination is requested.

Sub-paragraphs (a) and (b) do not apply if the requisitioning creditor's debt is alone sufficient, without the concurrence of others.

[FORM 6.56]

6.173(2) [Security for expenses of hearing] Before an application to the court is made on the request, the requisitionist shall deposit with the official receiver such sum as the latter may determine to be appropriate by way of security for the expenses of the hearing of a public examination, if ordered.

6.173(3) [Time for application] Subject as follows, the official receiver shall, within 28 days of receiving the request, make the application to the court required by section 290(2).

6.173(4) [Relief from unreasonable request] If the official receiver is of opinion that the request is an unreasonable one in the circumstances, he may apply to the court for an order relieving him from the obligation to make the application otherwise required by that subsection.

6.173(5) [Notice of relief order etc.] If the court so orders, and the application for the order was made without notice to any other party, notice of the order shall be given as soon as reasonably practicable by the official receiver to the requisitionist. If the application for an order is dismissed, the official receiver's application under section 290(2) shall be made as soon as reasonably practicable on conclusion of the hearing of the application first mentioned.

(See General Note after r.6.177.) References to ex parte hearings in para.(5) removed by I(A)R 2010 (SI 2010/686).

6.174 Bankrupt unfit for examination

6.174(1) [Application for stay etc.] Where the bankrupt is a person who lacks capacity within the meaning of the Mental Capacity Act 2005 or is suffering from any physical affliction or disability rendering him unfit to undergo or attend for public examination, the court may, on an application being made to it under this Rule, either stay the order for his public examination or direct that it shall be conducted in such manner and at such place as it thinks fit.

[FORM 6.57]

6.174(2)   [Who may apply] Application under this Rule shall be made–

(a)   by a person who has been appointed by a court in the United Kingdom or elsewhere to manage the affairs of, or to represent, the bankrupt, or

(b)   by a relative or friend of the bankrupt whom the court considers to be a proper person to make the application, or

(c)   by the official receiver.

6.174(3)   [Application not by official receiver] Where the application is made by a person other than the official receiver, then–

(a)   it shall, unless the bankrupt is a person who lacks capacity within the meaning of the Mental Capacity Act 2005, be supported by a witness statement of a registered medical practitioner as to the bankrupt's mental and physical condition;

(b)   at least 5 business days' notice of the application shall be given to the official receiver and the trustee (if any); and

(c)   before any order is made on the application, the applicant shall deposit with the official receiver such sum as the latter certifies to be necessary for the additional expenses of any examination that may be ordered on the application.

An order made on the application may provide that the expenses of the examination are to be payable, as to a specified proportion, out of the deposit under sub-paragraph (c), instead of out of the estate.

6.174(4)   [Application by official receiver] Where the application is made by the official receiver, it may be made without notice to any other party, and may be supported by evidence in the form of a report by the official receiver to the court.

(See General Note after r.6.177.) Note amendment by SI 2007/1898. Minor modifications are made by I(A)R 2010 (SI 2010/686). These include removing references to affidavits and ex parte hearings. The period specified in para.(3) has been reduced from seven days to five business days.

6.175   Procedure at hearing

6.175(1)   [Examination on oath] The bankrupt shall at the hearing be examined on oath; and he shall answer all such questions as the court may put, or allow to be put, to him.

6.175(2)   [Appearances etc.] Any of the persons allowed by section 290(4) to question the bankrupt may, with the approval of the court (made known either at the hearing or in advance of it), appear by solicitor or counsel; or he may in writing authorise another person to question the bankrupt on his behalf.

6.175(3)   [Representation of bankrupt] The bankrupt may at his own expense employ a solicitor with or without counsel, who may put to him such questions as the court may allow for the purpose of enabling him to explain or qualify any answers given by him, and may make representations on his behalf.

6.175(4)   [Record of examination] There shall be made in writing such record of the examination as the court thinks proper. The record shall be read over either to or by the bankrupt, authenticated by him, and verified by a statement of truth at a venue fixed by the court.

[FORM 6.58]

6.175(5)   [Record as evidence] The written record may, in any proceedings (whether under the Act or otherwise) be used as evidence against the bankrupt of any statement made by him in the course of his public examination.

6.175(6) **[Criminal proceedings etc.]** If criminal proceedings have been instituted against the bankrupt, and the court is of opinion that the continuance of the hearing would be calculated to prejudice a fair trial of those proceedings, the hearing may be adjourned.

(See General Note after r.6.177.) See I(A)R 2010 (SI 2010/686).

6.176   Adjournment

6.176(1) **[Adjourned by court]** The public examination may be adjourned by the court from time to time, either to a fixed date or generally.

[FORM 6.59]

6.176(2) **[Resumption]** Where the examination has been adjourned generally, the court may at any time on the application of the official receiver or of the bankrupt–

(a)   fix a venue for the resumption of the examination, and

(b)   give directions as to the manner in which, and the time within which, notice of the resumed public examination is to be given to persons entitled to take part in it.

[FORM 6.60]

6.176(3) **[Deposit for expenses re application]** Where application under paragraph (2) is made by the bankrupt, the court may grant it on terms that the expenses of giving the notices required by that paragraph shall be paid by him and that, before a venue for the resumed public examination is fixed, he shall deposit with the official receiver such sum as the latter considers necessary to cover those expenses.

6.176(4) **[Official receiver's application under s.279(3)]** Where the examination is adjourned, the official receiver may, there and then, make application under section 279(3) (suspension of automatic discharge).

6.176(5) **[Copies of order to be sent by court]** If, on the hearing of an application pursuant to paragraph (4), the court makes an order suspending the bankrupt's discharge, copies of such order shall be sent by the court to the official receiver, the trustee and the bankrupt.

(See General Note after r.6.177.)

6.177   Expenses of examination

6.177(1) **[Expenses paid out of r.6.173(2) deposit]** Where a public examination of the bankrupt has been ordered by the court on a creditors' requisition under Rule 6.173, the court may order that the expenses of the examination are to be paid, as to a specified proportion, out of the deposit under Rule 6.173(2), instead of out of the estate.

6.177(2) **[Official receiver not liable for costs]** In no case do the costs and expenses of a public examination fall on the official receiver personally.

GENERAL NOTE TO RR.6.172–6.177

These rules provide detailed guidance on the conduct of a public examination of a bankrupt under IA 1986 s.290. If the official receiver applies to the court, Form 6.55 is to be used, whereas if a creditor applies to the official receiver for a public examination, Form 6.56 is the appropriate document. A creditor seeking a public examination must provide security. If the bankrupt is not fit to be publicly examined, the court can excuse him. Note the use of Form 6.57 in this context. The hearing procedure is mapped out by rr.6.175 and 6.176. For an application under IR r.6.175(6) see *Rottmann v OR* [2009] B.P.I.R. 617 (which is discussed in the annotation to s.433). The solution of a private examination to be conducted before a judge was endorsed in [2009] EWCA Civ 473. The public examination is normally to be funded out of the estate, unless the deposit furnished by a requisitioning creditor is made use of. The fee on public examination was abolished in 1995.

6.178 Trustee's notice of disclaimer

6.178(1) **[Contents of notice]** Where the trustee disclaims property under section 315, the notice of disclaimer shall contain such particulars of the property disclaimed as enable it to be easily identified.

[FORM 6.61A]

6.178(2) **[Notice to be authenticated and dated]** The notice of disclaimer must be authenticated and dated by the trustee.

6.178(3) **[Copy of notice]** As soon as reasonably practicable after authenticating the notice of disclaimer, the trustee must–

(a) file a copy of the notice with the court; and

(b) in any case where the disclaimer is of registered land as defined in section 132(1) of the Land Registration Act 2002, send a copy of the notice to the Chief Land Registrar.

6.178(4) **[Date of notice]** For the purposes of section 315 the date of the prescribed notice is that on which the trustee authenticates it.

(See General Note after r.6.186.) Substantially modernised by I(A)R 2010 (SI 2010/686).

6.179 Communication of disclaimer to persons interested

6.179(1) **[Copy notices]** Within 7 business days after the date of the notice of disclaimer, the trustee shall send or give copies of the notice to the persons mentioned in paragraphs (2) to (5).

6.179(2) **[Leasehold property]** Where the property disclaimed is of a leasehold nature, he shall send or give a copy to every person who (to his knowledge) claims under the bankrupt as underlessee or mortgagee.

6.179(3) **[Property in a dwelling-house]** Where the disclaimer is of property in a dwelling-house, he shall send or give a copy to every person who (to his knowledge) is in occupation of, or claims a right to occupy, the house.

6.179(4) **[Giving notice]** He shall in any case send or give a copy of the notice to every person who (to his knowledge)–

(a) claims an interest in the disclaimed property, or

(b) is under any liability in respect of the property, not being a liability discharged by the disclaimer.

6.179(5) **[Unprofitable contract]** If the disclaimer is of an unprofitable contract, he shall send or give copies of the notice to all such persons as, to his knowledge, are parties to the contract or have interests under it.

6.179(6) **[Late communication]** If subsequently it comes to the trustee's knowledge, in the case of any person, that he has such an interest in the disclaimed property as would have entitled him to receive a copy of the notice of disclaimer in pursuance of paragraphs (2) to (5), the trustee shall then as soon as reasonably practicable send or give to that person a copy of the notice. But compliance with this paragraph is not required if–

(a) the trustee is satisfied that the person has already been made aware of the disclaimer and its date, or

(b) the court, on the trustee's application, orders that compliance is not required in that particular case.

6.179(7)   **[Notice to minor re dwelling-house]** A notice or copy notice to be served on any person under the age of 18 in relation to the disclaimer of property in a dwelling-house is sufficiently served if sent or given to the parent or guardian of that person.

GENERAL NOTE

Note the use of Pt 3 of Form 6.61 here. Modernised by I(A)R 2010 (SI 2010/686).

(See also General Note after r.6.186.)

6.180   Additional notices

6.180   The trustee disclaiming property may, without prejudice to his obligations under sections 315 to 319 and Rules 6.178 and 6.179, at any time send or give copies of notice of the disclaimer to any persons who in his opinion ought, in the public interest or otherwise, to be informed of the disclaimer.

GENERAL NOTE

Note the use of Pt 3 of Form 6.61 here. See I(A)R 2010 (SI 2010/686).

6.181   Duty to keep court informed [Deleted.]

6.181A   Records

6.181A   The trustee must include in that trustee's records of the insolvency a record of–

(a) the persons to whom that trustee has sent or given copies of the notice of disclaimer under the two preceding Rules, showing their names and addresses, and the nature of their respective interests;

(b) the dates on which the copies of the notice of disclaimer were sent or given to those persons;

(c) the date on which, as required by Rule 6.178(3)(a), a copy of the notice of disclaimer was filed with the court; and

(d) (where applicable) the date on which, as required by Rule 6.178(3)(b), a copy of the notice was sent to the Chief Land Registrar.

GENERAL NOTE

Substituted by I(A)R 2010 (SI 2010/686).

6.182   Application for permission to disclaim

6.182(1)   **[Applying without notice]** Where under section 315(4) the trustee requires the permission of the court to disclaim property claimed for the bankrupt's estate under section 307 or 308, he may apply for that permission without notice to any other party.

6.182(2)   **[Accompanying report]** The application must be accompanied by a report–

(a) giving such particulars of the property proposed to be disclaimed as enable it to be easily identified,

(b) setting out the reasons why, the property having been claimed for the estate, the court's permission to disclaim is now applied for, and

(c) specifying the persons (if any) who have been informed of the trustee's intention to make the application.

6.182(3)   **[Copy of consent to disclaimer]** If it is stated in the report that any person has consented to the disclaimer, a copy of that consent must be annexed to the report.

6.182(4)   **[Court may grant permission etc.]** The court may, on consideration of the application, grant the permission applied for; and it may, before granting permission–

(a)   order that notice of the application be given to all such persons who, if the property is disclaimed, will be entitled to apply for a vesting or other order under section 320, and

(b)   fix a venue for the hearing of the application under section 315(4).

(See General Note after r.6.186.) Modernised by I(A)R 2010 (SI 2010/686).

6.183   Application by interested party under s.316

6.183(1)   [Application if r.6.183] The following applies where, in the case of any property, application is made to the trustee by an interested party under section 316.

6.183(2)   [Delivery to trustee] The application must be delivered to the trustee–

(a)   personally;

(b)   by electronic means in accordance with Part 12A; or

(c)   by any other means of delivery which enables proof of receipt of the application by the trustee to be provided, if requested.

[FORM 6.62]

6.183(3)   [Where property cannot be disclaimed without permission of court] This paragraph applies in a case where the property concerned cannot be disclaimed by the trustee without the permission of the court.

If within the period of 28 days mentioned in section 316(1) the trustee applies to the court for permission to disclaim, the court shall extend the time allowed by that section for giving notice of disclaimer to a date not earlier than the date fixed for the hearing of the application.

(See General Note after r.6.186.) Substantially amended by I(A)R 2010 (SI 2010/686).

6.184   Interest in property to be declared on request

6.184(1)   [Notice to declare interest] If, in the case of property which the trustee has the right to disclaim, it appears to him that there is some person who claims, or may claim, to have an interest in the property, he may give notice to that person calling on him to declare within 14 days whether he claims any such interest and, if so, the nature and extent of it.

[FORM 6.63]

6.184(2)   [Failing compliance with notice] Failing compliance with the notice, the trustee is entitled to assume that the person concerned has no such interest in the property as will prevent or impede its disclaimer.

(See General Note after r.6.186.)

6.185   Disclaimer presumed valid and effective

6.185   Any disclaimer of property by the trustee is presumed valid and effective, unless it is proved that he has been in breach of his duty with respect to the giving of notice of disclaimer, or otherwise under sections 315 to 319, or under this Chapter of the Rules.

(See General Note after r.6.186.)

6.186   Application for exercise of court's powers under s.320

6.186(1)   [Application of Rule] This Rule applies with respect to an application by any person under section 320 for an order of the court to vest or deliver disclaimed property.

6.186(2)   [Time for application] The application must be made within 3 months of the applicant becoming aware of the disclaimer, or of his receiving a copy of the trustee's notice of disclaimer sent under Rule 6.179, whichever is the earlier.

6.186(3) **[Contents of witness statement]** The applicant shall with his application file a witness statement–

(a) stating whether he applies under paragraph (a) of section 320(2) (claim of interest in the property), under paragraph (b) (liability not discharged) or under paragraph (c) (occupation of dwelling-house);

(b) specifying the date on which he received a copy of the trustee's notice of disclaimer, or otherwise became aware of the disclaimer; and

(c) specifying the grounds of his application and the order which he desires the court to make under section 320.

6.186(4) **[Venue for hearing]** The court shall fix a venue for the hearing of the application; and the applicant shall, not later than 5 business days before the date fixed, give to the trustee notice of the venue, accompanied by copies of the application and the witness statement required by paragraph (3).

6.186(5) **[Directions for notice etc.]** On the hearing of the application, the court may give directions as to other persons (if any) who should be sent or given notice of the application and the grounds on which it is made.

6.186(6) **[Sealed copies of order]** Sealed copies of any order made on the application shall be sent by the court to the applicant and the trustee.

6.186(7) **[Leasehold property or property in a dwelling-house]** In a case where the property disclaimed is of a leasehold nature, or is property in a dwelling-house, and section 317 or (as the case may be) section 318 applies to suspend the effect of the disclaimer, there shall be included in the court's order a direction giving effect to the disclaimer.

This paragraph does not apply if, at the time when the order is issued, other applications under section 320 are pending in respect of the same property.

GENERAL NOTE TO RR.6.178–6.186

These rules complement IA 1986 ss.315–321 (disclaimer of property, etc. by the trustee). This disclaimer is to take the style of Form 6.61 and must be filed with the court. Rules 6.179 and 6.180 relate to the dissemination of the notice of disclaimer. Rule 6.182 develops IA 1986 s.315(4) (leave of court for certain notices of disclaimer). Section 316 must be read in the light of r.6.183 and Form 6.62. The trustee can, under r.6.184 and by using Form 6.63, compel persons to declare their interest in any property which he is considering disclaiming. The onus of proving that a disclaimer has been exercised improperly is naturally cast upon the person challenging it (r.6.185). Section 320 is to be viewed in the light of r.6.186. Note especially the time limitation upon applications under s.320. References in r.6.186 to affidavits have been removed and the period in para.(4) has changed from seven days to five business days as a result of I(A)R 2010 (SI 2010/686).

CHAPTER 15

REPLACEMENT OF EXEMPT PROPERTY

6.187 **Purchase of replacement property**

6.187(1) **[Time for purchase]** A purchase of replacement property under section 308(3) may be made either before or after the realisation by the trustee of the value of the property vesting in him under the section.

6.187(2) **[Sufficiency of funds in estate]** The trustee is under no obligation, by virtue of the section, to apply funds to the purchase of a replacement for property vested in him, unless and until he has sufficient funds in the estate for that purpose.

(See General Note after rr.6.188.)

6.188 Money provided in lieu of sale

6.188(1) [Application of Rule] The following applies where a third party proposes to the trustee that he (the former) should provide the estate with a sum of money enabling the bankrupt to be left in possession of property which would otherwise be made to vest in the trustee under section 308.

6.188(2) [Reasonableness of proposal] The trustee may accept that proposal, if satisfied that it is a reasonable one, and that the estate will benefit to the extent of the value of the property in question less the cost of a reasonable replacement.

GENERAL NOTE TO RR.6.187, 6.188

These rules provide further guidance on the operation of IA 1986 s.308, which is a novel provision in the Act. A third party can provide funds for the estate to prevent a sale and replacement of assets.

CHAPTER 16

INCOME PAYMENTS ORDERS

6.189 Application for order

6.189(1) [Court to fix venue] Where the trustee applies for an income payments order under section 310, the court shall fix a venue for the hearing of the application.

6.189(2) [Notice etc. to bankrupt] Notice of the application, and of the venue, shall be sent by the trustee to the bankrupt at least 28 days before the day fixed for the hearing, together with a copy of the trustee's application and a short statement of the grounds on which it is made.

[FORM 6.64]

6.189(3) [Contents of notice] The notice shall inform the bankrupt that–

(a) unless at least 5 business days before the date fixed for the hearing he sends to the court and to the trustee written consent to an order being made in the terms of the application, he is required to attend the hearing, and

(b) if he attends, he will be given an opportunity to show cause why the order should not be made, or an order should be made otherwise than as applied for by the trustee.

GENERAL NOTE

For the meaning of "venue" see r.13.6. The period in para.(3) has been changed from seven days to five business days by I(A)R 2010 (SI 2010/686).

(See also General Note after r.6.193.)

6.190 Action to follow making of order

6.190(1) [Copy of order to bankrupt] Where the court makes an income payments order, a sealed copy of the order shall, as soon as reasonably practicable after it is made, be sent by the trustee to the bankrupt.

[FORM 6.65]
or [FORM 6.66]

6.190(2) [Copy of order under s.310(3)(b)] If the order is made under section 310(3)(b), a sealed copy of the order shall also be sent by the trustee to the person to whom the order is directed.

(See General Note after r.6.193.)

6.191   Variation of order

6.191(1)   [Non-compliance with s.310(3)(a) order] If an income payments order is made under section 310(3)(a), and the bankrupt does not comply with it, the trustee may apply to the court for the order to be varied, so as to take effect under section 310(3)(b) as an order to the payor of the relevant income.

[FORM 6.67]

6.191(2)   [Application without notice] The trustee's application under this Rule may be made without notice to any other party.

6.191(3)   [Copy order to trustee and bankrupt] Sealed copies of any order made on the application shall, as soon as reasonably practicable after it is made, be sent by the court to the trustee and the bankrupt.

6.191(4)   [Variation, etc. of s.310(3)(b) order] In the case of an order varying or discharging an income payments order made under section 310(3)(b), an additional sealed copy shall be sent to the trustee, for transmission as soon as reasonably practicable to the payor of the relevant income.

(See General Note after r.6.193.) In para.(2) references to ex parte hearings have been changed by I(A)R 2010 (SI 2010/686).

6.192   Order to payor of income: administration

6.192(1)   [Compliance by payer] Where a person receives notice of an income payments order under section 310(3)(b), with reference to income otherwise payable by him to the bankrupt, he shall make the arrangements requisite for compliance with the order as soon as reasonably practicable.

6.192(2)   [Costs of compliance] When making any payment to the trustee, he may deduct the appropriate fee towards the clerical and administrative costs of compliance with the income payments order.

He shall give to the bankrupt a written statement of any amount deducted by him under this paragraph.

6.192(3)   [Where payer no longer liable etc.] Where a person receives notice of an income payments order imposing on him a requirement under section 310(3)(b), and either–

    (a)   he is then no longer liable to make to the bankrupt any payment of income, or

    (b)   having made payments in compliance with the order, he ceases to be so liable,

he shall as soon as reasonably practicable give notice of that fact to the trustee.

(See General Note after r.6.193.) I(A)R 2010 (SI 2010/686) relaxes the immediacy of the requirement in para.(1).

6.193   Review of order

6.193(1)   [Application to court] Where an income payments order is in force, either the trustee or the bankrupt may apply to the court for the order to be varied or discharged.

6.193(2)   [Application by trustee] If the application is made by the trustee, Rule 6.189 applies (with any necessary modification) as in the case of an application for an income payments order.

6.193(3)   [Application by bankrupt] If the application is made by the bankrupt, it shall be accompanied by a short statement of the grounds on which it is made.

6.193(4)   [Court may dismiss application etc.] The court may, if it thinks that no sufficient cause is shown for the application, dismiss it; but it shall not do so unless the applicant has had an opportunity to attend the court for a hearing, of which he has been given at least 5 business days' notice but which is without notice to any other party.

If the application is not dismissed under this paragraph, the court shall fix a venue for it to be heard.

6.193(5) **[Notice of venue etc.]** At least 28 days before the date fixed for the hearing, the applicant shall send to the trustee or the bankrupt (whichever of them is not himself the applicant) notice of the venue, accompanied by a copy of the application.

Where the applicant is the bankrupt, the notice shall be accompanied by a copy of the statement of grounds under paragraph (3).

6.193(6) **[Appearance etc. by trustee]** The trustee may, if he thinks fit, appear and be heard on the application; and, whether or not he intends to appear, he may, not less than 5 business days before the date fixed for the hearing, file a written report of any matters which he considers ought to be drawn to the court's attention.

If such a report is filed, a copy of it shall be sent by the trustee to the bankrupt.

6.193(7) **[Sealed copies of order]** Sealed copies of any order made on the application shall, as soon as reasonably practicable after the order is made, be sent by the court to the trustee, the bankrupt and the payor (if other than the bankrupt).

[FORM 6.66]

GENERAL NOTE TO RR.6.189–6.193

Once again these rules develop an innovation introduced by IA 1986 s.310, the income payments order. The trustee's application should adopt Form 6.64, whereas the court order should follow Forms 6.65 and 6.66. Variation of orders is provided for (see Form 6.67). Provision is made for third parties whose payments to the bankrupt may be diverted under IA 1986 s.310(3)(b). Note the special fee, which is 50p, under r.6.192(2): see r.13.11(a). We find the usual changes in paras (4) and (6) with regard to ex parte hearings and the period of seven days being translated into five business days by I(A)R 2010 (SI 2010/686).

CHAPTER 16A

INCOME PAYMENTS AGREEMENTS

6.193A Approval of income payments agreements

6.193A(1) **[Prior to discharge]** An income payments agreement can only be entered into prior to the discharge of the bankrupt.

6.193A(2) **[Where under IA 1986 s.310A(1)]** Where an income payments agreement is to be entered into between the official receiver or trustee and the bankrupt under section 310A(1), the official receiver or trustee shall provide an income payments agreement to the bankrupt for his approval.

6.193A(3) **[Duty of bankrupt]** Within 14 days or such longer period as may be specified by the official receiver or trustee (whichever is appropriate) from the date on which the income payments agreement was sent, the bankrupt shall–

(a) if he decides to approve the draft income payments agreement, authenticate the agreement and return it to the official receiver or trustee (whichever is appropriate); or

(b) if he decides not to approve the agreement, notify the official receiver or trustee (whichever is appropriate) in writing of his decision.

6.193B Acceptance of income payments agreements

6.193B(1) **[Official receiver to authenticate and date]** On receipt by the official receiver or trustee of the authenticated income payments agreement, the official receiver or trustee shall authenticate and date it.

6.193B(2) **[Entry into force, copy to bankrupt]** When the official receiver or the trustee authenticates and dates the income payments agreement, it shall come into force. A copy shall be sent to the bankrupt.

6.193B(3) **[Notice of agreement where third party payments]** Where the agreement provides for payments by a third person to the official receiver or trustee who is not the official receiver in accordance with section 310A(1)(b), a notice of the agreement shall be sent by the official receiver or trustee to that person.

6.193B(4) **[Contents of notice]** The notice shall contain–

(a)   the full name and address of the bankrupt;

(b)   a statement that an income payments agreement has been made, the date of it, and that it provides for the payment by the third person of sums owed to the bankrupt (or a part thereof) to be paid to the official receiver or trustee;

(c)   the full name and address of the third person;

(d)   a statement of the amount of money to be paid to the official receiver or trustee from the bankrupt's income, the period over which the payments are to be made, and the intervals at which the sums are to be paid; and

(e)   the full name and address of the official receiver or trustee and the address or details of where the sums are to be paid.

6.193B(5) **[Deduction of fee for clerical and administrative costs]** When making any payment to the official receiver or the trustee a person who has received notice of an income payments agreement with reference to income otherwise payable by him to the bankrupt may deduct the appropriate fee towards the clerical and administrative costs of compliance with the income payments agreement. He shall give to the bankrupt a written statement of any amount deducted by him under this paragraph.

6.193C   Variation of income payments agreements

6.193C(1) **[Application accompanied by copy of agreement]** Where an application is made to court for variation of an income payments agreement, the application shall be accompanied by a copy of the agreement.

6.193C(2) **[Notice where application by bankrupt]** Where the bankrupt applies to the court for variation of an income payments agreement under section 310A(6)(b), he shall send a copy of the application and notice of the venue to the official receiver or trustee (whichever is appropriate) at least 28 days before the date fixed for the hearing.

6.193C(3) **[Notice where application by official receiver or trustee]** When the official receiver or trustee applies to the court for variation of an income payments agreement under section 310A(6)(b), he shall send a copy of the application and notice of the venue to the bankrupt at least 28 days before the date fixed for the hearing.

6.193C(4) **[Form of order]** The court may order in Form 6.81 the variation of an income payments agreement under section 310A.

[FORM 6.81]

6.193C(5) **[Notice where third party to make payments]** Where the court orders an income payments agreement under section 310A(1)(a) to be varied, so as to take the form of an agreement under section 310A(1)(b) as an agreement providing that a third person is to make payments to the trustee or the official receiver, the official receiver or trustee shall send a notice in accordance with Rule 6.193B(3).

6.193C(6) **[Deduction of fee for clerical and administrative costs]** When making any payment to the official receiver or the trustee a person who has received notice of an income payments agreement with reference to income otherwise payable by him to the bankrupt may deduct the appropriate fee towards the clerical and administrative costs of compliance with the income payments agreement. He shall give to the bankrupt a written statement of any amount deducted by him under this paragraph.

GENERAL NOTE

This new chapter was introduced by the Insolvency (Amendment) Rules 2003 (SI 2003/1730) to provide further regulations for the income payments agreements regime, which was introduced by EA 2002. See the note to s.310A above.

CHAPTER 17

ACTION BY COURT UNDER SECTION 369 ORDER TO INLAND REVENUE OFFICIAL

6.194   Application for order

6.194(1)   [Application to specify documents etc.] An application by the official receiver or the trustee for an order under section 369 (order to HM Revenue and Customs official to produce documents) shall specify (with such particularity as will enable the order, if made, to be most easily complied with) the documents whose production to the court is desired, naming the official to whom the order is to be addressed.

6.194(2)   [Court to fix venue] The court shall fix a venue for the hearing of the application.

6.194(3)   [Notice of venue etc. to Commissioners] Notice of the venue, accompanied by a copy of the application, shall be sent by the applicant to the Commissioners for HM Revenue and Customs ("the Commissioners") at least 28 days before the hearing.

6.194(4)   [Whether Commissioners consent or object] The notice shall require the Commissioners, not later than 5 business days before the date fixed for the hearing of the application, to inform the court whether they consent or object to the making of an order under the section.

6.194(5)   [If Commissioners consent] If the Commissioners consent to the making of an order, they shall inform the court of the name of the official to whom it should be addressed, if other than the one named in the application.

6.194(6)   [If Commissioners object] If the Commissioners object to the making of an order, they shall secure that an officer of theirs attends the hearing of the application and, not less than 5 business days before it, deliver to the court a statement in writing of their grounds of objection.

A copy of the statement shall be sent as soon as reasonably practicable to the applicant.

GENERAL NOTE

For the meaning of "venue" see r.13.6. There are terminological changes made by I(A)R 2010 (SI 2010/686). The seven-day period formerly found in para.(4) has been converted to five business days.

(See also General Note after r.6.196.)

6.195   Making and service of the order

6.195(1)   [Powers of court] If on the hearing of the application it appears to the court to be a proper case, the court may make the order applied for, with such modifications (if any) as appear appropriate having regard to any representations made on behalf of the Commissioners.

[FORM 6.69]

6.195(2)   [Form and contents of order] The order–

(a)   may be addressed to an HM Revenue and Customs official other than the one named in the application,

(b)   shall specify a time, not less than 28 days after service on the official to whom the order is addressed, within which compliance is required, and

(c) may include requirements as to the manner in which documents to which the order relates are to be produced.

6.195(3)   **[Service of copy of order]** A sealed copy of the order shall be served by the applicant on the official to whom it is addressed.

6.195(4)   **[If official unable to comply]** If the official is unable to comply with the order because he has not the relevant documents in his possession, and has been unable to obtain possession of them, he shall deliver to the court a statement in writing as to the reasons for his non-compliance.

A copy of the statement shall be sent as soon as reasonably practicable by the official to the applicant.

(See General Note after r.6.196.)

6.196   Custody of documents

6.196   Where in compliance with an order under section 369 original documents are produced, and not copies, any person who, by order of the court under section 369(2) (authorised disclosure to persons with right of inspection), has them in his possession or custody is responsible to the court for their safe keeping and return as and when directed.

GENERAL NOTE TO RR.6.194–6.196

These rules provide further details on orders made under IA 1986 s.369. Form 6.69 is to be used for orders against the Inland Revenue under s.369. A maximum of 28 days after service is fixed for compliance with a s.369 order.

CHAPTER 18

MORTGAGED PROPERTY

6.197   Claim by mortgagee of land

6.197(1)   **[Application for order for sale, "land"]** Any person claiming to be the legal or equitable mortgagee of land belonging to the bankrupt may apply to the court for an order directing that the land be sold.

"Land" includes any interest in, or right over, land.

6.197(2)   **[Court may direct accounts to be taken etc.]** The court, if satisfied as to the applicant's title, may direct accounts to be taken and enquiries made to ascertain–

(a) the principal, interest and costs due under the mortgage, and

(b) where the mortgagee has been in possession of the land or any part of it, the rents and profits, dividends, interest, or other proceeds received by him or on his behalf.

Directions may be given by the court under this paragraph with respect to any mortgage (whether prior or subsequent) on the same property, other than that of the applicant.

6.197(3)   **[Powers of court]** For the purpose of those accounts and enquiries, and of making title to the purchaser, any of the parties may be examined by the court, and shall produce on oath before the court all such documents in their custody or under their control relating to the estate of the bankrupt as the court may direct.

The court may under this paragraph order any of the parties to clarify any matter which is in dispute in the proceedings or give additional information in relation to any such matter and CPR Part 18 (further information) shall apply to any such order.

6.197(4)   **[In like manner as in High Court]** In any proceedings between a mortgagor and mortgagee, or the trustee of either of them, the court may order accounts to be taken and enquiries made in like manner as in the Chancery Division of the High Court.

(See General Note after r.6.199.) In r.6.197 the words from "The court may" to the end substituted for the former words "The court may under this paragraph authorise the service of interrogatories on any party." by the Insolvency (Amendment) (No.2) Rules 1999 (SI 1999/1022) r.3, Sch. para.2 as from April 26, 1999.

6.198   Power of court to order sale

6.198(1)   [Order for sale etc.] The court may order that the land, or any specified part of it, be sold; and any party bound by the order and in possession of the land or part, or in receipt of the rents and profits from it, may be ordered to deliver up possession or receipt to the purchaser or to such other person as the court may direct.

6.198(2)   [Directions re sale] The court may permit the person having the conduct of the sale to sell the land in such manner as he thinks fit. Alternatively, the court may direct that the land be sold as directed by the order.

6.198(3)   [Contents of order] The court's order may contain directions–

(a)   appointing the persons to have the conduct of the sale;

(b)   fixing the manner of sale (whether by contract conditional on the court's approval, private treaty, public auction, or otherwise);

(c)   settling the particulars and conditions of sale;

(d)   obtaining evidence of the value of the property, and fixing a reserve or minimum price;

(e)   requiring particular persons to join in the sale and conveyance;

(f)   requiring the payment of the purchase money into court, or to trustees or others;

(g)   if the sale is to be by public auction, fixing the security (if any) to be given by the auctioneer, and his remuneration.

6.198(4)   [Sale by auction] The court may direct that, if the sale is to be by public auction, the mortgagee may appear and bid on his own behalf.

6.198(5)   [Rights in rem] Nothing in this Rule or the following Rule may affect the rights in rem of creditors or third parties protected under Article 5 of the EC Regulation (third parties' rights in rem).

(See General Note after r.6.199.) Rule 6.198(5) was inserted by the Insolvency (Amendment) Rules 2002 (SI 2002/1307) para.8(8) with effect from May 31, 2002 to cater for the advent of EC Council Regulation 1346/2000 on Insolvency Proceedings.

6.199   Proceeds of sale

6.199(1)   [Application of proceeds] The proceeds of sale shall be applied–

(a)   first, in payment of the expenses of the trustee, of and occasioned by the application to the court, of the sale and attendance thereat, and of any costs arising from the taking of accounts, and making of enquiries, as directed by the court under Rule 6.197; and

(b)   secondly, in payment of the amount found due to any mortgagee, for principal, interest and costs;

and the balance (if any) shall be retained by or paid to the trustee.

6.199(2)   [Where proceeds insufficient] Where the proceeds of the sale are insufficient to pay in full the amount found due to any mortgagee, he is entitled to prove as a creditor for any deficiency, and to receive dividends rateably with other creditors, but not so as to disturb any dividend already declared.

These provisions regulate the rights of mortgagees of the bankrupt's land. The court can order the sale of the mortgage property. Note the priority of claims against the proceeds of sale (r.6.199).

CHAPTER 19

AFTER-ACQUIRED PROPERTY

6.200   Duties of bankrupt in respect of after-acquired property

6.200(1)   [Time for bankrupt to give notice] The notice to be given by the bankrupt to the trustee, under section 333(2), of property acquired by, or devolving upon, him, or of any increase of his income, shall be given within 21 days of his becoming aware of the relevant facts.

6.200(2)   [Not to dispose of property] Having served notice in respect of property acquired by or devolving upon him, the bankrupt shall not, without the trustee's consent in writing, dispose of it within the period of 42 days beginning with the date of the notice.

6.200(3)   [To identify etc. disponee] If the bankrupt disposes of property before giving the notice required by this Rule or in contravention of paragraph (2), it is his duty as soon as reasonably practicable to disclose to the trustee the name and address of the disponee, and to provide any other information which may be necessary to enable the trustee to trace the property and recover it for the estate.

6.200(4)   [Property to which r.6.200(1)–(3) do not apply] Subject as follows, paragraphs (1) to (3) do not apply to property acquired by the bankrupt in the ordinary course of a business carried on by him.

6.200(5)   [If bankrupt carries on business] If the bankrupt carries on a business, he shall, when required by the trustee, furnish to the trustee information with respect to it, showing the total of goods bought and sold (or, as the case may be, services supplied) and the profit or loss arising from the business.

The trustee may require the bankrupt to furnish fuller details (including accounts) of the business carried on by him.

(See General Note after r.6.202.) See I(A)R 2010 (SI 2010/686). Note the temporal change made in para.(5).

6.201   Trustee's recourse to disponee of property

6.201(1)   [Trustee may serve notice on disponee] Where property has been disposed of by the bankrupt before giving the notice required by Rule 6.200 or otherwise in contravention of that Rule, the trustee may serve notice on the disponee, claiming the property as part of the estate by virtue of section 307(3).

6.201(2)   [Time for serving notice] The trustee's notice under this rule must be served within 28 days of his becoming aware of the disponee's identity and an address at which he can be served.

(See General Note after r.6.202.)

6.202   Expenses of getting in property for the estate

6.202   Any expenses incurred by the trustee in acquiring title to after-acquired property shall be paid out of the estate, in the prescribed order of priority.

The key provision on after-acquired property is IA 1986 s.307, which represents a new departure in bankruptcy law. Section 333(2) is also relevant. The bankrupt has 21 days after becoming aware that after-acquired property has become vested in him to notify the trustee. The bankrupt must then wait 42 days before disposing of that property. If property is wrongfully disposed of, it may be traced by the trustee at the expense of the estate.

CHAPTER 20

PERMISSION TO ACT AS DIRECTOR, ETC.

6.202A   In this Chapter a reference to a bankrupt includes a reference to a person in respect of whom a bankruptcy restrictions order is in force.

GENERAL NOTE

This was inserted by Insolvency (Amendment) Rules 2003 (SI 2003/1730) to widen the definition of a bankrupt to include those against whom a BRO or BRU is in force. A person may thus be discharged from bankruptcy but still be regarded as a bankrupt for the purposes of Chapter 20 if a BRO or BRU remains in force.

6.203   Application for permission

6.203(1)   **[Application supported by witness statement]** An application by the bankrupt for permission, under section 11 of the Company Directors Disqualification Act 1986, to act as director of, or to take part or be concerned in the promotion, formation or management of a company, shall be supported by a witness statement complying with this Rule.

6.203(2)   **[Contents of witness statement]** The witness statement must identify the company and specify–

(a)   the nature of its business or intended business, and the place or places where that business is, or is to be, carried on,

(b)   in the case of a company which has not yet been incorporated, whether it is, or is to be, a private or a public company,

(c)   the persons who are, or are to be, principally responsible for the conduct of its affairs (whether as directors, shadow directors, managers or otherwise),

(d)   the manner and capacity in which the applicant proposes to take part or be concerned in the promotion or formation of the company or, as the case may be, its management, and

(e)   the emoluments and other benefits to be obtained from the directorship.

6.203(3)   [Omitted.]

6.203(4)   [Omitted.]

6.203(5)   **[Venue and notice]** The court shall fix a venue for the hearing of the bankrupt's application, and give notice to him accordingly.

(See General Note after r.6.205.) I(A)R 2010 (SI 2010/686) clarifies para.(2)(b) and deletes paras (3) and (4).

6.204   Report of official receiver

6.204(1)   **[Notice of venue etc.]** The bankrupt shall, not less than 28 days before the date fixed for the hearing, give to the official receiver and the trustee notice of the venue, accompanied by copies of the application and the witness statement under Rule 6.203.

6.204(2)   **[Official receiver's report]** The official receiver may, not less than 14 days before the date fixed for the hearing, file in court a report of any matters which he considers ought to be drawn to the court's attention. A copy of the report shall be sent by him, as soon as reasonably practicable after it is filed, to the bankrupt and to the trustee.

6.204(3)   **[Where bankrupt disputes report]** The bankrupt may, not later than 5 business days before the date of the hearing, file in court a notice specifying any statements in the official receiver's report which he intends to deny or dispute.

If he gives notice under this paragraph, he shall send copies of it, not less than 4 days before the date of the hearing, to the official receiver and the trustee.

6.204(4) **[Appearances]** The official receiver and the trustee may appear on the hearing of the application, and may make representations and put to the bankrupt such questions as the court may allow.

(See General Note after r.6.205.) References to affidavits in para.(1) have been removed by I(A)R 2010 (SI 2010/686). There is the usual change in para.(3) from seven days to five business days.

6.205 Court's order on application

6.205(1) **[If court grants application]** If the court grants the bankrupt's application for permission under section 11 of the Company Directors Disqualification Act 1986, its order shall specify that which by virtue of the order the bankrupt has permission to do.

6.205(2) **[Powers of court]** The court may at the same time, having regard to any representations made by the trustee on the hearing of the application–

(a) include in the order provision varying an income payments order or an income payments agreement already in force in respect of the bankrupt, or

(b) if no income payments order is in force, make one.

6.205(3) **[Copies of order]** Whether or not the application is granted, copies of the order shall be sent by the court to the bankrupt, the trustee and the official receiver.

GENERAL NOTE TO RR.6.203–6.205

The placement of these provisions within the Insolvency Rules is puzzling. These rules relate to applications by a bankrupt for leave to participate in company management under CDDA 1986 s.11. The official receiver is to be notified to give him a chance to put his views to the court.

Rule 6.205(2)(b) was amended by I(A)R 2003 (SI 2003/1730) to cater for the advent of IPAs after April 1, 2004.

CHAPTER 21

ANNULMENT OF BANKRUPTCY ORDER

6.206 Application for annulment

6.206(1) **[Form of application]** An application to the court under section 282(1) for the annulment of a bankruptcy order shall specify whether it is made–

(a) under subsection (1)(a) of the section (claim that the order ought not to have been made), or

(b) under subsection (1)(b) (debts and expenses of the bankruptcy all paid or secured).

6.206(2) **[Witness statement in support]** The application shall, in either case, be supported by a witness statement stating the grounds on which it is made; and, where it is made under section 282(1)(b), there shall be set out in the witness statement all the facts by reference to which the court is, under the Act and the Rules, required to be satisfied before annulling the bankruptcy order.

6.206(3) **[Copy of application etc.]** A copy of the application and the witness statement in support must be filed with the court; and the court shall give to the applicant notice of the venue fixed for the hearing.

6.206(4) **[Notice of venue]** The applicant shall give to the official receiver and (if other) the trustee notice of the venue, accompanied by copies of the application and the witness statement under paragraph (2)–

(a) where the application is made under section 282(1)(a), in sufficient time to enable them to be present at the hearing, and

(b) where the application is made under section 282(1)(b), not less than 28 days before the hearing.

6.206(5) [Where application under s.282(1)(a)] Where the application is made under section 282(1)(a), paragraph (4) shall additionally be complied with in relation to the person on whose petition the bankruptcy order was made.

6.206(6) [Where applicant not bankrupt] In this Chapter, where the applicant is not the bankrupt all notices, documents and evidence required to be given, sent or delivered to another party by the applicant shall also be given, sent or delivered to the bankrupt.

GENERAL NOTE

The general 28-day limit originally fixed by r.6.206(4) was modified to deal with applications under s.282(1)(a).

Subparagraph (6) was added by the Insolvency (Amendment) Rules 2003 (SI 2003/1730). References to affidavits have been removed by I(A)R 2010 (SI 2010/686).

(See also General Note after r.6.215.)

6.207   Report by trustee

6.207(1) [Application of Rule] The following applies where the application is made under section 282(1)(b) (debts and expenses of the bankruptcy all paid or secured).

6.207(2)   [Contents of report] Not less than 21 days before the date fixed for the hearing, the trustee or, if no trustee has been appointed, the official receiver shall file in court a report with respect to the following matters–

(a) the circumstances leading to the bankruptcy;

(b) (in summarised form) the extent of the bankrupt's assets and liabilities at the date of the bankruptcy order and at the date of the present application;

(c) details of creditors (if any) who are known to him to have claims, but have not proved; and

(d) such other matters as the person making the report considers to be, in the circumstances, necessary for the information of the court.

6.207(2A)   [Additional contents where trustee not official receiver] Where the trustee is other than the official receiver, the report under paragraph (2) must also include a statement of–

(a) the trustee's remuneration;

(b) the basis fixed for the trustee's remuneration under Rule 6.138;

(c) the expenses incurred by the trustee.

6.207(3)   [Particulars of debts etc.] The report shall include particulars of the extent (if any) to which, and the manner in which, the debts and expenses of the bankruptcy have been paid or secured.

In so far as debts and expenses are unpaid but secured, the person making the report shall state in it whether and to what extent he considers the security to be satisfactory.

6.207(4) [Copy of report to applicant] A copy of the report shall be sent to the applicant at the same time that it is filed in court; and he may, if he wishes, file further witness statements in answer to statements made in the report.

Copies of any such witness statements shall be sent by the applicant to the official receiver and (if other) the trustee.

6.207(5)   [If trustee not official receiver] If the trustee is other than the official receiver, a copy of his report shall be sent to the official receiver at least 21 days before the hearing. The official receiver may then file an additional report, a copy of which shall be sent to the applicant at least 5 business days before the hearing.

GENERAL NOTE

This rule and its relationship with IR 6.209 was considered by Lewison J. in *Howard v Savage* [2006] EWHC 3693 (Ch); [2007] B.P.I.R. 1097. Amended by I(A)R 2010 (SI 2010/686)—new para.(2A) inserted.

(See also General Note after r.6.215.)

6.207A   Applicant's claim that remuneration is or expenses are excessive

6.207A(1)   [Application for order] Where the trustee is other than the official receiver and application for annulment is made under section 282(1)(b), the applicant may also apply to the court for one or more of the orders in paragraph (4) on the ground that the remuneration charged or expenses incurred by the trustee is or are, in all the circumstances, excessive.

6.207A(2)   [Time limit for application] Application under paragraph (1) must be made no later than 5 business days before the date fixed for the hearing of the application for annulment and be accompanied by a copy of any evidence which the applicant intends to adduce in support.

6.207A(3)   [Copy of application and accompanying evidence to trustee] The applicant under paragraph (1) must send a copy of the application and of any evidence accompanying it to the trustee at the same time that the application is made.

6.207A(4)   [Court order if application well-founded] If the court annuls the bankruptcy order under section 282(1)(b) and considers the application under paragraph (1) to be well-founded, it must also make one or more of the following orders–

(a)   an order reducing the amount of remuneration which the trustee was entitled to charge;

(b)   an order that some or all of the remuneration or expenses in question be treated as not being bankruptcy expenses;

(c)   an order that the trustee or the trustee's personal representative pay to the applicant the amount of the excess of remuneration or expenses or such part of the excess as the court may specify;

and may make any other order that it thinks just.

GENERAL NOTE

This is a new provision introduced by I(A)R 2010 (SI 2010/686).

6.208   Power of court to stay proceedings

6.208(1)   [Interim order] The court may, in advance of the hearing, make an interim order staying any proceedings which it thinks ought, in the circumstances of the application, to be stayed.

6.208(2)   [Application without notice] Except in relation to an application for an order staying all or any part of the proceedings in the bankruptcy, application for an order under this Rule may be made without notice to any other party.

6.208(3)   [Copies of application] Where application is made under this Rule for an order staying all or any part of the proceedings in the bankruptcy, the applicant shall send copies of the application to the official receiver and (if other) the trustee in sufficient time to enable them to be present at the hearing and (if they wish to do so) make representations.

6.208(4)   [Effect of staying order on annulment] Where the court makes an order under this Rule staying all or any part of the proceedings in the bankruptcy, the rules in this Chapter nevertheless continue to apply to any application for, or other matters in connection with, the annulment of the bankruptcy order.

6.208(5) **[Copies of staying order]** If the court makes an order under this Rule, it shall send copies of the order to the applicant, the official receiver and (if other) the trustee.

GENERAL NOTE

Rule 6.208 was substantially expanded in 1988 to enable the official receiver to have an early warning of an application to stay. There is also provision for annulment proceedings. References to ex parte hearings in para.(2) have been removed by I(A)R 2010 (SI 2010/686).

(See also General Note after r.6.215.)

6.209 Notice to creditors who have not proved

6.209 Where the application for annulment is made under section 282(1)(b) and it has been reported to the court under Rule 6.207 that there are known creditors of the bankrupt who have not proved, the court may–

(a) direct the trustee or, if no trustee has been appointed, the official receiver to send notice of the application to such of those creditors as the court thinks ought to be informed of it, with a view to their proving their debts (if they so wish) within 21 days, and

(b) direct the trustee or, if no trustee has been appointed, the official receiver to advertise the fact that the application has been made, so that creditors who have not proved may do so within a specified time, and

(c) adjourn the application meanwhile, for any period not less than 35 days.

GENERAL NOTE

For the significance of r.6.209 see the comments of Warner J. in *Re Robertson (a Bankrupt)* [1989] 1 W.L.R. 1139. In *Howard v Savage* [2006] EWHC 3693 (Ch); [2007] B.P.I.R. 1097 the link between this rule and IR 6.207 was considered by Lewison J.

(See also General Note after r.6.215.)

6.210 The hearing

6.210(1) **[Trustee to attend]** The trustee shall attend the hearing of the application.

6.210(2) **[Attendance of official receiver]** The official receiver, if he is not the trustee, may attend, but is not required to do so unless he has filed a report under Rule 6.207.

6.210(3) **[Copies of order]** If the court makes an order on the application or on an application under Rule 6.207A, it shall send copies of the order to the applicant, the official receiver and (if other) the trustee.

[FORM 6.71]

(See General Note after r.6.215.) See I(A)R 2010 (SI 2010/686).

6.211 Matters to be proved under s.282(1)(b)

6.211(1) **[Application of Rule]** This rule applies with regard to the matters which (a) must, in an application under section 282(1)(b), be proved to the satisfaction of the court; and (b) may be taken into account by the court on hearing such an application.

6.211(2) **[Debts paid in full]** Subject to the following paragraph, all bankruptcy debts which have been proved must have been (a) paid in full, or (b) secured in full to the satisfaction of the court.

6.211(3)   [If debt disputed etc.] If a debt is disputed, or a creditor who has proved can no longer be traced, the bankrupt must have given such security (in the form of money paid into court, or a bond entered into with approved sureties) as the court considers adequate to satisfy any sum that may subsequently be proved to be due to the creditor concerned and (if the court thinks fit) costs.

6.211(4)   [Advertisement in case of untraced creditor] Where under paragraph (3) security has been given in the case of an untraced creditor, the court may direct that particulars of the alleged debt, and the security, be advertised in such manner as it thinks fit.

   If advertisement is ordered under this paragraph, and no claim on the security is made within 12 months from the date of the advertisement (or the first advertisement, if more than one), the court shall, on application in that behalf, order the security to be released.

6.211(5)   [Payments court may take into account] In determining whether to annul a bankruptcy order under section 282(1)(b), the court may, if it thinks just and without prejudice to the generality of its discretion under section 282(1), take into account whether any sums have been paid or payment of any sums has been secured in respect of post-commencement interest on the bankruptcy debts which have been proved.

6.211(6)   [Security in r.6.211(2), (5)] For the purposes of paragraphs (2) and (5), security includes an undertaking given by a solicitor and accepted by the court.

6.211(7)   ["Post-commencement interest" in r.6.211(5)] For the purposes of paragraph (5), "post-commencement interest" means interest on the bankruptcy debts at the rate specified in section 328(5) in respect of periods during which those debts have been outstanding since the commencement of the bankruptcy.

GENERAL NOTE

For the significance of r.6.211 see *Re Robertson (a Bankrupt)* [1989] 1 W.L.R. 1139. On IR r.6.211 see the comments of Lewison J. in *Howard v Savage* [2006] EWHC 3693 (Ch); [2007] B.P.I.R. 1097. For the consequences of non compliance with r.6.211 see *IRC v Khan* [2005] B.P.I.R. 409. Significant changes have been made by I(A)R 2010 (SI 2010/686), including addition of new paras (5), (6) and (7).

(See also General Note after r.6.215.)

6.212   Notice to creditors

6.212(1)   [Notice of annulment] Where the official receiver has notified creditors of the debtor's bankruptcy, and the bankruptcy order is annulled, he shall as soon as reasonably practicable notify them of the annulment.

6.212(2)   [Expenses of giving notice] Expenses incurred by the official receiver in giving notice under this Rule are a charge in his favour on the property of the former bankrupt, whether or not actually in his hands.

6.212(3)   [Property in hands of trustee etc.] Where any property is in the hands of a trustee or any person other than the former bankrupt himself, the official receiver's charge is valid subject only to any costs that may be incurred by the trustee or that other person in effecting realisation of the property for the purpose of satisfying the charge.

(See General Note after r.6.215.)

6.212A   Annulment under s.261 [Revoked.]

GENERAL NOTE

Rule 6.212A (which was added in 1988) was intended to fill a lacuna in the case of annulments following acceptance of a proposal for an individual voluntary arrangement. It was revoked by I(A)R 2003 (SI 2003/1730) with effect from April 1, 2004.

6.213 Other matters arising on annulment

6.213(1) [Contents of s.261 or 282 order] In an order under section 282 the court shall include provision permitting vacation of the registration of the bankruptcy petition as a pending action, and of the bankruptcy order, in the register of writs and orders affecting land.

6.213(2) [Notice of order] The court shall as soon as reasonably practicable give notice of the making of the order to the Secretary of State.

6.213(3) [Requirement for gazetting/advertisement of notice of order] Within 28 days of the making of the order, the former bankrupt may require the Secretary of State to give notice of the making of the order. As soon as reasonably practicable such notice shall be–

(a) gazetted; and

(b) advertised in the same manner as the bankruptcy order to which it relates was advertised.

6.213(3A) [Additional contents of notice under r.6.213(3)] In addition to the standard contents, the notice under paragraph (3) must state–

(a) the name of the former bankrupt;

(b) the date on which the bankruptcy order was made;

(c) that the bankruptcy order against the former bankrupt has been annulled under section 282(1); and

(d) the date of the annulment.

6.213(4) [Requirement under r.6.213(3)] Any requirement by the former bankrupt under paragraph (3) shall be addressed to the Secretary of State in writing.

6.213(5) [Former bankrupt deceased etc.] Where the former bankrupt has died, or is a person incapable of managing his affairs (within the meaning of Chapter 7 in Part 7 of the Rules), the references to him in paragraphs (3) and (4) are to be read as referring to his personal representative or, as the case may be, a person appointed by the court to represent or act for him.

GENERAL NOTE

A 28-day limit was inserted into para.(3) by I(A)R 2004 (SI 2004/584). The wording in para.(4) was truncated by I(A)R 2004 (SI 2004/584) with effect from April 1, 2004 by the removal of the second sentence dealing with notification by the Secretary of State to the bankrupt of the cost of advertisement. Note the Insolvency (Amendment) Rules 2009 (SI 2009/642), which amended this provision from April 6, 2009 by substituting a new para.(3). A new para.(3A) has been introduced via I(A)R 2010 (SI 2010/686).

6.214 Trustee's final account

6.214(1) [Duty to account for all transactions] Where a bankruptcy order is annulled under section 282, this does not of itself release the trustee from any duty or obligation, imposed on him by or under the Act or the Rules, to account for all his transactions in connection with the former bankrupt's estate.

6.214(2) [Final account to Secretary of State etc.] The trustee shall submit a copy of his final account to the Secretary of State, as soon as practicable after the court's order annulling the bankruptcy order; and he shall file a copy of the final account in court.

6.214(3) [Contents of final account] The final account must include a summary of the trustee's receipts and payments in the administration, and contain a statement to the effect that he has reconciled his account with that which is held by the Secretary of State in respect of the bankruptcy.

6.214(4) [Release of trustee] The trustee is released from such time as the court may determine, having regard to whether–

(a) paragraph (2) of this Rule has been complied with, and

(b)   any security given under Rule 6.211(3) has been, or will be, released.

The key provisions on annulment of bankruptcy orders, IA 1986 ss.261 and 282, leave many questions unanswered. These rules provide the necessary answers. The form of the application to the court is prescribed and if the application is under s.282(1)(b), a full report from the trustee is required. Proceedings can be stayed where an annulment application is pending. Notice of the application may have to be sent to known creditors who have not proved. Public advertisements may also be required. The court order for the annulment should be in the style of Form 6.71, which has been amended by I(A)R 1991 (SI 1991/495) to remove the word "local" before "newspaper". Rule 6.211 explains further s.282(1)(b). Creditors must be notified of the annulment, entries in the Land Register, etc. will have to be vacated, the Secretary of State must be told and the former bankrupt can demand that the annulment be publicly advertised. Rule 6.214 is a necessary saving provision relating to the trustee's accounts. Note the amendments of rr.6.213 and 6.214 to include annulments under s.261.

Rule 6.212A was deleted by SI 2003/1730. Rules 6.213 and 6.214 were also modified by that same SI with effect from April 1, 2004.

CHAPTER 21A

NOTICE UNDER SECTION 279(2)

6.214A   Notice under section 279(2) that an investigation of the conduct and affairs of a bankrupt is unnecessary or concluded

6.214A(1)   [Duty of official receiver to give notice] Where the official receiver intends to file a notice that an investigation of the conduct and affairs of a bankrupt is unnecessary or concluded under section 279(2), he shall give notice in writing to all creditors of which he is aware and any trustee of his intention to file such a notice.

6.214A(2)   [Objections] Where a creditor or a trustee receives written notice of the official receiver's intention to file a notice under section 279(2) and he has any objection to the official receiver filing such a notice, he may, within 28 days of the date of such written notice, inform the official receiver in writing of his objection and give reasons for that objection.

6.214A(3)   [Period for objections] The official receiver shall not file a notice under section 279(2) until the period allowed for creditors or a trustee to object under paragraph (2) has expired.

6.214A(4)   [Form of notice where no objections] Where the official receiver receives no objection from either a creditor or a trustee he may file a notice under section 279(2) by sending to the court two copies of Form 6.82. The court shall endorse each copy with the date of filing and shall return one copy to the official receiver. The official receiver shall send a copy of the endorsed form to the bankrupt.

[FORM 6.82]

6.214A(5)   [Rejection of objection] Where the official receiver receives an objection under this Rule and he rejects that objection, he shall not file the notice under section 279(2) until he has–

(a)   given notice of the rejection (and his reasons) to the complainant; and

(b)   the period of time for an appeal by the complainant under Rule 7.50(2) has expired,

or an appeal under that Rule has been determined by the court.

Rule 6.214A was inserted by Insolvency (Amendment) Rules 2003 (SI 2003/1730) to cater for the liberal approach towards bankrupts favoured by EA 2002. It provides further details on how the new relaxed approach towards investigating the conduct of bankrupts will operate. The notification obligations of the OR under s.279(2) are explained and rights of objection outlined. A new para.(4) rule was substituted by I(A)R 2004 (SI 2004/584) with effect from April 1, 2004. This expands on the bureaucratic role of the court.

CHAPTER 22

DISCHARGE

6.215 Application for suspension of discharge

6.215(1) **[Application of r.6.215]** The following applies where the official receiver or any trustee who is not the official receiver applies to the court for an order under section 279(3) (suspension of automatic discharge), but not where the official receiver makes that application, pursuant to Rule 6.176(4), on the adjournment of the bankrupt's public examination.

6.215(2) **[Evidence in support]** The official receiver or any trustee who is not the official receiver shall, with his application, file evidence in support setting out the reasons why it appears to him that such an order should be made.

6.215(3) **[Court to fix venue]** The court shall fix a venue for the hearing of the application, and give notice of it to the official receiver, the trustee who is not the official receiver, and the bankrupt.

6.215(4) **[Copies of official receiver's report]** Copies of the official receiver's report under this Rule shall be sent by him to the bankrupt and any trustee who is not the official receiver, so as to reach them at least 21 days before the date fixed for the hearing.

6.215(5) **[Copies of the trustee's evidence in support]** Copies of the trustee's evidence in support under this Rule shall be sent by him to the official receiver and the bankrupt, so as to reach them at least 21 days before the date fixed for the hearing.

6.215(6) **[Where bankrupt intends to deny or dispute evidence]** The bankrupt may, not later than 5 business days before the date of the hearing, file in court a notice specifying any statements in the official receiver's or trustee's evidence in support which he intends to deny or dispute.

6.215(7) **[Copies of notice]** If the bankrupt files a notice under paragraph (6), he shall send copies of it, not less than 4 business days before the date of the hearing, to the official receiver and any trustee who is not the official receiver.

6.215(8) **[Copies of order]** If the court makes an order suspending the bankrupt's discharge, copies of the order shall be sent by the court to the official receiver, any trustee who is not the official receiver and the bankrupt.

[FORM 6.72]

GENERAL NOTE

Insolvency practitioners have been reminded of their obligations under IR 6.215(5)—see *Dear IP*, December 2007. The period specified in para.(6) has been converted from seven days to five business days under I(A)R 2010 (SI 2010/686).

6.216 Lifting of suspension of discharge

6.216(1) **[Bankrupt may apply to court]** Where the court has made an order under section 279(3) that the period specified in section 279(1) shall cease to run, the bankrupt may apply to it for the order to be discharged.

6.216(2) **[Venue and notice]** The court shall fix a venue for the hearing of the application; and the bankrupt shall, not less than 28 days before the date fixed for the hearing, give notice of the venue to the

1089

official receiver and any trustee who is not the official receiver, accompanied in each case by a copy of the application.

6.216(3)   **[Appearances etc.]** The official receiver and the trustee may appear and be heard on the bankrupt's application; and, whether or not they appear, the official receiver and trustee may file in court evidence in support of any matters which either of them considers ought to be drawn to the court's attention.

6.216(4)   **[Report on conditions in order]** If the court made an order under section 279(3)(b), the court may request a report from the official receiver or the trustee as to whether the conditions specified in the order have or have not been fulfilled.

6.216(5)   **[Copies of report]** If a report is filed under paragraph (3) or (4), copies of it shall be sent by the official receiver or trustee to the bankrupt and to either the official receiver or trustee (depending on which has filed the report), not later than 14 days before the hearing.

6.216(6)   **[Where bankrupt intends to deny or dispute report]** The bankrupt may, not later than 5 business days before the date of the hearing, file in court a notice specifying any statements in the official receiver's or trustee's report which he intends to deny or dispute.

If he files a notice under this paragraph, he shall send copies of it, not less than 4 business days before the date of the hearing, to the official receiver and the trustee.

6.216(7)   **[If court discharges order]** If on the bankrupt's application the court discharges the order under section 279(3) (being satisfied that the period specified in section 279(1) should begin to run again), it shall issue to the bankrupt a certificate that it has done so, with effect from a specified date and shall send copies of the certificate to the official receiver and the trustee.

[FORM 6.73]
[FORM 6.74]

General note to rr.6.215, 6.216

Rule 6.215 was substituted by I(A)R 2003 (SI 2003/1730) with effect from April 1, 2004. The reference to "report" in r.6.215(4) is unclear. On r.6.215(3) see *Dear IP* Issue 25 (December 2005). Rule 6.216 was substituted by Insolvency (Amendment) Rules 2003 (SI 2003/1730). It deals with the scenario where discharge has been suspended and the bankrupt seeks to have that suspension lifted. For the meaning of "venue" in r.6.216(2) see r.13.6. On alternative avenues open to the bankrupt see *Holmes v Official Receiver (Re a Debtor (No.26 of 1991))* [1996] B.C.C. 246. In r.6.216(7) the words from "and shall send copies" to the end added by the Insolvency (Amendment) Rules 1999 (SI 1999/359) r.1, Sch. para.7 as from March 22, 1999. I(A)R 2010 (SI 2010/686) changes the period in r.6.216(6) from seven days to five business days.

(See also General Note after r.6.233.)

6.217   Application by bankrupt for discharge

6.217(1)   **[If bankrupt makes s.280 application]** If the bankrupt applies under section 280 for an order discharging him from bankruptcy, he shall give to the official receiver notice of the application, and deposit with him such sum as the latter may require to cover his costs of the application.

6.217(2)   **[Venue and notice]** The court, if satisfied that paragraph (1) has been complied with, shall fix a venue for the hearing of the application, and give at least 42 days' notice of it to the official receiver and the bankrupt.

6.217(3)   **[Notice by official receiver]** The official receiver shall give notice accordingly–

  (a)   to the trustee, and

  (b)   to every creditor who, to the official receiver's knowledge, has a claim outstanding against the estate which has not been satisfied.

6.217(4)   **[Time for r.6.217(3) notice]** Notices under paragraph (3) shall be given not later than 14 days before the date fixed for the hearing of the bankrupt's application.

(See General Note after r.6.223.)

6.218   Report of official receiver

6.218(1)   **[Contents etc. of report]** Where the bankrupt makes an application under section 280, the official receiver shall, at least 21 days before the date fixed for the hearing of the application, file in court a report containing the following information with respect to the bankrupt–

   (a)   any failure by him to comply with his obligations under Parts VIII to XI of the Act;

   (b)   the circumstances surrounding the present bankruptcy, and those surrounding any previous bankruptcy of his;

   (c)   the extent to which, in the present and in any previous bankruptcy, his liabilities have exceeded his assets; and

   (d)   particulars of any distribution which has been, or is expected to be, made to creditors in the present bankruptcy or, if such is the case, that there has been and is to be no distribution;

and the official receiver shall include in his report any other matters which in his opinion ought to be brought to the court's attention.

6.218(2)   **[Copies of reports]** The official receiver shall send a copy of the report to the bankrupt and the trustee, so as to reach them at least 14 days before the date of the hearing of the application under section 280.

6.218(3)   **[Where bankrupt disputes report]** The bankrupt may, not later than 5 business days before the date of the hearing, file in court a notice specifying any statements in the official receiver's report which he intends to deny or dispute.

   If he gives notice under this paragraph, he shall send copies of it, not less than 4 days before the date of the hearing, to the official receiver and the trustee.

                                                [FORM 6.75]

6.218(4)   **[Appearances]** The official receiver, the trustee and any creditor may appear on the hearing of the bankrupt's application, and may make representations and put to the bankrupt such questions as the court may allow.

(See General Note after r.6.223.) I(A)R 2010 (SI 2010/686) changes the seven-day period in para.(3) to five business days.

6.219   Order of discharge on application

6.219(1)   **[Order to take effect when drawn up by court]** An order of the court under section 280(2)(b) (discharge absolutely) or (c) (discharge subject to conditions with respect to income or property) shall bear the date on which it is made, but does not take effect until such time as it is drawn up by the court.

                                                [FORM 6.76]

6.219(2)   **[Retrospective effect]** The order then has effect retrospectively to the date on which it was made.

6.219(3)   **[Copies of order]** Copies of any order made by the court on an application by the bankrupt for discharge under section 280 shall be sent by the court to the bankrupt, the trustee and the official receiver.

(See General Note after r.6.223.)

6.220   Certificate of discharge

6.220(1)   **[Where bankrupt is discharged]** Where it appears to the court that a bankrupt is discharged, whether by expiration of time or otherwise, the court shall, on his application, issue to him a certificate of his discharge, and the date from which it is effective.

[FORM 6.77]

6.220(2)   **[Requirement for gazetting/advertisement of notice of discharge]** The discharged bankrupt may require within 28 days of the order the Secretary of State to give notice of the discharge. As soon as reasonably practicable such notice shall be–

    (a)   gazetted; and

    (b)   advertised in such manner as the bankruptcy order to which it relates was advertised.

6.220(2A)   **[Additional contents of notice under r.6.220(2)]** In addition to the standard contents, a notice under paragraph (2) must state–

    (a)   the name of the former bankrupt;

    (b)   the date of the bankruptcy order;

    (c)   that a certificate of discharge has been issued;

    (d)   the date of the certificate; and

    (e)   the date from which the discharge is effective.

6.220(3)   **[Requirement in r.6.220(2)]** Any requirement by the former bankrupt under paragraph (2) shall be addressed to the Secretary of State in writing.

6.220(4)   **[Former bankrupt deceased etc.]** Where the former bankrupt has died, or is a person incapable of managing his affairs (within the meaning of Chapter 7 in Part 7 of the Rules), the references to him in paragraphs (2) and (3) are to be read as referring to his personal representative or, as the case may be, a person appointed by the court to represent or act for him.

(See General Note after r.6.223.) The Insolvency (Amendment) Rules 2009 (SI 2009/642), which took effect on April 6, 2009, amended this rule by substituting a new para.(2). Modernised by I(A)R 2010 (SI 2010/686)—new para.(2A) introduced.

6.221   Deferment of issue of order pending appeal

6.221   An order made by the court on an application by the bankrupt for discharge under section 280 shall not be issued or gazetted until the time allowed for appealing has expired or, if an appeal is entered, until the appeal has been determined.

(See General Note after r.6.223.)

6.222   Costs under this Chapter

6.222   In no case do any costs or expenses arising under this Chapter fall on the official receiver personally.

(See General Note after r.6.223.)

6.223   Bankrupt's debts surviving discharge

6.223   Discharge does not release the bankrupt from any obligation arising under a confiscation order made under section 1 of the Drug Trafficking Offences Act 1986 or section 1 of the Criminal Justice (Scotland) Act 1987 or section 71 of the Criminal Justice Act 1988 or under Parts 2, 3 or 4 of the Proceeds of Crime Act 2002.

These rules provide additional information on the effect of IA 1986 ss.279–281. Applications for suspension of automatic discharge under s.279(3) are explained. If the court orders suspension, Form 6.72 is to be used. Suspension orders can be varied by the court. Note the use of Forms 6.73 and 6.74 here. Rules 6.217 and 6.218 are specially referable to applications by the bankrupt to the court for discharge under IA 1986 s.280. The official receiver must be notified and he must file a report on the bankrupt's conduct. Form 6.76 is to be used for any court order under s.280. Certificates of discharge must normally adopt the style of Form 6.77. Rule 6.223 is a specialised provision dealing with the enforcement of sanctions against drug dealers, etc.: compare s.281(4).

Rule 6.223 was modified by I(A)R 2003 (SI 2003/1730) with effect from April 1, 2004.

CHAPTER 22A [REVOKED.]

REGISTER OF BANKRUPTCY ORDERS

Introductory note to Chapter 22A
Chapter 22A was inserted by the Insolvency (Amendment) Rules 1999 (SI 1999/359) with effect from March 22, 1999. Chapter 22A established a public register of bankruptcy orders and therefore alleviated the difficulties involving bulk searches of court records as illustrated by cases such as *Re Austintel Ltd* [1997] 1 W.L.R. 616. This Chapter was revoked by I(A)R 2003 (SI 2003/1730). These matters are now dealt with by Part 6A.

6.223A   *Register of bankruptcy orders [Revoked.]*

6.223B   *Specified bankruptcy information [Revoked.]*

6.223C   *Notification of changes [Revoked.]*

CHAPTER 23

ORDER OF PAYMENT OF COSTS, ETC., OUT OF ESTATE

6.224   General rule as to priority

6.224(1)   [Priority of expenses] The expenses of the bankruptcy are payable out of the estate in the following order of priority–

(a)   expenses or costs which–

    (i)   are properly chargeable or incurred by the official receiver or the trustee in preserving, realising or getting in any of the assets of the bankrupt or otherwise relating to the conduct of any legal proceedings which he has power to bring (whether the claim on which the proceedings are based forms part of the estate or otherwise) or defend;

    (ii)   relate to the employment of a shorthand writer, if appointed by an order of the court made at the instance of the official receiver in connection with an examination; or

    (iii)   are incurred in holding an examination under Rule 6.174 (examinee unfit) where the application was made by the official receiver;

(b)   any other expenses incurred or disbursements made by the official receiver or under his authority, including those incurred or made in carrying on the business of a debtor or bankrupt;

(c)   the fees payable under any order made under section 415 or 415A, including those payable to the official receiver (other than the fee referred to in sub-paragraph (d)(i) below), and any remuneration payable to him under general regulations;

(d) (i)   the fee payable under any order made under section 415 for the performance by the official receiver of his general duties as official receiver;

    (ii)   any repayable deposit lodged under any such order as security for the fee mentioned in sub-paragraph (i) (except where the deposit is applied to the payment of the remuneration of an insolvency practitioner appointed under section 273 (debtor's petition));

(e)   the cost of any security provided by an interim receiver, trustee or special manager in accordance with the Act or the Rules;

(f)   the remuneration of the interim receiver (if any);

(g)   any deposit lodged on an application for the appointment of an interim receiver;

(h)   the costs of the petitioner, and of any person appearing on the petition whose costs are allowed by the court;

(j)   the remuneration of the special manager (if any);

(k)   any amount payable to a person employed or authorised, under Chapter 5 of this Part of the Rules, to assist in the preparation of a statement of affairs or of accounts;

(l)   any allowance made, by order of the court, towards costs on an application for release from the obligation to submit a statement of affairs, or for an extension of time for submitting such a statement;

(la)   the costs of employing a shorthand writer in any case other than one appointed by an order of the court at the instance of the official receiver in connection with an examination;

(m)   any necessary disbursements by the trustee in the course of his administration (including any expenses incurred by members of the creditors' committee or their representatives and allowed by the trustee under Rule 6.164, but not including any payment of capital gains tax in circumstances referred to in sub-paragraph (p) below);

(n)   the remuneration or emoluments of any person (including the bankrupt) who has been employed by the trustee to perform any services for the estate, as required or authorised by or under the Act or the Rules;

(o)   the remuneration of the trustee, up to any amount not exceeding that which is payable under Schedule 6;

(p)   the amount of any capital gains tax on chargeable gains accruing on the realisation of any asset of the bankrupt (without regard to whether the realisation is effected by the trustee, a secured creditor, or a receiver or manager appointed to deal with a security);

(q)   the balance, after payment of any sums due under sub-paragraph (o) above, of any remuneration due to the trustee.

(r)   any other expenses properly chargeable by the trustee in carrying out his functions in the bankruptcy.

GENERAL NOTE

This is the normal priority regime though it is described in great detail here. Link this list with IA 1986 s.328. For "general regulations" see r.13.13(5). Rule 6.224(2) and (3) were omitted by the Insolvency (Amendment) (No.2) Rules 2002 (SI 2002/2712) r.1, 6(1) and Sch. Pt 4 para.25(d) as from January 1, 2003 subject to transitional provisions in r.6(2) of the 2002 Rules.

The reform to subpara.(1)(a) effected by the Insolvency (Amendment) (No.2) Rules 2002 (SI 2002/2712) mirrors that made to r.4.218 and allows recovery proceedings costs to be treated as bankruptcy costs. This amendment to r.6.224 needs to be viewed in the light of the enhanced control of recovery proceedings imposed by EA 2002 s.262, which introduces a new para.2A into Sch.5. Note also the insertion of subparas (la) and (r). Subparagraph (o) was modified by the Insolvency (Amendment) Rules 2005 (SI 2005/527) to include the specific reference to Sch.6.

The priority as between subparas (c) and (d) was in the reverse order prior to April 1, 1995: see SI 1995/586.

The reference to s.415A in para.(1)(c) was added by I(A)R 2004 (SI 2004/584) with effect from April 1, 2004. Fees orders are now being made under s.415A.

CHAPTER 24

SECOND BANKRUPTCY

6.225   Scope of this Chapter

6.225(1)   [Application of Ch.24 Rules] The Rules in this Chapter relate to the manner in which, in the case of a second bankruptcy, the trustee in the earlier bankruptcy is to deal with property and money to which section 334(3) applies, until there is a trustee of the estate in the later bankruptcy.

6.225(2)   [Definitions] "The earlier bankruptcy", "the later bankruptcy" and "the existing trustee" have the meanings given by section 334(1).

(See General Note after r.6.228.)

6.226   General duty of existing trustee

6.226(1)   [Duty to get in property etc.] Subject as follows, the existing trustee shall take into his custody or under his control all such property and money, in so far as he has not already done so as part of his duties as trustee in the earlier bankruptcy.

6.226(2)   [Power to sell perishable goods etc.] Where any of that property consists of perishable goods, or goods the value of which is likely to diminish if they are not disposed of, the existing trustee has power to sell or otherwise dispose of those goods.

6.226(3)   [Proceeds of sale] The proceeds of any such sale or disposal shall be held, under the existing trustee's control, with the other property and money comprised in the bankrupt's estate.

(See General Note after r.6.228.)

6.227   Delivery up to later trustee

6.227   The existing trustee shall, as and when requested by the trustee for the purposes of the later bankruptcy, deliver up to the latter all such property and money as is in his custody or under his control in pursuance of Rule 6.226.

(See General Note after r.6.228.)

6.228   Existing trustee's expenses

6.228   Any expenses incurred by the existing trustee in compliance with section 335(1) and this Chapter of the Rules shall be defrayed out of, and are a charge on, all such property and money as is referred to in section 334(3), whether in the hands of the existing trustee or of the trustee for the purposes of the later bankruptcy.

GENERAL NOTE TO RR.6.225–6.228

These rules supplement IA 1986 s.334 and deal with the complex relationship between the two successive bankruptcy regimes.

CHAPTER 25

CRIMINAL BANKRUPTCY

6.229   Presentation of petition

6.229(1)   [Presentation to High Court] In criminal bankruptcy, the petition under section 264(1)(d) shall be presented to the High Court, and accordingly Rule 6.9A in Chapter 2 (court in which other petitions to be presented) does not apply.

[FORM 6.79]

6.229(2)   [Effect of Rule] This does not affect the High Court's power to order that the proceedings be transferred.

(See General Note after r.6.234.)

6.230   Status and functions of Official Petitioner

6.230(1)   [Official Petitioner as a creditor] Subject as follows, the Official Petitioner is to be regarded for all purposes of the Act and the Rules as a creditor of the bankrupt.

6.230(2)   [Attendance, representation etc.] He may attend or be represented at any meeting of creditors, and is to be given any notice under the Act or the Rules which is required or authorised to be given to creditors; and the requirements of the Rules as to the lodging or use of proxies do not apply.

(See General Note after r.6.234.)

6.231   Interim receivership

6.231   Chapter 4 of this Part of the Rules applies in criminal bankruptcy only in so far as it provides for the appointment of the official receiver as interim receiver.

(See General Note after r.6.234.)

6.232   Proof of bankruptcy debts and notice of order

6.232(1)   [Effect of order] The making of a bankruptcy order on a criminal bankruptcy petition does not affect the right of creditors to prove for their debts arising otherwise than in consequence of the criminal proceedings.

6.232(2)   [Person suffering loss etc.] A person specified in a criminal bankruptcy order as having suffered loss or damage shall be treated as a creditor of the bankrupt; and a copy of the order is sufficient evidence of his claim, subject to its being shown by any party to the bankruptcy proceedings that the loss or damage actually suffered was more or (as the case may be) less than the amount specified in the order.

6.232(3)   [Non-application of Rules] The requirements of the Rules with respect to the proof of debts do not apply to the Official Petitioner.

6.232(4)   [Forms of proof] In criminal bankruptcy, forms of proof shall be sent out by the official receiver within 12 weeks from the making of the bankruptcy order, to every creditor who is known to him.

6.232(5)   [Notice to creditors] The official receiver shall, within those 12 weeks, send to every such creditor notice of the making of the bankruptcy order.

GENERAL NOTE

The new r.6.232(4) makes it clear that forms of proof do not have to be in a prescribed format. The deadline has been changed to within 12 weeks, which was what was originally intended but not conveyed by the language of the previous provision. I(A)R 2010 (SI 2010/686) makes a minor change to para.(4).

(See also General Note after r.6.234.)

6.233   Meetings under the Rules

6.233(1)   [Non-application of Ch.6 Rules] The following Rules in Chapter 6 of this Part do not apply in criminal bankruptcy–

> Rules 6.79 and 6.80 (first meeting of creditors, and business thereat);

> Rule 6.82(2) (the chairman, if other than the official receiver);

> Rule 6.88(2) and (3) (resolution for appointment of trustee).

6.233(2)   [Non-application of r.6.97] Rule 6.97 (supply of forms for proof of debts) does not apply.

(See General Note after r.6.234.)

6.234   Trustee in bankruptcy; creditors' committee; annulment of bankruptcy order

6.234(1)   [Non-application of Ch.10 Rules] Chapter 10 of this Part of the Rules does not apply in criminal bankruptcy, except Rules 6.136 (release of official receiver) and 6.147 (power of court to set aside transactions).

6.234(2)   [Non-application of Ch.11 Rules] Chapter 11 (creditors' committee) does not apply.

6.234(3)   [Application of Ch.21 Rules] Chapter 21 (annulment of bankruptcy order) applies to an application to the court under section 282(2) as it applies to an application under section 282(1), with any necessary modifications.

GENERAL NOTE TO RR.6.229–6.234

The criminal bankruptcy regime (see IA 1986 s.277) sits uneasily alongside the other facets of bankruptcy law. Further details of its operation are hereby provided. The form of the petition (Form 6.79) and the role of the official petitioner (see IA 1986 s.402) are described. Proof of debts, meetings or creditors, etc. are also regulated by these rules. The amendment to r.6.232(4) by I(A)R 1987 is discussed above. Typographical errors in r.6.234 have also been amended. The criminal bankruptcy regime is to be abolished by CJA 1988: see the note to IA 1986 s.277.

CHAPTER 26

MISCELLANEOUS RULES IN BANKRUPTCY

6.235   Bankruptcy of solicitors [Revoked.]

6.235A   Application for redirection order

6.235A(1)   [Application of r.6.235A] This Rule applies where the official receiver or trustee in bankruptcy applies to the court under section 371(1) (re-direction of bankrupt's letters etc).

6.235A(2)   [Application without notice] The application shall be made without notice to the bankrupt or any other person, unless the court directs otherwise.

6.235A(3)   [Applicant to set out reasons for order] The applicant shall with his application, where he is the official receiver, file a report, and where he is the trustee in bankruptcy, a witness statement, setting out the reasons why such an order is sought.

6.235A(4)   [Court to fix venue for hearing] The court shall fix a venue for the hearing of the application if the court thinks fit and give notice to the applicant.

6.235A(5)   [Order may be subject to conditions] The court may make an order on such conditions as it thinks fit.

6.235A(6)   [Order to identify person on whom served] The order shall identify the person on whom it is to be served, and need not be served on the bankrupt unless the court directs otherwise.

Rule 6.235A was inserted by the Insolvency (Amendment) Rules 2005 (SI 2005/527) in order to clarify procedures on redirection orders under s.371. See I(A)R 2010 (SI 2010/686).

6.235B Persons at risk of violence

6.235B(1) **[Application of r.6.235B]** The provisions of this Rule apply in any case where disclosure or continuing disclosure to other persons (whether to the public generally or to specific persons) of the current address or whereabouts of a debtor might reasonably be expected to lead to violence against the debtor or against a person who normally resides with the debtor as a member of the debtor's family.

6.235B(2) **["Current address", "debtor"]** For the purposes of this Rule–

"current address" means, in relation to any debtor, the address of the debtor's current place of residence and any address at which the debtor currently carries on business; and

"debtor" means a person who is subject to a bankruptcy order, a bankruptcy restrictions order or a bankruptcy restrictions undertaking.

6.235B(3) **[Court order]** The court may, on the application of the debtor, the official receiver, the trustee or the Secretary of State, order that–

(a) details of the debtor's current address be removed from any part of the court file of the proceedings in relation to the debtor which is open to inspection and be kept on a separate file not open to inspection;

(b) the details in respect of the debtor to be entered in the bankruptcy order must not include details of the debtor's current address;

(c) the full title of the proceedings must be amended by the removal of the details of the debtor's current address from the description of the debtor;

(d) the details of the debtor to be included in any notice gazetted or otherwise advertised must not include details of the debtor's current address;

(e) the details in respect of the debtor to be entered onto the individual insolvency register under Rule 6A.4 or the bankruptcy restrictions register under Rule 6A.6 must not include details of the debtor's current address; or

(f) the details of the debtor's current address kept on the individual insolvency register or the bankruptcy restrictions register must be removed from such register.

6.235B(4) **[Further order to r.6.235B(3)(b)–(f)]** Where the court makes an order under paragraph (3)(b) to (f), it may further order that–

(a) the description of the debtor to be inserted in the bankruptcy order,

(b) the full title of the proceedings,

(c) the details of the debtor required to be included in any notice to be gazetted or otherwise advertised, or

(d) the details in respect of the debtor kept or to be entered on to the registers referred to in paragraph (3)(d) and (e),

as the case may be, must instead include such other details of the debtor's addresses or whereabouts as the court thinks just, including details of any address at which the debtor has previously resided or carried on business.

6.235B(5) **[Notification where order under r.6.235B(3)]** Where the court makes an order under paragraph (3)(c)–

(a)   the official receiver must as soon as reasonably practicable send notice of it to the Chief Land Registrar, for corresponding amendment of the register; and

(b)   if official receiver thinks fit, the official receiver may cause notice of the order to be–

    (i)   gazetted, or

    (ii)   both gazetted and given in such other manner as the official receiver thinks fit.

6.235B(6)   [Contents of notice on amendment of title of proceedings] Any notice of the amendment of the title of the proceedings to be published in accordance with paragraph (5) must contain–

(a)   the standard contents with the exception of the current address of the debtor,

(b)   the amended title of the proceedings, and

(c)   the date of the bankruptcy order,

but must not include the description under which the proceedings were previously published.

6.235B(7)   [Contents of witness statement accompanying application] In any case where an application is made in respect of a debtor under or by virtue of this Rule, the application must be accompanied by a witness statement referring to this Rule and containing sufficient evidence to satisfy the court that paragraph (1) of this Rule applies to or in respect of that debtor.

GENERAL NOTE

This is a new provision introduced by I(A)R 2010 (SI 2010/686).

6.236   Consolidation of petitions

6.236   Where two or more bankruptcy petitions are presented against the same debtor, the court may order the consolidation of the proceedings, on such terms as it thinks fit.

GENERAL NOTE

This provision would have been better located perhaps towards the beginning of this Part of the rules.

6.237   Bankrupt's Home—Notification of property falling within section 283A

6.237(1)   [Form of notice] Where it appears to a trustee that section 283A(1) applies, the trustee shall give notice in Form 6.83 as soon as reasonably practicable to–

(a)   the bankrupt;

(b)   the bankrupt's spouse or civil partner (in a case falling within section 283A(1)(b)); and

                                                      [FORM 6.83]

(c)   a former spouse or former civil partner of the bankrupt (in a case falling within section 283A(1)(c)).

6.237(2)   [Contents of notice] A notice under paragraph (1) shall contain–

(a)   the name of the bankrupt;

(b)   the address of the dwelling-house; and

(c)   if the dwelling-house is registered land, the title number.

6.237(3)   [Time limit for notice] A trustee shall not give notice under paragraph (1) any later than 14 days before the expiry of the three year period under section 283A(2) or 283A(5).

6.237A   Application in respect of the vesting of an interest in a dwelling-house (registered land)

6.237A(1)   [Application of r.6.237A(2)] Paragraph (2) applies where–

(a)   property comprised in the bankrupt's estate consists of an interest in a dwelling-house which at the date of bankruptcy was the sole or principal residence of–

    (i)   the bankrupt;

    (ii)   the bankrupt's spouse or civil partner; or

    (iii)   a former spouse or former civil partner of the bankrupt; and

(b)   the dwelling-house is registered land; and

(c)   an entry has been made, or entries have been made, in the individual register or registers of the dwelling-house relating to the bankrupt's bankruptcy or the individual register or registers has or have been altered to reflect the vesting of the bankrupt's interest in a trustee in bankruptcy.

6.237A(2)   [Trustee to apply to register interest in bankrupt] Where an interest of a kind mentioned in paragraph (1) ceases to be comprised in the bankrupt's estate and vests in the bankrupt under either section 283A(2) or 283A(4) of the Act, or under section 261(8) of the Enterprise Act 2002, the trustee shall, within 5 business days of the vesting, make such application or applications to the Chief Land Registrar as shall be necessary to show in the individual register or registers of the dwelling house that the interest has vested in the bankrupt.

6.237A(3)   [Form of application] An application under paragraph (2) shall be made in accordance with the Land Registration Act 2002 and shall be accompanied by–

(a)   evidence of the trustee's appointment (where not previously provided to the Chief Land Registrar); and

(b)   a certificate from the trustee stating that the interest has vested in the bankrupt under section 283A(2) or 283A(4) of the Act or section 261(8) of the Enterprise Act 2002 (whichever is appropriate).

6.237A(4)   [Notification of application] As soon as reasonably practicable after making an application under paragraph (2), the trustee shall notify the bankrupt and if the dwelling-house was the sole or principal residence of his spouse or former spouse or civil partner or former civil partner, such person, that the application has been made.

6.237A(5)   [Further notification of application] The trustee shall notify every person who (to his knowledge) either claims an interest in the dwelling-house, or is under any liability in respect of the dwelling-house that an application has been made.

GENERAL NOTE

This deals with applications in respect of the vesting of an interest in a dwelling-house where the land is registered. The period in para.(2) has been changed from seven days to five business days by I(A)R 2010 (SI 2010/686).

6.237B   Vesting of bankrupt's interest (unregistered land)

6.237B(1)   [Certificate as to vesting] Where an interest in a dwelling-house which at the date of the bankruptcy was the sole or principal residence of–

(a)   the bankrupt;

(b)   the bankrupt's spouse or civil partner; or

(c)   a former spouse or former civil partner of the bankrupt,

ceases to be comprised in the bankrupt's estate and vests in the bankrupt under either section 283A(2) or 283A(4) of the Act or section 261(8) of the Enterprise Act 2002 and the dwelling-house is unregistered land, the trustee shall issue the bankrupt with a certificate as to the vesting in Form 6.84 as soon as reasonably practicable.

[FORM 6.84]

6.237B(2)   **[Certificate conclusive proof of interest]** A certificate issued under paragraph (1) shall be conclusive proof that the interest mentioned in paragraph (1) has vested in the bankrupt.

6.237B(3)   **[Notification of application]** As soon as reasonably practicable after issuing the certificate under paragraph (1) the trustee shall, if the dwelling-house was the sole or principal residence of the bankrupt's spouse or former spouse or civil partner or former civil partner, notify such person, that the application has been made.

6.237B(4)   **[Further notification of application]** The trustee shall notify every person who (to his knowledge) either claims an interest in the dwelling-house, or is under any liability in respect of the dwelling-house that an application has been made.

R.6.237B
This covers the same matters as r.6.237A but the land here is unregistered.

6.237C   The court may substitute for the period of three years mentioned in section 283A(2) such longer period as the court thinks just and reasonable in all the circumstances of the case.

R.6.237C
The three-year time-limit may be extended at the discretion of the court.

6.237CA   Vesting of bankrupt's estate—substituted period

6.237CA   For the purposes of section 283A(2) for the period of three years set out therein there shall be substituted, where the trustee in bankruptcy has sent notice to the bankrupt that he considers–

    (a)   the continued vesting of the property in the bankrupt's estate to be of no benefit to creditors; or

    (b)   the re-vesting to the bankrupt will facilitate a more efficient administration of the bankrupt's estate,

the period of one month from the date of that notice.

GENERAL NOTE

This new rule was inserted by I(A)R 2004 (SI 2004/584) with effect from April 1, 2004. It provides further fine tuning for this new regime in dealing with the family home.

6.237D   Charging Order

6.237D(1)   **[Application of r.6.237D]** This Rule applies where the trustee applies to the court under section 313 for an order imposing a charge on property consisting of an interest in a dwelling-house.

6.237D(2)   **[Respondents]** The respondents to the application shall be–

    (a)   any spouse or former spouse or civil partner or former civil partner of the bankrupt having or claiming to have an interest in the property;

[FORM 6.79A]

    (b)   any other person appearing to have an interest in the property; and

    (c)   such other persons as the court may direct.

6.237D(3)   **[Trustee's report to court]** The trustee shall make a report to the court, containing the following particulars–

(a)   the extent of the bankrupt's interest in the property which is the subject of the application;

(b)   the amount which, at the date of the application, remains owing to unsecured creditors of the bankrupt; and

(c)   an estimate of the cost of realising the interest.

6.237D(4)   [Terms of charge] The terms of the charge to be imposed shall be agreed between the trustee and the bankrupt or, failing agreement, shall be settled by the court.

6.237D(5)   [Rate of interest] The rate of interest applicable under section 313(2) is the rate specified in section 17 of the Judgments Act 1838 on the day on which the charge is imposed, and the rate so applicable shall be stated in the court's order imposing the charge.

6.237D(6)   [Court order] The court's order shall also–

(a)   describe the property to be charged;

(b)   state whether the title to the property is registered and, if it is, specify the title number;

(c)   set out the extent of the bankrupt's interest in the property which has vested in the trustee;

(d)   indicate, by reference to any, or the total, amount which is payable otherwise than to the bankrupt out of the estate and of interest on that amount, how the amount of the charge to be imposed is to be ascertained;

(e)   set out the conditions (if any) imposed by the court under section 3(1) of the Charging Orders Act 1979; and

(f)   identify the date any property charged under section 313 shall cease to be comprised in the bankrupt's estate and shall, subject to the charge (and any prior charge), vest in the bankrupt.

6.237D(7)   [Date in r.6.237D(6)(f)] Unless the court is of the opinion that a different date is appropriate, the date referred to in paragraph (6)(f) shall be that of the registration of the charge in accordance with section 3(2) of the Charging Orders Act 1979.

6.237D(8)   [Application for registration] Where the court order is capable of giving rise to an application or applications under the Land Charges Act 1972 or the Land Registration Act 2002, the trustee shall, as soon as reasonably practicable after the making of the court order or at the appropriate time, make the appropriate application or applications to the Chief Land Registrar.

6.237D(9)   ["Appropriate application"] In paragraph (8) an "appropriate application" is–

(a)   an application under section 6(1)(a) of the Land Charges Act 1972 (application for registration in the register of writs and orders affecting land); or

(b)   an application under the Land Registration Act 2002 for an entry in the register in respect of the charge imposed by the order; and such application under that Act as shall be necessary to show in the individual register or registers of the dwelling-house that the interest has vested in the bankrupt.

6.237D(10)   [Determining the value of interest in property for r.6.237D(6)(c)] In determining the value of the bankrupt's interest for the purposes of paragraph (6)(c), the court shall disregard that part of the value of the property in which the bankrupt's interest subsists which is equal to the value of–

(a)   any loans secured by mortgage or other charge against the property;

(b)   any other third party interest; and

(c)   the reasonable costs of sale.

GENERAL NOTE

This deals with applications for charging orders pursuant to s.313.

Paragraph (10) was added by I(A)R 2004 (SI 2004/584) with effect from April 1, 2004. Again this looks like a case of belated fleshing out of details.

6.237E   Interpretation

6.237E(1)   ["Registered land"] In Rules 6.237 and 6.237A, "registered land" has the same meaning as in section 132(1) of the Land Registration Act 2002.

6.237E(2)   ["Individual register"] In Rules 6.237A and 6.237D, "individual register" has the same meaning as in the Land Registration Rules 2003.

R.6.237E
This provides interpretation guidance.

GENERAL NOTE TO RR.6.237–6.237E

Rule 6.237 was substituted by Insolvency (Amendment) Rules 2003 (SI 2003/1730) to deal with the new law on the bankrupt's home. New rr.6.237A–E were also inserted. Rule 6.237 places the onus of notification on the trustee. Notification must be given before 14 days prior to the elapse of the three-year period. The references to civil partners and former civil partners found in rr.6.237, 6.237A, 6.237B and 6.237D are to be included with effect from December 5, 2005 by the Civil Partnership Act 2004 (Amendments to Subordinate Legislation) Order 2005 (SI 2005/2114). The relevant Forms will also reflect this change. The Insolvency Service has published guidance on the interface between IR r.6.237, s.283A of the Insolvency Act 1986 and Form 6.83—see *Dear IP*, September 2007.

CHAPTER 27

EC REGULATION—MEMBER STATE LIQUIDATOR

6.238   Interpretation of creditor and notice to member State liquidator

6.238(1)   [Application] This Rule applies where a member State liquidator has been appointed in relation to the bankrupt.

6.238(2)   [Interpretation] For the purposes of the Rules referred to in paragraph (3) a member State liquidator is deemed to be a creditor.

6.238(3)   [Rules referred to in r.6.238(2)] The Rules referred to in paragraph (2) are Rules 6.73(1) (duty of official receiver), 6.75(1) (report of official receiver), 6.76(2) (report of official receiver), 6.79(2) (creditors' meeting), 6.81 (power to call creditors' meeting), 6.83 (requisitioned meetings), 6.93 (entitlement to vote), 6.94 (admission and rejection of proof), 6.96 (meaning of "prove"), 6.97 (supply of forms), 6.98 (contents of proof), 6.100 (cost of proving), 6.101 (inspection of proofs), 6.104 (admission and rejection of proofs for dividend), 6.105(1) (appeal against decision on proof), 6.105(2), 6.106 (withdrawal or variation of proofs), 6.107(1) (expunging of proof), 6.108 (negotiable instruments, etc.), 6.109 (secured creditors), 6.110 (discounts), 6.111 (debts in foreign currency), 6.112 (payments of a periodical nature), 6.113 (interest), 6.114 (debt payable at future time), 6.126(1) (resignation of trustee), 6.136(1) (release of official receiver), 6.137(1) (final meeting), 6.142(1) (challenge to remuneration), 6.150(2) (creditors' committee), 6.160(3) (vacancy on creditors' committee), 6.172(3) (request for public examination), 6.212(1) (notice of annulment) and 6.217(3) (application by bankrupt for discharge).

6.238(4)   [Exercise of creditor's rights] Paragraphs (2) and (3) are without prejudice to the generality of the right to participate referred to in paragraph 3 of Article 32 of the EC Regulation (exercise of creditor's rights).

6.238(5) **[Notice, copies]** Where the trustee is obliged to give notice to, or provide a copy of a document (including an order of court) to, the court or the official receiver, the trustee shall give notice or provide copies, as the case may be, to the member State liquidator.

6.238(6) **[Duty to co-operate and communicate information]** Paragraph (5) is without prejudice to the generality of the obligations imposed by Article 31 of the EC Regulation (duty to cooperate and communicate information).

GENERAL NOTE

See note after r.6.239.

6.239 Interpretation of creditor and notice to member State liquidator appointed in main proceedings

6.239(1) **[Application]** This Rule applies, in addition to Rule 6.238, where a member State liquidator has been appointed in main proceedings in relation to the bankrupt.

6.239(2) **[Interpretation]** For the purposes of the Rules referred to in paragraph (3) the member State liquidator is deemed to be a creditor.

6.239(3) **[Rules referred to in r.6.239(2)]** The Rules referred to in paragraph (2) are Rules 6.18(3) (hearing of petition), 6.23(1) (notice of intention to appear), 6.28(4) (extension of time), 6.30(2) (substitution of petitioner), 6.31(1) (change of carriage of petition) and 6.218(4) (report of official receiver).

6.239(4) **[Exercise of creditor's rights]** Paragraphs (2) and (3) are without prejudice to the generality of the right to participate referred to in paragraph 3 of Article 32 of the EC Regulation (exercise of creditor's rights).

GENERAL NOTE

Chapter 27 (rr.6.238 and 6.239) was introduced by Insolvency (Amendment) Rules 2002 (SI 2002/1307) para.8(9) with effect from May 31, 2002 to cater for the introduction of EC Council Regulation on Insolvency Proceedings (1346/2000).

CHAPTER 28

BANKRUPTCY RESTRICTIONS ORDER

6.240 In this and the following two Chapters, "Secretary of State" includes the official receiver acting in accordance with paragraph 1(2)(b) of Schedule 4A to the Act.

R.6.240
This Chapter 28 was inserted by Insolvency (Amendment) Rules 2003 (SI 2003/1730) to support the legislation on bankruptcy restriction orders, which were an innovation in EA 2002. Rule 6.240 is a curiously located interpretation provision.

6.241 Application for bankruptcy restrictions order

6.241(1) **[Report by Secretary of State]** Where the Secretary of State applies to the court for a bankruptcy restrictions order under paragraph 1 of Schedule 4A to the Act, the application shall be supported by a report by the Secretary of State.

6.241(2) **[Contents of report]** The report shall include–

(a) a statement of the conduct by reference to which it is alleged that it is appropriate for a bankruptcy restrictions order to be made; and

(b)   the evidence on which the Secretary of State relies in support of the application.

6.241(3)   **[Witness statement in support by other persons]** Any evidence in support of an application for a bankruptcy restrictions order provided by persons other than the Secretary of State shall be by way of a witness statement.

6.241(4)   **[Venue and date of hearing]** The date for the hearing shall be no earlier than 8 weeks from the date when the court fixes the venue for the hearing.

6.241(5)   [Omitted.]

R.6.241
This outlines the procedure where an application is made for a BRO. Paragraph (5) omitted by I(A)R 2010 (SI 2010/686).

6.242   Service on the defendant

6.242(1)   **[Time limit]** The Secretary of State shall serve notice of the application and the venue fixed by the court on the bankrupt not more than 14 days after the application is made at court.

6.242(2)   **[Documents to accompany service]** Service shall be accompanied by a copy of the application, together with copies of the report by the Secretary of State, any other evidence filed with the court in support of the application, and an acknowledgement of service.

6.242(3)   **[Acknowledgement of service]** The defendant shall file in court an acknowledgement of service of the application indicating whether or not he contests the application not more than 14 days after service on him of the application.

6.242(4)   **[Failure to file acknowledgement of service]** Where the defendant has failed to file an acknowledgement of service and the time period for doing so has expired, the defendant may attend the hearing of the application but may not take part in the hearing unless the court gives permission.

R.6.242
Notice of the application must be served on the bankrupt within 14 days of the application being lodged.

6.243   The bankrupt's evidence

6.243(1)   **[Time limits etc.]** If the bankrupt wishes to oppose the application, he shall within 28 days of the service of the application and evidence of the Secretary of State, file in court any evidence which he wishes the court to take into consideration, and shall serve a copy of such evidence upon the Secretary of State within 3 business days of filing it at court.

6.243(2)   **[Time limit for Secretary of State's further evidence etc.]** The Secretary of State shall, within 14 days from receiving the copy of the bankrupt's evidence, file in court any further evidence in reply he wishes the court to take into consideration and shall as soon as reasonably practicable serve a copy of that evidence upon the bankrupt.

R.6.243
This outlines the responsibilities of the bankrupt if he wishes to oppose the application for a BRO. I(A)R 2010 (SI 2010/686) makes minor amendment to para.(1).

6.244   Making a bankruptcy restrictions order

6.244(1)   **[Power of court]** The court may make a bankruptcy restrictions order against the bankrupt, whether or not the latter appears, and whether or not he has filed evidence in accordance with Rule 6.243.

6.244(2)   **[Copies of order to Secretary of State]** Where the court makes a bankruptcy restrictions order, it shall send two sealed copies to the Secretary of State.

6.244(3)   **[Copy of order to bankrupt]** As soon as reasonably practicable after receipt of the sealed copy of the order, the Secretary of State shall send a sealed copy of the order to the bankrupt.

R.6.244
This deals with the making of the BRO and dissemination of the fact that it has been made.

CHAPTER 29

INTERIM BANKRUPTCY RESTRICTIONS ORDER

6.245 Application for interim bankruptcy restrictions order

6.245(1) **[Court to fix venue]** Where the Secretary of State applies for an interim bankruptcy restrictions order under paragraph 5 of Schedule 4A to the Act, the court shall fix a venue for the hearing.

6.245(2) **[Time limit for notice to bankrupt]** Notice of an application for an interim bankruptcy restrictions order shall be given to the bankrupt at least 2 business days before the date set for the hearing unless the court directs otherwise.

6.245(3) [Omitted.]

R.6.245
This Chapter 29 was inserted by Insolvency (Amendment) Rules 2003 (SI 2003/1730) to regulate interim BROs granted in cases of urgency before a full BRO hearing can be held. Rule 6.245 explains the mode of application. Paragraph (3) omitted by I(A)R 2010 (SI 2010/686).

6.246 The case against the defendant

6.246(1) **[Report by Secretary of State]** The Secretary of State shall file a report in court as evidence in support of any application for an interim bankruptcy restrictions order.

6.246(2) **[Contents of report]** The report shall include evidence of the bankrupt's conduct which is alleged to constitute the grounds for the making of an interim bankruptcy restrictions order and evidence of matters which relate to the public interest in making the order.

6.246(3) **[Witness statement in support by other persons]** Any evidence by persons other than the Secretary of State in support of an application for an interim bankruptcy restrictions order shall be by way of a witness statement.

R.6.246
This is how the case for an interim BRO is to be constructed. References to affidavits in para.(3) have been removed by I(A)R 2010 (SI 2010/686).

6.247 Making an interim bankruptcy restrictions order

6.247(1) **[Power bankrupt to file evidence and appear]** The bankrupt may file in court any evidence which he wishes the court to take into consideration and may appear at the hearing for an interim bankruptcy restrictions order.

6.247(2) **[Power of court to make order]** The court may make an interim bankruptcy restrictions order against the bankrupt, whether or not the latter appears, and whether or not he has filed evidence.

6.247(3) **[Copies of order to Secretary of State]** Where the court makes an interim bankruptcy restrictions order, it shall send two sealed copies of the order shall be sent, as soon as reasonably practicable, to the Secretary of State.

6.247(4) **[Copy of order to bankrupt]** As soon as reasonably practicable after receipt of the sealed copies of the order, the Secretary of State shall send a copy of the order to the bankrupt.

R.6.247
This explains the approach of the court to an application made under r.6.245 and the consequences of any order being made.

1106

6.248   Application to set aside an interim bankruptcy restrictions order

6.248(1)   [Power of bankrupt to apply] A bankrupt may apply to the court to set aside an interim bankruptcy restrictions order.

6.248(2)   [Witness statement in support] An application by the bankrupt to set aside an interim bankruptcy restrictions order shall be supported by a witness statement stating the grounds on which the application is made.

6.248(3)   [Documents to Secretary of State] Where a bankrupt applies to set aside an interim bankruptcy restrictions order under paragraph (1), he shall send to the Secretary of State, not less than 5 business days before the hearing–

     (a)   notice of his application;

     (b)   notice of the venue;

     (c)   a copy of his application; and

     (d)   a copy of the supporting witness statement.

6.248(4)   [Power of Secretary of State to attend hearing etc.] The Secretary of State may attend the hearing and call the attention of the court to any matters which seem to him to be relevant, and may himself give evidence or call witnesses.

6.248(5)   [Copies of order to Secretary of State] Where the court sets aside an interim bankruptcy restrictions order two sealed copies of the order shall be sent, as soon as reasonably practicable, to the Secretary of State by the court.

6.248(6)   [Copy of order to bankrupt] As soon as reasonably practicable after receipt of the sealed copies of the order, the Secretary of State shall send a sealed copy of the order to the bankrupt.

R.6.248
A bankrupt wishing to have the interim BRO set aside must follow this procedure. Note the discarding of references to affidavits in para.(2) by I(A)R 2010 (SI 2010/686). The seven-day period formerly used in para.(3) has been changed to five business days.

CHAPTER 30

BANKRUPTCY RESTRICTIONS UNDERTAKING

6.249   Acceptance of the bankruptcy restrictions undertaking

6.249   A bankruptcy restrictions undertaking authenticated by the bankrupt shall be deemed to have been accepted by the Secretary of State for the purposes of paragraph 9 of Schedule 4A of the Act when the undertaking is authenticated by the Secretary of State.

R.6.249
This Chapter 30 was inserted by Insolvency (Amendment) Rules 2003 (SI 2003/1730) to permit bankruptcy restrictions to be established consensually by an undertakings procedure. This procedure bears many of the features of the director disqualification undertakings regime, which was introduced by IA 2000. Rule 6.249 explains when a BRU is deemed to have been agreed.

6.250   Notification to the court

6.250   As soon as reasonably practicable after a bankruptcy restrictions undertaking has been accepted by the Secretary of State, a copy shall be sent to the bankrupt and filed in court and sent to the official receiver if he is not the applicant.

1107

R.6.250

The court and the OR must be told of any BRU.

6.251 Application under paragraph 9(3) of Schedule 4A to the Act to annul a bankruptcy restrictions undertaking

6.251(1) **[Witness statement in support]** An application under paragraphs 9(3)(a) or (b) of Schedule 4A to the Act shall be supported by a witness statement stating the grounds on which it is made.

6.251(2) **[Time limit for notice of application to Secretary of State etc.]** The bankrupt shall give notice of the application and the venue, together with a copy of the witness statement supporting his application to the Secretary of State at least 28 days before the date fixed for the hearing.

6.251(3) **[Power of Secretary of State to attend hearing etc.]** The Secretary of State may attend the hearing and call the attention of the court to any matters which seem to him to be relevant, and may himself give evidence or call witnesses.

6.251(4) **[Copies of order to Secretary of State and bankrupt]** The court shall send a sealed copy of any order annulling or varying the bankruptcy restrictions undertaking to the Secretary of State and the bankrupt.

R.6.251

This explains how and when a BRU may be annulled. Modernised by I(A)R 2010 (SI 2010/686).

CHAPTER 31

DEBT RELIEF RESTRICTIONS ORDER

6.252 Interpretation

6.252 In this Chapter and in Chapter 32, "Secretary of State" includes the official receiver acting in accordance with paragraph 1(2)(b) of Schedule 4ZB to the Act.

6.253 Application for debt relief restrictions order

6.253(1) **[Application to be supported by report]** Where the Secretary of State applies to the court for a debt relief restrictions order to be made in relation to a person in respect of whom a debt relief order has been made under paragraph 1 of Schedule 4ZB to the Act, the application shall be supported by a report by the Secretary of State.

6.253(2) **[Contents of report]** The report shall include–

(a)   a statement of the conduct by reference to which it is alleged that it is appropriate for a debt relief restrictions order to be made; and

(b)   the evidence on which the Secretary of State relies in support of the application.

6.253(3) **[Evidence in support by witness statement]** Any evidence in support of an application for a debt relief restrictions order provided by persons other than the Secretary of State shall be by way of a witness statement.

6.253(4) **[Date for hearing]** The date for the hearing shall be no earlier than 8 weeks from the date when the court fixes the venue for the hearing.

6.253(5) [Omitted.]

GENERAL NOTE

Modernised by I(A)R 2010 (SI 2010/686). References to affidavits in para.(3) have been changed and para.(5) has been deleted.

6.254   Service on the defendant

6.254(1)   [Date for service and venue] The Secretary of State shall serve notice of the application and the venue fixed by the court on the debtor not more than 14 days after the application is made at court.

6.254(2)   [Service accompanied by copy application, report, etc.] Service shall be accompanied by a copy of the application, together with copies of the report by the Secretary of State, any other evidence filed with the court in support of the application, and an acknowledgement of service.

6.254(3)   [Period for acknowledgement of service] The defendant shall file in court an acknowledge-ment of service of the application indicating whether or not he contests the application not more than 14 days after service on him of the application.

6.254(4)   [Service not acknowledged within period] Where the defendant has failed to file an acknowledgement of service and the time period for doing so has expired, the defendant may attend the hearing of the application but may not take part in the hearing unless the court gives permission.

6.255   The debtor's evidence

6.255(1)   [Period for evidence in opposition] If the debtor wishes to oppose the application, he shall within 28 days of the service of the application and evidence of the Secretary of State, file in court any evidence which he wishes the court to take into consideration, and shall serve a copy of such evidence upon the Secretary of State within 3 business days of filing it at court.

6.255(2)   [Period for evidence in reply] The Secretary of State shall, within 14 days from receiving the copy of the debtor's evidence, file in court any further evidence in reply he wishes the court to take into consideration and shall as soon as reasonably practicable serve a copy of that evidence upon the debtor.

6.256   Making a debt relief restrictions order

6.256(1)   [Power of court to make order] The court may make a debt relief restrictions order against the debtor, whether or not the latter appears and whether or not he has filed evidence in accordance with Rule 6.255.

6.256(2)   [Copies of order to Secretary of State] Where the court makes a debt relief restrictions order, it shall send two sealed copies to the Secretary of State.

6.256(3)   [Sealed copy of order to debtor] As soon as reasonably practicable after receipt of the sealed copy of the order, the Secretary of State shall send a sealed copy of the order to the debtor.

GENERAL NOTE

This new Chapter was added by the Insolvency (Amendment) Rules 2009 (SI 2009/642) with effect from April 6, 2009. It comprises IR rr.6.252–6.256. These rules deal with the procedure for obtaining a debt relief restrictions order (including service of proceedings) and the making of such an order. Note that only the Secretary of State can apply for a DRRO. These rules need to be read in the light of Sch.4ZB of the Act. For entry on and deletion from the register see IR rr.6A.5A and 6A.5B.

CHAPTER 32

INTERIM DEBT RELIEF RESTRICTIONS ORDER

Introductory note to Part 6, Chapter 32
This Chapter was introduced by Insolvency (Amendment) Rules 2009 (SI 2009/642) (effective April 6, 2009). It comprises IR rr.6.257–6.260. These rules deal specifically with an interim DRRO, the possibility of which is anticipated by para.5 of Sch.4ZB of the Act. Note that the application will be heard in public. A person who is made

subject to an interim DRRO can apply to have it set aside under r.2.260. For entry on and deletion from the register see IR rr.6A.7A and 6A.7B.

6.257   Application for interim debt relief restrictions order

6.257(1)   **[Court to fix venue]** Where the Secretary of State applies for an interim debt relief restrictions order under paragraph 5 of Schedule 4ZB to the Act, the court shall fix a venue for the hearing.

6.257(2)   **[Period of notice to debtor]** Notice of an application for an interim debt relief restrictions order shall be given to the debtor at least 2 business days before the date set for the hearing unless the court directs otherwise.

6.257(3)   [Omitted.]

GENERAL NOTE

I(A)R 2010 (SI 2010/686) deletes para.(3).

6.258   The case against the debtor

6.258(1)   **[Application to be supported by report]** The Secretary of State shall file a report in court as evidence in support of any application for an interim debt relief restrictions order.

6.258(2)   **[Contents of report]** The report shall include evidence of the debtor's conduct which is alleged to constitute the grounds for the making of an interim debt relief restrictions order and evidence of matters which relate to the public interest in making the order.

6.258(3)   **[Other evidence in support by witness statement]** Any evidence by persons other than the Secretary of State in support of an application for an interim debt relief restrictions order shall be by way of a witness statement.

GENERAL NOTE

I(A)R 2010 (SI 2010/686) removes references to affidavits in para.(3).

6.259   Making an interim debt relief restrictions order

6.259(1)   **[Power of debtor to file evidence and appear]** The debtor may file in court any evidence which he wishes the court to take into consideration and may appear at the hearing for an interim debt relief restrictions order.

6.259(2)   **[Power of court to make order]** The court may make an interim debt relief restrictions order against the debtor, whether or not the latter appears, and whether or not he has filed evidence.

6.259(3)   **[Sealed copies of interim order to Secretary of State]** Where the court makes an interim debt relief restrictions order, as soon as reasonably practicable, it shall send two sealed copies of the order to the Secretary of State.

6.259(4)   **[Sealed copy of interim order to debtor]** As soon as reasonably practicable after receipt of the sealed copies of the order, the Secretary of State shall send a copy of the order to the debtor.

6.260   Application to set aside an interim debt relief restrictions order

6.260(1)   **[Power to apply to court]** A person subject to an interim debt relief restrictions order may apply to the court to set the order aside.

6.260(2)   **[Application supported by witness statement stating grounds]** An application to set aside an interim debt relief restrictions order shall be supported by a witness statement stating the grounds on which the application is made.

6.260(3) **[Notice etc. to Secretary of State]** Where an application is made to set aside an interim debt relief restrictions order under paragraph (1), the person making the application shall send to the Secretary of State, not less than 5 business days before the hearing–

(a)   notice of his application;

(b)   notice of the venue;

(c)   a copy of his application; and

(d)   a copy of the supporting witness statement.

6.260(4) **[Power of Secretary of State to attend, etc.]** The Secretary of State may attend the hearing and call the attention of the court to any matters which seem to him to be relevant, and may himself give evidence or call witnesses.

6.260(5) **[Sealed copies of order to Secretary of State]** Where the court sets aside an interim debt relief restrictions order two sealed copies of the order shall be sent, as soon as reasonably practicable, to the Secretary of State by the court.

6.260(6) **[Sealed copy of order to applicant]** As soon as reasonably practicable after receipt of the sealed copies of the order, the Secretary of State shall send a sealed copy of the order to the applicant.

GENERAL NOTE

Modernised by I(A)R 2010 (SI 2010/686). The period in para.(3) has been changed from seven days to five business days.

CHAPTER 33

DEBT RELIEF RESTRICTIONS UNDERTAKING

6.261   Acceptance of debt relief restrictions undertaking

6.261 A debt relief restrictions undertaking authenticated by a person in relation to whom a debt relief order has been made shall be deemed to have been accepted by the Secretary of State for the purposes of paragraph 9 of Schedule 4ZB to the Act when the undertaking is authenticated by the Secretary of State.

6.262   Notification

6.262 As soon as reasonably practicable after a debt relief restrictions undertaking has been accepted by the Secretary of State, a copy shall be sent to the person who offered the undertaking and to the official receiver.

6.263   Application under paragraph 9(3) of Schedule 4ZB to the Act to annul a debt relief restrictions undertaking

6.263(1) **[Application supported by witness statement stating grounds]** An application under paragraph 9(3)(a) or (b) of Schedule 4ZB to the Act shall be supported by a witness statement stating the grounds on which it is made.

6.263(2) **[Notice etc. to Secretary of State]** The applicant shall give notice of the application and the venue, together with a copy of the witness statement supporting his application to the Secretary of State at least 28 days before the date fixed for the hearing.

6.263(3) **[Power of Secretary of State to attend, etc.]** The Secretary of State may attend the hearing and call the attention of the court to any matters which seem to him to be relevant, and may himself give evidence or call witnesses.

6.263(4) **[Sealed copy of order to Secretary of State and applicant]** The court shall send a sealed copy of any order annulling or varying the debt relief restrictions undertaking to the Secretary of State and the applicant.

GENERAL NOTE

Introduced by the Insolvency (Amendment) Rules 2009 (SI 2009/642) (effective April 6, 2009). This new Chapter comprises IR rr.6.261–6.263. It deals with debt relief restriction undertakings (DRRU). For entry on and deletion from the register see IR rr.6A.7A and 6A.7B. Note the large number of amendments made by I(A)R 2010 (SI 2010/686).

PART 6A

Introductory note to Part 6A
This major insertion of Pt 6A into the Insolvency Rules came about through the Insolvency (Amendment) Rules 2003 (SI 2003/1730). It seeks to bring together the scattered provisions in previous formulations of the rules and to enhance these in the light of the new information that now needs to be lodged on public registers.

CHAPTER 1

GENERAL

6A.1   The individual insolvency register; the bankruptcy restrictions register

6A.1(1)   [Duty of Secretary of State] The Secretary of State shall create and maintain a register of matters relating to bankruptcies, debt relief orders and individual voluntary arrangements in accordance with the provisions of this Part (referred to in this Part as "the individual insolvency register").

6A.1(2)   [Maintenance of bankruptcy restrictions and debt relief restrictions registers] The register–

(a)   referred to in paragraph 12 of Schedule 4A to the Act (referred to in this Part as "the bankruptcy restrictions register"), and

(b)   of the matters specified in paragraphs (b) and (c) of section 251W (referred to in this Part as "the debt relief restrictions register"),

shall be maintained in accordance with the provisions of this Part.

6A.1(3)   ["Registers"] In this Part the "registers" means the registers referred to in paragraphs (1) and (2).

6A.1(4)   [Register open to public inspection] The registers shall be open to public inspection on any business day between the hours of 9.00 am and 5.00 pm.

6A.1(5)   [Amendment of register] Where an obligation to enter information onto, or delete information from, the registers arises under this Part, that obligation shall be performed as soon as is reasonably practicable after it arises.

R.6A.1
This explains the obligations of the Secretary of State with regard to the register of individual insolvencies. Note the changes to paras (1) and (2) introduced by the Insolvency (Amendment) Rules 2009 (SI 2009/642) (in operation from April 6, 2009). These changes cater for the arrival of debt relief orders.

CHAPTER 2

INDIVIDUAL INSOLVENCY REGISTER

6A.2   Entry of information onto the individual insolvency register—individual voluntary arrangements [Deleted.]

6A.2A   Entry of information onto the individual insolvency register—individual voluntary arrangements

6A.2A(1)   [Application of r.6A.2A] This Rule applies where–

(a) a voluntary arrangement has been accepted by the debtor's creditors; and

(b) the Secretary of State has received–

    (i)   information under Rule 5.29(1) sent pursuant to paragraph (3) of that Rule; and

    (ii) notice under Rule 5.34, Rule 5.45 or Rule 5.50.

6A.2A(2)   [Details Secretary of State to register] Subject to paragraph (3), the Secretary of State must enter onto the individual insolvency register–

(a) the name and address of the debtor;

(b) the date on which the arrangement was approved by the creditors;

(c) the debtor's gender;

(d) the debtor's date of birth;

(e) any name by which the debtor was or is known, not being the name in which the debtor has entered into the voluntary arrangement;

(f) as regards an arrangement other than under section 263A, the name and address of the supervisor;

(g) as regards an arrangement under section 263A–

    (i)   that the official receiver is the supervisor; and

    (ii) the address of the official receiver; and

(h) a statement whether the arrangement–

    (i)   was completed in accordance with its terms; or

    (ii) failed.

6A.2A(3)   [Application of r.6A.2A(4)] Paragraph (4) applies where there is entered on the register information in respect of a voluntary arrangement–

(a) of which the Secretary of State had been notified prior to this Rule coming into force; and

(b) which has not been completed or terminated when this Rule comes into force.

6A.2A(4)   [Secretary of State to maintain register] The Secretary of State must maintain on the register the information that the Secretary of State was required to enter on to the individual insolvency register immediately prior to the coming into force of this Rule.

6A.2A(5)   [Rule 6A.2A(2), (4) subject to rr.5.67, 6A.3, 6A.8] Paragraphs (2) and (4) are subject to Rules 5.67, 6A.3 and 6A.8.

GENERAL NOTE

This replaces r.6A.2 as a result of I(A)R 2010 (SI 2010/686).

6A.3 Deletion of information from the individual insolvency register—individual voluntary arrangements

6A.3 The Secretary of State shall delete from the individual insolvency register all information concerning an individual voluntary arrangement where–

(a) he receives notice under Rule 5.30(5) or Rule 5.46(4) of the making of a revocation order in respect of the arrangement; or

(b) he receives notice under Rule 5.34(3) or Rule 5.50(3) of the full implementation or termination of the arrangement.

and in either case a period of 3 months has elapsed from the receipt of the notice.

R.6A.3
This covers deletion of entries with regard to IVAs. Modified by I(A)R 2010 (SI 2010/686).

6A.4 Entry of information onto the individual insolvency register—bankruptcy orders

6A.4(1) [Duty of Secretary of State] The Secretary of State shall enter onto the individual insolvency register any information that was required to be held on the register of bankruptcy orders maintained by the Secretary of State immediately prior to the coming into force of this Rule and which relates to a bankrupt who–

(a) has not received his discharge on or before the date that this Rule comes into force; or

(b) was discharged in the period of 3 months immediately preceding the coming into force of this Rule.

6A.4(2) [Duty of official receiver] Where the official receiver receives pursuant to Rule 6.34 or Rule 6.46 a copy of a bankruptcy order from the court, he shall cause to be entered onto the individual insolvency register–

(a) the matters listed in Rules 6.7 and 6.38 with respect to the debtor as they are stated in the bankruptcy petition;

(b) the date of the making of the bankruptcy order;

(c) the name of the court that made the order; and

(d) the court reference number as stated on the order.

6A.4(3) [Further duty of official receiver] The official receiver shall cause to be entered onto the individual insolvency register as soon as reasonably practicable after receipt by him, the following information–

(a) the name, gender, occupation (if any) and date of birth of the bankrupt;

(b) the bankrupt's last known address;

(c) where a bankruptcy order or debt relief order has been made in the period of six years immediately prior to the day of the latest bankruptcy order made against the bankrupt (excluding for these purposes any bankruptcy order that was annulled or any debt relief order that was revoked), the date of whichever is the latest of them;

(d) any name by which the bankrupt was known, not being the name in which he was adjudged bankrupt;

(e) the address of any business carried on by the bankrupt and the name in which that business was carried on if carried on in a name other than the name in which the bankrupt was adjudged bankrupt;

(f) the name and address of any insolvency practitioner appointed to act as trustee in bankruptcy;

(g) the address at which the official receiver may be contacted;

(h) the automatic discharge date under section 279; and

(i) where a bankruptcy order is rescinded by the court, the fact that such an order has been made, the date on which it is made and (if different) the date on which it has effect.

6A.4(4) [Duty of official receiver when discharge of bankrupt suspended] Where pursuant to Rule 6.176(5) or Rule 6.215(8) the official receiver receives a copy of an order suspending the bankrupt's discharge he shall cause to be entered onto the individual insolvency register–

(a) the fact that such an order has been made; and

(b) the period for which the discharge has been suspended or that the relevant period has ceased to run until the fulfilment of conditions specified in the order.

6A.4(5) [Duty to re certificate of discharge of suspension of bankruptcy] Where pursuant to Rule 6.216(7) a copy of a certificate certifying the discharge of an order under section 279(3) is received by the official receiver, he shall cause to be entered onto the individual insolvency register–

(a) that the court has discharged the order made under section 279(3); and

(b) the new date of discharge of the bankrupt,

but where the order discharging the order under section 279(3) is subsequently rescinded by the court, the official receiver shall cause the register to be amended accordingly.

6A.4(6) [Duty re discharge from bankruptcy] Where a bankrupt is discharged from bankruptcy under section 279(1) or section 279(2), the official receiver shall cause the fact and date of such discharge to be entered in the individual insolvency register.

6A.4(7) [Rule 6A.4 subject to r.6A.5] This Rule is subject to Rules 6.235B, 6A.5 and 6A.8.

R.6A.4
Registration of bankruptcy details is described. This provision was modified by the Insolvency (Amendment) Rules 2009 (SI 2009/642) (in effect from April 6, 2009). A new para.(3)(c) has been substituted. Modified by I(A)R 2010 (SI 2010/686)—note insertion of new subpara.(i) after (h) in para.(3).

6A.5 Deletion of information from the individual insolvency register—bankruptcy orders

6A.5 The Secretary of State shall delete from the individual insolvency register all information concerning a bankruptcy where–

(a) the bankruptcy order has been annulled pursuant to section 261(2)(a), 261(2)(b), 263D (3) or section 282(1)(b) and a period of 3 months has elapsed since notice of the annulment was given to the Secretary of State;

(b) the bankrupt has been discharged from the bankruptcy and a period of 3 months has elapsed from the date of discharge;

(c) the bankruptcy order is annulled pursuant to section 282(1)(a) and 28 days have elapsed since notice of the annulment was given to the Secretary of State under Rule 6.213(2); or

(d) the bankruptcy order is rescinded by the court under section 375 the Secretary of State has received a copy of the order made by the court and 28 days have elapsed since receipt of the copy of the order.

R.6A.5
Deletion of information on bankruptcies is dealt with here. The words "Subject to paragraph (2)," formerly appearing at the beginning were deleted by I(A)R 2004 (SI 2004/584) with effect from April 1, 2004. This is a sensible amendment in view of the fact that there is no para.(2)! Modified by I(A)R 2010 (SI 2010/686)—new timescales added to paras (a), (c) and (d).

6A.5A   Entry of information onto the individual insolvency register—debt relief orders

6A.5A(1)   [Rule 6A.5A subject to rr.5A.18, 6A.5B, 6A.8] This Rule is subject to Rules 5A.18, 6A.5B and 6A.8.

6A.5A(2)   [Duty of official receiver] The official receiver shall cause to be entered onto the individual insolvency register as soon as reasonably practicable after the making of a debt relief order the following information relating to the order or to the debtor in respect of whom it has been made–

(a)   as they are stated in the debtor's application–

    (i)   the name, gender, occupation (if any) and date of birth of the debtor;

    (ii)   the debtor's last known address;

    (iii) the name or names in which he carries or has carried on business, if other than his true name; and

    (iv) the nature of his business and the address or addresses at which he carries or has carried it on and whether alone or with others;

(b)   the date of the making of the debt relief order;

(c)   the reference number of the order;

(d)   the date of the end of the moratorium period; and

(e)   where a bankruptcy order or a debt relief order has been made in the period of six years immediately prior to the date of the latest debt relief order made against the debtor (excluding for these purposes any bankruptcy order that was annulled or any debt relief order that was revoked), the date of whichever is the latest of them.

6A.5A(3)   [Further duty of official receiver] Provided that information concerning a debt relief order has not been validly deleted under Rule 6A.5B, the official receiver shall also cause to be entered on the register in relation to the order–

(a)   where the moratorium period is terminated early, the fact that such has happened, the date of early termination and whether the early termination is on revocation of the debt relief order or by virtue of any other enactment;

(b)   where the moratorium period is extended, the fact that such has happened, the date on which the extension was made, its duration and the date of the new anticipated end of the moratorium period; or

(c)   where the debtor is discharged from all qualifying debts, the date of such discharge.

6A.5B   Deletion of information from the individual insolvency register—debt relief orders

6A.5B   The Secretary of State shall delete from the individual insolvency register all information concerning a debt relief order where–

(a)   the debt relief order has been revoked, or

(b)   the debtor has been discharged from his qualifying debts,

and a period of 3 months has elapsed from the date of revocation or discharge.

GENERAL NOTE

The above new rules were introduced by the Insolvency (Amendment) Rules 2009 (SI 2009/642), which took effect on April 6, 2009. They deal with entry on the register of information with regard to debt relief orders (IR r.6A.5A). The position on deletion is governed by IR r.6A.5B. See I(A)R 2010 (SI 2010/686).

CHAPTER 3

BANKRUPTCY RESTRICTIONS REGISTER

6A.6 Bankruptcy restrictions orders and undertakings—entry of information onto the bankruptcy restrictions register

6A.6(1) **[Duty of Secretary of State re order]** Where an interim bankruptcy restrictions order or a bankruptcy restrictions order is made against a bankrupt, the Secretary of State shall enter onto the bankruptcy restrictions register–

(a)   the name, gender, occupation (if any) and date of birth of the bankrupt;

(aa) the bankrupt's last known address;

(b)   a statement that an interim bankruptcy restrictions order or, as the case may be a bankruptcy restrictions order has been made against him;

(c)   the date of the making of the order, the court and the court reference number; and

(d)   the duration of the order.

6A.6(2) **[Duty of Secretary of State re undertaking]** Where a bankruptcy restrictions undertaking is given by a bankrupt the Secretary of State shall enter onto the bankruptcy restrictions register–

(a)   the name, gender, occupation (if any) and date of birth of the bankrupt;

(aa) the bankrupt's last known address;

(b)   a statement that a bankruptcy restrictions undertaking has been given;

(c)   the date of the acceptance of the bankruptcy restrictions undertaking by the Secretary of State; and

(d)   the duration of the bankruptcy restrictions undertaking.

6A.6(3) **[Rule 6A.6 subject to rr.6.235B, 6A.7, 6A.8]** This Rule is subject to Rules 6.235B, 6A.7 and 6A.8.

R.6A.6
Entry of details of BROs and BRUs is outlined. Amendments to paras (1) and (2) were made by I(A)R 2004 (SI 2004/584) with effect from April 1, 2004. The purpose of the change is to provide more information on the public register of the background of the bankrupt made subject to a BRO or BRU. See I(A)R 2010 (SI 2010/686).

6A.7 Deletion of information from the bankruptcy restrictions register—bankruptcy restrictions orders and undertakings

6A.7 In any case where an interim bankruptcy restrictions order or a bankruptcy restrictions order is made or a bankruptcy restrictions undertaking has been accepted, the Secretary of State shall remove from the bankruptcy restrictions register all information regarding that order or, as the case may be undertaking after–

(a)   receipt of notification that the order or, as the case may be the undertaking has ceased to have effect; or

(b)   the expiry of the order or, as the case may be, undertaking.

R.6A.7
Deletion of information about BROs and BRUs is regulated by this rule.

CHAPTER 3A

DEBT RELIEF RESTRICTIONS REGISTER

6A.7A   Debt relief restrictions orders and undertakings—entries of information onto the debt relief restrictions register

6A.7A(1)   [Rule 6A.7A subject to rr.5A.18, 6A.7B, 6A.8] This Rule is subject to Rules 5A.18, 6A.7B and 6A.8.

6A.7A(2)   [Duty of Secretary of State] Where an interim debt relief restrictions order or a debt relief restrictions order is made against a debtor, the Secretary of State shall enter onto the debt relief restrictions register–

(a)   the name, gender, occupation (if any) and date of birth of the debtor;

(b)   the debtor's last known address;

(c)   a statement that an interim debt relief restrictions order or, as the case may be, a debt relief restrictions order has been made against him;

(d)   the date of the making of the order and the order reference number; and

(e)   the duration of the order.

6A.7A(3)   [Further duty of Secretary of State re undertaking] Where a debt relief restrictions undertaking is given by a debtor, the Secretary of State shall enter onto the debt relief restrictions register–

(a)   the name, gender, occupation (if any) and date of birth of the debtor;

(b)   the debtor's last known address;

(c)   a statement that a debt relief restrictions undertaking has been given;

(d)   the date of the acceptance of the debt relief restrictions undertaking by the Secretary of State and reference number of the undertaking; and

(e)   the duration of the debt relief restrictions undertaking.

6A.7B   Deletion of information from the debt relief restrictions register—debt relief restrictions order and undertakings

6A.7B   In any case where an interim debt relief restrictions order or a debt relief restrictions order is made or a debt relief restrictions undertaking has been accepted, the Secretary of State shall remove from the debt relief restrictions register all information regarding that order or, as the case may be, undertaking after–

(a)   receipt of notification that the order or, as the case may be, undertaking has ceased to have effect; or

(b)   the expiry of the order or, as the case may be, undertaking.

GENERAL NOTE TO RR.6A.7A–6A.7B

IR r.6A.7A was inserted by the Insolvency (Amendment) Rules 2009 (SI 2009/642) with effect from April 6, 2009. See I(A)R 2010 (SI 2010/686). This deals with the registration of debt relief restriction orders and undertakings.
    IR r.6A.7B deals with deletion of entries with regard to DRRO and DRRU.

CHAPTER 4

RECTIFICATION OF REGISTERS

6A.8   Rectification of the registers

6A.8(1)   [Duty of Secretary of State re inaccurate information] Where the Secretary of State becomes aware that there is any inaccuracy in any information maintained on the registers he shall rectify the inaccuracy as soon as reasonably practicable.

6A.8(2)   [Duty of Secretary of State on death of bankrupt] Where the Secretary of State receives notice of the date of the death of a person in respect of whom information is held on any of the registers, he shall cause the fact and date of the person's death to be entered onto the individual insolvency register and, as the case may be, the bankruptcy restrictions register or the debt relief restrictions register.

R.6A.8
This explains rectification procedures where there are errors on the register. A new para.(2) was substituted by the Insolvency (Amendment) Rules 2009 (SI 2009/642) with effect from April 6, 2009.

THE THIRD GROUP OF PARTS

PART 7

COURT PROCEDURE AND PRACTICE

Introductory note to Part 7
Part 7 deals with the practice and procedure on all applications to the court, whether in corporate insolvency or individual bankruptcy, except for the three categories of petition listed in r.7.1. Several of the rules in this Part were amended or replaced by the Insolvency Amendment (No.2) Rules 1999 (SI 1999/1022) with effect from April 26, 1999 in order to bring insolvency proceedings into line with the CPR: see the note preceding r.0.1. Note further changes made by I(A)R 2010 (SI 2010/686).

CHAPTER 1

APPLICATIONS

7.1   Preliminary

7.1   This Chapter applies to any application made to the court under the Act or Rules except–

(a)   an application for an administration order under Part II,

(b)   a petition for a winding-up order under Part IV, or

(c)   a petition for a bankruptcy order under Part IX

of the Act.

(See General Note after r.7.18.)

7.2   Interpretation [Revoked by I(A)R 2010 (SI 2010/686).]

7.3   Form and contents of application

7.3(1)   [Contents etc. of application] Each application shall be in writing and shall state–

(a)   that the application is made under the Act;

(aa)   the names of the parties;

(ab) the name of the bankrupt, or the debtor who or company which is the subject of the insolvency proceedings to which the application relates;

(ac) the court (and where applicable, the division or district registry of that court) in which the application is made;

(ad) where the court has previously allocated a number to the insolvency proceedings within which the application is made, that number;

(b) the nature of the remedy or order applied for or the directions sought from the court;

(c) the names and addresses of the persons (if any) on whom it is intended to serve the application or that no person is intended to be served;

(d) where the Act or Rules require that notice of the application is to be given to specified persons, the names and addresses of all those persons (so far as known to the applicant); and

(e) the applicant's address for service.

7.3(2) [Omitted.]

7.3(3) [Application must be authenticated etc.] The application must be authenticated by the applicant if he is acting in person or, when he is not so acting, by or on behalf of his solicitor.

(See General Note after r.7.18.) See I(A)R 2010 (SI 2010/686)—para.(2) omitted.

7.3A Application under section 176A(5) to disapply section 176A

7.3A(1) [Application accompanied by witness statement] An application under section 176A(5) shall be accompanied by a witness statement by the liquidator, administrator or receiver.

7.3A(2) [Contents of witness statement] The witness statement shall state–

(a) the type of insolvency proceedings in which the application arises;

(b) a summary of the financial position of the company;

(c) the information substantiating the applicant's view that the cost of making a distribution to unsecured creditors would be disproportionate to the benefits; and

(d) whether any other office-holder is acting in relation to the company and if so his address.

R.7.3A
This was inserted by Insolvency (Amendment) Rules 2003 (SI 2003/1730) and deals with the obligations of the insolvency practitioner when seeking an order to disapply the special reserve fund for unsecured creditors—see the comment on s.176A. See I(A)R 2010 (SI 2010/686).

7.4 Filing and service of application

7.4(1) [Filing etc.] An application must be filed with the court, accompanied by one copy and a number of additional copies equal to the number of persons who are to be served with the application.

7.4(2) [Venue] Where an application is filed with the court in accordance with paragraph (1), the court must fix a venue for the application to be heard unless–

(a) it considers it is not appropriate to do so;

(b) the Rule under which the application is brought provides otherwise; or

(c) the case is one to which Rule 7.5A applies.

7.4(3) [Service] Unless the court otherwise directs, the applicant shall serve a sealed copy of the application, endorsed with the venue for the hearing, on the respondent named in the application (or on each respondent if more than one).

7.4(4) **[Directions]** The court may give any of the following directions–

(a) that the application be served upon persons other than those specified by the relevant provision of the Act or Rules;

(b) that the giving of notice to any person may be dispensed with;

(c) that notice be given in some way other than that specified in paragraph (3).

7.4(5) **[Time for service]** An application must be served at least 14 days before the date fixed for its hearing unless–

(a) the provision of the Act or the Rules under which the application is made makes different provision; or

(b) the case is one of urgency, to which paragraph (6) applies.

7.4(6) **[In case of urgency]** Where the case is one of urgency, the court may (without prejudice to its general power to extend or abridge time limits)–

(a) hear the application immediately, either with or without notice to, or the attendance of, other parties, or

(b) authorise a shorter period of service than that provided for by paragraph (5);

and any such application may be heard on terms providing for the filing or service of documents, or the carrying out of other formalities, as the court thinks fit.

(See General Note after r.7.18.) On r.7.4(6) see *Bagnall v Official Receiver* [2003] EWCA Civ 1925; [2004] B.P.I.R. 445. See I(A)R 2010 (SI 2010/686)—paragraph (1) is amended and new paras (2) and (5) substituted.

7.4A   Notice of application under section 176A(5)

7.4A   An application under section 176A(5) may be made without the application being served upon or notice being given to any other party, save that notice of the application shall be given to any other office-holder who is acting as such in relation to the company including any member State liquidator.

R.7.4A
This was inserted by Insolvency (Amendment) Rules 2003 (SI 2003/1730). This covers notice requirements where an application is made pursuant to s.176A to disapply the reserve fund for unsecured creditors. References to "insolvency practitioners" replaced by "office-holders" by I(A)R 2010 (SI 2010/686).

7.5   Other hearings *ex parte* [Deleted.]

7.5A   Hearings without notice

7.5A   Where the relevant provisions of the Act or the Rules do not require service of the application on, or notice of it to be given to, any person–

(a) the court may hear the application as soon as reasonably practicable without fixing a venue as required by Rule 7.4(2); or

(b) it may fix a venue for the application to be heard in which case Rule 7.4 must apply to the extent that it is relevant;

but nothing in those provisions is to be taken as prohibiting the applicant from giving such notice if the applicant wishes to do so.

GENERAL NOTE

Substituted for r.7.5 by I(A)R 2010 (SI 2010/686).

7.6   Hearing of application [Deleted.]

7.6A   Hearing of application

7.6A(1) [Hearing in open court] Unless the court otherwise directs, the hearing of an application must be in open court.

7.6A(2) [Application to district judge in county court] In the county court, the jurisdiction of the court to hear and determine an application may be exercised by the district judge (to whom any application must be made in the first instance) unless–

(a)   a direction to the contrary has been given, or

(b)   it is not within the district judge's power to make the order required.

7.6A(3) [Application to registrar in High Court] In the High Court, the jurisdiction of the court to hear and determine an application may be exercised by the registrar (to whom the application must be made in the first instance) unless–

(a)   a direction to the contrary has been given, or

(b)   it is not within the registrar's power to make the order required.

7.6A(4) [Reference to judge] Where the application is made to the district judge in the county court or to the registrar in the High Court, the district judge or the registrar may refer to the judge any matter which the district judge or registrar thinks should properly be decided by the judge, and the judge may either dispose of the matter or refer it back to the district judge or the registrar with such directions as that judge thinks just.

7.6A(5) [Application direct to judge] Nothing in this Rule precludes an application being made directly to the judge in a proper case.

GENERAL NOTE

Substituted for r.7.6 by I(A)R 2010 (SI 2010/686).

7.7   Use of affidavit evidence [Deleted.]

7.7A   Witness statements—general

7.7A(1) [Evidence in witness statement] Subject to Rule 7.9, where evidence is required by the Act or the Rules as to any matter, such evidence may be provided in the form of a witness statement unless–

(a)   in any specific case a Rule or the Act makes different provision; or

(b)   the court otherwise directs.

7.7A(2) [Cross examination of person making witness statement] The court may, on the application of any party to the matter in question order the attendance for cross-examination of the person making the witness statement.

7.7A(3) [Failure of person to attend] Where, after such an order has been made, the person in question does not attend, that person's witness statement must not be used in evidence without the leave of the court.

GENERAL NOTE

Substituted for r.7.7 by I(A)R 2010 (SI 2010/686).

7.8   Filing and service of witness statements

7.8(1) [Filing in court etc.] Unless the provision of the Act or Rules under which the application is made provides otherwise, or the court otherwise allows–

(a) if the applicant intends to rely at the first hearing on evidence in a witness statement, he shall file the witness statement with the court and serve a copy or copies on the respondent, not less than 14 days before the date fixed for the hearing, and

(b) where a respondent to an application intends to oppose it and to rely for that purpose on evidence in a witness statement, he shall file the witness statement with the court and serve a copy on the applicant, not less than 5 business days before the date fixed for the hearing.

7.8(2) [Omitted.]

(See General Note after r.7.18.) See I(A)R 2010 (SI 2010/686).

7.9 Use of reports

7.9(1) [Filing report instead of witness statement] A report may be filed in court instead of a witness statement–

(a) in any case, by the official receiver (whether or not he is acting in any capacity mentioned in sub-paragraph (b)), or a deputy official receiver, or

(b) unless the application involves other parties or the court otherwise orders, by–

    (i) an administrator, a liquidator or a trustee in bankruptcy,

    (ii) a provisional liquidator or an interim receiver,

    (iii) a special manager, or

    (iv) an insolvency practitioner appointed under section 273(2).

7.9(2) [Report to be treated as witness statement] In any case where a report is filed instead of a witness statement, the report shall be treated for the purposes of Rule 7.8(1) and any hearing before the court as if it were a witness statement.

7.9(3) [Omitted.]

7.9(3A) [Witness statement to state office-holder's capacity and address] Where in insolvency proceedings a witness statement is made by an office-holder, the witness statement must state–

(a) the capacity in which that office-holder is acting, and

(b) the address at which that office-holder works.

(See General Note after r.7.18.) See I(A)R 2010 (SI 2010/686)—new para.(3A) replaces (3).

7.10 Adjournment of hearing; directions

7.10(1) [Powers of court] The court may adjourn the hearing of an application on such terms as it thinks fit.

7.10(2) [Directions] The court may at any time give such directions as it thinks fit as to–

(a) service or notice of the application on or to any person;

(b) whether particulars of claim and defence are to be delivered and generally as to the procedure on the application including whether a hearing is necessary;

(c) [Omitted.]

(d) the matters to be dealt with in evidence.

7.10(3) [Directions as to evidence] The court may give directions as to the manner in which any evidence is to be adduced at a resumed hearing and in particular as to–

(a) the taking of evidence wholly or partly by witness statement or orally;

(b)   the cross-examination of the maker of a witness statement; or

(c)   any report to be made by an office-holder.

(See General Note after r.7.18.) On r.7.10(2) see *Re Gunningham* [2002] B.P.I.R. 302. See I(A)R 2010 (SI 2010/686)—para.(2) amended with subpara.(2)(c) omitted. Paragraph (3) added.

Chapter 1A

Block Transfer of Cases Where Insolvency Practitioner has Died Etc.

Introductory note to Part 7, Chapter 1A
This Chapter, inserted by I(A)R 2010 (SI 2010/686), is a welcome addition to the Insolvency Rules. It regularises the position where an office-holder leaves office with regard to multiple insolvencies. The underlying problem here is the position taken by English law that appointments are held by named individuals, rather than by the firms of which they are members. Thus an individual insolvency practitioner may hold scores of appointments and there is significant disruption when that individual leaves the firm, which is effectively managing the insolvency. Under the former law, the courts, drawing upon the inherent jurisdiction of the court as recognised by various provisions in the Act, were able to construct a set of working rules to deal with this scenario. The Insolvency Rules themselves did not offer any assistance. These judicial innovations were only finally free from doubt as a result of *Donaldson v O'Sullivan* [2008] EWCA Civ 879. The position for the future is much more secure.

7.10A   Preliminary and interpretation

7.10A(1)   [Rules for applications for block transfer order] The Rules in this Chapter relate to applications for a block transfer order.

7.10A(2)   [Definitions] In this Chapter–

"outgoing office-holder" has the meaning in Rule 7.10B(1),

"replacement office-holder" has the meaning in Rule 7.10B(1),

"block transfer order" has the meaning in Rule 7.10B(2),

"substantive application" is that part of the application in Rule 7.10C(1)(c) and (d).

General Note

Inserted by I(A)R 2010 (SI 2010/686), this provides useful definitions.

7.10B   Power to make a block transfer order

7.10B(1)   [Application of r.7.10B] This Rule applies where an individual who is acting as an office-holder ("the outgoing office-holder")–

(a)   dies,

(b)   retires from practice, or

(c)   is otherwise unable or unwilling to continue in office,

and it is expedient to transfer some or all of the cases in which the outgoing office-holder holds office to one or more office-holders ("the replacement office-holder") in a single transaction.

7.10B(2)   [Block transfer order] In a case to which this Rule applies the court has the power to make an order, ("a block transfer order"), appointing a replacement office-holder in the place of the outgoing office-holder to be–

(a)   liquidator in any winding up (including a case where the official receiver is the liquidator by virtue of section 136 of the Act),

(b) administrator in any administration,

(c) trustee in a bankruptcy (including a case where the official receiver is the trustee by virtue of section 300 of the Act), or

(d) supervisor of a voluntary arrangement under Part 1 or 8 of the Act.

7.10B(3) **[Replacement office-holder to be qualified]** The replacement office-holder must be–

(a) qualified to act as an insolvency practitioner, or

(b) where the replacement office-holder is to be appointed supervisor of a voluntary arrangement under Part 1 or 8 of the Act–

(i) qualified to act as an insolvency practitioner, or

(ii) a person authorised so to act.

GENERAL NOTE

Inserted by I(A)R 2010 (SI 2010/686), this provision explains when an application for a block transfer order can be made.

7.10C **Application for a block transfer order**

7.10C(1) **[Scope of order]** An application for a block transfer order may be made to the registrar or district judge for–

(a) the transfer to the High Court of the cases specified in the schedule under paragraph (8);

(b) the transfer of the cases back to the court from which they were transferred when a replacement office-holder has been appointed;

(c) the removal of the outgoing office-holder by the exercise of any of the powers in paragraph (2);

(d) the appointment of a replacement office-holder by the exercise of any of the powers in paragraph (3);

(e) such other order or direction as may be necessary or expedient in connection with any of the matters referred to above.

7.10C(2) **[Powers of removal in r.7.10C(1)(c)]** The powers referred to in paragraph (1)(c) are–

(a) section 172(2) and Rule 7.10B(2) (winding up by the court);

(b) section 108 (voluntary liquidation);

(c) section 19, paragraph 88 of Schedule B1 to the Act and Rule 7.10B(2) (administration);

(d) section 298 and Rule 7.10B(2) (bankruptcy);

(e) section 7(5) and paragraph 39(6) of Schedule A1 to the Act (voluntary arrangement under Part 1 of the Act); and

(f) section 263(5) (voluntary arrangement under Part 8 of the Act).

7.10C(3) **[Powers of appointment in r.7.10C(1)(d)]** The powers referred to in paragraph (1)(d) are–

(a) section 168(3) and (5) and Rule 7.10B(2) (winding up by the court);

(b) section 108 (voluntary liquidation);

(c) section 13, paragraphs 63, 91 and 95 of Schedule B1 to the Act and Rule 7.10B(2) (administration);

(d)   sections 298 and 303(2) and Rule 7.10B(2) (bankruptcy);

(e)   section 7(5) and paragraph 39(6) of Schedule A1 to the Act (voluntary arrangement under Part 1 of the Act); and

(f)   section 263(5) (voluntary arrangement under Part 8 of the Act).

7.10C(4)   **[Who may make application]** Subject to paragraph (5), the application may be made by any of the following–

(a)   the outgoing office-holder (if able and willing to do so);

(b)   any person who holds office jointly with the outgoing office-holder;

(c)   any person who is proposed to be appointed as the replacement office-holder;

(d)   any creditor in a case subject to the application;

(e)   the recognised professional body or recognised body by which the outgoing office-holder is or was authorised; or

(f)   the Secretary of State.

7.10C(5)   **[Where office-holder administrator]** Where one or more outgoing office-holder in the schedule under paragraph (8) is an administrator, an application may not be made unless a person permitted to apply to replace that office-holder under section 13 or paragraph 63, 91 or 95 of Schedule B1 to the Act is the applicant or is joined as applicant in respect of the replacement of that office-holder.

7.10C(6)   **[Minimum notice by applicant]** An applicant (other than the Secretary of State) must give notice of the application to the Secretary of State at least 5 business days before the hearing of the application.

7.10C(7)   **[Respondents to be served]** The following must be made a respondent to the application and served with it–

(a)   the outgoing office-holder (if not the applicant or deceased);

(b)   every person who holds office jointly with the outgoing office-holder; and

(c)   such person as the registrar or district judge directs.

7.10C(8)   **[Schedule of application]** The application must contain a schedule setting out–

(a)   the name of each case,

(b)   the identity of the court having jurisdiction when the application is made,

(c)   the case number (if any), and

(d)   the capacity in which the outgoing office-holder was appointed.

7.10C(9)   **[Supporting evidence]** The application must be supported by evidence–

(a)   setting out the circumstances which gave rise to it being expedient to appoint a replacement office-holder; and

(b)   exhibiting the written consent to act of each person who is proposed to be appointed as replacement office-holder.

7.10C(10)   **[Application to district judge where all cases in county court]** Where all the cases in the schedule under paragraph (8) are in a county court or more than one county court–

(a)   the application may be made to a district judge of a convenient county court having insolvency jurisdiction; and

(b)   this Rule applies with appropriate modifications.

GENERAL NOTE

Inserted by I(A)R 2010 (SI 2010/686), this outlines the procedure to be followed to obtain a block transfer order.

7.10D   Action following application for a block transfer order

7.10D(1)   [Consideration without hearing] The registrar or district judge may in the first instance consider the application without a hearing and make such order as the registrar or district judge thinks just.

7.10D(2)   [Power of registrar or district judge] In the first instance, the registrar or district judge may do any of the following–

(a)   make an order directing the transfer to the High Court of those cases not already within its jurisdiction for the purpose only of the substantive application;

(b)   if the documents are considered to be in order and that the matter is straightforward, make an order on the substantive application;

(c)   give any directions which are considered to be necessary including (if appropriate) directions for the joinder of any additional respondents or requiring the service of the application on any person or requiring additional evidence to be provided; or

(d)   if an order is not made on the substantive application, give directions for the further consideration of the substantive application by the registrar or district judge or a judge of the Chancery Division.

7.10D(3)   [Sealed copies of order to court] The applicant must ensure that a sealed copy of every order transferring any case to the High Court and of every order which is made on a substantive application is lodged with the court having jurisdiction over each case affected by such order for filing on the court file relating to that case.

7.10D(4)   [Costs as expense of insolvency proceedings] In any case other than an application relating to the appointment of an administrator, in deciding to what extent (if any) the costs of making an application under this Rule should be paid as an expense of the insolvency proceedings to which the application relates, the factors to which the court must have regard include–

(a)   the reasons for the making of the application;

(b)   the number of cases to which the application relates;

(c)   the value of assets comprised in those cases; and

(d)   the nature and extent of the costs involved.

7.10D(5)   [Costs as expense of administration] Where an application relates to the appointment of an administrator and is made by a person under section 13 or paragraph 63, 91 or 95 of Schedule B1 to the Act, the costs of making that application are to be paid as an expense of the administration to which the application relates unless the court directs otherwise.

7.10D(6)   [Notification of appointment] Any appointment made under this Rule must be notified–

(a)   to the Secretary of State as soon as reasonably practicable; and

(b)   to–

    (i)   the creditors, and

    (ii)   such other persons as the court may direct,

in such manner as the court may direct.

7.10D(7)   **[Where application to district judge under r.7.10C(10)]** Where the application was made to the district judge under Rule 7.10C(10) this Rule applies with appropriate modifications.

GENERAL NOTE

Inserted by I(A)R 2010 (SI 2010/686). This is a consequential provision that deals with a range of pragmatic issues, including the thorny issue of who foots the bill for the replacement of an insolvency practitioner via block transfer.

CHAPTER 2

TRANSFER OF PROCEEDINGS BETWEEN COURTS

7.11   General power of transfer

7.11(1)   **[Transfer to county court]** Where winding-up or bankruptcy proceedings or proceedings relating to a debt relief order are pending in the High Court, the court may order them to be transferred to a specified county court.

7.11(2)   **[Transfer to High Court etc.]** Where winding-up or bankruptcy proceedings or proceedings relating to a debt relief order are pending in a county court, the court may order them to be transferred either to the High Court or to another county court.

7.11(3)   **[Transfer to county court with jurisdiction to wind up companies]** In any case where winding-up proceedings are transferred to a county court, the transfer must be to a court which has jurisdiction to wind up companies.

7.11(3A)   **[Transfer to county court with jurisdiction in bankruptcy]** In any case where bankruptcy proceedings or proceedings relating to a debt relief order are transferred to a county court, the transfer must be to a court which has jurisdiction in bankruptcy.

7.11(4)   **[Power of High Court judge]** Where winding-up or bankruptcy proceedings or proceedings relating to a debt relief order are pending in a county court, a judge of the High Court may order them to be transferred to that Court.

7.11(4A)   **[Transfer for r.7.10D purposes of case in r.7.10C(8) schedule]** Solely for the purposes of Rule 7.10D (action following application for a block transfer order)–

    (a)   the registrar may transfer to or from the High Court; and

    (b)   the district judge of the county court to which the application is made may transfer to or from that county court,

any case in the schedule under Rule 7.10C(8).

7.11(5)   **[Order for transfer]** A transfer of proceedings under this Rule may be ordered–

    (a)   by the court of its own motion, or

    (b)   on the application of the official receiver, or

    (c)   on the application of a person appearing to the court to have an interest in the proceedings.

7.11(6)   **[Proceedings commenced before coming into force of Rules]** A transfer of proceedings under this Rule may be ordered notwithstanding that the proceedings commenced before the coming into force of the Rules.

GENERAL NOTE

See the *Practice Direction: Insolvency Proceedings* [2000] B.C.C. 927 (reproduced in App.IV to this *Guide*). The *Practice Direction* was republished in a more up-to-date form in 2007—see *Practice Direction: Insolvency Proceedings* [2007] B.C.C. 842. Various amendments were made to paras (1), (2), (3) and (4) by the Insolvency

(Amendment) Rules 2009 (SI 2009/642) with effect from April 6, 2009. A new para.(3A) was also inserted. These cater for the introduction of debt relief orders. See also General Note after r.7.18. A new para.(4A) has been added by I(A)R 2010 (SI 2010/686).

7.12 Proceedings commenced in wrong court

7.12 Where winding-up or bankruptcy proceedings or proceedings relating to a debt relief order are commenced in a court which is, in relation to those proceedings, the wrong court, that court may–

(a) order the transfer of the proceedings to the court in which they ought to have been commenced;

(b) order that the proceedings be continued in the court in which they have been commenced; or

(c) order the proceedings to be struck out.

(See General Note after r.7.18.) This rule was subject to a minor change by the Insolvency (Amendment) Rules 2009 (SI 2009/642), which took effect on April 6, 2009. This change merely recognised the advent of the possibility of proceedings relating to debt relief orders.

7.13 Applications for transfer

7.13(1) **[Official receiver's report]** An application by the official receiver for proceedings to be transferred shall be made with a report by him–

(a) setting out the reasons for the transfer, and

(b) including a statement either that–

(i) the petitioner, or

(ii) the debtor in proceedings relating to a debt relief order,

consents to the transfer, or that he has been given at least 14 days' notice of the official receiver's application.

7.13(2) **[More convenient conduct of proceedings]** If the court is satisfied from the official receiver's report that the proceedings can be conducted more conveniently in another court, the proceedings shall be transferred to that court.

7.13(3) **[Application not made by official receiver]** Where an application for the transfer of proceedings is made otherwise than by the official receiver, at least 14 days' notice of the application shall be given by the applicant–

(a) to the official receiver attached to the court in which the proceedings are pending, and

(b) to the official receiver attached to the court to which it is proposed that they should be transferred.

(See General Note after r.7.18.) A new para.(1)(b) was substituted by the Insolvency (Amendment) Rules 2009 (SI 2009/642) with effect from April 6, 2009.

7.14 Procedure following order for transfer

7.14(1) **[Copy of order etc. to transferee court]** Subject as follows, the court making an order under Rule 7.11 shall as soon as reasonably practicable send to the transferee court a sealed copy of the order, and the file of the proceedings.

7.14(2) **[On receipt]** On receipt of these, the transferee court shall as soon as reasonably practicable send notice of the transfer to the official receivers attached to that court and the transferor court respectively.

7.14(3) **[Non-application of r.7.14(1)]** Paragraph (1) does not apply where the order is made by the High Court under Rule 7.11(4). In that case–

(a) the High Court shall send sealed copies of the order to the county court from which the proceedings are to be transferred, and to the official receivers attached to that court and the High Court respectively, and

(b) that county court shall send the file of the proceedings to the High Court.

7.14(4) [Omitted.]

(See General Note after r.7.18.) Paragraph (4) was deleted by I(A)R 2010 (SI 2010/686).

7.15 Consequential transfer of other proceedings

7.15(1) **[Application of Rule]** This Rule applies where–

(a) the High Court has–

(i) made a bankruptcy order;

(ii) made a winding-up order;

(iii) appointed a provisional liquidator; or

(iv) appointed an interim receiver; or

(b) [Omitted.]

(c) winding-up or bankruptcy proceedings have been transferred to that Court from a county court.

7.15(2) **[Power of High Court judge]** A judge of any Division of the High Court may, of his own motion, order the transfer to that Division of any such proceedings as are mentioned below and are pending against the company or individual concerned ("the insolvent") either in another Division of the High Court or in a court in England and Wales other than the High Court.

7.15(3) **[Proceedings which may be transferred]** Proceedings which may be so transferred are those brought by or against the insolvent for the purpose of enforcing a claim against the insolvent estate, or brought by a person other than the insolvent for the purpose of enforcing any such claim (including in either case proceedings of any description by a debenture-holder or mortgagee).

7.15(4) **[Where proceedings are transferred]** Where proceedings are transferred under this Rule, the registrar may (subject to the directions of the judge) dispose of any matter arising in the proceedings which would, but for the transfer, have been disposed of in chambers or, in the case of proceedings transferred from a county court, by the district judge.

(See General Note after r.7.18.) Clarified by I(A)R 2010 (SI 2010/686)—para.(1)(a) and (1)(b) replaced with new para.(1)(a).

CHAPTER 3

SHORTHAND WRITERS

7.16 Nomination and appointment of shorthand writers

7.16(1) **[Nomination]** In the High Court the judge or registrar and, in a county court, a district judge may in writing nominate one or more persons to be official shorthand writers to the court.

7.16(2) **[Appointment]** The court may, at any time in the course of insolvency proceedings, appoint a shorthand writer to take down the evidence of a person examined under section 133, 236, 251N, 290 or 366.

7.16(3) **[Application by official receiver etc.]** Where the official receiver applies to the court for an order appointing a shorthand writer, he shall name the person he proposes for appointment.

(See General Note after r.7.18.) A minor change recognising the introduction of s.251N was made by the Insolvency (Amendment) Rules 2009 (SI 2009/642) with effect from April 6, 2009. Clarified by I(A)R 2010 (SI 2010/686).

7.17   Remuneration

7.17(1)   [Payment] The remuneration of a shorthand writer appointed in insolvency proceedings shall be paid by the party at whose instance the appointment was made, or out of the insolvent estate, or otherwise, as the court may direct.

7.17(2)   [Court's discretion] Any question arising as to the rates of remuneration payable under this Rule shall be determined by the court in its discretion.

R.7.17
The rates of remuneration for shorthand writers were formerly fixed by Sch.3. The court is now given a discretion to settle any disputed charge.

(See General Note after r.7.18.)

7.18   Cost of shorthand note [Revoked.]

GENERAL NOTE TO RR.7.1–7.18

Cross-examination was ordered under rr.7.7 and 7.10, and also discovery of documents, in *Re Bank of Credit and Commerce International SA (No.6)* [1994] 1 B.C.L.C. 450.

In *Re Cover Europe Ltd* [2002] EWHC 799 (Ch); [2002] B.P.I.R. 931 it was held that the Companies Court could, under r.7.10, deal with complicated issues of fact and give directions to the parties to serve details of statement of case and have witnesses cross-examined at trial; it was not necessary to remit the matter to the Queen's Bench Division.

IR rr.7.2, 7.5, 7.6, 7.7 and 7.18 revoked by I(A)R 2010 (SI 2010/686).

CHAPTER 4

ENFORCEMENT PROCEDURES

7.19   Enforcement of court orders

7.19(1)   [Orders enforced as judgments] In any insolvency proceedings, orders of the court may be enforced in the same manner as a judgment to the same effect.

7.19(2)   [Enforcement etc. by any county court] Where an order in insolvency proceedings is made, or any process is issued, by a county court ("the primary court"), the order or process may be enforced, executed and dealt with by any other county court ("the secondary court"), as if it had been made or issued for the enforcement of a judgment or order to the same effect made by the secondary court.

This applies whether or not the secondary court has jurisdiction to take insolvency proceedings.

7.19(3)   [Discharge of arrest warrant] Where a warrant for the arrest of a person is issued by the High Court, the warrant may be discharged by the county court where the person who is the subject of the warrant—

(a)   has been brought before a county court exercising insolvency jurisdiction; and

(b)   has given to the county court an undertaking which is satisfactory to the county court to comply with the obligations that apply to that person under the Act or the Rules.

(See General Note after r.7.25.) New para.(3) provided by I(A)R 2010 (SI 2010/686).

7.20   Orders enforcing compliance with the Rules

7.20(1)   [Application by competent person] The court may, on application by the competent person, make such orders as it thinks necessary for the enforcement of obligations falling on any person in accordance with–

(a)   paragraph 47 of Schedule B1 to the Act or section 47 or 131 (duty to submit statement of affairs in administration, administrative receivership or winding up),

(b)   section 143(2) (liquidator to furnish information, books, papers, etc.), or

(c)   section 235 (duty of various persons to co-operate with office-holder).

7.20(2)   [Who is competent person] The competent person for this purpose is–

(a)   under paragraph 47 of Schedule B1 to the Act, the administrator,

(b)   under section 47, the administrative receiver,

(c)   under section 131 or 143(2), the official receiver, and

(d)   under section 235, the official receiver, the administrator, the administrative receiver, the liquidator or the provisional liquidator, as the case may be.

7.20(3)   [Costs] An order of the court under this Rule may provide that all costs of and incidental to the application for it shall be borne by the person against whom the order is made.

(See General Note after r.7.25.)

7.21   Warrants (general provisions)

7.21(1)   [Address for warrant] A warrant issued by the court under any provision of the Act shall be addressed to such officer of the High Court or of a county court (whether or not having jurisdiction in insolvency proceedings) as the warrant specifies, or to any constable.

7.21(2)   [Prescribed officer of the court] The persons referred to in sections 134(2), 236(5), 251N(5), 364(1), 365(3) and 366(3) (court's powers of enforcement) as the prescribed officer of the court are–

(a)   in the case of the High Court, the tipstaff and his assistants of the court, and

(b)   in the case of a county court, the district judge and the bailiffs.

7.21(3)   [Definition] In this Chapter references to property include books, papers and records.

(See General Note after r.7.25.) Note the insertion of the reference to s.251N(5) by the Insolvency (Amendment) Rules 2009 (SI 2009/642) with effect from April 6, 2009. See I(A)R 2010 (SI 2010/686).

7.22   Warrants under ss.134, 364

7.22   When a person ("the arrested person") is arrested under a warrant issued by the court under section 134 (officer of company failing to attend for public examination), or section 364 (arrest of debtor or bankrupt)–

(a)   the officer apprehending the arrested person must give that person into the custody of–

(i)   the court in a case where the court is ready and able to deal with the arrested person, or

(ii)   where the court is not ready and able, the governor of the prison named in the warrant (or where that prison is not able to accommodate the arrested person, the governor of such other prison with appropriate facilities which is able to accommodate the arrested person), who must keep the arrested person in custody until such time as the court otherwise orders and must produce that person before the court at its next sitting; and

(b) any property in the arrested person's possession which may be seized shall be–

    (i) lodged with, or otherwise dealt with as instructed by, whoever is specified in the warrant as authorised to receive it, or

    (ii) kept by the officer seizing it pending the receipt of written orders from the court as to its disposal,

as may be directed by the court in the warrant.

(See General Note after r.7.25.) Modernised by I(A)R 2010 (SI 2010/686)—new para.(a) inserted.

7.23   Warrants under ss.236, 251N and 366

7.23(1) **[When person arrested]** When a person is arrested under a warrant issued under section 236 (inquiry into insolvent company's dealings), 251N (the equivalent in relation to debt relief orders) or 366 (the equivalent in bankruptcy) ("the arrested person"), the officer arresting him shall as soon as reasonably practicable bring him before the court issuing the warrant in order that he may be examined.

7.23(2) **[If not brought before court immediately]** If he cannot immediately be brought up for examination, the officer shall deliver him into the custody of the governor of the prison named in the warrant (or where that prison is not able to accommodate the arrested person, the governor of such other prison with appropriate facilities which is able to accommodate the arrested person), who shall keep him in custody and produce him before the court as it may from time to time direct.

7.23(3) **[Report of arrest etc.]** After arresting the person named in the warrant, the officer shall as soon as reasonably practicable report to the court the arrest or delivery into custody (as the case may be) and apply to the court to fix a venue for the person's examination.

7.23(4) **[Time for examination etc.]** The court shall appoint the earliest practicable time for the examination, and shall–

(a) direct the governor of the prison to produce the person for examination at the time and place appointed, and

(b) as soon as reasonably practicable give notice of the venue to the person who applied for the warrant.

7.23(5) **[Property in arrested person's possession]** Any property in the arrested person's possession which may be seized shall be–

(a) lodged with, or otherwise dealt with as instructed by, whoever is specified in the warrant as authorised to receive it, or

(b) kept by the officer seizing it pending the receipt of written orders from the court as to its disposal,

as may be directed by the court.

(See General Note after r.7.25.) Minor amendments have been made to this rule and its heading by the Insolvency (Amendment) Rules 2009 (SI 2009/642) with effect from April 6, 2009 to recognise the enactment of s.251N. Clarified by I(A)R 2010 (SI 2010/686).

7.24   Execution of warrants outside court's district

7.24(1) **[Application of Rule]** This Rule applies where a warrant for a person's arrest has been issued in insolvency proceedings by a county court ("the primary court") and is addressed to another county court ("the secondary court") for execution in its district.

7.24(2) **[Power of secondary court]** The secondary court may send the warrant to the district judge of another county court (whether or not having jurisdiction to take insolvency proceedings) in whose district the person to be arrested is or is believed to be, with a notice to the effect that the warrant is transmitted to that court under this Rule for execution in its district at the request of the primary court.

7.24(3) [Court receiving warrant] The court receiving a warrant transmitted by the secondary court under this Rule shall apply its seal to the warrant, and secure that all such steps are taken for its execution as would be appropriate in the case of a warrant issued by itself.

(See General Note after r.7.25.) Clarified by I(A)R 2010 (SI 2010/686).

7.25 Warrants under s.365

7.25(1) [Seizure] A warrant issued under section 365(3) (search of premises not belonging to the bankrupt) shall authorise any person executing it to seize any property of the bankrupt found as a result of the execution of the warrant.

7.25(2) [Seized property] Any property seized under a warrant issued under section 365(2) or (3) shall be–

(a) lodged with, or otherwise dealt with as instructed by, whoever is specified in the warrant as authorised to receive it, or

(b) kept by the officer seizing it pending the receipt of written orders from the court as to its disposal,

as may be directed by the warrant.

GENERAL NOTE TO rr.7.19–7.25

Chapter 4, as the title indicates, deals with the procedures for the enforcement of court orders, of statutory duties and of warrants issued under IA 1986. In particular, r.7.20 sanctions with the backing of the court the general duty of corporate officers and others to co-operate with the official receiver and with insolvency practitioners holding office as liquidator, etc. Rule 7.20 was amended by I(A)R 2003 (SI 2003/1730) with effect from September 15, 2003 to cater for the new mode of administration. Note I(A)R 2010 (SI 2010/686).

CHAPTER 5

COURT RECORDS AND RETURNS

7.26 Title of proceedings [Deleted.]

7.27 Court records [Deleted.]

7.28 Inspection of records [Deleted.]

7.29 Returns to Secretary of State [Deleted.]

7.30 File of court proceedings [Deleted.]

7.31 Right to inspect the file [Deleted.]

7.31A Court file

7.31A(1) [Court to open and maintain file] The court must open and maintain a file in any case where documents are filed with it under the Act or the Rules.

7.31A(2) [Documents to be placed on file] Any documents which are filed with the court under the Act or the Rules must be placed on the file opened in accordance with paragraph (1).

7.31A(3) [Who may inspect file or obtain copy] The following persons may inspect or obtain from the court a copy of, or a copy of any document or documents contained in, the file opened in accordance with paragraph (1)–

(a) the office-holder in the proceedings;

(b) the Secretary of State; and

(c) any person who is a creditor of the company to which, or the individual to whom, the proceedings relate if that person provides the court with a statement in writing by confirming that that person is a creditor.

7.31A(4) **[Proceedings where inspection or copying of documents exercisable]** The same right to inspect or obtain a copy of, or a copy of any document or documents contained in, the file opened in accordance with paragraph (1) is exercisable–

(a) in proceedings under Parts 1 to 7 of the Act, by–

(i) an officer or former officer of the company to which the proceedings relate; or

(ii) a member of the company or a contributory in its winding up;

(b) in proceedings with respect to a voluntary arrangement under Part 8 of the Act, by the debtor;

(c) in bankruptcy proceedings, by–

(i) the bankrupt;

(ii) any person against whom a bankruptcy petition has been presented;

(iii) any person who has, in accordance with Chapter 1 of Part 6, been served with a statutory demand;

(d) in proceedings relating to a debt relief order, by the debtor.

7.31A(5) **[Right to inspect by authorised representative]** The right to inspect or obtain a copy of, or a copy of any document or documents contained in, the file opened in accordance with paragraph (1) may be exercised on that person's behalf by a person authorised to do so by that person.

7.31A(6) **[Right to inspect/copy with permission of court]** Any person who is not otherwise entitled to inspect or obtain a copy of, or a copy of any document or documents contained in, the file opened in accordance with paragraph (1) may do so if that person has the permission of the court.

7.31A(7) **[File, document or copy not to made available]** The court may direct that the file, a document (or part of it) or a copy of a document (or part of it) must not be made available under paragraph (3), (4) or (5) without the permission of the court.

7.31A(8) **[Who may apply under r.7.31A(7)]** An application for a direction under paragraph (7) may be made by–

(a) the official receiver;

(b) the officer-holder in the proceedings; or

(c) any person appearing to the court to have an interest.

7.31A(9) **[Exercising right to inspect file]** Where any person wishes to exercise the right to inspect the file under paragraph (3), (4), (5) or (6), that person–

(a) if the permission of the court is required, must file with the court an application notice in accordance with these Rules; or

(b) if the permission of the court is not required, may inspect the file at any reasonable time.

7.31A(10) **[Exercising right to obtain copy of a document]** Where any person wishes to exercise the right to obtain a copy of a document under paragraph (3), (4), (5) or (6), that person must pay any prescribed fee and–

(a) if the permission of the court is required, file with the court an application notice in accordance with these Rules; or

(b) if the permission of the court is not required, file with the court a written request for the document.

7.31A(11)   [Application under r.7.31A(6), (7) without notice] An application for–

(a) permission to inspect the file or obtain a copy of a document under paragraph (6); or

(b) a direction under paragraph (7),

may be made without notice to any other party, but the court may direct that notice must be given to any person who would be affected by its decision.

7.31A(12)   [Where Secretary of State or official receiver requests file] If for the purposes of powers conferred by the Act or the Rules, the Secretary of State or the official receiver requests the transmission of the file of any insolvency proceedings, the court must comply with the request (unless the file is for the time being in use for the court's own purposes).

GENERAL NOTE

Inserted by I(A)R 2010 (SI 2010/686).

7.32   Filing of Gazette notices and advertisements [Omitted.]

CHAPTER 6

COSTS AND DETAILED ASSESSMENT

Introductory note to Part 7, Chapter 6
The whole of Chapter 6 (rr.7.33–7.42) was replaced by the Insolvency Amendment (No.2) Rules 1999 (SI 1999/1022) with effect from April 26, 1999 in order to bring these rules into line with the CPR. It was then substantially amended by I(A)R 2010 (SI 2010/686).

7.33   Application of the CPR [Deleted.]

7.33A   Application of Chapter 6

7.33A(1)   [Costs in insolvency proceedings] This chapter applies in relation to costs in connection with insolvency proceedings.

7.33A(2)   [Costs includes charges and expenses] In this chapter a reference to costs includes charges and expenses.

GENERAL NOTE

Substituted by I(A)R 2010 (SI 2010/686) for IR r.7.33.

7.34   Requirement to assess costs by the detailed procedure [Deleted.]

7.34A   Requirement to assess costs by the detailed procedure

7.34A(1)   [Where costs payable as insolvency expense] Where the costs of any person are payable as an expense out of the insolvent estate, the amount payable must be decided by detailed assessment unless agreed between the office-holder and the person entitled to payment.

7.34A(2)   [Office-holder to serve notice] In the absence of such agreement as is mentioned in paragraph (1), the office-holder–

(a) may serve notice requiring that person to commence detailed assessment proceedings in accordance with CPR Part 47; and

(b) must serve such notice (except in an administrative receivership) where a liquidation or creditors' committee formed in relation to the insolvency proceedings resolves that the amount of the costs must be decided by detailed assessment.

7.34A(3) [Assessment proceedings in court of insolvency proceedings] Detailed assessment proceedings must be commenced in the court to which the insolvency proceedings are allocated or, where in relation to a company there is no such court, any court having jurisdiction to wind up the company.

7.34A(4) [Payments on account] Where the costs of any person employed by an office-holder in insolvency proceedings are required to be decided by detailed assessment or fixed by order of the court, the office-holder may make payments on account to such person in respect of those costs provided that person undertakes in writing–

(a) to repay as soon as reasonably practicable any money which may, when detailed assessment is made, prove to have been overpaid; and

(b) to pay interest on any such sum as is mentioned in sub-paragraph (a) at the rate specified in section 17 of the Judgments Act 1838 on the date payment was made and for the period beginning with the date of payment and ending with the date of repayment.

7.34A(5) [Costs in any proceedings by detailed assessment] In any proceedings before the court (including proceedings on a petition), the court may order costs to be decided by detailed assessment.

7.34A(6) [Costs of trustee in bankruptcy or liquidator] Unless otherwise directed or authorised, the costs of a trustee in bankruptcy or a liquidator are to be allowed on the standard basis for which provision is made in–

(a) CPR rule 44.4 (basis of assessment); and

(b) CPR rule 44.5 (factors to be taken into account when deciding the amount of costs).

GENERAL NOTE

Substituted by I(A)R 2010 (SI 2010/686) for IR r.7.34.

7.35 Procedure where detailed assessment required

7.35(1) [Requirements of costs officer] Before making a detailed assessment of the costs of any person employed in insolvency proceedings by the office-holder, the costs officer shall require a certificate of employment, which shall be endorsed on the bill and authenticated by the office-holder.

7.35(2) [Information on certificate] The certificate shall include–

(a) the name and address of the person employed,

(b) details of the functions to be carried out under the employment, and

(c) a note of any special terms of remuneration which have been agreed.

7.35(3) [Detailed assessment proceedings] Every person whose costs in insolvency proceedings are required to be decided by detailed assessment shall, on being required in writing to do so by the office-holder, commence detailed assessment proceedings in accordance with CPR Part 47 (procedure for detailed assessment of costs and default provisions).

7.35(4) [Commencement of detailed assessment proceedings within three months] If that person does not commence detailed assessment proceedings within 3 months of the requirement under paragraph (3), or within such further time as the court, on application, may permit, the office-holder may deal with the insolvent estate without regard to any claim by that person, whose claim is forfeited by such failure to commence proceedings.

7.35(5)   [Failure to commence proceedings] Where in any such case such a claim lies additionally against an office-holder in his personal capacity, that claim is also forfeited by such failure to commence proceedings.

7.35(6)   [Assessment of costs by High Court] Where costs have been incurred in insolvency proceedings in the High Court and those proceedings are subsequently transferred to a county court, all costs of those proceedings directed by the court or otherwise required to be assessed may nevertheless, on the application of the person who incurred the costs, be ordered to be decided by detailed assessment in the High Court.

GENERAL NOTE

Clarified by I(A)R 2010 (SI 2010/686).

7.36   Costs of officers charged with execution of writs or other process

7.36(1)   [Detailed assessment of bill] Where an enforcement officer, or other officer, charged with execution of the writ or other process

  (a)   is required under section 184(2) or 346(2) to deliver up goods or money, or

  (b)   has under section 184(3) or 346(3) deducted costs from the proceeds of an execution or money paid to him,

the office-holder may require in writing that the amount of the enforcement officer's or other officer's bill of costs be decided by detailed assessment.

7.36(2)   [Application of r.7.35(4)] Where such a requirement is made, Rule 7.35(4) applies.

7.36(3)   [In case of r.7.36(1)(b) deduction] Where, in the case of a deduction under paragraph (1)(b), any amount deducted is disallowed at the conclusion of the detailed assessment proceedings, the enforcement officer shall as soon as reasonably practicable pay a sum equal to that disallowed to the office-holder for the benefit of the insolvent estate.

GENERAL NOTE

In r.7.36 former references to "sheriff" were replaced by the more anodyne "enforcement officer" by the Insolvency (Amendment) Rules 2005 (SI 2005/527). This reflects changes in the Courts Act 2003. Clarified by I(A)R 2010 (SI 2010/686).

7.37   Petitions presented by insolvents [Deleted.]

7.37A   Petitions presented by insolvents

7.37A(1)   [Application of r.7.37A] This Rule applies where–

  (a)   a winding-up petition is presented by a company against itself;

  (b)   a bankruptcy petition is presented by a debtor against that debtor,

and references in this Rule to "the insolvent" are to be read as a reference to the company or the debtor.

7.37A(2)   [Solicitor to give credit for deposit from insolvent] A solicitor acting in either of the cases mentioned in paragraph (1) must in the solicitor's bill of costs give credit for any sum or security received by the solicitor as a deposit from the insolvent on account of the costs and expenses to be incurred in respect of the filing and prosecution of the petition and the deposit must be noted by the costs officer on the final costs certificate.

7.37A(3)   **[No costs to insolvent where prior creditor's petition]** Where an order is made on a petition of a kind mentioned in paragraph (1) and prior to the presentation of that petition a petition had been presented by a creditor, no costs are allowed to the insolvent or that insolvent's solicitor out of that insolvent's estate unless the court considers that–

(a)   the insolvent estate has benefited by the insolvent's conduct; or

(b)   there are otherwise special circumstances justifying the allowance of costs.

GENERAL NOTE

Substituted by I(A)R 2010 (SI 2010/686) for previous IR r.7.37.

7.38   Costs paid otherwise than out of the insolvent estate

7.38   Where the amount of costs is decided by detailed assessment under an order of the court directing that those costs are to be paid otherwise than out of the insolvent estate, the costs officer shall note on the final costs certificate by whom, or the manner in which, the costs are to be paid.

7.39   Award of costs against official receiver or responsible insolvency practitioner

7.39   Without prejudice to any provision of the Act or Rules by virtue of which the official receiver is not in any event to be liable for costs and expenses, where an office-holder or the official receiver where that official receiver is not acting as an office-holder is made a party to any proceedings on the application of another party to the proceedings, he shall not be personally liable for costs unless the court otherwise directs.

7.40   Applications for costs

7.40(1)   **[Application of r.7.40]** This Rule applies where a party to, or person affected by, any proceedings in an insolvency–

(a)   applies to the court for an order allowing his costs, or part of them, incidental to the proceedings; and

(b)   that application is not made at the time of the proceedings.

7.40(2)   **[Serving of sealed copies of application]** The person concerned shall serve a sealed copy of his or her application–

(a)   in proceedings other than proceedings relating to a debt relief order–

    (i)   on the office-holder, and,

    (ii)   in a winding up by the court or a bankruptcy, on the official receiver;

(b)   in proceedings relating to a debt relief order, on the official receiver.

7.40(3)   **[Appearances re r.7.40(2)(a) application]** The office-holder and, where appropriate, the official receiver may appear on an application to which paragraph (2)(a) applies.

7.40(3A)   **[Appearances re r.7.40(2)(b) application]** The official receiver may appear on an application to which paragraph (2)(b) applies.

7.40(4)   **[Costs]** No costs of or incidental to the application shall be allowed to the applicant unless the court is satisfied that the application could not have been made at the time of the proceedings.

7.41   Costs and expenses of witnesses

7.41(1)   **[No allowance to bankrupt, etc.]** Except as directed by the court, no allowance as a witness in any examination or other proceedings before the court shall be made to the bankrupt or the debtor or an officer of the insolvent company to which the proceedings relate.

7.41(2) **[Petitioner's expenses]** A person presenting any petition in a company insolvency or bankruptcy proceedings shall not be regarded as a witness on the hearing of the petition, but the costs officer may allow his expenses of travelling and subsistence.

7.42 Final costs certificate

7.42(1) **[Certificate is final, etc.]** A final costs certificate of the costs officer is final and conclusive as to all matters which have not been objected to in the manner provided for under the rules of the court.

7.42(2) **[Duplicate certificate]** Where it is proved to the satisfaction of a costs officer that a final costs certificate has been lost or destroyed, he may issue a duplicate.

GENERAL NOTE TO RR.7.33–7.42

Chapter 6 was rewritten by the Insolvency (Amendment) (No.2) Rules 1999 (SI 1999/1022) r.3 with effect from April 26, 1999 in order to cater for the new terminology used in the Civil Procedure Rules (which replace the Rules of the Supreme Court and County Court Rules). The changes appear to be more a question of semantics than substance.

On costs under IR r.7.39 see the comments of Lewison J. in *Appleyard v Ritecrown Ltd* [2009] B.P.I.R. 235 at para.[55].

Note the changes made to r.7.40 by the Insolvency (Amendment) Rules 2009 (SI 2009/642) with effect from April 6, 2009. These reforms involve the substitution of new paras (1) to (3) and the introduction of a new para.(3A).

Minor amendments have been made to r.7.41 paras (1) and (2) by the Insolvency (Amendment) Rules 2009 (SI 2009/642) with effect from April 6, 2009.

Major restructuring and textual amendments have been made by I(A)R 2010 (SI 2010/686)—rr.7.33, 7.34 and 7.37 have been substituted.

CHAPTER 7

PERSONS WHO LACK CAPACITY TO MANAGING THEIR AFFAIRS

7.43 Introductory

7.43(1) **[Application of Ch.7 Rules]** The Rules in this Chapter apply where in insolvency proceedings it appears to the court that a person affected by the proceedings is one who lacks capacity within the meaning of the Mental Capacity Act 2005 to manage and administer his property and affairs either–

(a) by reason of lacking capacity within the meaning of the Mental Capacity Act 2005, or

(b) due to physical affliction or disability.

7.43(2) **["The incapacitated person"]** The person concerned is referred to as "the incapacitated person".

(See General Note after r.7.46.) Note amendment by SI 2007/1898.

7.44 Appointment of another person to act

7.44(1) **[Power of court]** The court may appoint such person as it thinks fit to appear for, represent or act for the incapacitated person.

7.44(2) **[General or particular appointment]** The appointment may be made either generally or for the purpose of any particular application or proceeding, or for the exercise of particular rights or powers which the incapacitated person might have exercised but for his incapacity.

7.44(3) **[Appointment by court or on application]** The court may make the appointment either of its own motion or on application by–

(a) a person who has been appointed by a court in the United Kingdom or elsewhere to manage the affairs of, or to represent, the incapacitated person, or

(b) any relative or friend of the incapacitated person who appears to the court to be a proper person to make the application, or

(c) the official receiver, or

(d) the person who, in relation to the proceedings, is the office-holder.

7.44(4)   [Without notice application, powers of court] Application under paragraph (3) may be made without notice to any other party; but the court may require such notice of the application as it thinks necessary to be given to the person alleged to be incapacitated, or any other person, and may adjourn the hearing of the application to enable the notice to be given.

(See General Note after r.7.46.) Minor changes of terminology are made by I(A)R 2010 (SI 2010/686).

7.45   Affidavit in support of application [Deleted.]

7.45A   Witness statement in support of application

7.45A   An application under Rule 7.44(3) must be supported by a witness statement made by a registered medical practitioner as to the mental or physical condition of the incapacitated person.

GENERAL NOTE

Substituted by I(A)R 2010 (SI 2010/686) for IR r.7.45.

7.46   Service of notices following appointment

7.46   Any notice served on, or sent to, a person appointed under Rule 7.44 has the same effect as if it had been served on, or given to, the incapacitated person.

GENERAL NOTE TO RR.7.43–7.46

The court is empowered by these rules to make special provision for any person subject to a disability who is affected by insolvency proceedings. In *Hunt v Fylde BC* [2008] B.P.I.R. 1368 Ashton D.J. indicated that the court can invoke IR r.7.43 on its own initiative.

IR r.7.44 attracted judicial comment by Ashton D.J. in *Hunt v Fylde BC* [2008] BPIR 1368 (see annotation to IR r.7.43 above).

IR r.7.45 replaced by IR r.7.45A via I(A)R 2010 (SI 2010/686).

CHAPTER 8

APPEALS IN INSOLVENCY PROCEEDINGS

7.47   Appeals and reviews of court orders in corporate insolvency

7.47(1)   [Powers of courts] Every court having jurisdiction for the purposes of Parts 1 to 4 of the Act and Parts 1 to 4 of the Rules, may review, rescind or vary any order made by it in the exercise of that jurisdiction.

7.47(2)   [Appeals to and from single judge of High Court] Appeals in civil matters in proceedings under Parts 1 to 4 of the Act and Parts 1 to 4 of the Rules lie as follows–

(a) to a single judge of the High Court where the decision appealed against is made by the county court or the registrar;

(b) to the Civil Division of the Court of Appeal from a decision of a single judge of the High Court.

7.47(3) **[County court not to be restrained etc.]** A county court is not, in the exercise of its jurisdiction for the purposes of Parts 1 to 4 of the Act and Parts 1 to 4 of the Rules, subject to be restrained by the order of any other court, and no appeal lies from its decision in the exercise of that jurisdiction except as provided by this Rule.

7.47(4) **[Application for rescission of winding-up order]** Any application for the rescission of a winding-up order shall be made within 5 business days after the date on which the order was made.

<small>GENERAL NOTE</small>

Significant changes are made by I(A)R 2010 (SI 2010/686). A new para.(2) has been substituted.

Appeals from a registrar's winding-up order go to the High Court, not the Court of Appeal: *Re Calahurst Ltd* (1989) 5 B.C.C. 318. This point was confirmed by the Court of Appeal in *Re Tasbian Ltd (No.2)* [1990] B.C.C. 322. This is also true in relation to an order made by a district judge in the county court: *Re Langley Marketing Services Ltd* [1992] B.C.C. 585; and the rule applies to an order made under CDDA 1986. It applies also to administration orders: *Cornhill Insurance plc v Cornhill Financial Services Ltd* [1992] B.C.C. 818. The appeal may take the form either of an appeal against the original decision of the registrar, or of an appeal from the registrar's refusal to review his original decision (*Re S N Group plc* [1993] B.C.C. 808). The jurisdiction under r.7.47 is very wide, and extends even to the review, rescission or variation by a High Court judge of a decision of any judge of that court: *Re W & A Glaser Ltd* [1994] B.C.C. 199 at 208, per Harman J. A judge can review his or her own decisions under r.7.47(1)—*Re Thirty Eight Building Ltd (No.2)* [2000] B.P.I.R. 158. The court has power to make retrospective orders under IR r.7.47(1)—see *Re Roches Leisure Services Ltd* [2005] EWHC 3148 (Ch); [2006] B.P.I.R. 453 (retrospectively extending date for expiry of administration). Leave is not required for an appeal to the High Court (*Re Busytoday Ltd* [1992] B.C.C. 480), but is necessary for a further appeal to the Court of Appeal (*Midrome Ltd v Shaw* [1993] B.C.C. 659). In spite of the wording of r.7.47(2) (and also r.7.48(2)) second appeals to the Court of Appeal require the leave of the Court of Appeal—Access to Justice Act 1999 s.55.

Appeals under r.7.47(2) are true appeals and do not require a hearing *de novo*. Thus a decision of the registrar will only be overturned if it was based on an error of law or wrongful exercise of discretion: *Re Probe Data Systems Ltd (No.3)* [1991] B.C.C. 428; and *Re Tasbian Ltd (No.3)* [1991] B.C.C. 435. See also *Re Industrial & Commercial Securities plc* (1989) 5 B.C.C. 320. The court will review an exercise of discretion only if it is satisfied that no judge, properly instructed as to the law with regard to the relevant facts, could have reached the conclusion that was reached in the court below: *Re MTI Trading Systems Ltd* [1998] B.C.C. 400. However, the court may rescind a winding-up order made by the registrar notwithstanding the fact that there is no ground to allow an appeal from his decision: *Re Dollar Land (Feltham) Ltd* [1995] B.C.C. 740. The High Court can hear both an appeal from and a request to review a registrar's order—*Re Piccadilly Property Management Ltd* [1999] B.P.I.R. 260.

The jurisdiction of the court under r.7.47 is not inconsistent with CPR r.40.12 (the "slip rule"); and an error in an order may be corrected under either provision, or under the court's inherent jurisdiction: *Re Brian Sheridan Cars Ltd* [1995] B.C.C. 1,035.

For limitations on the jurisdiction under IR r.7.47 see *Wilson v The Specter Partnership* [2007] EWHC 133 (Ch); [2007] B.P.I.R. 649 at [25]. Again, in *Eastaway v Secretary of State for Trade and Industry* [2007] B.C.C. 550 the Court of Appeal indicated that IR r.7.47(1) does not confer jurisdiction on the court to discharge a director disqualification *undertaking* because that rule applies only to court orders.

Paragraph (4) was considered by Mann J. in *Wilson v The Specter Partnership* (above) in which the point was made that the court enjoys discretion to extend the seven day period where the delay was justified and can be explained.

The procedure for appeals against orders under IR 1986 r.7.47 is governed by CPR r.52.11—*Jacob v UIC Insurance Co Ltd* [2007] B.C.C. 167.

See further the General Note to IA 1986 s.375.

(See also General Note after r.7.50.)

7.48   Appeals in bankruptcy by the Secretary of State

7.48(1) **[Appeal at instance of Secretary of State]** In bankruptcy proceedings, an appeal lies at the instance of the Secretary of State from any order of the court made on an application for the rescission or annulment of a bankruptcy order, or for a bankrupt's discharge.

7.48(2) [Omitted.]

An appeal under r.7.48(2) from either a county court judge or a registrar of the High Court to a single judge of the High Court is a true appeal and not a rehearing *de novo: Re Gilmartin (a Bankrupt)* [1989] 1 W.L.R. 513. On the former IR r.7.48(2) see the judgment of H.H.J. Hodge Q.C. in *Bailey v Dargue* [2009] B.P.I.R. 1. Reworded by I(A)R 2010 (SI 2010/686)—para.(2) has been omitted.

(See also General Notes to r.7.47 and r.7.50.)

7.49 Procedure on appeal [Deleted.]

7.49A Procedure on appeal

7.49A(1) [Permission of court required] An appeal against a decision at first instance may only be brought with either the permission of the court which made the decision or the permission of the court which has jurisdiction to hear the appeal.

7.49A(2) [Time limit for appellant's notice] An appellant must file an appellant's notice (within the meaning of CPR Part 52) within 21 days after the date of the decision of the court that the appellant wishes to appeal.

7.49A(3) [CPR Pt 52 procedure applies] The procedure set out in CPR Part 52 applies to any appeal to which this Chapter applies.

GENERAL NOTE

Substituted by I(A)R 2010 (SI 2010/686) for IR r.7.49.

7.50 Appeal against decision of Secretary of State or official receiver

7.50(1) [Time limit for appeal] An appeal under the Act or the Rules against a decision of the Secretary of State or the official receiver shall be brought within 28 days of the notification of the decision.

7.50(2) [Exceptions] In respect of a decision under Rule 6.214A(5)(b), an appeal shall be brought within 14 days of the notification of the decision.

GENERAL NOTE TO RR.7.47–7.50

The various procedures and time limits listed here govern reviews and appeals from decisions of the courts, the Secretary of State and the official receiver. For further details, see the General Note after r.7.47. Note also the Practice Direction in App.IV. Note changes made by I(A)R 2010 (SI 2010/686).

R.7.50

A new subpara.(2) was inserted by Insolvency (Amendment) Rules 2003 (SI 2003/1730) to fix a 14-day time limit for appeals against decisions made under r.6.214A(5)(b).

CHAPTER 9

GENERAL

7.51 Principal court rules and practice to apply [Deleted.]

7.51A Principal court rules and practice to apply

7.51A(1) [Provisions of CPR to certain insolvency proceedings] The provisions of the CPR in the first column of the table in this Rule (including any related practice direction) apply to insolvency proceedings by virtue of the provisions of these Rules set out in the second column with any necessary modifications, except so far as inconsistent with these Rules.

Provisions of CPR	Provisions of these Rules
CPR Part 6 (except 6.30 to 6.51) (service of documents)	Chapter 3 of Part 12A
CPR Part 18 (further information)	Rules 7.60 and 9.2(3)(b)
CPR Part 31 (disclosure and inspection of documents)	Rules 7.60 and 9.2
CPR Part 37 (miscellaneous provisions about payments into court)	Rule 7.59
Parts 44 and 47 (costs)	Chapter 6 of Part 7
CPR Part 52 (appeals)	Rule 7.49

7.51A(2)   [Other CPR provisions apply] Subject to paragraph (3), the provisions of the CPR (including any related practice direction) not referred to in the table apply to proceedings under the Act and Rules with any necessary modifications, except so far as inconsistent with these Rules.

7.51A(3)   [Allocation to CPR Pt 29 multi-track] All insolvency proceedings must be allocated to the multi-track for which CPR Part 29 makes provision, and accordingly those provisions of the CPR which provide for allocation questionnaires and track allocation do not apply.

7.51A(4)   [Application of CPR Pt 32 evidence rules to verified false statements] CPR Part 32 applies to a false statement in a document verified by a statement of truth made under these Rules as it applies to a false statement in a document verified by a statement of truth made under CPR Part 22.

GENERAL NOTE

Substituted by I(A)R 2010 (SI 2010/686) for IR r.7.51.

For the significance of the linkage between IR and the CPR see *Thakerar v Lynch Hall & Hornby (No.2) (Practice Note)* [2005] EWHC 2752 (Ch); [2006] 1 W.L.R. 1513 where Lewison J. ruled that a bankruptcy registrar enjoyed jurisdiction to make a third party debt order in relation to an order for costs made in insolvency proceedings in the High Court.

On the linkage with the CPR and the ability of the court to revisit its own judgment see *Paulin v Paulin* [2009] EWCA Civ 221. In *Re Beloit Walmsley Ltd* [2008] B.P.I.R. 1445 the court made the point that although r.7.51 incorporated the CPR regime, that procedural regime cannot be used to undermine time limits imposed by primary legislation in the Insolvency Act 1986.

7.52   Right of audience

7.52(1)   [Official receivers and their deputies] Official receivers and deputy official receivers have right of audience in insolvency proceedings, whether in the High Court or a county court.

7.52(2)   [Omitted.]

GENERAL NOTE

There appears to have been no express provision governing rights of audience in the former rules: the matter was presumably left to be settled by the ordinary rules of court and the common law. Paragraph (2) deleted by I(A)R 2010 (SI 2010/686).

7.53   Right of attendance (company insolvency) [Revoked by I(A)R 2010 (SI 2010/686).]

7.54   Insolvency practitioner's solicitor [Revoked by I(A)R 2010 (SI 2010/686).]

7.55   Formal defects

7.55 No insolvency proceedings shall be invalidated by any formal defect or by any irregularity, unless the court before which objection is made considers that substantial injustice has been caused by the defect or irregularity, and that the injustice cannot be remedied by any order of the court.

This rule appears to have been based on BA 1914 s.147(1), but is made to apply to all forms of insolvency proceedings. For its relevance in the context of setting aside a statutory demand, see *Re a Debtor (No.1 of 1987)* [1988] 1 W.L.R. 419. In the later case of *Re a Debtor (No.190 of 1987), The Times*, May 21, 1988, Vinelott J. held that r.7.55 did not apply to cure defects in the statutory demand. He thereby followed *Re Cartwright* [1975] 1 W.L.R. 573, which was decided under the old law. In *Re Awan* [2000] B.P.I.R. 241 Judge Boggis refused to allow r.7.55 to be invoked to justify failure to provide proof of service of petition as this was regarded as such a fundamental flaw. But in *Re Anderson Owen Ltd* [2009] EWHC 2837 (Ch) it was held by Norris J. that IR r.7.55 could be invoked to cure any defective service of proceedings instituted under s.212 of IA 1986.

Rule 7.55 only applies in the context of "insolvency proceedings"—this phrase has been somewhat narrowly defined by the courts so as to exclude the appointment of an administrator out of court pursuant to para.22 of Sch.B1—*Re Blights Builders Ltd* [2006] EWHC 3549 (Ch); [2007] B.C.C. 712. Rule 7.55 was also held not to be applicable in exactly the same circumstances in *Re G-Tech Construction Ltd* [2007] B.P.I.R. 1275. See also IR r.13.7.

In *Re a Debtor (No.340 of 1992)* [1996] 2 All E.R. 211 it was held that r.7.55 did not validate an improperly executed writ of *fieri facias* as in the circumstances of the case the irregularity was so serious as to mean that the writ could not be said to have been served at all. Here apart from knocking on a debtor's door the bailiff had left the premises without any serious attempt to gain access.

Rule 7.55 did, however, come into play in *Re a Debtor (No.22 of 1993)* [1994] 1 W.L.R. 46 (sometimes cited as *Focus Insurance v a Debtor*) where an omission by a creditor to state in his petition that there was an extant set-aside application by the debtor was waved through by Mummery J. See also *Re Continental Assurance Co of London plc (in liq.) (No.2)* [1998] 1 B.C.L.C. 583, where an application had been made in the wrong form but no prejudice had occurred. See also *Oben v Blackman* [2000] B.P.I.R. 302.

In *Foenander v Allan* [2006] B.P.I.R. 1392 the potential usage of this rule in addressing complaints about the constitution of the creditors' committee was noted.

Rule 7.55 could be used to correct a slip in a block transfer order that had incorrectly suggested that there was jurisdiction under IR r.6.132(5) to make an appointment of a trustee in bankruptcy—*Donaldson v O'Sullivan* [2008] EWHC 387 (Ch); [2008] B.P.I.R. 288 which was confirmed on other grounds—see [2008] EWCA Civ 879. But see now IR rr.7.10A–7.10D.

7.56 Service of orders staying proceedings

7.56 Where in insolvency proceedings the court makes an order staying any action, execution or other legal process against the property of a company, or against the property or person of an individual debtor or bankrupt, service of the order may be effected by sending a sealed copy of the order to whatever is the address for service of the claimant or other party having the carriage of the proceedings to be stayed.

Minor redrafting is carried out by I(A)R 2010 (SI 2010/686)—new heading provided.

7.57 Affidavits [Revoked by I(A)R 2010 (SI 2010/686).]

7.58 Security in court [Revoked by I(A)R 2010 (SI 2010/686).]

7.59 Payment into court

7.59 CPR Part 37 (miscellaneous provisions about payments into court) apply to money lodged in court under the Rules.

Rule 7.59 substituted by the Insolvency (Amendment) (No.2) Rules 1999 (SI 1999/1022) r.3, Sch. para.7 as from April 26, 1999. Reworded by I(A)R 2010 (SI 2010/686).

7.60 Further information and disclosure

7.60(1) **[Clarification, additional information, etc.]** Any party to insolvency proceedings may apply to the court for an order–

(a)   that any other party

      (i)   clarify any matter which is in dispute in the proceedings, or

     (ii)   give additional information in relation to any such matter;

     in accordance with CPR Part 18 (further information); or

(b)   to obtain disclosure from any other party in accordance with CPR Part 31 (disclosure and inspection of documents).

7.60(2)   **[Application under Rule]** An application under this Rule may be made without notice being served on any other party.

GENERAL NOTE

Rule 7.60 substituted by the Insolvency (Amendment) (No.2) Rules 1999 (SI 1999/1022) r.3, Sch. para.8 as from April 26, 1999. See *Highberry Ltd v Colt Telecom Group plc* [2002] EWHC 2503 (Ch); [2003] B.P.I.R. 311.

    The operation of the predecessor of this rule was considered in detail by Harman J. in *Re Primlaks (UK) Ltd (No.2)* [1990] B.C.L.C. 234. Here it was held that in an unfair prejudice application under s.6 of the Act arising out of a corporate voluntary arrangement, discovery should be ordered if it was in the interests of justice to do so; and clearly if a particular creditor was making an application under s.6 it was necessary for him to know the full facts of the transactions which he alleged were unfair.

7.61   Office copies of documents

7.61(1)   **[Right to require office copy]** Any person who has under the Rules the right to inspect the court file of insolvency proceedings may require the court to provide him with an office copy of any document from the file.

7.61(2)   **[Exercise of right]** A person's rights under this Rule may be exercised on his behalf by his solicitor.

7.61(3)   **[Form of copy]** An office copy provided by the court under this Rule shall be in such form as the registrar thinks appropriate, and shall bear the court's seal.

CHAPTER 10

EC REGULATION—CREDITORS' VOLUNTARY WINDING UP—CONFIRMATION BY THE COURT

7.62   Application for confirmation

7.62(1)   **[Application]** Where a company has passed a resolution for voluntary winding up, and no declaration under section 89 has been made (or is deemed not to have been made in accordance with section 96), the liquidator may apply to court for an order confirming the creditors' voluntary winding up for the purposes of the EC Regulation.

7.62(2)   **[Requirements]** The application shall be in writing supported by a witness statement by the liquidator (using [FORM 7.20A] the same form) and shall state–

(a)   the name of the applicant,

(b)   the name of the company and its registered number,

(c)   the date on which the resolution for voluntary winding up was passed,

(d)   that the application is accompanied by all of the documents required under paragraph (3) which are true copies of the documents required, and

(e)   that the EC Regulation will apply to the company and whether the proceedings will be main proceedings, territorial proceedings or secondary proceedings.

7.62(3) **[Filing]** The liquidator shall file in court two copies of the application, together with one copy of the following–

(a) a copy of the resolution for voluntary winding up referred to by section 84(3),

(b) evidence of his appointment as liquidator of the company, and

(c) a copy of the statement of affairs required under section 99.

7.62(4) **[Service not required]** It shall not be necessary to serve the application on, or give notice of it to, any person.

7.62(5) **[Confirmation]** On an application under this Rule the court may confirm the creditors' voluntary winding up.

7.62(6) **[Features of confirmation]** If the court confirms the creditor's voluntary winding up–

(a) it may do so without a hearing,

(b) it shall affix its seal to the application.

7.62(7) **[Authority]** A member of the court staff may deal with an application under this Rule.

7.62(8) **[Application of r.7.62]** This Rule shall also apply where a company has moved to a voluntary liquidation in accordance with paragraph 83 of Schedule B1 to the Act except that the material to be filed with the court under paragraph (3) must be a copy of the notice of moving from administration to creditors' voluntary liquidation sent by the administrator for the purposes of paragraph 83(3) that has been registered by the registrar of companies, together with the statement of affairs required under paragraph 47 of Schedule B1 to the Act.

GENERAL NOTE

Paragraph (8) was inserted by Insolvency (Amendment) Rules 2003 (SI 2003/1730). This extends the ambit of r.7.62 to cover cases where a company moves from new-style administration to voluntary liquidation. This mode of exit is likely to be widely used. Reworded by I(A)R 2010 (SI 2010/686)—see para.(8) in particular.

R.7.62(5)

The word "may" indicates that the grant of an order is discretionary, as was observed by Mr Registrar Baister in *Re TXU Europe German Finance BV* [2005] B.C.C. 90. In that case a confirming order was made only after assurances had been given satisfying the learned Registrar that foreign creditors would not be prejudiced. This leads to the question what the position would be if an order is refused. Since art.4(1) is expressed in mandatory terms, it must be the case that the Regulation will apply and that the insolvency will be conducted in accordance with the local (i.e. English) law. The liquidator's main problem is likely to be evidentiary and not substantive—in proving the liquidation and his own status to the authorities and other interested parties abroad, and in particular in securing a dissolution of the company if it is incorporated elsewhere. He would have the same difficulties if the Regulation did not apply.

7.63 Notice to member State liquidator and creditors in member States

7.63 Where the court has confirmed the creditors' voluntary winding up, the liquidator shall as soon as reasonably practicable give notice–

(a) if there is a member State liquidator in relation to the company, to the member State liquidator;

(b) in accordance with Article 40 of the EC Regulation (duty to inform creditors).

GENERAL NOTE

Chapter 10 (IR rr.7.62 and 7.63) was introduced by Insolvency (Amendment) Rules 2002 (SI 2002/1307) para.9(1) with effect from May 31, 2002 to cater for the introduction of EC Council Regulation 1346/2000 on Insolvency Proceedings. On the EC Regulation see Vol 2, p.125.

CHAPTER 11

EC REGULATION—MEMBER STATE LIQUIDATOR

7.64 Interpretation of creditor

7.64(1) [Application] This Rule applies where a member State liquidator has been appointed in relation to a person subject to insolvency proceedings other than proceedings relating to a debt relief order.

7.64(2) [Member State liquidator's rights to inspect, copy and appear] The member State liquidator has the same right to inspect or obtain from the court a copy of, or a copy of any document or documents contained in, the court file relating to the insolvency proceedings that is opened and maintained by the court under Rule 7.31A(1) as a creditor has under Rule 7.31A(3) and may appear at any hearing relating to those proceedings.

7.64(3) [Omitted.]

7.64(4) [Exercise of creditors' rights] Paragraph (2) is without prejudice to the generality of the right to participate referred to in paragraph 3 of Article 32 of the EC Regulation (exercise of creditor's rights).

GENERAL NOTE

Chapter 11 (IR r.7.64) was introduced via the same mechanism as Chapter 10 above and for a similar reason. The wording of para.(1) was added to by the Insolvency (Amendment) Rules 2009 (SI 2009/642) with effect from April 6, 2009.

   Substantially modified by I(A)R 2010 (SI 2010/686)—para.(2) reworked and para.(3) deleted.

PART 8

PROXIES AND COMPANY REPRESENTATION

8.1 Definition of "proxy"

8.1(1) [Definition] For the purposes of the Rules, a proxy is an authority given by a person (**"the principal"**) to another person (**"the proxy-holder"**) to attend a meeting and speak and vote as his representative.

[FORMS 8.1 to 8.5]

8.1(2) [Use of proxies] Proxies are for use at creditors', company or contributories' meetings summoned or called under the Act or the Rules.

8.1(3) [Giving proxies] Only one proxy may be given by a person for any one meeting at which he desires to be represented; and it may only be given to one person, being an individual aged 18 or over. But the principal may specify one or more other such individuals to be proxy-holder in the alternative, in the order in which they are named in the proxy.

8.1(4) [Chairman etc. as proxy-holder] Without prejudice to the generality of paragraph (3), a proxy for a particular meeting may be given to whoever is to be the chairman of the meeting; and for a meeting held as part of the proceedings in a winding up by the court, or in a bankruptcy, it may be given to the official receiver.

8.1(5) [Chairman etc. cannot decline] A person given a proxy under paragraph (4) cannot decline to be the proxy-holder in relation to that proxy.

8.1(6) [Conduct of proxy-holder] A proxy requires the holder to give the principal's vote on matters arising for determination at the meeting, or to abstain, or to propose, in the principal's name, a resolution to be voted on by the meeting, either as directed or in accordance with the holder's own discretion.

(See General Note after r.8.6.)

8.2   Issue and use of forms

8.2(1)   **[When forms are sent with notice]** When notice is given of a meeting to be held in insolvency proceedings, and forms of proxy are sent out with the notice, no form so sent out shall have inserted in it the name or description of any person.

8.2(2)   **[Forms of proxy]** No form of proxy shall be used at any meeting except that which is sent out with the notice summoning the meeting, or a substantially similar form.

8.2(3)   **[Proxy to be authenticated etc.]** A form of proxy shall be authenticated by the principal, or by some person authorised by him (either generally or with reference to a particular meeting). If the form is authenticated by a person other than the principal, the nature of the person's authority shall be stated.

(See General Note after r.8.6.)

8.3   Use of proxies at meetings

8.3(1)   **[Use at adjournment]** A proxy given for a particular meeting may be used at any adjournment of that meeting.

8.3(2)   **[Official receiver etc. as proxy-holder]** Where the official receiver holds proxies for use at any meeting, his deputy, or any other official receiver, may act as proxy-holder in his place.

Alternatively, the official receiver may in writing authorise another officer of the Department to act for him at the meeting and use the proxies as if that other officer were himself proxy-holder.

8.3(3)   **[Chairman etc. as proxy-holder]** Where the responsible insolvency practitioner holds proxies to be used by him as chairman of a meeting, and some other person acts as chairman, the other person may use the insolvency practitioner's proxies as if he were himself proxy-holder.

8.3(4)   **[Appointment of responsible insolvency practitioner]** Where a proxy directs a proxy-holder to vote for or against a resolution for the nomination or appointment of a person as the responsible insolvency practitioner, the proxy-holder may, unless the proxy states otherwise, vote for or against (as he thinks fit) any resolution for the nomination or appointment of that person jointly with another or others.

8.3(5)   **[Proposal by proxy-holder]** A proxy-holder may propose any resolution which, if proposed by another, would be a resolution in favour of which by virtue of the proxy he would be entitled to vote.

8.3(6)   **[Specific directions to proxy-holder]** Where a proxy gives specific directions as to voting, this does not, unless the proxy states otherwise, preclude the proxy-holder from voting at his discretion on resolutions put to the meeting which are not dealt with in the proxy.

GENERAL NOTE

Rules 8.3(4), (5) and (6) were inserted to improve the effectiveness of the proxy system allowing a proxy more discretion (if his principal desires).

(See General Note after r.8.6.)

8.4   Retention of proxies

8.4(1)   **[Chairman to retain proxies]** Subject as follows, proxies used for voting at any meeting shall be retained by the chairman of the meeting.

8.4(2)   **[Delivery]** The chairman shall deliver the proxies, as soon as reasonably practicable after the meeting, to the responsible insolvency practitioner (where that is someone other than himself).

(See General Note after r.8.6.)

8.5   Right of inspection

8.5(1)   **[Who may inspect]** The office-holder shall, so long as proxies lodged with him are in his hands, allow them to be inspected, at all reasonable times on any business day, by–

    (a)   the creditors, in the case of proxies used at a meeting of creditors, and

(b) a company's members or contributories, in the case of proxies used at a meeting of the company or of its contributories.

8.5(2)   [Who are r.8.5(1) creditors] The reference in paragraph (1) to creditors is–

(a) in the case of a company in liquidation or of an individual's bankruptcy, those creditors who have proved their debts, and

(b) in any other case, persons who have submitted in writing a claim to be creditors of the company or individual concerned;

but in neither case does it include a person whose proof or claim has been wholly rejected for purposes of voting, dividend or otherwise.

8.5(3)   [Who may also inspect] The right of inspection given by this Rule is also exercisable–

(a) in the case of an insolvent company, by its directors, and

(b) in the case of an insolvent individual, by him.

8.5(4)   [Person attending meeting] Any person attending a meeting in insolvency proceedings is entitled, immediately before or in the course of the meeting, to inspect proxies and associated documents (including proofs) sent or given, in accordance with directions contained in any notice convening the meeting, to the chairman of that meeting or to any other person by a creditor, member or contributory for the purpose of that meeting.

8.5(5)   [Confidentiality of documents] This Rule is subject to Rule 12A.51 (confidentiality of documents – grounds for refusing inspection).

(See General Note after r.8.6.) Note addition of new para.(5) by I(A)R 2010 (SI 2010/686).

8.6   Proxy-holder with financial interest

8.6(1)   [Limitation on voting by proxy-holder] A proxy-holder shall not vote in favour of any resolution which would directly or indirectly place him, or any associate of his, in a position to receive any remuneration out of the insolvent estate, unless the proxy specifically directs him to vote in that way.

8.6(1A)   [Written authorisation] Where a proxy-holder has authenticated the proxy as being authorised to do so by his principal and the proxy specifically directs him to vote in the way mentioned in paragraph (1), he shall nevertheless not vote in that way unless he produces to the chairman of the meeting written authorisation from his principal sufficient to show that the proxy-holder was entitled so to authenticate the proxy.

8.6(2)   [Application of Rule] This Rule applies also to any person acting as chairman of a meeting and using proxies in that capacity under Rule 8.3; and in its application to him, the proxy-holder is deemed an associate of his.

General Note to rr.8.1–8.6.

The use of proxies in insolvency proceedings is fairly strictly controlled by these rules. For the meaning of "associate" in r.8.6, see IA 1986 s.435. Rule 8.6(1A) was added to r.8.6 to restrict the possibility of a proxy profiting from his position unless expressly authorised to do so by his principal. A faxed form of proxy may be accepted for the purposes of these rules: *IR Commrs v Conbeer* [1996] B.C.C. 189.

In accordance with general principles, a proxy may be varied or revoked by the party who has given it at any time prior to the relevant meeting or decision: *Re Cardona, IR Commrs v Cardona* [1997] B.C.C. 697.

8.7   Company representation

8.7(1)   [Production of copy of resolution] Where a person is authorised to represent a corporation at a meeting of creditors or of the company or its contributories, he shall produce to the chairman of the meeting a copy of the resolution from which he derives his authority.

8.7(2) **[Copy of resolution to be sealed or certified]** The copy resolution must be under the seal of the corporation, or certified by the secretary or a director of the corporation to be a true copy.

8.7(3) **[Authority to authenticate proxy]** Nothing in this Rule requires the authority of a person to authenticate a proxy on behalf of a principal which is a corporation to be in the form of a resolution of that corporation.

GENERAL NOTE

Rule 8.7(3) was added to r.8.7 to remove any doubt regarding the formality for a corporate proxy. See I(A)R 2010 (SI 2010/686).

8.8 Interpretation of creditor

8.8(1) **[Application]** This Rule applies where a member State liquidator has been appointed in relation to a person subject to insolvency proceedings.

8.8(2) **[Interpretation]** For the purposes of rule 8.5(1) (right of inspection of proxies) a member State liquidator appointed in main proceedings is deemed to be a creditor.

8.8(3) **[Exercise of creditors' rights]** Paragraph (2) is without prejudice to the generality of the right to participate referred to in paragraph 3 of Article 32 of the EC Regulation (exercise of creditor's rights).

GENERAL NOTE

IR r.8.8 was introduced by Insolvency (Amendment) Rules 2002 (SI 2002/1307) para.9(2) with effect from May 31, 2002 to cater for the advent of the EC Council Regulation 1346/2000 on Insolvency Proceedings. On the EC Regulation see Vol 2, p.125.

PART 9

EXAMINATION OF PERSONS CONCERNED IN COMPANY AND INDIVIDUAL INSOLVENCY

9.1 Preliminary

9.1(1) **[Application of Pt 9 Rules]** The Rules in this Part apply to applications to the court for an order under–

(a) section 236 (inquiry into company's dealings),

(b) section 251N (debt relief orders – inquiry into dealings and property of debtor), or

(c) section 366 (inquiry into bankruptcy, with respect to the bankrupt's dealings – including section 366 as it applies by virtue of section 368).

9.1(2) **[Definitions]** The following definitions apply–

(a) the person in respect of whom an order is applied for is "the respondent";

(b) "the applicable section" is section 236, 251N or 366, according to whether the affairs of a company or those of a debtor in relation to a debt relief order or an application for a debt relief order or a bankrupt or (where the application under section 366 is made by virtue of section 368) a debtor in bankruptcy proceedings are in question;

(c) the company or, as the case may be, the debtor in relation to a debt relief order or an application for a debt relief order, the bankrupt or debtor in bankruptcy proceedings concerned is "the insolvent";

(d) "the applicant", in any application made under section 251N, means the official receiver.

(See General Note after r.9.6.) Amendments are made to paras (1) and (2) by the Insolvency (Amendment) Rules 2009 (SI 2009/642) with effect from April 6, 2009. A new para.(1) has been substituted by I(A)R 2010 (SI 2010/686).

9.2   Form and contents of application

9.2(1)   [In writing, specify grounds] The application shall be in writing and specify the grounds on which it is made.

9.2(2)   [Name of respondent] The application must specify the name of the respondent.

9.2(3)   [Purpose to be stated] It shall be stated whether the application is for the respondent–

    (a)   to be ordered to appear before the court, or

    (b)   to be ordered to clarify any matter which is in dispute in the proceedings or to give additional information in relation to any such matter and if so CPR Part 18 (further information) shall apply to any such order, or

    (c)   to submit witness statements (if so, particulars to be given of the matters to be included), or

    (d)   to produce books, papers or other records (if so, the items in question to be specified),

or for any two or more of those purposes.

9.2(4)   [Without notice application] The application may be made without notice to any other party.

GENERAL NOTE

The circumstances under which an order can be made under IR 9.2(4) are to be determined by case law—*Hill v Van der Merwe* [2007] EWHC 1613 (Ch); [2007] B.P.I.R. 1562. Rule 9.2(3)(b) substituted by the Insolvency (Amendment) (No.2) Rules 1999 (SI 1999/1022) r.3, Sch. para.9 as from April 26, 1999. Reworded by I(A)R 2010 (SI 2010/686).

(See also General Note after r.9.6.)

9.3   Order for examination, etc.

9.3(1)   [Powers of court] The court may, whatever the purpose of the application, make any order which it has power to make under the applicable section.

9.3(2)   [Venue] The court, if it orders the respondent to appear before it, shall specify a venue for his appearance, which shall be not less than 14 days from the date of the order.

9.3(3)   [Order to submit witness statements] If he is ordered to submit witness statements, the order shall specify–

    (a)   the matters which are to be dealt with in his witness statements, and

    (b)   the time within which they are to be submitted to the court.

9.3(4)   [Order to produce books etc.] If the order is to produce books, papers or other records, the time and manner of compliance shall be specified.

9.3(5)   [Service] The order must be served as soon as reasonably practicable on the respondent; and it must be served personally, unless the court otherwise orders.

GENERAL NOTE

For the meaning of "venue" see r.13.6. Modernised by I(A)R 2010 (SI 2010/686).
    (See also General Note after r.9.6.)

9.4 Procedure for examination

9.4(1) [Applicant may attend etc.] At any examination of the respondent, the applicant may attend in person, or be represented by a solicitor with or without counsel, and may put such questions to the respondent as the court may allow.

9.4(2) [Other attendances etc.] Unless the applicant objects, the following persons may attend the examination with the permission of the court and may put questions to the respondent (but only through the applicant)–

    (a) any person who could have applied for an order under the applicable section; and

    (b) any creditor who has provided information on which the application was made under section 236 or 366.

9.4(3) [Clarification, additional information] If the respondent is ordered to clarify any matter or to give additional information, the court shall direct him as to the questions which he is required to answer, and as to whether his answers (if any) are to be made in a witness statement.

9.4(4) [Omitted.]

9.4(5) [Representation of respondent] The respondent may at his own expense employ a solicitor with or without counsel, who may put to him such questions as the court may allow for the purpose of enabling him to explain or qualify any answers given by him, and may make representations on his behalf.

9.4(6) [Record of examination] There shall be made in writing such record of the examination as the court thinks proper. The record shall be read over either to or by the respondent and authenticated by him at a venue fixed by the court.

9.4(7) [Record as evidence] The written record may, in any proceedings (whether under the Act or otherwise) be used as evidence against the respondent of any statement made by him in the course of his examination.

(See General Note after r.9.6.) IR 1986 r.9.4(3) was replaced by Insolvency (Amendment) (No.2) Rules 1999 (SI 1999/1022) with effect from April 26, 1999. I(A)R 2010 (SI 2010/686) substitutes a new para.(2) and deletes para.(4).

9.5 Record of examination

9.5(1) [Record, witness statements not to be filed] Unless the court otherwise directs, the written record of questions put to the respondent and the respondent's answers, and any witness statements submitted by the respondent in compliance with an order of the court under the applicable section, are not to be filed with the court.

9.5(2) [Who may inspect documents without court order] The documents set out in paragraph (3) are not open to inspection without an order of the court, by any person other than–

    (a) the applicant for an order under the applicable section, or

    (b) any person who could have applied for such an order in respect of the affairs of the same insolvent.

9.5(3) [Documents in r.9.5(2)] The documents to which paragraph (2) applies are–

    (a) the written record of the respondent's examination;

    (b) copies of questions put to the respondent or proposed to be put to the respondent and answers to questions given by the respondent;

    (c) any witness statement by the respondent; and

(d)   any document on the court file as shows the grounds for the application for an order.

9.5(4)   **[Powers of court]** The court may from time to time give directions as to the custody and inspection of any documents to which this Rule applies, and as to the furnishing of copies of, or extracts from, such documents.

(See General Note after r.9.6.) Substantially redrafted by I(A)R 2010 (SI 2010/686).

9.6   Costs of proceedings under ss.236, 251N and 366

9.6(1)   **[Power of court]** Where the court has ordered an examination of any person under the applicable section, and it appears to it that the examination was made necessary because information had been unjustifiably refused by the respondent, it may order that the costs of the examination be paid by him.

9.6(2)   **[Further power]** Where the court makes an order against a person under–

(a)   section 237(1) or 367(1) (to deliver up property in his possession which belongs to the insolvent), or

(b)   section 237(2) or 367(2) (to pay any amount in discharge of a debt due to the insolvent),

the costs of the application for the order may be ordered by the court to be paid by the respondent.

9.6(3)   **[Applicant's costs]** Subject to paragraphs (1) and (2) above, the applicant's costs shall, unless the court otherwise orders be paid–

(a)   in relation to a company insolvency, as an expense of the liquidation,

(b)   in relation to an individual insolvency, but not in proceedings relating to debt relief orders or applications for debt relief orders, out of the bankrupt's estate or (as the case may be) the debtor's property.

9.6(4)   **[Travelling expenses etc.]** A person summoned to attend for examination under this Chapter shall be tendered a reasonable sum in respect of travelling expenses incurred in connection with his attendance. Other costs falling on him are at the court's discretion.

9.6(5)   **[No order against official receiver]** Where the examination is on the application of the official receiver otherwise than in the capacity of liquidator or trustee, no order shall be made for the payment of costs by him.

GENERAL NOTE TO RR.9.1–9.6

Rules 9.2(3)(b) and 9.4(3) were substituted by the Insolvency (Amendment) (No.2) Rules 1999 (SI 1999/1022) as from April 26, 1999, to coincide with the introduction of the CPR.

The examinations authorised by IA 1986 ss.236, 366, to which this Part refers, are private examinations, in contrast to the public examinations which may be ordered under IA 1986 ss.133, 134 and 290. For further discussion, see notes to those sections, and for the rules applicable in the latter case, see rr.4.211 et seq. In addition, ss.237 and 367, referred to in r.9.6, empower the court to order a person to deliver up property to the liquidator or other office holder, or to pay money in discharge of a debt.

The explanatory words "when it is, or is alleged to be, insolvent" in r.9.1(1)(a) are misleading. For the circumstances in which ss.236 applies, reference should be made to ss.236(1) and 234(1).

Under the former winding-up rules, it was the practice for an applicant seeking an order to support his application by a memorandum which was required to be verified by affidavit in every case except where the applicant, as a liquidator, was an officer of the court. Rule 9.2(1) has abolished this distinction, so that an unsworn statement is now sufficient in all cases. The statement is confidential: *Re Aveling Barford Ltd* [1989] 1 W.L.R. 360; (1988) 4 B.C.C. 548; but (in a departure from the previous practice) the court may order that it be disclosed in whole or in part to the person against whom the order is sought in a proper case: see the note to s.236.

An order requiring a person to give "an account of full particulars of all dealings" by him with the company may be open to objection on the grounds that it lacks the particularity called for by rr.9.2(3)(c) and 9.3(3)(a): *Re Aveling Barford Ltd* (above). It was held in the same case that the phrase "a person summoned to attend for examination under this Chapter" in r.9.6(4) includes a person required to give information by the alternative methods permitted under s.236. On the question of the examinee's costs, Hoffmann J. declined to make an order in advance or to say that there should be a presumption in favour of allowing costs, over and above the travelling expenses mentioned in r.9.6(4).

For comments on the exercise of the discretion conferred on the court by r.9.5(4), see *Hamilton v Naviede, Re Arrows Ltd (No.4)* [1995] 2 A.C. 75; [1994] B.C.C. 641.

There was an amendment made to IR r.9.6(3) introduced by the Insolvency (Amendment) Rules 2008 (SI 2008/737) with effect from April 6, 2008 to cater for the insertion of new rr.4.218A–4.218E.

For determination of costs under r.9.6 see Registrar Jaques in *Hunt v Renzland* [2008] B.P.I.R. 1380, where the point was made that there was a need to distinguish between the treatment of the costs of obtaining the order for the private examination and the costs of the examination itself.

The Insolvency (Amendment) Rules 2009 (SI 2009/642) (effective April 6, 2009) make a change to the heading of r.9.6 by inserting specific mention to s.251N and by including reference to debt relief orders in para.(3)(b).

See also I(A)R 2010 (SI 2010/686).

PART 10

OFFICIAL RECEIVERS

Introductory note to Part 10
The rules in this Part supplement IA 1986 ss.399–401.

10.1   Appointment of official receivers

10.1   Judicial notice shall be taken of the appointment under sections 399 to 401 of official receivers and deputy official receivers.

10.2   Persons entitled to act on official receiver's behalf

10.2(1)   [In absence of official receiver] In the absence of the official receiver authorised to act in a particular case, an officer authorised in writing for the purpose by the Secretary of State, or by the official receiver himself, may, with the permission of the court, act on the official receiver's behalf and in his place–

(a)   in any examination under section 133, 236, 251N, 290 or 366, and

(b)   in respect of any application to the court.

10.2(2)   [In case of emergency] In case of emergency, where there is no official receiver capable of acting, anything to be done by, to or before the official receiver may be done by, to or before the registrar or district judge.

GENERAL NOTE

The possibility of a person acting on behalf of the official receiver would appear to be in addition to the appointment of a deputy under IA 1986 s.401. Note the change made by the Insolvency (Amendment) Rules 2009 (SI 2009/642) with effect from April 6, 2009. This change merely involves specific reference to s.251N. Note minor change to para.(2) made by I(A)R 2010 (SI 2010/686).

10.3   Application for directions

10.3   The official receiver may apply to the court for directions in relation to any matter arising in insolvency proceedings.

GENERAL NOTE

This is a standard facility for all insolvency practitioners.

10.4   Official receiver's expenses

10.4(1)   ["Expenses"] Any expenses incurred by the official receiver (in whatever capacity he may be acting) in connection with proceedings taken against him in insolvency proceedings are to be treated as expenses of the insolvency proceedings.

"Expenses" includes damages.

10.4(2)   [Official receiver's charge except re debt relief order] In respect of any sums due to him under paragraph (1) in connection with insolvency proceedings other than proceedings relating to debt relief orders or applications for debt relief orders, the official receiver has a charge on the insolvent estate.

GENERAL NOTE

Note the wide definition of "expenses". Note the Insolvency (Amendment) Rules 2009 (SI 2009/642) which, from April 6, 2009, have supplemented the wording of para.(2) by including exclusionary reference to debt relief issues.

PART 11

DECLARATION AND PAYMENT OF DIVIDEND (WINDING UP AND BANKRUPTCY)

Introductory note to Part 11
The rules in this Part are to be viewed in light of the provisions of IA 1986—e.g. see ss.324 and 330.
    Note that I(A)R 2010 generally replaces references to "insolvency practitioner" with "office-holder".

11.1   Preliminary

11.1(1)   [Application of Pt 11 Rules] The Rules in this Part relate to the declaration and payment of dividends in companies winding up and in bankruptcy.

11.1(2)   [Definitions] The following definitions apply–

   (a)   **"the insolvent"** means the company in liquidation or, as the case may be, the bankrupt; and

   (b)   **"creditors"** means those creditors of the insolvent of whom the office-holder is aware.

11.1(3)   [Interpretation] For the purposes of this Part, a member State liquidator appointed in relation to an insolvent is deemed to be a creditor.

GENERAL NOTE

IR r.11.1(3) was inserted by Insolvency (Amendment) Rules 2002 (SI 2002/1307) para.10(1) with effect from May 31, 2002 to cater for the advent of EC Council Regulation 1346/2000 on Insolvency Proceedings. On the EC Regulation see Vol 2, p.125.

11.2   Notice of intended dividend

11.2(1)   [Before declaring dividend] Before declaring a dividend, the office-holder shall give notice of his intention to do so

   (a)   to all creditors whose addresses are known to him and who have not proved their debts, and

   (b)   where a member State liquidator has been appointed in relation to the insolvent, to that person.

11.2(1A)   [Notice of dividend by gazetting/advertisement] Before declaring a first dividend the office-holder shall give notice of the intended dividend. As soon as reasonably practicable such notice–

   (a)   shall be gazetted; and

   (b)   may be advertised in such other manner as the office-holder thinks fit.

11.2(1B)   [Non-application of r.11.2(1A)] Paragraph (1A) shall not apply where the office-holder has previously, by notice which has been gazetted, invited creditors to prove their debts.

11.2(1C)   **[Additional contents of r.11.2(1A) notice]** In addition to the standard contents, a notice under paragraph (1A) must–

  (a)   state that the office-holder intends to declare a first dividend; and

  (b)   specify the date by which and place at which proofs must be lodged.

11.2(2)   **["The last date for proving"]** Any notice under paragraph (1) and any notice of a first dividend under paragraph (1A) shall specify a date ("the last date for proving") up to which proofs may be lodged. The date shall be the same for all creditors, and not less than 21 days from that of the notice.

11.2(3)   **[Contents of notice]** The office-holder shall in the notice state his intention to declare a dividend (specified as interim or final, as the case may be) within the period of 2 months from the last date for proving.

GENERAL NOTE

This is to give tardy creditors a last chance to lodge their proofs. On late proof of debts see *Painter v Hutchison* [2007] EWHC 758 (Ch); [2008] B.P.I.R. 170.

   Notice need only be given under r.11.2(1) to known creditors or member state liquidator—this latter requirement was introduced by Insolvency (Amendment) Rules 2002 (SI 2002/1307) para.10(2) with effect from May 31, 2002 to cater for the advent of EC Council Regulation 1346/2000 on Insolvency Proceedings. Note that the Insolvency (Amendment) Rules 2009 (SI 2009/642) with effect from April 6, 2009 have modified this provision by substituting a new para.(1A) and inserting para.(1B). Reworked by I(A)R 2010 (SI 2010/686)—new para.(1C) added and the period specified in para.(3) reduced from four to two months.

11.3   Final admission/rejection of proofs

11.3(1)   **[Dealing with every proof]** The office-holder shall, within 5 business days from the last date for proving, deal with every creditor's proof (in so far as not already dealt with) by admitting or rejecting it in whole or in part, or by making such provision as he thinks fit in respect of it.

11.3(2)   **[Proofs lodged out of time]** The office-holder is not obliged to deal with proofs lodged after the last date for proving; but he may do so, if he thinks fit.

11.3(3)   **[Declaration of dividend]** In the declaration of a dividend no payment shall be made more than once by virtue of the same debt.

11.3(4)   **[Payment]** Subject to Rule 11.11, where–

  (a)   a creditor has proved, and

  (b)   a member State liquidator has proved in relation to the same debt,

payment shall only be made to the creditor.

GENERAL NOTE

Late proofs may be accepted at the discretion of the office-holder. With regard to late proof of debts see *Painter v Hutchison* [2007] EWHC 758 (Ch); [2008] B.P.I.R. 170. Rules 11.3(3) and (4) were inserted by the Insolvency (Amendment) Rules 2002 (SI 2002/1307) para.10(3) with effect from May 31, 2002 to cater for the advent of EC Council Regulation 1346/2000 on Insolvency Proceedings. In para.(1) note the change from seven to five business days made by I(A)R 2010 (SI 2010/686).

11.4   Postponement or cancellation of dividend

11.4   If in the period of 2 months referred to in Rule 11.2(3)–

  (a)   the office-holder has rejected a proof in whole or in part and application is made to the court for his decision to be reversed or varied, or

(b)   application is made to the court for the office-holder's decision on a proof to be reversed or varied, or for a proof to be expunged, or for a reduction of the amount claimed,

the office-holder may postpone or cancel the dividend.

GENERAL NOTE

An application to the court to have the decision of the office-holder on the admission or rejection of proofs varied is made, in the case of a winding up, under r.4.83(1) or (2) and in a bankruptcy, under r.6.105(1) or (2). There is a time-limit of 21 days in each case. If such an application has been made, the office-holder may postpone or cancel the dividend under this rule; but, if he proposes to pay a dividend, r.11.5(2) applies. The period has been reduced from four to two months by I(A)R 2010 (SI 2010/686).

11.5   Decision to declare dividend

11.5(1)   [Proceeding to declare dividend] If the office-holder has not, in the 2-month period referred to in Rule 11.2(3), had cause to postpone or cancel the dividend, he shall within that period proceed to declare the dividend of which he gave notice under that Rule.

11.5(2)   [Pending application re proof etc.] Except with the permission of the court, the office-holder shall not declare the dividend so long as there is pending any application to the court to reverse or vary a decision of his on a proof, or to expunge a proof or to reduce the amount claimed.

If the court gives permission under this paragraph, the office-holder shall make such provision in respect of the proof in question as the court directs.

GENERAL NOTE

If no application has been made to the court to challenge a decision on the admission or rejection of a proof, the dividend must be declared within the two-month period. If the office-holder wishes to declare an interim dividend pending the outcome of such an application, the leave of the court is required under r.11.5(2). Where this rule applies, the normal rules as to the payment of interim dividends (IA 1986 s.324, IR 1986 rr.4.180, 4.182) are displaced. For discussion see *Lomax Leisure Ltd v Miller* [2008] EWCA Civ 525; [2008] B.C.C. 686 where the point was made that the liquidator's obligations under IR r.11.5 with regard to payment of a declared dividend must be taken as being subject to his overriding duties under IR r.4.180 to ensure a proper distribution of assets. See I(A)R 2010 (SI 2010/686)—period in para.(1) reduced to two months.

11.6   Notice of declaration

11.6(1)   [Notice to all creditors who have proved] The office-holder shall give notice of the dividend to

(a)   all creditors who have proved their debts, and

(b)   where a member State liquidator has been appointed in relation to the insolvent, to that person.

11.6(2)   [Particulars in notice] The notice shall include the following particulars relating to the insolvency and the administration of the insolvent estate–

(a)   amounts realised from the sale of assets, indicating (so far as practicable) amounts raised by the sale of particular assets;

(b)   payments made by the office-holder in the administration of the insolvent estate;

(c)   provision (if any) made for unsettled claims, and funds (if any) retained for particular purposes;

(d)   the total amount to be distributed, and the rate of dividend;

(e)   whether, and if so when, any further dividend is expected to be declared.

11.6(2A)   [Value of prescribed part for unsecured creditors] Where, in a winding up other than a members' voluntary winding up, the liquidator proposes to declare a dividend to unsecured creditors, the notice must also state the value of the prescribed part, except where the court has made an order under section 176A(5).

11.6(3)   [Simultaneous distribution] The dividend may be distributed simultaneously with the notice declaring it.

11.6(4)   [Method of payment] Payment of dividend may be made by post, or arrangements may be made with any creditor for it to be paid to him in another way, or held for his collection.

11.6(5)   [Endorsement in negotiable instrument] Where a dividend is paid on a bill of exchange or other negotiable instrument, the amount of the dividend shall be endorsed on the instrument, or on a certified copy of it, if required to be produced by the holder for that purpose.

GENERAL NOTE

Creditors are to receive full information relating to the payment of dividends, etc. IR 1986 r.11.6(1) was expanded by Insolvency (Amendment) Rules 2002 (SI 2002/1307) para.10(4) with effect from May 31, 2002 to cater for the advent of EC Council Regulation 1346/2000 on Insolvency Proceedings. New para.(2A) inserted by I(A)R 2010 (SI 2010/686).

11.7   Notice of no, or no further, dividend

11.7   If the office-holder gives notice to creditors that he is unable to declare any dividend or (as the case may be) any further dividend, the notice shall contain a statement to the effect either–

(a)   that no funds have been realised, or

(b)   that the funds realised have already been distributed or used or allocated for defraying the expenses of administration.

11.8   Proof altered after payment of dividend

11.8(1)   [If amount claimed in proof increased] If after payment of dividend the amount claimed by a creditor in his proof is increased, the creditor is not entitled to disturb the distribution of the dividend; but he is entitled to be paid, out of any money for the time being available for the payment of any further dividend, any dividend or dividends which he has failed to receive.

11.8(2)   [Payments under r.11.8(1)] Any dividend or dividends payable under paragraph (1) shall be paid before the money there referred to is applied to the payment of any such further dividend.

11.8(3)   [Proof withdrawn etc.] If, after a creditor's proof has been admitted, the proof is withdrawn or expunged, or the amount of it is reduced, the creditor is liable to repay to the office-holder, for the credit of the insolvent estate, any amount overpaid by way of dividend.

GENERAL NOTE

Here we have a "heads I win, tails you lose" situation.

11.9   Secured creditors

11.9(1)   [Application of Rule] The following applies where a creditor re-values his security at a time when a dividend has been declared.

11.9(2)   [Reduction of unsecured claim] If the revaluation results in a reduction of his unsecured claim ranking for dividend, the creditor shall as soon as reasonably practicable repay to the office-holder, for the credit of the insolvent estate, any amount received by him as dividend in excess of that to which he would be entitled having regard to the revaluation of the security.

11.9(3)   [Increase of unsecured claim] If the revaluation results in an increase of his unsecured claim, the creditor is entitled to receive from the office-holder, out of any money for the time being available for the payment of a further dividend, before any such further dividend is paid, any dividend or dividends which he has failed to receive, having regard to the revaluation of the security.

However, the creditor is not entitled to disturb any dividend declared (whether or not distributed) before the date of the revaluation.

GENERAL NOTE

This again shows that the law will not disturb dividends that have already been declared.

11.10 Disqualification from dividend

11.10 If a creditor contravenes any provision of the Act or the Rules relating to the valuation of securities, the court may, on the application of the office-holder, order that the creditor be wholly or partly disqualified from participation in any dividend.

GENERAL NOTE

This is a useful sanction.

11.11 Assignment of right to dividend

11.11(1) **[Notice of assignment etc.]** If a person entitled to a dividend gives notice to the office-holder that he wishes the dividend to be paid to another person, or that he has assigned his entitlement to another person, the office-holder shall pay the dividend to that other accordingly.

11.11(2) **[Contents of notice]** A notice given under this Rule must specify the name and address of the person to whom payment is to be made.

GENERAL NOTE

The right to receive a dividend can be assigned.

11.12 Preferential creditors

11.12(1) **[Application of Pt 11 Rules]** Subject as follows, the Rules in this Part apply with respect to any distribution made in the insolvency to preferential creditors, with such adaptations as are appropriate considering that such creditors are of a limited class.

11.12(2) **[Rule 11.2 notice]** The notice by the office-holder under Rule 11.2, where a dividend is to be declared for preferential creditors, need only be given to those creditors in whose case he has reason to believe that their debts are preferential and notice of the intended dividend need only be gazetted if the office-holder thinks fit.

GENERAL NOTE

This makes necessary modifications to the above rules where the declaration is for the benefit of preferential creditors—see IA 1986 Pt XII. Note minor terminological changes made to para.(2) by I(A)R 2010 (SI 2010/686).

11.13 Debt payable at future time

11.13(1) **[Entitlement to dividend]** Where a creditor has proved for a debt of which payment is not due at the date of the declaration of dividend, he is entitled to dividend equally with other creditors, but subject as follows.

11.13(2) **[Calculation of amount of reduction]** For the purpose of dividend (and no other purpose) the amount of the creditor's admitted proof (or, if a distribution has previously been made to him, the amount remaining outstanding in respect of his admitted proof) shall be reduced by applying the following formula–

$$\frac{X}{1.05^n}$$

where

(a) "X" is the value of the admitted proof, and

(b) "n" is the period beginning with the relevant date and ending with the date on which the payment of the creditor's debt would otherwise be due expressed in years and months in a decimalised form.

11.13(3)   **[Relevant date]** In paragraph (2) "relevant date" means–

(a) in the case of a winding up which was not immediately preceded by an administration, the date that the company went into liquidation;

(b) in the case of a winding up which was immediately preceded by an administration, the date that the company entered administration; and

(c) in the case of a bankruptcy, the date of the bankruptcy order.

GENERAL NOTE

Rule 11.13 was substantially modified by the Insolvency (Amendment) Rules 2005 (SI 2005/527) to reformulate the mathematical calculation used for discounting future debts. This reformulation was in response to criticism made in the House of Lords in *Re Park Air Services plc* [2000] 2 A.C. 172 of the previous calculation methodology.

PART 12

MISCELLANEOUS AND GENERAL

12.1 Power of Secretary of State to regulate certain matters

12.1(1)   **[Power to make regulations]** Pursuant to paragraph 27 of Schedule 8 to the Act, and paragraph 30 of Schedule 9 to the Act, the Secretary of State may, subject to the Act and the Rules, make regulations with respect to any matter provided for in the Rules as relates to the carrying out of the functions of a liquidator, provisional liquidator, administrator or administrative receiver of a company, an interim receiver appointed under section 286, of the official receiver while acting as receiver or manager under section 287 or of a trustee of a bankrupt's estate, including, without prejudice to the generality of the foregoing, provision with respect to the following matters arising in companies winding up and individual bankruptcy–

(a) the preparation and keeping by liquidators, trustees, provisional liquidators, interim receivers and the official receiver, of books, accounts and other records, and their production to such persons as may be authorised or required to inspect them.

(b) the auditing of liquidators' and trustees' accounts;

(c) the manner in which liquidators and trustees are to act in relation to the insolvent company's or bankrupt's books, papers and other records, and the manner of their disposal by the office-holder or others;

(d) the supply–

    (i) in company insolvency, by the liquidator to creditors and members of the company, contributories in its winding up and the liquidation committee, and

    (ii) in bankruptcy, by the trustee to creditors and the creditors' committee, of copies of documents relating to the insolvency and the affairs of the insolvent company or individual (on payment, in such cases as may be specified by the regulations, of the specified fee);

(e)   the manner in which insolvent estates are to be distributed by liquidators and trustees, including provision with respect to unclaimed funds and dividends;

(f)   the manner in which moneys coming into the hands of a liquidator or trustee in the course of his administration are to be handled and invested, and the payment of interest on sums which, in pursuance of regulations made by virtue of this sub-paragraph, have been paid into the Insolvency Service Account;

(g)   the amount (or the manner of determining the amount) to be paid to the official receiver by way of remuneration when acting as provisional liquidator, liquidator, interim receiver or trustee.

12.1(2)   [Reference to trustee in r.12.1(1)] Any reference in paragraph (1) to a trustee includes a reference to the official receiver when acting as receiver and manager under section 287.

12.1(3)   [Contents of regulations] Regulations made pursuant to paragraph (1) may–

(a)   confer a discretion on the court;

(b)   make non-compliance with any of the regulations a criminal offence;

(c)   make different provision for different cases, including different provision for different areas; and

(d)   contain such incidental, supplemental and transitional provisions as may appear to the Secretary of State necessary or expedient.

GENERAL NOTE

This clarifies the power of the Secretary of State to make regulations to supplement the existing framework. Rule 12.1(1)(f) was amended by the Insolvency (Amendment) Rules 2001 (SI 2001/763) as from April 2, 2001 to cater for changes made by the Insolvency Act 2000. The Insolvency (Amendment) Rules 2009 (SI 2009/642) from April 6, 2009 have modified this provision by replacing the reference to "individual insolvency" in para.(1)(d)(ii) with a reference to "bankruptcy".

The limitations of IR r.12.1 have been exposed recently with regard to the introduction of the new reg.36A into the Insolvency Regulations 1994, a measure which seeks to provide a transparency mechanism with regard to time spent by office holders on cases. It seems that r.12.1 does not authorise regulations to be made with regard to nominees and supervisors of voluntary arrangements as they are not specifically mentioned therein—for background on this lacuna see R3 Technical Bulletin 73.2.

12.2   Costs, expenses, etc.

12.2(1)   [Incidence of costs etc.] All fees, costs, charges and other expenses incurred in the course of winding up, administration or bankruptcy proceedings are to be regarded as expenses of the winding up or the administration or, as the case may be, of the bankruptcy.

12.2(2)   [Prescribed part costs] The costs associated with the prescribed part shall be paid out of the prescribed part.

GENERAL NOTE

Instalments of rates on non-domestic property which fell due for payment after the liquidation date were held to be liquidation expenses in *Re Nolton Business Centres Ltd* [1996] B.C.C. 500, even though the local authority had fixed the rates prior to that date. Amendments were made by Insolvency (Amendment) Rules 2003 (SI 2003/1730) to reflect the more expanded role of administration as a distributional regime and the coming into operation of the reserved fund for unsecured creditors (see IA 1986 s.176A). Costs incurred with regard to the latter come exclusively out of that fund. For the meaning of "costs" in IR r.12.2(2) see H.H.J. Purle Q.C. in *Re International Sections Ltd* [2009] B.P.I.R. 297 at [16].

12.3 Provable debts

12.3(1) [What is provable] Subject as follows, in administration, winding up and bankruptcy, all claims by creditors are provable as debts against the company or, as the case may be, the bankrupt, whether they are present or future, certain or contingent, ascertained or sounding only in damages.

12.3(2) [What is not provable] The following are not provable–

(a) in bankruptcy, any fine imposed for an offence, and any obligation (other than an obligation to pay a lump sum or to pay costs) arising under an order made in family proceedings or any obligation arising under a maintenance assessment made under the Child Support Act 1991;

(b) in administration, winding up or bankruptcy, any obligation arising under a confiscation order made under section 1 of the Drug Trafficking Offences Act 1986 or section 1 of the Criminal Justice (Scotland) Act 1987 or section 71 of the Criminal Justice Act 1988 or under Parts 2, 3 or 4 of the Proceeds of Crime Act 2002.

"Fine" and **"family proceedings"** have the meanings given by section 281(8) of the Act (which applies the Magistrates' Courts Act 1980 and the Matrimonial and Family Proceedings Act 1984).

12.3(2A) [Postponed debts] The following are not provable except at a time when all other claims of creditors in the insolvency proceedings (other than any of a kind mentioned in this paragraph) have been paid in full with interest under section 189(2), Rule 2.88 or, as the case may be, section 328(4)–

(a) in an administration, winding up or a bankruptcy, any claim arising by virtue of section 382(1)(a) of the Financial Services and Markets Act 2000, not being a claim also arising by virtue of section 382(1)(b) of that Act;

(c) in an administration or winding up, any claim which by virtue of the Act or any other enactment is a claim the payment of which in a bankruptcy, an administration or a winding up is to be postponed.

12.3(3) [Effect of Rule] Nothing in this Rule prejudices any enactment or rule of law under which a particular kind of debt is not provable, whether on grounds of public policy or otherwise.

GENERAL NOTE

This provision complements IA 1986, ss.322 and 382. It must be read in the light of r.13.12. This was modified by Insolvency (Amendment) Rules 2003 (SI 2003/1730) to reflect the wider role of administration where issues of proof of debt will now become relevant. Note also the changes necessitated by POCA 2002. Not all debts are provable debts: see the discussion in *Woodley v Woodley (No.2)* [1994] 1 W.L.R. 1167 at 1175. Note that fines are now regarded as not provable in a bankruptcy (reversing the former position as declared in *Re Pascoe* [1944] Ch. 310). The Cork Committee (Cmnd. 8558, para.1330) recommended that the law should be changed for all insolvency proceedings, but the legislators have done so only for bankruptcies.

Criminal compensation orders are viewed in like fashion and are non-provable—*R. v Barnet JJ Ex p. Phillippou* [1997] B.P.I.R. 134. Confiscation order liabilities are treated in similar fashion—IR 1986 r.6.223. On the other hand, tax penalties are provable—*Re Hurren* [1983] 1 W.L.R. 183; *Count Artsrunik v Waller* [2005] B.P.I.R. 82—as are penalties imposed by professional associations which may be characterised as contractual debts (*Marcus v Institute of Chartered Accountants* [2004] EWHC 3010 (Ch); [2005] B.P.I.R. 413).

Rule 12.3(2A) further restricts the categories of provable debt. Subparagraph (a) was replaced and (b) deleted by the Financial Services and Markets Act 2000 (Consequential Amendments and Repeals) Order 2001 (SI 2001/3649) art.380 with effect from December 1, 2001.

The legal status of r.12.3 came under consideration in the Court of Appeal in *Woodley v Woodley (No.2)* [1994] 1 W.L.R. 1167. Here the suggestion that r.12.3 might be ultra vires the 1986 Act was considered and then dismissed. Authority for it was based upon para.17 of Sch.9 to IA 1986 and ultimately upon s.412(2)(a). In spite of this reassuring finding the Court of Appeal suggested that the Insolvency Rules Committee should look at the question of whether lump-sum orders made in family proceedings should be restored as provable debts, which was the position before the 1986 rules came into effect. Costs orders in matrimonial proceedings fall within r.12.3(2)(a)—*Levy v Legal Services Commission* [2000] B.P.I.R. 1065. Note also *Wehmeyer v Wehmeyer* [2001] B.P.I.R. 548. Compare

Cadwell v Jackson [2001] B.P.I.R. 966. On r.12.3 and foreign family proceedings see *Cartwright v Cartwright* [2002] EWCA Civ 931; [2002] B.P.I.R. 895. The Court of Appeal restated its criticism of the fact that lump sums were not provable in *Ram v Ram* [2004] EWCA Civ 1452; [2005] B.P.I.R. 616. As a result of the intervention of the Insolvency Rules Committee the position on proving for lump sums and costs in family proceedings was finally changed by the Insolvency (Amendment) Rules 2005 (SI 2005/ 527). For background see C. Brougham, [2005] 18 Insolv. Int. 106.

Foreign tax debts provide an example of a debt which is regarded as non-provable on policy grounds: see *Government of India, Ministry of Finance (Revenue Division) v Taylor* [1955] A.C. 491 which is discussed by Miller in [1991] J.B.L. 144. See also *QRS 1 Aps v Frandsen* [1999] 1 W.L.R. 2169. This rule cannot be maintained where the EC Regulation on Insolvency Proceedings (1346/2000) applies.

On future tort claimants see *Re T & N Ltd* [2005] EWHC 2870 (Ch); [2006] B.P.I.R. 532 and the subsequent legislative reforms introduced by SI 2006/1272 to IR r.13.12.

For consideration of the possibility of protective awards ranking as provable debts see the Court of Appeal judgment in *Haine v Day* [2008] B.P.I.R. 1343.

12.4   Notices [Revoked.]

12.4A   Quorum at meeting of creditors or contributories [Revoked.]

12.5   Evidence of proceedings at meetings [Revoked.]

12.6   Documents issuing from Secretary of State [Revoked.]

12.7   Forms for use in insolvency proceedings [Revoked.]

12.8   Insolvency practitioner's security [Revoked.]

12.9   Time-limits [Revoked.]

12.10   Service by post [Revoked.]

12.11   General provisions as to service [Revoked.]

12.12   Service outside the jurisdiction [Revoked.]

12.13   Confidentiality of documents [Revoked.]

12.14   Notices sent simultaneously to the same person [Revoked.]

12.15   Right to copy documents [Revoked.]

12.15A   Charge for copy documents [Revoked.]

12.16   Non-receipt of notice of meeting [Revoked.]

12.17   Right to have list of creditors [Revoked.]

12.18   False claim of status as creditor, etc.

12.18(1)   **[Offence]** Where the Rules provide for creditors, members of a company or contributories in a company's winding up a right to inspect any documents, whether on the court's file or in the hands of an office-holder or other person, it is an offence for a person, with the intention of obtaining a sight of documents which he has not under the Rules any right to inspect, falsely to claim a status which would entitle him to inspect them.

12.18(2)   **[Penalties]** A person guilty of an offence under this Rule is liable to imprisonment or a fine, or both.

GENERAL NOTE

This is a useful deterrent to restrict bogus claims to inspect. For the appropriate penalty, see r.12.21 and Sch.5.

12.19   Execution overtaken by judgment debtor's insolvency [Revoked by I(A)R 2010 (SI 2010/686).]

12.20   The Gazette [Revoked by I(A)R 2010 (SI 2010/686).]

12.21   Punishment of offences

12.21(1)   [Effect of Sch.5] Schedule 5 to the Rules has effect with respect to the way in which contraventions of the Rules are punishable on conviction.

12.21(2)   [First, second and third columns of Schedule] In relation to an offence under a provision of the Rules specified in the first column of the Schedule (the general nature of the offence being described in the second column), the third column shows whether the offence is punishable on conviction on indictment, or on summary conviction, or either in the one way or the other.

12.21(3)   [Fourth column] The fourth column shows, in relation to an offence, the maximum punishment by way of fine or imprisonment which may be imposed on a person convicted of the offence in the way specified in relation to it in the third column (that is to say, on indictment or summarily), a reference to a period of years or months being to a term of imprisonment of that duration.

12.21(4)   [Fifth column] The fifth column shows (in relation to an offence for which there is an entry in that column) that a person convicted of the offence after continued contravention is liable to a daily default fine; that is to say, he is liable on a second or subsequent conviction of the offence to the fine specified in that column for each day on which the contravention is continued (instead of the penalty specified for the offence in the fourth column of the Schedule).

12.21(5)   [Application of s.431] Section 431 (summary proceedings), as it applies to England and Wales, has effect in relation to offences under the Rules as to offences under the Act.

GENERAL NOTE

This explains the mechanics of Sch.5. Note the connection with IA 1986 s.431 for summary proceedings.

12.22   Notice of order under section 176A(5) [Revoked by I(A)R 2010 (SI 2010/686).]

PART 12A

PROVISIONS OF GENERAL EFFECT

Introductory note to Part 12A
This Part, which was introduced by I(A)R 2010 (SI 2010/686) deals with a number of general but important issues. This Part deals with notices, the provision of information, use of electronic communications and websites, service of proceedings, meeting requirements, notices to enforcement officers, Forms, the *Gazette* and other advertisement procedures, time limits and the security required of insolvency practitioners. It thus draws upon fresh ideas, but equally its debt to a number of substituted provisions in Pt 12 is clear—see in particular the deleted rr.12.4–12.17, 12.19–12.20 and 12.22.

CHAPTER 1

THE GIVING OF NOTICE AND THE SUPPLY OF DOCUMENTS—GENERAL

12A.1   Application

12A.1(1)   [Application of Pt 12A Ch.1] Subject to paragraphs (2) and (3), this Chapter applies where a notice or other document is required to be given, delivered or sent under the Act or the Rules by any person, including an office-holder.

12A.1(2)   [Non-application of Pt 12A Ch.1] This Chapter does not apply to the service of–

(a)   any petition or application to the court;

(b)   any evidence in support of that petition or application; or

(c)   any order of the court.

12A.1(3)   [Further non-application] This Chapter does not apply to the submission of documents to the registrar of companies.

GENERAL NOTE

This defines the scope of Ch.1. Note exclusions in paras (2) and (3).

12A.2   Personal delivery of documents

12A.2   Personal delivery of a notice or other document is permissible in any case.

GENERAL NOTE

This confirms the acceptability of personal service.

12A.3   Postal delivery of documents

12A.3   Unless in any particular case some other form of delivery is required by the Act, the Rules or an order of the court, a notice or other document may be sent by post in accordance with the rules for postal service in CPR Part 6 and sending by such means has effect as specified in those rules.

GENERAL NOTE

This explains where postal service is permitted.

12A.4   Non-receipt of notice of meeting

12A.4   Where in accordance with the Act or the Rules, a meeting of creditors or other persons is summoned by notice, the meeting is presumed to have been duly summoned and held, notwithstanding that not all those to whom the notice is to be given have received it.

GENERAL NOTE

This is a useful concession. There are sufficient safety valves in the system in the event of a material irregularity.

12A.5   Notice etc. to solicitors

12A.5   Where under the Act or the Rules a notice or other document is required or authorised to be given, delivered or sent to a person, it may be given, delivered or sent instead to a solicitor authorised to accept delivery on that person's behalf.

GENERAL NOTE

Solicitors can be authorised to accept service.

CHAPTER 2

THE GIVING OF NOTICE AND THE SUPPLY OF DOCUMENTS BY OR TO OFFICE-HOLDERS ETC.

12A.6   Application

12A.6(1)   [Application of Pt 12A Ch.2] Subject to paragraphs (2) to (4), this Chapter applies where a notice or other document is required to be given, delivered or sent under the Act or the Rules.

12A.6(2) **[Non-application of Pt 12A Ch.2]** This Chapter does not apply to the submission of documents to the registrar of companies.

12A.6(3) **[Non-application of rr.12A.10–12A.13]** Rules 12A.10 to 12A.13 do not apply to–

(a)   the filing of any notice or other document with the court; or

(b)   the service of a statutory demand.

GENERAL NOTE

This outlines scope of Ch.2.

12A.7   The form of notices and other documents

12A.7   Subject to any order of the court, any notice or other document required to be given, delivered or sent must be in writing and where electronic delivery is permitted a notice or other document in electronic form is treated as being in writing if a copy of it is capable of being produced in a legible form.

GENERAL NOTE

This deals with format issues. Legibility is the critical requirement.

12A.8   Proof of sending etc.

12A.8(1) **[Certificate by office-holder]** Where in any insolvency proceedings a notice or other document is required to be given, delivered or sent by the office-holder, the giving, delivering or sending of it may be proved by means of a certificate that the notice or other document was duly given, delivered or sent.

12A.8(2) **[Official receiver]** In the case of the official receiver the certificate may be given by–

(a)   the official receiver; or

(b)   a member of the official receiver's staff.

12A.8(3) **[Responsible insolvency practitioner]** In the case of a responsible insolvency practitioner the certificate may be given by–

(a)   the practitioner;

(b)   the practitioner's solicitor;

(c)   a partner or an employee of either of them.

12A.8(4) **[Person other than official receiver or responsible insolvency practitioner]** In the case of a notice or other document to be given, delivered or sent by a person other than the official receiver or a responsible insolvency practitioner, the giving, delivering or sending of it may be proved by means of a certificate by that person–

(a)   that the notice or document was given, delivered or sent by that person, or

(b)   that another person (named in the certificate) was instructed to give, deliver or send it.

12A.8(5) **[Certificate may be endorsed]** A certificate under this Rule may be endorsed on a copy or specimen of the notice or document to which it relates.

GENERAL NOTE

Proof of sending is dealt with. See former IR r.12.4.

12A.9   Authentication

12A.9(1)   [Signature on hard copy] A document or information given, delivered or sent in hard copy form is sufficiently authenticated if it is signed by the person sending or supplying it.

12A.9(2)   [Electronic form] A document or information given, delivered or sent in electronic form is sufficiently authenticated–

(a)   if the identity of the sender is confirmed in a manner specified by the recipient, or

(b)   where no such manner has been specified by the recipient, if the communication contains or is accompanied by a statement of the identity of the sender and the recipient has no reason to doubt the truth of that statement.

GENERAL NOTE
This rule covers modes of authentication.

12A.10   Electronic delivery in insolvency proceedings—general

12A.10(1)   [Form of delivery] Unless in any particular case some other form of delivery is required by the Act or the Rules or an order of the court and subject to paragraph (3), a notice or other document may be given, delivered or sent by electronic means provided that the intended recipient of the notice or other document has–

(a)   consented (whether in the specific case or generally) to electronic delivery (and has not revoked that consent); and

(b)   provided an electronic address for delivery.

12A.10(2)   [Presumption as to delivery] In the absence of evidence to the contrary, a notice or other document is presumed to have been delivered where–

(a)   the sender can produce a copy of the electronic message which–

　　(i)   contained the notice or other document, or to which the notice or other document was attached, and

　　(ii)   shows the time and date the message was sent; and

(b)   that electronic message contains the address supplied under paragraph (1)(b).

12A.10(3)   [Deemed time of delivery] A message sent electronically is deemed to have been delivered to the recipient no later than 9.00am on the next business day after it was sent.

GENERAL NOTE
This identifies where electronic delivery is acceptable.

12A.11   Electronic delivery by office-holders

12A.11(1)   [Statement for request of hard copy] Where an office-holder gives, sends or delivers a notice or other document to any person by electronic means, the notice or document must contain or be accompanied by a statement that the recipient may request a hard copy of the notice or document and specifying a telephone number, e-mail address and postal address which may be used to request a hard copy.

12A.11(2)   [Time limit for sending of hard copy] Where a hard copy of the notice or other document is requested, it must be sent within 5 business days of receipt of the request by the office-holder.

12A.11(3)   [No fee for hard copy] An office-holder must not require a person making a request under paragraph (2) to pay a fee for the supply of the document.

GENERAL NOTE
The office holder may be requested to provide hard copies of documents.

12A.12   Use of websites by office-holder

12A.12(1)   [Application of r.12A.12] This Rule applies for the purposes of sections 246B and 379B.

12A.12(2)   [Contents of notice re website] An office-holder required to give, deliver or send a document to any person may (other than in a case where personal service is required) satisfy that requirement by sending that person a notice–

(a)   stating that the document is available for viewing and downloading on a website;

(b)   specifying the address of that website together with any password necessary to view and download the document from that site; and

(c)   containing a statement that the person to whom the notice is given, delivered or sent may request a hard copy of the document and specifying a telephone number, e-mail address and postal address which may be used to request a hard copy.

12A.12(3)   [Period of availability on website and format of document] Where a notice to which this Rule applies is sent, the document to which it relates must–

(a)   be available on the website for a period of not less than 3 months after the date on which the notice is sent; and

(b)   must be in such a format as to enable it to be downloaded from the website within a reasonable time of an electronic request being made for it to be downloaded.

12A.12(4)   [Time limit for sending hard copy] Where a hard copy of the document is requested it must be sent within 5 business days of the receipt of the request by the office-holder.

12A.12(5)   [No fee for hard copy] An office-holder must not require a person making a request under paragraph (4) to pay a fee for the supply of the document.

12A.12(6)   [Deemed delivery] Where a document is given, delivered or sent to a person by means of a website in accordance with this Rule, it is deemed to have been delivered–

(a)   when the document was first made available on the website, or

(b)   if later, when the notice under paragraph (2) was delivered to that person.

GENERAL NOTE
Website use by office holders is covered—note the linkage with ss.246B and 379B of the Act.

12A.13   Special provision on account of expense as to website use

12A.13(1)   [Notice under r.12A.12 that documents on website only] Where the court is satisfied that the expense of sending notices in accordance with Rule 12A.12 would, on account of the number of persons entitled to receive them, be disproportionate to the benefit of sending notices in accordance with that Rule, it may order that the requirement to give, deliver or send a relevant document to any person may (other than in a case where personal service is required) be satisfied by the office-holder sending each of those persons a notice–

(a)   stating that all relevant documents will be made available for viewing and downloading on a website;

(b) specifying the address of that website together with any password necessary to view and download a relevant document from that site; and

(c) containing a statement that the person to whom the notice is given, delivered or sent may at any time request that hard copies of all, or specific, relevant documents are sent to that person, and specifying a telephone number, e-mail address and postal address which may be used to make that request.

12A.13(2)   **[Period of availability and format of document]** A document to which this Rule relates must–

(a) be available on the website for a period of not less than 12 months from the date when it was first made available on the website or, if later, from the date upon which the notice was sent, and

(b) must be in such a format as to enable it to be downloaded from the website within a reasonable time of an electronic request being made for it to be downloaded.

12A.13(3)   **[Time limit for sending hard copy]** Where hard copies of relevant documents have been requested, they must be sent by the office-holder–

(a) within 5 business days of the receipt by the office-holder of the request to be sent hard copies, in the case of relevant documents first appearing on the website before the request was received, or

(b) within 5 business days from the date a relevant document first appears on the website, in all other cases.

12A.13(4)   **[No fee for hard copy]** An office-holder must not require a person making a request under paragraph (3) to pay a fee for the supply of the document.

12A.13(5)   **[Deemed delivery]** Where a relevant document is given, delivered or sent to a person by means of a website in accordance with this Rule, it is deemed to have been delivered–

(a) when the relevant document was first made available on the website, or

(b) if later, when the notice under paragraph (1) was delivered to that person.

12A.13(6)   **[Relevant document]** In this Rule a relevant document means any document which the office-holder is first required to give, deliver or send to any person after the court has made an order under paragraph (1).

GENERAL NOTE

This is a cost saving measure.

12A.14   **Electronic delivery of insolvency proceedings to courts**

12A.14(1)   **[No electronic delivery to court]** Except where paragraph (2) applies or the requirements of paragraph (3) are met, no petition, application, notice or other document may be delivered or made to a court by electronic means.

12A.14(2)   **[Electronic delivery by another rule]** This paragraph applies where electronic delivery of documents to a court is permitted by another Rule.

12A.14(3)   **[Requirements]** The requirements of this paragraph are–

(a) the court provides an electronic working scheme for the proceedings to which the document relates; and

(b) the electronic communication is–

(i) delivered and authenticated in a form which complies with the requirements of the scheme;

(ii) sent to the electronic address provided by the court for electronic delivery of those proceedings; and

(iii) accompanied by any payment due to the court in respect of those proceedings made in a manner which complies with the requirements of the scheme.

12A.14(4)   ["An electronic working scheme"] In this Rule **"an electronic working scheme"** means a scheme permitting insolvency proceedings to be delivered electronically to the court set out in a practice direction.

12A.14(5)   [When electronic communication treated as delivered] Under paragraph (3) an electronic communication is to be treated as delivered to the court at the time it is recorded by the court as having been received.

GENERAL NOTE

This reflects the limits of electronic delivery where the court is involved.

12A.15   Notice etc. to joint office-holders

12A.15   Where there are joint office-holders in insolvency proceedings, delivery of a document to one of them is to be treated as delivery to all of them.

GENERAL NOTE

The position of joint office holders is addressed.

CHAPTER 3

SERVICE OF COURT DOCUMENTS

12A.16   Application

12A.16(1)   [Service of court documents] Subject to paragraph (2), this Chapter applies in relation to the service of–

(a) petitions,

(b) applications,

(c) documents relating to petitions or applications, and

(d) court orders,

which are required to be served by any provision of the Act or the Rules ("court documents").

12A.16(2)   [Non-application of r.12A17–12A.19 re service] Rules 12A.17 to 12A.19 do not apply to the service of–

(a) a winding-up petition,

(b) a bankruptcy petition,

(c) any document relating to such a petition, or

(d) an administration, winding-up or bankruptcy order.

12A.16(3)   [CPR Pt 6 service] For the purpose of the application by this Chapter of CPR Part 6 to the service of documents in insolvency proceedings–

(a) an application commencing insolvency proceedings (including a winding-up petition, a bankruptcy petition or an administration application), or

(b)   an application within insolvency proceedings against a respondent,

is to be treated as a claim form.

GENERAL NOTE

This defines the scope of Ch.3 (service of court documents).

12A.17   Application of CPR Part 6 to service of court documents within the jurisdiction

12A.17   Except where different provision is made in these Rules, CPR Part 6 applies in relation to the service of court documents within the jurisdiction with such modifications as the court may direct.

GENERAL NOTE

Linkage with CPR is explained.

12A.18   Service of orders staying proceedings

12A.18(1)   [Application of r.12A.12] This Rule applies where the court makes an order staying any action, execution or other legal process against–

(a)   the property of a company; or

(b)   the property or person of an individual debtor or bankrupt.

12A.18(2)   [Service by sealed copy of order] Service within the jurisdiction of such an order as is mentioned in paragraph (1) may be effected by sending a sealed copy of the order to the address for service of the claimant or other party having the carriage of the proceedings to be stayed.

GENERAL NOTE

Service of orders staying proceedings is covered by this rule.

12A.19   Service on joint office-holders

12A.19   Where there are joint office-holders in insolvency proceedings, service on one of them is to be treated as service on all of them.

GENERAL NOTE

This mirrors r.12A.15.

12A.20   Application of CPR Part 6 to service of court documents outside the jurisdiction

12A.20   CPR Part 6 applies to the service of court documents outside the jurisdiction with such modifications as the court may direct.

GENERAL NOTE

Service out of the jurisdiction is dealt with here. CPR Pt 6 applies. See former IR r.12.12.

CHAPTER 4

MEETINGS

12A.21   Quorum at meeting of creditors or contributories

12A.21(1)   [Quorum to be present] Any meeting of creditors or contributories in insolvency proceedings is competent to act if a quorum is present.

12A.21(2)   [Number for quorum] Subject to the next paragraph, a quorum is–

(a)   in the case of a creditors' meeting, at least one creditor entitled to vote;

(b)   in the case of a meeting of contributories, at least two contributories so entitled, or all the contributories, if their number does not exceed two.

12A.21(3)   [Persons present or represented by proxy] For the purposes of this Rule, the reference to the creditor or contributories necessary to constitute a quorum is to those persons present or represented by proxy by any person (including the chairman) and in the case of any proceedings under Parts 1 to 7 of the Act includes corporations duly represented.

12A.21(4)   [Where only chairman or one other person] Where at any meeting of creditors or contributories–

(a)   the provisions of this Rule as to a quorum being present are satisfied by the attendance of–

(i)   the chairman alone, or

(ii)   one other person in addition to the chairman, and

(b)   the chairman is aware, by virtue of proofs and proxies received or otherwise, that one or more additional persons would, if attending, be entitled to vote,

the meeting must not commence until at least the expiry of 15 minutes after the time appointed for its commencement.

GENERAL NOTE

This regulates quorum at meetings. Note differential requirements for creditor/contributory meetings. Formerly this was covered by IR r.12.4A.

12A.22   Remote attendance at meetings of creditors

12A.22(1)   [Request to convener to specify place for meeting] This Rule applies to a request to the convener of a meeting under section 246A(9) or 379A(8) to specify a place for the meeting.

12A.22(2)   [Request accompanied by concurrence] The request must be accompanied by–

(a)   in the case of a request by creditors, a list of the creditors making or concurring with the request and the amounts of their respective debts in the insolvency proceedings in question,

(b)   in the case of a request by contributories, a list of the contributories making or concurring with the request and their respective values (being the amounts for which they may vote at the meeting),

(c)   in the case of a request by members, a list of the members making or concurring with the request and their voting rights, and

(d)   from each person concurring, written confirmation of that person's concurrence.

12A.22(3)   [Time limit for request] The request must be made within 7 business days of the date on which the convener sent the notice of the meeting in question.

12A.22(4)   [Notice for attendance] Where the convener considers that the request has been properly made in accordance with the Act and this Rule, the convener must–

(a)   give notice to all those previously given notice of the meeting–

(i)   that it is to be held at a specified place, and

(ii)   as to whether the date and time are to remain the same or not;

(b)   set a venue (including specification of a place) for the meeting, the date of which must be not later than 28 days after the original date for the meeting; and

   (c)   give at least 14 days' notice of that venue to all those previously given notice of the meeting;

and the notices required by sub-paragraphs (a) and (c) may be given at the same or different times.

12A.22(5)   [Where request for final meeting or remuneration application pending] Where–

   (a)   a request to which this Rule relates is made in respect of a final meeting under section 106, 146 or 331;

   (b)   an application is made under Rule 4.131 or 6.142 in respect of remuneration or expenses reported in the draft report for that meeting; and

   (c)   the meeting cannot be held until the application (including any appeal) has been disposed of and any order of the court complied with,

paragraph (4)(a) does not apply and the duty to set a venue (including specification of a place) for the meeting applies in relation to the meeting when it is finally held.

12A.22(6)   [Chairman to attend remote meeting] Where the convener has specified a place for the meeting in response to a request to which this Rule applies, the chairman of the meeting must attend the meeting by being present in person at that place.

12A.22(7) [Non-application of expenses rules to remote meetings] Rules 2.37(3), (4), (5) and (6), 4.61 and 6.87 (expenses of summoning meetings) do not apply to the summoning and holding of a meeting at a place specified in accordance with section 246A(9) or 379A(8).

GENERAL NOTE

Remote attendance at meetings is dealt with—see ss.246A and 379A of the Act.

12A.23   Action where person excluded

12A.23(1)   ["Excluded person"] In this Rule and Rules 12A.24 and 12A.25 an **"excluded person"** means a person who–

   (a)   has taken all steps necessary to attend a meeting under the arrangements put in place to do so by the convener of the meeting under section 246A(6) or 379A(5); and

   (b)   those arrangements do not permit that person to attend the whole or part of that meeting.

12A.23(2)   [Power of chairman] Where the chairman becomes aware during the course of the meeting that there is an excluded person, the chairman may–

   (a)   continue the meeting;

   (b)   declare the meeting void and convene the meeting again;

   (c)   declare the meeting valid up to the point where the person was excluded and adjourn the meeting.

12A.23(3)   [Validity of continued meeting] Where the chairman continues the meeting, the meeting is valid unless–

   (a)   the chairman decides in consequence of a complaint under Rule 12A.25 to declare the meeting void and hold the meeting again; or

   (b)   the court directs otherwise.

12A.23(4)   [Suspension of meeting without adjournment] Without prejudice to paragraph (2), where the chairman becomes aware during the course of the meeting that there is an excluded person, the chairman may, in the chairman's discretion and without an adjournment, declare the meeting suspended for any period up to 1 hour.

Here we find explanation of the term "excluded persons" and the scenario where these persons arise.

12A.24 Indication to excluded person

12A.24(1) **[Request for indication by excluded person]** A person who claims to be an excluded person may request an indication of what occurred during the period of that person's claimed exclusion (an "indication").

12A.24(2) **[Time limit for request]** A request under paragraph (1) must be made as soon as reasonably practicable and, in any event, no later than 4.00 p.m. on the business day following the day on which the exclusion is claimed to have occurred.

12A.24(3) **[To whom request to be made]** A request under paragraph (1) must be made to–

 (a) the chairman, where it is made during the course of the business of the meeting; or

 (b) the office-holder where it is made after the conclusion of the business of the meeting.

12A.24(4) **[Time limit for indication]** Where satisfied that the person making the request is an excluded person, the person to whom the request is made under paragraph (3) must give the indication as soon as reasonably practicable and, in any event, no later than 4.00 p.m. on the business day following the day on which the request was made under paragraph (1).

12A.24(5) **["Office-holder"]** In this Rule and Rule 12A.25, **"office-holder"** has the meaning in Rule 13.9A.

This is a provision consequential upon r.12A.23—it enables excluded persons to obtain information.

12A.25 Complaint

12A.25(1) **[Right of complainant]** Any person who–

 (a) is, or claims to be, an excluded person; or

 (b) attends the meeting (in person or by proxy) and considers that they have been adversely affected by a person's actual, apparent or claimed exclusion,

("the complainant") may make a complaint.

12A.25(2) **[Relevant person to whom complain made]** The person to whom the complaint must be made ("the relevant person") is–

 (a) the chairman, where it is made during the course of the meeting; or

 (b) the office-holder, where it is made after the meeting.

12A.25(3) **[Duty of relevant person to take action]** The relevant person must–

 (a) consider whether there is an excluded person; and

 (b) where satisfied that there is an excluded person, consider the complaint; and

 (c) where satisfied that there has been prejudice, take such action as the relevant person considers fit to remedy the prejudice.

12A.25(4) **[Application of r.12A.25(5)]** Paragraph (5) applies where–

 (a) the relevant person is satisfied that the complainant is an excluded person;

 (b) during the period of the person's exclusion–

    (i)   a resolution was put to the meeting; and

    (ii) voted on; and

  (c)   the excluded person asserts how the excluded person intended to vote on the resolution.

12A.25(5) **[Excluded person's intended vote would change resolution]** Subject to paragraph (6), where satisfied that the effect of the intended vote in paragraph (4), if cast, would have changed the result of the resolution, the relevant person must–

  (a)   count the intended vote as being cast in accordance with the complainant's stated intention;

  (b)   amend the record of the result of the resolution; and

  (c)   where those entitled to attend the meeting have been notified of the result of the resolution, notify them of the change.

12A.25(6) **[Intended votes of more than one complainant]** Where satisfied that more than one complainant in paragraph (4) is an excluded person, the relevant person must have regard to the combined effect of the intended votes.

12A.25(7) **[Notification of any decision]** The relevant person must notify the complainant in writing of any decision.

12A.25(8) **[Time limit for compliant]** A complaint must be made as soon as reasonably practicable and, in any event, no later than 4 p.m. on the business day following–

  (a)   the day on which the person was, appeared or claimed to be excluded; or

  (b)   where an indication is sought under Rule 12A.24, the day on which the complainant received the indication.

12A.25(9) **[Time limit for complainant's application to court]** A complainant who is not satisfied by the action of the relevant person may apply to the court for directions and any application must be made no more than 2 business days from the date of receiving the decision of the relevant person.

GENERAL NOTE

Complaints by excluded persons are regulated here and procedures specified.

12A.26   Remote attendance at meetings of creditors' committees and liquidation committees

12A.26(1) **[Application of r.12A.26]** This Rule applies to any meeting of a creditors' committee or a liquidation committee held under these Rules.

12A.26(2) **[Remote attendance]** Where the office-holder considers it appropriate, the meeting may be conducted and held in such a way that persons who are not present together at the same place may attend it.

12A.26(3) **[Attendance by right to speak and vote]** Where a meeting is conducted and held in the manner referred to in paragraph (2), a person attends the meeting if that person is able to exercise any rights which that person may have to speak and vote at the meeting.

12A.26(4) **[How right to speak and vote exercisable]** For the purposes of this Rule–

  (a)   a person is able to exercise the right to speak at a meeting when that person is in a position to communicate to all those attending the meeting, during the meeting, any information or opinions which that person has on the business of the meeting; and

  (b)   a person is able to exercise the right to vote at a meeting when–

    (i)   that person is able to vote, during the meeting, on resolutions or determinations put to the vote at the meeting, and

(ii)   that person's vote can be taken into account in determining whether or not such resolutions or determinations are passed at the same time as the votes of all the other persons attending the meeting.

12A.26(5)   [Office-holder to make arrangements] Where a meeting is to be conducted and held in the manner referred to in paragraph (2), the office-holder must make whatever arrangements the office-holder considers appropriate to–

(a)   enable those attending the meeting to exercise their rights to speak or vote, and

(b)   ensure the identification of those attending the meeting and the security of any electronic means used to enable attendance.

12A.26(6)   [Where unnecessary or inexpedient to specify meeting place] Where in the reasonable opinion of the office-holder–

(a)   a meeting will be attended by persons who will not be present together at the same place, and

(b)   it is unnecessary or inexpedient to specify a place for the meeting,

any requirement under these Rules to specify a place for the meeting may be satisfied by specifying the arrangements the office-holder proposes to enable persons to exercise their rights to speak or vote.

12A.26(7)   [Office-holder to regards legitimate interests] In making the arrangements referred to in paragraph (5) and in forming the opinion referred to in paragraph (6)(b), the office-holder must have regard to the legitimate interests of the committee members or their representatives attending the meeting in the efficient despatch of the business of the meeting.

12A.26(8)   [When office-holder to specify a place for meeting] If–

(a)   the notice of a meeting does not specify a place for the meeting,

(b)   the office-holder is requested in accordance with Rule 12A.27 to specify a place for the meeting, and

(c)   that request is made by at least one member of the committee,

the office-holder must specify a place for the meeting.

12A.26(9)   ["The committee"] In this Rule, **"the committee"** means the creditors' committee or the liquidation committee.

G‌ENERAL N‌OTE

Again this deals with the issues connected with remote attendance at creditors' meetings.

12A.27   Procedure for requests that a place for a meeting should be specified under Rule 12A.26

12A.27(1)   [Application of r.12A.27] This Rule applies to a request to the office-holder of a meeting under Rule 12A.26 to specify a place for the meeting.

12A.27(2)   [Time limit for request] The request must be made within 5 business days of the date on which the office-holder sent the notice of the meeting in question.

12A.27(3)   [Duty of office-holder to set venue and give notice] Where the office-holder considers that the request has been properly made in accordance with this Rule, the office-holder must–

(a)   give notice to all those previously given notice of the meeting–

(i)   that it is to be held at a specified place, and

(ii)   as to whether the date and time are to remain the same or not;

(b) set a venue (including specification of a place) for the meeting, the date of which must be not later than 7 business days after the original date for the meeting; and

(c) give 5 business days' notice of the venue to all those previously given notice of the meeting;

and the notices required by sub-paragraphs (a) and (c) may be given at the same or different times.

12A.27(4) **[Chairman to be present in person]** Where the office-holder has specified a place for the meeting in response to a request to which this Rule applies, the chairman of the meeting must attend the meeting by being present in person at that place.

GENERAL NOTE

Again we have a consequential measure.

CHAPTER 5

EFFECT OF INSOLVENCY ON EXECUTION—SPECIFIC PROVISIONS FOR NOTICES TO ENFORCEMENT OFFICERS ETC

12A.28   **Execution overtaken by judgment debtor's insolvency**

12A.28(1) **[Application of r.12A.28]** This Rule applies where execution has been taken out against property of a judgment debtor, and notice is given to the enforcement officer or other officer charged with the execution–

(a) under section 184(1) (that a winding-up order has been made against the debtor, or that a provisional liquidator has been appointed, or that a resolution for voluntary winding up has been passed); or

(b) under section 184(4) (that a winding-up petition has been presented, or a winding-up order made, or that a meeting has been called at which there is to be proposed a resolution for voluntary winding up, or that such a resolution has been passed); or

(c) under section 346(2) (that a judgment debtor has been adjudged bankrupt); or

(d) under section 346(3)(b) (that a bankruptcy petition has been presented in respect of the debtor).

12A.28(2) **[Delivery to enforcement officer etc.]** Subject to paragraph (3) and Rule 12A.29, the notice must be delivered to the office of the enforcement officer or of the officer charged with the execution–

(a) by hand, or

(b) by any other means of delivery which enables proof of receipt of the document at the relevant address.

12A.28(3) **[Execution in county court]** Where the execution is in a county court and the officer in charge of it is a district judge in that court, then if–

(a) there is filed in that court in respect of the judgment debtor a winding-up or bankruptcy petition, or

(b) there is made by that court in respect of the judgment debtor a winding-up order or an order appointing a provisional liquidator, or a bankruptcy order or an order appointing an interim receiver,

section 184 or 346 is deemed satisfied as regards the requirement of a notice to be served on, or given to, the officer in charge of the execution.

GENERAL NOTE

This deals with substantive issues concerned with executions—see ss.184 and 346 of the Act. For former provision see IR r.12.19.

12A.29   Notice to enforcement officers

12A.29(1)   [Application of r.12A.29] This Rule applies in relation to any provision of the Act or the Rules which makes provision for the giving of notice to an enforcement officer.

12A.29(2)   [Notice by electronic means] Any such notice as is mentioned in paragraph (1) may be given by electronic means to any person who has been authorised to receive such notice on behalf of a specified enforcement officer or on behalf of enforcement officers generally.

GENERAL NOTE

The rules governing the giving of notices to enforcement officers are outlined. Electronic communication is permitted.

CHAPTER 6

FORMS

12A.30   Forms for use in insolvency proceedings

12A.30(1)   [Forms in Sch.4 to be used] Subject to the next Rule, the forms contained in Schedule 4 to these Rules must continue to be used in insolvency proceedings as provided for in specific Rules.

12A.30(2)   [Variations] The forms must be used with such variations, if any, as the circumstances may require.

12A.30(3)   [Barcodes, etc. in forms] The Secretary of State, the official receiver or an insolvency practitioner may incorporate a barcode or other reference or recognition mark into any form in Schedule 4 to these Rules a copy of which is received by any of them or is sent to any person by any of them.

GENERAL NOTE

On Forms see Sch.4. There is an interesting provision in para.(3) dealing with barcodes. Formerly this question of Forms was dealt with by IR r.12.7.

12A.31   Electronic submission of information instead of submission of forms to the Secretary of State, the Chief Land Registrar, office-holders, and of copies to the registrar of companies

12A.31(1)   [Application of r.12A.31] This Rule applies in any case where information in a prescribed form is required by the Rules to be sent by any person to the Secretary of State, the Chief Land Registrar, or an office-holder, or a copy of a prescribed form is to be sent to the registrar of companies.

12A.31(2)   [Satisfaction of requirement by electronic submission] A requirement of the kind mentioned in paragraph (1) is treated as having been satisfied where–

(a)   the information is submitted electronically with the agreement of the person to whom the information is sent;

(b)   the form in which the electronic submission is made satisfies the requirements of the person to whom the information is sent (which may include a requirement that the information supplied can be reproduced in the format of the prescribed form);

(c)   that all the information required to be given in the prescribed form is provided in the electronic submission; and

(d) the person to whom the information is sent can provide in legible form the information so submitted.

12A.31(3) **[Requirement for signature]** Where information in a prescribed form is permitted to be sent electronically under paragraph (2), any requirement in the prescribed form that the prescribed form be accompanied by a signature is taken to be satisfied–

(a) if the identity of the person who is supplying the information in the prescribed form and whose signature is required is confirmed in a manner specified by the recipient, or

(b) where no such manner has been specified by the recipient, if the communication contains or is accompanied by a statement of the identity of the person who is providing the information in the prescribed form, and the recipient has no reason to doubt the truth of that statement.

12A.31(4) **[Requirements as to copy information to other person]** Where information required in prescribed form has been supplied to a person, whether or not it has been supplied electronically in accordance with paragraph (2), and a copy of that information is required to be supplied to another person falling within paragraph (1), the requirements contained in paragraph (2) apply in respect of the supply of the copy to that other person, as they apply in respect of the original.

General Note

This deals with electronic submission of forms to designated official recipients.

12A.32   Electronic submission of information instead of submission of forms in all other cases

12A.32(1) **[Application of r.12A.32]** Subject to paragraph (5), this Rule applies in any case where Rule 12A.31 does not apply, where information in a prescribed form is required by the Rules to be sent by any person.

12A.32(2) **[Satisfaction of requirement by electronic submission]** A requirement of the kind mentioned in paragraph (1) is treated as having been satisfied where–

(a) the person to whom the information is sent has agreed–

(i) to receiving the information electronically and to the form in which it is to be sent; and

(ii) to the specified manner in which paragraph (3) is to be satisfied.

(b) all the information required to be given in the prescribed form is provided in the electronic submission; and

(c) the person to whom the information is sent can provide in legible form the information so submitted.

12A.32(3) **[Requirement for signature]** Any requirement in a prescribed form that it be accompanied by a signature is taken to be satisfied if the identity of the person who is supplying the information and whose signature is required, is confirmed in the specified manner.

12A.32(4) **[Requirements as to copy information to other person]** Where information required in prescribed form has been supplied to a person, whether or not it has been supplied electronically in accordance with paragraph (2), and a copy of that information is required to be supplied to another person falling within paragraph (1), the requirements contained in paragraph (2) apply in respect of the supply of the copy to that other person, as they apply in respect of the original.

12A.32(5) **[Non-application to statutory demand]** This Rule does not apply in respect of a statutory demand.

GENERAL NOTE

Electronic submission of forms to other non official recipients is covered here.

CHAPTER 7

GAZETTE NOTICES

12A.33   Contents of notices to be gazetted under the Act or Rules

12A.33(1)   [Content of notices as set out in Pt 12A Ch.7] Except when paragraph (3) applies, where under the Act or the Rules a notice is gazetted, in addition to any content specifically required by the Act or any other provision of the Rules, the content of such a notice must be as set out in this Chapter.

12A.33(2)   [Contents of all notices] All notices published must specify insofar as it is applicable in relation to the particular notice–

(a)   the name and postal address of the office-holder acting in the proceedings;

(b)   the capacity in which the office-holder is acting and the date of appointment;

(c)   either an e-mail address, or a telephone number, through which the office-holder may be contacted;

(d)   the name of any person other than the office-holder (if any) who may be contacted regarding the proceedings;

(e)   the number assigned to the office-holder by the Secretary of State; and

(f)   the court name and any number assigned to the proceedings by the court.

12A.33(3)   [Application to r.4.228(2)] This paragraph applies to notices under Rule 4.228(2) (first excepted case).

GENERAL NOTE

Contents of *Gazette* notices are specified. For previous position see IR r.12.20.

12A.34   Gazette notices relating to companies

12A.34   In addition to the information required by Rule 12A.33 a notice relating to a company must specify–

(a)   the registered name of the company;

(b)   its registered number;

(c)   its registered office, or if an unregistered company, the postal address of its principal place of business;

(d)   any principal trading address if this is different from its registered office;

(e)   any name under which it was registered in the 12 months prior to the date of the commencement of the proceedings which are the subject of the Gazette notice; and

(f)   any name or style (other than its registered name) under which–

(i)   the company carried on business; and

(ii)   any debt owed to a creditor was incurred.

GENERAL NOTE

Gazette notices relating to companies, and their contents, are the subject matter here.

12A.35   Gazette notices relating to bankrupts

12A.35   In addition to the information required by Rule 12A.33 a notice relating to a bankruptcy must state,–

(a)   the bankrupt's full name and residential address;

(b)   any other address at which the bankrupt has resided in the period of 12 months preceding the making of the bankruptcy order;

(c)   the bankrupt's date of birth;

(d)   the bankrupt's occupation;

(e)   any other name by which the bankrupt has been known;

(f)   any name or style (other than the bankrupt's own name) under which–

    (i)   the bankrupt carried on business; and

    (ii)   any debt owed to a creditor was incurred.

GENERAL NOTE

Contents of *Gazette* notices concerning individuals are covered by this rule.

12A.36   Omission of unobtainable information

12A.36   Information required under this Chapter to be included in a notice to be gazetted may be omitted if it is not reasonably practicable to obtain it.

GENERAL NOTE

This is a pragmatic concession.

12A.37   The Gazette—general

12A.37(1)   [Evidence of facts in notice] A copy of the Gazette containing any notice required by the Act or the Rules to be gazetted is evidence of any facts stated in the notice.

12A.37(2)   [Conclusive evidence of notice of date of court order] In the case of an order of the court notice of which is required by the Act or the Rules to be gazetted, a copy of the Gazette containing the notice may in any proceedings be produced as conclusive evidence that the order was made on the date specified in the notice.

12A.37(3)   [Variation of court order to be gazetted] Where an order of the court which is gazetted has been varied, and where any matter has been erroneously or inaccurately gazetted, the person whose responsibility it was to procure the requisite entry in the Gazette must as soon as is reasonably practicable cause the variation of the order to be gazetted or a further entry to be made in the Gazette for the purpose of correcting the error or inaccuracy.

GENERAL NOTE

This explains the significance of the *Gazette*, and in particular issues of evidential status.

CHAPTER 8

NOTICES ADVERTISED OTHERWISE THAN IN THE GAZETTE

12A.38   Notices otherwise advertised under the Act or Rules

12A.38(1)   [Content of notice in Pt 12A Ch.8] Where under the Act or the Rules a notice may be advertised otherwise than in the Gazette, in addition to any content specifically required by the Act or any other provision of the Rules, the content of such a notice must be as set out in this Chapter.

12A.38(2)   [Notice to specify re office-holder] All notices published must specify insofar as it is applicable in relation to the particular notice–

(a)   the name and postal address of the office-holder acting in the proceedings to which the notice relates;

(b)   the capacity in which the office-holder is acting; and

(c)   either an e-mail address, or a telephone number, through which the office-holder may be contacted.

GENERAL NOTE

This rule covers the use of notices and their contents where the *Gazette* is not involved.

12A.39   Non-Gazette notices relating to companies

12A.39   In addition to the information required by Rule 12A.38, a notice relating to a company must state–

(a)   the registered name of the company;

(b)   its registered number;

(c)   any name under which it was registered in the 12 months prior to the date of the commencement of the proceedings which are the subject of the notice; and

(d)   any name or style (other than its registered name) under which–

  (i)   the company carried on business; and

  (ii)   any debt owed to a creditor was incurred.

GENERAL NOTE

This covers contents of non-*Gazette* notices where companies are involved.

12A.40   Non-Gazette notices relating to bankrupts

12A.40   In addition to the information required by Rule 12A.38, a notice relating to bankruptcy must state–

(a)   the bankrupt's full name and address;

(b)   any other address at which the bankrupt has resided in the period of 12 months preceding the making of the bankruptcy order;

(c)   the bankrupt's date of birth;

(d)   the bankrupt's occupation;

(e)   any other name by which the bankrupt has been known;

(f)   any name or style (other than the bankrupt's own name) under which–

     (i)   the bankrupt carried on business; and

     (ii)   any debt owed to a creditor was incurred.

GENERAL NOTE

This covers non-*Gazette* notices featuring bankrupts.

12A.41   Non-Gazette notices—other provisions

12A.41(1)   **[Information capable of being read, heard or seen]** The information required to be contained in a notice to which this Chapter applies must be included in the advertisement of that notice in a manner that is reasonably likely to ensure, in relation to the form of the advertising used, that a person reading, hearing or seeing the advertisement, will be able to read, hear or see that information.

12A.41(2)   **[Omission of unobtainable information]** Information required under this Chapter to be included in a notice may be omitted if it is not reasonably practicable to obtain it.

GENERAL NOTE

This is a general miscellaneous provision.

CHAPTER 9

NOTIFICATIONS TO THE REGISTRAR OF COMPANIES

12A.42   Application of this Chapter

12A.42   This Chapter applies where under the Act or the Rules information is to be sent or delivered to the registrar of companies.

GENERAL NOTE

The scope of Ch.9 is defined.

12A.43   Information to be contained in all notifications to the registrar

12A.43   Where under the Act or the Rules a return, notice, or any other document or information is to be sent to the registrar of companies, that notification must specify–

(a)   the registered name of the company;

(b)   its registered number;

(c)   the nature of the notification;

(d)   the section of the Act or the Rule under which the notification is made;

(e)   the date of the notification;

(f)   the name and postal address of person making the notification;

(g)   the capacity in which that person is acting in respect of the company; and

the notification must be authenticated by the person making the notification.

GENERAL NOTE

This details the content of notices sent to the registrar of companies.

12A.44   Notifications relating to the office of office-holders

12A.44   In addition to the information required by Rule 12A.43, a notification relating to the office of the office-holder must also specify–

   (a)   the name of the office-holder;

   (b)   the nature of the appointment held by the office holder

   (c)   the date of the event notified;

   (e)   where the notification relates to an appointment, the person, body or court making the appointment;

   (f)   where the notification relates to the termination of an appointment, the reason for that termination (for example, resignation); and

   (e)   the postal address of office-holder.

GENERAL NOTE

This makes special provision for notifications concerning office holders. The alphabetical listing here has gone awry.

12A.45   Notifications relating to documents

12A.45   In addition to the information required by Rule 12A.43, a notification relating to a document (for example, a statement of affairs) must also specify–

   (a)   the nature of the document; and

   (b)   the date of the document; or

   (c)   where the document relates to a period of time (for example a report) the period of time to which the document relates.

GENERAL NOTE

Where the notification relates to a document the position as to contents is explained.

12A.46   Notifications relating to court orders

12A.46   In addition to the information required by Rule 12A.43, a notification relating to a court order must also specify–

   (a)   the nature of the court order; and

   (b)   the date of the order.

GENERAL NOTE

This prescribes rules where the notification relates to court orders—details are prescribed.

12A.47   Returns or reports of meetings

12A.47(1)   **[Additional content of return or report of meeting]** In addition to the information required by Rule 12A.43, the notification of a return or a report of a meeting must specify–

   (a)   the purpose of the meeting including the section of the Act or Rule under which it was convened;

   (b)   the venue fixed for the meeting;

   (c)   whether a required quorum was present for the meeting to take place; and

(d) if the meeting took place, the outcome of the meeting (including any resolutions passed at the meeting).

12A.47(2) [Where return re final meeting pre-dissolution] Where the return relates to the meeting required by section 94 or 106 (final meetings prior to dissolution), it must also specify the dates of the opening and close of the winding up.

GENERAL NOTE

This covers required details in cases where the notification relates to reports of meetings.

12A.48   Notifications relating to other events

12A.48 In addition to the information required by Rule 12A.43, a notification relating to any other event (for example the coming in to force of a moratorium) must specify–

(a) the nature of the event including the section of the Act or Rule under which it took place; and

(b) the date the event occurred.

GENERAL NOTE

This covers details required in other notifications.

12A.49   Notifications of more than one nature

12A.49 A notification which includes a notification of more than one nature must satisfy the requirements applying in respect of each of those notifications.

GENERAL NOTE

Multiple notifications may be required.

12A.50   Notifications made to other persons at the same time

12A.50(1) [Copy of notification to registrar] Where under the Act or the Rules a notice or other document is to be sent to another person at the same time that it is to be sent to the registrar of companies, that requirement may be satisfied by sending to that other person a copy of the notification sent to the registrar.

12A.50(2) [Non-application of r.12A.50(1)] Paragraph (1) does not apply–

(a) where a Form is prescribed for the notification to the other person; or

(b) where the notification to the registrar of companies is incomplete.

GENERAL NOTE

This covers notification to multiple parties.

CHAPTER 10

INSPECTION OF DOCUMENTS AND THE PROVISION OF INFORMATION

12A.51   Confidentiality of documents—grounds for refusing inspection

12A.51(1) [Power of office-holder to decline inspection] Where in insolvency proceedings the office-holder considers that a document forming part of the records of those proceedings–

(a) should be treated as confidential, or

(b) is of such a nature that its disclosure would be prejudicial to the conduct of the proceedings or might reasonably be expected to lead to violence against any person,

the office-holder may decline to allow it to be inspected by a person who would otherwise be entitled to inspect it.

12A.51(2) [Persons who may be refused inspection] The persons to whom the office-holder may under this Rule refuse inspection include members of a liquidation committee or a creditors' committee.

12A.51(3) [Application to court] Where under this rule the office-holder determines to refuse inspection of a document, the person wishing to inspect it may apply to the court for that determination to be overruled and the court may either overrule it altogether or sustain it subject to such conditions (if any) as it thinks just.

GENERAL NOTE

This explains where an office-holder may decline to disclose information on grounds of confidentiality or because of a threat to personal safety. Previously this was covered by IR r.12.13.

12A.52   Right to copy documents

12A.52 Where the Act or the Rules confer a right for any person to inspect documents, the right includes that of taking copies of those documents, on payment–

(a) in the case of documents on the court's file of proceedings, of the fee chargeable under any order made under section 92 of the Courts Act 2003, and

(b) in any other case, of the appropriate fee.

GENERAL NOTE

This indicates that a right to inspect embraces a right to seek copies of documents. See former IR r.12.15.

12A.53   Charges for copy documents

12A.53 Except where prohibited by the Rules, a responsible insolvency practitioner or the official receiver is entitled to require the payment of the appropriate fee for the supply of documents requested by a creditor, member, contributory or member of a liquidation or creditors' committee.

GENERAL NOTE

The office holder can charge for the cost of supplying documents. See former r.12.15A.

12A.54   Right to have list of creditors

12A.54(1) [Application of r.12A.54] This Rule applies in the following proceedings–

(a) administration;

(b) winding up (other than a members' voluntary winding up); and

(c) bankruptcy.

12A.54(2) [Right of creditor of member State liquidator] A creditor or a member State liquidator has the right to require an office-holder to provide a list of the creditors and the amounts of their respective debts unless paragraph (5) applies.

12A.54(3) [Duty of liquidator to furnish list] The office-holder on being required to furnish the list under paragraph (2)–

(a) as soon as reasonably practicable must send it to the person requiring the list to be furnished; and

(b) may charge the appropriate fee for doing so.

12A.54(4) **[Omission of name and address from list]** The name and address of any creditor may be omitted from the list furnished under paragraph (3) where the office-holder is of the view that its disclosure would be prejudicial to the conduct of the proceedings or might reasonably be expected to lead to violence against any person provided that–

(a)   the amount of the debt in question is shown in the list; and

(b)   a statement is included in the list that the name and address of the creditor has been omitted in respect of that debt.

12A.54(5) **[Non-application of r.12A.54(2)]** Paragraph (2) does not apply where a statement of affairs has been–

(a)   delivered to the registrar of companies, in a winding up or an administration; or

(b)   filed with the court, in bankruptcy proceedings.

GENERAL NOTE

Lists of creditors must be available.

CHAPTER 11

COMPUTATION OF TIME AND TIME LIMITS

12A.55 **Time limits**

12A.55(1) **[Application of CPR r.2.8]** The provisions of CPR rule 2.8 (time) apply, as regards computation of time, to anything required or authorised to be done by the Rules.

12A.55(2) **[Extension or shortening time for compliance]** The provisions of CPR rule 3.1(2)(a) (the court's general powers of management) apply so as to enable the court to extend or shorten the time for compliance with anything required or authorised to be done by the Rules.

GENERAL NOTE

With regard to computation, extension or shortening of time limits, the CPR rules apply. For previous position see substituted IR r.12.9.

CHAPTER 12

SECURITY

12A.56 **Insolvency practitioners' security**

12A.56(1) **[Duty of person making or certifying appointment]** Wherever under the Rules any person has to appoint, or certify the appointment of, an insolvency practitioner to any office that person must, before making or certifying the appointment, be satisfied that the person appointed or to be appointed has security for the proper performance of that office.

12A.56(2) **[Review of adequacy of security]** It is the duty–

(a)   of the creditors' committee in–

    (i)   an administration,

    (ii) an administrative receivership,

    (iii) a bankruptcy, and

1188

(b)   of the liquidation committee in a winding up,

to review from time to time the adequacy of the responsible insolvency practitioner's security.

12A.56(3)   [Expense in insolvency proceedings] In any insolvency proceedings the cost of the responsible insolvency practitioner's security shall be defrayed as an expense of the proceedings.

GENERAL NOTE

This deals with the security required of insolvency practitioners. Formerly covered by now substituted IR r.12.8.

CHAPTER 13

NOTICE OF ORDER UNDER SECTION 176A(5)

12A.57   Notice of order under section 176A(5)

12A.57(1)   [Sealed copies to applicant and any other office-holder] Where the court makes an order under section 176A(5), it must as soon as reasonably practicable send two sealed copies of the order to the applicant and a sealed copy to any other office-holder.

12A.57(2)   [Liquidator etc. to notify creditors] Where the court has made an order under section 176A(5), the liquidator, administrator or receiver must as soon as reasonably practicable, give notice to each creditor of whose address and claim the office-holder in question is aware.

12A.57(3)   [Non-application of r.12A.57(2)] Paragraph (2) does not apply where the court directs otherwise.

12A.57(4)   [Court may direct publication of notice] The court may direct that the requirement in paragraph (2) is complied with if a notice has been published by the liquidator, administrator or receiver which, in addition to containing the standard contents, states that the court has made an order disapplying the requirement to set aside the prescribed part. As soon as reasonably practicable the notice–

(a)   must be gazetted; and

(b)   may be advertised in such other manner as the liquidator, administrator, or receiver thinks fit.

12A.57(5)   [Copy of court order to registrar] The liquidator, administrator or receiver must send a copy of the order to the registrar of companies as soon as reasonably practicable after the making of the order.

GENERAL NOTE

Here we have a specific provision linked to applications/notifications under s.176A(5) of the Act (reserved fund for unsecured creditors). This replicates the former IR r.12.22.

PART 13

INTERPRETATION AND APPLICATION

Introductory note to Part 13
This interpretation Part should be viewed in the light of IA 1986 interpretation provisions, especially ss.247–251, 380–385, and 435–436.

13.1   Introductory

13.1   This Part of the Rules has effect for their interpretation and application; and any definition given in this Part applies except, and in so far as, the context otherwise requires.

13.2   "The court"; "the registrar"

13.2(1)   **[Power of judge, district judge, registrar]** Anything to be done under or by virtue of the Act or the Rules by, to or before the court may be done by, to or before a judge, district judge or the registrar.

13.2(2)   **[Authorisation by registrar or district judge]** The registrar or district judge may authorise any act of a formal or administrative character which is not by statute his responsibility to be carried out by the chief clerk or any other officer of the court acting on his behalf, in accordance with directions given by the Lord Chancellor.

13.2(3)   [Omitted.]

13.2(3A)   **["The registrar"] "The registrar"** means–

(a)   a Registrar in Bankruptcy of the High Court, or

(b)   where the proceedings are in the District Registry of Birmingham, Bristol, Caernarfon, Cardiff, Leeds, Liverpool, Manchester, Mold, Newcastle-upon-Tyne or Preston, a district judge attached to the District Registry in question.

13.2(4)   [Omitted.]

13.2(5)   [Omitted.]

GENERAL NOTE

The registrar handles much of the day-to-day business of insolvency work.

   See *Practice Direction: Insolvency Proceedings* [2000] B.C.C. 927. (The *Practice Direction* was republished in a more up-to-date form in 2007—see *Practice Direction: Insolvency Proceedings* [2007] B.C.C. 842 reproduced in App.IV in Vol.2 of this *Guide*.) Substantially amended by I(A)R 2010 (SI 2010/686)—paras (3), (4) and (5) omitted. New para.(3A) added.

13.3   "Give notice", etc.

13.3(1)   [Omitted.]

13.3(2)   [Omitted.]

13.3(3)   [Omitted.]

13.3(4)   **[Notice of venue in application to court]** Notice of the venue fixed for an application made to the court may be given by service of the sealed copy of the application under Rule 7.4(3).

GENERAL NOTE

This rule has been greatly cut down by I(A)R 2010 (SI 2010/686) only para.(4) left intact.

13.4   Notice, etc. to solicitors

13.4   Where under the Act or the Rules a notice or other document is required or authorised to be given to a person, it may, if he has indicated that his solicitor is authorised to accept service on his behalf, be given instead to the solicitor.

GENERAL NOTE

Solicitors have no implied authority to receive notices: *Re Munro* [1981] 1 W.L.R. 1358. See also *Re T & N Ltd* [2006] EWHC 842 (Ch); [2006] B.P.I.R. 1268.

13.5   Notice to joint liquidators, joint trustees, etc.

13.5   Where two or more persons are acting jointly as the responsible insolvency practitioner in any proceedings, delivery of a document to one of them is to be treated as delivery to them all.

13.6 "Venue"

13.6 References to the **"venue"** for any proceeding or attendance before the court, or for a meeting, are to the time, date and place for the proceeding, attendance or meeting or to the time and date for a meeting which is held in accordance with section 246A or 379A without any place being specified for it.

GENERAL NOTE

Clarified by I(A)R 2010 (SI 2010/686).

13.7 "Insolvency proceedings"

13.7 **"Insolvency proceedings"** means any proceedings under the Act or the Rules.

GENERAL NOTE

See *Jyske Bank (Gibraltar) Ltd v Spjeldnaes* [2000] B.C.C. 16—s.423 proceedings not insolvency proceedings. See also *Fourie v Le Roux* [2004] EWHC 2557 (Ch); [2005] B.P.I.R. 779 which proceeds along the same line of thought. See the note to r.7.55.

13.8 "Insolvent estate"

13.8 References to **"the insolvent estate"** are–

(a) in relation to a company insolvency, the company's assets, and

(b) in relation to a bankruptcy or a petition for bankruptcy, the bankrupt's estate or (as the case may be) the debtor's property.

GENERAL NOTE

Note the change made by the Insolvency (Amendment) Rules 2009 (SI 2009/642) with effect from April 6, 2009. This amendment involved removing the reference to individual insolvency in para.(8)(b) and replacing it with a more specific reference to bankruptcy.

13.9 "Responsible insolvency practitioner", etc.

13.9(1) **[Definition]** In relation to any insolvency proceedings, **"the responsible insolvency practitioner"** means–

(a) the person (other than the official receiver) acting in a company insolvency, as supervisor of a voluntary arrangement under Part I of the Act, or as administrator, administrative receiver, liquidator or provisional liquidator;

(b) the person (other than the official receiver) acting in an individual insolvency, as the supervisor of a voluntary arrangement under Part VIII of the Act, or as trustee or interim receiver;

13.9(2) [Omitted.]

13.9(3) **["Authorised person"]** A reference to an "authorised person" is a reference to a person who is authorised pursuant to section 389A of the Act to act as nominee or supervisor of a voluntary arrangement proposed or approved under Part I or Part VIII of the Act.

GENERAL NOTE

See IA 1986 Pt XIII. Amended by I(A)R 2010 (SI 2010/686)—para.(2) omitted.

13.9A Office-holder

13.9A **"Office-holder"** means in relation to insolvency proceedings any person who by virtue of any provision of the Act or the Rules holds an office in relation to those proceedings.

GENERAL NOTE

Introduced by I(A)R 2010 (SI 2010/686).

13.10 "Petitioner"

13.10 In winding up and bankruptcy, references to **"the petitioner"** or **"the petitioning creditor"** include any person who has been substituted as such, or been given carriage of the petition.

GENERAL NOTE

See rr.4.19, 6.30 and 6.31.

13.11 "The appropriate fee"

13.11 **"The appropriate fee"** means–

(a) in Rule 6.192(2) (payor under income payments order entitled to clerical etc. costs), or Rule 6.193C(4) (payor under income payments agreement entitled to clerical etc costs) 50 pence; and

(b) in other cases, 15 pence per A4 or A5 page, and 30 pence per A3 page.

GENERAL NOTE

Note the special higher fee for cases under r.6.192(2). This definition provision was modified by Insolvency (Amendment) Rules 2003 (SI 2003/1730) to deal with the new income payments agreements regime in bankruptcy which was introduced by EA 2002 (see s.310A of IA 1986).

13.12 "Debt", "liability" (winding up)

13.12(1) **[Definition]** "Debt", in relation to the winding up of a company, means (subject to the next paragraph) any of the following–

(a) any debt or liability to which the company is subject–

    (i) in the case of a winding up which was not immediately preceded by an administration, at the date on which the company went into liquidation;

    (ii) in the case of a winding up which was immediately preceded by an administration, at the date on which the company entered administration.

(b) any debt or liability to which the company may become subject after that date by reason of any obligation incurred before that date; and

(c) any interest provable as mentioned in Rule 4.93(1).

13.12(2) **[Liability in tort]** For the purposes of any provision of the Act or the Rules about winding up, any liability in tort is a debt provable in the winding up, if either–

(a) the cause of action has accrued–

    (i) in the case of a winding up which was not immediately preceded by an administration, at the date on which the company went into liquidation;

    (ii) in the case of a winding up which was immediately preceded by an administration, at the date on which the company entered administration.

(b) all the elements necessary to establish the cause of action exist at that date except for actionable damage.

13.12(3) **[Debt or liability]** For the purposes of references in any provision of the Act or the Rules about winding up to a debt or liability, it is immaterial whether the debt or liability is present or future, whether it is certain or contingent, or whether its amount is fixed or liquidated, or is capable of being ascertained by fixed rules or as a matter of opinion; and references in any such provision to owing a debt are to be read accordingly.

13.12(4) **["Liability"]** In any provision of the Act or the Rules about winding up, except in so far as the context otherwise requires, "liability" means (subject to paragraph (3) above) a liability to pay money or money's worth, including any liability under an enactment, any liability for breach of trust, any liability in contract, tort or bailment, and any liability arising out of an obligation to make restitution.

13.12(5) **[Application of r.13.12 to administration]** This Rule shall apply where a company is in administration and shall be read as if–

(a) references to winding up were references to administration,

(b) references to administration were references to winding up,

(c) references to going into liquidation were references to entering administration, and

(d) references to entering administration were references to going into liquidation.

GENERAL NOTE

Substantially modified by I(A)R 2010 (SI 2010/686). This important provision which had been remodelled in 2006 would have been better located in the Act itself. Compare IA 1986 s.382 ("debt" in bankruptcy cases), and see also r.12.3 (provable debts); and note that there are no corresponding definitions for other corporate insolvency proceedings, such as voluntary arrangements and administrations—a somewhat surprising omission in view of the references to "contingent and prospective creditors" in s.9(1) and to "debts for an unliquidated amount … or whose value is not ascertained" in rr.1.17(3) and 2.22(5). These omissions have had to be made good by the case law. For references to the relevant cases and a general discussion of the terms "debt" and "creditor", see the note to s.1(1), and also the notes to Sch.8 paras 12 and 14. This definition provision was amended by the insertion of r.13.12(5) to cater for the fact that these debt interpretation issues are now relevant in the context of administration because of the added distributional dimension of the new administration regime in the wake of the reforms introduced by EA 2002. In *Re T & N Ltd* [2005] EWHC 2870 (Ch); [2006] B.P.I.R. 532 David Richards J. held that future tort claimants could not be regarded as creditors with provable debts under IR 1986 r.13.12. In so deciding David Richards J. rejected the suggestion that such an exclusionary approach contravened either art.14 or the First Protocol of ECHR. In response to that decision r.13.12 was modified so as to specifically include such claimants within the concept of "creditor"—see the Insolvency (Amendment) Rules 2006 (SI 2006/1272). The key change is in r.13.12(2). The original wording of this rule was considered in *Re Beloit Walmsley Ltd* [2008] B.P.I.R. 1445.

In *Re Kentish Homes Ltd* [1993] B.C.C. 212 a rare example of non-provable debt arose. In this case a Law of Property Act receiver had incurred community charges in respect of premises which had been constructed by the receiver in order to fulfil contractual obligations of the insolvent company, but which had remained unoccupied until they were sold. This property development company had gone into liquidation after the commencement of a Law of Property Act receivership but the liquidator had not been allowed into possession. On the subsequent liquidation of the company it was held by Nicholls V.C. that the conditions laid down in r.13.12(1) had not been satisfied in respect of this sum and the local authority could not prove in respect of it. The liability to pay the community charge did not exist at the date of entry into liquidation nor did it arise in respect of a pre-liquidation obligation. The receiver was empowered to settle this debt but he had no legal obligation under s.109(8)(i) of LPA 1925 to do so nor would the court require him to do so. His Lordship made the point that the position would be the same in respect of the new council tax. These comments should be viewed with caution in view of *Re Toshoku Finance (UK) plc* [2002] UKHL 6; [2002] 1 W.L.R. 671.

By way of contrast it was held in *Tottenham Hotspur plc v Edennote plc* [1994] B.C.C. 681 that an order for costs was a debt for the purposes of r.13.12(1)(b) and (3) and so could form the basis of a winding-up petition.

In *Haine and Secretary of State v Day* [2008] EWCA Civ 626 the Court of Appeal, allowing an appeal from Sir Donald Rattee, held that a protective award made against an employer pursuant to s.189(2) of the Trade Union and Labour Relations (Consolidation) Act 1992 but after the entry into liquidation of that employer was a provable debt. Although the quantum of the award was a matter of judicial discretion which was exercised by the tribunal after the liquidation date, the underlying liability itself was triggered by the failure to consult about the job losses prior to liquidation. This interpretation was necessary to give effect to EC Council Directive 98/59. Also where there had been no attempt to consult the assumption would be that the full award would be made unless there were mitigating circumstances.

R.13.12(2)

This rule would appear to settle the inconsistency between *Re Berkeley Securities (Property) Ltd* [1980] 1 W.L.R. 1589; and *Re Islington Metal and Plating Works Ltd* [1984] 1 W.L.R. 14; (1983) 1 B.C.C. 98,933. The Cork Committee (*Report*, para.1310) favoured the former decision. This new rule is not ultra vires but is authorised by IA 1986 Sch.8 para.12.

13.12A "Authorised deposit-taker" and "former authorised deposit-taker"

13.12A(1) **["Authorised deposit-taker"]** **"Authorised deposit-taker"** means a person with permission under Part 4 of the Financial Services and Markets Act 2000 to accept deposits.

13.12A(2) **["Former authorised deposit-taker"]** **"Former authorised deposit-taker"** means a person who–

(a) is not an authorised deposit-taker,

(b) was formerly an authorised institution under the Banking Act 1987, or a recognised bank or a licensed institution under the Banking Act 1979, and

(c) continues to have liability in respect of any deposit for which it had a liability at a time when it was an authorised institution, recognised bank or licensed institution.

13.12A(3) **[Provisions r.13.12A(1), (2) to be read with]** Paragraphs (1) and (2) must be read with–

(a) section 22 of the Financial Services and Markets Act 2000;

(b) any relevant order under that section; and

(c) Schedule 2 to that Act.

R.13.12A

This rule was inserted by the Financial Services and Markets Act 2000 (Consequential Amendments and Repeals) Order 2001 (SI 2001/3649) r.381 with effect from December 1, 2001.

13.13 Expressions used generally

13.13(1) **["Business day"]** **"Business day"** means any day other than a Saturday, a Sunday, Christmas Day, Good Friday or a day which is a bank holiday in any part of England and Wales under or by virtue of the Banking and Financial Dealings Act 1971.

13.13(2) **["The Department"]** **"The Department"** means the Department for Business, Innovation and Skills.

13.13(2A) **["Duly authorised representative"]** **"Duly authorised representative"** means, in relation to a corporation, a person who is authorised by or under the constitution of the corporation to act on behalf of the corporation; and like expressions are to be construed accordingly.

13.13(3) **["File in court"]** **"File in court"** and file with the court means deliver to the court for filing.

13.13(4) **["The *Gazette*"]** **"The Gazette"** means the London Gazette.

13.13(4A) **["Gazetted"]** **"Gazetted"** means advertised once in the Gazette.

13.13(4B) **["Standard contents"]** **"Standard contents"** means–

(a) in relation to a notice to be gazetted, the contents specified in Rules 12A.33 to 12A.35; and

(b) in relation to a notice to be advertised in any other way, the contents specified in Rules 12A.38 to 12A.40.

13.13(5) **["General regulations"]** **"General regulations"** means regulations made by the Secretary of State under Rule 12.1.

13.13(6) **["Practice direction"]** **"Practice direction"** means a direction as to the practice and procedure of any court within the scope of the CPR.

13.13(7) **["Prescribed order of priority"]** **"Prescribed order of priority"** means the order of priority of payments laid down by Chapter 20 of Part 4 of the Rules, or Chapter 23 of Part 6.

13.13(8) **["Centre of main interests"]** **"Centre of main interests"** has the same meaning as in the EC Regulation.

13.13(9) **["Establishment"]** **"Establishment"** has the meaning given by Article 2(h) of the EC Regulation.

13.13(10) **["Main proceedings"]** **"Main proceedings"** means proceedings opened in accordance with Article 3(1) of the EC Regulation and falling within the definition of insolvency proceedings in Article 2(a) of the EC Regulation and

in relation to England and Wales set out in Annex A to the EC Regulation under the heading "United Kingdom", and

in relation to another member State, set out in Annex A to the EC Regulation under the heading relating to that member State;

13.13(11) **["Member State liquidator"]** **"Member State liquidator"** means a person falling within the definition of liquidator in Article 2(b) of the EC Regulation appointed in proceedings to which it applies in a member State other than the United Kingdom.

13.13(12) **["Secondary proceedings"]** **"Secondary proceedings"** means proceedings opened in accordance with Articles 3(2) and 3(3) of the EC Regulation and falling within the definition of winding-up proceedings in Article 2(c) of the EC Regulation, and

(a) in relation to England and Wales, set out in Annex B to the EC Regulation under the heading "United Kingdom", and

(b) in relation to another member State, set out in Annex B to the EC Regulation under the heading relating to that member State.

13.13(13) **["Temporary administrator"]** **"Temporary administrator"** means a temporary administrator referred to by Article 38 of the EC Regulation.

13.13(14) **["Territorial proceedings"]** **"Territorial proceedings"** means proceedings opened in accordance with Articles 3(2) and 3(4) of the EC Regulation and falling within the definition of insolvency proceedings in Article 2(a) of the EC Regulation, and

(a) in relation to England and Wales, set out in Annex A to the EC Regulation under the heading "United Kingdom", and

(b) in relation to another member State, set out in Annex A to the EC Regulation under the heading relating to that member State.

13.13(14A) **["Winding-up proceedings"]** **"Winding-up proceedings"** means winding-up proceedings within the meaning of Article 2(c) of the EC Regulation as listed under the United Kingdom entry in Annex B of that Regulation, except for bankruptcy and sequestration proceedings.

13.13(15) **["Prescribed part"]** **"Prescribed part"** has the same meaning as it does in section 176A(2)(a) and the Insolvency Act 1986 (Prescribed Part) Order 2003.

13.13(16) **["Certificate of service"]** A **"certificate of service"** means a certificate of service verified by a statement of truth.

13.13(17) **["Statement of truth"]** A **"statement of truth"** means a statement of truth in accordance with CPR Part 22.

13.13(18)   ["Witness statement"] A **"witness statement"** means a witness statement verified by a statement of truth in accordance with CPR Part 22.

13.13(19)   [When fee or remuneration charged] A fee or remuneration is charged when the work to which it relates is done.

GENERAL NOTE

Substantially modified by I(A)R 2010 (SI 2010/686). Modifications include provision of new definitions and insertion of paras (2A), (4B), (14A), (16), (17), (18) and (19). Rules 13.13(1), (6) and (7) were substituted by the Insolvency (Amendment) (No.2) Rules 1999 (SI 1999/1022) with effect from April 26, 1999. Rules 13.13(8)–(14) were introduced by Insolvency (Amendment) Rules 2002 (SI 2002/1307) para.10(7) with effect from May 31, 2002 to cater for the advent of EC Council Regulation 1346/2000 on Insolvency Proceedings as amended by EC Regulation 603/2005. Rule 13.13(3) was amended and r.13.13(15) inserted by I(A)R 2003 (SI 2003/1730) with effect from September 15, 2003. Note the modification of wording introduced by the Insolvency (Amendment) Rules 2009 (SI 2009/642) which took effect from April 6, 2009. This change involved the insertion of a new para.(4A) explaining what is meant by "gazetted".

For comment on IR 13.13(3) see *Re Blights Builders Ltd* [2006] EWHC 3549 (Ch); [2007] B.C.C. 712.

13.14   Application

13.14(1)   [Application of Rules] Subject to paragraph (2) of this Rule, and save where otherwise expressly provided, the Rules apply–

(a)   to receivers appointed on or after the day on which the Rules come into force,

(b)   to bankruptcy proceedings where the bankruptcy petition is presented on or after the day on which the Rules come into force, and

(c)   to all other insolvency proceedings commenced on or after that day.

13.14(2)   [Further application] The Rules also apply to winding-up and bankruptcy proceedings commenced before that day to which provisions of the Act are applied by Schedule 11 to the Act, to the extent necessary to give effect to those provisions.

13.15   Application of Insolvency Act 1986 and Company Directors Disqualification Act 1986

13.15   For the purposes of these Rules, any reference in the Act or the Company Directors Disqualification Act 1986 to "leave" of the court is to be construed as meaning "permission" of the court.

GENERAL NOTE

I(A)R 2010 (SI 2010/686) inserts this clarification.

SCHEDULES

SCHEDULE 1

SCHEME MANAGER'S VOTING RIGHTS

Rule 4.72(7)

1   This Schedule applies as does Rule 4.72.

2   In relation to any meeting at which the scheme manager is under Rule 4.72 entitled to be represented, the scheme manager may submit in the liquidation, instead of a proof, a written statement of voting rights ("the statement").

3   The statement shall contain details of–

(a)   the names of creditors of the company in respect of whom an obligation of the scheme manager has arisen or may reasonably be expected to arise as a result of the liquidation or proposed liquidation;

(b)   the amount of the obligation so arising; and

(c)   the total amount of all such obligations specified in the statement.

4   The scheme manager's statement shall, for the purpose of voting at a meeting (but for no other purpose), be treated in all respects as if it were a proof.

5   Any voting rights which a creditor might otherwise exercise at a meeting in respect of a claim against the company are reduced by a sum equal to the amount of that claim in relation to which the scheme manager, by virtue of its having submitted a statement, is entitled to exercise voting rights at that meeting.

6   The scheme manager may from time to time submit a further statement, and, if it does so, that statement supersedes any statement previously submitted.

SCHEDULE 2

ALTERNATIVE COURTS

Rules 5A.21(2) and 6.40(3)

Debtor's own county court	*Nearest full-time court*
ABERDARE	CARDIFF
ABERYSTWYTH	CARDIFF
AYLESBURY	LUTON
BANBURY	LUTON or GLOUCESTER or READING
BARNSLEY	SHEFFIELD
BARNSTAPLE	EXETER
BARROW IN FURNESS	BLACKPOOL or PRESTON
BATH	BRISTOL
BEDFORD	LUTON
BLACKBURN	PRESTON
BLACKWOOD	CARDIFF
BOSTON	NOTTINGHAM
BRIDGEND	CARDIFF
BURY	BOLTON
BURNLEY	BOLTON or PRESTON
BURTON ON TRENT	LEICESTER or DERBY or NOTTINGHAM
BURY ST. EDMUNDS	CAMBRIDGE
CANTERBURY	CROYDON or THE HIGH COURT (LONDON)
CARLISLE	PRESTON or BLACKPOOL
CARMARTHEN	CARDIFF
CHELMSFORD	SOUTHEND or THE HIGH COURT (LONDON)
CHELTENHAM	GLOUCESTER
CHESTERFIELD	SHEFFIELD
COLCHESTER	SOUTHEND or THE HIGH COURT (LONDON)
COVENTRY	BIRMINGHAM
CREWE	STOKE or CHESTER
DARLINGTON	MIDDLESBROUGH

Debtor's own county court	*Nearest full-time court*
DEWSBURY	LEEDS
DONCASTER	SHEFFIELD
DUDLEY	BIRMINGHAM
DURHAM	NEWCASTLE
EASTBOURNE	BRIGHTON
GREAT GRIMSBY	HULL
GUILDFORD	CROYDON
HALIFAX	LEEDS
HARROGATE	LEEDS
HASTINGS	BRIGHTON
HAVERFORDWEST	CARDIFF
HEREFORD	GLOUCESTER
HERTFORD	LUTON
HUDDERSFIELD	LEEDS
IPSWICH	NORWICH or SOUTHEND
KENDAL	BLACKPOOL or PRESTON
KIDDERMINSTER	BIRMINGHAM
KING'S LYNN	NORWICH or CAMBRIDGE
LANCASTER	BLACKPOOL or PRESTON
LINCOLN	NOTTINGHAM
MACCLESFIELD	STOKE or MANCHESTER
MAIDSTONE	CROYDON or THE HIGH COURT (LONDON)
MEDWAY	CROYDON or THE HIGH COURT (LONDON)
MERTHYR TYDFIL	CARDIFF
MILTON KEYNES	LUTON
MOLD	WREXHAM
NEATH	CARDIFF
NEWBURY	READING
NEWPORT (GWENT)	CARDIFF
NEWPORT (I.O.W.)	SOUTHAMPTON or PORTSMOUTH
NORTHAMPTON	LUTON
OXFORD	READING
PETERBOROUGH	CAMBRIDGE
PONTYPRIDD	CARDIFF
RHYL	BIRKENHEAD or CHESTER
SALISBURY	BOURNEMOUTH or SOUTHAMPTON
SCARBOROUGH	YORK or HULL or MIDDLESBROUGH
SCUNTHORPE	HULL or SHEFFIELD
SHREWSBURY	STOKE
ST. ALBANS	LUTON
STAFFORD	STOKE
STOCKTON ON TEES	MIDDLESBROUGH
STOCKPORT	MANCHESTER
STOURBRIDGE	BIRMINGHAM
SUNDERLAND	NEWCASTLE
SWANSEA	CARDIFF
SWINDON	GLOUCESTER or READING

Debtor's own county court	*Nearest full-time court*
TAMESIDE	MANCHESTER
TAUNTON	EXETER or BRISTOL
TORQUAY	EXETER
TRURO	PLYMOUTH
TUNBRIDGE WELLS	CROYDON
WAKEFIELD	LEEDS
WARRINGTON	CHESTER or LIVERPOOL or MANCHESTER
WARWICK	BIRMINGHAM
WELSHPOOL	STOKE or CHESTER
WEYMOUTH	BOURNEMOUTH
WIGAN	BOLTON or MANCHESTER or PRESTON
WINCHESTER	SOUTHAMPTON
WORCESTER	GLOUCESTER
WREXHAM	BIRKENHEAD or STOKE or CHESTER
YEOVIL	EXETER or BRISTOL

GENERAL NOTE

Changes to the heading for the list of alternative courts are made by the Insolvency (Amendment) Rules 2009 (SI 2009/642) with effect from April 6, 2009. Note also changes made by I(A)R 2010 (SI 2010/686).

SCHEDULE 3

SHORTHAND WRITERS' REMUNERATION

Rule 7.17

[Deleted by the Insolvency (Amendment) Rules 1993 (SI 1993/602) r.3, Sch. para.4 as from April 5, 1993.]

GENERAL NOTE

Shorthand writers' remuneration is now a matter to be determined by the court in its discretion: see r.7.17(2).

SCHEDULE 4

FORMS

Rule 12A.30

Index

PART 1: COMPANY VOLUNTARY ARRANGEMENTS

PART 5: INDIVIDUAL VOLUNTARY ARRANGEMENTS

PART 6: BANKRUPTCY

GENERAL NOTE

This Schedule sets out the prescribed forms referred to in the above list. The use of the new prescribed forms of statutory demand and creditor's petition was made mandatory after March 31, 1988: see *Practice Note (Bankruptcy: Prescribed Forms)* [1988] 1 W.L.R. 557. The forms are not reproduced here. Form 7.20 was added by Insolvency (Amendment) Rules 2002 (SI 2002/1307) para.11 with effect from May 31, 2002 to cater for the advent of EC Council Regulation 1346/2000 on Insolvency Proceedings. The 2002 Rules (ibid., para.13) also substituted several amended forms to address the implications of the EC Regulation. Forms 1.1–1.19 were substituted and new Form 5.5 inserted by the Insolvency (Amendment) (No.2) Rules 2002 (SI 2002/2712) as from January 1, 2003, and new Forms 2.1B–2.40B and 12.1 were added and Forms 3.2, 4.12, 4.17, 4.18, 4.19, 4.52, 5.2, 6.1, 6.2, 6.3 and 6.25 substituted by the Insolvency (Amendment) Rules 2003 (SI 2003/1730) r.14(1)(a), with effect from September 2003. The latter 2003 Rules, para.14(1) also insert new Forms 5.6–5.8 and new Forms 6.81–6.84 as from April 1, 2004. Further changes were made by the Insolvency (Amendment) Rules 2005 (SI 2005/527) to Forms 2.8B, 2.11B, 2.13B, 2.14B, 3.1A, 3.2, 4.17, 4.18, 4.19, 6.28, 6.83 and 6.84. Note SI 2007/1898 on Form 6.57. Changes to forms are made by the Insolvency (Amendment) Rules 2009 (SI 2009/642) with effect from April 6, 2009, the Insolvency (Amendment) (No.2) Rules 2009 (SI 2009/2472) and by the Insolvency (Amendment) Rules 2010 (SI 2010/686) which omits or amends many forms.

A number of the more important company insolvency forms are available on the Insolvency Service's website at *http://www.insolvency.gov.uk/information/forms.*

SCHEDULE 5

PUNISHMENT OF OFFENCES UNDER THE RULES

Rules creating offence	General nature of offence	Mode of prosecution	Punishment	Daily default fine (where applicable)
In Part 2, Rule 2.47(6).	Administrator failing to send a progress report.	Summary.	Level 3 on the standard scale.	One-tenth of level 3 on the standard scale.
Rule 2.111(3).	Administrator failing to file a notice of automatic end of administration and progress report.	Summary.	Level 3 on the standard scale.	One-tenth of level 3 on the standard scale.
Rule 2.129(2).	Failure to comply with administrator's duties on vacating office.	Summary.	Level 3 on the standard scale.	One-tenth of level 3 on the standard scale.
In Part 3, Rule 3.32(5).	Administrative receiver failing to send requisite accounts of receipts and payments as receiver.	Summary.	Level 3 on the standard scale.	One-tenth of level 3 on the standard scale.
In Part 12, Rule 12.18.	False representation of status for purpose of inspecting documents.	1. On indictment. 2. Summary.	2 years, or a fine, or both. 6 months or the statutory maximum, or both.	

GENERAL NOTE

This Schedule prescribes punishment for certain offences in various provisions of the Rules. It has been amended by IA 2000, EA 2002 and I(A)R 2010 (SI 2010/686). The "statutory maximum" means the prescribed sum under s.32 of the Magistrates Courts Act 1980—see the note to Sch.10 to IA 1986 at p.642.

SCHEDULE 6

DETERMINATION OF INSOLVENCY OFFICE HOLDER'S REMUNERATION

As regards the determination of the remuneration of trustees and liquidators the realisation and distribution scales are as set out in the table below–

The realisation scale

(i)	on the first £5000 or fraction thereof	20%
(ii)	on the next £5000 or fraction thereof	15%
(iii)	on the next £90000 or fraction thereof	10%
(iv)	on all further sums realised	5%

The distribution scale

(i)	on the first £5000 or fraction thereof	10%
(ii)	on the next £5000 or fraction thereof	7.5%
(iii)	on the next £90000 or fraction thereof	5%
(iv)	on all further sums distributed	2.5%.

Appendix I

Index to Statutory Definitions

The words and phrases listed below are given special meanings for the purpose of all or part of the insolvency legislation which is annotated in this *Guide*. The numbers shown refer to the section of IA 1986 (or where indicated, the EC Regulation, EA 2002 or CBIR) in which the statutory definition appears and, in most cases, is discussed in the note adjoining that section. References to the original Pt II of IA 1986 are given in italics.

An asterisk (*) means that the term has a special meaning for only a limited part of the legislation, as will be indicated in the section referred to. Some words or phrases have been used by the draftsman with more than one meaning and where this is the case, each reference has been separately asterisked or listed.

Where a definition applies to all the *bankruptcy* Parts of the Act, this is shown by *ᵇ; if it applies to all the *company* insolvency Parts, by *ᶜ; and if it applies to all the CDDA 1986, by *ᵈ.

An index to definitions in the Insolvency Rules 1986 is given in App.II.

Statutory definition	*Provision*
assurance	s.190(1)*
attachment completed	s.346(5)
authorised deposit taker	*s.8(1B)* Sch.B1 para.9(4)*
Authority (the)	Sch.A1 para.44(18)*
bankrupt	s.381(1),*b EA, s.268(9)*
bankruptcy debt	s.382*b
bankruptcy level	s.667(4)*
bankruptcy restrictions regime	EA, s.268(10)*
bankruptcy order	s.381(2)*
bankruptcy petition	s.381(3)*b
bankrupt obtaining credit	s.360(2)*
bankrupt's estate	ss.283,*b 385(1)*b
become insolvent	CDDA ss.6(2),* 9(2),* Sch.1*
before petition	s.351,* Sch.4A para.2(4)*
beginning of the moratorium	Sch.A1 paras.1,* 8(1)*
body	EA, s.268(11)*
body corporate	CDDA s.22(6)*d
bond	Sch.A1 para.4F(3),* Sch.2A para.3(2)*
British insolvency law	CBIR Sch.1, art.2(a)
British insolvency office-holder	CBIR Sch.1, art.2(b)
building	s.72DA(3)*
building operations	s.72DA(3)*
business	s.436
business day	s.251*c, CBIR Sch.2 para.1(1), Sch.3 para.1(1)
business document	Sch.B1 para.45(3)*
capital market arrangement	s.72B(2),* Sch.2A para.1(1)*
capital market investment	s.72B(2),* Sch.2A paras.2(1), 3(1)*
carrying on business	s.265(2)*
centre of main interests	s.1(5),* Sch.B1 para.111(1B) EC Reg. Preamble para.13
cessation	Sch.B1 para.99(1)*
charged value	s.313(2A)*
charitable purpose	s.242(5)*
chattel leasing agreement	s.251*c
collateral security	Sch.A1 para.23(6)*
collateral security charge	Sch.A1 para.23(6)*
commencement	EA Sch.19 para.2*
commencement of winding up	ss.86, 129, 185(3)*
commercial paper	Sch.A1 para.4F(3),* Sch.B1 para.3(2)*
communication services	ss.233(5)(d),* 372(5)(c)*
Companies Act	s.436; CDDA ss.22(7),*d 22A(4), 22B(4)*
Companies Acts	CDDA ss.22(7), (8)*d
companies legislation	CDDA s.22(7)
company	ss.70(1),* 111(4)(a),* 216(8),* 217(6),* 388(4),* 435(11);* CDDA ss.22(2),* 22A(2),*d 22B(2),* 22C(2)*d, Sch.B1 para.111(1A)*
company arrangement or administration provision	EA s.255(2)*
competent authority	ss.251U(2),* 392(2)*
competition disqualification order	CDDA s.9A

Statutory definition	Provision
competition undertaking	CDDA s.9B
condition	s.279(5)*
conditional sale agreement	s.436
conduct	CDDA s.9E(4)*
conduct and affairs of a bankrupt	s.289(4)*
conduct as a director of a company	CDDA ss.6(2),* 9(2),* Sch.1*
connected with a company	s.249*c
consent	Sch.B1 paras.78(1),* 78(2),* 108(2),* 108(3)*
contracts of insurance	CBIR Sch.1, art.1.3(a)*
contributory	ss.79, 83(2), 226(1),* 251*c
control of a company	s.435(10)*
convener	s.246A(3),* 379A(2)*
conveyance	s.190(3)*
correspondence	Sch.B1 para.111(1)*
court	ss.216(5),* 385(1),*b 423(4);* CDDA ss.2(2),* 3(4),* 4(2),* 6(2),* 8(3),* 8A(3),* 11(2),* 9E(3),* 17,* EC Reg. art.2(d),* CBIR Sch.1, arts 2(c), 14.4, Sch.2 para.63 (and see note below)
CPR	CBIR Sch.2 para.1(1)
create a preference… to the prejudice of the general body of creditors	s.243(1)*
creditor	ss.263B(3),* 383(1),*b Sch.B1 para.12(4)*
creditors' committee	*ss.26,* 49(1),* 68(1),* 301(1)*
creditors' meeting	Sch.B1 paras.50(1),* 111(1)*
creditor's petition	ss.264(1)(a),*b 385(1)*b
creditors' voluntary winding up	s.90
criminal bankruptcy order	ss.385(1),*b 402(5)*
daily default fine	s.430(4)
date of filing	Sch.A1 para.1*
day on which preference created	s.243(3)*
debt	s.385(1)*b
debt for a liquidated sum	s.267(3)*
debtor	ss.251R(2),* 251X,* 385(1),*b 386(2),* 423(5)*
debt or liability	s.382(3), (4)*b
debt relief order	ss.251A(1),* 251X,* 385*
debtor's petition	ss.264(1)(b),*b 385(1)*b
debtor's property	s.286(8)*
deductions of income tax	Sch.6 para.1
default fine	s.430(4)
default order	CDDA ss.3(3)(6), 5(4)(6)
designated disadvantaged area	s.72DA(3)*
develop	s.72DA(2)*
director	ss.214(7),* 251,*c CDDA s.6(3C),* 9E(5),* 22(4),* 22A(2),* 22B(2),* 22C(2)*
director or other officer employed by company	s.435(9)*
discharged	s.279ff.
disposing of property	s.359(5)*
disqualification order	CDDA s.1(1)
disqualification provision	EA s.268(2)*

Statutory definition	Provision
disqualification undertaking	CDDA s.1A(1)
dwelling house	s.385(1)*ᵇ
earlier bankruptcy	s.334(1),* Sch.11 para.16(1)*
EC (Insolvency) Regulation	s.436*ᶜ, CBIR Sch.1, art.2(d)
EEA State	s.436, CBIR Sch.1, art.1(3)(b)
effective date	ss.233(4),* 235(4),* 251E(7)*
electronic communication	CBIR Sch.4 para.1(1)
employment	*ss.22(2),* 47(3),* 66(3),* 131(6)*
enactment	s.426C(2)*
engineering operations	s.72DA(3)*
enforcement officer	ss.183(4),* 184(6),* 346(9),* 347(11),* CBIR Sch.2 para.1(1)
enters administration	Sch.B1 paras.1(2)(b),* 111(1)*
enters into a transaction at an undervalue	ss.238(4),* 339(3),* 423*
establishment	EC Reg. art.2(h),* CBIR Sch.1, art.2(e)
estate	ss.283,*ᵇ 385(1)*ᵇ
excepted petition	Sch.A1 para.12(5)*
excluded debt	s.251A(4)*
excessive pension contribution	Sch.4ZB para.2(4),* Sch.4A para.2(4)*
execution commenced/continued	*s.10(5)*
execution completed	s.346(5)
existing trustee	s.334(1)*
ex parte	CBIR Sch.2 para.1(5)
extortionate	ss.244(3),*ᶜ 343(3)*ᵇ
facts which a director ought to know or ascertain	s.214(4)*
family	s.385(1)*ᵇ
family proceedings	s.281(8)*
file in (with) the court	CBIR Sch.2 para.1(1)
filing	CBIR Sch.1, art.2(p)(i)
final date	s.330(2)*
financed	s.72E(2)(a)*
fine	s.281(8)*
fixed security	s.70(1)*
floating charge	ss.70(3),* 176A(9),* 251,*ᶜ Sch.B1 para.111(1)*
foreign court	CBIR Sch.1, art.2(f)
foreign main proceeding	CBIR Sch.1, art.2(g)
foreign market	Sch.A1 para.4E(3),* Sch.2A para.2(3)*
foreign non-main proceeding	CBIR Sch.1, art.2(h)
foreign proceedings	IA 2000 s.14(4),* CBIR Sch.1, art.2(1)
foreign representative	CBIR Sch.1, art.2(j), Sch.2 para.29(5),* Sch.3 para.3(5)*
former administrator	Sch.B1 para.99(2)*
former enactments	Sch.11 para.22,* CDDA Sch.3 para.1*
former foreign representative	CBIR Sch.2 para.12(2)*
former law	Sch.11 para.2(2),* 3(2),* 4(2)*
functions carried out in relation to a company by a director	s.214(5)*
Gazette	CBIR Sch.2 para.1(1), Sch.3 para.1(1)

Statutory definition	*Provision*
general assignment	s.344(3)*
general prohibition	Sch.B1 para.9(4),* CBIR Sch.2 para.1(7),* Sch.3 para.1(4)*
give a preference	ss.239(4),* 340(3)*
give notice	CBIR Sch.2 para.70
go into insolvent liquidation	ss.214(6),* 216(7)*
go into liquidation	s.247(2),*c CDDA s.22(3)*d
goods	ss.183(4),* 184(6)*
group	Sch.A1 para.3(5)*
guaranteed minimum pension	s.310(9)*
guilty of default	CDDA s.3(3)*
have no reasonable prospect of being able to pay a debt	s.268(2)*
hire-purchase agreement	*s.10,** 15(9),* 436, Sch.A1 para.1,* Sch.B1 para.111(1),* CBIR Sch.1, art.2(k)
holder of a floating charge	s.70(2)*
holder of a qualifying floating charge	Sch.B1 para.111(1)*
holder of a qualifying floating charge in respect of a company's property	s.72A(3)*
in administration	Sch.B1 paras.1(2)(a),* 111(1)*
inability to pay: see "unable to pay"	
incapacitated person	CBIR Sch.2 para.49(2)*
income of the bankrupt	s.310(7)*
income payments agreement	s.310A(1)*
income payments order	s.310(1)*
indictable offence	CDDA s.2(2)
individual	s.388(3),* CBIR Sch.1, art.2(o)
individual carrying on business	s.265(2)*
initial creditors' meeting	Sch.B1 para.51(1)*
initial period	s.351*
Inland Revenue Official	s.369(6)*
insolvency	s.247(1)*c; CDDA s.22(3)*d
Insolvency Act	Sch.13 Pt II,* CDDA ss.22(7),*d (8),* 22A(4),* 22B(4)*
insolvency administration order	s.421A(9)*
insolvency law	ss.426(10),* IA 2000 s.14(4)*
insolvency practitioner	s.388(1)
insolvency proceedings	EC Reg. art.1(1), 2(a)*
insolvency services	s.428(3)*
insolvent: see also "insolvency"	s.341(3)*
insolvent estate of a deceased person	s.421(4)*
instrument by which a floating charge was created	s.70(4)*
instrument creating a charge	s.70(3)*
instrument of appointment	ss.53(1),* 70(1)*
insurance company	s.8(4)(a)
interim liquidator	s.138(2)*
interim order	s.252*
interim relief application	CBIR Sch.2 para.1(1)
interim trustee	s.388(4)*

Statutory definition	*Provision*
office copy	s.251*c (Scotland)
office holder	ss.233(1),* 234(1),* 238(1),* 246(1),* 246B(3),* 372(1),* 379B(1),* CDDA s.7(3)
officer	ss.6A(3),* 206(3),* 208(3),* 210(3),* 211(2),* Sch.A1 paras.41(5),* 42(3),* CDDA ss.4(2), 22(6),*d 22A(2),*d 22B(2),*d 22C(2)*d
officer who is in default	s.430(5)*
official name of trustee	s.305(4)
official petitioner	s.402
official rate	ss.189(4), 251*c
official receiver	ss.399, 401,* CDDA s.21(1)*d
onerous property	ss.178(3),* 315(2)*
onset of insolvency	ss.240(3),* 245(5)*
opening of proceedings	EC Reg. art.2(f)*
order under	s.310, Sch.11 para.16*
ordinary application	CBIR Sch.2 para.1(1)
originating application	CBIR Sch.2 para.1(1)
other debt management arrangements	s.251F(3)*
owner's powers	CBIR Sch.1, art.1.7(a)*
party	Sch.A1 para.4D(3)*
party to an arrangement	Sch.2A para.1(3)*
pension-sharing transaction	s.342D(9)*
permanent trustee	s.388(4)*
persistently in default	CDDA s.3(2)*
person	Sch.A1 para.4K*
personal injuries	s.281(8)*
personally responsible for [all] relevant debts of a company	s.217(1),* CDDA s.15(1)
person connected with a company	s.249*c
person liable to contribute to the assets	s.79(2)*
person obtaining credit	s.429(4)*
person's affairs	s.385(2)*b
petitioning creditor	Sch.A1 para.10(2)*
postal packet	s.371(1)*
practice direction	CBIR Sch.2 para.1(1)
pre-commencement bankrupt	s.313A(7),* EA Sch.19 para.2*
preference	ss.239(4),* 243,* 340(3),* Sch.4A para.2(4),* Sch.4ZA para.2(4)*
preferential creditor(s)	ss.4(7),* 258(7),* 386(1), Sch.A1 para.31(8)*
preferential debt(s)	ss.4(7),* 59(2),* 258(7),* 386(1), Sch.A1 para.31(8),* Sch.6
prescribed	ss.38(4),* 70(1),* 176A(9),* 251,*c 342C(7),* 342F(9),* 384,*b 419*
prescribed amount	s.418(1)*b
prohibited name	s.216(2)*
project company	ss.72C(3),* 72D(2)(d),* 72DA(3),* 72E(2)(b),* Sch.A1 para.4H(1), (2),* Sch.2A para.7(1), (2)*
proper accounting records	s.361(3)*
property	ss.283(4),*b 307(5),* 351,* 436, 436A*
property comprised in the bankrupt's estate	s.351*

Statutory definition	Provision
property of the company	s.42(2)(b),* Sch.1*
property or goods of the bankrupt	s.285(6)*
property possession of which is required to be delivered up	s.351*
property vested in the existing trustee	s.307(3),* Sch.11 para.16
proposal	ss.1(2),* 253*
proprietor	ss.180(1),* 319(1)*
prosecuting authority	s.7A(8)*
protected rights	s.310(9)*
provision	EA s.268(11)*
public body	Sch.A1 para.4I(3),* Sch.2A para.9(1)*
public-private partnership project	s.72C(2),* Sch.A1 para.4I(1)*
public telecommunications operator	ss.233(5),* 372(5)*
purchaser	CBIR Sch.1, art.1.7(b)*
purpose of administration	Sch.B1 para.111(1)*
qualified to act as an insolvency practitioner	s.390
qualifying debt	s.251A(2)*
qualifying floating charge	Sch.B1 para.14(2)*
qualifying liability	*ss.19(7),* 44(2A)*
rated	Sch.A1 para.4E(2),* Sch.2A para.2(2)*
reasonable prospect that debtor will be able to pay a debt	s.271(4)*ᵇ
reasonable replacement	s.308(4)*
receiver	ss.51(6),* 70(1),* 72(2),* 251,*ᶜ Sch.A1 para.43(2)*
receiver or manager of the property of a company	s.29(1)(a)
recipient	CBIR Sch.3 para.12(3)
recognised investment exchange	Sch.A1 para.4E(3),* Sch.2A para.2(3)*
recognised professional body	s.391*
recognition application	CBIR Sch.2 para.1(1), Sch.3 para.1(1)
recognition order	CBIR Sch.2 para.1(1), Sch.3 para.1(1)
records	s.436
recovery provisions	s.342C(7)*
registered office	ss.117(6),* 126(4)*
register of charges	s.70(1)*
Registrar	CBIR Sch.2 para.1(3)
regulated activity	CBIR Sch.2 para.1(7),* Sch.3 para.1(4)*
regulated business	s.72D(2)(b),* Sch.2A para.10(1)*
regulated company	Sch.A1 para.44(18)*
regulations	ss.342C(7),* 342F(9)*
relative	s.435(8)*
relevant company	CBIR Sch.2 para.1(1), Sch.3 para.1(1)
relevant contributions	s.342A(5)*
relevant country or territory	s.426(11)*
relevant date	ss.131(6),* 387*
relevant day	ss.166(6),* 242(3),* 372(1)*
relevant debts	s.217(3),* CDDA 5.15(3)*
relevant deposit	s.8(1B)
relevant information about status	s.360(4)*

Statutory definition	*Provision*
trading record	ss.251P(5),* 355(5)*
transaction	s.436
transaction at an undervalue	ss.238(4),* 339(3),* 423*
UNCITRAL Model Law	CBIR reg.1(2)
transfer order	Sch.A1 para.23(6)*
transferee	s.342D(9)*
transferee company	s.110(1)*
transferor	s.342D(9)*
transferor company	s.110(2)*
transitional period	s.313A(7)*
Tribunal	s.396 Sch.7
trustee, trustee in bankruptcy, trustee of the estate of a bankrupt	s.385(1)*b
trustees or managers	s.342C(5)*
unable to pay a debt [individual]	s.268(1)*
unable to pay its debts [company]	*ss.8,* 123, 222,* 223,* 224,* Sch.B1 para.111(1)*
unapproved pension arrangement	s.342A(8)*
UNCITRAL Model Law	CBIR reg.1(2)
undervalue	Sch.4A para.2(4),* Sch.4ZA para.2(4)*
unregistered company	s.220(1)*
unsecured: see "secured"	
unsecured creditor	ss.67(9),* 248(a)*c
utility project	s.72D(2)(a)*
vacancy	s.300(8)*
value lost to the estate	s.421A(9)*
value of goods or services as consideration for floating charge	s.245(6)*
venue	CBIR Sch.2 para.1(4)
victim of the transaction	s.423(5)*
voluntary arrangement [company]	s.1(1)
voluntary arrangement [individual]	s.253(1)
wages or salary	Sch.B1 para.99(6)*
wages or salary payable in respect of a period of holiday/absence from work through sickness or other good cause	ss.19(9),* 44(2C)
waste	s.72DA(3)*
water authority	s.233(5)*
willing to act on instructions	s.217(5),* CDDA s.15(5)*
winding-up proceedings	EC Reg. art.2(c)
writing, thing in	s.436B

[Note that for the purposes of Pts I–VII of IA 1986, "the court" means, in relation to a company, the court having jurisdiction to wind up the company: CA 1985 s.744, as incorporated by IA 1986 s.251.]

Appendix II

Index to Definitions in the Rules

The words and phrases listed below have special definitions for all or part of the Insolvency Rules 1986. The numbers shown refer to the rule in which the definition appears. References to the original Pt 2 of the Rules are given in italics. An asterisk (*) means that the term has a special meaning for only a limited part of the Rules, as will be indicated in the rule referred to.

1218

Definition in the Rules	*Rule*
debt relief restrictions register	6A.1(2)(b)*
debtor	5A.18*
debtor, the	5A.15,* 6.35B(2)*
Department, the	13.13(2)
deponents	*2.11(2),* 3.3(2),* 4.32(3)**
due	2.85(4),* 4.90(4)*
duly authorised representative	13.13(2A)
earlier bankruptcy	6.225(2)*
eligible company	1.1(4)*
establishment	13.13(9)
examinee	4.212(1)
excluded debt	5A.2*
existing trustee	6.225(2)*
expenses	10.4(1)
family proceedings	5A.2,* 12.3(2)
file in court	13.13(3)
fine	5A.2,* 12.3(2)
first meeting of contributories	4.50(7)*
first meeting of creditors	4.50(7),* 6.79(7)*
first meetings in the liquidation	4.50(7)*
former administrator	2.109C(1)*
former authorised deposit-taker	13.12A(2)
Gazette, the	13.13(4)
gazetted	13.13(4A)*
general regulations	13.13(5)
incapacitated person	7.43(2)*
individual insolvency register	6A.1(1)*
individual register	6.237E(2)*
insolvency proceedings	13.7
insolvent, the	7.15(2),* 7.37A(1),* 9.1(2),* 11.1(2)*
insolvent estate	13.8
insolvent winding up	4.151(a),* 4.173(2)*
invalid resolution	2.28(1A)
land	6.197(1)
last date for proving	4.182A(2), 11.2(2)
later bankruptcy	6.225(2)*
legal proceedings	4.218A(1)(c)*
liability	13.12
liquidation committee	4.148A(5)*
litigation expenses	4.218A(1)(d)*
loan	5A.2*
main proceedings	13.13(10)
meeting of creditors	4.148A(5)*
Member State liquidator	13.13(11)
mutual dealings	2.85(2)*
NO CVL APPLICATION	4.1(4)*
nominated persons	3.3(2),* 4.32(3)*
obligation	2.85(9),* 4.90(9)*
office-holder	12A.22(5),* 13.9A
officer	1.30(2)*

Definition in the Rules	*Rule*
official exchange rate	2.86(2),* 4.91(2),* 6.111(2)*
other proceedings	2.38(1)*
outgoing office-holder	7.10B(1)
person	4.228(1)
petition, the	5A.23*
petitioner	13.10
petitioning creditor	13.10
practice direction	13.13(6)
prescribed officer of the court	7.21(2)*
prescribed order of priority	13.13(6)
prescribed part	13.13(15)*
primary court	7.19(2),* 7.24(1)*
principal	8.1(1)*
progress report	4.49B(1)*
proof, proof of debt	2.72(2),* 4.73,* 6.96*
proper address	*2.7(4),* 2.7(4A)**
proposal	5.36*
provable debts	12.3
property	7.21(3)*
prove, proving	2.72(2),* 4.73,* 6.96*
proxy	8.1(1)
proxy-holder	8.1(1)
recipient	2.109C(4)*
registered land	6.237E(1)*
registers	6A.1(3)*
registrar	13.2
relevant date	2.105(3),* 11.13(3)*
relevant person	1.55(1),* 2.28(1)*
replacement office-holder	7.10B(1)*
respondent	9.1(2)*
responsible insolvency practitioner	1.1(3),* 1.23(6),* 13.9
return day	4.22(2)
RSC	0.2(1)
Rules, the	0.2
secondary court	7.19(2),* 7.24(1)*
secondary proceedings	13.13(12)
Secretary of State	6.240,* 6.252*
solvent winding up	4.151(b),* 4.173(2)*
specified creditors	4.218B*
standard contents	13.13(4B)
statement	Sch.1 para.2*
statement of truth	13.13(17)
statutory demand	4.4(1)
substantive application	7.10A(2),* 7.10C(1)
successor company	4.228(1)
sum due	2.85(4),* 4.90(4)*
temporary administrator	13.13(13)
territorial proceedings	13.13(14)
venue	13.6
voluntary arrangement	5.36*

Definition in the Rules	*Rule*
winding-up proceedings	13.13(4A)
witness statement	13.13(18)

Appendix III

Insolvency Service Information

The Insolvency Service (an Executive Agency within the Department for Business, Innovation and Skills) is responsible for much of the administration of insolvency law and (through its Disqualification Unit) the law relating to director disqualification. The address of the Service's London headquarters is:

The Insolvency Service
PO Box 203
21 Bloomsbury Street
London WC1B 3QW
Tel. 0845 602 9848

The Disqualification Unit's address is the same; tel. 020 7291 6807.

Estate Accounts and the Insolvency Practitioner Unit (IPU) is based in Birmingham. Its address is:

The Insolvency Service
Cannon House
18 Priory Queensway
Birmingham B4 6BS
Tel. 0121 698 4000

The Service's website address is *http://www.insolvency.gov.uk.*

The Central Fax number for filing a notice of appointment of an administrator under IR 1986 r.2.19 (which may only be used when the court office is closed for business) is 020 7947 6607. If sent by email, the address is rcjcompanies.orders@hmcourts-service-gsi.gov.uk. In Scotland, the form should be sent directly to the relevant court. Details can be found on the Scottish Courts website, *http://www.scotcourts.gov.uk.*

[For Apps IV–XI, see Vol.2.]

Index

LEGAL TAXONOMY

FROM SWEET & MAXWELL

This index has been prepared using Sweet & Maxwell's Legal Taxonomy. Main index entries conform to keywords provided by the Legal Taxonomy except where references to specific documents or non-standard terms (denoted by quotation marks) have been included. These keywords provide a means of identifying similar concepts in other Sweet & Maxwell publications and online services to which keywords from the Legal Taxonomy have been applied. Readers may find some minor differences between terms used in the text and those which appear in the index. Suggestions to *sweet&maxwell.taxonomy@thomson.com*.

Where the provision is shown in *italics*, this denotes the administration regime prior to the introduction of the Enterprise Act 2002.

References within square brackets are located in Volume 2.

The following abbreviations are used to denote the location of entries:

[CBIR]	Cross-Border Insolvency Regulations 2006
[CDDA]	Company Directors Disqualification Act 1986
EA	Enterprise Act 2002
[ER]	EC Regulation on Insolvency Proceedings 2000
IA	Insolvency Act 1986
IA 2000	Insolvency Act 2000
IR	Insolvency Rules 1986
[UML]	UNCITRAL Model Law on Cross-Border Insolvency

Provision

A

Absconding
. bankrupts, ... IA 358
. contributories, ... IA 158

"Abstract of receipts and payments"
. administrative receivers, ... IR 3.32
. administrators, ... [IR 2.52]

Accounts
. administrative receivers, ... IR 3.32
. administrators, ... [IR 2.52]
. company voluntary arrangements
. . access for nominee, ... IR 1.6(3)
. . audits, ... IR 1.27(3)
. . production to Secretary of State, ... IR 1.27
. creditors' petitions for bankruptcy
. . requirement to submit, ... IR 6.64
. . submission and filing, ... IR 6.65
. debtors' bankruptcy petitions

Provision

. . requirement to submit, ... IR 6.69
. . submission and filing, ... IR 6.70
. individual voluntary arrangements
. . production to Secretary of State, ... IR 5.32
. . supervisor, ... IA 5.31
. public administration, ... IA 409
. receivers, ... IA 38
. special managers
. . bankruptcy, ... IR 6.170
. . winding-up, ... IR 4.209
. trustees in bankruptcy
. . annulment of bankruptcy orders, ... IR 5.61
. winding-up
. . creditors' voluntary liquidation, ... IR 4.40–4.41
. . further disclosure, ... IR 4.42
. . requests, ... IR 4.39

Adjournment
. court applications, ... IR 7.10
. creditors' bankruptcy petitions

1223

	Provision		Provision

Industrial and provident societies

Inland Revenue
See **Revenue and Customs**

Innocent intention

Insolvency

Provision

Provision